Education, Globalization, and Social Change

Edited by

Hugh Lauder, Phillip Brown,
Jo-Anne Dillabough,
and A. H. Halsey

OXFORD
UNIVERSITY PRESS

OXFORD
UNIVERSITY PRESS

Great Clarendon Street, Oxford OX2 6DP

Oxford University Press is a department of the University of Oxford.
It furthers the University's objective of excellence in research, scholarship,
and education by publishing worldwide in

Oxford New York

Auckland Cape Town Dar es Salaam Hong Kong Karachi
Kuala Lumpur Madrid Melbourne Mexico City Nairobi
New Delhi Shanghai Taipei Toronto

With offices in

Argentina Austria Brazil Chile Czech Republic France Greece
Guatemala Hungary Italy Japan Poland Portugal Singapore
South Korea Switzerland Thailand Turkey Ukraine Vietnam

Oxford is a registered trade mark of Oxford University Press
in the UK and in certain other countries

Published in the United States
by Oxford University Press Inc., New York

First published 2006

British Library Cataloguing in Publication Data

Data available

Library of Congress Cataloging in Publication Data

Education, globalization, and social change / edited by A. H. Halsey ... [et al.] – 1st ed.
p. cm.
ISBN-13: 978–0–19–927253–2
1. Educational sociology. 2. Education–Political aspects.
3. Globalization. I. Halsey, A. H.
LC191.E4247 2006
306.43—dc22

2006014915

Typeset by Newgen Imaging Systems (P) Ltd., Chennai, India
Printed in Great Britain
on acid-free paper by
Ashford Colour Press Ltd, Gosport, Hampshire

ISBN 978–0–19–927253–2

10 9 8 7 6 5 4

About the Editors

Hugh Lauder is Professor of Education and Political Economy at the University of Bath. His recent books include, *Trading in Futures: Why Markets in Education Don't Work* (1999) with David Hughes and others; *Capitalism and Social Progress: The Future of Society in a Global Economy* (2001); *High Skills: Globalisation, Competitiveness and Skill Formation* (2001) with Andy Green and Phil Brown. With A. H. Halsey, Phil Brown, and Amy Stuart Wells he edited *Education, Culture, Economy, and Society* (1997). He is currently undertaking an ESRC project with David Ashton and Phil Brown on the global skill strategies of multinational companies and is principal investigator of an ESRC project on composition effects in primary schools.

Phillip Brown is Research Professor in the School of Social Sciences, Cardiff University. His recent books include *Capitalism and Social Progress: The Future of Society in a Global Economy* (2001) with Hugh Lauder; *High Skills: Globalisation, Competitiveness and Skill Formation* (2001) with Andy Green and Hugh Lauder, and *The Mismanagement of Talent* (2004) with Anthony Hesketh. With A. H. Halsey, Hugh Lauder, and Amy Stuart Wells, he edited *Education, Culture, Economy, and Society* (1997). He is currently undertaking an ESRC project with David Ashton and Hugh Lauder on the global skill strategies of multinational companies.

Jo-Anne Dillabough is an Associate Professor in the Department of Educational Studies, a Faculty Associate (2005–6) at the Peter Wall Institute for Advanced Studies, University of British Columbia, Vancouver, Canada, and a Spencer Research Fellow. Her co-edited book (with Madeleine Arnot) is published by RoutledgeFalmer and is entitled *Challenging Democracy: International Perspectives on Gender, Education and Citizenship* (2000). Recent publications include numerous chapters in edited collections and articles in *Curriculum Inquiry, Sociology of Education, British Journal of Sociology of Education, British Journal of Educational Studies, International Studies in Sociology of Education* (with S. Acker), *Discourse*, and *Theory and Research in Social Education*. Prior to her post at UBC, she worked as a faculty member at OISE/UT (Toronto, Canada: 1997–2003) and was a post-doctoral fellow (SSHRC) at the School of Education and Lucy Cavendish College, University of Cambridge, UK (1996–8). She is currently the holder of two large-scale Social Sciences and Humanities Research Council (SSHRC) grants and a Spencer Foundation grant.

A. H. Halsey is Emeritus Professor and Fellow of Nuffield College, Oxford. He is a senior fellow of the British Academy and a foreign member of the American Academy of Arts and Sciences. He has been associated with the sociology of education since the 1950s, and, apart from the four readers, his main works in the subdiscipline are, *The British Academics* (1971) with Martin Trow; *The Decline of Donnish Dominion* (1992; 2nd edition, 1995); *Origins and Destinations* (1980) with Anthony Heath and John Ridge; and an autobiography, *No Discouragement* (1996). His latest books are *A History of Sociology in Britain: Science, Literature, and Society* (OUP), and *British Sociology from Without and Within*, with W. G. Runciman for the British Academy (OUP).

Acknowledgements

Extracts from 'Capitalism: The Global Reach', by Karl Marx and Friedrich Engels, are taken from *The Communist Manifesto*, ed. David McLellan (Oxford: Oxford University Press, 1998), 2–7. Reprinted with permission.

'Education: Its Nature and its role', by Émile Durkheim, is taken from *Education and Sociology*, trans. Sherwood D. Fox (New York: The Free Prees, 1956), 61–90. Reprinted with permission.

'The "Rationalization" of Education and Training', by Max Weber, is taken from *From Max Weber: Essays in Sociology*, ed. H. H. Gerth and C. Wright Mills (Oxford: Oxford University Press, 1946), 240–4. Reprinted with permission.

'The Democratic Conception in Education', by John Dewey, is taken from *Democracy and Education: an introduction to the philosophy of education* (New York: Macmillan, 1916), 81–99. Reprinted with permission.

'The Forms of Capital', by Pierre Bourdieu, is taken from J. G. Richardson (ed.), *Handbook of Theory and Research for the Sociology of Education* (Westport, Conn.: Greenwood, 1986), 46–58. Reprinted with permission.

'Thoughts on the Trivium and Quadrivium: The Divorce of Knowledge from the Knower', by Basil Bernstein, is taken from *Pedagogy, Symbolic Control and Identity: Theory, Research, Critique*, rev. edn. (Lanham, Md.: Rowman & Littlefield, 1996), 81–6. Reprinted with permission.

'The Means of Correct Training', by Michel Foucault, is taken from *Discipline and Punish: The Birth of the Prison*, English translation Copyright © Alan Sheridan 1977 (New York: Pantheon). Reproduced by kind permission of Penguin Books Ltd. (UK and Commonwealth rights) and Pantheon Books. Originally published in French as *Surveiller et Punir*, copyright © 1975 by Éditions Gallimard. Reprinted by permission of Georges Borchardt, Inc., for Éditions Gallimard.

'Orientalism Now', by Edward Said, is taken from *Orientalism* (London: Routledge & Kegan paul, 1980), 322–8. Reprinted with permission.

'Beyond Status and Class?', by Ulrich Beck and Elizabeth Beck and Elizabeth Beck-Gernsheim, is taken from *Individualization: Institutionalized Individualism and its Social and Political Consequences* (London: Sage), 30–41. Reprinted with permission.

Extracts from 'Multiculturalism and Gendered Citizenship', by Seyle Benhabib, are taken from *The Claims of Culture* (Princeton, NJ: Princeton University Press), 82–6, 92–102. Reprinted with permission.

'Feminist Politics and Democratic Values in Education', by Madeleine Arnot and Jo-Anne Dillabough, is taken from *Curriculum Enquiry* (Oxford: Blackwell), 159–89. Reprinted with permission.

Extracts from 'Disjuncture and Difference in the Global Cultural Economy', by Arun Appadurai, are taken from *Modernity at Large: Cultural Dimensions of Globalization* (Minneapolis: University of Minnesota Press, 1996), 27–9, 31–43, 201. Reprinted with permission.

Extracts from 'Education, Globalization, and the Nation State', by Andy Green, are taken from *Education, Globalization and the Nation State* (Basingstoke: Macmillan, 1997), 130, 169–72, 181–6. Reprinted with permission.

'Governmentality and the Sociology of Education: Media, Educational Policy, and the Politics of Resentment', by Cameron McCarthy and Greg Dimitriadis, is taken from the *British Journal of Sociology of Education* 21/2 (2000): 169–84. Reprinted with permission.

'Localization/Globalization and the Midwife State: Strategic Dilemmas for State Feminism in Education?', by Jill Blackmore, is taken from the *Journal of Educational Policy* 14/1 (1999): 33–54. Reprinted with permission.

'GATS and the Education Service Industry: The Politics of Scale and Global Reterritorialization', by Susan L. Robertson, Xavier Bonal, and Roger Dale, is taken from the *Comparative Education Review* 46/4 (2002): 472–96. Reprinted with permission.

'Globalization and the Changing Nature of the OECD's Educational Work', by Fazal Rizvi and Bob Lingard, was commissioned for this volume.

'Neoliberalism, Globalization, Democracy: Challenges for Education', by Mark Olssen, is taken from *Globalization, Societies and Education* 2/2 (2004): 238–73. Reprinted with permission.

'The Age of Human Capital', by Gary S. Becker, is taken from Edward P. Lazear (ed.), *Education in the Twenty-First Century* (Stanford, Calif.: Hoover Institution Press, 2002). Reprinted with permission.

'The Globalization of Rhetoric and Practice: The Education Gospel and Vocationalism', by W. Norton Grubb and Marvin Lazerson, was commissioned for this volume.

'Why the Rich are Getting Richer and the Poor, Poorer', by Robert B. Reich, is taken from *The Work of Nations* (New York: Knopf, 1991), 208–24. Reprinted with permission.

'The Myth of the Magnet Economy', by Phillip Brown and Hugh Lauder, was commissioned for this volume.

'Producing High-Tech: Globalization, the State, and Migrant Subjects', by Sangeta Kamat, Ali Mir, and Biju Mathew, is taken from *Globalization, Societies and Education* 1/2 (2004): 5–23. Reprinted with permission.

'What is Distinctive About the Knowledge Economy?: Implications for Education', by David Guile, was commissioned for this volume.

Extracts from 'The New Family and Flexible Work', by Martin Carnoy, are taken from *Sustaining the New Economy: Work, Family, and Community in the Information Age* (Cambridge, Mass.: Harvard University Press, 2000), 105–36, 140–3, 144–50. Reprinted with permission.

'The Opportunity Trap', by Phillip Brown, is a revised and abridged version of 'The Opportunity Trap: Education and Employment in a Global Economy', *European Educational Research Journal* 2/1 (2003): 142–80. Reprinted with permission.

'Social Inheritance and Equal Opportunity Policies', by Gosta Esping-Andersen, is taken from Simone Delorenzi, Jodie Reed, and Peter Robinson (eds.), *Maintaining Momentum: Extending Social Mobility and Life Chances from Early Years to Adulthood* (London: Institute of Public Policy Research, 2005). Reprinted with permission.

'Social Class and Cognitive Development in Childhood in the UK', by Leon Feinstein, is adapted from 'Inequality in the Early Cognitive Development of British Children', *Economica* 70 (2003): 73–97. Reprinted with permission.

'Signals of Success: Decoding the Sociological Meaning of Associations between Childhood Abilities and Adult Educational Achievement', by Roy Nash and Richard K. Harker, was commissioned for this volume.

'"Fitting In" and "Joining In": Social Relations and Social Integration', by Tess Ridge, is taken from *Childhood Poverty and Social Exclusion from a Child's Perspective* (Bristol: Policy Press, 2002), ch. 4. Reprinted with permission.

'Education and the Middle Class: A Complex but Crucial Case for the Sociology of Education', by Sally Power and Geoff Whitty, was commissioned for this volume.

Extracts from 'From Social Ties to Social Capital: Class Differences in the Relations between Schools and Parent Networks', by Erin McNamara Horvat, Eliot B. Weininger, and Annette Lareau, are taken from the *American Education Research Journal* 40/2 (2003): 319–27, 331–9, 343–5. Reprinted with permission.

'Producing Inequalites: Neo-Liberalism, Neo-Conservatism, and the Politics of Education Reform', by Michael Apple, is adapted from *Education the 'Right' Way: Markets, Standards, God, and Inequality* (New York: Routledge Falmer, 2001).

'The Politics of Bilingualism: A Reproduction Analysis of the Policy of Mother Tongue Education in Hong Kong after 1997', by Pak-Sang Lai and Michael Byram, is taken from *Compare* 33/3 (2003): 315–34. Reprinted with permission.

'Footsoldiers of Modernity: The Dialectics of Cultural Consumption and the Twenty-First Century School', by Paul Willis, is taken from the *Harvard Education Review* 73/3 (2003): 390–415. Reprinted with permission.

'Pedgogies that Bite/Byte Back', by Jane Kenway and Elizabeth Bullen, is taken from *Consuming Children* (Buckingham: Open University Press, 2001), 168–88. Reprinted with permission.

'Democracy, Education, and Multiculturalism: Dilemmas of Citizenship in a Global World', by Carlos Alberto Torres, is taken from the *Comparative Education Review* 42/4 (1998): 1–29. Reprinted with permission.

'Colonizing Knowledges', by Linda Tuhiwai Smith, is taken from *Decolonizing Methodologies: Research and Indigenous People* (London: Zed Books, 1999), ch. 3. Reprinted with permission.

'Toward a Critical Race Theory of Education', by Gloria Ladson-Billings and William F. Tate IV, is taken from *Teachers College Record* 97/1 (1995): 47–68. Reprinted with permission.

'Be Yourself: Race, Gender, and Sexuality in South African Schoolchildren's Accounts of Social Relations', by Elaine Untherhalter, Debbie Epstein, Robert Morrell, and Relebohile Moletsane, is taken from *Pedagogy, Culture, and Society* 12/1 (2004): 53–68. Reprinted with permission.

'Sexualities and Resistance: Queer(y)ing Identity and Discourse in Education', by Elizabeth Atkinson, is taken from J. Satterthwaite, E. Atkinson, and W. Martin (eds.), *Educational Counter-Cultures: Confrontation, Images, Vision* (Stoke-on-Trent: Trentham Books, 2004), 55–65. Reprinted with permission.

'"There is Something about Julia": Symptoms, Categories, and the Process of Invoking ADHD in the Swedish School: A Case Study', by Eva Hjörne and Roger Säljö, is taken from the *Journal of Language, Identity, and Society* 3/1 (2004): 1–24. Reprinted with permission.

'The Marketplace in Education', by Henry M. Levin and Clive R. Belfield, is taken from *Review of Research in Education* 27 (Washington, DC: American Educational Research Association, 2003): 1–24. Reprinted with permission.

'The Limits of Managerialist School Reform: The Case of Target-Setting in England and the USA', by Martin Thrupp and David Hursh, was commissioned for this volume.

'Schools in Disadvantaged Areas: Low Attainment and a Contextualised Policy', by Ruth Lupton, is taken from *Schools in Disadvantaged Areas: Recognising Context and Raising Quality*, Casepaper 76, Centre for the Analysis of Social Exclusion. Reprinted with permission.

'Four Ages of Professionalism and Professional Learning', by Andy Hargreaves, is taken from *Teachers and Teaching: History and Practice* 6/2 (2000), 151–82. Reprinted with permission.

'Performatitives and Fabrications in the Education Economy: Towards the Performative Society', by Stephen J. Ball, is taken from D. Gleeson and C. Husbands (eds.), *The Performing School: Managing, Teaching and Learning in a Performance Culture* (London: Routledge Falmer, 2001), 210–26. Reprinted with permission.

'Gender Politics and Conceptions of the Modern Teacher: Women, Identity, and Professionalism', by Jo-Anne Dillabough, is taken from the *British Journal of Sociology of Education* 20/3 (1999): 373–93. Reprinted with permission.

'Dichotamous Pedagogies and the Promise of Cross-Cultural Comparison', by Robin Alexander, was commissioned for this volume.

'Curriculum Studies and the Problem of Knowledge: Updating the Enlightenment?', by Michael Young, was commissioned for this volume.

'The Structure of Pedagogic Discourse', by Rob Moore, was taken from *Education and Society: Issues and Explanations in the Sociology of Education* (Cambridge: Polity Press, 2004), 119–46. Reprinted with permission.

'The Changing Discourse of Assessment Policy: The Case of English Primary Education', by Patricia Broadfoot and Andrew Pollard, is taken from A. Filer (ed.), *Assessment: Social Pratice and Social Product* (London: Routledge Falmer, 2000), 18–26. Reprinted with permission.

'The Framing of Performance Pedagogies: Pupil Perspective on the Control of School Knowledge and its Acquisition', by Madeleine Arnot and Diane Reay, was commissioned for this volume.

'Educational Triage and D–C Conversion: Suitable Cases for Treatment?', by David Gillborn and Deborah Youdell, is taken from *Rationing Education: Policy, Practice, Reform and Equity* (Buckingham: Open University Press, 2000), 132–69. Reprinted with permission.

'The Political Structuration of Assessment: Negotiating State Power and Legitimacy', by Luis Benveniste, is taken from the *Comparative Education Review* 46/1 (2002): 89–118. Reprinted with permission.

'Globalizing Empiricism: What, If Anything, Can Be Learned from International Comparisons of Educational Achievement?', by Harry Torrance, was commissioned for this volume.

Extracts from 'How Globalization Can Cause Fundamental Curriculum Change: An American Perspective', by Leonard J. Waks, are taken from the *Journal of Educational Change* 4 (2003): 383–405, 412–15. Reprinted with permission.

'The European University', by A. H. Halsey, draws on material from Hilde de Ridder-Symoens (ed.), *A History of the University in Europe* (Cambridge: Cambridge University Press, forthcoming), iv. Reprinted with permission.

Extracts from 'Building an Epistemic Regime', by Corynne McSherry, are abridged and adapted from *Who Owns Academic Work?: Battling for Control of Intellectual Property* (Cambridge, Mass.: Harvard University Press, 2001), 32–6, 46–50, 64–7. Reprinted with permission.

'Expowering Participants or Corroding Learning? Towards a Research Agenda on the Impact of Student Consumerism in Higher Education', by Rajani Naidoo, is taken from the *Journal of Educational Policy* 20/3 (2005): 276–81. Reprinted with permission.

'Educating for Privilege', by Robert Perrucci and Earl Wysong, is taken from *The New Class Society* (Oxford: Rowman & Littlefield, 1999), 194–200. Reprinted with permission.

'National and Global Competition in Higher Education', by Simon Marginson, is taken from the *Australian Educational Researcher* 31/2 (2004): 4–28. Reprinted with permission.

'Issues in the Expansion of Higher Education in the People's Republic of China', by Henry M. Levin and Zeyu Xu, is taken from *China Review* 5/1 (Spring, 2005): 33–59. Reprinted with permission.

'History, Biography, and Place in the Learning Society: Towards a Sociology of Life-Long Learning', by Gareth Rees, Ralph Fevre, John Furlong, and Stepthan Gorard, is taken from the *Journal of Educational Policy* 12/6 (1997): 485–97. Reprinted with permission.

'Adult Education and Cohesion', by Kjell Rubenson, is taken from *Lifelong Learning in Europe* 8/1 (2003), 23–31. Reprinted with permission.

'Poverty as Capability Deprivation', by Amartya Sen, is taken from *Development as Freedom* (Oxford: Oxford University Press, 2001), 87–110, 314–19. Reprinted with permission.

'What Poverty Does to Girl's Education: The Intersection of Class, Gender, and Policy in Latin America', by Nelly P. Stromquist, is taken from *Compare* 31/1 (2001): 39–56.

'Education Expansion and the Mediation of Discontent: The Cultural Politics of Schooling in the Arab States', by André Elias Mazawi, is taken from *Discourse: Studies in the Cultural Politics of Education* 23/1 (2002): 59–74. Reprinted with permission.

'Transnational Advocacy, Global Civil Society? Emerging Evidence from the Field of Education', by Karen Mundy and Lynn Murphy, is taken from the *Comparative Education Review* 45/1 (2000): 85–126. Reprinted with permission.

'From the Washington to the Post-Washington Consensus: The Influence of International Agendas on Education Policy and Practice in Malawi', by Pauline Rose, is taken from *Globalisation, Societies and Education* 1/1 (2003): 67–83. Reprinted with permission.

'Education for Positive Conflict and Interruptive Democracy', by Lynn Davies, is taken from *Education and Conflict: Complexity and Chaos* (London: Routledge, 2004), 203–24. Reprinted with permission.

We would like to thank the editors and staff at OUP for their enthusiasm and patience and Madeleine Arnot whose refreshing ideas about the shape of this book were invaluable. Of course the book may not now bear any resemblance to her ideas. As the formula has it, the responsibility is ours. We would also like to note with regret the death of two of the outstanding figures of the age in sociology of education, Pierre Bourdieu and Basil Bernstein.

Jo-Anne Dillabough would like to thank her family, Louis Lefebvre and Pascal and Dominique Dillabough-Lefebvre, for their forbearance and patience during the completion of this edition. Jo-Anne also wishes to extend a special note of thanks to Phil Gardner for his general support while she was engaged in the work on this book.

Hugh Lauder would like to thank Norma Adair, Maria Balarin, Alison Girdwood, Hugo Manson, Min-Cheng Lin, and Insub Park for providing him with an understanding of aspects of the sociology of education and the many subtle dimensions of globalization. Maria Balarin also demonstrated to him the compatibility of elements of post-structuralism with epistemic realism and non-relativism with respect to judgements between theories: the former being consistent with one interpretation of Foucault and the latter with aspects of Derrida's work. He also thanks his UK-focused Ph.D. students Ceri Brown and Amelia Hempel-Jorgensen for keeping his feet on the ground in Basingstoke. Finally but most importantly he would like to thank Sarah Hartshorn for whom nothing is too much trouble.

Contents

List of Contributors

PROFESSOR ROBIN ALEXANDER, University of Cambridge, UK
PROFESSOR ARUN APPADURAI, University of Chicago, USA
PROFESSOR MICHAEL W. APPLE, University of Wisconsin, Madison, USA
PROFESSOR MADELEINE ARNOT, University of Cambridge, UK
DR ELIZABETH ATKINSON, University of Sunderland, UK
ROFESSOR STEPHEN BALL, Institute of Education, University of London, UK
PROFESSOR ULRICH BECK, University of Munich, Germany
PROFESSOR GARY BECKER, University of Chicago, USA
PROFESSOR ELISABETH BECK-GERNSHEIM, University of Erlangen, Germany
ASSISTANT PROFESSOR CLIVE R. BELFIELD, Teachers College, Columbia University, USA
PROFESSOR SEYLA BENHABIB, Yale University, USA
DR LUIS BENVENISTE, Senior Education Specialist, World Bank, USA
PROFESSOR BASIL BERNSTEIN, Institute of Education, University of London, UK
ASSOCIATE PROFESSOR JILL BLACKMORE, Deakin University, Australia
PROFESSOR XAVIER BONAL, Autonomous University of Barcelona, Spain
PROFESSOR PIERRE BOURDIEU, Collège de France, Paris, France
PROFESSOR PATRICIA BROADFOOT, University of Bristol, UK
PROFESSOR PHILLIP BROWN, University of Cardiff, UK
ELIZABETH BULLEN, Deakin University, Australia
PROFESSOR MICHAEL BYRAM, Durham University, UK
PROFESSOR MARTIN CARNOY, Stanford University, USA
PROFESSOR ROGER DALE, University of Auckland, New Zealand
PROFESSOR LYNN DAVIES, University of Birmingham, UK
ASSOCIATE PROFESSOR JO-ANNE DILLABOUGH, University of British Columbia, Canada
ASSOCIATE PROFESSOR GREG DIMITRIADIS, University of Buffalo, USA
PROFESSOR DEBBIE EPSTEIN, University of Cardiff, UK
PROFESSOR GOSTA ESPING-ANDERSEN, University Pompeu Fabra, Spain
DR LEON FEINSTEIN, Institute of Education, University of London, UK
PROFESSOR RALPH FEVRE, University of Cardiff, UK
PROFESSOR JOHN FURLONG, University of Oxford, UK
PROFESSOR DAVID GILLBORN, Institute of Education, University of London, UK
PROFESSOR STEPHEN GORARD, University of York, UK
PROFESSOR ANDY GREEN, Institute of Education, University of London, UK
PROFESSOR W. NORTON GRUBB, University of California, Berkeley, USA
DR DAVID GUILE, Institute of Education, University of London, UK
PROFESSOR A. H. HALSEY, Nuffield College, Oxford, UK
PROFESSOR ANDY HARGREAVES, Lynch School of Education, Boston College, USA
PROFESSOR RICHARD HARKER, Massey University, New Zealand
DR EVA HJORNE, Göteborg University, Sweden
ASSISTANT PROFESSOR ERIN MCNAMARA HORVAT, Temple University, USA
ASSOCIATE PROFESSOR DAVID HURSH, University of Rochester, New York, USA
PROFESSOR IAN JAMIESON, University of Bath, UK

ASSISTANT PROFESSOR SANGEETA KAMAT, University of Massachusetts, Amherst, USA
PROFESSOR JANE KENWAY, Monash University, Australia
PROFESSOR GLORIA LADSON-BILLINGS, University of Wisconsin-Madison, USA
PAK-SANG LAI, Hong Kong Institute of Education, Hong Kong
PROFESSOR ANNETTE LAREAU, Temple University, USA
PROFESSOR HUGH LAUDER, University of Bath, UK
PROFESSOR MARVIN LAZERSON, University of Pennsylvania, Philadelphia, USA
PROFESSOR HENRY M. LEVIN, Columbia University, USA
PROFESSOR ROBERT LINGARD, University of Edinburgh, UK
DR RUTH LUPTON, Institute of Education, London University, UK
PROFESSOR CAMERON MCCARTHY, University of Illinois, USA
DR CORYNNE MCSHERRY, Electronic Frontier Foundation, USA
PROFESSOR SIMON MARGINSON, Monash University, Australia
ASSISTANT PROFESSOR BIJU MATHEW, Rider University, USA
DR ANDRÉ ELIAS MAZAWI, University of British Columbia, Canada
DR ALI MIR, William Paterson University, USA
DR RELEBOHILE MOLETSANE, University of Kwazulu-Natal, South Africa
DR ROB MOORE, University of Cambridge, UK
PROFESSOR ROBERT MORRELL, University of Kwazulu-Natal, South Africa
ASSOCIATE PROFESSOR KAREN MUNDY, University of Toronto, Canada
DR RAJANI NAIDOO, University of Bath, UK
PROFESSOR ROY NASH, Massey University, New Zealand
PROFESSOR MARK OLSSEN, University of Surrey, UK
PROFESSOR ROBERT PERRUCCI, Purdue University, USA
PROFESSOR ANDREW POLLARD, Institute of Education, University of London, UK
PROFESSOR SALLY POWER, Cardiff University, UK
PROFESSOR DIANE REAY, Cambridge University, UK
PROFESSOR GARETH REES, University of Cardiff, UK
PROFESSOR ROBERT B. REICH, University of California at Berkeley, USA
DR TESS RIDGE, University of Bath, UK
PROFESSOR FAZAL RIZVI, University of Illinois at Urbana-Champaign, USA
DR SUSAN ROBERTSON, University of Bristol, UK
DR PAULINE ROSE, Institute of Education, University of Sussex, UK
PROFESSOR KJELL RUBENSON, University of British Columbia, Canada
PROFESSOR EDWARD W. SAID, Columbia University, USA
PROFESSOR ROGER SALJO, Göteborg University, Sweden
PROFESSOR AMARTYA SEN, Harvard University
PROFESSOR NELLY P. STROMQUIST, University of Southern California, USA
PROFESSOR WILLIAM TATE, Washington University in St Louis, USA
PROFESSOR MARTIN THRUPP, University of Waikato, New Zealand
PROFESSOR HARRY TORRANCE, Manchester Metropolitan University, UK
PROFESSOR CARLOS ALBERTO TORRES, University of California, Los Angeles, USA
ASSOCIATE PROFESSOR LINDA TUHIWAI SMITH, University of Auckland, New Zealand
DR ELAINE UNTERHALTER, Institute of Education, University of London, UK
PROFESSOR LEONARD J. WAKS, Temple University, USA
ASSISTANT PROFESSOR ELLIOT B. WEININGER, Temple University, USA

PROFESSOR GEOFF WHITTY, Institute of Education, University of London, UK
PROFESSOR EARL WYSONG, Indiana University, Kokomo, USA
DR ZEYU XU, American Institutes for Research, Washington DC, USA
DR DEBORAH YOUDELL, Institute of Education, University of London, UK
PROFESSOR MICHAEL YOUNG, University of Bath, UK

Figures

Tables

Introduction: The Prospects for Education: Individualization, Globalization, and Social Change

Hugh Lauder, Phillip Brown, Jo-Anne Dillabough, and A. H. Halsey

Everywhere educationalists and statesmen are aware that the changes which have occurred in the structure of contemporary societies, in their domestic economies as in their foreign affairs require parallel transformations, no less profound in the special area of the school system.

Émile Durkheim (1904)[1]

Introduction

We live in an age when there is great optimism about the power of education to influence the well-being of individuals and nations. Parents and caregivers see education as a way for their children to improve on their own lives by building an understanding of their place in the world. It is also the principle means by which young people, by passing exams and gaining credentials, can gain an advantage in the labour market. Teachers, as they always have, hope to pass on the wisdom of generations in equipping students for the future.

Yet, while it can appear as if little has changed in education—students still walk through the school gates, university lecturers still speak to massed ranks of undergraduates—economic, political, and social changes over the past thirty years have fundamentally altered the nature and prospects for education. This book is about these changes and what they might mean for the future of education.

Education holds a unique position in modern societies because many people believe that it benefits society at the same time as meeting the aspirations of students and their parents. This faith in formal education has been strengthened in recent times as advances in knowledge and scientific understanding have been seen to play a decisive role in maintaining material and social progress both within developed and developing countries.

It is through science that we develop the technologies intended to improve our material well-being, while through the humanities it is hoped that moral and social progress can also be achieved. But what strengthens this faith is the idea that it is a source of social justice and national efficiency: that education offers students the promise of equality of opportunity irrespective of social background, gender, or ethnicity, while providing the economy with an educated workforce.

In this link between education and progress we see one of the key assumptions that many have held, that educational institutions are in some senses separate or removed from the rest of society. And, because of this relative autonomy individuals are able to develop their potential irrespective of the contrasting worlds that students inhabit beyond the school gates. It is thought that through disciplined study, students can learn to develop the foresight to transcend narrow self-interests or world-views. In part, such ideas reflect a tradition of thought that goes back to the Enlightenment in which reason, imparted through education, was seen as fundamental to the project of the 'perfectibility of man' (Passmore 2000).[2]

But we need to ask whether this faith in education can be repaid. Education in the form of schools, colleges, and universities, is a collection of institutions, policies, practices, and aspirations, as fallible as all other social institutions, such as healthcare or the legal system. The American conservative intellectual Allan Bloom has put his finger on a key problem confronting the education system when he writes:

> Every education system has a moral goal that it tries to attain. It wants to produce a certain kind of human being. This intention is more or less explicit, more or less a result of reflection; but even the neutral subjects, like reading, writing and arithmetic, takes their place in their vision of the educated person . . . Always important is the political regime, which needs citizens who are in accord with its fundamental principles. (Bloom 1997: 498–9)

Clearly, a major challenge for education is that different groups and political parties will have their own views as to what the qualities of the desirable human being should be: education may be the repository of hope for future generations but what form it should take is subject to fierce debate. It is for this reason that education will always be a source of political and social conflict.

Notice how deep these conflicts run. Bloom, for example argues that even apparently neutral subjects such as reading, writing, and arithmetic become embroiled in these debates because they are invested with social significance far beyond students' need to be literate and numerate. This tells us something important about education that is frequently forgotten in the heat of debate—as society changes so do the standards and aspirations for education.

Debates about the type of person the education system should be producing have been framed within a national context. Indeed, the idea of a 'system' of education is typically defined within national boundaries, although there are important national differences in how education is organized. In France there is a high degree of centralized state control over the curriculum whereas in the United States the federal state has had little control over curriculum or assessment, until the recent introduction of the No Child Left Behind legislation.

Despite such differences the development of formal education is never far removed from issues of nation building and national progress. Education systems have been funded, at least until the end of secondary school, by the taxpayer for good reason. The benefits accruing to education were not only seen to belong to the individual but also to the country as a whole. The economic gains from education were seen to be mutually beneficial. At the same time education could foster the dispositions required for a democracy such as rationality, tolerance, and empathy with others, strengthening the bonds of social cohesion between the individual and society (Dewey, Ch. 4 below).

While there has always been debate and struggle over how these private and public goods are to be achieved, the funding, organization, and purpose of 'national' education systems confront new challenges that remain unresolved. These include increasing individualization and social fragmentation; the death of certainty in the idea that there is 'one best way' of doing things revealed through the 'science' of society; and the processes, policies, and practices associated with globalization (Held et al. 1999). Education has therefore become a key battleground as nations attempt to understand the forces that have challenged the old certainties and as they seek to reinvent themselves in a context of globalization and late modernity (Beck 1992; Gidden 1998).

If we return to the inception of the nation-state and the role of education in its development, Green (1990) argues that there have been three factors involved in state formation: external military threat, the need for economic renewal, and internal unrest or revolution. Since Durkheim, the great French sociologist, first articulated the role of education in the national reconstruction of France after the Franco-Prussian war, the economic role of education has been seen as one among several. That has now changed and although policymakers will refer to the importance of the wider aims of education, there is little doubt that the economic role of education has assumed primacy.

That education should come to be seen as central to the reconstruction of the nation-state in modern times is not surprising for, as Liah Greenfield (2003) has argued, the project of the formation of nation-states was intimately connected to economic growth. It elevated the profit motive for individuals, which previously was seen as socially undesirable, and linked it to the legitimization of the state through economic growth. Now with the elevation of knowledge to a central position in economic competitiveness and the intensification of global economic competition, education's central economic role can be understood. Although we should not be blind to the importance of external threats of violence as a means of nurturing a form of nationalism as the example of 11 September 2001 and the subsequent 'war on terror' have made clear.[3]

The dominant view of the global knowledge economy (Guile, Ch. 24, below), at least from the vantage point of the developed nations, is of a competition between nations in which education plays a key role in outsmarting others in the competition for scientific knowledge and technologies that enable innovation. National prosperity, justice, and social cohesion are therefore seen to rest on the creation of a highly skilled workforce with the knowledge, enterprise, and insights required to attract the global supply of high-skilled, high-waged employment. This rhetoric is now taken as a matter of common sense, or what Grubb and Lazerson (Ch. 20, below) call 'the education gospel'.

However, the role ascribed to education in the reinvention of the nation-state is contradictory and often conflicts with more fundamental concerns that need to be addressed. It is with a consideration of these claims that we shall structure the introduction to this volume. It is important to elucidate these claims because they highlight several fundamental problems that now confront individuals and societies. Arguably these problems can be addressed only through collective rather than individual action, requiring international cooperation rather than a self-interested economic and nationalistic response as promulgated by the educational gospel. These problems include:

1. The Control of Technological and Economic Forces that Threaten Global Catastrophe

In focusing so heavily on the economic functions of education and the competition for credentials we may be reducing the potential of education to affect social progress in a much wider sense. Eric Hobsbawm (2005: 19) has written about the balance between 'the forces making for the transformation of homo sapiens from neolithic to nuclear humanity and the forces whose aim is the maintenance of unchanging reproduction and stability in human social environments'. And he notes that, 'For most of history, the forces inhibiting change have effectively counteracted open-ended change . . . Today this balance has been decisively tilted in one direction. And the disequilibrium is almost certainly beyond the ability of human, social and political institutions to control.'

Hobsbawm's point is that we could be entering a period which is defined by our inability to control the forces we have unleashed. This is not only to do with nuclear holocausts and the sustainability of the planet but with advances in genetics and the emergence of a global economy that threatens divisions between and within nations. A key role of education is to examine, critically, the nature of these forces and how we can individually and collectively bring them to democratic account.[4]

2. The Paradox of Prosperity

This paradox refers to the growing inequalities both within and between nations at a time when the global economy is wealthier than it has ever been. During the twentieth century the gross domestic product (GDP) of Britain increased more than sevenfold but income inequalities within Britain are as wide today as they were in the late nineteenth century (Halsey 2000). The gap has also widened between rich and poor nations. Landes (1999) suggests that the gap between Switzerland and Mozambique is roughly 400 to 1, whereas the gap between the richest and poorest 250 years ago was around 5 to 1.

For educationists the fundamental concern is how education is contributing to widening inequalities and whether it can be reformed in ways that contribute to its narrowing. At the heart of the debate about the future of education is the issue of child poverty that blights developing nations. Unicef reports that in developing countries every fourth child lives in abject poverty, in families with an income of less than $1 a day. Nearly 11 million children each year—about 30,000 children a day—die before reaching their fifth birthday, most from preventable or treatable causes. The scales of these global inequalities and their impact on children is also revealed in the following figures (Unicef 2005) which show that out of 100 children born in the year 2000:

- 30 are likely to be malnourished in their first five years of life,
- 26 will not be immunized against basic childhood diseases,

- 19 lack access to safe drinking water,
- 40 lack access to adequate sanitation, and
- 17 will never go to school.

(The numbers add up to over 100 because these are overlapping deprivations, often affecting the same disadvantaged children).

Relative child poverty has also increased dramatically in countries including the United States, Britain, New Zealand, and Canada over the past twenty years. The evidence shows that children living in poverty, whether it be absolute, as in developing countries, or relative as in the West, is a major handicap to educational achievement (Feinstein, Ch. 28, below).

But while many stakeholders and academics have become sensitized to cultural difference they are blind to inequalities. Education has an important role to play because individual life chances are often shaped by it. The conditions under which it has a significant influence on educational achievement vary between societies. In terms of absolute poverty, the example of the Asian Tiger economies suggests that rapid economic growth and a cultural commitment to education can do much to remove it. In developing countries, the condition of women appears crucial to economic and educational well-being (Unterhalter 2003). However, there are questions to be asked about the performance of key aid agencies such as the World Bank in helping to address these issues in developing countries (Rose, Ch. 70, below). In the West, flexible labour markets of the American and British kind have played a crucial role in increasing inequalities in wealth and income and in rising child poverty (Bradbury, Jenkins, and Micklewright 2001).

At the heart of these issues are two interrelated problems. The first, posed by Sen, (Ch. 66, below), is how do we create the economic, social and educational conditions by which individuals have the capacity to make considered choices about how to live meaningful lives. The second, is one of reflexive solidarity (Brown and Lauder 2001). How can people be educated not only to recognize and celebrate their own strengths and achievements, but also to acknowledge the debt they owe to society and the stewardship necessary to sustain the natural world? Human beings tend to take both the social and natural worlds for granted, yet as the chapters in this volume testify, it is society that shapes and elicits the potentials we have and which determines who will be the 'winners' and 'losers'. Clearly education has a role to play both in the construction of 'individual' achievement and in the ability to reflect upon our relationship to others.

3. The Opportunity Trap

The opportunity trap (Brown, Ch. 26, below) refers to the problem of how societies organize the distribution of life chances and rewards: who does what and who gets what and why within the division of labour, given the substantial differences in rewards attached to various occupations such as doctors, lawyers, and garbage collectors. This problem, which stands at the intersection between capitalism and democracy, was believed to be resolved through the tightening bond between education, jobs, and rewards. Opportunities could be extended to everyone through education so that jobs and rewards reflected differences in individual achievement. For much of the twentieth century a close relationship between education, jobs, and rewards was maintained in most of the developed economies primarily because education was used to 'cool out' the vast majority of students because access to higher education was severely restricted. Today, by contrast, higher education has become the norm for the middle classes and aspiring working classes in most of the developed economies.

However, the demand for 'knowledge' workers has failed to keep pace with the rapid increase in the supply of university graduates. This has led to increasing labour market congestion as university graduates struggle to distinguish themselves from other job-seekers with the same credentials. The result is credential inflation that makes it more difficult to cash in on educational success. As more of the leading employers recruit within the international job market, so the competition for credentials will intensify. There might be two consequences: wealthier parents might use their financial privilege to gain advantage for their children while the nation-state might no longer be able to control the rules of the credential competition in the interests of social justice.

This process raises questions about both the narrowing of educational aims and the economic opportunities that are promised if students engage in 'acquisitive' rather than 'inquisitive' learning.

These are just some of the issues that will impinge on those involved in education across the globe, but the educational institutions shaped by the dominant policy agenda seem wholly inadequate to meet the challenges that we now confront. However, our purpose is not to advocate a particular kind of education. Rather, it is to understand the economic, political, and social forces that now confront education and to assess their likely consequences in relation to the fundamental problems we have outlined.

Here the main question is whether education can be a source of progressive change or whether it must inevitably reflect and reproduce existing ways of thinking, doing, and dividing the spoils. Many will immediately respond pessimistically, and they may be right to do so, but before reaching that conclusion there is a great deal of analysis that needs to be undertaken. We can also point to achievements where some sense of social progress has been made. For example, in Western countries slavery is no longer condoned and the struggle against discrimination in relation to gender, ethnicity, and sexual orientation is more visible.

In industrial societies the history of education in the twentieth century was one of struggle in the progressive democratization of access to schooling. The guiding principles for expansion were, as one Minister of Education expressed it:

> The Government's objective, broadly expressed, is that every person, whatever his level of academic ability, whether he be rich or poor, whether he lives in town or country, has a right as a citizen, to a free education of the kind for which he is best fitted, and to the fullest extent of his powers. . . . It was necessary to convert a school system, constructed originally on the basis of selection and privilege, to a truly democratic form where is can cater for the needs of the whole population over as long a period of their lives as is found possible and desirable.[5]

The struggle for universal primary schooling was followed by a push for secondary schooling for all and finally, the opening up of higher education. These are steps forward that we often take for granted but are nevertheless important advances.

Now, however, the progress made through national educational systems in the twentieth century are in question. It is therefore important to explore the major issues that will shape the future of education. Underlying these issues is a fundamental question about the viability of national education systems as they have been understood. The problem is that we appear to be in an age that is struggling over the autonomy of nation-states and more global forms of organization that could address some of the fundamental problems outlined above. The institutions that have a remit to view education on a global scale, the World Bank, World Trade Organization (WTO), and the Organization for Economic Cooperation and Development (OECD), fall far short of having the kind of coordinating or intellectual capacity to think through these fundamental problems. Here there are several issues that need to be considered:

- The degree to which nation-states have autonomy over education in an era of economic and cultural globalization;
- the degree to which changes within nation-states, independent of various global policies and practices, affect their capacity to address issues such as child poverty and the competition for credentials which have a major impact on inequality of opportunity;
- the response of nation-states to what is seen as the demands of global economic competitiveness, which is exemplified in policies associated with the education gospel;
- the effectiveness of global (multilateral) agencies, such as the World Bank, the WTO, and the OECD to address issues of economic and educational inequality.

Understanding the Future of Education

To examine these issues the remainder of the chapter is divided into three parts followed by a conclusion. In Part One we examine the development of education and the nation-state in capitalist societies. This will include a discussion of 'consensus' and 'conflict' approaches to education and will examine some of the theoretical ideas that have challenged these structural theories that dominated the sociology of education until the 1990s. In Part Two we examine the challenges to national systems of education posed by individualization, social fragmentation, and the policies, practices, and agencies involved in contemporary globalization. This will include a discussion of the increasing importance attached to multilateral organizations such as the WTO, and the global influence of neo-liberalism sponsored by the United States of America. In Part Three we examine the role of education in the reinvention of the nation-state. Here we critically examine a 'state theory of learning' that supports the neo-liberal theory of educational progress based on parental choice, assessment, standards, and the new managerialism. In the Conclusion we review some of the key issues that are likely to shape the future of education around the world over the coming decade.

Part One: Education in Industrial Societies

The most striking feature of education in industrial societies[6] over the last century is the sheer scale of expansion. While it is clear that modern educational systems developed to enhance the nation-state (Gellner 1983; Green 1990, 1997), there are different interpretations of why education has expanded and its purpose within society. Here we begin by contrasting 'consensus' and 'conflict' theories as a way of thinking through the key challenges confronting education in the twenty-first century. Consideration of the historical context in which the education system has developed also helps us to separate the enduring conversation about education and the human condition from the chatter of the ephemeral and superficial.

Consensus Appoaches to Education

The *consensus* view is based on an evolutionary model of society from the primitive to the complex. In virtually all areas of life it is asserted that the particularities of everyday life—our relationships, economic activities, and social outlooks—have been superseded by universal ways of being, knowing, and relating to others. It is also assumed that society could be understood as a social organism, where different institutions such as the family, education, law, and state serve different functions in creating an organic social unity.[7]

The expansion of education is therefore explained in terms of its extended role in the *socialization* and *selection* of children for their future adult roles as workers and citizens (Durkheim 1956; Parsons 1961). In terms of socialization Gellner (1983: 34) argued that industrial societies require what he calls a common high culture in which students are taught a universal form of education that enables them to deal with the abstract symbol systems of literacy, maths, and science:

> The level of literacy and technical competence, in a common conceptual currency, which is required of members of this society if they are to be properly employable and enjoy full and effective moral citizenship is so high that it simply *cannot* be provided by the kin or local units (family and local community), such as they are. (emphasis added)

This transfer of responsibility to professional teachers and purpose-built schools, colleges, and universities reflected the increasing demand for an education which is impossible for families and local communities to teach. It also reflected the view that modern societies are highly mobile; as technology and skills change so too must workers uproot in order to seek new employment. Gellner (1983: 34) also notes that the role and status of knowledge changes dramatically in the modern industrialized state. He comments that: 'At the base of the modern order stands not the executioner but the professor. Not the guillotine, but the (aptly named) *doctorat d'état*, is the main tool and symbol of state power.' Hence, it is the modern professor, at the apex of the examination system, who administers justice and arguably maintains social control. 'The monopoly', he says, 'of legitimate education is now more important, more central, than the monopoly of legitimate violence' (ibid.).

What is central to the consensus view is that the state assumes the role of the bastion of efficiency and fairness. It does not serve special interests but represents a triumph of social democracy where all are equal before the law. Émile Durkheim (Ch. 2, below) argued that state education gives individuals both the means to life and the meaning of life. It also guards against the primitive instincts of egotism and self-interest. In his view the survival of society depends on adapting the child to the social milieu in which he or she is destined to live. It is therefore:

> up to the State to remind the teacher constantly of the ideas, the sentiments that must be impressed upon the child to adjust him [or her] to the milieu in which he [or she] must live. If it were not

always there to guarantee that pedagogical influence be exercised in a social way, the latter would necessarily be put to the service of private beliefs, and the whole nation would be divided and would break down into an incoherent multitude of little fragments in conflict with one another. One could not contradict more completely the fundamental end of all education. (Durkheim 1956: 79)

Along with the problem of socialization, the education system also takes increasing responsibility for what is assumed to be the *selection* of the most able individuals to ensure economic efficiency and social justice. As Halsey and Floud (1961: 1) observed, it is education that fuels technological innovation: 'Education is a crucial type of investment for the exploitation of modern technology. This fact underlies recent education development in all the major industrial societies ... education attains unprecedented economic importance as a source of technological innovation.' As technology reached further into the workplace so it was predicted that the number of unskilled jobs would decline while jobs that required expert knowledge would increase (Kerr, Harbison, and Myers 1973). Therefore the selective role of education became more important as employers required a system of certification to ensure that credential holders were competent in their chosen field. This applied to scientists, doctors, lawyers, and other professions as new expertise developed.

But the role of education in the selection process was also believed to resolve the age-old problem of how to link social justice to economic efficiency. Previously it had been assumed that efficiency required the majority to be involved in routine employment. Indeed, in the *Wealth of Nations*, Adam Smith thought that the primary role of education in the eighteenth century was to compensate for the 'almost entire corruption and degeneracy of the great body of the people' (Smith 1976: 781), that resulted from the mind-numbing jobs which most people were expected to undertake in return for increased wages.

The consensus view assumes that the process of industrialism has transformed the economy to the point where 'human capital' becomes more important than land, machines, or physical labour (Becker, Ch. 19, below; Drucker 1993). Consequently, efficiency relies upon selecting the apparently most able students for the most technically demanding jobs. It is only fair that all students should have the opportunity to achieve the jobs that carry the higher rewards in society. This 'meritocratic' competition is therefore based on the idea that individual ability cannot be predicted on the basis of social background, ethnicity, or gender.

In these terms, the expansion and increasing importance attached to education reflects its role as the key institution in administering meritocratic justice by attempting to equalize the opportunity for all students to demonstrate their individual worth, where 'worth' is understood as a combination of intelligence and motivation. Michael Young (1961), who coined the terms 'ideology of meritocracy', presented his famous formula:

$$\text{Intelligence} + \text{Effort} = \text{Achievement}.$$

The idea of meritocracy is the dominant aspiration that has drawn all the stakeholders in education towards a consensus because in socially mobile industrial societies it opens the way to educational and occupational success based on individual achievement rather than inherited privilege. Talcott Parsons (1961) argued that a commitment to meritocratic competition reflected the fact that industrial societies are based on an 'axis of achievement' rather than ascription, that inequalities in adult life must rest on differences in individual achievement that gives everyone an equal chance of achieving the best-rewarded jobs.

It was believed that the barriers to educational opportunities could be lifted by focusing on the performance of different social groups regardless of their social class, ethnicity, racial group, or gender. It is for this reason that James Coleman (1968) coined the concept of 'equality of results' by which he envisaged the aim of an equality of educational outcomes for different groups. This did not mean that everyone would end up with the same qualification, as some on the Right have claimed, but that each social group would achieve proportionately the same levels of educational qualifications.

However the question has remained as to whether, despite the opening up of education, social origins or inheritance still exert an undue influence in relation to social class (Halsey, Heath, and Ridge 1980; Esping-Andersen, Ch. 27, below), gender (Arnot, David and Weiner 1999; Arnot and Dillabough, Ch. 11, below) and race and ethnicity (Ladson-Billings and Tate, Ch. 39, below).

Consequently, *conflict* approaches to education were developed to explain why educational institutions had fallen so far short of the meritocratic ideal by examining how the conflict between social groups can advantage the winners and disadvantage the losers. That we should see education as a site of conflict is not surprising. We noted from Alan Bloom's quote that different groups in society have different ideals of the educated person. Equally, while some may agree, in principle, that educational success should be determined by talent, most parents will seek to maximize the benefits of education for their children.

Conflict Approaches to Education

At the heart of conflict approaches to education[8] are issues of social class. If it can be shown, as Halsey and colleagues have (Halsey, Heath and Ridge 1980) that there are systematic differences in the chances of students from different social backgrounds achieving highly rewarded professional and managerial jobs, then one inference to be drawn is that there are systematic blocks or barriers to upward social mobility, which generate social classes. Halsey and his colleague have coined the 1 : 4 rule in which those from professional and managerial backgrounds have four times the relative chances of someone from an unskilled manual background of achieving a highly rewarded job. This empirical evidence sets up the possibility of seeing education as deeply implicated in what is called the reproduction of social class advantage.

Within conflict theory there are two approaches to class that have been adopted in educational research, the neo-Marxist and Weberian. Neo-Marxist accounts have received less attention over the past twenty years, but current debates around globalization have once more demonstrated the contemporary relevance of Marx's (Ch. 1, below) view of global capitalism and its implications for society (Allman, McLaren, and Rikowski 2003). We provide a brief overview of both conflict theories before considering the implications of feminist and post-structuralist accounts.

The Neo-Marxist Approach

Neo-Marxists reject the characterization of 'industrial', 'post-industrial', or 'knowledge economy' because these labels obscure the realities of capitalist relations. It is economic relations based on the ownership and control of the means of production that are believed to determine the role of the state along with the education system. For Neo-Marxists the state serves the interests of the capitalist ruling class through the reproduction of privilege and a dominant ideology that enables it to share a common view and secures legitimacy for inequalities in education. Education is crucial in promoting this ideology (Althusser 1972; Dale 1989).

Marxists do not explain the educational failure of working-class students in terms of individual attributes which handicap them in their capacity to respond to educational opportunities, but point to the unequal nature of capitalist societies and seek to demonstrate the inevitability of working-class educational failure. From this standpoint the education system is primarily a means of reproducing the existing structure of social and educational inequalities. As Bowles and Gintis (1976: 265) assert: 'The education system ... neither adds to nor subtracts from the degree of inequality and repression originating in the economic sphere. Rather, it reproduces and legitimates a pre-existing pattern in the process of training and stratifying the workforce.'

Neo-Marxists reject the view that education has expanded to fulfil the dual functions of socialization and selection based on meritocratic competition. Rather than emphasizing socialization they use such concepts as 'ideology' and 'hegemony' to underline the view that the freedom, creativity, and capabilities of the majority are being sacrificed in the economic interests of the ruling classes. They also reject the idea of selection based on meritocratic competition as a myth. It is argued that the system is rigged in favour of the middle classes. As Bourdieu (1974: 32) has observed (*contra* Durkheim):

> It is probably cultural inertia which still makes us see education in terms of the ideology of the school as a liberating force ... and as a means of increasing social mobility, even when the indications tend to be that it is in fact one of the most effective means of perpetuating the existing social pattern.

From this perspective the education system is not the neutral arbiter of a meritocratic selection process but primarily serves to legitimate the unequal allocation of credentials, jobs, and rewards based on the reproduction of the social division of labour. But in capitalist 'democracies' this depends on creating a moral climate (hegemony) in which existing inequalities are seen as legitimate (Gramsci 1971). This includes getting students to believe that their success or failure in education is deserved. After all, if a modern society has one single pillar of legitimacy upon which it stands, it is that educational success is achieved on merit.

The alternative Weberian approach has focused on issues of social exclusion. But the use of exclusionary power is not seen to emanate from one source such as the ownership and control of the means of production. Other forms of power and privilege are also taken into account that include economic, political, or status differences that are subject to change over time (Parkin 1979).

Weberian scholars have focused on how professional groups have used exclusionary powers to control access to the professions in order to maintain or enhance their status and income (Collins 1979). They have also focused on the competition for a livelihood (Weber 1968: 341) as a conflict for positional advantage between groups of competitors, who will try to mobilize 'power in order to enhance or defend a group's share of rewards or resources' (Murphy 1984: 548). This would apply to both the way status groups seek to monopolize entry requirements into a 'profession' to restrict access, and the way that powerful social groups attempt to structure the competition for places in favour of family members (Collins 1979; Bourdieu and Passeron 1977).

Along with neo-Marxists, they reject the view that the contest for education and high-status jobs is based on merit, where all are given an equal opportunity to enter technical, managerial, and professional jobs. These theorists also reject the consensus view that the increasing demand for higher education is a response to the growth in high skills, as jobs become more technologically complex (Collins 1979).

The growth of modern examination systems represents what Weber saw as the bureaucratization of capitalism (Weber, Ch. 3, below). The demand for formally trained technicians and office workers increased the need for standardization that 'carries such examinations all over the world' (Weber 1948: 241). Weber (ibid.) argues that 'the universal clamour for the creation of educational certificates' has little to do with a thirst for knowledge:

> When we hear from all sides the demand for an introduction of regular curricula and special examinations, the reason behind it is . . . not a suddenly awakened 'thirst for education' but the desire for restricting the supply for these positions and their monopolization by the owners of educational certificates.

This competition for credentials as a source of positional advantage leads to 'credential inflation' that fuels the demand for certified study. In the competition for a livelihood one's position in education and job markets depends on the performance of others. The more people have access to university, the less a degree serves as a badge of distinction in the job market. This generates further demand for more advanced study and other forms of 'person capital' that give students an advantage over their peers (Brown and Hesketh 2004). Collins (2002: 24) notes that:

> The process of credential inflation is largely self-driven; it feeds on itself. A given level of education at one time gave access to elite jobs. As educational attainment has expanded, the social distinctiveness of that degree and its value on the occupational marketplace have declined; this in turn has expanded demand for still higher levels of education.

A strength of the Weberian approach is that it is not inherently 'reproduction bound', which has been a common weakness of 'conflict' theory in general. Although exclusionary tactics are embedded in social relations, there is always the prospect of less powerful or privileged groups mobilizing resources to break down exclusionary barriers. Moreover, there are no guarantees that the state will always operate in the economic interests of the elite over all other claims to influence and authority, but neither is the state viewed as a neutral agency. It is constantly engaged in conflict management as different interests vie for power and influence, and those that hold power adopt exclusionary tactics to maintain it. For neo-Weberians, the state is important in terms of education because it plays a key role as a moral regulator in setting the ground rules for the conduct of good citizenship. It also presides over how the competition for a livelihood is to be organized and the extent to which powerful interest groups are able to rig the rules of selection to their own advantage (Hirsch 1977; Brown 2000).

In contrast to neo-Marxist accounts, social class for neo-Weberians is about the structuration (Giddens 1984) of life chances in which they seek to study the structural and institutional factors that influence the extent of upward mobility in a society, and conversely the degree to which intergenerational privilege occurs.

While consensus theorists have overestimated the power of education to 'compensate' for society (Bernstein 1971) and to exaggerate the technological demand for a highly skilled workforce, conflict theories have underestimated changes in the relationship between credential competition and the occupational structure. The increase in employer demands for 'certified' labour cannot be explained solely in terms of the exclusionary tactics of professional enclaves seeking to restrict the number of entrants to a given profession by raising entry requirements (Collins 1979; Friedson 1986, Weedon 2002). The demand for higher educated labour increased in the twentieth century as a larger proportion of the workforce entered technical, managerial, and professional employment (Neef 1998). These changes in skill requirements reflect not only an increase in technological complexity but changes in models of organizational efficiency, leading to greater emphasis on problem-solving, communication, teamwork, and self-management skills (James, Veit, and Wright 1997; Thompson and Warhurst 1998). However, it is a matter of debate as to whether the increasing demand for skills will continue (Brown and Lauder, Ch. 22, below)

At the same time, it is important to see that school processes related to pedagogy, the curriculum, and assessment are intimately linked to the competition for credentials. For Bourdieu (Ch. 5, below) education is not about fairness but about the reproduction of privilege: the curriculum, pedagogy, and assessment reflect the norms, rituals, expectations, and practices consistent with the upbringing of professional middle-class children. His theory suggests that we should not separate the conflict over the kind of persons that education should produce from that relating to the competition for credentials.

Post-Structuralist Social Thought and Its Impact on Education: From Socialization to Identity

In the last twenty years structuralist theories, such as the neo-Marxist accounts of Althusser, and Bowles and Gintis, have been challenged by the 'cultural' turn expressed in post-structuralism and postmodernism.[9] This general theoretical shift can be characterized broadly as a move away from the earlier dominance of structuralism and the 'meta-narratives of modernity' towards more fluid and multifaceted approaches. From the 1980s, drawing on influential strands in French social thought and debates in social theory, among which the work of Michel Foucault was particularly prominent, such approaches to educational theory and social change began to gather force.[10] One of the most significant educational features of the cultural turn was the challenge it offered to the idea that the state can socialize individuals, through education, into a monocultural form of citizenship. Such a critique had also occupied some earlier neo-Marxist accounts, most notably in the seminal work of Willis (Willis 1977). Willis's work, however, did not reach beyond masculine resistance to education based upon class. The force of the cultural turn lay in the much wider resonances it established both with feminist concerns about gendered patterns of schooling practices and outcomes, and with claims by people of colour and post-colonial peoples to assert their rights in the face of colonizing systems of education. In both cases, the idea of difference emerged as a powerful contrast to the dominant notion of citizenship as founded upon the category of the white male. Difference therefore became a critical organizing concept for the struggles of women, people of colour, and post-colonial peoples.

The importance of the cultural turn also lay in its questioning of the established identity signifiers of social inequality—race, gender, class, and disability—widely used by researchers and government officials as definitive categories upon which research or policy could be established. These confident assumptions were assailed by new claims that identity categories as traditionally understood were simply unacceptable abstractions that could no longer usefully speak for all groups or individuals in the name of a straightforward economic relation to social inequality (Arnot and Dillabough, Ch. 11, below). In short, the cultural politics of difference and identity has brought the struggles of women and people of colour to the fore, explaining their oppression as a cultural artefact of the discourses of everyday life, including education.

From within the cultural turn, conflict perspectives on education in the modernist tradition could be criticized as no more than 'master narratives' of the nation-state, with neo-Marxist and Weberian conflict theories—focusing primarily upon the role of the political economy in reproducing social inequality—critiqued in the same terms. The modernist emphasis on class and material structures as the primary cause of social inequality was seen by many post-structuralists as obfuscating the interests and concerns of those gender and ethnic groups most affected by social stratification (Arnot and Dillabough, Ch. 11, below).

The cultural turn drew attention to a novel conceptualization of power tied to identity, language and cultural aspects of state life which challenged both consensus and conflict theories. This challenge represented a rethinking of the character of state power in education as fundamentally hidden in the accumulating surveillance mechanisms—the examination standing as a clear example—of the state.

This dramatic paradigmatic shift was concerned with moving away from apparently outdated theories of structural inequality and modern theories of the state towards more relevant cultural conceptions of power. Throughout the late nineteenth and early twentieth centuries, the focus within sociology had been on building grand theories of the state, the economy, and society. In this new theoretical moment, the goal became to obtain a greater understanding of how power—as a cultural phenomenon—operated discursively through the family, education, and the state.

Sociology of education came under growing pressure to accept the epistemological frameworks associated with the cultural turn and popularized, above all, by the work of Foucault. Foucault's most important contribution for the sociology of education lay in his analyses of discourse, hidden techniques of governance, and the formation of subjectivities through a process he describes as 'governmentality'. It is through the application of such a framework to the analysis of the state that Foucault is able to argue that truth and power are effectively inseparable.

Foucault (1980: 208–9) argued that whilst conceptualizations of power were not in themselves central to his work, modes of power needed to be understood in the making of the 'person':

> The goal of my work during the last twenty years ... has not been to analyze the phenomenon of power, nor to elaborate the foundations of such an analysis. My objective [...] has been to create a history of the different modes by which, in our culture, human beings are made subjects ... Thus it is not power, but the subject, which is the general theme of my research.

Post-structural theories of education operating under this rubric are critical of consensus accounts of socialization because in their concern for the material, they ignore the relationship between language and power formations. They also argue that cultural identity or citizenship per se do not comprise coherent or stable narratives which can be simply capitalized upon in efforts at nation-building.

The insistence on the problematic nature of social structures, combined with the Foucauldian critique of the 'person', resulted in a new concentration upon multiple sources of power, and not simply those derived from the state or the economy, together with their cultural impact on the 'making of citizens'. From this emerged a cultural politics that criticized the dominant white, male, metropolitan grand theories and images of the social and economic world that had pushed women and people of colour into positions of subjugation and oppression.

In this theoretical context, there can be no 'shared' understanding of citizenship or sense of common values acquired through socialization, as reflected in the position taken by Durkheim. Indeed, it was precisely Durkheim's conceptions of shared nationhood or national stability which many post-structuralists had criticized in their attempts to make issues of identity and diversity more explicit.

In the following sections, we elaborate some of the ways in which post-structuralist thought has been applied to education. However, before doing so, we identify a number of limitations which may be associated with the cultural turn in sociological theory and its impact on education. The most obvious of these is the substantial move away from a concern with class structures and theories of educational stratification, including the social distribution of educational opportunity. Some might argue that a growing preoccupation with various elements of discourse, culture, and idenitity/self has diverted attention from key social issues concerning social inequality. Educational stratification has, therefore, in many cases been substituted by Foucault's emphasis upon the 'subject'.

A second issue is that in an effort to chart and exercise an interest in the cultural turn in educational theory, theoretical links to a practical agenda in the sociology of education have been substantially weakened (see Shain and Ozga 2001; Lauder, Brown, and Halsey 2004).

A third concern is the difficulties raised for addressing the question of agency in education. It could be argued that an overemphasis on the cultural turn has resulted in the elision of structure and agency (Archer 1995), as well as the conflation of agency with freedom. This has led to the concept of agency being confused with identity rather than being viewed primarily as a modality of social life (McNay 2000) exercised within the complex web of cultural, political, and social institutions. In other words, the material conditions of work, income, and wealth which influence action are no longer seen as being central to a discussion of agency. Consequently those aspects of inequality related to economic conditions have been downplayed or ignored, especially in the context of the development of global markets. Blackmore (Ch. 15, below) argues that this is of particular importance to feminists because it is through the state, as opposed to the market, that progress for women has largely been made.[11]

Finally, the idea that knowledge is not about truth but is simply a weapon in the struggle between different groups has clearly been attractive to some feminists and post-colonial peoples. It counters the persistent tendency in liberal societies to see the 'disadvantaged' as a problem to be solved and as a victim of their own incompetence. Despite these attractions, the difficulties associated with linking truth to power may conflict with the claims of some indigenous peoples to a distinctive and authentic cultural past which is essential to their well-being. Similarly, a thoroughgoing relativism places in jeopardy those theories of oppression upon which the oppressed might draw in seeking to explain their position. After all, if knowledge is always viewed as a mere fiction of the powerful, then what status do theories of colonial oppression have?[12]

Gender and Education

The feminist critique began with the observation that state education reinforced traditional male and female roles which entrenched the split between the public realm of men (politics and the labour market) and the private role of women as homemakers. In turn this led to inequalities in the way women were treated in education and in the gendered patterning of the academic outcomes which it produced. Not only did the public/private split pose problems for women in terms of access to a more diverse set of educational opportunities but it also undermined the very premises of liberal equality in post-war democratic nation-states. From the perspective of the women's movement, education could thus be seen to support a 'patriarchal conception of civil society' (see Deitz 2003), both founded upon, and realized through, education. The key questions raised by women concerning the aims of education in the 1970s were:

- What might it mean to challenge liberal democratic models of education and their role in creating and sustaining gender hierarchies in contemporary nation-states?
- Does the democratic education project hold out the most effective mechanism for allowing women and girls to embrace new and more egalitarian forms of female citizenship?
- Would such a project lead the way to equality for all women? (Dillabough and Arnot, 2003).

In response to these questions, feminist critiques of education implied that schooling should create greater academic opportunities for women, that the curriculum should represent women fairly, and that they should be seen as legitimate and equal citizens of the state. In effect, schooling required transformation from a male-dominated structure to a more egalitarian one. Assuming such transformations could be made, it was thought that women's increased participation in education would constitute a progressive and profound feature of social change that would expand the meaning of democracy and conceptions of the nation-state.

While there is little doubt that progress has been made in this direction, many of the fundamental terms involved in the debate remain contested in feminist educational circles. Perhaps the most striking example of 'progress' is the apparent gender gap in girls' and boys' educational performance identified in many Western nation-states. This gap, now well documented by a number of educational researchers (Arnot et al. 1999), suggests that girls are now outperforming boys in every subject across the curriculum. In an earlier period, girls' success was defined in terms of the acquisition of domestic skills and a particular kind of femininity: 'femininity that could be taught to girls' (see Harris 2004: 3). More recently, young women have been incorporated into the public sphere through access to male-centred school subjects. The corresponding apparent 'failure of boys' against the apparent 'educational success of girls' is clearly beginning to shift the egalitarian premises of education in the 'West'.

This changing pattern of girls' academic achievement at school, coupled with increasing participation levels of women both at university and within the labour market, has prompted two broad analytical responses in relation to the role of education in shaping girls' and boys' futures against the background of increasing individualization and a new global political economy.

The first argument asserts that girls are the 'new winners' of twenty-first-century education in the West (Harris 2004). In this view, girls are perceived by the state as key actors in broadening the scope of society and in stabilizing the social order by increased participation in the labour market worldwide. In an earlier period, the regulation of adolescence, conceived in substantially Durkheimian terms, was seen to be the key to assuring the future of democracy. As Harris (2004: 2) writes:

> The behavior, attitudes, and development of adolescents were all monitored closely in the interests of producing rational, patriotic, and productive citizens for a modern nation-state. In the late nineteenth century, therefore, the state, scientists, and the community paid considerable attention to young people's moral and social development because they were meant to embody the ideas of national progress. [. . .] Young people were expected to personify modern civic values, such as responsibility, strength, and sacrifice, and model the new style of nation-defending citizenship.

However, in this new world order, Harris suggests that it is girls alone rather than adolescents as a whole who will come to be seen as the key to the nation-state's success in global competition and future stability. As such, women can no longer be viewed as vessels merely of domestic knowledge or as dependent upon the state; rather they are seen to be active, self-realizing, and capable of constant reinvention. According to Harris (2004), this conception of girls and young women is contingent upon the twentieth-century break with industrialization and an associated link to what Beck and Beck-Gernsheim (Ch. 9, below) refer to as late modernity. In many national contexts, educational aims have been reconfigured to adjust to the idea of girls forming the basis for a new, more flexible workforce—'the ideal flexible subject of the new economy' (Harris, ibid. 2). Young women in late modernity may therefore be seen as leading 'carriers and defenders of social change' (ibid.).

Such an analysis needs to be approached with some caution. The most obvious problem is that an individualized conception of women in the twenty-first century fails to recognize that individualization and the rejection of traditional roles implies a deeply classed perception of youth development. Such a perception can be seen as the product of an essentially middle-class conception of schooling and the state, drawing strongly from neo-liberal currents of thought. The idea of girls distancing themselves from traditional sex roles makes the assumption that all girls (regardless of their national, ethnic, class, and religious contexts) are in an equal position to exercise the autonomous decision to do so. More importantly, while it is also clear that young women are entering universities (and the labour market) in unprecedented numbers, this by no means implies that they have enjoyed corresponding gains in terms of employment equity and labour market success. Indeed, available evidence suggests that gender inequality in the labour market appears to be undermining girls' initial gains in educational success.

A second and quite different argument is that an educational agenda concerned with boys' *and* girls' educational failure has now replaced an earlier feminist concern exclusively with girls' and women's education (Arnot et al. 1999). As girls' improved academic achievement has loomed large across many national contexts, so too have public anxieties over the future of boys in the labour market. A key argument emerging from the education sector of many Western democracies has been that a renewed emphasis on boys' education will be necessary to break the cycle of their relative failure. Explanations for boys' apparent failures have been many. Among the most influential have been those which relate the impact of de-industrialization to an increase in service sector work and the decline in blue collar work (Harris 2004; Willis, Ch. 35, below). As boys have become distanced from traditional employment structures, so too have they become disengaged from the schooling system. A number of educational initiatives such as boy-centred literacy training and a renewed emphasis on male-centred sports activities have been proposed and practised in recent years. Arguably, however, the central problem for boys remains an intractable one—whilst the market economy favours the flexible and autonomous worker, some boys appear to remain tied to expectations of work and masculinities which may be seen as outmoded.

Clearly, girls' educational successes and women's increased participation in higher education and the labour market present many challenges in the twenty-first century. As new employment possibilities rise for women so too do barriers to employment security and equity. Women continue to earn less than men and are less likely to occupy permanent positions in the labour market (Lauder, Egerton, and Brown 2005). Women in these positions are often unable to obtain the education credentials necessary to transcend the casual forms of employment which distinguish flexible labour markets. Indeed, global changes in the nature of labour markets within which corporations will seek the cheapest workers, all other things being equal, have divided women according to occupation and class and many gains achieved as a result of the women's movement are threatened. This is especially the case in countries where feminism had less initial impact on debates about education, democracy, and job opportunities.

Benhabib's (Ch. 10, below) analysis offers a timely example of the widening of the gender debate in education in relation to social change. Her argument is that democracy must expand and deepen if it is to incorporate the political claims of all women. Benhabib's concerns have been supported by education feminists. For example, both Mirza (1992, 1997) and Brah and Minhas (1985) argue that national education systems have not only been insufficiently attentive to the relationship between culture, ethnicity, and race but also heterosexist. This has happened, as both Mirza (1992, 1997) and Deitz (2003) make clear: 'By presupposing the lives of white middle-class, heterosexual women as paradigmatic for the situation of all women' (Deitz 2003).

Such a recognition that not all women share the same social conditions and opportunities opens the way to a consideration of education in the wider context of race, ethnicity, and the impacts of globalization.

The Nation-State, Ethnicity, and Education

In recent educational debates over the post-colonial condition, the relationship between diversity, inclusion, and citizenship has been central. Within the British context, the post-war ideology of *welfarism* implied inclusion and equal citizenship through schooling, yet the disparities both in achievement and levels of inclusion for minority ethnic groups have remained profoundly and stubbornly evident (Gilborn and Youdell, Ch. 54, below). It is this recognition that has contributed to a scepticism towards notions of equal citizenship as attainable through education. A similar view has been evident in the US, particularly in relation to the outcomes of legal challenges to the segregation of schooling by race (e.g. *Brown* v. *the Board of Education*). As Gloria Ladson-Billings (2004: 10) puts it:

> Brown is more accurately characterized as a first step in a long and arduous process to rid the nation of its most pernicious demons—racism and White Supremacy. While we celebrate its potential, we must be clear about its limitations. The nation has never fully or honestly dealt with its 'race' problem. Our lack of historical understanding seems to obliterate some rather daunting facts. For example, slavery existed legally in North America for almost 250 years. An apartheid like social segregation existed legally for another hundred years. The United States as a nation is but 228 years old and existed as a slave nation longer than it has existed as a free one . . . Our attempt to deal with racial problems through our schools is an incomplete strategy . . . As long as residential segregation remains an issue, school segregation will be a particularly difficult reality.

Ladson Billings points outs that neither substantial social progress nor democratization through desegregation has been the necessary outcome of the ruling in favour of desegregation. Nor has the notion of equal citizenship, whether, for example, in the UK, New Zealand, Australia, or Canada, necessarily assured the protection of autonomous cultural identity through education. Indeed, the idea of civil rights or civil liberties, whether through legal or educational reform, has been seen as undermining majority rights in the nation-state.

We might summarize our discussion thus far by noting that contemporary societies are marked by deep tensions and contradictions between the notion of education and democratization and global economic change. Within this new context, two key theoretical and practical issues in education have emerged in relation to imperial/post-colonial systems of education.

First, it has become increasingly clear that a number of ideas associated with progressive schooling—such as inclusion—have lapsed as nation-states focus on the role of education in global economic competition and in particular with raising 'standards'. It is against this background that the neglect of issues of inclusion and equity emerge. Many would indeed argue that the cultural identity struggles of the late twentieth century have to some degree been subordinated to global economic competition (Cox 2003). Secondly, the focus on skills-based education has marginalized the diverse forms of cultural knowledge available to students in schools and higher education, excluding racial and ethnic communities who remain on the periphery of the labour market.

These concerns give rise to a number of important questions regarding an inclusive education for post-colonial peoples and more recent economic migrants. How might educational knowledge be more inclusive and relevant, thereby challenging the canon of colonial prescriptions? And how do increasing levels of migration challenge the aims of education in traditionally homogenous societies?

In this context, many have seen the rise of multiculturalism as an attempt to address the problems associated with segregation, the post-war concern over equity, and the promotion of the idea of 'tolerance'. Within the mainstream public education system, the key debate centred upon accommodation versus assimilation, in which multiculturalism came to be viewed by many as the panacea for both colonialist educational practices and post-war immigration. The emphasis on multicultural education, as a liberal attempt to eradicate intolerance, highlighted, as Torres (Ch. 37, below) has pointed out, the 'dilemmas of negotiating power' in increasingly diverse and plural states. Perhaps the most significant problem in this context turned on how citizenship was to be understood in relation to multicultural education. As Torres further argues, the notion of plurality presupposed by multiculturalism 'defies easy definitions of what the citizen is'. So while plurality could serve as the ideological basis for some aspects of multicultural education, it could not easily be incorporated into models of citizenship (particularly of the kind articulated by T. H. Marshall (1950)). It for this reason that struggles for cultural autonomy have proliferated worldwide in recognition of the failure of national education systems to engage in Fraser's (2000) 'politics of recognition'.

This concern has led to a renewed focus on culturally autonomous schools such as First Nations schools and higher education institutions, as well as the rise of Muslim and Orthodox Jewish schools, and other culturally autonomous forms of education. Yet such schools, not unlike the public school system itself, face acute challenges to survive. These include remaining financially viable and accommodating to the educational standards laid down by the state. In turn this creates pressures to follow mainstream schools in training students for tests, which, if poorly negotiated may result in parents opting out of culturally autonomous schooling in favour of mainstream schools.

When we place these views and theories within the context of the twin challenges of individualization and globalization, the question is whether these 'fractures' in society are exacerbated or ameliorated.

Part Two: The Twin Challenges of Individualization and Globalization

Our analysis of individualization and globalization raises questions about the aims, processes, and prospects for education in the twenty-first century. In considering these questions we need to further our understanding of the social, economic, and political transformation now confronting education. These changes are complex, uneven, and sometimes contradictory. Indeed, uncertainty and risk are a feature of the age. In order to capture the scale of these changes we will examine 'individualization' and 'globalization'.

Individualization focuses on individual differences and the way people are forced to construct their own biographies and identities. It also focuses our attention on issues of risk and uncertainty along with the threat it poses to the educational aims of solidarity and citizenship. Globalization threatens to drive a wedge between education and the nation-state. As we have noted, the nation-state provided a framework which brought together the economic and moral purposes of education and helped tie the individual to the wider society. It is this framework that is now being challenged by these processes.

Individualization

Individualization is not a new concept. It was central to the development, of sociology given its focus on the emergence, advancement, and critical destiny of industrial capitalism (Fletcher 1974: 3). At the beginning of the twentieth century Durkheim was preoccupied with the problem of how social integration could be maintained in a rapidly industrializing world. Durkheim described his work on *The Division of Labour in Society* as having 'its origins in the question of the relations of the individual to social solidarity'.[13] Increasingly complex societies posed a problem of social order because in the premodern condition they were achieved through established routines of daily life that were rarely subject to question. Durkheim defined this form of solidarity as 'mechanical', given that is was an integral feature of life which required little political justification: it was simply the way things were. As individuals broke away from established rules, roles, and rituals he assumed that a new 'organic' form of solidarity would emerge to regulate the behaviour of citizens.

In today's world this can perhaps be seen most clearly in the transformation of the economy. As the male breadwinners wage has declined and consumption increased women need to be employed, forcing a renegotiation of the domestic division of labour. However, research suggests that it is still a minority of men who carry out domestic roles on an equal basis, even when they are part of a family, but this may be changing. Connell (1997), in his discussion of changing masculinities, writes about the working-class men that now stand at the school gates waiting to pick up their children. However, structural shifts in employment and the renegotiation of domestic activities are only part of what can be seen as more profound changes in the nature of society.

Ulrich Beck explains these changes as a defining feature of late modernity (Beck and Beck-Gernsheim, Ch. 9, below; Giddens 1994). Beck suggests that individualization means, '*first*, the disembedding of industrial society ways of life and, *second*, the re-embedding of new ones, in which the individuals must produce, stage and cobble together their biographies themselves' (Beck 1997: 95). Therefore, individualization involves the disintegration of certainties and the need for new ones but at a time when such certainties no longer exist. As a result the construction of individual life projects has become both a reflexive and risky business.

However, the pervasive way in which science and technology now dominate everyday life is also a source of uncertainty. The old certainties associated with scientific truth and progress have gone as the unintended consequences of developments in nuclear power, military technologies, and genetic manipulation have been subject to increasing public debate over fears associated with global warming and other 'bads' (Beck 1997) that threaten the environment. We have more knowledge and conduct more scientific research than ever before but it is associated with greater uncertainty and contestation.

Both at an individual and institutional level there are decisions that are made about the use of scientific knowledge that often has consequences for others who live perhaps thousands of miles from where these decisions are taken. This has led to a greater need to reflect on our relations not only with such people, but also at home and in the workplace. These trends have led Giddens (1994) to argue that social reflexivity is a distinguishing feature of the late modern age. He suggests that: 'Decisions have to be taken on the basis of a more or less continuous reflection on the condition of one's action. 'Reflexivity' here refers to the use of information about the conditions of activity as a means of regularly reordering and redefining what activity is' (p. 86). These decisions no longer focus exclusively on 'goods' in the form of such things as income, jobs, status, and consumer choice, but also 'the denial, disposal of and redefinition of risks and danger' (Beck 1997: 30).

Individualization should not be equated with an extension of personal freedom. While people in Western democracies are freed from some of the constraints associated with rigid class expectations, gender stereotypes, sexual inhibitions, and choice of who to marry (or whether to marry at all), it creates greater dependency on social institutions such as education, employment, and consumer markets to deliver individual needs and wants. As Beck recognizes:

> individualization is not based on the free decisions of individuals. To use Sartre's term, people are condemned to individualization. Individualization is a paradoxical compulsion for the construction, self-design and self-staging of not just one's own biography, but also its commitments and networks as preferences and life phases change; all this, of course, occurs under the overall conditions and models of the welfare state, such as the education system (acquiring credentials), the labour market, labour and welfare law, the housing market and so on. Even the traditions of marriage and the family are becoming dependent on decision-making, and with all their contradictions must be experienced as personal risk. (1997: 96)

What Beck does not make clear is that there are different kinds of late modern society; not all conform to the Anglo-Saxon models of Britain or the United States (Estevez-Abe, Iversen, and Soskice 2001). In many countries there is greater continuity in employment and welfare states, designed to reduce risk. In contrast to the Anglo-Saxon models some, such as those of northern Europe, provide far greater insurance against some forms of risk. Of course this does not mean that contemporary risks associated with family arrangements are reduced but rather that the consequences of, say family breakdown, may not be as harsh. These societal differences also have a significant impact on the way education is organized and on its outcomes (Estevez-Abe, Iversen, and Soskice 2001).

Arguably, despite the accounts of late modernity offered by Beck, Giddens, and others, some of the most fundamental contemporary changes related to the rise of neo-liberalism and economic globalization that are clearly driven by the profit motive and the desire for market share that extends market forces into every aspect of our lives. If this analysis is correct it follows that many of the key conflicts in education will remain centred on the social classes that contemporary capitalism has created, rather than on issues of individual risk.

While the ties of deference to authority, education, employment, careers, marriage, and family structures have changed dramatically since the Second World War, inequalities in income and life chances have grown during the same period. The rich and the poor living in the same country are worlds apart in material wealth and life chances. In 1970 the chief executives of Fortune 100 companies in the United States received thirty-nine times the income of the average worker. By the end of the 1990s this had increased to 1,000 times (*The Economist* 2003).[14] At the same time marginal rates of tax have declined as top earners in Anglo-Saxon capitalist societies are far more reluctant to pay high marginal rates of tax than in that era (Reich 1991).

This calls into question Beck's (1997: 26) assertion that 'it is no longer possible to extrapolate the ways of life, life situations and lifestyles of people from their (vocational) position in the process of labour and production'.[15] Many people never break free of the influence and ties of social background through processes of individualization, reflexivity, and choice. Indeed, if anything the link between parental income and the education of children has strengthened. For example, Ermisch and Francesconi (2002) report that, on average, while 50 per cent of children's income can be explained by their parents' income, this rises to 70 per cent for the wealthy. In addition, what is not considered here is the possibility that individualization may be associated with new forms of class relations.

In a seminal paper Basil Bernstein (1997) argued that a distinction needed to be drawn within the middle classes between the old professional class and new symbol manipulators; the old professional class leads to an individual with relatively unambiguous role identities while the new class of symbolic manipulators leads to the concept of the person, with ambiguous personal identities and role performances. Bernstein suggests that this leads to conflict between these groups as they seek different types of education to enhance the respective foundations of their privilege. Brown and Hesketh (2004) also argued that there is increasing cultural confusion within the middle classes, as more students are adopting 'player' tactics as a way of winning a competitive advantage in the job market. These tactics undermine the principles of meritocratic competition that had previously served the interests of the middle classes because they rely on the personalities of the players.

Nevertheless, Beck and Giddens ask important questions for education by placing individualization and the management of scientific and technological risk at the heart of their social analysis. The relationship between 'goods' and 'bads' raises the issue of what should be taught and what a 'reflexive' education might look like (Dewey, Ch. 4, below). It questions an education based on the old certainties and 'the truth'. It suggests the need for an education based on active citizenship that not only informs students about the balance-sheet of 'goods' and 'bads' that technologies and economic growth policies have created, but also examines the economic and social conditions which give rise to them. For example, we need to understand why certain solutions and responses to the challenge of environmental sustainability are considered as official policy options and others are not.

Clearly, how we understand the nature and extent of individualization are theoretical and empirical issues that have far-reaching implications for our understanding of recent educational reforms. But in saying this we need to avoid the trap of assuming that education can, by itself, change thought and action, especially when it may demand a denial of the consumerism that often helps to define the identities of the young and old alike (Kenway and Bullen, Ch. 36, below). It will also depend on whether we see individuals as 'calculating pleasure machines'[16] or as citizens that understand that their immediate wants and desires may need to be tempered in the interests of the longer-term future if not survival of society.

Theories of individualization also initiate an important debate about how young people negotiate and construct family relationships and occupational careers (Ahier and Moore 1999). They raise new questions about the status and needs of the learner and how the educational system should be organized to respond to the challenges it presents.

At the same time social aspirations have been heightened, especially in terms of self-development. Inequality is no longer restricted to issues of income and material wealth as Giddens (1991: 6) has observed: 'class divisions and other fundamental lines of inequality, such as those connected with gender or ethnicity, can be partly defined in terms of differential access to forms of self-actualisation and empowerment'.

Individualization, Families, and Childhood

Educational inequalities have been strongly influenced by family resources, practices, and structures. Bourdieu (Ch. 5, below) has emphasized how the 'capitals' of the family (culture, social, and wealth) have influenced educational outcomes. But the nature of the family has been subject to significant changes. Carnoy (Ch. 25, below) charts a secular trend in OECD countries which documents the changing nature of the family, including: an increase in divorces, fewer children, and a decline in the support provided by extended families. While there are variations between countries the trends are discernible in all of them. Carnoy explains these changes by the challenge to traditional hierarchies of patriarchal dominance and by feminism and women's increased participation in the labour market.

Individualization has changed the nature of childhood (Holloway and Valentine 2000) and the way young people negotiate their role in the family (Ahier and Moore 1999). As youth cultures have become more independent of adult cultures we also need to pay attention to the relative influence of, for example, young people's interaction with global cultures of consumption (Kenway and Bullen, Ch. 36, below) because it is often through them and the commodities they offer that identities are constructed. In turn, how all these changes translate into educational achievement needs to be seen against the background of the structures of social class, gender, race, and ethnicity.

As women have entered the workforce in greater numbers there has been an increasing demand for state-supported early childhood education (ECE). This trend raises important questions about the degree to which ECE can provide the educational needs of children from disadvantaged families (see Part Five, The Family, Opportunity, and Social Mobility).

We should also take into account the many children around the globe who are subject to and live in conditions of conflict and danger (Davies, Ch. 71, below), and as refugees may no longer have families. Davies raises the profound question as to whether national systems of education exacerbate conflicts or help to ameliorate them.

Individualization and Market Individualism

There is a danger of confusing individualization with market individualism, that is, of conflating fundamental secular trends in post-industrial or late-modern capitalist societies with market deregulation that has been a feature of both developed and developing countries. The emphasis on individuals having to take responsibility for their own lives can be readily interpreted to mean that individuals are responsible for their employability, and if they cannot find the job they want, they have only themselves to blame. This is important because individualization creates new post-industrial possibilities for the way we think about education, work, and citizenship. Indeed, it could be argued that the stripping away of irrational forms of hierarchy and deference enable greater opportunities for reflection in education about the kinds of fundamental problem now confronting the world that we outlined earlier. However, market individualism severely constrains our understanding of individual freedom and the future of society. Education is reduced to employability; self-worth to market worth; citizens to consumers; and social solidarity to self-interest.

When we consider the forces that are driving education reform today it is difficult to escape the conclusion that market individualism is in the ascendancy. And if the model of market individualism that exists in Western societies is being exported to other parts of the world, then there clearly is a tension, if not outright contradiction, between 'reflexive' forms of democratic education and the model of the sovereign consumer.

Marx and Engels in the *Communist Manifesto* (Ch. 1, below) show that a feature of capitalism is that it never stands still 'all that is solid melts into air' in the search for new markets. Aspects of life that had previously been seen as outside the bounds of market exchange have become increasingly commodified, including our bodies, looks, dress, feelings and knowledge, and, of course, education. And this insatiable drive extends existing markets across the world.

Robert Skidelsky, despite being an eminent conservative political economist, has adopted a Marxian analysis to explain why capitalism has loosened the social glue of authority that had held societies together in the face of the disruptive forces unleashed by capitalism. As Marx and Engels asserted:

> The [ruling class] wherever it has got the upper hand, has put an end to all feudal, patriarchal idyllic relations. It has pitilessly torn asunder the motley feudal ties that bound man to his 'natural superiors' and has left remaining no other nexus between man and man than naked self-interest, than callous 'cash payment' . . . It has dissolved personal worth into exchange value . . . '

Market Individualism, Neo-Liberalism, and Educational Markets

Neo-liberalism, as an ideology, has a long history, but has enjoyed a renaissance in the last thirty years amongst politicians and policymakers in many, but certainly not all, countries.[17] Indeed, it is important to stress that the policy applications and responses to neo-liberal ideas take different forms in various countries. The neo-liberal revolution is aptly captured in the 'survival of the fittest', which is commonly associated with Charles Darwin and Herbert Spencer's ideas on evolution and natural selection.[18] It also assumes a return to 'primitive' capitalism (Brown and Lauder 2001), inspired by writers such as Adam Smith (1976), Friedrich Hayek (1976), and Milton Friedman (Friedman and Friedman 1980).[19]

There are a number of core assumptions:

- The economic system works best when individuals are allowed to seek their private interests. The pursuit of self-interest will foster free enterprise, and the operation of the market will always lead to superior outcomes to those achieved through government planning.
- Given that everyone is equal before the rule of law, the state should not try to intervene in the interests of any social group, rich or poor. The state should limit its involvement to enforcing contracts and to seeing to it that no one infringes upon the rights of others.
- Because people are primarily driven by self-interest, market competition will ensure that the 'fittest' businesses will survive and the 'fittest' people will prosper. This is the only efficient and fair way to organize society without infringing upon individual freedom.
- There are always natural differences in intelligence, motivation, moral character, etc.; this is a fact of life around which society must be organized. Any attempt to try to achieve equality of opportunity, let alone equality, will inevitably fail.[20]
- The cream will always rise to the top. But to be on the safe side, the best way to make sure this will happen is through individual competition, based on equal access to the markets for education, training, and jobs.
- Those who prove to be 'unfit' and require financial support from the state due to unemployment, poverty, etc., should receive a minimum level of support, because state support leads to a 'culture of dependency' among economically disadvantaged groups that weakens their incentive to be self-sufficient.
- Although people are best left to act in their own self-interest, the 'hidden hand' of the market, made up of the sum total of each person's planning, is helpful to all. Greed is a source of social progress.

Based on these tenets, neo-liberals reject the notion of a 'common' or 'comprehensive' education which developed in many countries during the twentieth century. The ideal behind the common school was that it enabled students from all walks of life to mix, rather than being segregated by class, gender, or ethnicity. In turn it was assumed that this would allow for tolerance and empathy to be fostered which are thought to be key dispositions required for a democratic society (Dewey, Ch. 4, below).[21] Equally, a common or comprehensive school enabled students to defer making early decisions about the kind of career they wanted to follow while also allowing 'late academic developers' to emerge, so providing the possibility of greater equality of opportunity (Turner 1961; Halsey and Floud 1961). However, neo-liberals assert that comprehensive schools depress educational achievement. The key to raising standards is greater competition between students and between schools. Through greater competition schools standards will rise because underperforming schools will close down while successful schools will be given more resources to build on their success.

The problem with state-funded and provided education is that there are no incentives for improvement because schools have a guaranteed supply of students due to 'zoning' or 'catchment' areas. Therefore, teachers are not spurred to perform well because they have a constant supply of students that ensures that their schools will not be closed and that they will not lose their jobs.

Notice the neo-liberal assumption that teachers are assumed to be little more than 'calculating pleasure machines'. What motivates them is their self-interest or the self-serving interests of their profession. It is assumed that teachers are primarily concerned with job security, status, and income. In other words, what motivates teachers is extrinsic to the activity of teaching. The pleasure and sense of fulfilment in seeing students develop over time or overcome behavioural and learning difficulties is simply discounted.

Neo-liberalism also calls into question the idea of meritocratic competition because it rejects state interference in the 'selection' process. While neo-liberals believe that each child should have the opportunity to succeed in education regardless of social circumstances, they insist parents have the right to 'choose' how their child is to be educated. They reject any attempt by the state to intervene in order to create a level playing field by making all children attend the school in the zone or catchment area where they live. Therefore, parental choice and 'diversity' are at the heart of the neo-liberal agenda for education.

In the United States charter schools, private providers and even home schooling have served to change the landscape of provision, while in Britain the introduction of specialist and privately sponsored state schools have served the same purpose. Such differentiation is integral to educational markets because, in principle, it offers parents greater choice.

The idea of applying market mechanisms to education has been the subject of intense debate, that has taken shape in three phases. In the first phase, as markets were introduced, market proponents argued that not only would educational achievement be raised across the board but it would also improve equity because minority ethnic groups, caught in the inner cities, would be able to escape the iron cage of zoning by choosing to send their children to more middle-class schools in the suburbs.[22]

Critics argued that educational markets would be inherently unfair because of the material and cultural assets possessed by middle-class parents. Such assets would give them greater opportunity to choose the best schools for their children and to exclude students from backgrounds they considered would hold their children back, including those who are economically disadvantaged, migrant, or from some ethnic groups. Therefore, critics of educational markets argued that selection to the best schools was governed by the wealth and wishes of parents rather than the talent of students (Brown 1997). Indeed, they argued that by applying pressure to change the rules of educational selection to those based on market principles, the professional middle class have moved the goalposts to their advantage (Wilson 1997).

The second phase saw a series of empirical studies designed to test these competing hypotheses. What became clear from these studies was that the outcomes of educational markets depended on specific contextual factors, although how complex these might be has only been revealed in the third phase of research. In some cases, as in Britain, many of the potential problems identified by critics of educational markets were mitigated by a lack of spare capacity in schools so that parents had little choice as to where to send their children and schools had to take on disadvantaged students when they might have preferred not to (Gorard, Fitz, and Taylor 2003). In New Zealand, often seen as an experimental laboratory for neo-liberal ideas, mainly working-class schools did enter spirals of decline because mainly middle-class students exited, leaving them with a rump of working class students (Lauder, Hughes, et al. 1999).

At the dawn of this educational revolution the proponents of neo-liberalism saw markets as a panacea to educational underperformance and inequality (Chubb and Moe 1997). Now in the third phase a clearer picture is beginning to emerge. A review of the evidence in the United States by Levin and Belfield (Ch. 43, below) suggests that in terms of the criteria of freedom to choose, raising educational outcomes, equity, and social cohesion, the introduction of educational markets has done little either to support the triumphalist neo-liberal case or the bleak scenarios of market critics: a similar conclusion is drawn by Nash and Harker (2005) in reviewing the New Zealand experience. However, we should treat such general conclusions with caution because they fail to take into account the fate of schools and communities in particular contexts.

Ruth Lupton (Ch. 45, below) highlights the complex interaction between choice, context, and competition. She shows how issues of context, especially in relation to social class and ethnic cultures, school organization, local geography, and competition interact to produce quite different outcomes in different contexts.

Lupton's account of why schools in apparently similar socioeconomic contexts emerge with radically different outcomes challenges the assumptions on which schools in market systems are judged. It has also been assumed that reliable quantitative measures of school context could be created so that the performance of schools in similar contexts could be judged, with those underperforming suffering a range of penalties (Thrupp and Hursh, Ch. 44, below). This practice is part of the wider system of market signals that has been created for parents and policymakers so that they can judge which schools are performing well and which are not.

League tables of school performance were the first and most well known of these market signals but they have been supplemented in England by a range of other indicators which now influence pedagogy and systems of learning in what can be described as a state theory of learning. The notion that a market system of education could, paradoxically, create a centralized theory of learning will be considered, by many, extraordinary but that in effect is what obtains in England and is being rolled out across the United States. It is so central to issues of teacher professionalism, school autonomy, and improvement that we shall be devoting a section to it later in the Introduction.

There are three aspects to the introduction of markets which are not fully addressed by the comprehensive reviews that have been undertaken on market policies in secondary education. The first concerns the impact of the compositional effects of the student body (Thrupp 1999). For example, do schools with a proportionately high number of students from deprived areas perform less well than might be expected from students' family backgrounds? Equally, do schools that recruit exclusively from professional and managerial families perform better than expected, given students' family backgrounds? The second concerns the impact of market policies on parental behaviour. The key question is, do they make parents pursue more self-interested choices in education so that where once they were content to send their children to the local comprehensive school, now they seek out the best performing school? As Le Grand (1997) has noted we tend to underestimate the impact of policies on people's thinking and behaviour. Finally, it is in the nature of markets that some schools will be winners and others losers. In such cases the basis for selection to the winning schools becomes a key issue. The question that needs to be addressed is whether under these circumstances students in the losing schools suffer just as those in the winning schools gain. In turn this raises the wider question relating to all selective systems of education, do successful schools gain at the cost of the less successful? In the New Zealand case Nash (Nash and Harkes 2005) has shown that, overall, there has been some gain in credential performance across the system but at the cost of polarization in credentials awarded between the least and most successful students.

Market Individualism, Learning Difficulties, and the Reconstruction of 'Normality'

While market individualism has made inroads into education through parental choice there are further limits to the kind of freedom associated with it. This is clearly seen in relation to those with learning difficulties when encountering the imperatives of the market. There are many kinds of learning difficulty stemming from a range of causes. Here we will focus on students seen to have behavioural problems which obstruct their learning. Although it is hard to obtain survey data, most researchers in this area recognize that many behavioural problems are a consequence of poverty and racism.

However, the influence of social conditions are ignored as the symptoms are treated rather than the causes. The strategy adopted to deal with the symptoms is to assume that students have problems rooted in the brain and hence that they have a medical condition. But there are several puzzles in such a diagnosis as Rose (2005) has pointed out. For a start, some of these apparent medical disorders have only recently been discovered, which raises questions as to what has occurred in the environment to trigger an increase in these behaviours or alternatively why they have been misdiagnosed in the past. Equally, Rose notes that a range of these 'disorders', such as Attention Deficit/Hyperactivity Disorder (ADHD)) were identified far earlier in the United States (in the 1960s) than in Britain. Why then should the former have so many more children with this disorder?

Part of the problem is the status of such diagnoses. The social world is created by the construction of categories, such as race, class, sexuality, and disability. Sometimes, as in the case of some disabilities, there is a clear correspondence between the diagnosis and brain function but in many there is not, which is why categories are contested (Hjorne and Saljo, Ch. 42, below). In the case of ADHD, Rose (2005: 254) points out that 'there needs to be a definition of normality against which the child is judged abnormal—and the narrower the range, the more children fall outside it. Almost certainly, the range of what is considered normal in British schools is broader than in the US—at least for white British children.' But he goes on to note that in the non-technical, statistical, sense what is 'normal' 'implies a value judgement—essentially subjective or socially determined—of how a child should, or is expected to, behave. A child who does not behave "normally" in this sense is clearly "abnormal"' (p. 255). While there is a medical opinion that 'the cause of ADHD is now unequivocally located in the brain', Rose takes the view that it may be better understood, 'not as a disorder but as a cultural construct in a society that seeks to relocate problems from the social to the individual' (p. 256).

Rose is one of Britain's leading biologists and he can find no medical evidence to support the condition. Yet the symptoms are treated by drugs such as Ritalin. In the United States the number of prescriptions for Ritalin has grown from a few hundred thousand in the 1980s to approximately eight million today. Between 1989 and 1997 those diagnosed as having 'learning disorders' increased by 37 per cent. This increase occurred at a time when class sizes increased, physical punishment in schools was banned, and special funding was made available for schools to identify and treat children with 'disabilities' such as ADHD (p. 260). While the benefits of drug treatments for children may be equivocal, the profits accruing to pharmaceutical companies are not.

By looking to those exiled to the 'margins' we often see what is most revealing about our societies, as Foucault has taught us. Here we may be witnessing the use of technologies and drugs to solve problems of social control in the classroom. In education, the key to understanding market individualism is the positional competition for credentials. In this intense competition any child that is seen to be inhibiting the learning of others is creating a problem that requires treatment, but the distinction between treatment and control is wafer thin. What we are seeing, in a period in which social 'difference' has become so prominent in educational debates, is the reconstruction of what it is to be 'normal' based on an individualized, asocial medical model of behaviour. It also reflects the growing anxieties within the middle classes to ensure that their children win in the competition for credentials as the costs of failure continue to mount.

Globalization

Education and Globalization

Part of the problem in thinking about the nature and effects of globalization is the term itself. There is no agreed definition of globalization for a number of reasons. It represents an uneven process that has no ending. It is mistaken to think of globalization as an evolutionary progression from simple to complex forms of social and economic organization. History tells us that the process could easily be reversed, especially in relation to free trade and financial markets (James 2001). Globalization is a political project. Anyone living in Europe will be fully aware of this at the regional level as the European Union struggles to embrace conflicting political and economic models of the welfare state.

Another problem is that most people writing and researching on globalization focus on specific aspects, such as international trade or cultural globalization. We lack a comprehensive understanding or agreement about the nature and implications of globalization and its consequences for individuals, groups, and nations in different parts of the world. Held and his colleagues (1999: 16) define globalization as: 'a process (or set of processes) which embodies a transformation in the spatial organization of social relations and transactions—assessed in terms of their extensity, intensity, velocity and impact—generating transcontinental or interregional flows and networks of activity, interaction, and the exercise of power'. Whatever definition is chosen it usually includes the following ideas:

- The transition from national 'walled' and regional economies towards global 'free' trade and markets;

- the declining importance of geographical, national, and cultural borders and boundaries leading to greater interdependence of people and countries worldwide;
- greater connection and interconnectedness through information technologies such as the internet, and cheaper transportation including shipping and air travel;
- more extensive global networks of companies, universities, students, migrants, faith groups, etc.;
- an exponential increase in global flows of goods, money, services, music, film, knowledge, people, information, ideas, tourists, etc.;
- more extensive and rapid diffusion of technologies, knowledge, and ideas;
- the compression of time and space across the planet.

A further consideration is that globalization has objective, subjective, and ideological dimensions. We can see globalization as an objective reality that can be clearly identified and shown to be quantitatively and qualitatively different from how things were organized in the past. There is also a subjective dimension that is captured in this definition from Waters (1995: 3) where globalization is seen as 'a social process in which the constraints of geography on social and cultural arrangements recede and in which people become increasingly aware that they are receding'. This subjective dimension involving people becoming increasingly aware of a changing world raises the issue of how globalization is experienced and impacts on individual identity and sense of belonging. To what extent is it changing the way people think about themselves and the world they live in? Does it lead to a weakening of national identity and loyalties that education has traditionally engendered and how will nation-states respond?

Debates about globalization are inevitably debates about the future of society. If, for instance, we assume that the nation-state has lost most of its powers of governance, it will have a profound impact on our understanding of the scope for national politics to promote the national 'interest' including its social and educational goals. This has led some commentators to suggest that globalization is primarily an 'ideological' construct that is being promulgated to support a neo-liberal agenda. Hirst and Thompson (1999: 2) argue that:

> The present highly internationalised economy is not unprecedented: it is one of a number of distinct conjunctures or states of the international economy that have existed since an economy based on modern industrial technology began to be generalized from the 1860s. In some respects, the current international economy is less open and integrated than the regime that prevailed from 1870 to 1914.

It is therefore difficult to assess the impact of globalization on education given a lack of agreement about the processes with which it is associated. While authors such as Hirst and Thompson underestimate the scale of economic globalization today, their assessment serves as an important corrective to the radical globalists who see the arrival of global free trade as the end of the nation-state (Ohmae 1996).

Despite these conceptual problems globalization remains a useful heuristic tool because it enables us to understand a range of policies, practices, and processes that constitute a new phase in capitalist development.[23] Equally, we need to avoid the tendency to use globalization as a catch-all explanation for all that is now happening in the world. It is not a force in its own right divorced from the multiple political and economic decisions that shape contemporary educational policies and institutions.

It is not surprising that we are tempted to think of globalization in this way: jobs are being transported from one country to another, the ethnic and cultural composition of nations are changing as people travel to find work. Go to a shopping mall in Shanghai and you will find the same stores and products as in San Francisco, Sydney, or London. Satellite television and the internet allow us 'to be' in other places and talk to friends, colleagues, and strangers, across the planet in real time. Equally, triumphs and tragedies are brought into our living rooms as they unfold. And in education, students will travel across countries, languages, and cultures for the opportunity to study. It is hardly surprising that the speed with which all these changes have occurred leaves us with the impression that some external force has been visited upon us.

We should also acknowledge that the consequences of political and economic decisions that have shaped globalization fall unevenly across the globe. While they have contributed to the prosperity of wealthy nations in Europe and North America, other countries have been excluded from this global web and have gravitated towards the 'black holes' of the global information society (Castells 1998: 345). A clear example of what is involved here, which has implications for education, concerns the digital divided (Castells 2001). Nations and regions that do not have sophisticated ICT infrastructures and a wide spread of usage are likely to be disadvantaged economically because they do not have access to the vast pool of knowledge and information or enjoy the *speed* of communication and knowledge transfer that more fortunate nations have. Those who live on the wrong side of the digital divide will find themselves left further and further behind.

A key reason for charting the politics, practices, and policies associated with global change is to examine their implications for national systems of education. Indeed, while there have been major public debates about the consequences of globalization for the economy and the nation-state, far less has been said about its impact on education. Here we will examine the consequences of globalization for social identity and the socialization and selection of future generations of worker-citizens. Moreover, given that education has been organized within nation-states we will also need to examine the changing relationship between education and the state. This requires a more detailed examination of some of the major factors currently shaping global change.

The Drivers of Globalization

There are at least three key factors shaping the politics and economics of globalization. These are Technology and the Knowledge Economy; Empire and the United States of America; and the Rise of Multinational Companies (MNCs). Most writers on globalization tend to emphasize one or more of these factors. How these factors are understood will determine whether we see the processes of globalization as progressive, giving rise to a consensus view of education's role in globalization, or as creating new forms of oppression and educational conflict.[24]

Technology and the Knowledge Economy

The creation of a global market for ideas, jobs, goods, services, and capital has been made possible both as an outcome of a neo-liberal political project and because of the revolution in information technologies.[25] The global wiring of the world's leading economies has led to the transformation of national into global capital. City brokers in New York, London, Frankfurt, Tokyo, Singapore, and Hong Kong are now able to trade in Japanese futures, Google shares, and euros, twenty-four hours a day, virtually anywhere in the world. Alone, the daily flow of foreign exchange stands in the region of 1.2 trillion dollars.

The idea that we are in the midst of a new economic revolution driven by technological innovation has become commonplace and is reinforced by global systems of production for everything from clothes to computers. Thomas Friedman (2005) describes how his Dell laptop computer is assembled in Malaysia from parts produced in Taiwan, Mexico, Thailand, India, Costa Rica, China, the Philippines, Germany, and Singapore. The computer was designed in Texas and Taiwan. Without a sophisticated system of global logistics, the internet, and little political interference in the movement of components across national borders, such just-in-time production would be impossible.

It is noticeable that the majority of parts for Friedman's computer are sourced from countries with low wages: it seems that for many goods the 'problem of production' has been solved as high-quality goods can be made anywhere as long as there is an adequate infrastructure and workers are motivated and willing to learn. As a result politicians see national competitiveness as lying in research and development and in upgrading the skills of workers to utilize new technologies.

In the developed economies prosperity is seen to depend on nations being able to create large numbers of high-skilled jobs that can no longer be delivered according to Fordist principles.[26] Jobs that can deliver a living wage to workers depend on the production of quality goods and services that meet the precise needs of customers and clients. And the creation of jobs offering a decent wage equally depends on new sources of productivity, investment, and innovation. Such jobs are most likely to be found in companies involved in microelectronics, telecommunications, biotechnology, financial services, consultancy, advertising, marketing, and the media. They can create customized niche markets for their goods and services, making it more difficult for competitors to mass-produce the same goods or to offer customers tailored services.[27]

Research and development are seen as crucial because by capturing intellectual property rights (IPRs) companies gain a monopoly that gives them an advantage over their rivals. In effect they are seen as the primary source of wealth in the knowledge economy. But, of course, making the intellectual breakthroughs that lead to property rights requires top-class research and development, much of which resides in universities.

There are clearly questions that educationists would want to ask about the nature of knowledge that is being created in today's economy. Guile (Ch. 24, below) argues that the knowledge economy is understood in a variety of ways that have different implications for education. Moreover, is this kind of knowledge in some sense qualitatively different from knowledge as it has been previously understood?

We also need to interrogate changes in culture and collective identities, given the importance of nation-building and the development of universalistic standards during the period of industrialization. What kind of culture enables the development and integration of the global economy?[28] Extending Anderson's (1984) idea of a socially 'imagined' nation-state, Appadurai (Ch. 12, below) has sought to analyse the ways in which our social imaginations have been extended by the possibilities of modern technology and travel. This presents the first charting of the cultural implications of the age in which we now live but he also emphasizes that this culture is fluid and irregular and can be seen from many perspectives.

There are clear implications in Appadurai's analysis for the aims of education as they were conceived in the development of the nation-state. One key outcome is that the new forms of social imagination may not conform to any particular view of citizenship. Rather different social groups within and between nations will form their own views regarding their allegiances and about how education may help to foster them (McCarthy and Dimitriadis, Ch. 14, below).

Finally, politicians claim that the combination of new technology and globalization will bring widespread benefits, so long as education can produce the appropriately skilled workers. But it is entirely appropriate to ask whether education can bear the weight of such expectations.

The Rise of Multinational Companies

The major beneficiaries of financial deregulation and the revolution in information technologies have been the multinational corporations (MNCs). Since the mid-1970s the multinationals have grown more rapidly than the world economy. The budget of MNCs is often larger than many small national economies. They have great political and economic power, which can determine the employment profiles of rich and poor nations alike. The United Nations found that 73 million people or 10 per cent of employment in non-agricultural activities are directly employed by the multinationals worldwide, and at least a further 130 million people have jobs indirectly controlled by these corporations.[29]

The MNCs are the conduits for the application of cutting-edge technology and organizational practices as they are amongst the leading employers of the world's labour. There is a debate about the nature, power, and global reach of multinational corporations and their impact on capitalist societies (Doremus et al. 1998; Hirst and Thompson 1999; Rugman and Verbeke 2004). But there is no doubt that the deregulation of global markets have enabled MNCs both to extend their access to new markets and spread cost and revenues across the world. As the multinationals seek to reduce their fixed costs by offloading as much of the 'risk' associated with fluctuations in demand for products and services onto suppliers, contractors, and workers, it has led to a greater use of outsourcing, off-shoring, subcontracting, franchising, licensing, and network production.

The global reach of MNCs has also led them to rethink every aspect of their activities on a global scale including sourcing, production, brand management, distribution, finance, governance, performance targets, talent management, and executive development.[30] Reich (1991: 95–6) suggests that this has transformed corporations into webs of smaller companies, business units, profit centres, partnerships, and new streams of entrepreneurial activities:

> the core corporation is no longer a 'big' business, but neither is it merely a collection of smaller ones. Rather, it is an enterprise web. Its center provides strategic insight and binds the threads together. Yet points on the web often have sufficient autonomy to create profitable connections to other webs. There is no 'inside' or 'outside' the corporation, but only different distances from its strategic center.

The creation of global webs or networks has blurred the traditional distinctions between 'indigenous' and 'foreign' companies, goods, jobs, and workers. It has also given the multinationals significant advantages in negotiations with organized labour. Although trade unions are able to exert a degree of pressure at the plant or national level, they lack cross-border organization and also find it difficult to coordinate actions when they are forced to deal with different companies even if they are 'owned' by the same parent company. This has greatly weakened the power of organized labour to stand up to the multinationals in support of the interests of workers and local communities (Fairbrother 2000).

Conversely, the multinationals have the capacity to pick and choose where they will locate production. Their aim is to produce in parts of the world where the labour costs of production are low and where the infrastructure supporting their production, in terms of workforce skills, transport, and communications, is most sophisticated. This has created a *global auction* for jobs, which threatens the living standards and job security of all Western workers (Brown and Lauder, Ch. 22, below). In reality, the global auction operates like a Dutch auction that enables corporate investors to play off nations, communities, and workers to increase their profit margins. Bidding spirals downwards, which impoverishes local communities and workers by forcing concessions on wage levels, rents, and taxes in exchange for investment in local jobs.

The implications for education are profound because the development of a global auction challenges the relationship between education, jobs, and rewards within specific countries. Reich (Ch. 21, below), argues that the fate of workers within the same country will depend on the value of their credentials, skills, and knowledge within the global labour market. According to the 'education gospel' the solution to this problem is to ensure that the education system delivers high standards to enable young workers in developed countries to compete for high skilled, high-waged jobs. But if the MNCs can trawl the world for skills at the cheapest price the rapid expansion of higher education in low-wage economies including China, India, and Russia pose a major challenge as we confront an era of high-skilled, low-waged work (Brown and Lauder, Ch. 22, below).

Empire and the United States of America

Since the attack on the twin towers in New York on 11 September 2001, the Republican administration of George W. Bush has led the invasion of Afghanistan and Iraq, which has raised the issue of the United States as an empire and its implications for the rest of the world.[31] Prior to 9/11 the Bush administration had already withdrawn from multilateral agreements such as Kyoto on climate change. However, such decisions, when linked to military responses in the Middle East, have led to speculation that the United States, as the one dominant military power in the world, was seeking to control oil and indeed trade while, as Marx put it (Ch. 1, below), creating, culturally, 'a world after its own image'.

This speculation has been reinforced by neo-conservative advisers to Bush, who talked of a 'new American Empire' and the 'new Rome'. The neo-conservatives place more emphasis on politics and culture than the neo-liberals who emphasize market freedom and free trade. The neo-conservatives are associated with an aggressive worldwide foreign policy agenda designed to impose a particular view of democracy and equal individual rights in other countries. They assert the use of state power to build patriotism and promote unilateral foreign policy given their dislike for multilateral organizations that may undermine national interest (Kristol 2003).

Part of the attempt to create a world in its own image by exporting American-style democracy, particularly in the Middle East, is motivated by a concern that the present authoritarian systems there are unstable. Paradoxically, they view democracy as creating political stability which serves as a prerequisite for maintaining oil supplies. The economic motives cannot be divorced from the political aspirations for democracy since, in the thinking of the neo-conservatives, the intended 'export' comes as a package: liberal democracy and free market economics.

The rhetoric, if not the practice, of spreading democracy may be considered laudable but the manner of its export is more deeply problematic, especially when it is administered through the barrel of a gun. The difficulties such a policy encounters have to do with the intricate nature of national institutions, practices, cultures, and customs of societies. For example, in relation to education Mazawi (Ch. 68, below) argues that conventional Western theories about the education–society relationship in Arab states simply do not apply. Nor do labels such as 'forces of tradition' versus 'forces of change'. The danger for politicians and academics is to fall into the trap of what Said (Ch. 8, below) calls 'Orientalism', viewing the East in images that reflect Western ways of thinking.

Imposing democracy on societies by force fails to address serious ethical and legal questions about US foreign policy interventions, but also the complex history, contested traditions, and vested interests (Todorov 2003) of a nation's people. It is this recognition that allows us to view more critically the relationship between neo-conservatives and neo-liberals, who often join forces in promoting the creation of market societies. In a disturbing book Amy Chua (2003: 6) has argued that in some countries in the developing world, characterized by multi-ethnic societies, ethnic minorities may dominate economically but when coupled with the development of democratic institutions in which the poorer majority have power, the result is likely to exacerbate conflict:

> In societies with a market-dominant ethnic minority, markets and democracy favour not just different people or different classes, but different ethnic groups. Markets concentrate wealth, often spectacular wealth, in the hands of the market dominant minority, while democracy increases the political power of the impoverished majority. In these circumstances the pursuit of free market democracy becomes an engine of potentially catastrophic ethnonationalism.

She cites a range of countries in East Asia, Africa, and South America where these tensions exist and in places have erupted into violence and genocide such as in Rwanda. However, South Africa offers an example of a nation that has successfully made the transition from domination by a wealthy white minority. Nevertheless, even here the clock is ticking since unemployment among black youth is high, although education is now seen as the route out of poverty (Unterhalter et al., Ch. 40, below).[32] But unless jobs can be found, the threat of conflict and high rates of crime will remain.

Chua seems to support liberal democracy and market economies. However, in the context of American neo-conservativism she has this to say (2003: 7):

> Global-anti-Americanism has many causes. One of them, ironically, is the global spread of free-markets and democracy. Throughout the world, global markets are bitterly perceived as reinforcing American wealth and dominance. At the same time, global populist and democratic movements give strength, legitimacy and voice to the impoverished, frustrated, excluded masses of the world.

The question of Empire extends into the developing world in more subtle ways than those advocated by neo-conservatives. While the current power of the United States derived from its economy as well as its military strength, Robert Wade (2003) has observed that America's economic power is paradoxical. The United States is the most indebted nation in history, yet the structure of the world economic system shores up its profligacy and extends its influence:

> Today's international economic architecture ensures that the ordinary operation of world market forces—the process we call globalization—tends to shore up American power by yielding disproportionate economic benefits to Americans and conferring autonomy on U.S. economic policymakers while curbing the autonomy of all others (ibid. 77).

An aspect of this strategy, that has the potential to influence educational systems, concerns the ideology of neo-liberalism and its influence on multilateral agencies such as the World Bank, World Trade Organization, and the Organization for Economic Development and Cooperation. Wade (2003: 80) argues that the neo-liberal agenda based on free trade has enabled the United States to pursue its national interests while giving the appearance of sponsoring open and fair competition through multilateral cooperation:

> To supervise this international framework you need a flotilla of international organizations that look like cooperatives of member states and confer the legitimacy of multilateralism, but that you can control by setting the rules and blocking outcomes you don't like.

If Wade is correct then what motivates the rhetoric of neo-liberalism is mercantilism rather than free trade. That is where the state advances its economic interests by rigging the rules of economic competition, such as exporting while restricting imports.[33] Wade is quick to point out that while this might be the objective of American economic policy, the practice of multilateral organizations and their outcomes might be quite different. This is because the United States is not so powerful as to dictate the terms on which all the rules and regulations associated with international trade are constructed. Other nation-states come with particular agendas that require horse-trading, such as the current trade dispute between the US company Boeing and Airbus (a European consortium). The prospect of China becoming the world's largest economy also represents a serious challenge to America's position as the dominant economic power, as do the advances made by Toyota, Honda, and BMW in the United States while General Motors and Ford are struggling to compete in their 'home' market.

Mundy and Murphy (Ch. 69, below) show that one of the new developments has been the forming of alliances between Non-Governmental Organizations (NGOs), citizen associations, and trade unions, which target multilateral organizations to lever change in the education systems of developing countries. What is significant about this development is that it may constitute part of the creation of a global civil society opposed to the excesses of market liberalism. However, neo-liberal ideas expounding the benefits of 'free trade' continue to dictate the policies and regulations of many of the multilateral agencies that govern trade, aid, and knowledge creation and distribution across the globe.

The Multilateral Agencies and Education

To understand the influence these multilateral agencies are currently exerting on national systems of education,[34] and because they rarely receive the same attention as educational policies sponsored by national governments, we will offer a brief summary of the World Trade Organization (WTO), The World Bank (WB), and the Organization for Economic Cooperation and Development (OECD).

The World Trade Organization

The relationship between the nation-state and multilateral agencies will depend on which agency and nation-states are involved. The literature on the WTO begins from the assumption that it is nation-states and regional trading blocs (Dale and Robertson 2002) that negotiate over trade agreements. Of course, some nations and trading blocs are more powerful than others and this is reflected in the agreements that have most relevance to education. Here it is, specifically, agreements on intellectual property rights and commerce in higher education that are of most relevance. Wealthy countries believe that they have dominance in research and development of high value goods in electronics, biotechnology, and related areas and are therefore keen to entrench their dominance in a system of intellectual property rights (IPRs) that ensures they have a monopoly in the manufacture and sale of the goods and services they produce. The impact of such a system has been contested by developing countries, especially in medicines and vaccines, such as treatments for HIV/AIDS, where matters of life and death turn on the monopoly prices charged by those with the IPRs. But as McSherry (Ch. 59, below) has shown, universities have become implicated and some would argue compromised by the race to claim IPRs.

Equally, the General Agreement on Trade in Services (GATS) organized within the forum of the WTO has relevance to extending global markets to higher education and private providers. The effects of this trade in higher education have also had a profound impact on the nature of higher education in terms of funding, equity (see Marginson, Ch. 62, below), and the autonomy of academics, and in the changing nature of teaching and learning (Naidoo and Jamieson, Ch. 60, below). However, the commercialization of higher education has gathered pace independently of multilateral agreements. As Mundy and Iga (2003: 286) note:

> The GATS for its part is an enormously uneven and ill-defined agreement. There is little doubt that the GATS predisposes nations to reframe their view of certain areas of human endeavour including the provision of health and education, as international competitive service industries . . . The GATS does not mandate compulsory liberalisation, but rather institutionalises rules within which governments can selectively open up specific markets.

This leaves education as a bargaining chip in multilateral discussions as to where commerce may make inroads into nationally protected services. In the meantime, there can be little doubt that the commerce involved in higher education students from developing countries now studying in Western universities has been of great financial benefit, especially to universities in English-speaking countries (Marginson, Ch. 62, below). But the wider benefits of this influx of students from developing countries into Western higher education is not unequivocal. For instance, Rizvi has asked how far the identities of these students are reconstructed by their experiences (Rizvi 2004). Do they identify with global elites or a transnational class or do they continue to see themselves as citizens of their home country?

While we have focused on the educational implications of the WTO we should not ignore the wider global trading system and its implications for entrenching poverty in developing countries. As Stromquist (Ch. 67, below) argues, to understand the relationship between poverty and girls' education we need to examine both nation-state and global policies. For, as she argues, 'In Latin America ... poverty is not a question of stubborn pockets of uneducated or untrained people but is rather inherent in the social and economic structure of the region.' The reason why global trading policies are influential in structuring poverty in South America and other regions of the world is precisely the mercantalist policies discussed above.

The consequence is that this manifestly unjust trading system makes it difficult for developing countries to trade their way out of poverty. This broad context is crucial because it explains why the expansion of education alone in these countries will not resolve problems of economic development, and may lead to high levels of frustration, if not social unrest, as educated youth are unemployed or locked into low-wage work.

The World Bank

If the WTO can be seen as a forum for bargaining between nation-states and trading blocs, the World Bank was founded to help reconstruction after the Second World War. However, in the 1980s on the back of the neo-liberal Reagan and Thatcher revolutions in the United States and Britain its mission has been transformed. As Stiglitz (2002: 13) notes, laconically:

> The IMF (the International Monetary Fund) and the World Bank became the new missionary institutions, through which these [neo-liberal] ideas were pushed on the reluctant poor countries that often badly needed their loans and grants.

The World Bank offers funds to developing countries conditional upon their satisfying certain demands. These demands are consistent with neo-liberal ideology and are known as Structural Adjustment Programmes. Broadly speaking they insisted upon the privatization of state services including welfare, health, and education, the decentralization of state services that could not be privatized, and the opening up of domestic markets to foreign competition. However, this neo-liberal formula for economic development is rarely applied in pristine form. In some cases negotiations have produced compromises. And while much of the literature critical of the World Bank assumes that its failures can be explained by a top-down, 'one size fits all' ideology, which to anyone outside the neo-liberal tradition would look inappropriate or perhaps even bizarre, case studies suggest that the internal politics and debates within developing countries have also influenced the way World Bank funds are used (see e.g. Girdwood 2004). However the weight of the criticisms of the Structural Adjustment Programme has led to some changes, although it remains a matter of debate as to how far the World Bank has moved (Rose, Ch. 70, below).

The inequalities between the Bank and those nations it seeks to 'support' are not just monetary. In an age when it is often claimed that knowledge is a key factor in creating economic wealth, the World Bank is seeking to develop a digital knowledge base that can be accessed by developing countries to aid their progress. As Samoff and Stromquist (2001: 632) note, in principle, 'the material poor need no longer be information poor. Information rich, they can improve their own and their country's material lives'. However, they argue that information is not the same as knowledge. Knowledge is structured by disciplines and theories in contrast to information which may be assimilated into knowledge structures but can equally have the status of an answer to a Trivial Pursuits question. In discussions of Information and Computer Technology (ICT) this is a crucial distinction because knowledge requires a broader understanding for its interpretation. This leads authors such as Samoff and Stromquist (ibid. 643) to raise questions about the efficacy of claims relating to information and knowledge creation and transmission for economically disadvantaged groups:

> First, what (and whose) information [or knowledge]? Acquired by whom, in what ways? Absorbed by whom, for what purpose? Communicated to whom, by whom and in what manner, for what purpose? . . . the generation of knowledge involves selection, sorting and filtering. People interpret and assign meaning.

They raise these questions in the context of the World Bank's policy to provide information for developing countries. However, because organizations such as the World Bank have the power to select, sort, and filter knowledge it defines as relevant to developing countries, this does not necessarily serve the interests of poor countries and may reinforce existing global inequalities. At stake here is a question that goes back to Marx and Said (see also Smith, Ch. 38, below) about the asymmetry of power and knowledge. Is it the powerful who define knowledge?

The Organization for Economic Cooperation and Development (OECD)

This multilateral agency is often seen as the global 'think tank' for wealthy nations and it has taken an increasing interest in education, as it has championed the idea of the knowledge economy (Rizvi and Lingard, Ch. 17, below). In the 1960s it championed educational expansion and equality of educational opportunity as an aid to economic growth, recognizing that much talent had traditionally gone to waste in industrial societies before the Second World War. In this respect, its current interest in the knowledge economy is consistent with its traditional concern with education and economic growth.

In education the OECD publishes country and thematic reviews of education, seeks to identify international 'best practice', and more recently to publish comparative data on school performance in the member countries. In contrast to the WTO and World Bank its influence is subtle. First, as a policy actor, the OECD forms part of an informal network of global contacts in which common presuppositions about education and the economy are reinforced. This is perhaps best seen in the way that the policy agenda appears to reflect neo-liberal priorities in stressing educational quality, diversity, flexibility, accountability, and equity. This does not mean that the papers they publish simply reflect or endorse neo-liberal assumptions but it does mean that the terrain for research and analysis marked out by the OECD reflects a neo-liberal agenda.

This brief review of multilateral agencies suggests that while the United States is able to exert influence in the form of 'soft' power through these institutions, that is a far cry from suggesting that they are puppet institutions. That said, at the time of writing one of the leading American neo-conservatives, Paul Wolfowitz, has been appointed President of the World Bank and it remains to be seen how its policies develop as a result.

There has been a global extension of trade in education but it is hard to place responsibility for this solely at the door of the WTO. What can be established is that the theories behind many of the policies favoured by such institutions have neo-liberal roots known as the Washington Consensus (Stiglitz 2002). There is a continued presumption that small states following orthodox economic policies—market and individual choice—offer a universal template for efficiency whether it be in education or in other spheres. Although softened at the edges, the approach has assumed the status of common sense amongst the elites that serve these organizations.

Globalization and the Benchmarking of Standards

One of the unique features of this round of globalization is that power in educational decision-making and governance, which was concentrated in the nation-state, has to some degree been diffused to supranational organizations such as the European Union, to regions, and to a range of agents, including the market, communities, and informal global networks (Robertson, Bonal, and Dale, Ch. 16, below).

Graham Room (2000) has examined elements of this diffusion in relation to universities which are seeking ways to benchmark their standards, as reflected in credentials, in order to facilitate the flow of international students, thereby enabling the development of a global market in education. As Room notes, this form of standard setting can be seen through both consensus and conflict views of education. From a consensus perspective the trend toward global standard setting is seen as industrial progress from the national to the international level. From a conflict perspective how standards are set will reflect the strategic interests of stakeholders, especially in relation to positional competition and the reputational competition between universities.

He identifies social, market, and political factors that have initiated the process of standard setting. Socially, he notes, 'Cross-national learning ... has been shaped by the global networks of cultural influence, based on former imperial connections and the more recent cultural dominance of the United States' (ibid. 109). Much of this learning has been established through informal networks and agreements between universities. Policy borrowing to develop best practice has also been encouraged by the OECD because the increasing flows of international students has increased the pressure for league tables to reflect the quality and reputation of universities in different countries. Room also documents the influence of regional blocs such as the European Union in stimulating the creation of one European market, which in turn has raised questions about the comparability of standards.

Room's (2000) analysis is important for two reasons. It draws attention to the complexities in grasping where power lies, as regards policy and practice in relation to university benchmarking, which, he argues, is a politically inspired account of best practice designed to serve market interests. However, he also argues that there are many actors involved in non-governmental inter-university agreements on benchmarking, all with their own agendas in promoting elements of a global standard-setting regime. Rather than painting a picture of an inevitable process, his analysis suggests a rather ill-fitting mosaic.

Globalization and the Challenge to Education

The discussion of the main drivers of globalization raises key issues for education. Whether because of impositions by the multilateral agencies, or corporate or consumer demand, there has been a loss of institutional autonomy. We have seen how the incorporation of universities into the knowledge economy has meant that much research is no longer disinterested but closely bound to the fortunes of corporations. Equally, as universities have been opened to global consumer demand the nature of pedagogy, knowledge, and learning may also be changing (Naidoo and Jamieson, Ch. 60, below).[35] More generally, the loss of autonomy will also be felt, particularly in developing countries that are subject to funding from the multilateral agencies, although, as we have seen, there may be more room for negotiation than critics of the World Bank have allowed.

The idea of meritocratic competition is challenged by globalization because nation-states are losing control of some key features of educational selection. Again the idea of meritocracy is that students compete in a common system usually defined by national boundaries.[36] In higher education, global consumerism raises questions about equality of opportunity in relation to access since it is wealth that becomes the key determinant of access (Marginson, Ch. 62; Levin and Xu, Ch. 63, below). In secondary schooling much of the debate about educational opportunities has focused on the strategies adopted by the middle class to sustain their advantage within a domestic competition (Ball 2003: Power and Whitty Ch. 31, below). This will remain a key area for future research, but we should also examine the global routes to advantage that are now being laid.

Here we should begin by looking at the credential system. One example of an international credential is the International Baccalaureate (IB) which is enjoying increasing popularity (Lowe 1999). It is taught in a variety of international schools which include those catering for a global elite of children whose parents work for governments, multinational companies, multilateral agencies, and NGOs. However, because it offers what is seen as a blue chip entry qualification to top universities in the world, aspirant local elites are also sending their children to these schools. Approximately half the students who are now studying for the International Baccalaureate are American, and a number of elite schools in the United States offer this qualification as an international standard of excellence.[37]

South Korea, one of the most strongly nationalistic of nations, formerly prohibited access to international schools on the grounds that the wealth and wishes of parents gave their children an unfair advantage in the competition for credentials and life chances, but has now lifted these restrictions. In Seoul, the city authorities encouraged the development of a new international school in order to attract foreign MNCs to the capital because MNC employees are asking for the provision of international school places as part of their work conditions.[38]

In the short term these trends do not substantially alter the national character of credential competition, where the vast majority of students remain firmly locked into national systems of assessment. Their academic performance will reflect the quality of local schools, colleges, and universities within a framework of national education (including the investment in school buildings, teacher expertise, staff-to-student ratio, and pedagogy). But if the outcome of the competition for credentials remains embedded in a national context, what happens if the middle classes in different countries see themselves in direct competition for the same jobs in the global labour market?

It is those elites who have been able to mobilize their material and cultural resources in the acquisition of credentials which are likely to benefit most from qualifications such as the IB in a global competition for high-skilled jobs (Lowe 1999). Competition systems based on meritocratic rules may extol the virtues of equality of opportunity in the domestic competition for a livelihood, but social elites (or those aspiring in that direction) may feel that they are being held back in the global competition, when compared to students in a market system who have received intensive hot-housing as part of an academic elite (Brown 2000).

Consequently, the professional middle classes from countries with a traditional commitment to state systems of education such as Germany, France, and Sweden may press for greater market freedom to maintain a level playing-field beyond their national boundaries. The alternative is to 'exit' into the international school system. Market reforms in education may therefore lead to greater equality between elites from different countries, but increase problems of social exclusion and polarization within societies. One of the key factors distinguishing elites in countries where English is not the major language is their access through education to English (Lai and Byram, Ch. 34, below). This has now become a major point of distinction because English has become the *lingua franca* of globalization. Many international schools teach in the medium of English and this is an added attraction for national elites.

Reich (Ch. 22, below) argues that economic globalization is generating a new class of symbolic analysts: those that are skilled in manipulating, networking, and marketing abstract symbol systems, which he sees as the highly paid core of the knowledge-based economy. They are the major players in the new economy because they are appropriating an increasing percentage of the costs of goods and services created. He cites the cost of a $10,000 car of which approximately 50 per cent goes to designers, engineers, lawyers, and advertisers. However, Reich argues that the symbolic analysts do not share the same fate as other Americans because they no longer depend on the domestic economy to make a living. This, he suggests, is leading them to secede from national educational and welfare systems because they have their own private systems of insurance, health, and education.[39]

These developments in the global economy have raised interest in neo-Marxist theories of a global or transnational class (Sklair 2001; Robinson 2004; Sassen 2005).[40] It will be recalled that neo-Marxists will have an interest in education because it is one means for the reproduction of privilege and enables closer bonding and a shared world-view to be sustained through the common experience of a privileged background and elite schooling. In this respect, the elite schools within the international school systems may provide not only blue chip credentials but the kind of common experience that could create a ruling consciousness.[41]

If symbolic analysts are the most high-profile in the global labour market, they are not the most numerous. Wealthier economies attract those with a range of skills where they have skill shortages. The advent of the jumbo jet and electronic communications has made it possible for a large outflow of migrants from poorer countries. Between 1970 and 1995, Mexico had the largest outflow of migrants with 6 million, followed by Bangladesh and Afghanistan with a little over 4 million, and the Philippines with a little under 3 million. The United States was the largest recipient of migrants.[42]

Western nations clearly gain from such migration, where it has been a factor in the increased productivity of the United States and arguably of Britain, but the loss of skilled workers from developing countries is a major issue. It is as if their education systems were supplying human capital to wealthier nations. While they gain a return in the repatriation of funds, they lose capacity to develop further with the loss of skilled workers. This is another form of educational selection in the global economy as it gives educated people from poorer countries the chance to achieve social mobility by moving to wealthier countries, but at a loss to their home countries.

The increased visibility of migrants in the West may testify to the increased flow of workers around the globe but their presence has had the effect of provoking xenophobia, exclusion, and resentment (McCarthy and Dimitriadis, Ch. 14, below; Gitlin et al. 2003). As Torres (Ch. 37, below) argues, it also poses problems for the nature of our democracies and for citizenship. The backlash against migration needs to be seen against de-industrialization, as manufacturing jobs have gone South and East (to Mexico and East Asia), because wage labour was cheaper and non-unionized in these countries, leaving behind 'rust-belt' communities of the jobless and demoralized.[43] The change in the nature of the labour market in Western societies with the decline of manual work and the rise of low-paid service work, or unemployment in the rust-belt areas has meant fundamental changes to youth culture and intensified problems for schools in working-class areas (Willis, Ch. 35, below; Thompson 2002). In an extended research programme Lois Weis and Michelle Fine (see e.g. Weis 1990; Fine and Weis 1998) have examined the educational and community effects of de-industrialization. Their results are disturbing, especially as regards inter-racial relations, with black men blaming the economy and racism for their situation, while white men blame black males (Weis and Fine 1996).

Globalization: Theorizing Its Impact on Educational Systems

So far we have looked at global trends in relation to education and equity issues. However education systems are complex and these trends are not likely to impact uniformly upon them. Rather, we need to consider the specific ways that these trends may be mediated by the way education is organized. For example, we have seen that higher education is most likely to be affected by global trends, but within any given system all universities are not likely to be affected equally. Naidoo and Jamieson (Ch. 60, below) argue that by using Bourdieu's (1986) concept of 'field' we can gain an understanding of why some universities will be much more vulnerable to change than others. A society, Bourdieu argued, comprises many 'fields' which are relatively autonomous and structured by particular power relationships. In higher education, it is the degree and reputation of academic capital that determines the power-holders within the field. The weaker the academic capital of an institution the more vulnerable it is to what Naidoo and Jamieson call 'consumerism'. Consumerism involves pressure by the state to introduce into higher education market mechanisms, quality assurance procedures, and greater curriculum choice through modularization and student feedback on courses. Through league tables relating to research and teaching, which act as market signals, it also enables domestic and international students to choose universities on the basis of their rankings.

The impact of these international and consumerist policies are likely to fall unevenly on universities because those with the greatest prestige nationally and globally are more likely to be able to resist change; they have a greater degree of autonomy. When Oxford and Cambridge in Britain, for example, are compared to the less prestigious 'new' universities, their argument appears plausible. It is the latter that have adopted many of the more conspicuous aspects of consumerism, especially in teaching and learning, whereas Oxford and Cambridge have the autonomy conferred by their global status.[44]

While the higher education sector appears particularly open to global forces, we should not ignore the possibility that global change will also affect education systems more broadly. Waks (Ch. 57, below) sketches a theory about the relationship between global policies and practices and fundamental educational change, arguing that while change in the last century was incremental, globalization is likely to produce radical change. He develops his theory by asking what political and economic institutions have maintained a system of education that has only changed at the margins and then examines how these institutions and interests may be realigned, in particular through changes in the labour market and the internet.[45]

In this section we have identified some of the key issues as regards the impact of various policies and practices associated with globalization. We have argued that in some respects the nation-state retains a degree of control over the powers it is prepared to derogate or relinquish in pursuit of its interests. However, there are aspects of globalization that are much harder for the nation-state to control. In most cases the effects of global policies and practices will be mediated by the nature of the educational system and the social and political interests that maintain it. In the next section we develop a view of the nation-state that sees it as neither passive nor autonomous in relation to global policies and practices.

Part Three: Education and the Reinvention of the Nation-State

Today education is under siege from above due to globalization and from below due to individualization. This section outlines some of the major challenges currently facing education, the state, and democracy under the dynamics of global change. Prior to this discussion we need to examine how nation-states are responding to these challenges. Central to these is the question of the autonomy of the nation-state when confronted by the policies and practices of globalization.

Broadly speaking there are three approaches to the key questions about the relationship between globalization and the autonomy of the nation-state. Following Held et al. (1999), we have identified the 'hyperglobalists' who argue that the nation-state has been rendered powerless by global forces (Ohmae 1996). The 'sceptics' argue that the nation-state has remained largely untouched by globalization (Hirst and Thompson 1999), and located between them are the 'transformationalists' who argue that 'sovereignty, state power and territoriality ... stand today in a more complex relationship than in the epoch during which the modern nation-state was being forged' (Held et al. 1999: 9). In our view, as national barriers to trade, communication, education, and knowledge have receded and regional governance and multilateral agreements have become more important (Dale and Robertson 2002) the state has needed to reinvent itself to address these changes. That is to say that the state has the autonomy to do so but within a new global framework. Education stands at the heart of this reinvention.

The transformationalists offer the most plausible account of the changing role of the state and for understanding its implications for education. Hobson and Ramesh (2002), for example, show how some power has been ceded by the nation-states as a result of trade-offs between national and supranational considerations.[46] Central to their account is the idea that states are 'spatially promiscuous', by which they mean that while they may be fixed in a territorial sense, 'they have the ability to dip into the global realm to circumvent, or adapt to, constraints faced at the domestic, regional or global levels' (p. 10). What they are drawing attention to is that policy-makers can trade-off national powers in order to address problems and possibilities at all these levels. What is significant is the idea that they may seek to overcome problems and/or gain advantage in their domestic politics by ceding power to the regional or global levels.

With this idea in mind they identify what they term 'exit' and 'adaptive' strategies. Exit strategies are employed when they are confronted by domestic constraints and they use the regional and global realms to reduce or overcome such constraints. An example is the underfunding of British universities, which led them to open the market to overseas students who now make a significant economic contribution to sustaining the British university system. Likewise, Singapore, in seeking to become a regional hub for research and development through the rapid expansion of world-class universities there, opted to attract some of the leading universities from around the world, who have established campuses in Singapore rather than relying on indigenous growth.

However, if nation-states employed only exit strategies it would suggest their primacy over global policies and practices. This is where their notion of adaptive strategies enters. Hobson and Ramesh give the example of pressure by domestic producers on the United States government to seek a global system that would enforce intellectual property rights (IPRs), as indeed the WTO agreement on Trade Related Intellectual Property Services (TRIPS) seeks to do.[47] Such a seemingly remote area from education should not blind us to its relevance. As we have seen, it has been argued that the emphasis on the development of IPRs in universities has fundamentally changed their role in society.

This is a case where even the most powerful nations have to negotiate with global partners in order to realize the trade potential of IPRs. But the knock-on effect in the changing role of universities sets up political problems domestically as McSherry (Ch. 59, below) argues, is the autonomy of the university system when confronted with the commercial pressures to generate IPRs. In turn this may give rise to another round of trading-off exit and adaptive strategies.

Hobson and Ramesh's theory provides a welcome advance in understanding the basis for negotiations and trade-offs that states undertake to deal with political and economic problems. However, what is needed in support of such an account is an explanation as to why some nation-states adopt some strategies and trade-offs and not others. For such an explanation we need to turn to the varieties of capitalism literature (Hall and Soskice 2001; Brown, Green, and Lauder 2001).

Capitalism and capitalist societies can take many forms. There are substantial differences between the organization of American and English Anglo-Saxon capitalism and that of Northern Europe or the East Asian Tigers. What is significant about these differences is that they have brought different kinds of 'solutions' to the classic problems that capitalism poses. These 'solutions' are at best partial and open to revision because of the relentless change endemic to capitalism of which current economic globalization is an example.

Durkheim, Marx, and Weber all posed the fundamental questions relating to capitalist societies: how can social justice be reconciled with the extremes of inequality that capitalism creates?; how can social solidarity be maintained in the face of the centrifugal forces of the market?; how can human freedom be realized in the face of alienation at work? What the 'varieties of capitalism' literature shows is that different nations and regions have devised various solutions to these problems. Some, such as the Northern European states, appear to have been able to reconcile capitalist efficiency, social justice, and human freedom better than others.

With these contextual issues in mind we will examine the implications of this analysis for education and the neo-liberal state. The reason for the focus on neo-liberalism is that while many countries either explicitly or more subtly reject neo-liberalism, it remains an issue across the globe, whether it be in France, which has been such an adamant opponent of Anglo-Saxon capitalism, or in Korea, Taiwan, or South America, where it has been the subject of intense debate. It also raises the question underlying the varieties of capitalist literature as to whether globalization leads to a convergence of thought and practice centred on neo-liberalism.

The Neo-Liberal State and Global Competitiveness

Hobson and Ramesh's (2002) account of the possible ways in which the modern nation-state interacts with the policies and practices of globalization takes us some way in understanding the continued centrality of the nation-state. In order to understand why the Anglo-Saxon states make certain trade-offs and not others we need a fuller account of how they see education in relation to the opportunities and threats presented by global policies and practices.

There are three aspects to the neo-liberal state's response to economic globalization. These are: (1) the view that education is central to economic competitiveness, (2) that the state provides the opportunities for employability, through what can be described as 'a state theory of learning'[48] and in so doing poverty, unemployment, and inequalities of income can be addressed but that (3) the individual is responsible for being employable. These deceptively simple ideas belie some fundamental changes in the role of the state and the way in which it manipulates power over education and its relationship to the labour market.

1. The View that Education is Central to Economic Competitiveness

Most politicians and policymakers will make the claim that their nation's competitiveness will depend upon the knowledge and skill of their workers (Becker, Ch. 19, below). As we have seen, this is because of the emergence of new technologies, such as those relating to genetics and electronics, information and communications, and collapsing barriers to international trade and investment. These changes, it is claimed, have accelerated the evolutionary path from low- to high-skills economies. Now wealth is to be based on new ideas that can be converted into money (commodified) through the possession of intellectual property rights and the skills to operate new technologies.

In neo-liberal states such as the United States and Britain the mission to augment human capital has much wider implications because it has been accompanied by reducing the welfare commitment to individuals and families on the assumption that if they possess the right qualifications, job opportunities will continue to exist. Consequently, neo-liberal states see it as important to prioritize education, at least in rhetoric if not always in practice, while spending less on protecting workers from the uncertainties inherent in capitalist economies (Brown and Lauder 2001). In this view, the state no longer guarantees employment as it did in the period after the Second World War or offers much support in times of unemployment. This is because neo-liberals argue that globalization makes it impossible for the state to commit to full employment because technologies and the tastes of consumers change so rapidly. What the state now offers is the opportunity to become employable through education. However, neo-liberals assume that most will want to make themselves employable because of the economic and social benefits that employment offers.[49] However, it recognizes that while all ought to seek employment, changing market structures will disrupt networks by which young working-class students in particular have found employment in the past. Therefore, it can step in to act as a surrogate for such networks (Strathdee 2005).

Education is at the heart of the new contract between the individual and the state not only because of the potential economic benefits but also because more highly educated individuals are less likely to be unemployed or find themselves in poverty, hence the logic behind reducing the commitment to social protection for workers. This idea is premised on two assumptions. The first is that high-skilled work will remain in the West because of the research and teaching record of its universities. The underlying vision being that 'brain' work will be done in the West while 'brawn' work in factories and in agriculture will be done in the rest of the world (Reich 1991).

What this view fails to acknowledge or address is the number of highly educated graduates from India (Kamat, Mir, and Mathew, Ch. 23, below) and the rise of Chinese universities (Levin and Xu, Ch. 63, below). Nor does it take into account the innovations of companies like Samsung, Sony, and Honda. The idea that the West will remain dominant in 'brainpower' already seems a slender hope. But even if it were true there are only so many jobs that can be created through research, development, and design work. And will those that cannot win such jobs have to compete at the same wage levels as those in China, India, and Vietnam? Looked at from the perspective of these countries, there must appear to be more than a whiff of neo-colonialist delusion in the pronouncements of Western politicians who have endorsed Reich's view.[50]

The second assumption is that the nature of work in the so-called 'knowledge economy' will continue to demand increasingly high-skilled workers, as the *consensus* approach predicts. However, there are many 'knowledge' jobs that are now becoming routinized with the help of computers because that is cheaper for companies. It means that they do not require more expensive, higher-skilled labour and they have greater control over the people they do employ (Brown and Lauder, Ch. 22, below).

If there are doubts about the economic rationale for the education gospel, then there are perhaps even more questions to be asked about the assumption that education can make a major contribution to the elimination of poverty, while promoting greater equality of opportunity by enabling individuals to become employable.

This brings us to the question of the conditions under which education can overcome the effects of poverty to provide students with what Sen (Ch. 66, below) refers to as the capability to make reasoned choices. Or to ask the question in another way, to what degree does poverty foreclose the possibilities of educational success? This question is complex as the factors involved in determining the degree to which people will escape poverty through education will vary between societies. For example, a combination of strong economic growth, family social capital, and arguably a traditional Confucian commitment to education, enabled a large proportion of the population in the Asian Tiger economies to escape poverty through education. Carnoy and Marshall (2005) consider three explanations concerning the performance of the Cuban education system: parental and family resources, quality of teaching, and what they call 'collective social capital'. They conclude that the collective social capital of the nation has an effect on educational performance, which is ranked as the best in South America. However, the relatively poor performance of the Cuban economy has meant that educational success has not been translated into economic success. When we take into account the greater social solidarity found in the Nordic countries and examine their records on inequality and educational performance, it is difficult to escape the conclusion that the greater the equality and social solidarity within nations, the better their educational performance (Esping-Andersen, Ch. 27; Rubenson, Ch. 65, below).

In contrast, in more individualist countries such as the United States and Britain, the focus has been on families and their resources. The Right has focused on research that shows low educational achievement to be related to parenting (Mayer 1997) while the Left has emphasized the institutional barriers to escaping poverty through education. What Mayer overlooks is the active engagement of middle-class parents in seeking the best advantage for their children at the expense of the disadvantaged (Power and Whitty, Ch. 31, below; McNamara Horvat, Weininger, and Lareau, Ch. 32, below; Ball 2003; Power et al. 2003). The evidence presented in this book suggests that some can escape poverty (Nash and Harker, Ch. 29, below) but that the intergenerational transmission of poverty is significant (Feinstein, Ch. 28, below). Education on its own, despite efforts to adopt best practice, can have only a limited impact (ibid.).

Finally, it is important to consider the 'statecraft' involved in engineering what is a fundamental change in the contract between the individual and the nation-state. This is not just a matter of changing policies or creating new agencies and forms of regulation, although these are all part of the process. Rather, it is, in fundamental ways, about regulating and changing individuals, their values, and their outlook on life.[51]

Consider the example of an immigrant family in the United States that form the case study at the centre of Richard Sennett's book, *The Corrosion of Character*. The father, Enrico was a janitor, his son Rico an IT consultant. Enrico worked in the same job for most of his life, had moved to the suburbs and paid for his children's education: a story of self-improvement based on the predictable structures of post-war American life. However, Rico and his partner have moved from job to job to gain advantage in America's flexible labour market. Consequently they have few lifetime friends because they are always uprooting. In this new economy everything is calculated in the short term, there is no commitment or loyalty and Rico sees the emphasis on teamwork and open discussion at work permeate the society to the detriment of his role as a father. To him open discussion and negotiation gives his children little of the scaffolding of values which would help them develop commitment, trust, obligation, and a sense of purpose. Instead they are free to challenge their parents and end up, in his view, disoriented. Yet as a role model he embodies the values he despises.

We may or may not share Rico's views about how children best develop but what this example illuminates is a paradox of modern societies: the decline of institutions that provide stability, such as trade unions and corporations that offer a job for life, and increasing individualization has led to a greater weight of expectations on education to make up for what the modern economy has removed. But if education is to instil the values that Rico feels he cannot, then it has a difficult task.[52]

The way in which the state as moral regulator has created the presumption that it is the individual's responsibility to become employable also entails changes in values and character.

2. Employability and the State Theory of Learning

The switch from the collective provision of employment to individual responsibility, as evidenced in Rico's case, is but one of the many ways in which we have seen the individual increasingly bearing the risks of market individualism and economic globalization. In transferring responsibility to the individual, the state has transformed the relationship between rights and responsibilities. Here the state not only acts as an administrator but also as a moral regulator.

In this new world the individual must internalize the need for self-regulation based on the individualistic assumption that if they are unemployed, then it must their fault. But, as Brown and Hesketh (2004) have argued, individuals also have to turn themselves into commodities that they can sell to employers, whatever their character and sensibilities. If they are to be successful, they may have to become 'players', prepared to play the game required by employers. When there is an excess of qualified talent, employers will look for those with the appropriate narratives of employability. Under such circumstances it is hard to see education as a process by which students seek to understand themselves and the world they inhabit, and easier to see it as a form of learning for self-promotion and trophy hunting.

The State Theory of Learning

Underpinning the doctrine of employability is the state guarantee that all will have the opportunity through education to make themselves employable. This has led to a focus on raising educational standards against the backdrop of a perceived global competition in education because the best educated will attract the best jobs. A range of policies and forms of global benchmarking have been introduced to raise standards, although what constitutes 'standards' is itself a matter of considerable debate. For example, if students can no longer spell as well as they did thirty years ago but have computer skills and better interpersonal communications, have standards risen or fallen?

For educationists, the problem is that standards are context-dependent: what is considered important in one era may not be as important in another. However, for sociologists there is another dimension to the debate on standards which concerns standardization. Within nation-states employers want credentials that signal a person's capabilities, but in global labour markets the standardization of qualifications has become even more important. Is an engineering degree from Tokyo University comparable to one from the Massachusetts Institute of Technology in the United States? It is for this reason that international league tables of performance have assumed such significance (Torrance, Ch. 56, below).

In order to drive up standards Britain and the United States have introduced a range of policies that have a direct bearing on the nature of teaching, what is learnt, and how it is learnt. We refer to this family of policies as a state theory of learning. These include parental choice, testing regimes, learning and knowledge, and the 'new managerialism' which assumes that educational institutions can and should be run as if they were businesses.

Teaching, Learning and Assessment

We have already seen that parental choice and market competition between schools is an attempt to drive up standards. Alongside market policies, a social technology has been implemented in which judgements are made about school performance on the basis of the repeated testing of children. Following Benveniste (Ch. 55, below) it can be argued that 'politics ... plays a fundamental role in shaping the design, implementation and impact of national assessment systems' and that testing and assessment are not just technical tools.

In England, repeated testing has been accompanied by a national curriculum and mandated periods of time in primary schools for teaching literacy and numeracy. For these periods and other elements in the curriculum the state also prescribes the form that teaching should take according to what it considers best practice. In the United States the testing regime has been introduced through the No Child Left Behind Act that requires every state to develop standardized tests and accountability systems. National targets are set to raise standards and there are, typically, penalties for those who do not meet the targets.

These testing regimes dovetail into market competition between schools because in England the test results are made public in the form of league tables which enable parents to make 'choices' about where to send their children. However, they change the nature of teaching and learning because they enable a system of surveillance of teachers' performance of a kind previously unknown. Where once teachers were seen as relatively autonomous professionals now, because of the demands for testing, we are entering what Hargreaves (Ch. 46, below) calls the 'post-professional' age. As Dillabough (Ch. 48, below) argues, we should see the concept of the professional in teaching as gendered and structured as much by political and social change as by teachers' narratives of their work.

It is worth looking at the implications of testing through the lens of the English case. In England, students are tested at ages 7, 11, 14, 16, 17, and 18. Initially the tests at 7, 11, and 14 were meant to reflect school performance, but they rapidly became instruments for sorting students by tracking or banding in secondary school. At the same time, they were also used to set targets for student achievement and to give senior managers in schools a diagnostic tool to see how departments and individual teachers were performing against so-called 'like schools'. In other words, an instrument that was initially used for one purpose rapidly came to be used for multiple purposes. It could be argued that when put to these uses it enables both students and teachers to reflect on their performance and to give both a much better idea of their progress. Alternatively, it can be seen as an overbearing machinery of surveillance and control, which is about sorting children and regulating their expectations while using what is in effect a statistical panopticon (Foucault 1991) to keep teachers in line.

The focal point for education thereby becomes 'the test' because the stakes are so high both for teachers and students. Inevitably, teachers spend a considerable time training students for tests or what is called 'exam technique'. It is important to see, from the perspective of government policy, how powerful the combination of market competition and the technology of testing is. As long as schools meet targets and educational standards, as defined by the tests, this combination of policies appears unassailable, especially to a public and media who typically take the reported statistics at face value.

But there are cracks appearing in the edifice that reveal serious problems of student learning and teacher competence (Thrupp & Hursh, Ch. 47). The broad assumption made by this social technology is that repeated high stakes testing provides students with the best possible form of learning, but we may doubt it. For a start, it assumes that rote memorizing is integral to learning because regardless of what attempts are made to encourage students to 'problem solve' in the tests, rote memory remains the key to success. In this educational climate, testing may encourage students to believe that rather than lifelong learning, there is a finite end to learning, the test. Equally, the work required in order to take the test successfully is heavily prescribed, arguably leaving little room for curiosity and an intrinsic desire to learn. Rather, the motivation for learning is externally imposed instead of intrinsically driven by students' curiosity and interest.

Broadfoot and Pollard (Ch. 52, below), formalize these observations by distinguishing between what they describe as 'liberal progressive' and 'performance' models of teaching, learning, and assessment, arguing that it is assessment based on regular testing which has given rise to what we are calling a state theory of learning. There are several further issues to emerge from their analysis, which is based on the work of Bernstein (Moore, Ch. 51, below). First, they ask whether students who have been subjected to the testing regime of the performance model will develop a desire to learn in the future, or if they think that learning is completed when they have sat the test. Their negative answer assumes greater importance when we consider the plea from many countries that people should engage in lifelong learning (Rubenson, Ch. 65, below).

Second, Bernstein saw changes in the framing of the curriculum, learning, and assessment as reflecting wider changes in society. In particular, he argued that the kind of fundamental changes that have been wrought by the state theory of learning could be seen as a reflection of changes in power that will advantage some students over others. Sociology of education has had little to say about theories of learning, but Bernstein provides the theoretical resources to make a start on this crucial area, as Arnot and Reay (Ch. 53, below) show. What their empirical research establishes is that the state theory of learning clearly advantages middle-class students and in some contexts girls over boys.[53]

Thirdly, in focusing on learning and testing, the state theory of learning has tended to downgrade issues concerning knowledge and the curriculum, yet knowledge is crucial to how students come to understand the world. The fundamental problem is the close link between knowledge and power. In the works of Marx, Said, Foucault, and Tuhiwai Smith, dominant groups are seen to promote their self-serving views of the world or impose silence instead of debate and analysis as in the case of gay students (Atkinson, Ch. 41, below). If it is imperative that the major threats now confronting the world are addressed in the core curriculum, and we believe they should be, then we need to treat knowledge claims with an appropriate degree of scepticism (Samoff and Stromquist 2001).[54]

Michael Young (Ch. 50, below), raises the question of the status of knowledge and its relationship to power in contemporary sociology of education, and comes to the view that while there are social foundations to knowledge, it has 'emergent properties that take it beyond the preservation of the interests of particular groups'.[55] He is acknowledging Bourdieu's point that in a certain sense the construction of knowledge is a 'cultural arbitrary', that it may be shaped by social practices and interests but that nevertheless it has value in helping us understand the world.[56] Knowledge in this sense is separate from the 'common sense' ways of knowing in everyday life. It is, for example, the knowledge associated with the sciences, mathematics, and history. But this presents the core pedagogic problem of how to enable students to move from common sense conceptions to those of the formalized disciplines of knowledge. Young notes that if, in educational institutions, we merely re-present common-sense knowledge we simply perpetuate inequalities. In raising these difficulties he asks some fundamental questions:

- Why do we want to persuade more young people to extend their schooling?
- What is distinctive about the kinds of knowledge that can be acquired in school or college?

Young's analysis is, in part, a critique of market-led policies in education because the state theory of learning ignores these hard questions. Rather, it is about developing the competencies necessary for the labour market and opposed to developing knowledge and understanding.

This is consistent with Bernstein's (Ch. 6, below) assertion that, for the first time in history, the focus on knowledge for the market has introduced a 'dehumanizing principle' into what he calls 'official' knowledge. Knowledge now is seen to flow like money to wherever it can create advantage and profit. It is dehumanizing because it is divorced from 'inwardness, from commitments, from personal dedication, from the deep structure of the self'. If we return to the fundamental tensions we identified at the beginning of this chapter, then if Bernstein is correct knowledge cannot be seen as a way of helping us develop a framework for living in which we can gain an understanding of the world and our place in it.

The New Managerialism and Accountability

The new managerialism makes several assumptions that distinguish it from previous practice in education. Broadly speaking it seeks to introduce some of the management techniques of private enterprise into state-funded and -provided forms of education on the grounds that it encourages initiative and a sense of professional control over educational policies and practices while also enabling sensitivity to local demands. At the same time it imposes financial disciplines on educational institutions because, not unlike businesses, there are clear limits to their spending. However, it also encourages private forms of fund raising. In borrowing from private enterprise it can be seen as consistent with the introduction of market competition in education.

Central to the new managerialism is the concept of performance (Ball, Ch. 47, below) in which the performance of teachers and lecturers is measured rather than judged (of course, this kind of measurement always involves judgement). As Ball notes, teachers are encouraged to value themselves and the work they do in terms of numerical targets. The bases of these measurements and calculations are the tests and targets discussed above. However, in the process educational values, which are always a matter of debate and deliberation, are being sidelined. As Ball (1994) noted, the management of education is becoming a technical issue divorced from those fundamental debates that Bloom (1997) saw as key to understanding the endemic conflict that underlies education. Instead the ends are determined by what the tests measure and the only issue that remains is to improve the means by which standards are raised. If this view is correct then it also means that it is not only students who are deprived of the potential of being able to reflect critically upon their place in the world, but also their teachers!

Against these views are those advocates of the system who defend these 'measures' because they create greater transparency within the business of education. However, this is to overlook the political dimensions of the system because it links educational accountability to political fortunes. Politicians determine targets so that, in principle, they are held responsible for the performance of the education system as a whole. However, as Pollitt (1990) argued, targets set for political purposes may not serve the interests of the public services for which they have been set. There is an assumption, underlying target setting, that social systems are like machines: once the target has been set, results will follow.

Social systems are not like machines and there are likely to be unintended consequences to setting targets in this high-stakes manner. In education, several have been identified. Equity may be one casualty. Gillbourn and Youdell (Ch. 54, below) coin the phrase 'educational triage' to demonstrate how target setting can generate unintended consequences. In England, the tests at 16 have five grades, A–E; however, the only grades that have broad legitimacy are A–C. These grades are a key mechanism of selection because it is only those with A–C grades in sufficient subjects who will be able to progress to university entry courses. In the schools that Gillbourn and Youdell studied, resources were spent on trying to move D level students up to C. Those judged to be performing at a lower standard and were sidelined many of them were from non-white ethnic groups.

It is not the case that all schools will follow such a triage strategy but it does demonstrate how educational values and decisions can be influenced and distorted by target setting of this kind. This may not be the only consequence of a system of education that operates with such rigid forms of target setting. Schools will also seek to rid themselves of those they consider most difficult or disruptive. However, as in the case of educational triage, it is hard to quantify the extent to which schools are 'off-loading' difficult students by buying places for them on courses run by other educational institutions. It is difficult to get a clear sense of how widespread these practices are and, therefore, what the trade-offs in improved performance, as measured by the tests, might be.

In its own terms, the system of targets is facing difficulties. Moreover, the initial improvements that accompanied this regime of accountability and testing have levelled off (Tymms 2004), while questions remain as to what is actually being learned by repeated testing. It is ironic that at the same time as England and the United States have embraced a regime of testing, East Asian societies such as Korea, Singapore, and Taiwan, highly successful in international comparative studies of educational performance, are attempting to turn their backs on examination-dominated systems to foster greater creativity and initiative in their students. Clearly, by focusing so intensely on student performance we can see that there is a dimension of the state theory of learning that is about social control: keeping students focused on the positional competition for credentials rather than searching for the key questions that are raised by contemporary life.

The state theory of learning is often seen as a key component of neo-liberal educational policy, although it could have applied equally in state socialist societies had the technology then been available. We think that it can also be understood as a genuine attempt to raise the performance of working-class students, at least in England. However, an audit of those less successful or failing may tell us that, at best, the results of this experiment in a state-imposed theory of learning are distinctly uneven (Feinstein, Ch. 28, below).

Education Under the Radar?

One of the dominant assumptions in the debate over the state theory of learning is that the kinds of issues and concerns raised here impact on the day-to-day reality of teachers' working lives. However, we also noted that it is difficult to obtain a comprehensive overview of how teachers negotiate the performance demands made upon them. Is it the case that debates over values and priorities are now redundant because the system of accountability predetermines them? Do teachers merely stick to the script or do they still exercise judgement as to how best to teach? Do students only learn what the tests demand?

Our view, and it is no more than a hypothesis, is that such an account is itself rather mechanistic, as teachers will seek to negotiate the system so that their values and skills are not wholly compromised. What is extraordinary about the state theory of learning is that the craft of teaching, where teaching styles need to be adjusted to classroom context, is undermined by a prescriptive system based on so-called 'best practice'. It suggests a confidence that is misplaced not only in identifying best practice but in the assumption that it can be transferred from one context to another with little difficulty.

However, even in these circumstances, we think that teachers will respond in different ways, given the conditions that they confront. And here, Bowles and Gintis's (1976) account of the different experiences of middle- and working-class schooling may still be relevant. They argued that the education of the middle classes was likely to be more expansive than that of the working classes: because working-class students do not have the cultural capital which creates an organic link between home and school, it is likely that schools will teach more to the test to improve their performances, while in middle class schools there may be time for a wider education because the students will already be better placed and more confident in taking the tests.

While we have considered the possibility of education taking place under the radar, we should also look at how other nations and cultures organize their educational systems. In a landmark comparative study Alexander (2001) has shown how the assumptions and practices underlying pedagogy and learning differ in a range of countries. In Ch. 49, below, he reflects further on some of the key issues he has raised. What he makes clear is that the state theory of learning is not the one best way to foster appropriate kinds of learning in primary schools. Indeed, the idea of a state-imposed single theory of learning is quite extraordinary. It assumes knowledge that we simply do not have about the nature of learning and its universal applicability.

Conclusion: 2020 Vision

One of the most striking features of formal education today is the unquestioning faith invested in it by individuals, families, communities, companies, governments, and nations. This chapter has attempted to assess whether such a faith is misplaced. In doing so it has posed some major questions concerning the future of education, especially in relation to the fundamental problems that we have outlined. Education is increasingly a servant of the economy but we have suggested that this is flawed in its own terms and for its blindness to the fundamental problems of the age.

In order to understand why nation-states have focused on the education gospel to the exclusion of other aims, we need to look at the fundamental changes in contemporary societies relating to individualization and to the many different impacts of globalization. It would be wrong simply to see the pursuit of the education gospel as the imposition of neo-liberal ideology without considering the conditions that have elevated this ideology to prominence. We tend to think of states as all-powerful, and indeed we have seen that there are different theories as to the power of the state but in our view there are limits within which states must operate. Here we assess the emergence of individualism, technology, and global policies and practices as defining some of the limits to state power before moving on to ask what many will consider the major question, which is whether there can be space in education to go beyond the education gospel to consider whether formal education has a role to play in helping to address the major problems that now confront us. These problems are intimately tied to economic questions: environmental survival, inequalities, and poverty cannot be understood without an appreciation of the political and economic factors that have led us into these desperate times. Of course there are different theories and views that will be taken on these problems, but what is important is that they can be debated in an informed way by everyone, because these problems will affect us all. This will involve a focus on an education for citizenship, which carries far greater weight than it is currently given. As we shall see, such an approach would require a fundamental transformation of education.[57]

Education, Technology, and Globalization

For most of the twentieth century, learning was understood to take place in formal educational institutions during a period of compulsory schooling, starting at about the age of 5 and finishing between the ages of 16 and 18. A proportion of students would stay on after that age to complete tertiary or higher education. Economic, social, and technological changes are now having a major impact on the nature and structure of educational institutions. Economically, there have been three profound shifts: the entry of women into the labour market in increasing numbers has raised the question of the availability of early childhood education; the move to a knowledge-based economy has led to the justification of a significant increase in the proportion of students going on to higher education; and intensified global competition, linked to technological innovations, has meant that the shelf-life of skills is reducing, leading to constant training and retraining. These developments have led to a redefinition of education from *education for life* to *education through life*. The boundaries between education and everyday life are collapsing.

Underlying these economic and social movements has been a new understanding of the nature of the learner and of learning signifying a fundamental change in our understanding of what education is for. 'Learning' signifies this change in at least two ways. First, the focus for education is on individuals, rather than a collective initiation into what a culture thinks is worthwhile. Second, what is learnt after secondary education is more open to individual choice, with the corollary that it does not need to take place in formal institutions.

The emphasis on individual learning has been reinforced by the advent of information technology. Hence, there are now many different ways in which learning can take place: the chat-room appears alongside the classroom: the face-to-face encounter between teacher and student can be replaced by e-mail: the textbook by the internet. Equally, schools, colleges, and universities are not the only places where people learn; in an era where lifelong learning has become an aspiration learning can as easily take place in the home or at work. The education system has lost its monopoly on information transmission, as the media, commercial software companies, and the internet all offer access to a bewildering array of information, although whether it is structured into the disciplines of knowledge remains an open question. What the education 'system' has not lost is the authority to 'certify' when learning, structured by forms of knowledge, has taken place, although this is likely to be subject to challenge in the future as private companies and international agencies seek to administer and brand their own credentials.[58]

These conceptual and technological changes in our understanding might appear to enable education to enter the glossy new technology revolution. While the consensus view of lifelong learning speaks to the growing opportunities for personal development and a broadening of the way we understand human capability, conflict theorists point to the dangers of increasing surveillance and disciplining of the individual (Foucault 1977), where every aspect of our lives comes under the formal gaze of the educational authorities, with the power to judge what constitutes 'prior learning' and 'real learning'.[59] In *Imprisoned in the Global Classroom,* Illich and Verne (1976: 14) reject the consensus view of what they call permanent education. They suggest that 'professional educators, through the institution of permanent education, succeed in convincing men [and women] of their permanent incompetence. The ultimate success of the schooling instrument is the extension of its monopoly, first to all youth, then to every age, and finally to all areas.' But this account is one in which educators are not seen as opening the doors to autonomy but of being complicit in a system of surveillance and control.

These contrasting interpretations of the shift from 'education for life' to 'learning through life' may represent two horns of an uncomfortable dilemma. While the increasing emphasis on individual learners, subjectivities, identities, and the self can be interpreted as an intensification of surveillance of which the state theory of learning is an exemplification, the same trends can also be interpreted as a prerequisite for democracy, freedom and self-actualization. The crucial question is how learning through life is interpreted. If students see it as a means to economic ends alone, then the outcomes of this increased investment in education is that we are producing ever more clever, calculating pleasure machines. In contrast, if the outcomes to education are that students become more conscious of what they owe to society and the environment, then we are one step towards an understanding of how the fundamental problems that confront us require collective solutions.

Here we need to appreciate that there are downsides to both individualization and market individualism. The social fragmentation that characterizes the United States and Britain are mirrored at the individual level. The downside of individualization has long been recognized; as Erich Fromm (1942: 29), observed,

> if the economic, social and political conditions on which the whole process of human individuation depends, do not offer a basis for the realization of individuality . . . while at the same time people have lost their ties which gave them security, this lag makes freedom an unbearable burden. It then becomes identical with doubt, with a kind of life which lacks meaning and direction.

This is the same tension that recently led Sennett to ask how human beings can develop 'a narrative of identity and life history in a society composed of episodes and fragments' (1998: 26).[60]

This takes us back to a consideration of Durkheim and the content of education. Durkheim (Ch. 2, below) argued that education consisted of a 'methodical socialization' of the young. This was intended to develop and unite the 'individual being' (personality, character, abilities) and 'social being' (ideas, sentiments, practices of the wider society), constituting 'the end of education'. For Durkheim the role of education was to give people meaning to their lives in order to overcome problems of alienation and insecurity:

> We need to believe that our actions have consequences which go beyond the immediate moment . . . Otherwise they would be too insignificant: scarcely more than a thread would separate them from the void . . . Only actions which have a lasting quality are worthy of our volition, only pleasures which endure are worthy of our desires.[61]

The question is whether education can compensate for the 'episodes and fragments' which seems to characterize much of life. It is into this void that market individualism may step by offering commodities as a substitute for the construction of a meaningful life or indeed sustainable life. To paraphrase the eminent economist J. K. Galbraith, would the American (and by extension European and Asian) middle classes defend their lifestyle to the point of extinction? The response given by consensus theorists, at least in regard to environmental sustainability, will be that technology will once more come to the rescue. There is an understandable assumption that technology can always produce 'win-win' outcomes without needing to challenge existing social classes or the power structures that sustain them. This has certainly been the hope of American presidents such as George W. Bush. Yet we should be cautious. David Noble (1999), one of the leading sociologists of technology, has drawn an explicit connection between Christianity and the origins of faith in technology in the United States. This time the problems identified by Hobsbawm seem too complex for a simple technological fix which is why the focus on the prospects for an education for citizenship is so important.

The Prospects for an Education for Citizenship

Today the complexity of individual aspirations, cultural differences, and social relations make the development of social solidarity problematic, although not impossible. The idea of the common school promoted by Dewey was designed to develop the understanding and solidarity required in a democracy. However, if students are to be separated in their education by class, gender, ethnicity, and religion, on what basis can they appreciate the wants and needs of strangers—those educated in different ways to their own? Here the writing of Kathleen Lynch and her associates may be important because they argue that all should have an equal right to an education which seeks to understand and foster what they call, 'care, love, and solidarity'. In their view, there is an inequality, typically based on gender, as regards emotional development, which recognizes that as human beings we are both vulnerable and interdependent (Baker, Lynch, Cantillon, and Walsh 2004: Lynch and Baker 2005). While such a view is clearly antithetical to the dominant vocational aims of education, nevertheless it is hard to argue that an understanding of the emotions in relation to vulnerability and interdependence is not crucial to citizenship, especially in a global context where our common humanity and suffering is beamed into our living rooms. In this regard, we have yet to achieve the promise of both individualization and globalization as understood by Dewey (Ch. 4, below) in the early twentieth century: 'Travel, economic and commercial tendencies, have at present gone far to break down external barriers; to bring people and classes into closer and more perceptible connection with one another. It remains for the most part to secure the intellectual and emotional significance of this physical annihilation of space.'

There are several constraints to an education for citizenship that would encourage students to reflect and act on the global consequences of their actions and those undertaken in the national interest. The first ties global migration to the education gospel. Mitchell's (2001) study of Chinese immigrants in Vancouver illustrates the point. She describes a conflict between the immigrants and locals over the purposes of schooling. For the locals it was as much to do with an initiation into the cultural context of society as it was with credentialism. However, the Chinese immigrants, who were keenly aware of global change and possibilities, were more concerned with grades and credentials. Mitchell understands this disagreement to reflect a tension between globalization and citizenship. Given that the Chinese were migrants, it is quite possible that what they wanted for their children was entry into the global labour market, where for locals context was as significant. For the Chinese migrants citizenship was perhaps secondary because a sense of identity could be gained through strong family ties that spanned the globe, rather than being situated in one place. Mitchell's identification of this tension is important for understanding the limits and possibilities in relation to formal education.

This discussion may offer a clue to why so much emphasis is placed on the relationship between education, employment, and economic growth. The focus on education as an individual investment in future employment and national prosperity sidesteps the difficulties inherent in identity politics. The need to make a living and replenish the national coffers is something that most people can agree about. In the early decades of the twentieth century Weber observed that 'behind all the present discussion of the foundations of the educational system, the struggle of the "specialist type of man" against the older type of "cultivated man" is hidden at some decisive point'. This struggle is now being played out on a new global stage.[62] Yet if we reinterpret the notion of a 'cultivated man' in terms of an education for understanding oneself and one's place in the world, then this is surely a prerequisite for citizenship.

Secondly, we have seen that national social solidarity was conceived on the basis of the white male model, but as ties of hierarchy and deference have been stripped away so many different groups—women, ethnic minorities, post-colonial peoples, gays, and those with disabilities—have all demanded a right to an equal education. As several contributors to this volume have noted, the power to name and represent is crucial to the education of those who were previously excluded. This conflict not only concerns the right to a democratic voice, but the idea that in order to be successful in education students need to be secure in their cultural identity. Students need to know where they have come from to be able to represent the world in their terms. This has led to calls for culturally autonomous schooling in which students from different groups are taught in their own language and culture.

However, as Torres has pointed out, the nature of democracy and citizenship needs to be rethought because the present system gives power to the majority enabling the aspirations of minorities to be ignored. These are difficult issues. In France, the notion of a strong state based on French traditions remains in education and this has been a cause for conflict between the state and Muslim women students who have sought to wear the hajib or the jilbab. The simple act of putting on a particular garment, by these young women, has ignited debates about the nature of multiculturalism, racism, and colonialism (Benhabib, Ch. 10, below). How are we to understand education's role in fostering social cohesion and citizenship in the light of debates such as these? Benhabib's suggestion that we are capable of developing multiple identities and allegiances is clearly possible, but not without a degree of tension. This is especially problematic now, when those of Muslim faith of middle or far Eastern heritage find themselves in a 'war on terror' in which they are often demonized. There is clearly an urgent need for comparative research into how students from different religious and ethnic backgrounds develop their identities under these conditions.

In turn this leads to the problem of whether education can promote equality of opportunity or whether it merely reproduces inequalities. The consensus view of meritocratic competition assumes that educational and occupational selection will be based on individual achievement, judged by tests, examinations, and credentials. However, the increasing emphasis on 'personal' capital—the extent to which the self can be packaged to capitalize on those personal qualities valued by employers (Brown, Ch. 26, below)—crucially depends on cultural capital rather than 'innate' differences between candidates. The veil of meritocratic expertise that shrouded the relationship between education, jobs, and rewards has been lifted. It has exposed a system of social selection, where social confidence, life experience, and access to cultural assets play a vital role in determining the outcome of the competition for a livelihood. These new processes of selection appear to be another turn of the screw in the reproduction of inequality in Western societies.

Gellner's (1983: 24–5) account of the rise of industrial societies led him to conclude that 'modern society is not mobile because it is egalitarian; it is egalitarian because it is mobile'. However, the development of a global labour market for some professional and middle-class workers also threatens the equation of mobility and egalitarianism because through the international school system and elite universities parents can buy much of their children's educational success. Therefore, the extent to which the education system is a source of opportunity not only relates to questions of social justice but also of citizenship. Those excluded from such privileged educational tracks may see the education system as inherently unfair and may therefore fail to commit to the kind of education and social solidarity that are necessary to address the fundamental problems we confront. In this respect, education for citizenship has not only assumed greater importance, but places new demands on the young and old alike. If students are to be encouraged to reflect critically and to act on the fundamental problems that we raised earlier, on what basis is 'global citizenship' to be understood?[63] There are legal rights and responsibilities in relation to the nation-state that every student can learn but there is no such global framework. Moreover, it requires a degree of imagination to see the connections between the local, national, and global. In what is an under-researched area, there are studies which show that young people can see how global change affects local conditions and vice versa (Manson 2004). Research on social solidarity or cohesion (Green, Preston, and Sabates 2003) also suggests that education may have a positive effect on some dimensions of civic and political participation.[64]

To capitalize on the insights gained from these studies, there is an urgent need to examine how individual and group differences can contribute to an understanding of our common humanity. We would take issue with Bloom's (1997) view that cultural assimilation is essential to democracy, but ways must be found to overcome the problem of what Paul Hirst calls the 'Ottomanization' of society where plural and largely self-regulating communities coexist side by side with different rules and standards. The account Hirst gives is to argue that the 'acceptance of a substantial measure of self-regulation' will be 'at the price of mutual tolerance', as 'no society has been devised that lets each do exactly as he or she will, contribute what he or she wishes, and yet have the enjoyment of the security and common advantages of a community'.[65] However, the difficulty with this view concerns the question of how, under these conditions, tolerance is to be engendered given the inequalities in gender (Arnot and Dillabough, Ch. 11, below), ethnicity, race, class, and disability. Moreover, even if such a project could succeed in one enlightened country, the fundamental problems we have addressed in this introduction are intimately tied to global developments. There is an urgent need to rethink the social, economic and political foundations for democracy in a global context (see Olssen, Ch. 18, below). Dewey (Ch. 4, below) suggests, 'since a democratic society repudiates the principle of external authority, it must find a substitute in voluntary disposition and interest', which he thinks, 'can be created only by education'.[66] In the present age Dewey's insight has particular resonance because as individualization and market individualism have eroded some of the important foundations for the promotion of democracy, such as the trade union movement, so education assumes greater importance.

Dewey's point brings us back to the social conditions that would enable an effective education for citizenship and to the question raised at the start of this chapter as to whether education is in some sense separate and removed from society so that it can act on it as an independent force for progress. However, the implications of our discussion are that if such an aim is to be realized in practice rather than just in rhetoric, it would require far greater equality and recognition of differences between social groups than is now the case. As we have seen, inequalities can undermine any possibility of the social consensus necessary for a collective approach to solving the fundamental problems we have outlined. But inequality is not just a matter for education but for the structuring of the labour market and the welfare state, as the research from the Nordic countries we have referred to shows.[67] Without the appropriate economic and social conditions issues of social justice and democracy will not be settled. And, arguably, these are the necessary conditions for addressing the most fundamental problem of all, the sustainability of the planet. It is with these concerns that an education for citizenship would be focused, and it is for this reason that we referred earlier to the idea that education for effective citizenship would require a fundamental transformation.[68]

Such a transformation, we have suggested, would require three conditions to be addressed: a change away from the neo-liberal reinvention of the state with its focus on the 'education gospel'; a greater equality within and between nations and finally, an education in terms of both processes and content that enabled greater understanding of oneself and one's place in the world, including the development of what Lynch calls, care, love and solidarity. Over and above these would be exposure to the best scientific and social scientific theories and debates concerning our continued existence.

When confronted with the problems we have outlined, it is difficult to avoid the conclusion that in neo-liberal nation-states education's role has been narrowed in ways that preclude all but the imperatives of personal and national economic growth. In turn this raises important questions: are the neo-liberal nation-states the model that all nation-states will need to follow if they are to survive global economic competition? Is there a logic of convergence to globalization that will drive nation-states in the same direction? If so what price will be placed upon the autonomy of the nation-state, of education, and the individual? More optimistically we can ask, what opportunities are there for alternatives that give greater emphasis to an education for citizenship? What social and economic conditions would have to change or could be changed in order to provide a more balanced education?[69]

Finally, we may note one of the many paradoxes of the current situation, as formal education has been extended in Anglo-Saxon societies, so its influence on the development of individuals' critical thinking may have declined; it may be that the media, NGOs, and global social movements may have more chance to foster critical thinking than formal education.[70] Yet as every teacher knows it is possible to spark a curiosity and passion that extends far beyond the calculation of economic benefit. In this human quality lies the possibility for progress.

Rethinking the Sociology of Education

It will be clear from this introduction that education has taken centre stage in policymaking. Yet the discipline has been marginalized both by policymakers and universities. The chapters included in this book all testify to the power of this area to provide and test explanations and to illuminate the key issues that should concern policymakers and our colleagues in education, so why doesn't the discipline have a higher profile? The answer to this question is complex and this is one of the reasons why policymakers do not turn to its explanations and prescriptions.

Policymakers prefer 'magic bullets', particularly in education, where simple ideas are superficially attractive. The introduction of markets in education is a good example as nothing seemed to be more obvious than to give parents greater choice in the schooling of their children and nothing could be more complex than to understand the outcomes. But if this is true then we owe it to students, citizens, and policymakers to ensure that complex ideas are presented clearly; it is not easy to do but it is essential in a democracy.

The alternative is that we create gurus and acolytes that speak a language that few outside a privileged circle can understand. Of course, each theory or more general intellectual approach to problems has its own terminology, but explaining the assumptions underlying theoretical terms in clear language should be something that we should strive towards. This book abounds with crucial ideas that challenge the rhetoric surrounding education. It also tackles fundamental questions about the causes of inequality and the conditions for effective education for citizenship. These are not obscure areas of investigation and they need a public airing.

There are times, however, when the discipline has taken its eye off the ball. Child poverty and income inequality have blighted both the developing and developed world. These should be issues that are central to the interests of sociologists of education but there are few papers on these subjects in our journals. Research on social deprivation and equality of opportunity once defined the sociology of education. Now it is economists and social policy analysts who have taken the lead. Equally, it might have been thought that the connections between education and the economy would have been central to the concerns of sociologists of education given the education gospel but while there has been more interest in this area, it remains under-researched by those trained in the discipline.

An area where sociologists of education have shown considerable strength concerns an ability to think reflexively about the discipline, and we could not complete this introduction without attempting to be reflexive ourselves. Connell (1997), in an important paper about the foundations of sociology, has argued that the approach in which the great founders, Durkheim, Weber, and Marx are given a central place is a product of forms of nineteenth-century colonial domination that excludes the key variables of gender, ethnicity, and imperialism. While there has been a debate about Connell's view, which has been challenged by Randell Collins (1997), he raises an important question, most sharply posed by Foucault (Tuhiwai Smith, Ch. 38, below), about in whose interests social science research is being conducted.[71]

It is the case that we have chosen to open this book with these three 'great' men. There are at least two reasons for doing so. Their concepts and intellectual ambitions remain indispensable aspects of the sociology of education: notions of class, exploitation, imperialism, and credential competition, remain central to our analyses. But Connell is right. We cannot do justice to our discipline by just drawing upon the foci of their lenses; we need to broaden our perspectives and view of the world from different vantage points. But we cannot do so, without engaging with them, and criticizing and updating their theories. In this process we need to acknowledge that we are standing on their shoulders.

NOTES

1. Durkheim (1977 [1904]), *The Evolution of Educational Thought* (London: Routledge & Kegan Paul) 7.
2. As we shall see, this is a view that has come under sustained attack by postmodernists and post-structuralists, some of whom deny there are any foundations to reason.

3. The United States and Britain make up half of all military spending comprising some half a trillion US dollars. They spend between them $26.8 billion in aid. (Stockholm International Peace Research Institute, June 2005). Much of the aid is related to security. See Woods (2005).

4. Jared Diamond (2005) has fleshed out Hobsbawm's concern by analysing historical examples where societies have failed to survive, sometimes through the destruction of the eco-systems that have sustained them. For approaches to environmental sustainability in education see Scott and Gough (2003) and Reid (2005).

5. These are quotes from speeches written by C. E. Beeby for the Minister for Education in New Zealand, Peter Fraser, in 1939. Quoted in Alcorn (1999). These views are representative of the struggle for the democratization of education in the West.

6. We use the term 'industrial society' because, while most modern societies are to varying degrees capitalist, the underlying change towards individualization, which we discuss subsequently, has to do with the processes of industrialization and the creation of conurbations. Anglo-Saxon capitalism in America and Britain has given a particular emphasis to individualism which we discuss under the heading of market individualism.

7. Durkheim also argued that the only way of grasping the full ramifications of an organic analysis of society was through the application of a truly scientific method for the social sciences.

8. The theories that we discuss in terms of consensus and conflict approaches often have fundamentally different world-views and are therefore not often open to synthesis. Rather we need to judge between them, where possible. This is as true of theories within the conflict tradition as those within the consensus tradition and it applies to theories of globalization as much as it does to those of the school–society relationship. See Burris (1987) for an attempt to reconcile Marxist and Weberian theories. Mouzelis (2000) examines the ways in which there may be a way of 'bridging' between theories. For a discussion of the issues involved in theory appraisal see Lauder, Brown, and Halsey (2004). Our thanks to Maria Balarin for drawing our attention to the above papers.

   Some have argued that the debate on class is no longer between neo-Marxists and Weberians but is about the relationship between class structure and culture. In this debate Bourdieu's theories have been central, see Devine, Savage, Scolt, and Crompton (2005). However, for analytic purposes we have retained the core distinctions between the two classical theories of class.

9. There are several reasons for this. Neo-Marxist structuralist theories could not account for agency; individuals were seen as passive in the face of the capitalist system. They also failed to take into account other forms of inequality such as gender and ethnicity and they failed to consider how identities are constructed in an increasingly multicultural world. Yet, if we assume as some do that security in one's heritage and identity are crucial to educational success, then this constitutes a major omission in Marxist thought. The exception lies in the work of Willis (1977) and Ch. 35 below. Willis combined agency, structure, and identity in his material and cultural analysis of working-class 'lads' in late-1970s Britain.

10. While many of these debates have been viewed by educational theorists as radical breaks with previous moments, they doubtless represent currents of thinking which have a more venerable historical provenance. For example, the conceptual apparatus, including 'discourse', 'regulation', or 'surveillance' used by sociologists of education following thinkers such as Judith Butler (1990), (see Bronwyn Davies 1989), Michel Foucault (1991) (see Julie McCleod 2005) or Nikolas Rose (1999) (see Kari Dehli 1996), could be seen to be intellectually linked to Althusserian or Gramscian formulations such as 'consensus

seeking' or 'hegemony' which remain more typically associated with modern or structuralist accounts of social inequality. The current emphasis on the cultural turn in the sociology of education is associated above all with a Foucauldian perspective. Once again, however, when we examine this more recent thinking on the subject of power, it is evident that new sociological concepts (discourse, surveillance, regulation, governmentality) have been derived in particular ways from earlier conceptualizations (Althusser, Gramsci, and above all, Nietzsche).

11. A final concern is that much of the creativity implicit in post-structural thought—such as the break with class conflict, economic formalism, or theoretical formalism more generally—had already been charted, at least in part, previously. Weber, for example, almost six decades before Foucault, had been interested in culture and its powerful role in shaping citizens and state life, which are evident in many of his writings. As Giddens (1976) writes: 'These writings took their inspiration in some substantial part from the so-called historical school of economics which, in conscious divergence from British political economy, stressed the need to examine economic life within the context of the historical development of culture as a whole.' The work of Tawney (1982) and T. H. Marshall (1950) can also be seen in this light.

12. There are reinterpretations of some of the leading postmodern thinkers which have challenged the common anti-realist interpretations of Foucault and Derrida. For example, Clark (2003) and Critchley (1999) in relation to Derrida and Olseen (2004) in relation to Foucault. We are indebted for these references to Maria Balarin.

13. Émile Durkheim, *The Division of Labour in Society*, trans. George Simpson (New York: Macmillan, 1933), Preface to the 1st edn., 37.

14. See also Larry Elliott, 'Pigs will not clean their own sties', *Guardian*, 22 November 2002. He reports figures presented by Paul Krugman that show that between 1970 and 1999 the average adjusted salary rose by around 10% from $32,522 to $35,864. By comparison the top 100 CEOs saw their remuneration increase from $1.3 m to $37.5 m, more than a 1,000 times the pay of the ordinary worker.

15. Beck suggests that the 'reflexive modernization' as he calls it 'disembeds and re-embeds the cultural prerequisites of social classes with forms of the *individualization* of social inequality. That means, on the one hand, that the disappearance of social classes and the abolition of social inequality no longer coincide. Instead, the blurring of social classes (in perception) runs in tandem with the exacerbation of social inequality, which now does not follow large identifiable groups in the lifeworld, but is instead fragmented across (life) phases, space and time' (ibid.). The key here is 'in perception' as most people would agree that perceptions of class identification have changed, especially as a consequence of de-industrialization. But this is very different from assuming that the material conditions in which people live are not shaped by our economic relations within capitalism.

16. We owe this phrase to Sean Hargreaves-Heap.

17. See, for a contemporary example, Jacques Chirac's rejection of the EU proposal to liberal services in Europe in which he refers to the threat of neo-liberalism.

18. Darwin borrowed this phrase from Herbert Spencer (1820–1903), an English sociologist who strongly advocated individualism and laissez-faire economics as the foundations for social progress. Summarizing Spencer's views on the evolution of society Carneiro wrote: 'He held that the rapid elimination of unfit individuals from society through natural selection would benefit the race biologically and that the state should therefore do nothing to relieve the condition of the poor, whom he assumed to be the less fit. Spencer also maintained that the economic system works best if each individual is allowed to seek his own private interests and that consequently the state should not intervene in the

economy except to enforce contracts and to see to it that no one infringes upon the rights of others. He believed that in the ensuing competition, the fittest business enterprises and economic institutions would survive' (R. Carneiro, *International Encyclopedia of the Social Sciences* (New York: Macmillan/Free Press, 1968), xv. 126.

19. There are significant differences between these thinkers; therefore neo-liberalism should not be considered a unified body of thought. However, the assumptions tend to be held in common between them.
20. There are some important differences here between Hobbes, Smith, and Hayek.
21. Conflict theorists have shown how far the reality is from the ideal with respect to class, race, gender, and disability. However, the problem is that in making these criticisms they may have opened the door to more selective forms of education as implied by market systems of education.
22. Not all proponents would consider themselves or be considered neo-liberals. See Lauder, Hughes, et al. (1999).
23. We say that 'globalization' constitutes a new phase of capitalist development. This assumes that capitalism and the nation-state also represented a phase in capitalist development, but to our knowledge the phases from feudalism to national capitalism to global capitalism remain to be theorized. Marx (Ch.1, below) certainly foresaw this phase of globalization but overlooked the significance of nationalism. The theoretical approaches taken in this section are similar to those outlined by Ngaire Woods (2001).
24. For a critique of the view that globalization in the form of increasing 'free trade' leads to a reduction in poverty see Wade (2004).
25. Ronald Reagan may have been exaggerating when he observed 'we meant to change a nation, and instead we changed a world', but he, along with Margaret Thatcher in the United Kingdom, did have a significant role to play in the neo-liberal drive to globalization (Brown and Lauder 2001).
26. Fordism is a technique based on breaking down production into its simplest component parts. It assumes a distinction between thought and execution in which executives and engineers do the thinking and production line workers execute simple repetitive tasks. It has been calculated that production workers exercise more skill driving to work than at work (Brown and Lauder 2001).
27. See Joseph A. Schumpeter, *The Theory of Economic Development* (New York: Oxford University Press, 1961); Randall Collins, *Weberian Sociological Theory* (New York: Cambridge University Press, 1986); Basil Blackwell and Samuel Eilon, *The Global Challenge of Innovation* (Oxford: Butterworth Heinemann, 1991). In such companies improvements in productivity depend upon the 'organic' integration of applied science, technological innovation, free-flow information networks, and high-trust relations between management and multiskilled workers. The increasing costs of errors, demand for quality control, and for multiskilled workers with a conceptual grasp of a large section of the production process or office activities has made the specialized division of labour in Fordism a source of organizational inefficiency.
28. See the discussion by Guile (Ch. 24, below) especially in relation to the work of Knorr-Cetina (1999, 2002).
29. John H. Dunning and Karl P. Sauvant, 'Introduction: Transnational Corporations in the World Economy, in United Nations Conference of Trade and Development (UNCTAD)', *Transnational Corporations and World Development* (Boston, Mass.: International Thompson Business Press, 1996), p. xi; United Nations Centre on Transnational Corporations, *Transnational Corporations in World Development: Trends and Prospects* (New

York: United Nations, 1988). See also Grazia Ietto-Gillies, *International Production: Trends, Theories, Effects* (Cambridge, Mass.: Polity, 1994).

30. See Peter Martin, 'The global company: the future depends on choice: global presence or local defense?' *Financial Times*, 7 November 1997.

31. For interesting educational responses to the consequences of 9/11 see Rizvi (2003) and Errante (2003). See also Kellner (2004). For more general accounts which show how difficult it is to pin down the concept of empire see Barber (2004), Ferguson (2004), Johnson (2004), and Mann (2003).

32. For an account of the difficulties in using education as the route to higher-skilled work in South Africa see Kraak and Young (2005).

33. We might see this strategy as one of Empire because of the more abrasive rhetoric and military adventures of the neo-conservatives but it also reflects America's perennial attempt to promote international democracy and free trade alongside its national interests (Ikenberry 2001).

34. The discussion focuses on education but for a more general analysis consistent with our argument that sees American influence as tempered by the interests of other nation-states see Woods (2003).

35. For further analysis of the implications of the international trade in higher education and lifelong learning see Heyneman (2001), Sidhu (2002), and Larsen and Vincent-Lancrin (2002).

36. When looking at globalization and education there is a series of questions that we should ask about selection, equality of opportunity, social class, changing educational practices, and the changing personal and professional identities of students and educators.

37. We are indebted to Professor Jeff Thomson, Department of Education at the University of Bath, for this information.

38. It might be argued that the educational conditions for the emergence of a transnational class (Sklair 2001; Robinson 2004) is being made possible by the international schools and a globalizing market for higher education. But the idea that a common form of schooling will give rise to a common perspective or consciousness assumes that the students from these schools see themselves as global citizens rather than having a commitment to the welfare of their country of origin or heritage. In so far as they are influenced by their family background, it should be noted that their parents comprise a heterogeneous community ranging from multinational and diplomatic employees to those working for NGOs. It would be surprising if the children from such a mixed community emerged with the same dominant view of globalization and its implications for solving fundamental problems. That said, this is an area that is greatly under-researched and more needs to be understood about how these emerging global factors, the labour market, and education systems are combining to (re)produce inequalities and different world-views.

39. This is one of the considerations that has lent some plausibility to the idea of the emergence a transnational ruling class.

40. There are substantial differences in the theories of the composition of such a global or transnational class between these authors.

41. This is a hypothesis that merits investigation, although it should be noted that students at these schools come from diverse national and cultural backgrounds. For a discussion of some of the key issues in relation to international schools see Hayden, Thompson, and Walker (2002).

42. Migrants do not work simply for individual gain. There are many poorer countries where the repatriation of funds by migrant workers forms a significant part of their national income. For example, Jordan receives 21.8 per cent, El Salvador 13.3 per cent, Jamaica 10.7 per cent, and Sri Lanaka 6.9 per cent of their Gross Domestic Product from remittances. For poorer countries these are significant sums. Data from *Financial Times*, 30 July 2003, p. 15.

43. For a discussion of the political economic changes in the 1980s and 1990s and their impact on the way social class has been restructured, see Brown and Lauder (2001).

44. We say 'conspicuous' because McSherry's point about the significance of IPRs also applies to these universities and questions are still appropriate as to how much intellectual freedom they have when tied to commercial interests.

45. Both the accounts by Naidoo and Jamieson and by Waks derive from a sociological/political economy tradition that sees educational systems as created and maintained by conflict between social groups. However, there is an alternative consensus account appraised by Dale (2000) which views the curriculum in education systems around the world as converging as part of a process of modernization within nation-states. He argues that the Common World Educational Culture (CWEC) theory, developed by John Meyer and colleagues, explains curricular models through universal models of education, state, and society. In their view, there is an international society made up of autonomous world states that are all progressing towards a common world educational culture. The values of this culture are those of Western modernity, in which the notions of progress and justice are central to determining the relationship between the individual and the state.

46. Hobson and Ramesh (2002) review these positions. We have stated them rather baldly for reasons of space; they characterize them more subtly.

47. For a critical analysis of TRIPS see the special issue of the journal *Globalisation, Societies and Education*, 1/3 (2003).

48. We owe this phrase to Harry Daniels.

49. In practice Keynesian policies to create jobs still operate. In Britain, since 2000, the fastest-growing sector has been the public sector, for high-skilled jobs in teaching and the health service.

50. Working out why some economies are successful when others are not has been one of the major endeavours of the past thirty years. If the secrets of success can be divined, then all that remains is to debate how the spoils of economic growth are to be allocated. But changing contexts make formulas for success difficult to replicate (see Landes 1999).

51. Foucault and Bourdieu may be particularly helpful in this respect. See Olssen, Codd, and O'Neill (2004) for an account of how Foucault can be used to understand the construction of the 'citizen' in a neo-liberal state. Foucault emphazises that subjectivity is not constructed only by the state, as has been implied by the analysis of the effects of globalization. However, we should not underestimate the state's power in this respect. As Bourdieu (2000: 175) notes, 'the State institutes and inculcates common symbolic forms of thought, social frames of perception, understanding or memory, State forms of classification or, more precisely, practical schemes of perception, appreciation and action'.

52. There is another side to Rico: he is a cultural conservative, intolerant of 'social parasites' such as welfare mothers and homosexuals, and a believer in 'Draconian standards of communal behaviour'. For Sennett, Rico's cultural conservatism fills a void in what is missing and it may explain aspects of recent political behaviour in the United States. But it also raises further profound questions for education. Part of education is about

challenging orthodoxy, of risk taking, yet this is the opposite of what Rico wants for his children; he wants education to instil certainties.

53. Over the past few years Bernstein's work has attracted even greater interest than before, in part because he does provide the promise of understanding both the intended and unintended effects of the state theory of learning.

54. Key to this view is the distinction between foundational and judgemental relativism. We would reject the idea that knowledge can be built on certain foundations such as observation, but also reject the idea that we cannot give good reasons for judging between theories. A thoroughgoing relativism entails both foundational and judgemental relativism. See Lauder, Brown, and Halsey (2004).

55. Young (1971) was the first to raise the question of the status of knowledge and its relationship to power in contemporary sociology of education, and has had a profound impact on the discipline. However, as will be clear from this chapter, he now rejects judgemental relativism, opening the way to asking some critical questions about the nature of the curriculum.

56. This is a position that has also been argued by Nash.

57. We stress the idea of an education for citizenship rather than citizenship education because while there have been worthy attempts to develop the latter, in many cases they appear to be band-aids for problems which are by-products of elements of globalization and market individualism. An education for citizenship would involve far more than just making time in the curriculum. See the discussion following.

58. This poses a fundamental dilemma for neo-liberal states. On the one hand they encourage corporations to make profit from education, and on the other education's role in the economy can only work if there is a standardization of qualifications.

59. The increase in the surveillance and control of teachers is often taken as indicating a lack of trust in professionals provoked by individualization and the decline of deference. However, another explanation we can infer from Bauman (2002) is that in an era of globalization the state is becoming separated from the nation, precisely because of the flow of people across borders and the loss of a national culture. A Foucaultian reading might suggest that the desire by the state to increase control over the population through various social technologies has been extended to education precisely because there is a lack of identity between the nation and the state. Hence a distrust of the nation by the state, including state workers such as teachers, and the attempt to reinvent the state to create an identity between state and nation.

60. The application of Sennett's thought to education is long overdue, especially in the light of his most recent book (2003).

61. Quoted from Émile Durkheim, *Selected Writings*, ed. and trans. Anthony Giddens (Cambridge: Cambridge University Press, 1972).

62. The importance attached to vocational purpose follows a secular trend as Floud and Halsey (1961: 9) observed, 'the striking development of secondary and higher education over the past quarter of a century has been accompanied by a strong trend towards vocationalism. Education increasingly takes on the character of 'training'; specialization takes place earlier, is more thorough-going, and is increasingly of a kind directly related to the requirements of modern trades and professions.' In some respects the distinction between the generally and vocationally educated is no longer as strong as it might have been. Employers have broadened the notion of employability to include the 'soft' currencies (interpersonal skills, drive, charisma, appearance, etc.) as well as the 'hard'

currencies (credentials, work experience, sporting achievements, etc.), the self has become the 'new vocational' (Brown and Hesketh 2004).

63. For an account which is critical of the idea of global citizenship see Miller (2000). However, see Marshall's (2003) review of research on global education for a different perspective.

64. While sociology of education has developed a robust understanding of the degree to which education reproduces inequalities, there is an urgent need for research on how education informs people's understanding of fundamental problems and their role in relationship to them. Sennett (1998) has opened up a window with a view that we need to exploit.

65. Paul Hirst, *Associative Democracy: New Forms of Economic and Social Governance* (Cambridge: Polity Press), 66, 61.

66. Dewey rightly emphasizes the individual in this context. Arnot (2004) notes in her discussion of Beck and Beck-Gernsheim's account of individualization that political action will no longer be based on traditional communities and organizations such as trade unions but on what are perceived to be shared risks. Individuals will act on the basis of alliances created to address those risks. What this analysis omits is the possibility of a collective backlash against aspects of globalization related to immigration.

67. Comparative analyses of the effects of globalization are crucial in this context although we should beware easy recipes that ignore the historical and institutional factors that structure the educational system.

68. For example, Hills (2004: 69) reports on research in the European Union ascertaining people's views as to why there are some that 'live in want'. The responses are significant. Respondents in more collective societies such as Sweden and Finland see injustice as a significant factor, whereas in Britain it is seen as relatively minor. In contrast, laziness is more likely to be cited in the latter than the former. The correlation is not perfect. Denmark for example does not conform to this model, but it raises a question as to whether the most unequal of the developed economies also have the least understanding of how poverty is structured, let alone any sense of solidarity with those in need.

69. There is clearly a chicken and egg issue here about causation. Do these economic and social conditions need to be fulfilled before any kind of effective education for citizenship could be developed? If the position we have advanced is correct, then effective practical outcomes involved in such an education may be dependent on changes in economic and social conditions within and between countries.

70. It may be that formal education is but one element of a much wider citizenship education provided through the media and many social movements; it is clear that our knowledge on how individuals develop ideas about active citizenship remains limited, but is another area for urgent research. See the point regarding the significance of Sennett's work in n. 64. For an important discussion of the implications of individualization for citizenship see Arnot (2004).

71. For an extended discussion of these see Lauder, Brown, and Halsey (2004).

Part One

Classic Texts

1 Capitalism, the Global Reach

Karl Marx and Friedrich Engels

Bourgeois and Proletarians

The history of all hitherto existing society is the history of class struggles.

Freeman and slave, patrician and plebeian, lord and serf, guild-master and journeyman, in a word, oppressor and oppressed, stood in constant opposition to one another, carried on an uninterrupted, now hidden, now open fight, a fight that each time ended, either in a revolutionary reconstitution of society at large, or in the common ruin of the contending classes.

In the earlier epochs of history, we find almost everywhere a complicated arrangement of society into various orders, a manifold gradation of social rank. In ancient Rome we have patricians, knights, plebeians, slaves; in the Middle Ages, feudal lords, vassals, guild-masters, journeymen, serfs; in almost all of these classes, again, subordinate gradations.

The modern bourgeois society that has sprouted from the ruins of feudal society has not done away with class antagonisms. It has but established new classes, new conditions of oppression, new forms of struggle in place of the old ones.

Our epoch, the epoch of the bourgeoisie, possesses, however, this distinctive feature: it has simplified the class antagonisms. Society as a whole is more and more splitting up into two great hostile camps, into two great classes directly facing each other: Bourgeoisie and Proletariat.

From the serfs of the Middle Ages sprang the chartered burghers of the earliest towns. From these burgesses the first elements of the bourgeoisie were developed.

The discovery of America, the rounding of the Cape, opened up fresh ground for the rising bourgeoisie. The East-Indian and Chinese markets, the colonization of America, trade with the colonies, the increase in the means of exchange and in commodities generally, gave to commerce, to navigation, to industry, an impulse never before known, and thereby, to the revolutionary element in the tottering feudal society, a rapid development.

The previous feudal or guild organization of industry, under which industrial production was monopolized by closed guilds, now no longer sufficed for the growing wants of the new markets. The manufacturing system took its place. The guild-masters were pushed on one side by the manufacturing middle class; division of labour between the different corporate guilds vanished in the face of division of labour in each single workshop.

Meantime the markets kept ever growing, the demand ever rising. Even manufacture no longer sufficed. Thereupon, steam and machinery revolutionized industrial production. The place of manufacture was taken by the giant, Modem Industry, the place of the industrial middle class, by industrial millionaires, the leaders of whole industrial armies, the modern bourgeois.

Large-scale industry has established the world market, for which the discovery of America paved the way. This market has given an immense development to commerce, to navigation, to communication by land. This development has, in its turn, reacted on the extension of industry; and in

This is an OUP version of the Communist Manifesto.

proportion as industry, commerce, navigation, railways extended, in the same proportion the bourgeoisie developed, increased its capital, and pushed into the background every class handed down from the Middle Ages.

We see, therefore, how the modern bourgeoisie is itself the product of a long course of development, of a series of revolutions in the modes of production and of exchange.

Each step in the development of the bourgeoisie was accompanied by a corresponding political advance. An oppressed class under the sway of the feudal nobility, an armed and self-governing association in the medieval commune; here independent urban republic, there taxable 'third estate' of the monarchy, afterwards, in the period of manufacture proper, serving either the estate or the absolute monarchy as a counterpoise against the nobility, and, in fact, corner-stone of the great monarchies in general, the bourgeoisie has at last, since the establishment of Modern Industry and of the world market, conquered for itself, in the modern representative State, exclusive political sway. The executive of the modern State is but a committee for managing the common affairs of the whole bourgeoisie.

The bourgeoisie, historically, has played a most revolutionary part.

The bourgeoisie, wherever it has got the upper hand, has put an end to all feudal, patriarchal, idyllic relations. It has pitilessly torn asunder the motley feudal ties that bound man to his 'natural superiors', and has left remaining no other nexus between man and man than naked self-interest, than callous 'cash payment'. It has drowned the most heavenly ecstasies of religious fervour, of chivalrous enthusiasm, of philistine sentimentalism, in the icy water of egotistical calculation. It has resolved personal worth into exchange value, and in place of the numberless indefeasible chartered freedoms, has set up that single, unconscionable freedom—Free Trade. In one word, for exploitation, veiled by religious and political illusions, it has substituted naked, shameless, direct, brutal exploitation.

The bourgeoisie has stripped of its halo every occupation hitherto honoured and looked up to with reverent awe. It has converted the physician, the lawyer, the priest, the poet, the man of science, into its paid wage-labourers.

The bourgeoisie has torn away from the family its sentimental veil, and has reduced the family relation to a mere money relation.

The bourgeoisie has disclosed how it came to pass that the brutal display of vigour in the Middle Ages, which Reactionists so much admire, found its fitting complement in the most slothful indolence. It has been the first to show what man's activity can bring about. It has accomplished wonders far surpassing Egyptian pyramids, Roman aqueducts, and Gothic cathedrals; it has conducted expeditions that put in the shade all former Exoduses of nations and crusades.

The bourgeoisie cannot exist without constantly revolutionizing the instruments of production, and thereby the relations of production, and with them the whole relations of society. Conservation of the old modes of production in unaltered form, was, on the contrary, the first condition of existence for all earlier industrial classes. Constant revolutionizing of production, uninterrupted disturbance of all social conditions, everlasting uncertainty and agitation distinguish the bourgeois epoch from all earlier ones. All fixed, fast-frozen relations, with their train of ancient and venerable prejudices and opinions are swept away, all new-formed ones become antiquated before they can ossify. All that is solid melts into air, all that is holy is profaned, and man is at last compelled to face with sober senses, his real conditions of life, and his relations with his kind.

The need of a constantly expanding market for its products chases the bourgeoisie over the whole surface of the globe. It must nestle everywhere, settle everywhere, establish connexions everywhere.

The bourgeoisie has through its exploitation of the world market given a cosmopolitan character to production and consumption in every country. To the great chagrin of Reactionists, it has drawn from under the feet of industry the national ground on which it stood. All old-established national industries have been destroyed or are daily being destroyed. They are dislodged by new industries, whose introduction becomes a life and death question for all civilized nations, by industries that no longer work up indigenous raw material, but raw material drawn from the remotest zones; industries whose products are consumed, not only at home, but in every quarter of the globe. In place of the old wants, satisfied by the productions of the country, we find new wants, requiring for their satisfaction the products of distant lands and climes. In place of the old local and national seclusion and self-sufficiency, we have intercourse in every direction, universal inter-dependence of nations. And as in material, so also in intellectual production. The intellectual creations of individual nations become common property. National one-sidedness and narrow-mindedness become more and more impossible, and from the numerous national and local literatures, there arises a world literature.

The bourgeoisie, by the rapid improvement of all instruments of production, by the immensely facilitated means of communication, draws all, even the most barbarian, nations into civilization. The cheap prices of its commodities are the heavy artillery with which it batters down all Chinese walls, with which it forces the barbarians' intensely obstinate hatred of foreigners to capitulate. It compels all nations, on pain of extinction, to adopt the bourgeois mode of production; it compels them to introduce what it calls civilization into their midst, i.e., to become bourgeois themselves. In one word, it creates a world after its own image.

2 Education: Its Nature and Its Role

Émile Durkheim

1. Definitions of Education: Critical Examination

The word 'education' has sometimes been used in a very broad sense to designate the totality of influences that nature or other men are able to exercise either on our intelligence or on our will. It includes, says John Stuart Mill, 'all that we ourselves do and all that others do for us to the end of bringing us closer to the perfection of our nature. In its most widely accepted sense, it includes even indirect effects on the character and faculties of men produced by things having quite a different objective: by laws, by forms of government, the industrial arts, and even by physical phenomena, independent of human will, such as climate, soil, and locality.' But this definition includes elements that are quite disparate, and that one cannot combine under a single heading without confusion. The influence of things on men is very different, in their processes and effects, from that which comes from men themselves; and the influence of peers on peers differs from that which adults exercise on youth. It is only the latter that concerns us here, and, therefore, it is this meaning that it is convenient to reserve for the word 'education.'

But what is the specific nature of this influence? Various answers have been given to this question; they can be divided into two main types.

Following Kant, 'the end of education is to develop, in each individual, all the perfection of which he is capable.' But what is meant by perfection? It is, as has often been said, the harmonious development of all the human faculties. To carry to the highest point that can be reached all the capacities that are in us, to realize them as completely as possible, without their interfering with one another, is not this an ideal beyond which there can be no other?

But if, to a degree, this harmonious development is indeed necessary and desirable, it is not wholly attainable; for it is in contradiction to another rule of human behavior which is no less cogent: that which has us concentrate on a specific, limited task. We cannot and we must not all be devoted to the same kind of life; we have, according to our aptitudes, different functions to fulfill, and we must adapt ourselves to what we must do. We are not all made for reflection; there is need for men of feeling and of action. Conversely, there is need of those whose job is thinking. Now, thought can develop only in detachment from action, only by turning in upon itself, only by turning its object entirely away from overt action. From this comes a first differentiation which is accompanied by a break of equilibrium. And behavior, in turn, as thought, can take a variety of different and specialized forms. Doubtless this specialization does not exclude a certain common base and, consequently, a certain balance of functions, organic and psychic alike, without which the health of the individual would be endangered, as well as social cohesion. We see, thus, that perfect harmony cannot be presented as the final end of conduct and of education.

Still less satisfactory is the utilitarian definition, according to which the objective of education would be to 'make the individual an instrument of happiness for himself and for his fellows' (James Mill); for happiness is an essentially subjective thing that each person appreciates in his own way. Such a formula, then, leaves the end of education undetermined and, therefore, education itself, since it is left to individual fancy. Spencer, to be sure, tried to define happiness objectively. For him, the conditions of happiness are those of life. Complete happiness is the complete life. But what is meant by life? If it is a matter of physical existence alone, one may well say: that without which it would be impossible; it implies, in effect, a certain equilibrium between the organism and its environment, and, since the two terms in relation are definable data, it must be the same with their relation. But one can express, in this way, only the most immediate vital necessities. Now, for man, and above all for the man of today, such a life is not life. We ask more of life than normal enough functioning of our organs. A cultivated mind prefers not to live rather than give up the joys of the intellect. Even from the material point of view alone, everything over and above what is strictly necessary cannot be exactly determined. The 'standard of life,' as the English say, the minimum below which it does not seem to us that we can consent to descend, varies infinitely according to conditions, milieux, and the times. What we found sufficient yesterday, today seems to us to be beneath the dignity of man, as we define it now, and everything leads us to believe that our needs in this connection grow increasingly.

We come here to the general criticism that all these definitions face. They assume that there is an ideal, perfect education, which applies to all men indiscriminately; and it is this education, universal and unique, that the theorist tries to define. But first, if history is taken into consideration, one finds in it nothing to confirm such an hypothesis. Education has varied infinitely in time and place. In the cities of Greece and Rome, education trained the individual to subordinate himself blindly to the collectivity, to become the creature of society. Today, it tries to make of the individual an autonomous personality. In Athens, they sought to form cultivated souls, informed, subtle, full of measure and harmony, capable of enjoying beauty and the joys of pure speculation; in Rome, they wanted above all for children to become men of action, devoted to military glory, indifferent to letters and the arts. In the Middle Ages, education was above all Christian; in the Renaissance, it assumes a more lay and literary character; today science tends to assume the place in education formerly occupied by the arts. Can it be said, then, that the fact is not the ideal; that if education has varied, it is because men have mistaken what it should be? But if Roman education had been infused with an individualism comparable to ours, the Roman city would not have been able to maintain itself; Latin civilization would not have developed, nor, furthermore, our modern civilization, which is in part descended from it. The Christian societies of the Middle Ages would not have been able to survive if they had given to free inquiry the place that we give it today. There are, then, ineluctable necessities which it is impossible to disregard. Of what use is it to imagine a kind of education that would be fatal for the society that put it into practice?

This assumption, so doubtful, in itself rests on a more general mistake. If one begins by asking, thus, what an ideal education must be, abstracted from conditions of time and place, it is to admit implicitly that a system of education has no reality in itself. One does not see in education a collection of practices and institutions that have been organized slowly in the course of time, which are comparable with all the other social institutions and which express them, and which, therefore, can no more be changed at will than the structure of the society itself. But it seems that this would be a pure system of *a priori* concepts; under this heading it appears to be a logical construct. One imagines that men of each age organize it voluntarily to realize a determined end; that, if this organization is not everywhere the same, it is because mistakes have been made concerning either the end that it is to pursue or the means of attaining it. From this point of view, educational systems of the past appear as so many errors, total or partial. No attention need be paid to them, therefore; we do not have to associate ourselves with the faulty observation or logic of our predecessors; but we can and must pose the question without concerning ourselves with solutions that have been given, that is to say, leaving aside everything that has been, we have only to ask ourselves what should be. The lessons of history can, moreover, serve to prevent us from repeating the errors that have been committed.

In fact, however, each society, considered at a given stage of development, has a system of education which exercises an irresistible influence on individuals. It is idle to think that we can rear our children as we wish. There are customs to which we are bound to conform; if we flout them too severely, they take their vengeance on our children. The children, when they are adults, are unable to live with their peers, with whom they are not in accord. Whether they had been raised in accordance with ideas that were either obsolete or premature does not matter; in the one case as in the other, they are not of their time and, therefore, they are outside the conditions of normal life. There is, then, in each period, a prevailing type of education from which we cannot deviate without encountering that lively resistance which restrains the fancies of dissent.

Now, it is not we as individuals who have created the customs and ideas that determine this type. They are the product of a common life, and they express its needs. They are, moreover, in large part the work of preceding generations. The entire human past has contributed to the formation of this totality of maxims that guide education today; our entire history has left its traces in it, and even the history of the peoples who have come before. It is thus that the higher organisms carry in themselves the reflection of the whole biological evolution of which they are the end product. Historical investigation of the formation and development of systems of education reveals that they depend upon religion, political organization, the degree of development of science, the state of industry, etc. If they are considered apart from all these historic causes, they become incomprehensible. Thus, how can the individual pretend to reconstruct, through his own private reflection, what is not a work of individual thought? He is not confronted with a *tabula rasa* on which he can write what he wants, but with existing realities which he cannot create, or destroy, or transform, at will. He can act on them only to the extent that he has learned to understand them, to know their nature and the conditions on which they depend; and he can understand them only if he studies them, only if he starts by observing them, as the physicist observes inanimate matter and the biologist, living bodies.

Besides, how else to proceed? When one wants to determine by dialectics alone what education should be, it is necessary to begin by asking what objectives it must have. But what is it that allows us to say that education has certain ends rather than others? We do not know *a priori* what is the function of respiration or of circulation in a living being. By what right would we be more well informed concerning the educational function? It will be said in reply that from all the evidence, its object is the training of children. But this is posing the problem in slightly different terms; it does not resolve it. It would be necessary to say of what this training consists, what its direction is, what human needs it satisfies. Now, one can answer these questions only by beginning with observation of what it has consisted of, what needs it has satisfied in the past. Thus, it appears that to establish the preliminary notion of education, to determine what is so called, historical observation is indispensable.

2. Definition of Education

To define education we must, then, consider educational systems, present and past, put them together, and abstract the characteristics which are common to them. These characteristics will constitute the definition that we seek.

We have already determined, along the way, two elements. In order that there be education, there must be a generation of adults and one of youth, in interaction, and an influence exercised by the first on the second. It remains for us to define the nature of this influence.

There is, so to speak, no society in which the system of education does not present a twofold aspect: it is at the same time one and manifold.

It is manifold. Indeed, in one sense, it can be said that there are as many different kinds of education as there are different milieux in a given society. Is such a society formed of castes? Education varies from one caste to another; that of the patricians was not that of the plebeians; that of the Brahman was not that of the Sudra. Similarly, in the Middle Ages, what a difference between the culture that the young page received, instructed in all the arts of chivalry, and that of the villein, who learned in his parish school a smattering of arithmetic, song and grammar! Even today, do we not see education vary with social class, or even with locality? That of the city is not that of the country, that of the middle class is not that of the worker. Would one say that this organization is not morally justifiable, that one can see in it only a survival destined to disappear? This proposition is easy to defend. It is evident that the education of our children should not depend upon the chance of their having been born here or there, of some parents rather than others. But even though the moral conscience of our time would have received, on this point, the satisfaction that it expects, education would not, for all that, become more uniform. Even though the career of each child would, in large part, no longer be predetermined by a blind heredity, occupational specialization would not fail to result in a great pedagogical diversity. Each occupation, indeed, constitutes a milieu *sui generis* which requires particular aptitudes and specialized knowledge, in which certain ideas, certain practices, certain modes of viewing things, prevail; and as the child must be prepared for the function that he will be called upon to fulfill, education, beyond a certain age, can no longer remain the same for all those to whom it applies. That is why we see it, in all civilized countries, tending more and more to become diversified and specialized; and this specialization becomes more advanced daily. The heterogeneity which is thus created does not rest, as does that which we were just discussing, on unjust inequalities; but it is not less. To find an absolutely homogeneous and egalitarian education, it would be necessary to go back to prehistoric societies, in the structure of which there is no differentiation; and yet these kinds of societies represent hardly more than one logical stage in the history of humanity.

But, whatever may be the importance of these special educations, they are not all of education. It may even be said that they are not sufficient unto themselves; everywhere that one observes them, they vary from one another only beyond a certain point, up to which they are not differentiated. They all rest upon a common base. There is no people among whom there is not a certain number of ideas, sentiments and practices which education must inculcate in all children indiscriminately, to whatever social category they belong. Even in a society which is divided into closed castes, there is always a religion common to all, and, consequently, the principles of the religious culture, which is, then, fundamental, are the same throughout the population. If each caste, each family, has its special gods, there are general divinities that are recognized by everyone and which all children learn to worship. And as these divinities symbolize and personify certain sentiments, certain ways of conceiving the world and life, one cannot be initiated into their cult without acquiring, at the same time, all sorts of thought patterns which go beyond the sphere of the purely religious life. Similarly, in the Middle Ages, serfs, villeins, burgers and nobles received, equally, a common Christian education. If it is thus in societies where intellectual and moral diversity reach this degree of contrast, with how much more reason is it so among more advanced peoples where classes, while remaining distinct, are, however, separated by a less profound cleavage! Where these common elements of all education are not expressed in the form of religious symbols, they do not, however, cease to exist. In the course of our history, there has been established a whole set of ideas on human nature, on the respective importance of our different faculties, on right and duty, on society, on the individual, on progress, on science, on art, etc., which are the very basis of our national spirit; all education, that of the rich as well as that of the poor, that which leads to professional careers as well as that which prepares for industrial functions, has as its object to fix them in our minds.

From these facts it follows that each society sets up a certain ideal of man, of what he should be, as much from the intellectual point of view as the physical and moral; that this ideal is, to a degree, the same for all the citizens; that beyond a certain point it becomes differentiated according to the particular milieux that every society contains in its structure. It is this ideal, at the same time one and various, that is the focus of education. Its function, then, is to arouse in the child: (1) a certain number of physical and mental states that the society to which he belongs considers should not be lacking in any of its members; (2) certain physical and mental states that the particular social group (caste, class, family, profession) considers, equally, ought to be found among all those who make it up. Thus, it is society as a whole and each particular social milieu that determine the ideal that education realizes. Society can survive only if there exists among its members a sufficient degree of homogeneity; education perpetuates and reinforces this homogeneity by fixing in the child, from the beginning, the essential similarities that collective life demands. But on the other hand, without a certain diversity all co-operation would be impossible; education assures the persistence of this necessary diversity by being itself diversified and specialized. If the society has reached a degree of development such that the old divisions into castes and classes can no longer be maintained, it will prescribe an education more uniform at its base. If at the same time there is more division of labor, it will arouse among children, on the underlying basic set of common ideas and sentiments, a richer diversity of occupational aptitudes. If it lives in a state of war with the surrounding societies, it tries to shape people according to a strongly nationalistic model; if international competition takes a more peaceful form, the type that it tries to realize is more general and more humanistic. Education is, then, only the means by which society prepares, within the children, the essential conditions of its very existence. We shall see later how the individual himself has an interest in submitting to these requirements.

We come, then, to the following formula: *Education is the influence exercised by adult generations on those that are not yet ready for social life. Its object is to arouse and to develop in the child a certain number of physical, intellectual and moral states which are demanded of him by both the political society as a whole and the special milieu for which he is specifically destined.*

3. Consequences of the Preceding Definition: The Social Character of Education

It follows from the definition that precedes, that education consists of a methodical socialization of the young generation. In each of us, it may be said, there exist two beings which, while inseparable except by abstraction, remain distinct. One is made up of all the mental states that apply only to ourselves and to the events of our personal lives: this is what might be called the individual being. The other is a system of ideas, sentiments and practices which express in us, not our personality, but the group or different groups of which we are part; these are religious beliefs, moral beliefs and practices, national or professional traditions, collective opinions of every kind. Their totality forms the social being. To constitute this being in each of us is the end of education.

It is here, moreover, that are best shown the importance of its role and the fruitfulness of its influence. Indeed, not only is this social being not given, fully formed, in the primitive constitution of man; but it has not resulted from it through a spontaneous development. Spontaneously, man was not inclined to submit to a political authority, to respect a moral discipline, to dedicate himself, to be self-sacrificing. There was nothing in our congenital nature that predisposed us necessarily to become servants of divinities, symbolic emblems of society, to render them worship, to deprive ourselves in order to do them honor. It is society itself which, to the degree that it is firmly established, has drawn from within itself those great moral forces in the face of which man has felt his inferiority, Now, if one leaves aside the vague and indefinite tendencies which can be attributed to heredity, the child, on entering life, brings to it only his nature as an individual. Society finds itself, with each new generation, faced with a *tabula rasa*, very nearly, on which it must build anew. To the egoistic and asocial being that has just been born it must, as rapidly as possible, add another, capable of leading a moral and social life. Such is the work of education, and you can readily see its great importance. It is not limited to developing the individual organism in the direction indicated by its nature, to elicit the hidden potentialities that need only be manifested. It creates in man a new being.

This creative quality is, moreover, a special prerogative of human education. Anything else is what animals receive, if one can apply this name to the progressive training to which they are subjected by their parents. It can, indeed, foster the development of certain instincts that lie dormant in the animal, but such training does not initiate it into a new life. It facilitates the play of natural functions, but it creates nothing. Taught by its mother, the young animal learns more quickly how to fly or build its nest; but it learns almost nothing that it could not have been able to discover through its own individual experience. This is because animals either do not live under social conditions or form rather simple societies, which function through instinctive mechanisms that each individual carries within himself, fully formed, from birth. Education, then, can add nothing essential to nature, since the latter is adequate for everything, for the life of the group as well as that of the individual. By contrast, among men the aptitudes of every kind that social life presupposes are much too complex to be able to be contained, somehow, in our tissues, and to take the form of organic predispositions. It follows that they cannot be transmitted from one generation to another by way of heredity. It is through education that the transmission is effected.

However, it will be said, if one can indeed conceive that the distinctively moral qualities, because they impose privations on the individual, because they inhibit his natural impulses, can be developed in us only under an outside influence, are there not others which every man wishes to acquire and seeks spontaneously? Such are the divers qualities of the intelligence which allow him better to adapt his behavior to the nature of things. Such, too, are the physical qualities, and everything that contributes to the vigor and health of the organism. For the former, at least, it seems that education, in developing them, may only assist the development of nature itself, may only lead the individual to a state of relative perfection toward which he tends by himself, although he may be able to achieve it more rapidly thanks to the co-operation of society.

But what demonstrates, despite appearances, that here as elsewhere education answers social necessities above all, is that there are societies in which these qualities have not been cultivated at all, and that in every case they have been understood very differently in different societies. The advantages of a solid intellectual culture have been far from recognized by all peoples. Science and the critical mind, that we rank so high today, were for a long time held in suspicion. Do we not know a great doctrine that proclaims happy the poor in spirit? We must guard against believing that this indifference to knowledge had been artificially imposed on men in violation of their nature. They do not have, by themselves, the instinctive appetite for science that has often and arbitrarily been attributed to them. They desire science only to the extent that experience has taught them that they cannot do without it. Now, in connection with the ordering of their individual lives they had no use for it. As Rousseau has already said, to satisfy the vital necessities, sensation, experience and instinct would suffice as they suffice for the animal. If man had not known other needs than these, very simple ones, which have their roots in his individual constitution, he would not have undertaken the pursuit of science, all the more because it has not been acquired without laborious and painful efforts. He has known the thirst for knowledge only when society has awakened it in him, and society has done this only when it has felt the need of it. This moment came when social life, in all its forms, had become too complex to be able to function otherwise than through the co-operation of reflective thought, that is to say, thought enlightened by science. Then scientific culture became indispensable, and that is why society requires it of its members and imposes it upon them as a duty. But in the beginning, as long as social organization is very simple and undifferentiated, always self-sufficient, blind tradition suffices, as does instinct in the animal. Therefore thought and free inquiry are useless and even dangerous, since they can only threaten tradition. That is why they are proscribed.

It is not otherwise with physical qualities. Where the state of the social milieu inclines public sentiment toward asceticism, physical education will be relegated to a secondary place. Something of this sort took place in the schools of the Middle Ages; and this asceticism was necessary, for the only manner of adapting to the harshness of those difficult times was to like it. Similarly, following the current of opinion, this same education will be understood very differently. In Sparta its object above all was to harden the limbs to fatigue; in Athens, it was a means of making bodies beautiful to the sight; in the time of chivalry it was required to form agile and supple warriors; today it no longer has any but a hygienic end, and is concerned, above all, with limiting the dangerous effects of a too intense intellectual culture. Thus, even the qualities which appear at first glance so spontaneously desirable, the individual seeks only when society invites him to, and he seeks them in the fashion that it prescribes for him.

We are now in a position to answer a question raised by all that precedes. Whereas we showed society fashioning individuals according to its needs, it could seem, from this fact, that the individuals were submitting to an insupportable tyranny. But in reality they are themselves interested in this submission; for the new being that collective influence, through education, thus builds up in each of us, represents what is best in us. Man is man, in fact, only because he lives in society. It is difficult, in the course of an article, to demonstrate rigorously a proposition so general and so important, and one which sums up the works of contemporary sociology. But first, one can say that it is less and less disputed. And more, it is not impossible to call to mind, summarily, the most essential facts that justify it.

First, if there is today an historically established fact, it is that morality stands in close relationship to the nature of societies, since, as we have shown along the way, it changes when societies change. This is because it results from life in common. It is society, indeed, that draws us out of ourselves, that obliges us to reckon with other interests than our own, it is society that has taught us to control our passions, our instincts, to prescribe law for them, to restrain ourselves, to deprive ourselves, to sacrifice ourselves, to subordinate our personal ends to higher ends. As for the whole system of representation which maintains in us the idea and the sentiment of rule, of discipline, internal as well as external—it is society that has established it in our consciences. It is thus that we have acquired this power to control ourselves, this control over our inclinations which is one of the distinctive traits of the human being and which is the more developed to the extent that we are more fully human.

We do not owe society less from the intellectual point of view. It is science that elaborates the cardinal notions that govern our thought: notions of cause, of laws, of space, of number, notions of bodies, of life, of conscience, of society, and so on. All these fundamental ideas are perpetually evolving, because they are the recapitulation, the resultant of all scientific work, far from being its point of departure as Pestalozzi believed. We do not conceive of man, nature, cause, even space, as they were conceived in the Middle Ages; this is because our knowledge and our scientific methods are no longer the same. Now, science is a collective work, since it presupposes a vast co-operation of all scientists, not only of the same time, but of all the successive epochs of history. Before the sciences were established, religion filled the same office; for every mythology consists of a conception, already well elaborated, of man and of the universe. Science, moreover, was the heir of religion. Now, a religion is a social institution.

In learning a language, we learn a whole system of ideas, distinguished and classified, and we inherit from all the work from which have come these classifications that sum up centuries of experiences. There is more: without language, we would not have, so to speak, general ideas; for it is the word which, in fixing them, gives to concepts a consistency sufficient for them to be able to be handled conveniently by the mind. It is language, then, that has allowed us to raise ourselves above pure sensation; and it is not necessary to demonstrate that language is, in the first degree, a social thing.

One sees, through these few examples, to what man would be reduced if there were withdrawn from him all that he has derived from society: he would fall to the level of an animal. If he has been able to surpass the stage at which animals have stopped, it is primarily because he is not reduced to the fruit only of his personal efforts, but co-operates regularly with his fellow-creatures; and this makes the activity of each more productive. It is chiefly as a result of this that the products of the work of one generation are not lost for that which follows. Of what an animal has been able to learn in the course of his individual existence, almost nothing can survive him. By contrast, the results of human experience are preserved almost entirely and in detail, thanks to books, sculptures, tools, instruments of every kind that are transmitted from generation to generation, oral tradition, etc. The soil of nature is thus covered with a rich deposit that continues to grow constantly. Instead of dissipating each time that a generation dies out and is replaced by another, human wisdom accumulates without limit, and it is this unlimited accumulation that raises man above the beast and above himself. But, just as in the case of the co-operation which was discussed first, this accumulation is possible only in and through society. For in order that the legacy of each generation may be able to be preserved and added to others, it is necessary that there be a moral personality which lasts beyond the generations that pass, which binds them to one another: it is society. Thus the antagonism that has too often been admitted between society and individual corresponds to nothing in the facts. Indeed, far from these two terms being in opposition and being able to develop only each at the expense of the other, they imply each other. The individual, in willing society, wills himself. The influence that it exerts on him, notably through education, does not at all have as its object and its effect to repress him, to diminish him, to denature him, but, on the contrary, to make him grow and to make of him a truly human being. No doubt, he can grow thus only by making an effort. But this is precisely because this power to put forth voluntary effort is one of the most essential characteristics of man.

4. The Role of the State in Education

This definition of education provides for a ready solution of the controversial question of the duties and the rights of the State with respect to education.

The rights of the family are opposed to them. The child, it is said, belongs first to his parents; it is, then, their responsibility to direct, as they understand it, his intellectual and moral development. Education is then conceived as an essentially private and domestic affair. When one takes this point of view, one tends naturally to reduce to a minimum the intervention of the State in the matter. The State should, it is said, be limited to serving as an auxiliary to, and as a substitute for, families. When they are unable to discharge their duties, it is natural that the State should take charge. It is natural, too, that it make their task as easy as possible, by placing at their disposal schools to which they can, if they wish, send their children. But it must be kept strictly within these limits, and forbidden any positive action designed to impress a given orientation on the mind of the youth.

But its role need hardly remain so negative. If, as we have tried to establish, education has a collective function above all, if its object is to adapt the child to the social milieu in which he is destined to live, it is impossible that society should be uninterested in such a procedure. How could society not have a part in it, since it is the reference point by which education must direct its action? It is, then, up to the State to remind the teacher constantly of the ideas, the sentiments that must be impressed upon the child to adjust him to the milieu in which he must live. If it were not always there to guarantee that pedagogical influence be exercised in a social way, the latter would necessarily be put to the service of private beliefs, and the whole nation would be divided and would break down into an incoherent multitude of little fragments in conflict with one another. One could not contradict more completely the fundamental end of all education. Choice is necessary: if one attaches some value to the existence of society—and we have just seen what it means to us—education must assure, among the citizens, a sufficient community of ideas and of sentiments, without which any society is impossible; and in order that it may be able to produce this result, it is also necessary that education not be completely abandoned to the arbitrariness of private individuals.

Since education is an essentially social function, the State cannot be indifferent to it. On the contrary, everything that pertains to education must in some degree be submitted to its influence. This is not to say, therefore, that it must necessarily monopolize instruction. The question is too complex to be able to be treated thus in passing; we shall discuss it later. One can believe that scholastic progress is easier and quicker where a certain margin is left for individual initiative; for the individual makes innovations more readily than the State. But from the fact that the State, in the public interest, must allow other schools to be opened than those for which it has a more direct responsibility, it does not follow that it must remain aloof from what is going on in them. On the contrary, the education given in them must remain under its control. It is not even admissible that the function of the educator can be fulfilled by anyone who does not offer special guarantees of which the State alone can be the judge. No doubt, the limits within which its intervention should be kept may be rather difficult to determine once and for all, but the principle of intervention could not be disputed. There is no school which can claim the right to give, with full freedom, an antisocial education.

It is nevertheless necessary to recognize that the state of division in which we now find ourselves, in our country, makes this duty of the State particularly delicate and at the same time more important. It is not, indeed, up to the State to create this community of ideas and sentiments without which there is no society; it must be established by itself, and the State can only consecrate it, maintain it, make individuals more aware of it. Now, it is unfortunately indisputable that among us, this moral unity is not at all points what it should be. We are divided by divergent and even sometimes contradictory conceptions. There is in these divergences a fact which it is impossible to deny, and, which must be reckoned with. It is not a question of recognizing the right of the majority to impose its ideas on the children of the minority. The school should not be the thing of one party, and the teacher is remiss in his duties when he uses the authority at his disposal to influence his pupils in accordance with his own preconceived opinions, however justified they may appear to him. But in spite of all the differences of opinion, there are at present, at the basis of our civilization, a certain number of principles which, implicitly or explicitly, are common to all, that few indeed, in any case, dare to deny overtly and openly: respect for reason, for science, for ideas and sentiments which are at the base of democratic morality. The role of the State is to outline these essential principles, to have them taught in its schools, to see it that nowhere are children left ignorant of them, that everywhere they should be spoken of with the respect which is due them. There is in this connection an influence to exert which will perhaps be all the more efficacious when it will be less aggressive and less violent, and will know better how to be contained within wise limits.

5. The Power of Education: The Means of Influence

After having determined the end of education, we must seek to determine how and to what extent it is possible to attain this end, that is to say, how and to what extent education can be efficacious.

This question has always been very controversial. For Fontenelle, 'neither does good education make good character, nor does bad education destroy it.' By contrast, for Locke, for Helvetius, education is all-powerful. According to the latter, 'all men are born equal and with equal aptitudes; education alone makes for differences.' The theory of Jacotot resembles the preceding.

The solution that one gives to the problem depends on the idea that one has of the importance and of the nature of the innate predispositions, on the one hand, and, on the other, of the means of influence at the disposal of the educator.

Education does not make a man out of nothing, as Locke and Helvetius believed; it is applied to predispositions that it finds already made. From another point of view, one can concede, in a general way, that these congenital tendencies are very strong, very difficult to destroy or to transform radically; for they depend upon organic conditions on which the educator has little influence. Consequently, to the degree that they have a definite object, that they incline the mind and the character toward narrowly determined ways of acting and thinking, the whole future of the individual finds itself fixed in advance, and there does not remain much for education to do.

But fortunately one of the characteristics of man is that the innate predispositions in him are very general and very vague. Indeed, the type of predisposition that is fixed, rigid, invariable, which hardly leaves room for the influence of external causes, is instinct. Now, one can ask if there is a single instinct, properly speaking, in man. One speaks, sometimes, of the instinct of preservation; but the word is inappropriate. For an instinct is a system of given actions, always the same, which, once they are set in motion by sensation, are automatically linked up with one another until they reach their natural limit, without reflection having to intervene anywhere; now, the movements that we make when our life is in danger do not at all have any such fixity or automatic invariability. They change with the situation; we adapt them to circumstances: this is because they do not operate without a certain conscious choice, however rapid. What is called the instinct of preservation is, after all, only a general impulse to flee death, without the means by which we seek to avoid it being predetermined once and for all. One can say as much concerning what is sometimes called, not less inexactly, the maternal instinct, the paternal instinct, and even the sexual instinct. These are drives in a given direction; but the means by which these drives are expressed vary from one individual to another, from one occasion to another. A large area remains reserved, then, for trial and error, for personal accommodations, and, consequently, for the effect of causes which can make their influence felt only after birth. Now, education is one of these causes.

It has been claimed, to be sure, that the child sometimes inherits a very strong tendency toward a given act, such as suicide, theft, murder, fraud, etc. But these assertions are not at all in accord with the facts. Whatever may have been said about it, one is not born criminal; still less is one destined from birth for this or that type of crime; the paradox of the Italian criminologists no longer counts many defenders today. What is inherited is a certain lack of mental equilibrium, which makes the individual refractory to coherent and disciplined behavior. But such a temperament does not predestine a man to be a criminal any more than to be an explorer seeking adventures, a prophet, a political innovator, an inventor, etc. As much can be said of any occupational aptitudes. As Bain remarked, 'the son of a great philologist does not inherit a single word; the son of a great traveler can, at school, be surpassed in geography by the son of a miner.' What the child receives from his parents are very general faculties: some force of attention, a certain amount of perseverance, a sound judgment, imagination, etc. But each of these faculties can serve all sorts of different ends. A child endowed with a rather lively imagination will be able, depending on circumstances, on the influences that will be brought to bear upon him, to become a painter or a poet, or an engineer with an inventive mind, or a daring financier. There is, then, a considerable difference between natural qualities and the special forms that they must take to be utilized in life. This means that the future is not strictly predetermined by our congenital constitution. The reason for this is easy to understand. The only forms of activity that can be transmitted by heredity are those which are always repeated in a sufficiently identical manner to be able to be fixed, in a rigid form, in the tissues of the organism. Now, human life depends on conditions that are manifold, complex, and, consequently, changing; it must itself, then, change and be modified continuously. Thus it is impossible for it to become crystallized in a definite and positive form. But only very general, very vague dispositions, expressing the characteristics common to all individual experiences, can survive and pass from one generation to another.

To say that innate characteristics are for the most part very general, is to say that they are very malleable, very flexible, since they can assume very different forms. Between the vague potentialities which constitute man at the moment of birth and the well-defined character that he must become in order to play a useful role in society, the distance is, then, considerable. It is this distance that education has to make the child travel. One sees that a vast field is open to its influence.

But, to exert this influence, does it have adequate means?

In order to give an idea of what constitutes the educational influence, and to show its power, a contemporary psychologist, Guyau, has compared it to hypnotic suggestion; and the comparison is not without foundation.

Hypnotic suggestion presupposes, indeed, the following two conditions: (1) The state in which the hypnotized subject is found is characterized by its exceptional passivity. The mind is almost reduced to the state of a *tabula rasa*; a sort of void has been achieved in his consciousness; the will is as though paralyzed. Thus, the idea suggested, meeting no contrary idea at all, can be established with a minimum of resistance; (2) however, as the void is never complete, it is necessary, further, that the idea take from the suggestion itself some power of specific action. For that, it is necessary that the hypnotizer speak in a commanding tone, with authority. He must say: *I wish*; he must indicate that refusal to obey is not even conceivable, that the act must be accomplished, that the thing must be seen as he shows it, that it cannot be otherwise. If he weakens, one sees the subject hesitate, resist, sometimes even refuse to obey. If he so much as enters into discussion, that is the end of his power. The more suggestion goes against the natural temperament of the subject, the more will the imperative tone be indispensable.

Now, these two conditions are present in the relationships that the educator has with the child subjected to his influence: (1) The child is naturally in a state of passivity quite comparable to that in which the hypnotic subject is found artificially placed. His mind yet contains only a small number of conceptions able to fight against those which are suggested to him; his will is still rudimentary. Therefore he is very suggestible. For the same reason he is very susceptible to the force of example, very much inclined to imitation. (2) The ascendancy that the teacher naturally has over his pupil, because of the superiority of his experience and of his culture, will naturally give to his influence the efficacious force that he needs.

This comparison shows how far from helpless the educator is; for the great power of hypnotic suggestion is known. If, then, educational influence has, even in a lesser degree, an analogous efficacy, much may be expected of it, provided that one knows how to use it. Far from being discouraged by our impotence, we might well, rather, be frightened by the scope of our power. If teachers and parents were more consistently aware that nothing can happen in the child's presence which does not leave some trace in him, that the form of his mind and of his character depends on these thousands of little unconscious influences that take place at every moment and to which we pay no attention because of their apparent insignificance, how much more would they watch their language and their behavior! Surely, education cannot be very effective when it functions inconsistently. As Herbart says, it is not by reprimanding the child violently from time to time that one can influence him very much. But when education is patient and continuous, when it does not look for immediate and obvious successes, but proceeds slowly in a well-defined direction, without letting itself be diverted by external incidents and adventitious circumstances, it has at its disposal all the means necessary to affect minds profoundly.

At the same time, one sees what is the essential means of educational influence. What makes for the influence of the hypnotist is the authority which he holds under the circumstances. By analogy, then, one can say that education must be essentially a matter of authority. This important proposition can, moreover, be established directly. Indeed, we have seen that the object of education is to superimpose, on the individual and asocial being that we are at birth, an entirely new being. It must bring us to overcome our initial nature; it is on this condition that the child will become a man. Now, we can raise ourselves above ourselves only by a more or less difficult effort. Nothing is so false and deceptive as the Epicurean conception of education, the conception of a Montaigne, for example, according to which man can be formed while enjoying himself and without any other spur than the attraction of pleasure. If there is nothing somber in life and if it is criminal artificially to make it so in the eyes of the child, it is, however, serious and important; and education, which prepares for life, should share this seriousness. To learn to contain his natural egoism, to subordinate himself to higher ends, to submit his desires to the control of his will, to confine them within proper limits, the child must exercise strong self-control. Now, we restrain ourselves, we limit ourselves, only for one or the other of the following two reasons: because it is necessary through some physical necessity, or because we must do it on moral grounds. But the child cannot feel the necessity that imposes these efforts on us physically, for he is not faced directly with the hard realities of life which make this attitude indispensable. He is not yet engaged in the struggle; whatever Spencer may have said about it, we cannot leave him exposed to these too harsh realities. It is necessary, then, that he be already formed, in large part, when he really encounters them. One cannot, then, depend on their influence to make him bow his will and acquire the necessary mastery over himself.

Duty remains. The sense of duty is, indeed, for the child and even for the adult, the stimulus *par excellence* of effort. Self-respect itself presupposes it. For, to be properly affected by reward and punishment, one must already have a sense of his dignity and, consequently, of his duty. But the child can know his duty only through his teachers or his parents; he can know what it is only through the manner in which they reveal it to him through their language and through their conduct. They must be, then, for him, duty incarnate and personified. Thus moral authority is the dominant quality of the educator. For it is through the authority that is in him that duty is duty. What is his own special quality is the imperative tone with which he addresses consciences, the respect that he inspires in wills and which makes them yield to his judgment. Thus it is indispensable that such an impression emanate from the person of the teacher.

It is not necessary to show that authority, thus understood, is neither violent nor repressive; it consists entirely of a certain moral ascendancy. It presupposes the presence in the teacher of two principal conditions. First, he must have will. For authority implies confidence, and the child cannot have confidence in anyone whom he sees hesitating, shifting, going back on his decisions. But this first condition is not the most essential. What is important above all is that the teacher really feels in himself the authority the feeling for which he is to transmit. It constitutes a force which he can manifest only if he possesses it effectively. Now, where does he get it from? Would it be from the power which he does have, from his right to reward and punish? But fear of chastisement is quite different from respect for authority. It has moral value only if chastisement is recognized as just even by him who suffers it, which implies that the authority which punishes is already recognized as legitimate. And this is the question. It is not from the outside that the teacher can hold his authority, it is from himself; it can come to him only from an inner faith. He must believe, not in himself, no doubt, not in the superior qualities of his intelligence or of his soul, but in his task and in the importance of his task. What makes for the authority which is so readily attached to the word of the priest, is the high idea that he has of his calling; for he speaks in the name of a god in whom he believes, to whom he feels himself closer than the crowd of the uninitiated. The lay teacher can and should have something of this feeling. He too is the agent of a great moral person who surpasses him: it is society. Just as the priest is the interpreter of his god, the teacher is the interpreter of the great moral ideas of his time and of his country. Let him be attached to these ideas, let him feel all their grandeur, and the authority which is in them, and of which he is aware, cannot fail to be communicated to his person and to everything that emanates from him. Into an authority which flows from such an impersonal source there could enter no pride, no vanity, no pedantry. It is made up entirely of the respect which he has for his functions and, if one may say so, for his office. It is this respect which, through word and gesture, passes from him to the child.

Liberty and authority have sometimes been opposed, as if these two factors of education contradicted and limited each other. But this opposition is factitious. In reality these two terms imply, rather than exclude, each other. Liberty is the daughter of authority properly understood. For to be free is not to do what one pleases; it is to be master of oneself, it is to know how to act with reason and to do one's duty. Now, it is precisely to endow the child with this self-mastery that the authority of the teacher should be employed. The authority of the teacher is only one aspect of the authority of duty and of reason. The child should, then, be trained to recognize it in the speech of the educator and to submit to its ascendancy; it is on this condition that he will know later how to find it again in his own conscience and to defer to it.

3 The 'Rationalization' of Education and Training

Max Weber

We cannot here analyze the far-reaching and general cultural effects that the advance of the rational bureaucratic structure of domination, as such, develops quite independently of the areas in which it takes hold. Naturally, bureaucracy promotes a 'rationalist' way of life, but the concept of rationalism allows for widely differing contents. Quite generally, one can only say that the bureaucratization of all domination very strongly furthers the development of 'rational matter-of-factness' and the personality type of the professional expert. This has far-reaching ramifications, but only one important element of the process can be briefly indicated here: its effect upon the nature of training and education.

Educational institutions on the European continent, especially the institutions of higher learning—the universities, as well as technical academics, business colleges, gymnasiums, and other middle schools—are dominated and influenced by the need for the kind of 'education' that produces a system of special examinations and the trained expertness that is increasingly indispensable for modern bureaucracy.

The 'special examination,' in the present sense, was and is found also outside of bureaucratic structures proper; thus, today it is found in the 'free' professions of medicine and law and in the guild-organized trades. Expert examinations are neither indispensable to nor concomitant phenomena of bureaucratization. The French, English, and American bureaucracies have for a long time foregone such examinations entirely or to a large extent, for training and service in party organizations have made up for them.

'Democracy' also takes an ambivalent stand in the face of specialized examinations, as it does in the face of all the phenomena of bureaucracy—although democracy itself promotes these developments. Special examinations, on the one hand, mean or appear to mean a 'selection' of those who qualify from all social strata rather than a rule by notables. On the other hand, democracy fears that a merit system and educational certificates will result in a privileged 'caste.' Hence, democracy fights against the special-examination system.

The special examination is found even in pre-bureaucratic or semi-bureaucratic epochs. Indeed, the regular and earliest locus of special examinations is among prebendally organized dominions. Expectancies of prebends, first of church prebends—as in the Islamite Orient and in the Occidental Middle Ages—then, as was especially the case in China, secular prebends, are the typical prizes for which people study and are examined. These examinations, however, have in truth only a partially specialized and expert character.

The modern development of full bureaucratization brings the system of rational, specialized, and expert examinations irresistibly to the fore. The civil-service reform gradually imports expert training and specialized examinations into the United States. In all other countries this system also advances, stemming from its main breeding place, Germany. The increasing bureaucratization of administration enhances the importance of the specialized examination in England. In China, the attempt to replace the semi-patrimonial and ancient bureaucracy by a modern bureaucracy brought the expert examination; it took the place of a former and quite differently structured system of examinations. The bureaucratization of capitalism, with its demand for expertly trained technicians, clerks, et cetera, carries such examinations all over the world. Above all, the development is greatly furthered by the social prestige of the educational certificates acquired through such specialized examinations. This is all the more the case as the educational patent is turned to economic advantage. Today, the certificate of education becomes what the test for ancestors has been in the past, at least where the nobility has remained powerful: a pre-requisite for equality of birth, a qualification for a canonship, and for state office.

The development of the diploma from universities, and business and engineering colleges, and the universal clamor for the creation of educational certificates in all fields make for the formation of a privileged stratum in bureaus and in offices. Such certificates support their holders' claims for intermarriages with notable families (in business offices people naturally hope for preferment with regard to the chief's daughter), claims to be admitted into the circles that adhere to 'codes of honor,' claims for a 'respectable' remuneration rather than remuneration for work done, claims for assured advancement and old-age insurance, and, above all, claims to monopolize socially and economically advantageous positions. When we hear from all sides the demand for an introduction of regular curricula and special examinations, the reason behind it is, of course, not a suddenly awakened 'thirst for education' but the desire for restricting the supply for these positions and their monopolization by the owners of educational certificates. Today, the 'examination' is the universal means of this monopolization, and therefore examinations irresistibly advance. As the education prerequisite to the acquisition of the educational certificate requires considerable expense and a period of waiting for full remuneration, this striving means a setback for talent (charisma) in favor of property. For the 'intellectual' costs of educational certificates are always low, and with the increasing volume of such certificates, their intellectual costs do not increase, but rather decrease.

The requirement of a chivalrous style of life in the old qualification for fiefs in Germany is replaced by the necessity of participating in its present rudimental form as represented by the dueling corps of the universities which also distribute the educational certificates. In Anglo-Saxon countries, athletic and social clubs fulfil the same function. The bureaucracy, on the other hand, strives everywhere for a 'right to the office' by the establishment of a regular disciplinary procedure and by removal of the completely arbitrary disposition of the 'chief' over the subordinate official. The bureaucracy seeks to secure the official position, the orderly advancement, and the provision for old age. In this, the bureaucracy is supported by the 'democratic' sentiment of the governed, which demands that domination be minimized. Those who hold this attitude believe themselves able to discern a weakening of the master's prerogatives in every weakening of the arbitrary disposition of the master over the officials. To this extent, bureaucracy, both in business offices and in public service, is a carrier of a specific 'status' development, as have been the quite differently structured officeholders of the past. We have already pointed out that these status characteristics are usually also exploited, and that by their nature they contribute to the technical usefulness of the bureaucracy in fulfilling its specific tasks.

'Democracy' reacts precisely against the unavoidable 'status' character of bureaucracy. Democracy seeks to put the election of officials for short terms in the place of appointed officials; it seeks to substitute the removal of officials by election for a regulated procedure of discipline. Thus, democracy seeks to replace the arbitrary disposition of the hierarchically superordinate 'master' by the equally arbitrary disposition of the governed and the party chiefs dominating them.

Social prestige based upon the advantage of special education and training as such is by no means specific to bureaucracy. On the contrary! But educational prestige in other structures of domination rests upon substantially different foundations.

Expressed in slogan-like fashion, the 'cultivated man,' rather than the 'specialist,' has been the end sought by education and has formed the basis of social esteem in such various systems as the feudal, theocratic, and patrimonial structures of dominion: in the English notable administration, in the old Chinese patrimonial bureaucracy, as well as under the rule of demagogues in the so-called Hellenic democracy.

The term 'cultivated man' is used here in a completely value-neutral sense; it is understood to mean solely that the goal of education consists in the quality of a man's bearing in life which was *considered* 'cultivated,' rather than in a specialized training for expertness. The 'cultivated' personality formed the educational ideal, which was stamped by the structure of domination and by the social condition for membership in the ruling stratum. Such education aimed at a chivalrous or an ascetic type; or, at a literary type, as in China; a gymnastic-humanist type, as in Hellas; or it aimed at a conventional type, as in the case of the Anglo-Saxon gentleman. The qualification of the ruling stratum as such rested upon the possession of 'more' cultural quality (in the absolutely changeable, value-neutral sense in which we use the term here), rather than upon 'more' expert knowledge. Special military, theological, and juridical ability was of course intensely practiced; but the point of gravity in Hellenic, in medieval, as well as in Chinese education, has rested upon educational elements that were entirely different from what was 'useful' in one's specialty.

Behind all the present discussions of the foundations of the educational system, the struggle of the 'specialist type of man' against the older type of 'cultivated man' is hidden at some decisive point. This fight is determined by the irresistibly expanding bureaucratization of all public and private relations of authority and by the ever-increasing importance of expert and specialized knowledge. This fight intrudes into all intimate cultural questions.

During its advance, bureaucratic organization has had to overcome those essentially negative obstacles that have stood in the way of the leveling process necessary for bureaucracy. In addition, administrative structures based on different principles intersect with bureaucratic organizations. Since these have been touched upon above, only some especially important structural *principles* will be briefly discussed here in a very simplified schema. We would be led too far afield were we to discuss all the actually existing types. We shall proceed by asking the following questions:

1. How far are administrative structures subject to economic determination? Or, how far are opportunities for development created by other circumstances, for instance the purely political? Or, finally, how far are developments created by an 'autonomous' logic that is solely of the technical structure as such?

2. We shall ask whether or not these structural principles, in turn, release specific economic effects, and if so, what effects. In doing this, one of course from the beginning has to keep his eye on the fluidity and the overlapping transitions of all these organizational principles. Their 'pure' types, after all, are to be considered merely as border cases which are especially valuable and indispensable for analysis. Historical realities, which almost always appear in mixed forms, have moved and still move between such pure types.

The bureaucratic structure is everywhere a late product of development. The further back we trace our steps, the more typical is the absence of bureaucracy and officialdom in the structure of domination. Bureaucracy has a 'rational' character: rules, means, ends, and matter-of-factness dominate its bearing. Everywhere its origin and its diffusion have therefore had 'revolutionary' results, in a special sense, which has still to be discussed. This is the same influence which the advance of *rationalism* in general has had. The march of bureaucracy has destroyed structures of domination which had no rational character, in the special sense of the term.

The Democratic Conception in Education

John Dewey

For the most part, save incidentally, we have hitherto been confused with education as it may exist in any social group. We have now to make explicit the differences in the spirit, material, and method of education as it operates in different types of community life. To say that education is a social function, securing direction and development in the immature through their participation in the life of the group to which they belong, is to say in effect that education will vary with the quality of life which prevails in a group. Particularly is it true that a society which not only changes but which has the ideal of such change as will improve it, will have different standards and methods of education from one which aims simply at the perpetuation of its own customs. To make the general ideas set forth applicable to our own educational practice, it is, therefore, necessary to come to closer quarters with the nature of present social life.

1. The Implications of Human Association

Society is one word, but many things. Men associate together in all kinds of ways and for all kind of purposes. One man is concerned in a multitude of diverse groups, in which his associates may be quite different. It often seems as if they had nothing in common except that they are modes of associated life. Within every larger social organization there are numerous minor groups: not only political subdivisions but industrial, scientific, religious associations. There are political parties with differing aims, social sets, cliques, gangs, corporations, partnerships, groups bound closely together by ties of blood, and so on in endless variety. In many modern states and in some ancient, there is great diversity of populations; of varying languages, religions, moral codes, and traditions. From this standpoint, many a minor political unit, one of our large cities, for example, is a congeries of loosely associated societies, rather than an inclusive and permeating community of action and thought.

The terms society, community, are thus ambiguous. They have both a eulogistic or normative sense and a descriptive sense; a meaning *de jure* and a meaning *de facto*. In social philosophy, the former connotation is almost always uppermost. Society is conceived as one by its very nature. The qualities which accompany this unity, praiseworthy community of purpose and welfare, loyalty to public ends, mutuality of sympathy, are emphasized. But when we look at the facts which the term *denotes* instead of confining our attention to its intrinsic *connotation*, we find not unity, but a plurality of societies, good and bad. Men banded together in a criminal conspiracy, business aggregations that prey upon the public while serving it, political machines held together by the interest of plunder, are included. If it is said that such organizations are not societies because they do not meet the ideal requirements of the notion society, the answer, in part, is that the conception of society is then made so 'ideal' as to be of no use, having no reference to facts; and in part that each of these organizations, no matter how opposed to the interests of other groups has something of the praiseworthy qualities of 'Society' which hold it together. There is honor among thieves, and a band of robbers has a common interest as respects its members. Gangs are marked by fraternal feeling, and narrow cliques by intense loyalty to their own codes. Family life may be marked by exclusiveness, suspicion, and jealousy as to those without, and yet be a model of amity and mutual aid within. Any education given by a group tends to socialize its members, but the quality and value of the socialization depends upon the habits and aims of the group.

Hence, once more, the need of a measure for the worth of any given mode of social life. In seeking this measure, we have to avoid two extremes. we cannot set up, out of our heads, something we regard as an ideal society. We must base our conception upon societies which actually exist, in order to have any assurance that our ideal is a practicable one. But, as we have just seen, the ideal cannot simply repeat the traits which are actually found. The problem is to extract the desirable traits of forms of community life which actually exist, and employ them to criticize undesirable features and suggest improvement. Now in any social group whatever, even in a gang of thieves, we find some interest held in common, and we find a certain amount of interaction and cooperative intercourse with other groups. From these two traits we derive our standard. How numerous and varied are the interests which are consciously shared? How full and free is the interplay with other forms of association? If we apply these consideration to, say, a criminal band, we find that the ties which consciously hold the members together are few in number, reducible almost to a common interest in plunder; and that they are of such a nature as to isolate the group from other groups with respect to give and take of the values of life. Hence, the education such a society gives is partial and distorted. If we take, on the other hand, the kind of family life which illustrates the standard, we find that there are material, intellectual, aesthetic interests in which all participate and that the progress of one member has worth for the experience of other members—it is readily communicable—and that the family is not an isolated whole, but enters intimately into relationships with business groups, with schools, with all the agencies of culture, as well as with other similar groups, and that it plays a due part in the political organization and in return receives support from it. In short, there are many interests consciously communicated and shared; and there are varied and free points of contact with other modes of association.

I. Let us apply the first element in this criterion to a despotically governed state. It is not true there is no common interest in such an organization between governed and governors. The authorities in command must make some appeal to the native activities of the subjects, must call some of their powers into play. Talleyrand said that a government could do everything with bayonets except sit on them. This cynical declaration is at least a recognition that the bond of union is not merely one of coercive force. It may be said, however, that the activities appealed to are themselves unworthy and degrading—that such a government calls into functioning activity simply capacity for fear. In a way, this statement is true. But it overlooks the fact that fear need not be an undesirable factor in experience. Caution, circumspection, prudence, desire to foresee future events so as to avert what is harmful, these desirable traits are as much a product of calling the impulse of fear into play as is cowardice and abject submission: The real difficulty is that the appeal to fear is *isolated.* In evoking dread and hope of specific tangible reward—say comfort and ease—many other capacities are left untouched. Or rather, they are affected, but in such a way as to pervert them. Instead of operating on their own account they are reduced to mere servants of attaining pleasure and avoiding pain.

This is equivalent to saying that there is no extensive number of common interests; there is no free play back and forth among the members of the social group. Stimulation and response are exceedingly one-sided. In order to have a large number of values in common, all the members of the group must have an equable opportunity to receive and to take from others. There must be a large variety of shared undertakings and experiences. Otherwise, the influences which educate some into masters, educate others into slaves. And the experience of each party loses in meaning, when the free interchange of varying modes of life-experience is arrested. A separation into a privilege and a subject-class prevents social endosmosis. The evils thereby affecting the superior class are less material and less perceptible, but equally real. Their culture tends to be sterile, to be turned back to feed on itself; their art becomes a showy display and artificial; their wealth luxurious; their knowledge overspecialized; their manners fastidious rather than humane.

Lack of the free and equitable intercourse which springs from a variety of shared interests makes intellectual stimulation unbalanced. Diversity of stimulation means novelty, and novelty means challenge to thought. The more activity is restricted to a few definite lines—as it is when there are rigid class lines preventing adequate interplay of experiences—the more action tends to become routine on the part of the class at a disadvantage, and capricious, aimless, and explosive on the part of the class having the materially fortunate position. Plato defined a slave as one who accepts from another the purposes which control his conduct. This condition obtains even where there is no slavery in the legal sense. It is found wherever men are engaged in activity which is socially serviceable, but whose service they do not understand and have no personal interest in. Much is said about scientific management of work. It is a narrow view which restricts the science which secures efficiency of operation to movements of the muscles. The chief opportunity for science is the discovery of the relations of a man to his work—including his relations to others who take part—which will enlist his intelligent interest in what he is doing. Efficiency is production often demands division of labor. But it is reduced to a mechanical routine unless workers see the technical, intellectual, and social relationships involved in what they do, and engage in their work because of the motivation furnished by such perceptions. The tendency to reduce such things as efficiency of activity and scientific management to purely technical externals is evidence of the one-sided stimulation of thought given to those in control of industry—those who supply its aims. Because of their lack of all-round and well-balanced social interest, there is not sufficient stimulus for attention to the human factors and relationships in industry. Intelligence is narrowed to the factors concerned with technical production and marketing of goods. No doubt, a very acute and intense intelligence in these narrow lines can be developed, but the failure to take into account the significant social factors means none the less an absence of mind, and a corresponding distortion of emotional life.

II. This illustration (whose point is to be extended to all associations lacking reciprocity of interest) brings us to our second point. The isolation and exclusiveness of a gang or clique brings its antisocial spirit into relief. But this same spirit is found wherever one group has interests 'of its own' which shut it out from full interaction with other groups, so that its prevailing purpose is the protection of what it has got, instead of reorganization and progress through wider relationships. It marks nations in their isolation from one another; families which seclude their domestic concerns as if they had no connection with a larger life; schools when separated from the interest of home and community; the divisions of rich and poor; learned and unlearned. The essential point is that isolation makes for rigidity and formal institutionalizing of life, for static and selfish ideals within the group. That savage tribes regard aliens and enemies as synonymous is not accidental. It springs from the fact that they have identified their experience with rigid adherence to their past customs. On such a basis it is wholly logical to fear intercourse with others, for such contact might dissolve custom. It would certainly occasion reconstruction. It is a commonplace that an alert and expanding mental life depends upon an enlarging range of contact with the physical environment. But the principle applies even more significantly to the field where we are apt to ignore it—the sphere of social contacts.

Every expansive era in the history of mankind has coincided with the operation of factors which have tended to eliminate distance between peoples and classes previously hemmed off from one another. Even the alleged benefits of war, so far as more than alleged, spring from the fact that conflict of peoples at least enforces intercourse between them and thus accidentally enables them to learn from one another, and thereby to expand their horizons. Travel, economic and commercial tendencies, have at present gone far to break down external barriers; to bring peoples and classes into closer and more perceptible connection with one another. It remains for the most part to secure the intellectual and emotional significance of this physical annihilation of space.

2. The Democratic Ideal

The two elements in our criterion both point to democracy. The first signifies not only more numerous and more varied points of shared common interest, but greater reliance upon the recognition of mutual interests as a factor in social control. The second means not only freer interaction between social groups (once isolated so far as intention could keep up a separation) but change in social habit—its continuous readjustment through meeting the new situations produced by varied intercourse. And these two traits are precisely what characterize the democratically constituted society.

Upon the educational side, we note first that the realization of a form of social life in which interests are mutually interpenetrating, and where progress, or readjustment, is an important consideration, makes a democratic community more interested than other communities have cause to be in deliberate and systematic education. The devotion of democracy to education is a familiar fact. The superficial explanation is that a government resting upon popular suffrage cannot be successful unless those who elect and who obey their governors are educated. Since a democratic society repudiates the principle of external authority, it must find a substitute in voluntary disposition and interest; these can be created only by education. But there is a deeper explanation. A democracy is more than a form of government; it is primarily a mode of associated living, of conjoint communicated experience. The extension in space of the number of individuals who participate in an interest so that each has to refer his own action to that of others, and to consider the action of others to give point and direction to his own, is equivalent to the breaking down of those barriers of class, race, and national territory which kept men from perceiving the full import of their activity. These more numerous and more varied points of contact denote a greater diversity of stimuli to which an individual has to respond; they consequently put a premium on variation in his action. They secure a liberation of powers which remain suppressed as long as the incitations to action are partial, as they must be in a group which in its exclusiveness shuts out many interests.

The widening of the area of shared concerns, and the liberation of a greater diversity of personal capacities which characterize a democracy, are not of course the product of deliberation and conscious effort. On the contrary, they were caused by the development of modes of manufacture and commerce, travel, migration, and intercommunication which flowed from the command of science over natural energy. But after greater individualization on one hand, and a broader community of interest on the other have come into existence, it is a matter of deliberate effort to sustain and extend them. Obviously a society to which stratification into separate classes would be fatal, must see to it that intellectual opportunities are accessible to all on equable and easy terms. A society marked off into classes need be specially attentive only to the education of its ruling elements. A society which is mobile, which is full of channels for the distribution of a change occurring anywhere, must see to it that its members are educated to personal initiative and adaptability. Otherwise, they will be overwhelmed by the changes in which they are caught and whose significance or connections they do not perceive. The result will be a confusion in which a few will appropriate to themselves the results of the blind and externally directed activities of others.

3. The Platonic Educational Philosophy

Subsequent chapters will be devoted to making explicit the implications of the democratic ideas in education. In the remaining portions of this chapter, we shall consider the educational theories which have been evolved in three epochs when the social import of education was especially conspicuous. The first one to be considered is that of Plato. No one could better express than did he the fact that a society is stably organized when each individual is doing that for which he has aptitude by nature in such a way as to be useful to others (or to contribute to the whole to which he belongs); and that it is the business of education to discover these aptitudes and progressively to train them for social use. Much which has been said so far is borrowed from what Plato first consciously taught the world. But conditions which he could not intellectually control led him to restrict these ideas in their application. He never got any conception of the indefinite plurality of activities which may characterize an individual and a social group, and consequently limited his view to a limited number of *classes* of capacities and of social arrangements.

Plato's starting point is that the organization of society depends ultimately upon knowledge of the end of existence. If we do not know its end, we shall be at the mercy of accident and caprice. Unless we know the end, the good, we shall have no criterion for rationally deciding what the possibilities are which should be promoted, nor how social arrangements are to be ordered. We shall have no conception of the proper limits and distribution of activities—what he called justice—as a trait of both individual and social organization. But how is the knowledge of the final and permanent good to be achieved? In dealing with this question we come upon the seemingly insuperable obstacle that such knowledge is not possible save in a just and harmonious social order. Everywhere else the mind is distracted and misled by false valuations and false perspectives. A disorganized and factional society sets up a number of different models and standards. Under such conditions it is impossible for the individual to attain consistency of mind. Only a complete whole is fully self-consistent. A society which rests upon the supremacy of some factor over another irrespective of its rational or proportionate claims, inevitably leads thought astray. It puts a premium on certain things and slurs over others, and creates a mind whose seeming unity is forced and distorted. Education proceeds ultimately from the patterns furnished by institutions, customs, and laws. Only in a just state will these be such as to give the right education; and only those who have rightly trained minds will be able to recognize the end, and ordering principle of things. We seem to be caught in a hopeless circle. However, Plato suggested a way out. A few men, philosophers or lovers of wisdom—or truth—may by study learn at least in outline the proper patterns of true existence. If a powerful ruler should form a state after these patterns, then its regulations could be preserved. An education could be given which would sift individuals, discovering what they were good for, and supplying a method of assigning each to the work in life for which his nature fits him. Each doing his own part, and never transgressing, the order and unity of the whole would be maintained.

It would be impossible to find in any scheme of philosophic thought a more adequate recognition on one hand of the educational significance of social arrangements and, on the other, of the dependence of those arrangements upon the means used to educate the young. It would be impossible to find a deeper sense of the function of education in discovering and developing personal capacities, and training them so that they would connect with the activities of others. Yet the society in which the theory was propounded was so undemocratic that Plato could not work out a solution for the problem whose terms he clearly saw.

While he affirmed with emphasis that the place of the individual in society should not be determined by birth or wealth or any conventional status, but by his own nature as discovered in the process of education, he had no perception of the uniqueness of individuals. For him they fall by nature into classes, and into a very small number of classes at that. Consequently the testing and sifting function of education only shows to which one of three classes an individual belongs. There being no recognition that each individual constitutes his own class, there could be no recognition of the infinite diversity of active tendencies and combinations of tendencies of which an individual is capable. There were only three types of faculties or powers in the individual's constitution. Hence education would soon reach a static limit in each class, for only diversity makes change and progress.

In some individuals appetites naturally dominate; they are assigned to the laboring and trading class, which expresses and supplies human wants. Others reveal, upon education, that over and above appetites, they have a generous, outgoing, assertively courageous disposition. They become the citizen-subjects of the state; its defenders in war; its internal guardians in peace. But their limit is fixed by their lack of reason, which is a capacity to grasp the universal. Those who possess this are capable of the highest kind of education, and become in time the legislators of the state—for laws are the universals which control the particulars of experience.

Thus it is not true that in intent, Plato subordinated the individual to the social whole. But it is true that lacking the perception of the uniqueness of every individual, his incommensurability with others, and consequently not recognizing that a society might change and yet be stable, his doctrine of limited powers and classes came in net effect to the idea of the subordination of individuality.

We cannot better Plato's conviction that an individual is happy and society well organized when each individual engages in those activities for which he has a natural equipment, nor his conviction that it is the primary office of education to discover this equipment to its possessor and train him for its effective use. But progress in knowledge has made us aware of the superficiality of Plato's lumping of individuals and their original powers into a few sharply marked-off classes; it has taught us that original capacities are indefinitely numerous and variable. It is but the other side of this fact to say that in the degree in which society has become democratic, social organization means utilization of the specific and variable qualities of individuals, not stratification by classes. Although his educational philosophy was revolutionary, it was none the less in bondage to static ideals. He thought that change or alteration was evidence of lawless flux; that true reality was unchangeable. Hence while he would radically change the existing state of society, his aim was to construct a state in which change would subsequently have no place. The final end of life is fixed; given a state framed with this end in view, not even minor details are to be altered. Though they might not be inherently important, yet if permitted they would inure the minds of men to the idea of change, and hence be dissolving and anarchic. The breakdown of his philosophy is made apparent in the fact that he could not trust to gradual improvements in education to bring about a better society which should then improve education, and so on indefinitely. Correct education could not come into existence until an ideal state existed, and after that education would be devoted simply to its conservation. For the existence of this state he was obliged to trust to some happy accident by which philosophic wisdom should happen to coincide with possession of ruling power in the state.

4. The 'Individualistic' Ideal of the Eighteenth Century

In the eighteenth-century philosophy we find ourselves in a very different circle of ideas. 'Nature' still means something antithetical to existing social organization; Plato exercised a great influence upon Rousseau. But the voice of nature now speaks for the diversity of individual talent and for the need of free development of individuality in all its variety. Education in accord with nature furnishes the goal and the method of instruction and discipline. Moreover, the native or original endowment was conceived, in extreme cases, as nonsocial or even as antisocial. Social arrangements were thought of as mere external expedients by which these nonsocial individuals might secure a greater amount of private happiness for themselves.

Nevertheless, these statements convey only an inadequate idea of the true significance of the movement. In reality its chief interest was in progress and in social progress. The seeming antisocial philosophy was a somewhat transparent mask for an impetus toward a wider and freer society—toward cosmopolitanism. The positive ideal was humanity. In membership in humanity, as distinct from a state, man's capacities would be liberated; while in existing political organizations his powers were hampered and distorted to meet the requirements and selfish interests of the rulers of the state. The doctrine of extreme individualism was but the counterpart, the obverse, of ideals of the indefinite perfectibility of man and of a social organization having a scope as wide as humanity. The emancipated individual was to become the organ and agent of a comprehensive and progressive society.

The heralds of this gospel were acutely conscious of the evils of the social estate in which they found themselves. They attributed these evils to the limitations imposed upon the free powers of man. Such limitation was both distorting and corrupting. Their impassioned devotion to emancipation of life from external restrictions which operated to the exclusive advantage of the class to whom a past feudal system consigned power, found intellectual formulation in a worship of nature. To give 'nature' full swing was to replace an artificial, corrupt, and inequitable social order by a new and better kingdom of humanity. Unrestrained faith in Nature as both a model and a working power was strengthened by the advances of natural science. Inquiry freed from prejudice and artificial restraints of church and state had revealed that the world is a scene of law. The Newtonian solar system, which expressed the reign of natural law, was a scene of wonderful harmony, where every force balanced with every other. Natural law would accomplish the same result in human relations, if men would only get rid of the artificial man-imposed coercive restrictions.

Education in accord with nature was thought to be the first step in insuring this more social society. It was plainly seen that economic and political limitations were ultimately dependent upon limitations of thought and feeling. The first step in freeing men from external chains was to emancipate them from the internal chains of false beliefs and ideas. What was called social life, existing institutions, were too false and corrupt to be intrusted with this work. How could it be expected to undertake it when the undertaking meant its own destruction? 'Nature' must then be the power to which the enterprise was to be left. Even the extreme sensationalistic theory of knowledge which was current derived itself from this conception. To insist that mind is originally passive and empty was one way of glorifying possibilities of education. If the mind was a wax tablet to be written upon by objects, there were no limits to the possibility of education by means of the natural environment. And since the natural world of object is a scence of harmonious 'truth,' this education would infallibly produce minds filled with the truth.

5. Education as National and as Social

As soon as the first enthusiasm for freedom waned, the weakness of the theory upon the constructive side became obvious. Merely to leave everything to nature was, after all, but to negate the very idea of education; it was to trust to the accidents of circumstance. Not only was some method required but also some positive organ, some administrative agency for carrying on the process of instruction. The 'complete and harmonious development of all powers,' having as its social counterpart an enlightened and progressive humanity, required definite organization for its realization, Private individuals here and there could proclaim the gospel; they could not execute the work. A Pestalozzi could try experiments and exhort philanthropically inclined persons having wealth and power to follow his example. But even Pestalozzi saw that any effective pursuit of the new educational ideal required the support of the state. The realization of new education destined to produce a new society was, after all, dependent upon the activities of existing states. The movement for the democratic idea inevitably became a movement for publicly conducted and administered schools.

So far as Europe was concerned, the historic situation identified the movement for a state-supported education with the nationalistic movement in political life—a fact of incalculable significance for sebsequent movements. Under the influence of German thought in particular, education became a civic function and the civic function was identified with the realization of the ideal of the national state. The 'state' was substituted for humanity; cosmopolitanism gave way to nationalism. To form the citizen, not the 'man,' became the aim of education.[1] The historic situation to which reference is made is the after-effects of the Napoleonic conquests, especially in Germany. The German states felt (and subsequent events demonstrate the correctness of the belief) that systematic attention to education was the best means of recovering and maintaining their political integrity and power. Externally they were weak and divided. Under the leadership of Prussian statesmen they made this condition a stimulus to the development of an extensive and thoroughly grounded system of public education.

This change in practice necessarily brought about a change in theory. The individualistic theory receded into the background. The state furnished not only the instrumentalities of public education but also its goal. When the actual practice was such that the school system, from the elementary grades through the university faculties, supplied the patriotic citizen and soldier and the future state official and administrator and furnished the means for military, industrial, and political defense and expansion, it was impossible for theory not to emphasize the aim of social efficiency. And with the immense importance attached to the nationalistic state, surrounded by other competing and more or less hostile states, it was equally impossible to interpret social efficiency in terms of a vague cosmopolitan humanitarianism. Since the maintenance of a particular national sovereignty required subordination of individuals to the superior interests of the state both in military defense and in struggles for international supremacy in commerce, social efficiency was understood to imply a like subordination. The educational process was taken to be one of disciplinary training rather than of personal development. Since, however, the ideal of culture as complete development of personality persisted, educational philosophy attempted a reconciliation of the two ideas. The reconciliation took the form of the conception of the 'organic' character of the state. The individual in his isolation is nothing; only in and through an absorption of the aims and meaning of organized institutions does he attain true personality. What appears to be his subordination to political authority and the demand for sacrifice of himself to the commands of his superiors is in reality but making his own the objective reason manifested in the state—the only way in which he can become truly rational. The notion of development which we have seen to be characteristic of institutional idealism (as in the Hegelian philosophy) was just such a deliberate effort to combine the two ideas of complete realization of personality and thoroughgoing 'disciplinary' subordination to existing institutions.

The extent of the transformation of educational philosophy which occurred in Germany in the generation occupied by the struggle against Napoleon for national independence, may be gathered from Kant, who well expresses the earlier individual-cosmopolitan ideal. In his treatise on Pedagogics, consisting of lectures given in the later years of the eighteenth century, he defines education as the process by which man becomes man. Mankind begins its history submerged in nature—not as Man who is a creature of reason, while nature furnishes only instinct and appetite. Nature offers simply the germs which education is to develop and perfect. The peculiarity of truly human life is that man has to create himself by his own voluntary efforts; he has to make himself a truly moral, rational, and free being. This creative effort is carried on by the educational activities of slow generations. Its acceleration depends upon men consciously striving to educate their successors not for the existing state of affairs but so as to make possible a future better humanity. But there is the great difficulty. Each generation is inclined to educate its young so as to get along in the present world instead of with a view to the proper end of education: the promotion of the best possible realization of humanity as humanity. Parents educate their children so that they may get on; princes educate their subjects as instruments of their own purposes.

Who, then, shall conduct education so that humanity may improve? We must depend upon the efforts of enlightened men in their private capacity. 'All culture begins with private men and spreads outward from them. Simply through the efforts of persons of enlarged inclinations, who are capable of grasping the ideal of a future better condition, is the gradual approximation of human nature to its end possible. . . . Rulers are simply interested in such training as will make their subjects better tools for their own intentions.' Even the subsidy by rulers of privately conducted schools must be carefully safeguarded. For the rulers' interest in the welfare of their own nation instead of in what is best for humanity, will make them, if they give money for the schools, wish to draw their plans. We have in this view an express statement of the points characteristic of the eighteenth century individualistic cosmopolitanism. The full development of private personality is identified with the aims of humanity as a whole and with the idea of progress. In addition we have an explicit fear of the hampering influence of a state-conducted and state-regulated education upon the attainment of these ideas. But in less than two decades after this time, Kant's philosophic successors, Fichte and Hegel, elaborated the idea that the chief function of the state is educational; that in particular the regeneration of Germany is to be accomplished by an education carried on in the interests of the state, and that the private individual is of necessity an egoistic, irrational being, enslaved to his appetites and to circumstances unless he submits voluntarily to the educative discipline of state institutions and laws. In this spirit, Germany was the first country to undertake a public, universal, and compulsory system of education extending from the primary school through the university, and to submit to jealous state regulation and supervision all private educational enterprises.

Two results should stand out from this brief historical survey. The first is that such terms as the individual and the social conceptions of education are quite meaningless taken at large, or apart from their context. Plato had the ideal of an education which should equate individual realization and social coherency and stability. His situation forced his ideal into the notion of a society organized in stratified classes, losing the individual in the class. The eighteenth century educational philosophy was highly individualistic in form, but this form was inspired by a noble and generous social ideal: that of a society organized to include humanity, and providing for the indefinite perfectibility of mankind. The idealistic philosophy of Germany in the early nineteenth century endeavored again to equate the ideals of a free and complete development of cultured personality with social discipline and political subordination. It made the national state an intermediary between the realization of private personality on one side and of humanity on the other. Consequently, it is equally possible to state its animating principle with equal truth either in the classic terms of 'harmonious development of all the powers of personality' or in the more recent terminology of 'social efficiency.' All this reinforces the statement which opens this chapter: The conception of education as a social process and function has no definite meaning until we define the kind of society we have in mind.

These considerations pave the way for our second conclusion. One of the fundamental problems of education in and for a democratic society is set by the conflict of a nationalistic and a wider social aim. The earlier cosmopolitan and 'humanitarian' conception suffered both from vagueness and from lack of definite organs of execution and agencies of administration. In Europe, in the Continental states particularly, the new idea of the importance of education for human welfare and progress was captured by national interests and harnessed to do a work whose social aim was definitely narrow and exclusive. The social aim of education and its national aim were identified, and the result was a marked obscuring of the meaning of a social aim.

This confusion corresponds to the existing situation of human intercourse. On the one hand, science, commerce, and art transcend national boundaries. They are largely international in quality and, method. They involve interdependencies and cooperation among the peoples inhabiting different countries. At the same time, the idea of national sovereignty has never been as accentuated in politics as it is at the present time. Each nation lives in a state of suppressed hostility and incipient war with its neighbors. Each is supposed to be the supreme judge of its own interests, and it is assumed as matter of course that each has interests which are exclusively its own. To question this is to question the very idea of national sovereignty which is assumed to be basic to political practice and political science. This contradiction (for it is nothing less) between the wider sphere of associated and mutually helpful social life and the narrower sphere of exclusive and hence potentially hostile pursuits and purposes, exacts of educational theory a clearer conception of the meaning of 'social' as a function and test of education than has yet been attained.

Is it possible for an educational system to be conducted by a national state and yet the full social ends of the educative process not be restricted, constrained, and corrupted? Internally, the question has to face the tendencies, due to present economic conditions, which split society into classes some of which are made merely tools for the higher culture of others. Externally, the question is concerned with the reconciliation of national loyalty, of patriotism, with superior devotion to the things which unite men in common ends, irrespective of national political boundaries. Neither phase of the problem can be worked out by merely negative means. It is not enough to see to it that education is not actively used as an instrument to make easier the exploitation of one class by another. School facilities must be secured of such amplitude and efficiency as will in fact and not simply in name discount the effects of economic inequalities, and secure to all the wards of the nation equality of equipment for their future careers. Accomplishment of this end demands not only adequate administrative provision of school facilities, and such supplementation of family resources as will enable youth to take advantage of them, but also such modification of traditional ideals of culture, traditional subjects of study and traditional methods of teaching and discipline as will retain all the youth under educational influences until they are equipped to be masters of their own economic and social careers. The ideal may seem remote of execution, but the democratic ideal of education is a farcical yet tragic delusion except as the ideal more and more dominates our public system of education.

The same principle has application on the side of the considerations which concern the relations of one nation to another. It is not enough to teach the horrors of war and to avoid everything which would stimulate international jealousy and animosity. The emphasis must be put upon whatever binds people together in cooperative human pursuits and results, apart from geographical limitations. The secondary and provisional character of national sovereignty in respect to the fuller, freer, and more fruitful association and intercourse of all human beings with one another must be instilled as a working disposition of mind. If these applications seem to be remote from a consideration of the philosophy of education, the impression shows that the meaning of the idea of education previously developed has not been adequately grasped. This conclusion is bound up with the very idea of education as a freeing of individual capacity in a progressive growth directed to social aims. Otherwise a democratic criterion of education can only be inconsistently applied.

Summary

Since education is a social process, and there are many kinds of societies, a criterion for educational criticism and construction implies a *particular* social ideal. The two points selected by which to measure the worth of a form of social life are the extent in which the interests of a group are shared by all its members, and the fullness and freedom with which it interacts with other groups. An undesirable society, in other words, is one which internally and externally sets up barriers to free intercourse and communication of experience. A society which makes provision for participation in its good of all its members on equal terms and which secures flexible readjustment of its institutions through interaction of the different forms of associated life is in so far democratic. Such a society must have a type of education which gives individuals a personal interest in social relationships and control, and the habits of mind which secure social changes without introducing disorder.

Three typical historic philosophies of education were considered from this point of view. The Platonic was found to have an ideal formally quite similar to that stated, but which was compromised in its working out by making a class rather than an individual the social unit. The so-called individualism of the eighteenth-century enlightenment was found to involve the notion of a society as broad as humanity, of whose progress the individual was to he the organ. But it lacked any agency for securing the development of its ideal as was evidenced in its falling back upon Nature. The institutional idealistic philosophies of the nineteenth century supplied this lack by making the national state the agency, but in so doing narrowed the conception of the social aim to those who were members of the same political unit, and reintroduced the idea of the subordination of the individual to the institution.

NOTES

1. There is a much neglected strain in Rousseau tending intellectually in this direction. He opposed the existing state of affairs on the ground that it formed *neither* the citizen nor the man. Under existing conditions, he preferred to try for the latter rather than for the former. But there are many sayings of his which point to the formation of the citizen as ideally the higher, and which indicate that his own endeavor, as embodied in the *Émile*, was simply the best makeshift the corruption of the times permitted him to sketch.

Part Two

Contemporary Theories of Social Change

In this book we are seeking to address some of the major questions in the sociology of education and some consideration of possible futures for education under the dynamics of globalization. In order to do so we need to examine the varieties of educational theory—both contemporary and past—available to us, and appraise the utility or persuasiveness of competing theoretical positions for understanding current educational issues and problems.

From the outset we encounter a major intellectual paradox. Theoretical orientations are not timeless or context-free. Like the phenomena for which they seek to account, they are themselves subject to the vicissitudes of social change. Sociological theories are designed to account for the character and directions of social change, yet they may themselves be seen to be influenced by, and influence, those very changes. For this reason any account of the sociology of education must present a reflexive dimension; it must be able to reflect upon its own internal tensions and theoretical presuppositions in relation to educational and global change. Each theoretical account of social change has its own history and each is also serendipitous to the extent that advances in social theory also reflect novel ideas. The combination of these differences results in the differential explanatory power of these theories. Here, we have taken the view that those sociological theories which attempt to explain the role of the nation-state in relation to individualization, market individualism, and globalization are best positioned to account for educational change.

The accounts in this section represent a challenge to earlier consensus accounts of the relationship between education and social change. Pierre Bourdieu's 'Forms of Capital' (Ch. 5) is perhaps one of the earliest post-war critiques of consensus accounts of social change. In this chapter he argues that inequality is reproduced not only through wealth but through education. Those families and individuals that have cultural and social capital gain an advantage in a context in which the education system is consistent with the values of the middle classes. A focus of his interest is in how individuals come to 'carry' the values and perspectives associated with cultural capital. He argues that what he calls embodiment is one mechanism, along with habitus, which represents the highly interconnected ways in which individuals internalize and transmit key aspects of social structure. This particular relationship is central in accounting for change in education. The key ideas here are that cultural reproduction emerges as an interaction between the institutionalized state and the embodied potentiality of individuals to carry forward elements of culture through habitus. Bourdieu's key contribution is to recognize the importance of both structure and agency in his account for social change in education. However, there is a certain irony in Bourdieu's basic premise that education is the major vehicle for the reproduction of privilege since with the recent dramatic increases in the polarization of income, the direct transmission of wealth remains a key factor in explaining inequality.

Bernstein (Ch. 6) addresses the connection of culture to language and ultimately to knowledge and pedagogy. His argument is that knowledge is heavily shaped not by a humanistic discourse but by culturally legitimated discourses of state power which are gleaned by an emphasis on, for example, market reforms. One way to account for social change in education is therefore to examine the very concept of knowledge and its changing forms in relation to state formation. He writes: 'there is a new concept of knowledge and its relation to those who create and use it. This new concept is a truly secular concept' and has been, over time, disassociated with the virtues of knowing for 'knowing's sake'. Such practices form the basis of social inequality for, as Bernstein writes, 'Once knowledge is separated from inwardness, from commitments, from personal dedication, from the deep structure of the self, then people may be moved about, substituted for each other and excluded from the market.'

By way of contrast, Michel Foucault's (Ch. 7) account of education represents a key paradigmatic shift in how state institutions, including education, are conceived. Foucault's main argument is that education expresses a form of discursive power through the classifying of students and the various institutional aspects of educational examination. Education thus draws upon specific 'techniques of power' which regard individuals not as meaningful beings within a larger social context but as objects through which power might be exercised. From this vantage point, social/educational institutions engage in forms of classification that do not necessarily resemble coercive forms of power in the ways asserted in conflict theories of education. Rather, as Foucault writes, they exert a 'modest, suspicious power'. Formal examinations and developed rituals of educational classification thus represent 'humble modalities' when 'compared with the majestic rituals of sovereignty or the great apparatuses of the state'. We therefore witness the 'effects of power rather than power itself'.

While Foucault's critique of the state is concerned with its form of classification and categorizing through institutions such as education, Edward Said's (Ch. 8) account of Orientalism addresses how such forms of classification shape the ways in which the West and especially academic institutions have constructed an imperial view of the 'Orient'. In coming to this conclusion he poses a key question 'is the intellectual designed to validate the culture and state of which he is a part?' Here Said is presenting in stark terms the problem of 'the scholar who is not vigilant, whose individual consciousness is not 'on guard' in challenging dominant perspectives of the state, and who becomes a medium through which state power is exercised. His account of social change thus moves the gaze of the macro nation-state towards the ways in which it represents or constructs issues of citizenship, and the study of the 'other'. It is in this sense that, as Massey (1994, 1995, 1999) suggests, power relations are exemplified through globalization.

In a radically different account of social change, Beck and Beck-Gernsheim (Ch. 9) consider the part that individualization and detraditionalization have played in shaping contemporary citizens, and the impact of such social and political processes on the changing nature of social relations. Their key argument is that late modernity is characterized by a distancing of individuals from traditional social roles and ritualistic elements of social life (such as family and class history). This distancing effect is changing the very nature of education and its forms: education being one of the many modernizing forces which lead to detraditionalization.

While less a theory of social change and more an examination of democratic principles in the modern world, Benhabib (Ch. 10) extends Beck and Beck-Gernsheim's account to the cultural realm of identity and its changing nature in political contexts. She argues, in particular, that questions of difference and culture can only emerge from a recognition of competing narratives that can be reconciled, in part, through 'a narrative view of actions and culture that inform it'. Accordingly, the key to an inclusive democratic framework which could ultimately apply to national education systems is its focus on the constructed and contested nature of culture and the necessity for debate over its significance. She argues for an 'intercultural justice between human groups'.

Whilst still concerned with the contested nature of identity and culture and their relevance for the nation-state, Arnot and Dillabough (Ch. 11) outline the impact of feminist thought on education and in particular democratic values relating to citizenship. The central argument is that feminist thought has an important role in understanding the gendered nature of a liberal democratic education. Here,the key contribution of feminist research to education has been its ability to assess women's relationship to the state and the state's success in women's incorporation through a study of their positioning in education. In doing so it seeks to challenge theoretical designs of the state and state education grounded in masculine domination.

Finally, in Appadurai's (Ch. 12) conception of the nation-state, social change is linked to the diasporic mobility of both commodities and people. This work implies that globalization is closely affiliated with the 'long-distance journey of commodities ... and of travelers and explorers of every type'. The key tensions in this model of social change is the pull between the idea of the nation-state as a form of homogenization and the post-colonial recognition of heterogeneity. What therefore becomes the legitimate model of education may therefore not be a national imaginary but a conception based upon the mobility of knowledge. However, Appadurai does not locate the central control of this mobility solely or necessarily in the hands of the state but through the effects of human motion and subtle forms of discursive power which are less visible than the state itself. The global state therefore becomes the primary mechanism by which social change may be accounted for. At the same time, this approach brings to the fore novel forms of diasporic cultural identification in the twentieth century along with a 'sociology of displacement' which is experienced through the contours of migration. It could be argued that he belongs to the school of hyper-globalists (see the main Introduction).

The Forms of Capital

Pierre Bourdieu

The social world is accumulated history, and if it is not to be reduced to a discontinuous series of instantaneous mechanical equilibria between agents who are treated as interchangeable particles, one must reintroduce into it the notion of capital and with it, accumulation and all its effects. Capital is accumulated labor (in its materialized form or its 'incorporated,' embodied form) which, when appropriated on a private, i.e., exclusive, basis by agents or groups of agents, enables them to appropriate social energy in the form of reified or living labor. It is a *vis insita*, a force inscribed in objective or subjective structures, but it is also a *lex insita*, the principle underlying the immanent regularities of the social world. It is what makes the games of society—not least, the economic game—something other than simple games of chance offering at every moment the possibility of a miracle. Roulette, which holds out the opportunity of winning a lot of money in a short space of time, and therefore of changing one's social status quasi-instantaneously, and in which the winning of the previous spin of the wheel can be staked and lost at every new spin, gives a fairly accurate image of this imaginary universe of perfect competition or perfect equality of opportunity, a world without inertia, without accumulation, without heredity or acquired properties, in which every moment is perfectly independent of the previous one, every soldier has a marshal's baton in his knapsack, and every prize can be attained, instantaneously, by everyone, so that at each moment anyone can become anything. Capital, which, in its objectified or embodied forms, takes time to accumulate and which, as a potential capacity to produce profits and to reproduce itself in identical or expanded form, contains a tendency to persist in its being, is a force inscribed in the objectivity of things so that everything is not equally possible or impossible.[1] And the structure of the distribution of the different types and subtypes of capital at a given moment in time represents the immanent structure of the social world, i.e., the set of constraints, inscribed in the very reality of that world, which govern its functioning in a durable way, determining the chances of success for practices.

It is in fact impossible to account for the structure and functioning of the social world unless one reintroduces capital in all its forms and not solely in the one form recognized by economic theory. Economic theory has allowed to be foisted upon it a definition of the economy of practices which is the historical invention of capitalism; and by reducing the universe of exchanges to mercantile exchange, which is objectively and subjectively oriented toward the maximization of profit, i.e., (economically) *self-interested*, it has implicitly defined the other forms of exchange as noneconomic, and therefore *disinterested*. In particular, it defines as disinterested those forms of exchange which ensure the *transubstantiation* whereby the most material types of capital—those which are economic in the restricted sense—can present themselves in the immaterial form of cultural capital or social capital and vice versa. Interest, in the restricted sense it is given in economic theory, cannot be produced without producing its negative counterpart, disinterestedness. The class of practices whose explicit purpose is to maximize monetary profit cannot be defined as such without producing the purposeless finality of cultural or artistic practices and their products; the world of bourgeois man, with his double-entry accounting, cannot be invented without producing the pure, perfect universe of the artist and the intellectual and the gratuitous activities of art-for-art's sake and pure theory. In other words, the constitution of a science of mercantile relationships which, inasmuch as it takes for granted the very foundations of the order it claims to analyze—private property, profit, wage labor, etc.—is not even a science of the field of economic production, has prevented the constitution of a general science of the economy of practices, which would treat mercantile exchange as a particular case of exchange in all its forms.

It is remarkable that the practices and assets thus salvaged from the 'icy water of egotistical calculation' (and from science) are the virtual monopoly of the dominant class—as if economism had been able to reduce everything to economics only because the reduction on which that discipline is based protects from sacrilegious reduction everything which needs to be protected. If economics deals only with practices that have narrowly economic interest as their principle and only with goods that are directly and immediately convertible into money (which makes them quantifiable), then the universe of bourgeois production and exchange becomes an exception and can see itself and present itself as a realm of disinterestedness. As everyone knows, priceless things have their price, and the extreme difficulty of converting certain practices and certain objects into money is only due to the fact that this conversion is refused in the very intention that produces them, which is nothing other than the denial (*Verneinung*) of the economy. A general science of the economy of practices, capable of reappropriating the totality of the practices which, although objectively economic, are not and cannot be socially recognized as economic, and which can be performed only at the cost of a whole labor of dissimulation or, more precisely, *euphemization*, must endeavor to grasp capital and profit in all their forms and to establish the laws whereby the different types of capital (or power, which amounts to the same thing) change into one another.[2]

Depending on the field in which it functions, and at the cost of the more or less expensive transformations which are the precondition for its efficacy in the field in question, capital can present itself in three fundamental guises: as *economic capital*, which is immediately and directly convertible into money and may be institutionalized in the form of property rights; as *cultural capital*, which is convertible, on certain conditions, into economic capital and may be institutionalized in the form of educational qualifications; and as *social capital*, made up of social obligations ('connections'), which is convertible, in certain conditions, into economic capital and may be institutionalized in the form of a title of nobility.[3]

Cultural Capital

Cultural capital can exist in three forms: in the *embodied* state, i.e., in the form of long-lasting dispositions of the mind and body; in the *objectified* state, in the form of cultural goods (pictures, books, dictionaries, instruments, machines, etc.), which are the trace or realization of theories or critiques of these theories, problematics, etc.; and in the *institutionalized* state, a form of objectification which must be set apart because, as will be seen in the case of educational qualifications, it confers entirely original properties on the cultural capital which it is presumed to guarantee.

The reader should not be misled by the somewhat peremptory air which the effort at axiomization may give to my argument.[4] The notion of cultural capital initially presented itself to me, in the course of research, as a theoretical hypothesis which made it possible to explain the unequal scholastic achievement of children originating from the different social classes by relating academic success, i.e., the specific profits which children from the different classes and class fractions can obtain in the academic market, to the distribution of cultural capital between the classes and class fractions. This starting point implies a break with the presuppositions inherent both in the commonsense view, which sees academic success or failure as an effect of natural aptitudes, and in human capital theories. Economists might seem to deserve credit for explicitly raising the question of the relationship between the rates of profit on educational investment and on economic investment (and its evolution). But their measurement of the yield from scholastic investment takes account only of *monetary* investments and profits, or those directly convertible into money, such as the costs of schooling and the cash equivalent of time devoted to study; they are unable to explain the different proportions of their resources which different agents or different social classes allocate to economic investment and cultural investment because they fail to take systematic account of the structure of the differential chances of profit which the various markets offer these agents or classes as a function of the volume and the composition of their assets (see esp. Becker 1964*b*). Furthermore, because they neglect to relate scholastic investment strategies to the whole set of educational strategies and to the system of reproduction strategies, they inevitably, by a necessary paradox, let slip the best hidden and socially most determinant educational investment, namely, the domestic transmission of cultural capital. Their studies of the relationship between academic ability and academic investment show that they are unaware that ability or talent is itself the product of an investment of time and cultural capital (Becker 1964*a*: 63–6). Not surprisingly, when endeavoring to evaluate the profits of scholastic investment, they can only consider the profitability of educational expenditure for society as a whole, the 'social rate of return,' or the 'social gain of education as measured by its effects on national productivity' (Becker 1964*b*: 121, 155). This typically functionalist definition of the functions of education ignores the contribution which the educational system makes to the reproduction of the social structure by sanctioning the hereditary transmission of cultural capital. From the very beginning, a definition of human capital, despite its humanistic connotations, does not move beyond economism and ignores, *inter alia*, the fact that the scholastic yield from educational action depends on the cultural capital previously invested by the family. Moreover, the economic and social yield of the educational qualification depends on the social capital, again inherited, which can be used to back it up.

The Embodied State

Most of the properties of cultural capital can be deduced from the fact that, in its fundamental state, it is linked to the body and presupposes embodiment. The accumulation of cultural capital in the embodied state, i.e., in the form of what is called culture, cultivation, *Bildung*, presupposes a process of embodiment, incorporation, which, insofar as it implies a labor of inculcation and assimilation, costs time, time which must be invested personally by the investor. Like the acquisition of a muscular physique or a suntan, it cannot be done at second hand (so that all effects of delegation are ruled out).

The work of acquisition is work on oneself (self-improvement), an effort that presupposes a personal cost (*on paie de sa personne*, as we say in French), an investment, above all of time, but also of that socially constituted form of libido, *libido sciendi*, with all the privation, renunciation, and sacrifice that it may entail. It follows that the least inexact of all the measurements of cultural capital are those which take as their standard the length of acquisition—so long, of course, as this is not reduced to length of schooling and allowance is made for early domestic education by giving it a positive value (a gain in time, a head start) or a negative value (wasted time, and doubly so because more time must be spent correcting its effects), according to its distance from the demands of the scholastic market.[5]

This embodied capital, external wealth converted into an integral part of the person, into a habitus, cannot be transmitted instantaneously (unlike money, property rights, or even titles of nobility) by gift or bequest, purchase or exchange. It follows that the use or exploitation of cultural capital presents particular problems for the holders of economic or political capital, whether they be private patrons or, at the other extreme, entrepreneurs employing executives endowed with a specific cultural competence (not to mention the new state patrons). How can this capital, so closely linked to the person, be bought without buying the person and so losing the very effect of legitimation which presupposes the dissimulation of dependence? How can this capital be concentrated—as some undertakings demand—without concentrating the possessors of the capital, which can have all sorts of unwanted consequences?

Cultural capital can be acquired, to a varying extent, depending on the period, the society, and the social class, in the absence of any deliberate inculcation, and therefore quite unconsciously. It always remains marked by its earliest conditions of acquisition which, through the more or less visible marks they leave (such as the pronunciations characteristic of a class or region), help to determine its distinctive value. It cannot be accumulated beyond the appropriating capacities of an individual agent; it declines and dies with its bearer (with his biological capacity, his memory, etc.). Because it is thus linked in numerous ways to the person in his biological singularity and is subject to a hereditary transmission which is always heavily disguised, or even invisible, it defies the old, deep-rooted distinction the Greek jurists made between inherited properties (*ta patroa*) and acquired properties (*epikteta*), i.e., those which an individual adds to his heritage. It thus manages to combine the prestige of innate property with the merits of acquisition. Because the social conditions of its transmission and acquisition are more disguised than those of economic capital, it is predisposed to function as symbolic capital, i.e., to be unrecognized as capital and recognized as legitimate competence, as authority exerting an effect of (mis)recognition, e.g., in the matrimonial market and in all the markets in which economic capital is not fully recognized, whether in matters of culture, with the great art collections or great cultural foundations, or in social welfare, with the economy of generosity and the gift. Furthermore, the specifically symbolic logic of distinction additionally secures material and symbolic profits for the possessors of a large cultural capital: any given cultural competence (e.g., being able to read in a world of illiterates) derives a scarcity value from its position in the distribution of cultural capital and yields profits of distinction for its owner. In other words, the share in profits which scarce cultural capital secures in class-divided societies is based, in the last analysis, on the fact that all agents do not have the economic and cultural means for prolonging their children's education beyond the minimum necessary for the reproduction of the labor-power least valorized at a given moment.[6]

Thus the capital, in the sense of the means of appropriating the product of accumulated labor in the objectified state which is held by a given agent, depends for its real efficacy on the form of the distribution of the means of appropriating the accumulated and objectively available resources; and the relationship of appropriation between an agent and the resources objectively available, and hence the profits they produce, is mediated by the relationship of (objective and/or subjective) competition between himself and the other possessors of capital competing for the same goods, in which scarcity—and through it social value—is generated. The structure of the field, i.e., the unequal distribution of capital, is the source of the specific effects of capital, i.e., the appropriation of profits and the power to impose the laws of functioning of the field most favourable to capital and its reproduction.

But the most powerful principle of the symbolic efficacy of cultural capital no doubt lies in the logic of its transmission. On the one hand, the process of appropriating objectified cultural capital and the time necessary for it to take place mainly depend on the cultural capital embodied in the whole family—through (among other things) the generalized Arrow effect and all forms of implicit transmission.[7] On the other hand, the initial accumulation of cultural capital, the precondition for the fast, easy accumulation of every kind of useful cultural capital, starts at the outset, without delay, without wasted time, only for the offspring of families endowed with strong cultural capital; in this case, the accumulation period covers the whole period of socialization. It follows that the transmission of cultural capital is no doubt the best hidden form of hereditary transmission of capital, and it therefore receives proportionately greater weight in the system of reproduction strategies, as the direct, visible forms of transmission tend to be more strongly censored and controlled.

It can immediately be seen that the link between economic and cultural capital is established through the mediation of the time needed for acquisition. Differences in the cultural capital possessed by the family imply differences first in the age at which the work of transmission and accumulation begins—the limiting case being full use of the time biologically available, with the maximum free time being harnessed to maximum cultural capital—and then in the capacity, thus defined, to satisfy the specifically cultural demands of a prolonged process of acquisition. Furthermore, and in correlation with this, the length of time for which a given individual can prolong his acquisition process depends on the length of time for which his family can provide him with the free time, i.e., time free from economic necessity, which is the precondition for the initial accumulation (time which can be evaluated as a handicap to be made up).

The Objectified State

Cultural capital, in the objectified state, has a number of properties which are defined only in the relationship with cultural capital in its embodied form. The cultural capital objectified in material objects and media, such as writings, paintings, monuments, instruments, etc., is transmissible in its materiality. A collection of paintings, for example, can be transmitted as well as economic capital (if not better, because the capital transfer is more disguised). But what is transmissible is legal ownership and not (or not necessarily) what constitutes the precondition for specific appropriation, namely, the possession of the means of 'consuming' a painting or using a machine, which, being nothing other than embodied capital, are subject to the same laws of transmission.[8]

Thus cultural goods can be appropriated both materially—which presupposes economic capital—and symbolically—which presupposes cultural capital. It follows that the owner of the means of production must find a way of appropriating either the embodied capital which is the precondition of specific appropriation or the services of the holders of this capital. To possess the machines, he only needs economic capital; to appropriate them and use them in accordance with their specific purpose (defined by the cultural capital, of scientific or technical type, incorporated in them), he must have access to embodied cultural capital, either in person or by proxy. This is no doubt the basis of the ambiguous status of cadres (executives and engineers). If it is emphasized that they are not the possessors (in the strictly economic sense) of the means of production which they use, and that they derive profit from their own cultural capital only by selling the services and products which it makes possible, then they will be classified among the dominated groups; if it is emphasized that they draw their profits from the use of a particular form of capital, then they will be classified among the dominant groups. Everything suggests that as the cultural capital incorporated in the means of production increases (and with it the period of embodiment needed to acquire the means of appropriating it), so the collective strength of the holders of cultural capital would tend to increase—if the holders of the dominant type of capital (economic capital) were not able to set the holders of cultural capital in competition with one another. (They are, moreover, inclined to competition by the very conditions in which they are selected and trained, in particular by the logic of scholastic and recruitment competitions.)

Cultural capital in its objectified state presents itself with all the appearances of an autonomous, coherent universe which, although the product of historical action, has its own laws, transcending individual wills, and which, as the example of language well illustrates, therefore remains irreducible to that which each agent, or even the aggregate of the agents, can appropriate (i.e., to the cultural capital embodied in each agent or even in the aggregate of the agents). However, it should not be forgotten that it exists as symbolically and materially active, effective capital only insofar as it is appropriated by agents and implemented and invested as a weapon and a stake in the struggles which go on in the fields of cultural production (the artistic field, the scientific field, etc.) and, beyond them, in the field of the social classes—struggles in which the agents wield strengths and obtain profits proportionate to their mastery of this objectified capital, and therefore to the extent of their embodied capital.[9]

The Institutionalized State

The objectification of cultural capital in the form of academic qualifications is one way of neutralizing some of the properties it derives from the fact that, being embodied, it has the same biological limits as its bearer. This objectification is what makes the difference between the capital of the autodidact, which may be called into question at any time, or even the cultural capital of the courtier, which can yield only ill-defined profits, of fluctuating value, in the market of high-society exchanges, and the cultural capital academically sanctioned by legally guaranteed qualifications, formally independent of the person of their bearer. With the academic qualification, a certificate of cultural competence which confers on its holder a conventional, constant, legally guaranteed value with respect to culture, social alchemy produces a form of cultural capital which has a relative autonomy vis-à-vis its bearer and even vis-à-vis the cultural capital he effectively possesses at a given moment in time. It institutes cultural capital by collective magic, just as, according to Merleau-Ponty, the living institute their dead through the ritual of mourning. One has only to think of the *concours* (competitive recruitment examination) which, out of the continuum of infinitesimal differences between performances, produces sharp, absolute, lasting differences, such as that which separates the last successful candidate from the first unsuccessful one, and institutes an essential difference between the officially recognized, guaranteed competence and simple cultural capital, which is constantly required to prove itself. In this case, one sees clearly the performative magic of the power of instituting, the power to show forth and secure belief or, in a word, to impose recognition.

By conferring institutional recognition on the cultural capital possessed by any given agent, the academic qualification also makes it possible to compare qualification holders and even to exchange them (by substituting one for another in succession). Furthermore, it makes it possible to establish conversion rates between cultural capital and economic capital by guaranteeing the monetary value of a given academic capital.[10] This product of the conversion of economic capital into cultural capital establishes the value, in terms of cultural capital, of the holder of a given qualification relative to other qualification holders and, by the same token, the monetary value for which it can be exchanged on the labor market (academic investment has no meaning unless a minimum degree of reversibility of the conversion it implies is objectively guaranteed). Because the material and symbolic profits which the academic qualification guarantees also depend on its scarcity, the investments made (in time and effort) may turn out to be less profitable than was anticipated when they were made (there having been a *de facto* change in the conversion rate between academic capital and economic capital). The strategies for converting economic capital into cultural capital, which are among the short-term factors of the schooling explosion and the inflation of qualifications, are governed by changes in the structure of the chances of profit offered by the different types of capital.

Social Capital

Social capital is the aggregate of the actual or potential resources which are linked to possession of a durable network of more or less institutionalized relationships of mutual acquaintance and recognition—or in other words, to membership in a group[11]—which provides each of its members with the backing of the collectivity-owned capital, a 'credential' which entitles them to credit, in the various senses of the word. These relationships may exist only in the practical state, in material and/or symbolic exchanges which help to maintain them. They may also be socially instituted and guaranteed by the application of a common name (the name of a family, a class, or a tribe or of a school, a party, etc.) and by a whole set of instituting acts designed simultaneously to form and inform those who undergo them; in this case, they are more or less really enacted and so maintained and reinforced, in exchanges. Being based on indissolubly material and symbolic exchanges, the establishment and maintenance of which presuppose reacknowledgment of proximity, they are also partially irreducible to objective relations of proximity in physical (geographical) space or even in economic and social space.[12]

The volume of the social capital possessed by a given agent thus depends on the size of the network of connections he can effectively mobilize and on the volume of the capital (economic, cultural or symbolic) possessed in his own right by each of those to whom he is connected.[13] This means that, although it is relatively irreducible to the economic and cultural capital possessed by a given agent, or even by the whole set of agents to whom he is connected, social capital is never completely independent of it because the exchanges instituting mutual acknowledgment presuppose the reacknowledgment of a minimum of objective homogeneity, and because it exerts a multiplier effect on the capital he possesses in his own right.

The profits which accrue from membership in a group are the basis of the solidarity which makes them possible.[14] This does not mean that they are consciously pursued as such, even in the case of groups like select clubs, which are deliberately organized in order to concentrate social capital and so to derive full benefit from the multiplier effect implied in concentration and to secure the profits of membership—material profits, such as all the types of services accruing from useful relationships, and symbolic profits, such as those derived from association with a rare, prestigious group.

The existence of a network of connections is not a natural given, or even a social given, constituted once and for all by an initial act of institution, represented, in the case of the family group, by the genealogical definition of kinship relations, which is the characteristic of a social formation. It is the product of an endless effort at institution, of which institution rites—often wrongly described as rites of passage—mark the essential moments and which is necessary in order to produce and reproduce lasting, useful relationships that can secure material or symbolic profits (see Bourdieu 1982). In other words, the network of relationships is the product of investment strategies, individual or collective, consciously or unconsciously aimed at establishing or reproducing social relationships that are directly usable in the short or long term, i.e., at transforming contingent relations, such as those of neighborhood, the workplace, or even kinship, into relationships that are at once necessary and elective, implying durable obligations subjectively felt (feelings of gratitude, respect, friendship, etc.) or institutionally guaranteed (rights). This is done through the alchemy of *consecration*, the symbolic constitution produced by social institution (institution as a relative—brother, sister, cousin, etc.—or as a knight, an heir, an elder, etc.) and endlessly reproduced in and through the exchange (of gifts, words, women, etc.) which it encourages and which presupposes and produces mutual knowledge and recognition. Exchange transforms the things exchanged into signs of recognition and, through the mutual recognition and the recognition of group membership which it implies, reproduces the group. By the same token, it reaffirms the limits of the group, i.e., the limits beyond which the constitutive exchange—trade, commensality, or marriage—cannot take place. Each member of the group is thus instituted as a custodian of the limits of the group: because the definition of the criteria of entry is at stake in each new entry, he can modify the group by modifying the limits of legitimate exchange through some form of misalliance. It is quite logical that, in most societies, the preparation and conclusion of marriages should be the business of the whole group, and not of the agents directly concerned. Through the introduction of new members into a family, a clan, or a club, the whole definition of the group, i.e., its fines, its boundaries, and its identity, is put at stake, exposed to redefinition, alteration, adulteration. When, as in modern societies, families lose the monopoly of the establishment of exchanges which can lead to lasting relationships, whether socially sanctioned (like marriage) or not, they may continue to control these exchanges, while remaining within the logic of laissez-faire, through all the institutions which are designed to favor legitimate exchanges and exclude illegitimate ones by producing occasions (rallies, cruises, hunts, parties, receptions, etc.), places (smart neighborhoods, select schools, clubs, etc.), or practices (smart sports, parlor games, cultural ceremonies, etc.) which bring together, in a seemingly fortuitous way, individuals as homogeneous as possible in all the pertinent respects in terms of the existence and persistence of the group.

The reproduction of social capital presupposes an unceasing effort of sociability, a continuous series of exchanges in which recognition is endlessly affirmed and reaffirmed. This work, which implies expenditure of time and energy and so, directly or indirectly, of economic capital, is not profitable or even conceivable unless one invests in it a specific competence (knowledge of genealogical relationships and of real connections and skill at using them, etc.) and an acquired disposition to acquire and maintain this competence, which are themselves integral parts of this capital.[15] This is one of the factors which explain why the profitability of this labor of accumulating and maintaining social capital rises in proportion to the size of the capital. Because the social capital accruing from a relationship is that much greater to the extent that the person who is the object of it is richly endowed with capital (mainly social, but also cultural and even economic capital), the possessors of an inherited social capital, symbolized by a great name, are able to transform all circumstantial relationships into lasting connections. They are sought after for their social capital and, because they are well known, are worthy of being known ('I know him well'); they do not need to 'make the acquaintance' of all their 'acquaintances'; they are known to more people than they know, and their work of sociability, when it is exerted, is highly productive.

Every group has its more or less institutionalized forms of delegation which enable it to concentrate the totality of the social capital, which is the basis of the existence of the group (a family or a nation, of course, but also an association or a party), in the hands of a single agent or a small group of agents and to mandate this plenipotentiary, charged with *plena potestas agendi et loquendi*,[16] to represent the group, to speak and act in its name and so, with the aid of this collectively owned capital, to exercise a power incommensurate with the agent's personal contribution. Thus, at the most elementary degree of institutionalization, the head of the family, the *pater familias*, the eldest, most senior member, is tacitly recognized as the only person entitled to speak on behalf of the family group in all official circumstances. But whereas in this case, diffuse delegation requires the great to step forward and defend the collective honor when the honor of the weakest members is threatened, the institutionalized delegation, which ensures the concentration of social capital, also has the effect of limiting the consequences of individual lapses by explicitly delimiting responsibilities and authorizing the recognized spokesmen to shield the group as a whole from discredit by expelling or excommunicating the embarrassing individuals.

If the internal competition for the monopoly of legitimate representation of the group is not to threaten the conservation and accumulation of the capital which is the basis of the group, the members of the group must regulate the conditions of access to the right to declare oneself a member of the group and, above all, to set oneself up as a representative (delegate, plenipotentiary, spokesman, etc.) of the whole group, thereby committing the social capital of the whole group. The title of nobility is the form *par excellence* of the institutionalized social capital which guarantees a particular form of social relationship in a lasting way. One of the paradoxes of delegation is that the mandated agent can exert on (and, up to a point, against) the group the power which the group enables him to concentrate. (This is perhaps especially true in the limiting cases in which the mandated agent creates the group which creates him but which only exists through him.) The mechanisms of delegation and representation (in both the theatrical and the legal senses) which fall into place—that much more strongly, no doubt, when the group is large and its members weak—as one of the conditions for the concentration of social capital (among other reasons, because it enables numerous, varied, scattered agents to act as one man and to overcome the limitations of space and time) also contain the seeds of an embezzlement or misappropriation of the capital which they assemble.

This embezzlement is latent in the fact that a group as a whole can be represented, in the various meanings of the word, by a subgroup, clearly delimited and perfectly visible to all, known to all, and recognized by all, that of the *nobiles*, the 'people who are known', the paradigm of whom is the nobility, and who may speak on behalf of the whole group, represent the whole group, and exercise authority in the name of the whole group. The noble is the group personified. He bears the name of the group to which he gives his name (the metonymy which links the noble to his group is clearly seen when Shakespeare calls Cleopatra 'Egypt' or the King of France 'France,' just as Racine calls Pyrrhus 'Epirus'). It is by him, his name, the difference it proclaims, that the members of his group, the liegemen, and also the land and castles, are known and recognized. Similarly, phenomena such as the 'personality cult' or the identification of parties, trade unions, or movements with their leader are latent in the very logic of representation. Everything combines to cause the signifier to take the place of the signified, the spokesmen that of the group he is supposed to express, not least because his distinction, his 'outstandingness,' his visibility constitute the essential part, if not the essence, of this power, which, being entirely set within the logic of knowledge and acknowledgment, is fundamentally a symbolic power; but also because the representative, the sign, the emblem, may be, and create, the whole reality of groups which receive effective social existence only in and through representation.[17]

Conversions

The different types of capital can be derived from *economic capital*, but only at the cost of a more or less great effort of transformation, which is needed to produce the type of power effective in the field in question. For example there are some goods and services to which economic capital gives immediate access without secondary costs; others can be obtained only by virtue of a social capital of relationships (or social obligations) which cannot act instantaneously, at the appropriate moment, unless they have been established and maintained for a long time, as if for their own sake, and therefore outside their period of use, i.e., at the cost of an investment in sociability which is necessarily long-term because the time lag is one of the factors of the transmutation of a pure and simple debt into that recognition of nonspecific indebtedness which is called gratitude.[18] In contrast to the cynical but also economical transparency of economic exchange, in which equivalents change hands in the same instant, the essential ambiguity of social exchange, which presupposes misrecognition, in other words, a form of faith and of bad faith (in the sense of self-deception), presupposes a much more subtle economy of time.

So it has to be posited simultaneously that economic capital is at the root of all the other types of capital and that these transformed, disguised forms of economic capital, never entirely reducible to that definition, produce their most specific effects only to the extent that they conceal (not least from their possessors) the fact that economic capital is at their root, in other words—but only in the last analysis—at the root of their effects. The real logic of the functioning of capital, the conversions from one type to another, and the law of conservation which governs them cannot be understood unless two opposing but equally partial views are superseded: on the one hand, economism, which, on the grounds that every type of capital is reducible in the last analysis to economic capital, ignores what makes the specific efficacy of the other types of capital, and on the other hand, semiologism (nowadays represented by structuralism, symbolic interactionism, or ethnomethodology), which reduces social exchanges to phenomena of communication and ignores the brutal fact of universal reducibility to economics.[19]

In accordance with a principle which is the equivalent of the principle of the conservation of energy, profits in one area are necessarily paid for by costs in another (so that a concept like wastage has no meaning in a general science of the economy of practices). The universal equivalent, the measure of all equivalences, is nothing other than labor-time (in the widest sense); and the conservation of social energy through all its conversions is verified if, in each case, one takes into account both the labor-time accumulated in the form of capital and the labor-time needed to transform it from one type into another.

It has been seen, for example, that the transformation of economic capital into social capital presupposes a specific labor, i.e., an apparently gratuitous expenditure of time, attention, care, concern, which, as is seen in the endeavor to personalize a gift, has the effect of transfiguring the purely monetary import of the exchange and, by the same token, the very meaning of the exchange. From a narrowly economic standpoint, this effort is bound to be seen as pure wastage, but in the terms of the logic of social exchanges it is a solid investment, the profits of which will appear, in the long run, in monetary or other form. Similarly, if the best measure of cultural capital is undoubtedly the amount of time devoted to acquiring it, this is because the transformation of economic capital into cultural capital presupposes an expenditure of time that is made possible by possession of economic capital. More precisely, it is because the cultural capital that is effectively transmitted within the family itself depends not only on the quantity of cultural capital, itself accumulated by spending time, that the domestic group possess, but also on the usable time (particularly in the form of the mother's free time) available to it (by virtue of its economic capital, which enables it to purchase the time of others) to ensure the transmission of this capital and to delay entry into the labor market through prolonged schooling, a credit which pays off, if at all, only in the very long term.[20]

The convertibility of the different types of capital is the basis of the strategies aimed at ensuring the reproduction of capital (and the position occupied in social space) by means of the conversions least costly in terms of conversion work and of the losses inherent in the conversion itself (in a given state of the social power relations). The different types of capital can be distinguished according to their reproducibility or, more precisely, according to how easily they are transmitted, i.e., with more or less loss and with more or less concealment; the rate of loss and the degree of concealment tend to vary in inverse ratio. Everything which helps to disguise the economic aspect also tends to increase the risk of loss (particularly the intergenerational transfers). Thus the (apparent) incommensurability of the different types of capital introduces a high degree of uncertainty into all transactions between holders of different types. Similarly, the declared refusal of calculation and of guarantees which characterizes exchanges tending to produce a social capital in the form of a capital of obligations that are usable in the more or less long term (exchanges of gifts, services, visits, etc.) necessarily entails the risk of ingratitude, the refusal of that recognition of nonguaranteed debts which such exchanges aim to produce. Similarly, too, the high degree of concealment of the transmission of cultural capital has the disadvantage (in addition its inherent risks of loss) that the academic qualification which is its institutionalized form is neither transmissible (like a title of nobility) nor negotiable (like stocks and shars). More precisely, cultural capital, whose diffuse, continuous transmission within the family escapes observation and control (so that the educational system seems to award its honors solely to natural qualities) and which is increasingly tending to attain full efficacy, at least on the labor market, only when validated by the educational system, i.e., converted into a capital of qualifications, is subject to a more disguised but more risky transmission than economic capital. As the educational qualification, invested with the specific force of the official, becomes the condition for legitimate access to a growing number of positions, particularly the dominant ones, the educational system tends increasingly to dispossess the domestic group of the monopoly of the transmission of power and privileges—and, among other things, of the choice of its legitimate heirs from among children of different sex and birth rank.[21] And economic capital itself poses quite different problems of transmission, depending on the particular form it takes. Thus, according to Grassby (1970), the liquidity of commercial capital, which gives immediate economic power and favors transmission, also makes it more vulnerable than landed property (or even real estate) and does not favor the establishment of long-lasting dynasties.

Because the question of the arbitrariness of appropriation arises most sharply in the process of transmission—particularly at the time of succession, a critical moment for all power—every reproduction strategy is at the same time a legitimation strategy aimed at consecrating both an exclusive appropriation and its reproduction. When the subversive critique which aims to weaken the dominant class through the principle of its perpetuation by bringing to light the arbitrariness of the entitlements transmitted and of their transmission (such as the critique which the Enlightenment *philosophes* directed, in the name of nature, against the arbitrariness of birth) is incorporated in institutionalized mechanisms (for example, laws of inheritance) aimed at controlling the official, direct transmission of power and privileges, the holders of capital have an ever greater interest in resorting to reproduction strategies capable of ensuring better-disguised transmission, but at the cost of greater loss of capital, by exploiting the convertibility of the types of capital. Thus the more the official transmission of capital is prevented or hindered, the more the effects of the clandestine circulation of capital in the form of cultural capital become determinant in the reproduction of the social structure. As an instrument of reproduction capable of disguising its own function, the scope of the educational system tends to increase, and together with this increase is the unification of the market in social qualifications which gives rights to occupy rare positions.

NOTES

1. This inertia, entailed by the tendency of the structures of capital to reproduce themselves in institutions or in dispositions adapted to the structures of which they are the product, is, of course, reinforced by a specifically political action of concerted conservation, i.e., of demobilization and depoliticization. The latter tends to keep the dominated agents in the state of a practical group, united only by the orchestration of their dispositions and condemned to function as an aggregate repeatedly performing discrete, individual acts (such as consumer or electoral choices).
2. This is true of all exchanges between members of different fractions of the dominant class, possessing different types of capital. These range from sales of expertise, treatment, or other services which take the form of gift exchange and dignify themselves with the most decorous names that can be found (honoraria, emoluments, etc.) to matrimonial exchanges, the prime example of a transaction that can only take place insofar as it is not perceived or defined as such by the contracting parties. It is remarkable that the apparent extensions of economic theory beyond the limits constituting the discipline have left intact the asylum of the sacred, apart from a few sacrilegious incursions. Gary S. Becker, for example, who was one of the first to take explicit account of the types of capital that are usually ignored, never considers anything other than monetary costs and profits, forgetting the nonmonetary investments (*inter alia*, the affective ones) and the material and symbolic profits that education provides in deferred, indirect way, such as the added value which the dispositions produced or reinforced by schooling (bodily or verbal manners, tastes, etc.) or the relationships established with fellow students can yield in the matrimonial market (Becker 1964*a*).
3. *Symbolic capital*, that is to say, capital—in whatever form—insofar as it is represented, i.e., apprehended symbolically, in a relationship of knowledge or, more precisely, of misrecognition and recognition, presupposes the intervention of the habitus, as a socially constituted cognitive capacity.
4. When talking about concepts for their own sake, as I do here, rather than using them in research, one always runs the risk of being both schematic and formal, i.e., theoretical in the most usual and most usually approved sense of the word.
5. This proposition implies no recognition of the value of scholastic verdicts; it merely registers the relationship which exists in reality between a certain cultural capital and the laws of the educational market. Dispositions that are given a negative value in the educational market may receive very high value in other markets—not least, of course, in the relationships internal to the class.
6. In a relatively undifferentiated society, in which access to the means of appropriating the cultural heritage is very equally distributed, embodied culture does not function as cultural capital, i.e., as a means of acquiring exclusive advantages.
7. What I call the generalized Arrow effect, i.e., the fact that all cultural goods—paintings, monuments, machines, and any objects shaped by man, particularly all those which belong to the childhood environment—exert an educative effect by their mere existence, is no doubt one of the structural factors behind the 'schooling explosion,' in the sense that a growth in the quantity of cultural capital accumulated in the objectified state increases the educative effect automatically exerted by the environment. If one adds to this the fact that embodied cultural capital is constantly increasing, it can be seen that, in each generation, the educational system can take more for granted. The fact that the same educational investment is increasingly productive is one of the structural factors of the

inflation of qualifications (together with cyclical factors linked to effects of capital conversion).

8. The cultural object, as a living social institution, is, simultaneously, a socially instituted material object and a particular class of habitus, to which it is addressed. The material object—for example, a work of art in its materiality—may be separated by space (e.g., a Dogon statue) or by time (e.g., a Simone Martini painting) from the habitus for which it was intended. This leads to one of the most fundamental biases of art history. Understanding the effect (not to be confused with the function) which the work tended to produce—for example, the form of belief it tended to induce—and which is the true basis of the conscious or unconscious choice of the means used (technique, colors, etc.), and therefore of the form itself, is possible only if one at least raises the question of the habitus on which it operated.

9. The dialectical relationship between objectified cultural capital—of which the form *par excellence* is writing—and embodied cultural capital has generally been reduced to an exalted description of the degradation of the spirit by the letter, the living by the inert, creation by routine, grace by heaviness.

10. This is particularly true in France, where in many occupations (particularly the civil service) there is a very strict relationship between qualification, rank, and remuneration (translator's note).

11. Here, too, the notion of cultural capital did not spring from pure theoretical work, still less from an analogical extension of economic concepts. It arose from the need to identify the principle of social effects which, although they can be seen clearly at the level of singular agents—where statistical inquiry inevitably operates—cannot be reduced to the set of properties individually possessed by a given agent. These effects, in which spontaneous sociology readily perceives the work of 'connections,' are particularly visible in all cases in which different individuals obtain very unequal profits from virtually equivalent (economic or cultural) capital, depending on the extent to which they can mobilize by proxy the capital of a group (a family, the alumni of an elite school, a select club, the aristocracy, etc.) that is more or less constituted as such and more or less rich in capital.

12. Neighborhood relationships may, of course, receive an elementary form of institutionalization, as in the Bearn—or the Basque region—where neighbors, *lous besis* (a word which, in old texts, is applied to the legitimate inhabitants of the village, the rightful members of the assembly), are explicitly designated, in accordance with fairly codified rules, and are assigned functions which are differentiated according to their rank (there is a 'first neighbor,' a 'second neighbor,' and so on), particularly for the major social ceremonies (funerals, marriages, etc.). But even in this case, the relationships actually used by no means always coincide with the relationships socially instituted.

13. Manners (bearing, pronunciation, etc.) may be included in social capital insofar as, through the mode of acquisition they point to, they indicate initial membership of a more or less prestigious group.

14. National liberation movements or nationalist ideologies cannot be accounted for solely by reference to strictly economic profits, i.e., anticipation of the profits which may be derived from redistribution of a proportion of wealth to the advantage of the nationals (nationalization) and the recovery of highly paid jobs (see Breton 1964). To these specifically economic anticipated profits, which would only explain the nationalism of the privileged classes, must be added the very real and very immediate profits derived from membership (social capital) which are proportionately greater for those who are lower down the social hierarchy ('poor whites') or, more precisely, more threatened by economic and social decline.

15. There is every reason to suppose that socializing, or, more generally, relational, dispositions are very unequally distributed among the social classes and, within a given class, among fractions of different origin.

16. A 'full power to act and speak' (translator).

17. It goes without saying that social capital is so totally governed by the logic of knowledge and acknowledgment that it always functions as symbolic capital.

18. It should be made clear, to dispel a likely misunderstanding, that the investment in question here is not necessarily conceived as a calculated pursuit of gain, but that it has every likelihood of being experienced in terms of the logic of emotional investment, i.e., as an involvement which is both necessary and disinterested. This has not always been appreciated by historians, who (even when they are as alert to symbolic effects as E. P. Thompson) tend to conceive symbolic practices—powdered wigs and the whole paraphernalia of office—as explicit strategies of domination intended to be seen (from below), and to interpret generous or charitable conduct as 'calculated acts of class appeasement.' This naively Machiavellian view forgets that the most sincerely disinterested acts may be those best corresponding to objective interest. A number of fields, particularly those which most tend to deny interest and every sort of calculation, like the fields of cultural production, grant full recognition, and with it the consecration which guarantees success, only to those who distinguish themselves by the immediate conformity of their investments, a token of sincerity and attachment to the essential principles of the field. It would be thoroughly erroneous to describe the choices of the habitus which lead an artist, writer, or researcher toward his natural place (a subject, style, manner, etc.) in terms of rational strategy and cynical calculation. This is despite the fact that, for example, shifts from one genre, school, or speciality to another, quasi-religious conversions that are performed 'in all sincerity,' can be understood as capital conversions, the direction and moment of which (on which their success often depends) are determined by a 'sense of investment' which is the less likely to be seen as such the more skillful it is. Innocence is the privilege of those who move in their field of activity like fish in water.

19. To understand the attractiveness of this pair of antagonistic positions which serve as each other's alibi, one would need to analyze the unconscious profits and the profits of unconsciousness which they procure for intellectuals. While some find in economism a means of exempting themselves by excluding the cultural capital and all the specific profits which place them on the side of the dominant, others can abandon the detestable terrain of the economic, where everything reminds them that they can be evaluated, in the last analysis, in economic terms, for that of the symbolic. (The latter merely reproduce, in the realm of the symbolic, the strategy whereby intellectuals and artists endeavor to impose the recognition of their values, i.e., their value, by inverting the law of the market in which what one has or what one earns completely defines what one is worth and what one is—as is shown by the practice of banks which, with techniques such as the personalization of credit, tend to subordinate the granting of loans and the fixing of interest rates to an exhaustive inquiry into the borrower's present and future resources.)

20. Among the advantages procured by capital in all its types, the most precious is the increased volume of useful time that is made possible through the various methods of appropriating other people's time (in the form of services). It may take the form either of increased spare time, secured by reducing the time consumed in activities directly channeled toward producing the means of reproducing the existence of the domestic group, or of more intense use of the time so consumed, by recourse to other people's labor or to devices and methods which are available only to those who have spent time learning

how to use them and which (like better transport or living close to the place of work) make it possible to save time. (This is in contrast to the cash savings of the poor, which are paid for in time—do-it-yourself, bargain hunting, etc.) None of this is true of mere economic capital; it is possession of cultural capital that makes it possible to derive greater profit not only from labor-time, by securing a higher yield from the same time, but also from spare time, and so to increase both economic and cultural capital.

21. It goes without saying that the dominant fractions, who tend to place ever greater emphasis on educational investment, within an overall strategy of asset diversification and of investments aimed at combining security with high yield, have all sorts of ways of evading scholastic verdicts. The direct transmission of economic capital remains one of the principal means of reproduction, and the effect of social capital ('a helping hand,' 'string-pulling,' the 'old boy network') tends to correct the effect of academic sanctions. Educational qualifications never function perfectly as currency. They are never entirely separable from their holders: their value rises in proportion to the value of their bearer, especially in the least rigid areas of the social structure.

6 Thoughts on the Trivium and Quadrivium: The Divorce of Knowledge from the Knower

Basil Bernstein

I am afraid that this will not be a paper[1] in the usual sense of that term. It will not be a systematic presentation or exposition of a particular thesis, nor an account of research, nor an overview of a relevant section of the intellectual field. I thought I would take this opportunity to explore some ideas which have arisen out of some recent work on the nature of pedagogic discourse. I am not entirely sure I can present these ideas, these intuitions, rather than worked-out positions, in the orderly way to which you are accustomed. This is not said as an academic strategy of defence but as an accurate assessment of my present state of knowledge. You may well ask—well, why don't you keep it to yourself until you have got the story right? Who wants to listen to a script where the plot is not worked out and half the characters are missing? The only answer I can give is that sometimes a script needs a little help and perhaps that is what will happen here, even if it means the script will have to be abandoned. The problem started many years ago when I read Durkheim's magnificent analysis of the evolution of education in France. It started with his analysis of the discourse, social structure and social relations of the medieval university. Durkheim was concerned to show how the discourse of the medieval university contained within itself *a tension, even a contradiction,* which provided the dynamics of the development of the university. This tension or contradiction he saw as a representation of the two discourses upon which the medieval university was founded, that of Christianity and that of Greek thought. These two discourses, he argued, produced the tension between faith and reason which he saw as providing the dynamic of the development of the university.

Durkheim was also interested in the origin of the abstract nature of the knowledge and this should not have been a problem to him. For if you recontextualise Greek thought you must have an abstract, idealised, essentialist discourse. Of course Durkheim was clear about the rapport, the harmony between Christianity and selected forms of Greek thought. However, he did say something else which set me thinking. To many of you it will be obvious. Durkheim said that the Christian God was a god you had to think about. It was a god that not only was to be loved, but also to be thought about. And this attitude created an abstract modality to the discourse. I am not concerned whether Durkheim is right here. I think (by the way) he is right, but not for the right reasons. I think he is right but his analysis is not sufficiently fundamental. Like many

From *Pedagogy, Symbolic Control and Identity: Theory, Research, Critique*, rev. edn. (Lanham, Md.: Rowman and Littlefield, 1996), 81–6.

abstract problems this one started with something which did not seem at first sight to be a real problem at all. The problem started with the first dislocation in official European knowledge. The first classification, the first, in Foucault's terms, archaeological flaw in the continuity of official knowledge. A dislocation which has had profound consequences for culture, a specialisation of two discourses to different time periods, the first progression, sequencing of official knowledge. I am of course referring here to that specialisation, that grouping of knowledge called the Trivium and that different specialisation of knowledge called the Quadrivium. The Trivium consisted of grammar, logic and rhetoric and the Quadrivium consisted of arithmetic, astronomy, geometry and music. Durkheim gives a very interesting account of how the emphasis on the elements of the Trivium changed with the development of a new bourgeoisie in the Renaissance. But this is not our concern here. Durkheim argued that this classification, dislocation, boundary, represented a split between the Trivium as exploration of the word and the Quadrivium as the exploration of the world; word and world held together by the unity of Christianity. Of course this is not quite right. It is not so much the Word but the means of understanding the principles behind the word and its realisation. Similarly it is not the World but the principles of understanding the material world. It was also the case that the Trivium was studied first and the Quadrivium second. Word before the World in Durkheim's terms. My version will be stronger, no world prior to the word. Durkheim, it seemed to me, had formulated and conceptualised a problem but had not explained it. Why was the Trivium first, what was the modality of the abstraction that Christianity gave to official discourse? And that was where I started.

Why was the Trivium first—it could be argued that the Trivium was first for material or pedagogic reasons; for example, you must first know how to think before you apply thought. It was also of interest that in the annual celebration it was the Quadrivium teachers who led the university parade and the Trivium teachers were last. A metaphoric realisation of the last shall be first. However, it was also the case that the Trivium dominated the university. The Trivium teachers had the power. Now, about the abstract orientation of the knowledge: is it enough to say: if you teach the Greeks you teach abstraction—you teach that the word is empty and is but a pointer to a concept? I am not sure either of those explanations is adequate but I am also not sure whether the one I shall offer is wholly adequate either.

I shall start where Durkheim left off in his discussion of the Trivium/Quadrivium and carry his analysis a stage further. I shall propose that there is another level below that of word and world. I shall propose that the Trivium is not simply about understanding the word, the principles which lie behind it, the mechanics of language and reasoning, but is concerned to constitute a particular form of consciousness, a distinct modality of the self, to set limits to that form of consciousness, to regulate the modality of the self. To constitute that self in the Word, yes, but the Word of God. A particular god. The Christian God. In other words, the Trivium is there to create a particular form of the outer (the world). The dislocation between Trivium and Quadrivium, then, is a dislocation between inner and outer. A dislocation as a precondition for a new creative synthesis between inner and outer generated by Christianity. Perhaps more than this. The Trivium comes first, because the construction of the inner, the valid inner, the true inner, is a necessary precondition that the understanding of the world will also be valid, will also be true, will also be acceptable, will also be legitimate in terms of the discourse of Christianity. The sacredness of the world is guaranteed or should be guaranteed by the appropriate construction of the inner, the truly Christian self. Thus, whereas the apparent form of the discourse is Greek, the message is Christian. More than this, the deep grammar of the Trivium, Quadrivium, that is, its paradigmatic and syntagmatic features, is a metaphor of the new dislocation between inner and outer that Christianity itself introduced and resolved. I shall argue that it is this new mediated relation between inner and outer which is the origin of the necessary abstract orientation of Christianity, a Christianity which appropriated Greek thought for its own message.

It is possible to illustrate both this abstract orientation and prior dislocation of inner and outer, so essential to the formation of the Christian self, by examining the process of conversion. In the early stages of the development and dissemination of the faith, conversion did not require a change of nationality. It did not require a change of culture. It did not require even a change of practice. It required a revolution of inwardness, a turning to a recognition of Christ, the meaning of Christ. Note here that Christianity takes a point outside the culture and practice of those to be converted as the basis for this conversion and then colonises from within. Christianity drives a wedge between inner self and outer practice. It creates a gap which becomes the site for a new awareness. To think and feel outside your culture and practice is intrinsically an abstract orientation. Although clearly the new feeling and thinking will be confined to the terms of the new modality. Thus the dislocation of inner and outer, to open up a new existential self, is intrinsic to Christianity. It is not Greek. There are dislocations in Greek thought, individual/society issues of distributive justice, the word and the concept, the ideal form and the particular representation, but I would not suggest reflection upon the dislocated self and its new synthesis.

In order to highlight further these tentative propositions, I want to make some comparison between Judaism and Christianity which will bring me nearer to the title of this lecture.

The crucial feature of Judaism I would argue is less that it is a monotheistic faith but more that the God is invisible. The God can only be heard. The Judaic God, unlike the Christian, is temporal not visual. If the Judaic God is invisible, then the distance between God and people is maximal. There is no way in which people can become God and God become human. The distance is uncrossable by both. How do people relate to this invisible God? How is the uncrossable crossed? Through relating to an attribute of that God. Holiness. Then how does the holiness of this God become material, become palpable? The holiness becomes material, becomes palpable through the daily cycles of prayer, ritual and through the classifications of the law. The holiness is realised in prayer, ritual and classifications which establish the fundamental nature of the social bond between men, women and community. Holiness, the attribute of the invisible God, establishes the unity of God and people through the nature of the social bond. There is no dislocation of inner and outer in Judaism. This does not mean to say that Judaism does not speak to the inner—the Psalms are sufficient testimony here—only that there is no dislocation of the self. Instead there is the complete and perfect community established by prayer, ritual and classification. The perfect community is the ultimate realisation of the Judaic God. Let us take this matter further before comparing the discourse of Judaism and Christianity. A consequence of the Invisible Judaic God is that exemplars are not possible. You cannot have an exemplar of something that is invisible. Judaism, unlike Christianity, is a non-exemplary religion. The Judaic God does not want mediation through exemplary figures. It is an unmediated religion, there are only two terms: God and Man, whereas Christianity, later, provides a metaphor of three. If we consider the Old Testament, we find that narratives of the major figures Moses, David, Solomon, the major prophets Elijah, Elisha seem to be predicated on one rule—all shall be shown to be fallible. Every great figure of the grand narratives commits great errors of judgement and practice. The rule that all must be shown to be fallible is the other side of the rule. 'There shall be no exemplars'. Such a rule emphasises, declares there is only one perfection, that of the invisible God. However, there is an implication here—God is Absolute—Man is relative, no man holds the truth—God is the principle of all things.

I want now briefly to look at Judaism as discourse. In Judaism we have a non-exemplary religion but with an incomplete text. This requires some explanation. There is the written law, the Torah, which is not only a blueprint of the universe but is a guide to most mundane and minute details of life, in which every minute detail connects with the whole. The particular carries the sanctity of the whole. Through proper interpretation, application and meaning, any contingency may be revealed. Thus the written law is subject to endless interpretation, interpretation which forbids generalisation, which proceeds from one particular to another. For generalisation, the holy principle is alive in every particular. Thus, in Judaism, a non-exemplary religion with an incomplete text, interpretation is through continuous elaboration of particulars and generalisation is abhorred. Such elaboration is only possible because of certainty of faith. Thus, in Judaism, we have a non-exemplary religion, an incomplete text but a *perfect* society, made perfect by the Torah. Christianity, on the other hand, is an exemplary religion, where the text is complete and perfect in Jesus, where generalisation and metaphor embrace the abstract. However, it is also a faith where faith cannot be taken for granted; it must be constantly re-won, revitalised, renewed. Thus the Christian self, unlike the Judaic self safe in its certainty, is subject to doubt, to questioning, to interrogation. In this sense Christianity creates a special modality of language, an interrogative mode which splits the self from its acts, intention from practice. At the same time language itself can both reveal and deceive. The very medium of communication can carry revelation or deception. No wonder language, communication, is so central to Christianity for it forms the authentic relation and its means of interrogation, and thus the true self in faith.

We can now at long last return to the Trivium/Quadrivium dislocation and Durkheim's insights. I have attempted to show that the abstract orientation and the dislocation of the two fundamental discourses of the medieval university have their roots in Christianity, in the original dislocation of the self which Christianity engendered as the prime condition for its own good news, the news of Christ. I have suggested that this dislocation of inner and outer, the condition for the establishment of the truly Christian self, is not a dislocation to be found in Greek thought. But Greek thought was selectively appropriated by Christianity and realised in a way to make Greek thought safe. In this it did not succeed.

Finally, I now want to make a rapid move from the principle of the organisation of discourse in the medieval period to the principles underlying the organisation of official discourse today. I have tried to show that in the medieval period we had two differently specialised discourses, one for the construction of the inner, one for the construction of the outer—the material world. The construction of the inner was the guarantee for the construction of the outer. In this we can find the origin of the professions. Over the next five hundred years there was a progressive replacement of the religious foundation of official knowledge by a humanising secular principle. I want to argue that we have, for the first time, a dehumanising principle, for the organisation and orientation of official knowledge. What we are seeing is the growing development of the specialised disciplines of the Quadrivium, and the disciplines of the Trivium have become the disciplines of symbolic control—the social sciences. In a sense the Trivium has been replaced by the social sciences for the management of feelings, thoughts, relations and practices. There is now less dislocation of knowledge. Genetic engineering and cognitive science reach across the natural, biological and social sciences. What of the principle underlying the new discourse? Today throughout Europe, led by the U.S.A. and the U.K., there is a new principle guiding the latest transition of capitalism. The principles of the market and its managers are more and more the managers of the policy and practices of education. Market relevance is becoming the key orientating criterion for the selection of discourses, their relation to each other, their forms and their research. This movement has profound implications from the primary school to the university. This can be seen in the stress on basic measurable skills at the primary level, vocational courses and specialisations at the secondary level, spurious decentralisation, and the new instruments of state control over higher education and research.

Of fundamental significance, there is a new concept of knowledge and of its relation to those who create it and use it. This new concept is a truly secular concept. Knowledge should flow like money to wherever it can create advantage and profit. Indeed knowledge is not like money, it *is* money. Knowledge is divorced from persons, their commitments, their personal dedications. These become impediments, restrictions on the flow of knowledge, and introduce deformations in the working of the symbolic market. Moving knowledge about, or even creating it, should not be more difficult than moving and regulating money. Knowledge, after nearly a thousand years, is divorced from inwardness and literally dehumanised. Once knowledge is separated from inwardness, from commitments, from personal dedication, from the deep structure of the self, then people may be moved about, substituted for each other and excluded from the market.

This orientation represents a fundamental break in the relation between the knower and what is known. In the medieval period the two were necessarily integrated. Knowledge was an outer expression of an inner relationship. The inner relationship was a guarantee of the legitimacy, integrity, worthwhileness and value of the knowledge and the special status of the knower as Christian. We know, however, how this special status in turn limited and distorted the knowledge, but this is not the point here. Today the market principle creates a new dislocation. Now we have two independent markets, one of knowledge and one of potential creators and users of knowledge.

The first dislocation between the Trivium and the Quadrivium constituted inwardness as a prior condition of knowing; the second dislocation, the contemporary dislocation, disconnects inner from outer, as a precondition for constituting the outer and its practice, according to the market principles of the New Right.

Durkheim stated that there was a contradiction at the heart of the medieval university, between faith and reason, and this was the key to the development both of knowledge and the university. Today perhaps there is not so much a contradiction as a crisis, and what is at stake is the very concept of education itself.

NOTE

Originally public lecture given to the University of the Aegian.

7 The Means of Correct Training

Michel Foucault

At the beginning of the seventeenth century, Walhausen spoke of 'strict discipline' as an art of correct training. The chief function of the disciplinary power is to 'train', rather than to select and to levy; or, no doubt, to train in order to levy and select all the more. It does not link forces together in order to reduce them; it seeks to bind them together in such a way as to multiply and use them. Instead of bending all its subjects into a single uniform mass, it separates, analyses, differentiates, carries its procedures of decomposition to the point of necessary and sufficient single units. It 'trains' the moving, confused, useless multitudes of bodies and forces into a multiplicity of individual elements—small, separate cells, organic autonomies, genetic identities and continuities, combinatory segments. Discipline 'makes' individuals; it is the specific technique of a power that regards individuals both as objects and as instruments of its exercise. It is not a triumphant power, which because of its own excess can pride itself on its omnipotence; it is a modest, suspicious power, which functions as a calculated, but permanent economy. These are humble modalities, minor procedures, as compared with the majestic rituals of sovereignty or the great apparatuses of the state. And it is precisely they that were gradually to invade the major forms, altering their mechanisms and imposing their procedures. The legal apparatus was not to escape this scarcely secret invasion. The success of disciplinary power derives no doubt from the use of simple instruments; hierarchical observation, normalizing judgement and their combination in a procedure that is specific to it, the examination.

Hierarchical Observation

The exercise of discipline presupposes a mechanism that coerces by means of observation; an apparatus in which the techniques that make it possible to see induce effects of power, and in which, conversely, the means of coercion make those on whom they are applied clearly visible. Slowly, in the course of the classical age, we see the construction of those 'observatories' of human multiplicity for which the history of the sciences has so little good to say. Side by side with the major technology of the telescope, the lens and the light beam, which were an integral part of the new physics and cosmology, there were the minor techniques of multiple and intersecting observations, of eyes that must see without being seen; using techniques of subjection and methods of exploitation, an obscure art of light and the visible was secretly preparing a new knowledge of man.

These 'observatories' had an almost ideal model: the military camp—the short-lived, artificial city, built and reshaped almost at will; the seat of a power that must be all the stronger, but also all the more discreet, all the more effective and on the alert in that it is exercised over armed men. In the perfect camp, all power would be exercised solely through exact observation; each gaze would form a part of the overall functioning of power. The old, traditional square plan was considerably refined in

From *Discipline and Punish: The Birth of the Prison*, trans. A. Sheridan (London: Penguin, 1977), 170–95.

innumerable new projects. The geometry of the paths, the number and distribution of the tents, the orientation of their entrances, the disposition of files and ranks were exactly defined; the network of gazes that supervised one another was laid down: 'In the parade ground, five lines are drawn up, the first is sixteen feet from the second; the others are eight feet from one another; and the last is eight feet from the arms dépôts. The arms dépôts are ten feet from the tents of the junior officers, immediately opposite the first tentpole. A company street is fifty-one feet wide ... All tents are two feet from one another. The tents of the subalterns are opposite the alleys of their companies. The rear tentpole is eight feet from the last soldiers' tent and the gate is opposite the captains' tent ... The captains' tents are erected opposite the streets of their companies. The entrance is opposite the companies themselves.'[1] The camp is the diagram of a power that acts by means of general visibility. For a long time this model of the camp or at least its underlying principle was found in urban development, in the construction of working-class housing estates, hospitals, asylums, prisons, schools: the spatial 'nesting' of hierarchized surveillance. The principle was one of 'embedding' ('*encastrement*'). The camp was to the rather shameful art of surveillance what the dark room was to the great science of optics.

A whole problematic then develops: that of an architecture that is no longer built simply to be seen (as with the ostentation of palaces), or to observe the external space (cf. the geometry of fortresses), but to permit an internal, articulated and detailed control—to render visible those who are inside it; in more general terms, an architecture that would operate to transform individuals: to act on those it shelters, to provide a hold on their conduct, to carry the effects of power right to them, to make it possible to know them, to alter them. Stones can make people docile and knowable. The old simple schema of confinement and enclosure—thick walls, a heavy gate that prevents entering or leaving—began to be replaced by the calculation of openings, of filled and empty spaces, passages and transparencies. In this way the hospital building was gradually organized as an instrument of medical action: it was to allow a better observation of patients, and therefore a better calibration of their treatment; the form of the buildings, by the careful separation of the patients, was to prevent contagions; lastly, the ventilation and the air that circulated around each bed was to prevent the deleterious vapours from stagnating around the patient, breaking down his humours and spreading the disease by their immediate effects. The hospital—which was to be built in the second half of the century and for which so many plans were drawn up after the Hôtel-Dieu was burnt down for the second time—was no longer simply the roof under which penury and imminent death took shelter; it was, in its very materiality, a therapeutic operator.

Similarly, the school building was to be a mechanism for training. It was as a pedagogical machine that Pâris-Duverney conceived the École Militaire, right down to the minute details that he had imposed on the architect, Gabriel. Train vigorous bodies, the imperative of health; obtain competent officers, the imperative of qualification; create obedient soldiers, the imperative of politics; prevent debauchery and homosexuality, the imperative of morality. A fourfold reason for establishing sealed compartments between individuals, but also apertures for continuous surveillance. The very building of the École was to be an apparatus for observation; the rooms were distributed along a corridor like a series of small cells; at regular intervals, an officer's quarters were situated, so that 'every ten pupils had an officer on each side'; the pupils were confined to their cells throughout the night; and Pâris had insisted that 'a window be placed on the corridor wall of each room from chest-level to within one or two feet of the ceiling. Not only is it pleasant to have such windows, but one would venture to say that it is useful, in several respects, not to mention the disciplinary reasons that may determine this arrangement' (quoted in Laulan, 117–18). In the dining-rooms was 'a slightly raised platform for the tables of the inspectors of studies, so that they may see all the tables of the pupils of their divisions during meals'; latrines had been installed with half-doors, so that the supervisor on duty could see the head and legs of the pupils, and also with side walls sufficiently high 'that those inside cannot see one another'.[2] This infinitely scrupulous concern with surveillance is expressed in the architecture by innumerable petty mechanisms. These mechanisms can only be seen as unimportant if one forgets the role of this instrumentation, minor but flawless, in the progressive objectification and the ever more subtle partitioning of individual behaviour. The disciplinary institutions secreted a machinery of control that functioned like a microscope of conduct; the fine, analytical divisions that they created formed around men an apparatus of observation, recording and training. How was one to subdivide the gaze in these observation machines? How was one to establish a network of communications between them? How was one so to arrange things that a homogeneous, continuous power would result from their calculated multiplicity?

The perfect disciplinary apparatus would make it possible for a single gaze to see everything constantly. A central point would be both the source of light illuminating everything, and a locus of convergence for everything that must be known: a perfect eye that nothing would escape and a centre towards which all gazes would be turned. This is what Ledoux had imagined when he built Arc-et-Senans; all the buildings were to be arranged in a circle, opening on the inside, at the centre of which a high construction was to house the administrative functions of management, the policing functions of surveillance, the economic functions of control and checking, the religious functions of encouraging obedience and work; from here all orders would come, all activities would be recorded, all offences perceived and judged; and this would be done immediately with no other aid than an exact geometry. Among all the reasons for the prestige that was accorded in the second half of the eighteenth century, to circular architecture, one must no doubt include the fact that it expressed a certain political utopia.

But, the disciplinary gaze did, in fact, need relays. The pyramid was able to fulfil, more efficiently than the circle, two requirements: to be complete enough to form an uninterrupted network—consequently the possibility of multiplying its levels, and of distributing them over the entire surface to be supervised; and yet to be discreet enough not to weigh down with an inert mass on the activity to be disciplined, and not to act as a brake or an obstacle to it; to be integrated into the disciplinary mechanism as a function that increases its possible effects. It had to be broken down into smaller elements, but in order to increase its productive function: specify the surveillance and make it functional.

This was the problem of the great workshops and factories, in which a new type of surveillance was organized. It was different from the one practised in the régimes of the manufactories, which had been carried out from the outside by inspectors, entrusted with the task of applying the regulations; what was now needed was an intense, continuous supervision; it ran right through the labour process; it did not bear—or not only—on production (the nature and quantity of raw materials, the type of instruments used, the dimensions and quality of the products); it also took into account the activity of the men, their skill, the way they set about their tasks, their promptness, their zeal, their behaviour. But it was also different from the domestic supervision of the master present beside his workers and apprentices; for it was carried out by clerks, supervisors and foremen. As the machinery of production became larger and more complex, as the number of workers and the division of labour increased, supervision became ever more necessary and more difficult. It became a special function, which had nevertheless to form an integral part of the production process, to run parallel to it throughout its entire length. A specialized personnel became indispensable, constantly present and distinct from the workers: 'In the large factory, everything is regulated by the clock. The workers are treated strictly and harshly. The clerks, who are used to treating them with an air of superiority and command, which is really necessary with the multitude, treat them with severity or contempt; hence these workers either cost more or leave the factory soon after arrival' (*Encyclopédie*, article on 'Manufacture'). But, although the workers preferred a framework of a guild type to this new régime of surveillance, the employers saw that it was indissociable from the system of industrial production, private property and profit. At the scale of a factory, a great iron-works or a mine, 'the objects of expenditure are so multiplied, that the slightest dishonesty on each object would add up to an immense fraud, which would not only absorb the profits, but would lead to a loss of capital ... the slightest incompetence, if left unnoticed and therefore repeated each day, may prove fatal to the enterprise to the extent of destroying it in a very short time'; hence the fact that only agents, directly dependent on the owner, and entrusted with this task alone would be able to see 'that not a sou is spent uselessly, that not a moment of the day is lost'; their role would be 'to supervise the workers, to inspect all the places of work, to inform the directors of everything that takes place' (Cournol). Surveillance thus becomes a decisive economic operator both as an internal part of the production machinery and as a specific mechanism in the disciplinary power. 'The work of directing, superintending and adjusting becomes one of the functions of capital, from the moment that the labour under the control of capital, becomes cooperative. Once a function of capital, it requires special characteristics' (Marx, *Capital*, vol. 1, 313).

The same movement was to be found in the reorganization of elementary teaching: the details of surveillance were specified and it was integrated into the teaching relationship. The development of the parish schools, the increase in the number of their pupils, the absence of methods for regulating simultaneously the activity of a whole class, and the disorder and confusion that followed from this made it necessary to work out a system of supervision. In order to help the teacher, Batencour selected from among the best pupils a whole series of 'officers'—intendants, observers, monitors, tutors, reciters of prayers, writing officers, receivers of ink, almoners and visitors. The roles thus defined were of two kinds: the first involved material tasks (distributing ink and paper, giving alms to the poor, reading spiritual texts on feast days, etc.); the second involved surveillance: the 'observers must record who left his bench, who was talking, who did not have his rosary, or Book of Hours, who did not comport himself properly at mass, who committed an impure act, who indulged in idle talk or was unruly in the street'; the 'admonitors' were placed in charge of those 'who talk or hum when studying their lessons and those who will not write and who waste their time in play'; the 'visitors' called on the families of pupils who had been absent or who had committed serious offences. The 'intendants' supervised all the other officers. Only the 'tutors' had a pedagogical role: their task was to teach the pupils reading, two by two, in low tones (M.I.D.B., 68–83). A few decades later, Demia favoured a hierarchy of the same type but almost all the functions of surveillance were duplicated by a pedagogical role: an assistant teacher taught the holding of the pen, guided the pupil's hand, corrected mistakes and at the same time 'marked down trouble-makers'; another assistant teacher had the same tasks in the reading class; the intendant who supervised the other officers and was in charge of behaviour in general also had the task of 'initiating newcomers into the customs of the school'; the decurions got the pupils to recite their lessons and 'marked down' those who did not know them.[3] We have here a sketch of an institution of the 'mutual' type in which three procedures are integrated into a single mechanism: teaching proper, the acquisition of knowledge by the very practice of the pedagogical activity and a reciprocal, hierarchized observation. A relation of surveillance, defined and regulated, is inscribed at the heart of the practice of teaching, not as an additional or adjacent part, but as a mechanism that is inherent to it and which increases its efficiency.

Hierarchized, continuous and functional surveillance may not be one of the great technical 'inventions' of the eighteenth century, but its insidious extension owed its importance to the mechanisms of power that it brought with it. By means of such surveillance, disciplinary power became an 'integrated' system, linked from the inside to the economy and to the aims of the mechanism in which it was practised. It was also organized as a multiple, automatic and anonymous power; for although surveillance rests on individuals, its functioning is that of a network of relations from top to bottom, but also to a certain extent from bottom to top and laterally; this network 'holds' the whole together and traverses it in its entirety with effects of power that derive from one another: supervisors, perpetually supervised. The power in the hierarchized surveillance of the disciplines is not possessed as a thing, or transferred as a property; it functions like a piece of machinery. And, although it is true that its pyramidal organization gives it a 'head', it is the apparatus as a whole that produces 'power' and distributes individuals in this permanent and continuous field. This enables the disciplinary power to be both absolutely indiscreet, since it is everywhere and always alert, since by its very principle it leaves no zone of shade and constantly supervises the very individuals who are entrusted with the task of supervising; and absolutely 'discreet', for it functions permanently and largely in silence. Discipline makes possible the operation of a relational power that sustains itself by its own mechanism and which, for the spectacle of public events, substitutes the uninterrupted play of calculated gazes. Thanks to the techniques of surveillance, the 'physics' of power, the hold over the body, operate according to the laws of optics and mechanics, according to a whole play of spaces, lines, screens, beams, degrees and without recourse, in principle at least, to excess, force or violence. It is a power that seems all the less 'corporal' in that it is more subtly 'physical'.

Normalizing Judgement

1. At the orphanage of the Chevalier Paulet, the sessions of the tribunal that met each morning gave rise to a whole ceremonial: 'We found all the pupils drawn up as if for battle, in perfect alignment, immobility and silence. The major, a young gentleman of sixteen years, stood outside the ranks, sword in hand; at his command, the troop broke ranks at the double and formed a circle. The council met in the centre; each officer made a report of his troop for the preceding twenty-four hours. The accused were allowed to defend themselves; witnesses were heard; the council deliberated and, when agreement was reached, the major announced the number of guilty, the nature of the offences and the punishments ordered. The troop then marched off in the greatest order' (Pictet). At the heart of all disciplinary systems functions a small penal mechanism. It enjoys a kind of judicial privilege with its own laws, its specific offences, its particular forms of judgement. The disciplines established an 'infra-penality'; they partitioned an area that the laws had left empty; they defined and repressed a mass of behaviour that the relative indifference of the great systems of punishment had allowed to escape. 'On entering, the companions will greet one another ... on leaving, they must lock up the materials and tools that they have been using and also make sure that their lamps are extinguished'; 'it is expressly forbidden to amuse companions by gestures or in any other way'; they must 'comport themselves honestly and decently'; anyone who is absent for more than five minutes without warning M. Oppenheim will be 'marked down for a half-day'; and in order to be sure that nothing is forgotten in this meticulous criminal justice, it is forbidden to do 'anything that may harm M. Oppenheim and his companions' (Oppenheim, 29 September 1809). The workshop, the school, the army were subject to a whole micro-penality of time (latenesses, absences, interruptions of tasks), of activity (inattention, negligence, lack of zeal), of behaviour (impoliteness, disobedience), of speech (idle chatter, insolence), of the body ('incorrect' attitudes, irregular gestures, lack of cleanliness), of sexuality (impurity, indecency). At the same time, by way of punishment, a whole series of subtle procedures was used, from light physical punishment to minor deprivations and petty humiliations. It was a question both of making the slightest departures from correct behaviour subject to punishment, and of giving a punitive function to the apparently indifferent elements of the disciplinary apparatus: so that, if necessary, everything might serve to punish the slightest thing; each subject find himself caught in a punishable, punishing universality. 'By the word punishment, one must understand everything that is capable of making children feel the offence they have committed, everything that is capable of humiliating them, of confusing them: ... a certain coldness, a certain indifference, a question, a humiliation, a removal from office' (La Salle, *Conduite* ... , 204–5).

2. But discipline brought with it a specific way of punishing that was not only a small-scale model of the court. What is specific to the disciplinary penality is non-observance, that which does not measure up to the rule, that departs from it. The whole indefinite domain of the non-conforming is punishable: the soldier commits an 'offence' whenever he does not reach the level required; a pupil's 'offence' is not only a minor infraction, but also an inability to carry out his tasks. The regulations for the Prussian infantry ordered that a soldier who had not correctly learnt to handle his rifle should be treated with the 'greatest severity'. Similarly, 'when a pupil has not retained the catechism from the

previous day, he must be forced to learn it, without making any mistake, and repeat it the following day; either he will be forced to hear it standing or kneeling, his hands joined, or he will be given some other penance'.

The order that the disciplinary punishments must enforce is of a mixed nature: it is an 'artificial' order, explicitly laid down by a law, a programme, a set of regulations. But it is also an order defined by natural and observable processes: the duration of an apprenticeship, the time taken to perform an exercise, the level of aptitude refer to a regularity that is also a rule. The children of the Christian Schools must never be placed in a 'lesson' of which they are not yet capable, for this would expose them to the danger of being unable to learn anything; yet the duration of each stage is fixed by regulation and a pupil who at the end of three examinations has been unable to pass into the higher order must be placed, well in evidence, on the bench of the 'ignorant'. In a disciplinary regime punishment involves a double juridico-natural reference.

3. Disciplinary punishment has the function of reducing gaps. It must therefore be essentially *corrective*. In addition to punishments borrowed directly from the judicial model (fines, flogging, solitary confinement), the disciplinary systems favour punishments that are exercise—intensified, multiplied forms of training, several times repeated: the regulations of 1766 for the infantry laid down that lance-corporals 'who show some negligence or lack of willingness will be reduced to the rank of private', and they will be able to rise to their former rank only after new exercises and a new examination. As Jean-Baptiste de La Salle put it: 'Of all penances, impositions are the most honest for a teacher, the most advantageous for the parents'; they make it possible to 'derive, from the very offences of the children, means of advancing their progress by correcting their defects'; to those, for example, 'who have not written all that they were supposed to write or who have not applied themselves to doing it well, one can give some impositions to write out or to learn by heart' (La Salle, *Conduite* . . . , 205). Disciplinary punishment is, in the main, isomorphic with obligation itself; it is not so much the vengeance of an outraged law as its repetition, its reduplicated insistence. So much so that the corrective effect expected of it involves only incidentally expiation and repentance; it is obtained directly through the mechanics of a training. To punish is to exercise.

4. In discipline, punishment is only one element of a double system: gratification-punishment. And it is this system that operates in the process of training and correction. The teacher 'must avoid, as far as possible, the use of punishment; on the contrary, he must endeavour to make rewards more frequent than penalties, the lazy being more encouraged by the desire to be rewarded in the same way as the diligent than by the fear of punishment; that is why it will be very beneficial, when the teacher is obliged to use punishment, to win the heart of the child if he can before doing so' (Demia, 17). This mechanism with two elements makes possible a number of operations characteristic of disciplinary penality. First, the definition of behaviour and performance on the basis of the two opposed values of good and evil; instead of the simple division of the prohibition, as practised in penal justice, we have a distribution between a positive pole and a negative pole; all behaviour falls in the field between good and bad marks, good and bad points. Moreover, it is possible to quantify this field and work out an arithmetical economy based on it. A penal accountancy, constantly brought up to date, makes it possible to obtain the punitive balance-sheet of each individual. School 'justice', rudiments of which are to be found in the army and the workshops, carried this system very far. The Brothers of the Christian Schools organized a whole micro-economy of privileges and impositions: 'Privileges may be used by pupils to gain exemption from penances which have been imposed on them . . . For example, a pupil may have been given four or six catechism questions to copy out as an imposition; he will be able to gain exemption from this penance by accumulating a certain number of privilege points; the teacher will assign the number for each question . . . Since privileges are worth a certain number of points, the teacher also has others of less value, which serve as small change for the first. For example, a child has an imposition from which he can redeem himself with six points; he earns a privilege of ten; he presents it to the teacher who gives him back four points, and so on' (La Salle,

Conduite . . . , 156 ff.). What we have here is a transposition of the system of indulgences. And by the play of this quantification, this circulation of awards and debits, thanks to the continuous calculation of plus and minus points, the disciplinary apparatuses hierarchized the 'good' and the 'bad' subjects in relation to one another. Through this micro-economy of a perpetual penality operates a differentiation that is not one of acts, but of individuals themselves, of their nature, their potentialities, their level or their value. By assessing acts with precision, discipline judges individuals 'in truth'; the penality that it implements is integrated into the cycle of knowledge of individuals.

5. The distribution according to ranks or grade has a double role: it marks the gaps, hierarchizes qualities, skills and aptitudes; but it also punishes and rewards. It is the penal functioning of setting in order and the ordinal character of judging. Discipline rewards simply by the play of awards, thus making it possible to attain higher ranks and places; it punishes by reversing this process. Rank in itself serves as a reward or punishment. At the École Militaire, a complex system of 'honorary' classification was developed; this classification was visible to all in the form of slight variations in uniform and more or less noble or ignoble punishments were associated, as a mark of privilege or infamy, with the ranks thus distributed. This classificatory, penal distribution was carried out at short intervals by the reports that the officers, teachers and their assistants made, without consideration of age or grade, on 'the moral qualities of the pupils' and on 'their universally recognized behaviour'. The first class, known as the 'very good', were distinguished by a silver epaulette; they enjoyed the honour of being treated as 'purely military troops'; they therefore had a right to military punishment (arrests and, in serious cases, imprisonment). The second class, 'the good', wore an epaulette of red silk and silver; they could be arrested and condemned to prison, but also to the cage and to kneeling. The class of '*médiocres*', had the right to an epaulette of red wool; to the preceding penalties was added, if necessary, the wearing of sackcloth. The last class, that of the 'bad', was marked by an epaulette of brown wool; 'the pupils of this class will be subjected to all the punishments used in the Hôtel or all those that are thought necessary, even solitary confinement in a dark dungeon'. To this was added, for a time, the 'shameful' class, for which special regulations were drawn up 'so that those who belonged to it would always be separated from the others and would be dressed in sackcloth'. Since merit and behaviour alone must decide the place of the pupil, 'those of the last two classes would be able to flatter themselves that they would be able to rise to the first two and bear its marks, when, by universal agreement, they will be recognized as having made themselves worthy of it by the change in their conduct and by their progress; and those of the top classes will similarly descend into the others if they become slack and if the various reports taken together are to their disadvantage and show that they no longer deserve the rewards and prerogatives of the higher classes . . . ' The penal classification should tend to disappear. The 'shameful' class existed only to disappear: 'In order to judge the kind of conversion undergone by pupils of the shameful class who behave well', they were reintroduced into the other classes, and given back their uniforms; but they would remain with their comrades in infamy during meals and recreation; they would remain there if they did not continue to behave well; they 'would leave it absolutely, if their conduct was considered satisfactory both in this class and in this division' (Archives nationales, MM 658, 30 March 1758 and MM 666, 15 September 1763). This hierarchizing penality had, therefore, a double effect: it distributed pupils according to their aptitudes and their conduct, that is, according to the use that could be made of them when they left the school; it exercised over them a constant pressure to conform to the same model, so that they might all be subjected to 'subordination, docility, attention in studies and exercises, and to the correct practice of duties and all the parts of discipline'. So that they might all be like one another.

In short, the art of punishing, in the régime of disciplinary power, is aimed neither at expiation, nor even precisely at repression. It brings five quite distinct operations into play: it refers individual actions to a whole that is at once a field of comparison, a space of differentiation and the principle of a rule to be followed. It differentiates individuals from one another, in terms of the following overall rule: that the rule be made to function as a minimal threshold, as an average to be respected or as an optimum towards which one must move. It measures in quantitative terms and hierarchizes in terms of value the abilities, the level, the 'nature' of individuals. It introduces, through this 'value-giving' measure, the constraint of a conformity that must be achieved. Lastly, it traces the limit that will define difference in relation to all other differences, the external frontier of the abnormal (the 'shameful' class of the École Militaire). The perpetual penality that traverses all points and supervises every instant in the disciplinary institutions compares, differentiates, hierarchizes, homogenizes, excludes. In short, it *normalizes*.

It is opposed, therefore, term by term, to a judicial penality whose essential function is to refer, not to a set of observable phenomena, but to a corpus of laws and texts that must be remembered; that operates not by differentiating individuals, but by specifying acts according to a number of general categories; not by hierarchizing, but quite simply by bringing into play the binary opposition of the permitted and the forbidden; not by homogenizing, but by operating the division, acquired once and for all, of condemnation. The disciplinary mechanisms secreted a 'penality of the norm', which is irreducible in its principles and functioning to the traditional penality of the law. The minor court that seems to sit permanently in the buildings of discipline, and which sometimes assumes the theatrical form of the great legal apparatus, must not mislead us: it does not bring, except for a few formal remnants, the mechanisms of criminal justice to the web of everyday existence; or at least that is not its essential role; the disciplines created—drawing on a whole series of very ancient procedures—a new functioning of punishment, and it was this that gradually invested the great external apparatus that it seemed to reproduce in either a modest or an ironic way. The juridico-anthropological functioning revealed in the whole history of modern penality did not originate in the super-imposition of the human sciences on criminal justice and in the requirements proper to this new rationality or to the humanism that it appeared to bring with it; it originated in the disciplinary technique that operated these new mechanisms of normalizing judgement.

The power of the Norm appears through the disciplines. Is this the new law of modern society? Let us say rather that, since the eighteenth century, it has joined other powers—the Law, the Word (*Parole*) and the Text, Tradition—imposing new delimitations upon them. The Normal is established as a principle of coercion in teaching with the introduction of a standardized education and the establishment of the *écoles normales* (teachers' training colleges); it is established in the effort to organize a national medical profession and a hospital system capable of operating general norms of health; it is established in the standardization of industrial processes and products (on this topic, one should refer to the important contribution of Canguilhem, 171-91). Like surveillance and with it, normalization becomes one of the great instruments of power at the end of the classical age. For the marks that once indicated status, privilege and affiliation were increasingly replaced—or at least supplemented—by a whole range of degrees of normality indicating membership of a homogeneous social body but also playing a part in classification, hierarchization and the distribution of rank. In a sense, the power of normalization imposes homogeneity; but it individualizes by making it possible to measure gaps, to determine levels, to fix specialities and to render the differences useful by fitting them one to another. It is easy to understand how the power of the norm functions within a system of formal equality, since within a homogeneity that is the rule, the norm introduces, as a useful imperative and as a result of measurement, all the shading of individual differences.

The Examination

The examination combines the techniques of an observing hierarchy and those of a normalizing judgement. It is a normalizing gaze, a surveillance that makes it possible to qualify, to classify and to punish. It establishes over individuals a visibility through which one differentiates them and judges them. That is why, in all the mechanisms of discipline, the examination is highly ritualized. In it are combined the ceremony of power and the form of the experiment, the deployment of force and the establishment of truth. At the heart of the procedures of discipline, it manifests the subjection of those who are perceived as objects and the objectification of those who are subjected. The superimposition of the power relations and knowledge relations assumes in the examination all its visible brilliance. It is yet another innovation of the classical age that the historians of science have left unexplored. People write the history of experiments on those born blind, on wolf-children or under hypnosis. But who will write the more general, more fluid, but also more determinant history of the 'examination'—its rituals, its methods, its characters and their roles, its play of questions and answers, its systems of marking and classification? For in this slender technique are to be found a whole domain of knowledge, a whole type of power. One often speaks of the ideology that the human 'sciences' bring with them, in either discreet or prolix manner. But does their very technology, this tiny operational schema that has become so widespread (from psychiatry to pedagogy, from the diagnosis of diseases to the hiring of labour), this familiar method of the examination, implement, within a single mechanism, power relations that make it possible to extract and constitute knowledge? It is not simply at the level of consciousness, of representations and in what one thinks one knows, but at the level of what makes possible the knowledge that is transformed into political investment.

One of the essential conditions for the epistemological 'thaw' of medicine at the end of the eighteenth century was the organization of the hospital as an 'examining' apparatus. The ritual of the visit was its most obvious form. In the seventeenth century, the physician, coming from the outside, added his inspection to many other controls—religious, administrative, etc.; he hardly participated in the everyday administration of the hospital. Gradually, the visit became more regular, more rigorous, above all more extended: it became an ever more important part of the functioning of the hospital. In 1661, the physician of the Hôtel-Dieu of Paris was called upon to make a daily visit; in 1687, an 'expectant' physician was to examine, in the afternoon, certain seriously sick patients. The eighteenth-century regulations laid down the hours of the visit and its duration (at least two hours); they insisted on a rotation of physicians, which would guarantee visits every day 'even on Easter Sunday'; at last, in 1771, a resident physician was appointed, charged with 'providing all the services of his state, at night as well as in the day, in the intervals between visits by an outside physician' (*Registre des déliberations du bureau de l'Hôtel-Dieu*). The old form of inspection, irregular and rapid, was transformed into a regular observation that placed the patient in a situation of almost perpetual examination. This had two consequences: in the internal hierarchy, the physician, hitherto an external element, begins to gain over the religious staff and to relegate them to a clearly specified, but subordinate role in the technique of the examination; the category of the 'nurse' then appears; while the hospital itself, which was once little more than a poorhouse, was to become a place of training and of the correlation of knowledge; it represented a reversal therefore of the power relations and the constitution of a corpus of knowledge. The 'well-disciplined' hospital became the physical counterpart of the medical 'discipline'; this discipline could now abandon its textual character and take its references not so much from the tradition of author-authorities as from a domain of objects perpetually offered for examination.

Similarly, the school became a sort of apparatus of uninterrupted examination that duplicated along its entire length the operation of teaching. It became less and less a question of jousts in which pupils pitched their forces against one another and increasingly a perpetual comparison of each and all that made it possible both to measure and to judge. The Brothers of the Christian Schools wanted their pupils to be examined every day of the week: on the first for spelling, on the second for arithmetic, on the third for catechism in the morning and for handwriting in the afternoon, etc. Moreover, there was to be an examination each month in order to pick out those who deserved to be submitted for examination by the inspector (La Salle, *Conduite* . . . ,160). From 1775, there existed at the École des Ponts et Chaussées sixteen examinations a year: three in mathematics, three in architecture, three in drawing, two in writing, one in stone-cutting, one in style, one in surveying, one in levelling, one in quantity surveying. The examination did not simply mark the end of an apprenticeship; it was one of its permanent factors; it was woven into it through a constantly repeated ritual of power. The examination enabled the teacher, while transmitting his knowledge, to transform his pupils into a whole field of knowledge. Whereas the examination with which an apprenticeship ended in the guild tradition validated an acquired aptitude—the 'master-work' authenticated a transmission of knowledge that had already been accomplished—the examination in the school was a constant exchanger of knowledge; it guaranteed the movement of knowledge from the teacher to the pupil, but it extracted from the pupil a knowledge destined and reserved for the teacher. The school became the place of elaboration for pedagogy. And just as the procedure of the hospital examination made possible the epistemological 'thaw' of medicine, the age of the 'examining' school marked the beginnings of a pedagogy that functions as a science. The age of inspections and endlessly repeated movements in the army also marked the development of an immense tactical knowledge that had its effect in the period of the Napoleonic wars.

The examination introduced a whole mechanism that linked to a certain type of the formation of knowledge a certain form of the exercise of power.

1. *The examination transformed the economy of visibility into the exercise of power.* Traditionally, power was what was seen, what was shown and what was manifested and, paradoxically, found the principle of its force in the movement by which it deployed that force. Those on whom it was exercised could remain in the shade; they received light only from that portion of power that was conceded to them, or from the reflection of it that for a moment they carried. Disciplinary power, on the other hand, is exercised through its invisibility; at the same time it imposes on those whom it subjects a principle of compulsory visibility. In discipline, it is the subjects who have to be seen. Their visibility assures the hold of the power that is exercised over them. It is the fact of being constantly seen, of being able always to be seen, that maintains the disciplined individual in his subjection. And the examination is the technique by which power, instead of emitting the signs of its potency, instead of imposing its mark on its subjects, holds them in a mechanism of objectification. In this space of domination, disciplinary power manifests its potency, essentially, by arranging objects. The examination is, as it were, the ceremony of this objectification.

Hitherto the role of the political ceremony had been to give rise to the excessive, yet regulated manifestation of power; it was a spectacular expression of potency, an 'expenditure', exaggerated and coded, in which power renewed its vigour. It was always more or less related to the triumph. The solemn appearance of the sovereign brought with it something of the consecration, the coronation, the return from victory; even the funeral ceremony took place with all the spectacle of power deployed. Discipline, however, had its own type of ceremony. It was not the triumph, but the review, the 'parade', an ostentatious form of the examination. In it the 'subjects' were presented as 'objects' to the observation of a power that was manifested only by its gaze. They did not receive directly the image of the sovereign power; they only felt its effects—in replica, as it were—on their bodies, which had become precisely legible and docile. On 15 March 1666, Louis XIV took his first military review: 18,000 men, 'one of the most spectacular actions of the reign', which was supposed to have 'kept all Europe in disquiet'. Several years later, a medal was struck to commemorate the event (cf. Jucquiot, 50–54). It bears the exergue, '*Disciplina militaris restitua*' and the legend '*Prolusio ad victorias*'. On the right, the king, right foot forward, commands the exercise itself with a stick. On the left, several ranks of soldiers are shown full face and aligned in depth; they have raised their right arms to shoulder height and are holding their rifles exactly vertical, their right legs are slightly forward and their left feet turned outwards. On the ground, lines intersect at right angles, to form, beneath the soldiers' feet, broad rectangles that serve as references for different phases and positions of the exercise. In the background is a piece of classical architecture. The columns of the palace extend those formed by the ranks of men and the erect rifles, just as the paving no doubt extends the lines of the exercise. But above the balustrade that crowns the building are statues representing dancing figures: sinuous lines, rounded gestures, draperies. The marble is covered with movements whose principle of unity is harmonic. The men, on the other hand, are frozen into a uniformly repeated attitude of ranks and lines: a tactical unity. The order of the architecture, which frees at its summit the figures of the dance, imposes its rules and its geometry on the disciplined men on the ground. The columns of power. 'Very good', Grand Duke Mikhail once remarked of a regiment, after having kept it for one hour presenting arms, 'only *they breathe*' (Kropotkin, 8; I owe this reference to G. Canguilhem).

Let us take this medal as evidence of the moment when, paradoxically but significantly, the most brilliant figure of sovereign power is joined to the emergence of the rituals proper to disciplinary power. The scarcely sustainable visibility of the monarch is turned into the unavoidable visibility of the subjects. And it is this inversion of visibility in the functioning of the disciplines that was to assure the exercise of power even in its lowest manifestations. We are entering the age of the infinite examination and of compulsory objectification.

2. *The examination also introduces individuality into the field of documentation.* The examination leaves behind it a whole meticulous archive constituted in terms of bodies and days. The examination that places individuals in a field of surveillance also situates them in a network of writing; it engages them in a whole mass of documents that capture and fix them. The procedures of examination were accompanied at the same time by a system of intense registration and of documentary accumulation. A 'power of writing' was constituted as an essential part in the mechanisms of discipline. On many points, it was modelled on the traditional methods of administrative documentation, though with particular techniques and important innovations. Some concerned methods of identification, signalling or description. This was the problem in the army, where it was necessary to track down deserters, avoid repeating enrolments, correct fictitious 'information' presented by officers, know the services and value of each individual, establish with certainty the balance-sheet of those who had disappeared or died. It was the problem of the hospitals, where it was necessary to recognize the patients, expel shammers, follow the evolution of diseases, study the effectiveness of treatments, map similar cases and the beginnings of epidemics. It was the problem of the teaching establishments, where one had to define the aptitude of each individual, situate his level and his abilities, indicate the possible use that might be made of them: 'The register enables one, by being available in time and place, to know the habits of the children, their progress in piety, in catechism, in the letters, during the time they have been at the School' (M.I.D.B., 64).

Hence the formation of a whole series of codes of disciplinary individuality that made it possible to transcribe, by means of homogenization the individual features established by the examination: the physical code of signalling, the medical code of symptoms, the educational or military code of conduct or performance. These codes were still very crude, both in quality and quantity, but they marked a first stage in the 'formalization' of the individual within power relations.

The other innovations of disciplinary writing concerned the correlation of these elements, the accumulation of documents, their seriation, the organization of comparative fields making it possible to classify, to form categories, to determine averages, to fix norms. The hospitals of the eighteenth century, in particular, were great laboratories for scriptuary and documentary methods. The keeping of registers, their specification, the modes of transcription from one to the other, their circulation during visits, their comparison during regular meetings of doctors and administrators, the transmission of their data to centralizing bodies (either at the hospital or at the central office of the poorhouses), the accountancy of diseases, cures, deaths, at the level of a hospital, a town and even of the nation as a whole formed an integral part of the process by which hospitals were subjected to the disciplinary régime. Among the fundamental conditions of a good medical 'discipline', in both senses of the word, one must include the procedures of writing that made it possible to integrate individual data into cumulative systems in such a way that they were not lost; so to arrange things that an individual could be located in the general register and that, conversely, each datum of the individual examination might affect overall calculations.

Thanks to the whole apparatus of writing that accompanied it, the examination opened up two correlative possibilities: firstly, the constitution of the individual as a describable, analysable object, not in order to reduce him to 'specific' features, as did the naturalists in relation to living beings, but in order to maintain him in his individual features, in his particular evolution, in his own aptitudes or abilities, under the gaze of a permanent corpus of knowledge; and, secondly, the constitution of a comparative system that made possible the measurement of overall phenomena, the description of groups, the characterization of collective facts, the calculation of the gaps between individuals, their distribution in a given 'population'.

These small techniques of notation, of registration, of constituting files, of arranging facts in columns and tables that are so familiar to us now, were of decisive importance in the epistemological 'thaw' of the sciences of the individual. One is no doubt right to pose the Aristotelean problem: is a science of the individual possible and legitimate? A great problem needs great solutions perhaps. But there is the small historical problem of the emergence, towards the end of the eighteenth century, of what might generally be termed the 'clinical' sciences; the problem of the entry of the individual (and no longer the species) into the field of knowledge; the problem of the entry of the individual description, of the cross-examination, of anamnesis, of the 'file' into the general functioning of scientific discourse. To this simple question of fact, one must no doubt give an answer lacking in 'nobility': one should look into these procedures of writing and registration, one should look into the mechanisms of examination, into the formation of the mechanisms of discipline, and of a new type of power over bodies. Is this the birth of the sciences of man? It is probably to be found in these 'ignoble' archives, where the modern play of coercion over bodies, gestures and behaviour has its beginnings.

3. *The examination, surrounded by all its documentary techniques, makes each individual a 'case'*: a case which at one and the same time constitutes an object for a branch of knowledge and a hold for a branch of power. The case is no longer, as in casuistry or jurisprudence, a set of circumstances defining an act and capable of modifying the application of a rule; it is the individual as he may be described, judged, measured, compared with others, in his very individuality; and it is also the individual who has to be trained or corrected, classified, normalized, excluded, etc.

For a long time ordinary individuality—the everyday individuality of everybody—remained below the threshold of description. To be looked at, observed, described in detail, followed from day to day by an uninterrupted writing was a privilege. The chronicle of a man, the account of his life, his historiography, written as he lived out his life formed part of the rituals of his power. The disciplinary methods reversed this relation, lowered the threshold of describable individuality and made of this description a means of control and a method of domination. It is no longer a monument for future memory, but a document for possible use. And this new describability is all the more marked in that the disciplinary framework is a strict one: the child, the patient, the madman, the prisoner, were to become, with increasing ease from the eighteenth century and according to a curve which is that of the mechanisms of discipline, the object of individual descriptions and biographical accounts. This turning of real lives into writing is no longer a procedure of heroization; it functions as a procedure of objectification and subjection. The carefully collated life of mental patients or delinquents belongs, as did the chronicle of kings or the adventures of the great popular bandits, to a certain political function of writing; but in a quite different technique of power.

The examination as the fixing, at once ritual and 'scientific', of individual differences, as the pinning down of each individual in his own particularity (in contrast with the ceremony in which status, birth, privilege, function are manifested with all the spectacle of their marks) clearly indicates the appearance of a new modality of power in which each individual receives as his status his own individuality, and in which he is linked by his status to the features, the measurements, the gaps, the 'marks' that characterize him and make him a 'case'.

Finally, the examination is at the centre of the procedures that constitute the individual as effect and object of power, as effect and object of knowledge. It is the examination which, by combining hierarchical surveillance and normalizing judgement, assures the great disciplinary functions of distribution and classification, maximum extraction of forces and time, continuous genetic accumulation, optimum combination of aptitudes and, thereby, the fabrication of cellular, organic, genetic and combinatory individuality. With it are ritualized those disciplines that may be characterized in a word by saying that they are a modality of power for which individual difference is relevant.

The disciplines mark the moment when the reversal of the political axis of individualization—as one might call it—takes place. In certain societies, of which the feudal régime is only one example, it may be said that individualization is greatest where sovereignty is exercised and in the higher echelons of power. The more one possesses power or privilege, the more one is marked as an individual, by rituals, written accounts or visual reproductions. The 'name' and the genealogy that situate one within a kinship group, the performance of deeds that demonstrate superior strength and which are immortalized in literary accounts, the ceremonies that mark the power relations in their very ordering, the monuments or donations that bring survival after death, the ostentation and excess of expenditure, the multiple, intersecting links of allegiance and suzerainty, all these are procedures of an 'ascending' individualization. In a disciplinary régime, on the other hand, individualization is 'descending': as power becomes more anonymous and more functional, those on whom it is exercised tend to be more strongly individualized; it is exercised by surveillance rather than ceremonies, by observation rather than commemorative accounts, by comparative measures that have the 'norm' as reference rather than genealogies giving ancestors as points of reference; by 'gaps' rather than by deeds. In a system of discipline, the child is more individualized than the adult, the patient more than the healthy man, the madman and the delinquent more than the normal and the non-delinquent. In each case, it is towards the first of these pairs that all the individualizing mechanisms are turned in our civilization; and when one wishes to individualize the healthy, normal and law-abiding adult, it is always by asking him how much of the child he has in him, what secret madness lies within him, what fundamental crime he has dreamt of committing. All the sciences, analyses or practices employing the root 'psycho-' have their origin in this historical reversal of the procedures of individualization. The moment that saw the transition from historico-ritual mechanisms for the formation of individuality to the scientifico-disciplinary mechanisms, when the normal took over from the ancestral, and measurement from status, thus substituting for the individuality of the memorable man that of the calculable man, that moment when the sciences of man became possible is the moment when a new technology of power and a new political anatomy of the body were implemented. And if from the early Middle Ages to the present day the 'adventure' is an account of individuality, the passage from the epic to the novel, from the noble deed to the secret singularity, from long exiles to the internal search for childhood, from combats to phantasies, it is also inscribed in the formation of a disciplinary society. The adventure of our childhood no longer finds expression in '*le bon petit Henri*', but in the misfortunes of 'little Hans'. The *Romance of the Rose* is written today by Mary Barnes; in the place of Lancelot, we have Judge Schreber.

It is often said that the model of a society that has individuals as its constituent elements is borrowed from the abstract juridical forms of contract and exchange. Mercantile society, according to this view, is represented as a contractual association of isolated juridical subjects. Perhaps. Indeed, the political theory of the seventeenth and eighteenth centuries often seems to follow this schema. But it should not be forgotten that there existed at the same period a technique for constituting individuals as correlative elements of power and knowledge. The individual is no doubt the fictitious atom of an 'ideological' representation of society; but he is also a reality fabricated by this specific technology of power that I have called 'discipline'. We must cease once and for all to describe the effects of power in negative terms: it 'excludes', it 'represses', it 'censors', it 'abstracts', it 'masks', it 'conceals'. In fact, power produces; it produces reality; it produces domains of objects and rituals of truth. The individual and the knowledge that may be gained of him belong to this production.

Is it not somewhat excessive to derive such power from the petty machinations of discipline? How could *they* achieve effects of such scope?

NOTES

1. *Règlement pour l' infanterie prussienne,* Fr. Trans., Arsenal, MS. 4067, fo. 144. For older plans see Praissac, 27–8 and Montgommery, 77. For the new plans, cf. Beneton de Morange, *Histoire de la guerre,* 1741, 61–4, and *Dissertations sur les Tentes*; cf. also the many regulations such as the *Instruction sur le service des règlements de Cavalerie dans les camps*, 29 June 1753.
2. Arch. nat. MM 666–9. Jeremy Bentham recounts that it was while visiting the École Militaire that his brother first had the idea of the Panopticon.
3. Demia, 27–9. One might note a phenomenon of the same kind in the organization of schools; for a long time 'prefects' were, independently of the teachers, entrusted with the moral responsibility for small groups of pupils. After 1762, above all, one sees the appearance of a new type of supervision, which was more administrative and more integrated into the hierarchy; supervisors, *maîtres de quartier, maîtres subalternes*. Cf. Duptont-Ferrier, 254 and 476.

Orientalism Now

Edward Said

The methodological failures of Orientalism cannot be accounted for either by saying that the *real* Orient is different from Orientalist portraits of it, or by saying that since Orientalists are Westerners for the most part, they cannot be expected to have an inner sense of what the Orient is all about. Both of these propositions are false. It is not the thesis of this [study] to suggest that there is such a thing as a real or true Orient (Islam, Arab, or whatever); nor is it to make an assertion about the necessary privilege of an 'insider' perspective over an 'outsider' one, to use Robert K. Merton's [1973] useful distinction. On the contrary, I have been arguing that 'the Orient' is itself a constituted entity, and that the notion that there are geographical spaces with indigenous, radically 'different' inhabitants who can be defined on the basis of some religion, culture, or racial essence proper to that geographical space is equally a highly debatable idea. I certainly do not believe the limited proposition that only a black can write about blacks, a Muslim about Muslims, and so forth.

And yet despite its failures, its lamentable jargon, its scarcely concealed racism, its paper-thin intellectual apparatus, Orientalism flourishes today in the forms I have tried to describe. Indeed, there is some reason for alarm in the fact that its influence has spread to 'the Orient' itself: the pages of books and journals in Arabic (and doubtless in Japanese, various Indian dialects, and other Oriental languages) are filled with second-order analyses by Arabs of 'the Arab mind,' 'Islam,' and other myths. Orientalism has also spread in the United States now that Arab money and resources have added considerable glamour to the traditional 'concern' felt for the strategically important Orient. The fact is that Orientalism has been successfully accommodated to the new imperialism, where its ruling paradigms do not contest, and even confirm, the continuing imperial design to dominate Asia.

In the one part of the Orient that I can speak about with some direct knowledge, the accommodation between the intellectual class and the new imperialism might very well be accounted one of the special triumphs of Orientalism. The Arab world today is an intellectual, political, and cultural satellite of the United States. This is not in itself something to be lamented; the specific form of the satellite relationship, however, is. Consider first of all that universities in the Arab world are generally run according to some pattern inherited from, or once directly imposed by, a former colonial power. New circumstances make the curricular actualities almost grotesque: classes populated with hundreds of students, badly trained, overworked, and underpaid faculty, political appointments, the almost total absence of advanced research and of research facilities, and most important, the lack of a single decent library in the entire region. Whereas Britain and France once dominated intellectual horizons in the East by virtue of their prominence and wealth, it is now the United States that occupies that place, with the result that the few promising students who manage to make it through the system are encouraged to come to the United States to continue their advanced work. And while it is certainly true that some students from the Arab world continue to go to Europe to study, the sheer numerical preponderance comes to the United States; this is as true of students from so-called radical states as it is of students from conservative states like

Saudi Arabia and Kuwait. Besides, the patronage system in scholarship, business, and research makes the United States a virtual hegemonic commander of affairs; the source, however much it may not be a real source, is considered to be the United States.

Two factors make the situation even more obviously a triumph of Orientalism. Insofar as one can make a sweeping generalization, the felt tendencies of contemporary culture in the Near East are guided by European and American models. When Taha Hussein said of modern Arab culture in 1936 that it was European, not Eastern, he was registering the identity of the Egyptian cultural elite, of which he was so distinguished a member. The same is true of the Arab cultural elite today, although the powerful current of anti-imperialist Third World ideas that has gripped the region since the early 1950s has tempered the Western edge of the dominant culture. In addition, the Arab and Islamic world remains a second-order power in terms of the production of culture, knowledge, and scholarship. Here one must be completely realistic about using the terminology of power politics to describe the situation that obtains. No Arab or Islamic scholar can afford to ignore what goes on in scholarly journals, institutes, and universities in the United States and Europe; the converse is not true. For example, there is no major journal of Arab studies published in the Arab world today, just as there is no Arab educational institution capable of challenging places like Oxford, Harvard, or UCLA in the study of the Arab world, much less in any non-Oriental subject matter. The predictable result of all this is that Oriental students (and Oriental professors) still want to come and sit at the feet of American Orientalists, and later to repeat to their local audiences the clichés I have been characterizing as Orientalist dogmas. Such a system of reproduction makes it inevitable that the Oriental scholar will use his American training to feel superior to his own people because he is able to 'manage' the Orientalist system; in his relations with his superiors, the European or American Orientalists, he will remain only a 'native informant.' And indeed this is his role in the West, should he be fortunate enough to remain there after his advanced training. Most elementary courses in Oriental languages are taught by 'native informants' in United States universities today; also, power in the system (in universities, foundations, and the like) is held almost exclusively by non-Orientals, although the numerical ratio of Oriental to non-Oriental resident professionals does not favor the latter so overwhelmingly.

There are all kinds of other indications of how the cultural domination is maintained, as much by Oriental consent as by direct and crude economic pressure from the United States. It is sobering to find, for instance, that while there are dozens of organizations in the United States for studying the Arab and Islamic Orient, there are none in the Orient itself for studying the United States, by far the greatest economic and political influence in the region. Worse, there are scarcely any institutes of even modest stature in the Orient devoted to study of the Orient. But all this, I think, is small in comparison with the second factor contributing to the triumph of Orientalism: the fact of consumerism in the Orient. The Arab and Islamic world as a whole is hooked into the Western market system. No one needs to be reminded that oil, the region's greatest resource, has been totally absorbed into the United States economy. By that I mean not only that the great oil companies are controlled by the American economic system; I mean also that Arab oil revenues, to say nothing of marketing, research, and industry management, are based in the United States. This has effectively made the oil-rich Arabs into huge customers of American exports: this is as true of states in the Persian Gulf as it is of Libya, Iraq, and Algeria—radical states all. My point is that the relationship is a one-sided one, with the United States a selective customer of a very few products (oil and cheap manpower, mainly), the Arabs highly diversified consumers of a vast range of United States products, material and ideological.

This has had many consequences. There is a vast standardization of taste in the region, symbolized not only by transistors, blue jeans, and Coca-Cola but also by cultural images of the Orient supplied by American mass media and consumed unthinkingly by the mass television audience. The paradox of an Arab regarding himself as an 'Arab' of the sort put out by Hollywood is but the simplest result of what I am referring to. Another result is that the Western market economy and its consumer orientation have produced (and are producing at an accelerating rate) a class of educated people whose intellectual formation is directed to satisfying market needs. There is a heavy emphasis on engineering, business, and economics, obviously enough; but the intelligentsia itself is auxiliary to what it considers to be the main trends stamped out in the West. Its role has been prescribed and set for it as a 'modernizing' one, which means that it gives legitimacy and authority to ideas about modernization, progress, and culture that it receives from the United States for the most part. Impressive evidence for this is found in the social sciences and, surprisingly enough, among radical intellectuals whose Marxism is taken wholesale from Marx's own homogenizing view of the Third World [...]. So if all told there is an intellectual acquiescence in the images and doctrines of Orientalism, there is also a very powerful reinforcement of this in economic, political, and social exchange: the modern Orient, in short, participates in its own Orientalizing.

But in conclusion, what of some alternative to Orientalism? Is this [study] an argument only *against* something, and not *for* something positive? [Elsewhere] I have spoken about 'decolonializing' new departures in the so-called area studies—the work of Anwar Abdel Malek, the studies published by members of the Hull group on Middle Eastern studies, the innovative analyses and proposals of various scholars in Europe, the United States, and the Near East[1]—but I have not attempted to do more than mention them or allude to them quickly. My project has been to describe a particular system of ideas, not by any means to displace the system with a new one. In addition, 1 have attempted to raise a whole set of questions that are relevant in discussing the problems of human experience: How does one *represent* other cultures? What is *another* culture? Is the notion of a distinct culture (or race, or religion, or civilization) a useful one, or does it always get involved either in self-congratulation (when one discusses one's own) or hostility and aggression (when one discusses the 'other')? Do cultural, religious, and racial differences matter more than socio-economic categories, or politico-historical ones? How do ideas acquire authority, 'normality,' and even the status of 'natural' truth? What is the role of the intellectual? Is he there to validate the culture and state of which he is a part? What importance must he give to an independent critical consciousness, an *oppositional* critical consciousness?

I hope that some of my answers to these questions have been implicit in the [earlier chapters of *Orientalism*], but perhaps I can speak a little more explicitly about some of them here. As I have characterized it in this study, Orientalism calls in question not only the possibility of nonpolitical scholarship but also the advisability of too close a relationship between the scholar and the state. It is equally apparent, I think, that the circumstances making Orientalism a continuingly persuasive type of thought will persist: a rather depressing matter on the whole. Nevertheless there is some rational expectation in my own mind that Orientalism need not always be so unchallenged, intellectually, ideologically, and politically, as it has been.

I would not have undertaken a [study] of this sort if I did not also believe that there is scholarship that is not as corrupt, or at least as blind to human reality, as the kind I have been mainly depicting. Today there are many individual scholars working in such fields as Islamic history, religion, civilization, sociology, and anthropology whose production is deeply valuable as scholarship. The trouble sets in when the guild tradition of Orientalism takes over the scholar who is not vigilant, whose individual consciousness as a scholar is not on guard against *idées reçues* all too easily handed down in the profession. Thus interesting work is most likely to be produced by scholars whose allegiance is to a discipline defined intellectually and not to a 'field' like Orientalism defined either canonically, imperially, or geographically. An excellent recent instance is the anthropology of Clifford Geertz, whose interest in Islam is discrete and concrete enough to be animated by the specific societies and problems he studies and not by the rituals, preconceptions, and doctrines of Orientalism.

On the other hand, scholars and critics who are trained in the traditional Orientalist disciplines are perfectly capable of freeing themselves from the old ideological straitjacket. Jacques Berque's and Maxime Rodinson's training ranks with the most rigorous available, but what invigorates their investigations even of traditional problems is their methodological self-consciousness. For if Orientalism has historically been too smug, too insulated, too positivistically confident in its ways and its premises, then one way of opening oneself to what one studies in or about the Orient is reflexively to submit one's method to critical scrutiny. This is what characterizes Berque and Rodinson, each in his own way. What one finds in their work is always, first of all, a direct sensitivity to the material before them, and then a continual self-examination of their methodology and practice, a constant attempt to keep their work responsive to the material and not to a doctrinal preconception. Certainly Berque and Rodinson, as well as Abdel Malek and Roger Owen, are aware too that the study of man and society—whether Oriental or not—is best conducted in the broad field of all the human sciences; therefore these scholars are critical readers, and students of what goes on in other fields. Berque's attention to recent discoveries in structural anthropology, Rodinson's to sociology and political theory, Owen's to economic history: all these are instructive correctives brought from the contemporary human sciences to the study of so-called Oriental problems.

But there is no avoiding the fact that even if we disregard the Orientalist distinctions between 'them' and 'us,' a powerful series of political and ultimately ideological realities inform scholarship today. No one can escape dealing with, if not the East/West division, then the North/South one, the have/have-not one, the imperialist/anti-imperialist one, the white/colored one. We cannot get around them all by pretending they do not exist; on the contrary, contemporary Orientalism teaches us a great deal about the intellectual dishonesty of dissembling on that score, the result of which is to intensify the divisions and make them both vicious and permanent. Yet an openly polemical and right-minded 'progressive' scholarship can very easily degenerate into dogmatic slumber, a prospect that is not edifying either.

My own sense of the problem is fairly shown by the kinds of questions I formulated above. Modern thought and experience have taught us to be sensitive to what is involved in representation, in studying the Other, in racial thinking, in unthinking and uncritical acceptance of authority and authoritative ideas, in the sociopolitical role of intellectuals, in the great value of a skeptical critical consciousness. Perhaps if we remember that the study of human experience usually has an ethical, to say nothing of a political, consequence in either the best or worst sense, we will not be indifferent to what we do as scholars. And what better norm for the scholar than human freedom and knowledge? Perhaps too we should remember that the study of man in society is based on concrete human history and experience, not on donnish abstractions, or on obscure laws or arbitrary systems. The problem then is to make the study fit and in some way be shaped by the experience, which would be illuminated and perhaps changed by the study. At all costs, the goal of Orientalizing the Orient again and again is to be avoided, with consequences that cannot help but refine knowledge and reduce the scholar's conceit. Without 'the Orient' there would be scholars, critics, intellectuals, human beings, for whom the racial, ethnic, and national distinctions were less important than the common enterprise of promoting human community.

Positively, I do believe—and in my other work have tried to show—that enough is being done today in the human sciences to provide the contemporary scholar with insights, methods, and ideas that could dispense with racial, ideological, and imperialist stereotypes of the sort provided during its historical ascendancy by Orientalism. I consider Orientalism's failure to have been a human as much as an intellectual one; for in having to take up a position of irreducible opposition to a region of the world it considered alien to its own, Orientalism failed to identify with human experience, failed also to see it as human experience. The worldwide hegemony of Orientalism and all it stands for can now be challenged, if we can benefit properly from the general twentieth-century rise to political and historical awareness of so many of the earth's peoples. If this [work] has any future use, it will be as a modest contribution to that challenge, and as a warning: that systems of thought like Orientalism, discourses of power, ideological fictions—mind-forg'd manacles—are all too easily made, applied, and guarded. Above all, I hope to have shown my reader that the answer to Orientalism is not Occidentalism. No former 'Oriental' will be comforted by the thought that having been an Oriental himself he is likely—too likely—to study new 'Orientals'—or 'Occidentals'—of his own making. If the knowledge of Orientalism has any meaning, it is in being a reminder of the seductive degradation of knowledge of any knowledge, anywhere, at any time. Now perhaps more than before.

NOTE

This chapter is taken from E. Said (1978), 'Orientalism Now', *Orientalism* (London: Routledge & Kegan Paul), 322–8.

1. See, for example, the recent work of Anwar Adel Malek, Yves Lacoste, and the authors of essays published in *Review of Middle East Studies 1 and 2* (London: Ithaca Press, 1975, 1976), the various analyses of Middle Eastern politics by Noam Chomsky, and the work done by the Middle East Research and Information Project (MERIP). A good prospectus is provided in Gabriel Ardant, Kostas Axelos, Jacques Berque, et al., *De l'impérialisme à la décolonization* (Paris: Éditions de Minuit, 1965).

Beyond Status and Class?

Ulrich Beck and Elisabeth Beck-Gernsheim

Are we now witnessing a historic change whereby people are 'released' from the forms of industrial society (class, social layer, occupation, family, marriage), as they were released during the Reformation from the secular domination of the Church? Is it possible that, amid the waning of traditional ways of life, new ones are taking shape for which we simply have no concept and therefore no perception? Are the forceful demands for self-determination and participation as much a sign of this as are the boundary crossing and new combinations of the private and the public?

Today, anyone who poses the key question of the reality of classes in Germany or other advanced societies is faced with an apparent contradiction. On the one hand, the structure of social inequality in the developed countries displays a surprising *stability*; research findings tell us that, despite all the technological and economic changes and all the attempts at reform, there has been no major change in the relations of inequality between major groups in our society—leaving aside isolated shifts and grey areas.

On the other hand, questions concerning inequality are no longer perceived and politically handled as class questions. In the wake of the unification of the two German states, unemployment and poverty have sharply increased and such phenomena as the struggle for women's rights, movements against nuclear power stations, and intergenerational, inter-regional and inter-religious conflicts also centrally involve issues of inequality. But if the public political debate is taken as a measure of real developments, the general conclusion would seem to be that we live in a country already *beyond* class society, in which the imagery of class is preserved only for want of a better alternative.

This contradiction is resolvable if we examine more closely the extent to which the *social significance* of inequalities has changed over the past three decades—a change that has largely escaped the attention of the relevant research. Our thesis is precisely that in the wealthy industrial heartlands of the West—and most plainly in the Federal Republic of Germany—the post-war development of the welfare state brought with it a social impetus toward individualization of unprecedented scale and dynamism, beneath the cover of largely constant relations of inequality. Against the backdrop of a comparatively high standard of living and social security, a break in historical continuity released people from traditional class ties and family supports and increasingly threw them onto their own resources and their individual fate in the labour market, with all its attendant risks, opportunities and contradictions.

A process of individualization has long been considered a feature of the newly developing bourgeoisie, but in another form it was also distinctive of the 'free wage labourer' of modern capitalism and of the labour market dynamic under the conditions of welfare state mass democracies. Entry into the labour market has repeatedly released people from fixed ties of family, neighbourhood and occupation, as well as from ties to a particular regional culture and landscape. These individualizing thrusts *compete* with such collective aspects of a labour market destiny as the social risks of wage labour (unemployment, deskilling etc.). But it is only insofar as these risks are reduced—through relative affluence and social protection—that individualization actually leads to a *dissolution* of lifeworlds associated with class and status group subcultures.

The implications for social structure are thus ambivalent. On the one hand, stratification theorists (and Marxist class theorists) may consider that nothing essential has changed, for distances in the income hierarchy and fundamental coordinates of wage labour have remained much the same. But on the other hand, ties to a social class (in Max Weber's sense) have typically been pushed into the background. A tendency to individualized lifestyles and life situations forces people—for the sake of material survival—to make themselves the centre of their own life plans and conduct.

Consequently, individualization should here be understood as a historically contradictory *process of socialization*. The standardized collective character of these individualized life situations is certainly difficult to comprehend. Yet it is precisely the breaking out of this contradiction and the consciousness of it as a contradiction, which can lead to the emergence of new socio-cultural commonalities: whether new class situations spanning different income and skill groups become visible along with the intensification of social risks; or whether, in the wake of individualization processes, expectations of 'a life of one's own' (conceived materially, spatially, temporally and as a pattern of social relations) are systematically awakened yet brought up against social-political limitations and resistances. This constantly gives rise to new quests, which may involve extreme experiments with social relations and with people's own lives and bodies in the various alternative scenes and youth subcultures (including the excesses of far-right violence). Commonalities are here cultivated not least in aggressive protest actions, sparked off by bureaucratic-industrial encroachments on people's own 'private lives'.

We may say that a wide-ranging social and cultural *process of erosion and evolution* has been unleashed by the ongoing individualization. The course and the consequences of individualization processes within society are therefore of general interest for an understanding of major social shifts in the phase of advanced modernity. There are strong indications that they tend to bring about a change in the social meaning and pattern of such central lifeworld structures as the family (marriage, parenthood), gender roles, community relations, labour relations and party affiliations and that they help to explain the 'new social movements' and political behaviour in general, including the question of consensus and governability in modern societies.

The Labour Market as 'Motor' of Individualization

'Individualization of social inequality'—does this not suggest that everything important is being forgotten, misunderstood or simply dismissed, including everything we have learned about the class character of society, its nature as a system, about mass society and the concentration of capital, about ideological distortions and alienation, about unchanging human traits and the complexity of social and historical reality? And does not the concept of individualization also spell the premature end of sociology, leading to the tolling of its bell?

This calls for a number of clarifications. The existence of individualization has been empirically verified in numerous qualitative interviews and studies. They all point to one central concern, the demand for control of one's own money, time, living space and body. In other words, people demand the right to develop their own perspective on life and to be able to act upon it. However illusory and ideological these claims may turn out to be, they are a reality which cannot be overlooked. And they arise from the actual conditions of life in Germany as they have developed in the past three decades. But today it is also becoming apparent that such processes of individualization can be quite precarious, especially where groups are suddenly hit or threatened by unemployment and forced to confront radical disruptions of their lifestyle precisely because of the individualization they have experienced and despite the protections provided by the welfare state.

How do such trends differ from the rise of bourgeois individualism in the eighteenth and nineteenth centuries? Processes of individualization among the bourgeoisie derived essentially from the ownership and accumulation of capital. The bourgeoisie developed its social and political identity in the struggle against feudal structures of domination and authority. In late modernity, by contrast, individualization is a product of the labour market and manifests itself in the acquisition, proffering and application of a variety of work skills. This argument can be elaborated by looking at three dimensions of the labour market—education, mobility and competition.

Education

As schooling increases in duration, traditional orientations, ways of thinking and lifestyles are recast and displaced by universalistic forms of learning and teaching, as well as by universalistic forms of knowledge and language. Depending on its duration and content, education makes possible at least a certain degree of self-discovery and reflection. Education, furthermore, is connected with *selection* and therefore requires the individual's expectations of upward mobility; these expectations remain effective even in cases where upward mobility through education is an illusion, since education is little more than a protection against downward mobility (as to some extent happened during the period of expansion of educational opportunities). For it is after all only possible to pass through formal education by individually succeeding by way of assignments, examinations and tests. Formal education in schools and universities, in turn, provides individual credentials leading to individualized career opportunities in the labour market.

Mobility

As soon as people enter the labour market, they experience mobility. They are removed from traditional patterns and arrangements and, unless they are prepared to suffer economic ruin, they are forced to take charge of their own life. The labour market, by way of occupational mobility, place of residence or employment, type of employment, as well as the changes in social location it initiates, reveals itself as a driving force behind the individualization of people's lives. They become relatively independent of inherited or newly formed ties (e.g. family, neighbourhood, friendship, partnership). By becoming independent from traditional ties, people's lives take on an independent quality which, for the first time, makes possible the experience of a personal destiny.

Competition

Competition rests upon the interchangeability of qualifications and thereby compels people to advertise the individuality and uniqueness of their work and of their own accomplishments. The growing pressure of competition leads to an individualization among equals, i.e. precisely in areas of interaction and conduct which are characterized by a shared background (similar education, similar experience, similar knowledge). Especially where such a shared background still exists, community is dissolved in the acid bath of competition. In this sense, competition undermines the equality of equals without, however, eliminating it. It causes the isolation of individuals within homogeneous social groups.

Education, mobility and competition, however, are by no means independent of one another. Rather, they supplement and reinforce one another—and it is only by doing this that they have led to the distinctive impetus towards individualization of the past three decades.

Individualization and Class Formation: Marx and Weber

The thrust toward individualization in the welfare state can be understood more precisely by examining Karl Marx's and Max Weber's theories of social inequality. It is quite possible to regard Marx as one of the most resolute theorists of 'individualization'. Marx often stressed that an unparalleled process of emancipation had been set in motion as a result of the development of industrial capitalism. In his view, emancipation from feudal relations was a precondition for the establishment of capitalist relations of production. But even within capitalism itself people are uprooted in successive waves and wrested loose from tradition, family, neighbourhood, occupation and culture.

Marx never followed up on this variant of a class society caught in the process of individualization. For him the capitalist process of isolation and 'uprooting' had always been cushioned by the collective experience of immiseration and the resulting class struggle. Marx thought that it was precisely the process of emancipation and uprooting and the deterioration of the living conditions of workers under capitalism that led to the transformation of the working class from a 'class in itself' into a 'class for itself'. He dismissed as irrelevant the question of how individual proletarians, qua market subjects, could ever form stable bonds of solidarity, given that capitalism systematically uprooted their lives. Marx always equated processes of individualization with the formation of classes. This still appears to be the basic position of many contemporary class theorists.

The thesis of the individualization of social inequality may be regarded as precisely mirroring the Marxian position. Processes of individualization, as already described, can only become entrenched when material immiseration, as the condition for the formation of classes predicted by Marx, has been overcome. Trends toward individualization are dependent on complex structural conditions which up to now have been realized in very few countries and even then only during the most recent phase of development. Among such trends are economic prosperity, the construction of a welfare state, the institutionalization of interests represented by trade unions, the legal underpinning of labour contracts, the expansion of education, the growth of the service sector and associated opportunities for mobility and the shortening of the working week.[1]

These analyses may now be at once broadened and clarified if we turn to a second tradition associated with the name of Max Weber. On the one hand, as is well known, Max Weber laid much greater stress than Marx on the wide range of modem lifestyles. On the other hand, he ignored the latent tendencies toward individualization within market society. Weber, in fact, argued that these could not succeed, but without sharing Marx's belief in class formation resulting from immiseration. Tendencies toward individualization were blocked, according to Weber, by the continuity and the authority of traditions and subcultures based on status. In industrial capitalism traditional 'status-bound' attitudes, Weber argues, have been combined with expertise and market opportunities into substantively differentiated 'social class positions'. Thus Weber's work already contained the basic arguments spelled out in detail by Marxist labour historians at the end of the 1960s: namely, that the characteristic norms governing lifeworlds, value orientations and lifestyles during the expansion of industrial capitalism are less the product of 'class structures' and 'class formation' (as understood by Marx) than remnants of *pre*-capitalist and *pre*-industrial traditions. 'Capitalist culture' is consequently a less autochthonous creation than is often assumed. It is rather of pre-capitalist origins, modernized and assimilated by a system of industrial capitalism which recasts and consumes it. Thus, although Weber recognized various trends toward 'disenchantment' and 'demystification' of traditional lifestyles, he still regarded the social dynamic of individualization processes as following the principle of community formation linked to status.

Historical studies suggest that this indeed applied up to the early 1950s, but I do not believe that it still held for post-war developments in Germany at least. At that point the unstable unity of shared life experiences mediated by the market and shaped by status, which Max Weber brought together in the concept of social class, began to break apart. Its different elements (such as material conditions dependent on specific market opportunities, the effectiveness of tradition and of pre-capitalist lifestyles, the consciousness of communal bonds and of barriers to mobility, as well as networks of contact) have slowly disintegrated. They have been changed beyond recognition by the increasing standard of living and the increasing dependence on education as well as by an intensified mobility, competition and the juridification of labour relations. The traditional internal differentiations and social environments, which were still real enough for industrial workers in Imperial Germany and in the Weimar Republic, have been increasingly dissolved since the 1950s. At the same time, differences within the industrial labour force and between rural and urban populations have been levelled. Everywhere educational reform is accompanied by a dependence on education. More and more groups get caught up in the race for educational credentials. As a result there emerge new *internal* differentiations. While these may still respond to traditional differences between groups, the impact of education makes them fundamentally different from traditional ones. Here we can employ Bernstein's distinction that the new generation must move from a 'restricted' to an 'elaborated' code of speech. In conjunction with novel patterns of upward and downward mobility and increasing local labour mobility as well, new hierarchies and differentiations develop which are internal to social classes.

During the same period, traditional forms of settlement have frequently been replaced by new urban housing projects. These changes have also generated new forms of individualization. They affect patterns of interaction dependent on housing and living arrangements. The modern metropolis as well as urban developments in the smaller towns replace traditional settlement patterns. People from a great variety of cultural backgrounds are mixed together and social relations in the neighbourhood are much more loosely organized. Thus traditional forms of community beyond the family are beginning to disappear. Often, the members of the family choose their own separate relationships and live in networks of their own. This need not imply that social isolation increases or that relatively private family life prevails—although this may happen. But it does imply that already existing (ascriptively organized) neighbourhoods are shattered, together with their limitations and their opportunities for social control. The newly formed social relationships and social networks now have to be individually chosen; social ties, too, are becoming *reflexive*, so that they have to be established, maintained and constantly renewed by individuals.

This may mean, to take an extreme example, that interaction is no longer present, that social isolation and loneliness become the major pattern of relationships, as often happens with elderly people. It may also mean, however, that self-selected and self-created hierarchies and forms of stratification develop in relationships with acquaintances, neighbours and friends. These relationships are no longer primarily dependent on 'physical' proximity. Whether they transcend the local sphere or not, they are formed by individuals who regard themselves as organizers of their own circles of contacts and relationships. In the passage from one generation to the next, this may also entail that opportunities arise for people to experiment and test out new modes of living with one another.

The ability to choose and maintain one's own social relations may explain, for example, the emergence of many different layers and aspects of the private sphere, including the new phenomenon of *political privatism*. By this I mean an internally consistent, externally provocative stretching of the social and legal limits to people's freedom of action; a way of experimenting with social relations and lifestyles at the edge of what is culturally 'permissible' which generates political disturbances as well as processes of identity formation and identity attribution. This may result in a division into culture and counterculture, society and alternative society (including a growth of far-right violence), such as we have repeatedly seen in the last 20 years.

These and other developments suggest that the unstable association of community and market society which Max Weber had in mind when he spoke of social class has been partially transformed or even dissolved in the course of post-war developments. People at any rate no longer seem to understand or to experience it. The new ways of living reveal dynamic possibilities for a reorganization of social relations, which cannot be adequately comprehended by following either Marx or Weber.

As a result, the following questions become paramount. What actually happens when, in the course of historical development, the identity of social classes rooted in the lifeworld melts away—that is, when class loses its basis in subcultures and people's own experience of the world, even as the conditions and risks of wage labour are becoming generalized? Is a class identity no longer shaped by status even conceivable? Can the inequalities persisting under conditions of individualization still be grasped by means of the concept of class or by means of even more general hierarchical models of social inequality? Perhaps all these hierarchical models categorically depend on traditional status dependency? But are there interpretations which can replace these models? It may, of course, also be the case that processes of individualization are embedded in contradictions which in turn produce new social groupings and conflicts. How then are processes of individualization transformed into their opposite, into a quest for new social identities and ties and the development of new ways of living? One can imagine three extreme variants which are by no means mutually exclusive and indeed may even overlap.

First, the waning of traditional lifestyles does not bring the end of class, but rather *emancipates* classes from regional and particularist limitations. A new chapter in the history of classes is beginning, but we still need to comprehend its historical dynamics. It can in any case no longer be said without further qualification that this still is a history of the formation of class solidarities.

Second, in the course of the developments just described, both the firm and the workplace lose their significance in conflict and identity formation. A new site arises for the formation of social bonds and for the development of conflicts: namely, the sphere of private social relations and of personal modes of work and life. It is here that new social formations and identities are moulded beyond class society.

Third, the end of class society is not some revolutionary 'big bang'. It is a collectively experienced process of individualization within a post-traditional society of employees.

Emergence of Non-Corporate Class Identities

Discussion about the working class and the workers' movement in the second half of the twentieth century was marked by a false alternative. On the one hand, more and more arguments are adduced to show that the situation of working people under capitalism has significantly improved (material prosperity, greater educational opportunities, trade union and political organization resulting in the acquisition of rights and social security). On the other hand, it is said that the lot of the working class—that is, the wage relationship with its associated dependence, alienation and risks—has remained the same as before or even grown sharper as a result of unemployment, deskilling and so on. The point of the argument is to demonstrate, in the former case, that the working class is being *dissolved* and in the latter case that it displays *continuity*—with all the political consequences that flow from this. What both sides fail to recognize, however, is that the symbiosis of occupation and class is being shattered, with the result that corporate subcultures melt away while basic features of class are generalized. Once this fact is grasped, the question arises of how far the detachment of classes from corporate rigidities marks the beginning of a new type of class formation.

With the waning of the corporate reality of social classes, it is less and less possible to relate the development of forms of solidarity in society to the historical model of the 'proletarian productive worker'. Talk of the working class, or the class of employees, no longer appears a matter of course in people's lifeworlds, so that the basic references cease to apply for arguments about whether the proletariat is becoming 'bourgeoisified' or employees 'proletarianized'. At the same time, the dynamic of the labour market—or unemployment!—has been encompassing ever wider layers; the group of those not dependent on a wage becomes ever smaller and the group of those dependent on a wage ever larger. For all the differences, common features—especially common risks—increasingly stretch across groups defined by income or education.

Consequently, the potential and actual clientele of the trade unions has markedly *increased*, while at the same time it is *endangered* in new ways. The image of proletarianization also involved the coming together of those affected by it through the facts of material impoverishment and alienation. Wage labour risks, however, do not necessarily set up *any* commonality. They call instead for social, political and legal measures which in turn bring about the individualization of demands; people have to be specifically made aware of the collective character of these demands, in contrast to individual-therapeutic ways of handling problems. Thus, trade unionist and political modes of perception and action enter into competition with individually centred legal, medical or psychotherapeutic remedies and compensations, which may sometimes appear much more apposite to those upon whom the harm has been inflicted.

From the Family to Political Privatism

In the 1950s and 1960s, a lot of social research in the industrialized West demonstrated that the way in which people related to their job could be understood only in the context of their family life and their general situation vis-à-vis work. It became apparent that, even for industrial workers, the central focus of life was their family and not their experience of industrial wage labour.

This thoroughly ambivalent development of the private sphere, intensified by means of the culture and leisure industry, is not only an ideology but a *real* process and a *real* opportunity for people to fashion the conditions of their own life. The process only began with the family-centred privatism so characteristic of the 1950s and 1960s. As can now be seen more clearly, it could assume many different forms and acquire an independent dynamic that eventually gave privatism a political charge or dissolved it from within (for example, through the altered significance of family and sexuality, marriage and parenthood, but also in the emergence of fast-changing alternative cultures). In a completely new manner that perhaps cut more ice than attempts at political reform, the constant erosion and evolution of lifestyles placed the social-political structure under pressure to change and adapt in the most detailed ways. In this sense, the detraditionalization of the last few decades has unleashed a learning process whose historical effects (on children's upbringing or gender relations, for example) may be tensely awaited.

In the 1950s and 1960s, people gave a clear and unambiguous answer to the question of their goal in life: it was a 'happy' family home, a new car, a good education for their children and a higher standard of living. Today many speak a different (inevitably less clear-cut) language, which revolves around issues of individuality and identity, the 'development of personal capacities' and 'keeping things moving'. This does not, however, apply equally to all sections of the population. It is essentially a change on the part of the better educated and more affluent younger generation, whereas older, poorer and less educated groups remain clearly tied to the value system of the 1950s. In the eyes of many, the conventional symbols of success (income, career, status) no longer fulfil their need for self-discovery and self-assertion or their hunger for a 'fuller life'.

People therefore end up more and more in a labyrinth of self-doubt and uncertainty. The (infinite) regress involved in this self-questioning—'Am I really happy?', 'Am I really fulfilled?', 'Who exactly is the I saying and asking this?'—leads to ever new kinds of response, which then often provide a market niche for experts, industries and religious movements. In their quest for self-fulfilment, people scour the travel brochures and go to the four corners of the earth; they throw away the best marriages and rapidly enter new ties; they undergo retraining, diet and jog; they shift from one therapy group to another and swear by quite different therapies and therapists. They pull themselves up by the roots, to see whether the roots are really healthy.

This value system of individualization also contains the elements of a new ethics, which is based on the principle of 'duty to oneself'. Of course, this completely contradicts the traditional view of ethics, in which duties are necessarily social in character and adjust the individual to the whole. The new value orientations are thus often seen as an expression of egoism and narcissism. But this is to misunderstand the essence of what is new about them: namely, their focus on self-enlightenment and self-liberation as an active process to be accomplished in their own lives, including the search for new social ties in family, workplace and politics.

The political strength of the labour movement rests upon its capacity to stop work in the organized form of the strike. By contrast, the political potential of the newly developing private sphere lies in the realization that it enables a degree of self-fashioning of people's lives which, through the direct act of making things different, challenges and overcomes deep-rooted cultural beliefs. To take one example, the strength of the women's movement also rests on the remoulding of everyday routines and certainties in all areas of formal work, the legal system and the various centres of decision making, where its policy of pinpricks is felt as painful by the closed male 'corporation'. In general, then, the trigger for today's social conflicts and movements (unlike in lifeworlds shaped by class cultures) is a perceptible threat to spaces of action and decision that were once confidently held in a spirit of expansion.

Toward an Individualized Society of Employees

There are a great many different attempts to develop new social groupings, but however strong the convulsions triggered by them may be, they are invariably qualified by the fact that they, too, are exposed to ever new thrusts toward individualization. The motor of individualization is going at full blast and it is not at all clear how new and lasting social arrangements, comparable in depth of penetration to social classes, can even be created. On the contrary, especially in the immediate future, it is very likely that, as a way of coping with unemployment and economic crises, social and technological innovations will be set in motion which will open up new opportunities for individualization processes, in particular with regard to greater flexibility in labour market relations and new regulations governing working hours. But this also applies to the new forms of communication. These technological and social revolutions, which either still lie ahead or are already in full swing, will unleash a profound individualization of lifestyles.

If this assessment is correct, a variant of social structure which neither Marx nor Weber foresaw will gain in importance. Class society will pale into insignificance beside *an individualized society of employees*. Both the typical characteristics as well as the dangers of such a society are now becoming increasingly clear. In contrast to class society, which is defined essentially in terms of tradition and culture, a society of employees must be defined in terms of labour law and by means of socio-political categories. The result is a peculiar stage of transition, in which persisting or intensifying inequalities coincide with elements of a no longer traditional, individualized post-class society (which bears no resemblance to Marx's vision of a classless society). This transitional society is distinguished by a variety of typical structures and changes.

First, processes of individualization deprive class distinctions of their social identity. Social groups lose their distinctive traits, both in terms of their self-understanding and in relation to other groups. They also lose their independent identities and the chance to become a formative political force. As a result of this development, the idea of social mobility (in the sense of individual movement between actual status classes), which until very late in the twentieth century constituted a social and political theme of considerable importance for social identity formation, pales into insignificance.

Second, inequalities by no means disappear. They merely become redefined in terms of an *individualization of social risks*. The result is that social problems are increasingly perceived in terms of psychological dispositions: as personal inadequacies, guilt feelings, anxieties, conflicts, and neuroses. There emerges, paradoxically, a new immediacy of individual and society, a direct relation between crisis and sickness. Social crises appear as individual crises, which are no longer (or only very indirectly) perceived in terms of their rootedness in the social realm. This is one of the explanations for the current revival of interest in psychology. Individual achievement orientation similarly gains in importance. It can now be predicted that the full range of problems associated with the achievement society and its tendency toward (pseudo-)legitimations of social inequalities will emerge in the future.

Third, in attempting to cope with social problems, people are forced into political and social alliances. These, however, need no longer follow a single pattern, such as the class model. The isolation of privatized lives, shielded against all other privatized lives, can be shattered by social and political events and developments of the most heterogeneous kind. Accordingly, temporary coalitions between different groups and different camps are formed and dissolved, depending on the particular issue at stake and on the particular situation. In this way, risks and risk conflicts, as far as they are personally experienced, are becoming an important issue as well. It is possible cheerfully to embrace seemingly contradictory causes, for example, to join forces with local residents in protests against noise pollution by air traffic, to belong to the metalworkers' union, and yet—in the face of impending economic crisis—to vote conservative. Such coalitions represent pragmatic alliances in the individual struggle for existence and occur on the various battlefields of society. A peculiar multiplication of areas of conflict can be observed. The individualized society prepares the ground for new and multifaceted conflicts, ideologies and alliances, which go beyond the scope of all hitherto existing schematizations. These alliances are generally focused on single issues, are by no means heterogeneous and are oriented toward specific situations and personalities. The resulting so-called structure is susceptible to the latest social fashions (in issues and conflicts) which, pushed by the mass media, rule the public consciousness just as the spring, autumn and winter fashion shows do.

Fourth, permanent conflicts tend to arise along the lines of ascribed characteristics, which now as much as ever are undeniably connected with discrimination. Race, skin colour, gender, ethnicity, age, homosexuality, physical disability—these are the major ascribed characteristics. Under the conditions of advanced individualization, such quasi-natural social inequalities lead to the development of quite specific organizing effects. These attempt to gain political muscle by focusing upon the inescapability and permanence of such inequalities as well as upon their incompatibility with the achievement principle, their tangibility, and the fact that—as a result of their direct visibility—they make possible independent social and individual processes of identification. At the same time, individual fate is increasingly determined in a new way by economic trends and by historical necessity, as it were,—for example, by economic crisis or boom, restricted admission to universities and to the professions, the size of age cohorts and so on.

Will it be possible to choose as a point of departure the claims and the promises of the process of individualization now under way together with its impulse toward social emancipation, thereby in a new way—beyond status and class—uniting individuals and groups as self-conscious subjects of their own personal social and political affairs? Or will the last bastions of social and political action be swept away as a result of that very process? Would the individualized society then not fall, torn apart by conflicts and displaying symptoms of sickness, into the kind of political apathy that precludes virtually nothing, not even new and insidious forms of a modernized barbarism?

NOTE

1. Under conditions of growing poverty and unemployment, 'individualization' means that poverty and unemployment less and less affect one group for a long period of time, but are distributed across society at particular phases of people's lives. To put this somewhat schematically, the conflicts involved in social inequality appear as conflicts between parts of a single life history. People's lives become more varied and discontinuous—which also implies that a growing section of the population is at least temporarily exposed to poverty and unemployment. Cf. U. Beck, *Risikogesellschaft.* Frankfurt/M. Suhrkamp 1986, pp. 143–51; Leisering and Zwick, 'Heterogenisierung der Armut?', *Zeitschrift für Sozialreform*, 1990, 11/12, pp. 715–45; P. A. Berger, *Individualisierung, Statusunsicherheit and Erfahrungsvielfalt.* Opladen: Westdeutscher Verlag 1996.

10 Multiculturalism and Gendered Citizenship

Seyla Benhabib

For as long as human societies and cultures have interacted and compared themselves with another, the status of women and children and the rituals of sex, marriage, and death have occupied a special place in intercultural understandings. Plato's discussion of the status of women and children in *The Republic* is one such memorable episode, situated at the very beginnings of the Western philosophical tradition. Socrates in bk. 5 of *The Republic*, exercising his characteristically cagey shyness, introduces the idea that the guardian classes will have their wives and children in common and will be asked to mate according to principles of eugenic selection (Plato 1968: 138). Aware of how deeply he was affronting prevailing views of the Greek household—the *oikos*—among his fellow citizens through his proposals, Socrates, in order to compensate for the loss of special feelings of attachment and loyalty between parents and their offspring that his proposals would generate, then avails himself of the myth that the earth is the mother of all.

Returning to this episode, Aristotle in his *Politics* voiced some of the common sentiments of Athenian citizens with respect to Plato's and Socrates' radical social experimentation. Aristotle objected that Plato had a faulty idea of the kind of unity appropriate to each sphere of human life. Plato, in Aristotle's view, tried to create a family-like unity in the *polis*, while dissolving familial unity for the sake of the impersonal solidarity of those 'born from the earth' at the end of a specific mating cycle (Aristotle 1941: 1261a, 10–25). For Aristotle, the fact that the Greeks did not treat their citizen-wives as slaves but distinguished carefully between their status and that of female slaves and concubines, who were usually non-Greek and non-Athenian, was a *point d'honneur*. The limited freedom of the Athenian citizen wife is for Aristotle clearly superior to the condition of female slavery he assumes to be prevalent among the Persians.

This philosophical exchange between Socrates, Plato, and Aristotle is one of the earliest instances of complex multicultural dialogue concerning the status of women and children. Not only such intercultural comparisons but also the 'traffic in women'—or the exchange of women through barter and marriage, war and conquest among the males of the human species—have been firm features of most known human societies everywhere. It should thus come as no surprise that the status of the private sphere,[1] broadly conceived to include women and children and the regulation of sex, birth, and death, leads to some of the most bitter and deeply divisive cultural struggles in our own days as well. When distinct cultural groups interact, the rifts of intercultural difference are most deeply felt along the boundaries demarcating the public from the private sphere.

In his comprehensive treatment of the puzzles of multicultural coexistence, Bhikhu Parekh lists twelve practices that most frequently lead to clashes of intercultural evaluation: female circumcision; polygamy; Muslim and Jewish methods of animal slaughter; arranged marriages; marriages within prohibited degrees of relationships; scarring children's cheeks or other parts of the body; Muslim withdrawal of girls from coeducational practices such as sports and swimming lessons; Muslim insistence that girls wear the *hijab*, or headscarf; Sikh insistence on wearing or taking off the traditional turbans; Gypsy and Amish refusal to send their children to public schools either altogether or after a certain age; Hindu requests to be allowed to cremate their deceased; the subordinate status of women and all that entails (2000: 264–65). Of the twelve practices listed by Parekh, seven concern the status of women in distinct cultural communities; two bear on dress codes pertaining to both sexes (the wearing of the turban and the *hijab*); two are about the lines separating private from public jurisdictional authority in the education of children; and one each concerns dietary codes and funeral rites. How can we account for the preponderance of cultural practices concerning the status of women, girls, marriage, and sexuality that lead to intercultural conflict?

The sphere of sexual and reproductive lives is a central focus of most human cultures (Okin 1999: 12–13). The regulation of these functions forms the dividing line between nature and culture: all animal species need to mate and reproduce in order to survive, but the regulation of mating, sexuality, and reproduction in accordance with 'kinship patterns' is, as Claude Lévi-Strauss argued in *The Elementary Structures of Kinship* (1969), the line that separates *fusis* from *nomos*. Nature does not dictate who should mate with whom; but all known human societies regulate mating for reproductive or nonreproductive purposes and create a symbolic universe of significations in accordance with which kinship patterns are formed and sexual taboos established. Women and their bodies are the symbolic-cultural site upon which human societies inscript their moral order. In virtue of their capacity for sexual reproduction, women mediate between nature and culture, between the animal species to which we all belong and the symbolic order that makes us into cultural beings.

Since Simone de Beauvoir's *Second Sex* (1949), feminist theory has dissected why this function of women as mediators between nature and culture also makes them the object of longing and fear, desire and flight.[2] The passages in and out of human life are usually marked by the presence of the female: always and inevitably in the case of birth; usually, but not necessarily, in the case of death, since male magicians, priests, and shamans can also play a significant role in the death ceremony. The female of the species, who presides over these functions, controls moments of the greatest vulnerability in human life: when we enter life we are helpless as infants, and when we leave it we are all equally helpless in the face of death. Such vulnerability generates emotions of intense ambivalence toward females, who are seen to be gatekeepers of these human passages. Ontogenetically—that is, in the life of the human individual—the private sphere is encountered the earliest, and thus leaves the deepest marks of ambivalence upon the psyche. Because processes in this sphere mark the human psyche during its earliest, formative stages, they also cut closest to core identity issues. Intercultural conflicts, which challenge the symbolic order of these spheres because they delve into the earliest and deepest recesses of the psyche, are likely to generate the most intense emotional response. Thus the loss of one's culture, cultural uprooting, and the mixture of cultures are often presented in sexualized terms: one's culture has been 'raped,' say primordialists, by the new and foreign customs and habits imposed upon it; cultural intermixture is very often described as mongrelization, or *mestizaje*. The use of these metaphors is not accidental: fundamentalist movements know very well the deep recesses of psychic vulnerability they tap when doing so (Kakar 1990).

These interconnections between psychic identity, the practices of the private sphere, and cultural difference assume a new configuration in modern liberal democracies. These societies demarcate the private from the public along the following lines: the political sphere, together with the economy and certain domains of civil society, is considered 'public' in multiple senses: accessible to all; shared by all; and in the interests of all. The household is considered private, in the sense that it strictly regulates access through kinship and marriage, and does not concern itself with the interest of all. In liberal societies, institutional patterns of regulating the private and the public spheres are undergirded by other assumptions as well. Liberalism is based on the conviction that privacy extends to those most deeply held beliefs pertaining to religion, culture, aesthetics, and lifestyle.

Liberalism not only respects 'the privacy' of the familial-domestic sphere; it also requires that the state not regulate matters of religious, cultural, and aesthetic belief. As Thomas Hobbes put it succintly many centuries ago, 'the liberty of the subjects is the silence of the laws' ([1651] 1996). Of course, matters are never that simple, and the line between the public and the private is always contested. From the standpoint of the liberal state, the family is a public institution in which practices governing marriage and divorce are defined and regulated by political as well as legal norms. The state confers fiscal and economic status upon the family in that it defines the tax status of those who are considered family members; in not recognizing same-sex unions as marriages, the state also upholds a specific conception of the family. Viewed as an institution within the modem state, then, the family has nothing 'private' about it. Likewise, the lines separating religion from the state, aesthetics from politics, are always hotly contested.

In this chapter I focus on a highly publicized multicultural dispute in the course of which traditional distinctions between the public and the private were contested and resignified. I then revisit the debate in feminist theory initiated by Susan Moller Okin's provocative question, 'Is multiculturalism bad for women?' (1999). I argue that this manner of posing the question has led to an unnecessary impasse and polarization, because both opponents and proponents of multiculturalism, despite disclaimers to the contrary, continue to defend a faulty understanding of cultures as unified, holistic, and self-consistent wholes. Therefore cultural processes of resignification and reinterpretation, which women in minority ethnic communities engaged in, are ignored. A deliberative democratic multicultural politics does not confine women and children to their communities of origin against their will, but encourages them to develop their autonomous agency vis-à-vis their ascribed identities.

[Elsewhere[3]] I elucidate several political and philosophical approaches toward multiculturalist dilemmas, all of which are attentive to the potential conflict between claims to cultural difference and universalist human-rights norms. I develop the philosophical argument supporting deliberative democracy in this context.

[. . .]

Multiculturalism, Laicité, and the Scarf Affair in France

Consider now what has been referred to as *l'affaire foulard*—the scarf affair—in France. Whereas in the cases of 'cultural defense' and Shah Bano, we have encountered the liberal-democratic state and its institutions reinscribing women's identities within their natal communities of faith and culture, in the foulard affair we encounter public officials and institutions that supposedly champion women's emancipation from these communities by suppressing the practice of veiling. The state here acts as the champion of women's emancipation from their communities of birth. Yet, as we shall see, some women resisted the state not to affirm their religious and sexual subordination as much as to assert a quasi-personal identity independent of the dominant French culture.

The practice of veiling among Muslim women is a complex institution that exhibits great variety across many Muslim countries. The terms *chador, hijab, niqab,* and *foulard* refer to distinct items of clothing worn by women from different Muslim communities: for example, the chador is essentially Iranian and refers to the long black robe and head scarf worn in a rectangular manner around the face; the niqab is a veil that covers the eyes and the mouth and leaves only the nose exposed; it may or may not be worn in conjunction with the chador. Most Muslim women from Turkey are likely to wear either long overcoats and a foulard (a head scarf) or a *carsaf* (a black garment that most resembles the chador). These items of clothing have a symbolic function within the Muslim community itself: women from different countries signal to one another their ethnic and national origins through their clothing, as well as their distance or proximity to tradition. The brighter the colors of their overcoats and scarves—bright blue, green, beige, lilac, as opposed to brown, gray, navy, and, of course, black—and the more fashionable their cuts and material by Western standards, the more we can assume the distance from Islamic orthodoxy of the women who wear them. Seen from the outside, however, this complex semiotic of dress codes is reduced to one or two items of clothing that then assume the function of crucial symbols of complex negotiations between Muslim religious and cultural identities and Western cultures.

L'affaire foulard refers to a long and drawn-out set of public confrontations that began in France in 1989 with the explusions from their school in Creil (Oise) of three scarf-wearing Muslim girls and continued to the mass exclusion of twenty-three Muslim girls from their schools in November 1996 upon the decision of the Conseil d'Etat.[4] The affair, referred to as a 'national drama' (Gaspard and Khosrokhavar 1995: 11) or even a 'national trauma' (Brun-Rovet 2000, 2), occurred in the wake of France's celebration of the second centennial of the French Revolution and seemed to question the foundations of the French educational system and its philosophical principle, *laicité*. This concept is difficult to translate in terms like the 'separation of Church and State' or even secularization: at its best, it can be understood as the public and manifest neutrality of the state toward all kinds of religious practices, institutionalized through a vigilant removal of sectarian religious symbols, signs, icons, and items of clothing from official public spheres. Yet within the French Republic the balance between respecting the individual's right to freedom of conscience and religion, on the one hand, and maintaining a public sphere devoid of all religious symbolisms, on the other, was so fragile that it took only the actions of a handful of teenagers to expose this fragility. The ensuing debate went far beyond the original dispute and touched upon the self-understanding of French republicanism for the left as well as the right, on the meaning of social and sexual equality, and liberalism versus republicanism versus multiculturalism in French life.

The affair began when on October 19, 1989, Ernest Chenière; headmaster of the college Gabriel-Havez of Creil, forbade three girls—Fatima, Leila, and Samira—to attend classes with their heads covered. Each had appeared in class that morning wearing her scarf, despite a compromise reached between their headmaster and their parents encouraging them to go unscarfed. The three girls had apparently decided to wear the scarf once more upon the advice of Daniel Youssouf Leclerq, the head of an organization called Integrité; and the former president of the National Federation of Muslims in France (FNMF). Although hardly noted in the press, the fact that the girls had been in touch with Leclerq indicates that wearing the scarf was a conscious political gesture on their part, a complex act of identification and defiance. In doing so, Fatima, Leila, and Samira on the one hand claimed to exercise their freedom of religion as French citizens; on the other hand they exhibited their Muslim and North African origins in a context that sought to envelop them, as students of the nation, within an egalitarian, secularist ideal of republican citizenship. In the years to come, their followers and supporters forced what the French state wanted to view as a private symbol—an individual item of clothing—into the shared public sphere, thus challenging the boundaries between the public and the private. Ironically, they used the freedom given to them by French society and French political traditions, not the least of which is the availability of free and compulsory public education for all children on French soil, to juxtapose an aspect of their private identity onto the public sphere. In doing so, they problematized the school as well as the home: they no longer treated the school as a neutral space of French acculturation, but openly manifested their cultural and religious differences. They used the symbol of the home in the public sphere, retaining the modesty required of them by Islam in covering their heads; yet at the same time, they left the home to become public actors in a civil public space, in which they defied the state. Those who saw in the girls' actions simply an indication of their oppression were just as blind to the symbolic meaning of their deeds as were those who defended their rights simply on the basis of freedom of religion. Like Antigone in Sophocles' tragedy, who uses obligations to her home and religion to bury and thereby honor her brother Polyneices, who had defied the polls, these young girls used the symbols of the private realm to challenge the ordinances of the public sphere.

The French sociologists Gaspard and Khosrokhavar capture these complex symbolic negotiations as follows:

> [The veil] mirrors in the eyes of the parents and the grandparents the illusions of continuity whereas it is a factor of discontinuity; it makes possible the transition to otherness (modernity), under the pretext of identity (tradition); it creates the sentiment of identity with the society of origin whereas its meaning is inscribed within the dynamic of relations with the receiving society. . . . it is the vehicle of the passage to modernity within a promiscuity which confounds traditional distinctions, of an access to the public sphere which was forbidden to traditional women as a space of action and the constitution of individual autonomy. (1995: 44–45, my translation)

The complexity of the social and cultural negotiations hidden behind the simple act of veiling elicited an equally ambigious and complex decision by the French Conseil d'Etat. On November 4, 1989, the French minister of education, Lionel Jospin, took the matter to the Conseil d'Etat (the French Supreme Court). The Conseil rendered a notoriously ambiguous decision. The minister of education asked three questions, two of which were related to the administrative handling of the answer, which would result from an answer to the first question: 'If, in view of the principles of the Constitution and the laws of the Republic and with respect to the totality of rules pertaining to the organization and functioning of the public school, the wearing of signs of belonging to a religious community is or is not compatible with the principle of laicité' (cited in Brun-Rovet 2000: 28). The court responded by citing France's adherence to constitutional and legislative texts and to international conventions, and invoked from the outset the necessity of doing justice to two principles: that the laicité and neutrality of the state be retained in the rendering of public services and that the liberty of conscience of the students be respected. All discrimination based upon the religious convictions or beliefs of the students would be inadmissable. The court then concluded that

> the wearing by students, in the schools, of signs whereby they believe to be manifesting their adherence to one religion is itself not incompatible with the principle of laicité, since it constitutes the exercise of their liberty of expression and manifestation of their religious beliefs; but this liberty does not permit students to exhibit [d'arborer] signs of religious belonging which, by their nature, by the conditions under which they are worn individually or collectively, or by their ostentatious or combative [*revendicatif*] character, would constitute an act of pressure, provocation, proselytizing or propaganda, threatening to the dignity or liberty of the student or to the other members of the educational community, compromising their health or their security, disturbing the continuation of instructional activities or the educational role of the instructors, in short, [that] would disturb proper order in the establishment or the normal functioning of public service.[5]

This Solomonic judgment attempted to balance the principles of laicité and freedom of religion and conscience. Yet instead of articulating some clear guidelines, the court left the proper interpretation of the meaning of these signs to the judgment of the school authorities. The decisive factors in curtailing the students' freedom of religion was not the individual students' beliefs about what a religious scarf (or for that matter yarmulke) meant to them, but how the school authorities interpreted the scarf's meaning, and whether or not it could be seen as a means of provocation, confrontation, or remonstration. It is not difficult to see why this judgment encouraged both sides to the conflict to pursue their goals further and led to additional repression through the promulgation on September 10, 1994, of the Bayrou Guidelines, issued by Minister of Education François Bayrou. Lamenting the ambiguities of the judgment of the court for conveying an impression of 'weaknesses' vis-à-vis Islamicist movements, the minister declared that students had the right to wear discrete religious symbols, but that the veil was not among them (*Le Monde*, September 12, 1994: 10).

The Bayrou declaration further hardened the fronts of various political actors: intellectuals, teachers' unions, various Islamic organizations, anti-immigrant groups, and the like. The French population was already highly polarized on the issues of Islam, immigration, and national security. In the summer of 1994, a bomb planted by Muslim fundamentalist groups exploded in the metro in Paris; thus it seemed that France, despite herself, was sucked into the vortex of violence coming from fundamentalist Islamic groups, and that its traditions of tolerance and pluralism were misused by these groups to further their own sectarian political goals.

The evolution of SOS-Racisme's attitudes in view of these developments is quite telling. During the Creil episode in 1989, SOS-Racisme—one of the most militant antiracist groups, drawing its membership particularly from among the young—led large sections of the French left into defending laicité and protesting the exclusion of the Muslim girls. But by 1994, the new president of the association called for a ban on all religious symbols; many had now come to see the recurrence of the wearing of the scarves not as isolated incidents, but as a provocation on the part of an organized Islam that had to be confronted clearly and unequivocally (Brun-Rovet 2000). L'affair foulard eventually came to stand for all dilemmas of French national identity in the age of globalization and multiculturalism: how to retain French traditions of laicité, republican equality, and democratic citizenship in view of France's integration into the European Union, on the one hand (see chap. 5 [of *The Claims of Culture*]), and the pressures of multiculturalism generated through the presence of second-and third-generation immigrants from Muslim countries on French soil, on the other hand. Would the practices and institutions of French citizenship be flexible and generous enough to encompass multicultural differences within an ideal of republican equality? Clearly, this affair is by no means over. As European integration and multiculturalist pressures continue, France, just like India and the United States, will have to discover new models of legal, pedagogical, social, and cultural institutions to deal with the dual imperatives of liberal democracies to preserve freedom of religious expression and the principles of secularism.[6]

Is Multiculturalism Bad for Women?

This case suggests that multicultural institutional arrangements and legal compromises very often work to the detriment of women. [. . .] They make women and girls objects of state regulation and punishment in order to teach the nation a lesson, as in the case of the scarf affair in France. It should thus come as no surprise that Susan Okin has raised the battle cry that 'most cultures are patriarchal, then, and many (though not all) of the cultural minorities that claim group rights are more patriarchal than their surrounding cultures' (1999: 17). When such groups demand special rights, it is to be expected that these rights would function to the detriment of women and imprison them in oppressive and inegalitarian gender structures. Certainly Okin was right in raising these issues, but the tenor with which she criticized cultures for being more or less all patriarchal and, above all, the militant insensitivity she showed in her depiction of many religious practices among Orthodox Jewish and Muslim groups, raised hackles.

Responding to Okin's opening salvo in this debate, Azizah Y. Al-Hibri coined the phrase 'Western patriarchal feminism.' Al-Hibri argued that while the questions raised by Okin were significant, her discourse reflected 'the perspective of the dominant cultural "I", a Western point of view burdened with immigrant problems and the human rights conflicts which they engender' (1999: 41).

Indeed, contemporary feminist discourse on these issues is strongly polarized: theorists like Okin and Martha Nussbaum who raise liberal concerns about women's equality and rights in multicultural contexts are accused of Eurocentrism, imperialism, patriarchal feminism, or simply arrogance, ignorance, and insensitivity vis-à-vis other cultures (see Okin 1999). Multicultural theorists of both genders are in turn charged with cultural relativism, moral callousness, the defense of patriarchy, and compromising women's rights in order to preserve the plurality of traditions (Wolfe 2001). The claims of moral and political autonomy contradict the pluralist preservation of multicultural traditions that seem to make no room for such autonomy. As was suggested in my considerations of Taylor and Kymlicka [*The Claims of Culture*, chap. 3] autonomy and cultural pluralism appear irreconcilable. But must this indeed be so? There is little doubt that women's concerns and the status of the private sphere expose the vulnerability of multicultural arrangements and reveal the unjust moral and political compromises, achieved at the expense of women and children, upon which they often rest. But what if both positions rest upon mistaken epistemological assumptions concerning cultures, which I have criticized throughout this book? If we were to adopt the perspective of complex multicultural dialogue I am advocating, might we be able to do justice both to women's aspirations for freedom and equality and to the legitimate plurality of human cultures?

On the basis of the epistemological model of culture developed in the previous chapters, I will defend the creation and expansion of deliberative discursive multicultural spaces in liberal democracies. I will contrast this approach with a defensive liberalism that wants to uphold the private/public distinction by placing multicultural issues on the privacy side of this divide. I will also consider proposals for legal pluralism or 'interlocking jurisdictional hierarchies,' which have been put forth to weaken the impact of permitting cultural groups alone to define privacy and family law (Shachar 2000: 387–426). I will argue that a legal pluralist model—consistent with the following principles, already outlined in the introduction: egalitarian reciprocity, voluntary self-ascription, and freedom of exit and association—can be a good complement to deliberative and discursive democratic multiculturalism.

Democratic Practices and Multicultural Spaces

Narrativity and narrative disagreement, I have argued, are rooted in the structure of human actions, which are made of deeds and words. Humans identify what they do in that they tell a story, give an account of *what* they do; furthermore, all cultures attribute evaluations to the world around us through a series of contrasts like good and bad, just and unjust, holy and profane. Not only are actions constituted narratively, but we also possess second-order narratives that lead us to qualify and classify what we do in the light of these cultural evaluations.

The view that cultures are unified, harmonious, seamless wholes that speak with one narrative voice is, I have argued, the view of cultures from the outside. By the locution 'the outside,' I do not mean the standpoint of the stranger and the nonmember. The outsider is the observer, as distinguished from the actor. The outsider who is a 'stranger' in the eyes of the group can also be very much an insider, in that he or she may have a full understanding of the complexities and perplexities of the culture to which he or she is denied admittance. The observer is the one who seeks to comprehend and to control, to classify and to represent the culture to the other(s). It is the epistemic interest in power, I want to suggest, that leads to the silencing of dissenting opinions and contradictory perspectives, and yields dominant master narratives of what the cultural tradition is, who is in, and who is out. This epistemic power interest can be exercised by the tribal chief as well as the enemy general, by the anthropologist in search of the truth as well as by the development worker in search of social control.

To the participants and actors, their culture presents itself as a set of competing as well as cohering accounts. In fact, when the accounts of traditions are not contested, it is because they are ossified and have already become meaningless even when they are adhered to. Cultural evaluations can be transmitted across generations only by creative and lively engagement and resignification. A story that is not well told will not be remembered.

Debates around feminism and multiculturalism get quickly polarized, because so little attention is paid to this aspect of cultures as riven by internal contestation. Although she recognizes gender as a cleavage, Okin writes as if cultures are unified structures of meaning in other respects. 'Many of the world's traditions and cultures, including those practiced within formerly conquered or colonized nation-states—which certainly encompass most of the peoples of Africa, the Middle East, Latin America, and Asia—are quite distinctively patriarchal' (2000: 14). Okin maps cultures onto nation-states and onto continents. No differentiations are made between cultural traditions, peoples, territories, and political structures. The absurdity of referring to one Middle Eastern or Latin American culture, except as a caricature or simplification, does not figure in this analysis. Whose culture? Which culture? When? Where? And as practiced by whom?

Yet the standpoint of the feminist critic, in this respect, is not all that different from the standpoint of the legislator. The U.S. courts reinscribe women and children in their communities of origin by upholding, against their rights of equal protection, the rights of the defendants to their own culture. The Indian courts are obliged to accept the jurisdictional division of labor between a unified criminal code and separate private and family law for India's Muslim and Hindu communities. The French Conseil d'Etat tries to do justice to the principles of laicité as well as the freedom of conscience and religion, but delivers the girls with the head scarves to the intensified scrutiny and authority of their school supervisors and disregards the students' own understanding of their actions. These cases suggest that, in considering the practices of minority cultural communities and the rights of their women and children, we get stuck between the Scylla of criminalizing and policing these communities and the Charybdis of multiculturalist tolerance, and often end up indifferent to their plight. Throughout this discussion, I have been suggesting that these alternatives can be avoided, in theory as well as in practice, by modifying our understandings of culture; rejecting cultural holism, and by having more faith in the capacity of ordinary political actors to renegotiate their own narratives of identity and difference through multicultural encounters in a democratic civil society.[. . .]

The cases discussed in this chapter illustrate what Ayelet Shachar has named 'the paradox of multicultural vulnerability' (2000: 386). 'Well-meaning accommodation policies by the state, aimed at leveling the playing field between minority communities and the wider society,' argues Shachar, 'may unwittingly allow systematic maltreatment of individuals within the accommodated minority group—an impact, in certain cases, so severe that it nullifies these individuals' rights as citizens' (386). The tension and, in many cases, the moral dilemma between accommodating difference and doing justice to all members of a minority group propels contemporary discussions of multiculturalism into a new phase. Having recognized how inevitably conflictual demands for multicultural accommodation may be within the liberal-democratic state, democratic and multicultural theorists must then address the question of *differentiated citizenship claims* in liberal-democratic societies. I want to distinguish between several normative models that have wrestled with these questions: liberal overlapping consensus; liberal egalitarianism; pluralist interlocking power hierarchies, and the deliberative democracy approach.[. . .]

NOTES

1. I distinguish three principal meanings of the *private sphere*. First and foremost, in liberal state privacy refers to the individual's right to determine and choose the dictates of his or her moral and religious conscience. A second set of privacy rights pertains to economic liberties, such as the freedoms of contract, commodity exchange, and wage labor. Third, privacy refers to the 'intimate sphere,' that is, the domain of the household, of meeting the daily needs of life, of sexuality and reproducation, of care for the young, the sick and the elderly. See Benhabib (1992: 107–9). There three meanings are not only frequently conflated; more significantly, legislators as well as individual citizens in the liberal state use one set of privacy rights to legitimize practices in other domains. In the multicultural conflicts considered in this chapter, privacy rights in the first sense (that is, the liberties of religion and conscience), have been used to protect and legitimize practices in the third sphere (that is, the domain of the household). When this occurs, the clash of rights and claims implicit between the liberty of conscience of the male subjects on the one hand and the equal treatment of their woman and children on the other more often than not gets obcured.

2. de Beauvoir (1949, 306 ff.); and Ortner, 'Is Male to Female as Nature Is to Culture?' (1974).

[3. In ch. 5 of *The Claims of Culture*.]

4. My discussion of these incidents relies primarily upon two sources: *Le Foulard et al République*, by Françoise Gaspard and Farhad Khosrokhavar (1995), and an excellent

seminar paper by Marianne Brun-Rovet, 'A Perspective on the Multiculturalism Dabate: "L'affaire foulard" and Laicité in France, 1989–1999' (2000).

5. The original decision is from the *Avis du Conseil d'État du 27 November 1989*. Excerpts from the decision can be found at <*http://www.unc.edu/depts/Europe/conferences/Veil2000/Annexes.pdf*>. More information on l'affaire foulard can be found at <*http://www.conseil-etat.fr/cedata/juris/jurisprudence/92/ensei92.htm*>.

6. The French scarf affair is being followed very closely in Turkey, a secular, multiparty democracy, the majority of whose population is Muslim. Throughout the 1980s Turkey confronted its own version of l' affaire foulard. As the Islamist parties, and in particular the Welfare Party, increased their power in parliament and in society at large, unprecedented numbers of Turkish Islamist woman began attending institutions higher learning, and they insisted on wearing the scarf to cover their heads. Their argument was the Islamic law forbade them to show their uncovered hair to men unrelated to them and in public. The scarf was seen as a symbol of female modesty and purity. From the standpoint of the Turkish state authorities, however, the scarf was seen as a challenge to the secularist and 'laic' principles, which Mustafa Kemkal Ataturk, the founder of the modern replublic of Turkey in 1923, had adopted, following, French republican principles. The wearing of the scarf by large numbers of young women was perceived as a direct threat to the separation of state and religion, and to the state guidance of the Muslim religion, practiced carefully by institutions like the Directorate General of Religious Affairs.

   As Yesim Arat presents it, 'In 1981, the Council of Ministers approved a statute, which required female employees in public institutions and students in schools tied to the Ministry of National Education to dress without headscarves. Following this decision, in 1982, the Council of Higher Education banned the use of headscarves in the universities. Islamist groups and woman with headscaves protested the decision. Under increasing pressure from the Islamists, in 1984, the Council of Higher Education allowed woman to cover their hair with a turban, a scarf tied at the back and covering only the hair' (2002: 8). After a series of interventions, including from the president of the Republic, who banned the turban in 1987, the Turkish Constitutional Court decided in 1989 that the use of the turban in the universities was unconstitutional and banned it. As in the French case, the students and Islamist organization representing them appealed. Article 24 of the 1982 Turkish Constitution guarantees freedom of religious expression, and Article 10 prohibits discrimination due to religious belief and differences in language, ethnicity, and gender; the Council to State and the Constitutional Court both claimed that 'rather than an innocent custom, it (the headscarf) has become a symbol of a world view opposed to the foundamental principles of the Republic' (cited in Arat 2002: 11; based on a circular distributed within the universities in 1998 and called 'Statutes and Legal Judgments Concerning Dress Codes in Institutions of Higher Education').

Feminist Politics and Democratic Values in Education

Madeleine Arnot and Jo-Anne Dillabough

In our period, the contemporary women's movement has forged a particularly powerful connection and, with its determined critique of hierarchy and sustained anti-authoritarianism, turned itself into a virtual testing ground for democracies most radical ideals.

(Phillips 1992: 2)

Introduction

Feminism and democracy, although apparently having a good deal in common, did not develop in tandem. In fact, it was only by the nineteenth century that the normative ideals of 'equality' united feminist and democratic movements in Western Europe and North America. One should not assume therefore that concerns about 'gender equality' are synonymous with the concept of democracy. Nor can it be legitimately argued that every and any form of democratic education would fulfil feminist educational ideals. Clearly, much depends upon how democratic education and questions of equality are defined, conceptualized and expressed in relation to gender politics and the authentic concerns of feminists. More significantly, some feminist theorising suggests that *gender equality*, as a goal, serves to obscure more complex explanations about the relationship of women to consideration of how, theoretically, we might unravel the contradictions which currently manifest the relationship between gender, education and democracy.

The tensions between democracy and feminism are no more clearly expressed than in feminist critiques of liberal democratic theories, structures and processes. One can identify important differences, for example, between feminist theories and the empirical tasks they have set for themselves; that is, critical distinctions which might explain the complexity of the relationship of women to liberal democratic politics, and the ways in which women's connection to the economy and family is circumscribed. Feminist political theorists have thus been inclined to examine the sources of, and complexity surrounding, female oppression and its manifestation in the language and practices of political liberalism. They have also exposed the illusions of 'political neutrality' which are central to many of the male-centred versions of traditional liberal democratic thought. These claims, along with related critical efforts, have led to the feminist position that a major

Madeleine Arnot and Jo-Anne Dillabough, 'Feminist Politics and Democratic Values in Education', *Curriculum Inquiry*, Blackwell Publishing.

transformation of the concept of democracy, as we understand it, is required before women can achieve full status as citizens, on par with that of men.

This kind of theoretical agenda offers us the possibility of re-assessing the contribution of *feminist educational thought* to our understanding of the political role of education in democratic societies. In this exploratory [chapter], we draw upon the insights of feminist political theorists to evaluate the ways in which feminist educational theorising in the last two decades has tackled the problem of a 'gendered' democracy. What contributions have been made to, and what theoretical insights are proffered on, the relationship between democracy and the gendering of values in schooling? Is there a need, for example, for a more systematic and structured approach to the study of democratic educational values through feminist theory? If so, what analytic framework and conceptual tools are required?

We begin by describing the key feminist debates which address the gendering of liberal democracy. In the first section, feminist critiques of liberal democracy, the gendered construction of the *nation* and *nationality*, and the notion of 'woman' as a political category are discussed. What is interesting about these debates is precisely what they expose about the complex nature of gender politics within and across the abstract terrain now identified as the 'democratic state'. They also provide novel insight into the ways in which feminist educational theorists might reconsider the links between gender and democracy.

In the second section, we revisit major but contrasting traditions of thought—that of liberal feminism, maternal feminism and socialist feminist educational theorising—to illustrate shifts in thinking about democracy and democratic education. We then go on to discuss the rise of new feminisms, in particular, examples of post-structuralist research, and their contribution to our understanding of democratic relations in education. In the final section [. . .] we describe the key levels of political analyses which have been drawn upon by feminists to examine the 'gendered' foundations of democratic education. In so doing, we suggest that feminists who are concerned with questions of democracy reconsider the value of theorizing *in novel ways* about women's agency and practices of resistance to new forms of gendered oppression in the state, of which education is a part. Such an approach may allow for a greater understanding of the contemporary terms upon which gender is constructed. However, in so doing, it must also ameliorate a condition of feminist theorizing that re-invigorates a structural and social analysis of gender politics which takes, as central, the particularity and heterogeneity of gendered experiences.

Feminist Political Theory

Feminist educational thought and its relevance to questions of democracy are more effectively scrutinised when considered against the work of feminist political and social theorists. Three themes emerge from a survey of recent writing in the latter tradition which provide some understanding of the relationship between gender and democracy.

Order and Disorder: The Basis of a Fraternal Pact

The work of Carol Pateman, a feminist political theorist, signals for many a new theoretical agenda. Her influential set of texts, such as *The Sexual Contract* (1988) and *The Disorder of Women* (1989), indicates the ways in which social concepts of order, disorder, civic society and the citizen have been constructed historically as gender dualisms—that is, the binary male and female divide—and an understanding of male power over women. She argues that the concept of liberal democratic citizenship developed by English philosophers was what Marx called a 'political lion's skin' worn only occasionally and somewhat reluctantly by women.

Pateman's central concern lies with the legitimacy of liberal theory, particularly since all concepts derived from the liberal tradition privilege the ontology of maleness and the 'epistemic' dominance of masculinity in liberal political thought. She argues that concepts like the 'political [or social] order' are, by definition, gendered. For example, mainstream political philosophy has equated the concept of *social order* with a rational, autonomous selfhood where individuals act according to universal and objective moral principles, thus transcending private interests. Yet at the source of such notions of the individual, Pateman (1989, 1992) argues, is a

Western European version of *masculinity*. Men, for the predominantly male European political philosophers, exemplified the potential of humans to create a social order which is based upon 'rationality' and 'truth'. 'Rational' thought and male versions of political autonomy are thus seen as central to the functioning of a pure democracy.

On the other side of the equation, that of *disorder*, we find women portrayed as psychologically unbalanced and therefore unable to articulate a political consciousness (Lloyd, 1986). Patemen (1992: 19) states, 'women, our bodies and distinctive capacities, represented all that citizenship was not. "Citizenship" has gained its meaning through the exclusion of women, that is to say (sexual) difference.' Thus, the 'lethal' combination of women's psychological 'disabilities' and sexual characteristics implied that they be excluded from the original social contract or, in effect, *the fraternal pact* (cf. Pateman, 1989). However, in constructing this civic brotherhood, men have legitimated their autonomic right to that power in public life, and at the same time, their sexual rights over women: 'The brothers make a sexual contract. They establish a law which confirms masculine sex right and ensures that there is an orderly access by each man to a woman' (Pateman, 1989: 109).

The 'sexual contract' is established through, for example, the separation of *public* and *private* spheres. This separation is representative of the historical distinction between 'male' and 'female' as antagonistic universalising categories. Women become symbols of emotion, natural feeling and caring for those related to them. Women *qua* women are not capable, it would seem, of the 'objectivity' and principled behaviour which characterises the soldier and the citizen.

This separation of public and private spheres has serious consequences for both men and women as 'citizens'. Men, by transcending the private domain, become social and public whilst women, who are constructed as symbolic of the private domain, are excluded by definition from the social (civilised) order. Therefore, while women are included within the liberal democratic project as symbols of morality and femininity (Yuval-Davis, 1997), they are *excluded* from possessing political power and, as it naturally follows, from the realm of citizenship (e.g., enfranchisement). Consequently, the greatest weakness of the liberal model is the very premise upon which women's citizenship has been constructed; in particular, a reliance on the gendered nature of the public/private split or what Phillips (1991*a*, 1991*b*) calls the 'political settlement'. In this 'settlement', gender inequality is embedded in the political principles and social relations which are legitimated by a theory of liberal democracy.

In short, feminist political theorists have raised questions which challenge the core of our understanding of citizenship and the civic sphere. Their analyses can be used to consider, for example, the challenge to the 'fraternal pact' put forward by social movements such as the international women's movement; the ways in which women have been inserted into the public sphere; and the shifting boundaries between public and private domains. Many questions too are raised about the role of education in relation to this political project—to what extent did the development of modern educational systems mirror and institutionalise the fraternal pact? We might also ask, just how is democracy taught to the young? Is it through a re-assertion of a gendered notion of citizenship—a privileging of male public spheres—which redefines democracy as a neutral and *degendered* entity (Phillips, 1991*a*)?

The Gendering of Nationhood and Nation States

In recent years, both feminist political and social theorists have turned their attention to a the study of state practices in response to questions of 'citizenship' and 'national identity'. Their primary concerns have centered around debunking myths about the egalitarian nature of democratic citizenship in the nation-state and exposing diverse forms of marginalization associated with, for example, civic nationalism. In this model of analysis, feminist political theorists do not simply view citizenship as a masculine entity, as it appears in the work of Carole Pateman. Rather, the goal is to examine how questions of nationhood and the 'civil society' impact upon the very nature and constitutive elements of women's marginalization in an era of increasing globalization and advanced modernization. Of particular significance within this tradition is the study of the 'ambivalent manifestation' of gender and male domination in nationalist and political rhetoric, in particular, those discourses which persistently function to marginalize women who are already defined as 'Other' in the state. The goal in much of this work [*Curriculum Inquiry*] is to explore the internal, gendered dynamics of national politics and its impact on the political and social identities (and experiences) of culturally oppressed and differently positioned women (e.g., class, sexuality).

Some of the most interesting work in this area has been conducted by Nira Yuval-Davis (1997), Yuval-Davis and Anthias (1989) and Pieterse and Parekh (1995). Yuval Davis (1997), for example, suggests that women are represented in nationalist discourses as romantic symbols of cultural morality who do not possess political agency, but who instead function as maternal catalysts of national identity in the broadest sense. She writes: 'women are "required to carry this burden of representation"—the symbolic bearers of the collectivity's identity and honour, both personally and collectively. [. . .] Girls did not need to act; they had to become the national embodiment' (Yuval-Davis, 1997: 105). In this 'identity' representation, there is no explicit conflict between gender and nation. In fact, as Yuval-Davis (1997) describes it, it seems very clear; women are not given any formal role in the development of the nation. They are instead seen as keepers and cultivators of it. This implies a certain responsibility which is placed upon women to reproduce and cultivate in democratic subjects those dominant cultural values which are endorsed by those who dominate the political machinery (and indeed political memory) of the state. This 'reproductive' process leads to a cultural privileging which not only exalts the state's position on national identity, but women's position within it. In so doing, however, nationalist rhetoric not only privileges the dominance of male super-ordinance in state hierarchies but represses, both epistemically and politically, the many cultural and national understandings which reside on the margins of the state.

This 'legitimized' practice of privileging also means that women who oppose or resist the dominant view of culture and nationhood[1] are viewed as 'non-persons' or 'non-citizens'. The 'non-citizen' is not only viewed as 'deviant', but is prevented from contributing to *formal* development of the nation. The 'non-citizen' then is that which signifies 'difference'. Yuval-Davis (1997: 5) writes: 'the study of citizenship should consider the issue of women's citizenship not only by contrast to that of men, but also in relation to women's affiliation to dominant or subordinate groups, their ethnicity, origin and urban or rural residence. It should also take into consideration global and transnational positionings of these citizenships.'

In summary, the work of Yuval-Davis (1997) and related feminist work (see Pieterse and Parekh, 1995) has raised questions about the role of national rhetoric and symbolism in the formation of gender identities. The project at this level of political analysis is to reveal the gendered peculiarities of national/cultural identity-formation and the 'particularities of their internationalization', or globalizing features (Robinson, 1997: 10). Yuval-Davis's (1997) work can be used to consider, for example, the ways in which civic nationalism (as educational discourse) or neo-colonialism simultaneously conditions and undermines the cultural identities and political representation of women (and girls and boys) in diverse educational contexts. It also sheds light on the ways in which national activity, as part of political socialization in education, is implicated in reproductive and sometimes traditional patterns of gender identity-formation.

Such work exposes a link between the liberal democratic schooling project, globalization, and gender in the broadest sense. It raises questions, for example, about the relationship between the social exclusion of women and girls in education and school restructuring as a response to modernization and globalization. It might also help us to question how national narratives concerning such issues as 'boys' and girls' achievement', 'standards' or 'school choice' (as liberal democratic practice) might lead to school exclusions when gender identities do not conform to a broader cultural narrative on identity and citizenship. Many questions too are raised about feminist theory and education outside 'Western' nations and the role of feminist politics there. Perhaps the most significant and enduring of these is: 'Why is neo-liberal democracy, as political education for the new "Civil Society", still the "operating system of global politics"' (see Pieterse and Parekh, 1995) in newly formed or reconstituted democracies (and the model for education elsewhere) in the wake of an international recognition of multiple views on gender, difference and identity-politics in the state,[2] one which cannot be maintained by neo-liberal or highly individualistic forms of liberal democratic sustenance.

'Woman' as a Political Category

A third conceptualization which has emerged in response to feminist critiques of liberal democracy is a concern with the ways in which women's roles/social practices have been represented as political categories in the polity, especially those associated with the democratic state. Does the state support a formal view of women as 'political agents', or do women have historically determined 'apolitical' roles in a democracy? Are women still seen, as they were at the early stages of the suffragist movement, as 'benevolent philanthropists'[3] or are they political actors who possess agency in their own right?

Such questions are addressed by feminist political theorists and philosophers who are concerned with the epistemological significance of women's representation in both political theory and the state. For example, the feminist political philosopher, Roland Martin, argues that the category 'woman' has been erased from politics and political theory:

> Women, children and the family dwell in the 'ontological basement', outside and underneath the political structure. This apolitical status is due not to historical accident or necessity but to arbitrary definition [. . .]. Since the subject matter of political theory is politics and since reproductive processes have been traditionally assigned to women and have taken place within the family, it follows that women and the family are excluded from the very subject matter of the discipline. (Roland Martin, 1994: 107–8)

Roland Martin's description of women's 'apolitical status' in the state leads to a historically determined and socially constructed vision of womanhood—that of *benevolent actor* and *virtuous being*. In this context, women, as mothers and caregivers, are constructed against the grain of formal political action and are therefore seen as outsiders to the political process.

By contrast, the category 'woman', as described by Iris Marion Young (1995), not only illuminates a vision of women as 'political' in the formal sense but points to women's collective resistance to more conventional definitions of political participation; to put this another way, women are seen as motivated political actors in their own right. She writes 'One reason to conceptualize women as a collective, I think, is to maintain a point of view outside of liberal individualism [. . .] Without conceptualizing women as a group in some sense, it is not possible to conceptualize oppression in a systematic, structured institutional process' (p. 192). Women are thus placed at the centre of democratic politics as a form of gendered resistance to masculine conceptions of the state. This oppositional practice is designed to challenge those liberal assumptions which view women as the 'victim', conflate the categories 'women' and 'domesticity' and ultimately function to exclude women from full political participation.

In such polarized representations, we find binary images of the category 'women': on the one hand, a daughter of the nation-state thought to instill a moral 'ethics of care' (Gilligan, 1982, 1986) in society through her connection to the private sphere; and on the other hand, an active *social* agent with membership in a political collectivity. At first glance, such contemporary visions appear somewhat irreconcilable and indeed contradictory. Nevertheless, they bear some relevance to current understandings of democracy. For example, the notion of women as daughters of the nation-state invokes symbolic images of care in the maintenance of democratic relations. At the same time, Young's description of the feminist collectivity points to an image of women as agents who actively participate in the reconstruction of a democracy.

Both modern and postmodern (and indeed post-structural) feminist political theorists have justifiably exposed both these images as problematic because they essentialize women in unacceptable ways. However, a feminist political/social analysis (rather than simply deconstructive analysis) of the varied and conflicting categories of 'womanhood' provide an alternative lens through which to examine the relationship between gender and democracy. It also implies a necessity for mapping the complex web of relations which underpin questions about women's inclusion and participation in a democracy. However, in confronting such issues, one must go beyond a simple examination of 'woman' as a gender category to address Iris Young's (1995) interest in *women's relation to the 'political'*. The simplest and arguably most powerful mechanism for achieving this end is to examine the potential links between the *feminist project* and *democratic principles*. In so doing, one learns that democratic concepts, such as equality, do not necessarily converge at the centre of all feminist projects and do not apply to the history of all women's struggles. Nor is it necessarily the case that all women define their politics in relation to the liberal democratic project. Wilson (1995: 8) writes: 'It is not [. . .] possible to say that [feminism] is a commitment to equality, since some feminists have argued, both in the past and today, for separate spheres of influence, emphasizing difference and complimentarity rather than equality.'

In short, feminist political theorists have raised questions about the suspected and elusive character of 'equality' and its contradictory role in the 'emancipation' of women. They have also exposed the gendered classifications which manifest the 'male-oriented' trajectory of liberal democratic thought. Indeed, such efforts have called into question the very structures of liberal democratic thinking and their role in the formation of gender identities. In our view, such insights can be used, for example, to critique state education and its regulation of women and girls' (and men and boys') political identities. We might also ask how a political/social, rather than simply deconstructive, analysis of gender categories (as manifested in liberal democratic thought) might force us question the very precepts of democratic educational practice and the manner in which feminists have examined 'gender and democracy' in education over time.

Feminist Analyses of Gender and Democracy in Education

The feminist critiques described thus far provide some insight into the ways in which gender and democracy have been examined in the social sciences. We draw indirectly upon these arguments to re-assess a range of contemporary feminist perspectives in education. We demonstrate how each theoretical stance provides some insight into the relation between education and the liberal democratic project, although not always making this agenda explicit nor central, nor necessarily building upon each others' work.

Feminist Research in Education

Feminist research originally achieved its status by demonstrating that state politics and institutions rested upon a patriarchal notion of civil society.[4] An assumption about the reality of women's oppression has always applied across feminist research, although sometimes reference is made to a normative concept of masculine control (i.e., the patriarchal state), and at other times a non-normative notion of female oppression is identified (e.g., contradictory state discourses, local power relations). Such discrepancies in feminist thought has led to educational research which draws upon different 'objects and subjects' of study and operates at different levels of political analysis; some studies are more highly focused on the ways in which the macro-structures of schooling (whether political or economic) shape the distribution of educational opportunities and privileges to male and female pupils, whilst others concentrate more upon the particularity of gendered experiences in education. Similarly, the epistemological and methodological standpoints of writers on gender and education are varied and even, on occasion, incompatible. Such standpoints range, for example, from the structuring of gender regimes and codes to analyses of the discursive framing of the educational project and its construction of particular subjects (e.g., 'the girl', 'the pupil', 'the teacher'). Often there is a tension between analyses which might highlight modes of social control, regulation and governance of educational 'subjects' or the disciplining of the body, or studies of youth cultures, rebellions and diverse coping strategies.

Other types of feminist research make claims about the potential for gender reform inherent in the liberal democratic project using the spaces and possibilities available in the educational system. Such possibilities may involve the deconstruction of educational texts and practices or the promotion of critical pedagogies (see Luke and Gore, 1989). Still other research has promoted the development of feminist values (e.g. caring) and female modes of authority (see Gilligan, 1986). Feminist pedagogies have also been defined, as have the strategies for the politicisation of young people's experiential knowledge. Such a diverse field represents precisely the contradiction of the liberal democratic educational project. It allows itself to become the subject of its own critique at the same time as obscuring its connections with political and economic conditions. In keeping with this concern, we begin with a critique of liberal democratic theory and its relationship to feminist models of democratic education.

Feminist Theory and Liberal Democratic Education

In many national contexts, the state has had to respond to increasingly confident feminist campaigns, many of which have drawn extensively from the discourse of liberal democracy (Heater, 1990). In the 20th century, such campaigns had intensified using the language of liberalism to struggle for women's equality. Some of the key assumptions which underlie liberal feminism are described below:

(1) The 'principle of political neutrality'[5] is viewed as sacrosanct in the liberal democratic state. Such neutrality serves to constrain the actions of government and individuals (see Whelehan, 1995), both of which may otherwise restrict women's potential for political agency in the state;

(2) Female autonomy is central to women's 'self-improvement and basic livelihood' in the liberal state since, as Whelehan (1995: 28) argues, 'men hold such rights naturally';

(3) Political equality between the sexes must be examined through the lens of opportunity, access, and self-determination. These female entitlements are to be achieved through various procedural forms of competition in a free society; and

(4) Women are capable of rational thought (Wollstonecraft, 1992, original publication, 1792). These rational capacities must be drawn upon to challenge the assumption that women are inferior to men in their ability to engage politically.

Each of these assumptions, in different ways, supports the notion of a free public society (with inherent liberties) open to women. Under liberalism, the long-term goal of feminism is to empower women to take up their rightful place in this 'open' society through the development of *female autonomy*. A secondary goal is to *de-gender*, as far as possible, the public sphere through the legal recognition of women's right to equality on a par with that of men. Liberal feminist analysis has thus highlighted the *importance of feminizing the male public sphere, whilst still retaining the social functioning of the female private sphere*. Paradoxically, however, it is the separation of public and private spheres which has protected the 'privacy' of the home and celebrated individualism and individual rights in the public domain. Unfortunately, this rather unnatural separation has meant that ideological concerns about the masculine dimensions of democratic life have yet to be applied (by liberal feminists) to a serious critique of women's positioning in the private domain. Nevertheless, the exposure by feminist political theorists of the divisions between such gendered spaces has made possible the liberal feminist critique of the public sphere.

The educational assumptions which are manifest in liberal feminist thought revolve around the notion of *opportunity*. That is, schooling, as the first point of entry into the economy, provides one of many opportunities through which men and women can achieve political equality in the public realm. According to the liberal feminist then, the opportunity structure of schools must accommodate the needs of women who wish to take up a place within a competitive economic sphere. As a consequence, liberal feminists have made numerous contributions towards the development of a particular form of democratic discourse (e.g., rights, equal opportunity) in schools, and at the same time, incurred some difficulties.

One such contribution emerged as a result of women's struggle to gain access to male forms of high status education. For example, liberal feminists provided statistical data which highlighted women's under-employment and under-representation in the public sphere. Such work exposed the failure of liberal democratic societies to give women anything other than secondary and marginal status and revealed the extent to which education was successful in ensuring the reproduction of a sex-segregated labour force. Liberal feminists also revealed how the state and the state education system, both of which should have been neutral arbiters, had been captured by men. Education was indeed, as Carole Pateman has suggested, a *fraternity*, with men dominating the machineries by which social justice was defined.

Another such target of analysis within liberal feminist thought was the assessment of official school knowledge and its representation of women. For example, several textbook and curriculum studies demonstrated how official knowledge was aligned with hegemonic male structures in society, thus legitimizing male-dominated public spheres and masculine forms of citizenry. The curricular traditions regulating women defined a female role which privileged the domestic and emphasised a vocational education which was service-oriented rather than subject-centred. Women were to be educated as daughters of the nation, imbued with an ethos of duty and service to both society and to their men folk (Brindle and Arnot, in press; Dyehouse, 1976; Davin, 1978). Whilst boys were differentiated along lines of social inequality (class differences), women were simply reduced to biological and/or psychological characteristics.

Women, despite their differences in social status and life experiences, were categorised in such educational discourses as more homogeneous than heterogeneous. Thus, despite the liberal feminists' over-arching concern with 'woman' and 'gender' as political categories, their own analyses exposed the 'gender essentialisms' (see Roman, 1992) of schooling. Significantly then, liberal democratic feminists turned the concept of rights 'against the patriarchal model of citizenship' and produced a 'powerful and sharp edged' (Connell, 1990) analysis of male dominance in education.

Whilst this model of education is worthy of *some* admiration, a number of key political issues which concern women's oppression have either been undermined or ignored. Firstly, liberal feminism has tended to accept the political, civic and economic sphere as unproblematic. For example, in merely accepting and thus defending 'equality' as the centre-point of liberal feminist thinking, the ideological premises upon which liberal democratic theory was structured went unchallenged. We also learned little about how liberal ideals function as part of a discourse of modern Western capitalism. Indeed, we failed to understand precisely how democratic schooling, as a political discourse, became a regulating force linked to the establishment, state agendas and the construction of gender identities.

Secondly, at this macro-contextual level, little attention is given to women's positioning in the domestic sphere. As a consequence, liberal feminism could not easily address the key constraints which have restricted women's participation in political, civic, economic and cultural decision making—the role, for example, of domestic labour, the lack of child care, the control of women and girls by 'husbands' and fathers, and the political regulation of sexuality. Democratic education therefore meant urging women to participate more fully in the public sphere, and to pursue non--traditional subjects and vocational courses. It has also meant releasing the intellectual potential of women into the economy. Much liberal feminist research has therefore focused on the 'presumed deficits' of girls, which relied on hopes of improving their achievement status rather than confronting the gendered nature of school structures.

Sexism within the curriculum, the classroom and the playground, (and indeed in the teaching profession)[6] could be left relatively unaffected, once more formal discriminatory practices had been removed. Freedom of subject choice, movement, play and action, freedom of expression in class, although allegedly liberating, later proved to be deeply problematic. In such 'spaces' could be found precisely those practices and gender conventions which shaped male and female identities and constrained the possibility of real equality between the sexes. Ironically, liberal feminists eventually found themselves arguing for the closure of options and of freedoms, such as 'freedom of choice' (Arnot, 1991), so that formal equality could be achieved (e.g., affirmative action).

The notion of female citizenship was also deeply problematic in the liberal feminist model of education. Women were to be educated towards greater autonomy and encouraged to work towards their own self-determination through education. Female citizenship therefore implied equal membership in masculinized subjects, more or less regulated by the sexist ethos of school subjects themselves. Taken in this light, democratic schooling was best understood as the 'training ground for the [female] entrepreneur' (see Dietz, 1985, our addition), and the institution capable of granting women an equal chance in the race towards individual achievement.

In short, liberal feminists focused on the most overt contradictions of capitalist democracy—the gap between, for example, equal opportunity as a principle and the reality of differential treatment. However, they failed to identify far deeper obstacles to gender equality. As a result, liberal goals for women's rights (now thought to have been achieved) were embedded in a neo-liberal agenda which focused on creating more competitive and rationalized performances in the market. The representation of the democratic school, from a strong liberal view, is an institutional form which touts its competencies, excellence, marketability, and technical skills, all of which (at least in theory) are thought to be equally applicable to men and women.

[...]

Democracy and Difference

Socialist and black feminists sought to address gender politics in terms of the *differences* between and among women rather than differences between men and women. They achieved this by demonstrating significant differences in the relationship between working-class and middle-class women, and of culturally oppressed to capitalist economies (see Barrett, 1980; Weis, 1983). These early interests in diversity and difference led to a critique of liberal feminist theories and called into question a degendered 'neutral' education system. In short, socialist feminists' efforts to politicise women's differences (albeit crudely) challenged the very possibility of a degendered liberal polity and led to an analysis of modern forms of male-directed economic power. Clearly, an increasing awareness of the extent of social inequalities between women of diverse backgrounds (and across national boundaries) belied the simplicity of both liberal and maternal feminist arguments.

Whilst this recognition of 'difference' has challenged much feminist thinking, it is more difficult to examine the relation between socialist feminist initiatives and democratic values in education. One could argue, for example, that socialist feminism never really engaged with the concept of democracy or democratic school movements (e.g. free schooling, open schooling). It has instead been concerned with a critique of our rather naive views of modern education and its links to capitalist social formations. This concern led to the exposure of schools as 'hegemonic' state institutions, which behind their illusions of neutrality (Bourdieu and Passeron, 1977; Bernstein, 1977) and their liberal guise (Bowles and Gintis, 1976), reproduced a highly diversified and stratified work force (e.g., Althusser, 1971). Socialist feminist initiatives have thus focused on developing politicised cultures of resistance to ensure a more democratic school environment. For example, Gramscian models of feminist education focused primarily on challenging male dominance and masculine 'gender codes' (Arnot, 1980) through 'counter-hegemonic' educational practices (see also Weiler, 1988).

This image of educational practice has implied the celebration of a radical consciousness, through alternative curricular forms and critical pedagogy. Unfortunately, much of this work stopped short of challenging male dominance in the private sphere or failed to prevent the celebration, by the male left, of the assertion of hegemonic masculinity in counter-school cultures (e.g., Arnot, 1982). It therefore seemed unlikely that the dominance of a masculinized bourgeois culture identified by French theorists such as Bourdieu and Passeron (1977) would be challenged in the classroom, nor were the forms of male authority which supported such culture necessarily challenged by a Marxist 'feminist pedagogy' (Luke and Gore, 1989). Instead, socialist feminism tended to reinforce the distinction between public and private spheres and failed to define what democratic participation would mean in the home. As Jagger (1983) argued, a more equal division of domestic labour and women's control over biological reproduction should be essential to the achievement of democracy. Many, however, argued for community control over biological reproduction in the name of the common good as a radical ideal. Deeply problematic issues such as public coercion versus private rights and the role of the state in relation to domestic relations were therefore never fully resolved.

In retrospect, socialist feminists scrutinised all analyses which presumed a unitary category of 'woman' and attempted to demarcate the lines of social exclusion, particularly for those at the economic periphery. Their analyses, together with related black feminist and lesbian feminist critiques (e.g., Brah and Minhas, 1985; Weis, 1983), began to expose other systems of identification (e.g., race, class, sexuality) as central elements at work in the production of female subordination. Consequently, this work has had much to offer in its early focus on difference and its recognition of the socially constructed nature of gender categories. Increasingly, therefore, academics became aware of the need to document the performative and gendered elements of difference. *Questions about difference*, by the beginning of the 1980s, were clearly on the agenda.

New Feminism(s) and the 'Deconstruction' of Democracy

In the period between 1980 to 1985, the debate between [. . .] feminism(s) escalated and its locus changed substantially. Increasingly, modern feminist perspectives were seen as historical responses to the inadequacies of rather totalizing discourse(s). A concern also arose that all feminism(s) in the modern period were defined, at least in part, by liberal discourse since many feminist advancements had taken place in national contexts where liberalism had substantial political credibility. These perspectives were thus challenged by diverse feminist communities (e.g., lesbian feminists) who argued that their identities could not be found in a liberal democratic discourse or in alternative radical and social frameworks. Liberal feminism, in particular, had not only failed to represent the diverse political interests of women, but had addressed women who had benefited primarily from membership in white, middle-class culture. Such concerns suggested that the category 'woman' was not only 'illusory' (see Butler, 1990), but repressed women's differences. Similar criticisms were directed at socialist feminism since class and political economy were central to its edifice as a modern political theory.

These 'master narrative(s)' had constructed a version of the social order which found causal explanations for women's inequality. Women's social positioning was the result of, for example, gender socialization patterns, capitalist exploitation, or men's oppression of women. Women's subjective experiences, in the case of liberal feminism or maternal feminism, had been largely ignored or universalised. In the case of socialist feminism, women's experiences were put down to class determination. Such explanations, it seemed, bore little relation to the complexity of women's identities and experiences.

Post-Structural Feminism

In the mid 1980s, a variety of new feminism(s) emerged which can be subsumed, albeit loosely, under the banner of post-structuralism. The terrain of post-structuralism within political theory is vast. However, two theoretical and empirical issues now manifest the realm of post-structural feminist work in relation to questions about liberal democratic practice: (1) the links between modern forms of governance in democratic states ('governmentality') and the regulation of gendered identities; and (2) the local expression of male dominance and its link to the production and regulation of the gendered citizen. We restrict our discussion here to the identification of features which have distinguished the *political* perspectives of feminist post-structuralists from other brands of feminism in their understanding of gender and democracy.

Over the last two decades, many post-structural (and, in some cases, post-modern) feminists (see Butler, 1995) have argued that the main task for feminism is to embrace three issues which are currently debated about theories of liberal democracy:

(1) that there is a false dichotomy between 'conceptual devices' thought to explain incontestable human experiences in liberal democratic discourse (e.g., state *vs* individual, man *vs* women, subject *vs* object, private *vs* public);

(2) that subjective, diverse and contradictory human experiences shape and thus reconstitute shifting gender relations and our understandings of the liberal state; and

(3) that societies depend upon both fluid and contradictory social forces, both of which are performative and unstable elements in the development of democratic society and the gender relations which prefigure it.

In keeping with these assumptions, democracy cannot be seen as something which is generated solely by state apparatuses or characterized as purely conceptual since its very foundations are thought to shift in line with context, its manifestations of power, and the shaping of subjective human experiences. Instead, one must view *democracy as one of many local sites where political power is both exercised over, and expressed by, individuals who are positioned differently within the polity*. This expression of power in language can only be understood as 'relational' or in dynamic tension. Such dynamic tensions lead to particular construction(s) of gender, which are historically-constructed and contextually-bound; hence, Foucault's emphasis on genealogy and 'the history of the present'. The 'conceptual devices' most commonly drawn upon by feminist post-structuralists in deconstructing democracy and democratic schools are 'identity', 'performativity', 'difference', and 'subjectivity'. Such terms provide an analytical device for assessing women's relationship to, or embeddedness within, democratic society.

While feminist post-structuralism appears incommensurate with the concrete goals of democratic schooling, some provocative research has emerged within this tradition. This research has confirmed the assumption that schools, as local sites, play a significant role in reconstituting the nature of gender politics in society (see Walkerdine and Lucey, 1989) and what we understand democracy to be. It has also challenged the normative and universalistic assumptions which characterise 'democratic' schooling and its apparent role in women/girls' emancipation. In that sense, it is responding precisely to the problematic which emerges in endorsing either a unitary category of womanhood (e.g., maternal feminism) or feminist positions which are more deterministic in their explanations about women's marginal status in the state (e.g., socialist feminism). In this section, then, we focus on what we believe to the most exemplary post-structural analysis of democratic schooling—the work of Valerie Walkerdine and her colleague Helen Lucey.

In their book entitled, *Democracy in the Kitchen*, Valerie Walkerdine and Helen Lucey (1989) illustrate how modern education fosters the development of normative liberal ideals which regulate women's and girls' identities, and ultimately, democratic citizenship. They suggest for example, that primary school teachers are positioned within liberal discourses which not only construct, but regulate, the 'good female teacher' and the 'pupil'. Using Foucault, they also describe the female teacher as one who must monitor the development of male-centered democratic concepts such as 'free-will' through gendered educational discourse, thus cultivating support for the democratic order drawing upon 'non-coercive strategies'. According to Walkerdine and Lucey (1989), the promotion and circulation of this discourse is a 'management technique' in which students come to accept as 'normal' modern forms of liberal democratic governance and the ideal of the 'bourgeois individual'. Such discourses develop as part of a history of educational ideas (i.e., educational knowledge) and are concerned with issues of gender and sexuality:

> It is women, whose sexuality itself is regulated to produce 'normal femininity', who become the central prop of the new form of pedagogy. Teachers trained in psychology, were to assume the entire responsibility for the 'freedom' of children, and for the continuous maintenance of the bourgeois democratic order. I want, therefore, to demonstrate that women, positioned as teachers, mothers, carers and caring professionals are held absolutely necessary for the moral order. [. . .] It places them as responsible for ensuring the possibility of democracy, and yet as deeply conservative. My argument is that [. . .] women of all classes have been placed as guardians of an order which is to difficult to escape. If you are told you are totally responsible for the nature of the child and with it, therefore, the possibility of freedom, of democracy—how much guilt and pain is involved resisting such a notion? (Walkerdine, 1986: 63).

In our view, the work of Walkerdine and Lucey (1989) signaled a new theoretical agenda for many feminists in education. It suggested, for example, that liberal democratic ideals (e.g., freedom) in schools positioned women teachers within a discourse of 'correct mothering' which ultimately served to reconstitute subordinate gender identities in schools, only one (the male) of which was 'the right citizen'. It thus became clear that the construction of democratic relations in schools was closely related to issues of sexuality, most notably the re-production of women's marginalized sexuality through educational practices.

In this model of democratic education, women teachers are 'used' to regulate liberal initiatives such as 'autonomy', 'freedom', and 'choice' even when they themselves are constrained by such discourses; that is, the liberal initiative offers only 'an illusion of choice'. According to Walkerdine and Lucey (1989), it is therefore within the particularity of gender struggles, as configured within democratic discourse, that women's constructed sexualities, social identities and political status can be found.

Critical Pedagogy and the Democratic School

An additional strand of work within the post-structural tradition is more explicitly concerned with pedagogy as a form of deconstructive practice. This work has developed primarily as a reaction to other radical forms of critical pedagogy which draw upon the language of liberal democracy to critique the role of schooling in the development of modern societies. Perhaps the best example of this work is a collection of feminist pedagogy edited by Carmen Luke and Jennifer Gore, entitled *Feminisms and Critical Pedagogy*. In this collection, Luke and Gore (1989) argue that a post-structuralist feminist pedagogy is needed to challenge those who draw upon the male-centred language of democracy as a so-called 'neutral' method of achieving gender equity in schools. Their greatest concerns are with male sociologists of education who merely advocate a commitment to critical pedagogy (as a form of democratic rationality) in the public sphere rather than tackle the statist divisions between the public and the private.

Feminists working along these lines tend to confront issues which male sociologists of education or other feminists have ignored or inadequately addressed such as: teaching and its role in the shaping of gendered subjectivities (Davies, 1989); pedagogical tools which can be used to 'deconstruct' the dominant heterosexual discourses of schooling (see Lather, 1992; Middleton, 1998); the pedagogical, regulating and gendered functions of contemporary educational reform (see Blackmore, 1996; Dehli, 1996; Kenway and Epstein, 1996); the gendered and racialized discourses of schooling (Connell, 1995; Davies, 1989; Walkerdine, 1981); and histories of sexuality, the body and discipline in schools (see Ellsworth, 1997; Middleton, 1998).

According to the post-structuralist, such issues should be continually addressed in order to 'keep things in process, to disrupt, to keep the system in play, to set up procedures which continuously demystify the realities we create, and to fight the tendency for our categories to congeal' (Caputo, 1987: 286, cited in Lather, 1992: 7). Deconstructing concepts such as democracy must therefore serve as a 'safeguard against dogmatism' (Lather, 1992: 7) and as a mechanism for rejecting the normalization of liberal democracy itself.

Making Alliances

Another strand of work which rests on the margins of post-structural/post-modern theorizing is the culturalist theory of schooling developed by Cameron McCarthy and Michael Apple (1988) and McCarthy (1990), which theorises the *dynamic relation between race, class, and gender* and its link to democratic practices in education. The main premise of this work is that schools, as sites of struggles over the meaning of democracy, take on a mediational role in both the construction and articulation of diverse political issues (such as gender) in the polity. Gender is therefore positioned within a complex matrix of social forces (e.g., 'race' and class)[7] which shape democratic relations in schools. This work is known as the *non-synchronous* model of schooling (McCarthy, 1990). McCarthy (1990: 118) writes: 'The concept of non-synchrony [. . .] raises questions about the nature, exercise and multiple determination of power within that middle ground of everyday practices in schooling [. . .]. The fact is that [. . .] dynamic relations of race, class and gender do not unproblematically reproduce each other. These relations are complex and often have contradictory effects in institutional settings.'

McCarthy's (1990) work on 'race' informs the gender and democracy debate in two ways. First, it speaks to the significance of 'building alliances' across diverse political communities to understand the very nature of democracy and democratic relations in schools.[8] Second, it points to the part played by 'difference' in both calling into question and 'opening up a kind of epistemological space' (see Robinson, 1998: 1) for rethinking the democratic educational project and its characterization of marginalized political identities. For example,

McCarthy suggests that any attempt to characterise the experience of marginality through recourse to a single social formation such as 'race' or 'gender' misrepresents the experience of marginality in a democracy; that is, questions about 'race' cannot be abstracted from their context while other social forces, such as gender, are kept in place. Democratic school relations and the struggle for equality must therefore be seen as a complex set of political acts which are linked to diverse forms of identification in the nation-state.

Although controversial, Giroux's now somewhat dated work on the politics of pedagogy and its implications for feminist practice should not be overlooked. His book, *Post-modernism, Feminism and Cultural Politics* (1991) intervened into the gender and democracy debate by suggesting that educ ators engage with women's identities, voice and experience—that is, privilege women epistemically—rather than focus solely on organised knowledge in schools; that is, the 'everyday' and the 'particular' of female experience should be the premise of democratic school since such an approach acts to counter the traditional narratives of 'abstract' and objective forms of rationalized knowledge.[9] Giroux (1991: 54) writes: 'Central to the notion of critical pedagogy is a politics of *voice* that combines a post-modern notion of difference with a feminist emphasis on the primacy of the political' (our emphasis).

By contrast, Connell's (1987, 1995), Mac an Ghaill's (1994, 1996) and Epstein and Johnson's (1998) work extends the feminist analysis by suggesting that 'heterosexual masculinities'[10] inform the construction of the so-called 'democratic schooling project'. The central goal of this work has been to extend our understanding of how gender relations and, ultimately, how sexual identities are socially constructed in relation to both state and social formations (e.g., race, class, sexuality). It also demonstrates how the democratic schooling project has sought recourse to 'heterosexuality' in shaping both student and teachers' gender identities, gender hierarchies, and gender relations in the state.

Levels of Feminist Political Analysis

In this section, we attempt, albeit experimentally, to bring together the analyses of liberal feminism, maternal and socialist feminism and post-structural feminisms to construct a more systematic base for theory development. In so far as each tradition has worked on, and with, particular gender problematics, they have offered their own descriptions of how power and politics operate, at which level such forces become significant, the key issues which educational research should address, and what we can assume about the relationship between individuals, structures and social forces. We now attempt to make sense of this extraordinary diversity by describing such problematics in terms of different *levels of feminist political analysis*. In so doing, we hope to offer some insight into those empirical/theoretical connections which still need to be made across feminist theories, and those issues which still remain underdeveloped in feminist educational research. We also attempt to illustrate how our earlier descriptions of key feminist debates in political theory bear some relevance to current questions still remaining in feminist educational thought.

In our view, one of the dangers which underlies the development of feminist thought thus far is precisely its non-cumulative line of development. For example, feminist thought is often based on critique rather than any systematic set of investigations, nor indeed based on any theory of gender relations or feminist educational initiatives, which could account for feminist critiques of liberal democracy. However, such a consideration might lead to feminist theories which embrace both normative (modern) ideals of social justice and political agency with non-normative (post-modern) questions of difference and particularity. For example, feminist theorists such as Fraser and Nicholson (1995) and Weir (1997) argue that we must counter the 'false antithesis' expressed about the distinctions between modern feminist thought (e.g., equality) and post-structural feminist thought (e.g., difference), and even more significantly, the fragmentation of the field. In other words, in promoting what Coole (1993) refers to as a 'refreshingly interdisciplinary approach' to the study of gender and democratic values in education, we must reconcile some of the contradictions within feminist educational thought. Therefore, not unlike feminist political and social theorists, we too must reconcile modernist questions of feminist solidarity and social structure with post-modern concerns about hierarchies of identification and difference (see Dillabough, 1998; Dillabough and Arnot, 1998).

Drawing upon the three theoretical traditions of feminist political theory described earlier, we suggest that feminists in education have been working primarily at three levels of political analysis. We identify these levels as the *Civic Spheres, Education and National Narratives*, and *Political Identities, Differences and Subjectivities*, respectively. Within these levels of political analyses, we identify how feminists in education might draw upon arguments made by political theorists to develop a more coherent feminist theory of democratic schooling.

Level 1: Civic Spheres

As we have seen, feminists in education, particularly since the late 1960s, have been working predominantly on what might be called the civic sphere. Broadly speaking, a feminist emphasis on the civic sphere has implied a certain normative commitment to the study of women's social positioning in the public sphere. Such work has been instrumental in exposing women's uneasy relationship to public decision making (cf. liberal feminism), to patriarchal machineries of education and forms of regulation, and, for example, male public discourses in schools. The organising principle in this domain is the notion that equal representation and participation in the public sphere is key to full citizenship. Women, as second-class members of the polity, have therefore made considerable efforts to 'assimilate' into the public sphere through liberal democratic initiatives in education. Such assimilation mainly takes the form of educational reforms (e.g. curricular initiatives, affirmative action), but it can also involve political activism, particularly around education (promoting concepts of the glass ceiling, for example).

While this kind of theoretical focus has led to a gendered restructuring of the public sphere, privileging the public dimensions of civil society poses a number of limitations for the study of gender and education. For example, one of the key tensions currently identified at this level by feminist political theorists and still inadequately addressed in education is the conflict between, on the one hand, the representation of women in the 'male' public sphere and on the other hand, male/gender dominance in the 'female' private sphere. In fact, much liberal feminist research still remains solely concerned with women's, girls' and boys' positions in state education,[11] in particular, their public achievement and success rather than the preparation of men for private life or a critique of the role that domestic discourses play in reconfiguring gender relations in the polity. However, as many feminist political theorists have argued (cf. Pateman, 1992), this obsession with gendered successes or failures is flawed precisely because gendered participation in the public sphere is still premised upon a patriarchal notion of civil society.

By contrast, maternal feminists have chosen to celebrate the private 'female' sphere over and above public patriarchy. The danger here, as feminist political theorists have suggested, is that they may celebrate private patriarchy through the diminution of femininity itself (see Arnot and Dillabough, 1988; Acker and Feureverger, 1997). Unlike maternal feminists, socialist feminists recognised the exploitative nature of the public/private distinctions, exposing its associations and functions within capitalist social formations. They nevertheless worked with the concept of the 'public' in education, failing on some level to investigate the political and social significance of the 'private'.

In seeking to address these limitations, one could argue that a creative association of public and private is to be found in the use of Foucault's concept of discourse, where political categories no longer represent true conceptual distinctions and language, knowledge, and power are seen as linked (Walkerdine and Lucey, 1989). However, whilst the public and private are seen as constituted through discursive practices and the construction of 'subjects'—whether mother, teacher, child—the danger here is that women and girls (in fact, all political subjects) are denied their political agency and the cultural, economic and structural basis of identity-formation in particular sites (the home, social institutions) remain under-theorized.

A novel way of addressing these concerns is to question how feminists might consider severing the *strong* boundaries between the public and private spheres in order to link the study of the fraternal social contract (i.e., the male public sphere) with the framing of the sexual contract (i.e., men's control of female sexuality). For example, liberal democracy's shaping of privacy, sexuality and the marriage contract are as significant to the analysis of modern educational systems as the framing, through state and local discourses, of the public citizen. Such efforts might reveal the limitations which emerge as consequence of over-emphasizing analyses of women's positioning in the civic sphere at the expense of understanding the performative nature of gender in the private sphere and its role in shaping democratic subjects, processes and actions.

Level 2: Education and National Narratives

As feminist political theorists argue, an analysis of the public sphere cannot but make some reference to the nation and nation-state (cf. Yuval Davis, 1997) and the gendered nature of citizenship and civic communities. Therefore, at this level of theoretical analysis, particular attention is given to the ways in which economic structures, nationalist rhetoric and cultural politics shape unequal relations between women of diverse social classes and ethnicities (e.g., socialist feminism). Related work has also been concerned with the impact of neo-liberalism (e.g., demise of the welfare state, token forms of democracy[12]) and globalization on both the formation of, and contestation about, national identities in late twentieth century democracies (see Brah, 1996).

Clearly, attention to such issues is not only necessary, but is a timely step forward in attempting to understand the relationship between contemporary feminist thought and democratic education. However, to date, related work in education has failed to resolve questions about the impact of nationalism on gender identity-formation and gendered notions of democratic citizenship in schools. As a consequence, the question of human rights, diverse forms of feminist activism, 'racial'/cultural struggles and movements, and identity politics (as civic activism) are often divorced from the analysis of educational inequalities, the shaping of gendered subjectivities in schools or the politics of difference. Educational equality or the study of *individual* subjectivity, rather than politicized forms of gender equity or justice, thus becomes the focus of feminist analysis. Consequently, serious and indeed *normative* concerns about 'identity' and 'difference', which are relevant to questions of justice and citizenship, still lurk on the margins of feminist educational research.[13]

The two key sites for the national education of the 'citizen' are teacher training and the school; the key principles being those which shape the structure of teacher training and the curriculum. For example, the circulation of professional and educational knowledge, discourses and pedagogic devices (cf. Bernstein, 1977) which shape the curriculum have privileged particular concepts of democracy (i.e., the liberal individual), and constructed the child as an educational subject and the teacher as its professional agent (cf. Walkerdine and Lucey, 1989). This privileging within curriculum theory is a mechanism drawn upon by the state to secure particular notions of national identity and political subjects. It is through the practice of liberal democracy that such ideals are legitimized, at least in part. As a consequence, questions about the contested nature of national/cultural identities and their impact on the construction of a gendered 'citizenry' in schools still remain largely unexplored. In fact, educational studies are only now beginning to address how identity, difference and differentiation, how normative values, and the construction of outsiders or the 'other', are gendered processes which concern the shaping of the 'citizen' (Holland et al., 1997).

Some current feminist work, for example, is examining the gendered nature of the 'ideal' citizen, particularly in relation to contemporary gender politics in schools and higher education (see Arnot et al., 1996; Dillabough, 1998). International and comparative work which examines the ways in which young people construct the gendered citizen and view themselves within the context of the gendered civic sphere (Bonder, 1997; Holland et al., 1997) is also in its inception. Such research attempts to capture the contested nature of 'citizenship' as it has been expressed in different political and economic phases, and through continuously transforming gender relations.

Despite this work, more comparative efforts are needed to examine how gender relations and gender politics evolve within dynamic educational cultures in the nation-state, especially those national contexts associated with rapid social and political change.[14] This could be achieved by focusing on the political concepts (and everyday assertions) any nation employs in relation to questions of gender and how such concepts (e.g., citizenship) are situated within a broader nationalist discourse of power relations. In our view, such an approach would contribute to the development of a novel analytic framework for assessing the relationship between cultural identity-formation and the shaping of the gendered 'citizen' in schools and higher education. We would therefore encourage feminists to question the role of national political formations on both the development of, and constraints placed upon, gender identities in diverse national schooling contexts.

Level 3: Political Identities, Differences and Subjectivities

School and classroom structures and experiences are central sites for research. It is here that feminists have developed their critique of male hegemony, seeing its operation in the interaction of teacher and pupil, and the gender conflicts between pupils. Perhaps more importantly, it is a site which many feminists have suggested can be reshaped along democratic lines. Therefore, understanding the political dimensions of classroom life is one which many have described as essential to the teaching of democracy, and inclusive education. At the same time, it is also in everyday interactions that pupils' identities and subjectivities are shaped and interpreted in ways which reinforce distinctions between masculinity and femininity, as well as those of, for example, sexuality, ethnicity and class.

Much post-structural and post-modern educational research has highlighted, through individualised narratives, the processes of social exclusion, particularly in relation to those constructed as 'other'. At the same time, such research has resisted using the categorization of public/private, or classifications such as male and female, preferring to report them as discursive entities, which permanently shift and are reconstituted. As a result, for feminist post-modernist and post-structuralists in education, to claim an identity, to lay the foundations of a new democratic project for women, or even engage in identity politics as part of democratic practice, may be (in some cases) to engage in an act of *repression*: 'the subject is an instance of mastery, of narrative closure, of the freezing of a process of difference/differance' (see Weir, 1997: 25). Identities must therefore be seen as discursively constructed through the language of democracy; gender identities are therefore a momentary outcome of a complex set of social and political relations. They must also be seen as sites of 'open political contest' (see Butler, 1995) and as a struggle to identify with political hierarchies which are framed by democratic discourse in school spaces. Such approaches are useful reminders of the none too simple relationship between the official *discourses* which underlie the democratic education project and the local construction of gender identities.

Despite post-structuralist scepticism about the modernist project of democratic schooling, problems still remain. For example, many critics of feminist post-structuralism argue that in endorsing 'illusory' conceptions of 'womanhood' and 'democracy', the potential for women to possess political agency is lost (see Dillabough, 1998; see also Weir, 1997). We may therefore be collapsing the original democratic project and the notion of women as a political actors into the realm of the unknown and conflating contemporary feminist politics with some of the worst excesses of neo-liberal individualism.[15] The ability of feminists to speak on behalf of, and in the name of, women thus becomes more difficult.

It may also be the case that feminist post-structuralists, by focusing almost exclusively upon individual rather than collective (yet heterogeneous) experiences in the study of women' identities, have inadvertently positioned themselves in the very discourse they wish to deconstruct (i.e., liberal democratic discourse about the importance of the 'self' and 'identity' over community). What still remains problematic then is the desire to take the study of the specificity of women's and girls' (and boys') subjectivity to its unnatural extreme (i.e., we reject in totality a notion of the abstract self), with less room for a rigorous analysis of education and its role in undermining women's potential for agency. As Weir (1997: 190) writes: 'once we get to the point where we reject any abstraction of the individual from contexts, and reject any postulation of the individual's capacity for reflection on contexts, we effectively deny any capacity of agents to criticize and change those contexts'.

Conclusions

What this [chapter] demonstrates is that it is no longer possible to take for granted definitions of democracy based upon liberal principles, nor can we base democratic politics on the interests of women *as* women in the simplest of senses. As Chantal Mouffe (1992*a*) argues, old versions of citizenship have become an obstacle to making democracy work for women in a more genuinely inclusive way. It is time to change the ways in which we struggle for democracy in education—to abandon the 'lion's skin' and construct new and more flexible definitions of citizenship which are not only inclusive at a social level, but are based upon the needs and concerns of contemporary women worldwide. If this is to be accomplished, feminist work must go beyond a feminist engagement with questions of voice, subjectivity and difference. It must also remain committed to the idea that women, as agents of knowledge (not foundationalist knowledge!!), need to make claims about their identity in order to effect broad social and political change. These agents are not uniform in character; they take multiple, dynamic positions which are often in tension. However, such agents should remain part of a heterogeneous community which is concerned with how new social and political formations (e.g., neo-liberalism) structure the relationship between gender and democratic education. In our view, then, the difficult task for feminists is to problematize the gendered premises of democratic education and the identities it constructs, whilst still defending a notion of 'radical democracy' (Fraser, 1996) which accords women's political agency without repressing multiple identities.

The nature of, and quest for, democratic life for women thus remains a key issue in the United Kingdom, North America and elsewhere. As Weiler (1993, 1994) suggests, we are now engaged in a battle over the meaning of education and democracy. The warring factions reside between those who wish to extend our understanding of democracy and those who would restrict access to knowledge and power to the elites. In these circumstances, neither 'equality' or 'difference', as isolated theoretical concepts, can meet the challenges of new gender oppressions in the state. As Phillips (1991*a*) argues, democracy and democratic education need to be 'engendered'.

In short, we have argued that the current state of education feminism and the study of democratic education would be greatly improved by drawing upon the work of feminist political theorists. This focus may provide us with novel conceptual tools for rethinking the role of feminist theory in the development of democratic education and its ability to confront questions about gender which still remain, as they have done since the beginning, as fundamentally political in nature.

NOTES

We are grateful for the support given to Dr. Dillabough by the Social Sciences and Humanities Research Council of Canada and the Leverhume Trust for the research fellowship granted to Dr Arnot for this work. We would also like to thank Jane Gaskell and Wendy Luttrell for comments on an early draft of this [chapter].

1. In the liberal democratic state, the dominant view of women is one which endorses white, middle-class notions of female citizenship.
2. The spread of liberal democracy (and advanced forms of political liberalism) has motivated the development of authoritarian style governments or mass economic deprivation in, for example, Southern and Eastern Europe, Africa, and South America.
3. See Ryan (1992) on the subject of 'benovolent philanthropy'.

4. This comment may appear as a very naive view of the history of feminist research. Indeed, feminist research has a much longer history than the type we refer to here. We refer here only to second wave feminist research.
5. See Whelahan (1995) on the question of liberal feminism.
6. See Acker and Feureverger's (1997) research on the experiences of female academics and their working conditions.
7. It is important to note that 'race', rather than gender, is the central element in this work. However, gender is seen as one facet of a complex set of dynamics which impact on the cultural politics of schooling.
8. We do not wish to suggest that other female scholars in education do not make such alliances. Clearly, scholars such as Elizabeth Ellsworth, Michelle Foster, Avtah Brah, Heida Safia Mirza and Anne Pheonix have all made links between race and gender in their efforts to understand social relations in schooling and the state. However, we refer here to Cameron McCarthy, Michael Apple, and Henry Giroux's work simply to highlight efforts made by male theorists in America to align, as far as possible, with the work of feminists concerned with democratic education.
9. Interestingly, Giroux's now dated view appears to resonate with the maternal view on the development of a women-centered epistemology.
10. This phrase was taken from Haywood and Mac an Ghaill's (1996) work on 'Schooling Masculinities'.
11. There is now a concern with boys' achievement and masculinity in the media and educational research.
12. See Stuart Robinson's work on globalization and the spread of liberal democratic foreign policies in Russia.
13. We do not wish to suggest that questions of identify and difference in educational research are not addressed. However, in the present theoretical; climate, such questions tend not to be addressed in relation to modernist political concerns.
14. Particularly interesting sites for this examination are those national contexts which are thought to be in the process of democratization (so-called 'developing' countries), those countries with less capital wealth than Western states or those states who have taken a neo-liberal stance on contemporary politics.
15. We are not suggesting that all post-structural theories are apolitical. Indeed, as the authors have argued elsewhere, they are not (see Dillabough and Arnot, 1998). However, the project of change for women is, in many cases, lost in the post-structural model.

12 Disjuncture and Difference in the Global Cultural Economy

Arun Appadurai

It takes only the merest acquaintance with the facts of the modern world to note that it is now an interactive system in a sense that is strikingly new. Historians and sociologists, especially those concerned with translocal processes (Hodgson 1974) and the world systems associated with capitalism (Abu-Lughod 1989, Braudel 1981–4, Curtin 1984, Wallerstein 1974, Wolf 1982), have long been aware that the world has been a congeries of large-scale interactions for many centuries. Yet today's world involves interactions of a new order and intensity. Cultural transactions between social groups in the past have generally been restricted, sometimes by the facts of geography and ecology, and at other times by active resistance to interactions with the Other (as in China for much of its history and in Japan before the Meiji Restoration). Where there have been sustained cultural transactions across large parts of the globe, they have usually involved the long-distance journey of commodities (and of the merchants most concerned with them) and of travelers and explorers of every type (Helms 1988, Schafer 1963). The two main forces for sustained cultural interaction before this century have been warfare (and the large-scale political systems sometimes generated by it) and religions of conversion, which have sometimes, as in the case of Islam, taken warfare as one of the legitimate instruments of their expansion. Thus, between travelers and merchants, pilgrims and conquerors, the world has seen much long-distance (and long-term) cultural traffic. This much seems self-evident.

But few will deny that given the problems of time, distance, and limited technologies for the command of resources across vast spaces, cultural dealings between socially and spatially separated groups have, until the past few centuries, been bridged at great cost and sustained over time only with great effort. The forces of cultural gravity seemed always to pull away from the formation of large-scale ecumenes, whether religious, commercial, or political, toward smaller-scale accretions of intimacy and interest.

Sometime in the past few centuries, the nature of this gravitational field seems to have changed. Partly because of the spirit of the expansion of Western maritime interests after 1500, and partly because of the relatively autonomous developments of large and aggressive social formations in the Americas (such as the Aztecs and the Incas), in Eurasia (such as the Mongols and their descendants, the Mughals and Ottomans), in island Southeast Asia (such as the Buginese), and in the kingdoms of precolonial Africa (such as Dahomey), an overlapping set of ecumenes began to emerge, in which congeries of money, commerce, conquest, and migration began to create durable cross-societal bonds. This process was accelerated by the technology transfers and innovations of the late eighteenth and nineteenth centuries (e.g., Bayly 1989), which created complex colonial orders

From *Modernity at Large: Cultural Dimensions of Globalization* (Minneapolis: University of Minnesota Press, 1996), ch. 2, pp. 27–9, 31–43, and notes p. 201. Reprinted with permission.

centered on European capitals and spread throughout the non-European world. This intricate and overlapping set of Eurocolonial worlds (first Spanish and Portuguese, later principally English, French, and Dutch) set the basis for a permanent traffic in ideas of peoplehood and selfhood, which created the imagined communities (Anderson 1983) of recent nationalisms throughout the world.

With what Benedict Anderson has called 'print capitalism,' a new power was unleashed in the world, the power of mass literacy and its attendant large-scale production of projects of ethnic affinity that were remarkably free of the need for face-to-face communication or even of indirect communication between persons and groups. The act of reading things together set the stage for movements based on a paradox—the paradox of constructed primordialism. There is, of course, a great deal else that is involved in the story of colonialism and its dialectically generated nationalisms (Chatterjee 1986), but the issue of constructed ethnicities is surely a crucial strand in this tale.

But the revolution of print capitalism and the cultural affinities and dialogues unleashed by it were only modest precursors to the world we live in now. For in the past century, there has been a technological explosion, largely in the domain of transportation and information, that makes the interactions of a print-dominated world seem as hard-won and as easily erased as the print revolution made earlier forms of cultural traffic appear. For with the advent of the steamship, the automobile, the airplane, the camera, the computer, and the telephone, we have entered into an altogether new condition of neighborliness, even with those most distant from ourselves. Marshall McLuhan, among others, sought to theorize about this world as a 'global village,' but theories such as McLuhan's appear to have overestimated the communitarian implications of the new media order (McLuhan and Powers 1989). We are now aware that with media, each time we are tempted to speak of the global village, we must be reminded that media create communities with 'no sense of place' (Meyrowitz 1985). The world we live in now seems rhizomic (Deleuze and Guattari 1987), even schizophrenic, calling for theories of rootlessness, alienation, and psychological distance between individuals and groups on the one hand, and fantasies (or nightmares) of electronic propinquity on the other. Here, we are close to the central problematic of cultural processes in today's world.

Thus, the curiosity that recently drove Pico Iyer to Asia (1988) is in some ways the product of a confusion between some ineffable McDonaldization of the world and the much subtler play of indigenous trajectories of desire and fear with global flows of people and things. Indeed, Iyer's own impressions are testimony to the fact that, if a global cultural system is emerging, it is filled with ironies and resistances, sometimes camouflaged as passivity and a bottomless appetite in the Asian world for things Western.

The crucial point, however, is that the United States is no longer the puppeteer of a world system of images but is only one node of a complex transnational construction of imaginary landscapes. The world we live in today is characterized by a new role for the imagination in social life. To grasp this new role, we need to bring together the old idea of images, especially mechanically produced images (in the Frankfurt School sense), the idea of the imagined community (in Anderson's sense); and the French idea of the imaginary (*imaginaire*) as a constructed landscape of collective aspirations, which is no more and no less real than the collective representations of Émile Durkheim, now mediated through the complex prism of modern media.

The image, the imagined, the imaginary—these are all terms that direct us to something critical and new in global cultural processes: *the imagination as a social practice*. No longer mere fantasy (opium for the masses whose real work is elsewhere), no longer simple escape (from a world defined principally by more concrete purposes and structures), no longer elite pastime (thus not relevant to the lives of ordinary people), and no longer mere contemplation (irrelevant for new forms of desire and subjectivity), the imagination has become an organized field of social practices, a form of work (in the sense of both labor and culturally organized practice), and a form of negotiation between sites of agency (individuals) and globally defined fields of possibility. This unleashing of the imagination links the play of pastiche (in some settings) to the terror and coercion of states and their competitors. The imagination is now central to all forms of agency, is itself a social fact, and is the key component of the new global order. But to make this claim meaningful, we must address some other issues.

The central problem of today's global interactions is the tension between cultural homogenization and cultural heterogenization. A vast array of empirical facts could be brought to bear on the side of the homogenization argument, and much of it has come from the left end of the spectrum of media studies (Hamelink 1983, Mattelart 1983, Schiller 1976), and some from other perspectives (Gans 1985, Iyer 1988). Most often, the homogenization argument subspeciates into either an argument about Americanization or an argument about commoditization, and very often the two arguments are closely linked. What these arguments fail to consider is that at least as rapidly as forces from various metropolises are brought into new societies they tend to become indigenized in one or another way: this is true of music and housing styles as much as it is true of science and terrorism, spectacles and constitutions. The dynamics of such indigenization have just begun to be explored systemically (Barber 1987; Feld 1988; Hannerz 1987, 1989; Ivy 1988; Nicoll 1989; Yoshimoto 1989), and much more needs to be done. But it is worth noticing that for the people of Irian Jaya, Indonesianization may be more worrisome than Americanization, as Japanization may be for Koreans, Indianization for Sri Lankans, Vietnamization for the Cambodians, and Russianization for the people of Soviet Armenia and the Baltic republics. Such a list of alternative fears to Americanization could be greatly expanded, but it is not a shapeless inventory: for polities of smaller scale, there is always a fear of cultural absorption by polities of larger scale, especially those that are nearby. One man's imagined community is another man's political prison.

This scalar dynamic, which has widespread global manifestations, is also tied to the relationship between nations and states, to which I shall return later. For the moment let us note that the simplification of these many forces (and fears) of homogenization can also be exploited by nation-states in relation to their own minorities, by posing global commoditization (or capitalism, or some other such external enemy) as more real than the threat of its own hegemonic strategies.

The new global cultural economy has to be seen as a complex, overlapping, disjunctive order that cannot any longer be understood in terms of existing center-periphery models (even those that might account for multiple centers and peripheries). Nor is it susceptible to simple models of push and pull (in terms of migration theory), or of surpluses and deficits (as in traditional models of balance of trade), or of consumers and producers (as in most neo-Marxist theories of development). Even the most complex and flexible theories of global development that have come out of the Marxist tradition (Amin 1980, Mandel 1978, Wallerstein 1974, Wolf 1982) are inadequately quirky and have failed to come to terms with what Scott Lash and John Urry have called disorganized capitalism (1987). The complexity of the current global economy has to do with certain fundamental disjunctures between economy, culture, and politics that we have only begun to theorize.[1]

I propose that an elementary framework for exploring such disjunctures is to look at the relationship among five dimensions of global cultural flows that can be termed (a) *ethnoscapes*, (b) *mediascapes*, (c) *technoscapes*, (d) *financescapes*, and (e) *ideoscapes*. The suffix *-scape* allows us to point to the fluid, irregular shapes of these landscapes, shapes that characterize international capital as deeply as they do international clothing styles. These terms with the common suffix *-scape* also indicate that these are not objectively given relations that look the same from every angle of vision but, rather, that they are deeply perspectival constructs, inflected by the historical, linguistic, and political situatedness of different sorts of actors: nation-states, multinationals, diasporic communities, as well as subnational groupings and movements (whether religious, political, or economic), and even intimate face-to-face groups, such as villages, neighborhoods, and families. Indeed, the individual actor is the last locus of this perspectival set of landscapes, for these landscapes are eventually navigated by agents who both experience and constitute larger formations, in part from their own sense of what these landscapes offer.

These landscapes thus are the building blocks of what (extending Benedict Anderson) I would like to call *imagined worlds*, that is, the multiple worlds that are constituted by the historically situated imaginations of persons and groups spread around the globe[...]. An important fact of the world we live in today is that many persons on the globe live in such imagined worlds (and not just in imagined communities) and thus are able to contest and sometimes even subvert the imagined worlds of the official mind and of the entrepreneurial mentality that surround them.

By *ethnoscape,* I mean the landscape of persons who constitute the shifting world in which we live: tourists, immigrants, refugees, exiles, guest workers, and other moving groups and individuals constitute an essential feature of the world and appear to affect the politics of (and between) nations to a hitherto unprecedented degree. This is not to say that there are no relatively stable communities and networks of kinship, friendship, work, and leisure, as well as of birth, residence, and other filial forms. But it is to say that the warp of these stabilities is everywhere shot through with the woof of human motion, as more persons and groups deal with the realities of having to move or the fantasies of wanting to move. What is more, both these realities and fantasies now function on larger scales, as men and women from villages in India think not just of moving to Poona or Madras but of moving to Dubai and Houston, and refugees from Sri Lanka find themselves in South India as well as in Switzerland, just as the Hmong are driven to London as well as to Philadelphia. And as international capital shifts its needs, as production and technology generate different needs, as nation-states shift their policies on refugee populations, these moving groups can never afford to let their imaginations rest too long, even if they wish to.

By *technoscape,* I mean the global configuration, also ever fluid, of technology and the fact that technology, both high and low, both mechanical and informational, now moves at high speeds across various kinds of previously impervious boundaries. Many countries now are the roots of multinational enterprise: a huge steel complex in Libya may involve interests from India, China, Russia, and Japan, providing different components of new technological configurations. The odd distribution of technologies, and thus the peculiarities of these technoscapes, are increasingly driven not by any obvious economies of scale, of political control, or of market rationality but by increasingly complex relationships among money flows, political possibilities, and the availability of both un- and highly skilled labor. So, while India exports waiters and chauffeurs to Dubai and Sharjah, it also exports software engineers to the United States—indentured briefly to Tata-Burroughs or the World Bank, then laundered through the State Department to become wealthy resident aliens, who are in turn objects of seductive messages to invest their money and know-how in federal and state projects in India.

The global economy can still be described in terms of traditional indicators (as the World Bank continues to do) and studied in terms of traditional comparisons (as in Project Link at the University of Pennsylvania), but the complicated technoscapes (and the shifting ethnoscapes) that underlie these indicators and comparisons are further out of the reach of the queen of social sciences than ever before. How is one to make a meaningful comparison of wages in Japan and the United States or of real-estate costs in New York and Tokyo, without taking sophisticated account of the very complex fiscal and investment flows that link the two economies through a global grid of currency speculation and capital transfer?

Thus it is useful to speak as well of *financescapes,* as the disposition of global capital is now a more mysterious, rapid, and difficult landscape to follow than ever before, as currency markets, national stock exchanges, and commodity speculations move megamonies through national turnstiles at blinding speed, with vast, absolute implications for small differences in percentage points and time units. But the critical point is that the global relationship among ethnoscapes, technoscapes, and financescapes is deeply disjunctive and profoundly unpredictable because each of these landscapes is subject to its own constraints and incentives (some political, some informational, and some technoenvironmental), at the same time as each acts as a constraint and a parameter for movements in the others. Thus, even an elementary model of global political economy must take into account the deeply disjunctive relationships among human movement, technological flow, and financial transfers.

Further refracting these disjunctures (which hardly form a simple, mechanical global infrastructure in any case) are what I call *mediascapes* and *ideoscapes,* which are closely related landscapes of images.

Mediascapes refer both to the distribution of the electronic capabilities to produce and disseminate information (newspapers, magazines, television stations, and film-production studios), which are now available to a growing number of private and public interests throughout the world, and to the images of the world created by these media. These images involve many complicated inflections, depending on their mode (documentary or entertainment), their hardware (electronic or preelectronic), their audiences (local, national, or transnational), and the interests of those who own and control them. What is most important about these mediascapes is that they provide (especially in their television, film, and cassette forms) large and complex repertoires of images, narratives, and ethnoscapes to viewers throughout the world, in which the world of commodities and the world of news and politics are profoundly mixed. What this means is that many audiences around the world experience the media themselves as a complicated and interconnected repertoire of print, celluloid, electronic screens, and billboards. The lines between the realistic and the fictional landscapes they see are blurred, so that the farther away these audiences are from the direct experiences of metropolitan life, the more likely they are to construct imagined worlds that are chimerical, aesthetic, even fantastic objects, particularly if assessed by the criteria of some other perspective, some other imagined world.

Mediascapes, whether produced by private or state interests, tend to be image-centered, narrative-based accounts of strips of reality, and what they offer to those who experience and transform them is a series of elements (such as characters, plots, and textual forms) out of which scripts can be formed of imagined lives, their own as well as those of others living in other places. These scripts can and do get disaggregated into complex sets of metaphors by which people live (Lakoff and Johnson 1980) as they help to constitute narratives of the Other and protonarratives of possible lives, fantasies that could become prolegomena to the desire for acquisition and movement.

Ideoscapes are also concatenations of images, but they are often directly political and frequently have to do with the ideologies of states and the counterideologies of movements explicitly oriented to capturing state power or a piece of it. These ideoscapes are composed of elements of the Enlightenment worldview, which consists of a chain of ideas, terms, and images, including *freedom, welfare, rights, sovereignty, representation*, and the master term *democracy*. The master narrative of the Enlightenment (and its many variants in Britain, France, and the United States) was constructed with a certain internal logic and presupposed a certain relationship between reading, representation, and the public sphere. (For the dynamics of this process in the early history of the United States, see Warner 1990.) But the diaspora of these terms and images across the world, especially since the nineteenth century, has loosened the internal coherence that held them together in a Euro-American master narrative and provided instead a loosely structured synopticon of politics, in which different nation-states, as part of their evolution, have organized their political cultures around different keywords (e.g., Williams 1976).

As a result of the differential diaspora of these keywords, the political narratives that govern communication between elites and followers in different parts of the world involve problems of both a semantic and pragmatic nature: semantic to the extent that words (and their lexical equivalents) require careful translation from context to context in their global movements, and pragmatic to the extent that the use of these words by political actors and their audiences may be subject to very different sets of contextual conventions that mediate their translation into public politics. Such conventions are not only matters of the nature of political rhetoric: for example, what does the aging Chinese leadership mean when it refers to the dangers of hooliganism? What does the South Korean leadership mean when it speaks of discipline as the key to democratic industrial growth?

These conventions also involve the far more subtle question of what sets of communicative genres are valued in what way (newspapers versus cinema, for example) and what sorts of pragmatic genre conventions govern the collective readings of different kinds of text. So, while an Indian audience may be attentive to the resonances of a political speech in terms of some keywords and phrases reminiscent of Hindi cinema, a Korean audience may respond to the subtle codings of Buddhist or neo-Confucian rhetoric encoded in a political document. The very relationship of reading to hearing and seeing may vary in important ways that determine the morphology of these different ideoscapes as they shape themselves in different national and transnational contexts. This globally variable synaesthesia has hardly even been noted, but it demands urgent analysis. Thus *democracy* has clearly become a master term, with powerful echoes from Haiti and Poland to the former Soviet Union and China, but it sits at the center of a variety of ideoscapes, composed of distinctive pragmatic configurations of rough translations of other central terms from the vocabulary of the Enlightenment. This creates ever new terminological kaleidoscopes, as states (and the groups that seek to capture them) seek to pacify populations whose own ethnoscapes are in motion and whose mediascapes may create severe problems for the ideoscapes with which they are presented. The fluidity of ideoscapes is complicated in particular by the growing diasporas (both voluntary and involuntary) of intellectuals who continuously inject new meaning-streams into the discourse of democracy in different parts of the world.

This extended terminological discussion of the five terms I have coined sets the basis for a tentative formulation about the conditions under which current global flows occur: they occur in and through the growing disjunctures among ethnoscapes, technoscapes, financescapes, mediascapes, and ideoscapes. This formulation, the core of my model of global cultural flow, needs some explanation. First, people, machinery, money, images, and ideas now follow increasingly nonisomorphic paths; of course, at all periods in human history, there have been some disjunctures in the flows of these things, but the sheer speed, scale, and volume of each of these flows are now so great that the disjunctures have become central to the politics of global culture. The Japanese are notoriously hospitable to ideas and are stereotyped as inclined to export (all) and import (some) goods, but they are also notoriously closed to immigration, like the Swiss, the Swedes, and the Saudis. Yet the Swiss and the Saudis accept populations of guest workers, thus creating labor diasporas of Turks, Italians, and other circum-Mediterranean groups. Some such guest-worker groups maintain continuous contact with their home nations, like the Turks, but others, like high-level South Asian migrants, tend to desire lives in their new homes, raising anew the problem of reproduction in a deterritorialized context.

Deterritorialization, in general, is one of the central forces of the modern world because it brings laboring populations into the lower-class sectors and spaces of relatively wealthy societies, while sometimes creating exaggerated and intensified senses of criticism or attachment to politics in the home state. Deterritorialization, whether of Hindus, Sikhs, Palestinians, or Ukrainians, is now at the core of a variety of global fundamentalisms, including Islamic and Hindu fundamentalism. In the Hindu case, for example, it is clear that the overseas movement of Indians has been exploited by a variety of interests both within and outside India to create a complicated network of finances and religious identifications, by which the problem of cultural reproduction for Hindus abroad has become tied to the politics of Hindu fundamentalism at home.

At the same time, deterritorialization creates new markets for film companies, art impresarios, and travel agencies, which thrive on the need of the deterritorialized population for contact with its homeland. Naturally, these invented homelands, which constitute the mediascapes of deterritorialized groups, can often become sufficiently fantastic and one-sided that they provide the material for new ideoscapes in which ethnic conflicts can begin to erupt. The creation of Khalistan, an invented homeland of the deterritorialized Sikh population of England, Canada, and the United States, is one example of the bloody potential in such mediascapes as they interact with the internal colonialisms of the nation-state (e.g., Hechter 1975). The West Bank, Namibia, and Eritrea are other theaters for the enactment of the bloody negotiation between existing nation-states and various deterritorialized groupings.

It is in the fertile ground of deterritorialization, in which money, commodities, and persons are involved in ceaselessly chasing each other around the world, that the mediascapes and ideoscapes of the modern world find their fractured and fragmented counterpart. For the ideas and images produced by mass media often are only partial guides to the goods and experiences that deterritorialized populations transfer to one another. In Mira Nair's brilliant film *India Cabaret*, we see the multiple loops of this fractured deterritorialization as young women, barely competent in Bombay's metropolitan glitz, come to seek their fortunes as cabaret dancers and prostitutes in Bombay, entertaining men in clubs with dance formats derived wholly from the prurient dance sequences of Hindi films. These scenes in turn cater to ideas about Western and foreign women and their looseness, while they provide tawdry career alibis for these women. Some of these women come from Kerala, where cabaret clubs and the pornographic film industry have blossomed, partly in response to the purses and tastes of Keralites returned from the Middle East, where their diasporic lives away from women distort their very sense of what the relations between men and women might be. These tragedies of displacement could certainly be replayed in a more detailed analysis of the relations between the Japanese and German sex tours to Thailand and the tragedies of the sex trade in Bangkok, and in other similar loops that tie together fantasies about the Other, the conveniences and seductions of travel, the economics of global trade, and the brutal mobility fantasies that dominate gender politics in many parts of Asia and the world at large.

While far more could be said about the cultural politics of deterritorialization and the larger sociology of displacement that it expresses, it is appropriate at this juncture to bring in the role of the nation-state in the disjunctive global economy of culture today. The relationship between states and nations is everywhere an embattled one. It is possible to say that in many societies the nation and the state have become one another's projects. That is, while nations (or more properly groups with ideas about nationhood) seek to capture or co-opt states and state power, states simultaneously seek to capture and monopolize ideas about nationhood (Baruah 1986, Chatterjee 1986, Nandy 1989a). In general, separatist transnational movements, including those that have included terror in their methods, exemplify nations in search of states. Sikhs, Tamil Sri Lankans, Basques, Moros, Quebecois—each of these represents imagined communities that seek to create states of their own or carve pieces out of existing states. States, on the other hand, are everywhere seeking to monopolize the moral resources of community, either by flatly claiming perfect coevality between nation and state, or by systematically museumizing and representing all the groups within them in a variety of heritage politics that seems remarkably uniform throughout the world (Handler 1988, Herzfeld 1982, McQueen 1988).

Here, national and international mediascapes are exploited by nation-states to pacify separatists or even the potential fissiparousness of all ideas of difference. Typically, contemporary nation-states do this by exercising taxonomic control over difference, by creating various kinds of international spectacle to domesticate difference, and by seducing small groups with the fantasy of self-display on some sort of global or cosmopolitan stage. One important new feature of global cultural politics, tied to the disjunctive relationships among the various landscapes discussed earlier, is that state and nation are at each other's throats, and the hyphen that links them is now less an icon of conjuncture than an index of disjuncture. This disjunctive relationship between nation and state has two levels: at the level of any given nation-state, it means that there is a battle of the imagination, with state and nation seeking to cannibalize one another. Here is the seedbed of brutal separatisms—majoritarianisms that seem to have appeared from nowhere and microidentities that have become political projects within the nation-state. At another level, this disjunctive relationship is deeply entangled with the global disjunctives discussed throughout this chapter: ideas of nationhood appear to be steadily increasing in scale and regularly crossing existing state boundaries, sometimes, as with the Kurds, because previous identities stretched across vast national spaces or, as with the Tamils in Sri Lanka, the dormant threads of a transnational diaspora have been activated to ignite the micropolitics of a nation-state.

In discussing the cultural politics that have subverted the hyphen that links the nation to the state, it is especially important not to forget the mooring of such politics in the irregularities that now characterize disorganized capital (Kothari 1989, Lash and Urry 1987). Because labor, finance, and technology are now so widely separated, the volatilities that underlie movements for nationhood (as large as transnational Islam on the one hand, or as small as the movement of the Gurkhas for a separate state in Northeast India) grind against the vulnerabilities that characterize the relationships between states. States find themselves pressed to stay open by the forces of media, technology, and travel that have fueled consumerism throughout the world and have increased the craving, even in the non-Western world, for new commodities and spectacles. On the other hand, these very cravings can become caught up in new ethnoscapes, mediascapes, and, eventually, ideoscapes, such as democracy in China, that the state cannot tolerate as threats to its own control over ideas of nationhood and peoplehood. States throughout the world are under siege, especially where contests over the ideoscapes of democracy are fierce and fundamental, and where there are radical disjunctures between ideoscapes and technoscapes (as in the case of very small countries that lack contemporary technologies of production and information); or between ideoscapes and financescapes (as in countries such as Mexico or Brazil, where international lending influences national politics to a very large degree); or between ideoscapes and ethnoscapes (as in Beirut, where diasporic, local, and translocal filiations are suicidally at battle); or between ideoscapes and mediascapes (as in many countries in the Middle East and Asia) where the lifestyles represented on both national and international TV and cinema completely overwhelm and undermine the rhetoric of national politics. In the Indian case, the myth of the law-breaking hero has emerged to mediate this naked struggle between the pieties and realities of Indian politics, which has grown increasingly brutalized and corrupt (Vachani 1989).

The transnational movement of the martial arts, particularly through Asia, as mediated by the Hollywood and Hong Kong film industries (Zarilli 1995) is a rich illustration of the ways in which long-standing martial arts traditions, reformulated to meet the fantasies of contemporary (sometimes lumpen) youth populations, create new cultures of masculinity and violence, which are in turn the fuel for increased violence in national and international politics. Such violence is in turn the spur to an increasingly rapid and amoral arms trade that penetrates the entire world. The worldwide spread of the AK-47 and the Uzi, in films, in corporate and state security, in terror, and in police and military activity, is a reminder that apparently simple technical uniformities often conceal an increasingly complex set of loops, linking images of violence to aspirations for community in some imagined world.

Returning then to the ethnoscapes with which I began, the central paradox of ethnic politics in today's world is that primordia (whether of language or skin color or neighborhood or kinship) have become globalized. That is, sentiments, whose greatest force is in their ability to ignite intimacy into a political state and turn locality into a staging ground for identity, have become spread over vast and irregular spaces as groups move yet stay linked to one another through sophisticated media capabilities. This is not to deny that such primordia are often the product of invented traditions (Hobsbawm and Ranger 1983) or retrospective affiliations, but to emphasize that because of the disjunctive and unstable interplay of commerce, media, national policies, and consumer fantasies, ethnicity, once a genie contained in the bottle of some sort of locality (however large), has now become a global force, forever slipping in and through the cracks between states and borders.

But the relationship between the cultural and economic levels of this new set of global disjunctures is not a simple one-way street in which the terms of global cultural politics are set wholly by, or confined wholly within, the vicissitudes of international flows of technology, labor, and finance, demanding only a modest modification of existing neo-Marxist models of uneven development and state formation. There is a deeper change, itself driven by the disjunctures among all the landscapes I have discussed and constituted by their continuously fluid and uncertain interplay, that concerns the relationship between production and consumption in today's global economy. Here, I begin with Marx's famous (and often mined) view of the fetishism of the commodity and suggest that this fetishism has been replaced in the world at large (now seeing the world as one large, interactive system, composed of many complex subsystems) by two mutually supportive descendants, the first of which I call production fetishism and the second, the fetishism of the consumer.

By *production fetishism* I mean an illusion created by contemporary transnational production loci that masks translocal capital, transnational earning flows, global management, and often faraway workers (engaged in various kinds of high-tech putting-out operations) in the idiom and spectacle of local (sometimes even worker) control, national productivity, and territorial sovereignty. To the extent that various kinds of free-trade zones have become the models for production at large, especially of high-tech commodities, production has itself become a fetish, obscuring not social relations as such but the relations of production, which are increasingly transnational. The locality (both in the sense of the local factory or site of production and in the extended sense of the nation-state) becomes a fetish that disguises the globally dispersed forces that actually drive the production process. This generates alienation (in Marx's sense) twice intensified, for its social sense is now compounded by a complicated spatial dynamic that is increasingly global.

As for the *fetishism of the consumer*, I mean to indicate here that the consumer has been transformed through commodity flows (and the mediascapes, especially of advertising, that accompany them) into a sign, both in Baudrillard's sense of a simulacrum that only asymptotically approaches the form of a real social agent, and in the sense of a mask for the real seat of agency, which is not the consumer but the producer and the many forces that constitute production. Global advertising is the key technology for the worldwide dissemination of a plethora of creative and culturally well-chosen ideas of consumer agency. These images of agency are increasingly distortions of a world of merchandising so subtle that the consumer is consistently helped to believe that he or she is an actor, where in fact he or she is at best a chooser.

The globalization of culture is not the same as its homogenization, but globalization involves the use of a variety of instruments of homogenization (armaments, advertising techniques, language hegemonies, and clothing styles) that are absorbed into local political and cultural economies, only to be repatriated as heterogeneous dialogues of national sovereignty, free enterprise, and fundamentalism in which the state plays an increasingly delicate role: too much openness to global flows, and the nation-state is threatened by revolt, as in the China syndrome; too little, and the state exits the international stage, as Burma, Albania, and North Korea in various ways have done. In general, the state has become the arbitrageur of this *repatriation of difference* (in the form of goods, signs, slogans, and styles). But this repatriation or export of the designs and commodities of difference continuously exacerbates the internal politics of majoritarianism and homogenization, which is most frequently played out in debates over heritage.

Thus the central feature of global culture today is the politics of the mutual effort of sameness and difference to cannibalize one another and thereby proclaim their successful hijacking of the twin Enlightenment ideas of the triumphantly universal and the resiliently particular. This mutual cannibalization shows its ugly face in riots, refugee flows, state-sponsored torture, and ethnocide (with or without state support). Its brighter side is in the expansion of many individual horizons of hope and fantasy, in the global spread of oral rehydration therapy and other low-tech instruments of well-being, in the susceptibility even of South Africa to the force of global opinion, in the inability of the Polish state to repress its own working classes, and in the growth of a wide range of progressive, transnational alliances. Examples of both sorts could be multiplied. The critical point is that both sides of the coin of global cultural process today are products of the infinitely varied mutual contest of sameness and difference on a stage characterized by radical disjunctives between different sorts of global flows and the uncertain landscapes created in and through these disjunctures.

NOTE

1. One major exception is Fredric Jameson, whose work on the relationship between postmodernism and late capitalism has in many ways inspired this essay. The debate

between Jameson and Aijaz Ahmad in *Social Text,* however, shows that the creation of a globalizing Marxist narrative in cultural matters is difficult territory indeed (Ahmad 1987). My own effort in this context is to begin a restructuring of the Marxist narrative (by stressing lags and disjunctures) that many Marxists might find abhorrent. Such a restructuring has to avoid the dangers of obliterating difference within the Third World, eliding the social referent (as some French postmodernists seem inclined to do), and retaining the narrative authority of the Marxist tradition, in favor of greater attention to global fragmentation, uncertainty, and difference.

Part Three

Education, Globalization, and the Nation-State

The central question of the age may be considered to be that of the impact of globalization on the nation-state and on education. Castells (2000) who is one of the leading commentators on globalization, argues that new technologies and the associated changes in the way we produce goods and services has produced a new capitalist era: the information age. He should be credited for a comprehensive survey of how changes in the technology and the economy have created a new phase in the global economy and how they are affecting nation-states (Castells 1997, 1998, 2000). However, while he puts great emphasis on knowledge in the knowledge economy and by implication, education, he has surprisingly little to say about either. (See Guile, Ch. 24, below, on education and the knowledge economy). In one way this book can be seen as dedicated to both tasks.[1] He may be on stronger and certainly more interesting ground in arguing that global changes in technology may also change identities (Castells 1997).

The degree to which this is true will largely turn on how the various dimensions of globalization will impact on the nation-state. We have seen that modern education systems had several purposes but that one was the creation of citizens and, relatedly, social solidarity. Green (Ch. 13, below) sets out the case that this aspect of education remains of importance. However, there are those such as McCarthy and Dimitriades (Ch. 14, below) who argue that globalization fundamentally challenges this view of education. In their opinion what is missing from accounts of the state and education is the way in which a popular global culture, educational policy, and classroom practice interact to reproduce inequalities and unintended outcomes. However, key to their theorizing is the need to understand the elements of stability that Green has identified with the more unpredictable outcomes and interruptions created by elements of globalization.

To understand what is at stake in this debate it may be helpful to clarify what is meant by social solidarity or cohesion and also to link it to issues of social justice. Green, Preston, and Sabates (2003) have helpfully identified six possible characteristics involved in social cohesion: (1) shared norms and values; (2) a sense of shared identity or belonging to a common community; (3) a sense of continuity and stability; (4) a society with institutions for sharing risks and providing collective welfare; (5) equitable distribution of rights, opportunities, wealth, and income; and (6) a strong civil society and active citizenry. This list doesn't distinguish between the sentiments and feelings involved in social solidarity (1)–(3) or, as they put it, social cohesion and the conditions that might create it (4–6). Not all of these conditions may be necessary to create a sense of shared norms and values or indeed identity. Conditions (4–6) may be not be necessary to create (1)–(3) as the counter-cases of the United States or Singapore might suggest.

Social justice or fairness in the selection of who wins or loses in the competition for credentials may also be related to social cohesion. Groups marginalized through inequality may not feel the same degree of solidarity as those that have done well. When we consider these conditions, the questions that underlie McCarthy and Dimitriades's criticisms appear clear. There are many young people who may well feel a closer identity to global cultures related to music, videos, and film than to any sense of shared norms or identity. Indeed, given the emphasis on identity politics, the role of state education in forging a sense of a common bond among young people is clearly being challenged. The example that we have referred to in the Introduction, of the way the French state has dealt with aspects of Muslim culture, points up the difficulties involved.

The carrier for much of global culture for young people is the market. However, Blackmore (Ch. 15, below) views the advent of neo-liberalism and the fostering of market conditions in areas that were once seen as the preserve of the state, such as education, with critical concern. For Blackmore, many of the advances that have been made by feminism have been associated with state policies, either through feminists working within the state or by pressure upon it. This is especially true in relation to education and the labour market. However, the more the state withdraws to allow the market to enter the less opportunities there are for women's rights to be developed.

Robertson, Bonal, and Dale (Ch. 16, below) continue the theme of how the role of the state has been changed by globalization, while elevating the role of markets in education. The question for them is how space, notions of territory, and governance are redefined by globalization. Having developed a theory as to how we might better understand how the state has changed in the light of these concepts they apply the analysis to the General Agreement on Trade in Services (GATS). The logic of the process that has been set in train by GATS is that ever more aspects of education that have been considered the preserve of the state for the reasons given by Green will become marketized.

The role of multilateral agencies has not only established the principles by which markets for education can be opened up but also provided some of the ideological justification for such policies. Rivzi and Lingard (Ch. 17, below) chart the ways in which the 'rich nations think tank', the Organization for Economic Cooperation and Development (OECD) has established a climate in which the default position is that current policies related to global economic competition should be prioritized and that markets are generally considered a 'good'.

Finally, in the light of the above debates, there is a need to reconsider not only the role of the state but also the role of education in fostering democracy. Olssen (Ch. 18, below) argues that there is still an important role for education and seeks to establish the social and philosophical grounding for this position. Given the kinds of concerns raised by McCarthy and Dimitriades this becomes an urgent project because, while economic and political interests may be a crucial determinant in the way education is reconstructed, unless there are alternatives to hand that we can consider critique of the present system will remain empty.

NOTE

1. See Guile, Ch. 24, below, for a discussion of the nature of the knowledge in the knowledge economy.

13 Education, Globalization, and the Nation State

Andy Green

Globalization has become a topic of great interest to social scientists, not only in the field of economics, but also in political and cultural studies. Despite the volume of theoretical work in this area, however, the issues it throws up have only recently begun to be taken up by educational theorists and, even here, somewhat one-sidedly within the postmodernist tradition. [. . .]

In its full-blown form (Reich, 1991; Ohmae, 1996; Waters, 1995), globalization theory predicts the end of the national economy and the end of the nation-state as the primary unit of political organization and loyalty. It also argues the emergence of a borderless world (Ohmae, 1990) where national cultures are transformed by global communications and cultural hybridization. The implications of all this for education are potentially immense. National governments would cease to control their education systems, which would gradually converge towards some regional or global norm, divested of any specific national characteristics. The historic functions of national education systems, to transmit national cultures and to reproduce national labour power, would become obsolete. The national education system, the historical product and key institutional support of the nation-state, would effectively cease to have a function in the new order.

[. . .]

In *The Work of Nations*, Reich paints a frightening picture of social fragmentation in America. The affluent fifth of society, the symbolic analysts, 'are selling their expertise on the global market', enhancing their standard of living 'even as that of other Americans declines' (1991, p. 250). They no longer depend on the economic performance of other Americans and are increasingly unwilling to support them. They exist in a hermetically sealed world of privatized transport, communications, education and health care and are fast retreating into residential enclaves which are privately maintained and policed (there are now more private security guards than police in America) (Reich, 1991, p. 269). The affluent American is increasingly seceding from the rest of society, and so too, in their different ways, are other, less privileged, groups who no longer have a real stake. Where are the bonds of social cohesion here? As Reich says: '[t]he question is whether the habits of citizenship are sufficiently strong to withstand the centrifugal forces of the new global economy' (1991, p. 304).

However, the very question, in a sense, answers the debate about political globalization. As global forces in economics and culture create more fissiparous and more individualistic societies, so the need for countervailing sources of social solidarity grows. Arguably, nation states cannot refuse this role—or at least if they do, the result will be a chaos which finally invades even the enclaves of the privileged. As Hirst and Thompson put it in unambiguous terms: 'In an individualistic and pluralist society, where there are few common standards, where strong binding collectivities have declined and been replaced by communities of choice, and where informal social sanctions have weakened,

From *Education, Globalization, and the Nation State* (Basingstoke: Macmillan, 1997), ch. 7, pp. 130, 169–72, 181–6. Reprinted with permission.

then the role of law is more rather than less necessary' (1996, p. 436).

Marx once wrote that 'socialism or barbarism' was the choice facing capitalist societies. Most governments in the advanced states today, needless to say, would not agree. However, under the impact of global capitalism, and despite the current neo-liberal vogue, governments may soon find themselves facing another dichotomy more redolent of Hobbes than Marx—between the state or barbarism. Let us hope that by then democracy is still part of the equation. The cohesive civic nation may still be the best guarantor of this.

Education and Internationalization

How has education been affected by these globalizing trends in political economy and culture? Globalization theory, together with its twin postmodernism, has to date elicited a number of responses to these questions within the field of education research, most of them pointing towards a fundamental shift in the very nature of education as a national or state 'project'. Jane Kenway (1992) has argued that economic globalization and the information revolution augur radical changes in the very nature of the learning process, promoting a new commodification of education and an uncoupling of learning from its traditional institutional locations. Donald (1992) has contended that postmodern, globalized societies have gone so far in cultural diversification and fragmentation that the old educational goal of transmitting common cultures is now obsolete and beyond reclaim. Most recently, Usher and Edwards (1994), also from a postmodern perspective, have argued that global postmodernity has brought both a 'crisis in rationality' and a pluralization of cultures that fundamentally undermines the modernist goals of national education as a unified 'project'. Education can no longer control or be controlled; it can 'no longer readily function as a means of reproducing society or as an instrument of large-scale social engineering' (p. 211). With the progressive replacement of universal and standardized education systems by virtual learning networks, schools will cease to act as dispensers of rational, disciplinary knowledge, and socialization will be reduced to the development and certification of individual competence. National objectives in education will be limited to 'fulfilling the requirements of the economy under conditions of global competition' (p. 175).

The arguments in this book are against such extreme scenarios of educational transformation; rather than a full-scale globalization of education, the evidence suggests a partial internationalization of education systems which falls far short of an end to national education *per se*. National education systems *have* become more porous in recent years. They have been partially internationalized through increased student and staff mobility, through widespread policy borrowing and through attempts to enhance the internationalized dimension of curricula at secondary and higher levels. They have also grown more like each other in certain important ways. However, there is little evidence that national systems as such are disappearing or that national states have ceased to control them. They may seem less distinctive and their roles are changing but they still undoubtedly attempt to serve national ends. The concluding sections of this chapter explore these themes.

Writers like Jane Kenway (1992) and Edwards (1994) have made much of the implications for education of new information technologies and the way these can interact with growing international markets. There is no doubt that the acceleration and enhancement of international communications through satellite, fibre-optic cable and the so-called 'information highway' opens up new possibilities for education. E-mail, internet, video-conferencing and the like now give access, to those who have the technology and the expertise, to the virtual college. Theoretically, learning need no longer be constrained by the limitations of time and space. Just as Gutenberg paved the way for the independent itinerant scholars of Renaissance Europe, so the global web can create a new generation of mental travellers, only this time they need not leave their terminals.

It seems unlikely that these developments will de-institutionalize education, at least at the compulsory levels. Minding, socializing and tutoring children still requires physical proximity and contact and institutions which support these processes (Erault, 1991). Computer-based, interactive learning software has yet to be developed to its full potential, but even when it is, it seems unlikely that it can replace the role of the teacher in the classroom since children still have to learn how to learn (EU Commission, 1996). The notion that schools can be entirely replaced by 'networks of information' (Usher and Edwards, 1994), where children engage only in virtual learning, is no more probable now than when Ivan Illich first proposed the de-schooling of society in 1971. However, at the higher education level, information technology may well lead to a substantial decoupling of learning from institutional spaces. Already university distance learning courses are conducted within and across many of the advanced nations, greatly increasing the international cross-fertilization of university studies. There are certainly limits to this process of virtualization in higher education not least because modern scientific and technological research requires the concentration of enormous resources in equipment and laboratories which must be located in physical spaces. The humanities, however, do not require this since the only physical plant is the library and this, in time, can also be made virtual with access through the internet. Non-research student learning, moreover, can, and no doubt will, increasingly adopt distance modes, which are both cheaper and more convenient for many adult students, and this will add to the internationalization of higher education.

[...]

Governments in the advanced states have invariably retained their control over the key areas of curricula, assessment and certification and have increasingly sought to steer their systems towards certain educational outcomes through the setting of targets. In those countries where there was formerly little government control over curricula and assessment this has been increased, as in England and Wales, where a national curriculum was introduced for the first time in 1988, and even in the USA, where the federal government has become more interventionist in relation to standards and assessment (Green and Steedman, 1993). In Japan, where there has been much talk about deregulation and diversification, the central education ministry, the Monbusho, seems to have lost few of its powers, and curriculum control is vigorously maintained through the national *course of study*, through the strengthening of the key areas of moral education, and through state controls over textbooks which have recently been simplified but not abandoned (Schoppa, 1991; Horio, 1988).

For all the postmodern protestations to the contrary, and despite the effects of globalizing trends, governments across the world still exercise considerable control over their national education systems and still seek to use them to achieve national goals. The nature of these goals, and the balance of priorities in different regions, has undoubtedly changed over time, as this chapter has sought to demonstrate. However, in the majority of countries governments still see education as a process of nation-building which involves both economic and social objectives. Education systems are still national institutions devoted, in varying degrees, to the preparation of future workers and the formation of future citizens.

Skills formation has been a major objective of education for governments both in the developing world and in the advanced nations. For the newly industrializing nations it is frequently seen as a condition of economic development. For the advanced nations it is seen as one of the principal means for maintaining high standards of living in the face of increasing global competition, particularly from the developing countries. The UK government 1994 White Paper, *Helping Business to Win* (HM Government, 1994), stated this in bald terms: 'The UK faces a world of increasing change; of ever-fiercer competition; of growing consumer power, and a world in which our wealth is more and more dependent on the knowledge, skills and motivation of our people.' This encapsulates a policy language now ubiquitous in official reports from governments in all advanced nations.

Economic 'globalization' has not only increased the pressure of competition but it has also changed its terms for the advanced states. As most developed nations now realize, in the face of increasing economic competition from low wage nations such as Vietnam, Thailand, Malaysia and China—not to mention the Latin American states as they come on stream—there is little mileage left in competing on wage costs for countries which seek to maintain a high standard of living. They have no alternative now but to move into areas of high value-added, knowledge-based production and services and these require, above all, high levels of skill and flexibility among their workforces (Finegold and Soskice, 1988). What is more, given the current difficulty of managing national economies through fiscal, monetary and trade regulations, where these are ever more difficult to impose, governments have found themselves increasingly interested in the area of skills formation because it is at least amenable to national control (Reich, 1991).

It may be said that the current obsession of western governments with education and training policy also owes something to political rhetoric and electoral pragmatism. As Avis et al. (1996) argue, education and training policy has been much hyped by governments because it is less contentious than employment and fiscal policies, because it allows them to make relatively risk-free election promises which few will oppose, and because it serves to mask the growing structural unemployment which is now endemic in most advanced economies (see also Ainley, Gokulsing and Tysome, 1996). Many economists see no proven link between skills and productivity and others argue that increasing the supply of skills is secondary to raising the demand for them, which is much more difficult (Keep and Mayhew, 1993). However, voters rarely question government claims that more education and training improves national economic competitiveness because they know that on an individual level, at least, human capital investment does pay dividends. Whatever the political calculations and however valid the economic reasoning, it remains the case that most governments see education and training as the critical factor in national economic performance and competitive advantage. As the CBI wrote in their influential 1989 report, *Towards a Skills Revolution*: 'Individuals are now the only sustainable source of competitive advantage' (CBI, 1989, p. 9). More perhaps than ever before, governments use education and training as an instrument for these—still very national—ends.

The situation as regards education and citizen formation is perhaps more complex. From a global perspective, it would appear that forming citizens and shaping national identities are still primary functions of education in most countries. National curricula still tend to place great emphasis on national languages and cultures. History is used to popularize national myths and to promote national identities; literature to celebrate the national language and literary achievements; and civic and moral education to instil national values and notions of good citizenship. Many schools still incorporate into their daily rituals the symbolic paraphernalia of nationhood, with the flying of flags, the singing of anthems and the recital of pledges and declarations. In Japan children clean classrooms, prepare meals and monitor each other's behaviour to develop the qualities of social cooperation and individual discipline and persistence which are seen as central to the nation's values (White, 1987). Governments frequently call on education to promote national values and culture as a source of social cohesion and national solidarity.

In some countries, such as Singapore, the emphasis is on a kind of civic nationalism which aims to integrate multiple ethnic cultures and religions into a single, though diverse, national identity. In other countries, more strident and ethnically based notions of nationalism have prevailed. Schools have one-sidedly promoted the culture and language of the dominant group, enhancing its sense of common identity while marginalizing and excluding minority groups and cultures. With the demise of the former communist regimes in Eastern Europe, a host of new ethnic nationalisms have emerged in the successor states. Dominant groups have frequently adopted exclusivist policies in education emphasizing particular languages and cultures at the expense of others, or—at the extreme—promoting ethnically segregated schooling, as in Latvia and Lithuania.

In the main, this use of education for national identity-building has been most prevalent historically among emerging nation states, and states reconstructing after wars and revolutions. As Christie Davies has written:

> Generally, we find a strong national focus in education in most early nation building processes as educational systems are established *pari passu* with the development of modern nation states, for example in Europe, the USA and Japan. In such periods education is not only organized and geared to national traditions and state interests, but is also expected to support national identity and expand national manpower resources. (1993, p. 332)

[...] In the postwar period nation-building through education has been most evident in the new states which have emerged through decolonization, the collapse of former 'empires' and other forms of national transition. Most conspicuously, it has been among the new nation states undergoing periods of accelerated economic development and state formation that education has been used most deliberately as an instrument for forming citizens and forging new national identities.

Among some of the older, advanced nation states this process has also been visible in the postwar period, particularly where countries have been engaged in major reconstruction as with Germany and Japan after the Second World War. However, these cases aside, there is a sense in which education systems in the advanced western states in the recent period have ceased to be so centrally concerned with questions of citizen formation and national identity. As Robert Cowen has recently written, there is an 'atonishing displacement of "society" within the late modern educational pattern' (Cowen, 1996). The reasons for this are complex. In part they derive from the overwhelming policy priority given by governments to questions of skills formation and economic performance, and this, as we have seen, is one consequence of the spread of global markets. However, they go beyond this. In all western states there has been a steady rise in individualistic and consumerist values and identities, and with it a gradual erosion of collective and community identities and beliefs. This has been enhanced, in many states, by the advance of neo-liberal ideologies and the encroachment of the market into every area of life. As national services and resources are increasingly privatized and subjected to the competitive forces of the market, so the public domain is diminished and the legitimacy of collective goals reduced (Ranson, 1994). Education has remained a public service, for the main part, and governments have continued to exercise powerful control over it. However, the scope of government ambitions in education has reduced in many countries. National economic goals are still held inviolate and education is instrumentally geared towards these ends. However, broader national educational objectives in terms of social cohesion and citizenship formation have become increasingly confused and neglected, in part because few western governments have a clear notion of what nationhood and citizenship mean in complex and pluralistic modern democracies.

The poverty of social vision in education in western countries does not necessarily imply, as some postmodernists have claimed, that education can no longer act as an integrating social force. Indeed in many ways, the conditions in modern western states are more conducive to this now than they were in the last century when this was the explicit and dominant function of the national education system (Durkheim, 1977). When national education was first developed in Europe it sought to integrate societies that were multiply divided not only by class, religion, gender and ethnicity, but also by geography and language. The gulf between urban and rural populations in early nineteenth-century Europe was massive both in spatial and temporal terms (Weber, 1979). Rural populations lived, quite literally, in different historical times from their modernizing urban counterparts. Of no less significance were the divisions of language, not only among populations in the immigrant societies like America, but also within Europe. At the time of the revolution in France, when national education was already firmly on the agenda, only 50 per cent of the population spoke French. At the moment of unification in Italy, when national education was first introduced, less than 3 per cent of the population spoke Italian (Hobsbawm, 1990, p. 60).

Modern western societies have in some ways, as postmodernists claim, become more pluralistic. In terms of lifestyles and values, there is greater individual diversity inasmuch as individuals are freer to make their own choices. However, in other ways contemporary societies are less structurally fragmented than their predecessors. Religion, language and geography do not divide them as much as they did formerly and there is now a common social experience provided by a ubiquitous consumer and media culture. The latter, to be sure, do not provide any clearly defined structure of moral values or national identities. They do, nevertheless, provide a common language for communication.

The postmodern world is, generally, both more diverse *and* more homogeneous than modernity. Globalization, as cultural theorists contend, has not only provided new means for local and particular cultures to express and identify themselves; it has *also* made them more present and more visible to other cultures, thus enhancing the opportunities for common discourse. The sharp divides between communities based on region, class, religion and language have arguably decreased leading to greater social uniformity. On the other hand, with the demise of these community and group identities, there has also been a loss of the solidarity and moral bonding which obtained within them. This leads to greater individuation and thus greater diversity at the individual level.

The scope for education to act as a socially integrative force in contemporary society is not necessarily diminished or impeded by the forces of globalization and postmodernity. What has diminished perhaps is the political will of governments, at least in the West, to pursue the goals of social cohesion and social solidarity. However, even this may change as the social atomization induced by global market penetration becomes increasingly dysfunctional. With the decline of socially integrating institutions and the consequent atrophy of collective social ties, education may soon again be called upon to stitch together the fraying social fabric. There are already signs that this is happening both in the UK and within the European Union with the burgeoning debate about the 'learning society' (EU Commission, 1996; Ranson, 1994). After many years of neglect the question of education and citizenship is coming back onto the agenda.

The major dilemmas for governments and educationalists in the coming decade will revolve around how to reconstruct cultures of citizenship and nationhood in ways which are appropriate to modern conditions and yet conducive both to a deepening of democracy and to a strengthening social solidarity. The question poses many difficult problems about the competing claims to loyalty of the local community, the region, the nation and the supra-national world. At the national level it requires the forging of notions of civic national identity which are both inclusive and mobilizing, which reconstitute the legitimacy of the public domain and the primacy of the public good. For the individual it means constructing identities and negotiating loyalties within the complex constellation of collectivities defined by geography, ethnicity, age and nationality as well as cultivating the skills and predispositions which enable active and conscious participation in democratic society at community and national levels.

Education has a major role to play in all this. 'The challenge of the modern era', as Stewart Ranson has written, is 'the creation of a moral and political order that expresses and enables an active citizenship . . . to regenerate and constitute more effectively than ever before a public—an educated public—that has the capacity to participate actively as citizens in the shaping of a learning society and polity' (1994, p. 102). Education must remain the public arena where tolerance, mutual respect and understanding and the ability to cooperate are cultivated. Just as it offers opportunities for individual development and advancement, it must also strive to promote civic identity and civic competence and to make possible a democratic and cohesive society. Education cannot ignore the realities of the global market. But nor can it surrender to global commodification.

Governmentality and the Sociology of Education: Media, Educational Policy, and the Politics of Resentment

Cameron McCarthy and Greg Dimitriadis

Introduction

As Arjun Appadurai (1996) has argued, social reproduction and integration have been inextricably complicated by the multiple contemporary pressures of globalization. New and unpredictable flows of people, money, technology, media images and ideologies are spreading out across the globe in often highly disjunctive ways. These developments must be understood both individually and in tandem. Indeed, these dynamics come together in radically different ways in different social sites and locales, inextricably complicating the idea that one can, ultimately, separate the local from the global. As James Clifford (1997) has stressed, the idea of the nation-state itself has come into question as a helpful construct for thinking about social reproduction. The nation-state, Clifford argues, is a fiction of the powerful, often overlaid on top of the heterogeneity of everyday practices. Social networks, cultural resources and institutions all play important roles in people's lives, in ways that exceed the predictive powers of those invested in the stability and the relevance of the nation-state.

All this has had important implications for education, as educational processes are at the very heart of social and economic reproduction; a point that has been made by numerous educational theorists and researchers operating in the field commonly called 'the sociology of education' (Bernstein, 1977, 1990; Bourdieu & Passeron, 1977; Apple, 1979, 1982; Arnot, 1981; Whitty, 1985). Although often differing on questions of structure and agency, this work has traditionally been concerned with how class, race and gender reproduce themselves across generations by way of pedagogical texts and institutions, often serving to maintain the normative underpinnings of the nation-state. Yet, with the conceptual status of the state itself increasingly thrown into doubt, new questions and complexities emerge here.

Most importantly, researchers and theorists can no longer assume that schools can be studied as isolated and autonomous structures, nor can one

Cameron McCarthy and Greg Dimitriadis, 'Governmentality and the Sociology of Education: media, educational policy and the politics of resentment', *The British Journal of Sociology of Education*, 21, 2, 169–187 http://tandf.co.uk/journals.

simply assume *a priori* the imperatives of a bounded state. The interconnectedness of local and global forces has, again, posed new questions for those attempting to talk about social and cultural reproduction. In a key example, popular culture is coming to play an increasingly important part in the lives of the young (see, for example, Steinberg & Kincheloe, 1997), complicating questions about cultural reproduction and the curriculum. Yet, popular culture itself is clearly very much a part of a global entertainment industry, with multiple international connections between capital and points of production, distribution, advertising, etc. Texts and tropes circulate widely and are coming to reflect a material and cultural hybridity that does not fit neatly into pre-existing modes of nationalist thinking and planning. We now live at the nexus of multiple 'power geometries', unpredictable and transnational lines of connection between local and global forces (Massey, 1994).

The responses to these tensions have been varied. Some critics have called for more sober interrogations of the state and its power. Andy Green (1997), most notably, has argued that the nation-state will remain a relevant construct for thinking about the role of education in this age of globalization, that the state will continue to serve its Durkheimean functions. Hence, he argues, state educational planners should be more prescriptive about planning their public education systems; that common curricula can foster some semblance of social cohesion and can be wedded to the imperatives of industry. His work, by and large, assumes that the state will continue to exert its power. Others, however, have taken a more explicitly anti-state stance. Indeed, Green posits his work in counter-distinction to the work of critical pedagogues like Henry Giroux who have been, he argues, too quick to assume that the state is no longer a relevant construct. These critics, he maintains, argue for the importance of locally negotiated curriculum, for the dismissal of any notion of a 'common' public in this age of intense globalization and ethnicization. According to Green, these critics have abdicated any investment in the state at all.

Both responses—the unified and unifying permanent state of Green and the post-state society of Giroux—we feel, are inadequate, as neither is a compelling model of the state to draw on in these challenging political times. For functionalists and comparativists like Green, the state is a monolithic entity that is a reality forevermore. For critical pedagogues like Giroux, the state can simply be wished away in the ecstasy of the local embrace. What is missing here is a model of the state that is sensitive to both its durability and its permeability, a model that can account for the massive interconnections between local and global forces and different material and discursive sites. We argue here that Michel Foucault's notion of 'governmentality' proves helpful in addressing these concerns, providing a fruitful avenue of inquiry for those in education today (Foucault, 1991, p. 87). Also, we argue that the related discursive practice of resentment or the mobilization and deployment of affect is a vital element of governmentality, a vital response within the state and the body politic, and across social institutions to the challenges of multiplicity and diversity and instability precipitated by globalization.

Offering a new direction for thinking about state reproduction, Foucault argued that the 'state' should not be seen as immutable, nor as a reified entity. The 'state' is a result of multiple—although very real and very powerful—discursive practices taking place across a range of sites. Elaborating on Foucault's claims, Nikolas Rose writes that:

> The 'power of the State' is a resultant, not a cause, an outcome of the composing and assembling of actors, flows, buildings, relations of authority into relatively durable associations mobilized, to a greater or lesser extent, towards the achievement of particular objectives by common means. This is not a matter of the domination of a 'network' by 'the State' but rather a matter of translation. The translation of political programmes articulated in rather general terms—national efficiency, democracy, equality, enterprise—into ways of seeking to exercise authority over persons, places and activities in specific locales and practices. The translation of thought and action from a 'centre of calculation' into a diversity of locales dispersed across a territory—translation in the sense of a movement from one place to another. Through a multitude of such mobile relays, relations are established between those who are spatially and temporally separated, and between events and decisions in spheres that none the less retain their formal autonomy. (1996, p. 43)

Hence, the 'state' and its power derives from various 'relatively durable' associations of 'persons, places, and activities' which take place across and between specific local sites and in interaction with particular global settings. These associations gel together around specific modalities such as 'efficiency, democracy, equality [and] enterprise', which tend to operate in specific, although unpredictable, ways (p. 43). This is not the stuff of top-down state planning, but rather, indexes the ways that these discursive constructions come to infuse themselves in institutions as such, orchestrating cohesion and elaborating affect, sensibility, feeling and association in complex ways. The goal of educational theorists here is to map out relations between specific sites, and the ways these constructs translate between and across these sites. Contemporary educational theorists, however, have not interrogated these kinds of interconnections and interrelations as clearly as they might, tending, instead, to take less relational and more formal and instrumental approaches. As such, much of this work is limited in its effectivity, its ability to address the mutual imbrication of the various sites that inform educational practice today. Much of this work fails to engage with a power that does not simply prohibit or repress, a power that is dispersed, that circulates—a power that does not exist outside relations but produces relations (Foucault, 1980). Indeed, the locus of power struggles in the modern society is not now to be found pure and simple in the classic sites of state politics, including in labor–capital arm wrestling, or bulldozing actions of civil rights and union-based political actors and their detractors. Modern power struggles are also to be located in the deeply contested arena of the popular, the domain of struggles over social conduct, popular commitments, anxieties and desires, and, ultimately, the disciplining of populations (Miller, 1998).

Yet, work on popular culture and education has tended not to engage with such notions of power, assuming instead that popular culture can be looked at as an autonomous set of affectively invested texts that exert repressive power on young people. Two approaches, as David Buckingham (1996) makes clear, tend to dominate here. First, critical pedagogues like Henry Giroux and Douglas Kellner argue that media and popular culture play important roles in young people's lives and must be explored as a kind of alternative 'lived' curriculum. Yet, as with much curriculum history and theory, textual analysis has reigned supreme here, much of which simply demonstrates how these texts reproduce dominant cultural imperatives, assuming high levels of predictability from text to subject. Second, theorists of 'media literacy' such as Len Masterman (1990) have stressed the ways young people can be taught to resist these seemingly deleterious effects of contemporary media cultures. This has tended to be, as David Buckingham (1996) writes, a '*defensive*' position, one that attempts 'to inoculate students against or protect them from what are assumed to be the negative effects of the media' (p. 644). Both approaches assume that popular culture is a site of oppression for the young.

Missing, however, is a sense of how different sites—for example, popular culture, educational policy, classroom practices—mutually inform each other in ways that help reproduce contingent state imperatives. Also missing is a sense of how the local and the global are entirely interrelated in the 'relatively durable' associations between these sites. Investigating these seemingly common-sense connections, we argue, is a first step towards a more fruitful approach to popular culture, education and state power.

Taking Foucault's notion of 'governmentality' as a starting point, we will interrogate one of its forms of elaboration, a complex of technologies of truth, a set of discursive practices that operates across multiple contemporary sites. This can be summarized in Friederich Nietzsche's term 'resentment'. Resentment is understood here as the deployment of moral evaluation in political life—a technology of truth that is generated within the reciprocal relationship between the state and the body politic. As an expression of governmentality, resentment performs the ideological and discursive work of managing the complexities and challenges of diversity and multiplicity, and social, cultural and economic change generated by globalization. Resentment is directly linked to governmentality in the sense that resentment is deeply imbricated in the techniques and processes of self-management and the self-regulation of modern populations. This is what Foucault (1980) describes as 'rule at a distance'. These practices of self-management shift accountability and responsibility for the welfare of the poor and disadvantaged, for example, from a centripetal state to its capillary systems extended in the body politic.

These developments do not displace the state, neither do they herald its ultimate demise. Instead, they help to re-constitute the state as a de-centered system of networks—one in which everyday practices in social institutions such as education and in popular culture help to broker contemporary change. In this sense, we seek to disabuse readers of the notion of the state as a unitary material object. The notion of a centralized state is, in our view, an ideological construct—a project of legitimation (Coffey, 1999). As Philip Corrigan & Derek Sayer (1985) argue, 'the repertoire of activities and institutions conventionally identified as the "state" are cultural forms' and regulations (p. 3). They further maintain that:

> Out of the vast range of human social capacities—possible ways in which social life could be lived—state activities more or less forcibly 'encourage' some whilst suppressing others ... this has cumulative and enormous cultural consequences for how people identify (in many cases, have to identify) themselves and their 'place' in the world. (Corrigan & Sayer, 1985, p. 84)

The link between the state as legitimized administrative apparatuses and the state as one of the crucial sites of the production of identities in the body politic leads us to the wide-open spaces of the public sphere, in which civic order is built from discourses that manage the needs, interests and desires generated by and within the socially combatant populations that make up society. These discourses are increasingly overtaken by the language and practice of resentment. Like 'efficiency, democracy, equality [and] enterprise', resentment is informing many and different sites today, and is, as such, an important way to think about the relations and associations between what happens in school, what happens in the media and how public policy is being informed. We cannot, following Foucault, think, about these things separately anymore. Power operates in multiple and discursive ways, in ways that must be understood with a flexible set of tools. As such, this article is both methodological and substantive. We wish to both suggest a new direction for the sociology of education as well as to deconstruct 'resentment' as a powerful way that education is being formed and reformed, and, as such, open a space to resist it.

Resentment, Popular Culture and Educational Practice

A key insight to be gleaned from Foucault and his notion of 'governmentality' is that educational institutions are always in synch with popular culture in terms of strategies of incorporation and mobilization of racial identities. Thus, the vast field of meaning making is opened up, in which the tasks of educating about group differences, the management of diversity, etc. have been absorbed within an ever-expanding arena of simulation generated by and through electronic mediation. Television, film, radio and the internet are now the most powerful sites for educating about difference and the production of resentment. We live in a time when 'pseudo-events' fomented in media-driven representations have usurped any relic of reality beyond that which is staged or performed, driving, it is crucial to note, incredibly deep, and perhaps permanent, wedges of difference between the world of the suburban dweller and his/her inner-city counterpart. Daniel Boorstin writes, 'we have used our wealth, our literacy, our technology, and our progress, to create a thicket of unreality which stands between us and the facts of life' (1975, p. 3). These Durkheimian 'facts of life'—notions of what, for example, black people are like, what Latinos are like—are invented and reinvented in the media, in popular magazines, in newspapers and in television, music and popular film. As critics such as Len Masterman (1990) point out, by the end of his/her teenage years, the average student will have spent more time watching television than he/she would have spent in school. In the US, it is increasingly television and film that educates American youth about race, as evidenced by the so-called 'hood' or 'reality' films of the early 1990s (McCarthy, 1998).

Because reality itself has been redefined by and through media cultures, it is increasingly difficult to separate what happens in the realm of the popular from what happens in schools. Both are in synch in terms of cultural reproduction. We therefore want to take the subject of diversity, knowledge and power to a place that is normally considered outside the circuit of the education field itself, to the end point and margin of education, to the terrain of popular culture and its pedagogies of wish fulfillment and desire. In so doing, we wish to shift attention from the multiculturalist complaint over current modes of teaching and curriculum, *per se*, to the broader issue of the cultural reproduction of difference and the coordination of racial identities, foregrounding the connections between the production and reproduction of popular cultural form and the operation of power in daily life. We see resentment as a powerful organizing trope here, one that operates across multiple sites.

In *On the Genealogy of Morals*, Friedrich Nietzsche (1967) conceptualized resentment as the specific practice of identity displacement, in which the social actor consolidates his identity by a complete disavowal of the merits and existence of his social other. Here, one becomes 'good' by constructing the 'other' as evil. Nietzsche writes, 'picture "the enemy" as the man of ressentiment conceives him—and here precisely is his deed, his creation: he has conceived "the evil enemy", "*the Evil One*", and this in fact is his basic concept, from which he then evolves, as an afterthought and pendant, a "good one"—himself!' (1967, p. 39). A sense of self, thus, is only possible through an annihilation or emptying out of the other. Indeed, while all processes of identity construction are relational, processes of resentment are explicitly nihilistic and reactive. The world is conceived of as 'hostile' and all one's energies are directed 'outward' towards the annihilation of the other. Hence, one's identity becomes pure, good and coherent. These practices of ethnocentric consolidation and cultural exceptionalism—evident on a global scale—now characterize much of the tug-of-war over educational reform and multiculturalism—and the stakes could not be any higher, for all parties involved.

Indeed, these discourses now dominate the public—popular—sphere and involve the critical process of the renarration of social identities in a time of ever-widening economic and cultural anxiety with clear implications for education. These discourses help to manage feelings of uncertainty, and to articulate and mobilize needs, desires and interests in these complicated times. Resentment enters normatively into the space of social realignments, corporate downsizing and state disinvestment in public works. This is a space in which the state increasingly sheds itself of social welfarism, thereby allowing or even encouraging the reinterpretation and rearticulation of issues of inequality as matters of individual will, volunteerism and community goal orientation and moral fiber. The problem of inequality has been reassigned as a problem of individual and group success or failure in navigating the shoals of contemporary life. In what follows, we will briefly look at the mise-en-scene of these resentment discourses or technologies of truth associated with the tug-of-war of racial and cultural strife in the educational life of a divided society—the US. We will limit our discussion to three such discourses.

Origin and Nation

First, we would like to call attention to the '*discourse of origin and nation*' as revealed, for example, in the Eurocentric/Afrocentric debate over curriculum reform in the US. Discourses of racial origins rely on the simulation of a pastoral sense of the past, in which Europe and Africa are available to American racial combatants without the noise of their modern tensions, contradictions and conflicts. For Eurocentric combatants such as William Bennett (1994) or George Will (1989), Europe and America are a self-evident and transcendent cultural unity. For Afrocentric combatants, Africa and the diaspora are one 'solid identity', to use the language of Molefi Asante (1993). Proponents of Eurocentrism and Afrocentrism are themselves proxies for larger impulses and desires for stability among the middle classes in American society in a time of constantly changing demographic and economic realities. The immigrants are coming! Jobs are slipping overseas into the third world! Discourses of Eurocentrism and Afrocentrism travel in a time warp to an age when the gods stalked the earth.

This discourse of origin and nation is foregrounded in a spate of recent advertisements by multinational corporations such as IBM, United, American Air lines, MCI and General Electric (GE). These advertisements both feed on and provide fictive solutions to the racial anxieties of the age. They effectively appropriate multicultural symbols and redeploy them in a broad project of coordination and consolidation of corporate citizenship and consumer affiliation. The marriage of art and economy, as Stuart Ewen (1988) so defines advertising in *All Consuming Images*, is now commingled with the exigencies of ethnic identity and nation. One moment, the semiotic subject of advertising is a free American citizen abroad in the open seas sailing up and down the Atlantic or the translucent aquamarine waters of the Caribbean sea. In another, the free American citizen is transported to the pastoral life of the unspoiled, undulating landscape of medieval Europe. Both implicate a burgeoning consumer culture undergirded by the triumph of consumer capitalism on a global scale.

Hence, there is the GE 'We Bring Good Things to Life' advertisement (which is shown quite regularly on CNN and ABC), in which GE is portrayed as a latter-day Joan of Arc fighting the good fight of American entrepreneurship overseas, bringing electricity to one Japanese town. In the advertisement, GE breaks through the cabalism of foreign language, bureaucracy and unethical rules in Japan to procure the goal of the big sell. The American nation can rest in peace as the Japanese nation succumbs to superior US technology.

On the terms of its present trajectory, multiculturalism can be properly diagnosed as one such discourse of resentment, a discourse that attempts to manage the extraordinary tensions and contradictions existing in modern life that have invaded social institutions including the school. At the heart of its achievement, multiculturalism has succeeded in freezing to the point of petrification its central object: 'culture'. Within the managerial language of the university, culture has become a useful discourse of containment, a narrow discourse of ascriptive property in which particular groups are granted their nationalist histories, their knowledges and, alas, their experts. Cultural competence then becomes powerfully deployed to blunt the pain of resource scarcity, and to inoculate the hegemonic knowledge paradigms in the university from the daylight of subjugated knowledges and practices.

This discourse of racial origin as it is infused in multiculturalism provides imaginary solutions to groups and individuals who refuse the radical hybridity that is the historically evolved reality of the US and other major Western metropolitan societies. The dreaded line of difference is drawn around glittering objects of heritage and secured with the knot of ideological closure. The university itself has become a playground of the war of simulation. Contending paradigms of knowledge are embattled as combatants release the levers of atavism holding their faces in their hands as the latest volley of absolutism circles in the air. In this sense, multicultural education is articulated to popular culture in ways which implicate broader cultural imperatives.

Hence, critical pedagogues like Steinberg & Kincheloe (1997) are correct to note the ways popular texts and their complex pleasures and pedagogies are elided from dominant classroom culture today, an insight under-scored by an important body of work in cultural studies and education (see, for example, Giroux, 1996). In this sense, school life is largely divorced from the realities of the popular. However, in another and equally important sense, schools are, in fact, entirely implicated in the kinds of market logics and imperatives so intrinsic to popular culture. Movements for 'school choice', for example, index the ways schools are accommodating, not contesting, dominant discourses of consumer capitalism. These discourses are implicated at all levels of the educational process—from decisions about policy and administration to the situated realities of the classroom. As such, Ruth Vinz calls attention to the 'shopping mall' approach to multicultural education so prevalent today, giving a most compelling (hypothetical) example:

> On Monday of a given week, students begin their unit on Native Americans. They learn that Native Americans lived in teepees, used tomahawks to scalp white folks, wore headdresses, and danced together around a fire before eating their meal of blue corn and buffalo meat. By Wednesday of the same week, literature is added as an important cultural

> artifact; therefore, one or two poems (sometimes including Longfellow's 'Hiawatha') represent tribal life of the past and present. By Friday, students take a trip to The Museum of the American Indian with its unsurpassed collection of artifacts and carry home their own renditions of teepees, tomahawks, or headdresses that they made during their art period. (Vinz, 1999)

The following week, she notes, students might continue their virtual tour of the globe, moving to, for example, Latin American cultures, i.e. 'During the second week, students study Latinos ... '. As Vinz makes clear, dominant approaches to multicultural education evidence a kind of market logic, putting multiple and fabricated cultural products at the fingertips of students to consume in very superficial ways. This 'we are the world' approach to education elides the complexity and tension of the emerging global reality, making it one more product for consumers to consume in simple and simply unproductive ways. This is one example of how media culture is in synch with educational practice and policy. Recall the GE advertisement mentioned earlier.

Popular Memory, History and Nostalgia

Second, there is *'the discourse of popular memory, history and nostalgia'*. This kind of discourse is clearly evident in much contemporary curriculum proposals, proposals that attempt to use education policy as a key site to re-suture an historical, social cohesion inextricably called into question by the multiple pressures of globalization. This attempt to rewrite the cultural landscape is evidenced in all manners of educational practice—from hiring decisions to curricula construction to textbook selection—all of which help call students into a kind of common heritage narrated from a middle-class bourgeois perspective. Of course, right-wing educators like William Bennett, Dinesh D'Souza and George Will have been quite explicit about their efforts to narrate US history from a Eurocentric position—a project that has been roundly criticized by historians of oppressed groups, including African Americans (e.g. Lerone Bennett), Asian Americans (e.g. Ronald Takaki), the working class (e.g. Howard Zinn) and women (e.g. Alice Echols), all of whom have attempted to narrate a kind of nondominant historical knowledge.

This is common well-documented knowledge, a debate that has been raging for several years and culminated around the 'PC (Politically Correct) Wars' of the early 1990s. Less often discussed, however, is the role of popular media in buttressing these narratives with all the force of common sense. Indeed, this discourse suffuses the films of the past decade or so. Films such as *Dances with Wolves* (1990), *Bonfire of the Vanities* (1990), *Grand Canyon* (1993), *Falling Down* (1993), *Forrest Gump* (1994), *A Time to Kill* (1996), *The Fan* (1997), *Armageddon* (1998) and *Saving Private Ryan* (1998) foreground a white middle-class protagonist who appropriates the subject position of the persecuted social victim at the mercy of myriad forces—from 'wild' black youth in Los Angeles (*Grand Canyon*), to Asian store owners who do not speak English well (*Falling Down*), to a black baseball player, living the too-good life in a moment of corporate downsizing (*The Fan*). All hark back to the 'good old days' when the rules were few and exceedingly simple for now-persecuted white men.

These films are seeped in nostalgia, enmeshed in the project of rewriting history from the perspective of bourgeois anxieties and the feelings of resentment which often drive them. This project is realized perhaps most forcefully in the wildly successful *Forrest Gump*. A special-effects masterwork, this film literally interpolates actor Tom Hanks into actual and re-created historical footage of key events in US history, renarrating the latter part of the twentieth century in ways that blur the line between fact and fiction. Here, the peripatetic Gump steals the spotlight from the civil rights movement, the Vietnam War protesters, the feminist movement, etc. Public history is overwhelmed by personal consumerism and wish fulfillment. Individual needs, interests and fantasies replace collective struggle, and the narrative ground of America's contemporary history is rewritten from the point of view of the disadvantaged white middle class.

This nostalgia for the good old days is associated with a set of discourses that recode white middle-class identity as the identity of the oppressed. The professional middle-class suburban dweller has appropriated the radical space of difference, the space of social injury, of social victim—denying avenues of social complaint to the inner-city poor and their immigrant counterparts. The suburbs and their gated communities have become the new barometers of public policy as pro-suburban discourses now displace issues of poverty and inequality, replacing these issues with demands for tax cuts, crime control, and the greater surveillance and incarceration of minority youth. All of this is accompanied by a deeply nostalgic investment in Anglo-American cultural form and its European antecedents.

These shifting currents of association are quintessentially represented in Joel Schumaker's *Falling Down* (1993). The film features a white suburban male protagonist, D-fens, who enters the inner city to settle moral scores with the socially deprived minority poor. D-fens is the prosecuting agent of resentment. He has a very expansive sense of the social other—a vision that embraces Latinos who are gangbangers, Asian store owners who are portrayed as compulsively unscrupulous and African Americans who are plain low-life and losers.

What is fascinating about a film like *Falling Down* is that it is centered around a proto-normative, anomic protagonist who, as James might put it, is 'out there'. He is the purveyor of what Jacques Lacan in his 'mirror stage ...' essay calls 'paranoiac alienation' (Lacan, 1977, p. 5). In this sense, D-fens' character is very closely based on real-life characters whose paranoia leads them to office massacres and school murders. We learn, for example, D-fens is a disgruntled laid-off white-collar employee—a former technician who worked for many years at a military plant. Displaced as a result of the changing economy of the new world order—displaced by the proliferation of different peoples who are now flooding Los Angeles in pursuit of the increasingly illusive American dream—D-fens is a semiotic prototype of a paranoid, single, white male who is frustrated by failure in the job site and in personal relations with women. He is the kind of individual who we are encouraged to believe a displaced middle-class person might become. As Joel Schumaker, the film director, explains: 'It's the kind of story you see on the six o'clock news, about the nice guy who has worked at the post office for twenty years and then one day guns down his co-workers and kills his family. It's terrifying because there's the sense that someone in the human tribe went over the wall. It could happen to us' (Morgan, 1993). D-fens is the post-civil rights scourge of affirmative action and reverse discrimination. Nostalgic films like *Falling Down* promote a new kind of social didacticism—one that seeks to expose the depravity of a social system which coddles the slackers and criminal elements among society's minority poor and working class. These films also offer individual agency and determination as the way forward in winning back our communities and society.

Individual Enterprise, Volunteerism and the Conversationalization of Public Life

Finally, we wish to call attention to resentment discourses facilitating a redirection of whole areas of governmental responsibility and public life towards '*individual enterprise and volunteerism and a general pattern of the conversationalizing of public discourse*'. First, we will discuss that aspect of the individualization of public life which manifests itself in the promotion of new forms of corporate and state-supported volunteerism. This generalized pattern of individualization of social and political problems generally affects the young. White youth growing up in the 1980s and 1990s in the age of Reagan/Bush regimes—the age of junk bonds, the ruthless pursuit of self-interest, and the icy abandonment of racial minorities—have within the past few years developed a deep sense of a lack of fulfillment that manifests itself in a loss of faith and a crisis of identity (Popkewitz, 1998). This has led to at least two developments within the drama of race relations in the US. On the one hand, there is the increasing declaration of victim status by the white middle classes, as we saw in the discourse of popular memory and the rise of nostalgia films such as *Falling Down* (1993) and *Forrest Gump* (1994). This deployment of hostile moral evaluation targets immigrants and minorities for containment and restriction. It is also expressed in public policy, for example, in proposition 227 (the anti-immigrant, 'English Only', initiative passed by a 2 : 1 majority of Californian voters).

On the other hand, there has been, in some quarters, among the young, an outpouring of a new idealism that serves to reconstruct new millennium youth identities. This new idealism propounds a form of volunteerism that rearticulates the 1960s notion of service overseas as represented by, for example, the Peace Corps, to a sense of rescue mission at home now needed in our times. This form of volunteerism is linked to a sense of national mission and patriotism that seeks to boost America's economic fortunes in the rough and tumble of global capitalism. This idealism feeds on state and business neo-liberal agendas aimed at universalizing the principle of enterprise, bringing entrepreneurial initiative to the inner city, and redirecting inner-city problems away from the public purse and back into the community through a discourse of self-help and volunteerism. This is a form of altruistic resentment. A condescension to help those you fear on your own terms, for your own peace of mind.

This sense of service is deeply racialized. While in the 1960s, the target of this idealism was the dispossessed in the Third World, the new found idealism at the dawning of the twenty-first century targets the black and Hispanic minority poor of America's inner cities, who are seen as the tragic ballast weighing down the forward motion of the ship of state. This type of idealism is now being encouraged by the state and corporate interests as a new form of volunteerism and communalism. For instance, corporate organizations such as Nike have promoted the initiative known as P.L.A.Y. or Participate in the Lives of America's Youth, using sport as a vehicle to promote a clean up of the inner city. Similar initiatives have been promoted by the Bush and Clinton administrations such as The Points of Light Foundation, America's Promise and Americorps—the latter gives young people tuition relief and a stipend in return for volunteering in some area of public need (e.g. working inner-city community centers, old people homes, etc.).

Perhaps the best example, and certainly one of the most publicized of these volunteeristic projects, is the alternative teacher certification organization, 'Teach for America' (TFA). A study of TFA tells us more about the ideological, even psychological, needs of today's middle-class white and minority youth than it does about the underclass to whom the project is targeted. TFA is the 1990s brainchild of a Princeton graduate out of Texas, who dreamed up the idea of a youth service corps of teachers comprising the best and the brightest, interestingly, noneducation majors of the top white and black universities in the country. TFA depends on heavy infusions of money from corporate sources interested in a 'partnership' with the inner city. Also, executives from America's leading companies such as IBM, XEROX and Union Carbide, sit on the TFA's executive board. The selected students or corps members are taken on a fast-track to their social rescue goals. In batches starting at 500 and increasing by 500 every year, these corp members are put through a 'highly intensive Summer Institute'—in reality, an 8-week program that hacks the 4- or 5-year preservice preparation of teacher education departments down to the barest of essentials. After they have been given their survival tool kit to teach in the urban and rural classroom, these youngsters are placed in classrooms of the most needy school districts across the country, from New York to Los Angeles, to New Orleans and rural Mississippi in the South.

For this analysis, we look at TFA recruitment literature, one of its main policy documents and its application form for prospective recruits. What is interesting about these documents is their use of the language of resentment. There is a complex of discourses that informs the TFA project as illustrated in its anti-intellectual, deregulation, anti-bureaucracy themes, its media-produced images of the sense of threat and danger that the inner city represents, and, furthermore, the projection in this TFA literature of the corps member as a special species of green-beret educator. The latter, given his/her intellectual capacity and social pedigree, is armed (*sui generis*) with the antidote for minority underachievement in the urban and the rural classroom. TFA's thinly disguised objective is to exposed the bankruptcy and incompetence of teachers, and the system of education preparation and certification that is now centered in the university. Themes of social efficiency and curriculum essentialism that led to the displacement of educators in the post-sputnik curriculum reform movement of the late 1950s and early 1960s now percolate through TFA's policy discourse. What we wish to do very briefly is to take a look at the construction of identity and the other in the literature and TFA's manuals.

For instance, on the front cover of TFA's recruitment brochure *America Needs Both of You* (Teach for

America, 1994a), the object of the mission appears: a black inner-city female student, shot in extreme close up, next to a locker, number '136', outside the urban classroom. Half of the sixth-grader's face is completely shadowed, and the other half is in light. What we can see inscribed on this child's face is the play of contradictory attributes that are imputed to the inner-city child by TFA. She is the embodiment of rebellion, helplessness and abandonment. She is standing next to her locker because she has been presumably expelled from the classroom by her real teacher, whom we never see. Just above her head and just to the right of the locker, is the classroom door, number '104'. It is closed, shut. The 'America Needs You' caption that runs underneath this photograph interpellates or addresses the corps member. The latter's role is to open the door and let the child back in. The corps member will replace the teacher in this abandoned classroom. To underscore the call to patriotic duty and service, the brochure is produced on white card stock and the text is printed in red and blue. Service to inner city is, therefore, service to country.

Later, on page 3 of the brochure, under the sub-heading 'America Needs You', TFA sketches the nature of the educational problem and the task at hand:

Foremost among the factors that threaten America's future is the state of the public school system. Consider the following statistics:

- on average, 3,600 students drop out each school day.
- students in the United States consistently score below those of almost all other industrialized nations in math and science.
- 75% of 17-year-olds are unable to write an adequate analytic essay.
- 1/3 of the U.S. population is functionally or marginally illiterate.

This challenge calls for attention and commitment of the nation's best minds. It calls in particular for an increase in the quality and quantity of teachers. Too few Teachers come from the top ranks of academic achievers. Some inner-city and rural areas have trouble attracting teachers. (Teach for America 1994a, p. 3)

These statistics are then further interpreted more elaborately in TFA's literature directed at helping the TFA recruiter prepare for her interview with prospective corps members recruits who will compete for one of the limited corps member slots. One of the most interesting questions in the interview format is the following:

Let's . . . pretend that I'm one of your students, named [use your name] and we're going to act out a scene. So, don't tell me what you would do, just do it. Don't tell me what you would say, just say it. I'm going to take out a knife [your pen] in a non-threatening manner. School rules prohibit knives in the building, but some teachers look the other way. Begin. (Teach for America, 1994b, p. 22)

As this passage from the interview format indicates, TFA reproduces the sense of danger that the inner-city school has been branded with in the popular media. Interestingly, this sense of danger is recoded in the TFA discourse. It is reproduced in a new way—the danger and the threat of the inner city is now associated with a sense of high-minded pleasure, a re-energized and re-vivified sense of mission that, in turn, marks off the fortunate middle-class corps member from the object of her duty: the 'at-risk' inner-city child.

TFA offers an activist program of intervention in the inner city that again illustrates the extent to which the terms of public discourse have been redirected towards the idea of universalization of entrepreneurial spirit and individual initiative. TFA offers its model of the school as an enterprise zone. Within this framework, the inner-city school is both feared and loved. It is a site of altruistic resentment—a critical site in the battle to save the nation's poor from self-destruction and, ultimately, to preserve America's place in the New World Order of globalization. In this high moment of de-intellectualization, teacher education programs in the University are linked to the general educational bureaucracy as targets of moral and affective reform in the world of globalization that is dawning. Inner-city schools, TFA has figured, need emancipatory corporate values. The inner-city child needs moral renovation in order to be made ready for a capitalist future as part of the international reserve army of labor. Resentment discourses that foreground the new volunteerism make social anxieties manageable through the process of marketing the other as a site of intervention and consumerist change.

These resentment discourses also have a conversationalizing dimension, as we pointed at the beginning of this section—the new medium for rendering the difficult problems of political and social life accessible and amenable to individual agency and wish fulfillment. From the television and radio talk shows of Oprah Winfrey and Jenny Jones to the rap music of Tupac Shakur to pseudo-academic books like *The Bell Curve, The Hot Zone* and *The Coming Plague,* to self-improvement texts like *Don't Sweat the Small Stuff ... and its All Small Stuff,* these examples from popular culture all psychologize and seemingly internalize complex social problems, managing the intense feelings of anxiety so much a part of contemporary cultural life. Television talk shows, for example, reduce complex social phenomena to mere personality conflicts between guests, encouraging them to air their differences before staging some kind of denouement or resolution. Histories of oppression are thus put aside as guests argue in and through the details of their private lives, mediated, as they often are, by so-called experts. Racial harmony becomes a relative's acceptance of a 'bi-racial' child. Sexual parity is reduced to a spouse publicly rejecting an adulterous partner. Psychologistic explanations for social phenomena reign supreme, and are supported by a burgeoning literature of self-improvement texts, texts which posit poor self-esteem as the pre-eminent societal ill today. These popular texts and media programs are pivotal in what Deborah Tanner calls 'The Argument Culture' (1998), in which the private is the political, and politics is war by other means.

The increasing importance of conversationalizing discourses has had clear influences on school practice. We are thinking here, specifically, of that most important and universally embraced of current educational reforms—the effort to bring computer technology into every classroom. Communication itself, it is important to note, has come to be the dominant trope for much of these reform efforts in schools. We recall here the AT&T 'reach out and touch someone' advertisement campaign that so infused the popular imagination several years ago, a campaign which opened a discursive space for many of its future efforts. Indeed, as discussed elsewhere, AT&T recently sponsored a program entitled 'Learning Circles', a program which sought to bring (first as gift, then as commodity) computers into classrooms to encourage 'problem solving' between different groups (Dimitriadis & Kamberelis, 1997). Importantly, this technology was supposed to wipe away all social and cultural barriers (after all, no one knows what you look like) and promote uninhibited conversation across geographic and cultural sites. This was a seeming good in and of itself, and is a clear example of how tropes of media culture—tropes of resentment—can serve to dictate educational policy on the right and left.

In short, then, resentment discourses that emphasize the individualization and the conversationalization of public life facilitate the further penetration of global capital into the under-capitalized sections of society. Much educational policy has become complicit with this project of normalizing the problems of poverty and inequality as the objects of the management of diversity and the individual wish fulfillment of the inner-city other.

Educational Policy and the Pedagogy of Resentment

The notion of 'governmentality', particularly its expression in the discourses of resentment, it is important to note, allows us to make these kind of connections—connections between public policy, educational practice and the work of popular media forms. While educational theorists and practitioners have tended to look at these realms as autonomous, as we have stressed throughout and will show now, they cannot be looked at separately. We now turn to questions of policy.

Educational policies dictated by resentment have had, in point of fact, very real material effects on the dispossessed, those quickly losing the (albeit meager) benefits of affirmative action (e.g. California's Proposition 209), bilingual education (e.g. California's Proposition 227—the so-called 'English for the Children' initiative) and need-based financial aid. The idea of high-quality (public) education as the great potential equalizer—a good in and of itself—is now being lost to the bitter resentments at the heart of contemporary culture, lost to petty market logics and the free-standing subject-positions so enabled by them. The pressures of globalization—for example, new patterns of immigration, the proliferation of media images or the ravages of de-industrialization—have been met here and elsewhere by calls for the weakest kinds of self-serving 'diversity'. This diversity, as noted, is encouraged by a consumer capitalism that is entirely linked to the imperatives of resentment explored throughout. In a particularly stark example of this process, Martin Luther King Jr's revolutionary dream of the day when his 'four little children will ... live in a nation where they will not be judged by the color of their skin, but by the content of their character', has been appropriated by right-wing commentators like Shelby Steele (1990) to contest the advances of affirmative action.

How the discourse of resentment has (explicitly) propelled the conservative agenda here is fairly obvious. A new and seemingly beleaguered middle class is looking to recapture its once unquestioned privilege by advocating 'color blind' hiring and acceptance policies (in the case of affirmative action) while forging a seemingly unified—and, of course, white Anglo—cultural identity through restrictive language policies (in the case of bilingual education). Indeed, the consolidation of seamless and coherent subjects so at the heart of contemporary cultural media flows (as already explored) has enabled and encouraged the overwhelming public support and passage of bills like California's Propositions 209 and 227. These evidence the popular feelings of resentment that Michelle Fine & Lois Weis (1998) so powerfully document among white working-class men in *The Unknown City*.

Yet, these resentments run deep and operate on numerous levels with respect to the efforts of modern Americans to manage the contradictions and material constraints of everyday life. These tensions are being foregrounded as the logic of globalization impacts the local, and greater diversity within the US urban centers has begun to strain resources and access to education, health care, etc. Hence, the tensions now erupting between African Americans and Latinos vis-à-vis many such bills. In a recent *Time* magazine article entitled 'The Next Big Divide', the author explores burgeoning conflicts between African Americans and Latinos in Palo Alto over bilingual education, noting that these disputes,

> arise in part from frustration over how to spend the dwindling pot of cash in low-income districts. But they also reflect a jostling for power, as blacks who labored hard to earn a place in central offices, on school boards and in classrooms confront a Latino population eager to grab a share of these positions. (Ratnesar, 1997, p. 1)

It has been suggested, in fact, that efforts to institute 'ebonics' (Black English) as a second language in Oakland, CA was prompted by competition for shrinking funds traditionally allotted to bilingual (Spanish) programs. Resentment, spawned by increasing competition for decreasing resources, is key to unraveling the complexities of these struggles, for, as Joel Schumaker tells us, its power transcends both race and class lines.

Perhaps more importantly, however, the discourse of resentment is also informing more seemingly liberal responses to these issues and bills. The importance of public education in equalizing the profound injustices of contemporary American society is increasingly downplayed in favor of discourses about self-interest and the rigid feelings of resentment which under-gird them. Affirmative action, thus, is a good because education will keep dangerous minorities off 'our streets' by subjecting them to a lifetime of 'civilizing' education, crafting them into good subjects for global cultural capitalism. Furthermore, the story goes, affirmative action really helps middle-class women more than blacks or Latinos, so it should—quite naturally—remain in place.

These discourses inform the debate on bilingual education as well; a debate that has similarly collapsed liberal and conservative voices and opinions. Indeed, bilingual education, many argue, should be supported (only) because it will prepare young people for an increasingly polyglot global cultural economy, hence keeping immigrants and minorities off public assistance, allowing them to compete in an increasingly diverse (in the sense already developed) global community. Cultural arguments are also elided from within these positions, for, as many so eagerly stress, bilingual education really helps immigrants learn English and become assimilated faster—a bottom-line supported by an ever-present spate of quantitative studies.

Market logics are all-pervasive here, and are deeply informed by self-interest and resentment. These forces have shown themselves most clearly in recent decisions to provide less need-based financial aid for higher education to the poor, apportioning the savings to attract more so-called qualified middle-class students (Bronner, 1998). Competition for the 'best' students—seemingly without regard for race, class and gender—has become a mantra for those wishing to further destroy educational access for the dispossessed. Indeed, why, many argue, should poor minorities take precious spots away from the more qualified wealthy? The resentment of the elite has now come full circle, especially and most ironically, in this moment of unmatched economic wealth. As Jerome Karabel, professor of sociology at UC Berkeley (the site of key roll-backs in affirmative action) comments, 'College endowments are at historically unprecedented heights, so the number of need-blind institutions should be increasing rather than decreasing' (p. 16). As we all know, these are not lean, mean times for everybody. We also live in an era of unbridled wealth, won in large measure, for the elite, through, in part, divide and conquer strategies, and the triumph of resentment and its ability to dictate public policy.

Conclusion

Resentment, in summary, is produced at the level of the popular, at the level of the textual. Yet, its implications run deep, across myriad contexts, including in public policy which is increasingly defined by the logics of resentment. Thus, those of us on the left, those wishing to help keep the promise of public education a real one, must question the terms on which we fight these battles. We must question if our responses will further reproduce a discourse with such devastating and wholly regressive implications. As Foucault reminds us, we must choose what discourses we wish to engage in, the 'games of truth' we wish to play. Indeed, what will be our responses to the burgeoning trend of eliminating need-based financial aid policies? What game will we play? And towards what end?

Such questions are crucial and pressing, as this moment is replete with both possibility as well as danger. This period of intense globalization and multinational capital is witness to the ushering in of the multicultural age—an age in which the empire has struck back, and first-world exploitation of the third world has so depressed these areas that there has been a steady stream of immigrants from the periphery seeking better futures in the metropolitan centers. With the rapid growth of the indigenous minority population in the US, there is now a formidable cultural presence of diversity in every sphere of cultural life. Clearly, as Appadurai reminds us, social reproduction and integration have been inextricably complicated by globalization and the new and unpredictable flows of peoples as well as money, technology, media images and ideologies it has enabled (Appadurai, 1996). All these dynamics, he stresses, must be understood individually and in tandem if we are to understand the emerging cultural landscape and its imbrication in a multifaceted global reality. Foucault's notion of 'governmentality', as we have stressed throughout, provides us with a way to address these concerns, an important critical tool to begin to deconstruct these seemingly immutable and all-pervasive forces operating, as they do, in numerous social, cultural, and material sites.

Indeed, if this is an era of the post, it is also an era of difference—and the challenge of this era of difference is the challenge of living in a world of incompleteness, discontinuity and multiplicity. It requires generating a mythology of social interaction that goes beyond the model of resentment which seems so securely in place in these times. It means that we must take seriously the implications of the best intuition in the Nietzschean critique of resentment as the process of identity formation that thrives on the negation of the other—the dominant response from those facing a new and complex global and local reality. The challenge is to embrace a politics that calls on the moral resources of all who are opposed to the power block and its emerging global contours.

This age of difference thus poses new, although difficult, tactical and strategic challenges to critical and subaltern intellectuals as well as activists. A strategy that seeks to address these new challenges and openings must involve, as a first condition, a recognition that our differences of race, gender and nation are merely the starting points for new solidarities and new alliances, not the terminal stations for depositing our agency and identities or the extinguishing of hope and possibility. Such a strategy might help us to better understand the issue of diversity in schooling and its linkages to the problems of social integration and public policy in modern life. Such a strategy might allow us to 'produce' new discourses as well, especially and most importantly in this highly fraught and exceedingly fragile moment of historical complexity.

Localization/Globalization and the Midwife State: Strategic Dilemmas for State Feminism in Education?

Jill Blackmore

This [chapter] explores the implications of the processes of globalization/localization for state feminism, with a focus on Australia. Superficially, localization appears to be one response to globalization, exemplified by devolution to self managing schools and in the public sector. But globalization and localization are merely different aspects of the same phenomenon, and the processes articulating local/global relations have particular gendered effects which while locally specific in their articulation, resonate in highly patterned ways cross nationally. There has been in many Western liberal democracies a fundamental change in the role of the welfare state with a shift from a more protectionist position to one where the 'midwife' state mediates, rather than regulates, global markets. But the shift to the smaller or more selectively interventionist state, although a common global policy 'response' to the 'logic' of globalization, is not an inevitable consequence of economic globalization. Rather, it is an ideologically informed position which has gained legitimacy by calling upon dominant (if not deterministic) orthodoxies about economic globalization. Furthermore, the shift in the role of the state, as with educational restructuring generally, is as much about cultural reconstruction as it is about economic reconstruction. Feminists are wary of such moves as they provide discursive spaces to undermine past successes and future claims for gender equity. I briefly point to the significance of state feminism in select Western nation states, and then elaborate upon some of the strategic dilemmas arising out of the dynamics of globalization/localization for the delivery of gender equity reform.

Feminism and the Logic of Globalization

Globalization has provided the justification for the restructuring of the workplace, and of educational

Jill Blackmore, 'Localization/Globalization and the Midwife State: Strategic Dilemmas for State Feminism in Education?', *The Journal of Educational Policy*, 14/1: 33–54 © 2000 Taylor & Francis Ltd. http://tandf.co.uk/journals.

The author is very grateful for the careful and insightfull editorial suggestions provided by Sandra Taylor and Suzanne Franzway.

work more specifically, in most Western liberal capitalist nation states in the past decade. The general logic of most theories of globalization is that globalization is a threat to national and cultural identity due [to] the totalizing impact of information technologies and global markets and the demands of more culturally diverse and shifting populations (Waters 1995, Green 1996). Paradoxically, the typical policy 'response' in most Western liberal nation states to globalization is that of localization (Lawton 1992). The global pattern in educational restructuring has been marked by a shift to self management to produce greater flexibility at the level of the local in order to be 'responsive' to global markets (Taylor *et al.* 1997). More optimistic post-Fordist readings of the labour market and work organization see this as producing flatter, more democratic, organizations in which responsibility is devolved to individuals, thus enabling them to work collaboratively, productively, reflexively and creatively in teams. Such readings are seductive to feminists who have communitarian proclivities. More pessimistic neo-Fordist readings of post-modernist theory confirm feminist materialist accounts of workplace reform. They focus upon the apparent re-assertion of executive prerogative arising from the strong centralizing mechanisms of accountability back to the centre so typical of devolved systems of management, and upon the arising anomie and individualizing nature of life in self managing institutions informed by the principles of market liberalism (Harvey 1989, Hargreaves 1994, Brown and Lauder 1997, Blackmore and Sachs 1997). 'To describe these changes as "cultural" is not just rhetoric: the aim is to produce new cultural values and workers who are "enterprising", or self motivating, or, as Rose has put it, "self steering"' (Fairclough 1992: 7).

From whatever perspective, it is evident that the new global order is marked by 'widespread tensions between increasingly international imported practices and local traditions' (Fairclough 1992: 7), tensions particularly evident in education reform. While state education systems and organizations have devolved responsibility for implementation decisions to smaller localized units of production 'at the chalkface' (e.g. self managing schools, teams or departments) in culturally specific ways (site based management in the USA, self governing schools in New Zealand, self managing schools in Australia, grant maintained schools in the UK), the pattern has also been for governments to retain strong central coordination of policy and funding at the core (Ball 1994, Wylie 1995, Whitty 1996). This core–periphery model of organizational governance, and the tensions it produces, has implications for feminist work in education, both theoretically and strategically.

Theoretically, both post-modernism and feminist post-structuralism have displayed a fetish with the local, exemplified in their interest in Foucault and their emphasis on the differentiating rather than universalizing tendencies of globalization (Ramazanoglu 1993, Hekman 1996). But feminist post-structuralism's rejection of universalizing metanarratives (including that of universal womanhood), and its emphasis on the partiality and 'situatedness' of knowledge, the historically contingent nature of subjectivity and a politics of difference around issues of race, class and gender, as well as sexuality, produces moral and political dilemmas for feminism (Haraway 1988, Fraser and Gordon 1994, Yeatman 1994). Feminist post-structuralism questions whether there is any normative dimension upon which a feminist politics can ground its claims for equity in a liberal state (Young 1990, 1994). Indeed, feminist post-structuralism's concentration on the local, the cultural, the linguistic and the aesthetic, has often been at the expense of attending to the historical and material aspects of globalization and therefore a more systemic understanding of the politics of difference, at the very instance that global restructuring has undermined many feminist achievements (Grewal and Kaplan 1994). Kathleen Jones (1993) cautions us that to:

> . . . dispense with the female subject at this point is particularly dangerous . . . Having money permits one to fantasise escaping corporeality and history. It also enables one to ignore the political-economic system of global inequality that constructs differential opportunities . . . the political-economic context remains, fantasies of paranoic floating signifiers not withstanding, and is more extraordinarily fixed and materially more powerful, than ever . . . Systems of law, global economic inequalities, the structured disenfrachisement of most women and most men in the world, the influence of the

military-industrial complex ... are working to constitute and to fix very specific subjects in very confined and inegalitarian geo-political spaces ... (Jones 1993: 10–11)

Strategically, feminism, as a social movement, is also caught. On the one hand, there is the temptation to call upon universal metanarratives of human rights acceptable to an emerging global political 'community' or networks of global and regional governmental and non-governmental organizations (eg. UN, UNESCO, European Community) (Bradley and Ramirez 1996). On the other, post-colonial feminists suggest that such metanarratives privilege white middle class Western women's position, 'othering' that which is non-white or non-Western, and thus failing to address the temporal and spatial particularity of women's experience (Mohanty 1990).

To view global/local relations as a binary subverts any capacity to see how the global and local infiltrate each other. To focus only on the local is reductionist, as well as non-strategic as it masks any similarities and links attributable to globalization. Grewal and Kaplan (1994) suggest that the global and the local should be viewed as different aspects of the same phenomenon. You cannot consider one without the other as analyses of the 'micro' always contain some understanding of the larger, the societal, the enveloping 'macro' (Anyon 1994: 125). Indeed, the local exists within larger, often multinational organizations or education systems, through systems of communication networks, themselves manifestations of the often standardizing processes of globalization. The trend towards self management of schools and the new vocationalism, for example, 'disguises the globally dispersed forces that actually drive the production process' which demands new organizational forms and a tighter education–work nexus (Appadurai 1990: 307). The promise of seemingly more democratic, local self management, as espoused in policy texts cross-nationally, masks the overarching framework in which democratic politics and notions of public responsibility are being re-defined in the reduced public sectors of most Western liberal democracies. Similarly, the desire for flexible, multi-skilled workers masks the reality of the attack on the material and professional conditions of teachers' work as governments simultaneously seek greater control, but also more creative responses, to markets in the context of international monetary/market pressures in a deregulated global economy.

Gender is notably absent from mainstream discussions of globalization, either as an organizing principle or a category of analysis. Yet the logic of globalization should raise warning signals for feminists, because globalization is generally associated with the reduction of nation-state power and political intervention; the supplantation of politics by the market; an emphasis on the competitive individual rather than community; and the exacerbation of management/worker divides at a time of increased employment insecurity. Feminists in most Western liberal democracies have, in varying degrees, relied upon the welfare state for gender equity reform. To supplant the state with the market is dangerous for women, as the market has never recognized merit or favoured women, and has no obligation to do so. Nor do women tend to fit the model of the self maximizing autonomous individual of competitive social relations central to market theory because, in general, women have responsibilities to others due to their social location in the wider community as 'carers'. And men continue to manage while women remain concentrated on the margins in the paid workforce, despite their increasing presence. Feminist educators and policy makers should therefore consider whether the nation-state is being put at risk by globalization, or merely being re-invented to mediate market relations. And if so, how will the state mediate local/global relations and with what repercussions, if any, for the delivery of gender equity?

'State' Feminism at Risk?

The state is central to matters of gender equity, although women have always had an 'ambiguous relationship' with the state (Franzway *et al.* 1989, Gordon 1990). Since the late nineteenth century, the 'dependence' of women in such Western liberal democracies as Australia, New Zealand, Scandinavia, USA and the UK has increasingly shifted from individual men onto a paternalistic welfare state (Fraser and Gordon 1994, Koven and Michel, 1994).

The state has both promoted gender equity through legislation on equal pay parity, child care and employment safety nets etc. and simultaneously undermined such initiatives, through marriage bars, administrative regulations, and discriminatory work and labour market practices. Most feminists no longer view the state as being a monolithic set of structures. The state is conceived to be a range of practices, processes, procedures and structures which work, often in contradiction to each other, but which can provide openings for feminist interventions (Franzway *et al.* 1989). Yet there is still a level of internal coherence to any state's processes of regulation which could be described as patriarchal (Connell 1990).

The second wave of the women's movement has produced a sense of 'global feminism' and policy borrowing between nation states in areas of gender equity policies and equal opportunity. Yet global discourses of human rights, and Western feminist discourses of equal opportunity and affirmative action, articulate differently at the level of the local. To illustrate this point, I make comparison between Australia, Sweden, New Zealand, the USA and England. Historically, these nation states have all had strong feminist movements which have engaged differently with the state. I also explore the implications for the different state feminisms of the general shift from the welfare to the competitive state. Gender reform strategies vary considerably cross-nationally due to the different federal state political structures; industrial relations systems; level and strength of union activism; labour market structures; and cultural differences in emphasis upon different institutions as avenues of social change (e.g. the courts in the USA and the public sector in Australia) (Edwards and Magarey 1995).

The feminist movement in Australia significantly differs from the American, for example, in that there has been a stronger sense of collective action and egalitarianism, a greater focus on schools than on universities, and a pattern of institutionalization of gender equity policies in the public sector, and education in particular (Eisenstein 1992). Australian women's lobby groups began to work in uneasy alliances with male dominated federal and state Labor parties and unions to position feminists within the state bureaucracies (femocrats) after Labor won the federal election in 1972 (Yeatman 1992). Women's Advisers, supported by Equal Opportunity Units, openly worked for gender equity reform in most states, although with uneven success depending upon state politics (Burton 1990, Poiner and Wills 1990, Eisenstein 1992). Australia, during the 1980s, was unique for its combination of strong 'top down' national and state gender equity policies legislated upon nationally and locally, and enacted through Action Plans. These policies both legitimated and provided a language of reform for 'bottom up' feminist grass roots activities in schools (Kenway *et al.* 1997). While there has been significant debate about whether feminists should engage with, or work outside, the state, both strategies persisted throughout the 1970s and 1980s. State feminism meant working nationally as well as locally. These approaches arose out of, and were facilitated by, a history of social liberalism originating in the late nineteenth century and the postwar labour settlements between labour and capital which legitimated state intervention in economic and social life, a strong union movement and a centralized wage system which provided a safety net for women workers comparable to that of Sweden rather than the localized system of funding education and collective bargaining in Canada and USA (Probert 1995).

Whereas American gender equity policy making has focused upon legislative means and weak intervention in the economy, state feminism in Australia, as in New Zealand and Sweden, has relied heavily on strong state interventions in the economy, and as Canada, on resourcing EO infrastructure within the bureaucracy for promoting the status of women (Lewis and Astrom 1992). While in each instance, equity discourses have competed against late 1980s global discourses of managerialism and economic orthodoxies of market liberalism about balanced budgets which position equity as a cost, how feminists engage with the state still differs among nations. Canadian feminists view the state as 'containing feminist activity', and have developed a more activist non-governmental professionalized feminist lobby than Australia. Yet the emphasis in Australia, as Canada has been on wage justice (unions) and not social justice as in Sweden (Barlow and Robertson 1994, Sawer 1994). While Australia,

Canada and the UK have strong radical and socialist feminist traditions which have worked for gender equity through grass roots activities and the unions, Canada's provincial orientation has undermined the emergence of national gender policies typical of Australia or Sweden (Sawer 1994). Swedish feminist political success lay in grounding the welfare state settlement on developing women's economic independence This meant the integration of social and labour market issues as the basic precondition of welfare state citizenship. Yet in education, because gender was subsumed under the general rubric of social justice, gender specific policies have not been as institutionalized as in Australia (Lewis and Astrom 1992). So while Australia was renowned for its 'state feminism' in terms of government funded services run by women for women similar to those in Sweden, Australia still lags behind Sweden in terms of social policy outcomes, with a lower average wage for women relative to men and lower level of political representation of women than in Sweden (Sawer 1991, 1994).

In the UK, Canada and the USA, where gender equity built on race and class legislation (e.g. Anti-Discrimination Act 1975 in England), gender equity policy formation and implementation was more fragmented and localized without the legitimating and resource support of the state (Stromquist 1992, Arnot 1993). Local alliances between feminist teachers, progressive Local Education Associations, teacher unions and parent organizations, similar to the provincially based activities in Canada, 'took principal responsibility for the delivery of equal opportunities' (Weiner 1995: 75). While many English feminists see interest in the state as being less important, American feminists have either depicted the state as the villain or as gender neutral. Nancy Fraser and Linda Gordon suggest this is because the US state has been relatively less 'welfarist', less protectionist and less economically interventionist state, and, even more importantly, less visible than its European counterparts. This tendency is reinforced by the high level of state decentralization due to the federal system, the mystification accomplished by labelling as 'welfare' only some programs that contribute to a citizen's well being and not others, and the tradition of hostility marking the women's liberation movement in the USA toward the state (Fraser and Gordon 1994: 9). Segal points to the irony that:

> In the countries where there have been longer periods of social-democratic government and stronger trade unions there is far less pay-differential and occupational segregation (both vertical and horizontal) between women and men, and far greater expansion of welfare services ... Despite the existence of the largest and most vociferous feminist movement in the world, US women have seen the least overall change in the relative disadvantages of their sex compared to other Western democracies. (1990: 90)

What is clear from the above, is that the nation state continues to be important to gender equity in most instances, but that particular traditions in state feminist practice are more under threat in some states than others, due the move away from a paternalistic (and in the case of Sweden maternalistic), welfare state to a 'midwife' state which mediates global/local markets. Australia's tradition of state feminism has meant there is not the same alternative feminist non-governmental political infrastructure, as say Canada or the USA, through which to mount claims for women if the state withdraws from promoting, even if only symbolically, issues of gender equity.

The Midwife State: Policy Responses to the Globalization Logic

Paradoxically, policy responses by governments to globalization discourses have tended to be more neo-Fordist than post-Fordist. Premised upon principles of competitive individualism, market liberalism in the context of neo-conservative politics, the effect has been in public sector reform to tighten control over the workplace, rather than democratize, due to the strong bottom up accountability to the centre, and moves to deskill workers and reduce living standards (Brown and Lauder 1997). The convergence of conservative political and liberal market orthodoxies towards 'pure' versions of economic rationalism and public choice theory (compared to earlier, 'soft' versions of human capital theory invoked by Labor governments in Australia), has been facilitated by strong international links between conservative economic think tanks (Hyman 1994). The new economic orthodoxy which tends to be replicated in many nation states is to maximize exports, reduce social spending, curtail state economic regulations, and empower capital to reorganize national economies along transnational trading blocs. There is a strong element of anti-statism, which results in weak domestic policy in the face of globalization. Educational restructuring globally, informed by policy borrowing between nation states, has marked similarities across 'developed' and 'developing' states. The trend is for a shift from welfare to more contractual or competitive states, the privatization of educational costs, workplace restructuring based on more decentralized wage fixing processes, devolution towards self managing organizations, and the corporatization of education as the market penetrates educational organizations, linking them more closely to the economy (Gordon 1991, Codd 1993, Yeatman 1992, Kenway *et al.* 1993, Gewirtz *et al.* 1995, Dale and Robertson 1996, Whitty 1996, Watkins 1996).

Whereas the Keynesian state asserted primacy over the market with its regulatory tendencies, the competitive state tends to mediate the market, intervening only to reduce its excesses (Yeatman 1992, Delhi 1996). The public sector is dismantled or 'corporatized', so that it no longer 'services the welfare state, but instead, services a state which defines its primary objective as one of fostering a competitive economy', thus abandoning the 'rhetoric of social citizenship' which 'underpins the core discourses of the welfare state' (Yeatman 1994: 3–4). The state is thus increasingly withdrawn from its traditional welfare obligations, defining them as merely a domestic problem. With the interpenetration and crystallization of transnational markets and structures, 'the state itself has to act more like a market player, that shapes its policies to promote, control, and maximize returns from market forces in international settings' (Cerny 1990: 230). Indeed, 'Governments are acting as the midwives of globalization', as they deregulate along free market lines (Brodie 1996: 386).

This shapes what Guy Neave (1988) refers to as the shift in the terms of the global debate over education since the 1970s in most Western capitalist democracies. Neave describes it as a shift away from a sense of 'collective social responsibility' and the desire to 'democratize' knowledge, towards a view of education as a 'national enterprise' concerned about output; a highly technical view imbued with notions of managerial rationality. Sally Power and Geoff Whitty (1996: 1) suggest that the 'almost simultaneous emergence of comparable reforms across different continents has led some to suggest that the marketization of education needs to be understood as a global phenomenon'. It is evident in the more instrumental views of education underpinning national trends to 'vocationalize' and 'regulate' the curriculum through national curriculum frameworks, often with highly prescriptive content (Blackmore 1997*a*, Lingard and Porter 1997). Embedded in new national curricula, Whitty and Power argue, is a hidden curriculum which is reshaping the nature of cultural consumption and the messages imparted to students, i.e. the MacDonaldization of curriculum. Market liberal ideologies also re-define education as a private good more than a public good, while educational costs are shifted away from the state and onto the individual and 'self managing educational institutions' through privatization and marketization (Marginson 1997). In Australia, recent national reports argue for 'up-front' full fees for university students combined with pseudo-vouchers, and many policy makers advocate compulsory school fees in a single education market because public/private distinctions are 'dysfunctional'. Furthermore, the internationalization and marketization of tertiary and secondary education means on the one hand, all education sectors seek business sponsorship. The other side of privatization is that schools now demand increased 'voluntary' parental contribution of funds and labour. Ironically, all the above is occurring at the moment when women now constitute a majority of students in education, and indeed when their academic achievements are being lauded. Yet it is women who largely constitute the expanding 'voluntary' education labour force. Citizens are converted, through the above processes reconstituting education/state relations, into clients of a competitive 'midwife' state which mediates the education market. Students are 'delivered' as consumers to be sold a customized product. The shift towards the competitive state thus suggests a fundamental change to individual/state relations.

This shift towards a competitive state has implications for 'state feminism'. Most evident in many Western liberal democracies has been the marginalization of key concepts of equality of opportunity and disadvantage, and an emphasis on 'quality', 'effectiveness' and 'the competitive edge' in national educational policy statements (Neave 1988: 277). Values of social justice are now being supplanted by values of individual choice, and democratic notions of a rights based citizenship, a key element to feminist claims on the state, is now being replaced by the economic conceptualization of community as the arbitrary aggregate of rational, self maximizing individual choosers (Peters and Marshall 1996, O'Neill 1996). In Australia, Labor governments maintained an uneasy tension between claims for efficiency, effectiveness and equity during the 1980s. Now the radically conservative governments of recent years are supplanting the more socially egalitarian traditions of gender equity policy of the 1980s, with their focus on group disadvantage and systemic inequality, with a view that equity can be achieved by merely improving any individual's access to a range of market choices. On the premise that we are now on a level playing field, any 'special' treatment is deemed as unfair. In part, this shift has been made possible because the women's movement and multicultural movement during the 1980s have themselves put difference amongst women and cultural diversity on the policy agenda. It was easy for conservative governments to make the move from the growing recognition of the fluidity of the category of woman, 'race' and 'multicultural' as categories of disadvantage to a more individualized notion of diversity. And the notion of diversity conservative governments have promoted, contrary to the concept as it originated in the civil rights movement in the USA in the 1960s, does not rank gender, race and class as first order differences, but merely as equivalent to other individual differences in a range of behaviours, attitudes and skills (Morrison 1992, Bacchi 1997, Blackmore 1998).

At the same time, the globalizing politics of [the] more leftish governments of Blair and Clinton is increasingly evident in the cross-fertilization of ideas, as for example, between the federal Australian Labor Party and Blair in higher education, with Blair copying Australian Labor's funding mechanisms. Previously the left in most Western liberal states was receptive, although to differing degrees, to arguments about group inequality and systemic disadvantage/discrimination, and the social policies of such welfarist states actively encouraged women and children's dependency upon a paternalistic and protectionist state. Now, working within the frame of the midwife state, leftish governments take the worrying position that *all* forms of dependency on the state are bad (Fraser and Gordon 1994). Increasingly, education and training for both official 'left' and 'right' politics is expected to produce an entrepreneurial individual totally independent from the state. This is at the moment that the state is shifting responsibility onto the family for education, health and welfare and self-funding of self managing educational institutions. As many feminist economists suggest, this assumes human capital and neoclassical economic theory's notion of the atomistic individual who emerges like a mushroom fully-grown, with preferences, capacities and identity fully developed without parental nurturance or socialization through schooling (Ferber and Nelson 1993, Kuiper and Saps 1995).

So there is a fundamental process of re-privatization and re-gendering of social relations underway which has contradictory effects for gender equity. Structural adjustment policies, so enthusiastically endorsed by international monetary bodies, simultaneously promote access to education and training for women as necessary for economic growth, but demand reduced public expenditure to balance national budgets. Yet the attack on public expenditure undercuts the social wage and capacity of women to exercise choice (Unterhalter 1996: 389). Global market economies demand deregulation of the public, but at the same time re-regulate the private by 'radically shrinking the realm of political negotiation' of social movements and 'expanding the autonomy of the market and the family' by returning social welfare to the home, 'thereby creating the illusion that they are being returned to some place they naturally belong' (Brodie 1996: 389). The state raises expectations of democratic involvement in local self managing schools, but makes self managing schools increasingly dependent upon voluntary parental labour for funds. Parents, largely women, now 'take up the slack' as the state withdraws from education by acting as surrogate teachers in classrooms and pseudo-administrators on school councils (Blackmore 1998, Dehli 1996). There is a re-commodification underway in that all services (public and private) are relegated to the market, and in so doing are removed from politics, as the market is seen to be value free. These services are thus being reconstituted, but with the family, not the state, as the fundamental building block in society. Thus, state systems of education are constructed as an 'unnecessary interposition between consumers (students and parents) and providers (teachers)' (O'Neill 1996: 406). This is not only a form of economic reconstruction, but, by undermining those very institutions which have historically tempered market relations (e.g. the welfare state, the unions and education), it is cultural reconstruction. This reconstruction is achieved by corporatizing these very same institutions, and re-organizing them on the basis of market principles of individual choice, demand/supply, and competition (Bryson 1996).

The imposition of public sector reform on education has produced particular tensions between markets and equity, between localized responsiveness and centralized accountability (Gewirtz *et al.* 1995, Wylie 1995). The state has devolved to sub units such as schools decisions to prioritize between a restricted range of options and within budgetary constraints, such prioritizing being well contained within regulatory strategic management, policy and financial management frameworks (e.g. national curriculum). At the same time, strong accountability mechanisms have been imposed to supply feedback to the centre, a process facilitated by new information technologies. The competitive state thus steers increasingly more complex systems from a distance, in many instances by faxing the crises down the line to seemingly more deregulated local units, while simultaneously re-regulating (Cerny 1990, Ball 1994, Watkins 1996). Equally crucial, states seek to simultaneously manage the balance between democratic processes and the reality of increasingly executive style management. This balancing act is achieved, at least rhetorically, by drawing upon discourses which argue that local or devolved systems of educational management are more democratic, more responsive to local need, and more participatory than centralized, bureaucratic systems of governance. Re-regulation for the global economy therefore means that such anti-statist discourses jar against increased state policy mandates, e.g. national curriculum, standardized testing. Thus individuals, as citizens, suffer withdrawal of state support; but, as workers, individuals are expected to submit to greater state control to increase national productivity through enterprise agreements and to self surveillance through performance management contracts.

As I have argued elsewhere (Blackmore 1997*b*), this shift in individual/state relations, in response to the globalization logic, plays out in education in highly gendered ways. Teaching, as a numerically feminised caring occupation located in the public sector, has been particularly susceptible to attacks upon the welfare state and the deregulation of the labour market (Acker 1996, Blackmore 1997b). In Australia, feminist unionists' promotion of affirmative restructuring after 1987 sought to create opportunities to re-define skill, to revalue women's work, and to develop a new regulatory framework. Their aim was to facilitate more flexible working arrangements and enable work and social responsibilities to be more readily combined, while still ensuring that women were not confined to poorly paid and dead end jobs (Baldock 1990, Davis and Pratt 1993). But recent research indicates that decentralization of administration and industrial relations (usually accompanied by 'outsourcing' and 'downsizing'), has worked against women. Part time women workers tend not to be covered by collective bargaining or unionised and therefore, more susceptible to being 'downsized'. Those in more secure jobs under industrial awards tend to sacrifice personal benefits (recreation leave, superannuation) for family reasons (part time work, flexible hours) under enterprise bargaining agreements (Zetlin and Whitehouse 1996). The move to more individualized contractual employer/employee relations has further exacerbated the gender wage gap in an increasingly casualized education labour market (Blackmore 1997*b*). The normative principles of industrial regulation under the welfare state, which saw such forms of state regulation as promoting a public good, are now lacking as the midwife state mediates the market (Zetlin and Whitehouse 1996).

Furthermore, feminization, casualization and de-professionalization are highly inter-connected historical processes actively reconstituting the social relations of gender. The competitive individualism, outcomes orientation and surveillance aspects of the strong accountability mechanisms not only reduce the professional autonomy of teachers locally, but the strong policy frameworks of corporate managerialism have led to the reassertion of hierarchy within teaching such that professional judgement is subordinated to management prerogative, both locally and centrally, under performance management contractual arrangements (Blackmore *et al.* 1996). At the same time, there is a de-skilling process occurring within the profession, with, in Victoria, the new position of 'instructor'. Teacher instructors, without teacher qualifications, will serve under fully qualified teachers in the classroom to deliver curriculum, a position which will most likely be feminized. Thus the polarization effects of globalization which play out locally with the re-gendering of the authority relations between employer/employee in education as control is re-asserted by re-masculinized central units of policy and finance and the feminization of an increasingly casualized and deprofessionalized teaching workforce (Edwards and Magarey 1995, Westergaard 1995, Bryson, 1996). Anne Marie O'Neill's comment about New Zealand has wider application: 'Operational devolution and institutional market responsiveness occur within a context whose parameters are increasingly shaped by decreasing levels of centralized funding and increasing levels of centralized control and surveillance' (1996: 406). Devolution driven by market principles also changes the nature of the delivery of social justice at the local level. The New Zealand case is an example of the potentially detrimental impact on women of the combination of devolved education systems and free market economic policies (Gordon 1994*a*, *b*, Court 1993). The first to introduce school charters to regulate the relations between the state and self governing schools, the New Zealand government initially devolved considerable authority to boards of trustees, but with a strong equity provision targeting women, Maoris, people of ethnic and other minorities. Schools were expected to include specific equity goals for equal educational and employment opportunity. But political commitment to equity has been superseded by competition between schools, and as elsewhere there has been an increase in gender pay gap within five years and a reduction of women in leadership (Pringle and Timperley 1995). This division of labour is also racially as well as gender biased, with Maoris also under-represented in leadership. Ultimately, a conservative government repealed the equity act and rejected pay equity because it was 'social engineering by the state' (Court 1993). The EEO requirement laid down for charters remained, largely, because they did not demand pay equity, but they did 'enhance' business as women gained flexible hours to do the 'double shift' of family and paid work in return for lower pay (Court 1993). Responsibility for equity policies, when largely devolved to local communities, is often ignored, treated as a luxury or a cost, or viewed instrumentally and not as a human right. Nor is equity as an indicator of success as marketable as good academic results, technologically well resourced educational institutions, or strong entrepreneurial leadership. The market can promote particular norms (e.g. competitive individualism) within schools which, when played out in organizational forms and through curriculum, be neither inclusive or equitable (Gewirtz *et al.* 1995, Power and Whitty 1996).

As a commitment to economic globalization has come to be seen as a national matter of survival since the late 1980s, there has been a rejigging of both the content and nature of policy formation itself which has re-positioned both feminists and educators in the policy production process. First, there has been a closer linking of state education systems to the world market in national policies framed in terms of economic rationalism (albeit with different national versions e.g. Thatcherism, Reaganism, Rogernomics) to improve national productivity and international comparative advantage. This vocationalization and internationalization of education is represented in the dominant readings of global discourses of gender equity encouraging more women and girls to go into science, maths and technology, an emphasis which tends to reinforce high status knowledges of science and maths, and define success narrowly as being largely located in male domains, areas where women are usually not rewarded in the workplace for their educational achievement (Yates 1993, Kenway *et al.* 1997). It has also produced competency and outcome based approaches to curriculum which are seen to disadvantage girls and women pedagogically (Taylor and Henry 1994). Globalization pressures to balance budgets and be more competitive have also led to reduced public expenditure. Thus in Australia, education and training providers have been opened up to national and international market forces and individual students compete in an increasingly expensive user pays system, which again works against women who tend not to be supported in on-the-job training by employers or the state (Blackmore and Angwin 1997). Leaving equity to the market ignores the evidence that women's educational achievement is not rewarded equally to that of men in the labour market.

At the same time, the nature of policy formation within the competitive state has itself changed, affecting the capacity of feminists to influence state policies. Indeed, the voices of feminist educators have been remarkably absent in the re-formation of Australian education after 1987. In times of greater political and economic volatility, policy is increasingly viewed as a solution to public media generated problems as much as a seeking of a solution for social or economic problems (Wallace 1993). One response to the immediacy of managing perceived political crises has been the 'Ministerialization of policy' which has occurred as the power to initiate policy has shifted during the late 1980s largely from bureaucrats to Ministers (Taylor *et al.* 1997, Blackmore 1998). More specifically, gender equity policy has shifted into the hands of state premiers under the Ministerial Committee for Employment, Education, Training and Youth Affairs and out of the hands of public servants, many of them femocrats, as well as feminist academics who had acted as policy advisers. The effect of this is exaggerated by institutional memory loss and de-legitimation of equity discourses. This has occurred first, due to the supplanting of a public service discourse imbued with a notion of service, professional advocacy and the public good, to one in which the bureaucracy serves the government. And second, many femocrats have fled the chilly climate or shifted out of specialist equity policy areas, to be replaced by multiskilled managers without expertise in, or commitment to, gender equity. Not only is possession of knowledge and experience in gender equity (or any other field for that matter) likened to producer capture, but the new managerialism emulating business equates success to doing much more for much less. Third, gender equity policy production is increasingly being outsourced on a contractual basis to consultants who are less likely to speak truth to power due to their reliance upon delivering the goods to continue in business. Finally, loyalty upward to the Minister is deemed more important than any commitment to any constituency e.g. women (Blackmore 1998). The corporatist state, both conservative and social democratic, has, in privatizing the business of state policy making, withdrawn it from open debate and accountability.

Such responses to globalization cannot be separated out from particular ideological readings or contextual differences. Gender equity policies in Australia, as elsewhere, have often operated at the level of the symbolic than actually effecting change. Policy has not been effectively or easily translated into practice, largely due to lack of political will, even under Labor. But a regression has begun under the neo-conservative Federal Coalition, with their dis-investment in gender equity both symbolically, for example, with the abolition of gender neutral language guidelines in government documents, and in reducing the resourcing of gender equity infrastructure established during the 1980s. Nationally, the Office for the Status of Women and the Equal Opportunity and Human Rights Commission have been undermined with 40% funding reductions, the Women's Budget has been abolished, as has the Women's Section of the Bureau of Statistics, and now Affirmative Action policies (as with multiculturalism in 1997) are under review for 1998. What is left of gender equity infrastructure has been devolved to the states in the looser Commonwealth state relations of Liberal policy structures which emphasize state rights. Not only are the structures and processes of state feminism at the federal level being dismantled, but its representational voice is being de-legitimated by suggestions that 'feminists' do not represent the 'true voice of women'.

Even while there is a convergence of neo-conservative and market liberal ideologies which circulate in what are universalizing global discourses, these discourses are articulated locally in highly differential ways within nation states (Hyman 1994, Kenway and Epstein 1996). In the state of Victoria, for example, one finds the radical conservatism of the Kennett government actively exploiting feminist discourses about women as new agents of change and sources of productivity, thus channelling individual women's energy towards market ends by promoting discourses of individual competitiveness and success at a time when there is increased social and gender inequality (Blackmore 1998). At the same time, while the *neo*-conservative Howard federal government and Kennett government deregulate the labour market by seeking to move to individual contractualism and wipe out the safety net, Howard intervenes in conservative moral agendas in actively promoting a narrow view of the family. Equity discourses are being reconstituted around 1950s modernist notions of the nuclear family and homogenist, assimilationist and hegemonic (i.e. sexist and racist) notions of citizenship. Both governments, as conservative governments in the USA, England, Canada, New Zealand and Sweden, continue to dismantle the welfare state, restructure and individualize industrial relations and employment contracts, and shift educational and welfare costs onto the family and individual. So there gender equity policy is being refrained within a more conservative framework at the very moment that the citizen claims of women upon the polity have been de-politicized through increased managerialism and the abandonment of the normative principles of the welfare state premised upon citizenship, publics and public goods.

Thus structural adjustment policies promoted by global financial bodies claiming to address *economic* globalization which circulate globally amongst particular elite communities (politicians, academics, big business) have provided an environment for a political backlash against feminism. But the imperatives implicit in such instrumental and deterministic readings of globalization have been both ideological and economic. Policy 'responses' have not been an inevitable consequence of economic globalization, but reflect particular ideological positions which have been made orthodox through the legitimacy imparted to them by international monetary bodies and other global discourses (Brodie 1996). The logic of globalization, as played out through the restructuring discourses, has thus produced the very effects they assumed to describe at the level of the local through processes of both cultural and economic reconstruction. The issue now is what are the strategic implications of the changing nature and role of a more conservative midwife state for the 'delivery' of gender equity in education?

Implications for Gender Equity Policy of Globalization Logics

For Australia, where gender equity has been especially reliant upon state feminism, the discursive power of the logic of globalization has raised particular strategic problems.

While globally circulating policies appear to provide common responses to the logic of globalization—workplace restructuring, devolution, a shift from welfare to the competitive state, privatization of educational costs, market liberalism, competitive individualism—these articulate differently in specific contexts (Neave 1988, Peters and Marshall 1996, Gewirtz *et al.* 1995). The dynamics of globalization and localization are occurring simultaneously, but often in contradictory ways, requiring a range of gender equity strategies operating at different levels—at the level of the nation, the state (in federated systems such as Australia, Canada and the USA) and locally, but also at the supra-national level.

At the national level, feminist equity claims have focused upon notions of modern citizenship held in most Western liberal democratic societies. Challenges to the nation-state have come from without (e.g. internationalization and globalization, migration and refugee patterns, supra-national bodies of trade and governance and international law). Claims upon the state have also come from within, from previously marginalized groups such as women and indigenous groups (e.g. Maoris in New Zealand, Aboriginal Reconciliation in Australia, Native Indians in USA, and First Nation peoples in

Canada), now making claims for more inclusive notions of citizenship. The destabilization of the national community, itself an effect of feminist and post-colonial critiques of the white masculine citizen underpinning nationhood, requires us to ask:

> what happens to citizenship claims when the internationalisation or globalization of finance, production and labour markets is working to erode the self determining properties of the nation state . . . as the state is less a unit of governance and more a unit of political management with respect to how its internal subjects and their economic activities articulate with transnational markets and institutions? (Yeatman 1994: 449)

While the nation-state is not a polity necessarily, the corporatization of state policy and the infiltration of the market has oriented the nation-state to a new globalized context. Modern citizenship—with all its trappings of a social welfare network and public education infrastructure—has been premised upon a national society which is self determining (Yeatman 1992, 1994). This national-societal approach has produced public policy on gender equity, equal opportunity, equal pay claims and and discrimination. Now globalization threatens both national geographical boundaries and national sovereignty, with multilateral trade agreements and formation of new regional blocs, many of which ignore social equity in their reconstitution (with the exception of the European Community). Furthermore, the orthodoxy that market deregulation is the only response to globalization puts pressure on governments to further deregulate industrial relations systems which have historically been premised upon the national entity of the labour market. Australia, as Sweden, has had a strongly centralized wage system which has protected women workers, and imparted significant power to peak trade union bodies under corporatist state arrangements in the 1980s. The declining popularity of unions coincides with, and indeed is a consequence of, a casualized, feminized and polarized labour market, itself a factor of globalization in more service oriented economies (Lash and Urry 1994). The transformation of state/individual relations away from a sense of the collective good is exemplified in the supplanting of highly centralized, public, free education systems premised upon the view that state investment in education is a public good (socially as well as economically) by self managing, increasingly privatized, educational organizations serving a range of education markets in which individual clients exercise choice as a private matter (Marginson 1997). Neither individual or school has a strong sense of obligation to 'the public' in this scenario, or to acting on issues of equity which may be associated with citizenship or group disadvantage other than those which come within an individual rights claim. And what happens to nationally based pay claims, affirmative action or national equity policies premised upon equity as a principle of a democratic nation-state, when the basis is not the territorially based and legally oriented jurisdiction of the nation-state? Given that social organizations have been culturally and organizationally structured in terms of the national political economy (unions and women's lobby groups etc.), globalization has the capacity to reshape the national polity with: 'a shift to both sub national (logics of devolution and decentralisation) and supranational (transitional institutions of governance) levels where the historically achieved nation-state in most instances remains a critical node of political management mediating between these levels of governance' (Yeatman 1994: 451).

Tactics

So how can feminists working for gender equity respond to the above conditions both substantively (i.e. how gender is raised as an issue), and strategically (in terms of ways of working with/through/against/upon the state)? Generally, there is a need for both strategic essentialism and strategic pluralism. Spivak's (1993) notion of 'strategic essentialism' requires women to continue to be viewed at particular times and in particular contexts as a class or the universal category of woman in order that local and global patterns of gender inequality are continually foregrounded. It is not an either/or situation. Strategic essentialism does not necessarily lead to conservative politics, nor does recognition of the continuity and ambiguity of each identity render a shared feminist politics across class, race and culture helpless. The agent can be in an ensemble of subject—race, class, gender—positions in which, in one instance, they are dominant, and in others dominated. It is the *articulation* and shifting relations between class, race and gender, local and global, state and individual, which need to be focused upon theoretically and in empirical research, and just the shared common universal experience of womanhood. There is a need therefore to consider the 'situated knowledge' which can inform and be informed by a globalized gender politics. 'Strategic pluralism' means that feminists must work on a range of fronts simultaneously; using a multiplicity of feminist theories and strategies (Taylor 1991); maintaining short term and long term objectives (Cockburn 1992); working at the level of the local but watching for global patterns and articulations (Anyon 1994); and working from the margin and within the mainstream (Eisenstein 1995).

In the short term, at the level of the state and individual local educational institutions in devolved systems, a feminist politics for globalized times would require thinking about how particular contemporary discourses can be reworked in more progressive ways. This may involve tactics which mean working simultaneously with/against managerialist and market value systems, policy frameworks and self managing institutions. It means working from both the top down and the bottom up. It means both co-opting the language of the market, while seeking to shift its meaning. Arnot (1993) argues that the capacity for the women's movement in England to mobilize and argue against New Right notions about the family in the 1980s tempered its conservative effects. As producers and consumers, women can make powerful claims on the market, both individually and collectively. And, as I have argued elsewhere, women principals have indicated a capacity within their own local education markets, to seek to work collectively and individually in a socially responsible way premised upon a strong sense of 'the public' and community (Blackmore 1996).

Others have argued, such as Luke (1997) in the case of universities, that accountability measures, the 'institutional economies' of quality assurance, and the new contractualism can be appropriated for equity ends. This can be achieved by arguing (even if within the parameters of managerialism) for the inclusion of equity objectives, procedures and outcomes in performance management contracts, outsourcing contracts, organizational profiles, institutional charters and outcomes based measures of performance so critical to self governing institutions. While advocating such a tactic, there is a need to recognize that the delegation of responsibility for outcomes to individual managers and the lack of transparency of quality assurance and of accountability structures have a tendency to control educational workers through self-management or self surveillance (Luke 1997). Equity can be built into all contractual arrangements between individuals (line managers, executive and at the chalkface) and between individual institutions, as well as between the centre and the periphery, in a form of two way accountability to ensure implementation and outcomes. Top management commitment can be gained on the grounds that equity is more 'productive', which in turn sets up organizational expectations that individuals, particularly those in positions of power, take on responsibility about equity issues in an informed and transparent way (Cope and Kalantzis 1997). And this can be achieved, preferably through consent (professional development/incentives) rather than coercion (performance contracts/withdrawal pay). Consumers (parents and students) can also collectively and individually exert pressure upon organizations to be more inclusive and equitable (Deem *et al.* 1995).

Strategies

These are short term tactics working within parameters not of our own making, yet seeking to address the fastly moving agendas of globalization. A longer term strategy would be to undertake a feminist critique of the underlying assumptions of restructuring in ways which bring together theories of cultural and economic globalization and structural adjustment with concrete local examples in education. Restructuring policies have largely been informed by normative theoretical paradigms derived in a large part from economics, a field which feminists have only recently begun to deconstruct e.g. public choice theory, human capital theory, structural adjustment (Kuiper and Saps 1995, Ferber and Nelson 1994,

Hyman 1994). Feminist economics comes from a range of theoretical perspectives, for example, liberal, Marxist, institutional. But there is agreement that mainstream economists have a particular world view which can be summarized as the atomistic individual making rational choices within a neutral market to maximize their material gain. Theories of rational choice which assume that individuals have the equal capacity, resources and knowledge to make 'rational' choices disregard differential power relations and social relationships of responsibility, and indeed the *social* interdependencies which make *market* relations possible. There is need for more empirical research which highlights how the mainstream economic theory fails to adequately explain either global or local features of globalization: persistent income inequality, higher rates of poverty amongst women and children, occupational segregation, discrimination, undervaluing of domestic labour and women's work and the ongoing institutional division of labour along gender lines. If economics actually took into account empirical evidence which indicated that the assumptions underpinning its models did not reflect experience (and particularly women's experience), it may lead to an overturning of such central concepts (Bakker and Miller 1996).

A second long term strategy would be to undertake more cross national research which takes in a broader range of factors than previous studies. Unterhalter (1996) argues that while there is a growing feminist critique of structural adjustment as a policy response to globalization (e.g. Hyman 1994), they have not considered an alternative discourse which conceptualizes the state as well as the household in the reconfiguration of the public and the private. Such research could offer alternative locally specific policy responses to global metanarratives. As Brodie suggests, 'globalization is a paradigm shift of governing practices' and not some deterministic external inevitable force (Brodie 1996: 386). Yet the standard response by governments has to be less interventionist in the market i.e weak domestic policy by the state. Yet it could well be argued that stronger domestic economic policies are more necessary on economic grounds in consumption oriented states such as Canada, Sweden and Australia. For these countries, one 'solution' would be to follow the 'high road' of high wage, high skills model, innovation and technology so as to value add on human resources and thus maintain competitive advantage while preserving the standard of living and wages. The high road of strong domestic policy could be expected to benefit women both in terms of their public and private activities (Brodie 1996). But it requires public investment in education and training, not state dis-investment (Marginson 1997).

A third consideration is to undertake more cross national research to highlight the resonances and variations within specific labour markets e.g. educational labour markets, to understand how educational, economic and social policies—localized labour markets, industrial relations conditions, different forms of school governance and administrative structures—impact on teaching as a 'feminized' profession. Such research can better inform local labour policies, but also suggest the types of international and national strategic responses which unions and women's organizations can develop to improve women's work situations. Sandra Acker comments:

> Teacher's salaries are determined locally in the United States but nationally in Great Britain. Elementary school principals are mostly male in the United States and Canada but female in Mexico and Israel. Salaries and levels of satisfaction vary widely. Theories that rest in observations about the extent to which teachers lack status, possess autonomy, or experience control also need to be more sensitive to national contexts. (Acker 1996: 141)

Fourth, analyses in which gender is an organizing principle must also consider other first order differences of race, ethnicity and class. Social polarization arising out of crystallization of centre–periphery arrangements of global, national and organizational labour markets are racialized, classed as well as gendered. While traditional notions of class, always troublesome for women anyway, have been disturbed they are also being solidified (Westergaard 1995). To factor in class also raises issues for feminism about shared citizenship claims, given the polarization between the few individual women who are managerial professionals and who enjoy privileged access to transnational modes of distribution of goods as global citizens compared to class position of the young female instructor with minimal training and a one year contract in a school region.

Feminist Claims

Given the reliance upon state feminism in Australia in particular for gender equity reform since the 1970s, it is relevant to consider whether this reliance has impeded the growth of strong independent feminist institutions outside the state. This reliance now suggests future problems as the state withdraws from its progressively interventionist stance. In Australia, there are no obvious alternative institutional frameworks evident as there are, for example, in Canada, to take the state's place as sites of feminist activism (Sawer 1994). How will Australian feminists work for social justice outside the state? What can they learn from feminists in Canada, the UK and USA where there have been weaker state interventions in more decentralized contexts? Another aspect of this problem is to consider where any appeal for equity would best be focused, and how it should be mounted, given that the nation-state is less receptive to such appeals. Linda Gordon (1990: 13) talks about: 'the changing legalistic arrangements necessary to facilitate new political organizational frameworks and networks to work at both the supranational and sub-national levels, and a revitalisation of imagined communities at the level of the local and the global, and not total reliance upon the national'. There is already evidence of new forms of local, national and global activism. Globally, the Beijing Women's Conference in 1996 and the recent condemnation of the UNESCO Women's Committee of Australia's failure to report on equal opportunity signalled the capacity for feminists internationally to put pressure on national governments. Locally, in Victoria, alliances are being formed between women's groups and union welfare, environmental and multicultural interest groups, for example, in defence of 'the public', and in particular, in defence of public education (e.g. Education Coalition in Victoria and the national movement to Defend Public Education with a former CEO of Victorian state education, a committed feminist, as a key initiator). But as yet, these lack the same infrastructure and legitimizing discourses that state feminism had provided in the 1980s.

A further strategic issue is the grounds upon which future claims are to be made against the state or for that matter supra-national or local bodies, in the context of globalized social relations. In substantive terms, the shift from the paternalistic to the midwife state has significantly altered the basis upon which women, individually and collectively, can make claims upon the state in most Western liberal democracies (Orloff 1993). Feminist claims on the welfare state have largely been premised upon needs and rights rather than interests, given that claims on the basis of interest has positioned women as 'connoting selfishness, materialism and essentialism' (Pringle and Watson 1992: 64). Needs discourses centred around the maternalistic and caring state inevitably convey a sense of lack, or of marginality. The effect of this strategy has been that the state offers freedom to men, but protection to women. As Fraser and Gordon (1994) perceive, this produces the mythology of women as dependent rather than emphasizing the interdependence between male autonomy and women's work in maintaining the economic infrastructure.

The rights discourse has largely been operationalized by those seeking equality in the workplace to gain access to power e.g. feminist discourses about women's styles of leadership have been exploited by individual women to gain access to middle management or getting more middle class girls into non traditional male dominated subject areas (Bacchi 1997, Blackmore 1998). But the rights discourse evokes, if not possessive individualism, at least a demarcation of the citizen's realms of freedom from the state. It tends to ignore systemic disadvantage and undermines the sense of the collective interests amongst women. The needs discourse has a whole set of assumptions about the role of the state in meeting certain fundamental needs. The rights discourse of the welfare state has been too easily appropriated by market liberal discourses as exercising client choice within a market state which provides no such guarantee of fundamental needs. The market is treated unproblematically as the mechanism by which to respond both to rights (i.e. individual preference exercised through consumer choice) and needs (education, welfare, health services). This is exemplified in increasingly more individualistic versions of human capital economic theory and public choice theory. The market is also the means by which to manage diversity in a pluralistic society, where diversity is treated as a new source of both consumption (emergence of niche markets), and productivity (managing diversity through flexible specialization to respond to niche markets). One possible strategy for feminists is to explore what social justice policies and claims upon the state might be if based upon interests, a claim which respects difference, rather than needs and rights (Young 1990, 1994).

In conclusion, feminists must work not just with and through, but also on and against the state, by engaging with all levels of political activity locally and globally. These multiple approaches are not to be rejected, but extended, given the volatility of post-modern politics. While national and state gender equity policy units have called upon international conventions as normative models, increasingly, the appeal will be to the global notions of human rights (e.g. United Nations and ILO) and not national legislative norms (Cohen 1996). There is what Mohanty (1990) calls an 'imagined community' of feminism to which women can appeal which can influence governmental policies, nationally and internationally so that, for example, intra-state trade agreements (as in the EU social contract) can include principles of equity. At the same time, while post-colonial feminists sensitize us to how international bodies such as the World Bank and OECD can promote global solutions to local problems which can work to the detriment of women as a group (e.g. reduced public expenditure accompanying balancing national budgets and repaying international debt in the face of financial crisis impacting hardest on women and children e.g. Indonesia 1998), such bodies can be pressured to build in gender and race as part of their analysis of national and global policies as well as their own policy recommendations (e.g. devolution) (Taylor *et al.* 1997). This imagined community would be one which recognizes that there is not some homogenous entity which can be called Western or third world feminists—but can work through strategic essentialism and strategic pluralism forming alliances and collaborations where there is a shared commitment, though not necessarily a common experience, due to shared interests. Thus the category of woman can be used with a sense of irony, conscious of time and place, recognizing the systemic and structural gender inequality but the politics of difference amongst women.

16 GATS and the Education Service Industry: The Politics of Scale and Global Reterritorialization

Susan L. Robertson, Xavier Bonal, and Roger Dale

Introduction

One consequence of the hype around globalization and education—and debates on global political actors such as the World Bank, International Monetary Fund (IMF), and World Trade Organization (WTO)—is that there has not been sufficient attention paid by education theorists to the development of a rigorous set of analytic categories that might enable us to make sense of the profound changes now characterizing education in the new millennium.[1] This is not a problem confined to education. Writing in the *New Left Review*, Fredric Jameson observes that debates on globalization have tended to be shaped by 'ideological appropriations—discussions not of the process itself, but of its effects, good or bad: judgements, in other words, totalizing in nature; while functional descriptions tend to isolate particular elements without relating them to each other.'[2]

In this [chapter] we start from the position that little or nothing can be explained in terms of the causal powers of globalization; rather, we suggest that globalization is the outcome of processes that involve real actors—economic and political—with real interests. Following Martin Shaw, we also take the view that globalization does not undermine the state but includes the transformation of state forms; 'it is both predicated on and produces such transformations.'[3] Examining how these processes of transformation work, however, requires systematic investigation into the organization and strategies of particular actors whose horizons or effects might be described as global.[4]

One subject of globalization—and the focus of this article—is the growing importance and power of the WTO in promoting the liberalization of trade. Of particular interest to us in relation to education is the General Agreement on Trade in Services (GATS)—a process begun in 1994 that aimed at a multilateral agreement over the liberalization of trading in services, which had emerged with renewed vigor in the Millennium Round.[5] The major reasons for making GATS the object of investigation here are that (1) it is less well known than other supranational organizations that affect

Susan L. Robertson, Xavier Bonal, and Roger Dale, 'GATS and the Education Service Industry: The Politics of Scale and Global Reterritorialization', *Comparative Education Review*, 46, 4.

national education policies, such as the World Bank, the Organization for Economic and Cooperative Development (OECD), and UNESCO; (2) it operates in a quite different manner from those organizations in that it works through binding rules, rather than persuasion or leverage; and (3) it has the potential to affect education systems and practices across a greater range of their activities than have any of the other supranational organizations we have become used to reading about in the comparative education literature.

Space, Scale, and Territorialization

In this [chapter] we address these issues through an initial attempt to analyze the potential effect on the orientation and control of national education systems that is inherent in the development of GATS. This involves setting out, briefly, three rather abstract sets of concepts—space, scale, and territorialization—being developed by a number of globalization theorists around the production of space and scale, and its sociopolitical contestation.[6] We then draw on these sets of concepts to enable us to examine critical current and potential shifts in GATS's activity in education. Each of these sets of concepts has proven effective in analyzing the nature and consequences of globalization and its relationships with the national level, and for that reason we deploy them to help us better understand both the nature of the shifts that are occurring within national systems of education and what might be at stake.

Fixity and Motion in Space

The first of these concepts is that of the fixity and motion of capital. This is a key idea introduced to debates on globalizing capital and globalization by David Harvey and developed further by Neil Brenner.[7] Quoting both Karl Marx and Harvey, Brenner describes the dynamics of fixity and motion, and the tensions between the two: 'On the one hand, in its drive to accumulate surplus value, capital strives 'to annihilate space through time' and therefore to overcome all geographical barriers in its circulation process. Yet, to pursue this continual dynamic of deterritorialization and 'time-space' compression, capital necessarily depends upon relatively fixed and immobile territorial infrastructures, such as urban, regional agglomerations and territorial states.'[8]

What Brenner is emphasizing here is that for capital to continue accumulating, both its perpetual motion and points of fixity are necessary. At its very simplest, what this means is that to ensure its constant expansion, capital has to be mobile, seeking out new means and places to make profit. However, that profit can only ultimately be both generated and realized at and through fixed points. Thus, while we are often told that the celebrated flow of capital around the world financial system is so great and rapid as to escape the possibilities of control by any nation-state, including the most powerful, at the same time that flow can only be realized through institutions that are relatively fixed—as in, for instance, stock exchanges. This is not to say, to anticipate one of our major arguments, that those institutional fixes must, or will, take place at a national level or on national territory, though that has typically been the assumption until the past 10 years or so. Rather, it is to say that they are essential. It is also to point out that the points of fixity might be seen as necessary evils from the point of view of the motion of capital, whose logic is to minimize any obstacles in its way.

One of the defining characteristics of globalization is the enormously accelerated expansion of capital—especially of financial capital. However, even in these circumstances, and even in the case of financial capital, points of fixity are essential. This is because (1) capital cannot guarantee the conditions of its own existence and (2) it always has to be institutionally embedded. In other words, capitalist social relations must be set in a configuration of social institutions that is supportive of, or at least not obstructive to, its continuing expansion. The key point for our argument here is that education as a social institution is deeply implicated in both of these elements of fixity. In terms of the former, it contributes to the array of means addressing capital's need for infrastructural support to enable its continuing accumulation, brings about the necessary degree of social order for that accumulation to proceed, and provides the system as a whole with legitimation.[9] These three contributions of education systems are the key means through which education is associated with the continuing expansion of capital.

The key point here, of course, is that this fixity has typically been achieved at a nation-state level. However, it is also the case that while capital needs points of fixity, it is also driven by its own logic to minimize them, as they constitute obstacles to the free movement of goods and services, finance and labor. This is especially important in the present stage of globalization, where motion above all takes the form of free trade whose logic is to remove any barriers to its further expansion. And this is also the case with state education, which is the most national of institutions and charged with embedding and defining at the level of the social formation, rather than at the mode of production more narrowly conceived, ideas such as national identity, democracy, and citizenship—none of which is in any direct way crucial to the continued accumulation and expansion of capital but which indirectly stabilize and regularize capitalist regimes of accumulation. In sum, we are arguing that the logic of capital in an era of globalization takes the form of increased pressure of motion on fixity, or of the forces of economic change on the institutions of political stability.

Globalization and Scale

A key direction taken by the pressure of motion involves a second concept that we introduce here—the notion of scale.[10] Broadly, scale refers to nested layerings of territories, for example, territories we might call local, subregional, national, supraregional, or global levels.[11] A central feature of scale, argues Erik Swyngedouw, is that it is not ontologically given, a priori, or a definable feature of geographic territories. Rather, scale is constructed with particular activities taking place on different scales, where one of those scales might be dominant over others, as in the post-World War II period and the national scale. Harvey calls this a scalar fix, a particular configuration of various overlapping forms of territorial organization that includes all circuits of capital and multiple entwined geographical scales.[12] The scales are fixed through social processes such as legal codes, monetary regimes, networks, state regulatory institutions, and so on.

While scales appear fixed, over the medium term and long haul, we can see that they are fluid and dynamic; they are produced, contested, and transformed through a range of sociopolitical and discursive processes, strategies, and struggles over what that social space contains.[13] Struggles take place at different scales engaging an array of actors and interests, for example, capital, national states, para-state organizations, labor unions, local social movements, and supranational organizations. Summarizing these debates, Brenner notes that scale

1. is methodologically important as a spatio-temporal unit of analysis;
2. involves a critical dimension in the unfolding wave of global capitalist restructuring—referred to as rescaling;
3. is a key strategy of social and political transformation; and
4. is a metaphorical weapon in the struggle for hegemony over social and political space.[14]

Territorialization

The third concept attempts to grasp hold of the idea of struggles over space and scale—referred to by Harvey as territorialization.[15] This is the strategic action taken by social actors over space in efforts to command and govern space. The development of both cities and territorial states are examples for Brenner of territorialization: they are the result of imperial powers seeking to lay claim to territories, their resources, and subjects. In Brenner's words, 'The central hypothesis that emerges from these considerations is that the tension between fixity and motion in the circulation of capital has periodically triggered major transformations in the scalar organization of the territorial state.'[16]

Shifts in scale and processes of reterritorialization, in response to crisis and crisis displacement, are recognizable at the current time as strategies such as devolution, centralization, regionalization, decentralization, internationalization, and so on. In drawing these ideas together, we can argue that shifting scales involves the active construction and reconstruction of territories for the purposes of governing. In particular, issues that appear fundamental at one scale disappear entirely from view at another; factions that are active participants at one scale can fade from the scene or even change at another.[17]

Space, Scale, and the Governance of Education

A crucial part of our argument is that these three processes of fixity and motion, scale, and territorialization are important analytical windows through which to view the changing governance of education. Bringing these in, we argue, moves us toward a more nuanced understanding of the relationship between globalization and education. We will develop this part of the argument based on the work of Bob Jessop and his analysis of the dominant regime in the post-World War II period in advanced capitalist societies: the Keynesian Welfare National State (KWNS).[18]

Jessop argues that following the world crisis in the 1970s, a series of rescaling efforts have been underway in advanced capitalist societies as a means of managing the crisis. The outcome has been, according to Jessop, the emergence of a new type of institutional fix—the Schumpeterian Workfare Post-National Regime (SWPNR). In other words, what has been disembedded are the institutional arrangements and social relations of the post-World War II period, which secured full employment through a relatively closed national economy, demand-side management, and economic and social rights, which were, in turn, attached to citizenship of a national territorial state. Education provision within this settlement was a major social policy item largely, but not exclusively, funded and provided by the state, where conditions of universal access were linked to a right of citizenship. These regimes were primarily national in that economic and social policies were pursued within a national matrix—a national state, a national economy, a society of national citizens, a national system of education, and so on. They were also statist in that state institutions—operating at a number of hierarchical scales—augmented market forces to secure, on the one hand, economic growth and, on the other, social cohesion through a notion of citizenship as a form of social contract.

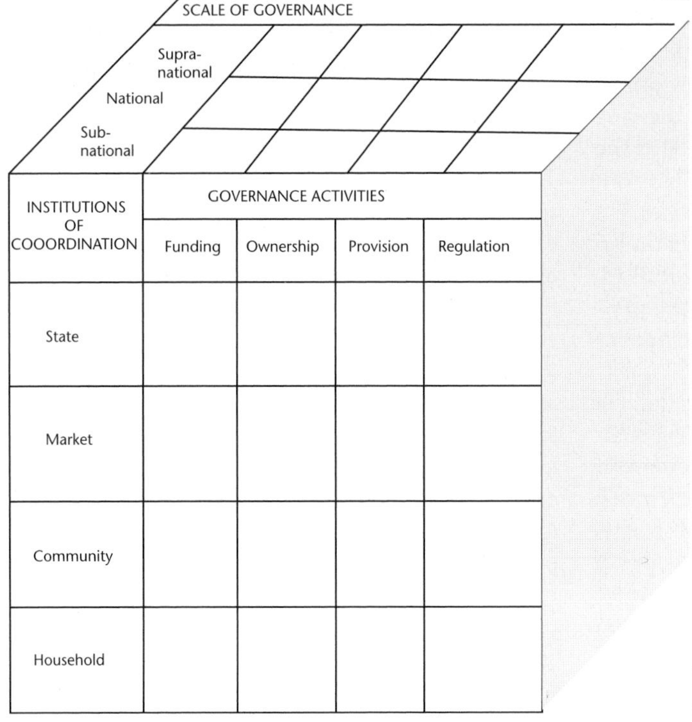

Fig. 16.1 Pluri-scalar governance of education

While the first two components of Jessop's typology—the idea of Keynesianism and especially the second, welfare—have been recognized in a number of contributions in education, the notion of the national state and postnational regime's elements have had considerably less airing. These two elements are particularly significant to our argument in that they usefully enable us to capture the consequences for education of the combination of the changing relations between fixity and motion and rescaling. The consequences of this shift from the national state to the postnational regime in education are represented in figure 16.1. The shift from national to postnational is reflected in the change in scale of governance of education—from national to either or both supranational and subnational—and the shift from state to regime is reflected in the changes in the configurations of coordination of educational governance, from assumed state monopoly over all aspects to a bewildering range of possibilities in which regulation seems to be the only necessary element of state monopoly, though we suggest that even that cannot be assumed.

Finally, we note that the strategy adopted by the KWNS was essentially, albeit in different ways and to different degrees, one of decommodification, driven basically by the state's need to supply public goods. This had two consequences. On the one hand, as has been widely recognized, it entailed the state raising taxes—from capital as well as from citizens—to pay for the decommodified services. On the other, decommodified services are by definition not tradable. When, as in the case of education, they represent an enormous expenditure, the pressure of capital is to make them subject to the rules of the market and free trade.

Pressure for the increased commodification of education is one consequence of a globalizing competitive economy where states can no longer act as if national economies are closed and their growth dynamics are predominantly domestic. In response, advanced economies have sought to develop a competitive advantage through the development of what are widely referred to as knowledge-driven economies. 'Its growth dynamic depends on how effectively a given economic space—not necessarily a national economy—is inserted into the changing global division of labour.'[19] New economic spaces can be seen with the rapid growth in the global nongovernmental services sector, which represents over 60 percent of Gross Domestic Product (GDP) in the industrialized countries and 50 percent in developing countries. By 1997, global trade in services amounted to US$1.295 trillion—around 25 percent of the overall figure for global trade in commodities.[20] For some observers, given that services account for almost two-thirds of the economic activity in industrialized economies, it was not surprising that this would eventually be regarded as an area to be opened to the world market. Indeed, there had been considerable pressure on areas such as financial services, telecommunications, transport, education, and health, with a view to expanding their horizons of operation beyond the borders of the national territory.[21]

Throughout this period, the education sector, from compulsory to higher education and training, given its role in the reproduction of labor power and in structuring national identity, has been the target of restructuring. Further, education has also been viewed as a potentially lucrative service, from compulsory schooling to higher education, which can be sold in the global marketplace. For example, by the early 1990s, the export of education services from New Zealand to Asia had risen to become a greater foreign exchange earner than the wine industry.[22] By 1996, the United States provided exports of education and training services that reached $8.2 billion, and it had a trade surplus in education services of $7 billion.[23] Education, in other words, was fast becoming viewed as an area that might yield substantial profits in the global economy. However, disembedding the post-World War II institutional fix, with its particular governance arrangements, and setting into motion the forces of capital accumulation in the form of the knowledge-driven economy involves old and new economic and political actors engaged in a process of rescaling and territorialization. It is precisely this process that we now detail in the study of a particular case of globalization: the rise of the WTO, promoted by powerful national states and capital, and the attempt to rearticulate the nature and form of education and its governance through GATS to make education systems and education provision within nation-states more amenable to a global accumulation strategy.

The WTO and GATS—Global Actors, Global Strategies

In the post-World War II period, the task of monitoring and regulating international trade was undertaken by a permanent negotiating forum: the General Agreement on Tariffs and Trade (GATT). Under this agreement, member states had the status of contracting parties. The role of GATT was to be a forum for negotiations and to lay down the rules of conduct for international trade. It was regarded, however, as a weak organization institutionally, with optional codes and a nonbinding dispute settlement mechanism.[24]

In 1995, GATT was replaced by the WTO, an international organization, which now has over 140 members. In contrast to GATT, where negotiations took place over pluri-lateral codes, the new WTO had a much stronger capacity to enforce rules as member countries commit themselves to all of the codes already negotiated. The WTO is the only international or global body mandated to establish binding rules governing trade between member countries that extend into many areas of domestic legislation.

Specifically, the WTO became responsible for the implementation of the 'tripod' of agreements reached during the Uruguay Round in 1994—GATT, GATS, and Trade-Related Aspects of Intellectual Property Rights (TRIPS). In this respect, the WTO agreements play a central role in constituting the basic regulatory framework for international trade and the development of trade policies. Collectively, these agreements have three main objectives:

1. promoting trade liberalization where possible,
2. progressively increasing liberalization through negotiations, and
3. establishing mechanisms for dispute settlement.

What was remarkable about the Uruguay Round was that, for the first time, investments, services, and copyrights were to be regarded as commodities. Initiated in the first instance by the United States at the Uruguay Round, GATT was expanded to become GATS and, potentially, the first multilateral, legally enforceable set of rules to be concluded on trade in services as a whole, cross-border as well as all possible means of supplying a service, including establishing a commercial presence in the export market. In essence, GATS sets out a work program normally referred to as the built-in agenda. According to Article 19, WTO members 'shall enter into successive rounds of negotiations to achieve a progressively higher level of liberalization.'[25]

The two basic principles of GATT were preserved and adapted in GATS. The first principle, most-favored nation, requires any GATS member country that grants most-favored nation treatment to another country over imports and exports to grant the same treatment to all GATS signatories. The second principle, national treatment, states that foreign companies who are present in the market of a given country must benefit from treatment at least as favorable as the national companies operating in the same market.

There are three levels to GATS: (1) the main text, displayed on the WTO website, contains general principles and obligations; (2) annexes that deal with rules for specific sectors; and (3) individual countries' specific commitments to provide access to their markets. There is also a fourth element to GATS; lists showing where specific countries are temporarily not applying the most-favored national principle of nondiscrimination as well as temporary withdrawals from most-favored nation treatment. However, while many service areas are not complete because of continuing negotiations and thus exemptions, governments are nonetheless committed to phasing in these commitments within 10 years. Indeed, all exemptions should not exceed a period of 10 years and are subject to periodic review by the Council for Trade in Services or renegotiation every 5 years.

According to Ngaire Woods and Amrita Narlikar, this type of agreement makes the process of liberalization almost irreversible: 'The WTO was created on an all or nothing basis whereby countries had to commit to full membership in a "Single Undertaking", binding themselves to a rule-based system, not just for the short term periods of loans or negotiations as is the case of the Fund or Bank conditionality. Withdrawal from any WTO commitment is extremely difficult, a temporary withdrawal requiring an appeal for a waiver to the organization.'[26] When a country violates a rule, the WTO can legitimately retaliate against that member unless all consensually agree to veto a decision of the Disputes Settlement Body. And the extreme difficulty of withdrawing once committed may help account for the relatively few commitments in the area of primary and secondary education.

These developments in the governance of economic activity in a national territory, increasingly by international economic institutions, and in particular the WTO, the IMF, and the World Bank, now address issues that were previously dealt with at the level of national governments, that is, 'decisions and policies taken at the international level are increasingly affecting groups and people within states.'[27] On the one hand, not all WTO member countries have been enthusiastic about lifting restrictions on foreign investment and market access, particularly developing countries that may not have a competitive advantage in these areas. On the other hand, economies such as Canada, the United States, Australia, and New Zealand have sought to promote the services sector, with an eye to its enormous export potential.[28]

That the decisions favor some countries more than others is a consequence of the way in which the agendas that emerge are the result of political struggles over the rules of the game and how they work. The governing process of the WTO is directly representative of member states because decision making at all levels is member driven and all states enjoy an equal vote. As a result, the Czech Republic, the United States, Hungary, and Canada all have the same value vote. However, in the WTO, the decision-making process occurs through consensus, and this process generally takes the form of informal meetings in what is referred to as the Green Room process.[29] Meetings are dominated by four countries—the Quad—made up of the United States, the European Union (EU), Japan, and Canada. These countries all have large market shares in the services area and enjoy significant input and influence over WTO decisions—not least because they can afford to staff a permanent presence in the WTO headquarters in Geneva, enabling attendance at more than 1,200 informal and formal meetings a year, and because they are deemed to have an interest in the issues under discussion.[30] Their influence is bolstered by the active presence of interest group coalitions, which can promote the economic interests of particular factions of capital. Not being a member, not being deemed to have a vital interest even if a member, not being able to afford a presence in meetings even if a member, and not having the resources to keep abreast of matters under negotiation to develop a more complex understanding of the issues and how they are emerging and being shaped result in even further disadvantages for the least developed countries.

Some nations and interest groups, including, until recently, the EU, have sought to slow the pace of implementation of GATS in the face of pressure from the United States and representatives from the private sector. In the case of GATS, for instance, these representatives included the U.S. Coalition of Services Industries and British Invisibles.[31] The differential capacities to fix the rules of the game thus institutionalize particular economic and political interests on a new global scale. As a result, the governance mechanisms deployed by the WTO issue in an uneven process of transformation of state power across nations, and conditions for uneven development within and across territories.

GATS: Scalar Shifts and Territorialization in the Governance of Education

How is education viewed as an activity by the WTO under GATS? We begin by noting that the definition of services covered by GATS excludes services provided under government authority and without commercial purpose.[32] While this means that tertiary education falls very largely within the ambit of GATS—which is why it is by far the most extensively commercialized sector—on the face of it, the compulsory sector, which is very widely taken to be a public sector activity, might be expected to be exempt. However, in order to meet the criteria fully and be excluded from the scope of the application of GATS, the education system of a country in question must be completely financed and administered by the state and must have no commercial purposes. However, 'few—if any—education systems remain which fulfil these conditions, most if not all of them fall within the scope of application of the Agreement. In fact, the vast majority of countries have mixed systems, in which the private sector plays a more or less significant role and competes with the public sector.'[33]

Indeed, on closer scrutiny, the public-private test is inadequate in determining whether the agreement applies. For instance, any institution that requires the payment of fees, even in a public system, falls within the category of private commercial activity and is then covered by GATS. If that argument holds, there are few public education systems in the world that could argue that GATS did not apply to them. Not only that, the direction of restructuring has been to pressure education systems to increase fees as a result of shortfalls in government expenditures on public education over the past 2 decades; others have sought to implement a system of fees in line with public choice theory—a line pushed strongly by the World Bank in the 1990s.[34] In these cases, education becomes a potentially private and therefore commercial activity rather than an exclusively public one, bringing it inside the ambit of a tradable service that could be subject to a request-offer process. This is not to suggest that as a result of this, a particular sector of a nation's education system that meets the criteria for inclusion as a trade is then immediately open for trade. Rather, if the process of progressive liberalization continues, such sectors will be vulnerable to pressure to open them to trade over the next decade.

Following the WTO-GATT principles outlined above, GATS is applied to services in education in two ways. First, it provides a general framework of obligations that applies to all countries in the WTO. This framework stipulates that there should be no discrimination in favor of national providers, that is, the national treatment principle is invoked, and there should be no discrimination between other members of the agreement, in other words, the most-favored nation principle. Second, it identifies the specific commitments of member countries, indicating on a sector-by-sector basis the extent to which foreigners may supply services to a country. There are certain basic principles that all countries must follow; however, the extent to which some services, such as education, are fully open at present to free trade has been a matter of individual choice of nations—the so-called voluntary bottom-up strategy. While this is referred to as a 'voluntary bottom-up strategy' by the WTO, it is difficult to see what is voluntary about this process. While a member country can seek exemptions from aspects of the application of the GATS agreement prior to entry, these exemptions should not exceed a period of 10 years and will nonetheless be reviewed after a 5-year period. Further, the 'voluntary' concept appears to refer to decisions that member countries themselves might make as to how they tailor their commitments in a process that involves them in progressively higher levels of liberalization. They may then be open to requests for trade that, if there is a disagreement as to whether a measure falls within the scope of the GATS agreement, involve the Dispute Settlement Body of the WTO.[35] Thus, while at present GATS is, in part, a voluntary agreement under which countries can decide, through what are known officially as request-offer negotiations, which service sectors they agree to cover under GATS rules, the U.S. government and business organizations have placed change high on the agenda in the new rounds of negotiation.

That education is a huge potential income-generating item is immediately apparent from the following crude figures on global public spending on education offered by Education International; on the threshold of the twenty-first century, global public spending on education had topped $US1 trillion dollars and 'represented the costs of over 50 million teachers, one billion pupils and students, and hundreds and thousands of educational establishments.'[36] It is therefore not surprising that education activity, as a potentially tradable commodity in the global arena, should come into view. And, while much of the export market.in education has until recently been centered on the tertiary sector, the WTO has a more expansive view of what constitutes education services. In the background papers prepared by the WTO for ongoing negotiations, education services are viewed as falling into five main categories:

1. *Primary education.*—Includes the normal notion of primary education and preschool education services but excludes child day-care services and adult literacy services.
2. *Secondary education.*—Includes high school education, technical and vocational education, and school-type services for handicapped students.
3. *Higher education.*—The teaching of practical skills in postsecondary, subdegree technical, and vocation services provided by universities, colleges, and specialized professional schools.
4. *Adult education.*—All education services not in regular schools and universities, including general and vocational programs, literacy programs, and correspondence schools.
5. *Other educational services.*—Anything not mentioned except recreational matters.

From this list, there are few subsectors within the overall 'education sector' that do not fall into the ambit of GATS. To date, 42 WTO members have made commitments for at least one education subsector, such as primary, secondary, or higher education. Interestingly, this figure of 42 includes, as one member, the European Community (EC) states—an interesting turn of events given the notion of subsidiarity that structures EU relations between the EC and member states. Further, among the 42 members, 25 have included commitments for at least four of the five education sectors.[37]

In terms of the nature of the activity that is then legally protected under GATS, there are four main categories of trade in education:

1. *Cross-border supply.*—Includes any type of course that is provided through distance education or the Internet, any type of testing service and education materials that can cross borders.
2. *Consumption abroad.*—Involves the education of foreign students and is the most common form of trade in education services.
3. *Commercial presence.*—The actual presence of foreign investors in a host country. This would include foreign universities setting up courses or entire institutions in another country.
4. *Presence of natural persons.*—The ability of people to move between countries to provide education services.

At present, education remains one of the sectors, along with the energy sector, where WTO members have been least inclined to schedule liberalization commitments—though there is clearly considerable pressure exerted to do so by organizations such as the OECD. In a recent report tabled by the OECD, it is noted that most of the OECD countries (25 out of 30) have made commitments in educational services, but a significant number of developing countries have not made commitments. Among the non-OECD countries, China, Chinese Taipei, and Thailand are the only countries among the main importers of educational services (i.e., that send their students abroad most frequently) that have made commitments. The report goes on to note that 'on the other hand there are some low-income countries such as the Kyrgyz Republic, Lesotho, Moldova, and Sierra Leone that have made a high level of commitment, most likely,' as the OECD suggests, 'in order to attract foreign educational investments.'[38]

In the following section, we signal, broadly, the existing practices and social relations of education institutions that would now constitute barriers to trade and would be subject to change following the progressive liberalization process. Concerning cross-border supply, countries would be regarded as having barriers in place if they, for example, restricted the import of certain types of education materials (e.g., teaching texts based on creation science) or restricted the use of national satellites for beaming educational activity to nationally based firms or state activity. Countries, whether large or small, have sought to foster their own research and teaching materials, where possible. However, making this a formal monopoly would be viewed as an inhibition of the cross-border supply of a service.

Barriers concerning consumption abroad are those that restrict student mobility—that is, the education of foreign students—abroad. It is here that the most visible tip of the education services market can be recognized. As noted earlier, the advanced economies, such as the United States, Canada, Australia, New Zealand, France, and Germany, have all sought to educate foreign fee-paying students in publicly funded institutions where the student pays a significant if not a total portion of the costs of their education. This is not restricted to tertiary education. Rather, such education activity might include primary, secondary, tertiary, specialist learning such as languages, or professional learning such as teacher training, social work, engineering, and so on. Barriers that have been identified as restricting consumption abroad are problems with visas, the amount of currency that can be taken out of the country, the difficulties in attaining the translation of degree of equivalents, and unequal access to resources within the country of study. Griffin Cohen observes that the sensitive issues are not likely to be those associated with visas and the like. Rather, it will be the 'way in which the removal of these barriers to "consumption abroad" is applied in distinct circumstances. For example, any country that highly subsidizes students may find a requirement to provide equal access to these resources to students from another country an intolerable strain on public finances. The result could be the elimination of public subsidies to all students.'[39]

Identified barriers to establishing a commercial presence include (1) the inability to be recognized as a degree- or certificate-awarding institution, for instance, institutions cannot get status from the state to be recognized as a university; (2) measures that limit direct investment by foreign providers, for example, because of equity ceilings (hence, some type of financial twinning is required); (3) national requirements about setting up an institution, including national advantages such as establishment grants; (4) nationally or professionally controlled needs tests—controlling the supply of particular types of labor and therefore their value—as in the case of medicine; (5) restrictions on foreign teachers—the WTO singles out the case of Greek teachers, or of France and the regulation of foreign professors; (6) the existence of government monopolies—making it difficult to establish a commercial presence; and (7) (as Cohen points out above) high levels of government subsidization of local institutions—which are not available to foreign providers.

Finally, barriers related to the presence of natural persons refer to matters such as the different approval processes for national and foreign educational providers, difficulties in the recognition of foreign educational credentials, and needing to obtain visas in order to study, teach, or establish a firm in another country. While some aspects of this agenda need to be examined further—for instance, the difficulties some educators face, particularly those from developing countries who take up posts in wealthier ones—there are other issues at stake. This not only exposes former colonies to a preference for academics from the former colonizing country but, as education becomes viewed as a private tradable commodity, foreign providers may well want to import educators rather than using local educators.

Two key potential outcomes for national states emerge if the barriers, as identified by the WTO under GATS, are to he removed in the area of education services. The first of these is that, if a country volunteers to commit itself to GATS rules in a particular education sector, this would require that foreign education service providers be guaranteed the right of access and operation, including the right to invest, to be given degree-granting authority, to be eligible for government grants for their own operations or for their students, or to send in their own labor. This would pose significant pressure on a system that was publicly funded and at the very minimum profoundly affect the public nature of education. The important issue here, too, is that once settlement of various issues is codified in GATS, any changes will need to be settled through the disputes process.

Second, if barriers to free trade were to be eliminated in the area of education services, the private sector would be in a position to undermine public delivery of education services through challenging government monopolies. Given that GATS is about securing the conditions for creating and expanding private markets in the education services area, whenever governments operate in what is—or potentially could be—a market, their actions are barriers to the creation of private markets and therefore need to be controlled. Included in the challenge to government monopolies is the notion that government funded institutions are given unfair advantages through either direct subsidies or cross-subsidization within an institution. These subsidies would either have to be removed or applied to the private sector as a matter of equal and fair treatment. Either way, the pressure would be to encourage public institutions to behave more like commercial enterprises and to have profit making rather than other motives—such as the valuing and protection of some disciplinary areas of knowledge for their own unprofitable sake—as their primary objective. These brief elaborations of the implications of GATS for education services highlight the complexity of globalization as a product or an outcome of the complex processes of territorialization and rescaling that are at work in relation to a country's education activities.

So far we have argued that through GATS, the conditions are being created for disembedding education activity from its fixed institutionalized location as a nationally regulated redistributional and legitimatory decommodified public good, forcing it into motion and into the global marketplace to be fixed through processes of successive liberalization as a part of the built-in GATS agenda. In essence, the WTO, through the GATS process, has the potential to establish a new set of global rules of the game for the governance of education within national territories, in the process transforming states' power and therefore the processes of development within and across nation-states.

In the following and final section, we examine the likely consequences for national states and their territories of this process. While this might be viewed as speculative, we, first, argue that—given the nature of the agreement as a binding commitment—such speculations are critical if we are to have an informed debate on this. Second, as indications of the likely outcomes of a process of liberalizing education, including making it more open to global interests, we can look at the social effects of the liberalization and globalization of education in countries like New Zealand, or the effect of the North American Free Trade Agreement (NAFTA) on the Canadian and Mexican education systems.[40]

Contradictions and Displacements in the Process of Rescaling

The above arguments suggest significant potential implications that rescaling will have on the governance of education as well as its social, economic, and political consequences for societies and individuals. In this section, we are particularly concerned with the potential contradictions that might emerge with resealing and the possible effects on the politics of education. Given the crucial role that education plays in ensuring both the economic and the extra-economic conditions of capital accumulation process, rescaling the politics of education is particularly important.

A hypothetical world education system, free of barriers, might entail not only an internationalization of educational credentials or a possible globalization of knowledge production and consumption but also would affect central aspects that have been largely under the control of nation-states in the KWNS regime. The process of rescaling the governance of education to the global level, and specifically to the WTO, raises a number of crucial questions. For instance, how might national human capital planning be altered if a national education system was now governed by the rules of GATS rather than a nationally specific set of rules? Further, how might one of the post-World War II roles of education, to construct national identity, be nationally secured in a global educational market place? Finally, would nation-states continue to allocate a central role to education as the central institution ensuring social mobility and meritocracy?

A key point that we want to make is that the contradictions and displacements would not be homogeneous; rather, they would be differentiated along several dimensions—the result of differing capacities and interests of nation-states to both participate in the global agenda and influence its outcomes. One dimension is procedural, that is, the mode of political and operating calculation.[41] A second dimension is substantive, that is, the social functions assigned to educational policy aspects of the politics of education.[42] The potential displacements can also be differentiated by considering which of the core problems of the state—creating conditions for capital accumulation, providing a context for its reproduction, and legitimating the capitalist mode of production—would be challenged by, the processes of rescaling and global territorialization.[43] A third possible dimension of difference lies in the capacity—or indeed an awareness of the capacity—of the implications of particular decisions in the negotiation process to control the nature of the effects caused by the process of rescaling. This capacity varies as a result of the differing economic and political powers of nation-states. These are key questions whose answers will be no doubt shaped by the crucial changes that may occur under GATS rules. An awareness of some of these questions is discernible in localized pockets of resistance in countries like Canada where similar processes have been underway as a result of NAFTA.[44] Such concerns may well account for some of the hesitation around offering the sub-sectors. As we have already indicated, the process appears to be an uneven one among actors, which is partly a result of the substantial differences in the capacity of nation-states to set the rules of the game (as there are differences in the influence capacity of private organizations over an institution like the WTO) and partly because of the differing strengths of the economies of the countries involved and the need they have to attract foreign investment—a point recognized in a recent set of papers released by the OECD.[45] The consequences of GATS both emerge from and reinforce the differing capacities of nation-states to deal with the new rules of the game in an interstate system of decision making.[46] These three dimensions do not exhaust the possible implications of the process of displacement, but they are useful instruments to analyze the potential contradictions and tensions in the movement from the national to the global level of decision making.

Setting Rules for a World without Rules: Constitutionalizing the Neoliberal Agenda

A first possible consequence of rescaling upward can be observed in what Jessop identifies as a central contradiction in the neoliberal doctrine, that is, the need to extend the scope of regulations in order to guarantee larger market access and, at the same time, to avoid all the barriers to the free, circulation of capital.[47] The GATS rules are a clear example of the need to establish political rules that have a compulsory character for its members. Interestingly, these rules of the game have to be highly codified in order to be effective. So do the modes of conflict resolution as found in the Dispute Settlement Body. A review of recent disputes on the WTO website reveals that the United States receives most of other countries' complaints, suggesting that the country that is the major player in promoting progressive liberalization through the WTO also has the capacity to disobey the rules that it has previously encouraged. Codification, however, reveals the rules and makes them evident and therefore susceptible to critique around their construction or application.

In the educational field, we might distinguish those aspects of a free market that may be quickly encouraged in the process of negotiating GATS, such as commercial presence or cross-border supply, and those that will be subject to more difficult bargaining as a result of their political sensitivity, such as the presence of natural persons, because they are more likely to have an effect, whether direct or indirect, on the immigration laws. On the other hand, the high level of rule codification in the WTO indicates a different mode of political procedure. While nation-states operate in a more flexible regulative framework that leaves scope for political decisions on issues such as creating higher education institutions and grant-system policy, sanctioning educational credentials, and so on, the WTO procedures are based on the strict accomplishment of rules leaving little margin for political flexibility.[48] This may have a decisive impact on a nation-state that has often used its education system to absorb the problems within its territory—such as social cohesion, legitimation, and support for accumulation.

Undermining the Role of Education for Social Cohesion—or a Permanent Educational Crisis?

A second effect of rescaling may be located in the structural role of education systems as important institutions for social cohesion. These distortions may take place on several levels. On the one hand, because the WTO—unlike the EU, the World Bank, and the OECD—has no social agenda, there are substantial aspects of the social function of education that, structurally, the WTO does not address. While the role of education as a means to distribute equality of opportunity may—indeed, must if legitimation is to be assured—remain on national and local state's education policy agendas, states will increasingly face the dilemma of not having the fiscal and regulatory resources to address these issues. The state's capacity to deal with the failure of the trickle-down effect of markets as a mechanism to distribute wealth may disappear in the process of displacement of the powers over education on a global scale. Some emergency strategies to react to educational crises may simply not be possible within the WTO-GATS framework, given that it sets strict rules on the state's intervention capacity. In addition, discursive resources about meritocracy may lose their rhetorical power in a global educational marketplace where the purchasing power of individuals becomes a legitimate means of acquiring a high-quality education.

Rescaling may also reduce the capacity of the national state to deal with one its core problems—its legitimation problems. While the audience for what counts as legitimation remains basically national, under GATS rules the national state may have more difficulties in generating discourses and practices to manage educational crises. It might be anticipated that a range of processes will emerge to deal with these problems. This might include recontextualization—that is, an attempt to achieve legitimation through transforming or rescaling the process to remove from view and therefore limit and manage struggles—as is the case of many restructuring states' devolution strategies.[49] However, neither recontextualization nor rescaling will ultimately fully absorb the displacement of the legitimation burden unless the WTO itself moves toward developing mechanisms to deal with these problems—like the EU. This is particularly the case at the current conjuncture. As William Robinson argues, 'even if the global financial system can be brought under regulation the mechanisms simply do not exist for absorption strategies, nor does the system provide the material basis for a project of legitimation. It is not clear in the new epoch how these new contradictions will be played out or to what extent we may expect a transnational state to acquire the capacity to resolve them.'[50]

Interestingly, the for-profit discourse of an organization like the WTO leaves little space for the development of discursive and political strategies to deal with the potential and inevitable contradictions and displacements of capital accumulation and, thus, problems of legitimation. To date, the WTO has relied almost exclusively on the discourse of neoliberalism and arguments about the trickle-down effect. However, as the WTO meeting in Seattle in 2000 showed, the WTO will require more in its regulatory armory to absorb the evident problems that have emerged in unequal trading relations. In other words, in the context of a growing world-watching civil society, the WTO has until recently shown little internal capacity to deal with social and political conflict. Its reactive strategies, as exemplified by tactics such as having meetings in remote places like Qatar or using crude slogans, are not at all sophisticated. Rather, these have become easy targets for the new global social movements.

From Investment to Consumption: The Business of Education and the Human Capital Problem

We have already suggested that under GATS, education may be regarded as a for-profit service. Although we have already referred to some of the implications of this, a further crucial aspect still remains unexplored. If education becomes a key industry for the process of capital accumulation in the knowledge-based economy, this possibility would transform states by entailing a crucial shift in the economic functions assigned to educational systems under the KWNS regime. Supported by human capital theory, education has played a central role in the process of capital accumulation and economic development. That is, education has been understood by states as a key investment to improve labor productivity and economic growth. Indeed, the human capital paradigm has been given as the rationale for educational planning. Although based on neoclassical economics, this paradigm has oriented educational policy making in national governments as well as in international organizations like the World Bank.[51] Priorities and strategies concerning educational investment are established in national ministries and supranational organizations as means for economic growth and for absorbing the problems of potential market failure.[52]

However, if the primary leitmotiv of the rescaling and territorializing processes for global capital is about market access, then it follows that, by setting into motion and commodifying education, GATS rules undermine the strategic and economic functions, as well as the social functions, of education in national systems. Through GATS, education becomes a goal rather than a means in the process of capital accumulation. Although the goals and the means of the economic functions of education are not necessarily mutually exclusive, those aspects that may guide the expansion of education in the search of consumers may contradict those that guide education as an area of strategic investment for economic development.

Moreover, the attack on the state sovereignty has the effect of limiting the state's ability to invest strategically in education; it can also affect the strategic decisions of nation-states in considering education as another area of foreign capital attraction. In a highly competitive global market, attracting foreign educational capital may well become a means of solving a country's balance of payments problems and a strategy to deal with the state's fiscal deficit. Indeed, this appears to be a reason, as we have noted earlier, for some countries signing all of their education sectors onto all modes of educational trade.

The Localization of Globalisms: The Emergence of New Forms of Cultural Imperialism

The final possible consequence of rescaling to be considered here is concerned with the possible cultural implications of GATS on national education systems.[53] The scope of these effects may be diverse and may not be able to be predicted but would include all possible forms of cultural imposition, for example, U.S. texts on science, cultural hybridization as a result of global education channels such as Channel One, or the process of production and circulation of cultural commodities. Analyzing these possible effects is beyond the objectives of this [chapter]; however, we can point to the likely consequences for nations of cultural functions assigned to educational institutions by post-World War II nation-states—many of which have a public-good character. These include the building of national identity, the use and development of national language, a certain national policy of knowledge production, and the production and reproduction of specific forms of cultural capital appropriated by the emerging new middle classes. Whatever the form of the consequence, what is important to register is that because of GATS constraints, nation-states will lose a considerable capacity to direct these outcomes in ways that they might previously have done. Language and national identity are vulnerable social functions in a global marketplace dominated by multinational educational corporations. Indeed, the basis of a national policy for knowledge production, its national appropriation and its distribution, may be eroded in a free-market context of a knowledge-driven economy.[54] Along with the importance of knowledge and information as key inputs for economic productivity and growth, the struggle over its production, appropriation, and dissemination becomes a critical aspect for the structuring of the unequal global social structure.

Finally, even the role of schooling for cultural and social reproduction will face important challenges. Middle classes have historically tried to influence, participate in, or even appropriate some state institutions to ensure the basis of their privileged position through the production and reproduction of cultural capital.[55] Rescaling crucial aspects of the governance of education upward might potentially undermine the role of cultural capital in the reproduction of social structure while stressing the economic capacity of individuals to access the top global higher-education institutions. Mechanisms of social and cultural reproduction may be altered as a consequence of a changing educational market that affects the patterns of educational aspirations and educational consumption.

Conclusions

In this analysis, we have attempted to make a number of points. First, we sought to move the analysis of globalization and education forward by introducing a series of concepts—fixity and motion, space, scale, and territorialization—that we believe give greater purchase on this complex process of change in the governance of education through the WTO-GATS process. Further, we argued that identifying key political and economic actors like the WTO as subjects of globalization and examining the mechanisms through which they both exert power and respond to pressures moves us away from the ideological appropriations of globalization. In essence, we used this as a window on complex processes at work to reveal real actors and interests. Examining the politics of rescaling and the emergence of the WTO as a global actor (and the mechanisms like GATS through which rescaling works on national territories and education systems) enables us to see how education systems are both offered as a new service to trade in the global economy and pressured into responding to the logic of free trade globally. We are also able to see processes of territorialization at work, particularly through the way in which particular countries have been very powerful in promoting liberalization in ways that suit their own interests. We have argued that the WTO becomes a site where powerful countries are able to dominate and shape the rules of the game, and in a global economy some countries increasingly view opening up their education systems to the global marketplace as a means of attracting foreign investment. At the same time we have tried to be careful to not suggest that the WTO is simply an instrument of global capital, though this is surely a part of the story. Rather, we have shown that many states—though not all in the same way and not for the same reasons—are at least willing if not eager players in the WTO processes, as they seek to advance their own national interests in the global knowledge economy. Further, the process of rescaling aspects of the governance of education upward to the global level will, we believe, pose considerable problems in the short and medium terms for national states. That is, national states will find it increasingly difficult to manage both the conditions that ensure the expansion of capitalism and the means to absorb its contradictions because their technical and political capacity will be curtailed. Diminished state autonomy—particularly in the provision and regulation of traditionally public goods—without the possibility of constructing at the same time global political structures to account for market failures may locate education at the forefront of national and global political battles. If this happens, the role of national education system in fixing, albeit indirectly, the conditions for the expansion of global capitalism—in the face of no alternative—will be eroded. This will, surely, create a much shakier terrain than it has been to date, and that new terrain will inevitably threaten its legitimatory base.

NOTES

This [chapter] draws on work on globalization and the state funded by the Royal Society of New Zealand, Marsden Award VOA-918. The argument was inspired by a course taught by Bob Jessop and Ngai-Ling Sum at the University of Oslo's 2001 Comparative Social Sciences Summer School. We are indebted to the insightful and incisive comments on an earlier version of the article made by Bob Jessop and Mark Ginsburg, as well as the critical comments of three anonymous reviewers.

1. For important accounts, see Martin Carnoy, 'Globalization and Educational Restructuring' (International Institute for Educational Planning, Paris, 2000); Phillip Jones, 'Globalization and Internationalism: Democratic Prospects for World Education,' *Comparative Education* 34, no. 2 (1998): 143–55; Roger Dale, 'Specifying Globalization Effects on National Policy: A Focus on the Mechanism,' *Journal of Education Policy* 14, no. 1 (1999): 1–17, and 'Globalization and Education: Demonstrating "A Common world Educational Culture" or Locating "A Globally Structured Educational Agenda"?' *Educational Theory* 50, no. 4 (2000): 427–48; and Sandra Taylor and Miriam Henry, 'Globalization and Educational Policy-making: A Case Study,' *Educational Theory* 50, no. 4 (2000): 487–504.
2. Fredric Jameson, 'Globalisation as Political Strategy,' *New Left Review* 4 (July–August 2000): 49–68, quote on 49.

3. Martin Shaw, 'The State of Globalization: Toward a Theory of State Transformation,' *Review of International Political Economy* 4, no. 3 (1997): 497.
4. Bob Jessop, 'The Changing Governance of Welfare: Recent Trends in Its Primary Functions, Scale and Modes of Coordination,' *Social Policy and Administration* 33, no. 4 (1999): 348–59.
5. The Millennium Round refers to the new round of negotiations that opened at the meeting in Seattle in November 1999 and that replaced the previous Uruguay Round. In essence, this takes negotiations into the new millennium over a 10-year period. See World Trade Organization, *Services: Agreement* (Geneva: World Trade Organization, 1994).
6. See David Harvey, *The Limit to Capital*, 2nd ed. (London: Verso, 1999), and *The Condition of Postmodernity* (Oxford: Blackwell, 1989); H. Lefebvre, *The Production of Space* (Oxford: Blackwell, 1991); Neil Brenner, 'Between Fixity and Motion: Accumulation, Territorial Organisation and the Historical Geography of Spatial Scales,' *Environment and Planning D. Society and Space* 16, no. 1 (1998): 459–81, and 'Globalization as Reterritorialization: The Re-scaling of Urban Governance in the European Union,' *Urban Studies* 36, no. 3 (1999): 431–51; Chris Collinge, *Spatial Articulation of the State: Reworking Social Relations and Social Regulation Theory* (Birmingham: Centre for Urban and Regional Studies, 1996); Jessop, 'The Changing Governance of Welfare.'
7. See Harvey, *The Limits to Capital*; Brenner, 'Between Fixity and Motion.'
8. See Brenner, 'Between Fixity and Motion,' p. 461.
9. See Roger Dale, *The State and Education Policy* (Milton Keynes: Open University Press, 1989).
10. As early as the 1970s, Henri Lefebvre posed the 'the scale question'—in particular its social production and sociopolitical contestation.
11. Harvey, *The Limit to Capital*, p. 423.
12. Ibid., pp. 422–24.
13. Erik Swyngedouw, 'Neither Global nor Local: Globalization and the Politics of Scale,' in *Spaces of Globalization: Re-asserting the Power of the Local*, ed. K. Cox (New York: Guilford, 1996), p. 96.
14. Brenner, 'Between Fixity and Motion,' p. 460.
15. See Harvey, *The Limit to Capital*, pp. 398–405.
16. See Brenner, 'Between Fixity and Motion' (n. 6 above), p. 472.
17. See Harvey, *The Limit to Capital* (n. 6 above), pp. 422–23.
18. See Bob Jessop, 'Reflections on Globalization and Its (Il)Logics,' in *Globalization and the Asia Pacific: Contested Territories*, ed. Kris Olds, Peter Dicken, Paul E. Kelly, and Henry Wai-Chung Yeung (London: Routledge, 1999). pp. 19–38.
19. Jessop, 'The Changing Governance of Welfare' (n. 4 above), p. 352.
20. See Education International, 'The WTO and the Millennium Round: What Is at Stake for Public Education?' (Educational International, Brussels, 1999), p. 4. Available at http://www.ei-ie/pub/eng/epbeipsiwto.html.
21. See, e.g., the OECD-US Forum on Trade in Educational Services, Washington, D.C., May 23–24, 2002.
22. See the Ministry of Education website—and documents such as 'Export Education in New Zealand: A Strategic Approach to Developing the Sector' (New Zealand Ministry of Education, Wellington. 2001). The report notes that in New Zealand there are over 700

export providers (New Zealand has a population of 3 million), which in 2000 contributed $700 million to the economy. It is noted that the export of education services had the potential to realize $1 billion. For an analysis of the early stages of this development, see Roger Dale and Susan Robertson, '"Resiting" the Nation, "Reshaping" the State: Globalization Effects on Education Policy,' in *Education Policy in New Zealand: The 1990s and Beyond*, ed. Mark Olssen and Kay Morris-Matthews (Palmerston North, New Zealand: Dunmore, 1997), p. 224.

23. See Robert E. Quinn, 'The WTO and Education 180/MDE' (Earthsystems, 1999), p. 2. Available at http://www.earthsystems.org/seac/seac-discussion/0767.html. Earthsystems is a nonprofit 501(c)3 organization, originally based at the University of Virginia.

24. See Jagdish Bhagwati, 'After Seattle: Free Trade and the WTO,' *International Affairs* 77, no. 1 (2001): 15.

25. See http://www.wto.org.

26. This section of the WTO agreement, Article 9, secs. 3–5, establishing the WTO is discussed by Ngaire Woods and Amrita Narlikar, 'Governance and the Limits of Accountability: The WTO, the IMF and the World Bank,' *International Social Science Journal* 53, no. 170 (2001): 569–83, quote on 572.

27. Ibid., p. 572.

28. The whole of the Asian region is regarded as a huge potential market for services; almost 3.1 billion people—over 60 percent of the world's population—lives in Asia. A number of these economies have high rates of growth that are predicted to continue well into the twenty-first century—with a growing middle class and growing discretionary income to spend (Singapore, Taiwan, Malaysia, and Hong Kong). These markets have proved lucrative ('World Investment Report' [United Nations Conference on Trade and Development, New York, 1995]). See, e.g., WTO-GATS, 'Communication from New Zealand—Negotiating Proposal for Education Services' (World Trade Organization, Geneva, June 26, 2001)—where the export of education is promoted as critical for generating revenue for public and state sector institutions—and 'vital' for the development of human capital (available at http://www.wto.org).

29. See Woods and Narlikar; Chakravarthi Raghavan, 'After Seattle, World Trade System Faces Uncertain Future.' *Review of International Political Economy* 7, no. 3 (2000): 495–504.

30. See Bernard Hoekman and Michel Kostecki, *The Political Economy of the World Trading System: The WTO and Beyond* (Oxford: Oxford University Press, 2001).

31. In the Seattle Round of the WTO, the Coalition of Service Industries (CSI) outlined their goals: (i) ensure the right of U.S. companies to establish operations in foreign markets, including the right to wholly own these investments; (ii) ensure that U.S. companies get 'national treatment' so that foreign investors have the same rights as domestic companies in a given market; (iii) promote procompetitive regulatory reform focused on an inadequacy of appropriate and consistent rules as well as transparency and impartiality of regulatory administration; (iv) remove barriers to cross-border trade; and (v) remove obstacles to the free movement of people and business information. A second group—British Invisibles—have also been prominent in the WTO forums. Otherwise known as International Financial Services London (IFSL), British Invisibles are a London-based organization who work for the removal of barriers to trade in the global market for 'invisible' financial services. British Invisibles played an important role in the negotiations that led up to the 1997 Agreement on Financial Services under the WTO (see IFSL website: http://ifsl.org.uk).

32. Article 1.3 of GATS.

33. See Education International (n. 20 above), p. 6.

34. Using public-choice theory, the New Zealand government has argued—successfully—that the private benefits of education arising from higher education should be paid for privately through a fee structure. For an account of this, see Robert Stephens, 'Financing Tertiary Education,' in Olssen and Morris-Matthews, eds., pp. 190–208. For a discussion on World Bank policy in this regard, see Christopher Colclough and Keith Lewin, *Educating All the Children: Strategies for Primary Schooling in the South* (Oxford: Clarendon, 1993).

35. While it might be inferred that this has arisen as a result of particular players attempting to put a 'brake' on the process in the face of U.S. pressure, it should be noted that at the time of writing the United States had only offered one sector—the adult sector—in the voluntary negotiations over education services.

36. See Education International, p. 3.

37. These are the Czech Republic, Hungary, Japan, Mexico, Norway, Poland, the Slovak Republic, Switzerland, Turkey, the EU, Albania, China, Chinese Taipei, Croatia, Estonia, Georgia, Jordan, the Kyrgyz Republic, Latvia, Lesotho, Liechtenstein, Lithuania, Moldova, Oman, and Sierra Leone.

38. See OECD/CERI, 'Current Commitments under the GATS in Educational Services' (a background document prepared for the OECD/US Forum on Trade in Educational Services, Washington, D.C., May 23–24, 2002), p. 7.

39. See Marjorie Griffin Cohen, 'The World Trade Organization and Post Secondary Education: Implications for the Public System' (British Columbia Teachers' Federation, Vancouver, 2000), p. 4. Available at http://bctf.bc.ca/social/globalization/CohenPaper.html.

40. See Susan Robertson and Roger Dale, 'Local States of Emergency: The Contradictions of Neo-Liberal Governance in Education in New Zealand,' *British Journal of Sociology of Education* 23, no. 3 (2002), in press. For a discussion of NAFTA on the Canadian and Mexican education systems, see Roger Dale and Susan Robertson, 'The Varying Effects of Regional Organizations as Subjects of Globalization of Education,' *Comparative Education Review* 46, no. 1 (2002): 10–36.

41. See Bob Jessop, *State Theory: Putting Capitalist States in Their Place* (University Park: Pennsylvania State University Press, 1990), p. 343.

42. Ramesh Mishra, *Globalization and the Welfare State* (Cheltenham: Elgar, 1999).

43. Roger Dale, The State and Education Policy (n. 9 above).

44. See, e.g., the work of the Canadian Centre for Policy Alternatives, a research group formed in reaction to NAFTA. They currently publish widely on GATS—e.g., see Scott Sinclair, *GATS: How the World Trade Organization's 'New Services' Negotiations Threaten Democracy* (Ottawa: Canadian Centre for Policy Alternatives, 2000).

45. OECD/CERI.

46. See John Dunning, 'The Future of the WTO: A Socio-Relational Challenge?' *Review of International Political Economy* 7, no. 3 (2000): 473–83, on the differential capacities of member nations in the negotiation process; he refers to difference of intellectual capital and social relational capital that mediate and thus produce uneven outcomes for different members.

47. See Bob Jessop, 'The Changing Governance of Welfare' (n. 4 above).

48. See Saskia Sassen, 'Servicing the Global Economy: Reconfigured States and Private Agents,' in Olds et al., eds. (n. 18 above), p. 159.

49. See Basil Bernstein, *Pedagogy, Symbolic Control and Identity: Theory, Research, Critique* (London: Taylor & Francis, 1996). See also Xavier Bonal, 'Managing Education Legitimation Crises in Neo-Liberal Contexts: Some Semi-peripheral Evidence' (paper presented at the Travelling Policy/Local Spaces: Globalisation, Identities and Education Policy in Europe conference, University of Keele, U.K., June 27–29, 2000).

50. See William Robinson, 'Social Theory and Globalization: The Rise of the Transnational State,' *Theory and Society* 30, no. 2 (2001): 189.

51. See Phillip Jones, *World Bank Financing of Education: Lending, Learning and Development* (London: Routledge, 1992); Woods and Narlikar (n. 26 above).

52. See, e.g., the need for the Australian government to regulate the provision of private education services following financial losses by some companies; this was seen by key Asian countries to be an international political issue to be dealt with by the national state.

53. See seminal works such as Michael Young, ed., *Knowledge and Control: New Directions for the Sociology of Education* (London: Collier-Macmillan, 1971); Apple, ed. (n. 9 above); Pierre Bourdieu, 'The Forms of Capital,' in *Education, Economy and Society*, ed. Albert H. Halsey, Hugh Lauder, Phillip Brown, and Amy Stuart Wells (Oxford: Oxford University Press, 1997).

54. For an excellent analysis of knowledge production and appropriation, see John Frow, 'Knowledge as Gift and Commodity,' *New Left Review*, no. 219 (1996): 108.

55. Bourdieu.

Globalization and the Changing Nature of the OECD's Educational Work

Fazal Rizvi and Bob Lingard

Introduction

In recent years, intergovernmental organizations (IGOs) have become highly influential in shaping educational policy at the national level. They have played a prominent role in charting the policy agendas of nation-states; in turn national governments have looked to IGOs to construct their strategies for developing, legitimating, and implementing programs of educational reform. Developing countries have of course always been subject to the dictates of IGOs, such as the World Bank and other lending bodies, through mechanisms of accountability attached to loans and aid, such as the structural adjustment schemes. But more recently, governments of developed countries too have ceded some of their autonomy in public policy development to IGOs. For example, the Bologna Process, supported by the European Union (EU), has compelled national policymakers to restructure their systems of higher education to ensure a fairer and more efficient system of credit transfer, enabling students to become more mobile across national systems, something which is considered highly desirable for the global economy. As Martens et al. (2004) have pointed out, IGOs have become increasingly important in national policymaking in education by developing new governance mechanisms involving policy and program coordination, opinion formation, and the development of other instruments of both legal requirements and financial support.

Among the intergovernmental organizations affecting educational policy development, the OECD plays a pre-eminent and distinctive role, especially in the developing countries, but increasingly in the rest of the world as well. More and more, the OECD has developed alliances with other intergovernmental organizations such as UNESCO, EU, and the World Bank not only to explore the contours of policy options in education, but also actively to promote its policy preferences. The case of the OECD is interesting because it neither has the legal instruments at hand nor financial means at its disposal actively to promote policymaking at the national level; yet over the past decade its influence over its member countries and others has increased markedly. Through its Indicators in Education project, through the Programme for International Student Assessment (PISA), and through its thematic policy reviews, its educational agenda has become an important reference point for assessment of policy initiatives and programme effectiveness at the national level, while also contributing to the constitution of a global policy space in education (Lingard, Rawolle, and Taylor 2005).

In this chapter we explore some of the reasons for the increasing international influence of the OECD in education; and suggest that a part of the explanation lies in the way the OECD has utilized the ideology of globalization, speaking consistently of 'the imperatives of globalization' and of the need to reformulate educational purposes and governance in line with the requirements of the global economy. From its very beginning, the OECD has had to negotiate a central tension at the heart of its educational policy work between the economic and cultural ends of education, between the promotion of social equity on the one hand and social efficiency on the other. We will argue that over the past decade or so, the OECD agenda in education has increasingly become tilted towards social efficiency, as it has promoted a particular ideological view of educational aims linked to the requirements of a global knowledge economy and a range of ideas about educational governance derived from the new theories of public management, which increasingly promote corporatized and privatized administration of education, outcome measures, and knowledge as commodity.

The OECD

As an intergovernmental organization affecting the seeming convergence of education policy thinking around the world (see Rizvi 2005), the OECD occupies an important place. Its educational policy work is widely used by national governments to guide their reform agendas. Its statistical compilations provide a reference point for benchmarking and for promoting policy debates. Governments look to the OECD to define policy options; and are increasingly prepared to fall in line behind its recommendations. This has not always been the case. The OECD has traditionally viewed itself as a unique forum, which enables the governments of the industrialized economies to examine and formulate their own distinctive policies in both economic and social spheres. However, its outreach and impact are now greater than this, through its work with 'non-member economies' and its contribution to global policy discourse in education. Its Directorate for Education, for example, has a Unit for Co-operation with Non-member Economies (NME), the terminology used by the OECD to refer to non-member countries.[1]

The OECD has variously and simultaneously been described as: a think-tank, a geographic entity, an organizational structure, a policymaking forum, a network of policymakers, researchers, and consultants, and a sphere of influence (Henry et al. 2000: 1). In formal terms, the OECD describes itself as: . . . 'a club of like-minded countries. It is rich, in that OECD countries produce two thirds of the world's goods and services, but it is not an exclusive club. Essentially, membership is limited only by a country's commitment to a market economy and a pluralistic democracy' (OECD 1997).

Established in 1961 out of the Organization for European Economic Cooperation (OEEC) funded under the Marshall Plan for the economic reconstruction of Europe, the OECD has remained essentially a US-backed initiative, with the United States still contributing 25 per cent of the Organization's budget. This is not to say the relationship between the US and the OECD's European members has always been an easy one. Indeed, the European countries have always sought to 'tone down' the dominant US versions of market liberalism, with their own distinctive social democratic agendas. The US interventions in key appointments and in the formulation of work plans have also been resisted from time to time. For example, in relation to education, it was largely at the insistence of the US and against considerable internal opposition that the controversial project on educational indicators was initiated in the mid-1980s (Henry et al. 2000: Ch. 4). Perhaps, then, Haas's description (1990: 159) of the founding of the OECD as 'a rather incoherent compromise between the United States and the European members' retains salience, as does his observation that most international organizations have their own superpower 'capable of playing a hegemonic role if it chose to do so' (p. 57).

It should be noted however that the OECD's capacity to contain its members is limited, because unlike many other international agencies, the OECD has no prescriptive mandate over its member countries. Rather, it operates through a process of 'consensus building' and through 'peer pressure'. It is proud of its 'traditions of transparency: of providing explanations and justifications for policy, and of engaging in critical self-appraisal' (OECD 1998: 102). As Martens et al. (2004: 15) point out, the OECD does not have any legally binding mandate over its members; nor does it have the financial resources at its disposal to encourage policy adoption. It thus seeks to exert influence through processes of 'mutual examination by governments, multilateral surveillance and peer pressure to conform or reform'. Structurally, this is done through an elaborate system of directorates, committees, and boards, at the apex of which is a Council comprising representatives from each member country, normally at ambassadorial or ministerial levels. In this way, the OECD asserts its agenda in rather informal ways though the processes of opinion formation and coordination, in a manner that is dynamic and constantly shifting.

Over the past decade or so, however, its proud record as a debating forum has seemingly been undermined by the triumph of neo-liberal precepts of economic activity. As we have already noted, within the OECD there has always been a tension between support for US-style market capitalism with a minimal welfare state and the stronger European social-market model framed by social-democratic ideology. The OECD encouraged debates between Keynesian thinking and views critical of its assumptions. In more recent years, however, this debate, once conducted in philosophical terms, seems to have vanished, replaced by a more technocratic discourse concerning the ways neo-liberal policies of free trade and competition are best promoted. Ideological debates have thus been replaced with technical questions of how to promote trade and monitor neo-liberal reforms in the entire range of the OECD's policy concerns from industrial relations and infrastructure to immigration and education. It thus appears to be the case that, while some ideological tensions remain, the framework of much of the OECD's policy work has shifted decidedly towards the US neo-liberal model.

The OECD's Educational Work

Nowhere is the shift in the recent OECD's policy orientation more evident than in the growing importance it now attaches to education. Such is its emphasis on the knowledge economy in the new century that, in 2002, the OECD established a separate Directorate for Education, something it had resisted for most of its history (Papadopoulos 1994). In establishing the Directorate, the secretary-general of the OECD stressed that 'education is a priority for OECD Member countries and the OECD is playing an increasingly important role in this field. Society's most important investment is in the education of its people.' He noted in particular how the internationally comparable statistics and indicators underpin much of the work of the OECD, and that the ultimate outputs of its policy recommendations are designed to increase both the quality and equity of education systems. He went on to list equity in access and outcomes, quality, choice, public and private financing, and individual and social returns to investment in learning as major areas of concern for the OECD. In presenting the OECD's educational work in such terms, he appeared to commit the Organization to a neo-liberal instrumentalist conception of education, viewed as a major factor in contributing to human capital formation and economic growth.

Of course, this should hardly be surprising, since the OECD is after all an organization concerned primarily with economic policy; and in so far as it has an interest in education, this must clearly be linked to its overall economic objectives. This is in line with the OECD's original charter in which there was no independent structural location for education within the Organization, though there was always an 'inferred role' (Papadopoulos 1994: 11), deriving from early human capital formulations of links between economic productivity and educational investment, then somewhat narrowly conceived in terms of boosting scientific and technological personnel capacity and, by extension, of improved and expanded science and mathematics education in schools. Hence, initially education-related activities were carried out under the rubric of the Office for Scientific and Technical Personnel, which in turn grew out of the former OEEC's pivotal work in mapping the technological gap between Europe and North America, against the broader backdrop of geopolitical issues relating to the Cold War (Papadopoulos 1994).

It was not until 1968 that the Centre for Research and Innovation (CERI) was established within the OECD, partly as a result of a growing recognition within the Organization of the 'qualitative' aspects of economic growth 'as an instrument for creating better conditions of life' and, along with that, of a more comprehensive view of education's multiple purposes. By 1970, then, the Organization had come to the realization that 'the full range of objectives of education had to be taken into account if the educational activities of the Organization were to make their rightful contribution to economic policy' (Papadopoulos 1994: 64). According to Papadopoulos (p. 122), this marked the triumph of a more comprehensive, less economistic, view of education policy within the OECD, enabling the Organization to attach equal, if not more, importance to education's social and cultural purposes.

This was clearly evident in the educational work the OECD pursued, organized under four programmes: two of them emerging from the Education Committee and the CERI Governing Board, with the other two being the more specialist programmes of Educational Buildings (PEB) and Institutional Management in Higher Education (IMHE). An illustrative list of the projects sponsored by the OECD during the 1970s and 1980s suggests a much more than simple relationship between education and economic development. Included in this list are reports and analyses of: school pedagogy and curriculum; the use of school buildings; educational disadvantage and advantage; multicultural education; girls and education; linguistic diversity; alternative education; school improvement and effectiveness; early childhood education; links between school and work; school–community relations; youth employment; youth at risk; people with disabilities; teacher education; educational and performance indicators; the economics of education; educational policy; educational technology; educational planning; educational management; mass higher education; vocational education and training; recurrent education and lifelong learning; adult literacy.

Two further points should be made about these programmes. First, they were largely supportive of national agendas, brought to the OECD by the member countries. They pointed to an organizational politics characterized essentially by consensual processes of decision-making in which nation-states retained a great deal of power in defining the ways they wished to use the resources of the OECD. The OECD responded to national priorities and did not wish its own perspective imposed upon them. Second, these programmes indicated the OECD to be a broad ideological church respectful of the diversity of ideological positions. According to Papadopoulos (1994) to view the OECD as a homogeneous unit with a narrow, static agenda was to fail to capture its educational reach, the contestations within its various forums and the ideological layers that underpin its charter aimed at both economic and social development.

However, this is not to deny the existence of deep ideological tensions within the Organization. Any analysis of the debates until the mid-1990s both within the OECD's committees and its secretariat reveals an ideological cleavage between social-democratic and neo-liberal policy stances. The ideological divide still tends to be referred to within OECD parlance as 'European' versus 'Anglo-Saxon', though these descriptors hardly convey (nor were they really meant to convey) the variegations within these two camps. While much of the internal politics remains cloistered, given the Organization's essentially consensual decision-making and extenuated report-writing processes, this analysis also shows—from the Organization's publications, its programmes of work, and their historical accounts—how the discourses of social and economic concerns have been rearticulated over time.

Papadopoulos (1994) traces the ideological tensions between social efficiency and equity in the OECD's educational work from its foundation. Until the late 1980s and early 1990s, he demonstrates the dominance of the social justice agendas until the economic transitions which occurred following the OPEC oil crisis of the mid-1970s. By the 1980s, while the tensions remained, education was now conceived as a central element of economic policy. Since that time with greater policy awareness granted to globalization and the knowledge economy, we would argue that the social efficiency perspective has begun to dominate the educational work of the OECD. This is manifest in support for a human capital account of education, new forms of educational governance and a global space of comparative educational performance. Equity remains on the agenda, but has been rearticulated away from a strong definition of social justice towards social capital and social inclusion concerns. Concerns about social class correlations with educational performance are less evident in this rearticulated equity agenda, with more emphasis given to special needs education, gender and ethnicity. In what follows, we attempt to show this ideological ascendancy of a particular view of education linked to a neo-liberal conception of globalization and the educational requirements of the global economy and of the knowledge economy.

Imperatives of Globalization: the OECD's perspective

In recent years, the OECD has made considerable use of the idea of globalization in both redefining its programme of policy work and reconceptualizing its relationship to member countries. It has sought not only to examine but also to prescribe the manner in which its members should respond to the pressures of globalization, as well as take advantage of the opportunities the emerging global economy has created for them. It has suggested that:

> OECD has evolved greatly in the globalising world economy. It has been 'globalising' itself, notably through new Members and dialogue activities ... Further, analysing the many facets of the process of globalization, and their policy implications, has become the central theme in OECD's work, as the challenges and opportunities of globalization have become a high priority of policy-makers in OECD countries. (OECD 1996*a*: 15)

It has also asserted that 'a broad consensus exists on many aspects of the policy requirement for a globalizing world economy'. In articulating the logic of globalization in this manner, the OECD appears to 'objectify' the economic relations it regards as 'globalizing', treating them as self-evident. This has the effect of masking some of the normative assumptions underlying its conception of globalization, treating them as if they were beyond political debate.

Yet, globalization is a highly contested political term, referring to a whole range of social processes. Indeed, it is possible to interpret globalization from three distinct perspectives. First, the term 'globalization' has been used to describe the ways in which the world is becoming increasingly interconnected and interdependent, referring to a set of social processes that imply 'inexorable integration of markets, nation-states and technologies to a degree never witnessed before—in a way that is enabling individuals, corporations and nation-states to reach round the world farther, faster, deeper and cheaper than ever before' (Friedman 1999: 7). In this way, globalization is widely associated with technological revolutions in transport, communication, and data processing. These developments, it is argued, have transformed the nature of economic activity, changing the modes of production and consumption. The global economy is now characterized as informational, networked, knowledge-based, post-industrial, and service oriented (Porter 1990; Castells 2000). The global economy has also led to a new conception of governance, requiring a radically revised view of the roles and responsibilities of national governments, minimizing the need for their policy intervention, with greater reliance on the market (Strange 1996). Yeatman (1998) has argued that this view suggests that the old centralized bureaucratic state structures were too slow and sclerotic and 'out of sync' with the emergent needs of transnational capital, and that new, devolved forms of governance are more compatible with the demands of the global economy. Culturally, this naturalized view of globalization is linked with enduring or even increasing cultural interactions across national and ethnic communities (Appadurai 1996).

A second perspective on globalization does not so much highlight its descriptive aspects as an objective set of social processes, but represents it instead as a subjective or phenomenological awareness by people and states of recent changes in global economy and culture. This view of globalization is reflected in the 'values which take the real world of 5 billion people as the object of concern ... everyone living as world citizens ... with a common interest in collective action to solve global problems' (Albrow 1996: 34). Important here is our collective consciousness of the world as a single space in which our problems are seen to be interconnected; involving a cosmopolitanism that requires us to recognize our interconnectivity and interdependence across the globe.

And finally, an increasing number of scholars and activists view globalization not as an inexorable process, but as a deliberate, ideological project of economic liberalization that subjects states and individuals to more intense market forces (e.g. Bourdieu 1998, 2003). Such a perspective is based on a politics of meaning that seeks to accommodate people to a certain taken-for-grantedness about the ways the global economy operates and the manner in which culture, crises, resources, and power formations are filtered through its universal logic. It thus 'ontologizes' the global market mentality, creating global subjects who view policy options through the conceptual prism within which it is located. From this perspective, the term 'globalization' designates certain power relations, practices and technologies, playing a 'hegemonic role in organizing and decoding the meaning of the world' (Schirato and Webb 2003: 1).

The OECD's perspective on globalization is a synthesis of these three perspectives. Its descriptions of global processes are informed by its assumed normative commitment to its ideological forms, articulated in terms of the neo-liberal logic of markets. Its ideological commitment to neo-liberalism is, in turn, based on its description of what it often refers to as 'the imperatives of globalization'. And it promotes forms of social subjectivities that encourage people to view the world as an interconnected space in which informational networks play a crucial role in sustaining market activity. In this way, the OECD combines its empirical assertion about globalization with its prescriptive judgements; objective dimensions of globalization are elided with a subjective orientation towards the new conditions it describes.

Bourdieu (2003) writes about this slide from the descriptive usage of globalization to a normative or performative one. The performative usage constitutes globalization as simply neo-liberal economics encompassing the globe and in so doing elides the politics of the creation of a global economy, including the role of IGOs such as the OECD in its constitution. As Bourdieu argues, the creation of a global economy framed by neo-liberalism is a political project. He elaborates:

> Economic globalization is not a mechanical effect of the laws of technology or the economy but the product of a policy implemented by a set of agents and institutions, and the result of the application of rules deliberately created for specific ends, namely trade liberalization (that is, the elimination of all national regulations restricting companies and their investments). (Bourdieu 2003: 84)

The OECD, while it no doubts views itself as presenting a very complex characterization of globalization, nonetheless provides a predominantly neo-liberal reading. Other social policies are then structured so as to complement this neo-liberal account of globalization. In what follows, we will attempt to demonstrate this structuration by examining the ways in which it now addresses the purposes of education within and for the knowledge economy, the OECD's perspective on educational governance and its changing discourse in relation to the internationalization of education.

Knowledge Economy and Changing Purposes of Education

Since the 1990s, the OECD has changed the balance of focus within its educational policies. Increasingly education has come to be seen as central to human capital formation for the health of national economies in the face of international competition and global pressures. Furthermore, the economy for which individuals were being educated is now characterized as a knowledge economy with knowledge being the central, indeed intrinsic component of economic production and activity, reflecting developments in economic theory. Not only is human capital, including dispositions of individuals, important economically, but so too are knowledge and innovation at the workplace. The OECD has been centrally important in articulating and spreading policy talk about the knowledge economy and the role of education, innovation, and research in relation to it. Indeed, its document, *The Knowledge Based Economy* (1996) has been highly influential in promoting the concept and its associated policy developments. Within this knowledge economy frame, the economic goals of education are thus given priority over its social and cultural purposes and some emphasis is given to the need for different organizational arrangements in education. Additionally, the meaning that the OECD now attaches to the idea of lifelong learning is located within its broader discourse of knowledge economy, which it now shares with other IGOs such as UNESCO and EU.

Lifelong Education for all became a major term of reference for UNESCO in 1994; and it was not until in 1996 that the OECD adopted 'Making Lifelong Learning a Reality for All' as a theme of its mandate for 1997–2001. However, during the mid-1990s there were different emphases attached to the concept of lifelong learning between the humanistic, social-democratic opportunity construction of lifelong learning and the individualistic, neo-liberal self-capitalizing individual construction (Rose 1999) within the work of these two organizations. Increasingly, however, the neo-liberal construction of the purposes of lifelong learning has taken precedence. This work has witnessed a refocusing of the goals of education on preparing people for the world of work and a life of self-capitalization, as indicated in two very influential OECD reports, *The Knowledge Based Economy* (OECD 1996*c*) and *Lifelong Learning for All* (OECD 1996*b*). In these documents, education is considered necessary to develop dispositions amongst all citizens towards ongoing learning across the life cycle. What is required now are flexible, mobile lifelong learners who have cosmopolitan dispositions and are able to deal effectively with cultural diversity, endemic change, and innovation. This emphasis has weakened the focus on social justice and social-democratic purposes of education, thus complementing the neo-liberal underpinnings of the OECD's broad approach to economic policy.

This emphasis is reiterated in the most recent approved program of work of CERI for 2005–6, which sits within the overarching theme of Lifelong Learning and includes four sub-themes of Innovation and Knowledge Management, Human and Social Capital, a Futures Focus, and Learning and Teaching. A look at a listing of recent CERI publications shows the way, even within this relatively autonomous arm of OECD's educational work, concerns of knowledge economy have become prominent. Recent CERI publications include: *Innovation in the Knowledge Economy: Implications for Education and Learning* (2004*a*), *Measuring Knowledge Management in the Business Sector: First Steps* (2004*b*), *Knowledge Management: New Challenges for Educational Research* (2003*a*), *Schooling for Tomorrow—Networks of Innovation* (2003*b*), and *The Well-Being of Nations: The Role of Human and Social Capital* (2001). The ubiquitous idea of knowledge economy, interpreted in neo-liberal terms, has thus become the defining concept with which the OECD has suggested the need for educational reform, providing a framework within which it has rearticulated the social and cultural purposes of education.

This much is evident from a look at the OECD website, where the current mission of its Directorate of Education is described thus: 'To assist members and partners in achieving high quality lifelong learning for all, contributing to personal development, sustainable economic growth and social cohesion'. The Directorate currently has six strategic objectives which frame its program of work for 2005–6. These are: promoting lifelong learning and improving its linkages with other socio-economic policies; evaluating and improving outcomes of education; promoting quality teaching; rethinking tertiary education in a global economy; building social cohesion through education; and building new futures for education.

This list is clearly based on an instrumental view of education, as serving the needs of the global knowledge economy. Not only is its emphasis on lifelong learning, but also its focus on equity and social cohesion is based on this economic instrumentalism. This can be seen from the view of Barry McGaw (OECD 2005: 7), the Director of Education, who suggests that 'Building only human capital is insufficient', but rather, 'Social capital—networks together with shared norms, values and understandings that facilitate co-operation within or among groups—is also essential to the development and maintenance of cohesive societies.' Here, the focus on human capital is clearly evident, but is complemented by a rearticulation of social justice (or equity concerns) as social capital. The OECD's definition of social capital is available in its publication, *The Well-Being of Nations* (2001*b*), positing a functionalist account of social inclusion as formal access to education. Contrast this with a tougher definition as utilized, for example, by Bourdieu (1986), which demands more than simply equality of access to educational opportunity, and suggests the need to address the issue of how schools reproduce inequalities, particularly in relation to social class of origin.

That the social efficiency and economic framing of education has usurped the goals of educational equity and has rearticulated it in the OECD's recent work can be further demonstrated by looking in more detail at the Organization's recent educational programs and its six key strategic objectives. Its Strategic Objective 1, 'Promoting lifelong learning and improving its linkages with other socio-economic policies' is informed by the premise that 'The contribution of education to economic development features in much of the work of the OECD as a whole.' Not surprisingly, therefore, its project on, for instance 'Improving early childhood education and childcare' is linked to lifelong learning and labour market policies, while 'Developing and measuring adult competencies' is designed to 'strengthen the linkages between learning, enterprise training and the labour market'. Its 'Enhancing the economic impact of human capital' project is concerned to 'improve understanding of the role of human capital and intellectual assets in economic performance'. In seeking to understand the social outcomes of learning, the project on 'Investigating the social outcomes of learning' is also interested in linkages to other social and economic policies.

If we move to consider Strategic Objective 2, 'Evaluating and improving outcomes of education', we again see clearly the emphasis on economic and social efficiency. Thus it is stated: 'The prosperity of countries now derives to a large extent from their human capital and individuals need to advance their knowledge and competencies throughout their lives in order to succeed in a rapidly changing world'. Strategic Objective 4 on 'Rethinking tertiary education in a global economy' speaks of the need for an appropriate balance of public and private sources of funding and also about the need for indicators regarding the individual and social returns from tertiary education. Returns to the individual are seen as 'labour market earnings', eschewing the broader liberal educational purposes of tertiary education.

Strategic Objective 5, 'Building social cohesion through education' speaks of improving equity and opportunities, but here the primary focus is on students with special needs, an emphasis on ethnic and cultural diversity of the student population as a result of the flows associated with globalization. All of this is worthwhile, as is the focus on bullying and violence, but social class issues are nowhere to be seen—equity has been rearticulated narrowly as concerned largely with issues of access to institutions and as social cohesion, an idea which in itself is highly ambiguous and may in fact be viewed as a residualization of a stronger social justice approach evident in the earliest work of the OECD (Papadopolous 1994). Strategic Objective 6, 'Building new futures for education' deals, *inter alia*, with knowledge management, which is in turn framed by knowledge economy discourse. Thus it is argued that 'In advanced 21st century societies, the management of knowledge is as fundamental as the management of more fundamental educational resources (personnel, finance and facilities), but knowledge management in education tends not to be well developed.' Absent from this discourse are issues concerning the ethics and politics of knowledge production and dissemination, and how various strategies of knowledge management could be used to reproduce global inequalities.

OECD's Perspective on Educational Governance

With its growing emphasis on a more instrumental approach to education purposes, linked to the requirements of the knowledge economy, the OECD has also been pursuing a vigorous agenda about the need to rethink state structures and forms of educational governance. It has viewed the reform of educational governance as central to a nation's capacity to ensure accelerated economic productivity and growth. It has been at the forefront of a wave of public sector reform that has seen the structures and practices of all public sector departments transformed under the rubric of 'corporate managerialism' or 'new public management'. This transformation has been based upon the take-up of private sector management practices in the public sector. The emphasis has changed from the old bureaucratic stress on correct procedures to an emphasis upon outcomes achieved at the lowest possible costs.

The twin goals of greater efficiency—doing things at the lowest cost—and greater effectiveness—achieving the goals set—have underpinned the new structures that are less hierarchical and much flatter, with greater management prerogative for policy steering. The old pyramidal structure has thus been replaced by a flatter coat-hanger-like arrangement. Relations between the policy-producing strategic centre of the organization and the practice periphery have also been reset. The strategic centre establishes the strategic plan and desired policy outcomes, while the policy-practising periphery is responsible in whatever ways for achieving these goals. As such, any new autonomy at the periphery is in relation to means rather than policy ends, which are set more tightly by the centre as part of a new regime of outcomes accountability.

This new regime of governance is perhaps most evident in a highly influential OECD report, *Governance in Transition: Public Management Reforms in OECD Countries* (OECD 1995), which exemplifies the typical OECD genre of disinterested academic description attached to exhortations to change, combining descriptive with normative elements in its discourse. It notes, in a not too muted criticism of old-style state bureaucracies, that 'highly centralized, rule-bound, and inflexible organizations that emphasise process rather than results impede good performance' and that the efficiency of the public sector 'has a significant impact on total economic efficiency' (p. 7). It articulates a new discourse on educational governance that the OECD has vigorously promoted over the past decade. This discourse is constituted by such concepts as strategic planning, cost-efficiency, human resource allocation, competition and choice, optimizing information technology, performance management, and accountability. It provides the basis for an approach to public administration that redefines the relationship between the state and its institutions and individuals and civil society. It implores public institutions to restructure the way in which they make decisions and to re-imagine the manner in which they fund programmes, relate to their clients, and manage their resources.

It is important to note that, in promoting this view of governance, the OECD does not use a language of exploration of policy options to which it is committed, but acts instead as a strong advocate for these reforms; not as a facilitator of political debates among member countries, but as a political actor in its own right. It highlights the relevance of these governance principles for all its member countries, regardless of their local histories and traditions, and for the entire public sector, including education. In the process of implementation, educational systems thus lose their *sui generis* character. As a consequence, the organizational structures and basic practices look similar now in educational, health, welfare, and other public-sector bureaucracies. This outcome has also been achieved through, and expressed in some cases by, the appointment of generic managers to the various public sector bureaucracies and through contract employment linked to achievement of targets and goals. In a sense, this new arrangement is post-bureaucratic and is the result of the attempt to pull state structures and practices into line with the perceived needs of global capital.

What we have seen in educational systems across all the OECD countries, as a result of this public sector restructuring, is a centralization of policy setting and devolution of responsibility to achieve the goals set at the centre. The OECD has been thus been a strong advocate of the idea of devolution. However, its commitment to devolution does not rest on assumptions of social democracy, but on a set of corporate management principles. Its perspective on devolution has been framed not only by corporate managerialism, but also by market ideologies. In describing the recent wave of worldwide school-based management reforms, Whitty, Power, and Halpin (1998: 3) have argued that 'central to these initiatives are moves to dismantle centralized educational bureaucracies and to create in their place devolved systems of education entailing significant degrees of institutional autonomy'. These changes have also been 'linked to enhanced parental choice' designed to introduce a market element into the provision of educational services. A similar logic for the reform of higher education systems has been articulated by the OECD's program on the Institutional Management of Higher Education (IMHE).

Indeed, the ideology of privatization, the notion that services are best delivered by the private sector within a competitive market, has become something of a mantra within the OECD. It has come to symbolize a new way of looking at public institutions and the role of the state in managing the affairs of its citizens. Under this broad philosophical orientation, many possible activities are construed as eligible for privatization, ranging from selling state-owned enterprises to contracting out public services to private contractors, be they individuals or corporations. According to Bray (1996), privatization of education takes at least three forms: transferring ownership of public institutions, shifting sectoral balance without redesignating existing institutions, and increasing government funding and support for private institutions. Bray might have added to this list contracting out functions and services. At various times and contexts, the OECD has advocated each of these forms. It is important to note, however, that the debate within the OECD forums now is not whether to privatize, but which of its many forms might best produce the greatest amount of efficiency and effectiveness. The discourse is no longer normative, but technical—no longer about the capacity of the private sector to deliver public goods in a fair and equitable fashion, but about social efficiency with which educational markets operate.

This concern for social efficiency is encapsulated in Lyotard's concept of 'performativity' (1984). Over the past two decades, the OECD has been at the forefront of promoting a new culture of performativity, which is linked to proof of policy outcomes as an important element of the steering-at-a-distance mechanism (Kickert 1991) of the restructured state. This culture of performativity pervades restructured educational systems through the imposition of a raft of performance indicators to hold accountable those who are responsible for service delivery. It represents a triumph of instrumental reason, which prioritizes the operational and measurable over substantive moral claims about truth and justice. As Yeatman (1994:110) puts it, such '[p]erformativity is a systems-orientation: instead of the state appearing as the enlightened and paternal command of shared community, the state is equated with the requirements of a system for ongoing integrity and visibility'. Performativity simplifies the tasks of governments and effectively works as a 'principle of selective closure in respect of the information overload and social complexity' (Yeatman 1994: 117) confronting the contemporary state.

Given this ideological shift towards a culture of performativity, it is not surprising that a large proportion of the OECD's educational work now pivots around its Indicators in Education project. Developed in highly controversial circumstances (see Henry et al. 2000), its annual publication *Education at a Glance: OECD Indicators* is disseminated widely not only across the OECD countries, but elsewhere as well, and sets the agenda for its deliberations. These data are collected in conjunction with the European Commission and UNESCO, under the title, 'World Indicators Project'. The categories around which the project collects comparative data reveal much about its educational priorities, as being linked to the imperatives of performativity and social efficiency. Its focus on issues of transition from school to work, student participation and progressions, and labour-market outcomes of education derive their significance from the OECD's instrumental view of education linked to the needs of the global knowledge economy. The OECD argues that international comparison is designed to assist in the processes of policy formation in member countries and to contribute to the public accountability of education systems; to provide a better understanding of 'the internal processes that determine the relationship between educational expenditures and educational outcomes is particularly important' (CERI 1995: 7).

However, this is a somewhat understated view of the purposes and significance of the OECD's work on indicators; that this work not only provides relevant comparative information to member countries, but also helps shape their policy agendas and priorities. There is a broader politics of change associated with the Indicators project, based as it is on a particular view about the policy directions and approaches needed to reform education. In this way, the project plays a normative and legitimation role in the promotion of what could be called a global ideology of educational management and change linked to broader public sector reform across member countries. It also serves to illustrate recent shifts in the OECD's role as a policy instrument and forum, that is, as a catalyst facilitating policy development in member countries and assisting processes of policy dissemination, adaptation, and borrowing—to that of an international mediator of knowledge and global policy actor. Along with PISA, the Indicators work as a significant 'magistrature of influence' above the nation (Lawn and Lingard 2002), enhancing the policy effects of the OECD.

And in so far as its work on educational indicators now encapsulates countries beyond its member countries, and is conducted in association with other IGOs such as the European Commission and UNESCO, this work is part of a project of global rationalization, setting up a set of standardized educational measurements with which to assess the competitive advantage of nations within the global economy in terms of the quality of their human capital. The OECD was involved in November 1999 in the creation of the PARIS21 Consortium, consisting of the UN, OECD, World Bank, IMF, and EC. Its purpose is to 'boost statistical capabilities especially in poor countries'. One can speculate on the effects of this policy-as-numbers approach in contributing to a global policy space of comparison. Viewed in these terms, the Indicators in Education project cannot simply be represented as a collection of comparative data on the relative performance of member countries, but is clearly part of a broader ideological agenda designed to make their educational systems more responsive to what the Organization regards as the human capital needs of the global economy. The Programme for International Student Assessment (PISA) also works in this way. PISA now encompasses almost as many non-member as member countries and constitutes an emergent global policy space in education, which encourages policy convergence and which sees the OECD as a powerful policy actor in the constitution of this space. It accounts for about 30 per cent of the Directorate for Education's budget. The emphasis on international comparative outcome measures such as PISA is complementary to the new forms of governance in education.

Internationalization: From Student Mobility to Educational Trade

The broad elements of this shifting neo-liberal ideological agenda are also evident in the recent shifts in the OECD's work in relation to the internationalization of higher education. The Organization's work on this stretches back to the mid-1980s, and was linked to study abroad programs of the European Union. It involved an exploration of rationales for student mobility. In an influential report, published in the early 1990s, two consultants to the OECD, Jane Knight and Hans de Wit defined internationalization of education as a complex set of processes designed to integrate an international dimension into most aspects of the work of universities. They argued that a comprehensive understanding of internationalization must involve a commitment to the development of new skills, attitudes, and knowledge in students, faculty, and staff. Accordingly, they note: 'Internationalisation of higher education is the process of integrating an international/intercultural dimension into the teaching, research and service of the institution' (Knight and de Wit 1995).

In a more focused way, Knight and De Wit (1995) argued that the rationales for internationalization fall into two broad overlapping rationales:

1. Economic and political rationales, such as economic growth and investment in the future economy; to be competitive with the international labour market; to foster diplomacy through educational cooperation; financial incentives (e.g. contract education, recruitment of foreign students and international education advisory services can generate income); and the national demand for higher education is so great that nations stimulate study abroad;
2. Cultural and educational rationales, which may either be to export national, cultural and moral values, or to increase intercultural knowledge, skills and research; to expand the social learning and development of the individual; to provide an international dimension to research and teaching; to strengthen the core structures and activities of higher learning institutions through international cooperation; and to improve the quality of education and research.

Whatever their validity, these rationales suggest the OECD, in its earlier mode of analysis of internationalization, to be committed to an exploration of the diversity of approaches relevant to the purposes of education. There is a refusal to embrace a reductionist view of education, giving equal weight to economic and cultural concerns. This view was reinforced in the 1990s by a number of other OECD documents examining the idea of internationalization, which suggested that internationalization was important to the development of universities partly because of labour market stipulations, but also because of social and cultural developments in general, which were heading towards multicultural and cosmopolitan sensitivities.

Through the 1990s, there were attempts within the OECD to define the complex idea of the internationalization of curricula, with the recognition that commercial and economic issues had to be reconciled with issues of cultural diversity and interpersonal dimensions of global relations. There was on the one hand a realization that the changes associated with technological innovation and the globalization of the economy, together with the post-Fordist vision of flatter organizational structures and flexible work, demanded a different set of cognitive and communication skills, multi-skilling and lifelong learning, and attitudes of teamwork and tolerance towards other cultures. Radical re-thinking of curriculum and pedagogy was thus deemed to be necessary.

Yet, towards the end of the 1990s, these curriculum conversations within the OECD became increasingly marginal, replaced by a different set of considerations regarding the internationalization of higher education, marked more by concerns about the coordination and regulation of international trade in education than by the issues of cross-cultural understanding and global imagination. The OECD's August 2004 policy illustrates its shifting concerns in this area. The OECD's original interest in internationalization was informed by issues to do with the educational benefits of student mobility. Mobility is no longer examined in educational terms, but in commercial terms, concerned with the ways to generate additional revenue from international education for universities in member countries from non-member countries such as China and India.

The OECD has thus looked closely at the developments in higher education in China, as a way of exploring how greater cooperation can be forged between the OECD members and the world's fastest-growing economy. Its work on expanding access to higher education in China in 1999–2001 and on financing higher education and quality in China in 2004 has highlighted the need to improve the interface between the public and private education sectors and the national and regional education authorities; and has also offered policy recommendations for increasing equity of access. The interest by the OECD countries in privately funded higher education in China is barely masked. That this work on China is informed largely by the OECD's economic interest in clearly revealed in the fact the Organization has shown little interest in developmental issues of higher education in Africa and South America.

The OECD's interest in issues of cross-border trade in higher education is further revealed in its support for the General Agreement on Trade in Services (GATS) currently being negotiated by the World Trade Organization (WTO), the principles of which, the OECD argues, are consistent with its own advocacy for 'Coded Liberalization of Capital Movements and Current Invisible Operations', issued in 1995. In its policy brief on the *Internationalization of Higher Education* (2004*b*), the OECD presents four main policy rationales for cross-border education: mutual understanding, skilled migration, revenue generation, and capacity building. It argues however that these rationales are not mutually exclusive and have a strong economic drive. It recognizes that cross-border trade in education runs the risk of undermining public education and quality, but suggests that such fears can be overcome by a vigorous regime of transnational regulation and coordination. However it insists upon the veracity of the GATS mandate for the development of 'any necessary disciplines to ensure that measures relating to qualification requirements and procedures, technical licensing requirements do not constitute unnecessary barriers to trade'.

The other rationale for cross-border education highlighted by the OECD relates to skilled migration. Over the past decade, the OECD has paid a great deal of attention to the issues of skilled migrants needed within its member countries to retain competitiveness within the global economy. It has viewed international education as a major source of recruitment, even if this means 'brain drain' from the developing countries. The Organization seems to regard as perfectly understandable the aim by the developed countries to recruit talented students from the developing countries 'to work in the host country's knowledge economy, or render its higher education and research sectors more competitive' (OECD 2004*b*: 4). Indeed, it advocates an easing of the relevant visa or immigration restrictions on the one hand and providing specific services to help international students stay abroad on the other. Its report on *Science and Technology Labour Markets* (2001) argues that highly skilled persons are driven by different push-and-pull factors. 'In addition to immigration legislation, other factors, such as taxation, studying abroad, quality of work, openness in communication, business expansion overseas, labour market supply and demand signals, etc. play an important role in the choice of highly skilled migrants to relocate overseas.' Largely technical in its discourse, absent from the report is any discussion of moral considerations pertaining to the global inequalities created by such policies of skilled migration via internationalization of higher education.

Conclusion

The educational work of the OECD has always been linked to the broad economic purposes of the Organization. In respect of its policy framework, there has been a tension between the neo-liberal and the social democratic. We have argued that at the current moment in the context of globalization considered in particular ways in the work of the OECD, and given the global hegemony of the USA, the neo-liberal perspective now dominates. Indeed, we have suggested that the OECD has been an important institution and actor in the constitution of a global economy framed by neo-liberalism. Policies, we know, often discursively create the contexts to which they are purportedly a response (Taylor et al. 1997). The OECD, while working with competing definitions of globalization, has largely constituted globalization in a performative way as neo-liberal ideology applied to the whole globe. The impact of the work of the OECD is also now much wider than in its member countries. Along with other international organizations, it has created particular economic 'policy talk' about a knowledge economy, which has contributed to policy convergence in respect of economic policy and organizational arrangements and practices across the globe. In all of this, the OECD has become more of a policy actor than it once was.

Since its inception, ongoing tensions between social efficiency and equity goals of education have existed in the OECD's educational work. In his historical overview of the OECD's educational work during the 1970s and 1980s, Papadopoulos (1994) provided an account of these tensions. Some years later, Henry et al. (2000) demonstrated these tensions in the late 1990s, between quality and equality, between the economic, social, and cultural purposes of education, and in an emergent stress on social cohesion set against the recognition of the growing inequality associated with neo-liberal globalization. In this chapter we have argued that, more recently, the discourse of knowledge economy, in the context of a particular construction of gobalization, has pushed the balance between equity and social efficiency firmly towards the latter and focused on the production of the self-capitalizing, flexible, neo-liberal subject. In the process, there has been a rearticulation of equity, through the use of the concepts of social capital and social cohesion, rather than stronger social-democratic concerns about social justice in provision and outcomes in education. Through its statistical and assessment work in education (e.g. Indicators, Education at a Glance, PISA) and more generally (e.g. PARIS21), the OECD is also promoting a policy agenda for reforming educational governance, based on neo-liberal precepts of marketization and privatization on the one hand and strong systems of accountability on the other. The OECD has thus contributed to the creation of a global policy space in education. Here it now works as a 'magistrature of influence'.

In this chapter we have argued that the OECD has been a dynamic institution, simultaneously expressing, responding to, and promoting particular policy ideas in education. In its current phase it insists that 'The development of modern knowledge economies has increased the importance of education policy.' In creating a separate Directorate for Education within the OECD in 2002, it has both underlined the importance of education and also made education a function of economic policy in the knowledge economy. It is interesting to speculate therefore whether this new arrangement simply reinforces the neo-liberal economic hegemony, especially through its cross-sectoral work, or allows some more space for a re-emphasis upon the equity aspects of educational policy, particularly in a context where the neo-liberal uptake of globalization seems to have exacerbated inequalities within and between nations.

NOTES

This chapter is based partly on an Australian Research Council supported research published as M. Henry, B. Lingard, F. Rizvi, and S. Taylor (2000), *The OECD, Globalization and Education Policy* (Oxford: Pergamon). The arguments presented here are based on extension of this work over 2000–4 by the authors, who gratefully acknowledge the significant contributions of Miriam Henry and Sandra Taylor.

1. Chile, Estonia, Israel, the Russian Federation, and Slovenia participate in the Education Committee as observers, Chile and Israel also participate on the Governing Board of the Centre for Education Research and Innovation (CERI), while for PISA 28 non-member countries are involved along with the 30 member countries.

18 Neoliberalism, Globalization, Democracy: Challenges for Education

Mark Olssen

[...]

Globalization

In seeing an important role for the state, it need not be disputed that that what is called the 'globalization thesis' does refer to a process with certain ascertainable effects. We would agree with Castells (1996, p. 97) that the global economy has shown some marked patterns of integration, including:

- the increasing interpenetration of markets, which received further impetus after the Uruguay Round of GATT;
- the birth of WTO;
- the slow but steady progress in European integration/unification;
- the signing of NAFTA (North American Free Trade Agreement);
- the intensification of economic exchanges in Asia;
- the gradual incorporation of Eastern Europe and Russia into the global economy;
- the quasi legal integration of capital markets; and
- the growing role played by trade and foreign investment in economic growth everywhere.

Castells notes (1996, p. 97) that the global economy is internally diversified into three major regions:

- North America, including Canada and Mexico (after NAFTA);
- the European Union (EU); and
- the Asia-Pacific region, centred on Japan.

Regionalization corrupts, or at least substantially modifies, the version of globalization theory advocated for by neoliberals in that it constitutes a context for the emergence of new regulatory controls within particular regions. Naomi Klein (2003) tells the story of the emergence of 'fortress continents' which she says is the model being employed by NAFTA and the European Union. After September 11 this model has taken on a new urgency:

> A fortress continent is a block of nations that join forces to extract favourable trade terms from other countries, while patrolling their shared external borders to keep people from those countries out. But if a continent is serious about being a fortress it also has to invite one or two poor countries within its walls, because someone has to do the dirty work and heavy lifting. It is a model being pioneered in Europe, where the European Union is currently expanding to include 10 poor eastern bloc countries, at the same time as it uses increasingly aggressive security methods to deny entry to immigrants from even poorer countries, like Iraq and Nigeria.

Mark Olssen, 'Neoliberalism, Globalisation, Democracy: Challenges for Education', *Globalisation, Societies and Education*, 2, 2, 238–273

Regionalization makes the relationship of the nation-state to globalization more complex. Regional blocks with an assortment of institutions, associations and accords create a new constraint on the nation-state, and both erode and confirm its sovereignty in important respects. The relation of Britain to the European Union, for instance, in accepting European conventions and accords, and even in accepting the Euro as currency, surrenders certain aspects of sovereignty, and means that sovereignty of the state is no longer, in all matters, coincident with the national borders of its territory. But, of course, the acceptance of such 'constraints' and 'conditions' also enables new possibilities in conformity with national development, in the context of existing regional and global economic and political exigencies.

It is important, however, not to misrepresent what globalization *means* in this sense. In that Held and McGrew (2000) distinguish between the 'hyperglobalizers' and the 'skeptics', I have difficulty with either view. In that 'skeptics' emphasize the uneven patterns of integration of countries to the world economy, and deny that 'globalization' is a novel development, emphasizing the origins of 'transnational flows' prior to 1914, I would concur. Globalization cannot be seen as a qualitatively new development, but rather as the intensification of a process that that is age-old.[1] What needs to be pointed out, however, is that this does not mean that globalization is not effecting new changes. With the 'globalizers' and 'hyperglobalizers' it can be argued that states have a diminished capacity to protect their borders against private international decision-making, but this is so *only in some arenas*, and *only on some issues*. This is as much because certain issues (environmental issues, trade issues, health issues) have become global issues of concern, as it is that states have been divested from control. Where states traditionally had control, we consider they still have it; where states were weak in the face of international pressure, or from a particular country or block of countries, they continue to be so. Sometimes, too, as Pheng Cheah (1998, p. 31) points out, global institutions 'can become an alibi for economic transnationalism, which is often US economic nationalism in global guise'.

If at the level of governance, globalization is complex and fragmented, at the cultural level we can also agree that globalization is having a marked effect. We can agree with Pheng Cheah (1998, p. 32) that an 'alternative spatialisation of politics' is underway. We can also agree with Arjun Appadurai that contemporary 'global culture flows' create conflict between existing global forms and the separateness of the nation-state. Appadurai's (1993, p. 418) thesis of growing interconnectedness through travel, technology and communications, where global institutional forms are 'both instances and incubators of a post-national global culture' is we think largely correct. However, I would maintain that Appadurai's thesis needs careful qualifying. Just as national and global governance can co-exist, I would maintain that global culture can *coalesce* with national identity, and compromises national consciousness only in certain respects, not all of which can be seen as negative; e.g., in relation to norms of democratic justice, which can be supported as warranted and important. Furthermore a plausible argument could be maintained that there is no contradiction, or pressures toward mutual exclusivity, between the global and national domains in relation to culture.

The view presented here is not one of 'globalization *or* the nation-state', but of 'globalization *and* the nation-state'. By this is meant that while globalization is effecting major changes, the role of the state is changing, but this doesn't mean that it is diminishing. It still has a highly significant role in relation to work, welfare, education and defence. It is still the superior agency, hierarchically relating to all other constituents in a definite territory with clear boundaries. While it is affected to a greater extent in the twenty-first century by international pressures and greater interdependence this is not a qualitatively new form of development. What has emerged, as Hirst (2000, p. 178) argues, is a 'division of labour between local, national and supranational levels and between public and private government'. As Hirst (2000, p. 185) argues, 'we still have a world of states. The change is that we now have many other agencies too'. Although sovereignty is a changing relation, and is frequently sold on one issue to be retained or strengthened on another, over most governance capacities states still retain sovereignty, or they control the conditions in terms of which it is transferred. In this sense Hirst argues that while sovereignty is not total, it never was, for state power has never existed *independent* of an international context. As governance becomes more complex and multi-levelled, so too, sovereignty alters both its scope and domain. Sovereignty is not then, Hirst (2000, p. 183) says, a 'zero-sum game': the existence of global agencies and regional blocks does not substantially weaken the nation-state.

Having said this, it can still be agreed that globalization is a significant phenomenon. Significant governmental functions are undergoing relocation and the forms of governance are changing from state to global, to inter-state, to non-governmental and to private market mechanisms. As a process, then, more sense can be made of globalization by defining two interrelated phenomena: (1) as a high degree of global *inter-connectedness*, as a consequence of changes in science and technology; and (2) as a discursive system, pursued at the policy level by powerful states and international capital. This enables us to distinguish two senses of globalization which I will call 'Globalization I' and 'Globalization II'. The essential features of Globalization I are:

- Increased speed and volume of private trans-border transactions, especially related to capital and communications systems.
- New developments in technology, which have assisted mobility of cross border flows (electronic clearing systems, the internet).
- The increasing possibility of transport (cheaper air fares, etc).

The essential features of Globalization II are:

- The replacement of the Bretton Woods agreement with neoliberal orthodoxy (open borders, floating exchange rates, abolition of capital controls, etc).
- Deregulation and liberalization of government policy and establishment of highly integrated private transnational systems of alliances.
- Privatization and marketization: the establishment of central banks (e.g., the European Central Bank) which reside inside countries but adopt a market-independent monetary policy and which are largely autonomous from political interference.[2] Also, the growth of private international authorities, including consultants, advisors and arbitration specialists.

These two forms of globalization, while related, can be seen as conceptually distinct. Globalization I leads to growing *interconnectedness* between countries. As McGrew (2000, pp. 3–4) states:

> Globalisation has been variously concerned with action at a distance (whereby the actions of social agents in one locale can come to have significant consequences for 'distant others'); time-space compression (referring to the way in which instantaneous electronic communication erodes the constraints of distance and time on social organization and interaction); accelerating interdependence (understood as the intensification of enmeshment among national economies and societies).

Not all of these developments necessarily 'undermine' the state, however. New technologies, although they may undermine the nation-state in a cultural sense, may not unduly affect it in a political sense, or may even enhance it. Instant forms of recording and transcription enable the documenting of abuses in new important senses. In this sense, what technology can do is provide new possibilities in relation to democracy. As Castells (1997, p. 300) notes:

> What the power of technology does is to extraordinarily amplify the trends rooted in social structure and institutions: oppressive societies may be more so with the new surveillance tools, while democratic participatory societies may enhance their openness and representativeness by further distributing political power with the power of technology . . . thus the direct impact of new information technologies on power and the state is an empirical matter, on which the record is mixed.

The point of distinguishing two types of globalization is that neoliberalism structures the character of globalizing processes that have already taken place. Competition, for instance, is increased as a consequence associated with neoliberal endorsement of free trade, open economies and marketization. In this sense, Globalization II requires a great deal of state power to drive it. The creation of markets have been engineered by particular policies. As Hirst (2000, p. 179) notes, it was public policy, not market pressures, which led to deregulation of capital markets and removal of exchange controls in the late 1970s and early 1980s. As he states: 'What is supposed to be an inevitable market-driven global process is actually substantially a product of public policy... it was influential economic policy elites and state officials in advanced states that shaped the deregulatory free-market vision of world trade.' States are not however surrendering their sovereign capacities. Rather they are implementing control mechanisms to adapt to the changing architecture of global power. Regulatory controls operate to offset or negate competitive effects. One means of doing this, as Wiener (2001) points out, is by *harmonizing* governance and legal arrangements with the transnational. In this process states are disciplining transnational systems as much as the other way round.[3] Another mechanism of state adaptability is through *privatization of responsibility*. Thus, criminal responsibility over use of financial resources, which has become an issue linked with terrorism post September 11, has been devolved to (or imposed on) private sector banks, just as the governance issues connected with intellectual property rights has placed liability on internet service providers, and tends to stress 'self-enforcement'. What results, says Wiener, is a form of neoliberal multi-level governance which acts through domestic law, where state borders are losing practical relevance. This is not a response to the technological imperatives, but to deliberate state policies. Whereas Bretton Woods insulated national economies from shock, and provided for greater control, under neoliberalism, interdependence alters this protection system. One of the major effects means that states act in concert, seeking to harmonize policies and laws to ensure the effectiveness of measures taken at the national level.

Kanishka Jayasuriya (2001) maintains that globalization has also ushered in a new form of economic constitutionalism which has changed the role of nation states as concerns its legal institutions and the rule of law. This is to say, there has been a changing *architecture* of power both globally and within the state which is serving to *transform* the processes of governance and the nature of sovereignty. Crucial in this transformation is the shift from political constitutionalism to a 'kind of economic constitutionalism' (Jayasuriya, 2001, p. 443). As Jayasuriya (2001, p. 452) continues: 'Economic constitutionalism refers to the attempt to treat the market as a constitutional order with its own rules, procedures and institutions that operate to protect the market order from political interference.' The nub of this thesis is that the interlinking between law and the state is being uncoupled as aspects of sovereignty are being taken up by global and regional bodies. This, claims Jayasuriya (2001, p. 443), 'gives a juridical cast to economic institutions, placing these institutions beyond politics'. Because multinational corporations act beyond the control of individual nation-states, this demands a new model of global democracy constructed along republican lines with a strong emphasis on public autonomy and responsible ethical behaviour. If globalization shapes and alters the form of sovereignty, sovereignty must be seen as a historically dynamic concept whose boundaries 'move' between the global order and nation-state. In the process of globalization, some of the governance roles of the state become uncoupled from the state and taken up by international institutions. They become fragmented within global civil society. This involves the growth of private and public international authorities (e.g., the increasing importance of trade associations, independent 'central' banks, and other domestic regulatory bodies that operate relatively autonomously from the structures of political accountability). Such changes call for the development of global governance structures, as individual states are less able to regulate economic and societal issues.

Thus although the impacts of globalization are pervasive, it would be precipitous to consider the nation-state as an outmoded form of identity. The nation-state performs different functions than the global institutions, and relates to different forms of consciousness and concern. So while it can be agreed that relations between the state and the global are changing, this does not spell the end, or even the demise, of the nation-state. States are coping with such processes, through processes like *harmonization, localization*, and *privatization*, within and between domestic and international agencies. These processes require vigilance by states in relation to international institutions. Although, regional organizations (e.g., NAFTA) and global agencies (e.g., IMF) will often force states to accept specific decisions, or adopt the rules of structural adjustment, at other times states will successfully resist such developments.[4] What is clear, although states will continue to be important, it will not be possible, as Jaysuriya (2001, p. 448) states, to put 'the sovereignty genie back in the conventional state bottle'. Many decisions of importance—economic, environmental, human rights, health—will be global in nature. Issues such as climate change, Aids, international debt, the dominance of the G-7 countries, the depletion of natural resources, poverty, nuclear proliferation, defining the rules of world trade, policing world financial markets, evolving common standards for all sorts of activities (e.g., nuclear power), will increasingly become argued about and resolved in the global arena. In this sense many aspects of sovereignty will increasingly be global. Autonomous regional and global agencies will replace the state in relation to specific areas of control.

Cosmopolitan Democracy

In the context of this more fragmented state and global order, writers such as McGrew (2000) and Jayasuriya (2001) question the applicability of liberal democratic models of democracy. These models were developed in the context of autonomous state system that has largely ignored the impact of globalization. The established territorial patterns of liberal democracy appear as increasingly unable to deal with the complex issues and problems which transcend state's borders. In this sense, as McGrew (2000, pp. 404–405) states, the scale of human social organization no longer corresponds with the nation-state. If this is so, then the nation-state can no longer be seen as the repository of democratic life, and new forms of global democracy must be entertained.

Jayasuriya advocates a republican cosmopolitan order. Republicanism is a conception of political order and government modelled on classical models of the Greek and Greco-Roman polis. Although the republican assumption of a uniform public sphere needs adjusting, the idea of democracy working in and through a global civil society is not unfeasible, given the proliferation of new technologies of communication. Jayasuriya draws off MacCormick's work on the European Union which refers to diffused but interlocking networks of democracy in which participation and citizenship are developed. MacCormick uses the concept of 'subsidiarity' to explore the possibilities for democracy in a more fragmented political environment. As Jayasuriya (2001, p. 455) summarizes it, there are four:

> The familiar *market subsidiarity*, which allows for the operation of the market in the provision and production of certain goods; . . . a *collective subsidiarity*, which emphasizes the participation of individuals in a range of collectivities such as work places, associations or political parties; . . . a rational *legislative subsidiarity*, which endorses the need for effective representative democracy expressed through legislatures at provincial, federal, and all Europe levels . . . and . . . a *comprehensive subsidiarity* through which deliberation 'may come to be constitutive of a common good, or of the common perception of a shared good' by fostering institutions.[5]

Although Jayasuriya is a legal theorist, such an analysis is useful as a starting point when seeking to understand how democracy can be modified to operate effectively at the global level. Essentially what is being suggested is the creation of alternative authority structures to the nation-state where groups and social movements can represent effective citizen mobilization within the global arena, policing governance through the establishment of public democratic organizations. In Jayasuriya's (2001, p. 455) words, it 'seeks to build not a managerial civil society, but a political civil society composed of publicly accountable associations and regulatory entities'. Although Jayasuriya develops such a model in relation to Habermas, such a conception is equally compatible with the Foucauldian notion of the public sphere, based and deliberative processes, which we have outlined. Similar to Jayasuriya and Habermas, it fits too, within a 'neo-republican' conception of the political order as 'freedom from domination', which is one of the central elements of republican thought.

That republican principles of political organization can include national state, regional, and global levels has a long history in political thought. Immanuel Kant (1932) developed such a conception in his *Perpetual peace*, first published in 1795, which was an extension and development of his 1784 essay 'Idea toward a universal history in a cosmopolitan respect'. According to Kant, the ideal of republican government is extendable to the international arena, and represents the Enlightenment ideal of 'perpetual peace' through a free federation of states. Kant proposed a federation of republican states on the basis that peace might be achieved between states under a system of international law. Kant himself pays debts for the conception to early modern thinkers like Hugo Grotius and Samuel Pufendorf but his more immediate sources of inspiration are Rousseau and Charles-Irénée Castel (Wood, 1998, p. 60). As Allen Wood (1998, p. 62) states:

> Kant's philosophical project... is truly cosmopolitan in intent, not limited by any geographic or cultural borders. Its articles are meant not merely as precepts of a *ius gentium*, applying to the relations between sovereign states, but beyond this also as principles of a *ius cosmopoliticum*, which regards *all* peoples of the earth as a 'single universal community' or 'universal state of humankind' founded on a 'universal right of humanity'.[6]

For Kant, then, the solution to the relations between states resided in the development of republican states and their organization into a peaceful federation of states operating under the rule of the cosmopolitan law. Such a conception has clearly provided a model for those like Daniele Archibugi (1998) or David Held (1995) in their models of cosmopolitan democracy. Held argues that contemporary patterns of globalization are undermining existing patterns of liberal model, centred as they are on the nation-state. Held (1995, pp. 279–280) argues that because there is no global *demos*, there is no locus for decisions beyond or between states. Conventional democratic theory applies to life *within*, but not *between*, states. In Held's view democracy is threatened by being confined to the national level. According to Held (1995, p. 237) national democracies require safeguarding 'by elaborating and reinforcing democracy from the "outside" through a network of regional and international agencies and assemblies that cut across spatially limited locales'. Through such interlinking global networks individual nation-states are rendered accountable in relation to transnational democratic norms. Such proposals do not involve a conception of world government but rather a common framework of interlocking and overlapping institutions and agencies. As Anthony McGrew (2000, p. 414) states: 'The implications of this model for the nation-state and individual citizenship are profound. It proposes the end of sovereign statehood and national citizenship as conventionally understood and their re-articulation within the framework of cosmopolitan democratic law.' While the cosmopolitan ideal expresses some important insights, the approach needs serious modification. In Kant's original formulation, it expresses the overly abstract faith that international relations and global governance can be run according to deontological principles of universal reason. Not only does it fail to relate issues of global justice to the lives and communities of actual contexts, but also it potentially ignores the realities concerning the global power of transnational capital, and the 'uneven' development that is the inevitable consequence. As Bellamy and Castiglione (1998, p. 154) point out, it champions a 'free-standing' conception of human rights based on 'individualism, universality and generality'. Additionally, there is inadequate understanding of how democracy works in and through communities and agencies at the global or national levels.

This is not to say that cosmopolitan conceptions should be entirely discarded. Bellamy and Castiglione (1998, p. 162) maintain that 'it would be mistaken to regard the cosmopolitan and the communitarian arguments as totally at odds with each other... Rather, they offer contrasting but to some degree compatible accounts of how we should think about individuality, rights and their relationship to the societies that embody them'. They maintain (1998, p. 162) that 'cosmopolitan morality only makes sense to the extent that it is embedded within a communitarian framework', a position they dub as 'cosmopolitan communitarianism'.

That community, as I envisage it, is 'without borders'; while this means they are characterized by differences of custom, tradition and practice, they are also characterized by certain commonalities in structure and belief, networked throughout and across them. Such commonalities are expressed by Jana Thompson (1998, p. 191) as constituting universal cosmopolitan principles regarding peace and security, the self-determination of communities, the freedom of individuals and individual well-being. In this sense, as I conceptualise community, the limits to a particular community are not the limits of justice and democracy. This is to say, that communities without borders permit 'bridgeheads' that enable transnational democracy based on certain shared ends and values. My conception also recognizes an idea of 'multiple overlapping' communities in that individuals can identify with many different communities—ethnic, religious, political, and social—at the same time. In a global world identity becomes more complex, and the processes of identity attachment cannot be confined to a single territorial state. At the same time, my conception recognizes that individuals derive their identities from socially embedded communities that they do not themselves choose.

Just as all communities have some common interests, and in this sense belong to a 'community of communities', so there is a common good for humanity expressing the core of these values and species necessities. In an age of terrorism the necessary objectivism of the good becomes more evident. Such a conception of the good can harbour general principles of right, just as communitarianism can harbour certain cosmopolitanism principles.

Clearly a modified conception of cosmopolitanism could in this sense contribute to democratic practice. Recent debate over the proposed war with Iraq, concerning UN resolution 1441, has demonstrated that dominant states do not always intimidate or silence smaller states. The contestation against support for war led by France, Germany and Russia not only amplified the debate to a world audience, but it also stimulated citizen involvement and delayed and possibly prevented war from obtaining legitimacy under international law. Democracy at this level is by no means perfect. Political leaders may or may not heed public opinion. While their actions may well not be checked democratically, there is an element of democracy in the fact that the careers of those who disregard public opinion carry potentially serious political risks.[7] Foucauldians do not object to this sort of development, imperfect as it is. Similarly, they don't reject attempts to strengthen international institutions such as the United Nations. But, they have no illusions that such institutional processes are subject to abuse or coercion, and sometimes reveal the idea of democracy as hardly worthy of its name. In addition, although global institutions should abide by democratic justice, this should not be seen as residing in a deontological conception of universal reason to be applied like a blueprint to all nations and peoples. Rather, as the traditional communitarians maintained, the means of resolving arguments in morality and challenging domination are context-dependent and embedded in communities. Moving beyond traditional communitarianism, however, 'thin communitarianism' maintains that this need not entail relativism because outcomes can be assessed in terms of success or failure in solving problems they confront, or in relation to-democratic standards. As communities are only partially bounded, this also establishes the possibilities of 'bridgeheads' which can constitute a basis from which issues concerned with moral relativism can be addressed.

In accord with a 'thin' communitarian stance, a somewhat different approach to global politics and change has been advanced by writers like John Burnheim (1985, 1986, 1995) and Rob Walker (1988, 1991, 1994, 1995). Although sometimes presented in opposition to cosmopolitan ideas, I regard such approaches as *supplementary* if appropriately modified along the lines indicated above. Rather than emphasize reform, or rule based upon a federation of nation-states, organized at different levels, such approaches are premised on a model of *radical global democracy* based on active participation and the rights of citizens to contest policies within the global political process. As McGrew (2000, p. 410) summarizes them, such approaches stress:

> The creation of alternative forms of global social, economic and political organization based generally upon communitarian principles: that is principles which emerge from the life and conditions of particular communities, from local communities to communities of interest or affection e.g. environmental, religious, gender. It combines a commitment to direct forms of democracy and self-governance together with new structures of functional governance.

Burnheim's advocacy of what he calls '*demarchy*' offers a specific practical means by which democracy can be extended and organized at the level of regional and global politics. As Burnheim expresses it, demarchy refers to a governance arrangements organized along *functional* as opposed to territorial lines, which aims to ensure more adequate representation of interests and participation. In this scenario, as McGrew (2000, p. 411) puts it, 'democracy... [is] not to be sought in geographically-bounded entities like nation-states, but rather in functional authorities of varying geographical scope'.[8] Demarchical control means control by independent bodies—organizations rather than individuals or states—which represent specific interests—the environment, women, labour—on a genuinely representative basis. Demarchy aims to establish public control in a decentralized arena, establishing organizations which rule over functionally specific areas. In a demarchical system, representatives are nominated, selected and replaced on a representative democratic basis. Hence, Burnheim (1985, p. 184) says that demarchy is: 'A form of organization appropriate to a very complex society that generates a host of structures, of interests and possibilities. It is equipped to handle complex problems and is propelled by social forces and movements.' Although Burnheim (1985, pp. 19–30) sees demarchy as an alternative to governance by the nation-state, and as operational at both the national and global levels, I would argue that it need not supplant governance structures (like the state) which are organized on a territorial basis. In addition, while it may operate at any level, I would argue that it is peculiarly suited to regional and global contexts. In my view, the basis for a form of demarchical governance already operates in *co-existence* with states, and could be extended, at the global level.[9] Demarchy in this conception is rather like an international community of organizations, premised on concepts of *interdependence, community,* and *reciprocity,* which can be appropriately operationalized at the global and regional levels of governance. In this sense it is based on the idea of overlapping partial communities, and involves different kinds of bodies functioning at different levels. It also reinforces, if guided and supported by states, a conception of the separation of powers between and within national, regional and global levels. It is well-suited where there is a pre-existing requirement for a democratic will, a ready made environment of institutional structures and resources which enable deliberative politics, where established structures and mechanisms already exist to permit participation, and where it is desirable to avoid concentrations of power. It seems well-suited to global politics, where it could be argued even non-democratic nation-states want decentralized democratic governance in relation to pressing world problems and issues.

In summary, then, demarchical governance could institute modes of institutionalization, representation, and rules of replacement for agencies and bodies operating at either regional or global levels. In my view, because this sort of governance can *co-exist* with already established structures of power, such as states, it permits a multiplicity of forms and types of democratic governance. Such a pattern of governance is not self-establishing or self-maintaining, as Burnheim (1985, p. 13, pp. 19–50, pp. 156–80) claims, but can best operate alongside of other structures, and indeed would be strengthened by an independent system of nation-states which have specific interests in how global agencies operate, and constitute a check and guarantee on such a process. Contra Burnheim (1985, pp. 19–30), therefore, I would argue that nation-states are also important to, and do not necessarily contradict, forms of demarchical governance operating regionally and globally in a successfully democratic way.

Importantly, however, the ultimate support for democracy at all levels, and in all contexts, whether in the nation-state or the global polity, resides in the active participation and willingness of citizens to contest policies. This timeless theme in democratic theory is developed in recent work by Rob Walker (1988, pp. 8–9; 1995, pp. 311–14), who emphasizes the role of critical social movements as a theory of radical democracy 'beyond borders'. In this, as McGrew (2000, p. 413) summarizes it, such movements constitute 'a "bottom up" theory of the democratization of world order'. As a theory of progressive politics, this form of radical democracy operates through 'grassroots' social movements, such as women's movements, environmental or peace movements, which express resistance to international as well as national institutions and authorities. Social movements energize publics, forge solidarities, develop critical consciousness, define injustice and justice in specific contexts, expose domination and oppression, clarify alternatives, and enhance the prospects for a just world peace. Social movements also work for redistributive policies in favour of the disadvantaged, and keep governments and demarchical agencies 'in line'. Such a view of global justice also constitutes a check on nation-states at a number of levels. It puts nation-states under an obligation to respect human rights in line with critical debate and policies formulated at the regional or global levels. In addition, it puts nation-states under obligations not to exploit or oppress individuals, or other communities. Finally, it creates the conditions whereby all nations' actions are monitored, and accountable at supra-national levels, and where they have the chance to achieve their own regime of justice internally, *in conformity with global principles.*[10]

Democracy, Justice and the 'Thin' Community

These models of cosmopolitan and radical global democracy are in direct opposition to the standard model of international relations as an anarchic system of states each pursuing their own interest. This standard view of international relations accords with the Westphalian model of free independent states, organized and run on the basis of autonomy and non-interference. Such a conception is essentially Hobbesian. That is, it represents an extrapolation from Hobbes views about individuals in the state of nature to ethical scepticism concerning relations between states in the international arena.[11] For Hobbes (1968), there were no *effective* moral principles in the state of nature.[12] The fact that one individual cannot trust another individual to abide by a moral rule or norm, makes it pointless acting in such a way oneself—which is why life in the state of nature is 'solitary, nasty, brutish and short'. In the international system of states, ethical scepticism means that there are no moral restrictions on a state's interpretation of its own interests. Hence, as moral rules would be inappropriate, the system is seen as 'anarchic'. Each state should pursue their own interests, as Beitz (1979, pp. 51–2) puts it, 'in the absence of reliable expectations of reciprocal compliance', i.e., given there is no possibility of a community of states acting in accord with a moral rule or principle at all. Since the Peace of Westphalia, which ended the Thirty Years War in 1648, the anarchic conception of independent states is seen as the ruling view.[13]

Kant rejected such a conception, as did Grotius and Pufendorf before him. Rather than support an anarchic conception of international relations based on individual state interests, they supported an ethical view of the role of the state acting in accord with an objective moral rule.[14] Initial plausibility of a such a view can be seen in the existence of human rights accords, international charters, and initiatives towards international peace, which would seem to suggest that some conception of international morality does exist, and does influence states in their actions towards each other. Before the Peace of Westphalia, Grotius had defined international relations as a moral community of states.[15] Pufendorf also developed a conception of the 'morality of states', interpreting international relations from within a natural law tradition.[16]

Globalization, terrorism and WMD make such a model, based on an 'ethical' conception of the global order, even more plausible in the twenty-first century. A number of factors reinforce this. The rise of international terrorism and WMD alters the 'equation', for it makes individual and collective survival an important ethical concern. The possibilities of nuclear terrorism together with the democratization of knowledge, and of access to nuclear knowledge and technology, make the challenges facing humanity formidable. It could be argued that crises associated with climate change, or with conditions like Aids or SARS, contribute similarly to such an argument. In this situation, survival constitutes a new basis to justify a global law of morality amongst nations. It is worthwhile acting according to principles if by doing so acts of terrorism are *minimized,* and the possibilities for survival are *enhanced.* Similarly, the possibility of AOT or of violence increases the need for a discourse of safety and security. We may not agree with Hobbes on very much, but the importance of *security* as opposed to *freedom,* was indeed a profound insight. Globalization and terrorism raise the issue of 'survival' both for individuals and nations. It is in my interests to treat you fairly and impartially on the basis of respect if it reduces the chances for terrorism and enhances those of survival. It is in the interests of my country to act similarly.

Such a thesis would argue that given these new realities of AOT and WMD, the *self-interest* of states, like the *self-interest* of individuals, is a poor basis for action and ethics. Indeed actions calculated in terms of short-term interests may not be realized as in the long-term interests of either. The interests of survival are normative in that it imposes requirements of action in the interests of all. The self-interests of humanity cannot be calculated on the basis of the interests of each, however, but must involve a collective consideration. This necessitates a conception of democracy, as Beitz (1979, p. 58) puts it, which expresses a 'moral point of view':

> The moral point of view requires us to regard the world from the perspective of one person among many rather than from that of a particular self with particular interests, and to choose courses of action, policies, rules, and institutions on grounds that would be acceptable to any agent who was impartial among the competing interests involved... From the moral point of view... one views one's interests as one set of interests among many and weighs the entire range of interests according to some impartial scheme.

Democracy must in this light be seen as a comprehensive discourse of (1) safety and security; (2) freedom and autonomy; (3) inclusion; (4) fairness and justice; and (5) equality of resources and capabilities. Safety and security express themselves in children's telephone 'help-lines', women's refuges, or human rights accords for the treatment of ordinary citizens, or prisoners, or so on. Inclusion warrants that no one is excluded from democratic entitlement, and constitutes the basis on which safety and security can be assured. Freedom incorporates freedom from domination and freedom for the development of capabilities. Justice and fairness promise treatment in a public arena according to publicly stated criteria embodied in constitutional laws and rules. Equality of resources and capabilities ensure opportunities and conditions for development for all. In that treating people fairly and reasonably on the basis of respect minimizes terrorism and increases the chances for survival, democratic justice based on an equalization of power and non-domination becomes an objective good. It is in the interests of both the individual and the collectivity. In an age of terrorism, where a Hobbesian global Leviathan is clearly undesirable, a comprehensive discourse of democracy becomes the best answer to the Hobbesian problem of order.

The effective operation of such a theory requires an alternative to the prevailing view of conflict in international relations, in that the prevailing principle of non-interference that has been the basis of international law since the Treaty of Westphalia is incompatible with such a broadly humanitarian vision of world order. If the state is to be trusted to regulate and maintain sovereignty in particular domains, state sovereignty must itself be qualified. Although as Wolff argued in relation to Grotius, no state has the right to interfere in another state's sovereign affairs, the entire community of states 'as a whole' had such a right.[17] In contemporary terms we might understand this as saying that it is the 'community of states' acting through the United Nations, and through international agencies such as the World Bank and the World Trade Organization, that must assume the role of auditors and custodians of democracy in international affairs.

Such a conception requires institutions committed to conflict resolution, ongoing debate and communication, as well as the mutual survival of different traditions. Such a democratic conception is not utilitarian, but presupposes rights and entitlements which are universally given to all. Rights in this conception are not natural but are given by the state as the collective expression of the democratic will of the people. Such rights are necessary to self-creation and constitute recognition that a space of autonomy is necessary to self-development of both individuals and groups. If the new challenges that face humanity focus our attention on the way *collective action* and *individual interests* are *inextricably linked*, it is also imperative that a concern for individual rights and other entitlements within liberal constitutionalism, is not compromised.

Compared to traditional conservative versions of communitarianism, such a conception constitutes a 'thin' communitarianism of the sort that is evident in Foucault's work (Olssen, 2002; Olssen et al., 2004). In his analysis of the Greeks and

Greco-Romans, for instance, Foucault reinstates a form of communitarianism which, ultimately, is necessitated by the social *conditions* of selfhood and which underlies his conceptions of self-creation and ethics. Such a communitarianism is 'thin' in the sense that, contra Spinoza, Hegel, Herder, Rousseau and Marx, it has no common bond or goal which is characterized by integration or consensus. Community in this sense is definable as an all-encompassing arena without fixed borders or unity, which comprises an assortment of different ways by which life is lived. In this sense, the 'thin' community does not eclipse liberty or autonomy of individuals in preference for belonging, social cohesion, or co-operation. The model of community is, as William Corlett (1993) describes it, 'without unity'. This is to say, the model is not a *totalizing* one, which presupposes unity between individual and collective. Rather, it is a *detotalizing* one, where society comprises a minimal structure of norms, rules, understandings, practices and agreements necessary to permit individual agency and social difference to take effect and function.

There are, of course, substantive constraints on individuals according to the pressing concerns of collective action which underpins individual interests and liberty—the need to solve global warming, to maintain security, and health. These collective issues, which underpin individual liberty and interests, become the basis upon which rights and duties are extended. In this sense thin communitarianism differs also from modern natural law liberalism in that the individualist language of claims is supplemented by a more cosmopolitan concern with both rights and duties which rather than seen as natural, constitute a global ethics orientated to survival. Within such a socio-historical conception, a richer sense of liberty and autonomy consistent with the requirements of survival are the entitlement of all so long as they abide within the rule of law. Conceptions of democratic citizenship will develop as a consequence of such a model.

In this conception, the 'thin' community still posits an irreducible conception of the common good. Such a conception is compatible with maximum liberty of each consistent with the extension of like liberty to all, and with the necessary tasks of survival in the global age. In ontological terms, such a conception displays affinities to the Aristotelian conception of 'the good' espoused by Martha Nussbaum (1992, 2000*a*, 2000*b*). Nussbaum's conception incorporates 'an account of the most important functions of the human being, in terms of which human life is defined' (1992, p. 214). It recognizes that all individuals and all cultures have certain developmental and lifestyle needs. Such a conception, she says, is 'vague, and this is deliberately so . . . for it admits of much multiple specification in accordance with varied local and personal conceptions. The idea is that it is better to be vaguely right than precisely wrong' (p. 215). Such a conception is not metaphysical in that it does not claim to derive from a source exterior to human beings in history. Rather, it is as 'universal as possible' and aims at 'mapping out the general shape of the human form of life, those features that constitute life as human wherever it is' (p. 216). Nussbaum calls this her 'thick vague theory of the good' (p. 214). Hence, her list of factors constitutes a formal list, allowing for difference or variation within each category. Amongst the factors are: (1) mortality: all human beings face death; (2) various invariant features of the human body, such as 'nutritional, and other related requirements' regarding hunger, thirst, the need for food and drink and shelter; (3) cognitive: 'all human beings have sense perception . . . the ability to think'; (4) early development; (5) practical reason; (6) sexual desire; (7) affiliation with other human beings; and (8) relatedness to other species and to nature (pp. 216–19). Nussbaum classifies such a conception, following the influential writings of W. V. O. Quine, Donald Davidson, Hilary Putnam and Nelson Goodman, as an 'internalist essentialism' (p. 208) which is 'an historically grounded empirical essentialism' (p. 208). Within its broad end, and subject to the limits necessary for its realization and continuance, it permits and recognizes a multitude of identities and projects and ways of life.[18]

This sort of 'capabilities' approach has not only been advanced by Nussbaum but by Sen (1979, 1985, 1992, 1993, 1999, 2002). For Sen (1999, p. 295), the development of capabilities is part of the expansion of freedom. Criticizing Human Capital theory for narrowly considering human beings as part of the productive economic process, Sen (1999, p. 295) maintains that:

> The acknowledgement of the role of human qualities in promoting and sustaining economic growth—momentous as it is—tells us nothing about why economic growth is sought in the first place. If, instead, the focus is, ultimately, on the expansion of human freedom to live the kind of lives that people have reason to value, then the role of economic growth in expanding these opportunities has to be integrated into that more foundational understanding of the process of development as the expansion of human capability to lead more worthwhile and more free lives.

The form of 'thin' communitarianism being advocated is broadly compatible with such an approach. Foucault's emphasis on 'self-creation' can be held to *presuppose* a range of capabilities as *necessary*. Such an approach, as Nussbaum argues, enables both international comparisons, and concentrates on the actual conditions which provide for the functional needs of individuals and groups. Such an approach also provides for education, for a politics based on the capabilities approach presupposes that a society provides necessary public education by which capabilities can be developed. Under such an approach it is the business of education to provide for the production of such capabilities. Taking Foucault's emphasis on 'self-creation' as fundamental, we can say that a number of things are clearly required. These include: (1) basic material and institutional supporting structures and resources; (2) training and knowledge; (3) non-humiliation, respect and dignity; (4) a protected space where autonomy can be practiced; and (5) structures that permit dialogue and communication. Unlike Nussbaum, we have replaced Rawls with Foucault as the major influence on justice and ethics. Foucault's is a non-liberal conception, yet one which protects traditional liberal ideals as regards 'liberty' and 'autonomy' in the context of the development of the virtues necessary for a global community.[19] By stressing 'capabilities' such an approach is not advocating a utilitarian ethics, nor a traditional rights-based approach, nor a teleology of functioning in the Aristotelian sense, nor even a Kantian approach, but simply focuses on the political virtues and collective arrangements wherein survival can be assured and individual development and self-creation can take place.[20]

In addition, a Foucauldian-inspired 'thin' community has other characteristics. Importantly, it is established and reproduced by voluntary acts of free and equal citizens. In addition, to speak of 'community', is to speak of an all-encompassing arena, *without fixed borders*. In this sense, it is not to be understood as a 'bounded' territory or region, but rather it moves across borders—globally—and links politically to forms of republicanism and cosmopolitanism. Also important, such a community is not incompatible with universalism. 'Thin' communitarianism thus overcomes the relativism whereby ethical reasoning must be *internal* to a particular community tradition.[21] Further, common values and practices are only required to the extent they are necessary for democratic continuity and survival. Finally, it comprises antecedent values, norms and institutions that recognize the social nature of the individual.

In terms of its social ontology such a conception is therefore more coherent than liberalism. Given that human beings can only make meaningful choices for their lives against a background context of alternatives constituted in a community, it can be argued further that a stress on self-creation and liberty as the basis. of ethics would require a strong state that could protect these conditions. Individual autonomy to choose presupposes, in this sense, the existence of structures that are institutionally embodied. As a consequence, 'thin' communitarians stress balancing the rights and freedoms of individuals to pursue their own interests with an equal interest in the rights and interests of the community as necessary to the realization of individual claims. Such a conception is 'thin' in that the plurality of ends, goals and values are either institutionally permitted or, in that they conflict, democratically negotiated. In this conception, the reciprocal or inter-related links between individual and collective are kept clearly in balance. It is this retheorisation of relations between individual and collective which gives thin communitarianism its distinctive stance. What it acknowledges is that collective and individual interests each depend on the other. Individual liberty is not possible, or is certainly not meaningful, except where collective action is undertaken to ensure security, and intervene over such impending crises as climate change,

Aids, SARS and other potential global crises. To trust the future of the world to the forces of 'spontaneous evolution', or the supposedly beneficent effects of the 'invisible hand' of nature, as Frederick Hayek, and the classical Political Economists would do, is in the global era a recipe for disaster of catastrophic proportions. While liberals will be uneasy about the extension of collective power, what they must recognize is that such a colossal extension *has emerged anyway,* as a consequence of the sheer complexity of government in a global era, as well as of impending global crises that need attention. To call for a minimal state in the face of impending global catastrophes around climate change, or global violence, not only overlooks the fact that any individual state is only one of many centres of power in a global *network of power centres,* but fails to grapple with the *necessary* size and complexity of the collective power in the global era if the liberty and security of individuals is to be secured. What is called for today is not to abolish or reduce the size of the state, or of global collective power, but to bring it under greater democratic control. It must make it as difficult as possible for abuses to occur, and where they do occur, their identification and correction must be as speedy as possible.

The fact that collective agents may sometimes abuse their power should not cause us to seek neoliberal solutions based on *laissez-faire,* for in a world of huge technological capacity for good and ill, and other impending crises never hitherto previously witnessed, there is no option but collective agency. The dependence of individuals on common rules and collective agency should not cause liberals fear because collective agency is compatible with individual self-interest, and more successful in achieving goals on their behalf. Indeed, by following common rules, and approaching problems through collective agency, each individual is able to do better for him/herself. This is to say, collective agency and cooperative strategies overcome Prisoner's Dilemmas of strategies based on individual self-interested choice. At the same time collective agency aids in the survival of each and all in that it assists to secure the continuance and reproduction of valued traditions and ways of life. Collective agency is also important in securing action against 'free riders' and therefore gives *assurance of fair treatment* for all. There is, in addition, a historically contingent dimension to this relation, for in a complex and dangerous world, the need to rely on collective agency is becoming far greater than it was in the past. In a global age of massive technological potential, the prospects for relying, as Frederick Hayek argued for, on the supposedly 'self-regulating' forces of 'spontaneous evolution' is simply not a viable option at all.

Community, Liberty and Justice

Such a view also effects a conception of freedom as encompassing both positive duties and negative rights. In this, liberty and autonomy are seen as constituted by society in terms of meaningful civic functioning. Only in society is freedom realizable and determinate. As human beings are socially and historically constituted it is not possible to conceive of liberty except in society. And once the individual is seen as socially and historically constituted, active expressions of liberty become necessarily forms of participation. And hence, freedom as participation needs re-theorizing once again. As an extension of this, as in the classical view, it is held that liberty cannot operate in the absence of law. To speak of 'natural liberty', as liberals do, is in my view to enter a realm of logical and empirical. incoherence. On my view, it is only through the civil law of society that liberty becomes definite and bounded. In his *Commentaries on the Laws of England,* the eighteenth-century legal and political philosopher, William Blackstone (1979) depicted liberty in such a way seeing 'civil liberty' as consisting in 'protecting the rights of individuals by the united force of society' (cited in Heyman, 1992, p. 85). Civil liberty must be supplemented by 'political liberty', which is more collective, and can be defined as the power of a community to govern itself, and for its citizens to participate in self-government. Such a conception is both positive and negative: the positive freedom of a community is its power to make and enforce laws for the public good; the negative conception entails that it is free to the extent that it is not interfered with. As Heyman (1992, pp. 87–8) points out, in such a classical conception, both senses of freedom are governed by the laws of the constitution which both confers and limits governmental power. Political liberty, thus, enables individuals to achieve goals through collective action, e.g., the protection of rights, as requiring in Blackstone's sense, 'the unified force of society'. For these purposes, the economy would be regulated necessary to increase civil liberty of individuals to pursue their own good (see Blackstone, 1979). Crucially, in this 'quasi-Foucauldian' approach, unlike for Rawls or Habermas, there is no Kantian tribunal of trans-cultural transcendental reason that could ground moral decisions or justify policy outcomes. There are, however, pragmatic factors, like the importance of peaceful co-existence for survival or stability that can justify policy outcomes. Certain common rules and collective action will be necessary if individual liberty and security is to mean anything at all. Just as individual action will have to be constrained if liberty is to given to all, so collective action will be necessary to secure those conditions. It can be agreed too, as Martha Nussbaum (2000*b*, p. 124) has stated, that the core capabilities and basic needs of humans can be the object of an 'overlapping consensus' 'among people who otherwise have very different comprehensive conceptions of the good'. Here she is accepting Rawls's way of reconciling individual autonomy with collective action. The area of 'overlapping consensus' constitutes for Rawls the common rules that exist between individuals if cooperation over the realizations of societal interests is to be achieved. Comprehensive beliefs on the other hand, are those beliefs (in religion, culture, or philosophy) where individuals may be autonomous to exercise their liberty as they see fit. My only objection to this way of conceptualizing things is the individualism which it entails, for it fails to accord full significance in global or national politics to collective action, and the sense today in which collective action is increasingly necessary to the liberty and security of all. Rather than an 'overlapping consensus' which for Rawls expresses the common 'agent-neutral' interests of self-interested beings, I would rather simply recognize the 'common good' or the 'public interest', and I would ontologically recognize those common interests in *objective* terms. This area of commonness is the area that all self-interested beings share for security, liberty, sustenance and opportunity for developing their lives as they wish compatible with the ongoing survival of the planet and the like liberty, security and development of all. This area of common concerns is in the global era of far greater proportions than in earlier periods and concerns security, sustenance, safety and citizenship. It constitutes a global *Leviathan*, yet it can be harnessed democratically, for each single (King's) head is less powerful than the collective might of all the others.

In addition, while the new concerns of the global age require surveillance and scrutiny on a scale never previously thought likely, let alone desirable, a certain *essential* measure of rights and autonomy, which must be given to all as a mark of inclusion, can continue to operate, subject to responsible conduct within the rule of law[22] as the litmus test of legitimacy of collective power.

There is also present within Foucault's approach a general conception of *democratic justice* that could underpin such a model of community in a normative sense.[23] In his discussions about 'domination', and the 'equalization of power relations', Foucault (1991) is advancing a political principle that speaks to both liberty and equality. In terms of equality, equalizing power would mean fighting for marginalized and oppressed groups. In relation to liberty, it presupposes the irreducible moral status of each person and would oppose governmental policies that conflicted with or inhibited self-creation. As Mitchell Dean (1999, p. 184) puts it, the law is important in Foucault's political conception according to whether 'it allows rather than inhibits the self-directed use and development of capacities'. This echoes Foucault's view that liberty requires a certain political structure, given that liberty itself involves the exercise of power. Under certain situations, the power relations in terms of which liberty is realized make its expression impossible. In this situation, there results a *state of domination*, says Foucault (1991, p. 12), in which power relations become fixed 'in such a way that they are perpetually asymmetrical [in which case] the margin of liberty is extremely limited'. Foucault gives the example of the traditional conjugal relation in the eighteenth and nineteenth centuries:

> We cannot say that there was only male power; the woman herself could do a lot of things; be unfaithful to him, extract

money from him, refuse him sexually. She was, however, subject to a state of domination, [...] where all that was finally no more than a certain number of tricks which never brought about a reversal of the situation.

Such states of domination entailed relations of power that:

Instead of being variable and allowing different partners a strategy which alters them, find themselves firmly set and congealed. When an individual or social group manages to block the field of relations of power... to prevent all reversibility of movement... we are facing what could be called a state of domination. (p. 3)

In his criticism of Habermas, Foucault (1991, p. 18) proceeds to state a conception whereby power relations can be 'equalized' in order: 'To give oneself the rules of law, the techniques of management, and also the ethics, the ethos, the practices of self, which would allow these games of power to be played with a minimum of domination.' As against totalizing approaches, such as Marxism, Hegelianism and liberalism, the normative emphasis of Foucault's position is that all power relations must be characterized by *openness* (i.e., not be 'set' or 'congealed'). As a consequence, such principles give a normative basis to a conception of democratic justice, while recognizing that justice may require different things at different times and places. Such a conception is universal, in Rorty's (1998, p. 52) sense, in terms of 'reach', but not in terms of 'validity'. This is to say, unlike Rawls and Habermas, it does not seek to encourage deliberation in order to arrive at a supposed 'rational consensus', but simply to achieve a 'settlement'. In Rawls's terms, the outcomes of deliberation would bare the character of a 'treaty' or 'modus vivendi', rather than a 'consensus'. It is necessity that makes collective action important, for the interests of individuals would not be realized except that they are collectively addressed. What results is a new 'settlement', or 'pact' or agreement', or 'accommodation' which enables life to be lived in the presence of fundamental disagreements over practices, values and ways of life. Such a conception, based upon power relations that must remain dialogically open, and, through *resistance*, is normatively skewed towards power equalization, is also *context-sensitive* to the specific contingencies of historical circumstance.

Democracy and Multiculturalism

Such a conception of democracy also underpins multicultural rights by recognizing different group aspirations yet underpinning them with a rights culture. Notwithstanding liberal fears that conceptions of the common good overly constrain individual liberty, it is not insensitive to diversity and doesn't seek cultural homogeneity through the uniform application of a single standard or rule. Although rights are not recognized as natural, they are a mark of inclusion, and hence underpin constitutional regimes' legitimacy. On this basis, collective powers are legitimate only to the extent that individual rights and entitlements are recognized and constitutionally provided for. The violation of constitutional principles and individual rights delegitimates collective power. In the most obvious sense, this can lead to defeat in elections; in situations of oppression, where democratic principles are themselves violated, it can lead to protracted organized resistance, or revolution. Such a commitment to the rule of law becomes in effect the *sine qua non* of collective powers' *right to rule*. Such a principle must not become a slogan or mantra that means simply conforming to laws which have been conveniently rushed through to justify action. The rule of law must mean, as British QC Helena Kennedy (2004) puts it, 'adherence to human rights standards—equality before the law, fairness, respect for human dignity and due process. There cannot be hierarchies of human rights'.[24]

If democracy must respect constitutional principles and accord equal rights, it must also respect the diversity of group interests within the global order. This is to say it must respect multiculturalism. By the same token, multiculturalism must respect democracy. Democratic norms must necessarily cross-cut multicultural groups to protect three conditions: (1) the basic rights of all citizens individually and as groups (freedom of speech, thought, assembly, expression, lifestyle choice, etc.); (2) that no person or group is manipulated into accepting values represented by public institutions; and (3) that public officials and institutions are democratically accountable in principle and practice.

Democracy in this sense must constitute a new universal.[25] This is to say that it is a more basic set of procedural norms and rules than are the rights of any minority to do what they like. We must move away from any conception of multiculturalism whereby cultural minorities can be completely unresponsive to outside cultures, or where prohibitions against group members leaving the culture can be enforced. No minority and no culture can guarantee their own survival forever, as openness to the world outside is a necessary principle of democracy. This openness is indeed a core principle of cosmopolitanism, which must infuse citizenship education post-September 11. The point here is that a democratic rights culture must underpin any conception of multiculturalism, so defined.

By making a 'rights culture' fundamental, in this sense, limits are placed upon the 'discourse of diversity' that multiculturalism entails. This does not mean that the recognition of distinct identities and differences, as argued for by multiculturalists, are not important. Liberalism has clearly failed to sufficiently acknowledge such insights from 'the politics of recognition', tending to represent justice as the *imposition of a single standard or rule* to all of the diverse groups within the social structure. Yet, while we can accept that multiculturalists have contributed something important in arguing for the recognition of distinct cultural identities, based on ethnicity, race, religion, gender or class, as Kymlicka (1999) has argued, such arguments cannot be used to legitimate 'internal restrictions' (e.g., prohibiting group exit) which violate or contradict democratic principles, or interfere with the rights of other individuals or groups. By the same token, multicultural advocacy may result in 'external protections' to counter group disadvantage or marginalization. Such claims may themselves vary from one historical period to another, and should thus be deliberated and enacted through the democratic process itself.

Although multiculturalism advances a 'discourse of diversity', it is different from, and largely unrelated to, the 'discourse of diversity and devolution' advanced by neoliberalism. In relation to neoliberalism, diversity is sponsored by the market mechanism, which results in compounding and cumulative inequalities. With multiculturalism, diversity may also be dysfunctional to the extent that it undermines the degree of societal cohesion necessary for different groups to work and live together. The extent to which multicultural diversity reinforces norms of intolerance and conflict also takes on a new and altered significance post 9/11. Clearly the balance of contending forces between the common interests of society, and the sub-groupings within it, and the overall extent to which diversity is recognized and permitted, is itself a question of democratic deliberation and adjudication, which may alter in different places and times.[26]

It can also be argued that such a view of democracy is not only compatible with, but strongly coerces a conception of *distributive justice*. If anything threatens survival, it is cumulative and compounding inequalities driven by neoliberal reason. Both Charles Beitz (1979) and Onora O'Neill (1988, 2000) have inquired into applying principles of distributive justice to the international arena. In Beitz's (1979, p. 144, pp. 149–50) view:

> International economic cooperation creates a new basis for international morality. If social cooperation is the foundation of *distributive justice*, then one might think that international economic interdependence lends support to a principle of global distributive justice... In an interdependent world, confining principles of social justice to democratic societies has the effect of taxing poor nations so that others may benefit from living in 'just' regimes.

Central to Beitz's (1979, p. 151) argument is that national boundaries should not be seen as having 'fundamental moral significance' for '[s]ince boundaries are not coextensive with the scope of social cooperation, they do not mark the limits of social obligations'.

Although Beitz seeks to apply Rawls's 'justice as fairness' conception, O'Neill acknowledges that liberalism's abstract principles are incompatible with the specificity required to apply to the international community. The very abstractness necessary to be relevant transnationally, she states, makes it irrelevant to the ideals of a concrete *Sittlichkeit*. Because deontological solutions are universalist they ignore context. This is the problem with Rawls. He subordinates *Sittlichkeit* (ethical life) to *Moralität* (abstract individualist principles). Hence, his deontological principles cannot be linked to the 'discourse and experience of particular communities' (O'Neill, 1988, p. 718).[27] In prioritizing distribution over recognition, he is unable to achieve policy flexibility. Although Rawls in his later 'political/not metaphysical' writing sought to correct the problem, he paid a heavy price for trying to accommodate his critics.[28] My conception of 'thin communitarianism' answers this criticism, because it is structured along republican/global lines. It can retain an internationalist focus, can be related to specific communities, and is concerned with survival. It is not as abstract as Rawls, for *Moralität* operates in and through *Sittlichkeit*. It also avoids the problems of utilitarianism, in that it can explain 'rights', can explain why majorities shouldn't tyrannize minorities, and can explain why some groups, and some countries, shouldn't be sacrificed to benefit others.

In addition to this, the principles of non-domination and power equalization, or dispersal, do not determine outcomes in specific instances. They present a guide but they don't dictate the solution. In this sense, they can be sensitive to both 'distribution' and 'recognition'. What fills the void is *deliberation*. If principles do not determine outcomes but *underdetermine* them, then deliberation in an open contestable environment becomes crucial. That is, it is through deliberation that the outcome is achieved, and sometimes constructed (Miller, 2000, chapter 1). The final solution will be an accord prevailing in the communities involved, and represent a 'reasonable' settlement.[29] It will also be consistent with global principles of justice, however.

This is where the deontological liberals like Rawls need amendment. They remain tied to universalizing theory unrelated to context. As O'Neill (1988, p. 720) says, 'the move from abstract principles to determinate situation is part and parcel of all ethical reasoning, indeed of all practical reasoning'. Deontological liberals have little to say about the processes of history or differences of situation or demands for recognition. They seek merely to 'apply principles', prefer abstract accounts, and apply a single standard to all situations.

Similarly with Habermas's discourse ethics. As with Habermas the resolution of conflict occurs according to norms inherent in language and communication in the public sphere, there is a naive overlooking of strategic relations of power. Foucault agrees with Habermas that the misuse of power is the central problem of our era. But whereas Habermas seeks resolution through universals and context-independent standards of the ideal speech situation, in a way similar to Rawls,[30] Foucault concentrates his attention upon the historically contingent context-dependent inequalities in power that seek strategic redress. In this he posits a series of strategies and tactics of resistance as power acts against power. Thus we disagree with Habermas's Kantian argument that there is a universal trans-historical foundation for determining truth claims or policy claims (Habermas, 1987, p. 294). Our view is that his theory of communicative action is idealist in the sense that it introduces the reality of a non-contextualized, trans-historical reason, which introduces a fatal problem into Habermas's work. Because Foucault's position posits power as always present in terms of which all communication works, communication is always, inevitably, a conversation of non-rational rhetoric which involves the issue of interests. For Foucault, democratic norms have historical validity to the extent they are historically valued. While it makes little sense to ask if these norms are 'universally true', the value of democratic deliberation and communication is constituted in a settlement anchored in norms of the historical present. Thus, Foucault's work is anchored by contextualism in the norms of the present. While he rejects metaphysical universals as anchoring democracy, he seeks recourse to norms of power, resistance, and criticism. In this sense, it is historically conditioned situations that form the basis for analysis, not metaphysical universals. To correct Habermas, Foucault introduces the centrality of *power* and *phronesis*.

Foucault's approach supports a more republican conception of political organization. Republicanism is committed to a substantive conception of society and to the good. Freedom is seen as non-domination, which links to equality, community, civic virtue and an emphasis on constitutionalism and checking the power of government. Such a conception of freedom developed in a republican tradition from the time of the Roman Empire, and was further developed after the English Civil war by writers like James Harrington. In the eighteenth century republican thought became popular in

England, France and America.[31] Such a view rejects the liberal conception of negative freedom as non-interference. By focusing on freedom of some over others, freedom is seen as immunity from arbitrary control. By focusing on freedom as non-domination also means that it is not necessary to see freedom exclusively linked to civic participation.[32] Pettit (1997, p. 38) also maintains that it is different to 'interference' because one can be enslaved without interference. For Pettit (1997, p. 35) interference does not necessarily mean loss of liberty, if it is not arbitrary, but accepted by legitimate authority. As for William Blackstone, for James Harrington, in *Oceana*, says Pettit (1997, p. 39) 'liberty... is the liberty *by* the laws'. Freedom depends *on the law*, and hence, *on the constitution*.[33] As Pettit (1997, p. 173) says: 'We find constitutionalism in place whenever there are legally established ways of constraining the will of the powerful, even if the constraints are not recorded in a formal constitution.' Non-domination also entails that powers should be dispersed, or 'equalized' as we have been saying. For Montesquieu (1900) and republicans that followed him, it was this principle of dispersion, or equalization, that entailed the separation of powers. Such a principle becomes a core political principle which can support policies of bicameral arrangements for two houses of parliament, decentralization of power in federal systems, binding governments to international covenants or conventions, or permitting semi-autonomous institutions or associations within the polis (Pettit, 1997, pp. 178–79; Majone, 1996).

Learning Democracy through Education

Such a principle can also function economically to support policies of redistribution and 'equalization'. Not according to Rawls's formula, but according to a formula that is context-appropriate. Non-domination also supports two educationally important processes: *deliberation* and *contestation*, which are important for how principles are put into practice in determinate historical settings. Both affirm the importance of education in that both constitute skills that must be learnt. Contestation underpins and qualifies consent in such a schema and becomes an open democratic entitlement. The concept of deliberation, as Miller (2000, p. 9) puts it, 'starts from the premise that political preferences will conflict and that the purpose of democratic institutions must be to resolve this conflict'. Deliberation presupposes a different conception of democracy to traditional 'realist' liberal models, which refers to a narrow system of representative government and a means of changing governments through a system of elections.[34] The deliberative model also implies a different regulative ideal. In this sense, it is part of a variety of mechanisms aiming to *deepen* democracy, and presupposes a different conception of human nature. Whereas the liberal model gives weight to each person's preferences as a rational decision-maker, each with 'pre-formed' beliefs and opinions, the deliberative conception of democracy requires seeing outcomes as being fashioned, and seeing beliefs and values as being moulded, in the process of discussion (Miller, 2000, p. 9). In Miller's (2000, p. 17) view, the cooperative strategies entailed in deliberation override self-interest.[35] In his view (p. 18), there are: '... good reasons to expect the deliberation process to transform initial policy preferences (which may be based on private interest, sectional interest, prejudice, and so on) into ethical judgments on the matter in hand... individual preferences are transformed into ethically-based judgments about matters of common concern.' In a deliberative democracy, openness of debate is an insurance against knowingly strategic action, or collusion in agenda setting or making decisions, says Miller (2000, p. 18). Thus, a deliberative democratic community is ideally one where the participants not only contribute freely, but also where they are prepared to change their views in the light of evidence and cogent argument. It is a community in which 'the decisions reached reflect not simply the prior interests or prior opinions of the participants, but the judgments they make after reflecting on the arguments made on each side, and the principles or procedures that should be used to resolve disagreements' (Miller, 2000, p. 142). In deliberation, an understanding of the need for exceptions, the recognition of differences, or the need for modifications can be brought to light and assessed.

The aim of deliberation, says Miller (2000, p. 4) is not *epistemic consensus,* but should represent: 'A fair balance between the different views expressed in the course of the discussion, and to the extent that it does, even those who would prefer some other outcome can recognize the decision as legitimate.' Contestation is central to deliberation and to freedom in republican conceptions of democracy. As Philip Pettit (1997, p. 180) observes public decisions can be held to be legitimate 'so far as they are capable of withstanding individual contestation... under procedures that are acceptable to all concerned'. The right to contest thus replaces arbitrariness in decision-making. In Pettit's (1997, p. 185) words 'to require public decision-making to be contestable is to insist that decision-making satisfy a democratic profile'. Hence, the decision-making model is premised on contestation before consent. A government will be democratic to the extent that people can contest whatever it decides. To stop contestation is to undermine its legitimacy.

Essentially, here, is the idea of democracy as self-rule. Foucault's notion of 'speaking the truth to power' captures this idea of contestability as well. For Foucault (2001, p. 11) such a right is embodied in the classical Greek notion of *parrhesia,* which means 'frankness in speaking the truth'.[36] But someone is said to use *parrhesia* 'only if there is a risk or danger for him in telling the truth... the *parrhesiastes* is someone who takes a risk' (2001, p. 16). In addition: 'The function of *parrhesia*... has the function of criticism... *parrhesia* is a form of criticism, either towards another or towards oneself, but always in a situation where the speaker or confessor is in a position of inferiority with respect to the interlocutor. The *parrhesiastes* is always less powerful than the one with whom he speaks.' Finally, 'in *parrhesia,* telling the truth is regarded as a duty'. Foucault (2001, pp. 19–20) draws these elements together thus:

> *Parrhesia* is a kind of verbal activity where the speaker has a specific relation to truth through frankness, a certain relationship to his own life through danger, a certain type of relationship to himself or other people through criticism... and a specific relation to moral law through freedom and duty. More precisely, *parrhesia* is verbal activity in which a speaker expresses his personal relationship to truth, and risks his life because he recognizes truth telling as a duty to improve or help other people (as well as himself). In *parrhesia,* the speaker uses his freedom and chooses frankness instead of persuasion, truth instead of falsehood or silence, the risk of death instead of life and security, criticism instead of flattery, and moral duty instead of self-interest and moral apathy. That, then, quite generally, is the positive meaning of the word *parrhesia* in most of the Greek texts... from the fifth century BC to the fifth century AD.

Contestability, then, is a pre-condition for democracy in the republican ideal. The right to contest decisions presupposes that decision-making is conducted in such a way that a basis for contestation exists, and that there are channels, mediums and forums by which views can be expressed and conflicts resolved. Such a principle supports a 'debate-based' society whereby communities can move towards agreed outcomes, whereby settlements can be reached and preferences formed. As such, to emphasize contestation is to accept conflict and abandon the quest for an unobtainable ideal of consensus. Politics in this sense is agonistic in that it is conceived as the non-antagonistic resolution of the political. As a consensus without exclusion is not possible, it warns against the possibility of a final harmonious form of democracy. As Chantal Mouffe (2000, p. 128) writes: 'Agonism forces us to nurture democratic contestation, to accept responsibility for our actions, and to foster the institutions in which political action, with all its limitations, can be pursued. Only under these conditions is pluralist democracy possible.' Education is pivotal in the formation of a deliberative contestatory democracy. Such a conception of society depends upon the creation of a normative culture, which can make constitutional and legal codes operative. Pettit (1997, p. 245) cites Philip Selznick (1992, pp. 398–390) who talks about the need for 'habits of civility'. The purpose of education is to help construct a socially established normative culture that provides security and builds the *capabilities* for democracy. These might include techniques of debate and legal eristic, of meeting procedure and political activism. In addition, norms of trust and civility are necessary to underpin law, and to satisfy the constraints associated with contestability and deliberation. Trust in democratic principles must cut across a wide range of groups—gender, ethnic, prisoners, war widows, gays, those with special needs. Common democratic principles must cut across group differences, and practices based on tolerance and trust are commonly required by all groups. As Pettit (1997, pp. 248–49) says:

> It is extremely doubtful that governments would have been forced to take account of environmental considerations, even in the inadequate measure to which they currently do so, if people were not generally responsive to a norm requiring concern for the common good: a norm requiring efforts on behalf of that good even when free-riding looks like the rational self-interested response... If the law is to be kept on track... then there has to be a form of civility available that will drive not just a politics of difference but a politics of common concern.

Pettit (1997, p. 249) notes with respect to the politics of difference:

> That, while it requires partial forms of civility in order to be effective, it also requires a disposition on the part of people, even people of quite different perspectives, to display a civility that relates to the society as a whole. Let people cease to countenance society-wide norms in their enthusiasm for more local affiliations, and the republic will degenerate into a battlefield of rival interest groups.

Pettit's point is that state action is fundamental in the engineering of trust and other 'habits of civility'. From our point of view these are democratic capabilities which education is fundamental in providing. Such capabilities involve not only norms of tolerance and civility, but the skills of deliberation in all its complex forms. Education lies between what Pettit (1997, p. 255) calls the 'stark choice between the invisible hand and the iron hand: between the strategy of marketing and a strategy of management'. Education is the 'third estate' between the free market and the autocratic hand of regulation and management. Such collective norms become central to personal identity, to personal aims and ambitions, and to dreams, which are only possible within a community. Such communitarian *civicness* attests to the irrepressibly social nature of selfhood. Without cultural models and normative values—of care, of solidarity, of compromise, of negotiation, of tolerance, of legal debate and eristic—there can be no global society or polity. Trust and civility become part of the 'conditions of liberty' as Gellner (1994) states. Yet, what enables trust and civility is prior reliance on the rules and laws. That is, the prior existence of a comprehensive discourse of democracy.

Conclusion

The principle of democracy being talked about here is non-foundational but universal. By this is meant that it is not based upon any fixed conception of human nature, or of a premise, as with Habermas, of universal rationality whereby conflicts can be redeemed dialogically through communicative action in the ideal speech community. Rather, the principle of democracy being suggested insists on the protection of human rights, recognizes the distinctiveness of sub-cultures, ensures the principles of inclusion and openness, and ensures the universal application of the rule of law, and of open dialogue, not based upon any faith in rationality, but based purely on a principle of a mutual interest in universal survival. Thus, while such a conception of democracy is 'deliberative', it is pragmatically rather than epistemologically based.[37] This is to say that the safety of all is guaranteed in the final analysis on the basis of an interest in survival, and it is the same grounds which justify the culture of reasonableness, as well as liberal values such as freedom of association, expression, and the like. In an age of terrorism democracy is the condition upon which survival can best be assured. Such a conception is universal to the extent that it is willed. The inspiration is Nietzschean rather than Kantian. It is also very Foucauldian in the sense that it constitutes a universalism of democracy as a contingent discourse of open protection and facilitation in a world of danger.[38]

Although survival may justify democracy, as an end or goal it is too thin to be fully adequate, of course, for mere survival cannot possibly satisfy a complete account of life's ends and aims. And it may not be universally agreed to, if we mean by universal 'agreed to by all', for there are no doubt some, including 'suicide bombers', for whom it holds no sway at all. Ultimately, that is the choice of course, and certainly it focuses the concentration. For if democracy is the precondition of survival, then it requires a democratic mandate to be effective, even so.

Beyond this, it is possible to build a much richer conception of democracy on this basis. If survival is a final justification, and focuses our attention as to why democracy is important, survival with dignity resonates of a more traditional concern with ends. This of course is the classic conception of democracy as a doctrine based on the ultimate worth and dignity of the human being, as espoused in the republican tradition. Thus, it is not the narrow 'realist' theory of democracy that has been articulated and advocated by post-war American political science, commonly associated with the writings of Joseph Schumpeter's (1976) *Capitalism, socialism and democracy*, which refers to a narrow system of representative government and a means of changing governments through a system of elections (Hindess, 2000). Rather, if safety, dignity, and survival are to be possible, it must be deepened, once again, to refer to a substantive end which is something more than mere utility, but encompasses the well-being and safety of each and all.

If post-September 11 makes democracy of more pressing concern; this conception has moved a long way from a narrow theory of universal enfranchisement. To the extent that counter-terrorist action now constitutes an important item, it must itself be subject to the democratic norms of public visibility and critical scrutiny, together with open processes of deliberation and debate, as well as traditional rights of contestation in terms of the rule of law. If my substantive conception posits certain general ends, which allow for a degree of diversity and pluralism, the procedural view of democracy is as a multifaceted array of mechanisms and processes instituted to ensure the inclusion, security or safety (including sexual safety) as well as development and opportunities of all individuals and groups. In this respect research needs to focus on the means of deepening democracy to satisfy these goals. As a way of concluding this [chapter] it might look to include research on all or any of the following themes:

- *The concern with equality*: the development of any conception of democratic justice must seek to deal with rather than avoid issues to do with distribution of resources and life chances. Given a rejection of the classical liberal fiction regarding entitlement to property based on a model of pre-social, possessive individuals who 'owe nothing to society', it is important to theorize the implications of a social ontological framework of community for considerations of democratic justice as it pertains to distributional ethics. Community in this sense is definable as an all-encompassing arena without fixed borders or unity, which comprises an assortment of values, norms and institutions that enable life to be lived. Such a conception of community recognizes social ties and shared values, as well as practices of voluntary action and public institutions like education which constitute the conditions for stability and reproduction of society. Although neoliberal philosophers like Nozick (1974) have shifted political philosophy away from a concern with issues of distributive justice in recent years, my own view is similar to the nineteenth-century social democrat L. T. Hobhouse (1911), who held that one's entitlement to rewards and gain must be balanced by one's obligation to society. What liberal conceptions of democracy obscured, in Hobhouse's view, was the inter-dependence between individuals and the social structure or for the social and moral obligation of the society (acting through the vehicle of the state) to assist in arranging the social futures of each rising generation. As he argued in his book, *Liberalism* (1911, pp. 189–190), in his justification for re-distributive policies of progressive taxation, the state has an obligation to enforce reasonable conditions of equality on the basis that while a society should provide the conditions for enterprise, all individuals are correspondingly indebted to society for the conditions and structures provided, and on this basis, individuals should contribute in direct proportion to the luck or good fortune they experience.
- *The role of the state*: the role of the state should be concerned with guaranteeing both negative freedom and positive freedom. Negative freedom involves the state's responsibility for ensuring the universal entitlements to safety and reasonable autonomy for all. The trade off in respect to privacy will be necessitated to the extent that these obligations are threatened. To the extent that greater surveillance is deemed necessary, the proposals must be themselves subject to democratic processes that ensure visibility, openness, deliberation and debate. The state's obligations as regards positive freedom involve it in developing opportunities based on people's rights to inclusion and the

development of their capacities. This obligation gives the state a role in the provision of social services, health care, and education. In brief, the role for the positively geared state lies in relation to socially directed investment decisions, to provide for the general conditions for all species needs and development, including education and training, and to create and maintain quality infrastructure such as schools, hospitals, parks and public spaces.

• *The development of civil society*: a vibrant civil society can constitute a check on the powers of government. Civil society refers to that sector of private associations relatively autonomous from the state and economy, which spring from the everyday lives and activities of communities of interest. Clearly, one principle of democracy is the idea of multiple centres of power and of their separation, as suggested by writers like Montesquieu and de Tocqueville. Another principle of democracy is the right to contest, challenge or oppose. Institutions of civil society, as writers like Paul Hirst have maintained, can be seen to constitute an important powerful network of quasi-independent associations, which can strengthen democratic rule through checking the power of the state. If democracy is rule by the people, the ability and opportunity to 'speak the truth to power', in Foucault's (2001) sense, is itself one of democracy's crucial rights, indeed its very condition. According to Cohen and Arato (1992) civil society strengthens democracy in both a defensive and offensive sense. The defensive aspect refers to the way that associations and social movements develop forms of communicative interaction that support the development of people's identities, expand participatory possibilities and create networks of solidarity. The offensive aspect refers to how associational networks and institutions come to exert influence on, and constitute checks to, the state, and to each other.

• *The role of education*: the role of education is crucial for democracy, as educational institutions, whether compulsory or post-compulsory intersect with, and therefore mediate between, institutions like the family and those of the state and the economy. Although formal institutions of education have been in the main public institutions, there is an important sense in which they are semi-autonomous from the state. This is not the neoliberal sense where management and administration are devolved to the local school, but the sense in which the schools are located in, and represent local community groups. In this sense, schools are important as democratic organizations, through the particular way that they are connected to communities, through their ability to empower families, and involve minority groups in participatory projects. Education also is crucial as the central agency responsible for the production of democratic norms such as trust and political decision-making. This is to say, as Mill (1975) recognized in *Representative government*, educational institutions are important as sites where democracy and self-government are learnt. Deliberative democracy is especially complex, for it involves not just norms and procedures of debate but norms and procedures of contestation, inclusiveness, tolerance, compromise, solidarity with others, generosity, care, the operations of forums, and of checks and balances, the use of sanctions and screens, and the separation of powers. In the republican tradition, schools are instrumental in the development of civic virtue and habits of good citizenship. This is what signals the real importance of the 'knowledge economy'. For education is essentially important in its role of constructing democratic civic norms, and this must become one of the central aims of government policy in this regard. It is not a case of 'brainwashing' or 'socialization' but of teaching skills and establishing models of civic conduct based on tolerance, deliberation, conflict resolution, give and take, and trust. While educational processes depend upon fairness of political processes, and in the distribution of economic resources, education is necessary to construct the network of norms that permit both the market and democracy to function. As Pettit (1997, p. 255) puts it, education represents a 'stark choice between the invisible hand and the iron hand: between a strategy of marketing and a strategy of management'. It is for this reason of course why education should ideally be public, universal, compulsory and free. For if education is vital in constructing norms that nurtures the market, it cannot be itself subject to the market's disorganizing effects.

NOTES

1. Globalization can be seen as spreading or developing with technological changes, effected no doubt initially by the invention of such instruments as the alphabet and the printing press. Twentieth-century developments in transport and electronic communications have obviously had a major impact in intensifying globalization.
2. The European Central Bank acts independently, has its own 'legal' personality, is not responsive to any immediate local community, and is protected under Article 106(2) of the EC Treaty.
3. In this process, the contours and size of a new welfare state is being negotiated globally, as 'excessive' welfare states will lead to capital flight, tax competition and uncompetitiveness.
4. The Ethyl Corporation forced Canada to allow it to sell MMT (methylcyclopentadienyl manganese tricarbonyl) in Canada through the authority of NAFTA. In July 1988 the Canadian government agreed to allow the Corporation to resume its sales of MMT in Canada. It also agreed to pay compensation and issued statements assuring the population that there were no risks to health. On the other hand, the French government pulled out of critical negotiations over the Multi-Lateral Agreement of Investment being proposed in 1998 in response to direct public pressure, thus preventing attempts to introduce it to Europe (see Monbiot, 2001, pp. 310–313).
5. Jayasuriya is citing MacCormick (1999, p. 155).
6. Cited from Kant's original German edition of *Perpetual peace* (1795).
7. Robert Dahl (1999) notes the difficulties of making international organizations democratic. One must be cautious in talking about global organizations as 'democratic'. They are clearly only democratic in the limited sense that such global organizations result from treaty agreements between nations which have equal voting power regardless of whether each nation-state is organized democratically. Dahl argues with respect to decisions taken over NAFTA that 'a recognizably democratic political system is unlikely to develop' (1999, p. 23) in international organizations. He argues that 'it is notoriously difficult for citizens to exercise effective control over many key decisions on foreign affairs'. His case illustration regarding NAFTA indicates that most of the citizenry in America 'did not know whether their Congressional representative favoured or opposed NAFTA' (1999, p. 24) and he generalizes this point to other instances and countries. Dahl's argument is important in that it shows up the limitations of democracy. We would dispute Dahl's conclusions however. Firstly, democracy is not just a system of immediate and direct popular control. It is also a discourse of rights, or security and safety, of inclusion, a free press, and so on. Secondly, even in the sense that Dahl is specifically referring to, as a system of popular control, it is not true to say because the vast majority of the population are not aware at the time of specific issues over NAFTA, that there is no democratic check on actions of national leaders at the international or global level. Leaders take 'risks' in acting without proper consultation with their electorates, or subjects, *in retrospect*, should the policy choice later be seen as unfair, or unmandated. They may be subject to investigations by the media, or to not being returned to office. It can be noted here, too, that the consequences for actions exercised at the global level, reside both *at the global level* (international courts of justice) and, as Hirst and Thompson (1996) and Hirst (2000*b*) maintain, within *individual nation-states*.
8. McGraw is citing Dryzek (1995).

9. It may, of course, operate imperfectly. In this context the task becomes to deepen democracy by instituting appropriate mechanisms of accountability and control.

10. A good example of a grassroots movement is the continued existence of the Global Justice Movement, which has shown signs of growing in numbers and strength. As George Monbiot (2003) notes, in 2002 40,000 members gathered at the World Social Forum in Porto Alegre, Brazil, and in 2003 more than 100,000 from 150 countries attended. Another meeting, in 2003, held in Florence, titled 'Another Europe is possible' and organized by the European Social Forum, attracted some 40,000 intellectuals, students, social activists, radical economists and concerned individuals, expressing solidarity with those who had attended similar meetings and protests in Genoa, Prague, Seattle, and London over the preceding three years. The meeting expressed 'anti-globalization' protests against agencies like the IMF, WB, WTO, and NAFTA. At Florence in 2002, says John Vidal (2002), they advocated open borders, a universal right to work and to have a home, the regulation of MNCs, a Tobin tax on financial markets, no GM foods or pollution, no privatisation of public services, the public ownership of the media, and an end to racism. In addition 'there was almost complete consensus on three issues: that "neo-liberalism"—the free market ideas espoused by the IMF and G7—is a violent political and economic doctrine, that trade with poor countries should be fair, and that one vote every four years given to political parties run by self-serving elites is no way to run modern, complex democracies in a globalised economy' (Vidal, 2002, p. 18).

11. Many writers, like Charles Beitz, have based their critique of this model of international relations and ethics on the inappropriateness of this analogy (see Beitz, 1979, p. 64).

12. As Charles Beitz (1979, p. 146) notes, Hobbes did maintain that there were natural principles and he proposes nineteen laws of nature (see Hobbes, *Leviathan*, ch. 15). The difficulty in international relations, as in the state of nature, as Hobbes held it to be, was in the difficulty in being sure that others would act on them.

13. Stephen Krasner (1993) maintains that this Westphalian system was not in fact inherent in the treaties signed in 1648.

14. For contemporary work in this tradition, see the English School of Martin Wright (1992) and Hedley Bull (1977).

15. Grotius's was a 'pre-liberal' conception, and notably, he argued against the principle of 'noninterference', arguing that it is sometimes justifiable (see Beitz, 1979, p. 71). It was Wolff and Vattel who later argued for an absolute principle of non-interference, arguing that unlimited respect for another state's autonomy upheld stability. Wolffs view marked the application of 'pure' classical liberal principles ('autonomy', 'non-interference', etc.) to international relations. Although Wolff argued that no state had a right to interfere in another state's sovereign affairs, the entire 'community of states' had such a right (see Beitz, 1979, pp. 70–73).

16. Although he argued against Hobbes, as Beitz (1979, p. 60) notes, he produces similar conclusions about the weakness of moral rules in international relations.

17. See Christian Wolff, *Jus gentium methodo scientifica pertractatum* (1749, section 2, p. 9). See also Beitz (1979, p. 75).

18. Nussbaum (1992, p. 215) refers to her approach as a 'soft version of Aristotelian essentialism'. Her faithfulness to Aristotle's thought has been questioned however (see Arneson, 2000; Mulgan, 2000). In her defence against these charges, Nussbaum (2000*b*) makes it clear that her relation to Aristotle is 'inspirational' and works at the level of a commitment to basic postulates rather than in terms of a detailed commitment to the detail [*sic*] of Aristotle's positions on particular topics. Foucault's approach incorporates a Nietzschean emphasis on 'self-creation' and rejects the Aristotelian stress on essentialist

teleology concerning the subject. The two approaches are otherwise quite compatible in terms of the relations between the individual and the social, and of the individual as a social being.

19. Although 'liberty' and 'autonomy' are central to such a community, they are politically provided for rather than being the essential attributes of persons. The notion of autonomy is also heavily qualified in the Foucauldian sense, for given the degree of interdependence between persons and community, *autonomy* is *precisely what individuals do not have.* While a certain level of self-reliance is attainable, it can only be achieved through education and knowledge, and even then it will always be *partial* and *limited,* for individuals are far more dependent upon the structures of social support than the liberal conception acknowledges. It is in this sense, that the liberal conception of 'autonomy' has been integrally tied to 'non' or 'pre-social' conceptions of the self that were integral to the discourse of classical liberalism. Failure to recognize these historical constraints in terms of which the liberal notion of autonomy was developed has led to inappropriate recent attempts to recast autonomy in a social constructionist light (e.g., Reich, 2002).

20. Although Nussbaum's work is insightful, I find her own position with regard to the representation of the good problematic in several respects. By focusing on 'vagueness' or 'thickness' (her 'thick, vague conception') she attempts to reconcile collective power and individual interests and goals. At one level she is right to represent the good as abstract and therefore capable of allowing for diversity within it, but she doesn't specify any principles by which such a reconciliation could take place, or which could allow us to differentiate the appropriate domain of state action with respect to individual discretion. What she does do, however, is ground the ethical justification of collective power in 'human flourishing' or 'capability', and it would seem that this provides a basis for a more detailed articulation of human rights and entitlements. While this is unlikely to provide us with a single 'one-off' principle, like John Stuart Mill's 'harm principle' which can reliably adjudicate the appropriate domain of state action *vis à vis* individual discretion, it does permit some basis for the assessment of the responsibilities and limits of collective power in relation to individuals. States, as the collective agency of individuals are responsible to serve their interests and needs, and their violation of this responsibility de-legitimises their warrant to rule.

21. This was one of the criticisms of early forms of communitarianism. See O'Neill (2000, p. 445).

22. Failure of collective power to express the valid goals of the citizenry risks anarchic violence and threatens survival at all levels.

23. Although Foucault never really was interested in normative political philosophy, we are extending his approach in this direction, because we consider it a weakness of the Foucauldian approach. In this sense our model of a republican thin communitarianism can only really be said to be 'inspired' by Foucault, in the same sense as Nussbaum is 'inspired' by Aristotle (see note 18, above). We would claim that our approach is broadly consistent with Foucault's thought in terms of ontological and epistemological commitments.

24. The effect of conditionally grounding the legitimacy of collective action in human interests in survival is to introduce a form of 'contract' which looks forward to survival, and is conditional on the wish to survive, but is not metaphysically grounded in an original origin or covenant. It is to say, in effect, that co-operating citizens agree to associate on the basis of a mutual award of equal rights to life, liberty, access to resources and opportunity, in the interests of survival.

25. It is constructivist in the sense that it is necessary that the contract includes a universal entitlement to survival.

26. Sharon Gewirtz (2002) suggests that official government support towards state funding of 'faith-based' schools in England has altered post-September 11, suggesting that forms of religious separatism over education are being seen as socially dysfunctional for the production of democratic values, such as tolerance.

27. Although O'Neill defines *Sittlichkeit* as 'concrete community', I have maintained 'ethical life' as closer to Hegel's intended use.

28. See Lamore (1999). O'Neill (2000, p. 445) refers to his 'nearly communitarian writing' with specific reference to Rawls (1985).

29. The reference to the word 'reasonable' is Rawls's of course. The concept is apt for a settlement will invariably be a mix of factors, reflecting principles of justice, the potential effects of a policy on the stability of the community, and its acceptance by the majority of those affected. In this sense any particular policy settlement reflects a mix of pragmatic, moral and political factors.

30. Richard Rorty (1998, p. 53) argues there is a great deal of similarity.

31. Amongst some of the republican writers on these continents are Machiavelli, Montesquieu, Rousseau, de Tocqueville, Harrington, Price, Wollstonecraft, Madison, Hamilton, Jay, Paine. See Pocock (1975), Skinner (1978), Pettit (1997) and Honohan (2002).

32. Participation needs more extensive theorization within political theory than it has had to date. It must be seen also as a continuum of action, varying in terms of extent and kind. Our view would be that nearly all people participate to some degree in an active sense of joining voluntary civic groups and associations. It need not be seen as the only good in relation to citizenship, however. We would agree with McLean (1986, p. 143), however, that traditional arguments between realist liberals who support a narrow conception of representative democracy based on elections, and more classical versions of democracy based on participation in the public sphere often represent little more than a 'dialogue of the deaf'. While we believe that democracy needs 'deepening' and that participation in the public life is an important component of citizenship, we simply do not accept realist arguments against such a position, as should be now obvious.

33. This is a crucial difference between republicanism and liberalism. For liberals' freedom is 'noninterference' because it is 'pre-social' or 'natural' and hence it exists outside of society. Hence, for Hobbes (1968, p. 264), freedom resides 'in the silence of the law', and for Filmer perfect liberty would require an absence of laws. As Filmer (1991, p. 268) states, 'for it is no law except it restrain liberty'.

34. Such a model can be seen associated with Joseph Schumpeter's (1976) *Capitalism, socialism and democracy*, especially pp. 250–283 ('Two concepts of democracy').

35. Miller (2000, p. 17) gives the example of a game strategy where individual self-interest dictates that each group member keeps money and invests it on their own, but when pursued cooperatively as a collective, when the money is pooled, far greater wealth is produced. His major focus is in critiquing neoliberal theories of democracy, especially Arrow's general possibility theorem that denies the possibility of amalgamating voter preferences to reach a collective social decision. Essentially, Arrow maintained that no collective rule could be rational. All decision rules are arbitrary which means all outcomes reflect strategic manipulation. The interesting point here is the thesis that collective endeavour produces higher and better outcomes for the individuals and the group, than individual endeavour. This maxim could also be applied to learning theory.

36. Foucault (2001, p. 11) explains that '*Parrhesia* is ordinarily translated into English by "free speech" (in French by *franc-parler*, and in German by *Freimüthigkeit*). *Parrhesiazomai* or

parrhesiazesthai is to use *parrhesia*, and the *parrhesiastes* is the one who uses *parrhesia*, i.e., the one who speaks the truth.'

37. It thus has the character of a 'settlement', rather than a 'consensus', or a 'reflexive equilibrium', although the latter concept (which is Rawls's) may, in this view, form part of a broader conception of citizenship, which the state seeks to democratically promote.
38. My view is that 'survival' is a better basis to justify democracy than 'social contract'. However, it is not possible to explore the differences in this [chapter].

Part Four

Education, Knowledge, and the Global Labour Market

Over the last century greater significance has been attached to the economic contribution of formal education and training. It is widely believed that the developed economies have entered an 'age of human capital', as knowledge, innovation, and individual creativity have become the major sources of competitive advantage in a knowledge economy. Gary Becker (Ch. 19), who was awarded a Nobel Prize in Economics for his contribution to human capital theory, argues that the economic success of individuals, companies, and nations depends on the scale and effectiveness of people investing in themselves. He suggests that 'technology may be the driver of a modern economy, especially of its high-tech sector, but human capital is certainly the fuel'.

Becker also argues that the economic value of education increases over time. He supports this claim with evidence from the United States that purports to show that the income differentials between high school and college graduates doubled during the 1980s, but what he does not show is whether this is due to a decline in the earnings of high school graduates which would make it appear that the value of a college degree was increasing. Equally, because these are based on average earnings they obscure the fact that 'rates of return' vary considerably amongst college graduates in the United States as some have witnessed a rapid increase in earnings while others have not.

The contribution by Grubb and Lazerson (Ch. 20) shows that whatever critics may argue they have not prevented the globalization of what they call the 'education gospel'. In both developed and developing countries the same ideas about education expansion and reform are to be found in the belief that education is the source of individual, economic, and social salvation. Despite this spread of the education gospel, Grubb and Lazerson show that important differences remain in the way 'vocationalism' is understood and that it has led to different policy responses due to the particular histories, institutions, politics, and cultural values in different countries.

They highlight these national differences through a comparison of how countries attempt to maintain connections between schooling and employment, the extent to which the vocational is reduced to a utilitarian conception of behavioural competence, and the extent to which vocationalism contributes to social inequalities. They conclude by arguing that state regulation and intervention will be required, even in countries that pride themselves on free markets and limited government, 'otherwise it will prove impossible to have forms of schooling, and schooling in preparation for work, that live up to the noblest ambitions of the Education Gospel'.

The chapter by Robert Reich (Ch. 21) represents an important development of human capital ideas given his focus on the impact of economic globalization on skills, employment, and wages. He suggests that in a global economy it is no longer possible for countries to protect workers from the full force of international competition. Like Becker, he sees the development of human capital as the main weapon that individuals and governments now have in the fight for economic prosperity. This leads him to explain why the 'rich are getting richer and the poor, poorer' in terms of their relative ability to sell their skills, knowledge, and insights in the global labour market.

What he calls the 'symbolic analysts' have enjoyed a significant increase in earnings precisely because the market for their services become global, whereas those workers who remain locked into national or local markets have experienced stagnation or a decline in income. He also argues that those without marketable skills within the global economy face increasing competition for jobs from low-waged economies. Therefore the solution to wage inequalities is to raise the educational standards and skill levels of all American workers so that they can compete for the global supply of high-skilled, high-waged jobs.

Brown and Lauder (Ch. 22) critically assess the way writers such as Becker and Reich have understood the changing relationship between education, jobs, and rewards in the global knowledge-driven economy. They claim that the research evidence does not support the idea of a rapid increase in the demand for 'knowledge' workers although there has been a rapid expansion of tertiary education. They also point to increasing attempts to routinize and standardize knowledge-work driven by the global integration of business activities, that reflect a trend towards business 'outsourcing' and 'offshoring'. One of the conclusions draw from their analysis is that 'human capital' is increasingly subject to the laws of diminishing returns as more people gain access to tertiary education both at home and abroad, and 'knowledge' workers in the developed economies are forced to compete with well-educated employees willing to work for much lower incomes in developing economies.

The role of the state is a key issue in the chapter by Kamat, Mir, and Mathew (Ch. 23). Basing their study on an analysis of Indian IT workers, they examine both the role of the Indian state in the creation of high-tech migrants, and analyse historical shifts in US immigration policies. They show how the Indian state has sponsored what they call 'techno-managerial migration' by encouraging private provision of education and abandoning a commitment to equal educational access to all Indians. This empowered socially advantaged groups to benefit from new opportunities to develop the knowledge and skills needed to gain visas to work in the IT industry in the United States.

They also show how US immigration policies since the 1960s have permitted certain categories of skilled labour to enter the IT industry at the same time as protecting the economic interests of indigenous workers by offering opportunities to upgrade their skills to meet the labour shortages filled by Indian IT specialists. In conclusion, they reject the view that the nation-state has become powerless in the wake of globalization as migrant workers continue to be subject to 'one sovereign state or the other so as to ensure the continued viability of the systems of states'.

The final chapter in this Part is David Guile's account of the nature of knowledge in the knowledge economy (Ch. 24). Despite much talk about the rise of a 'knowledge' or 'informational' economy there is surprising little discussion of what constitutes such an economy. His analysis suggests that there is little agreement about what is distinctive about the 'knowledge' economy, which has led to 'theoretical incoherence' and often contradictory conclusions for education policy and practice. This led him to compare those theorists that emphasized the importance of 'codified' theoretical knowledge associated with the application of scientific method, with those that emphasized the 'subjective, bodily, and tacit aspects' of knowledge production. Rather than seeing these as competing models he argues that Knorr Cetina's concept of 'epistemic cultures' offers a way of building on the strengths of both approaches. Therefore, the defining feature of knowledge economies/societies as opposed to previous forms of economic and social organization is the spread of knowledge (epistemic) cultures which work across the boundaries of expertise and professional capabilities. This he argues raises 'fundamentally different questions about the way in which education policy should support the development of the knowledge economy', including such issues of how to build a culture of lifelong learning and a critique of our obsession with academic grades and qualifications.

19 The Age of Human Capital

Gary S. Becker

The Age of Human Capital

Human capital refers to the knowledge, information, ideas, skills, and health of individuals. This is the 'age of human capital' in the sense that human capital is by far the most important form of capital in modern economies. The economic successes of individuals, and also of whole economies, depends on how extensively and effectively people invest in themselves.

Studies suggest that capital invested in men and women constitutes over 70 percent of the total capital in the United States. The total invested in schooling, on-the-job training, health, information, and research and development is surely over 20 percent of gross domestic product. Technology may be the driver of a modern economy, especially of its high-tech sector, but human capital is certainly the fuel.

An economy like that of the United States is called a capitalist economy, but a more accurate term is *human* capital or a *knowledge* capital economy. While all forms of capital are important, including machinery, factories, and financial capital, human capital is the most significant.

Stock Market Crashes and Human Capital

More than a decade ago, I used the significance of human capital to make one of my more useful short-term business forecasts. You may recall that on October 17, 1987—so-called Black Monday—the value of the stocks listed on the New York Stock Exchange fell by 22 percent. On one day alone, equity wealth declined 22 percent. There was chaos in Washington and in the media. Financial magazines were predicting another Great Recession like the one in 1929, when the stock market also crashed.

I happened to be working on my regular monthly *Business Week* column during the day of the 1987 crash. So on Black Monday, I scrapped the column I was preparing and wrote one that predicted no major recession for the United States. This column ran about the same time as an issue of *Business Week* in which the cover story focused on a possible major depression due to the crash.

My argument was very simple. I began by emphasizing that human capital is three-fourths, or so, of the wealth in the United States, and that the value of human capital did not seem to have been much affected by the stock market crash. It is known that financial returns and human capital returns generally vary largely independently of each other. If so, the crash would only affect the value of the nonhuman capital, a fraction of all wealth. By multiplying the fraction of wealth that crashed in value by the size of the fall, I showed that the total wealth of the economy declined by only a few percentage points, perhaps as little as two percent. That could cause trouble, but not by itself a major recession. This is why I predicted difficult times only for luxury goods and the like—which did happen. Three months after the crash, the economy was back on course, and quarterly time series on stock prices show little evidence of the crash.

The Growing Return to Human Capital

The modern economic environment places more of a premium on education, training, and other sources of knowledge than was true even fifty years ago. This can be inferred from changes in the relation between education and earnings. In the United States during most of the past forty years, college graduates earned on the average about 50 percent more than high school graduates, and the latter earned about 30 percent more than high school dropouts. (See Figure 19.1 for the college–high school earnings gap.)

Wage differences between typical college and high school graduates increased from 40 percent in 1977 to 60 percent in the 1990s. The gap between high school graduates and persons with at least a college education grew even faster, from 50 percent in the late 1960s to about 75 percent in recent years. These are probably the largest increases in U.S. history.

Similar trends are found elsewhere toward greater demand for more skilled workers, although in Europe this has taken the form of increased unemployment of less educated and less trained workers. The gap in wage differentials by education is large in European nations for both men and women.

The global economy cannot succeed without considerable investment in human capital by all nations. Richer countries specialize in high-knowledge products and services, while poorer nations specialize in lower-skilled and raw material-intensive products. Still, investments in human capital are also necessary in poorer nations if they are to have a chance of growing out of poverty.

Almost without exception, studies of the economic growth of different nations show a close relation during the past several decades between economic performance and schooling, life expectancy, and other human capital measures. In particular, although on the average Third World nations grew a little less rapidly than richer ones, poorer nations with more educated and healthier populations managed to grow faster than average. Especially important for these nations are their investments in elementary and secondary education.

Of course, machines and other physical capital are important. But alone they are far from sufficient to produce growth because skilled workers and managers, and innovative entrepreneurs, are needed to operate complicated machinery, to produce efficiently, to develop new products and processes, and to utilize innovations from other countries. Neglect of human capital and world markets by most economists after World War II, and their emphasis on import substitution and protected markets, was a seriously distorted view of the growth process. Ultimately it was a failed vision of what is essential to achieve economic progress and reductions in poverty.

Distance Learning

Modern economies require that people invest in the acquisition of knowledge, skills, and information not only when young but throughout most of their lives. Yet the basic methods of acquiring human capital have hardly changed since the time of Socrates. For 2,500 years, teachers and students have met face to face for lectures and discussions. However, the growth of the Internet will revolutionize the system of teaching and learning by allowing 'distance learning,' where teachers and students may interact closely even though they are separated physically and in time.

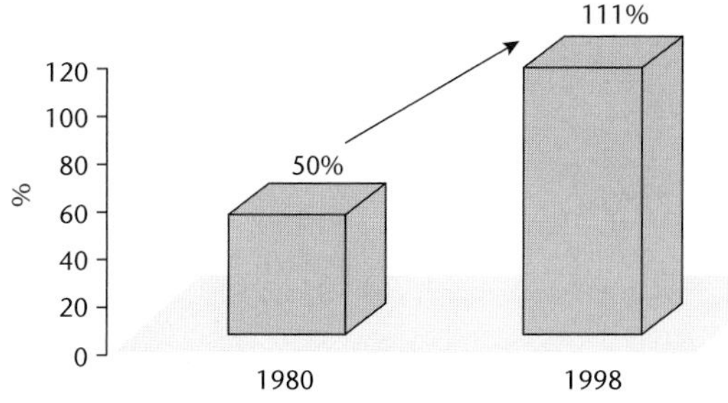

FIG. 19.1. Widening pay-gap between high school and college graduates

Source: 1980: U.S. Census Bureau. 1999: ML Growth Stock Research).

The key economic advantage of distance learning over traditional on-site learning is that it saves students time. Studies show that the value of time spent learning is the principal cost of investment in human capital among teenagers and adults with even moderate actual or potential earnings. It is especially important for executives and highly skilled employees. Web-based instruction eliminates regular commutes to schools and other teaching facilities, which can amount to more than an hour each way for persons with jobs. On-line instruction also allows greater time flexibility for students to interact with course materials, 'chat' with other students, take quizzes, and submit reports. People with full-time jobs can choose the most convenient time to do their coursework, including during weekends, before work, and after.

Thousands of Internet students could take a single, popular course, instead of the small numbers in a typical classroom. The spread of faster and, ultimately, broadband access to the Web enables the use of colorful graphics and attractive simulations. On-line instruction may well widen the market and raise the popularity of superstar teachers who command high audiences and very high salaries.

Distance learning appeals mainly to adults who want to take courses toward a bachelor's or master's degree or maintain and upgrade job skills that have grown outdated. Highly skilled professionals, such as doctors, have always had to keep up with change in their fields by reading and by taking short courses. But the continual introduction of new technologies makes skills obsolescence a serious prospect for all professionals and for many other working adults.

On-the-job training and learning offer a particularly promising on-line market. Companies have long invested in employee education, although mostly in-house to eliminate travel time to off-site schools. Distance learning offers an opportunity to outsource teaching to specialized companies without taking employees away from their work. Web-based courses are rapidly developing in information technology, finance, accounting, marketing, management, the global economy, and many other subject areas.

How well companies manage their human capital is a crucial factor in their success. Bill Gates said, 'Take our 20 best people away and ... Microsoft would become an unimportant company.'

Unfortunately, the huge amounts invested by companies are not on their balance sheets because typically they are costed as current spending rather than capitalized. They are part of 'goodwill' and other residual accounting categories. Increased investments in human capital and knowledge by companies partly explains the enormous rise in the ratio of market price to book value of the assets of publically traded companies.

Conclusions

I conclude by listing several main points of this [chapter]:

1. Human capital is of great importance in the modern economy.
2. Human capital has become of much greater significance during the past two decades.
3. Human capital is crucial to the international division of labor.
4. Much unmeasured learning goes on in companies and by adults.
5. People need to invest in themselves during their whole lives.
6. Distance learning will become of crucial importance to the teaching and learning process.
7. Human capital stimulates technological innovations and the high-tech sector.

The Globalization of Rhetoric and Practice: The Education Gospel and Vocationalism

W. Norton Grubb and Marvin Lazerson

Introduction

An orthodoxy about the role of schooling has developed in many countries. Rhetoric about the failure of schools has come first: in the US where a report called *A Nation at Risk* blamed the educational system for a 'rising tide of mediocrity'; in the UK, where a series of reports such as *Skills for All* and *21st Century Skills* have argued for massive changes in schooling; in Korea, calling for an Edutopia; in China, with the 'Action Plan for the 21st Century' declaring that 'education will be more and more strategically important in positioning the nation on a par with the advanced world's economy'; in Australia with reports such as *Sleepers, Wake!* an effort by its prime minister to dispel Australians' complacency and to develop a 'clever country'. International agencies have picked up this rhetoric too, particularly with the European Union promoting the Europe of Knowledge, and the OECD (2001*a*) emphasizing the implications of the Knowledge Revolution. Many countries have promoted 'key' or 'core' skills, or *Schlüsselqualifikationen* (key qualifications) in Germany and *qualificaciones quiaves* in Spanish, or the 'skills of the 21st century'—higher levels and new forms of learning as ways of competing in the new millennium. A few countries seem to have escaped this rhetoric, to be sure: Finland continues to espouse a mixture of economic and non-economic goals for schooling, and Austria appears too concerned with the aging of the labour force to emphasize the role of the Knowledge Revolution. But in many countries, an amazingly similar rhetoric has developed, one that first stresses the failures of schools and universities and then proceeds to reform them with more economic and utilitarian goals.

We call this rhetoric the Education Gospel because it has become an article of faith. Starting from a critique of schooling, it brings glad tidings about the potential of educational expansion and reform, leading to social and individual salvation. Like a gospel, it has been accepted by an extraordinary range of policymakers, reformers, many (but not all) educators, the business community, most students wanting to get ahead, and much of the public. Its essential vision insists that the Knowledge Revolution is changing the nature of work, shifting toward occupations associated with knowledge and information, enhancing the importance of 'higher-order' skills, and increasingly requiring some tertiary education, a practice that OECD (1998) has labelled Tertiary Education for All. Individuals are more likely to find their skills becoming obsolete because of the pace of technological change, and therefore workers must engage in lifelong learning.

While much of the Gospel's rhetoric emphasizes national needs such as competitiveness and growth, it also incorporates the individual goals of 'getting ahead'. The Education Gospel thus balances the public purposes of an expansive education system with the private intentions of using education for personal ends. The two are best combined, and the public goal noblest, in the effort to make schooling more inclusive and equitable—when more schooling is promoted to enhance equity or social inclusion.

The most obvious consequences of the Education Gospel effects have been changes in the purposes of schooling toward preparation for occupations, a process we call vocationalism. This is an awkward but useful term referring not primarily to traditional secondary vocational education but to preparation for *vocations*—the only word in English denoting occupations as careers or callings rather than mere jobs, employment that provides personal meaning, economic benefits, continued development, social status, and connection to the greater society. The shift to occupational goals has taken place at many levels of education, from secondary education to pre-baccalaureate institutions such as community colleges and technical institutes to universities. We therefore refer to a vocationalized education system, in preference to VET or TVET systems, because vocationalism has extended to many forms of schooling not usually considered part of VET—to forms of academic or general secondary education that are necessary for upward mobility and that might be considered pre-vocational, and to universities that prefer to call themselves 'professional'.

Several international developments have fostered the globalization of both rhetoric and practice. International competition has increased; and because no developed country wants to fall into the ranks of underdeveloped countries relying on raw materials and unskilled labour, the need for greater levels of skill and education has become more compelling. Other forms of international competition and national domination have been exhausted—colonialism, the dominance of trade by just a few countries, the importance of raw materials—and education as a form of competition can build on older ideas about the value of education, highly valued in many countries though not necessarily for economic purposes. The international exchange of ideas has been promoted by the global communications, and emulation of other countries—sometimes of Germany's dual system, sometimes of American higher education, sometimes of Japan and Korea's success in math and science, and often of market-like practices including deregulation and liberalization—seems to have increased. China represents an interesting example: at different times it has adopted elements from Soviet higher education, from the US comprehensive universities, and from the German dual system, resulting in a particularly complex system of tertiary education. International organizations have both spread information about national practices and—as with OECD and the European Union—promoted certain practices; for many transitional and developing countries agencies such as the World Bank and USAID have been influential. In developed countries, vocationalism has been self-reinforcing as more occupations depend on school-based routes of access, and as competition among students for access to employment exacerbates the use of schooling for occupational reasons. Many transitional countries have become increasingly market-oriented, and the emergence of more structured labour markets—for example, the development of 'two-way choosing' (individuals choosing employers and employers choosing among applicants) in China replacing the directive allocation of labour—has enhanced the role of educational qualifications in employment opportunities. So many different features, somewhat independent of each other, have reinforced both the Education Gospel and vocationalism

In this essay, we consider the consequence of vocationalism in different countries. There have been many common features among countries, like the expansion and differentiation of tertiary education and the efforts to create linkages between schooling and employment. But the specific forms that these responses take, and the particular solutions to the problems created everywhere by vocationalism, are influenced by the particular histories, institutions, and values of different countries. In particular, after we describe the main ways that educational institutions have become vocationalized in the next section, we examine three general problems that emerge whenever vocationalism overtakes educational institutions: maintaining connections between schooling and employment; preventing overly narrow and utilitarian conceptions of schooling; and fostering equity instead of inequality. Finally we examine possible directions for vocationalism in the future.

We regard this chapter as a work in progress. It draws first on our analysis of the US (Grubb and Lazerson 2004); the US has the advantage for comparative work of having been one of the first countries to vocationalize its schooling system, around 1900. We have extended this analysis to England (Grubb 2004); and we also draw on our experiences in Germany; in Austria, Canada, and Finland engaging in county studies for OECD; in Australia, comparing its VET system to that of the US; in China and Korea;[1] and in those countries that have adopted forms of tertiary education subordinate to universities (Grubb and Sweet 2005). But we have much more to do before we can fully understand the various forms that vocationalism has taken.

The Process of Vocationalizing Schools and Universities

Several commonalities among countries help define vocationalism. In many countries there has been a broad movement away from apprenticeships and other forms of work-based preparation. This happened in the US during the nineteenth century, in England not until the 1960s, in France over the past few decades; work-based learning in China has declined since the 1980s with decreases in state enterprises that ran state enterprise schools, with more conventional schooling taking their place. Some countries like the Scandinavian countries never had strong apprenticeship traditions. Vocationalism is first and foremost an approach in which *educational institutions* provide preparation for occupations, rather than employers themselves, or unions, or non-governmental organizations, or profit-making training ventures, or churches, or families—even though all of these may exist around the margins. In turn, the institutional histories and purposes of the dominant institutions that provide occupational preparation continue to exert their own influences, leading to the conflicts we explore in the following sections.

The great exceptions to the decline of apprenticeship, of course, are the countries with strong dual systems combing work-based learning in apprenticeships with school-based learning, in Germany, Austria, and Denmark. These have been the envy of many other countries wanting to develop stronger forms of vocational education and apprenticeship, in part to strengthen weak forms of vocational education and in part to follow romanticized conceptions of apprenticeship spun by Lave and Wenger (1991), Collins, Brown, and Newman (1989), and others. But apprenticeship as a form of work-preparation suffers from some inescapable weaknesses. It can easily become routine production rather than learning through production; it may not facilitate well-rounded learning about work. It is suitable more to stable conditions of skill and employment, and often deteriorates under changing conditions. It's not a good setting for teaching abstract and theoretical material, including that associated with the Knowledge Revolution; and apprenticeships often replicate the gender divisions of the workplace, the class biases of family selection, and the discriminatory patterns of employers—unless there are strong institutional controls. And, under pressures to make it easier and simpler, as well as cheaper, for people to enter labour markets, even the traditionally strong *Ausbildung* system has been criticized. So the efforts to revive apprenticeship in many countries have faltered—in the US, England, China with its German-funded pilot projects—or have been relegated to minor efforts in second-chance programs, as in Finland.[2] And the current 'crisis' in the German *Ausbildung* system, with government support declining, fewer employers willing to offer apprenticeships, and more students trying to enter the university, can be interpreted as symptomatic of the pressures against apprenticeship, even in countries with strong traditions.

A second feature of vocationalism has been the transformation of secondary schooling. A common pattern has been to develop academic education for those bound for university, separate from vocational education or VET for those bound for employment—a restructuring of educational systems that exemplifies the differentiating power of vocationalism. In many European countries these two strands have taken place in separate institutions; in China three kinds of vocational schools have developed, varying in the amount of academic content and internships; in the US and Canada, because of an ideology of common schooling, these streams usually took place within comprehensive secondary schools. But in virtually all countries the hierarchical relationship of academic and vocational education—the first leading to university and the professions, and second leading to immediate employment in lower-paid jobs, often with few prospects for advancement—has led to a wide status gap between them and a tendency for the quality of vocational programs to erode. Then many countries (and the EU) have tried to re-establish 'parity of esteem' between the two (Lasonen and Young 1998). But most of these have failed to work well—with some exceptions in the US (National Research Council 2003: ch. 7; Grubb 1995)—because they have failed to grapple with the employment conditions underlying the status gap, the essence of vocationalism. As a result many countries have been left with a problem of what to do with weak secondary vocational education, and the choices have been limited: either to abandon secondary vocational education and introduce it into tertiary institutions such as community colleges and technical institutes (the implicit route of the US and England); or to strengthen vocational education, for example by increasing requirements or tightening connections to employers (the route China has taken), or making other marginal changes (*Achieving the Lisbon Goal*, 2004); or to try some form of integrating vocational preparation with academic preparation; or to emulate the German system, a difficult route for countries without the requisite institutional structure. While there are infinite varieties of VET systems, then, there are few conceptually distinct directions for reform.

Where academic secondary education becomes a route into universities and professional preparation, then a different transformation takes place: learning becomes subordinated to the competitive and instrumental process of enhancing university entry. Certainly in the US, this has almost emptied the intellectual content from the high school, as students understand its purpose as preparation for the university and access to professional and managerial jobs; in England too secondary education has sometimes been described as a 'bare-knuckled struggle for access to elite schools, colleges, universities, and jobs', particularly among the anxious middle class (Brown and Hesketh 2004). Under these conditions it is more accurate to call academic secondary education pre-vocational. This has not happened universally, of course; the Finnish system, although quite concerned about international competition and the Knowledge Revolution, has nonetheless managed to preserve a great variety of subjects and purposes, as have the other Scandinavian countries and France with its emphasis on preserving its particular culture. But the pressures are to transform secondary academic education too, even if it is not as overtly vocational as VET is.

A third common feature—perhaps the most powerful effect of the Education Gospel—has been to expand tertiary education. At this level the connections to the Knowledge Revolution, to technological developments, and to high-status professions are the most obvious. The twin pressures in the Education Gospel—for educational changes that appear to enhance a country's competitiveness and growth, and that provide routes to individual mobility—are well served by expanding tertiary education. In most countries this has come not simply from expanding universities, but by simultaneously differentiating tertiary education—often by creating (or expanding) sub-university institutions,[3] and sometimes by creating another tier of universities, such as the former polytechnics in England, the regional universities in the US, the second-tier universities in Australia, the distinctions between the elite *Grandes Écoles* and the universities in France. Typically the lower tiers of tertiary education are more overtly vocational (or *professional*) than are the upper tiers (except in France). Technical institutes are explicitly dedicated to professional areas of study, and the comprehensive tertiary institutions (like community colleges in the US and Canada) usually transfer academic students to professional programs in second-tier universities, and so are often pre-vocational. The regional and second-tier universities in the English-speaking countries usually are dominated by highly professional programs in business, IT, health, education, engineering, and other such subjects, and then an undercurrent of sarcasm develops about certain fields of study: golf course management, leisure studies, fashion accessories merchandising, and other subjects that would never have been part of the traditional universities. Overall, tertiary education has become much more overtly vocationalized, or professionalized.

Of course non-vocational purposes persist in education, and they differ among countries—from education for civic purposes, to more overtly nationalist goals, to efforts to develop a cadre of leaders, to conceptions of the well-rounded individual, to ideals of the liberal arts. And so many educational institutions are hybrids, with a mixture of goals of which vocational purposes are only one, creating battles among different conceptions of what an educational institution should be. Similarly, different conceptions of what it means to be vocational have developed, not necessarily consistent with one another. Student intentions define one kind of vocational purpose, not only in overtly vocational programs but also in these we have called pre-vocational. An overtly vocational curriculum, with subjects defined by their future utility, is another. Rates of placement in related occupations is a third; if an institution is overtly vocational in the sense that its curriculum is vocational, but it fails to place its graduates in related employment, then its legitimacy is undermined and its standing among students will be eroded. So many of the battles over the vocational status of education institutions involve the fact that vocational transformations are never complete, and that the meaning of vocationalism itself remains contested.

Maintaining Connections between Schooling and Employment

One unavoidable problem, when preparation for work shifts from apprenticeship or simple work experience into educational institutions, is that preparation for work and work itself become institutionally separated, leading to the danger that the two might become independent of one another. This critique of vocationalism appears in many forms: in the charge of employers that students are not being adequately prepared, or are prepared in outmoded techniques; in the suspicion that schooling can never be a substitute for the 'school of hard knocks' and experience; in the view of credentialism (e.g. Collins 1979) that diplomas and qualifications are empty pieces of paper rather than markers of competencies; in the observation that over-education rather than under-education is the more serious problem in developed countries, with too many individuals having more education than their jobs require.[4] If all these critiques were valid, then vocationalism would lose much of its power since educational institutions would be dysfunctional.

All countries following the path of vocationalism have therefore developed mechanisms to narrow the distance between education institutions and employment. The specific forms these mechanisms take have been enormously varied, and it's sometimes difficult to see the commonality among them. One mechanism is the attempt to inform students about employment options and the educational routes to employment, in career information and guidance (CIG), so that they might make informed decisions about their schooling paths and then their employment choices. But, apart from the fact that this places the burden on *students* (rather than *employers* and *educational institutions* themselves) for matching school and work, countries have taken very different approaches to CIG (OECD 2005). Often CIG have been peripheral, with funding low and variable. In many cases, these services have been transformed by educational imperatives—the need to have students complete programs—and have become forms of academic counselling concerned with the appropriate courses to take rather than career counselling. Where counselling and guidance are the responsibilities of individual schools and universities, institutional self-interest may distort the advice given, and there is no source of information about the variety of educational institutions and occupations available. There are exceptions, of course: England's Careers Service provided advice in a non-school setting to all individuals, and avoided the problems of institutional bias, the dilution of career-related counselling, and the common inaccessibility of guidance and counselling to non-students—until the Blair government demolished it. Similarly Germany has a comprehensive career guidance service, independent of any particular type of schooling, that works closely with employers. But complaints about CIG are ubiquitous, and its institutional location helps explain why this is so frequently the case.

A second linkage mechanism relies on direct connections between schools and workplaces, like school–business partnerships, advisory committees, or co-operative education where schools and employers jointly prepare workers. There's no question that such mechanisms can be quite strong, particularly in countries with tripartite decision-making about apprenticeship systems; again, Germany and Austria are exemplars. But many developed countries have weak unions and employer associations, and therefore tripartite discussions are difficult. In countries where employers have given up apprenticeships and other ways of providing employment preparation, it is often difficult to get them to discuss employment preparation, since they see it as no longer their responsibility. And schools and colleges, with their concerns for the development of students, are often at odds with employers, who are primarily concerned with immediate productivity and short-run profit. So these partnerships are often episodic, and the efforts of governments haven't always been helpful—for example, the English government's predilection for changing the structure of advisory committees every few years.

A third linkage includes a variety of credentials, licenses, and qualifications, ranging from highly formalized to informal. When an educational credential works as intended, it provides uniform expectations among all participants. Employers can specify the competencies they need; education and training programs use credential requirements to shape their curriculum; and students know what competencies they must master to become marketable. This is the positive sense of credentials, as market-making devices coordinating the activities of employers, education providers, and students. However, credentials (unlike prices) are not set by the invisible hand of the market. They require considerable institutional effort to create and to enforce: competencies or standards must be established; a method of assessing competencies must be created; and a mechanism for policing the process must be developed. Each of these is complex and potentially controversial, and can be implemented in many different ways ranging from laissez-faire to highly bureaucratized. But if any of these three are inconsistent with the others, then the value of a credential becomes uncertain and 'credentialism' takes on the negative connotation of educational requirements not rationally related to employment requirements (Collins 1979).

Credentials are one of the crucial markers of vocationalism, since a pre-vocational education system need not certify results to employers. The structure of credentials varies enormously among countries, often reflecting historical patterns and national policy objectives. Germany, with its dual system, has a trio of qualifications, from employers, from schools, and from the national government, all carefully developed. England has an elaborate system of credentials, but there's no coherent conception underlying them, and they usually fail to consider employers' views, so many of them are worthless; elaborate systems are not necessarily effective systems. Many countries, particularly the English-speaking countries, have developed competency-based credentials based on task analysis and the Canadian DACUM system; but such approaches treat work as a series of independent tasks rather than a social activity requiring more complex understanding, and therefore fail to encourage some important competencies. Many countries have credentials whose content is specified by education providers, leading to complaints of 'supply-driven' content. And many countries have developed multiple systems of qualifications, like Finland with its education-based credentials and then an independent system of Nautecoy qualifications for other VET and adult programs, widely promoted but whose economic effects are poorly understood. In the vast variety of qualifications, what is sometimes amazing is how infrequently participants ask why any particular qualification ought to have an effect on employment, even though that is the purpose of most credentials.

Overall, the mechanisms linking schooling and employment are often quite weak—again, with some clear exceptions. The academic goals of schools and universities often take priority over occupational goals; employers who have abandoned any role in occupational preparation are unwilling to participate actively; and the governments often don't think systematically enough about what might bridge the two. This is one of the inevitable costs of locating preparation for employment within educational institutions.

Utilitarian Conceptions of Education

The creation and expansion of credentials is itself one form of a larger problem with vocationalism: the tendency to turn education into a commodity with economic value. This is the dark side of giving education a usefulness that is simultaneously reason for the expansion of education.

The negative consequences of such utilitarian conceptions takes several different forms, some of which are self-defeating—that is, vocationalism may itself undermine occupationally-relevant learning. One is a persistent debate about what kinds of skills and competencies are valuable in employment. The debates over credentials, particularly over narrow and behaviourist conceptions of credentials versus broader and more expansive conceptions, represents one version of this conflict. Another is whether vocational forms of schools should prepare individuals for immediate employment, or for employment over the long run—not an issue for a stable economy, but crucial in economies where jobs change, where individuals change their occupations, and where the upward trajectories associated with careers require ever-expanding and ever-different competencies. And issues of narrow and specific training versus broad and general preparation fuel a great deal of discussion, including most of the debate about occupational curricula (Achtenhagen and Grubb 2001). Broader forms of preparation require either far-sighted employers, far-sighted providers and instructors, or students aware of how their lives may unfold in dynamic ways; but where employers are concerned with immediate employability, providers are unable to resist the pressures of employers, and students are generally uninformed about their possible life courses, then overly narrow training might ensue. The result might satisfy short-term needs but not long-run developments, and complaints in the Education Gospel that workers lack the 'higher-order skills' and the flexibility required in modern jobs is really a complaint about the heart of vocationalism.

In addition, students in vocationalist systems might themselves adopt attitudes toward learning that are counterproductive. In many countries—the English-speaking countries are good examples—students have adopted highly utilitarian and credentialist views of their schooling: utilitarian in the sense that they see their schooling as useful only to future employment, and credentialist in the sense that they concentrate on accumulating the credentials they think necessary, rather than the learning that credentials are supposed to represent. Under such conditions, there's a great deal of talk about the practical side of education over theory, of 'hands-on' approaches in preference to book learning, about 'learning by doing'—though John Dewey would be aghast at how his ideas have been misused.[5] As Cox (2004) has shown for community college students in the US, such attitudes can get in the way of learning if students avoid any instruction that seems to be 'academic' or 'not relevant', because they start to see learning in terms of accumulating facts and discrete skills rather than broadening understanding, and because instructors are often unaware of their students' attitudes and may conflict with their conceptions about the purposes of schooling and the nature of learning. Paradoxically, then, the constant insistence in the Education Gospel on 'skills' for occupations may undermine the effort to develop a broader variety of conceptual abilities and other higher-order competencies.

Finally, and perhaps most obviously, the development of utilitarian approaches threatens to overwhelm the many other purposes of education that have been articulated for schooling, including civic and moral purposes, purely intellectual goals, nation-building, the promotion of national character, literacy in the service of religion, and other goals too numerous (and too country-specific) to catalogue easily. Again, this takes numerous forms in different countries: in the debates over universities in China, and the balance of 'redness' (political socialization) versus 'expertness'; in somewhat similar debates in the US over the roles of liberal or general education versus professional education; in the sarcastic comments about utilitarian fields of study—golf course management and leisure studies—since such discussions assume that education should serve loftier goals than simple work preparation. Of course, occupational goals need not displace other purposes, and often there are older models of schooling that continue to exert some power: the old elite university in China, designed to prepare the intelligentsia; the liberal arts colleges in the US, intended to prepare generations of leaders; the Oxbridge tradition in England, with its distaste for subjects such as business and education that seem too commonplace; the university of Helsinki with its links to early nation-building. In other countries, a principled stand in favour of broad education has helped prevent an overly utilitarian approach, as in Finland's national curriculum, with its broad array of subjects at every level, and the attempts to preserve the broad disciplinary learning in the German *Gymnasium*. But the pressure from vocationalism is to transform education thoroughly, leading *in extremis* to a world we have described as HyperVoc. In this grim world, narrow work skills for routinized work are all that matter; the search among students for fast access to employment leads them to avoid other 'frills' including the arts, the humanities, or any version of general education; employers seek specific skills narrowly tailored to their production, certified through specific qualifications; and both broad occupational programs and broad academic programs disappear—except perhaps for elite students—because they are not seen as useful. The world of HyperVoc may seem exaggerated, but each of its features can be found in the English-speaking countries, and—as part of globalization—some of these ideas threaten other countries as well.

Vocationalism and the Promotion of Inequality

Vocationalism does not, of course, create inequality among the citizens of a country—in earnings, income, status, health, and every form of consumption—and in particular cannot be blamed for the high levels of inequality that prevail in many countries. However, vocationalism has changed the mechanisms underlying inequality, by shifting from a world in which parents directly fostered the success of their children—through apprenticeships or inheritance of a farm or a family business—to indirect sponsorship of success through formal schooling. As schools and universities have developed clearer connections to occupations, struggles over access to and success in formal schooling have become more critical because the consequences for earnings, class standing, and upward mobility have become so enormous.

Vocationalism has had distinctly ambiguous effects on equity. Most obviously, by replacing family-based sponsorship of success by formal schooling—particularly publicly sponsored schooling which allows for debates about who should benefit—it creates the possibility that access to occupations could be made equitable. Even if inequality in a country were high, *patterned* inequality—in which class and status are reproduced from generation to generation, or racial minorities or immigrants or residents of certain regions are more likely to be poor—might be replaced by with inequality that is more nearly random, or related only to personal characteristics (like motivation and ambition) that are widely admired. Indeed, debates over equality of educational opportunity and outcomes are prominent in virtually all developed countries, and many transitional countries as well, and all of them use a vocationalist measure of inequality—for example, differences in access to higher levels of schooling, now a proxy for access to earnings and status.

But a number of factors reproduce inequality under vocationalism. One is that the structures of schooling tend to mirror the differences of labour markets. The differentiation of education institutions along roughly occupational lines has been both *horizontal*—in the division of academic from vocational education, or engineering majors distinct from education majors—and *vertical* in differences among institutions preparing for different occupational levels like the distinctions between universities and technical colleges or institutes. Indeed, it's hard to imagine a vocationalized system of education that is not differentiated in this way, as long as doctors and lawyers require different amounts and kinds of schooling than do accountants and teachers, clerks and auto mechanics. But these different institutions create tracks or streams, in contrast to comprehensive forms of schooling. Sometimes they create dead-ends, for example where there is no provision for students in vocational tracks to enter tertiary education, or where technical institutes do not permit transfer to universities (as in China). Tracks, streams, dead-ends, and differentiated institutions by definition create inequalities—the inequalities associated with a differentiated labour market—and then they allow for patterned inequalities to develop.

Then every analysis of schooling practice has found powerful effects of family background on educational outcomes, much more powerful than the influences of schooling resources. These operate in many different ways: through the ability of high-status parents (especially professionals) to teach their children both the cognitive abilities and the non-cognitive behaviours necessary in schools; through the role models and values parents (and their communities) provide children; through the income differences that allow some parents to provide more books and computers, travel and recreation, private tutoring and college tuition; through the greater ability of some parents to negotiate the formal education system on behalf of their children, partly because of the cultural compatibility between well-educated families and educational institutions. These processes seem biased and unfair to partisans of equity, but it's hard to imagine a vocationalized schooling system in which powerful effects of family background do not exist. When the high-status tracks of schools and universities prepare students for high-status occupations—particularly professional and managerial positions—then they inevitably favour (or 'privilege') those cognitive abilities, values, and behaviours associated with such occupations. Inevitably, these are learned earliest by the children of well-educated professionals and managers, and reinforced most powerfully by their parents. If educational practices developed abilities and norms that favoured children from working-class backgrounds, this could occur only in programs or tracks preparing for working-class jobs; inevitably these would be second-class alternatives like traditional vocational education or the occupational programs in technical colleges criticized for 'cooling out' non-traditional students. Inequality begets inequality in so many ways, now through the mechanisms of vocationalized schooling rather than direct transmission of wealth.

In addition, creating greater equality in schooling requires substantial institutional effort to overcome the benefits of family background—and it requires *sustained* institutional effort, over the entire (and lengthening) trajectory of education. Many countries have strengthened their programs of early childhood education, in the hopes that they could equalize 'school readiness' and the ability of children to take advantage of primary schooling (OECD 2001*c*); but no country has managed to attain such levels of equality, and then differentiating processes start recreating inequality in the primary grades. Finland provides an exemplary case of developing practices within its comprehensive schools (years 1 to 9) that prevent some students from falling behind others; but powerful as these practices are they fail to eliminate family-linked inequality by the end of year 9, and the process of transition to upper secondary education and then tertiary education recreates familiar patterns of inequality (OECD 2005). Sustaining equity-related practices in early childhood programs, throughout elementary and secondary education, through all of the transitions into and through differentiated forms of secondary and tertiary education would be a formidable task indeed. And higher-status parents with greater political power would surely not stand for it; on the contrary: all parents under vocationalism have powerful incentives to make sure that only their own children do well in school. The dominant pattern is for parents to pressure for privileges for their own children, not efforts benefiting other people's children—and in this political battle upper-status and well-educated parents have considerable advantages. So while some countries have been more successful than others in reducing the effects of family background on school attainment, familiar patterns emerge almost everywhere.[6]

Even the vocationalist expansion of education has had at best ambiguous effects on inequality. On the one hand, the expansion of access, particularly to tertiary education, has increased schooling for groups who previously did not have much chance at higher education including more working class students, minority, and immigrant students. But two problems may intervene. One is simply that elites, or middle-class families and students, will take more advantage of expanded opportunities than do working-class and low-income students. In England, for example, the proportion of students from the bottom three social classes attending university increased from 1.5 to 18.2 per cent between 1940 and 2000. But the proportion from the top three social classes increased from 8.4 to 47.8 per cent, so the absolute difference in attendance rates (though not the relative difference) increased over this period; the steady expansion of higher education has benefited higher classes substantially more than lower classes (Chevalier and Conlon 2003: table 1). Similarly in Finland, one would expect that the expansion of both universities and polytechnics would have reduced the effect of family background on children's education levels; but many effects of family background have been reduced only by trivial amounts (Asplund and Leijola 2005).

In addition, *greater* access to tertiary education has not meant *equitable* access. In Finland and England, middle- and upper-income parents tend to send their students to universities, while working-class parents send theirs to second-tier universities and (in Finland) polytechnics, with lower levels of resources, higher rates of dropping out, and access to a lower tier of occupations. So the simultaneous expansion and differentiation of tertiary education may mean that greater access does not mean equal access to the same kind of institution, the same levels of resources, or the same kinds of occupational outcomes. To be sure this need not be true: whether expansion and differentiation enhance or diminish equity is an empirical issue, turning on the probabilities of attending different types of institutions, and this almost surely differs among types of institutions and among countries.[7] But our point is that expanding tertiary education does not automatically enhance equity, despite the promises of the Education Gospel.

Finally, in several ways the equity of a country's educational system depends on the nature of its welfare provision.[8] Generous welfare states, like those of Scandinavian countries (Esping-Anderson 1990), enhance the equity of education in several ways: by reducing the overall level of inequality in a country, and therefore reducing the differences among children that they bring to the early grades; by providing various complements to schooling—early childhood programs, nutrition programs, health and mental health services, family support programs—to reduce some barriers to learning; and by providing support (housing, transportation, income, etc.) to tertiary students who need to support themselves. In contrast, in countries with weak welfare provision, such as the US, the differences that children come to school with are enormous; their schooling is often interrupted by health, housing, and family problems, and the dropout rates from tertiary education are high partly because many students need to support themselves. In turn, the equity of a country's education affects the demands made on its welfare provision, since there are fewer individuals with such low levels of schooling that they are unemployable and therefore social burdens. Obviously many other factors influence the relationships between education systems and welfare states, but in general the countries with generous welfare provision can anticipate a virtuous circle, with more equitable schooling systems reducing the population needing such support; countries such as England and the US with weak and declining welfare states have created vicious circles, in which inequitable education creates more poverty, greater demands from the poor, lower welfare spending per person, and weaker effects on educational equity.

Inequality reasserts itself in so many ways. Even though vocationalism has changed the mechanisms of generating inequality, the same patterns of inequality persist. These can be moderated, particularly by trying to create more equitable structures of schooling, by paying close attention to practices within each level of schooling, and by expanding welfare states. But under vocationalism the essential inequalities of labour markets are necessarily manifest in schooling systems, and so the struggle for equity must be constant.

Conclusions: The Future of Vocationalism

Overall, the consequences of vocationalism are at best ambiguous. Certainly its practices represent some substantial advances over pre-vocational forms of preparing the workforce: a greater attention to learning, including conceptual forms of learning, rather than placing learning in competition with production; an attention to both the private and public consequences of education; an expansion of public support for education; the potential to shift issues of equity into a public forum, for debate and potential improvement. On the other hand, even while vocationalism seems to be a rational and utilitarian approach to preparing the labour force, it creates it own excesses and irrationalities.

It's also clear that vocationalism varies among countries, and that these problems are more serious in some countries that in others. It's tempting to articulate at least three models or approaches to vocationalism:[9] (1) One is an Anglo-American approach in the English-speaking countries, with extreme narrowing of the purposes of schooling; little use of work-based learning and low participation of employers overall; low-quality and low-status vocational education contrasting with high-status professional education; an extreme differentiation of tertiary institutions, reinforcing inequality; many poorly structured qualifications leading to charges of credentialism; high levels of inequality, weak welfare states, and schooling as the mechanisms of transmitting inequality. (2) A second is the dual system of the German-speaking countries plus Denmark, which has traditionally relied on apprenticeship mechanisms, high-quality vocational education, better-developed tripartite planning, efforts to narrow the variation among tertiary institutions, highly rationalized credentials, and moderate levels of inequality supported by corporatist welfare states and by wage-setting mechanisms. (3) A third might be a Scandinavian approach, with fewer efforts to narrow the purposes of education, more equitable schooling systems, more generous welfare states and much lower levels of inequality, but still with low-quality vocational education, few apprenticeships, little participation among employers, and uncertain qualifications. But this three-part approach leaves out many countries, including developed Asian countries and transitional countries such as China, and we're not sure that we or anyone else know enough about the varieties of vocationalism to be sure that it is useful. In addition, vocationalism is relatively new in many countries and still in flux, so historical perspectives in many other countries are quite short. Over the longer run, however, a useful exercise would be to understand the varieties of vocationalism, just as there has been progress in understanding the varieties of capitalism (Hall and Soskice 2001) and the varieties of welfare states (Esping-Anderson 1990), and to understand somewhat better how forms of vocationalism depend on and shape capitalism and welfare states.

But while our comparative understanding of vocationalism is still underdeveloped, some issues are relatively clear. One is that the rhetoric of the Education Gospel is often exaggerated, and more moderate and realistic claims should be the basis for future developments. For example, the claims in the Education Gospel of serious levels of under-education have in practice been replaced by serious levels of over-education in many (though not all) countries. While individuals need more and more schooling to gain access to the best jobs, it is not true that the majority of jobs in the near future will require tertiary qualification, as is sometimes claimed; even in the most developed countries, there remain huge numbers of moderately-skilled and unskilled jobs, and they are dwindling in relative terms only slowly. And the rhetoric about the effects of education on growth is surely over-blown: the assumptions necessary to link more education to higher growth are suspect (Wolf 2002), and the examples of sharp growth and decline over the past thirty years—Asian countries, the US from the 1980s to the 1990s, Finland after its depression in the early 1990s, the decline of many African countries—have been caused by many more factors than simply education (Grubb and Lazerson 2004: ch. 6). From the perspective of micro-economic growth theories, a huge variety of factors affect growth including national governance and stability; macro-economic policies; institutional settings including financial, legal, and corporate institutions; supportive policies including education, labour relations, science and technology policy; regulatory and environmental policies; and developments in specific industries (Landau, Taylor, and Wright 1996). It's simply foolish to isolate one of these factors—education—and give it the prominence that the Education Gospel does over all the others.

Another relatively clear trend is that vocationalism is self-reinforcing, and that more and more countries will adopt more free-market policies that encourage vocationalism. If vocationalist pressures continue to intensify, then countries need to consider how they might shape or constrain some of its negative features—in particular, preventing overly narrow forms of vocationalism we have caricatured as HyperVoc. There are many ways to do this, by insisting on a broad range of educational goals, preventing the development of overly narrow curricula, creating broader qualifications, trying to link occupational programs with academic content, and enhancing alternative routes into employment including revived forms of apprenticeship. But taking any of these steps requires first understanding how the narrowing effects of vocationalism work, in order to create defences against them.

Finally, the inequality that vocationalism brings is not inevitable. The variation among countries in the extent of both economic and educational inequality is proof that both economic and educational policies—including the practices of welfare states—can enhance equity, however measured. But doing so requires both national consensus and consistent implementation of equity policies. Otherwise the 'natural' or unimpeded effect of vocationalism is to mirror the inequalities of labour markets, and to reproduce the inequalities of groups with different positions in those markets.

Vocationalism and the Education Gospel are already powerful forces around the globe, and they are likely to become even more powerful if we are right about the self-reinforcing trends in vocationalism. Just as pre-vocational forms of work preparation had their problems, so too the shift to school-based preparation has created different problems. Preventing the worst features of vocationalism from expanding will therefore continue to require state regulation and intervention, even in countries that pride themselves on limited governments and free markets. Otherwise it will prove impossible to have forms of schooling, and schooling in preparation for work, that live up to the noblest ambitions of the Education Gospel.

NOTES

1. We thank Juan Do for research on China and Jongsoon Jung for reviewing information about Korea.
2. The big exceptions have been South American countries, which have developed VET programs in cooperation with employers following SENAI in Brazil, but we know too little about these countries to include them in this analysis.
3. These include a wide variety of institutions such as community colleges, further education colleges in the UK, state colleges in Norway, polytechnics in Finland, *Fachhochschule* in German-speaking countries, the *Instituts Universitaires de Technologie* (IUTs) in France, and *da zhuan* in China, with differences reviewed in Grubb and Sweet (2005).
4. On over-education see Daly, Buchel, and Duncan (2000), table 1, the review in Hartog (2000), especially Tables 1 and 2, and the special issue of *Economics of Education Review* 19 (2000), on over-education.
5. Dewey's own argument called for integrating classroom-based 'knowing' and experience-based 'doing'—'learning and doing', not 'learning by doing'; as he wrote, 'Learning by doing does not, of course, mean the substitution of manual occupations or handwork for textbook studying' (Dewey and Dewey 1915: 74).
6. See, for example, the variation among countries in the effects of family background on PISA scores, in OECD (2001*b*).
7. For example, in the US there has been a long-running debate about whether community colleges have enhanced equity by increasing college-going rates among individuals who would others have little access to tertiary education, or reduced equity by luring individuals into two-year colleges who would have otherwise earned a baccalaureate

degree. Rouse (1995, 1998) has shown that the former effect ('educational advancement') outweighs the latter ('cooling out'), though this is an empirical question that may differ among types of institutions and countries.

8. Most analyses of welfare states ignore education completely. Esping-Anderson (1990) clearly views education as part of a broad conception of a welfare state, but neither he nor any other theorists whom we know integrate education and the welfare state. For some efforts along these lines for the US, see Grubb and Lazerson (2004: ch. 9).

9. The first two of these have been articulated by Soskice (1994).

Why the Rich Are Getting Richer and the Poor, Poorer

Robert B. Reich

[T]he division of labour is limited by the extent of the market.

Adam Smith, An Inquiry into the Nature and Causes of the Wealth of Nations (1776)

Regardless of how your job is officially classified (manufacturing, service, managerial, technical, secretarial, and so on), or the industry in which you work (automotive, steel, computer, advertising, finance, food processing), your real competitive position in the world economy is coming to depend on the function you perform in it. Herein lies the basic reason why incomes are diverging. The fortunes of routine producers are declining. In-person servers are also becoming poorer, although their fates are less clear-cut. But symbolic analysts—who solve, identify, and broker new problems—are, by and large, succeeding in the world economy.

All Americans used to be in roughly the same economic boat. Most rose or fell together, as the corporations in which they were employed, the industries comprising such corporations, and the national economy as a whole became more productive—or languished. But national borders no longer define our economic fates. We are now in different boats, one sinking rapidly, one sinking more slowly, and the third rising steadily.

The boat containing routine producers is sinking rapidly. Recall that by midcentury routine production workers in the United States were paid relatively well. The giant pyramidlike organizations at the core of each major industry coordinated their prices and investments—avoiding the harsh winds of competition and thus maintaining healthy earnings. Some of these earnings, in turn, were reinvested in new plant and equipment (yielding ever-larger-scale economies); another portion went to top managers and investors. But a large and increasing portion went to middle managers and production workers. Work stoppages posed such a threat to high-volume production that organized labor was able to exact an ever-larger premium for its cooperation. And the pattern of wages established within the core corporations influenced the pattern throughout the national economy. Thus the growth of a relatively affluent middle class, able to purchase all the wondrous things produced in high volume by the core corporations.

But, as has been observed, the core is rapidly breaking down into global webs which earn their largest profits from clever problem-solving, -identifying, and -brokering. As the costs of transporting standard things and of communicating information about them continue to drop, profit margins on high-volume, standardized production are thinning, because there are few barriers to entry. Modern factories and state-of-the-art machinery can be installed almost anywhere on the globe. Routine producers in the United States, then, are in direct competition with millions of routine producers in other nations. Twelve thousand people are added to the world's population every hour, most of whom, eventually, will happily work for a small fraction of the wages of routine producers in America.[1]

The consequence is clearest in older, heavy industries, where high-volume, standardized production continues its ineluctable move to where labor is cheapest and most accessible around the world. Thus, for example, the Maquiladora factories cluttered along the Mexican side of the US border in the sprawling shanty towns of Tijuana, Mexicali, Nogales, Agua Prieta, and Ciudad Juárez—factories owned mostly by Americans, but increasingly by Japanese—in which more than a half million routine producers assemble parts into finished goods to be shipped into the United States.

The same story is unfolding worldwide. Until the late 1970s, AT&T had depended on routine producers in Shreveport, Louisiana, to assemble standard telephones. It then discovered that routine producers in Singapore would perform the same tasks at a far lower cost. Facing intense competition from other global webs, AT&T's strategic brokers felt compelled to switch. So in the early 1980s they stopped hiring routine producers in Shreveport and began hiring cheaper routine producers in Singapore. But under this kind of pressure for ever lower high-volume production costs, today's Singaporean can easily end up as yesterday's Louisianan. By the late 1980s, AT&T's strategic brokers found that routine producers in Thailand were eager to assemble telephones for a small fraction of the wages of routine producers in Singapore. Thus, in 1989, AT&T stopped hiring Singaporeans to make telephones and began hiring even cheaper routine producers in Thailand.

The search for ever-lower wages has not been confined to heavy industry. Routine data processing is equally footloose. Keypunch operators located anywhere around the world can enter data into computers, linked by satellite or transoceanic fiber-optic cable, and take it out again. As the rates charged by satellite networks continue to drop, and as more satellites and fiber-optic cables become available (reducing communication costs still further), routine data processors in the United States find themselves in ever more direct competition with their counterparts abroad, who are often eager to work for far less.

By 1990, keypunch operators in the United States were earning, at most, $6.50 per hour. But keypunch operators throughout the rest of the world were willing to work for a fraction of this. Thus, many potential American data-processing jobs were disappearing, and the wages and benefits of the remaining ones were in decline. Typical was Saztec International, a $20-million-a-year data-processing firm headquartered in Kansas City, whose American strategic brokers contracted with routine data processors in Manila and with American-owned firms that needed such data-processing services. Compared with the average Philippine income of $1,700 per year, data-entry operators working for Saztec earn the princely sum of $2,650. The remainder of Saztec's employees were American problem-solvers and -identifiers, searching for ways to improve the worldwide system and find new uses to which it could be put (Maxwell Hamilton 1989).

By 1990, American Airlines was employing over 1,000 data processors in Barbados and the Dominican Republic to enter names and flight numbers from used airline tickets (flown daily to Barbados from airports around the United States) into a giant computer bank located in Dallas. Chicago publisher R. R. Donnelley was sending entire manuscripts to Barbados for entry into computers in preparation for printing. The New York Life Insurance Company was dispatching insurance claims to Castleisland, Ireland, where routine producers, guided by simple directions, entered the claims and determined the amounts due, then instantly transmitted the computations back to the United States. (When the firm advertised in Ireland for twenty-five data-processing jobs, it received 600 applications.) And McGraw-Hill was processing subscription renewal and marketing information for its magazines in nearby Galway. Indeed, literally millions of routine workers around the world were receiving information, converting it into computer readable form, and then sending it back—at the speed of electronic impulses—whence it came.

The simple coding of computer software has also entered into world commerce. India, with a large English-speaking population of technicians happy to do routine programming cheaply, is proving to be particularly attractive to global webs in need of this service. By 1990, Texas Instruments maintained a software development facility in Bangalore, linking fifty Indian programmers by satellite to TI's Dallas headquarters. Spurred by this and similar ventures, the Indian government was building a teleport in Poona, intended to make it easier and less expensive for many other firms to send their routine software design specifications for coding (Gupta 1989).

This shift of routine production jobs from advanced to developing nations is a great boon to many workers in such nations who otherwise would be jobless or working for much lower wages. These workers, in turn, now have more money with which to purchase symbolic-analytic services from advanced nations (often embedded within all sorts of complex products). The trend is also beneficial to everyone around the world who can now obtain highvolume, standardized products (including information and software) more cheaply than before.

But these benefits do not come without certain costs. In particular the burden is borne by those who no longer have good-paying routine production jobs within advanced economies like the United States. Many of these people used to belong to unions or at least benefited from prevailing wage rates established in collective bargaining agreements. But as the old corporate bureaucracies have flattened into global webs, bargaining leverage has been lost. Indeed, the tacit national bargain is no more.

Despite the growth in the number of new jobs in the United States, union membership has withered. In 1960, 35 percent of all nonagricultural workers in America belonged to a union. But by 1980 that portion had fallen to just under a quarter, and by 1989 to about 17 percent. Excluding government employees, union membership was down to 13.4 percent (US Government Printing Office 1989). This was a smaller proportion even than in the early 1930s, before the National Labor Relations Act created a legally protected right to labor representation. The drop in membership has been accompanied by a growing number of collective bargaining agreements to freeze wages at current levels, reduce wage levels of entering workers, or reduce wages overall. This is an important reason why the long economic recovery that began in 1982 produced a smaller rise in unit labor costs than any of the eight recoveries since World War II—the low rate of unemployment during its course notwithstanding.

Routine production jobs have vanished fastest in traditional unionized industries (autos, steel, and rubber, for example), where average wages have kept up with inflation. This is because the jobs of older workers in such industries are protected by seniority; the youngest workers are the first to be laid off. Faced with a choice of cutting wages or cutting the number of jobs, a majority of union members (secure in the knowledge that there are many who are junior to them who will be laid off first) often have voted for the latter.

Thus the decline in union membership has been most striking among young men entering the work force without a college education. In the early 1950s, more than 40 per cent of this group joined unions; by the late 1980s, less than 20 per cent (if public employees are excluded, less than 10 percent) (Katz and Revenga 1989). In steelmaking, for example, although many older workers remained employed, almost half of all routine steelmaking jobs in America vanished between 1974 and 1988 (from 480,000 to 260,000). Similarly with automobiles: During the 1980s, the United Auto Workers lost 500,000 members—one-third of their total at the start of the decade. General Motors alone cut 150,000 American production jobs during the 1980s (even as it added employment abroad). Another consequence of the same phenomenon: The gap between the average wages of unionized and nonunionized workers widened dramatically—from 14.6 per cent in 1973 to 20.4 per cent by end of the 1980s.[2] The lesson is clear. If you drop out of high school or have no more than a high school diploma, do not expect a good routine production job to be awaiting you.

Also vanishing are lower- and middle-level management jobs involving routine production. Between 1981 and 1986, more than 780,000 foremen, supervisors, and section chiefs lost their jobs through plant closings and layoffs (US Dept of Labor 1986). Large numbers of assistant division heads, assistant directors, assistant managers, and vice presidents also found themselves jobless. GM shed more than 40,000 white-collar employees and planned to eliminate another 25,000 by the mid-1990s (*Wall Street Journal 1990*). As America's core pyramids metamorphosed into global webs, many middle-level routine producers were as obsolete as routine workers on the line.

As has been noted, foreign-owned webs are hiring some Americans to do routine production in the United States. Philips, Sony, and Toyota factories are popping up all over—to the self-congratulatory applause of the nation's governors and mayors, who have lured them with promises of tax abatements and new sewers, among other amenities. But as these ebullient politicians will soon discover, the foreign-owned factories are highly automated and will become far more so in years to come. Routine production jobs account for a small fraction of the cost of producing most items in the United States and other advanced nations, and this fraction will continue to decline sharply as computer-integrated robots take over. In 1977 it took routine producers thirty-five hours to assemble an automobile in the United States; it is estimated that by the mid-1990s, Japanese-owned factories in America will be producing finished automobiles using only eight hours of a routine producer's time (International Motor Vehicles Program 1989).

The productivity and resulting wages of American workers who run such robotic machinery may be relatively high, but there may not be many such jobs to go around. A case in point: In the late 1980s, Nippon Steel joined with America's ailing Inland Steel to build a new $400 million cold-rolling mill fifty miles west of Gary, Indiana. The mill was celebrated for its state-of-the-art technology, which cut the time to produce a coil of steel from twelve days to about one hour. In fact, the entire plant could be run by a small team of technicians, which became clear when Inland subsequently closed two of its old cold-rolling mills, laying off hundreds of routine workers. Governors and mayors take note: Your much-ballyhooed foreign factories may end up employing distressingly few of your constituents.

Overall, the decline in routine jobs has hurt men more than women. This is because the routine production jobs held by men in highvolume metal-bending manufacturing industries had paid higher wages than the routine production jobs held by women in textiles and data processing. As both sets of jobs have been lost, American women in routine production have gained more equal footing with American men—equally poor footing, that is. This is a major reason why the gender gap between male and female wages began to close during the 1980s.

The second of the three boats, carrying in-person servers, is sinking as well, but somewhat more slowly and unevenly. Most in-person servers are paid at or just slightly above the minimum wage and many work only part-time, with the result that their take-home pay is modest, to say the least. Nor do they typically receive all the benefits (health care, life insurance, disability, and so forth) garnered by routine producers in large manufacturing corporations or by symbolic analysts affiliated with the more affluent threads of global webs.[3] In-person servers are sheltered from the direct effects of global competition and, like everyone else, benefit from access to lower-cost products from around the world. But they are not immune to its indirect effects.

For one thing, in-person servers increasingly compete with former routine production workers, who, no longer able to find well-paying routine production jobs, have few alternatives but to seek in-person service jobs. The Bureau of Labor Statistics estimates that of the 2.8 million manufacturing workers who lost their jobs during the early 1980s, fully one-third were rehired in service jobs paying at least 20 per cent less (US Dept of Labor 1986). In-person servers must also compete with high school graduates and dropouts who years before had moved easily into routine production jobs but no longer can. And if demographic predictions about the American work force in the first decades of the twenty-first century are correct (and they are likely to be, since most of the people who will comprise the work force are already identifiable), most new entrants into the job market will be black or Hispanic men, or women—groups that in years past have possessed relatively weak technical skills. This will result in an even larger number of people crowding into in-person services. Finally, in-person servers will be competing with growing numbers of immigrants, both legal and illegal, for whom in-person services will comprise the most accessible jobs. It is estimated that between the mid-1980s and the end of the century, about a quarter of all workers entering the American labor force will be immigrants (Federal Immigration and Naturalization Service 1986–7).

Perhaps the fiercest competition that in-person servers face comes from labor-saving machinery (much of it invented, designed, fabricated, or assembled in other nations, of course). Automated tellers, computerized cashiers, automatic car washes, robotized vending machines, self-service gasoline pumps, and all similar gadgets substitute for the human beings that customers once encountered. Even telephone operators are fast disappearing, as electronic sensors and voice simulators become capable of carrying on conversations that are reasonably intelligent, and always polite. Retail sales workers—among the largest groups of in-person servers—are similarly imperiled. Through personal computers linked to television screens, tomorrow's consumers will be able to buy furniture, appliances, and all sorts of electronic toys from their living rooms—examing the merchandise from all angles, selecting whatever color, size, special features, and price seem most appealing, and then transmitting the order instantly to warehouses from which the selections will be shipped directly to their homes. So, too, with financial transactions, airline and hotel reservations, rental car agreements, and similar contracts, which will be executed between consumers in their homes and computer banks somewhere else on the globe (Deutsch 1989).

Advanced economies like the United States will continue to generate sizable numbers of new in-person service jobs, of course, the automation of older ones notwithstanding. For every bank teller who loses her job to an automated teller, three new jobs open for aerobics instructors. Human beings, it seems, have an almost insatiable desire for personal attention. But the intense competition nevertheless ensures that the wages of in-person servers will remain relatively low. In-person servers—working on their own, or else dispersed widely amid many small establishments, filling all sorts of personal-care niches—cannot readily organize themselves into labor unions or create powerful lobbies to limit the impact of such competition.

In two respects, demographics will work in favor of in-person servers, buoying their collective boat slightly. First, as has been noted, the rate of growth of the American work force is slowing. In particular, the number of younger workers is shrinking. Between 1985 and 1995, the number of eighteen- to twenty-four-year-olds will have declined by 17.5 per cent. Thus, employers will have more incentive to hire and train in-person servers whom they might previously have avoided. But this demographic relief from the competitive pressures will be only temporary. The cumulative procreative energies of the postwar baby-boomers (born between 1946 and 1964) will result in a new surge of workers by 2010 or thereabouts (Johnson, Packer *et al.*, 1987). And immigration—both legal and illegal—shows every sign of increasing in years to come.

Next, by the second decade of the twenty-first century, the number of Americans aged sixty-five and over will be rising precipitously, as the baby-boomers reach retirement age and live longer. Their life expectancies will lengthen not just because fewer of them will have smoked their way to their graves and more will have eaten better than their parents, but also because they will receive all sorts of expensive drugs and therapies designed to keep them alive—barely. By 2035, twice as many Americans will be elderly as in 1988, and the number of octogenarians is expected to triple. As these decaying baby-boomers ingest all the chemicals and receive all the treatments, they will need a great deal of personal attention. Millions of deteriorating bodies will require nurses, nursing-home operators, hospital administrators, orderlies, home-care providers, hospice aides, and technicians to operate and maintain all the expensive machinery that will monitor and temporarily stave off final disintegration. There might even be a booming market for euthanasia specialists. In-person servers catering to the old and ailing will be in strong demand.[4]

One small problem: The decaying baby-boomers will not have enough money to pay for these services. They will have used up their personal savings years before. Their Social Security payments will, of course, have been used by the government to pay for the previous generation's retirement and to finance much of the budget deficits of the 1980s. Moreover, with relatively fewer young Americans in the population, the supply of housing will likely exceed the demand, with the result that the boomers' major investments—their homes—will be worth less (in inflation-adjusted dollars) when they retire than they planned for. In consequence, the huge cost of caring for the graying boomers will fall on many of the same people who will be paid to care for them. It will be like a great sump pump: In-person servers of the twenty-first century will have an abundance of healthcare jobs, but a large portion of their earnings will be devoted to Social Security payments and income taxes, which will in turn be used to pay their salaries. The net result: no real improvement in their standard of living.

The standard of living of in-person servers also depends, indirectly, on the standard of living of the Americans they serve who are engaged in world commerce. To the extent that *these* Americans are richly rewarded by the rest of the world for what they contribute, they will have more money to lavish upon in-person services. Here we find the only form of 'trickle-down' economics that has a basis in reality. A waitress in a town whose major factory has just been closed is unlikely to earn a high wage or enjoy much job security; in a swank resort populated by film producers and banking moguls, she is apt to do reasonably well. So, too, with nations. In-person servers in Bangladesh may spend their days performing roughly the same tasks as in-person servers in the United States, but have a far lower standard of living for their efforts. The difference comes in the value that their customers add to the world economy.

Unlike the boats of routine producers and in-person servers, however, the vessel containing America's symbolic analysts is rising. Worldwide demand for their insights is growing as the ease and speed of communicating them steadily increases. Not every symbolic analyst is rising as quickly or as dramatically as every other, of course; symbolic analysts at the low end are barely holding their own in the world economy. But symbolic analysts at the top are in such great demand worldwide that they have difficulty keeping track of all their earnings. Never before in history has opulence on such a scale been gained by people who have earned it, and done so legally.

Among symbolic analysts in the middle range are American scientists and researchers who are busily selling their discoveries to global enterprise webs. They are not limited to American customers. If the strategic brokers in General Motors' headquarters refuse to pay a high price for a new means of making high-strength ceramic engines dreamed up by a team of engineers affiliated with Carnegie-Mellon University in Pittsburgh, the strategic brokers of Honda or Mercedes-Benz are likely to be more than willing.

So, too, with the insights of America's ubiquitous management consultants, which are being sold for large sums to eager entrepreneurs in Europe and Latin America. Also, the insights of America's energy consultants sold for even larger sums to Arab sheikhs. American design engineers are providing insights to Olivetti, Mazda, Siemens, and other global webs; American marketers, techniques for learning what worldwide consumers will buy; American advertisers, ploys for ensuring that they actually do. American architects are issuing designs and blueprints for opera houses, art galleries, museums, luxury hotels, and residential complexes in the world's major cities; American commercial property developers, marketing these properties to worldwide investors and purchasers.

Americans who specialize in the gentle art of public relations are in demand by corporations, governments, and politicians in virtually every nation. So, too, are American political consultants, some of whom, at this writing, are advising the Hungarian Socialist Party, the remnant of Hungary's ruling Communists, on how to salvage a few parliamentary seats in the nation's first free election in more than forty years. Also at this writing, a team of American agricultural consultants are advising the managers of a Soviet farm collective employing 1,700 Russians eighty miles outside Moscow. As noted, American investment bankers and lawyers specializing in financial circumnavigations are selling their insights to Asians and Europeans who are eager to discover how to make large amounts of money by moving large amounts of money.

Developing nations, meanwhile, are hiring American civil engineers to advise on building roads and dams. The present thaw in the Cold War will no doubt expand these opportunities. American engineers from Bechtel (a global firm notable for having employed both Caspar Weinberger and George Shultz for much larger sums than either earned in the Reagan administration) have begun help in the Soviets design and install a new generation of nuclear reactors. Nations also are hiring American bankers and lawyers to help them renegotiate the terms of their loans with global banks, and Washington lobbyists to help them with Congress, the Treasury, the World Bank, the IMF, and other politically sensitive institutions. In fits of obvious desperation, several nations emerging from communism have even hired American economists to teach them about capitalism.

Almost everyone around the world is buying the skills and insights of Americans who manipulate oral and visual symbols—musicians, sound engineers, film producers, makeup artists, directors, cinematographers, actors and actresses, boxers, scriptwriters, songwriters, and set designers. Among the wealthiest of symbolic analysts are Steven Spielberg, Bill Cosby, Charles Schutz, Eddie Murphy, Sylvester Stallone, Madonna, and other star directors and performers—who are almost as well known on the streets of Dresden and Tokyo as in the Back Bay of Boston. Less well rewarded but no less renowned are the unctuous anchors on Turner Broadcasting's Cable News, who appear daily, via satellite, in places ranging from Vietnam to Nigeria. Vanna White is the world's most watched game-show hostess. Behind each of these familiar faces is a collection of American problem-solvers, -identifiers, and -brokers who train, coach, advise, promote, amplify, direct, groom, represent, and otherwise add value to their talents.[5]

There are also the insights of senior American executives who occupy the world headquarters of global 'American' corporations and the national or regional headquarters of global 'foreign' corporations. Their insights are duly exported to the rest of the world through the webs of global enterprise. IBM does not export many machines from the United States, for example. Big Blue makes machines all over the globe and services them on the spot. Its prime American exports are symbolic and analytic. From IBM's world headquarters in Armonk, New York, emanate strategic brokerage and related management services bound for the rest of the world. In return, IBM's top executives are generously rewarded.

The most important reason for this expanding world market and increasing global demand for the symbolic and analytic insights of Americans has been the dramatic improvement in worldwide communication and transportation technologies. Designs, instructions, advice, and visual and audio symbols can be communicated more and more rapidly around the globe, with ever-greater precision and at ever-lower cost. Madonna's voice can be transported to billions of listeners, with perfect clarity, on digital compact disks. A new invention emanating from engineers in Battelle's laboratory in Columbus, Ohio, can be sent almost anywhere via modem, in a form that will allow others to examine it in three dimensions through enhanced computer graphics. When face-to-face meetings are still required—and videoconferencing will not suffice—it is relatively easy for designers, consultants, advisers, artists, and executives to board supersonic jets and, in a matter of hours, meet directly with their worldwide clients, customers, audiences, and employees.

With rising demand comes rising compensation. Whether in the form of licensing fees, fees for service, salaries, or shares in final profits, the economic result is much the same. There are also non-pecuniary rewards. One of the best-kept secrets among symbolic analysts is that so many of them enjoy their work. In fact, much of it does not count as work at all, in the traditional sense. The work of routine producers and in-person servers is typically monotonous; it causes muscles to tire or weaken and involves little independence or discretion. The 'work' of symbolic analysts, by contrast, often involves puzzles, experiments, games, a significant amount of chatter, and substantial discretion over what to do next. Few routine producers or in-person servers would 'work' if they did not need to earn the money. Many symbolic analysts would 'work' even if money were no object.

At midcentury, when America was a national market dominated by core pyramid-shaped corporations, there were constraints on the earnings of people at the highest rungs. First and most obviously, the market for their services was largely limited to the borders of the nation. In addition, whatever conceptual value they might contribute was small relative to the value gleaned from large scale—and it was dependent on large scale for whatever income it was to summon. Most of the problems to be identified and solved had to do with enhancing the efficiency of production and improving the flow of materials, parts, assembly, and distribution. Inventors searched for the rare breakthrough revealing an entirely new product to be made in high volume; management consultants, executives, and engineers thereafter tried to speed and synchronize its manufacture, to better achieve scale efficiencies; advertisers and marketers sought then to whet the public's appetite for the standard item that emerged. Since whitecollar earnings increased with larger scale, there was considerable incentive to expand the firm; indeed, many of America's core corporations grew far larger than scale economies would appear to have justified.

By the 1990s, in contrast, the earnings of symbolic analysts were limited neither by the size of the national market nor by the volume of production of the firms with which they were affiliated. The marketplace was worldwide, and conceptual value was high relative to value added from scale efficiencies.

There had been another constraint on high earnings, which also gave way by the 1990s. At midcentury, the compensation awarded to top executives and advisers of the largest of America's core corporations could not be grossly out of proportion to that of low-level production workers. It would be unseemly for executives who engaged in highly visible rounds of bargaining with labor unions, and who routinely responded to government requests to moderate prices, to take home wages and benefits wildly in excess of what other Americans earned. Unless white-collar executives restrained themselves, moreover, blue-collar production workers could not be expected to restrain their own demands for higher wages. Unless both groups exercised restraint, the government could not be expected to forbear from imposing direct controls and regulations.

At the same time, the wages of production workers could not be allowed to sink too low; lest there be insufficient purchasing power in the economy. After all, who would buy all the goods flowing out of American factories if not American workers? This, too, was part of the tacit bargain struck between American managers and their workers.

Recall the oft-repeated corporate platitude of the era about the chief executive's responsibility to carefully weigh and balance the interests of the corporation's disparate stakeholders. Under the stewardship of the corporate statesman, no set of stakeholders—least of all white-collar executives—was to gain a disproportionately large share of the benefits of corporate activity; nor was any stakeholder—especially the average worker—to be left with a share that was disproportionately small. Banal though it was, this idea helped to maintain the legitimacy of the core American corporation in the eyes of most Americans, and to ensure continued economic growth.

But by the 1990s, these informal norms were evaporating, just as (and largely because) the core American corporation was vanishing. The links between top executives and the American production worker were fading: An ever-increasing number of subordinates and contractees were foreign, and a steadily growing number of American routine producers were working for foreign-owned firms. An entire cohort of middle-level managers, who had once been deemed 'white collar,' had disappeared; and, increasingly, American executives were exporting their insights to global enterprise webs.

As the American corporation itself became a global web almost indistinguishable from any other, its stakeholders were turning into a large and diffuse group, spread over the world. Such global stakeholders were less visible, and far less noisy, than national stakeholders. And as the American corporation sold its goods and services all over the world, the purchasing power of American workers became far less relevant to its economic survival.

Thus have the inhibitions been removed. The salaries and benefits of America's top executives, and many of their advisers and consultants, have soared to what years before would have been unimaginable heights, event as those of other Americans have declined.

NOTES

1. The reader should note, of course, that lower wages in other areas of the world are of no particular attraction to global capital unless workers there are sufficiently productive to make the labor cost of producing *each unit* lower there than in higher-wage regions. Productivity in many low-wage areas of the world has improved due to the ease with which state-of-the-art factories and equipment can be installed there.
2. US Department of Commerce, Bureau of Labor Statistics, 'Wages of Unionized and Non-Unionized Workers', various issues.
3. The growing portion of the American labor force engaged in in-person services, relative to routine production, thus helps explain why the number of Americans lacking health insurance increased by at least 6 million during the 1980s.
4. The Census Bureau estimates that by the year 2000, at least 12 million Americans will work in health services—well over 6 per cent of the total work force.
5. In 1989, the entertainment business summoned to the United States $5.5 billion in foreign earnings—making it among the nation's largest export industries, just behind aerospace. US Department of Commerce, International Trade Commission, 'Composition of US Exports', various issues.

Globalization, Knowledge and the Myth of the Magnet Economy

Phillip Brown and Hugh Lauder

Introduction: The Rise of the Magnet Economy

The dominant view today is that we have entered a global knowledge economy, driven by the application of new technologies and collapsing barriers to international trade and investment. This has accelerated the evolutionary path from low to a high skills economy. Becker (2002) has depicted an 'age of human capital', where the prosperity of individuals and nations rests on the skills, knowledge, and enterprise of all rather than the elite few that drove industrial capitalism in the twentieth century. This view is reflected in the central role of education in national economic and social policy. Not only is education seen to hold the key to a competitive economy but it is also seen as the foundation of social justice and social cohesion: 'Our future success depends upon mobilizing even more effectively the imagination, creativity, skills and talents of all our people. And it depends on using that knowledge and understanding to build economic strength and social harmony' (DfES 2003: 2). This view echoes the prophets of the post-industrial economy (Bell 1973; Drucker 1993). Bell predicted that the growing importance of 'knowledge' work, reflected in the historical shift from blue-collar to white-collar work, would significantly raise the demand for educated workers, who would enjoy greater autonomy in their work. The expansion of tertiary education and lifelong learning reflects this growing demand for high skilled workers.

Drucker (1993) went further by arguing that we have entered a new stage of post-capitalist development, where it is no longer ownership of capital that generates wealth creation but knowledge. This, he argues, has led to a power shift from the owners and managers of capital to knowledge workers, thereby marking a new stage of capitalist development. In these terms, the prosperity of individuals, companies, and nations have come to depend on human and intellectual capital rather than on issues of ownership that defined Marxist accounts of the capitalist system.

This evolutionary model of an inexorable shift from physical to mental labour is not limited to the changing relationship between education and the occupational structure within specific societies. It is extended to include the relationship between nation-states. The rise of the global knowledge-based economy is believed to remove much of the source of conflict and strife between nations. Trade liberalization is presented as a 'win–win' opportunity for both developing and developed nations.[1] The territorial disputes that drove nations to war in pursuit of land and material wealth become less important in terms of power, privilege, and wealth. According to Rosecrance (1999: p. xi):

> In the past, material forces were dominant in national growth, prestige, and power; now products of the mind take

Reproduced from Globalization, Societies and Education, vol. 4. I. pp. 25–57, 2006.

precedence. Nations can transfer most of their material production thousands of miles away, centring their attention on research and development and product design at home. The result is a new and productive partnership between 'head' nations, which design products, and 'body' nations, which manufacture them.

This shift from *bloody wars* to *knowledge wars* represents the highest stage in evolutionary development as nations put down their weaponry to concentrate on the competition for ideas, skills, and knowledge that contribute to economic advantage. This represents a logical extension of muscle to mental power, given that 'it is knowledge, not cheap labor; symbols, not raw materials, that embody and add value' (Toffler 1990: 82)

These new rules of wealth creation rest on 'outsmarting' economic rivals. Schools, colleges, universities, think tanks, design centres, and research laboratories are now on the front line in the search for competitive advantage. This is reflected in current attempts by organizations such as the OECD's PISA studies and the International Education Association (IEA) to develop comparative measures of academic performance. And as 'standards of organisational performance have gone global' (Carnevale and Porro 1994: 13), the quality of a nation's human resources are judged on relative rather than absolute criteria. Therefore, it is not only the qualities of individual students that are being assessed, but the quality of national systems of education and training as a whole.[2]

As Gordon Brown (2004), the UK's Chancellor of the Exchequer has suggested: 'if we are to succeed in a world where offshoring can be an opportunity . . . our mission [is] to make the British people the best educated, most skilled, best trained country in the world'. This mobilization of the people to the common 'educational' cause has many of the features of conscription. In short, it is asserted that there is no other source of individual, family, or national welfare as nation-states are largely powerless to protect domestic markets from international competition or the strictures imposed on interest rates and public spending by the financial markets. Moreover, state support of uncompetitive businesses will, so the argument goes, hinder economic prosperity as competitiveness is best achieved through open competition within the international arena. Indeed, some view 'national' labour markets as an impediment to the operation of a global market for labour, within which workers are rewarded according to their contribution, based on skills and productivity rather than national political settlements between government, employers, and trade unions (Reich 1991).

There are, therefore, no British, German, or American jobs, only British, German, or American workers who confront the ultimate judgement of the global market-place. The problem this poses for workers in the developed economies is that the Fordist settlement of the last century based on low skills for relatively high wages is no longer an option as routine production can now be fulfilled in low-wage economies for a fraction of the cost. Therefore, jobs that can deliver a living wage to 'affluent' workers depend on the creation of high-quality goods and services within niche markets that meet the precise needs of customers and clients.[3]

Robert Reich (1991) explained the growth in income polarization in the United States in the 1980s—that continued to grow into the twenty-first century—in terms of the relative ability of workers to sell their skills, knowledge, and insights in the global job market. He argues that the incomes of the top 20 per cent have pulled away from the rest because of their ability to break free of the constraints of local and national labour markets. The global labour market offers far greater rewards to 'symbolic analysts' or 'knowledge workers' precisely because the market for their services has grown, whereas those workers who remain locked into national or local markets have experienced stagnation or a decline in income.

Reich, amongst others, interprets rising wage inequalities as proof of both the realities of the global labour market and as evidence of the failure of the existing education system. The reason why income inequalities have grown is not explained as a 'structural' problem—that the proportion of high-skilled, high-waged jobs is limited by the occupational structure in which many people are not required to use many of their talents for a living—but due to the failure of the education system to make a larger proportion of the workforce employable in the global competition for high-skilled, high-waged work. As Reich (1991: 247) suggests:

> Unlike America's old hierarchical and somewhat isolated economy, whose white-collar jobs were necessarily limited in proportion to the number of blue-collar jobs beneath them, the global economy imposes no particular limit upon the number of Americans who can sell symbolic-analytic services worldwide. In principle, all of America's routine production workers could become symbolic analysts and let their old jobs drift overseas to developing nations.

It is believed, therefore, that there is now a global auction for jobs. Low-skilled jobs will be auctioned on price and will tend to migrate to low-waged economies such as those in Asia or Eastern Europe, while high-skilled jobs will continue to attract higher wages. These jobs will be auctioned on 'quality' rather than price, including the skills, knowledge, and insights of employees. The main bidders for 'quality' jobs are assumed to be today's leading economies. This offers the potential for countries such as the Britain, France, and the United States to become *magnet* economies, attracting a disproportionate share of these high-skilled, high-waged jobs (Brown and Lauder 2001).

The proponents of the magnet economy also assume a transformation in the relationship between education and social justice. In the second half of the twentieth century the ideology of meritocracy was premised on the idea that a fair and efficient society depended on the creation of a level playing field that would give all within that society the chance to compete on equal terms regardless of social class, gender, or ethnicity. Today, it is assumed that the nature of this competition has changed. The occupational structure is no longer restricted as noted in the above quotation from Reich. The children from wealthy backgrounds no longer have an unfair advantage over children from disadvantaged backgrounds because of the international character of the labour market. What holds back the children from disadvantaged background is not the fact that those from privileged backgrounds enjoy all the educational advantages, but their lack of credentials, knowledge, and skills, which prevents them from competing in the global competition for high-skilled, high-wage employment.

Therefore, a 'fair' educational system is no longer one that attempts to create a level playing field but one dedicated to raising the standards of all, and facilitating greater access to higher education in order to arm the workforce with the credentials, knowledge, and skills that are valued in the global labour market. Hence, competition for the best jobs is not between neighbours but nations. Holding back the most talented or preventing parents from investing in private education is likely to damage national competitiveness as these are the people most likely to drive the economy. This does not prevent other students fulfilling their aspirations because the same jobs are available to all those with the energy, talent, and commitment to develop marketable skills within the global economy.

While the policy implications of the magnet economy have focused on the job prospects of the existing population, this may also work in reverse. In other words, the developed economies are not only in competition for quality jobs but also for the most talented workers; this has been a feature of competitive strategies of both the United States and Singapore (Alarcon 1999; Low 2002). It has also become a more prominent feature of UK policy in an attempt to overcome skill shortages and to redress the tendency for it to be a net exporter of inventors, scientists, and entrepreneurs.

An Assessment

This chapter will now assess[4] the underlying assumptions of the magnet economy and especially the changing relationship between education, jobs, and rewards. We will argue that while there has been a fundamental change in the relationship between education, economy, and society it is far removed from the policy rhetoric of the knowledge economy described above. Our account of the social and economic realities of the early twenty-first century will focus on four facets of the dominant policy discourse.

First, we examine the idea that countries such as Britain and America can become high-skilled, high-waged 'magnet' economies, able to resolve problems of labour demand and income inequalities through educational reform. We will argue that it fails to understand how multinational companies are developing human resource strategies that increase the likelihood of a larger proportion of high-skilled jobs being established in relatively low-waged economies. Governments in the developed economies have yet to acknowledge the full consequences of countries such as China and India expanding their educational systems to compete for high-skilled work within key sectors of the global economy or trends towards the 'offshoring' of skilled along with semi-skilled and unskilled jobs.

Secondly, the official policy discourse is driven by a view of human capital that assumes a tightening bond between education, jobs and rewards, with a rising wage dividend for those who invest in higher education.[5] We will argue that the basic premise of the rhetoric concerning human capital—that investments in education and training lead to rising wages—is not a universal law of economic development but a 'transitional' case where there are no guarantees that the educational system will meet the expectations of students, families, or governments.

The global economy cannot keep pace with the individual demand for high-skilled work as access to tertiary education becomes more widespread both within and across countries. The global expansion of tertiary education leads to downward pressure on the incomes of skilled workers in the developed economies along with some upward pressure on those in developing economies. But at the same time there are trends towards 'winner-takes-all' markets that reveal that people with similar qualifications in the same occupations, organizations, and countries experience increasing polarization in earnings and future career prospects.

Thirdly, the anticipated powershift from employers to 'knowledge' workers has not materialized. The view that there will continue to be an exponential increase in the demand for knowledge workers who will be encouraged to use their creative energies to the full, is ahistorical. It fails to take account of the tendency for periods of rapid technological innovation to be followed by standardization (Weber 1945). This is as true for 'knowledge' workers today as it was for craft workers in the fledgling automobile industry at the beginning of the twentieth century. A feature of paid work under capitalism is that the nature of jobs and skills change. There is no credential ladder-to-heaven which once climbed leads to guaranteed high status and rewarding work. The competitive pressures created by economic globalization have led companies to limit the discretion of knowledge workers and 'devalue' the contribution of many. It is, therefore, not just a matter of the oversupply of skills that threatens the equation between high skills and high income, where 'knowledge' is routinized it can be substituted with less-skilled and cheaper workers at home or further afield.

Fourthly, it will be argued that the emphasis on individual employability and raising the educational standards of all ignores increasing 'positional' conflict in access to education and tough-entry jobs (Hirsch 1977; Brown 2003). As the oversupply of graduates forces many to enter employment that does not utilize their knowledge, skills, or creativity, the competition for elite jobs intensifies, leaving employers with problems of how to select between large numbers of highly qualified candidates and how to legitimate their selection decisions (Brown and Hesketh 2004). It has also led social elites to find new forms of social closure to give them a competitive advantage.

Therefore the question of 'who does what job' will continue to depend on a competition for credentials that will reflect material, cultural, and educational inequalities in the social background of students unless strenuous attempts are made to create a level playing field. Issues of equality of opportunity have become more rather than less important. But these questions can no longer be restricted to the politics of individual nation-states but have increasingly global ramifications. In sum, this analysis challenges the major tenets of the dominant discourse of education, knowledge, and the global economy. To grasp its full implications each of the above points will be discussed in more detail.

Magnet Economy or Global 'Dutch' Auction?

From a Western perspective the idea of the magnet economy offers a comforting picture of a global economy in which low-skill, low-wage work is shipped to developing countries while prosperous Western workers make good incomes through their knowledge and creativity (Reich 1991). This is based on the assumption the most of the foreign direct investment (FDI) in research, development, design, marketing, legal services, and other areas of high-skilled activity will be concentrated in those developed economies at the forefront of the knowledge revolution.

A major weakness of this view is its failure to understand how multinational companies are transforming their corporate strategies to take advantage of the global potential not only to sell products and services but to transform how and where they produce, and this is no longer restricted to locating 'screwdriver' production plants or 'back office' data processing in low-wage economies. It also fails to understand the skill formation strategies being adopted by countries including China, India, and Russia. The comparative advantage of a high-skilled workforce in the developed nations is understood as a comparative disadvantage in less-developed economies, and many developing economies are determined to close the skills gap. In China, an official policy statement on employment prospects to 2020 states:

> It is necessary to fully utilize various education resources, strengthen the improvement in human resources quality, direct major efforts to the promotion of quality-oriented education, stress cultivation of practical abilities, and make efforts in improving education quality, so as to train millions of high-caliber workers, thousands of special talents and a large number of outstanding innovative talents for the socialist modernization drive.[6]

This has led to the rapid expansion in the global supply of high-skilled workers that also has major implications for the future of high-skilled, high-waged work in Western nations. Table 22.1 shows that China had six times as many university students as the UK and almost as many as the US in 2001. It also has plans to increase university numbers to 16 million by 2005, including 600,000 engaged in postgraduate studies. This amounts to 15 per cent of age cohort. Even more ambitious is the plan to increase enrolment to Chinese senior high schools from 27 million in 2000 to 46 million in 2005.[7] The expansion of higher education in India is following a similar path. There are plans to increase the participation rate of 18–23-year-olds in higher education from 6 per cent in 2002 to 10 per cent in 2007.[8]

While of degree of scepticism is required with respect to the accuracy of these statistics they show that in six years higher education numbers in China, India, and Russia have almost doubled from a combined total of 15.8 to 30 million students. This is almost double the combined total for the US and the UK at 15.7 million. There is therefore a good supply of highly qualified Indian, Chinese, and Russian workers entering the global labour market.

Rather than a magnetic attraction to a specific location, global economic integration has enabled companies to create a new spatial division of labour for high-skilled activities including research, innovation, and product development, as well as for low-skilled, low-waged work. Given the importance attached to knowledge-intensive industries as a source of new high-skilled employment in the

Table 22.1 The expansion of tertiary education in selected emerging and developed economies

	Tertiary education (ISCED 5 and 6): Total enrolment (000s)					
	1970	1980	1990	1995	1999/2000	2000/2001
United States	8,498	12,097	13,710	14,261	13,202	13,596
France	801	1077	1,699	2,092	2,015	2,032
United Kingdom	601	827	1,258	1,821	2,024	2,067
India	2,472	3,545	4,951	5,696	9,404	9,834
Brazil	430	1,409	1,540	1,869	2,457	2,781
China	48	1,663	3,822	5,622	9,399	12,148
Russia	n/a	5,700	5,100	4,458*	n/a	8,030

*1994

Source: UNESCO See Brown et al., (2005).

developed economies, we will use the electronics industry to expose the problems underlying the idea of the magnet economy.

In the 'take-off' of the electronics industry in the United States during the 1980s, the two major regional areas, Silicon Valley and Route 128, attracted $12 billion in venture capital (Saxenian 1994). At today's prices that is a considerable sum, if thought of in terms of potential Foreign Direct Investment (FDI). Investment of this magnitude can certainly produce high rewards and productivity for those who create intellectual property. However, the nature of globalization in the electronics industry has meant that such investment does not translate into the employment of large numbers of skilled workers concentrated in the West, far less one country.

In the 1960s and 1970s companies such as Ford, IBM, or Siemens were characterized as 'national champions' as they not only paid taxes that contributed to the public exchequer but also offered mass employment within the home nation. However, the IBMs and Siemens of the post-war period that controlled all elements of hardware and software production have given way to a fragmented horizontal structure across national boundaries that combine speed and flexibility, while off-loading corporate risk. Facilitated by the personal computer, the internet, and an increasing supply of highly qualified employees in developing countries, these networks extend across the globe, particularly to the Pacific Rim, India, and Eastern Europe.

Saxenian (2002) has charted the development of this industry.[9] The story starts with an increasing numbers of Taiwanese, Indian, and Chinese students enrolled in Ph.D. programmes in the United States.[10] During the 1980s Taiwan sent more doctoral students to the United States than did any other country. The first generation of these students tended to stay in the United States, working in the semi-conductor industry before returning home to establish their own businesses. Encouraged by government policies approximately 6,000 doctoral engineers were returning home each year by the mid-1990s (Saxenian 2002). The combination of the knowledge and networks established in the United States by the first generation of IT entrepreneurs, coupled with the critical mass of expertise of returnee graduates, enabled Taiwan to capitalize on the possibilities of a horizontally structured industry operating across national borders.

The emergence of the electronics industry in Bangalore in India also demonstrates how less-skilled employment in the IT industry was exported from Western economies to enclaves in the developing world (Kobrin 2000). The education and training of electronic engineers provided the necessary human capital for the electronics industry in Bangalore to take off. But contrary to the view that only lower-skilled work would be subject to price competition, the IT industry suggests that this is at best wishful thinking. India's tertiary education system now trains over 67,000 computer science professionals annually and another 200,000 enrol each year in private software training institutions.

The cost advantage to companies employing software professionals in India in comparison to the United States is presented in Table 22.2.

It can be seen from Table 22.2 that Indian programmers are around fourteen times cheaper than

Table 22.2 Salaries of software professionals in the United States and India, 1997

	United states (USD per annum)	India* (USD per annum)
Help desk support technician	25,000–35,500	4,400–7,000
Programmer	32,500–39,000	2,200–2,900
Network administrator	36,000–55,000	15,700–19,200
Programmer analyst	39,000–50,000	5,400–7,000
Systems analyst	46,000–57,500	8,700–10,700
Software developer	49,000–67,500	15,700–19,200
Database administrator	54,000–67,500	15,700–19,200

Note: Figures are starting salaries for large establishments employing more than 50 software professionals. They may be marginally lower for small firms. Salaries for a particular designation vary owing to factors such as educational and experience profile of the professional; platform of operation; nature of the assignment (contract/full-time); location of the employer; and the additional technical/professional certification.

* Converted at exchange rate of INR 41.50/USD.

Source: INFAC, Bombay (1998). OECD Information Technology Outlook, (Paris: OECD, 2000): 140.

those in the United States. But much of the work of Indians in the past has been at the low end of the market. Saxenian (2000*a*) has shown that the annual revenue per employee in the Indian software industry was $15,000–20,000 whereas in Israel and Ireland the corresponding figure was $100,000 per employee. However, wages have risen in Bangalore and there is now concern that, with increasing competition from China, Russia, and Romania, amongst others, the industry will price itself out of the market unless it moves into higher value added production (Yamamoto 2004). This may be facilitated by the large numbers of Indian entrepreneurs in Silicon Valley where in 1998 they were running more than 775 technology companies, accounting for $3.6 billion in sales and 16,600 jobs (Saxenian 2000*a*).

This example highlights the flip side of the magnet economy. If the latter assumes a virtuous circle of high skills and high-waged employment contributing to national prosperity, the converse is that of a global auction. This operates as a Dutch auction, where unlike at an art or antique auction where the highest bidder wins, in a Dutch auction corporate investors are able to play off nations, communities, and workers as bidding spirals downwards and MNCs win concessions such as cheap rents and tax holidays in exchange for investments in jobs, technology, and commercial property (Brown and Lauder 1997: 2).

The policy discourse of the knowledge economy assumes that the competition for high-skilled employment would be fought out between the developed economies as low-skilled, low-waged work would migrate to less-developed economies (Reich 1991). However, a number of less-developed countries including India, China, and Malaysia are increasingly competing for high-skilled work that could reduce the bargaining power of high-skilled workers in the West. Hence, high-skilled workers in the developed economies may be subject to the same price competition that has to date been limited to those in routine occupations. The consequence is that many of the jobs undertaken by university graduates in Britain and America may be done cheaper elsewhere.

This analysis of the IT industry shows that even when there is a concentration of technology firms such as in Silicon Valley the cost of training and labour can be reduced by hiring qualified workers from low-waged economies. In the United States, 55,000 qualified workers from India were granted temporary visas in 1999 (Saxenian 2000*b*). Hence, there does appear to be a magnetic effect, where qualified workers in less-developed economies are attracted to work in the developed economies. But here it is high-skilled workers rather than high-skilled jobs that are being attracted: precisely the opposite effect to that assumed in the official discourse surrounding the magnet economy.

While the importance of 'talent' has been a key component of American capitalism for over a century, in the current economic climate it may reduce the incentives for companies to invest in the training of indigenous workers and lead employers to reduce the cost of indigenous knowledge workers. 'Guest' workers typically do the same jobs for fewer rewards and inferior contracts of employment. Hence, even in areas where there is increased demand for high-skilled workers there is a growing propensity to import qualified labour rather than invest in the skills of the less qualified and socially disadvantaged.[11]

It might be argued that the electronics industry, although clearly significant, is but one, perhaps atypical, example. However, a characteristic of knowledge-intensive industries is that they do not require large numbers of skilled workers (Keep 2000). In 2004, the internet company Google had a market capitalization of around $30bn. but employed just 2,000 people. At the same time Ebay had a capitalization of around $54bn. and employed 4,400. Tesco, a leading UK retail company, had a capitalization similar to Google (£19bn.) but employed 240,000 worldwide.

It is also important not to exaggerate the impact of globalization, as not all knowledge work is structured by industries across the globe. For example, research and development for multinationals tends to remain in the home country of multinationals (Brown, Green, and Lauder 2001), although there is evidence that this has begun to change in some MNCs.[12] There is a significant number of managers and professionals whose livelihood depends more on the state of domestic rather than global markets, especially those working in the public sector. But this does not undermine our argument that income inequalities and positional conflict cannot be resolved through the creation of a high-skill, high-wage magnet economy.

It might also be claimed that while knowledge-intensive industries do not require vast armies of skilled workers, they have downstream effects in terms of knowledge and wealth, that generate new business enterprise and support services. But this does not follow. It is clear, for example, that Bangalore is an enclave and that its success has had a limited 'knock-on' effect for the rest of India (Kobrin 2000).

Equally, while extolling the virtues of Silicon Valley as the high temple of the knowledge economy, Finegold (1999: 65) recognized that knowledge workers live side by side with:

> a large much lower skilled and lower-paid workforce ... income inequality between these high and low skilled workers appears to be widening in these regions, even more than in the USA as a whole; in Silicon Valley the average earnings of the top 20 per cent of households rose steadily from 1991 to 1997 to over $130,000 while the earnings of the bottom 20 per cent fell 8 per cent to under £35,000.

The contrasting fortunes of employees in Silicon Valley brings into relief Castells's (1998: 1) view that the knowledge-based, network economy can link up 'valuable people and activities from all over the world, while switching off from the networks of power and wealth, people and territories dubbed as irrelevant'.[13] Britain, along with America, is not a high-skilled, high-waged economy but one in which this accurately reflects the fortunes of a minority of workers, who stand alongside an increasingly large proportion of well-qualified but low-waged workers, who in turn stand beside the low-skilled and low-waged.

This analysis suggests that the imperative to stimulate demand for high-skilled, high-waged employment will remain a key policy objective in all the developed economies. However, against a backdrop of mass higher education, the dominant discourse overestimates the extent to which even the most successful nations within the global economy can create mass high-skilled employment (see Table 22.3).

Indeed, the emphasis on high-skilled work and labour-market flexibility as a means to survival in

Table 22.3 Employment by education and training category, United States, 2000–2010

Most significant source of education or training	Number		Distribution %	
	2000	2010	2000	2010
Total, all occupations (thousands)	145,954	167,754	100.0	100.0
Bachelor's or higher	30,072	36,556	20.7	21.8
First professional degree	2,034	2,404	1.4	1.4
Doctoral degree	1,492	1,845	1.0	1.1
Master's degree	1,426	1,759	1.0	1.0
Bachelor's or higher degree, plus work experience	7,319	8,741	5.0	5.2
Bachelor's degree	17,801	21,807	12.2	13.0
Associate degree or postsecondary vocational award	11,761	14,600	8.1	8.7
Associate degree	5,083	6,710	3.5	4.0
Postsecondary vocational award	6,678	7,891	4.6	4.7
Work-related training	103,760	116,597	71.3	69.5
Work experience in a related occupation	10,456	11,559	7.2	6.9
Long-term on-the-job training	12,435	13,373	8.5	8.0
Moderate-term on-the-job training	27,671	30,794	19.0	18.4
Short-term on-the-job training	53,198	60,871	36.5	36.3

Source: Daniel E. Hecker, 'Employment Outlook: 2000–10 Occupational Employment Projections to 2010', *Monthly Labor Review*, November 2001, 83.

the global economy only holds true if the supply of relevant skills is limited. Once there is an oversupply, the competition shifts to a global auction based on price and the assumption that skill can provide workers with a shelter from the drive to lower wage costs no longer holds.

The implication of the analysis so far is that the expansion of higher education may lead to the creation of a substantial wastage of talent amongst college and university graduates leading to a greater dispersion in incomes as graduates accept subgraduate work. It is to the evidence on this question that we now turn.

The Death of Human Capital?

The idea of the magnet economy is based on the view that we live in an 'age of human capital' where, 'the economic successes of individuals, and also of whole economies, depends on how extensively and effectively people invest in themselves' (Becker 2002: 3). It is assumed that within the knowledge economy wages will rise in line with the academic profile of the workforce. The more people invest in their education and training the more they will earn and the more the economy will prosper through improvements in productivity. The equation, high skill = high income, also serves to justify inequalities as people are believed to earn what they are worth, as reflected in their credentials. It also holds out the prospect of widespread prosperity because the only limit to raising incomes is inadequate investment in education and training rather than the economic and social realities of work in the twenty-first century. The political appeal of the rhetoric of human capital is obvious and its consequences are far-reaching. The worldwide expansion of higher education has taken place behind the slogan 'learning is earning'. In Britain, as elsewhere, the learning dividend has also been used to justify increased fees for university education.

Evidence on rates of return to education are often based on differences in the incomes of university-level graduates and non-graduates. Figure 22.1 presents OECD (2002) figures that suggest that Britain and the US have larger graduate premiums than other OECD countries, with over double the premium achieved by graduates in countries such as Italy and Japan. Figure 22.1 also shows that the returns for men are greater than those for women in most of the countries surveyed with the exception of Canada, France and the Netherlands.

There are a number of problems with this kind of evidence. First, while a university education is on 'average' associated with earning a higher income than that for non-graduates, it is misleading to conclude that this reflects the increasing value of

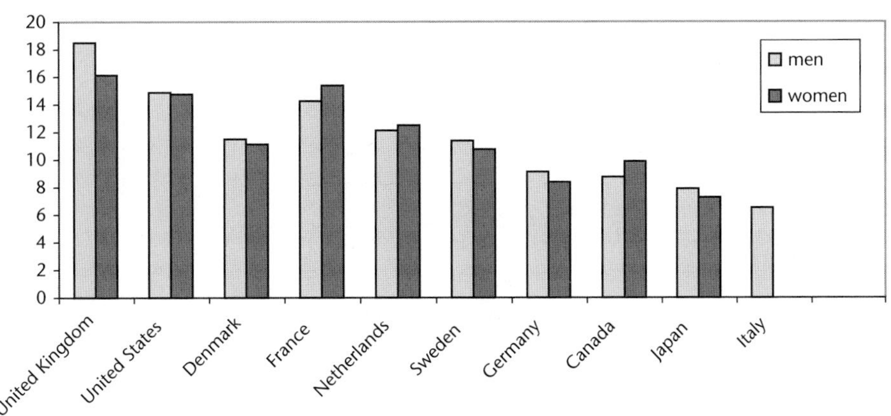

Fig. 22.1 Returns to education: private real rates of return, university-level education, 1999–2000

Note: The rates of return to tertiary education are calculated by comparing the benefits and costs with those of upper-secondary education. In Sweden, the theoretical length of standard tertiary courses is used in the calculations rather than the average theoretical length of different programmes. In Italy, reliable data on earnings for women were not available. The data for Italy is from 1997, the data for the Netherlands is from 1998.

knowledge work rather than a decline in the incomes of those without a university education. Secondly, focusing on the average earnings of graduates might hide growing disparities in graduate incomes, where a relatively small number of high earners pull up average earnings. Thirdly, it is misleading to assume that past returns offer an accurate guide to future returns. Finally, we also need to make greater use of trend data rather than rely on snapshots of differences in the incomes of graduates and non-graduates at a specific point in time.[14] Mindful of these problems, Mishel, Bernstein, and Boushey (2003) have examined evidence from the US that focuses on difference within the college graduate population as well as between graduates and non-graduates. They also present trend data from 1973 that provides an assessment of whether the value of a college degree has increased over time, as assumed in the rhetoric of the knowledge economy.

Figures 22.2 and 22.3 present a different picture to the mantra of 'learning is earning'. Indeed, if the graduate premium was calculated on the economic value of a college degree in 1973 as opposed to its current market value the 'headline' story of rising graduate returns would look very different. Mishel, Bernstein, and Boushey show that it is only male and female college graduates in the 'higher earner' category who have enjoyed any growth in real income since 1973. In other words, the vast majority of college graduates have received no additional 'premium' on their investments in their human capital compared to college graduates in the 1970s, although they continue to earn more that those without a college education. But even here the picture is equivocal as the high earning category of those who left high school before going to college were better paid than the median income for college graduates (although the differential has narrowed in recent years).

This evidence suggests that with the exception of the high-earning graduates, there is a degree of substitution between graduate and non-graduate jobs which manifests itself in many graduates being over-qualified (Livingstone 1998; Pryor and Schaffer 2000). In this respect, the story in the United States parallels that of Britain.[15]

In Britain, a recent study has suggested that contrary to the claim made by the prophets of the post-industrial economy, the first jobs taken by young people today may have less income and status associated with them than when their fathers first entered the labour market. Brynin (2002*a*) compared the social status of fathers' occupations over time

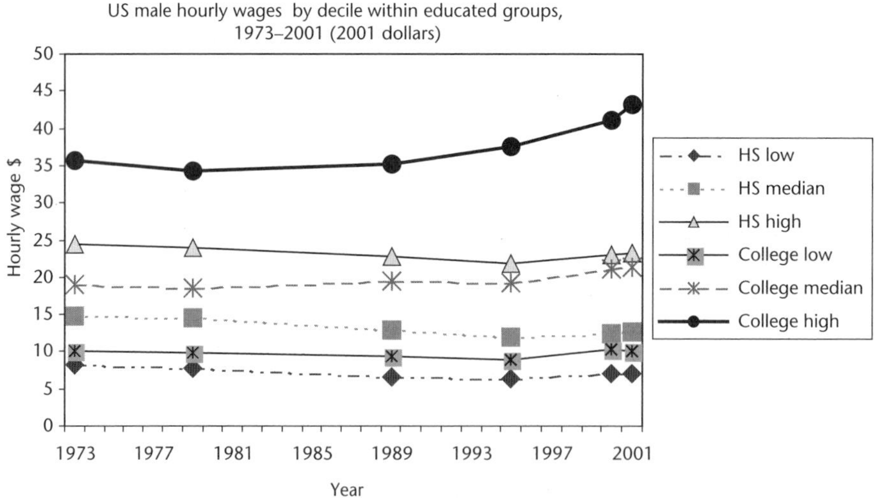

Fig. 22.2 US male hourly wages by decile within educated groups, 1973–2001

Note: Low, median, and high earners refer to, respectively the 10th, 50th, and 90th percentile wage.
Source: Mishel, Bernstein, and Boushey (2003: 167).

with those of their sons and daughters. While fathers' occupations increased in status over time, those of sons and daughters' (from the 1955 or 1972 cohorts) first and second jobs showed a decline in status relative to their fathers. This research directly challenges one of the more optimistic elements in the post-industrial literature that as jobs in the manufacturing sector declined, more high-skilled jobs would be created in the service sector.[16]

Brynin's (2002*a*) macro findings are supported by a study of key service sectors. Mason (2002) found that around a third of graduates were undertaking non-graduate jobs and that, for many, it was not expected that these jobs would be upgraded. Battu and Sloane (2000), estimating the numbers of overqualified workers, suggest that approximately 40 per cent of graduates are in non-graduate jobs.[17]

Returning to Figures 22.2 and 22.3, they also reveal that female college graduates continue to earn less in each of the earning categories than males, but perhaps the most striking difference is the way male and female top earners have raced away from the rest. They now earn over twice as much as the median college graduate of the same sex. This underlines the need to avoid talking about the 'average' college or university graduate, for when it comes to rewards within the job market some are far more equal than others.[18]

Further evidence of major differences in the rates of return to those with the same level of education is also provided when race as well as gender differences are factored into the equation of high skills = high wages. Table 22.4 shows that white men with a bachelor's degree earn around $10,000 a year more than black or Hispanic men with the same qualification. The difference between white men and Hispanic females widens to virtually $20,000.

This evidence on the rate of returns to education does not destroy the thesis of the magnet economy, even if it challenges the rhetoric of the human capital model of rising skills and incomes in the evolutionary drive to technological progress. It can still be argued that the widening income inequalities that characterize top-earning college graduates reflect their ability to market themselves within the global labour market. However, if increasing income polarization was a consequence of the neutral operation of the global economy we should find the same trend in all the advanced economies. Figure 22.4 shows that this is not the case as the increasing polarization in income is far more pronounced in America and the UK than in any other OECD country (Gardiner 1993: 14). Figure 22.4 shows that during the period of rapid economic globalization in the 1980s and early

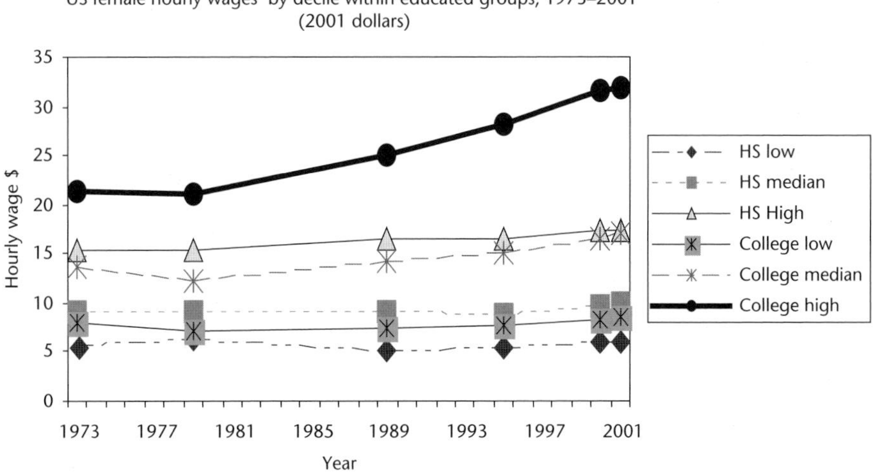

Fig. 22.3 US female hourly wages by decile within educated groups, 1973–2001

Note: Low, median, and high earners refer to, respectively the 10th, 50th, and 90th percentile wage.
Source: Mishel, Bernstein, and Boushey (2003: 167).

Table 22.4 Median annual earnings (US$) by educational attainment, race, and sex, 1999

	All races		White		Black		Hispanic	
	Men	Women	Men	Women	Men	Women	Men	Women
No high school diploma	24,279	16,330	27,611	17,819	21,499	15,396	20,225	14,552
High school diploma	32,098	21,970	34,839	22,469	27,408	20,609	25,291	19,923
Some college	37,245	26,456	39,817	27,136	31,961	25,209	31,446	24,236
Associate's college	40,474	30,129	41,186	30,547	31,206	27,198	36,212	24,744
Bachelor's degree	51,005	36,340	51,884	36,909	40,805	34,692	41,467	31,996
Master's degree	61,776	45,345	61,904	45,914	52,308	41,780	50,419	43,718
Doctorate	76,858	56,345	80,697	59,010	55,700	41,593	60,690	55,425
Professional degree	96,275	56,726	100,000	59,098	67,449	39,371	60,432	56,666

Note: Limited to year-round, full-time workers aged 25 years and older.
Source: US Census Bureau, Current population Survey, March 2000.

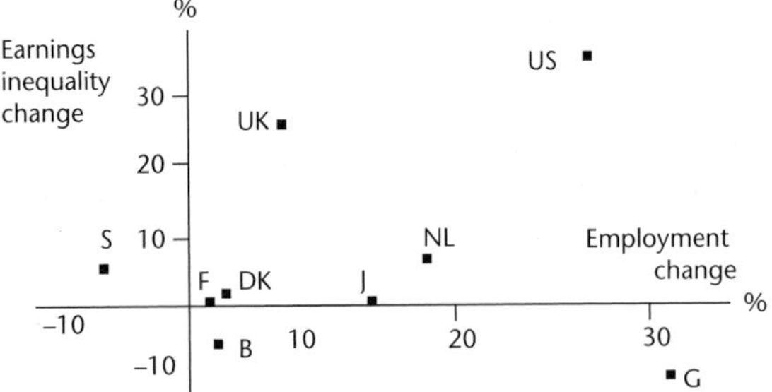

Fig. 22.4 Employment growth and changes in earnings inequality in the Netherlands and selected OECD countries, 1982–95

Source: Visser and Hemerijk (1997).

1990s, income differentials actually fell in Germany (OECD 1993).

This evidence suggests that income inequalities in the United States and United Kingdom cannot be explained by the creation of a global labour market as Reich and others have suggested, but in the way the United States and Britain have *responded* to global economic conditions. This response, like the global economy itself, has been shaped by the political dominance of neoclassical economics in both countries that extol the virtue of flexible labour markets and competitive individualism. The debate about what is distinctive about America and Britain takes us beyond the confines of this chapter, but the polarization in income can be explained more convincingly in terms of differences in labour market power rather than returns to skills (although they are not mutually exclusive). Howell (2002) subjects what he calls the unified theory which predicts that inequalities in income and differences in levels of employment are determined by levels of skill and labour market rigidities, to a comparative analysis. The unified theory explains income inequalities in terms of skills: those with high skills have higher incomes, correspondingly those with low skills have low and falling incomes because they cannot operate with the new technology. Equally, labour rigidities, such as those assumed to exist in mainland Europe, that protect workers create greater unemployment than in flexible labour markets of the American and British kind. The solution to the analysis posed by the unified theory is to create labour market flexibility and greater educational opportunities for the less skilled. He finds that the data do not support the unified theory and argues that we need to look at issues of labour market power and ideology.

A consequence of Howell's (2002) analysis is that income polarization in the US and UK can be seen to enable company executive and senior managers, along with those who worked in the financial markets, to engage in 'wealth extraction' rather than the development of sustainable forms of 'wealth creation' (Lazonick 1993). This largely explains why a study reported by Bound and Johnson (1995) found that in America a large part of the increase in the returns to a university degree was due to an increased premium put to use in the business and law fields. The wages of computer specialists and engineers actually *fell* relative to high school graduates.

The official view of human capital has become a victim of its own success, at least in its influence over government policy. Human capital is itself subject to the laws of diminishing returns. It is losing its capacity as a source of competitive advantage for both individuals and nations because the 'positional' advantage of those with higher education and skills is not only declining domestically (as higher education is expanded) but also globally.

Therefore, while much current thinking about the relationship between education, jobs, and rewards is based on an evolutionary model of rising skills and incomes this now looks more like a 'transitional' case limited to the twentieth century where access to higher education was limited to a few. In mass, if not universal, systems of higher education and at a time when vast numbers of highly-skilled workers are available in developing economies, the global expansion of tertiary education has outstripped the demand for high-skilled workers, creating downward pressure on the incomes of skilled workers in the developed economies along with some upward pressure on those in emerging economies.

The paradox of human capital is that at a time when human knowledge is being taught, certified, and applied on a scale never witnessed previously in human history, the overall value of human capital is likely to decline, apart from in the case of leading-edge knowledge that has clear market application. For the few, investments of effort, time, and money will continue to be handsomely rewarded but for most it will take the form of defensive expenditure: it is a necessary investment to have any chance of getting a decent job. We will return to the issue of positional competition but our next task is to examine the idea of a powershift from those who owned and controlled the means of production in the twentieth century to the 'knowledge workers' of today.

Knowledge without Power

The imagery of the knowledge economy centres on a power shift (Bell 1973; Drucker 1993) resulting from a fundamental change in the means of wealth creation. As the economy comes to depend on human ingenuity, knowledge, and creativity, the most important corporate asset is its intellectual capital (Stewart 2001). It is argued that this has given knowledge workers greater control and autonomy over the nature and pace of their work. The rhetoric of the knowledge economy assumes that innovation and creativity are enduring features of the new economy but such assumptions are both static and ahistorical. Brint (2001: 116) cautions against such a view:

> Theorists of the knowledge economy have often missed the historical dimension of industrial growth and maturation. Are the insurance or the automobile industries knowledge-intensive? Most of the theorists would likely say they are less knowledge-intensive than the computer industry. However, both the concept of life insurance and actuarial studies on which contracts were based were intellectual innovations in their time. The internal combustion engine was, of course, a marvellous breakthrough in its time. Our sense of the computer software industry as particularly knowledge-intensive reflects the rapid growth and turbulence in the industry and the constantly upgraded products the industry has been producing in recent years . . . Many years in the future, we shall see the same standardization in the computer software industry that a previous generation witnessed in the insurance and automobile industries.

Based on these observations Brint draws out three characteristics of knowledge-centred industries. These are (1) speed of change is an important factor suggesting that research and development are at a premium in creating a competitive edge; (2) new issues susceptible to expert analysis regularly emerge; (3) the knowledge necessary for operating in-service industries is embedded in the providers themselves. But as in goods-producing industries, if services become standardized and commodified they no longer constitute knowledge-centred industries.

This analysis is helpful because it defines what may be constituted as knowledge-centred industries at any given time. It enables us to distinguish such industries that are likely to be subject to routinization from those that are not. For example, research-based activities in the pharmaceuticals industry are unlikely to be routinized because of the creativity involved, while many activities within the banking industry are (see below). It also helps us to understand why there has not been a 'democratization' of the workplace as knowledge is being managed in ways that stand in stark contrast to the proponents of the knowledge economy.

John Burgoyne has made a useful distinction between the activities of knowledge workers and 'knowledge worked' (Brown and Hesketh 2004: 55). While companies have an increasing demand for knowledge workers capable of crossing existing knowledge boundaries in the creation of integrated products and services such as the mobile phone that doubles as a camera or MP3 player, most of these higher-level activities can be transformed into occupational activities where the knowledge has been 'worked' in advance, leaving people to apply knowledge captured in computer software, work manuals, or written procedures.

This analysis draws attention to the fact that regardless how the economy is characterized, in terms of knowledge, information, or post-industrialism, it is based on the principles of capitalism and the profit motive. While innovation and the exploitation of new ideas is a key aspect of today's global economy, it is also driven by the need to standardize knowledge so that it can be rapidly processed and reproduced at lower cost and with greater predictability than when it is in the hands and minds of highly specialized knowledge workers (experts). This drive to standardization, as much as innovation, has become an integral part of the competitive strategy of many multinational companies for the simple reason that it not only offers them greater control over the 'product' but also enables them to reduce costs by off-shoring activities to countries where labour costs are significantly lower. Furthermore, as companies develop people strategies at an international, if not global level, the integration of activities involves the application of common standards that erode national differences in employment practices. For global companies it is less of a question of 'when in Rome' because 'we are all in Rome'!

Standardization shifts the priority from creativity to control. It enables greater control of the workforce by closely prescribing tasks while reducing its costs.[19] The key distinction here is one that we can adapt from Bernstein (1997), between strong and weak classification and frames. Strong classification and frames emphasize existing states of knowledge and received problems, whereas weak classification and framing emphasizes the importance of ways of knowing, of constructing problems, rather than solving problems with appropriate routines. This enables us to chart changes in the nature of knowledge work such that while it may, initially have been weakly classified and framed, as standardization is established so it becomes more strongly classified and framed. As jobs change in this way we might expect to see workers' autonomy or discretion downgraded or removed while the complexity involved in their routines is maintained or indeed increased.[20]

The distinction between discretion and complexity merits some discussion because it is used in empirical analyses of changes in the demand for skill and it highlights the way university graduates may be used for non-graduate work. It was noted in the previous section that about 30 per cent of graduates in Britain undertake non-graduate work. The question then is how the skills of this 30 per cent are used. Brynin (2002*b*: 366) suggests that:

> We are, therefore, seeing an increasing demand for graduates but perhaps for work not traditionally at the graduate level. There is no general upgrading of labour but a complex redistribution of skills and their rewards . . . We can, therefore, perhaps see the use of graduates not merely as a response to oversupply, nor only as a reaction to the demand for ever rising educational skills, but as a tool in the armoury of methods for redistributing labour and reducing its average costs.

He goes on to hypothesize that graduates are being used to fill the demand for intermediately skilled work because of weaknesses in the supply of intermediately skilled workers.[21] However, graduates may be preferred for intermediately skilled workers because the division of labour has been reconstructed in ways that suit some of the skills that graduates acquire at university. The major influence on this change in the division of labour concerns the process of management de-layering that started in the 1980s. This enabled many middle-management jobs to be stripped out with closer communications between senior managers and workers. What facilitated this process was the new technology related to the introduction of the personal computer (Aronowitz and De Fazio 1994).

In turn, this has meant that many in intermediate positions as well as those in lower positions now have to cope with greater complexity and it is this that employers may believe graduates are better able to deal with than non-graduates. But one of the hallmarks of being a graduate in the past was the ability to exercise autonomy in the work undertaken. In order to study for a degree, a high level of autonomy is required. Since employers are not asking these graduates to exercise judgement or discretion regarding key decisions about the job, they do not pay them as much as those undertaking graduate-level work. Hence we would expect to see a widening dispersion in graduate incomes as more graduates come onto the jobs market. The utilization of graduate skills in this attenuated way does give employers greater flexibility at cheaper cost than if they made full use of the skills graduates have to offer.

This analysis is supported by statistical evidence. Felstead, Gallie, and Green (2002), found a significant decline in the level of discretion over job tasks, especially among managers and other professionals. It was also particularly notable in 'Education', 'Public Administration', 'Finance', 'Real Estate', and 'Business Services'. They concluded their survey of skills in Britain by suggesting that:

> more skilled jobs typically require higher levels of discretion over job tasks. Despite this, the rise in skills among employees has *not* been accompanied by a corresponding rise in the control they can exercise over their jobs. Rather there has been a marked decline in task discretion. For example, the proportion of employees reporting a great deal of choice over the way they do their job fell from 52 percent in 1986 to 39 percent in 2001. This decline occurred for both men and women. (p. 73)

An everyday example may help to clarify the processes involved. In the 1990s many retail banks in Britain and America divided their market between the mass 'Fordist' segment in which the majority experienced electronic banking with call centres to address specific problems, while those earning a relatively high income could be assigned a personal relations manager with whom they dealt face to face. These managers had the discretion to loan a substantial amount unsecured and even more with security. Judgement and experience were required successfully to loan money unsecured. More recently, this form of discretion with all the experience and acquired knowledge that it presupposes has been removed in some of the major clearing banks. Now loans have to be agreed by a 'credit controller'. This credit controller is, in the first instance, a computer programme that automatically assesses a loan application according to pre-specified criteria. Only in appealing against the credit controller's judgement, as represented by the computer programme, does the manager have a role. But even here there is no indication that his or her judgement will carry weight. Effectively, the role of the personal relations manager is no more than one of 'front of office' sociability. As one manager put it to us, 'a junior with a ready smile could do my job now'. And, in this particular case, juniors on far lower salaries are being introduced to do the job.

The education required to learn a series of routines and to make a limited set of strongly classified and framed judgements is not at the same level as that required of individuals whose work requires creativity and the freedom to work unsupervised for long periods. Hence, it is possible to see why this type of white-collar Fordism does not require high levels of education, although this does not mean that companies will curtail the use of university graduates in the banking sector. University graduates will continue to be valued for their social and communication skills alongside any technical requirements of the job. Their behavioural competence in working with colleagues, customers, and clients is more important that the use of creative intellect. The problem is that the jobs on offer are far removed from the expectations harboured by most graduates as they enter the labour market.[22]

One of the basic tenets of the shift from Fordist to Post-Fordist forms of work organisation (Brown and Lauder 1997) was that accountability and control of workers would focus on outcomes rather than constant supervision and surveillance. So long as targets were met, how those targets were achieved would be a matter of human creativity and ingenuity. Now, process as well as product can be micro-managed through the use of software programs that monitor emails and telephone conversations, along with the use of electronic manuals that prescribe many aspects of the job that can be easily updated to meet changing circumstances. Consequently, the potential for individual discretion and creativity to be exercised can be squeezed out, which is precisely what has happened in the example of the bank manager.

We need to emphasize two points about this argument. First, these control strategies will not be implemented uniformly across the globe. Shoshana Zuboff (1988) demonstrated that the introduction of computer technology could be used to reduce skill, discretion, and judgement or alternatively to complement them. Hunter et al. (2001) have also stressed that how technology and skill are structured within an organization will be key to understanding the wider roles of education and skill in the economy.[23]

There are also some forms of knowledge work that are more susceptible to standardization than others. Work based on expert scientific knowledge, creativity, and individual enterprise, especially where it involves highly profitable networks, are likely to escape standardization, but this leaves a large number of professional and managerial workers vulnerable.[24]

Secondly, this discussion of knowledge without power has focused on the modern workplace, but it equally applies to market situation. A further paradox of the knowledge-driven economy is that the more widespread access to expert knowledge becomes, the less it offers a source of power either to define the work context or within the job market.

While there is a tendency to focus on the technical requirements of work it is important to recognize that the power that derives from individual certification and knowledge will increasingly depend on 'social' considerations. As Mats Alvesson (2001: 863) has suggested:

> the ambiguity of knowledge and the work of knowledge-intensive companies means that 'knowledge', 'expertise' and 'solving problems' to a large degree become matters of belief, impressions and negotiations of meaning. Institutionalized assumptions, expectations, reputations, images, etc. feature strongly in the perception of the products of knowledge-intensive organizations and workers.

The value added associated with many knowledge-intensive industries (i.e. consultancy, financial services), stems from convincing clients that large fees or high prices are legitimate when professional knowledge is utilized. The 'personal' *is* the product that is being sold as it represents the embodiment of corporate value (Rose 1999). Management consultants, for instance, not only have to be convincing to colleagues but to clients and customers. They must define and epitomize valued knowledge. This involves standards of appearance, speech, deportment, and social confidence that demonstrate that one is in tune with clients, customers, and partners, as firms are entrusting the individual with the knowledge claims of the organization. The extent to which this embodiment of the firm matters will obviously depend on the nature of the business, but the more businesses are encouraged to get closer to clients and customers the more important 'personal' capital will become (Brown and Hesketh 2004).

The link between the 'branding' of companies as world class, leading edge, upmarket, etc. and the people who work for them furthers our understand of why, for many, knowledge is not power. As the numbers entering the job market with higher degrees continue to increase, being good is no longer good enough. Companies with ambitions to 'be the best' also want to be seen to recruit the 'best' talent. This involves companies competing for managers and professionals with established 'reputations' within the market-place, and for graduates from universities reputed to be world class. For those defined as part of this talented elite (Michaels et al. 2001) the rhetoric of the knowledge economy is close to reality, as they are the most likely to enjoy greater levels of discretion within their jobs and a high level of market power should they decide to seek alternative employment. But this is far removed from the realities of the knowledge economy for most.

Employability for most is not an expression of market power but a constant reminder of economic vulnerability as they are continually faced with the fact that there is not such thing as a job for life. Along with a growing recognition of the contrasting fortunes of those with the same formal credentials, this has led to an increasing intensification in the competition for education and jobs that has become global.

Standards of Justice: Getting Ahead in Education and the Labour Market

The protagonists of the knowledge economy have focused much of their attention on issues of individual employability. This reflects employer complaints that many of those entering the workforce, including the highly qualified, lack the social and self-management skills that are required. They also assume that the barriers to opportunity that characterized the Fordist era have been lifted and the nature of competition transformed. We have noted that the major issue for policymakers is no longer one of how to equalize the national competition for education and jobs but rather how to 'outsmart' other nations in a bid to capture a lion's share of high-skilled, high-waged jobs. Issues of inclusion and exclusion are defined solely in terms of raising educational standards and extending access to university.

Trends in education, employment, and income distribution do not support this view that the historical conflict between justice and efficiency has been resolved, but points to an intensification of the struggle for credentials and tough-entry jobs (Hirsch 1977; Brown 2000). The focus on individual employability (supply side) rather than a political commitment to job creation (demand side) is a political sleight of hand that shifts the responsibility for employment firmly onto the shoulders of individuals rather than the state.

While there is no doubt that the technical and social requirements of knowledge work have changed, the increasing focus on a broader range of employability skills such as drive, resilience, or interpersonal sensitivity offer employers a convenient way of legitimating their recruitment decisions when large numbers of applicants can no longer be rejected because they lack the appropriate credentials or technical expertise. Any class, ethnic, or gender bias in these decisions is extremely difficult for individual candidates to contest, even though they reflect a growing chasm between what is required to get the job as opposed to what is required to do the job (Brown and Hesketh 2004).[25]

The issue of equality of opportunity in recruitment raises broader concerns about the official emphasis on lifting educational standards rather than on narrowing inequalities in the performance of different classes and social groups. It is not that raising standards is unimportant but that it cannot provide a solution to the problem of positional conflict. Rather than dampen competitive tensions in education and the labour market, social conflict has intensified in the scramble to secure a competitive advantage. When there are more contestants than jobs, how one stands relative to others becomes important. Positional considerations also become more important when access to higher education is extended, at the same time that there is growing differentiation within the same occupation. In the mid- to late twentieth century a job title was closely related to job entitlements. Most of those in the same profession or of the same managerial status received similar remuneration packages and career opportunities. Frank and Cook (1995) argue that this is no longer the case as the fortunes of those in occupations such as law, management, medicine, journalism, and academia have significantly diverged: hence the wide disparity in income documented in the previous discussion. This, they suggest, has led to the creation of winner-takes-all markets.[26]

A consequence is increasing competition for the glittering vocational prizes. This leads not only to a major misallocation of human capabilities, but to increasing market congestion that has important repercussions for individuals, families, and society. For individuals and families the fundamental problem posed is that while students attempt to raise their game, resulting in higher levels of credential achievement, this does little to improve their relative chances of entering tough-entry colleges, universities, or jobs. If everyone adopts the same tactics in the competition for positional advantage no one secures an advantage. This creates an *opportunity trap* that is forcing people to spend more time, effort, and money trying to access the education, certificates, and jobs they want, with few guarantees that their aspirations will be realised (See Brown, Ch. 26).[27]

The focus on raising standards rather than equity ignores the fact that some individuals and families are much better placed to mobilize their material, cultural, and social assets to increase their chances of winning the competition for elite credentials and jobs. The emphasis on parental choice and market competition within education serves to legitimate, as least in political terms, the huge inequalities in the quality of educational experiences (Lauder, Hughes, et al. 1999).

At the societal level this congestion has already led to intense conflict amongst the middle classes (Ball 2003; Power et al. 2003). However, a clear implication of our argument is that access to elite employment, increasingly open to international competition, will be restricted to those transnational and national elites that can gain access to the globally most prestigious universities (Lowe 2000). To put it provocatively, within the foreseeable future the children from middle-class backgrounds that fail to gain access to these universities will be left to fight over the scraps.

This argument finds support in recent trends within higher education which suggest the emergence of a global hierarchy of 'world-class' universities (Wolf 2002). In such a market, the 'best' students are attracted to the universities with the highest reputations that in turn attract the best academics because they can pay for them.[28]

Consequently, the elite American and European universities are likely to provide the international benchmark for academic excellence for the foreseeable future. It is only those universities that follow such practices that will enable students into the competition for elite jobs. We know already that these leading universities recruit largely from high-earning families. The richer their background, the more likely students will be to attend the 'Harvards' and 'Oxfords' of the higher education system (Power et al. 2003), contributing to a pattern of exclusion which is manifest in recent studies of social mobility in both Britain (Ermisch and Francesconi 2002; Galindo-Rueda and Vignoles 2003) and the United States (Perrucci and Wysong 1999).

Although educational systems retain strong national characteristics, the early steps towards global integration are likely to have a profound impact on the future of positional competition. It is those international elites that have been able to mobilize their wealth and cultural resources in the acquisition of credentials that will benefit most in a global competition for high-skilled jobs.[29] While national elites in countries that have maintained meritocratic rules in an attempt to equalize educational opportunities will increasingly be viewed as holding back their children in the global competition. Consequently, not only will market rules be endorsed by social elites who already play by these rules, but the social elites from other countries such as Germany, France, Sweden, and Korea[30] may also break free of the restraints imposed on wealth through national rules of meritocratic competition to gain positional advantage for their offspring (Brown 2000: 646).

Faced with these developments centre-left governments have avoided one of the most important questions to confront them at the start of the twenty-first century, that is, how to organize the competition for a livelihood in such a way that genuinely equal opportunity is available to all. Avoiding this problem by appeals to the need to raise educational standards for all in the global market offers little insight into how the question of social justice is to be addressed.

Conclusion

This chapter has argued that the idea of a magnet economy is the latest version of an evolutionary model of technological, economic, and social change in which issues of inequality, opportunity, and social conflict are resolved through increasing investment in education and human capital. We have come to a different conclusion.

The research evidence does not support the idea of a rapid increase in the demand for highly skilled workers although there has been a rapid expansion of tertiary education. Indeed, there are increasing numbers of highly educated people in jobs for which they are overqualified. What growth there has been in the demand for skills within the economy has also been uneven across occupations and industries. Equally, much of the change in skill sets demanded by employers focuses on changes in the personal and social context of work rather than on the technical demands of the job. Employers want people with drive, commitment, and business awareness. They want new employees who can hit the ground running and who have the social confidence and emotional intelligence to get on with colleagues and customers. They want people who are able to work without close supervision and who are willing to embrace change rather than resist it.

These personal characteristics are associated with higher levels of education regardless of the technicalities of the job. Therefore, the demand for skills within a knowledge-driven economy cannot be understood in a linear way from low to high skills based on a model of technological evolution. It has also been argued that the demand for technical skills may have reached a ceiling under present economic conditions for the reasons we have discussed.

There is evidence of increasing attempts to routinize and standardize knowledge work driven by the global integration of business activities. Such evidence also endorses the trend towards business outsourcing. Standardization is a necessary precondition for the relocation of increasingly complex work to developing economies that have a ready supply of high-skilled workers willing to work for relatively low wages. The consultancy firm ATKearney have predicted that over 500,000 US jobs in the financial sector (approximately 8 per cent of the workforce in that sector), will be moved offshore by 2008. They also note that until recently most offshore transfers have entailed back office functions such as data entry and transaction processing, but that these new transfers will involve 'a wide range of high-end internal functions ... including financial analysis, research, regulatory reporting, accounting, human resources and graphic design' (ATKearney 2003: 1). These transfers are anticipated to reduce annual operating costs in the United States by more than $30 billion.

This analysis suggests that the overriding problem confronting governments is not deficiencies in the employability skills of graduates, but problems of demand and skill utilization: there are not enough good quality jobs available, and employers fail to exploit the potential for higher productivity and growth that mass education now offers.

We have also argued that the problem of domestic demand for high skills cannot be resolved through the operation of the global labour market. We reject the win–win scenario, as developing nations such as China and India have entered the competition for high-skilled employment that may depress rather than increase the demand for highly skilled workers in the developed economies.

A paradox of the knowledge economy is that human capital is increasingly subject to the laws of diminishing returns as more people gain access to tertiary education both at home and abroad, and knowledge workers in the developed economies are forces to compete with well-educated employees willing to work for much lower incomes in developing economies.

Therefore, further investments in human capital will not narrow income inequalities, as Georg Simmel observed at the turn of the twentieth century, a rise in the level of knowledge in a society, 'does not mean by any means ... a general levelling, but rather the opposite' (1978: 440). There will not be a general levelling of incomes in an upward or downward direction. For the fortunate fifth and especially the very fortune 5–10 per cent at the apex of occupational pyramids, whether as lawyers, designers, consultants, or academics, those defined as outstanding talent are likely to prosper as market competition has a propensity to exaggerate the rewards of success and the price of failure.

But if globalization cannot resolve long-standing issues of 'who does what' and 'who gets what', it has contributed to both the intensification of positional conflict and to a transformation in the nature of the competition for a livelihood (Brown 2000). Increasing inequalities in occupational rewards and career prospects place a premium on gaining access to internationally recognized schools, colleges, and universities. The middle-class families in Britain and the United States, along with those from elite backgrounds, have abandoned any lingering commitment to 'meritocratic' competition in education that characterized the 1960s and 1970s. Elite credentials are now an essential commodity that must be fought for through the mobilization of all the financial, cultural and social capital that families can muster in the market for elite education and occupations. And as multinational companies and intergovernmental agencies recruit 'cosmopolitans' rather than 'locals' (in every sense of these terms) social elites from around the world are demanding a level playing field in competition with elites from other countries, which further undermines national policies committed to equality of educational and occupational opportunity.

An unintended consequence of the application of human capital ideas to public and economic policy is that it is creating increasing problems in the management of expectations. The developed economies are in danger of creating a heady cocktail of discontent: students and their parents may find that a degree fails to deliver the standard of living they have been led to expect and employers will have too many overqualified and disgruntled employees. This has wider political ramifications. A disillusioned middle class may well flex its political muscles to gain a better deal for family members as it invests increasing amounts of time, effort, and money in maintaining the status and standard of living to which it has become accustomed.

In the past, it has been assumed that middle-class youth might turn to the left (Bowles and Gintis 1976). A more likely scenario today is that the situation might lead to pressure towards the national protection of jobs and greater restrictions on the global movement of labour. In the United States measures have already been taken by some states to ensure that public-sector employment is kept within America rather than being exported overseas. If we were to forecast the source of political debate and change over the next decade, it would be the disenchantment of the middle class in Western societies with the promises held out for education and labour market opportunities.[31]

Finally, this analysis highlights the need to reframe the issues examined in this chapter. It calls for the development of a conceptual framework that encompasses changes not only within education, work, and the labour market, but also in the relationship between the local, national, and global. The labour market outcomes described in this chapter cannot be explained by the national profile of the education system in question. They reflect changes in the production, reordering, and reproduction of the global division of educated labour. How individuals, families, companies, and nation-states respond to these challenges is in urgent need of knowledge work of the most creative kind.

NOTES

1. See for example, <http://www.dti.gov.uk/ministers/speeches/hewitt200904.html>.
2. Economists used to treat national economies as hermetically sealed units which limited international comparisons to rates of economic growth. Educational investment was important only in so far as it appeared to correlate to such differences in growth rates. There was little sense of an international labour market within which differences in the quality of education could have a decisive impact on the livelihoods of workers within different countries.
3. It is also more difficult for competitors to mass-produce the same goods or to offer customers tailored services.
4. Of course, if we are in the midst of an economic revolution then it may be that the trends we identify constitute no more than a short-lived blip, so this chapter is best seen as an attempt at social forecasting (Bell 1977) designed to question the present orthodox view of the education-knowledge-economy relationship. For if our alternative account proves to be the more accurate then it strikes at the heart of current educational, economic, and social policy.

5. This view of human capital gains its legitimacy from human capital theory. However, in the formal theory it would be possible for the incomes of highly qualified graduates to fail to keep increasing if supply exceeded demand. (Krugman, 1997; Lauder, Brown, and Egerton, 2005).
6. Government White Paper, China's Employment Situation and Policies, section VI. Employment Prospects for the Early Part of the 21st Century, People's Republic of China, Beijing, April, 2004. See <http://www.china.org.cn/e-white/20040426/6.htm>.
7. See 'Chinese University Students to Top 16 Million' at <http://www.edu.cn/20010903/200991.shtml>.
8. The figures on China and India where compiled with the assistance of Gerbrand Tholen. For a broader statistical analysis of these issues see P. Brown et al. 2006.
9. See also Saxenian 1994, 2000*a*, 2000*b*, 2002.
10. See also Alarcon, (1999).
11. This magnetic effect is not restricted to the IT industry. There are examples of qualified teachers, doctors, and nurses being attracted to countries such as Britain at the same time that indigenous workers are unemployed or in low-skilled employment. But the causes for increased recruitment in these cases do not lie in the rise of the knowledge-based industries in the first instance but in the electoral politics related to increased education and health expenditure. However, under GATS state workers may be subject to increased overseas competition.
12. Preliminary Evidence from the Global Skills Webs ESRC Research Project conducted by Phillip Brown, David Ashton and Hugh Lauder.
13. The process by which exclusion or irrelevance occurs will not be random, explanations will require theories of hegemony, imperialism and post-colonialism in the context of globalization.
14. For an earlier analysis of this kind that draws the key distinction between cross-sectional and longitudinal data see Levin and Kelley (1997).
15. There are difficulties in comparing and explaining income trends across countries, especially in terms of one factor such as skill; however, in both the United States and Britain the evidence suggests the data are inconsistent with the hypothesis of an accelerated demand for university graduates. On the problems of comparing the links between income and skill see Devroye and Freeman (2002).
16. Time has proved two problems with the white-collar scenario. The first is that although the proportion of white-collar workers has increased dramatically, the numbers entering white-collar work is now stable (Mishel, Bernstein, and Schmitt 2003). The second is that there was an expectation that white-collar work would be equated with skills upgrading but in fact as Esping-Andersen (1999) has shown, after the first wave of increase in white-collar workers subsequent waves have experienced low-skill, low-income work.
17. Graduate as opposed to non-graduate work can be defined in at least three ways. Workers can be asked whether their jobs use the kinds of skills that qualified them to become graduates; employers can be asked the same type of question, or a system of job classification that defines jobs in relation to educational levels can be used to assess the demand and supply of graduates relative to it. See Felstead et al. (2002), Mason (2002), and Battu and Sloane (2001) respectively for research using these strategies.

18. The within-group inequality in earnings for college graduates is not only far greater than that of the lower skilled, it has also been growing more rapidly, whereas non-graduates experienced slow or no growth in within-group variance in earnings. See: T. Lemieux (2003), 'Residual Wage Inequality: A Re-examination', University of British Columbia, *CLEER Working Paper* 2, <http://www.econ.ubc.ca/cleer/papers/cleer002.pdf>.

19. This highlights the inherent conflict between 'knowing' as part of the work experience and 'knowledge' as an economic commodity (Scarbrough 1999: 5). In other words, the advent of the knowledge-based economy has not resolved the enduring problem of how to convert the employment potential of knowledgeable and creative individuals into productive activities that contribute to bottom-line profits (Marx 1976).

20. The utility of Bernstein's distinction is that classification and framing enable us to chart the change in the nature of knowledge work. The distinction between complexity and autonomy is to be found in de Witte and Stein (2000) while Evetts (2002) emphasizes the accuracy of 'discretion' over that of 'autonomy'.

21. However, we need to distinguish carefully between issues concerning the utilization of skill from those of demand and supply of credentials (Livingstone 1998). There is a debate about the levels of demand and supply of intermediately skilled workers that has produced conflicting results. While surveys of employers suggest that there are skill shortages for intermediately skilled workers (Mason and Wilson 2003), surveys of workers Felstead et al. (2003) suggest that there is an oversupply of the intermediately skilled, relative to demand. Mason (2000, 2002) has argued that the problem is not one of oversupply but the supply of *appropriately* skilled workers at this level. Hence the need for two-year Foundations rather than three-year degrees. However, surveys of employers are likely to be inaccurate for two reasons. First, they focus on what employers would *ideally* like, but even this ideal may reflect current ideologies about best practice rather than what actually occurs. For example, Mehralizadeh (1999) has shown that, for a leading car manufacturer in the UK, while senior management emphasized the importance of process or key skills, workers on the shop floor did not believe they were of significance in practice. Middle managers acknowledged that there had been a major debate about the significance of key skills. There is an additional problem confronting researchers of the knowledge-based economy in that there is often a hiatus between macro-level studies that seek to take into account national-level data on, say, the relationship between new technology, work practices, and pay on the one hand, and case studies which may often lead to contrary findings on the other (Brown and Campbell 2002). The problem is that there are not sufficient case studies employing the same methodology, and theories to aggregate up to the macro level. This means that we have to rely on quantitative studies of skills to identify the macro trends with qualitative studies illuminating particular choices and strategies.

22. The above example is one of several strategies that can be employed to standardize knowledge work. Much of the focus has been on technology and related tools such as manuals. These, as we have seen, include the use of electronic technology to limit the discretion of what were once seen as weakly classified and framed professional occupations. If we think of the way that our personal relations manager's job has been reclassified, then computer technology has become central. Its effect is intended to increase the decision-making power of those at the top of the organization, reduce inconsistency in performance, and enhance predictability, precisely what Fordism in car assembly was intended to achieve (Taylor/Braverman).

23. In looking at graduate jobs, one of the trends that we have not taken into account is that of the creation of what Elias and Purcell (2003) call new and niche graduate jobs: these

include entertainment and sports, hospitality, and occupational hygienist professions. They report that on average these types of graduate jobs earn less than what they term modern graduate occupations, e.g. management, IT, and the like. These jobs are an example of what Meyer (1997) described as the creation of professions through education. This leads to a more complex analysis of how occupations are structured than suggested by assuming that demand elicits supply; it is an example of 'demand' being constructed.

24. It could be argued that as the pace of innovation increases so the demand for knowledge workers will not decline because new innovations require loosely classified and framed jobs that give workers a high degree of discretion over problem-solving. In other words, our more pessimistic prognosis is unjustified; however, the trends identified here suggest the opposite. A further consideration beyond the remit of this chapter would be to examine the specific factors that have driven many corporations down the road of routinization and cost-cutting. Clearly economic globalization has a part in this account. One of the major economic forces unleashed by globalization has been an intensification of competition due to the advent of improved information flows through the internet and the speed in which production facilities can be established or closed down. This has intensified competition on price. Buyers can trawl the internet for products, large companies can set up auctions amongst their suppliers, and the ease with which factories and offices can be established and closed down around the globe has meant that MNCs can determine where they will direct their investment based on, amongst other things, the quality and price of labour as we have seen in the discussion of the magnet economy.

25. Economists seek to explain selection for elite graduate jobs in rational terms, albeit they acknowledge that some of these 'intangible' qualities are hard to measure (see Acemoglu 2002, and Pryor and Schaffer 2000). In contrast, we are suggesting that recruitment to these elite jobs is based on group conflict presupposed by positional competition. (See below.)

26. The notion of a winner-takes-all labour market suggests that globalization can lead to distortions in the rational workings of the labour market, as musicians, authors, consultants, etc. increasingly gain global exposure. Equally, as the labour market for employees, including managers, consultants, accountants, and lawyers, extends beyond national borders, those who are able to develop international reputations can leverage greater market power when it comes to negotiating their salaries and benefit packages.

27. The knock-on effect of a congested graduate market may be downward occupational mobility. In the United States this appears to have had a significant impact on joblessness among poorly educated men of prime working age (Pryor and Schaffer 2000), although such an effect is not apparent in Britain (Battu and Sloane 2001).

28. It is important not to overemphasize the shift to a winner-takes-all market for higher education at the present. Room (2000: 111) has, for example, noted that the market for overseas students is segmented: 'International flows of students follow well-defined routes which in many cases are underpinned by traditional linguistic and cultural links between the former imperial powers and their colonial territories.' However, we are suggesting that the conditions for the creation of such a market now exist.

29. These differences in the rules of competition reflect contrasting social priorities. Meritocratic rules, for instance, involve restrictions on the middle classes in the use of their superior market power in the interest of social cohesion or state legitimation.

30. Korea is an interesting example of a country which until recently prevented its indigenous students from attending international schools that offer qualifications such as the IB.

31. Capitalism, however, has always offered scope for progressive reform just as it has the potential to widen inequalities and undermine social justice. There remain important

differences in the way nation-states seek to develop 'high-skilled' strategies and differences in the way employers utilize the skills and capabilities of their workforce. These are crucial issues because, while the aspiration to high-skills economies (Brown et al. 2001) is unlikely to solve the distributional question, high-skilled work is necessary to generate a 'social dividend' that can advantage all in society.

Producing Hi-Tech: Globalization, the State, and Migrant Subjects

Sangeeta Kamat, Ali Mir, and Biju Mathew

[...]

Introduction

The study of migration and migrant populations has, in recent times, seen a new dynamism as the rate and diversity of communities that have begun to migrate across the world has increased dramatically in the last two decades. Understanding the nature and politics of migration has become important to theorizing globalization. This is in sharp contrast to earlier studies of globalization that focused on the flow of capital as against labour across national borders. The attention to migration, may in part, be attributed to the increased visibility of Third World communities in the First World and the attendant cultural tensions produced in the mainstream national culture as well as internally within immigrant communities. Filipina domestic workers in Long Island homes, Somalian refugees in Minneapolis, Mexican farm labour communities spread across the US, the growing Chinese presence in the retail sector, South Asian cab drivers in New York City, and Indian software professionals in Silicon Valley are images of immigrant communities that have come to the fore in the last ten years. Research on migrants and migration has contributed much to our understanding of the cultural implications of globalization, in particular to its unstable and ambiguous effects. Scholars have explored the contradictions of diasporic culture (Boscagli, 1996; Levy, 2000; Prashad & Mathew, 2000), traced new categories of global or transnational culture (Appadurai, 1996; Pollock *et al.*, 2000) or studied changing race relations in the context of such large-scale migrations (Prashad, 2000).

While the study of diasporic and transnational cultural flows, with the migrant as the subject of such cultural productions, has provided invaluable insights, the political-economic context and implications of migration have received less attention. Most specifically, the role of the State in producing migrants as cultural subjects of globalization is largely unexamined. Given the ease with which cultural production travels, aided by an ever-expanding mediascape (including telecommunication technologies), the relevance of the nation-state as a category of analysis is treated with some ambiguity (Tölölyan, 1996). This is best exemplified by the work of Appadurai (1996) who argues that his effort 'is explicitly transnational—even post-national. As such it moves dramatically away from the architecture of classical modernization theory, which one might call fundamentally realist, insofar as it assumes the salience, both methodological and ethical, of the nation-state'. (p. 9). Other theorists have been far more cautious and have resisted the

Sangeeta Kamat, Ali Mir, and Biju Mathew, 'Producing hi-tech: globalization, the state and migrant subjects', *Globalisation, Societies and Education*, 2, 1, suggestion that the nation-state is becoming irrelevant. Brenner (1997) for instance argues that such approaches result in the 'neglect [of] the major role of State level processes' resulting finally in a situation where 'the national-state scale vanishes almost entirely. In their haste to escape from the territorial trap, therefore, many globalization researchers veer toward an equally problematic inversion of State-centric approaches, culminating in a kind of global-babble' (138).

Taking our cue from this debate, in this [chapter] we locate the role of the State in the 'real' processes of migration and show how it is integral to not only structuring the nature of migration across borders but also to shaping migrant cultures. In other words, we argue that the State influences not only the 'fact' of migration but is also part of constructing the 'mental space' of migrant subjects. An analysis of the State as a critical actor in the formation of transnational culture provides important insights into our understanding of globalization. In this [chapter], we focus on one specific migrant group—the Indian high-tech worker in the US. The following sections of this [chapter] examine the relation between Indian software professionals and the two nation-state forums they interface—the Indian State on the one hand and the US on the other. In outlining the role of particular States in producing transnational processes and cultures, we suggest a new theoretical oeuvre that locates state policies and national cultures as integral to theorizing globalization. The work of comparative education scholars on education, the State and globalization underscores this particular point well (Green, 1997; Burbules and Torres, 2000; Morrow and Torres, 2000; Stromquist and Monkman, 2000). For instance, the edited collection by Burbules and Torres (2000) shows that 'nation-states have become increasingly internationalized, in the sense that their agencies and policies become adjusted to the rhythms of the new world order' (p. 7). The work of each of these scholars makes a persuasive case for how 'the nation-state is changing but in ways that do not necessarily reduce the scope or importance of its functions' (Green, 1997, p. 165).

In this [chapter], we discuss the large-scale migration of the Indian high-tech worker and show how this migration would not be possible without the education policies of the Indian State and the immigration policies of the US government. Equally salient, the policies of the two States are shaped not only by the demands of the global economy but also by the peculiarities of national history and politics of each country. The case of high-tech migrant workers illustrates the complex intersections of caste politics in Indian society and race politics in the US reflected in the education and immigration policies of each country respectively. Our discussion of the historical and political legacies of each country that are implicated in the migration of the high-tech worker raises equally interesting questions about the political and cultural effects of the sudden growth of this labour sector in both countries. Unfortunately, we cannot address the complex question of these effects in this [chapter], though our work on the Indian diaspora shows that the nation-state and nationalism are ever-present in the transnationalism of the high-tech Indian.[1]

The Indian State and the High-Tech Migrant

India's success in the information technology sector in the 1990s is celebrated as the fulfilment of the dream of modern India.[2] The post-colonial Indian State in its initial moments of emergence invested in large river valley dams and hydroelectric projects that, in Prime Minister Nehru's words, were the 'temples of modern India'. These dams were emblematic of the trajectory to which the new nation was committed. This was an early defining moment in the Indian State's technological imaginary—the new nation was visualized as one where technological miracles in the form of large dams, large public sector infrastructure projects in iron and steel, nuclear fuel, ship building, and aeronautics would be the central concerns and the driving force behind its progress. This technological project would need a technically sophisticated workforce that could build and maintain these 'temples'. Thus in the State's imaginary, India's great leap forward was to come through an elite technological workforce. From that early moment onwards, the success of the Indian State's project of modernity has been most significantly evident in its sophisticated and high-skilled labour force in the domestic as well as foreign labour markets.

We argue that this workforce is not homogenous and that we need to produce a more complex understanding of the Indian State's relation to the production of this migrant technological workforce. In addition, we need to examine the systemic role of the nation-state as a form in the differential mediation and management of this heterogeneous workforce within the phenomena we call globalization. We argue that the role of the Indian State has changed considerably vis-à-vis the production of this global workforce. We suggest that there is not just one original moment that is represented by developmentalist modernity, but three distinct moments in the production of this workforce and that these three moments articulate with and respond to different aspects of the global technological labour market as it evolved from the 1960s to today. The limitations of the developmentalist phase in which the state was the only player in the production of technologically skilled labour, led to a private sector in technology education that accentuated the caste and class divisions in Indian society. In the Nineties, the phenomenal growth of the computer and information technology sector in Western industrialized countries led the Indian State to build and invest in the private education institutes that facilitated the upward mobility of ascendant caste and class groups. In its current phase, the technological education policy of the Indian State is subservient to the global service sector. Though we analyse these moments as distinct from each other we see them as intertwined and their engagement is itself reflective of the larger contradictions that the Indian State has negotiated since independence. In other words, the story of the high-tech migrant labour force is to some extent the story of the contradictions faced by the post-colonial Indian State.

The Compact of Technological Modernity

Higher education policy in post-colonial India reflects the emergent structures of power within the nation-state. The formation of the early technology education infrastructure echoed the particular trajectories established within the nationalist movement. Khilnani (1997), reflecting on the nature of the Indian State and politics that came out of the nationalist struggle (a 'precarious balance'), concludes that: 'Politics at once divides the country and constitutes it as a single, shared, crowded space, proliferating voices and claims and forcing negotiation and accommodation' (p. 9). India thus emerged from its nationalist movement not as a bourgeois democratic nation-state in the image of the Euro-American capitalist democracies but as a 'coalitional' State—where the State drew its mandate from multiple forces such as its caste and class elites alongside a mobilized stratum of subaltern communities that constituted the struggle for independence.[3] The upper caste political elite that came to operate the State structures held in place what in hindsight was an impossible coalition—one fraught with irresolvable contradictions. The developmentalist regime that was inaugurated within the logic of Nehruvian modernity operated primarily through the idea of State socialism, that seemed to respond to the aspirations of both the national bourgeoisie on the one hand and the large segment of lower caste and Dalit communities on the other.[4] The national bourgeoisie were protected under State socialism—the State provided infrastructural development for building its productive capacities and protected its markets from international competition. For the masses of urban and rural poor, the affirmative action programmes (known as 'reservations' in India), the promise of land reform, employment generation schemes, and subsidies in essential commodities provided a brief but ultimately empty resolution. We argue, as Corbridge and Harriss (2000) do, that the post-colonial developmentalist regime was not a unique moment but one that exhibited a series of continuities from the colonial regime with the trajectory of development being defined by a national elite who spoke 'in the name of' the people.

The educational infrastructure created out of this regime reflected the same dominant logic. The dream of technological modernity concretized through a national technological education infrastructure that produced an elite engineering workforce. The Indian Institutes of Technology (IITs) were the elite science and technology institutes directed by the Central (i.e. Federal) government while the regional engineering colleges (RECs) were the second tier elite colleges administered at the regional (i.e. State) level; though the RECS also received substantial aid from the Central government. Further, at the regional level, local universities mimicked this structure by establishing sub-regional engineering colleges. In addition, the Central and State funded Indian Technological Institutes (ITIs) were created as diploma-granting institutions that trained the bottom-end of the labour market for this technological dream. The dozens of ITIs were generating a large mass of low-level workforce that was to enter the State sector as technicians, machinists, plumbers and electricians. On a smaller scale, specialized and elite institutions were also established in medicine (the All India Institute of Medical Sciences, the Armed Forces Medical College), management (the Indian Institutes of Management) and pure and applied science (the Indian Institute of Science, ISIs). That this project of technological modernity was hegemonic was evident at multiple registers. It largely reproduced the structures of power that constituted the post-colonial nation—the educational elite that graduated from these institutions was primarily high caste (largely Brahmin and other allied castes that already enjoyed a legacy of elite education).[5]

The success of this project, the garnering of further power by the upper caste elite, also discursively established the hegemony of technological modernity in the minds of large segments of the Indian middle caste/class who had no real access to this educational infrastructure. In less than two decades of independence, the technological imaginary had become hegemonic, so much so that most popular movements of the time referenced the importance of technological education in one way or the other.[6]

If the first moment of State formation—the Nehruvian—had yielded to a social compact that kept the emergent techno-managerial regime locked within the circuits of upper caste domination, the early 1970s saw the beginnings of the breakdown of this compact. The beginnings of the breakdown are best captured in what is presumed to be an inexplicable and deviant moment of Indian realpolitik—the state of Emergency that lasted for two years between 1975 and 1977. Far too often, the Emergency (imposition of authoritarian rule) is understood as an aberration in the otherwise perfect record of Indian democracy, one that was caused by a power hungry politician. An alternative reading, such as the one put forth by Prashad (1996) argues that the crisis of Indian democracy was already in formation in the 1960s and 1970s. The nation was rocked by a large-scale Maoist upsurge in the East and South-east, strikes in the urban centres, the resurgence of lower caste mobilizations in Southern India (example, the Telangana movement and the Dravidian movement) and the Sarvodaya (Gandhian self-government) movement along Northern India. In other words, the late-60s and early-70s witnessed a series of agitations against the failure of the developmentalist State to provide for large segments of the nation's middle and lower castes. The Emergency can thus be read as a response to the crisis in post-colonial democracy and the failure of the Nehruvian imaginary of a technologically modern State.

The Privatization of Technological Education and the Rise of the Middle-Castes

The breakdown of the coalitional State and the resurgence of sectional caste interests also manifests in new developments in the higher education sector. The 1970s saw the establishment of what came to be dubbed 'donation engineering colleges'—private educational institutions where entering students could by-pass the highly competitive public entrance examinations and join engineering (and later medical) colleges by paying a steep 'donation' or fee to the institution. The Siddaranga Institute of Technology (SIT) was one of the many private engineering colleges that mushroomed in the decade of the Seventies, mostly across the southern states of Karnataka and Andhra Pradesh.[7] Beginning in Karnataka the trend spread quickly to the two neighbouring states of Andhra Pradesh and Maharashtra. In the mid-1970s, several similar institutions had been formed in Karnataka such as the M. S. Ramaiah Engineering College in Bangalore, the Basava Kalyan Engineering College in Bidar, the Sri Jaychamarajendra College of Engineering (SJCE) in Mysore, the Khaja Banda Nawaz College of Engineering in Gulbarga, the Prodadevaraya Institute of Technology of the Veerashaiva Vidyalaya Sanhga in Bellary, and the B. V. Bhoomireddy Engineering College in Hubli. The caste basis of these colleges was clear from the naming of the institutions. The two dominant middle-caste communities of Karnataka—the *Lingayats* and the *Vokkaligas*—accounted for a large number of these colleges.[8] If SIT and SJCE were the *Lingayat* identified institutions, Ramaiah Engineering, the largest and the most prestigious of the lot, was a *Vokkaliga* institution. In Andhra Pradesh, the earliest example of the above formation was the Siddartha Engineering and Medical Colleges in Vijaywada that symbolized the emergence of the *Kamma* community into the technological workforce. The naming of the institutions (e.g. Siddartha) points to the strong non-Brahmin sensibility of the community, and an identification with an alternative route to knowledge and modernity. The development of Siddartha in Vijaywada followed a spate of caste-based institutions in the city of Hyderabad such as the Chaitanya Bharati Institute of Technology, the Vasavi Engineering College and the Matrusri Engineering College. It is important to note the following similarity between these institutions: almost all were formed under the patronage of caste-based trusts that then spun off Educational Societies that came to dominate the techno-managerial education sector in the 1980s.[9]

These institutions openly claimed their caste basis and their caste specific educational goals. For instance, the Kammavari Trust announced that: 'The Kammavari Sangham ... [has] diversified its activities to many folds. The Sangham provides scholarships and free hostel facilities to the poor and meritorious students of the Kamma community ... The Sangham also started the Kammavari Credit Cooperative Society to mobilize deposits, to lend loans for productive purposes, encourage small entrepreneurs and social causes ... '.

The organization of caste groups into 'secular' trusts had its origins in the nationalist movement. Most of these trusts started in the 1930s and 1940s, diversified into primary and secondary education in the 1950s and engaged in large-scale expansion of techno-managerial education in the 1970s. This strategic caste-based mobilization was a conscious strategy that dates back to the colonial period.[10]

It is useful to note that not all the beneficiaries of this private education wave were caste or class elites. While the institutions were, for the most part, controlled by the elite within such community formations, the beneficiaries came from different socio-economic backgrounds. The hegemony of the Nehruvian moment one could argue was so total that many lower middle class families put themselves through severe hardships just to ensure an engineering education for their children. Thus while as a trend, the 'donation engineering college' was clearly an elite strategy of ascendant caste groups to wrest some control from the State, its effects were more distributed. The State too had a tricky role to play in this transformation. Since the ascendant caste groups had come to occupy centre stage in politics, the State had to find a way to accommodate them while keeping in place a veneer of its socialist credentials.

The advent of the donation colleges led to a growing criticism that the State was not only cooperating with the strategy that allowed the rich to by-pass the socialist agenda and further their own interests but also that this was at the expense of quality. The response of the State to this crisis was interesting in as much as it set the stage for the model for future techno-managerial education. The State re-entered the space of the private donation engineering colleges by insisting on a common entrance examination for the private techno-managerial educational institutions. In the 1980s, the State revived a body that was itself a product of the post-colonial nation's early technological infrastructure—the All India Council for Technical Education (AICTE)—and gave it the charge of certifying the private engineering colleges. In return for regulatory powers over the private engineering colleges that included the entrance exam and monitoring the curriculum, the State diverted some of its educational subsidies towards the private institutions through the Grants-in-Aid programme and consolidated such institutions under a common administration such as the Visvesariyya Technological University in Karnataka.

New Educational Forms and the Globalization of High-Tech Labour

Given the justifiable concerns about the quality of the emergent workforce from the new institutions, the integration of this workforce into the national and international high-tech labour market raised some problems. The easiest solution for the graduates was to join the second rung of the international labour market. While the IITs and the RECs continued to export their graduates to the elite North American research environments, the new engineers chose to enter the lower rung labour markets such as those of the Middle East, Australia, Canada, and more recently South Africa, New Zealand and Botswana. Their mass integration into the US corporate sector had to wait until larger shifts in the global labour market created the space for their skills through a new set of structural arrangements.

By the mid-1980s corporate America had discovered subcontracting. The large-scale shifts in the global economy away from manufacturing in the advanced capitalist countries and the revolution in computing technologies that began in the early 1980s created a demand for new skills. In response, the Indian high-tech workforce began to 'retool' using the technological education at its disposal. The microcomputer revolution generated an enormous demand in the US for a technical workforce with a certain kind of mid-level skill (for example, translating the functionality of large legacy systems to the microcomputer level). Several Indian corporations (Tata Burroughs Limited, for example) provided labour for these projects at less than a fifth of the cost of US labour. By the late-1980s, the international labour market was shifting and a regime of subcontracting and information technology-based service industry work came into maturity. The new engineers, whose skills did not permit them to enter research spaces with ease, found themselves in a unique position to exploit this new market.

In many ways, we argue that this second (post-Nehruvian) moment was a period of transition that led to a new form of globalization—the globalized service sector. As the rationalization of this sector proceeded, it became evident that not all engineering skills were of equal value. Fewer and fewer of the new colleges offered a standard engineering college curriculum and instead started focusing on electronic and computer engineering domains. The same caste-based trusts that had deployed their resources towards large engineering colleges began to invest in a mushrooming segment of Masters of Computer Applications degrees. This led to further privatization of technical education as the State gave up all pretences towards providing leadership in broad technical education, confining itself to producing elite engineers who joined the research and development departments of US corporations. As private capital that was in tune with the emergent globalization phenomena entered the field of technical education, the State imposed no standardization and instead allowed the market to determine the skill sets and the quality of skills produced. Indian firms began offering two year 'diplomas' in software engineering with euphemistic names such as National Institute of Information Technology (NIIT). A franchise network of NIITs mushroomed all over the nation followed in less than a decade by a large base of new corporations entering the field of software training, especially in the Southern States.[11]

These new corporations changed the notion of technical education by taking not a broad based approach but by focusing on a narrow set of skills condensed into certification programmes of six months or a year. This phase signified a transition from 'education' to 'training' along with an attendant reduction in skill sets. As a senior NIIT manager said:[12] 'We pushed the WAP (Wireless Access Protocol) market for a while, took leadership in training in that domain and then moved out of that market quickly enough ... because it was clear to us that the market was not going to be a sustainable one'.

In other words, short-term skills became the primary focus of technical education programmes, though advertised as providing a lifelong career. The State's role is this process is relevant to our discussion of globalization. The State abdicated its role of providing public education in order to facilitate the demands of a new global labour market. In the NIIT manager's words: 'to the government's credit, it has simply stopped interfering. Its greatest contribution lies in the fact that it saw its role as facilitating the flow of labour to the US and encouraging companies such as NIIT ... '.

The primary mode of 'encouragement' was the flexibility of the government in creating favourable conditions for these new IT firms. For instance, when Texas Instruments set up its operations in Bangalore, the government went to great lengths to assist the process, and one Department of Energy official claimed that the Department had broken 26 separate rules to accommodate Texas Instruments and was willing to break more (Evans, 1992).[13]

In the process of interfacing its citizens with technological modernity, the State steadily abandoned its role as the grand equalizer, a mission the leaders of the new nation had committed to in 1947. In its place, the State chose to respond to an international labour market, even if that meant changing the very definition of technical education to imply a narrow range of skills training and the simultaneous privatization of the same, thus allowing for the reproduction of caste and class inequality. The super elites—the highest castes—continue to have access to the best quality of comprehensive technology education and the ascendant middle castes have their share of the pie as they deploy themselves as the new labour of the globalized service sector. Meanwhile, the marginalized communities—the lower castes, the Dalits and tribal communities—have little or no access to the dream of technological modernity. If the social compact of the 1950s produced a veneer of socialism that aimed to create access for the lowest end of society, the contemporary social compact is one of elites—old and new—the bourgeoisie, the upper-castes and the new middle-castes.

The American State and the High-Tech Migrant

In the previous sections, we have argued that the Indian state has historically played a central role in the creation of conditions that permit, facilitate and control the emigration of the nation-state's subjects. In the following sections, we examine the role of the receiving state in the process of migration of Indians to the US over the past four decades, particularly in the context of the legal reforms that permitted and facilitated the migration of a particular class of people.

Much of the scholarship documenting the experiences of Indians migrating to the US focuses on the early years of this process. Studies on Indian migration to the US show the early arrival of Indians as indentured labourers and servants of British visitors, or the late 19th century migration of Punjabi peasants to California who took up employment in steel factories, lumberyards and railroad-laying (Leonard, 1997). Their accounts provide a compelling analysis of the racial reproduction of the state and the policies that guided this process,[14] the attempts by Indian migrants to claim naturalization by contending that they were 'white',[15] and the Thind case, which closed the door on such attempts[16] (Jensen, 1998). There is very little systematic research available of the new wave of the post-60s migration that not only accelerated the flow of Indians into the US but also transformed the demographic character of this community.

According to the latest report of the US Census Bureau, there are 1.7 million Indians and Indian Americans living in the US. Placed in a historic perspective, this figure indicates a dramatic increase in this population. The records indicate that there were little more than 500 Indians in the US in 1898, about 7,000 in 1913, 2,400 in 1940, 7,000 in 1965, over 387,000 in 1980 and more than 815,000 in 1990. This increase in numbers was possible due to the nature of legislation enacted over the past several decades that reflects the changing attitude of the US towards foreign workers.

Following the Thind verdict, Indians faced a period of discrimination,[17] resulting in a rapid decline in the rate of their migration. By 1940, only 2,400 Indians remained in the US, a mere 3% of whom were professionals, while the vast majority continued to work in agriculture related occupations. Between 1923 and 1946, a mere 3,000 Indians were admitted into the US. On 2 July 1946, Congress passed the Luce-Cellar Act, which repealed the 'barred zone' clause of the 1917 Act and granted 'the privilege of admission to the United States' along with the 'ability for naturalization' to 'races indigenous to India'. However, the quota system allowed only a small number of Indians to migrate and their population in the US increased at an extremely slow rate.

The grounds for a significant change in this pattern of migration were laid by the 1952 Immigration Act (the McCarran-Walter Act), through which the prohibitions against contract workers were first lifted.[18] Although only a small number of skilled workers entered the US under the provisions of this legislation, the Act set the precedent for the migration of high-skill temporary workers from different parts of the world. The passage of the Immigration and Nationality Act (also called the Hart Cellar Reform Act) in 1965 represented the most significant overhaul of immigration policy since 1924, abolished the national-origins quota system and eliminated race, national origin, or ancestry as a basis for immigration. Its biggest impact was the reduction of discrimination against Asians, opening the door for a new wave of migration to the US. The Act created an annual quota of 170,000 immigrants from the Eastern Hemisphere, with a limit of 20,000 for any one country. Visas were issued to immigrants from all over the world based on their skills or to effect family reunification. Most South Asian immigrants of this time arrived under the category of occupational preference. They tended to be urban, English-speaking, highly educated, skilled professionals. Reports indicate that 83% of Indians who migrated to the US between 1966 and 1977 were scientists (around 20,000), engineers (40,000) and doctors (25,000).

The Arrival of the Professional Class

While enacting legislation concerning immigration, the lawmakers in the US have attempted to walk a fine line between providing the skilled foreign labour that was needed (and demanded) by US corporations and protecting the interests of local labour. Consequently, the 1952 Immigration and Nationality Act created the category of an H-1 visa, which could be offered to 'an alien having a residence in a foreign country which he has no intention of abandoning'. Further, the law required that the resultant demand for the overhaul of the immigration rules led to the passage of the Immigration Act of 1990, which instituted a series of measures that attempted to streamline the immigration process for skilled workers in a manner that protected qualified US workers from discrimination. First, the new law created the category of H-1B visas specifically for workers in specialty occupations, defined as those that require 'a theoretical and practical application of a body of highly specialized knowledge' (INA 214). Second, a cap of 65,000 visas was placed on this category. Third, the law required prospective employers to file Labor Condition Applications with the Department of Labor (not with the Department of Justice which governs the INS) to ensure that the hired aliens adhered to wage standards, and that the working conditions of the hired aliens would not 'adversely affect the working conditions of similarly situated US workers'. Fourth, the law stipulated that H-1B workers would be admitted into the US for a maximum initial stay of three years, which could be extended for a maximum of another three years. Unless the status of such workers changed (for instance, if they were approved for permanent residency), they would be required to leave the country after the expiry of the six-year period. The Immigration Subcommittee that worked on this legislation explicitly contended that immigration rules were adequately tightened 'for the benefit of American workers'.

The nature of the demands required of an H-1B application succeeded in dampening the inflow of temporary foreign workers initially. The figures released by the Visa Office of the Department of State place the numbers of H-1 visas issued at 58,673 in 1990, 59,325 in 1991, 51,667 in 1992, 42,206 in 1993, 49,284 in 1994, and 59,093 in 1995. The share of Indian workers in this category rose from a modest 2,697 in 1990 (the largest contingents at this time were from the Philippines and the UK) to 19,203 in 1996 (the largest group by far; the UK being a distant second at 5,601).

As the decade progressed, the numbers of aliens arriving to work for the information technology industry rose dramatically. The explosion of the Information Technology (IT) sector and a chronic shortage of skilled workers created a tight labour market. In the meantime, the transformation of the Indian political economy (discussed in the first section of this [chapter]) had generated large pools of appropriate labour skills for the American market. However, the entry of workers was restricted by the 65,000/year ceiling imposed by the 1990 law. The demand for skilled foreign workers first outstripped the supply in 1997. By September of that year, the cap was reached leaving several prospective employers with unfilled positions. The labour shortage spurred by the continuing growth of the IT industry was significantly exacerbated by the Y2K crisis and the pressure on Congress to raise the ceiling for temporary workers started mounting. By early May 1998, the limit of 65,000 for the fiscal year was again exhausted. The popular press was replete with stories of dire prognostications of the potential disasters unleashed by the Y2K bug. The public imagination suffused with visions of collapsing security systems, airline mishaps, vanishing bank accounts, and IRS nightmares visited on citizens. It further contended that the high-tech sector was the driving force behind the resurgent US economy and that any roadblock that slowed it down would be against national interest.

Against this backdrop, Congress found it easy to enact the American Competitiveness and Workforce Improvement Act (ACWIA) in 1998, which increased the H-1B visas quota to 115,000 for 1999 and 2000, and to 107,500 for 2001. The bill also decreed that the cap would return to 65,000 in 2002. Interestingly, the ACWIA passed by an overwhelming majority with limited discussion about its potential impact on US labour (Carney, 1998). Once again though, the government had to resolve the (in this case, muted) tension between serving the interests of the corporations (and by extension, the national economy) and the local workers. It sought to do this by imposing a $500 fee per H-1B petition and earmarked those funds for the training and development of displaced workers and for low-income student scholarships.

The pent-up demand for skilled foreign workers manifested itself through the increase in H-1B visas issued: 80,608 in 1997, 91,378 in 1998 and 116,695 in 1999 (the last number exceeded the cap due to an 'oversight' at the INS). Correspondingly, the number of Indian workers arriving in the US went up to 31,686 in 1997, 40,247 in 1998 and 55,047 in 1999. In other words, over 47% of the visas issued in 1999 were awarded to Indian workers, most of them in the IT sector.

The new act, while welcomed by the IT industry, failed to satisfy its huge appetite for foreign labour. The roaring economy spurred by the booming stock market had resulted in a proliferation of dot-com businesses. Simultaneously, every corporation was beefing up its IT operations, subcontracting them for the most part to specialized firms. Incidentally, subcontracting was spurred by the current managerial logic that firms ought to focus their energies on their 'core competencies' (Hamel and Prahalad, 1994), not on the aspects of the business that could be better handled by the market.

Pressure from various industry quarters led to the introduction of the American Competitiveness in the 21st Century Act (ACTFCA),[19] a bill proposed by a group of US Senators[20] that would raise the cap on H-1B visas to 195,000 a year and welcomed by the stewards of the IT industry.[21] Once again, there were a few provisions in the bill that allowed the lawmakers to claim that the H-1B programme was merely a temporary measure that would exist until local labour was available to meet the demand. Among other things, the bill sought to 'establish a new High Tech Scholarships and Grants programme to be administered by NSF to improve pre-college math and science education (apply new technologies, train teachers, develop innovative curricula, improve student skills and motivation)'. It also earmarked $20 million annually for Boys and Girls Clubs of America to help pay for computer facilities, and funds to hire and train instructors to teach disadvantaged students in inner city neighbourhoods. In addition, a separate bill (HR 5362) introduced an increase in the application fee for the H-1B visas to $1,000.

Retaining Control over Migration

One can identify two axes around which US policy facilitating Indian migration have evolved. On the one hand, immigration laws were written to permit the entry of appropriate (skilled) labour for the benefit of local corporations and the local economy. On the other hand, the State has had to temper these policies by ensuring that the laws contained sufficient provisions that sought to both protect local labour and offer it opportunities to increase its skill level. Through the latter, the State has allowed itself to contend that its encouragement of migration was a temporary measure, designed to alleviate short-term labour shortages while appropriate local labour was being trained and developed. In this manner, the state resolves the tension between serving the seemingly contradictory demands of its various constituencies.

Therefore, in terms of the migration of Indians to the US, we notice that both the sending and the receiving States successfully position themselves as agents that react to the pressures of a global labour market. The changing demands of the market lead to a corresponding shift in the legal framework that, in this context, is the handmaiden in the service of the corporate economy. The shortage of professionals in the US first opened the doors for doctors and engineers to cross its national borders to seek employment in the country. As the demand abated, the Immigration and Nationality Act Amendments of 1976 insisted that potential migrants demonstrate proof of firm job offers before they migrated to the US while the Health Professionals Educational Assistance Act of 1976 did the same for health workers. Currently, as the American Medical Association seeks to regulate the relationship between demand and supply among doctors, only a very limited number of physicians from India have the wherewithal to negotiate the very tricky and complicated road to employment in the US. On the other hand, software professionals whose skills were hugely in demand in the late 1990s discovered that the migratory process, at least in terms of finding H-1B employment and obtaining travel documents, has been a relatively easy one.[22]

The changing dynamic of the legislation around the H-1 visa has allowed the state to determine and construct the 'desirable' immigrant. It also decides the terms of migration and the duration of stay of the immigrant.[23] As Prashad (2000) argues, the authority of the state allows it to exercise a control reminiscent of the colonial doctrine 'we want your labour, not your bodies'.

Migration and the Reproduction of the State

In his book '*In an Antique Land*' the novelist/anthropologist Amitav Ghosh (1993) explores the contemporaneity of the idea of the nation-state. Through the shifting fortunes of an 'Egyptian' Jewish trader, his slave from south India, MS 131 and Ghosh's own experiences in Egypt in search of the story of MS 131, the author brings to life a world were the conditions of migration were not determined by the nation-state. Over time, the lucidly mobile cultures of the Arabian Sea and the spice route were transformed by the power of the nation-state into Egyptian or Indian national cultures. Today, it appears we have come full circle with pronouncing the death of the nation-state. In this age of unmediated mediascapes and deterritorialized cultural flows the nation-state appears less a political reality and more a methodological problem. Does the idea of a nation-state then have a short shelf life? Our discussion shows that the converse is true. In as much as the acceleration of migration is an important aspect of the larger phenomenon called globalization (Sassen, 1996), the question then is whether the nation-state has lost some of its relevance even on this count. Are we witnessing a slow but significant process of erosion of the nation-state and its powers? Or have entirely new sets of powers become visible? When examined from within the standard frames of globalization, the evidence for a disappearing nation-state is clearly ambiguous. The central trope of globalization thus far has been the explosive expansion of capital and its unrestricted mobility across national boundaries, overseen in part through international bodies such as the WTO, the IMF/World Bank and other inter-state treaties. The emergence of these supra-national bodies is the basis for the argument of a collapsing nation-state. However, as Smith (1997) and others argue, the global regime of capital is made possible only through an interaction of a 'system of states'. The history of emigration and immigration of Indians to the US convinces us that this is indeed so. Organizations such as the WTO exist and acquire legitimacy precisely because they build on the fundamental assumption of stable nation-states. The issue of labour migration is even more muddied, especially given the silence that surrounds the topic at international forums. The silence should not however be read as an exclusion or inaction but as a reflection of the different valence that labour has in the specific configuration of globalization that we are currently witnessing.

Our [chapter] points out that both the US and the Indian State have hardly been inactive on the question of migration. The US immigration policies since the 1960s have created a regime of immigration that clearly privileges a global techno-managerial workforce while carefully and diligently managing a set of contradictions. These policies of the past two decades indicate the growing complexity of rules with differential frameworks that make visible the nature of the immigrant population that is desired for American citizenship.

The Indian State's relation to techno-managerial migration is just as well articulated and systematic. The State's withdrawal from the domain of techno-managerial education points to transforming notion of citizenship within India. The quasi-socialist mode of State-sponsored higher education was intended as a structural intervention to ensure equal access for all Indians. This aspiration was abandoned and the State withdrew from even making such a notional claim and allowed for caste-based capital to be the fundamental mode of mobilization towards a wider techno-managerial education. First, the State's empowerment of some segments of the population in terms of facilitating their entry into the techno-managerial domain—the narrow modernity that it had defined for its citizens—is indicative of who are the 'more equal' citizens. Second, as global capital enters India, there is the question of how the State deals with those who do not fit in with this narrow modern-citizen that the Indian State has constructed. One could argue that given the violent suppression of these 'non-modern' subjects—the repression of peoples' movements and the increase in State violence against labour—we are beginning to see the emergence of a new relation between the Indian State and its 'populations' in the era of globalization. It is here that we note the similarities between the two States. The phenomenon of the high-tech migrant worker makes clear that 'globalization dramatically alters many of the ways in which states mediate power at both the substate and transnational levels' (Morrow and Torres, 2000, p. 29). Both the American and the Indian States work towards the empowerment of specific social groups of labour, indicating an implicit agreement on the management of a global labour regime. In this sense therefore, the well articulated international laws of the WTO are not very different from the system of documentation categories that have universal acceptance—the engineering degree and the H-1B visa. The sole difference between the management of capital and that of labour is that the latter, given the history of the relation between States and populations, must continue to be the subject of one sovereign State or the other so as to ensure the continued viability of the system of States. Each individual must remain a governable object under the aegis of a particular State for the idea of the nation-state to remain viable.

In the words of Henri Lefevbre (1991), who wrote extensively on theories of the modern State, the State in this system tends to the 'control of flows' and 'assures their coordination' of international resources for the capitalist system. The State thus is a social architecture that is constantly engaged in the production of matrices of international control creating what Lefevbre calls the 'State Mode of Production' where the State as a unit is central to a whole array of global networks, flows and practices of managing space. Thus, globalization can no longer be understood as a discrete set of disconnected histories but must be seen as a unified trajectory of a global network of States through which the political space is subdivided, parcelized and territorialized (Brenner, 1997). Globalization then is not a departure from the State System but instead represents the normalization of its form.

NOTES

1. See Aihwa Ong's (1999) impressive ethnography of Hong Kong and Chinese entrepreneurs in the US for similar insights.
2. We use the term technological modernity to specify a limited aspect of Euro-American modernity that seems to have had a special valence in the imaginary of India in its postcolonial phase. We point to this specific aspect of Indian modernity as one relevant to our discussion. The debate as to what constitutes Indian modernity is too vast a subject to be addressed here. For various distinct lines of argumentation on the larger issue, see Chatterjee, 1993; Appadurai, 1996; Khilnani, 1997; Pollock et al., 2000.

3. We use the term 'coalitional' to signify the composite and negotiated character of the State and not in the technical sense suggested by some theorists of State formation such as Kalecki (1993).

4. Dalit literally translates into 'downtrodden' and refers to the group deemed by the caste system as outside of the caste system and hence 'untouchable' or impure. In the post-independent period, Dalits organized as a political and cultural category distinct from Hindus and other religious and social groups. Corbridge and Harriss (2000) detail the developmentalist regime (also referred to as the Nehruvian phase) immediately following independence and the various political coalitions that sustained it.

5. This techno-managerial workforce was sought most vigorously not just by the Indian State and corporate sectors but also by American universities in search of highly skilled researchers—a demand that exploded in the 1960s as cold war hysteria gripped the US and the fear of falling behind the Soviet bloc in the domain of technology became a dominant concern. By the mid-1960s large segments of American elite technology institutes had already identified the Indian educational infrastructure as a significant part of their answer to the cold war demand for technological research.

6. For instance, the demand for a separate Telangana state in the late 1960s and the early 1970s framed access to education for the 'mulki' (the local) as one of its specific concerns.

7. The introductory document of the SIT states that 'The Siddaranga Institute of Technology [which] was established in 1963 is one among the over 100 institutions run by the Siddaranga Educational Society under the patronage of the Siddaranga Math'. The southern region of India has had a longer history of rulers investing in education in its people since pre-colonial times. There are undoubtedly other reasons for the rapid development of technical education in the South as opposed to the Northern region of India that require a separate study.

8. In some categorizations these are referred to as the upper-caste in contradistinction with the backward castes, the dalits and the tribal communities. In this [chapter] we use the term middle-caste so as to clarify the distinctions between the Brahminical upper-castes and these emergent elite middle-castes.

9. Minority elite groups in the south also reproduced the non-Brahmin middle-caste foray into techno-managerial education. The above-mentioned Khaja Banda Nawaz Engineering College in Gulbarga, the Ghousia Engineering College in Ramanagram, the Hazrat Khwaja Bhaktiar Khaki Engineering College of the Karnataka State Muslim Federation and the Muffakam Jah Institute of Technology in Hyderabad spoke to the concerns and the aspirations of the elite Muslim communities in the South.

10. Clearly, these caste-based organizational forms have been mobilized to different ends in different parts of the country—the success of the Gujarati *Patidar* (Patel) community in mobilizing internal credit resources is well known as is the enormous power of the *Kunbi* community which controls the Sugar Cooperatives in Maharashtra. The emergent non-Brahmin upper castes are mostly those that have a strong agrarian base and which during the Seventies managed to mobilize significant amounts of agrarian surplus. In Andhra Pradesh, the two most powerful non-Brahmin upper-caste communities—the *Kammas* and the *Reddys*—invested in agro-businesses such as fertilizer, seed or pesticide agencies on the one hand and in techno-managerial education on the other.

11. We also argue that the entry of private capital into this domain of information technology training is linked to the earlier wave of caste-based mobilization of resources. For example, the largest investor and long time President of NIIT—Shiv Nadar—is himself from such a middle caste South Indian community (the *Nadars* whose initial foray into the domain of

a new IT industry was based as much on caste-based resource mobilization as any of the private engineering colleges).

12. In an interview with one of the authors, 27 May 2002, NIIT headquarters, Bangalore, India.

13. As the NIIT manager says: 'The government has consistently cooperated with the demands put forth by IT professional bodies, IT industry trade bodies etc. ... mostly by way of loosening up the rules that make for an export oriented units ... such definitions have become very loose ... NIIT may not export much but simply because we are in the domain of IT we receive favourable treatment from the government.' (In an interview with one of the authors, 27 May 2002, Bangalore, India.)

14. The first Congress had decided that in order to become a naturalized citizen, a person had to be 'white' (a statute that was amended after the Civil War to include persons of African nativity or descent).

15. Indian petitioners argued that they were of 'Caucasian stock' and therefore were, technically, white. In March 1908, a court in New Orleans accepted this argument and admitted two Indians to citizenship. A number of such cases followed over the years, the best known of which is US versus Balsara, 1910 in which the courts ruled that the Parsi applicant was indeed Caucasian and therefore eligible for citizenship.

16. Bhagat Singh Thind's claim, which was originally granted by the district court, was subsequently refused by the Supreme Court which ruled that the meaning of 'white' should be interpreted on the basis of the understanding of the 'common man', and that therefore, Indians were ineligible for naturalization.

17. The Alien Land Law had prohibited Asian migrants from owning land. Indians had been exempt from this stipulation and had managed to purchase land considered marginal or worthless by Californians and had, through effort, turned these properties into productive farms. When the court announced the Thind verdict, California's attorney general commenced proceedings to revoke Indian land holdings.

18. There were several reasons for the passage of this Act. The Vietnam War had generated a shortage of physicians in the US and the indulgent 1950s had resulted in relative disinterest among many Americans in the arenas of science and technology, leading to a concern that the US was not producing enough top-notch engineers and scientists. This, coupled with an apprehension that the US was losing out in the space race to the Soviet Union, persuaded President John F. Kennedy to ask the US Congress to overhaul immigration laws so that 'highly trained or skilled persons' who might be 'be helpful to our economy' could migrate to the US. In addition, there was some pressure on the Congress to end the racially discriminatory nature of earlier immigration laws.

19. The Information Technology Association of America (ITAA), the leading trade association on the IT workforce shortage issue suggested through its President, Harry N. Miller that 'increasing the availability of highly skilled workers to American technology firms is one of the most positive steps Congress can take this year toward continuing the robust growth of the New Economy. Such an expansion of the H-1B programme will grow the American economy, build American businesses, and protect American competitiveness in world markets—all while working to assure fairness for the information technology industry's most important asset—the American worker'. The ITAA claimed that 'when Congress raised the H-1B annual ceiling to 115,000 in 1998, no one anticipated an even greater escalation in the demand for IT workers', Miller stated. 'Now that the evidence of a dramatic IT workforce shortage continues, it is time for Congress to increase the cap again.'

20. By Senators Abraham (R-MI), Gramm (R-TX) and Hatch (R-UT).

21. In a hearing before the Subcommittee on Immigration held on 21 October 1999, Senator Spencer Abraham invited a panel of five industry CEOs to testify that the Act would help American industry and help reduce the huge gap between supply and demand. Objections from groups such as the IEEE which claimed that the more pressing need was to 'make fundamental improvements in pre-college math and science education, to have lifelong learning and retraining to keep our workers in the cutting edge and better access for underrepresented groups: women, minorities, handicapped, economically disadvantaged and especially older Americans' were largely ignored.

22. The numbers released by the INS are indicative of this: over 60% of all visas allocated in 1999 were in occupations related to systems analysis and programming (53.3%), electrical and electronics engineering (4.9%) and computer-related occupations not classified elsewhere (3.4%).

23. The number of 'green cards' that can be offered to citizens of any given country are limited by law to 9,600 a year; the influx of 50,000 or so Indian temporary workers makes it structurally impossible for all of them to obtain permanent residency. Yet the passage of various INS regulations allows this to be contingently bypassed and the ACTFCA gives INS the authority to extend the maximum six-year stay of an H-1B worker on a case by case basis.

What Is Distinctive About the Knowledge Economy? Implications for Education

David Guile

Introduction

The idea that we live and work in a knowledge economy/society has gained increasing prominence in UK and EU economic and educational policies over the last decade. The conventional wisdom is that knowledge now constitutes the most important factor of production in the economies of advanced industrial societies; and as a corollary, that the populations of these countries require greater access to knowledge as represented by qualifications.

However, in both sociological and philosophical terms the nature of the knowledge economy has been under-theorized. Leading sociologists such as Bell (1973) and Castells (1996) have defined the knowledge economy in terms of knowledge as the key factor of and technology as the key resource for production. Yet, the nature of the knowledge involved has been contested by other social scientists, for example, Gibbons and colleagues (1994) and Nonaka and Takeuchi (1995) who offer very different accounts of what constitutes the distinctive nature of knowledge in the knowledge economy. This leads not only to theoretical incoherence but also to educational policies and practices that are often contradictory. A further problem with these accounts of the knowledge economy is that Bell and Castells do not consider the changing nature of the social relationships within which technology is embedded while Gibbons and colleagues and Nonaka and Takeuchi do not even discuss the question of technology. Yet there has been rapid change since the inception of the industrial revolution, so the question remains as to what is distinctive about this apparent new phase in the development of capitalist societies.

The aim of this chapter is to redress the under-theorization of the knowledge economy by sociologists and to identify the implications of the analysis developed here for education. The chapter starts by distinguishing between and accounting for the different explanations of the role of knowledge in the knowledge economy; it then argues that connections can be made between these two conceptions of knowledge and the knowledge economy though the concept of *epistemic cultures* (Knorr Cetina 1999); it then concludes by considering the implications of *epistemic* cultures for education.

Theoretical Knowledge as the *sine qua non* of Knowledge Economy

The widespread consensus amongst social scientists since the mid-1950s is that epochal economic and technological changes have been occurring in advanced industrial economies. One particular strand of epochalism that has been very influential in social theory is the 'knowledge economy' thesis (Osborne 1998). The concept of the knowledge economy was first coined by Drucker (1969) to refer to the application of knowledge from any field or source, new or old, to spur economic development. However, the figure who is best known for drawing attention to the impact of knowledge in the economies of advanced industrial societies is Daniel Bell.

Bell (1973) accepted that some form of knowledge had always been central to the functioning of any society (in the sense that knowledge is an anthropological universal). He argued that what was distinctive about advanced industrial societies was that theoretical knowledge—'organized statements of facts or ideas, presenting a reasoned judgement or an experimental result', now constituted the 'axial principle' of development (p. 175). Theoretical knowledge had acquired this new role because the shift from a manufacturing to service economy meant that: 'when knowledge becomes *involved* in some systematic form in the *applied transformation of resources* then one can say that knowledge, not labour, is the source of value' (Bell 1979: 169). Thus, the character and wealth of advanced industrial societies is now determined by a 'knowledge theory of value' because theoretical knowledge served two key purposes: its application through the R&D process constituted the main source of innovation; and it was central to policy formation to aid planning. Furthermore, this new role for theoretical knowledge called for, according to Bell (1974: 29) an 'intellectual technology' to guide its application in the research and policy process. So instead of maintaining the usual understanding of technology as to do with tools or machines, Bell invoked the term 'intellectual technology' to refer to the substitution of algorithms (problem-solving rules) for intuitive judgement in policy and research.

Bell's ideas about the new role of knowledge in the economies of advanced industrial societies have provided a dominant metaphor over several decades by helping many social scientists and policymakers to indicate what was distinctive about economic change. Moreover, his ideas have continued to influence thinking about knowledge economies/societies because they have been reinvigorated and given a new lease of life as a result of the extension and elaboration of its core argument in Manuel Castells's trilogy *The Information Age: Economy, Society and Culture* (1996; 2000).

Castells's trilogy, which has been heralded as the most important sociological analysis of recent times (Calhoun 2000), contains three main lines of argument. The first is a continuation of Bell's argument that knowledge (in Castells's terms, information generation, processing, and transmission) has superseded land, labour, and capital as the fundamental sources of productivity, and power. Castells extends his analysis by introducing two further propositions about this new paradigm: it is 'global' and 'networked'.[1] By virtue of the fact that he was writing twenty years after Bell, Castells focuses on Information and Communication Technology (ICT) and its impact on society, rather than on the contribution of intellectual technology to economic development. Castells (2000: 30) argues that ICT is characterized by: 'incomparable memory storage capacity and speed of combination and transmission of bits. . . . [thus, they offer] . . . substantially greater flexibility, feedback, interaction and reconfiguration of data [and] on-line communication, combined with flexibility of text, [which] allows for ubiquitous space/time programming'.

Thus, Castells introduces a new dimension to Bell's original argument. He maintains that the widespread deployment of ICT has resulted in the emergence of a new economic paradigm—an 'informational' economy, whose core feature is an increased demand for, and production of, information. The reason for this demand for information is the dual shift that has occurred in the principle of economic development in advanced industrial societies (Castells 1996: 61–5). The first is the move away from a mode of production whose primary aim was to maximize output in order to produce surplus profit, towards an 'informational mode of development' concerned with technological development and the generation of data. The second is a logical consequence of the first: the constant accumulation of wealth through the continuous transformation of existing technologies themselves and through the continuous transformation of ICT means that success in the global economy is dependent on the generation, processing and application of information to enhance business performance.

So in summary, the common link between Bell and Castells is that they both accept that knowledge is critical for economic development in advanced industrial societies. However, whereas Bell focused exclusively on the application of science as a spur to economic prosperity, Castells is chiefly concerned with the technological application of science in the form of ICT and the application of the data ICT generates.

Tacit Knowledge as the *sine qua non* of the Knowledge Economy

The relationship between science and society that lies at the heart of Bell's claims about the role of theoretical knowledge in the economy and partly underlies Castells's claims about the link between ICT and information, has changed over the past half-century in ways that they do not appear to acknowledge. Instead of conceiving of science as the major source of 'enlightenment' and 'technological innovation', many social scientists have increasingly viewed science in more modest and instrumental terms (Osborne 1998). This change in its status can be attributed to a number of factors:

- the emergence of the 'triple helix' between universities, industry, and the state that has significantly broadened the range of interest groups that are concerned with the production of knowledge in advanced industrial societies (Etzkowitz and Leydesdorff 1997);
- the process of global competition which emphasizes the 'performativity' of knowledge, that is, its instrumental capacity to address everyday problems (Lyotard 1988);
- the increased 'risks' associated with the commercial exploitation of science which have led societies to become more distrustful of science and to contest its knowledge claims (Beck 1992).

One manifestation of this new relationship between science and society has been a debate in other branches of social science, for example, science policy and management studies, about the emergence of a new mode of knowledge production, a new conception of knowledge and its contribution to the knowledge economy/society.

Michael Gibbons and his colleagues (1994) offer one of the most widely discussed accounts of the emergence of new modes of knowledge production. They distinguish between Mode 1—disciplinary-based research conducted in universities—and Mode 2 knowledge—transdisciplinary and heterogeneous modes of knowledge created in 'contexts of application' and 'characterised by a constant flow back and forth between fundamental and the applied, between the theoretical and the practical' (p. 18). This new form of knowledge is, according to Gibbons et al. (p. 24), a 'mixture' of codified and tacit components. This distinction was originally coined by Polanyi (1958) to reveal the philosophical limitations of conceiving of scientific knowledge in purely abstract, formal terms, and failing to acknowledge the 'personal element' of scientific knowledge. Gibbons and colleagues use the distinction between codified and tacit knowledge to identify what is distinctive about Mode 2 knowledge. They argue that it is the tacit dimension of scientists' knowledge that enables them to reconfigure the 'diverse array of knowledge resources' available amongst communities of practitioners according to the problem in hand.

This emphasis on tacit knowledge shifts the locus of R&D. Instead of R&D being viewed as an exogenous process carried on in university laboratories, it is now conceived of as an endogenous process carried out inside firms. From Gibbons and colleagues' perspective, therefore, it is tacit knowledge which is less susceptible to codification, rather than codified knowledge which provides firms with the distinctive capabilities that would give them a competitive edge in the global economy. Hence, surviving in the global economy involves firms discovering the configurations of tacit knowledge that will convey a commercial advantage on a recurrent basis (Gibbons et al. 1994).

The idea that firms constitute sites for innovation is not an entirely new proposition. Writers in management science such as Drucker (1969), Penrose (1959), and Nelson and Winter (1972) first pointed out in the 1960s that firms were repositories of quite specific types of knowledge which they to a greater or lesser extent were able to exploit successfully. This 'epistemological dimension' of firms' activities, that is, the way in which they contribute to the wider stock of ideas about what constitutes knowledge creation and knowledge sharing, has been comprehensively analysed by Nonaka and Takeuchi (1995). From their perspective, new knowledge is not exclusively created by scientists nor through the disembodied process that they maintain is a central feature of scientific methodology. Knowledge can be created by professionals facilitating a 'spiral of interactions' between explicit knowledge—in Nonaka and Takeuchi's terms information that has been communicated orally or in written form—and the tacit knowledge which they have developed intuitively and naturalistically at work.

Nonaka and Takeuchi, like Gibbons et al., invoke Polanyi's arguments about the 'tacit dimension' to justify their claims about the crucial role of tacit knowledge to economic development. Based on case study evidence of new product development in Japanese companies, Nonaka and Takeuchi maintain that the spiral of interactions between workers' codified and tacit knowledge constitutes a quintessential knowledge-creation process. It enables tacit knowledge to be made explicit as we represent intuitive understandings in the form of 'metaphors, analogies, concepts, hypotheses or models'. Once tacit knowledge has attained this state of explicitness, it can be shared and become part of the wider repertoire of knowledge that workers use to transform product and service design and delivery.

So in contrast to Bell and Castells who accepted the primacy of theoretical knowledge even though they focused on different aspects of its production and application in the economy, Gibbons and colleagues and Nonaka and Takeuchi place far greater emphasis on tacit knowledge as the key knowledge resource. The main reason for such different explanations about the type of knowledge required in the knowledge economy being put forward is because Bell, Castells, Stehr, Gibbons et al., and Nonaka and Takeuchi adopt fundamentally different views of knowledge: scientific realist and postmodern conceptions, respectively.

Scientific Realist and Postmodern Conceptions of the Knowledge Economy

It is widely accepted that Bell's views about the primacy of theoretical knowledge rests on an unquestioned assumption about the nature of scientific knowledge and scientific inquiry (Muller 2000; Stehr 1994). This leads Bell to accept two ideas about theoretical knowledge: that it is independent of contingent conditions; and that its application is a linear process (Stehr 1994: 67). Thus, by accepting the givenness of reality, the legitimacy of scientific knowledge, and a linear flow between discovery and application, of scientific ideas, Bell was able to endorse that knowledge constitutes the 'axial principle' of economic development. Castells, unlike Bell, does not engage in any epistemological discussion about the status of knowledge because he feels that he had 'no compelling reason' to improve on Bell's own definition of knowledge. The net effect of this silence about epistemological issues is that Castells ends up, by default, sharing a similar philosophical position with Bell about the character of knowledge (Muller 2001: 276–7).

By embracing a rather strong version of scientific realism, Bell and Castells disregard a number of issues about the character of and the application of knowledge which are central to their own theses. The first issue is that they both accept scientific knowledge as a given rather than the outcome of external influences or debates within disciplines. The implication of this assumption manifests itself in the work of each writer in different ways. Bell uses knowledge as an independent variable to explain the changes occurring in post-industrial societies in terms of the increased knowledge component of a nation's Gross National Product, while Castells uses information as an independent variable to explain the link between the deployment of ICT and productivity as 'knowledge acts upon knowledge'. The second issue is that they both treat theoretical knowledge and information as though they are discernible cultural objects that can be acquired easily and applied to produce solutions to problems. For Bell, theoretical knowledge possesses intrinsic qualities that can be easily applied to address economic or social problems so long as the application of knowledge is guided by the appropriate intellectual algorithms (Schiller 1997). While the information generated by ICT, for Castells, is a malleable resource and it is a fairly straightforward matter to transform it into usable knowledge to foster economic development (Webster 1997: 120).

One consequence of accepting the scientific realist assumption about the giveneness of and applicability of scientific knowledge is that Bell and Castells assume that science, by itself, is the 'engine' that impels technological and social change. In doing so, they implicitly adopt what Dennett (1987) has referred to as a 'design strategy' notion of social transformation. They assume that it is the design of the technological features of any system that is responsible for producing a specific set of outcomes, for improving and securing the results of that system and which is primarily responsible for generating new information, products, and services. Thus Bell and Castells maintain that the process of modernization can be gauged by looking at the transformative impact of science on advanced industrial societies. Each writer points to their structural features, the final output of knowledge inputs (i.e. new products and services) within the economy, and the transformative effects of scientific knowledge on different aspects of social and cultural life, on personal life and identity, industrial organization and market expansion, etc.

It is perfectly reasonable for Bell and Castells to maintain, up to a point, that modernization can be gauged by looking at the transformative impact of science and technology on advanced industrial societies. It has long been recognized that there has always been a close relation between technological specialization, technological cultures, and technological development in capitalist economies (Noble 1979). However, to understand why the changes that Bell and Castells have identified have occurred, it is necessary to take more explicit account of the contribution that culture makes to the development and application of science and technology. Before addressing this issue, the chapter highlights the postmodern conceptions of knowledge that characterize the work of Gibbons and colleagues and Nonaka and Takeuchi.

The postmodern influence can be detected in Gibbons et al.'s work from the polemic tone that permeates their observation that the emergence of Mode 2 knowledge fundamentally calls into question the whole edifice of scientific realism because, unlike Mode 1, it is incomplete:

> no longer in the conventional sense that it will eventually be superseded by superior science (for Popperians) or by a new scientific paradigm (for Kuhnians), but also in the sense that it is sharply contested (and no longer within the controlled environment of scientific peers but in the wider *agora*); and second, this shift involves re-negotiating and re-interpreting these boundaries'. (Nowotony, Scott, and Gibbons 2002: 199)

For Gibbons and colleagues this continued weakening of the insulation of science from society constitutes incontrovertible evidence of a trend that will perpetuate a growing demand for Mode 2 knowledge not only in scientific fields, but also more widely in society. Furthermore, the general acceptance of a more pluralistic conception of knowledge will, according to Gibbons and colleagues, also fuel a demand for new standards against which knowledge can be assessed, and this development will consolidate the shift towards a 'Mode 2 society'.

At first sight it is more difficult to trace a postmodern influence on the work of Nonaka and Takeuchi. They view their theory of knowledge conversion as an attempt to overcome one of the key scientific realist assumptions that the mind and world are separate, and they eschew any explicit references to postmodernism in their writings. For this reason, they, and other scholars familiar with their work, may be surprised, even startled, to discover that their work is interpreted as evincing a postmodern sensibility and as remaining trapped in the dualism. Nevertheless, there is clear evidence of the postmodern inflection of Nonaka and Takeuchi's thinking in their advocacy of a pluralistic conception of knowledge.

In a determined effort to distance themselves from the 'epistemological decorum' (Shapin 1994) that is the dominant characteristic of the scientific realist mode of knowledge production, Nonaka and Takeuchi (1995: 64) emphasize the inescapable 'subjective, bodily, and tacit aspects' of knowledge production. Thus they maintain that their spiral of knowledge conversion is as valid as scientific methodology as a method for producing new knowledge in the context of the workplace, and that the resulting knowledge is equally as valuable as science in supporting organizations' competitive advantage in the knowledge economy.

Whilst there is a reasonable argument to be made that organizations do not rely solely on science to secure competitive advantage and that knowledge production and application is determined by contextual factors, in making this argument Nonaka and Takeuchi introduce a radically new debate about tacit and theoretical knowledge. They claim that they are equally important forms of knowledge in the knowledge economy, thus they follow the postmodern tradition of symmetricalizing all forms of knowledge and methods of knowledge production. Where postmodernists tend to cite Nietzche and his rejection of the idea of foundational truth and rational subject to establish the philosophical basis for the symmetricalization of knowledge (Ward 1996: 18), the justification for symetricalizing tacit and scientific knowledge lies, according to Nonaka and Takeuchi, in the work of Polanyi. As we shall see, although Polanyi does not provide the justification for the symmetricalization of knowledge, his ideas about the relation between scientific practice and scientific culture do pave the way for a cultural account of the relationship between knowledge, society, and the economy.

Knowledge, Culture, and the Knowledge Economy

When Polyani originally invoked the notion of tacit knowledge his concern was to present the case for a holistic understanding of scientific knowledge, rather than to introduce another category of knowledge (Thorpe 1999). Put simply, his argument was that the way in which scientists used and developed knowledge could not be explained solely through reference to its propositional basis. Hence, his famous phrase 'we know more than we can tell' (Polanyi 1966: 4). For Polanyi, this was the natural starting point to address the relationship between the 'articulatable' and 'inarticulatable' elements of knowledge. So, unlike Nonaka and Takeuchi, tacit knowledge is not, for Polanyi, an informal, inchoate, or obscure form of knowledge whose nature calls for it to be made explicit in order to be understood or useful in practice; his formulation was much more subtle.

Polanyi also acknowledged that science has always had a tacit dimension and that skilful performance in the world of science, just as in art or any other field, is not achieved solely through following explicitly formulated rules based on propositional knowledge. It also requires that a number of other factors are taken into account in practice which are left out in the 'formulation of [explicit] rules' (Polanyi 1958: 49). Polanyi invoked the idea of 'indwelling' to explain scientists' immersion or enculturation in a set of theoretical presuppositions and physical skills related to their disciplinary field (Thorpe (1999: 25–35). He conceived indwelling as entailing a tacit transmission of scientific culture whereby meaning is established in scientific practice in two ways—sentiently and sapiently.[2]

The former is a fairly limited form of tacit knowledge which is established as scientists become aware of the impact of practical actions on the body as they manipulate laboratory resources. The latter is a more comprehensive form of tacit knowledge which is established as scientists become conscious of what follows from their thoughts and actions as they generate hypotheses, identify possible avenues of inquiry, and interpret the results of experiments. This sapient conception presupposes the interdependence between theoretical and tacit knowledge (Guile forthcoming *a*). Thus, in contradistinction to how he is often interpreted Polanyi stressed the interdependent dimensions of scientific knowledge rather than maintaining that there were two different types of knowledge (Seely Brown and Duguid 2001: 203–4).

By overlooking this aspect of Polanyi's argument, Gibbons and colleagues and Nonaka and Takeuchi lose sight of his original position about the interdependence between tacit and theoretical knowledge. This oversight has theoretical consequences for their respective ideas about tacit knowledge as well as for our understanding of what knowledge is required in the knowledge economy. In affirming the importance of tacit knowledge over theoretical knowledge, Gibbons and colleagues and Nonaka and Takeuchi sever the link between these two forms of knowledge. This severing happens in slightly different ways in each case. In privileging scientists' tacit knowledge over their disciplinary knowledge, Gibbons and colleagues play down the extent that the tacit thoughts and actions of scientists working in transdisciplinary settings are underpinned and informed by the disciplinary knowledge that they have already acquired formally and subsequently developed through living in scientific communities.

Equally, in conceiving of tacit knowledge as though it is an intuitive and unconscious form of knowledge that is developed sentiently, Nonaka and Takeuchi end up claiming that a fairly limited form of tacit knowledge is the most important resource in the knowledge economy. Yet a careful reading of their text reveals that the tacit knowledge that they claim is the vital knowledge resource is both a form of 'personal knowledge' that has not been shared with others (Eraut 2004), and a form of 'social knowledge' held by workplace communities of practice (Spender 1996). It is, in other words, sapient tacit knowledge and its distinguishing feature is that it constitutes a resource which allows scientists and other professional to infer what follows from what.

The link between culture, practice, and inference introduces a radically different conception of the relation between theoretical and tacit knowledge compared to Nonaka and Takeuchi and Gibbbons and colleagues' ideas about that relation. One way to highlight this is through reference to Zuboff's (1988) classic discussion of the new challenges of operating in technological environments. Zuboff analysed ICT in the context of its implementation by taking explicit account of how organizational context, managerial intent, and work structures influence the deployment of information technology in firms. This approach allowed her to identify the way in which the introduction of ICT can fundamentally alter the nature of knowledge and skill in commercial and industrial settings. In doing so, she shed light on the way in which different conditions foster the development of different types of tacit knowledge.[3]

Zuboff introduced the concepts of 'action-centred' and 'intellective' skill to encapsulate the nature of the different types of knowledge and skill required for working with machine technology compared with working with information technology. The former refers to an 'experiential' mode of skill formation that has been typically been acquired through a sentient engagement with the work process prior to the introduction of ICT. The latter referred to the mode of thinking that is required when working in computer-mediated environments and which involves the interpretation of symbolic data where meaning is not a given value, rather, it must be constructed.

These distinctions allowed her to contrast traditional sentient work cultures and practices with the growing 'textualization of work' ushered in through the deployment of ICT in commercial and industrial settings. In the world of action-centred skill, the context of action sensitizes workers as to what kind of details to look for and what kinds of data to expect. In contrast, in computer-mediated environments workers were forced to ask questions about the data generated by the computerization of the work process, for example, 'What is happening?' and 'What does this mean? (Zuboff 1988: 196). Answering the type of questions that arise from working in a symbolic medium raises issues of dialogue, visualization, collaboration, and risk-taking in the workplace. Accomplishing work came to depend, as Zuboff concludes (p. 95), more upon a capacity for 'theoretical' or 'system thinking' to assist workers to think about and respond to an electronically presented symbolic medium than upon 'acting out know-how derived from sentient experience'.

The shift in the quality of knowledge required for working in computer-mediated environments is, however, rather more complex than it may at first seem. It is not simply the replacement of one type of knowledge (tacit) by another (codified or explicit) knowledge. Zuboff (p. 192) acknowledges that tacit knowledge continues to play a role in intellective skill development. One of the main reasons tacit knowledge is still important, according to Zuboff, is that our long-term memory is based on the apprehension of meaning rather than on responding to precise verbal or visual context. This means that our 'intellective mastery will depend upon being able to develop a tacit knowledge that facilitates the recognition of decision alternatives and frees the mind for the kind of insight that could result in innovation and improvement. Such tacit recognition depends upon first being able to explicitly construct the significance of patterns and relationships in the data.' It is only possible, in other words, to interpret textual data about the performance of technological systems and to respond to the interpretations of others, when we know what course of action follows from knowing that something is the case. This entails grasping what Brandom (2000: 158) refers to as the 'representational' and 'inferential' form of a text or utterance; that is, the ability to articulate what is happening in the production process, to communicate that understanding to others, and to engage in collective discussions about what follows.

So, in contrast to Gibbons et al. and Nonaka and Takeuchi, Zuboff identifies the way in which different technological contexts facilitate the development of different types of skill and knowledge. In traditional contexts, we develop action-centred skill that relies on a sentient form of tacit knowledge, whereas in ICT-based contexts we develop intellective skill that is based on a sapient form of tacit knowledge which builds on our prior theoretical and practical knowledge. Thus Zuboff establishes not only, like Polanyi, the interdependence of theoretical and tacit knowledge, but also that the capability to interpret, share, and create knowledge is developed as we call upon both types of knowledge when we form judgements about what is happening in the production process.

This allows Zuboff to take the link between culture, practice, and knowledge production a step further than Gibbons and colleagues and Nonaka and Takeuchi. She acknowledges that certain cultural conditions have to be met if workers are to develop the tacit knowledge associated with intellective skill. The first condition is the provision of some from of 'training' to assist workers to understand the data the technological system provides. The second condition is opportunities in the workplace to use ICT to: (1) identify the significance of patterns and relationships in data; (2) construct meaning through dialogue and participation in workplace cultures; and (3) apply conceptual frameworks to interpret data to clarify and resolve problems.

Her insights leave us therefore with the thorny problem of learning how to relate different forms of knowledge to one another. Elsewhere I have argued that it is possible to formulate a holistic theory of knowledge in which these two apparently disparate forms of knowledge can be integrated (Guile 2006). However, in social and practical terms it can be argued that connections can be made between these two conceptions of knowledge through the concept of knowledge cultures.

Epistemic Cultures and the Knowledge Economy

The significance of the relationship between culture and knowledge production has only recently been appreciated in the debate about the knowledge economy. This is partly because writers such as Knorr Cetina have started to give greater prominence to a hitherto neglected aspect of that debate—the contribution that knowledge or *epistemic* cultures make to knowledge societies/economies. The expanding role of expert systems, as Knorr Cetina (1997: 8) points out, does not only result in the massive presence of technological and informational products of knowledge processes, it also means that epistemic cultures have 'spilled and woven their tissue into society'. The concept of an 'epistemic culture' refers to:

> Those amalgams of arrangements and mechanism—bonded through affinity, necessity, and historical co-incidence—which, in a given field, make up *how we know what we know*. Epistemic cultures are cultures that create and warrant knowledge, and the premier knowledge institution throughout the world is, still, science. (ibid.)

Hence, from Knorr Cetina's perspective:

> A knowledge society (knowledge economy) is not simply a society [economy] of more experts, more technological gadgets, more specialist interpretations (it is also) a society [and economy] permeated with knowledge cultures, the whole set of structures and mechanisms that serve knowledge and unfold with its articulation.[4] (ibid.)

Knorr Cetina employs two different, but related, approaches to illustrate the crucial role that *epistemic cultures* make to the production and application of science. One is by a comparison of the way in which two scientific fields—high-energy physics (HEP) and molecular biology—organize their strategies for acquiring knowledge. This allows her to reveal the link between scientific practice, that is, the diverse aggregation of patterns and dynamics that are displayed in expert scientific practice and how they differ from setting to setting, and scientific outcomes. Furthermore, it follows from Knorr Cetina's argument, even though she does not explicitly discuss it, that the way in which scientists are enculturated in these epistemic practices that enables them to infer with one another what follows from the scientific research process.

It is the spread of epistemic cultures, for Knorr Cetina, that makes knowledge economies/societies distinctively different from previous types of economies/societies. She pursues this insight by arguing that some of the structural forms traditionally found in epistemic cultures are gradually becoming more prevalent in the economies of advanced industrial societies. The paradigmatic example is, according to Knorr Cetina (ibid.), an extension of the 'object-centred relationships' which are characteristic of scientific settings. The defining feature of these object-centred relationships in scientific settings is the interplay between the 'question-generating' aspect of the research process and the increasing use of technological objects to stabilize that process and to provide 'answers' to research questions. Whereas in science this process is structured and guided the disciplinary field in which scientists are working,

Knorr Cetina argues that there is growing evidence of the spread of these object-centred relationships in fields other than science. She explores the implications of her argument through a detailed analysis of the operation of global financial markets and identifies the distinctive epistemic culture and forms of epistemic activity associated with trading (Bruegger and Knorr Cetina 2000). She concludes that traders are constantly engaged in a struggle to understand the operation of financial markets through a process of collecting and discounting relevant information. This involves them continually questioning what is happening in the market and making a determined effort to try to find information about the likely performance of financial markets. Thus financial markets (and by extension other forms of work based on the collection and discounting of information) are, in theory, knowledge objects for those who participate in them.

These observations about the spilling over of epistemic cultures in occupational fields other than science raise a number of issues that Knorr Cetina does not address. The first one is that whereas in science the 'question-generating/answer-providing' process is structured and guided in the disciplinary field in which scientists are working, the framework for this epistemic process has to be established in other professional fields. Working across the boundaries that define accepted areas of expertise in transdisciplinary teams and in inter-professional collaborations presupposes new types of professional capability. This can be defined as the ability to present data to experts in different fields as well as to their own clients who are not familiar with its meaning, to respond to their interpretation, of that data, to establish connections between respective interpretations, and to agree appropriate courses of action (Guile forthcoming). These capabilities are of a very different magnitude from the current emphasis in educational policy on the mastery of subject knowledge and the acquisition of key skills. Moreover, they raise new and fundamentally different questions about the way in which educational policy should support the development of the knowledge economy.

The second issue is the link between knowledge cultures and knowledge work may be more complex and not as automatic and inevitable as Knorr Cetina's metaphor of 'spilling over' assumes. This suggests that the concept of the knowledge economy/society needs tighter boundaries. Instead of describing the economy *sui generis* as a knowledge economy, it may be more helpful to differentiate between organizations and networks within industrial sectors that have established cultures that foster knowledge production. It may also be helpful for researchers and policymakers to identify the epistemic preconditions that are required to foster the spread of knowledge cultures. This would allow researchers and policymakers to differentiate more carefully between the roles that education and business play in fostering the growth of epistemic cultures. It would also allow policymakers to revisit and reappraise the assumed link between educational policy and the knowledge economy.

Educational Implications of 'Knowledge' in the Knowledge Economy

Educational policy has been increasingly premised on the basis of the link between education and national competitiveness since the early 1990s

(Brown and Lauder 1991). This link has been given a new twist in recent UK and EU educational policies. In both cases the concept of the knowledge economy has been deployed in two senses: as a vision of future economic activity and as a rationale for lifelong learning policies. This twin emphasis can be seen quite clearly in the words of David Blunkett, then UK Secretary of State for Education, who observed: 'Learning is the key to prosperity—for each and everyone of us as individuals, as well as for the nation as a whole. Investment in human capital will be the foundation of success in the knowledge-based global economy of the twenty-first century' (DfEE 1998: 7).

Furthermore a similar link between education and the knowledge economy is expressed in the European Union *Lifelong Learning Memorandum* which states that the aim of EU's educational policers should be to identify 'coherent strategies and practical measures with a view of fostering lifelong learning for all in order to help Europe become the most competitive and dynamic knowledge-based society in the world' (EC 2001: 3). One of the results of taking the link between knowledge, learning, and economic development for granted is that policymakers have followed Bell and Castells and adopted a design strategy conception of policy implementation. They have assumed that policy measures such as widening participation, frameworks to assure the quality of learning, and standards of qualifications can be 'designed' to produce the desired set of outcomes. One consequence of this emphasis on frameworks is, as Moore and Young (2001: 445) have presciently observed, that there is not only very little clarity within educational policy about what type of knowledge is required, there is also very little discussion as to how it should be acquired. The implications of this issue have not been addressed in educational policy terms. Yet they are profound, perhaps an example from higher education may illustrate the point.

Higher education is seen as the focal point for the knowledge economy. However, it too is marked by the distinction between the two types of knowledge rather than an appreciation of their interdependence. One way to illustrate this issue is to distinguish between a number of conceptions of knowledge—the 'traditional', the 'utilitarian', and the 'postmodern'[5] that are embedded in educational policy for higher education. The traditional conception represents a combination of ideas. It endorses the view that there is a given body of foundational knowledge (i.e. literary and scientific knowledge) that should feature in the curriculum, and which universities have a responsibility to transmit. It also consolidates the foundational and canonical status of disciplines by accepting that they and the scientific method constitute the only foundation for conducting research. The 'utilitarian' conception conceives of knowledge as a means to an end. From this perspective, the role of the university curriculum is held to be a contribution to realizing the particular 'form of society' desired by policymakers while the role of research is deemed to be to support the growth of industrialization. Finally, the postmodern conception is based on the idea that the world and knowledge are always a product of different ideological standpoints. For postmodernists, any curriculum based on the traditional and utilitarian conceptions is relying on essentially arbitrary assumptions about knowledge and culture. Thus, from this position it follows that the values, interests, and perspectives that inform the 'local' or 'tacit' knowledge should be granted equal status in universities.

These three distinctions can be used to reveal the tensions about knowledge that have been generated in higher education as policymakers have exerted constant pressure on universities to make their curriculum relevant to the knowledge economy. One tension is the result of the clash between the firm emphasis from the QAA on specifying the subject knowledge that is to be taught and assessed within university degrees, and its equal firm emphasis on ensuring that all degrees develop learners' key skills. The former perpetuates the idea that all knowledge is based on forms of generalization (i.e. abstract representations of the world) that are rooted in well-established disciplinary or multidisciplinary traditions, so that they can use knowledge in ways that have traditionally been expected, for example, written assignments. In contrast, the latter assumes that any form of knowledge is malleable so long as learners have developed the key skills necessary to apply it in different contexts. Consequently, universities are now expected to assist learners to acquire subject knowledge as well as to enable them to acquire context-free skills (i.e. key skills) in context-specific situations (i.e. lectures, laboratories, work placements) (Guile 2002). This places qualifications in a tricky position: they are expected to guarantee standards of knowledge acquired and serve as a proxy measure for employers to use to assess learners likely performance in the workplace.

A second tension is the clash between the traditional emphasis on the acquisition of 'subject knowledge' and the postmodern emphasis in higher educational policy on the heterogeneity of knowledge as represented by measures to accredit prior 'experiential' and/or 'tacit' knowledge and to recognize the cultural diversity of discourse. This tension places learners in a contradictory position. On the one hand, acquiring subject knowledge presupposes the development of the capabilities to grasp the system of connections that structure and inform disciplines. On the other hand, presenting experiential and tacit knowledge for accreditation through systems of assessment such as learning logs and portfolios appears to negate the importance of grasping connections.

The net effect of these tensions is that learners are left with an acute pedagogic dilemma (Guile forthcoming). This dilemma following Prawat (1999: 60) can be defined as a question of 'head fitting' or 'head splitting'. Learners oscillate between being expected to fit their head into clearly defined subject-based programme specifications or to split their mind into a multitude of minds in order to engage with and respond to heterogeneous forms of knowledge now accepted in higher education.

The pressure to modernize higher education has brought the two accounts of knowledge, in the knowledge economy that Bell, Castells, Gibbons and colleagues, and Nonaka and Takeuchi centre-stage, into the higher education curriculum, without recognizing the epistemological inadequacy of those accounts of the knowledge economy. The irony is that the attempt to modernize the higher education curriculum and to adopt a more inclusive stance towards the forms of knowledge that are taught and accredited leaves learners bereft of any way to relate these different forms of knowledge. Yet, it is increasingly apparent as the discussion of epistemic cultures revealed that the knowledge economy is making the longstanding interdependence between theoretical and tacit knowledge more explicit, and that this presupposes pedagogies that support learners to mediate different forms of knowledge, not oscillate between them (Guile forthcoming *a*).

Conclusion

This chapter has argued that the social scientists who have promulgated the knowledge economy thesis have failed to grasp the linkages between two conceptions of knowledge in the knowledge economy. This has led them to offer conflicting accounts as to whether theoretical or tacit knowledge is the most important economic resource in the knowledge economy. It then argued that, in treating theoretical and tacit knowledge as separate and different types of knowledge, social scientists have failed to detect what is distinctive about the knowledge economy in two senses. Sociologically they have failed to understand the interdependence between knowledge and culture, and philosophically how it is possible to see these kinds of knowledge as interdependent.

In educational policy terms there are at least two consequences to this kind of analysis. The first concerns the structuring of HE knowledge, the second the need to consider how educationists can foster the appropriate capabilities for learners to participate in knowledge cultures. However, in the light of the cultural basis to the knowledge economy major questions need to be raised about treating qualifications as a proxy measure for the knowledge required in that economy. Knowledge and culture in this sense cannot be tested directly in the way assumed by batteries of exams and tests. Rather more focus should be put on developing the forms of knowledgeability for a particular way of life in which collaboration and communication are seen as key aspects of an education for working and living in a knowledge economy/society. The consequence is that if policymakers are serious about considering the relation between education and the knowledge economy, they would move away from the emphasis on credentials acquired through batteries of tests and exams.

Finally, it should be said that while distinctive features of the knowledge economy have been identified, it is unlikely that they constitute a different kind of capitalism in terms of its focus on profits and markets (see Brown and Lauder in this volume). Nevertheless, this analysis does have implications for the role of education in this new phase of capitalist development.

NOTES

1. Since the focus of this chapter is the new role of knowledge in the economies of advanced industrial societies, I have only concentrated on the first of Castells's arguments about the Network Society.
2. I have used Brandom's (2000) discussion of the difference between sentience and sapience in two ways: to clarify the relation that Polanyi claimed existed between theoretical and tacit knowledge; and, to make a link to the distinction Zuboff (1988) drew between 'action-centred' and 'intellective' skill.
3. My interpretation of Zuboff is very different from how her text has been perceived by many other social scientists. I have focused on her ideas about how different conditions foster the development of different types of tacit Knowledge whereas many other writers have concentrated on the implications of her analysis for the organization of work.
4. There is a parallel between Knorr Cetina's concern with establishing a broader definition of the role of knowledge in 'knowledge societies' and the concern of this chapter to establish a broader definition of the role of knowledge in the economy. For this reason, I have highlighted the parallels between the respective arguments by inserting the references to the knowledge economy into her original text.
5. These conceptions of knowledge are partly influenced by the knowledge distinctions formulated by Moore and Young (2001) to clarify the different conceptions of knowledge that inform the current debates about the 14–19 curriculum. They are also partly influenced by my interpretation of Delanty's (2000) argument about the 'cognitive shifts' that have occurred in industrial societies.

Part Five

The Family, Opportunity, and Social Mobility

The issue of equality of opportunity has long been a central concern of policymakers and sociologists of education. Modern capitalist societies gain legitimacy from the claim that while there may be inequalities in income and wealth, everyone has the opportunity given the appropriate ability and character to aspire and to achieve high-earning jobs. However, there has been a debate about how equality of opportunity should be understood. Broadly speaking, there are at least four accounts of equality of opportunity that can be given. The first three relate to education and can be grouped into concepts of equality of educational opportunity: (1) Equality of access to education which was a primary concern during the twentieth century as education was progressively opened up to children whatever their social background. In so far as private education has become a significant factor internationally and nationally this issue has re-emerged because access to private education is determined by family income and wealth. (2) Equality of treatment referred to the idea of equal access to the same curriculum so that children from one ethnic, gender, or social class background were not discriminated against in the curriculum choices they were offered. Hence girls should be offered the same curriculum in maths and science as boys. However, the question of equality of treatment has now been raised in a new guise because, as school systems become increasingly differentiated, by charter schools in the United States or specialist schools and city academies in England, so there are questions about the quality of the education students will receive. Will those who are have the fortune or influence to be admitted to these new kinds of school gain a better education than those who do not? (3) Equality of results derives from the central finding of studies of equality of opportunity that it is social groups, in terms of social class, gender, ethnicity, or disability rather than individuals who suffer inequalities.

James Coleman (1968), a leading researcher on inequality in education developed the idea of equality of results as one in which groups in society should achieve in education in proportion to their numbers in the population as a whole. For example, if 40 per cent of the white population in the United States gained a degree so should 40 per cent of those of Afro-Caribbean heritage. This is the strongest sense of equality of opportunity but it remains relevant today as inequalities remains based on social class, gender, race, ethnicity, and disability. Finally (4) it is now recognized that, even when students complete education with the same qualifications there is discrimination in the labour market in terms of gender, class, and ethnicity. Educational qualifications are not an automatic passport to jobs in the labour market equating to the educational qualification (see, for example, Heath and McMahon 1997).

The task of sociology of education has been to assess to what extent the claims based on these definitions of equality of opportunity are borne out in reality. In order to do so, the dominant strategy has been to calculate the life chances of individuals from different social classes (Halsey, Heath, and Ridge 1980). In other words, given a children's social background at birth, what are his or her chances of achieving the highest educational qualifications and the best-paying jobs? Or to put it another way, as Esping-Andersen (Ch. 27) does in this Part, how strong is the influence of social inheritance on children's education and subsequent life chances?

The studies presented in this Part all point to inequalities in educational and subsequent job outcomes as being significant and all the more shocking since the links between parental background and educational achievement have been understood for some time (Halsey, Heath, and Ridge 1980; Jencks 1972; Bowles and Gintis 1976).

The question is, then, given the persistence of these gross inequalities how can they best be explained? It is here that the chapters in this Part make a considerable contribution based on theoretical and empirical advances in the past five years.

There have been two general orientations to explaining the persistence of inequalities of opportunity, the first is that of geneticists who argued that intelligence, which is claimed to determine educational and job outcomes, is largely genetically inherited and fixed, that is, subject to little change in the face of the experiences of a lifetime (Murray and Herrnstein 1994). Moreover Murray and Herrnstein also argued that there is a racial component to this genetic inheritance so that a 'league table' can be identified ranking the intelligence of races. However, these rather crude, genetically based theories face several problems. For a start, the empirical evidence does not support their claims. The reinterpretation of Herrnstein and Murray's data by Fischer et al. (1996) clearly demonstrates the strength of social background in educational achievement. The advent of longitudinal studies which show the development of cohorts from birth through to middle age (see for example the chapters by Feinstein and Nash and Harker in this section) enable us to gain a clearer understanding of the powerful social effects on educational and subsequent occupational achievements. Figure 28.1 in Feinstein's chapter is startling in illustrating just how powerful these effects are. Clearly, we need a far more complex understanding of the interaction between genetic and environmental influences, and that work is now being undertaken. See Flynn (2004) for an account of the thinking behind some of his work in this area.

Given that there is a significant social component to educational achievement, it remains to explain the factors that generate this inequality. Esping-Andersen points to the success of the Nordic countries in reducing inequality. He notes that these countries have high levels of redistribution, well-developed welfare states, and good early childhood education. While he acknowledges that all three are likely to be influential in producing more egalitarian societies he focuses much attention on the importance of early childhood education. Feinstein (2003) certainly took a similar view but on reconsideration (Ch. 28, below) he points to the persistent inequalities that disadvantaged students face throughout their education. In contrast, Nash and Harker (Ch. 29), using the same longitudinal data base as Feinstein, ask how it is possible that inequalities that show up so early in a child's life seem, on average, to persist through education and into adulthood. They hypothesize that reading to children, in particular, has a lasting impact on their cognitive development, although they leave open the possibility that children's subsequent educational experiences may also be influential. Their analysis addresses some difficult questions. For example, we know that there has been a high degree of upward social mobility, how then is this to be explained by reference only to early childhood experiences? Here an answer that can be gained from their data is that there is a wide disparity of reading practices amongst working-class families, although on average, they read less often and consistently to their children relative to professional middle-class families. However, this analysis cannot fully account for the phenomenon of late developers and we therefore need to look at additional explanatory accounts of the kind that are provided throughout this book.

One aspect of inequality relates to the experiences of students in school and the degree to which those in poverty consider themselves as 'outsiders' who feel excluded from the life of the school. Ridge (Ch. 30) reports on interviews with students and parents who live in poverty about their school experiences, charting many ways in which they find it difficult to participate fully in school life. In turn this provides additional understanding of Feinstein's quantitative analysis.

The other side of the coin to the exclusion felt by some students in poverty are the strategies and aspirations of the middle class. Power and Whitty (Ch. 31) seek to subject the notion of middle-class dominance in education to critical analysis, arguing that some of the key sites of conflict over education are between those considered middle class, rather than between the middle and working class. In undertaking this analysis they identify many of the taken for granted assumptions made about the middle class as a homogeneous category.

However, McNamara Horvat, Weininger, and Lareau (Ch. 32) show how middle-class parents use their social capital to advantage the interests of their children at school. Social capital is a contested concept and they are careful to review the literature prior to their analysis of how it works in the favour of middle-class parents in education.

It has been argued that a cause of inequality lies in the resources and practices of families (Nash and Harker, Ch. 29). Families are themselves positioned by the labour market, yet the structure of families, as Carnoy (Ch. 25) documents, has undergone radical change as a result of the secular trends related to individualization. Partly as family size has reduced and women have entered the labour market and partly to make up for what are perceived to be the lack of resources amongst low-income families, some states have entered to support early childhood education.

In policy terms, early childhood education has been established as improving educational performance, but we need to be careful in considering it a panacea. For a start, the idea that early childhood education could compensate for society has persisted since the late 1960s when compensatory education programmes were developed in the United States. A look at Esping-Andersen's data tells us that inequalities have not been reduced, despite the benefits of this type of intervention. Moreover, there is confusion between the idea that early childhood education may improve education performance and that it will help to foster equality of results. This is because the competition for credentials, which many chapters in this volume argue are weighted towards the middle class, needs to be distinguished from any sense of raising absolute standards. The competition for credentials is about the relative advantage that some groups gain in education over others. In this context Brocker's (2003) impressive analysis of the creation of inequality through the labelling of young children by teachers is an important corrective to the more starry-eyed expectations of some policy analysts and politicians.

One of the key factors that has been overlooked in the debate over the importance of early childhood education has been the question of hope. Neither disadvantaged parents nor children as they grow older will engage with education if they believe they have no future other than the grinding poverty that they are enduring. Charlesworth's (2000) striking analysis of the response to education in a northern British city with high unemployment makes this clear. It is for this reason that the multiple strategies to reduce poverty seen in the Nordic countries is so important.

In this context Mike Apple (Ch. 33) critically examines the influence of neo-liberal policies and their impact, especially in relation to the creation of inequalities through the introduction of markets in education. When judged against the policies and outcomes in the Nordic countries it makes for dismal reading. But his chapter also has a clear lesson, that if greater equality of opportunity is an aim, then the focus for change should be on the State whether at the federal or local level because of the wider popular influence that its policies can create. In effect it can take the views and aspirations of a coalition of interests and elevate them into a dominant ideology.

Finally, Pak-Sang Lai and Michael Byram (Ch. 34) look at the influence of the role of English in the creation of inequality. As English has become the *lingua franca* of globalization, so those that have access to learning English have a major advantage in the job market, globally. But this plays back into education because while parents, particularly those from the professional middle classes, will demand that English be taught or will pay for their children to go to schools where English is the medium for learning, others will emphasize the importance of their indigenous tongues because it is so crucial for the development of their identities. In turn this raises questions about how resources for language teaching should best be allocated. There is perhaps no clearer fault-line in the development of education throughout the globe than that between those students who can gain access to English and those who cannot.

In this Part we focus primarily on inequalities in educational outcomes, but Brown (Ch. 26) explains why we also need to investigate how the 'opportunity' structure is being transformed and why it is likely to heighten positional conflict in both education and the job market.

The New Family and Flexible Work

Martin Carnoy

[...]

The Changing Family Structure

[...]

In 1970, more than 40 per cent of US households were composed of married couples with children. By 1995, this percentage had fallen to one-quarter (see Figures 25.1 and 25.2). More than half (54 per cent) of all Americans in 1995 still lived in a nuclear family, meaning a married couple with or without children, but that was down from 70 per cent in 1970 and 75 per cent in 1960 (US Bureau of the Census 1992, 1996). One-fourth of Americans were living as singles in 1995, up from 13 per cent in 1960 and 17 per cent in 1970.

Further down the spectrum, about one-half of all Danes in 1997 lived in single-person families, and 45 per cent lived within a nuclear family. Only 22 per

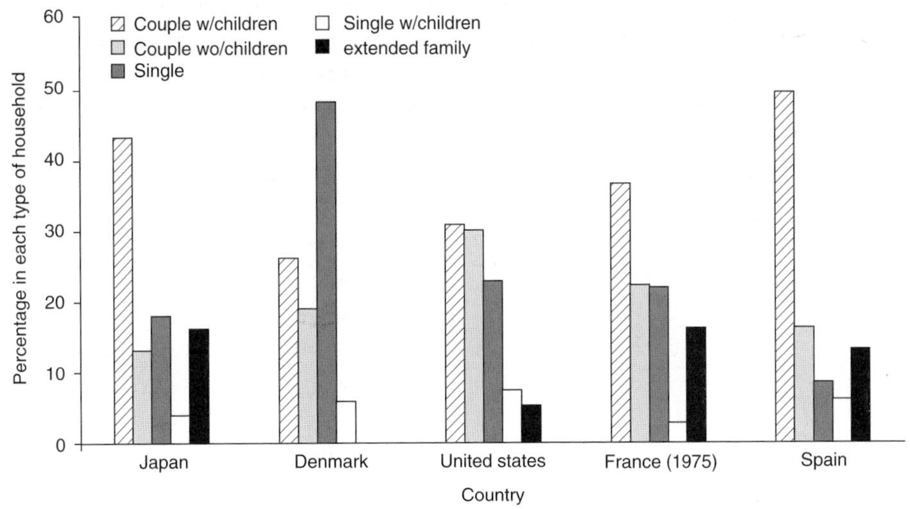

Fig. 25.1 Family Structure, by country, 1975 to 1980
Sources: Denmark: Danmarks Statistik, Socialforskningsinstitutet 1992, table 4.4. France: INSEE 1996, 298. Japan: Ministry of Social Welfare 1997, figures 4.12a and 4.12b.

cent of Danes, whether married or not, had children under the age of eighteen in the household, and only 14 per cent were married with children. Even if we add unmarried couples with children, the figure is only 18 per cent. Excluding adult children (above the age of eighteen) living at home underestimates the total number of married and unmarried nuclear families by as much as 8 per centage points, but this still means that the 'traditional' nuclear family of a married couple with children of any age represents a maximum of about one in five families in Denmark.

At the other end of the spectrum, the composition of Spanish households has also changed, but much less so than in the United States or Denmark. The dominant living arrangement in Spain, as in the United States, is the nuclear family. In 1970, almost 70 per cent of Spaniards lived within a married-couple family, with or without children, and in 1991, the figure had dropped only slightly, to 65 per cent. Of this proportion, about one-fourth in 1991 were married without children. This means that somewhat less than one-half (48 per cent) of all Spanish households consisted of married couples with children, almost double the US proportion. This was down from about 53 per cent in 1970 (Alberdi 1994, 149–55).

One reason for the slow decline in the category of married couple with children is high youth unemployment. Because young people cannot get jobs, they continue to live with their families well into their twenties and even early thirties. In the 1990s, the average age at which a Spanish child left his or her parents' household was about twenty-eight. The family is assisted in this arrangement by 'indirect' government assistance. Many Spanish (and European) men in their late fifties are already generously pensioned and can continue to support a family. Publicly provided medical care is also available through the family to all members in the household, regardless of age. Beyond these incentives for children to stay at home, in Spain (and Italy and even France), it is culturally acceptable for children in their twenties to live with parents, well beyond the age at which parents need to care for them. Although many Spanish parents may live in households with children, a high proportion of them have little parental child-rearing responsibilities beyond helping their children financially.

If we adjust for the fact that in about one-third of Spanish nuclear families all the children are above eighteen years of age, and if, instead, we count only families with minor children, only 32 per cent of Spanish families could be called nuclear, not much more than in the United States. The family categories that have grown most rapidly are the

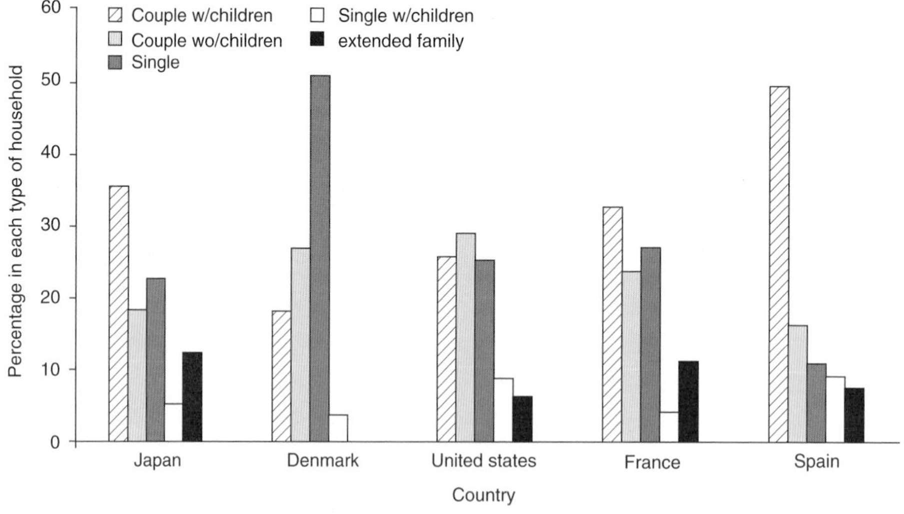

Fig. 25.2 Family Structure, by country, mid-1990s
Source: Denmark: Danmarks Statistik, Socialforskningsinstitutet 1997, table 75. Other countries: see figure 25.1.

same as those in the United States: individuals living alone and households headed by single parents. Single-parent households in Spain increased from 6 per cent of all households in 1981 (there was no measure of this category in 1970) to almost 10 per cent in 1991, a figure that is even higher than in the United States. Between 1970 and 1991, the number of individuals living alone increased from 7 to 11 per cent of all households, still far lower than the 25 per cent in the United States. These last two figures can also be accounted for, at least in part, by the tendency of adult children in Spain to continue to live in the households of their parents.

Thus, the direction of change in Spanish households is the same as in the United States, but the household structures remain far different. In Spain, the married couple with children remains the dominant form of family life, in part for economic reasons. At the same time, we see the structural changes occurring in Spain that have so transformed American families: older people tending to live alone rather than in extended families, more unmarried people living alone, more households headed by single parents, and more married couples living together but without children.

The family trends in France are similar to those in the United States and Spain but fall somewhere between the two. Even in 1968, only 36 per cent of French families could be considered nuclear families. By 1990, this figure had dropped to 33 per cent, a slow decline. One reason that a higher percentage of French families are nuclear families rather than couples living without children is that their children, like those of Spain, tend to stay in the family until a much later age than adult children in the United States. At least part of the slower French decline in nuclear families can be explained by rising unemployment rates and the increased probability that older children in France live at home.[1]

The data also show that no matter how much the French family shares this commonality with Spain, many fewer French than Spaniards live in nuclear families, and more French than Spaniards live as couples without children. The proportion of couples without children in France rose from 1968 to 1990, from 21 to 24 per cent of family units or families, about twice the Spanish proportion. More men and women live alone in France than in Spain, at a level similar to that in the United States. The per centage of those living alone in France also rose from 1968 to 1990, from 20 to 27 per cent of families (INSEE 1996, 298). The share of extended (complex) French families declined from almost 20 per cent to 12 per cent, about the same as the level and decline in Spain, and that of single-parent families increased from a low 2.9 per cent of all families in 1968 to a still low 4.5 in 1990. This suggests that the changes in family structure happening elsewhere are also happening in France, and they are fairly close to the changes in the United States, though they are not quite as rapid or as acute. There is no denying, however, that a much smaller proportion of French women than American (or Spanish) women raise their children alone. Thus, growing divorce rates and increasing out-of-wedlock births in France make for a disintegrating traditional family, but excellent public day-care and preschool systems, combined with long postpartum family leaves and long paid vacations, greatly cushion the decline of the traditional family.

Like the Spanish, the Japanese are heading toward fewer traditional family arrangements, but much more slowly than the United States or even Spain. The main change in Japan (as in Spain) has to do with the number of children in the typical Japanese family, not with radical shifts in lifestyle or even high divorce rates. As everywhere else in the OECD, increasing life spans and smaller families have meant more couples without children. In 1975, only 12 per cent of Japanese couples had no unmarried children living with them. Twenty years later, this figure had increased to 18 per cent. The proportion of married couples with and without children, however, remained constant, at almost 36 per cent. The prevalence of the extended family as a living arrangement declined, and the proportion of single-person households increased to 23 per cent, still only one-half the Danish figure. As in France and Denmark, the proportion of households headed by single parents is only 5 per cent, half that in the United States (see, for example, Saboulin and Thave 1993).

In sum, the traditional family is on the decline in all these countries, yet significant differences remain. These differences are related to national culture, labor markets, and public policies regarding family support. The changes in family structure also affect what happens in labor markets. The persistence of more traditional families in Spain and Italy, for instance, allows for high rates of youth unemployment to be absorbed by families willing to continue supporting their children at home even in adulthood. The persistence of traditional, rigid labor markets supported by traditional family structures has, in turn, unintended effects on future families. Today's low fertility rates in southern Europe and Japan means fewer children and fewer nuclear families in the future.

[. . .]

Changing Work and the Changing Family: An Ecocultural Global Phenomenon?

The changing family is part of a changing structure of work and a changing labor market. With more intense global competition and a more globalized worldview, time takes on greater importance. A more flexible work structure is one that better utilizes an individual's time in performance of a greater number of tasks. A more flexible work structure also affects family life in positive and negative ways. Today's young woman wants a life that includes wage work and professional accomplishment. For most, staying home and tending to children is not enough. Labor market flexibility has the positive effect of allowing men and women greater possibilities for combining their competing desires to work and to raise children. On the negative side, because flexible work is acutely time sensitive, it puts increased pressure on workers to be available for work as they are needed. It also makes workers more concerned about their total commitment to their work, which necessarily relegates family life to a much lower priority.

On the positive side, flexible labor markets in countries such as the United States, Great Britain, Scandinavia, and, to some degree, Japan allow a high percentage of men and women from fifteen to fifty-four to find jobs. Where flexibility includes relatively easy exit from and reentry into the job market, couples have the greatest choice about having children, especially regarding questions of when and how many. From this standpoint, labor market flexibility has a positive effect on fertility rates. The situations in Italy and Spain, in which formal labor markets are highly rigid, provide a good contrast. There, unemployment among youth (from fifteen to twenty-four years of age) is above 35 per cent, the ratio of employment to population for young women is only about 20 per cent (compared with 55 per cent in the United States, 59 per cent in the United Kingdom, and 44 per cent in Japan), and exit from and reentry into employment is difficult at any age for both men and women. High unemployment among youth delays marriage and family formation, and once a Spaniard or Italian gets a job, he or she is likely to keep it at all costs, even if the wage allows only a very small family or none at all. Labor market rigidity restricts family choices in Italy and Spain, even though other aspects of their societies, such as close ties with grandparents willing to help with child rearing, favor larger families. Greater labor market flexibility could have a positive effect on family size.

Flexibility also has a major downside for family life, however. In his famous time and motion studies, Frederick Taylor was able to extract more output from each worker by breaking down a single task into parts; the worker could thereby be made to speed up, producing more in a given amount of time (Taylor 1911). An efficient assembly line requires that each worker do one repetitive task as quickly as humanly possible during the eight hours on the line. Today, the production problem is different. Each employee has to do many different things, often at different times. The question is how to organize the company's workforce to accomplish these complex tasks most effectively and at the lowest cost. Usually, this means having workers move from task to task and varying the number of working hours, depending on the company's needs that day or that week. From the company's standpoint, the best employees are those that can do many different things on constantly changing schedules. Because many workers are not willing to fit into such schedules, companies are hiring more temporary workers for specific tasks to be done in specific time periods, downsizing part-time workers, and eliminating certain divisions and/or expanding others. Many larger companies, like the one in which Arlie Hochschild conducted her interviews for *Time Bind*, simply want more time on demand from their workforce and favor those employees who are regularly willing to sacrifice other activities, including time with family, to the company's needs. Hochschild concludes that 'while the mass media so often point to global competition as the major business story of the age, it is easy to miss the fact that corporate America's fiercest struggle has been with its local rival—the family' (Hochschild 1996, 203–4).

The family in today's flexible production environment has to struggle with its employers for time, but even if couples did not have this conflict, those that Hochschild interviewed seem to prefer spending time in the workplace to spending it in the family. This is a product of many forces, but high among them has to be the value that Americans have always placed on material gain as the sovereign, or even sole, measure of status and success. It is telling that in the late 1970s and 1980s, as the average wages of American men fell, average family income rose, mainly because the proportion of wives and mothers working full time increased significantly (Bluestone and Rose 1997). Barry Bluestone and Stephen Rose have shown that between 1973 and 1988 the average working family purchased an 18.5 per cent increase in real earnings with a 16.3 per cent increase in hours worked. The average family earnings, in the absence of such increase in hours worked, increased only 1.8 per cent. Another way to look at this phenomenon is that of the more than 13 million women in the United States who entered the labor market—that is, as 'new' workers—between 1979 and 1993, 73 per cent went to work full time.[2] The US average real wage (corrected for changes in the cost of living) fell (for men and women combined) 9.7 per cent between 1975 and 1995, and the median income for all males with income fell 8.2 per cent. Median real income for families, however, rose 9.2 per cent during the same period. This suggests that married women, working at lower average wages than men, more than made up the difference in family income by working more hours, on average, than in 1975.

[...]

[...]

Flexible Workplaces and the New Family

The other side of this story is that relying on traditional family structures to sustain flexible production is risky. Far from losing its fundamental importance to work, the family will be even

Table 25.1 Average annual hours worked per person in employment and self-employment, by country, various years

Country	1973	1979	1983	1990	1994	1996	1998
Australia	—	1,904	1,852	1,869	1,879	1,867	1,861
France	1,904	1,813	1,711	1,668	1,635	1,645	1,634
Germany	—	—	—	—	1,602	1,576	1,580
West Germany[b]	1,868	1,764	1,724	1,610	1,580	1,557	1,562
Italy[c]	1,842	1,748	1,724	1,694	1,682	—	—
Japan	2,201	2,126	2,095	2,031	1,898	1,919[a]	1,879[c]
Netherlands[c]	1,724	1,591	1,530	1,433	1,388	1,374	1,365[a]
Spain	—	2,022	1,912	1,824	1,815	1,810	1,821
United Kingdom	1,929	1,821	1,719	1,773	1,728	1,738	1,737
United States	1,924	1,905	1,882	1,943	1,945	1,951	1,957

[a] 1997.

[b] West Germany series is shown for continuity with period before early 1990s.

[c] Data are for dependent employment only.

Source: OECD 1997*a*, table G; OECD 1999*b*, table F.

more crucial as the economy shifts to flexible, knowledge-based production. Not only is an ever increasing proportion of jobs in the OECD organized around 'knowledge' rather than physical skills, but today's younger workers are likely to need to acquire new kinds of knowledge at different points in their working lives as they move through different kinds of jobs.

The family in a flexible work system is a central hub of productive and reproductive activity. When it is potentially 'strong' (with two highly educated adults at its core) it serves as a risk hedge against periods of unemployment and as a source of child development support for its offspring, of investment capital for adult and child education and job training, of networking for job searches and upward mobility, and of personal security and growth. Networked into larger information and communication systems, the family can also become a production unit.

Yet low birthrates can threaten population reproduction and future economic growth. Divorce rates throughout the OECD, even in more traditional societies, will almost certainly increase and then stay as high as those in the United States or Scandinavia. Increased stress on families, even on those with traditional supports, as they try both to raise children and to satisfy the need of both women and men for status and social interaction as wage earners in remunerated work, could have a serious negative effect on adult productivity and the well-being of children. The combined effect of flexible production, with its demands for individualized, work-focused activities, women's fight for greater equality in the family and labor market, and the increased importance of the family as an investment unit now shapes the emergence of the next stage of family life. The family could and should be the social institution that tempers the stress induced by the processes of disaggregation of labor and individualization of social and economic life. For the family to be able to play its fundamental role of sustaining work, it has to be redefined and strengthened under the new cultural and technological conditions of our societies.

The US model is appealing to employers and many politicians in Europe because its potential for job creation and low unemployment stand in stark contrast to Europe's frustrating struggle to create jobs and reduce unemployment. American-style flexible markets, however, have a downside that makes them understandably unappealing to the average European and Japanese: flexibility not only expands job growth, but it is characterized in the highly deregulated economy of the United States by stagnant or falling wages for a significant percentage of workers. Most workers have to pay much more attention to keeping their jobs because of the continuing threat that they might lose them. Flexibility also tends to increase the number of hours family members work. In lower-skill jobs, American-style flexible markets encourage people to work more in order to earn more rather than lobby for a higher wage for the hours they do work. In high-skill jobs, high pay is the norm, but only for those who are willing to commit themselves to a supercharged work schedule, meeting crucial deadlines at all costs and outcompeting other workers in the do-or-die global economy. In some of these higher-skill occupations, the financial incentives are great: workers who make the right moves may earn a lot in a few years. Thus the long hours have a potentially high payoff. All this promotes higher profits, economic growth, and higher average family income but at the cost of job security, more intensified family work schedules, and increased individual stress and isolation.

Europeans and Japanese may admire the vitality of the current US 'job machine,' but consider the American system of work and family relations too socially costly. They read about high levels of open poverty, deteriorating living conditions, lack of child care, stressful dual workdays, long commuting hours, downgraded schools, social violence, and a high fraction of the young male black and Latino populations in prison. Americans tend to live either in cities that are no longer very safe for children and adolescents or in suburbs, with their own risks for young people, as indicated by the increasingly frequent and shocking killings in suburban schools. According to a 1994 national survey, child care in America is of such poor quality that children's development is at risk (Fuller et al. 1997). All political parties and leaders invoke a strengthened family as a solution to the nation's social ills, but social legislation supporting the family lags behind that of all other industrialized countries. Most children in the United States not only live in families broken by divorce (Susan Chira, 'Struggling to Find Stability When Divorce Is a Pattern,' *New York Times*, March 19, 1995), but more than a third also live in or near the poverty line. In some ethnic minorities the crisis of the family is very deep, playing a major role in perpetuating the underclass status of a significant segment of the minority population (Wilson 1987). About one-half of all African American children are conceived out of wedlock, and many do not know their fathers (Jaynes and Williams 1990). Not only do less educated mothers in the United States have more children than higher-educated mothers, just as in other OECD countries, but they are likely to raise their children in relatively worse economic conditions, with less access to child development and early educational services than in most of the rest of the OECD.

The third issue for Europeans concerned with the American model of flexible work is that it puts ever increasing emphasis on work and earnings themselves as the be-all and end-all of human existence. This is not a completely new phenomenon in America. Yet with increased competition in the globalized economy and the rapidly rising capacity to use 'world time' to enhance productivity, the very best workers are now those who never sleep, never consume, never have children, and never spend time socializing outside of work. As Hochschild argues, it is in the employer's interest to make the workplace more socially congenial for workers because they will then be willing to spend more time there. It is also in the employer's interest to make workers believe that if they do not spend more time there, the employer will find someone else who will.

[...]

Some Policy Implications

The policy implications lie, at least partly, in the shift to more knowledge-intensive work for all. The developed countries are quickly becoming knowledge societies in which communicative, cooperative, and cognitive skills rather than raw materials, human strength, and machines form the basis for the production of wealth. Because knowledge is more important in work, and because women's identities are increasingly associated with income-earning capacity, family formation (including the age at marriage, the number of children, and the timing of the children) is increasingly determined by the pattern of knowledge acquisition, such as the length of professional development and career formation. The quality of family life will increasingly be gauged by learning opportunities for adults and the capacity of the adults in the family to provide learning opportunities for their children. The intense emphasis on learning as a factor in life decisions has already occurred in upper-middle-income groups (more highly educated men and women), whose women are choosing to establish careers (to pursue higher levels of education and to take jobs with high levels of learning opportunities) before having children. The availability in Europe and Japan of subsidized child development centers that care for youngsters of all ages—and, in the United States, the lack of such centers—shapes the sustainability of marriages and the number and timing of children, especially for professional couples. Such learning-driven behavior as a dominant shaper of family formation, now limited to better-educated young people (who are necessarily more fully sensitized to the implications of flexible labor markets), will move into the rest of the population, just as reduction of fertility rates among the middle class moved into the working class at the beginning of the twentieth century.

With knowledge and information playing such potentially important roles in flexible work, family formation, and family relations, support systems consistent with improving both individual productivity and family life should be increasingly organized around enhancing access by both children and adults to high-quality learning opportunities. The integration of households into learning networks is the linchpin of a flexible, knowledge-based work system. Government family policies are fundamental to this integration, because the state, whether local or national, is the only institution that has both the material resources to support the household's investments in its members and the political motivation to do so. Such policies need to enhance the family's capacity to invest in learning without interfering in the privacy of its decisions. The state can do this by helping the family acquire education for its children even as parents are on flexible work schedules; giving parents new opportunities to further their own education and training; guaranteeing family health care even when family members are unemployed or studying; providing widely available training on child care and child development to youth, prospective parents, and parents, using fiscal policies to reward families that invest in education; and strictly enforcing laws that ensure that parents, whether they are divorced or married, living together or not, contribute financially to the support of their children.

The acquisition of knowledge depends heavily on early childhood development, and early childhood takes place in families. Not only are most parents uneducated about child development, but in the free market Anglo-American model, collective society pays little attention to the crucial early years of a child's learning. Again, this is an attitude left over from preindustrial and industrial society, when how much knowledge children acquired in school was far less important to their work lives.

Those OECD countries that have been especially conscious of children's welfare when both parents or a single parent work, or even as a respite for women who do not work, provide all-day, high-quality subsidized day care. In Scandinavia and France, day care is the centerpiece of family policy, and is beginning to be so in Japan. In all these countries, day care is organized by the state around well-trained, certified teachers who specialize in early childhood development.

With individuals in families facing more intense pressures in their work lives yet still having children, governments need to take the issue of child development even more seriously. Child development centers are the key to meeting the household's need for parents' job flexibility and children's early enriched learning. They are expensive, and as in the case of higher education, parents who can afford to pay should. In France, parents do contribute on the basis of ability to pay, and in the United States, where publicly supported child-care centers are the exception, financial responsibility for high-quality childhood development is borne almost entirely by the families themselves. This means that low-income parents are denied access to high-quality care with an enriched development focus. Thus, from such early care on, knowledge development in a market model is highly unequal—precisely the opposite of what a flexible, knowledge-based society needs for sustained development.

The state (again, because it is the only institution that has the resource mobilization power to do so) also has to insure high-quality health care for all children, even before they are born, and has to invest in the education of parents regarding the responsibilities and skills of parenthood. Because most early childhood education takes place in families, even where the state subsidizes child development centers, parents are children's main teachers; yet most parents are hardly prepared for that role. Secondary schools and universities need to require parenting courses and need to emphasize child development responsibilities of parents. If anything, an educational focus of this kind will convince many young people to delay parenting until they can fulfill their children's learning needs.

Beyond early childhood development, governments need to make schools into community learning centers, where parents can leave their children in a learning environment during parents' working or education hours and during school vacation periods when parents do not have vacation time. The community learning center should also be a place where parents and seniors can engage in learning activities—some related to their children's education and some to adult activities, including community-run business courses for the self-employed. (I discuss this in more detail in the next chapter, in which I deal with the changing nature of community in the new, individualized, disaggregated labor society.)

Currently, parents in Europe and the United States are induced to have more children through family income entitlements, tax deductions for dependents, and welfare for mothers with dependent children. In the knowledge economy, fiscal inducements should be tied to investment in education and training, not simply to having children. The Clinton administration's proposed middle-class tax cut, which provides tax deductions for the costs of children's college education and for adult training, are a step in this direction. A similar deduction should be allowed for children's preschool and parents' education toward a degree. The part of the middle-class tax cut that gives an additional tax credit of five hundred dollars just for having a child, with no restrictions on how that money is used, is a step in the wrong direction.

This focus on state support for families through investment tax credits for education and training and the direct provision of high-quality early childhood development also means that the state needs to reconceive the way it views and delivers education. Local existing educational institutions—from primary and secondary schools to community colleges and universities—are the logical sites around which the state can build all-day, all-year, cradle-to-grave learning networks for households to hook into, whether parents have jobs or are self-employed. Yet these institutions have to evolve to meet varying needs in various communities. The demand for both full-day children's education and adult education, for example, may be far greater in low-income areas than high-income communities. Government allocation of resources for education should be responsive to such unequal needs as part of equalizing opportunities and social protection, particularly in light of the fact that less educated families have more children but a weaker capacity to provide them with the information and networks needed to be productive in a flexible, knowledge-intensive economy.

Which model is more likely to be able to respond to this integrative challenge? The US version has the distinct advantage of a highly flexible educational system that allows young people and adults to leave and reenter, change majors, and retrain for new careers at just about any age. Americans also have a high propensity to form voluntary associations responsive to new demands in the society. These are taking on many of the organizational responsibilities for new learning systems, even though they usually have to rely on state funding, particularly in low-income communities. Flexible education and voluntary, private local organizing is consistent with labor market flexibility, lifelong education, and responses to the need for knowledge formation in a rapidly changing economy. American women have been especially inclined to use this flexibility to shape their reentry into the labor force after raising young children or divorcing. The greatest growth in college enrollment in the 1970s and 1980s came from women thirty or more years of age returning to school to train for better jobs. Flexibility has also allowed for modular add-ons to basic public education, such as private after-school tutorial programs.

The US model has major drawbacks, however, in meeting knowledge needs for a flexible economy. Americans and America's political leadership seem unwilling to confront the public crises of the family and related child poverty. One way to deal with these crises is to invest heavily in early, high-quality, publicly funded education for low-income children. Child development centers, so central to Europe's 'public-family' approach to poverty, are virtually absent in the United States. Beyond early childhood education, the schools of the future will probably have to serve as dawn-to-late-evening community knowledge centers. I discuss this concept in greater detail [elsewhere (Carnoy 2000: ch 5)], but I want to mention here that under the actual US model, families unable to pay privately for 'extra' educational services privately are at a tremendous disadvantage. For that to change, the larger community has to be willing to publicly pay for new forms of knowledge provision. In the current environment, this may not be easy to achieve politically.

Europe and Japan have much more rigid educational systems than the United States. Adult education is not readily available in France, Italy, and Germany, and it is unusual for young people to leave the educational system and reenter later. Even changing majors in university can be difficult. Women seeking to redefine themselves are hardly well served by an educational system that is youth-centered and highly linear. This makes educational responses to the crisis in the traditional family more difficult. It is hard to imagine the present French or Italian educational system, or even the local state-run German system, for example, being sensitive and responsive to changing wage-earner family needs. Although voluntary associations in continental European countries (where the state is expected to 'take care of things') are rarer than in the United Kingdom or the United States, they do exist, but they are not taken as seriously by public officials. I recently interviewed a parents' council at a Bergamo, Italy, primary school. Their major complaint was that the school would not change its timetable to eliminate half-day Saturdays to accommodate family needs, even when the parents' council presented a well-thought-out plan to teachers and the administration. No reason was given. This is typical of these systems, and it reflects the rigidity and arrogance of teachers' unions and centralized bureaucracies, whatever their advantages in student achievement might be.[3]

However, despite growing disillusionment with the nation-state at many levels, continental Europeans (and the educationally more flexible Scandinavians) are much more willing than Americans (or the British or Australians) to acknowledge the role of the public sector in equalizing opportunity and providing important services. Japan relies less on government agencies than on corporate organizations for lifelong support systems, but the Japanese, like the continental Europeans and Scandinavians, have a relatively homogeneous society and a sense of collective responsibility for each other. Voters in all these countries support public funding for child-care centers and early childhood education. Continental Europe, Scandinavia, and Japan provide generally high-quality subsidized programs for young children, and these, together with other family support programs, have contributed to a significant reduction in child poverty in the past three decades.

Can this sense of collective responsibility and willingness to organize and spend substantial public funds on early childhood education be extended to developing lifelong, flexible systems that provide education in response to changing family needs? Or is it more likely that Americans and American political leadership will extend their current advantage in flexible education by taking responsibility for high-quality, publicly funded early education and other forms of family education and networking support systems?

This is a fundamental issue for the viability of these societies in our high-speed future. Obviously, the capacity of an economic system to innovate and organize the production of goods and services is crucial in a competitive global system. Social cohesion is also crucial, however, and the family as the main institution of social cohesion needs help in an age of flexible production and changed gender roles. The capacity and willingness of a society to provide this help, especially in the form of support for learning and learning networks for families that have limited capacity to provide them privately, will be major elements in sustaining innovation and work systems over the long haul.

NOTES

1. In 1982, 45 per cent of French people aged 22–24 lived at home with their parents and 30 per cent lived as a couple; in 1995, 54 per cent lived with their parents and 19 per cent as a couple.
2. The proportion of mothers in the United States whose children were under the age of 6 and who were employed climbed from 14 per cent in 1950 to just over 60 per cent in 1991.
3. French and Italian teenagers scored higher in math than US teenagers on the Third International Mathematics and Science study (TIMMS).

26 The Opportunity Trap

Phillip Brown

Introduction

The opportunity to make a better life is enshrined in democratic societies. It is one of the few constants in a maelstrom of technological, economic, and social change. Virtually everyone believes in it. It does not rob the rich and offers hope to the poor. It has been the social glue that binds the ambitions of diverse peoples. In recent decades the rise of mass higher education, the increasing emphasis on individualization, and the policy focus on the knowledge-driven economy, have all contributed to the belief that all have the 'opportunity' to enter fulfilling and rewarding careers.

Such ideas have pushed education to the centre-stage of social and economic policy agendas. Widening access, higher standards, and the expansion of tertiary education are part of the official mantra believed to deliver opportunity, prosperity, and justice. The growing importance attached to grades and credentials are taken to symbolize the tightening bond between education, jobs, and rewards. We are told that 'the more we learn the more we earn' at the same time offering an efficient and fair means of social selection based on individual achievement. In these terms, credentials are the currency of opportunity.[1]

This chapter challenges such accounts of education, opportunity, and the labour market in the knowledge-driven global economy. It points to social inequalities in the competition for a livelihood and to an intensification of 'positional' conflict (Hirsch 1977; Brown 2000), as 'success' depends on gaining access to tough-entry schools, universities, and jobs.

Within the social sciences there is a vast literature that has demonstrated long-term patterns of inequalities in educational and occupational opportunity (Halsey et al. 1980; Goldthorpe et al. 1987). This focus on the *opportunity gap* between the fortunes of the rich and poor has made an invaluable contribution to our understanding of education and social stratification. It has offered conclusive evidence of the relationship between social inequalities and future life chances. There is also little doubt that the opportunity gap has widening for those from disadvantaged backgrounds in countries such as the United States, Britain, and Australia, which have experienced a polarization in income and wealth.

However, a distinction needs to be drawn between this traditional focus and what we will call the *opportunity trap*. Its root cause cannot be explained solely in terms of how socially disadvantaged groups enter the competition for a livelihood on unequal terms. We must return to a consideration of the role of education in the social structure of competition, as there are too many contestants chasing credentials, jobs, and rewards that only a few can achieve.

Throughout the twentieth century the education system served to 'cool out' the vast majority of students that limited social expectations of reaching university and of coveting the rewards it could bring. Today, the rise of mass higher education has fuelled expectations of middle-class lifestyles, which has become more important as welfare provision has been cut and the stakes attached to winning and losing have increased with a widening of wage inequalities, especially in the Anglo-Saxon economies (Gray 1998).

This is a revised and abridged version of 'The Opportunity Trap: Education and Employment in a Global Economy' (2003), *European Educational Research Journal* 2/1: 142–80.

This has led to increasing positional competition as individuals seek ways of getting ahead or avoiding the social 'congestion' that has built around popular nurseries, schools, universities, and employers. The price of success (and failure) is mounting as individual 'opportunities' become harder to cash in. Middle-class families are running faster, for longer, just to stand still, as Boudon (1973) observed:[2]

> It is well known that all industrial societies are characterized by a high level of inequality of educational opportunity. Thus individuals who have a better educational level are also more likely to have a better social background. But it is also more difficult for them to reach a higher social status than their fathers, simply because the father's status is more likely to be high in the first place. (p. 6)

As the proportion of middle-class families has grown since the 1950s they are adopting more desperate measures to win a positional advantage, such as through the use of elite prep-schools, private tutors, and remortgaging homes to fund the trappings of elite education. Yet if all adopt the same tactics nobody gets ahead, it simply raises the entry requirements and the price of success (Hirsch 1977). But anyone aspiring or expected to 'get on in life' is compelled to take up the opportunity to enter this competition because it's the only game in town. This is the *opportunity trap* as few can afford to opt out of the competition for a livelihood.

This chapter will examine the opportunity trap in education and the job market, but it is important to note that it is not restricted to the experiences of young people. There are few labour market shelters from the 'risk' culture of global capitalism (Beck 1992). Insecurity has been democratized, as the competition for career advancement has intensified in 'lean' organizations constantly looking to reduce labour costs. As Robert Jackall has observed, 'The real task for the ambitious manager . . . becomes how to shape and keep shaping others' perceptions of oneself . . . so that one becomes seen as "promotable".'[3] Therefore the price of success may be the experience of self-denial, the suppression of feeling, interests, and activities that do not conform to the perceived requirement of an occupational career (Bunting 2004). Equally, in the absence of permanent employment, people are forced to exploit their 'opportunities' for permanent employability (Kanter 1995; Carnoy 2000).

Equally, the opportunity trap is not limited to individuals or families. It exposes an inherent tension, if not contradiction, in the relationship between capitalism, democracy, and the nation-state. Opportunity, delivered through expanding education and social mobility, has kept the democratic dream of individual achievement and social justice alive throughout the twentieth century, at the same time as fulfilling the imperatives of economic growth. This chapter will argue that the legitimate foundations of opportunity, based on credentials, jobs, and rewards are unravelling. Within education, this not only represents further symptoms of the diploma disease (Dore 1976), but a social revolution that fundamentally challenges our understanding of efficiency and social justice.

Education, Opportunity, and Positional Competition

Émile Durkheim (1956) believed that the education system had two key roles, the *socialization* of the young for their future adult roles, and their *selection* into employment based on individual achievement. The rise of the credential over the last century owes a lot to the fact that it captures elements of both. On the one hand, the credential represents a measure of the quality of educational experience. It signifies the acquisition of knowledge and 'expertise' (at least on the day of the examination). On the other hand, by extending the opportunity for all to take common examinations, the credential also offers a way of assessing the relative performance of individual students in academic examinations, and therefore their relative 'position' within the hierarchy of talent. Over the last century this led employers to extend the use of credentials to screen potential employees, on the assumption that the credential offered a way of assessing the relative merits and capabilities of candidates (Bourdieu and Boltanski 1978).

This dual quality of the education system is vital to an understanding of the opportunity trap, because it explains why expanding access to higher education will not improve job opportunities for credential holders, unless it is matched by the expansion of high-skilled, high-wages jobs. Fred Hirsch describes this duality of education in these terms, 'there is an absolute dimension, in which quality is added by receptive students, good teachers, good facilities, and so on; but there is also a relative dimension, in which quality consists of the differential over the educational level attained by others' (1977: 6). This led him to conclude that 'To the extent that education is a screening device . . . the possibility of general advancement is an illusion' (p. 6).

The same is true when thinking about individual employability because the chance of getting a specific job will not only depend of having the appropriate certified expertise, but on the number of applicants competing for the same job. If five well-qualified lawyers apply for the same job, four will be rejected regardless of their suitability for the job. Therefore, one's employability, along with the market value of one's credentials, depends on the employability and the credentials of others.

To further our understanding of this duality we can say that the absolute dimension refers to the *performance* imperatives of individuals, institutions, or societies. This highlights the way schools, companies, or governments try to meet their goals, by improving the quality of teaching, learning, and examination results; through raising productivity and profit margins; or through increasing economic growth. *Positional* imperatives refer to relative performance, to how one stands compared to others within an implicit or explicit hierarchy (Hirsch 1977). Again, this can refer to individuals, organizations, or nations, such as when universities or companies seek to enhance their 'reputational' capital (Brown and Scase 1997), or national governments their international economic competitiveness. Scarcity value is an inherent feature of positional goods, such as credentials.

Opportunities for education, therefore, can be extended by widening access and through improving the quality of teaching and learning, but as long as the educational system has a selective role, inequalities in outcome are inevitable. This is a key point as it recognizes that equality of outcome is impossible, if we mean by this that everyone ends up with similar credentials or jobs. Within the social sciences 'equality of opportunity' usually refers to the degree to which the distribution of education, qualifications, or jobs reflects the class, gender, and ethnic make-up of society (Halsey 1975; Arnot et al. 1999). It is for this reason that social mobility studies frequently refer to odds ratios (Marshall et al. 1997). Hence, the rhetoric of expanding educational opportunities should not disguise the fact that the value of credentials is strengthened by exclusion and weakened by inclusion. Success is meaningless without failure. While we can all be encouraged to do our best, we cannot all be the best.

Any weakening of the selective value of credentials would simply mean that selection is delayed until entry into the labour market where candidates are screened and sorted by other criteria. Our understanding of these issues has also been challenged by trends in economic globalization. To date, education and labour market opportunities have been based on 'closed' competitions limited by national boundaries (Brown and Lauder 2001). The nature of opportunity in a context of increasing globalization will be considered in the following discussion of two theories of education and labour market opportunities. We begin with *positional consensus theory* as it captures many of the ideas that inform 'official' international policy debates.[4]

Positional Consensus Theory

The global integration of financial markets, advances in information and communication technologies, corporate restructuring, and the increasing significance of multinational companies within the world economy all herald a transformation in the means of production, where knowledge, skills, and human capital are seen to be more important than capital or natural resources (Drucker 1993; Stewart 2001). Societies can be defined by their 'stage' of technological development, as it is technological innovation that is viewed as the driving force of social change.[5] Today, the shift towards a knowledge-based economy represents a further, more complex stage in the technological evolution of capitalist economies.

The more technologically advanced a society becomes the greater the demand for technical, scientific, and professional workers who require extensive periods of formal education and training, whilst the proportion of semi- and unskilled jobs declines over time (Kerr et al. 1973). The rapid expansion of higher education since mid-century reflects the exponential increase in scientific and technical knowledge, which has led to greater investment in tertiary education to supply the 'knowledge' workers required in today's economy.

It is also argued that the technological upgrading of the economy is characterized by high rates of social mobility because inequalities in the opportunity for education and employment are inconsistent with the assignment of occupational roles: 'Industrialisation . . . is against tradition and status based upon family, class, religion, race, or caste' (ibid. 1973: 53). The political determination to achieve economic efficiency and social justice is reflected in what Parsons (1959) described as the 'axis of achievement' in industrial societies. Here, efficiency and justice are seen to work with the grain of knowledge capitalism. It is concluded that getting the most talented people into senior managerial, professional, and executive positions has become even more crucial as the knowledge base of the economy expands (Michaels et al. 2001).

The role of the labour market is to match the supply and demand for technical skills and competence, based on objective measures of future productive capacity. Technological progression will lead to a growing number of workers establishing technical, managerial, and professional careers, which had previously been restricted to a small elite. This has led to a further democratization of capitalism. In the previous era, power and control were almost exclusively in the hands of employers. Some entered white-collar work in large private or public organizations that offered the prospect of career progression based on time-serving and sponsorship by senior managers. This ensured a high degree of dependency on the company as career progression depended on long-term loyalty to the company. Today, there has been a power shift because intellectual capital can no longer be controlled by organizations. This has led to a significant increase in the economic power of knowledge professionals. The knowledge-driven economy not only transforms the nature of work but also transforms the nature of capitalism (Cortada 1998).

Freed from the emasculating powers of the corporation, new ways need to be found to attract and retain talent without the aid of bureaucratic careers, which are judged to be inappropriate for both individuals and companies (Bridges 1995; Arthur and Rousseau 1996). This has led to the redefinition of the 'career', from a stepped progression within the same organization over an extended period, to that of the 'boundaryless' career that is less concerned 'with the availability of standard jobs than it is with the marketability of cumulative personal skills. Employment increasingly focuses less on filling predetermined work roles, and more on cultivating and using skills and capabilities. In the process, employment is coming to mean something at once more exciting and more temporary, driven by shifting personal competencies . . . by project activities . . . and by discovery' (Arthur and Rousseau 1996: 373).

This is believed to generate new opportunities for jobs that offer excitement, creative fulfillment, and personal development. Work is the new consumption. From this perspective there is an emphasis on expanding opportunities for education and fulfilling jobs, and a tightening bond between education, jobs, and rewards that highlights the technological imperative of individual achievement. Although the spread of opportunities will lead to inequalities in income and status, these inequalities reflect legitimate differences in talent, achievement, and contribution. Indeed, they create the necessary incentives to ensure that the most talented are motivated to engage in intensive and extensive periods of education and training (Davis and Moore 1945).

For our purposes, it is interesting to note that widening opportunities within education are not identified as a problem because the demand for skilled workers is assumed to increase, creating more room in the middle if not at the top of the occupational ladder (a form of technological trickle-down). This obviously has an impact on the way the positional competition is understood. It is a competition in the sense that all should be given an opportunity to express their innate potential in comparison with others, rather than a power struggle over access to education, credentials, and jobs.

We also need to consider how the consensus view interprets recent trends towards global integration, as it assumes that the domestic competition for education and jobs has become less relevant, and that good jobs can be achieved by most of those entering domestic labour markets in the developed economies, if nations can become 'magnet' economies (Brown and Lauder 2001), attracting a disproportion share of the global supply of high-skilled, high-waged jobs. Equally, widening income inequalities are believed to reflect the value of human capital within a global labour market (Reich 1991).

This is seen not only to increase opportunities but to transform established thinking about the link between opportunity and social justice. Given that good jobs were in short supply and the education system was assigned the role of deciding who should do what (at least in the limited sense of feeding the job market with graded human products), the basis of opportunity was to give people an equal chance to gain the top vocational prizes. This led to much discussion about class, gender, and racial inequalities in educational outcomes.

In the context of globalization, such issues are viewed as secondary to raising the overall performance of the national education system relative to the standards achieved by competitor nations. The problem is no longer one of equalizing opportunities within domestic competitions for education and jobs but of outsmarting other nations in the global knowledge wars (Brown and Lauder, this volume). It is also believed that the role of government is limited to providing all with the opportunity to enhance their employability, as national governments can no longer guarantee employment in a competitive global environment.

Positional Conflict Theory

If consensus theory focuses on increasing educational and occupational opportunities for all, conflict theorists have traditionally focused on positional issues such as the exclusionary tactics of elites and the reproduction of educational and occupational inequalities.[6] One of the most important critiques of the consensus view derives from Weber's writings on social closure (Parkin 1979; Murphy 1988). Here the competition for a livelihood is explained as a conflict between groups of competitors who will use whatever resources or powers they can muster to maintain or enhance an advantageous position, such as in gaining access to elite education or high-waged employment.

These exclusionary tactics include the way status groups seek to monopolize entry requirements into a 'profession' by restricting access, and to the way powerful social groups attempt to structure the competition for places to favour those with the appropriate cultural capital (Collins 1979; Bourdieu 1986). The increase in employer demand for 'certified' labour is therefore explained in terms of the exclusionary tactics of professional enclaves seeking to restrict the number of entrants to a given profession by raising entry requirements (Collins 1979; Friedson 1986).

This focus is evident in Weber's explanation of the popularity of credentials in Germany at the beginning of the twentieth century:

> The development of the diploma from universities, and business and engineering colleges, and the universal clamor for the creation of educational certificates in all fields make for the formation of a privileged stratum in bureaus and in offices. Such certificates support their holders' claims for intermarriages with notable families... claims to be admitted into the circles that adhere to 'codes of honor', claims for a 'respectable' remuneration rather than remuneration for work done, claims for assured advancement and old-age insurance, and, above all, claims to monopolize socially and economically advantageous positions. (Weber 1945: 241)

Hence, the rise of industrial bureaucracy and the increasing importance attached to academic credentials is not explained by the need for a meritocratic system to give all an opportunity to compete for the growing number of professional and managerial jobs, but the equivalent of a 'land grab' (as in the historical example of those who took the land of evicted Irish tenants), where those from privileged backgrounds attempted to 'certify' their privileges (Offe 1976).

From this perspective much of the recent expansion of higher education does not reflect changes in the demand for high-skilled workers, but credential inflation (Collins 2002). The idea of credential inflation is akin to that of monetary inflation. If the supply of money is greater than the supply of goods and services it leads to an increase in the cost of those goods and services (inflation). In other words the Euro or dollar in your pocket buys less. Equally, if more people gain the qualifications previously required for professional or managerial jobs, and if the numbers of these jobs does not expand to meet the supply of qualified people, there is credential inflation. Where inflation occurs the exchange value weakens (Berg 1970). As a result:

> Students who want to get ahead are forced to go back to school for longer periods, to get advanced degrees and professional specializations. One can predict that the process will continue to repeat itself at the more advanced level too. If in the future everyone had a Ph.D., law degree, M.B.A., or the like, then these advanced degrees would be worth no more than a job in a fast food restaurant, and the competition would move on to still higher degrees. (Collins 1994: 146)

Credential inflation is also seen to reinforce the opportunity gap because it will favour those with the personal and family resources that are able to meet the costs associated with an extended competition (Hirsch 1977).

While these ideas make an important contribution to understanding positional conflict they need to be modified and extended if we are to understand the causes and consequences of the opportunity trap. Earlier conflict accounts have underestimated changes in the relationship between credential competition and the occupational structure. Positional Conflict Theory (Brown 2000) also needs to give greater attention to how positional competition is experienced by individuals and social groups. Again Hirsch (1977) makes a useful distinction between forms of positional power that derive from mobilizing material, cultural, and social capital to stay ahead in the race, from the mobilization of social groups seeking to change the rules of the game. Market power, for instance, can mean the 'command over economic resources *in* the marketplace' or 'influence over markets (of a monopolistic kind)' (p. 153).

This distinction between competition *ranking*, that involves the use of resources in the marketplace, and competition *rigging*, that focuses on influences over markets (Brown 2000: 637), assumes additional importance in a context of economic globalization. Indeed, the trend towards international integration can itself be seen as an example of how power elites have extended their influence over markets (Korten 1996). The MNCs have been the major benefactors of market deregulation as they are able to achieve economies of scope and scale on a worldwide basis (Reich 1991).

But while it has increased the market power of the MNCs, it challenges the power of professional interest groups to rig domestic markets as they are exposed to international competition. Moves toward the globalization of professional services including management consultancy and financial and legal services will make it more difficult for the 'professions' to maintain monopolistic controls over domestic markets. This is leading professional organizations to develop international alliances with similar groups in other countries to find ways of sheltering from increased competition. A consequence of the professional classes feeling that their exclusionary powers over markets (rigging) are threatened, is that it heightens the importance of being able to capitalize on their material, cultural, and social assets within 'ranking' tournaments.

We need to understand both rigging practices and ranking tournaments in order to develop a comprehensive theory of the social structure of competition. Such analyses need to include an understanding of how individuals and social groups mobilize their cultural, economic, political, or social assets in positional power struggles, whatever form they take. Within the English education system, for instance, the shift from 'meritocratic' to 'market' rules (Brown 1990) can, in large part, be understood as a consequence of middle-class attempts to lift barriers that previously limited the use of material and cultural assets in credential competitions. This does not give them monopolistic powers that guarantee success, but it greatly increases their chances of a high ranking (Ball 2003; Power et al. 2003).

Thus rigging and ranking are not mutually exclusive. Even if those who have the power to define the rules of the game and are the most likely to win it, they still need to take part in order to develop their intellectual capital and to proclaim the legitimacy of their success. When this is applied to the competition for a livelihood, success for individuals and their families is not guaranteed (Erikson and Goldthorpe 1992; Devine 1999). For the middle classes this problem stems from a basic fact of life and death—it reflects the limits to inheritance. Children from affluent or wealthy backgrounds can inherit the car, television, house, or mansion, but they cannot directly inherit cultural capital (Bourdieu 1986).

Positional conflict theory needs to show how competitions are structured and how individuals and social groups fare within the 'rules of the game'. We need to incorporate the insights of social researchers such as Bourdieu and Bernstein.[7] Bourdieu's work on forms of capital, for instance, offer important insights into how individuals and social groups play out a ceaseless competition for positional advantage in many spheres of contemporary life (Bourdieu 1986, 1998).

This approach remains firmly grounded in the neo-Weberian tradition that rejects the consensus view of a politically neutral, open, and fair contest within education and the labour market in the advanced economies. The organization of positional competition will inevitably reflect a power struggle between competing interest groups. This has led to significant variations in the way competition rules are drawn up and how they relate to labour market opportunities in different countries (Esping-Andersen 1999; Hall and Soskice 2001).

Explaining the Opportunity Trap

Taking this approach to the study of education, employment, and the labour market in the twenty-first century can throw conceptual light on the social structure of opportunity and how this has changed over time. It can help us to understand why positional conflict has intensified and why it cannot be resolved through educational reform or economic globalization. Our argument is that as opportunities for education increase, they are proving harder to cash in. The problem is rooted in the relationship between capitalism, democracy, and the nation-state. The mass ranks of the middle classes and those from aspirational working-class families have high hopes of what the knowledge economy has to offer, fuelled by the expansion of higher education. At the same time people are more dependent on the job market for their economic welfare as the gap between winners and losers has grown (Frank and Cook 1996). The problem is that the labour market cannot keep pace with social expectations of work, rewards, and status.

The opportunity trap has exposed further limitations to individual freedom. It is often assumed that the process of 'individualization' (Durkheim 1933; Beck 1992) over the last century has led to greater freedom as individuals have broken free of ascribed roles within the family, employment, and wider community. But this opportunity to create one's own 'life project' makes people more, rather than less, dependent on educational and labour market success, because they are the life-support system upon which everything else depends, at least for those who are not 'independently' wealthy.

With this 'right' to opportunities comes the responsibility of 'make something of one's self'. To be judged by our own efforts is sacrosanct, but the problem many confront today is that doing one's best may not be good enough. Even extraordinary efforts to improve one's performance will count for little if everyone else does the same thing. This is something my university students understand. I asked them whether they would prefer to gain a first-class degree along with half of all university students in the country, or an upper-second class degree, if they were in the top 25 per cent of achievers. Only one out of over a hundred students opted for the first-class degree, because they saw the necessity to gain an advantage in the hunt for tough-entry employment.

What these students understood was that opportunity depends on the opportunities of others. Absolute performance is not sufficient, because cashing in one's opportunities depends on access to scare credentials, jobs, and networks. For societies, this means that what can be offered to the winners cannot be offered to the population as a whole. There are simply not enough good jobs to go around. An important part of the attraction of elite universities or blue-chip companies is the fact that they offer social status and lifestyles that are in short supply. They are sought after because they are exclusive rather than inclusive.

Not Enough Good Jobs?

A major trend since the early 1980s has been an increased demand for technical, managerial, and professional workers *and* a more intensive struggle for competitive advantage in education and the labour market. This is because the increase in the absolute number of middle-class occupations has not kept pace with current demand (Brynin 2002; Green 2006).

The American and British economies have failed to raise skill levels throughout the economy. They are characterized by enclaves of 'knowledge' work alongside large swathes of low-waged, low-skilled jobs (Brown et al. 2001: 240). A recent study of work skills in Britain found that the proportion of degree-level jobs rose from 10 per cent in 1986 to 17 per cent in 2001 (Felstead et al. 2002). But is also found that whereas there are under three million economically active people aged 20–60 who possess no qualification, there are 6.5 million jobs that require no formal qualifications to obtain them (p. 11).

There are also increasing within-group differences, both in terms of the quality of employment and rates of return (Mishel et al. 2003). Moreover, if those with higher education continue to expand at the same time that the demand for skilled labour weakens, returns may not be as clear-cut as the rhetoric of 'learning is earning' would have us believe (Levin and Kelly 1997; Wolf 2002). Previous returns may not be an accurate guide to future income. Indeed, data for the United States on education and income offers a surprising finding. Much of the difference in financial returns from investments in education does not stem from differential increases in income that conforms to the human capital idea that learning pays, but due to the decline in the earning power of non-university graduates. While educational levels have been improving in the US many students at the end of the 1990s were earning little (or no) more than they did in the 1970s (Mishel et al. 2003).

Moreover, changes in skill requirements not only reflect an increase in technological complexity but changes in models of organizational efficiency and control (Thompson and Warhurst 1998). The shift from bureaucratic to flexible paradigms of organizational efficiency (Atkinson 1985), does not necessarily mean that workers are being given greater opportunities to use their initiative and creative skills. The primary concern of employers is rarely the release of the creative energies of the workforce but how to maintain managerial control in flatter, leaner, and more flexible organizations. The inculcation of corporate mission statements, teamwork techniques, and staff appraisal schemes tied to remuneration are all ways of controlling the workforce (Rose 1999).

The power shift in the direction of knowledge workers has been greatly exaggerated. Most 'knowledge' workers are only able to capitalize on their knowledge within employment. Power remains decisively with the employers. As Georg Simmel (1990 [1907]) observed a century ago, the freedom of employees is invariably matched by the freedom of employers in a money economy. While employees are free to change employers, they are not free from the need to make a living in a wage economy.

The modern idea of employability frees employers from the moral and social obligations to employees. The insecurity that this imposes on the workforce limits their sense of freedom, precisely because they are not free from the necessity to earn a living. In a buoyant labour market the balance of power between employees and employers is disguised by a healthy supply of job opportunities, but when the economy begins to slow and unemployment increases, the realities of flexible labour markets are thrown into sharp relief. Even the winners now live under a permanent stewards' enquiry.

Rising Stakes and Insecure Ladders

Differences in the lifestyles and life chances of winners and losers within employment have always existed. But the race to inequality in the 1980s and 1990s in the United States and Britain has led to a dramatic increase in the stakes.[8] This is exacerbated by the obsession with waged work as the only meaningful way to improve one's life chances or expression of social contribution. Rather than alleviate the problems associated with unemployment the government has removed the safety blanket that offered social welfare to the losers within the capitalist system. But the costs of failure have been exaggerated by downgrading the quality of welfare support.

Nevertheless, there was an assumption that extending the opportunity for market competition within education would regulate supply and demand following the tenets of neo-classical economics. It was assumed that people would adjust their expectations according to available employment, but this ignores two things. First, that educational and occupational goals are guided not only by income, but also by self-development, self-esteem, and social status, as well as ignorance about available vacancies and the numbers applying for them. Secondly, the more waged work is the mainstay of everyday life and the more unequal earnings have become, the more academic credentials are akin to the oxygen of life rather than a commodity you can take or leave like a new television, mobile phone, or MP3 player.

The ladder of opportunity is distinctly unstable. For much of the twentieth century, when there was an economic downturn it was unskilled blue-collar workers who bore the brunt of redundancies. The downsizing of companies in recent decades has had a dramatic impact on the job tenure of knowledge workers, including engineers, managers, administrators, and executives. They have experienced a democratization of job insecurity, and must now constantly defend their position if in employment. This is associated with an intensification of work leading to a culture of long hours, and a lack of clearly defined career opportunities (Sennett 1998; Bunting 2004). This has left them worrying not only about their own future but also about that of their children. There are few guarantees that children from the middle and professional classes will maintain, let alone surpass, the social positions of their parents. Their positions are not guaranteed. This is true for all categories of workers, who are required to stay fit in their present job, if they have one, and to remain fit to compete in the wider job market. This transforms the progressive idea of lifelong learning, as the expansion of advanced programmes such as professional doctorates can be interpreted as an extension of the opportunity trap.

Too Many Contestants

The qualitative shift in the nature of waged work is also coupled with the problem of too many contestants chasing too few prized jobs. Mass higher education and the decline of blue-collar work has led to rising expectations of middle-class lifestyles. Giddens (1991: 6) has noted that 'class divisions and other fundamental lines of inequality, such as those connected with gender or ethnicity, can be partly *defined* in terms of differential access to forms of self-actualisation and empowerment'. But this depends on finding ways to exploit their opportunities in education and the labour market, at the same time that there has been an influx of serious contestants due to changes in the class structure and gender relations (Crompton 1999; Devine 1999).

The growth of the middle classes since the 1950s has increased the proportion of the student population that not only aspired to a middle-class career, but expect to make one. This has served to intensify competition for the 'best' schools, colleges, and universities that are judged to give access to the most prestigious vocational prizes.

In the United States there is evidence of the 'seriously rich' attempting, and succeeding, to rig inheritance laws to make it easier for them to pass wealth on to their offspring. In a context of increasing positional competition they are seeking to reproduce their advantage through wealth and ownership rather than credential competition. This is not to say that they will not buy access to elite kindergartens, schools, colleges, and universities, as this is an important source of cultural and social capital, but economic security has been bought in advance. The extent to which this is happening and whether it represents a precedent that other developed economies will follow remains unclear.

This is not an option for the middle classes that need to translate their cultural advantage into marketable knowledge, certificates, experience, and networks. They may inherit some material wealth but usually this represents a fringe benefit. It pays for skiing holidays, a second home, or private education, but it is inadequate to support a middle-class lifestyle. This depends on a reasonable degree of success in the job market. Failure for the middle class is not met with a material springboard, but the threat of poverty. The middle classes have little option other than to capitalize on their cultural assets via education, given the need to acquire credentials from tough-entry schools, colleges, and universities as employers introduced formal entry and promotion procedures throughout the twentieth century (Bourdieu and Boltanski 1978).

For the lower socio-economic classes the limitation of inheritance is altogether different. The digital divide, lack of money for 'extracurricular' activities, cramped housing conditions, and poor job prospects placed them at a distinct disadvantage (Shipler 2005). A commitment to equal opportunities and positive discrimination offers virtually the only chance of breaking the cycle of disadvantage through the formal economy. The decline of bureaucratic work organization has made the access to credentials even more important, as there is less scope for occupational mobility within lean organizations.

Competition has also become more intense as women are encouraged to compete on equal terms with men (Dillabough and Arnot 2001). Although inequalities in subject choices, pay, and promotion prospects remain, women, especially from middle-class backgrounds, are serious contenders for professional and managerial employment (Osborne et al. 2000; Crompton 1999). The academic performance of women, especially from middle-class backgrounds, has intensified the competition for elite credentials (Arnot et al. 1999).

This has made it difficult for Western governments to resist calls for wider access to higher education. In an elite system of higher education the possession of a graduate qualification represents a passport into professional and managerial occupations. The recent move towards mass higher education in a number of European countries has removed the problem of access to higher education from middle-class families. It has also opened new opportunities to working-class, 'mature', and ethnic-minority students to gain graduate qualifications.

This has resulted in a significant increase in the numbers of university graduates entering the labour market. But while the expansion of higher education appears to extend access to professional and managerial employment to more people, and raises expectations of middle-class lifestyles, 'more means different' as it has led to a greater differentiation in the perceived 'quality' of both students and universities. In short, the rapid expansion of higher education and lifelong learning is a symptom of the opportunity trap, not its resolution.

The Globalization of Positional Competition

Finally, the view that workers now have to operate in a global rather than a national market is a simplification of existing realities for most workers. This is because the global labour market does not operate as a 'free' market (Castells 2000; Held et al. 1999). Nationality continues to operate as a vital tool for restricting the competition for jobs by excluding millions of well-qualified workers from other parts of the world such as skilled software engineers from India competing for IT jobs within the European Community or North America (Kobrin 2000). These restrictions are sometimes loosened when there are national labour or skill shortages, such as the use of temporary visas in the United States for IT workers, or the foreign talent scheme in Singapore. This also applies at the other end of the labour market for those who are willing to work as 'guest' workers to undertake the jobs that the indigenous workforce is unwilling to consider given the long hours, poor remuneration, and bad conditions involved in a lot of this work (Sassen 1988; Fevre 1998).

There are already a number of bilateral agreements that extend labour-market opportunities (and risks) but these by definition are intended to limit the competition to 'club members' rather than to make it global in scope. The free movement of labour is enshrined in the statutes of the European Community, where people are able to compete for jobs in other EU countries on the basis of their knowledge, skills, and experience. Graduates for Britain, France, Germany, Spain, and Portugal may find themselves in increasing competition for technical, managerial, and professional jobs in international agencies and MNCs (Brown 2000). But these graduates are largely sheltered from direct competition from graduates from Moscow, Lahore, and Beijing, at least within their domestic job markets. The rich and the poor within national societies are still related. Access to elite schools, colleges, and universities along with the credentials they bestow remain a key factor in determining future life chances. Therefore, the question of social justice will continue to depend on how individual nations-states frame the competition for a livelihood.

For most workers, most of the time, where they are born and grow up continues to structure their labour-market opportunities within local or national contexts. This does not mean that limitations on the physical movement of labour undermine the importance attached to the global economy. Capital has greater mobility than workers. Workers from different countries come into competition when companies make decisions about where to invest in new plants, offices, or research capability. The decision to 'offshore' will include a number of considerations such as proximity to markets, political stability, communication networks, social overheads, wage costs, incentives in the form of cheap rents, tax holidays, and government grants, as well as skill levels and the quality of education and training systems.

The globalization of labour markets cannot resolve the opportunity trap, although political leaders continue to pronounce education as the best economic policy they have, based on the assumption that as low-skilled, low-waged jobs migrate to newly industrializing nations, high-skilled, high-waged jobs will migrate in the other direction, leading to a concentration of knowledge work in the developed economies.

The reality is different. The developed economies confront an exponential growth in the global supply of high-skilled workers eager to work for a fraction of the salaries of professionals and managers in the United States or Western Europe. China, India, and Russia have all doubled the numbers in higher education since 1995 and China now has more university students than the United States (Brown and Lauder, this volume).

Some Sociological Implications

Credentials: The Currency of Opportunity

People are encouraged to invest time and effort to become qualified on the assumption that it will pay off in terms of a good job and high incomes (Collins 1994; Ashton and Green 1996). Although academic success never came with a job guarantee, restrictions on access to higher education gave university graduates the status of a labour-market elite. It has been argued here that the opportunity bargain has been seriously strained if not broken. This has led to a spiral of inflation as more enter the labour-market with better grades and higher qualifications, leading employers to lift their entry requirements in an attempt to reduce the flood of applicants. But these inflationary pressures can lead to a different outcome. For many jobs more advanced forms of education and training may be seen as counter-productive (i.e. too academic, too specialized, or leading to 'unrealistic expectations'). Rather than constantly lift entry requirements, employers may increasingly differentiate in terms of the 'quality' of the credential (this is rarely the case with money among people holding the same currency). Does it, for instance, carry the imprimatur of an 'elite' or a 'second chance' institution?

These inflationary pressures can also lead employers to place less emphasis on credentials by extending their recruitment criteria.[9] As one employer explained, 'paper qualifications are the first tick in the box and then we move onto the real selection'.[10] This suggests a change in the way companies appropriate credentials. Previously, they were seen as a certificate of cultural suitability (Bourdieu and Passeron 1977). However, employers argue that the kind of people they are looking for has changed and the credential tells them less about what they need to know about a candidate when making their recruitment decisions. The credential represented discipline, perseverance, and rule-following behaviour, highly valued in bureaucratic organizations.

Today, there is more emphasis on personal drive, self-reliance, and interpersonal skills (Brown and Scase 1997). The devaluation of credentials increases the value of *barter* between the individual and the recruiter. For tough-entry jobs individuals not only need the required credentials, but must sell themselves to the employer by demonstrating, through interview, psychometric tests, and group exercises, that they are more employable that other candidates. Success in the labour market depends on 'personal capital' both in the form of 'hard' currencies (credentials, sporting achievements, etc.) and the 'soft' currencies (personal qualities) to be exchanged in the market for jobs. Personal capital does not refer to the size of one's bank balance, but to the extent the self can be packaged to capitalize on those personal qualities valued by employers (Brown and Hesketh 2004: 34).

The rise of personal capital reflects a rupturing of the 'meritocratic' link between education, jobs, and rewards. It exposes the 'social' realities of selection that were shrouded in the mythology of innate differences in productive potential. Social confidence, appearance, ambition, and narratives of the productive self, have always been important but are now critical when employers are confronted with large number of applicants armed with the same credentials. The rhetoric of employability has been introduced to bridge this chasm between education and jobs. Personal responsibility for employment is the price for widening opportunities to education. Opportunities have to be paid for because governments are finding it increasingly difficult to manufacture the connection between credentials and jobs creation.

Employability becomes an inevitable feature of a knowledge-driven economy not because it reflects the high levels of knowledge and skills required by most of the workforce and the demand for rapid retraining and lifelong learning, but because mass higher education has undermined the claim that the occupation structure reflects differences in knowledge and expertise (Weber 1945). Differences in 'expertise' between university graduates and other workers were used by employers to justify differences in training, rewards, and career development. The problem today, as the participation rate in higher education moves towards 50 per cent in a number of countries, is that many graduates may find themselves in inferior jobs, despite having the same 'knowledge' as their senior colleagues. This has weakened the differentiating power of knowledge (credentials) in the legitimation of labour market and workplace inequalities.

We have entered a period of 'educational stagflation', where inflationary pressures mount as more credentials are awarded, at the same time the job market cannot create enough of the jobs that many expect. This is not necessarily a bad thing from an employer perspective as flexible labour markets depend on a reserve army of knowledge workers. As most of the employment growth is in the service sector, university graduates are invaluable not because of their knowledge of a particular field but because of their communication skills in dealing with customers, although this is obviously not the case of all graduates! However, the wages, jobs, and intrinsic rewards associated with many of these jobs are not commensurate with the opportunity bargain that graduates bought into. The knock-on effect is that as more graduates are underemployed opportunities for the less qualified becomes ever more limited (Keep and Mayhew 2004).

New Strains of the Diploma Disease

Ronald Dore (1976) argued that the 'diploma disease' not only led to wasteful competition, but infected the very purpose of liberal education. When education is dominated by grading competitions:

> the pupil is concerned not with mastery, but with being certified as having mastered. The knowledge that he gains not for its own sake and not for constant later use in a real life situation—but for the once-and-for-all purpose of reproducing it in an examination. And the learning and reproducing is all just a means to an end—the end of getting a certificate which is a passport to a coveted job, a status, an income. If education is learning to *do* a job, qualification is a matter of learning in order to *get* a job. (1976: 8)

We can therefore distinguish *inquisitive learning* from *acquisitive learning*. Inquisitive learning is driven by an interest in knowledge and learning for its own sake, whereas acquisitive learning is consumer driven. It involves learning what is necessary to pass examinations. It is based on a model of individual rational calculation where the moral foundations of education have been lost (Dewey 1916; Lawn 2001).

Since Dore's original diagnosis of the diploma disease in the 1970s the symptoms have worsened. Acquisitive learning is now widely believed to define the purpose of education. There is a considerable wastage of effort and resources as many compete for the prizes that only a few can achieve (Frank and Cook 1996). The opportunity trap lures people into 'fashionable' areas of study at the same time as there are skill shortages in less-popular fields often based on science and engineering. But these are modest problems when set against the individual and social costs associated with the social limits to opportunity.

More and more effort, time, and money is being spent doing what is necessary rather than for any intrinsic purpose. Rather than 'opportunities' extending our freedom and fulfilling our dreams, they are making people increasingly self-centred, stressed, and unfulfilled. The pursuit of success harbours the danger of turning the self into a commodity (Rose 1999). If the diploma disease signifies a shift in the purpose of education, employability is a shift in the meaning of life. We are, in short, being economically enslaved by our opportunities. It has been argued that even the winners now live under a permanent stewards' enquiry, as their positions are not guaranteed for life. One must enter a lifelong campaign to stay fit in one's present job and to remain fit in the wider job market in case one joins the ranks of surplus employees.

This has a significant impact on the way we bring up our children. The priority is to treat and train our children in ways that are demanded for success in this new rat race, rather than in ways that benefit the child as an intelligent and well-rounded member of society. Many of our young are 'growing up absurd' (Goodman 1956). They now confront batteries of tests from the time they leave their pushchairs, a lengthening obstacle course that extends into their late twenties, and intense supervision giving children little room for creativity, freedom, or individual expression. We are creating hordes of smart conformists. They know what they have to do to get ahead, but they have little understanding of why they do what they are doing. In England, a student can expect over 100 formal examinations before her or his eighteenth birthday.

The Hobbesian Condition in the Twenty-First Century

In the seventeenth century Thomas Hobbes (1881, 1961) argued that unless societies can find a cohesive force to bring people together they confront an unending war of 'all-against-all'. Hobbes believed that although humans may vary in terms of strength, ability, or energy, such differences were less apparent than their common human capabilities. The result is a constant struggle between equals that offers little prospect of a solution. Hobbes's answer was to impose the will of the state as the only authority able to command the obedience of the people.

Subsequently, the Scottish economist Adam Smith and the French sociologist Émile Durkheim, had other ideas. They believed that the organization of work held the key to resolving the problem of social order. Through a commitment to economic growth it was assumed that both efficiency and justice were possible. Indeed, Durkheim argued that efficiency would come to depend on extending individual opportunities to all. By matching individual capabilities to work roles on the basis on personal achievement, everyone could agree about the question of 'who does what?' and 'who gets what?' However, he also observed that 'labour is divided spontaneously only if society is constituted in such a way that social inequalities exactly express natural inequalities' and this rests on 'absolute equality in the external conditions of the conflict' (Durkheim 1933: 377).

In the second-half of the twentieth century they seemed to be vindicated. Old class antagonisms were destroyed as new opportunities for education and skilled employment were extended to all classes. Many appeared to benefit from improvements in productivity and working conditions along with the expansion of white-collar work. This led Dahrendorf (1990: 159) to conclude that 'wherever possible, people will try to make headway by their own efforts. In the United States, this has long been the dominant mode of conflict. Today the same is true in most countries. Individual mobility takes the place of the class struggle.'

At the beginning of the twenty-first century the Hobbesian problem has returned. Opportunity, rather than being the glue that bonds the individual to society, has become the focus for intense social conflict. This in turn presents a serious threat to efficiency, justice, and social cohesion. Instead of a normative commitment to equality of opportunity (Parsons 1959) there are civil and international knowledge wars that have incited a scramble for tough-entry schools, universities, and jobs.

The post-war commitment to 'comprehensive' education has been sacrificed in the battle for positional advantage. The parents of elites and the middle classes have mobilized whatever material or cultural resources they can bring to bear on the outcome of this competition. The use of private education, tutors, counsellors, and career specialists has become *de rigueur*. It is an expression of doing the best for one's child, rather than cheating on society. It has brought *merit* and the *market* into a head-to-head. In the age-old battle between family and merit described by Michael Young (1961) the commitment to meritocracy has been defeated by a new form of ascription, where millions are being excluded from any chance of receiving an education that would allow them an equal chance of competing with the sons and daughters of the wealthy.[11]

There is also increasing cultural confusion within the middle classes as the rules of meritocratic competition, that legitimated their 'achievements' in the past, have crumbled under the competitive strain without any widely accepted alternative. The consequences are being felt in the 'graduate' labour market where a growing number of those competing for tough-entry jobs are adopting 'player' tactics. Here, employability is viewed as a positional game in which the meritocratic ideal of matching the right person to the right job based on the presentation of abilities, achievements, and the authentic self are rejected. The players seek a positional advantage by marketing themselves in ways that conform to the behavioural competences desired by employers. They use careers information and social contacts to 'decode' the winning formula, attend workshops that simulate group exercises at assessment centres, read books on how to answer difficult interview questions, and 'practise' psychometric tests. They understand the task as learning to be competent at being competent (Brown and Hesketh 2004).

This increase in player behaviour, which also extends to parents who suddenly discover religion in order to get their child into the local church school with a good reputation, is based on the recognition that rather than offering unprecedented opportunity and prosperity to all, we have entered a zero-sum game where the winners take most, if not all. While millions join the paperchase for marketable skills and strive for a decent job, many have failed to stay in touch with the democratic dream, while others live in gratuitous affluence.

Positional conflict has, therefore, not only cast the rich against the poor, but has led to internecine struggles within the professional classes (Brown 1995; Ball and Vincent 2001). The losers are not only the disadvantaged who find themselves excluded from attaining a decent life for themselves and family members, but also many of those from more affluent backgrounds who may have done all they can to get ahead but have little to show for their efforts. But the extent of entrapment will continue to reflect the opportunity gap—social inequalities in the power of social groups to rig competition rules in their favour and to prosper in ranking tournaments.

This analysis also raises the question of whether social elites are increasingly defining the competition for credentials and jobs in international, if not global, terms. We cannot rule out the possibility that as the middle classes become more aware of the opportunities and threats posed by economic globalization, it will lead them to mobilize resources to compete at a global level (Brown 2000).

At this point it is easy to miss the broader significance of the Hobbesian problem. While some cling to the idea of an 'aristocracy of talent', and believe that mass higher education reflects the 'dumbing down' of education and cultural standards (Murray and Herrnstein 1994), this analysis leads us to a different conclusion. While there is clear evidence of credential inflation, what the opportunity trap also reflects is a silent revolution. The overheated competition for credentials and jobs reflects the fact that the capabilities of a few have been greatly exaggerated, while those of the major have been greatly underestimated. The opportunity trap reflects the fact that the hierarchy of jobs does not conform to a hierarchy of talent as Durkheim envisaged. Nor does the hierarchy of job-holders give us much confidence that it reflects innate differences rather than the product of class, gender, racial, or spatial inequalities in opportunities.

The opportunity trap can be explained by rising expectations and the economic limits to high-skilled, high-waged employment, that exposes the dim view of intelligence for what it is, a social fiction (Brown and Lauder 2001). It is the social rather than the human limits to opportunity that represent the main problem in developed economies. The issue here is not simply that some people may be better than others at some tasks, but that academic study reflects general intelligence. This conflates relative performance with absolute capability. Indeed, employers recognize that those with the highest grades are not necessarily the 'best' employees. It is time to rethink the basic assumptions that inform our understanding of justice, opportunity, and efficiency.

This conclusion also offers an explanation of why the educational and social inequalities identified by social scientists have not had more profound economic consequences. These inequalities have not seriously dented productive efficiency because human capability is not in reality how it is commonly understood, as characterized by a limited pool of talent, that places a premium on getting the most talented into the most intellectually demanding jobs. An alternative explanation is that with the appropriate motivation and training most people could perform most jobs reasonable well.

The problem this poses for governments of all persuasions it that the wealth of human capability that is being nurtured within schools, colleges, and universities; the explosion of knowledge via new technologies and the internet; and an exponential increase in the global supply of high-skilled, low-waged workers challenge the 'legitimate' foundations of how capitalist democracies have resolved the questions of 'who does what' and 'who gets what'. They have become victims of their own success!

Conclusion

The opportunity trap has become a defining feature of the risk society (Beck 1992). The problem is not only how to find decent jobs but how to maintain them. We have argued that people have been forced to depend on gaining a positional advantage, as more and more people are chasing the same rewards and the inequalities between winners and losers have increased.

The opportunity trap can be applied to governments was well as individuals, groups, or classes. 'Opportunity' represented the democratic solution to the distributional questions of what education, what jobs, and what rewards. But what looks like an extension to personal freedom, limits freedom. The division of labour can no longer bear the aspirations of individuals, families, and social classes. Democracy has exceeded the limits of knowledge-driven capitalism as 'opportunity' has become disorganized (Lash and Urry 1987).

Governments, especially in America and Britain, have not been passive bystanders. For over two decades they have pursued policies that greatly exacerbate the trends identified in this chapter. They deliberately sought to increase the stakes, given a blind commitment to market individualism. Some conservative thinkers believed that greater market competition would attune aspirations with available job opportunities and education would 'diversify as society required' (Scruton 1984). However, market reforms had exactly the opposite consequence because they have made people more and more dependent on credential competition.

Equally, if the market is to be the arbiter in the competition for a livelihood, there is little scope for the state to limit access to credentials in the 'national' interest. In other words, the moral foundations of opportunity, justice, and efficiency have been reduced to the logic of the market. What this leaves unresolved is that self-interest is not the grassroots equivalent of the common good (Bell 1953; Fevre 2003). It then becomes an act of faith that the number of decent jobs will grow commensurate with the supply of qualified people entering the labour market.

This has not stopped governments printing paper qualifications at an alarming rate, in ways they could not do with money because of the financial markets that take a dim view of inflation. In education there are no such concerns. Indeed, the increasing numbers of credentials in circulation is seen to reflect a widening of access and opportunities. Governments are reluctant to admit that this has led to a growth in wasteful competition and a weakening of the opportunity bargain, as they persist with slogans such as 'learning is earning' and the 'opportunity society'. Yet we need to be wary of defining this as 'over-education' as it smuggles in a utilitarian view of education, that its only purpose is to prepare people for the job market or to increase lifetime earnings. It denies the value of education and learning as an end in itself. The problem is that given the way we have organized our life-support systems (work, incomes, dignity, quality of life), these broader goals of education remain but lip-service in a world that hardly exists.

This chapter also raises the issue of whether the opportunity trap, as characterized here, is to be found in all the developed economies or whether there are important national differences in the social structure of positional competition. It raises the issue of whether societal differences in competition rules will converge or diverge from the Anglo-Saxon model. The prospect of enduring societal differences in the way the competition for a livelihood is organized and experienced needs to be fully explored in a context of increasing European and global integration.

Comparative differences in university graduation rates suggest that important differences remain in the organization of education, employment, and the labour market. The graduation rate in Germany, for instance, is far below that found in the United Kingdom or the Netherlands. The 'dual system' in Germany channels large numbers of young adults into training programmes that offer access to decent job opportunities without the requirement of higher education. But whether the dual system can continue to perform this role is a moot point (Streeck 1997; Lauder 2001).

In conclusion, we have shown that the opportunity trap is not simply an educational problem but it does pose problems for education. The education system reflects rather than 'compensates' for society (Bernstein 1970). The solution cannot be found within the confines of education, but requires little short of a social revolution (Brown and Lauder 2001). However, there is a high degree of collusion with the rhetoric of 'learning is earning' within the educational establishment, as schools, colleges, and universities try to pursue their own positional advantage in the competition for students, resources, and reputational capital. But unless a realistic re-evaluation of the role of education, efficiency, and justice is mounted, another political denunciation of the failings of education is inevitable.

NOTES

1. This is far removed from debates about the 'diploma disease' (Dore 1976; Collins 1979) and class reproduction (Bowles and Gintis 1976) in the 1970s. The 'diploma disease' highlights problems of credential inflation caused by the failure of the jobs market to meet the rising demand for technical, professional, and managerial jobs, as educational opportunities have expanded (Breg 1970). It also focused on how the paper-chase has undermined the ideals of a liberal education as this chapter will go on to argue.

2. Boudon was interested in the fact that the 'distribution of social status has changed less rapidly than the distribution of levels of education' (1973: 4). He draws on C. Arnold Anderson's (1961) paper, 'A Skeptial Note on Education and Mobility', in J. Floud and A. H. Halsey's edited collection, *Education, Economy and Society*. Boudon notes, 'It is well known that all industrial societies are characterized by a high level of inequality of educational opportunity. Thus individuals who have a better educational level are also more likely to have a better social background. But it is also more difficult for them to reach a higher social status than their father, simply because the father's status is more likely to be high in the first place' (1973: 6).

3. R. Jackall (1988), *Moral Mazes: The World of Corporate Managers* (New York: Oxford University Press), 64. See also <*http://www.suhyit.edu/~harell/_billeyiack/book_reviews.htm*>.

4. Within the social sciences the positonal quality of education has been widely acknowledged. The main focus has been on the extent to which the competition for credentials is fair and efficent (Bell 1978). As we have noted, a large body of research has highlighted persistent inequalities in the competition for a livelihood and patterns of social mobility based on class, gender, and race (although writers such as Herrnstein and Murray (1994) in America and Saunders (1995) in Britain have argued that much of these differences in academic performance can be explained in terms of innate rather than social inequalities).
5. This interpretation of the relationship between education and employment conforms closely to 'technocratic' theory (Kerr et al. 1973; Collins 1979).
6. These ideas are outlined in the 'Introduction' to this volume.
7. See, for example, the Special Issues of the *British Journal of Sociology of Education*, 23/4 (2002), devoted to the contribution of Basil Bernstein.
8. The same trend has not been found in continental Europe, where neo-liberalism is less evident.
9. Unlike money, credentials are not a currency of exchange but one of entitlement. If you have the appropriate qualifications you are entitled to enter the competition for specific kinds of employment. It confers an entitlement to barter.
10. See Brown and Hesketh (2004).
11. As I have noted elsewhere, educational selection is increasingly based on the wealth and wishes of parents rather than the abilities and efforts of students. Here the equation, 'ability + effort = merit' is reformulated into 'resources + preferences = choice' (Brown 1995, 2000).

Social Inheritance and Equal Opportunity Policies

Gosta Esping-Andersen

In a world of genuine equal opportunity our life chances would largely depend on effort, motivation, and skills and very little on the luck of birth. For very good reasons, social scientists over the past half century were confident that social inheritance of life chances, or ascription, would wane. For one, the democratisation of education should eliminate perhaps the most important filter of traditional class privilege, namely parents' unequal ability to invest in their children's human capital. For another, as postindustrial theorists like Daniel Bell (1977) insist, the knowledge intensive economy will prioritise merit and ability over ascriptive characteristics. And, thirdly, since economic want and insecurity in families have adverse effects on schooling, the expansion of the welfare state ought to have contributed decisively in levelling the playing field.

We confront, therefore, a major puzzle because a cumulation of social scientific evidence suggests that individuals' life chances remain as powerfully determined by their social origins as in the epoch of our fathers and grandfathers. This is cause for worry if we care about social justice, and also quite problematic if we are concerned with our future economy. The evolving knowledge economy will up the ante in terms of the skills and qualifications necessary for a good life. Those who acquire insufficient human capital today will, with growing likelihood, find themselves locked into a life of low pay and precariousness. And, if a large share of today's youth fails to realise its full productive potential, tomorrow's retirees will be less well off.

This chapter opens with a review of what we know about social inheritance and life chances, focusing especially on the key mechanisms that perpetuate unequal opportunities. The bad news is that social inheritance has not, in any meaningful way, abated. But there is some good news because recent research has uncovered a few non-trivial exceptions to the rule. If we can identify the precise mechanisms at work, this might help us redefine the pursuit of more equality of opportunity. The last part of the chapter is therefore devoted to an assessment of policy alternatives. To anticipate my conclusions, I am sceptical about the standard assumption that generational inheritance is driven primarily by unequal investments in education. Instead, the decisive mechanisms probably concentrate in conditions prior to children's first encounter with the classroom. It is in early childhood that parental transmission is key. Poverty and economic insecurity are very problematic but the 'cultural capital' of families is arguably decisive. This would indicate that research and public policy need to change the focus from education systems towards families and early childhood welfare.

In a rare example of disciplinary convergence, sociologists and economists study inter-generational inheritance (or mobility) pretty much the same way and produce similar conclusions. The only real difference is that economists focus on earnings and incomes, while sociologists mainly examine

From Simone Delorenzi, Jodie Reed, and Peter Robinson (eds.), *Maintaining Momentum: Extending Social Mobility and Life Chances from Early Years to Adulthood* (London: IPPR). Reprinted with permission.

educational, occupational, or social class attainment.[1] In reality the difference of focus matters little since the main mobility variables—income or occupational destiny—are pretty much two sides of the same coin. Earnings and occupational status are, unsurprisingly, highly correlated (Erikson and Goldthorpe, 1992), as are earnings and class (Wright, 1979).[2]

Both disciplines also assume a similar causal logic. Both agree that education is the crucial site where social inheritance is transmitted. Human capital theory, as developed by Becker (1964), and more recently by Becker and Tomes (1979; 1986), argues that offsprings' income correlates highly with parental income because parents are unequally able to invest in their children's education. It is therefore not surprising that social scientists believed so readily that opportunities would become more equal. The impact of parental investments should logically diminish if access to education is democratised and if government investment in education is to the greatest benefit of lower income families. In most advanced countries, postwar education reforms were designed to accomplish precisely that. Hence the emphasis on comprehensive school systems, late (if any) streaming, scholarships, and bridges between the branches of the educational system.

Early US research on inter-generational income mobility produced fairly optimistic results. Parent–child correlations were found to hover around 0.2 to 0.3, and this suggested a fairly modest degree of social inheritance (Solon, 1999). These studies, however, were riddled with methodological problems and recent, more robust, estimates now converge around a far higher core figure (of about 0.4) for the United States. There is credible support for the prediction that changes in income distribution and/or in government investment in education will affect the elasticity. Harding *et al.* (2002) demonstrate a continuous decline in the US correlation that is related both to government expenditure and to declining household income dispersion during the 1960s and 1970s. Interestingly, rising inequalities thereafter have produced a reversal.

Comparisons with other countries are, of course, better suited to test the effects of differing educational policies. In one of the early studies of income mobility between generations, Atkinson *et al.* (1983) showed very strong parent–child correlations for Britain. More recent research pretty much confirms this picture (Solon, 1999; Corak, 2004). Indeed, Blanden *et al.* (2004) show that government policy may actually reinforce—rather than weaken—the social origins effect if, as in Britain, the expansion of higher education has mainly been to the benefit of the privileged classes.

Within the comparative literature, the US, followed by Britain, emerge as substantially less mobile than other countries. Bjorklund and Jantti (1997) compare Sweden and the US and find substantially greater inter-generational income mobility in the former (a correlation around 0.2). Estimates for Germany also suggest more mobility than in the US or Britain (Corak, 2004). Comparatively speaking, the Nordic countries (Denmark and Sweden) exhibit systematically more inter-generational income mobility while the UK and US (and Italy) fall at the other extreme (Jorgensen 2001).

That the US is far less mobile than Germany and Sweden may come as a surprise considering the unregulated nature of its labour markets and the prevailing mobility myth. It also contradicts one of the main theoretical premises of sociological research, namely the thesis that modernisation, i.e. economic growth and industrialisation, will, in the long run, increase mobility opportunities—and thus undo the class divide.[3] It was assumed, rather than demonstrated, that the United States—as the vanguard of economic development—boasted substantially more social fluidity than elsewhere. And it was predicted that Europe, and even Third World nations, would eventually exhibit similarly high mobility rates once the economic catch-up process caught on.[4] Clearly, the comparative research on inter-generational income mobility has given this thesis the death-knell.

Turning to sociological research, the new consensus, as far as long-run historical evolution is concerned is best captured by Erikson and Goldthorpe's notion of the 'constant flux'. That is, the correlation between social origins and achievement appears extraordinarily stable and trendless over long historical periods in just about all societies.[5] And this holds for occupational class mobility (Erikson and Goldthorpe, 1992), and for educational attainment

(Shavit and Blossfeld, 1993). Yet, these very same studies do identify exceptions to the constant flux, particularly among the youngest cohorts in Sweden, and arguably also in the Netherlands. Subsequent analyses corroborate this (Erikson and Jonsson, 1996). In brief, just as the economists find exceptionally low inter-generational correlations in Sweden, so the sociologists identify Sweden as a unique case of diminishing social inheritance.

Virtually all inter-generational mobility research shows strong asymmetries across social classes or income groups. Atkinson *et al.* (1983) found that there was far more immobility at the very top and at the bottom of the social hierarchy: most of the mobility that does occur is concentrated in the middle. Ermisch and Francesconi (2004) suggest that, in Britain, downward mobility from the top of the class structure is far less likely than is upward mobility from the bottom. A Danish study illustrates the logic well. Denmark is also in the vanguard in terms of income mobility. Indeed, within the second, third and fourth quintiles there is virtually no correlation between parents' and children's incomes. In other words, virtually the entire social inheritance effect for Denmark is concentrated within the two extremes (Jorgensen 2001: table II.17). But the mobility disadvantage that the poorest face (and the advantage that the richest enjoy) in Denmark is far less than in other countries. The core problem of social inheritance lies buried in the extremes. Children of the poor face exceptionally tough barriers to move up in the hierarchy; children of the rich appear unusually protected. The challenge is to understand the mechanisms at work.

Sociologists have always been preoccupied with the mechanisms that connect origins and destinations, especially with those that may jointly explain both educational and job inheritance. Most sociologists will interpret inter-generational mobility correlations in terms of two main kinds of social interactions: firstly, the social milieu of the family during childhood and youth (such as family stability, poverty, or 'cultural capital') and, secondly, the characteristics of the social community (neighbourhood class or race segregation, or social networks).[6]

The Mechanisms of Inter-Generational Transmission

In the postwar era there has been an almost perfect consensus that education is the chief mechanism through which origins are linked to destinations. Reformers put their faith in educational reform, but their faith was largely misplaced, and this requires explanation.

We can look at the effect of education at a micro or macro level. In the former case, the system is a given and research focuses on the processes of social selection within that system. In the latter, as in cross-national mobility comparisons, research focuses on educational systems, with whether one model promotes more or less opportunity than another.

Many of those studies that compare across systems present puzzling national differences. For example, Shavit and Blossfeld (1993) find that Sweden, alone among a large number of countries, has managed to rupture the constant flux.[7] Swedish (and Danish) public expenditure on education does lie a couple of percentage points above the OECD mean. But comparative educational attainment research, as well as international evaluation studies, suggest that differences in public educational spending matter very little (Shavit and Blossfeld, 1993; Erikson and Jonsson, 1996; OECD, 2001).

System design might conceivably be of greater importance. It is, for example, an established fact that early streaming in schools reinforces social inequalities. And the Swedish reform of its comprehensive school system was explicitly designed to augment equal opportunities. But Denmark never embarked on comprehensiveness. Educational system characteristics (such as tracking, or the mix of public and private schools) may help account for group-specific mobility patterns, but they generally fail to explain overall mobility differences. Hence, the constant flux of occupational or educational attainment prevails in countries with distinctly different educational systems—such as the United States, Germany, Italy and the UK, four countries that pretty much represent the global diversity in education systems.[8] Nor is it easy to explain the two deviant cases by reference to system attributes. Danish education is quite similar to the German dual system while Sweden (since the 1960s) boasts a comprehensive school system that, in many respects, recalls the American—although it is far less heterogeneous in terms of quality and financing.[9]

When we move to micro-analyses, the education variable comes closer to the individualised investment-logic that drives economic theory. But if we doubt that it is all money-driven, we need to broaden our search for the smoking gun. In fact, since education hardly ever explains more than a fifth of the variation in log-earnings (Card, 1999), the gun is bound to be located elsewhere.

Sociologists generally prefer to study educational attainment in terms of transitions rather than years of education (Mare, 1993). This is so for two principal reasons. One, the social origins effect is not monotonic by years of schooling. It is stronger at earlier key transitions (in particular transitions into secondary education) and tapers off later on. Put differently, if 'poor' kids make it through the hurdles, their performance is more on par with 'rich' kids. There is, in other words, a potential problem of selection bias when we measure education simply in terms of years of schooling.[10] Two, the important selection occurs at the moment youth face transitions, because it is at this point that they (and their parents) will calculate the potential gains, risks, and opportunity costs associated with additional schooling (Breen, 2001). The risk calculus is, itself, likely to co-vary with the mechanisms (such as income, social networks or cultural capital) that link social origins to educational outcomes. What, then, determines educational choices and outcomes?

An important clue comes from research on remedial education (Heckman, 1999). One solid finding is that attempts to correct for skill-deficiencies later in life are ineffective if people do not already possess adequate motivational or cognitive resources to begin with. This, as developmental psychologists have established, all begins in early childhood, in particular in the ages nought to six, which is when the basic abilities for learning are most intensely developed (Danziger and Waldfogel, 2000; Duncan and Brooks-Gunn, 1997).[11] This said, one would expect that family effects will overshadow community or neighbourhood effects (which are more likely to assert their influence at later stages).[12]

There is now consistent evidence that the family milieu during early childhood is decisive for later achievement, and also for later social problems, such as school drop-out and criminality. One factor that has been studied extensively is the impact of poverty and, more generally, of family resources (Duncan *et al.*, 1998; Duncan and Brooks-Gunn, 1997; Machin, 1998; McCulloch and Joshi, 2002). Indeed, the effects can be very powerful, as illustrated by American estimates that show that poverty in childhood is associated with an average of two years less schooling and substantially lower earnings as adults (Mayer, 1997; Duncan, *et al.*, 1998). There is also strong evidence that family instability, unemployment, and alcoholism seriously impair children's educational attainment. Additionally, there is some evidence that mothers' employment may be harmful for children's development, but this is a disputed issue (Ermisch and Francesconi, 2002; Duncan and Brooks-Gunn, 1997).

Since many of these family characteristics, like unemployment, are correlated with parental income it is not easy to disentangle the real mechanisms. Financial security within the family no doubt plays a key role for how parents and their children make decisions at the moment of educational transitions. The perceived risks associated with continuing education are likely to be more intense in families that feel financially insecure. But other characteristics are not necessarily correlated with income. Inspired by Bourdieu's (1983) notion of 'cultural capital', there is a growing literature which suggests that social skills, personality traits, and cultural capital may be as important as educational certificates in career progression (Jencks *et al.* 1972; DiMaggio 1982; DiMaggio and Mohr, 1985; de Graaf *et al.*, 1998; for an overview, see also Bowles *et al.*, 2001); and also that the cultural and educational resources of parents are vital for children's cognitive development and school performance (OECD, 2001). Cultural resources may also be decisive in allowing parents to better 'navigate' the educational system in the best interests of their offspring (Erikson and Jonsson, 1996).

That cognitive skills compete with education in dictating life chances is fairly well established. What comes as a surprise is that the two are only weakly correlated—in other words they capture different dimensions of human capital.[13] There is evidence that cognitive abilities, independently of educational attainment, affect life chances. Bowles *et al.*'s (2001: 1154) review of the econometric evidence from twenty-four studies concludes that 'a standard deviation difference in cognitive performance is associated with something less than a ten per cent increase in wages, and is in this respect roughly equivalent to a year of schooling'. Warren *et al.* (2002) show that formal educational qualifications matter in the early career stage (and then decline in importance) while cognitive skills assert a persistent effect throughout the career. Green and Riddell (2000) and Esping-Andersen (2004) find that cognitive abilities account for about a third of the 'returns to education' in earnings equations. There is strong support for the possibility that a good part of the inter-generational class inheritance effects we observe is mediated via parents' impact on children's cognitive development.

If that is so, we obviously need to examine a broader menu of parental characteristics, and we also need to focus more on what happens before children even start school. Some recent work has deepened the family context considerably by including direct information on cultural assets, such as literature, reading, and cultural consumption (de Graaf *et al.* 1998; OECD 2001; Esping-Andersen 2004).

To the extent that cognitive abilities and education measure distinct attributes, and to the extent that the former are importantly determined in preschool ages, we are in a position to account for the 'constant flux' of educational attainment. The selection mechanisms that occur in school systems are, in large part, already prefigured in that cognitively and motivationally strong children will profit far more from any given curriculum and teaching than will their weaker counterparts, regardless of what kind of school system prevails or of how well-financed it is.[14] In other words, if we want to identify the smoking gun behind the constant flux, parental influence on cognitive development may be a good place to start.

In previous work I have estimated, for eight countries, the impact of social origins (using parents' education and socioeconomic status as measures) on their childrens' educational attainment and cognitive performance. In these kinds of estimations it is vital that we control for gender and especially for immigrant status. Girls normally perform better than boys and non-natives are at a disadvantage in terms of administered cognitive tests. A summary of the results is presented in Table 27.1.

There are stark differences across countries in how much social origin influences schooling and cognitive skills. At one end we find (as usual) the UK and the US, with Canada, where the parental impact is unusually strong, especially with regard to children's cognitive performance. At the other end we find the three Scandinavian countries where, uniformly, parents' social status has a far more modest impact on their children's fate. To illustrate, the impact of parents' status is almost twice as strong in the US as it is in Denmark.

The analyses above focused on a single cohort (in their thirties). If we look at educational attainment for distinct cohorts we can identify whether there is any trend towards a weakening of the social inheritance effect. This amounts to a replication—and update—of the Shavit and Blossfeld (1993) studies. The great advantage of the International Adult Literacy Survey (IALS) data is that they include also the youngest generations born in the 1970s. It is this generation that, far more than any preceding one, will have drawn the benefits, if any, from postwar welfare state policies. As shown in Esping-Andersen (2004), most countries conform to the prevailing 'constant-flux' consensus. If we begin with the oldest cohorts, born around 1940, we find a uniform and strong impact of parents' education on children's attainment. Across all countries children of parents with upper secondary level education are roughly two and a half times as likely to also attain the same level as those whose parents did not. As we move to the youngest cohorts, convergence turns to a sharp divergence. In one group of countries—the US, the UK, Germany, and Italy—the parental impact remains unchanged. But in the Nordic countries—and now Denmark is in the vanguard—the parental effect begins to weaken with the

Table 27.1 The impact of social origins on educational attainment and on cognitive performance in eight countries (ages 30–40)

	Coefficients for			
	Child's years of education*		Child's cognitive score	
	β	Standard beta	β	Standard beta
Canada	.080	.423	5.055	.411
US	.206	.424	10.251	.364
UK	.489	.331	11.247	.284
Sweden	.085	.339	6.203	.338
Norway	.105	.328	6.064	.286
Denmark	.277	.259	4.397	.204
Germany	.803	.403	4.051	.105
Netherlands	.319	.377	4.987	.251

Note: All estimates are significant at .001 or better. The cognitive performance variable is the mean individual score on the three literacy items tested in the IALS (document, prose, and quantitative abilities). Note also, that the age bracket for Canada is 25–35. All estimates include controls for gender and immigrant status.

* β is adjusted for the differing variance in fathers' and children's education, i.e. $\beta = \beta[\sigma^2 y \sigma^2 x]$

Source: IALS microdata [second wave].

cohorts born in the 1960s and even more so with those born in the 1970s.

Since social inheritance is especially strong at the top and bottom of the social hierarchy it would be especially illuminating to focus on children of less educated parents, i.e. those with only primary level or less. Indeed, when we look at children from this social background, the uniqueness of the Nordic countries is even more accentuated. In line with our earlier results, the 'constant flux' best describes most countries but, led again by Denmark, the children of less-educated parents in Scandinavia do continue to have a disadvantage but this disadvantage has been sharply reduced for the cohorts born since the 1960s. The odds that UK children of such parents will make it through upper secondary level is 2 : 10 compared to children of parents with secondary education. In Denmark, the odds are 5 : 10.[15]

However, this data does not help us to disentangle the precise mechanisms at work. Do children of higher status parents do better because parents invest more in their education, or is it the result of cultural transmission? The recently released PISA data, examining the cognitive abilities of fifteen to sixteen year olds in a large number of countries, permit a far more detailed seperation of income and culture factors.[16] The study does not include information on parental income, but does include a 'wealth' variable based on a composite of information on the size, standards, and quality of the parental home—arguably a reasonable proxy for income. It also includes an indicator score variable, weighting parents' occupation and income, information on father's and mother's education and employment status, and a range of variables that indicate the family's cultural milieu.

In the above-mentioned study I attempt to estimate the relative importance of culture versus money (Esping-Andersen, 2004). The analyses also address the debate on whether mothers' employment may have adverse consequences for children's cognitive development. The results point systematically to 'culture' as being the smoking gun we are looking for.

It is, first of all, evident in all countries studied that children's cognitive performance is far more powerfully related to the family's cultural capital than to income variables. The cultural capital variable (a composite measure of the quantity of books in the home, of frequency of discussing cultural themes, and of frequenting cultural events) explains roughly twice as much of the variation in cognitive abilities as do the income variables. Interestingly, the correlation between family income and family culture is quite low.

The impact of mothers' employment is, as noted, a controversial issue. In a study using British data, Ermisch and Francesconi (2002) conclude that the effect can be quite damaging. American research comes to more ambiguous findings and suggests, tentatively, that adverse effects—if any—are mainly acute when mothers work full-time and especially when their job is stressful (Duncan and Brooks-Gunn 1996). What emerges from my analyses of the PISA data is that part-time employment is nowhere problematic and in a few countries, basically the Nordic, neither is full-time work. But, and this is worth noting, the impact is opposite for boys and girls. Indeed, for girls the effect is generally positive while for boys it is largely negative. Again, this gender-specific pattern is far less accentuated in Scandinavia than elsewhere.

If we now try to pull the evidence together, two sets of conclusions emerge. One, the transmission mechanisms are fairly similar across all countries. Family income matters but, if anything, it would appear that parental cultural capital is rather more decisive—at least as far as cognitive development and school success are concerned. Still, when we add that cognitive skills explain a substantial proportion of earnings variations, the effect is most likely present throughout the life course. Basically, as Mayer (1997) argues, money alone cannot buy equal opportunities.

All this would invite profound pessimism among reformers bent on creating a world of equal opportunities. While it is easy to forge policies to reform education systems it seems difficult to imagine how government can equalise families' cultural capital, let alone influence parents' cognitive stimulus. The national comparisons, however, suggest that the world is not necessarily preordained to a perpetual constant flux. There are three countries that systematically deviate: Denmark, Norway and Sweden. Inter-generational income mobility is far greater, occupational destinies and educational attainment are substantially less determined by the luck of birth and, most interestingly, cognitive abilities depend less on parental background. To this we might add that inequalities of cognitive abilities are markedly smaller than elsewhere. If we compute a Gini coefficient for cognitive test scores, the Danish coefficient is exactly half the American. The US and UK may not exactly deviate in the other direction, but they do stand out as being quite immobile in terms of life chances.

We are then left with the one overriding puzzle: why is the social inheritance of life chances so much weaker in Scandinavia than elsewhere? And why, starting from basically the same initial level, has it declined so significantly over the past twenty years?

Public Policy and Equality of Opportunity

Since it would be difficult to explain Scandinavia's egalitarianism in terms of public investment in education, an alternative economic explanation might lie in their unusually compressed wage distributions which, de facto, implies that earnings are only weakly linked to human capital or gender. The US has one of the OECD's most unequal wage distributions, and hence one would expect that skill or other worker attributes play a far greater role in dictating individual incomes. No doubt there is some truth to this. Yet it fails to explain the fact that Scandinavia is also more egalitarian in terms of educational attainment, occupational mobility, and cognitive development.

It is very tempting, in fact, to explain it all tautologically: very inegalitarian societies beget very inegalitarian results. But the tautology disappears when we add to this that very inegalitarian societies also beget more ascription and less mobility.[17] This pattern emerges clearly in a comparison of national Gini coefficients and inter-generational income mobility (Table 27.2).

This quite astounding covariation runs counter to the prevailing thesis that income inequality stimulates incentives for mobility. In fact, all the data we have examined suggest that mobility is negatively related to levels of overall inequality. The causal

Table 27.2 Income inequality and social inheritance (countries ranked by Gini)

	Social mobility	Gini coefficient
Denmark	0.81	.22
Sweden	0.85	.23
Germany	0.75	.28
UK	0.71	.31
US	0.71	.34
Italy	0.67	.35

Note: Social mobility refers to the association between parental and child income. A coefficient of 1.00 would denote perfect mobility and the lower the number, the less mobility.

Source: Jorgensen [2001: Table 11.18].

direction is unclear. It may be that pervasive social inheritance predestines a society to be more unequal on all dimensions of distribution. It may also be that causality goes in the opposite direction: if income inequalities are huge the poor will have to travel a greater distance to reach the middle. For policy making it would be futile to speculate on which is the real chicken and egg because if inequality and mobility co-vary, an effective policy intervention in one or the other would have effects on both. The great policy challenge is to identify the crucial point that will untie the Gordian Knot.

One important conclusion is that we must abandon our faith in education policy as the great leveller because the inequalities are to a great extent established prior to school age. Of course, education systems can contribute to strengthening or weakening these and as the OECD's (2001) review of the evidence makes clear, any overall strategy for equal opportunities must also include attributes of the school system—in particular avoiding early tracking, class or ethnic segmentation, favouring comprehensive schools, and promoting bridges between educational branches. In brief, the main egalitarian aim of education policy is probably to see that schools do not simply reproduce or even worsen the inequalities that already have been created.

The second important conclusion is that 'money' may be important but that it is not a sufficient precondition for good life chances. We know that economic hardship in childhood has potentially very negative effects on educational attainment and later life chances. How precisely it works is not fully evident but it is safe to say that the impact is pervasive throughout childhood and probably most acute at moments of transition from compulsory to non-compulsory levels. Income-poor families are less resourceful, less able to plan ahead and 'navigate the school system', and poor parents are more likely to spur their children to abandon school in favour of a job. A policy of guaranteeing against child poverty would no doubt be very effective and, as it turns out, it is financially cheap. If we were to peg the guarantee to fifty per cent of median income, the additional public outlay would not exceed 0.2 per cent of GDP in most countries (Esping-Andersen and Sarasa, 2002).[18]

When we more closely examine why there is so little child poverty in Scandinavia it turns out that public income transfers are far less important than the mere fact that just about all mothers are employed. Child poverty in two income families is everywhere modest and declines precipitously among employed lone mothers, too. Swedish lone mothers boast an employment rate near 80 per cent and a poverty rate of only four per cent.

Encouraging mothers' employment necessitates affordable child care which in Scandinavia is practically universal for the nought to six age bracket. There is no a priori reason for publicly provided child care if our sole aim is to facilitate women's employment. American mothers are also now typically employed and use daycare. But American daycare is almost exclusively privately provided and the quality of care will correlate strongly with parental income (Blau, 2001). American day care is of extremely uneven quality, and children from disadvantaged families are likely to find themselves concentrated at the low end. This contrasts with Scandinavian care which is basically of uniform, high standards, meaning that children from disadvantaged families will benefit disproportionately.

The upshot is that a policy designed for altogether different objectives, namely to reconcile work and motherhood, has the potential of equalising the stimulus structure for pre-school children. Indeed, the uneven distribution of cultural capital among families is greatly neutralised if, as in the Nordic countries, virtually all children from age one to six participate in a child care system that is of homogeneously high quality. As long as cognitive and motivational stimulus is predominantly internalised in the family, as is the case in almost all societies, the effect is to reproduce the cultural differentials of the parental generation. The market model, exemplified by the US, will also reproduce differentials, in this case due to uneven quality in care. The uniqueness of the Scandinavian model, at least in the last two to three decades is that a crucial part of pre-school stimulation is shifted from parents to centres *that do not replicate social class differences*.

Recent evaluation research concludes similarly. As Waldfogel's (2002) review of both American and European research shows, child care programs that are intensive, intervene early, and that promote high standards contribute very effectively to raise the cognitive performance of children from disadvantaged milieux. In turn, this helps children start and proceed on a much more equal footing once they enter formal education. Although we have little longitudinal research, what evidence there is suggests that early quality care continues to exert positive emotional and cognitive results throughout childhood (Waldfogel 2002: 539).

High quality and universal child care is, in tandem with low child poverty, likely to be a key explanatory factor behind Scandinavia's success in reducing social inheritance. It is difficult to prove conclusively but all the data point in this direction. Most importantly, the decline in social inheritance effects on educational attainment coincides almost perfectly with the period (1970s–80 s) in which child care attendance became the norm. The fact that the inheritance effect begins to drop for the cohorts born in the 1960s and then drops even further for those born in the 1970s adds credence to the argument. It was not until the 1980s that Denmark and Sweden arrived at near-universal coverage.

Therefore a promising strategy for equal opportunities will require a broad-based approach that encompasses educational policy, income redistribution and, as its flagship, major investments in pre-school institutions. There exist, however, several important caveats that may raise doubts as to its feasibility and effectiveness.

The exchequer will undoubtedly be the first to protest, arguing with reason that the financial costs of universal, high quality care are prohibitive. The per child cost of the Danish system is roughly 10,000 euros per year. But one thing is the up-front expenditure, another the long-term financial dynamics. If mothers have access to day care their work interruptions will be far shorter and this translates into far superior lifelong earnings (and tax payments). Calculations based on the Danish system indicate that working mothers will actually reimburse the initial cost over their lifetime career. Price-Waterhouse has undertaken a similar study for Britain and arrives at the same conclusion.

A second serious caveat has to do with the potential behavioral consequences of generous income guarantees to child families. A basic income guarantee will almost certainly not affect the labour supply of high income mothers, but it is likely to encourage low educated, low paid mothers to stay at home. If this occurs the upshot may be social polarisation. As I have argued the core problem of social inheritance is concentrated at the top and bottom of the social hierarchy. Scandinavia is successful on the equal opportunity front probably because children of low educated parents come to enjoy middle class cognitive stimulus via day care. This will not come about if there are incentives for low educated mothers to stay home with the children.

And this brings me to the third caveat. A strong argument against the child care formula is that mothers' (and parents') employment intensity may have adverse effects on their children's well being and school performance. Even if mothers' work may be positive because it reduces poverty, this should be weighed against the loss of quality and intensity in the parent–child interaction. As my brief review of the evidence suggested there are no unambiguous answers to this question. Mothers' part-time employment appears generally to be unproblematic. The main problems tend to be associated with long and stressful workdays—and it would seem that it is mainly boys that suffer.

It is also clear that the impact of parental employment varies by the phase of childhood. Negative effects are most visible in the youngest ages, zero to five. In the first years the key issue has mainly to do with the child's emotional security and there is accordingly a clear case to be made in favour of adequate maternity and parental leave time. In any case, parental employment effects will interact strongly with the quality of external care, asserting themselves far more negatively if children are placed in poor quality care. And there is also evidence that the gender of the parent matters little. What matters is that one of the parents is present. In other words, here is additional ammunition in favour of parental leave schemes and flexible work schedules that encourage take-up among both fathers and mothers.

In any case, the issue is not whether we should encourage a return to traditional familialism because women's lifelong paid employment is becoming the norm everywhere. This we must take for granted and, as such, we inevitably must address the challenge of making motherhood and careers compatible. The day care formula, if pursued along the Scandinavian line of universal coverage and high standards, will both enhance welfare and maybe also efficiency on two fronts simultaneously. It will help women pursue careers just when our ageing society needs their employment. It will equalise the life chances of children while benefiting our economy by producing a more homogeneously productive and capable future workforce.

NOTES

1. But this distinction is far from perfect. Sociologists such as Robert Hauser and Christopher Jencks have studied earnings determination intensively; economists, such as Freeman, and Bowles and Gintis have studied educational attainment.
2. For general overviews, see Featherman and Hauser (1976), Erikson and Goldthorpe (1992), Hauser and Warren (1997) and Sorensen (2001).
3. A subsequent revision of the thesis argued that rising mobility would mainly occur in the initial stages of industrialisation, after which mobility flows would stabilise (Featherman, Jones, and Hauser, 1975). For an overview, see Grusky and Hauser (1984).
4. In practice the modernisation hypothesis that guided sociological mobility research has a close kinship to the thesis in economics that earnings begin to regress to the mean as countries become rich (Solon, 1999: 1779).
5. It is important to note here that we are referring to net mobility rates, i.e. net of changes in the marginals of parent–child mobility matrices.
6. Economists like Borjas (1995) and Corcoran *et al.* (1992) have begun to move in similar directions. In this chapter I will not address the community effects, mainly because they are empirically less salient than the family effects.
7. Their study did not include any of the other Scandinavian countries.
8. The main results from OECD's (2001) PISA study corroborate this. It shows that variations in youth (aged about fifteen) educational and cognitive performance are predominantly related to family-of-origin variables. National differences in school systems, or even intra-national variations in the quality of teachers and schools, make little difference.
9. Erikson and Jonsson (1996) suggest the possibility that the comprehensive Swedish system may have helped create more educational equality. Yet they remain quite sceptical as to whether this is what accounts for the declining social inheritance effects found for Sweden. In fact, also Denmark and Norway (previously unstudied) exhibit a similar (and

very strong) declining inheritance effect, and their education systems are not of the comprehensive type. Echoing the growing consensus in the literature, we must probably look elsewhere for explanations.

10. Considering that early transitions, such as between elementary and lower secondary education, are near-universal, there is a good case to be made for a quadratic specification if years of education is used.
11. The decisiveness of early childhood is also highlighted in Jencks and Phillips' (1998) analysis of the black–white score gap.
12. Solon *et al.*'s (2000) attempt to distinguish the impact of family over neighbourhood effects show clearly that the latter are, by far, the most important (by 5 : 1).
13. Using IALS data, the simple bi-variate correlation hovers between 0.4 and 0.5, depending on country.
14. This, in fact, is also the main conclusion from OECD's (2001) PISA study, which includes detailed information on children's cognitive performance, knowledge, and social background as well as on the schools and on neighbourhood effects.
15. In this case, the UK performs rather better than the US and Germany (where the odds are only 1 : 10).
16. For a description of the PISA study, see OECD (2001).
17. Corak (2001) has also argued that inter-generational correlations will be higher in more unequal societies, and his study also stresses the centrality of non-monetary factors, such as parents' cultural stimulation.
18. Our calculations suggest an additional expenditure of 0.22 per cent of GDP for the UK.

Social Class and Cognitive Development in Childhood in the UK

Leon Feinstein

This chapter is concerned with equality of opportunity. It reproduces earlier research (Feinstein 2003) that is concerned with the strong and enduring effect of parental background on children's cognitive development in the UK. The key point is not that there are social class effects on life chances, which is well known (see, for example, Acheson 1998; Black et al. 1980; Chadwick 1842; Haveman and Wolfe 1995; Jencks 1972); the point is about the timing of those effects within the lifecourse. The analysis is epidemiological in its concern to describe the patterns of longitudinal change in the achievement scores in school tests of children in different social class groups as those children mature. The analysis brings out very clearly the way social class effects are not once and for all stratification impacts but are incremental in impact, compounded through childhood.

It is not the case that social class effects are set in stone at an early age. There is great discontinuity in academic or cognitive test scores as children move up and down the distribution of scores but there are also continuities, and there are strong and deepening relationships between social class and test scores such that as children get older it gets harder and harder for low social class children to draw on their own capabilities and resilience (Rutter 1990; Sameroff et al. 1998) to escape the effects of their social contexts on their school achievements, although a small proportion do.

In this chapter, I first present the clear, simple, stylized fact from the earlier research and then set out a number of caveats and further reflections, putting the results within the context of theoretical and conceptual debates about the importance and meaning of social class and discussing the implications for policy.

Method and Data Resources

The data for the analysis come from the British Cohort Study (BCS). The sample frame for this dataset was all the children born in Great Britain in the week of 5–11 April 1970. To date, five follow-up surveys have been completed at ages 5, 10, 16, 26, and, most recently, at age 30. A further study is currently in the field (2004/5). The achieved sample at birth was 17,196, approximately 97 per cent of the target birth population. Attrition has reduced the sample to 11, 200 at the age 30 survey. The data are available on-line to all approved users through the ESRC Data Archive.

Particularly relevant constructs for this study include measures of the cognitive and personal development of cohort members at ages 22 and

Adapted from Leon Feinstein, 'Inequality in the early cognitive development of British children', *Economica* 70 (2003), 73–97, by permission of Blackwell Publishing.

42 months for a random 10 per cent sub-sample of the cohort and a further 10 per cent at risk of fetal malnutrition. At 22 months the children were asked by the health visitors administering the survey to complete a range of different tasks, for example: pointing to their eyes to illustrate understanding of language; putting on their shoes, indicative of personal development; stacking cubes and drawing lines as tests of locomotor ability. These tests, together with those at 42 months, were intended to indicate the general development of children based on the tests used for screening in child health clinics (Chamberlain and Davey 1976.) A pilot study found high correlation between the BCS tests and similar, standard tests of development such as the Bayley Scale of Infant Behaviour or the Newcastle Survey (Neligan and Prudham 1969). At 42 months counting and speaking could be tested, and further copying tests were administered such as drawing simple geometrical shapes. At age 5 copying was again assessed, together with tests of basic vocabulary. Harris (1963) and Koppitz (1968) show these scores to have good properties of discrimination and reliability. Standard age 10 scores for maths and reading are also available. All these scores are appropriate for the age of the children being tested.

Although there were over 17,000 children in the full cohort, the research presented here only makes use of information about 2,457 children in the preschool sub-sample. This includes test scores at four ages (22, 42, 60, and 120 months old) for 1,292 of these children, who form the sample frame used. Analysis suggests that this is a reasonably representative sample of the population. The random element in the sub-sample can be used to test whether the 10 per cent of cases at risk of fetal malnutrition lead to biases in the results and this has been shown not to be the case (Feinstein 2003).

There is one major issue concerning the preschool sub-sample that cannot be overcome. It only included children from two-parent families, for reasons pertinent at the time of data collection. This is a potentially serious limit to the representativeness of these results, particularly for those concerned with family breakdown. Nonetheless, these data still shed light on questions of the importance and explanation of early ability differences between children of different backgrounds.

Principal components analysis was used to combine scores and create a single index of development at each age, the set of developmental indicators being each child's position in the distribution at each age. Thus, what is being compared at each age is not the absolute score in maths say, but each child's position relative to other children in the distribution of scores of measures appropriate for that age. As some groups of children rise in the distribution others must necessarily go down.

It is important also to consider here what is meant by social class. Three groups were constructed based on the Registrar General's sixfold, 1966 Classification of Occupations. I use the term socio-economic status (SES) here to refer to the position of the family in this occupational classification. High SES refers to children where the father is in a professional or managerial job and the mother is similar or out of the labour force. Low SES refers to children where the father is in an unskilled or semi-skilled manual job or unemployed and the mother is similar or out of the labour force. Medium SES is defined here as all other combinations. For this study I equate SES with social class though in doing so I recognize that I ignore important sociological issues. I consider SES, however, as a powerful indicator of many aspects of economic, cultural, human, and social capital and intend it only as a proxy for such assets.

Results

There are three points to emphasize. First, the 22-month scores matter in the particular sense that by themselves they predict final educational attainments at school exit. It is important to emphasize that this is a matter of prediction and not determination. There is considerable discontinuity over time so that, for example, a child in the bottom quartile at 22 months in these data still has a 15 per cent chance of being in the top quartile at age 10. However, 15 per cent of children in the bottom quartile had achieved no general academic qualifications by age 26 compared to only 8 per cent of those in the top quartile (the difference being statistically significant at $p<0.01$). Thus age 22-month scores are not by any means decisive but they matter.

Secondly, there is already a social class differential at 22 months. The gap between the top and bottom SES groups at 22 months is already 13 percentage points (13 places in the distribution that ranges from 0 to 100.) This is statistically significant as well as substantial in magnitude. The difference between top and middle groups at 8 percentage points is also significant and substantial. Moreover, as we have already seen, this class gap matters because early scores matter. This does not mean that social class determines early ability. There are low SES children who do well early on and high SES children who attain low scores. What is indicated is a correlation such that on average a high SES child will out-score a low SES child.

The third point is about bringing the first two together, as in Figure 28.1. The graph presents the average scores at the four points in time of four particular groups of children; two groups from high social class backgrounds and two groups from low social class backgrounds (medium SES children are omitted.) For each type of background we consider children who scored in the top or bottom quartiles in the index of cognitive development at 22 months, giving rise to the four groups.

What is observed at Figure 28.1 is the change over time of the relative positions in the distribution of cognitive skills of four groups of children, represented by the four lines in the graph. Considering the points on the vertical axis the highest two points indicate the high initial scores of the two groups of children who were scoring well at 22 months, the groups distinguished according to the occupation of parents. Those in the high SES group continue to score well on average, still having an average position in the distribution of just under the 70th percentile at age 10. The decline of the low SES group is apparent in the graph as the downward sloping line. Their average position in the distribution at age 10 is the 40th percentile, down 46 points from the 86th percentile at 22 months.

The two lowest points on the vertical axis represent the two groups scoring in the bottom 25 per cent at 22 months. Again, the low SES group is distinguished from the high SES group. We see that the low SES group continued to score poorly with an average rank position at the 27th percentile at age 10, compared to the 58th percentile for the high SES children in the same bottom quartile at 22 months.

Thus, there is discontinuity after 22 months but it is heavily socially determined. The advantageous upward mobility is overwhelmingly for children from advantaged backgrounds, the downward mobility for children from disadvantaged backgrounds (the low SES children). The high early achievers from disadvantaged backgrounds (and as already emphasized there are such children) are overtaken between ages 5 and 10 years by poor early achievers from advantaged backgrounds. This is not because the early scores are just random noise. As we have seen they predict adult-level outcomes and, moreover, whatever children's social class their age 10

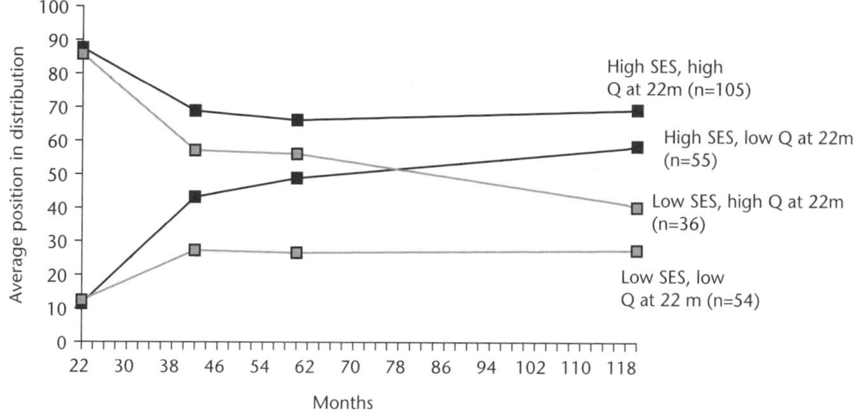

Fig. 28.1 Average rank of test scores at 22, 42, 60 and 120 months by SES of parents and early rank position

Source: Feinstein (2003: 73–98).

scores are predicted to be substantively higher if they did well early on. However, equality of opportunity is constantly and heavily influenced by the background of parents. This is not a one-off experience but one repeated over time in a compounding way.

Caveats and Contextual Factors

1. *These are individual level data and the analysis is very much at the individual level.* The social class attainment gap is a social-level construct but there is no analysis here of social-level phenomena. In a text on education and globalization this is clearly an important issue. By focusing on the attainment of individual children does the analysis risk emphasizing individual responsibility at the expense of collective, social, or structural forces that may in fact be more important and that the focus on the individual obscures? This is a risk that must be taken seriously. Yet the analysis does not in itself indicate anything at all about cause so there is no actual allocation here of responsibility for the pattern of social class inequality. The underlying causes of the pattern of child development observed may include structural and social factors such as labour markets, schooling systems, assessment biases, educational discrimination, and housing effects. What the analysis highlights is that the assessed cognitive development of the child is not independent of the important factors that influence assessed attainment *at any point in childhood*, even in the early verbal stages.

This can be considered distinctly from the question of the benefit that follows from cognitive advantage. A great deal of economic literature on the importance of human capital (e.g. Becker 1981; Card 1999) has emphasized the importance of cognitive capabilities of children for their ultimate labour market success but this is not despite the importance of social context but in a sense because of it. In the standard economic model of wage determination, human capital earns a premium because of the increase in firm productivity and profits that result from it. Thus the impact of human capital on the level of social equality depends on the economic and sociological system by which resources are allocated between firms and households.

One of the striking features of globalization in recent years is how the process of skill-biased technological change has increased to diminish employment opportunities and earnings for those with low literacy and numeracy (Bynner and Parsons 1997; Berman and Machin 2000; Nickell and Bell 1996) even beyond the effects of deindustrialization and the erosion of manufacturing industry that was occurring even in the inter-war period leading up to and through the Great Depression (Rowthorne and Wells 1987; Singh and Weisse 2001). Thus, even though there has been a major expansion of higher education in the UK since the mid-1980s such that the supply of skilled labour has increased in the period since then, the income gain that follows such education has continued to rise. The implication is that the demand for labour with HE skills has outreached the expansion in supply even though the expansion might have been associated with a decrease in the signalling advantage of a degree and with a potential reduction in the unobserved skill of those with HE qualifications.

Globalization as an economic phenomenon is associated in economic terms with increases in international competition in trade and therefore with a focus on comparative advantage as a source of profit and hence employment opportunities for industries open to external forces. The low relative capital/labour cost ratio of richer nations and their greater educational investments go hand in hand with a comparative advantage in production requiring high levels of skills. This has increased the labour market premium on those skills and marginalized those without human capital. The response to this could be to restrict trade or to enhance human capital. The policy of the UK in line with that of all OECD nations has been to attempt to maximize human capital investment. Yet what Figure 28.1 highlights is that a focus on human capital as an engine of growth at the national level risks: (1) marginalizing those whose family circumstances during childhood and/or personal attributes are not auspicious for their educational success, and (2), failure or at best low efficiency if the current allocation of resources of human and financial capital is allowed to limit the potential for human capital formation of the next generation.

Theory that emphasizes the importance of individual capabilities for individual outcomes need not reify those capabilities. What this analysis suggests (but does not prove) is that these capabilities are malleable and so policy that waits until children reach adulthood before it attempts to redress social class inequalities will be dealing with a bolted horse.

2. *Tests of school attainment are taken as the outcome variable: (a) The validity of measurement.* Some may object to the notion of ability as a measurable construct at all given its perceived association with the politics of the Right and the behavioural genetic literature on intelligence (Gillborn and Youdell 2000). There is a concern that the term 'ability' is a cover for uni-dimensional notions of intelligence (Spearman 1904) that are seen by some as biological in origin (Jensen 1998) and so both fixed and linked to simple and politically regressive constructions of ethnicity and race.

The use in Figure 28.1 of a single index at each age to describe age-standardized ability has the advantage of simplicity of presentation. How ever, for many purposes it is an oversimplification. Modern theories of intelligence, such as the multiple intelligences of Gardner (1983) or the triarchic model of Sternberg (1985) are more concerned with understanding the different aspects of intelligence, such as practical, analytical, and creative intelligences, and considering how these different aspects interact. These elements of cognition also interact with others such as attention and self-regulation (Alexander et al. 1993; Hinshaw 1992) in the psychology of school achievement. The measures used in this study are a very raw slice at each point in time of the broader development of the sample children.

However, the Figure makes apparent that relative ability is not fixed. The claim that the use of measurement is inherently linked to the thesis of non-malleability is specious. Measurement enables the testing of hypotheses and so supports the evolution of thinking.

2. *Tests of school attainment are taken as the outcome variable: (b) Reliability and bias in measurement.* The term 'bias' is used here in its technical, statistical sense, i.e. as the systematic deviation of a manifest statistic (such as a mean score) from the true, population score, although there are of course other meaningful definitions in social research (Hammersley and Gomm 1997). There may be important social class differences in the capability of these measures to identify the 'true' scores at each age. It is plausible that the earlier measures in Figure 28.1 are less biased by social class than the later measures. Thus, one might view age 10 maths tests as suffering more heavily than the earlier measures such as cube-stacking at 22 months from the effects of social class biases in children's engagement in the testing process, biases in teaching and class biases in the socialized nature of the knowledge content. According to this interpretation the trends in the Figure are due to changes in bias, not changes in ability.

However, the key trends in the Figure are already apparent in the measures at 42 months and age 5. There are large social class disparities in the age 5 copying score, a particularly predictive measure of subsequent school success (Feinstein and Duckworth 2005). Children were asked to copy eight basic designs and the test is one of pattern recognition and locomotor skill, very little to do with use of language and language codes which are more easily seen as socially contextual and biased.

According to the interpretation of the Figure by which the trend is nothing to do with real ability but is simply reflecting changes in the degree of social class bias, it is nonetheless important that children from the low SES group who at 22 months were scoring highly on the cube-stacking and cognitive/locomotor tests were less likely to score highly on similar tests at age 5 than high SES children with similarly high 22 month scores. This may not reflect any change in actual ability but simply a socially structured deterioration in performance on tests. However, it is clearly the case that observations of success in such tests are very strong indicators of subsequent life chances across a very wide range of outcomes and so it is important to consider the question of the allocation of success in these measures. The benefits of school success may be due to signalling effects in the labour market and not due to real differences in ability or skill and it would still be the case that social class bias in measurement would lead to effects on life chances. That is one explanation of Figure 28.1 but does not diminish its importance as an indication of the extent to which unspecified processes related to social class lead to social class disparity in school success.

To conclude, although the changing bias interpretation may have some slight explanatory power, I do not find this a convincing explanation of the Figure. The scores of children in these later tests are not only explained by social class but also by other factors. Amongst working-class children, those from smaller families or with higher parental aspirations or higher income will on average score more highly than others on the age 10 and earlier tests. It is harder to explain these systematic variations by social class bias in testing, more likely that they indicate a valid and reliable measure of cognitive functioning.

3. *Is this just random measurement error or regression forwards the mean?* First, it is worth re-emphasizing the correlation of scores at 22 months with final educational achievement at school exit as this demonstrates considerable convergent validity in the scores. The scores measure quite well what they are supposed to measure. It is conceptually feasible that the shape of the graph is caused by systematic or non-random measurement error such that low SES children who scored well early on were overrated by the score, and high SES children who scored badly were underrated. This would be a sensible hypothesis if one believed that the early gap is actually far greater than that observed in these data and that it is unlikely that low SES children could exhibit early signs of intelligence, presumably because the 'sorting mechanism' by which parents are allocated to occupations was very strongly linked to their uni-dimensional genetically transmitted capabilities. For those tending to that view it is worth pointing out that scores at 22 months predict subsequent outcomes even within social class groups. So, there is validity in the age 22 month and subsequent scores for both high and low SES children and no evidential basis for the assumption of systematic measurement error.

There is likely to be some degree of regression towards the mean in the results but the key issue there is the substantially lower long-term mean of low SES children compared to that for high SES children so that the middle two lines cross. Thus, it is still the case under this interpretation that social class origin overrides the protective power of high early test scores. This effect could be genetic or environmental in origin or more realistically genetic and environmental, involving an interaction between genes and environment, with the environmental elements the only candidates for policy response.

4. *The definition of social class and the problem of causality (again).* The measure of social class used here is based on the RGO categorization of the occupation of parents in the period before the birth of the child. The results are purely descriptive and don't provide evidence on the size of social class 'effects' in any causal sense since such a claim would depend on a conceptualization in which social class was randomly allocated, in other words there was no relationship at all between genetic inheritance and occupation. That would be a very strong claim to make.

The results are not open to a simple causal interpretation because social class is not a straightforward 'treatment' in the manner of an experimental intervention. Social class is correlated with every aspect of family background from income to parenting (Bornstein and Bradley 2003; Hobcraft 2002) making it hard to distinguish its effects from that of its observed and unobserved correlates, depending on the definition used. I return to this issue in the conclusions in which I describe a model from developmental psychology which is useful in clarifying the possible causal pathways and resulting policy implications.

Holding the issue of causality aside, the results are informative in epidemiological terms, describing the size of the raw, relative gap between children in different social class groups at different points in time and clarifying the probabilistic implications of success/failure at one age for success/failure at subsequent ages.

5. *It is not just the early years that matter.* There are good empirical and theoretical grounds for the view that the early years are particularly vital as a period for social intervention, support, and policy if the social class attainment gap is to be reduced (Cunha, et al. 2005). There are important complementarities between early and subsequent attainment such that if the appropriate support is not

available early on it will become progressively more difficult to remedy disparities. Nonetheless striking social class effects continue to impact on children who are achieving well even at age 14. This is shown in Table 28.1 taken from Feinstein (2004) but originally from the Department for Education and Skills (DfES 2003) drawing on the National Pupil Database.

Table 28.1 reports the probability for children with and without free school meals status of achieving the target attainment level at each key stage in 2000, given that they achieved the previous key stage target. Family background continues to be related to school progress and the developmental pathways of pupils long after entry to school, in fact exerting an influence at each stage of pupil's educational careers in each subject at every key stage, even in these more recent data. Thus, the lower educational performance of low-income pupils is not experienced only before entry to school but also in terms of transitions and progress throughout school. The effect is repeated and compounding and to be offset will require substantive intervention throughout schooling.

6. *It is not just standard cognitive skills that matter for adult life chances.* If one is to make predictions of which children will suffer as adults from low income or become parents in workless households then reading and maths scores will matter but so will psychosocial development and behaviour (Cooper and Farran 1988; McClelland and Morrison 2003; Caspi et al. 1998; Feinstein and Bynner 2004). These latter factors are important as indicators of psychological well-being but also as an influence on choices made and on relationships with peers and teachers at school, with colleagues and employers in employment, or with peers and families at home and in neighbourhoods, influencing pathways through adolescence and emerging adulthood (Arnette 2004).

7. *These results are only of historical interest as the data are from the 1970s.* It is important to note this criticism of the application of these findings to more recent policy debates. However, one might wonder what historical shifts before 1997 might have led to a different pattern in more recent data. There is certainly no evidence to suggest that inequality fell substantially over this period nor much policy change to suggest that social class or family background will have become less important since the 1970s.

A more interesting question concerns the issue of what will have happened to this pattern of social class disparities since 1997, as there has been a considerable shift of policy since that date with, in particular, a great increase in recent years in resources for early years' programmes. This began with the targeting of resources through the Sure Start programme on the most deprived areas of the country. Alongside the wide-ranging parenting and child support services provided through Sure Start there has been a major increase in national resources for education and health and ongoing reorganization of the provision of services for children. Key

Table 28.1 Probability of successful progression through school

Progression	Subject	Time period	Percent of those who achieved earlier target who achieve next target		
			All	Free school meals	Not free school meals
Key stage 1 to Key stage 2	English	1998–2002	68	59	70
Key stage 1 to Key stage 2	Mathematics	1998–2002	65	58	66
Key stage 2 to Key stage 3	English	1999–2002	78	66	80
Key stage 2 to Key stage 3	Mathematics	1999–2002	83	73	85
Key stage 3 to Key stage 4	5 A*–C GCSEs	2000–2002	51	41	52

Note: Table 28.1 reports the probabilities of achieving the target level at each Key stage given prior success, 2002.

Source: National Pupil Database.

recent features of this have included: (1) the integration of education and social work services set out in the UK's Every Child Matters Green Paper (HM Government 2003), (2) reform of the regulations, standards, and training for those working with children, set out in the Children's Workforce Strategy (HM Government 2004), (3) a 5 Year Plan for the provision of education (Department for Education and Skills 2004), (4) a Children's Act (2004) leading to the creation of a Children's Commissioner and greater integration of services, (5) a 10-year strategy for childcare (HM Treasury 2004) that sets out the long-term goal of universalizing the benefits of the Sure Start programme with nationally rolled out Children's Centres, with the aim of providing by 2010 20 hours a week of free high-quality care for 38 weeks for all 3- and 4-year-olds and an out of school childcare place for all children aged 3–14 between the hours of 8 a.m. to 6 p.m. each weekday, and, (6) the introduction and expansion of the working families tax credit (Hills 2004) that provided increased subsidization of families on low income where children are present, and has been responsible for a substantial reduction in the incidence of absolute child poverty (Paxton and Dixon 2004). In relation to this last point although the decline in childhood poverty is very welcome, it should be emphasized that the UK (1) still has a poor record compared with other European nations, (2) has experienced slightly *increasing* levels of relative income inequality since 1997, (3) has increasing levels of wealth inequality that may be greater than income inequality, and, (4) has considerable levels of poverty amongst pensioners and those in work without children.

Each of these policy elements is born of the recognition that the welfare state has failed to meet the needs of modern parents and children and in failing to invest sufficiently early in the lives of children is leaving it too late to create even the possibility of equality of opportunity. It is still the case that the UK spends three times as much on each student in Higher Education as it does on each child under the age of 5 years (Alekeson 2005). The fact that students from lower social class groups represent a lower proportion of total entrants to full-time undergraduate study than they do of the UK population as a whole (28% versus 39%, Connor and Dewson 2001), creates a very large subsidization of the education of middle-class children. In particular institutions and subjects, the proportion of HE students from lower social class groups can be as low as 10 per cent. Thus, it is not surprising that the most rigorous evaluation of the changing pattern of transmission of inequality from one generation to the next in the UK (Blanden et al. 2004) finds that the degree of social mobility fell between the cohort born in 1958 and that in 1970 and that the major reason for this was that middle-class children benefited most from the expansion of participation in HE between the cohorts.

Another crucial piece of evidence here is that once school attainment at age 16 is accounted for there is no or little effect of social class on participation in school beyond age 18 (Galindo-Rueda et al. 2004). In other words, the damage to equality of opportunity is done before age 16. This does not prove that reforms to funding to HE don't matter because if students have already internalized credit constraints before age of 16 this will affect their engagement in learning long before they have the explicit choice of staying on in school or not. However, it does suggest that a focus on inequality of attainment before age 16 must be a vital element in a progressive strategy to offset inequality in HE participation as in other aspects of education and in other domains of adult life.

However, as to whether these policies will have shifted the pattern observed in Figure 28.1 for more recent cohorts of children is an empirical question that will be addressed when the children surveyed in the Millennium Cohort Study (MCS) are followed through their childhoods. The age 7 data is forecast to be available for analysis in 2008. It is to the Government's credit that it has supported this investment in data so that its record can be assessed. The reason why it has not possible to test the change in relationship between social class and cognitive development since the 1970s is that the planned 1982 and 1994 cohort studies were not funded by the governments of the day.

Policy Discussion

This chapter makes what is intended as a policy-relevant point that even if one accepts the noble version of meritocracy according to which individual 'merit' is of wider value to society and should earn a return in the labour market, merit doesn't fall from the sky or follow one-to-one from genes, unrelated to personal circumstances. Hence there would be an intergenerational transmission of disadvantage even in a meritocratic society in which the rewards earned by adults matched, in some sense, their talents. In the simple version of meritocracy, merit would be genetic and so to be meritocratic the society would simply have to ensure that the most talented rose to the top. In reality, however, although there may be important genetic elements, merit is sufficiently influenced by the actions of families, schools, and the wider culture that advantage reproduces itself through its effects on merit as well as through structural constraints to social mobility. That is why equality of opportunity is a hard target and should be recognized as such. Imaginative and subtle interventions are required if we are to enhance the capacity of families and communities to nurture their talents and capabilities in the face of the wide-ranging and compounding effects of economic, social, educational, and psychological risk factors that appear strongly to benefit middle-class children over working-class children in the education system.

This chapter does not offer simple prescriptions for how to respond to the cognitive disparities in Figure 28.1 because of the complex and interactive sources of the pattern observed. Social class effects on childhood cognitive development are large because of the great range of protective resources that accompany high SES status in these data, features that have all been shown to be associated with positive outcomes for children and young people such as income (Gregg et al. 1999), low stress (Yeung et al. 2002), high parental interest in education (Feinstein and Symons 1999), motivated and able peers (Robertson and Symons 2003), and beneficial school (Rutter et al. 1979) and out of school contexts (Eccles and Gootman 2002).

Policy is difficult because all of these features interact. Box 1 describes a framework for classifying the salient features of the family environment as they impact on children's cognitive development. Here the focus is on the family context but other contexts are also important in childhood, namely, preschool settings, schools, peer-groups, and neighbourhoods. Similar models have been developed for these other contexts and for the interactions between contexts, though there is not space to discuss them here.

The framework is based on a distinction between proximal and distal processes, a distinction that has its origins in developmental psychology, more specifically in ecological models of development (e.g. Bronfenbrenner 1979, 1986; Bronfenbrenner and Crouter 1983). Income, for example, is a distal factor if one hypothesizes that there are important mediating factors that explain the raw, distal correlation between family income and child attainment. These mediating factors can be thought of as pathways, interceding reasons why the distal factor exerts an influence on the outcome. Proximal factors are those mediating elements. These are factors closer to the lived experience of the child that impact directly on attainment, factors in the example such as the instruction provided by a teacher, safe and healthy housing conditions, parental emphasis on the importance of learning, and so on. What is proximal and what is distal is entirely contextual.

Characteristics within the family are more closely related to the environmental factors that impact on

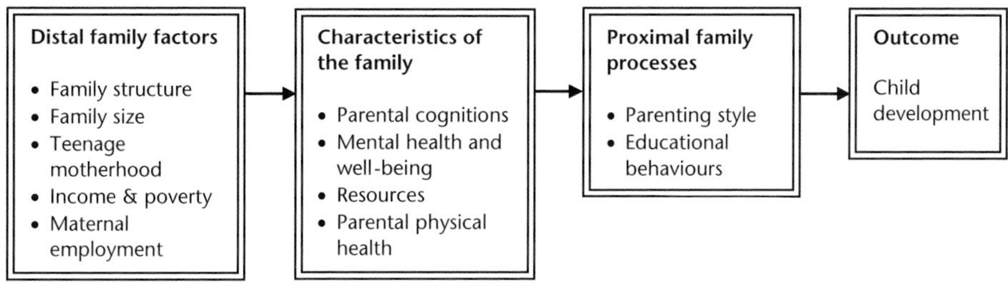

Fig. 28.2 Conceptual model for the related influences on child development

children. Here important factors include the availability of cognitively enriching and stimulating materials and activities, parental attitudes, network supports, and the physical infrastructure of the home. The final category of environmental measure is family process. The term process refers to the actual interactions experienced by the child. Process is the most proximal element in the model as it refers to the day-to-day life of the child. Examples of family process variables include aspects of parent–child relationships such as warmth and affection, the use of discipline, control, and punishment, as well as the educational content of language use in the home environment.

A number of caveats must be recorded. First, it is not implied that a specific factor (distal or proximal) causes a given child outcome through a unique one-way causal pathway that would operate for all parent child dyads with those specific aspects of an environment. Rather, there is a complex process of interaction between children and contexts. Secondly, the attention to proximal factors as the most central elements of the framework does not relegate distal factors or indicate a lower concern for their importance. Some aspects of the social class attainment gap may be explained by the proximal factors and characteristics of the family but that does not mean that the class effect is not real. Rather, this framework helps in understanding the elements of the class effect and the interactions between them. For example, Yeung et al. (2002) are concerned with the effects of stress and low income on child attainment but the model applied is one in which the effects of low income are strongly mediated by stress. Thus stress is the more proximal feature for the child but that does not imply that policy intervention should be targeted at stress reduction rather than income amelioration.

Thirdly, the framework in the form presented is a simple, static model, not referring explicitly to the important reciprocal feedback effects from child to family. The model is also uni-dimensional in its specification of the outcome but in theory and practice it makes a tremendous difference whether one is considering educational achievement, IQ, or pro-social behaviour as the developmental outcome of interest, to name but three. For each of these outcomes the nature of the relationships between the factors in the model will be different. Moreover, the outcomes themselves will interact in the real, transactional, dynamic process of development. It should also be emphasized that the nature of the relationships in the model will be heavily moderated by structural factors such as ethnicity, gender, and historical context. What is specified is a set of relationships not a fixed set of parameters indicating universal effect sizes.

The model is described briefly here because it is helpful as theoretical background for thinking about policy interventions. Programmes that target single features of the model without consideration of the interaction between elements are unlikely to lead to sustained effects because of the importance of the contextual effects of the other factors. For example, parenting programmes that focus on the proximal features of the model may have temporary effects and may be advantageous and worthwhile but if they aren't integrated with interventions to ease the contextual determinants of some parenting problems then these benefits are unlikely to endure. The nature of the benefits will also be moderated by the effects of structure and context.

Other models are available for those who wish to consider the problem of the causes of social class disparities in attainment in the tests used in Figure 28.1. Terms such as habitus, cultural capital, socialized intelligence, and family resources may be more familiar to many readers of this chapter. Nevertheless I describe the ecological model briefly here because I find it useful and intriguing as a theoretical framework that supports reflection, empirical investigation, and analysis.

There is not space here to consider the implications of this model in detail or to address the many cautionary notes and caveats that will occur to readers. As a final conclusion, however, I would like to remind readers that the key fact of the Every Child Matters legislation referred to above and made law in the UK in 2004 is that the needs and interests of children should be the central concern of practitioners and policymakers working in the area of childhood, particularly in education and children's social services. The needs of each child are different, though there may be common patterns. One of the main policy implications of the complexity of this model are that interventions need to be very well targeted to the specific needs and contexts of the child and family. This calls for a considerable degree of personalization of policy as well as integration of services. There is no magic bullet in this model or universal factor that should be the single focus of public-sector investment. What is implied by the ecological model is the provision of structures and processes that are appropriate to the developmental needs of children. What the high quartile low SES children in Figure 28.1 require may be different to what the low quartile children require and the needs of each may differ from those of the children in each high SES group. There will also be individual heterogeneity within these groups. This makes the public-sector service providers who work with children and families and know them best key agents in the delivery of policy. How well the UK Government is able to fund, train, and work with the children's workforce, sponsoring and enhancing genuinely cross-cutting implementation will be a major factor in determining their success in offsetting the profound structural and systemic conditions that lead to the pattern observed in Figure 28.1.

NOTE

I owe a debt of gratitude to many people for their help in the development and communication of the ideas contained in this paper. In particular I would like to thank James Symons, Marco Manacorda, and Peter Holmes for their comments and support on the original Economica paper; Alice Sullivan and Peter Stevens for their guidance on relevant sociology literature; Jacquelynne Eccles and Pam Davis-Keen for their help with the psychology literature; and Neville Butler and John Bynner for their vision and steadfastness in creating this fantastic data in the first place, without which this chapter would not exist. I would also like to thank Kirsti Norman for her excellent administrative assistance.

Signals of Success: Decoding the Sociological Meaning of Associations between Childhood Abilities and Adult Educational Achievement

Roy Nash and Richard K. Harker

Introduction

What are we to make of the fact that the performance of children on everyday tasks of verbal and non-verbal behaviour at 22 months of age is associated with their educational qualifications at age 26? The public attention given to the rediscovery of the significance of 'psychological capital' by an economist is worth serious reflection. Although the detection of this *signal* across the span of two decades, as Feinstein (2003) acknowledges, is unlikely to surprise early childhood specialists, the sociology of education has a deep-seated reluctance to accept theories of social disparity in education that afford a central place to early-developed individual differences in cognitive ability. The theory of general intelligence, which offers a notorious explanation of this kind, has been subjected to relentless critique by sociologists of education. Most of the now classical texts in our discipline (Boudon 1973; Bourdieu and Passeron 1990; Bowles and Gintis 1976; Willis 1977; and Halsey, Heath, and Ridge 1980), have endeavoured to show, by a variety of approaches, that differences in measured intelligence are a minor cause of inequality of educational opportunity. The fact that class differences in cognitive abilities can be detected before children are 2 years old and shown to be related to class variance in adult educational achievement is, therefore, one that presents a challenge to an influential orthodoxy in the sociology of education. Many sociologists, engaged tooth and nail in the struggle against IQ theory, have endorsed an explanation of class differences in access to education as an effect of the discursive formations that constitute the educational system.

In this intellectual doctrine, any explanatory account of social disparities in education that refers to family resources and practices, particularly as these influence the development of cognitive and non-cognitive dispositions associated with educational attainment, is dismissed as a 'deficit theory' that blames the victims of class and cultural oppression for their conditions of life and modes of response to it. Ball (1990: 4), for example, adopts a characteristically distanced tone to the sociological theories of only a generation ago, which he sees as being organized around and reinforcing the problem of 'working-class underachievement', and thus constructing 'a sophisticated and powerful social pathology of working-class family life as deficient and culturally deprived—abnormal.' Ball's contemporary account describes how, '[i]n the processes of schooling the student is compiled and constructed both in the passive process of objectification, and in an active, self-forming subjectification, the latter involving processes of self-understanding mediated by ... the teacher', in such a way that difference is understood as the product of discourse. The 'techniques and forms of organization' of the school lead to the 'creation of separate and different curricula, pedagogies, forms of teacher–student relationships', so that 'identities and subjectivities are formed, learned and carried'. Social inequality in educational achievement is thus understood in terms of 'power-knowledge the single, inseparable configuration of practices and ideas that constitute a discourse'. This position may be taken to its ultimate extreme by Gillborn and Youdell (2000), who argue that the educational system is plainly responsible for the inequitable distribution of qualifications, as shown by the fact that A to E GCSE passes are awarded to 75 per cent of professional workers' and to only 15 per cent of unskilled workers' children, and suggest with little more 'evidence' that the effective mechanism must be located in teachers' taken-for-granted theories of 'ability'. There is clearly no escape from the need to confront theories of ability in the explanation of class and cultural differences in educational achievement.

This chapter attempts a realist break with these postmodernist tendencies and proposes a return to a more traditional approach to the explanation of inequality of educational opportunity (Coleman 1969; Jencks et al. 1972).[1] If variance in early cognitive performances transmits a perceptible signal to adult educational achievement, then it seems reasonable to enquire not only into the strength of the signal, but also into the mechanisms of its transmission and its substantive content. The sociology of education may be able to help decode a message containing some important news.

We take another look at the 1970 British Cohort Study (BCS70) on which Feinstein's analysis is based in order to extend the structural level of explanation, where variables such as social class and parental education carry the explanatory burden, to the level of process and practice where the effective mechanism is to be found.[2] If there are sociological explanations of group variance in cognitive development to be had, then they will need to be grounded, as Bernstein (1990) argued, in a close analysis of class-cultural modes of socialization within the family. There is something about a literacy-directed socialization that imparts a cognitive *habitus* in the form of dispositions exercised in the conduct of schoolwork. Such, at least, is the hypothesis to be considered.[3] The major difficulty facing this hypothesis is, of course, its entry onto ground staked out by IQ theory. Whether it is possible, in fact, to use the concepts and techniques of mental measurement in a neutral discourse is a matter in itself that merits comment. To employ factor analysis, for example, in order to detect a signal, as if the nature of this signal was a matter of indifference, would not be regarded by all observers as consistent with neutrality. There is uncontestable evidence, however, that the literacy resources of families are significantly associated with educational achievement. This is the structural evidence that sociology regards as its own, but here, too, are signals that need careful interpretation if they are to be incorporated into a full process level explanation.

This chapter thus sets itself a considerable task. It will build on Feinstein's contribution in an attempt to show how the signal from early competence to adult qualifications is almost certainly transmitted through classed practices of literate socialization. The argument will proceed through the examination of quantitative evidence, the analysis of an episode in the early development of a literate cognitive *habitus*, and a conceptual engagement with the theory of general intelligence. We deal with a complex problem and only through the application of a multidisciplinary 'numbers and narratives' approach to the construction of realist explanations, with an account of process mechanisms, will substantive progress be made.

Some Evidence of Class Disparities in Educational Achievement

The existence and generous availability of the BCS70 data are facts of which British social science may be proud. There is just one point on which objections might be raised: the data on child performance and class location are about thirty years old. As it is the connection between childhood abilities and adult status that makes them interesting, this could hardly be otherwise. It may be worth reporting, nevertheless, some recent evidence that the patterns of association found in the 1970s continue to be a contemporary reality. Some pertinent data on educational performance can be obtained from the international PIRLS 2000 survey and will serve to establish a point of reference for the arguments to be developed (Gonzalez 2003). Table 29.1 reports English data for 10-year-olds' reading achievement showing the associations between father's occupational group, number of children's books in the home, and reading scores at age 10.

The association with socio-economic status—the correlation is actually .269—is evident from the data presented in Table 29.1. The difference in mean reading scores between children whose fathers report their occupations as 'professional' and those who describe themselves as operators or labourers, is 6.3 points, a little less than the standard deviation (*SD*) for this sample of 8.6:[4] the effect size *d* is 0.73.[5] The difference associated with high and low numbers of children's books in the home, 5.6 points ($d = 0.65$) is also statistically significant. The proportion of homes with more than 100 children's books ranges from professionals with 54 per cent to operators with 20 per cent. It will be observed that working-class students from homes with more than 100 children's books have reading scores more or less equal to those from professional homes with fewer than fifty children's books. This information is worth some consideration. The

Table 29.1 Reading mean scores, father's occupation, and number of children's books in household, 10-year-olds, PIRLS England sample

Father's occupational group	Reading mean	SD	N	Reading mean with 0–50 children's books	SD	N	Reading mean with more than 100 children's books	SD	N
Professional	155.6	8.0	280	152.7	9.0	50	156.4	7.9	150
Senior official	154.0	7.7	210	150.6	8.1	49	155.8	7.7	96
Technician	153.4	7.4	131	151.9	6.2	36	155.0	8.3	41
Clerk	153.5	7.1	40	152.9	8.0	17	154.8	6.7	15
Busn. owner	151.6	8.5	157	148.0	8.5	55	155.5	7.4	48
Sales worker	151.1	9.8	119	149.9	9.4	55	154.4	9.4	31
Trade worker	150.9	7.6	278	148.7	8.3	101	153.3	6.2	97
Fishery wrker	150.8	9.3	21	151.4	11.7	4	150.7	10.4	9
Operator	149.3	8.4	148	147.9	8.3	65	152.3	6.5	30
Labourers	149.3	8.4	81	147.4	8.3	39	152.1	10.4	21
Not applicable	148.2	10.1	102	146.1	10.2	57	152.9	5.5	18
TOTAL	152.1	8.6	1,567	149.2	8.7	528	154.8	7.7	556

Note: Source PIRLS (Programme for International Reading Literacy Study) England dataset. Reading achievement is assessed using the average score on all blocks. The standard deviation for this restricted sample is 8.6. (see n. 4.) Occupational groups, which have been reordered, are from a parental questionnaire and represent self-classification into these categories. The category 'never worked outside home', with 8 respondents, is omitted. The PIRLS category 'not applicable', in most cases, indicates a household with no father present, and the scores may be interpreted as *applicable* in that sense. Information about the number of children's books is also from the parental questionnaire. The original five-point scale has been collapsed into three categories, 0–50, 51–100, and 101+. About a third of families that responded to this item are in each category: only the high and low values are given in the table.

interaction effect is such that with 41 per cent of the top half of the SES categories in households with more than 100 children's books, and just 28 per cent of those in the bottom half, some of the effect on reading associated with social class will be accounted for by these resources of household literacy. Nothing more, however, will be said about the PIRLS data. Although the survey is extensive, it provides no longitudinal information and thus has limited value for the causal analysis of social disparities in educational achievement. It has been drawn on here simply to establish the fact that the associations discussed are a contemporary reality and thus to support the decision to make a systematic use of BCS70 on which Feinstein's analysis is based.

It so happens that the BCS70 dataset, for all its richness, includes few *direct* indicators of educational practices within the family. The variable most suited to this purpose, arguably, can be derived from the mother's report, in the 5-year-old survey, of the number of days children were read to at that time. This proves, in fact, to be an exceptionally informative variable. It is now possible to show that reading scores are associated with social class and, furthermore, are associated within class fractions in direct relationship to the level of reading young children have received at home as 5-year-olds. This is a process variable that one can consider along with the resource variables described in the PIRLS data presented above.

The pattern revealed by Table 29.2 is indeed broadly similar to that of Table 29.1. There is a clear association between social class and reading scores at age 10, the correlation of .292 is once again moderate, but there is a difference of 10.8, an effect size of 0.98, between the means of professional and low-skilled workers' children, and there is an average within class difference of 5.8 points, about one half *SD* ($d = 0.53$), linked to the number of days their mothers reported reading to them at age 5. The number of days children are read to is clearly associated with social class: the range for 'read to every day' extends from 63 per cent in professional homes to 29 per cent in low-skilled homes. It seems reasonable to conclude from these comparisons of the contemporary and historical patterns of associations between social class, educational achievement, and indicators of family literacy practices and resources, that an analysis based on BSC70 data will not be irrelevant to our understanding of the current situation.

The discussion has begun to explore the relationships between educational achievement, social class, and family literacy. It is important to understand that social class and indicators of literacy are not treated here as variables having the same status and employed in a model that seeks to account for

Table 29.2 Reading mean scores age 10, social class, days read to at age 5, BCS70

Social class	Reading mean	N	SD	Reading mean, read to 0–3 days	SD	N	Reading mean, read to 7 days	SD	N
Professional	39.7	479	9.1	36.8	9.3	83	40.6	8.7	302
Large business	37.8	614	10.2	34.7	10.0	150	39.8	9.5	343
Lower service	37.4	624	10.0	34.9	10.4	166	38.3	9.9	328
Small business	33.9	1,656	10.6	31.3	10.6	630	36.3	10.2	711
Inter. non-manual	34.5	441	10.0	32.0	10.8	159	35.7	9.3	196
Skilled manual	30.6	3,045	10.8	28.7	10.5	1,425	32.9	10.7	1,029
Low skilled manual	28.9	1,133	10.7	27.1	10.3	604	31.6	10.9	328
TOTAL	32.9	7,992	11.0	29.9	10.7	3,217	35.7	10.6	3,237

Note: Source 1970 British Cohort Study. Reading scores are from the Edinburgh Reading Test administered to cohort members when they were 10 years old. For this sample the mean is 32.9 and the standard deviation 11.0. Social class derived from father's occupational group 1980 recoded to an eight-point scale in accordance with the model proposed by Savage and Egerton (1997), excepting that professional occupations are placed above those graded as large business. The number of days each week someone in the family read to children when they were five, as reported by their mothers, has been recoded to give approximately equal proportions in the sets 0–3 days and 7 days used in the table.

the overall variance in educational achievement. The point is rather to consider to what extent the difference between social classes might be a consequence of family-based early childhood activities functional in the acquisition of literacy. We have established that the reading achievement gap between professional and low-skilled workers' children is close to one *SD* at age 10, and that the greater the level of household literacy resources and practices the higher the mean achievement. A good proportion of the class achievement difference is likely to be due to the classed distribution of literate resources and associated practices. Indeed, it seems that 13 per cent of the variance in adult educational achievement can be accounted for by tests of cognitive performance administered two decades earlier at a time when they had been at school for no more than a few months. This can be compared directly, for example, to the 8.5 per cent of the variance accounted for by household income. Some theoretical implications of these facts will be considered. It will first be useful to present evidence on the strength of the signal between early and later performance. This can be assessed from the pattern of correlations reported in Table 29.3.

The analysis provided by Feinstein includes only those cases for which information is available at ages 22, 42, and 60 months. There are no doubt good methodological reasons for that decision, but there are clearly advantages in using the entire sample when the data are present. The associations between tests of childhood abilities and educational qualifications are quite remarkable. They become perhaps even more remarkable when the nature of the tests is understood. It may be of interest to note that many of the tasks included in the performance assessments up to the age of 10 would not be out of place in conventional IQ tests.

It is difficult to assess intellectual capabilities in early childhood, and 22 months is very early indeed. The Stanford-Binet test (Roid and Barram 2004), which has a respectable claim to be definitive in this field, does not begin to assess children until age 3½, and scores derived from the age 22-month tests should not be recognized, therefore, as directly comparable with those that might be obtained from intelligence tests. Correlations between the items at this level, as Feinstein observes, are low or moderate and although a principal component can be extracted it does not have the technical features of the psychometric *g*. The more comprehensive tests administered to children at 42 months do include, however, a number of items commonly found in standard instruments developed for the purpose of intellectual assessment. The 42-month tests also generate two distinct but highly correlated factors,

Table 29.3 Correlations between early cognitive performance and educational achievement, with sample size

	ECP22	ECP42	ECP60	BAS10	Read10	Maths10	OLEngl.	OLMaths
ECP42	.338 (2204)							
ECP60	.294 (1839)	.352 (1839)						
BAS10	.287 (1557)	.354 (1557)	.499 (8779)					
Read10	.305 (1601)	.353 (1601)	.476 (8995)	.738 (9723)				
Maths10	.278 (1604)	.331 (1604)	.450 (8986)	.738 (7918)	.738 (9969)			
OLEngl.	.169 (767)	.281 (767)	.344 (4466)	.517 (3897)	.585 (3975)	.519 (3973)		
OLMaths	.114 (716)	.214 (716)	.345 (4199)	.526 (3664)	.513 (3738)	.616 (3735)	.658 (4322)	
Hqual26	.146 (1070)	.235 (1070)	.354 (6234)	.505 (5388)	.498 (5517)	.496 (5517)	.572 (3524)	.613 (3338)

Note: Source BSC70. ECP22, ECP42 and ECP60 (Early Cognitive Performance at 22, 42 and 60 months) are principal component scores derived from performance tests administered at those ages. BAS10 is the total score for the four British Ability Scales administered at age 10. Read10 and Maths10 are scores from the Edinburgh Reading Test and the Friendly Mathematics Test taken by10-year-olds. OLEngl and OLMaths are scores derived from English and mathematics O-Level/CSE achievement coded to an eight-point scale using examination grade data at 16-years (McNiece, Bidgood & Soan, 2004). Hqual26 is the BSC70 derived variable of that name which codes highest educational qualification at 26 into a six-point scale from none to degree level. The sample numbers are given in brackets. All correlations are significantly different from zero $p. < .001$.

the first rotated factor accounts for 41 per cent of the variance and seems to reflect the ability to count, whereas the second accounts for 17 per cent of the variance and has to do with language proficiency. The second of these is reported as ECP42 in Table 29.3. Although few of the tasks at 42 months exactly match those found in the Stanford-Binet test—and those that do, in general, omit the problem-solving element characteristic of intelligence tests even at this age—a distinct family resemblance can be detected. The tests administered at 5 years can be divided into two broad categories. The English Peabody Picture Vocabulary Test (EPVT) assesses word knowledge by asking children to name a pictured object or activity. The other tests include copying designs, a human figure drawing exercise, and a test that requires children to add features to an outlined face shown in profile. All of these items, with the limited exception of the profile test (which adds relatively little to the principal factor), are commonly included in tests of mental ability designed for young children. The British Ability Scales (BAS), administered at age 10, were obviously designed within the tradition of mental measurement. The four sub-scales used in the BCS70 study, two verbal (word definitions, verbal similarities) and two non-verbal (progressive matrices, digit span), are all recognizable elements of standard intelligence tests. It has already been noted that the combined score accounts for rather more than a quarter of the variance in adult qualifications. This is, of course, a much greater proportion than can be accounted for by social class of origin. The reading and mathematics attainment tests were designed to be familiar to students in British primary schools and are not problematic in this respect. There may be little justification for the assumption that the continuity observed in the rankings of these childhood performances is due to a common mental property, but it would be unreasonable to deny that these performances reveal the existence of related skills constituting the cognitive *habitus*.

Feinstein has demonstrated that rank orders of relative ability established in the earliest years are more stable than otherwise and, also, that mobility in rank over time is associated with social class. This aspect of his analysis is worth the effort of replication. The current analysis uses changes between performance quintiles at 5 and 10 years. This is a substantial period in a child's life and as data are available for a sample many times larger than that used by Feinstein the findings may to that extent be more informative. The first point to note is that stability is more common than mobility. A third of all children occupy the diagonal position and thus have exactly the same relative status at 10 as they had at 5. A further 37 per cent differ by only one quintile, many of which movements will be within the margin of error, and it can thus be concluded that in these years about three-quarters of all students retain their broad status on these indicators of cognitive performance throughout their primary schooling. Table 29.4 shows the extent of the changes observed between the ages of 5 and 10 in relation to social class.

The evidence that working-class children are more likely than middle-class children to decline in their relative level of performance, and that middle-class children are more likely to improve than working-class children, is clearly demonstrated by the data presented in Table 29.4. The odds of children from unskilled backgrounds being in the high rather than the low quintile at age 5, relative to those from professional backgrounds, are about 11 : 1, but at age 10 the odds ratio has climbed to 41 : 1. These values are calculated from the raw data. The highest ability quintile at 5 years is actually the modal category for children from the professional to the intermediate non-manual classes, but the reversal is abrupt, and for those with manual origins the modal category is the lowest quintile. The average standardized gain on these tests made by professional class children between 5 and 10 years approaches half an *SD*, whereas unskilled working-class students show an average decline of a third of an *SD*. It seems that the gap in this respect between the upper- and lower-class fractions has expanded by about three-quarters of an *SD* during the stage of primary education. It is impossible, without further information, to attribute this relative shift to resources and practices at specific sites, but the likelihood that home and school have independent and interactive effects is high.

The movement in relative status given by these assessments that takes place between 5 and 10 years is evidently not random. It is possible to explore the causes of relative decline in more detail by examining the patterns between indicators that point to specific agents, organized sites, and established practices by the use of logistic regression. We are interested in students who improve or decline between 5 and 10 as shown by their movement between quintiles at those ages. The odds of being in the gain rather than the loss group are improved by social class, for example, children of professional origin are 3.4 times more likely to be in the gain group when compared with those of unskilled origin. The odds are further increased by 23 per cent by mother's education, for each step on a four-point scale, and by 7 per cent for each day children were read to when they were 5-years-old. These odds are additive, and it is interesting to note that when reading at age 5 is examined independently, the odds are improved by 31 per cent for each day children are read to (if they are read to at all). This relationship is evidence of a direct link between practices of literacy within the family and relative improvement in performances in the cognitive domain during the years of primary education. We are entitled to suppose that the more reading 5-year-old children in the low to mid-quintiles get from their parents, the more likely it is that they will reach the mid- to high quintiles at 10 years.

A correlation between educational achievement and a structural property of the family environment indicated by number of books in the home, or by mother's educational level, enables what Pettit (1993) has called a programme explanation to be constructed. Such structural explanations are useful in that they suggest that there is something about the conditions indicated that generates the observed effect. An association between father's occupation and progress at school provides, for example, the basis for a structural or programme explanation because there is no process account of how that association is generated. An association between the number of days parents read to their children and the children's progress at school provides, on the other hand, adequate basis for the construction of a process explanation. There is every reason, in fact, to suppose that the mechanism generating relative shifts in childhood performance levels is to be found in the interactions that generate a cognitive *habitus* constituted in such a way that abstract problem-solving, mediated by symbolic tools, is more or less facilitated.

What intellectual skills do middle-class children typically acquire to a greater degree of proficiency when compared to working-class children? If there is to be a vital sociology of cognitive development with realist foundations, then it will, perhaps, make extensive use of those methods that clinical psychology has developed for its own. It is not, however, *method* that determines what is proper to

Table 29.4 Changes in relative position on tests at 5 and 10 years

Social Class	Low quintile at 5 yrs (%)	Low quintile at 10 yrs (%)	High quintile at 5 yrs (%)	High quintile at 10 yrs (%)	Large loss 5–10 yrs (%)	Large gain 5–10 yrs (%)	Mean residual score	Total N
Professional	8.0	3.4	42.6	43.2	4.5	36.8	0.47	474
Large bus.	9.3	8.2	39.4	32.7	8.5	17.2	0.39	624
Lower serv.	10.3	8.1	34.7	32.1	8.8	25.0	0.31	620
Small bus.	16.3	14.9	27.2	21.2	17.5	20.5	0.12	1676
Int. non-man.	19.2	14.3	24.8	19.4	12.6	10.1	0.09	448
Skilled man.	25.4	25.1	19.4	12.2	18.8	9.3	−0.14	3,118
Low skilled	32.6	31.4	15.7	9.0	30.1	8.4	−0.34	1,165

Note: Source BCS70. The derived variables Early Cognitive Performance at 60 months and the British Ability Scale are divided into quintiles. The percentage of students in the low and high quintiles is given for the tests at each age. Gains and losses between ages five and 10 are calculated by classifying children in the low quintile at five who reached the high-average or high quintile at 10 as having made a large gain, and those in the high quintile at five who were in the low or low-average quintile at 10 as having made a large decline. ECP60 also is regressed on BSC10 to obtain a standardized residual. This statistic indicates the extent to which children have improved or worsened their relative status at age five. Positive scores represent a relative gain, and negative scores a decline, in *SD* units.

sociology, but the provision of *explanations* of a certain kind, in order to account for the causes of social events, the nature of social processes, and the maintenance of collective states of affairs. These remarks will establish a context for the following illustrative observation and analysis of a literate cognitive *habitus* in the early processes of formation.

Towards a Sociology of Cognitive Development

The recording presented in this section shows Miriam, who is almost exactly 3 years and 3 months old, playing with construction bricks in the company of her grandfather. The bricks are of different sizes and there are a few play figures, Piglet and Pooh are mentioned, and some special pieces including a birthday cake with four candles, or strawberries as they are called at one point. Miriam and her grandfather have been involved in the game for a few minutes and it has been established, by the child, that it is Pooh's birthday and that he is 5. Miriam's grandfather is building a wall of bricks around the play board, which is the garden, and the little girl is placing things in it. She has put Pooh in the middle of the garden with the birthday cake before him. The extract begins with her observation that only large bricks can be used to join together the smaller bricks. Her grandfather confirms that remark by using the concept of length and making her reasoning explicit. The conversation then takes another direction as Miriam declares a new condition of the game. It is also Piglet's birthday.

[M] See, only these ones join *[points to a two by four stud brick that has been placed so that it joins a couple of two by two stud bricks underneath it]*.

[GF] That's right. Only these ones can join.

[M] Piglet's on the edge *[places Piglet at the edge of the play board]*.

[GF] These ones—these are long enough to join, aren't they? Only these ones can join because they're *[the]* longest. They're long.

[M] Piglet's saying to Piglet ... And it's Piglet's birthday today!

[GF] It's Piglet's birthday as well?

[M] Yeah.

[GF] Is he five as well?

[M] No, he's four.

[GF] He's four. So he must have four candles on his cake.

[M] Yeah *[dubiously]*.

[GF] That's a good idea.

[M] One, two, three, four, five. That's Pooh's cake because it's five *[points to the cake before Pooh]*.

[GF] Yeah, that's actually got four on it.

[M] Must be Piglet's—must be Piglet's one.

[GF] Do you want to count them again? Because I don't think there are five candles on that cake.

[M] There should be this many? *[spreads the fingers on her right hand and holds it up palm facing her grandfather]*.

[GF] Yes, there should be. There should be as many as on your hand. But I don't think there are. Can you count them again? On the cake?

[M] On Piglet's birthday cake?

[GF] Yeah, on Piglet's birthday cake.

[M] On Piglet's ... *[moves the cake in front of Piglet]*.

[GF] Yeah, put Piglet's birthday cake in there. Can you count the strawberries on it?

[M] One, two, three, four.

[GF] That's right, four. Not five. So he must be four.

[M] But Piglet's four.

[GF] Piglet is four, yes. So, he must have that birthday cake.

[M] But where is Pooh's birthday cake?

[GF] Well, that's tricky. We need one—if Pooh—if Pooh is five he must have a birthday cake with five candles, and I'll have to make one. Shall I make a special birthday cake with five candles?

[M] Yes.

[GF] Okay. Right. And ... *[gets to his feet with the intention of getting some paper and sticky tape with which to make candles]*.

[M] Five. Five. Let me get up because I'm going to help you.

At one level this conversation is about a child being taught to count. But the play is actually about making rules, acting within their constraints, and accepting their consequences. Miriam has begun the game by establishing that it is Pooh's birthday, stating that he is 5, and placing the cake in front of him on the play board. Then she decides—presumably because two birthdays must be more fun than one—that it is also Piglet's birthday and that he is 4. She knows that if you are 4 you are not as big as those who are 5 and this is, in that sense, perhaps a birthday of somewhat secondary importance. When her grandfather points out that Piglet must have a cake, with four candles, she agrees doubtfully, and her reservation may be due to the fact that there is only one cake and it has already been allocated to Pooh. She then counts the candles on the cake—making a motivated error perhaps—and declares that the cake belongs to Pooh because there are five. Her grandfather, disconcertingly, then informs her that the cake actually has four candles. Miriam knows that if the cake is to be Pooh's there should be five candles, which is as many fingers as there are on her hand, and she accepts at once, even before being encouraged to recount, that if there are only four then the cake must be Piglet's. She then does count the candles correctly and confirms with her grandfather that as Piglet is 4 this must be his cake. It should also be noted that when Miriam's grandfather argues, somewhat over enthusiastically, that Piglet must be 4 because the cake has four candles she points out that Piglet *is* 4, thus stating the application rule in its correct form (for it is age that determines the number of candles, not the other way round), and her grandfather's response confirms that this is so. The reallocation of the cake, however, has the consequence that Pooh, who is older and whose birthday was declared first in the game, is now without a cake, and Miriam puts this problem to her grandfather who proposes a solution.

The conversation is worth at least this much attention. The mathematics the child is learning in this episode are not so much to do with the mechanics of counting (although her grandfather will not accept her incorrect counting), but with how material objects (candles) and abstract properties (ages) can be mapped in a one-to-one relationship. What is also being learned, and this is a parallel matter of great importance, are the processes of syllogistic reasoning. The social rule is that when it is one's birthday one shall have a cake with as many candles as one is years old. If Piglet is 4 then he must have a cake with four candles. And if that leaves Pooh without a cake for his birthday then the consequences of that must be accepted. A cake with the correct number of candles must be provided. This bit of imaginative play provides Miriam, helped by the not too expert participation of her grandfather, with an opportunity to develop capacities of social thought—for the syllogism is a social product of a literate community—that are fundamentally literate in character (Luria 1978; Olson 1994; Hasan 2002).

By the time Miriam goes to school it is likely that she will be well on the way to reading. She already knows the names of most letters and their phonetic values, learned to write 'M' for Miriam some months ago, and can usually count accurately at least to ten. There is no reason to suppose that this head start, as it might be called, will not be consolidated into a lasting advantage as she proceeds through school. What she will also be able to do, and this is much less easy to test than skills like reading and counting, is to think about abstract relations in the sequential, logical manner revealed in this episode. These are powerful and effective mental tools to have. As Bourdieu and Passeron (1990: 73) note, language provides 'a more or less complex system of categories, so that the capacity to decipher and manipulate complex structures, whether logical or aesthetic, depends partly on the complexity of the language transmitted by the family'. Miriam's parents (and grandparents) are located in the professional middle-class. The relative educational advantage in manipulating complex logical structures from which she will surely benefit is one held largely in comparison with children of working-class parents. There are crucial questions that still need to be settled. Are the effective cognitive dispositions acquired in early childhood through interactions of this character such that they continue to develop with a durable effect on scholastic attainment? What is the capacity of the educational system to teach children with relatively limited experience of these modes of socialization to the same level of attainment in, for example, reading and mathematics, as those with a more intensive experience? The available research into these matters tends to be conducted within a psychological rather than a sociological disciplinary framework and this is an area where collaboration might be productive.

The task for sociological theory is to make the connection between processes at this level and the programme explanations with which it must so often be satisfied. The most complete form of sociological explanation will arguably include a reference to the structural properties of social organizations, the habituated dispositions that enable individuals to conduct themselves as social agents, and the collective practices that reveal the causal processes necessary to complete our explanatory narratives (Nash 2003, 2004). Although it is not always easy, or sometimes even possible, to discover the connection of process between structural properties and an observed event for which an explanation is sought, the ideal should be retained. The scientific procedure is to hypothesize what the generative process might be, establish a research programme to test for its existence, and show how it has the effects attributed by theory. This is exactly what the empirical aspects of Bernstein's project in this area were intended to do, and there is every reason to encourage the continuation of this sociological research into the nature of the cognitive *habitus*. This may be the moment to point out that if there is one obstacle to that programme more formidable than all others it is that posed by IQ theory. It is crucial that the sociology of education should confront IQ theory with a rigorous conceptual critique rather than, as is all too common, a somewhat casual ideological dismissal.

How is the Signal Transmitted?

The argument that 'ability' can be treated as an element in a discursive formation so that its causal effects on social practice can be analysed has been criticized as an inadequate model. The 'big idea' behind discourse theory is, nevertheless, one that compels attention. Is it possible to adopt the discourse of mental measurement without reproducing the theoretical assumptions that constitute it? Feinstein insists that his approach is neutral with respect to the general theory of intelligence. His use of 'signal' is an appeal to the independent domain of information theory. At the same time, however, Feinstein writes of 'qualitative changes in the ability being proxied at different stages of development' (p. 77), and this phrase might be interpreted as a signal that a rather familiar concept of ability is being employed after all. It may be argued that this is to construct 'ability' as a durable state of being that endures through different stages of development and is assessed by performances accepted as proxies for that effective property of mind or brain. In this discourse, the object of measurement is deemed to be a functional 'ability', and even if this is accepted as the neutral language of information technology, it establishes a position fully consistent with orthodox IQ theory. The appeal to communications theory cannot prevent certain questions arising. What is the nature of the instrument transmitting the signal? Inasmuch as the signal is sent by a human being, then a biological entity is involved, and inasmuch as a single factor is isolated, then the object of reference is by definition one-dimensional. By virtue of what property are children aged 22 or 36 months able to send more or less strong signals about their future qualification status? In the transcendental question of Bhaskar's (1993) critical realism: what property needs to exist in order that such a signal can be sent? These are, indeed, central and unavoidable questions.

The general theory of intelligence was originated by Spearman (1927) a little over a century ago: the seminal paper actually appeared in 1904. In its present, remarkably unmodified form, it continues to find support from what seems to be a growing number of influential advocates, including Jensen (1998), Macintosh (1998), Deary (2000), and Bartholomew (2004), among several others. This orthodox theory of general intelligence, or *g* theory, is dismissed as a pseudo-science by some critics (Howe 1990; Richardson 1998), and yet treated by others, most notably Flynn (1987), whose opposition may even be the more effective in consequence, with almost exaggerated intellectual respect. The great difficulty in overthrowing *g* theory, for if it were no better than a pseudo-science it would surely by now have been relegated to the status of phrenology or palm-reading, is that it attempts to explain patterns of intellectual achievement that manifestly exist. There is irrefutable evidence that intellectual development follows a growth curve much like that of physical development, that intellectual development is to a marked degree influenced by genetic endowment, and that, like it or not, the tests designed by Binet, from which all subsequent IQ tests stem, have a definite practical value in the assessment of intellectual performance. This is not to say that *g* theory is sound, but the irremediable flaw in *g* theory, its central incoherence, is only made apparent by a critique of its conceptual foundations, and criticism within the sociology of education tends to be concerned with other matters (Brown and Lauder 2000).

The basic problem with the theory of general intelligence is just that ambiguity which makes it so difficult to pin down. To many of its proponents it seems that *g* can refer to a mathematical factor (and scores so derived), a cluster of related skills, a property of a test described in terms of content, and to an unspecified, and so 'hypothetical', property of the brain. Moreover, when *g* is described as an 'ability', or some sort of proxy for an ability, which word itself is used sometimes to refer to a skill that can be exercised in given contexts and sometimes to a capacity to acquire such a skill by education, it is necessarily then 'reified', that is treated as an object. If *g* is referred to as marking *an* ability, perhaps one disclosed by factor analysis, and given a causal role in the explanation of variance in educational achievement, then such an entity can only be a functional mental operator for which the traditional term is 'faculty'. It is perhaps not so much that *g* is reified in this fashion, but that *ability* is treated as an object of measurement and as a causal property of the organic system. For at least 100 years *g* theory has maintained these ambiguous references while asserting its right to have *g* accepted as a scientific refinement—a concept under construction much as, for example, it is asserted that 'electricity' once was—of the ordinary language concept of 'general intelligence'. The positivist discourse in which intelligence is a 'construct', that is, a postulated object of measurement; normally distributed; gaining its empirical validation from technical procedures, its meaning from operations; and given causal status in the explanation of cognitive activity, is an incoherent position for a realist philosophy of science to maintain. Intelligence is not a 'concept' or a 'construct' given meaning by its 'operational definition', rather it is a property of people (or their brains) at which certain indicator scales may be hypothesized to point; constructs are not objects of measurement, rather certain properties of things can be scaled or measured; and constructs are not subject to 'validation', rather the existence of actual things hypothesized to be such can be demonstrated by appropriate methods. The formal adherence to the Humean constant conjuction view of causality; the idea that statistical explanations are somehow different in principle from other explanations; and the untenable distinction between 'observable' and 'non-observable' entities or 'constructs', and so on, are all further related obstacles to clarity and good sense in the investigation of individual differences (Nash 1990, 2001, 2005*a*).

The best case to be made for *g* is that the principal factor extracted from a correlation matrix that represents performances on cognitive tests of a certain kind is a complex indicator that may, at that level, mark a discrete neural property, and which may be treated as the effective causal mechanism of the forms of thought exercised in such performances. The question 'is *g* real?', often posed in the literature, can be answered affirmatively if and only if there is some neural property by virtue of which the complex skills exercised in problem-solving of the kind included in the Stanford-Binet test are more or less readily acquired and displayed in appropriate contexts (Bock, Goode, and Webb 2000). That hypothesis may, in principle, be tested. If such a property of an appropriate sort is ever discovered, which is not inherently fantastic, then *g* theory will to that extent be vindicated but, in the meantime, the explanation of population variance in educational achievement by reference to *g* can only be regarded as hypothetical in the sense that some neural property of the right kind is hypothesized to exist. At this moment there is little convincing evidence that it does.

This critique, however, may be of limited use to the sociology of education. A realist theory of intellectual development, should one ever emerge, will have to explain the facts of intellectual development that *g* theory confronts and the individual differences it admittedly tends to celebrate. It may well be that proficiency in certain performances is caused by some discrete state of the brain, but what concerns sociology is how cognitive *habitus* are differentially formed as a consequence of specific forms of education, and that can be investigated without much reference to neural states. There is obviously no contradiction in a theory that encompasses the idea that the brain is a tool of thought and that it is shaped by its social environment. The most plausible explanation of the steady rise in IQ test scores observed in the mid-decades of the twentieth century—the Flynn effect—has been given in terms of genetic-environment matching (Dickens and Flynn 2001). What seems to be happening, in summary, is that children are increasingly likely to be offered a specifically literate socialization, and those genetically predisposed to respond to such stimulation are likely to gain the most. The concept of a 'trigger mechanism' may be a useful metaphor in this context. It is just the nature of a genetically guided developmental process to respond to environmental triggers, but exactly what genes are 'switched on' or suppressed by environmental conditions with consequential distinct and lasting effects on cognitive development remains a matter for scientific investigation. Such triggers, of course, may be expected to occur throughout development, and the role of the school in providing appropriate environments, as one sees most clearly in screening for sporting talent, is potentially large. Nevertheless, that the forms of gene–environment matching proposed by Dickens and Flynn, with respect to cognitive formation, will benefit middle-class more than working-class children is a safe prediction given the classed distribution of literacy resources and associated dispositions, the extent of which has been illustrated here with empirical data.

Sociologists have no need to be bogged down in critiques of a thoroughly ambiguous *g* theory. What matters is to gain a greater understanding of how cognitive skills are acquired in the early years of life and how variance in scholastic achievement resulting from their differential exercise is realized in the educational system. That work cannot be accomplished, however, merely through the ideological critique of IQ theory. Research into the nature of the cognitive *habitus* should be conducted in terms of specific skills and described with reference to performances, where the ability to exercise a skill is nothing more than to have a skill, and does not refer to an effective neural property. That certain skills are associated, however, is not a state of affairs to be taken for granted. On the contrary, the social conditions of skill acquisition and development are of critical importance to a theory of cognitive socialization. The most satisfactory foundations for a theory of cognitive development in this field may be those established by Vygotsky (1994), but it is arguable that sociology may see the elaboration of intellectual structures, their identification by suitable test performances, and the functional relationship between their possession and school learning, as matters primarily for cognitive and educational psychologists. The investigation of the social contexts of their acquisition, however, is a matter in which sociologists of education have a distinctive contribution to make. If effective cognitive structures, or mental formations, are acquired differentially, with respect both to rate of development and relative level of effective capacity, in social and educational environments marked by the material and symbolic resources of socio-economic class, then it can be expected that this will make some contribution to the generation of inequality/difference (Nash 1997, 1999*a*).

Conclusion

The political attention won for early childhood education as result of the emphasis given to the significant relationships established between cognitive performance at the age of 2 or 3 years and adulthood might result in concrete benefits to this sector. Feinstein's research does imply, among other things, that upward social mobility by working-class children may to a considerable extent be accounted for by the literate resources of their families. The recent PIRLS data presented in Table 29.1 show that about a quarter of all children with a father in the category 'operator' and 'labourer' are from homes with more than 100 children's books: our theories of the relationship between class and literacy need at least to be sophisticated enough to acknowledge that reality (Nash 1999*b*). The sociology of education has been notably reluctant to listen to psychological research on the emergence of those dispositions that might be regarded as constituting the cognitive *habitus*, and if the contribution of an economist is heard with less suspicion then it must be the more welcome. The idea that social differences in educational achievement are adequately explained as a consequence of the 'separate curricula, pedagogies, forms of teacher–student relationships', and so on, should be recognized, at best, as a hypothesis in search of evidence. The fact is that class disparities in education can be detected, in the form of a strong signal, long before children enter school, and how much children get from the educational system is linked by a chain of evidence to structures of the cognitive *habitus* acquired largely within the family. It is argued that this position is not a deficit theory and can be maintained without endorsing the general theory of intelligence.

The explanations of events, processes, and states of affairs offered by sociologists must always be considered, on the basis of the evidence and logical forms of argument provided, and either accepted or rejected as more or less correct or incorrect. No scientist can do other than present evidence and argument in explanation of some event or state of affairs. This is not to say that good explanations are easily come by, on the contrary, in this field their acquisition presents considerable difficulties. One can demonstrate an association between structural properties and class variance in reading scores, such as that between the number of books in the home and reading scores; one can demonstrate an association between structural properties and practices, such as that between the number of books in the home and the number of days children are read to; and one can demonstrate a relationship between practices and class variance in reading scores, but it is surprisingly difficult to demonstrate that this constitutes a causal process, in which structural properties, dispositions of conduct, and established practices are all incorporated in a complex causal sequence. Statistical models are not necessarily suited to this form of explanatory narrative and it is necessary to transcend the orthodox discourse of statistical explanation, which is both positivist and nominalist in this respect, in favour of a realist alternative. This does not mean abandoning quantitative methods, but it does mean making a different use of them in explanations. In the last resort, however, the plausibility of an explanatory account is for individuals to weigh up: one can plead only that more weight be given to scientific rather than extra-scientific considerations.

It is not irrelevant in this context to insist again that the ideological impulse in the sociology of education to minimize the influence of early socialization into literate modes of thought as a source of durable cognitive dispositions and to downplay the long-term consequences of such capacities for educational achievement, is as wrongheaded as it is worthy. Although it may seem that the policy goal of equality of educational opportunity is more likely to attract material support given the theory that working-class children are no less competent at school entry than middle-class children, and are denied access to education by the structures of the educational system, there are compelling intellectual and political reasons to believe that this position is misguided. If it is the case that a durable cognitive *habitus* is developed in the early years, then the implications of that fact must be faced and realistic policies to counter its effects need to be devised.

It is true that keeping IQ theory at arm's length requires a degree of intellectual agility. In essence, it is not satisfactory to propose that a concept of intelligence is an appropriate object of measurement in a science of human capabilities. The theory that a commonsense concept can be measured by ranking individuals by their performance on tasks deemed to require the exercise of intelligence and validated by its correlation with scholastic achievement has an attractive simplicity, and may have proved adequate as the basis for a technology of mental measurement, but at a deeper intellectual level it is staggeringly defective. The construction of a discourse in which the term *g* codes for 'intelligence', moreover, is a matter that calls for constant vigilance. Of even more importance than this scholastic reality, however, may be the practical reality that children differ in their performance of tasks—ones that often happen to be included in tests of intelligence—which do afford a good indication of their possession of durable skills, differentially acquired in classed environments, more or less specialized for literacy. One can, indeed, detect a strong signal, and the modes of its transmission, and its message, may be accessible to sociological decoding.

Sociologists of education can find many useful things to do, but investigating the extent of social disparities in education, explaining their causes, and evaluating policies by which they might be reduced, have a good claim to be among their definitive professional activities. This chapter has, accordingly, reported some data on the extent of inequality/difference in education, presented some evidence that this may, to no small degree, originate in families as a consequence of the varying emphasis given to literate socialization, and it remains only to play out the hand by considering what might be done. Successful policies will almost certainly include the provision of community-based early childhood education and direct attention to the importance of resources and cultural conditions of cognitive development. It is a matter, as Flynn (2004) points out, of making more effective the social multipliers through which cognitive skills can be brought to a higher level of development. The differential progress children make between the ages of 5 and 10 is a consequence of structures of relations, dispositions, and practices that characterize and define both home and school. What happens to children should be regarded on theoretical grounds as being due to interactions between these institutions, and may be detected in some statistical models as interaction effects. How might the school, as an instutition with formal responsibility for the education of all, develop processes to teach new entrants whose intellectual formations have emerged in a range of different learning environments? In conditions of such inherent complexity, policy formulation is not exactly straightforward. One may, for example, entertain no serious doubt that children whose cognitive *habitus* is developed in highly literate families will enter school with those skills demanded by its necessary function and, in consequence, tend to outperform other children, but what might be done to increase the number of those whose intellectual formation is so constituted is a long way from being self-evident. Whether resources would more effectively be directed at early childhood education, community development projects, or income-maintenance schemes such as a caregiver wage, for example, are all matters that merit careful assessment.

NOTES

1. Scientific realism maintains that the entities and properties investigated by science have an existence that is not limited to the theoretical discourse within which they are discussed. Realism claims, in other words, that the objects of the physical and social world do exist: that 'desks' and 'chairs' are actual physical things, that 'classes' and 'nation-states' are real social entities that emerge as such in being constituted by social relations of a specific kind, and so on. The purpose of a scientific theory, as discussed with respect to educational research by Nash (2005*b*), is to provide explanatory narratives that reveal the causal mechanisms of operation. This philosophy, although it might be regarded as consistent with common sense, can be distinguished from the idealist theses of both classical positivism and contemporary postmodernism.
2. The 1970 British Cohort Study data are used with acknowledgements to the UK Data Archive and the Centre for Longitudinal Studies, Institute of Education, University of London.
3. We use the concept of *habitus* in a broad sense to refer to dispositions to act that have been acquired as durable tendencies of an individual as a consequence of their socialization within a social group. This seems consistent with Bourdieu's own practice and embraces the concept of *habitus* as a structured ensemble of cognitive and non-cognitive dispositions giving tendencies that allow a non-determined and socially variable range of possibilities for action. In this respect, Bourdieu's (1996: 148 ff.) *manifesto* is expressed in these words: 'We need to escape the mechanistic vision which would reduce agents to simple particles swept up in a magnetic field, by reintroducing not rational subjects working to fulfil their preferences as far as circumstances permit, but socialized agents who, although ideologically individuated, are endowed with transindividual dispositions, and therefore tend to generate practices which are objectively orchestrated to objective requirements, that is irreducible either to the structural forces of the field or to individual dispositions.' An interesting discussion of

the value, or otherwise, of Bourdieu's concept of *habitus* is presented by Robbins (1991). The collection of Bourdieusian commentaries edited by Grenfell and Kelly (1999), with specific reference to education, may also be useful.

4. The standard deviation is a measure of the dispersion in a set of scores. It has useful mathematical properties in that the normal curve of distribution is interpreted using the standard deviation. Such approximations are subject to error, but in concrete terms, one *SD* on the PIRLS test will be the equivalent of about a year in standardized reading ages.

5. The effect size *d* used here reports the observed differences as a ratio of the total sample standard deviation, being the best indicator of the population standard deviation.

'Fitting In' and 'Joining In': Social Relations and Social Integration

Tess Ridge

[...]

To understand the multidimensional impact of poverty on children's lives, an analysis of poverty that embraces the social relational aspects of children's lives is also needed. The notion of social exclusion has the potential to broaden our understanding of poverty from a narrow issue of inadequate material resources to a more comprehensive and dynamic analysis (Berghman, 1995). The relational impact of poverty, outlined by Room (1995), as inadequate social participation, lack of social integration and lack of power has a particular resonance in children's lives. Childhood is a social experience in itself, with its own norms and customs, where the costs of inclusion may be great, likewise the cost of exclusion. Friendships and social interactions with peers are key locations where children develop their social identity and enhance their social capital. This chapter provides an opportunity to understand the social lives and experiences of children in poverty, through the medium of their own voices. It reveals the children's interpretations and constructions of their social relationships and it explores the children's perceptions of their ability to participate in the social world of their peers.

The chapter focuses on three key areas:

- The capacity of children to *fit in* with their peers. This is examined through an exploration of social relationships bounded by friendship and bullying.
- The importance of *clothes* as a key signifier of peer inclusion, this was a particular area of concern identified by children during the interviews.
- Children's opportunities to *join in* shared social activities with their peers. This focuses in particular on children's social experiences at school and on the children's perceptions of their capacity to join in with shared social activities.

'Fitting In': Friendships

The importance of friendships and the value of developing and sustaining satisfactory social relationships have only recently been acknowledged as significant factors in the development of social capital and in the maintenance of secure social identities. With modern society increasingly characterised by risk and uncertainty (Beck, 1992). the value of friendships as a source of support in the face of breakdown of other traditional forms of support has only recently been explored (Pahl and Spencer, 1997; Pahl, 1998; Silva and Smart, 1999). In a complex and demanding social environment, friendships and informal relationships can act as a 'social glue', binding us into the social structure (Jerrome, 1984). Friendships, and by extension social networks, are also increasingly recognised as powerful social assets, playing an important role in the development and maintenance of social capital (Pahl and Spencer, 1997; Pahl, 2000), has

From *Childhood Poverty and Social Exclusion from a Child's Perspective* (Bristol: Policy Press, 2002), ch. 4. Reprinted with permission.

argued that 'network poverty', a lack of secure social networks, can play a critical role in people's vulnerability to poverty and social exclusion.

Friendship for children has generally been seen as an essential part of cultural reproduction, and the development of secure social identities (Rubin, 1980; James et al., 1998). The importance of friendship for children lies not just in the growth and development of social skills and social identity, but also in learning to accept and understand others. Children need to learn not just how to make friends, but also crucially how to be a friend (Furnham, 1989). However, friendship for children, as for adults, also creates an entry point into wider social relationships; it plays a role as a social asset—a source of social capital—both in childhood and in the future. Conversely, difficulties in maintaining social relationships can leave children vulnerable to social exclusion (see Ridge and Millar, 2000).

An exploration of the meaning and value of friendships among children from low-income families may provide an important insight into the role of friendships in children's well-being and social integration. Previous research has shown that friendships can have diverse meanings for children (James, 1993; Brannen et al., 2000), and this was reflected in the variety of different reasons that children in this study gave about why they felt friendship was important. As well as the more obvious reasons for children valuing friends for play and sociability, they also identified considerably more complex reasons.

The Value of Friends

As with previous research, the friendships in this study were strongly gendered (Archer, 1992; Hartup, 1992; James, 1993; Jamieson, 2001). Girls were generally more articulate about their friendships, and were much more likely to see friends as confidants and as supportive and valued alternatives to family. Boys were more likely to see friendship as an opportunity for having fun and a good time, but they also valued the protective effect of friendship in the face of bullying. These are in line with Hartup's findings (1992), that girls' relationships tend to be more 'intensive' and boys' more 'extensive'.

For many children, having the companionship of friends ensured fun and happiness. This was a view of friendship that was more likely to be articulated by the boys, although the girls also appreciated good times with friends. Friends staved off boredom and without friends, they felt they would not be happy:

> Like if you ain't got no one to speak to or anything then it will be like sort of borin' and all that. If you've got a problem and you ain't got anybody to speak to, if you've got a friend then you 'ave and they can sort things as well. (Cally, 14 years, two-parent family)

> I go round my friends' houses quite a lot and there would be no one to talk to and I would get really bored if I had no friends. (Kevin, 12 years, lone-parent family)

Although friends were undeniably valued for fun and enjoyment, many children and young people identified the importance of friendship as a source of social and emotional sustenance. This was an aspect of friendship that was articulated most often by girls. For many children and young people, the family is not necessarily the ideal site for sharing problems; alternative sites of support are sought and often found in friendships:

> They are as important as your family especially when you are this age. because your family can help you to a certain extent but for the things you don't want to tell your family, friends are so important to have. (Amy, 15 years, two-parent family)

> It's someone to talk to and rely on, and go out with. . . . Some things that happen[s] you can't just go along and tell your mum, can you, or your dad. and say like this happened. (Colleen, 13 years, lone-parent family)

Friends were supportive and discreet confidants, and reciprocity played an important part in maintaining and nurturing friendships:

> Just to talk to and to tell 'em things and you know they are going to keep it a secret, not tell anyone else. (Charlene, 12 years, two-parent family)

> Like I'm there for them and they're there for me, and we're all really close and get on really well, and I just think its really important. (Carrie, 15 years, lone-parent family)

For many of the children, friendship also performed a valuable social function, averting the dangers of loneliness and social isolation. Clarke summed up the general feeling:

> If you haven't got friends you haven't got a lot really have you, you know. (Clarke, 15 years, lone-parent family)

[. . .]

Friendships Bring Wider Social Networks

Friendships also open the door to other relationships with friends' parents and siblings, a whole social milieu. For some children this was particularly valuable where their own home life was stressed, or where they were socially restricted. Lisa spent every weekend away from home that she could, staying with her friends and their families:

> It gives me a break from here as well, 'cos we're not like the perfect family who get on all the time and stuff. Because it's been hard with [step-mother's] children and her, and her way of living and us mixing in. ... There are like the arguments and the rows, especially at my age and being a teenager and stuff. So it's nice to be able to get out ... 'cos it's like a different living. (Lisa, 15 years, two-parent family)

It was evident from the children's accounts that they valued friendship highly, and that it performed several important social functions for them; many of the functions belie the everyday simplistic impressions of children's friendships as mere extensions of playground society. However, although their perceptions of friendship involved feeling happy, secure and supported, their social realities were very different. Many of the children were experiencing bullying and problems making and sustaining their friendships.

Bullying

Previous research has shown that around one quarter of children have been bullied in school (Whitney and Smith, 1993). Bullying can affect children's self-esteem and social values; it may also affect learning (Smith and Sharp, 1994) and lead to truancy (Carlen et al., 1992). Nearly half of the children talked about being bullied, either currently or in the past. This had had a marked effect on how they felt about their school and, in some cases, about themselves. There was no substantial difference between genders or by family type. However, there were signs of difference between rural and urban locations. Rural children seemed more likely to report having been bullied—14 rural compared to five urban children. This may well reflect different school practices, or the possibility that children from families on a low income stand out more in a rural environment than urban children from low-income families. Most of the bullying revolved around school where children came into regular contact with their peers. Nell suffered years of bullying at her school and highlighted the importance of developing secure friendships for protection and improved self-esteem:

> I used to get bullied constantly because of my attitude to things. ... If you're not entirely confident about your appearance then people are bound to pick on you. It was one of my friends who stopped me from being bullied because she was trying to build my confidence up for ages. (Nell, 17 years, two-parent family)

Some of the children in the study had been bullied for several years, and had developed strategies to protect themselves:

> If you haven't got a friend in school you feel more lonely, and you feel like sometimes school work can be much harder. ... I was bullied for a couple of years but I got used to it and ignored 'em and got on with my work. (Stewart, 16 years, lone-parent family)

Children who were being bullied had little faith in the school system or in its ability to stop their unhappiness. One 10-year-old had reported his bullying at school but nothing had been done about it. Another felt that there was nobody he could tell. Bella was particularly unhappy and wanted to change her school:

> I want to change to a new school, because I don't like it up there no more. I got bullied and well, the police officer used to come and see me, and a girl found out and she's told everyone at the school, now I just want to move school.
> (Bella, 12 years, lone-parent family)

Her experiences at school had also undermined her confidence in her school friendships, which had left her feeling very isolated; she now felt she had no one to talk to if she had problems:

> No I can't tell 'em 'cos they go and tell their friends or something. (Bella, 12 years, lone-parent family).

Transitions from one school to another can also be daunting for children who have been bullied. Milly had been bullied and did not like school because people were 'horrible' to her; she was worried about what was going to happen to her when she went to secondary school:

Because you hear stuff like they flush your head down toilets and stuff, so I don't want to go. (Milly, 10 years, lone-parent family)

Difficulties Making and Sustaining Friendships

As well as the experiences and fears of bullying, nearly half of the sample were experiencing difficulties either making or sustaining their friendships. There was an underlying assumption that all children have friends in their immediate neighbourhood; however, this was not reflected in children's accounts and 14 children said they did not have friends living nearby. They, along with four others (making nearly half of the sample), had difficulties in seeing school friends, and sustaining the friendships they had made at school. School friends lived too far away to meet after school, and the children in the sample found weekends and holidays quite isolating. Difficulties in accessing transport and the cost of transport were also major factors mentioned by children. In common with many of the children and young people in the study, Carrie rarely got to see her friends out of school because of problems with transport. She wished that she could move nearer to her school friends as she had no friends near to where she lived. Here she explained why she was never able to see her friends out of school:

Because they live so far away and I can't get to them and they can't get to me. 'Cos it's like so much money on the bus to get to their homes, it's really expensive. (Carrie, 15 years, lone-parent family)

Some children felt very isolated and did not feel that they had friends at home or at school. For them friendship was a shifting and insecure thing. Shamus had experienced the loss of friends and the social insecurity this can bring:

Once you lose one friend then you lose the rest of them. (Shamus, 12 years, lone-parent family)

Most of the children had friends but were experiencing great difficulty in maintaining their friendships in the way they thought fit. However, a few of the children appeared particularly socially isolated. Kim had very few friends, and was quite isolated in her home environment. Her family lived in a rural area and there had been some difficulty fitting into the neighbourhood. In general, she did not associate with the children in her area and spent little time outside of the house:

We sometimes play at the park, but without other kids ... I normally play on my own or with my brothers. I hardly ever play with them. (Kim, 11 years, lone-parent family)

For rural children, village life can also be isolating and children can find that they have few children of their own age living in their village. Children and young people are often bused long distances to their rural schools and, without adequate after-school transport, children from low-income families in particular are effectively trapped and contained within their villages (Davis and Ridge, 1997). Sian had few friends of her own age in the village and saw very little of her friends from school; she wished she could see them more:

I've got one [friend] that lives down the road, but she's two years younger than me, I've got no one really my age in the village. (Sian 16 years, two-parent family)

One way in which children [could] see friends who live further away and develop their friendships was to have them to stay the night, quite a common practice in childhood. However, this was not possible for all the children and many of the children said that they were not able or allowed to have friends to stay. In some cases it was a question of space; they were living in crowded conditions and sharing bedrooms, where a visitor would be considered too much extra. For some of the children in the two-parent families, the special needs of the parent of child with a disability meant that having friends to stay was problematic. One of the parents explained how her children were increasingly restricted in their capacity to have friends over even to play:

I'd like to move to a bigger house. I know we've got a roof over our heads and we're very lucky in that respect ... but their father has got a progressive disease in his nervous system and he finds it difficult having them around sometimes, and we haven't really got anywhere they can sort of get away. ... They're having to be quiet a lot of the time and not have their friends round so much as other kids do. (Jackie, two-parent family)

Without space and/or transport, the issue of reciprocity was raised. Parents may be reluctant to let children stay away from home with friends when they are unable to return the gesture. Having children to stay was also costly, and there are not always extra resources to go around. Kevin felt that having less money had made a difference to his friends when they came to stay:

> They've got nicer houses than this one and they like found it cold when they stay in my house because I haven't got central heating. (Kevin, 12 years, lone-parent family)

Stability was important in maintaining friendships and moving can be very disruptive to children's social relationships. Bella had moved five times in her life, and found it very difficult to sustain supportive and lasting friendships. She also suffered from a painful period of bullying at school. She said she would not want to move again because she needed to make friendships that would last, and this was more likely if she could stay in one place:

> I've moved so many times that I like to keep set on one place where I can make new friends, I like to stay here. (Bella, 12 years, lone-parent family)

The significance of friendship for children lies not just in the growth and development of social skills, but also in learning to accept and understand others and to foster social belonging and integration. It is a precious social asset, and one that many of these children and young people, through the effects of poverty and inadequate space and resources, are evidently finding it hard to sustain. The harsh realities of problematic peer relationships are bullying and exclusion. Ambert (1995) argues that bullying can happen simply because children 'do not belong to the proper race, religion, social class, or, even do not wear "appropriate" clothing, do not belong to the "in" groups and do not share in the values and pastimes of their peers' (1995, p. 186). The next section explores one of these factors, the need to wear the 'appropriate' clothing for peer acceptance.

'Fitting In': The Importance of Clothes

Young people use fashion and clothes as a means of making and expressing their identities (Willis et al., 1990). As children get older the relationship between peer inclusion and individuality becomes more complex (Miles, 1996), but for younger children the need to fit in and to feel part of the prevailing peer culture was strong. Previous research has shown that children are under considerable pressure to wear 'acceptable' clothes from an early age (Middleton et al., 1994).

In this study, children themselves identified the importance of clothes, and highlighted their efforts to maintain the 'right' appearance to fit in with their peers. They talked about their relationship with clothes, how important they felt clothes were, and what the implications were for them if they could not sustain an 'appropriate' appearance according to their peers. Carrie sets the scene:

> If you don't wear the right stuff you're like different and that of the crowd, just different. It's right to have the right clothes. (Carrie, 15 years, lone-parent family)

The majority of the children and young people felt that clothes were an important issue for them and those that did not were mainly younger children. Clothes appeared to be marginally more important for girls than for boys, and there were also signs that children in urban areas would be more likely to feel that clothes were important than rural children and young people. This may indicate that urban life might be more socially demanding for children. Age was an important factor in children's perceptions of clothes and the age of 12 seems to be a critical age for self-awareness and self-esteem. Colleen explained how she has changed over time, and how clothes are now much more important than when she was younger:

> When I was about 10 I didn't really care, I just went out and wore whatever, it didn't really matter. But as you grow up you're more conscious about what you're wearing and everything, as you get older it's different. (Colleen, 13 years, lone-parent family)

There were only five children over the age of 12 who were apparently unconcerned about clothes, and their responses revealed that this was not necessarily a comfortable area for them. Stewart was aware of the importance of clothes for self-image and acceptance but he was also realistic about what clothes he was able to afford:

> Some people, what you wear is more like what you are sort of thing. I try to keep myself looking kind of neat sort of thing,

but 'cos I got no choice to wear certain clothes an' that. ... I'm not really worried about what sort of names and things I wear, I just wear what I can get. (Stewart, 16 years lone-parent family)

Why Clothes Are Important

Children were very clear about why they felt that clothes were important, and several reasons were given for needing to have the 'right' clothes. Clothes were needed for children to be able to 'fit in' and be part of a social group. They were also identified as important for protection from bullying and exclusion. Children and young people also talked about the role of clothes in developing their self-esteem and building their confidence. These were not discrete reasons but interlocked and they reinforce each other. It was both reassuring and self-affirming for children to feel that they fitted into the social groups to which they aspired. Many children outlined the consequences of not having the right clothes, either for themselves, or for other children:

If you don't wear trendy stuff ... not so many people will he your friend 'cos of what you wear. (Charlene, 12 years, two-parent family)

You've got to keep going with the trend otherwise you kind of get picked on kind of thing. (Peter, 12 years, lone-parent family)

If they, like, have clothes that they had for quite a while and they've grown out of it, and be, like, sort of too short for them and all, then people call them tramps and smelly and all that. (Cally, 14 years, two-parent family)

As we have seen, the fear of being bullied was very real, and the flipside of being part of the group was being apart. Designer labels were particularly singled out as signifiers of fashion and inclusion, and this was clearly a difficult area to negotiate. Nicole and Amy outlined the perils of not having the right labels on your clothes:

They might have trainers but it would be like, um, like Gola or something like, like really sad make, that people think are sad anyway. And they like get the mickey taken out of them. (Nicole, 13 years, lone-parent family)

Some kids can be really cruel even about what you're wearing. It's sort of like they can be friends with someone and then disown them because they haven't got say Adidas track suit bottoms on. (Amy, 15 years, two-parent family)

Being fashionable was clearly considered important by some children; however, underlying the desire to be fashionable were also worries that their friends would have better clothes than them and the fear of being singled out and different:

If you are like wearing fashion clothes people don't stare at you. If you are wearing like scruffy clothes people just go 'Look, look at him, scrub!', or something like that. (Kevin, 12 years, lone-parent family)

You don't really want like not very nice things, you don't want like holey things. You want like nice clean things and new things. So you don't really want old things. (Nigel, 10 years, two-parent family)

Overall, children and young people did not mention the desire to have all designer label clothing, and this was in some part likely to be a realistic reflection of their inability to get them. Their concern was directed at ensuring that they did not make social gaffes and were not singled out in any way. On the whole, clothes seemed to be an area where these children struggled particularly hard to attain the things they felt that they needed. One child said he would not go out if he did not have the right clothes because he would be too embarrassed; another that he always made sure he had the right clothes.

The Cost of Clothes

Many of the children and young people who were not able to get the clothes they felt they needed were keenly aware that their parents could not afford them:

I would ask my parents to buy me things and then I realized that my parents couldn't afford things. 'Cos I'd sit down and listen to their conversations and then I stopped asking for things and saved up for them. And that's been ever since I was about D's age, since I was about eight because I was a quick learner. (Nell, 17 years, two-parent family)

It's like all the fashion and like sports stuff and that. And it's really expensive and mum won't be able to afford it so I wouldn't be able to have it. (Nicole, 13 years, lone-parent family)

Clearly the cost of buying new clothes was prohibitive and children and young people were keenly aware of the cost; many had devised a variety of strategies to get the clothes. Some children would save up and buy their own clothes through catalogues, and for the young people who were working, this had made a considerable difference in their ability to get such clothes:

> I'd rather buy for myself 'cos I like to be the same as my friends and my mum can't afford it. So I just save up for myself, so my mum don't have to pay. (Laura, 15 years, lone-parent family)

However, as we saw in the previous chapter, many children were not working and they were also not able to access regular pocket money to be able to save. For these children the disadvantages of having the wrong clothes appeared to be particularly acute:

> I just want to fit in the group, 'cos it's like I get . . . people take the mick out of me because I can't afford things. Like my trainers are messy and they don't suit me and I need new trainers and new clothes . . . I can't get decent clothes like everyone else does. (Bella, 12 years, lone-parent family)

> If you haven't got the right clothes and all your friends have got all the nice clothes you feel left out like, 'cos like you think to yourself, 'Oh they've got all the good clothes and they've got all the money to buy them' and that and you feel left out . . . I sometimes like get really worried if like I've got all these old fashioned clothes and I don't like them and everyone else has fashionable ones. (Sue, 11 years, lone-parent family)

Gaining Confidence from Looking Good

Where children and young people had managed to dress in a way that pleased them and conformed to the prevailing fashion demands, they singled out the feelings of self-confidence and self-esteem that followed; looking good was an important part of feeling good:

> It's all about my confidence really, if I feel good in what I'm wearing I can talk to people better and stuff. (Amy, 15 years, two-parent family)

> I'm very fussy about clothes . . . I don't know why but I can't go out and look horrible, 'cos I feel like people are watching me and that and I have to go out looking presentable. I can't go out and look scruffy or anything like that. I won't go out if I look scruffy, I won't do it. (Colleen, 13 years, lone-parent family)

The importance of clothes, and in particular the capacity to wear the 'right' clothes, to maintain a degree of social acceptance within peer groups, has been plainly revealed. Children maintained that suitable standards of clothing were needed in order to 'fit in' and to feel part of their social groups. The disadvantages of not having the 'right' clothes were revealed through children's fears of isolation, bullying and exclusion. However, the cost of buying the 'right' clothes was prohibitive, and children showed a keen awareness of the tensions between needing to have the 'right' clothes and being able to afford them.

'Joining In': Social Experiences at School

Recent anti-poverty policy measures intended to address children's social and developmental needs have been directed mainly through school, and have focused almost entirely on improving literacy and numeracy standards (DSS, 1999*b*), and tackling truancy and school exclusions (SEU, 1998*c*). While these are critical and important issues in children's lives, the degree of social inclusion that children experience at school and at home is also vital. There is an underpinning assumption of parity of opportunity and experiences between children within school that is rarely challenged. There has been little interest or debate about the potential for education to be exclusionary and divisive between children and young people from low-income families and their more affluent peers.

Current education policy is increasingly driven by demands to improve academic standards. But school also plays a particularly significant role in children's lives as a site of social as well as pedagogical learning. There is increasing interest in school as an environment for developing 'soft skills'[1] for future employability. Children's learning intersects with their home and community environment, and this consequently leads to different experiences and outcomes (Pollard and Filer, 1996). Therefore, how children from low-income families experience school may well be mediated by the constraints of their home environment. Yet there is very little knowledge or understanding of how children in poverty might experience school, or the impact of low income on their school lives. This section explores with children their social experiences at school, and their capacity to engage with school life and participate in school social activities.

[. . .]

School Uniforms

The previous section has shown the importance attached to wearing the 'right' clothing, particularly for fitting into the social groups to which children and young people aspire. This awareness of clothing codes also extended to the school environment where children and young people spend a large part of their day in social interaction with their peers. The insistence of schools on a uniform has long been recognised as having a protective effect for children. However, although children acknowledged and confirmed the value of school uniform, they also revealed a sharp awareness of the subtler nuances of clothing codes that can override those protective effects. Several children pointed to things that could jeopardise that:

Well it's important to have a decent school uniform because like you see some people going there and they haven't got enough money to buy like the uniform so they are in like different things. (Sue, 11 years, lone-parent family)

[Uniform is] quite good yeah because they can't take the mick out of you if you've got like no named stuff. But you still 'ave to 'ave good trainers or good shoes. (Charlene, 12 years, two-parent family)

'Mufti Day'

Children and young people also identified certain occasions when they were particularly vulnerable. One such occasion highlighted by many was 'mufti day' (a day free of school uniform), when they found it difficult to find the right clothes to wear, and in some cases were really anxious leading up to the day and on the day itself. The common experience was of not having enough of the 'right' clothes to wear:

Sometimes I don't know what to wear 'cos I ain't got much stuff. (Charlene, 12 years, two-parent family)

You spend about two weeks planning what you are wearing, discuss it with everyone just to make sure you are wearing the right things. (Carrie, 15 years, lone-parent family)

Amy found mufti day particularly worrying, and she explained why she was so against having them at school:

When I was younger I wore something in one time, and then a couple of months later we had another non-uniform day, I wore it again and I was worried about that but no one noticed. But I was very 'Oh my God, what if everyone notices I've worn it twice' sort of thing. . . . I don't think [we] should have to pay for non-uniform days. In fact, I don't think we should have non-uniform days. Because I like the idea of a uniform 'cos everyone's the same and you ain't got to worry about what other people are wearing and it's so much better. I just don't think it's right. (Amy, 15 years, two-parent family)

As well as needing to ensure that they had the 'right' kind of uniform and shoes, there were other demands on children and their families to provide school bags, equipment and stationery:

People were always on top of each other like 'Oh you've got that bag, why haven't you got Umbro or Nike or something like that'. Which I did 'cos I would make sure dad would like get them for me. I wouldn't be out. (Lisa, 15 years, two-parent family)

Like we've got to work out all this money for school bags and stationery, and then you've got a uniform that when it gets too small for you as well you've got to keep paying every two years or something. It gets expensive. (Nicole, 13 years, lone-parent family)

[. . .]

Not Going on School Trips

Half of the children in the study did not go on school trips with any regularity; some of these children were also not going on any holidays with their families. [. . .] In these cases, a trip away with the school could have played an especially significant role in the children's social lives. One child had only ever been on one holiday and that was with his school. Cost was cited as a major cause of children missing out. Several of the more expensive trips involved children going to Germany or France to improve their language skills and to experience life in countries which they were studying. However, these children were also being excluded from the more general cheaper options:

I wanted to go to Germany and it was about a hundred odd quid and mum goes 'No'. It's like we go on a ferry, coach, really posh ferry, hotel, we get to meet friends there. And mum she said no. So I missed that. ... I always miss out on the school trips and everything. (Bella, 12 years, lone-parent family)

There was like Alton Towers trips and things like that that I couldn't go on ... School trips were quite expensive, like we had this week at school where you could do different activities each day, and I'd end up doing like the free ones or the ones that didn't cost much 'cos everything else was too expensive. (Cherry, 17 years, lone-parent family)

When children did not go on school trips with their peers the social repercussions rippled far wider than the immediate impact of not sharing in the experiences of others on the day. School trips, particularly special occasions when children stay away, have a social excitement about them from the outset, and this can extend well past the actual event, enriched and informed by the retelling of memories and stories of the trip. Amy describes how she missed out on a special school trip and how she still feels uncomfortable and excluded from her friends' shared experiences of the trip:

Year 7 there was a French trip, it was one day and you stayed overnight on the ferry and most people went but I didn't go. ... I don't know it was a lot of money for one day. ... But even now my friends sometimes bring it up and I'm like 'Oh I didn't go. I can't talk about it'. (Amy, 15 years, two-parent family)

Alternative sources of income to help children from lone-parent families go on trips would seem to be absent parents; however, only one child talked about receiving any help from her absent mother to go on a trip:

When people are talking about it I feel quite 'Oh I wonder if dad's going to let me go ... '. We went to London, that was the last trip we went to. That was the thing I was really worried because I knew within me that I really wanted to go, 'cos it was drama. It was going to see Miss Saigon and we also got to go to the Tate Gallery ... I wanted to go, and I knew I wanted to go and I was determined to go. So I was like well if dad says he can't then I'm going to write to my mum and ask her to send me the money. (Lisa, 15 years, two-parent family)

Schools generally provide a range of trips, some of which might be free or very cheap. However, having cheaper alternative options does not necessarily mean that children do not feel left out. For some children not going on trips also meant that they had to stay in school working, while their peers went away, and this was seen as particularly isolating and unfair.

Children Who Were Excluding Themselves

Of greatest concern must be the children who are excluding themselves from school trips. Several of the children in the study who were not going on any school trips indicated that they were very disillusioned with the process. In these cases children indicated that they felt there was no point even asking to go on trips so they didn't. In effect, these children were excluding themselves. Martin attended a large school where there were a lot of regular trips away and activities; here he talks about being resigned to not sharing in them:

I don't usually go on trips 'cos they are expensive and that ... At our school they do loads of activities and they go to loads of different places ... I don't bother asking. (Martin, 11 years, two-parent family)

Finding Resources to Participate Effectively at School

Another area of difficulty mentioned by children and young people in the study was ensuring adequate resources for school to be able to participate fully. As we have seen, access to school uniforms was constrained; however, children and young people also highlighted difficulties obtaining books, stationery and bags for school, particularly in comparison with other children.

GCSE projects were also mentioned as an area where young people were struggling to sustain themselves, and where they felt having less money coming in was affecting them. School projects which are part of assessed course work caused particular difficulties, and young people were very aware of the need to keep up with others in the year, who would be examined alongside them. Amy had difficulty finding the money she needed for her textiles project, and then had to find more for an enterprise project:

Projects, it's just I got to do this business enterprise and you've got to make it as much as a business as you can. ... I mean I was with a group, I put in my money and they weren't getting the stuff, so me and my friend split from them and we've done our own now. But I had to put in more money. (Amy, 15 years, two-parent family)

Brad had also had problems, and explained that he was especially aware of the differences between him and some of the other young people in his year. He had to find a suitable project to make for design technology GCSE, with a limited budget. This was something he would be marked on and given a final grade for, and he was afraid that he would be disadvantaged and his work viewed less favourably:

Like we're now doing this thing for my design technology GCSE, and you've got to design something and make it. And like there's people designing like things that will cost them like £300 and things like that, and mine cost £12.99 to build. ... There's people building things for their cars that they'll get when they're 17. Things like that. I'll be lucky if I get one by the time I'm 19 I expect. (Brad, 15 years, two-parent family)

As well as material resources, social costs were also evident, particularly where children were likely to arrange to do things as a group. Shared social activities at school, such as school discos and fetes, can be particularly exposing for children who are trying to manage on a low income:

Like my friends are like saying are you doing this or are you doing that and I say no, 'cos I haven't got enough money or something like that. If they arrange to do something and I haven't got the money I say 'No I can't do it I ain't got enough money'. (Laura, 15 years, lone-parent family)

Well say I cancel like if they are sort of having a school fair there or something. My friends ... they are really good and they sort of like give me money and say 'There, go and get something with this'. (Sue, 11 years, lone-parent family)

[...]

Parents' Concerns about the Cost of Education

The cost of ensuring that their children are receiving an equitable education with their peers was a matter of considerable concern for parents on a low income. On top of the costs of providing a school uniform, and paying for school trips, parents are also increasingly asked for contributions towards their children's schooling (Middleton et al., 1997). For parents in the study these extra costs add worry and strain. As Tilly explained, even a seemingly reasonable sum, like £2, can strain an over-tight budget:

All the time they're bringing home something that wants money and even things they're doing in school wants money ... they did a medieval thing and you had to pay for that to cover food. Which obviously it's a contribution so you don't have to pay, but you have to give it to them otherwise he's singled out, see what I mean, then he's the one who feels awful. It might only be £2 but £2 is £2. Then there is cooking, he's started cooking now and that's ingredients every week. (Tilly, two-parent family)

For families like Jen's, where there were several children at school, the cost burden was even greater, and hard choices had to be made about priorities:

In sewing they had to have £2.50 for a cushion. I know it's not a lot but out of every week's money it is a lot, and then school photos, and then my middle one is making a box, like an ottoman box and he keeps, mum I need this, and it's costing me well up to now £30 just for wood and screws. So that week we have to have not a lot of shopping I'm afraid. (Jen, lone parent)

It was evident that increasing demands from schools were making some parents feel very frustrated and angry, and in some instances were creating tensions between children and their parents. In Hannah's case it was her children who had to explain to the school why she was unable to pay the full amount:

It's just that I can't pay that much. All right if it's a pound, two pound. But swimming they want like ten pounds. So all right maybe I try to give like two to three pound like a donation or something, but that's it. K ... comes home and says 'mum they want to know why you've not paid a lot of money'. [I say] 'Tell 'em to sod off' sort of thing you know. They're forever asking for money at K's school for this that and the other. (Hannah, lone parent)

It was evident that the costs of adequate school participation were increasing and both children and their parents were aware of the pressures maintaining school appearances create. Solutions to some of these issues may lie in increased in-kind provision of goods and services in schools for children from low-income families. One of the few instances of this kind of provision was the free school meals service. [...]

Summary

Peer relationships play a critical role in children's lives in the development of self and social identity. Friendships and social relationships are valuable social assets, furthering social and material interests, providing support and enhancing social identity and social status (Allan, 1989). These values are reflected in the children's accounts of their friendships. However, friendships are rarely unproblematic, and the flipside of having friends and feeling socially included can be exclusion and bullying. Bullying was a significant issue for these children and nearly half of them had experienced bullying, either ongoing or in the recent past, and for some children it was sustained over a long duration. Their fears and their negative experiences of exclusion and bullying are apparent from their accounts.

Being able to wear adequate and suitable clothing also emerged as an important issue, and one that was identified by children themselves as socially significant. Their accounts reveal a high sensitivity to the nuances of fashion and the implications of being seen as not conforming to current fashion. Wearing the right clothes gave them the capability to sustain themselves within the clothing expectations of their peers and to avoid stigma, bullying and exclusion that could follow from 'inappropriate' clothing. However, the cost of getting the right clothes was prohibitive, and the children's accounts reveal some of the pressures they experienced in their endeavours to ensure that they were socially included.

By children's own accounts, schools are manifestly failing to provide them with a sufficiently inclusive social environment for their needs. They revealed school life to be fraught with the problems of bullying, material disadvantage and structural exclusion from shared activities through financial hardship. Half of these children were not going on school trips with their peers, some of them were self-excluding, feeling that the cost was too high even to approach their parents. As well as the dangers of exclusion from shared social activities, children were also keenly aware that material costs were affecting their school involvement, particularly during examination years when there were extra demands related to project costs and educational trips.

[...]

NOTE

1. Employers in the UK are increasingly stressing the importance of 'soft skills'. These are poorly defined at present but include personal qualities, friendliness, teamwork, communication skills, the ability to fit in and so on (Sparkes, 1999).

Education and the Middle Class: A Complex but Crucial Case for the Sociology of Education

Sally Power and Geoff Whitty

Introduction

Until recently, remarkably little had been written explicitly about the relationship between education and the middle class. In part, this reflects a broader absence within sociology. As Butler and Savage (1995: p. vii) point out, 'traditionally, the social scientific gaze has been directed either downwards, to the working classes, the poor and the dispossessed, or upwards, to the wealthy and powerful'. However, it is an absence that is becoming increasingly problematic for the study of education as the number of people deemed to be 'middle class' grows and as the conventional indicators of success and failure shift upwards and become harder to define.

While we are some way short of Blair's (1999) vision of a one-class Britain in which the 'old establishment' is replaced by 'a new, larger, more meritocratic middle class ... that will include millions of people who traditionally see themselves as working class', there is little doubt that the middle class has expanded. Thirty years ago, only 14 per cent of the adult population were classed as belonging to professional or managerial groups and 36 per cent of the population were in non-manual occupations (Punt 1975). More recent figures show that half the population are now in non-manual jobs and about 30 per cent are classed as being in managerial or professional positions (Mills 1995).

This expansion is likely to be especially significant for our understanding of the relationship between schooling and social reproduction. Unlike the very few 'wealthy and powerful', whose assets are such that privilege can be passed down irrespective of external accreditation, members of the middle class have largely depended upon the credentials bestowed by the education system in order to acquire or hold on to their position. Although there is some evidence to suggest that educational qualifications are even more crucial for the working class in securing middle-class status (Goldthorpe 2003), the middle class has traditionally been defined by education inasmuch as its market power is based principally upon credentials (Giddens 1973).

And just as the hard line distinguishing 'white-collar' and 'blue-collar' workers is blurring, or at least is becoming less relevant as the principal means of classifying socio-economic differences, so the expansion of educational qualifications has rendered what counts as educational success and educational failure less straightforward. There was a time when obtaining any qualifications and staying on beyond the legal school leaving age indicated educational success. But the expansion of credentials, together with the limited number of employment opportunities for unskilled school-leavers, mean that the majority of school leavers now obtain some form of qualification and increasingly go on to higher education. Analysis of the 9,000 young people still remaining in the 1970 British Cohort Study shows that 21 per cent went on to get degrees compared to only 12 per cent from the 1958 National Child Development Survey Cohort (Bynner et al. 1997). The expanding numbers staying on in the education system means that the possession of qualifications may not in itself be enough to secure the desired occupational destination.

A sociology of educating the middle class is important not only because of demographic and educational changes such as these, it is also important analytically. The relative lack of a visible presence for the middle class reflects the extent to which it has been 'normalized' within the field. In much the same way as 'whiteness' has only recently been granted the same attention as 'blackness', and gender studies focus on masculinity as well as 'women's issues', issues concerning a relational concept such as class cannot be properly illuminated without looking at the middle class as well as the working class. Of course, much of the existing literature on education and the working class is implicitly about the educational strategies of the middle class. However, more explicit sociological exploration of the middle class as a social category will not only extend our understanding of the reproduction of an increasingly large section of the population, but will also enrich our understanding of the processes of social and cultural reproduction overall.

Representations of the Middle Class

In claiming that sociologists have largely overlooked the education of the middle class, we are not suggesting that the middle class is absent from sociological accounts. It has, however, rarely been the *focus* of the investigation—but rather the background against which the perspectives and experiences of the working class have been contrasted. The middle class exists in many studies predominantly as the symbol of success against which the structural disadvantages of others are compared. This has led to a partial and somewhat oversimplified version of the complex but crucial relationship between education and the middle class. In this chapter, we explore some of these oversimplifications: (1) the dominance of the middle class; (2) middle-class homogeneity; (3) schools as middle-class institutions; (4) the inevitability of educational success; and (5) representations of middle-class attributes and orientations.

The Dominance of the Middle Class

The contrast between middle-class success and working-class failure within much sociology of education has led to the impression of middle-class omnipotence. Coming from very different positions, both Holly (1974) and Musgrove (1979) have critiqued this position. Over thirty years ago and drawing on a Marxist perspective, Holly (1974: 107) complained that 'a class system which has a bottom and a middle but no top makes nonsense. How strange that we hear so much of the "working" class and "middle" class while we hear almost nothing about any "upper" class.' He cites moves away from selection and streaming in schools as evidence of the lack of power of the middle class to prevent progressive change. But Musgrove (1979: 114), in a blistering attack on such neo-Marxist perspectives in general (and Holly's support for comprehensive schools in particular), comes to the very same conclusion, claiming that 'Clerks and teachers are not "hegemonic", and it is patent logical absurdity to put the middle at the top.'

It is clear that the position of the middle class is problematic. Confusion is compounded by language. As Williams (1983) notes, the concept of a middle class is based on an image of a ranked social hierarchy where it is squeezed between an upper and a lower class. The term 'lower class' has largely become obsolete, particularly in sociology where the term 'working class' is far more common. However, the concept of a working class (set against a ruling class) derives from a strong relational (and conflictual) understanding of social structure. The two contrasting conceptions of social structure do not sit easily together. With reference to strong relational understandings of class, as Mann (1993) argues, the 'problem' of the middle class is usually seen as a subset of a different class 'problem'—that of the relationship between the capitalist and working classes. Orthodox Marxism (which would include Holly's position) would place some members of the middle class within the working class. It is somewhat surprising then that the sociology of education, despite Holly's and Musgrove's pleas, usually seems to place the middle class within what Mann (1993: 547) refers to as 'an occasional pessimistic Marxian response' and make them part of the ruling bourgeois or capitalist class. According to Musgrove (1979: 114) this is not only a 'patent logical absurdity', it may have unfortunate consequences in that it: '... simply diverts attention from the great, commanding heights of power, wealth and privilege. And the almost incredible irony is that this facile, ill conceived, and really very foolish analysis undermines the only serious opposition that real power and dominance have recently faced.' Of course, dimensions of 'power, wealth and privilege' are relative and complicated. Social class differences in educational attainment can be explained in terms of three forms of capital: economic capital, social capital, and cultural capital. It may be that the middle class has considerable cultural capital, although, as we shall see, even this is probably limited to particular fractions of the middle class.

The Assumed Homogeneity of the Middle Class

Because middle-class students are often only points of contrast against which the various experiences of working-class students are set, they are typically treated as a relatively undifferentiated group. However, as the middle class has expanded it has become increasingly internally differentiated—in terms of both vertical and horizontal distinctions. Our own research, like that of the very few other empirical studies focusing on the middle class (Delamont 1984*a*, 1984*b*; Aggleton 1987; Ball 2003; Brooks 2003), indicates that these distinctions are intimately connected to education provision.

Our own ongoing research (Edwards et al. 1989; Power et al. 2003, 2005) based on a cohort of some 350 academically able middle-class students shows how, even within this group, different educational pathways consolidate vertical differentiation within the middle class. Although the overwhelming majority of our respondents are 'getting on', most of those who are getting on 'famously' attended private schools and elite universities. Some schools, notably those that are private and academically selective, feed a greater proportion of their students into high-status universities which then provide pathways into high-status occupations and high incomes.

In addition to vertical differentiation, though, there is horizontal differentiation. Indeed, some argue that the extent of differentiation is such that we should refer to the middle class*es*. Savage et al. (1992), for instance, identify lines of horizontal differentiation that are based upon the ownership of distinctive types of asset. They identify three distinct middle classes; the petite bourgeoisie holding property assets, managers holding organisational assets and professionals holding cultural capital.[1] The first of these, the petit bourgeoisie, has been relatively unimportant a grouping in the UK, but the divide between the managerial and professional class is, they argue, fundamental to any understanding of the middle classes. Indeed, Hanlon (1998) argues that we are currently seeing a struggle between the managerial and the professional classes and between managerial and professional elements within both groups. To some extent this has led to a blurring of the distinction as the 'professions' have become more managerialized and management roles more professionalized.

In our own middle-class cohort there have been high levels of movement between those in managerial and those in professional roles. Moves from professional to managerial roles appear to be largely associated with upward progression within a career. However, movement from managerial to professional occupations was often the result of 'sideways' movement. This may relate to Fielding's (1995) claim that managerial occupations are riskier than professional careers and it might be particularly the case for women as they cope with the contingencies of increasing domestic responsibilities.

Others have claimed to identify other sources of division. Dunleavy (1980) and Perkin (1989) argue that one main cleavage in the middle class is based on the sector of employment. Those in the public sector derive their economic and ideological support from the state while those in the private sector derive their support from the market. As both the state and the market compete for resources, the economic and ideological positionings of each group remain distinctive and conflictual. We certainly identified evidence of this distinction in our cohort. Students whose parents worked in the private sector were more likely to have attended private schools and were more likely to be working in the private sector than those who had been to state schools. This sectoral allegiance was also evident in voting preferences. However, as with the distinction between professional and managerial sections of the middle class, this relation between sector of schooling, occupational differentiation, and political allegiance may well be blurring. This is partly the result of changes in the employment structure, such as the 'contracting' out of public services to private-sector providers. If the sector of employment is a crucial factor in middle-class cleavages, there may well be significant shifts in the relative strength and allegiances of fractions of the middle class.

A similar, but rather different, cleavage has been identified in terms of the field of production. In 1987, Berger commented that '[c]ontemporary Western societies are characterised by a protracted conflict between two classes, the "old" middle class (occupied in the production and distribution of material goods and services) and a "new" middle class (occupied in the production and distribution of symbolic knowledge)'. Education provided one of the main battlegrounds for this 'protracted conflict' and it is possible to argue that many of the skirmishes around progressive or traditional education and comprehensive or selective schooling were driven by the oppositional values and preferences of these two 'classes' as they struggled to define an education system that would privilege their respective socialization practices (see Bernstein 1977; Power and Whitty 2002). With reference to our own cohort, there were clear preferences amongst 'new' middle-class parents for schools that were non-selective and more progressive; in contrast, 'old' middle-class parents tried to find schools that were more selective and traditional.

Schools as Middle-Class Institutions

Another common assertion which relates to the assumed homogeneity of the middle class and the assumed success of middle-class students (considered next) is the often-made claim that schools are 'middle-class' institutions.

Reay (1998: 52) for instance, talks about working-class women being silenced through 'not being able to speak the language of middle-class institutions'. Inasmuch as teachers are, by definition, middle class then it can be argued that the schools they teach in are middle-class institutions. It is also the case that the middle class gets more out of schools than the working class—but then it probably does out of all organizations—whether they be hospitals or shops. However, it is true that schools are more explicitly involved in the transmission of the dominant culture than many other institutions (Whitty 1985).

Nevertheless, calling schools 'middle-class institutions' glosses over important differences between them. Willis's (1977) Hammertown Boys and Corrigan's (1979) Cullingham Secondary and Municipal Comprehensive do not feel particularly middle class and are certainly very different from Delamont's (1984*a*) St Luke's or even Lacey's (1970) Hightown Grammar. Even within those schools that might be seen to cater specifically for the middle class, there is huge variation. Bernstein comments on the

> spectrum of British public schools, which over the last hundred years has created a range of social types out of the beatings of Harrow and the subtle spontaneity of Summerhill. The British middle class can not only ensure its privileged position in education, but through the public school system it can select which social type. In a way the British public school system is a system for generating not a finite range of sentences, but *social types*. I know of no other middle class which has the possibility of such a differentiated form of socialization. (1977: 18, his emphasis).

The statement that schools are 'middle class' can therefore be an unhelpful shorthand unless we know precisely how and in what ways. Schools are institutions that have their own cultures and their own rules which are, as Bernstein's body of work argues, underpinned by complex relations to social class. Undoubtedly there is greater congruence of values between some homes and some schools, but this cannot merely be presumed in particular cases.

As already mentioned, the schools our middle-class respondents attended had very different cultures. Using Bernstein's (1977) distinction between the expressive order (to do with conduct, character, and manner) and the instrumental order (concerned with the acquisition of specific skills and bodies of knowledge) we were able to map out the dimensions of variation and show how different schools were 'open' or 'closed' with social relations that were respectively 'differentiated' or 'stratified' (Power et al. 1998). By mapping these properties against family attributes, we were able to show how middle-class children grew to be variously 'committed', 'detached', 'estranged', or 'alienated' throughout their educational careers. These complex responses lead one to question another commonly held assumption about the middle class—that success is guaranteed.

The Inevitability of Middle-Class Success

There is often an implicit assumption within the sociology of education that for the middle-class student academic progress is painless and a successful path through higher education into a prestigious occupation assured. That this is not always so, and the implications of this 'failure', is one of the most neglected areas of sociological research. There is no doubt that proportionately middle-class children do better than working-class children—but the extent of middle-class 'underachievement' is larger than is often assumed. For instance, even if we look back to the tripartite system which was seen to sanction class advantages institutionally, we find sizeable middle-class failure. Comparison of 11+ pass rates from two LEAs (Swift 1965) shows that while it is the case that only 2 per cent of children from Social Class VI passed the test, it is also true that 46 per cent of those from Social Class I failed the test. If we look at Social Class II, the majority of children (61%) failed the test. In connection with staying-on rates, one-fifth (22%) of boys from Social Class I and nearly two-thirds (61%) from Social Class II left schools at 15 years of age or before (obtained from the 1961 census and cited in Meighan 1981).

Even those who 'succeed' in conventional terms, though, may experience 'failure' in relative terms. Our own respondents' profiles revealed high levels of success in school and university examinations, but many achieved less than had been predicted for them. Their retrospective accounts communicate disappointment, regret, and even outright hostility towards their schools. Their narratives certainly indicate that the translation of educational promise into educational success is rarely easy or straightforward—irrespective of socio-economic background or kind of school attended. Half the interviewees had some form of 'troubled' or 'broken' progression, even though the majority 'got there' in the end. A significant minority had to retake their A-levels to achieve required entry qualifications, dropped out of their initially chosen degree programme, entered or returned to higher education after an unplanned period of casual employment, or failed to find the kind of employment which they believed their graduate qualifications merited.

These findings suggest that we need to have more sophisticated definitions of what counts as 'success'. The expansion of higher education and increasing credentialization has led to a more explicit demarcation of the 'educated' from the 'uneducated', but it has simultaneously led to more implicit demarcation between the 'educated' and the 'well-educated'. Additionally, there are clearly different levels of expectations of educational success within different sections of the middle class that render what would count as considerable achievement in one group a notable failure in another. The greater the expectations, the higher the risks. As one of our respondents, who struggled to come to terms with not getting into Oxford, commented: 'it was further to fall from ... Failure from ordinary life is bad enough, but failing from such a high point makes it even worse'. As Ehrenreich (1990) has argued, it is 'fear of falling' that is the distinctive feature of 'the inner life of the middle class'.

Of course, it could be argued that middle-class failure does not merit significant attention because it is less of a 'problem' than working-class failure. This is certainly true in terms of a presumption that being middle class is a desirable attribute. Social mobility data suggest that middle-class families are more successful in maintaining their position inter-generationally than working-class families are in improving theirs (Goldthorpe 2003; Blanden et al.

2005). But, while middle-class failure may be exceptional (though less so than is often assumed), on an individual level this can make it particularly wounding.

There are strong analytical reasons for exploring such cases. Sociological approaches to understanding education are strong in explaining (albeit in divergent ways) the unexceptional success of middle-class students and the unexceptional failure of working-class students. But they are much less developed in explaining exceptional success and failure—which is often, therefore, accounted for in terms of individual rather than social factors. Exceptionality can then become evidence against sociological interpretations. For instance, the construction of the 'bright' working-class and the 'dull' middle-class student (Saunders 1996) promotes asociological accounts of ability and intelligence. The scope of sociological explanation within education would be significantly broadened and strengthened if it extended beyond accounting for unexceptional outcomes to unravel exceptional outcomes too.

Middle-Class Attributes

Another by-product of using the middle class as a backdrop to studies of the working class is that they take on characteristics only in contrast to those attributed to the working class. This creates some interesting inconsistencies in sociological accounts.

In studies of school choice, for example, the middle class is seen to be strategic and calculating: the 'skilled' choosers (e.g. Gewirtz et al. 1995; Macrae et al. 1996; Ball 2003). Middle-class parents, and in particular middle-class mothers (see Power forthcoming), are portrayed in a manner which is often pejorative. Branlinger and her colleagues (1996: 586) from the US, for instance, interviewed a number of mothers in the mid-1990s about school choice and concluded:

> It was evident that the mothers we interviewed wanted to perceive themselves—and be perceived—as liberals who were just and compassionate people. On the other hand, they harbored illiberal views related to desire for privileged status for their children. Ideological modes of operation maintained liberal image and disguised self-interested school preferences . . .

Working-class parents are seen as less self-interested. In relation to school choice, for instance, '[t]here is a collectivity to choosing, in contrast to the individuality of the child-matching strategies of the privileged' (Gewirtz et al. 1995: 48). They are 'disconnected' from the market and tend to choose local schools 'partly as a result of a positive attachment to the locality and to going to school with friends and family' (p. 183).

It is sometimes implied that their attributes are not just different, but that working-class values and practices are *better*. This might be explained as an attempt to value and validate the accounts and experiences of the disadvantaged. As Gillborn (1998) argues, there is a frequent misreading of Becker's (1967; Becker cited in Verhoeven 1989) 'Whose side are we on?' which suggests that sociologists have a 'kind of sentimental and quasi-political imperative . . . to side with "the underdog"'. So that while the working class in these studies is described warmly in terms of community and solidarity, the middle class is seen as calculating and competitive. The working class thinks and acts collectively, whereas the middle class is individualistic.

Because the middle class is defined in opposition, however, other accounts present them differently. Where the working class are attributed with 'savvy', the middle class are presented not as percipient strategists, but as blinkered conformists. In Willis's account, for instance, it is the working-class 'lads' whose understandings: ' . . . involve a partial penetration of the really determining conditions of existence of the working class which are definitely superior to those official versions of their reality which are proffered through the school and various state agencies' (Willis 1977: 3). Although Willis acknowledges that these penetrations work against rather than for the success of individual students, it is the working-class students who gain his respect.[2] The disdain with which the middle-class or aspiring middle-class conformists are held is apparent in the following passage: 'the term "ear 'ole" itself connotes the passivity and absurdity of the school conformists for "the lads". It seems that they are always listening, never *doing*: never animated with their social internal life, but formless in rigid reception.' (p. 14). Like the parental choice studies cited, Willis holds that the working class act and think collectively. Indeed, he claims that their grasp of the difference between *individual* and *group* logic leads them to understand that conformism has no rewards for the working class as a whole—'a profound critique of the dominant ideology of individualism in our society' (1977: 129). While the distinction between an individualistic middle class and a collective working class has the attraction of analytical simplicity, it is often hard to discern. It is difficult to know what the difference is between 'collective' and 'individual' practice—as most social practices involve the latter even if they arise out of, or have consequences for, the former. Moreover, the distinction is often difficult to support empirically. Willis himself concedes that working-class 'collectivism' is only partial—in that 'individuals are still behaving perhaps individualistically and competitively in some things and in the private spheres of their lives' (ibid.). Conversely, Reay found middle-class mothers were very effective at networking and working together (e.g. organizing a petition) to achieve their ends. Indeed she goes so far as to claim that 'contemporary *collective* middle-class action has led to increasing class and racial segregation' (p. 161, our emphasis).

Such work sometimes makes it appear that working-class disadvantage can be directly attributed to middle-class desires for maintaining advantage. In some accounts of parental choice, middle-class parents are presented as the key instigators of recent policies which have further damaged educational equity. For instance, Gewirtz et al. (1995) and, more recently, Ball (2003) seem to imply that the creation of an education market was itself a middle-class strategy designed to preserve middle-class advantages that had been eroded over recent years. While the relational nature of class and the importance of education as a positional good mean that we do need to consider middle-class advantage and working-class disadvantage as connected, the nature of the connection is over-simplified.

First, the concept of 'a middle-class strategy' is again based on an assumption of a relatively homogenous middle class disadvantaging the working class. As we have already argued, many of the battles over education are better interpreted as battles between sections of the middle class for ascendancy. In doing so, they adopt different strategies. While some of the most recent arrivals have followed the example of the 'old' middle class by making use of the private sector, the majority of middle-class parents have—in different ways—made state-maintained schools 'safe' for their children (see Whitty 2001). Secondly, there is little evidence to suggest that middle-class advantages were actually in any serious danger of being eroded before the introduction of market-oriented reforms. Elements of the middle class have always shown themselves remarkably adept at benefiting from successive reforms—including, and despite Holly's (1974) fears, the shift from selective schooling to comprehensivization. Thirdly, while the middle-class vote is certainly important in securing electoral victory, the ways in which middle-class anxieties influence state policy is far from straightforward. The attribution of agency in these processes needs to be handled carefully if it is not to be confused with malice or bad faith.

Conclusion

This chapter has sought to argue that the lack of an adequate sociology of the middle class has created a number of absences and analytical inconsistencies within contemporary sociology of education. Some of the problems we have identified probably lie in the inadequate conceptualization of the middle class within contemporary sociology of education to which we alluded earlier. While it is unsatisfactory, especially in relation to education, to take the orthodox Marxist approach of placing the employed middle class within the working class, it is equally unsatisfactory to make them part of the ruling class. It is perhaps more accurate to see them as occupying contradictory class locations and adopting ambiguous class positions (Wright 1982; Ehrenreich and Ehrenreich 1979).

A more fine-grained analysis of the crucial relationship between education and the middle class and the complex ways in which schools foster differentiated middle-class identities can throw new light on some of the enduring issues within the sociology of education. In particular, it can help illuminate how 'success' is constructed and distributed and how this success contributes to social and cultural reproduction. The picture may become more complex, but it is surely an important task for the sociology of education to unravel such complexity rather than to ignore it or to use it to celebrate indeterminacy.

NOTES

This chapter draws upon Power (2001) 'Missing: a sociology of educating the middle class', in J. Demaine (ed.), *Sociology of Education Today* (Basingstoke: Palgrave), and the findings of our ongoing research on education and the middle class (Power et al. 2003; Power et al. 2005).

1. These are somewhat similar to Mann's (1993: 549) threefold division of the middle class into the petit bourgeoisie (proprietors of small, familial businesses), careerists (employees moving up corporate and bureaucratic hierarchies), and professionals ('learned', collectively organized occupations licensed by the state).
2. Although Willis does distance himself from the 'lads' on occasions, his allegiance is, at least implicitly, with them.

From Social Ties to Social Capital: Class Differences in the Relations Between Schools and Parent Networks

Erin McNamara Horvat, Elliot B. Weininger, and Annette Lareau

[...]

The concept of social capital has undergone a meteoric rise to prominence over the last 15 years, as even a brief search of publication databases throughout the social sciences will document. Moreover, above and beyond its prominence in various subspecialties of sociology, political science, and neighboring disciplines, the concept's reach now extends into more distant fields such as public health (Hawe and Schiell, 2000; Morrow, 1999, 2000) and public housing research (Lang and Hornburg, 1998); it has also been placed on the agenda in various policy debates (see, for example, Woolcock, 1998).

This prominence is clearly reflected in educational research. James Coleman (1988, 1990) and Pierre Bourdieu (1986), the figures most frequently credited with theoretical development of the notion of social capital, both displayed an abiding interest in the sociology of education, thus ensuring that the concept would make itself known in that field of inquiry.[1] Nevertheless, in the context of educational research, studies elevating the concept of social capital to a prominent position have exhibited a restricted methodological scope, primarily using quantitative techniques. We argue that ethnography can make an important contribution by providing insights into the underlying actions that produce or expend social capital, thereby complementing quantitative research.

We take as our point of departure one of the most frequently invoked kinds of social capital—that of parental networks—to examine its impact on children's schooling. Using a large ethnographic dataset, we describe variations in the architecture of such networks. We also examine how they facilitate particular actions affecting children's school experiences. In doing so, we are particularly interested in assessing how social capital comes into play when problematic issues arise at school. Our data suggest

Erin McNamara Horvat, Elliot B. Weininger, and Annette Lareau, 'From Social Ties to Social Capital: Class Differences in the Relations Between Schools and Parent Networks', *American Educational Research Journal*, Summer 2003, 40, 2, 319–351.

that there are important class-specific differences in the architecture of parental networks and, associated with this, in parents' capacity to effectively intervene in school matters. On the basis of this result, we suggest certain reformulations that may render the concept of social capital more useful in the context of educational research.

In what follows, we first briefly review the various conceptions of social capital that have animated educational research. After a short discussion of methodology, we demonstrate that parental networks vary across class categories. Our findings imply that the form of 'intergenerational closure' identified by Coleman (1988, 1990) as one of the paradigmatic instances of educationally relevant social capital—network ties connecting parents of school peers—is primarily a middle-class phenomenon. In the case of working-class and poor families, by contrast, closure is organized predominantly along kinship lines. The data further indicate that the presence of professionals in parental networks is substantially more prevalent in the middle class. We follow with a discussion of how problems at school are dealt with by middle-class parents, on the one hand, and by poor and working-class parents, on the other, focusing on the manner in which these networks may play a role. Here we show that the resources that are made available to middle-class parents through their networks affect various aspects of their children's schooling, including teacher behavior, track placement, and program participation. We conclude by arguing that in the educational context, social capital may be just as likely to function as a mechanism that facilitates the intergenerational transmission of advantage as one that ameliorates its effects.

Social Capital and Education

Use of the term 'social capital' has been plagued by conceptual murkiness. The 'foundational' statements in the social capital literature—primarily those of Coleman (1988, 1990) and Bourdieu (1986)—were relatively brief and imprecise, leaving subsequent researchers free to develop discrepant meanings of the same term. Moreover, as Portes (1998) noted in a review, some of the most widely cited uses of the concept—including those of Coleman (1988, 1990) and Putnam (1996)—failed to distinguish adequately between the constitutive elements of social capital, the various manners in which it can be put to use, and the manifold consequences it brings about. The upshot of this, Portes argued, was analyses that often did not live up to their explanatory ambitions, punctuated from time to time by tautological declarations or equations that did little more than attach new labels to familiar variables.

Consequently, the most recent research has devoted considerable attention to the development of a theoretically clarified, broadly oriented, and analytically rigorous conceptualization of social capital (Lin, 2001; Portes, 1998; Portes and Sensenbrenner, 1993; Woolcock, 1998). However, with occasional exceptions (discussed later), educational research has not been involved in this conceptual work. Instead, studies of the (hypothesized) importance and role of social capital in educational contexts have proceeded largely on the basis of examples provided by Coleman (1988, 1990) and, in particular, examples of intergenerational closure (networks connecting the parents of school peers) and parent–child relations (and more specifically, parental involvement in children's schooling). In the case of intergenerational closure, social capital is understood in terms of a set of social relations that enables the reciprocal monitoring of children by the parents of peers, thereby increasing adherence to behavioral norms that are presumed to affect school performance. In the case of parent–child relations, social capital denotes the intensity—construed affectively or normatively—with which parents undertake behaviors that contribute to their children's schooling, such as studying together. (See Dika and Singh, 2002, for a review of educational research on social capital.) The outcomes of studies proceeding from these definitions have not, by and large, triggered theoretical reconsideration of the notion of social capital.[2]

The majority of studies examining social capital in school settings have used quantitative methodologies to address outcomes such as test scores and grades, study habits, or high school dropout patterns and college attendance. The results have been less than decisive. Taking up the question of familial social capital, Goyette and Conchas (in press) reported modest effects for a parent–child interaction index on the amount of time devoted to homework among Mexican and Vietnamese youth. Likewise, Smith, Beaulieu, and Seraphine (1995)—using indicators such as maternal employment, number of siblings, and (self-reported) parental monitoring practices—have registered associations between familial social capital and the likelihood of college attendance; however, these associations were partially contingent on location (i.e., urban, suburban, town, or rural residency). Using different data and measures, McNeal (1999) found that familial social capital is only efficacious in keeping children from dropping out of high school in combination with high socioeconomic status—that is, when parents have a high income, education, and/or occupational prestige.[3]

The literature on intergenerational closure (that is, networks connecting parents of school peers) has been even more mixed. Both Muller (1995) and Carbonaro (1998) reported effects on mathematics achievement; the latter study also discerned an impact on high school dropout rates. However, Morgan and Sørensen (1999) subsequently presented data implying that the results for mathematics were spurious, a claim Carbonaro (1999) assented to. Muller and Ellison (2001) have also reported a modest negative effect on class cutting. In contrast, however, Goyette and Conchas (in press) found no association between a Colemanesque measure of closure and time devoted to homework among Mexican or Vietnamese youth. It is interesting that Teachman, Paasch, and Carver (1997), taking up the subject of high school dropout rates, discerned a significant interaction between income and a measure of whether parents know the parents of their child's friends.[4] The work of Stanton-Salazar (1997) and Stanton-Salazar and Dornbusch (1995) constitutes something of an exception to the literature because it moves away from the general orientation toward Coleman's theoretical premises. Drawing on Bourdieu, Stanton-Salazar renders central class and race differences in the architecture and function of interpersonal networks: '[W]hereas working class community and networks are organized on the basis of scarcity and conservation, the cosmopolitan networks constructed by middle-class members are oriented toward maximizing individual (and group) access to the mainstream marketplace' (1997, p. 4). Indeed, Stanton-Salazar insists on the stratified character of social networks strongly enough to define social capital in terms of the 'degree and quality of middle-class forms of social support' transmitted through social ties (1997, p. 5). From this perspective, social capital is largely implicated in the reproduction of stratification—an argument that finds at least provisional support in the quantitative studies (mentioned earlier) that exhibit a positive effect for social capital only in combination with an indicator of social position.

The institutional conditions under which schooling occurs generally fall outside the scope of the studies just discussed. Others, however, take a more critical edge. Some of these highlight resources that low-income families provide for their children but which go unrecognized by school officials. Delgado-Gaitan (1992), for example, in a study of six Mexican-American families, finds that neither resources inside the home, such as parents assisting with homework, and resources outside the home, such as parents procuring information from co-workers on how to manage a problem at their child's school, are presently not recognized in the school. Similarly, Villanueva (1996), in a study of three generations of Latino families, stresses the 'wisdom' of grandparents who are not formally educated yet provide important lessons to children and grandchildren. The work of both Delgado-Gaitan and Villanueva thus highlights the important role played by the school in selectively legitimating family resources.

In a related vein, Mehan and his colleagues (1996) studied an untracking effort in San Diego called Advancement Via Individual Determination (AVID), in which a sample of underperforming minority students was placed in a special class and provided with additional support services (i.e., help in procuring college applications, visiting campuses, and negotiating the application process). Mehan and his colleagues argue that if social and cultural capital can be inculcated and activated by institutional agents, then schools need not merely be reproducers of class cultures but can assist in transformation (see also Moll, Amanti, Neff, and Gonzales, 1992). Similarly, Valenzuela (1999) reported that the recent immigrants in her study of Latino students in a Texas high school had higher levels of social capital than their U.S.-born counterparts, but also found that the social capital held by these students was no match for the exclusionary tracking practices of the school. Thus, although this work is useful in directing us to consider the strengths to be found in low-income immigrant families and communities, the fact remains that the school has an independent and critical role in deciding crucial aspects of children's educational advancement. In this context, the literature suggests that the social networks accessible by working-class and poor families are less valuable than those of middle-class families for negotiating the particular institutional environment formed by the school.

In this article we approach social capital in terms of the emergent consensus (Lin, 2001; Portes, 1998; Stanton-Salazar, 1997) that the concept must be taken to refer to the material and immaterial resources that individuals and families are able to access through their social ties. In contrast to Stanton-Salazar, whose work focuses primarily on the network ties that profitably connect students with key institutional agents such as teachers and guidance counselors, we return to one of the 'canonical' implementations of the concept of social capital by asking whether informal parental networks differ by class in their basic architecture and whether parents differ in how they put their network ties to use in resolving problems with schools to secure advantageous outcomes for their children.[5] In particular, we take up the question of whether and how social capital can enable certain actors to *contest* the judgments or behavior of agents who occupy positions of institutional authority—in this case, educators and school officials. On the basis of our results, we subsequently return to questions of theory, arguing that, consistent with the work of Lin (2001) in particular, it is necessary to give a central place to the theme of *inequality* in efforts to re-conceptualize social capital.

Data and Method

The findings reported here are based on interviews with and observations of 88 third-and fourth-grade children and their families. The interviews were carried out in phases as part of a larger study that intensively examined children's lives both in and out of school. The study was designed to provide an in-depth comparison of parents' relationships with schools as well as other institutions, including health care and organized leisure activities such as organized sports, Brownies, and Boy Scouts. Third and fourth graders were selected because at that stage parents are still heavily involved in children's lives, yet children also begin to display some autonomy regarding their leisure time. All names used in this article are pseudonyms.

The third author of this article, a White middle-class woman, began the study by locating a pool of children in a third-grade classroom in the Midwestern university community of Lawrenceville (population approximately 25,000). She conducted participant observations and in-depth interviews at Quigley school, a mixed-race and mixed-class environment. In conducting the interviews she was assisted by a Black graduate student. In addition, she observed children in out-of-class activities such as sporting events. These data were collected in 1989–1990. After a move to a large Northeastern city, the third author continued data collection. Here, because of residential segregation, schools tended to be homogeneous by race and class. In the end, she settled for including a predominantly White suburban school with some Black middle-class families in it (Swan) and a city school in a White working-class neighborhood (Lower Richmond) that drew a number of poor Black families from an adjacent housing project.[6] These data were collected from 1993 to 1995. During data collection in the Northeast, a mixed-race and mixed-gender team of graduate students assisted the third author.[7] The third author conducted almost all of the classroom observations and was assisted by the team for the interviews and observations of school and community events. Thus the study was organized around classrooms in three different schools: Quigley, Swan, and Lower Richmond (see Table 32.1). It was primarily from these classrooms that the families were recruited. It is important to note that the project was conceived of as a single study. Although the data collection spanned multiple sites over a relatively long period of time, the same core interview protocol

Table 32.1 Summary of school characteristics

School characteristic	Quigley	Lower Richmond	Swan
Type of school and grades served	public 1–3	Public K–5	Public K–5
No. of students enrolled	200	475	450
Racial composition of student body	52% White[a]	54% White	90% White[b]
	44% Black	44% Black	8% Black
	3% Asian	1% Asian	2% Asian
	1% Hispanic	1% Hispanic	
Percentage of school population eligible for free lunch	40%	64%	n/a[c]
Surrounding area	Midwestern university town	Residentially stable, White working-class neighborhood close to a Black poor area in a large Northeastern city	Predominantly White, suburban middle-class area in a large Northeastern city

Note: n/a = not applicable.

[a]The ethnic breakdown is for the entire school district, which included four elementary schools, one junior high school, and one high school. The elementary schools were racially balanced.

[b]Estimated by the researcher on the basis of conversations with the principal.

[c]The school did not offer a free lunch program.

was used throughout (with modest additions and deletions), and the sampling techniques remained consistent. Most important, the research questions and aims of the study remained fundamentally the same for the duration of the project.

In all three schools, observations included both in-class and out-of-classroom activities. The classroom observations included routine classroom activities and lessons. Researchers also observed parent-teacher conferences, PTA meetings, and special events such as graduation, school fairs, book fairs, Back-to-School Night, and classroom celebrations of Halloween and Valentine's Day. During these informal school activities, visible differences in the density of the parental networks were observed. As in Lareau's 2000 study showing that middle-class parents were more connected to one another and to the school, the middle-class parents observed for this study were involved in the life of the school (for example, they ran the book fair and school fair) and connected to one another. The parents at Lower Richmond did not know each other. On Back-to-School Night the classroom was quiet before the start of the program. Few greetings were exchanged among parents. The reverse was true at Swan. Before the beginning of the formal program on Back-to-School Night the room was alive with parents' conversations about children's organized activities. The room was noisy. In addition, parent-run school events at Swan were more elaborate. For example, the school fair at Swan had more booths and fancier rides than the fair at Lower Richmond. Following up on the patterns observed at the schools, the third author and her assistants carried out interviews—averaging about 2 hours each—with 137 parents or guardians of the various children. It is these data, in particular, that we draw on here.

The families in each school were allocated to class categories on the basis of criteria widely used in contemporary sociology (e.g., Wright, 1997; Zipp and Plutzer, 1996), although the relatively small number of cases precluded highly differentiated schemes similar to those developed for quantitative class analysis. On the basis of detailed information concerning respondents' jobs, we grouped some families in the middle-class category in which at least one adult was employed in an occupation that entailed some kind of managerial (as opposed to merely supervisory) authority or presupposed some type of highly credentialed skill.[8] Correlatively, families in which adult members' jobs did not exhibit either of those attributes were grouped in the working-class category. We broke with the tendency of most sociological studies of class, however, by adding a category for 'the poor' to our data, under which were grouped families for whom government assistance, rather than participation in the labor market, constituted the primary means of subsistence. Our reason for doing so was that one of our schools included a substantial number of children from such families, and their exclusion would have been arbitrary. To select interviewees, students at each school were grouped by race and social class. Then every third student was selected and a letter was sent home explaining the study and requesting one interview each with the mother and the father (the parents were interviewed separately). In these classrooms (which ranged from 26 to 30 students) more than 90% of the parents agreed to participate. The classrooms did not, however, yield sufficient numbers of children in some key categories (i.e., middle-class Black children and poor White children). These children were recruited elsewhere.[9]

As was indicated earlier, most of the families in the study were recruited from three schools. Given the significant impact of school culture and norms on the behavior of students and families, it is reasonable to question whether our results are due to school effects. That is, it could be argued that some of the class effects that we report are actually the result of differences between the schools. Because of the high degree of class homogeneity in the schools from which most of our sample was drawn, it is difficult to put this concern to rest. Thus, although our results clearly point to the power of the middle-class parents to harness social capital in their interactions with schools, this finding could also be affected by the school context. Further research that samples students from a wide selection of school settings is needed to disentangle these effects.

Although social class is the central focus of this article, the roles of race and family structure are worthy of comment. Briefly, we found comparable social class patterns interwoven across race boundaries; we consider the role of race later in the [chapter]. Similarly, reflecting a national pattern, we found social-class differences to be interwoven with differences in family structure (see Table 32.2). Middle-class children were far more likely to come from two-parent households. In the sample of 36 middle-class children, only three came from single-parent families. Although some of the poor children had regular contact with their fathers, none resided together. The working-class families had a mixed family structure with both two-parent and single-parent households. Although family structure is not the focus of this article, it may be confounded with the class differences we report.

[...]

Table 32.2 Family structure, by race and class

	Intact, two-parent, original family		Blended family[a]		Single-parent family		Family run by grandparent or guardian	
Social Class	Black	White	Black	White	Black	White	Black	White
Middle	13	17	2	1	3	0	0	0
Working	6 1 bi-racial	6	0	1	3	5	2	2
Poor	0	3	0	0	12	9	2	0

[a] 'Blended families' include single- and two-parent households where a parent has remarried or there are other live-in adults who are romantically attached.

Social Capital in Action

We now take up the question of how parents' social capital may affect their children's school experiences. We address this issue through an analysis of situations in which parents may feel compelled to intervene in their children's schooling. Our data imply that middle-class networks frequently make available various resources that parents can (and do) use to deal with such situations, thereby attaining a desired outcome for their children. For example, when confronted with inappropriate behavior on the part of a teacher, parents' ties to other parents often enabled them to function as 'guardian angels,' descending on the school en masse and quickly bringing about change. In contrast, working-class and poor parents inevitably responded to such situations in a purely individualized fashion. Likewise, middle-class parents' networks provided resources that made it possible to customize their children's educational careers in important ways—for example, by contesting a placement decision or obtaining additional resources for a learning-disabled child. In contrast, working-class and poor parents, lacking these resources, were considerably less likely to dispute the school's authority.

Responding to Inappropriate Teacher Behavior

In the schools that we studied, teachers occasionally acted inappropriately, either by losing their temper with a student and yelling or by striking or pushing a student. Middle-class parents responded in a very different fashion to these incidents than did working-class and poor parents. Middle-class parents mobilized resources to respond collectively. By contrast, in working-class and poor families, these incidents were treated as the behavior of an individual teacher with a student and were addressed at the individual level. Although kinship networks were often aware of the difficulty, other parents in the school community were not.

The case of Garrett Tallinger, a White middle-class boy, provides an example. In the course of what was supposed to be a noncompetitive football game, a dispute broke out with the physical education teacher over whether Garrett had scored a touchdown. According to Garrett's mother,

> Carl [the teacher] evidently pushed Garrett away, I mean, he just lost it. He just didn't want these kids in this big argument with him. And he must have thrown down the football, but it bounced up and hit one of the kids. Although one of the kids said he just threw it right at him. [He] pushed Garrett, picked up another kid, I mean, one of the kids, he picked [him] up and threw him down, sent the girls inside, apologized evidently, who knows, ... and kept the boys out. But it really frightened the kids. It frightened the girls, because they were very upset, when they got to class. Carl went in, apologized to the girls. ... He apologized on the spot and then left. The school. This was the last period of the day. But the boys were really shaken. Well, some of the boys.

Ms. Tallinger did not learn about these events from her son. Instead, she returned home that day to find a slew of phone messages already awaiting her:

> I had come home with this major traffic jam ..., walk in the door, Garrett's in the basement, ... and I had all these phone messages, Georgia Finley, Midge Bartlett, Rick's mother. [Before I could even say hello to the children I got another phone call.] Sarah says, 'Have you talked to Garrett?' I said, 'No.' I could tell by her tone of voice. She said, '*Well* ...,' and then she proceeded to tell me that Don [her son] was practically bruised. ... At this point, I still hadn't talked to Garrett.

By then members of the school board were getting calls. The parental network facilitated a quick and collective response. The teacher and the principal called the Tallingers that weekend. There was a meeting with the parents the following Tuesday. The teacher was suspended for a week.

In stark contrast, working-class and poor families handled these same types of incidents in a more individual fashion. In the following example, the live-in boyfriend of the mother of Wendy Driver, a White working-class girl, describes what occurred after a school bus driver pushed Wendy. Their intervention was restricted to the individual level; only the family, principal, and bus driver were involved:

> The bus driver pushed her back into her seat and we feel that the bus driver has slips that he fills out. If the kids are not behaving, he's supposed to fill them out and turn them in and then let the school handle it, not touch the children. That's not what he's there for. So we went up. Well, I went up. I was off that day. And I took her up and spoke to one of the counselors and she said that the principal wasn't in yet, so I said OK and I let her go to class and I came home. I went back up when the principal came in and I sat down and I

talked to the principal. She seemed like a real nice person. She said she'll see what's going on. He is supposed to fill out slips and not touch students. So ever since then, she hasn't come home and said anything about the bus driver touching her.

In a similar, though more serious, example, a poor Black girl had her hair pulled by a teacher. The girl's aunt (also her guardian) responded by writing the teacher a 'very nasty note.' When asked to relay what the note said, she replied:

I told him you put your damn hands on my daughter's head one more fuckin' time and I'll be there to fuck you up, period. Keep your hands off her. You don't have to pull her hair because she's not doing anything that bad. I know Kadija. Kadija don't do nothin'—she said somebody was messin' with her. You keep your hands off her, so I had no more problems out of him for the whole year [laughs].

In both cases, only immediate family members undertook the intervention. Although both actions were successful in the sense that they prevented future misbehavior, neither, to the best of our knowledge, resulted in formal disciplinary sanctions on the order of the one brought about by the Tallingers and their acquaintances.

In addition, among many working-class and poor parents there was knowledge that teachers would 'hit kids' from time to time. For instance, Ms. Yanelli, a White working-class mother, had 'heard' this:

Well, I heard that Mr. Tier hits kids. And, uh, do you believe that? I don't know. I mean, there's talk in the neighborhood and I thought, what do you mean, he hits kids? He wouldn't get away with that so I kind of didn't believe it. And I asked Billy about it and he said once in a while he'll give him a noggin on the head, you know.

Nevertheless, despite this information, she liked the teacher because her son liked him:

But, I really like Mr. Tier. He got Billy real interested this year and that means a lot to me because in Ms. Green's class he would daze out, just daze out, and that was our problem last year. ... But he was so excited about having Mr. Tier this year he came home and said, I've got the best teacher in the whole school.

Our observations confirm that, on occasion, school officials or teachers would manhandle a student, by shoving or vigorously shaking him or her, or twisting an arm. Thus events that created an explosion of collective outrage among middle-class families tended to generate isolated anger or even resigned acceptance within working-class and poor families.[10]

Customizing Children's School Careers

Special Services

One very clear difference between the working-class and poor families and the middle-class families was in the way that parents handled any special educational needs their child might have. Whether the issue was a possible learning disability or inclusion in a 'gifted' program, middle-class parents were much more proactive about the (perceived) educational needs of their children. Mobilizing network members to provide testing and gather information was the norm when a family was presented with a problem of this sort. Parents routinely talked about discussing these types of issues with family and friends who were in the field of education. For example, the mother of Melanie Handlon, a White middle-class girl, tapped into her networks when the school suggested that Melanie might have a learning disability.

Well, [the school] decided at the end of last year that they didn't think [testing] was necessary. She had improved in all of her subjects. And now when this year started they again suggested that we have her tested, and we are going to do it this year. Uh, I've been watching and observing her. My sister-in-law, who is a teacher, has been watching her and observing her. We don't see any of the classic things that, you know, they diagnose for learning disabilities.

A similar process took place in the case of children potentially eligible for inclusion in a gifted program. In the case of the Marshalls, a middle-class Black family, we can again see how a parent collected information through network ties and then used it to secure the desired outcome for her daughter. Stacey Marshall had applied for admittance to the gifted program but had scored slightly below the minimum threshold on the entrance exam. She subsequently enrolled in a school activity called Problem Solving that was run by the teacher who administered the gifted program. Encountering Ms. Marshall in the hall one afternoon, the teacher declared, 'You really should get her tested. She's an extremely bright child.' After discussing the matter with her husband, Ms. Marshall determined that they should 'scrape together the money' (about $200) to have Stacey tested by a private psychologist. In the following excerpt Ms. Marshall details her use of community contacts to locate a psychologist:

I found out about Terry Hoffman [the psychologist] from ... a White friend of mine ... whose son had been at the same ... school with [Stacey's older sister]. They live in a different school district and, as it turns out, they had gone through the same thing with her son. Her son had not made the screening test at his elementary school. And June [the mother] is very, um, ... aggressive and assertive and she kinda hit the roof. You know, 'Well wha'd'ya mean?' If you don't make it, you can challenge it. And she decided, 'I'm takin' Drew [her son] some place else.' And she had found this Terry Hoffman.

Networks were pivotal both in making the decision to have Stacey tested and in locating a psychologist to conduct the testing. Stacey was tested by Dr. Hoffman and scored high enough that her parents were able to push to have her admitted to the gifted program.

Also interesting in this respect is the case of Marcus Baldwin, a Black middle-class boy. Two months into his third-grade year, Ms. Baldwin heard from his teacher that 'he wasn't learning anything, wasn't makin' any gains.' The teacher and the counselor called a conference to deliver this information, in which they said that they thought Marcus had 'serious delays.' The educators proposed testing him for learning disabilities. Ms. Baldwin was upset that it had taken them so long to notify her. Drawing on her extensive professional networks, she decided to have him evaluated herself:

I'm in the field of mental health so I know psychologists. I have a Master's in clinical [psychology]. ... I've done almost everything. I've worked all the settings: community mental health, school, residential, ... all of that, individual ... therapy, group therapy, testing. I—I've done it all. So I got a psychologist to evaluate him. It was someone I know that I have worked with in the past. We were in the same organization. ... He was a school psychologist, certified school psychologist.

Ms. Baldwin was able to use the assessment provided by her colleague to challenge the educators' conclusions:

He evaluated him and Marcus tested out above-average intelligence. Well what's goin' on? So, we had a big conference: the principal, the teacher, [the psychologist] came—presented the test, everything. And then they're like: We have to figure out what's—what has happened. If you've got a kid who has above-average intelligence and the performance is—is totally different: Where are things?

Thus Ms. Baldwin's network ties provided her with the leverage that allowed her to contest the school officials' view of her child's abilities.

In contrast, working-class and poor families rarely used network ties to try to intervene in placement processes or to dispute assessments—whether the families were sanguine about the results or not. They did not, by and large, mobilize networks to challenge gatekeepers in schools. Indeed, some parents were wary of contact with professionals and also felt that they should be able to 'handle it themselves.' This sentiment is apparent in the response provided by Ms. Nelson, a Black working-class mother, when asked whether she and her husband would take their child to a counselor or psychologist:

Well, there's nothing wrong with them [counselors and psychologists]—if you can't do it, you go find somebody else. If you can't handle it. But I shouldn't have to go somewhere. I don't send mine anywhere else when I can deal with the situation or we can deal with the situation.

In combination with the fact that their networks included so few professionals, this ethos rendered working-class and poor parents highly dependent on the school in the area of assessment and considerably more deferential than their middle-class counterparts in matters pertaining to placement. In one example, Wendy Driver, a White girl from a working-class family, was unable to read by fourth grade. Her mother was very concerned but felt that she could depend on the school to advise her on a course of action:

I think they just want to keep it in the school [for] now, and when they get to a point where they can't figure out what it is, ... then I guess they'll send me somewhere else. ... So I figured I'd wait until the first report card to see what they'd say and then take it from there.

Nor did she have any idea what she might do to address the issue herself:

I wouldn't even know where to start going. On the radio there was something for children having problems reading and this and that call and I suggested it to a couple different people and they were like, wait a second, it's only to get you there and you'll end up paying an arm and a leg. So I said to my mom, no, I'm going to wait until the first report card and go up and talk to them up there [at the school].

Whereas Ms. Baldwin could and did turn to colleagues for information, Ms. Driver's source of information was a radio advertisement. Later in the year, Ms. Driver knew that the teachers disagreed about how to proceed with her daughter. At a conference the fourth-grade teacher recommended retention, but the reading specialist argued that Wendy should be promoted. Ms. Driver felt incapable of adjudicating between them and ultimately left the decision to the school, on the grounds that she '[didn't] want to jump into anything and find out that it's the wrong thing.'

Middle-class parents also used their networks to exert control over another critical aspect of their children's educational lives: selection of a teacher.[11] In the course of our interviews, parents were asked if they had ever requested a particular teacher for their child. As can be seen in Table 32.3, the results indicate that the middle-class parents were more than twice as likely to have made such a request as the working-class parents.[12]

To know which teacher to request, these middle-class parents used their connections with other parents and with professional educators. The following response from Mr. Conner, the father of a middle-class White boy, provides another example of the importance of professional connections:

I don't think I [sought out such information] specifically. My wife probably did—she's more involved in the whole educational process. She's been a teacher, and she probably takes a much more active role researching about school, talking to other parents, finding out about teachers for the upcoming year, and requesting a teacher for the next year.

This remark reveals a general middle-class orientation toward the quasi-strategic customization of children's school careers ('the whole educational process')—that is, a careful scrutiny of potential opportunities to 'improve,' 'correct,' and render more 'fulfilling' their children's school experience. (Also typical is the fact that the majority of the actual work is done by the mother.)

Informal conversations with other parents that touched on the subject of teachers often took place at school events or at community events such as church functions or children's activities. When asked where she gathered information on prospective teachers, Ms. Hughes, a White middle-class mother who had made many such requests, replied, 'Oh, from parents—just out on the soccer field or, you know, you kind of scout around.' Ms. Irving, the mother of a Black middle-class girl, offered the following account:

Well, I have several friends who are teachers in the school district. And I have several friends that have kids who go to the school. . . . So you talk to someone who has an older kid who had her [the teacher]. What did you think of her, ya know? And usually when you do that you go, you talk to someone whose child had the same learning ability. Or whose child you would like to see [your child] do as well as. I've done that before. I've asked people, you know, What do you think of her? Or just in talking to people. . . . You hear about other teachers, just in associating with other parents.

Thus Ms. Irving not only perceived a need to gather information that could be useful in improving her child's school experience but also exhibited a deft awareness of the variable relevance of information provided by various sources. An analogous sensitivity is apparent in the remarks of Ms. McNamara, a middle-class White mother who also described

Table 32.3 Proportion of parents/guardians who requested a teacher, by class

Parental requests	Middle-class	Working-class
Requested a teacher	34.4%	15.8%
N	32	19

Note: This table is based on information provided by each child's primary caregiver. The poor group is excluded because most poor White families had to be recruited from outside the schools being studied. Because we did not have extensive information about those schools, we did not ask the same questions about the school experiences of respondents whose children attended them. The study included 36 middle-class families and 26 working-class families. Lower numbers are reported here as a result of missing data. We did not subdivide the results by race because cell sizes become very small.

teacher selection in strategic terms: 'I try to not request very often. ... Because if you do ... it's like, you get ignored. It's better to, like, save your ammunition for when you really need it.'

In contrast, working-class and poor parents tended to accept the luck of the draw in their children's teacher assignments. This attitude presumably was due, at least in part, to the distinct character of their interpersonal networks, which typically lacked the type of contacts used by their middle-class counterparts for gathering the information that fueled teacher requests. Nevertheless, even when working-class and poor parents did have more or less compelling information regarding a teacher, they were much less likely to make a request. Rather, if they heard about an undesirable teacher at the bus stop grocery store, or laundromat, they simply 'hoped' that their child would avoid him or her. As Ms. Doerr, a Black working-class mother, put it:

> What's her name for next year? I sure hope she don't get her. What's her name, Ms. Worthingham or something like this, she's a fourth-grade teacher. I've heard horrible things about her. ... It seems that she's not very friendly and she doesn't like children at all. In fact, I've been told that she's a real redneck.

Indeed, it appeared that many working-class and poor parents assumed that they had neither the capacity nor the right to intervene in such matters under the gatekeepers' jurisdiction.

Contesting the Curriculum

The occasional furors that erupted over curricular issues gave rise to processes similar to those that we have already examined. Middle-class parents, for example, shared concerns about aspects of the curriculum with other parents. Thus when her child's school decided to hold an AIDS awareness week, Ms. Hopewell, the mother of a middle-class White girl, brought the matter before the PTA, arguing that it was inappropriate for young children and instigating a wide-ranging discussion. Although no consensus emerged among the parents, the school decided to send home formal notification of the program, offering parents the opportunity to hold their child out if they wished.

The full range of resources that middle-class parents have at their disposal becomes apparent in the case of the Kaplans, a middle-class Jewish family. In early fall, their son's class began practicing for the winter holiday program. The Kaplans were offended by a Christian song that the choir teacher had selected (as part of a multicultural holiday program) that included the lyrics 'come let us bow and worship Him now.' They were offended not for religious reasons but because they felt the lyrics blurred the distinction between church and state. Ms. Kaplan complained to the choir teacher, but the teacher felt that the song was in keeping with the overall diversity of the holiday program. Ms. Kaplan then went to the principal. Although usually highly attuned to parents' concerns, the principal sided with the choir teacher in this instance.

Mr. and Ms. Kaplan first attempted to mobilize other parents. They circulated a petition but found some parents unsupportive and unwilling to sign. They also wrote a letter on their own to the district superintendent, triggering a districtwide policy review. The offending song was removed from the holiday program. (The principal was 'counseled' on issues of sensitivity as well.) The Kaplans were satisfied with this outcome but found that it had strained their relationships with some of the other parents. It is important to note that, in the process of contesting the school's authority, they did not expend all of the resources at their disposal. An old college friend of Ms. Kaplan's, who happened to work for a major television network on a national show, called to say hello in the middle of the drama. The friend offered to send down a camera crew to do a story; Ms. Kaplan declined, preferring to hold that option in reserve.

Alternative Network Functions

Our discussion thus far has presented an image of working-class and poor networks that verges on privation: Lacking extensive ties both to other parents in their child's school and to professionals, we have suggested, these parents tend to handle the problematic situations that arise in the course of their children's schooling on a purely individual basis, if they don't concede authority to the school altogether. Nevertheless, we do not wish to create the impression that working-class and poor familial networks are irrelevant. What is striking about our dataset is precisely the fact that these networks appear to offer working-class and poor families so little purchase on matters pertaining to *schooling*. They do, however, fulfill important functions in other areas of daily life.

[. . .]

Discussion

For this article we have used an ethnographic dataset, composed of extensive information on the families of 88 children, to examine the nature of parental networks and their impact on schooling. Our aim has been to describe variation in the architecture of social networks and to explore class differences in the mobilization or activation of network ties by parents in school settings. Given our methodology, systematic outcomes are hard to measure; however, our data do point to several important findings regarding the shape of the networks, their function in school settings, and the theoretical implications for social capital theory.

We find that Coleman's (1988, 1990) school-based 'intergenerational closure'—that is, networks that link parents of school peers—is primarily a middle class phenomenon. Moreover, these networks appear to form, at least in part, as a result of children's participation in organized activities, which is itself far more frequent in the middle class. In contrast, working-class and poor families exhibit a form of intergenerational closure that is often circumscribed or delimited by kinship (see Fischer, 1982). In general, the social networks that we observed among working-class and poor families did not include ties to school or children's activity-based contacts.

We also find that the parental networks of middle-class families are far more likely to include professionals of various sorts than are those of their working-class and poor counterparts. Moreover, parental networks tend to be homogeneous with respect to class, in the sense that middle-class networks do not encompass working-class or poor parents, and working-class and poor networks do not encompass middle-class parents; in other words, informal networks tend to be 'homophilous' (Lin, 2001). This network homogeneity is generally unrecognized in the tradition of social capital research stemming from Coleman (1988, 1990). And although it is to some degree a function of school homogeneity, we believe it extends beyond that.

These network differences are clearly associated with differences in the way that problems with the school are handled. Working-class and poor parents tend to undertake individual responses and do not receive much concrete support through their networks in doing so. By contrast, middle-class parents sometimes react collectively; at other times they act individually but maintain the possibility of collective involvement in reserve. In yet other instances, middle-class parents draw on ties to individuals unconnected with the school who can provide the information, expertise, or authority necessary to compel the school to follow a preferred course of action. In short, both the architecture of parental networks and their use vis-à-vis the school vary dramatically by class.

Parents must decide how to handle the various problems, small or large, that inevitably crop up in the course of their children's schooling, as well as whether to try to intercede in the school's routine practices. To be sure, our data do not enable us to establish unequivocally whether the types of interventions we have documented tend to cumulate and whether they thereby have definite consequences for educational outcomes. Nevertheless, even if forms of parental involvement such as teacher requests are judged unlikely to dramatically affect children's educational attainment, interventions in issues such as teacher behavior, track placement, and program participation are a different matter. Indeed, Lucas (1999) has described a contemporary tracking regime in which placements in different subject areas are uncoupled from one another, resulting in an increase in the significance of parental interventions as determinants of tracking location (see also Baker and Stevenson, 1986; Lareau, 2000; Useem, 1992). Thus, although we lack longitudinal data, there is good reason to suspect that the forms of parental behavior that we have documented are relevant to student outcomes.

What do these findings suggest for future research examining social capital in educational settings? The most comprehensive general theory of social capital produced to date is that of Lin (2001), and it is largely against the background of this theory that our results can best be understood. From our perspective, Lin's fundamental insight (consistent with Bourdieu, 1986, before him) is that a theory of social capital that focuses on the resources that are transferred or pooled through social networks must necessarily include the social-structural location of the actors involved in its purview. This implies that any such theory is simultaneously a theory of *inequality in* social capital (see Lin 2001 [esp. pp. 243–249], 2000). Thus, the working-class and poor parents we observed and spoke with were often able to draw on their networks for crucial forms of assistance. In particular, childcare needs were frequently satisfied through the support of extended family members; from time to time, financial needs could also be met through kin networks. Nevertheless, important though they undoubtedly were for the lives of the children in working-class and poor families, these resources were both qualitatively and quantitatively distinct from those that were pooled or transferred through middle-class networks. Educational researchers who draw on the social capital concept would thus do well to specify the nature and social distribution of the resources that are identified by means of this concept.

[. . .]

NOTES

An earlier version of this [chapter] was presented at the annual meeting of the American Educational Research Association, New Orleans, April 2002. Annette Lareau gratefully acknowledges the financial support of the Spencer Foundation. We thank Nikki Johnson for her research assistance and the anonymous reviewers for their many helpful suggestions. All errors are the responsibility of the authors.

1. Indeed, the inclusion in the National Education Longitudinal Survey of questions intended to allow for testing of hypotheses drawing on Coleman's (1988, 1990) account of social capital reflects well the importance ascribed to the concept in the field of educational research.
2. It is important to note the theoretical foundations underlying the conceptions of social capital and how they implicate the actions of both families and schools. In our work, we find the theoretical perspective of Pierre Bourdieu to be particularly useful in understanding the dynamic between schools and families. Bourdieu has produced a vast body of work, which is accompanied by a large and growing secondary literature that explains and extends his ideas. Readers who would like to explore Bourdieu's work in this area are directed to consult Bourdieu (1977, 1984, 1986, 1990, 1994) as well as Bourdieu and Passeron (1977), Bourdieu and Wacquant (1992), and the secondary works by Calhoun, Lipuma, and Postone (1993), Robbins (1991), and Swartz (1997). Bourdieu's notion of social capital is part of a larger framework that uses the concepts of *habitus*, *field*, and *symbolic violence*, as well as various forms of capital (economic, cultural, social, and symbolic). Social capital can be conceived of as the set of valuable connections of an individual. Unlike Coleman, Bourdieu recognizes the unequal value of various network ties. In the school setting, the ties that are valuable are by-and-large middle-class. Bourdieu (Bourdieu & Passeron, 1977) and others (Bernstein, 1974; McLaren, 1998; Mehan et al., 1996; Stanton-Salazar, 1997) have argued that schools are essentially middle-class institutions that reward middle-class behaviors. That is, the behaviors that most easily map onto the expectations of teachers and others at school are those that are most likely to be rewarded. In the realm of social capital, the connections or parental networks that are the most valued in school settings are those that provide leverage in this middle-class environment. Parent's connections to middle-class professionals thus provide them with valuable capital in the school setting.

3. Valenzuela & Dornbusch (1994) report an interesting, positive association between familism—understood in terms of culturally specific phenomena of proximity to, contact with, and emotional affinity with adult kin—and school grades among Mexican students. Valenzuela and Dornbusch proffer an account based on Coleman's notion of social capital. But once again, it turns out that social capital is efficacious only in combination with an indicator of social position—in this case, parental education (Valenzuela & Dornbusch, 1994, pp. 30–31).
4. We leave out of this discussion works, such as Bankston and Zhou (1995), that use alternative conceptions of social capital (in this case, subjective identification with an ethnic community).
5. Because it focuses so exclusively on membership in voluntary organizations, the tradition of social capital research established by Putnam (2000) ends up excluding a variety of forms and instances of social capital from its purview—that is, precisely those in which the transfer or sharing of resources occurs on an informal basis. We thank an anonymous reviewer for drawing our attention to this implication of our research.
6. This approach to data collection does in fact echo the general pattern of class segregation in the nation (Massey & Denton, 1993) but did result in a limitation to the study. It is impossible to know if parents would have behaved differently had they resided in a community that was different in terms of class.
7. The first and second authors were not part of the data collection team, coming to the project only after it had been completed. Their participation was therefore limited to analysis of the data.
8. The schools from which we recruited the families included very few children of employers or self-employed workers, rendering moot the perennial question of whether these categories belong to the middle class.
9. District statistics indicated that a vast a majority of the White and Black children were on school lunch, from which we surmised that they were poor. Interviews, however, revealed that most of the White families had unreported income that boosted them out of the poverty level. As a result, we needed to recruit additional White poor families. These families were generally recruited by using flyers in social service offices and posting flyers on telephone poles in another neighborhood; as an incentive, these white poor families were paid ($25 per interview). No other families were paid for interviews. But we did bring a pie with us to all of the other interviews, and we followed up (for the entire sample) with a handwritten thank you note. A number of the Black middle-class families, again where the schools did not provide a sufficient number of cases to fill this category, were recruited through informal networks.
10. In our sample, working-class and poor parents were themselves considerably more likely to use corporal punishment in disciplining their children.
11. An extensive literature highlights the importance of teacher quality in enhancing student outcomes. See, for example, Darling-Hammond (2000) and Haycock (1998).
12. We were unable to tabulate responses for the poor group. The tabulations suffer from certain problems: further implying that they should be read with caution. In particular, all of the tabulations are beset (with varying degrees of severity) by missing data, usually as a result of time constraints on interviews. In addition, in some tabulations it was impossible to include figures for the poor group. The reason, as explained above, is that all of the poor White families were recruited from schools other than those on which the study was focused, thus entailing changes in the questions posed by the interviewer.

Producing Inequalities: Neo-Liberalism, Neo-Conservatism, and the Politics of Educational Reform

Michael W. Apple

Gritty Materialities

In this chapter, I raise serious questions about current educational 'reform' efforts now underway in a number of nations. I use research on the English, US, and New Zealand experience(s) to document some of the hidden differential effects of two connected strategies—neo-liberal inspired market proposals and neo-liberal, neo-conservative, and middle-class managerial-inspired regulatory proposals. In the process, I examine the interrelations among class, gender, and race. All three must be taken up *together* since, for example, in the United States 70 per cent of working-class positions are held by women and persons of color.[1] I also suggest that the rhetorical flourishes of the discourses of critical pedagogy need to come to grips with these changing material and ideological conditions. Critical pedagogy cannot and will not occur in a vacuum. Unless we honestly face these profound rightist transformations and think tactically about them, we will have little effect either on the creation of a counter-hegemonic common sense or on the building of a counter-hegemonic alliance.

Thus, I examine the ways in which the social and cultural terrain of educational policy and discourse has been altered 'on the ground' so to speak. I argue that we need to make closer connections between our theoretical and critical discourses on the one hand and the real transformations that are currently shifting educational policies and practices in fundamentally rightist directions on the other. Part of my discussion will need to be conceptual; but part of it will appropriately need to be empirical in order for me to pull together what is known about the real and material effects of the shift to the right in education.

My focus on the 'gritty materialities' of these effects is not meant to dismiss the importance of theoretical interventions. Nor is it meant to suggest that dominant discourses should not be constantly interrupted by the creative gains that have emerged from various neo-Marxist, postmodern, post-structural, post-colonial, queer, and other communities. Indeed, critical and revolutionary pedagogies *require* the fundamental interruption of common sense. However, while the construction of new theories and utopian visions is important, it is equally

A different version of this chapter appears in Michael W. Apple, *Educating the 'Right' Way: Markets, Standards, God, and Inequality* (New York: Routledge Falmer, 2001).

crucial to base these theories and visions in an unromantic appraisal of the material and discursive terrain that now exists. Common sense is already being radically altered, but not in directions that any of us on the left would find comforting. Without an analysis of such transformations and of the balance of forces that have created such discomforting alterations, without an analysis of the tensions, differential relations of power, and contradictions within it, we are left with increasingly elegant new theoretical formulations, but with a less than elegant understanding of the field of social power on which they operate.[2]

Hence, while much of the literature on 'critical pedagogies' has been politically and theoretically important and has helped us make a number of gains. However, it too often has not been sufficiently connected to the ways in which the current movement toward what might best be called 'conservative modernization' both has altered common sense and has transformed the material and ideological conditions surrounding schooling. It, thereby, sometimes becomes a form of what best be called 'romantic possibilitarian' rhetoric, in which the language of possibility substitutes for a consistent tactical analysis of what the balance of forces actually is and what is necessary to change it.[3] This is the task in which I engage in this chapter.

Right Turn

In his influential history of curriculum debates, Herbert Kliebard has documented that educational issues have consistently involved major conflicts and compromises among groups with competing visions of 'legitimate' knowledge, what counts as 'good' teaching and learning, and what is a 'just' society.[4] That such conflicts have deep roots in conflicting views of racial, class, and gender justice in education and the larger society is ratified in even more critical recent work as well.[5] These competing visions have never had equal holds on the imagination of educators or the general citizenry nor have they ever had equal power to effect their visions. Because of this, no analysis of education can be fully serious without placing at its very core a sensitivity to the ongoing struggles that constantly shape the terrain on which education operates.

Today is no different than in the past. A 'new' set of compromises, a new alliance and new power bloc has been formed that has increasing influence in education and all things social. This power bloc combines multiple fractions of capital who are committed to neo-liberal marketized solutions to educational problems, neo-conservative intellectuals who want a 'return' to higher standards and a 'common culture', authoritarian populist religious fundamentalists who are deeply worried about secularity and the preservation of their own traditions, and particular fractions of the professionally oriented new middle class who are committed to the ideology and techniques of accountability, measurement, and 'management'. While there are clear tensions and conflicts within this alliance, in general its overall aims are in providing the educational conditions believed necessary both for increasing international competitiveness, profit, and discipline and for returning us to a romanticized past of the 'ideal' home, family, and school.[6]

In essence, the new alliance has integrated education into a wider set of ideological commitments. The objectives in education are the same as those that guide its economic and social welfare goals. They include the dramatic expansion of that eloquent fiction, the free market; the drastic reduction of government responsibility for social needs; the reinforcement of intensely competitive structures of mobility both inside and outside the school; the lowering of people's expectations for economic security; the 'disciplining' of culture and the body; and the popularization of what is clearly a form of Social Darwinist thinking, as the recent popularity of *The Bell Curve* so obviously and distressingly indicates.[7]

The seemingly contradictory discourse of competition, markets, and choice on the one hand and accountability, performance objectives, standards, national testing, and national curriculum have created such a din that it is hard to hear anything else. As I have shown in *Cultural Politics and Education* and *Educating the 'Right' Way*, these tendencies actually oddly reinforce each other and help cement conservative educational positions into our daily lives.[8]

While lamentable, the changes that are occurring present an exceptional opportunity for serious critical reflection. In a time of radical social and educational change, it is crucial to document the processes and effects of the various and sometimes contradictory elements of the conservative restoration and of the ways in which they are mediated, compromised with, accepted, used in different ways by different groups for their own purposes, and/or struggled over in the policies and practices of people's daily educational lives.[9] I shall want to give a sense of how this might be happening in current 'reforms' such as marketization and national curricula and national testing in this chapter. For those interested in critical educational policies and practices, not to do this means that we act without understanding the shifting relations of power that are constructing and reconstructing the social field of power. While Gramsci's saying, 'Pessimism of the intellect, optimism of the will,' has a powerful resonance to it and is useful for mobilization and for not losing hope, it would be foolish to substitute rhetorical slogans for the fuller analysis that is undoubtedly required if we are to be successful.

New Markets, Old Traditions

Behind a good deal of the New Right's emerging discursive ensemble was a position that emphasized 'a culturalist construction of the nation as a (threatened) haven for white (Christian) traditions and values'.[10] This involved the construction of an imagined national past that is at least partly mythologized, and then employing it to castigate the present. Gary McCulloch argues that the nature of the historical images of schooling has changed. Dominant imagery of education as being 'safe, domesticated, and progressive' (that is, as leading toward progress and social/personal improvement) has shifted to become 'threatening, estranged, and regressive'.[11] The past is no longer the source of stability, but a mark of failure, disappointment, and loss. This is seen most vividly in the attacks on the 'progressive orthodoxy' that supposedly now reigns supreme in classrooms in many nations.[12]

For example, in England—though much the same is echoed in the United States, Australia, and elsewhere—Michael Jones, the political editor of the *Sunday Times*, recalls the primary school of his day. 'Primary school was a happy time for me. About 40 of us sat at fixed wooden desks with ink wells and moved from them only with grudging permission. Teacher sat in a higher desk in front of us and moved only to the blackboard. She smelled of scent and inspired awe.'[13] The mix of metaphors invoking discipline, scent (visceral and almost 'natural'), and awe is fascinating. But he goes on, lamenting the past thirty years of 'reform' that transformed primary schools. Speaking of his own children's experience, Jones says: 'My children spent their primary years in a showplace school where they were allowed to wander around at will, develop their real individuality and dodge the 3Rs. It was all for the best, we were assured. But it was not.[14] For Jones, the 'dogmatic orthodoxy' of progressive education 'had led directly to educational and social decline'. Only the rightist reforms instituted in the 1980s and 1990s could halt and then reverse this decline.[15] Only then could the imagined past return.

Much the same is being said on this side of the Atlantic. These sentiments are echoed in the public pronouncements of such figures as William Bennett, E. D. Hirsch, Jr., and others, all of whom seem to believe that progressivism is now in the dominant position in educational policy and practice and has destroyed a valued past. All of them believe that only by tightening control over curriculum and teaching (and students, of course), restoring 'our' lost traditions, making education more disciplined and competitive as they are certain it was in the past—only then can we have effective schools. These figures are joined by others who have similar criticisms, but who instead turn to a different past for a different future. Their past is less that of scent and awe and authority, but one of market 'freedom'. For them, nothing can be accomplished—even the restoration of awe and authority—without setting the market loose on schools so as to ensure that only 'good' ones survive.

We should understand that these policies are radical transformations. If they had come from the other side of the political spectrum, they would have been ridiculed in many ways, given the ideological tendencies in our nations. Further, not only are these policies based on a romanticized pastoral past, these reforms have not been notable for their grounding in research findings. Indeed, when research has been used, it has often either served as a rhetoric of justification for preconceived beliefs about the supposed efficacy of markets or regimes of tight accountability or they have been based—as in the case of Chubb and Moe's much publicized work on marketization—on quite flawed research.[16]

Yet, no matter how radical some of these proposed 'reforms' are and no matter how weak the empirical basis of their support, they have now redefined the terrain of debate of all things educational. After years of conservative attacks and mobilizations, it has become clear that 'ideas that were once deemed fanciful, unworkable—or just plain extreme' are now increasingly being seen as common sense.[17]

Tactically, the reconstruction of common sense that has been accomplished has proved to be extremely effective. For example, there are clear discursive strategies being employed here, ones that are characterized by 'plain speaking' and speaking in a language that 'everyone can understand'. (I do not wish to be wholly negative about this. The importance of these things is something many 'progressive' educators, including many writers on critical pedagogy, have yet to understand.) [18] These strategies also involve not only presenting one's own position as 'common sense', but also usually tacitly implying that there is something of a conspiracy among one's opponents to deny the truth or to say only that which is 'fashionable'.[19] As Gillborn notes,

> This is a powerful technique. First, it assumes that there are no *genuine* arguments against the chosen position; any opposing views are thereby positioned as false, insincere or self-serving. Second, the technique presents the speaker as someone brave or honest enough to speak the (previously) unspeakable. Hence, the moral high ground is assumed and opponents are further denigrated.[20]

It is hard to miss these characteristics in some of the conservative literature such as Herrnstein and Murray's publicizing of the unthinkable 'truth' about genetics and intelligence or E. D. Hirsch's latest 'tough' discussion of the destruction of 'serious' schooling by progressive educators.[21]

Markets and Performance

Let us take as an example of the ways in which all this operates one element of conservative modernization—the neo-liberal claim that the invisible hand of the market will inexorably lead to better schools. As Roger Dale reminds us, 'the market' acts as a metaphor rather than an explicit guide for action. It is not denotative, but connotative. Thus, it must itself be 'marketed' to those who will exist in it and live with its effects.[22] Markets are marketed, are made legitimate, by a depoliticizing strategy. They are said to be natural and neutral, and governed by effort and merit. And those opposed to them are by definition, hence, also opposed to effort and merit. Markets, as well, are supposedly less subject to political interference and the weight of bureaucratic procedures. Plus, they are grounded in the rational choices of individual actors.[23] Thus, markets and the guarantee of rewards for effort and merit are to be coupled together to produce 'neutral', yet positive, results. Mechanisms, hence, must be put into place that give evidence of entrepreneurial efficiency and effectiveness. This coupling of markets and mechanisms for the generation of evidence of performance is exactly what has occurred. Whether it works is open to question.

In one of the most comprehensive critical reviews of all the evidence on marketization, Geoff Whitty cautions us not to mistake rhetoric for reality. After examining research from a number of countries, Whitty argues that while advocates of marketized 'choice' plans assume that competition will enhance the efficiency and responsiveness of schools, as well as give disadvantaged children opportunities that they currently do not have, this may be a false hope.[24] These hopes are not now being realized and are unlikely to be realized in the future 'in the context of broader policies that do nothing to challenge deeper social and cultural inequalities'. As he goes on to say, 'Atomized decision-making in a highly stratified society may appear to give everyone equal opportunities, but transforming responsibility for decision-making from the public to the private sphere can actually reduce the scope of collective action to improve the quality of education for all.'[25] When this is connected to the fact that, as I shall show shortly, in practice neo-liberal policies involving market 'solutions' may actually serve to reproduce—not subvert—traditional hierarchies of class and race, this should give us reason to pause.[26]

Thus, rather than taking neo-liberal claims at face value, we should want to ask about their hidden effects that are too often invisible in the rhetoric and metaphors of their proponents. Given the limitations of what one can say in a single chapter, I shall select a few issues that have been given less attention than they deserve, but on which there is now significant research.

The English experience is apposite here, especially since proponents of the market such as Chubb and Moe rely so heavily on it[27] and because that is where the tendencies I analyze are most advanced. In England, the 1993 Education Act documented the state's commitment to marketization. Governing bodies of local educational authorities (LEAs) were mandated to formally consider 'going GM' (that is, opting out of the local school system's control and entering into the competitive market) every year.[28] Thus, the weight of the state stood behind the press towards neo-liberal reforms there.[29] Yet, rather than leading to curriculum responsiveness and diversification, the competitive market has not created much that is different from the traditional models so firmly entrenched in schools today.[30] Nor has it radically altered the relations of inequality that characterize schooling.

In their own extensive analyses of the effects of marketized reforms 'on the ground', Ball and his colleagues point to some of the reasons why we need to be quite cautious here. As they document, in these situations educational principles and values are often compromised such that commercial issues become more important in curriculum design and resource allocation.[31] For instance, the coupling of markets with the demand for and publication of performance indicators such as 'examination league tables' in England has meant that schools are increasingly looking for ways to attract 'motivated' parents with 'able' children. In this way, schools are able to enhance their relative position in local systems of competition. This represents a subtle, but crucial shift in emphasis—one that is not openly discussed as often as it should be—from student needs to student performance and from what the school does for the student to what the student does for the school. This is also accompanied too uncomfortably often by a shift of resources away from students who are labelled as having special needs or learning difficulties, with some of these needed resources now being shifted to marketing and public relations. 'Special needs' students are not only expensive, but deflate test scores on those all-important league tables.

This makes it difficult not only to 'manage public impressions', but it also to attract the 'best' and most academically talented teachers.[32] The entire enterprise does, however, establish a new metric and a new set of goals based on a constant striving to win the market game. What this means is of considerable import, not only in terms of its effects on daily school life but in the ways all of this signifies a transformation of what counts as a good society and a responsible citizen. Let me say something about this generally.

I noted earlier that behind all educational proposals are visions of a just society and a good student. The neo-liberal reforms I have been discussing construct this in a particular way. While the defining characteristic of neo-liberalism is largely based on the central tenets of classical liberalism, in particular classic economic liberalism, there are crucial differences between classical liberalism and neo-liberalism. These differences are absolutely essential in understanding the politics of education and the transformations education is currently undergoing. Mark Olssen clearly details these differences. It is worth quoting the passage in its entirety.

> Whereas classical liberalism represents a negative conception of state power in that the individual was to be taken as an object to be freed from the interventions of the state, neo-liberalism has come to represent a positive conception of the state's role in creating the appropriate market by providing the conditions, laws and institutions necessary for its operation. In classical liberalism, the individual is characterized as having an autonomous human nature and can practice freedom. In neo-liberalism the state seeks to create an individual who is an enterprising and competitive entrepreneur. In the classical model the theoretical aim of the state was to limit and minimize its role based on postulates which included universal egoism (the self-interested individual); invisible hand theory which dictated that the interests of the individual were also the interests of the society as a whole; and the political maxim of

laissez-faire. In the shift from classical liberalism to neo-liberalism, then, there is a further element added, for such a shift involves a change in subject position from 'homo economicus,' who naturally behaves out of self-interest and is relatively detached from the state, to 'manipulatable man,' who is created by the state and who is continually encouraged to be 'perpetually responsive.' It is not that the conception of the self-interested subject is replaced or done away with by the new ideals of 'neo-liberalism,' but that in an age of universal welfare, the perceived possibilities of slothful indolence create necessities for new forms of vigilance, surveillance, 'performance appraisal' and of forms of control generally. In this model the state has taken it upon itself to keep us all up to the mark. The state will see to it that each one makes a 'continual enterprise of ourselves' ... in what seems to be a process of 'governing without governing'.[33]

The results of Ball and his colleagues' research document how the state does indeed do this, enhancing that odd combination of marketized individualism and control through constant and comparative public assessment. Widely publicized league tables determine one's relative value in the educational marketplace. Only those schools with rising performance indicators are worthy. And only those students who can 'make a continual enterprise of themselves' can keep such schools going in the 'correct' direction. Yet, while these issues are important, they fail to fully illuminate some of the other mechanisms through which *differential* effects are produced by neo-liberal reforms. Here, class issues come to the fore in ways that Ball, Bowe, and Gewirtz make clear.

Middle-class parents are clearly the most advantaged in this kind of cultural assemblage and not only, as we saw, because schools seek them out. Middle-class parents have become quite skilled, in general, in exploiting market mechanisms in education and in bringing their social, economic, and cultural capital to bear on them. 'Middle class parents are more likely to have the knowledge, skills and contacts to decode and manipulate what are increasingly complex and deregulated systems of choice and recruitment. The more deregulation, the more possibility of informal procedures being employed. The middle class also, on the whole, are more able to move their children around the system.'[34] That class and race intersect and interact in complex ways means that—even though we need to be clear that marketized systems in education often *expressly* have their conscious and unconscious *raison d'être* in a fear of 'the Other' and often are hidden expressions of a racialization of educational policy—the differential results will 'naturally' be decidedly raced as well as classed.[35]

Economic and social capital can be converted into cultural capital in various ways. In marketized plans, more affluent parents often have more flexible hours and can visit multiple schools. They have cars—often more than one—and can *afford* driving their children across town to attend a 'better' school. They can as well provide the hidden cultural resources such as camps and after-school programs (dance, music, computer classes, etc.) that give their children an 'ease', a 'style', that seems 'natural' and acts as a set of cultural resources. Their previous stock of social and cultural capital—who they know, their 'comfort' in social encounters with educational officials—is an unseen but powerful storehouse of resources. Thus, more affluent parents are more likely to have the informal knowledge and skill—what Bourdieu would call the habitus[36]—to be able to decode and use marketized forms to their own benefit. This sense of what might be called 'confidence'—which is itself the result of past choices that tacitly but no less powerfully depend on the economic resources to actually have had the ability to make economic choices—is the unseen capital that underpins their ability to negotiate marketized forms and 'work the system' through sets of informal cultural rules.[37]

Of course, it needs to be said that working class, poor, and/or immigrant parents are not skill-less in this regard, by any means. (After all, it requires an immense amount of skill, courage, and social and cultural resources to survive under exploitative and depressing material conditions. Thus, collective bonds, informal networks and contacts, and an ability to work the system are developed in quite nuanced, intelligent, and often impressive ways here.[38]) However, the match between the historically grounded habitus expected in schools and in its actors and those of more affluent parents, combined with the material resources available to more affluent parents, usually leads to a successful conversion of economic and social capital into cultural capital.[39] And this is exactly what is happening in England.

These claims both about what is happening inside schools and about larger sets of power relations are supported by even more recent synthetic analyses of the overall results of marketized models. This research on the effects of the tense but still effective combination of neo-liberal and neo-conservative policies examines the tendencies internationally by comparing what has happened in a number of nations—for example, the United States, England and Wales, Australia, and New Zealand—where this combination has been increasingly powerful. The results confirm the arguments I have made here. Let me rehearse some of the most significant and disturbing findings of such research.

It is unfortunately all too usual that the most widely used measures of the 'success' of school reforms are the results of standardized achievement tests. This simply will not do. We need constantly to ask what reforms do to schools as a whole and to each of their participants, including teachers, students, administrators, community members, local activists, and so on. To take one set of examples, as marketized 'self-managing' schools grow in many nations, the role of the school principal is radically transformed. More, not less, power is actually consolidated within an administrative structure. More time and energy is spent on maintaining or enhancing a public image of a 'good school' and less time and energy is spent on pedagogic and curricular substance. At the same time, teachers seem to be experiencing not increased autonomy and professionalism, but intensification.[40] And, oddly, as noted before, schools themselves become more *similar*, and more committed, to standard, traditional, whole class methods of teaching and a standard and traditional (and often monocultural) curriculum.[41] Only directing our attention to test scores would cause us to miss some truly profound transformations, many of which we may find disquieting.

One of the reasons these broader effects are so often produced is that in all too many countries, neo-liberal visions of quasi-markets are usually accompanied by neo-conservative pressure to regulate content and behavior through such things as national curricula, national standards, and national systems of assessment. The combination is historically contingent; that is, it is not absolutely necessary that the two emphases are combined. But there are characteristics of neo-liberalism that make it more likely that an emphasis on the weak state and a faith in markets will cohere with an emphasis on the strong state and a commitment to regulating knowledge, values, and the body.

This is partly the case because of the increasing power of the 'evaluative state'. This signifies what initially may seem to be contradictory tendencies. At the same time as the state appears to be devolving power to individuals and autonomous institutions which are themselves increasingly competing in a market, the state remains strong in key areas.[42] As I claimed earlier, one of the key differences between classical liberalism and its faith in 'enterprising individuals' in a market and current forms of neo-liberalism is the latter's commitment to a regulatory state. Neo-liberalism does indeed demand the constant production of evidence that one is in fact 'making an enterprise of oneself'.[43] Thus, under these conditions not only does education become a marketable commodity like bread and cars in which the values, procedures, and metaphors of business dominate, but its results must be reducible to standardized 'performance indicators'.[44] This is ideally suited to the task of providing a mechanism for the neo-conservative attempts to specify what knowledge, values, and behaviors should be standardized and officially defined as 'legitimate', a point I shall expand upon in the next section of this chapter.

In essence, we are witnessing a process in which the state shifts the blame for the very evident inequalities in access and outcome it has promised to reduce, from itself onto individual schools, parents, and children. This is, of course, also part of a larger process in which dominant economic groups shift the blame for the massive and unequal effects of their own misguided decisions from themselves onto the state. The state is then faced with a very real crisis in legitimacy. Given this, we should not be at all surprised that the state will then seek to export this crisis outside itself.[45]

Of course, the state is not only classed, but is inherently *sex/gendered* and *raced* as well.[46] This is evident in Whitty, Power, and Halpin's arguments. They point to the gendered nature of the ways in which the management of schools is thought about, as 'masculinist' business models become increasingly dominant.[47] While there is a danger of these claims degenerating into reductive and essentializing arguments, there is a good deal of insight here. They do cohere with the work of other scholars inside and outside education who recognize that the ways in which our very definitions of public and private, of what knowledge is of most worth, and of how institutions should be thought about and run are fully implicated in the gendered nature of this society.[48] These broad ideological effects—e.g. enabling a coalition between neo-liberals and neo-conservatives to be formed, the masculinization of theories, policies, and management talk—are of considerable import and make it harder to change common sense in more critical directions. When these tendencies are combined with dominant and new middle-class discourses associated with the new managerialism, the results can be very damaging.

For example, other, more proximate, effects inside schools are equally striking. For instance, even though principals seem to have more local power in these supposedly decentralized schools, because of the cementing in of neo-conservative policies principals 'are increasingly forced into a position in which they have to demonstrate performance along centrally prescribed curricula in a context in which they have diminishing control.'[49] Because of the intensification that I mentioned before, both principals and teachers experience considerably heavier workloads and ever escalating demands for accountability, a never-ending schedule of meetings, and in many cases a growing scarcity of resources both emotional and physical.[50]

Further, as in the research in England, in nearly all the countries studied the market did *not* encourage diversity in curriculum, pedagogy, organization, clientele, or even image. It instead consistently devalued alternatives and increased the power of dominant models. Of equal significance, it also consistently exacerbated differences in access and outcome based on race, ethnicity, and class.[51]

The return to 'traditionalism' led to a number of things. It *delegitimated* more critical models of teaching and learning, a point that is crucial to recognize in any attempt to think through the possibilities of cultural struggles and critical pedagogies in schools. It both reintroduced class and race re-stratification within the school and lessened the possibility that de-tracking would occur. More emphasis was given to 'gifted' children and 'fast track' classes, while students who were seen as less academically able were therefore 'less attractive'. In England, the extent of this was nowhere more visible than in the alarming rate of students being excluded from schools. Much of this was caused by the intense pressure to constantly demonstrate higher achievement rates. This was especially powerful in marketized contexts in which the 'main driving force appeared to be *commercial* rather than *educational*'.[52]

In their own analysis of these worrisome and more hidden results, Whitty, Power, and Halpin and others demonstrate that among the dangerous effects of quasi-markets are the ways in which schools that wish to maintain or enhance their market position engage in 'cream-skimming', ensuring that *particular* kinds of students with particular characteristics are accepted and particular kinds of students are found wanting. For some schools, stereotypes were reproduced in that girls were seen as more valuable, as were students from some Asian communities. Afro-Caribbean children were often clear losers in this situation.[53]

So far I have focused largely on England. Yet, as I mentioned in my introductory points, these movements are truly global. Their logics have spread rapidly to many nations, with results that tend to mirror those I have discussed so far. The case of New Zealand is useful here, especially since a large percentage of the population of New Zealand is multiethnic and the nation has a history of racial tensions and class and race inequalities. Furthermore, the move toward New Right policies occurred faster there than elsewhere. In essence, New Zealand became the laboratory for many of the policies I am analyzing. In their exceptional study, based in large part on a conceptual apparatus influenced by Pierre Bourdieu, Lauder and Hughes document that educational markets seem to lead to an overall decline in educational standards. Paradoxically, they have a negative, not a positive, effect on the performance of schools with large working-class and minority populations. In essence, they 'trade off the opportunities of less privileged children to those already privileged'.[54] The combination of neo-liberal policies of marketization and the neo-conservative emphasis on 'tougher standards', about which I shall say more in the next section, creates an even more dangerous set of conditions. Their analysis confirms the conceptual and empirical arguments of Ball, Phil Brown, and others that markets in education are not only responses by capital to reduce both the sphere of the state and of public control. They are also part of an attempt by the middle class to alter the rules of competition in education in light of the increased insecurities their children face. 'By changing the process of selection to schools, middle class parents can raise the stakes in creating stronger mechanisms of exclusion for blue collar and post-colonial peoples in their struggle for equality of opportunity.'[55]

The results from New Zealand not only mirror what was found elsewhere, but demonstrate that the further one's practices follow the logics of action embodied in marketizing principles the worse the situation tends to get. Markets *systematically* privilege higher SES families through their knowledge and material resources. These are the families who are most likely to exercise choice. Rather than giving large numbers of students who are working class, poor, or of color the ability to exit, it is largely higher SES families who exit from public schools and schools with mixed populations. In a situation of increased competition, this in turn produces a spiral of decline in which schools populated by poorer students and students of color are again systematically disadvantaged and schools with higher SES and higher white populations are able to insulate themselves from the effects of market competition.[56] 'White flight' then enhances the relative status of those schools already advantaged by larger economic forces; schooling for the 'Other' becomes even more polarized and continues a downward spiral.[57]

Having said this, however, we need to be cautious not to ignore historical specificities. Social movements, existing ideological formations, and institutions in civil society and the state may provide some support for countervailing logics. In some cases, in those nations with stronger and more extensive histories of social democratic policies and visions of collective positive freedoms, the neo-liberal emphasis on the market has been significantly mediated. Hence, as Petter Aasen has demonstrated in Norway and Sweden, for instance, privatizing initiatives in education have had to cope with a greater collective commitment than in, say, the United States, England, and New Zealand.[58] However, these commitments partly rest on class relations. They are weakened when racial dynamics enter in. Thus, for example, the sense of 'everyone being the same' and hence being all subject to similar collective sensibilities is challenged by the growth of immigrant populations from Africa, Asia, and the Middle East. Greater sympathy for marketized forms may arise once the commonly understood assumptions of what it means to be, say, Norwegian or Swedish are interrupted by populations of color who now claim the status of national citizenship. For this reason, it may be the case that the collective sensibilities that provide support for less market-oriented policies are based on an unacknowledged *racial contract* that underpins the ideological foundations of a national 'imagined community'.[59] This, then, may also generate support for neo-conservative policies, not because of neo-liberalism's commitment to 'perpetual responsiveness', but rather as a form of cultural restoration, as a way of re-establishing an imagined past when 'we were all one'. Because of this, it is important that any analysis of the current play of forces surrounding conservative modernization is aware of the fact that not only are such movements in constant motion, but once again we need to remember that they have a multitude of intersecting and contradictory dynamics including not only class, but race and gender as well.[60]

Most of the data I have drawn upon come from schools outside the United States, although they should make us stop dead in our tracks and give some very serious thought to whether we want to proceed with similar policies here. Yet, the United States still sits at the center of much of the discussion in this literature. For example, charter schools and their equivalents in the US and England are also put under critical scrutiny. In both places, they tend to attract parents who live and work in relatively privileged communities. Here too, 'it would appear that any new opportunities are being colonized by the already advantaged, rather than the "losers" identified by Chubb and Moe'.[61]

In the process, this critical research suggests that there are hidden similarities between advocates of school effectiveness research and those committed to neo-liberal 'reforms.' Both tend to ignore the fact that external characteristics of schools such as poverty, political and economic power, and so on consistently account for much more of the variation in school performance than things like organizational features or those characteristics that supposedly guarantee an 'effective school'.[62]

The overall conclusions are clear. '[In] current circumstances choice is as likely to reinforce hierarchies as to improve educational opportunities and the overall quality of schooling'.[63] As Whitty, Power, and Halpin put it in their arguments against those who believe that what we are witnessing in the emergence of 'choice' programs is the postmodern celebration of difference:

> There is a growing body of empirical evidence that, rather than benefiting the disadvantaged, the emphasis on parental choice and school autonomy is further disadvantaging those least able to compete in the market ... For most disadvantaged groups, as opposed to the few individuals who escape from schools at the bottom of the status hierarchy, the new arrangements seem to be just a more sophisticated way of reproducing traditional distinctions between different types of school and the people who attend them.[64]

All of this gives us ample reason to agree with Henig's insightful argument that 'the sad irony of the current education-reform movement is that, through over-identification with school-choice proposals rooted in market-based ideas, the healthy impulse to consider radical reforms to address social problems may be channelled into initiatives that further erode the potential for collective deliberation and collective response'.[65]

This is not to dismiss either the possibility or necessity of school reform. However, we need to take seriously the probability that only by focusing on the exogenous socio-economic features, not simply the organizational features, of 'successful' schools can all schools succeed. Eliminating poverty through greater income parity, establishing effective and much more equal health and housing programs, and positively refusing to continue the hidden and not so hidden politics of racial exclusion and degradation that so clearly still characterize daily life in many nations (and in which marketized plans need to be seen as partly a structure to avoid the body and culture of 'the Other')—only by tackling these issues together can substantive progress be made. Unless discussions of critical pedagogy are themselves grounded in a recognition of these realities, they too may fall into the trap of assuming that schools can do it alone.

These empirical findings are made more understandable in terms of Pierre Bourdieu's analysis of the relative weight given to cultural capital as part of mobility strategies today.[66] The rise in importance of cultural capital infiltrates all institutions in such a way that there is a relative movement away from the *direct* reproduction of class privilege (where power is transmitted largely within families through economic property) to *school-mediated* forms of class privilege. Here, 'the bequeathal of privilege is simultaneously effectuated and transfigured by the intercession of educational institutions'.[67] This is *not* a conspiracy; it is not 'conscious' in the ways we normally use that concept. Rather it is the result of a long chain of relatively autonomous connections between differentially accumulated economic, social, and cultural capital operating at the level of daily events as we make our respective ways in the world, including as we saw in the world of school choice.

Thus, while not taking an unyieldingly determinist position, Bourdieu argues that a class habitus tends to reproduce the conditions of its own reproduction 'unconsciously'. It does this by producing a relatively coherent and systematically *characteristic* set of seemingly natural and unconscious strategies—in essence, ways of understanding and acting on the world that act as forms of cultural capital that can be and are employed to protect and enhance one's status in a social field of power. He aptly compares this similarity of habitus across class actors to handwriting.

> Just as the acquired disposition we call 'handwriting,' that is a particular way of forming letters, always produces the same 'writing'—that is, graphic lines that despite differences in size, matter, and color related to writing surface (sheet of paper or blackboard) and implement (pencil, pen, or chalk), that is despite differences in vehicles for the action, have an immediately recognizable affinity of style or a family resemblance—the practices of a single agent, or, more broadly, the practices of all agents endowed with similar habitus, owe the affinity of

style that makes each a metaphor for the others to the fact that they are the products of the implementation in different fields of the same schemata of perception, thought, and action.[68]

This very connection of habitus across fields of power—the ease of bringing one's economic, social, and cultural resources to bear on 'markets'—enables a comfort between markets and self that characterizes the middle-class actor here. This constantly *produces* differential effects. These effects are not neutral, no matter what the advocates of neo-liberalism suggest. Rather, they are themselves the results of a particular kind of morality. Unlike the conditions of what might best be called 'thick morality' where principles of the common good are the ethical basis for adjudicating policies and practices, markets are grounded in aggregative principles. They are constituted out of the sum of individual goods and choices. 'Founded on individual and property rights that enable citizens to address problems of interdependence via exchange,' they offer a prime example of 'thin morality' by generating both hierarchy and division based on competitive individualism.[69] And in this competition, the general outline of the winners and losers *has* been identified empirically.

National Curriculum and National Testing

I showed in the previous section that there are connections between at least two dynamics operating in neo-liberal reforms, 'free' markets and increased surveillance. This can be seen in the fact that in many contexts, marketization has been accompanied by a set of particular policies for 'producers', for those professionals working within education. These policies have been strongly regulatory and have been quite instrumental in reconstituting common sense. As in the case of the linkage between national tests and performance indicators published as league tables, they have been organized around a concern for external supervision, regulation, and external judgement of performance[70] and have increasingly been colonized by parents who possess what is seen as 'appropriate' economic, social, and cultural capital. This concern for external supervision and regulation is not only connected with a strong mistrust of 'producers' (e.g. teachers) and to the need for ensuring that people continually make enterprises out of themselves. It is also clearly linked both to the neo-conservative sense of a need to 'return' to a lost past of high standards, discipline, awe, and 'real' knowledge and to the professional middle class's own ability to carve out a sphere of authority within the state for its own commitment to management techniques and efficiency. The focus on efficient management plays a prime role here, one which many neo-liberals and neo-conservatives alike find useful.

There has been a shift in the relationship between the state and 'professionals'. In essence, the move toward a small, strong state that is increasingly guided by market needs seems inevitably to bring with it reduced professional power and status.[71] Managerialism takes center stage here. Managerialism is largely charged with 'bringing about the cultural transformation that shifts professional identities in order to make them more responsive to client demand and external judgement'. It aims to justify and to have people internalize fundamental alterations in professional practices. It both harnesses energy and discourages dissent.[72]

There is no necessary contradiction between a general set of marketizing and deregulating interests and processes—such as voucher and choice plans—and a set of enhanced regulatory processes—such as plans for national curricula and national testing.[73] 'The regulatory form permits the state to maintain 'steerage' over the aims and processes of education from within the market mechanism.'[74] Such steerage has often been vested in such things as national standards, national curricula, and national testing. Forms of all of these are being pushed for in the United States currently and are the subject of considerable controversy, some of which cuts across ideological lines and shows some of the tensions within the different elements contained under the umbrella of conservative modernization.

I have argued that paradoxically a national curriculum and especially a national testing program are the first and most essential steps toward increased marketization. They actually provide the mechanisms for comparative data that 'consumers' need to make markets work as markets.[75] Absent these mechanisms, there is no comparative base of information for 'choice'. Yet, we do not have to argue about these regulatory forms in a vacuum. Like the neo-liberal markets I discussed in the previous section, they too have been instituted in England; and, once again, there is important research available that can and must make us duly cautious in going down this path.

One might want to claim that a set of national standards, national curricula, and national tests would provide the conditions for 'thick morality'. After all, such regulatory reforms are supposedly based on shared values and common sentiments that also create social spaces in which common issues of concern can be debated and made subject to moral interrogation.[76] Yet, what counts as the 'common', and how and by whom it is actually determined, is rather more thin than thick.

It is the case that while the national curriculum now so solidly in place in England and Wales is clearly prescriptive, it has not always proved to be the kind of straitjacket it has often been made out to be. As a number of researchers have documented, it is not only possible that policies and legislative mandates are interpreted and adapted, but it seems inevitable. Thus, the national curriculum is 'not so much being "implemented" in schools as being "recreated," not so much "reproduced," as "produced".'[77]

In general, it is nearly a truism that there is no simplistic linear model of policy formation, distribution, and implementation. There are always complex mediations at each level of the process. There is a complex politics that goes on within each group and between these groups and external forces in the formulation of policy, in its being written up as a legislative mandate, in its distribution, and in its reception at the level of practice.[78] Thus, the state may legislate changes in curriculum, evaluation, or policy (which is itself produced through conflict, compromise, and political maneuvering), but policy writers and curriculum writers may be unable to control the meanings and implementations of their texts. All texts are 'leaky' documents. They are subject to 'recontextualization' at every stage of the process.[79]

However, this general principle may be just a bit too romantic. None of this occurs on a level playing field. As with market plans, there are very real differences in power in one's ability to influence, mediate, transform, or reject a policy or a regulatory process. Granted, it is important to recognize that a 'state control model'—with its assumption of top-down linearity—is much too simplistic and that the possibility of human agency and influence is always there. However, having said this, this should not imply that such agency and influence will be powerful.[80]

The case of national curriculum and national testing in England and Wales documents the tensions in these two accounts. It was the case that the national curriculum that was first legislated and then imposed there, was indeed struggled over. It was originally too detailed and too specific, and, hence, was subject to major transformations at the national, community, school, and then classroom levels. However, even though the national curriculum was subject to conflict, mediation, and some transformation of its content, organization, and its invasive and immensely time-consuming forms of evaluation, its utter power is demonstrated in its radical reconfiguration of the very process of knowledge selection, organization, and assessment. It changed the entire terrain of education radically. Its subject divisions 'provide more constraint than scope for discretion'. The 'standard attainment targets' that have been mandated cement these constraints in place. 'The imposition of national testing locks the national curriculum in place as the dominant framework of teachers' work whatever opportunities teachers may take to evade or reshape it.'[81]

Thus, it is not sufficient to state that the world of education is complex and has multiple influences. The purpose of any serious analysis is to go beyond such overly broad conclusions. Rather, we need to 'discriminate degrees of influence in the world', to weigh the relative efficacy of the factors involved. Hence, although it is clear that while the national curriculum and national tests that now exist in England and Wales have come about because of a complex interplay of forces and influences, it is equally clear that 'state control has the upper hand'.[82]

The national curricula and national tests *did* generate conflict about issues. They did partly lead to the creation of social spaces for moral questions to get asked. (Of course, these moral questions had been asked all along by dispossessed groups.) Thus, it was clear to many people that the creation of mandatory and reductive tests that emphasized memory and decontextualized abstraction pulled the national curriculum in a particular direction—that of encouraging a selective educational market in which elite students and elite schools with a wide range of resources would be well (if narrowly) served.[83] Diverse groups of people argued that such reductive, detailed, and simplistic paper and pencil tests 'had the potential to do enormous damage', a situation that was made even worse because the tests were so onerous in terms of time and record keeping. Teachers had a good deal of support when as a group they decided to boycott the administration of the tests in a remarkable act of public protest. This also led to serious questioning of the arbitrary, inflexible, and overly prescriptive national curriculum. While the curriculum is still inherently problematic and the assessment system does still contain numerous dangerous and onerous elements within it, organized activity against them did have an impact.[84]

Yet, unfortunately, the story does not end there. By the mid-1990s, even with the government's partial retreat on such regulatory forms as its program of constant and reductive testing, it had become clearer by the year that the development of testing and the specification of content had been 'hijacked' by those who were ideologically committed to traditional pedagogies and to the idea of more rigorous selection.[85] The residual effects are both material and ideological. They include a continuing emphasis on trying to provide the 'rigor [that is] missing in the practice of most teachers ... judging progress solely by what is testable in tests of this kind' and the development of a 'very hostile view of the accountability of teachers' that was seen as 'part of a wider thrust of policy to take away professional control of public services and establish so called consumer control through a market structure'.[86]

The authors of an extremely thorough review of recent assessment programs instituted in England and Wales provide a summary of what has happened. Gipps and Murphy argue that it has become increasingly obvious that the national assessment program attached to the national curriculum is more and more dominated by traditional models of testing and the assumptions about teaching and learning that lie behind them. At the same time, equity issues are becoming much less visible. In the calculus of values now in place in the regulatory state, efficiency, speed, and cost control replace more substantive concerns about social and educational justice. The pressure to get tests in place rapidly has meant that 'the speed of test development is so great, and the curriculum and assessment changes so regular, that [there is] little time to carry out detailed analyses and trialing to ensure that the tests are as fair as possible to all groups'.[87] The conditions for 'thin morality'—in which the competitive individual of the market dominates and social justice will somehow take care of itself—are reproduced here. The combination of the neo-liberal market and the regulatory state, then, does indeed 'work'. However, it works in ways in which the metaphors of free market, merit, and effort hide the differential reality that is produced. While on the one hand this makes a socially and culturally critical pedagogy even more essential, it also makes it much more difficult to actually accomplish.

Basil Bernstein's discussion of the general principles by which knowledge and policies ('texts') move from one arena to another is useful in understanding this. As Bernstein reminds us, when talking about educational change there are three fields with which we must be concerned. Each field has its own rules of access, regulation, privilege, and special interests: (1) the field of 'production' where new knowledge is constructed; (2) the field of 'reproduction' where pedagogy and curriculum are actually enacted in schools; and, between these other two, (3) the 'recontextualizing' field where discourses from the field of production are appropriated and then transformed into pedagogic discourse and recommendations.[88] This appropriation and recontextualization of knowledge for educational purposes is itself governed by two sets of principles. The first—delocation—implies that there is always a *selective* appropriation of knowledge and discourse from the field of production. The second—relocation—points to the fact that when knowledge and discourse from the field of production is pulled within the recontextualizing field, it is subject to ideological transformations due to the various specialized and/or political interests whose conflicts structure the recontextualizing field.[89]

A good example of this, one that confirms Gipps and Murphy's analysis of the dynamics of national curricula and national testing during their more recent iterations, is found in the process by which the content and organization of the mandated national curriculum in physical education were struggled over and ultimately formed in England. In this instance, a working group of academics both within and outside the field of physical education, headmasters of private and state-supported schools, well-known athletes, and business leaders (but *no* teachers) was formed.

The original curriculum policies that arose from the groups were relatively mixed educationally and ideologically, taking account of the field of production of knowledge within physical education. That is, they contained both critical and progressive elements and elements of the conservative restoration, as well as academic perspectives within the specialized fields from the university. However, as these made their way from report to recommendations and then from recommendations to action, they steadily came closer to restorational principles. An emphasis on efficiency, basic skills and performance testing, on the social control of the body, and on competitive norms ultimately won out. Like the middle-class capturing of the market discussed earlier, this too was not a conspiracy. Rather, it was the result of a process of 'overdetermination'. That is, it was not due to an imposition of these norms, but to a combination of interests in the recontextualizing field—an economic context in which public spending was under severe scrutiny and cost savings had to be sought everywhere, government officials who were opposed to 'frills' and consistently intervened to institute only a selection of the recommendations (conservative ones that did *not* come from 'professional academics' preferably), ideological attacks on critical, progressive, or child-centered approaches to physical education, and a predominant discourse of 'being pragmatic'. These came together in the recontextualizing field and helped insure in practice that conservative principles would be reinscribed in policies and mandates, and that critical forms were seen as too ideological, too costly, or too impractical.[90] 'Standards' were upheld; critical voices were heard, but ultimately to little effect; the norms of competitive performance were made central and employed as regulatory devices. Regulatory devices served to privilege specific groups in much the same way as did markets. Thus goes democracy in education.

Thinking Strategically

So far in this chapter, I have raised serious questions about current educational 'reform' efforts now underway in a number of nations. I have used research largely, but not solely, on the English and Welsh experiences to document some of the hidden differential effects of two connected strategies—neo-liberal inspired market proposals and neo-liberal, neo-conservative, and middle-class managerial-inspired regulatory proposals. Taking a key from Herbert Kliebard's historical analysis, I have described how different interests with different educational and social visions compete for dominion in the social field of power surrounding educational policy and practice. In the process, I have documented some of the complexities and imbalances in this field of power. These complexities and imbalances result in 'thin' rather than 'thick' morality and in the reproduction of both dominant pedagogical and curricular forms and ideologies and the social privileges that accompany them. I have suggested that the rhetorical flourishes of the discourses of critical pedagogy need to come to grips with these changing material and ideological conditions. Critical pedagogy cannot and will not occur in a vacuum. Unless we honestly face these profound rightist transformations and think tactically about them, we will have little effect either on the creation of a counter-hegemonic common sense or on the building of a counter-hegemonic alliance. The growth of that odd combination of marketization and regulatory state, the move towards pedagogic similarity and 'traditional' academic curricula and teaching, the ability of dominant groups to exert leadership in the struggle over this, and the accompanying shifts in common sense—all this cannot be wished away. Instead, it needs to be confronted honestly and self-critically.

Having said this, however, I want to point to a hidden paradox in what I have done. Even though much of my own and others' research recently has been on the processes and effects of conservative modernization, there are dangers in such a focus of which we should be aware. Research on the history, politics, and practices of rightist social and educational movements and 'reforms' has enabled us to show the contradictions and unequal effects of such policies and practices. It has enabled the rearticulation of claims to social justice on the basis of solid evidence. This is all to the good. However, in the process, one of the latent effects has been the gradual framing of educational issues largely in terms of the conservative agenda. The very categories themselves—markets, choice, national curricula, national testing, standards—bring the debate onto the terrain established by neo-liberals and neo-conservatives. The analysis of 'what is' has led to a neglect of 'what might be'. Thus, there has been a withering of substantive large-scale discussions of feasible alternatives to neo-liberal and neo-conservative visions, policies, and practices, ones that would move well beyond them.[91]

Because of this, at least part of our task may be politically and conceptually complex, but it can be said simply. In the long term, we need to 'develop a political project that is both local yet generalizable, systematic without making Eurocentric, masculinist claims to essential and universal truths about human subjects'.[92] Another part of our task, though, must be and is more proximate, more appropriately educational. Defensible, articulate, and fully fleshed out alternative critical and progressive policies and practices in curriculum, teaching, and evaluation need to be developed and made widely available. But this too must be done with due recognition of the changing nature of the social field of power and the importance of thinking tactically and strategically. Let me be specific here.

For example, in the United States the increasingly popular journal *Rethinking Schools* has provided an important forum for social and educational criticism and for descriptions of critical educational practices in schools and communities. At times influenced directly by the work of Paulo Freire and by educators who have themselves elaborated and extended it, and at other times coming out of diverse indigenous radical educational traditions specific to the US, *Rethinking Schools* and emerging national organizations such as the National Coalition of Educational Activists have jointly constructed spaces for critical educators, cultural and political activists, radical scholars, and others to teach each other, to provide supportive criticism of each other's work, and to build a more collective set of responses to the destructive educational and social policies coming from the conservative restoration.[93]

In using the phrase 'collective responses', however, I need to stress that this phrase does not signify anything like 'democratic centrism' in which a small group or a party cadre speaks for the majority and establishes the 'appropriate' position. Given the fact that there are diverse emancipatory movements whose voices are heard in publications such as *Rethinking Schools* and in organizations such as the National Coalition of Educational Activists—anti-racist and post-colonial positions, radical forms of multiculturalism, gays and lesbians, multiple feminist voices, neo-Marxists and democratic socialists, 'greens', and so on—a more appropriate way of looking at what is happening is to call it a *decentered unity*. Multiple progressive projects, multiple 'critical pedagogies', are articulated. Like Freire, each of them is related to real struggles in real institutions in real communities. We, of course, should not be romantic about this. There are very real differences—political, epistemological, and/or educational—in these varied voices. Yet, they are united in their opposition to the forces involved in the new conservative hegemonic alliance. There *are* tensions, but the decentered unity has remained strong enough for each constituent group to support the struggles of the others, as long as key issues such as class are not neglected.

This is not all. At the same time as these critical movements are being built, critical educators are also attempting to occupy the spaces provided by existing 'mainstream' publication outlets to publish books that provide *critical* answers to teachers' questions about 'What do I do on Monday?' during a conservative era. This space has too long been ignored by many theorists of critical pedagogy. Some of these attempts have been remarkably successful. Let me give one example. One very large 'professional' organization in the United States—the Association for Supervision and Curriculum Development (ASCD)—publishes books that are distributed each year to its more than 150,000 members, most of whom are teachers or administrators in elementary, middle, or secondary schools. ASCD has not been a very progressive organization, preferring to publish largely technicist and overtly depoliticized material. Yet it has been concerned that its publications have not sufficiently represented socially and culturally critical educators. It, thus, has been looking for ways to increase its legitimacy to a wider range of educators. Because of this legitimacy problem and because of its large membership, it became clear to a number of people who were part of the critical educational traditions in the United States that it might be possible to convince ASCD to publish and widely circulate material that would demonstrate the actual practical *successes* of critical models of curriculum, teaching, and evaluation in solving real problems in schools and communities, especially with working-class and poor children and children of color.

After intense negotiations that guaranteed an absence of censorship, a colleague of mine and I agreed to publish a book—*Democratic Schools*[94]—with ASCD that provided clear practical examples of the power of Freirian and similar critical approaches at work in classrooms and communities. *Democratic Schools* was not only distributed to all 150,000 members of the organization, but it has gone on to sell an additional 100,000 copies. Thus, nearly 250,000 copies of a volume that tells the practical stories of the largely successful struggles of critically oriented educators in real schools are now in the hands of educators who daily face similar problems.[95] This is an important intervention. While there is no guarantee that teachers will always be progressive (nor is there any guarantee that those who are progressive around class and union issues will be equally progressive around issues of gender, sexuality, and race), many teachers do have socially and pedagogically critical intuitions. However, they often do not have ways of putting these intuitions into practice because they cannot picture them in action in daily situations. Due to this, critical theoretical and political insights, then, have nowhere to go in terms of their embodiment in concrete pedagogical situations where the politics of curriculum and teaching must be *enacted*. This is a tragic absence and strategically filling it is absolutely essential. Thus, we need to use and expand the spaces in which critical pedagogical 'stories' are made available so that these positions do not remain only on the theoretical or rhetorical level. The publication and widespread distribution of *Democratic Schools* provides one instance of using and expanding such spaces in ways that make Freirian and similar critical educational positions seem actually doable in 'ordinary' institutions such as schools and local communities.

Although crucial, it is then not enough to deconstruct restorational policies in education. The Right has shown how important changes in common sense are in the struggle for education. It is our task collectively to help rebuild it by reestablishing a sense that 'thick' morality, and a 'thick' democracy, are truly possible today.

This cannot be done without paying considerably more attention to two things. The first—the material and ideological transformations that the right has effected—has been a key topic of this chapter. Yet, there is another element that needs to be stressed—the building of large-scale counter-hegemonic movements that connect educational struggles to those in other sites and also assist both in creating new struggles and defending existing ones within educational institutions themselves. In the current conservative context, there are characteristics of some of the material on critical pedagogy that make this an even more difficult act, however.

In the past, I have warned that the stylistic politics of some of our most 'advanced' work forces the reader to do all of the work.[96] Neologism after neologism reign supreme. As Dennis Carlson and I have argued elsewhere,[97] the discourse of critical pedagogy in its Freirean and feminist forms has increasingly been influenced by postmodern theories. While this has proved very useful in reconceptualizing the field and its politics, it has also opened up the discourse to the criticism that it has become too theoretical, abstract, esoteric, and out of touch with the conflicts and struggles that teachers, students, and activists act on. Furthermore, it has often led to the constitutive nature of class dynamics, a major loss in a time of global economic transformation and a rearticulation of national and international class relations and divisions. Henry Giroux and others have defended these largely abstract discourses as necessary in critical pedagogy, since to reconstruct the world one must first learn to speak a new language and 'new ideas require new terms'.[98] This is undoubtedly correct. Indeed, such a position is one I self-consciously took when I first introduced Gramscian and Habermasian theories into education in the early 1970s.

Yet, having said this, given the very real success of the strategy of 'plain speaking' by neo-liberals and neo-conservatives, some of the criticisms of material on critical pedagogy do have power. Even though a good deal of it is rich and provocative, some of it *is* conceptually and politically confused and confusing. Some of it *is* disconnected from the gritty materialities of daily economic, political, and educational/cultural struggles. Some of it *does* romanticize the cultural at the expense of equally powerful traditions of analysis based in political economy and the state. And some of it *does* place so much emphasis on 'post' that it forgets the structural realities that set limits on real people in real institutions in everyday life.

Thus, as many commentators have argued repeatedly, much more effort must be given to ground the discourse of critical pedagogy in the concrete struggles of multiple and identifiable groups.[99] Much of it needs to be considerably less dismissive of previous critical traditions that—rightly—continue to influence educational and cultural activists. Just as importantly, as I just noted, what critical pedagogies actually look like when put into practice—not only their theoretical elaborations—needs to be made much more visible than we have been apt to do. Unfortunately, when rightist mobilizations have had no small measure of success in creating a reactionary common sense about education (and even among many educators), the linguistic styles of all too much critical work gets labelled as 'arrogant' (sometimes appropriately) and cuts itself off from many of the radical teachers and activists it wants to support.

It is *hard* work not to be sloppy. It is hard work to write in such a way that theoretical and political nuance are not sacrificed on the altar of common sense, but also in a way that the hard work of reading can actually pay off for the reader her- or himself. And it is hard and time-consuming work to write at multiple levels. But if we don't, neo-liberals and neo-conservatives will. And we will be much the worse for it. In this time of conservative restoration, the multiple projects of critical education are indeed crucial. A good dose of reality will do no harm, and I believe will actually make them more effective in the long run.

NOTES

1. See Michael W. Apple, *Cultural Politics and Education* (New York: Teachers College Press, 1996).
2. Pierre Bourdieu, *Distinction* (Cambridge, Mass.: Harvard University Press, 1984).
3. Geoff Whitty, 'Sociology and the Problem of Radical Educational Change', in Michael Flude and John Ahier (eds.), *Educability, Schools, and Ideology* (London: Halstead, 1974), 112–37.
4. Herbert Kliebard, *The Struggle for the American Curriculum*, 2nd edn. (New York: Routledge, 1995).
5. John Rury and Jeffrey Mirel, 'The Political Economy of Urban Education', in Michael W. Apple (ed.), *Review of Research in Education* (Washington, DC: American Educational Research Association, 1997), xxii. 49–110; Kenneth Teitelbaum, *Schooling for Good Rebels* (New York: Teachers College Press, 1996), and Steven Selden, *Inheriting Shame* (New York: Teachers College Press, 1999).
6. Michael W. Apple, *Official Knowledge*, 2nd edn. (New York: Routledge, 2000); *Cultural Politics and Education* (New York: Teachers College Press, 1996).

7. Richard Herrnstein and Charles Murray, *The Bell Curve* (New York: Free Press, 1994). See also Joe Kincheloe, Shirley Steinberg, and Aaron Greeson (eds.), *Measured Lies* (New York: St Martin's Press, 1997).
8. Apple, *Cultural Politics and Education*, 227–41, and Michael W. Apple, *Educating the 'Right' Way: Markets, Standards, God, and Inequality* (New York: Routledge Falmer, 2001). See also Michael W. Apple, et al., *The State and the Politics of Knowledge* (New York: Routledge Falmer, 2003).
9. Stuart Ranson, 'Theorizing Educational Policy', *Journal of Education Policy* 10 (July 1995): 427.
10. David Gillborn, 'Race, Nation, and Education', unpublished paper, Institute of Education, University of London, 1997, 2.
11. Gary McCulloch, 'Privatising the Past', *British Journal of Educational Studies* 45 (March 1997): 80.
12. See E. D. Hirsch, Jr., *The Schools We Want and Why We Don't Have Them* (New York: Doubleday, 1996).
13. Quoted in McCulloch, 'Privatising the Past', 78.
14. Quoted ibid.
15. Ibid.
16. John Chubb and Terry Moe, *Politics, Markets, and American Schools* (Washington, DC: Brookings Institution, 1990), and Geoff Whitty, 'Creating Quasi-Markets in Education', in Apple (ed.), *Review of Research in Education*, xxii. 3–47.
17. David Gillborn, 'Racism and Reform', *British Educational Research Journal* 23 (June 1997): 357.
18. Michael W. Apple, *Power, Meaning, and Identity* (New York: Peter Lang, 1999); *Teachers and Texts* (New York: Routledge, 1988). Of course, there has been a considerable amount of literature on the question of 'clarity' in critical educational writings, with contributions on both sides made by Burbules, Giroux, Lather, Gitlin, myself, and a number of others. My own position on this is that such a debate is essential and that while there is a danger in sacrificing theoretical elegance and the richness and subtlety of language in our attempts to be clear, there is still a good deal of arrogance and truly sloppy and merely rhetorical writing within the multiple communities of critical educational work. Obviously, there is a need to respond to complexity; but there is also a need not to marginalize sympathetic readers.
19. Gillborn, 'Racism and Reform', 353.
20. Ibid.
21. Herrstein and Murray, *The Bell Curve*, and Hirsch, *The Schools We Want and Why We Don't Have Them*.
22. Roger Dale quoted in Ian Mentor, Yolande Muschamp, Peter Nicholls, Jenny Ozga, with Andrew Pollard, *Work and Identity in the Primary School* (Philadelphia: Open University Press, 1997), 27.
23. Mentor, et al., *Work and Identity in the Primary School*, 27.
24. Whitty, 'Creating Quasi-Markets in Education', 58.
25. Ibid.
26. Ibid. See also, Geoff Whitty, Tony Edwards, and Sharon Gewirtz, *Specialization and Choice in Urban Education* (London: Routledge, 1993), and Apple, *Cultural Politics and Education*.

27. Chubb and Moe, *Politics, Markets, and American Schools.*
28. Sally Power, David Halpin, and John Fitz, 'Underpinning Choice and Diversity', in Sally Tomlinson (ed.), *Educational Reform and Its Consequences* (London: IPPR/Rivers Oram Press, 1994), 27.
29. Whether there have been significant changes in this regard given the victory by 'New Labour' over the Conservatives again in the last elections is open to question. Certain aspects of neo-liberal and neo-conservative policies have already been accepted by Labour, such as the acceptance of stringent cost controls on spending put in place by the previous Conservative government and an aggressive focus on 'raising standards' in association with strict performance indicators. See, for example, David Gillborn and Debbie Youdell, *Rationing Education* (Philadelphia: Open University Press, 2000).
30. See Power, Halpin, and Fitz, 'Underpinning Choice and Diversity', and Gillborn and Youdell, *Rationing Education.*
31. Stephen Ball, Richard Bowe, and Sharon Gewirtz, 'Market Forces and Parental Choice', in Sally Tomlinson (ed.), *Educational Reform and Its Consequences* (London: IPPR/Rivers Oram Press, 1994), 39.
32. Ibid. 17–19.
33. Mark Olssen, 'In Defense of the Welfare State and of Publicly Provided Education', *Journal of Education Policy* 11 (May 1996): 340.
34. Ball, Bowe, and Gewirtz, 'Market Forces and Parental Choice', 19.
35. See the discussion of the racial state in Michael Omi and Howard Winant, *Racial Formation in the United States* (New York: Routledge, 1994), and the analyses of race and representation in Cameron McCarthy and Warren Crichlow (eds.), *Race, Identity, and Representation in Education* (New York: Routledge, 1994) and Cameron McCarthy, *The Uses of Culture* (New York: Routledge, 1998).
36. Bourdieu, *Distinction.*
37. Ball, Bowe, and Gewirtz, 'Market Forces and Parental Choice', 20–2.
38. Michelle Fine and Lois Weis, *The Unknown City* (Boston: Beacon Press, 1998) and Michael Dunier, *Sidewalk* (New York: Farrar, Straus, and Giroux, 1999).
39. Pierre Bourdieu, *The State Nobility* (Stanford: Stanford University Press, 1996) and David Swartz, *Culture and Power* (Chicago: University of Chicago Press, 1997).
40. Apple, *Teachers and Texts; Official Knowledge*, 113–36.
41. Whitty, Power, and Halpin, *Devolution and Choice in Education*, 12–13.
42. Ibid. 36.
43. Olssen, 'In Defense of the Welfare State and Publicly Provided Education'.
44. Whitty, Power, and Halpin, *Devolution and Choice in Education*, 37–8. See also the discussion of managerialism and the state in John Clark and Janet Newman, *The Managerial State* (Thousand Oaks, Calif.: Sage, 1997).
45. This is discussed in greater detail in Michael W. Apple, *Education and Power*, 2nd edn. (New York: Routledge, 1995).
46. See Omi and Winant, *Racial Formation in the United States*; Debbie Epstein and Richard Johnson, *Schooling Sexualities* (Philadelphia: Open University Press, 1998); and Sue Middleton, *Disciplining Sexualities* (New York: Teachers College Press, 1998).
47. Whitty, Power, and Halpin, *Devolution and Choice in Education*, 60–2.

48. Among the best work here is Nancy Fraser, *Unruly Practices* (Minneapolis: University of Minnesota Press, 1989) and Nancy Fraser, *Justice Interruptis* (New York: Routledge, 1997).

49. Whitty, Power, and Halpin, *Devolution and Choice in Education*, 63.

50. Ibid. 67–8. See also Gillborn and Youdell, *Rationing Education.*

51. Gillborn and Youdell, *Rationing Education*, demonstrates this clearly. What is also important here is the fact that this has consistently happened even in the face of overt attempts to use such policies to alter existing inequalities. See also, Whitty, Power, and Halpin, *Devolution and Choice in Education*, 119–20.

52. Whitty, Power, and Halpin, *Devolution and Choice in Education*, 80.

53. Ibid. See also, Gillborn and Youdell, *Rationing Education*, and Sharon Gewirtz, Stephen Ball, and Richard Bowe, *Markets, Choice, and Equity in Education* (Philadelphia: Open University Press, 1995).

54. Hugh Lauder and David Hughes, *Trading in Futures* (Philadelphia: Open University Press, 1999), 2.

55. Ibid. 29. See also Phil Brown, 'Cultural Capital and Social Exclusion', in A. H. Halsey, Hugh Lauder, Phil Brown, and Amy Stuart Wells (eds.), *Education: Culture, Economy, and Society* (New York: Oxford University Press, 1997), 736–49.

56. Lauder and Hughes, *Trading in Futures*, 101.

57. Ibid. 132.

58. Petter Aasen, 'What Happened to Social Democratic Progressivism in Scandinavia?: Restructuring Education in Sweden and Norway', in Apple et al., *The State and the Politics of Knowledge.*

59. On the issue of a racial contract that underpins nearly all social arrangements in our kind of society, see Charles W. Mills, *The Racial Contract* (Ithaca: Cornell University Press, 1997). I am drawing as well on Benedict Anderson's position that nations are themselves based on 'imagined communities'. See Benedict Anderson, *Imagined Communities* (New York: Verso, 1991).

60. See, for example, the analysis of the gender dynamics surrounding neo-liberal policies in Madeleine Arnot, Miriam David, and Gaby Weiner, *Closing the Gender Gap* (Cambridge: Polity Press, 1999). The ways in which neo-conservative policies act on and through the politics of sexuality and the body as well are nicely described in Epstein and Johnson, *Schooling Sexualities.*

61. Whitty, Power, and Halpin, *Devolution and Choice in Education*, 98. See also Amy Stuart Wells et al., *Beyond the Rhetoric of Charter School Reform* (Los Angeles: University of California at Los Angeles, Graduate School of Education and Information Studies, 1999). For more discussion of the results of neo-liberal and neo-conservative policies in the United States, see Apple, *Educating the 'Right' Way*; Linda McNeil, *The Contradictions of School Reform* (New York: Routledge, 2000); Pauline Lipman, *High Stakes Education* (New York: Routledge Falmer, 2004); and Angela Valenzuela (ed.), *Leaving Children Behind* (Albany: State University of New York Press, 2005).

62. Whitty, Power, and Halpin, *Devolution and Choice in Education*, 112–13.

63. Ibid. 14.

64. Ibid. 42.

65. Jeffrey R. Henig, *Rethinking School Choice: Limits of a Market Metaphor* (Princeton: Princeton University Press, 1994), 222.

66. See especially the discussion of the role of the state in this in Bourdieu, *The State Nobility*.
67. Loïc Wacquant, 'Foreword' to Bourdieu, *The State Nobility*, p. xiii.
68. Bourdieu, *The State Nobility*, 273.
69. Ball, Bowe, and Gewirtz, 'Market Forces and Parental Choice', 24.
70. Menter et al., *Work and Identity in the Primary School*, 8.
71. Ibid. 57.
72. Ibid. 9.
73. Ibid. 24.
74. Ibid.
75. Apple, *Cultural Politics and Education*, 22–41.
76. Ball, Bowe, and Gewirtz, 'Market Forces and Parental Choice', 23.
77. Power, Halpin, and Fitz, 'Underpinning Choice and Diversity', 38.
78. Ranson, 'Theorizing Educational Policy', 436.
79. Ibid. See also Misook Kim Cho and Michael W. Apple, 'Schooling, Work, and Subjectivity', *British Journal of Sociology of Education* 19 (Summer 1998): 269–90.
80. Ranson, 'Theorizing Educational Policy', 437.
81. Richard Hatcher and Barry Troyna, quoted ibid. 438.
82. Ranson, 'Theorizing Educational Policy', 438.
83. Philip O'Hear, 'An Alternative National Curriculum', in Sally Tomlinson, (ed.), *Educational Reform and Its Consequences* (London: IPPR/Rivers Oram Press, 1994), 66.
84. Ibid. 55–7.
85. Ibid. 68.
86. Ibid. 65–6.
87. Catherine Gipps and Patricia Murphy, *A Fair Test* (Philadelphia: Open University Press, 1994), 204.
88. See Basil Bernstein, *The Structuring of Pedagogic Discourse* (New York: Routledge, 1990); *Pedagogy, Symbolic Control, and Identity* (Bristol, Pa.: Taylor & Francis, 1996); and Apple, *Official Knowledge*, 61–88.
89. J. Evans and D. Penney, 'The Politics of Pedagogy', *Journal of Education Policy* 10 (January 1995): 27–44. See also, Ting-Hong Wong and Michael W. Apple, 'Rethinking the Education/State Formation Connection', *British Journal of Sociology of Education* (forthcoming).
90. Ibid. 41–2.
91. Terri Seddon, 'Markets and the English', *British Journal of Sociology of Education* 18 (June 1997): 165–6.
92. Alan Luke, 'Series Editor's Introduction', to Jay Lemke, *Textual Politics* (Bristol, Pa.: Taylor & Francis, 1995), pp. vi–vii.
93. *Rethinking Schools* is one of the best examples of the ways critical academics, elementary/middle/high school teachers, students, and community activists can work together in non-elitist ways. Information can be obtained from *Rethinking Schools*, 1001 E. Keefe Avenue, Milwaukee, Wisconsin 53212, USA. For faxes, the number is 414-964-7220. The email address is: rethink@execpc.com.

94. Michael W. Apple and James A. Beane (eds.), *Democratic Schools* (Washington: Association for Supervision and Curriculum Development, 1995).

95. Translations of this volume have been or are due to be published in Japan, Spain, Argentina, Brazil, Spain, Portugal, and elsewhere. A Commonwealth edition for the UK, Australia, New Zealand, and other nations has also recently appeared. See Michael W. Apple and James A. Beane (eds.), *Democratic Schools: Lessons From the Chalk Face* (Buckingham: Open University Press, 1999). Thus, it is clear that providing critical answers to the pressing issues of 'What do I do on Monday?' is seen as crucial in a number of nations.

96. Apple, *Teachers and Texts; Power, Meaning, and Identity*.

97. Dennis Carlson and Michael W. Apple, 'Critical Educational Theory in Unsettling Times', in Dennis Carlson and Michael W. Apple (eds.), *Power/Knowledge/Pedagogy* (Boulder: Westview Press, 1998), 1–38.

98. Henry Giroux, *Border Crossings* (New York: Routledge, 1992), 219.

99. One of the clearest discussions of the ethical and political dilemmas of doing critical theoretical and empirical work with due recognition of the importance of connecting this work to the lived culture of social actors in their everyday lives can be found in Fine and Weis, *The Unknown City*, 264–88. See also the chapters in Carlson and Apple, *Power/Knowledge/Pedagogy*.

The Politics of Bilingualism: A Reproduction Analysis of the Policy of Mother Tongue Education in Hong Kong after 1997

Pak-Sang Lai and Michael Byram

[...]

Introduction

The sovereignty transfer of Hong Kong in 1997 led to an abrupt change of language policy in school education as revealed by the immediate reinforcement of the Guidelines on Mother Tongue Education. The new Hong Kong Special Administrative Region government (HKSAR) pushed to make Chinese the principal medium of instruction (MOI) in part because of the ineffectiveness of English in students' learning and in part with the aim of restoring the status of Chinese by eliminating the place of English as an influential language both in school and in society at large. Language in education is not only a school issue but also a social issue. In a language ideological debate, Blommaert (1999) has pointed out that language has an important role to play in a society at least for the six 'target domains', namely social change, the nation, building process, the symbolic power of hegemony, language change, language and political process and lastly ideological discourse. In this [chapter], class analysis and the politics of bilingualism in Hong Kong education is examined. Reproduction theories are used to unravel the social events, structures and functions, as well as conflicts of language in class dominance and perpetuation through school education.

Policy of Bilingualism: Colonial Days

In the old colonial days, Hong Kong had had a laissez-faire approach to language policy in school education. Government schools were English-medium schools whilst private schools run by local Chinese [provided] basically vernacular education. The English-medium education was more elitist and aristocratic than the Chinese-medium education as English at that time was treated as the high language of the diglossia (Fishman, 1980, p. 37) in

Pak-Sang Lai and Michael Byram, 'The Politics of Bilingualism: a reproduction analysis of the policy of mother tongue education in Hong Kong after 1997', *Compare*, 33, 3, 315–34 the colonial society. In 1878, the colonial government decided to expand the English-medium education in order to meet fast developing needs of trade and the civil service (Ng-Lun, 1984). Thereafter, bilingual schools gradually out-numbered and out- performed Chinese schools and bilingual education became the mainstream education. In 1984, the year the Sino-British Joint Declaration was proclaimed, which marked the commencement of political transition of Hong Kong, bilingual schools, formally known as Anglo-Chinese schools, were five times more [numerous] than the Chinese Middle schools and more than 90% of daytime secondary school students attended class with English as the medium of instruction, either fully or partly (So, 1992; Hong Kong Education Commission, 1994, p. 16; Chan, 1995; Government Information Services, various issues). Many CMI schools had in fact been making substantial moves to change to EMI pending acquisition of the full status.

The main features of the bilingual education were that English as a subject was learned as early as the first class in primary school; English was the teaching medium in secondary and higher education; contemporary Chinese history was learnt in the subject of World History and was taught in English; and the subject of Chinese Language and Literature was offered and taught in Chinese. Basically, the bilingual education so evolved looked much like, in Baker's sense, a transitional programme of a weak form of education for bilingualism (Baker, 1997, pp. 174, 175). Vernacular schools became less popular and the colonial education became more English-based, which institutionally produced a cultural assimilationist effect on the people and strengthened the diglossic status of English as the high language. Students of low language (i.e. Chinese) were discouraged from using their home language in learning and the high language (i.e. English) was increasingly used in the classroom. It was such a gradual, incremental and total socialization that people of Hong Kong deeply believed that English, 'the language to learn' was the language of power and prestige, and Chinese, 'the language to forget' was the language of servitude, stigma and shame (Baker, 1997, p. 179).

Policy of Bilingualism: Present Time

In 1997, immediately after the resumption of sovereignty, the HKSAR government of China began to take proactive steps to raise Chinese to the status of the high language of society. In this context, Chinese here means either Cantonese, the dialect originating from Guangzhou, Guangdong Province, and widely spoken in the southern provinces of China, including Hong Kong with some variation, or Putonghua (formerly known as Mandarin), the national language which is the dialect largely spoken by people of the northern provinces and the spoken form of Standard Modern Chinese. Cantonese and Putonghua 'are varied in syntax, lexis and phonology' (Pierson, 1992, p. 186) despite adherence to similar Chinese characters. The government started a new drive on vernacularisation and on a new language policy of bi-literacy (i.e. mastering written Chinese and English) and trilingualism (i.e. speaking fluent Cantonese—the home language of majority people of Hong Kong, Putonghua—the national language and standard spoken language, and English). This new language policy is basically limited bilingualism. Unlike [under] the former colonial government, it is Chinese not English which is the major language that matters. The policy intent of the government on bilingual education is clear and overt. It is multi-purpose. From an educational and pedagogical viewpoint, learning in Chinese is more effective. Globally speaking, a bilingual citizenry, particularly taking English as the second language, will be an asset that Hong Kong wishes to secure as Hong Kong positions itself as Asia's world city for development in the twenty-first century. Politically, learning Putonghua will help [in] building a new citizenship, fostering national identity and integration with China. In socio-cultural terms, it is to revitalise Chinese, local culture and ethnic heritage, and secure close links between Western and Oriental cultures with effective media of communication. As part of de-colonisation, it is to revive Chinese as the high language in schools and in society at large. Last but not least, it helps build a more inclusive society with class ascension not discriminated against by exploitative linguistic social groups of elite, i.e. English speaking elites of the colonial past.

Vernacularisation was taking place in its fully-fledged form yet at a creeping pace as 1997 approached. After 1997, the new HKSAR government stepped up the pace and set out the new language policy of trilingualism under which English has been stripped away as the language of the ruling class, yet remains as an active medium of communication in many sectors of the society, notably in trade and business, finance and banking service, hotels and tourism. Cantonese takes the place of English as the regular and formal language in civic matters and is used widely at home and in schools, in media and social and cultural activities, with friends and in government. For example, in September 1997, just two months after the sovereignty transfer, the educational authorities enforced mother tongue education in school. Next, the government officials were instructed to write their circulars and formal documents in Chinese wherever and whenever possible. Vernacularisation in law and the courts has been speeded up. However, the new diglossia (Fishman, 1980) is not confined only to Cantonese and English. Putonghua also has a role to play in social formation upon return to China. In areas like government and law, Putonghua has been made the legal and official language, together with English and Cantonese, of society. Putonghua has acquired its instrumental and transactional values in the local economic and business sectors as contacts across the border are intensified with China opening up more to the outside world (Kwo, 1992). Radio and television programmes in Putonghua have increased and very recently Hong Kong has acquired its own Putonghua TV station. The HKSAR government is hoping for trilingualism with 'Putonghua the language of politics and administration, English the language of technology, commerce and finance and Cantonese the language of the family and intimacy' (Pierson, 1992, pp. 183–184). In its language shift plan, Putonghua as the national spoken language of China is boosted to become the high language of the three languages. More importantly, politically speaking, Putonghua helps people of Hong Kong to affirm their Chinese ethnic identity (Pierson, 1992, p. 195) and culturally and socially to reintegrate with people in China. In many respects, Putonghua and Cantonese are in conflicting roles when diglossic situations of official, ceremonial, and symbolic functions are involved.

Mother Tongue Education

In school, vernacularisation now takes the form of mother tongue education. Broadly speaking, the language-majority students [receive] their education [via] their home language. Since the majority of the Chinese people in Hong Kong are from the southern provinces of China, the spoken Chinese used in school is the regional dialect of Cantonese, which has long been used during the colonial years. Unlike the practice on the Mainland, the national spoken language of Putonghua is learnt only as [an] optional [...] subject. Also, Hong Kong schools keep the old practice of teaching students to write in traditional Chinese characters and not simplified Chinese characters or pinyin as in Mainland schools. [...] English is learnt as a second language. In specific terms, the HKSAR government announced a language policy for schools, which had and has three elements (Hong Kong Education Department, 1997, pp. 5–9):

1. The MOI in secondary schools will be Chinese, the mother tongue, except [for] English lessons.
2. Schools with English as the medium of instruction (EMI) will change to schools with Chinese as the medium of instruction (CMI) unless they prove with substantial evidence that both students and teachers are capable of using English in class. Use of mixed codes, i.e. a mixture of Chinese and English in teaching and learning is not allowed in these EMI schools.
3. CMI schools could apply to switch to English medium for certain subjects in some classes in secondary 4 and 5 grades and schools are free to decide the teaching medium for their students in secondary 6 and 7.

Under this current policy of mother tongue education, Anglo-Chinese schools are no longer the mainstream schools. The move made, at one blow, 223 EMI secondary schools switch to CMI schools.[1] Before that, only 77 out of the total of 401 secondary schools were CMI schools. Now CMI schools have increased to 300 and EMI schools reduce to 101.[2]

These EMI schools will be monitored regularly to see whether they should keep the EMI status or not.

Recently, to the surprise of many people, the HKSAR government seems to have slowed down the vernacularisation move as [is shown] by [its] allowing the EMI schools to keep their status for another three years until 2003.[3] In the meantime, the government is seriously considering a two-mode teaching system, which allows some subjects to be taught in Chinese and some others in English. Moreover, there appears to be a rising demand from some sectors of society for Putonghua learning and use of Putonghua as MOI in school [thus] compet[ing] with Cantonese as the sole variety of Chinese in the mother tongue education.

Politics of Bilingualism

The politics of bilingualism changes with changes in politics in society and in government policies, the effects of which permeate [. . .] every [area] of society [and] affects the established interests and rules [of] various social groups that constitute the basis of social order or socially constructed reality. Different social groups compete with each other for securing their groups' social basis and interests in language shift, despite the call for support from the government, which is supposed to play a 'neutral' role in capitalistic democratic politics (Gramsci, 1971; Poulantzas, 1973). In Hong Kong after 1997, the politics of bilingualism has been involved in the language shift in general and specifically in the implementation of mother tongue education and has become the everyday life of the people of Hong Kong, and its outcome, in one way or another, will shape the future bilingual education of Hong Kong. With respect to the role of education in the training of a political leadership, the new HKSAR government would like education to produce a new type of ruling elite who are bi-literate and trilingual and drawn openly from all walks of life in the society, which we shall refer to as a new local ruling elite group hereafter. However, it does not want such ruling elites to be members of a self-preserving and exclusive social class who speak fluent English and have close and strong ties with the former colonial authorities, which we shall refer to as the old local ruling elite group (Tung, 2001). Under the 'one country, two systems' principle, the national ruling elite, i.e. central government leadership, will not interfere with the internal affairs of the HKSAR and the use of school language is one clear example of non-interference. Nevertheless, there are local ruling elites, comprising government officials, politicians in affiliation with China, and social activists who are supporters of the national policy, who put state interests first and act closely along the lines of the national ruling elite; we shall refer to these as patriotic groups. They are also core members of pro-Putonghua speaking groups. At the other pole, there are local ruling and political elites whose prime concern is the interests of [the] people of Hong Kong and local problems; we shall refer to these as liberal groups and many are active in pro-Cantonese speaking campaigns. Collins (1979) holds that school is a place of struggle for class domination as education plays an important part in political predominance, economic advantages and social prestige. Also, school is one important place where these class-dominated privileges or benefits will replicate, be remade and passed on to children of dominant classes (Bernstein, 1971; Bourdieu and Passeron, 1977; Bourdieu and Boltanski, 1978; Williamson, 1981; Harrison, 1993; Brown, 1997; Lareau, 1997). Early reproduction theories argued that school life resembles and thus helps consolidate and transmit the hegemonic socio-economic structure of the dominant class; see, for example, on aspects of school organisation Sharp (1980), on ideology and curriculum Apple (1990), Bowles and Gintis (1976) and Young (1971), and on linguistic codes Bernstein (1975). This correspondence principle in relation to reproduction analysis has been criticised mainly for its economic determinism and structural reductionism without identifying 'both the incorporation of concepts of agency and resistance, along with the diversification of the causal nexus of power to include non-class forms of exclusion and domination' (Morrow and Torres, 1998*a*, p. 20). Also, the role of the government is not defined clearly enough in the struggle of group hegemony in a democratised capitalist society where autonomous civil society has grown to begin to limit the power of the state which focuses mainly on mediation functions (Gramsci, 1971; Poulantzas, 1973; Pun,

1997). This will be a society of plurality that different social groups with diverse interests actively struggle to dominate, to exclude others from securing the social privileges and benefits, and to reproduce or transform existing relations between society and education (Collins, 1979; Parkin, 1979; Murphy, 1988). A society in advanced capitalism is more a credential society where social relations are pivoted on status competition (Collins, 1979) and credentialisation (Bourdieu and Passeron, 1977). In this sense, reproduction takes on new dimensions with the theory of cultural capital and links closely with school and education. Cultural capital in the form of educational qualification and certification is more on personal- and merit-basis, which thus has made the politics of reproduction or social exclusion more individualist and focused on individual, family and group levels (Parkin, 1974; Bourdieu and Passeron, 1977; Collins,1979; Brown, 1997; Morrow and Torres, 1998*b*). Parental involvement, for instance, in school reproductive processes is being studied for its class-based criteria when marketisation of education becomes the main trend of educational development and change (Brown, 1997; Lareau, 1997; Wells and Serna, 1997; Reay, 1998). School is the site where the interplay of group politics for domination or hegemony, in Gramscian terms (Gramsci, 1971), for reproduction (Bourdieu and Passeron, 1977; Bourdieu and Boltanski, 1978; Harrison, 1993) and for contestation and resistance (Giroux, 1983) takes place.

Reproduction analysis when studied in its historical specificity and unique contextual developments can give a clearer picture of how and why such a reproduction relationship exists in that society (Aronowitz and Giroux, 1985; Morrow and Torres, 1998*a*). For example, complications and complexities in cultural reproduction analysis with particular emphasis on ex-colonial language are seen in national societies in Asia, Africa, South America and the Arab world, which are undergoing de-colonisation and globalization. In his case studies, Anderson (1991) shows that ex-colonial language, and ex-colonial education at large, which formed a bridge leading 'creole' political elite people to a nationalism of the 'imagined community', were and are important cultural capital for ascension, dominance and rule. The politics of bilingualism in post-colonial times will become more complex, discursive and elusive in the sense that the national language is promoted together with the internationalised colonial language as the second language, and yet proficiency acquisition in the latter is made difficult by the bilingual ruling elite class using the legitimised 'cloak' of boosting the learning of the national language for political ends such as national identity and consolidation. This policy move is likely to change the role of the government as the mediator in group politics (Porio, 1988; Pun, 1997) and engender a new exclusive bilingual and internationalised elite class in a decolonised and globalised national society.

Social/Linguistic Groups in Hong Kong Context

Class analysis in the Marxian sense may not fully or accurately reflect the current socio-economic situation of Hong Kong since numbers of 'blue collar' workers are shrinking rapidly and the manufacturing sector has dwindled both in terms of economic value and in terms of employment; [it] now constitutes only 6% of total domestic earnings and 7% of total employment in 2000 (Government Information Services, 2001). Instead, the tertiary sector is expanding rapidly, producing a rise in the total earnings from 67.5% in 1980 to 85.6% in 2000 and an increase in the percentage of the total workforce from 50.2% in 1980 to 83.4% in 2000 (Government Information Services, 2001). The rise of 'white collar' workers and competition for credentials has turned social exclusion into individualist rather than collectivist (Brown, 1997, p. 737; Parkin, 1974). Social differences are based more on professional qualifications and occupational groups (Collins, 1979; Parkin, 1979) and social and cultural resources (Bourdieu & Passeron, 1977; Lareau, 1997). Also, class-based features are not evident in Hong Kong schools because basically the school system is simple, uniform and homogenous. The majority of schools are subsidised or run directly by the government. These schools are put in compliance with the same set of education ordinances and treated alike by educational officials in discharging their formal duties. Secondary schools provide free education and teach the same curriculum and get their students from the same central allocation scheme, which is coordinated by the government. Children of different social backgrounds will come together and mix as placement is centralised and based on meritocracy principles, i.e. high achievers will first be allocated to schools of their first priorities in the annual central allocation exercise.

Despite the principles of meritocracy, this institution in school education, largely inherited from colonial times, has produced a batch of elite schools, which usually are EMI schools and have high caliber students, a good name and long history of schooling, and a good track record of student success. In the new education system reform after 1997, the structural formation of these elite schools shows signs of changes with the introduction of mother tongue education and elite schools' opting out of central allocation under the direct subsidy scheme in which, basically, the amount a school can obtain from the government funding will depend on how many students choose to study in that school. In return, that school is allowed to charge a school fee and select its new students and English as its teaching medium freely. In the change of language policy in school, together with other related changes in the education system reform after 1997, parents of different social groups are getting involved in the reproductive politics and language and ideology of parentocracy plus market power (e.g. 'user pays' principle) comes into play and will divide, in a loose manner, parents into upper and middle social groups on the one side and lower social groups on the other side (Brown, 1997). For example, in response to elite schools opting for the direct subsidy scheme, one of the reform changes listed in the *Education Blueprint for the 21st Century* (Hong Kong Education Commission, 2000), upper and middle social groups are willing to pay for better quality education for their children in these elite schools if they de-link from the existing 'no-need-to-pay' school system based on the liberal democratic principle of equality of opportunity. Linguistically speaking, in broad terms, parents of the lower social group are less educated and competent in English, while the upper and middle social groups have many parents who are professional elites and are better linked to the outside world with English as the major medium of communication; we shall refer to these as the elite group hereafter.

Parental Choice and School

Upon return to China in 1997, the HKSAR government officially commenced its process of decolonisation that Hong Kong had long awaited. With respect to language, it is natural and logical to raise the social status of Chinese among people in the society. The new language policy of bi-literacy and trilingualism is said to properly reflect the language needs for Hong Kong as a Chinese and an international society. In education, there are no huge disagreements in principle between the government and the people over the issue that use of mother tongue can enhance learning (Kwok, 1998; Hong Kong Education Commission, 1999). For instance, a survey conducted immediately after the introduction of the mother tongue education policy showed that 89.6% of students and 90.1% of parents felt that classroom learning can be more effective in Chinese and 96.8% of students and 93.2% of parents believe that the motivation for learning can be raised (Hong Kong Federation of Youth Groups, 1997). There were, however, inherent worries about the language shift in school education. First, students feared the switch to Chinese 'would hurt their chances of finding a job or getting a place at university'.[4] Second, parents showed great concern about the negative labelling effects of CMI schools on their children when some elitist schools are still allowed to continue to use English as MOI (Kwok, 1998). Third, some people suggested using Putonghua, instead of Cantonese, in the teaching of Chinese while some others insisted on using English as MOI since Hong Kong is an international city.

In practice, the policy of mother tongue education turns out to be an unpopular policy when the interests of parents are at stake. It failed to address parents' concerns and worries about their children's acquisition of English at school. It was particularly so when they learned some competent EMI schools would be exempted from shifting into CMI schools. Weighing all the possible benefits and costs, parents in general were hesitant in making their choice for mother tongue education despite its pedagogical and communicative advantages in children's study. Their hesitation was unfortunately contributory to an unsupportive or uncooperative approach to the implementation of the new language policy when its implementation seemed to be accomplished by limiting the chance of most children from learning in English. The government report on enhancing language proficiency in 1995 noted the ambivalence of parents to the government action on extensive use of Chinese in schools: 'It is very difficult to change parents' preference for sending their children to English-medium schools because they believe that such schools lead to a relatively more successful career than Chinese-medium schools' (Hong Kong Education Commission, 1995, p. 21). Postiglione (1997) examined the relationship of social stratification and schooling in Hong Kong, hypothesising that family, school and classroom are linked together and that 'the key element in the process of social reproduction is the culture of status groups, an important element of which is language' (p. 152). He illustrated the situation using civil service English as an example of cultural capital and reproduction:

> Schools expect students to possess cultural knowledge and styles (e.g. knowledge of high culture and an ease in using formal language) that are most often found among members of the dominant class ... During Hong Kong's colonial period, the children of high-level government servants were often exposed to situations in which their parents interacted with high culture colonials usually through the medium of civil service English. This was reinforced not only in the government-funded University of Hong Kong, but also through the territory-wide examinations. Hence, these dominant class students were much more likely to do well in examinations, graduate from upper secondary school and go on to university than their less advantaged peers. (Postiglione, 1997, p. 145)

Class hegemony of this kind which Read (1974) describes as linguistic imperialism was a common practice in the old colonial days as seen, for example, in Cambodia under Vietnamese occupation in the twentieth century (Clayton, 2000), and in earlier years, as pointed out by Anderson (1991), seen in the Anglicised Australia, New Zealand, Canada, South Africa and India (pp. 93, 110), the Japanified Korea, Burma and Taiwan (pp. 98–99), and the Magyarized Slovaks (p. 110).

English in Hong Kong was, is and will be a valuable cultural capital of elite social groups that parents want to transmit to their children through schooling because English will give them more symbolic capital and more economic, social and political advantages, and power in the society. It becomes even more so when Hong Kong strives to become a world city of Asia in the wake of globalization and internationalisation in the era of ICT. Through the practice of schooling, English proficiency is made the cultural symbol of intelligence, which is used as the major criterion for grading and streaming of students similar to the operation of the standardised test score in American schools (Wells and Serna, 1997).

Primary children of high banding in the scholastic aptitude test and school results will enter English-medium schools to go on with their secondary education whilst those of low banding are forced to study in Chinese-medium schools. English-stream students are labelled as 'able' students and Chinese-stream students as inferiors. An EMI school is a 'gifted entitlement' (Wells and Serna, 1997) to students since when they acquire this entitlement they are considered superior to CMI school counterparts. In order to make their children enter an English-medium school, parents of a powerful elite and wealthy class desperately find ways to get their children placed in the English-medium schools when their children fail in the centralised secondary school placement exercise. Under the present enrolment arrangement, schools are allowed to recruit students of their 'taste' for some school places. Parents of advantageous social class can then make use of this flexibility and choice by schools to find a place not gained through the placement test. They make the best possible use of their social and economic privileges to secure a school place for their children, for example, by submitting recommendation letters, making donations and personal requests. By so doing, elite parents, as pointed out by Wells and Serna (1997), 'rationalize their children's entitlement to better educational opportunities based upon the resources that they themselves bring to the system' (p. 725). They maintain 'the strong sense of giftedness entitlement' by attaching their children to English-medium schools despite 'the evidence that the gifted label may be more a form of symbolic capital than a true measure of innate student ability' (Wells and Serna, 1997, p. 727).

Lower social class parents also want their children to study in English-medium schools as this gifted label, they think, can help their children meet keen competition on the job market in the future. This is particularly true for those whose children are talented students who can study effectively in either language and will get themselves well prepared for a life in the English-speaking elitist community. Strangely enough, parents of average children who learn better in Chinese than English also want to keep English-medium education. They seemingly are unaware of the fact that mother tongue education will save their children from limited cultural inheritance of English and allow them to move higher up the social ladder through university education in Chinese. Although they do not have much family and cultural resource to get their children into English-medium schools, they turn to the government, making strong demands for better English education for their children.

There is therefore a strong bias against Chinese-medium education. Despite the accumulated evidence that the use of mother tongue as the teaching medium is beneficial to most students (Street, 1984, 1994; Wells, 1986; Friere and Macedo, 1987; Lanauze and Snow, 1989; Swain and Lapkin, 1991), especially to less able ones, parents and schools are, however, more concerned with the highly valued symbol of English that attaches to an English-medium school. No one would like to lose it. It was no secret that in the past before the strong enforcement of mother tongue education in 1997, many English-medium schools seldom used English but Chinese or a mixed code of Chinese and English to teach their students. To them, English-medium teaching was just the token but the English-medium label could mean fame, success and talent, and they did not like to let go of this 'gifted' label. They learned too well from a regrettable case that the results would be disastrous if a school abandoned the name (Morris, 1996; Adamson and Auyeung-Lai, 1997). During the political transition, a prestigious English-medium secondary school, which once attracted most Band One[5] primary pupils to enrol took the lead voluntarily to switch to mother tongue education and ended in an awful situation. Able children of elite social groups left the school and the school's public examination results dropped greatly and rapidly. Fewer of its students got into local universities to continue their study. The prestige of the school soon waned. The poor university admission rate discouraged parents of Band One primary pupils [from] enrol[ling] in that school. Since Band One pupils had the privilege on merit to be first allocated to prestigious and high-performing elite schools, their parents, naturally, avoided putting that school as top priority in their preference list. In three years, the school fell to the bottom and became a school attracting only Band Four to Band Five pupils, many of whom were from lower social classes. In [the] eyes of most elite parents, the school was an ill-performing school and degraded into [a] non-elite school. It was not until the school switched back to English-medium education that the situation gradually improved. Since then, few English-medium schools have dared to try to change the teaching medium to Chinese.

It is therefore apparent from all this that Chinese-medium schools have long had a lower status, in terms of social recognition if not in students' achievement. This social prejudice against Chinese-medium schools as second-class schools has its colonial as well as social and economic roots, which cannot be corrected overnight. The HKSAR government finds it easy to reverse the language policy by forceful means but it is not easy to remove the inferiority label of Chinese-medium school from the minds and hearts of the parents. Despite government's major efforts to emphasise the pedagogical advantages and learning effectiveness in mother tongue education, parents, particularly of elite classes, expressed persistently their concerns about government's forceful implementation and reiterated that the government should leave the choice of language medium to individual schools where they find it easier to exert influence and to secure an English label for their children.

The strong and highly individualised consumer–provider relationships between schools and parents have often made schools comply with elite parents' specific demands as they can use their political power and cultural capital to influence schools' decisions (Lareau, 1989; Wells and Oakes, 1998), for instance, in the form of threat of withdrawal of their children, or in extensive participation in the school process (Wells and Serna, 1997). Wells and Oakes (1998) pointed out that 'in more deregulated and decentralised educational systems in which schools compete with each other for clients, the demands of these parents could have even greater political and economic consequences for the future of each school' (pp. 168–169). Parental power has been felt in the US where elite parents posed strong resistance to national educational de-tracking reform in racially mixed schools in the 1980s (Wells and Serna, 1997; Wells and Oakes, 1998). In the UK and New Zealand, the marketisation of school education, which reformed public funding of schools by student head count made the fate of a school dependent on parental choice and the school headship needed to respond to parents' demand in running a school (Ball, 1994; Grace, 1994). Schools are sometimes torn between individual preferences and national educational goals and are more often inclined to accommodate the interests of powerful clients at the expense of national ones.

In 1997, the HKSAR government undertook a bold act to reinforce the policy of mother tongue education. All EMI schools were required to change to CMI, on grounds that nobody denied the claim that school children can understand better in their home language. But, in real life, no single EMI school could afford to lose any elite client in the recent consumer-oriented reform changes laid down in the *Education Commission Report No.7* (Hong Kong Education Commission, 1997) for quality education and later in the *Education Blueprint for the 21st Century* (Hong Kong Education Commission, 2000) focused on school-based reform and market competition principles. Despite the early consensus they made with the government in promoting mother tongue education, many elitist schools applied for an exemption on the grounds that the schools' inheritance of and parents' wish for English education should be respected. The HKSAR government blamed them for hypocrisy and warned that their hypocritical move would put the language reform policy in jeopardy. Taking an unprecedented step in history, some EMI schools, which were not on the list of exemption from language change, joined hands with parents openly to organise campaigns against the government's decision. They understood so well that 'the socially constructed status' (Wells and Serna, 1997, p. 721) of a school relied more heavily on the family background of students and students' performance than on close relationship with the government. They knew so well that without the trust and backing of the elite parents, the prestige of a school was difficult to maintain when it became vernacularised and lost the socially 'gifted' language label. Nevertheless, the tension was uncompromisingly resolved by the government's action that schools had to use CMI unless they got an approval from the education authorities for keeping the EMI status and had to wait for an evaluation on the efficacy of the mother tongue education reform to be conducted at a later time.

National vs. Local Ruling Elite

The politics of bilingualism becomes even more complex when the interests of [the] national ruling elite are involved in the class reproduction struggle among local elite groups and lower social classes. When the local community is furious at the language shift from English to Cantonese in [. . .] mother tongue education, the local patriotic ruling elites (allegedly acting in the interests of the national ruling elites) are eager to introduce Putonghua to the society of Hong Kong. Liberal groups of local elites (putting local interests first in public disputes), however, [place] more emphasis on English and Cantonese. National interests seemingly clash with local interests, if not in principle or value, at least with respect to implementation of the language policy of trilingualism. On the one hand, the HKSAR government aims to put in place a new institutional framework, which enables new local ruling elites who are bi-literate and trilingual with Chinese, specifically Putonghua, as the high language to grow and proliferate. Instead of a diglossia, a triglossia (Adamson and Auyeung-Lai, 1997) of English, Cantonese and Putonghua is more likely and the change is subtle (Kwo, 1992; Pierson, 1992; Adamson and Auyeung-Lai, 1997). On the other hand, since the ethnic Chinese in Hong Kong are largely Cantonese-speaking, it is natural that they would like the Beijing central government to respect their will and treat Cantonese as the high and majority language of the HKSAR, arguing that if

Beijing keeps its promise to maintain Hong Kong's way of life for 50 years after the handover, then the current socio-linguistic structure should not be altered and Putonghua will not be imposed unless instigated by the people of Hong Kong (Pierson, 1992; Adamson and Auyeung-Lai, 1997).

Thus, with regard to Chinese, complexity arises as the patriotic groups (and national ruling elites) and the liberal groups do not share the same view on which Chinese variety is adopted [where] mother tongue education is concerned. In the politics of bilingualism, the patriotic groups would like Putonghua, the national language, to be the high language, and be used in class teaching. The liberal groups, however, would like to keep 'the present independent development in language and communication' (Pierson, 1992, p. 185) and see their majority language, Cantonese, be formally used at all levels of society and be used as the principal medium of instruction in school. They are of the strong view that with regard to the language policy of the school curriculum, Hong Kong should be treated differently from other parts of China under the 'one country, two systems' framework. They do not want the language issue be politicised in school, like that in Guangdong Province on the mainland, for instance, with a centrally imposed Putonghua as a national lingua franca and as a means for ideological indoctrination (Adamson and Auyeung-Lai, 1997, p. 97). In practice, they and the general public take a more pragmatic approach towards the nationalisation policy of language in the sense that so long as their life and immediate interests related to English or Cantonese are not affected, they will not oppose the use of Putonghua. They are convinced they should have a trilingual policy for Hong Kong in which there should be a voluntary but not compulsory adoption of Putonghua in local schools.

The inclusion of a Putonghua component into the controversial mother tongue education has made the local social situations of language difficult and complex. Across the society, there are people with strong pro-China sentiments who often press for making Putonghua the important lingua franca and these 'activists' within the local ruling elite class and from various sectors of the community not only make the English-speaking elite become more and more isolated, but also aggravate a polarisation of the local elite into pro-Putonghua speaking and pro-Cantonese speaking groups. There had been a movement of learning Putonghua in school since a pilot scheme was conducted between 1981 and 1984 and now nearly every school has at least some Putonghua learning in one of the following ways: an extracurricular activity, or an optional subject, or an independent subject or part of the Chinese language curriculum (Kwo, 1992). Recently, the chairman of a language policy advisory group to the government openly suggested using Putonghua as MOI in the secondary education in the next 10 years.[6]

As Putonghua, the national spoken language, is seen to rise as the hegemonic language of society and to be the choice of the national ruling elite (Cheung, 2001), the preference for Putonghua over Cantonese, the indigenous language, is a delicate and politically sensitive issue. This could be, as suggested by Bourdieu (1991), a symbolically powerful change of social institution: 'Through a complex historical process, sometimes involving extensive conflict (especially in colonial contexts), a particular language or set of linguistic practices has emerged as the dominant and legitimate language, and other languages or dialects have been eliminated or subordinated to it' (Bourdieu, 1991, p. 5). In school education, while it is said that Cantonese is good for classroom learning, the government admits that use of Putonghua in school will be an irresistible trend when Hong Kong's integration with China deepens. Postiglione (1997) identified the conflicts between Cantonese-speaking and Putonghua-speaking social groups by applying Collins' status group concept to analyse the relationship between schooling, status group culture and social stratification:

> For many years in Hong Kong, for example, most schools transmitted a common Hong Kong culture and identity and reinforced Cantonese cultural status groups through their resistance to using Putonghua as a medium of instruction. At the same time, other schools were more committed, through using Putonghua as a medium of instruction, to reinforcing a national status culture more closely aligned with Beijing. As speaking Putonghua has come to offer an economic as well as a political advantage (similar to speaking English), the status culture being transmitted by these schools will become more valuable in social stratification. (Postiglione, 1997, p. 144)

Role of Government

In examining the issue of Hong Kong's mother tongue education between 1982 and 1994, Pun (1997) theorises that in the last days of colonial rule, the politics of bilingualism was largely the struggle for hegemony in the language policy development among various social groups in a capitalist society under democratisation. She has found that the colonial government of Hong Kong was cautious not to be involved directly or intervene in the political discourse on language use in school. On the other hand, since the mother tongue education at that time had an effect on the tracking of students into either English-stream or Chinese-stream based on their English ability, it was not well received by the general public as their interests in [the] linguistic capital of English might be greatly affected. Unless and until the state changed its political leadership, mother tongue education was but a token reform and English remained the dominant language in school.

After 1997, the new HKSAR government evidently assumed a direct and active role in the controversial language reform despite opposition and resentment of most parents who have different vested interests in the three languages as used in the society. Conflicting and contrary developments are apparent. Firstly, the modified mother tongue education creates more controversies rather than pacification. People feel that the way the government enforces the policy of trilingualism reflects largely the interests of national ruling elite and the local business and professional elite class with close China connections, and benefits the local general public very little. People of lower social class find that they get lost in it because what Cantonese is promoted in school is not valued as the high language in society, which looks more to English and Putonghua. Secondly, state intervention, in the sense that Putonghua is made one of three official languages after 1997, adds complexities of bilingual politics by bringing Putonghua into the local linguistic community, the people of which, once again, feel humiliated with another 'external' language imposed on top of its local language, Cantonese. Thirdly, the SAR government would like to see Putonghua be accepted and adopted, in the similar manner to English, by the people of Hong Kong because this will fall in line with the national language policy of China advocated by the national ruling elite who aim at championing Chinese (Putonghua, in the understanding of the central government in Beijing), as the formal principal medium of instruction in schools all across the country, including also autonomous regions of ethnic minorities like Tibet and Xinjiang. Fourthly, as [an icon of] struggle for symbolic power, English is still highly valued by both the ordinary people and elite classes, either old or new, which is, however, what the government would like to have changed for Putonghua, on which a new symbolic order is built.

Political takeover is often followed by a 'linguistic unification', which will be a hegemonic political process of institutionalising a new symbolic order (Bourdieu, 1991). In the process, the national language takes over the dominant role of previous local influential languages. Indigenous people who acquire the new 'dominated linguistic competencies' are rewarded under the new symbolic institution and in this way the old influential linguistic social class will gradually lose its privilege and power (Bourdieu, 1991, p. 49). The politics of bilingualism of patriotic groups (and the national ruling elite) and liberal groups (and the pro-Cantonese speaking public) after 1997 is, in fact, a struggle for 'linguistic unification' as explained by Bourdieu. The HKSAR government is caught in a dilemma when its active engagement in promoting the trilingual policy is accused of lending a helping hand to the national ruling elite in their national project of 'linguistic unification', instead of safeguarding the local linguistic interests. Under the principle of 'one country, two systems', the HKSAR government is supposed to act independently to secure the best interests of the local community, but the facts reveal that this is not quite the case. The mother tongue education has been shown to be undermining the long established foundation of a credential system based on English and hence to be annoying the local public.

In view of the fact that the local public is not fully represented by HKSAR government under the existing limited democracy, even though this is subject to change to an eventual popular election, i.e. both the Chief Executive of the government and the councillors to the Legislative Council will be directly elected under a 'one man, one vote' system, the current direct government involvement in the language politics invites criticism of the imposition of a national hegemony against local interests.

New Local Ruling Elite

The people of Hong Kong post-1997 anticipate a new class politics in its transformation from a colonial to a national society. The reform of bilingual education as a social transformation aims at a new social institution of symbolic entitlements for a new local elite class (who are brought up in trilingual environments) to grow and to take the place of the old elite class (who are brought up in English-speaking environments) which has long been a group of 'closed, self-perpetuating and self-serving' (Tung, 2001) privileged people interwoven with the exclusionary nexus of the colonial power, language, education and culture. Amidst class polarisation problems, local and national ruling elite conflicts, and language reform pitfalls, the HKSAR government strives to make society a more open and socially inclusive institution within which members of the new elite class, according to Tung (2001), will be drawn from talented people of all walks of life, who will have enjoyed an education in a trilingual environment of Cantonese, Putonghua and English provided by the government on egalitarian principles, such as nine-year free and compulsory basic education and progression to higher education by scholastic ability and achievement.

The politics of bilingualism, however, may lead the society in different directions. For example, faced by severe resistance from the public, the HKSAR government revised the initial mother tongue policy in order to balance the interests of political forces by switching many but not all existing EMI schools to CMI schools which meant that prestigious, elitist EMI schools would continue to possess their privileged status. The English creole local elite can still maintain its reproduction mechanism of English symbolic entitlements inherited from the colonial past (Anderson, 1991). In the meantime, the strife of patriotic and liberal groups over the local language reform contributed primarily to the poverty of Putonghua-medium education in [the] schools of Hong Kong, and will be the obstacle to formally [instituting] an entitlement mechanism based on Chinese. The reproductive politics of linguistic capital becomes more difficult and complex with these changes of social, conditions and environments after the political transition. Juxtaposed now with the hegemonic struggle of non-elite versus elite classes and of local versus national ruling elites in the society is the conflict between the old elite class and the new elite class. The linguistic capital in question is no longer confined to English or Cantonese but extends to include Putonghua as intended by the HKSAR government.

Globalisation and Cultural Politics

Both the national and local ruling elites value English and adopt pragmatism and utilitarianism in repositioning of English in the new HKSAR society undergoing decolonisation and internationalisation. Unlike Japanese in Korea and Taiwan in contemporary history, which had been stopped from use as an official language when the people of Korea and Taiwan gained back their national rule, English retains its status as the official language of Hong Kong though it is ceasing to be the language of the ruling class. Similar to the cases of Singapore and India where English shares with the major ethnic language(s) the opportunity to become one of the legitimate lingua francas of the newly formed national societies when the British withdrew the colonies, the HKSAR government chose Putonghua and Cantonese but also kept English as the formal and legal language. Under the grand education system reform for the twenty-first century in pursuit of internationalisation goals and lifelong learning, English is treated as a core language subject or learning language in school and constituted to form one of the nine key learning areas in the new curriculum (Hong Kong Education Commission, 2000; Curriculum Development Council, 2001). In the advent of [a] globalised ICT society, [. . .] English [. . .] is highly valued as an internationalised language whereas its past legacy as a colonial language is cautiously downplayed by the ruling elites.

Looking from this global perspective, the internationalisation of English, by virtue of its nature, helps boost free and equal access for English learning in school locally. But, the linguistic politics is no longer a question of access but of the amount and proficiency in English. In practice, English learning is, however, not expanding as supposed, but restricted by the mother tongue education, which, as explained in the earlier paragraphs, turns nearly all EMI schools into CMI schools, leaving only elitist ones to keep the English label. Access becomes even more difficult when some of these elitist English-medium schools change to a new mode of subsidisation by which a school is allowed to freely recruit its students and charge extra school fees on top of public funding in pursuit of quality education (Hong Kong Education Commission, 2000). By this Direct Subsidy Scheme, parents of lower social classes are anxious that they could not afford such expensive school fees and thus their children will be deprived of English-medium education in these renowned elitist schools. Furthermore, parents [from] elite classes can afford more and better English learning for their children [by], for example, sending their children to study in an international school, [employing] private and paid tuition after school, and [utilising] immersion language programmes abroad. In the light of these subtle changes, English becomes even more a scarce cultural capital and its acquisition depends more on 'user pays' arrangements, as Brown (1997) explains, which changes 'the rules of engagement' to be based on market power and not genuinely on an ideology of meritocracy and free comprehensive education as in the past. 'With the increased importance of material capital required to meet escalating costs involved in acquiring the appropriate forms of cultural capital', English learning ends up as discriminatory action, which extends the social engagement of the elite class in the school contexts of vernacularisation, in terms of 'superior market power' and thus 'social basis' (Brown, 1997, p. 745) and English proficiency becomes a means of tightening of the grip of the elite class.

In addition, the English benchmarking exercise serves as another example of elitist discrimination. The English benchmark, on the technical and practical side, is supposed to mediate the competition for credentials but now is used by the elite classes as the rule of engagement which is 'designed to control and monitor entry to key positions in the division of labour' (Parkin, 1979, pp. 47–48). Using an excuse of rapidly dropping English standards with the implementation of changes of mother tongue education, the elite class, particularly the business and professional groups, strongly demand that the competencies of graduating students in the use of English need to be tested and, if possible, rated on an absolute score,[7] and credentialled. The decision on benchmarking is, however, elitist, political and strategic because the test is oriented to English of native-speaker standard, penalising the 'creole' English spoken and developed by the local majority (Graddol, 1997). When this sort of non-scholastic English competence is credentialled through the school process, it is definitely advantageous to children brought up in English-rich families of middle and upper social classes and disadvantages those from lower social classes whose home life environment is Chinese but not English.

English benchmarking thus scares parents of lower social class who see their children being put in CMI schools for reasons mainly of ineffectiveness in learning in English. They turn to the government again, making claims that choice of mother tongue education should reflect the preference of parents and children, and school's discretion and should be less about children's linguistic competence or scholastic performance. Many parents tend to hold the common sense view that the more exposed to [an] English-speaking environment their children are, the greater their chance of learning English well. To link English proficiency with access to economic success and professional career advancement cannot but help politicising the issue on benchmarking which itself is largely a technical and instrumental device concerned with occupational skill competence.

The politics of the post-1997 mother tongue education faces a dilemma with English learning. On the one hand, restrictive English-medium education helps the global development of an elite group that 'mastery of English will lead to the prosperity and glamorous hedonism that the privileged in this world have access to' (Phillipson, 1996, p. 2). On the other hand mother tongue education at the expense of English proficiency hinders such growth for the local majority, whose majority language is Chinese. A government-commissioned study group on language education warned in 1995, before the handover, that it cannot do both well under the same one roof: 'However if the aim of the education system is to produce students with a high level English language proficiency, then English medium instruction can achieve that aim. Chinese medium instruction will not' (Hong Kong Education Commission, 1995, p. 10). There are supplementary measures like native-English teachers schemes and extra resources for schools switched to CMI but they can do very little to remove this institutional inequality, which will be a disadvantage to children of lower social class and prevent them from becoming internationalised on the one hand and on the other hand from competing with people in both local and world markets where English is definitely an advantage.

The intricacy of local–international conflicts over the language choice in school between English, the internationalised language, and Cantonese, the home language, involves also the ambivalent role of Putonghua as the national language and as the regional language. As globalization takes on its local forms leading to diversity and fragmentation (Graddol, 1997), there are arguments that it is more beneficial, economically speaking, to use Putonghua instead of Cantonese as the mother tongue in classroom learning, not to mention its political and regional importance. Also, the rise of Putonghua as a language of oligarchy in the Asian region will diminish the hegemony of English in Hong Kong (Graddol, 1997, p. 3). Undoubtedly, Putonghua learning grows in its relative local and regional and even global importance with juxtaposition of English.

There is now a tendency of to accommodate different views of the language row that captures many people's attention: the education system 'should concentrate on Cantonese and Putonghua and strive for a working level of English'.[8] If this is what it meant by mother tongue education under the present trilingual language policy, then the discourse which takes into account the nature of complexity, discursiveness, multiplicity, diversity, incoherence and the context and change of issues suggests that such a compromise approach to the bilingualism of Hong Kong after 1997 is more like wishful thinking. It goes against what has emerged in the early post-transition years on the one hand and on the other hand it addresses rather than resolves the conflicts and problems uncovered in the earlier discussions.

Conclusion

Mother tongue education in post-1997 Hong Kong will have a long, hard way to go. First, the parents are ambivalent towards the use of home language as medium of instruction in school education because on the one hand Cantonese is more effective in learning for their children and yet both Putonghua and English will definitely be valuable cultural and political as well as economic capital in a Hong Kong society undergoing political transformation and globalization. Social differentiation by linguistic capital becomes apparent.

Second, the policy of trilingualism reveals the internal contradictions rather than brings in complementary advantages because the interests of national and local ruling elites and of various social groups in the society are at stake in its implementation. Polarisation of local ruling elite class in language politics becomes acute. Inconsistency and indecisiveness in policy action reflects the interplay of various local social forces, which in one way or another, involves also the interests of national ruling elite. In addition, the HKSAR government has been criticised for not sufficiently representing the interests of the local public, which it should have done it under the principles of 'one country, two systems'.

Third, the new linguistic changes subsequent to political changes give rise to a new local elite class, which, defined in linguistic capital terms, is trilingual and alludes to a social networking different from the old elite class which, to a great extent, was exclusively interwoven with the British colonial power, and with the language, education and culture of English.

Fourth, the colonial legacy of English does not prevent both the HKSAR government and people of Hong Kong from considering its communicative and instrumental value as an important internationalised language in the globalised world, particularly when the decolonising society is also heedful of globalization and internationalisation. Proficiency in English, as revealed in the analysis, for example, of language benchmarking, remains as valuable linguistic capital, and Chinese [. . .] will not be able to take its place in the language politics at either the indigenous or international, [perhaps] not at the national, level for the time being. The politics of bilingualism thus escalates the tensions between different social groups in the society and between the local elites and national ruling elites in the mother tongue education. The HKSAR government's policy of bi-literacy and tri-lingualism addresses, rather than resolves the problems in the first post-handover years after 1997.

NOTES

Correspondence should be addressed to: Pak Sang Lai, Educational Policy and Administration Department, Hong Kong Institute of Education, 10 Lo Ping Road, Tai Po, New Territories, Hong Kong.

1. See 'Reprieve for English schools', *South China Morning Post,* 12 June 2000.
2. See the story by Y. Shum, 'The Chief Executive reiterates the importance of using CMI', *Ta Kung Pao,* 12 December 1997.
3. See 'Mother-tongue policy diluted', *South China Morning Post,* 2 September 2000, p. 6.
4. See the story by S. Kwok, 'Students voice fear on switch to Chinese', *South China Morning Post,* 19 September 1997, p. 8.
5. The 'Banding' system is a device in the central allocation of secondary school places. First, a territory-wide scholastic aptitude test is conducted on a school basis so that each primary school can be assessed. Based on the results, schools are assigned a certain quota of Band One to Band Five. The given quota is then distributed to students according to their subject performance assessed internally in their school in their last two years of primary school. High achievers will be granted Band One quota and low achievers Band Five quota. Before the placement, all primary school graduates fill in a preference list of schools. Students with the Band One quota will have their preference considered first under the centralised allocation mechanism run by the government. Students who get the Band Five quota are the last to have their school assigned. To lessen the negative labelling effects on school and students, the five bands are reduced to three from 2001 onwards.
6. See 'No mother tongue in the next 10 years', *Oriental Daily News,* 18 November 2001.
7. See the story by Q. Chan, 'English benchmark test for students floated', *South China Morning Post,* 27 May 2002, p. 1.
8. See ibid.

Part Six

Power, Culture and the Politics of Identity

The essays brought together in this section represent some of the most timely and incisive interventions into current debates over the limits of democracy and national education systems in relation to claims for social justice in the nation- state. In Paul Willis's contribution (Ch. 35) culture is seen as central to a critique of national education. For Willis, culture is not at the heart of an autonomous identity with the potential to resist colonial forms of education. In Willis's view culture represents the process by which resistance to dominant norms of the state and state education becomes possible. Willis presents collective, class cultural expressions in schooling as the predominant medium through which responses to modernization and social divisions are undertaken by young people. A key resource in this resistance to the effects of modernity is the utilization of youth culture. Indeed, the cultural role of young people in transforming the very conditions under which they are expected to produce and consume, as Willis demonstrates, stands at the heart of political legitimacy in democratic education models.

Kenway and Bullen (Ch. 36) have a different take on culture. They are concerned with the global commodification of culture and the way young people use it to construct identities. The major question for education is how this process of the commodification of identities can be turned to more reflective and critical purposes in education.

Torres (Ch. 37) is concerned with the problematic relationship between multiculturalism and democracy. For him, citizenship and multiculturalism still remain largely at odds with each other because of the unique history of their distinctive development within the hegemony of liberalism. Citizenship, Torres argues, is a concept emerging largely from a masculinist political history—embodied in the so-called 'great men'—of the Enlightenment. By contrast, multiculturalism and multicultural education emanated from a much more recent concern over rising immigration and diversity in US schools. It was drawn upon to recognize difference without admitting inequalities in power between different cultures. To this extent, education for multiculturalism bears little relationship to the potential for citizenship and further democratization because such ideals remain founded upon highly exclusionary political principles of political legitimacy.

Tuhiwai-Smith (Ch. 38) views the critique of colonial knowledge as central to an emancipatory education for indigenous peoples. Her discussion of colonialism and its historic grip upon the education system in New Zealand serves to illustrate the fundamental problems attending the notion of education as a nation-building project when the history and identity of subjugated peoples are not recognized.

Although starting from a different vantage point, a similar concern with the essentially mythical character of egalitarianism emerges in Ladson-Billings and Tate's (Ch. 39) account of desegregation, race, slavery, and education in the United States. The key issues raised here are that while class and gender have reshaped the ways in which we view state education in relation to democracy, race remains highly undertheorized as a central idea for the reconstruction of the nation-state. Their argument is that white privilege and property ownership remain the central organizing forces in determining racial inequality through education. As de Toqueville remarked nearly two centuries ago: 'I know of no other country where love of money has such a grip on men's hearts or where stronger scorn is expressed for the theory of permanent equality of property.' Despite efforts (most famously expressed in Brown versus the Board of Education) to challenge racial segregation through education, the long history of white dominance in property rights undermines democratic attempts to challenge the principle that 'separate is inherently unequal'. Multiculturalism and anti-racist programmes, whilst potentially helpful, remain unable to address the most fundamental of education's current problems—the relationship between race and achievement in US schools. From their viewpoint, insights derived from critical race theory should serve as the basis for exposing the racist premises of liberal educational politics.

Unterhalter et al.'s (Ch. 40) account of educational exclusion in South Africa offers a graphic illustration of the theoretical problems of class reductionism in nations such as South Africa where race, class, and gender have long stood as the cornerstone of a national system of exclusion based on apartheid. In their critique of South African education, they show how exclusion is sustained through educational structures. From this theoretical vantage point, inequality cannot be understood in narrowly economic terms but is closely tied to the cultural politics of apartheid as a distinctive strategy for nation-building. Students' accounts of their exclusion through education expose the forms of internalized apartheid still experienced by marginalized groups.

In broadening the concept of masculinity to masculinities, the concept of 'sexuality' is itself opened out. This is most evident in Atkinson's (Ch. 41) work. The central premise of her argument is that sexuality constitutes an organizing principle of educational life. The school system is premised on 'compulsory heterosexuality'. In particular, schools are premised historically upon compulsory heterosexuality (and hegemonic masculinities) and this historical reality continues to shape masculinities and femininities today; not unlike Connell's position, there are multiple masculinities and femininities rather than straightforward sexed identities; that aspects of sexuality frame school culture and reproduce hidden cultural inequalities; and that other forms of masculinity, such as 'queer theory', ought to be admitted to the work of framing gender inequality in education.

Hjorne and Saljo (Ch. 42), not unlike Atkinson, argue that schools serve to categorize people, especially those identified as having disabilities on grounds that are suspect. The idea here is that 'personal identity' has an irreducibly intersubjective basis because the acquisition and maintenance of a sense of self depends on the structures of reciprocity and recognition that are built into the presuppositions for communicative action. Rather than helping to diagnose and support 'disabilities', schools become the mechanism of surveillance over classifications which are deemed problematic. This view of education accords well with Foucault's analysis of state power.

Foot Soldiers of Modernity: The Dialectics of Cultural Consumption and the Twenty-First-Century School

Paul Willis

[. . .]

Young people are unconscious foot soldiers in the long front of modernity, involuntary and disoriented conscripts in battles never explained. In particular, subordinate and working-class students are rendered by state-mandated education into the compulsory living materials of future imaginings and moldings. These institutional imaginings have immense social power but are usually undertaken by one generation for the next without the rudiments of a sociological or ethnographic imagination. The theories and qualitative methods of the social sciences are necessary to represent local experience at the grassroots and to understand its connections to the operations of larger institutional and macro forces. Power brokers and policy planners are transfixed by the internal logic of their 'top-down' practices and initiatives; however, they fail to ponder the frequently ironic and unintended consequences of these practices and the creative cultural ways in which subordinate and working-class groups respond to them. These 'bottom-up' responses are often informed by quite different social perceptions, practices, and assumptions.

What is crucial but missed is the recognition that the waves of attempted economic and technical modernization 'from above' are often antagonistically related to waves of cultural modernization 'from below,' which are usually misunderstood. In part, technical modernization is fighting not chaos, a recalcitrant past, or the wrong type of future, but its own alter ego of late cultural modernism as articulated by working-class, dominated, and subordinated groups—what I will henceforth refer to as the popular classes. While often appearing to stand in the way of progress, the latter most often tend to believe in this goal and they profoundly condition, in unexpected ways, how it is played out socially and culturally.

Youth are always among the first to experience the problems and possibilities of the successive waves of technical and economic modernization that sweep through capitalist societies. Young people respond in disorganized and chaotic ways,

Paul Willis, 'Foot Soldiers of Modernity: The Dialectics of Cultural Consumption and the Twenty-First Century School', *Harvard Educational Review*, Volume 73:3 (Fall 2003), pp. 390–415.

but to the best of their abilities and with relevance to the actual possibilities of their lives as they see, live, and embody them. These responses are actually embedded in the flows of cultural modernization, but to adult eyes they may seem to be mysterious, troubling, and even shocking and antisocial. Schools are one of the principal sites for the dialectical playing out of these apparent disjunctions and contradictions, which, while misunderstood, underlie some of the most urgent education debates—from traditionalism versus progressivism to the canon versus multiculturalism.

In this [chapter], I argue that a social understanding of education needs to consider both top-down practices and bottom-up responses, and the ways in which they interact 'on the ground' to produce the complex eddies, waves, and flows of modernization. The activities and processes I discuss in this article have currency throughout Western industrialized countries and exist in highly varied and often compressed versions in newly industrialized and industrializing countries. However, I draw on ethnographic arguments taken primarily from my own research in England. I deal with three waves of what I am calling cultural modernization 'from below,' which I discuss in the chronological order of my work. This order does not necessarily reflect their real occurrence in time, certainly not across all countries.

The first wave of modernization from below is based on the cultural responses of working-class and subordinate groups to 'top-down' state programs and initiatives aimed at competitive modernization. The most important feature of these schemes has been the vastly expanded scale of compulsory education. This wave of modernization is disrupted by the effects of the second and third waves described below, and the subsequent responses of the popular classes to these waves. The social and cultural dislocations and crises resulting from the emergence of a postindustrial society drive the second wave of modernization. This wave brings a catastrophic decline in the demand for manual labor in industrialized Western countries and transforms the role of the state in the regulation of the youth labor market. We can understand this deindustrialization as one aspect of globalization whereby economic restructuring triggers the brutal arrival of the postindustrial society in the 'first' world as industrial society finally takes root—unevenly—in the 'third.' The third wave of modernization from below arises from the common cultural responses of young people to the arrival of the global 'commodity and electronic society.' Young people creatively respond to a plethora of electronic signals and cultural commodities in ways that surprise their makers, finding meanings and identities never meant to be there and defying simple nostrums that bewail the manipulation or passivity of 'consumers.'

Although my main focus here will be on the third wave, all aspects and themes of the three waves continue as simultaneous and intertwined forces. In different ways, they continue to have broad relevance to the current conjunctures in various countries. The basic argument of this [chapter] is that the third wave cannot be understood except within the context of, and dialectical links with, the first two waves. Common cultural forms must be understood with respect to their interaction with other major forces sweeping through society and with the responses of the popular classes to these forces.

First Wave: Cultural Responses to Universal Schooling

Part of the political settlement between forces representing 'capital' and 'labor' in the United Kingdom (UK) after World War II was to give, at least theoretically, equal education rights to all children. In 1972, the UK raised the minimum school-leaving age from fifteen to sixteen. This marked the coming to full fruition of the early modernist drive to secure compulsory full-time education for all. Émile Durkheim (1956) comments on education as the instrument of modernization *par excellence* that is mobilized to raise the skill levels of workers in an internationally competitive industrial world. Always inherent in this drive is the tension between the socially integrative ideologies of aspiration and egalitarianism and the obvious practical logic of the continuing delivery of social agents into gendered hierarchies severely divided by skill, remuneration, and disposition. This tension helps us understand that even the extended support across the organized left in the UK for raising the school-leaving age failed to hide the disappointing response of a good section of the working class to the prospect of another year of enforced school attendance. Many working-class kids did not accept their new privilege with good grace. Instead, they simply wanted the earliest possible access to the wage. They did not want to be in school at all, never mind another year of it (Willis, 1977).

The Lads

Learning to Labour describes the informal school culture and interactions of a group of young White working-class boys in an English industrial midlands school in the mid-1970s (Willis, 1977). The 'lads' resisted the mental and bodily inculcations of the school and rejected students who showed conformist attitudes to the school authorities. Their culture borrowed and recycled elements of traditional working-class culture and embodied an assertive masculine style, which was often aggressive and predicated on being able to 'handle yourself' in a fight. The lads deployed a particularly concrete and sharp way of speaking and were devoted to a certain kind of omnipresent humor—'having a laff'—often directed cruelly against conformists and teachers. Their devotion to 'the laff' was central to the culture, and its deployment was an ubiquitous form capable of turning almost any situation into material for jokes and ribbing: 'It's the most important thing in life, even communists laff' (p. 29).

In *Learning to Labour*, I wanted to get at the inside story of this phenomenon, to try to see the world as the lads did, to get a feel for their social games and their fields of power from their point of view. They had little or no interest in studying and were not interested in gaining academic qualifications.[1] Vigorous opposition to the teachers' authority was the central vertical dynamic organizing the lads' lived culture: 'Who are they, tellin' us what to do when they're no better than us?' The central horizontal dynamic that organized and arranged their cultural assumptions and practices was a rejection of conformist pupils labeled as 'ear'oles':[2] 'They'm prats, they never get any fun do they?' This rejection was felt as a kind of distinction and superiority: 'We can make them laff, they can't make us laff.' These positions and orientations were enacted and embodied through a strong 'rough' masculine set of strategies, embellished in various ways through smoking, drinking, and stylish dressing.

From an educational point of view, the strangest thing about the lads' attitudes and behavior was their low interest in and/or hostility toward academic work and the gaining of qualifications. From a sociological point of view, the most interesting thing about their culture was the indifference it induced among the lads to the actual kind of work they thought of undertaking, ranging from readily available factory work to tire fitting and bricklaying. I argued in *Learning to Labour* that their own culture helped induct them voluntarily into the low-status jobs that most would shun. Their own culture was involved in processes of social reproduction, understood as the generational replacement of individuals in unequal class positions. There was a tragic irony at the heart of their culture; it was surprisingly more effective than any intended ideological mechanism aimed at promoting social reproduction.[3]

'Modern' Social Functions of Resistance

Although resistant cultures continue to be condemned in schools with teachers and administrators increasingly seeing them as pathological, they actually show some clear elements of rationality. In particular, these resistant cultures supply cultural forms and shields from stigma to blunt the cruel edge of individualism and meritocracy in capitalist societies. These ideologies and their associated mechanisms and practices can have only limited meaning for the majority of the working class who cannot all hope to attain the privilege of well-paid and high-prestige jobs at the end of the educational process. Individual logic says that it is worth working hard at school to gain qualifications to get a good job. However, this cannot be the case for all working-class individuals, even though all are asked to behave as if it were so.[4] Only a substantial minority from the working class can hope for mobility, and their cultures and dispositions are adapted accordingly. No one else discusses this, but the lads' culture, despite its disorders and chaos, tells them that no amount of extra qualification will improve the position of the whole class; that would constitute, in fact, the dismantling of the whole class society.

Meanwhile, the dominance of the individualistic and meritocratic ideology produces for the middle class a functional legitimacy for enjoying their privilege—they are there because they have passed exams. The capacities of the popular classes are subject to stultification in hopeless obedience to an impossible dream. Credentialism, or the proliferation of educational qualifications, works to prevent the working class from pursuing either alternative flowerings of their capacities or subversive courses of growth. It seeks to enslave their powers and trap them in the foothills of human development and can stand only as a fraudulent offer to the majority of what can really mean something only to the few. The student population is graded in a descending status order, from whose lowest ranks escape is usually impossible. The educational offer is to join an ever-multiplying classificatory system in which every increase further depresses its bottom layers (Gilborn and Mirza, 2000). The lads' culture exposes this dynamic, releasing them from collusion in their own exclusion and freeing up their potential for an alternative cultural expressivity.

Ironically, the lads' culture also had a stabilizing effect on the hierarchical social order. In their 'tumble out of' and 'escape' from what they felt was the oppressive atmosphere of the school, they went into manual work quite voluntarily, subsequently helping to reproduce the whole social order at its most difficult point. The lads also found a 'culture of the shop floor' on arrival at work that was welcoming and familiar to them because it displayed many of the same qualities as their own counter-school culture. It gave them a collective and human means—even if sexist, anti-intellectual, and often racist—of surviving the harsh conditions and authority regimes of work. The lads' transition from school to work was, in part, a cultural vote with their feet for the working-class adult world of work. In this informal socialization process, there was also an enthusiastic taking up of rights to the only working-class inheritance bequeathed upon the lads—the wage. The power of the wage created possibilities for which their own culture had already precociously and only too well prepared them: smart dressing, pubbing and clubbing, and crosstown driving.

Hugely important to understand here is the antimental animus of the counter-school culture. While highly relevant in opposing and penetrating the demands of the school, it also becomes a kind of second nature that continues to orient bodily style, attitudes, and values during the transition from school to work and long after. This pattern impels them toward a certain kind of culturally mediated and experiential form of meaning-making throughout their lives. The danger is that this antimental attitude could lead to the whole world being divided into two—the mental and the manual. This makes hope for a 'second chance' return to higher education much more difficult and unlikely. The lads' antimentalism reconciles them and those like them to manual work and often to job-hopping between dead-end jobs—now interspersed with long spells of unemployment, or even permanent unemployment—for the rest of their lives. It makes all jobs involving mental work, now and for the future, seem to be simply boring paperwork—'Who wants to spend their day pushing paper around?'

The Articulations of Gender with Antimentalism

Gender meanings and resources are also important elements within the articulations of cultural forces and practices resistant to the school. Symbolic structures of masculinity in the lads' culture help to embody and give an extra force to their school resistance. Masculinity gives them an axis of power over women, but it also gives them a realistic basis for feeling at least some ambiguous superiority over other less successful males, such as teachers and ear'oles. This response has a definite logic and is effective against the attempted domination of the school, and it gives alternative nonmental grounds for valuing the self and a whole solid, sometimes formidable, presence to resist belittling. As I argue in *Learning to Labour*, once formed, 'hard' or 'tough' masculine identities and the patterning of social relations that follow prove highly inflexible, intractable, and durable. This is perhaps especially so when they have been formed through the winning back of identity and dignity lost in inescapable institutional tensions in which they are trapped on the losing/receiving end. Masculinity and its reflexes henceforth help to organize the same repertoire of defensive/offensive responses no matter what the situation—as if all social sites and social relations contained somehow a mandatory threat. This produces an obvious danger for women in and out of the home, where a compensatory masculinity may seek proof and to exercise a felt superiority. Furthermore, shop floor and manual work relations are suffused with masculinity and masculinized social relations. These relations blunt the oppositional possibility of recognizing how specifically capitalist forms subordinate labor power.

There is a further twist here where the anti-mentalism and masculinity of the lads become intertwined with their sense of themselves and their own vital powers. For the lads, a manual way of acting in the world is a manly way, while a mental way is effeminate. These gendered associations reinforce and lock each other, producing a disposition and sensibility that may, quite literally, last a lifetime. In a final sealing of their subordinate future, mental work becomes not only pointless 'paper pushing' but also 'sissy' work for the lads. Teachers are seen as inferior because they are 'sissies.' Even higher paid mental work is considered sissy from the lads' point of view. Exhausting, exploited, and increasingly low paid, manual work can still somehow be seen in a masculine register, which prevents its true brutality from showing through.

Learning to Labour gives an account of the cultures of White, male, working-class resistance in school. It offers a perspective for understanding a particular stability in the first wave of cultural modernization in the UK and its contribution to the maintenance of a relatively peaceful class-divided society. Even after the advent of the Welfare State and formal educational equality for all, there was a settled—though unequal—relation between classes, where no over-ambition from the working class threatened either capitalist organization or the interests of the middle class. At the same time there was some real autonomy allowed to students and young workers, including, at least for an important section, their own transitions from childhood to adulthood. Arguably, this limited autonomy effectively sidelined, or at least profoundly modified, 'modernizing' institutional attempts at controlling and regulating the passage into adulthood. Working-class and informal cultural forms and activities, while seen as antisocial by some, could take root and flower in inhospitable circumstances. This made those circumstances more livable and provided collective and mutual relations, communications, and meanings that sustained working-class identity and informal activity on a wider scale.

Although the social and political landscape has changed over the last twenty-six years, there continues to be very hard and persistent elements of resistant culture in schools. Despite their sometimes antisocial nature and the undoubted difficulties they produce for classroom teachers, these cultures continue to pose, in living form, crucial and collective questions from the point of view of the working class: What is 'progress' for? What can I/we expect from the sacrifice of hard work and obedience in school? Why am I/are we compelled to be in school if there appears to be nothing in it for me/us?

Second Wave: Responses to the Postindustrial Society

In the early 1980s the UK became the first industrialized country to experience massive losses of the manual industrial work that had previously been available to the working classes. This trend is now firmly established across the old industrialized world. In the UK, over half of the manufacturing jobs that existed in the 1970s have been destroyed with a slightly larger reduction in related trade union membership (Roberts, 2001). At the same time, there has been a virtually epochal restructuring of the kind of work available. From the point of view of the working class, work opportunities have shifted away from well to reasonably paid skilled or semi-skilled industrial work to much lower-paid service and out-of-reach white-collar work.

Taken together, the new customer service call centers and the hotel and catering industries now employ more than double the number of workers as the old 'smoke-stack' industries—cars, ship building, steel, engineering, coal mining (Roberts, 2001). The whole working class has been badly affected by the diminution in both the quality and quantity of jobs available, especially young people, older workers, and ethnic minorities. Recently, unemployment has dropped considerably to a general rate of 5.1 percent (Office of National Statistics, 2003). This figure, however, conceals a high turnover in part-time, casual, and insecure low-paid work. It also masks huge geographic variations, with large, predominantly middle-class areas enjoying virtually full employment while the older industrial areas and inner cities suffer from overall unemployment rates of 20 percent and more. One in two less-skilled men are without work and one in five households lack access to earned income (Gregg and Wadsworth, 1999; Willis, Bekenn, Ellis, and Whitt, 1988). Clearly, not everyone will find a role in the new weightless economy, and many continue to expect, against increasing odds, to be remunerated and respected for an ability and disposition to work in traditional manual ways.

The objective probabilities of a reliable and decent wage through manual work have been radically decreased for substantial parts of the working class, and the threat of its removal has become a permanent condition for all workers. This has to be understood as a threat, not only to the wage as an amount of money, but also to the wage as a particular kind of social inheritance and cultural, even moral, enfranchisement (Willis, 2000; Willis, Jones, Canaan, and Hurd, 1990). The wage provides access to cultural commodities and services and to the forms of informal meaning-making that these commodities and services frame and facilitate. It also provides the means to independent living, a place separate from the patriarchal dependencies of the parental home, and from the vicissitudes of the marketplace. The wage enables the formation of the couple and preparation for the nuclear family. Gaining access to the male family wage is still one of the important material bases for the courtship dance, romance, and 'love-pairing.'

In the UK, we have been suffering from the breaking of these transitions for over two decades. The old processes and expectations often continue in some form but have been thrown into permanent crisis. There are still plenty of male working-class kids, like the lads, who are perhaps more willing than ever to take on exploited manual work in traditional masculine and antimentalist ways, but there is not enough work to go around, and many are left in suspended animation.[5] The lucky ones, at least to start with, feel grateful for any work. Even though the uncertainties associated with job insecurity—or the deceptive lure of job hopping—may seem like an antidote to the wearing down of repetitive or heavy labor, they threaten to throw workers back into a stagnant pool of labor at any moment. Nevertheless, simple gratitude and escape from vertiginous despair have become important reproductive mechanisms for those finding or holding on to work (Willis et al., 1988). The dramatic changes brought about by this second wave of modernization have destroyed or substantially weakened traditional forms of transition from school to work and have shaken the material foundations of traditional working-class cultural forms. While unemployment is seen from above as a price worth paying for competitive economic restructuring, economic adaptation produces continuing social and cultural crises at the bottom of social space.

The View from Below[6]

The young unemployed are much less physically mobile than the employed. They cannot afford cars and, therefore, have no access to the 'crosstown car culture' of visits to pubs, clubs, and friends. In the Wolverhampton survey conducted for the *Youth Review* (Willis et al., 1988), half of the unemployed say that their activities are limited by the costs of travel, while three-quarters say that they are limited by lack of cash. A good proportion of them visit town centers and shopping malls during the day. They are attracted to the consumer meccas but have no economic role to play. Rather, they simply hang out or engage in activities that put them into conflict with shoppers, shop owners, and the police.

The dominant experience of the young unemployed is one of very limited sociability. They are isolated and homebound, traversing acres of boredom by themselves or in conflict with parents for whom their enforced dependence is often wholly unwelcome. The young unemployed have more free time than any other social group but, ironically, they are excluded from leisure activities, which overwhelmingly now require consumption and commercial power. For instance, whether we like it or not, drinking is by far the most popular activity among young people in the UK, where three-quarters of them go to pubs nearly four times a week. However, only one-third of the long-term unemployed go drinking, and much less often. Furthermore, they do not spend the extra time engaging in sports or outdoor hobbies, nor do they participate in state-provided community and sports infrastructures any more than the employed. Another vivid aspect of this isolation, according to the *Youth Review* findings, is that, for the unemployed, courtship seems to lose the centrality that it holds for the employed. The young unemployed are much less likely to have a 'steady' relationship, and thoughts of marriage or settling down seem very far away for most of them. They are prone to alienation, depression, and pessimism about their future prospects and are plagued by feelings of social shame and suspicions that other people blame them for their condition. Young people who experience long-term unemployment are uniquely open to drug abuse, often seen in distorted ways as forms of self-medication.

A whole succession of training programs and special labor market measures have been developed by the state to bridge the gaping holes left by the collapse of the old transitions between school and work. In 1998, the British government introduced the New Deal program, which provides unemployed young people with two years of work experience, training, or work in the voluntary and charitable sector (Unemployment Unit, 1999). For the first time with such schemes, refusal to participate is not an option, and benefits are withdrawn if a young person fails to commit to one of these options. Essentially, the means of subsistence are made contingent upon flexibility and obedience, a qualitatively new coercive stage in the disciplining of labor power and attitude.

A significant minority of young people refuses this contractual submission to their own subordination. They are not accounted for in official figures and become invisible to the programs and to the state (Unemployment Unit, 1999; 'One in five young people,' 2003). Despite such refusal and widespread discontent, there is surprisingly little outright public or organized opposition. This may be explained in part by some bleak, internalized, and individualistic additions to the reproduction repertoire whereby many individuals blame themselves for their lack of work and for the lack of success attendance to state schemes brings. Individualizing and internalizing a structural problem, they shamefully reproach themselves for their inability to find work. Having been given so many training opportunities to develop their individual employability and having been told repeatedly that finding work is a question of permanent individual job search, it must be their individual fault when they cannot find work.

These are just some of the forces that corrode the main elements of the first wave modernist cultural settlement. The pride, depth, and independence of a collective industrial cultural tradition, forged from below and neither reliant on patronage nor punished for its cultural impertinence, is giving way to the regulated indignities of becoming a client to a reprimanding state. As the research for the *Youth Review* illustrates, young workers are forced into a reenvisioned reserve army of flexible and obedient labor. This army of workers is supposed to stand ready to occupy, at rock-bottom wages, the new menial functions of the postindustrial economy and to service the growing personal and domestic needs of a newly ascendant middle class. For those who refuse to join state schemes and the legitimate labor market, begging from parents and others, drug dealing, prostitution, hustling, and benefit fraud offer some income. They also lead to entanglements with youth justice systems and possible incarceration, which finally destroys any hope of a 'proper' job. But for some, the highly ambiguous and self-defeating freedoms of the streets seem to offer a viable alternative to the mental incarceration of endless state schemes.

Schools in the Second Wave

The school is and will be a principal site for the early playing out of these contradictions and social tensions, thus placing students at the frontlines of these conflicts. A further condition is now added to devalue and question the role of schools at the level of cultural practice. Not only are young people able to challenge its underlying individualistic and meritocratic ideologies, but they can also expose the practical inability of schooling to connect many students to real prospects in the world of work.

In these conditions, it is no longer possible to believe in a universal and positive role for the educational system in promoting benign and emancipatory effects for the popular classes. Are schools to prepare their students for unemployment? Are they to engage in remedial programs to equip individuals to fight each other for the very chance of low-paid service work? Are they to abandon altogether any hope of interrupting processes of social reproduction?

Meanwhile, many of the cultural experiences and disarticulations of the late adolescent or early adult unemployed find their way back into the school, importing with them their own hidden and not so hidden injuries and reinforcing attitudes of cynicism, detachment, and gender crisis. These cultural expressions are articulated within different formations of school culture, heightening the negative potential of an already existing atmosphere of disorder, violence, and social fear (Devine, 1997; Johnson, 1999; Paulle, 2003). Singular racial oppressions, exacerbated and magnified through even higher expected unemployment rates, can add further impulses of anger and opposition (Sewell, 1997). School cultural practices have to be understood within this general context of disaffection with oppositional forms termed and understood as displaying 'disassociated' or 'disaffected' resistance, rather than the 'simple' resistance of wave one. Resistance takes on a kind of futility, even potential pathology, when disassociated from traditional first wave cultural resources, from their sense of a future. After all, first wave resistance is solidified by a well-grounded social bet on capital's need for labor. It assumes and relies on a future of collective labor albeit actively and culturally formed to be relatively free from individualistic and meritocratic distortions and false promises. Even if not fitting official templates, there is a consequent materiality here to be worked on for economic, social, and cultural betterment, which still gives continuity to working-class forms. Second wave modernization deconstructs this working-class inheritance, and resistance spins freely without the context of any socially imagined future. It is hard to detect any link of disaffected or disassociated resistance with any kind of emancipatory political project.

Second Wave Gender Articulations

As in the first wave, gender registers and plays a part in these fundamental social and cultural shifts. In particular, forms of working-class masculinity are being thrown into crisis by the second wave of modernization, uprooted from their secure and central lodgings within proletarian relations of manualism, 'pride in the job,' and breadwinner power. This shift in the meaning of masculinity undermines the specific logic of masculinized resistance in school, as well as the continuities between male counter-school culture and what remains of shop floor culture. Further, the anti-mentalism of the counter-school culture cannot be securely cloaked in traditional proletarian masculinity. Antimentalism loses the counterpoint with a viable predictable future in manual work.

As the relationship between the wage and traditional meaning of masculinity shifts, the material base for the courtship dance disappears. For many young women, there is no longer the realistic prospect of gaining access to the family wage and to transition into a separate household through male earning power.[7] Questions of gender identity and sexuality may be rendered into matters of immediate attraction or non-attraction, rather than being informed by long-term expectations of commitment. Where a collective apprenticeship to a respectable future fails, for some young men a strategy for maintaining a sense of manhood may entail, and perhaps demand, immediate gender tributes extracted through heavy sexist language and humor and physical intimidation or its threat. This practice can be taken up into whole bodily dispositions, attitudes, and presence. Where masculinity cannot be about assuming the mantle and power of the wage, it can become a claim for power in its own right.[8]

Under conditions of chronic unemployment, social stability and reproduction may require that some of the young and potentially most disruptive of the unemployed of both sexes withdraw themselves into more or less self-pacified or marginalized positions. By excluding themselves permanently from the labor market, they withdraw from society the seeds of non-cooperation and rebellion. The development of an 'underclass' (especially the degeneracies of its public imagery; see Adair, 2002), vastly expanding prison populations (the new 'welfare' means for the poor), and the further economic victimization of single mothers may also provide socially reproductive object lessons in destitution *pour encourager les autres*, thereby enabling coercive control of working populations, present and future, without the use of explicit force. Substantial proportions of the student body may be influenced by oppositional cultures, but calculate that a state-regulated chance of a low-paid job beats incarceration or the tender mercies of the street. These are raw and open forms of social reproduction that are very different from the more settled, if mystified, forms associated with first wave modernization. But even through ambiguous and dis-associated means, collective questions gain cultural articulation again: What's the point of school if there ain't no jobs to follow? If 'progress' is so great, why is all I/we see at school, and in the schemes to follow, increased containment and discipline?

Third Wave: Commodity and Electronic Culture

Along with the upheavals in the material conditions of the subordinate classes described above come enormous changes at the cultural level that bring about disorganization to settled forms of working-class culture. New global electronic forms of communication are sidelining old sensuous communities—face-to-face interactions with known others—with now literally hundreds of TV channels available through digitalization. This is furthered by the huge growth of commercial leisure forms and the mass availability of cultural commodities. The postmodern cultural epoch is characterized by this qualitative expansion of commodity relations from the meeting of physical needs—food, warmth, and shelter—to the meeting and inflaming of mental, emotional, expressive, and spiritual needs and aspirations. You could say that the predatory productive forces of capitalism are now unleashed globally not only on nature but also on human nature.

At the level of culture, young people are becoming less defined by neighborhood and class than they are by these new relations of commodity and electronic culture. Even as their economic conditions of existence falter, most young working-class people in the UK would not thank you now for describing them as working class. They find more passion and acceptable self-identity through music on MTV, wearing baseball caps and designer shoes, and socializing in fast-food joints than they do through traditional class-based cultural forms.[9]

We should not underestimate the cultural offensive of capitalism against the young consumer. Young people may believe that they are free to choose, but the marketers have different ideas. Simon Silvester, executive planning director for Young & Rubicon Europe, writes recently in the 'Creative Business' section of the *Financial Times*, 'Marketers have concentrated on youth for 50 years for good reason—they [young people] are forming their brand preferences and trying out new things. ... In 40 years, there'll be a generation of pierced grannies telling you they're brand-promiscuous and adventurous' (Silvester, 2002, p. 6). Ralph Nader (1996) writes in *Children First*:

> A struggle different than any before in world history is intensifying between corporations and parents over their children. It is a struggle over the minds, bodies, time and space of millions of children and the kind of world in which they are growing up. ... The corporate marketing culture stresses materialism, money, sex, the power of violence, junk food and the status they bring; its power crowds out or erodes the values of the inherent worth and dignity of the human being. (pp. iii, vii)

Common Culture and the Expressive Subject

Such arguments are well known and, oddly enough, made with equal vigor from the Left and the Right.[10] There is much to be agreed with in Nader's pungently expressed views. However, my purpose is not so much to join a moral crusade as to establish the nature of an epochal shift in the symbolic order and its forms. It is crucial to better understand the consequences of these shifts on young people from a social scientific and ethnographic perspective.

The market, which provides an encompassing and saturating cultural environment through its electronic forms, supplies the most attractive and useable symbolic and expressive forms that are consumed by teenagers and early adults. Perhaps political parties, public cultures, or even properly functioning educational institutions should be the principal and principled source of symbolic forms and meanings. It is certainly necessary to continue to battle for the maintenance of the roles and influence of these institutions, but as Margaret Thatcher once said, 'You cannot buck the market.' Once penetrating the realm of culture and consciousness, a market economy of commodity relations must exert the same formative powers there as it does in the material realm. It drives out craft production and feudal relations of symbolic dependence and brings in an avalanche of commodity goods for consumers constituted as citizens (so long as they have money) who are free to choose and consume as they wish—now with their spirits as well as their bodies. It is not possible to throw out this influence without now throwing out market relations tout court.

My position is that the undoubted market power of capitalist cultural provision certainly determines the forms of production of cultural commodities, but that this cannot be seen as necessarily enforcing an isomorphic consumption reflecting only intended uses or meanings as coded within the production, advertising, and distribution of commodities. As the research reported in *Common Culture* (Willis et al., 1990) illustrates, the commodity form is certainly dominant. But while constricting and structuring the field, the commodity form does not determine it. Within bounds, the commodity form's built-in desperation to find use at any price incites and provokes certain kinds of appropriation. This appropriation is also not necessarily along standard lines: no two people look the same; no two living rooms look the same; no two people think the same; and yet they are all products of a social existence within a market economy. What the production-oriented pessimists overlook is the other half of the equation—the processes and activities of the acculturation of consumer items. Acculturation refers to the processes and activities whereby human beings actively and creatively take up the objects and symbols around them for their own situated purposes of meaning-making. This process is well known to cultural anthropologists who have observed and commented on it in other contexts (see Clifford, 1997). But while anthropological dignity is accorded to the uses and contextual meanings of objects and artifacts in societies beyond far shores, the proximity and banality of commodity forms 'at home' seem to have robbed them of such dignity. I would insist that no matter how disreputable their provenance, commodities and electronic messages are still subject to grounded processes, not only of passive consumption but also of active appropriation. Against the grain of dominant assumptions that aesthetics belong only to High Art and legitimate culture, I have argued that there is a 'grounded aesthetics' in everyday practice whereby meanings are attributed to symbols and artifacts, now mostly commodities, in creative ways that produce new orders of symbolic meaning (Willis et al., 1990). These grounded aesthetics reset the possibilities for how every day is experienced and how the selection and appropriation of cultural materials will take place in the future.

Young and working-class people are caught up in the front line of engagement. They acculturate the materials of commodity culture almost as a matter of cultural life and death, not least because they find themselves with ever-diminishing inherited folk cultural resources and with little or no access to legitimate and bourgeois forms of cultural capital. In light of the multiple and complex possibilities of the grounded uses of new environmental resources—commodity and electronic—there is a strange emergence from subordinate cultural relations of a new kind of expressive subject. I would argue that it would have been better if this had occurred without exploitation and in planned developmental ways with more democratic control at the point of formal cultural production. But our hopes for an institutionally led and mutually cooperative cultural program for the popular classes have been rendered quaint and parochial by the new relations of desire brokered through the commodity.

The emergence of a subordinate expressive subject concerns members of the majority popular classes taking for themselves—on the alien and profane grounds of the commodity—something that only the elite have enjoyed as part of their sacred privilege. This privilege entails the formation of sensibilities to mark oneself culturally as a certain kind of person—rather than simply an unconscious carrier of traditional markers of class, race, and gender—or to 'choose' to belong to these categories in distinctive, mannered, celebratory, or self-conscious ways. This is to take part in self-formation on relatively autonomous expressive grounds, rather than to be formed from outside on automatically ascribed grounds. The connection of the 'given self' to variable external symbolic forms reflects the desire not just to take up social or material space in a way governed by others, but to matter culturally (Willis, 2000). Without some cultural marking, youth feel in danger of being culturally invisible, which increasingly means socially invisible. The choice to wear body jewelry may well last a lifetime, but it is a choice furnished in the conditions of a whole experienced life and life stage. It marks the self-consciousness of one's biography, a sense of self and specific social situation that simply cannot be reduced to the successful marketing of earrings.

It is crucial here to recognize the blurring of the lines between production and consumption in what I call *Common Culture* (Willis et al., 1990). Active consumption is a kind of production. Formal production—as in learning to play an instrument by listening to CDs—often arises first in relation to creative consumption. This is part of what separates the acculturation of popular cultural items from the usual notion of popular culture as materials that have their own inherent meanings and values. Selecting and appropriating popular cultural items for one's own meanings is a kind of cultural production. Though mediated through alien commodity materials, the attachment of an expressive identity to—or its workings through—a socially given mere existence is now a popular, and in its own way democratic, aspiration. While the continuing educational question for first wave modernization concerns whether state education is a means of liberation or ideological confinement for the unprivileged majority, the late modernist question for the same social group concerns whether the commodification and electrification of culture constitute a new form of domination or a means of opening up new fields of semiotic possibility. Are the young becoming culturally literate and expressive in new ways, or are they merely victims of every turn in cultural marketing and mass media manipulation?

However we judge the general tide of influence on this new front, it is incontestable that all school students are drawn in to the field of force of popular cultural provision. The basic point I want to make with respect to the overall theme of this [chapter] is that commodity-related expressive consumption—or common culture—does not take place in a vacuum or simply repeat the exploited meanings of commodity production. Furthermore, the acculturations that arise have to be understood as grounded in and informing other inherited social categories and positions as well as antagonisms between them. We must grant the freedoms of consumption that pedagogists begrudge, political economists deride, and antihumanists deny, but we must locate them at material and social interconnections and historical conjunctures that constrain and channel these freedoms in all kinds of ways. In the school, this points to the importance of understanding popular cultural consumption with respect to previously existing themes of school conformism, resistance, disaffection, variations, and points between them.

We must be alive to how cultural commodities are used to 'body out'—give specific bodily expression to—the nature and practice of previously existent or socially articulated positions still organized ultimately by elementary class, race, and gender factors. Of particular importance is how the body-oriented and somatic emphasis of common cultural practices chime with, resonate with, and show an elective affinity with the antimentalism and manual emphases of working-class and subordinate bodily cultures. Bodybuilding, rave, and hip-hop dancing are some of the fields being opened up for the cultural exercise of the body, emphasizing its physical presence and showing its expressivity and superiority over desiccated mental ways of being. Commodity related cultural practices are also producing new fields for the expression of gender in and out of the school. These practices include the trying on of new cloaks for the expression of masculinized resistance or independence from the school. This masculinity is no longer guaranteed by a proletarian industrial inheritance but is still targeted toward the school.

Common cultural practices can also wrap themselves up with second wave disaffected resistance producing a doubly articulated emphasis on the 'now' of immediate consumer gratification to go along with the heavy extra weight placed on the present by the lack of a predictable social future. Where the moral and cultural benefits that flow from the proletarian inheritance of the wage are denied, a cultural expressivity through commodities may supply an instant social and cultural imaginary for resistance and alternatives to the felt oppressions of the school, providing, so to speak, something to resist 'with.' We must recognize that these practices include amplifications and resonances of misogyny and homophobia, as well as criminal and violent themes (hooks, cited in Marriott, 1993). The apparently boundless horizons of consumption have done little to remove the unconscious foot soldiers from their struggles, and have only added another front on which to contend.

These amplifications and resonances of opposition through common cultural means carry their own ironies for social reproduction and negation of subordinate interests. They remove students farther from what school might offer them and diminish the chances of a shot at a 'proper' job (Sewell, 2002). Meanwhile, many students from less privileged backgrounds are inexorably drawn to exploited, dead-end, low-paid, intermittent, and part-time work in order to gain or maintain access to this world. The interest in any kind of paid work, no matter how exploited, can be motivated not by any intrinsic interest or delayed gratification, but by the necessity to earn the wages that allow access to the things that really energize and impassion them beyond the boring world of work. Unemployment, or the prospect of it, produces oppression by excluding young people from forms of identity-making and satisfaction provided by these new leisure and consumption fields. The old categories of judging a fair wage and a decent job are being capsized. The individualism inspired by cultural market relations can give a generalized sense of power and autonomy, often entirely misplaced with respect to the objective lack of real choice on youth labor markets, therefore concealing and mystifying it.[11]

Status Systems and Schools

[...]

I argue that popular culture should be understood in relation to the strong urge of young people to make and maintain a viable informal cultural identity acknowledged by others in shared social space. Commodity consumption and display (trainers, music, appearance, etc.) are major raw materials for the development of such expressive subjectivity and for the symbolic public marking of identity for self and others. But these forms of cultural expression are not simply about developing identity; they are also about putative, comparative, and hierarchical social placing of identity.[12] However, this comparative social dimension cannot be achieved within consumer relations themselves. Knowledgeable manipulations of symbolic markers of identity do not confer status on their own. While a necessary condition, these manipulations need to be part of an identity founded on other grounds. The school is a crucial site for these grounds where an over-mapping of distinctions takes place, with common culture positions and identities mapping onto distinctions within the school and these distinctions themselves mapping onto wider social distinctions.

There is not necessarily an automatic connection between basic social elements (class, race, and gender), school resistance or nonresistance (first wave), disaffection (second wave), and particular kinds of common cultural expression (third wave). Within the site of the school, each of these factors has a relatively independent life and can attach itself to other elements so that there is the possibility, among other things, for class and 'ethnic cross-dressing' (McCarthy, 2002). However, there are likely to be some tendencies of strong association, which is the ethnographer's task to uncover. For instance, lower-working-class students are likely to be located at the bottom of the official school status system. From this position they are likely to be inclined to exploit popular culture and other resources to embody their resistance or disaffection with alternative status markers, mobilizing cultural 'positional goods' that they can control.

Perhaps it is the singular nature of the modernist school, where people of the same age are forced into a common arena, that compels individuals and groups to find a place and identity within a single complex matrix. No matter how heterogeneous their backgrounds or how different their cultural destinies would have played out without the unnatural social atmospherics of the school, it is within the constraints of this institution that young people negotiate their identities. The previous section looked at some elements of the common cultural status system within the school and some of its points of contact with other systems. There are, in fact, several status systems in play at once in the school. The urgent and sometimes sulphurous social pressures built up in the pressure cooker of the school fuse and force into lived articulation a number of status-conferring symbolic relations derived from without and within the school. For example, the official academic status measures within the school create hierarchical levels among students, which reinforce the external cultural capital systems that confer likely status and advantage on middle-class students. Team sports provide a powerful system of status measurement and achievement,[13] and perceptions of sexual attractiveness provide a status system both inside and outside of schools. Furthermore, systems based on perceived bodily hardness and toughness provide working-class and Black students greater chances for privilege, while opposition to authority, derived from both the resistance of the first wave and the disassociation of the second, produce their own kinds of status systems. Lastly, but by no means least, new patterns of popular cultural consumption confer separate bases for evaluation and prestige.

Though forced into a common matrix, these symbolic relations are not aligned and do not point uniformly to common high-status positions. Conflict is ensured in the cauldron of the school, where students are competing for place and identity with reference to all of these positionalities. To change the metaphor, here is a complex cultural microecology, requiring considerable bravery and skill. On the one hand, failure in navigation skills may lead to victimhood, suffering, and even tragedy, while on the other, it may lead to involvement in serious crime and violence stretching beyond the school.

All schools are likely to manifest all or most of the themes discussed here, although there is likely to be wide variability in the cultural microecologies of particular schools and variation in the combination and alignment of systems. In different ways, common cultural systems are likely to become more central, inflecting how variations in the mix of social class, race, and ethnicities take root and grow in school ecologies. None of this can be read out automatically from social determinants, which again indicates a wide research agenda for ethnographic study.

There is a real autonomy and unpredictable chemistry in how status systems will mix in any given school. Successive and continuing waves of modernization and responses to them have added new layers of pressure and confusion. The contemporary school has been turned into a strange kind of hybrid, incorporating, under the same roof, the very different past and likely future trajectories of their very different students and the weighting of their stakes in different kinds of modernization, and whether these come from above or from below.

'Dominant Populars' in Schools

In predominantly working-class schools there is likely to be a polarization of the official culture and its hierarchies of status from the subterranean one. The latter develops and maintains its dominance by gathering for itself privileged positions within informal status systems that would include, most importantly, the status system of common culture. For instance, 'popular' boys are likely to be tough, oppose the school, and be seen as stylish in their music and clothing tastes. To drop one of these attributes would be to drop out of the 'dominant popular'—the status system configuration that commands the most student prestige in a given school. To a greater or lesser extent, other social groups are likely to seek justifications for their own positions in relation to the dominant popular in the magnification of the mappings of distinction that are beneficial to them.

Of course, such dominant populars are socially subordinate in the wider frame. They invert not only the school's official hierarchies, but also some of the wider social hierarchies by appearing to confer on students deceivingly dominant roles even when they occupy subordinate economic and social positions outside the school. Unless they can convert informal skills and knowledge to market advantage in the informal or formal cultural industries, marked reproductive consequences are likely to continue for the members of such inverted fixings of the official cultural systems of the school. They may enjoy the ambiguous superiority of symbolic dominance only as a short prelude to and ironic preparation for extended economic disadvantage in the labor market. Middle-class students in predominantly working-class schools may take up positions within such subordinate dominant populars. If so, interesting competitions of influence will ensue between likely poor academic performance and effects flowing from inherited economic and cultural capital.

In schools with predominantly middle-class students, the weight of cultural capital is likely to give informal qualitative and quantitative ballast to the official system and its status prizes. Other systems are more likely to be aligned with this official system so that 'popular' boys, for instance, are likely to achieve at least some academic success, get along with staff, and be seen as attractive and stylish. This produces a dominant popular more aligned with the school and with hierarchies outside of it, so to speak, a truly dominant dominant popular. Status systems that are out of line with the official system are likely to be attenuated in their power. A central point I wish to make is that the contents and meanings of the common cultural status system are likely to be very different when aligned with a dominant popular articulated in line with, rather than in opposition to, the school. In general, though, the conflicts and overlaps of various symbolic systems result in a cumulatively rising social atmosphere within the singular institution of the school. There are likely to be negative social and psychological effects associated with being excluded from the dominant popular in any given school.[14]

The School as Instrument and Site

The school is the direct instrument of the first wave; it suffers disorientation from the second wave; and it is an important site for the playing out of the third wave of modernization. You could say that all cultural forms and experiences now have an element of cultural diaspora. Even if you stop in the same place, change flows over you; when the young are still, symbolic borders pass them.

In this [chapter], I have described three themes of cultural modernity 'from below': continuing threads of institutionally based informal cultural resistance; responses of disaffection and depression to the continuing effects of postindustrial unemployment and tougher forms of state-regulated school-to-work transitions; and the new cultural and bodily relations and possibilities arising from grounded consumption and leisure. The combinations of these three themes are unstable and different in their implications for different social groups. Each wave affects the others and has to be understood in light of the others. In particular, issues of popular culture are too often treated for themselves and in their own vectors of effect on identity. These issues can be seen much more productively through the play and effect of preceding and continuing cultural and structural forces of modernization. These forces continue to play over particular groups still constituted in traditional categories of class, race, and gender. Thus there are multiple ways in which resistance (first wave) and disaffection (second wave) are given expression and development within common cultural practices (third wave).

It is true that in the last wave of modernization we can observe the cultural unconscious pushing back; that which was automatic seems willed. The tragedy is that what is sometimes called the aesthetization of experience does not actually change the material relation between freedom and necessity, between the chosen and the determined. These relations are actually tightening for the worse in the life space of the subordinate classes at the hands of second wave modernization, even as third wave modernization indicates symbolic space without borders. Cultural and material vectors seem to be out of kilter as never before. We must not overlook that the superabundance of images and imaginary possibilities of apparently free-floating and classless forms of consumption intersect with materially worsening conditions for large sections of the working class. This is especially true, given the brute facts of youth unemployment and exploitative underemployment in low-wage service jobs for masses of young people. The blurring of consumption and production in third wave modernization might offer some young people hope of embarking on alternative 'twilight' careers in the provision of cultural goods and services. But second wave conditions also produce heightened attractions to crime and to illegal activities in the informal economy. Meanwhile, schools continue to struggle, still formed by the ambitions and illusions of the first wave of modernization now breaking on very different shores.

In schools we can see a blunt, culturally mediated form of negotiation between young people and adults, both uncomprehending the meaning and effects of modernity. Antisocial behavior and associated common cultural forms can be vehicles for expression and for seizing space and autonomy where words fail. It must be understood that schooling is not only an instrument for producing modernity, but is also a site for the playing out of its contradictory forces and forms. Accepting popular culture does not mean a lazy throwing open of the school doors to the latest fad, but rather committing to a principled understanding of the complexity of contemporary cultural experience.

There is a wider set of issues here concerning the fullest understandings of cultural formations and the determinants of their direction for emancipation or alienation. The school is a social field as well as an instrument of social development. Therefore, educators, educational organizations, and their progressive allies should speak up unequivocally on behalf of young people in the middle and bottom of social space who are embroiled in the flux of this dialectical modernization. They can take up clues and themes from young peoples' emergent cultures, pains, and experience. If the consciousness, actions, and cultures of students need to change, so do the wider conditions and structural possibilities that help to structure those very responses. As this [chapter] addresses throughout, consciousness and structure are the two intertwined poles of continuous cultural processes. If consciousness has to change, so does structure. At the very least there are firm 'voluntarist' limits on how far consciousness can be asked to change if questions of structure are firmly off the agenda. Rather than ever-more individualistic economic competition for the good life driven by the first wave, where are the means for the majority to find a collective place in the sun free from ideological straitjackets? Rather than shaming individualized insecurity and the state disciplining of working poverty described in the second wave, where are the guarantees for enhanced security and greater choice that globalized economic advance is supposed to bring? Rather than predatory market provisions of the third wave enflaming immediate desire, where are the means for the democratic production of new symbolic and informational goods?

The social impulses embodied in these arguments may have an ideological and utopian tinge. Although in different ways, this is no more so than in the idealist figures of the top-down imaginary—dutiful students, an ever-retraining reserve army of the unemployed, passive grateful consumers—forced to progress through educational and economic institutions. These top-down efforts seek to bend consciousness to unremittingly inflexible and harsh structural conditions. It is the internal contradictions and social impossibility of these idealist figurations that unleash cultural modernization from below to forcibly demonstrate in return that everything cannot be as tidy and convenient for the powerful as the official ledger would have it. In this [chapter], I have examined the counter effects, folding loops of irony, and unintended consequences unleashed from dominant imaginings and moldings of 'progress,' unavoidably set in motion by the institutional and economic power that backs them up. Maintaining a critique and indicating alternative views of 'progress' are fundamental educational issues that are umbilically connected to debates over the canon and multiculturalism, or traditionalism and progressivism.

As for the specific questions of how to address issues of popular culture in the curriculum, I would argue that we should look beyond the products of popular culture to their uses in context—to the field of what I term common culture. Educators fret over the predatory view of popular culture, fearing the exploitations of the vulnerabilities and immoderate desires of the young. I am certainly not endorsing the ways market production scales away the remnants of organic community and institutional responsibility with imaginary relations and desires. Rather, I am trying to understand the processes of common culture to shed light on the grounded forms in which the young acculturate commodities into their everyday lives. In this way we may be able to separate the predatory from the creative and entertain a practical hope for practical action.

For all the predatory dangers of popular culture, within common cultural practices lies a new growth of awareness and identity within the individual or group. This growing awareness is a kind of variable and unpredictable mind-full-ness about individual choices and their limits and lodgings within complex social relations and structural determinants. These new, yet nondominant, forms of identity and expression are precarious and open to further rounds of commodification. They also turn within new complexities and flows of social reproduction in situ. But there is nevertheless a dialectical site to be mined for clues to new kinds of public sphere. Within these public spheres, the subordinate mind-full-ness associated with consumer culture might become a purposeful self-conscious mindfullness of individual and collective action.

Educators and researchers within informal settings might explore a variety of ways that cultural consumption and production might be encouraged to operate in less exploitative ways. Their exploration might open new public realms that are seen not as compensating for or attacking commercial imperatives and their erosion of traditional values, but as going along with the flow of actually existing energies and passions. The conditions of existence within these new public realms would make young people more visible and give them more control over what is expressed and how.

Within formal settings, educators and researchers can use the resource of critical ethnographic texts to explore the meanings and rationalities of common cultural practices close to home. They may consider the products of popular culture not simply for their fetishized, immediate identities, but for their common cultural histories, and ask: How did these expressions become commodities and with what effects? How are they de-fetishized and turned into cultural possessions in situ? What do these appropriated expressions say about social position and location?

Pedagogic voices can be shockingly quiet about issues of social context, as if the four walls of the classroom, sanctuary-making as they can be, contain all that is necessary to understand and direct what goes on within them. Educators and researchers should utilize the cultural experiences and embedded bodily knowledge of their students as starting points, not for bemoaning the failures and inadequacies of their charges, but to render more conscious for them what is unconsciously rendered in their cultural practices. The experiences and knowledge of the students—foot soldiers of modernity—can help us, and them, to understand their own place and formation within flows of cultural modernization. This knowledge provides practical grounds for critical self-understandings of social reproduction and even perhaps for an appreciation of how far, under what conditions, and for whom Bourdieu's elusive enigma might hold true: 'Resistance can be alienating and submission can be liberating' (quoted in Bourdieu and Wacquant, 1992, p. 24). While celebrating the 'freedoms' of consumption, we must always locate them on the front lines where they are exercised.

NOTES

I am extremely grateful for close and detailed critical comments on an earlier draft and suggestions generously offered by Philip Corrigan and Bowen Paulle. Thanks also for the detailed comments and suggestions from editors at *HER*, and especially for the close editorial attentions of Rubén Gaztambide-Fernández and Lionel C. Howard.

1. Not all working-class students failed. However, like today, middle-class students were about six times more likely to go into higher education than were working-class pupils.
2. 'Ear'oles' is slang for the exterior bit of the human ear; the lads saw them as always listening and never doing.

3. Other forms of resistance and behavior leading to social reproduction have since been documented. Working-class girls perform more 'silent' forms of resistance and disaffection, with similarly ironic processes of reproduction to be observed with respect to their destiny in unpaid domestic work and within low-paid 'feminized' occupations (e.g., Anyon, 1983; Llewellyn, 1980; Payne, 1980). In the era of politically driven diaspora following and merging with continuing economic migration, other variants of informal and resistant cultures of school borrow from, recycle, and adapt to elements of various traditional race, ethnic, and national cultures (e.g., Fordham, 1996; Mac an Ghaill, 1988; Portes, 1995; Raissiguier, 1995).
4. Despite a marked spreading out and increase in the 'nominal rate' of paper qualifications in the UK over the last twenty-five years, patterns of unequal attainment between the classes have remained remarkably constant (Arnot, 2002).
5. This job trend is compelling evidence of the inflexibility and long duration of locked cultural forms.
6. The following is based mainly on my work on *The Youth Review* (1988), Furlong and Cartmel's (1997) *Young People and Social Change*, and Starrin, Rantakeisu, and Hagquist's (1997) 'In the Wake of Recession.'
7. Single mothers may or may not find some mileage in the manipulation of an increasingly mean, disciplining, and coercive state to provide bare housing and subsistence, but various kinds of limitations on total lifetime welfare entitlements mean that they are running out of road on their way to a crossroads of enforced choice between workfare subservience and the dubious freedoms of subsistence in the informal economy (see Hofferth, Stanhope, and Harris, 2002).
8. On 'hyper-masculinity' see Mac an Ghaill (1994).
9. For an overview of popular culture in the United States, see Traube (1996).
10. For a discussion of these arguments, see the articles by N. Dolby, D. Buckingham, and D. Trend (2003) in *Harvard Educational Review* 73/3: 258–84, 309–27, 285–308.
11. See discussion of the 'epistemological fallacy of late modernity' in Furlong and Cartmel (1997).
12. For an interesting parallel argument about the comparative importance of subcultural capital, see Thornton (1995).
13. This is especially true in the United States (see Holland & Andre, 1994; Spady, 1970).
14. For a biographic and life history ethnographic exploration of some of these issues, see Ortner (2002).

Pedagogies that Bite/Byte Back

Jane Kenway and Elizabeth Bullen

Introduction

The pedagogical strategies outlined in this chapter plunder the corporate vernacular and also anti-corporate activist practices. They are more overtly political than those outlined previously. They explicitly blend the playful and the earnest and are intended to both delight and bite.

We begin with a consideration of strategies designed to come to grips with students' affective investment in the commodity and consumer form. We have called this section 'Cool hunting and cool criticism'. Whereas the carnivalesque in the classroom turns standard practice on its head, in this section we turn marketing and media production strategies on their heads. Our object is to offer students ways of understanding how they use consumer culture as a resource in identity building and how, at the same time, *they* are used by consumer-media culture. The second pedagogical approach we describe here builds on kids' inscriptions in consumer culture but also encourages them to adopt an insider-outsider standpoint. We call the young activist who adopts this standpoint the *cyberflâneur*. The youthful *cyberflâneur* conducts his or her life politics and accepts his or her global citizenship 'responsibilities' in the interwoven webs of the Internet and the corporate world—the 'branded web' as Klein calls the latter. Both are prime sites for the youthful *cyberflâneur*, as we will explain. We build on the focus on identity and on multimedia technologies when we consider teens and zines and culture jamming in the final section. These strategies once again appropriate popular cultural forms but with more agency and edge. They offer popular paradigms for kids to make their own media, using the same tools as the media uses but promoting their own ideas and policing 'their own desires' (Klein 2000: 293). Culture is understood as a prime site for citizenship and multimedia technologies come to be viewed as machinery for action.

Cool Hunting and Cool Criticism

Consumer-media culture is a *'pedagogical machine'* (Sholle and Denski 1995: 21, original emphasis) and consumer-media education invites students to prise open its covers, peer inside and see how its mechanics work. Ultimately, it invites them to recognize that 'The overwhelming objective of the media is neither to entertain nor to inform but, rather, to deliver audiences to advertisers' (Davies 1996: 177). Such a recognition involves a number of others. As we [have already] explained (Kenway and Bullen 2001: ch. 1), the media is used by producers to sell products to consumers and equally, media audiences have become commodities sold by media organizations to producers, thus creating a process of double exchange (Jhally 1990). At the same time, there is a process of exchange between the media and its audience that relates particularly to young people. In discussing 'adolescent consumer socialization' and MTV, Davies (1996) points to the contention of Schultze *et al.* (1991) that: 'To survive economically, the electronic media need a consumer youth market. On the other hand, young people derive guidance and nurturance from the media because other social institutions do not shape youth culture as powerfully as they once did' (Davies 1996: 177–8). This exchange, however, neither provides equal benefits to both parties nor makes transparent its operations. So, looking inside at the workings of the 'pedagogical machine' becomes an important component of consumer-media education. Equally, looking at the 'pedagogical machine' at work producing meaning and identity is another important component.

Students 'need' to see how consumer-media culture produces both meanings and identities. They need to look at how these meanings construct a certain 'version of reality' and at how 'they hook up with emotional (affective) commitments that are historically situated' (Sholle and Denski 1995: 22). For schools and teachers, this means recognizing both students' agency as producers of their own identity *and* their emotional or affective investment in, and consumption of, media culture and advertising images in the process of identity construction. As Sholle and Denski (1995: 25, original emphasis) explain, this investment is best understood, not as rational decision-making, but as '*emotional and bodily* commitments'. The young are 'vulnerably preoccupied with their self-image' and 'issues of social impression management' (Cohen 1998: 165). Consumer-media culture, likewise concerned with impression management, seeks to exploit this vulnerability and in so doing masks or mystifies its marketing intent. All this makes for pedagogical challenges of some magnitude.

As indicated [Kenway and Bullen 2001: ch. 3], there are many aspects to the work and workings of consumer-media culture. For the purposes of this section, though, we take the marketing concept known as 'cool hunting' and the media production strategy which Gow (1993) calls 'pseudo-reflexive impression management' as stepping-off points to theorize a postcritical pedagogy which invites students to call into question their affective investments without devaluing them. The hunted become the hunters and the pseudo-reflexive becomes the authentically reflexive. We call this 'cool criticism by the cool hunted'.

That kids buy image when they buy products, and that brands are inextricably tied to young people's identity-building, is now common knowledge. Along with this, many corporations have identified themselves as cool, alternative and defiantly young. Brand-name fashion, music and magazines are used as instantly recognizable codes of identity. For instance, 'ravers' wear clothing labels like Snug, Fiction and Porn Star, listen to techno music and read magazines like *Vice* and *Tribe*. Hard core (skate) 'boarders' listen to bands like Korn and Offspring; they wear Vans sneakers and punk-band T-shirts (*Maclean's* 1999). Yet it is less well-known that image-based brands create youth cultural style or attitudes partly through tapping into or resonating with those that already exist. According to Klein, when 'the baby boomers dropped their end of the consumer chain' in the early 1990s, 'Advertisers, brand managers, music, film and television producers raced back to high school, sucking up to the in-crowd' in search of street credibility (2000: 67–8). In other words, they went 'cool hunting'. Cool consultants such as Sputnik do not use market research techniques; they infiltrate, they are 'in with the in-crowd' (Klein 2000: 72). Here, too, we see the looting of such identity politics as green, feminist and black, gay and ethnic pride.

Under such circumstances we see the corporate plundering of the vernacular, of any as yet uncommodified styles with marketable possibilities. Just as consumer-media culture helped to disaggregate youth as we [have shown (Kenway and Bullen 2001: ch. 2)], it also contributed to a general notion that the young as a group have many tribes. In turn, this led to the young inventing their own subcultures and subcultural styles, drawing on an eclectic range of resources and blending them in extraordinary ways. Many big brands have zeroed in on the increasing number of youth subcultural groups or tribes which make up the Y Generation. The subcultural styles of the young from poor neighbourhoods have often been creative 'choices of necessity', and it is an irony that such choices are often those most sought by cool hunters.

Explaining that young and often poor urban African-American males have been the market most 'aggressively mined' for cool, Klein (2000: 74) says that in America, 'cool hunting simply means black-culture hunting'. It is a clear example both of how race is reduced to a matter of style and of the 'plagiaristic commerce' between black and white. Nike is preeminent among brands that have appropriated the vernacular cultural styles, forms and discourses of African-Americans and Latinos and packaged and sold them back to them. These young consumers have a colossal emotional stake in the identities they have been invited to construct around corporate logos. [. . .] [T]he commodification of race as style is complicated by issues of authenticity and its location in 'the long transactional history of white responses to black culture, of black counter-responses, and of further countless and often traceless negotiations, tradings, raids and other compromises' (Ross 1989: 67).

Klein (2000: 370–1) explains that

> Everyone pretty much agrees that brands like Nike are playing a powerful surrogate role in the ghetto, subbing for everything from self-esteem to African-American cultural history to political power. What they are far less sure of is how to fill that need with empowerment and a sense of self-worth that does not necessarily come with a logo attached.

With a huge emotional investment in such products, kids are usually resistant to criticism—until they find that they have been played for suckers. Klein (2000) reports that the discovery that the Nike shoes they had bought for up to $180 a pair had been manufactured in Indonesia for only $5 a pair resulted in a demonstration by African-American and Latino kids outside Nike's Fifth Avenue store in 1997. This example points to the benefits of tracing the history of corporate cool hunting and its theft of identities and identity politics.

The practice of cool hunting reminds us of Appadurai's (1986) notion that things have cultural biographies and social histories. In turn, this points to the possibilities of a pedagogy based on the notion that *things have social lives* (Lury 1996: 19). They move or transform their meanings, acquire and lose value, create social identities and carry interpersonal influence (Lury 1996). According to Appadurai, different kinds of things are commodified at different times and in different contexts or 'commodity situations' in their social lives. He proposes '*the commodity situation in the social life of any "thing" be defined as the situation in which its exchangeability (past, present, or future) for some other thing is its socially relevant feature*' (Appadurai 1986: 13, original emphasis). Studying this historical trajectory, as Lury points out, 'draws attention to the different pathways along which objects travel' in their particular social history (1996: 20). This involves tracing the biography of the commodity and its particular cultural significance or exchange value. Hebdige (1988) provides a methodological model here, his study of the social significance of the scooter being a well-known example. The sequence of the biography begins with the design and production of the object and Hebdige recommends attending to the larger economic and social frames. His methodology also draws attention to the status of objects in terms of their 'gendering' and aestheticization in the context of the consumer market.

We suggest that students undertake a similar cultural and social biographical analysis of the objects of cool in their own consumer culture. Cool hunting of this sort also needs to take into account subcultural, cross-cultural and retro influence, in addition to asking the simple questions of who made the object and where it originated. For instance, the current cult of body piercing might be examined in the light of ethnic cultural rituals and practices and their often highly gendered significance, as well as in relation to the currency it has for the young 'tribes' of today. What significance do we read into a pierced nose, a baseball cap worn backwards or a Winnie the Pooh lunchbox? When does an object lose its coolness and why? What is its exchange value in terms of the identity, solidarity or pleasure the consumer derives and how does this equate with the functional uses of the product? Are there stereotypes involved? Has the use of the product changed over time? Cool hunting aims to disclose both the appropriation of objects as in the case of Nike's plundering of African-American street culture and, conversely, the way consumer-media objects and identities are used by consumer groups—the African-American expropriation of Bart Simpson (Fiske 1996) being already mentioned. This is cool hunting turned into 'urban anthropology' (Klein 2000: 88).

Students may also elect to study the full life cycle of things by choosing objects (in particular objects associated with earlier youth cultures) which are now obsolete. Opportunity shops, garage sales or family memorabilia provide sources of material objects of this kind and, in some cases, opportunities to learn about the social context and significance of these objects by interviewing parents or previous owners. Such objects can be used as props for classroom displays or fashion parades. Tracing the travels of things across time and space, watching to see who uses what and with what effects, the self-conscious adolescent becomes conscious of the self and other. They watch themselves and their friends to see how they use cultural goods to communicate and they identify the 'masquerades' involved. Turnbull (1998: 102) offers a variation on these themes when she suggests students 'engage in a form of practical work which ask[s] them to create an image of *themselves* in the past, present and the future using a variety of already existing or especially created media forms'.

Clearly, the social life of things must also be considered in the light of the way in which objects are represented in film, print and broadcast media texts and in terms of marketing and advertising strategies. Lury argues that the 'methodological "animation" of objects can reveal new aspects of material culture, aspects which remain hidden if only one moment of an object's life is privileged' (1996: 26). However, there is an irony to this, given the current trend in entertainment and advertising towards reality programming or what has come to be known as 'voyeur TV' or V-TV—programmes like *Survivor* or *Shipwrecked* which do not use professional actors (Romei 2000: 6). A further dimension of this is the pretence of offering viewers the behind-the-scenes, hidden reality by calling attention to the 'constructedness' of much advertising and TV. Gow (1993) calls the latter production strategy 'pseudo-reflexivity' and it is designed to mask marketing intent. Cool hunters, therefore, must also be cool critics or, as Klein (2000) puts it, the Y Generation must be the why generation.

According to Gow (1993), media has become a positioning tool. This means that it sells products and personalities by 'creating, maintaining, or changing consumer perceptions of a product' (p. 319). Thus, it is not about the product so much as it is about the mind of the prospective consumer. Music videos are a good example of this. Impressions are created through the juxtaposition of aural, visual and narrative imagery which together become more than the sum of their individual parts. Together they create the persona/e of the performer or performers and manage the audience impressions of it/them by associating with desirable images and disassociating from undesirable ones. It is Gow's case that while sets, cast, lighting, camera angle and so forth can be used to create desirable associations, it is far more difficult to overcome the undesirable association between video music clips and commercialism.

Gow (1993: 320) cites Frith's contention that 'The belief in a continuing struggle between music and commerce is the core of rock ideology' (1981: 40–1). As Gow points out, commercialization has not harmed the careers of many pop stars, but then the market for pop music tends to be quite young. Youth, however, tend to want to express nonconformist or rebel identities (for young people's perspectives, see also Alvermann and Hagood 2000). Gow argues that in order to avoid giving the impression that they have sold out to consumer culture, many bands employ a pseudo-reflexive impression management strategy. By this he means the practice of employing: 'imagery that demystifies some, but not all, of the aspects of the video making process in order to draw audience attention away from the promotional motives underlying video production and enhance the anti-commercial stance typically adopted by hard rock musicians' (Gow 1993: 318). Rather than concealing the constructed nature of media products, this is deliberately foregrounded.

Authentic reflexivity in this instance involves shattering the 'illusion of reality' by making the codes of production transparent. It is potentially a subversive practice and, like much critical media education, invites a questioning of the ideological nature of the messages and of the social relationships they construct. By contrast, 'pseudo-reflexivity' is not deconstructive and, in fact, makes these things more difficult for the consumer to detect. The reflexivity or self-referentiality of commercials which parody themselves, for instance, 'is calculated to mystify rather than disenchant' (Stam 1992: 16). 'Videos structured along pseudo-reflexive lines', Gow argues, 'demystify one type of fiction, music video, in order to enhance the illusions surrounding another, sound recording' (1993: 322). In other words, viewers are encouraged to believe that 'the video makers—and, by virtue of the association principle, the band members themselves—are avoiding the usual practice of conjuring up a fantasy world in order to address their audience in an "honest" fashion' (Gow 1993: 322). However, only the production of the visual images is demystified, not the production of the music itself, and the reflexivity or interrogation of the one makes the other seem more authentic.

Examples of pseudo-reflexivity in video music clips include documentary style, behind-the-scenes glimpses of performers, production crew and hangers-on; juxtapositions of edited and 'raw' footage and of backstage and on-stage performances; and images involving audiences or fans. The hybridization of the reality and myth appears to invert convergences like the entertainment and advertising blend, because it foregrounds the difference between them. Its end, however, is identical, likewise intending to mask selling intent. What is particularly significant about Gow's research is that these production strategies are linked with the affective responses of the audience. They create a bond with the performers by inviting the members of the viewing audience 'backstage', by allowing them 'in' on the various technologies of production. They offer the consumer the pleasures of voyeurism. However, 'in the world of commercial entertainment such pleasures are often "bought only at the price of a corresponding blindness"' (Gow 1993: 325, quoting Altman 1987: 223). We wish to exploit and invert some of these pseudo-reflexive strategies in order to offer ways for young people to view and to consider their affective investment in consumer culture.

Students need a 'backstage pass' which offers them access to authentic reflexivity. By this we mean that students should be encouraged to look beyond the glamour and glitz of surface appearances and, by the same token, behind seemingly raw and spontaneous representations of consumer objects and identities. We propose that these not be confined to music. Backstage images of models preparing for the catwalk, for instance, offer an insider view merely to distract the viewer from the fact that the model's entire *raison d'être* is to sell fashion. Blockbuster movies are now sold to audiences using documentary-style promotions purporting to show the making of the movie. They condense a shoot of months into less than an hour, suppressing the tedious reality.

In making the backstage reality the object of investigation, it is not necessary to have access to supermodels, rock bands or sporting heroes, although print, TV and radio interviews and documentaries, biographies or autobiographies may offer insights. Far more accessible and far more useful are the experiences and impressions of sound technicians, makeup artists, photographers and camera crew, set designers, publicists, graphic designers and bit players in entertainment and advertising. Some of these may make themselves available to students for interviews. Others may be invited as guest speakers or as cultural intermediaries-in-residence. Other ways of accessing the backstage reality are industry publications as opposed to music, sport or fashion magazines which function as commercials targeting a youthful readership. Secondary materials, in particular social commentary aimed at a popular audience, are also sources of alternative perspectives. Kaz Cooke's *Real Gorgeous* (1994) reveals the reality behind the beauty myth in an engaging and humorous fashion.

However, as we have already indicated, there is another deeper and darker reality which exists behind the scenes: the 'night-time of the commodity'. In the following section, we look at how kids might become critical observers of the social and economic forces which drive, and are driven by, consumer-media culture.

The Youthful *cyberflâneur* as Global Citizen

The capacity 'To recognize yet disregard the invisible boundaries of the cityscape—this is the desire of the child and the regret of the adult' (Gilloch 1996: 85). For Benjamin, transgression is very much linked to the crossing of physical and spatial boundaries. It is linked with the pleasures of losing oneself in the streets of the metropolis. These are the pleasures of the *flâneur*, the male stroller or street reader. The pleasures of the *flâneur* have been described as those of 'just looking' (see Bowlby 1985). According to Nixon (1997: 334), 'the flâneur [is] an allegorical representation of the new relationship between the display of commodities and consumers' and, thus, of 'a new spectatorial consumer subjectivity'. In this regard, it refers not merely to the pleasures of window-shopping, but those of looking at oneself in the midst of this spectacle. Bowlby (1985) and Nixon (1997) have each considered the *flâneur* in relation to gender identity. Representations of gender identity in consumer culture act as a mirror to, and a model for, the production of gender identity. Although they contest the highly gendered nature of this figure and its association with the male gaze and, thus, visual mastery over women, these readings do not entirely reflect the *flâneur*—or the possibility of the *flâneuse*—as originally conceived.

Wilson (1992: 93), identifying references to the *flâneur* as early as 1806, describes him as a 'key figure in the literature of modernity and urbanization'. He is originally figured as 'a solitary onlooker' who 'stands wholly outside production' (Wilson 1992: 95). As initially interpreted by Benjamin, he is a cultural critic and literary producer whose 'object of inquiry is modernity itself' (Buck-Morss 1991: 304). Admittedly always an ambivalent figure, his existence seemingly inconsequential, his engagement with the city apparently superficial, the 'blend of excitement, tedium and horror' the urban world evokes for him points to the ambivalence of urban life itself. He recognizes 'the enormous unfulfilled promise of the urban spectacle, the consumption, the lure of pleasure and joy which somehow seemed destined to be disappointed, or else are undermined by the obvious poverty and exploitation of so many who toil to bring pleasure to so few' (Wilson 1992: 108). Ultimately, the *flâneur* comes to epitomize these very things. Benjamin's *flâneur* falls under the spell of 'the dreaming collective created by consumer capitalism' (Buck-Morss 1991: 312). He sells out. He becomes the 'prototype of a new form of salaried employee who produces news/literature/advertisements for the purpose of information/entertainment/persuasion' (Buck-Morss 1991: 306). In charting these changes, McLaren and Hammer conclude that 'The postmodern *flâneurs* of today are corporate individuals cunningly managing and shaping the world of mass-produced images, superannuated servants of the state whose forms of knowledge production are mediated by and fastened securely to the logic of consumption' (1995: 175). Finally, the *flâneur* 'advertise[s] not simply commodities but ideological propaganda' (McLaren and Hammer 1995: 174).

We wish to redeem the concept of the *flâneur*, to rescue it from its gendered connotations (if not the actual linguistic constraints of the French language in this regard) and to reconstitute the relationship between the pleasures of looking and cultural criticism. Further, we wish to relocate the *flâneur* from the embodied and lustrous streets of the metropolis to the disembodied nooks and crannies of the 'virtual Rialto', the Internet, described here by Nunberg (1995):

> It's urban, close, interior. Forget about cyberspace; this is cyberville, cyberstadt, cyber-ciudad. You want a good metaphor for the Internet, go to Venice in February. You thread your way down foggy streets and over bridges till you lose all sense of compass direction, and then all of a sudden you break into some glorious piazza. The rusty gate on the alley over there might open into a lush garden, and behind that might be a palazzo with long enfilades of rooms and galleries, but you can't see anything from the street. It's a place you get to know as an accumulation of paths and hidden passages, the way a woodsman knows the forest ... That's perfect for the Internet: the virtual Rialto. Except that Venice is too permanent—you come back after 50 years and everything's right where it was when you left. Whereas on the Internet addresses and connections change daily. Maybe we want to think of it as the Venice that Italo Calvino might have invented as one of his imaginary cities, a fantastic place where houses move over night from one quarter to another, where bridges disappear and canals reroute themselves with no warning ... Or maybe the model isn't an old-world city at all, but one of those shantytowns that spring up overnight on the outskirts of Latin American cities—the barriadas of Lima, the favelas of Rio.

Ultimately, we want the youthful *cyberflâneur* to come to see that the threads of online networks that constitute the virtual Rialto are intermingled with those of what Klein (2000: 357) calls the 'branded web'. With its 'fiber optic cables and shared corporate cultural references', the branded web has 'provided a basis for meaningful global communication' and laid 'the foundations for the first truly international people's movement' (Klein 2000: 357). Through its networks, the connections between the theatrical spectacle of the virtual Rialto or marketplace and the sweatshops and shantytowns not only of Latin America, but Indonesia, China, Vietnam, the Philippines and other free trade zones, are revealed.

The Internet has become a common theme of much discussion of anti-corporate activism. Klein (2000: 356–7) points to the irony of this when she says:

> Now that the corporations have spun their own global rainbow of logos and labels, the infrastructure for genuine international solidarity is there for everyone to see and use. The logo network may have been designed to maximize consumption and minimize production costs, but regular people can now turn themselves into 'spiders' . . . and travel across its web as easily as the corporations that spun it . . . It's like the Internet in general: it may have been built by the Pentagon, but it quickly becomes the playground of activists and hackers.

Klein (2000: 357) goes on to explain that the branded web connects people who in one way or another are associated with a commodity. For instance,

> McDonald's workers around the world are able to swap stories on the Internet about working under the arches; dub kids in London, Berlin, and Tel Aviv can commiserate about the corporate co-optation of the rave scene; and North American journalists can talk with poor rural factory workers in Indonesia about how much Michael Jordon gets paid to do Nike commercials.

There are strong synergies between the branded web and the Internet. In Turkle's (1995: 243) view, 'The Internet carries a political message about the importance of direct, immediate action and interest-group mobilization. It is the symbol and tool of a postmodern politics.' In addition to talking about resignification, as discussed above, we are talking here about networking, political organization and advocacy for just causes—global citizenship, if you like.

We have coined the term *cyberflâneur* to refer to the child who transgresses the spatial, physical and temporal boundaries of the corporate world through technology. The child 'is an apprentice in this "art of straying", in the still self-conscious crossing of the spatial limits of his or her class' (Gilloch 1996: 85). Our youthful *cyberflâneurs* are not limited by geography in making their connections on the web to the 'branded web'; as investigative activists, they stray where they may. They 'lose' themselves online in their search for information about corporate behaviour and for corporate activist sites and communities that they might learn from and belong to. They are spectators at the corporate bazaar, both real and virtual, but they are spectators of the 'watchdog' variety—they look back, not in wonder but with a sceptical and quizzical eye. Their object of inquiry is consumer-media culture. In short, the *cyberflâneur* is an excellent metaphor to deploy to point to the possibilities of youthful online activism on the 'branded web'.

Being a *cyberflâneur* is likely to be attractive to young people for several reasons. First, as noted, for postmodern youth, play and pleasure are often associated with adult-free zones and with the technologies that kids have seemed to 'master' much more adroitly than many of their parents. The conventional hierarchical adult/child politics of kids' everyday school lives are directly challenged in cyberspace. It has no government and in many ways is ungovernable. The key slogan of 'netiquette' is 'Information wants to be free'. Indeed, among many youthful users, there is an antipathy to any form of authority, be it governmental or commercial. Cyberspace offers webs and networks with multiple and shifting centres of power and authors of meaning. Fluidity, seamlessness, heterogeneity, interactivity, interconnectedness, reciprocity, community and freedom typify the medium and, as we have seen, its young consumers.

A second reason why being a *cyberflâneur* is likely to appeal to kids is because of the potential it provides to further build peer–peer communities. As we have shown, commodities and brands have provided a means by which kids have already forged bonds with each other. Kids like to connect with other kids and build on shared interests. Building online activist communities is simply an extension of this rapidly growing trend. But the point about kids' online communities does not stop there. Agre (1997) argues that, as the collective life of the Internet community unfolds, communities are being rebuilt and the rules of social life are being renegotiated: 'Concepts of identity, civility, and community [have been] suddenly transformed beyond recognition' (1997: 13), Agre says. Rebuilding community and renegotiating the rules of social life are likely to be attractive propositions for young people, particularly for those who have been alienated and disadvantaged by the maxim that the commodity rules—OK! Turkle (1995: 239) draws on her studies of Net participation to argue that downwardly mobile young middle—class people in the USA are using MUDS (Multiple User Dungeons—text-based virtual reality) as 'a vehicle of virtual social mobility'. Feeling that 'they have no political voice, they look to cyberspace to help them find one' (p. 241).

The youthful *cyberflâneur* will note that there are many Net activists who argue that the easy replication and distribution of digitalized information provides a powerful resource for political activism. Klein (2000: 396) quotes environmentalist Tony Juniper who describes it as 'the most potent weapon in the toolbox of resistance'. This technology is seen as providing unprecedented opportunities for distributing subversive information, for resistance and for the development of alliances across differences. There are numerous examples of political activism online and, as Klein shows, many anti-corporate activists, ranging from reclaim the streets party organizers to human, worker and environmental rights groups, employ the Internet as a tool for awareness raising, information sharing, organization and strategy. Information sharing involves distributing facts, figures and real-life anecdotes. A prominent example of such sites is www.mcspotlight.org which exposes not only corporate practices of McDonald's, but retailers like Tesco and K-Mart, and corporations like Coca-Cola, Nike and the Body Shop.

McSpotlight is an information network run by volunteers from 16 countries. Begun in 1996, the site originally gave coverage of the notorious McLibel trial. McDonald's sued two members of a small activist group for defamation over a pamphlet which, according to Klein (2000: 388), 'used a single brand name to connect all the dots on the social agenda'. These included environmental issues, Third World poverty, nutrition, the exploitation of child consumers and youth employees, waste and animal cruelty. Like many such sites, McSpotlight offers links to other activist sites as well as to corporate homepages. For instance, the NikeWatch Campaign link connects to the Community Aid Abroad Australia site which contains reports, educational resources, lists of organizations campaigning for workers' rights and other campaign websites including United Students Against Sweatshops (USA), the Alberta Nike Campaign site and Adbusters (Canada). Adbusters, for example, in turn provides links to Global Exchange with its 'reality tours', and the youthful and less earnest Urban75 with its parodic Boycott Top Five:

> NEW ENTRY! In with a bullet at Number Four is BP Amoco for their continued sponsorship of government death squads in Columbia as long as they help to keep the environmentalists off their back.
>
> The fastest new climbers are Pepsi Co for their continuing business relationship with Burma, in defiance of an international boycott. The Burmese Government has an appalling human rights record. Extra points were scored for their sponsorship of Latin American Cockfighting . . . and for their sponsorship of bullfighting in Mexico, with their dodgy banners festooned all around bullrings.

Other corporate entries in the Boycott Top 5—and contenders for a spot in the chart—are distinguished by their records in relation to the environment, human rights, testing on animals, child and sweatshop labour and so forth.

Sites like these offer opportunities for our *cyberflâneurs* to make the workings of the 'branded web', and its connections to youthful consumer-media culture, the object of their gaze. They reveal the reality behind many of the consumer goods and services we take for granted. How many children—and their parents and teachers—know that toys given away in McDonald's Happy Meals are made by children working in Chinese sweatshops, who earn $5.25 a day, work seven days a week and sleep 15 to a room on wooden bunks with no mattresses (*Sydney Morning Herald* 2000)? How many consider the possibility that a much-coveted object, a Nike soccer ball for instance, might have been made by a child as young as 6 for as little as 6 cents an hour? Certainly not many of the press reporting on the S11 protest at the World Economic Forum held in Melbourne in September 2000. Little front page coverage reflected on what Bigelow (1997: 114) describes as 'the glib premise, which underlies so much economic discussion, that foreign investment in poor countries is automatically a good thing'. This is what Bigelow asked of his students when he trialled a global studies curriculum.

Among the classroom strategies he used was what he called the Transnational Capital Auction. Students, divided into seven different 'countries', 'submitted bids for minimum wage, child labor laws, environmental regulations, conditions for worker organizing, and corporate tax rates' (Bigelow 1997: 114). In this corporate 'Game of Survival', economic and ethical imperatives were pitched against one another. Bigelow reports that 'in the frenzied competition of the auction', the students 'created some pretty nasty conditions because the game rewarded those who lost sight of the human and environmental consequences of their actions' (1997: 114). The students were subsequently invited to reflect on the impact on their 'country' of not having corporate taxes or child labour, minimum wage or environmental laws. What Bigelow did not do, but on later reflection realized he should have, was to bring the students back together and conduct the auction again. He believes that had the students done so, they 'could have practiced organizing *with* one another instead of competing *against* one another. They could have tested the potential for building solidarity across borders. At the very least, replaying the auction would have suggested that people in Third World countries aren't purely victims; there are possible routes for action, albeit enormously difficult ones.'

In the final section of this chapter we explore the potential of the Internet and multimedia technologies as mechanisms for political activity and building solidarity within and between school and youth communities. Using them, though not constrained by them, the *cyberflâneur* becomes not merely a critical observer of culture, but a producer. Culture work is understood as political play.

Teens, Zines and Culture Jamming

'The mouse is more powerful than the remote control' (Weston 1994) and as such it offers new possible orientations to consumer-media culture. Students can readily recognize the different qualities of interactivity between the Internet and other media forms such as video on demand or video games. Given half a chance, they can also understand and benefit from the fact that 'Information is no longer constrained by the traditional mass media' (Storm 1995) with its highly stylized gender and racial modalities that we have discussed. The pleasures of 'just looking' can be accompanied by the pleasures of joining others who are doing life politics online, exposing corporate greed and calling on corporations to be good global citizens and to conduct their affairs ethically.

Online, students can self-publish and, in so doing, capitalize on the very different relationship between the author and the reader that the Internet offers. They can thus develop a strong sense of agency as producers of culture. This also allows them to move beyond a reliance on the few centralized corporations and to capitalize on this 'from many to many' paradigm of communication. Clearly, then, the Internet is not only a source of information and games for students. It offers children and youth a means to 'distribute' their voices and views in ways that they enjoy. It also offers them the opportunity to blend the playful and earnest. In this final section, we look at the ways that kids might capitalize on the distributed self-publishing opportunities now available to them.

In saying this, we are well aware that many schools now have their own websites where they publish student newspapers as well as provide links to galleries and libraries of student projects. We are also aware that by 2000, nearly 12,000 high schools in 72 countries used HighWired.com to publish their student newspapers and school news on the Internet. The content of these newspapers is entirely student-generated and varies in terms of its local and international significance. Claims about the number of hits registered at various sites and top ten lists under various categories are indicative of some of the personal pay-offs for participants. Participation comes at no cost to schools. Online publishing is a considerably cheaper alternative to print media and HighWired's costs are underwritten by sponsorship. Arguably involved in the commodification of schools, HighWired clearly engages students—or is that teachers?

If HighWired has regenerated the concept of the school newspaper by adapting it to the new technologies, the result seems otherwise conventional, if not old-fashioned. The standardized format clearly makes it easy for the schools to publish but it also makes it difficult for schools to give any initial impression of their particular student culture. We argue that much cyberpublishing originating in schools continues to reflect the centrality of print in education culture. It also reproduces other elements of the traditional school. While HighWired offers the opportunity for students to publish information relating to all aspects of school life and the curriculum, there is no sense that these newspapers address themselves to many tribes of young consumers or to youth subcultural style. The target audience, like the format, is homogenized. Further, although we have found some insightful articles on social justice issues and exposés of corporate practices, they were often earnest in tone and conventionally journalistic in style.

This raises two important questions. First, do these student journalists write with a view to informing and engaging a peer audience or do they anticipate the judging prerogative of adults, given that teachers are their ultimate editors/censors? Second, do such newspapers offer students an opportunity to produce their own culture and their own cultural criticism in their own 'voice', or do links with traditional English, media and journalism curricula lead them to recreate the degraded version of the *flâneur* who, as we saw above, merely 'produces news/literature/ advertisements for the purpose of information/entertainment/persuasion' (Buck-Morss 1991: 306)? The fact that we did not find much that was feisty, subversive, politicized, alternative, celebratory, impassioned, fun or youthful suggests that the latter is the case in both instances.

There are, of course, a burgeoning number of youth interest/ rights/activist websites and e-zines. Oblivionnine ('conglomerating youth angst through corporate buyouts and media mergers since 1995' at www.oblivion.net) and BRAT ('because your school newspaper sucks' at www.brat.org) are examples of the way e-zines promote young people's virtual communities around such shared interests as film, games, music and politics. However, drawing on Kenway and Langmead (2000), we take the new generation of feminists who seek 'girl power' or more accurately 'Grrrl power' in and through new technology as an alternative model for online publishing for schools. These groups include such suitably insurgent titles as 'riot grrrls', 'guerrilla girls' and 'bad grrrls'. Grrrl power is an offspring of consumer/techno culture which venerates speed and change, the new, the novel, virtuality, simulation. The relevant sites online offer a wide range of cultural and sexual representations and interventions which take various forms and foci. They showcase prominent 'cybergrrrls' and act as 'guides to the wired world' with regard to such things as 'zines and comics, cyberpunk and gothic looks (nanofash)'. Their diversity is indicated by sites like chickclick.com with its network of links to 'girl sites that don't fake it'. These sites include the Riotgrrl and Riotgrrl websites; Wired Woman ('explores how technology affects women's lives'); Smarty-Pants ('mixes style with substance'); Bohos (a comic about four teenagers and 'what it means to be cool in a world gone mad'); as well as Lawgirl, Teengrrl, Disgruntled Housewife, Breakup Girl, Hissyfit, GrrlGamer and DjDazy. These sites are quirky, smart and slick, fun and pop. They offer feisty articles and chic images which glorify new technologies, technological savvy and linguistic Netspeak panache. They are youth-orientated and aim for wide popular appeal.

These publications are part of a broader subcultural movement which combines politics with style through appropriation and subversion of the forms and genres of popular mass media and culture. Exploiting the new 'democratized technologies' to produce 'hybrid political texts such as zines' (Garrison 2000: 144), they subvert practices like cool hunting which we defined above. As Garrison (2000: 163) explains:

> Like the major recording labels who 'plunder' music subcultures and 'indies' (independent bands and labels) for 'talents and trends', subcultures 'plunder' mainstream

> media, but their purposes are different: one is geared to profit margins and sustaining markets; the other to finding constructive meaning in a time of crisis and uncertainty. At a time when the mainstream mass media scripts politics as bumper stickers, soundbites, and tabloid sensationalism, it seems especially important to look for and foster (sub)-cultural spaces that insist on political content and intent in members' activities and in the objects they create. These include the tactical subjectivities employed to counter and subvert the depoliticized politics of conspicuous consumption.

The website for *Bitch*, a magazine offering a feminist response to popular culture, puts it this way when it says its mission is about

> forging connections between the sociocultural messages we get and the commercial agendas of who's behind them. It's about asking ourselves and each other questions: where are the girl-friendly places in the mass media? Where are the things we can see and read and hear that don't insult our intelligence? How can we get more of them?
>
> We can make them.

Taking Riot Grrrl as typical of the youth or 'third wave' feminist movement, Garrison (2000: 142–3) explains that it is 'an alternative subculture built around the opposition to presuppositions that young (usually white) US girls and women are too preoccupied with themselves and boys to be interested in being political, creative, and loud'. It is 'The tensions between this expectation and the political desires of members', she argues, that 'offers a powerful opportunity to learn different ways of resisting in a consumer-oriented culture' (Garrison 2000: 143). Indeed, as Garrison (2000: 143) goes on to add,

> For more and more subcultures (youth or otherwise), the ability to intertwine politics and style is a risky and necessary tactic in a cultural-historical period marked by 'the logic of late capitalism' in which the commodification of resistance is a hegemonic strategy. The hybrid political texts and distribution networks produced by feminists like Riot Grrrls are- ... both 'popular' and subcultural, they provide spaces for youth-controlled conversations, and they can operate as an interface between different Third Wave cohorts.

We believe that this emphasis on style is crucial if students are to invest in the production and politicization of elements of their own learning culture and to take pleasure in it.

As the Grrrl power story suggests, this need not mean an insistence on particular versions of citizenship. Grrrl power celebrates multiple ways of being female and disparate feminine cultures, sexualities, styles and pleasures. As Williams (n.d.) says, 'net chicks come in all varieties', they celebrate a 'feisty individuality' and even assert 'a girl's right to be feminine'. According to the Riot Grrrl Europe Manifesto (Riot Grrrl Europe n.d.), 'Amongst us are now grrrls and bois, ages fourteen or twenty seven, geeks and cheerleaders, dykes, punks. Try to call us all by name, you can't, cause we are everywhere. In every thinkable shape and form'.

While passionate, angry and aggressive tirades against Net-nerds and cowboys are in evidence, old-style rational and 'serious' feminist critiques are largely off the agenda. Racist, sexist, homophobic, classist and other derogatory material are also off the agenda if the code of conduct laid down by the Riot Grrrl ring mistress at the <http://skapunx.net/SallyTampon/grrrl/riotring> website is any indication. She accepts 'personal pages, band pages, distro pages, zine pages, grrrl-friendly product pages, anything as long as you are a grrrl at heart and yr page shows creativity and insight'. It says to grrrls, 'Do it yourselves (DIY) and Do what you like'.

As the Riot Grrrl Europe Manifesto indicates, riot grrrls take a critical stance towards the world around them 'and not only in a feminist way'. The civic sphere for such groups is culture particularly and their tools of citizenship are often humour, irony, mimicry, parody, burlesque and transgression. They do not necessarily seek to unsettle gender and sexual binaries so much as to play with or mock, exaggerate and distort them. The 'Feed the Model' found at adiosbarbie.com offers an arcade -style interactive game. A more sophisticated version called 'Feed the Super-model' at the official riotgrrl.com website allows visitors to plump up photographic images of real models and actors 'by feeding them more than Carr's water cracker and a bottle of Evian'. When we visited, the featured 'superskinny model' was Jennifer Love Hewitt.

The ironical, iconoclastic and critical sensibilities of these grrrls have much in common with those of the anti-corporate activity known as 'culture jamming'. Klein (2000: 280) defines this consumer activist strategy—a kind of 'semiotic Robin

Hoodism'—as 'the practice of parodying advertisements and hijacking billboards to drastically alter their messages'. More broadly, it refers to anything 'that mixes art, media, parody and the outsider stance' (Klein 2000: 283). The object of culture jamming is to reclaim public space (including schools) which has been colonized by corporate messages. Klein says that 'The most sophisticated culture jams are not stand-alone ad parodies but interceptions—counter-messages that hack into a corporation's own method of communication to send a message starkly at odds with the one that was intended' (2000: 281).

The term culture jamming was coined in the 1980s by the technoyippie band, Negativland, with 'jamming' referring to CB radio slang for the illegal electronic disruption of radio or TV transmissions. Today, culture jamming involves graffiti, vandalism, spamming (junk e-mail) and computer hacking. Some culture jamming practices are not merely subversive, they are blatantly illegal. Nevertheless, the principles behind them offer the opportunity for some pedagogical lateral thinking in relation to consumer-media education. Like e-zines, culture jamming offers a paradigm for kids to make their own media, using the same tools and techniques as the media. The 'newly accessible technologies that have made both the creation of and the circulation of ad parodies immeasurably easier' (Klein 2000: 285) are one means of translating culture jamming strategies to the classroom—with the irony that these technologies may have been made available to schools through corporate sponsorship. Original versions of advertisements can be downloaded and reworked on the desktop. The 'Photoshop' program offers the facility to match colours and fonts. There is the potential to create parodies as flashy, fun and visually arresting as the media created for them.

According to Juliet Beck, ad parodies are an effective way of subverting the hold of corporate consumer culture over people's fantasies and desires, precisely because the corporations are so dependent on advertising and brand image (Straus 2000). They are especially effective, moreover, because as the popularity of satires like *The Simpsons* with its ample use of parody indicates, parody is pleasurable. As Dery (Dery n.d.) puts it, 'culture jammers are Groucho Marxists, ever mindful of the fun to be had in the joyful demolition of oppressive ideologies'. At the same time, because parody manipulates and mocks elements of genre, form, language, image and structure, it also demands a consideration of the function of each of these in the parodic target, thus revealing 'the deeper truth hiding beneath the layers of advertising euphemisms' of the original corporate strategy (Klein 2000: 282).

If the technologicalization of the classroom means that students will soon be able to create their own computer-generated parodies, they need not be limited by this. Fake ads can be created using time-honoured techniques like collage and juxtaposed or combined with counterimages of environmental destruction or child labour. As ad spoofs like 'Absolut Nonsense Vodka' suggest, a simple word pun can be effective enough. Parodies of media genres like award ceremonies, game shows, magazine quizzes, news reports, soaps etc. can also be co-opted for the classroom. Moreover, we suggest that the notion of culture jamming be extended to the imagining of an alternative culture which 'jams' the stranglehold of consumer-media culture, not only over kids' fantasies and desires, play and pleasure, but over the needs and wants of cash-strapped schools. To this end, education and activist websites offer a rich range of activities which can be adapted to the school domain. Examples of pleasurable strategies designed to promote a critical awareness of consumer culture and perhaps even to raise funds for school communities include 'recycle fashion' parades, swap party and barter auctions, boycotts, kid-coordinated fairs or carnivals in which amusements and products are made by and for the kids, and variations on Buy Nothing Day and No TV Day.

Conclusion

We began [Kenway and Bullen (2001)] with a discussion of the generalized sense of unease that parents and teachers often feel about young people today. We mentioned that many fear that childhood itself is ending, that children themselves are developing out of order, that adults have lost control of children to the media. It can be inferred from such concerns that some adults feel that it is possible to reverse-engineer children, to change them back to the way children are *meant* to be, and that if school education is retraditionalized, proper adult/child authority relations can be restored. In response to this way of thinking we have offered an alternative, suggesting that such concerns and such nostalgia have arisen because of the destabilizing effects of wide-scale social and cultural change.

We made the case that the 'overdeveloped' countries of the West are going through another historical period in the invention of the child. We argued that current versions of Western childhood are very much the product of what we called consumer-media culture, and that this culture is underpinned in part by the sweated work of the 'othered' children of the so-called Third World. We explained how, with the aid of various media, the commodity form has increasingly become central to the life of the young of the West, constructing their identities and relationships, their emotional and social worlds. In so doing, we showed how adults and schools have been negatively positioned in this matrix to the extent that youthful power and pleasure are construed as that which happens elsewhere—away from adults and schools and mainly with the aid of commodities. In telling this story, we also told its parallel, the story of the changing face of capital as it redesigns institutions and people for profit. We showed how old institutional and cultural distinctions have given way to new uneven fusions between entertainment, advertising and education. Here we pointed to the seepage of the market form into more and more aspects of children's lives, even to the extent that schools are no longer understood as commercial-free zones run along market-free lines. Indeed, we showed how adults hope that the marketed school run according to traditional authority patterns will return children to their proper place—under adults' control. But as we indicated, it is far too late for that. Many kids have consigned schools to the periphery of their identities and concerns.

The scenario we have sketched clearly challenges many current notions of policy, curriculum and pedagogy, and notions of students and teachers. We hope that it will provoke people to ask, 'What new notions of schools, teachers, pedagogy and curriculum do these changes necessitate?' We have begun to answer part of this question by laying out some grounds for a pedagogy for young people who have grown up in 'the age of desire'. We have offered this example because we think these times require educators to look at schools and kids very differently, to ask new questions, to work in new ways and with different ideas but also to keep the notion of educating to the fore.

It is the responsibility of adults—teachers, parents, policy makers—to ensure that school education is not absorbed into the 'vortex of the commodity' (Sharp 1985) and that it makes powerful connections with the young people of today who, in many ways, have 'no choice' about their image- and commodity-drenched surroundings. At the very least, school could teach them to understand the differences between data, information, knowledge, education, entertainment and advertising. But can the marketized school tell the difference? Schools can play a role in alerting the young to matters of life politics in addition to matters of lifestyle. But if kids are to listen, we also need to re-enchant the school.

Democracy, Education, and Multiculturalism: Dilemmas of Citizenship in a Global World

Carlos Alberto Torres

The Theoretical Problem

The questions of citizenship, democracy, and multiculturalism are at the heart of the discussion worldwide on educational reform, deeply affecting the academic discourse and the practice of comparative and international education. Cloaked in different robes, questions about citizenship, the connections between education and democracy, or the problem of multiculturalism affect most of the decisions that we face in dealing with the challenges of contemporary education. In this [chapter] I outline some of the problems that occur in trying to reconcile the tensions among theories of citizenship, democracy, and multiculturalism in the context of capitalist societies, and I try to pinpoint some of the gaps and omissions in the discussion. In the closing section, I focus on one key aspect of this exploration: the question of the canon, culture, and the constitution of a democratic multicultural citizenship.

Theories of citizenship and theories of democracy mark the advent of modern political science and reflect, in their complexities, the theoretical and practical challenges to democracy in contemporary societies. Both also underline the dilemmas of negotiating power in democratic societies.

Theories of citizenship relate to every problem of the relations between citizens and the state and among citizens themselves, while theories of democracy relate clearly to the connection between established—hidden and explicit—forms of social and political power, the intersection between systems of democratic representation and participation with systems of political administrative organization of public governance, and with political party systems. Ultimately, theories of democracy need to address the overall interaction between democracy and capitalism.

Finally, theories of multiculturalism, so prevalent in the educational field in the last twenty years, have emerged as a particular response not only to the constitution of the pedagogical subject in schools or to the interaction between the pedagogical subject and the political subject in democratic societies but also as a way to identify the importance of multiple identities in education and culture. In short, theories of multiculturalism are intimately connected to the politics of culture and education.

Carlos Alberto Torres, 'Democracy, Education, and Multiculturalism: Dilemmas of Citizenship in a Global World', *Comparative Education Review*, 42, 4.

Thus, theories of multiculturalism relate to the main analytical purpose of theories of citizenship. Both attempt to identify the sense and sources of identity and the competing forms of national, regional, ethnic, or religious identity. Yet theories of multiculturalism have addressed the implications of class, race, and gender for the constitution of identities and the role of the state in a way that, by and large, mainstream theories of citizenship have not. While the interconnections between identity and citizenship are not at all evident in the specialized bibliography, they have a practical grounding that also brings them closer to theories of democracy. This is so because, not only are theories of democracy preoccupied with participation, representation and checks and balances of power, but some brands also are concerned with ways to promote solidarity beyond particular interests of specific forms of identity.

Theories of citizenship, democracy, and multiculturalism, in their specific spheres of influence and empirical locus, not only strive to identify a sense of identity (for the notion of a democratic citizen and a multicultural political subject) including all its contradictory sources but also seek to define vigorously the limits and possibilities of forms of sociability that will promote the ability of individuals to tolerate and work together with people who are different from themselves. Likewise, these theories may enhance people's (or in a more restricted formulation, citizens') ability and desire to participate in the political process of promoting the public good and accountability. Finally, these theories will help individuals' willingness to exercise self-restraint and personal responsibility in their economic demands and in personal choices that affect the health and wealth of society and the environment as well as the process of community(ies) formation. This is so because as Jürgen Habermas so aptly has argued, 'The institutions of Constitutional freedom are only worth as much as a population makes of them.'[1]

The dilemmas of citizenship in a democratic diverse multicultural society can be outlined, at the beginning of our analysis, as follows: Theories of citizenship had been advanced—in the tradition of Western political theory—by white, heterosexual males who identified a homogeneous citizenship through a process of systematic exclusion rather than inclusion in the polity.[2] That is, women, identifiable social groups (e.g., Jews, Gypsies) working-class people, and members of specific ethnic and racial groups—in short, people of color—and individuals lacking certain attributes or skills (i.e., literacy or numeracy abilities) were in principle excluded from the definition of citizens in numerous societies.

Theories of democracy, while effective in identifying the sources of democratic power, participation, and representation in legitimate political democratic systems, had been unable to prevent the systemic exclusion of large segments of the citizenship. Thus, formal democracy drastically differs from substantive democracy. More worrisome still is the fact that theories of democracy had been unable to differentiate the roots of representative democracy (based on the notions of equal representation, equity, and equality) from their immersion in the foundational principles that articulate capitalist societies. By definition, capitalism requires differential representation in power and politics, fostering inequity formation through hierarchies and competing interests and inequality through the workings of a profit-seeking system.

Theories of multiculturalism, while effective in discussing the politics of culture and identity and the differential sources of solidarity across and within specific forms of identity, and even insightful in showing the remarkable complexity of multiple identities, had been unable or unwilling to embrace a theory of citizenship and a theory of democracy that could be workable, in practical, procedural terms; ethically viable, in moral terms; and politically feasible in the context of capitalist civil societies.

We need a theory of multicultural democratic citizenship that will take seriously the need to develop a theory of democracy that will help to ameliorate, if not eliminate altogether, the social differences, inequality, and inequity pervasive in capitalist societies and a theory of democracy able to address the draconian tensions between democracy and capitalism, on the one hand and among social, political, and economic democratic forms, on the other. Finally, we really need a theory of democratic multicultural citizenship that can provide a reasonable theoretical answer to the neoconservative cry about the ingovernability of modern democracies in capitalist societies.

Citizenship and Education

In discussing theories of citizenship and their importance to education, it is important to move beyond historical or legal considerations. Likewise, it is important to move beyond the notion of citizenship as a kind of personal status, a combination of rights and duties that all legal members of a nation-state hold. The discussion of theories of citizenship requires stating a premise from the outset: a theory of a 'good citizen' should be relatively independent from the formal premises of the legal question of what it is to be a citizen. This is so because of the dual theoretical concerns of citizenship: as identity and as civic virtues. However, without considering the political economy dimension and the need for a historical-structural analysis of citizenship, any suggestion that citizenship is primarily a function of civic virtues could be seen as an idealistic undertaking. Civic virtues need a civil minimum that can only be found in a historical-structural context where these civil minimums overlap with basic material conditions.

The Enlightenment as the Foundation of Citizenship and the Proposal of T. H. Marshall

The movement of the Enlightenment suggests a historical and social construction of human identities, and therefore socialization in rational principles is considered important, with educational institutions—as key institutions of the Enlightenment—playing a central role.

There are three elemental aspects of a theory of citizenship for the Enlightenment. First, the Kantian proposal that sustains the hypothesis that socialization processes, especially as related to cognitive thinking, have a place within structures that preceded individuals becoming knowledgeable. Second, the Hegelian proposition that suggests the capacity to be socialized should be recognized as a civilizing technique—that is, as part of a process that largely depends on the circumstances that inhibit or facilitate progressive social change.[3] Third, the Marxist contention that suggests that without access to the production and distribution of resources—the material benefits of the economy—it is impossible to sustain citizenship in political terms.

The most significant development in citizenship theory in this century undoubtedly has been linking the welfare state and its network of services with the full expression of democratic citizenship, T. H. Marshall's celebrated and much-cited 1949 article 'Citizenship and Social Class' articulates, like few other works, the new postwar consensus about the notion of the liberal welfare state as a precondition for the exercise of citizenship in capitalist societies.[4]

For Marshall, citizenship developed over 250 years in England as three elements emerged: civil, political, and social rights. Western civil society obtained civil rights in the eighteenth century, political rights in the nineteenth century, and social rights in the twentieth century. Civil rights encompass all rights required for individual freedom (e.g., the right to own property, freedom of speech, and the right to justice). Political rights include all rights surrounding the electoral process (e.g., the right to vote, to elect and be elected, etc.). Finally, social rights are those that appear as the most controversial of all, including not only a modicum of economic welfare and security but also what is necessary for individuals to live a full life: 'To share to the full in the social heritage and to live the life of a civilized being according to the standards prevailing in society. The institutions most closely connected with welfare are the educational system and the social services.'[5] Marshall's arguments on citizenship are embedded in the arguments of the ongoing democratization of society, which illustrates a central, principle of the Enlightenment. Yet, as Carole Pateman points out, citizenship is not synonymous with democracy. Traditional theories of citizenship are challenged by different forms of social theory.[6]

Feminism

Marshall along with many other scholars took for granted that all people in England during the eighteenth century were legally free and therefore enjoyed civil citizenship. A most serious challenge to this assumption, however, is the idea that adult English males had enjoyed their legal freedom and citizenship because of the commodification of women's labor and women's lack of legal power in households controlled through patriarchal practices.[7] As Pateman put it: 'Despite the increasing volume and range of criticism, his commentators typically fail to appreciate the peculiar narrowness of Marshall's interest in citizenship, which runs in one direction only ... He fails to ask whether rights are of equal worth to all citizens, or to make the point in another way, whether citizenship means the same for all individuals. He asked about the social integration, and the material and cultural conditions of the male working-class. He did not consider whether there were other citizens who might be described as second class.'[8]

This commentary points to three interesting criticisms of Marshall; (*a*) that his analysis, with the drastic ideology of the (male) working class may no longer account for changes in citizenship due to a restructured globalized capitalism; (*b*) that he failed to take into account the issue of ethnicity (which describes a sizable segment of what Pateman chose to call 'second-class citizens'); and (*c*) that he obviously failed to account for the subordination of women in his analysis of citizenship. Hence, it is the importance of the feminist challenge to citizenship to which I turn briefly.

Feminism has been important to the deconstruction of the prevailing inherent 'maleness' of the traditional conceptions of citizenship. Let us take, as a case in point, the contribution of Chantal Mouffe's discussion of identity. Mouffe's position is that relations of subordination are multilayered, and in fact, individuals may play a dominant role in one relationship and a subordinate role in another.[9] In part, this has to do with the material and symbolic positionality of subjects and with the fact that identity is not a fixed essence but an assemblage of positions (i.e., status/role), narratives, and discourses constructed by the subject from his or her relations (and therefore experiences) and from her or his own positionality.

The basic implication of Mouffe's analysis is that the notion of the identity of a subject should not be approached simply as the coexistence of a plurality of positions. This assertion is a most important challenge for the notion of citizenship. Since the agent cannot be singled out as formed by a basic identity, and since the notion of plurality defies easy definitions of what is a citizen, this analysis seriously challenges any simplistic definition of citizenship based on legal or territorial notions. But there is more. While a plurality of identities does exist, they cannot be simply understood as an aggregate of factors or as an amalgam of properties.

The feminist discussion highlights three rather intractable themes for the traditional liberal conception of citizenship. First, there is the notion of identity as an elusive, disputed, ever-changing assemblage of narratives and positions that will make it very difficult to speak of citizenship as a single identity correlated either with a territory, culture, or experience. Hence, Mouffe's criticisms of essentialized positions are based on the premises of 'conceptualizing identities and differences as discursively constructed instead of as objectively given.'[10] Second is the notion of the patriarchal foundations of liberal democracies and the indispensable criticism and changes in those foundations if all men and women are to be considered full citizens. As Pateman instructs us, 'By a genuinely democratic citizen, I mean that both sexes are full citizens.'[11] This, in turn, invites one to criticize the political usage of the notions of the public and the private. The feminist criticism of the 'public' as a male, patriarchal concept, and the need to understand democracy as method as well as content encompassing the private and public domains—a distinction that should incorporate the value of caring as related though not necessarily exclusive to, motherhood—are important challenges to the traditional notion of citizenship measured as voting patterns and participation rates. And third, Mouffe suggests that finding a democratic equivalence in incorporating the diverse struggles is built in the very notion of postulating alternative identities into the construction of democratic citizenship and community. Mouffe's posture assumes the need of discussing citizenship, not as one single identity enmeshed with others, or as a sum of identities, but as an articulating principle 'that affects the different subject positions of the social agent, while allowing for a plurality of specific allegiances and for the respect of individual liberty.'[12]

Critical feminist perspectives help in understanding the constitution of the subject as constructed through different discourses and positions. This is a view that is more adequate than the reduction of identity to one single position—such as class, race, or gender—and appears a prerequisite to understanding how relations of power are constructed and what forms of exclusion, despite the claims of liberal citizenship, prevail.

Debates within feminism, however, show the importance of the new contributions of border feminists, most predominately Chicana feminists who criticize as cultural imperialism white Eurocentric feminism for its inability to imagine the needs, desires, and rights of their women of color counterpart: 'Feminism affects and influences Chicana writers and critics, but feminism as practiced by women of the hegemonic culture oppresses and exploits the Chicano in both subtle and open ways.'[13]

The complexity of race, gender, and class dynamics, particularly through the contributions of border feminism, needs to be situated in the life-world of globalized postcolonial societies, hence the importance of discussing the contribution of postcolonial analysis for citizenship, especially if we take into account the title of the well-known poem of Gloria Alzandúa: 'To Live in the Borderlands Means You.'

Postcolonialism

As the 'adult English male' subject was the citizen par excellence for Marshall, looking back at his contribution we need to recognize that the citizen he had in mind is British. But, as Pateman points out, Marshall does not draw in detail the notion of the 'British subject' nor does he look at the implications of a three-staged citizenship built in England fully supported by the expansion of British imperialism in the world.[14] For instance Pateman notes the 1948 Act separated those acquiring British nationality by virtue of birth or naturalization in the United Kingdom from those acquiring it as part of the status of Commonwealth countries.[15] Hence the importance of discussing postcolonialism as a challenge to citizenship.

Colonialism is linked to the expansion of control by mostly European metropolitan societies over Third World societies, a historical process that Lenin defined as imperialism, a superior phase of capitalism.[16] Colonialism also was an attempt to force modernization through territorial, political, and technological invasion from industrial advanced societies over less technologically developed societies. This process was not a product of authoritarian philanthropy of bringing modernity to 'traditional' people but an attempt to solve some of the looming social problems of the colonial powers themselves and to exploit the untapped natural and human resources of the country being colonized.

For instance, the expansion toward 'new territories'—Africa and Asia most prominently, but Latin America as well—served as a 'safety valve' for Europe given the overpopulation and political crises of the last quarter of the nineteenth century and years leading up to World War I. It also addressed the superabundance of labor as well as the declining rates of return to capital in need of new markets for investments and raw materials. Finally, colonialism was based on geopolitical considerations of European nation-states and elites trying to enhance their planetary reach while trying to settle, militarily and diplomatically, their differences in European nation building.

Postcolonialism, connected with liberation movements fighting against colonialism, emerged as an attempt to criticize the rational foundations of colonialism and to decolonize 'the mind,' as Frantz Fanon liked to say, 'Postcolonial thought is, above all, criticism of the Enlightenment and its legacy of modernity.' Joining the criticism of feminism, postcolonialism critiques the notion of an unqualified reason and universality, the progressive unfolding of history, ideas of national sovereignty, or the integrity of a self-identity subject that holds specific, self-reflective interests.

For postcolonialism, analysis of the various dimensions of transnationalization, of what constitutes a nation, and what role territorial spaces play in the articulation of the notion of national sovereignty are central. This also implies a serious challenge to the notions of political community and political identity. Ray Rocco claims that it is precisely the type of changes that he analyzed among nation, identity, community, territory, and state that the discourse on citizenship tries to articulate. In his study of Los Angeles Latino communities, Rocco finds that Latinos, particularly new immigrants, engage in practices that fall within the notion of citizenship building:

> They engage in practices within relational settings of civil society that under specific conditions, can be construed as in effect making claims that are about membership in the community, about having access to institutional settings, resources, and opportunities ... about the freedom to develop and maintain culturally based associational networks, that challenge the criteria of inclusion/exclusion, and affirmations of spaces of cultural identities. [Rocco's studies] revealed a number of such practices, which although not necessarily understood nor intended by the actors to be 'political,' nevertheless are in effect contestations of established boundaries, rules, and constructions of citizenship.[17]

'Under specific conditions.' This is the crux of theorizing citizenship from the postcolonialist perspective of hybridity, borders, and subaltern spaces. What specific conditions would facilitate that the contestations of established boundaries, rules, and the construction of citizenship can be incorporated into a discussion of how subaltern identities in multicultural societies may constitute a comprehensive, dynamic, and complex notion of citizenship?

Critical Race Theory

Despite Marshall's contribution to a theory of citizenship, a glaring omission in his analysis was the consideration of ethnicity and race. Today this is more important than ever. Race and racism continue to be central concepts in understanding the US racial formation. Despite much lip service paid to discussions on race and the liberal discourse of tolerance, race and racism are perceived by critical race theorists as muted and utterly marginalized in the analysis of public policy and citizenship.[18]

Critical race theory was born in the United States within legal studies attempting to address the differential treatment of people of color by the courts and in prison. For many, critical race theory is the result of work by progressive legal scholars of color who see American law as permeated by racism and who make the elimination of racism in American jurisprudence a central goal in the elimination of all forms of subordination.

Critical race theory, as outlined by one of its key proponents, Derrick Bell, views civil rights achievements in the United States during this century with growing skepticism: 'In our era, the premier precedent of Brown vs Board of Education promised to be the twentieth century's Emancipation Proclamation. Both policies, however, served to advance the nation's foreign policy intent more than they provided actual aid to Blacks.'[19] Bell argues that, in the United States, the legal rights framework has been sacrificed on behalf of whiteness: 'Even those whites who lack wealth and power are sustained in their sense of racial superiority by policy decisions that sacrifice black rights. The subordination of blacks seems to reassure whites of an unspoken, but no less certain, property right in their 'whiteness.' '[20]

Critical race theory, as Daniel Solorzano and Octavio Villalpando explain, is related to five key insights: (1) the primary focus on race and racism; (2) the challenge to dominant ideology; (3) the commitment to social justice; (4) the importance of experiential knowledge, and (5) the use of an interdisciplinary perspective.[21] Critical race theory, then, will be useful to prove that racism is endemic and deeply ingrained in American life. These culturally sanctioned beliefs, no matter how symbolically concealed, involve the defense of pre-established social, cultural, and economic advantages. Therefore, the challenge to racism entails a serious challenge to the superordinate position of whites over racial minorities. To address this racial inequality, Gloria Ladson-Billings and William Tate claim that civil right acts have been ineffective because, ultimately, having not challenged the basis for property subordination, whites have, paradoxically, benefited from school desegregation. Even more, when desegregation was launched, new models of resegregation through ability grouping emerged, reproducing the conditions for a learning imbalance between whites and colored people.[22]

A third important insight of critical race theory, one prominent in the discussion of citizenship, is that claims of neutrality, objectivity, meritocracy, and the goal of a color-blind society need to be challenged.[23] Thus, 'for the critical race theorist, social reality is constructed by the formulation and exchange of stories about individual situations. These stories serve as interpretative structures by which we impose order on experience and it on us'.[24]

For critical race theorists, racism is so deeply ingrained in the United States that a rethinking of citizenship needs to incorporate systematic challenges to the practice of racism in the legal system and, by extension, in the school system. This rethinking should challenge not only racism but also the prevalence of the logic of property rights over the logic of personal rights and the foundation of human rights as the basis for equality and justice. Given the magnitude of the task, there are no naive assumptions that antiracist positions can be easily organized in a coalition to challenge prevailing racist structures, sentiments, and values.

By putting the question of race first, critical race theorists argue that the discussion of citizenship can no longer be treated as a homogeneous identity in search of the exercise of rights and obligations. Along the same lines as critical race theorists, another important claim on the state and the constitution of citizenship is provided by old and new social movements.

New Social Movements

If we understand politics as a struggle for power, new social movements should not be interpreted exclusively in political terms, as they also represent cultural and moral practices centered on the construction of collective identities and spaces. They originate around certain demands and specific social relations, becoming increasingly autonomous from traditional institutions of political representation of interests. This is so, argues Ernesto Laclau—joining other proponents of social movement theory—because individuals no longer exclusively define their identity in relation to the means and relations of production but also as consumers, residents of a particular neighborhood, members of churches, ethnic or gender groups, and participants in the political system.[25]

New social movement theory has provided the basis for a dramatic shift in understanding the relationship between social movements and education. A distinctive characteristic of new social movements is their cognitive and ideological focus on rethinking preexisting social and cultural paradigms as part of a politics of identity. As a consequence, one of their key strategies is broadly educational, as opposed to a focus on gaining power, and its implications for citizenship are numerous. To cite just a few, consider the gains that the environmental movement has made in schools, promoting a democratic citizenship that is responsible—at a collective and even planetarian level—for the protection of endangered species, for the levels of pollution in the air and water, or for the control of dangerous substances in food. Consider the role of the Zapatista movement in Chiapas, redressing the inequality built into the interaction of Mexican aboriginal people and the postrevolutionary Mexican state, and its consistent and impetuous political program linking those ethnic and political demands to the constitution of a true radical democracy in Mexico and the constitution of a democratic citizenship without exclusions. Consider the impact of the antitobacco movement in schools, challenging the notions of the glamour of smoking and linking advertisements to the powerful tobacco lobby and multinational tobacco corporations. By challenging the consumption of tobacco, all sorts of connections between the political system, the mode of production, and the risks to the quality of life of the citizens are critically exposed. Consider the case of the racially based civil rights movement in the United States. The dismantling of segregated schools constituted, despite its obvious limitations, perhaps the most fundamental and far-reaching demands linking race and education and eventually remaining a central tenet of American citizenship.[26] Consider the growing importance of the feminist movement in affirming unequivocally the political, social, cultural, and economic equality between men and women, and drastically changing the spectrum of social relations in schools by promoting the principles and methods of feminist pedagogy and by promoting a new level of social exchange among students, teachers, and parents in defending feminist goals.

The praxis of social movements offers potentially fertile ground for a 'conscientization' approach à la Paulo Freire. Social movements typically build on the knowledge base and previous struggles of people, taking into account their organizational capabilities and grievances. This allows for the building of programs *with* and *from* the communities rather than *for* them, as the late Paulo Freire illustrated in countless writings.

In short, new theories of critical modernism—including feminism, critical race theory, and subordinate social spaces theory nested within the theoretical net of postcolonialism—and the practice of new social movements have enhanced the possibilities of citizenship, particularly in multicultural democratic societies. The question, then, is how citizenship relates to the notion of democracy and education.

Democracy and Education

The prevailing notion of democracy at the beginning of the twenty-first century is liberal representative democracy, with its principle of the active citizen. As it is defined by David Held, it constitutes 'a cluster of rules, procedures and institutions permitting the broadest involvement of the majority of citizens, not in political affairs as such, but in the selection of representatives who alone can make political decisions.[27]

Yet it is convenient to distinguish at the outset, as the Italian political scientist Humberto Cerroni does, between democracy as content and democracy as method. Democracy appears to be primarily a method of political representation, a cluster of rules that include elected government; free and fair elections; universal suffrage; freedom of conscience, information and expression; the right of all adults to oppose their government and stand for office; and the right to form independent associations. As a principle democratic governments seek to develop parliamentary and judicial systems free from the control of the executive by using a system of checks and balances. Finally given the liberal impetus, liberal democracy upholds the belief in the predominance of individual rights over collective rights, which implies a serious recognition of the potential tyranny of majorities.

The notion of democracy as content is related to the notion of democracy as a system of political participation by the people in public affairs. It is related to the power of the people over any other regulatory institution such as kinship), the idea of equal rights for all citizens, and, particularly in the US Constitution, a political philosophy of egalitarianism. However, a motion of radical democracy goes beyond the attempt to prevent forms of exclusion that preclude political and social participation. Radical democracy postulates radical equality in racial/ethnic, class, and gender interactions, both in the public sphere and in the intimacy of the household. Thus, a first important tension occurs between democratic regimes that uphold formal rules but fail dramatically to uphold democracy in terms of class, race/ethnicity, and gender interactions.

A second important tension, then, is to explain how the notion of democracy became intimately intertwined with the notion of capitalism as the most conducive mode of production for the development of democratic systems. Samuel Bowles and Herbert Gintis persuasively argue that the dynamics of democracy rely on two logics of expansion of the capitalist system: personal rights and property rights, which are often opposed.[28] The conflict between these two logics—represented perhaps in the clash between business ideology and social movements in advanced industrial capitalism and independent-development capitalism—is over the use and appropriation of social resources and also about the question of setting ethical standards of social behavior. However, capitalism as an economic and social system of accumulation, production, reproduction, and distribution of commodities is intrinsically conflictual and marked by internal contradictions.

If capitalism is a conflictual system and democracy has two logics of development, then the question is why democracy and capitalism became intermingled and why this working relationship of politics and economics does not fall apart. Bowles and Gintis claim that the connection between democracy and capitalism occurred through four historical accommodations of the system: (*a*) in Europe, the Lockean proposal that accommodates the system limiting the political participation of the propertied; (*b*) in the United states the Jeffersonian proposal that distributing property widely among the citizenry (of Anglo-Saxon origin) reaccommodates the system in the face of increasing political strains; (*c*) the political proposal of James Madison to foster a sufficient heterogeneity of interest among citizens to prevent the emergence of a common political program of the nonpropertied; and (*d*) the Keynesian model, in which economic growth and distribution of income generate a communality of interests between the dispossessed and the wealthy.

Is there a new accommodation of the system in the face of the current crisis of democracy? What is the situation of democracy and capitalism at the end of the millennium? It can be characterized as the problem of governability of democracy in capitalist societies or, to put it in the terms of Bowle and Gintis, as the lack of a new historical accommodation of the system—a risky impasse. Yet, it seems that a new accommodation is emerging with the notion of citizen as consumer and the predominance of globalization from above.[29]

Democracy and Multiculturalism

The connections between democracy and multiculturalism are among the most contested polemics of our time. Let me start with the prophetic voice of Cornel West, who argues that

> the new cultural politics of difference are neither simply oppositional in contesting the mainstream (or *male* stream) for inclusion nor transgressive in the avant-gardist sense of shocking conventional bourgeois audiences. Rather they are distinct articulations of talented, (and usually privileged) contributors to culture who desire to align themselves with demoralized, demobilized, depoliticized, and disorganized people in order to empower and enable social action and if possible, to enlist collective insurgency for the expansion of freedom, democracy and individuality.[30]

West sets the right tone for the discussion. Multiculturalism, in any form, shape, or color relates to the politics of difference and the emerging social struggles over racialized, gendered, and classist societies. Yet discussions on multiculturalism in the United States should start with a subtle but important differentiation among notions of multiculturalism as a social movement and a theoretical approach, multicultural education as a reform movement, and citizenship education as a curriculum-oriented specialty that, particularly given the characteristics of the US racial formation, needs to take into account issues of racial identity and cultural diversity for citizenship building as antiracist pedagogy.

As a social movement, multiculturalism is a philosophical, theoretical, and political orientation that goes beyond school reform and tackles the issues of race, gender, and class relations in society at large. As multicultural education, however, the landscape in the United States has been dominated by liberal multiculturalism.

The proponents of liberal multiculturalism will argue that it will increase fairness by representing the range and richness of America's different ethnicities and tolerance by exposing students to multiple perspectives on the meaning of history. 'In this view, multiculturalism pluralizes the notion of an American identity by insisting on attention to African-Americans, Native Americans, and the like, but it leaves in place a unified concept of identity.'[31]

Within the pluralist framework, *identity* 'is taken as the referential sign of a fixed set of customs, practices, and meanings, an enduring heritage, a readily identifiable sociological category, a set of shared traits and/or experiences.'[32]

From an existentialist, and not merely a sociological standpoint, identity also is related to key feelings and experiences of protection, association, and recognition. As West so forcefully claims,

> People identify themselves in certain ways in order to protect their bodies, their labor, their communities, their way of life; in order to be associated with people who ascribe values to them; and for purposes of recognition, to be acknowledged, to feel as if one actually belongs to a group, a clan, a tribe, a community. So that any time we talk about the identity of a particular group over time and space, we have to be very specific about what the credible options are for them at any given moment.[33]

In contrast, *diversity*, Joan Scott argues, 'refers to the plurality of identities, and it is seen as a condition of human existence rather than as the effect of an enunciation of differences that constitute hierarchies and asymmetries of power.'[34] West will agree since he argued that 'this historical process of naming is part of the legacy not just of white supremacy but of class supremacy.'[35]

Power and difference in multiculturalism narratives are always interrelated with a discussion of identity. Yet, *national identity*—the most important form of territorial solidarity based on notions of a single nation-state and the experience and feeling of patriotism and a common cultural heritage—not a fixed marker that guides citizens in their choices of loyalties and solidarities. Historically, the concept of national identity is better defined in opposition to 'others' (i.e., another national identity or an enemy of the nation) rather than in reference to a set of uncontested historical properties of a nation and the national experience of its people as a homogenous group.

Therefore, identities are constructed in a process of contestation and struggle and are subject to multiple interpretations. Identities are social constructions with material and historical bases, and indeed they are based on (or, if one allows for the Althusserian lapse, are interpellated by) perceptions of knowledge, experience, and power, particularly what knowledge is (or should be considered) legitimate and should count, what experiences should be celebrated and learned from, and how power can be negotiated among different knowledge and experiences. Yet, the same notion of experience that seems to underlie the notion of identity, as Scott has so forcefully argued, is something historically, culturally, and discursively produced. Once again, as Michael Apple has so aptly argued for more than two decades, connections between power and knowledge become central to any practical agenda of research and policy making in education, particularly in this new phase of the conservative restoration.[36]

Identity, as I have argued, is not a fixed marker, an essential substance that some people share in virtue of their origin, race, religious affiliation, sexual preference, gender, or class, but a process of learning that is context-dependent and, indeed, open to interpretation. As such, it also depends on the historicity of the struggles that impinge on social consciousness at a given moment in time, making experience and the consciousness of the experience a salient process of understanding and meaning making by the individuals attempting to understand the conditions of their lives.

The poet T. S. Eliot said that 'we had the experience but missed the meaning,/And approach to the meaning restores the experience.'[37] 'Eliot's dictum tells us that the notion of identity built on a given experience is as elusive as the notion of consciousness of identity, and this consciousness cannot be separated from processes of oppression, discrimination, and exclusion that constitute people's lives.

Key Democratic Issues for a Democratic Multicultural Citizenship

Let us take as a premise that the suffrage movement at the turn of the century, the civil rights movement in the sixties, affirmative action, as well as the First Amendment, helped the renewal of citizenship in the country, enhancing American democracy by creating a more level playing field and emphasizing the central role of diversity.[38] As Walter Feinberg rightly points out, affirmative action 'uses group membership to identify and correct past acts of discrimination against individuals, acts that have resulted in inadequate educational, economic, and social positioning.'[39]

Attacks on affirmative action and cultural diversity, particularly in higher education, may undermine the foundations of citizenship in the United States. Why? First, because affirmative action reminds us of a historical debt that needs to be repaid to specific groups. Second, and moving from the importance of race-based affirmative action to the need to be complemented with a need-based affirmative action, we should be reminded that there cannot be equality of political opportunity without equality of social opportunity.

Economic citizenship cannot be accomplished without bare essentials, as Todd Gitlin has suggested, including 'the right to a job, education, medical care, housing, retraining over the course of life—these are the bare elements of an economic citizenship that ought to be universal.'[40] Finally, in the context of US democracy, affirmative action reaffirms the importance of the critique of public policy and the history of a given social formation. Not surprisingly, many people have identified African-Americans as the major subject of affirmative action despite the fact white women have become the principal beneficiaries of these policies.[41] West said it so passionately: 'One of the reasons why black people are so integral a part of American civilization is because black people have raised a lot of hell. That is very important, especially in a society in which power and pressure decide who receives visibility. By raising hell I mean organization, mobilization, chaos-producing capacity, as in rebellion.'[42] The black struggle in the United States shows that criticism and rebellion emerge as two key factors in the constitution of citizenship for a democracy of content and not merely a democracy of method.

No doubt, the capacity to generate criticism and rebellion against mainstream ideas that may represent the powers that be has long been a central component of any political democratic education for citizenship. In fact, we cannot understand citizenship without understanding the role that education, particularly higher education, plays in the constitution of the democratic pact. Moreover, we cannot understand the democratic pact without considering affirmative-action policies and cultural diversity as indissolubly linked.

Freire argued that few human encounters are exempt from oppression of one kind or another because by virtue of race, class, or gender, people tend to be victims and/or perpetrators of oppression. He stressed that racism, sexism, or class exploitation are the most salient forms of dominance but he also recognized that oppression exists based on religious beliefs, political affiliation, national origin, age, size, and physical and intellectual handicaps. Starting from a psychology of oppression, influenced by the works of psychotherapists such as Freud, Jung, Adler, Fanon and Fromm, Freire developed a 'Pedagogy of the Oppressed.' He believed that education could improve the human condition, counteracting the effects of a psychology of oppression and ultimately contributing to what he considered the 'ontological vocation of mankind': humanization. In the introduction to his widely acclaimed *Pedagogy of the Oppressed* he wrote, 'From these pages I hope at least the following will endure: my trust in the people, and my faith in men and women and in the creation of a world in which it will be easier to love.'[43]

Following Freire, one may argue that the central question of education today is what role, if any, educational institutions and practices should play in the constitution of the social pact that articulates democracy. This brings us to the dilemma of a democratic culture: the construction of a democratic citizen. To put it simply, democracy implies a process of participation in which all are considered equal. However, education involves a process whereby the 'immature' are brought to identify with the principles and forms of life of the 'mature' members of society. Thus, construction of the democratic citizen is a process of cultural nurturing, but also it involves articulating principles of pedagogic and democratic socialization in individuals who are neither tabula rasa in cognitive or ethical terms nor fully equipped for the exercise of their democratic rights and obligations.

This central problem of education—how to contribute to the democratic pact—is compounded by the fact that teachers relate to the demand of a common public school increasingly segregated by race and class, in a society with a growing gap between the haves and have-nots, and in which gender distinctions continue to be central to school discrimination. In this context, several issues stand out clearly as central themes in the discussion on public policy in the minds of policy makers, teachers, researchers, and citizens, among them diversity and multiculturalism.

Citizenship can be predicated in terms of civic virtues or legal status. Civic virtues point to a sense of solidarity that unites individuals around common goals. These goals are, at the very least, how to survive and live together in our contemporary diverse society, but they also can be accomplished with a more ambitious agenda: how to thrive as a community of communities, as a culture of cultures, drawing from our cultural diversity as a cultural strength, and affirmative action, broadly understood, as a useful policy. Yet, as Gitlin cautions us, 'The question is how to cultivate the spirit of solidarity across the lines of difference—solidarity with 'anyone who suffers'. For surely that spirit cannot be expected to generate spontaneously inside fortified groups, each preoccupied with refining its differences from other groups.'[44]

For a framework of solidarity and common ground across cultures, ethnicities, classes, and gender, the goals of cultural diversity are central. We need to develop flexible frameworks for solidarity in schools that take seriously the need for democratic reform. Cultural diversity is a major byproduct of the growing process of economic, cultural, and political globalization that has no parallel in history. Globalization has produced all sorts of implications for the multicultural, multilingual, and multiethnic configurations of local communities in the United States and elsewhere.

In terms of the social covenant, not surprisingly, diversity is a key challenge for any institution of higher education in complying with federal and state statutes for affirmative action and in facing the growing social and educational demands.

Higher education institutions are at the center of the storm in terms of diversity and affirmative action and, I must say, in terms of promoting a renewal of citizenship. A commitment to, diversity and multiculturalism implies a commitment to diversify the faculty, resembling, to the extent possible and given the available resources, the demographic traits of schools and universities in the United States. Diversity also implies the diversification of the student body, so demands from different intellectual, ethnic, gender and underrepresented groups and constituencies will be appropriately addressed in the classroom. To achieve the goals of diversity and multiculturalism, universities should be able to attract the best and brightest, the most qualified scholars, undergraduates, and graduates who can explore in their teaching, research, and outreach the frontiers of knowledge without prejudice, approaching their work with creativity, with joy, with enthusiasm and dedication, with a sense of utopian hope.

Achieving such goals is not easy. Tensions will always arise between growing social and intellectual demands and diminishing fiscal resources. There will also be tensions among diverse intellectual, ethnic, and social constituencies and among faculty desires to serve the ideals of equity coupled with the imperatives of equality in the context of the perennial academic quest for excellence and community. There will be also serious criticisms of policies oriented to equity and equality in education, including affirmative action policies. Affirmative action should not be considered as a moral absolute, but it should be included in a democratic conversation of how affirmative action and cultural diversity enhance citizenship and what role higher education institutions should play in this respect.

I believe that in order to achieve the missions of higher education, the construction of an academic consensus based on diversity is essential. This consensus building, however, should begin with a recognition of the importance of these tensions, should take into account the precariousness of many of the managerial solutions available, and should recognize the limitations of the many intellectual paradigms in vogue. These are some of the intellectual challenges of discussing citizenship, cultural diversity, and affirmative action in higher education. This, in turn, brings us to the question of canon versus culture in the construction of a democratic multicultural citizenship.

Canon, Culture, and Democratic Multicultural Citizenship: Conclusions

The impossibility of an uncontested canon results from the impossibility of defining a single, integrated, non-problematic, and descriptive social and pedagogical identity in the culture of the West.

(Morrow and Torres)[45]

In a sense, this is a game of never-ending mirrors.

(Wallerstein)[46]

Canon(s) and culture(s) are not, in principle, opposed, but they have a difficult time in cohabitation, more so when a given canon is made as a set of metaphysical principles that cannot be historically examined, and therefore changed. Metaphysical canons become, in principle, opposed to cultural negotiation.

Foundational canons, however, are ongoing processes of cultural negotiations, taking as their precedents key foundations for dialogue and open-ended interpretations of history and community experiences. They also enjoy what Freire would like to term an 'epistemology of curiosity': an endless need to define what cultural principles make the life of people more harmonious, the cultural exchanges more self-reflective, and the ethical underpinnings of the culture closer to the cultural imperatives of social justice, individual responsibility, and caring.

Foundational canons are changed through cultural negotiation, as Gitlin puts it: 'Negotiation may take place—does take place—on the edges of a canon, so that Whitman was brought in the '40s, while Whittier was booted out (Leo Marx has made that point), and during recent years Ellison's Invisible Man is effectively canonized. In other words, once a foundation is clear there's plenty of room for divergences and plurality.'[47]

Any cultural canon, as long as it is made into a metaphysical condition of being, is in principle opposed to cultural negotiation. As such, a metaphysical cultural canon—a canon revered as the encapsulation of virtue, wisdom, and truth—must have several authority sources or legitimacy claims which may include, for instance, the sheer power of a given group establishing legal restrictions that become the law of the land (e.g., the South African white power before the establishment of a racial democracy in 1994, or the legislation of slavery in the American South); claims to enjoy racial purity (e.g., Nazism); claims to being the original founding fathers of the nation (e.g., Caucasian and Eurocentric immigrant-bashing groups); claims to control the language that constitutes identity and make social, political, and economic exchanges possible (i.e., English-only movements); or claims to moral or ethical superiority based on a religious mandate, 'Beruf' or 'Call' (e.g. Christian bigotry, movements to establish the biblical superiority of men over women, and homosexual-bashing movements based on Christian faith).

The liberal pluralist call to recognize the richness of 'otherness' and diversity in a society otherwise characterized by shared historical foundations based on cultural consensus (e.g., the notion of 'togetherness' as an essential pragmatic principle for the social pact to work) can be confronted with a more radical perception of multiculturalism, a historically nuanced vision of multiculturalism. 'Oddly enough, given the charges of incoherence and anarchy made against multicultural approaches, historicizing the question of identity also offers the possibility of a more unified view than that of the liberal pluralists ... An alternative to pluralism is to make difference and conflict the center of a history 'we' all share.'[48]

Now, if national identity is not a fixed marker but a process of learning as I have defended, this creates another conundrum. The first question is to consider whether it is possible that exposure to similar processes of learning creates different conclusions. This is certainly the drama of democratic education and democratic life. What we pursue in democracy is to allow the process of learning to go on and, at the same time, to accept that the conclusions could, and indeed will be, divergent. People will have different views, and political disagreements will be the bread and butter for education as much as coalition and alliance politics is for democratic governance.

This has implications at the level of the knowledge base of the society and the democratization of knowledge. The next question is whether some explanations are more powerful than others. In other terms, is one type of social science more useful (I am tempted to say more truthful) than others? Discussing the impact of deconstructionism in the social sciences, Immanuel Wallerstein warns us that 'we are clearly involved here in a very complex activity, one in which equilibria (canons) are at best transient and one in which there can be no determinate future, since the aleatory elements are too vast.'[49]

The problem, it seems, is the consideration that, because reality is a social construction, everything goes, and therefore that every explanation is as valuable as the next, that there are no particular criteria from which to ascertain which explanation is more truthful or powerful or which is a better approach to understand and explain the complexity of the real. Wallerstein is very clear in this respect:

> The role of the scholars is not to construct reality but to figure out how it has been constructed and to test the multiple social constructions of reality against each other. In a sense, this is a game of never-ending mirrors. We seek to discover the reality on the basis of which we have constructed reality. And when we find this, we seek to understand how this underlying reality has in turn been socially constructed. In this navigation amidst the mirrors, however, there are more correct and less correct scholarly analyses. Those scholarly analyses that are more correct are more socially useful in that they aid the world to construct a substantively more rational reality. Hence the search for truth and the search for goodness are inextricably linked to each other. We are all involved, and involved simultaneously, in both.[50]

Three points should be retained here. First, despite the deconstructionist storm and the fact that we can think of reality as a social construction, this social construction is not just the product of our imagination but the product of real people interacting in complex ways, and hence not all explanations have the same quality (i.e., logical coherence, analytical insights, empirical documentation), explanatory power, or truthfulness. Second, even if all explanations, by their very nature, are transient—that is, they are works in progress until a better explanation is constructed—they are all to be judged against their ability to explain, and in turn, their ability to help the construction of a more rational society. Hence, there is an element of usefulness in each validity construct that cannot be overlooked. While the previous comment can be read as overtly pragmatic, it, in itself, points to the third implication of Wallerstein's analysis—that the notion of the truth and the goodness in society are intimately and inextricably intertwined. Hence, a more constructive, useful rational society refers to Wallerstein's suggestion of looking at the social sciences as part of the quest for a just society. Wallerstein thus is proposing a categorical imperative of justice and goodness to inspire, if not to guide, the analytical endeavor.

In politics and social struggles, however, disagreements could be even more drastic than the implications of debates in the social sciences about causality or explanatory validity. Consider, for instance, the situation in Algeria. If democratic elections are granted (as happened in 1992), fundamentalist Islamic movements are likely to win. Considering their platform of basing the social order in a peculiar vision of strict literal adherence to the Koran and their practice of intimidation of citizens—the death toll from massacres in small towns has been estimated to be at least 100,000 in [1993–7]—this victory would not only result in many people losing their civil liberties—particularly women, as demonstrated in the Taliban government in Afghanistan—but would also put the democratic structure at peril. Here the government of the majority that could be achieved through democracy as a method will undoubtedly destroy democracy as practice and content. The constitution of a democratic political culture is then a foundational premise for the continuation of democracy and the exercise of democratic life.

The idea of democracy is to learn to live with challenges and tensions and to learn about the process of learning about democratic differences. Democratic disagreements will take place everywhere, from dinner-table discussions in which families disagree passionately over public and private issues to political pulpits in which leaders and coalitions try to capture the imagination of most people and to constitute electoral majorities. These coalitions, however, will always be temporary, fragile, and subject to disintegration—in one word, ephemeral.

The notion of democracy as a method facilitates the process of differential representation and participation in which some conclusions through the voting process, alliance making, and the notion of majority coalitions may prevail in a particular moment of time. Thus, some majorities may push for a particular vision that is not, by definition, shared by all the inhabitants of the given polity. As I have argued, however, democracy as a method does not and cannot totally encapsulate the notion of democracy as content.

The notion of democracy as content, however, places some limits on what is expected and acceptable for democratic behavior and highlights civil minimums that go beyond the formalities of the democratic methodology, reaching a more radical understanding of democratic representation and participation—in short, of democratic interactions in the public and private spheres. Thus, considering identity as a process of learning, we are back to the unpleasant question of how to establish that some views are more plausible than others. This question is made even more uncomfortable if, as I have discussed elsewhere,[51] science can be related to power and therefore cannot be used, without qualifications, to settle the disputes. There is no metaphysical answer to this question, but there are procedural and methodical answers as well as historical answers. The procedural and methodical answers attempt to expand, to push the democratic envelope to its limits but to respect the rules of confrontation and negotiation, to try to understand how democratic life may accommodate a diversity of interests, a diversity of identities and experiences, and a diversity of ideologies without damaging the fabric of the democratic discourse and without accepting the premise that a final solution for a problem will be arrived at in the deliberations. We know what the implications of metaphysical notions such as a 'final solution' are.

The historical answer is partly what we have defined as historical accommodations between capitalism and democracy. The period in which we are living shows that the process of globalization may in fact be creating the conditions for a new historical accommodation. Yet, as has been clear in the past with the previous historical accommodations, the viability of the social pact is always suspect with sizable segments of the population. Tensions and conflicts will continue to arise, more prominently where the ability to redistribute resources diminishes. Consensus building and consensus politics are always fragile, and democracy continues to be a dream as much as a system of radical political representation and participation.

The notion of consensus should be differentiated from the notion of the democratic social pact. Social pacts are more enduring than historical consensuses, which are by nature ephemeral. The paradox is that social pacts are made up of historically consensual agreements that generations create, sustain, and transform into laws, routines, customs, practices, habits, regulations, and even cultures. What cannot be changed, unless we are willing to do away with the notion of democracy, is the notion of a prevailing social pact that, by its mere existence, in the long run, will prevent the polity from falling into chaos or authoritarianism. A social pact that strives to accommodate diversity and sameness as the keystones of the government of the people, by the people, and for the people. Or as Freire so often reminded us, the ability to agree to disagree is fundamental for a politics of democratic dialogue as much as the ability to live with tensions and contradictions is fundamental for democratic politics.

Another important question falls squarely in the dimension of education: is there an opposition between identity formation (which should be a remarkable part of the educational agenda) and the formation of citizenship through the establishing of a knowledge floor? Identity formation has always been part of the liberal state ideology, the first duty of the state—as historian Ted Mitchell reminds us, and as Governor Clinton DeWitt told his constituency in 1882.[52] Paradoxically, identity building has always been, consciously or unconsciously, blended in educational policy with the notion of citizenship building, as if identity and citizenship are fixed markers and, moreover, both will always coincide, assuming that citizenship can be predicated as a cultural representation with an acute degree of homogeneity and historical accuracy.

At the beginning of a new millennium, it is clear that identity formation takes place in many diverse spheres, including education, but that formally citizenship building has been confined mostly to the educational domain. The question, which certainly goes beyond the limits of this [chapter], is whether they should both be treated as processes of lifelong learning (with potential divergent conclusions), whether both—identity and citizenship—should be treated as discrete theoretical entities, which may intersect at some point (and hence the need to rethink their contradictions and correspondences), and whether this interaction (between identity and citizenship) can be accomplished at all in the context of late capitalism and the criticism of democratic ingovernability.

Thus, identity is a never-secured effect of a process of enunciation of cultural difference. Taken to the extreme, however, this epistemological premise may seem impractical for pedagogy or political mobilization. Yet, from a progressive perspective, it would be simplistic to think of cultural difference as the difference between dominant and subordinate cultures. The fact is that critical multiculturalism also should address the ideological cleavages and differences within subordinate cultures, not only as the negotiation between peoples of color and the oppressive networks of power, but also among people of color themselves. Here, the words of critical race theorists resonate with peculiar force: 'Unfortunately, the tensions between and among these differences are rarely interrogated, presuming a "unity of difference"—that is, that all difference is both analogous and equivalent.'[53]

Membership and experience in a given identity does not guarantee the accurate recollection of the experience—for instance, using the analytical tools of social sciences and humanities—and hence the political risks are many, including the fact that in many multiculturalist quarters 'personal testimony of oppression replaces analysis, and this testimony comes to stand for the experience of the whole group. The fact of belonging to an identity group is taken as authority enough for one's speech; the direct experience of a group or culture—that is, membership in it—becomes the only test of true knowledge.'[54]

Despite the growing literature on multiculturalism, only recently has the discussion shifted to address the connections between multiculturalism and citizenship, exploring the limits and possibilities of multiculturalism in democratic societies. Perhaps it is fair to argue that the multitude of tasks confronting multiculturalism is overwhelming. They include the attempt to develop a sensible, theoretically refined, and defensible new metatheoretical and theoretical territory that would create the foundations for multiculturalism as a paradigm; the attempt to establish its epistemological and logical premises around the notions of experience, narrative, voice, agency, and identity; the attempt to pursue empirical research linking culture/power/knowledge with equality/inequality/discrimination; and the need to defend multiculturalism from the conservative right that has demonized multiculturalism as an antipatriotic movement, opposing the need for a canon that can regulate the cultural exchanges from a principle of order. These multifaceted tasks and the concrete political experience of the eighties and nineties in the United States have forced the different proponents of multiculturalism onto the defensive, both in theoretical and political terms. This means that they have been so far unable fully to address the need for a theory of multicultural citizenship, a theory that should be instrumental in advancing democratic goals in the context of theories of democracy, despite the fact that they operate within the capitalist framework. Yet a final dilemma for multiculturalism is the understanding of the connections between diversity and the commons, that is, the question of unity in diversity.

There are certainly many analytical and political alternatives in confronting the dilemma of unity in diversity. First and foremost is the need to explore the degree of hybridization of cultures and the notion that every social subject is constituted by multiple identities and multiple affiliations. Recognition of the complexities posed by the process of hybridization, and the notion of multiple identities in the social and psychological construction of the pedagogical subject should challenge any attempt to essentialize differences based on race, gender, class, nationality, ethnicity, religion, or sexual preference. Second, rather than dealing with differences in ethical and political commitments as primary contradictions, one may see them as secondary contradictions, or as conflicting loyalties in the social construction of identity. This opens up areas of negotiation in the context of progressive alliances based on multiple identities and learning communities. A fundamental premise is the avoidance of any essentialization of cultural struggles. Yet it is also important to recognize that there are a number of insights in neoconservative and neoliberal arguments. For instance, from a very different vantage point than neoconservatives, West and a number of black intellectuals are concerned with the 'cultural breakdown and escalating self-destructive nihilism among the poor and very poor.'[55] Nihilism offers certainly poor foundations for the advancement of democracy and the attainment of citizenship.

West has said that people do not live on arguments, although they might be influenced by arguments. Reading his *Prophetic Thought in Postmodern Times* helped me to revisit, once again, why we all conduct educational research, or at least why we should, and why we should take seriously the contradictions among education, citizenship, and democracy. West argues that there is an undeniable cultural decay in America that frightens him more than anything else: 'By unprecedented cultural decay I mean the social breakdown of the nurturing system for children. The inability to transmit meaning, value, purpose, dignity, and decency to children.'[56]

While historically situated, his remarks, I believe, apply to many societies. Facilitating the nurturing and learning of children, youths, and adults is what public education—jointly with the family and a few other societal institutions—is supposed to do. That is what educational research should be about: understanding the indissoluble linkages of theory and practice. This is another practical reason that, periodically, we should revisit theoretically, the relationship among state, education, citizenship, democracy and multiculturalism and why we should strive, as Freire has told us on innumerable occasions, to build a world that is 'less ugly, less cruel and less inhumane.'

Democracy is a messy system, but it has survived because there is a sphere for debates and a set of rules that people follow even if they do not benefit from them. Schools and universities within democratic communities cannot be less committed to expand the democratic discourse. Without a serious exploration of the intersections among cultural diversity, affirmative action, and citizenship, the plural bases of democracy and the democratic discourse per se are at risk. Without a technically competent, ethically sound, spiritually engaging, and politically feasible theory and practice of democratic multicultural citizenship, the people will perish.

Where there is no vision, the people perish.[57]

NOTES

1. Jürgen Habermas, 'Citizenship and National Identity: Some Reflections on the Future of Europe', *Praxis International* 12 (1992): 1–19, esp. 7.
2. While I am aware that the 'classics' of political philosophy reflect primarily male, European, and heterosexual views, thus making it impossible to uncritically accept them as a cultural canon, I do contend that—properly deconstructed and analyzed with a nuanced historical sense—they continue to be an invaluable source for thinking and praxis. A similar argument is made by Carole Pateman discussing the pertinence of these works for feminist political science. 'It is impossible to completely turn our backs on the classics or on contemporary methodology, because all modes of discourse reflect and are implicated in the past to a greater or lesser degree. Moreover, there are valuable insights to be gained and lessons learned from male-stream theory.' Carole Pateman, 'Introduction: The Theoretical Subversiveness of Feminism', in *Feminist Challenges: Social and Political Theory*, ed. Carole Pateman and Elizabeth Gross (Boston: Northeastern University Press, 1986), 3.
3. R. A. Morrow and Carlos Alberto Torres, *Reading Freire and Habermas: Critical Pedagogy and Transformative Social Change* (New York: Teachers College Press, 2002).
4. See T. H. Marshall, *Citizenship and Social Class and Other Essays* (Cambridge: Cambridge University Press, 1950), *Sociology at the Crossroads* (London: Heinemann Educational Books, 1963), *Social Policy in the Twentieth Century* (London: Hutchinson, 1965), *The Right to Welfare and Other Essays* (London: Heinemann Educational Books, 1981), and 'Citizenship and Social Class', in *States and Societies*, ed. David Held et al. (Oxford: Oxford University Press, 1983), 248–60.
5. Marshall, Sociology at the Crossroads, 74.
6. Carole Pateman, 'Democratization and Citizenship in the 1990s: The Legacy of T. H. Marshall', Vilhelm Aubert Memorial Lecture (Oslo: University of Oslo, Institute for Social Research and Department of Sociology, 1996), 6.
7. See the collection of papers in Linda Gordon, ed., *Women, the State and Welfare* (Madison: University of Wisconsin Press, 1990).
8. Pateman, 'Democratization and Citizenship in the 1990s', 7–8.
9. Chantal Mouffe, *The Return of the Political* (London and New York: Verso, 1993).
10. Nancy Fraser, *Unruly Practices: Power, Discourse, and Gender in Contemporary Social Theory* (Minneapolis: University of Minnesota Press, 1989), 183.
11. Carole Pateman, 'Equality, Difference, Subordination: The Politics of Motherhood and Women's Citizenship', in *Beyond Equality and Difference: Citizenship, Feminist Politics, and Female Subjectivity*, ed. Gisela Bock and Susan James (London: Routledge, 1992), 17–31, esp. 28.

12. Mouffe, 84.
13. Sonia Saldivar-Hull, 'Feminism on the Border: From Gender Politics to Geopolitics', in *Criticism in the Borderlands: Studies in Chicano Literature, Culture, and Ideology*, ed. Hector Calderon and José David Saldivar (Durham, NC: Duke University Press, 1994), 204.
14. Pateman, 'Democratization and Citizenship in the 1990s' (n. 6 above), 9.
15. Ibid. 10–11.
16. Discussions of colonialism also must include the United States and its experiences in the Philippines, Cuba, and Puerto Rico and the former Soviet Union and its relationship with Eastern Europe and Afghanistan. To the dismay of many conservative analysts, and given its historical peculiarities, socialist Cuba continues to be an exception to colonialist doctrine.
17. R. A. Rocco, 'Refraining Postmodernist Constructions of Difference: Subaltern Spaces, Power, and Citizenship' (paper presented at the Symposium on the Challenge of Postmodernism to the Social Sciences and the Humanities, University Complutense, Somosaguas campus, Madrid, April 22–25, 1997), 14.
18. Gloria Ladson-Billings and William F. Tate IV, 'Toward a Critical Race Theory of Education', *Teachers College Record* 97 (Fall 1995): 47–68.
19. D. Bell, 'Racial Realism—after We're Gone: Prudent Speculations on America in a Post-racial Epoch', in *Critical Race Theory: The Cutting Edge*, ed. Richard Delgado (Philadelphia: Temple University Press, 1995), 2.
20. Ibid. 7.
21. Daniel G. Solorzano and Octavio Villapando, 'Marginality and the Experience of Students of Color in Higher Education', in *Sociology of Education: Emerging Perspectives*, ed. Carlos A. Torres and Ted Mitchell (Albany: State University of New York Press, 1998).
22. The classic text of how ability grouping structures inequality continues to be Jeannie Oakes, *Keeping Track* (New Haven, Conn.: Yale University Press, 1995).
23. Ladson-Billings and Tate, 55–59.
24. Ibid. 57.
25. Ernesto Laclau, 'New Social Movements and the Plurality of the Social', in *New Social Movement and the State in Latin America*, ed. D. Slater (Amsterdam: Centrum voor Studie en Documentatie van Latijns Amerika [CEDLA], 1985), 27–42. See also Henry Pease Garcia et al., *America Latina 80: Democracia y movimento popular* (Lima: Centro de Estudios y Promoción del Desarrollo [DESCO], 1981); Norbert Lechner, ed., *Cultura politica y democratización* (Santiago: Facultad Latino-americana de Ciencias Sociales [CLASCO] and Instituto de Cooperación Iberoamericana, 1987).
26. Ron Eyerman and Andrew Jamison, *Social Movements: A Cognitive Approach* (Cambridge: Polity Press, 1991).
27. David Held, 'Democracy and the New International Order', in *Cosmopolitan Democracy: An Agenda for a New World Order*, ed. Daniele Archibugi and David Held (Cambridge: Polity Press, 1995), 97.
28. Samuel Bowles and Herbert Gintis, *Democracy and Capitalism: The Contradictions of Modern Political Life* (New York: Basic, 1986).
29. Globalization has been defined as 'the intensification of worldwide social relations which link distant localities in such a way that local happenings are shaped by events occurring many miles away'. See David Held, ed., *Political Theory Today* (Stanford, Calif.: Stanford

University Press, 1991), 9. Held suggests, among other things, that globalization is the product of the emergence of a global economy expansion of transnational linkages between economic units creating new forms of collective decision making, development of intergovernmental and quasi-supranational institutions, intensification of transnational communications, and the creation of new military orders. I have suggested elsewhere that globalization puts limits to state autonomy and national sovereignty. These limits are expressed in tension between global and local dynamics in virtually every decision and policy domain in the social cultural, and economic spheres. See Carlos Alberto Torres, *Democracy, Education and Multiculturalism: Dilemmas of Citizenship in a Global World* (Lanham, Md.: Rowman & Littlefield, 1998). Globalization therefore not only blurs national boundaries but also shifts solidarities within and outside the national state. Globalization cannot be defined exclusively by the post-Fordist organization of production but emerges as a major characteristic of a global world economy. Issues of human rights, regional states, and cosmopolitan democracy will play a major role affecting civic minimums at the state level, the performance of capital and labor in different domains, and particularly the dynamics of citizenship, democracy, and multiculturalism in the modern state.

30. Cornel West, 'The New Cultural Politics of Difference', in *Race, Identity and Representation in Education*, ed. Cameron McCarthy and Warren Crichlow (New York and London: Routledge, 1993), DD. 11–23. esp. DD. 11–12.
31. Joan W. Scott, 'Multiculturalism and the Politics of Identity', in *Feminist Theory in Practice Process*, ed. Micheline R. Malson, Jean F. O'Barr, Sara Westphal-Uhl, and Mary Wyers (Chicago: University of Chicago Press, 1989), 13.
32. Ibid. 14.
33. Cornel West, Kloe de Alba, and E. Sheris, 'Colloquy: Our Next Race Question: The Uneasiness between Blacks and Latinos', *Harper's* (April 1996), 55–63, esp. 57.
34. Scott, 14.
35. West, 'Colloquy', 57.
36. Michael W. Apple, *Education and Power* (Boston and London: Routledge, 1982), *Teachers and Text: A Political Economy of Class and Gender Relations in Education* (New York and London: Routledge, 1986); *Official Knowledge: Democratic Education in a Conservative Age* (New York and London: Routledge, 1993), and *Teoria Critica y Educación* (Buenos Aires: Miño y Davila Editores, 1997).
37. T. S. Eliot,' The Dry Salvages', in *The Four Quartets* (1943; reprint, New York: Harcourt, Brace & Co., 1971), 24.
38. 'Affirmative action began with Title VII of the Civil Rights Act of 1954, which prohibited discrimination on the basis of race and sex and which was later augmented by a number of executive orders that regulate federal contracts and set goals and timetables for hiring minorities.' See Walter Feinberg, 'Affirmative Action and Beyond: A Case for Backward-Looking Gender- and Race-Based Policy', *Teachers College Record* 97/3 (Spring 1996): 363–97, esp. 363.
39. Ibid. 378.
40. Todd Gitlin, *The Twilight of Common Dreams: Why America Is Wracked by Culture Wars* (New York: Henry Holt, 1995).
41. Feinberg, 366–7.
42. West, 'Colloquy', 58.

43. Paulo Freire, *Pedagogy of the Oppressed* (Montevideo: Editorial Tierra Nueva, 1972), 19. See also Carlos Alberto Torres's preface, 'The Political Pedagogy of Paulo Freire', in *Paulo Freire, Politics and Education,* by Paulo Freire (Los Angeles: University of California, Latin American Center, 1998).

44. Gitlin, 217.

45. Morrow and Torres (n.3 above), 428.

46. Immanuel Wallerstein, 'Social Science and the Quest for a Just Society', *American Journal of Sociology* 102/5 (March 1977): 1241–57, esp. 1254.

47. Gitlin, personal communication.

48. Scott (n. 3 above), 16.

49. Wallerstein, 1253.

50. Ibid. 1254.

51. Torres, *Democracy, Education, and Multiculturalism* (n. 29 above). See esp. Ch. 7.

52. Ted R. Mitchell, *'The Republic for which it Stands': Public Schools, the State, and the Idea of Citizenship in America* (Angeles: University of California Press).

53. Ladson-Billings and Tate (n. 18 above), 62.

54. Scott, 18.

55. Cornel West, *Prophetic Thought in Postmodern Times* (Monroe, Maine: Common Courage Press, 1993), 196.

56. Ibid. 16.

57. Proverbs 29:18 (AV).

Colonizing Knowledges

Linda Tuhiwai Smith

We have a history of people putting Maori under a microscope in the same way a scientist looks at an insect. The ones doing the looking are giving themselves the power to define.

Merata Mita[1]

In the previous chapter the metaphor of an archive was used to convey the sense by which the West drew upon a vast history of itself and multiple traditions of knowledge which incorporate cultural views of reality, of time and space. This chapter argues that the form of imperialism which indigenous peoples are confronting now emerged from that period of European history known as the Enlightenment. The Enlightenment provided the spirit, the impetus, the confidence, and the political and economic structures that facilitated the search for new knowledges. The project of the Enlightenment is often referred to as 'modernity' and it is that project which is claimed to have provided the stimulus for the industrial revolution, the philosophy of liberalism, the development of disciplines in the sciences and the development of public education. Imperialism underpinned and was critical to these developments. Whilst imperialism is often thought of as a system which drew everything back into the centre, it was also a system which distributed materials and ideas outwards. Said's notion of 'positional superiority' is useful here for conceptualizing the ways in which knowledge and culture were as much part of imperialism as raw materials and military strength. Knowledge was also there to be discovered, extracted, appropriated and distributed. Processes for enabling these things to occur became organized and systematic. They not only informed the field of study referred to by Said as 'Orientalism' but other disciplines of knowledge and 'regimes of truth'. It is through these disciplines that the indigenous world has been *re*presented to the West and it is through these disciplines that indigenous peoples often research for the fragments of ourselves which were taken, catalogued, studied and stored. It is not the intention of this chapter to tell the history of Western knowledge but rather to draw that history down into the colonized world, show the relationship between knowledge, research and imperialism, and then discuss the ways in which it has come to structure our own ways of knowing, through the development of academic disciplines and through the education of colonial elites and indigenous or 'native' intellectuals. Western knowledge and science are 'beneficiaries' of the colonization of indigenous peoples. The knowledge gained through our colonization has been used, in turn, to colonize us in what Ngugi wa Thiong'o calls the colonization 'of the mind'.[2]

Establishing the Positional Superiority of Western Knowledge

The project of modernity signalled the end of feudalism and absolutist authority, legitimated by

From Linda Tuhiwai Smith, *Decolonizing Methodologies: Research and Indigenous People* (London: Zed Books, 1999), ch. 3. Reprinted with permission.

divine rule, and announced the beginning of the modern state. The new state formation had to meet the requirements of an expanding economy based on major improvements in production. The industrial revolution changed and made new demands upon the individual and the political system. The modern state was wrested from the old regime of absolutist monarchs by the articulation of liberal political and economic theories.[3] As a system of ideas, liberalism focuses on the individual, who has the capacity to reason, on a society which promotes individual autonomy and self-interest, and on a state which has a rational rule of law which regulates a public sphere of life, but which allows individuals to pursue their economic self-interest. Once it was accepted that humans had the capacity to reason and to attain this potential through education, through a systematic form of organizing knowledge, then it became possible to debate these ideas in rational and 'scientific' ways.

The development of scientific thought, the exploration and 'discovery' by Europeans of other worlds, the expansion of trade, the establishment of colonies, and the systematic colonization of indigenous peoples in the eighteenth and nineteenth centuries are all facets of the modernist project. Modernism is more than a re-presentation of fragments from the cultural archive in new contexts. 'Discoveries' about and from the 'new' world expanded and challenged ideas the West held about itself.[4] The production of knowledge, new knowledge and transformed 'old' knowledge, ideas about the nature of knowledge and the validity of specific forms of knowledge, became as much commodities of colonial exploitation as other natural resources.[5] Indigenous peoples were classified alongside the flora and fauna; hierarchical typologies of humanity and systems of representation were fuelled by new discoveries; and cultural maps were charted and territories claimed and contested by the major European powers. Hence some indigenous peoples were ranked above others in terms of such things as the belief that they were 'nearly human', 'almost human' or 'subhuman'. This often depended on whether it was thought that the peoples concerned possessed a 'soul' and could therefore be 'offered' salvation and whether or not they were educable and could be offered schooling. These systems for organizing, classifying and storing new knowledge, and for theorizing the meanings of such discoveries, constituted research. In a colonial context, however, this research was undeniably also about power and domination. The instruments or technologies of research were also instruments of knowledge and instruments for legitimating various colonial practices.

The imaginary line between 'east' and 'west', drawn in 1493 by a Papal Bull, allowed for the political division of the world and the struggle by competing Western states to establish what Said has referred to as a 'flexible positional superiority' over the known, and yet to become known, world.[6] This positional superiority was contested at several levels by European powers. These imaginary boundaries were drawn again in Berlin in 1934 when European powers sat around the table once more to carve up Africa and other parts of 'their' empires. They continue to be redrawn. Imperialism and colonialism are the specific formations through which the West came to 'see', to 'name' and to 'know' indigenous communities. The cultural archive with its systems of representation, codes for unlocking systems of classification, and fragmented artefacts of knowledge enabled travellers and observers to make sense of what they saw and to represent their new-found knowledge back to the West through the authorship and authority of their representations.

Whilst colonialism at an economic level, including its ultimate expression through slavery, opened up new materials for exploitation and new markets for trade, at a cultural level, ideas, images and experiences about the Other helped to shape and delineate the essential differences between Europe and the rest. Notions about the Other, which already existed in the European imagination, were recast within the framework of Enlightenment philosophies, the industrial revolution and the scientific 'discoveries' of the eighteenth and nineteenth centuries. When discussing the scientific foundations of Western research, the indigenous contribution to these foundations is rarely mentioned. To have acknowledged their contribution would, in terms of the rules of research practice, be as legitimate as acknowledging the contribution of a variety of plant, a shard of pottery or a 'preserved head of a native' to research. Furthermore, according to Bazin, 'Europeans could not even imagine that other people could ever have done things before or better than themselves'.[7] The objects of research do not have a voice and do not contribute to research or science. In fact, the logic of the argument would suggest that it is simply impossible, ridiculous even, to suggest that the object of research can contribute to anything. An object has no life force, no humanity, no spirit of its own, so therefore 'it' cannot make an active contribution. This perspective is not deliberately insensitive; it is simply that the rules did not allow such a thought to enter the scene. Thus, indigenous Asian, American, Pacific and African forms of knowledge, systems of classification, technologies and codes of social life, which began to be recorded in some detail by the seventeenth century, were regarded as 'new discoveries' by Western science.[8] These discoveries were commodified as property belonging to the cultural archive and body of knowledge of the West.[9]

The eighteenth and nineteenth centuries also constituted an era of highly competitive 'collecting'. Many indigenous people might call this 'stealing' rather than 'collecting'. This included the collecting of territories, of new species of flora and fauna, of mineral resources and of cultures. James Clifford, for example, refers to ethnography as a science which was

> [a] form of culture collecting . . . [which] highlights the ways that diverse experiences and facts are selected, gathered, detached from their original temporal occasions, and given enduring value in a new arrangement. Collecting—at least in the West, where time is generally thought to be linear and irreversible—implies a rescue of phenomena from inevitable historical decay or loss.[10]

The idea that collectors were actually rescuing artefacts from decay and destruction, and from indigenous peoples themselves, legitimated practices which also included commercial trade and plain and simple theft. Clearly, in terms of trade indigenous peoples were often active participants, in some cases delivering 'made to order' goods. The different agendas and rivalries of indigenous groups were also known to have been incorporated into the commercial activities of Europeans. Hence, muskets could be traded and then used to pursue traditional enemies or one group of people could be used to capture and assist in the enslavement of another group who were also their traditional rivals. Indigenous property is still said to be housed in 'collections', which in turn are housed either in museums or private galleries, and art and artefacts are often grouped and classified in the name of their 'collector'. These collections have become the focus of indigenous peoples' attempts to reclaim ancestral remains and other cultural items (known in the West as 'artefacts') belonging to their people.

It is important to remember, however, that colonialism was not just about collection. It was also about re-arrangement, re-presentation and re-distribution. For example, plant species were taken by Joseph Banks for the Royal Botanic Gardens at Kew. Here they could be 'grown, studied, and disbursed to the colonial stations, a centre of plant transfers on the scientific level, and of the generation and publication of knowledge about plants'.[11] The British Empire became a global laboratory for research and development. New species of plants and animals were introduced to the colonies to facilitate development and to 'strengthen' indigenous species. This point is worth remembering as it contrasts with the view, sometimes referred to as a diffusionist explanation, that knowledge, people, flora and fauna simply disbursed themselves around the world. This botanical colonization had already been successfully carried out in other places: for example, maize, sweet potatoes, and tobacco from South America had been widely distributed. In the centre of this collection and distribution network was the imperial 'home' country. The colonies were peripheral satellites which gained access to these new knowledges and technologies through 'recourse to the writings of authors in the centre'.[12] One effect of this system of redistribution was the interference caused by new species to the ecologies of their new environments and the eventual extinction of several species of bird and animal life.[13] In the case of New Zealand, Cherryl Smith argues that, ecologically, the indigenous world was colonized by weeds.[14]

Among the other significant consequences of ecological imperialism—carried by humans, as well as by plants and animals—were the viral and bacterial diseases which devastated indigenous populations. This devastation or genocide was, in the accounts of many indigenous peoples, used deliberately as a weapon of war. Stories are told in

Canada, for example, of blankets used by smallpox victims being sent into First Nation communities while the soldiers and settlers camped outside waiting for the people to die. There were several ideologies which legitimated the Western impact on indigenous health and well-being. These supported racial views already in place but which in the later nineteenth century became increasingly legitimated by the 'scientific' views of social Darwinism. The concept of the 'survival of the fittest', used to explain the evolution of species in the natural world, was applied enthusiastically to the human world. It became a very powerful belief that indigenous peoples were inherently weak and therefore, at some point, would die out. There were debates about how this could be prevented, for example, through miscegenation and cultural assimilation, and whether this, in fact, was 'desirable'. Judgements on these issues circled back or depended upon prior considerations as to whether the indigenous group concerned had souls, could be saved, and also could be redeemed culturally. Influential debates on these matters by Catholic scholars such as Bartolomé de Las Casas took place during the sixteenth century. In nineteenth-century New Zealand some of the debates delved right down into the supposed fecundity rates of indigenous women and the better prospects for racial survival if miscegenation occurred. There were very serious scientific views put forward to account for the demise of the indigenous populations. Some views included: sterility caused by the 'licentiousness' of the women, a vegetable diet, infanticide and abortion. Other causes were put down to a sense of 'hopelessness' and lack of spirit, which came about through contact with 'civilization'.[15]

But there were also state policies (federal, provincial and local) of 'benign neglect' which involved minimal intervention (the 'infected blanket' strategy) while people suffered and died. There were also more proactive policies based around such ideas as 'Manifest Destiny' which sanctioned the taking of indigenous lands by any means.[16] Ward Churchill and other indigenous writers classify these actions as part of the Columbian legacy of genocide.[17] In relation to the diseases and disease which the West is said to have introduced to indigenous peoples, the bigger question has always been the extent to which the impact of disease is an inevitable consequence of contact with the West. The significance of the issues which this question raises emerges when we examine, in a later chapter, the world-wide search currently being undertaken amongst indigenous populations for genetic solutions to Western diseases. Aborigine activist Bobbi Sykes has an 'acid test' for the Western impact on indigenous health which consists of two lists: one a list of diseases introduced by Europeans to Aboriginal people, the other a list of diseases introduced by Aboriginal people to Europeans. There are no items listed on the second list. That empty space tells a very potent story.[18]

The globalization of knowledge and Western culture constantly reaffirms the West's view of itself as the centre of legitimate knowledge, the arbiter of what counts as knowledge and the source of 'civilized' knowledge. This form of global knowledge is generally referred to as 'universal' knowledge, available to all and not really 'owned' by anyone, that is, until non-Western scholars make claims to it. When claims like that are made history is revised (again) so that the story of civilization remains the story of the West. For this purpose, the Mediterranean world, the basin of Arabic culture and the lands east of Constantinople are conveniently appropriated as part of the story of Western civilization, Western philosophy and Western knowledge.[19] Through imperialism, however, these cultures, peoples and their nation states were repositioned as 'oriental', or 'outsider' in order to legitimate the imposition of colonial rule. For indigenous peoples from other places, the real lesson to be learned is that we have no claim whatsoever to civilization. It is something which has been introduced from the West, by the West, to indigenous peoples, for our benefit and for which we should be duly grateful.

The nexus between cultural ways of knowing, scientific discoveries, economic impulses and imperial power enabled the West to make ideological claims to having a superior civilization. The 'idea' of the West became a reality when it was re-presented back to indigenous nations through colonialism. By the nineteenth century colonialism not only meant the imposition of Western authority over indigenous lands, indigenous modes of production and indigenous law and government, but the imposition of Western authority over all aspects of indigenous knowledges, languages and cultures. This authority incorporated what Said refers to as alliances between the ideologies, 'clichés', general beliefs and understandings held about the Orient and the views of 'science' and philosophical theories.[20]

For many indigenous peoples the major agency for imposing this positional superiority over knowledge, language and culture was colonial education. Colonial education came in two basic forms: missionary or religious schooling (which was often residential) followed later by public and secular schooling. Numerous accounts across nations now attest to the critical role played by schools in assimilating colonized peoples, and in the systematic, frequently brutal, forms of denial of indigenous languages, knowledges and cultures. Not all groups of indigenous peoples, however, were permitted to attend school—some groups being already defined in some way as 'ineducable' or just plain troublesome and delinquent. Furthermore, in many examples the indigenous language was used as the medium of instruction and access to the colonizing language was denied specifically. This policy was designed to deny opportunities to participate as citizens.

Colonial education was also used as a mechanism for creating new indigenous elites. It was not the only mechanism for producing elite groups, as the traditional hierarchies within an indigenous society who converted to the colonial ideology also formed part of the elite group. Schooling helped identify talented students who were then groomed for more advanced education. Many of these students were sent away to boarding schools while others were sent to the metropolitan centre in Europe for their university studies. In these settings, and through their learning, students acquired the tastes, and sampled some of the benefits and privileges, of living within the metropolitan culture. Their elite status came about through the alignment of their cultural and economic interests with those of the colonizing group rather than with those of their own society.

School knowledge systems however, were informed by a much more comprehensive system of knowledge which linked universities, scholarly societies and imperial views of culture. Hierarchies of knowledge and theories which had rapidly developed to account for the discoveries of the new world were legitimated at the centre. Schools simply reproduced domesticated versions of that knowledge for uncritical consumption. Although colonial universities saw themselves as being part of an international community and inheritors of a legacy of Western knowledge, they were also part of the historical processes of imperialism. They were established as an essential part of the colonizing process, a bastion of civilization and a sign that a colony and its settlers had 'grown up'. Attempts to 'indigenize' colonial academic institutions and/or individual disciplines within them have been fraught with major struggles over what counts as knowledge, as language, as literature, as curriculum and as the role of intellectuals, and over the critical function of the concept of academic freedom.[21]

Colonizing the Disciplines

Academic knowledges are organized around the idea of disciplines and fields of knowledge. These are deeply implicated in each other and share genealogical foundations in various classical and Enlightenment philosophies. Most of the 'traditional' disciplines are grounded in cultural world views which are either antagonistic to other belief systems or have no methodology for dealing with other knowledge systems. Underpinning all of what is taught at universities is the belief in the concept of science as the all-embracing method for gaining an understanding of the world. Some of these disciplines, however, are more directly implicated in colonialism in that either they have derived their methods and understandings from the colonized world or they have tested their ideas in the colonies. How the colonized were governed, for example, was determined by previous experiences in other colonies and by the prevailing theories about race, gender, climate and other factors generated by 'scientific' methods. Classification systems were developed specifically to cope with the mass of new knowledge generated by the discoveries of the 'new world'. New colonies were the laboratories of Western science. Theories generated from the exploration and exploitation of colonies, and of the people who had prior ownership of these lands, formed the totalizing appropriation of the Other.

Robert Young argues that Hegel

> articulates a philosophical structure of the appropriation of the other as a form of knowledge which uncannily simulates the project of nineteenth century imperialism; the construction of knowledges which all operate through forms of expropriation and incorporation of the other mimics at a conceptual level the geographical and economic absorption of the non-European world by the West.[22]

David Goldberg claims that notions of the Other are more deeply embedded in classical philosophy but became racialized within the framework of liberalism and the ideas about people and society which developed as disciplines through liberalism.[23] In an interesting discussion on the discourses which employ the word 'civilization', John Laffey suggests that the word 'civilization' entered Anglo-French usage in the second part of the eighteenth century, enabling the distinction to be drawn between those who saw themselves as civilized and those who they then regarded as the 'savages' abroad and at home.[24] As a standard of judgement, according to Laffey, the word 'civilized' became more defined with the help of Freud and more specialized in the way different disciplines employed the concept. One such use was comparative and allowed for comparisons between children and savages or children and women, for example. This way of thinking was elaborated further into psychological justifications for the distinctions between the civilized and the uncivilized. Freud's influence on the way disciplines developed in relation to colonialism is further explored by Marianna Torgovnick, who examines the links between Freud and anthropology in her analysis of Malinowski's book 'The Sexual Life of Savages'.[25] According to Turgovnick, 'Freud's explanation of the human psyche in terms of sexuality under-girded their endeavors and influenced the structure of many ethnographic enquiries at this stage of the discipline's development even when those enquiries suggested (as they often did) modifications of Freudian paradigms, such as the Oedipus complex.'[26] Other key intellectuals have also been referred to as not so innocent philosophers of the truth. Henry Louis Gates Jr. names Kant, Bacon, Hume, Jefferson and Hegel as 'great intellectual racialists' who have been influential in defining the role of literature and its relationship to humanity, 'The salient sign of the black person's humanity ... would be the mastering of the very essence of Western civilization, the very foundation of the complex fiction upon which white Western culture has been constructed ... '[27]

Of all the disciplines, anthropology is the one most closely associated with the study of the Other and with the defining of primitivism.[28] As Adam Kuper argued, 'The anthropologists took this primitive society as their special subject, but in practice primitive society proved to be their own society (as they understood it) seen in a distorting mirror.[29] The ethnographic 'gaze' of anthropology has collected, classified and represented other cultures to the extent that anthropologists are often the academics popularly perceived by the indigenous world as the epitome of all that it is bad with academics. Haunani Kay Trask accuses anthropologists of being 'takers and users' who 'exploit the hospitality and generosity of native people'.[30] Trinh T. Minh-ha makes similar references to anthropology and anthropologists, including those whose intent now is to train Third World anthropologists. 'Gone out of date,' she says, 'then revitalised, the mission of civilizing savages mutates into the imperative of "making equal".'[31] In writing a history of geography, Livingstone refers to this discipline as the 'science of imperialism par excellence'.[32] His comment relates to geographical studies into such things as the mapping of racial difference, the links which were drawn between climate and mental abilities, the use of map makers in French colonies for military intelligence and the development of acclimatization societies.[33] [...] [H]istory is also implicated in the construction of totalizing master discourses which control the Other. The history of the colonies, from the perspective of the colonizers, has effectively denied other views of what happened and what the significance of historical 'facts' may be to the colonized. 'If history is written by the victor,' argues Janet Abu-Lughod, 'then it must, almost by definition, "deform" the history of the others.'[34] Donna Awatere claims that, 'The process of recording what happened automatically favours the white occupiers because they won. In such a way a whole past is "created" and then given the authority of truth.'[35] These comments have been echoed wherever indigenous peoples have had the opportunity to 'talk back' to the academic world.

While disciplines are implicated in each other, particularly in their shared philosophical foundations, they are also insulated from each other through the maintenance of what are known as disciplinary boundaries. Basil Bernstein has shown how this works in his paper on the 'classification and framing of knowledge'.[36] Insulation enables disciplines to develop independently. Their histories are kept separate and 'pure'. Concepts of 'academic freedom', the 'search for truth' and 'democracy' underpin the notion of independence and are vigorously defended by intellectuals. Insularity protects a discipline from the 'outside', enabling communities of scholars to distance themselves from others and, in the more extreme forms, to absolve themselves of responsibility for what occurs in other branches of their discipline, in the academy and in the world.

In the context of research and at a very pragmatic level researchers from different projects and different research teams can be in and out of the same community (much in the way many government social services are in and out of family homes), showing 'as a collective' little responsibility for the overall impact of their activities. At other levels criticism of individual researchers and their projects is deflected by the argument that those researchers are different in some really significant 'scientific' way from others. How indigenous communities are supposed to work this out is a mystery. There are formal organizations of disciplines, researchers and communities of scholars, many of which have ethical guidelines. These organizations are based on the idea that scholars consent to participate within them as scholars, as professionals, or as ethical human beings. Not all who carry out research in indigenous communities belong to, or are bound by, such collegial self-discipline.

Disciplining the Colonized

The concept of discipline is even more interesting when we think about it not simply as a way of organizing systems of knowledge but also as a way of organizing people or bodies. Foucault has argued that discipline in the eighteenth century became 'formulas of domination' which were at work in schools, hospitals and military organizations.[37] Techniques of detail were developed to maintain discipline over the body. The colonizing of the Other through discipline has a number of different meanings. In terms of the way knowledge was used to discipline the colonized it worked in a variety of ways. The most obvious forms of discipline were through exclusion, marginalization and denial. Indigenous ways of knowing were excluded and marginalized. This happened to indigenous views about land, for example, through the forced imposition of individualized title, through taking land away for 'acts of rebellion', and through redefining land as 'waste land' or 'empty land' and then taking it away. Foucault suggests that one way discipline was distributed was through enclosure. This is the other side of exclusion in that the margins are enclosures: reserved lands are enclosures, schools enclose, but in order to enclose they also exclude, there is something on the outside. Discipline is also partitioned, individuals separated and space compartmentalized. This allowed for efficient supervision and for simultaneous distinctions to be made between individuals. This form of discipline worked at the curriculum level, for example, as a mechanism for selecting out 'native' children and girls for domestic and manual work. It worked also at the assessment level, with normative tests designed around the language and cultural capital of the white middle classes.

The deepest memory of discipline, however, is of the sheer brutality meted out to generations of indigenous communities. Aborigine parents in Australia had their children forcibly removed, sent away beyond reach and 'adopted'.[38] Native children in Canada were sent to residential schools at an age designed to systematically destroy their language and memories of home. There is a growing body of testimony from First Nations people in Canada which tells of years of abuse, neglect and viciousness meted out to young children by teachers and staff in schools run by various religious denominations.[39] These forms of discipline were supported by paternalistic and racist policies and legislation; they were accepted by white communities as necessary conditions which had to be met if indigenous people wanted to become citizens (of their own lands). These forms of discipline affected people physically, emotionally, linguistically and culturally. They were designed to destroy every last remnant of alternative ways of knowing and living, to obliterate collective identities and memories and to impose a new order. Even after the Second World War, when the post-colonial period was beginning according to some cultural studies theorists, many indigenous peoples around the world were still not recognized as humans, let alone citizens. The effect of such discipline was to silence (for ever in some cases) or to suppress the ways of knowing, and the languages for knowing, of many different indigenous peoples. Reclaiming a voice in this context has also been about reclaiming, reconnecting and reordering those ways of knowing which were submerged, hidden or driven underground.

Colonialism and 'Native' Intellectuals

The position within their own societies of 'native' intellectuals who have been trained in the West has been regarded by those involved in nationalist movements as very problematic. Much of the discussion about intellectuals in social and cultural life, and their participation in anti-colonial struggles, is heavily influenced by Marxist revolutionary thought, is framed in the language of oppositional discourse, and was written during the post-war period when struggles for independence were under way.[40] Included within the rubric of 'intellectual' by liberation writers such as Frantz Fanon are also artists, writers, poets, teachers, clerks, officials, the petit bourgeoisie and other professionals engaged in producing 'culture'. Their importance in nationalist movements is related to their abilities to reclaim, rehabilitate and articulate indigenous cultures, and to their implicit leadership over 'the people' as voices which can legitimate a new nationalist consciousness.

At the same time, however, these same producers and legitimators of culture are the group most closely aligned to the colonizers in terms of their class interests, their values and their ways of thinking. This view was restated in 1984 by Donna Awatere who wrote that '[Colonial Maori] ... are noticeable because they have succeeded as white in some section of white culture; economically, through the arts, at sport, through religion, the universities, the professions.'[41] There were concerns that native intellectuals may have become estranged from their own cultural values to the point of being embarrassed by, and hostile towards, all that those values represented. In his introduction to Cesaire's *Return to My Native Land* Mazisi Kunene wrote that, 'those [students] who returned despised and felt ashamed of their semi-literate or illiterate parents who spoke inelegant patois'.[42] In New Zealand the few Maori who were trained at universities in the last part of the nineteenth century are generally viewed positively as individuals who retained a love for their culture and language and who were committed in the context of the times to the survival of indigenous people. What is problematic is that this group of men have been named by the dominant non-indigenous population as individuals who represent 'real' leadership. They have been idealized as the 'saviours of the people' and their example remains as a 'measure' of real leadership.

As Fanon has argued, the problem of creating and legitimating a national culture 'represents a special battlefield'[43] and intellectuals are important to this battle in a number of different ways. In recognizing that intellectuals were trained and enculturated in the West, Fanon identifies three levels through which 'native' intellectuals can progress in their journey 'back over the line'.[44] First there is a phase of proving that intellectuals have been assimilated into the culture of the occupying power. Second comes a period of disturbance and the need for the intellectuals to remember who they actually are, a time for remembering the past. In the third phase the intellectuals seek to awaken the people, to realign themselves with the people and to produce a revolutionary and national literature.[45] In this phase the 'native writer progressively takes on the habit of addressing his [*sic*] own people'.[46]

Fanon was writing about Algeria and the structure of French colonialism in Africa. He himself was trained in France as a psychiatrist and was influenced by European philosophies. One of the problems of connecting colonialism in New Zealand with its formations elsewhere is that New Zealand, like Canada and Australia, was already privileged as a white dominion within the British Empire and Commonwealth, with the indigenous populations being minorities. Whilst geographically on the margins of Europe, they were economically and culturally closely attached to Britain. Within these states the indigenous people were absolute minorities. The settlers who came arrived as permanent migrants. For indigenous peoples in these places this meant a different kind of experience with colonialism and different possibilities for decolonization. What it also points to is that indigenous intellectuals have emerged from different colonial and indigenous systems. In the Pacific Islands, for example, scholars come from majority cultures and independent island nations but they have also been incorporated at a regional level into the metropolitan cultures of Australia and New Zealand.[47] Hau'ofa argues that 'the ruling classes of the South Pacific are increasingly culturally homogeneous. They speak the same language, which is English; they share the same ideologies and the same material life styles . . . .[48]

Currently the role of the 'native' intellectual has been reformulated not in relation to nationalist or liberationary discourses but in relation to the 'post-colonial' intellectual. Many intellectuals who position themselves as 'post-colonial' move across the boundaries of indigenous and metropolitan, institution and community, politics and scholarship. Their place in the academy is still highly problematic. Gayatri Spivak, who writes as a post-colonial Asian/Indian intellectual working in the United States, argues that Third World intellectuals have to position themselves strategically as intellectuals within the academy, within the Third World or indigenous world, and within the Western world in which many intellectuals actually work. The problem, she argues, for Third World intellectuals remains the problem of being taken seriously. 'For me, the question "Who should speak?" is less crucial than "Who will listen?" "I will speak for myself as a Third World person" is an important position for political mobilisation today. But the real demand is that, when I speak from that position, I should be listened to seriously; not with that kind of benevolent imperialism . . . '[49] Spivak acknowledges that the task of changing the academy is difficult: 'I would say that if one begins to take a whack at shaking the structure up, one sees how much more consolidated the opposition is.'[50]

The role of intellectuals, teachers, artists and writers in relation to indigenous communities is still problematic, and the rhetoric of liberation still forms part of indigenous discourses. Indigenous communities continue to view education in its Western, modern, sense as being critical to development and self-determination. While criticizing indigenous people who have been educated at universities, on one hand, many indigenous communities will struggle and save to send their children to university on the other. There is a very real ambivalence in indigenous communities towards the role of Western education and those who have been educated in universities. This is reflected in many contexts in struggles over leadership, representation and voice between those perceived as 'traditional' and those seen either as the 'radicals' or simply as having Western credentials. In Australia, the term 'flash blacks' encompasses both those who are well educated and those who have high-flying jobs. In New Zealand one struggle over the value of Western education was played out in the 1980s through a process of reprivileging of 'elders' and a reification of elders as the holders of all traditional knowledge and a parallel deprivileging of the younger, frequently much better educated members (in a Western sense) of an *iwi* (tribe). Maori academics who work away from their tribal territories can easily be criticised because they live away from home, and are perceived therefore as being distanced from the people. At the same time they are drawn into tribal life whenever a crisis occurs or there are additional demands for specialist knowledge and skills. The bottom line, however, is that in very fundamental ways they still remain members of an *iwi* with close relations to families and other community ties.

The 'Authentic, Essentialist, Deeply Spiritual' Other

At a recent international conference held in New Zealand to discuss issues related to indigenous intellectual and cultural property rights, the local newspapers were informed and invited to interview some of the delegates. One news reporter thought it would be a good idea to have a group photograph, suggesting that it would be a very colourful feature for the newspaper to highlight. When she and the photographer turned up at the local *marae* (cultural centre) they were so visibly disappointed at the motley display of track suits, jeans and other items of 'modern' dress, that they chose not to take a photograph. 'Oh, I forgot to come as a native', joked one of the delegates. 'My feathers got confiscated at the airport when I arrived.' 'I suppose my eyes are too blue.' 'Are we supposed to dress naked?' As we have seen, the notion of 'authentic' is highly contested when applied to, or by, indigenous peoples. 'Authorities' and outside experts are often called in to verify, comment upon, and give judgements about the validity of indigenous claims to cultural beliefs, values, ways of knowing and historical accounts. Such issues are often debated vigorously by the 'public' (a category which usually means the dominant group), leading to an endless parading of 'nineteenth century' views of race and racial difference. Questions of who is a 'real indigenous' person, what counts as a 'real indigenous leader', which person displays 'real cultural values' and the criteria used to assess the characteristics of authenticity are frequently the topic of conversation and political debate. These debates are designed to fragment and marginalize those who speak for, or in support of, indigenous issues. They frequently have the effect also of silencing and making invisible the presence of other groups within the indigenous society like women, the urban non-status tribal person and those whose ancestry or 'blood quantam' is 'too white'.[51] In Tasmania, where experts had already determined that Aborigines were 'extinct', the voices of those who still speak as Aboriginal Tasmanians are interpreted as some political invention of a people who no longer exist and who therefore no longer have claims.

Recent poststructural and psychoanalytical feminist theorists have argued against the claims made by earlier generations of feminists that women as a group were different, because their essence as women was fundamentally, undeniably different, and that therefore their 'sisterhood' would be a natural meeting place for all women. Pedagogically, essentialism was attacked because of its assumption that, because of this essence, it was necessary to be a woman and to experience life as a woman before one could analyse or understand women's oppression. Third World women and women of colour also attacked this assumption because it denied the impact of imperialisms, racism and local histories on women, who were different from white women who lived in First World nations. The concept of authentic, which is related to essentialism, was also deconstructed but more so from psychoanalytic perspectives because the concept assumed that if we strip away the oppressions and psychological consequences of oppression we would find a 'pure' and authentic 'self'. One of the major problems with the way words are defined is that these debates are often held by academics in one context, within a specific intellectual discourse, and then appropriated by the media and popular press to serve a more blatant ideological and racist agenda.[52] As Trinh T. Minh-ha put it when writing of anthropologists in particular, 'But once more *they* spoke. *They* decide who is "racism-free or anti-colonial", and they seriously think they can go on formulating criteria for us . . . '[53]

In the colonized world, however, these terms are not necessarily employed in the same way that First World academics may have used them. The term 'authentic', for example, was an oppositional term used in at least two different ways. First, it was used as a form of articulating what it meant to be dehumanized by colonization; and, second, for reorganizing 'national consciousness' in the struggles for decolonization. The belief in an authentic self is framed within humanism but has been politicized by the colonized world in ways which invoke simultaneous meanings; it does appeal to an idealized past when there was no colonizer, to our strengths in surviving thus far, to our language as an uninterrupted link to our histories, to the ownership of our lands, to our abilities to create and control our own life and death, to a sense of balance among ourselves and with the environment, to our authentic selves as a people. Although this may seem overly idealized, these symbolic appeals remain strategically important in political struggles. Furthermore the imputing of a Western psychological 'self, which is a highly individualized notion, to group consciousness as it is centred in many colonized societies, is not a straightforward translation of the individual to the group, although this is often the only way that Westerners can come to understand what may constitute a group. The purpose of commenting on such a concept is that what counts as 'authentic' is used by the West as one of the criteria to determine who really is indigenous, who is worth saving, who is still innocent and free from Western contamination. There is a very powerful tendency in research to take this argument back to a biological 'essentialism' related to race, because the idea of culture is much more difficult to control. At the heart of such a view of authenticity is a belief that indigenous cultures cannot change, cannot recreate themselves and still claim to be indigenous. Nor can they be complicated, internally diverse or contradictory. Only the West has that privilege.

The concept of essentialism is also discussed in different ways within the indigenous world. It is accepted as a term which is related to humanism and is seen therefore in the same way as the idea of authenticity. In this use of the word, claiming essential characteristics is as much strategic as anything else, because it has been about claiming human rights and indigenous rights. But the essence of a person is also discussed in relation to indigenous concepts of spirituality. In these views, the essence of a person has a genealogy which can be traced back to an earth parent, usually glossed as an Earth Mother. A human person does not stand alone, but shares with other animate and, in the Western sense, 'inanimate' beings, a relationship based on a shared 'essence' of life. The significance of place, of land, of landscape, of other things in the universe, in defining the very essence of a people, makes for a very different rendering of the term essentialism as used by indigenous peoples.

The arguments of different indigenous peoples based on spiritual relationships to the universe, to the landscape and to stones, rocks, insects and other things, seen and unseen, have been difficult arguments for Western systems of knowledge to deal with or accept. These arguments give a partial indication of the different world views and alternative ways of coming to know, and of being, which still endure within the indigenous world. Concepts of spirituality which Christianity attempted to destroy, then to appropriate, and then to claim, are critical sites of resistance for indigenous peoples. The values, attitudes, concepts and language embedded in beliefs about spirituality represent, in many cases, the clearest contrast and mark of difference between indigenous peoples and the West. It is one of the few parts of ourselves which the West cannot decipher, cannot understand and cannot control . . . yet.

NOTES

1. M. Mita (1989), 'Merata Mita on . . . ', in the *New Zealand Listener,* 14 October, p. 30.
2. Ngugi Wa Thiong'o (1986), *Decolonizing the Mind: The Politics of Language in African Literature,* James Currey, London.
3. Jaggar, A. (1983), *Feminist Politics and Human Nature,* Harvester Press, Sussex.
4. Hall, S. (1992), 'The West and the Rest: Discourse and Power', ch. 6 of *Formations of Modernity,* eds. S. Hall and B. Gielben, Polity Press and Open University, Cambridge, pp. 276–320.
5. S. Goonatilake (1982), 'Colonies: Scientific Expansion (and Contraction)', in *Review,* Vol. 5, No. 3, Winter, pp. 413–36.
6. E. Said (1978), *Orientalism,* Vintage Books, New York, p. 7.
7. M. Bazin (1993), 'Our Sciences, Their Science', in *Race and Class,* Vol. 34, No. 2, pp. 35–6.
8. Goonatilake, 'Colonies'.
9. M. Adas (1989), *Machines as the Measure of Man. Science, Technology and Ideologies of Western Dominance,* Cornell University Press, Ithaca.
10. J. Clifford (1988), *The Predicament of Culture, Twentieth Century Ethnography, Literature, and Art,* Harvard University Press, Cambridge, p. 231. See also on the topic of collection, M. Ames (1986), *Museums, The Public and Anthropology,* University of Columbia Press, London.
11. Brockway, L. H. (1979), *Science and Colonial Expansion. The Role of the British Royal Botanical Gardens,* Academic Press, New York, p. 187.

12. Goonatilake, 'Colonies', p. 432.
13. Crosby, A. W. (1986), Biotic Change in Nineteenth Century New Zealand', in *Review*, Vol. 9, No. 3, Winter, pp. 325–37.
14. C. W. Smith (1994), 'Kimihia te Matauranga, Colonization and Iwi Development', MA thesis, University of Auckland, p. 23.
15. D. L. Pool, (1977), *The Maori Population of New Zealand 1769–1971*, Auckland University Press and Oxford University Press, Auckland, pp. 75–105.
16. W. Churchill (1994), *Indians Are Us? Culture and Genocide in Native North America*, Common Courage Press, Maine.
17. Ibid. 28–42.
18. R. B. Sykes (1989), *Black Majority*, Hudson Hawthorn, Victoria, p. 185.
19. Bernal, M. (1991), *Black Athena, The Afroasiatic Roots of Classical Civilization*, Vintage, London.
20. Said, *Orientalism*, 205–6.
21. See, for examples of these debates in relation to indigenous issues, Ngugi wa Thiong'o (1986), *Decolonizing the Mind. The Politics of Language in African Literature*, James Currey, London, and Haunani Kay Trask (1993), *From a Native Daughter*, Common Courage Press, Maine.
22. R. Young (1990), *White Mythologies, Writing, History and the West*, Routledge, London, p. 3.
23. D. T. Goldberg (1993), *Racist Culture: Philosophy and the Politics of Meaning*, Blackwell, Oxford.
24. J. F. Laffey (1993), *Civilization and its Discontented*, Black Rose Books, New York.
25. M. Torgovnick (1990), *Gone Primitive: Savage Intellects, Modern Lives*, University of Chicago Press, Chicago.
26. Ibid. 7.
27. H. L. Gates (1994), 'Authority (White) Power and the (Black) Critic: It's All Greek to Me', in *Culture/Power/History*, eds. N. Dirks, G. Eley and S. B. Ortner, Princeton University Press, New Jersey.
28. G. Stocking Jr. (1987), *Victorian Anthropology*, The Free Press, London.
29. A. Kuper (1988), *The Invention of Primitive Society*, Routledge, London, p. 5.
30. H. K. Trask (1993), *From a Native Daughter*, Common Courage Press, Maine.
31. Trinh T. Minh-ha (1989), *Woman, Native, Other*, Indiana University Press, Bloomington, p. 59.
32. D. Livingstone (1992), *The Geographical Tradition*, Blackwell, Oxford.
33. Ibid. 216.
34. J. Abu-Lughod (1989), 'On the Remaking of History: How to Reinvent the Past', in *Remaking History*, Dia Art Foundation, Bay Press, Seattle, p. 118.
35. D. Awatere (1983), 'Awatere on Intellectuals: Academic Fragmentation or Visionary Unity', article in *Craccum*, Auckland University Students' Association, 3 May, Auckland, pp. 6–7.
36. B. Bernstein (1971), 'On the Classification and Framing of Knowledge', in *Knowledge and Control: New Directions for the Sociology of Education*, ed. M. F. D. Young, Collier Macmillan, London, pp. 47–69.

37. M. Foucault (1977), *Discipline and Punish: The Birth of the Prison*, trans. A. Sheridan, Penguin, London, p. 137.

38. This practice is known popularly as the 'stolen children' policy but an official inquiry was conducted by the Australian government called 'A National Inquiry into the Separation of Aboriginal and Torres Strait Islander Children from Their Families'. This was completed in 1997.

39. A government commission to investigate the abuses in the residential school system for 'First nations' children was recently completed by the Canadian government. For further background read E. Furness (1995), *Victims of Benevolence: The Dark Legacy of the Williams Lake Residential School*, Arsenal Pulp Press, Vancouver; C. Haig-Brown (1988), *Resistance and Renewal: Surviving the Indian Residential School*, Tillacum Library, Vancouver, in L. Taine, ed. (1993), *Residential Schools: The Stolen Years*, University of Saskatchewan Press, Saskatoon.

40. Gramsci's views on the intellectual have been influential, among other Marxist views. So too have the existentialist views of Jean Paul Sartre who wrote the introduction to Fanon's book, *The Wretched of the Earth*. A critique of these influences on Fanon, in particular, can be read in Young, *White Mythologies*.

41. D. Awatere (1984), *Maori Sovereignty*, Broadsheet, Auckland, p. 83.

42. A. Cesaire (1969), *Return to My Native Land*, translated by John Berger and Ana Bostock, introduction by Mazisi Kunene, Penguin Books, Harmondsworth, p. 24.

43. F. Fanon (1990), *The Wretched of the Earth*, Penguin, London, p. 193.

44. Ibid. 178–9.

45. Ibid. 179.

46. Ibid. 193.

47. E. Hau'ofa (1987), 'The New South Pacific Society: Integration and Independence', in *Class and Culture in the South Pacific*, eds. A. Hooper, S. Britton, R. Crocombe, J. Huntsman and C. Macpherson, Centre for Pacific Studies, University of Auckland, Institute for Pacific Studies, University of the South Pacific, pp. 1–15.

48. Ibid. 3.

49. G. Spivak (1990), 'Questions of Multiculturalism', in *The Post-Colonial Critic: Interviews, Strategies, Dialogues*, ed. S. Harasayam, Routledge, New York, pp. 59–60.

50. G. Spivak (1990), 'Criticism, Feminism and the Institution', in *The Post-Colonial Critic*, p. 6.

51. 'Blood quantum' refers to the 'amount' of native blood one has and is used in places such as Hawai'i to determine eligibility access to Hawai'ian lands and identity. It is based on racial beliefs that the more indigenous peoples intermarried the more assimilated or 'watered down' they became. Conversely if they did not intermarry they remained 'pure'.

52. Similar debates occur over a word such as 'invention', where anthropologists may talk to each other about the invention of culture; the media can then accuse indigenous people of inventing culture to serve their own interests *at the expense of the dominant group*. This occurred in New Zealand over an article written by A. Hanson (1991), 'The Making of the Maori: Culture Invention and its Logic', in *American Anthropologist*, pp. 890–902. One of the larger daily newspapers took the article and turned it into the following headline: 'US EXPERT SAYS MAORI CULTURE INVENTED', *Dominion*, Saturday, 24 February.

53. Trin T. Minh-ha, *Woman, Native, Other*, p. 59.

Toward a Critical Race Theory of Education

Gloria Ladson-Billings and William F. Tate IV

[. . .]

The presentation of truth in new forms provokes resistance, confounding those committed to accepted measures for determining the quality and validity of statements made and conclusions reached, and making it difficult for them to respond and adjudge what is acceptable.

Derrick Bell, *Faces at the Bottom of the Well*

I am not included within the pale of this glorious anniversary! Your high independence only reveals the immeasurable distance between us. The blessings in which you this day, rejoice, are not enjoyed in common. The rich inheritance of justice, liberty, prosperity and independence bequeathed by your fathers, not by me . . .

Frederick Douglass, *My Bondage and My Freedom*

In 1991 social activist and education critic Jonathan Kozol delineated the great inequities that exist between the schooling experiences of white middle-class students and those of poor African-American and Latino students. And, while Kozol's graphic descriptions may prompt some to question how it is possible that we allow these 'savage inequalities,' this [chapter] suggests that these inequalities are a logical and predictable result of a racialized society in which discussions of race and racism continue to be muted and marginalized.[1]

In this [chapter] we attempt to theorize race and use it as an analytic tool for understanding school inequity.[2] We begin with a set of propositions about race and property and their intersections. We situate our discussion in an explication of critical race theory and attempt to move beyond the boundaries of the educational research literature to include arguments and new perspectives from law and the social sciences. In doing so, we acknowledge and are indebted to a number of scholars whose work crosses disciplinary boundaries.[3] We conclude by exploring the tensions between our conceptualization of a critical race theory in education and the educational reform movement identified as multicultural education.

Understanding Race and Property

Our discussion of social inequity in general, and school inequity in particular, is based on three central propositions:[4]

1. Race continues to be a significant factor in determining inequity in the United States.
2. US society is based on property rights.
3. The intersection of race and property creates an analytic tool through which we can understand social (and, consequently, school) inequity.

In this section we expand on these propositions and provide supporting 'meta-propositions' to make clear our line of reasoning and relevant application to educational or school settings.

Race as a Factor in Inequity

The first proposition—that race continues to be a significant factor in determining inequity in the United States—is easily documented in the statistical and demographic data. Hacker's look at educational and life chances such as high school dropout rates, suspension rates, and incarceration rates echoes earlier statistics of the Children's Defense Fund.[5] However, in what we now call the postmodern era, some scholars question the usefulness of race as a category.

Omi and Winant argue that popular notions of race as either an ideological construct or an objective condition have epistemological limitations.[6] Thinking of race strictly as an ideological construct denies the reality of a racialized society and its impact on 'raced' people in their everyday lives. On the other hand, thinking of race solely as an objective condition denies the problematic aspects of race—how do we decide who fits into which racial classifications? How do we categorize racial mixtures? Indeed, the world of biology has found the concept of race virtually useless. Geneticist Cavalli-Sforza asserts that 'human populations are sometimes known as ethnic groups, or "races." ... They are hard to define in a way that is both rigorous and useful because human beings group themselves in a bewildering array of sets, some of them overlapping, all of them in a state of flux.'[7]

Nonetheless, even when the concept of race fails to 'make sense,' we continue to employ it. According to Nobel Laureate Toni Morrison:

> Race has become metaphorical—a way of referring to and disguising forces, events, classes, and expressions of social decay and economic division far more threatening to the body politic than biological 'race' ever was.
>
> Expensively kept, economically unsound, a spurious and useless political asset in election campaigns, racism is as healthy today as it was during the Enlightenment. It seems that is has a utility far beyond economy, beyond the sequestering of classes from one another, and has assumed a metaphorical life so completely embedded in daily discourse that it is perhaps more necessary and more on display than ever before.[8]

Despite the problematic nature of race, we offer as a first meta-proposition that race, unlike gender and class, remains untheorized.[9] Over the past few decades theoretical and epistemological considerations of gender have proliferated.[10] Though the field continues to struggle for legitimacy in academe, interest in and publications about feminist theories abound. At the same time, Marxist and Neo-Marxist formulations about class continue to merit consideration as theoretical models for understanding social inequity.[11] We recognize the importance of both gender- and class-based analyses while at the same time pointing to their shortcomings vis-à-vis race. Roediger points out that 'the main body of writing by White Marxists in the United States has both "naturalized" whiteness and oversimplified race.'[12]

Omi and Winant have done significant work in providing a sociological explanation of race in the United States. They argue that the paradigms of race have been conflated with notions of ethnicity, class, and nation because 'theories of race—of its meaning, its transformations, the significance of racial events—have never been a top priority in social science. In the U.S., although the "founding fathers" of American sociology ... were explicitly concerned with the state of domestic race relations, racial theory remained one of the least developed fields of sociological inquiry.'[13]

To mount a viable challenge to the dominant paradigm of ethnicity (i.e., we are all ethnic and, consequently, must assimilate and rise socially the same way European Americans have), Omi and Winant offer a racial formation theory that they define as 'the sociohistorical process by which racial categories are created, inhabited, transformed and destroyed. ... [It] is a process of historically situated *projects* in which human bodies and social structures are represented and organized.' Further, they link 'racial formation to the evolution of hegemony, the way in which society is organized and ruled.' Their analysis suggests that 'race is a matter of both social structure and cultural representation.'[14]

By arguing that race remains untheorized, we are not suggesting that other scholars have not looked carefully at race as a powerful tool for explaining social inequity, but that the intellectual salience of this theorizing has not been systematically employed in the analysis of educational inequality. Thus, like Omi and Winant, we are attempting to uncover or decipher the social-structural and cultural significance of race in education. Our work owes an intellectual debt to both Carter G. Woodson and W. E. B. Du Bois, who, although marginalized by the mainstream academic community, used race as a theoretical lens for assessing social inequity.[15]

Both Woodson and Du Bois presented cogent arguments for considering race as *the* central construct for understanding inequality. In many ways our work is an attempt to build on the foundation laid by these scholars.[16] Briefly, Woodson, as far back as 1916, began to establish the legitimacy of race (and, in particular, African Americans) as a subject of scholarly inquiry.[17] As founder of the Association for the Study of Negro Life and History and editor of its *Journal of Negro History*, Woodson revolutionized the thinking about African Americans from that of pathology and inferiority to a multitextured analysis of the uniqueness of African Americans and their situation in the United States. His most notable publication, *The Mis-education of the Negro*, identified the school's role in structuring inequality and demotivating African-American students:

> The same educational process which inspires and stimulates the oppressor with the thought that he is everything and has accomplished everything worthwhile, depresses and crushes at the same time the spark of genius in the Negro by making him feel that his race does not amount to much and never will measure up to the standards of other peoples.[18]

Du Bois, perhaps better known among mainstream scholars, profoundly impacted the thinking of many identified as 'other' by naming a 'double consciousness' felt by African Americans. According to Du Bois, the African American 'ever feels his two-ness—an American. A Negro; two souls, two thoughts, two unreconciled strivings.'[19] In a current biography of Du Bois, Lewis details the intellectual impact of this concept:

> It was a revolutionary concept. It was not just revolutionary; the concept of the divided self was profoundly mystical, for Du Bois invested this double consciousness with a capacity to see incomparably further and deeper. The African-American—seventh son after the Egyptian and Indian, the Greek and Roman, the Teuton and Mongolian—possessed the gift of 'second sight in this American world,' an intuitive faculty (prelogical, in a sense) enabling him/her to see and say things about American society that possessed a heightened moral validity. Because he dwelt equally in the mind and heart of his oppressor as in his own beset psyche, the African American embraced a vision of the commonweal at its best.[20]

As a prophetic foreshadowing of the centrality of race in US society, Du Bois reminded us that 'the problem of the twentieth century is the problem of the color line.'[21]

The second meta-proposition that we use to support the proposition that race continues to be significant in explaining inequity in the United States is that class- and gender-based explanations are not powerful enough to explain all of the difference (or variance) in school experience and performance. Although both class and gender can and do intersect race, as stand-alone variables they do not explain all of the educational achievement differences apparent between whites and students of color. Indeed, there is some evidence to suggest that even when we hold constant for class, middle-class African-American students do not achieve at the same level as their white counterparts.[22] Although Oakes reports that 'in academic tracking ... poor and minority students are most likely to be placed at the lowest levels of the school's sorting system,'[23] we are less clear as to which factor—race or class—is causal. Perhaps the larger question of the impact of race on social class is the more relevant one. Space limitations do not permit us to examine that question.

Issues of gender bias also figure in inequitable schooling.[24] Females receive less attention from teachers, are counseled away from or out of advanced mathematics and science courses, and although they receive better grades than their male counterparts, their grades do not translate into advantages in college admission and/or the work place.[25]

But examination of class and gender, taken alone or together, do not account for the extraordinarily high rates of school dropout, suspension, expulsion, and failure among African-American and Latino males.[26] In the case of suspension. Majors and Billson argue that many African-American males are suspended or expelled from school for what they termed 'non-contact violations'—wearing banned items of clothing such as hats and jackets, or wearing these items in an 'unauthorized' manner, such as backwards or inside out.[27]

The point we strive to make with this meta-proposition is not that class and gender are insignificant, but rather, as West suggests, that 'race matters,' and, as Smith insists, 'blackness matters in more detailed ways.'[28]

The Property Issue

Our second proposition, that US society is based on property rights, is best explicated by examining legal scholarship and interpretations of rights. To develop this proposition it is important to situate it in the context of critical race theory. Monaghan reports that 'critical race legal scholarship developed in the 1970s, in part because minority scholars thought they were being overlooked in critical legal studies, a better-known movement that examines the way law encodes cultural norms.'[29] However, Delgado argues that despite the diversity contained within the critical race movement, there are some shared features:

> an assumption that racism is not a series of isolated acts, but is endemic in American life, deeply ingrained legally, culturally, and even psychologically;
>
> a call for a reinterpretation of civil-rights law 'in light of its ineffectuality, showing that laws to remedy racial injustices are often undermined before they can fulfill their promise';
>
> a challenge to the 'traditional claims of legal neutrality, objectivity, color-blindness, and meritocracy as camouflages for the self-interest of dominant groups in American society';
>
> an insistence on subjectivity and the reformulation of legal doctrine to reflect the perspectives of those who have experienced and been victimized by racism firsthand;
>
> the use of stories or first-person accounts.[30]

In our analysis we add another aspect to this critical paradigm that disentangles democracy and capitalism. Many discussions of democracy conflate it with capitalism despite the fact that it is possible to have a democratic government with an economic system other than capitalism. Discussing the two ideologies as if they were one masks the pernicious effects of capitalism on those who are relegated to its lowest ranks. Traditional civil rights approaches to solving inequality have depended on the 'rightness' of democracy while ignoring the structural inequality of capitalism.[31] However, democracy in the US context was built on capitalism.

In the early years of the republic *only* capitalists enjoyed the franchise. Two hundred years later when civil rights leaders of the 1950s and 1960s built their pleas for social justice on an appeal to the civil and human rights, they were ignoring the fact that the society was based on *property rights*.[32] An example from the 1600s undescores the centrality of property in the Americas from the beginning of European settlement:

> When the Pilgrims came to New England they too were coming not to vacant land but to territory inhabited by tribes of Indians. The governor of the Massachusetts Bay Colony, John Winthrop, created the excuse to take Indian land by declaring the area legally a 'vacuum.' The Indians, he said, had not 'subdued' the land, and therefore had only a 'natural' right to it, but not a 'civil right.' A 'natural right' did not have legal standing.[33]

Bell examined the events leading up to the Constitution's development and concluded that there exists a tension between property rights and human rights.[34] This tension was greatly exacerbated by the presence of African peoples as slaves in America. The purpose of the government was to protect the main object of society—property. The slave status of most African Americans (as well as women and children) resulted in their being objectified as property. And, a government constructed to protect the rights of property owners lacked the incentive to secure human rights for the African American.[35]

According to Bell 'the concept of individual rights, unconnected to property rights, was totally foreign to these men of property; and thus, despite two decades of civil rights gains, most Blacks remain disadvantaged and deprived because of their race.'[36]

The grand narrative of US history is replete with tensions and struggles over property—in its various forms. From the removal of Indians (and later Japanese Americans) from the land, to military conquest of the Mexicans,[37] to the construction of Africans as property,[38] the ability to define, possess, and own property has been a central feature of power in America. We do not suggest that other nations have not fought over and defined themselves by property and landownership.[39] However, the contradiction of a reified symbolic individual juxtaposed to the reality of 'real estate' means that emphasis on the centrality of property can be disguised. Thus, we talk about the importance of the individual, individual rights, and civil rights while social benefits accrue largely to property owners.[40]

Property relates to education in explicit and implicit ways. Recurring discussions about property tax relief indicate that more affluent communities (which have higher property values, hence higher tax assessments) resent paying for a public school system whose clientele is largely non-white and poor.[41] In the simplest of equations, those with 'better' property are entitled to 'better' schools. Kozol illustrates the disparities: 'Average expenditures per pupil in the city of New York in 1987 were some $5,500. In the highest spending suburbs of New York (Great Neck or Manhasset, for example, on Long Island) funding levels rose above $11,000, with the highest districts in the state at $15,000.'[42]

But the property differences manifest themselves in other ways. For example, curriculum represents a form of 'intellectual property.'[43] The quality and quantity of the curriculum varies with the 'property values' of the school. The use of a critical race story[44] appropriately represents this notion:

> The teenage son of one of the authors of this article was preparing to attend high school. A friend had a youngster of similar age who also was preparing to enter high school. The boys excitedly pored over course offerings in their respective schools' catalogues. One boy was planning on attending school in an upper-middle-class white community. The other would be attending school in an urban, largely African-American district. The difference between the course offerings as specified in the catalogues was striking. The boy attending the white, middle-class school had his choice of many foreign languages—Spanish, French, German, Latin, Greek, Italian, Chinese, and Japanese. His mathematics offerings included algebra, geometry, trigonometry, calculus, statistics, general math, and business math. The science department at this school offered biology, chemistry, physics, geology, science in society, biochemistry, and general science. The other boy's curriculum choices were not nearly as broad. His foreign language choices were Spanish and French. His mathematics choices were general math, business math, and algebra (there were no geometry or trig classes offered). His science choices were general science, life science, biology, and physical science. The differences in electives were even more pronounced, with the affluent school offering courses such as Film as Literature, Asian Studies, computer programming, and journalism. Very few elective courses were offered at the African-American school, which had no band, orchestra, or school newspaper.

The availability of 'rich' (or enriched) intellectual property delimits what is now called 'opportunity to learn'[45]—the presumption that along with providing educational 'standards'[46] that detail what students should know and be able to do, they must have the material resources that support their learning. Thus, intellectual property must be undergirded by 'real' property, that is, science labs, computers and other state-of-the-art technologies, appropriately certified and prepared teachers. Of course, Kozol demonstrated that schools that serve poor students of color are unlikely to have access to these resources and, consequently, students will have little or no opportunity to learn despite the attempt to mandate educational standards.[47]

Critical Race Theory and Education

With this notion of property rights as a defining feature of the society, we proceed to describe the ways that the features of critical race theory mentioned in the previous section can be applied to our understanding of educational inequity.

Racism as Endemic and Deeply Ingrained in American Life

If racism were merely isolated, unrelated, individual acts, we would expect to see at least a few examples of educational excellence and equity together in the nation's public schools. Instead, those places where African Americans do experience educational success tend to be outside of the public schools.[48] While some might argue that poor children, regardless of race, do worse in school, and that the high proportion of African-American poor contributes to their dismal school performance, we argue that the cause of their poverty in conjunction with the condition of their schools and schooling is institutional and structural racism. Thus, when we speak of racism we refer to Wellman's definition of 'culturally sanctioned beliefs which, regardless of the intentions involved, defend the advantages Whites have because of the subordinated positions of racial minorities.' We must therefore contend with the 'problem facing White people [of coming] to grips with the demands made by Blacks and Whites while at the same time *avoiding* the possibility of institutional change and reorganization that might affect them.'[49]

A Reinterpretation of Ineffective Civil Rights Law

In the case of education, the civil rights decision that best exemplifies our position is the landmark *Brown* v. *Board of Education of Topeka, Kansas*. While having the utmost respect for the work of Thurgood Marshall and the National Association for the Advancement of Colored People (NAACP) legal defense team in arguing the *Brown* decision, with forty years of hindsight we recognize some serious shortcomings in that strategy. Today, students of color are more segregated than ever before.[50] Although African Americans represent 12 percent of the national population, they are the majority in twenty-one of the twenty-two largest (urban) school districts.[51] Instead of providing more and better educational opportunities, school desegregation has meant increased white flight along with a loss of African-American teaching and administrative positions.[52] In explaining the double-edge sword of civil rights legislation, Crenshaw argued that

> the civil rights community . . . must come to terms with the fact that antidiscrimination discourse is fundamentally ambiguous and can accommodate conservative as well as liberal views of race and equality. This dilemma suggests that the civil rights constituency cannot afford to view antidiscrimination doctrine as a permanent pronouncement of society's commitment to ending racial subordination. Rather, antidiscrimination law represents an ongoing ideological struggle in which occasional winners harness the moral, coercive, consensual power of law. Nonetheless, the victories it offers can be ephemeral and the risks of engagement substantial.[53]

An example of Crenshaw's point about the ambiguity of civil rights legislation was demonstrated in a high school district in Northern California.[54] Of the five high schools in the district, one was located in a predominantly African-American community. To entice white students to attend that school, the district funded a number of inducements including free camping and skiing trips. While the trips were available to all of the students, they were attended largely by the white students, who already owned the expensive camping and skiing equipment. However, these inducements were not enough to continuously attract white students. As enrollment began to fall, the district decided to close a school. Not surprisingly, the school in the African-American community was closed and all of its students had to be (and continue to be) bused to the four white schools in the district.

Lomotey and Staley's examination of Buffalo's 'model' desegregation program revealed that African-American and Latino students continued to be poorly served by the school system. The academic achievement of African-American and Latino students failed to improve while their suspension, expulsion, and dropout rates continued to rise. On the other hand, the desegregation plan provided special magnet programs and extended day care of which whites were able to take advantage. What, then, made Buffalo a model school desegregation program? In short, the benefits that whites derived from school desegregation and their seeming support of the district's desegregation program.[55] Thus, a model desegregation program becomes defined as one that ensures that whites are happy (and do not leave the system altogether) regardless of whether African-American and other students of color achieve or remain.

Challenging Claims of Neutrality, Objectivity, Color-blindness, and Meritocracy

A theme of 'naming one's own reality' or 'voice' is entrenched in the work of critical race theorists. Many critical race theorists argue that the form and substance of scholarship are closely connected.[56] These scholars use parables, chronicles, stories, counterstories, poetry, fiction, and revisionist histories to illustrate the false necessity and irony of much of current civil rights doctrine. Delgado suggests that there are at least three reasons for naming one's own reality in legal discourse:

1. Much of reality is socially constructed.

2. Stories provide members of outgroups a vehicle for psychic self-preservation.
3. The exchange of stories from teller to listener can help overcome ethnocentrism and the dysconscious conviction of viewing the world in one way.[57]

The first reason for naming one's own reality is to demonstrate how political and moral analysis is conducted in legal scholarship. Many mainstream legal scholars embrace universalism over particularity.[58] According to Williams, 'theoretical legal understanding' is characterized, in Anglo-American jurisprudence, by the acceptance of transcendent, acontextual, universal legal truths or procedures.[59] For instance, some legal scholars might contend that the tort of fraud has always existed and that it is a component belonging to the universal system of right and wrong. This view tends to discount anything that is nontranscendent (historical), or contextual (socially constructed), or nonuniversal (specific) with the unscholarly labels of 'emotional,' 'literary,' 'personal,' or 'false.'

In contrast, critical race theorists argue that political and moral analysis is situational—'truths only exist for this person in this predicament at this time in history.'[60] For the critical race theorist, social reality is constructed by the formulation and the exchange of stories about individual situations.[61] These stories serve as interpretive structures by which we impose order on experience and it on us.[62]

A second reason for the naming-one's-own-reality theme of critical race theory is the psychic preservation of marginalized groups. A factor contributing to the demoralization of marginalized groups is self-condemnation.[63] Members of minority groups internalize the stereotypic images that certain elements of society have constructed in order to maintain their power.[64] Historically, storytelling has been a kind of medicine to heal the wounds of pain caused by racial oppression.[65] The story of one's condition leads to the realization of how one came to be oppressed and subjugated and allows one to stop inflicting mental violence on oneself.

Finally, naming one's own reality with stories can affect the oppressor. Most oppression does not seem like oppression to the perpetrator.[66] Delgado argues that the dominant group justifies its power with stories—stock explanations—that construct reality in ways to maintain their privilege.[67] Thus, oppression is rationalized, causing little self-examination by the oppressor. Stories by people of color can catalyze the necessary cognitive conflict to jar dysconscious racism.

The 'voice' component of critical race theory provides a way to communicate the experience and realities of the oppressed, a first step on the road to justice. As we attempt to make linkages between critical race theory and education, we contend that the voice of people of color is required for a complete analysis of the educational system. Delpit argues that one of the tragedies of education is the way in which the dialogue of people of color has been silenced. An example from her conversation with an African-American graduate student illustrates this point:

> There comes a moment in every class when we have to discuss 'The Black Issue' and what's appropriate education for Black children. I tell you, I'm tired of arguing with those White people, because they won't listen. Well, I don't know if they really don't listen or if they just don't believe you. It seems like if you can't quote Vygotsky or something, then you don't have any validity to speak about your own kids. Anyway, I'm not bothering with it anymore, now I'm just in it for a grade.[68]

A growing number of education scholars of color are raising critical questions about the way that research is being conducted in communities of color.[69] Thus, without authentic voices of people of color (as teachers, parents, administrators, students, and community members) it is doubtful that we can say or know anything useful about education in their communities.

The Intersection of Race and Property

In the previous sections of this [chapter] we argued that race is still a significant factor in determining inequity in the United States and that the society is based on property rights rather than on human rights. In this section we discuss the intersection of race and property as a central construct in understanding a critical race theoretical approach to education.

Harris argues that 'slavery linked the privilege of Whites to the subordination of Blacks through a legal regime that attempted the conversion of Blacks into objects of property. Similarly, the settlement and seizure of Native American land supported White privilege through a system of property rights in land in which the "race" of the Native Americans rendered their first possession right invisible and justified conquest.' But, more pernicious and long lasting then the victimization of people of color is the construction of whiteness as the ultimate property. 'Possession—the act necessary to lay the basis for rights in property—was defined to include only the cultural practices of Whites. This definition laid the foundation for the idea that whiteness—that which Whites alone possess—is valuable and is property.'[70]

Because of space constraints, it is not possible to fully explicate Harris's thorough analysis of whiteness as property. However, it is important to delineate what she terms the 'property functions of whiteness,' which include: (1) rights of disposition; (2) rights to use and enjoyment; (3) reputation and status property; and (4) the absolute right to exclude. How these rights apply to education is germane to our discussion.

Rights of disposition. Because property rights are described as fully alienable, that is, transferable, it is difficult to see how whiteness can be construed as property.[71] However, alienability of certain property is limited (e.g., entitlements, government licenses, professional degrees or licenses held by one party and financed by the labor of the other in the context of divorce). Thus, whiteness when conferred on certain student performances is alienable.[72] When students are rewarded only for conformity to perceived 'white norms' or sanctioned for cultural practices (e.g., dress, speech patterns, unauthorized conceptions of knowledge), white property is being rendered alienable.

Rights to use and enjoyment. Legally, whites can use and enjoy the privileges of whiteness. As McIntosh has explicitly demonstrated, whiteness allows for specific social, cultural, and economic privileges.[73] Fuller further asserts that whiteness is both performative and pleasurable.[74] In the school setting, whiteness allows for extensive use of school property. Kozol's description of the material differences in two New York City schools can be interpreted as the difference between those who possess the right to use and enjoy what schools can offer and those who do not:

> The [white] school serves 825 children in the kindergarten through sixth grade. This is approximately half the student population crowded into [black] P.S. 79, where 1,550 children fill a space intended for 1,000, and a great deal smaller than the 1,300 children packed into the former skating rink.[75]

This right of use and enjoyment is also reflected in the structure of the curriculum, also described by Kozol:

> The curriculum [the white school] follows 'emphasizes critical thinking, reasoning and logic.' The planetarium, for instance, is employed not simply for the study of the universe as it exists. 'Children also are designing their own galaxies,' the teacher says. . . .
>
> In my [Kozol's] notes: 'Six girls, four boys. Nine White, one Chinese. I am glad they have this class. But what about the others? Aren't there ten Black children in the school who could *enjoy* this also?'[76]

Reputation and status property. The concept of reputation as property is regularly demonstrated in legal cases of libel and slander. Thus, to damage someone's reputation is to damage some aspect of his or her personal property. In the case of race, to call a white person 'black' is to defame him or her.[77] In the case of schooling, to identify a school or program as nonwhite in any way is to diminish its reputation or status. For example, despite the prestige of foreign language learning, bilingual education as practiced in the United States as a nonwhite form of second language learning has lower status.[78] The term *urban*, the root word of *urbane*, has come to mean black. Thus, urban schools (located in the urbane, sophisticated cities) lack the status and reputation of suburban (white) schools and when urban students move to or are bused to suburban schools, these schools lose their reputation.[79]

The absolute right to exclude. Whiteness is constructed in this society as the absence of the 'contaminating' influence of blackness. Thus, 'one drop of black blood' constructs one as black, regardless of phenotypic markers.[80] In schooling, the absolute right to exclude was demonstrated initially by denying blacks access to schooling altogether. Later, it was demonstrated by the creation and maintenance of separate schools. More recently it has been demonstrated by white flight and the growing insistence on vouchers, public funding of private schools, and schools of choice.[81] Within schools, absolute right to exclude is demonstrated by resegregation via tracking,[82] the institution of 'gifted' programs, honors programs and advanced placement classes. So complete is this exclusion that black students often come to the university in the role of intruders—who have been granted special permission to be there.

In this section we have attempted to draw parallels between the critical race legal theory notion of whiteness as property and educational inequity. In the final section we relate some of the intellectual/theoretical tensions that exist between critical race theory and multicultural education.

The Limits of the Multicultural Paradigm

Throughout this [chapter] we have argued the need for a critical race theoretical perspective to cast a new gaze on the persistent problems of racism in schooling. We have argued the need for this perspective because of the failure of scholars to theorize race. We have drawn parallels between the way critical race legal scholars understand their position vis-à-vis traditional legal scholarship and the ways critical race theory applied to education offers a way to rethink traditional educational scholarship. We also have referred to the tensions that exist between traditional civil rights legislation and critical race legal theory. In this section we identify a necessary tension between critical race theory in education and what we term the multicultural paradigm.

Multicultural education has been conceptualized as a reform movement designed to effect change in the 'school and other educational institutions so that students from diverse racial, ethnic and other social-class groups will experience educational equality.'[83] In more recent years, multicultural education has expanded to include issues of gender, ability, and sexual orientation. Although one could argue for an early history of the 'multicultural education movement' as far back as the 1880s when George Washington Williams wrote his history of African Americans, much of the current multicultural education practice seems more appropriately rooted in the intergroup education movement of the 1950s, which was designed to help African Americans and other 'unmeltable' ethnics become a part of America's melting pot.[84] Their goals were primarily assimilationist through the reduction of prejudice. However, after the civil rights unrest and growing self-awareness of African Americans in the 1960s, the desire to assimilate was supplanted by the reclamation of an 'authentic black personality' that did not rely on the acceptance by or standards of white America. This new vision was evidenced in the academy in the form of first, black studies and later, when other groups made similar liberating moves, ethnic studies.[85]

Current practical demonstrations of multicultural education in schools often reduce it to trivial examples and artifacts of cultures such as eating ethnic or cultural foods, singing songs or dancing, reading folktales, and other less than scholarly pursuits of the fundamentally different conceptions of knowledge or quests for social justice.[86] At the university level, much of the concern over multicultural education has been over curriculum inclusion.[87] However, another level of debate emerged over what became known as 'multiculturalism.'

Somewhat different from multicultural education in that it does not represent a particular educational reform or scholarly tradition, multiculturalism came to be viewed as a political philosophy of 'many cultures' existing together in an atmosphere of respect and tolerance.[88] Thus, outside of the classroom multiculturalism represented the attempt to bring both students and faculty from a variety of cultures into the school (or academy) environment. Today, the term is used interchangeably with the ever-expanding 'diversity,' a term used to explain all types of 'difference'—racial, ethnic, cultural, linguistic, ability, gender, sexual orientation. Thus, popular music, clothes, media, books, and so forth, reflect a growing awareness of diversity and/or multiculturalism. Less often discussed are the growing tensions that exist between and among various groups that gather under the umbrella of multiculturalism—that is, the interests of groups can be competing or their perspectives can be at odds.[89] We assert that the ever-expanding multicultural paradigm follows the traditions of liberalism—allowing a proliferation of difference. Unfortunately, the tensions between and among these differences is rarely interrogated, presuming a 'unity of difference'—that is, that all difference is both analogous and equivalent.[90]

To make parallel the analogy between critical race legal theory and traditional civil rights law with that of critical race theory in education and multicultural education we need to restate the point that critical race legal theorists have 'doubts about the foundation of moderate/incremental civil rights law.'[91] The foundation of civil rights law has been in human rights rather than in property rights. Thus, without disrespect to the pioneers of civil rights law, critical race legal scholars document the ways in which civil rights law is regularly subverted to benefit whites.[92]

We argue that the current multicultural paradigm functions in a manner similar to civil rights law. Instead of creating radically new paradigms that ensure justice, multicultural reforms are routinely 'sucked back into the system' and just as traditional civil rights law is based on a foundation of human rights, the current multicultural paradigm is mired in liberal ideology that offers no radical change in the current order.[93] Thus, critical race theory in education, like its antecedent in legal scholarship, is a radical critique of both the status quo and the purported reforms.

We make this observation of the limits of the current multicultural paradigm not to disparage the scholarly efforts and sacrifices of many of its proponents, but to underscore the difficulty (indeed, impossibility) of maintaining the spirit and intent of justice for the oppressed while simultaneously permitting the hegemonic rule of the oppressor.[94] Thus, as critical race theory scholars we unabashedly reject a paradigm that attempts to be everything to everyone and consequently becomes nothing for anyone, allowing the status quo to prevail. Instead, we align our scholarship and activism with the philosophy of Marcus Garvey, who believed that the black man was universally oppressed on racial grounds, and that any program of emancipation would have to be built around the question of race first.[95] In his own words, Garvey speaks to us clearly and unequivocally:

> In a world of wolves one should go armed, and one of the most powerful defensive weapons within the reach of Negroes is the practice of race first in all parts of the world.[96]

NOTES

1. Jonathan Kozol, *Savage Inequalities* (New York: Crown Publishers, 1991). For further discussion of our inability to articulate issues of race and racism see Toni Morrison, *Playing in the Dark: Whiteness and the Literary Imagination* (Cambridge: Harvard University Press, 1992): Cornel West, 'Learning to Talk of Race', *New York Times Magazine*, 2 August 1992, 24, 26; and Beverly Daniel Tatum, 'Talking about Race, Learning about Racism: The Application of Racial Identity Development Theory in the Classroom', *Harvard Educational Review* 62 (1992): 1–24.
2. Throughout this [chapter] the term *race* is used to define the polar opposites of 'conceptual whiteness' and 'conceptual blackness' (Joyce King, 'Perceiving Reality in a New Way: Rethinking the Black/White Duality of our Time' [Paper presented at the annual meeting of the American Educational Research Association. New Orleans. April 1994]). We do not mean to reserve the sense of 'otherness' for African Americans: rather, our discussion attempts to illuminate how discussions of race in the United States positions *everyone* as either 'white' or 'nonwhite.' Thus, despite the use of African-American legal and educational exemplars, we include other groups who have been constructed at various times in their history as nonwhite or black. Readers should note that some of the leading legal scholars in the critical race legal theory movement are of Latino and Asian-American as well as African-American heritage.
3. See, for example, Patricia Hill-Collins, *Black Feminist Thought* (New York: Routledge, 1991); Joyce King and Carolyn Mitchell, *Black Mothers to Sons: Juxtaposing African American Literature and Social Practice* (New York: Peter Lang, 1990); and Patricia Williams, *The*

Alchemy of Race and Rights: Diary of a Law Professor (Cambridge, Mass.: Harvard University Press, 1991).

4. These propositions are not hierarchical. Rather, they can be envisioned as sides of an equilateral triangle, each equal and each central to the construction of the overall theory.
5. Andrew Hacker, *Two Nations: Black and White, Separate, Hostile, Unequal* (New York: Ballantine Books, 1992); and Marian Wright Edelman, *Families in Peril: An Agenda for Social Change* (Cambridge, Mass.: Harvard University Press, 1987).
6. Michael Omi and Howard Winant. 'On the Theoretical Concept of Race', in *Race, Identity and Representation in Education*, ed. C. McCarthy and W. Crichlow (New York: Routledge, 1993), 3–10.
7. Luigi Luca Cavalli-Sforza, 'Genes, People and Languages', *Scientific American*, November 1991, 104.
8. Morrison, *Playing in the Dark*, 63.
9. This assertion was made forcefully by the participants of the Institute NHI (No Humans Involved) at a symposium entitled 'The Two Reservations: Western Thought, the Color Line, and the Crisis of the Negro Intellectual Revisited', sponsored by the Department of African and Afro-American Studies at Stanford University. Stanford, Calif., 3–5 March 1994.
10. See, for example, Nancy Chodorow, *The Reproduction of Mothering* (Berkeley: University of California Press, 1978); Simone de Beauvoir. *The Second Sex* (New York: Bantam Books, 1961); Vivian Gornick. 'Women as Outsiders,' in *Women in Sexist Society*, ed. V. Gornick and B. Moran (New York: Basic Books, 1971), 70–84; Nancy Hartsock, 'Feminist Theory and the Development of Revolutionary Strategy', *Capitalist Patriarch and the Case for Socialist Feminism*, ed. Z. Eisenstein (London and New York: Monthly Review Press, 1979); and Alison Jagger, *Feminist Theory and Human Nature* (Sussex: Harvester, 1983).
11. See, for example, Samuel Bowles and Herbert Gintis. *Schooling in Capitalist America* (New York: Basic Books, 1976); Martin Carnoy, *Education and Cultural Imperialism* (New York: McKay, 1974); Michael W. Apple, 'Redefining Inequality: Authoritarian Populism and the Conservative Restoration', *Teachers College Record* 90 (1988): 167–84; and Philip Wexler, *Social Analysis and Education: After the New Sociology* (New York: Routledge & Kegan Paul, 1987).
12. David Roediger. *The Wages of Whiteness* (London: Verso, 1991), 6.
13. Michael Omi and Howard Winant, *Racial Formation in the United States from the 1960s to the 1990s*, 2nd edn. (New York: Routledge, 1994), 9.
14. Ibid. 56.
15. Carter C. Woodson, *The Miseducation of the Negro* (Washington, DC: Association Press, 1933); and W. E. B. Du Bois. *The Souls of Black Folks* (New York: Penguin Books, 1989; first published in 1903).
16. Our decision to focus on Woodson and Du Bois is not intended to diminish the import of the scores of African-American scholars who also emerged during their time such as George E. Haynes, Charles S. Johnson, E. Franklin Frazier, Abram Harris, Sadie T. Alexander, Robert C. Weaver, Rayford Logan, Allison Davis, Dorothy Porter, and Benjamin Quarles. We highlight Woodson and Du Bois as early seminal thinkers about issues of race and racism.
17. See John Hope Franklin, *From Slavery to Freedom*, 6th edn. (New York: Alfred A. Knopf, 1988).

18. Woodson, *The Miseducation of the Negro*, p. xiii.
19. Du Bois, *The Souls of Black Folks*, 5. Other people of color, feminists, and gay and lesbian theorists all have appropriated Du Bois's notion of double consciousness to explain their estrangement from mainstream patriarchal, masculinist US culture.
20. David Levering Lewis, *W. E. B. Du Bois: Biography of a Race, 1868–1919* (New York: Henry Holt, 1993), 281.
21. Du Bois. *The Souls of Black Folks*, 1.
22. See, for example, Lorene Cary, *Black Ice* (New York: Alfred A. Knopf, 1991); and Jeannie Oakes, *Keeping Track: How Schools Structure Inequality* (New Haven: Yale University Press, 1985).
23. Oakes, *Keeping Track*, 67.
24. American Association of University Women. *How Schools Shortchange Girls: A Study of Major Findings on Gender and Education* (Washington, DC: Author and National Education Association, 1992).
25. Myra Sadker, David Sadker, and Susan Klein, 'The Issue of Gender in Elementary and Secondary Education', in *Review of Educational Research in Education*, ed. G. Cerant (Washington, DC: American Educational Research Association, 1991), xix. 269–334.
26. Hacker, *Two Nations*, puts the dropout rate for African-American males in some large cities at close to 50 percent.
27. Robert Majors and Janet Billson, *Cool Pose: The Dilemmas of Black Manhood in America* (New York: Lexington Books, 1992).
28. Cornel West, *Race Matters* (Boston: Beacon Press, 1993); and David Lionel Smith, 'Let Our People Go', *Black Scholar* 23 (1993): 75–6.
29. Peter Monaghan, '"Critical Race Theory" Questions the Role of Legal Doctrine in Racial Inequity', *Chronicle of Higher Education*, 23 June 1993, A7, A9.
30. Delgado, cited in Monaghan, 'Critical Race Theory'. Quotations are from p. A7. For a more detailed explication of the first item in the list, see Bell, *Faces at the Bottom of the Well*.
31. Manning Marable, *How Capitalism Undeveloped Black America* (Boston: South End Press, 1983).
32. Derrick Bell, *And We Are Not Saved: The Elusive Quest for Racial Justice* (New York: Basic Books, 1987).
33. Howard Zinn, *A People's History of the United States* (New York: Harper & Row, 1980), 13.
34. Bell, And *We Are Not Saved*.
35. William Tate, Gloria Ladson-Billings, and Carl Grant, 'The *Brown* Decision Revisited: Mathematizing Social Problems', *Educational Policy* 7 (1993): 255–75.
36. Bell, *And We* Are *Not Saved*, 239.
37. Ronald Takaki, *A Different Mirror: A History of Multicultural America* (Boston: Little Brown, 1993).
38. Franklin, *From Slavery to Freedom*.
39. Clearly, an analysis of worldwide tensions reinforces the importance of land to a people—Israel and the Palestinians, Iraq and Kuwait, the former Soviet bloc, Hitler and the Third Reich, all represent some of the struggles over land.
40. Even at a time when there is increased public sentiment for reducing the federal deficit, the one source of tax relief that no president or member of Congress would ever consider is that of denying home (property) owners their tax benefits.

41. See, for example. Howard Wainer, 'Does Spending Money on Education Help?' *Educational Researcher* 22 (1993): 22–4; or Paul Houston, 'School Vouchers: The Latest California Joke', *Phi Delta Kappan* 75 (1993): 61–6.

42. Kozol, *Savage Inequalities*, 83–4.

43. This notion of 'intellectual property' came into popular use when television talk show host David Letterman moved from NBC to CBS. NBC claimed that certain routines and jokes used by Letterman were the intellectual property of the network and, as such, could not be used by Letterman without permission.

44. Richard Delgado, 'When a Story Is Just a Story: Does Voice Really Matter?' *Virginia Law Review* 76 (1990): 95–111.

45. See, for example, Floraline Stevens, *Opportunity to Learn: Issues of Equity for Poor and Minority Students* (Washington, DC: National Center for Education Statistics, 1993): idem, 'Applying an Opportunity-to-learn Conceptual Framework to the Investigation of the Effects of Teaching Practices via Secondary Analyses of Multiple-case-study Summary Data', *The Journal of Negro Education* 62 (1993): 232–48; and Linda Winfield and Michael D. Woodard, 'Assessment, Equity, Diversity in Reforming America's Schools', *Educational Policy* 8 (1994): 3–27.

46. The standards debate is too long and detailed to be discussed here. For a more detailed discussion of standards see, for example, Michael W. Apple, 'Do the Standards Go Far Enough? Power, Policy, and Practices in Mathematics Education', *Journal for Research in Mathematics Education* 23 (1992): 412–31; and National Council of Education Standards and Testing, *Raising Standards for American Education: A Report to Congress, the Secretary of Education, the National Goals Panel, and the American People* (Washington. DC: Government Printing Office, 1992).

47. Kozol, *Savage Inequalities.*

48. Some urban Catholic schools, black independent schools, and historically black colleges and universities have demonstrated the educability of African-American students. As of this writing we have no data on the success of urban districts such as Detroit or Milwaukee that are attempting what is termed 'African Centered' or Africentric education. See also Mwalimu J. Shujaa, ed., *Too Much Schooling, Too Little Education: A Paradox of Black Life in White Societies* (Trenton, NJ: Africa World Press, 1994).

49. David Wellman, *Portraits of White Racism* (Cambridge: Cambridge University Press, 1977). Quotations are from pp. xviii and 42.

50. See, for example, Gary Orfield, 'School Desegregation in the 1980s', *Equity and Choice*, February 1988, 25; Derrick Bell, 'Learning from Our Losses: Is School Desegregation Still Feasible in the 1980s? *Phi Delta Kappan* 64 (April 1983): 575; Willis D. Hawley, 'Why It Is Hard to Believe in Desegregation', *Equity and Choice*, February 1988, 9–15; and Janet Ward Schofield, *Black and White in School: Trust, Tension, or Tolerance?* (New York: Teachers College Press, 1989).

51. James Banks, 'Teaching Multicultural Literacy to Teachers', *Teaching Education 4* (1991): 135–44.

52. See Karl Taeuber, 'Desegregation of Public School Districts: Persistence and Change', *Phi Delta Kappan* 72 (1990): 18–24; and H. L. Bisinger, 'When Whites Flee', *New York Times Magazine*, 29 May 1994, 26–33, 43, 50, 53–4, 56. On loss of professional positions, see Sabrina King, 'The Limited Presence of African American Teachers', *Review of Educational Research* 63 (1993): 115–49; and Jacqueline Irvine, 'An Analysis of the Problem of Disappearing Black Educators', *Elementary School Journal* 88 (1988): 503–13.

53. Kimberle Williams Crenshaw, 'Race Reform, and Retrenchment: Transformation and Legitimation in Antidiscrimination Law', *Harvard Law Review* 101 (1988): 1331–87.
54. Ibid. 1335.
55. Kofi Lomotey and John Statley, 'The Education of African Americans in Buffalo Public Schools' (Paper presented at the annual meeting of the American Educational Research Association, Boston, 1990).
56. Richard Delgado, 'Storytelling for Oppositionists and Others: A Plea for Narrative', *Michigan Law Review* 87 (1989): 2411–41.
57. See Richard Delgado et al., 'Symposium: Legal Storytelling', *Michigan Law Review* 87 (1989): 2073. On dysconsciousness, see Joyce E. King, 'Dysconscious Racism: Ideology, Identity and the Miseducation of Teachers', *Journal of Negro Education* 60 (1991): 135. King defines dysconsciousness as 'an uncritical habit of mind (including perceptions, attitudes, assumptions, and beliefs) that justifies inequity and exploitation by accepting the existing order of things as given. ... Dysconscious racism is a form of racism that tacitly accepts dominant White norms and privileges. It is not the *absence* of consciousness (that is, not unconsciousness) but an *impaired* consciousness or distorted way of thinking about race as compared to, for example, critical consciousness.'
58. These notions of universalism prevail in much of social science research, including educational research.
59. Williams, *Alchemy of Race and Rights*.
60. Richard Delgado, 'Brewer's Plea: Critical Thoughts on Common Cause', *Vanderbilt Law Review* 44 (1991): 11.
61. For example, see Williams, *Alchemy of Race and Rights*; Bell, *Faces at the Bottom of the Well*; and Mari Matsuda, 'Public Response to Racist Speech: Considering the Victim's Story', *Michigan Law Review* 87 (1989): 2320–81.
62. Delgado, 'Storytelling'.
63. Ibid.
64. For example, see Crenshaw, 'Race, Reform, and Retrenchment'.
65. Delgado, 'Storytelling'.
66. Charles Lawrence. 'The Id, the Ego, and Equal Protection: Reckoning with Unconscious Racism', *Stanford Law Review* 39 (1987): 317–88.
67. Delgado et al., 'Symposium'.
68. Lisa Delpit, 'The Silenced Dialogue: Power and Pedagogy in Educating Other People's Children', *Harvard Educational Review* 58 (1988): 280.
69. At the 1994 annual meeting of the American Educational Research Association in New Orleans, two sessions entitled 'Private Lives. Public Voices: Ethics of Research in Communities of Color' were convened to discuss the continued exploitation of people of color. According to one scholar of color, our communities have become 'data plantations'.
70. Cheryl I. Harris, 'Whiteness as Property', *Harvard Law Review* 106 (1993): 1721.
71. See Margaret Radin, 'Market-Inalienability', *Harvard Law Review* 100 (1987): 1849–906.
72. See Signithia Fordham and John Ogbu, 'Black Student School Success: Coping with the Burden of "Acting White"' *The Urban Review* 18 (1986): 1–31.
73. Peggy Mcintosh, 'White Privilege: Unpacking the Invisible Knapsack', *Independent School*, Winter 1990, 31–6.

74. Laurie Fuller, 'Whiteness as Performance' (Unpublished preliminary examination paper, University of Wisconsin-Madison, 1994).

75. Kozol, *Savage Inequalities*, 93.

76. Ibid. 96: emphasis added.

77. Harris, 'Whiteness as Property', 1735.

78. David Spener, 'Transitional Bilingual Education and the Socialization of Immigrants', *Harvard Educational Review* 58 (1988): 133–53.

79. H. G. Bissinger, 'When Whites Flee', *New York Times Magazine*, 29 May 1994, 26–33, 43, 50, 53–54, 56.

80. Derrick Bell, *Race, Racism, and American Law* (Boston: Little, Brown, 1980).

81. We assert that the current movement toward African-centered (or Africentric) schools is not equivalent to the racial exclusion of vouchers, or choice programs. Indeed, African-centeredness has become a logical response of a community to schools that have been abandoned by whites, have been stripped of material resources, and have demonstrated a lack of commitment to African-American academic achievement.

82. Oakes, *Keeping Track.*

83. James A. Banks. 'Multicultural Education: Historical Development, Dimensions, and Practice', in *Review of Research in Education*, ed. L. Darling-Hammond (Washington, DC: American Educational Research Association, 1993), xix. 3.

84. George Washington Williams, *History of the Negro Race in America from 1619–1880: Negroes as Slaves, as Soldiers, and as Citizens* (2 vols.) (New York: G. P. Putnam & Sons, 1882–3). On the intergroup education movement, see, for example, L. A. Cook and E. Cook, *Intergroup Education* (New York: McGraw-Hill, 1954); and H. G. Traeger and M. R. Yarrow, *They Learn What They Live: Prejudice in Young Children* (New York: Harper & Brothers, 1952).

85. See, for example, Vincent Harding, *Beyond Chaos: Black History and the Search for a New Land*, Black Paper No. 2 (Atlanta: Institute of the Black World, August 1970); J. Blassingame, ed., *New Perspectives in Black Studies* (Urbana: University of Illinois Press, 1971); James A. Banks, ed., *Teaching Ethnic Studies* (Washington, DC: National Council for the Social Studies, 1973); and Geneva Gay, 'Ethnic Minority Studies: How Widespread? How Successful?' *Educational Leadership* 29 (1971): 108–12.

86. Banks, 'Multicultural Education'.

87. In 1988 at Stanford University the inclusion of literature from women and people of color in the Western Civilization core course resulted in a heated debate. The university's faculty senate approved this inclusion in a course called Cultures, Ideas, and Values. The controversy was further heightened when then Secretary of Education William Bennett came to the campus to denounce this decision.

88. In the 'Book Notes' section of the *Harvard Educational Review* 64 (1994): 345–7, Jane Davagian Tchaicha reviews Donaldo Macedo's *Literacies of Power* (Boulder: Westview, 1994) and includes two quotes, one from noted conservative Patrick Buchanan and another from Macedo on multiculturalism. According to Buchanan, 'Our Judeo-Christian values are going to be preserved, and our Western heritage is going to be handed down to future generations, not dumped into some landfill called multiculturalism' (quoted in Tchaicha, 345). Macedo asserts that 'the real issue isn't Western culture versus multiculturalism, the fundamental issue is the recognition of humanity in us and in others' (quoted in Tchaicha, 347).

89. In New York City, controversy over the inclusion of gay and lesbian issues in the curriculum caused vitriolic debate among racial and ethnic groups who opposed their issues being linked to or compared with homosexuals. Some ethnic group members asserted that homosexuals were not a 'culture' while gay and lesbian spokespeople argued that these group members were homophobic.

90. Shirley Torres-Medina, 'Issues of Power: Constructing the Meaning of Linguistic Difference in First Grade Classrooms' (Ph.D. diss., University of Wisconsin-Madison, 1994).

91. Richard Delgado, 'Enormous Anomaly; Left–Right Parallels in Recent Writing about Race', *Columbia Law Review* 91 (1991): 1547–60.

92. See Bell, *And We Are Not Saved.*

93. See Cameron McCarthy. 'After the Canon: Knowledge and Ideological Representation in the Multicultural Discourse on Curriculum Reform', in *Race, Identity and Representation*, ed. C. McCarthy and W. Crichlow (New York: Routledge. 1994), 290; and Michael Olneck, 'Terms of Inclusion: Has Multiculturalism Redefined Equality in American Education?', *American Journal of Education* 101 (1993): 234–60.

94. We are particularly cognizant of the hard-fought battles in the academy waged and won by scholars such as James Banks, Carlos Cortez, Geneva Gay, Carl Grant, and others.

95. Tony Martin, *Race First: The Ideological and Organizational Struggles of Marcus Garvey and the Universal Negro Improvement Association* (Dover, Mass.: The Majority Press, 1976).

96. Marcus Garvey, cited ibid. 22.

Be Yourself: Class, Race, Gender and Sexuality in South African Schoolchildren's Accounts of Social Relations

Elaine Unterhalter, Debbie Epstein, Robert Morrell and Relebohile Moletsane

[. . .]

Introduction

This [chapter] aims to examine South African schoolchildren's understandings of social relationships and to show how class and race are articulated through gender and sexuality. It also considers how education is positioned in representations that children make of the social divisions in their society. Class, race and gender are complex concepts in any context, but the particular history of segregation, apartheid, political repression and emergent democracy in South Africa has made them both fixed and changeable. This mutability requires a peculiarly multi-layered form of analysis. We attempt this through a review of theoretical writings on class, race, gender and South African education, and use some of the silences we identify in this literature to examine empirical data collected in two working-class schools in Durban.

The first part of the [chapter] presents a brief overview of debates concerning social divisions in South Africa and the ways in which these have influenced writings on education. The second section sketches aspects of the education system in South Africa and gives a brief outline of the research project which generated the data for this [chapter]. The last section explores young people's views of social relationships, recorded in letters to an 'agony aunt'.

We did not set out to investigate narrowly formulated understandings of class, but were interested in the diverse ways class might be expressed through comments on race, gender and sexuality. Anoop Nayak has argued, writing about white youth in the north-east of England, that they 'do gender' through class, race or sexuality and vice versa (Nayak, 1999). In the writings by youth in Durban working-class schools we found class and race similarly expressed through portrayals of gender and sexuality.

From Elaine Unterhalter, Debbie Epstein, Robert Morrell, and Relebohile Moletsane, 'Be Yourself: Class, Race, Gender, and Sexuality in South African Schoolchildren's Accounts of Social Relations', *Pedagogy, Culture, and Society* 12/1 (2004). Reprinted with permission.

Class, Race, Gender, Sexuality, and Education in South Africa

Theorising the intersections of class and race was a major political and theoretical project in South Africa throughout the twentieth century. Work in this area can be divided into two phases. Up to the late 1980s, a major concern was the ways in which these social divisions were intrinsic to relations of production and the form of the state (Simons and Simons, 1969; Davies et al., 1976; Davies, 1979; Wolpe, 1988; Saunders, 1988; Gelb, 1991, Michie and Padayachee, 1997). The key focus in these debates was whether the South African political economy could or should be analysed in terms of race or class. As neither race nor class reductionism was satisfactory, the major contention was what new theoretical formulation could be developed that provided both a satisfactory account of the society and, implicitly, pointed towards strategies to change it. Much of this work was silent with regard to gender, although a number of historical accounts indicated how control of women's labour and women's sexuality was a feature of new class formations that came into being with colonialism. These persisted with particular racialised contours through the segregation and apartheid eras (Cock, 1980; Bozzoli, 1983; Gaitskell et al., 1983; Kimble, 1983; Walker, 1990).

In these accounts the particular forms of exploitation and political exclusion that characterised relations of production and the nature of the state were largely explained in terms of the intersections of class, race and gender, that is, social relationships that embodied and perpetuated inequality. Louis Althusser's writings were influential in their stress on the reproduction of class power and the coercive nature of the state and its institutions, portrayed as ideological and repressive state apparatuses. These generally included schools. The issues raised by this approach continue to influence analysis in South Africa (see, for example, Marais, 1998) because post-apartheid South Africa has the highest level of income inequality in the world, with significant levels of inequality both between racial groups and within some groups (May, 2000; Bhorat et al., 2001, p. 39).

A second phase began in the mid-1980s (Marks and Rathbone, 1982) and gathered pace in the 1990s when a number of commentators began to examine the ways in which race, class and gender were features, not only of relations of production, but also of social status and ascribed and assumed identities (Vail, 1989; Comaroff and Comaroff, 1992; Howarth and Norval, 1998; Nuttall and Coetzee, 1998). In our work on this theme, some of us have highlighted how gendered identities, that is particular formations of masculinity or femininity, have characterised particular race and class positions at key historical moments, rendering political projects ambiguous (Epstein and Unterhalter, 1999; Morrell, 2001*a*; Unterhalter, 2000).

Much of the politics of the last phase of opposition to apartheid and the post-apartheid era in South Africa highlighted the complex and contradictory political formations and alliances linked to both relations of production and other identities. This latter was expressed through ethnicity, community-based organisations, 'stakeholder' groups, single-issue campaigns such as the Treatment Action Campaign (TAC) formed in response to the HIV/AIDS epidemic, or the lesbian and gay rights organisations which formed to lobby for gay rights to be recognised in the Constitution. These have subsequently mobilised against discriminatory legislation relating to the workplace and families. Thus a complex politics concerned with redistribution, transformation of relations of production and the affirmation of subordinated identities has begun to emerge (Gevisser and Cameron, 1994; Murray, 1994; Marais, 1998).

Writers responding to these new political formations have been concerned with social relations in a somewhat different way to the first, older group of commentators. The move away from state-centred, class-focused, economistic and reproductionist analyses has been fuelled by enhanced understanding of the complex processes by which identities are constituted, the capacity of subjects to occupy multiple subject positions and some of the contradictory political consequences of these processes. These insights have exposed the limitations of simple formulations based on causal connections between race, class, and gender inequalities.

The new generation of analysts have been particularly concerned with the ways cultural and political dimensions of class, race and gender might restructure relations of production, making inequality highly complex. This writing, influenced by the intellectual movements of the 1980s and 1990s, particularly poststructuralism, postcolonial theorising, feminism, queer theory, normative democratic theory and Gramscian engagements with Marxism, has highlighted how realising projects linked to the redistribution of power is exceptionally complex and often contradictory (Nuttall and Coetzee, 1998; Howarth and Norval, 1998; Giliomee and Simkins, 1999; Unterhalter, 2003).

Writing about education in South Africa has been strongly influenced by the wider sociological and political debates concerning race, class and gender we have sketched above. A first wave of scholarship set out to examine how the education system reproduced the class, race and sometimes gender hierarchies of society (Kallaway, 1984; Cross, 1986; Chisholm, 1990; Unterhalter, 1991). One major project was to show how the exclusionary and exploitative features of the political economy were sustained by features of the education system, where inequalities of race, class and gender were solidified. Over two decades this approach was subjected to critiques which sought to show the complexity of conditions within the education system and how different strategies in education policy were associated with a range of social forces (Nkomo, 1990; Unterhalter et al., 1991; Kros, 1990/1; Kallaway et al., 1997; Hyslop, 1999; Kallaway, 2002). But the overarching assumption remained that education policies and practices contributed to and helped sustain class, race and gender inequalities primarily understood in terms of relations of production. Despite acknowledging complex dimensions of the political economy that impinged on conditions within schools, a foundational assumption in these analyses was that relations of production were mirrored (sometimes accurately, sometimes in distorted shapes) in the form of the state and thus in state policy with regard to education.

However, just as a number of sociological studies started to focus on issues of status, identity and cultural political aspects of social positioning, similar concerns became evident in the writing on education in South Africa. At least two trends are evident: first, the discovery of identity as an important focus in the analysis of education, entailing a conscious move away from the macro level class perspectives of the 1980s and early 1990s. Work began to document conditions in particular schools and among particular groups of learners (Soudien et al., 2001; Dolby, 2001). Second, there was an acknowledgement that the interaction of 'society' and the individual was more complex than the earlier analysis had suggested (Muller, 2000; Carrim, 2001). In this writing much more complexity and fluidity were conceded to the concept of identity than hitherto. For example, Carrim commented how ethnicity began to be a feature of educational aspiration as the fixity of apartheid relations broke down, but ethnicity itself was neither fixed nor untouched by complex individual positionings (Carrim, 2001). The ways that masculinity and femininity intersected with class, race, gender and generation in how schooling was understood and some of the policy implications of these understandings began to be documented using new methods, including the analysis of published autobiographies and social history (Unterhalter, 1999; Morrell, 2001*b*; Chisholm, 2001; Unterhalter, 2002*a*).

Much of this new work, implicitly or explicitly, saw itself as amplifying, rather than supplanting, the understandings of social divisions of the first group of writers. The locus of analysis for both phases was the education system or the school, and the chief concern the ways that these either reproduced class, race or gender divisions and contributed to the maintenance of hegemonic social relations or were sites of struggle. Although questions of identity or more nuanced readings of the link between individual and society have come to the fore in the last ten years, the context remains how education articulates with the formations of inequality in South Africa.

In this [chapter] we take a different approach. We are concerned, not with how schools and the education system as a whole are implicated in the reproduction or erosion of inequalities in South Africa, but with what aspects of social relations with respect to schooling we have not yet paid attention to. This requires the focus of our question to be, not the education system as a whole, or particular schools, teachers or learners, but rather the forms of aspiration young people express, their discourses and subjectivities and the ways they see these interact with the school, family, political, economic and cultural environment. We are particularly concerned with the ways race, gender and class are framed in these narratives. We have not proceeded deductively to prove reproduction or transformation of inequalities in education, but rather inductively to establish emergent themes, the *petits recits* of the everyday lives of children growing up after the establishment of democratic government in South Africa.

Gender, Class and Schools in an HIV/AIDS Environment

The education reforms put in place after the first democratic elections in South Africa sought to end the segregation and discrimination in schooling linked to race, class and gender inequalities of the apartheid era. Schooling was brought under a single legislative framework and policies were put in place to provide for local governance and to link resources to the needs of the poorest school districts (Sayed and Jansen, 2001; Motala and Pampallis, 2001). A Gender Equity Task Team commissioned research and reported to the Education Department on strategies to redress some of the gendered inequalities in the school system (Wolpe et al., 1997). These initiatives represented important steps to transformation, but by 2000, while redress of past inequalities had not disappeared from government priorities, it had come to be set in the context of the horrors of the HIV/AIDS epidemic, which was foremost in the Tirisano Action Plan drawn up by the new Minister of Education. This set out detailed planning objectives for four to five years relating to curriculum change, the conditions of work in school, and the establishment of a culture of learning that might challenge the spread of the virus (Department of Education, 2000).

The HIV/AIDS epidemic represented one significant constraint on the government's ability to realise its aspirations for a more equal education system. Another was the sheer enormity of the inequalities in resources (both human and financial) and the complex effects of discrimination, poverty, and restrictions on opportunities. Thus, nearly ten years after concerted work began to transform the apartheid education system, class inequalities remain in many areas, with fiscal austerity exacerbating the dramatic differences between schools in terms of numbers and level of training of teachers, quality of classrooms and equipment, and the success of school leavers, measured crudely by school leaving (matriculation) results. There are marked differences in performance at this level by the location of school, so that state schools in more affluent areas, or schools which enrol children of professional parents, have dramatically different results from those in poorer areas (Motala and Perry, 2001; Motala, 2002). Gender inequalities are also evident in matriculation results (Unterhalter, 2002*b*). Much attention has focused on the climate of sexual violence in schools, often unchecked by teachers or managers, which undermines the achievements of girls (Human Rights Watch, 2001).

The realisation of educational equity thus remains elusive. A survey conducted in 1999 by the Human Sciences Research Council looked at the views of a representative sample of the adult population regarding service delivery in social development. One-third felt that the delivery of education had improved since 1994, one-third felt it had stayed the same and nearly one-third thought it had worsened (Khosa, 2001, p. 381). Much larger proportions of those surveyed felt there had been more substantial improvements in access to running water, electricity and public transport. This article is concerned not so much with an evaluation of what the government has and has not been able to achieve towards its goals of equality and redress in education, but how education appears in the understandings of social relationships formulated by young people in African working-class townships in Durban, who have received some benefit from the new education policies.

The research project on which we draw was based in two coeducational secondary schools located in the two largest townships in the Greater Durban Area, with predominantly working-class African populations. The schools in the study each have approximately 1,000 students with equal numbers of boys and girls, and a significant proportion of learners over 20. Lillian Ngoyi school is located in KwaMashu township, established in the 1960s after the forced removal of Africans from residential areas close to white suburbs of Durban. Dingiswayo High is in Umlazi, a township that grew up on land under the control of the Kwazulu bantustan during the apartheid era. Both schools are poorly resourced compared to middle-class, former white, suburban schools, though by national standards they have reasonably good facilities. Both schools are headed by African, Zulu-speaking male teachers who have been in office for over a decade. Both are relatively orderly, with school bells signalling the beginning and end of lessons and with learners mostly in class during stipulated teaching periods. In terms of exam results the two schools are very similar. (See Moletsane et al., 2002, for more detailed analysis.)

From 2000 to 2002 data were collected in both schools using a wide range of methods to understand the social background of the learners and teachers and document gender regimes. A particular concern was to explore responses to pedagogic strategies aimed at building awareness about the HIV/AIDS epidemic and enhancing the capacity of learners and adults in their communities to take action with regard to gender equality and HIV/AIDS prevention. Research methods included surveys, individual and group interviews, ethnographic style observations, and reviews of school documents. Findings from this work is reported in a number of papers (Morrell et al., 2001; Moletsane et al., 2002; Morrell, 2002; Thorpe, 2002; Kent, 2002).

A survey conducted in 2000 of 450 students at the two schools revealed aspects of class by highlighting household employment. In this survey learners reported that 27% of fathers and 42% of mothers were unemployed (i.e. neither employed nor self-employed), while 51% of fathers and 41% of mothers were wage-earners. Amongst the fathers, 'driver' was the most common occupation (16%), followed by 'builder' (6%), 'farmer' and 'security officer' (each 4%). Amongst mothers, 'teacher' (10%), 'clerk' (4%), 'driver' and 'security officer' (each 2%) were the most common. Parents with jobs were concentrated in the semi-skilled areas, with women teachers perhaps the exception. One hundred learners (22% of those surveyed) indicated that they had no income earner in their homes. The fragile nature of employment in production, transport and services in South Africa was revealed by the 1995 Income and Expenditure Survey of 30,000 households, which indicated that these households were most vulnerable to losing an income earner (Adelzadeh et al., 2001, p. 234). This survey also revealed that 50% of households in the first quintile and almost 40% in the second quintile had no income earners (Adelzadeh et al., 2001). Thus, the children attending both schools have features in common with many South Africans classified as poor or working-class: low incomes, insecure work conditions and high levels of unemployment.

In this [chapter] we analyse the thoughts and hopes of these young people from working-class backgrounds in order to consider the ways in which they frame their understandings of social relations. The data come from the analysis of ideas expressed in essays, written for a competition at the request of the research team in response to the following prompt: 'Write a letter to "Sis Dolly" about a problem in your life. It can be your own problem, or something about other people, but it must be something real in your life. Then write a reply giving Dolly's advice'. 'Sis Dolly' is the agony aunt for the popular magazine *Drum*, established specifically for African readers in 1951 and still aimed at a black urban readership. Learners were briefed by one teacher at each school who facilitated the competition, with members of the research team present. It was stressed that the letters could be fictional but must deal with problems that learners felt to be real, about either their personal lives or their social circumstances.

Letters were received from 59 learners in Grades 10 and 11 (the higher grades in the school) written in English or IsiZulu; most were in English. Ten letters were from Lillian Ngoyi High School and 49 from Dingiswayo High School. Only ten were written by boys, all in their very late teens. The age range of authors was 15 to 20 years, with the majority being 15, 16 or 17.

Problem page letters, like those to 'Sis Dolly' in *Drum*, demand a particular genre of writing. An identifiable problem, normally of a personal nature, is explained, and the answer given nearly always appears to offer a solution. The genre suggests a dialogue between the worried questioner and the problem-solving respondent. Problems are often, but not exclusively, related to relationships, romance or their failures, and sexuality, often in its least desired or desirable forms. We are aware that the form of problem requires attention to intertextuality. Further work, beyond the scope of this [chapter], is required on how far the key issues we have identified link with themes constantly stressed in the weekly Sis Dolly column, in other forms of popular culture, in churches and in school. The analysis we make of the narratives is thus tentative and provisional, and the conclusions we draw are indicative rather than definitive.

The objection may be made that this genre is not appropriate to elicit the wider concerns of youth regarding social relationships. However, other genres for eliciting children's views used in research projects in other parts of the country (for example the freeform essay, the survey, or the structured discussion in school) yield material with many similar elements. That is, children tend to represent ideas in the form of problems with relationships or questions of identity located in family, neighbourhood and national contexts (Jones, 1993; Barbarin and Richter, 2001; Parkes, 2002). We do not think any one genre or method of data collection is sufficient for understanding the complexity of children's views on social relations, but we do feel the problem page genre is one of a number of ways which helps us gain access to the representations children make and is particularly appropriate for looking at the ways children might represent class and race through accounts of gender and sexuality.

Representing Class through Gender and Sexuality

In schools where poverty and a scarcity of resources are evident, we expected the letters to be particularly eloquent on this theme. But very few were concerned with material conditions and none showed a conventionally politicised perception of class, race, or gender. However three issues, largely neglected in much of the writing on class and education in South Africa, emerged as particularly salient in the aspirations articulated in the letters. The first was a strongly voiced injunction, appearing over and over again in the answers young people gave to themselves, to 'believe in yourself', have confidence, or often simply 'be yourself'. This theme was frequently intertwined with aspirations to be educated (i.e. to complete matriculation and/or some tertiary education). A second theme was the importance of relations with parents. A third theme concerned the terms on which sexuality was negotiated. In the shadow of the HIV/AIDS epidemic, this has already received considerable attention (Adams and Marshall, 1998; Baylies and Bujra, 2000; MacPhail and Campbell, 2000; Harrison et al., 2001), but the depiction in the letters of some of the ways sexuality impinges on social relations provides a number of new insights.

Only three of the 59 letters received documented hardship experienced by children because of lack of income. A 15-year-old girl at Lillian Ngoyi wrote:

> Well I've got a huge problem. It starts like this: my dad died two years ago and he was the only one who was working at home. We are five children at home and my mom. My older sister had finished her matriculation [school leaving examination] and she's not working and she's not continuing with her studies because of the money. My mother had tried so many times to find temporary work, but she can't work because of the last born baby who is disabled. He is blind. He can't even, talk, walk or sit properly. His pension money is helping us at home. We pay our school fees, buy food and pay people we owe their money. Now my problem is like this: My neighbours and my friends always have new beautiful and expensive clothes. Sometimes I just wish I can quit school and go to work so I can buy those nice things and help my family with things that we are running short of especially food.

Strikingly, the answer to herself, formulated in the words of Sis Dolly, expresses particular links between self-confidence and education that were a feature of many of the letters:

> You really need help, but you know what, there are only two people who can help you. The first is God; if you believe in Him everything will go the way you like it to be. The second person is you; if you believe in yourself and never give up anything you do . . . everything will be alright. *But please don't quit school because of the way you think your family is. Be sure educated and you're the one who will help your family and be the way you like it to be.* (Italics added)

The letter illustrates a number of themes evident in the writing by economists on poverty in South

Africa: the fragile incomes of wage-earning households, their heavy dependence on pension and other welfare payments, the lack of employment opportunities for those with relatively little education, and the importance of neighbourhood networks that provide credit and other services crucial for survival. The answer this teenager provides to herself, however, emphasises neither help from the state nor the community, but rather from God and individual effort. Education is invested with a particular power to transform personal motivation into concrete assistance for her family. Within the letter is a struggle over meaning with regard to class and schooling. The young girl feels herself an outsider in a world where there are sufficient material resources, a world she feels she can enter only through paid work, that is, by removing herself from school. But simultaneously she feels the only way to become an insider to that world of sufficiency is to remain in school. Class identities are both fixed through existing forms of relations of production and highly mutable, as the self-dialogue shows.

In many other letters the exhortation to self-confidence is connected with education. For example, education is stressed in Sis Dolly's response about what to do when friends suggest a teenage girl drops out of school because school certificates do not yield high financial rewards:

> My girl, I will like to say to you Education Is The Key To Success. Go to school and depend to yourself . . . Stealing people's things you'll end up in jail . . . But education, your certificate always represents yourself. (Girl, Grade 10, Lillian Ngoyi)

In another example, schooling and self-belief are suggested as the answer to choosing between two boyfriends proposing different styles of love:

> Just now you better focus on your studies and afterwards see where you stand. You go girl! Do what's right for you. (Girl, Grade 11, Dingiswayo)

Schooling and pride in oneself are suggested in the answer to a letter from a teenage boy, who wishes to be a doctor but is ashamed because he is short and suffers ridicule from his classmates who say he is just a child:

> In school, if you are proud of yourself and you believe in yourself you can do what you like. In my opinion there is no child who is doing grade 11. (Boy, Grade 11, Dingiswayo)

In these children's accounts schooling is the process through which they realise themselves, are able to affirm pride in their efforts, and through which, even though benefits may not be immediate, aspirations to earn more or achieve status will be realised. Doubtless the children's replies articulated through Sis Dolly represent orthodoxies presented to them by teachers, church ministers and other Sis Dolly columns. What is interesting, however, is the stress on individual, rather than communal achievement, and on education as a vehicle for realising, rather than thwarting aspiration.

All the letters, except one, utilised the personal voice of the problem page genre. However, one letter from a boy at Lillian Ngoyi presents a more impersonal view of education and futures:

> Dear Dolly—My only problem is education. I still think it must be improved. Particularly in rural areas where is a shortage of resources . . . and there are no sport facilities because we all know sport is part of education . . . What are they doing for us to keep us going to school? We need equipment to have best education money can buy and for a better future. *I want to emphasize that education is the key to a better success.* . . .
>
> [Sis Dolly replies:] . . . To be honest I wish our government to realise that we don't need weapons, we need to be educated . . . Just imagine if that money they used on weapons was invested on this project we are going to turn *this dream* to reality. (Boy, age unknown, grade unknown, Lillian Ngoyi; italics added)

Despite its difference in tone from the other letters, here too we see the familiar connection between education and self-realisation, with a stress on success and dreams fulfilled that schooling is believed to bring. This contrasts with the sociological literature discussed above, which is much more pessimistic on this theme. The children thus appropriate symbolic meanings about education, that to date have been largely ignored in the scholarship on South African schooling.

A second major theme in the letters is the importance of parents and family. In virtually all the problems the setting is the family, and Sis Dolly generally urges that the young protagonists should turn to members of their family for help with their problems. In these two examples from Dingiswayo School a girl and a boy experience pressures from peers and difficulties at home. But in both instances the solution suggested by Sis Dolly is to talk to parents, and to realise personal aspiration through this relationship *combined with* commitment to schooling:

My mother is treating me like a baby. When I get back from school I have to hurry and I don't get a chance to walk back with my friends ... [My mother doesn't] let me sing in the school choir because the practice ends late ... I realise that my mother thinks that I spend all that time with boys but it's not like that. I know how to behave well like a woman. ...

[Sis Dolly writes:] ... *You must explain to your mother that you sometimes have to stay after school and study* ... You should do things that will make your mother happy so that she can let you do a lot of other things and let you study with your friends. You should be happy that your mother wants you to be respected in the community ... so that you can have a bright future. (Girl, 16, Grade 10, Dingiswayo; translated from Zulu; italics added)

I live with my father and my elder brother. My father do not have much time with me. He has not given me advice since I was born. I do not blame him though because he is working for me. My problem is that peer pressure is more than I can take. I have 6 girlfriends ... I have slept with 5 of them ... and my home boys praise me. They think I am one big charmer ... However I am not sure whether I like what I am doing. Last month I told myself that I am going to abstain.

[Sis Dolly writes:] ... You are going through adolescence stage ... There is no need to blame yourself. That will make it more worse than it is. ... I am glad that you do realise that being a womaniser is not good. *It is even worse for you because you are a scholar* and you are too young. My advice to you is talk to your father. Try to close the gap between you and him. It's your life. Be in control of it ... (Boy, 16, Grade 10, Dingiswayo; translated from Zulu; italics added)

In both of these examples the imaginary dialogue between child and parent resolves itself with the child seeking the approval of the parent and investing the parent and commitment to study with considerable powers for good.

This is not always the case, however. Parents or other close relatives are, in some letters, a source of pain. There are letters about fathers who are violent to children, a long account by a young girl of how she was treated as a servant by her mother and other relatives during the many months her grandmother lay dying in their house, anxieties about parents' responses to pregnancy and the stresses brought about when parents separate. But time and again Sis Dolly enjoins:

You must come together as a family and talk about the issue.

Mom was the first person I should have talked to [in response to a letter about sexual abuse by a father].

Sit down and talk to your aunt.

You should try to talk to one of your parents [in response to a letter about not having money to buy sanitary pads].

You must take it easy and relax and think positively. Your father is trying to close that gap ... Tell your father that you love him.

Only in two letters did Sis Dolly suggest talking to teachers, rather than parents, and in two she recommends an approach to a counsellor. It is evident that in children's stories of their lives, while schooling appears as an abstract process through which one passes to obtain success and realise dreams, it is in the real negotiated relationships with parents that children believe the conditions are laid down for them to go to school and prosper.

While it is not surprising that parents are a major feature of youth accounts of their lives, their important role points up how little relations between family and school have been considered in the sociology of education in South Africa. In the handful of studies on this theme parents have been identified as tyrannical and unsupportive. Morrell's study of corporal punishment in sixteen Durban schools highlighted how most parents still beat their children (Morrell, 2001*c*). A national survey of adolescent sexual behaviour drew attention to the inability or refusal of parents to talk to their children about emotional and sexual problems (NPPHCN/UNICEF, 1997). In contrast, the letters indicate working-class youth constructing accounts where relations with parents (rather than teachers, community organisations or peers) are believed to provide the emotional resources for study. Education is invested with meaning as a process through which they can surmount material disadvantage and their feelings of inadequacy linked to class.

The last theme that emerges powerfully from the letters is that of teenage sexuality. The largest number of letters were concerned with romantic relationships and their attendant anxieties, nearly all situated within discourses of normative heterosexuality. Here there are considerable differences in the themes that concern young girls and young boys. The largest proportion of letters from girls were about problems with boyfriends regarding fidelity, whether or not to have sex, whether they are beautiful enough, and the consequences of pregnancy. Four letters reported experiences of rape. By contrast, a much smaller proportion of letters from boys were concerned with sexuality. Those that were raised problems about the pressures that came from having a large number of sexual partners, difficulties boys experienced in attracting girlfriends, and the consequences of a girlfriend becoming pregnant. One confided a homosexual experience with a classmate. Interestingly, however, although the problems varied widely and showed sharp differences with regard to masculinity and femininity, the answers given by Sis Dolly were very uniform: attend to your schooling and confide in your parents if you can.

A striking feature, however, is that in any one letter there are multiple gendered perspectives concerning sexuality, which itself becomes a vehicle for expressing class and race. Here is an example from Dingiswayo School:

> I am a girl of 18 years. I was seriously abused in the past. I was in grade I and I was 6 years old.
>
> This started like this. Some boy took my lunch money at school. If I had some lunch he ate it. He was in grade 4. He looked much older.
>
> I was scared to tell them at home because my dad is very aggressive. When time went by he [the school boy] said I'm his girlfriend . . . One day when I was walking to school he took me into the woods. He asked me if [I knew] anything about sex. I said no. He said we'd do it anyway even if I don't know he'll teach me. He took my panties off and raped me for several times. I was afraid to tell because I didn't know what he was doing to me. This went on for quite some time until my teacher noticed that there's something wrong . . . This still hurts because my mom says I'm a whore and I started [at] a young age. She says that boys are using me and I'm their ball . . . This boy has come back again and wants me to be his girl because he loved me a long time ago. He apologised for what he did and said that he is a grown man now. This is really troubling me because I got raped again last year.
>
> Now I don't know if I got the virus. I'm terrified. I tried killing myself but didn't succeed. (Grade 11)

In this letter a boy has abused a girl and she has suffered long-term trauma. But later he says he wants her to 'be his girl' and apologises. The girl describes the boy in at least these two guises and herself as victim, but also as a confused lover. Her mother is portrayed as accusatory, but also as potentially forgiving. Sis Dolly, having said that 'your mother shows clearly that she doesn't care about her children. A mother like that is killing our nation', advises her (fictional) self that she and her mother should 'sit and talk to each other'.

The multiple perspectives here present a new dimension in thinking about teenage sexuality. Much of the research on this theme in Southern and Eastern Africa has been conducted under the shadow of the HIV/AIDS epidemic and has sought to understand gendered features of teenage sexuality and ways to talk openly with teenagers so that they can have knowledge and take appropriate action (Morrell et al., 2001; Kaim, 2002; Burns, 2002). However, missing from this work has been an acknowledgement that teenage girls may be both the victims of sexual violence, and for complex reasons complicit with it (Kent, 2002). The source of their complicity may lie in their family relationships, an area about which we know virtually nothing. It may also be that aspects of race and class are affirmed through certain sexualised identities, themselves linked to shifting family and community forms and insecure labour market conditions.

Conclusion

The themes which emerged from the children's writings contrast with issues addressed in the sociology of education literature on South Africa. Young people, invited to express opinions, frame their aspirations for themselves in terms of a future offered through the institution of schooling. They encourage themselves not to 'lose hope' and to attend to their studies. This contrasts with the sociological literature on equity in education, which focuses on the lack of resources, and race, class and gender divisions in the education system. The young people in these two schools wish for any education, any certificate which they see as the way out of poverty and hardship.

Young people portray their education and social relationships as mediated not through organisations of civil society, community or forms of the state, but through families. While early feminist scholarship in South Africa noted links between patriarchy and race and class hierarchies, scant attention was paid to relations within families. This theme has been largely ignored in writings on race, class and education before and after 1994. The letters to Sis Dolly point to the need for a careful scholarship of South African families and education, sensitive to issues raised by thinking about race, class and gender.

The narratives that youth make about sexuality and the mutability of subject positions highlight the complexity of representation. Much research on teenage sexuality in South Africa to date has worked with issues of grave concern, like the high levels of sexual violence. But there is also a need to learn about social relations through these accounts. We suspect the children's narratives which stress mutability are important not only as discursive forms, but also because they have real referents and may have much to tell us about class and race and the way these relations are enacted.

From the meanings the young people struggle over in the letters, it is evident that they position schooling and the family as transformative spaces. A major common discourse constructs study, schooling and parental support as the means through which the hardships of young people's daily experiences of race, class and gender division will be overcome. But the youth in this study portray social relationships much less in terms of class and race, and much more in terms of sexuality and gender. This may be an outcome of the development of democracy in South Africa which has led to changes in the education system. While these are not extensive, they appear to have created conditions for working-class children to articulate aspirations in which individual hopes and the needs of their families play a major role. These letters suggest working-class children do not wish to be 'comrades in struggle', or victims of the HIV virus, but someone 'learned', who can 'think about going forward'. We need to attend to theorising these accounts of social relations, revisiting our older ideas in the light of the concerns of Mandela's grandchildren.

Sexualities and Resistance: Queer(y)ing Identity and Discourse in Education

Elizabeth Atkinson

[...]

Introduction

Where do you start when you start with silence? In spite of the growing literature in queer theory, the long history of gender studies as a subject in its own right and the increasing recognition of heteronormative forces in educational contexts by a small but significant body of educational researchers, there is a deafening silence on sexualities in education. The sort of sexual anonymity demanded of teachers and researchers within all phases of education is representative of a wider silencing, or neutralising, of identity for those involved in the teaching profession, which contrasts oddly with the discourses of sexuality embedded in the interactions of children and young people within and beyond the context of schooling. While colleagues in sociology, cultural studies and psychology continue a long tradition of both teaching and researching sexuality, those of us who are 'inside' education, and particularly those involved in working with teachers and children, find that attempts to address these issues within our own field are met with anxious questions, raised eyebrows or ribnudging jokes, along with an assumption that research and teaching in this area can only be a sort of personal flag-waving that has little to do with serious academic study. This [chapter] aims to offer a recognition of sexualities as a form of resistance to these assumptions and as a way of developing a significant but under-recognised dimension of what bell hooks (1994) describes as 'education as the practice of freedom'.

On Writing, Toothache, Trains and Sexuality

I planned this [chapter] on a train, and wrote it with a toothache. Why is this relevant to a [chapter] on sexualities and resistance? There are three reasons. The first is my dilemma over whether or not to take *Schooling Sexualities* (Epstein and Johnson, 1998) to read in the dentist's waiting room. After a tussle between pride and fear, I stuffed it into a bag and rehearsed my answers to curious questions all the way to the dentist's surgery, where it remained safely hidden for the duration of my visit. The second is the insult, 'Faggot', shouted by a young man to the bartender as he came into my carriage on the recent rail journey during which I was planning this chapter, and my subsequent public defence of the bartender's right to complain: my first public involvement in a homophobic incident. Together, these two snapshots present two of the key reasons, silence and stigma, why we need to insist that sexualities become a site of open inquiry in education. The third reason is the very fact that this sort of

Elizabeth Atkinson, (2004), 'Sexualities and Resistance: Queer(y)ing Identity and Discourse in Education', in J. Satterthwaite, E. Atkinson, and W. Martin, (eds.), *Educational Counter-Cultures: Confrontations, Images, Vision* (Stoke-on-Trent: Trentham Books).

intrusion of the private into the public arena, my reference to my own experiences, especially if they concern intimate or personal events, is seen as inappropriate, excessive, and indulgent.

As Debbie Epstein (1994) points out, it is exactly this refusal to cross the boundary between public and private life that maintains and perpetuates the status of sexuality in education as silent and silenced. Liz Kelly (1992) states that this public–private divide has been maintained by the distinction between an authoritarian political stance in relation to *social policy*—that is, private life as constructed by authoritarian populism—and the emphasis on freedom of choice in the *economic sphere*—that is, public life as constructed by economic liberalism. And it is by maintaining this public–private divide, by reinforcing these secrets and signs hidden behind silences, that we allow ourselves to keep up the pretence of the *absence* of sexuality in education, while its embodiment in the day-to-day educational experience of ourselves and our students impacts on everything we do. As Kelly puts it: 'sexuality in the late twentieth century [and, I would add, the early twenty-first] is both visible yet invisible, spoken about yet silenced, designated as private yet pervasively public' (1992: 26–27). I could go on. I could cite the warning of a colleague that my focus on sexuality in a paper to be presented at a British Educational Research Association conference would attract unwanted press attention; the nudges and winks received by another colleague in response to her announcement of a research focus on sexuality and sex education; the statement from an anxious headteacher, when approached about researching attitudes in his school towards gay, lesbian and bisexual students, that 'It's like asking about wife battering'; the nervous and excited *frisson* that ran through my group of fifty final year Early Childhood Studies undergraduates when I showed them the gay kiss between two teenage boys in *Beautiful Thing* (Channel Four Corporation, 1996), one of the few British films in existence (outside the field of pornography) which portrays a same-sex romance between teenagers.

But why is it that if we choose, as educators, whether in schools, colleges or universities, to resist the silence, we are branded as having an unnatural and inappropriate interest in issues beyond the realm of propriety? Don't just take my word that it happens: here's the word of the President of the Midwest Sociological Society, Joane Nagel:

> The study of sexuality has been a stigmatised one in sociology and elsewhere. In the past two years that I have been working in this area, I have been challenged and heard skeptical comments from a number of colleagues about my research, comments whose text and subtext questioned my motives, my sexuality, and the value of my work on such a 'frivolous' topic, one so marginal to the 'important' problems with which sociology should be grappling. (2000: 13)

And if it is so 'frivolous' and 'unimportant', why is it that it pervades every area of educational life? 'Gender' has become such a respectable area of inquiry that the key figures of second wave feminism find themselves at the core of university reading lists across a host of disciplines whilst sexualities remain silenced, marginalised and taboo, supported by repeated moral panics fuelled in recent years in the UK, first by the Conservative backlash in the 1980s and early 1990s against the 'Loony Left' (Jones and Mahony, 1989; Epstein, 1994; Smith, 1994) and then by the determination of New Labour to appeal to a wide spectrum of the electorate to endorse its centrist policies.

Sites of Education; Sites of Sexuality

As Epstein and Johnson state in the introduction to *Schooling Sexualities* (1998: 2):

> As places of every-day-life activity as well as public or state institutions, schools are sites where sexual and other identities are developed, practiced and actively produced. Pupils, but also teachers and to a lesser extent other participants (parents, usually mothers, and other carers for example), are 'schooled' there, as gendered and sexual beings. Sexual and other social identities, as possible ways of living, are produced in relation to the cultural repertoires and institutional conditions of schooling.

Kelly echoes this view (1992: 27):

> Whatever conservative ideologues might say, schools are places where sex talk, sexual behaviour, sexual relationships, sexual abuse and harassment, sexual identity, sexual divisions and sexual politics are threaded throughout the warp and weft of interactions between students, staff and students and staff. This reality exists alongside the cautious inclusion or the deliberate exclusion of sexuality in the formal taught curriculum.

This silencing of sexualities is, of course, social and political as well as anti-educational. Epstein and Johnson draw a link between concepts of sexuality and concepts of nationhood, whereby only that form of sexuality which is normalised and accepted both within and beyond educational settings, constitutes legitimate 'Englishness'. The links between notions of 'race' and notions of sexuality are also explored by Anna Marie Smith (1994), Joane Nagel (2000) and bell hooks (1989). Epstein and Johnson identify the ways in which this sort of construction of nationhood extends beyond boundaries of race, to the exclusion of any sort of sexuality which does not meet the heterosexual norm, while Epstein, O'Flynn and Telford (2003) explore the naturalisation of heterosexuality and the silencing of transgressive sexualities from the early years to post-compulsory educational settings. The lesson to be learnt from all these studies is that by continuing to close our eyes to the implicit sexualities embedded in the formal and informal processes of schooling, and by maintaining silence in relation to sexualities in educational research, we contribute to the perpetuation of dominant discourses of sexuality. This not only denies significant aspects of teachers' and learners' identities, but leads to very real physical risks for those whose sexual identity, however silenced, is perceived as transgressive (see, for example, Trenchard and Warren, 1984; Mason and Palmer, 1996).

There is nothing new, of course, about researchers' concern over the hegemony of specific sexual norms. In 1989, for example, Carol Jones and Pat Mahony brought together accounts of the embodied nature of schooling and of the promotion of specific forms of sexuality within educational contexts, and expressed their concern (p. ix) that schools and education authorities fail to recognise 'the links between equal opportunities (gender) and issues of sexuality', and between certain forms of hegemonic masculinity and sexual violence. They make a clear link between the state's control of sexuality through education and the social control of women and girls, through what they describe as 'a highly laundered and mythologised version of heterosexuality' (p. xii). In a more recent study, Mac an Ghaill (1994) identifies the carefully restricted boundaries of masculinity through which boys learn to be men in the context of schooling.

Francis and Skelton (2001:10) identify 'the problematics of heterosexual discourses for heterosexual students and teachers' as a current and contentious issue in schooling. This goes beyond issues of sexism and sexual oppression, to the recognition, or lack of recognition, of the presence of sexuality within the processes of education, particularly in relation to motivation and passion for teaching and learning. We are not only dealing with discourses of oppression here, then, but also with discourses of *desire*.

Normalisation and Resistance

The conflation of gender, sex and desire within the heterosexual matrix (Butler, 1999) renders *all* gendered behaviours in educational sites sexual, whether implicitly or explicitly. And the 'heterosexual assumption' (Foucault, 1979; Weeks *et al.*, 2001) leads to the construction of heterosexuality as a cultural norm, carrying its opposite, deviance, like a shadow: 'normalcy becomes produced and sexualised as heterosexuality, that is . . . normalcy becomes inserted into sex . . . the term "heteronormativity" begins to get at how the production of deviancy is intimately tied to the very possibility of normalcy' (Britzman, 1995). This is not, of course, unique to schooling. As Valerie Walkerdine's analysis of the sexualisation of young girls in popular culture shows (1997), classed and sexualised notions of childhood, and specifically girlhood, are deeply embedded in the representations of media and popular culture, and contribute to the maintenance of certain forms of masculinity through their opposition to a subordinate femininity. Drawing on Foucault (1979), Weeks, Heaphy and Donovan (2001) state: 'the apparatus of sexuality lies at the heart of the workings of power in modernity, and the heterosexual assumption, based on a binarism of domination and submission, is central to this.' Mac an Ghaill (1994), drawing on the work of Wolpe (1988), emphasises the fluidity and complexity of this productive process, and argues that gender and sexualities are constructed, reconstructed and negotiated in specific sites and in response to specific circumstances. They are also constructed against, and with, a range of other discourses, both public and private, a point I have explored myself elsewhere

(Atkinson, 2001). And if gender and sexualities are constructed in, through, against and with discourses, then they can be turned back against those discourses as forms of resistance.

Part of this resistance might lie in a greater recognition of sexual boundary crossing, whereby marginalised and transgressive sexualities might be re-stated as productive and powerful rather than destructive and threatening. Judith Butler explores this idea of boundary crossing in relation to the work of Mary Douglas (1969): 'Douglas suggests that all social systems are vulnerable at their margins, and that all margins are accordingly considered dangerous. If the body is synecdochal for the social system per se or a site in which open systems converge, then any kind of unregulated permeability constitutes a site of pollution and endangerment' (Butler, 1999: 168).

Pillow quotes a school administrator she interviewed in the course of her research on teen pregnancy as stating, 'Bodies are dangerous' (2003: 145). A greater awareness of how boundaries are inscribed on and in bodies in educational settings, coupled with a desire to question and interrogate sexualised norms, might open up a whole new field in the realm of what Andy Sparkes (1996) calls 'body projects'.

Interrupted Body Projects and Flexible Narratives of the Self

What I would like to suggest, drawing on the work of Sparkes, is that what we are experiencing in education, both through silenced sexualities and through the dominance of normalising forces, is the continuing effect of a series of 'interrupted body projects'. This means that attempts to create, negotiate or validate our sexual identity come up against barriers which constrain and limit us, and which reduce our capacities as teachers and learners. While Sparkes focuses on teachers whose identity has been interrupted by bodily injury or the prospect of decreasing fitness, I would like to broaden this concept of 'body projects' to embrace the wider field of teachers and learners in general. We are *all* experiencing 'interrupted body projects', by virtue of being involved in education.

Sparkes' analysis (1996: 181) identifies the way in which the absence of a range of narratives from which teachers might choose to represent their bodily identity leads to the construction of *disciplined* and *docile* bodies that, according to Frank (1991), become predictable through their regimentation. He goes on to state: 'there is a constant need for identities to be reflexively created, recreated and sustained by the individual through flexible narratives of the self' (Sparkes, 1996: 184). Sparkes' concern, however, is that these flexible narratives are not available to those working in educational contexts, and that there is an urgent need to interrogate this silence: 'This would necessitate a consideration of the manner in which body stories operate to serve both conservative functions that maintain the dominant order, and also how they might have the potential to act as sites of resistance so as to transform individual lives and cultures within teaching' (1996: 186).

Body Projects in Educational Settings

While the sexual identities of teachers, particularly female teachers, and researchers, have been neutralised in educational contexts, a rash of recent significant research has demonstrated the *sexualised* nature of the gendered exchanges between pupils and pupils, and between pupils and teachers (Mac an Ghaill, 1994; Epstein, 1997; Kehily and Nayak, 1997; Epstein and Johnson, 1998; Renold, 1999, 2000, 2002; Francis and Skelton, 2001; Halstead and Waite, 2001; Reay, 2001; Atkinson, 2002).

This recent research literature abounds with telling examples. To cite just a few, Diane Reay (2001) describes how the children in her study made a clear distinction between 'girlies', 'heavily involved in gender work which even at the age of seven inscribed traditional heterosexual relations' and therefore made them legitimate targets of sexual harassment and 'nice girls', hard-working, well-behaved and therefore, as traitors to the heterosexual norm, constructed by some of the boys as 'a polluting, contagious "other"'(p. 159). Emma Renold (2000) describes the preoccupation of the ten-to-eleven year old girls in her study with physical appearance, and the difficulties they had in negotiating a public identity that was 'tarty, but not too tarty' (p. 313); and Kehily and Nayak (1997), researching the role of humour in the production of heterosexual hierarchies among teenagers, describe the way in which 'young women and subordinate males can be seen as targets for comic displays which frequently blur the boundaries between humour and harassment' (p. 81). A particularly interesting dimension of this research is what it reveals about the differential status of male and female sexualities for adults in schools. While Epstein and Johnson (1998), for example, highlight the invisibility and neutralisation of women teachers through specified codes of dress and behaviour, the work of Skelton (2001), Francis and Skelton (2001) and Swain (2000, 2002) shows how visibly sexualised masculinities play a major part in the gendered behaviour of both male teachers and male pupils in primary schools.

A significant body of research has linked the dominance of particular forms of hegemonic masculinity within educational settings to sexual violence, linking Jones and Mahony's collection of women's narratives (1989) to more recent explorations of the violent discourses of children and young people in school, especially boys (see, for example, Kehily and Nayak, 1997; Halstead and Waite, 2001). As Swain puts it, (2000: 96): 'Although [hegemonic masculinity] does not necessarily involve physical violence, it is often underwritten by the threat of violence'. This is echoed in the work of Halstead and Waite (2001), who identify the way in which sexual violence forms a theme in boys' sexualised joking in the context of sex education lessons. While Halstead and Waite recognise the use of humour as a defence mechanism among these boys, they are also aware of the darker undertones of these violent discourses and their relationship to certain dominant forms of heterosexuality.

Kelly states (1992:37):

> Each time it is raised, just what this so called 'natural' family and 'normal' sexuality consists of must be highlighted: supporting 'traditional values' means supporting, rather than challenging, the existence of child sexual abuse, domestic violence, rape, sexual assault and sexual harassment. We need approaches to sexuality in education that enable children and young people [and teachers and researchers] to question, rather than accept, these realities.

Embodied Learners and Leaky Bodies

Ironically, where sex and sexuality *have* been made the explicit focus of government policy and/or classroom teaching, the aim has been largely to reduce the effects of what has been perceived as premature sexual activity, with the specific objective of reducing teenage pregnancy figures. As Kelly puts it (1992: 32–33, drawing on Lenskyj (1990)): 'The implicit message in the traditional "plumbing and prevention" approach is that it is girls' knowledge and activity which is both the problem and the target'. This objective has tended to obscure wider aims for a broadening of sexuality education, although there is the beginning of a recognition, embedded in the Department for Education and Employment guidelines on Sex and Relationship Education (DfEE, 2000) of the need to support and reflect young people's developing sexual identity, whatever form it might take. In contrast to this liberal approach, the neutralising of young women's and men's sexual bodies within the school environment, through the silencing of discourses of sexuality and desire, denies their sexual maturity, and is deeply embedded within discourses of class and power. Pillow reminds us of this (1997, 2003) when she considers the classed nature of state teen pregnancy programmes, in which girls identified as having low socio-economic status are constructed as having 'made mistakes' and as needing to demonstrate their potential for responsible behaviour to school and society. In the context of these programmes, sexual activity is perceived as lower-class, and not something in which middle-class girls are expected to indulge. This assumption plays a significant part in the way in which teenage girls choose to use their bodies as sites of resistance (Pillow, 1997; Hey, 1997; Epstein and Johnson, 1998).

Sexualities and Resistance: Queer(y)ing Identity and Discourse in Education

Nagel (2000: 3) draws our attention to the 'sometimes conspicuous, sometime concealed ways in which sexuality underpins the logic of social life, political policies, and personal and public political decisions' and suggests that the interrogation of sexuality as 'the intimate substructure of social life' (p. 2) offers 'the same promise that unveiling gender did a generation ago—the promise to reveal to us our own presumptions and prejudices and to allow us to think the unthinkable' (p. 3). Similarly, Leslie Bloom

(1999: 331) states: 'interpreting sexuality must be as salient to educational qualitative research as interpreting gender, race, and ethnicity have become'.

As Butler (1999) and hooks (1994) remind us, harnessing sexuality as a site of resistance challenges the Cartesian dualism which for centuries has rationalised the separation of mind and body. As hooks puts it (1994: 192): 'Entering the classroom determined to erase the body and give ourselves over more fully to the mind, we show by our beings how deeply we have accepted the assumption that passion has no place in the classroom'. I have suggested that the recognition of sexualities and sexual identities constitutes a valid and valuable form of resistance to the normalisation of identity which constitutes an often implicit, and sometimes explicit, part of the grammar of teaching and learning. In seeking to promote a safe and neutral environment for the promotion of learning, we have generated an educational world in which real, embodied selves have little place. In doing so, we have sanctioned and institutionalised the normalisation of nothingness, the assumption that those who teach are not actually people at all, and that those who learn can only resume their full identities once they leave the classroom. At the same time, we turn a blind eye to the explicit sexualisation of young children's identity, especially that of girls, through fashion, toys and popular culture and to the ways in which this affects the development and reinforcement of specific bounded, sexed and gendered identities from the earliest years of schooling.

I would like to suggest, however, that queer(y)ing identity and discourse in education allows us to achieve three possibilities: (1) a recognition that sexuality—and its place in education—is deeply political; (2) a refusal to erase the body in conducting education as the practice of freedom; and (3) a resistance to the unquestioned dominance of often oppressive sexual norms.

There is hope for the future.

'There Is Something about Julia'—Symptoms, Categories, and the Process of Invoking ADHD in the Swedish School: A Case Study

Eva Hjörne and Roger Säljö

Introduction

Categorization is fundamental to human existence. It penetrates every context of collective social action and individual reasoning. We simply cannot describe, reflect on, or deal with reality without invoking categories and, thus indirectly, systems and traditions of categorization by means of which we render events and objects intelligible. Categories are codified in language and largely invisible to us. We treat them as transparent and rarely run into situations where we have to doubt their relevance. Many categories undergo naturalization (Bowker and Star 1999: 294), and appear as self-evident, even though they may in fact have been problematic in the past. But there is also the opposite process. Categories referring to race, ethnicity, or gender have passed unnoticed as indicative of a natural state of affairs in the past, but later they emerged as cultural constructions contingent on a certain social order and/ or world view. And as such, they can be contested.

In a sociocultural perspective (Wertsch 1991, 1998), categories serve as mediational means, as cultural tools that are fundamental to our making sense of what we encounter. They exist in the reasoning of individuals as well as between people in social interaction. Categories are not just names for things and relationships, they do a real job by signifying and informing us about how to classify and act in specific contexts. Social action is contingent on classifications, they are essential in the 'doing' of social life, to use ethnomethodological parlance (Heritage 1984). 'We hang murderers, we lock up the insane man, we free the victim of circumstances, we pin a medal on the hero', as Hayakawa (1965: 217) puts it. And we argue by means of such tools. Are the actions committed by a political and military elite in a region in a state of war to be construed as a 'heroic defence' of the country against enemies, or as 'genocide' and instances of 'crimes against humanity'? At the time of writing, this is exactly what is being argued about at the International Court in the Hague.

'" There is something about Julia" — Symptoms, catogories, and the process of invoking ADHD in the Swedish School: A Case Study', *Journal of Language, Identity and Education* (2004) 3,1, 1–24.

In institutional settings, categories and classifications are central as they mediate between individuals and collectives. The social worker or the officer at the employment agency uses classifications of people and their situations in order to determine whether they are entitled to specific kinds of support. The issue of the interplay between categories and institutional action is classical in social science (cf. Mäkitalo and Säljö 2002). In the present study, this problem will be addressed within the context of how schools categorize and deal with children, who, for some reason, find it difficult to adapt to the norms and expectations of the institutional activities that by tradition are offered in such settings. The main focus of this chapter is on analysing how categories are introduced in institutional practices as resources for making decisions and talking about life at school, and what implications they have for the children and for the school.

At present, biomedical, psychiatric, and neuropsychological categories offering neuropsychiatric diagnoses play an important role in schools in many countries, including Sweden, where this line of research has been very active. Labels such as MBD (minimal brain dysfunction), DAMP (deficit in attention, motor control, and perception), ADHD (attention deficit and hyperactivity disorder),[1] Aspergers, dyslexia, dyscalculia, etc. are used widely in schools as categories for classifying children, for organizing teaching and learning opportunities, and for the distribution of economic and other kinds of resources. This practice has resulted in a rapid increase in the number of children in Sweden who are categorized as in some sense handicapped. Kadesjö (1998, 2000), a specialist with a medical background, claims that 21 per cent of all schoolchildren have some kind of neuropsychiatric problem (1998: 799). Considering that the number of people who have 'classical' handicaps (physical handicaps, blindness, deafness, etc.) is but a fraction of this (about or slightly below 2 per cent[2]), these claims regarding the relative frequency of neuropsychiatric disorders are dramatic. If correct, there will be profound effects on school policy and school practices, as we will return to.

The aim of this chapter is to analyse the *in situ* use of diagnoses of this kind within the Swedish school. This implies that we are not taking a stand on the controversial issues of the nature and aetiology of these conditions, or whether these diagnoses can be seen as valid and reliable indicators of identifiable medical and/or psychological conditions. In this chapter we will focus on how the neuropsychiatric classifications are used in the school setting, and in particular how they are introduced as categories relevant for understanding what are perceived as problems in the daily practices. The latter is our primary research question. We base our analyses on audio-recorded data from institutionalized meetings where professionals in a school discuss and make decisions on how to handle situations when children are reported as having difficulties accommodating to school practices. In our empirical work, we have followed the regular meetings of the pupil welfare team (PWT) in a Swedish comprehensive school during one year.

Classification Systems as Institutional Artefacts

> The question, 'What is it really?' 'What is its right name?' is a nonsense question [. . .] one that is not capable of being answered. [. . .] When we name something, then, we are classifying. *The individual object or event we are naming, of course, has no name and belongs to no class until we put it in one* [. . .]. What we call things and where we draw the line between one class of things and another depend upon the interest we have and the purposes of the classification. [. . .] Most intellectual problems are, ultimately, problems of classification and nomenclature. (Hayakawa 1965: 215–20)

Categories emerge as outcomes of the activity that the philosopher Nelson Goodman (1978) refers to as 'kind-making'. Categories and classifications are relative to human practices, they are embedded in various discourses, and they *re*-present the world in manners that are relevant for a certain activity. They enable shared understandings among people operating in social practices, who can communicate efficiently by identifying objects and events in standard terms (cf. Goodwin and Opper 1992). Animals, for example, are classified in one way by the meat industry, in another way by the leather industry, in a third manner by a zoologist, in a fourth manner by a conservationist, and in still a different way by an economist. Categories are the basic working tools of institutional actors in their mundane and undramatic daily activities. As Douglas (1986) points out, institutions 'think' in terms of categories. Thus, the social worker, the bank manager, the physician and many others, rely on categories when analysing a situation and when making a decision.

In school, which is one of society's oldest institutions catering to the needs of the entire population, categories referring to entities such as age, abilities, handicaps, academic subjects, and many other dimensions have played, and continue to play, an important role at many levels. They are used when discussing the practices pursued in such settings as well as in our argumentation about the objectives and responsibilities of schooling (Mehan 1992). Calhoun (1973), for instance, gives an interesting illustration of how the shift from one category ('teaching problems') to a different one ('learning problems') in the United States during the nineteenth century was a critical element in what was to be a radical change in how schools defined their responsibilities. Thus, during the eighteenth century and well into the nineteenth, 'schoolmasters' had 'teaching problems, but children seemed not to have what the twentieth century would call "learning problems"'. Thus, and as a concrete illustration, 'whatever blocks arose in the way of transmitting simple reading and arithmetic to children, the people who reported these blocks almost never blamed them on stupidity or dullness' (p. 72). As soon as the ideas of early intelligence testing began to penetrate institutionalized schooling, 'learning problems' entered the stage as the preferred category in terms of which responses by groups of children to the activities characteristic of schools were understood. By and large, the problems came to be localized in the child and seen as indicative of a lack of (usually innate) intellectual resources. The subsequent development of the intelligence test naturalized this assumption and made it almost invisible in many school systems (cf. Stevenson and Stigler (1992: 97)), who discuss the differences between American and Japanese schools (and parents) when it comes to using assumed intellectual capacities among children as explanatory factors of school success).

The critical factor we point to is, thus, the circularity between the categories we use and how we perceive the world. This circularity implies that 'discourses do not simply describe the social world', rather 'they bring phenomena into sight' (Parker 1990: 191). Or, even more strongly, discourses and categories are best conceived as 'practices that systematically form the objects of which they speak' (Foucault 1972: 49). Attending to categories, and the manner in which they constitute phenomena in institutional settings, thus, is an important research task in modern society.

Naming Diversity in School—Ideologies in Action

In the context of schooling, the categories used for describing various groups have changed over the years. In Sweden, the compulsory school attendance law appeared in the middle of the nineteenth century. As a consequence, a large number of pupils, many from families with little or no prior exposure to schooling as an institutional activity, entered the classroom. Not surprisingly, a range of new problems arose. Reports from frustrated teachers fuelled the debate about how to bring order to classrooms through various strategies that would imply segregating pupils into those who fitted in and those who were to be given special treatment or even excluded (Trent 1994; Sundqvist 1994). To manage this task, classifications that could serve as instruments for making distinctions between pupils were urgently needed. The categories produced during this period to a large extent reflect what Hacking (1986) refers to as the 'analyse moral'. Children were described by means of terms grounded in religious and moral assumptions of what constituted normality and deviance. Thus, and as has been described by Sundqvist (1994) and Börjesson (1997), one finds categories such as vicious, lazy, slow, nail-biters, sons/daughters of vagrants, and so on for describing children who did not fit into the system.

Categories generated from the psychological discourse of ability testing subsequently replaced these terms. Schools for 'idiots' and 'feeble children' were launched, and psychometric tests such as the famous Stanford-Binet and Terman-Merrill tests were widely used as tools for sorting pupils. The categories that emerged from this psychometric breakthrough were diverse and included a fine-grained set of concepts, especially for describing the lower end of the scale. Terms such as feeble-minded, mentally deficient, ill-balanced, idiot, imbecile, moron, moral imbecile, subnormal, mentally retarded were among those suggested and used in practice. Since some of these terms soon after their introduction became pejorative, new ones were introduced. Each new classification was supposed to improve on the previous one used for, more or less, the same type of characteristic. The point of this discursive technology, some authors argue, 'was to control difficult children, divert them away from schools' and send them 'into institutions or regimens of treatment' (Hacking 1999: 111). As a consequence, various kinds of remedial classes and special schools increased dramatically during the first fifty years of the twentieth century (Ohlander 1956; Trent 1994).

In our opinion, the use of categories such as ADHD (or, in Sweden, the equivalent DAMP) must be related to the changes in public schooling in Sweden. The nine-year comprehensive school was introduced in the decades following the Second World War. The ideological premise was that it was supposed to be a school catering to the needs of the entire population and it should operate without streaming.[3] All pupils should fit in, even those who were previously separated into various types of remedial classes and special clinics. Another important feature of this transformation was that drop-outs were not tolerated. Considering that previously only a minority of children would proceed beyond Grade 6 (38 per cent of an age cohort at the end of 1940s, cf. Lindensjö and Lundgren 2000), this was a radical change in expectations regarding schools. This implies that a broad variation of abilities and interests on the part of children was represented in the same classroom. This heterogeneity, of course, was a pedagogical challenge, and inevitably once again introduces the issue of how to handle differences in academic performance, motivation, social background, and so on among the children.

So, the interesting question arises, where does one look for the categories that will be used to debate, analyse, and work with diversity? The immediate predecessor of ADHD/DAMP was MBD (Minimal Brain Dysfunction) (see Gillberg 1991 for an in-depth account of the transition from MBD to ADHD/DAMP). The use of MBD, a brain injury so small it could not be detected when examining the brain, represents a return to biomedical categories and explanations as the more dominant voice in a living tradition of argumentation oscillating between biological, social, and moral/religious positions (Billig 1987; Shotter 1993; Mäkitalo 2002). During the 1960s and 1970s, family relationships and psychological explanatory models had been widely used to account for symptoms such as hyperactivity, concentration difficulties, and school failure. But in the 1970s, the concept of MBD entered the stage and quickly established itself as a diagnosis relevant for explaining children's difficulties in Swedish schools (Hagberg 1975; Rydelius 1999). During the 1980s this concept fell into disrepute in many parts of the world. This process followed a massive critique from researchers arguing that there was no homogeneity in terms of symptoms among the children classified in this manner (Schmidt et al. 1987). New terms were introduced, and these varied somewhat across countries. In Sweden (and some other Scandinavian countries) the term DAMP came to be widely used. In the US, the same syndrome was referred to as ADHD, and in UK the acronym HKD (HyperKinetic Disorder) was adopted.

An important general point to keep in mind is that categories (like all linguistic expressions) can never be absolutely neutral. Communication always implies contextualizing, and in this process perspectivizing is necessary and inevitable. Thus, issues that relate to the 'politics of representation' (Mehan 1993) can always be raised. In our opinion, categorization in the school context should be studied as a practice; it is something that people *do* in order to manage their daily chores. As categories are part of institutional practices, they are also material in their consequences. It matters whether we describe people in one way or the other. The material consequences of categories implies that it is meaningful and relevant to study the use of categories, even if their ontological status may be questioned. Thus, even if many would argue that concepts such as ADHD and DAMP have no reliable or uniform definition (cf. Kärfve 2000, who very explicitly makes this claim), their use in school practices and in the rhetoric about school failure must be attended to. It is a social fact that ADHD/DAMP is part of a living tradition of argumentation and that this syndrome serves as a widely accepted explanation of children's learning disabilities and school performance. ADHD/DAMP as a category, thus, has established itself within schooling, and in this sense it is both a social fact and a resource that is actively used for dealing with problems. It has implications for the manner in which teaching is organized and for the use of limited resources. It will also have consequences for the students' educational career, and obviously, a neuropsychiatric diagnosis, indicative of a brain injury, will play a critical role in identity formation of young people.

Empirical Setting and Method

In our opinion, it is important to highlight the process through which children are diagnosed with ADHD/DAMP. And, as we will show, this is a process. A critical, early phase in the process towards being diagnosed in the Swedish context can be found in the discussions and decisions made in the so-called pupil/student welfare team meeting (PWTM).[4] This is an institutional arena where, amongst other things, various problems are discussed. The participants in the meetings vary somewhat between schools, but generally the principal, the vice-principal, teachers, special teachers, the school psychologist, school nurse, and/or a social worker will be present. In the school we have studied there was also a speech therapist, who would often participate in these meetings.

The institutional procedure for conducting PWTMs implies that one of the participants, for instance a teacher or the school psychologist, decides that problems experienced by a child should be discussed at an upcoming meeting. In the session, the child's situation is presented and decisions are made on how to proceed. This setting, thus, is critical in the sense that it is here that institutional categories and accounting practices will play a decisive role in interpreting what happens in school, and in initiating the kind of process that eventually may result in a child being diagnosed as ADHD/DAMP.

The findings reported derive from a field study. The empirical setting in which the study has been carried out is a school—West Valley Comprehensive School—situated in a village close to a city. The village is in an agricultural area. Most inhabitants live in single-family houses. West Valley has 800 children from preschool to grade 9. About 2 percent of the children are immigrants (which is substantially below the national average).[5] The study is limited to children in grades 1 to 5. There are about 475 pupils in these grades, and seventy-six of these children were discussed in the PWTMs during the school year of 2000–2001, i.e. the period we have followed.

The school has a pupil/student welfare team (PWT), consisting of the principal (PR),[6] the assistant principal (AP), the school-psychologist (SP), the school-nurse (SN), the speech therapist (SE), and the special needs teacher (ST). There are three assistant principals, each of whom is responsible for about six classes. This team meets twice a month for discussions and decision-making about how to handle various kinds of problems. The data used for the present study were generated during these meetings, which we have followed through participant observation over one year. During this year, there were a total of fourteen meetings. These have been audio-recorded and later transcribed. In total, there are 35 hours of recorded material. In addition, some of the conferences involving the parents have been recorded. Field notes were taken throughout the year, and we also have access to the relevant documentation including protocols from PWTM's. Transcription conventions are given in the Appendix. The study reported here was preceded by a pilot in the same school carried out by one of the authors (E.H.). During this pilot study, the contacts with the school and the staff were established. The purpose of the research, i.e. studying how the staff handled children with various problems, was explained. This implies that when the data reported here were collected, the researcher was well known to the staff and the children.

It should also be pointed out that this study follows a process longitudinally. This implies that we did not know at the start what children would be discussed at the PWTMs, nor when the category of ADHD/DAMP would be invoked by members of the team.

Results

Among the seventy-six children (fifty boys and twenty-six girls) who were discussed during the PWTMs during this period, nineteen already had an ADHD/DAMP diagnosis or were thought to have this problem. These children were (the figures in brackets indicate the number of times that each of these children were discussed during the 14 meetings): Julia (10), Axel (9), James (9), Lukas (7), Kenny (6), Robert (5), Peter (5), Karl (4), Patrick (3), Melvin (3), Noa (3), Sandy (3), Tony (3), Jonas (3), Tom (2), Penny (1), Gloria (1), Leo (1), and Frederic (1). The remaining pupils were defined as having various kinds of problems, for example, other medical diagnoses such as Aspergers (three pupils) or dyslexia (twelve) or, alternatively, they were defined as having social/relational problems or more general learning disabilities.

The focus of our study is on scrutinizing how the category of ADHD/DAMP is used and in what situations it is introduced as a resource for understanding and managing the problems experienced in school.

The Process of Invoking ADHD/DAMP

The first step in the process of categorizing pupils is taken in the classroom. The teacher has to report a pupil to the assistant principal, and thus bring the perceived problem to public attention. The next step is that the pupil and his/her problems are discussed in the context of the PWTM. Here, a further decision on how to proceed is made. Various options are available (see Fig. 42.1). One frequent solution is that it is decided that the regular teacher should try to resolve the problem within the normal classroom context. Other options are that it is decided that a special needs teacher should attend to the matter, or that the social authorities should be contacted. But it is also in the context of the PWTM that the suggestion that the problem might be of a neuropsychiatric nature will be voiced publicly and discussed. Following such a suggestion, a decision to go ahead with a full assessment may be taken. Before starting a psychological assessment, however, the parents have to be informed and give their consent (see Fig. 42.2). After the child has been tested, the psychologist informs the parents of the results before reporting back to the PWTM. Here, the team has to decide how to take the matter further. Usually the assistant principal informs the teacher, and the result will sometimes be to have a personal assistant assigned to the student or, alternatively, extra educational staff in the classroom. Another solution, though less frequent, is to transfer the child to a special group in another school. Yet another outcome of this process is that nothing at all happens. The problems disappear from view as far as the PWTM process is concerned.

Figure 42.1 gives an overview of the complexities involved in this process of handling difficulties, which are discussed in the PWTMs. At various stages, the process can go in different directions depending on the problem experienced by the teacher or the child, but also on the traditions and experiences within a particular school. For instance, already at the first and second stages a teacher might define the problem very differently. Similar behaviours in the classroom may be dealt with differently, and they may or may not be reported to the assistant principal.

Classroom	**Teacher**	**Assistant principal**	**PWTM**	**Measures suggested**
a pupil is perceived to have difficulties	reports the problem to his/ her superior for discussion in PWTM	reports the teacher's observations	discussions of how to proceed	a) testing for ADHD/DAMP b) testing for dyslexia/Aspergers c) an extra school-year d) skip a school-year e) learning disability group f) special teaching group g) personal assistant h) social services i) child guidance clinic j) back to teacher's concern
Step 1	Step 2	Step 3	Step 4	Step 5

Fig. 42.1 The institutional process of decision-making in West Valley comprehensive School

Table 42.1 Overview of pupils discussed discussed in the PWTMs

Pupils	Categories used for describing school difficulties		
	ADHD/DAMP	Other problems	TOTAL
Boys	15	35	50
Girls	4	22	26
Total	19	57	76

When it has been decided that the child should preferably be assessed for ADHD/DAMP, additional steps are taken, as shown in Figure 42.2. The first step in this second phase (Step 6) is to gain the parents' consent to test the child, as we have already mentioned. After the child has been assessed and maybe thought to have ADHD/DAMP different solutions, mostly connected to financial resources, are discussed during the PWTM. The proposed measure could be, for instance, to send the child to a special teaching group or to send the child back to the classroom for the teacher to deal with. The latter option implies that the problems are handled as part of the regular school practices.

For our purposes, the critical point is when, and in what circumstances, the ADHD/DAMP concept is invoked in this process by the participants and publicly discussed. What are the problems and behaviors that are considered indicative of this diagnosis? In order to understand this, we turn to the discussion in the PWTM.

'What About the DAMP, Then?'—ADHD/DAMP as a Discursive Category in School

The general purpose of the PWTM is to come to a decision about what to do when children have difficulties and do not fit into the regular system. From an analytical point of view, the discussion can be seen as a series of attempts to classify what is reported in a manner that will resolve the matter by suggesting a solution. In the following excerpt, the team members are discussing Julia, 8 years of age, who reportedly has had problems in accommodating to life in school (and who is the pupil most frequently discussed during this year, in ten meetings of the fourteen, but she did not at the time of discussion have a confirmed diagnosis). The excerpt illustrates the dramaturgy of the most typical manner of arguing in the sense that a series of behaviours and/or events are presented. This is followed by a suggestion that there must be 'something about Julia' or some similar conclusion.

Excerpt 1: *Julia, 8 years old, first meeting*

1. [AP] she finds it difficult to break off a task, she has difficulties in
2. start working, and when she's working she finds it difficult to
3. stop, she has difficulties with [changes]
4. [ST] [mmm]
5. (. . .)[7]
6. [SP] is she able to co-operate [at all now] (?)
7. [AP] [no she has difficulties co-operating
8. as well
9. [AT] she has almost no friends . . . and she can't [subordinate] herself
10. [AP] [mmm]
11. [AT] . . . and then there was this business of the mother who is very worried
12. that this could be some kind ehhh . . . of letter[8] or something
13. (. . .)
14. [AT] Julia has no learning disabilities and that's usually a part of this thing . . .
15. and there is something about Julia, but what (?)

According to this analysis, Julia 'has difficulties with changes'. She reportedly finds it difficult to start working but she is also unwilling to interrupt what she is doing and start on something new (1, 2), and she is unwilling to subordinate herself (9). She also has problems with her peer relations (9), and she reportedly finds it difficult to co-operate (7). It is reported that the mother has explicitly mentioned her worry about her daughter suffering from a neuropsychiatric disorder (11). Through this mode of reasoning, and the contributions of the various parties who provide direct and indirect information, the suspicion of ADHD/DAMP is implicitly confirmed as the relevant categorization.

In this excerpt, the special needs teacher argues that she has no learning disabilities (which should

Step 6	Step 7	Step 8	Step 9	Step 10	Step 11
Parents' Conference Reporting to the parent with the intention of gaining consent to test the child for suspected neuropsychiatric disorder	**Psychological assessment** testing	**Medical expert** motor-test, confirmation of diagnosis	**Parents' conference** psychologist reports the results of the tests	**PWTM** psychologist reports the tests to the team and a decision about how to proceed is made	**Outcome of process** Personal assistant special teaching group medical treatment back to teacher's concern

Fig. 42.2 Steps in the second phase of an ADHD/DAMP-assessment

be expected, given the diagnosis suggested in (12) by the special needs teacher, i.e. the special needs teacher includes learning disabilities in the ADHD concept). This is one of the few occasions in our material where a counterargument, or some kind of disconfirming information, to the suspicion of an ADHD/DAMP diagnosis is given. Yet the special needs teacher implicitly confirms the potential relevance of the category by arguing that still 'there is something about Julia' (15).

In another case, the team again describes a child's problem through a series of categories and they end up by suggesting that it could be DAMP.

Excerpt 2: *Robert, 7 years old*

1. [SN] (...) at the slightest problem he needs extra time ... and you have to
2. explain very carefully ... and prepare him for what will happen ...
3. [PR] He needs planning in advance all the time (!)
4. (...)
5. [AP] his mother has been wondering if it could be DAMP or something ... she
6. has also said that there is something wrong with him ... that [something]
7. is the matter
8. [Many] [mmm]
9. [SP] but here I guess we should start an [assessment] ... of this
10. [Many] [mmm]

Robert reportedly, according to the school-nurse, needs extra time 'at the slightest problem' (1). He also needs explanations (2) and extensive preparations (2) to handle changes. In addition, the principal establishes that he needs planning in advance (3). In this case, the conclusion again is that 'there is something wrong with him' (6), and that this 'something' is causing his problematic behaviour. Again, the suggestion that it might be ADHD/DAMP is reported as coming from the mother. From this description, the psychologist establishes that the boy ought to be assessed for ADHD/DAMP (9).

In the third case, Axel, the team members also talk about 'something' that has been disturbing the boy for quite some time. Again, the presupposition is that there is something inside the boy that is disturbing him. In this case, the psychologist, indirectly and without using the term, introduces the category ADHD/DAMP.

Excerpt 3: *Axel, 7 years old*

1. [SP] it seems like this business of the concentration problems, that what we
2. have is a boy who should be assessed
3. (...)
4. [SP] this is a boy who has been considered for an assessment at ... his day-
5. care center ... that's an indication that there has been something wrong
6. for a long time

Some interesting features of these discussions are obvious, and one can argue that they represent a particular accounting practice. The child and his/her behaviours are targeted fairly quickly as objects of discussion. A central feature of the accounts is that the child has difficulties with 'changes'. There is an implicit commitment to the assumption that there is a cause that can be found within the child. The disturbing overt behaviours are generally not contextualized in relation to concrete events in the classroom that might be relevant to understanding them. Even in cases where one points to relatively concrete factors such as that children need extra time or careful explanations of what to do, these problems are generally contextualized as symptoms of something that resides within the child. Within this framing, the categories for understanding child behaviour offered by biomedical discourse seem to come to mind easily, and they are obviously considered practically useful within the school context. The team continues during another meeting to discuss Julia's behaviours in a rather open manner. The professionals negotiate about the explanations of her conduct, and the ADHD/DAMP category seems to be the answer, which everybody finds relevant to pursue.

Excerpt 4: *Julia, 8 years old, second meeting*

1. [AP] (. . .) as soon as things change or something well, . . . she's very
2. sensitive to that . . . it must always be on Julia's terms . . . if you
3. sort of keep things calm, nothing happens . . . if you don't provoke her in
4. any way then everything is quiet and all right but you have to
5. like . . . something can very very easily [happen] . . .
6. [Many] [mmm]
7. [AP] the problem is with the peer relations and to do what the others are
8. doing . . . like when you say 'now we're going to do maths' and she insists
9. on writing ehh . . . a story or something then that's what she wants to do
10. [and then you can't] . . .
11. [PR] [((inaudible)) everything is on her terms] (?)
12. [AP] yes [yes]
13. [PR] [(deep sigh)]
14. ((Pause, 11 sec.))
15. [AP] but . . . but there's so much more to it . . . now she's doing a lot of
16. schoolwork but sometimes she refuses to show things she has done or she
17. doesn't always do . . . ((laughters))
18. [PR] the right things (?)
19. [AP] no . . . she can easily get stuck on doing something she wants to do . . . she
20. works on page eight or thirty-seven way ahead in the book although they
21. should be on page two or something like that
22. [PR] what about the DAMP then (?)
23. [AP] yes that's just the thing . . . like the mother ehh . . . had felt that there
24. were some things she had seen on a TV program that fitted into this . . .
25. like difficulties in following rules and things [like that]
26. [SP] [mmm] the mother was
27. supposed to phone me . . .
28. [AP] yes (?)
29. [SP] but she has[n't]
30. [AP] [no] (?)
31. [PR] but if a DAMP-assessment is to be carried out, it's high time to start
32. on it now when she is in, in . . . second grade

The assistant principal here points to a range of different, sometimes rather contradictory, behaviors on the part of Julia; refusing to do things (16), insisting on an activity (8, 19), having problems with peer-relations (7). She also suggests a tendency towards aggressive behaviour (3, 5). Different characteristics of the girl also become important in the discussion. The assistant principal mentions that the girl is obstinate (2, 11), dominant (2, 11, 19), that she has difficulties in following rules and instructions (16, 19, 25), and that she is very sensitive to changes (2). These different kinds of problems in Julia's conduct are connected to her inner characteristics, and the principal suggests that Julia should be assessed for ADHD/DAMP (22, 31). The assistant principal supports this by referring to the mother's opinion (23). It can be observed that the language is both sociological and social when the assistant principal speaks about Julia's problems with peers and working in school. However, the principal refers to the biomedical category and the suspicion from the previous meeting by saying 'What about the DAMP then?' (22). Here, the biomedical language enters the stage, and it is obviously seen as a relevant category for understanding Julia. From a rhetorical perspective, this is the nature of the transformation that is occasioned by the introduction of the category of ADHD/DAMP. When the assistant principal re-enters into the discussion (23), she confirms the potential relevance of this category by referring to the mother's reactions to a television programme she has seen, where behaviours of the kind ascribed to Julia ('difficulties in following rules') were described as indicative of a neuropsychiatric disorder. The psychologist closes the discussion by saying that the mother has not called her as yet. Through this move, she supports the principal's suggestion and implicitly confirms that the next step in the procedure is to talk to the parents and get their permission for the child to be assessed for a suspected neuropsychiatric disorder.

Again, and as we will return to in the final discussion, the discussions of the problems experienced to a large extent have the character of enumerations of observations that have been made concerning Julia's behaviours. Julia is described as 'doing a lot of schoolwork', but still not following the expected work patterns by changing tasks when she is supposed to, and she is also described as 'sensitive'. There are few systematic attempts to contextualize Julia's activities and problems in the pedagogical setting or to view them as relative to some concrete circumstance or some identifiable type of challenge. Instead, using generalized and ambiguous descriptions of the girl's behaviour dominate the discussion. A key part of this accounting practice, apparent in most cases when ADHD/DAMP is considered, is the claim that these children have difficulties with 'changes' and/or with changing from one activity to another in the manner expected. Viewing these discussions in terms of their discursive properties, it seems as if the category ADHD/DAMP is easily available and is perceived as creating closure in the discussion by somehow pointing in the right direction.

In the next excerpt, the assistant principal presents Peter's difficulties by explicitly referring to them as a relational problem. However, the initial account is transformed during the discussion, and it soon becomes a problem of Peter himself. Also in this case, the team express a concern that there is 'something else' disturbing the boy (18).

Excerpt 5: *Peter, 9 years old*

1.	[AP]	then let's see ... Peter in the third grade (...) he has worked a lot with
2.		the special needs teacher and there are some problems between them
3.		((between the special needs teacher and Peter, our comment)) they find
4.		that ... or, yes I've been talking to the special needs teacher as well,
5.		and she says that the chemistry between them isn't [very good]
6.	[SP]	[between] the
7.		special needs teacher and Peter (?)
8.	[AP]	the special needs teacher and Peter yes ... so it's ... not only that Peter
9.		says so but the special needs teacher feels the same
10.		(...)
11.	[ST]	wasn't he all over the place last year and ... fell over a lot and bustled
12.		[about] ...
13.	[AP]	[mmm]
14.	[ST]	and walked on crutches and ehh ... all those [kinds of thi-]
15.	[AP]	[yes, that's] him
16.	[ST]	yes I think ... clumsy even though he doesn't look clumsy [and then]
17.	[AP]	[mmm]
18.	[ST]	you may sort of start thinking whether there's something else that's
19.		disturbing [him]
20.	[Many]	[mmm]
21.	[ST]	... when he's kind of generally diffi[cult]
22.	[AP]	[mmm]
23.	[ST]	well ... he seems like that ... should a DAMP- assessment be underta- (?)
24.		(...)
25.	[Many]	[((inaudible))]
26.	[SP]	[WE TALKED] probably about this a year ago ... in these terms too ... with
27.		lack of concentration and [such things]
28.	[ST]	[yes exactly]

In this excerpt the problem of the boy is first described as relational (2) between the special needs teacher and Peter (the special needs teacher talked about is not the one attending the meeting). However, the discussion does not continue along these lines but, rather, recontextualizes the problem by focusing on Peter (11 and onwards). His conduct and the alleged motor function problems are discussed as problematic in general terms. Thus, he was 'all over the place' last year, he 'fell over' (11), he 'walked on crutches' (14), is 'clumsy' (16), 'generally difficult' (21), and shows a 'lack of concentration' (27). Also in this case it is reported that there is 'something else that's disturbing him' (18), and this seems to be the decisive factor for suggesting a biomedical diagnosis as ADHD/DAMP. Thus, from this rather general description of the boy's conduct, the team members decide to initialize an ADHD/DAMP-assessment (23). In this case, it is the special needs teacher who initiates the suggestion of a suspected ADHD/DAMP and leads the discussion towards a solution, which in this case is a diagnosis of the child.

The accounting practice used here again illustrates the de- and recontextualizing elements that seem to be an underlying premise in the PWTMs. The team does not see it as relevant to include in its analyses the role and actions of teachers and other relevant actors. The assumption somehow seems to be that teachers are fulfilling their duties in the manner that can be expected, and the analyses in this sense do not have to embrace the system in which the various actors operate. Learning problems of individual pupils are legitimate targets of discussion while teaching problems are not. The very design of the PWTM, in which the staff meets to discuss 'problems', seems to induce such a perspective of the matters to be talked about.

In the case of Axel, the school nurse presents the problems experienced in class, and she strongly emphasizes a series of difficult behaviours.

Excerpt 6: *Axel, 7 years old*

1. [SN] I met Axel this morning and right now it's a dis [aster] (!)
2. [SP] [mmm]
3. [SM] he stands out in all kinds of ways ... lack of concentration, anxious ...
4. has difficulties with peer [relations]
5. [SP] [mmm]
6. [SN] ... he can't sit still won't listen to instructions goes and
7. screams, slams the [doors]
8. [SP] [mmm]
9. [SN] ... very (!) provocative (...)
10. (...)
11. [SP] what's the reason (?) ... should we consider a diagnosis, or (?)

In this case, the biomedical diagnosis is immediately suggested as a next step. By introducing a diagnosis, closure seems to be created and the team members obviously consider this a relevant solution. So, when Axel some time later finally, and in the local jargon, 'gets' a diagnosis, the news is greeted with relief.

Excerpt 7: *Axel, 7 years old—some meetings later*

1. [AP] The psychologist talked about him being in line for the small
2. group[9]
3. [SN] Yes (!)
4. [AP] ... but if he gets a place I don't know ... so as the situation is right
5. now we need ... there's got to be an [assistant]
6. [SN] [mmm] ... what kind of diagnosis was
7. it (?)
8. [AP] ADHD
9. [SN] I see, that was just as [well]
10. [AP] [mmm]
11. [SN] ... I mean that it [finally] happened
12. [AP] [mmm]

The comment made by the school nurse that 'it finally happened' (11) testifies to the manner in which the diagnosis is construed as the end point of an institutional process. The diagnosis provides a platform on which the demands for additional resources (normally a personal assistant) can be successfully claimed.

Discussion and Conclusions

The process of categorizing is a practice of engaging in sense-making within the context of a particular institutional practice and its accounting practices. From an analytical perspective, it is, we argue, legitimate to ask what these accounting practices are like, how they operate, and why they are used as resources for mediating between the interests of collectives and individuals. The problem for the team we have studied is to continuously solve institutional dilemmas by means of closing the gap between a problem and possible solutions through categories available to the members. The accounts of the problems provided by the staff indicate that there are many different kinds of problems. In spite of the diversity in behaviours and problems observed, it is fascinating to see that the discussion of these children leads to one specific biomedical category, ADHD/DAMP. This category—as an inference-rich member's category in Sacks's (1992) sense—seems to close the gap between the descriptions of children's behaviours and the probable causes in a satisfactory manner for the team members.

There is a high degree of consensus in the meetings, which indicates that the accounting practices employed are well established and accepted. Expressed differently, the neuropsychiatric category of ADHD/DAMP is reflexively used in the constitution of normality and deviance in the meetings. As a member's category it 'can be seen to presume that the features of the object (...) being categorized are pregiven, i.e. they are presumed to exist independently of the activity of categorization itself' (Hester 1991). The communicative strategy utilized implies enumerating a number of problems that have occurred and that are associated with a particular child. The participants contribute by adding illustrations that confirm and extend the account that is evolving. This is followed by implying that there is a cause within the child itself that is likely to produce inappropriate behaviours. This is a very clear, and powerful, rhetorical figure in the reasoning employed. The logic and some of the central categories used in the discussion are illustrated in Figure 42.3.

The transformation of the various observations into a claim that there is some clearly definable problem inside the child, which is captured in the category ADHD/DAMP, testifies to the appeal of the biomedical model of diagnostic reasoning in this discourse community, and the 'things ontology' (Shotter 1993) it builds on. This model localizes the cause of the problems in the child's brain as an organic structure, and posits problems in behaviour as a direct outflow of biological dysfunctions. No further analysis of the relationship between the alleged brain injury and the broad range of behaviours described is made at the meetings. The correlation is presumed rather than challenged. Expressed differently, the basic metaphor underlying the discussion is not a developmental and contextual one, where children's actions are seen as contingent on previous experiences and local practices. The analyses preferred effectively make the role of the teachers and a broad range of contextual elements invisible as ingredients in the problems observed.

One of the most salient features of the discussions is the lack of argumentation and critical analysis. Consent within the team is easily produced and maintained. The general comments and claims made by the participants regarding the behaviours of students are never challenged in a concrete sense by asking when and where the events took place, or by clarifying details of the circumstances. No contributor is held accountable for the claims they make regarding the children's problems. Counterarguments offering alternative interpretations of events are almost completely absent. Invoking parents' suspicions of a neuropsychiatric disorder, a strategy employed in several cases, adds to this picture of consent regarding the nature of the problem. In this context, it is interesting to note that even though the team is multidisciplinary, and the members represent different competencies, this does not result in any apparent variations in the manner in which the problems experienced are presented and discussed.

The accounts of children are ambiguous, at times even contradictory. A child can be described as too focused on what he/she is doing, while another child is unable to concentrate and 'all over the place'. A child may be disruptive but show no problems in her learning capacities, even though this should be expected. Other children are introverted and passive. Even when accounting for the behaviours of the same child, and sometimes even during the same PWTM, the categories used may be incompatible. Figure 42.4 gives a presentation of some of the contradictory terms used by team members to back up their suggestion that a particular pupil should be tested for ADHD/DAMP (the items on the same row in the two columns refer to the same child).

If one looks at these terms, and the manners in which they are used in the discussion, they are not only contradictory but also quite vague. But even though they may appear vague and general, they operate, we argue, with a high level of precision in the institutional context. When children are accounted for in this vague manner at the meetings, the outcome is that a process to instigate an assessment into a possible neuropsychiatric disorder will be considered and, in most cases, also decided on. The vagueness, thus, is only apparent. When the discussion reaches a stage where the child is described as suffering from 'something', or, alternatively, when it is claimed that there is something 'disturbing' him or her, these comments are read in a fairly specific way. In the context of institutional reasoning, the kinds of terms listed in Figure 42.4, contradictory as they may seem, are inference-rich and move the discussion in a specific direction.

In passing, let us comment briefly on two observations that conflict with what has been reported in the literature. In contrast to what has been argued in other studies (cf. Mehan 1993), the neuropsychiatric categories seem to resonate with parents' views. As we have already pointed out, in several instances in our material, the parents are quoted by staff as having suggested to teachers and other representatives of the school that they suspect that ADHD/DAMP (or some other similar 'letter' symptom) is the problem that their child is suffering from. The category thus serves as a meeting ground for the various parties involved and as a bridge between professional, semi-professional, and lay discourse. There is very little resistance on the part of parents in our material to having their children diagnosed for a neuropsychiatric disorder, which *per se* is an interesting observation.

Also, when invoking ADHD/DAMP in the meetings, the social background and the immediate family conditions seem to be effectively bracketed. This is at odds with what is often claimed with respect to how school failures are accounted for. For instance, Lubeck and Garrett (1990), in their study of the social construction of the 'at risk' child, argue that the 'concept of children at risk defines the nature of the social problem: certain children are unable (...) to avail themselves of the opportunities that schools present'. Thus, the 'problem of poor school performance resides not in social, political, economic, and educational institutions, but rather in the child, and, by extension, in the family' (p. 327). In our material, and specifically in relation to this group, the interest in pursuing issues of the relationship between family, socializing practices, and schooling seem almost non-existent. This contrasts with how the team members reason in the context of other problems that children may have (for instance, dyslexia and emotional problems). In our interpretation, this decontextualization of the child from her/his life circumstances is produced by this category through the adoption of a biomedical voice, which points to factors held to be of a different nature. And perhaps

The child 'has'	**The child 'is'**	**The child 'behaves'**
concentration problems	provocative	is shutting her/himself out
problems with peer relations	anxious	refuses to do things
difficulties to follow rules	obstinate	insists on doing things
relational problems	stubborn, alone and sullen	falls over
difficulties with changes	sensitive	is all over the place
something	generally difficult	bustles about
introvert DAMP	introvert	

Fig. 42.3 Terms used as descriptions of child behaviour by staff

The pupil

is provocative	is sensitive
can't concentrate	is shutting her/himself out
is all over the place	is difficult to get through to
is clumsy	doesn't look clumsy
shows signs of LD	does not show signs of LD

Fig. 42.4 Contradictory categories of children's behaviours/problems used in discussions that precede the decision to initiate an ADHD/DAMP assessment (all terms are used in our corpus)

this is also why the category of ADHD/DAMP serves as an attractive meeting ground for school staff and parents in the discussion of children's problems.

But on yet another level, the meetings are very interesting because of the kinds of analyses and discussions not present. Thus, there is almost no professional pedagogical discussion involved in the meetings we have recorded. For instance, there are few, if any, analyses of the kinds of situations that elicit the problematic behaviours reported, and that would be conducive to producing an understanding of what is common to or characteristic of the contexts where the child reacts in a disruptive or unpredictable manner. In other words, there are no attempts to understand the child and his/her problems as they surface in the attempts to adapt to the role of being a pupil and acting in an educational setting. Also, there are no discussions of the kinds of measures that have been taken to deal with the problems, and what the effects have been. This is also confirmed by the abstract nature of the written documentation, which does not document in any detail the analyses made or the progress of the work with the child. In this sense, there is no systematic and cumulative problem-solving process that focuses on the child and his/her problems in school.

At a general level, our results illustrate how a specific accounting practice is employed within a particular institutional system. And, to use Wittgenstein's (1953: §106) groundbreaking insight, the findings also demonstrate the profound manner in which we 'predicate of the thing what lies in the method of representing it'. In this tradition, behavioural problems are understood in terms of brain dysfunctions rather than as responses to concrete events in the school situation. This testifies to a basic assumption of medicalization: brain injuries are real while other kinds of explanations referring to the child's biography or contextual factors are seen as vague. In fact, the participants in the meetings are forced to be quite flexible when connecting the broad range of contradictory behaviours and attitudes to this particular syndrome. In spite of this, the idea of the appropriateness of ADHD/DAMP as a solution to the problems experienced seems to be shared by all the parties in our material. The category does a concrete job on many levels; it is a link in the process of attracting resources by classifying the child as handicapped, it relieves all the parties, including parents, of responsibility, and it creates closure in the situation by offering a reasonable explanation of problematic behaviours, thus avoiding going into issues that have to do with the child's biography. And it allows the institutional process to go on; the decision to initiate an assessment of a suspected neuropsychiatric disorder is seen by the team members as a concrete outcome and a step forward towards resolving the problem. But, as Mehan, Hertweck, and Meihls (1986: 164) in a study of a similar problem have pointed out, disability 'exists neither in the head of educators nor in the behaviours of students'. Instead, it is 'a function of the interaction between educators' categories, institutional machinery, and students' conduct'. The ADHD/DAMP diagnosis is symptomatic but our results indicate that it is read as pointing to a clear and definite cause that is indisputable, and that in a deterministic manner limits the possibilities of children to participate in, and profit from, school practices. Considering the growing number of children who are claimed to suffer from such handicaps, the acceptance by educators of medical categories of this kind is indirectly a powerful statement with regard to who fits into mainstream schooling in late-modern society. In this manner, the medical categories do a concrete job by placing this particular discussion outside political and ideological considerations.

Appendix: Transcript Symbols

[ ]	Simultaneous talk
–	Interruption, the speaker interrupts himself at the end of a word
–	Untimed pause
(. . .)	Indicates that some talk is left out
?	Marks intonation of a question
!	Indicates an animated tone
,	Continuing intonation
UPPER-CASE	Loud talk
(( ))	Comments on how something is said for example 'inaudible'

NOTES

The research report here has been financed by The Bank of Sweden Tercenentary Foundation

1. A note on classification of classifications. In Sweden, the acronym DAMP has been frequently used as a neuropsychiatric diagnosis. DAMP, to a large extent, replaced the previous term MBD (the English acronym was used in Swedish as well). Today, there is a tendency to use DAMP and ADHD as more or less identical in terms of their symptomatic features (Socialstyrelsen 2002). Sometimes, the combined expression ADHD/DAMP is used, and this is another indication that the categories have in fact been collapsed. In order to facilitate the reading of this text, we will use the expression ADHD/DAMP, except in quotes, where the transcript reproduces the category used by the speaker.
2. It is very difficult to estimate the number of children who are handicapped, since handicaps do not appear in public records. Also, and relating to our topic, the definitions of what exactly constitutes a handicap are not clear. The figure of 2 per cent of a cohort as handicapped (in the classical sense) is taken from a government report, where it is claimed that 0.5 per cent of a cohort have vision or hearing impairments (including those who are deaf) or have physical disabilities. Slightly more than 1 per cent have severe learning disabilities and attend special schools, and another small number of children have other medical problems (SOU 2000: 19, p. 188).
3. This was (and still is) the political ambition, but there were exceptions and special arrangements for various groups. Special schools were kept for children with some types of handicaps, for instance, those with severe learning difficulties.
4. The Swedish term is either EVK (short for elevvårdskonferens) or EVT (short for elevvårdsteamsmöte). The latter acronym is used in this school.
5. This is an estimate of the proportion of children who are first- and second-generation immigrants. The criterion used is that they are entitled to mother-tongue teaching. The difficulty in establishing who is an immigrant is in itself an illustration of the problem of using categories in a uniform manner, which we are addressing in this chapter.
6. Abbreviations used in excerpts below.
7. Some dialogue not relevant to this analysis has been left out.
8. The term 'letter' refers to an expression in Swedish: *bokstavsbarn*, which literally translates into 'letter children'. This term is frequently used in schools (and elsewhere) for this group of children who have a diagnosis expressed in the form of an acronym (DAMP, ADHD, MBD, etc.)
9. A special teaching group with few students.

Part Seven

Changing Education and Teachers' Work

Part Seven begins with a consideration of the determinants of educational outcomes. Following Carnoy and Marshall (2005) we can broadly consider three hypotheses that address the relationship between equality of educationl opportunity and educational outcomes: that family resources and motivation are key to success in education (see Bourdieu, Ch. 5 above; Nash and Harker, Ch. 29; above); that the quality of schools and teaching may also play a role in promoting greater equality; and, finally, what Carnoy and Marshall call 'collective social capital' may also assume significance in this context. This latter idea may well be novel in highly individualized societies. What they mean by this is 'the way individuals and families are organized socially and politically—particularly in the collective commitment to reduce (through the state) the most pernicious effects of socio-economic difference' (p. 231). This variable may be of particular significance in countries where there is a high degree of social solidarity or consensus as to the aims of education. The particular focus of their study is Cuba but the same may also apply to some of the Asian Tiger societies such as South Korea or Taiwan. What Carnoy and Marshall find is that this latter variable plays a significant role in explaining Cuba's educational performance. In turn this raises broad questions in comparative education about the social conditions necessary to achieve relatively egalitarian outcomes in education.

In the Anglo-Saxon societies, which we have seen privilege market individualism over social solidarity, the major attempt to raise educational standards and to reduce inequality has been through the introduction of market mechanisms such as parental choice into state education. Some of these systems have now been in existence for over a decade and it is timely that they should be reviewed to see what evidence there is for the claims made by pro-market advocates. Since the introduction of markets in education was canvassed there has been a major debate about their effects on equity, educational achievement, and questions of social cohesion. Levin and Belfield (Ch. 43) seek to summarize the available evidence in the case of the United States. This is an extraordinarily detailed review set against a helpful conceptual framework, and while they acknowledge that on many counts the data is not adequate to the task they have set themselves the outcomes do not favour either the advocates or the critics of markets in education.

Market systems in education have been introduced because it is assumed that, in accordance with Carnoy and Marshall's second hypothesis, schools under the right systemic conditions can improve educational outcomes by, among other means, providing greater equality of opportunity (see Lauder and Hughes et al. 1999). However, it has not been considered sufficient to provide an appropriate market system: schools themselves also have to change. Therefore, alongside the introduction of markets in education has been a system of management called 'the new managerialism', which seeks to copy the private sector in the way schools are organized (Thrupp and Hursh, Ch. 44). That is to say that great emphasis is placed on leadership and management teams who are seen as distinct from teachers in their decision-making capabilities, work conditions, and pay. It is a very much a top-down system, although there will be varying degrees of consultation with teachers. More recently, this style of management has been linked to the social technologies of target setting providing an extremely powerful architecture for the control of teachers and students alike. However, there are problems associated with both the new managerialism and target setting which Thrupp and Hursh (Ch. 46) identitfy.

A key assumption of recent educational policy associated with the new managerialism has been that if the management structures and teaching are following best practice, then schools in similar circumstances should perform equally well. In a detailed case study of four schools, all in disadvantaged areas, Lupton (Ch. 45) shows that their different exam results and evaluations by school inspectors are a result of being positioned quite differently in their communities. In this context, there is a place for explaining the differences in performance through the leadership in the schools but this is only a minor part of her explanation which looks to wider contextual factors and the way educational policy has impacted on the schools. This research is a major step forward in understanding how schools in deprived areas are shaped by their contexts, and by implication is a major criticism of the policy assumption that schools in apparently similar areas should perform similarly.

It is often said that changes in education are superficial, that if one looks beneath the rhetoric and policies one will find a teacher with a black- or whiteboard talking to thirty students: that teaching has not changed in generations. Those that assert this view have failed to understand how wider social changes have also affected the roles of teachers and students. However, it will be apparent that the changes we have described have inevitably had a major impact on teachers. Hargreaves (Ch. 46) outlines how the teaching profession has been dramatically tranformed and raises questions about its nature today. There is no doubt that the profession has lost considerable autonomy in what it teaches and how.

Ball (Ch. 47) elaborates on some of these key changes through the concept of performativity. This is a system that links teachers' identity and work to targets and measured outcomes which reflect a 'truth' about their performance. They judge themselves and their work in relation to these targets and consequently the many other aspects of the work they do is either undervalued or ignored. It is assumed that the complex daily interactions by which teachers may improve children's morale or help them to solve problems not directly related to the curriculum can all be summed up by the figures that are embodied in test outcomes. There are two further helpful aspects to the notion of performativity that help to throw light on teachers' work. The first is that the process is not unique to education but tends to extend across the state sector, including health. The assumption is that the same management techniques can be applied in all areas with similar success. In other words, there is nothing unique to education that requires a different approach to decision-making, governance, and management.

However, Ball has always had a concern that contemporary education policies deny teachers, and indeed students, the right to debate the ends of education as well as the means, precisely because education is unique in that the ends are embodied in the means. If we want to develop students as citizens it might be thought that a command and control system of education, which by definition denies debate about ends, would be inimical to an education for citizenship. This reflects the second point, which is that performative practices leave no room to debate values.

Dillabough (Ch. 48) argues that we cannot see teaching and the concepts of professionalism related to it in gender-neutral ways, but rather that the dominant view of the teacher is as someone who is a rational and instrumental actor. This is a view associated with masculinity and not far distant from the conception of the teacher embodied in the new managerialism and performative practices. This leads her to identify the gendered dualisms at the heart of what it is to be a teacher. Such a view forecloses on the many valuable teaching identities that could be possible in education. In this way, she argues, that concepts of professional identity and teacher professionalism are shaped by political considerations which require challenge.

At the centre of the changes in teachers' identity and autonomy is the state's view that the educational system can raise educational standards and compensate for the inequalities of society though the imposition of social technologies such as new management techniques, parental choice, and target setting. The resulting pressures on teachers and students have been considerable. The balance sheet on all these policies will soon be drawn up and it is doubtful that it will emerge in credit. The problem is that we now have cadres of head teachers and senior management teams that are committed to this particular process of education. Fundamental change to a system that gives students the space to learn and reflect and teachers a greater degree of autonomy will not be easy to create.

The Marketplace in Education

Henry M. Levin and Clive R. Belfield

In this chapter we wish to address the educational marketplace by describing the principal reform proposals and the assumptions about market behavior that motivate them. We will show that all educational arrangements, including market approaches, face a conflicting set of goals, and they require tradeoffs—that is, sacrifice of some goals in order to obtain others. The movement to an educational marketplace must confront this dilemma, particularly the conflicts that may arise between the private and public purposes of education. We will review the tools that can be used to orient educational market approaches towards specific goals and their consequences. Finally, we will provide a brief review of the available evidence on the impacts of educational markets.[1] Although there are many ways to introduce markets into the education system, we pay particular attention to educational voucher programs because these programs typically would introduce multiple features of a market simultaneously.

Market Reforms in Education

Voucher Programs

The most prominent market reform in education is that of educational vouchers. The concept is found as early as the eighteenth century in a plan proposed by Thomas Paine (West 1967). However, the present discussions on vouchers date back to an important essay published by Milton Friedman (1962) which asked what the government role should be in education. Friedman concluded that: 'a stable and democratic society is impossible without a minimum degree of literacy and knowledge on the part of most citizens and without widespread acceptance of some common set of values' (p. 86). Since education contributes substantially to these goals, Friedman agrees that some minimal public subsidy is justified. But, he argues that public funding for schooling is not an argument for government schools. Rather, the operation of a private marketplace of schools will provide greater benefits in efficiency and technical progress by promoting choice and competition. To combine public funding with private provision, Friedman proposed that: 'Governments could require a minimum level of schooling financed by giving parents vouchers redeemable for a specified maximum sum per child per year if spent on "approved" educational services' (Friedman 1962: 89). All educational voucher plans utilize this basic concept, although each may contain different provisions with respect to the size of the voucher, the opportunities for parents to add to the voucher, and other details.

An attempt was made to establish an educational voucher demonstration in the early seventies by the US Office of Economic Opportunity (Center for the Study of Public Policy 1970; Weiler 1974). No state was willing to use public funds for private schools even with federal assistance, so the demonstration was modified to an exercise in public school choice by creating mini-schools within existing public schools in a California school district, and allowing parents to choose among mini-schools within the district. The public discussions of vouchers also led to attempts by partisans to establish statewide voucher plans during the decades of the seventies and eighties (e.g. Coons and Sugarman, 1978). Historically, smaller districts in Maine and Vermont had used a voucher-like mechanism to pay tuition to private schools and other public school districts to educate their children in lieu of establishing schools in the home district (Hammons, 2001). By 2003, publicly funded voucher programs had been implemented in several US cities, and proposed in several others (e.g., Washington, DC). But, the total number of participants is very small as a proportion of public school enrollments. (There is also a network of privately funded voucher programs, providing scholarship grants to over 100,000 students, see Howell and Peterson, 2002, table 2.1).

Milwaukee Parental Choice Program

A formal voucher program for K-12 schooling did not exist in the US until the State of Wisconsin established one for Milwaukee in 1990. The Milwaukee Parental Choice Program was limited to low income families and to no more than 1 percent of students from the Milwaukee Public Schools (raised later to 1.5 percent and more recently no cap on enrollment). The amount of the voucher rose from $2,446 in 1990 to $4,894 in 1998 and $5,882 in 2003–4, amounts predicated upon the amount of state aid to local school districts. Until 1995 the Milwaukee voucher was limited to attendance in non-religious schools and only about a dozen schools and about 830 students participated by the fifth year. In 1998 religious schools were declared eligible by state law for the voucher, an action that was upheld subsequently by Wisconsin courts and the U.S. Supreme Court. This broadening of school eligibility promoted a large expansion: By 2003–4, 107 schools were enrolling almost 12,778 voucher students and two-thirds of voucher recipients were enrolled in religious schools.

Evaluations of the impact of the Milwaukee voucher plan on academic achievement cover only the period from 1990–95 (Witte, 1999). The evaluations of the earlier period were controversial and contradictory, complicated by a problematic data set (missing data, considerable attrition, instability among comparison groups). The initial evaluation for the State of Wisconsin showed no difference in achievement between voucher and non-voucher students (Witte, 1999). A re-analysis by Greene, Peterson, and Du (1998) using a somewhat different approach found achievement advantages for longer-term, voucher students in both mathematics and reading. A third evaluation that made considerable adjustments for the data problems showed no difference in achievement for reading and a slight advantage for the voucher students in mathematics (Rouse 1998).

Because the earlier period was characterized by relatively few schools and students, a more valid evaluation of the impact of the Choice Program would ideally build on the present situation. Unfortunately, after 1995, schools receiving vouchers were not required to report test results (or even pertinent information on the characteristics of enrollees), so no such analysis could be done.

Cleveland Opportunity Scholarship Program

The second of the existing voucher plans was established by the State of Ohio for the city of Cleveland beginning in 1995. Known as the Cleveland Scholarship and Tutoring Program, it has particular prominence because it was the focus of a US Supreme Court decision which resulted in the legal approval (at the Federal level) of inclusion of religious schools in a voucher plan (*Zelman* vs. *Simmons-Harris* 2002). Low income families were given preference for vouchers in Cleveland, with those below 200 percent of the poverty level (about $36,000 for a family of four) provided with 90 percent of tuition or $2,250, whichever is lower. Families above 200 percent of the poverty level were provided with 75 percent of tuition or $1,875, whichever is lower. About one-quarter of the students came from the latter group.

The vast majority of students in the program chose religious schools; this was not surprising, since such schools represent three-quarters or more of existing private enrollments more generally and are the only ones available at the tuition levels of the Cleveland voucher. There were no differences in achievement in any subject between voucher and non-voucher students over the period of evaluation, Kindergarten to Fourth Grade (Metcalf et al., 2003).

Florida Opportunity Scholarship Program

The Florida voucher program was established in 1999 and has two components. Schools that receive an F for two years out of four on the Florida educational assessment system must allow their students to select another public school or to receive a voucher to go to a private school. The voucher has a value of up to about $4,500. Some 542 students were using the voucher in 2002–3.

Florida also sponsors the McKay Scholarships for students with disabilities, a voucher approach. Parents who decide that their handicapped child is not progressing in public schools can use what is spent in the public school to apply towards private schools. In 2002–3 almost 9,000 out of 375,000 students with disabilities were taking advantage of this finance mechanism. The amount that could be allocated to the voucher was a maximum of more than $21,000, depending upon the services that were being provided in the public school for that child. Parents could add on to the voucher amount to pay for a more expensive placement. No evaluations of the impact of vouchers on student performance have been done other than a general analysis that argues that schools that might have met the failure criteria succeeded to improve because of their fear of the voucher (Greene, 2001). But, other incentives were also in place, making it very difficult to disentangle the impact of the voucher threat from the stigma of failure or from the effects of special state assistance for schools at the precipice of failure (Kupermintz, 2001; Camilli and Bulkley, 2001).

Colorado Opportunity Contract Pilot Program

In Spring 2003 the State of Colorado passed a voucher plan to take effect in the Autumn of 2004. It would provide vouchers to students from low income families with low academic performance if they are in districts where 8 or more schools in 2001–2 had low or unsatisfactory performance (or are in a district which participates in the program voluntarily). The amount of the voucher would depend upon the grade level and district expenditure: it would amount to the lesser of the actual cost of educating the child in the private schools or 37.5 percent of district expenditure at kindergarten; 75 percent of district expenditure at grades 1–8; and 85 percent of district expenditure for grades 9–12. The plan would start with a maximum of 1 percent of student enrollments in eligible districts and rise to no more than 6 percent by 2007 (see Lenti, 2003). In December 2003 the Colorado plan was struck down, being judged to violate the Colorado Constitution by depriving local school boards of control over instruction in their districts. Legal challenges are likely to continue, however.

Tuition Tax Credits

An alternative way of encouraging a private educational marketplace is a tuition tax credit (TTC) (James and Levin, 1983; Belfield and Levin, 2003). A TTC provides a reduction in tax burden equal to a portion of tuition paid to a private school. For example, a TTC on income tax could be enacted that reduces the tax liability of the taxpayer by some sum, e.g. up to $1,000 a year. Since 1997, six states have enacted tuition tax credits for education, and 13 states have tax deduction programs (for schooling expenditures). A tax credit is different from a tax deduction: some states allow a portion of tuition to be deducted from income in computing a tax, but this only reduces the tax burden by the tax rate on the allowable deduction rather than providing a reduction in the tax burden of that amount. Some states also permit businesses to contribute up to some maximum amount to cover the tuition of students in private schools. The TTC serves as a subsidy to households with children in private schools, reducing the effective tuition cost to them, thus increasing the demand for private enrollments. Poorer households can take less advantage of a tax credit because they have less tax liability, although it is possible to design a plan that refunds the credit if tax liability is not adequate to offset it.

Charter Schools

Charter schools are public schools that are able to waive compliance with state and local regulations in exchange for adhering successfully to a specific mission, their charter. In 2002–3 there were 2,556 charter schools serving 685,000 students in 36 states and Washington, DC, according to the Center for Educational Reform (www.edreform.org). These schools simulate some of the dynamics of a market by increasing the supply of alternatives to parents and by competing with existing public schools. In addition, many of them contract with for-profit, educational, management organizations (EMOs) to operate their schools (Miron and Nelson, 2002: 170–93).

Typically they also have their own boards of trustees and considerable autonomy relative to public schools in their states. Although they are not components of a private marketplace, they contain features of choice and competition which some analysts believe are good predictors of behavior in such a marketplace (see Kane and Lauricella, 2001; Sugarman, 2002).

Because the intention of charter school legislation is to encourage flexible educational provision in response to local needs, charter schools themselves are heterogeneous (on virtual/cyber charter school laws, see Huerta and Gonzalez, 2003). As well as exemption from regulations in hiring unionized teachers, charter schools can choose a non-traditional pedagogy and or curriculum; they can also select the mode of delivery (classroom-based or through distance-learning) and school facilities. Given this heterogeneity, the evidence on charter schools' performance (at least as reflected in test score comparisons) is mixed (on charter schools in California, see Zimmer, 2003). For advocates, the charter school movement represents a freedom from government intrusion—not only in how the education is provided, but also in how it should be assessed.

Educational Management Organizations

In the last decade, for-profit businesses have risen to manage schools. Businesses have long sold products and services and managed some operations of schools such as transportation, cafeterias, maintenance, and construction as well as school textbooks, supplies, and equipment such as furnishings and computers (even to include curricular packages and assessment systems). But, the rise of educational management organizations (EMOs) has represented a marketplace in itself where such entities compete to manage entire schools under contract to school districts or to charter school boards. In general, the EMOs and their schools are in competition because they typically are premised upon school choice of clientele and promise to out-perform comparable schools administered by the school district. In fact, school districts often contract with EMOs to operate schools that have done poorly under district administration (for insights into the challenges of establishing and maintaining a profitable educational management organization, see Levin (2001*a*, 2002)). Thus, they provide two major dimensions of a market, choice and competition, features that we will discuss in the next section.

Internal Anatomy of Markets

What is a market and what is assumed about its behavior?[2] Markets are places (literally or figuratively) where buyers and sellers come together to establish purchase of goods and services at an agreed upon price. The purely competitive market is considered the ideal. In such a market there are a very large number of buyers and sellers so that no one buyer or seller can influence the price. There is perfect information on the alternatives open to market participants. There is freedom of entry into the market by either buyers or sellers meaning that there are no obstacles to either producing or purchasing the good or service. Buyers wish to maximize total satisfaction or utility subject to the limitation of their resource capacity or income. Sellers wish to maximize profits.

Given these assumptions it can be shown that a supply curve can be depicted that shows the amount of a particular good or service that will be supplied at each and every price at any point in time. Each supply curve refers to a given quality of the good or service. Multiple supply curves can denote different qualities offered. The supply curve will be upward sloping or increasing with price because the industry must divert resources from other uses at an increasing cost to increase output,especially over the short run. The demand curve will be downward sloping or inversely related to price because as prices rise they reduce the amount of other goods and services that might be purchased and encourage the purchase of relatively cheaper substitute goods and services. Under these conditions, there is an intersection of the supply and demand curve and an equilibrium price for clearing the market. All suppliers and consumers pay the market price. See Figure 43.1 for the basic schema of supply and demand.

Although suppliers may want a price that is higher than the market price, competition for clientele will push down the price to that point where firms simply cover all of their costs plus a minimal profit, enough to stay in business. Firms have a choice of which goods or services to produce, so they can decide to enter or leave the industry if they cannot succeed at the equilibrium price. Firms that are less efficient and cannot produce their output at the market price will fail and will leave the marketplace. Consumers may wish to get a price below the market equilibrium, but they will be unable to purchase goods at a below market price in the long run because firms will not be able to sustain themselves at a price below the cost of production. The key dynamics of the market are choice and competition. Households have a choice of suppliers, so firms must compete for their business by providing goods or services at the lowest price.

This is not to say that prices will be invariant over a period of time. Prices may change as a function of overall supply and demand conditions such as the technology of production or changes in household preferences and income. But, the competitive market equilibrium will assure that the new price is consistent with efficient production. For example, Figure 43.2 shows what happens when there is a technology breakthrough that lowers the cost of production: the supply curve shifts to the right (to S2) which establishes a new and lower equilibrium price. Presumably, competition provides incentives to improve productivity to be able to gain larger profits at the market equilibrium. However, such competitive advantages may be short-lived since other competitors may be able to emulate the conditions that lead to gains, so market prices will fall as in Figure 43.2 to ensure only a competitive market return.

It is this model that provides claims for those that seek to shift the production of schooling from governments to the private marketplace. They believe that by providing choice and competition, the quality of schooling will rise when costs are constant or the costs will fall for a given quality. In addition, advocates may wish to provide greater choice in types of schooling, providing a range of sub-markets for families because of differences in educational preferences (values, religion, philosophy) rather than requiring each school to provide a uniform type of education (Chubb and Moe, 1990). By replacing a local school monopoly with market competition, efficiency can be brought to the consumer in two ways.[3] First, there will be incentives to compete by providing schooling services at the lowest possible costs. Second, households will be better matched to the types of schooling that meet their needs because of the variety of schools that will emerge and the incentives of schools to be responsive to the needs of clientele.

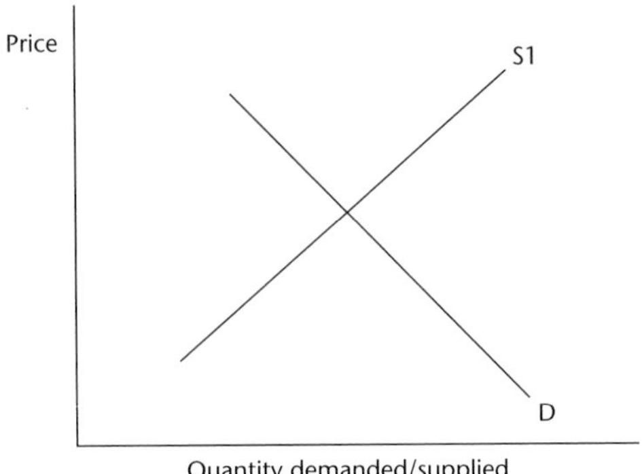

Fig. 43.1 Competitive market equilibria: model 1

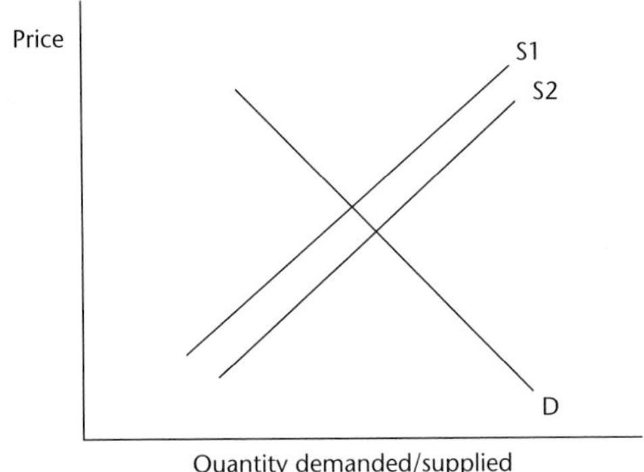

Fig. 43.2 Competitive market equilibria: model 2

Market advocates would argue that the market approach leads to choice and competition overall, increasing productive behavior on the part of parents and students as well as schools. Parents and students have incentives to choose schools wisely. They also have incentives to keep schools attentive with the implicit option of switching to other schools if they are dissatisfied. Schools have incentives to be responsive to student needs to both attract and retain students and to get to the maximum size consistent with good education (it should be noted that most private schools are considerably smaller than their public school counterparts; see Andrews et al., 2002). At the same time they have incentives to innovate over the long run to gain market advantages, a dynamic that can make the industry technologically and organizationally progressive as other competitors imitate those improvements to increase their own effectiveness. These incentives arise primarily from choice and competition promoted by the marketplace.

Finally, even in markets where there is considerable competition, government regulation is necessary. Governments should set basic standards to capture the public interest in schooling, a matter which will be addressed below. At issue is how extensive this regulatory framework should be, not whether it should exist.

Imperfect Competition

Few markets are perfectly competitive. In many cases there are few suppliers of a particular product or service, and even these firms may choose to collude rather than compete. Further, a key resource used by firms may be controlled by a single entity such as another firm or a union. Consumers may not have good information, and the nature of the good or service may make accurate information difficult to acquire. Certainly, all of these factors are a reality in education. Particularly in rural areas there may be too few potential students to establish competitive schools that can operate efficiently. For example, in Chile about one-quarter of the municipalities were too small to have even a single competitor to the community's school (McEwan and Carnoy, 2000). Teachers unions may constrain the ability of schools to adjust employment, benefits, and salaries to market realities or to change the organization of educational services. And, parents may have difficulties obtaining and evaluating school quality with schools providing information that is designed primarily for marketing and promotional goals rather than for useful comparisons. Though each of these may reduce the efficiency of the marketplace, the issue is whether greater choice and competition is introduced that improves educational processes and outcomes, not whether the improvement is optimal.

As long as there is some choice and competition, it is believed that the outcomes will be better than when there are no choices at all. This does not mean that only competition can be used to obtain efficiency in the use of educational resources to gain maximal performance. In his classic book, *Exit, Voice, and Loyalty*, Albert Hirschman (1970) suggests that both exit (market choice) and voice (informing the provider of how to improve) are important to efficiency and that the easy option of abandoning a supplier may undermine the incentive to guide and pressure them directly to improve services. In the case of education, such school involvement may also be key to student and family engagement that contributes to learning. McMillan (2000) has found some evidence of this in reviewing the impact of choice on parental participation and student achievement.

In order to make appropriate choices families need to have good information. In part, this is the motivation for more prescriptive standards and testing in schools—so that families will have information about school quality and will be able to compare schools and hold them accountable. However, there has been considerable debate over whether school quality can be easily codified and quantified (or even manipulated), leading to the possibility that parents will be making choices based on false information (for discussion, see Kane and Staiger, 2002). In addition, although the intentions of most families are aligned toward their children's well-being, some families may make poor or inappropriate choices.

Market Failure and Externalities

Probably the greatest challenge to the view of market efficiency in education is created by the presence of externalities. Externalities refer to effects that 'spillover' to the larger society from the individual transactions of the marketplace. That is by virtue of producing and selling goods and services, firms may have an impact that extends beyond the internal production and sale of products to consumers. At the same time, the choice of such services and their consumption by consumers may also have effects beyond the purchasers. Externalities can be divided into those that represent social costs and social benefits. An example of the former is the spewing of pollution by firms in their quest to be narrowly efficient in the production of goods or services. An example of the latter is the reduction in risk of contracting communicable diseases for all society as more and more individuals receive inoculations that reduce the incidence of such diseases. That is, the probability of contagion is reduced, even for those who do not receive inoculations, by the acts of those who do get vaccine protection.

Schooling is considered to be a primary source of external social benefits because the results of an education benefit not only the individual, but the society of which she is a part. That is, even those who are not in school are expected to benefit from a more highly educated society. It has long been held that one of the central purposes of schools is to improve the cohesion and stability of society through the provision of a common experience that prepares the young for adult roles and responsibilities (Guttman, 1987). Schools are expected not only to educate students as individuals, but also to contribute to the overall effectiveness of society through creating competent adult citizens. Even Friedman (1962: 86), a prime advocate of replacing government schools with those of the marketplace, has acknowledged this external benefit of schools by asserting that a democracy requires a minimal level of literacy and knowledge and a common set of values to function effectively. This supposition underlies Friedman's argument for public funding of education. He asserts that this externality (or 'neighborhood' effect) can be addressed by setting 'minimum standards' for schools in a marketplace without further government intervention. Friedman does not attempt to suggest what these minimum standards might be or how they might be satisfied, providing a blank canvas on which other designers have sketched their own interpretations. That there is broad agreement that schools must meet not only the narrower requirements of individual students and their families is evident. The larger question is how to reconcile the private choices of families with the public requirements of education for democratic knowledge and values.

Education and the Public–Private Nexus

When families choose the type of education that they want for their offspring, the decision revolves primarily upon their values as well as their perception of their child's needs. That education yields private benefits to the child and her family is obvious. More and better education is closely associated with higher income and status and greater access to worldly knowledge, both technical and cultural. Since parents want their children to succeed, they will prefer schools that meet high standards. Beyond that, parents usually have political, religious, and philosophical values that they believe are important and should be transmitted to their children. Accordingly, they will seek schools that reflect these values or, at least, do not undermine them. The range of household choices for schooling will be largely predicated on the diversity of backgrounds and educational beliefs of the heterogeneous populations that are found in the US (Hochschild and Scovronick, 2003). Increasingly, this diversity is reflected in other nations as immigration and religious radicalism increase throughout much of the world.

If the market responds only to these diverse demands, it will not seek a homogeneous set of school offerings with substantially common experiences for all students. Instead it will tend to divide into market segments or niches that appeal to a particular group of households, segments based upon religion, child philosophy, instructional approaches, and so on. James (1987, 1993) has found that diversity in the population is an important statistical predictor of the extent of private schooling internationally. Coons and Sugarman (1978) and Chubb and Moe (1990) argue that this is the most appropriate way to serve competing needs rather than expecting a single institution to serve all needs. Under a market approach, schools will seek market niches through product differentiation. That is, they will compete by matching their appeal to particular educational preferences of parents rather than trying to produce a standardized educational product. The problem is that serving well a wide variety of different values and preferences is likely to undermine the social goals of providing a unifying educational influence around societal institutions and values.

In general, the social purpose of schools is to prepare the young for democratic participation in the political, social, and economic institutions that unite society into nations, regions, and communities. Successful citizen participation in a free and democratic society requires a common language, values and knowledge for economic and political understanding and participation, and an acquaintance with a common set of social goals. In addition, democratic societies are also concerned with the provision of fairness in access to life's rewards so that effort and talent, rather than private privilege, are the determinants. These goals argue for a common educational experience rather than one that is differentiated according to family political, religious, and philosophical preferences. That is, the very externalities of education that justify public support argue in favor of a common educational experience rather than one premised upon private choice.

How are these conflicting goals to be reconciled? That conflict is at the heart of all educational systems. On the one hand, the right to influence the way in which one's child is reared means that parents should have the options of choosing the school that matches most closely their childrearing preferences. On the other hand, the right of a society to maintain an effective and stable democracy and a fair society requires that children have a common educational experience. The existing educational system in the US, in which 90 percent of students are in government-sponsored schools, has faced this historic challenge. But, even more so, a market system that bases its appeal on differentiation and choice must adopt a mechanism to ensure common experiences across schools to prepare students for their civic rights and responsibilities.

Clearly, there is no perfect system as much as a search for a 'best system' in providing a balance among these and competing aims (Tyack 1974). In this context, one can denote four major criteria for addressing an effective educational system: (1) freedom of choice; (2) productive efficiency; (3) equity; and (4) social cohesion.

(1) *Freedom to Choose*. This criterion places a heavy emphasis on the private benefits of education and the liberty to ensure that schools are chosen that are consistent with the child-rearing practices of families. Voucher advocates typically place great weight on this criterion relative to detractors.

(2) *Productive Efficiency*. This criterion refers to the maximization of educational results for any given resource constraint. Educational voucher advocates assume that market competition among schools for students will create strong incentives, not only to meet student needs, but to improve educational productivity. Voucher detractors believe that the assumptions that make competition effective will not be present in the educational marketplace.

(3) *Equity*. This criterion refers to the quest for fairness in access to educational opportunities, resources, and outcomes by gender, social class, race, language origins, handicapping condition, and geographical location of students. Voucher advocates argue that the ability to choose schools will open up possibilities for students who are locked into inferior neighborhood schools and that the competitive marketplace will have great incentives to meet the needs of all students more fully than existing schools. Challengers argue that vouchers will create greater inequities because parents with education and income are better informed and have greater resources such as access to transportation. Also, they believe that the choices, themselves, will further segregate the poor and disenfranchised as those with power and status will select schools with students like themselves and schools will also select students by such criteria.

(4) *Social Cohesion*. This criterion refers to the provision of a common educational experience that will orient all students to grow to adulthood as full participants in the social, political, and economic institutions of our society. This is usually interpreted as necessitating common elements of schooling with regard to curriculum, social values, goals, language, and political institutions. Voucher advocates believe that this will take place in schools without making special provisions or that it will only require minimal regulations.

Vouchers by Design

There is not a single voucher plan, but many different ones, each with emphases on a somewhat different mix of priorities among the four criteria. Although some refer to 'the voucher plan', differences among voucher plans can have profoundly different results. Within limits, educational voucher arrangements are highly malleable. Plans can be constructed with particular features to address each of the four criteria by using three design instruments: (1) finance; (2) regulation; and (3) support services.[4]

(1) *Finance.* Finance refers to the overall magnitude of the educational voucher, how it is allocated and whether schools can add tuition charges to the government voucher for families willing and able to purchase a more costly education. A larger voucher will promote more options in the marketplace with greater freedom of choice and competition. If the educational voucher is differentiated by educational need such as larger vouchers for those with handicaps and from poverty backgrounds, some issues of equity will be addressed. Schools will have greater incentives to attract such students and provide the resources and programs to address their needs. If families can add-on to vouchers from their private resources as Friedman proposed, there will be advantages for families with higher incomes in the educational marketplace who are able to send their children to more expensive and restrictive schools with potential increases in inequities relative to the present system.

(2) *Regulation.* Regulation refers to the requirements set out by government for eligibility of schools to participate in the voucher system as well as any other rules that must be adhered to by schools and families in using educational vouchers. Presumably, only schools that meet certain standards will be eligible to redeem vouchers. Some voucher plans have emphasized a common curriculum and uniform testing as a condition of school participation to ensure that students are meeting goals of social cohesion and that schools can be compared for their productive efficiency along common measures of student achievement. Admissions requirements have also been a matter of scrutiny where schools with more applicants than available places would be required to choose a portion of students by lottery to assure fairness in selection procedures. Eligibility for vouchers may be restricted to certain populations in the name of equity. For example, public and private voucher programs in Milwaukee and Cleveland have been limited to children from poorer families in order to give them choices outside of their neighborhoods. The Florida legislation limited vouchers to children in failing public schools.

(3) *Support Services.* Support services refer to those types of publicly provided services designed to increase the effectiveness of the market in providing freedom of choice, productive efficiency, and equity. Competitive markets assume that consumers will have access to a wide variety of choices as well as useful information for selecting among them. In the United States the availability of public transportation is very limited, necessitating a system of school transportation from children's neighborhoods to schools of choice. In the absence of school transportation, school choices and competition for students will be limited, reducing both the competitive efficiency of schools and creating inequities for those who cannot afford private transportation.

Information must be widely available for families to make informed choices about the schools that they select for their children. Accurate information on school programs and effectiveness as well as other important aspects of school philosophy and practice would need to be collected and disseminated to parents to assist in making decisions (Schneider et al., 2000). It could be argued that the schools will provide their own information through promotional materials and informational sessions to parents. However, there is little assurance that the information will be accurate and balanced, and it may be especially difficult to process for less-educated parents.[5] Technical assistance might also be provided by government agencies through information and training to new schools to advance the productivity of the entire sector.

Different Voucher Plans

Different voucher plans have incorporated specific designs that utilize these three policy instruments to achieve particular goals. Depending upon the specifics, a given voucher plan may differ from another plan in its impact on choice, efficiency, equity, and social cohesion. In essence, each plan uses the design tools to construct a plan which either implicitly or explicitly places greater weight on some goals rather than others.[6]

(1) *Designs for Freedom of Choice.* A voucher plan that maximized choice would allow for a very broad definition of education that would encompass most types of schools and schooling; would provide either a large voucher to all or a smaller voucher with parents permitted to add to it out of private resources; would minimize regulation of curriculum, admissions, and other dimensions of school

operations; and would provide a good system of comparative information on schools as well as an adequate system of transportation. Such a design would ensure a large number of alternatives on the supply side that parents could choose from. This type of plan is especially attractive to libertarians who prefer to see the least government interference in the marketplace, especially if the voucher is modest and parents are able to add to it. Libertarians may believe that the support services of information and transportation are unwarranted because the cost of government intervention exceeds its value, and they would favor add-ons rather than a large basic voucher from public funding.[7]

(2) *Designs for Efficiency*. Productive efficiency is maximized when schools produce a given level and type of education for the least cost. That is, they are operating at the lowest point on their average cost curve. This is somewhat difficult to assess because under a system of freedom of choice, schools may be producing very different types of education. It is the matching of these educational offerings to the preferences of families in a competitive environment that is viewed as the heart of efficiency. Accordingly, designs that focus on efficiency would have a voucher that is high enough (including parental add-ons) to attract many competitors into the marketplace. Regulations would be minimal because they would tend to inhibit competition. However, some would argue that academic achievement is so central to the productivity of all schools that testing of student achievement should be required and reported. Support services such as information and transportation would raise efficiency through increased competition, but the cost of those services would have to be taken into account relative to the efficiency gains.

(3) *Designs for Equity*. Equity in education refers to equality in access, resources, and educational outcomes for groups that have traditionally faced differences on these dimensions. From a finance perspective, an equitable design would seek compensatory vouchers where more funding was available for students with greater educational need such as those in educationally at-risk and handicapped categories. In addition, families could not add-on to the voucher so that income differences would be neutralized. The most fundamental regulation on equity is the question of who is eligible to receive and use a voucher. Thus far all of the voucher plans in the US have been limited to students from low income families or those enrolled in failing schools. Thus, the voucher has been accessible to students who are worst off educationally, providing greater equity in choice for them as it has been provided traditionally through residential location and private schools for those who are more affluent. Equity-oriented regulations would also embrace a provision of non--discrimination in admissions. Schools would be required to choose some portion of their students by lottery if there were more applicants than openings. Provisions encouraging or requiring that schools not limit themselves to a narrow social or ethnic population are likely, given the evidence that peers have an important impact on educational outcomes (Zimmer and Toma, 2000). Transportation and information would be required support services to provide access to those who are less advantaged and an informed basis for choosing schools.

(4) *Designs for Social Cohesion*. Social cohesion connotes a common educational experience, one that prepares all students for civic responsibilities and participation (see the discussions in Wolfe, 2003). The voucher would have to be large enough to provide a common educational experience beyond specialized and elective subjects and activities. The voucher would have to be structured so that all students could gain access to schools where they would be exposed to peers from a variety of backgrounds. This means that parental add-ons to the voucher would probably be proscribed because they would tend to place students from different income strata into different schools. Regulations would focus on establishing common elements in curriculum and certain school activities including the possibility of all students engaging in community service. Support services might focus on the provision of technical assistance in helping schools develop a common educational core as well as the information and transportation to enable families to find and gain access to schools with a heterogeneity of students.

Incompatibilities and Tradeoffs

Moe (1995) has suggested that molding particular objectives into voucher plans is a matter of design. To some degree he is correct, but such a perspective does not acknowledge the tensions and conflicts among criteria and goals in themselves that suggest that gains in fulfilling one criterion may reduce the ability to fulfill others. This means that intrinsically there must be tradeoffs. Some goals cannot be attained without sacrificing others.

A plan such as Friedman's focuses on freedom of choice and productive efficiency through heightened competition, arguably at the expense of equity and social cohesion. Recall that Friedman would provide a modest, flat voucher at public expense. Parents could add to the voucher out of private resources and schools could set their own tuition. Regulation would be minimal, and there would be no provision for transportation and information. This would promote a very large number of alternatives at different levels of tuition, *for those who could afford them*, with few restrictions on schools that enter the marketplace, promoting a large supply of alternatives. Clearly, social cohesion and equity goals would not be paramount.

Conversely, plans that emphasize social cohesion and equity tend to reduce freedom of choice and productive efficiency by establishing a variety of regulations and support services. For example, the Jencks plan (Center for the Study of Public Policy, 1970) would regulate admissions and curriculum and require standardized testing and reporting of results (see also the proposal by Godwin and Kemerer, 2002). It would also provide larger vouchers for the poor—compensatory vouchers—and a system of transportation and information. And, vouchers could not be augmented from private resources. The regulations and a fixedgovernment voucher with no private augmentation would reduce freedom of choice relative to the Friedman plan. The high costs of providing information and transportation and monitoring the regulations for eligible schools would add considerably to the costs of the voucher system and reduce productive efficiency (Levin and Driver, 1997). But, the larger vouchers for the poor, regulations on admissions, and information and transportation services would increase equity. The common curriculum and testing requirements would be expected to improve social cohesion.

Although some design provisions would improve outcomes along more than one criterion, almost all would also reduce outcomes on other criteria. Provision of information and transportation will improve choice options for all participants, but especially for those from families with the least access to information and transportation, the poor. But, such provision would also raise the costs of the overall educational system, probably reducing productive efficiency unless gains from competition due to better information and access offset the costs of the transportation and information. The establishment of regulations with continuous monitoring and enforcement could be used to increase equity and social cohesion, but at the sacrifice of freedom of choice and productive efficiency.

This means that there is no optimal system that provides maximal results among all four criteria. Ultimately, the choice of design features will depend upon specific preferences and values as transmitted through democratic institutions. Those who place a high value on freedom of choice will probably be willing to sacrifice some equity and social cohesion provisions by eschewing regulations and support services and allowing parental add-ons to vouchers. Conversely, those who place a high value on social cohesion will be willing to sacrifice some freedom of choice through establishing a common curriculum core and other standardized features of schools. Ultimately, much of the debate over the specifics of educational voucher plans revolves around the political power and preferences of the stakeholders.

It is an understatement to say that advocates of vouchers may agree on the general case for vouchers, but may disagree profoundly on specifics. There are even strong differences among persons who are often placed in the same general political category. Thus, many liberals want to see greater freedom of choice for students in the inner-city through educational vouchers, even though liberals are usually viewed as antagonistic to marketplace solutions for government services. At the same time, cultural conservatives are deeply committed to a common curriculum and knowledge framework that should be required of all students and the schools where they are enrolled, a very substantial commitment to regulation (Bennett, 1987; Hirsch, 1987). Political conservatives with libertarian views reject regulatory requirements entirely in favor of market accountability, that is letting consumers decide what they want.

Evidence on Vouchers and Choice

Educational vouchers and tuition tax credits apply to a very small proportion of school populations in the US. Even among these situations, there have been relatively few evaluations, and virtually none that address consequences for all four of the criteria that we have set out. Nevertheless, it is possible to provide the contours of findings for each area.

Freedom of Choice

Advocates of the marketplace emphasize that parents will have greater freedom of choice than they would under a government system. In an open market families will have the right to choose schools for their children that are premised on their values, educational philosophies, religious teachings, and political outlooks. Where there are varied preferences and/or abilities across students, this freedom of choice becomes especially important: it is too expensive and complicated for a government provider to collect and process all the information needed to allocate students to their most preferred school. For libertarians, allowing families to make their own choices should—almost by definition—improve educational outcomes.

The evidence on choice favors the view that vouchers will increase choice considerably in terms of the numbers and diversity of options and that those who take advantage of choice will express higher satisfaction with their schools than comparable groups. Doubters of the expansion of choice often start out with the existing numbers of openings at private schools in a particular region, showing that the available openings are miniscule in comparison with the potential number of vouchers. Certainly, in the short run this is likely to be true with little expansion of openings in response to voucher demands. Existing schools have capacity limitations which can only be relieved through longer run expansion, and there is a time lag between the stimulus to establish new schools and the ability to plan, construct, and staff them. However, in response to the new private market demand, the long-run supply of school places will increase (as evidenced in Milwaukee between 1998 and 2002). But, there is another reason that the number of school choices should expand under a market system relative to government sponsorship of schools. Private schools (and charter schools too) tend to be about half of the size of public schools in the US (NCES, 2003). This means that for any given population there are likely to be twice as many schools under a market regime.

The US evidence strongly supports the conclusion that parents value freedom of choice (Peterson and Hassel, 1998). Many families report higher satisfaction from participation in voucher programs (Howell and Peterson, 2002), and from being able to choose charter schools over regular public schools (Zimmer, 2003). Indeed, the very fact that parents in large numbers choose different types of schools when given options is *prima facie* evidence of the benefits of choice, and guaranteeing freedom of choice is an important way to raise satisfaction levels within the education system (Teske and Schneider, 2001).

But, there are several caveats to bear in mind when depending on increased choice to improve substantially the quality of education. One is that some families may not have the resources or the capacity to make choices that are in their children's best interests; there may be a role for education professionals to guide, monitor, or regulate these choices. Also, in sparsely populated areas the limited population size may preclude the establishment of alternatives. For example, in Chile where educational vouchers have been available for more than two decades, about one-quarter of municipalities, mostly in rural areas, do not have a single alternative to the municipal school (McEwan, 2003). A second is that some families may choose schools that will lead to *de facto* segregation of groups; individual families may feel better off, but society as a whole may be worse off. A third caveat is that there may be only limited options to increase the range of choices: in the US, many families already have as much choice as they feel they need—fully three-quarters of families appear satisfied with their choice of school (Henig and Sugarman, 1999). And, when a sample of low-income families was offered a voucher of $1,400 toward attendance at private school, only between 29% and 70% used the voucher for at least three years (Howell and Peterson, 2002: 44). Fourth, private schools might deny some students access. A religious private school is likely to bar enrollment to students with atheist beliefs (or belief in an alternative faith), for example (around 75 percent of all US private schools currently in operation are religiously affiliated). The final caveat is that private schools may be subject to increased regulations if they accept vouchers: these regulations may discourage new supply (as found by Muraskin and Stullich, 1998: 49).

So, parents may be 'free to choose' in principle, but not in practice. Each of these factors suggests that the gains from enhanced freedom of choice in a market—although positive overall—may not be profound and may be particularly limited for some groups.

Efficiency

Some economists have questioned whether the resources spent on public schools has been invested efficiently. For example, over the period 1973 to 1996 Hanushek (1998) charts falling NAEP Science scores and stable NAEP Math scores in US schools, even as real current expenditure per pupil increased by around 45 percent (although this debate is controversial: compare Hanushek (1994) and Grissmer et al. (1998)). Many commentators attribute this alleged decline in performance to inefficiencies in government provision of education and a lack of competition. They contend that an educational system with a greater reliance on the marketplace through choice and competition would be more efficient.

Competitive Pressures

Economists believe that marketplace competition forces providers of a service to be more efficient. Competition exists when multiple, separate providers—facing the same legal rules and regulations—are available to meet the demands of consumers. Where there is more competition between providers (schools/districts), then consumers (parents/children) will face lower prices for services and/or higher quality services; providers must accept lower 'profits', such that only efficient firms will remain in business. More competition should mean higher quality schooling and enhanced educational outcomes in the education market.

The impact of competition can be assessed in terms of test scores and other outcomes from the education system. Belfield and Levin (2002) review over 40 published studies from 1972 to 2002 which explicitly test for a link between competition and educational outcomes in US schooling. These studies use large-scale cross-sectional datasets, employing over 400 individual tests for the impact of competition. Competition is measured either between schools within districts, between districts, or between the public and the private sectors. The impact is measured as the effect on educational outcomes when the extent of competition is increased by one standard deviation.

Their results are summarized in Table 43.1. The first row indicates that the evidence from over 200 tests in 25 separate studies shows that competition does have a beneficial effect on the academic outcomes of students in public schools. In general, test scores rise with the extent of competition. However, the effects are substantively modest: around three-fifths of the tests show no correlation, and the mean effect of increasing competition by 1 standard deviation is to raise academic test scores in public schools by approximately 0.1 standard deviations, equivalent to about 10 points on the verbal SAT or one-tenth of the test score gap between Anglo and African-American students.

If competition presses schools to offer more effective schooling, students may respond by enrolling longer or by applying to college in greater numbers. No effect of competition on dropout rates is evident, but a 1 standard deviation increase in competition from private schools is associated with public school graduation rates of approximately 0.08 to 0.18 standard deviations. The effects of competition on spending are harder to predict. From the evidence, there is no clear link between educational expenditures and competition.

Fundamentally, competition in the marketplace should raise educational efficiency (see Hoxby 2000). Indirectly, the evidence suggests that competition raises test scores modestly, but does not raise expenditures. There is also some direct support: the evidence given in Table 43.1 shows an increase of 1 standard deviation in private-school enrollments raises public-school efficiency (ratio of test scores to per-pupil spending) by as much as 0.2 standard deviations.

Overall, this evidence supports the argument in favor of introducing more marketplace competition into education: increasing competition—either intradistrict, interdistrict, or from private schools—may raise effectiveness and efficiency of public schools, as well as address other educational objectives. It is important to note that the substantive effect is modest and does not support the contention that market competition will produce radical improvements in educational results. Also, the magnitude of the reform is important. Case studies of Cleveland and San Antonio show very few pressures to improve when the competitive stimuli are limited to small-scale reforms (Hess et al., 2001).

However, this evidence only establishes the benefits of competition, and does not consider any necessary reorganizational costs to foster, regulate, and monitor competition, or to promote competition broadly across the education system. For example, Levin and Driver (1997) estimate the additional costs of a statewide voucher system for record-keeping and monitoring of students, transportation, adjudication, and information services and conclude that these added costs would be substantial, perhaps as much as one-fourth of existing per-pupil expenditures. Bear in mind that the centralized administration of an extremely decentralized activity (funding and regulating household and school choice) entails a huge increase in transactions and their costs. For example, in the case of California, the State would have to shift its attention from monitoring somewhat over 1,000 school districts to concerning itself with the establishment of individual accounts for almost 7 million individual students and a doubling of existing numbers of schools to 25,000 or more.

More Efficient School Managers and Owners

The second argument that the marketplace may deliver higher quality education rests on the belief that private owners and managers of schools will be more efficient than government ownership and management. Government-run education systems are often heavily criticized (Bok, 2000): public schools may have excessive rules, or rules applied to

Table 43.1 Summary of the effects of increases in competition by one standard deviation

Outcome variable	Stat. sig. estimations (*n*)[a]	Competition measure	Effect of increasing competition by 1 standard deviation
Academic outcomes	38% (*206*)	Herfindahl Index	Outcome scores in public schools rise by 0.1 s.d.
		Private school enrollments or other proxies for competition	Outcome scores in public schools rise by <0.1.s.d.
Attainment, graduation rates, drop-out rates	42% (*52*)	Number of districts or schools	Drop-out rates are not affected
		Private school enrollments	Graduation rates are higher by 0.08–0.18 s.d.
Spending	42% +ve 22% –ve	Number of districts in state	Spending is lower by 12%
	(*33*)	Private school enrollments	Spending effect is ambiguous (higher by 0.2–0.4 s.d. *or* lower by 7%
Efficiency	66% (*64*)	Herfindahl Index	Efficiency is higher, only in concentrated markets
		Private school enrollments	Efficiency is higher, by approximately 0.2 s.d.

Note: [a] Number of separate studies: academic outcomes, 25; attaiment, graduation rates, drop-out rates, 6; spending, 11; efficiency, 13; teaching quality, 8; private school enrollments, 6. Final column effects are calculated using all studies, where both significant and insignificant coefficients are reported.

Source: Belfield and Levin (2002).

all schools regardless of circumstance, and they may be run 'democratically', making them fraught with conflicts and compromises to appease the demands of special interest groups which have little connection to students' educational needs (Chubb and Moe, 1990). Costs may be inflated, because politicians feel that spending on public services is electorally popular and because of corruption, fraud and waste (which taxpayers cannot escape from as easily as shareholders can divest themselves of stock in a wasteful company). In contrast, private owners have incentives—profits, typically—to monitor closely their companies to make sure that they are meeting their objectives. With more market freedom, private schools could be taken over by more efficient providers, or a for-profit company could franchise its schooling technology for example. Whichever development takes place in the open educational marketplace, the profit motive or educational mission will induce owners and managers to raise educational quality and efficiency to attract an optimal number of students.

The evidence on the relative effectiveness in producing academic achievement of private schools over public schools has been reviewed by McEwan (2001). The evidence for Catholic schools is summarized in Table 43.2 (the results for nonreligious schools are similar). Overall, it shows only small differences between private and public school types (when student intake differences are accounted for), indicating that there are not large differences in results across management and ownership structures (see also Figlio and Stone, 1999). For achievement, there appear to be modest effects for mathematics of poor, minority students in grades 2–5 (but not in grades 6–8 or among non-black students) from attendance at Catholic schools, and no consistent effects for reading. For educational attainment (i.e. years of schooling), Catholic schools increase the probability of high school completion and of college attendance (particularly for minorities in urban areas).[8]

Other studies have compared the school effectiveness of specific types of choice arrangements such as charter schools or magnet schools (Gamoran, 1996). A recent comprehensive review by Miron and Nelson (2002) compares charter schools with traditional public schools. Summarized in Table 43.3, the evidence indicates that, although results vary from state to state, charter schools appear on average to be no more (but also no less) effective than traditional public schools. Evidence on charter schools is continuing to accumulate.[9]

Table 43.2 Summary of Catholic school effects

Academic Outcome	No. of positive and significant estimates/Total number of studies	Average effect (all studies)
K–8 Math:		
Full sample	1/4	0.02
Minority	2/7	0.05
White	1/7	0.04
K–8 Reading:		
Full sample	1/3	0.03
Minority	0/7	0.00
White	2/7	0.10
Secondary Math:		
Full sample	2/5	−0.05
Minority	1/6	0.00
White	3/4	0.10
Secondary Reading:		
Full sample	1/4	−0.05
Minority	0/2	0.00
White	1/2	0.00
High school graduation:		
Full sample	4/5	−0.07
Minority	5/6	0.14
White	5/6	0.06
College attendance:		
Full sample	3/4	−0.06
Minority	5/6	0.15
White	5/6	0.06

Source: McEwan (2001: table 5).

Another potential school type that might be expected to take advantage of an educational marketplace is for-profit schooling. As of summer 2003, the largest for-profit provider of education in the US is Edison Schools, which educates approximately 80,000 students across 150 schools. However, many of the private for-profit companies have faced difficulties in achieving profitability and in competing with non-profit religious schools. In general, the for-profit companies have not been able to innovate more efficiently than public schools, and have had difficulties in establishing brand equity (Levin, 2001b). Overall, private for-profit schools have not established themselves as clearly superior to public schools, and the evidence on improved managerial competence is ambiguous.

Educational Effectiveness from Voucher Programs

Evidence from existing voucher programs and randomized field trials is relevant to the question as to whether a marketplace is more efficient than a state-run system. (Most of these evaluations focus on test scores, although it may be more appropriate to consider the effect on student attainment). Evaluations of the small-scale voucher programs in the US show largely neutral effects. For the Milwaukee Parental Choice Program, the results vary from no effect to an effect on mathematics, but not reading, to an effect for both mathematics and reading (compare Witte, 1999; Rouse 1998; Greene et al., 1998). For the Cleveland Scholarship and Tutoring Program, there are no significant differences between scholarship and public school students on any set of educational outcomes, although those students who accept the voucher but then return to the public schools report the lowest test scores (Metcalf et al., 2003). The Florida Opportunity Scholarship Program involves so few students that it is not possible to identify an educational impact as yet.

Experimental evidence also shows weak educational effects from participation in a voucher program. Using an experimental design, Howell and Peterson (2002) randomly assigned educational vouchers among a group of voucher applicants from low-income families, forming a group of voucher recipients and a similar control group. The voucher amount of about $1,400 a year was applied mainly to tuition at low-cost Catholic schools for up to three years in three cities (New York, Washington DC, and Dayton, Ohio). The full results are reported in Howell and Peterson (2002) for voucher recipients who used their voucher at a private school; the test score impacts are summarized in Table 43.4. Overall, no achievement advantages were found for educational vouchers after three years. Although the authors report positive gains for one specific group, African Americans, after three years of voucher enrollment, these results have been challenged on methodological grounds and non-robustness when statistical corrections are made.[10]

Table 43.3 Summary of charter school effects

Academic outcome	Grade level	State	Results for charter schools relative to comparison group
Math	2–11	AZ	+ve (very weak)
Reading			+ve (weak)
Reading	3,4 and 7	CO	+ve (2/3rds outperformed comparison schools)
Writing		CO	+ve
Math		CO	No difference
Reading/Math	4,6,8 and 10	CT	+ve
Reading/Math		DC	−ve (less likely to have improved; more 'below basic')
Reading/Math	3,5+	GA	No difference
Reading/Math	4,5,7,8, and 11	MI	−ve
Reading/Math	5, 6, 8, 9, and 11	PA	−ve (lower scores in cross-section) +ve (faster gains)
Reading/Math	3–8	TX	−ve, all schools +ve, at-risk schools

Source: Miron and Nelson (2002: table 3).

Table 43.4 Summary of impact of voucher experimental trials

City	Impact of switching to a private school on test score performance			
	Year I (NPR)	Year II (NPR)	Year III (NPR)	Year III (*N*)
Full Sample				
New York City	1.1	0.6	1.4	*1,250*
Dayton	2.2	4.2	..	
Washington, DC	−0.3	7.5**	−2.1	*687*
African Americans				
Three-city average	3.9	6.3**	6.6**	*1,172*
All Other Groups				
Three-city average	−1.0	−1.4	−3.5	*760*

Notes: NPR is National Percentile Ranking. **Statistical significance at $p < 0.05$. '..' indicates no statistically significant difference.

Source: Howell and Peterson (2002: table 6–1).

Considering all the evidence on the efficiency and effectiveness of markets in education, the following conclusion appears to be robust: markets do improve educational quality over what would be provided in a fully public system, but the size of this improvement is probably modest and appears to be found for some groups and not for others. To the degree that students are stratified into schools with more nearly homogeneous student populations, the peer effects of diversity on achievement may be reduced for some groups of students as well. The educational marketplace has advantages in matching students to the types of schools that their families prefer relative to traditional assignment by attendance area. This advantage is less evident where intra-district or inter-district or extensive charter school choice exists. The additional costs of the infrastructure required to monitor and administer a voucher system are substantial and may outweigh the modest achievement advantages.

Equity

The concern that school systems—whether provided by markets or the state—be fair and equitable is an important one. Equity can be assessed in terms of inputs—do all students get an appropriate amount of funding and resources, commensurate with their needs? Equity can also be assessed in terms of outcomes—do all students finish their schooling with sufficient skills and a fair opportunity to progress in life?

Those who challenge education markets argue that they will produce greater social inequities, as parents with higher incomes may benefit most. First, families already paying for private schooling may receive a government subsidy for tuition fees, which previously they were willing to pay for independently. This windfall is intrinsic to universal voucher programs, for example, and is also likely with the introduction of a tax credit or deduction. Second, wealthier families will have the most resources to purchase educational services in a private market, allowing them to purchase more education if 'add-ons' are permitted, resulting in greater inequities in inputs.[11] Also, highly educated parents may gain extra benefits when choices are expanded: as Schneider et al. (2000) have shown, these parents are probably better informed about what is available to them in the market, and will be best placed to take advantage of new school services. The likely result is that children from wealthy families will use the marketplace to greater advantage. Social stratification will increase. However, there is little direct evidence that this source of advantage is significantly greater in practice than the inequities of a public school system with local financing where families with adequate income can choose school neighborhoods.

Moreover, markets can be regulated so as to avoid inequities and, in fact, help low-income families or students in failing schools. Many voucher programs—particularly the small-scale programs—have an income threshold applied to them: only families below a certain income level are eligible for a voucher. Similarly, tuition tax credits can be allocated on a merit-based or income-based criterion. The general idea is to enable low-income and minority families to enter the market with more 'purchasing power' given to them from government subsidies. Furthermore, markets may make the education system more equitable through open enrollment (Godwin and Kemerer, 2002). Advocates argue that the ability to choose schools will open up possibilities for students who are locked into inferior neighborhood schools, and that the competitive marketplace will produce greater incentives to meet the needs of all students more fully than existing government schools.

More general concerns about broadening the scope of the market and the implications for educational equity should also be noted. First, private schools may refuse to admit some types of students, denying them an appropriate education. (It is difficult to find direct evidence that private schools do this overtly, see Lacireno-Paquet et al., 2002). Second, families may seek schools that enroll students from their backgrounds with the direct or subtle exclusion of other types of students. Simply creating a curriculum and marketing appeal that is friendly to some types of ethnic and social groups can discourage others from applying. There is a reasonable amount of evidence that—where families are given school choice—they prefer enrollment at schools that are the same racial and socio-economic group as their own (Witte, 1999; Martinez et al., 1996; Schneider et al., 2000; Fairlie and Resch, 2002; Weiher and Tedin 2002). As well, many families wish to enroll their children with peers of as high as possible ability and social class backgrounds. If families sort themselves according to ability, high-achieving students will help each other, and gain further advantages over other students.[12] Persistent and significant educational inequities may result. Recent literature has emphasized the impact that different peer groups have on the education of fellow students, and the peer consequences of choice would appear to be negative (Levin 1998; Zimmer and Toma 2000). Given the largely neutral impact of vouchers on participants' test scores, these sorting effects may be critical in a full evaluation of the educational marketplace.

Social Cohesion

Schools should promote the social good; this is the main reason they are publicly funded. What constitutes the 'social good' will vary across societies, but in a democracy the purpose of schooling is usually interpreted as necessitating common elements of schooling with regard to curriculum, values, goals, language, and political orientation. After compulsory schooling, citizens should possess the skills and knowledge necessary for civic and economic participation in society. By introducing markets and choice into the education system, therefore, there is a risk that these common elements will be undermined.[13]

There are two routes through which an education system can generate social cohesion and order. One is by the design of the system itself: social goods are created when collective action is undertaken, i.e. when all students are offered the same system of education. This is the idea of 'common schooling': social goods are created through communal activities. Clearly, reliance on the market would undermine this 'common schooling'; where families can opt out of public schools, or when they can provide extra funds for their children's education, they will not be part of this communal activity (see Levinson and Levinson, 2003). Where richer families can buy more elitist and exclusive education for their children, social cohesion may be adversely affected. However, it is difficult to find empirical research that substantiates the importance of common schooling in promoting social order.

The second route to producing social goods is through the instruction that students receive within school. When students are taught socialization skills and the importance of civic virtues, social cohesion may be enhanced. Some schools may include courses such as Civics or Political Science or Religious Education as part of the curriculum; others may encourage charitable acts by the students or offer instruction on (for example) environmental issues.[14] At issue is whether private schools can inculcate more of these capacities than public schools; whether families would—if schooling choices were more open—demand more of this type of education; and whether schooling does influence social cohesion.

Opponents of the marketplace are concerned that individual families are more likely to stress private advantages to them than broader benefits to society. Indeed, the pressure for greater freedom of choice derives from the preferences of families. Precisely how to measure the student behavior that connotes these social benefits is not settled. For example, some would measure student knowledge of political and economic institutions and modes of participation in civic life. Others would measure attitudes towards civic participation. Others yet might measure orientations towards contributing to society.

When measuring some of these dimensions, research evidence for the US suggests that private schools offer more 'civic education' than public schools do.

Table 43.5 summarizes the empirical evidence from two cross-sectional analyses of civic education in the US, controlling for other factors including family background. Students in assigned public schools are compared with those in four other types of school: magnet public, private Catholic, private religious but non-Catholic, and private independent. Although not fully consistent, the results broadly indicate that private schools produce more community service, civic skills, civic confidence, political knowledge, and political tolerance than is available in public schools. The explanatory power of the school type on actual levels of civic-mindedness is, however, very low. Nevertheless, there is certainly no direct evidence that, were families to choose a private school from the marketplace of providers, social cohesion would fall.[15] However, this analysis is based upon existing samples of private schools, not the kinds that would arise under a voucher plan. Analysis of the expansion of the supply of private schools accepting vouchers in Milwaukee indicates 30 percent are secular, with the rest religiously affiliated: around half of these religious students are Catholic and half are from other faiths. But there was a reasonable expansion of new schools: just under half of the participating schools were founded after the Program was introduced, suggesting the need for caution in extrapolating from existing provision (see Belfield et al., 2003).

Table 43.5 Summary of correlations between school type and civic education

Facet of civic education	Relative to assigned public school results in 1996/1999: Magnet Public	Catholic	Religious, non-Catholic	Private secular
Community service	../..	+ve/+ve	+ve/..	+ve/..
Civic skills	../..	+ve/+ve	../..	../..
Civic confidence	../..	../+ve	../+ve	+ve/+ve
Political knowledge	../..	../+ve	../..	+ve/..
Political tolerance	+ve/..	../+ve	../−ve	../+ve

Notes: Results are from probit and ordered probit estimations (details available from author). +ve or −ve indicates that there was a statistically significant difference (p<0.10) from the assigned public school category; '..' indicates no statistically significant difference.

Sources: Estimates for 1999 are taken from Belfield (2003). Estimates for 1996 are taken from Campbell (2001: table 12–7).

Future Developments

What are the prospects for market approaches to education, and where are the needs for research? The market approach to education is proceeding apace in elementary and secondary education. Much of the momentum derives from the political tides that have swept in privatization more generally in recent decades. But, other reasons are the quest for many different forms of school choice and the search for radical alternatives to counter the failure of inner-city schools. The federal legislation under No Child Left Behind is also an important force for privatization as an extension of school choice. At present, schools that fail to meet achievement targets must provide opportunities for their students to choose successful schools. At the same time, it is possible to use federal funding under Chapter I to obtain educational services in the private marketplace, especially tutoring services. Given the impossibility of meeting NCLB standards over time, especially for highly mobile students who do not attend a particular school long enough to benefit from enriched services, it seems likely that more and more schools will be declared 'failures'. This will provide political ammunition to push for educational market approaches and privatization as a promising alternative to that 'failure'.

The evidential base is far from complete. About the only conclusions that we can draw at this time are: (1) market approaches increase choice considerably; (2) competition and choice are associated with small improvements in academic achievement, but nothing approximating the revolutionary changes argued by advocates; (3) there is some evidence that universal market approaches will lead to greater inequalities, but restricted ones limited to the poor may have the opposite impacts; and (4) the effects of educational markets on social cohesion are unknown and depend heavily on how social cohesion is defined and measured and what types of schools will emerge in a market expansion.

Why Is So Little Known?

Although we have been able to set out a policy and evaluation framework for educational vouchers with some confidence, the evidence needed to fill in that framework is much less comprehensive. There are a number of reasons for this:

(1) *Lack of Market Experience*. Educational vouchers and tuition tax credits as well as charter schools and for-profit educational management organizations are a relatively recent phenomenon. They embrace only a tiny fraction of schools and students in the US. This has meant that the empirical universe from which one can derive evidence is extremely limited. Thus, much of the evidence is derived from other forms of educational competition, international settings such as Chile, and public/private school comparisons rather than from extensive market competition. Even the applications of educational markets are relatively small in scale and are difficult to generalize to more extensive applications.

(2) *Chicken vs. Egg Dilemma*. In the absence of more solid and persuasive evidence of superiority and the complications of trade-offs among goals, it is difficult to initiate more extensive market demonstrations. That is, in order to encourage dramatic departures from the traditional organization of schools, it is necessary to show that the alternatives are demonstrably superior. But, in the absence of larger scale applications of educational markets, it is not possible to derive that evidence.

(3) *Too Many Variants*. Clearly the outcomes of an educational marketplace depend crucially on the specifics. There are many different combinations of arrangements for finance, regulation, and support services, each with potentially different consequences on the four criteria that have been delineated. Therefore, generalization is limited from the few implementations that exist today in the US or in other countries. In reality, evidence must be limited to a particular application of educational vouchers or other forms of the educational marketplace, and the existing variants are too limited from which to draw extensive generalizations.

(4) *Evaluations are Extensive and Expensive*. It is one thing to do research on modest interventions in education. It is quite another to evaluate a system-wide change. Holding other things constant statistically or experimentally becomes less feasible as one expands the scope of the intervention, and market approaches to education represent extensive interventions. Thus, costly evaluations of educational vouchers that have adopted experimental designs have found that even after three years of assessment, a timeline that many think is too short, serious challenges to validity arise (e.g. see Peterson and Howell, 2004; Krueger and Zhu, 2004*a,b*). Further, even these evaluations typically address only matters of student achievement and parental satisfaction, ignoring the other important dimensions. The significant advantages in using randomized field trials to produce very precise answers and accurately identify impacts may come at the cost of relevance to broader policy questions and issues of program implementation. Although much more can be done in ascertaining the probable impact of market reforms in education on different educational outcomes, the multiplicity of educational goals and the thinness of the evidence suggests that *a priori* views and ideological stances will probably dominate in terms of educational policy on this topic.

NOTES

1. There is now a considerable amount of evidence on education markets, from researchers in political science, law, education, sociology, and economics (e.g., Godwin and Kemerer, 2002; Wolfe, 2003; Hoxby, 2003). It is therefore only possible to provide an overview of the issues (for an earlier, book-length review, see Gill et al., 2001).

2. The brief exposition that follows is designed only to provide the uninformed reader with the most rudimentary picture of a market and price determination. It is not a substitute for a more thorough presentation. Detailed expositions at an introductory level can be found in Pindyck and Rubinfeld (2000).

3. It is important to note that a large number of households exercise choice among schools and school districts in their choice of neighborhood. For some detail on existing school choice, see Henig and Sugarman (1999). For the theory on why choice of community may lead to efficient production of schooling and other public goods in local communities, see the classic article by Tiebout (1956).

4. More detail is provided in the Appendix to Levin (2002: 170–1) presenting 'Questions for Analyzing Design Dimensions of Vouchers'.

5. The dearth of knowledge and understanding by parents is heavily underlined in Public Agenda (1999). Schneider, Teske, and Marschall (2000) also found class and race differences in knowledge of schools. For a detailed investigation of public attitudes, see Moe (2001).

6. Levin (1999) with greater elaboration in Levin (2002). Also see Godwin and Kemerer (2002).

7. For example, E. G. West, an important supporter of private markets in education, has argued that public benefits or externalities of education are largely mythical or are not worth the burden of tax support because of the deadweight loss of public welfare created by that level of taxation. His views imply that the provision of payment for education should be privately arranged rather than being a matter for the government. See West (1991).

8. There have been a number of attempts to identify alternative outcomes for schooling besides test scores, and to compare these across school types. Comparisons between private religious and public schools show the former reduce teen involvement in sexual activity, arrests, and the use of hard drugs, but there is no difference in alcohol, tobacco or soft drug usage (Figlio and Ludwig, 2000).

9. Recent micro-level analysis from four states indicates that charter school students may perform better (WI), broadly equivalent (TX), or worse (CA, NC) than students in other school settings (Bifulco and Ladd, 2003; Witte, 2003: Hanushek et al., 2003; and Buddin and Zimmer, 2003). These micro-level analyses also find considerable variation in academic achievement across types of charter school.

10. These findings have been challenged by a re-analysis that concludes that these gains may not be robust to more consistent racial classification and alternative sampling schemes (see Krueger and Zhu, 2004*a, b*; and in rebuttal, see Peterson and Howell, 2004). Notwithstanding, on either set of assumptions there is very little evidence that voucher programs make a large difference to educational outcomes for participating students.

11. Much of the present system of funding public education permits greater funding of schools in wealthier areas through the property tax. However, by basing this type of decision on individual families rather than communities, it can be shown that the inequalities are likely to increase.

12. There is more international evidence on sorting according to ability levels. For New Zealand, there is evidence of ethnic partitioning after decentralization: the proportion of minority students increased in lower performing schools and fell in higher performing schools (Fiske and Ladd, 2003). Similar evidence has been found in studies of schools in Scotland and the Netherlands (Willms, 1996; Karsten, 1994). For the United Kingdom, families—when given new school choice options—selected schools with similar socioeconomic status to their own (Gorard and Fitz, 2000). However, the overall effect on the socioeconomic partitioning of the system was slight.

13. Often, the assumption that a government system does generate social cohesion is taken for granted. Given the substantial involvement of local, state, and federal governments in education over the past century, there has been very little specific evidence adduced as to how social cohesion is being promoted and what indicators can be used to ensure that it continues to do so. (We appreciate the comments of a reviewer on this issue).
14. A related approach is to compare the educational processes (e.g. pedagogies, cultures, classroom interactions, and textbooks) of private versus public schools (see Peshkin, 1986; Brint et al., 2001).
15. From data from the 1996 Youth Civic Involvement survey, Smith (2003: 114) reports higher levels of tolerance, civic capital efficacy, and participation in private schools, although when these correlations are adjusted for student and community characteristics only private independent schools show an advantage. Further, this conclusion depends heavily on which schools might predominate in market expansion. Evangelical schools, which are the most rapidly growing segment at present, show less political tolerance among their students than Catholic or public schools (Godwin et al., 2001).

The Limits of Managerialist School Reform: The Case of Target-Setting in England and the USA

Martin Thrupp and David Hursh

For many years now school reform has been the focus of policy and academic debate in education on both sides of the Atlantic and elsewhere. Much of the debate has been about how to close the 'achievement gap' between (typically white, middle-class) high-achieving students and (typically working-class and minority ethnic group) low-achieving students. While the last decade has seen the focus of this debate shift from an emphasis on market solutions to an emphasis on managerialist solutions, at its heart a tension between two broad perspectives continues to be apparent.

The first is a *problem-solving* perspective on school reform which stresses that schools and student achievement can be improved through developments in social technology and organization. A problem-solving perspective tends to run through policy and be favoured by policymakers because it holds out the hope of finding a ready solution to the problem of 'under-performance'. It also dominates academic research and writing in school management areas such as school effectiveness, improvement, leadership, and change (see Thrupp and Willmott 2003).

The alternative broad perspective, favoured in the sociology of education and policy sociology, is more critical, emphasizing that there are powerful social and political constraints on the feasibility of boosting student achievement through school reform (Gewirtz 2002; Thrupp 1999; Tomlinson 2005). The critical perspective on student achievement allows that the professional middle class will, through electoral pressures and more direct strategies, use schools and education systems to maintain their social and political dominance, for instance by choosing schools in ways which place their children in advantageous school contexts, requiring a formal and informal curriculum which favours middle-class culture, and reifying academic hierarchies in the competition for credentials. Those taking a critical perspective tend to be less optimistic about the potential of recent school reforms to improve student achievement, arguing that reforms lack the authenticity and depth to address the effects of structural inequalities or in some cases (for instance market competition between schools), will themselves be able to be exploited by the middle class in pursuit of positional advantage (Thrupp 2005; Thrupp and Tomlinson 2005).

At its most extreme the problem-solving perspective extends to a belief in the plausibility of 'failure free' schooling (Reynolds and Stringfield 1996), while the critical perspective can lead to the view that 'the only solution to educational resignation and failure in the inner city is the ultimate elimination of poverty and racial degradation' (Anyon 1995: 8). Yet since many who take an essentially problem-solving position allow for *some* influence of social structure and since those who take a critical perspective generally allow for *some* mediation of structure through schools and teachers, it is more helpful to think of a *spectrum* of perspectives than any clear dichotomy. Nevertheless where the thinking of policymakers, practitioners, and academics lies on this spectrum has important implications for shaping education research, policy, and practice. Thus Dale (1992: 206) has criticized 'problem-solving' research which 'takes the world as it finds it' rather than 'standing back from the existing social order and asking how that social order comes about'. Similarly Grace (1995) has advocated 'policy scholarship' over 'policy science', Moore (1996) has called for 'sociology of education', over 'sociology for education', and Thrupp and Willmott (2003) have criticized 'textual apologists' for failing to challenge managerialist reform while applauding the work of 'textual dissenters' who have. Finally Grace (1994: 59) has called for 'complex hope' as 'an optimism of the will that recognises the historical and structural difficulties which need to be overcome', comparing this favourably to the 'naive' and 'simple' hope which usually dominates education policy discourses.

In this chapter we focus on the critical limits of *target-setting* as a managerialist technique. Setting targets against which to monitor performance is a key New Public Management tool (Boston et al. 1996) and an important regulatory technique for 'steering from a distance'. It is really a form of central regulation but it is one in which local authorities are heavily implicated, as they are both responsible for relaying targets into schools and have their own (often related) targets to meet. Under New Labour target-setting has become a key feature of public policy in England, and schooling has become saturated with required targets at every level.[1] With the passing of the federal No Child Left Behind (NCLB) Act, it is also becoming increasingly important in the US.

Our discussion here will consider target-setting in both England and the US, concentrating on England where it most developed and moving to the US where the NCLB is now having a major impact on schools across the nation. We begin by noting how target-setting has been central to New Labour's school reform programme since it was elected in 1997. Second, drawing on a range of studies, we look at the likely impact of target-setting in England both in terms of the statistical evidence on levels of student achievement as well as more direct qualitative evidence of school processes. Finally, we turn to the US where there is growing evidence of target-setting leading to outcomes similar to those in England.

What becomes clear from reviewing the impact of target-setting in these ways is how damaging it is. Although target-setting (and its related testing and accountability regimes) may often seem to deliver higher student performance, in fact there are problems with both the sustainability and authenticity of its impact. On balance, the evidence on target-setting supports a critical reading of managerialist school reform, the implications of which we return to in our conclusion.

Target-Setting in England

Target-setting has become pervasive in England's schools over the last decade. Given New Labour's emphasis on improvement and standards, most school targets are related to academic achievement but targets are also set and monitored in other areas where student or school performance is regarded as an issue, for instance, truancy and school exclusions, meeting the education of minority groups, organizational targets related to delivering quality education services, achieving stakeholder representation, and so on. Within schools, teachers negotiate targets with students, teachers negotiate student achievement targets with school's senior management teams as part of the performance management process, and headteachers and governors negotiate school targets with LEA advisers which are in turn required to take account of national targets (DfEE 1998). LEAs also have to set targets with the DfES, again centred on student achievement but including many other aspects of LEA work. The government itself publicly sets targets against which to monitor its own performance. At all of these levels there is an expectation to improve year-on-year and hence target-setting has become an integral element of government micromanagement of the education system.

While there are many targets, not all receive the same focus. Targets related to particular 'headline' achievement benchmarks feature much more in policy and media discussion and debate than others. During New Labour's first term the stakes became high as New Labour sought to persuade the electorate that it was being tough on underperformance and improving the school system. In 1997 the then Education Secretary David Blunkett set targets for 75 and 80 per cent of students reaching level 4 in numeracy and literacy respectively in Key Stage (KS) 2 tests and promised to resign if these targets were not met by 2002 (they weren't—but by 2002 Blunkett had moved out of education). In more recent years attention has shifted to secondary school level where the headline figure has been the proportion of students gaining five A*–C grades in GCSE exams (see below). The stakes are also high for schools and local authorities. The DfES sets 'floor targets'—minimum performance levels which have to be achieved by all secondary schools regardless of intake characteristics. Floor targets were initially outlined in March 2000 when Blunkett (2000) insisted that 'by 2004 there should be no secondary school anywhere with less than 20 per cent; of its pupils achieving 5A*–Cs. And by 2006 there should be none achieving less than 25 per cent.' Floor targets continue to put pressure on the generally low socio-economic schools near the bottom of the exam league tables and on the local authorities which are charged with helping to improve these schools (see below).

Target-setting has never been intended to stand alone but alongside various other processes such as development planning, performance management and performance pay, LEA and DfES monitoring, action planning, OFSTED inspections and special measures, as well as the numerous other initiatives of the DfES Standards and Effectiveness Unit.[2] For instance each year LEA staff monitor target-setting in schools, hold 'stock take' meetings with DfES staff (schools directorate advisers) to review progress against their targets, make new ones, and lay out their targets in Education Development Plans (EDPs). The sophistication of target-setting technology has also grown over time. Whereas the first targets were little more than best guesses—Tomlinson (2001) described the Parent Charter targets as 'wildly over-optimistic'—targets are now forecast much more systematically. Schools and LEAs have been able to set achievement targets on the basis of information provided in the government's 'autumn package' published annually by the DfES which contains national pupil performance data taken from the results of statutory and optional National Curriculum tests. It is used to examine aspects of a school's performance against all schools nationally or to a group of similar schools. There is also the Pupil Achievement Tracker (PAT) system intended to facilitate more detailed and better informed discussion about pupil progress.

Target setting—along with associated national testing, performance management, and monitoring regimes—has invoked both support and criticism in the English media. In 2003 the *Times Educational Supplement* ran a unprecedented campaign against primary-level key stage testing and target-setting. This appears to have had some effect, as *Excellence and Enjoyment* (DfES 2003*a*) resulted in primary schools setting their own targets with LEA targets set afterwards (rather than the other way around as had previously been the case). The DfES described this as being 'in response to concerns expressed by headteachers and others' (DfES 2003*b*: 6) because 'it is important that schools are able to feel confident that they have been given sufficient control over the targets which they set for their pupils and that LEAs are not determining the process and the eventual outcome' (ibid. 8).

While more emphasis on a bottom-up rather than top-down target-setting process could be viewed as a softening up of target-setting policy, there remains little evidence of a fundamental shift. The approach whereby the DfES agrees LEA targets which inform the target-setting process at school level continues at secondary level and new targets continue to be set for both primary and secondary schools. The current (2005) national targets are as follows. At KS 2, the target is for 85 per cent of 11-year-olds to achieve Level 4 or above in English and mathematics, by 2006, with this level of performance sustained to 2008. At KS 3 the target is for 85 per cent of 14-year-olds to achieve at least Level 5 in English, mathematics, and ICT, with 80 per cent achieving Level 5 in science, with this level of performance sustained to 2008. At KS 4 60 per cent of pupils are to achieve five or more A*–C GCSEs or equivalent by 2008. Floor targets in 2005 are: at KS2 to reduce by 40 per cent the proportion of schools where fewer than 65 per cent of pupils achieve Level 4+ in English and fewer than 65 per cent achieve Level 4+ in mathematics (with the reduction measured against the number of schools that were below 65 per cent in 2003). At KS 3 all schools need to have at least 50 per cent of pupils achieve Level 5 or above in English, mathematics, and science by 2005. In KS 4 the floor target is that at least 25 per cent of pupils achieve five or more A*–C GCSEs or equivalent by 2006 and 30 per cent by 2008. Target-setting is also central to new 'compacts' the DfES now agrees with individual LEAs.

The Impact of Target-Setting in England

Figure 44.1 shows national targets set and results achieved on a year by year basis since 1997. Two problems stand out. The first is how modest the secondary targets are, especially at KS 4. Only about 50 per cent of students have been expected to get five A–C grades (i.e. pass grades) at GCSE, rising to 60 per cent as a target in the near future (2008). Put another way, it is accepted that some 50 per cent, or at best 40 per cent, of the student population will fail. As Torrance (2003) has commented 'if we assume a reasonable indication of a sound secondary education is 5 GCSE A*–C grades, including English and Maths … then around 50 per cent of the school population is still not achieving this'.

The scale of this failure and its links to social class and school composition have been highlighted by OFSTED Chief Inspector David Bell who has noted that only 32 per cent of children whose parents have 'routine occupations' are likely to leave school with five good GCSE passes compared with 81 per cent of children from more advantaged homes (Bell 2003). The same year, Bell noted that while 'improvement in schools with the highest levels of social disadvantage has been greater than that of any group of schools', nevertheless 'the gap between the average achievement in the highest performing schools and the lowest continues to widen' (OFSTED 2003: para 79). Clearly floor targets are intended to address this problem but there is no sign yet that they will be able to. As Bell argued, 'There remain some groups of pupils and some schools for whom raising standards remains an almost intractable challenge' (ibid., see also Curtis 2003).

The second, related point is that test gains are clearly proving unsustainable over time—i.e. they are 'plateauing'. This is particularly obvious from the KS 2 results which rose steadily from 1995 to 2000 but then plateaued such that by 2005 the number of students reaching level 4 in numeracy and literacy has still not reached the 75 and 80 per cent respectively expected by 2002. A frequent interpretation of this plateauing trend is that it suggests the 'using up' of capacity to improve due to to 'teaching to the test' rather than improved learning and teaching per se. For instance Tymms (2004) has argued that test data have been used in a very high-stakes fashion so that the pressure created makes it hard to interpret the data. 'Teaching test technique must surely have contributed to some of the rise, as must teaching to the test'(p. 492). Similarly Wiliam (2001: 14) has argued that 'rising test scores demonstrate little more than teachers' increasing abilities to teach to the tests, and to the power of high-stakes tests to distort the curriculum'. Certainly even before looking in detail at relevant school processes the pattern of test results supports the 'teaching to the test' thesis. Over the late 1990s when Maths and English results were rising, the other core subject, Science, rose at a similar rate. This was despite having no 'science hour', in fact teachers reported they were teaching less science because of the 'literacy hour' and 'daily Maths lesson'. So the similar rates of improvement for Maths, Science, and English are unlikely to have been because of government strategies, because there were none in Science, but because teachers were getting better at teaching to the tests.[3]

These are the most obvious problems indicated by patterns in the test results data, but there are others. Tymms (2004) has used results from several different studies and an analysis of the standard-setting procedures to provide a comprehensive analysis of the officially reported gains in achievement at KS 2. His key conclusion is that national testing has failed to monitor standards accurately over time because statistical procedures were faulty and not corrected until 2000/1, the form of the national tests has changed over time, and that curriculum has

	1997	1998	1999	2000	2001	2002	
	Results	Results	Results	Results	Results	Targets	Results
KS2 L4+							
English	63	65	71	75	75	80	75
Mathematics	62	59	69	72	71	75	73
KS2 L5+							
English	16	17	22	29	29	-	29
Mathematics	18	17	24	25	25	-	28
KS3							
English	57	65	64	64	65	-	66
Mathematics	60	59	62	65	66	-	67
Science	60	56	55	59	66	-	66
ICT (teacher assessment)	-	-	58	62	65	-	66
KS4							
5 A*–C GCSE	45.1	46.3	47.9	49.2	50	50	51.2
1 A* – C GCSE	92.3	93.4	94	94.4	94.6	95	95
5 A* – G including			85.8	86.8	86.9		86.8

	2003	2004		2006		2007		2008	
	Results	Targets	Results	Targets	Results	Targets	Results	Targets	Results
KS2 L4+									
English	75	85		85					
Mathematics	73	85		85					
KS2 L5+									
English	27	35		-	-	-	-	-	-
Mathematics	29	35		-	-	-	-	-	-
KS3									
English	68	75				85		50*	
Mathematics	70	75				85		50*	
Science	68	70				80		50*	
ICT (teacher assessment)	67	58				85			
KS4									
5 A*– C GCSE	52.6	20**		25**				60 (30)**	
1 A* – C GCSE	-								
5 A* – G	86.3								

Fig. 44.1 England's national school test results and targets 1997–2008

* In all schools at least 50% of pupils achieve Level 5 or above in English, Mathematics and Science.

** In all schools at least 20% of pupils will achieve five or more A*–C GCSEs or equivalent by 2004, 25% by 2006 and 30% by 2008.

Source: DfES website.

inevitably changed and therefore so has test content. Furthermore Wiliam (2001) has pointed out that curricula are always changing and that what is actually taught in schools changes even if the 'official' curriculum is not changed.

All of this should be enough to warn against taking achievement gains, and hence the success of target-setting and associated technologies at face value, but this view is reinforced further by considering the school processes underlying the achievement figures. A key concern is that increased emphasis on narrow targets has reduced the curriculum in various ways. To begin with, target-setting has required a closer specification of formal content and teaching methods from central government. This is most obvious in the core primary subjects of English and Maths when a National Literacy Strategy (NLS) was introduced followed by a National Numeracy Strategy (NNS) (subsequently the NLS has been extended to KS3).[4] Second, there is much evidence that schools and teachers focus on the test/target. Indeed Gillborn and Youdell (2000: 12) discuss what they call the 'A-to-C economy' in which 'almost every aspect of [secondary] school life is re-evaluated for its possible contribution to the headline statistic of the proportion of pupils attaining at least 5 higher grade GCSE passes'.

The pressure to meet targets has a variety of unjust and perverse consequences. It encourages schools to recruit bright, middle-class, 'able' children and avoid taking on 'expensive' SEN and excluded students wherever possible (Ball 2003; Bagley et al. 2001). Once in schools, children are seen to be similarly commodified or marginalized through decisions around setting and testing. For instance Gillborn and Youdell (2000) note the occurrence of 'educational triage' where decisions are made to focus on some students at the expense of others depending on whether or not they are seen to have the potential to enhance their school's A–C position. Pressure to meet targets may also often lead to impression management by way of fabrication (Ball 2001) and contribute to a general decline in the vitality and creativity of teaching (Gewirtz 2002).

Other criticisms revolve around intensification of teacher and management workloads, the demotivating effect of ambitious targets on the students and schools which cannot reach them and the difficulty of targets which rise year on year when the characteristics of student year groups can vary markedly. There are concerns too that 'the overdetermined New Labour classroom may well produce a generation of young people marred by what Hugh Lauder calls "trained incapacity"' (cited in Ball 1999: 202). Target-setting and testing may represent a considerable opportunity cost in terms of time, energy, and funding which could be better used towards more clearly educational and social justice goals.

Findings about target-setting from an EU-funded research project set in the inner-London borough of Wyeham (Ball et al. 2006; Thrupp et al. 2004) prove recent insights into practitioners' thinking about target setting. This research illustrated how very particular academic targets have become the 'bread and butter' of school management:

> In our school improvement plan we've got targets, which I can read them off there, actually. So, this year we had a target of five A to Cs of 45, up from 41. In 2002/3 we had 49, this year we've got 49, which will be hard to get. And then we got 53%, 54%, 58%. ... The national expectation is for children of level 12 and above, at, well, average—the expectation is level 4 at KS 2. So, the aggregate is 12. Aggregate KS scores are the best indicator of GCSE performance at 16+. So, the expectation is to go from aggregate 12, targeted 15. The students are supposed to move in one level in KS 3. And then if they get aggregate 15s, you'd expect them to get five A to Cs. Although you wouldn't necessarily expect them to get five A to Cs, but that's what I'm saying. (Head, Tennyson School)

Nevertheless there was no simple or uniform take-up of the language and practices of target-setting. There was support from school staff, especially heads, but it was usually heavily qualified. For instance:

> I mean, I was reading in the paper yesterday that they're now declaring, or want to declare, the government, that if you are twenty-five percent or below, you're automatically a serious weakness school. Automatically ... I think I'd like to talk to them about that, and say, 'okay, we've hit our target this year, which is—we said we'd be thirty-two percent and we got thirty-two percent five A to Cs.' But I argue what's more important—I'm more worried not about the five A to Cs, I'm more worried about that every single one of my children has a qualification. (Head, Merchant School)

Staff other than heads usually expressed indifference ('Target setting is a, is a kind of legal requirement. You know, the government says we've got to do it, but hey', teacher, Hazlett) or they expressed concerns about target-setting. In line with the critiques mentioned earlier, the main concerns included required achievement targets being unrealistic, pointless, and demotivating, for instance:

> I actually think [targets] are, you know, almost worthless. They're based on a model that simply says about, you know, a one percent or two percent improvement. So, if it's 43% this year, it'll be 45% next year and 47% the—you know, it's just an ideal 'let's get better'. (Deputy Head, Hazlett School)

Nevertheless school staff have little choice but to work with targets. The head of McCaulay School suggested that while there may be good educational reasons for setting targets, setting and meeting targets is also necessary in order for schools to avoid central government and local authority pressure:

[There is] the right of the pupil to be involved in their own learning, and therefore they needed to know what you are aiming for them. You know, the rights of the parents to be involved ... But also, critically, if you want to come out of special measures this is the only way. ... Until you've hit these percentages, you know, you're going to be continuing to see it, I suppose ... Or, unless you can justify what your target, you know, why you're where you are, and you only do that by having knowledge of your data. So, that's the argument really. (Head, McCaulay)

The service managers who worked for the Wyeham local authority also had much to say about target-setting, nearly all of it critical. To some the oversaturation of schools with targets and too much emphasis on particular targets at the expense of others for political reasons had become major problems in New Labour's education policy: 'I've been told, and I can't verify the number, but it might involve individual schools in having more than eighty targets as a result of those—just those four policies ... So, I don't think that's rational' (Mrs Gordon). Specific concerns on behalf of schools was the time wasted in meetings (Ms Mansell: 'you're taking teachers out of school. And, actually, teachers are far better off in schools'), the difficulty of year on year and between-school comparisons and unrealistic targets. Service managers had to work between mostly sceptical school staff and an insistent government and also try to deliver programmes which were marginalized by schools because they didn't fit the headline targets:

Mr Jones: It is just unrealistic. The trouble is Headteachers look at it and just say 'this is just ridiculous' and the LEA say: 'I know it is unrealistic', and when we get the Minister in we tell them 'the targets are unrealistic' ...

Ms Mansell: Again we have also got this thing where there is this incredible focus on the C/D borderline because that's the grades that schools are interested in, converting the Ds to Cs, and they are less interested in having As and A*s, because floor targets for that sort of thing are much more important than the floor targets that we have in the gifted and talented strand.

There were also problems with targets at the local authority (EF) level:

Mr Ramsay: But you know, I sat in a meeting with the DfES where they had the research and statistics and said, you know, this is the progress we've made, that's where you want us to get to. To do that, we will actually have to improve at a faster rate than any Education Authority has in the whole history of testing or whatever. And they sat there and said 'you've got to do it'. And it can't be done.

Target-Setting and its Effects in the United States

Although the terminology used in the US is more around 'standards' than targets, it has also been moving towards a national target-setting regime which has numerous similarities to England's. Until 2002 states varied in the extent to which they were willing to implement standards, standardized testing and in the significance given to the tests. For instance, while Iowa entirely resisted developing standards, standardized testing and accountability systems, Texas passed legislation making high school graduation contingent on passing more difficult 'criterion-referenced' tests after 1994. Moreover, Texas schools that receive high ratings became eligible for cash awards and those that receive low ratings face sanctions, including possible closure (Haney 2000). At the same time as Texas secondary schools came under pressure to raise test scores, they became rated on the percentage of students graduating and faced sanctions for high dropout rates.

In 2002 the No Child Left Behind (NCLB) Act was passed into law with overwhelming congressional support. NCLB extended what states such as Texas had begun by mandating that *all* states conduct standardized tests in reading and math in grades 3 though 8 and by 2008, add science and grades 9 through 12. Schools now face severe penalties for failing to increase test scores sufficiently, including potentially being converted into charter (privately administered, publicly funded) schools.[5] Most of the Act's requirements immediately went into effect, including requiring all states to develop standardized tests and assessment systems in order to determine whether schools are making 'adequate yearly academic progress' (AYP). Under NCLB, schools must not only develop and assess students; they must make public the aggregated test scores for groups of students delineated by gender, race, and ethnic group, and with or without disability. Because schools may have several ethnic and racial groups, all of whom must be represented by gender and ability status, schools typically have to generate and report the scores for dozens of subgroups. The test scores for each group are then compared to the state's testing requirements to determine whether the group is making AYP.

If any *one* group fails to make AYP, the entire school is designated as failing. Sometimes, shifting a single child's score from one group to another (for example, by changing a student's disability status) can mean the difference between a school failing or passing. Schools that fail to make AYP face significant sanctions which become more severe year by year unless there is an improvement (US Department of Education, 2002a). If schools do not make AYP for two consecutive years, they must be identified as 'in need of improvement' and students allowed to transfer to another public schools with transportation provided by the failing school. By the fourth year 'failing schools' must take corrective action that includes one of these options: replacing the school staff, implementing a new curriculum, 'decreasing management authority at the school level, appointing an outside expert to advise the school, extending the school day or year, or reorganizing the school internally' (US Department of Education 2002*b*: 6). Further, if a school fails to make progress for five years the school district must initiate plans for fundamental restructuring: 'This restructuring may include reopening the school as a *charter school,* replacing all or most of the school staff who are relevant to the failure to make adequate progress, or turning over the operations either to the state or to a *private* company with a demonstrated record of effectiveness' (US Department of Education, 2002*b*: 7, emphasis added).[6]

The consequences of target-setting in the US have many parallels to the evidence from England. One extensive review of anecdotal evidence from all states concludes 'that the over-reliance on high-stakes testing has serious negative repercussions that are present at every level of the public school system' (Nichols and Berliner 2005: p. i). Our discussion here employs evidence from New York, Chicago, Texas, and Florida, as well as what is known to date about the consequences of the NCLB.

In New York almost every recent standardized exam has been criticized for having poorly constructed, misleading, or erroneous questions, or for using a grading scale that either over- or understates students' learning. Critics argue that an exam's degree of difficulty has varied depending on whether the State Education Department (SED) has wanted to increase the graduation rate and therefore makes the exam easier or appear rigorous and tough and therefore makes the exam more difficult. The passing rate for the exam can be increased or decreased simply by adjusting the cut score, turning a low percentage of correct answers into a pass or a high percentage of correct answers into a failure (see Hursh 2005 for further details). The SED has also been criticized for how they construct the test questions. For example, a recent English exam received national censure for removing from literary passages references 'to race, religion, ethnicity, sex, nudity, alcohol, even the mildest profanity and just about anything that might offend someone for some reason' (Kleinfield 2002: 1; see Hursh 2005 for further details).

However, even if the tests were well constructed and valid, the yardstick by which schools are measured—adequate yearly academic progress (AYP)—often discriminates against schools serving students of colour and living in poverty. The determination of whether a school is making AYP tells us little about whether a school is improving. Not only can the validity of the tests be questioned but the determination of success or failure may have little to do with whether the school is improving. Under NCLB, every state, with the approval of federal Department of Education, determines, for every test, what knowledge and skills students need to demonstrate proficiency. States can, therefore, make achieving proficiency more or less difficult. However, for all states and every school, all students (regardless of ability or proficiency in the English language) are to achieve proficiency by the year 2014.

Contrary to a common-sense interpretation of AYP, schools are *not* evaluated on whether their test scores are improving but on whether their aggregated and disaggregated test scores exceed a minimum yearly threshold that gradually increases over the next decade. Consequently, a school is considered to be passing as long as their scores exceed the threshold, even if their scores fall. Similarly, schools that begin with initially low test scores may be considered failing even if they significantly improve their test scores, as long as those scores remain below the threshold. Therefore, achieving AYP may have nothing to do with whether a school's test scores rise or fall; achieving AYP depends only on exceeding the minimum threshold.

Because test scores strongly correlate with a student's family income, a school's score is more likely to reflect their students' average family income rather than teaching or the curriculum. Consequently, most failing schools in New York are found in poor, urban school districts. Almost all (83 per cent) of the failing schools are located in the big five urban districts: New York City, Buffalo, Rochester, Syracuse, and Yonkers (NYSSBA 2002). Most of the remaining failing schools are in smaller urban districts. The failure rate of schools in the urban districts is high, particularly at the middle-school level. In Rochester, for example, all the middle schools failed. To NCLB's testing requirement that schools demonstrate improvement for all disaggregated groups of students on all the tests, Florida added the further stipulation that no school that had been assigned by the state a grade of a D, E, or F (per the annual rating of A through F) could meet AYP. Not surprisingly, 90 per cent of Florida's public schools were designated as failing to meet AYP, and 100 per cent of districts failed (Pinzur 2003).

Because of the pressure to raise test scores, particularly in the urban school districts, teachers are compelled to teach the skills and knowledge that will be tested, neglecting other usually more complex aspects of the subject and some subjects altogether. In an ethnographic study of schools in Chicago, Lipman (2004) documents how the testing requirements undermined the critical literacy goals of a bilingual school and frustrated creative, dedicated teachers. She describes how an elementary school, with a student population of over 90 per cent Mexican-American, had to shift their focus away from using the students' own culture to develop critical literacy, and focus instead on test preparation. One teacher stated that she devoted the first half of the school year to the students writing intensively and reading sophisticated literature but then, for the third quarter, shifted to test preparation. Test preparation included getting students 'used to the format of a short, mediocre selection of writing ... to get them to recognize this type of question is asking you for some really basic information you can go back to look for' (Lipman 2004: 110–11). The teachers, Lipman writes, experience 'the contradictions and conflicts ... between their efforts to help students see knowledge as a tool to analyze the world and the process and practice of preparing for standardized tests' (p. 111).

In Chicago, as in England (Gillborn and Youdell 2000), administrators instruct teachers to put their efforts into raising the test scores of those students who are closest to passing the standardized tests. As one teacher said:

> They tell us ... 'We don't want high kids and we don't want the lowest kids, we want the kids that are just about to pass the IOWA [standardized] test.' So here you have a third or a fourth of your classroom really needs help to be ready for that next grade level and they don't get to go. (Lipman, 2004: 82)

Such educational 'triage' (Gillborn and Youdell 2000) exacerbates educational inequality as the students who either pass or are close to passing the test become valued commodities and those students who need the most help are left to fend for themselves.

McNeil (2000) illustrates how the emphasis on tests and test scores undermined exemplary schools and teachers in Houston, Texas. She documented how after the Texas standardized testing requirements (TAAS) were implemented, previously successful schools began to expect less of their students as they prepared them to pass the more basic skills required on the tests. Rather than, for example, teaching students to write well, teachers taught students to write the five-paragraph essay with five sentences in each paragraph that would receive passing grades on the standardized tests. Because culturally advantaged middle- and upper-class students are likely to rely on their cultural capital to pass the exams, it is disadvantaged students who receive the additional drilling. Unfortunately, learning to write five-sentence five-paragraph essays does not transfer well to literacy required beyond the test and outside of school. By expecting less of disadvantaged students, they fall further beyond.

Lowered expectations are not the only problem. Schools emphasizing test preparation are likely to devote most of their curriculum budget to test-prep materials rather than the enriched resources students need. Further, schools, in focusing on test preparation, are likely to reduce or eliminate subjects that are not being tested, including the arts and sciences. In Texas, because science is not tested in the early grades, it is no longer taught.

Rather than ensuring that more students do well, the pressure to raise test scores also encourages schools to force weak students out of school before they take the required exam. In Texas, urban students are more likely to be retained in school, especially in ninth grade, the year before the required TAAS exam is first given. Students who are repeatedly retained are likely to give up and drop out of school. Haney (2000), in his study of the Texas education reforms, concludes that for the year 1996–7, 17.8 per cent of students were being retained in ninth grade (24.2 per cent of African-American and 25.9 per cent of Hispanic students) and that only 57.57 per cent of African-American and 52.11 per cent of Hispanic ninth-grade students were in twelfth grade four years later (ibid. 5, pp. 8–9).

As noted earlier, schools in Texas have faced a double-edge sword: they need to raise test scores but face possible sanctions for high dropout rates. Rodney Paige, superintendent of the Houston Independent School District (HISD) since 1994, found a fabricating 'solution' to this problem. He ordered principals not to list a student as dropping out but as having left for another school or some reason other than dropping out. Such creative book-keeping resulted in the district claiming a greatly reduced dropout rate and winning awards for excellence (Winerip 2003). Eventually critics claimed that the dropout rate was covered up and research has revealed the rate to be much higher than the official one. Significantly, 'almost all of the students that were being pushed out were at-risk students and minorities' (Kimball cited in Capello 2004). A state investigation into sixteen high schools revealed that of 5,000 students who left school, 2,999 students should have been reported as dropouts and were not (Winerip 2003). States other than Texas have also responded to the pressure to raise test scores by surreptiously pushing students out of school. In New York, students are being pushed out of schools to raise test scores and, then, rather than being counted as dropouts, they are listed as having transferred to an alternative school or working on a Graduate Equivalency Diploma (GED), a diploma achieved not by attending school but by passing an exam (Lewin and Medina, 2003: 1).

We might expect that when the curriculum is narrowed and simplified, students who score low on tests are abandoned, poorly constructed tests lead to mass failures, and students are pushed out of schools, the achievement gap will grow rather than reduce. Evidence from New York supports this conclusion. From 1998 to 2000, the number of students dropping out increased by 17 per cent. A recent report for the Harvard Centre for Civil Rights concluded that New York now has the lowest graduation rate of any state for African-American (35 per cent) and Latino (31 per cent) students (Orfield et al. 2004). In New York City only 38 per cent of *all* students graduate on time, fifth worst of the 100 largest cities in the nation (Winter 2004). According to another recent study, New York's graduation rate ranks 45th in the nation (Haney 2003). The tests have also negatively affected English language learners, who moved from the highest diploma-earning minority in 1996 to the highest dropout minority in 2002 (Monk, Sipple, and Killen 2001). Lastly, dropouts among students with disabilities have increased from 7,200 in 1996 to 9,200 in 2001.

The quantitative evidence from Texas is more contradictory and contested. The state reports that the mean student test score and percentage passing the TAAS exam has increased, the differences between the mean tests score for White, African-American, and Hispanic students have decreased, and school drop-out rates have declined. However, Haney (2000) investigated the Texas data and revealed how the higher test scores were achieved. First, while students who are in special education must take the TAAS, their scores are not included in those reported by the school. Therefore, if students, whose scores might negatively affect the overall school's score can be excluded by placing the student into special education, we might expect, after TAAS was implemented, the percentage of students in special education to increase. Haney (2000) shows that for the first four years in which TAAS was implemented, the percentage of special education students increased from 4.5 to 7.1 per cent.

A second way to increase test scores has been to retain students in grades previous to tenth grade, the grade in which students first take the TAAS, providing students another year to prepare for the test. Haney's data reveal that the retention rate for previous grades has increased significantly, particularly for ninth grade. In 1996–7 25.9 per cent of Hispanic, 24.2 per cent of African-American and 17.8 per cent of White students were retained in ninth grade. Of course, grade retention also increases the likelihood that a student will drop out of school. Rather than relying on the dropout out rate reported by schools and school districts, Haney (2000) compared the percentage of students in ninth grade with the number of students in twelfth grade four years later. His data reveal that in fact there has been a significant increase in the dropout rate in Texas. Therefore, Haney concludes, the Texas 'miracle' was really the Texas 'mirage'. Test scores have increased because students are increasingly likely to be retained in previous grades or have become so discouraged that they have quit school altogether. Further, other students have been placed in special education so that their lower scores would not be included in the reported scores. In Texas, schools have raised test scores by retaining students or removing them from the pool of test-takers. Rather than increasing education achievement, fewer students have the opportunity to receive an education.

Even as schools have manipulated the scores by limiting who takes the exams, the higher average score might only mean that the students are performing better on the tests, not that they are learning more. While students' scores on the TAAS exam have been increasing, their scores on nationally administered tests, such as the university admissions exams, have been decreasing. Researchers investigating explained: 'The discrepancy in performance has a lot to do with the differences in the tests. TAAS was designed to make sure that students learned at least the basics of the state curriculum. The [university admissions tests], on the other hand, assess students on advanced academic skills needed for college'. (Markley 2004).

Conclusion

With the development of the NCLB, there are growing similarities between England and the US in their experience of target-setting as a managerialist school reform. In terms of the nature of policy there are numerous targets at a variety of levels with similarly punitive consequences for failing to improve no matter how unrealistic the targets may be. In terms of the impact of policy there are problems with the reach, sustainability, authenticity, and credibility of target setting. The targets imply an acceptance of continued student failure, there are weaknesses in the content of the tests and their assessment, and there is evidence of plateauing as the gains due to 'teaching to the test' are used up. The pressures of target-setting towards narrowing the curriculum and fabrication of results are difficult to avoid. Externally set targets are generally perceived by practitioners as forced or inorganic and hence often inappropriate. Moreover there is much evidence in both settings that those worst affected are students from low SES and minority backgrounds as well as those who have special needs of various kinds.

To return to the distinctions drawn at the outset between problem solving and critical perspectives on education reform, it is clear that the evidence on target-setting supports a highly critical reading of managerialist school reform as it becomes increasingly unlikely that such reforms will genuinely deliver the improvements in school and student achievement sought by their problem-solving architects. But quite how target-setting will develop in the future remains to be seen. One possibility in the US is that the targets set under the NCLB will prove so extreme that they will restrict the social mobility of middle-class families and the policy will implode. This is because the rising test score requirements place an increasing number of middle-class schools at risk of failing. Over the next ten years NCLB's test score requirements rise until 2014 when *all* students, whether they are English language learners, have a disability, or are homeless and poor, must demonstrate proficiency on every test (an educational impossibility) or their school fails. Consequently, each year more middle-class, white schools are likely to fail. In fall 2004 'In North

Carolina ... more than 32 schools rated excellent by the state failed to met Washington's criteria for academic progress' (Dillon 2004). In Florida, three-quarters of the state's high performing schools were rated as low performing under NCLB. Such contradictory information leaves students and families confused and angry. Middle-class parents from prestigious schools in prosperous suburbs are concerned that the low federal rating makes it more difficult for their children to be admitted to university. Other parents have more pecuniary worries; they fear that if their schools are listed as failing, their property values will decline (Dillon 2004).

A more likely and in many ways more disturbing scenario is that over time the targets will be whittled back so that they mostly end up placing pressure only on those low SES areas where many individuals and schools do not meet the basic floor targets for achievement. Yet the problem in low SES areas is that the causes of 'underachievement' will be unable to be addressed by target-setting and hence, as in 'Wyeham', it is likely to proves more problematic and 'unrealistic' than in middle-class areas where schools and districts are able to hit more of their targets, more of the time. In such contexts a critical perspective points to quite different solutions including policies which would create more balanced school intakes and those which would provide extra resources to allow the different organizational designs that would enable higher quality to be consistently delivered in high-poverty circumstances (Thrupp 1999; Lupton 2005).[7] The difficulty with managerialist reforms such as target-setting is that not only do they divert attention from more fundamental solutions, they are themselves deeply damaging. They are very much part of the problem, rather than of any solution.

NOTES

1. Although league tables of raw exam results were first published under the Conservatives in 1992 and the first headline targets for GCSE passes appeared in the 1994 Parents Charter, it was after New Labour was elected in 1997 that the range of targets set increased massively.
2. Some examples include City Academies, Advanced Skills Teachers, Beacon Schools Education Action Zones, Excellence in Cities, Federations, Gifted & Talented, the Innovation Unit, Personalised Learning, the Primary Strategy, School Diversity, School Improvement and Specialist Schools.
3. We are grateful to Margaret Brown for this observation.
4. On the other hand from 2004 the targets for Key Stage 4 include a wider range of qualifications in order to reflect the achievements of pupils taking qualifications other than GCSEs and GNVQs.
5. NCLB also restricts schools regarding which curricula they may use, increases teachers' and paraprofessionals' (aides) qualification requirements, prohibits schools from denying access to or discriminating against the Boy Scouts of America or other 'patriotic societies', requires school districts to provide military recruiters with contact information on secondary school students, and limits what research the government will fund to that using the 'medical model' of control groups. However, in this chapter we limit our analysis to target-setting and testing and their implications.
6. There are similar levels of sanctions for failing school districts, see US Department of Education (2002*b*: 6–7).
7. For example Lupton (2005) suggests smaller teaching groups, more teachers in the classroom, more non-contact time for front-line staff, a higher ratio of managers to staff, and substantially more investment in learning support, language teaching, pupil welfare, and parental liaison roles.

Schools in Disadvantaged Areas: Low Attainment and a Contextualised Policy Response

Ruth Lupton

Schools in disadvantaged areas present a problem for policymakers in England. Their academic performance is well below the national norm. 2001 data show that on average only a fifth of pupils in schools with the poorest intakes achieved five GCSE passes at grades A*–C, compared with 50% nationally (DfES 2002*a*). At Key Stage 3 (age 14) in 2000, the median for schools with more than 40% FSM[1] was that no pupil (0%) achieved the expected performance level in English, compared with 83% in schools with less than 5% FSM (Glennerster 2002).

This is a long established pattern (Floud and Halsey et al. 1956; Douglas 1964), principally because poverty presents barriers to children's education which mean that they enter secondary school with lower than average attainment and dealing with social and economic problems that inhibit their learning. School effectiveness research has consistently shown that only about 8–15% of the attainment difference between schools is accounted for by what they actually do, rather than by intake variations (Reynolds et al. 1996; Sammons 1999). There is a 'profoundly close' relationship between poverty and attainment, such that 'the more socially disadvantaged the community served by a school, the very much more likely it is that the school will appear to underachieve' (Gibson and Asthana 1998).

While this evidence strongly suggests that, in the long run, broader social policies will contribute more to reducing school attainment differences than educational interventions, educational policy clearly has a part to play (Whitty 2000). Since the 1970s, successive governments in Britain have, within a broad framework of standardised provision within the state sector, provided a range of compensatory measures to assist children from disadvantaged backgrounds. These have taken various forms, including welfare interventions such as free school meals and on-site pupil or family support services, and additional educational provision such as homework clubs and reading recovery programmes. Compensatory measures have been a particular feature of New Labour education policy since 1997. Resources for schools in deprived areas have been increased through area-targeted programmes (Education Action Zones (EAZs) and Excellence in Cities (EiC)) and through initiatives such as Pupil Learning Credits,[2] and the 'extended schools' programme. These measures appear to be having an impact, with GCSE higher grade attainment levels rising more quickly in EiC areas than others (OFSTED 2003), and while it is not universally agreed that they are sufficient (DfES 2003*a*; Johnson 2003), they nevertheless represent a recognition that context matters, and that something

This paper was written while the author was at the ESRC Centre for the Analysis of Social Exclusion (CASE) at the London School of Economics, and was originally published as CASEpaper 76 in the centre's working paper series.

different and extra is needed for schools in poor areas if attainment is to reach expected levels.

Schools in Disadvantaged Areas: Low Quality and a Decontextualised Policy Response

There is, however, also another problem with schools in poor areas: they typically do less well in inspections by OFSTED,[3] central government's principal mechanism for checking the quality of schooling.

Under the OFSTED inspection system, all schools are inspected regularly, on average once every four years. Those with unsatisfactory performance are described as having 'serious weaknesses', or put into special measures if they are 'failing or likely to fail to give pupils an acceptable standard of education' (School Inspections Act 1996 Section 13(9)). In 1998, the Social Exclusion Unit (SEU) found that five times as many secondary schools in 'worst neighbourhoods' were in special measures than was typically the case (SEU 1998). In more detailed analyses, OFSTED (2001) combines its inspection grades into four areas: 'standards' (attainment and progress); 'quality of education' (teaching and the curriculum); 'climate and ethos'; and 'management and efficiency'. Figure 45.1 shows that, as might be expected, it is standards that are most strongly associated with FSM. But high levels of FSM are associated with worse inspection grades on all the other measures as well—measures of what schools actually do as well as measures of attainment and progress. There is an apparent quality problem as well as an attainment problem: a matter for concern not just because of its consequences for attainment but for equity reasons, and more broadly because discrepancies in school quality can influence the dynamics of housing markets and reinforce residential social segregation (Gibbons 2001). It is the quality problem that is the focus of this [chapter].

Explanations for the poor quality of schools in disadvantaged areas are contested. The dominant one has been that the problem is internal to schools. Not all schools in poor areas offer a poor education. Figure 45.1 shows that five out of six high FSM schools are *not* adjudged to need substantial improvement in their quality of education, climate, or management and efficiency. This would seem to suggest that a deprived socio-economic context (at least one that is measured by FSM eligibility) does not in itself determine school failure, and that the explanation for the low quality problem in many schools in deprived areas lies within the schools

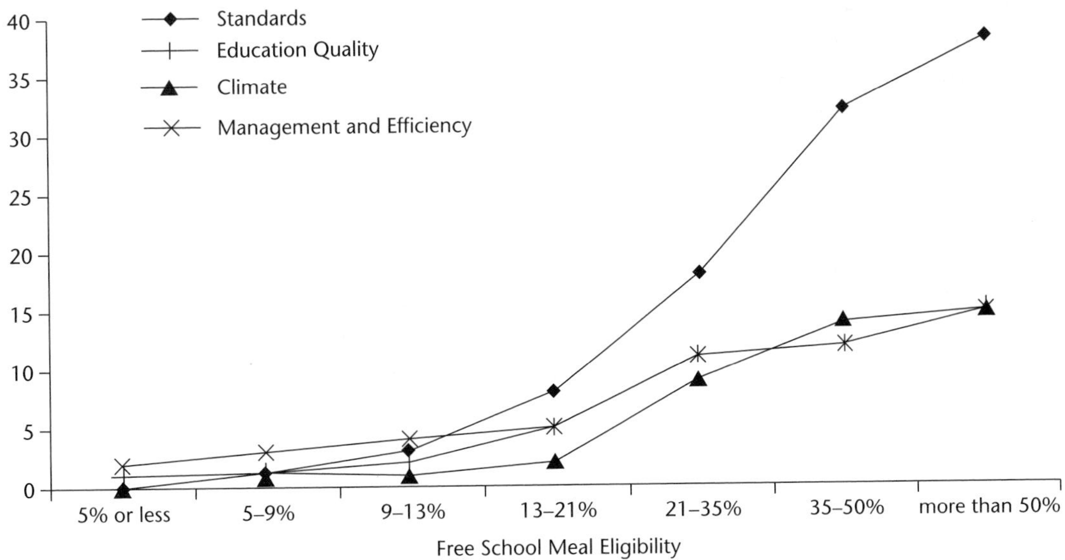

Fig. 45.1 Relationship between OFSTED inspection outcome and FSM eligibility
Source: National summary data report for secondary schools 2001 data (OFSTED 2001).

themselves, accounted for by poor management and professional practice. School effectiveness and improvement research (SEI) has tended to support this view, by producing generic notions of good practice and failing to identify contextual factors that might foster or impede their implementation (Angus 1993; Thrupp 1999; Willmott 1999). The major UK studies of schools in disadvantaged areas have focused on successful or improving schools, in order to identify what they do well (OFSTED 1993; NCE 1996), and perhaps unsurprisingly have identified exemplary schools where good leadership and teaching appear to overcome the problems of a disadvantaged context, rather than bringing out the effects of context on practice.

This internal focus has led to an emphasis in policy on fixing the problem by attempting to get staff in schools in disadvantaged areas to improve: in other words to get them to implement the practices that are successful elsewhere. There has been a reluctance to acknowledge contextual influences for fear that these might be used as an excuse for poor practice. As a result, there has been little attempt to tailor school improvement policies to particular contexts. While policies to raise attainment have consistently featured additional support measures for disadvantaged pupils, school improvement policies have tended to be generic. Under the New Labour government, good practice advice has been disseminated through measures such as the Beacon Schools scheme, web-based resources, and by more direct measures like the standardisation of numeracy and literacy teaching. Scrutiny through the inspection system has been lightened for successful schools but tightened for struggling schools, which are also subject to closure and a 'Fresh Start' if they consistently fail to improve. These school-level interventions have been underpinned by efforts to strengthen the teaching profession, such as pay increases, recruitment incentives and training bursaries, and workforce reform. However, these are all policies that apply across the board, simply with more pressure for those schools that are failing. Only recently has there been a recognition that additional or different measures may be needed in schools in disadvantaged areas. In 2001, the government launched its 'Schools in Challenging Circumstances' initiative, incorporating extra funds along with additional inspection visits, support from specialist recruitment managers, and trainee headship posts. Even so, the government's analysis of the problem is still dominated by references to the poor practice of heads and teachers (DfES 2001: 49) and the initiative dominated by 'access to good practice and advice' (p. 50) and support to schools to 'turn themselves around' (p. 51). A more significant departure is an associated pilot project in eight schools looking at different organisational designs, such as much smaller classes and integration of activities with community regeneration programmes.

Meanwhile, the neglect of context has been increasingly criticised, on the basis of growing evidence that being located in a disadvantaged area has an impact on school processes, which is precisely what is being measured by the OFSTED inspection. Early work on poverty and schooling pointed to exactly this problem (Plowden 1967; Hargreaves 1967; Halsey 1972; Willis 1977; Rutter et al. 1979; Ball 1981), and a fresh body of work has emerged in the late 1990s, again indicating that concentrated poverty has an impact on what schools do, as well as directly on what pupils achieve (Gewirtz 1998; Bishops' Conference 1999; Clark et al. 1999; Thrupp 1999; OFSTED 2000). These studies have highlighted three main issues: resources (including staff); relationships; and the impact of both resources and relationships on school practice, on curriculum coverage, classroom practice, teachers' activities and time allocation, and organisation and management. They do not contradict the notion that some contextual difficulties can be overcome by excellent management and highly skilled and hard working teachers, nor do they claim that difficult contexts necessarily lead to school failure. However, they do suggest that achieving success is difficult, even where good professional practice is in place, and that it may require additional resources, and tailored practices, rather than attempts to apply the same organisational models within broadly the same funding framework.

Aims of this [chapter]

This [chapter] reports on new research looking at contextual effects on school processes. It aims to explore directly the link between such effects and quality differences as measured by the OFSTED inspection. It also focuses on differences *between* schools in different disadvantaged contexts (rather than on differences between 'rich' and 'poor' schools as most of the existing research has done), in order to illuminate whether it is poverty per se that matters, or whether there are differences between similarly high poverty areas with varying locational characteristics, housing, amenities or culture.

[. . .]

The study incorporated two parts. One was a quantitative analysis of the relationship between OFSTED inspection results and area deprivation. This used OFSTED inspection grades (known as Judgement Recording Scores) as a measure of school quality and analysed these in conjunction with a range of contextual measures including FSM, area deprivation measures, census data and institution type variables. This part of the research drew on a sample of schools in eleven Local Education Authorities (LEAs)[4]. Its purpose was to identify relationships between quality and different contextual variables for further qualitative exploration.

The second part of the study involved case studies of four schools, selected from within the eleven LEAs. It is the second part of the study that is reported here. All served neighbourhoods within the top 3% most deprived wards in the country using 1991 Census data,[5] and as Table 45.1 demonstrates, all had intake characteristics that reflected high levels of deprivation in the area. All had FSM levels more than twice the national average, and two, both inner city schools, had exceptionally high FSM eligibility, in the top 5% of schools in the country. All of the schools had higher than average numbers of pupils with special educational needs (SEN), two of them twice the national average. Two schools had a majority of pupils for whom English was a second language and all had lower than average prior attainment (as reported by their OFSTED reports).

The aim was to select schools which, although all disadvantaged, varied in their local contexts, in terms of region, area type as defined by the Office for National Statistics (Wallace and Denham 1996), ethnic mix and housing type and tenure. Table 45.1 demonstrates that this was achieved. Southside Grange School[6] was a co-educational comprehensive in an industrial area in the North East of England, with pockets of deprivation among the most severe in the country. Middle Row High School was also a co-educational comprehensive, in an inner area of a large Midlands city. It had recently been awarded specialist sports college status. West-City High School for Girls was a single sex comprehensive, in Inner London, with technology college status, and The Farcliffe School was a co-educational secondary modern school in a seaside town in the South East of England. It is important to note that the schools were not selected because they were failing schools. The intention was to observe schools across the quality continuum, in order to be able to explore relationships between context and quality. In practice, it proved impossible to gain access to a failing school, but, as Table 45.1 shows, the selected schools did have varying quality assessments by OFSTED, and varying levels of academic attainment. In the simplest terms, there were two inner city schools, West-City HSG and Middle Row HS, in very deprived areas of mixed ethnicity, which also had relatively high attainment (for high FSM schools) and were judged by OFSTED to be good schools, and two schools outside major conurbations both with predominantly white populations and lower aggregate levels of deprivation. These two schools had lower attainment than the first two and were less highly rated by OFSTED, although neither was regarded as a bad school.

In each school, an initial phase of work was carried out to establish the context of the school, based on interviews with head teachers and LEA representatives, collection and analysis of socio--economic data, and mapping of pupil postcodes. A second phase then explored the impact of context on school organisation and practice. This involved qualitative interviews with each head teacher and a sample of teaching staff (6 to 8 in each school), as well as teaching and support staff with specific roles in relation to attendance, behaviour or learning support. Unstructured observations were also carried out, and supporting documentation (such asattendance and prior attainment data) were collected.

The findings are summarised in this [chapter] in the following sections:

- The distinctive features of schools in disadvantaged areas;

Table 45.1 Case study schools

	Southside Grange School	Middle Row HS	West-City HSG	The Farcliffe School
Region	North-East	Midlands	London	South-East
Area type	Industrial area in semi-rural LEA	Inner city	Inner city	Seaside town
Ethnic mix of area	Mainly white	Mainly Asian	Mixed	Mainly white
Housing type and tenure	Mixed	Victorian street terraces, mainly private	Medium to high rise flats, mainly Council	Mixed
School status	Comp	Comp. Sports College	Comp. Technology College	Sec. Modern
Sex	Mixed	Mixed	Girls	Mixed
No. on roll (Jan. 2001)	670	843	892	626
% Eligible for FSM (Jan. 2001)	37	61	62	36
Nat. ave. = 16				
% with SEN (Jan. 2001)	24	48	30	44
Nat. ave. =23				
% with English as additional language (Jan. 2001)	1	95	56	1
Nat. ave. = 8				
OFSTED	An improving school	A good school	A good school	More strengths than weaknesses
GCSE 5 A*–C 2000 Nat. ave. = 49	19	36	41	3

Sources: DFES, OFSTED reports.

- The differences between schools and the importance of local context;
- How schools respond;
- The relationship between context and practice;

A final section draws implications for policy.

Poverty Matters: The Distinctive Features of Schools in Disadvantaged Areas

The primary aim of this work was to explore differences between schools in disadvantaged areas, not to make comparisons with more advantaged schools. Nevertheless, an important initial finding was that, consistent with the findings of Thrupp (1999) and others, all of the case study schools had features that were viewed by their staff as being distinctive from those of schools in less disadvantaged areas. About half of the interviewees made direct comparisons with other schools in which they had taught, and others referred to contrasting experiences as parents or pupils in middle class schools, giving a strong indication that what was being described in these schools was not the norm elsewhere. The disadvantaged contexts of the schools appeared to be influential for classroom practice and teaching resources, and for school organisation more broadly, generating numerous relatively small process effects that together contributed to school environments that were described as being characteristically different from those found in more advantaged settings. Here I have briefly outlined these effects under five headings: additional learning needs; material poverty; the emotional climate and disturbed behaviour; reluctant participation; and the unpredictable school.

Additional Learning Needs

The first distinctive feature was the wide range of abilities and prior attainment within the schools and in particular the extreme learning needs of the lowest attainers. These were difficult to meet, even where additional learning support was provided, and generated additional demands on mainstream teaching staff. Teachers reported a lack of appropriate books and worksheets for lower ability pupils, meaning that they had to create their own resources, a disproportionately time-consuming activity. At both of the inner city schools which had large numbers of ethnic minority pupils, the same was also said of resources for pupils at the early stages of English. Not all the teachers interviewed were confident of their ability to create appropriate resources for pupils at the very early stages of learning, or with limited English. They saw this as a specialist job for which their general teacher training had not equipped them.

Where the majority in a class were low attainers, teaching approaches were often adapted. In some cases, these appeared to be adaptations appropriate to the learning styles and prior attainment of the pupils. For example, teachers made greater use of telling rather than writing when they gave their instructions. However, in some cases, adaptations arose out of the need to control classes. A tendency towards less challenging tasks was noted where controlling the classroom was difficult. Some teachers admitted that it was easy to slip into feeling that a good lesson was one in which most of the pupils had been on task for most of the time, and major disruption had been avoided. The quality and the challenge of the task could be seen as secondary. Worksheets and copying exercises were used more commonly with lower classes. Subject content was simplified and discussion was limited. These findings add to a substantial body of research (see Hallam 2002 for a review) suggesting that teaching for groups with many lower ability pupils tends to be insufficiently challenging.

Material Poverty

A second issue was the adjustments that were made to deal with material poverty. Considerable resources went into making sure that poverty did not interfere with the core curriculum. For example, none of the schools expected financial contributions from parents and pupils for equipment and materials. What was more at issue was the impact of pupils' lack of resources on the range of extracurricular activities offered and its impact on minor organisational and administrative processes. Enrichment activities had to be carefully chosen so that parents could afford to pay, and major trips had to be subsidised heavily and planned well in advance so that parents had time to save. Homework was another issue that had to be carefully considered. Few pupils in any of the schools could be assumed to have learning resources like reference books and computers at home. All the schools provided access to libraries and computers after school, and homework clubs. Even on a daily basis, lack of resources made a difference. Pupils did not always come to lessons with basic equipment like a pen or ruler, which necessitated time being spent in lessons giving it out or collecting it in.

The Emotional Climate and Disturbed Behaviour

Third, and possibly most distinctively, all the schools had a charged emotional environment. The number of pupils who were anxious, traumatised, unhappy, jealous, angry or vulnerable was reported to be much greater than in schools where parents were materially well off, less stressed themselves and more able to secure a stable and comfortable environment for their children.

In each school, there was a minority of children (probably no more than about twenty) who had severely disturbed behaviour. These pupils were disruptive in lessons, found it difficult to concentrate, were sometimes aggressive towards other pupils and staff, found it hard to accept rules, and struggled to get through the school day smoothly on a regular basis.

Apart from these pupils, the emotional needs of the pupils more generally had a wider impact on the schools. Pupils tended to share their emotions with staff, creating a distinctive teacher/pupil relationship, not just one of educator/learner, but significant adult/child. Teachers talked about 'mothering', 'caring' and 'social work' as well as about teaching and learning. This extract is typical:

> I think you feel more sort of motherly. It's the wrong word but you feel you ought to protect them and look after them . . . You do tend to take more care of them I think because you know they don't have that care at home. Maybe care's the wrong word but maybe their parents just don't have time or the money or know-how sometimes to give them that attention. Some of them, you can tell they really like the attention and you make a fuss of them. (Class Teacher 6, Southside Grange School)

This had three main implications for teachers' work. Firstly, they had to develop strategies for dealing with pupils' emotional needs in the classroom. At West-City HSG for example, one teacher described limiting the amount of time he spent on whole group instruction, in order to spend more time walking around the classroom to give emotional support to individual pupils. Several teachers referred to the need to develop clear routines and to introduce new challenges carefully and with reassurance because children with insecure or disrupted home lives sometimes felt threatened by change. Some teachers felt that dealing with the emotional issues and helping pupils to work on handling their emotions more positively, developing their abilities to interact well with each other and to listen and concentrate, were valuable in themselves as lesson outcomes, even if short-term academic learning was limited.

The second implication was that supposed non-contact time was taken up with pupils' emotional and behavioural problems. Form tutors, particularly, seemed to 'spend forever on pastoral issues' (Class Teacher 3, West-City HSG), including contacting parents. In the schools with the greater behavioural problems, filling in incident sheets and discussing difficult pupils with other staff also ate into non-contact time, such that planning and marking had to he done before or after school.

The third implication was a more general one relating to the nature of the work and teachers' motivations. These were draining atmospheres in which to work, more demanding on a personal level than simply delivering the subject. Teachers had serious pupil welfare issues to worry about as well as academic outcomes. They were also regularly dealing with situations of drama, tears, or conflict in which it was difficult to find the right response, and hard not to feel attacked personally nor drawn in too closely. This was rewarding work. With only one exception, all the staff I interviewed enjoyed this aspect of their work and were motivated by it. However, it was energy-sapping.

Reluctant Participation

Low attendance was a problem in all the schools (Table 45.2). At all four, a significant proportion of absences was accounted for by small numbers of persistent non-attenders or pupils who took whole weeks off at a time. This suggests that schools dealing with a higher than average number of

Table 45.2 Percentage of pupil half days missed through absence 2000/1

	Authorised	Unauthorised	Total
Southside Grange	8.6	3.5	12.1
Middle Row HS	9.7	3.8	13.5
West-City HSG	10.0	1.3	11.3
The Farcliffe	10.0	3.0	13.0
England	7.8	1.1	8.9

extremely disaffected pupils will tend to have low overall attendance rates, even if the vast majority of pupils attend most the time, because of the effect on statistics of the virtual non-attendance of a small group.

Similarly, formal parental participation through consultation evenings and parents' meetings was said to be low in all the schools. There are no national data with which to compare, and not all of the schools kept data. The estimates of staff suggested that attendance rates of about 50% were considered to be good. A further issue for schools in these disadvantaged contexts was, therefore, the need for strenuous efforts to increase participation rates. All of the schools had invested additional resources in increasing attendance and in home-school liaison, and these are discussed later in the [chapter]. There were also, however, day-to-day issues for teaching staff arising from the low participation level: encouraging and cajoling pupils to complete homework and return it and bring the relevant books and equipment to lessons. None of these problems were intractable, and staff reported that clear and consistent policies within departments and across the school, and the provision of homework clubs, all helped. But they demanded constant reinforcement. As one manager put it, it was easy to design initiatives but 'it's the energy to sustain these things that's difficult' (Deputy Head teacher, Middle Row HS).

The Unpredictable School

These issues, together, added up to an unpredictable working environment. Incidents could erupt at any time, such that neither lessons nor free time could be relied upon to go according to plan. Unplanned events impacted on senior managers as well as teachers. The head teacher at The Farcliffe School compared her daily work with her experience in more advantaged schools. At The Farcliffe, she was 'doing things I haven't done in twenty years': pupil counselling, staff support and involvement in daily discipline or welfare issues. As a result, strategic issues and planning were disrupted. At Southside Grange, the head teacher's typical day involved seeing pupils into the school in the morning, taking assembly, standing in the corridor between lessons, doing backup behaviour patrol, talking to pupils and staff in the dining hall at lunchtime, dealing with several disciplinary incidents or counselling children with emotional outbursts, supervising pupils leaving at the end of the day and (on some days) teaching. Paperwork and planning were usually done in the evenings.

Moreover, at the most basic level pupil mobility meant that it was never clear how many pupils, with what needs, would be in the school at any time. New arrivals had to be catered for at short notice. At The Farcliffe School, so many new pupils were arriving that the school was running an admissions day each month, followed by an assessment day, rather than having to deal with new admissions on an ad hoc basis. At the time of the fieldwork in December 2001, 37 new pupils were expected at an upcoming admissions day. Meanwhile, existing pupils could suddenly disappear. This level of mobility meant that setting and achieving academic targets was difficult, as was planning class and ability groupings. It also meant that performance measures might be misleading, if much of the teaching of GCSE pupils had taken place in other schools, prior to their arrival.

Differences between Schools: The Importance of Local Context

These findings applied to all of the schools in the study. However, there were also different process effects depending on the socio-economic and cultural characteristics of each area. One poor area was not the same as another. Staff commented primarily on two groups of factors. One group related to pupils' social and economic characteristics. These included family income, ethnic origin, gender, family structure and relationships, and family resources such as housing, transport, books and computers. These are referred to here as *pupil characteristics*. The second set of issues, more commonly mentioned, related to the *cultures* and *attitudes* of pupils and their families. This is in some senses an artificial distinction since culture and attitudes cannot properly be divorced from social and economic structures, but for this purpose it provides a useful way of distinguishing what were for teachers practical issues that could be addressed by pragmatic interventions, and those which were less tangible and in many respects harder to influence because they were about the deep-seated attitudes that pupils and parents carried in their approach to school.

Pupil Characteristics

It has already been observed that all the schools had intakes with high levels of material poverty and additional learning needs. However, in terms of other pupil characteristics, a general distinction could be made between the two inner city schools, West-City HSG and Middle Row HS, and the two schools in white working class areas outside major cities. In the latter schools, Southside Grange and The Farcliffe, staff drew attention to the emotional and practical needs of pupils who came from disrupted or violent families. Some children were perceived to be lacking consistent love, attention and support at home, while a minority were actually neglected or abused.

Difficulties at home played themselves out at school in concentration problems, attention-seeking behaviour, difficulties adapting to a consistent rule structure, unwillingness to trust and the need for emotional support and reassurance. Although behaviour at both The Farcliffe School and Southside Grange was generally good, staff at both referred to the frequency of minor disruption. At Southside Grange, they also spoke about the very disturbed behaviour of a minority of pupils, whose emotional outbursts could be extraordinarily disruptive to the general order of the school. Managing such pupils and engaging them was a daily struggle in which progress was slow and success could never be taken for granted.

Different issues were raised in the inner city schools. These schools both had small numbers of children who arrived at the school with no English, and large numbers who did not speak any English at home, or have access to English media. Outside the school, many pupils from non-English speaking families were expected to help with translation and to take adult responsibilities for their parents, activities that impinged upon their school work. Among Muslim families there were expectations on girls to undertake domestic chores, as well as restrictions on their social activities. In general it was these kinds of issues that were raised most commonly by staff, rather than concerns about emotional relationships and support within families, although there were, of course, specific cases of abuse, neglect, intergenerational tensions or family conflict.

'Culture' and Attitudes to Learning

The majority of teachers' remarks about local context, however, related to pupils' culture and attitudes. They suggested that these were influenced by five main contextual factors: ethnicity and cultural difference; gender and prior attainment; economic opportunity; the nature of social networks; and the reputations of the areas and the schools.

Striking contrasts were observed between the predominantly white areas (Southside and Farcliffe) and the inner city areas with high ethnic minority populations (West-City and Middle Row). At both Southside Grange and The Farcliffe School, pupils were perceived as having different behavioural expectations at home than at school. Several staff in both schools spoke about children having 'different sets of rules' at home, governing their manners towards adults and other children, their use of language, aggression or physical violence, and the acceptability of adult behaviours (smoking, drinking and sex) and illegal behaviours. In some instances, this was seen as an issue of different norms of behaviour, as illustrated by this description of the school attempting to enforce a ban on gambling:

> We took one bairn home one day for playing pitch and toss, which is a local gambling game . . . took the bairn home in the middle of the afternoon, took them in and there was a gambling school going on in the house. All these people in their underwear, sitting there drinking beer, playing poker

> and the father just said 'what's the problem?' and in the end we brought the kid back to school because we thought he'd be better off at school. And the father wasn't being awkward. He simply could not understand why I didn't want these kids gambling, because it was part of their life. (Head teacher, Southside Grange School)

In other cases, the problem was seen to arise from the structures of family and society, which failed to provide children with any constant set of rules. Children were perceived to have a lot of freedom and unsupervised leisure. Some only had one parent at home or alternated between different step-families and grandparents who had different behavioural expectations. As a result, they found it hard to adjust to the disciplined environment of school.

Teachers in the white working class areas also alluded specifically and frequently to negative or indifferent attitudes towards learning and towards school, among both children and parents. This disinterest in school was seen as stemming largely from parents, who did not share the school's orientation towards learning and in some cases were seen as giving clear messages to children that their school work was unimportant. Parents were seen as willing to condone absence from school, keeping children off to go shopping, work on the market, or take holidays during term time, and unwilling to participate actively in their children's education, helping with homework or collaborating with school over homework and discipline. As previous research (Lareau 1987) has found, some teachers were inclined to interpret lack of parental participation as a parental failing, indicating lack of interest in education and sometimes lack of interest in the children themselves. However, there were other staff who offered more structural explanations, noting that white working class areas contained many families whose expectations of social mobility through education were small, conditioned by their own experiences over several generations.

Reviewing these cultural issues, the head teacher at The Farcliffe School reflected that 'it must be easier at inner city schools where they have ethnic minority pupils whose parents think education is important and also where there's a work ethic', and on the face of it this was borne out by the observations of teachers at West-City HSG and Middle Row HS. Family life certainly played a bigger part within the Islamic culture than in liberal western families. Many children attended evening Islamic school, worked in family businesses, or were expected to visit or receive family members in the evening and at weekends, rather than having unsupervised leisure time. This created its own problems. Some children had little homework time as well as little leisure time, and in some cases, parental restrictions on children, and their expectations of being able to enforce these with punishment, were uncomfortably authoritarian for staff accustomed to a more liberal culture. However, because respectful behaviour towards adults was expected from children, parents were more likely to be supportive of school behaviour policies and sanctions.

Orientations towards learning were also developed in a different context. Many families in the inner city areas were new to British education and the British labour market. If a low value on education arose in white working class communities from generations of manual labour or unemployment and low expectations of social mobility, this was not the case among many immigrant families, who saw education as a way up in society. Again this was perceived to create its own problems because parents lacked knowledge of the education system, or of the range of jobs that were potentially available. Nevertheless staff referred to a commitment to academic success and a positive attitude towards schooling.

In both the inner city schools, staff reported practical difficulties dealing with parents, such as lack of translation, parents not understanding the educational system, or not being on the telephone. However, they rarely mentioned lack of support for the school's values. Behaviour was generally good, with several staff remarking that most pupils were focused on learning and that 'you're not firefighting all the time and dealing with behavioural problems. You are dealing with issues to do with the socio-economic area and environment but I think it's an orderly environment. Teachers feel that they can teach most of the time' (Deputy Head, West-City HSG). As one teacher at Middle Row HS said 'most of the children really want to learn' (Class Teacher 3, Middle Row HS). Thus although the socio-economic context created barriers to learning, the cultural context in these areas appeared in some respects to be beneficial to the school.

On the basis of this evidence, it appeared that differences between areas in attitudes towards learning were a reflection of ethnic differences. But this was not the only explanation, nor does it explain differences between schools in 'white' areas and between schools in 'ethnic' areas.

One obvious point was that teachers were observing area cultures through their dealings with the pupils in the school, whose behaviour and orientation towards learning were also influenced by individual characteristics. West-City HSG was a girls' school, and several staff observed that this was a key factor determining attitudes to learning and to school in general. Even in the other schools, staff commented on gender mix within classes and year groups as impacting on levels of disruptive behaviour and on teaching strategies. More boys tended to mean more disruption. Prior attainment also made a difference. In all the schools, staff noted that that it was the lower attaining pupils who most easily became disaffected and who reacted by non-participation or disruptive behaviour. Thus it was not surprising that pro-school attitudes were less commonly reported in the secondary modern school, The Farcliffe, than the higher attaining comprehensive, West-City HSG, which had prior attainment close to the national average in some years.

Another factor shaping aspirations and future expectations was the structure of economic opportunity in each area. All of the areas in the study had suffered major employment decline between the 1970s and the mid-1990s, impacting on expectations of work. But current opportunity structures also mattered. As it happened, both of the white working class areas in this study were peripheral—physically isolated from the wide range of opportunities and high-achieving role models that large urban areas could provide. Each had relied on specific geographically-based industries that had seriously declined: tourism in Farcliffe and steel and chemicals in Southside. Southside had since experienced virtually no economic recovery. Farcliffe had gained jobs principally in other low paid sectors, notably care. Both economies offered limited opportunities in the formal labour market, with high unemployment and a predominance of low wage employment for the lower skilled, and they had well-established illegal economies.

Illegal economies were established in the other two areas as well, but these neighbourhoods were also closer to the opportunities afforded by major urban centres. Although both of these economies had suffered major manufacturing decline, the nearby city centres had, from the mid to late 1990s, experienced growth in professional and financial service jobs and in retail and hospitality industries. In theory, at least, there was a wider world of opportunity to connect to. West-City HSG was best placed and was making particular attempts to make these links. The school had an expansive programme of careers education from Year 7, and had developed relationships with a large firm of City solicitors, whose staff provided mentoring, visits, careers talks and work experience. This situation could be contrasted with that of Southside Grange School, which had no large white-collar firms to connect with. Industrial structure and its change over time, not just ethnicity, must therefore be considered as a factor in shaping attitudes and aspirations. Whether the orientations of white working class pupils in areas in major urban centres, with booming service economies, would be the same as in the economically marginalised ones in this study is not clear.

Nor is it clear that the location of economic opportunity, on its own, is enough to influence perceptions of futures. As Putnam (2000) has suggested, people in low income communities do not necessarily benefit from the proximity of wider opportunity structures unless they also have 'bridging' social networks that give them 'word of mouth' access to employment or shared leisure interests. 'Bonding' networks, within communities, are valuable for social and practical support but may serve to keep people embedded within these communities rather than connected to others.

'Embeddedness' was certainly a feature of the white working class areas in this study, but the notion emerged most strongly in interviews with staff from Middle Row HS, in a predominantly Muslim inner city area. They pointed to three issues. Firstly, many marriages were to people from Pakistan, so marriage did not extend links to other areas of the city or country. Secondly there were strong links and time-consuming family and religious networks within the area. Thirdly, local families were investing in property and businesses, demonstrating a commitment to staying in the area. Racism was a deterrent to reaching out into other areas, but it was also the case that one of the strengths of the area for Pakistani families was its cultural homogeneity and the familiarity and support that it offered. Several teachers commented that the biggest difficulty that pupils faced was the insularity of their environment:

> Middle Row is a ghetto for the kids of this area. They very seldom get out. . . . If you take white middle class kids, they're quite cute. They know about things, they know about the world. These kids don't. They live in a closed society. If you put them down anywhere else in England they're be totally lost. They'd have no support, no nothing. (Class Teacher 6, Middle Row HS)

By contrast, West-City did not have one ethnic community but many. As well as having strong in-group networks, particularly within the sizeable Turkish and Bangladeshi communities, it was also a 'melting pot' of different ethnic groups, that did not necessarily see themselves as settled in the area. Anecdotal evidence suggests that some African groups were demonstrating patterns of traditional white migration: aspiring to move out to the suburbs and to Essex as they became more upwardly mobile. Some staff referred to the determination of families to succeed in British society and not necessarily to make their lives within the community of West-City.

A final, connected, issue was the extent to which the images that schools and areas conveyed contributed to feelings of self-esteem. In this study, both of the inner city schools were institutionally stable and well regarded, and had a local image that pupils could be proud of. The other schools were not in this position. The Farcliffe School, particularly, had a very poor reputation and little distinctive to offer pupils in the way of facilities and curriculum. Moreover, rejection in the selective system also conveyed to pupils a sense that learning was something they were not very good at. One member of staff said that failing the 11-plus and being allocated to the 'worst school' meant that some pupils 'just walk through the door and just give up'. Another noted that 'kids come here because no-one can be bothered to get them into somewhere else . . . those kids come in with those chips very firmly on their shoulder'.

Neighbourhood images, as well as school ones, were important. As Howarth (2002) has demonstrated, living in a stigmatised neighbourhood can engender low self-esteem, presenting particular challenges for schools in helping pupils to develop positive identities and take their place confidently in society. In the schools in this study, there were certainly issues of racial stigmatisation in the inner city schools, perhaps particularly in Middle Row, which had a strong identity as an 'Asian' area, often poorly regarded by those outside it (Lupton 2003*b*). In the predominantly white areas, stigma was also an issue, especially in Southside, where low housing demand contributed to a marked polarisation between neighbourhoods, and the labelling of certain neighbourhoods as 'sink areas', where no-one would want to live if they had a choice.

More or less favourable contexts

In combination, these factors meant that although all the schools were in disadvantaged areas, some were in areas that might be seen as being more pro-school than others. In fact, the more disadvantaged areas within this study, the mixed ethnic inner city areas, appeared to offer an environment that was more conducive to running a teaching and learning organization than the less disadvantaged areas, which were predominantly white and outside major conurbations. Parents and pupils were more inclined to see the instrumental value of education, and to meet disciplinary expectations. This is a fairly crude point and in a longer version of this [chapter] (Lupton 2003*a*), I discuss at length two important issues that must also be considered in the interpretation of these findings. I note the importance of teachers' subjective interpretations of their context, observing particularly that educational and organizational difficulties arising from ethnic differences tended to be interpreted by staff as practical problems that could be overcome to some extent by efforts on their part (and that current good practice supported these efforts), whereas those arising from social class differences tended to be interpreted as problems of cultural deficit, where changes would have to come from parents and children (and where it was difficult to see how schools and teachers could adapt within the confines of the current educational system and curriculum). I also note that area contexts were mitigated by the institutional contexts of schools (their history, resources, reputations and position in the organizational life cycle) and their position in the competitive market for pupils. Schools could have relatively favourable area contexts, but be constrained by a relatively unfavourable position in the market, or institutionally.

These contextual factors could affect their organization and processes directly. For example, resources might need to be devoted to marketing, or it could be difficult to recruit experienced staff. They could also impact by skewing intakes towards the more socially disadvantaged pupils in the area. The aim in this [chapter] is not to imply that area context alone is important, but to emphasise that the organizational impacts on schools in different kinds of disadvantaged areas can be significantly different, in ways which are not fully recognized by the mechanisms used to allocate funds and to form judgements on their quality.

How Schools Respond

Thus far, this [chapter] has highlighted how context impacts upon schools, without considering the attempts of governors, head teachers and staff to respond. However, there are of course deliberate adaptations made by school managers in order to deal with different contexts, which impact upon school practices and processes.

In the four schools in this study, these adaptations extended to almost every aspect of organisation: lesson lengths, class sizes, ability groupings, additional learning support, behaviour and attendance management, pastoral care, extracurricular activities and so on. For reasons of space, I do not document all of these [here], but try to give a flavour of the kinds of responses by focusing on the critical issues of attendance and behaviour, and also to highlight the apparently complex relationship between context and organisation.

I have already indicated that one of the striking features of the schools was the effort that needed to be made to secure the participation of pupils and parents and to manage behaviour. All of the schools had implemented a first-day contact system for non-attendance and all had also invested in additional staff specifically to monitor and follow up attendance. At Middle Row HS, efforts to improve attendance had recently been upgraded, with registration at the end of the afternoon, spot checks and home visits as well as attendance boards and rewards for good attenders. Two of the schools had specific home-school workers, over and above the teaching staff. All four schools had well-developed systems for behaviour management, with clear standards, policies and procedures for the reporting of incidents. At the two schools in the white working class areas, where behaviour was more problematic, behaviour management involved a considerable investment of resources. The head teacher at Southside Grange School had opted for a system of back-up support, with a senior member of staff patrolling the school at all times dealing with behavioural incidents and providing support to staff, while at The Farcliffe School, where there was a shortage of senior staff, a similar role was carried out by non-teaching staff known as Key Stage Pastoral Assistants.

Dealing with the problematic behaviour of a small minority of pupils was a major organisational issue, disproportionate to the numbers of such pupils in the schools. A critical issue was the extent to which these pupils were retained within the school, provided for in specialist schools, educated off-site or excluded. The schools' strategies in relation to this issue are discussed in the longer work upon which this [chapter] is based. Here I concentrate on the implications for the school of the pupils who were left. The need to make appropriate provision for these pupils while minimising disruption to others had primarily resulted in the establishment of specialised learning support units, although there were other initiatives, such as the creation of a separate tutor group at Southside Grange School. Learning support units enabled pupils to be withdrawn for periods ranging from two weeks to more than one term, for help with their behaviour and often to provide extra help with basic skills and core curriculum areas. They were funded by Excellence in Cities and provided in addition to learning support for pupils with special educational needs or language needs, whose funding was directly related to the number of such pupils in the school.

Table 45.3 briefly summarises these various additional mechanisms for securing a learning environment. In one sense they are unremarkable. In a school in a more advantaged area, one might perhaps expect a different range of additional activities, such as extension activities for pupils with above average attainment. In other words, some contextualisation of schooling, over and above the core product, is perhaps to be expected. The critical difference here was that, in the case of attendance and behaviour initiatives, the organisational adaptations had to take place in order to enable basic curriculum delivery to go on. Whereas in schools where attendance and behaviour could be taken for granted, contextualised adaptations might be seen as being additional, in these cases they were not added extras; they were essential in order to enable the schools to offer the standard education that would be expected in any school in the country.

A further point is also worth mentioning: the striking variation in approaches between schools that were apparently dealing with similar problems. A good example is the differences between learning support units. At Middle Row HS, for example, pupils attended the centre for two weeks only, with a focus on learning rather than behaviour, and with core subjects taught by senior mainstream staff. At The Farcliffe School, they attended for a term, focusing on behavioural issues and group work, as well as basic skills. At Southside Grange, most pupils attended for certain lessons only, while also attending those mainstream lessons in which they could cope. While in the learning support unit, they attempted to keep up with their curriculum subjects, bringing work from those lessons. West-City

Table 45.3 Organisational adaptations to context

Issue	Southside Grange School	Middle Row HS	West-City HSG	The Farcliffe School
Day-to-day management of attendance	Registers checked and followed up by two part-time attendance officers (school funded).	Registers checked and followed up by Home/School Liaison Officer (school funded).	Initially dealt with by tutors and year heads. Then by school-based EWO (half funded by school).	Registers checked by Pastoral Assistants and followed up by Family Liaison Officer (school funded).
Day-to-day management of behaviour	Incidents recorded by staff and passed to head of house and tutor. Senior staff on back-up patrol.	Incidents recorded by staff on green slip and passed to form tutor.	Class teacher expected to deal with incidents. Senior staff on call if necessary. If repeated, referral system through senior staff.	Key Stage Assistants patrol school. Refer to head of year if necessary.
In-school provision for the most disruptive pupils	Classroom known as 'the Base'. Mornings only. 1 member of staff. Pupils attend for some or all lessons and attempt to keep up with curriculum, prior to reintegration when ready.	Learning Support Centre, 2 staff (learning mentors). Pupils from all years spend two weeks full time before reintegration and follow-up mentoring. Focus on helping with learning problems.	Learning Support Centre, 2 staff. Used for 1:1 programmes on return from exclusion and for proactive group work. Pupils not in centre full time.	Learning Zone for KS3 Teacher and 1 LSA. KS3 pupils, full time. Pupils spend one term. Focus on behaviour, plus basic skills KS4 group on modified timetables.
Number of pupils accessing this provision	15 (tutor group) of which 12 attend Base	5 (one from each year)	n/a	10 in KS3, 10 in KS4

HSG had no system of withdrawal for particular groups of pupils. Its learning support unit provided support for individuals returning for exclusion or offered proactive group work.

Pupil groupings were another example, with a striking contrast between the systems adopted at Southside Grange School and The Farcliffe School, both schools that operated in white working class areas and had a recent history of low attainment. Southside Grange had a banding and setting system for all teaching, except for Key Stage 4 subjects with small numbers of pupils. Higher sets were taught in larger groups, typically about 27 to 30 pupils, and lower sets in smaller groups which could be as small as 10 pupils. According to the head teacher, who described mixed ability teaching as 'anathema', this allowed able pupils to learn at their own rate, but also enabled teachers to develop specialisms in teaching pupils of lower ability. Teachers had their own classrooms, so that they could customise these according to the groups they most commonly taught. The Farcliffe School had a very different approach. A banding system was abolished by the new head teacher, principally to counter problems of low self-esteem among pupils in the lower band. Within the context of the selective system and the school's poor performance and reputation, mixed ability teaching was seen as an important way to give all pupils the message that they were equally valued. Most classes were fairly small, about 20 pupils, while under the previous system top sets had been larger and bottom sets smaller. Ostensibly, therefore, both schools had introduced systems that they believed would bring maximum benefit to pupils of lower ability, given their contexts, yet their strategies were polar opposites.

A similar contrast existed in their responses to the social needs of pupils through the involvement, or otherwise, of external agencies. While both head teachers agreed that social problems should not be allowed to interfere with pupils' learning, and that the objective was to provide a kind of haven from the outside world, their implementation of this strategy was very different. The head teacher at Southside Grange School argued that the school should concentrate on its educational role, and not become involved in trying to resolve other problems associated with poverty. He promoted compensatory measures that were clearly within the school's remit, such as making sure pupils could have hot meals, investing in pastoral care and trying to broaden educational experiences by organising holidays and educational visits. However, a deliberate decision had been made not to have external agencies on the school site, in order to focus organisational resources on the core area of work, education, and on the core performance indicator, attainment. Involvement in social issues was seen as detracting from the school's ability to fulfil its unique role. By contrast, the head teacher at The Farcliffe School argued that although efforts to engage other agencies in tackling social problems might take some energy away from core educational tasks, this was a worthwhile trade-off. because the gain in pupils' ability to learn would offset the loss of learning time and energy devoted to it.

'This isn't a school; it's a family, a social services department, and the rest. If we're going to improve on education, these other things have got to be dealt with' (Head Teacher, The Farcliffe School). This school had held a multi-agency conference and was systematically attempting to involve other agencies. A social worker visited the school for half a day each fortnight, offering a drop-in for pupils at lunchtime and a 'by appointment' service in the afternoon, open to parents by self referral or at the suggestion of the school. There was a counsellor in school four days a week. The police also started a monthly drop-in at the school, but at the time of the fieldwork it was temporarily discontinued due to staff illness. A local voluntary organisation worked once a week in lesson time with a small number of vulnerable students who were known to be neglected at home, teaching them practical skills like sewing, cooking and ironing. It was also hoped that a site-based school nurse could be provided, running a drop-in health service. Again, apparently similar contexts had resulted in very different responses.

[...]

The Contribution of Management Responses

Quality, therefore, looks more difficult to achieve in disadvantaged areas than in others, and more difficult in some disadvantaged areas than in others. But it may still be argued that good management and professional practice can overcome these difficulties, since some schools do offer a good quality education and since staff themselves insist that quality is doable. While this is clearly true to a certain extent, three caveats need to be offered on the basis of evidence from this study.

First, it is not always apparent what constitutes good practice in these unusual and challenging circumstances, as the wide variation between the schools indicated. Differences in context may give rise to the need for differentiated strategies. For example, it may be argued that, since research shows that mixed ability groups tend to benefit lower attaining pupils both socially and educationally (Hallam 2002), mixed ability teaching is the right grouping strategy for a school with a large number of low ability pupils (such as The Farcliffe). On the other hand, since pupils themselves report that the benefit of setting is that the most disruptive pupils are all removed into bottom sets, leaving others to learn (Ireson and Hallam 2001), one could argue that setting is the right strategy for a school like Southside Grange which attracts some aspiring pupils with above average prior attainment, but also serves some of the most disadvantaged neighbourhoods in the country and has a minority of pupils with extremely disturbed behaviour. A quality education may conceivably be achieved in different ways in different settings. In other respects, it may be argued that we do not yet know what are the optimum strategies to follow, for example in the design and use of learning support units or the deployment of external agencies. Where educational research has provided insufficiently differentiated information about good practice in different contexts, it may be difficult for school managers to make the right decisions that would enhance quality in specific areas of school practice.

Second, it is not clear that school managers are always in a position to implement quality-enhancing strategies. Despite the more generous funding of schools in disadvantaged areas, resources in the case study schools were clearly insufficient to meet some of the additional needs that they faced. Two specific issues were raised. The first was the need for smaller teaching groups or greater LSA support, because of the large numbers of pupils with educational or emotional needs. The second was the need for greater numbers of language support staff in the inner city schools. Most of the support went to pupils at the very early stages of English, in the form of direct tuition, but there were also large numbers of pupils whose only use of English was at school, and whose lack of fluency inhibited their access to the curriculum. At Middle Row HS, a senior teacher involved in language support estimated that about two-thirds of the pupils would benefit from some support with English. At both of the inner-city schools, mainstream teaching staff felt that language support within departments, helping with the development of teaching and learning resources, would be a valuable addition. It is likely that further resource issues would be raised in a study focusing particularly on budgeting and financial issues.

There were, however, also other constraints preventing the schools from implementing what they might have considered to be optimum strategies. One was lack of flexibility in provision for the minority of pupils who found it difficult to cope with school and had extreme behavioural problems and/or non-attendance. Because of their legal obligations, the schools' efforts were directed into getting these pupils to come to school, attend lessons and learn the national curriculum. However, many teachers felt that school, the nature of the curriculum, and the environment of academic pressure was part of the problem for certain pupils at certain stages of their learning careers, and that alternatives might work better: smaller groups or individual tuition in less formal settings, and less academic curricula that valued other skills and qualities, for example. Although the schools could exercise a certain amount of curriculum flexibility, they did not have the flexibility to offer a substantially different educational experience for pupils who were likely to fail in the current system because of social and psychological problems. As a result, a disproportionate amount of each school's time went on managing the needs of these pupils and minimizing the disruption to others. Another issue was that strategies that would enhance educational quality were subject to the constraints of market and institutional pressures. For example, at The Farcliffe School, half the staff were unqualified teachers and the unpopularity of the school was such that staff turnover was extremely high. There were insufficient staff to fill Head of Year positions. At

Southside Grange, the pressure of falling rolls and an unbalanced intake had led the head teacher and governors to pursue an aggressive marketing strategy to attract more middle class parents, an imperative that undoubtedly influenced educational decisions such as the move towards banding and setting. In other words, there were systemic constraints on the ability of head teachers to adapt to their particular contexts, a finding that suggests that relying on the agency of head teachers to improve quality, in the absence of systemic changes is unlikely to be wholly successful.

Third, good practice in one respect may have detrimental organisational impacts in another. For example, dealing with welfare issues or behaviour may detract from preparing lessons or planning new initiatives. This is a difficult point to substantiate in the absence of a comparison with schools in less pressurised circumstances, and certainly respondents in this study were at pains to emphasise that their efforts in areas of behaviour, attendance, and additional learning needs did not prevent them from carrying out other duties such as preparation, marking or planning, rather that these activities were pushed into evenings and weekends. However, it is clear that disadvantaged contexts generate additional time implications, both for mainstream teaching staff and in particular for senior staff. In the case study schools, heads of year, deputy heads and head teachers took responsibility for serious incidents and for liaison with parents and other agencies, and were also responsible for the management of additional non-teaching staff such as LSAs and attendance workers and for bidding for and monitoring projects funded from specific funding streams. This was a significant time commitment. At Middle Row HS, for example, one deputy head estimated that she spent between half a day and one day per week on attendance issues, including managing the home/school liaison worker, administering the rewards system, and liaising with the LEA's education welfare officer over extreme cases. Logic would suggest that at the very least, this level of senior management commitment must mean that other tasks have to be carried out after school hours, creating additional pressure on staff.

Thus while it seems clear that, even in the most difficult circumstances, good managers can deliver quality schooling, they have to do so despite a range of constraints: lack of contextualised good practice knowledge: insufficient resources in some areas; lack of flexibility; market pressures: inability to attract and retain staff; and the knock-on effects of additional efforts in one area upon practice in another.

What Can Be Done?

In summary, the research reported in this [chapter] does three things:

(1) Supports earlier research findings that disadvantaged contexts have process implications for schools, and provoke management responses in the form of additional systems for managing behaviour and attendance, additional provision for pupils with particular needs, and additional welfare roles. These are all seen as necessary responses in order to facilitate essential teaching and learning, not as 'icing on the cake' provision.

(2) Suggests that these process implications are likely to make it more difficult for schools in disadvantaged areas to achieve a high quality of education than schools in other areas, particularly in relation to school climate, and in the provision of an environment conducive to teaching and learning. Low quality is not an inevitable consequence of high levels of disadvantage, but is more likely, even where good management is in place.

(3) Suggests that different kinds of deprived area have different implications for schools, with some high FSM schools enjoying an environment more conducive to delivering a high quality education than others.

There are a number of implications for policy. One is that differences between schools in different kinds of disadvantaged areas need to be reflected in funding mechanisms. Current mechanisms are too crude, with the proportion of extra funding allocated to schools in poor areas determined by the proportion of families on means-tested benefits and the proportion from ethnic minorities. Yet this study suggests that some high FSM, high ethnic minority areas may actually offer more favourable environments for schooling than white, lower FSM areas, with implications for organizational resource needs, although they may of course also face extreme pressures in terms of the language and welfare needs of their pupils. Either better measures of context are needed, or funding mechanisms based on an assessment of the roles and activities needed, rather than on crude measures of intake. Simple poverty and ethnicity measures are not sufficient, and may even be misleading.

A second implication is that policies to improve schools need to be contextualised to take account of the different circumstances in which they are operating. Transparently, trying to encourage heads and teachers to work towards generic 'good practice' is not ensuring that the quality of schooling is consistently as good in disadvantaged areas as in others. But what would a contextualised school improvement policy look like?

First of all, it would need to recognise that some of the practices in schools in disadvantaged areas are necessarily different from those in other areas and that differentiated provision is needed, adapted to the specific needs in each school. This would mean adjusted curriculum, learning resources and pedagogic approaches, to enable effective teaching and learning to take place. At the level of the classroom, teachers need to be equipped with suitable resources for working with low ability pupils, and mechanisms need to be developed to transfer expertise from special needs to mainstream education, in recognition of the fact that some lower sets are effectively special needs groups, requiring teaching techniques with which mainstream teachers are not necessarily equipped. At the level of the school, we need a better understanding of effective practice in particular circumstances, in addition to the generic practice lessons that are already available. For example, what is the optimum size of groups for pupils with emotional and behavioural needs? What are the benefits to different groups of pupils (for example those with high ability but behavioural problems or those with low attainment and self-esteem) from mixed ability or streamed groups? What is the most effective way to run learning support centres for different groups of pupils? How are parents most effectively engaged in different circumstances? Where this knowledge is available, we need to make sure that it is known and implemented, regardless of market pressures. At a wider level still, we may need to consider more radical models of schooling for some disadvantaged pupils who find it difficult to learn within the standard organisational framework of a school, who struggle with the pace of curriculum or the form of assessment, or who are unmotivated by a curriculum that seems to bear little relationship to their life experiences and opportunities.

It could certainly be argued that on this front, government policy is moving in the right direction, with policies like Education Action Zones and Excellence in Cities enabling additional provision in low-income areas and the recent 14–19 Green Paper (DfES 2002*b*) and subsequent policy document 14–19: *Opportunity and Excellence* (DfES 2003*b*) recognising the need for the development of a wider range of curricular options, and for the need for local variation relevant to local labour markets and training opportunities. However, on the other hand, certain initiatives, such as the literacy strategy, are explicitly decontextualised, requiring teachers to adopt standard practices regardless of circumstance.

Second, a contextualised school improvement policy would need to recognise, systematically, that differences in practice have implications for organisational design. For example, smaller teaching groups may be needed (and therefore more teachers), or more learning support staff or units. Additional staff may be needed in pupil welfare or parental liaison roles. Here again, progress is beginning to be made through Excellence in Cities and other government initiatives. But more needs to be done. Funding for these initiatives needs to be secure, not provided through short term competitive funding streams. The sums needed are far in excess of what is currently provided. For example, if it is the case that at schools like Middle Row HS two-thirds of pupils would benefit from additional help with English in the classroom, levels of language support staffing would need to be about ten times their current level. Critically, additional management time needs to be provided, so that the burden of running new projects and managing new staff does not overload already overloaded heads and deputies.

Third, contextualised school improvement would also need to recognise that there are organisational design implications in relation to the delivery of core teaching and learning activities, not just in relation to additional provisions. Regardless of the additional welfare roles that are needed, the basic work of teachers in schools in poor areas is different from those in other, more advantaged schools. The constant mixing of pastoral and educational roles as emotional needs are met within and outside the classroom are energy-sapping, and time that could be used for preparation and marking is used for following up incidents, completing paperwork, counselling pupils, contacting parents and other agencies, and consulting with colleagues. We need more systematic efforts to redesign teachers' jobs accordingly, for example by altering the balance between contact and non-contact time for mainstream teachers (and by implication altering staffing ratios), and offering sabbaticals or secondment opportunities. This is a key issue which is as yet unaddressed in government policy.

Fourth, beyond the level of the individual school, a contextualised school improvement policy would recognise that quality can only be ensured if there are sufficient good teachers attracted to and retained in schools in poor areas. Financial incentives and job and career re-design may need to be considered. Moreover, since many staff in this study reported that the classroom management challenges posed in these schools were beyond what they were prepared for, whether moving from initial teacher training or from other more advantaged schools, there may also be a need for more specific training and support to prepare teachers for the particular challenges of disadvantaged schools.

Recent policy developments suggest that the current government is not entirely oblivious to the need to develop different models of schooling for poor areas nor of the need for extra funding. It is inching towards a contextualised school improvement policy through increasingly valuable small-scale initiatives. This research suggests these efforts are not enough and that the government needs to take the plunge and implement more wide-ranging reforms that could really enable schools in poor areas to work as well as schools anywhere else.

NOTES

1. Free School Meal eligibility. Pupils are eligible for Free Schools Meals if their parents claim Income Support or Income-based Job Seeker's Allowance.
2. Pupil Learning Credits were funds for schools in deprived areas to spend on enrichment activities. They were introduced in 2001 and have subsequently been withdrawn and absorbed within schools' core funding.
3. OFSTED is the Office for Standards in Education.
4. These 11 LEAs are the English LEAs in CASE's wider study of disadvantaged areas, which is reported on in Lupton (2001 and 2003*b*).
5. This analysis was conducted in order to select neighbourhoods for CASE's wider study and is explained in Glennerster et al. (1999).
6. Not its real name. The names of all the schools have been changed to protect their identities.

Four Ages of Professionalism and Professional Learning

Andy Hargreaves

[. . .]

Introduction

Teaching in many parts of the world is in the midst or on the edge of a great transformation. The expectations of teachers to get their students to high standards of performance, to ensure that all of them are literate and can and do learn, are escalating. Contexts of rapid change and uncertainty are drawing, and sometimes forcing, many teachers together to work more collaboratively in order to respond to such change effectively. Pressures and demands in some countries for students to learn new skills such as teamwork, higher order thinking and effective use of new information technologies, call for new styles of teaching to produce these skills—meaning that more and more teachers are now having to teach in ways they were not themselves taught. Teachers have been encouraged to work more with their colleagues and access the expertise they need to improve. Schools are having to reach out more to parents and communities, and this raises questions about teachers' expertise and how they can share it with people beyond their schools.

At the same time, shrinking public-sector finances and tightening policy controls have been pushing teachers to do more work, more compliantly and for limited reward. Overworked and underpaid teachers have had to master and comply with centrally imposed learning standards, detailed curriculum targets and pervasive testing regimes—and they have seen their work and their worth become broken down and categorized into checklists of performance standards or competencies. All these conflicting pressures and tendencies are leading teachers and those who work with them to re-evaluate their professionalism and to make judgements about the kinds of professional learning they need to get better in their job.

Ask teachers what it means to be professional and they will usually refer to two things (Helsby, 1995). First, they will talk about *being professional*, in terms of the quality of what they do; and of the conduct, demeanour and standards which guide it. The literature usually refers to this conception as *professionalism* (Englund, 1996).

Teachers will also talk about being *a professional*. This normally has to do with how teachers feel they are seen through other people's eyes—in terms of their status, standing, regard and levels of professional reward. Attempts to improve this status and standing of teaching are usually presented in the literature in terms of *professionalization*. Professionalism (improving quality and standards of practice) and professionalization (improving status and standing) are often presented as complementary

Andy Hargreaves, 'Four Ages of Professionalism and Professional Learning', *Teachers and Teaching: History and Practice*, 6, 2, 151–82 projects (improve standards and you will improve status), but sometimes they are contradictory. For example, defining professional standards in high-status, scientific and technical ways as standards of knowledge and skill, can downgrade, neglect or crowd out the equally important emotional dimensions of teachers' work in terms of being passionate about teaching, and caring for students' learning and lives (Hargreaves & Goodson, 1996). In teaching, stronger professionalization does not always mean greater professionalism.

The concepts of professionalism and professionalization are 'essentially contested', as philosophers say. Outside education, professions have been represented theoretically, in the image of those who belong to them, and who advance their interests as having a strong technical culture with a specialized knowledge base and shared standards of practice, a service ethic where there is a commitment to client needs, a firm monopoly over service, long periods of training, and high degrees of autonomy (for example, Etzioni, 1969). Larson (1977) identifies the criterion of autonomy as a crucial one that helps distinguish professional from proletarian work. Friedson (1994) argues that common-sense discourses of professionalism and behaving like a professional have been captured by managerialism as a way to control white-collar workers. Meanwhile, Schön (1987) has re-cast professional action as comprising distinctive, reflective, practical judgement rather than esoteric knowledge.

In addition to the impact of these wider debates about the professions, teacher professionalism in particular has taken on very different meanings over the past century or so (Murray, 1992). Many parts of the world have witnessed several stages in the evolution of the idea of professionalism in teaching, each phase carrying significant residues and traces from the past.

Images of and ideas about teacher professionalism, and even about the nature of teaching itself, linger on from other agendas and other times—remaining as real forces to be reckoned with in the imaginations and assumptions of policy-makers, the public and many parts of the teaching profession itself. Teaching is not what it was; nor is the professional learning required to become a teacher and improve as a teacher over time. This [chapter] identifies four broad historical phases in the changing nature of teachers' professionalism and professional learning.

These phases are not universal, but are relatively common across Anglophone cultures—although there are differences even there (for example, teaching is far from being an all-graduate profession in New Zealand). The phases are ones with which many other nations are now engaging, however, although not necessarily in the same order. For example, Chile is trying to move more towards being an all-graduate profession (a characteristic of the second age of professionalism; see later), while at the same time experiencing more school-based staff development (a third-age phenomenon).[1] The ages should therefore be seen as a contingent history of Anglophone nations that now contribute a collage of opportunities with which other cultures engage, rather than being viewed as discrete stages with an evolutionary necessity that all other cultures must follow.

The four ages are:

- the pre-professional age
- the age of the autonomous professional
- the age of the collegial professional
- the fourth age—post-professional or postmodern?

I will argue that the fourth age, which we are now entering, is marked by a struggle between forces and groups intent on de-professionalizing the work of teaching, and other forces and groups who are seeking to redefine teacher professionalism and professional learning in more positive and principled postmodern ways that are flexible, wide-ranging and inclusive in nature.

The Pre-Professional Age

Teaching has always been a *demanding* job, but it has not always been a technically *difficult* one. Even in the earliest incarnations of mass education, teachers struggled alone in their own classrooms to cover content with large groups of often-reluctant learners, with few textbooks or resources to help them, and with little reward or recognition. Teaching and learning could never be pursued without reference to the necessities of classroom control, and teachers' success and survival depended on their ability to balance the two.

In their investigation of the history of educational change efforts in the US, Tyack and Tobin (1994) point to the emergence of what they call a grammar of schooling. Like language, they argue, schooling has a fundamental grammar. Just as the grammar of language frames how we can speak, so the grammar of schooling frames how we can educate. Each grammar has its origins. But once established, each grammar also becomes highly stable, slow to change. Two of these—the graded school (with its batch-processing of age-graded cohorts divided into 'classes') and Carnegie course credits that have constituted the subject-based criteria for high-school graduation and university entrance—became institutionalized decades ago and now form the contemporary grammar of schooling.

In England and Wales, the contemporary system of accepted secondary school subjects was established and institutionalized through the 1904 Secondary Regulations that defined the academic subject base of secondary schooling (excluding more vocational 'subjects' at which working-class students were starting to excel!) (Goodson, 1988). Other educational changes enjoyed only temporary or localized success because they contravened the fundamental grammar of schooling. They were like localized dialects of change, used only for a short time, or on the experimental margins of educational life.

Public (state) education actually evolved as a factory-like system of mass education (later extended to secondary schools, which first emerged as small academies for subject-specialized elites), where students were processed in large batches and segregated into age-graded cohorts or *classes*. These were taught ('instructed') through standardized and specialized curricula (courses of instruction) (Cuban, 1984; Curtis, 1988; Hamilton, 1989).

What has come to be regarded as 'real school' to many people, as the seemingly normal, natural and given way to organize teaching and curriculum, is therefore a highly specific socio-historical invention, rooted in the needs and concerns of generations past (Meyer and Rowan, 1978; Metz, 1991). At the heart of this historical legacy is a particular set of practices that, for decades, defined the essence of teaching itself.

The basic teaching methods of mass public education were most commonly ones of recitation or lecturing, along with note-taking, question-and-answer, and seatwork (Cuban, 1984). Traditional, recitation-like patterns of teaching enabled teachers working with large groups, small resources and students whose motivation was often in question to meet four fundamental demands of the classroom: maintaining student attention, securing coverage of content, bringing about some degree of motivation, and achieving some degree of mastery (Hoetker and Ahlbrand, 1969; Westbury, 1973; Abrahamson, 1974).

Funnelling classroom talk through the teacher reduced a potentially chaotic 'babble' to the carefully structured, question-and-answer pattern of two-party talk, where selected students acted as proxy representatives for the whole class, where the teacher initiated lines of inquiry and students merely responded, and where the teacher evaluated the accuracy, quality and appropriateness of student contributions, but not *vice versa* (Sinclair and Coulthard, 1974). The 'hands-up' pattern of student participation was carefully orchestrated by the teacher—competition was encouraged, attention sustained, some semblance of involvement secured—in the process of getting the pre-decided point across (Hammersley, 1974, 1976). This avoided excesses of boredom and inattention that would accompany straight lecturing—especially where false questioning trails could be set in the early stages, and the 'answer' or 'point' of the lesson could be delayed so that students had to work hard to discover it (Hammersley, 1977).

Within lesson structures of this kind, teachers do not orient themselves so much to the needs of individual students, but tend to treat the whole class as a kind of collective student (Bromme, 1987). The progress of groups of students in the higher (but not the highest) parts of the class achievement range is often monitored especially closely by the transmission teacher, and used to 'steer' his/her judgements about the management and development of the lesson for the class as a whole (Dahloff and Lundgren, 1970). The teacher's predominant practical concern is not with the learning experiences of individual students, but with the overall instructional 'flow' of the lesson—with how well it is proceeding to its intended conclusion and maintaining order as it does so (Clark and Peterson, 1986).

At the heart of traditional patterns of teaching in Western societies, therefore, are fundamental problems of order and control. In her study of four junior high schools, Metz (1978, p. 67) remarked that 'school staffs are preoccupied with order because order is constantly threatened'. In his classic text on the *Sociology of Teaching*, Willard Waller memorably depicted the school as 'a despotism in a state of perilous equilibrium ... capable of being overturned in a moment' (1932, p. 10). The successful teacher in this setting, he said was 'one who knows how to get on and off his high horse rapidly' (p. 385). Traditional patterns of teaching were understandable coping or survival strategies for teachers in the first six decades of this century, given the purposes, constraints and demands that teachers had to meet (A. Hargreaves, 1977, 1978, 1979; Woods, 1977; Pollard, 1982; Scarth, 1987).

For a century or so, transmission teaching formed the accepted and largely unquestioned wisdom of what teaching really was. In this pre-professional view, teaching was technically simple. Once you had learned to master it, you needed no more help after that point. Schools where teachers continue to believe teaching is basically easy, where the pre-professional view persists, are ones that Rosenholtz (1989) has described as 'learning impoverished'. With teachers who feel there is little else to learn in teaching, they achieve poorer results in basic skills achievements than their more professionally oriented counterparts.

In this context of pedagogical certainty, professional learning for new teachers was largely seen as a matter of apprenticing oneself as a novice to someone who was skilled and experienced in the craft. In reality, much of that apprenticeship was served in the thousands of hours observing one's own teachers while being in their classes as a student (Lortie, 1975). To this experience was usually added a period of teaching practice or practicum, served at the side of an experienced cooperating teacher (as they later came to be called) as part of a wider programme of teacher preparation (D. Hargreaves, 1994).

Such teacher preparation programmes within American Normal Schools, for example, began humbly, given the limited visions of teaching for which new entrants to the occupation were then being trained; although teacher educators fought hard to improve the status of their courses and programmes over time. David Labaree (1992, pp. 136–7) describes this historical trajectory in the case of the US.

> The rapid proliferation of high schools at the end of the nineteenth century posed a competitive threat to normal schools, but also gave normal school faculties the opportunity to raise admission standards and pursue college status. By the 1920s, normal schools were being converted wholesale into state teachers colleges, which in turn transformed the faculty members into college professors ... Students tended to treat these institutions as mechanisms for acquiring the educational credentials needed to get ahead as much as for acquiring a teaching certificate. After the Second World War, state teachers' colleges continued to adapt to this demand and to the professional aspirations of their faculties by rapidly converting themselves into full-service state colleges.

As teacher education programmes and institutions ascended the ladder of status and acceptance, a more philosophical and theoretical base was made available to new teachers. But so tenacious was the grip of traditional teaching within the grammar of schooling, that even those teachers who appeared to espouse new philosophies of teaching and learning during their teacher education programmes quickly reverted to transmission and recitation patterns when they took up their first positions. And when, in hindsight, they evaluated their teacher pre-service education experience, it was usually only the practicum that retained any value for them (Hanson and Herrington, 1976; Lacey, 1977; Hargreaves and Jacka, 1995; Sugrue, 1996).

Practice made practice (Britzman, 1991). The unquestioned grammar of teaching was passed on from experienced teachers to novices. And once they had served their brief apprenticeship, experienced teachers saw no more of their colleagues in the classroom, received no feedback on their practice, and changed and improved mainly by trial and error, in their own isolated classes. This individual, intuitive and incremental approach to improvement and professional development confined teachers in the pre-professional age to what Hoyle (1974) calls 'restricted professionalism'—scarcely a form of professionalism at all.

Summary and Implications

In the pre-professional age, teaching was seen as managerially demanding but technically simple, its principles and parameters were treated as unquestioned commonsense, one learned to be a teacher through practical apprenticeship, and one improved as a teacher by individual trial-and-error. The 'good' teacher was the 'true teacher' who 'devoted herself to her craft', demonstrated loyalty and gained personal reward through service, 'whatever the costs'. In this age, teachers were virtually amateurs: they 'only needed to carry out the directives of their more knowledgeable superiors' (Murray, 1992, p. 495).

These pre-professional images and discourses of teaching and teacher development are not just items of historical curiosity. They persist, for example, in pockets of the profession today, especially among teachers in their later career who started their work in the pre-professional age (Huberman, 1993; Sugrue, 1996; Weber and Mitchell, 1996). As McCulloch (1997) has shown in Britain, pre-professional images are also highly influential among many Ministers or Secretaries of State for Education, who tend to draw on their own biographical (and sometimes sentimental) memories of schooling as children, instead of referring to broader histories of education as a public project, as they go about the business of formulating educational policy. Pre-professional images also figure prominently in public perceptions of teaching among adults whose own schooling and experiences of teachers took place in the pre-professional age, and whose nostalgia-tinted ideas about teaching often remain rooted there (Hargreaves and Fullan, 1998).

Finally, pre-professional images of teaching continue to be dominant in many East Asian countries, partly because of the constraints of class sizes and other factors mentioned earlier, but also because of the cultural importance of Confucian conceptions of teaching and authority within schools and families. In these contexts, the designation 'pre-professional' may be a derogatory misnomer, since certain Asian whole-class teaching methods such as 'sticky probing' (questioning an individual's understanding at some length in front of the rest of the class) are often explicitly refined and reflected upon by educators themselves (Watkins and Biggs, 1996). However, the grave danger is that when these precise whole-class methods are lifted out of their Asian context and transposed to the West (as some have advocated for whole class, primary teaching in Britain), they may not be added as one more technique to teachers' existing repertoires, but may amplify existing Western assumptions about and attachments to pre-professional versions of whole-class teaching among the public, and among those parts of the profession least interested in their own learning.

In the still pervasive and influential pre-professional view, teachers are (at best) enthusiastic people, who know their subject matter, know how to 'get it across', and can keep order in their classes. They learn to teach by watching others do it, first as a student, then as a student teacher. After that, barring a few refinements gained through trial-and-error, they know how to teach and they are on their own! If one holds to a simple, pre-professional image of teaching, teachers need little training or ongoing professional learning, preparation time is relatively expendable (since the demands of preparation are not so great), and budget cuts that reduce contact with colleagues outside the classroom are seen as having little impact on the quality of what goes on within it (because it is assumed that teachers control everything within their individual classroom domain and keep all their work confined to it). If the task of teaching is seen as basically simple, why do we need to invest in continuous professional learning beyond a few inservice sessions connected to the government's latest policies?

Given the growing diversity of our classrooms and of students' learning needs within them, it is important to confront these images and discourses of professionalism that deny the difficulty of teaching. Combatting the pre-professional view of teaching means challenging the nostalgia that many policy-makers, members of the public and teachers themselves have for 'real teaching' and 'real schools'! As the novels of Gabriel Garcia Marquez (1982, 1988) portray so superbly, a strong dose of reality can be a powerful cure for nostalgia—whether this involves exiles returning to their actual homeland, or adults being led through focus group discussions to remember the gritty details (and not merely the ideal images) of their own schooling. Against this, policy-makers and the public need to be persuaded of how complex and difficult teaching is today in an age of cultural diversity and new technology, why teaching needs to become more sophisticated still, and what kinds of supports and learning opportunities teachers need to improve their work even further.

Governments who are largely interested in keeping costs down, demeaning teaching and tightly controlling it have little chance of being persuaded of this view. Arrogance is even more impervious than ignorance as an obstacle to dialogue. Instead, educators everywhere would do best to realize that when the arteries of communication to government are blocked, it is best to build a by-pass around them and capture the imagination of the public on whose votes governments ultimately depend—by opening up schools and teaching in all their complexity to the community, making what educators do more visible, and thereby countering the pervasive nostalgia for 'real teaching' that keeps the pre-professional prejudices on which governments can feed alive (Hargreaves and Fullan, 1998).

The Age of the Autonomous Professional

From the 1960s onwards, the status and standing of teachers in many countries improved significantly, compared with the pre-professional age. Canadian teachers, for example, achieved substantial salary raises in the 1970s—as did British teachers through the Houghton pay award of 1973. Almost everywhere, teacher education became increasingly embedded within the universities, and teaching moved closer and closer to becoming an all-graduate profession (Labaree, 1992). In England and Wales, especially, teachers enjoyed unprecedented autonomy over curriculum development and decision-making—especially where they worked with courses or age groups that were not constrained by the requirements of external examinations (Lawton, 1980; Lawn, 1990). With the international space race, and the commitment to investing in developing scientific and technological expertise, educational innovation mushroomed in mathematics, sciences and other subjects as well. Governments and charitable foundations invested in imaginative and ambitious curriculum projects and packages that stimulated excitement about curriculum development. Developed by 'experts' in Higher Education, Regional Laboratories and similar organizations, these projects encouraged individual schools and teachers everywhere to take up the projects' ideas, and experiment with the new approaches to student-centred learning that they contained. This was the era of curriculum innovation, of designer projects, and of appeal to individual teacher initiative as the levers for educational change (Weston, 1979). Although projects were often formally adopted, however, they were rarely implemented faithfully in the classroom, still less institutionalized into the routines of teachers' practices (Fullan, 1991). Paradoxically, this was because of the very autonomy of teacher judgement that these projects presumed—subject department heads might agree on purchasing the materials, but how classroom teachers taught them was ultimately left to their individual 'professional' judgement—with the effect that the innovations were often used in very different ways than their designers intended (for example, Atkinson and Delamont, 1977).

In this post-war period, the words 'professional' and 'autonomy' became increasingly inseparable among educators. Over time, many teachers were granted a measure of trust, material reward, occupational security and professional dignity and discretion in exchange for broadly fulfilling the mandates the state expected of them (Helsby and McCulloch, 1997). Teachers enjoyed a kind of 'licensed autonomy', as some writers called it (Dale, 1988). In what Hobsbawm (1994) calls the 'golden age' of history in the twentieth century (at least in the industrialized North and West), full employment, futures for school leavers to go to, the favourable demographics of a baby-boom expansion in the school population, and the belief that an expanding economy provided the wherewithal to treat education as an investment in human capital, all helped to relieve teachers from external pressures on their pedagogical freedom.

Meanwhile, pedagogy itself was losing its sense of singularity. While very many teachers continued to teach in the same broadly didactic way, how teachers taught was no longer beyond question. From the 1960s onwards, classroom pedagogy started to become an ideological battleground between child-centred and subject-centred education, open classrooms and closed classrooms, traditional methods and progressive methods. Heady accounts of the explosive success of open education in England were brought back to, and widely disseminated throughout, North America (Silberman, 1970). Deschooling and freeschooling commanded broad and popular readerships (Holt, 1969, 1971; Postman and Weingarter, 1969; Illich, 1971). Experimental and alternative schools sprang up at the elementary and secondary levels (Smith and Keith, 1971). The child-centred, developmentalist theories increasingly espoused in Faculties of Education were now extending their influence into the world of educational practice. Pedagogical expertise was no longer something that could be passed on as an assumed tradition from expert to novice. For more and more teachers, pedagogy was becoming an ideological decision; an object of judgement and choice. Unquestioned routines and traditions were being replaced by an ideological conflict between two great metanarratives of traditionalism and progressivism.

In reality, the claims of open education (as of innovative curriculum projects) were often exaggerated. Actual incursions of progressive practice into the traditional grammar of teaching seemed modest at best. There was little evidence of discovery learning or cooperative groupwork (Galton *et al.*, 1980), and basic skills continued to receive exceptionally high emphasis (Bassey, 1978). The problem, as school surveys showed, was not that teachers needed to go back to basics, but that they never really got away from them in the first place (Goodlad, 1984; Tye, 1985).

In all this, the precepts of teacher pre-service education corresponded exceptionally poorly with the realities of classroom practice as most new teachers experienced them, and tragic tales of how new teachers lost their ideals and complied with existing definitions of classroom reality in order to ensure their very survival, persisted for many years and continue today (for example, Hanson and Herrington, 1976; Lacey, 1977; Bullough *et al.*, 1991; Schempp *et al.*, 1993; Hargreaves and Jacka, 1995).

Similar problems afflicted the growth and impact of continuing professional development and inservice education. While expansion of inservice education during this period was remarkable (Fullan and Connelly, 1990), the shape it took was less impressive. Workshops and courses were delivered off-site by experts, and received by teachers as individuals, who were then unable to integrate what they had learned into their practice when they returned to workplaces that did not understand or support their efforts (Little, 1993).

One of the overriding characteristics of teaching at this time was its individualism (D. Hargreaves, 1980). Most teachers taught in a box. They instructed their classes in isolation, separated from their colleagues. In the 1970s and 1980s, individualism, isolation and privatism were identified as widespread features of the culture of teaching (Zielinski and Hoy, 1983; Rosenholtz, 1989). Johnson's (1990) study of 115 'good' teachers (among whom one might expect higher than usual rates of collaboration) still found an important minority of isolated teachers within the sample. Of those who did collaborate, the majority maintained close relationships with only a very small number of colleagues. One of her respondent's comments is especially poignant. 'Teachers are isolated people. They don't know what others are doing. Things that work for them, they keep year after year. You don't have the time to sit down and discuss with each other from different areas. As small as this school basically is, I don't know all the people who are here' (Johnson, 1990, p. 151). When teachers did interact, this tended to be around materials, discipline, and individual student problems rather than about curriculum goals, teaching behaviour, or classroom learning (Lortie, 1975; Little, 1990).

The consequences of teachers' classroom individualism, and the individualistic ways in which they experienced inservice courses off-site and away from their immediate colleagues, were extensive and disturbing. They included:

- lack of confidence and certainty about effectiveness because of limited feedback on performance (Rosenholtz, 1989);
- impaired improvement as a teacher, because of lack of opportunities to learn from colleagues (Woods, 1990);
- limited senses of efficacy, and of self-belief in the power to change children's lives and futures, because of lack of feedback and support (Ashton and Webb, 1986);

- tendency to focus on short term improvement that makes a difference in one's own classroom, with one's own students, rather than on more fundamental forms of long-term or school-wide change (Lortie, 1975);
- proneness to self-defeating guilt and frustration, especially among exceptionally committed teachers (A. Hargreaves, 1994; Johnson, 1990);
- lack of consistency and coherence between teachers in expectations and programmes that are created for students (Campbell, 1985);
- lack of professional dialogue that might cause teachers to reflect on and reshape their practice in ways that could serve students better (Little, 1990);
- the irony that isolation does not create a kaleidoscope of individuality and iconoclastic eccentricity in teachers' classes, but dull routine and homogeneity (Goodlad, 1984);
- an atmosphere of uncaring and indifference in relation to students' needs in large secondary schools because teachers do not share students in common (Hargreaves *et al.*, 1996).

The causes of teacher individualism were equally various and included:

- the physical, egg-crate structure of schooling that divided teachers from one another and which efforts at collaboration always had to overcome (Lortie, 1975);
- the habit and routine of teachers having already worked within an existing grammar of schooling for decades; the impossibility for many teachers of imagining anything else (A. Hargreaves, 1994);
- economizing of effort in the face of unwanted multiple innovations and accelerated educational reform (Flinders, 1988; McTaggart, 1989; Dow, 1996);
- anxiety and self-doubt about competence, whose flaws would be exposed by observation and inspection—a point that has been widely asserted but not empirically proven (D. Hargreaves, 1980; Joyce and Showers, 1988; Rosenholtz, 1989);
- strong emotional bonds with students from whom primary or elementary teachers in particular get valuable 'psychic rewards', that they do not want to weaken by sharing those students with other colleagues (Lortie, 1975).

Summary and Implications

The age of professional autonomy was marked by a challenge to the singularity of teaching and the unquestioned traditions on which it is based. While the challenge was often rhetorical, it nonetheless justified the principle that teachers had the right to choose the methods they thought best for their own students. Pedagogical choice was polarized and permissive. As these first chinks of choice opened up in the occupation of teaching, autonomy and protection from interference had to be guarded more than ever. The spread of teacher pre-service education in the universities and the growth of inservice education provided by experts added weight to the claims to expertise on which the rights to autonomy would rest.

While modernistic models of *professionalization* in teaching—in terms of lengthening training, extending accreditation, and making the knowledge base in teacher education more academic—might have helped enhance the status of teachers in the community and of teacher educators in the university (Labaree, 1992), the 'licensed autonomy' with which this strategy was associated often did little to further the *professionalism* of teaching in terms of the quality of the work (Hargreaves and Goodson, 1996). This strategy insulated teachers from the community by keeping teachers on pedestals above the community, it isolated teachers from one another, and it subordinated teachers' professional learning to academic agendas, which often had only tenuous connections to their practice. Professional autonomy might have stimulated many innovations, but with no support structures for teachers, few innovations moved beyond adoption to successful implementation, and fewer still became institutionalized throughout the system as a whole (Fullan, 1991). The benefits of inservice education seldom became integrated into classroom practice, as individual course-goers returned to schools of unenthusiastic and uncomprehending colleagues who had not shared the learning with them. Finally, pedagogy largely stagnated as teachers were reluctant or unable to stand out from their colleagues and make anything more than modest changes of their own. The age of professional autonomy provided teachers with poor preparation for coping with the dramatic changes that were headed their way and against which their classroom doors would offer little protection.

The Age of the Collegial Professional

By the mid to late 1980s, individual teacher autonomy was becoming unsustainable as a way of responding to the increased complexities of schooling. The world in which teachers worked was changing, and so was their own work. More and more teachers faced the prospect of having to teach in ways they had not been taught themselves (McLaughlin, 1997). Yet, the persistence of individualism in teaching meant that teachers' responses to the challenges they faced were often *ad hoc*, uncoordinated with the efforts of their colleagues and based on rates of development in their own knowledge and skill that just could not keep pace with the constantly changing demands they had to meet (Fullan and Hargreaves, 1996).

In an age of increasing uncertainty, teaching methods are now proliferating far beyond simple distinctions between traditional and child-centred methods. Administrative mandates to teach in particular ways are being imposed and overturned at an ever increasing rate. As the authority of external scientific expertise is being eroded, and course-based professional development delivered by experts outside the school is also being questioned (Day, 1999), many teachers are starting to turn more to each other for professional learning, for a sense of direction, and for mutual support. The role of the teacher has expanded to embrace consultation, collaborative planning and other kinds of joint work with colleagues. In a world of accelerating educational reform, this kind of working together can help teachers to pool resources, and to make shared sense of and develop collective responses towards intensified and often capricious demands on their practice. It also calls for new skills and dispositions, and for more commitments of time and effort, as teachers rework their roles and identities as professionals in a more consciously collegial workplace.

Not all teachers are being drawn to their colleagues, of course. Many remain ignorant about or indifferent to the possibilities of collaboration, and some cling tightly to their classroom autonomy when others try to force collaboration upon them (Grimmett and Crehan, 1992). While there is little solid evidence about the extent to which teachers in general are now working more collaboratively, numerous case studies and interview-based inquiries point to growing commitments to collaboration, and testify to its mounting importance in the landscape of teaching (for example, Nias *et al.*, 1989, 1992; Campbell and Neill, 1994; Acker, 2000; Lieberman and Miller, 2000), not least as a way of making sense of and responding to new external curriculum and assessment demands (Helsby and McCulloch, 1997). What factors have been responsible for the emergence of collaborative teacher cultures? Why have they started to gain such prominence in recent times?

No one factor can be regarded as the crucible of collaboration. Many influences have forged it into existence. These include the following.

- *Expansion and rapid change in the substance of what teachers are expected to teach.* This makes it harder and harder for individual teachers to keep up with developments in their subjects, and makes teamwork and coordination of knowledge increasingly essential (Campbell, 1985; Hargreaves *et al.*, 1992).

- *Expansion of knowledge and understanding about teaching styles and methods.* How teachers teach is no longer an amateur assumption (Soder, 1990), an unquestioned tradition. Nor is it a matter of taking ideological sides between progressives and traditionals, Left and Right. The knowledge base on teaching strategies has expanded dramatically in the past decade and a half, with metacognition, situated cognition, cooperative learning, computer-based inquiry, student self-assessment and portfolio assessment all influencing the field (Joyce and Weil, 1980). No one teacher can be a virtuoso performer of all of the strategies. And no one method can be conclusively or comprehensively shown to be scientifically superior to the rest. What matters is how the strategies are selected and combined to meet the needs of particular and unique groups of students in any setting. Drawing judiciously on the knowledge base, teachers working together in one school or department can fulfil this task collectively much better than they can alone.

• *Addition of increasing 'social work' responsibilities to the task of teaching.* Teachers say their job is more and more packed with social work responsibilities (A. Hargreaves, 1994). They have to deal with and they worry about escalating violence in their schools (Barlow and Robertson, 1994). Changing family structures and growing poverty are widely seen as a source of difficulties (Elkind, 1997; Levin and Riffel, 1997). Guidance or pastoral care is now viewed as every teacher's responsibility, not just that of a specialized few (Levi and Ziegler, 1991) and teachers must work together more to resolve the learning and discipline problems they face (Galloway, 1985).

• *Integration of special education students into ordinary classes.* Teachers today have to deal with a much wider range of abilities and behaviours than many once had. This requires individualized learning programmes, additional planning, and more consultation with special education resource teachers, to draw on extra expertise that classroom teachers do not always have themselves (Wilson, 1983).

• *Growing multicultural diversity.* This also challenges teachers to acknowledge the wide range of understandings, prior knowledge and learning styles that exist in their classes, and to modify their teaching practice accordingly (Ryan, 1995; Cummins, 1998). Teachers must learn how to individualize their teaching and create more opportunities for *all* their students to be included in classroom conversation (Hargreaves and Fullan, 1998; Nieto, 1998). This places high demands on their expertise, which they can mainly improve only through interaction with colleagues (Newmann, 1994; Lieberman, 1996).

• *The structural limits to improving classroom teaching.* Existing structures and cultures of secondary schooling are poorly designed to accommodate new teaching strategies. When teachers in an individualized culture work against ingrained structures of subjects, time periods and single-teacher classes, they may find themselves having to try new methods several times a day for fixed time periods with different classes, rather than having longer time frames and other teachers of other subjects alongside to assist them (Hargreaves *et al.*, 1996). Such teachers may also feel unnecessarily vulnerable (Kelchtermans, 1996) when they take risks, or experience early setbacks, if they believe that they are innovating alone. In reality, however, other colleagues, who could otherwise be powerful sources of learning and moral support, may actually be engaged in similar struggles in other classrooms (but perhaps in other subjects) elsewhere in the school (Hargreaves *et al.*, 1992).

• *The alienating nature of secondary school structures for many students in early adolescence.* This leads either to physical dropout or to less visible but equally important psychological disengagement from school. Secondary schools have often failed to become real communities for their students (A. Hargreaves, 1982). Secondary school students at risk often feel there is no adult in school who really knows them or cares for them. In order to rectify these problems of alienation and impersonality in secondary schools, efforts have been made in a number of places (but not including countries with a strong subject-based National Curriculum) to create what are variously called mini-schools, sub-schools or schools-within-schools for early adolescents which bring together groups of 80–100 or so students, taught by a small team of four or five teachers, so that the teachers and students know each other well, and the students develop a sense of attachment to their community. In the process, schools-within-schools also bring teachers together to talk about and work with students they hold in common, and not just plan around subject matter together (as is the more customary emphasis within secondary school subject departments) (Sizer, 1992; Hargreaves *et al.*, 1993; Meier, 1998).

• *Changing structures, procedures and discourses of school management and leadership.* Changes in patterns of management, decision-making and leadership, introduced in part because of fiscal stringency, and in part because of the influence of trends in organizational restructuring in the corporate sector, have led to heightened emphases on teamwork and collaborative decision-making among school staffs (Hannay and Ross, 1997).

• *There is increasing evidence of the vital contribution that cultures of collaboration make to widespread improvements in teaching and learning, as well as successful implementation of change*. From the mid-1980s, evidence has accumulated that cultures of collaboration are not just a self-indulgent teacher luxury, but have positive and systematic connections to teachers' senses of efficacy about being able to make a difference with their students. Such cultures also influence teachers' willingness to take risks, and the likelihood of their being committed to continuous improvement (Ashton and Webb, 1986; Rosenholtz, 1989; Talbert and McLaughlin, 1994; Newmann and Wehlage, 1995; Ross, 1995; McLaughlin, 1997). When this collaboration extends beyond talk into practice and joint work among teachers, when the ties between teachers are strong and professionally meaningful, then the benefits are likely to be especially positive (Little, 1990). Moreover, peer coaching between teachers has been shown to add greatly increased value to the successful implementation of new teaching strategies (Joyce and Showers, 1988). Teachers normally learn better together than they do alone. 'Like students, teachers learn by doing, reading and reflecting, collaborating with other teachers, looking closely at students and their work, and sharing what they see' (McLaughlin, 1997).

In this respect, professional development is usually most effective when it is not delivered by extraneous experts in off-site locations, but when it is embedded in the life and work of the school, when it actively secures the principal's or head teacher's support and involvement, and when it is the focus of collaborative discussion and action (Little, 1993). Accordingly, this period has witnessed a shift in patterns of professional learning, inservice education, and pre-service teacher education, to more school-based forms.[2] Teachers often learn best in their own professional learning communities. Many of these are often on-site, built into ongoing relationships and teams within departments, in interdisciplinary teams across them, in specific projects and task groups, and so forth (Little and McLaughlin, 1994; Siskin, 1994; Grossman, 1996). A strong collaborative culture (Nias *et al.*, 1989) or professional community (Talbert and McLaughlin, 1994) can even make highly effective use of external input—including the much-maligned one-shot workshops and inspirational speeches by 'experts'—because teachers process it together in ways that have value and make sense for the school community in which they work (Wideen *et al.*, 1996).

The forms of collaboration that have emerged during this age are quite different from those that have been initiated in the fourth age as a specific and episodic response to imposed curriculum reform, which, the research shows, tends to fade away fast once the initiatives have been implemented and individual business can resume as usual. This has demonstrably been the case in the implementation of the English and Welsh National Curriculum, for example, confounding predictions of David Hargreaves (1994) that it would unintentionally herald a 'new professionalism' in teaching (Woods *et al.*, 1997; Helsby, 2000).

Summary and Implications

In the still emerging age of the collegial professional, there are increasing efforts to build strong professional cultures of collaboration to develop common purpose, to cope with uncertainty and complexity, to respond effectively to rapid change and reform, to create a climate which values risk-taking and continuous improvement, to develop stronger senses of teacher efficacy, and to create ongoing professional learning cultures for teachers that replace patterns of staff development, which are individualized, episodic and weakly connected to the priorities of the school.

Professionalism here is 'new' rather than 'old' (D. Hargreaves, 1994); collegial and collective, rather than autonomous and individual (Hargreaves and Goodson, 1996). However, if collegiality is 'forced' or 'imposed', teachers can quickly come to resent and resist it (Grimmett and Crehan, 1992; A. Hargreaves, 1994). Also, the flattened management structures, that are sometimes represented as empowerment, can easily turn into using collaboration as a form of exploitation and enslavement (Renihan and Renihan, 1992). In England, for example, while the National Curriculum initially created more teacher consultation and collaboration, 'the deluge of directives' that fell upon teachers reduced much of this collaboration to technical tasks of coordination rather than working together for fundamental change (Webb and Vulliamy, 1993; also Helsby, 1995). Not surprisingly, collaboration of this sort began to be abandoned once the urgency of implementation had passed (Helsby, 2000). All too often, teachers are finding themselves in circumstances where they are losing possession of their purposes to central governments and other outside interest groups, while being offered the carrot (or is it the stick?) of professional collaboration to determine the means of delivering these purposes. Moreover, collaboration is often encouraged in working conditions that provide teachers with little time to meet each other in the school day—and, in some cases, what little time teachers already have is targetted for cutbacks and economies (A. Hargreaves, 1998).

Many teachers caught up in educational reform and change are experiencing increasing role expansion and role diffuseness, with no sense of where their commitments and responsibilities should end. In this context, professional collaboration can help them marshall their resources, conserve their energy, and sift their way through the plethora of requirements and demands; or it can be a strategy to get teachers to steer themselves towards implementing the dubious policy ends of others, sacrificing their ideals and their energy as they do so (Smyth, 1995). In this respect, moving teachers' professional learning and preparation more towards the school site may increase its collaborative and practical potential, but in excess, if it is severed from the academic world altogether, this strategy will de-professionalize the knowledge base of teaching and dull the profession's critical edge.

Teacher professionalism and professional learning are at the crossroads—becoming more extended and collegial in some ways, more exploitative and overextended in others. The puzzle and the challenge for educators and policymakers is how to build strong professional communities in teaching that are authentic, well supported, and include fundamental purposes, and benefit teachers and students alike (collegial professionalism), without using collaboration as a device to overload teachers, or to steer unpalatable policies through them. I will return later to how teachers might best negotiate their way through these alternatives.

The Fourth Age: Post-Professional or Postmodern Professional?

Changes and developments in education and in society at large at the turn of the millennium, suggest that teacher professionalism and professional development may be entering, or perhaps may even already be embedded in, a new era—the era of postmodernity. The fate of teacher professionalism in this era is by no means fixed, but is being and will be argued about, struggled over and pulled in different directions in different places at different times. One possible outcome of these processes is a new, postmodern professionalism that is broader, more flexible and more democratically inclusive of groups outside teaching and their concerns than its predecessors. This outcome, I will argue, will not arise by chance, nor will it even come into being as a gift from enlightened policy-makers. A widespread, postmodern professionalism that is open, inclusive and democratic will come about only through a conscious *social movement* (Touraine, 1995) of committed people—teachers and others—who work together for its realization.

The forces ranging against this possibility are considerable. They are forces that portend a post-professional age where teacher professionalism will become diminished or abandoned. This can occur and is already occurring in many places either by returning teachers to the hands-on, intuitive, learn-as-you-go approach of the pre-professional age, or by subjecting them to the detailed measurement and control of narrowly conceived competence frameworks; or both.

The Post-Professional Scenario

What is it about the postmodern social condition that poses challenges and threats to professionalism and professionalization in teaching? I have written about educational change and the postmodern condition in considerable detail elsewhere (A. Hargreaves, 1994), so will present only a brief summary here.

At root, the postmodern age—a period beginning in earnest somewhere around the 1970s—is driven by two major developments in economics and communications. First, there are new patterns of international economic organization where corporate and commercial power is extensively globalized; national economies (and other nation-state policies that are dependent on them) are less autonomous; nations and their policies are market oriented and frantically competitive economically, while being more inward and anxious about their identity culturally; and workplaces and other organizations are more flexible and less stable as company plants are closed down, relocated or restructured to remain competitive and respond quickly to the opportunities and demands that new technologies can detect and communicate more rapidly.

The second driving force of postmodernity is the electronic and digital revolution in communications, leading to instantaneous, globalized availability of information and entertainment. The communications revolution has conquered geography, compressing space and time. With more migration and international travel, it has created a proliferation, even a glut of knowledge and information, as well as increased contacts between of diverse cultural and belief systems.

One of the consequences of these postmodern developments has been a set of assaults on professionalism in universities, medicine, teaching and elsewhere. Market principles have become embraced so strongly by many governments, that schools (like many other public institutions) have been rationalized, cut-back, made more economically efficient, less of a tax burden and set in competition against one another for 'clients'. As the most expensive budget item, teachers, their salaries and their working conditions (such as preparation time and professional development opportunities) have been made a major target for economies. Teachers and their professional organizations (along with other members of what is sometimes derisively termed the educational establishment) have also been regarded as obstacles to the marketization of education—so they have been weakened through legislated changes in the conditions of union membership; restricting the scope of their decision-making; prescribing centralized curricula; shifting them towards more temporary contracts; and generally lowering their status through 'discourses of derision' that repeatedly hold them responsible for the alleged ills of public or state education (Ball, 1990). Efforts have also been made to limit the period and level of certification for initial teacher education (New Zealand) or shift most of the burden of 'professional' preparation (and therefore of opportunities for critical reflection) from higher education to the already overburdened world of schools (England) (Barton *et al.*, 1994). The effect of all this is to return teaching to an amateur, de-professionalized, almost premodern craft, where existing skills and knowledge are passed on practically from expert to novice, but where practice can at best only be reproduced, not improved. In the area of continuing professional development, self-managing schools (and the accompanying absence of system-level support) have created huge vacuums of professional development at the local level (Bullough and Gitlin, 1994; D. Hargreaves, 1994). Managers in the new neo-liberal scenario appear to be receiving more professional development, while teachers get less (Helsby, 1995).

The assault on professionalism is also a product of a gathering sense of uncertainty in the postmodern age and of how governments have chosen to respond to that uncertainty. A profusion of knowledge and information (including widely circulated claims and counterclaims about medical and scientific knowledge itself) is challenging assumptions about what is most essential to teach, and growing cultural diversity is challenging the established canons of Western (and also colonial) knowledge and belief that have underpinned the curriculum. As a result, schooling is becoming assailed by disputes and uncertainties. While some governments (especially in North America) have rolled with and embraced these uncertainties and complexities, valuing multiple intelligences, diverse learning (and teaching) styles, and a process-based rather than content-based curriculum, others have countered the spread of uncertainties with an emphatic assertion and imposition of false certainties.

The results, with which teachers have had to deal, have been centralized curricula and testing regimes that have trimmed back the range and autonomy of teachers' classroom judgement, and a market-inspired application from the corporate sector, of systems of administration by performance management (through targets, standards, and paper trails of monitoring and accountability). These may have comforted governments and others with 'procedural illusions of effectiveness' (Bishop and Mulford, 1996), but they have also subjected teachers to the micro-management of ever-tightening regulations and controls that are the very antithesis of any kind of professionalism.

Not surprisingly, in a deepening context of de-professionalization, which these developments represent, particular initiatives like collaborative planning or rewarding teachers for excellent classroom performance (that could in other circumstances be professionally positive) are instead interpreted and responded to cynically by teachers. If they are weighed down by obese reform demands, teachers are unlikely to exercise their talents wholeheartedly in collaborative planning. They will construe it as a time-consuming ruse to have them steer through the details of policies which have been predecided centrally (and for which they, not the policy-makers, will be held accountable) (Webb and Vulliamy, 1993). Similarly, when teachers work within an overall climate where the profession generally is subjected to public blaming, shaming and intrusive inspection, then any moves to establish a higher paid cadre of 'advanced skills teachers' are perceived as at best tokenistic, and at worst divisive. As research on advanced skills teachers in Australia has shown, one common reaction when new initiatives and their coordination are required in a school is that teachers turn to their newly elevated colleagues and in effect say, 'you're the advanced skills teacher—you do it!' (Ingvarrson, 1992).

If teachers are to maintain and pursue their professionalism at this point, they will at the very least need to defend themselves against these powerful forces of de-professionalization. This means maintaining and reasserting many (although not all) parts of the modernistic project of teacher professionalization that were most prominent in the age of the autonomous professional.

- Teachers must continue to struggle for substantial and *competitive salaries for all teachers* that will attract and retain highly qualified people in the profession—*and not just for a few* in positions of responsibility or with 'advanced skills' status. This also entails persuading politicians and the public of the value of modestly increasing taxes to fund this strategy—in order to benefit the children that teachers teach.

- Teachers must *counter* the discourses of derision, of *blaming and shaming,* among politicians and the media, that have helped create and sustain a loss of public faith in, and regard for, teachers and their work. This does not mean that teachers should bury their mistakes or gild the lily when evaluating their own or their colleagues' performance. Indeed, as Scheff (1994) argues in his extensive writings on the sociology of shame, shame is not all bad. Healthy individuals acknowledge both pride and shame in their past actions. Only when we deny shame, he says (as is common in Western societies) and project it on to others as blame, do negative consequences arise in the form of conflicts and standoffs—whether among nations, within families, or between unions and governments. For the public regard of teachers to be increased, politicians must be pressed to balance their criticisms of teachers with stronger displays of authentic pride in their efforts and achievements. More than this, Scheff argues, if parties are to move beyond bitter conflict, each must first acknowledge and exchange their own sense of shame for past actions with one another in rituals of apology and purification. Each party, in other words, must commit to and engage in a kind of Truth and Reconciliation Commission. Only then can they move forward together and take shared responsibility for improvement. In education, this might involve governments publicly acknowledging that they have often actively weakened public education by providing insufficient financial support for it, and that they have managed the implementation of reform very badly in ways that have sometimes damaged rather than improved the quality of teaching and learning. Teachers' unions might similarly participate in the ritual by conceding their past inabilities to deal adequately with incompetence and mediocre performance in the profession, as well as their inclination to oppose rather than initiate change that demands extra effort from them (even when there are benefits for students). As I shall argue shortly, this proposal is not so fanciful as it might initially sound.

• *Teachers must regulate,* although not eliminate, *the introduction of more unlicensed and uncertificated adults performing educational work in schools.* Given advances in teaching and learning, the diversity of students' learning needs and the sheer complexity of teachers' work these days, it is vital that more and better use is made of adults (paid and unpaid) from the community to work alongside teachers in schools and classrooms (Hargreaves and Fullan, 1998). There may even be some tasks which teachers now do (e.g. clerical, administrative or routine) that can be performed by less qualified individuals in their stead (Mortimore and Mortimore, 1994). But using people less qualified (and costly) than teachers to do complex work that only teachers can uniquely do (e.g. guidance or pastoral work that involves classroom teaching, or librarianship that involves curriculum planning and understanding students' learning differences), is something that the profession and the public should guard against at all costs if educational quality is to be protected.

• *All teachers must value and defend* their entitlement to and their education in *a rigorous knowledge base that undergirds their professionalism.* Engaging with this knowledge base on a continuing basis should be regarded as an individual obligation of all teachers, as well as an institutional entitlement. Engaging with such a knowledge base is what lifts teachers out of the pre-professional prejudice that only practice makes perfect. Such a knowledge base must be integrated with practice—indeed, it will be all the more effective for that. It must also be treated as providing forms of educational understanding, and ways of accessing and filtering educational research, rather than falsely deifying and uncritically applying a body of incontrovertible scientific 'fact' on effective teaching, learning, management and change strategies. What is clear, however, is that calculated attacks on the quality of educational research (for example, by England's Chief Inspector, Chris Woodhead, 1995), and attempts to dismantle or destabilize the university basis of teacher education, must be interpreted and resisted as constituting not just an assault on teacher education, but on the professional status of teaching itself.

Successfully defending themselves against de-professionalization will require not only that teachers retain and return to parts of the modernistic project of professionalization, but also that they extend and enrich the idea and practice of collegial professionalism in ways which will genuinely improve the quality of teaching, rather than merely delivering and easing the implementation of government policies. What this means for teachers and those who work with them is as follows.

• As far as possible, teachers ensure that their *collaborative energies* are *directly* connected *to* the task of *improving teaching, learning and caring* in school—and that those connections are made obvious not only to teachers, but to parents and students as well.

• A convincing public case has yet to be made as to why *teachers need time for collaboration within the school day*—and not just after school or during the long vacations. To teachers, time to plan, prepare, mark and meet is never sufficient. To the public, especially when compared with their own official hours of work, it seems almost endless. The research evidence for the benefits of increased teacher time for working together seems almost incontestable (for example, Fullan, 1991). Meanwhile, the gap between professional and public perceptions of the need for such time seems largely unbridgeable. This is a gap that teachers must start to close—one parent, one school at a time.

• Teachers must direct their collaborative efforts toward positive change not only within their own schools but also with their colleagues elsewhere, across the profession as a whole. One of the key initiatives here for teachers' professional effectiveness and public credibility is for them *to set and meet an exacting set of professional standards of practice.* Although there is increasing support across the world for this idea, these standards are often viewed as things that other people set for teachers (as with the Teacher Training Agency in England), as something that an elite of appointed teachers sets for a minority of their colleagues who voluntarily commit to them (as with the National Board of Professional Teaching Standards in the United States), or as something that teacher representatives of a unionist tradition use to describe and justify existing levels of practice instead of trying to raise them to a higher level (Ontario College of Teachers). No professional self-regulatory body in teaching seems yet to have developed the stomach or teeth to raise professional standards among all its members. Until such commitment is made, teaching will continue to lack professional credibility in the public's eyes, and teachers will continue to be the victims rather than being in the vanguard of educational reform.

Pushing Professionalism Further

Marshalling a more effective defence against de-professionalization is still not enough to protect and promote the professionalism of teaching; however, in the postmodern age, the context of teaching is changing dramatically, and older modernistic versions of professionalism and professionalization will not be sufficient to address these significant changes.

For good or ill, one effect of the marketization of education is that teachers and principals are now having to turn outwards toward wider publics as they plan, prepare and defend what they teach (Hargreaves and Fullan, 1998). Teachers are also having to relate differently to communities beyond their school because of increasing multiculturalism and the impact of changing family structures on education. Schools can no longer pretend that their walls will keep the outside world at bay. They are already becoming more porous and permeable institutions (Elkind, 1997). Teachers are having to learn to work with more diverse communities, to see parents as sources of learning and support rather than interference, to communicate more with social workers and second language teachers, and so on. New technologies are further breaking down the barriers of schooling. Schools are losing their monopoly on learning, as students and parents can access more and more information independently of them. In Ontario, for example, when parent councils were recently established as a new form of school governance, involved parents often outflanked and outran school principals by communicating with each other about how the new councils should be run, on the Internet.

The need for closer relations between professionals inside the school and people 'out there' beyond it, is especially pressing given the experience of what many regard as a crisis of community in the postmodern age (Etzioni, 1993; Sergiovanni, 1994). This has been brought about by modernization and rational planning; the effects of urban design on distancing workplaces from residences; the sacrifice of neighbourly closeness to private lot-space and manicured lawns among the affluent; the individualizing effects of the automobile; the consuming seductions of shopping and of home entertainment; and, throughout all this, the eating up of relationships by the carnivorous consumption of work and time (A. Hargreaves, 1994; Hochschild, 1997). In the middle of all this, schools are increasingly seen as providing a possible focal point for retaining and regenerating community. This raises questions about how teacher professionalism can and should be redefined so that professionals do not stand on pedestals above parents and the community, but develop more open and interactive relationships with them (Hargreaves and Fullan, 1998).

The new relationships that teachers are having to form with parents is one of the greatest challenges to their professionalism in the postmodern age. Of course, communication with parents has always been a part of teachers' work and responsibility. Teachers often stress the importance of support at home for student success at school. Parent involvement in school has traditionally taken many forms, including parent–teacher interviews, parent nights, special consultation on student problems, parent councils, and parent volunteer help in the school and classroom (Young and McGheery, 1970; Midwinter, 1972; Epstein, 1995). In recent years, however, teachers' relationships with parents in our more permeable schools have become more extensive, and they have developed more edge.

Teachers face great emotional and intellectual demands as they extend their work out beyond the classroom. Vincent's (1996) research indicates that most teachers prefer parents to work with the school as *supporters* or *learners*, since this enlists parental support but leaves existing versions of the teacher's professional authority intact. In these sorts of roles, parents basically support the teacher, by raising funds, organizing special lunches, preparing materials, and so on. They may even undertake practical tasks in the classroom like mixing paints or hearing children read (and in doing so, come to observe how complex the teacher's job is). They may be helped to understand new developments in the curriculum through workshops or classes, or they may be asked to participate in and co-sign homeschool contracts about their children's learning and behaviour.

These relationships, however, are all too often professionally controlling and defensive. Vincent shows that 'support' often amounts to co-optation and surveillance with the home's contract commitments being very specific, while the schools' contract commitments are evasively general. Also, because professionals often disagree about preferred teaching methods, teachers work to exclude parents from the core issues of teaching, learning and assessment that perhaps should concern them most—in an effort to minimize or stave off potential threats or embarrassment (Brito and Waller, 1993). In other words, the strength of relationships that teachers have with parents outside the school around core issues of teaching and learning may depend on the consistency of professional understanding about teaching and learning issues within it. In this respect, postmodern professionals who interact with people beyond the school must also be collegial ones inside it—postmodern professionalism includes and depends on collegial professionalism.

Teachers and parents tend to be especially diffident about issues of discipline. Unlike cultures such as Japan, where schools and families collaborate closely on behavioural and disciplinary issues (Shimahara and Sakai, 1995), teachers in many Western countries are caught in the paradox that parents often judge schools by their disciplinary record, but that, in teachers' eyes, they disapprove of teachers interfering with their own disciplinary judgements (Wyness, 1996; Blase, 1987).

Assessment is another area in which teachers often feel insecure when talking to parents. Many teachers suspect that they may be assessment impostors, that their technologies of grading are unsophisticated, subjective and suspect—making them open to parental criticisms which they tend to avoid. More responsive and open processes of assessment and reporting to parents can conversely reduce anxiety among teachers whose practices increase understanding and trust with parents (Earl and LeMahieu, 1997)—especially, when, once again, teachers routinely discuss assessment issues and particular examples of student work among themselves.

One other problem area in parent–teacher relations is that teachers are often inclined to have assumptions and expectations about parental interest and support that are socially or ethnoculturally biased. Studies over many years have pointed to educators' misjudgements about parental involvement—for example, misconstruing failure to attend meetings as failure to support their children or the school (for example, Central Advisory Council for Education, 1967). Professionals are often inclined to impose their own culturally skewed values about good parenting onto social groups different from themselves (Burgess *et al.*, 1991; Levin and Riffel, 1997). Dehli and Januario (1994) recommend that schools and classrooms should be organized so that parents have easy and regular access, so that communication with parents takes a variety of forms and so that parent–teacher communications can be conducted in different languages (also Henry, 1994).

The literature on parent–teacher relations suggests that considerable strides have yet to be made beyond parent–teacher relationships that sustain teachers' senses of professional superiority (parents as supporters or learners), to ones of genuine partnership where relationships between teachers and parents are both open and authoritative (Hargreaves and Goodson, 1996)—where, in Vincent's (1996) terms, they are relationships of reciprocal learning.

In postmodern professionalism, teachers should try to learn from parents as well as having parents learn from them. There are many ways to do this, including two-way student reports (Earl and Le Mahieu, 1997), having students run interviews with their parents on parents' night in relation to portfolios of work they have accumulated (rather than teachers trying to run and control all the communication themselves) (A. Hargreaves, 1997), setting homework assignments to be shared with a family member (Epstein, 1995) and setting up focus groups of parents to talk about their concerns, where the role of teachers in each group is primarily to listen and learn, and not to argue or defend (Beresford, 1996).

If postmodern professionals should be authoritative yet open in their relations with parents, and prepared to work with them in conditions of reciprocal learning, it is important that these partnerships are not idealized and that those who advocate them do not represent all parents as being altruistic and perfect. Just like children, parents can be a pain sometimes—they can try and get special deals for their own children (lenient grades, assignment to the best teacher, movement out of mixed ability tracks, etc.) (Oakes *et al.*, 1997), or rifle through papers on the teacher's desks when he/she is out of the classroom (Acker, 2000).

But it is even and especially when parents are critical, suspicious and difficult that partnerships are essential in the age of postmodern professionalism. Teachers must move towards the danger here, rather than closet themselves away (Maurer, 1996). It is in teachers' own interests to treat even imperfect parents not just as irritants or as targets for appeasement, but as the most important allies teachers have in serving those parents' own students and in defending themselves against the widespread political assaults on their professionalism.

The public is yet to be convinced that teachers need more time to work with each other, and not just their students. It has, in large part, yet to understand how and why teaching, and the students whom the teachers teach, have changed since the time most parents were themselves at school. It is not yet persuaded to commit to the kind of tax increases that would benefit the public education system and the quality of those who teach in it. For too long, the public has been a fragmented body of individuals—prone to nostalgia in an age of uncertainty, impressionable in the face of political and media-driven derisions of schools and teachers today, and easily bought by the market ideology of parental choice which helps them believe that, in times of chaos, at least their own individual choices can benefit their own children in their own schools. It is now vital that the teaching profession works in partnership with the public, to become a vigorous *social movement* of acting subjects rather than fragmented individuals (Touraine, 1995), who work together to improve the quality and the professionalism of teaching.

When the arteries of communication to government are blocked—as they are where governments remain under the sway of neo-liberal market ideologies, and have minimal commitment to public education and public life—then teachers must build a by-pass around governments, and capture the public imagination about education and teaching today, on which governments and their electability ultimately depend. Developing a postmodern professionalism that opens schools and teachers up to parents and the public—one classroom, one school at a time—where learning runs authentically in both directions, is most likely to build the trust, the commitment and the support for teachers and teaching on which the future of their professionalism in the postmodern age will depend.

Conclusion

So we are now on the edge of an age of postmodern professionalism where teachers deal with a diverse and complex clientele, in conditions of increasing moral uncertainty, where many methods of approach are possible, and where more and more social groups have an influence and a say. Whether this postmodern age will see exciting and positive new partnerships being created with groups and institutions beyond the school, and teachers learning to work effectively, openly and authoritatively with those partners in a broad *social movement* that protects and advances their professionalism, or whether it will witness the de-professionalization of teaching as teachers crumble under multiple pressures, intensified work demands, reduced opportunities to learn from colleagues, and enervating discourses of derision, is something that is still to be decided. That decision, I believe, should not be left to 'fate', but should be shaped by the active intervention of all educators and others in a social movement for educational change which really understands and advances the principle that, if we want better classroom learning for students, we have to create superb professional learning and working conditions for those who teach them.

The conditions for such a social movement to grow and flourish are now starting to take shape at the turn of the century. The teacher demographics are favourable—a rash of retirements (hastened by teachers' demoralization with the effects of educational reform) is leading to a crisis of teacher recruitment in many parts of the world. Governments are consequently having to make strides (albeit small ones at first) to improve the public image of teaching so as to attract more people into the profession—by, for example, holding impressive commissions on the status of teaching (Australia) and the future of the profession (US), committing to higher pay rises than usual (New Zealand), or devising schemes to reward 'advanced skills teachers' (England and Australia). Governments are already beginning to bend. The public demographics are also favourable—with the aging boomer generation seeing their own offspring leave home, and starting to become involved in their later years less with their own private interests and their own families, and more with volunteering and participating in the wider community.

The forces of de-professionalization in teaching have cut deep. But the objective prospects for a reinvigorated postmodern professionalism, and the creation of a broad social movement that would support it, are strong. If teachers want to become professionally stronger, they must now open themselves up and become more publicly vulnerable and accessible. That is their paradoxical challenge in the postmodern age.

NOTES

1. It is interesting that in recent years, perhaps because of an increasingly globalized discourse of educational reform, even those countries without a specific history of professionalism are beginning to engage with projects of professionalism and professionalization in education—for example, Chile, Argentina, Hong Kong and Japan.
2. Although there is a long record of examples of school-based curriculum development and professional development, it becomes a concentrated centre of activity, initiative and research from the late 1970s onwards in the Anglophone world, Scandinavia and elsewhere—see Hargreaves (1982) for a review.

Performativities and Fabrications in the Education Economy: Towards the Performative Society

Stephen J. Ball

Each time I have attempted to do theoretical work it has been on the basis of elements from my experience—always in relation to processes that I saw taking place around me. It is in fact because I thought I recognised something cracked, dully jarring or disfunctioning in things I saw in the institutions in which I dealt with my relations with others, that I undertook a particular piece of work, several fragments of autobiography.

(Foucault, cited in Rajchman, 1985 p. 36)

This chapter joins in a burgeoning conversation concerned with performativity in education and social policy. It looks at both the capillary detail and the bigger picture of performativity in the public sector. Ideally it should be read in relation to the multitude of performative texts and 'texts of performativity' with which we are continually confronted and which increasingly inform and deform our practice. The chapter is intended to be both very theoretical and very practical, very abstract and very immediate.

Performativity is a technology, a culture and a mode of regulation, or even a system of 'terror' in Lyotard's words, that employs judgements, comparisons and displays as means of control, attrition and change. The performances—of individual subjects or organisations—serve as measures of productivity or output, or displays of 'quality', or 'moments' of promotion or inspection. They stand for, encapsulate or represent the worth, quality or value of an individual or organisation within a field of judgement. 'An equation between wealth, efficiency, and truth is thus established' (Lyotard, 1984 p. 46). The issue of who controls the field of judgement is crucial. 'Accountability' and 'competition' are the lingua franca of this new 'discourse of power' as Lyotard describes it. A discourse which is the emerging form of legitimation in post-industrial societies

From D. Gleeson and C. Husbands (eds.), *The Performing School: Managing, Teaching and Learning in a Performance Culture* (London: Routledge Falmer, 2001), 210–26. Reprinted with permission.

for both the production of knowledge and its transmission through education. My aim is to begin work on and towards an analytics of this discourse of power, and the resistances and accommodations to it. This is both an exercise in critical ontology and the analysis of new regulative forms.

In referring to various texts or data, I am not attempting in any simple sense to mobilise proof of my arguments. I am trying to establish the existence of an attitude and an ethical framework within which teachers and researchers in schools, colleges and universities are having to work and think about what they do and who they are. I am interested in the way in which these texts play their part in 'making us up' (Hacking, 1986 p. 231) by providing 'new modes of description' and 'new possibilities for action'. Thus are new social identities created—what it means to be educated; what it means to be a teacher or a researcher. This remaking can be enhancing and empowering for some but this has to be set over and against the various inauthenticities discussed below.[1] It is productive as well as destructive. There are 'winners' and 'losers' in the 'struggle for the soul of professionalism' (Hanlon, 1998), which is embedded in this remaking. We make ourselves up within the information we provide and construct about ourselves. We articulate ourselves within the representational games of competition, intensification and quality.

The argument focuses upon a struggle over visibility. I shall explore a paradox, arguing that tactics of transparency produce a resistance of opacity, of elusivity; but that this resistance is also paradoxical and disciplinary. In general terms I want to outline a new mode of social (and moral) regulation that bites deeply and immediately into the practice of state professionals reforming and 're-forming' meaning and identity, producing or making up new professional subjectivities. This new mode involves, as Deleuze (1992) puts it, a shift from 'societies of discipline' to 'societies of control': 'controls are a modulation, like a self-deforming cast that will continuously change from one moment to the other, or like a sieve whose mesh will transmute from point to point' (Deleuze, 1992).

Within this new mode of regulation, the organisation of power within definite forms of time-space (e.g. factory or office production systems) is now less important. It is the database, the appraisal meeting, the annual review, report writing and promotion applications, inspections, peer reviews that are to the fore. There is not so much, or not only, a *structure* of surveillance, as a *flow* of performativities both continuous and eventful—that is *spectacular*. It is not the possible certainty of always being seen that is the issue, as in the panopticon. Instead it is the uncertainty and instability of being judged in different ways, by different means, through different agents; the 'bringing off' of performances—the flow of changing demands, expectations and indicators that make us continually accountable and constantly recorded—'giving the position of any element within an open environment at any given instant' (Deleuze, 1992 p. 7). This is the basis for the principle of uncertainty and inevitability; it is a recipe for ontological insecurity, posing questions such as—are we doing enough? are we doing the right thing? how will we measure up?

Nonetheless, clearly, controls overlay rather than displace disciplines in most educational organisations even if the emphasis is shifting. There is at work here a combination of two things: first, of *rituals* (grandiloquent pronouncements and spectacular events) which serve to naturalise the discourses of control (such as inspections, audits, promotion applications, job interviews); second, of *routines* (record-keeping, committee and taskforce meetings, interactions) which address forms of identity by treating people in terms of the identities of the discourses of performativity (Corrigan and Sayer, 1985).

Different identities and performances are more or less possible, more or less available, in different locations (Blackmore and Sachs, 1999). However, whatever our location, we now operate within a baffling array of figures, performance indicators, comparisons and competitions—in such a way that the contentments of stability are increasingly elusive, purposes are contradictory, motivations blurred and self worth slippery. Constant doubts about which judgements may be in play at any point mean that any and all comparisons have to be attended to. What is produced is a state of conscious and permanent visibility (or visibilities) at the intersection of government, organisation and self-formation. And one key aspect of the steering effects of judgement and comparison is a gearing of academic production to the requirements of national economic competition, which are in turn supported by: 'Policies which pursue the general goal of reorganizing, maintaining and generalising market exchange relationships' (Offe, 1984 p. 125).

Performativity works from the outside in and from the inside out. As regards the latter, performances are, on the one hand, aimed at culture-building, the instilling of pride, identification with and 'a love of product or a belief in the quality of the services' provided (Willmott, 1992 p. 63). On the other hand, ratings and rankings, set within competition between groups *within* institutions, can engender individual feelings of pride, guilt, shame and envy—they have an emotional (status) dimension, as well as (the appearance of) rationality and objectivity. As regards the former, we can consider a teacher who appears in Jeffrey and Woods' powerful, moving and indeed terrifying book *Testing Teachers* which deals with the UK regime of school inspections and examines teachers' experience of these inspections as a conflict of values, a colonisation of their lives, and deprofessionalisation of their role:

> I don't have the job satisfaction now I once had working with young kids because I feel every time I do something intuitive I just feel guilty about it. 'Is this right; am I doing this the right way; does this cover what I am supposed to be covering; should I be doing something else; should I be more structured; should I have this in place; should I have done this?' You start to query everything you are doing—there's a kind of guilt in teaching at the moment. I don't know if that's particularly related to Ofsted but of course it's multiplied by the fact that Ofsted is coming in because you get in a panic that you won't be able to justify yourself when they finally arrive. (Jeffrey and Woods, 1998 p. 118)

Here then is guilt, uncertainty, instability and the emergence of a new subjectivity[2]—a new kind of teacher. What we see here is a particular set of 'practices through which we act upon ourselves and one another in order to make us particular kinds of being' (Rose, 1992 p. 161). Crucially, and this is central to my argument, together, these forms of regulation, or governmentality,[3] have a social and interpersonal dimension. They are folded into complex institutional, team, group and communal relations—the academic community, the school, the subject department, the university, for example. *We* sit on peer reviews, *we* write the accountability reports, *we* assign grades to other departments, *we* berate our colleagues for their 'poor' productivity, *we* devise, run and feed departmental and institutional procedures for monitoring and improving 'output'.

Within this economy of education, material and personal interests are intertwined in the competition for resources, security and esteem and the intensification of public professional labour—the changing conditions of and meanings for work.[4] The focus here is primarily on performance itself as a system of measures and indicators (signs) and sets of relationships, rather than on its functions for the social system and the economy. The starting point is Lyotard's concept but my use of the concept of performativity moves beyond his presentation of the principle of performativity 'as the optimising of performance by maximising outputs (benefits) and minimising inputs (costs)'. For I also want to differentiate between perform*ativity* in Lyotard's sense, to 'be operational (that is, commensurable) or disappear' (Lyotard, 1984 p. xxiv); and in Butler's (1990) sense, as enactment or perform*ance*. That perverse form of response/resistance to and accommodation of performativity that I call *fabrication* is also a major concern.

While at times I will talk about schools and school teachers in this chapter, and refer to other public sector organisations, I can claim no luxury or objectivity of distance in all this. My daily practice within a university is the most immediate reality for what I am attempting to analyse. Thus, some of my illustrations are taken from documents, events and observations within my own institution. Some of the oppressions I describe are perpetrated by me. I am agent and subject within the regime of performativity in the academy. As signalled by the opening quotation, this is in part an exercise in autobiography.

Social Relations of Practice

As represented by Lingard and Blackmore (1997 p. 13) the policy duality of accountability and enterprise in higher education produces tensions which 'are played out in the everyday/everynight lives of individual academics, in the form of demands made upon their time to provide feedback and accountability upwards to their institutions, through performance management, quality assurance and research quantums and productivity agreements under enterprise bargaining'. Two points follow from this. First, there is the contradiction—what Lyotard calls the law of contradiction. This arises between intensification, as an increase in the volume of first-order activities, and the 'costs' of second-order activities themselves, like performance monitoring and management. Thus, as a number of commentators have pointed out, acquiring the performative information necessary for perfect control, 'consumes so much energy that it drastically reduces the energy available for making improvement inputs' (Elliott, 1996 p. 15; also Blackmore and Sachs, 1997). Survival and competitive advantage in the economy of education rests equally upon the energy of first-order activities and the energy of second-order activities—producing what Blackmore and Sachs (1997) call 'institutional schizophrenia'. However, there is no simple 'realist' relationship between the former and the latter and they are mediated by the effort devoted to the production of personal and institutional 'fabrications'. Furthermore, as noted already, it is important to recognise the extent to which these activities enter into our everyday relations. These are most apparent in the pressures on individuals, formalised by appraisals, annual reviews and databases, to make their contribution to the performativity of the unit. Again in this there is a real possibility that authentic social relations are replaced by judgemental relations wherein persons are valued for their productivity alone. In Deleuze's terms, 'individuals have become "dividuals" and masses, samples, data, markets or "banks"' (Deleuze, 1992 p. 5). This is part of what Lash and Urry (1994 p. 15) call the 'emptying out' of relationships, which are left flat and 'deficient in affect'.

In relation to individual practice we can also identify the development and ravages of another kind of 'schizophrenia'. There is the possibility that commitment, judgement and authenticity within practice are sacrificed for impression and performance. There is a potential *splitting* between the teacher's own judgements about 'good practice' and students' 'needs' on the one hand and the rigours of performance on the other. Again this can be illustrated by quoting teachers from Jeffrey and Woods' study of UK school inspections. One teacher, Veronica, talked about resenting 'what I've done. I've never compromised before and I feel ashamed. It's like licking their boots'; and another, Diane, talked about a. loss of respect for, herself:

> My first reaction was 'I'm not going to play the game', but I am and they know I am. I don't respect myself for it; my own self respect goes down. Why aren't I making a stand? Why aren't I saying, 'I know I can teach; say what you want to say', and so I lose my own self-respect. I know who I am; know why I teach, and I don't like it: I don't like them doing this, and that's sad, isn't it? (Jeffrey and Woods, 1998 p. 160)

There is a lot here. There is an indication of the particular performativity—the management of performance—which is called up by the inspection process. What is produced is a spectacle, or what we might see as an 'enacted fantasy' (Butler, 1990), which is there simply to be seen and judged. And as the teacher also hints the heavy sense of inauthenticity in all this may well be appreciated as much by the inspectors as the inspected; Diane is 'playing the game' and 'they know I am'. Nonetheless, the effects here in terms of discipline and control are powerful indeed; as are the costs to the self. Jeffrey and Woods note the 'most dramatic' example of Chloe:

> She was the only year 6 teacher at Trafflon and after criticism of their SATs results she resolved to go down the path of 'improvement of results'. She changed her curriculum, and achieved her aim by getting the second best results the following year in her LEA. She justified this by saying that she was 'now just doing a job'; and had withdrawn her total involvement to preserve her 'sanity'. 'The results were better because I acted like a function machine'. (Jeffrey and Woods, 1998 p. 163)

Again the alienation of self is linked to the incipient 'madness' of the requirements of performativity: the result, inauthentic practice and relationships. We also see here the emergence of 'new forms of social relations'—social structures are replaced by 'information structures' (Lash and Urry, 1994 p. 111).

We might find a similar splitting and personal and social inauthenticity as teachers and researchers in higher education when we apply for grants in which we have no academic interest but will look good on departmental returns or earn income; or give conference papers or submit journal articles which are unready or unoriginal in order to chalk up another count in the annual output review. This may exemplify a situation that Giddens sees as endemic in late modernity, where there is an institutionalised 'existential separation' from 'the moral resources necessary to live a full and satisfying existence' (Giddens, 1991 p. 91). He suggests as a result the individual may experience personal meaninglessness. However, there are mixed motives at work here—we tell ourselves 'necessary fictions' which rationalise our own intensification or legitimate our involvements in the rituals of performance.

Nonetheless, this tension, this structural and individual 'schizophrenia', and the potential for inauthenticity and meaninglessness is increasingly an everyday experience for us all. The activities of the technical intelligentsia drive performativity into the day to day practices of teachers and into the social relations between teachers. They make management ubiquitous, invisible, inescapable—part of, embedded in, everything we do. We choose and judge our actions and they are judged by others on the basis of their contribution to organisational performance. And in all this the demands of performativity dramatically close down the possibilities for 'metaphysical discourses', for relating practice to philosophical principles like social justice and equity. And 'fables' of promise and opportunity such as those which attend democratic education are also marginalised. Even so, we are all expected to make our contribution to the construction of convincing institutional performances. Which brings us to the issue of fabrication.

Fabrications

The fabrications that organisations (and individuals) produce are selections among various possible representations—or versions—of the organisation or person. Complex organisations like schools and universities are multi-faceted and diverse, indeed they are sometimes contested and often contradictory. Clearly, particular groups or individuals will be able to privilege particular representations. However, these selections and choices are not made in a political vacuum. They are informed by the priorities, constraints and climate set by the policy environment. To paraphrase Foucault, fabrications are versions of an organisation (or person) which does not exist—they are not 'outside the truth' but neither do they render simply true or direct accounts—they are produced purposely 'to be accountable'.

Truthfulness is not the point—the point is their effectiveness, in the market or for the inspection, as well as the work they do 'on' and 'in' the organisation—their transformational impact. As Butler (1990 p. 136) puts it, in a rather different context: 'Such acts, gestures, enactments, generally construed, are *performative* in the sense that the essence or identity that they otherwise purport to express are *fabrications* manufactured and sustained through corporeal signs and other discursive means.' However, as Butler is swift to point out, such fabrications are paradoxical, and deeply so. In one sense organisational fabrications are an escape from the gaze, a strategy of impression management that in effect erects a façade of calculation. But in another sense the work of fabricating the organisation requires submission to the rigours of performativity and the disciplines of competition—resistance *and* capitulation. It is, as we have seen, a betrayal even, a giving up of claims to authenticity and commitment. It is an investment in plasticity. Crucially and invariably acts of fabrication and the fabrications themselves act and reflect back upon the practices they stand for. The fabrication becomes something to be sustained, lived up to. Something to measure individual practices against. The discipline of the market is transformed into the discipline of the image, the sign.

All of this keeps the gaze in place—the 'professional' teacher and lecturer are here defined by their grasp of and careful use of systems and procedures, and by the particular rewards and new identities that this delivers through a regressive self-regulation. It is in these ways that we become more capable, more efficient, more productive, more relevant; we become user-friendly; we become part of the 'knowledge economy'. We learn that we can become more than we were. There is something very seductive about being 'properly passionate' about excellence, about achieving 'peak performance'.[5]

Apart from their official functions, as responses to accountability, both main aspects of educational performativity—comparison and commodification—are linked to the provision of information for consumers within the education market forum. And they are thus also different ways of making schools and universities more responsive or appear to be more responsive to their consumers.

However, the work of fabrication points to a second paradox. Technologies and calculations which appear to make public sector organisations more transparent may actually result in making them more opaque, as representational artefacts are increasingly constructed with great deliberation and sophistication.

Within all this (some) educational institutions will become whatever it seems necessary to become in order to flourish in the market. The heart of the educational project is gouged out and left empty. Authenticity is replaced by plasticity. Within the education market institutional promotion and representation take on the qualities of postmodern depthlessness—yet more floating signifiers in the plethora of semiotic images, spectacles and fragments that increasingly dominate consumer society. Indeed, the particular disciplines of competition encourage schools and universities to fabricate themselves—to manage and manipulate their performances in particular ways. Increasingly educational institutions are taking the position that part of what they offer to choosers/consumers is a physical and semiotic context which is no longer 'left to chance, but has to be heavily designed' (Lash and Urry, 1994 p. 204). Certainly, schools have become much more aware of and attentive to the need to carefully organize the ways in which they present themselves to their current and potential parents through promotional publications, school events, school productions, open evenings, websites (Abbott, 1999)[6] and local press coverage. Furthermore, there is a general tension or confusion in the education market between information-giving and impression management and promotion. This blizzard of hype and (pseudo) information also contributes to opacity rather than transparency.

Again, individually, we also fabricate ourselves. We produce versions of ourselves for and at job interviews—and increasingly may have to 'perform' a presentation for our potential colleagues—for promotion and for grant-getting.

Let me try to be even more specific with some more examples, and in doing so begin to develop an analysis of the 'poetics of fabrication'. This might allow us to think about how plausibility and believability are achieved, or brought off, both tactically and creatively. It might be useful to distinguish between trivial or *representational* fabrications (which is not meant to underplay their effects) and those which are *constitutive* and arise from *organising* principles.

The Routine Selection (or Manipulation) of Statistics and Indicators

Systems of calculability almost always leave latitude for representational variation (Ball 1997):

> I'm rushing around like a loony today trying to put together this exam results display she [the headteacher] wants . . . I didn't have any data to do it with and I've had to collect that and then I've had to find a way of presenting the results in a way that looks good . . . GCSEs and A level results against the national average . . . that's presented us with some problems, because obviously with four subjects the results are uneven . . . I've found a way of doing the A-level that looks alright, I'm struggling a bit with the GCSE. (Secondary School Head of Faculty)

In higher education the dual-authoring of papers with less productive colleagues is another fairly innocuous method of massaging publications returns. Leo Walford, Journals Editor at Sage Publications, has recently talked about the research assessment exercise (RAE) in the UK leading to what he calls the 'salami-slicing of strong research papers in several thinner articles' (Headline 'RAE can "corrupt" research', *THES*, 26 March 1999). In addition the republication of just slightly different versions of essentially the same paper seems to be becoming more common. Publishers are harassed to organize their production schedules to ensure publication before the RAE cut-off date. The choice of indicators, where more than one is available, is another routine act of fabrication. And in the UK the run-up to each RAE is now marked by a flurry of transfers of star performers to institutions wanting to boost their chances of a better grade—another form of instant fabrication.

In the school sector we can point to the introduction of baseline testing in UK schools as another point of struggle over and manipulation of indicators. Primary schools are eager to test early—despite advice to 'let the children settle down'—to produce maximum 'under-performance', against which 'value-added' gains can be made, and attributed to the schools. Some parents on the other hand are preparing their children for the tests to ensure a good showing, or are shocked by the poor performance of their 'unprepared' children. The interests of good schooling and good parenting are made antithetical by the demands of performativity. And the way in which performativity can easily become totally divorced from service is dramatically demonstrated by a UK private rail company which on several occasions has reportedly run trains without stopping at scheduled stations to ensure that they meet their punctuality targets. Or we might note the impact of the publication of the morbidity rates of individual surgeons in the USA which has led to many doctors refusing to operate on difficult or high-risk cases. The same may happen in the UK—'Surgeons may refuse high-risk cases' was a headline in *The Independent* newspaper (*The Independent*, 7 October 1999).

The Stage Management of Events

A colleague in London described to me a situation where two schools rented extra computers for their open evening, the idea being to give parents the impression of a hi-tech learning environment. Another colleague at the Chinese University of Hong Kong described a practice in mainland China in which schools about to be inspected rented plants and bushes from local nurseries, in order to meet the requirement that they should provide a pleasant and conducive learning environment for students. In both cases, the rented items were returned once the event was finished. Jeffrey and Woods (1998) again, describe a school preparing for inspection by rehearsing the inspectors' questions: 'We practised ensuring that we presented a consensus for any interviews we had. It was very helpful. I want them to say that the Senior Management Team has a shared clear view' (Grace, quoted p. 155). School open evenings are now typically carefully choreographed events, sometimes with professional support.

Constructing Accounts of the Institution

Increasingly, public sector institutions are required to construct a variety of textual accounts of ourselves in the form of development plans, strategic documents, sets of objectives etc. (as are individuals). Symbolism is as important as substance here, in at least two senses. First, such texts symbolise and stand for the corporate consensus of the institution, and indeed these exercises in institutional extrapolation can also work as a means of manufacturing consensus (Ball, 1997), the focusing of activities around an agreed set of priorities. Second, they provide a touchstone of shared endeavour which displaces or subsumes differences, disagreements and value divergences. Of course they are also a version of the institution constructed for external audiences. They may deploy discursive tactics to convey order and coherence, consensus and dynamism, responsiveness and careful self-evaluation or, to other audiences, a synthetic personalism, 'a caring institution'. By such means the organisation is written into being.

Performance as Performativity

All of these examples of what I have called *representational* fabrications do in different ways have *organising* effects. As I argued more generally earlier fabrications act back on their producers. And indeed as technologies of accountability some of the requirements referred to here are intended to work as much as formative interventions as they are as summative indicators. The other sense of fabricating an institution as *constitutive*—in relation to certain organising principles—is the way in which performativities are achieved by the adoption of particular policies and practices. One way in which we can see this, which also points up the relationship between market incentives, market values and market information, is in the generation of GCSE examination results and league table positions in certain UK schools. The logic of market incentives would suggest that any school or university which can select its clients will do so—either formally or informally. Those schools which do select their students, either formally or informally, are more able to control their league table position and their reputation generally. Furthermore, those students who offer the best chance of GCSE success tend to be the cheapest to teach, and easiest to manage. Students who threaten the reputation or performance of the school will be deselected (excluded) and indeed we have seen a massive growth in the number of students excluded from school in the UK since 1991. Generally, as explained by headteachers in our research on many occasions, the most effective long-term strategy for improving GCSE performance is to change the student intake. Thus, GCSE attainment percentages and local league table positions do not in any simple sense represent the outcomes of 'good' teaching and 'effective' learning; they are instead artefacts produced out of a complex set of policy strategies and practical tactics which underpin the fabrication of performance.

Individual Fabrications

In addition to these organisational fabrications, as noted earlier, we are increasingly required to fabricate ourselves. While there have always been performance and 'impression-management' aspects of rituals like interviews and lectures, they are increasingly a part of organisational routines, in annual appraisal interviews, in students' assessments of their tutors, and in promotion and job applications. The point is to make yourself different and, in the case of representational texts, to express yourself in relation to the performativity of the organisation. This is an aspect of what Blackmore and Sachs call self-management—'the issue was as much what was seen to be done, rather than substantively what was done' (Blackmore and Sachs, 1999 p. 10).

The application or promotion text is increasingly an artifice of high order. A career is reconstructed within these texts as a seamless, developmental progression to the present, with lines of further development, a potential value-added, streaming off into the future. We rehearse our national and international reputation, quote from reviews of our books, highlight the excellence of our teaching and our contributions to administration and the institutional and academic communities. We become rounded paragons with multiple strengths and infinite possibilities for further work, adept in the studied art of convincing exaggeration. We make fantasies of ourselves,[7] aestheticise ourselves. Appraisal documents can be equally fantastical in setting and reporting on personal targets. But again we are increasingly caught up in the logic of our own representations. We are engaged in an indexing, a tabularising, of the self. Increasingly we represent and enact our academic selves in terms pf productivities and tables of performance. We work on ourselves and each other, through the micro practices of representation/fabrication, judgement and comparison. A new kind of practical ethics is articulated and realised. In all this, what we are seeing, I want to argue, is 'a general change in categories of self-understanding and techniques of self-improvement' (Rose, 1992 p. 161).

The Performative Society

> ... the generalisation of an enterprise form to all forms of conduct may of itself serve to incapacitate an organisation's ability to pursue its preferred projects by redefining its identity and hence what the nature of its project actually is. (du Gay, 1996 p. 190)

This is also Lyotard's point. It is not that performativity gets in the way of real academic work, it is a vehicle for changing what academic work is! At the heart of Lyotard's thesis is his argument that the commodification of knowledge is a key characteristic of what he calls 'the postmodern condition'. This involves not simply a different evaluation of knowledge but fundamental changes in the relationships between the learner, learning and knowledge, 'a thorough exteriorization of knowledge' (Lyotard, 1984 p. 4). Knowledge and knowledge relations, including the relationships between learners, are desocialised.

Underlying this is the dissemination of the market or enterprise form as the master narrative defining and constraining the whole variety of relationships within and between the state, civil society and the economy. As far as public sector activities are concerned: 'the emphasis shifts from the state as provider to the state as regulator, establishing the conditions under which various internal markets are allowed to operate, and the state as auditor, assessing their outcomes' (Scott, 1995 p. 80). As Bernstein (1996 p. 169) puts it 'contract replaces covenant'. Within the public sector this process of exteriorisation also involves a profound shift in the nature of the relationship between workers and their work. Service commitments no longer have value or meaning and professional judgement is subordinated to the requirements of performativity and marketing; though obviously there is an important element of cynical compliance at work in the processes of individual and institutional fabrication. This is part of a larger process of ethical retooling in the public sector which is replacing concern for client need and professional judgement with commercial decision-making. The space for the operation of autonomous ethical codes based on a shared moral language is colonised or closed down. Embedded here is what Hanlon calls 'a struggle for the soul of professionalism' (Hanlon, 1998 p. 50)—'a contest over the meaning of professionalism which has at its centre the issue of trust—'who is trusted, and why they are trusted is up for grabs' (Hanlon, 1998 p. 59). The ethos of traditional professionalism is no longer trusted 'to deliver what is required, increasing profitability and international competitiveness' (Hanlon, 1998 p. 52) and is being replaced by a 'new commercialised professionalism' (Hanlon, 1998 p. 54).

The new structures and roles for organisational management with a central core for policy, audit and regulation and separate 'service delivery units'—the rim and the hub—increasingly mirror the steering-at-a-distance role of the 'small state' or what Neave (1988) calls 'the new evaluative state'. In this way, the state also provides a new ethical framework and general mode of regulation, a much more hands-off, self-regulating regulation, which nonetheless enables and legitimates the dissemination of the commodity form as we are required to commodify ourselves and our academic productions. This is, in Aglietta's (1979 p. 101) terms, a new 'regulative ensemble' or a 'particular mode of social coherence', a historically distinct form of labour organisation. This ensemble of performative technologies is an improvised and polyvalent mix of physical, textual and moral elements which 'make it possible to govern in an "advanced liberal" way' (Rose, 1996 p. 58).

Within the framework of performativity, academics and teachers are represented and encouraged to think about themselves as individuals who calculate about themselves, 'add value' to themselves, improve their productivity, live an existence of calculation. They are to become 'enterprising subjects', who live their lives as 'an enterprise of the self' (Rose, 1989). This is not simply a set of changes in the nature of public sector professionalism and social relations. Rather these changes encapsulate a more general and profound shift in the way we are coming 'to recognise ourselves and act upon ourselves as certain kinds of subject' and 'the nature of the present in which we are' (Rose, 1992 p. 161); and thus a certain form of life in which 'one could recognise oneself' (Foucault, 1988 p. 49) is threatened or lost. Instead we are presented with other ways of saying who we are and representing ourselves. We have an opportunity to be enthused. We also have everyday opportunities to refuse these ways of accounting for ourselves, not as apathy, rather as 'a hyper- and pessimistic activism'. As Foucault puts it: 'I think that the ethico-political choice we have to make every day is to determine which is the main danger' (Foucault, 1983, p. 232).[8]

NOTES

1. The idea of authenticity, as a discursive practice in its own right, needs to be worked upon. It is deployed here in a neutral sense or at least as a 'nonpositive affirmation ... an affirmation that affirms nothing' (Foucault, 1997 p. 197)—an act of exiting. However, I might go as far as saying that while 'authenticity' is certainly not intended as a normative

condition it is intended to indicate a stance towards, an anticipation of the effects of, the discourses we employ 'a refusal to be mindlessly complicitous' (Pignatelli, 1993 p. 430), the generation of 'inventive responses' and an honouring of 'disqualified knowledges' (Foucault, 1980; see also Ball, 1999).

2. Subjectivity is: 'patterns by which experiential and emotional contexts, feelings, images and memories are organized to form one's self-image, one's sense of self and others, and our possibilities of existence' (de Lauretis, 1986 p. 5).
3. As Mitchell Dean explains: 'The notion of governmentality implies, then, first a project for the analysis of the state which would no longer rely on the juxtaposition of micro and macrolevels of power, and the conceptual autonomy of an analytics of micropower and the theory of sovereignty' (Dean, 1994 p. 160).
4. The pressures of performativity and performance act, in particular and heightened forms, on those academic workers who are without tenure or on fixed-term contracts.
5. Erica McWilliam pointed out to me the importance of trying to capture a sense of the seductive possibilities of performativity. See McWilliam, Hatcher *et al.* (1999) on the role of awards in higher education.
6. Abbott distinguishes between those sites which are promotional and those which are educative.
7. A colleague in another university recently described her application for promotion to me 'as a form of prostitution'.
8. An extended version of this [chapter] was given as the Frank Tate Memorial Lecture at the Australian Association for Research in Education conference in Melbourne, 1999. It was later published in the *Australian Educational Researcher* 27/2: 1–24.

Gender Politics and Conceptions of the Modern Teacher: Women, Identity and Professionalism

Jo-Anne Dillabough

When the idea for reason was conceived, it was intended to achieve more than the mere regulation of the relation between the means and the ends; it was the instrument for understanding the ends, for determining them.

(Horkheimer, 1947, p. 10; original emphasis)

[. . .]

Introduction

For at least a decade, sociologists have claimed that British teacher education and the field of teaching have been restructured in line with a kind of neo-liberal rationalism which positions education more effectively within the capitalist hierarchy (see Gewirtz, 1997; Mentor *et al.*, 1997; Whitty, 1997). In consequence, the modern teacher and teacher educators are now viewed as the pivotal agents of educational reform. For example, the notion of the teacher as a rational and consumer-oriented professional is heralded by the state and mainstream scholars alike as key to the success of 'education in the market place' and thereby central to the transformation of the nation as a global economic force.

Paradoxically, while a strong neo-liberal emphasis on schooling is emblematic of new capitalist formations, the '*rational*' vision of the modern teacher is not. Indeed, the notion of the rational actor in the state has an extensive history in philosophical and political traditions, most notably, in Kantian and Cartesian traditions of thought. Nevertheless, twenty years ago, it may have been difficult to argue that 'teacher professionalism' (as a potentially progressive idea) had any similarities to idealized Cartesian and/or Kantian notions of the rational individual. Yet, it is clear that many of the constituent elements from which contemporary models of teacher professionalism are constructed resonate with the same sort of Kantian and Cartesian assumptions about the modern political subject that have plagued liberal democratic societies for three centuries; most notably, the notion of the teacher as a 'rational,

Jo-Anne Dillabough, 'Gender Politics and Conceptions of the Modern Teacher: women, identity and professionalism', *British Journal of Sociology of Education*, 20, 3, 373–94 © 1999 Taylor & Francis Ltd. <http://tandf.co.uk/journals>.

instrumental actor'. Within education, these elements frame, albeit problematically, the state project of reforming the public's vision of the modern teacher.

There has been enormous scholarly interest in the dynamics of educational reform and its link to the state's conception of the modern teacher. However, two key issues pertaining to this debate still remain unexplored. The first of these concerns the relationship between male power and the construction of the rational teacher. The second relates to the part played by feminist theory in exposing the gendered nature of contemporary educational concepts such as 'teacher professionalism'. Until such questions are addressed, attempts to critique or theorize the relation between teacher professionalism and gender will remain rare.[1] In this [chapter], I therefore attempt to pursue such issues on exploratory and critical grounds.

The [chapter] will seek to demonstrate that questions of gender and the history of male dominance in political thought are central to our understanding of contemporary teaching and its character. To do this, I engage in two related forms of feminist critique which permit an analysis of the role of gender in the formation of the teacher as professional. The first section, entitled 'The Gendering of Teacher Professionalism', draws upon feminist critiques of liberal democracy—in particular, feminist concerns about the 'rational individual' in the state—to critically assess the gendered construction of the modern teacher. The central goal here is to illustrate how liberal concepts, which are most closely associated with Kantian and Cartesian notions of the 'self', resonate with dominant conceptions of 'teacher professionalism' in the fields of teaching and teacher education. I argue that these conceptions not only endorse particular forms of masculinity, but serve, at least in part, to regulate the production of the modern teacher.

The second section, entitled 'Women and Teacher Professionalism', deals less with grand theoretical concepts and more with substantive educational concerns about the gender dualisms which lie at the heart of 'teacher professionalism'. Consequently, seminal feminist critiques of the relation between the concept of rationality and women's marginal position in the teaching profession are described and explored.

In the third section, 'Gender Politics and the Teaching Profession', I draw upon existing feminist research and my own preliminary empirical data to illustrate the ways in which rational and instrumental notions of teaching frame the often exploitative conditions of women teachers' work. Since the [chapter] is based largely on research with three different groups of women teachers in the UK, I refer here to teaching in the broadest sense, including female university teachers in teacher education and female student teachers.[2]

In the final section, 'Alternative Feminist Conceptualisations of Identity Formation in Teaching', I draw extensively upon feminist political and social theory to construct an alternative conceptual model for assessing the role of gender in the identity formation of teachers. I justify the development of this exploratory model on two levels: first, it is essential to unravel the ways in which dominant knowledge forms in any field bear resemblance to a historical narrative which most scholars assume are long-forgotten memories of the past. This involves critique in the first instance rather than simply charting the actual pragmatics and discursive practices of liberal democracy itself. Second, since feminist critiques of male epistemology are linked to questions of women's identity and gender identity in the broadest sense, it is useful to draw upon them in order to rethink the part played by gender in the identity formation of teachers.

The Gendering of Teacher Professionalism: A Conceptual Analysis

In recent years, there has been renewed interest in the notion of the teacher as a professional. For example, Nixon *et al.* (1997) have argued that the 'identity category', which has the widest popular support in contemporary teacher education, is the notion of the teacher as 'professional'. Despite this support, a uniform notion of 'teacher professionalism' does not exist. There is, however, a more general view which circulates about teacher professionalism, at least with regard to the way it is defined by central government, related agencies in Britain (e.g. Teacher Training Agency (TTA)), and expressed within teacher education reform initiatives. Broadly speaking, this more general view of 'professional identity' is characterized in terms of the teacher's 'rational' capacity to 'behave competently' in the name of student achievement, and social and economic change.[3] This conception tends to be defined in terms of the instrumentality of the teacher as reform agent and his/her role in subverting personal interests (e.g. political concerns, personal wisdom) to accord with objective standards of practice. Carr (1989) writes:

> Technical rationality continues to provide the dominant epistemology of practice, and central government's predilection for technological views of teaching is inevitably creating conditions under which a reflexive approach to professional development becomes impossible. (p. 5)

> Teaching is portrayed as an unreflective technical process and 'quality' as synonymous with meeting pre-specified standards through a system of supervision, inspection and control. Teaching Quality may use the rhetoric of professionalism, but in reality this amounts to giving teachers a little more than the right to exercise a limited technical discretion [...]. Education is seen as something which serves extrinsic purposes such as national interest, the economic needs of the society, or the demands of the labour market. (pp. 2–3)

Within this model of teacher professionalism, the liberal discourse most commonly associated with the modern teacher is the rational, instrumental actor.

Many sociologists in education have critiqued this rational view of teacher professionalism, arguing that it represents one attempt by the state to marginalize egalitarian principles in practice. For example, Mahoney and Hextall (1997) argue that teachers' notions of professional practice are constrained by the now abstract and so-called 'neutral' descriptions of the new Standards Teacher. Similarly, Jones and Moore (1993) argue that a mainstream neo-liberal culture of 'professionalism' now dominates education and serves to constrain educational professionals' authenticity in practice. This culture serves to undermine the political authenticity of teachers and leads to instrumental forms of 'technical control'. Jones and Moore (1993) write: 'the effectiveness of "competency" resides in the manner in which it codifies and regulates behaviour through constructs of "skills" and the manner in which its methodology, active within a particular policy and institutional context, facilitates technical control' (p. 387). Similar ideas have been put forward by Lawn and Ozga (1981), suggesting that 'teacher professionalism' is used by the state as a political device which gives the impression of liberation (e.g. collaboration, 'empowerment'), but simultaneously de-skills and de-professionalizes teachers to the point of exploitation. Taken together, this work has exposed the formidable links between teachers' professional identities and the changing, and increasingly centralized, modes of state regulation over teachers' labours. It has also pointed to the underlying ideological orientation of 'teacher professionalism' as expressed in educational knowledge and discourse.

While this line of reasoning is valuable, critics within this discourse have ignored questions of gender. Consequently, the stress within sociology on 'neo-liberal' politics or restructuring as sole motivations for understanding 'teacher culture' (see Gewirtz, 1997) or the 'professional teacher' is limited insofar as the goal of scholarship is simply to expose state practices, rather than relate such practices to broader sociological concerns such as gender relations. In the next section, I attempt to redress this imbalance. I do so in the first instance by summarizing feminist political and social theorists' concerns about the gendered nature of 'idealized' Kantian and Cartesian inventions such as the 'rational, instrumental actor', and their relevance to current debates about the modern individual. An engagement with this body of work is pertinent because it affords the conceptual refinement needed to reinstate gender as a key issue in the construction of teacher professionalism. Having drawn upon feminist political theory in this way, I shall be in a position to illuminate some of the gendered tensions which arise as a consequence of relying, within an abstract liberal conception of identity, upon two concepts—rationality and instrumentalism—in the development of the teacher as professional.

The Problem of Rationality in Liberal Democratic Theory

> Like Western thought generally, political theory [...] relies on and reproduces its dualistic foundations, where knowledge and citizenship are equally grounded in hierarchical oppositions that value mind over body, culture over nature, reason over emotion, order over chaos, transparency over opacity. The feminine, a metaphor or identity for the denigrated terms, emerges as anarchic and wild; a threat to clear thought, self-discipline and political order. (Coole, 1993, p. 18)

Theoretical debates which concern the gendering of liberal democratic discourse now have a lengthy history in feminist political and social theory. The most notable of these debates is the now longstanding feminist concern with Kantian and Cartesian notions of the 'rational man'—the 'disembedded' political subject—as expressed in liberal democratic theory. For example, as feminist political theorists argue, both the Kantian and the Cartesian view of the rational political subject reflected a certain disdain for anything 'coded as feminine' (see Coole, 1993, p. 1), and conflated femininity with the subjective element of political participation. As a consequence, the objective and reasoned elements of political participation were privileged and thus dominated the construction of the active citizen. In such a context, women could not possess political identities because their 'emotionality' and sexuality were viewed as a threat to the rational state (see Coole, 1993). Male rationality and reason have thus emerged as normative political ideals in liberal democratic societies.

One contribution of feminist political theory to our understanding of the gendered nature of liberal democratic practices is feminist critiques of both Kantian and Cartesian philosophies, and the concept of reason. For example, both Coole (1993) and Braaten (1997) have argued that 'reason', although a rather idealized political concept, is still revered as the centre-piece of liberal democratic practice and remains central to the success of the modern individuals, that is, to possess reason is to know, and to be a knowing subject is to possess political power. However, as feminist theorists argue, in conceding to rationality as the sole foundation for a political identity, women must remain (at least in abstract terms) outside the domain of the polity since they are constructed symbolically as that which stands in opposition to rationality. As such, women cannot 'know' in the purest sense; they are instead viewed as the medium through which the rational individual is cultivated. Women stand outside the political process as 'Other': 'From Plato to Descartes to Kant the self is the unitary substratum; reason reigns over the passions, the I reigns over the will; otherness must be suppressed' (Benhabib, 1995*b*, p. 198).[4] 'Identity' viewed in this manner reproduces dominant notions of masculinity in two ways. On the one hand, it gives rise to a cultural vision of 'inclusive' political participation which favours a masculine conception of the modern subject/individual. It achieves this through the formation of stable gender categories which differentiate, as if natural and legitimate, between the 'rational' man and 'irrational' women.[5]

On the other hand, this strand of political thought constructs an 'exclusionary' notion of the modern identity which can only justify itself through the practice of reason. In such a case, men stand as legitimate representatives of the public sphere, while women, as Clark (1976) suggests, remain in the 'ontological basement' of political life. As a consequence, women can only achieve political status on par with that of men if they fully embrace the symbolic gender dualisms which frame state practice and have their roots in the European philosophical tradition, that is, they must *separate* from the 'self' when it is entrenched in any formal attachment or intimate connection with another (see Weir, 1997).

The Problem of Instrumentalism in Liberal Discourse

The Kantian focus on the separation of 'self' from experience in the search for a legitimate political identity exposes another gendered tension which underlies traditional conceptions of rationality. This tension is best expressed as follows: by conceptualising the 'self' as detached, the individual symbolizes a position of complete independence where he/she no longer appears 'to have intrinsic needs for others' (see Weir, 1997). Weir (1997) views this strong liberal characterization of the individual as an unrealistic abstraction. Such a view 'runs against the structural features of the self as a being who exists in a space of concerns' (Taylor, 1989, p. 51). An over-reliance on this instrumental conception of identity does, however, lead to two problems which are central to the reproduction of Weir's (1997) 'disembedded subject' in the state.

First, this view of the modern individual negates the role of social context, structure and particularity in the formation of gender identities, i.e., it fails to view identity as an embedded political construct which 'always depends upon larger social meanings' (see Benhabib, 1997; Weir, 1997) for self-definition. Second, the language of instrumentalism (e.g.

detached political subject, freedom, autonomy) falsely implies that women will acquire the necessary freedom to act politically in their own name if they extract themselves from their social experience.[6] Consequently, in this model, the social element of identity formation is denied; unrealistic expectations are thus circulated about the capacity for women to be 'free' despite the now obvious and well-documented social constraints placed upon them.

Liberal Discourse, Gender and the Construction of the Modern Teacher

On first examination, feminist critiques which have exposed the idealized modern individual as a masculine entity may seem unrelated to educational concepts, in particular, teacher professionalism and women's position within it. However, as discussed at the outset, in recent years 'teacher professionalism' has been redefined by the state to reflect a certain strain of rationality which privileges male theories of the polity. Therefore, on any systematic application of feminist critiques of the modern subject to dominant views of teacher professionalism, a number of tensions arise which pose particular difficulties for feminists.

The first tension emerges when the part played by Kantian or Cartesian representations of the 'rational man' are rendered visible in contemporary notions of teacher professionalism. For example, state-centred notions of 'teacher professionalism', such as the Competent Teacher or the Standards Teacher, are closely associated with Kant's idea that personal perspectives (e.g. emotions, experience) should not inform political action in the public sphere, and in this case, the actions of teachers. Instead, it is now advocated that teachers' identities should conform to a more objective and procedural account of professionalism, as expressed by, for example, government agencies (e.g. TTA).[7] However, if we accept feminist critiques of the Kantian position as valid, one could argue that women's (and men's) diverse emotional experiences and political beliefs (and, hence, differences) are repressed in this abstract model of teacher professionalism. As such, this model gives a misleading picture of teaching by attending to what has been traditionally viewed as the masculine sphere of the political spectrum (i.e. the rational public sphere). The other sphere—the realm of the private[8]—is not viewed as politically relevant in this model of teaching (see Noddings, 1996), at least as far as abstract knowledge structures about professionalism are concerned.

Second, the dominant notion of 'professional identity' appears to be premised on a rather simplistic and instrumental model of teacher development. This abstract model of professionalism characterizes teachers as individuals who do not make meaningful connections with students or other 'professionals', but instead respond to the instrumental goals of the state (see Mahoney and Hextall, 1997). Thus, the teaching self is not constituted through complex and meaningful social interactions; it simply asserts itself in the name of progress. This notion highlights a 'forging of a concept of profession with the quest for order in a period of rapid social change and with middle-class male anxiety about proving one's self, in ways that are highly reminiscent of the themes of the masculine cultural project as is already visible in relation to bureaucracy' (Davies, 1996, p. 669). Since, as Davies (1996) argues, women are typically associated with 'feminine' codes, they are often excluded from, or controlled by, this 'masculine cultural project'. Consequently, a discursive notion of the teaching 'self' is lost, and the complexity of education and its socializing mechanisms remain unexplored.

A third tension emerges when one considers the instrumental forms of training currently in operation in teacher education. Whereas earlier perspectives on professional teacher training emphasized the idea of meaningful student–teacher relationships, school communities and progressive pedagogical approaches, current approaches point to a return to traditional assessment methods and idea of the teacher as the transmitter of knowledge (e.g. whole-class teaching). As Gewirtz (1997) writes:

> there is a decline in the sociability of teaching; and there is pressure on teachers to adopt more traditional pedagogies, with a focus on output rather than the process and on particular groups of high-attaining students [...] These shifts are in large part a consequence of a deliberate strategy on the part of the policy makers attempting to ameliorate particular problems of the state—problems of capital accumulation, legitimation and control. (p. 230)

Paradoxically, this legitimate 'authority' and control is not gained through creative and authentic insight nor through shared social experience in the classroom. Rather, it is achieved through teachers' and teacher educators' individual efforts to commit to standardized procedures which are created by an objective body of so-called 'experts'. If a teacher succeeds at this task, she will be labelled 'competent'. However, such notions are constrained by masculine ideals of professional autonomy and agency, 'an ideal that can be achieved—in a world of "hostile strangers"—[. . .] through impersonal relations that are distant and emotionally detached' (Davies, 1996, p. 672). Since knowledge about teaching appears to be tied to very particular gender codes and categories, the reproduction of masculine ideals through the concept of 'teacher professionalism' leads to the devaluation of those gender codes which are typically associated with the 'feminine'. This not only means that gender dualisms are re-represented in educational thought. It also implies that dominant conceptions of teacher professionalism yield to gendered teaching identities which are always unequal.

In summary, feminist critiques of the modern subject provide the necessary analytical tools for exposing the relation between gender and rationality, and their complementary roles in the gendering of professional knowledge. They also problematize the gender dualisms which underlie a notion of teaching as rational, instrumental action. This view reconstitutes the teacher as Kant's individuated 'rational man'—a teacher devoid of meaningful connections to those whom she is expected to educate. Feminist critiques of concepts such as 'teacher professionalism' also point to the implicit theories of gender identity deployed in educational and professional discourses, and their representation within hierarchical systems of educational knowledge.

Women and Teacher Professionalism

The contradictions inherent in the liberal concepts of 'rationality' and 'instrumentality' can be more clearly understood when one examines how their deployment in teacher education over time has led to a diminished view of women teachers as 'professionals'. Therefore, at this level of analysis, the problem moves beyond that of the simple exclusion of women's knowledge from a dominant and, indeed, abstract notion of teacher professionalism. Rather, it is concerned more directly with the contradictory and problematic nature of women's inclusion in the teaching profession itself.

Interestingly, not unlike feminist political theorists, feminist educationalists are also concerned with rationality and its gendered manifestations. However, their arguments move beyond a concern with political thought to professional knowledge and its implications for women teachers. In this section, therefore, I address the ways in which feminist educationalists have critiqued the application of male-centered concepts (e.g. rationality) to the teaching profession, and in particular, to the lives of women teachers.

Inclusion, Rationality and Women Teachers' Experiences

> We are arguing that the proof of masculinity as rational, as possessing knowledge, as superior, has constantly to be reasserted and set against its equal and opposite proof of the failure and lack of femininity. To say this is not to collude with the idea that women, and all other excluded groups, really 'are' lacking, but to demonstrate the great investments in proving this to be the case. (Walkerdine and Lucey, 1989, p. 201)

In 1989, Valerie Walkerdine and Helen Lucey published an important book entitled *Democracy in the Kitchen*. In this work, the authors were concerned with the question of how liberal democratic ideals (e.g. freedom) framed the lives of girls and women, both normatively and symbolically, outside the domain of rationalism. Consequently, as was the case in feminist critiques of liberal democratic theory, Walkerdine and Lucey (1989) argued that women's political identities had been constructed against, and in subordination to, male theories of the rational individual. Women were thus seen as both conditioned and constrained by essentializing images of 'irrationality'—an image of women dating back to the Enlightenment.

Their work also served to illustrate just how Enlightenment concepts, as a largely male enterprise, continued to re-emerge in education over time. According to Walkerdine and Lucey (1989), for example, it is still the bourgeois male teacher or student who is honoured with the title 'rational being' because it is he who is 'endowed with reason' (p. 200) in the purest sense. By contrast, women teachers and female students cannot possess knowledge in their own right because they are viewed as moral vessels through which liberal democracy and the rational society are cultivated. At the same time, however, women teachers and female students are still seen in the abstract as 'free' and equal to men in their capacity to explore the possibilities and opportunities of liberal democracy in practice.

It is within these debates that concerns about the role of 'rationality' have emerged in the field of teaching and teacher education, particularly as they concern the lives of women teachers who work in the 'feminized' professions (e.g. teaching, teacher education). Many feminists have suggested, for example, that an over-reliance on 'rationality' within dominant educational discourse in both schools and higher education masks the historical constraints imposed upon women teachers and their capacity to be 'rational' agents within the profession (see Blackmore, 1996). As Casey (1990) and Steedman (1985) argue, the very structure of teaching has been shaped by biologically determined gender dualisms which have led to the coding of women as 'feminine' and, hence, the representation of 'women teachers as mothers' (see Casey, 1990, 1993). As a consequence, the professional status of women teachers is closely tied to domestic work in the private sphere. This linking of women teachers to the private sphere remains dependent, at least in part, upon traditional distinctions within political consciousness between 'public man' and 'private woman'.

The now seminal work of Walkerdine and Lucey (1989) and others (see Steedman, 1985) has been key to feminist critiques of women's social positioning in education. Not only has it pointed to the part played by the rhetoric of 'rationality' in marginalizing women teachers (and girls), it also suggests that women teachers are represented as symbolic of the private sphere, and deemed responsible for the cultivation of the 'rational' ideal of freedom through their role as moral regulators of the state (see Walkerdine, 1990). The historical role of teacher thus becomes one of regulating and governing liberal democratic subjects who uncritically support the 'freedoms' that are thought to underlie modern capitalism and its gendered manifestations. Walkerdine (1990) writes:

> the primary school forms an important place where this 'free-will' is established. It is in this sense that we can begin to understand the position of the teacher as 'the responsibility and the spur of freedom'. The freedom which she has to foster is, I would argue, the notion of bourgeois individuality ... The teacher, then, is responsible for freedom. (p. 61)

Paradoxically, this responsibility for ensuring the 'freedom' of students often contradicts that which is articulated about the professional identity of teachers, that is, the professional is ultimately one who is free to the extent that rational and independent choices about educational practice can be made. However, women teachers are at the same time constrained by the very 'illusion of freedom' as they are continually reconstituted as 'mothers' and 'guardians' of the nation. These constraints are clearly linked to identity narratives which concern women's reproductive capacity rather than their ability, as it were, to be 'rational'.

As these arguments imply, educational discourse which pertains to women teachers is often essentialized by traditional notions of the female identity. However, at the same time, such notions are often construed as irrational, driven by emotions and/or deemed inappropriate by society (see Blackmore, 1996). As such, the social construction of women's professional status points to the naturalization of women's teaching identity as inferior to that of men. It also suggests that women teachers' professional identity can only be found amid the so-called 'virtues' of the private sphere, which is ultimately viewed as contemptible in the context of a 'real' profession. Consequently, the only remaining option for women teachers is to take up an instrumental stance where 'mothering' is replaced with procedural forms of quality control or an identification with masculine forms of competence as the sole mechanism for achieving professional autonomy. Arguably, however, this formal identification with masculinity becomes a position of dominance rather than a position of reflection or female agency: 'the self becomes all too proficient at the domination of nature, at the repression of drives, at defending identity against otherness, against difference' (Weir, 1997, p. 66).

Consequently, as was the case with the representation of women in political thought, some of the most difficult questions concerning the significance of women teachers' professional identities are collapsed into an oppositional view of gender categories, which lead to the defense of one essentialized teaching 'self' over another. However, the dominance of an essentialized teaching 'self' in teacher education—the rational teacher—functions to mask the reality that most women teachers are situated on the inferior side of the gender binary. This position ultimately leads to women's exclusion from the formal language of teacher professionalism, yet simultaneously defines their inclusion on the basis of female subordination.

Gender Politics and the Teaching Profession

The dual obsession with polarized identity discourses which concern teacher professionalism—'teacher as mother' or the 'rational' teacher—has very specific consequences for understanding the institutionalization of the gender order in the teaching profession. These consequences are bound up in the gender relations and political formations which lead to women's experiences of exclusion in the teaching profession. Within education, the most obvious of these exclusions is the often subtle exploitation of women teachers' labours in education.

At this point, therefore, I turn to a consideration of the many and varied aspects of female exploitation in the teaching profession, drawing upon current examples of feminist educational research together with some preliminary work of my own. In reviewing my own work, I focus largely on women teacher educators and, to a lesser extent, female student teachers since their gendered positioning in teacher education still remains unexplored.[9] However, I also draw upon research which concerns the experiences of female academics who teach in the feminized professions. I do this with the intention of forging links between the working experiences of women teachers in those academic professions which 'institutionalize women's labours' and the lives of women (both students and academics) in teaching and teacher education. In so doing, I hope to illustrate how educational institutions function within a broader gender order which supports the essentialization of male and female identities, yet remains committed to a rational notion of teacher professionalism in both schools and teacher education.

Gender, Exploitation and the Contemporary Teacher

There is now a detailed, if limited, body of feminist research which attempts to expose the exploitation of women's labours in the teaching profession, some of which includes the study of women teachers in the academy and the work of women teachers more broadly. Much of this work has exposed the gender hierarchies and Kantian dualisms which continue to shape knowledge production about the role of women teachers and their subordinate status. For example, both Acker and Feuerverger (1997) and Brooks (1997) have provided evidence to suggest that female university teachers are exploited as workers; they are overloaded with administrative responsibilities, encouraged to function as caregivers, and given responsibilities which may lead to their exclusion from an equal chance of success as 'professionals'. In referring to empirical work conducted with female university teachers, Acker and Feuerverger (1997) write:

> *[Women academics]* experience a 'bifurcated consciousness' (Smith, 1987) or 'segmented self' (Miller, J. L., 1983) or 'outlaw emotions' (Jagger, 1989) as they try to live up to the contradictory prescriptions for 'caring women' and productive academics. They see themselves working too hard, with high levels of anxiety, in reward systems that they dislike and without sufficient recognition for the aspects of the work they care about or have to do. Although self-selection may play a part in producing the anxiety and perfectionism demonstrated by many of these women, we have argued that their 'outsider status' in academe, combined with narrow institutional criteria for success, result in a situation where they suffer considerable pain. (p. 418; emphasis added)

Acker and Feuerverger (1997) also provide some illustrative and provocative examples of women teachers' concerns about the nature of their own exploitation in practice. They quote Lucille, a female academic in their study:

I sort of am used: as a departmental resource, like the fire extinguisher ... And I'm the shoulder for students to cry on. And I'm the person who can be counted on to teach well. Who can be called on to do whatever needs to be done ... I don't mind, I mean those are things that I would do anyway because they're what one does. But, certainly, as far as recognition for it, or the rest of it goes, forget it. (*Lucille*, quote extract taken from Acker and Feuerverger, 1997, p. 414)

Other feminists have pointed to the significance of the gender binary in the exploitation of women teachers' labours. For example, Luttrell (1996) argues that women educators are more often employed in non-tenured, part-time or contractual posts, where teaching and pastoral responsibilities are greater than they would be in permanent positions. This kind of employment status often leads to a situation where women are sometimes overwhelmed by the extent to which they have been conceptualized as service providers in education. Recent evidence for this claim in the everyday work of female teacher educators is also present in my own research. In the words of one female teacher educator participating in an interview which I conducted in the UK on educational restructuring and women in teacher education:[10]

I was asked to be a year tutor. I was asked and I remember feeling valued when I was asked. Then I got told that 'they only asked you because you're the only one that will do it. Everyone else has said no', but I didn't know that then [...] A year tutor is like everyone's *mother*. You'll be stuck with everything [...] It was difficult to cope with.[...] One set of problems after another [...] So I was seen as a *mother figure* [...] I just didn't realize how I became everybody's *dogsbody* [...] So I did that for two years and I wouldn't do it anymore. It stopped me from doing any research [...] I remember saying I wanted to go back and engage in research [...] I was getting really fed up with that and I remember sitting in the staff room and somebody said 'you're year tutor' and I said 'I'm not' but I let them do that to me. Now I think why? [...] *Is it because I'm a woman?* (*Sylvia*, Interview 1; emphasis added)

Sylvia's comments relate directly to issues which concern the conflation of the categories 'teaching' and 'motherhood', where the latter category emerges as symbolic of diminished status and working conditions which further marginalize women. Consequently, any institutional attempts to demonstrate 'inclusion' through role status or professional responsibilities such as year tutor may lead to experiences of marginalization, which may ultimately constrain women teachers' professional agency in practice. This is largely because inclusion as a 'professional' (i.e. the position of year tutor) may be premised upon female submission, male hierarchies of knowledge, or a conceptualization of teaching as 'motherhood'. It thus becomes clear that certain understandings of 'inclusion' take priority over others, such that the exploitation of women's labours is legitimized within a formal political structure.

Sylvia's remarks also expose what Luttrell (1996) identifies as the illusions of 'maternal omnipotence' (p. 352), which form part of the structured gender relations of labour in teaching, and their conscious and unconscious manifestations in the everyday language of individuals in the workplace. These 'illusions' are not restricted to Sylvia's experience. They emerge as significant in the lives of other women teachers. As Helen, another female teacher educator, remarked:

There is always this feeling that if you're a woman I think that you do your work for the sake of your job. Then you wish somebody will appreciate you. But they're *(men)* not in it for the job. They only appreciate you if you're servicing them. Somewhere there is a serious conflict. I don't know what it means. Because sometimes it's like slavery. (*Helen*, Interview 3, 1998; emphasis added)

As is evident in Helen's remarks, there is a tendency to invoke very particular and indeed dichotomous understandings of gender identity. However, such understandings serve to elucidate the paradoxical nature of women teachers' work. This paradox emerges when the history of women's service role re-emerges in contemporary practices and invokes both conscious and unconscious feelings about one's social positioning more generally. According to Helen, for example, the act of service should lead (at least in theory) to a certain appreciation for the work women do. However, as she suggests, appreciation can only emerge as a response to the conflation of women and service. Women teachers therefore emerge as a devalued entity unless they are serving others. Clearly, this process of devaluation not only has serious consequences for women teachers, but also invokes a particular understanding of the structural dimensions of gender inequality in higher education:

When I came here *(to the university)* I still saw a very male, white middle class power structure which shocked me. It all seemed so male. I went to exam boards and it was all me and these males making the decisions [. . .] All the people who seemed to be in a position of authority were men, like principle lecturers. It seemed that there were very few women, and they were all middle class, and I saw the world as a female tutor and I couldn't believe how few [. . .] female tutors there were. There were hardly any [. . .] But I am still shocked and I am still pretty peeved when I sit in exam boards and meetings where you see who holds the power. (*Janine*, Interview 2, 1996; emphasis added)

Emergent Feminist Political Identities and the Sociological Constraints of Gender Relations in Teaching[11]

The empirical work cited reveals some of the complex ways in which the teaching profession is both modelled on, and illustrative of, the broader gender order. In other words, as was particularly noted in the first section of the [chapter], women's labours in teaching cannot be separated from the historically constructed knowledge claims which circulate about gender relations in society. However, such assumptions contradict many of the new modes of regulating the 'competent' teacher. And so the paradox re-emerges: notions of the 'good teacher' are premised upon rational action and instrumental forms of expertise. Nevertheless, women teachers and teacher educators are still constructed outside this dominant view of the professional, despite the demands placed upon them to conform to it. Consequently, the search for a meaningful and coherent 'professional [and political] identity' thus becomes a fraught, complex and ambiguous process:

I'm trying to reclaim my identity now. I felt as soon as I'd come here, I'd been turned into some sort of workhorse and that is a gendered position to be in [. . .] So I'm very much trying to reclaim and establish a way of working here that isn't at odds with my political situation. I haven't done it yet but that's what I am trying for. However, I am going about gaining political control in a fragmented way. (*Sylvia*, Interview 2, 1997)

I was doing an executive job and that was all I could do but I couldn't be responsible for both ends, so then we were inspected for the second time and it was exactly the same situation I realised I was going to have to protect myself [. . .] I made it very clear that I was not going to take responsibility for that [OFSTED inspection results]. I said [to OFSTED] that's not my job, that's somebody else's job. I learned the second time around not be in the great catch all area. I laid down precisely where I was going to walk and what I was prepared to take responsibility for. (*Helen*, Interview 3, 1998)

And so the battle for women to assert themselves as 'professionals' continues. Yet, in many cases, such political assertions appear to be based on women's desires to both protect and set themselves apart from any blame for institutional failure; in other words, such assertions seem necessary for survival in the teaching profession. The need for self-protection, as expressed by both Sylvia and Helen, point to the struggle women teachers engage in to both resist and get beyond their marginal positioning in the profession. In exposing this struggle, the gender dualisms which frame the construction of the professional teacher come sharply into view. These dualisms are represented in multiple forms; women teachers as subordinates, as 'mothers', and as scapegoats for what has not been achieved in teacher education. What is significant is that each of these images is consonant with the kind of Cartesian and Kantian dualisms which form the history of women's representation in political thought.

In charting teachers' struggle to gain political status, one also achieves some insight into the ways in which gender hierarchies are implicated in the production of knowledge about the 'professional teacher' and her role in tackling gender inequality in the school classroom. One also begins to see how gender dualisms manifest the lives of women teachers across diverse domains of education. As one female student teacher, Louise, commented in response to a question about her own 'feminist practice' in the classroom:

I've thought about it. I see it in the classroom, in the sort of cliché of the girls being very conscientious and having beautifully presented pages and taking endless trouble and the boys have got very different agendas. There seems to be a maturity gap so I sort of thought as a teacher of my subject I could overcome that and focus on the boys because one feels it is fairly close to a loss of face to show much willingness with a young woman teacher when they're working hard to establish that they're men and all the rest of it. These poor skinny lads. They're like tadpoles. You have to kind of grace that and do whatever. So the line I've taken on the class really is to try and focus them by subject material that they won't feel is too girlie to talk about or too wet. (*Louise*, Interview 2, 1996)

As Louise's remarks imply, it is here that the manifestations of gender dualisms—codes of masculinity and femininity—have both influenced, yet rendered problematic, the possibility of feminist practice in teaching. Indeed, the very idea of tackling gender inequality may lead to the reproduction of a professional stance which impugns the significance of women. Such a stance emerges in multiple forms. As Carry, another student teacher, comments:

Carry: The boys always draw more attention to themselves than girls. Girls are a lot more subtle.

JD: How would you describe their tactics of getting attention?

Carry: Well, they're vocal. They call out [. . .] The girls are a lot quieter. They tend to talk amongst themselves whereas boys will shout across a room. They have a more physical presence. They will pull you by the arm and drag you back to their chair . . .

JD: When the boys do that in the classroom how does it make you feel? If you were monitoring all that?

Carry: Well I tend to get annoyed because my time is being taken up in an unproductive way . . . I've noticed that if you are not careful and not aware you will spend all your time with the boys and that's really bad. (*Carry*, Interview 2, 1996)

Carry's difficulties, of which she herself is well aware, are not confined to the classroom. Even the most politically aware feminist teachers find the struggle to identify with women's concerns a formidable challenge. It is a challenge which not only involves the problem of gender relations, but which is also a broader political struggle over the recognition of women's work in the labour force. The following extract from an interview with Sylvia, a teacher educator, serves to illustrate this:

JD: How would you characterise your feminist strategies in practice?

Sylvia: Well I don't think on my own I can change anything. I can listen to other women. I do see parts of my job as constantly looking at this [. . .] I came into education on a political trip. I wanted to change things and I wanted to say that it's OK to be you and it is OK to recognise that you are you, although you might not be able to affect institutional change. You've got the right to have a personal view and I very much think that has to be fought for [. . .] I want to be in a position to say that what you are fighting for is worth fighting for. It's worth having. I see it as a fight.

JD: If there was anything that held you back (constrained your agency) as someone who wanted to express your feminist beliefs, what would that be?

Sylvia: OFSTED for instance. Well they are policing. I stood in front of them and told them there was a race and gender issue and I didn't know how they would react. But I did it anyway. I thought it was the right thing. I was shocked that none of the students could see it. None of them [. . .] I am aware that I can't pursue my own agenda here because my agenda is too radical. I am aware that I am working in the market economy. I am aware of the pressure on management. I suppose I am aware of the tensions—the reality is the same . . . To at least keep a position and still to recognise that my position is not going to be achieved in one institution. (*Sylvia*, Interview 3, 1998)

The social constraints which limit women teachers' political agency are complex. It appears, for example, as though women construct their political identities (and agency) in *relation* to broader social structures, including those exploitative structures which equate women teachers with subordination in the polity. More significant, however, is the link between gender relations and capitalist restructuring in the broadest sense, along with the manifestation of market thinking in the everyday lives of women teachers. This link, while seemingly peripheral to Sylvia's larger discourse about the maintenance of a feminist position in practice, is absolutely central to both the reconfiguration of the polity and the teaching profession in late modernity.

Alternative Feminist Conceptualisations of Identity Formation in Teaching

In the previous sections, I have been arguing for a need to understand the complex ways in which historically determined gender dualisms serve as identity-framing devices in the field of teaching.

I have therefore sought to illuminate, either through critique or through the representation of data, how gender dualisms which reach back to the Enlightenment continue to inform the construction of the modern teacher. These dualistic forms are not only linked to a crude and abstract form of gender determinism in political theory, but are manifest in educational concepts (i.e. the rational, competent teacher) which privilege masculine 'gender codes' in shaping ideas about the modern teacher and their practices. As I have argued, these concepts presume a de-gendered, 'disembedded' and de-contextualized notion of teacher professionalism. Therefore, I now turn to explore an alternative conceptual framework for assessing the role played by gender in the formation of teachers' identities. Such an approach does not resolve all of the problems identified thus far. It does, however, offer a feminist sociological response to instrumental and rational conceptualizations of the modern teacher. It also makes a case for understanding teachers as discursively formed, as individuals who construct meaning through social mediation, and as agents who are 'embedded, embodied, localised, constituted, fragmented, and subject to systems of power and exploitation' (Weir, 1997, p. 184).

As a point of departure, I wish to argue that we move away from an instrumental assessment of teacher identities and focus instead on a social and political analysis of their development. Such a shift calls for the elucidation of an alternative feminist framework which embraces two antithetical notions in identity theorizing; (1) the post-modern notion of the authentic and discursive self; and (2) the modern conception of the embedded or collective self (see Fraser, 1997; Fraser and Nicholson, 1990; Benhabib, 1995; Weir, 1997). Any over-arching theory of identity formation must therefore consider the relationship between, for example, teacher authenticity,[12] the social mediation of gender relations and the capacity of teachers to reflect critically upon their social positioning as gendered subjects within the state. I would therefore like to posit an 'intersubjective' theory of identity formation (and 'teacher professionalism')[13] whereby teachers can be seen as embedded in relationships 'between *active* subjects' (see Weir, 1997); they are, in other words, bounded individuals who possess some degree of political agency. This view stands against the now dominant view of the 'disembedded' professional as an 'object of knowledge' or as a passive and de-professionalized object of discourse (the 'professional') whose identity is merely reconstituted through neo-liberal political forces.

It thus becomes necessary to move beyond the instrumental study of identity formation in teaching, where concepts such as 'voice' or 'narrative' are drawn upon as the only explanatory tools for theorizing the teaching 'self'. Instead, I suggest we view identity as something which is not solely determined by one's own narrative, but which is also shaped by social and structural relations both within and beyond education. Such an approach suggests that identity formation (in education) be studied, at least in part, through an examination of what feminist critical theorists (see Braaten, 1995; Benhabib, 1995*b*; Weir, 1997) refer to as 'communicative thinking' or what Habermas refers to as 'communicative action'. According to Habermas (1993) and his contemporary feminist followers, we can only know ourselves and recognize others when we have come to terms with, and reflected upon, our structural 'embeddedness' in formal and informal political and language structures. As a consequence, the 'embedded' subject is one who communicates, negotiates and acts upon difference in relation, and response, to meaningful social interactions with others. This social position of the 'embedded subject' is thus said to be situated 'intersubjectively'—in social and dialectical relation to others. Gender, both as a social construct and a powerful social force, is therefore also situated 'intersubjectively'.

In emphasizing an adapted, yet novel, feminist version of the embedded 'self', one can begin to view teachers as political agents who reveal and act upon their differences through a shared and meaningful process of critical reflection. This process does not just imply a negotiation of one's identity with those of others. It also involves the negotiation of larger political meanings in language across a variety of diverse social contexts (Habermas, 1974; Weir, 1997). However, as is expressed in frameworks such as contemporary hermeneutics, the meaning ascribed to identity formation is never fixed or predetermined. It arises out of the relation between those who interpret and ascribe meaning to action, language and everyday practices in varied social contexts and circumstances. Such a framework provides more complex theoretical tools for challenging two critical, yet oppositional, views of the modern teacher, both of which form part of the socially constructed nature of women's subordination: (1) the teacher as an instrumental and unmediated form of masculinity; and (2) the 'teacher as mother'.

In adopting a more sociologically driven feminist framework, we may get closer to challenging and thus transforming the 'real' existence of the gender binary, as expressed through formal knowledge structures in education.[14] This approach might also allow us to see ways forward in theorizing a conceptual understanding of the role of gender in teachers' identity formation which combines both critical modernist conceptions of the self as reflective agent and post-modern notions of the 'self' as authentic and discursive (see also Apple, 1996; Gewirtz, 1997). In my judgement, three conceptual notions which have their roots in contemporary versions of feminist critical theory will be most helpful in rethinking the role of gender in the study of identity formation in teaching. It is to these themes which I now turn.

Intersubjective Identities

As many feminist theorists have argued, self-definition is contingent upon diverse and 'sometimes conflicting contexts of meaning' (see Weir, 1997). Such contexts condition the processes which underlie identity formation: 'my identity is produced through a complex process through which I am identified, and identify myself, in terms of intersubjective contexts of meaning' (Weir, 1997, p. 185). Clearly, such a position on identity formation begs a more complex story about the modern political subject than many of the male-centred traditions of philosophy which have preceded it. Such complexity, as expressed through feminist dialogue, has much to offer in understanding the gendered nature of identity formation in teaching. For example, in applying the notion of intersubjectivity to identity formation, educational researchers might consider studying women teachers' political 'identity' not as a rational entity, but as a complex, subjective and multi-faceted phenomenon which is embedded in the tension between the desire for political agency and the necessity for mutual recognition (see Benhabib, 1995*b*; Weir, 1997) in diverse and social contexts.

It is through the study of this tension that we might better understand the gendered nature of 'intersubjectivity' as central to identity formation in teaching. Studying how teachers reconcile multiple and often conflicting gender identities in the struggle to engage in politically motivated educational practice would be an important contribution to study of identity formation in teaching. However, such tensions can only be examined in relation to the institutional and social contexts within which women currently operate, and have encountered in the past. Such efforts should therefore consider a study of the 'gender regimes' and hierarchies (Connell, 1985, 1990) of educational institutions from diverse perspectives (e.g. differently positioned women) and their impact on the gendered experiences of teachers over time.

Difference and 'Narrativity' as Normative

Difference has become the heralded concept of late modernity. It is posited as the definitive term upon which modern narratives about identity have been crushed. However, feminist critical theorists have argued that 'difference' carries enormous power as a normative concept, which explains, theoretically and empirically, how one comes to identify oneself and others within the state. The work of such theorists has important implications for the study of women's political identity in teaching because it assumes that teachers, in order to identify and reflect on their position in the profession, need to recognize others (e.g. teachers, students) as different from themselves. This commitment to difference in the study of teaching avoids the difficulty of universalizing the 'rational teacher' as masculine, while simultaneously recognizing the value of particularity in women's lives. It also avoids the trap of equating difference with marginality and allows for a novel understanding of teaching as an act of social mediation and reflection in which difference sits at the centre of identity rather than lurking on the margins. The binary is thus challenged and the category of the teacher and its representations can shift. However, identity is not simply a recognition of difference as a part of oneself, that is, the authentic individual as expressed in liberal theory. It is a recognition that teachers are embedded in a meaningful social and political context where multiple selves meet within a dialectical frame. It is at this moment of 'meeting' that one can identify with difference as part of oneself and others. At the same time, one can also view difference as a discursive entity which is heavily regulated in fragmenting social spaces.

Within this framework, one might also consider what Benhabib (1995*b*) refers to as 'narrativity' in the study of identity. In Benahabib's view, narrativity—the self telling the story—becomes the medium through which the embedded individual expresses himself/herself as a gendered identity in the state. However, this self must be seen as embedded in a 'web of *gendered* narratives' (Benhabib, 1995*b*; emphasis added) which constrains teachers' autonomy to merely express a singular and authorial view of their professional role. In so doing, the teacher identity transcends the gender binary and becomes a more complex and multi-faceted entity.

Human Agency and Political Identity

One of the most salient yet neglected aspects of identity formation in education is the assessment of teachers' beliefs about human agency. I would therefore argue for a greater focus on the study of human agency in educational theorizing in relation to gender and the professional lives of women teachers. However, in so doing, we must redefine human agency as a phenomenon which is not simply concerned with the exercise of freedom in the struggle for political status, but as a bounded and gendered construct which can only exist in relation to other social structures and human relations.

As a further step, we may also wish to draw upon feminist critiques of human agency which concern the masculinization of women's freedoms in the state and argue that human agency is not simply that which exerts power with some effect, but something which cannot be fully exercised without a recognition of others in the act of meaningful communication. My own research suggests that women often see themselves as agents, yet they are incapable in many social circumstances of achieving the kind of agency they have described themselves as possessing. This observation suggests the necessity for dismantling the liberal notion that agency simply represents unconstrained action. Rather, it suggests that 'agency' be reconstructed to include an understanding of how the gendered 'self' is constrained, and how such constraints impact on the construction of political identities which then attempt to make claims to agency as a form of political liberation. This implies identifying, for example, the psychological, political and sociological forces which influence one's capacity to be a reflective 'agent', rather than simply assuming that in a liberal world all individuals are agents in their own right. It also implies attending to the ways in which women teachers reflect upon the contexts in which they work and attempt to resolve identity conflicts which emerge as a consequence of their contradictory and gendered position within education. This view of agency is similar to Connell's (1985) theoretical assumptions about how identities are shaped by the 'gender regimes' of social institutions—the communicative symbols and 'gender codes'—of everyday life. Three general assumptions about agency which could form the basis of a feminist analysis of teacher identities can now be sketched.

(1) Educational theorists need to return to the idea that the teacher *'agent'* may serve both as a form of social constraint and a reflective and active agent in the process of change (see Apple (1996) and Gewirtz (1997) on the question of simultaneity). However, this conceptualization of agency must take into consideration the gendered positioning of teachers and the role that structural inequality plays in constraining women teachers' agency in practice. It must also consider the many ways in which the teaching profession (and the men and women who work within it) reflects the complex and contradictory nature of contemporary gender relations. It must therefore break with oppositional and narrow-minded views of teacher professionalism, such as the caring subject or the abstract and rational object. Such views of teaching should not be conceptualized as separate entities, but instead seen as two of many interdependent forces which condition the formation of teachers' professional identities in practice. Consequently, there is no ultimate need to reject Kant's rational self for Steedman's (1985) 'mother made conscious' or vice versa. Rather, one is in the position to theorize a feminist form of teacher identity which cuts across such crude gendered distinctions, thereby providing a theoretical basis for assessing the complex ways in

which teacher identities are formed through everyday practices.

(2) Women teachers are still constrained by what Arnot (1982) identified almost two decades ago as 'dominated gender codes' that are embedded in human interaction. It may therefore be more relevant to study the actual gender codes embedded in the language of political agency and related forms of 'communicative action/thinking' than it is to define an abstract, idealized or universal notion of teacher agency. This implies observing the ways in which teachers construct meaning in everyday action and 'internalise the objective structure' (see Arnot, 1982) of gender relations, rather than simply assessing the ways in which they express themselves in isolation from others (e.g. narrative accounts). Such an approach may challenge the notion of the teacher as the 'disembedded' and neutral actor, and bring into relief the part played by gendered subjectivities in the construction of teachers' political agency.

(3) Agents are constrained by new modes of regulation and 'governance' (e.g. educational reform) which lead to the development of differently positioned forms of agency and political self-expression. New educational structures and modes of regulation must therefore be assessed in order to expose their gendered manifestations (e.g. gendered nature of new teacher education reforms) and the role they play in shaping teachers' political agency in practice. This suggests a novel interpretation of the agent which accounts for the gendered trajectory of the teaching profession and the 'recontextualization' of gender relations over time as taking a leading rather than a marginal role in the formation of teachers' professional identity.

Conclusion

I have offered a feminist re-reading of the concepts of 'professional identity' and 'teacher professionalism' and attempted to chart their 'exclusivity' as gendered terms. I have also sketched a preliminary conceptual framework for assessing the gendered nature of identity formation in teaching and teacher education. This work points toward a feminist perspective critical of mainstream conceptions of teacher professionalism as relying too heavily upon traditional liberal concepts, as failing to provide adequate recognition for the multitude of potential teaching identities in education and, consequently, as incapable of comprehending the gendered tensions to which they give rise.

What has also become clear is the manner in which an acceptance of the gender order as natural is manifest in, and aggravated by, such mainstream conceptions in the field of teaching. These views not only represent teachers' 'professional identity' as a form of human agency closely tied to masculinity, but are also linked to women's contradictory and devalued position in relation to the state. To put this another way, educational concepts which concern the modern teacher are not simply free-floating, de-gendered entities. They are social constructs which yield to, and are located within, broader and more powerful state structures which serve to legitimize what Taylor (1989) has called 'disengaged instrumentalism'—a state committed to instrumental goals and individual progress over and above any concern for marginalized peoples, human exploitation or the welfare of a community. As a result, identities conditioned by the forces of individualism are, by necessity, operating under a 'logic of exclusion' (Butler, 1990) where the 'other' in teacher education becomes what the prescribed identity is not.

In conclusion, the principles of rationality which underlie state-centred views on the modern teacher may provide an outline of what constitutes teacher professionalism but, simultaneously, they also, serve to define its epistemological boundaries. A failure to challenge this reality merely justifies, rather than critically examines, what are no more than the educational conceptions of a particular time. Sociologists of education have derided this approach because it commits to an uncritical acceptance of instrumental goals which lead to further, yet newly reconstituted, forms of inequality. However, beyond this, as I have attempted to argue, it also leads to a retreat from a feminist analysis of the social and political dimensions of identity formation in teaching. The fundamental effect is that teachers are no longer seen as political participants, and are once again removed from contesting the very meanings which are attributed to their professional identities in practice. It is now up to feminists to reclaim the political and social dimensions of teaching. The ongoing struggle to engage with feminist theory as a way forward in the study of teaching constitutes one vital attempt to achieve this goal:

> We need new models of identity, of individuation, of agency and autonomy, which will take account of the important critiques of these concepts which have been generated by feminist theorists [. . .] We need to uphold a commitment to women's struggles for identity and autonomy, in the context of feminist critiques of defensive, atomistic individualisms and critiques of the disembedded subject as the free and unfettered author of his destiny. We need to make a space for an understanding of self-identity which will not clash with our conviction that individuals must be understood as embedded, 'embodied', localized, constituted, fragmented and subjected to systems of power, oppression and exploitation. We need still to understand ourselves clearly as actors capable of learning, of changing, of making the world, and ourselves, better. (Weir, 1997, pp. 184–5)

NOTES

I am greatly indebted to Madeleine Arnot for her ongoing mentorship in the development of the ideas which underlie the work of this [chapter]. I am also grateful to Phil Gardner, Wendy Luttrell, Patrick Brindle and the anonymous reviewers for their helpful comments on an earlier draft of this [chapter]. I also wish to thank the women teacher educators who participated in this study. Without their commitment, this study would not have been possible. I gratefully acknowledge the financial support of the Social Sciences and Humanities Research Council of Canada.

Correspondence: Jo-Anne Dillabough, Department of Curriculum, Teaching and Learning, OISE/University of Toronto, 252 Bloor Street West, Toronto, Ontario M5S IV6, Canada.

1. I know of only one serious attempt to examine the relationship between teacher professionalism and gender as it relates to educational change (see Mahoney and Hextall, 1997).
2. I refer here to women teachers' lives in the broadest sense. The reasons for this are twofold. First, the women involved in my study were from three different yet related domains of teaching: (1) women teacher educators in the academy; (2) female mentors in schools; and (3) female student teachers. Interestingly, many of the key issues concerning these women teachers were similar regardless of where they were placed professionally. For example, the intensification of work seemed to be comparable across each of the groups. In addition, experiences of exploitation were congruous across the three different professional groups. Second, recent work on women teachers in the academy (in particular, service professions) suggests that the working conditions of female teachers in the 'education professions' are also similar. As a result, in this [chapter], I attempt to link this literature to my current work in teacher education.
3. I do not wish to argue that there is only one view of 'professional identity' in teacher education. I merely point to the dominant view of the teacher as professional and argue that this view has gained public appeal at the cost of marginalizing women teachers (as will be discussed later in the [chapter]).
4. Benhabib is reflecting upon the concerns of feminist political theorists who have been influenced by post-modern critiques of the 'self'.
5. These categories are indeed illusory, as many feminist theorists have argued, yet it remains vital to recognize that they maintain a very real presence in rational theories of identity, such as those expressed in traditional Kantian and Cartesian view points. They also shape the nature of gender identity formation, at least in part.

6. See Phillips' (1991) notion of the degendered subject.
7. See the recent work of Mahoney and Hextall (1997) on this issue.
8. I do not wish to make distinctions between the public and private spheres as a theoretical goal. However, since such distinctions are made in formal educational discourse, I do wish to map out which 'abstract spheres' are neglected in educational knowledge.
9. I do not outline any methodological details of this study here since the representation of quotes from teachers is merely intended to illustrate, in preliminary fashion, issues which concern the relation between gender and teacher professionalism.
10. As part of the larger study described earlier, I am also investigating the formation of feminist political identities in teacher education. This work involves interviews with women teacher educators, student teachers, and mentors, both individually and in focus groups in a rural and urban English context. It also involves extensive observational work in both the university setting and the school-based context to determine the social and political forces which impact on the formation of feminist political identities in teaching.
11. I do not deal extensively with the theme of 'emergent political identities' in teacher education practice. I am currently exploring these issues in another paper in progress (Dillabough, 2000) and in relation to other sociological issues (e.g. race, class). Consequently, the empirical data presented here is merely drawn upon to illustrate a concern about the representation of gender dualisms in the everyday lives of women teachers.
12. I am referring here to what teachers, as authentic individuals, bring to the practice of teaching (history, narrative, subjectivity, positioning).
13. Intersubjective theory is a conceptual position on identity formation which has it origins in the Frankfurt School of Critical Theory. Within the feminist wing of this school, a form of feminist perspective taking is argued for whereby it is assumed that individuals always have multiple and competing identities which are grounded in social circumstances and reflected upon through social mediation.
14. Unlike theorists who take an extreme post-modernist position, I argue for the existence and manifestation of the gender binary in historical and contemporary thought. I do so for two reasons. First, I believe it is essential to chart and critique the representation of gender dualisms in contemporary thought, i.e. male power over women and its presence in knowledge forms. I argue such a position on the basis of the now detailed body of work charting women's exploitation in many national contexts. To deny the existence of the binary (as part of the gender order) is, in my view, to deny women's struggles for social and political change. On the other hand, I also believe it is necessary to expose the illusory nature of the binary. In other words, we need to examine representations of the gender binary on multiple levels and expose its illusory nature. On a theoretical level, for example, one can assess how women have been conceptualized historically as non-citizens in traditional philosophical thought. On an empirical level, however, it is also possible to challenge false representations of the gender binary—the categorical separation of masculinity and femininity—through a study of diverse women's lived experience. Such approaches force feminists to consider simultaneously both the 'real' and illusory nature of the gender binary.

Part Eight

Curriculum, Learning, and Assessment

We open this section with the work of Robin Alexander (Ch. 49). Alexander draws attention to the importance of stepping outside localized ways of thinking about pedagogy arguing that cross-cultural comparative enquiry can offer 'a more rounded and coherent basis for reconceptualizing curriculum and pedagogy'. He makes this comment in recognition of the urgency with which we need to rethink the implications for pedagogy and the curriculum of what in the Introduction we have called the state theory of learning. He frames such a comparative analysis by identifying a continuum between pedagogy, equated with classroom processes and procedures, and Bernstein's (1990) notion that pedagogy is a relay for relations of class, gender, religion, and region and above all power relations. His concern, then, is to fill out the conceptual space that this continuum represents.

Alexander is unusual in the theoretical scope and comparative dimensions he brings to the searching questions about pedagogy that he poses. Young (Ch. 50) is equally adept at crossing borders in this case, between philosophy and sociology in raising the issue of what knowledge should be taught. It is a question that Plato asked and one which will remain. However, it is a particularly pressing question today because the present emphasis on an education for paid work emphasizes assessment and learning but omits the crucial question of what should be learned. In this chapter Young provides an important response to his classic (1971) book in which he and colleagues argued that the knowledge taught in schools was an expression of power relations because knowledge was defined by the dominant groups in society for their own advantage. Now he acknowledges that knowledge, although socially produced, has emergent properties so that it cannot be reduced to power relations. This enables him to argue that equality of opportunity will not be served by a curriculum which merely reproduces common sense, as in, for example, many courses on the leisure industry. Students need to grasp the structures and disciplines of knowledge if inequalities are to be addressed.

Moore (Ch. 51) seeks to interpret and elucidate the work of Basil Bernstein in the context of Durkheim's writings on education and society. Bernstein is perhaps the most original thinker in recent sociology of education and is particularly important within the context of the commodification of knowledge and the state theory of learning because he seeks to show how wider social forces are transmitted through to the processes of pedagogy and learning. However, his work is not easy to read, often presenting a series of startling ideas in little more than an extended set of notes. Moore's interpretation of both Bernstein and Durkheim shows how these thinkers can be understood in a range of ways and is an exemplar of the kind of theoretical exegesis that is so important to scholarship in the discipline.

Broadfoot and Pollard (Ch. 52) utilize elements of Bernstein's analysis to provide a critique of the assumptions underlying the state theory of learning. Critique of the theory and practice of the state theory of learning is difficult because there has been no attempt to compare it to a sample of children who have undergone a different experience of learning. There are therefore at least two ways in which criticisms of it can be made. The first is the route taken by Alexander who seeks to compare this theory of pedagogy and learning with those from other countries. The second adopted by Broadfoot and Pollard is to provide an alternative account of pedagogy and learning and ask how likely both are to fulfil the aims of lifelong learning. Here they contrast performative and liberal theories of pedagogy, arguing that the former is likely to discourage future learning.

Arnot and Reay (Ch. 53) seek to develop Bernstein's theory to the processes of learning. This is an important area because sociological theories ought to have something to contribute to the development of theories of learning. What emerges from their chapter is an account which shows that the state theory of learning creates different kinds of experience for students based on their gender and social class. This is a far cry from the more extravagant official claims made about its success.

Gillbourn and Youdell (Ch. 54) take a different theoretical approach to this dominant theory of learning by examining the trade-offs that schools and teachers need to consider when seeking to boost their league table scores, so as to be considered 'successful'. What they show is that a process of what they call 'triage' took place in the schools that they studied, in which the weakest students were considered a lost cause so that resources could be focused on those who could be trained to pass the exams at a level which reflected well on the school. Underpinning these judgements was an ideology about 'ability' levels which assumed that 'ability' cannot be easily improved, thereby justifying the decision to give up on the least able.

What drives the state theory of learning is assessment. It can be argued that in any modern education system assessment is the key because of the significance of the assessment to the positional competition for credentials. However, as Benveniste (Ch. 55) argues, assessment is not just a technical issue but one which invariably has social and political dimensions relating to the state's power and legitimacy. In turn modes of assessment will have an impact on the rules on the competition for credentials. Benveniste demonstrates this argument with case studies from Latin America, but the conclusions he draws have more general applicability.

Torrance (Ch. 56) looks at the comparative assessment of the performance of national educational systems through studies such as those conducted by the OECD and the International Educational Association. He shows how these studies have technical problems in the way they are constructed and how they are used to make political capital. This chapter is a salutary reminder that the headlines about national educational performance should be treated sceptically. Ideologically they can be seen as reinforcing the idea that education is central to economic performance while avoiding the difficult questions of who wins and who loses within national education systems.

Waks (Ch. 57) continues the theme of the way globalization has become inextricably tied to the fortunes of national education systems. His is one of the first studies to establish a theoretical framework to assess the conditions under which global changes may produce fundamental change within educational systems. His approach is that of the classical political economy strategy of identifying the political and institutional factors that hold the education system to a particular path of dependency. Having identified them he then asks how globalization may reconfigure these political and institutional factors to bring about fundamental change. It is an arresting analysis that may help us to understand the impact of globalization.

Dichotomous Pedagogies and the Promise of Cross-Cultural Comparison

Robin Alexander

The Problem

In 1981 Brian Simon published an article with the quotably provocative title 'Why No Pedagogy in England?' (Simon 1981). Simon argued that unlike most countries of continental Europe England had developed no 'science of teaching' worthy of the name, but instead had locked itself into rationales for classroom practice in which pragmatism might be sustained by a generalised ideology but there was no discernible grounding in principle or other than highly selective psychological evidence. He traced the problem back, in part, to the Victorian public (i.e. private) school view that education should be concerned with 'character' rather than the intellect, a view which also kept the academic study of education firmly out of Britain's two oldest and most influential universities, Cambridge and Oxford, until the latter part of the twentieth century. Though Simon readily acknowledged the impact of psychology on educational theory and research as these developed elsewhere, he did not concede—even when he revisited his 'Why No Pedagogy?' article in the 1990s (Simon 1994)—that it or its cognate disciplines yet offered anything approaching the coherent pedagogy he could point to in other European countries. This was in part, too, because for much of the post-war period British educational psychology was deployed to buttress the prevailing doctrine of individualism, which frustrated Simon's agenda of a pedagogy of general principles, grounded in what children have in common and directed to the achievement of collective goals.

The severity of Simon's stricture has challenged many UK researchers over the years, especially the growing number who have devoted their energies to studying learning, teaching, and life in classrooms, occasionally even generating titles in which Simon is consciously echoed (Hamilton 1999; Alexander 2004). In this sense, pedagogic research, if not a coherent and principled pedagogy, is now fairly well established in England.

In 1995, while collecting data for a comparative study of primary education in England, France, India, Russia, and the United States (Alexander 2001), I found, prominently displayed on a Michigan classroom wall, this teaching manifesto:

Important issues to me—
Process orientation vs product orientation
Teaching students vs teaching programs
Teacher as facilitator vs teacher as manager
Developing a set of strategies vs mastering a set of skills
Celebrating approximation vs celebrating perfection
Respecting individual growth vs fostering competition
Capitalizing on student's strengths vs emphasising student's weaknesses
Promoting independence in learning vs dependence on the teacher

It could as well have come from an English primary classroom during the 1960s–1980s heyday of Plowdenite progressivism, the American version of which was celebrated as 'open education'. I was reminded of this manifesto, and of Simon's critique of what he deemed the unrealistic individualism and 'pedagogic romanticism' of the English progressive movement, when I heard that the title of the AERA session for which this chapter was originally written was to be 'Getting beyond dichotomous notions of inquiry vs didactic instruction'. I also recalled Israel Scheffler's brilliant deconstruction of the slogans, shibboleths, and metaphors which saturate this kind of discourse (Scheffler 1971); but recalled, too—following Argyris and Schön's distinction between 'espoused theory' and 'theory-in use'—the need to understand its rhetorical function and distinguish between its public and private purposes (Argyris and Schön 1974).

All very *déjà vu,* in fact. However, it must be acknowledged that such language may be nurtured by politicians and the press long after more discerning educators have abandoned it. In a context where political rhetoric—more than ever since 9/11—is bounded by the atavism of us and them, the free and the oppressed, the chosen and the damned, to corral educational ideas and practices into the warring camps of 'traditional' and 'progressive' appeals not just to lazy minds but also to more alert calculations about how the world is best represented for the purposes of selling newspapers and winning elections.

One way of slowing if not reversing the downward slide of this oppositional discourse, I have found, is to replace the exclusive 'versus' in slogans like those from the Michigan classroom by an inclusive 'and'. That way you open a debate rather than close it. However, another frequently-observed elementary school poster—'101 ways to praise a child ... Wow! ... Nice job! ... Way to go ... You're cute ... ' etc. is less easily tackled, for its entire vocabulary blossoms from the belief that praise is the only kind of feedback which children can cope with. (The UK equivalent is the robotically genial 'fantastic ... brilliant ... good girl/boy ... ' which greets every student response regardless of quality.)

The belief, of course, manifests the familiar polarisation: in this case, relentless condemnation is deemed the only conceivable alternative to fulsome praise. The idea that feedback can be both critical *and* supportive lies beyond reach, and this in turn sustains the barely productive hegemony of recitation teaching dominated by 'test' rather than 'authentic' questions (Nystrand et al. 1997; Alexander 2005). Dichotomous pedagogies, from the mind-boggling 'child, not curriculum' onwards, can harm the very people whose interests they claim to serve.

By stepping outside such localised ways of thinking and the histories which have made them all but impermeable, cross-cultural comparative enquiry can offer a more rounded and coherent basis for reconceptualising curriculum and pedagogy. At the very least, a comparative perspective offers if not a conceptual solution then certainly alternative practices which, with any luck, will lodge themselves conspicuously and untidily between the poles of 'process' and 'product' or 'child-centred' and 'subject-centred'.

But we must also note that there are two senses in which comparative enquiry may actually feed the polarising tendency. First there is the ethnocentric risk of carrying local conceptualisations into the international arena—witness, for example, the opposition of 'ability' and 'effort', as supposedly culture-neutral concepts, in discussions about Asian and American education (Bempechat and Drago-Severson 1999), when in truth in different countries within these regions each of these terms, and indeed other pivotal educational concepts like 'development' and 'potential', let alone 'achievement', are culturally and linguistically charged in very specific ways (Alexander 2001: 369–71). Second, bipolarity is an inevitable hazard when just two countries are being compared. Even a three-country comparison risks what Tobin (1999) calls the 'Goldilocks effect' (this teaching is too formal, this teaching is too informal, but this teaching is just right; this system is too centralised, this one too decentralised ... and so on). I chose to compare five countries, and so while over such a broad canvas I risked being superficial or just plain wrong, I could at least avoid being ambushed by pernicious dichotomies and indeed Goldilocks.

But the problem reaches deeper than this. Naive dichotomous representations of complex realities persist in part because there is unfilled political and conceptual space in which they can flourish. People polarise either when it serves their personal or collective interests to deny the possibility of a middle ground, let alone of the kind of complexity for which even Goldilocks is inadequate, or when they know no other way. So, if the problem is as real here as the AERA symposium organisers appeared to believe, dare we ask without risk of causing offence 'Why no pedagogy in the United States?' And if the implied proposition is admitted, then the reasons must be historical, cultural, and political as well as conceptual. I leave others to address the matter of causality: I shall concentrate on the possibilities, drawing on comparative research, for attacking the problem empirically and conceptually.

Pedagogy I define as the discourse which attends the act of teaching. Teaching and pedagogy are not the same. Teaching is a practical and observable act. Pedagogy encompasses that act *together with* the purposes, values, ideas, assumptions, theories, and beliefs which inform, shape, and seek to justify it.

In acquiring this penumbra pedagogy also connects teaching with the wider culture. Hence the continuum of intellectual preoccupations which it provokes within the research community: at one end the quasi-scientific minutiae of lesson structure, student grouping, time on task, opportunity to learn, initiation-response-feedback (IRF) exchanges and all that follows from the everyday equating of 'pedagogy' with classroom processes and procedures; at the other end we find the grander questions of culture, structure, agency, policy, and control, and the Bernsteinian notion of pedagogy as a 'relay' for the relations of class, gender, religion, region, and above all power, coming together tellingly in Freire's title *Pedagogy of the Oppressed* (Bernstein 1990; Freire 1973).

How can one begin to fill the conceptual space which this continuum signals, quite apart from attending to the problem of pedagogical polarities with which we started? Many have been working for years to do the latter, at least. Indeed, to complain about the persistence of the old dichotomies is to run the risk of ignoring the by now considerable literature, both conceptual and empirical, on the art, or craft, or science, or (*pace* Gage 1978) the science-of-the-art of teaching, not to mention the emergence of a literature which explicitly uses the term 'pedagogy' itself, albeit sometimes—as in 'poisonous pedagogy' (Macedo 1999)—pejoratively.

In considering what a comparative perspective might offer to the development of a non-dichotomising pedagogy, I'd like to take three propositions from my own comparative research. First, across cultures one can find a recurrence of many more than two contrasting bedrock views of what teaching is all about, which by surfacing not in their pure form but in different combinations extend the range of pedagogical orientations and possibilities still further. Second, beyond these are primordial values about the relationship of individuals to each other and to society which have a direct bearing not just on how teachers think but on how they act. Third, the identification of such values and value concordances and dissonances in everyday classroom practice is greatly aided if we have a coherent framework or model for conceptualising teaching itself. In running briefly through each of these suggestions, I can of course only touch on ideas and findings which are developed and explored in detail elsewhere (Alexander 2001).

In sum then, I'm proposing that one way of breaking free of bipolar models of teaching is to devise frameworks for making sense of educational values and practices which make such bipolarity as difficult as possible.

Conceptualising Teaching

To start with the third proposition above. In my own research, one of the challenges I faced when confronted with a large quantity of qualitative and quantitative data from schools and classrooms in five countries was to find frameworks which encouraged me to make sense of disparate data in ways which showed no obvious bias towards particular cultural contexts. Relatedly, I was interested in seeing how far I could tease out the universal or generic in teaching from the culturally specific—an overweening ambition perhaps, but worth entertaining.

In the literature on culturally located views and models of teaching, generalised 'Asian', 'Pacific Rim', 'Western', 'non-Western', and 'European' 'models' of teaching and learning feature prominently and perhaps over-confidently (Reynolds and Farrell 1996; Stevenson and Stigler 1992; Clarke 2001). If we readily recognise that the geographical and cultural coverage of 'Asian' is simply too broad to have descriptive validity for the analysis of teaching, we should be no less aware of the hegemonic overtones of 'Western'. Does 'Western' encompass South as well as North America? Does it include some European countries while excluding others? With its implied validation of a particular worldview, tellingly captured since 2003 in the Old/New Europe name-calling of the Bush administration, 'Western' may well exacerbate rather than supplant the pedagogy of opposition, fuelling a self-righteous occidentalism every bit as pernicious as Said's orientalism (Said 1979).[1]

I also reminded myself of the many studies of teaching and classroom effectiveness, many of them within an acknowledged or tacit input-process-output paradigm, which seek to represent the whole as the sum of its myriad observable parts (Reynolds et al. 1994). For the absence of a genuinely holistic framework was one of the problems: we are good at dissecting and atomising teaching for the purposes of correlating the variables thereby revealed, but poor at reconstituting it as coherent and recognisable events located in time and space.

Eventually, I built up a framework from two simple and irreducible propositions, the second an extension of the first:

- Teaching, in any setting, is the act of using method x to enable students to learn y.
- Teaching has structure and form; it is situated in, and governed by, space, time and patterns of student organisation; and it is undertaken for a purpose.

These translated into a model containing three broad analytical categories—the immediate context or *frame* within the act of teaching is set, the *act* itself, and its *form*—and a set of elements within each such category. The core acts of teaching (*task, activity, interaction,* and *judgement*) are framed by *space, student organisation, time,* and *curriculum,* and by *routines, rules, and rituals.* They are given form, and are bounded temporally and conceptually, by the *lesson* or teaching session. (See Figure 49.1.)

The next stage was to devise subsidiary analytical frameworks. For reasons of space these cannot be filled out in detail here: they are developed and applied in the full account of this research (especially Alexander 2001: pp 267–528). Taken together, they enabled me to apply both quantitative and qualitative techniques to a mixture of fieldnotes, interview transcripts, videotapes, and lesson transcripts, and to show how the different elements related to each other (or not). More recently, the framework has been extended further into the key pedagogical domain of that teacher–student and student–student interaction through which both learning and culture are mediated (Alexander 2005).

Versions of Teaching

If pedagogy combines the act of teaching and its attendant discourses, then the explication of values and ideas will be essential to the process of making sense of observable practice. The *Culture and Pedagogy* research yielded, alongside the expected differences in the goals and orientations of the five education systems, differences no less marked in how schools and teachers were perceived, and how they perceived themselves.

At classroom level (the research offered three 'levels' of data and analysis, state, school, and classroom) these differences can be grouped most obviously within six constellations of pedagogical values, or versions of teaching:

1. Teaching as *transmission*
2. Teaching as *induction*

A generic model of teaching

Frame	Form	Act
Space Student organisation Time Curriculum Routine, rule and ritual	Lesson	Task Activity Interaction Judgement

Fig. 49.1 A generic model of teaching

Source: Alexander (2001: 325).

3. Teaching as *negotiation*
4. Teaching as *facilitation*
5. Teaching as *acceleration*
6. Teaching as *technology*.

In a basic transmission model teachers see their task as passing on information, and it is to information rather than reflective understanding that knowledge tends to be reduced. In India, many of whose primary classrooms until recently illustrated an extreme version of transmission teaching—the data preceded the more reciprocal approaches encouraged by the Government of India's DPEP (District Primary Education Programme) and SSA (Sarva Shiksha Abhiyan) reforms—teachers responded with heavily reiterative interactions and lesson structures in order to move their forty or sixty pupils along, more or less, together. There was little opportunity for fine judgements about the proper balance of different kinds of learning tasks, since the spread of prior pupil attainment was so wide. Instead, rote served as a kind of cognitive blunderbuss which, if fired often enough, eventually had some kind of impact on the learning of most pupils, if not all of them. The pre-DPEP/SSA Indian classrooms, though, represented an extreme case but not a unique one. In fact, transmission teaching is ubiquitous, not just as a matter of historical memory and habit, but because there are undoubtedly circumstances in which the transmission of information and skill is a defensible objective, in any context.

Disciplinary induction elevates knowledge from information to something which is both a cultural good—or, in the much-quoted and indeed much-abused phrase from Matthew Arnold's *Culture and Anarchy*, 'the best that has been thought and said'—and is seen to confer powers of intellectual precision, agility, and discrimination as well as a civilised disposition and outlook. It is usually associated with expository and recitation teaching—as, typically, in our French data—but also with a high degree of structured and sometimes argumentative talk, for the essence of the discipline is that it is a living paradigm for making sense of the world rather than, as in the transmission model, an inert bundle of facts.

Democratic pedagogy (teaching as negotiation) continues to retain its hold on the thinking of many American and English teachers, though few of the latter may have heard of John Dewey, its progenitor. It also flowered briefly in the Soviet Union during the 1920s period of educational experimentation. Democratic pedagogy rejects the traditional domination–subordination relationship between teacher and taught, makes knowledge reflexive rather than disciplinary, the child an active agent in his or her learning, and the classroom a workshop or laboratory. In all these respects the classroom seeks to enact the ideals of the wider democratic society. Negotiation thus stands in conscious antithesis to both transmission and induction.

Developmental facilitation and its adjunct 'readiness' are key concepts in the Western progressive movement, and they connote the Rousseauesque principle that children have their own ways of thinking, seeing, and feeling, the Piagetian idea that children go through the same stages of development but at different rates, Froebel's use of organic imagery and the metaphor of growth, and the presumed corollary of all these that children must not be 'pushed' and will learn only when they are 'ready'. The teacher's task therefore becomes facilitation rather than direction. In England, this idea reached its apogee in the 1960s and 1970s, following the publication of the Plowden report (CACE 1967), and in the United States it remains influential long after the demise of 'open education', where it is usually authenticated by reference to Piaget rather than Rousseau or Froebel.

Acceleration derives from Vygotsky's famous maxim that 'the only good teaching is that which outpaces development' (Vygotsky 1978) and is diametrically opposed to the principle of readiness. When one combines this with the arguments of Vygotsky, Luria, and their fellows about the critical role of language in learning, the teaching imperative is clear: the momentum of a lesson must be secured and maintained, it must drive forward, and its engine is what in the *Culture and Pedagogy* project we came to call a proper balance of 'interactive' and 'semantic' (or 'cognitive') pace (Alexander 2001: 423–6). Acceleration is as antithetical to developmental readiness/facilitation as democratic pedagogy is to transmission and disciplinary induction.

Finally, the idea that teaching is first and foremost a technology, guided by principles of structure, economy, conciseness, and rapidity, and implemented through standardised procedures and materials, reaches back to a much older central European tradition. These principles were first adumbrated in 1632 by Jan Kamensky (Comenius) in chapter 19 of his *Great Didactic* (Keatinge 1896), and they found their way to Russia and much of eastern and central Europe via Bohemia and Germany. In these countries, long before the emergence of modern psychology, there was a prior commitment to economy and pace in teaching, and this fitted as well with the later theories of Vygotsky as, in the contrary tradition, Piaget complemented the earlier ideas of Rousseau.

With this last version I follow Simon in claiming that there is a distinctly continental European pedagogic tradition. In my own data, the cultural divide in 'Western' pedagogy seemed to be the narrow stretch of water separating France from England rather than the vastness of the Atlantic Ocean. There was a discernible Anglo-American nexus of pedagogical values and practices centring on developmentalism and democratic pedagogy, just as there was a discernibly continental European one rooted in the Comenian tradition, with Russia at one highly formalised extreme combining Comenian structure, graduation, and pace with Vygotskian acceleration, and France—procedurally more eclectic and less ritualised, but firmly grounded in epistemic structure and the cultural primacy of *les disciplines*—at the other. India's pedagogy was both Asian and European, as its history would suggest: an amalgam of Brahmanic, colonialist, and post-Independence traditions and values (Kumar 1991).

This, of course, cannot be the whole story. Comparative pedagogical analysis reveals, alongside the obvious national differences, a subtle shading of commonality and variation which reflects the international trade in educational ideas which preceded globalisation by many centuries. It also shows how ideas are domesticated and indeed recreated as they cross national borders, so that, for example, Prussian and American Herbartianism ended up rather different from each other, and different again from Herbart's initial adaptation of the Pestalozzian idea of *Anschauung*. In the same way, more recently, it is interesting to see how Vygotsky's socio-cultural perspective has, in Britain, been reconfigured with its cultural and historical elements played down, to generate a pedagogy closer to the dominant individualism.

Further—it goes without saying but it should perhaps be said anyway—the six versions of teaching adumbrated here constitute a continuum of tendencies and not a set of discrete national descriptors.

Primordial Values

Buttressing these specifically pedagogical positions are three primordial values—

- *individualism,*
- *community,*
- *collectivism*

—which are concerned with that most fundamental human question, the relationship of humans to each other and to the communities and societies they inhabit. These are familiar enough in social and political theory, though less so in accounts of pedagogy.

Within the classroom a commitment to *individualism* manifests itself in an emphasis on freedom of choice, individualised learning tasks, diverging rather than uniform learning outcomes, and a view of knowledge as personal and unique rather than imposed from above in the form of disciplines. *Community* is reflected in an emphasis on collaborative learning, often in small groups, in the concern given to developing a climate of caring and sharing rather than competing, and indeed in an emphasis on the affective rather than the cognitive. *Collectivism* is reflected in common knowledge, common ideals, a single curriculum for all, an emphasis on national culture rather than pluralism and multiculture, and on learning together as a class rather than in isolation or in small groups.

In the 'five cultures' data these values were highly pervasive at both school and classroom levels, and could be traced right through to patterns of teaching and classroom organisation, in which context it seems to me not at all accidental that so much discussion of teaching methods should have centred on the relative merits of whole class teaching, group, and individual work. In France this debate can be traced back to arguments at the start of the nineteenth century about the relative merits of *l'enseignement simultané, l'enseignement mutuel,* and *l'enseignement individuel* (Reboul-Sherrer 1989). As a post-revolutionary instrument for fostering civic commitment and national identity as well as literacy, *l'enseignement simultané*—whole class teaching—won. Only recently, in conjunction with the decentralising movement of the 1980s and the rising tide of individualism, has its hegemony begun to be questioned.

Individualism, community, and collectivism are—as child, group, and class—the organisational nodes of pedagogy because they are the social and indeed political nodes of human relations. Compare this, for example, with Shweder's contrast of 'holistic, sociocentric' cultures like India, and what he terms 'Western' cultures with their concept of 'the autonomous distinctive individual living in society' (Shweder 1991). Note too the American survey that found that only Britain was within striking distance of American respondents' insistence that freedom is far more important than equality and that personal welfare far outweighs responsibility to society (German respondents voted a balance of both sets of commitments) (Wattenberg 1991). Or even consider the cultural conditions which make it possible for a British head of government to assert, as Margaret Thatcher infamously did during her period of Reaganite infatuation, that 'there's no such thing as society: there are only individual men and women, and there are families'. Such a sentiment would be inconceivable in France or Russia. In the United States, however, there's much more talk of nation than of society: an important distinction and a telling discrepancy. Britain, being a still muddled historical confection of rampant England and suppressed Wales, Scotland, and Northern Ireland, finds it difficult to conceive of either of these notions.

However, divorcing teaching as technique from the discourse of pedagogy as we so often do, we may have failed to understand that such core values and value-conflicts pervade social relations inside the classroom no less than outside it; and hence we may have failed to understand why it is that undifferentiated learning, whole class teaching, and the principle of bringing the whole class along together 'fit' more successfully in many other cultures than they do in England or the United States, and why teachers in these two countries regard this pedagogical formula with such suspicion. For individualism and collectivism arise inside the classroom not as a clinical choice between alternative teaching strategies so much as a value-dilemma which may be fundamental to a society's history and culture.

I should add that as the six versions of teaching and the three primordial values emerged from data collected in England, France, India, Russia, and the United States, a comparable study in other countries might well yield additional versions of teaching, and weaken still further the hegemony of Anglo-American pedagogical dichotomies of the kind which prompted a group of AERA members to propose the symposium to which this chapter originally contributed. Indeed, Jin Li's study of American and Chinese beliefs appears to do just that. She contrasts American students' view of knowledge as 'out there', set apart from the learner and available to be willingly or unwillingly acquired, with the Chinese view which sees knowledge as integral to what it means to be a person. By this view socialisation, education, knowledge, and morality are inseparable. And especially pertinent to our starting-point of dichotomous pedagogy, and indeed to the particular dichotomies illustrated earlier, she comments: 'These different construals of knowledge may be one reason why there are so many US concepts referring to mental processes on the one hand and the external body of school subjects on the other.' (Li 2003).

Discussion

Let us return to the proposition or hope that the persistence of a dualist teaching discourse can be weakened by the introduction of pluralist frameworks for conceptualising the act of teaching and its informing values, and that comparative study may open the door to these.

The immediate and predictable consequence of this approach is that we confirm that pedagogy, as the purposive amalgam of educational practice, ideas, and values, is vastly more complex than those 'process vs product' slogans can possibly entertain.

That much we knew already. But I'd also suggest that the approach casts doubt on the value and validity of comparativists' current efforts to portray ostensibly monolithic national patterns of teaching. In this matter, though I find Stigler's and Hiebert's idea of culturally rooted 'teaching scripts', which they apply to the TIMSS and TIMSS-R video data, immensely suggestive, I believe that it underplays the dissonances which these contain, certainly in the United States (Stigler and Hiebert 1999; Stigler, Gallimore, and Hiebert 2000; Le Tendre et al. 2001). For though our Michigan teachers had recourse to what Stigler and Hiebert call the culturally-evolved 'core beliefs' about knowledge, learning, and teaching, their interviews and our classroom observation told a different story. There we found not the coherence of 'teaching scripts ... consistent with the stable web of beliefs and assumptions that are part of the culture' (Stigler and Hiebert 1999: 87–8), nor the purity of that either/or polarisation with which we started, but contradictory thinking and mixed messages.

The 'teaching scripts' hypothesis prompts other reservations. It ignores the gap between teachers' espoused theory and their theory-in-use (Argyris and Schön 1974), or the public and private languages of teaching, and it reduces the complex relationship between teachers' beliefs and observable practice to a simple linear one when in truth teaching is more about compromise and the imperfect reconciliation of competing imperatives than the implementation of ideals.

More fundamentally, the 'teaching script' is ahistorical. Educational ideas and practices reflect a long process of accretion and sedimentation, or hybridisation, and the past (and its tensions and contradictions) is always observable within the present.[2] This is another reason why dichotomies are so unsatisfactory, for there is a sense in which education is—if we must use these terms—at the same time both 'traditional' and 'progressive'. Thus, contemporary English primary education displays the simultaneous residues of (1) nineteenth-century mass elementary education (the 'cheap but efficient' class teacher system, the dominance of curriculum 'basics' defined as reading, writing, and number), and (2) the 1960s progressive backlash (small groups, affectivity, the visual environment, resistance to the hegemony of the 'basics'), alongside (3) the current neo-elementary rubric of the UK government's 'standards' strategies in literacy and numeracy.

Further, the 'teaching script' idea is conceptually and empirically weak, for in terms of our earlier model of teaching it penetrates thus far into teaching but no further: it contents itself, that is to say, with certain aspects of pedagogical 'frame' and 'form' but not with the deeper layers of the teaching 'act', notably the exchange and negotiation of meanings through teacher–student discourse. Once one reaches that layer of teaching the script idea begins to break down. In any case, no script is merely read: it is interpreted, misread, and in other ways re-created (always assuming that it is readable in the first place).

For if we take our three primordial values of individualism, community, and collectivism, the scenario is not one of singularity. Human consciousness and human relations involve the interplay of all three values. Though one may be dominant, they may in reality all be present and coexist in uneasy and unresolved tension. In the *Culture and Pedagogy* data nowhere was this tension more evident than in the United States, where we found teachers seeking to reconcile—and indeed to foster as equivalent values—individual self-fulfilment with commitment to the greater collective good; self-effacing sharing, and caring with fierce competitiveness; environmentalism with consumerism; altruism with self-absorption; childhood innocence with a television-fuelled consciousness of society's dangers and horrors that spilled over into classroom conversations among 6-year-olds on child abuse and the relative merits in judicial execution of gas, the bullet, lethal injection, and the electric chair. Meanwhile, in the world outside the school individualism competed with the traditional American commitment to communal consciousness and local decision-making; and patriotism grappled with anti-statism. Such tensions were manifested at every level from formal educational goals to the everyday discourse of teachers and children.

In those classrooms where the ambiguities and unresolved dissonances of American elementary pedagogy were most marked, negotiated pedagogy was compromised by the imperative of transmission, not always admitted and sometimes in disguise. Developmental facilitation and readiness competed with the clock and the sheer impossibility of allowing the degree of divergence of student work patterns and learning outcomes that this belief logically dictates. Physically, classrooms might speak of considerable ambiguity of purpose. With their mix of desks, blackboards, easy chairs, table lamps, carpets, and flags it was not clear whether they were places of work, play, rest, relaxation, or worship. And though invariably organised for collaborative group work the centre of gravity veered between the group, the class and the individual. The celebration of choice, autonomy and self-discipline sat not always comfortably with the imposed rules and routines which most teachers find essential. Grouping encouraged talk, but the generic learning activities were dominated by individual tasks involving reading and writing. Talk was overwhelmingly conversational in structure, syntax, and lexis, and had a casual surface ambience, but was often managed as a kind of recitation teaching and was therefore not conversation at all, and communicative rights veered between the negotiated and the imposed. On the other hand such talk lacked the structure and follow-through of recitation at its most effective. The espoused Brunerian commitment to scaffolded dialogue (Bruner and Haste 1987) foundered on the rock of the belief that every child must have his or her say, so interactions tended to be brief, random, and frequently interrupted. In any case, the purposes of such interactions were often social more than cognitive, about acquiring confidence more than learning to think (like other pairings these, emphatically, are not mutually exclusive) (Alexander 2001: 490–508).

And so we could go on. In contrast, most of the lessons observed in France and Russia displayed somewhat greater clarity of purpose, procedural coherence, and above all consistency in message. Where different values and ideas were simultaneously espoused, they usually managed to reinforce rather than subvert each other. But also, and crucially—as, in both countries, in the area of the treatment of ethnic minorities—value issues and conflicts might be concealed under a blanket of imposed consensus.

I see this situation as not simply a case of 'Why no pedagogy?' For this is the country of 83,000 governments (McKay 1994), whose constitution requires education to be decentralised; and it is the country whose history and political ideology shout plurality and diversity. Perhaps the problems of both pedagogic discourse and classroom practice are in part the price which American educators must pay for democracy, pluralism, and the tenth amendment of their constitution, as well as for the much-vaunted celebration of individualism and personal freedom. Perhaps, too, as Berliner and Biddle (1995) have pointed out, the problems relate to the massive disparities in finance, policy, and provision between states and districts, and the way that teachers' roles, already broader and more diffuse than in many other countries, have somehow to combine instruction with socialisation, community enlightenment, and indeed social reform. Within the classroom, it was clear, the aggregation of instructional and social purposes, and the many tensions within and between these, could yield patterns of organisation and teaching which were exceptionally complex and professionally demanding.

Yet by the same pluralist token, nothing is inevitable. Cutting through all this were other teachers who displayed clarity of purpose and coherence of practice of a kind which was no less American. Thus, one teacher neatly manifested a commitment to individualised, collaborative, *and* collective pedagogy by getting her 6-year-old students to move the furniture—sometimes several times in a day—between three dispositions: separate tables for individual assignments, combined tables for collaborative group work, and all the tables in a horseshoe for whole class activity. These moves, by dint of training and habit, took just 90 calm seconds to achieve, and the deeper layers of her teaching—lesson structure, task design, assessment, and above all the quality of the classroom talk which she fostered—all displayed the same clarity and coherence. Not surprisingly, our video and transcript discourse analyses showed that she, together with several teachers in France and Russia, came closest to realising the goal on which much psychological and pedagogical research converges: dialogic teaching in pursuit of scaffolded learning.

This teacher explained her approach in both principled and pragmatic terms. Her range of educational goals included fostering children's capacities to work individually, collaboratively, and collectively. Though she did not express the matter thus, her ideas and practices convincingly manifested the principle that in teaching—returning to our earlier model—*frame* (in this case classroom and student organisation), *form* (lesson structure and sequence), and *act* (task, activity, and mode of interaction) must be precisely aligned both with each other and a lesson's objectives. Thus she achieved what in England was once applauded, before the imposition of government-sanctioned 'best practice', as 'fitness for purpose' (Alexander, Rose, and Woodhead 1992: para. 101).

But this example raises another and more sensitive issue. For when I described this teacher's work to an American colleague, he immediately and correctly, without further clues, identified the teacher as African American. This, I think should prompt us to consider how far the more acute pedagogical ambiguities and dissonances which our research uncovered in this country are a function of specific kinds of socialisation and consciousness rather than a general condition of American society. The case should also encourage those with an interest in comparative pedagogy to look as closely at—and learn from—differences *within* cultures as between them (Ladson-Billings 1991; Foster 1997).[3]

Once we move beyond the simple nostrums of comparative school effectiveness research which in its adulation for teaching practices elsewhere largely ignores culture or at best treats it as just another variable to be number-crunched, and indeed—as Berliner and Biddle remind us (1995: 1–2) with respect to the claimed superiority of Japanese education over American—rarely engages either with the downside of what it urges us to emulate, we come to a more qualified conclusion. Yes, there is much that we can learn from education elsewhere, but this example from a Michigan elementary school suggests that the answers may be closer to home than we think.

Whether we compare locally, nationally, or internationally, the matter of values must be kept centre-stage. We know that it is a mistake to presume that we can wrench a policy or practice from its context of values and transplant it as it stands; or that we can change teaching without attending to the values underpinning the practice which we seek to transform. If individualism, freedom, choice, community, affectivity, caring, sharing, discovery, negotiation, and reflexive knowledge are important, relevant, and valid, as many in the United States insist, then they can't simply be swept aside in pursuit of something called 'school effectiveness'. The values must be engaged with in the same spirit of seriousness as the observable practice.

We must look no less carefully at the values which inform the practices elsewhere which impress us. Thus, the oral pedagogy of the observed Russian classrooms, with its carefully structured and sequenced lessons, its brisk yet somehow unhurried management of time and pace, and its heavy emphasis on public and dialogic talk in a whole class context, achieves its undoubted efficiency—albeit across a relatively narrow spectrum of objectives—by being part of a package which includes central prescription on curriculum, deference to the authority of the teacher, a belief in knowledge as given rather than negotiable, a commitment to rules and regulation in the domains of knowledge, language, and behaviour, a belief in collectivism emblematised in the class and the idea that its members should progress together rather than be encouraged to diverge, and allegiance to the Vygotskian principle of education as accelerated development. Similarly, the drive and precision of the dialogue which many admire in French classrooms is rooted in an unquestioning belief that *les disciplines* are central to a notion of what it is to be educated and indeed civilised, and that it is they, rather than children's 'natural' modes of understanding, which should dictate the structure of lessons and of learning tasks and activities. If it is felt that US teachers could profitably emulate teaching of the kind which one can observe in these two countries, then a lot more than classroom practice will need to change.

Aside from those supposedly quintessential American values such as individualism, community, freedom, and choice, two highly influential strands of more specifically *educational* thinking surfaced and resurfaced in the Michigan teacher interviews and to some extent in the English ones. One, shorthanded earlier as 'teaching as negotiation', was democratic pedagogy (sharing, negotiation, choice, enquiry, reflexive knowledge); the other ('teaching as facilitation') was developmentalism (individualism, readiness, activity, manipulation of materials).

The Piagetian legacy seems to be as deeply rooted as the Deweyan one, notwithstanding all the talk of constructivism, partly I suspect because it fits the wider ideology. For all that the US and the UK now have a substantial neo-Vygotskian industry and the derived 'activity theory' has become deeply fashionable (Daniels 2001), there is no disguising the fact that the principle that education outpaces development is diametrically opposed to the Anglo-American principle of readiness, and that Vygotsky's Marxian goal of taking the child from the 'natural' to the 'cultural' line of development sits at best uncomfortably with the rhetoric of personal knowledge, critical pedagogy, and cultural reproduction. These are the kinds of issue which must be sorted out first.

I suggested at the beginning of this chapter that in England there is now no shortage of pedagogic research but as yet no coherent pedagogy in Simon's sense of an empirically and ethically grounded theory of teaching. We need, then to differentiate *descriptive* and *prescriptive* pedagogies.

But cross-cutting these there are *pragmatic* and *political* pedagogies. Indeed in England, now that the UK government has all but completed its takeover of pedagogy—first, under Thatcher, by prescribing a national curriculum and now, under Blair, by prescribing teaching methods and ensuring strict professional compliance by policing from the national school inspectorate—this is the prevailing mix, and while academics can and do extend their pedagogical descriptions and analyses, the scope for applying these to the development of grounded pedagogical principles becomes ever more restricted. For the UK government now advances as the sole touchstone for what it calls 'best practice' not those ethical and empirical concerns which ought to lie at the heart of pedagogical discourse in a democracy, but the deceptively simple nostrum 'what works'. The message is clear: government takes care of values, teachers put them into practice.

This, then, is the old theory–practice divide—the ultimate dichotomy—redefined by centralisation. Disingenuously, the UK government also insists that practice should be 'evidence-based' but clearly the evidence, to be acceptable, must fit the policy. 'What works' seamlessly and shamelessly privileges the pragmatic and political in the guise of respecting the empirical. In fact, evidence is the first casualty of this approach, while ethical considerations are nowhere in view (Alexander 1997, 2004).[4]

In the United States, too, there is no shortage of descriptive pedagogies, Moreover, the effort to devise a grounded prescriptive pedagogy, or a coherent and principled practical theory of teaching, stretches both backwards and forwards from Jerome Bruner's seminal and tellingly entitled *Toward a Theory of Instruction* (Bruner 1968). But we may not be there yet, and one reason may be the complexity of the value questions which, in this almost aggressively plural society, remain unreconciled. Another, of course, is the way the Tenth Amendment prevents even authoritarian federal governments from stepping in and imposing their own solutions, though this is a gap which state governments have been increasingly inclined to plug. It is perhaps symptomatic of the American educational condition that over the years during which I have served on the editorial board of the journal *Teaching and Teacher Education*, most of whose contributors are American, there have been many more articles on teachers' values and beliefs than empirical accounts of learning and teaching, and very few indeed which have sought to reconcile values, beliefs, evidence, learning, and teaching within a principled pedagogy.

Perhaps, in this particular country, that is how it has to be. French pedagogy manifests collective beliefs about language, culture, knowledge, identity, and civic responsibility largely through collective methods. Russian pedagogy marries four main legacies: the pre-Soviet and Soviet idea of *vospitanie* (personal, social, moral, and civic upbringing); ideas from Soviet psychology about human development, learning, and the relationship between thought, language, and culture; post-Soviet humanist curricular values; and the much older Comenian tradition of highly structured, graduated, and predominantly oral teaching. I defined pedagogy earlier as the performance of teaching *together with* the purposes, values, ideas, assumptions, theories, and beliefs which inform it. An American pedagogy, we must therefore accept, generates its principles by addressing the values, conflicts and all, which go with the territory, not by wishing they would go away. As those who planned the AERA symposium imply, a dualist, dichotomising pedagogy is no answer, least of all in a country which purports to defend individual voices, no matter how many there be. Nor, clearly, is an imposed monolithic one. A pedagogy which is both pluralist and consensual, individualist and collective, local and national, is of course a much tougher proposition. But out there are teachers who have achieved it.

NOTES

This chapter originated as a contribution to the 2002 annual conference of the American Educational Research Association (AERA) in New Orleans, where it was presented at the symposium 'Defamiliarising our notions of pedagogy and curriculum: getting beyond dichotomous notions of enquiry vs didactic instruction'. This somewhat ponderous title signalled a tendency which in Britain and the United States, and indeed elsewhere, is real, familiar, and deeply seated: the reduction of complex educational debates to bipolar slogans cast in a state of permanent and irreconcilable opposition. This chapter draws on a large-scale macro-micro comparative study of culture and pedagogy in England, France, India, Russia, and the United States to posit an approach which attends to a greater variety of educational orientations than the old rhetoric allows, conceives of continua rather than dualities, locates these in the context of broader cultural values, and offers conceptual coherence by framing them within a comprehensive model of teaching.

1. This analysis preceded by some years US Defense Secretary Donald Rumsfeld's excoriation of the contrary political allegiances of 'old' and 'new' Europe in the run-up to the 2003 invasion of Iraq. Since that conflict, and the Manichaean rhetoric which fuelled it, the use of geographical-cultural pedagogic descriptors such as 'Western', 'European', or 'Asian' seems even more suspect.
2. Anderson-Levitt (2001) uses the idea of hybrid across space, to show how the local is embedded in the transnational. I use it here more to connote a historical process. In fact, as *Culture and Pedagogy* demonstrates by reference to all five of the education systems in that study, the continuities are both temporal and spatial. Anderson-Levitt is also critical of the 'teaching script' idea.
3. The practice of this teacher provides a case study in *Culture and Pedagogy*: Alexander (2001: 508–15).
4. Alexander 1997 develops the idea that notions of 'good practice' must attend to and reconcile conceptual, ethical, empirical, pragmatic, and political considerations. The UK government's 2003 'strategy' for primary education (DfES 2003) provides a good example of the sleight of hand described here, and is critiqued in detail in Alexander 2004, as is the UK government's misuse of evidence in support of educational policy.

Curriculum Studies and the Problem of Knowledge; Updating the Enlightenment?

Michael Young

Introduction

In this chapter I want to do two things, after which I will to make brief reference to a broader more philosophical issue implicit in my subtitle: why the Enlightenment, and in what sense does it need updating?

First I want to argue for a central role for the curriculum in educational policy in opposition to the recent trend to emphasize targets, outcomes, and widening participation at almost any cost. I will elaborate on this point as it applies to policies for 14–19-year-olds in England. Secondly, I seek to reinstate the issue of knowledge as integral to curriculum theory, in contrast to such issues as assessment, evaluation, and guidance that MA programmes increasingly seem to focus on. It is not that these issues are unimportant, but that how they are dealt with depends on prior attention to the question of knowledge. My assumption is that *the acquisition of knowledge* is the key feature that distinguishes education (general or vocational) at any level from all other activities. It is for this reason that debates about knowledge are crucial; by this I do not mean specific knowledge contents, although they are important, but the concepts of knowledge that underpin curricula.

A number of trends in educational theory, not only in the sociology of education, have contributed to the marginalization of knowledge in curriculum studies. I will mention three:

1. The first is my own and others' work in the sociology of knowledge from 1970 (Young 1971). Ironically the intention of this work was to give centrality to the role of knowledge in education. However the issue was conceptualized as identifying the interests of those with power to select knowledge for the curriculum. The problem with this kind of sociology of knowledge is not that it is wrong as some critics claimed at the time—social interests are always involved in curriculum design—but that it is only a partial perspective on the curriculum. There are social interests involved but, on its own an interest-focused approach leaves us with no independent criteria for the curriculum, *only competing interests*.
2. The second trend has been in the philosophy of education and is symbolized in the later writings of Paul Hirst, in which he rejected his earlier *forms of knowledge* thesis and argued that the curriculum must be based on *social practices*. However, as with the 1970s sociology of knowledge, the idea of social practices provides no grounds for distinguishing curriculum knowledge from the knowledge we acquire in the course of our everyday lives—all are products of social practices.

3. The third trend has been the influence on curriculum studies and the humanities and social sciences generally of postmodernist ideas. The writings of the French philosophers Michel Foucault and Jean-François Lyotard are used to critique the subject-based curriculum on the basis that they exclude all voices except those of the professional or academic elite (Moore and Muller 1999). Like the earlier sociology of knowledge, this appears to offer a radical challenge to existing concepts of knowledge. However, in challenging the very idea of knowledge, like the earlier trends I mentioned, postmodernism leaves the curriculum theorist on the sidelines of any real debate.

It is these developments together with the not unrelated social and political changes associated with globalization which have contributed to the crisis in curriculum theory. In policy terms we have a national curriculum, a post compulsory curriculum, a vocational curriculum, and even a higher education curriculum all of which take for granted the assumptions about knowledge on which they are based. On the other hand we have a marginalized curriculum theory which offers critiques of the interests involved in existing curricula but no alternatives.

There are three starting assumptions for the rest of my argument. First, each of these three developments that I have referred to collude, albeit unintentionally, with the marketization that now drives educational policy and which is in a deep sense anti-educational. Second, in denying a distinctive role for knowledge that transcends social practices, interests, or specific contexts these approaches remove the grounds for a critical relationship between theory and curriculum policy and practice. Third and positively, I will argue for a knowledge-based theory of the curriculum that recognizes a distinction between the type of knowledge that can be acquired at school, college, or university and the common-sense or practical knowledge that we acquire in our everyday lives. To put it more generally, because the world is not as we experience it, curriculum knowledge must be discontinuous, not continuous with everyday experience. The difficult pedagogic issue of developing strategies for overcoming this discontinuity is not something that I will be concerned with. It is most fruitfully discussed within the framework of recontextualization, suggested by Basil Bernstein among others (Bernstein 2000). Judith Williamson, in a recent article in the *Observer*, expressed this point about knowledge most lucidly:

> Whether in astrophysics or literature, *there is a body of knowledge* to be learned and renewed. Most would like (it) to be useful and many would like it to be easy. However it is not often the former and rarely the latter. What really matters about knowledge is that it is true or rather that we can learn or find the truth or truths as best we can, in any field. This is what education and more specifically, universities are for. (emphasis added)

In other words, education presupposes the possibility of both knowledge and truth.

Concepts of Knowledge and the 14–19 Curriculum

Let me take an example of the problem that arises from neglecting the question of knowledge from current policy on 14–19 education. The government proposes that:

- The National Curriculum at Key Stage 4 should be reduced to three compulsory subjects: English, Maths, and Science (it began in 1988 with ten)
- Modern Languages and Design Technology, like History, Geography, and all other subjects, will become optional
- 14-year-olds will be able to take GCSEs in areas such as Engineering, Health and Social Care, and Leisure and Tourism.

The hope is that as a result of such reforms, (1) more students will achieve more GCSEs at higher grades; (2) they will benefit from the opportunity of a wider range of choices; and (3) they will be better prepared for future employability.

There have been a number of responses to these proposals, e.g.

1. They have been welcomed by the serious press and respected educationalists such as Ted Wragg as at last giving a proper value to vocational subjects and the importance of student choice.

2. From a more radical position (as in the recent Royal Society of Arts report on the Future of Schooling), the new proposals appear as a half-hearted attempt to move towards the fully skills-based curriculum the report advocates.
3. The emphasis on vocationalizing the 14+ curriculum together with the target of achieving 50 per cent participation in HE has been sharply criticized by those on the right such as Chris Woodhead as 'dumbing down' and 'giving in to anti-elitist dogmas'. However the only alternative such critics offer is a return to a mythic 'golden age' when vocational education took the form of craft apprenticeship, academic studies followed in the footsteps of Thomas Arnold's Rugby, and the majority left school at 15 or earlier for unskilled factory jobs which of course no longer exist.

There has, as far as I am aware, been little critical comment from educationalists. This, I suggest, reflects the marginalization of the issue of knowledge in curriculum studies that I referred to earlier. Without a theory of what knowledge is important and its role in the curriculum one is left with little more than an unease about the likely consequences of premature vocationalism and a reluctance to appear elitist by defending the subject-based curriculum, but with no viable alternative. The space has been vacated by curriculum theory and the only serious alternatives to government curriculum policies appear to come from the right.

My problem with the government proposals is that they focus almost entirely on the *extrinsic* purposes of education and assume that future employment is the main motivator of young people's willingness to go on learning. Quite apart from whether they are correct about what motivates young people and whether as a country we want growing numbers with GCSEs in Leisure and Tourism, such a policy seriously neglects the *intrinsic* purposes of education. By this I do not mean the old idea of 'education for its own sake' but the need to consider a number of more fundamental questions. For example:

- Why do we want to persuade more young people to extend their schooling?
- What is it that is distinctive about the kinds of knowledge that can be acquired in school or college?
- Is it just that we want more young people to participate in full-time study, regardless of what they are learning?

The official reason for allowing 14-year-olds to choose Leisure and Tourism instead of, for example, Geography or History, is presumably that employment-related knowledge will be more meaningful to them. However, this assumes that differences between the kind of knowledge acquired in studying geography or history and the knowledge that might be acquired in a course in Leisure and Tourism, such as how to book a flight or a holiday, are not significant. What does such an assumption signify?

- Does it, like the 1944 Education Act, assume that only some students have the ability to acquire disciplinary knowledge in subjects such as History or Geography, or is there an assumption that knowledge differences are no longer important?

Few would openly endorse the assumptions of the 1944 Act and its spurious reference to parity of esteem, so I will not consider them further. The argument that knowledge differences between subjects and sectoral fields such as Leisure and Tourism are not important has wider implications which I want to examine in the rest of this chapter. I shall move beyond the specific case of Geography and Leisure and Tourism to more general questions concerning the knowledge basis of the curriculum.

I do not seek to defend any particular expression of a subject-based curriculum and in particular not the one that was established, initially in the public schools, in the last decades of the nineteenth century. This would in effect be endorsing the position of right-wing conservatives such as Chris Woodhead who focus on the list of subjects associated with the academic curriculum and neglect the principles and form of social organization that such a list presupposes. The subject-based curriculum established at the end of the nineteenth century had credibility not just from its association with elite institutions but from three more fundamental principles on which it was based that were not necessarily made explicit at the time and that arguably transcend the particular historical context. These were :

- A clear separation was accepted between the knowledge that can be acquired at school and the knowledge that people acquire in their everyday life.
- It was assumed that the knowledge acquired through the curriculum is cognitively superior to people's everyday knowledge—in other words that the curriculum could take people beyond the everyday knowledge available to them through their experience.
- School subjects were located within communities of specialists whose members included not only schoolteachers but university teachers and researchers (often linked within subject associations, many of which were first established in England at the turn of the last century).

Whereas right-wing conservatives focus only on the list of subjects, radical educationists concentrate on the extent to which the specialist subject communities were located in privileged sections of society and excluded the voices of the majority. Both neglect that there may be crucial social conditions for knowledge acquisition and production that are independent of the specific social contexts in which they are located.

The radical criticisms of a knowledge-based curriculum have a contemporary importance because they have gained a new and wider credibility that has not been associated with movements of the left. Policymakers, supported by some educationalists, have recognized a tension between the flexibility and openness to innovation of leading sectors of the economy and the rigidity of divisions in the curriculum. Curriculum divisions can be seen, by reformers, as barriers to change and to access to learning, especially for disadvantaged groups, and are associated with elite institutions. The question is whether we are left in the trap of two unacceptable alternatives. The first is the right-wing view that knowledge is essentially a given and that attempts to change the disciplinary structure of the curriculum are doomed to lead to dumbing down. The second, modernist view is that we have no alternative but to allow the curriculum to respond to market pressures for more choice, and more employment-related options, whatever the consequences for learners. If this is a trap, my view is that it is a trap partly of our own making—a product of inadequate theorizing.

Insularity and Hybridity in the Curriculum

I want to sharpen the issue by characterizing this tension between 'past' and possible 'future' curricula in terms of the principles of 'insularity' and 'hybridity' (Muller 2000). Let us take first the principle of *insularity*—it goes back a long way—to the establishment of research laboratories in the eighteenth century and to the disciplines that became the basis of the university curriculum in the early nineteenth century. It emphasizes the *differences* rather than the *continuity* between types of knowledge— and specifically the differences between theoretical and everyday or common-sense knowledge. It rejects the view that the divisions and classifications between types of knowledge in the curriculum are a mere reflection of traditions established in earlier times. Curriculum classifications, it is argued, not only have social and political origins; they also have *epistemological* and *pedagogic* significance. In other words they relate in fundamental ways to *how people learn* and *how they produce and acquire new knowledge.*

The principle of insularity asserts that the conditions for new knowledge production and acquisition put limits on the possibilities for curriculum innovation, in particular:

1. the crossing of disciplinary boundaries,
2. the incorporation of everyday knowledge into the curriculum, and
3. the involvement of non-specialists in curriculum design.

There will be, it is argued, a pedagogic price to pay for dispensing with such boundaries.

Not surprisingly, this principle of insularity can be invoked uncritically in defence of the curriculum status quo. However there are two points to make here. First, insularity refers to *relations between contents* of knowledge, not to the specific contents themselves. In other words insularity is not an argument for a particular list of subjects, but only for the necessity of boundaries between different fields of knowledge and between theoretical and everyday knowledge.

Second, insularity is not primarily a political principle, although it may be used for political purposes. It is based on the view that knowledge cannot be equated solely with social needs or interests or as Dewey and the pragmatists argued, with its uses or purposes. As Descartes put it nearly four centuries ago, real knowledge is 'beyond all custom and example'. My argument is not that we have to agree with Descartes that true knowledge is achieved though introspection but that, like him, we need to ask, what are the conditions for knowledge acquisition, and production? What, in other words, is our *discourse on method?* This implies not accepting uncritically the Enlightenment philosophers' claims for knowledge and truth or, like the postmodernists, rejecting them, but going beyond their limitations—in particular their individualistic and ahistorical view of knowledge and reason and their tendency to equate knowledge only with the natural sciences.

The principle of hybridity is a more recent idea. It rejects the claim that the boundaries and classifications between subjects and disciplines reflect features of knowledge itself and sees them as always a product of particular historical circumstances and interests. It stresses, and here I quote Joe Muller, the South African social theorist, the 'essential unity and continuity of all forms and kinds of knowledge (theoretical and everyday) ... [and] the *permeability* of all classificatory boundaries' (Muller 2000). In other words, for hybridizers, anything goes with anything else—a kind of modular utopia!

The principle of hybridity is frequently defended in terms of its consistency with what is seen as the increasingly boundary-less character of modern economies and societies. A curriculum based on hybridity is no more than a recognition of contemporary reality, it is claimed. It challenges the tendency for school or academic knowledge to become 'for its own sake' and offers a way of making the curriculum relevant to more young people. At the same time, by being more inclusive and adaptable, a curriculum based on the principle of hybridity is seen as supporting the political goals of equality and social justice.

In the 1970s the principle of hybridity was expressed in ideas such as interdisciplinary studies and an integrated curriculum. In the more market-dominated period since the 1990s, it has been expressed differently—with a far greater emphasis on individual access and choice. Practical examples of the principle of hybridity are:

- modular or unitized curricula;
- the University for Industry's adoption of the slogan that learning must be in 'bite-sized chunks';
- the incorporation of experiential learning and workplace knowledge into the curriculum;
- the blurring of distinctions between academic and vocational knowledge.

The principle of hybridity assumes a fundamentally relativist view of knowledge that has always appealed to radicals as a basis for exposing the vested interests associated with existing knowledge boundaries and divisions.

There are, however, specific political reasons why a curriculum based on the principle of hybridity appeals to education policymakers today; it appears to converge with the new policy goals of social inclusion and accountability. Inclusion requires the curriculum to recognize the knowledge and experience of those traditionally excluded from formal education. Likewise, accountability requires limitations to be placed on the autonomy of subject specialists to define what counts as knowledge.

The insularity of academic knowledge can therefore be set against the social and economic arguments for a more 'responsive' curriculum that could be the basis for new kinds of skills and knowledge that transcend current boundaries. In rejecting the links between specific knowledge classifications and either pedagogic requirements or epistemological principles, the hybridity principle implies that decisions about the curriculum will (and should) depend, ultimately, on market pressures; in other words on political not educational priorities. What is the likely outcome of the tension between these two principles?

One outcome follows from treating insularity as a form of conservatism and a defence of privilege that has to give way to the hybridizing pressures of the new global economy. According to this scenario, we can expect the progressive disappearance and replacement of the disciplinary curriculum and, it might be argued, the weakening of an autonomous critical role for educational institutions. To put it more starkly, the principle of hybridity treats those features of the curriculum that set it apart from everyday reality as fundamentally out of date. The future is assumed to be one of increasing homogeneity in which the acquisition and production of knowledge are not distinct phenomena—just two among many diverse social practices.

A more likely outcome, however, is that new divisions will emerge between *elite institutions* which are able to maintain discipline-based curricula and *mass institutions* which are under pressure to develop curricula geared to immediate economic and political demands.

An Alternative Approach

The alternative approach which I want to argue for rests on very different assumptions:

1. It rejects the conservative view that knowledge is given and somehow independent of the social and historical contexts in which it is developed.
2. It assumes a view of knowledge as socially produced and acquired in particular historical times and in a world characterized by competing interests and power struggles. At the same time it recognizes knowledge as having emergent properties that take it beyond the preservation of the interests of particular groups. In other words we have to be prepared to speak about and argue for cognitive or intellectual interests.
3. It rejects a view of knowledge *as just another set of social practices*. It sees the differentiation both between fields and between theoretical and everyday knowledge as fundamental to what education is about even though the form and content of the differentiation is not fixed and will change.

The challenge for curriculum theory is to identify the nature of this differentiation, and to explore how to develop curricula that are based on it but not inconsistent with the wider goals of greater equality and participation. The approach to differentiation that I have found most useful draws on Bernstein's distinction between Vertical and Horizontal knowledge structures (Bernstein 2000). This is not the place to go into his analysis. Suffice to say, his argument is that knowledge boundaries and classifications are not only 'prisons ... (they can also be) tension points condensing the past and opening up possible futures'.

As I suggested earlier, the curriculum established in the late nineteenth and early twentieth century was both a list of subjects and a set of codes, rules, practices, and forms of association developed by those involved in specialist fields of enquiry. What Bernstein's analysis offers is a way of distinguishing those conditions that are necessary for the acquisition and production of knowledge and those associated with the social interests within which these processes were located—for example the Public School/Oxbridge link at the turn of the last century. Such an approach depends on a number of assumptions. It assumes that (*a*) the codes and practices associated with subjects and disciplines such as geography, history, and the sciences set the curriculum apart from the everyday knowledge that students bring to school; (*b*) these rules and codes are explicitly associated with educational institutions which are separated from the demands of family and everyday life; and (*c*) it is this separation of the curriculum from everyday life that gives the knowledge acquired through it an explanatory power and capacity for generalization that is not a feature of everyday knowledge tied to practical concerns. Certain principles for guiding curriculum policy necessarily follow. For example:

- The curriculum cannot be based on everyday practical experience. Such a curriculum would only recycle that experience.
- The content and forms that the curriculum takes is not and should not be static; new curriculum forms and content will always emerge.
- It is important to be cautious about replacing a curriculum based on specialist research and pedagogic communities with one based on the immediate practical concerns of employers or general criteria for employability such as key skills.
- Providing access to concepts with explanatory power is not something limited to school subjects as we know them. However it does depend, as in the case of fields such as engineering, architecture, medicine, and accountancy—on

knowledge shared by specialist teachers, university researchers, and professional associations. Not to rely on such forms of organization—as in the case of pre-vocational fields such as Leisure and Tourism—is to seek a short cut to increasing participation which can only perpetuate inequalities.

- A curriculum of the future needs to treat knowledge as a distinct and non-reducible element in the changing resources which people need access to in order to make sense of the world. The task of curriculum theory from the point of view argued here is to reassert this priority in the new circumstances that we face.

The 'Curriculum of the Past' and the 'Curriculum of the Future'

I want to draw my argument together with reference to a distinction that I proposed in my book *The Curriculum of the Future* (Young 1998) between a *curriculum of the past* and *a curriculum of the future*. I see the two concepts rather differently within the framework I have developed in this chapter than I did in 1998. It can be summarized in terms of a number of key dimensions on which the organization of knowledge in the curriculum can vary:

- between the insulation of disciplines and subjects *and* the forms of connectivity between them;
- between the separation of the acquisition of knowledge from its application *and* their integration;
- between the assumption that knowledge forms a coherent whole in which the parts are systematically related *and* the assumption that knowledge can be broken up (modularized) into separate elements and put together by learners or teachers in any number of different combinations.

The *curriculum of the past* took for granted that knowledge is best transmitted and acquired through insulated, specialist forms that are consistent with its disciplinary coherence. It disregarded the possible impact of political and economic changes which call these principles into question as well as the inequalities of access that were associated with them. However, despite this, the 'curriculum of the past' was located in a history of real social networks, and real trust among specialists which gave it an objectivity and a concept of standards which transcended its social origins in elite institutions. The idea of a *curriculum of the future* has yet to establish an equivalent basis for objectivity. It will not only have to be consistent with the circumstances of the twenty-first century; it will also have to establish new forms of association and trust and rely on new types of specialists if it is to fulfil the claims made for it.

The present unresolved tension between the two curriculum models leaves us with, at best, pragmatic modifications of the *curriculum of the past*. They avoid fundamental questions of how the new networks of specialists will be established which take account of global economic changes but do not lose the crucial autonomy that was provided by the old subjects and disciplines.

Before returning to my subtitle, 'Updating the Enlightenment', I quote the French philosopher Paul Valery who, though he wrote sixty years ago, expresses an important strand of my argument about knowledge and the curriculum: 'the rules of classic art teach us by their arbitrary nature that the thoughts arising from our daily needs, sentiments and experiences are only a small part of the thoughts of which we are capable' (Paul Valery 1943).

End Note

Originally I had thought that I would begin this chapter with the theme of its subtitle 'Updating the Enlightenment'. However that turned out to be a project for the future. Instead I offer an end note, no more than a little background to remind readers that the questions about knowledge and the curriculum with which I have been concerned are far from new. My interest in going back to the Enlightenment arose from trying to understand what it was about the Enlightenment ideas, and especially its ideas about knowledge and truth, that led to the postmodernist critiques. Debates around postmodernism tend to polarize between a defence of reason and knowledge as in some way beyond history and society and a totally relativist position that rejects any objective view of knowledge or any so-called meta-narrative of progress in history. I want to make several preliminary points in linking this debate to issues in curriculum studies. First, in contrast to prevailing tendencies to polarize positions, I think we have to work with the tension between the objective claims of reason and knowledge and their inescapably contextual and historical character. Second we are not limited, like most Enlightenment thinkers were, to equating real knowledge only with the mathematical sciences. Third it is difficult, I would say impossible, to formulate any sort of debate in the field of curriculum as in any other area of policy, without some idea about progress, however cautious we need to be about its specific expression. Finally, there is Hegel; I am a late beginner in trying to take Hegel seriously. I don't think we can afford to forget him if we want to get beyond the kind of polarities that he attempted to reconcile but are still very much with us; obvious examples are those between the particular and the universal and between the objectivity of knowledge and its rootedness in history. Let me explain briefly why I think Hegel is important for curriculum theory. It was Hegel who most fully recognized the dramatic implications of the Enlightenment; for the first time in history, it was no longer necessary to rely on tradition or divine revelation in dealing with issues of epistemology, ethics, and aesthetics. As Habermas put it, 'Hegel inaugurated the discourse of modernity' that we are still part of. Modernity for Hegel was unique because it was *self-grounding* and it is the implications of this momentous development that we are still grappling with in curriculum theory—one example is in English literature and the debate about the canon, another is what on earth should be taught in school history? Hegel's idea that dialectical reason is the driving force of history is somewhat alien to us today. However, his legacy was not a position in the sense this is usually understood: it provided a framework for a debate.

Callinicos (1998), in his excellent book on social theory, states that Habermas distinguishes three positions staked out by those following Hegel. First, there were the the left Hegelians, the most famous being Marx. They retained Hegel's concept of history as a dialectical process but moved it from the realm of ideas to the revolutionary tendencies of the working class. Second, there were the right Hegelians, who associated Absolute Reason with the state of their time (and therefore with the end of history). They were the forerunners of modern liberalism (both John Stuart Mill and New Labour?). Finally and much later there was Nietszche's response to Hegel; he set out to unmask both right and left as mere expressions of the will to power. In his total rejection of the Enlightenment he was the forerunner of today's postmodernists.

The point of this digression from curriculum issues is that Hegel's identification of the self-grounding of reason and knowledge and the difficulties that are posed by no longer being able to rely on tradition or divine revelation are still with us today in relation to the curriculum as much as in other contemporary policy debates. Some, successors to the right Hegelians now seen as technocrats, want to halt history; some, like the left Hegelians, invoke popular voices as expressions of social contradictions, and others claim that there is no rational resolution to problems, only power. I think that I am trying to find a way between the first two.

My conclusions to this digression are first that the Enlightenment changed everything—we cannot go back to tradition or God in deciding what to teach: we have only reason, knowledge, and history. Second, although the circumstances have changed since the time of Hegel and his successors, and we know more about how knowledge is acquired and produced than they did, the fundamental issues have not changed. Hence in rethinking curriculum theory we have to keep going back to the questions that they raised.

NOTE

This chapter was originally presented as a paper to the *Rethinking Curriculum Studies* series at the Institute of Education, University of London, 11 March 2003, and later to a staff seminar at the University of Bath.

The Structure of Pedagogic Discourse

Rob Moore

Introduction

This chapter considers issues raised by the distinction that Durkheim makes when he writes: 'underlying the particular condition of our intelligence and sensibility there is in each one of us a more profound condition which determines the others and gives them their unity; and it is this more profound condition which we must get at if we are truly to do our job as educators and have an effect which will be durable' (Durkheim 1977: 28). It is this 'more profound condition' that is now the central concern, as it was for Durkheim himself (for reasons to be given below). In order to provide a sense of what is at issue here, another distinction drawn by Basil Bernstein can be considered:

> It is a matter of some interest that the sociology of education has rarely turned its attention to the analysis of the intrinsic features constituting and distinguishing the specialised form of communication realised by the pedagogic discourse of education. Many of the analyses of the sociology of education, especially those carried out by the diverse group of theories of reproduction, assume, take for granted, the very discourse which is subject to their analysis. These theories, in particular, see pedagogic discourse as a medium for other voices: class, gender, and race. The discourses of education are analysed for their power to reproduce dominant/dominated relations external to the discourse but which penetrate the social relations, media of transmission, and evaluation of pedagogic discourse. It is often considered that the voice of the working class is the absent voice of pedagogic discourse, but we shall argue here that what is absent from pedagogic discourse is its own voice. (Bernstein 1990:165)

'It is as if', Bernstein says, 'pedagogic discourse is itself no more than a relay for power relations external to itself; a relay whose form has no consequences for what is relayed' (ibid. 166). He asks the question: 'How is it possible to make a distinction between a relay and what is relayed?' This distinction is not identical to Durkheim's, but both are of the same form and have to do with the same thing.

Basil Bernstein, until his death in 2000, was the pre-eminent British social theorist working in the sociology of education, and his work is likely to remain for many years its most substantial intellectual achievement. It is not possible here to adequately summarize the complexity of Bernstein's system and its development from his first published paper in 1958. Rather, the focus will be upon two issues: (*a*) what is distinctive about Bernstein's theory and (*b*) what that can tell us about the production of knowledge and the structuring of intellectual fields (Moore and Muller 2002). The first question will be pursued by considering two seminal papers from the 1970s, respectively on 'classification and framing' and 'visible and invisible pedagogies' (Bernstein 1977: chs. 5 and 6), and the second question will be examined through his later writings concerning 'languages of description' and 'vertical and horizontal knowledge structures' (Bernstein 2000). Bernstein stands out amongst social theorists in that his theory has generated an impressively wide range of *empirical* work amongst researchers across the world (e.g. Morais et al. 2001; Power et al. 2001; Arnot 2002: ch. 11; *British Journal*

From Rob Moore, *Education and Society: Issues and Explanations in the Sociology of Education* (Cambridge: Polity Press, 2004), ch. 5. Reprinted with permission.

of Sociology of Education 2002). This was made possible because his theory sought to generate concepts that enable a close engagement with data (Bernstein 2000: ch. 6), and the particular character of that theory is what requires examination.

The implication of Bernstein's statement above is that the sociology of education has been in a significant manner one-sided. It has paid considerable attention to the ways in which forces such as class and gender differences are present within or relayed through education, but has neglected something that is intrinsic to education itself: the *voice* of pedagogic discourse. The 'voice of pedagogic discourse' and the 'more profound condition' are aspects of the same thing, but, unfortunately, it is not possible to give a simple and immediate illustration of what this is. However, an everyday observation might provide an initial sense of what is involved. As I am writing, my television set is showing the play between the English and South African cricket teams. I can see the pictures and hear the commentary—they are *what* is being relayed by the broadcast. But there is also something else, a *relay* (a signal), that makes this possible, and this I cannot see or hear, but without it I would see or hear nothing at all! It is this invisible condition for that which *is* visible that Durkheim and Bernstein are concerned with.

The problems here are compounded, alas, by others to do with the 'visibility' of Durkheim and Bernstein themselves! Bernstein throughout his work emphasizes his debt to Durkheim:

> Durkheim's work is a truly magnificent insight into the relationship between symbolic orders, social relationships and the structuring of experience. In a sense, if Marx turned Hegel on his head, then Durkheim attempted to turn Kant on his head. For in *Primitive Classification* and in *The Elementary Forms of the Religious Life,* Durkheim attempted to derive the basic categories of thought from the structuring of the social relation. It is beside the point as to his success. He raised the whole question of the relation between the classification and frames of the symbolic order and the structuring of experience. (Bernstein 1973: 194)

Bernstein speaks of Durkheim's 'truly magnificent insight', but he was also very much aware of the way in which Durkheim's thought had been successively recontextualized through a series of reinterpretations that fundamentally misrepresented his concerns and his theory—he was (and is) commonly presented as a conservative and a positivist, whereas he was actually a socialist and a rationalist. Bernstein's former tutor at the London School of Economics, Donald MacRae, in his Foreword to the 1973 edition of the first volume of *Class, Codes and Control*, says of Bernstein's work:

> Its concerns, but not its procedures, are Durkheimian and the relation of Bernstein to Durkheim—and not the Durkheim of the textbooks—would be worth serious exploration. For Durkheim raises questions that the other great sociological theorists from Ferguson to the present have either not seen or have avoided. In a way what Bernstein does is to attack the questions of *The Elementary Form of the Religious Life* but in terms of categories forged not out of Kantian categories but out of categories derived from the half-century of sociology since Durkheim's death, from the author's own thought and feeling, from his researches, and, by a circuitous route, from the neo-Kantianism of Ernest Cassirer. (Bernstein 1973: p. xiv)

Bernstein also had a 'truly magnificent insight'—an insight into Durkheim and his project that is very far removed from the 'Durkheim of the textbooks', and in order to properly understand Bernstein, it is necessary to recover Durkheim in something like the sense that Bernstein had of him, which involves reversing the movement that in the early 1970s positioned Durkheim at the conservative, positivist pole of the intellectual field.

Durkheim and the Science of Education

Of the founding thinkers of sociology, it was Émile Durkheim (1858–1917) who devoted most attention to education. Furthermore, education was at the core of his theory. Karabel and Halsey, in their authoritative 1977 review of the sociology of education, say of *The Evolution of Educational Thought* (Durkheim 1977) that 'No sociologist of education has yet surpassed—in depth or in breadth—this investigation of the relationship between social structure and the process of educational transmission' (Karabel and Halsey 1977: 74; also 87–8). This verdict remains valid today. Durkheim's theory does not have just historical priority; it maintains a powerful intellectual claim on the centre of the sociology of education. But there are considerable difficulties in pressing this claim on his behalf, given the various ways in which his thought was refracted and recontextualized in the major sociological debates in the post-war period.

Durkheim's influence on the sociology of education has been extensive, and has sometimes assumed contradictory forms. He provided a major source for the American normative functionalism that was the dominant sociological paradigm of the 1950s—the time when sociology was struggling to become institutionalized in British universities. Associated with this was a particular model of 'advanced industrial society' [...] related to his ideas on 'organic solidarity', which powerfully influenced thinking about education in sociology. This functionalist model became the object of intense criticism in the late 1960s and early 1970s with the rise of subjectivist, humanist sociologies such as phenomenology and ethnomethodology (associated with the New Sociology of Education). These approaches portrayed Durkheim as a conservative positivist, and formulated their own positions in *opposition* to his. In this sense, Durkheim's influence was negative, in that this school constructed their approaches on the grounds that they were *not* Durkheimian, as they understood and represented him. In a more specialized way, his classic work *Suicide* (1952) provided, via the work of Robert Merton, the basis for a set of classic studies of pupil subcultures in English secondary schools [...]. These studies played a pivotal role in shifting attention from the macro-level concerns of structural theories to the micro-processes of schooling. However, this set of influences only partially represent Durkheim—filtered as they are through secondary, Anglophone, reinterpretations.

There is a more authentic, though less frequently acknowledged, influence reflecting Durkheim's seminal position in the development of French social science. Despite recent enthusiasm for structuralist and post-structuralist thinkers, it is rarely recognized that, through what Bourdieu called 'a strange ruse of intellectual reason', these ideas (e.g. of Claude Lévi-Strauss, Louis Althusser, Michel Foucault) have their roots in 'the Durkheimian philosophy of man' (Bourdieu 1988: p. xxiii). This alternative, but more 'subterranean' influence (Alexander 1990: 4–6), surfaces in crucial ways throughout the sociology of education. Understanding Durkheim in this way enables us to see, for instance, the manner in which Foucault's concerns range across the terrain mapped by Durkheim in *The Division of Labour in Society* (1933) and what his thinking owes to Durkheim's critique of humanism (Cladis 1999). From this perspective, Durkheim can be presented in a way very different from the received conventions of 'the textbooks'.

Context and Background

In locating Durkheim, it is important to have a sense of his time and the circumstances of the French Third Republic. They bear directly upon the particular ideas that he chose to develop and the manner in which he did so. Durkheim's writing is deeply polemical (though this is not necessarily obvious to us as contemporary readers; Lukes 1973). He took as his major task that of establishing sociology as a *science*. The particular model of science that he supported (an 'emergent' model [...]) was one which enabled him to advance the claim that 'the social' exists as a distinct domain of the real requiring its own distinctive discipline: sociology. His attacks upon empiricism and utilitarianism are made on behalf of sociology as an aspiring science. These arguments are also *political*, in that he saw a direct link between 'the science of society' and the anti-clerical, secular morality that he supported within the Third Republic and promoted through his thinking on education (Durkheim 1973).

Durkheim was a deeply committed and passionate defender of individual liberty and dignity: he possessed a strong sense of social justice, was an egalitarian republican, militant anti-clerical rationalist, and an internationalist. These attitudes were channelled into his academic work and informed both his own teaching and his approach to education and its role in society. He was, by all accounts, a dedicated and inspired teacher, who placed his immense intellectual powers at the service of educational reform in France, for the purpose of improving the general social condition.

> Let us therefore make use of our liberties to seek out what we must do and to do it, to smooth the functioning of the social machine, still so harsh on individuals, to place within their

reach all possible means of developing their abilities without hindrance, to work finally to make a reality of the famous precept: to each according to his labour! Let us even recognise that in a general way liberty is a delicate instrument which one must learn to handle; and let us train our children accordingly. All moral education should be oriented to this end. (Durkheim 1973: 55–6)

It is no accident that the great theorist of *la république des professeurs* should put education at the centre of his thinking and activity. Durkheim's theory of knowledge underpinned the secular rationalism that Clark (1973) describes as the 'predominant cultural pattern' of the militant supporters of the Third Republic.

Education, Society, and the Problem of Knowledge

Durkheim was in the first place a *rationalist*. His rationalism has its origins in the ideas of the great German Enlightenment philosopher Immanuel Kant (1724–1804; see Scruton 1997). This must be the starting point for understanding the centrality of education to his theory and the character of that 'profound condition which determines the others and gives them their unity'. Kant attempted to reconcile the ancient conflict in Western philosophy between *empiricists* and *rationalists* (or 'apriorists'; Durkheim 1995: Introduction). The basis of this distinction can be summarized as follows. Empiricists are those who believe that *experience* is prior to knowledge, and that knowledge is ultimately based upon sensory experience. In many cases (especially for the 'logical positivists' of the early twentieth century; [...]), such sensory phenomena (or sense data) are seen as the objective basis of scientific knowledge. One important consequence of this belief is that it disallows any knowledge claims that cannot ultimately be grounded in sensory experience.

The problem with empiricism is in accounting for the remarkably orderly and structured nature of thought in the light of the disorderly and potentially random character of empirical (or experiential, subjective) association. Following Kant, Durkheim was concerned with the 'compulsive' way in which human beings invariably experience reality in terms of basic *categories* (concepts and intuitions) such as space, time, causality and extension. As Ernest Gellner says, 'The empiricists could not account for this compulsion. They have great trouble with *any* compulsion: their world is, so to speak, floppy and *loose*. It coagulates by accident, like a snowball' (Gellner 1992: 31–2). In essence, the logic (or rather, illogic) of associationism is simply not sufficient to account for the enduring structured regularities of human thought. 'Association is lawless, it can establish links *anywhere*. Our concepts, by contrast, are astonishingly well disciplined. How on earth could anarchic association engender such well-drilled concepts and produce such an orderly and stable world?' (ibid. 34).

Whereas empiricists see knowledge as *a posteriori*, as coming *after* experience, rationalists see its crucial dimensions as *a priori*, as *preceding* experience (Scruton 1997: 32–3). That is, the fundamental categories of experience such as time and space that *structure* our experiences exist prior to experience, and provide experiences with their basic organizing principles. Kant referred to these basic, *a priori* categories as 'transcendental', meaning that they are the universal and necessary pre-conditions for any experience and for knowledge, and are revealed by means of *deduction* rather than being empirically established (see [...] Scruton 1997: 39–42). Although both culturally and individually *time* can be known and subjectively experienced in many ways, we cannot but experience reality in terms of time in some form or other. The *category* is fundamental and necessary, though its form is open to variation. Kant views these categories as a universal property of the human mind (a 'transcendental ego'), and they are the condition for our individual experiences.

Durkheim shared this basic Kantian *a priorism*. However, he also saw a fundamental problem in Kant. The 'apriorists' are genuine rationalists; however, 'they have to ascribe to the intellect a certain power to transcend experience. But for this singular power, they offer neither explanation nor warrant. Merely to say that it is inherent in the nature of human intellect is not to explain that power' (Durkheim 1995: 14). In the final analysis, the transcendental ego explains nothing, because how can we explain the transcendental ego itself? The solution offered by Kant is simply that (as Gellner puts it: 1992: 36) 'the mind did it'. Durkheim addresses this problem through the radical suggestion that the basic categories of thought are *social* in origin: essentially, the transcendental categories of Kantian epistemology are derived from the principles of social order. In these terms, the 'social self' (see below) in Durkheim stands in place of Kant's 'transcendental ego'. As he says: 'Philosophers have often speculated that, beyond the bounds of human understanding, there is a kind of universal and impersonal understanding in which individual minds seek to participate by mystical means; well, this kind of understanding exists, and it exists not in any transcendent world but in this world itself' (1977: 340).

Durkheim's Definition of Education

Durkheim's definition of and approach to education have, in the first instance, to be understood in these Kantian terms. Education is defined as the 'methodical socialization of the young generation'.

> *Education is the influence exercised by adult generations on those that are not yet ready for social life. Its object is to arouse and to develop in the child a certain number of physical, intellectual and moral states which are demanded of him by both the political society as a whole and the special milieu for which he is specifically destined.*
>
> ... It follows from the definition that precedes, that education consists of a methodical socialization of the young generation. In each of us, it may be said, there exist two beings which, while inseparable except by abstraction, remain distinct. One is made up of all the mental states that apply only to ourselves and to the events of our personal lives: this is what might be called the individual being. The other is a system of ideas, sentiments and practices which express in us, not our personality, but the group or different groups of which we are a part; these are religious beliefs, moral beliefs and practices, national or professional traditions, collective opinions of every kind. Their totality forms the social being. To constitute this being in each of us is the end of education. (Durkheim 1956: 71–2)

We must note here that this is a broad definition of 'education', and is not restricted to what happens within modern education systems or schools. Durkheim associates this process with the formation of a 'social self' that owes its origins entirely to society: socialization 'creates in man a new being'. Education, in this broad sense, mediates between society and the self, and is the process whereby the 'outer' (social) becomes the 'inner' (self). Education is the process (the formation of *habitus*) whereby the social comes to be inscribed within the individual as the structuring principles of consciousness that provide the framework and conditions for the individual, 'personal' self. Durkheim (or at least his English translators) uses the term *habitus* relatively rarely, but once the character of his project is properly understood as the sociologizing of Kant in the manner described, the *concept* is seen to be fundamental to his theory and ubiquitous in his writing.

Understood with reference to Durkheim's Kantianism, we can see that his central concern is not so much with the *content* of knowledge and beliefs, as with the fundamental *generative* categories of thought [...]. It is by virtue of being generative that these categories carry the possibilities of creativity, reflexivity and innovation. These possibilities find their fullest expression in what Durkheim called 'reflection', and are most highly refined within the sciences. By seeing these principles as social in origin, Durkheim also sees them as socially and historically variable, rather than universal. He expresses this view in the following, where he also makes a fundamental distinction (echoing that considered earlier) between societies' 'external forms of life' and 'the fundamental substance of their way of conceiving the world'.

> Far from being immutable, humanity is in fact involved in an interminable process of evolution, disintegration and reconstruction; far from being a unity, it is in fact infinite in its variety, with regard to both time and place. Nor do I mean simply that external forms of life vary, that men do not everywhere speak the same language, wear the same clothes, or observe the same rituals. Rather I mean that *the fundamental substance of their way of conceiving the world* and conducting themselves in it is in a constant state of flux, which itself varies from place to place. The view that there is one single moral system valid for all men at all times is no longer tenable. (Durkheim 1977: 324, my emphasis)

The main features of Durkheim's approach to sociology of education, and his historical materialism, can be summarized as follows:

- humanity is socially and historically developed;
- education is the process whereby the young are made into social beings under particular historical circumstances;

- central to that process is the inscription of the basic generative categories of thought;
- these categories are principles of social order translated, through education, into the structuring principles of consciousness;
- because these principles vary as societies vary, and because there is no universal human nature, there can be no universal pedagogy;
- the purpose of the science of education is to explicate the links between particular forms of social order, forms of education and forms of consciousness.

The sociologizing of the Kantian categories brings into play the concept of *habitus*—'the fundamental substance of their way of conceiving the world'—as that which mediates between the inner and the outer and that transcribes the principles of social order as the generative principles that structure consciousness through the medium of pedagogy.

The Duplex Self

The formation of *habitus* through pedagogy must be seen in terms of Durkheim's distinctive model of the self (a 'duplex' Self) and of the relationship between the self and the social. Durkheim's definition of education (above) includes the following:

> In each of us, it may be said, there exist two beings which, while inseparable except by abstraction, remain distinct. One is made up of all the mental states that apply only to ourselves and to the events of our personal lives: this is what might be called the individual being. The other is a system of ideas, sentiments and practices which express in us, not our personality, but the group or different groups of which we are a part. (Durkheim 1956: 71–2)

The distinction being made here between the social and the personal self constitutes the 'duplex' model of Self (e.g. Durkheim 1977: 325–40). He relates his model to the traditional division between the body and the soul that he sees as an intuitive awareness of this state ('The old formula *homo duplex*'). 'Far from being simple, our inner life has something that is like a double centre of gravity. On the one hand is our individuality—and, more particularly, our body in which it is based; on the other is everything in us that expresses something other than ourselves' (Durkheim 1973: 154–5). Durkheim's preoccupation with the *social* side of the equation is probably the cause of the main criticisms of his work: that he reifies society and produces an objectified, deterministic model of the person. If it is society that constitutes the self, is there any space left for individual freedom and voluntaristic social action? It is important, especially in relation to education, to understand properly Durkheim's view of the relationship between individuality and the social.

Paradoxically, it is precisely because Durkheim *does* define the social as a reality in its own right that his theory opens up an effective space for both individual freedom and collective human influence over society and history. The starting point is the fact that 'the social' is both external to us and also 'within' us. The social 'within', however, is not identical with our subjective experiences or the *content* of our values and beliefs (it is, as it were, 'tangential' or 'refracted' in the way that speech and language are not identical). The generative structure of *habitus* should not be confused with the *output of habitus* any more than language should be confused with speech. This 'gap' between experience (personal subjectivity) and generative principle opens the space for what Durkheim calls 'spontaneity', and enables a voluntaristic view of the individual. The point has been well made by Poggi (1972: 223–4), who differentiates between 'norms' and 'instincts' by saying that the latter are both 'within', and '*from within*', whereas norms are 'within' but do not *come* from within—their source is external. However:

> The externality of norms is the externality of mental things and they can only affect action by being continually transformed into 'internalities' through the *mediation of the individual's active subjectivity*. This mediation involves an irreducible element of freedom in the relationship between the norm and the behaviour that the norm evokes. It cannot be said, in a strict sense, that the norm *determines* the behaviour, although Durkheim's treatment of this point sometimes seems to suggest that it does. To this extent, some degree of 'spontaneity' is a necessary element of compliant behaviour, but one that Durkheim construes in a rather austere manner. (Poggi 1972: 225–6, my emphasis)

What Poggi refers to as the continual transformation of the external into the internal through the mediation of the individual's active subjectivity is fundamental to Durkheim's view of education. In a sense, education is the socially legitimated and regulated form of this process. Experience and subjectivity are *structured* by the social (the social self), but not determined by it. Precisely because the 'personal self' (the self of individual subjective experience) is not identical with the 'social self', there is an irreducible space within the Self that is the space of individuality, spontaneity and creativity. The tangential relationship between consciousness and experience (between the social and the personal self) constructs an arc that is continually mediated by active subjectivity. Durkheim's view, Poggi says, is that 'society is at bottom a 'conditional' reality, inescapably dependent on norms that in principle can only be observed freely, and by the same token need not be observed at all' (ibid. 228). Durkheim's 'sociologism' leads not to a determined but to a 'conditional reality'. From this point of view, the 'problem of order' is endemic to society, because its roots are intrinsic to the ontology of the duplex Self. The individual is both socially constituted but also continually at a distance from and with inclinations often in deep conflict with the social. Social order is never given, but always needs to be worked at to be sustained because of this 'inner contradiction' in our nature.

Human beings, for Durkheim, are socially *contained* rather than determined, and this condition becomes an increasingly urgent issue in modern societies in which social change actively requires innovative 'spontaneity' and the space of individuality is continually enlarged. Because of the way in which 'spontaneity' figures in the relationship between norm and behaviour, 'in a sense all societies are suspended over the abyss of chaos; they possess a purely conditional existence' (Poggi 1972: 266). Durkheim's personal experiences and his perceptions of his own time (the political instability of the previous decades in France and the cataclysm of the First World War) led him (not unreasonably) to fear that the 'abyss of chaos' loomed all too near. When his son André was reported missing in action, he wrote of 'the image of this exhausted child, alone at the side of a road in the midst of night and fog... that seizes me by the throat' (Lukes 1973: 555). This poignant image condenses Durkheim's fears of the consequences of the breakdown of social order. Historical circumstances, both general and deeply personal, do much to explain what Poggi aptly describes as Durkheim's 'austere' approach, but can also, unfortunately, make his style and priorities initially less than convivial to modern readers.

Durkheim's sociological translation of Kant locates his categories within social order. But they reappear in the social self as the constitutive principles of consciousness and experience. This continual translation between the outer and the inner is the work of *habitus*: the pedagogic formation and regulation of the self in the mediation of the individual and society. In the context of Durkheim's project for sociology and the science of society, it should also be noted that the duplex model and the idea of a *social* self resists the possibility of psychological reduction—crucially, the self, in this respect, is as much an object for sociology as for psychology, and in the distinctive way appropriate to it as an autonomous science of society.

The Structuring of Order

Following on from the sociologizing of the transcendental categories of Kant's philosophy and the observation that rather than being universal, they will differ as societies differ in terms of social order, it then becomes necessary to theorize and model the transformations of social order. Durkheim attempts this task through the concepts of 'mechanical' and 'organic' solidarity. However, the terms appear only in his first major work, *The Division of Labour in Society* (1933), where he associates these two forms of solidarity with simple and complex societies at the opposed points of an immense arc of human social evolution. It only takes a moment's reflection to see that neither mechanical nor organic solidarity could ever exist in an exclusively pure form. Durkheim is describing two contrasting *principles* of social integration that must always be present to varying degrees and always together. Schmaus argues that the *concepts* denoted by 'mechanical' and 'organic' reappear in his next work, *Suicide*, as 'social integration' and 'regulation', and, similarly, the term 'social representations' replaces 'collective consciousness' in the later book. Schmaus sees these changes as 'terminological' (1994: 174), in order to avoid certain confusions that arose concerning the argument in *Division of Labour*.

Consider how Durkheim describes the different situations of primary and secondary school teachers:

In the first place, secondary education is a more complex organism than primary education. Now, the more complex an organism is, the more it needs reflection in order to adapt itself to its environment. In the elementary school, at least in theory, every class is in the hands of one and only one teacher; consequently his teaching tends to have a quite natural unity which is very straightforward and therefore does not need to be intellectually planned: it is indeed the unity of the person teaching. The same is not true of secondary schools, where the same pupil is generally taught by a variety of teachers. Here there is a genuine division of pedagogic labour... How, short of a miracle, can unity emerge from this diversity, unless it is contrived? How can all these different teachers adapt to one another and complement each other so that they create a unified whole if the teachers themselves have no notion of what the whole is? It is not a question, especially in secondary schools, of producing mathematicians and men of letters, physicists and naturalists, but of developing the mind through the medium of literature, history, mathematics and the natural sciences. But how can each teacher fulfil his function, as he regards his own specialised part in the total enterprise, if he does not know what this enterprise is and how his various colleagues are supposed to collaborate with him in it, in such a way that all his teaching is related to it? People often argue as if all this went without saying, as if everybody knew instinctively what is involved in developing a mind. (Durkheim 1977: 6)

In the first place, the basic distinction that Durkheim is making between the elementary school and the secondary school is a form of the distinction between those principles initially termed 'mechanical' and 'organic' solidarity. But here they are co-present at different levels within the same institution in the same society at the same time in history. The point at issue has been well made by Randall Collins:

To grasp this, it is necessary to treat Durkheim's theoretical statements analytically rather than concretely. That is to say, when he speaks of the principles of a 'society' and its integration, we should not take this to mean that *empirically* this necessarily refers to a 'whole society' as conventionally defined (which in practice usually means a political unit, especially a nation-state). Instead, we should take 'society' in its generic sense, as any instance of prolonged sociation, whatever its boundaries in space or time. In this sense, a social class may well be a 'society', though it need not always be; in fact, the Durkheimian theory shows us the variable conditions under which its integration and moral solidarity is greatest or weakest. (Collins 1990: 109)

So, Collins suggests, 'society' should be understood in the 'generic sense' as 'any instance of prolonged sociation' (society in the sense given by 'I belong to the College Debating Society' or, more loosely, in the phrase 'high society' or the statement 'He craved the society of others'). Durkheim uses the term 'society' in this way, for instance, in *Moral Education* (1961: 79) in relation to the family and the manner in which the school provides the link between the family and the nation. Collins concludes that 'we arrive at a conception of modern stratification, in which the entire stratification order is a line-up of different types of 'societies' (1990: 110).

Secondly, having identified the complex division of labour in the secondary school, Durkheim raises the key issue of how to *theorize* it. What kind of 'unity' should emerge from the diversity of the teachers' specialized pedagogic roles? What should be the social form of their complementary activities? Durkheim argues that this issue is central to educational theory, and that the need to answer it in a 'methodical' and scientific manner justifies 'educational theory' and its teaching to student teachers.

Thirdly, he makes a distinction between teaching subjects in order to produce 'mathematicians and men of letters; physicists and naturalists' and 'developing the mind through the *medium* of literature, history, mathematics and the natural sciences' (my emphasis). Remembering that the crucial issue here is how to form the complementary relationships between the specialized subjects and that each teacher, through his or her specialism contributes to 'the total enterprise', it is the *structuring* of this enterprise that 'develops the mind' through the 'medium' of the disciplines—the formation of *habitus*, 'a more profound condition which determines the others and gives them their unity'.

Social Order and Individuality

The general historical movement in social evolution is towards greater complexity in the social division of labour. The key point is where the balance between the 'shared' and the 'idiosyncratic' element of consciousness shifts from the former to the latter, tipping the principle of solidarity towards the organic pole. The development of complexity within the social division of labour is realized through:

1. *differentiation* of institutions,
2. *specialization* of their activities,
3. *autonomization* of their fields,
4. *interdependence* of their relationships.

A consequence of this is that the principle of the self is increasingly detached from any particular, localized social base, and becomes concomitantly more abstract and 'universal' (see Lukes 1973: 155–7; Poggi 1972: 185–9). This is associated with the rise of what Durkheim refers to as a 'cult of personal dignity' (Lukes 1973: 156) that transcends the crude individualistic egotism of utilitarianism, empiricism and those he refers to as 'the economists'. This higher form of individualism has three main features.

- First, it is *abstract*: it elevates humanity in general, as a principle, rather than identifying any *particular* category of person. It is universal and egalitarian.
- Secondly, despite its individualism, it maintains a strong sense of the *collective*. It is not an egoistic individualism of the utilitarian type. All its great thinkers (Kant and Rousseau, Fichte, Hegel, Marx) asserted both the individual and the collective, and Durkheim associates this with an inherent socialism.
- Thirdly, it has the aura of the *sacred*. It not only proclaims the rights of the individual but inspires the individual with a sense of higher purpose and a source of moral value and worth extended to all humankind. '[I]ndividualism thus extended is the glorification not of the self but of the individual in general. It springs not from egoism but from sympathy for all that is human, a broader pity for all sufferings, for all human miseries, a more ardent need to combat them and mitigate them, a greater thirst for justice' (Durkheim 1973: 48–9).

However, these great prophets of the higher form of individualism, each in his own way, fail to properly reconcile or integrate the *individualist* and *collectivist* dimensions of their systems. It is at this point that the argument takes a distinctively original, but typically Durkheimian, twist. That these two things so frequently occur together within the same philosophy suggests that they 'must depend on a single social state of which they are probably only different aspects' (ibid. 48). The reconciliation occurs when it is recognized that individualism itself is social in origins and character. Individuation comes about as 'societies become more voluminous and expand over vaster territories' (ibid. 51), and is the culmination of the evolution of social complexity.

Hence, in just the way that Durkheim sees his theory as providing a solution to the problem of Kantian epistemology, so he sees it as reconciling the tension between the individual and the social in the theorists of the higher form of individualism. A particular historical development of the social is the *condition* for the emergence of the individual, and this is crucial for modern education.

> [I]ndeed, once the individual personality has become an essential element of the intellectual and moral culture of humanity, the educator should take into account the germ of individuality that is in each child. He should seek to foster its development by all possible means. Instead of applying to all, in an invariable manner, the same impersonal and universal set of rules, he should, on the contrary, vary and diversify his methods according to the temperaments and the configuration of each intelligence. But to be able properly to adapt educational practices to the variety of individual cases, it is necessary to know what they are, what are the reasons for the different processes that constitute them, the effects which they produce in different circumstances; in a word, it is necessary to have them submitted to pedagogic reflection. An empirical, mechanical education cannot be other than repressive and levelling . . . Now, the only way to prevent education from falling under the yoke of habit and from degenerating into mechanical and immutable automatism is to keep it constantly adaptable by reflection . . . Reflection is the force *par excellence* antagonistic to routine, and routine is the obstacle to necessary progress. (Durkheim 1956: 105–6)

For Durkheim, there is no inherent conflict between the collective and the individual. A particular historical development of the collective is the condition for the emergence of the individual self in its modern form. The individual and individualism are the quintessential expressions of the complexity of modern society. The manner in which the modem education system solves the problem of configuring the relationship between specialization and totality is crucial, because, as the paradigm of the more general social order, the structuring and processes of its *habitus* ('of developing the mind through the medium of literature, history, mathematics and the natural sciences') constitute the principle whereby the individual manages in practice the complexity of modernity. And for educators to properly meet this end, sociology must deliver a 'science of education'.

Returning to Bernstein's comments on Durkheim's 'magnificent insight' quoted above, he says that 'Durkheim attempted to derive the basic categories of thought from the structuring of the social relation', and adds that 'He raised the whole question of the relation between the classification and frames of the symbolic order and the structuring of experience' (Bernstein 1973: 194). In the first instance he acknowledges the Kantian character of Durkheim's sociological project in the manner described above, but in the second he embeds terms of his own—'the classification and frames of the symbolic order'—within the account as if they are quite naturally at one with Durkheim's own thinking, as if he has simply given those names to concepts at work in Durkheim's thinking, rather in the way that the concept of *habitus* is a recurring motif even when not named in that manner. Bernstein's own magnificent insight was to read Durkheim, apparently at the very beginning of his own intellectual career, in a manner quite at odds with 'the textbooks' of his time and for long after, to highlight and conceptualize principles at work in Durkheim's system and continue with his own distinctive and original elaboration of that project. The above reading of Durkheim is through a Bernsteinian lens and attempts to recover Durkheim in a manner that makes sense of Bernstein's own Durkheimianism, in order to read on now into Bernstein himself.

Bernstein: Class, Codes and Control

There is a crucial difference between the concerns of Durkheim and those of Bernstein. As an educationalist, Durkheim was seeking to define the type of educational system appropriate to French society in his day—a task he believed to be of some urgency—whereas Bernstein's major focus has been the ways in which symbolic resources are differentially distributed amongst groups and within and through education. In this respect *power* is a central concern in his work in a way that it is not in Durkheim's. Del Hymes has observed that 'Bernstein, a sociologist working in a complex society, recognised both linguistic form and social relations, but necessarily in terms of a plurality of styles and social positions. Styles and social positions are only sometimes side by side. More often, they are superimposed, stratified. Some control others' (Hymes 1995: 3–4). Hymes's essential point is that Bernstein is looking at the ways in which different modes of 'solidarity' (principles of order) interact and are *differentially* distributed in complex, modern societies. This comment by Hymes resonates with the way in which Collins (above) defines Durkheim's 'generic' use of the term 'society'. In this respect, Bernstein's interest was in the distribution of modes of sociality and their regulative principles and relationships.

It is not easy to classify Bernstein's theory, and he was dismissive of what he called 'epistemological botany' that attempts to pigeon-hole theories (2000). Commentators who know his work well stress how it weaves together threads from various disciplines and approaches. Hasan suggests that his is 'a type of theory whose primary allegiance is not to the mores of some recognised discipline: rather it is committed first and foremost to the investigation and explication of its central problematic' (2001: 128; Bernstein 2000: 125). Similarly, Diaz says that 'Bernstein cuts across paradigmatic positions in his concern with how society is inscribed within the individual and how what is written becomes a grammar for society' (Diaz 2001: 84). The question of the inscription of the social within the individual is at the centre of the problematic. In this respect, as Bernstein continually stressed, the starting point is in Durkheim. Bernstein summarizes his problematic as follows:

> Basically the theory addresses forms of symbolic control as regulators of cultural reproduction and of its change. In particular it addresses those forms of symbolic control institutionalised formally or informally as pedagogic practices. It seeks to understand how such practices, directly or indirectly, relay power and control and, more specifically, relay the

distribution of power and principles of control which are a function of class relations. Thus there are two elements: one modelling agencies, agents, practices and specialised forms of communication, so as to reveal varieties or modalities of regulation and their organising principles as cultural relays; the second showing how such principles are themselves, directly or indirectly, media for the reproduction of class relations. (Bernstein 1996: 126)

Diaz argues that Bernstein 'provided a model for the understanding of how social class and power distribution become internally shaped means of recognition and cognition', and that 'mediating these relations was a *semiotic device* that implies a socially produced potential of meanings, contexts of internalisation, and unequally distributed realisations' (Diaz 2001: 84, my emphasis). This 'semiotic device' mediates between the inner and the outer in the process of inscription/realization, and its principles and forms are what Bernstein sought to describe and model. It constitutes the central focus of his analysis, and the concepts he develops are designed to delineate its variations and modalities: 'Irrespective of the question of the intrinsic logic of the various forms of public thought, the *forms* of their transmission, that is their classification and framing, are social facts' (Bernstein 1977: 87). Hence, Bernstein's theory has a distinctive *object* ('forms of transmission'), and the purpose of his theory is to make this object visible.

Bernstein created a radically new language for talking about the curriculum and pedagogic processes: a theoretically grounded, conceptual language the terms of which would engage with both underlying principles and the ways in which those principles manifest themselves in systematically varying, but conceptually specifiable, forms of social practice. At one level, *particular* concepts must be able to describe empirical instances as examples of their type (in order that we may know that type when we see it, or recognize its absence), and at another, principles must be described theoretically such that they can be modelled as the *generative* principles of those types actualized in particular instances. These aspects of the theory were explored by Joseph Solomon in an interview with Bernstein (Bernstein 2000: Postscript).

Solomon suggests that the 'position of interpretation' in Bernstein's theory is 'rather weak'. 'Instead, the need to produce accurate 'descriptions' of practices of educational and cultural production and reproduction, and especially of educational practices, is permanently stressed' (ibid. 274). He goes on to say that 'you work very much by creating models of relations, mechanisms and transformations. In your texts, very often, concepts and their meanings are condensed, expressed in the form of an actual diagram. What is the function of these models? How do they link with the empirical research that is supported by the theory?' Solomon posed here a crucial set of questions, and elicited from Bernstein one of the most explicit statements of this fundamental dimension of his approach (2000: 209; see also 114–15).

In an earlier paper Bernstein described his type of 'model' when discussing certain interpretations of his theory:

It is often said that the theory works by producing opposing dichotomies in which each side functions as an ideal type: elaborated/restricted, positional/personal, stratified/differentiated, open/closed, visible/invisible, collection or serial/integrated. That these are opposing forms (models) I certainly agree. That they are ideal types I certainly disagree. Classically the ideal type is constructed by assembling in a model *a number of features* abstracted from a phenomenon in such a way as to provide a means of analysing the presence or absence of the phenomenon, and a means of analysing the 'workings' of the phenomenon from an analysis of the assembly of its features. Ideal types constructed in this way cannot *generate* other than themselves. They are not constructed by a principle that generates sets of relations of which any one form may be only *one of the forms* the principle may regulate. (Bernstein 1996: 126)

Bernstein's theoretical language is always attempting to move in two directions at the same time: crossways, as it were, between concept and description, and also vertically between levels.

Classification and Framing, Visible and Invisible Pedagogies

In volume 4 of *Class, Codes and Control* (1990), Bernstein developed a distinction between approaches that treat education as a 'relay' for power relations external to education (mainly reproduction theories—standpoint, interest, voice theories, etc.) and an approach that focuses upon the *intrinsic features of pedagogic discourse*. The difference is between perspectives that are concerned with *relations* to and those concerned with *relations within* pedagogic discourse. This is not simply to do with differences in interests or foci of concern (Moore and Maton 2001). It is to do with perspectives operating in distinctive theoretical modes and using different 'languages of description' (Bernstein 1977: ch. 7; 2000: chs. 7 and 9). The distinction is between what is relayed and an underlying 'pedagogic device' (Bernstein 2000: 114) that structures and organizes the content and distribution of what is relayed. The key process is recontextualization, whereby knowledge produced at one site, that of knowledge *production* (mainly, but not exclusively, the university), is selectively transferred to sites of *reproduction* (mainly, but not exclusively, the school). This process is not straightforward and cannot be taken for granted. Bernstein's distinction is between the message (that relayed) and the 'grammar' of the pedagogic device (the relay) that makes the message possible by drawing into a specialized relationship knowledge and people, time and space, context and performance according to rules of distribution, recontextualization and evaluation (ibid.).

Bernstein describes the 'pedagogic device' as a 'symbolic ruler, ruling consciousness, in the sense of having power over it, and ruling in the sense of measuring the legitimacy of the realisations of consciousness' (ibid.). It is through its realizations that the pedagogic device reveals itself, and the theorization of its form and principles entails the production of concepts that can describe realizations as phenomena of its generative possibilities. Diaz indicates how:

> In essence, boundaries are the critical point for definitions of knowledge and practice, as well as for the subject. The more the boundaries, the more the distribution of unequal spaces and the more the distribution of inequalities between positions, discourses, and practices. Thus, there is a close relation in Bernstein between boundaries, power, social groups, and forms of identity. Bernstein's analysis of power and boundaries provokes questions about their force, duration of spacing, ordering of internal forms and sites for knowledge, flows of identity, and relations with changes in the collective basis of society. (Diaz 2001: 84–5)

The concepts of classification and framing are crucial. The device is approached through categories and boundaries, the explicit and the implicit. It is not the *content* of pedagogic discourse that concerns Bernstein, but the structuring of relations *within* the field of discourse and the manner in which it associated with the contextual regulation of practice and consciousness for groups differentially positioned in terms of family, work and state. From this point of view, the content of a progressive and a traditional curriculum may be similar, but the structuring of their *forms* is radically different. These differences are expressed in relations between *context, meaning* and *practice*, and Bernstein defines *code* as 'a regulative principle, tacitly acquired which selects and integrates' these three features.

> From this general definition it is possible to conceptualise specific code modalities by a process of translation of the above three elements.
>
> • *context* translates as interactional practices
>
> • *meanings* translate as orientation to meanings
>
> • *realisation* translates as textual productions.
>
> Different distributions of power and principles of control differentially shape interactional practices according to different classification and framing values and thus give rise to different orientations to meaning, forms of realisations and so 'texts'. The formulation, above, shows visually the possibility of the produced text having consequences for expected meanings and their generating interactional practices. (Bernstein 1996: 194)

The differential regulation of context, meaning and realization through tacitly acquired codes active within an educational transmission process regulated by the principles of a particular pedagogic device generates a complex position system and its relations of power and control. The issue of 'translation' will be returned to below.

The possibilities or forms of regulation are given by the relationships of classification and framing. 'Classification' refers to the *relationship* between contents or contexts and the degree of boundary maintenance or insulation between them. 'Framing' is to do with the pedagogical relationship between the teacher and the taught, and the amount of control and the range of options each possesses over the '*selection, organisation, pacing and timing of the knowledge transmitted and received*' (Bernstein 1977: 88–9). Classification and framing can vary independently (+C/+F, +C/−F, −C/+F, −C/−F) and are *relative* in terms or strength or weakness (hence, this does not mean that there are only four given types of pedagogy). Strong classification and framing can be represented by a 'traditional' curriculum and pedagogy, with well-defined subjects and the pupil having little control over selection, organization, pacing and timing of the knowledge. Where both principles are weak, there is low insulation between subject categories, and pupils have a higher degree of control over the pacing of acquisition.

The key difference between 'strong' and 'weak' classification and framing is *not* to do with the presence or absence, or number or flexibility, of rules regulating a teaching situation. It has to do with the degree to which the rules are *explicit* or *implicit* from the point of view of the *pupil* or *student*. On this basis, Bernstein also distinguishes between 'traditional' and 'progressive' in terms of 'visible' and 'invisible' pedagogies (Bernstein 1977: ch. 6). The difference between the two is that the rules governing the hierarchical relationships between teacher and taught, control of sequencing of transmission, and the criteria used to evaluate the success of acquisition are *more* or *less* visible (or explicit). Bernstein's theory and its concepts aim to model (and reveal the principles giving rise to) systematic variations in the configuration and appearances of a complex set of relational properties structuring pedagogic discourses and codes.

> I started with classification because classification, strong or weak, marks the distinguishing features of a context. For example, some children when they first go to school are unaware or unsure of what is expected of them. They fail to recognise the distinguishing features which provide the school/classroom with its unique features and so particular identity. Such a failure in recognition will necessarily lead to inappropriate behaviour. On the other hand, some children are extensively prepared and are aware of the difference between the family context and the school context. In this case they are able to recognise the distinguishing features of the school, or class, even if they are not always able to produce the range of behaviour the school expects. Inasmuch as some children recognise the distinguishing features of the school, relative to the children who do not, those that do are in a more powerful position with respect to the school. It is likely that those who do recognise the distinguishing features of the school are more likely to be middle-class children than lower working-class children. The basis of such recognition is a strong classification between the context of the family and the context of the school. In our example the strong classification between the family and the school is a product of the symbolic power of the middle-class family. This power is translated into the child's power of recognition with its advantageous outcomes. . . . We can therefore set up a relationship between the principle of the classification and the *recognition rules* for identifying the specificity *or* the similarity of contexts. As the classification principle is established by power relations and relays of power relations, then recognition rules confer power relative to those who lack them. (Bernstein 2000: 104–5)

This illustrates how Bernstein typically attempts to refine his concepts by a process of 'translation' that drives concepts from initially abstract to increasingly more substantive forms such that they can be recognized and recovered in the world (effectively displayed at the beginning of the paper on visible and invisible pedagogies (Bernstein 1977: 116–20)). Hence, in the first instance, classification has to do with the degree of insulation between family and school (strong classification); but in order for this to be a differentially effective property of context, pupils must possess 'recognition rules' which identify the *specialized* character of the educational situation and its demand for an appropriate response (appropriate, that is, to the evaluation criteria operating in the school). Further, pupils must be equipped with the 'realization rules' that enable them to perform in the appropriate manner. Bernstein (2000: 106–8) describes work by Harry Daniels and others in which the concepts of recognition/realization rules are translated into research devices enabling their substantive investigation in the classroom—where these ideas can be recovered in terms of what teachers and pupils actually *do*. It is this feature of Bernstein's work that, in contrast to that of many other high theorists, enables it to ground such an impressive array of independent empirical research.

Bernstein (see above) describes *two* ways in which groups of pupils might be positively oriented towards the school context in the case of invisible pedagogies. The school might be recognized as either *similar* to the context of the home (weak classification between them) or in terms of its *specialized* character *vis-à-vis* the home (strong classification). It is the *recognition rule* that is important. Certain groups, at certain points in time, are *doubly* advantaged in that their children are symbolically equipped to operate effectively in both the progressive primary school (similar context, −C/−F) and the selective, academic secondary school (specialized context, +C/+F). These children are primarily those of the 'new' middle class, the 'agents of symbolic control'. Such children are able to recognize differences *between* contexts of different types and also to realize performances appropriate to criteria *within* contexts of different types (Power et al. 2003).

The subtlety of Bernstein's approach relates not so much to differences *between* classes, but to variations *within* classes and the ways in which those variations are contextually regulated. At no point, for instance (contrary to some interpretations), did he argue that working-class people speak only in a 'restricted' code, and middle-class people only in an 'elaborated' code favoured by the school. Rather, his concern was to identify the conditions under which members of different groups (class *fractions*) tend to realize restricting or elaborating variants and potentials—what are the orienting conditions whereby particular groups come to recognize the specialized features of *contexts* that call for elaborating discourses and how effectively can they meet the criteria (Bernstein 1973: chs. 8 and 9).

The distinction between elaboration and restriction relates to that between the explicit and the implicit, and to (Durkheimian) modes of sociality grounded in principles of difference and similarity. The 'restriction' upon restricted codes is not cognitive, but cultural and contextual: meaning is restricted to those 'in the know', who share basic cultural values, assumptions and understandings. Meanings can be conveyed in ways that are highly condensed symbolically, in few words or in gestures that 'speak volumes'. Formal religious ritual, for example, is an intensely condensed code through which complex layers of profound meaning can be conveyed through stylized gesture or display to those who *know* the rules. A lecture, by contrast, works by unpacking or expanding meaning, by making explicit (elaborating) what is unclear (from the point of view of the listeners): 'Today I am going to talk about Bernstein's concept of elaborated code. What he means by this is...' Ideally, the exposition progresses through moves that successively break down broad abstract concepts into constituent elements that enable the listeners to configure what they do know with what they formerly did not. What are differentially distributed between groups are the recognition and realization rules and orientations to meaning whereby they can successfully distinguish between that which can be assumed and taken for granted and that which is calling for a *demonstration* of understanding within a specialized context such as a classroom, tutorial or examination. These issues of recognition and realization become problematic for many children when the *ideology* of the pedagogy (as with progressivism) denies that such demands are being made, as if the child itself is free to be the 'author' of the text (Bernstein 2000: 110). In this respect, pedagogic processes regulate 'normativity' (Cladis 1999). The pedagogic regime requires continual display—display that is always measured against the calibration of the 'symbolic ruler'. But not all know that they are, in fact, on display!

Against the conventional view that aligns 'traditional' education (strong classification and framing) with the dominant classes and presents it as inherently conservative, and 'progressive' education (weak classification and framing) with the subordinated classes and presents it as inherently emancipatory, Bernstein's model produces a more nuanced perspective.

I argued that the conflict between visible and invisible forms was an ideological conflict between different fractions of the middle class about the forms of control. One fraction, located in the field of production, carried out functions directly related *to the economic base* of production, circulation and exchange. The other fraction was located in what I called the field of symbolic control. Members of this fraction related directly to *specialized forms of communication....* Agents of symbolic control could be said to control discursive codes, where as agents of production (circulation and exchange) dominate production codes. It also follows that agents of symbolic control could function in specialised agencies of symbolic control or in the economic field. Similarly agents of production could function in the economy or in specialised agencies of symbolic control (e.g. accountants, managers). I propose that location, hierarchical position in the field of symbolic control or in the economic field would regulate distinct forms of consciousness and ideology *within* the middle class. In essence I was distinguishing between a complex division of labour of symbolic control and a complex division of labour in the economic field. (Bernstein 1996: 112–13)

Bernstein's focus has mainly been on mapping intra-class variations and contradictory positionings (see also Bernstein 1977: ch. 8, and Bernstein 2001) of groups and families between the private and public sectors and between material and symbolic production and control. Progressivism (at least in the form it took in Britain in the 1960s and 1970s) comes to be seen as a pedagogy promoting the interests of new middle-class and *liberal* professional groups against those of both working-class and *managerial*-based middle-class fractions (Power et al. 2003). This is linked to the culturally conferred capacity of the children of these 'agents of symbolic control', with their expertise in 'specialized forms of communication', to successfully read (decode) the often contradictory and implicit messages of progressive pedagogy. That is, what these pupils possess is a capacity to see through appearances to that which is rendered ideologically or rhetorically *implicit* in invisible pedagogy—the demand for highly specialized performances by pupils requiring equally specialized recognition and realization rules, as expressed in *appropriate* forms of play, for example. They can 'see' the rules that *implicitly* regulate the pedagogy by virtue of principles tacitly acquired in the family, but which remain invisible to other children who lack such tacit cultural resources. By focusing upon (modelling) the *structure* of pedagogic discourse rather than *interpreting* its content (as in constructionist approaches), Bernstein reveals invisible pedagogy, in this particular form, to be a highly specialized code favouring and sponsored by the new middle class, rather than the universalistic, emancipatory project that it claims itself to be.

By contrast, visible pedagogies, precisely by making their rules explicit (even if the rules themselves are arbitrary), are *more* open and available to children from a variety of social backgrounds. The explicit character of the rules also clearly delineates the 'space' of consciousness that is the concern of the school. For example, in a 'traditional' pedagogy, there is strong classification and insulation between work and play, whereas in 'progressive' pedagogy—especially for young children—play (or, rather, a specialized construct of 'play') is a central category of the theory of learning and is incorporated into the field of the teacher's surveillance and evaluation of the child. In this respect, progressivism both extends the scope of education's regulation of the subject (its symbolic ruler) and intensifies its normative demands (Hargreaves 1989; Walkerdine 1984). Because the rules and criteria are *implicit* ('invisible'), they are not available to *all* pupils and their families in the same way. This concern with normativity in Bernstein's work parallels that in Foucault and, for both, that in Durkheim (Gephart 1999).

Bernstein's distinction between the relay and that which is relayed, and his theorization of the relations *within* pedagogic discourse, provide a critical model of relations *to* pedagogy that radically revalorizes the conventional ideological default settings of the curriculum debate. It calls into question received views of the relationships between particular pedagogies and social groups and the potentials of different pedagogies for emancipation or control. He rejects simple dichotomizing, essentialist models of curriculum and pedagogy, such as middle-class/working-class, male/female, black/white, etc., and the view that any given curriculum form has automatic effects by virtue of its *intrinsic* character. There is a *complex* interplay between pedagogic discourse and positioning.

Languages of Description and Knowledge Structures

Bernstein's method distinguishes between two qualitatively different (though not *radically* discontinuous) languages in theory and research (2000: ch. 7). On the one hand, there is the language of a theory itself—a language *internal* to it—and, on the other, the language that describes those things outside the theory within the field it investigates, an external language of description. Crucially, it must be possible to read one language in terms of the other—to specify what it is in the world that corresponds to terms and operations in the theory. It is within this space that Bernstein's theory is most methodologically demanding.

There must be a 'discursive gap' (Bernstein 2000: 125–6, 209) between the internal language of the theory and the language that describes things outside it (otherwise, as with constructionism or discourse theory, descriptions are merely circular, and theory simply constructs its own objects). This second language must not only be able to describe what is outside the theory in terms relevant *to* the theory, but also be capable of recognizing what is *beyond* the theory. It must submit to an external *ontological* imperative (the principle of ontological realism [...]) that allows that which is outside to 'announce itself' (ibid. 316) in such a way that the theory is independently tested against reality and open to systematic modification in the light of that testing—a principle of falsification. As Bernstein says in the interview with Solomon:

> When the model is referred to something other than itself, then it should be able to provide the principles which will identify that something as falling within the specification of the model and identify explicitly what does not so fall. Such principles we can call the *recognition rules* for identifying an external relevant something. However, this something will always generate, or have the capacity to generate, greater ranges of information than the model calls for. The *realisation rules* of the model regulate the descriptions of the something. They transform the information the something does, or can put out, the language of enactment, into data *relevant* to the model. However, if the realisation rules produce descriptions which are limited to transforming only that information into data *which at that time* appear consonant with the model, then the model can never change and the whole process is circular. Nothing exists outside the model. (Bernstein 2000: 209)

The discipline that Bernstein imposed upon his theory was exceptionally rigorous. Within the research context, this means designing research instruments that are sufficiently precise and robust that they can engage with data in such a way that (*a*) the theory can 'recognize' its concepts in the world, and (*b*) the world can 'announce' itself to the theory in such a way that the theory can be modified in the light of experience. Bernstein (2000: chs. 6 and 7) provides detailed examples of this method in practice from his own research and that of collaborators (see also Morais et al. 2001, especially the papers by Hasan (ch. 2), Daniels (ch. 4), Morais and Neves (ch. 8) and Singh (ch. 10)). Understanding the discipline imposed by the requirement of a 'discursive gap' between the internal and external 'languages of description' (of describing what is *outside* the theory in terms that can acknowledge what is *beyond* the theory) is central to understanding Bernstein's method, and also to locating his system within the broader context of current debates in social theory. It is precisely the discipline of the 'discursive gap' that is denied by constructionism and abandoned across a wide range of post-modern, feminist, multiculturalist and post-colonialist standpoint approaches. As the anti-realists say, 'there is nothing but the text'. For Bernstein, however, the quest for validity must extend, as Habermas puts it in a strikingly similar analysis in critique of Foucault, 'beyond the boundaries of the text' (Habermas 1995: 223; Moore and Muller 1999, 2002).

The distinction that Bernstein makes between those sociologies that treat education simply as a relay for forces outside it and that which is concerned to theorize the internal forms and principles of pedagogic discourse operate in different theoretical *modes* (Moore and Maton 2001). Essentially, 'relay' approaches, through reduction, redescribe education *empirically*: Bowles's and Gintis's correspondence principle is a device that takes the liberal account of education (as meritocratic, open, universalistic, etc.) and translates its language into an alternative set of terms (as anti-egalitarian, closed, particularistic). In a similar fashion, feminist accounts redescribe it as patriarchal, androcentric, sexist, etc. But these translations are at the *same* level—one empirical description replaces another. They operate through processes of alternative *interpretation*, rather than through modelling in the sense described above. Educational processes are not translated into a *theoretical* language the terms of which are internal to the theory itself. Liberal becomes 'bourgeois' or 'male', but not +C/+F or −C/−F. In reductionism, the mind, in Durkheim's terms, does not go 'outside itself' through theory, but takes a step to the side, as it were, and sees a familiar object from a less familiar angle—it claims that we have simply misrecognized the object; we thought it was one thing (a duck), in fact it is another (a rabbit). The *principles* of pedagogic discourse cannot be translated in this manner. They can *only* be expressed conceptually in terms that are discontinuous with empirical descriptors: e.g. the way that Bernstein produces the concept of 'invisible pedagogy' as −C/−F through a set of transformations that *begin* with an empirical description that is then theoretically translated into a term wholly conceptual in character, a term within an *internal* language of description.

Through the concepts of 'vertical' and 'horizontal knowledge structures' Bernstein (2000: ch. 9) provides a means of understanding these 'differences of modality in terms of the structuring (and possibilities) of intellectual fields. Initially, there are two observations to be made regarding these concepts. First, although they appear formally in his final volume, these ideas clearly have their descriptive origin in a paper from the early 1970s ('The sociology of education: a brief account'; Bernstein 1977: ch. 7). Secondly, it is interesting that Bernstein's fellow Durkheimian Randall Collins employs much the same language in *The Sociology of Philosophies* (2000). To begin with Collins:

> At times the density of debating factions floods the attention space with contending positions; this excess of horizontal density is fateful for the abstraction-reflexivity sequence too, because it generates epistemological scepticism. This faction takes the meta-stance of 'a plague on all houses', denying on reflexive grounds the very possibility of knowledge. This in turn provides a foil for a cognitive move, providing new transcendental grounding for epistemological-metaphysical systems. This 'horizontal' crowding of the network's collective conscience has a counterpart in the 'vertical' crowding which takes place if continuing factional wars are kept up across the generations. Such long-term debates drive up the abstraction-reflexivity sequence by raising the level of reflexivity concerning the categories of argument: names, universals, particulars, radical contingency. (Collins 2000: 845)

The condition of 'horizontal crowding' and 'epistemological scepticism' that Collins describes corresponds to the field of post-modernism and to post-structuralism's proliferation of hyphenated identities. In Bernstein's terminology, this is a 'horizontal knowledge structure with a weak grammar'. Bernstein (2000: ch. 9) makes two distinctions: (*a*) between vertical and horizontal *discourses*, and (*b*) between vertical and horizontal *knowledge structures*. The distinction between discourses has to do with that between 'common-sense' knowledge that is local, context-dependent, specific and tacit (essentially, that which operates with a *restricted* code) and vertical discourse that 'takes the form or a coherent, explicit and systematically principled structure, hierarchically organised as in the sciences, or it takes the form of a series of specialised languages with specialised modes of interrogation and specialised criteria for the production and circulation of texts as in the social sciences and humanities' (ibid. 157). Vertical discourse, consequently, entails the distinction between vertical and horizontal knowledge structures, and this difference, in turn, is expressed in terms of *strong* and *weak* grammar (Moore and Muller 2002).

The crucial difference between vertical and horizontal knowledge structures has to do with their relative capacities for *integration* and *abstraction* (the strengths of their 'grammar')—in Collins's terms, to generate 'abstraction-reflexivity sequences' in which knowledge is systematically integrated at successively higher levels of abstraction and generality. The exemplar of a vertical knowledge structure with a strong grammar is physics, and of a horizontal knowledge structure with a weak grammar, the sociology of education (Moore and Maton 2001). How is this so?

Bernstein illustrates the difference between the two structures visually (ibid. 161). The strong grammar form is represented by a triangle the apex of which signifies abstraction/integration. The weak form has a *segmented* structure—it is a series of cells, and in this respect reproduces the form of a horizontal *discourse* (where L = 'language'):

$$L^1L^2L^3L^4L^5L^6L^7\dots L^n$$

> Thus in the case of English Literature, the language would be the specialised languages of criticism, in Philosophy the various languages of this mode of inquiry, and in Sociology... the languages that refer for example to functionalism, post-structuralism, post-modernism, Marxism, etc. The latter are the broad linguistic categories and within them are the ideolects (theories) of particular favoured or originating speakers. *Horizontal Knowledge Structures, unlike Hierarchical Knowledge Structures* which are based on integrating codes, are based upon collection or serial codes; integration *of* language in one case and accumulation of *languages* in the other. (Bernstein 2000: 161–2)

In the earlier paper (1977) Bernstein refers to these 'broad linguistic categories' as 'approach paradigms' (p. 158). In this language and in the above, approaches are identified as theoretical perspectives. Today, they could be personified as the 'particular favoured or originating speakers' of post-modern discourse theory—in terms of the hyphenated identities of post-structuralism. These segmented knowledge forms with their specialized, and exclusive grammars are congenitally restricted in their capacities to generate cumulative, progressive knowledge integrated at successively higher levels of abstraction—in their post-modern version this possibility is systematically denied. Post-modern voice discourses can *proclaim* a position, but they create little 'news' (Bernstein 1977: 157). Under such conditions of 'horizontal crowding', it is not that more gets said, but that more come to say the same thing ('integration *of* language in one case and accumulation of *languages* in the other').

The manner in which Bernstein's theory *works* is represented in research by others across a range of areas. People *other* than Bernstein can take it, or aspects of it, and apply and develop it in their own ways for their own purposes. This capacity for the theory to detach itself from its originator has to do with the process of 'translation' whereby concepts at the most general theoretical level come to be systematically redefined as terms which engage with the world and which initiate a research process in which the world can 'announce' itself to theory. It is in this respect that Bernstein's thought stands out from that of so many other theoreticians.

Conclusion

This chapter has attempted a number of things: first, to examine the manner in which education is *central* to Durkheim's theoretical system and his project. This follows from the manner in which that project was concerned with sociologizing Kant. In order for the outer (principles of social order) to become inner (as the generative principles of consciousness), there must be a 'device' that achieves that transformation and structures the process whereby it is achieved and sustained over time—a *habitus*. Durkheim repeatedly points to this through distinctions concerning that 'more profound condition which determines the other [aspects of consciousness] and gives them their unity'. Within the complexity of his thinking, this condition is associated, on the one hand, with his 'duplex' model of the self and, on the other, with his determination to establish sociology as an autonomous science, and the social as a distinctive domain of the real. The way in which Durkheim places education at the centre of his system could, at the same time, be seen as placing Durkheim at the centre of the sociology of education through the sheer scale, ambition and originality of his thought. But, as Karabel and Halsey (1977) indicated, and as Bernstein was very much aware, this requires a major programme of recovery.

A second objective was to understand Durkheim in a manner that informs the sense in which Bernstein declared himself to be a Durkheimian, so as to better understand Bernstein himself. Bernstein's own project systematically conceptualized principles that are, as it were, at work below the surface of Durkheim's writing (in the way that *habitus* is), and to do so in such a way that those concepts could be refined into research devices that can engage with the world. His success in this respect, as measured by the quality and extent of the research inspired by his ideas, is remarkable.

Thirdly, in his concern with the 'voice' of pedagogy, he was not simply exploring a particular area of sociology of education, he was exploring it in a distinctive theoretical mode. In his last papers he began to construct a new theoretical language for analysing intellectual fields—fields of knowledge *production*. In doing so (in the distinctions between vertical and horizontal knowledge structures and strong and weak grammars), he was also producing a description of his own mode of theorizing (Moore and Muller 1999, 2002). This can be explicated through his accounts of the 'languages of description'. The sociology of education conducted in this Durkheimian/Bernsteinian manner indicates differences in the ways in which fields of knowledge production can be organized and *be* productive (Moore and Maton 2001). The broader context for these considerations is to be found in the underlying epistemological concerns [. . .].

The Changing Discourse of Assessment Policy: The Case of English Primary Education

Patricia Broadfoot and Andrew Pollard

[. . .]

Assessment, the 'Pedagogic Device' and Instrumentalism

From the outset of the PACE project[1], the work of Basil Bernstein (see Bernstein 1996) has proved particularly apposite as a framework for our theoretical interpretations. The capacity of Bernstein's conceptualization to embrace curriculum, pedagogy and assessment, and its concern with power, knowledge and consciousness as key variables, enabled us to successfully integrate the diverse perspectives of the PACE project. This integration has been achieved through the emergence of three core PACE themes, which we have identified as values, understanding and power. We have also used Bernstein's well-established concepts of the 'classification and framing of educational knowledge' to portray the inter-related trends that have taken place in primary schools over the period (Pollard et al. 1994).

The argument that schools, as well as teachers and pupils, are embedded in a dynamic network of personal identity, values and understandings (Pollard et al. 1994: 156) is central to the analysis of the PACE project. Personal identities, values and understandings 'are constantly developing in the light of internal and external interaction, pressure and constraints' (1994: 156) upon schools. Because of these dynamics, policy directives are translated into classroom practice through a series of 'mediations'. That is, at each successive stage of the process of delivering education, actors are involved in a process of creative reinterpretation. In this too, Bernstein's analysis of the power of pedagogy to define and control the reconceptualization of the original message provides a powerful theoretical model for examining the significance of the changes documented in the PACE data.

The overall findings from the PACE study suggests that, through the 1990s, teachers have become more instrumental, moving from a 'covenant' to a 'contract'-based work ethic. However, at the same time they appear to be preserving a good measure of their traditional personal and moral accountability. The findings also suggest that teachers have developed new curriculum expertise, while at the same time losing confidence in their ability to deliver. What then is the significance of these changes for primary pupils who are themselves also becoming more instrumental and 'performance'-oriented?[2] These pupils are all too aware of the hurdles that lie before them and the skills they must acquire if they are to jump them. We believe that as different controlling groups within the education system seek to accommodate the new requirements on them, through a series of mediations, they are gradually changing the discourse through which the ideology and practice of primary education is expressed. This process of mediation, shaping a changing educational discourse, is conceptualized by Bernstein in terms of the 'pedagogic device' which he describes as 'the symbolic ruler for consciousness—the fundamental system for both creating and controlling the unthinkable' (1996: 50). It is possible to use this concept of the 'pedagogic device' (or mediating process) to analyse the significance of the changes that have taken place in policy and in pedagogy, curriculum and evaluation.

Bernstein locates that discourse of primary education which is now being progressively eroded within a number of broad social science traditions of the 1960s. These had a common emphasis on 'competencies' and are characterized by a 'universal democracy of acquisition'. He cites, for example, the psychology of Piaget, the linguistics of Chomsky and the sociology of Garfinkel as instances of social scientific conceptualizations which in turn came to underpin the creation of educational approaches based on 'competencies'. These identified the subject as active and creative in the construction of a valid world of meaning and practice; and an educational approach which 'celebrated what we are rather than what we have become'. In such models, learning is conceptualized as accomplishments which are intrinsically creative and tacitly acquired, rather than instilled through formal instruction.

Radical as these educational ideas may seem, Bernstein argued that they found 'official' expression in the 1967 (DES) Report of the Plowden Committee, *Children and Their Primary Schools*, and in the next twenty years of primary school practice which the report's ideas profoundly shaped. He contrasts that 'competence'-based pedagogic model with one based on 'performance' which emphasizes a specific output from the acquirer, a particular text that the learner is required to construct and the acquisition of the specialized skills necessary to the creation of the required output. It is through the operation of explicit assessment procedures that learners will be made aware of the learning outcomes that will be valued. Their performance will in turn be a means of locating them in terms of a hierarchical judgement. In this power of assessment to control social and learning outcomes, we see the relevance of Bernstein's assertion that assessment is the 'purest form' of pedagogic control.

Tables 52.1 and 52.2 display, to contrastive effect, some important patterns related to 'liberal progressive' and 'performance' models. They are displayed in contrastive ways for analytic purposes, though of course the situation is more complex than this device allows. This form of modelling derives from Bernstein (1996: 58), though he is in no way responsible for our adaptation and extension. The characteristics of Bernstein's 'performance' pedagogic model are readily recognizable in the developments currently taking place in primary schools as documented by the PACE project. As Tables 52.1 and 52.2 illustrate, the increasingly tight classification of the curriculum into clearly delineated subjects; the growing strength of the framing of both teachers' and pupils' work so that they have less autonomy and choice; and the designation of times and spaces for particular purposes, are all clear indicators of the change towards a 'performance' pedagogic model.

The issues illustrated by the contrastive pedagogies in Tables 52.1 and 52.2 can be perceived to be embedded in two interrelated educational discourses. That is, they reflect a 'regulative discourse' (concerned with the creation of social order) and an 'instructional discourse' (Bernstein 1996). Changes in these 'regulative' and 'instructional' discourses are perhaps most powerfully brought into being through changes in assessment practices. Thus recent profound changes to the language and practices associated with 'levels' and 'standards' in the evaluation of pupils, and with 'target setting', 'league tables' and 'value added' in the evaluation of schools, can be expected to create, through the 'regulative' discourse, profound changes in the social order, in social relations and social identities. Through the 'instructional' discourse, a change in such assessment language and practices can be expected to create changes in the ways in which particular knowledge and skills are inculcated.

The PACE data reflects just such a gradual but inexorable change in both the 'regulative' and 'instructional' discourses of English primary education. The concepts, vocabulary, perceptions, concerns and commitments of primary school teachers have been changing through the decade. While

Table 52.1 Some contrastive aspects of competence and performance models in relation to schools and teachers

	A 'competence model' LIBERAL PROGRESSIVE EDUCATION	*A 'performance model' PERFORMANCE EDUCATION*
Schools and teachers	*'Invisible management' with relative professional autonomy*	*'Visible management' with relative professional regulation*
Organizational form	Professional, with flat management structure. Control through self-regulation, socialization and internalization of norms.	Mechanistic, with hierarchical structure and bureaucracy. Standardization for control and co-ordination.
Management style	Collegiate, with emphasis on proficiency, dialogue and consensus. Informality in relationships.	Managerial, with emphasis on efficiency and target setting for results. Greater formality in relationships.
Teacher roles	Teachers as facilitators, with affective dimensions seen as intrinsic to the teaching role.	Teachers as instructors and evaluators, with emphasis on cognitive and managerial skills.
Teacher professionalism	Professional covenant based on trust, and commitment to education as a form of personal development. Confidence and sense of fulfilment and spontaneity in teaching.	Professionalism is the fulfilment of a contract to deliver education, which is seen as a commodity for individuals and a national necessity for economic growth. Teacher confidence and fulfilment are less.
Teacher accountability	Personal and 'moral' accountability.	External and contractual accountability.
Whole school co-ordination	Relative autonomy and informal teacher collaboration.	Formal school planning with 'contrived' collegiality.
Economic costs	Expensive, because of sophisticated teacher education and time-consuming school practices.	Cheaper, because of more explicit teacher training and systematized school practices.

imposed assessment practices were once an affront to their values, professionalism and sense of self, they are increasingly seen as a taken for granted part of the job, with the achievement of 'targets' becoming a new vehicle for self-satisfaction and professional fulfilment.

Whither Lifelong Learning?

One interesting aspect of the performance discourse concerns whether it is consistent with the New Labour government's other educational aims and policies. This may be examined in terms of two broad issues.

First, it can be argued that there is a deep tension between the rhetoric of the much vaunted 'learning society' and the reality of the 'performance' culture which is being promoted by current policy making and by the accountability requirements which are being placed on schools.

The educational ideology of the learning society is one in which learners are empowered to want and be able to manage their own learning in an individualistic manner; where there will be more openness and opportunity and fewer prescribed spaces and times for learning, or defined outcomes or prescribed bodies of knowledge. One manifestation of this is a 1998 set of proposals from the Labour government on lifelong learning, *The Learning Age: A Renaissance for a New Britain* (DFEE 1998). However, we believe that the call for resilient and flexible learners, whose intrinsic motivation and mastery orientation will provide the foundation of future national economic and social development, is in tension with the systemic, performance-oriented changes which are being strengthened within the schools system. As was argued in a paper for the National Curriculum agency (Pollard 1997), the aims and structure of the National Curriculum for primary schools could helpfully be reconceptualized to enable teachers to achieve a new balance between basic skills, subject knowledge, learning dispositions and personal, social and moral development. Our analysis of the broad trends of change in primary education suggests that, if the performance orientation

Table 52.2 Some contrastive aspects of competence and performance models in relation to classrooms and pupils

	A 'competence model' *LIBERAL PROGRESSIVE EDUCATION*	*A 'performance model'* *PERFORMANCE EDUCATION*
Classroom and pupils	*'Invisible pedagogies', with weak classification and frame*	*'Visible pedagogies', with strong classification and frame*
Autonomy	Considerable.	Limited.
Space	Flexible boundaries and use.	Explicit regulation.
Time	Flexible emphasis on present experiences.	Strong structuring, sequencing and pacing.
Activity	Emphasis on the realization of inherent learner capabilities through subject-integrated and learner-controlled activities, such as projects.	Strong control over selection of knowledge and explicit promotion of specialized subjects and skills.
Evaluation	Emphasis on immediate, present qualities using implicit and diffuse criteria.	Emphasis on inadequacies of the product using explicit and specific performance criteria.
Control	Relatively 'invisible', with control inhering in interpersonal communications and relationships.	Explicit structuring and systems for classification and differentiation through instruction.
Pupil products	Pupil products are taken to indicate a stage of cognitive, affective or social development. Teachers 'read' and interpret learner products using specialized professional judgement and knowledge.	Pupil products are simply taken to indicate performance, as objectified by grades. Teachers instruct and assess using established procedures and criteria.
Pupil learning	Highlighting intrinsic motivation and encouraging mastery orientation. Potential for 'deep learning', but tendency to produce routinization and evasion.	Highlighting performance orientation. Tendency to produce instrumentalism and 'surface learning' or learned helplessness and withdrawal.

underpinned by high-stakes assessment continues to dominate, it may become increasingly difficult to encourage many pupils to adopt positive dispositions to learning. A narrow performance orientation, while satisfying short-term indicators, may thus have the unintended consequence of actually undermining longer term dispositions to learn through life, especially for those who are least successful in the current system. Ironically, it is just such school 'underperformers' that the lifelong learning initiatives are particularly designed to address.

Second, the trend that we have identified suggests the likelihood of growing tensions in the social fabric and towards the social exclusion of certain groups. This appears to be coming about as the instrumental 'performance'-oriented means to the end (of economic performance) becomes elevated into the end in itself. In such circumstances, society begins to lack any more fundamental basis for social solidarity than mutual competitiveness (Broadfoot 1996). We can already see some of these tensions manifest in contemporary debates about discipline in schools, crime and moral decline and in a climate in which schools increasingly feel the need to exclude certain pupils and compete with their neighbours for others. This climate of competitiveness and social polarization is reflected in PACE evidence that points to teachers' increasing concern about the performance and behaviour of children from particular social groups.

In short, both in its own terms of raising standards for the purposes of economic competitiveness and in relation to more profound issues of social solidarity, the current 'performance' emphasis, which is an increasingly defining feature of English schooling, may ultimately prove to be seriously counter-productive.

Conclusion

The PACE study as a whole has focused on a particular sector of English society, primary education, which is located within the broader sweep of history and social, cultural, economic and political change as we engage with new forms of modernity and postmodernity. Within the multi-faceted design of the PACE study, one particular focus echoes that of this book as a whole in being concerned with assessment as a social product. In this, it is seen as being moulded and fashioned by the ebb and flow of historical tradition, cultural assumptions and the changing social and economic and political contexts of English society at the [beginning] of the [third] millennium. In this chapter, our particular concern has been with assessment policy. We have [referred to] some of the factors that have underpinned its recent evolution in the English context and the impact these policy changes have had on primary schools. The focus of our discussion has been the significance for pupils' learning of the new priorities now being required in primary schools. Of course, English primary schools were formerly famous for their embrace of a very different ideological tradition, but these have now been forced to come to terms with the imposition of assessment practices which embody fundamentally different assumptions about both the means and ends of education.

Above all, our analysis has focused on the significance of policy developments, not just for the immediate future of English primary schooling but in terms of the educational project as a whole, its role in society and its potential capacity to meet the challenges of a rapidly changing world. We have argued, in the words of Gray, that:

> the rhetoric about 'driving up standards' can be read as an attempt to realign education to the commodity values that increasingly define worthwhile or legitimate knowledge in post-industrial societies', i.e. 'the task of education is not the dissemination of a general model of life, not to transform students' minds but to supply the system with the merchandise it needs in the form of information and skills. (Gray 1990: 10)

We have progressed, almost imperceptibly, beyond the concerns articulated in the 'Great Debate' in England in the 1970s about standards and the need for more accountability within the education system. Indeed, the development of assessment as a policy device has also gone significantly beyond its role as a means of holding schools (and other institutions) accountable for educational standards. Nor is the concern fundamentally about raising standards, as central as this discourse apparently appears to be in current policy initiatives. Rather, we have entered an era in which the use of a particular application of assessment policy has led to a fundamental redefinition of the goals of education itself in terms of economic commodity values. As a result, it is becoming increasingly difficult for any of the players in the system even to articulate an alternative set of priorities, an alternative vision of desirable educational outcomes. As Elliott (1996: 76) suggests, contemporary assessment policies have played a central role in 'changing the rules which shape educational thought and practice. They are part of a language game which serves the interests of power and legitimates those interests in terms of the performativity criterion.' As a result, he suggests, 'the more marginalized and silenced are the voices who would articulate, given the social space to do so, a different vision of quality in education, of the pedagogical conditions which make it possible.'

To the extent that such voices are silenced, however, the likelihood of developing the type of educational institution that is needed to foster 'lifelong learning for all' is correspondingly reduced. In this chapter we have presented data that begin to suggest that the growing 'performance' orientation of English primary schools may lead to a substantial number of learners who are put off the business of learning at a relatively young age by the experience of failure. It is a pattern that is likely to be repeated at the level of secondary and higher education. Yet institutions find themselves increasingly powerless to remedy the situation, condemned as they are to pursue perpetually those elusive learning outcomes which form the basis of 'league tables' and other external quality assessments on which they will be judged.

This book as a whole explores the socio-cultural origins and implications of assessment practice. It does so through the successive contexts of policy formation, technological development, classroom practice and the lived experiences and perceptions of those who are assessed. The particular goal of this chapter has been to demonstrate that the current English obsession with a performance assessment policy is not, and cannot be, simply the application of a neutral technology: that tests are not 'valid irrespective of human expectation, ideas attitudes and wishes' (Feyerabend 1987: 5) but rather must be understood as a 'social technology' (Madaus 1994) rooted in contemporary power relations. Citing Hanson (1993), Madaus writes: '"They [tests and assessments] are not, and cannot be, measures or indicators of some purely objective, independently-existing state of affairs" writes Hanson, rather they "act to transform, mould and even to create, what they supposedly measure"' (Madaus 1994: 222; see also chapters 3–4).

Thus as a policy device, the growing recourse to measures of 'performativity' (Lyotard 1979) has had, first the effect of silencing alternative voices concerning the goals of education and how these goals may best be achieved. Second, when translated into practice, these policies mould individuals' views of themselves, both as learners and as people more generally in defining notions of success and failure and the reasons for it.

Thus, at the very moment when public education needs to break free of its familiar organizing principles and assumptions if it is to respond to the opportunities and challenges of the information revolution, it has become subjugated as never before to the educational assumptions of an earlier, modernist, industrial age. At the very time when the traditional role of educational assessment in providing for selection, legitimation and control needs to be replaced by an emphasis on assessment to support 'lifelong learning', there seems less chance than ever of such a change being realized. At present this contradiction lies largely buried beneath the rhetorical weight of the 'standards' agenda. Sooner or later, however, the tensions inherent in the profound changes in assessment discourse that have taken place in recent years will become apparent. The PACE study has revealed the beginning of the story; it is difficult to predict the end.

NOTES

1. The Primary Assessment, Curriculum and Experience (PACE) project was established in 1989 to monitor educational change in primary schools. It was funded by the Economic and Social Research Council (UK) in three phases: 1989–92; 1992–94; 1994–97.
2. It is important to note that the terms 'performance' and 'competence' as used by Bernstein (1996) and in this chapter have distinctly different meanings from those associated with 'performance' (authentic) and 'competence' testing as more generally understood in the field of assessment and as used elsewhere in this book.

The Framing of Performance Pedagogies: Pupil Perspectives on the Control of School Knowledge and Its Acquisition

Madeleine Arnot and Diane Reay

It should be quite clear that the specific application of the concepts [of classification and framing] requires at every point empirical evidence . . . . We have, for example, little first-hand knowledge which bears upon aspects of framing.

(Bernstein, 1977: 112, original emphasis and our addition)

There are few developed sociological theories of learning that can successfully combine an analysis of the social relationships of the classroom with the processes of learning acquisition. Bernstein's theory of pedagogy is unique in formulating connections between the organization and structuring of knowledge, the means by which it is transmitted, and the ways in which acquisition is experienced. Here we use Bernstein's theoretical concepts to begin to understand the nature of pupils' pedagogic experiences in contemporary English education. We consider the significances for pupil learning of the imposition of a state-regulated national curriculum and a market-oriented pedagogy (Bernstein 1990). Drawing on findings from research in two differently organized and located state secondary schools, we suggest that the control over classroom learning associated with these educational reforms has privileged those who have already had the advantage of being able to exercise discretion within strongly controlled environments. Even within the strongly framed contexts, such as that now found in English secondary education, there are spaces in which the most successful can gain control of their learning. Yet those pupils who most need to be supported in their learning are likely to find the least opportunities for so doing in this highly structured environment. The consequences of the strong framing of the English version of performance pedagogy becomes the mechanism for sustaining rather than reducing class and gender inequalities.

The Restructuring of English Secondary Education: Market-Oriented Performance Pedagogies

Bernstein's analysis of neo-liberal reforms of schooling draws heavily upon his theory of pedagogic transmission that he developed over a period of twenty years. Mainstream sociology of education, in his view, was seriously constrained in its analysis of the depth of social stratification and inequality by the fact that it 'rarely turned its attention to the analysis of the intrinsic features constituting and distinguishing the specialised form of communication realised by the pedagogic discourse of education'. He commented:

> Many of the analyses of the sociology of education, especially those carried out by the diverse group of theories of reproduction, assume, take for granted, the very discourse which is subject to their analysis. These theories, in particular, see pedagogic discourse as a medium for other voices: class, gender, and race. The discourses of education are analysed for their power to reproduce dominant/dominated relations external to the discourse but which penetrate the social relations, media of transmission, and evaluation of pedagogic discourse. It is often considered that the voice of the working class is the absent voice of pedagogic discourse, but ... what is absent from pedagogic discourse is its own voice. (Bernstein 1990: 165)

If pedagogic discourse is seen as only a relay for patterns of discourse external to itself then its form has no consequences for what is relayed. As a result, 'theories of culture reproduction are essentially theories of communication without a theory of communication' (ibid. 170).

Bernstein's own analysis of 'the inner structure of the pedagogic' offers such a theory of communication. Drawing on an important Parsonian distinction between the expressive and instrumental orders (Bernstein 2000: 102) he developed an understanding of the ways in which the moral order and the instructional order work in the context of the school, and the relationship between them. He made the important distinction between *what* is and *how* it is transmitted. Initially he referred to these elements as the classification and framing of knowledge which together make up an educational code (Bernstein 1977). By the 1990s, Bernstein had developed these concepts further. The classification of knowledge was now referred to as the *instructional discourse* and framing was defined as the *regulative discourse* (the rules of the social order which frame order, conduct, character, manner, relations, and identity (Bernstein 2000: 13). By separating out the rules which govern the instructional from the regulative discourse, the transmission of knowledge from the transmission of the moral order, Bernstein offered researchers the possibility of analysing the complex different social class assumptions built into different aspects of pedagogic practice and the possibility of mapping empirically significant shifts in pedagogy and its 'products'.

Initially the concept of framing only referred to the degrees of control which teachers or pupils had over the mode of transmission (the ways in which knowledge was being taught and learnt) but, in his later writings, Bernstein developed the concept of framing so as to focus on the teacher–pupil relationship and its role in 'creating the pedagogic arena, game ... or specific practice' (Bernstein 2000: 180). In his final volume, Bernstein (2000) moved 'from rules which distinguish the practice to the *particular* interactional practice and its *specific locational and communicative realisations*'. Framing in his view came to represent the 'inner logic' of a pedagogy (Bernstein 1990: 63), determining how knowledge was to be transmitted. As a result, it plays a critical role in his understanding of how social class inequalities are both shaped, affected, and resisted within the processes of learning (not just within the processes of educational distribution). He therefore explored in great detail the social class assumptions which underlay strong and weak versions of framing (Bernstein 1990, 2000). He privileged the role of the regulative discourse in which instructional discourses were embedded in his theory of social class reproduction within the English educational system.[1]

Bernstein argued that the English education system had previously been distinguished from the mainstream European models by its strong classification but weaker framing (Bernstein 1977: 98). Historically, pupils in the UK had been allowed more discretion and negotiation in relation to their learning than those found in central European systems but since the 1990s, the English educational system has now shifted far more towards the strong state control of pedagogy found in other European systems (Bernstein 1990: 85). This new form of visible pedagogy is strongly associated with 'selective class based acquisition'—in this case, with those fractions of the middle classes located within the field of economic production (entrepreneurial professions and those opposed to rises in public expenditure) and with a swing back from the invisible competence-based pedagogies of the 1970s associated with the new middle classes in the field of symbolic control. Although the entrepreneurial/capital classes are not dependent upon such pedagogies for their privilege, nevertheless such pedagogies especially with their emphasis on performance in national assessments provided, whether unintentionally or not, opportunities for the 'reproduction and advancement' of this class fraction.

Whilst the principles of classification are still as strong as those represented by the traditional grammar school curriculum, neo-liberal and neo-conservative reforms of schooling introduced in the Education Reform Act (1988) has led to the strengthening of framing. This can be seen in the explicit principles of selection, sequencing, and criterial/assessment rules found in the state-controlled programmes of study for main subjects, the normative assumptions built into QCA lesson schemes, and the tight sequencing rules (what is learnt in which order) applied through national assessments. The use of national league tables based upon success in GCSE examination performance puts added pressure on schools and teachers to ensure that pupils' learning is in line with government expectations.

The new pedagogic practices that have been put in place are a complex market-oriented visible pedagogy which, Bernstein argues, appears to address left critiques of neo-liberalism and unequal educational systems whilst at the same time meeting the needs of the capitalist formation for a communicative society and a flexibilization of learning a veritable 'pedagogic janus' (Bernstein 1990: 87). The new performance pedagogies offer a confusing, almost schizoid pedagogic regime which introduces extensive, seemingly democratic choices for parents while encouraging individual ownership through student profiles, life skills courses, etc. Bernstein located the hybrid model of schooling within a range of performance-based pedagogic modes.[2] Key to such performance-based models are strongly classified space, time, and discourse, explicit forms of control, performance as the pedagogic text, different degrees of autonomy, and a low-cost schooling. Evaluation of student's work (the text) is explicit and has to meet certain criteria. The key for pupils was to learn how to recognize or realize what constitutes a legitimate text especially since evaluations are often based on what is missing from the text.[3] These structuring principles which have the effect of differentiating and dividing learners, however, are often hidden in the rhetoric of what is euphemistically called 'independent learning' or what the UK government is now calling 'personalized'. Behind this socially neutral rhetoric is likely to be found the social stratification of learners.

Beck (1999), Bourne (2000), and Moss (2004) have explored various aspects of this regime. Beck, for example, highlighted the shift it represented between knowledge and the knower through a dehumanizing and more secular pedagogic approach. Knowledge is thus 'divorced from persons, commitments and personal dedication, separated from inwardness' and the inner self. It becomes competences and skills which are meant to be transferable into different market settings but without personal meaning. Moss (2004) uncovers the elements of the National Literacy strategy which restructure teachers' work, reducing both teachers' and students' control over the selection and pacing of knowledge, while Bourne (2000) outlines the development of a new pedagogic culture in creating new definitions of literacy.

Bernstein speculated about the consequences for marginalized and disadvantaged groups of such strong framing within a performance model of schooling. On the one hand, strong *external* frames of pedagogy by the state (such as we have seen in England) are likely to aggravate social disadvantage: 'social class may play a crucial role ... where the external frames are strong it often means that images, voices and practices the school reflects make it difficult for children of marginalised classes to recognise themselves in the school' (Bernstein 2000: 5). Similarly, the strengthening of *internal* framing of performance pedagogy is likely to hinder the academic progress of such children. The key element of strong framing here is the element of pacing (Bernstein 1990). Greater teacher control over the pacing of learning is encouraged through the pressure which school inspectors (Ofsted) bring to bear. The quality of teachers' practice is judged in part in terms of the pacing of their lessons and the successful acquisition of pre-ordained knowledge. Such is the strength of pacing that new initiatives such as the Literacy hour even provide a diagrammatic clock which teachers are expected to adhere to when teaching the programme (Moss 2004).

Bernstein's analysis of shifts in educational policy is central to our project on the social conditions of learning. We employ his concept of framing to investigate the social consequences of contemporary performance pedagogies in two educational sites. Using two secondary schools with different political and pedagogic histories, we explore the ways in which different groups of male and female, higher- and lower-achieving pupils from different social and ethnic backgrounds currently experience learning. Pupils' accounts reveal the 'nature of social relationships' which are associated with these new framings of educational knowledge—the forms by which the curriculum is made public. Of especial concern are the different degrees of control which learners have over the pedagogic 'communication and its social base'.

Research Context and Design

The two secondary schools in which we conducted our research differ substantially in ideological ethos and in pupil organization. Nevertheless both have been affected by the strengthening of the framing of educational knowledge. Each school, although from very different starting points and trajectories, has had to introduce the increasing 'tight framing' of performance pedagogies, geared to nationally assessed performance goals.

The delivery of the National Curriculum and its standardized assessments, while not easy, was always likely to be less problematic for Greenfield school, located in a predominantly white city. Grammar school traditions were part of its history and the presence particularly of the professional middle-class students meant that successful educational results could be achieved. The strongly framed instructional discourse in this school which organized its pupils into ability sets (groups) for different subjects provided a relatively strongly framed regulative discourse even though the resulting stratification of learners was masked by the emphasis on individualized and independent learning. In contrast, the teaching of a strongly segmental curriculum in a predominantly working-class and multi-racial urban secondary school which we call Mandela was highly disruptive of its ethos. Since 1988, the school's traditionally weak framing with its egalitarian concerns has had to respond with a stronger discourse of regulation. The pupils here were taught in mixed ability classes, with only limited differentiation of learners. Teachers in this school spoke with anxiety about the consequences of the imposition of state-controlled curriculum and pedagogy, and new testing regimes on social inequalities on working-class pupils who came to the realization that trying hard was no longer enough to ensure that they did well.

Using Bernstein's framework, we set out to elicit pupil voices, not as independent (client) assessors who might expose underlying social practices, but rather as products of the educational codes operating within the school. Our project involved the creation of discussion groups of male and female, higher- and lower-achieving pupils (aged 12–13 years) from different ethnic and class backgrounds. The aim was to hear collective rather than individual voices, using the categories often relayed through pedagogic discourse itself (see Reay and Arnot 2004 for a reflexive account of methodology). At a later point we observed and interviewed individual pupils in English and Maths classes and asked the teachers to build in strategies of pupil consultation in their lessons (ibid.)

In Arnot and Reay (forthcoming 2005) we suggest that the sort of pupil voice we elicited could be called 'code talk'.[4] We asked pupils to tell us about the social conditions of their schooling—the regulative discourse which frames their instruction—by describing the ways in which they experienced their own learning and their confidence in themselves as learners, their sense of social inclusion in the classroom, and the degree to which they felt they could control their learning. Pupils tried therefore to express their understanding of the principles which governed their learning, and the moments of conflict, negotiation, engagement, and disengagement. Put sociologically, their 'code talk' illuminated the tension between transmission of knowledge within contemporary classrooms and the possibilities of their own agency.

As Bernstein (2000) argued, the social/moral order of the school 'is prior to and a condition for, the transmission of competences'. We are interested therefore in the role of social class, ethnic, and gender relations in embedding the contemporary instructional discourse associated with performance pedagogies and how the principles which regulate the selection and transmission of educational knowledge are experienced by these different groups. Below we present a small slice of our findings. We begin our analysis by focusing on the degrees of control different groups of pupils feel they have over the curriculum content and their degrees of freedom to negotiate their own learning.

Pupils' Understandings of the Principles Governing the Selection of Knowledge

As Bernstein (1977: 99) asserts, 'educational knowledge is uncommonsense knowledge ... freed from the particular, the local through the various languages of the sciences and forms of reflexiveness of the arts which make possible either the creation or the discovery of new realities'. Of central importance in the pedagogical relationship is the relationship between the 'uncommonsense knowledge' of the school and the 'commonsense knowledge, every day community knowledge of the pupil, his [*sic*] family and his peer group' (ibid.). The criteria for selection of knowledge and the evaluation of knowledge and successful acquisition (realization) places great emphasis, particularly today upon the attainment of 'states of knowledge rather than ways of knowing' (ibid. 98). Strong classifications of the sort found in the National Curriculum ensure that pupils are socialized not just into the appropriate forms of knowledge but also into the boundaries, hierarchies, and forms of identity which position individuals within specialized discourses.

When we asked groups of secondary pupils in Greenfield and in Mandela who they thought controlled the school curriculum, they revealed their understanding of the strength of framing associated with government control over teachers' work, and teachers' control over pupil learning. All the Greenfield pupils in our study experienced the overt power of the teacher to regulate the curriculum and the ways in which it was taught because of the form of pupil organization. Whilst some pupils were critically reflective about the constraints on teachers themselves (strong external framing), most pupils thought the source of authority rested with teachers themselves. The experience of strong framing over the selection of knowledge, however, did not necessarily generate similar or identical responses from different groups of pupils. Ability, gender, and ethnicity worked in complex ways in shaping the strategies pupils used to relate to what was seen as the teachers' transmission project. All, however, recognized the power relations embedded in the structure and content of the curriculum.

Higher-achieving boys and girls, for example, were clear about who controlled what to learn, and whether what was selected was of value. However, where the former talked about the fact that teachers had not let them decide what to work on, the latter seemed more aware of teachers' position *vis-à-vis* the government (external framing). Although, schools had some discretion in their view in terms of the 'softer subjects' such as RE and PSE and in determining the length of lessons, these girls saw teachers were viewed as 'working to a set plan', they were assumed to be as strongly controlled as were pupils. When asked about who controlled what they learnt, they responded thus:

Alice: The government I guess
Jenny: yeah, the government ...
Caroline: The teachers?
Q: You think the teachers? The government?
Caroline: Well I guess the teachers get it across in a different way but the government, yes

Rebecca: I think the school plays a part in it as well because some schools don't do PSE . . .

Alice: Some schools don't do RE

Jenny: I think the school does play a part but there . . . like every school has to do English and Maths and Science. Every school has to do that and that's the government whose given the rule and then the school is like given the opportunity to make the lessons shorter or longer and stuff like that.

However, the idea that the state controls learning conflicts with the view promoted by the school that pupils are responsible for their own learning. The discussions of a group of low- to medium-achieving (mainly middle-class) girls on the balance of power between government, the teaching profession, and their own independence is illuminating. Kelly introduced the idea that pupils themselves can control what they learn by co-operating or not with the school agenda. Control of learning was discretionary on co-operation (an awareness in Bernsteinian terms that the instructional discourse was at the mercy to some extent of social relations). The reality of the setting structure (strong framing) is juxtaposed with her belief in the principle of pupil agency and choice. Jemima, on the other hand, sees pupils' lack of power:

Kelly: I think the government has a little tiny inch but we have that much to decide what we do. If we want to be naughty and not do nothing and just do like . . . if we really know what we're doing if we concentrated and really tried our hardest we could be in the top set.

Jemima: No offence to Kelly or anything but I disagree. I think the teachers like, the teachers and government decide our education so we don't go to miss, to our teachers and say 'Can we have drama for all six periods . . . all the lessons and go the next day'. 'Oh do we have to do maths today? Can we have drama again?'

Later in the discussion, Jemima moved to agree with Kelly *''cos you're the one who's doing the work . . . and you're like the one who's writing it down and everything'*. The tensions between pupil agency and government and teacher control were clearly difficult for them:

Kelly: I agree with Jemima there. I do think that we . . . it's up to us. Nobody made our lives, nobody says you have to think this and you have to think that, it's your own mind. You're allowed to think what you want but I do agree, you don't say 'Oh I am allowed to do this today! Like you're a queen and you have stuff done at your feet 'cos nobody does . . .

The girls also perceived that, although teachers had the power to determine the curriculum, if they had not got anything planned for the lesson, they might offer pupils choice over activities. Yet these choices (moments of weaker framing) are illusionary, since, as the girls notice, teachers set the knowledge terrain and the choices were proscribed by external structures. As Claire commented: 'If we have to choose A B or C, we don't have a choice obviously in the work, its just A, B and C.' Criticisms of the 'teacher's choice' of subject matter ranged from its parochial perspective to 'boringness':

Emily: It's very Christian.

Victoria: It's so much about here, Britain. The history, language, geography—we should do other stuff.

Claire: Boring, art is boring, boring, boring. Art is not what you are given but what you want to do.

These views were not similar to those put forward by the three Muslim girls, who clearly saw that not only were teachers in control of what they learnt, but that they should be.

Joti: it's her who decides because she is the one who is teaching you.

When it came to the evaluation of knowledge itself, pupils revealed the tensions between instrumentality (relevance) and interesting/boring (fun) criteria. Higher-achieving boys and girls at both Mandela and Greenfield thought that teachers might keep control about what is worth learning, but they also argued that the knowledge should be related to pupils' interests. In Greenfield, Robert comments that 'maybe there's a good deal of trust' about letting teachers decide what should be learnt at school. But at the same time, he admitted to liking academic topics such as history lessons about Henry VII and Henry VIII.

The context in which control could be delegated to teachers for these boys was school knowledge that was considered interesting. The most academically successful boys at Mandela also mentioned art as interesting 'all of the time'; 'science is quite interesting because you get to do experiments' (Timi); 'French, games and PE and drama's good most of the time because you get to act' (Hasmi);

'technology's good too' (Timi). Although knowledge gleaned outside school could also be just as important: 'Like Pokemon you learn hand–eye co-ordination and making your brain quicker, stuff like that, that's just as important.'

At Greenfield, a more instrumental approach to knowledge appeared important to higher-achieving pupils, especially if linked to university education. Maths, English, and IT were considered relevant to jobs in the future, backed by parental assertions that they had to work hard at these subjects to guarantee 'a certain job' as an adult. Concerns about relevance, however, were also shaped by many criticisms. High-achieving girls, for example, expressed doubts that the knowledge they were being taught prepared them adequately for a high technological world.

Rebecca: I suppose for later life, but you know, like in history and like the humanities sorts of things and obviously maths and English are relevant and stuff but in like some of the lessons you just think what's this got to do with anything?

Alice: Like when I came home on the first day when we got home the first day and I had my timetable I said to my mum. 'We only do IT once a fortnight and we do drama twice a fortnight' and my mum said that doesn't make sense because IT . . . computers is going to be really, really important in the future as we are already using them a lot and drama—it's important to like express yourself but it's not as important as IT which is going to help you in the future . . .

A much deeper ambivalence towards curricular knowledge was expressed particularly by working-class boys. Although some boys, such as Carl, could see the value of studying history if you want to become an archaeologist, there was much debate about the school emphasis on English and music:

Carl: They don't tell you anything about the outside world. Because you are in school and they teach you one times one is one. And they teach you all the maths and all the English but you should already know English from our parents but like, in maths . . . The maths is OK but the English, you should know English and why do you need to read a book? I mean it's not exactly important.

Sean: It is.

Neil: They can teach you how to read because you might need that later on and like, what's the point of music? I mean there's not many people who want to do music when they get older.

There are glimmers of oppositional stances to mainstream educational discourses which sanctify school-based knowledge. Craig agreed: 'Because if you learn one thing and that then you get so good at one and then go to . . . and you try and get a job of it and then you don't and you think "What was the point of that?"' They wanted more practical knowledge linked to employment; however, if not, there is always leisure-based knowledge:

Kenny: A lot of what you learn in school isn't relevant, like it doesn't help you with your life.

Andy: Like you learn loads of important stuff out of school like catchphrases and stuff off the television and how to improve your football skills.

Jason: And technology things and I'm learning Chinese.

Paul: I'm learning to do tricks on bikes. BMXing.

The only time these working-class boys at Mandela articulated a positive relationship to school knowledge was to valorize the active, stressing those aspects of learning which engage the body as well as the mind:

Andy: Drama's still fun but most of the other work is boring.

George: Yeah, drama's good.

Andy: It's mostly acting and there's more focus on doing something rather than writing something down and copying from a book.

George: Yeah, you get to move around and do stuff so that's more fun.

It is almost as if school-based learning is only acceptable in disguised forms. Learning has to be served up as if it is not learning for these boys to take any pleasure in it. Competition was important for these working-class boys but only if disarticulated from serious study and converted into less threatening 'fun and games'. As Craig commented: 'And they should make it more fun. Like about history. Blackadder[5] or something like that. And they never show it.' Learning here is constituted for boys as a competition they have to win, posing problems in particular for working-class, low-achieving boys. As they assert, this results in a self-sabotaging scenario of 'can't win, won't win, and don't want to play'.

Of central importance to this discussion then is the value which pupils ascribed to the forms of school knowledge. Most pupils in Greenfield sought instrumental value in the relevance of school curriculum to adult life and a changing world. As in

Mandela, working-class boys challenged the value of school knowledge, its relevance for adult work. In contrast, middle-class girls and boys tended to both recognize and be able to work with and negotiate the curriculum as given, although in the case of the middle-achieving girls' group, such negotiation depended more on personal mood rather than status or coercion. For many pupils the curriculum was something served up by teachers and government that they themselves had little control over, and, in particular for the working-class pupils, was perceived to be of limited relevance to their everyday lives.

Pupils' Experience of Boundary-Maintaining Procedures

Another facet of strong framing associated with performance pedagogies is the boundary between the instructional discourses of the home and school. Bernstein argues that strong internal framing (such as its strong pacing rules) requires two sites of acquisition—the school and the home. The curriculum 'cannot be acquired wholly by the time spent at school': 'pacing of the acquisition is such that time at school must be supplemented by official pedagogic time at home, and the home must provide a pedagogic context and control of the pupils to remain in that context. There must be an official pedagogic discipline in the home' (Bernstein 1990: 77).

As Bernstein commented, the middle-class home provides an effective second site of acquisition with effective official pedagogic context and support. 'The curriculum practice of the street' which often is related to the use of time to work for money by poor children (ibid.), cannot provide such an official pedagogic context. Without such domestic pedagogic work, the working-class child cannot easily find support for the modes of acquisition used by the school. Therefore homework is not supplementary to the pacing of acquisition; it is integral to a strongly framed pedagogy such as the market-oriented pedagogies established in English secondary schools.

In our study, working-class pupils were clearly constrained and affected by the boundary-maintaining procedures of the classroom which segregate and distance the culture of their homes from the school. In the context of a state-defined curriculum and the powerful mechanisms to ensure normative notions of pupil progress built into its work schemes and syllabi, pupils struggled to negotiate the expectations, knowledge, and judgements of their families and those of teachers. Homework in this context becomes the critical interface between the instructional and regulative discourses, between the nature of education and the social order in which it is located. Further, their experiences of homework tasks could be critical to the valuing of school-based learning.

For some, such as the Asian girls at Greenfield, the boundary-maintaining procedures were less problematic since their parents took an active interest in what was happening at school and supported the role of teachers in defining appropriate schoolwork. One girl's elder sister even went through all her homework. Belief in school by parents meant that knowledge was also seen as valuable by Sunara and Joti:

Sunara: My parents they are interested because if I don't go to school they will be like 'Why aren't you going to school? What are you trying to skive off for?' and they are like telling you off and then if you do go to school they are like 'That's good. They are going to school they are going to learn a bit' and that kind of stuff . . .

On the whole though, working-class pupils appeared to be affected by the boundaries which segregate and distance the culture of their homes from that of the school. In the context of powerful normative notions of pupil progress built into its work scheme and syllabi, working-class pupils in our study struggled to negotiate the expectations, knowledge, and judgements of their families and those of their teachers. Parents were reported in some cases to challenge the principles behind the relevance of school knowledge. Claire's mum, for example, said, '*What the heck are you learning about that for, you don't need that!*' One working-class father commented, '*You don't need history, just sit here and watch Discovery Channels*,' while another pupil reported, '*My Dad doesn't like RE thinks its stupid learning about RE.*' Similarly Natalie and Jemima described the limited intervention by their parents in their school lives.

Natalie: Sometimes we talk about school and they ask how I got on.

Jemima: Sometimes I go home from school, mum goes 'How was school?' and I go 'All right' and mum goes 'Is that it?' And I go 'Yeah, that's it really.' I did my work and that and sometimes mum asks me and sometimes I say to mum I did have a good day at school.

Carry saw the boundary between home and school as institutionalized:

I think school's ... the school and home's home. It's completely different. At home I don't think anybody even wants to talk about school. I mean parents don't want to talk about work ...

In our discussions with these pupils, the ways in which knowledge was defined through homework and the responses of teachers to the help offered by their parents represented not just a poignant moment of conflict between the home and school—pupils perceived it as a breach of trust by the school. Sean and Craig reveal the shame they felt at an incident relating to their history homework.

Craig: That's really annoying when Mr Smith sets you homework and I don't know much about Henry VIII and all the wives and everything but he always sets us homework about that.

Q: So he gives you homework about that and you don't know much about it?

Sean: No but he didn't give as much like ... and he gives you this like little sheet and it has got 'What can you say about this bloke?' it's got like 'He's got a beard'. 'Sorry Sean, detention. You have just put 'he has got a beard'.

Sean and Craig also recognize the gap between the different instructional modes promoted by their families and the school. Sean found 'My mum tells me something and teacher tells me different'. Craig comments:

Like your parents give you like different methods of learning and then when you come in school, they say something different and you get confused and then you mix it like together and then you get it wrong because you get confused.

Particular homework aggravates this tension.

Sean: Yeah and sometimes the homework is so stupid. Like the other day it was 'What can you tell from this?' and I asked my Dad about it and he goes 'Well what's the point of setting this? It's just a picture.'[6] What can you tell from it? That he wears clothes and he has got a hat.

Teachers can suggest that pupils ask parents to help with their homework but in Maths this may not work because their parents are not necessarily good at Maths. Although some of these working-class boys claimed they asked their dads about schoolwork, if they did not know the answer, the boys were likely to get another detention the next day at school:

Carl: And the next day you say and they say 'Well then they must have been stupid' or something like that.

Performance pedagogies employ particularly strong boundary-maintaining procedures between the school and society. They redefine not just legitimate, relevant knowledge but also as we see here, appropriate and inappropriate domestic pedagogic work. The strengthening of framing associated with market-oriented pedagogies such as that found in the UK aggravates rather than reduces the distance between home and school and differentiates between social class family cultures.

The Successful Learner

Also integral to the instructional discourse of contemporary performance pedagogy is the notion of the successful learner. In our discussions with pupils we asked them a crude but effective question about whether there was a distinction between the 'good' and 'bad' learner, how they described themselves and how they knew what sort of learner they were. We also asked pupils to discuss what might help them be more successful in the classroom and whether they thought they could be more successful at learning school knowledge.

In both schools most pupils we consulted associated successful learners with features such as listening, hard work, being good at responding, concentrating, giving work in, making an effort, being liked by the teacher, and doing well. The pupils in the top set in Greenfield, however, were more likely to associate the concept of the 'good learner' with enjoyment and 'being challenged', being liked by the teacher, knowing most subjects, and being interested in school work. This particular group of pupils talked about the act of learning rather than just gaining knowledge. In contrast, lower-achieving boys at Greenfield were much more circumspect about the distinction between good and bad learners. They associated good learners with classroom learning behaviour—paying attention, not talking, and doing the homework. Within these definitions they were able to rank themselves in terms of the amount they worked and the amount they talked in class. So long as they made an effort, paid attention, and did the work (even while talking during class) they classified themselves as good learners. In Greenfield, pupils from various sets positioned themselves as independent learners ('I' the learner) as if the school had not already positioned them differentially in a hierarchy of learners.

The language of learning in Mandela, however, was different. Here most pupils appeared ambivalent about this distinction and only the three middle-class boys were prepared to position themselves as good learners. In comparison with Greenfield pupils who could draw information about themselves as learners from their position in various sets, the Mandela pupils were used to mixed ability classrooms and were able to experience 'difference' on a daily basis. They appeared to be less likely to use the classifications of learners and to place more emphasis on social variables such as gender and ethnic group (the visible dominance of regulative discourses). There were more references to 'we' as a social grouping of learners in this school. The ways in which these pupils constructed differences between learners also had implications for their confidence as learners. If learning was about effort then there is much that can be gained by hard work. The lower-achieving group of boys in Mandela underlined this point: 'It's important to focus' 'Yeah, you need to focus a lot', and persist—'you need to read over and over to get it done'. Thus the rewards, as Bernstein had argued, of this performance pedagogy still had to be achieved. The mythological discourse operating in this school, that of egalitarianism, masks the reality of differential success in achieving this goal.

Working-class boys appeared to operationalize the principles which underlay the performance pedagogy but in ways that undermined their own position. For example, they used the concept of intelligence to underscore the differences between learners. Working-class boys, in particular, articulated a painful awareness of the readiness of schools to attribute successful learning to 'ability': they catalogued a range of innate factors which combined to exclude themselves. For example: 'You've got to be clever', 'you have to be intelligent to be a good learner', 'you have to be clever to get jobs, important jobs'—although, for Ricky, there seemed to be an element of individual volition 'you've got to be in a good mood to be clever'. The danger for these low-achieving working-class boys was the power such intrinsic qualities played in shaping their confidence as learners. They were the only ones to describe invidious evaluations of their own intelligence:

Rick: Other people saying you are thick.
Robbie: Yeah, telling you you're stupid.
Dean: People undermine your confidence by putting you down.
Danny: People putting you down makes you feel like you are thick and then you feel like just don't want to try. Your feelings are hurt.

The undermining of their confidence as learners, which all four boys articulated, was further exacerbated by 'being picked on' by teachers because, as Ricky pointed out: 'It makes you think—what's the point of trying?' These boys vividly described how they were made to feel stupid and childlike in classroom encounters with teachers:

Kenny: Some teachers are a bit snobby, sort of. And some teachers act as if the child is stupid. Because they've got a posh accent. Like they talk without 'innits' and 'mans', like they talk proper English. And they say, 'That isn't the way you talk'—like putting you down. Like I think telling you a different way is sort of good, but I think the way they do it isn't good because they correct you and make you look stupid.
Martin: Those teachers look down on you.
Kenny: Yeah, like they think you're dumb . . . we don't expect them to treat us like their own children. We're not. But we are still kids. I'd say to them, 'You've got kids. You treat them with love but you don't need to love us. All you need to do is treat us like humans.'

Pupils in the lowest sets at Greenfield had similar experiences. The hierarchical organization of pupils also had the effect of making some pupils 'feel stupid'. The working-class boys in the lowest English sets also wondered whether there was any point in trying hard at their learning:

Neil: It's too easy, it's like they think you're stupid or something.
Sean: Yeah, like 'How do you write "the"?'

Rather than using their own assessment of their learning (something which higher-achieving pupils felt confident to do), the lower-achieving groups sought reassurance for their quality of their work from their teachers, other pupils, and their parents. They indicated their reliance on others to motivate them and assess whether they were doing well at school. Lower-achieving working-class boys reported feeling most successful at learning when the teacher or their parents said 'well done'.

As we have argued elsewhere, the experiences of regulation are most acutely felt by those who cannot easily work with the model of the independent learner being promoted as the means by which 'performance' is secured (Arnot and Reay 2004; Arnot et al. 2004). The model of the independent learner is one which involves students having the maturity to engage with teachers and negotiate their own learning progress. As such, the concept of the independent learner represents the mythological aspect of market-oriented performance pedagogies (an attempt to represent such pedagogies as having weak rather than strong frames). However, whilst some pupils were able to work with the notion of being responsible for their own learning, for others these demands were associated with disengagement, confusion, shame, and alienation.

We found that the class gap between pupils was expressed most clearly when we asked them about whether they wished to be consulted by a teacher about their learning. Middle-class girls in both schools appeared to have achieved greater levels of opportunities for consulting teachers in the classroom and therefore did not require new consultation mechanisms (Arnot et al. 2004). However, working-class pupils reported far fewer and less successful discussions with teachers. For example, Sean and Neil, both working class, were given discretion about when to finish off their work in the lessons rather than being asked what to learn. They commented.

Neil: It would be good if they said something like 'Oh what do you want to do in the lesson today?' or something.
Sean: Yeah.

The group of lower-achieving boys at Greenfield appeared to know that not only were the teachers in command of their education, but that even when teachers asked them what they would like to do that day, far more was at stake than just choice of topic. Their experiences of strong framing was reflected in their frustrations with their lack of control over what is transmitted and assessed and the ways in which teachers interpreted their work. The role of discipline and shame, rather than reflection or opportunities to choose activities, played a major part in their understanding of how strong framing works. Control over their learning meant gaining control over what was seen as largely pointless curriculum content. As a result, even if they were consulted, they replied they would respond thus:

Q: If that happened, what would you say?
Neil: nothing.

The experience and approach of these boys appears to be that teachers rarely listen to them, or respect their views. Similarly, a significant number of working-class boys at Mandela were already switched off from seeing themselves as learners:

Q: If you had a choice what would you choose to learn?
Jason: Nothing.
George: Nothing.
Andy: No idea.
Paul: Definitely nothing!

These working-class boys are positioned in a similar education space to that of Willis's 'lads' in the 1970s even though the form of performance pedagogy was substantially different (the autonomous knowledge-based version). They are clearly alienated from academic learning and see themselves as powerless in relation to the selection of knowledge. More than the other groups in our study, they fit Bernstein's suggestion that 'The stronger the classification and the framing, the more the educational relationship tends to be hierarchical and ritualised, the educand is seen as ignorant, with little status and few rights. These are things which one earns, rather like spurs, and are used for the purpose of encouraging and sustaining the motivation of pupils' (Bernstein 1977: 98).

Performance Pedagogies and Social Inequalities in the Classroom

In this chapter we have explored, through the voices of pupils, how performance pedagogies are experienced by different social groups. If strong frames control what can and cannot be said, then the pedagogic relationship between teachers and pupils is always likely to be hierarchical, although often disguised, mystified, or masked. Similarly knowledge will not be experienced as permeable, nor open. Socialization will be into an existing order, another form of alienation (Bernstein 1977: 98). In strengthening the frames, the government has strengthened the notion of discipline, or 'accepting a given selection, organisation, pacing and timing of knowledge' (ibid.).

The teaching of the National Curriculum, with its strong specialist subject discourses, strong boundaries between educational and common-sense knowledge, and its neo-liberal performance pedagogies, transmits messages about the social order. Our data suggest that this 'pedagogical Janus' will, as Bernstein predicted, give special significance to those pupils who possess educational knowledge and who are able to work successfully with its transmission rules. But these differentiations must be seen in context.

In Greenfield, for example, the strong classificatory principles underlying contemporary market-oriented performance pedagogies were supported by the differentiation of learners in Year 8 according to their achievement in particular subjects. The setting structure therefore sent explicit messages to pupils about how their learning was to be controlled and how it reflected, at least in principle, their abilities. Teachers had the power to shape their learning experiences, the content of their learning, and their trajectory through the school structure. In this context pupils' control of their own learning was strongly circumscribed by structures rather than the social dynamics of the classroom. The instructional discourse had shaped the organization of pupils, whilst in Mandela the regulative discourse provided the criteria for mixed ability teaching. Here, the competitive performance pedagogies were delivered within a quasi-egalitarian setting in which pupils battled against the lack of control over both their own status and their success in the performance culture. Their success involved relational work in ways that were not found in Greenfield. In Greenfield, the instructional discourses appeared dominant whilst in Mandela, the regulative discourse was more visible.

In Mandela and Greenfield middle-class children appeared to have gained access to the principle of the discourse. Our data suggest that particularly higher-achieving middle-class girls experience weaker frames in the controls over knowledge and they were able, it seems, to exploit those small opportunities for creativity and the possibilities of their own agency even within a strongly segmented and hierarchized knowledge structure. In both Greenfield and Mandela, Year 8 pupils appeared to accept the principle that the forms of knowledge they are being taught should be in the hands of the school and mostly in the hands of teachers, although some recognized that teachers themselves are strongly controlled (framed) by government policy. In both sites, there is evidence of an instrumental desire for 'useful knowledge' defined in social class terms. For working-class boys in particular, this instrumentality, especially for the modern technological world, is tempered by a desire to break down the boundaries between educational and community and cultural knowledge. These class and gender differences in the valuation of school knowledge and its interpretation are noticeable in both schools.

The evidence we have collected also suggests that strong framing of educational knowledge is experienced differentially. As Bernstein argues, what is relayed by strong framing is the notion of *difference* amongst pupils (Bernstein 2000). The assumptions about learners underlying the strengthening of pacing in visible pedagogies is more likely to be met by middle-class children who can 'exploit the possibilities of pedagogic practice' (Bernstein 1990: 74). The working-class child is likely to have greater dependency on the teacher and on oral forms of discourse.

There is always the chance that strong framing can be responded to and negotiated. Strong framing creates particular voices but also the strategies for responding to and challenging such controls. In our study, we found only those who have 'shown signs of successful socialization' (Bernstein 1977: 98) have access to relaxed frames within the strongly structured learning environment. Higher-achieving pupils, for example, found small arenas of discretion in what they studied, but for the most part, pupils had little feeling of being in control. In our other reports on the data (Arnot and Reay 2004) we concluded that higher-attaining middle-class girls were able to employ both strong and weakened frames. They express a desire and are at moments able to gain more control over the pacing and sequencing of their learning (more relaxed frames). They work with notions of individual choice in terms of when to co-operate, when to slow down or speed up (or zoom) through their work. They can work independently, but they can also make considerable demands on the teacher to deal with their needs for extension work. High-achieving middle-class boys speak less about the pace, difficulty, and ease of their work.

In contrast, lower-achieving working-class pupils clearly experience strong controls over the selection and pacing of knowledge in ways that lead to disengagement from learning and a celebration of peer-group bonds (Arnot and Reay 2004). Their lack of control within the new regulative discourses leads to behaviour responses rather than 'independent learning', a heavy reliance on friendship support, and a desire for teachers to 'get it right'. These boys experience high levels of surveillance and control and, from their point of view, no discretion over their learning and restricted help or sympathy from teachers. In Mandela, despite an earlier commitment to pupil autonomy and control, the working-class pupils appear to consider their learning as largely the responsibility of others—namely teachers.

The data from these two school settings suggest that we need to examine the extent to which a positive pedagogic identity is achievable for, in particular, working-class boys in the current, strongly framed learning environment. Bernstein writes about how socialization within schooling can be 'deeply wounding' either for those who wish for, but do not achieve a pedagogic identity, or for the majority for whom the pursuit of an identity is early made irrelevant (Bernstein 1975: 250). If, as Bernstein suggests, an increase in the strength of framing often means that the images, voices, and practices that the school authorizes makes it even more difficult for working-class children to recognize themselves in schooling, this is likely to be particularly problematic for working-class boys who experience daily the strong regulative culture of the classroom and confrontational relations with teachers. This clearly has profound consequences for the production of positive pedagogic identities so desired by the new goals of lifelong learning.

Bernstein (2000: 190) argued that every pedagogy has a voice, one that is never heard. We can hear only its realizations, and its messages. In the context of the curriculum, this pedagogic voice is expressed through the regulative discourse which embeds the teaching of knowledge and skills. Bernstein urges sociologists of education to make the pedagogic voice the 'fundamental theoretical object of sociology of education'. Our research on contemporary performance pedagogies makes a small contribution to that project.

NOTES

1. He devoted a chapter in vol. iv to exploring the social class assumptions of strong frames within visible pedagogies.
2. Bernstein calls these singulars, regions, and generic. (1990: v. ch. 3).
3. In contrast to what he called competence models where only what is present in the text is evaluated.
4. Other forms of pupil talk are classroom talk, subject talk, and identity talk (see Arnot and Reay forthcoming 2005).
5. A British TV satirical comedy.
6. This was a picture of Henry VIII.

Educational Triage and the D-to-C Conversion: Suitable Cases for Treatment?

David Gillborn and Deborah Youdell

***triage** n. of action f. trier to pick, cull ... 1. The action of assorting according to quality ... 2. The assignment of degrees of urgency to wounds or illness in order to decide the order of suitability of treatment.*

(*Oxford English Dictionary*)

The demands of the A-to-C economy are felt across our schools, in each year group and by all teachers. We have already seen how so many areas of activity, throughout secondary schooling, have come to reflect a concern with maximizing the proportion of pupils who eventually attain the benchmark level of five or more higher-grade passes in their GCSE examinations. The multiple selection and setting practices, that we have described above, represent the main school-wide strategies adopted (with varying degrees of enthusiasm, regret and concern) within our case-study institutions. The pressures of the A-to-C economy are such, however, that both Clough GM and Taylor Comprehensive have sought to identify additional means by which they can further target resources on a limited number of pupils in one last push to maximize their scores in the nationally published school performance 'league tables'. In practice these strategies often focus on pupils seen as heading towards grade D passes, where an improvement of a single grade could potentially figure significantly in the school's final results. In effect, the schools seek to convert likely grade Ds into grade Cs.

In this chapter we will examine the D-to-C conversion strategies utilized in each of our case-study schools. These strategies appear to be very different, reflecting the ethos and established practices and procedures within each school. As we will show, however, at a deeper level the strategies share similar characteristics and can be understood as a form of *educational triage*—a means by which scarce resources are rationed, leaving some to perish while others survive. As we will show, like medics in a crisis, teachers are increasingly seeking to identify those individuals who will benefit most from access lo limited resources. In a medical emergency *triage* is the name used to describe attempts to direct attention to those people who might survive (with help), leaving other (less hopeful) cases to die. In school, educational triage is acting systematically to neglect certain pupils while directing additional resources to those deemed most likely to benefit (in terms of

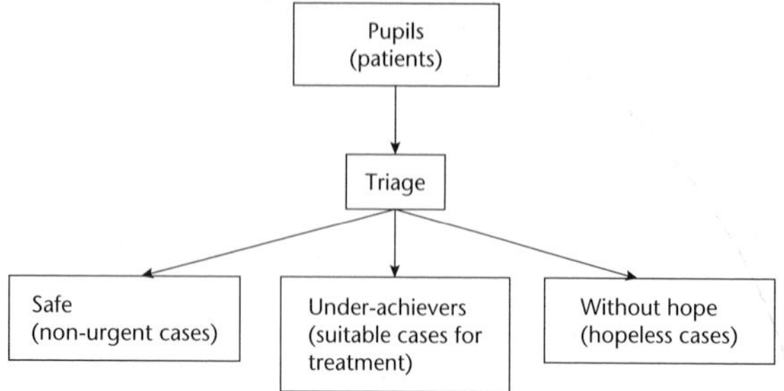

Fig. 54.1 Educational triage: the rationing of educational opportunity

the externally judged standards). These strategies seek to maximize the effectiveness of scarce resources but their effect, in practice, is to privilege particular groups of pupils marked especially by social class and 'race'.[1] The process is represented schematically in Figure 54.1.

In making sense of the processes of educational triage, it is useful to draw on Foucault's understanding of disciplinary power. Foucault suggests that, rather than being something that is held or possessed by one individual or group over or against another individual or group, power should be understood as something that circulates through the deployment of discourses. No particular discourse is intrinsically imbued with more or less power than another. Yet, through drawing on particular discursive practices, in the specific context and in the light of the exigencies faced, certain discourses do become dominant and, therefore, come to bound what counts as legitimate knowledge and, indeed, what is knowable. The making of individuals, who are knowable and known, is central to this technique of power. Foucault identifies a series of technologies or instruments of disciplinary power—specifically, hierarchical observation, normalizing judgement, and the examination—which enable the simultaneous making and surveillance of the individual who is, in turn, self-surveillant (Foucault 1991).

Three key discourses, and a set of concomitant technologies, are essential to the functioning of educational triage. First, a particular understanding of 'ability' as fixed and measurable. Second, the predictability and subsequent prediction of pupils' likely GCSE grades, which are underpinned by, and draw heavily upon, this understanding of ability. Third, the notion of 'under-achievement', again underpinned by a particular understanding of ability as fixed and measurable, and the subsequent identification of, and intervention with, 'under-achieving' pupils. In subsequent sections of this chapter we examine each of these discourses in turn. We begin, therefore, by returning to the notion of 'ability', a discourse that has already featured heavily in our account of life in Clough GM and Taylor Comprehensive.

'Ability' in Teacher Discourse

[...]

Clough operates with an underpinning discourse of ability as a fixed and generalized academic potential. In turn, a series of technologies for the measurement of ability are mobilized, including 'IQ' testing and reading and spelling 'ages', that feed into (and help shape) the school's understandings of individual pupil's performance throughout their school careers. On the basis of this understanding of ability, and the concomitant techniques for measuring it, we saw that the notion of 'under-achievement'—performance below the level expected—is a staple of the school's discourses surrounding ability and attainment.

A similar situation persists in Taylor. While the school does not make use of generalized-ability testing, it does draw upon a range of other measurement tools. We have already mentioned, for example, the banding system used by the now abolished ILEA and still current in several London authorities: this assigned pupils into one of three ability bands, on the basis of tests undertaken in year 6, with an optimum 'comprehensive' banding ratio of 1:2:1. Taylor, in line with its LEA, continues to make extensive use of these bands and, in these terms, continues to argue that it is 'truly comprehensive'.[2] Alongside these bands, which act as the key general indicator, Taylor utilizes year 9 SATs levels and tests within individual subject areas to assess the 'ability' of each member of its population. As in Clough, these tests, and the ongoing reference made to them, indicate an adherence to an overarching notion of ability as fixed, generalized and measurable. No single or precise relationship between 'ability' (as defined by banding on entry) and potential GCSE outcomes is explicitly offered by the school. This does not mean, however, that no such relationship is thought to exist. Taylor's headteacher, for example, believes that band on entry acts as a good general predictor of eventual GCSE outcome. As in Clough, however, this relationship is far less clear at the level of individual pupils:

> We analyse their GCSE results also by banding on entry. And, not surprisingly, there are very big differences in the overall performance, the average performance of band 1, band 2, band 3. If you [look] at individuals then you get a much cloudier picture. You know, you get the occasional child who entered in band 3 and finishes up getting five-plus As-to-Cs. You get children who entered in band 1 who drop out completely. Not many, but you get one or two each year. (. . .) On average they are pretty good predictors (. . .) After all, that banding is done on their London Reading Test, their reading is a fairly basic skill, their reading age at 11, or 10 when they take the test, also correlates quite well with their social background, parental income level, the whole lot. (Headteacher, Taylor Comprehensive)

For this headteacher, therefore, there is a clear and predictable relationship between reading on entry to Taylor (tested at age 10 or 11 and translated into bands) and subsequent GCSE outcomes at age 16. The reliability of this relationship is not seriously disrupted by the 'one or two' pupils whose performance contradicts it. For band 1 pupils, low performance is understood in terms of 'able' pupils 'dropping out'. For band 3 pupils, 'finishing up' with benchmark grades remains an unexplained anomaly. Significantly, the headteacher also views these differences as marked by social class. He does not assert that pupils from different social class backgrounds have different levels of 'ability', nor does he suggest that this relationship highlights a possible area of inequity which the school might endeavour to redress, rather he simply states that a correlation exists—its origins and wider consequences go unremarked.

In this 'truly comprehensive' school, in line with the old ILEA banding system, band 1 pupils make up roughly 25 per cent of the population, but, in line with the national average, over 45 per cent of the school population actually attain benchmark grades (of five or more higher-grade passes). We have seen that the headteacher subscribes firmly to the banding system and its relationship with GCSE outcomes. As such, we might expect the school to include at least the upper quartile of band 2 pupils in those it anticipates will attain the benchmark level. It seems, however, that this is not the case. Drawing comparison with the educational opportunities and subsequent outcomes available within the old tripartite system (where test performance at 11 placed pupils into different types of school) the headteacher points out that the many band 2 pupils who now attain the benchmark would not have enjoyed access to the equivalent GCE O-level examinations in a selective grammar school:

> [If] we go back to the days of the old grammar school, strictly speaking no child in band 2 or band 3, no child should finish up with five A-to-C grades. They wouldn't have got to the grammar school so they wouldn't even have taken the old O level. As it is, lots and lots of them do. And you do see advances in children who entered in band 2 and finish up performing as if they were in band 1. (Headteacher, Taylor Comprehensive)

This might be taken to indicate a belief that inequitable opportunities and outcomes, along with gross underestimations of the potential maximum performance of large groups of pupils, were embedded in the old tripartite structure. Yet the headteacher's assertion that these pupils are 'performing as if they were in *band 1*' (emphasis added) illustrates a continued belief in a particular set of relationships between 'ability' bands and GCSE outcomes—namely, that it is only really band 1 pupils who can be expected to attain the benchmark. This view persists despite evidence to the contrary within the school itself. As such these related practices of labelling, differential treatment and contrasting teacher expectations remain intact (through the measuring of 'ability' via reading ages, allocating pupils to bands and the assumed relationship between bands and GCSE outcomes).

Heads of year [. . .] play a key role in applying these judgements of 'ability' to real-life questions such as setting, options allocations and, as we discuss below, identifying pupils for additional support. In comparison with senior staff, especially the headteacher, year heads appear less confident of the relationship between early test scores and likely GCSE outcomes—nevertheless, they ultimately continue to subscribe to it. Asked 'does a particular reading age tell you a particular kid should be getting certain grades?', Taylor's head of year 9 replied: 'Not necessarily. I mean, it depends [on the] subject. But certainly a kid with a reading age, taking on GCSE English for instance, with a [current] reading age of 9.6, 10 or lower is going to have difficulty achieving a benchmark of E, which is just below the national average.' This reference to variation across subjects could be viewed as a move *away* from a notion of generalized ability. However, it might also reflect a subscription to the division of (high-status) 'academic' subjects and (lower-status) 'practical' or 'arts' subjects. Furthermore, the identification of reading as the means of access to one particular (high-status, academic) curricular area is easily extended to all such curricular areas, thereby reducing dramatically the range and nature of subject areas across which this variation might be seen. Ultimately, despite the assertion that reading age does not 'necessarily' relate to anticipated GCSE outcomes, this head of year feels confident in drawing a relationship between a specific reading age and a specific GCSE outcome. The head of year 11, when asked whether it is possible to relate ability bands to expected GCSE grades, answered:

> Loosely. Very loose. I mean it is loosely 'cause don't forget that was five years, well four years ago. That gives you a rough idea. And they are compared back to that in some of the figures, how the girls have achieved in [band] 1, 2 and 3 and how the boys have achieved. So they are, they do refer back to them. (. . .) It's roughly. There's the odd hiccups, but not that many.

It appears initially that this teacher does not subscribe to a notion of fixed ability; pupils' performance can change over time, thereby diminishing the utility of bands on entry. Yet the description of this relationship is shifting—'loosely' becomes 'roughly' and, ultimately, the relationship seems fairly secure: there are 'the odd hiccups but not that many'.

The situation appears to be further confused when we look specifically at the GCSE outcomes of pupils in band 2. We have seen the headteacher attempt to explain the benchmark attainments of many band 2 pupils while simultaneously retaining the notion that such grades 'should' be restricted to band 1 pupils. We find a similar lack of clarity and consistency with this head of year:

> *Researcher*: So you can't say that sort of [band] 2 will get between . . . ?
>
> *Head of year 11 (Taylor Comprehensive)*: No, I don't think so. No. I mean they are average, [band] 2. So the average is meant to be, I think it's an E isn't it? For GCSE? Which, some of those will get, a lot of those will get higher than that.

Here we find the incommensurability of 'average' in terms of band on entry and 'average' in terms of GCSE outcomes: an 'average' band position does not translate into the official 'average' GCSE outcome. Yet the discursive strength of these measures/labels is such that this teacher, and indeed the school, is unable to either separate or discard them. Furthermore, this lack of 'fit' does not mean that the teacher cannot ascribe GCSE outcomes on the basis of bands, rather, it means that the outcomes might not be the ones most readily expected. It seems, therefore, that understandings of the nature of the relationship between band and GCSE outcome vary both within and across key members of school staff. Yet despite this apparent incoherence and inconsistency, the overarching belief in the relationship itself remains intact.

Predicting GCSE Grades

So far, in this and [in Gillborn and Youdell 2000: chs. 1–5] we have detailed numerous contradictions, incongruities and potential inequities bound up in discourses of 'ability', and the tools used to measure it, in our case-study schools. Despite the problematic nature of these discourses, whether acknowledged or unacknowledged, both schools continue to predict GCSE outcomes for their year 11 pupils based substantially (though not exclusively) on these measures of ability.

Making Predictions in Taylor Comprehensive

Given the relationship that is believed to exist between band on entry and GCSE outcomes, it is not surprising that these bands are the starting point for the year head charged with the task of assessing pupils' predicted grades in year 11 (their final year of compulsory schooling). The predicted GCSE grades utilized in Taylor are supplied in the first instance by individual subject teachers and collated by the head of year. This is done following 'mock' GCSE examinations taken in the autumn term of year 11. Given the time and effort expended on 'mock' examinations, however, it is perhaps surprising that the 'mock' results do not translate directly into predicted grades. Rather, these are used in conjunction with a range of other indicators of varying degrees of formality:

Well it's a gut feeling for a start, I have to say, in all honesty. But then there's [a system used across the school for evaluating pupils' effort and performance] (. . .) And there's also comments you get back from staff. It's just an overall picture you get. And reports, I mean you get the yearly reports. And year 10s' were only done at the end of last year so they're quite new. So it's quite interesting to see. I mean it is a gut feeling. (Head of year 11, Taylor Comprehensive)

In view of these other indicators, therefore, pupils' predicted grades may differ from the actual grades they have only recently achieved in subject specific 'mock' examinations.

Making predictions in Clough GM

As we have already seen, NFER test results (referred to by some teachers as 'IQ' results) and reading and spelling 'ages' on entry are considered to be effective indicators of GCSE outcomes in Clough: the headteacher argues strongly that 'for a significant proportion you can be confident that the thing *is* a good predictor of their GCSE results'. As in Taylor, these sources are drawn upon when predicting GCSE outcomes. While Taylor predicts GCSE grades only once during year 11, however, in Clough the GCSE predictions are revised throughout the year. Again, no single indicator is relied upon totally. Rather, a variety of data are drawn upon in an attempt to divine the future: 'we use all the data that's available so we use, we use their SATs testing in year 9, we use their NFER scores, where they're tested internally, we use their reading ages and spelling ages, any data' (Head of technology, Clough GM).

Problems with Predictions

Both schools make considerable use of predicted grades, but they are not universally seen as unproblematic. In Taylor, as we have seen, the use of 'gut feeling' in predicting grades is clearly acknowledged. And whereas the accounts of teachers in Clough tend to emphasize the range of tests drawn upon, in interview one head of faculty (technology) also cites 'gut feeling' while another (modern languages) describes predicted outcomes as a 'shot in the dark at the moment'. One of the difficulties identified is the range of approaches taken, and different intended impacts, when individual teachers predict GCSE grades:

different teachers use different ploys for estimating the grades as well. So you get that inaccuracy built into it as well. 'Cause if you look at it there are very few As. Teachers won't commit themselves to giving a grade A as an estimated grade 'cause they're wanting to err on the side of caution. Then you've got the teachers who use them to underestimate to try and motivate. So, although you've got a kid that you think might get a grade C, you think if you tell him he's going lo get a C he'll sit back and won't do any more work. So you give him a D in the hope . . . So some teachers use that as a ploy. (Head of technology, Clough GM)

The use of such 'ploys' renders predicted grades even more uncertain than would otherwise be the case. Notwithstanding doubts about the validity, reliability and usefulness of predictions based on particular test results (of different styles and ages), the range of approaches among teaching staff serves to render predicted grades of even less use as a serious measure of pupils' attainment and guide to future achievement. Despite teachers' willingness to acknowledge such problems in certain circumstances, it is nevertheless the case that predicted grades carry very real significance within schools. Predicted grades are not only a tool used by school managers or faculty heads: wide-ranging discussions concerning individual pupils are suffused with references to such predictions. In both our case-study schools, tutors who were asked to briefly describe members of their tutor group readily offered such predictions (without reference to the basis on which they were being made) alongside references to family background, relationships with teachers and peers, and judgements about personality, motivation and behaviour.

Racism and Problems with Predictions

In preceding chapters we have already raised several concerns about the possibility that pupils of minority ethnic backgrounds might be especially disadvantaged in processes of selection and the attribution of different academic categories. This can occur through the use of formal tests as well as featuring in a range of informal judgements about 'ability' and 'motivation'. The production of 'predicted grades' provides yet another context within which such processes might come into play. The apparently concrete nature of each predicted grade, when presented in written form on reports and elsewhere, belies the uncertain and subjective nature of the processes that lie behind its production. There is considerable scope for racialized interpretations of 'ability', motivation and effort inadvertently to influence the kinds of grade produced, quite apart from any discrete 'ploys' adopted by individual teachers. This infuses the process with additional possibilities for predictions that are inequitable or even discriminatory. This is clearly demonstrated by the following account, by a senior teacher in Clough, which concerns black pupils' attempts to improve these predictions:

> I found that quite strange that the kids had their estimated grades because they then came back at you and gave you earache, you know, would challenge you in the corridor and so you were under threat. You know, 'why have you only given me that grade', you know? Because kids, you know, have different perceptions of themselves, they have no understanding, you know, and some of them live in Cloud-cuckoo-land. I mean we've got, we had a whole period where we had Afro-Caribbean kids running around with gold rimmed glasses on with plain glass in them because they thought it made them look more intelligent, you know, they really had highly inflated opinions of themselves as far as academic achievement, and this is fact. I mean there were a whole group of kids that put on glasses and wandered round the corridors with gold rimmed glasses on because they really fell that they were sort of A/B ... (A faculty head, Clough GM)

On the basis of this teacher's account it is clearly impossible to discern whether black pupils were wearing non-prescription glasses and, if they were, what their motivations for doing so might have been. Nor is this quotation evidence that this or any other teacher was actively or unwittingly making poorer predictions for black pupils than for their peers from other ethnic groups. Nevertheless, this account does give a worrying insight into several issues relevant to the production and use of predicted grades. It shows quite clearly, for example, that this teacher recognizes that the predicted grades are important to pupils but that he is dismissive of their protests that the estimates are too low: 'kids, you know, have different perceptions of themselves, they have no understanding'. The quotation seems especially dismissive of protests by black pupils: 'they really had highly inflated opinions of themselves as far as academic achievement'. Furthermore, it is noticeable that the pupils' concerns (which *could* have been interpreted as a sign of motivation, a thirst for achievement and success) are experienced negatively as 'challenge' and 'threat'. There is a strong echo with previous research that has suggested teachers' readiness to impute a challenge into the actions of black pupils (cf. Gillborn 1990; Gillborn and Gipps 1996; Sewell 1997; 1998; Wright 1992).

It is clear that the processes of GCSE grade prediction are multiple and inconsistent. Even if we were to accept the particular view of 'ability' (as fixed, measurable and generalizable) that underlies so much of the schools' approach, we would still surely have to accept that these predictions are of limited utility in view of the numerous, uncoordinated and personal judgements and ploys that come into play. Nevertheless, these predictions are formally the key to the D-to-C conversion strategies mobilized in both of the schools, that is, they are the core means by which triage assessments are made.

'Under-achievement'

We have seen that understanding ability as a fixed, generalizable and measurable attribute underlies schools' attempts to predict levels of performance and eventual GCSE outcomes for individual pupils. In this and [in Gillbourn and Youdell 2000: chs. 1–5] we have discussed the problematic nature of this notion of 'ability', the tools used to measure it and the subsequent prediction of pupil performance. Yet despite all the contradictions and inconsistencies, both of our study schools continue to draw heavily upon these techniques. More worrying still, they are mobilized to support the notion of 'under-achievement', to identify pupils who are considered to be 'under-achieving' and who are seen, therefore, as ripe for additional support.

Before examining the forms of additional support that are provided, it is important to understand the ways in which the case-study schools construct and mobilize notions of 'under-achievement'. In educational contexts where demands for equality of opportunity continue (albeit in sometimes diluted forms), any disproportionate allocation of resources to particular groups of pupils can be called to account. If pupils are identified as *already* suffering or losing out in some way within the current system of resource distribution, however, a justification for 'special treatment' becomes available. In this way, within the particular constraints and demands of the A-to-C economy, discourses of 'under-achievement' serve to justify the privileging of particular pupils by presenting the action as remediating existing disadvantage, thereby allowing inequitable resource allocation while retaining a construct of equity and comprehensiveness. As we will see, the schools operate quite specific notions of 'under-achievement' that do not replicate previous academic understandings of that term. In both Taylor and Clough, two pupils could have identical attainments and yet only one of them might be seen as 'under-achieving' and therefore deserving additional support.

'Under'-achievement in Clough GM

In [Gillborn and Youdell 2000: chs. 3 and 4] we explored notions of ability and 'under-achievement' as they are understood within Clough. We saw that ability is seen to be fixed, generalized and measurable and that assessments of performance are compared with measured ability in order to identify 'under-achievement'. We also saw that, in making sense of performance that *exceeds* expectations based on measured ability, the school was not able to consider seriously any possibilities that challenged either its understanding of fixed ability or the utility of the measurement tools it employs. It is in this context that assessments of 'under-achievement' are made in the upper school:

> [As one of] the heads of department, I would then go through the estimated grades and look where I feel that kids are under-achieving within the department, so they're identified. So the pupils that are on Ds and they're getting Bs and As anywhere else, I then identify those children, we'd discuss them at a meeting and look to see if individual teachers, because when you do your estimated grades you do it isolated. So you, once you can get an overall picture of how a kid's performing elsewhere, you may look at a pupil and think well that's a, he's only ever going to achieve a level D, but then by looking at his other grades and maybe he's picking up As and Bs in history and English, that can then raise teacher expectations of the kid. 'Cause we're all only human. (Head of technology, Clough GM)

Here again we see the significance of the teachers' belief in 'ability' as fixed and generalizable. If a pupil's predicted grade in one subject does not match the profile of grades elsewhere, there is an assumed under-achievement. Because ability is thought to operate across subject boundaries, a pupil predicted a grade D can be elevated in teachers' eyes through attainment elsewhere: 'by looking at his other grades (. . .) that can then raise teacher expectations of the kid'. Being identified as 'under-achieving', therefore, is not simply a matter of performing badly in a subject: performance elsewhere can influence such decisions (confirming or challenging expectations). Other aspects of pupil identity can also come into play. We examine these in detail below with reference to decisions made in Taylor.

'Under-achievement' in Taylor Comprehensive: Gender, Class and 'Race'

When teachers in Taylor talk about 'under-achieving' pupils, it is clear that ideas about several indicators are in play simultaneously. For example, notions of 'ability' and gender interact in important ways, and the precise consequence for different groups of pupils is not always as clear as first described by senior teachers. The headteacher suggests that under-achievement is found most commonly among boys from band 2: 'severely under-achieving is something we have seen among pupils of all levels of ability, our biggest concentration of such problems being among boys who entered the school in [ability band] 2'. Turning to the description of 'under-achievers' offered by one head of year, however, we see a somewhat different picture of which pupils might be allocated to this group. Boys are once again focused upon, but issues of social class and 'race' are also brought into play. The notion of boys' under-achievement is given authority and validity through recourse to national examination patterns and prominent coverage in the popular media (see, for example, Woodhead 1996).[3] However, the ways in which ability and identity categories are drawn into and out of the frame indicate a sense of contradiction and confusion. In the following quotation, for example, the teacher switches continually between class and ethnic categories:

And boys generally are under-achieving. *White middle-class boys*. (. . .) And *Black Afro-Caribbean boys*. I think there's been a fair amount of energy put into the problem, you know the challenge of *Black middle-class, um, Black Afro-Caribbean boys*, but I think *white working-class boys* have been kind of a little bit left behind. (. . .) I am very aware that *boys* do under-achieve (. . .) of those 23 boys [whose parents/carers did not attend parents' evening] they're nearly all under-achievers, they're nearly all *middle, um, working-class white boys*, I think there were two *Afro-Caribbean boys* in that group. The rest were *white working-class boys* with poor attendance whose parents we very rarely see, for whatever reasons. (Head of year 9, Taylor; our emphasis)

From this quotation it can be seen that the *gender* of under-achievers remains stable while their *'race'* and *social class* is shifting. The class background of under-achieving white boys is frequently identified as being middle-class and then changed (corrected?) to working-class. In addition, a racialized understanding of social class also appears to be expressed. The social class of white boys, while unstable, *is* continually expressed. However, the social class of African Caribbean boys is all but absent: 'blackness' appears to act as a totalizing signifier (of a homogenous group) of which further elaboration is unnecessary (or one in which social class is understood as self-evident) (cf. Mac an Ghaill 1989). Ultimately it seems that African Caribbean boys are assumed to be uniformly classed: it is only in the case of white pupils that social class emerges as a key axis of differentiation in the teacher's eyes.

The situation becomes increasing complex (and revealing) when teachers are invited to give concrete examples of these general patterns of experience. The movement from the general to the particular can reveal processes of which the teacher may be only partially aware: in this case, the head of year offers an example of an individual boy from year 9 who has been identified as under-achieving. While it was not claimed that this boy was necessarily representative of all under-achievers, it is interesting to note that the example concerns a white, middle-class boy from ability band 1, who is deemed to be performing to the level of ability associated with band 2 and therefore under-achieving in relation to the school's expectation of a band 1 pupil:

It's a bit subjective really. But it means, for instance, in science, say, that he's coming up to taking science SATs and they're undergoing science assessments which, potentially, they could be at level 6 [of attainment] if they're at the very top, level 6 or level 5 in science. *I would expect this boy to be somewhere in level 5 or 6 because he's intellectually, you know, one of the top echelon. He's actually performing at below 4*. So I picked that up from his science reports. Now if that's happening across the board then, and I know it is because I've looked at his books. So I know, as an English teacher, what a year 9 student achieving level 5, say, which is the higher end of the National Curriculum, what he should be writing and the kind of level of his writing and the level of his oral work. And that boy is not producing it, in terms of effort, it's just not going down on paper, and I think it is mainly effort. (Head of year 9, Taylor Comprehensive; our emphasis)

As we discussed earlier, test results that act as indicators for ability, combined with teachers' own judgements, enable the identification of particular groups of pupils who are assumed to be capable of attaining A*-to-C grades in GCSE examinations. Hence, while this ability band 1 boy is *under*-achieving (in relation to teachers' expectations for his ability band), a peer classified as ability band 2 performing *to the same level* in their SATs would be deemed to be achieving appropriately to their potential (that is, *not* under-achieving).

It should also be noted that while the headteacher asserts that under-achievers are primarily *band* 2 boys, and the head of year appears to have the intention of suggesting that they are primarily white *working-class* boys, the pupil in the proffered example is a white, *middle-class* boy from *ability band 1*. In the particular instance that the teacher chooses to use as an exemplar, therefore, strategies to achieve D-to-C conversions are reworked from an imagined target clientele of working-class pupils in ability band 2, and refocused (via the particular definition of under-achievement) to highlight a middle-class pupil in band 1. While the ability and class nature of the clientele may have shifted upward, however, the ethnic and gendered character of the target group remain stable: white boys.

The racial and social class dimensions of 'under-achievement' (as defined by the school) go largely unremarked and unexplained by teachers: however, its gendered nature is discussed. Extending the code of pupil pathology and deficit to families, one head of year suggests a connection between boys' under-achievement and parental interest—a connection that might be read as simultaneously indicating that these boys are positioned as being working-class—and uses this to absolve the school of any active role in pupil failure by asserting 'there's a strong link between parental interest and boys'. Furthermore, when there is an acknowledgement that the school, or at least the education system more generally, might be culpable in boys' under-achievement, this is related not to current school-level practice but to earlier curricular changes that are said to have disadvantaged boys:

> there's a lot of research that says that, you know, the curriculum has moved in the '70s and '80s when there was that whole feeling that girls needed to, we needed to address the curriculum in comprehensive schools for girls. And then they did skew it slightly then. (. . .) But, the curriculum is now perhaps more girl-biased. I don't know, I don't. (Head of year 9, Taylor Comprehensive)

It is interesting that in this teacher's commentary on curricular change the pre- and post-National Curriculum eras are conflated, with pre-National Curriculum practices presented as continuing to impact within the very curricular reorganization that was, at least in part, designed to undo those changes associated with the 'progressivist' project (cf. Ball 1994). This teacher claims authority for his claim that the current curriculum favours girls by reference to 'a lot of research', in contrast to the 'feeling' which led to the earlier moves to enhance girls' access to the curriculum. This juxtaposing of the researched-based 'facts' of boys' current curricular disadvantage, with the implicit questioning of the basis upon which earlier efforts to improve girls' access to the curriculum were made, acts to validate the subsequent claim that it is this which has led to boys' under-achievement. Hence, even where educational practices are identified as being a partial cause of boys' under-achievement, it is not current practice that is responsible. At fault, rather, are the supposedly over-zealous changes of earlier progressivists (and by extension even girls themselves). Despite the contradictions within the analysis offered by this teacher, therefore, it is a discourse that operates to give further credence to the category of 'under-achieving boys'.

These assertions of under-achievement act to validate the school's focus upon, and demand for, D-to-C conversions. Through the practice of identifying pupils as under-achieving, the school avoids the appearance that it is attempting to get 'natural' grade D pupils to convert their grades to Cs—a move that would, of course, deny the very notion of 'ability' enshrined in the school's actions. Rather, within the dominant view of fixed and generalized ability, the school sees itself as attempting to get 'natural' A*-to-C grade pupils to increase their performance so as to fulfil their intellectual potential. As such, implicit to the school's notion of 'under-achievement' is an understanding of 'ability' as stable and predictable, while also being mutable enough to be unfulfilled or unmet. It is already clear that targeting pupils on the D/C borderline intersects conveniently with the school league table demands for higher-grade passes in the A-to-C economy. The key to understanding the iniquitous effects of these processes lies in the nature of the interventions made with appropriate 'under-achieving' (but supposedly capable) pupils. The understanding of 'ability' mobilized by the school enables those pupils thought to be most likely to make the D-to-C conversion (that is, those pupils considered most valuable to the league tables) to receive particular attention. In practice, it is an approach that embodies familiar biases against pupils of working-class background, black young people (regardless of class) and girls.

These decisions represent a central element in the processes that we identify as educational triage. The school is seeking to identify those for whom additional resources might prove the difference between life and death/success and failure. In this instance, however, it is clear that the professional judgements that identify 'suitable cases for treatment' are deeply scarred by social class, gendered and racialized perspectives on the health/ability/potential of pupils.

In order to understand the ways in which triage, underpinned by these notions, is constructed and deployed, we will examine one key strategy in each school: the 'Achievement Initiative' in Taylor and the target setting and internal competition embodied by the 'pupil league table' in Clough.

The 'Achievement Initiative' in Taylor

We have seen that in Taylor Comprehensive, as in Clough GM, there are key interrelated discourses that circulate within the staff body and inform decisions on pupils. Ability is believed to be fixed and generalized, it is 'assumed to be measurable and is, therefore, measured. Similarly, GCSE grades are seen as predictable and so they are predicted. Finally, and relatedly, 'under-achievement' is both identifiable and identified. These interconnected discourses, and their facilitating technologies, provide both the conceptual and practical basis for those strategies deployed in the pursuit of D-to-C conversions and maximum school attainment at the five A-to-C benchmark.

Since the 1995/6 academic year, one strategy by which Taylor has sought D-to-C conversions has been through an *Achievement Initiative*. The main component of this initiative is the establishment of 'Achievement Groups' in which final-year pupils (selected by their head of year) are mentored by individual teachers and given additional support and assistance in preparation for the GCSE examinations. Selected pupils are invited to attend these groups, which meet outside school time and are led by members of the teaching staff on a voluntary basis. It is interesting to observe in this regard that the pastoral is 'ministering' to the demands of the academic.[4] An indicator of the importance attached to this initiative is the status of the teachers involved; in addition to some year 11 tutors, the volunteers also include the headteacher, both deputy headteachers and the head of year 11.

For the headteacher, the express aim of the Achievement Groups is to raise the number of pupils attaining five higher-grade passes. Recall his assertion that 'the best thing that we can do for our pupils is to strive to get the greatest possible proportion achieving that five high-grade benchmark' [Gillborn and Youdell 2000 ch. 3]. He goes on to say: 'In this regard, our Achievement Initiative is being tested in its first year of operation.'

The processes whereby pupils are identified for inclusion in the initiative draw upon the notion of fixed and measurable ability and the subsequent prediction of GCSE grades and assessment of 'under-achievement'. As such, triage principles are applied in order to identify those pupils who are 'safe' (non-urgent cases), those who are 'without hope' and those for whom treatment might make the difference (pupils defined as 'under-achieving' in the school's particular sense of that term). These processes, however, are neither straightforward nor uniformly applied. Analysis of teachers' accounts of these groups and the actual membership of them shows that both formal and informal selection criteria are in operation. Furthermore, the head of year's resistance to the dominating focus on five A*-to-C grades adds a further dimension of inconsistency to these groups.

Officially, the criteria for selection are based on the intersection of pupils' predicted grades and teachers' assessments of 'under-achievement'. The following constellation of characteristics formally marks out a pupil for inclusion in the initiative:

1. The pupil is *entered* for five or more GCSE examinations.
2. The pupil is assessed as having the *ability* to attain five or more higher-grade passes.
3. The pupil is currently predicted to *fall short* of the five A*-to-C benchmark by one grade in one or more subject(s).
4. This predicted shortfall is seen as an indication that the pupil is 'under-achieving'.

These criteria for inclusion and the objective of the initiative are illustrated by an extract taken from a memo sent to the deputy head (curriculum) by the head of year 11 (see Figure 54.2).

The central concern of the Achievement Groups is to maximize the proportion of the school population attaining the benchmark level through the D-to-C conversion. Formally, this implies that outside the Achievement Groups will be pupils in two categories: a 'safe' group of pupils already predicted to

Thank for the lists predicted grades for pupils whose grades fall below the 5 A–C threshold. (. . .). I have also picked out a further 29 pupils who could achieve the 'target' if they raised their levels by one grade—

[pupil name] [tutor group]	B C C C D D D
[pupil name] [tutor group]	C C D D D D
[pupil name] [tutor group]	A A B C D D
[pupil name] [tutor group]	B C C C D D D
[pupil name] [tutor group]	A C D D D D D D
[pupil name] [tutor group]	A C C D D D
[pupil name] [tutor group]	B C C C D D D D
[pupil name] [tutor group]	C C C C D D D
[pupil name] [tutor group]	C C C C D D D D
[pupil name] [tutor group]	C C C C D D D D D
[pupil name] [tutor group]	C D D D D D
[pupil name] [tutor group]	A C C D D
. . .	

Fig. 54.2 Extract from a memo by the head of year 11 identifying pupils for inclusion in the Achievement Initiative, Taylor Comprehensive

attain at least five higher-grade passes (non-urgent cases in the metaphor of medical triage); and those pupils (seen as hopeless cases) who are not expected to attain the benchmark even with extra support. The latter group will include a wide range of pupils: some may he expected to attain no pass grades at any level, while others may be predicted to attain a string of D grades but *not* be assessed as 'under-achieving' in the school's terms (see above).

Our analysis of the actual composition of the groups, however, shows that both the third and fourth criteria for selection, that is, those restricting selection to pupils performing *below* the benchmark and concerned with 'under-achievement', are frequently discarded. In addition, pastoral heads of year move through the school with the same cohort of pupils. This means that the head of year 11 (a key player in implementing the Achievement initiative) changes annually. A recent head of the year 11 makes it clear that effecting D-to-C conversions was the original aim of the Achievement Initiative (and remains an important aspect of it) but, in selecting pupils from her year group, she broadened the scope of the Achievement Groups to include pupils from across the perceived ability range, thereby effectively refusing the dominant definition of 'under-achievement' in Taylor. Furthermore, she states that she selected pupils to ensure that the groups had an equal gender balance:

> They're kids who are under-achieving (. . .) it tends to be across the curriculum (. . .) on my list it was mainly kids who are not getting five A-to-Cs, but there are other kids who are under-achieving, and kids with special needs who'll get a little extra attention, and I tried to make it equal boys and girls (. . .) the intention is to improve their grades, it's not just about A-to-Cs (. . .) to me there's more to achievement than five A-to-Cs.

By the early part of year 11, a proportion of pupils (42 per cent of the year group: n = 88) are defined as safe/non-urgent cases, that is, they are predicted by teachers to be on track to attain five or more A*-to-C grades without further need for any formal additional or special support.[5] While this group includes boys and girls and individuals from the range of ethnic and social class groups, it is the case that girls, white pupils and those not in receipt of free school meals are disproportionately represented (see Table 54.1 and Figure 54.3).

By the same point, and in stark contrast, a proportion of pupils (17 per cent of the year group: n = 36) are treated as *beyond help*, that is, five or more A*-to-C grades are predicted by teachers to be beyond their reach. Again, this group of pupils encompasses both boys and girls and the range of ethnic and social class groups. In this case, however, it is boys, black pupils and those in receipt of free school meals who are disproportionately represented (see Figure 54.4).

Table 54.1 Educational triage by ethnic origin, free school meals and gender (Taylor Comprehensive)

	Safe (non-urgent cases)		Suitable cases for treatment		Without hope		total	
	N	%	N	%	N	%	N	%
White	43	(64)	41	(60)	16	(24)	100	(148)
Black	29	(6)	52	(11)	19	(4)	100	(21)
FSM	25	(14)	49	(28)	26	(15)	100	(57)
Non-FSM	49	(74)	37	(56)	14	(21)	100	(151)
Boys	33	(34)	45	(46)	22	(23)	100	(103)
Girls	51	(54)	36	(38)	12	(13)	99	(105)

Source: Based on the composition of the Achievement Groups in Taylor.

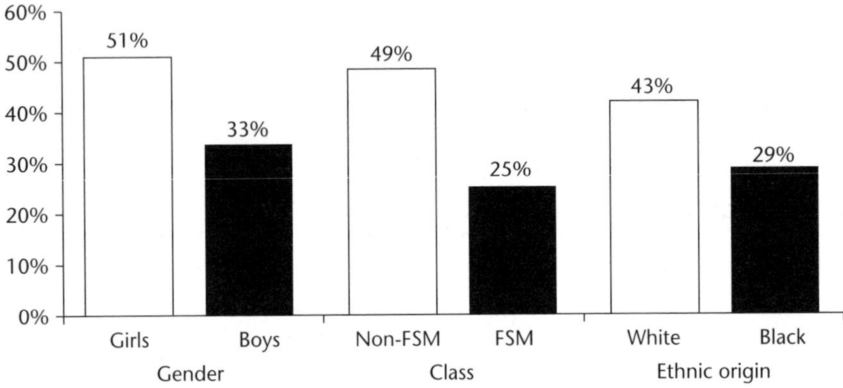

Fig. 54.3 Pupils designated 'safe' by triage at Taylor Comprehensive

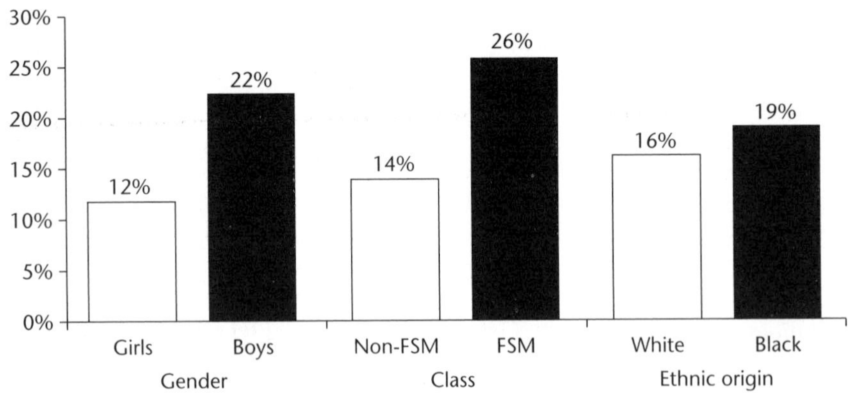

Fig. 54.4 Pupils designated 'without hope' by triage at Taylor Comprehensive

Together these two groups represent 60 per cent (n = 124) of the year group. The remaining pupils are included in the Achievement Initiative. Given the multiple processes by which pupils are identified for inclusion, it is unsurprising that few of these pupils actually fulfil the official inclusion criteria outlined above.

Superficially, membership of the Achievement Groups appears to be relatively equitable, that is, no particular groups of pupils (in terms of class, gender or ethnicity) dominate.[6] Given the inclusion criteria and the ethnic and class profile of the 'safe' group, we should expect to see a disproportionately high representation of black pupils and pupils in receipt of free school meals in the initiative. Pupils in these groups are somewhat more likely to appear; in practice however, entry into the group does not make good the under-representation of black pupils and pupils in receipt of free school meals in the 'safe' group. Furthermore, it also includes 28 pupils (33 per cent of those in the Initiative) who are *already* predicted to attain the five higher-grades benchmark. In this way we can see that the Achievement Initiative (equivalent within the triage model to a 'treatment' group) does not make up for the disproportionately small chance of being 'safe' experienced by black pupils and those in receipt of free school meals. In addition, some pupils judged 'safe' (non-urgent cases) according to the school's own criteria are included in any case as an insurance policy.

We have seen that, at the point of prediction and inclusion, the composition of the treatment group reflects the range of ethnic and social class groups, but that this does not of itself denote equity (since some groups are markedly under-represented in the 'safe' category). More revealing still is an examination of the *outcomes* of the process. As we have noted, some teachers (like the recent head of year 11) are not only aware of inequalities in the identification of likely candidates for D-to-C conversion, but are also prepared (so far as is possible given their location in the staff hierarchy) to modify (subvert?) the systems. It is equally clear, however, that such individuals are in the minority and that their views (of under-achievement and the school's priorities) are out of step with the dominant position that currently informs most academic and pastoral moves in the school.

Our analysis of outcomes in the school suggests that of all the pupils included in Achievement Groups, white pupils and pupils not in receipt of free school meals are more likely to attain the benchmark (five higher grades) than black pupils and pupils in receipt of free school meals. Furthermore, the majority of those who do finally achieve the benchmark have in fact already been predicted to do so. Of those in the initiative, 18 pupils attained five or more higher-grade passes; of these 16 had been predicted to do so. Of these pupils only a minority were black and/or in receipt of free school meals.[7] In total, only two Achievement Group pupils achieved the benchmark in contradiction of teachers' previous predictions. Even here, where it might reasonably be suggested that the initiative had helped support a D-to-C conversion, both of these beneficiaries were boys, one white and one defined officially as 'other'. Not only did the Achievement Initiative fail to make good existing inequality in its composition, therefore, it also delivered results that replicated existing trends in the disproportionate success of white pupils and those not in receipt of free school meals.

It appears that despite the best efforts of teachers and a high-profile formal concern with those on the C-D borderline, in practice Taylor's Achievement Initiative is neither concerned with effecting D-to-C conversions nor able to do so. Rather, it is an insurance measure, that is, it acts to ensure that pupils already expected to attain the benchmark do indeed do so. Although the year head's personal concerns over inclusivity extended the catchment of the group somewhat, it had little or no impact in terms of D-to-C conversions. These outcomes seem to confirm that the Achievement Initiative, despite laudable intentions, does little to equalize opportunities in the school; indeed, it is implicated in further cementing, or at least playing out, existing inequalities.

Surveillance and Self-Surveillance in Clough

In Clough a very different technique is deployed in pursuit of the same outcome—maximizing attainment of the benchmark through D-to-C conversions.

In contrast to the Achievement Initiative in Taylor, which is predicated on notions of comprehensiveness and equity (however flawed) and delivered within an ethos of supportive pastoral care, in Clough the strategies are predicated on a market model of individualized competition that does not pay even rhetorical attention to issues of equity and diversity. In Clough the strategies and their underpinning discourses are resolutely blind to issues of 'race', class, gender and the differential outcomes between such groups.

Target Setting and the Monitoring of Teachers

This internal marketization in Clough is manifest through targets pertaining to the proportion of pupils attaining A*-to-C grades at GCSE. These targets are set by the school's governing body and the headteacher. The targets are multiple and include:

- the proportion of pupils attaining the five A*-to-C benchmark across all subjects, responsibility for which lies with the headteacher;
- the proportion of pupils attaining A*-to-C grades across the subjects making up each faculty, responsibility for which lies with the relevant faculty head;
- the proportion of pupils attaining A*-to-C grades within each individual subject within each faculty, responsibility for which lies with the head of faculty and the subject coordinator, where one exists;
- the proportion of pupils attaining A*-to-C grades across groups taught by each teacher, responsibility for which lies with the individual teacher;
- and the proportion of pupils attaining five A*-to-C grades within each group taught by each teacher, responsibility for which again lies with the individual teacher.

The level of disciplinary surveillance is clear. In addition, these targets are not static; teachers and faculties are under pressure to produce year-on-year improvements:

> So we're not naive enough to not think that, you know, the pressure's not on to improve those. 'Cause, you know, that stops the teacher sitting back thinking . . . well I don't, see I personally hit 66 per cent last year which is well above national [A*-to-C] average (. . .) So that's well above national average. The national average is what, something like 50, isn't it? So I could actually sit back and say well, you know, I'm above, but I haven't I've had to set 70 per cent this year . . . (Head of faculty, Clough GM)

Faculty heads and teaching staff within Clough take a range of positions in relation to these targets. The head of technology traces the pressure for benchmark grades from the headteacher, to the school's governing body and ultimately to education policy nationally:

> I don't think we're getting much understanding from senior management over that sort of thing but, you know, they've got targets to hit 'cause they're set targets by the governors. So they then put the pressure on us (. . .) the whole thing's motivated by league tables now, isn't it? That's what's motivated everybody. (Head of technology, Clough GM)

Within Clough it is made explicit that the targets might be met through concentrating on 'borderline' pupils (again, the D-to-C conversion):

> Well if you look at my estimated grades now, my estimated grades are about 51, 52 per cent. So that means to hit those targets I've got to put the pressure on, on the Ds, what I've estimated to be a D. And I won't hit my 70 per cent [target] unless I can *convert those Ds into Cs*. (Head of faculty, Clough; emphasis added)

Not all teachers, however, see this conversion as a real possibility. The head of English at once confirms the school's understanding of ability and alludes to its implicit shift in focus from D grade 'under-achievers' to *all* D grade pupils:

> You give them [senior managers] the names of the Ds, the borderline people, who if they whip themselves a bit harder possibly could go to a C, but the other thing is this, a lot of those Ds they're there, that's as high as they can go. (Head of English, Clough)

While still confirming the school's notion of fixed ability, the head of year 11 goes further in identifying the contradictions and-incoherence of the demands for A*-to-C grades in general and the D-to-C conversion in particular:

> you're teaching for results, it's almost, you know, you must get the results. I think you've always wanted to get the results but I think there's more pressure on pushing everybody and I think if you push everybody at the same speed some aren't going to make it. I mean, does that make sense? (. . .) And

this is something which, as a teacher, you know. You are always going to have a proportion of children who aren't going to reach the average. Or you bring the average down so low that everybody, you know, it is, that's the problem isn't it? You can't do it, you're never going to be able to get everybody to achieve the average, it's unrealistic. But you in the classroom can understand, and you presumably looking at statistics can understand that but some people can't. They think that every child coming into school, every child coming in must get five A-to-Cs. And if you try and explain to them that it's not possible for some to get that they say, well, it's because you're not teaching them well enough. And that's soul-destroying as a teacher because you can get them up to a certain level but you can't get them all to get A-to-Cs, it's meant for everybody to reach an A-to-C. (. . .) So, you know, you're on a, whatever you do you're going to be judged as not succeeding. And that, to me, is crazy. (Head of year 11, Clough GM)

Expected performance in relation to each of the staff targets in Clough is subject to ongoing monitoring through repeated analysis of pupils' predicted grades throughout Key Stage 4 and during year 11 in particular. These are compared across faculties, subjects (with the core areas of English, maths and science subject to particularly heated competition) and individual teachers. This is understood to allow 'discrepancies' in performance between faculties, subjects and teachers to be identified. Furthermore, it facilitates the identification of 'discrepancies' in the performance of individual pupils across and within faculties and subjects. Again, the process takes for granted that 'ability' is relatively fixed and generalized:

So [the senior teacher] calculates all the deviation scores. We do a deviation for individual teachers and we do it for, for, you know, teaching groups, so I can look at each teacher's deviation score. And then whole department, the whole of food [part of the faculty] will be looked at as a deviation score or the whole of resistant materials [another part of the faculty] (. . .) to see whether kids are scoring a grade lower or a grade higher. (. . .) and then when you get kids like who are performing in art and get two grades higher than they've got everywhere else, you know, that puts you under the cosh a little bit. (. . .) we can get a kid who is maybe performing at a grade B with us and, but he's only achieving Es and Fs in English and . . . so you can get that skew, you know. Which can be a pain in the neck because when you look at the final grades, 'cause then departments are actually compared, so you have, every grade a kid gets is awarded a number so I think if he gets an A, A* it's 10, 9. And then you'd get, the norm is worked out, you know, from that listing. (Head of technology, Clough GM)

This same head of faculty goes on to put these results into the context of performance nationally:

But then what we found interesting is that last year the *Daily Mail* published the deviation scores across the whole country and technology and physics and I think mathematics are scoring 0.8 of a grade lower nationally, across the whole country. And the same with art and drama are scoring, you know, I think it was one-plus, one point something above deviation. I found that quite interesting. So I think really, to get a true deviation score you should take those into deviation. So, for example, if I come out −0.8 I'm doing okay 'cause . . . It's at the national level 'cause that's across the whole country, they're scoring a lower grade in our subject than in English, maths or . . .

It is important to recognize what all this calculation and recalculation represents so far as issues of power and control within education are concerned. Here we see attempts to instigate complex and multiple systems of hierarchical observation, examination and categorization, that is, *surveillance*, through the establishment of multiple parameters of internal competition within the school. These permeate all levels and sections of the school community (literally from the headteacher, through every member of staff, to any given individual pupil) and engender an unprecedented degree of *self-surveillance*. These technologies find their most public and extreme expression in a regularly updated league table of year 11 pupils.

A League Table of Pupils

The Clough 'pupil league table' reflects the performance indicators deployed in the nationally published league tables of schools and LEAs; it is posted in a key public space within the school. This league table ranks year 11 pupils on the basis of their predicted GCSE outcomes, as collated through the teacher/subject/faculty/school target monitoring processes already outlined (above). A ranking of the entire year group is produced but only the top 150 pupils are listed on the publicly posted version, with the bottom 40 pupils being omitted. As the table is regularly updated pupils may, in principle, not only move up and down the rank order, but actually move on and off the public version. An extract from the table is reproduced in Figure 54.5.

The rank placement on the pupil league table is based on a mean score calculated on each pupil's *predicted* GCSE performance. Calculating exam scores (for GCSE in this instance) involves the assignment of a numerical score to each grade (eight points for an A*, seven for a grade A and so on down to one point for a grade G) which can then be added together to derive an overall exam score for each pupil. It has been noted that calculating exam scores in this way enables examination passes at all grades to be included in assessments of performance. At the same time, however, a single overall exam score might be arrived at through varying collections of grades. A score of 25 might indicate attainment of five higher grades (by achieving five passes at grade C) but it can also indicate a combination of GCSE passes that does *not* meet the five A*-to-C criterion (such as one grade B, three Ds, two Es and a G); see Gillborn and Gipps (1996: 15). In Clough these predicted overall exam scores are then transformed into an average grade score across all subjects for each individual pupil: where an average grade score of five is assumed to be equivalent to a grade C (i.e. the grade for which five points would be allocated). However, this technique does not alter the range of possible routes to single scores: an overall exam score average of 5 may or may not reflect the benchmark criterion in exactly the same way as an overall raw score of 25. This means that it is technically possible, though unlikely practically, for a pupil not predicted to attain five higher-grade passes to appear higher on the table than one who is expected to reach the benchmark.[8]

The various routes through which a single exam score can be attained (be it a raw figure or an average) means that ranking in the Clough pupil league table does not reflect directly predicted performance in terms of the single most important measure of the A-to-C economy. Nevertheless, the influence of the A-to-C economy is clear; the use of an aggregate exam score measure does not mean that Clough has rejected this economy in favour of an arguably more inclusive mode of monitoring and representing predicted performance. Although ranking on the table is based on exam score averages, the table also includes a number of other indicators of pupils'

Rank	*Given name*	*Family name*	*GCSE average*	*A*	*B*	*C*	*D*	*A–C*	*Attendance*	*NFER score**
53			4.70	0	1	5	4	6	93.4	121
54			4.67	0	2	4	2	6	99.3	92
55			4.67	0	2	3	3	5	98.1	97
56			4.67	1	0	3	4	4	98.1	0
57			4.67	0	3	2	3	5	93.9	0
58			4.63	0	3	1	3	4	94.6	97
135			3.29	0	0	0	4	0	54.7	0
136			3.25	0	0	0	3	0	97.5	103
137			3.25	0	0	1	4	1	93.1	75
138			3.25	0	0	0	3	0	79.5	95
183			1.88	0	0	0	0	0	91	77
184			1.88	0	0	0	2	0	64.9	101
185			1.83	0	0	0	0	0	87.7	94
186			1.75	0	0	0	1	0	98.7	72

Fig. 54.5 Extract from Clough pupil league table

* NFER test results are included in the version used by senior teachers but omitted from the table that is displayed publicity in the school. A score of 0 denotes that no test was taken (usually because the pupil joined the school later in secondary education).

predicted performance (see Figure 54.5). Pupil by pupil predicted grade score averages are supplemented by the number of GCSEs predicted at each grade between grades A and D (D being the conversion grade) and the total number of GCSEs predicted at grades A-to-C. Predicted GCSE passes at grades E-to-G do not appear on the table. Pupils' NFER scores (or 'IQ' results as many staff refer to them) also appear on the version of the table retained by senior managers but are removed from the version that is publicly displayed in the school. It is interesting to note that, in guiding us through the table, the senior teacher with a leading role in its production highlighted as evidence of 'under-achievement' those cases (pupils) where there were 'discrepancies' between high NFER scores and low GCSE averages. He did not, however, either highlight or attempt to explain those cases where there were 'discrepancies' between low NFER scores and high GCSE averages.[9]

The inclusion of multiple yet selective indicators of predicted performance belies Clough's overriding concern: the A-to-C economy. Ranking by predicted grade averages rather than the benchmark could reflect a push for greater inclusivity within the competitive model. It could also reflect a 'failure' to make best use of the available information within the terms of the market model employed. As already noted, ranking by grade averages allows some pupils to occupy an 'artificially' high rank in terms of the A-to-C economy. This may function to 'keep hold' of pupils who might otherwise become disillusioned and 'drop out' of the race for benchmark grades. It should also be noted that the information technology used to generate the pupil league table has the capacity to sort and resort by any of the indicators included in it. Ultimately, it is clear that Clough GM is utilizing every available and 'relevant' technology (in both statistical and Foucauldian terms) to survey, judge and classify each individual pupil and, in turn, promote pupils' self-surveillance.

In discussing the basis for inclusion in the public version of the pupil league table, and the rationale for making it public, the headteacher restates the school's mobilization of particular notions of fixed ability, 'under-achievement' and the implicit adoption and extension to pupils of a market model of competition:

> Well, we reckoned that that left about 30 kids or so, 30-plus who, for one reason or another, were never going to change their position in that they were always going to be right at the bottom, not necessarily through their fault. (. . .) there are kids down in the sort of 120s who really with, in terms of their ability, could easily be in the top 25 or 30. So the idea was to provide a spur to all those who had it in them to do a bit better really. There is always a group of kids who can't, for one reason or another.

The head of year 11 also explicitly says that the table was designed to engender competition between pupils inside the school. She also suggests that the table seeks to raise pupils' and teachers' sense of competition with other schools. In this way, this head of year notes a lack of consensus among staff concerning the extent to which pupils should be exposed to their own educational 'success' and 'failure':

> It was to get them, the ones who are not being so successful, to get them to realize that they could do better and that they were letting themselves down. And the other problem is that schools don't realize that they're in competition with other schools. (. . .) So it's to try and place them within society as well as within the school I think. You might think that getting five GCSEs, yeah five A-to-Cs here is good but if you went to somewhere else you'd be down the bottom. (. . .) there are still within the school those who want to cushion the children and only let them see their successes and those who say, 'Yes, let them see their successes but also prepare them for the fact that there are also failures', that you aren't going to achieve necessarily what you want to.

The headteacher is confident that pupils have received the table well and that it has succeeded in engendering competition and prompting further effort from pupils, as demonstrated by improved grade averages when the table was updated:

> They certainly found it interesting and are keen to see where they are. Most of the kids in year 11 will tell you where they are in the league table and who's top and where their friends are relative to them and when the tables were revised most kids, the vast majority of the kids had better estimated grades than previously.

The headteacher reports that he was unaware of the responses of those pupils whose ranking was too low to be featured in the table. In discussing this he shifts from his previous assertion that these pupils are almost certainly not able to improve their position to suggesting that withholding their ranking is simultaneously a protective and a motivating factor. Finally, he moves his attention back to the top of the table:

Well the message that went to the year group as a whole was that we would put up the top 150, we didn't say the rest of you are duffers, or useless, or whatever. (. . .) And I guess that's the sort of message that they received. So the fact that they don't know whether they're 151 or 150-something or other might be an encouragement to some of them to try and leap into the table. What we didn't want to do was to put up a list which had, I remember [pupil name] was 190, and have it there all the time, you know, and that person become the object of some ridicule amongst his peers or whatever. Being 150 isn't quite so bad, is it? For some of those kids being first would be quite bad as well.

The head of year for these pupils does not share the headteacher's confidence concerning the impact of the table:

The 50 that don't appear on there are going to be ridiculed, I feel. Now you can ask them, maybe you can come back and tell me what they say. I feel that they're maybe being ridiculed a little bit. Some of them who have got the ability and see themselves as 147 think 'Oh God that's shameful', and hopefully . . . So that's obviously where it's going to work. Some of them will make excuses, 'Oh the computer's wrong', 'Oh I mean really interesting', 'Oh that's a mistake'. They won't face up to the fact that they're not achieving. I've got one boy who, you'll probably not meet him. He is the greatest, he's amazing, he's got such an impression of himself and he just thinks he's wonderful and he didn't appear on the lists. I think he was 152nd. And he was just so outraged, he just said, 'Oh well the system doesn't work because I should be there. The machine's wrong'. And that was it. You know, he has no recognition of the fact that he was under-achieving at all.

Dominant models of an inclusive school ethos, embedded through pastoral care and the development of a collective and cohesive school community, are difficult to reconcile with the explicit institution of such overt competition between pupils (and teaching staff). Yet as the discussions of the pupil league table outlined above demonstrate, at the level of senior managers at least, such a notion has been sacrificed to the greater demands of the A-to-C economy. While resistance to this move remains among some pastoral middle managers, many members of teaching staff appear to have accepted, if not embraced, this internal market. As we will see when we move on to examine pupils' experiences of the A-to-C economy, it is the pupils themselves (in formal terms the least powerful members of the school community) who represent the main locus of resistance, however ineffectual, to such market strategies.

Drawing once again on the notion of rationing opportunity through the practice of educational triage, we can identify three relatively discrete zones or areas within the Clough pupil league table (see Table 54.2):[10] first, a 'safe' group, where all pupils are predicted to attain the benchmark of five or more A*-to-C passes (this would include ranks 1 through 55: n = 55: 29 per cent of pupils); second, a group without hope, pupils who cannot attain the benchmark level because they are entered for too

Table 54.2 Educational triage by ethnic origin, free school meals and gender (Clough GM)

	Safe (non-urgent cases)		Suitable cases for treatment		Without hope		Total	
	%	N	%	N	%	N	%	N
White	33	(38)	38	(43)	29	(33)	100	(114)
Black	4	(1)	58	(14)	38	(9)	100	(24)
FSM	7	(3)	44	(19)	49	(21)	100	(43)
Non-FSM	35	(52)	42	(62)	22	(33)	99	(147)
Boys	23	(23)	49	(49)	28	(28)	100	(100)
Girls	36	(32)	36	(32)	29	(26)	101	(90)

Based on positions in the pupil league table and GCSE predicted grades as formulated by Clough.

few subjects (ranks 137–190: n = 54: 28 per cent of the year group). This produces a maximum size 'treatment' group of 81 pupils (ranks 56–136, 43 per cent of the year group) for whom attaining the benchmark grades is seen to remain at least a possibility, that is, they are entered for at least five GCSE examinations. In the light of the conceptual contradictions between notions of inclusivity and competition, the inequalities played out through setting and selection in the school, and the broader evidence concerning differential outcomes at GCSE nationally (Gillborn and Gipps 1996), it is perhaps not surprising that pupils' positions within this league table and their eventual actual GCSE outcomes are marked by 'race', class and gender. Dividing the table into these triage groups once again highlights considerable inequalities of experience and outcome.

Black pupils and pupils in receipt of free school meals are unlikely to be predicted grades that allocate them to the 'safe' group (see Figure 54.6). And while this under-representation is made up to some extent in the treatment group, black pupils and those in receipt of free school meals are over-represented in the group judged as without hope (see Figure 54.7).

Furthermore, those black pupils who do feature in the treatment group are far less likely than their white peers ultimately to attain five or more higher-grade passes. Almost all pupils in the safe group ultimately attain the benchmark—the exception to this being pupils in that category who were also in receipt of free school meals: only one of three such pupils did so. In addition, there is a strong general correspondence between pupils' position in the league-table groups and their 'ability' ranking as defined through the NFER tests administered on entry to year 7.

The pupil league table in Clough GM, therefore, embodies the processes, products and outcomes of those inequitable setting and selection practices discussed [elsewhere: see Gillborn and Youdell 2000: chs. 3–5]. Given the strength of the school's adherence to notions of unequal and fixed ability, which guide its practices, it is not surprising that its measurements of ability and subsequent GCSE grade predictions prove to be so prophetic. Indeed, based on our data and analyses in this and previous chapters, we suggest that these discursive practices *produce* the very effects that they claim to *predict*.

Conclusions

Despite pockets of staff unease and even resistance, both Taylor Comprehensive and Clough GM have largely succumbed to the demands of the educational market place and its A-to-C economy. They exist in a marketized situation where they compete not only with other schools (for pupils and resources) but also with themselves (striving for year-on-year improvements in the performance tables both overall and within each subject area). Amid all this, the percentage of pupils attaining at least five higher-grade passes has become the paramount concern. Schools' responses, however, are not predetermined; Taylor and Clough are very different schools, and in pursuit of improved performance against the national benchmark they mobilize different technologies, reflecting the broader ethos, mechanisms, skills, capacities, and beliefs within

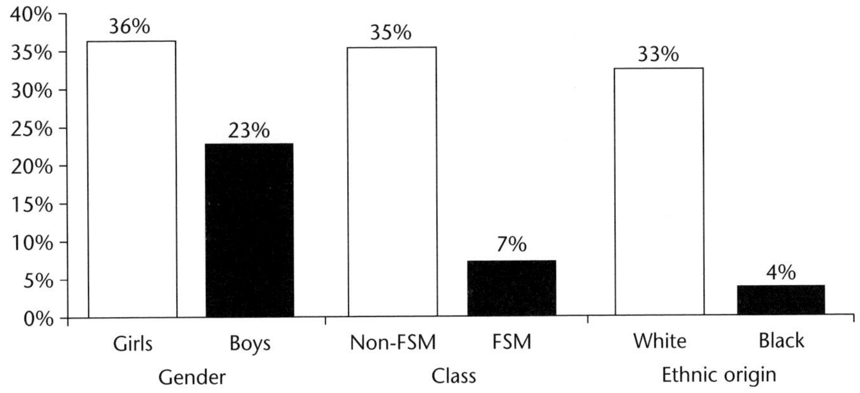

Fig. 54.6 Pupils designated 'safe' by triage at Clough GM

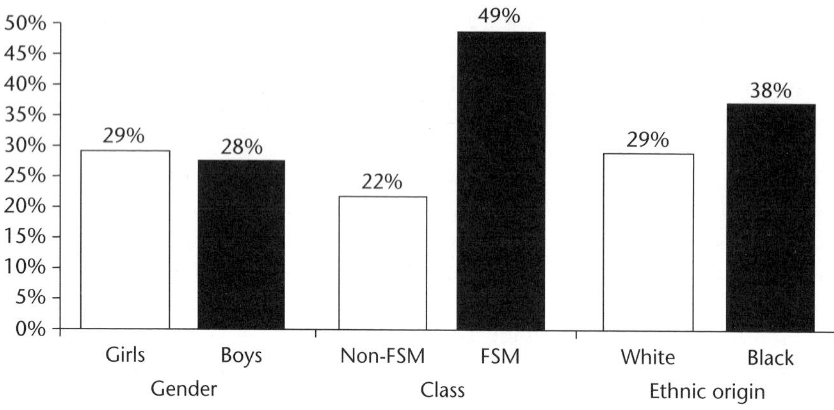

Fig. 54.7 Pupils designated 'without hope' by triage at Clough GM

and about each school. Nevertheless, there are strong similarities between the underlying assumptions and discourses that shape the measures taken in each school in pursuit of converting predicted grade D passes into final grades of C and above.

First, both schools adopt a view of 'ability' as if it were fixed, generalized and measurable. There is often an interesting contradiction when teachers speak of the relationship between 'ability' and outcome. Initially they seem reluctant to sanction a clear and reliable relationship; they speak of 'loose' fits and do not accept simple relationships when posited. Nevertheless, when they discuss the situation further it emerges that, at heart, these simple and predictable relationships are exactly the kind of assumption that lies at the centre of their dealings with issues of selection and maximizing performance at grades A*-to-C. Beyond superficial uncertainties lies an apparently deep-seated belief in the simple, unitary version of 'ability'/intelligence that many teachers appear to question but ultimately support through their actions. Hence, a head of year 11 can describe the association between school measures of 'ability' and outcomes as 'very loose', but go on to conclude that there are only 'the odd hiccups' where it does not work out and, at the next stage in the process, play a pivotal role in translating such criteria into differential expectations and treatment.

Second, both schools produce a range of detailed subject-by-subject predictions for the eventual GCSE results of every pupil. The schools use a range of criteria and adopt different procedures but, once again, the similarities arc clear. In both schools the underlying view of 'ability' as fixed and measurable informs the production of GCSE predictions that involve a range of criteria beyond the pupils' actual performance in 'mock' examinations. Judgements about 'ability', effort and the best way to motivate pupils all come into play as the schools produce their own forecasts of future performance. These predictions are presented with an air of authority and certainty that belies their production. Teachers admit to using 'gut feeling' and adopting different 'ploys'. There is clearly great scope for such predictions to reflect assumptions based on pupils' gender, class and ethnic origin; we noted, for example, that a faculty head viewed Black pupils' concerns about low predicted grades as a 'challenge' and 'threat' rather than evidence of high aspirations and motivation to succeed.

Third, these notions of 'ability' and the predicted grades are combined to identify pupils who are 'under-achieving'. In both schools a particular and divisive notion of 'under-achievement' is mobilized. Here two pupils may be predicted exactly the same GCSE grades but only one might be identified for special treatment, where her/his predicted grades do not match the school's idea of appropriate performance for their level of 'ability'. In Taylor Comprehensive an Achievement Initiative has been launched, involving staff mentoring and special classes. In Clough GM the response has a sharper disciplinary edge, with elaborate surveillance of staff and pupils' performance meant to bolster effort through target setting and self-motivation. The latter includes the production (and regular update) of a public league table of pupil performance based on GCSE predictions. In many respects this can be seen as the ultimate working through of the internal logic that has driven British educational reform for the last two decades: the glorification of academic results above all else, the individualization of competition and the philosophy of 'naming and shaming' are all present here, encapsulated for all to see on a league table of pupils.

It is here, as the schools seek to generate one last push towards maximum success in terms of the GCSE higher grades so central to the A-to-C economy, that we can see most clearly the operation of educational triage. In both schools the particular definition of 'under-achievement' is mobilized to allow the targeting of additional support and resources on to a limited pool of pupils where the most reward is expected: these are the suitable cases for treatment in the final rationing of education. At either extreme there are safe/non-urgent pupils, who can be relied upon, and 'hopeless' cases whose teachers believe that five higher-grade passes is simply not a credible aim. In both schools white pupils and those not in receipt of free school meals are over-represented among the 'safe' group. At the other extreme, black pupils and those in receipt of free school meals (a proxy for poverty) are over-represented among those believed to be beyond help.

The attempt to target resources and draw maximum benefit might have been expected to redress some of the previous inequities in the system. After all, since black pupils and those in receipt of free school meals are less likely to be considered a safe bet, we might reasonably have assumed that they would be over-represented in the treatment group and draw considerable benefit. The opposite is the case. Not only are black pupils and those in receipt of free school meals most likely to be condemned to the group of lost causes, even when they gain entry to the 'treatment' group, there is evidence that they do not draw equal benefit. In both schools, black pupils in the 'treatment' group were markedly less likely to achieve five or more higher-grade passes than their white peers.

In [Gillborn and Youdell 2000: ch. 2] we discussed the dominant linked trends of changes in achievement and educational reform in contemporary Britain. We noted that as overall 'standards' have improved, so the relative inequalities between groups (especially those related to 'race' and social class) have widened. Here, in a microcosm, we see those trends under construction in the myriad decisions, selections and interactions between teachers and pupils. Some black pupils and their peers in receipt of free school meals *do* gain entry to the treatment groups and a very small number draw tangible benefits: but overwhelmingly the processes provide a second chance for those already predicted success. Pupils thought to possess 'ability' (on the basis of a previous test score and/or in relation to social criteria) are given a second chance to fulfil their privileged destinies through the mobilization of higher teacher expectations and additional resources. In Taylor, for example, the whole time-consuming machinery of the Achievement Initiative seems actually to provide an elaborate insurance policy for those already predicted to attain the all-important benchmark of five or more higher-grade passes. In all of this, as we have shown, pupils are positioned as passive recipients: recipients of others' judgements about their 'ability', motivation and the treatment best suited to their needs. But pupils are not passive. They experience the pain and uncertainty of these processes as much as, if not more than, any teacher. As we show in the next chapter, pupils understand their education in different ways but the processes of selection and differentiation do not pass them by. Pupils see triage at work; they perceive some of the principles and inequalities that shape the process; and, on occasion, they seek actively to resist and reshape the dominant labels and processes.

NOTES

1. We recognize that the use of such a metaphor might be considered masculinist. But we feel that it accurately captures both the nature and severity of the relevant processes. Educational triage is a process by which schooling does violence to the opportunities afforded different groups of pupils: it is systematic, deliberate and inequitable.

2. A phrase used by a member of the school's Equality and Achievement Working Party and echoed by several colleagues.

3. See [Gillborn and Youdell 2000: ch. 2] for a discussion of these debates in public policy and educational discourses.

4. See Power (1996) for a full exploration of the historically competing, yet shifting, relationship between the pastoral and the academic. In the instance discussed here, the pastoral can be seen to have shifted into a position where it is not merely subordinate to the academic, but actually colonized by it.

5. This is not to say that these pupils have not *already* experienced favourable treatment. On the contrary, various selection and setting practices are used by some subject departments in Taylor, each associated with differential educational expectations, experiences and opportunities.

6. This may well be attributed to the year head's explicit attempt to ensure a gender balance in the groups.

7. Of pupils included in the Achievement Initiative, 20 per cent (n = 12) of white pupils attained the benchmark in comparison to 9 per cent (n = 1) of Black pupils. Similarly, 25 per cent (n = 14) of pupils not in receipt of free school meals attained the benchmark in comparison to 14 per cent (n = 4) of pupils in receipt of free school meals.

8. This would require that the pupil not meeting the benchmark nevertheless went on to attain pass grades (of G and above) in a greater number of subjects.

9. See [Gillborn and Youdell 2000: ch. 3] for a detailed discussion of how these different cases are explained within the school's dominant conception of 'ability'.

10. As with our analysis of Taylor (above), here we apply the language of triage to the school's own classification and hierarchization of pupils. The terms are ours but the distinctions are the schools'.

The Political Structuration of Assessment: Negotiating State Power and Legitimacy

Luis Benveniste

Introduction

The systematic measurement of student performance has become part of a standard 'education policy package' sponsored by multilateral organizations and international aid agencies. The research literature on national assessment systems has centered primarily on the technical merits, purposes, and challenges of measuring student academic achievement as well as the symbolic legitimating meanings that have promoted their diffusion worldwide. This body of work, however, overlooks the national policy context of the assessment debate by treating national evaluations independently from the political, social, and cultural environments in which they are embedded. Thus, it does not fully explain why countries or regions appraise student performance the way that they do.

In this [chapter], I argue that politics and the nature of state–polity relations play a fundamental role in shaping the design, implementation, and impact of national assessment systems. In other words, the evaluation of student achievement is not just a technical tool for the diagnosis of conditions that may afflict the education sector. Assessment is also a political phenomenon that reflects the agendas, tensions, and nature of power relations between political actors.

The national assessment systems of Argentina, Chile, and Uruguay are presented to illustrate the appropriateness and pertinence of this paradigm. I posit that in these countries the formulation and organization of national evaluation policies cannot be fully understood without taking into consideration the political environment that gave birth to them and the nature of the power relations between relevant educational actors. Through these cases in three countries, I explore the relationships between assessment, legitimacy, and state power. I propose that these relationships are important determinants of the characteristics adopted by national assessment systems and their influence on educational actors.

The first section frames the rapid spread of national assessment systems worldwide in the context of globalization processes. It presents the evaluation of student achievement as part of a global culture that champions decentralization, accountability, and market competition as engines of educational quality. While globalization forces can explain the diffusion of assessment systems worldwide, national politics play a central role in shedding light on the local configurations that these systems adopt.

The second section describes briefly the origins and characteristics of the national assessment systems of Argentina, Chile, and Uruguay. These cases illustrate a general framework that can be used to help

Luis Benveniste, 'The Political Structuration of Assessment: Negotiating State Power and Legitimacy', *Comparative Education Review*, 46, 1.

understand the political structuration of assessment systems and its relationship to legitimacy and state power. Assessment systems can reveal deficiencies in schooling. This may potentially pose a challenge to state legitimacy, particularly where the central state is responsible for providing educational services. In this scenario, central states will attempt to diffuse attention to student outcomes for face-saving purposes.

By contrast, in a decentralized educational environment, central states may afford to reveal inefficiencies in schooling, as they are not necessarily formally responsible for poor performance. In these contexts, national assessments may seek to promote change in the behavior of educational actors by linking student outcomes to public accountability or performance incentive schemes—without these outcomes or schemes necessarily representing an affront to state legitimacy. This ability to command change may also place the central state in a privileged position. The regulatory and allocative ability of assessment can run counter to the devolution of authority in decentralization and can preserve the concentration of power. This situation implies that central states may command authority yet bear limited responsibility over education processes and outcomes.

Globalization and the Measurement of Student Academic Performance

Explaining International Trends in Student Assessment

In recent years, there has been remarkable growth in the creation and advancement of national assessment systems. In Latin America, prior to 1991, only four countries—Chile, Colombia, Costa Rica, and Mexico—had experience with systemic evaluations of academic attainment at the basic education level. During the 1990s, national assessment systems flourished throughout the entire continent. Within the last decade, almost every Latin American country has sought to develop an instrument to monitor student learning.[1] In addition, many Latin American countries have participated in international comparative studies of student achievement, such as the Third International Mathematics and Science Study (TIMSS), the Programme for International Student Assessment (PISA), and Latin America's own comparative experiment sponsored by UNESCO's Regional Office for Latin America and the Caribbean (OREALC).

The rapid spread of national assessment systems is part of a global culture that has embraced the evaluation of student achievement as a powerful instrument that monitors and stimulates education reform worldwide. The World Declaration on Education for All, adopted in Jomtien, Thailand, in 1990 and ratified in Dakar, Senegal, in 2000, recognized that periodic student assessments make a valuable contribution toward the improvement of educational quality. As Article 4 of the declaration states: 'It is, therefore, necessary to define acceptable levels of learning acquisition for educational programs and to improve and apply systems of assessing learning achievement.'[2]

Multilateral and bilateral agencies have played a central role in promoting and supporting national assessment systems within less-developed countries. In Latin America, the World Bank, the Inter-American Development Bank, UNESCO, and the United States Agency for International Development have made critical investments in the design and implementation of national assessments. In 1994, OREALC established the Latin American Laboratory for the Evaluation of Educational Quality to appraise student achievement in mathematics and language across the Americas, identify standards of quality, and encourage member countries to reach those standards.[3] The Organization of Iberoamerican States also launched another hemispheric initiative to furnish Latin American ministries of education with technical support on educational quality assessment matters.[4]

This enthusiasm over national assessments is nurtured by the belief that quality education is an indispensable element for national development within a globalized economic environment that thrives on highly skilled labor. We live in a 'knowledge economy,' in which human capital has gained ascendancy over both labor and raw materials as a vehicle for increased productivity and economic growth. Countries' ability to attract foreign capital and remain competitive in the global marketplace is considered to pivot on their capacity to have a ready supply of highly qualified labor. The demands of this new institutional environment have prompted nations to shift governmental concern away from mere control over the resources and contents of education toward a focus on outcomes. National assessments have come to epitomize this accent on academic performance.[5]

The demand for high-quality educational services has underscored a burgeoning generalized perception that educational systems are in crisis. This crisis, in turn, is ascribed to the fact that the public sector has been unable to manage social services effectively.[6] Governmental administration of schooling is increasingly blamed for the inability of the educational system to meet social expectations. Public schools are considered bogged down by generic and centrally driven bureaucratic requirements that constrict the capacity of schools to address the needs of their student population.[7] National assessments have been championed on the grounds that they can supply schools with up-to-date information in order to support local management and greater school autonomy.[8] In this sense, evaluation upholds decentralization processes and buttresses the devolution of power from the center to the periphery with the purpose of fostering greater efficacy in the administration of schooling services.

Finally, Thomas Kellaghan and Vincent Greaney posit that assessment systems reflect current economic thinking in the context of globalization by embodying ideas of corporatism and managerialism.[9] In addition to prescribing the use of performance indicators and concentrating on standards and results, the measurement of student achievement is closely linked to business ideas of competition and accountability. Evaluations foster a more efficient allocation of resources by identifying how resources are being appropriated and how they ought to be redistributed for a more efficient yield.[10] Reward systems tied to testing outcomes may also prompt educators to direct greater efforts toward teaching practices that increase student achievement. Furthermore, evaluation can augment efficiency by making principals and teachers more accountable to parents. In the face of test results, parents-consumers can voice their discontent and demand better services.[11] Finally, assessment systems can act as 'signaling devices' that encourage competition among educational establishments. Test scores may serve as a gauge for consumers of educational services to exercise choice. Successful schools will thrive in a competitive environment, while those with low results will be driven out of business.

In short, the swift expansion of national assessment systems worldwide reflects a global culture that has espoused student testing as a critical state function. National assessment systems support a new vision for a lean, non-interventionist state model in which the responsibility for the provision of services is devolved to localities. The role of the central state is mainly circumscribed to monitoring and promoting minimum performance standards, making data available to educational actors so as to inform local decision making, and ensuring equity in the distribution of knowledge. The logic underpinning this model of assessment is the promotion of decentralization, market competition, and consumer accountability.

Explaining National Perspectives in Student Assessment

Globalization trends unveil the motor behind the rapid spread of assessment systems and reveal the rationales that have inspired the international community to support, promote, and exhort countries to adopt those systems. However, while transnational trends may elucidate why national assessment systems have entered the international policy stream, they cannot explain divergences in national implementation. Globalization cannot account for the different guises that national assessment systems have assumed across nations.

From the perspective of nation-states, the research literature has highlighted two distinct frames for the absorption of these world models. First, there are technical motivations. Assessment systems are rational-functional instruments that assist educators and policy makers in identifying inefficiencies in education provision and in suggesting avenues for their remediation. Assessments are a pathway to solutions for policy dilemmas. Second, sociological institutional theorists posit that assessment systems play primarily a symbolic role whose purpose is legitimating state action by embracing internationally accepted models of modernity (and hence rational-functional policy making). Student testing is a ritual activity inspired by a global culture.

In the former case, assessment systems are espoused for operative purposes. Student tests are devices for the scientific collection of objective data designed to support rational decision making at the classroom and policy levels.[12] Evaluations may also be associated with incentive schemes that encourage greater productivity and effectiveness in the provision of schooling.[13] This perspective emphasizes that national assessments will be shaped by the desire to inform policy making, resource allocation, classroom practices, or parental perceptions. Information is one of a variety of means for supporting the educational system in its drive toward greater quality, equity, and efficiency.

In the latter case, the measurement of student achievement is not necessarily related to an attempt by nation-states to implement change. Assessment systems, instead, play largely a symbolic role. According to this paradigm, nations do not evaluate academic performance to uncover the deficiencies in education but, rather, to appear as if they do. The primary purpose of assessment is to align state practices with accepted global models of policy making.[14] The absorption of assessment systems is motivated by a drive for legitimation. The emphasis on the symbolic aspects of assessment is founded on the fact that, as institutional sociologists rightly highlight, assessment itself can pose a threat to the legitimacy of state action. The appraisal of educational outcomes can draw attention to deficiencies in education provision and expose governmental action to public criticism. As Jeffrey Puryear underscores, 'evaluation is politically unpopular. ... Comprehensive, reliable assessments of educational systems may threaten important groups, including politicians, teachers, school administrators, government bureaucrats and policy makers. Evaluation, after all, involves judgment and may bring change. Measuring efficiency and output may expose some to criticism; others may risk losing their jobs. It may uncover political patronage, inefficiency, incompetence and low standards.'[15]

For this reason, institutional sociologists advocate that assessment systems must play primarily a figurative role. Governments must decouple evaluative processes from their outcomes in order to blur the inefficiencies in the educational system and preserve their legitimacy.[16] Form takes precedence over function. Hence, national assessments become organized so that the act of testing per se has more salience than the functional purposes of assessment data.

In summary, from the perspective of institutional sociologists, states adopt national assessment systems because they are induced by a world cultural model to align themselves with evaluative practices. Assessment systems are structured to serve primarily a ceremonial function that can legitimize state action to the international community and its domestic constituencies without threatening the state's legitimacy. In this way, evaluation systems can herald the central state's commitment to high-quality educational services while circumventing liability over educational outputs.

It becomes apparent from this description that the rational-functional and symbolic rationales for the national adoption of assessment systems operate at crosscurrents. Rational-functional explanations focus on testing outcomes, while symbolic justifications emphasize the act of testing per se. Rational-functional explanations are based on the assumption that evaluations have the express objective to shape policy making and classroom behavior. Symbolic justifications assume that evaluations have a ritualistic character that endorses ex ante state-sponsored educational practices. Rational-functional explanations aim to couple educational conditions with test results. Symbolic justifications highlight the decoupling between schooling inputs and outputs.

An important dimension has been left out of this analysis: the political context of assessment. Politics underpin how central states shape their national assessments around rational-functional and symbolic justifications. Recognizing the political environment of assessment is essential for elucidating how educational systems resolve the tensions inherent between these two approaches and the motivations that inspire them to do so.

The Political Nature of Assessment

The role of politics in shaping the nature of student testing has been largely absent from the international scholarly literature. This silence has overemphasized rational-functional and legitimacy explanations by treating them in a vacuum, disregarding the role of contextual forces.[17] An awareness of political and organizational power relations is vital for (*a*) contextualizing transnational trends in assessment within a specific national framework and (*b*) explaining the dynamics of national education organization and reform.

Assessment is a political act, and, as such, it is subject to contestation.[18] Testing arises from a political process, oftentimes inspired and molded by political motivations. It is the product of the competition and negotiation among social actors who vie to influence the determination of norms and values that the state will uphold over others.[19] Additionally, national assessment systems can structure patterns of social relations. Testing is a means to exercise power. 'The major problem with national data collection schemes,' asserts Ernest House, 'is that they are used to attempt to control educational results rather than to seek information.'[20] Authority over the disposition and interpretation of testing outcomes signifies authority to sway policy making, resource allocation, and public perceptions.[21] Furthermore, assessment instruments denote mechanisms for regulation and holding social actors implicitly or explicitly accountable for outcomes. The organizational arrangements of assessment systems can delineate who is (and, perhaps equally important, who is not) responsible for student achievement.

Understanding the political dimensions of assessment is essential for shedding light on the diffusion of global models of assessment, the motivations of central states in espousing the measurement of academic achievement, and the configurations that these systems adopt. The national assessment systems of Argentina, Chile, and Uruguay are presented below to explore the following broad principles:

1. Nations adopt and adapt global models of assessment for rational-functional and symbolic reasons in order to address and satisfy political priorities laid out by the central state.
2. National assessment systems may be important conduits for the exercise of state power. By drawing attention to test scores and outcomes, central states can highlight education efficacy concerns and exert significant influence (through mechanisms such as public accountability or performance incentive schemes) to steer educational actors and affect their behavior.
3. In a decentralized context, central states may afford to reveal inefficiencies in educational services, as they are not necessarily formally responsible for poor performance. Schools and regional governance levels will be held accountable.
4. By contrast, where the central state bears responsibility over the provision of educational services, unveiling inefficiencies in schooling may potentially pose a challenge to its legitimacy. In this context, the central state will attempt to safeguard its legitimacy by highlighting educational inputs over outputs and by diffusing responsibility over deficiencies in education.
5. Assessment systems may run counter to the power-sharing logic of decentralization. The regulatory and allocative dimensions of assessments may privilege the core position of central states. In a decentralized context, this may signify that central states can command, yet bear limited responsibility over, education processes and outcomes.

We now turn to examples from three countries to delve into these tenets further.

National Assessment Practices in Southern Cone Countries

The national assessment systems of Argentina, Chile, and Uruguay bear some striking resemblances.[22] They appraise student achievement at regular intervals in their primary and secondary education cycles. The subjects prioritized are mathematics and language. In addition to achievement measures, assessment instruments collect detailed background information from students and their educational establishments in order to explore the relationship between children's learning and contextual variables. Exams are administered by independent proctors and are graded centrally. Schools receive individualized reports comparing their test outcomes to the national average and a regional average. In Chile and Uruguay, school performance is also compared with that of other educational establishments within the same socioeconomic stratum (see Table 55.1).

The Argentine national assessment system is rooted in the 1993 Federal Education Law. The Federal Education Law established the creation of SINEC, the national assessment, under the jurisdiction of the Ministry of Culture and Education (MoCE), for the permanent evaluation of education provision.[23] Between 1993 and 1995, the MoCE carried out a series of pilot tests to validate the instruments of SINEC. The program is now fully operational, and nationwide evaluations are conducted on an annual basis. In February 2001, a presidential decree established the creation of the Institute for the Development of Educational Quality (IDECE) as a semiautonomous agency responsible for the administration of SINEC.

Students are tested yearly in grades 3, 6–7, 9, and 12 in math, language, science, and social studies. Starting in 1997, all grade-12 students are evaluated; in the other grades, only a sample of schools participates in the examination. The test includes both public and private schools. Data are also collected on socioeconomic background variables, and surveys are distributed to teachers and school principals. Schools receive a brief report regarding their average aggregate performance by subject relative to other schools in the region, and teaching guides are designed to strengthen those areas in which students scored poorly.

The first sustained and systematic evaluation effort in Chile took place in 1978, when the Ministry of Education commissioned the Pontificia Universidad Católica, the Catholic university, to design and implement an information system for the education sector. This solicitation would give birth to the Programa de Evaluación del Rendimiento Escolar, better known as PER. This evaluation program would operate for three years but was later discontinued. In 1988, the national assessment

Table 55.1 National assesment systems: general characteristics

	Argentina	Chile	Uruguay
Evaluation agency	IDECE; also some jurisdictions have developed regional assessment systems	PER (1982–4); SIMCE (1988-present)	UMRE (primary level); MESyFOD (secondary level)
Administrating unit	Ministry of Education	PER; SIMCE	National Administration of Public Education, through project implementation units of World Bank-funded project (grades 3–6) and IDB-funded project (grade 9)
First national evaluation	1993	PER in 1982; SIMCE in 1988	1996
Schools tested	Public and private	Public, state-subsidized private, and private	Public and private
Grades tested	Sample: grades 3, 6, 7, and 9; universal: grade 12	Universal: grades 4 and 8 (occasionally grade 10)	Universal: grade 6 (UMRE) and grade 9 (MESyFOD); controlled sample: grade 3 (UMRE)
Subjects tested	Language and math; also social studies and natural sciences for grades 6 and 12	Language and math; also social studies, history, and geography to a subsample	Language and math

Note: IDB = Inter-American Development Bank; IDECE = Institute for the Development of Educational Quality; MESyFOD = Programa de Modernización de la Educación Secundaria y Formación Docente; PER = Pontificia Universidad Católica; SIMCE = Ministry of Education (for Chile); UMRE = Unidad de Medición de Resultados Educativos.

program was reborn as SIMCE, and now it is managed directly by the Ministry of Education.[24]

Chile's SIMCE tests all children in grades 4 and 8 in language and mathematics, and a 10 percent sample of the children is tested in the natural sciences, history, and geography. Each grade is evaluated every other year. Exams are conducted in all municipal, state-funded but privately managed schools, and private schools; SIMCE also collects data on family and school background. Individual classrooms receive a detailed report about their performance, and school rankings are published in the press.[25]

The appraisal of educational outcomes in Uruguay was launched in 1993. The evaluation of educational quality at the primary level is managed by Unidad de Medición de Resultados Educativos (UMRE), which operates through the project implementation unit of a World Bank-funded project. At the secondary level, MESyFOD is responsible for the national evaluation; MESyFOD operates through the project implementation unit of an Inter-American Development Bank-funded project.[26] Both assessment agencies report to the National Administration of Public Education (ANEP). They are semiautonomous entities and transitory in character; that is, there is not yet an official permanent assessment structure in Uruguay.

In the case of Uruguay, students in public and private schools are evaluated approximately every three years in math and language in grades 3, 6, and 9. The first nationwide evaluation of students in grade 6 was carried out in 1996. The first national evaluation of students in grade 9 took place in 1999. As in the previous two countries, data on school and family socioeconomic variables are collected, and schools receive individualized reports regarding their performance level. Unidad de Medición de Resultados Educativos has also organized workshops with principals and teachers to design test items or obtain feedback regarding the characteristics and appropriateness of the assessment. This approach has sought to build consensus and support from teachers and policy makers for the evaluation.[27]

Argentina, Chile, and Uruguay have received substantial financial backing from multilateral organizations to underwrite past and current evaluative experiences. The World Bank and the Inter-American Development Bank have been keen supporters of their national assessments. The Chilean assessment system has oftentimes been featured and promoted by international organizations as a model for emulation.[28]

As laid out in their official pronouncements, the national assessment systems in all three nations have been espoused as technical instruments for informing the policy design and planning process. Testing schemes have formally sought to provide a continuous stream of data about student academic performance in order to inform policy makers and other educational actors about the conditions of the education sector. In particular, assessment has been associated with two distinct rationales: the promotion of educational quality and equity (see Table 55.2). Argentina's SINEC, Chile's SIMCE, and Uruguay's UMRE concur that the measurement of student achievement is a necessary tool for moving the educational system toward higher academic performance. Test data can diagnose the deficiencies that afflict the education sector and point toward avenues for their remediation. Moreover, testing outcomes are a means to identify those sectors of the population that are in greatest need of additional support and direct compensatory resources that may foster social equalization.

The responsibilities assumed by assessment agencies are not restricted to the appraisal of academic performance. In all three countries, they dedicate significant efforts—particularly in Argentina—to the production of pedagogical and methodological support materials, such as manuals and videos. These materials are intended to motivate educators and school supervisors to apply the lessons learned from analyzing test outcomes and, ultimately, to bring about a transformation in educational practices that can enhance the quality of learning. In Argentina and Uruguay, the assessment units have also organized several workshops, tailored to supervisors, principals, and teachers, that address issues of concern to these constituencies.

In addition, assessment outcomes have prompted governmental involvement in the formulation of specific compensatory programs for enhancing student learning. Chile's '900 Schools Program' (P-900) and 'Projects for Educational Improvement' (PMEs) stand out as national initiatives that have linked test

Table 55.2 National assessment systems: mission statement

	Assessment system's mission statement
Argentina	(1) To strengthen the process of decentralization by providing each jurisdiction with relevant data about its educational situation within the national context, (2) to produce comparable statistics at the national level in order to integrate and articulate the educational system as well as to prevent excessive segmentation or differentiation across jurisdictions, (3) to provide information for the formulation and appraisal of compensatory policies that allocate resources to disadvantaged sectors, and (4) to portray the performance of the various actors involved in the administration and management of schooling services.*
Chile	(1) To facilitate the guiding and normative functions of the central government in educational matters, and (2) to channel technical and economic assistance to the neediest sectors of the educational community.†
Uruguay	(1) To produce information about the extent to which primary school graduates have been able to develop skills and fundamental understandings in language and mathematics that every Uruguayan child ought to have incorporated regardless of his social origin, economic condition, or local context.‡

* Argentina—Ministerio de Cultura y Educación, 'Sistema Nacional de Evaluatión de la Calidad: El caso Argentine,' *Revista Latinoamericana de Innovaciones Educativas* 6 (1994): 111–54.

† Josefina Olivares, 'Sistema de Medición de la Calidad de la Educatión de Chile: SIMCE, algunos problemas de la medición,' *Revista Iberoamericana de Educación* 10 (1996): 177–96

‡ UMRE, *Evaluación censal de aprendizajes en lengua materna y matemática. Material informativo para maestros y directores. Fundamentos* (Montevideo: Administración Nacional de Educación Pública, 1996).

results and remediation activities closely. The P-900 is a comprehensive remediation program that includes teacher-training modules, special interventions for at-risk children, community support strategies, and strengthened school management. This program is designed for municipal and government-subsidized private schools that score in the lowest 10 percent of the mathematics and language SIMCE. The PMEs consist of cash grants to publicly funded schools for the implementation of their own educational projects. Projects are selected for their technical merit, but some preference is given to schools with low SIMCE scores and rural establishments. In Argentina and Uruguay, test results have been an input for channeling government resources to needy schools; however, socioeconomic factors or repetition rates, rather than attainment levels in a strict sense, have weighed more heavily in determining participation in educational remediation programs (see Table 55.3).

Finally, student testing in Argentina, Chile, and Uruguay has come to symbolize a public commitment for high quality and equitable educational opportunities. Even those groups that have been most vociferous against current evaluative practices, such as teachers' unions, recognize and regard assessment as an important governmental function (see Table 55.4).

The Political Structuration of Assessment in South America

Notwithstanding these shared features, the Argentine and the Chilean assessment systems differ from the Uruguayan evaluation scheme in significant ways; most saliently, in the use and treatment of assessment results. The former two systems have organized themselves around the ample dissemination of average test scores and fostering an assessment for public accountability model, while the latter has restricted widespread access to test data.

The Chilean government has relied on student assessment scores as a means to hold teachers accountable for student outcomes. Since 1996, the National Evaluation System of Schools' Performance (SNED) has utilized SIMCE data for the allocation of school-wide rewards for excellence in academic performance. Cash awards are distributed among all professional staff. School effectiveness, measured by the absolute SIMCE mathematics and language scores, and school improvement,

Table 55.3 National assessment systems: pedagogical and compensatory activities

	Argentina	Chile	Uruguay
Sociocultural and contextual data collection	Yes	Yes	Yes
Pedagogical support initiatives	Methodological guides and training workshops for school supervisors, teachers, and principals (on jurisdictional request)	Methodological guides	Methodological guides and training workshops for school supervisors, teachers, and principals
Compensatory activities	Yes, indirectly via national compensatory plans such as Plan Social Educativo	Yes, in particular for the lowest-scoring schools (in the tenth percentile)	Yes, indirectly for schools from unfavorable sociocultural contexts or with high repetition rates

Table 55.4 National assessment systems: support by teachers' unions

	Official discourse on role of state-sponsored assessment
Argentina	The educational system needs without doubt to organize a permanent and systematic assessment system. But this must be realized with greater rationality, with a model that guarantees the proper use of scarce resources, that takes advantage of the knowledge contributed by teachers and principals after years of classroom practice and school management experience, and that includes them actively in transformational processes. Otherwise, we only add a new element of control that teachers will learn how to bypass in order to carry on with their work. And resources will be wasted when they are greatly needed to cover the many urgencies schools face.*
Chile	[The Chilean state] is responsible to society for the management of an objective and trustworthy audit of the resources it invests, evaluating the [educational] system's goals and objectives.†
Uruguay	[The UMRE ended up] inspiring satisfaction. That is, it supplied schools with a depiction of their [academic] situation cross-referenced to sociocultural variables, repositioning results in terms of their contexts. This allows for a type of public stance that is congruous with the trade union's habitual position. ... In short, there was a national test and there were results of that test that did not merit objections.‡

* Instituto de Investigaciones Pedagógicas Mariana Vilte-CTERA, 'Para qué sirven los operatives de evaluación de la calidad?' *SUTEBA* 6 (1997), 27.
† Colegio de Profesores de Chile, *Primer congreso nacional de educación: Inform final* (Santiago: Colegio de Profesores de Chile, 1997), 56.
‡ Personal interview. UGN37, 1998.

measured by the difference in scores of two consecutive SIMCE tests, are two of the variables employed to calculate these monetary premiums.[29] In Argentina, the use of assessment data as an input for a teacher evaluation scheme has been under consideration for some time but has not yet been articulated. Cash and in-kind awards to high-scoring schools have been the federal government's main instruments for rewarding academic excellence.

Parental accountability schemes have also been favored by both nations, particularly in the case of Chile. Chilean schools are required to forward their official SIMCE report cards to the parent community. Since 1995, average school test scores have also been widely publicized in newspapers. Student achievement data is meant to inform parent-customers about the quality of service provision and to assist them in the selection of an educational establishment for their children. Argentine newspapers provide coverage of average achievement scores by jurisdiction and list the highest-scoring schools in the country. The Argentine government makes school-by-school results available on the Internet as an initial step to promote parental accountability. It is expected that the grade-12 assessment will become a requirement for high school graduation in the coming years.

In contrast, Uruguay has adopted a cautious strategy regarding the treatment of assessment results. Test data is intended primarily for consumption within the education community. The authorities have made a commitment to release to the public only global results at the national level. Moreover, the presentation of test outcomes is disaggregated and couched in terms of the relationship between student performance and sociocultural environmental variables. Uruguay has espoused an explicit policy to abstain from using student assessment data for accountability purposes.

At first sight, it would appear that Argentina and Chile have emphasized a rational-functional program that relies on assessment as a means of fostering public accountability and providing specific reward mechanisms to encourage quality-enhancing behavior. Alternatively, the Uruguayan assessment would seem to favor a largely symbolic function, as test results receive limited diffusion. Its emphasis on the relationship between student learning and the socioeconomic context in which learning occurs may also be interpreted as an attempt by the central government to shift responsibility for test outcomes to variables beyond its control. Additionally, the evaluation system was a product of a conscientious consensus building process—including central government officials, regional and local school inspectors, teacher representatives from the Technical-Pedagogical Assemblies, trade union leaders, and private sector delegates—that, once again, would point toward a focus on processes rather than outcomes. The consequences that derive from these two approaches are not slight. It would follow that the approach favored by Argentina and Chile could entail significant risk. Public accountability in Argentina and Chile would come at the expense of domestic state legitimacy, as test results tend to inevitably call attention to the shortcomings in the education sector.

As highlighted above, the political context of assessment is a vital element for explaining and understanding the differences in the evaluative strategies espoused among the three countries. First, tracing how evaluation intersects with the political model of the central state reveals the reasons for the national advancement of assessment systems and the forces that have shaped their configuration. The assessment paradigms favored in Argentina, Chile, and Uruguay sought to sustain specific visions of state-polity relations. These state models underlie the nature of assessment and the guises that assessment systems assume.

Second, the impact of assessment strategies on state legitimacy rests on the nature of the relationship between the central state and lower governance levels. Revealing or blurring inefficiencies in service provision responds to explicit political objectives that shed light on the role of evaluative practices as currency for the exercise and transaction of state power. These two themes are the focus of the sections below.

National Assessments and State Models

In the early 1980s, the ruling Chilean military regime spearheaded a dramatic transformation of the educational system that would alter the administrative and financial management of schooling. First, the governance of education provision, until then highly concentrated, was transferred to the municipal level. Second, the private sector became a provider of tate-subsidized educational services. The changes promoted in the finance and administration of schooling sought to promote choice and competition as well as a reduction in government intervention consistent with free market philosophies.[30] Decentralization and privatization—the availability of public funding for private schools—went hand in hand as instruments for reducing public bureaucracy and empowering the market mechanism. The free market was conceived of as the motor propelling greater efficiency and quality in educational service provision, as schools—public and private—competed with each other to attract and retain student-clients.

The establishment of the Chilean national assessment sought to galvanize the military government's vision of educational reform and to act as a guarantee for the survival and maintenance of its educational policies into the future. With the successful transfer of public school governance from the central government to municipalities in 1988, and in the wake of a plebiscite that would put an end to General Augusto Pinochet's administration, the military regime wished to prove to the public that this new state model had improved educational services. The military regime also sought to ensure the preservation of the education privatization reform initiatives that it had spearheaded.[31]

On March 10, 1990, a day prior to the transfer of power to democratic authorities, the military regime promulgated the Constitutional Organic Law of Education (LOCE). This law delineates the juridical framework for the operation and management of the educational system. Article 19 of the LOCE determines that it is the obligation of the Ministry of Education 'to design such instruments that will allow the institution of a system for the recurrent evaluation of the achievement of fundamental objectives and minimum curricular contents in basic as well as middle education.' This article also specifies that the Ministry of Education 'must elaborate statistics of its results, by region and by educational establishment, which must be published in some of the newspapers of national and regional circulation and must be affixed in visible places in each establishment evaluated.'[32] Thus, LOCE mandated student achievement testing as a state function and legislated the mechanism devised to nourish an educational free market system.

The assessment system was fashioned to bolster a consumer sovereignty paradigm in education in which public rankings of test results would encourage parental choice and school competition. Student achievement data, ideally, would act as a signaling device that drives teachers and principals to implement change and improve their performance with the objective of attracting a consumer base.[33] According to this model, test scores operate as a measure of educational worth for consumers. For producers, in turn, test scores operate as direct and indirect incentive mechanisms for guiding educational actors toward higher achievement For example, assessment outcomes are directly linked to the allocation of compensatory resources, the apportioning of financial awards for distinguished performance, and the determination of merit pay scales for school teachers.

Like SIMCE, the establishment of SINEC in Argentina was embedded in a larger education reform effort: SINEC was part of a policy package that decentralized secondary educational governance and finance to provincial jurisdictions.[34] The 1993 Federal Education Law ascribed a subsidiary role to the federal government in education and cemented the decentralization of the educational system to provincial jurisdictions. It mandated changes in five distinct arenas: (*a*) the reorganization of the education system's academic structure, (*b*) the adoption of common curricular matrices, (*c*) the sponsorship of teacher training opportunities, (*d*) the evaluation of educational quality, and (*e*) an increase in public investments in education for a five-year period.[35] The perceived risks of the decentralization process were (*a*) potential curricular contradictions in the national educational system, (*b*) disengagement between the central government and provincial jurisdictions, and (*c*) the deepening of regional educational inequalities. Hence, the strategic responses from the central government to address these hazards were to promote basic curricular guidelines, to monitor and assess educational performance, and to provide financial and technical assistance to the jurisdictions with the lowest levels of socioeconomic development.[36]

Assessment embodied the redefinition of a central state that now found itself 'school-less.' Thus, SINEC represented a new era in state-societal relations where the central state reconfigured itself from provider of schooling services to helmsman in educational policies. As provincial ministries assumed responsibility for the administration and financing of schools within their jurisdictions, the national Ministry of Culture and Education became a guarantor of the quality, equity, and cohesiveness of the educational system across the country. The national assessment system would be a key vehicle for the central government to fulfill this mission.

Moreover, SINEC would play another key role in this political reorganization. Assessment data would not only inform policy change but would actually serve as a conduit to justify and mobilize public opinion around the incipient Argentine educational transformation. The implementation of the decentralization of both the secondary education provision and finance had become a priority for President Carlos Saul Menem and federal authorities, and this initiative had inspired some trepidation among provincial governments. The national government sought to supply public opinion with immediate, conclusive, and objective evidence that the education sector was in crisis and that this crisis demanded the wide-sweeping reforms inscribed in the Federal Education Law. The appraisal of student performance would furnish proof that education reform was a national imperative by exposing the fissures within the educational system. According to a high-level government official, the national assessment was a means for the central government to show that 'everything was bad, that everything was falling apart, and that everything was rotten.'[37]

In Uruguay, the introduction of assessment is embedded within a state model that advocates governmental intervention in the production and distribution of social welfare. Renato Opertti asserts that the Uruguayan education reform efforts of the 1990s have been a 'vindication of the Welfare State.'[38] The transformation of the Uruguayan educational system is founded on four pillars: (*a*) the consolidation of social equity, (*b*) the appreciation of teacher professionalism and training, (*c*) the improvement of educational quality, and (*d*) the strengthening of institutional management.[39] The central state plays a vital role in this reform process, both as the visionary of educational change and as its enactor.

Unidad de Medición de Resultados Educativos is organized around this conception of governmental responsibility for educational services. In particular, the assessment system was designed to bolster the central state as an interventionist agency supporting and tending for the neediest children. 'What we endeavor is to produce information regarding ... which skills [students] have mastered and which ones they have not, what pedagogical and institutional strategies have succeeded to instill fundamental learning in students from the neediest sectors and, finally, where it is still necessary to invest and provide technical assistance to attain a more democratic educational system that benefits all Uruguayan children without socioeconomic distinctions.'[40] Within this operational framework, the national government accepts 'responsibility for the permanent improvement of the quality of learning.'[41] This assumption of responsibility has meant accepting accountability for student results and circumscribing liability for test outcomes. 'There is not going to be an index finger accusing anybody,' declared Germán Rama, the former National Director of ANEP, on the dissemination of the first set of test results in 1996.[42]

Unidad de Medición de Resultados Educativos has made explicit that the eyes of the assessment system are cast on systemic variables affecting student performance.

> Obviously, the deterioration [of the educational system] was not the unique or principal responsibility of teachers. **A multiplicity of factors external to the educational system has been in operation for this to occur**: the mass expansion of education, the deterioration of the quality of life of families, the retraction in educational investments during the military regime, etc. **However, it is necessary to recognize that there are variables internal to the system that affect the quality of student learning**: the pertinence of pedagogical strategies, the relevance of the curriculum, the modalities and expectations inherent in academic evaluations, the fact that schools from the poorest areas are the gateway to the teaching profession, among others.[43]

This approach underscores the structural conditions of schooling. Teachers or schools cannot be held exclusively accountable for learning outcomes.[44]

Finally, the organization of assessment was also an avenue for the Uruguayan government to make a public statement about the type of state-polity relations that it was going to pursue: one in which assessment data would not be an avenue to foster market competition or privatization. The Uruguayan Federation of Teachers and the Technical-Pedagogical Assemblies had expressed opposition to UMRE 'because of its international perspective,' in reference to policies often associated with multilateral organizations that seek to reduce central government intervention in the provision of social services.[45] The national government, in turn, sought to underscore its independence from multilateral organizations and to reaffirm to the public its defense of public intervention in the social sectors. 'We are not dominated by [the World Bank],' declared a former senior ANEP official, 'We are an underdeveloped country where state involvement is vital. ... Education is a competency of the State,'[46] In order to avoid the perception of alignment with privatization or free market policies, governmental authorities committed to maintaining secrecy about individual school test results. The ANEP guaranteed that only national data would be made available to the public.

National Assessments and the Negotiation of State Legitimacy and Power

In the Uruguayan education system, the central government officially bears the obligation for the conditions of the education system. In this institutional context, assessment outcomes are a direct reflection of central government efficiency. Thus, the central state has a vested interest in safeguarding its own legitimacy and blurring deficiencies in educational provision. This objective, as indicated directly above, is accomplished principally through two means: (*a*) limiting the salience and circulation of student performance data and (*b*) highlighting constraining environmental factors in academic achievement.

Unidad de Medición de Resultados Educativos has played down the significance of achievement scores by directing attention to the linkages between socioeconomic variables and academic performance. In its reports, the government refrains from furnishing straight averages of academic achievement. Instead, student outcomes are consistently presented in terms of levels of performance by sociocultural level. Emphasizing the impact of contextual forces in education mitigates the responsibility ascribed to policy makers and educators for schooling outcomes.

This focus on level of performance by sociocultural performance bolsters the message of the central state's commitment to providing high-quality educational services and caring for the neediest sectors of the population, and, consequently, such a focus endorses the state's privileged position at the core of the organization of society. Assessment operates as a mechanism of social accountability that buttresses state intervention and regulation in social affairs, while it simultaneously diffuses the state's liability for results by highlighting educational inputs over outputs. That is to say, evaluation reifies and validates the central state's involvement in the education sector as it nuances the inefficiencies that the assessment system may uncover, which in turn can threaten the state's legitimacy.

By contrast, Argentina and Chile have championed student assessment instruments that, largely through the logic of market competition and public accountability, are meant to operate as engines to promote educational quality. Public accountability, however, may signify a high political risk by calling attention to public policy inefficiency.[47] Although desirable and politically advantageous at the inception of the program, as in the case of Argentina, the structuration of these assessment systems exerts lasting and profound effects. Argentina and Chile must now confront an evaluative apparatus tailored to reveal inefficiencies and, potentially, question state legitimacy.

The Argentine and Chilean governments find themselves under increasing pressure to demonstrate progress in the provision of educational services. They face the challenge to defend public sector performance through a system designed to uphold public accountability. A strategy embraced in both countries has been to utilize assessment results to showcase specific policy successes, such as test score improvements in educational establishments participating in state-sponsored compensatory programs like the 900 Schools Program or the Plan Social Educativo (see Table 55.5).[48] Average test score gains over time have also been awarded primacy over substandard absolute results in public policy parlance.

Most important, the evaluative paradigm in Chile and Argentina is largely sustained by a fundamental reformulation of the relationship among centralized

Table 55.5 SIMCE scores comparison between public and P-900 schools

	1990	1992	1994	1996	Difference: 1990–6
State-funded schools	58.98	66.37	67.74	67.93	8.95
P-900 schools	52.11	60.91	61.62	64.34	12.23
Difference	– 6.87	– 5.46	– 6.12	– 3.59	3.28

Source: Chile—Ministerio de Educación, *Programa de las 900 escuelas: Procao de ingreso 1998* (Santiago: Ministerio de Educación, Division de Educación General, 1988), 9.

authorities, regional governments, and educational actors. In their postreform educational landscapes, the central state can in fact afford to display inefficiencies in educational services and preserve its own legitimacy by reducing its liability and displacing accountability over teaching and learning to lower governance levels. As the central state relinquishes responsibility over the administration of education, it enjoys greater discretion to call attention to assessment results and recouple educational processes and testing outcomes.

In Chile, the underlying logic behind the assessment of educational quality was to bestow on schools the responsibility for securing the patronage of their clientele. It is educational establishments and municipalities—not provincial or central authorities—that must be accountable to the public for their evaluation outcomes. In other words, in the Chilean educational system, the expectation is that schools are the primary agents responsible for the quality of education they provide as well as for taking the necessary steps to enhance student attainment. The central government's duty in the provision of education is circumscribed, and one of its main direct engagements is through providing remedial support to the neediest school population.

In Argentina, there is an analogous phenomenon, albeit at a different level of governance. In the new, decentralized Argentine educational landscape, provinces bear the official responsibility for the conditions in the education sector. The federal government has relinquished its traditional role as provider of education. Assessment results are a means to track regional academic performance. The public disclosures of jurisdictional scores are expected to inform and pressure local authorities into devising relevant strategies that address deficiencies in schooling and raise educational quality.

This relationship between the character of assessment and accountability is corroborated by Argentina's and Chile's earlier evaluative experiences. The PER, SIMCE's predecessor, operated between 1982 and 1984, just as the Chilean educational system was embarking on the process of municipalization. The central ministry, however, remained largely in charge of the provision of educational services during this period. Test outcomes never received ample dissemination at this time, and the PER was later disbanded. According to a high-level government official, 'the Ministry of Education thought that it was responsible for the low achievement results and ... it preferred to safeguard the information.'[49]

Likewise, the Argentine government conducted a student achievement study in 1991–2 just prior to the decentralization of educational services from the federal to the provincial governments. The Ministry of Education decided against releasing the outcomes of this evaluation publicly. 'The results were so disastrous that [former] Minister Salonia did not want to publish them,' attests a high-ranking government officer.[50] He kept the results 'under 7 keys' because he considered them 'unpresentable.'[51]

Hence, as the central state relinquished its traditional responsibility over educational services, the Argentine and Chilean central authorities also began to afford to direct public attention to the outcomes of education and to foster public accountability over them. This disclosure plays an important political role.

In Argentina and Chile, the establishment of national assessment systems occurred in the context of wider decentralization reforms. Decentralization strives to reduce the size of the central government and shift the responsibility for the provision of educational services to lower governance levels. Much of the academic literature has portrayed national assessments as key promoters for the effective redistribution of power. In a decentralized system—and particularly in countries where significant regional socioeconomic disparities exist—evaluation becomes a tool to track and ensure equity in the distribution of knowledge. The growing desire for school autonomy entails greater need for quality control in order to guarantee minimum universal standards of teaching and learning.[52] Information can empower local actors to 'promote their responsibility and their improvement in a climate of greater autonomy.'[53] The Chilean SIMCE, for example, has been hailed 'as a strong tool for implementing a reform program fostering decentralization, accountability and increased learning.'[54] Similarly, the Argentine SINEC is described as a conduit for newly decentralized schools to assume responsibility over the provision of high-quality education and to strengthen their capacity to do so by providing relevant information.[55]

Yet, decentralization implies that the central state relinquishes some of its ability to exercise control. This redistribution of central state power defies its position of privilege and reduces its sphere of influence. In the middle of a contraction in the central state's sphere of influence, national assessment systems may in fact act as a conduit to counterbalance this diffusion of power. In other words, decentralization and assessment can work at cross-currents. While decentralization programs devolve control from the core to the periphery, national assessments may reconcentrate power back to the core. And while decentralization limits the sphere of influence of the central state, assessment vests the state with the normative authority to assert its privileged position.[56] The reduction of the role of the central state as architect and provider of educational services is counteracted by an increased role of the central government as regulator and guarantor of educational quality.[57] Thus, although assessment has been extolled as a tool for local empowerment and decision making, evaluation can actually operate as a centralizing mechanism of control and administration.

In Chile, the SIMCE was conceived to support the transfer of responsibility for educational establishments over to municipalities. In theory, assessment data would encourage and enable schools to respond to and satisfy the demands of local consumers. In practice, assessment has prompted teachers and principals to align themselves with the national test. The SIMCE has proved to exert a powerful influence in curricular and pedagogical activities. 'Teaching to the test,' despite being widely criticized by educators as a stratagem to improve children's scores in order to secure a higher position in the public rankings, is commonplace. For instance, an educator from a low-income, subsidized private school avows, 'they [the teaching staff at the school] have never worked for SIMCE in order to obtain better results.' On the other hand, this school dedicates one period of classroom practice every day to a program entitled 'Let's Improve Our Scores.' A municipal school in Santiago reports that, in testing years, students in grades 4 and 8 receive supplementary instruction in mathematics and language after the regular school day. Even those educational establishments that manifest opposition to teaching with SIMCE in mind report escalating pressure from central and district authorities to align themselves closer to the test. Some municipalities organize mock tests to give schools an opportunity to prepare children for the national evaluation. Others offer financial incentives for high-scoring schools. Some teachers fear their jobs might be at risk if their students do not perform adequately in the evaluation. In summary, SIMCE has proved to exert a commanding presence in the organization of Chilean schooling, steering the national attention toward test scores and public rankings.[58]

In Argentina, the national assessment system plays a distinct role as the nature of traditional federal-provincial relations adopts a new configuration in a decentralized environment: SINEC redefined the function of the central government after relinquishing its power over the provision of education. In light of greater regional autonomy, the evaluation of student performance intends a 're-articulation of the [educational] system' that preserves national cohesiveness around shared educational quality objectives and that guarantees equity in the fulfillment of these goals.[59]

Initially, the federal government dedicated significant effort to building consensus with provincial jurisdictions. Test content and items were painstakingly developed and approved by all provincial representatives in the Federal Council of Culture and Education. But over time, assessment has become a site where the contention between national and provincial levels is increasingly acted out. A national newspaper depicted SINEC as 'a battle for space' led by 'the Ministry without schools' in order to 'prevent provinces from snatching its lead role.'[60]

As provincial jurisdictions defined their own spheres of influence, the national assessment became increasingly perceived as an infringement of their institutional domain. Moreover, the national assessment bears a threat to the legitimacy of the subnational state by exposing and comparing testing outcomes across jurisdictions. Provincial leaders as well as educators describe the SINEC as a centralizing force in the Argentine educational landscape. A government official in the city of Buenos Aires remarks that the evaluation is not a collaborative effort but is largely a top-down imposition. 'Jurisdictions have no margin to decide on any issue. . . . Our participation is at best bounded and restrained.'[61] Similarly, a public school teacher in the province of Entre Ríos underscores that decentralization and assessment are not necessarily complementary functions. 'This is not a decentralized system. It has been recentralized. The evaluation of [educational] quality, the curricular basic contents, professional training are all symptomatic of a recentralization of the system beyond educational establishments. And this is much stronger than our previous situation. The features of control are stricter.'[62]

Some provinces have adopted a series of strategies to counter the centralizing pressures of the national evaluation. Some jurisdictions are developing regional assessment initiatives that respond to their own programmatic and curricular priorities. This is an attempt to encourage educational establishments to attune themselves with local mandates. Other jurisdictions have attempted to attack the technical integrity and the credibility of the national tests' results.[63] And in some instances, a few jurisdictions have engaged in a strategy of passive resistance to the national evaluation. The neglect from provincial authorities and school supervisors signals to teachers and educators that the national evaluation bears little significance. As a government officer in the province of Buenos Aires admits, 'the federal government sends materials [to schools] . . . but if your authorities do not give you the go ahead, you have to be a very independent teacher to decide to use them.'[64]

In Argentina and Chile, the national assessment has been a means for the central government to exert regulatory and allocative authority. Evaluation has played a salient role in preserving the primacy of the national state at center stage in the context of the deconcentration of power. Evaluating per se, however, is not a sufficient condition to bring schools or districts into alignment with central mandates. The central government must tie evaluative practices to schemes that will foster educational actors to accommodate and abide by governmental directives. Some of these schemes include publicizing test scores, providing performance incentives, marrying attainment to teacher merit pay scales, or making the exam an accreditation requirement. The lower the stakes of the evaluation, the less likely that it will exercise any consequential impact on schooling practices. The higher the stakes, the more likely the assessment is to shape the behavior of educational actors.[65]

The case of Uruguay offers an interesting counterpoint. Education administration is organized in a highly centralized fashion. In the words of a high-ranking government official, 'teachers in Uruguay behave like an army. If you give them an order they will follow it.'[66] The UMRE does reinforce the regulative authority of the National Administration of Public Education, but there is already an extensive apparatus of normative and allocative control in operation. For instance, the central government makes budgetary appropriations, determines curricular programs, decides teacher appointments, and manages the school supervisory cadre. Indeed, the assessment system is one of various existing mechanisms of regulatory control, but there is no impetus to utilize assessment outcomes as a means to encourage alignment with centralized mandates.

Contrary to appearances, the Uruguayan assessment model defies the characterization of strictly top-down or centralized control. The UMRE was built cooperatively with a wide array of regional and local educational actors, including teachers, supervisors, private sector representatives, teachers' union advocates, and government officers. This direct popular exchange bolstered the legitimacy of the central state's regulatory power. Moreover, it deepened the penetration and impact of the assessment initiative.

Conclusion

The diffusion of national assessment policies in the Southern Cone is a product of the interplay of globalization forces and national politics. The globalization of assessment is embedded in the globalization of a new state paradigm. The modern state, in its ideal model, is not a provider of educational services but, rather, a guarantor of their quality and equity in their distribution. It breaks away from monolithic administration as it introduces flexibility, responsiveness to grassroots conditions, and democratic participation into governmental policy. The logic of public accountability and market competition will support the educational system in driving educational actors toward greater allocative efficiency and the delivery of higher quality services. The *estado docente*—the state as teacher—represents an outdated archetype equated with centralized, bureaucratized, and inefficient management. It is deemed top-heavy and insensitive to local variation and initiative. The modern state, rather, is concerned with consensus building, information dissemination, evaluation, and the compensation of inequities.[67]

Cristian Cox, for example, uses the following imagery to describe the transformation of the Chilean state: 'A State that is not an "oarsman" (producer of services) but a "helmsman"; that adds to its traditional normative and budgetary tools an increasing use of information, evaluation and incentive instruments; that externalizes functions and creates support networks in civil society; and that conceives as one of its essential functions working proactively for the quality of the entire system through explicit and long-term programs and strategies, and for its equity through positive discrimination practices.'[68] Similarly, Cecilia Braslavsky and Gustavo Cosse posit that Latin American nations have embraced a conception of the *estado promotor*—the promoter state. The *estado promotor* is an 'empowering' state whose purpose is identifying the educational needs of districts and regions and supporting them to redress their 'dark facets.'[69]

According to this perspective, state action focuses on guiding social services toward higher performance and organizing compensatory activities for at-risk populations. National assessments support governments in these tasks by focusing the attention of educational actors on student outcomes, supplying information on variations in the conditions of education that may suggest avenues for remediation purposes, and providing a framework to link performance to a reward system that steers educational services toward improvement. The enthusiasm over national assessment systems is grounded on their potential (*a*) to foster a more efficient use of resources, (*b*) to promote the constant improvement and to safeguard the fair distribution of goods and services, and (*c*) to encourage regional autonomy.

The diffusion and absorption of this idealized paradigm of assessment at the national level responds to technical and rational-functional as well as symbolic-legitimation motivations. In the three examples described in this article, assessment systems have been construed with the explicit goal to forward two main goals: the promotion of educational quality and the preservation of equity. Assessment is both an avenue for achieving these goals through technical means and an embodiment of the central state's commitment to reach them.

Yet, as the cases that I describe illustrate, these goals are mediated by the character of national politics. Evaluative processes and instruments are shaped by and come to represent the particular political agendas of national authorities. In Chile, SIMCE was intended to advance a central state project with a clear model of state-polity relations: the institution of a consumer sovereignty paradigm that would grant parents greater opportunities for choice through market competition. In Argentina, SINEC was part of the reinvention of the role of the central state vis-à-vis the decentralization of educational services to provincial jurisdictions. In Uruguay, UMRE is a reaffirmation of a state model in which the central government privileges its obligation as purveyor of educational services and protector of the most underprivileged sectors of the population. The plight for the improvement of educational quality incarnates the duty of the national government to secure and open avenues for upward social mobility. In all three cases, the central government is responsible for monitoring standards, managing resources (sometimes in the form of performance incentives), and enabling schools' higher achievement through compensatory programs.

An important difference between these countries stands out. Uruguay has adopted a strict policy to limit the public dissemination of test results, and it has highlighted the relationship between student outcomes and the sociocultural factors that condition them. This approach has signaled the central state's rejection of free market or privatization policies. But it has also been a way of denoting its commitment to high-quality education while blurring deficiencies in educational service provision. The central state, as purveyor of educational services, must account for student outcomes. Thus, diffusing accountability for test results safeguards its legitimacy to its constituents.

By contrast, in Argentina and Chile assessment systems were designed to ground and validate state-societal reform initiatives by revealing, rather than concealing, shortcomings in educational performance. Public accountability is meant as a means of encouraging schools and regional governments toward enhanced performance. School or provincial outcomes are publicized so that parents and educators can scrutinize them. Test scores are tied to reward schemes so as to elicit changes in the behavior of educational actors. These strategies embody exhortations to action.

In light of the public display of educational deficiencies, assessment does not affront the legitimacy of the central state. In a decentralized educational environment, schools or regional governance structures must account for student outcomes. The legitimacy of the central state may be in fact bolstered through its involvement in compensatory activities, such as the 900 Schools Program or the Plan Social Educativo.

In this institutional context, an interesting paradox arises. On one hand, evaluation is promoted on the grounds that it supports grassroots decision making and education decentralization. Information is meant to empower local actors and foster a climate of greater autonomy. On the other hand, national assessments can yield significant normative and allocative power to the central state. This authority can command a strong presence in the educational system. Its influence may be felt all the way into the classroom. The regulatory dimension of assessment can place the central government in a comfortable position where it can command authority over educational services without formal or official responsibility for them. If not carefully reined in, assessment may stand for a top-down imposition rather than the realization of a joint vision.

Assessment and decentralization operate under competing logics. National assessments incarnate a centralizing force that mandates universal normative criteria. Central prescriptions can and often do supersede site-specific formulations. In a decentralized environment, national assessments may signify a way for the central state to preserve its core position and offset the power-sharing logic of decentralization. As Hans Weiler suggests, 'reconciling the two may well turn out to be an exercise in contradiction.'[70] Correct that there should be a question mark at the end of this title?

NOTES

1. Carlos Rojas and Juan Manual Esquirel, *Los sistemas de medición del logro académico en Latinoamérica* (Washington, DC: World Bank, 1998); Laurence Wolff. Educational Assessments in Latin America: Current Progress and Future Challenges (Santiago: PREAL, 1998).
2. World Conference on Education for All, Meeting Basic Learning Needs: A Vision for the 1990s (New York: Inter-Agency Commission for World Conference on Education for All, 1990), 5.
3. Juan Casassus, Violeta Arancibia, and Juan Enrique Froemel, 'Laboratorio Latinoamericano de evaluación de la calidad de la educación', *Revista Iberoamericana de Education* 10 (1996): 231–61.
4. Organización de Estados Iberoamericanos, Programa evaluation de la calidad de la educatión: Reseña, 1991–1997 (Buenos Aires: OEI, 1997).
5. Organisation for Economic Co-operation and Development, *Education at a Glance—Analysis* (Paris: OECD, 1996); World Bank, *Education Sector Strategy* (Washington, DC: World Bank, 1999).
6. Benjamin Levin, 'The Lessons of International Education Reform', *Journal of Educational Policy* 12 4 (1997): 255–66; Joao Oliveira, *Educational Reform in Latin America: Towards a Permanent Agenda* (Washington, DC: World Bank, 1991).

7. Marlene Lockheed and Emmanuel Jimenez, 'Public and Private Schools Overseas: Contrasts in Organization and Effectiveness', in *Who Chooses? Who Loses?* ed. Bruce Fuller and Richard Elmore (New York: Teachers College Press, 1996), 111–28; John Chubb and Terry Moe, *Politics, Markets, and America's Schools* (Washington, DC: Brookings Institution, 1990).
8. Benjamín Alvarez, 'Contribución de la evaluación al aprendizaje de las naciones', in *Evaluación y reforma educativa: Optiones de politico*, ed. Benjamin Alvarez and Monica Ruiz-Casares (Washington, DC: Academy for Educational Development, 1997).
9. Thomas Kellaghan and Vincent Greaney, 'The Globalisation of Assessment in the Twentieth Century', *Assessment in Education* 8 1 (2001): 87–102.
10. Marlene Lockheed and Eric Hanushek, 'Improving Educational Efficiency in Developing Countries: What Do We Know?' *Compare* 18 1 (1988): 21–38.
11. Martin Carnoy and Claudio de Moura Castro, *Improving Education in Latin America: Where to Now?* (Washington, DC: Inter-American Development Bank, 1996); Laurence Wolff, Ernesto Schiefelbein, and Jorge Valenzuela, *Improving the Quality of Primary Education in Latin America and the Caribbean: Toward the Twenty-First Century* (Washington, DC: World Bank, 1994).
12. Rojas and Esquivel (n. 1 above); Wolff (n. 1 above): Alvarez.
13. Carnoy and de Moura Castro; Alejandro Tiana, 'La evaluación de los sistemas educativos,' *Revista Iberoamericana de Education* 10 (January–April 1996): 37–61.
14. John Meyer, John Boli, George Thomas, and Francisco Ramirez, 'World Society and the Nation-State', *American Journal of Sociology* 103 1 (1997): 144–81; Hans Weiler, 'Decentralisation in Educational Governance: An Exercise in Contradiction?' in *Evaluation as Policymaking: Introducing Evaluation into a National Decentralised Educational System*, ed. Marit Granheim, Maurice Kogan, and Ulf Lundgren (London: Kingsley, 1990).
15. Jeffrey Puryear, 'International Education Statistics and Research: Status and Problems', *International Journal of Educational Development* 15 (1995): 79–91, quotation on 88.
16. John Meyer and Brian Rowan, 'The Structure of Educational Organizations', in *Environments and Organizations*, ed. Marshall Meyer (San Francisco: Jossey-Bass, 1978); Karl Weick, 'Education Organizations as Loosely Coupled Systems', *Administrative Science Quarterly* 21 1 (1976): 1–19.
17. Charles Perrow, *Complex Organizations: A Critical Essay* (New York: McGraw-Hill, 1993); Thomas Popkewitz, 'Some Problems and Problematics in the Production of Evaluation', in Granheim, Kogan, and Lundgren, eds., 103–18.
18. George Noblit and Deborah Eaker, 'Evaluation Designs as Political Strategies', in *The Politics of Reforming School Administration: The 1988 Yearbook of the Politics of Education Association*, ed. Jane Hannaway and Robert Crowson (New York: Falmer, 1989).
19. Doug Archbald and Fred Newmann, *Beyond Standardized Testing: Assessing Authentic Academic Achievement in the Secondary School* (Reston, Va.: National Association of Secondary School Principals, 1988).
20. Ernest House, 'Decentralised Evaluation for Norway', in Granheim, Kogan, and Lundgren, eds., 215.
21. George Noblit, 'The Prospects of an Applied Ethnography for Education: A Sociology of Knowledge Interpretation', *Educational Evaluation and Policy Analysis* 6 1 (1984): 95–101; Peter Airasian and George Madam, 'Linking Testing and Instruction: Policy Issues', *Journal of Educational Measurement* 2 2 (1983): 103–18.

22. This account is based on policy documents and over 100 individual and group interviews conducted in 1998 with national government education officials, regional government representatives, school supervisors, principals, teachers, and union leaders.

23. Maria Lucrecia Tulic, 'Una aproximación a la evaluación de las potíticas públicas: El caso del SINEC,' *Revista Iberoamericana de Educación* 10 (1996): 159–76; Argentina—Ministerio de Cultura y Educación, 'Sistema Nacional de Evaluación de la Calidad: El caso Argentine', *Revista Latinoamericana de Innovaciones Educativas* 6 (1994): 111–54. The acronym SINEC stands for Sistema Nacional de Evaluación de la Calidad, or National Program for the Evaluation of Educational Quality. At present, the Ministry of Culture and Education is known as the Ministry of Education.

24. The acronym SIMCE stands for Sistema de Medición de la Calidad Educativa, or National Program to Measure Educational Quality.

25. Josefina Olivares, 'Sistema de Medición de la Calidad de la Educación de Chile: SIMCE, algunos problemas de la medición', *Revista Iberoamericana de Educación* 10 (January–April 1996): 177–96; Erika Himmel, 'National Assessment in Chile', in *National Assessments: Testing the System*, ed. Paud Murphy, Vincent Greaney, Marlene E. Lockheed, and Carlos Rojas (Washington, DC: World Bank, 1996).

26. The acronym UMRE stands for Unidad de Medición de Resultados Educativos, or Center for the Measurement of Educational Results. The acronym MESyFOD stands for Programa de Modernización de la Educación Secundaria y Formatión Docente, or Secondary Education and Teacher Training Modernization Project.

27. UMRE, *Evaluación censal de aprendizajes en lengua materna y matemática. Material informativo para maestros y directores. Fundamentos* (Montevideo: Administratión Nacional de Educación Pública, 1996).

28. See, e.g., Benjamín Alvarez and Monica Ruiz-Casares, eds. (n. 8 above); Helena Bomeny, ed., *Avaliação e determinação de padrões na educação Latino-Americana: Realidades e desafios* (Rio de Janeiro: Editors Fundação Getulio Vargas, 1997); Murphy, Greaney, Lockheed, and Rojas, eds.; Organization de Estados Iberoamericanos, *Evaluatión de la calidad de la education* (Madrid: OEI, 1996); Rojas and Esquivel (n. 1 above); Wolff (n. 1 above).

29. Other variables considered in SNED include (*a*) *initiative*, measured by teacher-training activities and institutional educational projects; (*b*) *labor conditions*, measured by whether the school cadre is complete and substitute teachers are readily available; (*c*) *equality of opportunities*, measured by student retention and promotion rates; and (*d*) *parental integration*, measured by parent approval rates in SIMCE surveys and their participation in parent-teacher associations.

30. Osvaldo Larrañaga, 'Descentralización de la educación en Chile: Una evaluación económica,' *Estudios Públicos* 60 (Spring 1995): 243–86.

31. Himmel, 'National Assessment in Chile'.

32. Diario Oficial de la República de Chile, *Ley número* 18.962, *ley orgánica constitutional de enseñanza* (Santiago: Presidencia de la Nación, 1990), 6.

33. Himmel, 'National Assessment in Chile', 14.

34. The management and finance of primary education had been decentralized already in 1978 by former president Jorge Rafael Videla's military junta. The transference of primary schools to provincial jurisdictions had been initiated in the late 1960s by another military government, but it was interrupted during a brief democratic interregnum between 1973 and 1976. Despite the decentralization of educational management, the central government had retained authority for dictating curricular programs and supervising

school performance (Adriana Puiggrós, ed., *Historia de la educación en la Argentina*, iv [Buenos Aires: Editorial Galerna, 1993]).

35. Argentina—Ministerio de Cultura y Educación, *Conozcamos la ley* (Buenos Aires: Ministerio de Cultura y Educación, 1995).

36. Argentina—Ministerio de Cultura y Educación, *Perfil estratégico del nuevo ministerio y aspectos clave de la nueva estructura* (Buenos Aires: Ministerio de Cultura y Educación, 1993).

37. Personal interview, AGN8, 1998.

38. Renato Opertti, 'La reforma educativa: Reinvindicación del estado benefactor', *Cuadernos del CLAEH* 22 (1997): 146–7. José Batlle y Ordóñez was President of Uruguay twice, in 1903–7 and 1911–15. He spurred a social movement that is still vigorous today, and his political philosophy is at the core of the Colorado Party. *Battlismo* is grounded on the state as an agent of interventionist practice in the economic and social spheres.

39. German Rama, *La reforma educativa en Uruguay* (Montevideo: Administración Nacional de Educación Pública, 1998).

40. UMRE, *Manual del aplicador* (Montevideo: Administración Nacional de Educación Pública, 1996), 1–2.

41. UMRE, *Fundamental y objetivas de la evaluation muestral de aprendizajes en 3er aña educacion primaria* (Montevideo: Administración Nacional de Educación Publica, 1997), 6.

42. 'Los resultados no son satisfactorios', *El Observador* (Montevideo; 29 November 1996).

43. UMRE, *Manual del aplicador*, 1, bold in the original.

44. UMRE, *Material informativo para maetros y directores: Fundamental* (n. 27 above). The containment of school accountability has been an important factor in securing support from the teacher cadre for state-sponsored evaluative practices. 'The teacher-run Technical-Pedagogical Assemblies have been vocal advocates of this doctrine. Neither schools' nor teachers' sustained efforts can revert the motivational problems in learning that emerge from the socioeconomic crisis that a great number of our students and their families are undergoing. Critical living conditions and family insecurity determine that these children lack minimum vital necessities (food, lodging, hygiene, etc.) to guarantee their subsistence. To think that schools and teachers can revert this situation would be to deposit a large degree of omnipotence on them and ascribe responsibilities for situations and problems that overcome them' (Asamblea Nacional Técnico Docente, 'Resoluciones' [Asamblea Nacional Técnico Docente, Montevideo, 1998, mimeographed], 29).

45. Personal interviews, UGN6, UGNS7, 1998.

46. 'Estado no puede entregar la educación a manos privadas', *El Diario* (Montevideo; 6–7 November 1996).

47. In fact, during the PER period, the Chilean military regime was concerned about being blamed for mediocre test outcomes. Hence, PER results were largely treated as if they were 'a state secret' (C. Escobar Cáceres, 'Impacto del Programa de Evaluatión del Rendimiento Escolar [PER] a nivel macroinstitucional' (Masters thesis, School of Engineering, Pontificia Universidad Católica de Chile, 1989). In Argentina, the press heralded the appraisal of student competencies as providing irrefutable evidence of 'the decay of the Argentine education' ('Burrolandia no será vagolandia? Falta de cultura del trabajo en Argentina', *Àmbito Finandero* [Buenos Aires; 23 February 1994], 16).

48. Chile—Ministerio de Educación, *Programa de las 900 escuelas: Orientaciona 1998, rediseno y metas del P-900* (Santiago: Ministerio de Educación, División de Educación General, 1998).

49. Escobar Cáceres, 213–14.

50. Personal interview, AGN1, 1998.

51. 'Los chicos aprenden mal y poco en escuelas y colegios de codo el país', *Clarin* (Buenos Aires; 4 February 1994), 12–13.

52. Juan Prawda, 'Educational Decentralization in Latin America: Lessons Learned', *International Journal of Educational Development* 13/3 (1993): 253–64; Anton Luyten, 'The Role of Testing Agencies in International Education,' in *International Perspectives on Academic Assessment*, ed. Thomas Oakland and Ronald Hambleton (Boston: Kluwer Academic, 1995).

53. Alvarez (n. 8 above), 6.

54. Wolff (n. 1 above), 8.

55. Lilia Toranzos, 'Evaluatión y calidad', *Revista Iberoamericana de Educatión* 10 (January–April 1996): 63–78.

56. Hans Weiler, 'Control versus Legitimation: The Politics of Ambivalence', in *Decentralization and School Improvement: Can We Fulfill the Promise*? ed. Jane Hannaway and Martin Carnoy (San Francisco: Jossey-Bass, 1993), p. 78; Sverre Kvale, 'Evaluation and Decentralisation of Knowledge', in Granheim, Kogan, and Lundgren, eds., 119–38.

57. Cecilia Braslavsky and Gustavo Cosse, *Las actuales reformas educativas en America Latina: Cuatro actores. Ires lógicas y ocho tensiones* (Santiago: PREAL, 1997).

58. Personal interviews, CESS1, CESM9, CGM6, and CGN11, 1998.

59. Toranzos, 70.

60. *Clarin* (n. 51 above), 12.

61. Personal interview, AGP3b, 1998.

62. Personal interview AER14, 1998.

63. For instance, a former minister of culture and education of San Luis discredited the 1995 results of SINEC that positioned this province among the four lowest in the country. He accused the federal government of 'blasting a low and treacherous blow' by conducting a biased sample that favored private over public establishments ('Objetó el Ministro de Educación puntano la evaluación nacional de ren-dimiento escolar', *La Nación* [Buenos Aires; 11 July 1995]). Similarly, the former director general of schools of the province of Buenos Aires lambasted the reliability of SINEC and offered as proof the fact that her jurisdiction jumped from fourteenth to first place in the provincial ranking tables ('Adiós al promedio en el secundario', *La Natión* [Buenos Aires; 3 March 1999], 8). The press has also given coverage to claims of possible wrongdoing in the correction of exams, unclear grading schemes related to open-ended questions, and exam graders that had not been paid ('El 5 y el 6 de Julio evaluaran la calidad en el secundario', *La Natión* [Buenos Aires; 31 March 1999], 10). Newspapers have reported as well about irregularities in test-taking procedures, principals who gained access to tests in advance, and the disclosure that the highest ranking private school in the province of Buenos Aires had actually provided students with the answers to the exam beforehand ('Un colegio jaqueado por machetes', *La Natión* [Buenos Aires; 19 November 1998], 12).

64. Personal interview, AGP2, 1998

65. Lorrie Shepard, *Will National Tests Improve Student Learning*? (Los Angeles: National Center for Research on Evaluation, Standards, and Student Testing, 1991); A. LaPointe, 'Assessing the Quality of Education over Time: The Role of the National Assessment of Educational Progress (NAEP)', in *University Examinations and Standardized Testing*, ed. Stephen Heyneman and Ingemar Fägerlind (Washington, DC: World Bank, 1988).

66. Personal interview, UGNS, 1998.

67. Daniel Filmus, *Estado, sociedad y educación en la Argentina de fin de siglo: Procesos y desafios* (Buenos Aires: Troquel, 1996); Juan Carlos Tedesco, *El desafío educativo: Calidad y democracia* (Buenos Aires: GEL, 1987)

68. Cristian Cox, *La reforma de la educación Chilena: Contexto, contenidos, implemencatión* (Santiago: PREAL, 1997), 20.

69. Braslavsky and Cosse (n. 57 above); Cecilia Braslavsky, 'Reconversion of the Argentine Educational System, 1984–1995', in *Argentina: The Challenges of Modernization*, ed. Joseph Tulchin and Allison Garland (Wilmington, Del.: SR, 1998).

70. Weiler, 'Control versus Legitimation' (n. 56 above), 78.

56 Globalizing Empiricism: What, If Anything, Can Be Learned from International Comparisons of Educational Achievement?

Harry Torrance

Introduction

This chapter seeks to evaluate international comparisons of educational achievement both as research studies in their own right and as instruments of policy. Such studies variously claim that they can accurately measure the achievement of students in key subjects (usually maths, science, and language), at different ages and across many countries, and from this draw lessons about what comparative standards are being achieved by each country's education system and what governments should do to raise educational achievement. Thus for example the 'Trends in International Maths and Science' (TIMSS) programme, organized, conducted, and managed by Boston College, in collaboration with the International Association for the Evaluation of Educational Achievement (IEA), claims to 'help countries all over the world improve student learning in mathematics and science. [TIMSS] collects educational achievement data at the fourth and eighth grades to provide information about trends in performance over time together with extensive background information to address concerns about the quantity, quality, and content of instruction' (TIMSS 2003*b*).

The 'Programme for International Student Assessment' (PISA), organized and managed by the Organisation for Economic Cooperation and Development (OECD) through subcontracts to research organizations to conduct the studies claims to 'measure how well young adults, at age 15 ... are prepared to meet the challenges of today's knowledge societies ... Key features ... of PISA have been: its policy orientation, with design and reporting methods determined by the needs of governments to draw policy lessons ... ' (PISA 2003, 'Overview' from OECD 2004*a* 20).

These are extraordinarily ambitious claims, and in reality the 'policy debate', at least in the public domain in England and similar English-speaking countries, rarely seems to get far beyond the headline report that we are fourth, fourteenth, or whatever, in the latest league table, and furthermore that this is an unsatisfactory state of affairs. But what do these reports actually contain—are they valid and reliable studies and could they inform policy if they were read carefully? This chapter seeks to explore these questions with respect to both their methodological problems and their potential policy implications.

The chapter will focus on the most recent publications from TIMSS 2003 (published December

2004), PIRLS 2001 (the 'Progress in International Literacy Study' also run from Boston College to parallel TIMSS, published in 2003), and PISA 2000 and 2003 (both published in 2004). TIMSS 2003 involved twenty-five countries at 4th grade Maths and Science (*c*.9 + years of age) and forty-six countries at 8th grade Maths and Science (*c*.14 + years). PIRLS 2001 involved thirty-five countries in assessing Reading at 4th grade. PISA involved forty-three countries in assessing Reading (2000), and subsequently Maths (2003) at age 15 + years. In addition to the testing programmes each survey also gathers background questionnaire data from students, teachers, and principals/administraters about hours of instructional time, curriculum coverage, students' home background and attitudes to learning, and so forth.

This chapter will not attempt to evaluate each study individually, as this would be well beyond its scope, but rather treat them as a single phenomenon, as a manifestation of the global empiricism which seem to be driving public policy in education, with each new published league table bringing with it the necessity for governments to be seen to be doing something about educational standards. Methodological issues and the socially constructed research reality that lies behind the headline figures will be reviewed, before we identify what, if anything, despite their flaws, these studies might tell us about educational systems and processes.

Defining Education

A significant issue to note right at the start of this discussion is that the definition of what counts as important in these studies is always drawn very narrowly. TIMSS, as the name implies, focuses on Maths and Science. PIRLS focuses on reading (despite the word 'literacy' in its title) and has been introduced to the TIMSS 'portfolio' only recently. PISA focused initially on Reading (2000), with a subsample of students taking some Maths and Science tests, and has embarked on a rolling programme whereby Maths takes precedence in 2003, with a minor focus on reading and science, then Science will take centre-stage in 2006 with a minor focus on reading and maths. While it is obviously not the case that achievement in Maths, Science, and Reading is unimportant, either for individual students or for governments investing in education systems, neither is it self-evident that achievement in these subjects necessarily constitute the most important outcomes of education. Learning to read and write might be considered absolutely fundamental to the pursuit of individual achievement and social mobility, and indeed to the protection of individual liberty, but most people get by most of the time with a pretty rudimentary knowledge of maths and science, and in any case testing reading came rather late to these international studies. Maths, Science, and latterly Reading are clearly being taken as proxies, as indicators of the more general 'health' of our education systems, and proxies moreover, that are closely related to the (assumed) economic purpose of education. The assumption seems to be that economic prosperity depends on technological advance and this in turn depends on the production of mathematicians and scientists. None of these assumptions are discussed or justified in the reports of TIMSS, PIRLS, or PISA however. Indeed, in so far as they are even mentioned they are taken as axiomatic (cf. the quotation from PISA 2003 above). There is an immediate danger then, of these studies falling into the first trap of assessment—assessing what you can assess, what it is (relatively) easy to assess, rather than what you should assess—for example progress in the arts and humanities, the vitality of student–teacher relationships which might engender an orientation to lifelong learning, or the understanding of democratic processes and participation that 15-year-olds might have. These international studies, and governments presumably, just seem to hope that such important outcomes of education are indeed fostered by systems that also teach maths, science, and reading.

Key Methodological Issues

Can We Compare Like with Like Across Languages and Test Formats?

Looking in more detail at the technicalities of the studies, it is interesting to reflect on what the press and policymakers think the headline league table figures might mean. When we hear that England has come fifth in Science (TIMSS 2003, 4th grade) or the United States ninth in Reading (PIRLS 2001, 4th grade) it is reasonable to assume that the tests are basically comparing like with like, i.e. that these rankings derive from scores that are not just comparable, in terms of statistical scaling, but actually derive from similar samples of students sitting the same test. Moreover, we probably also assume that the samples of students taken from each country are big enough and representative enough to ensure that scores are accurate representations of a whole country's performance. In fact none of these assumptions pertain, at least not in any straightforward sense.

TIMSS, PIRLS, and PISA are very carefully designed within their own terms, but still depend to a large extent on key underlying assumptions being combined with statistical techniques to produce their findings. Test questions (items) are developed by central teams working with individual country collaborators. Thus individual countries submit items; these are pooled and further developed in English to produce a general item bank. The items are then translated back into individual languages and piloted. They are then finalized in English before being translated back into individual languages for administration by in-country coordinating organizations (Ministries of Education or research organizations such as the National Foundation for Educational Research (NFER) in England). Thus the 'master copy' is always in English (though PISA also conducts this process in French, English and French being the two official languages of the OECD). Students take the test translated into the 'official' language or languages of their own country but this is not always the language they speak at home.[1] Clearly major issues are raised by this whole process with respect to curriculum fidelity, and the extent to which different topics are included in country-specific syllabuses and/or treated in different ways within those syllabuses. The studies themselves note this problem and report for example that 'the curricula of some countries align more closely than others with the TIMSS frameworks' and, moreover that 'it was notable that several of the higher performing countries reported high levels of emphasis on the ... topics in their ... curriculum' (Mullis et al. 2003*b*: 180, 182). However, even if we assume that country coordinators have done their best to ensure curriculum validity, and we simply leave this major issue to one side, we are nevertheless still faced with immense problems of how individual items are translated and to what extent they can really be said to be measuring the same thing in every country (especially with respect to reading which will vary enormously with the context of interpretation that students are used to). The international studies go to considerable lengths to try to overcome such problems in advance, but do not report on what translation problems they may or may not have come across in piloting, and do not conduct (or at least do not publish in their main substantive reports) post hoc studies of how items have performed or what biases have been encountered. Individual countries occasionally do, however, and a recent analysis in France indicated that 'French pupils obtained better results than the average OECD score for all the items about a literary piece which France had proposed' (Bonnet 2002: 394).

Beyond translation problems there are also more general validity and reliability issues to do with whether or not particular test approaches and formats really do test what they claim to be testing. These international studies all use various combinations of open response, limited response, and multiple choice formats which may be more or less fit for the purpose. Thus it is hard to see how PISA can be really be assessing 'the challenges of today's knowledge societies ... [and] the capacity of students to apply knowledge and skills ... and to analyse, reason and communicate effectively' (OECD 2004*a*: 20) when 50 per cent of the weighting of its tests are closed response and multiple choice formats (p. 27). It might be argued that this fitness-for-purpose issue is not directly relevant to variation in performance since at the level of format and weighting the test-taking experience is the same for everyone sitting the test. However, some observers argue that the reliance on psychometric theory and Western test development expertise will inevitably adversely influence the results of those students who are not so familiar with such formats (Bonnet 2002; Goldstein 2004). Indeed even those directly involved with assisting in administration and analysis note that final overall mean scores are constructed from different performances on different tasks and by different assessment methods, so that, for example, 'The overall high performance of the top three countries [in PIRLS] Sweden, the Netherlands and England, resulted from very divergent patterns of response ... England ... showed distinctly better performance on constructed response items ... The Netherlands showed notably better performance on multiple choice items' (Sainsbury, Schagen, and Hammond 2004: 14). Thus even good overall scores will be produced by *different* specific performances. Knowing what these differences are may be helpful to policymakers, but this same report goes on to conclude that 'it has not been possible to make simple statements about the differing reading skills of students' (ibid. 20) and the implications for policy are rarely straightforward or unequivocal (see below).

In addition, the actual tests which students sit also differ. Matrix sampling, combined with a reliance on Item Response Theory or Modelling (IRM), means that students sit permutations of the test from a bank of items that are considered to be of similar difficulty. They do not all answer the same questions. In the most recent PISA test for example, 'The total assessment time of 390 minutes of testing was organized in different combinations of test booklets with each individual being tested for 120 minutes' (OECD 2004*a* 27; cf. also Mullis et al. 2003*a*: 24 re PIRLS; and Mullis et al. 2003*b*: 31 re TIMSS). The developers claim that their statistical scaling, deriving from IRM, render the end results comparable; critics disagree (Goldstein 2004). The key point here however, is that that in terms of public perception and the presumed legitimacy of 'evidence-based policy-making', these studies are not comparing what most people would consider to be 'like with like'.

Sampling

Nor does this problem begin and end with the tests themselves. The sample of students taking the tests is also problematic. Sample size has to reflect the scale of the systems being sampled and is determined at school and individual student level in order to try to ensure that particular in-country policies such as selection and streaming do not bias the sample towards particularly high or low achievers. Other issues of stratification such as ethnic background, socio-economic status, language spoken at home, and so forth also have to be taken into account. Certain minimum levels of response are set, but given these, actual sample size can vary enormously from country to country. Thus for example in TIMSS 2003, 9,891 students from the USA were included in the original sample of identified schools in the 8th grade, and 8,912 were actually tested. At the other end of the range 3,243 were originally included in Morocco, and 2,943 were tested (Mullis et al. 2004*b*: 356). In PISA 2003 the range was much wider with 30,000 students tested in Mexico, but only 3,350 in Iceland (OECD 2004*a*: 28). Interestingly enough, not all countries manage to persuade enough schools to be involved so that, for example, the Netherlands was not included in the analyses for PISA 2000 (OECD 2004*b*: 4), while England could not be included in the 8th grade analyses for TIMSS 2003, nor for the PISA 2003 analyses (though this hasn't stopped official bodies such as DfES and NFER from making claims about England's performance from the excluded data, see Ruddock et al. 2004).

Even within an appropriately constructed sample (i.e. one that meets the designers' guidelines) there will be great variation from country to country with respect to the ages of students included and the years of schooling they have had (at ostensibly the same grade level). Thus for example in PIRLS 2001, focusing on 4th grade, ages ranged from an average of 9 years 7 months in Cyprus to 11 year 2 months in Morocco. Scotland's sample averaged 9 years 8 months, while England's and the United States' was 10 years 2 months. Most students had four years of schooling but those from Slovenia and the Russian Federation had three years while England, New Zealand, and Scotland had five years (Mullis et al. 2003*a*: 26). In TIMSS 2003 at 8th grade, ages ranged from 13 years 7 months (Scotland) to 15 years 5 months (Ghana) with years of schooling varying from seven in Norway, Slovenia, and the Russian Federation to nine in Australia, New Zealand, and Scotland (and England, though as noted above, England was excluded from the final analysis for failing to satisfy the 'guidelines for sample participation rates', Mullis et al. 2003*b*: 34). In PISA 2003 ages ranged from 15 years 3 months to 16 years 2 months though no summary is provided of grades or years of schooling since 'Differences between countries in the nature and extent of pre-primary education and care, in the age of entry to formal schooling, and in the structure of the education system do not allow school grades to be defined so that they are internationally comparable' (OECD 2004*a*: 27). Perhaps the OECD should let Boston College in on this secret.

A further complicating factor here is that the length of a 'school year' differs from country to country, as does the proportion of time within it spent on Maths, Science, and Reading. Thus for example the total 'instructional hours' recorded in the PIRLS data for 4th grade ranged from a minimum of 602 per year in Slovenia to a maximum of 1,082 in the Netherlands. The international average was 837 hours. Within this the time devoted to Reading varied from 1 hour per week in Macedonia to 9 hours in the United States (Mullis et al. 2003*a*: 146). TIMSS 2003 reports that the time spent on science in 4th grade ranges from 33 hours per year in the Russian Federation to 176 hours in the Philippines (Martin et al. 2004: 10). It might be argued that it is important to know that students in Slovenia had only around 1,800 hours of instruction by 4th grade, as compared with 4,000 in the Netherlands, and that this might help to explain why the Netherlands' mean score was 52 points higher than Slovenia (though at 502, Slovenia was still higher than the international average). However, many other factors intervene in the production of educational achievement and in any case not all comparisons are so straightforward. New Zealand students had even more instruction, five years compared to Slovenia's three, but scored only 27 points higher. Later in the chapter we will see that two years less schooling for Finnish students does not impede their attainment at all, quite the reverse.

The key point for the moment however, is that the sample of students and the amount of instruction that they are exposed to varies enormously from country to country; likewise the tests they sit are not the same. Statistical techniques allow scores to be recorded on a single rank-ordered scale but, as we have seen, the mean scores and league table positions are very much a construction of the testing process itself rather than some sort of absolute indicator of what similar children in different countries can do.

Policy Implications

Given these caveats is there anything that *can* be learned from such comparative studies, especially for policymaking, the ostensible purpose of the exercise? The answer is a clear 'no' with respect to the basic league table headlines, but 'perhaps' when it comes to looking at some of the detail that emerges from analyses of scores in relation to other background data (such as curriculum access, student attitudes to study, and home resources). Certainly there are some intriguing correlations. For example in PIRLS 2001, where England came 'third' in the league table, 'ten year old pupils in England have a poorer attitude towards reading and read less often for fun than pupils of the same age in other countries' (Twist et al. 2003: p. vi; PISA 2000 also confirms this). So pupils in England *can* read, but don't want to: three cheers for the government's National Literacy Strategy. Moreover 'children in England tend to play computer games more frequently than their international peers, watch television more frequently and for longer' (ibid. p. vi). Now, of course, the fact that such activity coincides with a high mean score for England probably says more about the socio-economic status of English children in comparison with others (and the enduring correlation of socio-economic status with educational achievement) than it does about whether or not watching television and playing computer games helps develop reading. But such juxtapositions certainly give the lie to the usual media (and teacher) cry of 'they can't read because they're too busy watching television'.

The League Tables

But to get a little more focused, and take the league tables first, one obvious question might be whether or not the results of these various international studies actually correlate in any way with each other? In other words, is there some consistency in the league table positions that countries occupy and could governments draw lessons from this? To begin with we can note that not all countries have taken part in all five of the surveys reviewed here (i.e. PISA 2000 (Reading), PISA 2003 (Maths), PIRLS 2001, and TIMSS 2003 4th grade and 8th grade[2]). Given that these are the most recent surveys, we might expect that any country likely to want to become involved in such surveys will have done so by now, and certainly the total list of countries now involved in one or more of the surveys is a long one, beginning with Argentina and ending with Uruguay. Counting duplications such as 'Belgium' and 'Belgium Flemish', and 'UK', 'England', and 'Scotland' as single countries for purposes of simplicity; and excluding regional level participants such as 'Basque Country, Spain', 'Canada Ontario', and 'Canada Quebec', a total of 71 countries have taken part in one or more of the surveys. Of these 71 countries only *five* have taken part in all five surveys and had their results analysed and reported: Hungary, Italy, New Zealand, Norway, and the USA. Additionally, the Netherlands took part in all five but, as noted above, their results were not included in PISA 2000 because of low sample response. Similarly, if we treat 'UK' and 'England' as one country for present purposes, England took part in all five surveys but their results were excluded from PISA 2003 and TIMSS 2003, 8th grade, because of low sample response rates. So only five countries have the full set of data on which to draw, though as we can see in Table 56.1, obvious policy implications are very hard to discern.

It would appear that if Hungarian policymakers are worried about unflattering headlines they would be best advised to buy into the Boston College programme (i.e. PIRLS and TIMSS) rather than that of the OECD (PISA). The same would appear to be true for the United States. Other than that ... New Zealand might be a little concerned that 'standards have dropped' since 2000 (though of course these surveys cannot be compared in any direct sense); while Italian and Norwegian policymakers would appear to be very slow learners indeed. No matter how many tests their students sit to 'help ... improve student learning ... ' (TIMSS 2003*a*, cited above), the rankings don't improve.

If we focus instead on surveys which, on the face of it, ought to be at least a little more directly comparable than those in different subjects at different age groups, i.e. the studies of reading at ages 15+and 9+, and maths at 15+and 14+in PISA, PIRLS, and TIMSS 8th grade, the picture doesn't get much clearer. Tables 56.2 and 56.3 list the top six countries in each of the studies, plus selected others in the English-speaking world who took part in the particular studies and appear to be so enamoured of these league tables.

Only Canada appears in the first six of both PISA and PIRLS (Table 56.2). The correspondences in Table 56.3 are rather better, with Hong Kong, South Korea, and Japan appearing in the first six of both, but again the policy implications are rather

Table 56.1 Rankings for countries which have taken part in all five surveys

Country	PISA 2000 (Reading)	PISA 2003 (Maths)	PIRLS 2001 (Reading)	TIMMS 2003			
				8th Grade		4th Grade	
				Mths	Sci	Mths	Sci
Hungary	22nd	25th	8th	9th	7th	11th	8th
Italy	20th	31st	10th	22nd	22nd	15th	14th
New Zealand	3rd	12th	13th	20th	13th	17th	12th
Norway	13th	22nd	25th	27th	20th	21st	20th
United States	15th	28th	9th	15th	9th	12th	6th

Sources: PISA, PIRLS, and TIMSS reports cited in references.

Table 56.2 Selected comparisons of international assessment rankings and scores in reading

Reading PISA 2000 (15+year-olds)		Reading PIRLS 2001 (9+year-olds)	
1. Finland	546	1. Sweden	561
2. Canada	534	2. Netherlands	554
3. New Zealand	529	3. England	553
4. Australia	528	4. Bulgaria	550
5. Ireland	527	5. Latvia	545
6. South Korea	525	6. Canada	544
7. UK	523	9. USA	542
15. USA	504	13. New Zealand	529
International average	500	International average	500

Sources: PISA, PIRLS and TIMSS reports cited in references.

Table 56.3. Selected comparisons of international assessment rankings and scores in maths

MATHS PISA 2003 (15+year-olds)		MATHS TIMSS 2003 (8th grade: 14+year-olds)	
1. Hong Kong	550	1. Singapore	605
2. Finland	544	2. South Korea	589
3. South Korea	542	3. Hong Kong	586
4. Netherlands	538	4. Taiwan	585
5. Lichstenstein	536	5. Japan	570
6. Japan	534	6. Belgium (Flemish)	537
7. Canada	532	14. Australia	505
11. Australia	524	15. USA	504
12. New Zealand	523	18. Scotland	498
28. USA	483	20. New Zealand	494
International average	500	International average	467

Sources: PISA, PIRLS and TIMSS reports cited in references.

nebulous. Teach Maths as they do in the Pacific Rim? This was certainly a position that seemed to be taken in England in the mid-1990s, but whether and if so in what ways this particular moral panic has impacted on the standards of Maths teaching in England is not possible to judge from the figures above, since, in the meantime, English secondary schools have become so sick of testing that they did not take part in these 2003 surveys in sufficient numbers to be included in the analyses.[3] The figures from Scotland however, for TIMSS, do not indicate any obviously positive impact on the UK as a whole (cf. also further discussion below of Singapore and Hong Kong).

However, one of the biggest problems of dealing with this issue at the level of the headline score is that the sample sizes and scaling techniques used mean that, in any case, there are very rarely significant differences between the mean scores of adjacent countries in any particular league table. Thus in PIRLS 2001, England 'came third', but could as easily have come second or fourth—the range of adjacent countries who had scores which were not statistically different from England. The United States came ninth but could as easily have come as high as fourth of as low as twelfth. Thus either England (actually third) or the USA (actually ninth) could both have come fourth (Mullis et al. 2003*a*: 27). In other studies similar transpositions could have occurred. In TIMSS 2003, England came fifth in 4th grade science but could have come third or sixth. The United States came sixth but could have come fourth or ninth (Martin et al. 2004: 42). The range can be still wider when larger numbers of countries are involved. Thus in TIMSS 2003 in 8th grade science the United States came ninth but could have come eighth or thirteenth; New Zealand came thirteenth but could have come eighth or twentieth (Martin et al. 2004: 40).

A further important element in interpreting the leagues tables, and here we do get a little closer to useful information, is to look at the distribution of scores as well as the means. Thus for example, in PIRLS 2001, where England came third overall, it had the highest individual student scores in the whole table, but also *lower* scores (i.e. a much longer 'tail') than the lowest scores of ten countries below it, right down to France in eighteenth place (Mullis et al. 2003*a*: 26). Thus the overall mean score for England averaged out the best of individual student scores with some of the worst. A similar picture emerges with respect to Singapore's first place in all four of the TIMSS 2003 surveys. On the face of it such a ranking implies that Singapore must be the most effective country in the world at teaching Maths and Science. Yet its 'tail' is as long or longer than the next five countries below it at grade 4 Maths, longer than the next three countries below it at grade 4 Science, and longer than the next seven countries below it in grade 8 Science (Mullis 2004: 34, 35; Martin 2004: 36, 37). Thus excellence at the top seems to carry less positive implications for lower achievers. In other studies and countries the situation is reversed. Finland, South Korea, and Canada rank second, third, and seventh in PISA 2003 *and* have a narrow spread of scores, as do Denmark and Iceland which are lower in the table but still well above the international average (OECD 2004*a*: 95). This would seem to imply that countries do not have to sacrifice excellence in the pursuit of generally good levels of achievement, that narrow notions of 'high' and 'low' ability do not determine the spread of scores and that different systems can make a difference to student achievement across the board. Overall the range of scores achieved is an issue that could stand further investigation and, especially if combined with additional qualitative data, could potentially provide policymakers with useful advice.

What is Claimed by the Reports Themselves?

Summaries of research findings always tend towards the simplistic or the commonplace or both. The puzzle and the fascination and is usually to be found in the detail—irrespective of whether or not the data is quantitative or qualitative. So we should not be too harsh on these surveys for the banality of their summaries, but banal they most certainly are. Thus PISA 2000 reports that 'Socio-economic difference is the strongest single factor associated with performance in PISA' (OECD 2004*b*: 6). Well, it is interesting that such an enduring finding of educational research is still being confirmed, after 50 to 100 + years of educational development in most of the countries involved, and always helpful to have educational policymakers reminded of it, but we hardly need multi-million dollar international surveys to verify it. Similarly PIRLS tells us that 'there was a positive relationship between engaging in early literacy activities and performance in PIRLS reading assessment in every country' (Mullis et al. 2003: 96); while TIMSS reports that 'higher levels of parents' education are associated with higher ... student achievement in mathematics' (Mullis et al. 2003*b*: 127). Furthermore: 'At both eighth and fourth grades students from homes where the language of the tests is always or almost always spoken had higher average achievements than those who spoke it less frequently' (ibid. 131). We also learn that higher achievement was correlated positively with numbers of books in the home (ibid. 134) and with a study desk and computer at home (ibid. 135). Again, all this is modestly informative, but hardly tells us anything that we don't already know.

TIMSS also very specifically claims to be able to report progress from one TIMSS study to another, i.e. to provide definitive evidence as to whether or not standards in individual countries are improving over time. In principle TIMSS should be able to do this in a much more convincing way than simply looking across a range of surveys, as above, because the studies retain and reuse a proportion of items. Thus Maths in TIMSS in 1995 and 1999 ought to be comparable with Maths in TIMSS in 2003. However, as the reports themselves acknowledge, actually producing any worthwhile comparisons is still very difficult to achieve, because of changes in country-specific policy and curriculum content, as well as all the methodological problems reviewed above. Furthermore the numbers of countries for which it is even possible in principle is limited by differential participation. Only twelve countries took part in both TIMSS 1999 and 2003; only five took part in 1995, 1999, and 2003. Of these the 'standard error' reported, i.e. the confidence with which we can assume the scores are correct, can in any case wipe out apparent trends. Thus the United States had a mean of 492 in 8th grade Maths in 1995, 502 in 1999, and 504 in 2003—on the face of it a modest improvement. But the standard error also recorded indicates that that 1995 could have been as high as 497 and 2003 as low as 501—still an improvement, but only just (Mullis et al. 2003*b*: 42). These tables do repay closer scrutiny, however. We also learn that Hong Kong improved over the same period *and* significantly reduced its tail. Singapore on the other had pretty similar scores at the top of the table (609, 604, and 605) but by 2003 had a much longer tail than in 1995—maintaining good levels of achievement seems to have cost them something in equity (ibid. 42). The crude lesson of Hong Kong and Singapore's success is that we should do as they do; closer analysis suggests that there are subtle differences in what they are doing and we would probably learn more from Hong Kong than Singapore. To take the analysis further however, would require closer classroom level study and different sorts of data.

The Intrigue is in the Detail

What this example from TIMSS 2003 demonstrates, however, is that closer investigation can reveal some interesting details. We have already noted that PIRLS and PISA 2000 indicated that English students can read but don't want to and that higher achievement is correlated with watching more television than their international counterparts. We learn from TIMSS 2003 that England made 'significant gains' in 4th grade Maths between 1995 and 2003 but also 'significant improvement' in 4th grade Science (TIMSS 2003*b*). Further investigation reveals that scores in Science started higher and finished higher than those in Maths, while the range of scores achieved in Science decreased and the tail got shorter (Mullis et al. 2003*b*: 45; Martin et al. 2004: 47). On the face of it then standards in Science started better, finished better, and with less of a tail than in Maths. There are potentially chastening lessons here for English policymakers. I have already noted that England has a 'National Literacy Strategy' designed to raise standards in reading and writing, which, apparently, puts children off reading. England also has a 'National Numeracy Strategy' designed to raise standards in Maths. Yet such investment apparently achieves no more, and in some respects rather less, than in Science where there is *no* national strategy. Interestingly enough these figures also accord with similar achievement statistics from the English National Testing system. Results in Key Stage 2 Science (age 11+) started higher in the mid-1990s than in Maths and have remained higher, without the benefit, or impediment, of a 'national strategy' (Torrance 2004).

What other gems can we spot? Finland came top in PISA 2000 (Reading) and second in PISA 2003 (Maths). Canada came second in PISA 2000 and New Zealand third. The UK was seventh. Yet we also learn from other sources that Finland starts school one year later than Canada and two years later than New Zealand and the UK (i.e. Finns have seven years of schooling by 8th grade, as against eight (in Canada), and nine (in New Zealand and the UK); Mullis et al. 1999: 32[4]). The pressure in the UK is to start school even earlier, with a pre-school 'Foundation' curriculum now being implemented in nurseries and infant school 'reception' classes from the age of 3+. Yet the evidence from Finland is that high achievement can be accomplished by *fewer* years of schooling, not more.

From TIMSS 2003 we learn that most countries involved have some form of National Curriculum and some element of periodic national testing in their systems. But interestingly enough we also learn that Australia, one of the few countries with *no* national curriculum or testing system and public exams only at grade 12 (i.e. probably the least formally controlled system in the programme) came fourteenth in 8th grade Maths, while Malaysia, with a national curriculum and formal public testing at grades 6, 9, 11, and 13 (i.e. probably the most formally controlled system) came tenth, with no significant difference in their respective mean scores (Australia range 10th–21st, Malaysia range 10th–19th: Mullis 2003*b*: 38, 166). Of course many other factors will intervene in the production of achievement in maths, but on the face of it a very tightly centralized and controlled curriculum and testing system does not in and of itself produce better results than a much more decentralized and voluntaristic system. One is tempted, once again, to reflect on the implications for policy, especially for England, which, with a National Curriculum and formal testing and/or public examinations at ages 7, 11, 14, 16, 17, and 18, is even more centrally controlled than Malaysia, but, as we have seen earlier, could not produce sufficient returns to meet the TIMSS 2003 guidelines and be included in the rankings. It may well be *because* English schools and students are so heavily tested that a sufficient sample of schools could not be found to collaborate. Certainly there is evidence from the Australian experience that the shackles could be loosened in England, were policymakers interested in reflecting on evidence which contradicts their current predilections, rather than just confirming them.

Perhaps the most generally informative and useful findings from these various studies concern gender. The evidence again largely confirms what we already know, as with the data on socioeconomic background, but nevertheless it is not unhelpful to have it deriving from very large-scale international surveys and with the details available for further scrutiny. In particular both PISA 2000 and PIRLS confirm that in reading girls perform consistently and significantly better than boys (OECD 2004*b*: 12; Mullis et al. 2003*a*: 29). In Science and Maths the evidence is more equivocal. In Science, TIMSS 2003 reports that 'Boys outperformed girls ... often by a substantial margin ... mainly attributable to higher performance in physical and earth sciences, although girls had on average higher achievement in life science' (Martin et al. 2004: 4–5). But PISA 2003 indicates that while there is a tendency for boys to perform better than girls, the difference is only significant in thirteen of the participating countries (OECD 2004*a*: 296).

Likewise boys generally perform better than girls at Maths but not consistently, and not necessarily to a significant extent. Thus in TIMSS 2003, Maths: 'On average, across all countries, there was no significant difference in achievement between boys and girls at either 8th or 4th grade' (Mullis et al. 2003*b*: 47).

PISA 2003 similarly found that boys generally did better than girls at Maths but that 'gender differences tended to be small and are certainly much smaller than the gender differences that were observed by PISA 2000 in the area of reading literacy' (OECD 2004*a*: 99). The top two countries in the rankings, Hong Kong and Finland, and the fourth, the Netherlands, had no significant differences between boys and girls in Maths, but the third, South Korea did have. The report concludes: 'The wide variation in gender gaps among countries suggest that current differences are not inevitable ... and that effective policies and practices can overcome what were long taken to be ... differences ... in underlying capacities' (OECD 2004*a*: 99).

Conclusion: The Rage for Control Rather than Understanding

One could go producing interesting nuggets. These studies are admirable in their scale and scope, and in the wealth of detail that they present for further investigation. The individuals involved in producing the reports deserve congratulation for their ambition and expertise in research design and their sheer hard work in analysing the data. Or perhaps one should say in partially analysing it—since it is the background material, the large-scale survey findings about curriculum coverage, student attitudes to learning, and so forth, that are most of interest. The core of the studies—the basic test results and rankings—are almost meaningless since they could be used to argue virtually any case that one wanted to present.

More problematic still is the contribution that such studies make to the tidal wave of neo-empiricism that seems to be sweeping over educational research at the present time. There seems to be an assumption among some policymakers and indeed some educational and social researchers themselves that if only one could gather enough large-scale, ideally experimentally based, data, one could provide unequivocal evidence for policy (cf. Hargreaves 1996; Oakley 2003; National Research Council 2002; US Dept. of Education 2003). The above discussion demonstrates that this is not the case. Indeed the reverse is probably nearer the mark—making sense of large amounts of data is very difficult and requires some prior theoretical understanding of how the data might link together. Far from providing unequivocal evidence, large-scale studies which are not also well theorized simply provide data which can be presented in any number of ways and which can be cherry-picked by media and policymakers alike to support whatever is the current agenda.

Thus, for example, comparing and contrasting Hong Kong, Finland, and South Korea with respect to gender differences in Maths achievement is certainly illuminating with respect to demonstrating that gender differences are neither inevitable nor immutable. But such an analysis requires that questions deriving from gender studies, concerning how and why gender differences occur, are asked in the first place; they do not arise unbidden from the data. Answering them fully would involve further investigation and iteration dependent on our theories of teaching and learning and how institutions change. In turn, exploring the data in this way will raise further questions for investigation (which would probably involve more localized qualitative enquiry about school organization and classroom processes). It is not that large-scale studies such as TIMSS and PISA are necessarily unhelpful, but they are inadequate without these further enquiries, and their overwhelming presence in the policy discourse probably does more harm than good.

Why then are policymakers so enamoured of them? Perhaps 'love' is the wrong metaphor, perhaps fear is closer to the truth. There is much in these studies that presents a challenge to current policy but despite the current rhetoric about research informing policy, evidence informing practice, only a fraction of the data is ever focused on and it is interpreted within a completely unchallenged discourse of comparing and raising test scores. Avoiding and/or responding to damaging headlines seems to be the main concern for policymakers, rather than developing policy on the basis of evidence. League tables make good headlines and usually they can be written to suggest that problems persist even when the news is good. PISA 2000, which ranked the UK seventh in Reading and fourth in the subsample in Maths, was greeted by the headline 'Are our students really this bright?' (BBC News website accessed 24 Sept. 2003). Policymakers have to respond to headlines and have to be seen to be doing something, anything, rather than nothing. Not taking part in these surveys is not an option, even when it backfires, as in England, and not enough schools take part. Not being able to respond at all, to whether or not England is doing well or badly compared to others, is probably more politically unacceptable than being able to respond, with yet another policy initiative, yet another 'strategy', to bad news. And of course sometimes it's good news.

However real damage is done by the nature of these knee-jerk reactions. As we have seen, scores in Science in England have been as good if not better than scores in Maths and Reading, even without a 'national strategy'. Yet schools have had to struggle with the massive training and implementation disruption that such strategies have caused and the deficit model of teachers and teaching that the government works with. Successive research studies and even reports by the government's own Chief Inspector of Schools now testify to the decline in arts and humanities in the English primary school curriculum, as schools concentrate on what is tested (in the National Testing system, as well as international studies) rather than what is important (Bell 2003; Earl et al. 2001; OfSTED 2002; Osborn et al. 2000). Research studies have a responsibility to interpret and explain, in the light of prevailing theory, both using theory and developing it as appropriate. Just producing the league tables and the screeds of background data is not enough. Likewise policymaking has a responsibility to demand and respond to such interpretative explanation, not just pick a result or two (good or bad) that suits the prejudice of the current minister. Producing knowledge on which we can act requires an interpretative framework and a value orientation by which choices can be defended. The facts do not speak for themselves. To paraphrase Marx, policymakers may attempt to change the world, but the prerequisite is, first and foremost, to understand it.

NOTES

1. For example, in PIRLS 2001, while 79% of the sample 'always', or 'almost always' spoke the language of the test at home, 16% did so only 'sometimes', and 6% 'never' (Mullis et al. 2003: 99).
2. As noted above, each PISA survey focuses on one subject area while also including subsample studies of the subjects not focused on. For simplicity here I am treating PISA 2000 and PISA 2003 as single surveys and concentrating on the primary focus of the surveys in each case—Reading (2000) and Maths (2003). TIMSS 2003 tested Maths and Science. All countries involved at each grade took part in both Maths and Science tests though not all countries took part at both grades. For present purposes therefore I am treating them as two, rather than four, surveys, though results are presented separately for Maths and Science in Table 56.1.
3. In England all schools are involved in administering National Curriculum Tests to students at ages 7, 11, 14, and (via public examinations) 16. Small wonder that they do not wish to be involved in further testing around ages 14–15.
4. This reference is to TIMSS 1999; although Finland did not take part in TIMSS 2003, it did take part in TIMSS 1999.

How Globalization Can Cause Fundamental Curriculum Change: An American Perspective

Leonard J. Waks

I. Globalization and Curriculum Change

The field of educational change has until recently concentrated on schools and school systems as units of analysis, glossing over macro-forces driving change at the institutional level. But scholars in the field now acknowledge the need to extend their reach. In the Introduction to the 'Pushing the Boundaries of Educational Change' section of the *International Handbook of Educational Change*, editor Andy Hargreaves argues that by 'extending and deepening our understanding of educational change beyond the boundaries of what is usually addressed in the field (we) can really strengthen how we think about change and deal with it in action' (p. 283).

In the introduction to the Handbook's chapter on 'Globalization and Educational Change' (Wells et al., 1998) the editors add: 'there is no greater context for educational change than that of globalization, nor no grander way of conceptualizing what educational change is about' (p. 322). But in that chapter Wells and her co-authors acknowledge up front that 'few educational researchers or theorists have attempted to make connections between the economic, political and cultural dimensions of globalization and the policies and practices of education' (p. 343). Thus they aim merely to provide a 'broad overview' of interpretations of globalization and their implications for education, leaving it to other scholars to think 'more carefully... about "globalization"... (and the) various ways it affects the educational change process' (p. 344).

In this [chapter] I discuss the impact of globalization upon *curriculum* change, arguing that unlike earlier social and economic developments, globalization will cause fundamental rather than merely incremental change. This topic is not as narrow as might initially be thought because fundamental curriculum change has implications not merely for subject matter selection, but also for instructional methods, technology utilization, organization and administration.

As the term 'globalization' is vague and contested, it will be useful in this introduction to situate my argument within the field of competing interpretations of globalization before considering its fundamental impact on curriculum change.

1. Globalization

I will be using the term 'globalization' as a carry-all term referring to an interacting complex of forces including (a) an economic dimension, comprised of a rise in the ratio of cross-border trade and direct foreign investment to total economic activity, and global integration of product markets increasing competition between providers from different nations, as well as (b) a technological dimension, the spread of global communication technology networks. Globalization in this sense has resulted in a reorganization of trans-national enterprises: large, vertically organized firms have been transformed to global business 'networks' of downsized flagship firms, small supplier firms, competitor firms, government agencies, and universities.[1] To enhance competitiveness, many American firms have re-engineered their work systems to include worker participation in cross-functional teams using knowledge and information in novel ways for rapid response to global opportunities. Telecommunications networks have enabled this shift, and have also spread to homes, generating new opportunities for home-based enterprise, learning, and consumption. These changes, I will argue, constitute powerful forces for curriculum change.

There is widespread agreement that globalization in the indicated sense is taking place, though commentators differ about its extent, variability and societal consequences. Wells et al. (1998) divide these commentators into four groups, three of which agree that globalization is a significant driving force of change, though they differ on the predictions and evaluations they make of its societal effects. For them 'Neo-liberals' such as Milton Freidman see globalization in terms of open markets. Because goods and financial assets are sold on an open global market, nation states have lost control of their economies and the power to control the value of their currencies. This decreased power of the state will, in their view, remove economic inefficiencies, resulting in economic growth and consequently, greater prosperity. They prescribe that public education be privatized via charter schools, voucher programs, or out-sourcing of educational services to private, for-profit firms to take advantage of market efficiencies.

'Liberal progressives' such as Robert Reich (1992) agree that global economic liberalization will result in efficiencies in both the public and private sectors. But they contend that it will also result in social inequalities and environmental destruction unless economic liberalization is accompanied by international agreements protecting basic social, political and environmental rights. They seek to strengthen public education to preserve education as a universal right, but they also seek to reform it so that it may provide occupational skills relevant in the global economy. Thus they also support charter schools as one way of using market mechanisms to support these school reforms.

Neo-Marxists, such as Stanley Aronowitz, agree that globalization generates social inequalities. But they are skeptical about the efficacy of action by the liberal state to ameliorate these, and seek instead to challenge the global capitalist order and its state apparatus through direct action organized by trans-national alliances of labor and human rights activists—a 'Seattle' approach to resisting globalization. In education some neo-marxists advocate 'critical pedagogy' to encourage the resistance of young people and the formation of personal identities specific to their ethnic, gender and class positions. Some also support charter schools, where workers and ethnic minorities can gain control over the education of their children and break the pattern of social reproduction through schooling.

A subtle tension in the neo-marxist position is worth noting. On the one hand it rejects the progressive faith in ameliorative social action by the liberal state. On the other, its educational program (critical pedagogy, charter schools), like those of neo-liberals and liberal progressives, depends on the existence of spaces for ameliorative action within the state's educational machinery. In any event, commentators from right, center, and left all have positive things to say about charter schools.

The fourth group in the framework of Wells et al., the 'realists', have presented a skeptical or carefully qualified view about globalization, either denying that it has significantly expanded in the recent period (Hirst and Thompson, 1996), or emphasizing that it is an uneven process playing out differently in different kinds of nation states and regions. Brown, Green and Lauder (2001), for example, demonstrate how the different histories and institutional forms of different societies shape distinct education, training, and labor market responses. They conclude that there is no simple global 'convergence' of education and training, or of labor markets, among different kinds of nation states. They grant, however, that global forces are pressing many other societies to move closer to the 'liberal society' model of the US and UK. 'Realists' are not tied to prescriptions for education; their research studies are conducted on descriptive and theoretical planes distanced from policy and practice.

The definition of 'globalization' embedded in my argument is sufficiently broad to be shared by neo-liberals, progressives and neo-marxists; I also accept the 'realist' qualification that globalization, even in this broad sense, is playing out differently in different societies. Consequently, an important qualification, reflected in the [chapter] title, is that as my argument is drawn primarily from American materials, it applies most directly to the American situation and that of other 'liberal' societies including the United Kingdom. But it retains relevance for those societies whose education and labor market regimes are moving in this 'liberal' direction.

2. Curriculum Change

My contention is that globalization can cause fundamental, as opposed to merely incremental, curriculum change. 'Curriculum' refers in the first instance to the knowledge and information content of formal education and its translation into teachable subject matter. For Smith, Stanley and Shores (1957) curriculum represents a 'sequence of potential learning experiences... set up in the school for... disciplining children and youth in group ways of thinking and acting.' For Good (1959) it stands for the 'overall plan of content or... materials of instruction the school should offer the student by way of qualifying him for graduation or certification or the entrance into a professional or vocational field.' For Tanner and Tanner (1980) it means the 'planned and guided learning experiences and related learning outcomes... under the auspices of the school'. These standard textbook definitions all point to three *logical core* elements of the curriculum concept: (1) predetermined subject matter content, presented in a (2) planned sequence of experiences, leading to (3) certifiable completion.

But the definitions also tie curriculum to features of its *institutional* context. All refer to (4) the institution of schooling, within whose structures some social actors have the capacity to issue the authoritative prescriptions of scope of content, the sequence of learning, and criteria of completion implied in the three core elements. Curriculum thus implies institutionalized and prescribed learning. As Goodson puts it, 'the bond between curriculum and prescription was forged early' (Goodson, 1997, p. 13). Reid goes further, claiming that 'regulation, uniformity, hierarchy were there from the start... these were the features that gave curriculum its identity as something different from teaching and learning' (Reid, 1999, p. 36). Finally, two extrinsic or contextual notions are implied: (5) socialization in the thought and action of a group (usually the nation), and (6) allocation of social benefits: access to favorable social and occupational positions upon completion.

The field of curriculum has for the most part conceived curriculum makers as rational actors who organize subject matters in a deliberate sequence to achieve societal goals and objectives; this conception is embedded in the curriculum paradigms advanced by such leaders as Franklin Bobbit and Ralph Tyler. Elements (1)–(3) have thus dominated attention; curriculum has been understood in terms of technical efficiency, the rational adjustment of curricular means to learning ends. In this 'technical' view curriculum change is a two-stage process: (a) changes in the goals and objectives of society as perceived by elites are brought to bear upon curriculum makers, who then (b) adopt new means of shaping and sequencing subject matters to adjust them better to the new ends.

But recently the field of curriculum has been influenced by an 'institutional' trend affecting many social science disciplines. Institutional approaches emphasize that social actors are embedded in institutional environments that define the meaning of their situations, establish rules (explicit or tacit) of appropriate action, and thus shape or constrain action. The institutional research program thus involves a tendency to abandon or qualify models of social action in which agents employ unbounded rationality in the technical adjustment of means to ends (see Rowan and Miskel, 1999).[2]

There is a growing consensus that an adequate understanding of the curriculum change process will have to draw upon both political-economic components to explain the pressures elites impose upon curriculum making at the boundary of the educational institution, and institutional components to explain how the institution's internal processes respond to these pressures. The work of Larry Cuban, Ian Westbury, and William Reid has been important in shaping this consensus.[3]

For Cuban (1992) political actors are responsive to pressures from economic and social elites who are in turn responding to broad changes in economic and social life. To maintain public support and legitimacy, educational leaders must demonstrate responsiveness to the needs of society, as represented by elites and imposed by public opinion and legislation. To do so they must be perceived as promoting educational change. But while they can directly forge a change in what Cuban calls the 'intended' curriculum of a school or system, their directives are only loosely coupled with day to day curriculum delivery in classrooms, called by Cuban the 'taught' curriculum. School principals, department chairs and grade leaders depend on the day-to-day support of teachers. Teachers in turn must negotiate day-to-day interactions with students to maintain control and effectiveness; teachers cannot push students beyond the limits they establish in striving for their own multiple ends. Thus on Cuban's institutional model, curriculum change does not result from curriculum makers adjusting new means to new ends. Rather, change results as elites apply pressures at the boundary of the school institution that are buffered by school leaders, and resisted or transformed by teachers as they negotiate their roles with students.

Curriculum is seen here as embedded in an institutional context consisting of rules for how physical space is organized, time is allotted to tasks, and subject matters are translated into teachable topics. These rules constitute what Cuban calls the institutional 'grammar' of schooling. This notion sets up his key distinction between 'incremental' and 'fundamental' curriculum change. Incremental changes correct deficiencies or imbalances in existing practice, making it more effective without altering its basic organizational features, its standard grammar. Fundamental changes, by contrast, seek to alter the grammar, the standard organizational ways of doing things. Fundamental change is not concerned merely with introducing new curricular means and ends, however significant, but, as noted earlier, with introducing new institutional rules that establish new organizational patterns, new configurations of space and time utilization, new roles and authority relations (Cuban, 1992, p. 218).

Cuban provides support for this distinction by analyzing change processes during the progressive and cold war eras, and his case studies provide useful comparisons with our era of globalization. Progressive reformers sought to introduce active, problem-based learning in projects grounded in conditions approximating those of 'real life'. Cold war reformers promoted new science curricula with advanced content and problem-solving of the sort engaged in by real scientists. Both reforms aimed at fundamental change because they involved significant changes in instructional content and method that required complementary changes in roles assigned to teachers and pupils.

On Cuban's account, while economic and social changes were the primary external factors driving these changes, school practitioners played the role in both cases of 'softening, selecting and modifying' the larger changes, 'fashioning a fit' between the external changes and the existing contours of the system of schooling (Cuban, 1992, p. 232). The proposed new forms of learning that required transformed roles for teachers and students never took hold. Instead, demands for rational management in the progressive era and enriched disciplinary content in the cold war era led to a broad adoption of standardized tests that, instead of fundamentally changing the curriculum, locked in defining features of the school grammar: discipline-based, textbook based teaching of standardized curriculum content geared to the test items, and courses linked to college admission requirements.

Standard textbooks, achievement tests, and college admission requirements formed an institutional array surrounding the curriculum that became ever more solid—locked in and inflexible. This solidification of the external context, its conversion from a responsive environment to a fixed and rigid set of constraints, has been captured in Westbury's oft-quoted phrase: 'curriculum is an idea that becomes a thing.' Reid (1999), drawing on the formulations of Meyer, adds the twist that this 'thing' over time itself becomes a new 'idea', a set of shared curriculum 'categories' or meanings, deeply entrenched in the public mind, that dictate the terms within which education as a public concern may be discussed. 'Education' comes to *mean* the standard curriculum practices: e.g. 'science education' comes to mean standard school and college courses in science disciplines.[4]

It is a central insight of institutional theory of curriculum that the enclosure of curriculum within an inflexible institutional environment, and the generation of fixed terms and meanings for discussion of education, create an 'institutional exoskeleton' preventing fundamental change.

For Cuban, the progressive and cold war era reforms achieved merely incremental, not fundamental change. There were changes in the intended curriculum, the official theory of what the curriculum was about. But the actual patterns of curriculum organization and teaching stayed more or less the same. New curriculum content was introduced, enhancing the legitimacy of the system by demonstrating its capacity for 'change.' But the 'changes' remained superficial—meager modifications of the contents in the same old bottles (Cuban, 1992). Cuban (1990) argues that this process has been repeated 'again and again and again' and will continue to obstruct fundamental change.

Bidwell and Dreeben (1992) offer a parallel analysis of curriculum change processes from the colonial era to the middle of the nineteenth century, when the current institutional pattern took shape, and project conclusions similar to Cuban's to the present and foreseeable future:

> Curricular content is revised, new ways to teach are proposed, and different boundaries between levels of schools are established. Nevertheless, the basic structure of schools, as organized around interchangeable content-based subjects, has remained remarkably durable ... In the United States the results of the processes of institutionalization ... have been in place for more than a century and it is not easy to foresee substantial changes in them (p. 360).

The question addressed here is whether globalization can unleash change factors sufficiently powerful to overturn this grammar of interchangeable content-based subjects?

II. The Conditions of Fundamental Curriculum Change

I argue that globalization can cause fundamental change. It will be useful to consider what sort of argument might sustain this sort of claim. It is one thing to argue that fundamental changes are necessary to bring curriculum practice into alignment with new patterns of knowledge production and utilization in the workplace—to make the curriculum technically efficient; this would be a forceful argument that fundamental change *should* occur. But it is quite another thing to argue that fundamental changes *can* actually occur. Institutional theory has so far emphasized the persistence of established patterns of schooling despite technical inefficiencies and external pressures for change; it has accentuated the factors *constraining* fundamental change. But fundamental change sometimes occurs. The Roman Empire and the Soviet Union both collapsed, and institutional theorists must be able to account for such events by specifying conditions under which existing institutions are destabilized and new institutions can emerge[5]. It would be foolish to insist that entrenched curriculum patterns simply cannot disintegrate, or that fundamentally different ones cannot emerge.

Fortunately, identifying the major constraints to fundamental change is tantamount to specifying the conditions for fundamental change; the removal of the constraints is equivalent to the establishment of the change conditions. In the remainder of this section I consider four constraints which must be removed for fundamental change to take place. In the following sections I argue that these constraints are in fact being removed in the process of globalization.

> Constraint 1. Powerful elites generally support entrenched practices and are sustained by them. Fundamental change thus requires that *external* elites withdraw this support and join with critical masses of citizens to form a *powerful constituency* for change.

On the one hand, not all reforms call for *fundamental* change. The 'back to basics' reforms of the 1970s, for example, demanded merely the strengthening of features of the entrenched pattern that had been weakened by progressive reforms. The cold war reforms called for discipline-based content, increased tracking by ability groups, and even more bureaucracy in school organization. Except for changes in teaching-learning methods in classes for the brightest children, the cold war reforms called for merely incremental change.

More to the point, even calls for fundamental reform are rarely supported by sufficiently powerful constituencies to forge a new consensus. The progressive education reformers' demands for fundamental change were supported by influential intellectuals and social leaders, but were opposed by corporate and political elites as well as many traditional educators. In the inevitable political end game of negotiation and compromise, advocates of fundamental change had to yield the more fundamental features of their program and settle for incremental change. Fundamental change cannot occur unless powerful elites withdraw support from the *status quo*.

> Constraint 2. Internal school processes are capable of buffering external pressures by elites for change. Fundamental change thus requires *destabilizing* the *internal processes* buffering the school from external pressures, motivating internal actors to innovate.

Internal responses to external pressures for change generally buffer pressures for change. Practitioners within the institutions 'soften, select and modify' proposed changes and 'fashion a fit' between them and existing contours of practice. But despite these stabilizing behaviors, internal processes may nonetheless be affected by the very same factors as are exerting pressure at the organizational boundary. For example, teaching may encounter new levels of student resistance, due to changing student perceptions of connections between schooling and expected careers. Teachers' 'coping' patterns may become ineffective as student motivation to cooperate wanes. Both students and teachers responding to external changes may discover themselves ripe for innovation.

> Constraint 3. The entrenched pattern is held in place by both its forming of tight linkages with other institutions, and its generation of fixed ideas for discussion of appropriate practice in public consciousness. The two processes generate a tight institutional exoskeleton that holds the pattern in place. Thus fundamental change requires erosion of this institutional exoskeleton—removal of external props and wearing away of fixed public ideas that lock in the *status quo*.

Standard textbooks, achievement tests and college admission requirements all prop up standard operating procedures and place a straitjacket upon the terms of public discourse about education. But over time innovations coming from either the grass roots or elites and can loosen these constraints, creating room for further, more radical, experimentation leading to more enduring change. In a turbulent world, when e.g. assumptions about cognitive requirements for the workplace are being turned upside down, teachers and curriculum leaders can experiment, and administrators can make system adjustments, without arousing as much opposition from parents and citizens anxious that their kids won't be prepared for college or won't be getting a 'real' education.

> Constraint 4. Visions of change and innovative practices introduced by reformers are generally fragmented. Fundamental change requires a setting forth of more coherent visions of curriculum organization, that are consistent with emerging popular models of rational action. Such visions can bring previously unconnected innovations together into a cohesive new pattern of standard practice.

A lot of experimentation produces only experimental particles floating around the core of established practice. For the particles to converge to form a fundamentally changed practice, a synthetic vision—a mental model linking new conceptions of subject matter units, administrative divisions, funding patterns, personnel credentials, lines of authority—must be advanced by credible leaders.

My argument for fundamental change is that (1) globalization *is* creating a powerful external alliance for fundamental change. (2) It *is* destabilizing school participation and classroom interaction, and (3) weakening the external props holding the system up, promoting more room for legitimate experiments which are now forming a 'shadow institution' with its own practices and ideas. Finally, (4) credible leaders *are* formulating new coherent visions of a new curricular organization towards which these 'shadow' innovations may converge, one that is in harmony with the changing social reality. Therefore the conditions for fundamental curriculum change are now falling into place.

III. Globalization, Work, Knowledge, Learning and Education

Earlier I distinguished between the globalization of markets and the globalization of information networks, and noted that these were complementary components of globalization. In this section I trace the lines of force connecting these dimensions of globalization to organizational restructuring, the emerging American occupational structure, knowledge production and utilization in the workplace, and finally to learning and education.

1. Globalization of Markets and Global Competition among Multi-National Enterprises

The Imperial powers laid the groundwork for a system of global trade in the nineteenth century, but competition for resources and markets engendered conflicts. The first world war slowed down the globalization process. The current stage of economic globalization began after World War II, when the economies of Europe and Asia were shattered by the war and the United States had surplus capital for investment. In the preceding 80 years abundant natural resources, large domestic markets, a strong legal structure for contracts and patents, and an ideology of progress through science and technology had propelled the growth of American firms utilizing mass production methods.

After World War II the world economy was in a state of chronic under-supply, and American firms faced little competition in international trade. They increased their direct foreign investments, creating subsidiaries throughout the world making mass produced products for global markets—a process that generated the slogan 'America makes and the world takes', and the idea that globalization meant Americanization. Under these non-competitive conditions American firms could set world prices for mass-produced goods, and could secure labor cooperation by passing along some part of their excess profits to unionized industrial workers as wages and benefits above world levels.

American direct foreign investment grew from \$2.9 billion in 1960 to \$27 billion by 1990. But by the 1970s European and Asian economies had recovered sufficiently to compete with American firms on a global scale. Foreign direct investment in the United States, a meager \$364 million in 1960, had by 1990 expanded to \$48 billion, as foreign-owned companies competed for a market share in the large and affluent domestic American economy (Milberg, 1994). In 1960 1.3% of American GDP was produced by foreign firms, while by 1990 they were producing 8.4% of GDP (Karrier, 1994). European and Asian firms competed successfully with their American counterparts in global markets on the basis of both price and quality.

American firms responded to this competition during the 1970s and 1980s by initiating aggressive anti-union practices, by out-sourcing low skilled manufacturing jobs to reduce wages, and by greatly expanding low wage service sector industries. The AFL-CIO, which represented 30% of those employed in the non-farm sector in 1954, represented fewer than 12% by the 1990s. More than 90% of the new jobs in the American economy in the 1970s and 1980s were in the service sector, while manufacturing suffered a net loss of almost 1 million jobs (World Book Knowledge Source). Firms also demanded trade protection measures, government loans, and reductions of federal corporate taxes as well as state and local subsidies.

Despite these measures, they continued to lose domestic and global market share, and productivity remained stagnant (Milberg, 1994); the annual rate of productivity growth, which had exceeded 4% in the postwar period dropped to 1.1% in the 1970s and 1980s (Appelbaum et al., 2000, p. 227). Americans experienced a severe 'crisis of competitiveness'.

2. The Competitiveness Crisis and Education: Two Periods of 'Excellence' Reforms

Economic and political elites blamed the crisis on the low skill levels of American workers, and by implication, on the poor performance of the American educational system. A 1980 report showed that American students were performing below those of the top group of nations, including such major global competitors as Japan, South Korea, and Germany on tests of math and science achievement. In response, elites pressed for educational change to make Americans competitive with the low-wage, high skill workers in developing nations.[6] The first phase of what came to be known as the 'excellence' reform movement began with the distribution of the national blue ribbon report, 'A Nation at Risk'. In clear and dramatic language, the report stated: 'Our nation is at risk. Our once unchallenged preeminence in commerce, industry, science, and technological innovation is being overtaken by competitors around the world . . . What was unimaginable a generation ago has begun to occur . . . other (nations) are matching or surpassing our educational attainments' (p. 5). The report linked our competitive crisis to the alleged failure of the educational system, lamenting that in international comparisons on 19 academic tests, American students were never first or second, and in comparison with other industrialized nations, were last seven times (p. 8).

The recommendations of the report were touted as 'revolutionary' but in Cuban's terms they were merely incremental, even conservative. They proposed an intensification of the academic curriculum: more required courses in science, mathematics, and computer literacy and imposition of 'world class standards' monitored with standardized tests. No changes were proposed in the basic organizational format of curriculum beyond making wider use of computers in instruction.

Many states issued their own excellence reports and adopted the recommendations of 'A Nation at Risk.' But the results were disappointing. There were changes in the 'intended' curriculum, but day-today practice did not change very much. The reforms had taken place without participation by, and consequent ownership of, the recommendations by teachers and community leaders; they were opposed by many credible public education leaders (e.g. Ernest Boyer, Harold Howe), by teachers' groups, and by minority group leaders fearing that 'higher standards' would be used to exclude them.

A second phase of the excellence reform movement started in the mid-1980s, when reformers responded to the indifference of teachers and community members by granting a degree of professional autonomy and parental influence through site-based management and school choice. The community emphasis brought many educational and minority group leaders into the alliance for change. At this stage the public policy discourse continued to stress 'excellence', defined largely in terms of academic standards and test scores. And new educational technologies were still key ingredients, though in this second phase of reform technology was no longer to be imposed in a top-down fashion; teachers were assigned responsibility for selecting specific uses based on training in technology utilization.

Despite the initial focus of 'excellence' reforms on student performance, test scores have not changed much. Fifteen years after 'A Nation at Risk' research showed 'essentially flat achievement and longstanding academic problems in U.S. schools' (Murphy and Adams, 1998, p. 441).

But market competition between schools was now also touted as a major new engine of change As the consensus for reform grew, diverse social groups, including ethnic minorities, feminists, environmentalists, Roman Catholics, and high-tech professionals added their support for 'choice.' Some of these groups were much less committed to 'excellence'—defined in terms of standards and standardized tests—than the initial reformers. As a result, 'choice' became less exclusively tied to enhancing academic achievement, and increasingly linked to the theme of promoting 'diversity'.

'School Choice' thus became a contradictory policy aimed both at achieving 'common' goals and at letting different groups seek their own quite different goals. This phase of educational reform directed change efforts away from the mainstream system, with consequences to be discussed later.

3. The Global Spread of Information Networks

What we now refer to as the 'Internet' was begun in the late 1960s as the ARPA-net, a US defense network that accepted its first international connection in 1973. Meetings between ARPA and the National Science Foundation led in the 1980s to the building of NSF-net, linking American scientists and academics, in 1986, and the closing of ARPA-net in 1990. In the early 1990s digital information networks began to spread rapidly throughout the globe. The first commercial Internet Service Provider opened for business in 1990, and the World-Wide Web was introduced at CERN in 1991, the same year in which many foreign countries were connected to NSF-net. The next year the World Bank went on-line, followed by the White House and United Nations in 1993 (Howe, 2001).

The growth of the World-Wide Web and its commercial use were phenomenally rapid in the mid 1990s. In June 1993 there were 130 web sites, of which only 1.5% had 'dot.com' domain names. By the end of 1993, 4.6% of the 623 sites were commercial; by the end of 1994 18% of the 10,000; by 1995 50% of the 100,000; and by the end of 1996 over 60% of the 650,000 sites (Gray, 1997).

The driving forces of the growth of digital networks included the rapid technical advances and price declines in computer chips, satellites, and fiber optic cables which facilitated growth in television, telephony, FAX, and the Internet, turning the information grid into a seamlessly integrated resource, 'the biggest machine ever made' (Dizard, 1997, p. 1). Electronics replaced automobiles as the world's largest industry, and telecommunications technologies and their peripherals became the largest share of the electronics product sector (p. 7). Software supplanted hardware as the key to global information convergence, and became the fastest growing sector in the global economy, with the market value of software firms expanding from $663 billion in 1994 to $1.8 trillion in 1996.

By 1995 digital networks were penetrating American homes. NSF-net once again became a research network, while AOL, Prodigy, and Compuserve offered popular Internet services for families. (Howe, 2001). Since that time the growth of the Internet has continued. At the end of 2001 the Internet was growing in the United States at the rate of two million users a month. 143 million Americans were on-line (54% of the population), an increase of 26 million in 13 months. Schools and colleges were on-line, and 75% of 14–17 year olds and 65% of 10–13 year olds were Internet users (NTIA, 2002). The increase in tele-workers and home-based consultants enabled more families to consider home schooling.[7]

4. Economic and Technical Convergence: Business Networks and Network Enterprise

By the mid 1980s many American business leaders were realizing that their main competitive strategies—cost cutting, trade protection, tax breaks and subsidies, were not preserving their share of domestic or global markets or improving productivity. Their customers wanted high quality products, customized features, consistent on-time delivery, and short lead times, and these could not be provided merely by cutting costs or improving mass production methods.

The spread of information networks facilitated a further 're-engineering' or organizational restructuring of vertically integrated multi-national corporations in the early 1990s. American and European firms, in competition with Asian counterparts sharing and coordinating strategies, resources and competencies in their network structures—Japanese *keiretsu*, Korean *chaebol*, and Chinese family networks—came to realize that they too must compete as business networks. Rapid product development cycles, technology diffusion, proliferation of quality producers, and diversity of markets, have forced major firms increasingly to collaborate with their global customers, suppliers, and selected competitors (Rugman and D'Cruz, 2000). Large, vertically integrated firms were broken apart, and non-core aspects of their businesses were sold off. Many professionals in the legal, accounting, information services and other departments were either laid off, or left the firms voluntarily to work as 'knowledge workers' in small partnership firms or as independent consultants, taking advantage of the wider availability and lower costs of network technologies.[8]

As early as 1983 Turoff and Hiltz (1983) had observed that the emerging information and communications technologies were making the notions of centralization and decentralization largely outmoded, as vertically integrated bureaucratic hierarchies were giving way to structures based on fluid networks by means of which connected workers could join ad hoc groupings formed around specific projects. Grosse and Kujawa (1988) spoke of the new multi-national enterprises as 'international contractors', relying not upon subsidiaries but 'joint ventures, licensing or servicing contracts.' These 'meta-national' firms, unlike the traditional transnational firms rooted in a distinct 'home' country, do not take knowledge from the corporate center in the US, Western Europe, or Japan, incorporate it into a product, and ship it to markets in 'less developed areas.' Rather, they draw upon knowledge (in the form of public technical and managerial knowledge, experience and insight, and market intelligence) from employees and network associates all over the world, via in-person and electronic links, to shape products rapidly for the highly differentiated global markets (Doz, Santos and Williamson, 2001).[9]

5. Globalization and Workforce Re-organization

The formation of global networks and network enterprises to compete in global markets has brought about changes in workforce organization in all societies. But as Brown, Green, and Lauder (2001) demonstrate, different societies have employed different competitive strategies.[10] The primary contrast is between nations like the US and UK with a bi-polar skill distribution, able to leverage advantages of both high skilled elite workers and low cost producers, vs. high skill societies like Germany and Japan, seeking to leverage the advantages of their wide skill distribution (p. 144). For the latter, the education and training problem is maintaining cutting edge skills throughout the workforce. For the former, this problem does not arise, as large segments of the workforce are excluded from skilled jobs (p. 162). In this section I consider this bi-polar skill and income distribution, consisting of knowledge workers and skilled production workers, vs. routine workers.

Knowledge Workers

Peter Drucker originated the term 'knowledge worker' in the 1960s, to refer to workers holding diplomas from technical institutes and universities. He based this idea on the rapidly growing proportion of diploma holders in the advanced economies, and the increasing inputs from these workers.[11] Today, however, the term 'knowledge worker' refers more to a mind-set adjusted to the 'smart' work space of the network enterprise than to holders of specific diplomas or bearers of discipline-based scientific or technical knowledge.

The primary capabilities of such workers are knowing how to access, interpret, and apply new knowledge and information to add value to an organization. They see themselves as professionals, but are not limited by narrow professional identities; an intellectual property lawyer, for example, may define himself as a 'problem-solver in the media industry.' They are time-sensitive, oriented to working on specific projects with time deadlines. In this regard they function, when employed, more like independent professionals than like salaried employees. They are learning-oriented, because their unique human capital derives from continuous learning in their professional endeavors. Although each project is time-bound, the knowledge work process does not end with the project, because the worker must integrate the lessons learned to enrich and refine his tacit knowledge. They apply knowledge to knowledge to create new knowledge and information that can combined and permuted to create new products or services (Castells, 1996). The knowledge and information created throughout the process are converted by the processes of the knowledge management system into documents available for knowledge re-use. Even when working for the same employer they play different roles in different projects, as members of different teams. They identify more with professionals in the network than with other employees in the firm. Because network technologies are widely available in work centers and homes, these workers have fewer incentives to remain permanently employed; they are increasingly working as contractors in similar projects for different companies rather than as employees.[12]

Network enterprises depend upon continuous accessing of globally distributed knowledge and information by such workers. It thus needs systems for sensing this mass of information, selecting what is needed and converting it into inputs for new products and services. The knowledge work space is frequently a 'smart' environment, with 'smart machines' programmed with expert systems providing immediate inputs for rapid learning; constantly improved 'hyper-media' including on-line data bases and search engines that make needed information immediately available, with continuously expanded and upgraded libraries of real-time network-specific knowledge, provided by members of the network for so-called'knowledge re-use'. Firms in the network employ 'digital knowledge management systems', including software tools for the management of information by individual workers, such as the programs created by IBM's Lotus division and Microsoft's 'Digital Dashboard.'[13] Some systems also include programs that can automatically integrate fax, phone, voice mail, e-mail, graphics, video and audio throughout the system into digital 'documents' that can be indexed and analyzed and further operated upon, and even translated into foreign languages to create yet more documents, *ad infinitum*. This process known as 'integrated messaging' Because of their use of such knowledge management systems, network organizations are also sometimes called 'alert organizations'.

Grantham (2000) projects a continuing disintegration of the corporation and growth of the network of flexible small companies and freelance workers. He sees an evolution over the next five years toward a 'team of teams' approach in which workers 'come together, blending interdisciplinary skills focusing on a particular project, completing the project, then disbanding the team as each of its workers move on to other projects.' The most important asset in the process is no longer the production capital but the knowledge that moves with the workers from one project to another. Knowledge workers relate in a new way to the means of production, becoming a *'knowledge class.'*

High Skill Production Workers

In the environment of business networks, innovations in the organization of production workers have also become 'increasingly common' (Appelbaum et al., 2000, pp. 3–4). American managers had been borrowing 'quality circles'—off-line, after-the-fact discussions among workers and managers to improve production processes—from the Japanese. But by the late 1980s the term became unfashionable as this sort of give and take came to be seen as only one element in a total management system. Quality circles were supplanted by 'total quality management' (TQM) systems attending to customer satisfaction, employee input, close links to suppliers and customers, management by data. TQM was geared to improve inventory management, just-in-time delivery, statistical quality control, and systematic problem-solving, including follow-up assessment and the dissemination of best practices throughout the system.

The late 1980s also saw modest introduction of more substantive forms of worker participation, in the form of self-directing work teams that make and implement decisions without top-down control. The term 'process re-engineering' has been used to refer to such innovations. Other terms include 'continuous improvement systems' and 'high-performance work systems'. Employee participation of all forms grew but workers in self-directing work teams remained a small minority in 1990, when among 6.5 million workers in companies responding to a survey, 1.2 million (20%) were involved in quality circles but only 300,000 (5%) in self-directing teams (Levine, 1995, pp. 3–7). Since then, many firms have introduced at least some self-managing teams. Lawler compared Fortune 1000 companies in 1987 and 1995, finding that the proportion reporting some use of these teams increased in that period from 28% to 68% A 1995 survey conducted by the Bureau of the Census and the University of Pennsylvania found that 13% of non-managerial workers in their sample were placed in self-managing teams (Appelbaum et al., 2000, pp. 9–10). Productivity growth, stagnant since the early 1970s, increased to 2%, bolstered by the rapid growth of manufacturing productivity (Appelbaum et al., 2000, p. 228).

The spread of digital information technologies converged in the 1990s with these workplace organization practices. Information technologies are fundamentally different than earlier innovations. Information-based tools are highly malleable. They are re-programmable; the same equipment can perform a wide variety of functions. They reduce re-tooling time, and create opportunities for economies of scope. They have a built-in capacity for data collection and analysis, to support decision-making (Ducatel, 1994, pp. 1–4; Appelbaum et al., 2000, p. 14).

Overall, there has been an increase in skills needed in the workplace as a result of the adoption of information technologies and worker participation practices. In firms adopting these techniques skills sets shift from manual and craft skills to higher level cognitive skills including abstract reasoning, because the workers are removed from the physical processes of moving and making. They are system controllers, who must be able to program and maintain their machines, as well as to interpret the data read-outs that the machines produce, which often requires some grasp of the concepts upon which these messages are based. Information technologies fit best in workplace situations where workers and managers cooperate directly in production processes and expertise across multiple functional specialties is available, that is, in flatter, multi-functional teams (Ducatel, 1994, p. 4; see also Ostroff, 1999). Workers in these teams require additional 'soft' skills in communication and group decision making.

Appelbaum et al. (2000) studied the impact of workplace systems combining worker participation with high skills and training on productivity and worker earnings. In the 'high performance work systems' (HPWS) front line workers participate in gathering and analyzing information, and hence require both information processing and communications skills (p. 8); HPWS also require workers to 'become familiar with and carry out a wider range of tasks, to develop better interpersonal and behavioral skills, to take on supervisory and coordination functions, and to interact effectively with other workers and managers' (p. 208). Appelbaum et al. found that HPWS had a positive effect on performance in each of the industries studied (p. 129); HPWS organizations were significantly more likely to have high value added products, reduced costs, high perceived quality of products, lower inventory costs and more rapid inventory turnovers (p. 159). The workers in such organizations earned significantly more that those in traditional production contexts (p. 223).

But Cappelli and his co-authors (1999) noted that despite the benefits of such forms of organization in particular market segments, the advantages of mass production using low cost labor have remained strong in other segments of American industry. Some successful firms have retained lower cost methods, while others have aimed at improved quality, product diversity, and rapid turn-around time. American producers, in comparison with their foreign competitors, have moved more slowly toward high skill, high performance systems, because the larger scale of American production accommodates mass production, and long-established traditions of top-down management have been difficult to change.

The Bi-polar Structure of the American Workforce

The overall result has been a widening division between high skills and low skills segments in the American manufacturing sector. Robert Reich (1992) divided future workers into three categories: highly skilled 'symbolic analysts' who access, combine, and permute knowledge and information to create new products and services, and relatively unskilled, low wage routine production workers and in-person service providers. The above analysis suggests a somewhat different categorization: elite knowledge workers providing professional services, high skill workers organized in information-rich, high performance workplaces, and providers of routine, low skill production and in-person services. The 'routine worker' category contains a high proportion of women, minorities and recent immigrants (including illegal aliens). Unlike routine industrial workers of the 1950s, a large proportion of today's routine workers work in temporary or part time 'contingent' work without union protection, job security or health and pension benefits.[14] From 1970 to 1992 the total payroll of temporary employees rose an astounding 3000% (Weinbaum, 1999). A high school diploma thus no longer provides American students a ticket to a decent job with benefits. With welfare rolls and transfer payments declining, and permanent jobs for unskilled unionized workers in the manufacturing sector disappearing, more Americans are now grouped together in an expanding *'working poor class'*.

6. Workforce Re-organization, Learning, and Education: Failure of the Standard Curriculum

The class situations of 'knowledge' and 'routine' workers differ from those of former managerial-professional and industrial workers, the 'typical' clients of American schools and colleges in the industrial era. Those destined for knowledge work and high skill production work—and their future employers—understand that the established curriculum grammar does not provide the human capital for knowledge work. To point to the most obvious contradictions: students remain individuated in school learning, but graduates are expected to work in groups. Students learn cognitive routines sorted into distinct subject matter disciplines, and are taught by professionals with discipline-specific credentials, but graduates are expected to connect and permute materials from multiple disciplines in non-routine ways. Schools present subject matter in an orderly sequence, unconnected to real world applications, but graduates must acquire and process information 'just-in-time' for immediate use.[15]

John Dewey (1976/1910) argued that educators must consider how the content and mature organization of knowledge grows out of the practical demands of social life, and how that content is used, tested, and modified in its actual use. The series of curricular activities gradually must approximate mature knowledge-in-use just as the young people themselves gradually approximate maturity in their life roles and consequent knowledge needs.[16] Cole (1990) showed that schooling employing the standard curriculum grammar is a specific learning environment that produces a specific sort of learning in which memory, classification, and routine verbal-logical problem solving plays a large role. Snow and his associates[17] have shown that the learning associated with the standard curriculum grammar is linked to 'crystallized', not 'fluid' knowledge. Students undergoing the standard kind of curricularized learning may efficiently acquire information and rote cognitive routines, but this is simply not the sort of learning needed by the high skilled workers in today's global network economy.

IV. From Globalization to Fundamental Curriculum Change

This leaves the question whether the American educational institution can respond to this technical inefficiency in standard curricular schooling practices, by instituting fundamental curriculum change. I argue that constraints to fundamental change are being removed, that a powerful alliance for change, a disruption of mainstream practice, a 'shadow' educational institution built from innovations, and a coherent vision of a new system, are now forming.

There is Potentially a Powerful Alliance for Fundamental Change

In the late industrial period, despite intellectual critiques and periodic incremental reforms, no constituency for fundamental change existed. Secondary education was the gateway to full participation in society, allocating positions in the workplaces of industrial society. Some graduates went on to college and professional or managerial careers. Others went directly into the industrial workplace, earning union wages and enjoying job security, health insurance, and pension benefits. Even those excluded from equal participation viewed the school as the gateway, and fought for equal educational opportunity. Capital, the working class, and even the excluded poor thus achieved a working consensus on the form and content of education. The battles were over access.

Today the potential for change exists, in a powerful alliance of corporate capital, middle class managerial, professional and industrial knowledge workers, and the working poor. The corporate sector wants a steady supply of knowledge professionals and high skill workers. It has not been satisfied with the products of mainstream education. The 'excellence' reforms have left it skeptical about the possibility of reforming established schools through the political process. Instead, it is either imposing its own educational projects upon the schools through 'partnerships' involving high-tech academies, or providing counterpart experiences in its 'corporate universities'.[18]

Highly skilled production workers and professional knowledge workers will demand educational opportunities for their children connected with the new economy. Suburbanites pressure for school change: more Internet connections and more problem solving in groups. Many appear content with the current pace of change, sensing that their communities have the will and resources to make necessary curriculum adjustments over time. But few middle class parents remaining in the cities, regardless of their ethnic group, have much remaining hope for school reform. Some are demanding 'school choice', both to avoid having their kids placed in schools serving the working poor, and to provide them with knowledge and skills for contemporary workplaces. Some are opting for private or parochial schools and they support vouchers; others are choosing charter schools, hoping that they will attract middle class families and academically motivated students. A rapidly increasing number among the knowledge professional group are now home-schooling their children.

The working poor no longer believe that the established schools can provide access even to dignified working class status. The academic achievement of their children is frequently insufficient for subsequent training for knowledge or high skill production work. Their children appear stuck at the bottom of the social ladder, their life chances deteriorating rather than improving. They are 'at risk' for crime, incarceration or self-destruction. There is increasing support among the working poor for charter schools and voucher programs.[19]

These groups have yet not forged a consensus on the direction of educational change. But there is movement in this direction. Right now they are demanding a variety of new schools—from aviation and African-centered to zoo-based schools–and the charter framework is well adapted to this diversity. But the social movements motivating some of these first generation charter schools are losing steam, because they have lacked coherent programs for economic and social renewal. An inner city African-American child, for example, may feel better in an African-centered school, but the African curriculum content will not supply the knowledge and skills needed for entry into high skill or knowledge work.

These skills—in information technology, but also in ill-structured problem-solving and decision-making, communications and group relations—provide the common denominator amidst today's curriculum diversity, and hence the predictable convergence point for durable curriculum content innovations.

[...]

NOTES

1. The 'flagship—five partners' model is developed in Rugman and D'Cruz (2000).
2. Seminal articles of Meyer (1977, 1978) and Meyer and Rowan (1978) are viewed as setting forth a new institutional 'paradigm' in educational studies.
3. See Cuban, 1984, 1990, 1992; Tyack and Cuban, 1995; McKinnon and Westbury, 1975; Westbury, 1973; Reid, 1999.
4. This idea parallels Ivan Illich's notion of institutionalized schooling obtaining a 'radical monopoly' over socially legitimate learning (see Illich, 1971).
5. For further discussion see Rowan and Miskel, (1999: 380).
6. For a discussion of American performance on international comparisons of science and math achievement, see Baker (1997).
7. See Qvortrup (1998), for a recent review of home-based tele-workers.
8. Karen Vander Linde, partner in charge of learning services at Price Waterhouse Coopers' business process outsourcing group, one of the fastest growing units at Price Waterhouse, claims that firms are outsourcing their knowledge professionals so that when they work on projects as 'partners' they can compel the employees to adopt appropriate knowledge work attitudes and alleviate the transition to a networked, e-learning environment (PR News Wire, 2001). Albert and Bradley (1997: 10) however, claim that knowledge professionals are more frequently leaving employment in large firms voluntarily, to take advantage of the greater discretion, flexibility, productivity and enhanced income derived from operating as a consulting professional. The terms 'necessity entrepreneurs' and 'opportunity entrepreneurs' are used to distinguish those who start their own firms after being laid off from those who initiate their firms voluntarily to take advantage of entrepreneurial opportunities.
9. In March 2000 both the *New York Times* and *USA Today* ran cover stories spotlighting *Fast Company*, the trendy new magazine that has captured the spirit of network enterprise.
10. According to Brown, Green and Lauder (2001), the United States and United Kingdom have adopted 'high skill–low skill' strategies, with high skilled professional elite 'knowledge workers' and a wide spread of skill levels and incomes in the working

population. Germany has maintained a 'high skill' strategy, with relative income and skill equality for domestic workers; low skill jobs are confined to foreign guest workers and high levels of unemployment are accepted. Japan has combined a 'high skill' workforce strategy with long working hours and labor discipline.

11. Drucker's insight has been verified by the growing number of college graduates in skilled production jobs (Holusha, 1995) making the distinction I am suggesting between knowledge professionals and skilled production workers fuzzy.
12. These characteristics of contemporary knowledge workers are reported by Disney (2001); Seang (2001); and Seebach (2001).
13. Microsoft unveiled its vision to 'enable the knowledge worker' in 1999, reorganizing its operations into four customer groups: IT managers, knowledge workers, software developers, and consumers. Bob Maglia, previously in charge of applications software, was re-assigned to the division targeting knowledge workers (Taft and Glascock, 1999). Lotus introduced products for its Domino Notes platform incorporating such concepts as 'locating appropriate people and resources through directory services' and 'aggregating information from diverse sources.' The management literature at the turn of the century has identified 'knowledge sharing' as among the major issues facing the global corporation, and has begun to explore 'best practices' for knowledge sharing (Verespej, 1999: 10; Comedu-Kirschner, 2000: 8). 'Knowledge management' has entered a new phase in the late 1990s, in which instead of merely training existing workers to use knowledge assets, jobs are re-designed from scratch to assume knowledge work processes. A detailed chronicle of knowledge work in many sectors is chronicled in Cortada (1998).
14. See Sassen (1994), for a more detailed account of the jobs in the service economy and their role in the workforce of today's 'global' cities.
15. Shukor (2001) maintains that the standard curriculum (in Malaysia) is based around 'spoon feeding' and 'an exam-oriented school environment,' and adds that the 'entire system needs major tweakings if not a complete overhaul' (p. 17) to produce knowledge workers. Commenting on the Malaysian government's 'smart school initiative', Shukor comments that 'computers are just tools,' and the real problem is freeing students to think and make decisions.
16. Dewey is worth quoting at length on this point. He says 'there is all the difference in the world whether the acquisition of information is treated as an end in itself, or is made an integral portion of the training of thought. The assumption that information that has been accumulated apart from use in the recognition and solution of a problem may later on be, at will, freely employed by thought is quite false. The skill at the ready command of intelligence is the skill acquired with the aid of intelligence' (1976/1910: 163).
17. Cited in Rowan and Miskel (1999: 377).
18. On the rapid growth and operating principles of corporate universities, see Meister (1998). Their threat to the mainsteam tertiary sector is discussed by Nurden (1999). Authers (1999), discusses their crucial role in creating a corporate culture that spans the flagship corporation and its 'partners.' Prestoungrange (2000) provides a detailed account of the role of problem based action learning in corporate university programs.
19. Fine and Weis (1998) in a study of de-industrialized workers in Buffalo New York and Jersey City New Jersey, provide useful case examples. Jersey City's poor broke with the public schools, supported the state takeover of the district, and were sympathetic to a voucher initiative (p. 10). Black males in particular rejected public schools. 'Eddie' dissented from a 'system that has failed a generation of people.' 'Lawrence' complained about an outdated curriculum that 'doesn't mean nothin' to nobody' and added 'our concepts of schools are antiquated . . . they need to be transformed.' Julius said 'its not about degrees anymore . . .' (pp. 230–2).

Part Nine

Universities, Higher Education, and Lifelong Learning

The advent of mass higher education in which over 50 per cent of an age cohort attend university, the opportunities for lifelong learning so that many 'mature' students can enter university, and changing forms of governance and global competition have had a major impact on higher education. Halsey (Ch. 58) charts the social, cultural, and economic factors that have brought about change in the European university which, he reminds us, has a history 'only slight shorter than that of the Roman Catholic church' and which remains the model for higher education in many countries.

Higher education, he argues is built into the fabric of the modern social project with its aims of increasing command over nature, prolonging life, and promoting economic growth and a degree of equality of opportunity. In the present era the democratic needs of access have given way to mass higher education but at some cost to the degree of control that university teachers had over their institutions and indeed the curriculum of upper secondary schools. Now he argues control has passed to 'politicians, courts, and budgetary administrators'.

McSherry (Ch. 59) extends this theme by arguing that the space for disinterested enquiry and research is closing because of university links to corporations who seek to gain a competitive advantage by buying the research and knowledge generated by universities. This process creates major questions about university research and teaching autonomy and in her view is fundamentally altering the character of the university.

Naidoo and Jamieson (Ch. 60) pick up this theme in relation to what they call consumerism. Here they focus on new commercial systems of governance that have been introduced to many, although not all universities. In particular this form of governance has introduced various mechanisms to give students greater choice and control over the learning process. However, they raise serious questions about the teaching–learning relationship under consumerist conditions. Here they acknowledge that some universities, the less powerful, are more likely to subject themselves to the whole package of consumerist policies while the more powerful may have the autonomy to resist. In developing the theoretical framework for this analysis they also provide a way of understanding the differential impact of global consumer demand on university systems. There are few papers that seek to examine the implications of policy for teaching and learning because the links are so complex. But they set an ambitious agenda to research these links.

Perucci and Wysong (Ch. 61) examine the inequalities in higher education in the United States, focusing on the way universities reproduce social inequalities. They chart how this occurs from the school system and into a higher education sector, effectively divided on class lines. We should see their argument against a backdrop of growing income and wealth inequality in the United States.

Marginson (Ch. 62) takes up the theme of inequality but seeks to explore it in the context of an emerging global market for higher education and its impact on local populations. By comparing Australian and American higher education systems he shows that the markets in both countries are vertically organized and segmented according to prestige. The overall effect of neo-liberal policies has been to accentuate the differences within and between market segments. However it has also been part of neo-liberal policy in Australia to open the sector to the global market. This, he argues, has introduced several undesirable consequences. The first is that it has led to the introduction of business cultures into the management of universities. It has also compromised the project of creating greater equality of opportunity through higher education because those Australians with the wealth can now move to more prestigious universities overseas, although for the elites in developing countries the opening up of higher education has benefited them.

This latter point is particularly relevant in relation to the fast developing economies of Asia. Levin and Xu (Ch. 63) chart the rapid expansion of higher education in China. While many Chinese are going overseas for their education, there will come a time in the not too distant future when their own universities will be equal in standing to those in the West. Nevertheless, this expansion has encountered many difficulties, especially in relation to equity and the positional competition for credentials. Higher education is for the most part fee-paying and this means that only those who can find the money can attend. While there is no doubt that the number of those entering the middle class in China has accelerated due to this expansion, questions remain as to how much the present policy favours the families of the ruling party and the ruling economic elites.

While there have been major changes in the nature of higher education, new paths are being laid in relation to the idea of lifelong learning. The impetus towards lifelong learning has undoubtedly been economic. As flexible labour markets have been introduced in which workers can be hired or fired depending on the vagaries of the trade cycle or changes in tastes or technology so there has been a need to reskill the workforce. It is in this context that the idea of lifelong learning has taken off. Rees, Fevre, Furlong, and Gorard (Ch. 64) argue that the dominant human capital theory which has motivated the development of lifelong learning, more honoured in rhetoric than practice, is fundamentally flawed. They take the example of pit closures in South Wales and show how, after initial promises that retraining would lead to jobs, workers became disillusioned and disinclined to re-engage with formal learning processes.

Rubenson (Ch. 65) examines another aspect of the social conditions that may effect the motivation for lifelong learning. He argues that there are 'crucial differences in what adult education attempts to do and can do in different social political structures'. What is interesting about Rubenson's account in looking at the Nordic adult education model are the number of social and economic factors that he believes underpin its success. These include the relative equality in income distribution, active labour market policies, and a corporatist model of industrial relations. It is clear that how lifelong education is structured and understood will depend on economic, social, and political factors.

The European University

A. H. Halsey

Expansion

In the foreword to the first of the four-volume history of the university in Europe the general editor, Walter Ruegg, describes it as 'the European institution *par excellence*'.[1] It has a history only slightly shorter than that of the Roman Catholic Church: it is older than any European nation-state. Rooted in the religious life of Christendom, it survived as an essentially ecclesiastical organisation until the nineteenth century when first the French and second the German secular variants emerged to be spread, especially in the German form, throughout the world. But sociologists of education would necessarily set this elite tertiary stage of education in the wider context of arrangements for learning in human society as a whole.

The history of popular communication from the usable alphabet of the Ancient Greeks through the printing press to modern information technology has been a very slow process, albeit accelerating in our own time. The process has been slow because to democratize communication also requires transformation of virtually every aspect of social structure. People are bound together by power and authority, by interest and sentiment, by habituation and learning, as well as by words and numbers. Vast changes of human society were therefore required to work out all the implications of this original linguistic revolution. Nor is the journey complete. The scope and reach of higher learning never ceases to unfold. It is built into the modern social project of ever-increasing human command over nature, prolonging life, ceaselessly hungering after economic growth, and permitting more widespread leisure. The pull of professional needs and the push of democratic demands for access continually press for expansion in face of limited public and private resources. Higher education came at the end of the process as the conspicuous international growth industry of today. It is a worldwide phenomenon with ancient roots. The background of transition out of pre-industrial to industrial society is now, following Max Weber, the standard interpretation of social development among sociologists of education.[2]

Behind this interpretation lies the yet wider one of a general characterization of industrial society by contrast with an earlier agrarianism. Agrarian society was characteristically static, segmented in its structure and with separate special languages attached to its various functions. Hunting, cooking, tool-making, ritual, and territorial defence all had identified groupings and specialized knowledge passed on and made personal by apprenticeship. Each unit was capable of perpetuating its own social reproduction. Training and education therefore, as Weber emphasized, was also segmented and hierarchical. The family and quasi-familial community organizations passed on the common culture, smiths taught their children special skills, and a class of priests and literati were the guardians of high culture, working in the interests of the dominant strata.

Modern industrial societies aim to turn everyone into a member of the educated class of participating workers and citizens. The distinction between the clerisy and the laity is eroded and institutionally, the university has a monopoly of nothing. In that context the decline of donnish dominion[3] is simply the inverse of the rise of meritocracy.

This chapter draws on material from A. H. Halsey, in Hilde de Ridder-Symoens (ed.), *A History of the University in Europe*, volume 4, Cambridge University Press (In Press), reproduced with permission.

Ernest Gellner's macroscopic view of the evolution of industrial society has nationalism as its focus. He presents a model of modernity with education and mobility built in as essential features. 'A society has emerged based on a high-powered technology and the expectancy of sustained growth, which requires both a mobile division of labour, and sustained, frequent, and precise communication between strangers involving a sharing of explicit meaning, transmitted in a standard idiom and in writing when required ... The level of literacy and technical competence ... required of members of this society, if they are to be properly employable and enjoy full and effective moral citizenship, is so high that it simply cannot be provided by the kin or local units.' Only a modern national education system will serve. 'At the basis of the modern social order stands not the executioner but the professor' (Gellner 1983: 34). An industrial society requires universal literacy and general sophistication. Since members are normally required to be able to deal with strangers, communication has to be explicit, impersonal, context-free, and in a shared and standardized language.

In agrarian medieval Europe the conditions for international communication were established by the lingua franca of Latin in advance of the industrial conditions which required and facilitated mass participation. Abelard or Erasmus could be famous and peripatetic teachers. Students could travel between *studia generale* by donkey, barge, and bark from Edinburgh to Rome. The 'nations' of a university campus prefigured the retreat to nationalism of a culture extending throughout Christendom in the Middle Ages and there were struggles between kings and pope for authority over the curriculum and organization of originally ecumenical institutions. But by and large and for the time being, the dons were masters of their own house, essentially because they lived on the economic margins of a society where the nation-state had yet to intervene as the main strategic agent of economic growth and popular participation.

The subsequent development of science lay at the centre of successive industrial transformations. A shared and standardised language linked researchers into global networks permitting competitive co-operation in the advance of physical, chemical, and biological knowledge. The university was the major instrument of this development; the academic was accordingly held in high esteem. But scientific advance translated into technological development in industry meant breaching the walls of the academy and extending knowledge, or at least its use, throughout society.

Thus Gellner emphasizes that:

> The educational system which guarantees this social achievement becomes large and is indispensable, but at the same time it no longer possesses monopoly of access to the written word: its clientele is co-extensive with the society at large, and the replaceability of individuals within the system by others applies to the educational machine at least as much as to any other segment of society, and perhaps more so. Some very great teachers and researchers may perhaps be unique and irreplaceable but the average professor and school master can be replaced from outside the teaching profession with the greatest of ease and often with little, if any loss.
> (Gellner 1983: 35–6)

In short, the academic becomes both indispensable and also deprived of his former privileged position. This is something of a paradox. The highly educated are both central to the working of a dynamic, endlessly innovating, mobile, and wealthy society, but graduates and cognitive activity are dispersed to all the other institutions of society—business enterprise, recreational organizations, social administration, even the family and local social groups. So the university, as Daniel Bell has argued, has become the gatekeeper to the higher occupational positions in a complex society in which new technical elites reshape the class structure and the populist reaction is to demand greater 'equality', usually meaning educational expansion, as a defence against social exclusion (Bell 1973).

Gellner's version of the Weberian thesis is that the universal necessity of high standards of education is not only national but must be of a generic character preceding and topped by further specialist training. This is indisputable, but Gellner then claims that the additional skills consist only of a few techniques that can be learned fairly quickly. That gloss is arguable. The implication that there has been a narrowing of the distance between the most advanced modern specialist and the comprehensive schoolchild by comparison with the university medieval schoolman and the peasant of late agrarian Europe is contentious. Cognitive possession of difficult intellectual work at the frontier of the natural and social sciences is one thing, while power to use this body of knowledge in daily life is quite another. And the problem of the institutional means for developing and passing on scientific knowledge is yet a third question which has been left open.

Certainly a generalized scientific culture must exist in modern industrial society with the implications for both the structure of knowledge and the organization of social relations which Gellner so brilliantly sketches. He shows convincingly that a cognitive epistemological revolution was necessary, and supplied by the philosophers Hume and Kant, as a pre-condition for the development of both the knowledge itself and its social use. He is equally convincing in his argument that a necessary consequence was the superimposition of national and indeed international ordering of both production and reproduction in industrial society. In that context the decline of academic power is what Weber referred to as the disenchantment of the world.

Weber illustrated how easy it is to misinterpret modern scientific culture when he pointed out that its existence did not mean that his audience in the lecture room in Munich in 1914 knew more of the conditions of life under which they existed than had an American Indian or a Hottentot. 'Unless he is a physicist, one who rides on the street car has no idea how the car happened to get into motion. And he does not need to know. He is satisfied that he can "count" on the behaviour of the street car ... The savage knows incomparably more about his tools' (Gerth and Mills 1947: 139).

Who dominates either in the academy or in the society at large is a question that can only be resolved in the political and organizational context. The organization and passing of such a culture rests on traditional structures of kinship and community as well as the inventions of the national institutions which have allowed it to emerge. A place for the *cognoscenti* has to be found within it. Both traditional and 'scientific' learning are embodied in it at all levels; and some pattern of transition for individuals out of learning into occupation has to be fashioned.

Moreover and above all, Durkheim's preoccupation with *l'éducation morale* is highly relevant to the understanding of the transmission of modern culture from one generation to another. The ancient and the modern institutions work in complex interaction. The external mark of certification is an outcome of both ascription and 'achievement', which explains the stubbornly persistent inequality of the social distribution of the certificates of entry into an ever-changing and more specialized division of labour. The efficient worker has to acquire appropriate attitudes to punctuality, duty, the calculation of reward for effort, and so on, and these attributes pass from fathers to sons and mothers to daughters through every kind of social encounter and not solely through the formal educational system. Here again lie the roots of continuing social inequality. And against a background of declining religious belief, increasing frailty of family and community, and the search for new legitimacies in the social order, the role of the professional expert at the apex of the education system is both strengthened and undermined. The question of how these moral as well as cognitive authorities are to be socially organized cannot possibly be appropriately resolved by simple market solutions. Only a complex process of politics can properly determine the duties and privileges of professions, including the academic professions. Contemporary enthusiasm for the use of the market disguises a politics which permits a wide range of alternatives.

Similar arguments apply to organizing research and its application. Market competition is no guarantee of innovation. It may explain the success of the German universities in the middle of the nineteenth century,[4] but equally fails to explain the remarkable successes of British academic innovators in the period between Hume and Rutherford. Humility about the conditions that foster creativity should give us pause before we apply any simplistic reform.

Experience should have taught us that institutions of higher education have multiple ends. Yet contemporary argument is frequently narrowed on to problems of efficient and economical means towards the ends of innovation and the formation of 'human capital'. These are important considerations. Parsons and Platt have portrayed the university or polytechnic as the institutionalization of rationality ('the core value of the university is cognitive rationality'), and few would reject that definition (Parsons and Platt 1973: 26). Nevertheless many different values have hitherto been sought.

Efficiency is one, but apart from the debatable question about its relation to market organization, other ends, such as fair access and freedom of research and teaching, also have legitimate claims. Thus, for example, efficient management might settle the struggle between the dominant form of monolithic departmental hierarchy and the alternative form of producer co-operation. But even if this were so, it could still be argued that self-government is an end in itself which ought to be preserved, even at some cost to efficient decision-making.

Another prized value in higher education, especially perhaps with respect to women, ethnic minorities, and disadvantaged classes, is equality. Should poor chances in lower education be compensated in higher education by some form of quota or positive discrimination, for example? Should the strict principle of meritocracy be modified by recognizing that women rarely compete on equal terms in research because of childbearing and persisting habits of domestic division of labour?

The transformation of tertiary education in Europe with respect to equality has been a major preoccupation since the Second World War. In 1945 the European Universities were largely if not exclusively finishing schools for a minority of well-to-do or meritocratic young, mostly men. A secondary stage of socially selected young people took matriculation examinations, usually widely based in science and arts, and some then went on to the universities to complete a degree. But the system was to be transformed. Throughout Europe since 1945 the number of students enrolled in universities and other institutions of tertiary education rose more or less continuously. Beginning with the American GI Bill which enabled thousands of veterans from the Second World War to be funded by the state through tertiary education, and with the absorption of Eastern Europe into the Soviet sphere, it became more or less normal practice to engage in one form or another of what we might now see as a historic exercise in retrospective equalizing of educational opportunity. The British FET grant was a typical imitative scheme and all over the Continent, the devastation of war notwithstanding, expansion of education became the order of the day and continued, albeit at varying speeds, through the post-war period and on to the end of the twentieth century.

Growth can only be described as spectacular. In Britain for example the number of students in universities in 1950 was outstripped by 1990 by the number of university teachers! Though it slowed in the 1980s, there was a doubling of student numbers between 1970 and 1980 in Finland, Austria and the former West Germany. Average annual growth rates were over 8 per cent per annum in the 1970s and over 4 per cent per annum in the 1980s. Women account for a lot of the increase and were by 1990 half of the total except in Portugal and Switzerland.

Experience differed in the East as against the West. In the Eastern European countries in the 1970s growth was slower, at 3 per cent per annum with Czechoslovakia, Poland and Yugoslavia in the lead and the Soviet Union and Bulgaria in the rear. Then, in the 1980s development in Eastern Europe was virtually halted. In Hungary, Poland, Czechoslovakia, Romania and Yugoslavia, numbers actually declined in the economic and political crisis years at the end of the decade. Thus the gap in participation between East and West Europe widened.

Behind this European-wide educational movement we can detect three motors and at least three resistances. The motors were in the first place social and economic, the aspirations and the financial capacity of increasing numbers to find wealth and welfare. Yet they were expressed in Europe for the most part politically because the East and the West lived under one of the two main versions of democracy, and both electorates across Europe believed that the state was the main instrument for delivering both prosperity and justice. True the West assumed that private enterprise was essential to liberty but state-dominated educational systems were the legacy of centuries and in recent experience the nation-state had triumphantly defeated fascism.

Governments inspired by Keynesian liberalism knew how to deliver full employment by macroeconomic planning. The collapse of this belief in the 1980s is, of course, part of the very different atmosphere in which tertiary systems of education and training are managed in the twenty-first century. In the 1950s however, spurred on by progressive propaganda, in the East by Soviet-style planning and in the West by OECD, which was designed to resuscitate the West European economy, labour force efficiency was the first and most obvious motor.

Second, and closely connected to the same recent experience, was confidence in the capacity of universities to improve technical and technological efficiency. The campus had produced the atomic bomb, penicillin and the map of the human genome. Future prosperity depended on the enthronement of academia rather than the business enterprise as the central institution of a modern economy.

Third, and perhaps most powerful, was the drive by nation states to enlarge access to tertiary education. Historically the problem had been phrased in both East and West Europe as one of class. Initially it took the form of redress of some of the inequality of the pre-war period. Later it took the more surprising form of widening access for women, ethnic minorities, and mature students. Only much later did it become clear that the traditional class project, in the sense of equalizing *relative* class chances, had failed in both its Marxist and liberal versions.

Such were the motors: but the resistances were formidable. Despite the urge to reform, the autonomy of existing institutions put up spirited defences. The universities themselves tended to remain attached to Humboldtean and Newmanesque conceptions. Bruce Truscot was a best seller,[5] essentially championing the Oxbridge idea of an enlightened elite of scholars. Not until Clark Kerr sent a message across the Atlantic in 1963 from his Gifford lectures at Harvard did a genuinely new picture emerge of the university as the intellectual centre of the economic and cultural life of the nation.[6] Moreover in Europe the grip of the selective secondary schools on the mind of the aspiring parent remained strong—the *lycée* in France, the *Gymnasium* in Germany. And an ideology of 'the pool of ability' rationalized the continuing resistance to new provision for wider passage from secondary to tertiary institutions.

Second and not at all surprising were the forces of class and status defence. Nothing motivates parents more, be they bourgeois or party functionaries, than the question of how to pass on their advantages to their own children. Fortunately economic advance was opening more jobs and careers to more educated people so that the defence of the grammar school and the college was eased. But class and status struggles centred on the university admissions office increasingly.

A third and powerful resistance emerged later in the shape of governmental reluctance to spend on higher education. Three root causes can be identified—the competing claims of warfare over welfare, the unwillingness of electorates to vote higher taxes, and the growing popularity of economic-liberal doctrines of minimal government. It all seemed paradoxical in the light of immediate post-war experience. Yet ageing populations do tend to give first priority to spending on health and are disinclined to allow governments to spend their money for them in the face of evidence that bureaucracies are inefficient. One might have supposed a rational basis to reluctance in the recognition that spending on higher education by government is socially regressive. In fact the determined resistance of suburban parents to attempts by economic liberals as well as socialists to cut back student subsidies attests the opposite. The gathering flow of women into the economy, the rise, that is, of the two-earner family, generated increased demand, even within education, for pre-school and nursery provision rather than university funding.

Fourth there was the resistance stemming from anti-market or guild or public service organization of schools, colleges and faculties which came into play when the economic-liberal doctrines became paramount in the polities of Europe. The guild and civil service forms of organization of teachers and researchers were powerful but in the end impotent to stem the reorganization of education along market lines.

The background of demographic changes must also be mentioned. These too, including fluctuations in fertility which occurred in unexplained concurrence, were Europe-wide. The whole region was gradually transformed after the baby boom period following the Second World War into a region of unprecedented incipient population decline. By 1990 the typical total period fertility rate had dropped to 1.8 whereas a stable population requires 2.1. The combination of fluctuating fertility and secular decline might have led to pessimistic if not catastrophic long-run prospects for the universities. But in fact the demography and relative prosperity of this advanced industrial region have created a regime of 'the third age' in which health and leisure and income are relatively evenly distributed to those who have retired from active labour participation and form in effect a new and powerful political class with resources and the appetite for further education. Hence the formation of the university of the third age in France, the support for the Open University in Britain, the introduction of the *Seniorunivérsitat* in German-speaking countries and similar institutions in Europe generally.

Properly understood the class handicap is by no means a peculiar feature of modern Europe. It pertains to other countries and other periods. Yossi Shavit and Hans-Peter Blossfeld have edited and summarized a study in comparable terms of thirteen countries which supplies crucial evidence.[7] The 'comparable terms' are essentially statistical, being defined by Robert Mare[8] to distinguish between two processes, viz. the expansion of the educational system and the selection and allocation of pupils and students. In order to clarify the distinction, Mare uses the notion of transitions, what Boudon had labelled 'branching points', at which children can choose or be selected to proceed to a further stage of education.[9] The odds of making the transition are obviously determined by exogenous factors such as the gender, class background, ethnicity, parental education and income, family size, geographical location, etc. of the potential student population. The odds are also an outcome of the given structure of opportunity at the time. Thus, instead of asking the simple question as to how educational attainment processes have changed historically we can ask separately about the effects of expansion (or contraction) of opportunity and about the effects of shifts in the exogenous factors. Mare's method or model makes the answers possible through logit regressions.

Empirically he shows that when education expands as it has done in Europe since 1945, the regressions decline across successive cohorts unless the association between social class and educational transitions (the logit effects) increases. We should also note the characteristic empirical pattern that logit effects tend to decrease in successive transitions. In an expansive period the growing proportions of successive cohorts reaching higher levels of the educational system have less selectivity and the homogeneity of unmeasured factors becomes lower than it had been for previous cohorts. Thus the logit effects of social origin on higher educational transitions tended to increase. The end result of this interactive process was a reduction in the variance of schooling, an increase in its mean, but little change in the distribution of relative chances for education between social strata. Does this generalization apply to all the countries of Europe in the post-war period?

The countries covered by the study are the Federal Republic of Germany, the Netherlands, Sweden, England and Wales, Italy, Switzerland, Poland, Hungary, and Czechoslovakia. Some non-European countries are also included (USA, Taiwan and Japan). The spread, though not comprehensive, enables us to see the general European development in a wider context and particularly to look at the experience of the communist reforms in Eastern Europe compared with the more capitalistic social structures of Germany or Britain, or with the social democratic regimes of Sweden or the Netherlands.

Experience leads us to expect educational inequality. In a period of economic and political reconstruction and growth we would expect to find growing wealth, better health and attempts to respond to popular aspirations towards a better society and a more elevated and peaceable civilization occasioned by the vicissitudes of war. Moreover we are interested to know how far the different political regimes were able to respond, specifically with respect to access to university or tertiary education. Did the relationship between parental political and economic characteristics and educational opportunity change after the war, after the demise of fascism and national-socialism and with the rise of communism and social democracy?

Persisting inequality of educational attainment between class and ethnic groups as well as between the sexes is an old feature of European history. Modes of explaining the pattern have been of two basic kinds—cultural capital theory and the thesis of economic constraint. Cultural capital theory postulates that the poor, by and large, lack the advantages of language, motivation and skill which select pupils in school and equip them with the wherewithal to proceed successfully to the university. The alternative (though not necessarily incompatible) theory of economic constraint, advanced for example by Boudon,[10] insists that in most countries education has to be financed from family resources to include both direct costs and foregone earnings. Thus, as Diego Gambetta has argued using Italian evidence, poorer families need to make higher sacrifices and to have stronger ambitions than rich families if they are to negotiate a passage through tertiary studies.[11] In this way cultural and financial inequalities between classes and status groups combine to produce educational inequalities among their children.

The idea of meritocracy is also familiar as a feature of the broad trend towards modernity and the substitution of achieved for ascriptive roles in response to the requirements of an ever more technological economy. Therefore the connection between social origin and educational qualification should diminish over time, despite the determination of most if not all countries to expand the numbers and the duration of those *in statu pupillari*. Whether theorists take the modernization or the reproduction view of education, they tend to agree that educational expansion whether responding to the functional requirements of a modern economy or to the competition between status groups for scarce educational, resources, will lead to greater equality at the lower levels of education. But the two schools tend to differ as to the consequences for tertiary education. Modernization theorists expect that the effects of class origin will evaporate over time: reproduction theorists by contrast predict stability or even increase in the in egalitarian influences of class hierarchy. Certainly the expansion of tertiary institutions, in one way or another, produces a new and enlarged hierarchy of prestige and power to place alumni in the professional and managerial structure so as to make possible both a rising proportion of graduates and a stable differential advantage of those with advantaged class origins.

Models of Higher Education

From 1945 to 1989 there emerged two contrasted models of the organization of higher education. In the Soviet Union and the countries of Eastern Europe post-compulsory schooling was dominated by the state, seen as an antechamber to the modern economy, and as the finishing school of the new socialist man or woman. Consequently the array of appropriate studies was narrow and vocational and the further ranges of 'useless' subjects like the classics were neglected.[12] In the West the movement was also towards science and technology but less markedly so and the traditional curricula retained their place. In the West also the private college or university was dwarfed in importance by the rapidly growing state institutions but was tolerated. Only outside Europe in the USA and Japan was there a serious development of private universities and these were mostly of religious origin, especially of new American Protestant sects. In Western European practice, though tending towards the American model (which itself was largely imported from the German universities after the period of their great success in the 19th century), there remained a state-dominated system of colleges and universities with government as the obvious prime source of funding for post-war expansion.

We should hesitate to attribute expansion solely to a political drive to satisfy popular desire for egalitarian widening of opportunities. At least comparable weight must be given to governmental resolve to modernize through research and through the education and training of a modern labour force. In the Soviet Union the definition of post-compulsory education as a vast apparatus of production of the labour force required for a modern industrialized economy and a centralized plan seems to have led the political response to what otherwise might have expressed itself as individual aspirations for upward mobility.

We should also note the slow withdrawal of religious influences which had so clearly shaped the evolution of the medieval European university. We have here the triumph of a secular version of university life, least perhaps in Spain, clearly in France and with the special case of Oxford and Cambridge in England where foreign observers were often puzzled by the coexistence of monastic colleges and anachronistic admission to close tutorial relations alongside modern laboratory departments where Nobel prizes and famous scientific exploits were frequently to be observed. In the USA the separation of church and state had facilitated the expansion of private colleges, in France Napoleonic revolution had given pride of place to the *grandes écoles* and in England the integration of the Church of England into the state apparatus had led to the development of socially but not academically inferior 'red brick' universities with, among other things, separate admission procedures. So the picture is more of a spectrum than of a binary division. In the Soviet Union and the eastern bloc the separation of church from state was in effect constituted after the Second World War by the abolition of the former. The ancient church foundations of Hungarian universities are a typical example.

In one sense the intrusion of the state in Eastern Europe can legitimately be seen as a recrudescence of the religiously based controls over matriculation and membership which were previously practised in the Christian medieval and early modern universities of the West. It is worth recalling that penalties on opinion and entry were still in force in England until the Test Acts repealed them in 1870. In Hungary after the 1956 uprising some hundreds of teachers and many more students were expelled from the universities, and in 1957 organizations like KISZ (Communist Youth Association) were set up and eventually exercised monopolistic control over student life; and ideological subjects transmitting Marxism-Leninism became compulsory in such a way as to influence belief as had Christian doctrine in medieval Europe.

Only much later, in the 1980s, did the rise of market liberal doctrines and the drive towards privatization and government at arm's length begin to make serious inroads into systems of a public character (whether dominated by an established state or an established church) culminating in the collapse of the communist command economies of Eastern Europe at the end of that decade. Only in the 1990s did new bargains and balances between private and state organizations begin to emerge.

Many of the consequences of the communist revolutions and the counter-revolution of 1989 are outside our scope here. In the context of matriculation deliberate intrusion by the Communist Party through the state attempted to change the social composition of the student intake and thus the levels of social fluidity in society at large. Thus history affords (at a price) an opportunity to compare the efficacy of different social changes to bring about transformation through education. The attempted socialist transformation in Eastern Europe accordingly becomes our main focus of attention.

Did the socialist transformation work? In fact the use of social classification was abandoned in 1963 and success in examinations substituted. We cannot know how far it was successful in achieving its aims. The period was short, there was a good deal of cheating, and the party apparatchiks were bound to look for ways of awarding opportunity to their own children; and they found them through 'side doors' including the right to intervene in the appeal procedures through the ministry. All in all it may be remarked that the system of information and competition for prestige and the pursuit of modernity puts great pressure on national university systems. News from the West was of paramount significance to both researchers and to students seeking new revolution. The importance of this aspect of university life is that a student revolution was inconceivable in East Germany for more than four decades after it began in Hungary in 1956.

Meanwhile the period after the Second World War saw a growth in enrolment, a diversification of curricula, a crisis in relation to the labour market destination of alumni (from both the education and the training systems and at both the secondary school and the tertiary college level) in the mid-1970s. Then finally there was a phase of reconstruction in the 1980s in which access and selection were increasingly influenced by the manifold difficulties in the political economies of Western as well as the political upheaval of Eastern Europe, including sharp rises in public expenditure and unemployment and the rise or resurgence of economic-liberal doctrines of state management. Put crudely the 1980s were the decade of the market and the expansion of higher education had to proceed under conditions of fiscal constraint which led to much redefinition of the structure and purposes of the university.

Conspicuous among these developments was a pronounced weakening of the traditionally close link between the academic secondary school and the university. The upper secondary school in all countries became in effect and instead a freestanding institution rather than a conveyance of selected minorities from common elementary schooling to elite advanced education. Of course, in the forties, fifties and sixties, selective secondary schools continued to select, though Sweden became internationally famous in Europe as an experimental pioneer in the development of the comprehensive or common school. The crucial 'branching point' was the upper secondary course to prepare for the *baccalauréat* or the *Abitur* or their equivalents in Italy or elsewhere. In Britain it was the sixth-form of the grammar school where pupils prepared for university entrance. This upper secondary stage remains important but its curricula afterwards became more varied in relation to gradually elaborating arrangements in most European countries for vocational training as well as for academic education. By 1990 most secondary pupils left at 18 years, many postponing entry to higher education, others choosing part-time or full-time attendance at some other form of tertiary education, and still others going straight into employment. However the patterns varied between countries either from tradition or from adaptation to new demands or new terms of financial support.

Entry to higher education in Europe and in most developed countries was generally straight from school, sometimes from a particular type of school at which the student had concentrated on academic subjects. Italy had a very specialized structure, particular types of school leading to certain higher education categories. In the United Kingdom, as in Japan and USA, the examination required for higher education entry could be taken at any type of establishment which provided for post-compulsory schooling, including the rapidly growing sixth form colleges. In other countries (and in Northern Ireland and some other parts of the UK), children could be selected for entry to different types of secondary education although there was provision for transfer at later stages: the higher education entry examination was then usually taken in the more academic schools.

Matriculation

Each country had a specific national education qualification which formed the main basic requirement for entry to higher education. The qualification generally covers at least five subjects, some compulsory, and usually including mathematics, the native language and one foreign modern language. England, Wales and Northern Ireland were unusual in limiting the number of subjects more narrowly and thus specializing earlier. At least five passes at GCE (usually taken at age 16) are required for degree level courses, of which two must be of Advanced level (usually taken at 18), although most candidates for entry attempt three A-level subjects and already have at least 6 O-level passes.

There is a passionate controversy over the special position of the A level examination in England, which guards entry to the university as does the *Abitur* and the *baccalauréat* in France, Germany and elsewhere. Behind it lie the status and class battles for possession of educational property which were intensified by the reform and expansion movements of the period with which we are dealing. Special arrangements meanwhile exist for the growing body of mature students and those lacking 'traditional' qualifications.

Matriculation into higher education depends mainly on gaining the appropriate entry qualification, although limits on places may mean that a further selection process takes place either for certain types of course, or for certain institutions which experience strong demand from students. In the United Kingdom entry to all institutions is competitive. In East and West Europe more generally the state has increasingly controlled entry to higher education since Napoleonic times, either through defining examination content and standards or through varied means of student financial support or through special schemes of encouragement for particular social categories of student by positive discrimination or, more usually, by setting up barriers to entry. The conquest of Eastern Europe by the Red Army in 1945 brought with it a determined effort to change the terms of admission to higher education in Poland, Hungary, Albania, Yugoslavia, Czechoslovakia, Romania, Bulgaria and East Germany. Old bourgeois conceptions and domination were to be overthrown and a new era of opportunity for workers and peasants was to dawn. The failure of the original movement within the Soviet Union did not become common knowledge until after Khrushchev's attack on Stalin at the twentieth congress in 1956.

The Hungarian experience was typical. Admission restrictions had to yield before a huge social demand for admission to a relatively small tertiary sector. Temporarily quotas were abandoned and the gates were opened to all, including women. But the number of places was too small to cope with the demand and quotas had to be reintroduced and entrance examinations imposed. There was naturally pressure to change the class composition of the student body given that so many sons and daughters of workers and peasants had previously been denied opportunity to match their talents either for reasons of finance or qualification from secondary schools.

In part the new movement was a continuation of pre-war liberal developments towards popular democracy. As early as 1945 in the Communist countries, two-year evening courses for workers were introduced in the universities. After 1947 evening courses were offered alongside the normal day courses. After 1949 candidates for entry were classified with the intention of giving priority to those of peasant or worker origin. And since the number of such children in the secondary schools was insufficient, special matriculation courses were organized. Debate continues about the effectiveness as well as the justice of this method. But there can be little doubt that large numbers of talented and diligent youth were able to take advantage of the chances thus offered by social revolution.

In the West some countries like Belgium and France used one uniform national examination. Sweden attempted the ranking of students by marks weighted according to the courses taken and work experience (which tacitly modifies age as a selective barrier) The American system of standardized attainment tests is not used in Europe. Positive discrimination in favour of candidates with working-class backgrounds was used in Poland and Czechoslovakia, as well as in Hungary, though examination performance was also part of the entrance procedure. Entrance examinations were been widely used with higher requirements in medicine, science and law. Such procedures obtained in the highly prestigious institutions such as Oxford and Cambridge in England and the *grandes écoles* in France, but also in the East European Communist states where, at the same time, at least a quarter of the places were reserved for working-class students. Even the lottery is not unknown. In the Netherlands the problem of excessive demand was overcome by its use. A lottery operated in which an individual's chances were weighted by marks attained in the secondary school leaving examinations.

Nevertheless the automatic right of entry to the university which is the traditional privilege of those who obtain a *baccalauréat* or the *Abitur*, still gives admission in France and Germany, though not to other forms of higher education. The consequences are seen in high failure or drop-out rates in the first two years of undergraduate study. Even in England and Scotland this phenomenon is appearing since the expansion of the system of higher education to include the former polytechnics in 1992. It is an inevitable consequence of the transformation to mass higher education. In other words it is possible to use the first years of university study as a selective device in place of the traditional upper secondary school. It is therefore not surprising that as late as 1994 there was fear of rioting in Paris and reports of long queues for admission in Bologna. Other countries, like Belgium or Spain, never granted the prerogatives of the *Abitur*. In France, however, in spite of several university reforms, including the *Loi Savary* of 1984, the right of entry of a *bachelier* has never been modified. Of course, selective *grandes écoles* continue to cream off the best 15 per cent of the candidates. And the *numerus clausus* has been increasingly applied in France and Germany so that the right became nominal. It did not guarantee a place in any particular faculty of any particular university.

In summary it appears that the evolution of matriculation and the admissions system has been to move the point of selection upwards from the upper secondary school and its examinations to the admissions offices of the institutions of higher education. The traditional system was essentially controlled by teachers in universities. Control now is much more in the hands of politicians, courts, and budgetary administrators. Diversity is to be found at both the secondary and tertiary levels and the unique role of the *baccalauréat*, the *Abitur* and their equivalents in other European countries as the *rite de passage* to university education, is no more.

Instead there have developed alternative modes of entry to a diverse set of post-compulsory educational and training institutions with the parallel development of vocational equivalents to A level, the *baccalauréat* and the *Abitur*. In France there was a technical *baccalauréat* with 12 options as well as the traditional one with 8 sections and a proposed 30-option practical *baccalauréat* which was expected to be taken in one form or another by 80 per cent of the secondary school leavers by the end of the twentieth century.

In most countries most students first enter full-time higher education aged between 18 and 21. At the end of the 1980s the rate of full-time enrolment in this age group was more than 10 per cent in over half of the OECD countries. However, older students are also admitted everywhere; in Germany a quota of places in *numerus clausus* branches is reserved for them. In the Nordic countries, Austria, West Germany and Switzerland full time enrolment was higher among persons aged 22 to 25 than among those aged 18 to 21 in 1990. Reasons for starting first study in higher education later in life are many. In some countries there is compulsory military service, some students pursue lower level further education full-time or enter employment; others may retake entry examinations and so increase the range of institutions which will accept them.

All in all the articulation of the formal education system to the labour market in Europe is entering a new state of flux. It was not only that the macro-economic management associated with Keynes, Bretton Woods, and the left-wing-planning governments of the 1950s and 1960s was collapsing. Nor was it only that the command economies of Eastern Europe were rapidly eroded at the end of the 1980s. It was also that the sexual division of labour was now being comprehensively renegotiated, that the 'career' to which university admission had been traditionally a key with its life-long employment in a superior trade or profession, was disappearing. Part-time and temporary contract were becoming normal, and not only for casual, unskilled and unschooled work but for professional and technical appointments. Europe, along with the rest of the advanced industrial world, was entering a profoundly different phase of the development of its economy and society.

In future there was to be not admission or rejection but widening opportunity for readmission, for recurrent education and serial partnership or cohabitation in a two-earner family, sometimes living apart, often migrating between insecure jobs. Structured youth unemployment was to accompany much greater investment in university study. Easier capital flows portended much less stable regional division of labour. A new world was emerging in which admission to higher education was destined to take an enlarged but different role in the distribution of life chances.

The percentage of women in higher education has increased in all countries, most markedly in the Netherlands. In the Netherlands and Germany the percentage of women pursuing postgraduate studies in 1982 was not below the percentage of their overall enrolment in 1972. By 1991 half of European women aged 25–64 years had attained some kind of tertiary education.

It may turn out, as we have suggested, that a principle feature of the post-war history of higher education in Europe is the elaboration of alternatives to the University. Ambitious expansion, 'doubling in a decade' as the progressive slogans of the 1950s had it, altered the terms of entry and the definition of what was to be learned in a university all over Europe. The old stereotype of entry through completion of the *baccalauréat* or equivalent leaving certificate from a *lycée* or other upper secondary school into a full-time course of three or, in Continental countries, more years in pure science or pure arts was to be transformed into a large variety of courses, typically vocational or preparatory to professional training, and offered in a wider range of institutions, residential and non-residential. The development of mass higher education is dawning in Europe, increasing participation to significant proportions of the young and, in effect, replacing the older idea of the university by a much more expansive and, as some traditionalists would argue, a diluted conception of tertiary rather than higher education.

The first half of this [chapter] draws heavily on my *Decline of Donnish Dominion* (Oxford 1995) and the second half on my contribution (Chapter 6) to the fourth volume of *A History of the University in Europe*, (Cambridge University Press, forthcoming).

1. H. De Ridder-Symoens (ed.) *A History of the University in Europe*, Vol. 1, *Universities in the Middle Ages*, xix.
2. The latest and highly informative work in this tradition is Philip Brown and Anthony Heskith, *The Mismanagement of Talent: Employability in the Knowledge Economy* (Oxford: Oxford University Press, 2004).
3. A. H. Halsey, (1995), *Decline of Donnish Dominion* (Oxford: Oxford University Press).
4. See J. Ben-David (1962), *Scientific Growth*, ed. Gad Freudental (Berkeley: University of California Press, 1991).
5. B. Truscot (Edgar Allison Peers), *Redbrick University* (London: Penguin, 1943).
6. C. Kerr, *The Uses of the University* (Cambridge, Mass.: Harvard University Press, 1963).
7. Y. Shavit and H. P. Blossfeld (eds.) *Persistent Inequality: Changing Educational Attainment in Thirteen Countries* (Boulder, Colo.: Westview, 1993).
8. R. D. Mare, 'Change and Stability in Educational Stratification', *American Sociological Review* 46 (1982), 72–87.
9. R. Boudon, *Education, Opportunity, and Social Inequality: Changing Prospects in Western Society* (New York: Wiley, 1974).
10. Boudon, ibid.
11. D. Gambetta, *Were they Pushed or Did they Jump?: Individual Decision Mechanisms in Education* (Cambridge: Cambridge University Press, 1987).
12. Cf. N. de Witt, 'Basic Comparative Data on Soviet and American Education', *Comparative Education Review* II (June, 1958).

59 Building an Epistemic Regime

Corryne McSherry

The 'Second Academic Revolution'

[...]

The university is 'in crisis,' and this, too, is nothing new.[1] The contours of the present crisis look like this: The research university is being rapidly repositioned as a site of commodity production in an information economy. With the end of the Cold War and the emergence of a knowledge-based global economy, commentators suggest, a 'new social contract' is being negotiated between the university and the public (Etzkowitz and Leydesdorff 1997*a*: 1). Under the terms of this contract, (1) the transfer of knowledge from the academic to the 'productive sector' is being accomplished through direct rather than indirect means; and (2) that transfer process is becoming a central part of the university's *raison d'être* and the professoriate's self-definition.

In this 'second academic revolution,' contends the sociologist Henry Etzkowitz, the university's traditional interest in the 'advancement of knowledge' is matched by its interest in the 'capitalization of knowledge' (1997*b*: 141).[2] Through consulting arrangements, patenting of 'fortuitous by-products of research,' and, in some places, the formation of 'incubators' for new technology companies, entrepreneurial professors and their universities have become active rather than passive actors in the information economy. Industrial corporations, meanwhile, are sponsoring scientific conferences and setting up in-house 'universities' to train and improve their stock of human capital. This activity, Etzkowitz contends, generates a 'triple helix' of knowledge production, in which the three institutional spheres of liberal capitalism (public, private, and academic) are intertwined rather than distanced.

As Etzkowitz notes, this revolution is facilitated by the academy's own practices. Drawing on Bruno Latour and Steve Woolgar's (1979) work on credit and credibility, Etzkowitz suggests that 'entrepreneurial' universities are an outgrowth of academic scientists' own efforts to translate reputation into financial support for further research. The ever-present pressure to find research funds, exacerbated by perceived and real declines in federal and state spending on research, socializes faculty to 'capitalize knowledge,' or find ways for research to generate income as well as more knowledge (Collins and Tillman 1988). Federal funding of non-defense university research, once adjusted for inflation, leveled off or began to decrease by 1988, with similar trends evident in defense-related projects by the early 1990s. State support of public research universities is also declining (Slaughter and Leslie 1997). Small wonder, then, that many scientists are more willing to pursue industrial support for their research, including funding derived from the licensing of patents, consulting, and sponsored research projects. In 1996, royalties paid to 131 universities on licensed inventions alone reached $336 million (Blumenstyk 1998).

These activities are validated, in turn, by universities' own rhetoric, particularly the increasingly common definition of higher education's traditional public service mission as 'support for economic growth.' The stated premise of this argument is that the academy's survival depends upon its ability to move from a 'reactive' to a 'proactive' approach to society's problems (Leydesdorff and Etzkowitz 1997*a*; Collins and Tillman 1988). The sociologist and university administrator Mary Walshok (1995) has characterized this challenge as a 'crisis of relevance.' Walshok seeks to make the university 'relevant' by promoting social as well as economic initiatives, but for many analysts of the new social contract between university and society, social impact means economic impact. University presidents, for example, point to a series of studies by 'new growth theorists' showing that university research has been responsible for 50 percent of new economic growth since 1945 and use those studies to promote the idea that 'the university means business' (Atkinson 1996*a*, 1996*b*). This justificatory rhetoric, combined with industrial pressures on the federal government, gives sense to research policies that reward institutions for 'transferring' research to the private sector.

Sheila Slaughter and Lawrence Leslie (1997) present a less sanguine view of the triple helix, arguing that new practices of 'academic capitalism' threaten the autonomy that sets professors apart from other information workers. Academic capitalism, they suggest, involves more than 'entrepreneurial activity,' for this phrase implies that a researcher's primary motive is still finding support for 'curiosity-driven' research. In reality, they argue, profit itself has become a significant imperative within the professoriate. In the 1980s, moreover, as federal and state science policy began to emphasize technology transfer and applied research, the ability of the professoriate to define research agendas that responded to 'pure' as opposed to economic imperatives was curtailed. For Slaughter and Leslie, the academy does indeed face a 'crisis,' but the problem is not relevance. Rather, the problem is the decline of academic freedom.

Yet it is not clear just what is new about the 'new social contract' that Slaughter and Leslie, Etzkowitz, Walshok, and others identify. The land grants that helped found many public universities in the late nineteenth century were justified in large part by the idea that universities would produce research for the agricultural sector. Both the University of California and the Massachusetts Institute of Technology, among others, had small but viable patenting programs in the 1920s, encouraged faculty to consult with industry, and relied on private industry for research support (Matkin 1990). Further, if academic researchers were ever truly free to ignore political and economic imperatives, they have not been so for several decades (see Mukerji 1989; Lowen 1996). Scientists' dependence on state and federal funding agencies for support helped clear a space, in fact, for the practices of academic capitalism that Slaughter and Leslie document. Even scientists doing research that still counts as 'basic' serve government interests by helping to ratify political decisions about what constitutes 'quality research' (Mukerji 1989). These historical and contemporary practices suggest, at least, the need for a closer examination of the 'revolutionary' claims made by surveyors of the so-called knowledge frontier (Faulkner and Senker 1995).

What is new, or at least newly visible, is the proliferation of contests for the meaning of intellectual work. Slaughter and Leslie offer a telling description of such a contest. Focusing specifically on the introduction of new management practices in the university, such as the use of standardized evaluation mechanisms across disciplines, they note that 'as decisions about professors' performance of academic work were moved outside the purview of professional expertise, professors became more like all other information workers and less like a community of scholars' (1997: 60). The linkage of professional autonomy to peer review dates to the medieval university, and in this sense Slaughter and Leslie are correct that the deployment of administrative technocratic practices to define high-quality research directly challenges the traditional prerogatives of the professoriate. The result? A blurred boundary between academic and other information workers.

Autonomy, Freedom, and Property

This blurred boundary is nominally defended by the discourse of academic freedom. The starting premise of this defense is that scholars are defined by their ability to disseminate the results of their research. At [the University of Washington], for example, the freedom to publish, or to refuse to do so, may not be contractually rescinded (though it may be informally abandoned) in research agreements. Ironically, perhaps, this starting premise is invoked repeatedly by proponents of technology transfer, who can legitimately claim that the capitalization of university research does not prevent (though it may delay) publication of results. A related argument emphasizes protection of faculty autonomy, defined as the ability to set one's own research and teaching agenda and manage one's own time. Under these criteria, which set faculty apart from knowledge workers in private industry, academics are the true liberal individuals: freely choosing, radically autonomous, hampered only by voluntary obligations.

What seems strange, however, is that academic 'freedom' and 'autonomy' are invoked to defend opposite positions. Thus, for example, critics of university-industry liaisons insist that research contracts with the private sector subordinate free inquiry to the interests of capital. Proponents of such liaisons reject this 'ivory tower syndrome,' arguing that diversity of inquiry should permit free choice of research partners—including industrial partners.[3] The right to manage one's own time and research interests includes the ability to market one's intellectual labor to private industry as a consultant.[4] Following this line of reasoning, new modes of knowledge production would seem to be perfectly consonant with 'traditional academic values.'

Which brings us to the final and strangest development in this 'crisis': the use of intellectual property discourse to define and defend academic freedom. Simply put, professors are deciding that they would rather be knowledge owners than knowledge workers. In overlapping debates over academic intellectual property—including rights in written materials, software, lecture materials, research data, and useful inventions—academic autonomy, equality, and freedom are increasingly treated as commensurate with individual property rights. Lecturers and administrators square off in a battle for control of ownership of courses and 'the classroom,' a struggle that turns on the real difficulty of delineating 'the class' and its legal author. Scientists are asked by their administrators to retain copyrights in their articles rather than assigning them to the journals in which they are published (in order to ensure educational access to those works), yet are pitted against those same administrators in disputes over licensing arrangements. Further down on the food chain, graduate students scheme to avoid their contractual obligation to share intellectual property rights with the university—keeping in mind perhaps that a student was once sent to a prison camp for 'stealing' intellectual property from his university.[5] Participants on all sides of these debates insist that they are struggling to preserve academic freedom.

In this context, the only question really worth asking, indeed the question most often asked by 'revolutionaries' and critics alike, seems to be, Who will own the properties in question and on what terms? The trouble is, the more faculty look like property owners, the more their work looks like a potential commodity and their institution looks like the knowledge factory Clark Kerr once was accused of celebrating.[6] As an engineering professor declared at a [University of Washington] retreat on university–industry relations, 'It really does change the nature of the place when you can look around and see someone, not very much older than you *or better than you*, driving around in expensive cars' (italics mine). The nested claims that (1) professors do not labor for money (or expensive cars) but for recognition; (2) academic knowledge is not proprietary; and (3) academia rewards brilliance rather than luck and/ or marketing acumen remain crucial pillars of the professoriate and the academy itself, for they ground the university's claim to the space of disinterested reason. Former Stanford president Donald Kennedy has argued that the spectacle of a wealthy professor 'just gets under people's skin' (1997: 261). I would go further and suggest that the 'spectacle' directly challenges the university's theoretico-political hierarchy based on the superiority of impractical knowledge—a hierarchy the university simultaneously defends through its repeated characterization of intellectual properties as accidental 'by-products' of research. As we shall see, the stakes of the university's struggle to retain its status are very high, for the institution and for the information economy.

[...]

Public and Private Domains

The concept of the public domain was imported from tangible property law, and, in the seventeenth and eighteenth centuries as now, it was most often construed negatively, as that space of expression which could not be owned. Copyright law was organized around a three-tiered separation of public and private discourse: (1) between protectible and unprotectible works; (2) between 'idea' and 'expressive' elements of protected works; and, eventually, (3) between public and private uses of the work (Rose 1993). Copyright was constructed as an intermediary between public and private, a channel that both secured private rights and ensured the continued availability of literature to the public.[7] The battle over copyright could then turn on the terms of this mediation—such as the length of time an expression was permitted to remain private (subject to copyright)—while the incommensurability of these two poles went unquestioned. In patent law, practical ideas were susceptible to ownership, but ideas coded as 'philosophical' or as 'laws of nature' still eluded patentability. The latter form of knowledge, plus ideas on which patents had expired, constituted a public commons from which the private domain of patented mechanical inventions could be derived.

The conceptual organization of creative work around the public/private split lay at the heart of what Mark Rose calls the shift from a 'regime of regulation' to a 'regime of property' (1993: 15). As we have seen, under the regime of regulation the state was directly involved in policing, or regulating, the circulation of ideas and expression. This regulation meant, among other things, that the creation and expression of knowledge were seen as explicitly political and potentially dangerous activities. Property claims could still be construed as contingent privileges rather than natural rights. As the law became concerned with the preservation of an individual's property rather than with the state, however, the basic premises of property claims were no longer seen as sites of political contestation. As Paul Goldstein notes, copyright was 'about enabling an individual to craft [works] out of thin air and intense devouring labor' (1992: 80). Patents, in turn, rewarded the crafting of mechanical things out of the raw material of nature. Both doctrines firmly located creators and their works in the private sphere, where cultural production continually referred back to owners and disputes over the circulation of meaning could continually be recoded as struggles for property rights.

Karl Marx (1843/1972) developed the ramifications of the public/private opposition for liberal theories of property and subjectivity, and his observations hold for the subcategory of creative owner-subjects as well. In *On the Jewish Question*, Marx characterizes the liberal subject as a natural, authentic, sensuous, and 'real' but also nonpolitical individual. In contrast to the autonomous, disembodied, rational persons who assert political rights in the public sphere, the private individual's rights are seen as natural rights, with which the state should only minimally interfere. Secluded in a private sphere, individuals may look solely to their own self-interest. In this context, Marx argues, 'the only bond between men, is natural necessity, need and private interest, the preservation of their property and their egoistic persons' (p. 43). Indeed, the pursuit of self-interest is seen as the natural activity of man. Socioeconomic relations are thereby naturalized and individuals figured as sources of power rather than effects (Brown 1995).

Having relegated various characteristics to the nonpolitical realm (the private), the state could then treat all its subjects as equal in the political realm (the public). That 'nonpolitical' distinctions continue to work in the 'private' sphere to produce most subjects as unequal is not, in this definition, an acceptable political question. Thus, as Wendy Brown puts it, 'the subject [was] *ideally emancipated* through its anointing as an abstract person, ... and is *practically resubordinated* through this idealist disavowal of the material constituents of personhood, which constrain and contain our freedom' (1995: 106).

This observation is as relevant to IP [intellectual property] law as it is to other arenas of political struggle, and it brings into sharp relief one source of IP law's instability. Consider, for example, the political consequences of the line between idea and expression. The legal scholar James Boyle suggests that the idea/expression split requires and helps conceal the tension between 'private' authors and 'the public as audience': 'Information is [both] the lifeblood of the noble disinterested citizens of the public world and a commodity in the private sphere to which we must attach property rights if we wish our self-interested producers to continue to produce. By disaggregating the book into 'idea' and 'expression,' we can give the idea ... to the public world and the expression to the writer, thus apparently mediating the contradiction between public good and private need' (1996: 57–8). In the late twentieth century, 'free expression' is often treated as expression that is protected from state regulation, while private regulation of information is not only a lesser concern but considered one of the necessary preconditions for creativity (Goldstein 1992; Gordon 1993). Because 'free speech' in the United States is usually understood to require protection from the power of the state, the law ignores how property rights discourse may be deployed to limit the information commons (see Boyle 1996). A copyright suit may be brought for the sole purpose of obtaining a preliminary injunction against a publication. A patent on a method of golf putting can be used to prevent golf instructors from teaching the latest innovations in the sport.[8] A trademark action can be brought to prevent use of the word 'olympics' to refer to a national sports competition involving gays and lesbians.[9] And so on.

Yet the force of the idea/expression—or, in the case of patents, the nature/culture—dichotomy depends on the construction of a public domain. And if the only bond between persons is a mutual interest in the defense of property, who is left to preserve the commons? It is no wonder that this arena has been so frequently treated as a kind of conceptual placeholder, a barely discernible realm of unprotectable, and therefore unprotected, expression (Gaines 1995; Litman 1990).

If we look more carefully at the history of patents, however, it appears that the task of preserving the commons was *not* left unassigned. The public domain was neither entirely empty nor entirely uncultivated in the seventeenth and eighteenth centuries. In fact, as the laws of nature shifted from God's hands to those of the scientist, nurturing the public domain became his special obligation as well. Scientists were the self-proclaimed 'ingenious heads' from which inventions were most likely to spring, at least according to the natural philosophers Robert Boyle and Thomas Sprat, because they were skilled in the use of reason (MacLeod 1988). For followers of Francis Bacon, those ingenious heads were also the least likely to claim property in invention. The force of science relied on its claim to facts about nature, and the status of those facts as 'true' depended upon their location outside of the realm of artifact, or manufactures—the realm of human invention. In other words, as readers of the Book of Nature, scientists had no business claiming its expression as their personal property (Shapin 1996). This attitude was also inherited, in part, from Plato and Aristotle, who argued that any scientific claim had to be publicly justified and openly shared (McMullin, 1985).[10]

Robert Hooke, among others, did advocate rewards for invention, but in the form of pensions, awards, or monuments 'proportionable to the worth of the invention and the merits of the person' (quoted in MacLeod 1988: 191). Honor and a lump sum reward, he suggested, were compensation enough for ingenious persons.[11] In the seventeenth and eighteenth centuries members of scientific societies tried to develop alternatives to patents. Scotland's Society of Arts, for example, offered cash prizes in exchange for submitting new inventions to the Society, thereby making them, in effect, public property. Legal scholars also saw a bright line between patent holders and scientists. William Blackstone was explicit on this point in 1760, declaring in *Tonson* v. *Collins:* 'Mechanical inventions tend to the improvement of the arts and manufactures, which employ the bulk of the people ... but as to science, the case is different. That can and should be the employment of a few' (quoted in Rose 1993: 119). The creator of patentable (that is, commercially useful) inventions, then, was very clearly not a scientist.

Thus, just as patent-holders were establishing a special relationship to commodified knowledge, scientific societies and some individual scientists were busily laying claim to 'public knowledge.' This claim was not universally endorsed: many scientists did seek to gain financially from their inventions and worried about 'practical' problems (Etzkowitz 1997). Nevertheless, the construction of the laws of nature, facts, and rational knowledge was the principal activity of science, and that activity was defined as not only 'public' but specifically in tension with the interested realm of private property. Ironically enough, then, disinterested science both provided the conceptual justification for patent rights by underscoring the domination of man over nature and helped legitimate the private ownership of knowledge by building a contrasting space of communal ownership. Meanwhile, intellectual property law helped affirm the credibility of science—the refusal to patent supported scientists' claim that their creative work was a matter of fact rather than artifact.

Recognizing this ironic operation, we can begin to trace the outlines of an epistemic regime comprising two mutually constitutive economies of creation. To fill in those outlines, however, we need to investigate the 'public' economy of knowledge.

[...]

Knowledge Owners and Knowledge Workers

I began this chapter by telling a story of 'crisis' in intellectual property law and the academy. I want to revisit this story and reassess its possible meanings and stakes. Thorstein Veblen insisted in 1918 that the higher learning 'is the only end in life that indubitably justifies itself' (1918/1965: 10–11). In fact, the higher learning helps justify a great deal more than itself. Truths generated by the university are, by definition, universal truths, assigned to the public domain. Thus the university's *raison d'être* situates it, in principle, as a primary arbiter of the public domain that balances a 'real world' defined by utility and self-interest.

At a minimum, the academy, and especially academic science, certifies knowledge and knowledge workers (Larson 1977). Modern universities are crucial 'knowledge resources' precisely because of their 'reputations for neutrality' (Walshok 1995: 191). Clinical trials of new drugs, for example, are partially validated by the scientific integrity of the laboratories conducting the trials. Investment decisions are based in large part upon faith in the results of those trials. Universities acknowledge that faith by carefully policing the use of their names for advertising purposes. Even industrial partners, though they grumble mightily about the 'bureaucratic red tape' that limits their access to university research and researchers, recognize their interest in maintaining the fiction of university neutrality. As a senior executive of a major corporation noted at a [University of Washington] conference on university-industry relations, 'the university shouldn't be afraid to say no.' Why not? Because if it says yes too often the university loses the basis of its credibility, and the products it certifies lose value. Indeed, the stakes are higher still. The university works to guarantee the intellectual property system as well by assuming and defending a public domain of knowledge to balance the private realm of knowledge commodities (Young 1992; Biagioli 1998).

In sum, the university's reason for being is inextricably tied to that of the intellectual property system. The relationship between IP law and academia is not a simple one, and IP law, by itself, no more defines the 'crisis' in the university than academia, by itself, defines the public domain. But the emergence of IP discourse in the university does challenge the constitutive boundaries of a shared epistemic regime. As with the fundamental dualisms upon which academic and legal discourses rest (public/private, idea/expression, fact/artifacts, nature/culture, science/utility), the rearticulation of one demands the reconstitution of the other. Hence the enormous political, social, and economic stakes of maintaining and policing the boundary between these discursive formations.

Parallel border skirmishes are happening all over the world, from Uruguay to Britain to China (Webster and Packer 1997; Turpin and Garrett-Jones 1997; Sutz 1997). The features of these battles vary considerably, but they reflect a common struggle by universities, industrialists, governments, and judiciaries to intermediate but maintain the boundaries between their respective domains. These struggles are sometimes international in scope. For example, the Digital Millennium Copyright Act—which required, among other provisions, that universities more actively police use of intellectual property by students, faculty, and staff—was ostensibly passed to bring the United States into line with international rules concerning intellectual property. The Copyright Term Extension Act that lengthened the duration of copyright by twenty years was voted in and signed on the same rationale. In addition, the needs of transnational corporations are pushing the development of a for-profit learning industry in which traditional US colleges and universities are active players (Schiller 1999). This industry relies heavily on proprietary distance-learning programs to deliver instruction around the world, and the production of these programs necessarily involves the commodification of professorial skills and training.

Thus the IP disputes arising in the context of 'the second academic revolution,' though they often seem local, in fact respond directly and indirectly to the emergence of a global information market and mode of development. At the same time, in the United States at least, debates over specific issues such as technology transfer are framed by distinctly nationalist rhetoric. Legislation facilitating the patenting of federally funded research was promoted as a strategy for ensuring that US companies and consumers benefited from US-taxpayer-funded inventions. US universities have also been subject to periodic public criticism for assigning to foreign-based companies patent rights in research partially funded by taxpayers (Hilts 1993*a, b*; Rosenblatt 1993). In short, the production of academic IP involves the subversion and reconstruction of multiple political borders.

One commonly noted effect of these subversions is the diminution of cultural resources for creative works, including new commodifiable products (Lange 1981; Gaines 1991; Boyle 1996). Critics of this effect often argue for re-establishing a balance by sharply limiting the reach of intellectual property claims and/or investing in public creative resources. While I am sympathetic with these arguments, the proposed strategy ultimately reinstalls a public/private binary, thereby restabilizing an epistemic regime in which we might be strategically intervening. To take a concrete example, the logical extension of a limit-based argument is that conflict-of-interest offices should more actively police university-industry relationships, ensuring that the public/private divide is maintained rather than taking advantage of the blurring of that divide to rethink its underlying premises.

Equally conservative but more tactically interesting are efforts of university inhabitants to claim property rights. These efforts, too, leave virtually unexamined the central categories upon which the intellectual property system relies. Yet these property claims are also a powerful destabilizing maneuver, for they call attention to the multiple investments in locating intellectual labor in the public rather than private domain. Not surprisingly, these claims make jurists uncomfortable. Note, for example, a 1987 comment by the Seventh Circuit in a legal dispute between three academics regarding the ranking of names on a scientific publication: 'Many disputes may be compromised by converting the stakes to a common denominator such as money and splitting the difference. Few commercial disputes end up in court, because the disputants may readily compromise and move on. Other disputes are harder to resolve because they seem to involve principles for which no compromise is readily apparent. The result may be a private war. A dispute that would be resolved quickly in the commercial world may fester.'[12] The academy, the court suggests, is the site of 'principles,' and it would do well to handle its disputes itself. The fact that the academy is unable (or unwilling) to do so suggests that a battle over the standards by which particular meanings will be accepted as official definitions is under way. At stake in this contest are the truth claims of law and the academy and, by extension, the epistemic regime those claims assume and produce.

[. . .]

NOTES

1. In the past five decades alone, the American research university has gone through at least three distinct 'crises'. In the 1950s the university was thrown into 'crises' by McCarthyite threats to academic freedom and specifically efforts by many administrators to require faculty to sign loyalty oaths. In the 1960s the 'crisis' was ostensibly provoked by student protests against pedagogical and disciplinary practices, university involvement in military research, and the Vietnam war. These protests fueled intense antagonism between

university administrators and faculty and government entities as well. In the 1980s the 'crisis of the university' was pictured as a moral problem with universities attacked from within and without as bastions of 'cultural relativism' rather than reason.

2. The first academic revolution, with I will discuss later, involved the rationalization of the academy and the concomitant prioritization of research over teaching as the university's primary mission (Hofstadter and Metzge, 1955, Jencks and Reisman, 1968)

3. This argument was cited, for example by Arizona State vice-provost Jonathan Fink in defense of a faculty member, Robert Balling, who received funding from the fossil-fuel industries for several years but did not acknowledge that support in his publications on climate change. Fink admitted that the support looked 'a little funny' but insisted any university interference in that relationship would constitute a violation of Balling's academic freedom (Blumenstyk, 1998*a*).

4. Which raises another problem: How is time to be defined? At one major research university, policy requires that professors devote four-fifths of their working week to the university—the one-day-a-week rule. It is not clear, however, whether the 'working week' lasts five or seven days.

5. In a 1992 University of South Florida case, a student was sent to a work camp for patenting in his own name research conducted under industrial contract. Petr Taborsky, an undergraduate in biology and chemistry, worked as a lab assistant for Professor Robert P. Carnahan on a research contract for a utility holding company, Floriada Progress, Inc. Taborsky allegedly 'disappeared' with several research notebooks and used information in them to file and win two patents on a sewage cleanser. But the university had long since ceded IP rights in any research arising from the contract to the utility company. Taborsky himself did not sign an agreement to this effect until months after the discovery, and he insists the invention was the product of independent research unrelated to the contract itself. Thus far he has retained the patent rights, but USF was able to have him sentenced to three and a half years of work camp for his 'theft' of the notebooks.

6. Kerr (1963/1995) insists that the term was actually coined by the student activist Mario Savio.

7. I am thinking here of Latour's (1993) distinction between mediation and intermediation. The discourse of modernity, Latour suggests, is organized around dichotomies and the operation of intermediaries between the poles of these dichotomies. Mediation implies compromise and thus slippage from the pure forms of these poles, while intermediation implies instead a negotiation between these poles—but they, in their pure form, are left intact.

8. US Patent no. 6, 004,230.

9. *San Francisco Arts and Athletics, Inc., v. United States Olympic Committee* 107 S. Ct. 2971 (1987).

10. The public domain was not unbounded. Proprietary practices common in the Renaissance, for example, were replicated in the seventeenth century. Galileo Galilei used codes and anagrams to keep his discoveries secret until publication and to establish priority for them. In the seventeenth century the Royal Society secretary Henry Oldenburg persuaded scientists to write up their discoveries and deposit them in a sealed box at the Royal Society until they could be published. Thus the publicness of scientific findings was temporally bounded. It was determined by the community as well: the members of Francis Bacon's mythical House of Salomon, which provided the model for modern scientific societies, were required to share discoveries among themselves but to keep secret the ones members chose not to publish. In other words, scientists were obligated to be open with one another but were not yet under a special obligation to the general public.

11. Indeed, many inventors received little more than that prior to the eighteenth century, for patent law was highly volatile, and the strength of the patent depended primarily on the financial resources available to defend it. MacLeod has suggested that in many cases patents were pursued as marks of recognition: as the text confirmed the author, in other words, so patents confirmed inventors.
12. *Weinstein v. University of Illinois*, 811 F. 2d 1091, 1092 (1987).

Empowering Participants or Corroding Learning? Towards a Research Agenda on the Impact of Student Consumerism in Higher Education

Rajani Naidoo and Ian Jamieson

[. . .]

Introduction

The implementation of funding and governance regimes based on a model of consumption has emerged as a major theme in the New Labour Government's programme of 'modernization' of the public services in the UK. Understood as an attempt to transform relations between various stakeholders and prise open the public sector to market forces (Rouse and Smith 1999), consumerist mechanisms have been applied relatively recently to one of the most important and intimate functions of higher education: the development and 'delivery' of academic programmes. The Government's rationale for the introduction of a consumerist framework in higher education has been linked to a variety of factors, notably the introduction of tuition fees and the need to maintain and enhance 'quality' in a system that has shifted from an elite to a mass higher education system (DfEE 1998*a*; Blackstone 1999; DfES, 2003). New Labour has also linked the introduction of consumerism to the high skills policy discourse through which economic success in the context of the knowledge economy is perceived to rely on the production of higher, value-added products and services, which are in turn dependent on scientific and technological knowledge, and on continual innovation. New Labour has argued that in this context, the responsibility of higher education is to contribute to Britain's competitive edge in the global marketplace by producing, transferring and disseminating economically productive knowledge. In relation to teaching and learning, universities are expected to increase the total proportion of graduates and equip such graduates with specialized and generic high

Rajani Naidoo and Ian Jamieson, 'Empowering participants or corroding learning? Towards a research agenda on the impact of student consumerism in higher education', *Journal of Educational Policy*, 20, 3, 276–81 premium skills including the capacity to innovate and the ability to learn how to learn (DfEE 1998*b*).

Academics have been portrayed as resisting these pressures and protecting their own professional interests against both the national economic interest and the interests of other stakeholders. Consumerist mechanisms in learning and teaching are therefore expected to apply pressure on academics to become more responsive to external demands by reducing their power to define the curriculum, determine acceptable standards of student achievement and decide on appropriate pedagogic strategies. Various consumerist levers to enhance student choice and control over the education process have been introduced or strengthened in England over the last ten years. Examples of such levers include the modularization of the curriculum and the assignment of uniform levels and credits to courses to facilitate choice (Middleton 2000); the requirement that universities publish detailed information on academic programmes so that students can be assured of what they are to receive at the outset of their studies, and the publication of performance indicators evaluating institutional functioning. In addition, consumer rights have been strengthened by the elaboration and institutionalization of complaints and redress mechanisms (See QAA Code of Practice, QAA 2000) and there is currently a national pilot of a student satisfaction survey, and proposals for the compulsory publication of information relating to the quality of academic programmes such as external examiner reports—all of which will be placed in the public domain. The assumption is that students will utilize such mechanisms to demand high quality provision and will apply pressures on universities to make courses more relevant to the skills they require for the workplace. The related assumption is that consumerist forces will have a positive impact on the professional practices of academic staff since the increased competition within and between universities will force providers to respond to student pressure or lose out on 'customers'.

It is apparent that contemporary government policy is seeking to change, fundamentally, the terms on which teaching and learning take place in higher education. Indeed, if these policies are taken to their logical conclusion the impact could be so profound that it could change popular understanding of the aims and nature of education. In relation to the introduction of consumerism, these changes could have an effect on some of the key constituent elements of higher education including: the professional identities of academics; the curriculum and teaching; the nature and outcomes of student learning; inequality and labour market skills. While there is a small amount of research on how students act as consumers in relation to choosing universities and programmes (Bredo et al. 1993; Connor et al. 1999; Hesketh and Knight 1999) little research has been conducted on the effects of consumerism on learning and teaching in the UK. This absence in part reflects two tendencies in social science: The first tendency is for in-depth studies of student learning to be conducted in isolation from the macro context, and the second is to focus on the structural conditions and social effects of higher education while relegating academic practices to the proverbial black box. In this respect the research programme outlined below seeks to link more explicitly than has previously been the case, the structural and the institutional to learning outcomes. We examine the possible impact of consumerism on the teaching–learning nexus by analyzing possible interactions between certain key changes. First, in academic professional identity, teaching and the curriculum; secondly, on student identities and their impact upon teaching and assessment and their consequent learning outcomes. By engaging in this task the aim is to develop hypotheses in order to articulate a research agenda capable of evaluating these fundamental changes. To this end the [chapter] interrogates the assumptions underlying consumerism by drawing on the work of Bourdieu (1986, 1988, 1996) to establish a theoretical model of the impact of consumerism on higher education and draws upon some empirical studies, conducted in a variety of national settings, to confirm the plausibility of the model. This strategy then enables us to hypothesize the potential consequences of the consumerist turn in higher education.

In addition, a further purpose of this [chapter] is to raise some important questions about the consequences for the labour market of consumerism in higher education. Here the assumption made by the UK Government is that improved learning in a mass higher education system will provide the skilled workers required for a knowledge-based economy. This is because learning at this level will involve high order skills relating to autonomous learning in the workplace as well as the ability to exercise initiative and judgement in decision-making. However, as Lloyd and Payne (2003) indicate, more sceptical analyses which have focused on the uneven nature of capitalist development and the availability of both high and low skills routes to competitive success have cast doubt on the view that the knowledge economy automatically gives rise to the demand for a high level of skills amongst significant proportions of the workforce. In the view of Brown and Lauder (2003), such learning is only required for an elite in the current knowledge economy, since many 'knowledge' jobs are now being routinized. These views are consistent with the analysis of consumerism, which we develop below, and its consequences for learning.

Towards a Theoretical Understanding of Consumerism

We begin by outlining a framework which situates consumerism within the context of the introduction of neo-liberal market and new managerialist principles to higher education. In the next section, we draw on Bourdieu's theoretical concepts to develop an understanding of how consumerism is likely to impact on learning and teaching. Consumerism may be seen to be part of a broader policy shift away from the Keyne-sian welfare state settlement towards a new settlement based on neo-liberalism which introduced mechanisms of the market and new managerialism into higher education. Researchers such as Williams (1997), Dill (1997), Deem (2001) and Naidoo (2003) have indicated how the development of quasi-markets linked to managerialist frameworks in higher education have altered relations within and between institutions as well as the nature of rewards and sanctions in academic life. In particular, consumerism operates within a regulatory policy framework which is based on the notion that competition between higher education institutions for limited resources will produce a more effective, efficient and equitable higher education system. The underlying assumption is that higher education services that are below standard will be rejected, thus forcing higher education providers to improve or lose out on 'customers' and revenue. The student–consumer thus emerges as the focus of competition and a modernizing force that will bring about increased efficiency, diversity and flexibility to the higher education sector. Consumerism can also be seen to be related to 'new managerialism' through the deployment of performance indicators and league tables which strengthen the hand of consumers by providing information to aid choice. As the current White Paper (DfES 2003) makes clear, these mechanisms can also provide students with the means to evaluate teaching and learning. The outcomes of such measures when made public are highly influential since they result in both symbolic and material rewards and sanctions.

Commodifying Teaching and Learning

In order to understand the effects of consumerism on learning and teaching in higher education, it is useful to turn to the work of Pierre Bourdieu. Bourdieu (1988) has conceptualized society as consisting of numerous 'fields' which are structured social spaces which function in a relatively autonomous manner in relation to other fields. The activities in each field revolve around the acquisition and development of different species of capital, which may be defined as particular resources that are invested with value (Bourdieu 1986). Bourdieu has characterized universities as existing in 'the field of higher education' which has its own specialized structure, value system and modes of operation and which functions relatively autonomously from other fields such as the field of politics and the field of economics. The 'capital' invested with value in the field of higher education is termed 'academic capital' and consists in the first instance of intellectual or cultural, rather than economic or political assets. The logic underlying practice in the field of higher education is therefore shaped by deeply ingrained rules, cultures, values and professional protocols that revolve around the struggle for, and acquisition of, academic capital (Bourdieu 1988, 1996; Naidoo, forthcoming).

Consistent with analyses such as Slaughter and Leslie (1997), our argument is that consumerist and other market related pressures which have led to the unmediated influence of economic forces on higher education are likely to lead to the erosion of academic capital and the valorization of economic capital. We believe that this shift may in turn lead to the commodification of higher education, which can be understood as the transformation of educational processes into a form that has an economic worth of its own and has an 'exchange', rather than an intrinsic 'use-value'. Clearly, in the past educational credentials have had an exchange-value but, arguably, this has been a by-product of the values, processes and ethos of universities. What has now changed, as Bernstein (1990) has remarked, is that 'knowledge, after nearly a thousand years, is divorced from inwardness and is literally dehumanised' (p. 155). The 'devalorization' of academic capital is likely to shift the underlying logic shaping academic practices. Under these conditions, the pedagogic relationship is likely to be transformed into one that is dependent on the market transaction of the commodity. Education is likely to be reconceptualized as a commercial transaction, the lecturer as the 'commodity producer' and the student as the 'consumer'. In this way, previously integrated relationships between academics and students are likely to become disaggregated with each party invested with distinct, if not opposing, interests. In other words, rather than merely stipulating new procedures to enhance the functioning of higher education, consumerist mechanisms may be seen as a device to reform academic values and pedagogic relationships to comply with market frameworks.

The Uneven Impact of Consumerism

We hypothesize, however, that consumerist levers will have an unequal impact across the higher education sector. Within the field, universities will be placed in a hierarchy structured by the distribution of academic capital and their associated reputational capital (Brown and Scase 1994), which will determine their degrees of autonomy from political and economic fields. While all universities will be influenced by consumerist mechanisms, their position in the 'field of university education' will determine to what degree the former penetrate and restructure core university practices. Universities that are in the upper levels of the hierarchy with high levels of academic, reputational and financial capital are likely to draw on superior resources to engage in practices intent on conserving the academic principles structuring the field of education, thereby maintaining their dominant position. Institutions in a more vulnerable position in the field are more likely to experience the forces of consumerism in pristine form (see also Bernstein 1996). There are also likely to be differences in relation to academic subjects. Subjects that have strong classification and framing (Bernstein 1996) will tend to be more insulated against consumerist forces relative to subjects with weaker classification and framing. In addition, in elite universities and departments students are least likely to push for changes because they understand that a combination of the university and the subject has a very high exchange value in the external job market. By contrast, students studying loosely framed and classified subjects in less elite universities are more likely to exert pressure on faculty for change, and faculty are more likely to be receptive. What this means is that the consequences of consumerism are likely to be felt more strongly at the more vulnerable institutions which admit students from disadvantaged backgrounds. This is a crucial point not only in relation to inequality, but also as regards a higher education system that contributes to a contemporary labour market dominated by the rhetoric of a knowledge economy and one to which we shall return to in the final sections of the [chapter].

In the next section [. . .] we discuss the impact of consumerism on the learning/teaching nexus. At this point, we should enter a caveat. It is important, but not always possible, to distinguish the impact of consumerism from other contemporary changes such as the increase in numbers of students or the impact of quality assurance mechanisms. Part of the research agenda for which we seek to lay the basis in this [chapter] would be to see if we can separate out the influence of various forces leading to changes in learning and teaching. In addition, preliminary analysis that we have carried out indicates that there are some indications that measures implemented through consumerist pressures have improved basic and measurable conditions for good teaching and learning, such as the quality of the physical environment and greater transparency in academic procedures, such as the stipulation of deadlines for the return of academic work. However, our argument is that such developments are necessary but not sufficient for high quality learning which is based on intrinsic and hard to measure factors such as commitment, professional responsibility, empathy and knowledge and enthusiasm for the subject. In the next section, we will highlight various areas of concern in relation to changes in pedagogic relationships and academic identities, the erosion of trust and risk in teaching and the changing structure of knowledge.

The Distortion of Pedagogic Relations

Research on teaching and learning (see Fabos and Young 1999; Hall 2001) has illustrated the pivotal role of the quality of the pedagogic relationship on effective learning. One of the most important consequences of the grafting of a framework derived from the commercial sector onto an institutional sector driven by a different set of values and rewards is that the pedagogic relationship between teacher and learner may be compromised. While there has been little in-depth analysis of consumerism on student learning, the limited findings arising from various national contexts has indicated that the reconceptualization of the complex relationship between students and teachers to that of 'service provider' and 'customer' is likely to be corrosive of both sides of the relationship.

In relation to students, the North American literature, in particular, has indicated that when students are encouraged to view themselves as consumers, they are more likely to view the act of learning as a commercial transaction. Since customers are generally external to an organization, students who internalize a consumer identity in effect place themselves outside the intellectual community and perceive themselves as passive consumers of education. King (1993) and Sacks (1996) point to a growing culture of 'entitlement' through which students perceive educational success as a right. Consistent with this mentality is a loss of responsibility for their learning and a resistance to engaging in education as a process rather than a purchasable product that is simply appropriated. In addition, more instrumental attitudes are exhibited through increasing demands for short pre-packaged courses and little real interest in what is actually being taught and learnt (Shumar 1997). These new identities and rationalities assumed by students have the potential to transform learning into a process of picking up, digesting and reproducing what students perceive of as an unconnected series of short, neatly packaged bytes of information. Under these conditions, the student disposition generated may have negative ramifications for the development of higher order skills and more importantly, the dispositions and attitudes required for autonomous, lifelong learning.

The Impact of Consumerism on Concepts of Academic Professionalism

A further issue that needs to be addressed is that of the nature and degree to which consumerism has an impact on academics' notions of professionalism, especially in terms of their pedagogic relations with students. Here we are not seeking to contrast the possible impact of consumerism with a previous golden age for academics. For example, Bourdieu (1988, 1996) has argued that while higher education can be conceptualized as existing in an institutional field which is relatively autonomous from political and economic forces and as such has its own structures and laws of functioning, academic practices can nevertheless be placed in a 'general science of the economy of practices' (Bourdieu 1977: 183). This includes an analysis of all forms of reward and competition including those purporting to be 'disinterested' and hence non-economic as practices, which are nevertheless aimed at placing some institutions and individuals in a position of advantage over others. He illustrates how intellectual conflict and development in the academic world can be viewed as struggles to improve or defend one's position in the academic hierarchy.

However, Bourdieu emphasizes that this does not mean reducing such activity within the field of higher education to the logic of economism. In many Western countries and in most disciplines, financial considerations have been traditionally one step removed from the exigencies of the market. The stakes expressly fought for and gained in these struggles are therefore in the first instance academic stakes such as recognition, status and publication rather than struggles expressly for economic gain.

However, consumerism may reduce traditional academic struggles to one solely over income for institutions and individuals. Arguably, the struggles for prestige outlined by Bourdieu could be seen as consistent with elite university education. This is because many of the virtues associated with academic practice including originality, intrinsic interest and theoretical and empirical rigour are directly related to high standards of research and publication. Similarly, as regards potential research students, pedagogic practice would have had to impart these virtues. But consumerism was designed to change academic priorities to create high quality teaching for all, not just the elite of research students, by reducing the rewards and sanctions of the struggle within the higher education field from one based on status and prestige to those of the cash nexus. In other words, in an era of mass higher education the status accorded to research and publication has to be placed on a par with teaching. However, it is an open question as to whether consumerist levers can extend the virtues associated with high status academic work to all students precisely when the terms of academic competition for prestige have been changed. The point being that pedagogic activities based on the academic virtues described above may be displaced by a managerial and market ethic which stresses income generation and reconceptualizes students primarily as potential income generation units and as customers to be satisfied.

The potential undercutting of professional knowledge and virtues by consumer demand and satisfaction may, perversely, also have the effect of undermining, rather than enhancing, pedagogical relationships. The micro-auditing of professional activities in order to comply with the extensive monitoring procedures required by a consumerist framework may damage the very activity which it intends to enhance (also see Lyotard 1984.) One of the ways in which this could happen is through organizational resources shifting from what Power (1999) has termed 'first order' to 'second order' functions. In the context of higher education, there are likely to be tensions in the extent to which valuable resources such as time and energy are invested in second order functions, such as documenting and accounting for professional activity, rather than in first order functions such as developing innovative academic programmes and working directly with students. The threat of litigation may also elicit security-seeking tactics (Troman 2000), which could lead to negative pedagogical consequences. There are some indications that the pressures of greater student numbers as well as the fear of student complaints and litigation has led to a shift from individually tailored feedback relying on professional judgement to minimal and standardized feedback that meets official criteria and protects academics against student complaints. In addition, performance indicators and league tables, which have become part of the higher education landscape to give students information and choice, may also invoke a particular pathology since they function as powerful market currencies. First, rather than investing in achieving missions, universities invest valuable resources in attempting to move up rankings as the development of an industry around the Quality Assurance Agency activities such as institutional and subject review indicates. But league tables can also have more direct effects. These rankings may become so crucial that universities are put under pressure to 'manage' data, or even in extreme cases to falsify it. Whilst there is little direct evidence of this happening in higher education to date, there is evidence of this happening in comparable public sector organizations like schools and hospitals which are under a very similar regime. Universities may, for example, come under pressure to award more first class passes and to lower the failure rate. What these concerns point to is a contractual model of human relations governed by market incentives and sanctions, itself dependent on a low trust view of human nature. The danger is that such extrinsic rewards and sanctions based on a one-dimensional view of human nature (see Ball 2003) may erode intrinsic, 'hard to measure' emotional attributes such as commitment to the pedagogic process, enthusiasm for the subject and flexibility in dealing with different needs of students, all of which we would argue are essential for high quality learning. Indeed, many commentators have argued that the commodification of relations between individuals removes some of the key underpinnings to society (Hirschman 1989; Wolf 1989; Brown and Lauder 2001). The question is whether an analogous point can be made with respect to higher education. We believe it can.

The Erosion of Trust and Risk-Taking

In order to understand what is at stake here we need to say something about the nature of learning and teaching in higher education and also about the nature and transmission of knowledge. If we take academic research as a paradigm of best practice for learning, then one of the key lessons from post-positivist philosophy of science is that research problems are initially ill structured. Hence one of the key requisites of autonomous learners is that they can think through ill-structured problems and use research and scholarship to sharpen the definition of problems, better to address them (Haig 1987). The point here, and it has been made by many commentators in rather different ways (see Seltzer and Bentley 1999), is that advanced forms of learning require risk-taking on the part of learners because there is no guarantee of success. Learning requires trust, or more precisely an act of faith, by learners that they can address, if not solve, problems successfully and that their teachers will act as reliable guides in this process of discovery. Faith, trust and risk-taking do not sit easily with the commodification of the learning relationship in which there now may be an assumption that, in return for a fee and a specified level of work on behalf of both teachers and taught, that qualifications will follow.

In addition, advanced learning of this kind has not traditionally occurred in a vacuum but within the context of established disciplines with attendant insights, conventions and procedures that may help in defining, addressing and solving problems. Philosophers of education have made the point that the experience of education can be life changing, that once inside a discipline or form of knowledge, the unique perspective it offers can fundamentally alter the way learners view themselves and the world. However, to get students to this point requires guidance, facilitation and initiation. Unlike the products on a supermarket shelf that can be sampled relatively quickly, to be on the 'inside' of a discipline takes time, hard work and persistence. When these attributes are linked to acts of faith and trust we are some distance from the type of commodification exemplified by the supermarket model. The same may hold true for academics. The constant threat of student litigation and complaints, together with requirement to comply with extensive external monitoring procedures may encourage them to opt for 'safe teaching' which is locked into a transmission mode where pre-specified content can be passed on to the student and assessed in a conventional form.

The Changing Structure of Knowledge

Underlying the points made above is the view that close and sustained engagement with the content and internal structure of a discipline may be crucial in enabling students to master complex conceptual structures and modes of analysis for purposes of knowledge creation (Bernstein 1996). It has also been argued that this form of disciplinary induction creates both the skills and critical orientation, as well as the relevant dispositions, for independent lifelong learning and innovation. However, the learning of this form of disciplinary knowledge is under threat from mechanisms of choice which have introduced modularization and which have privileged movement across departments, disciplines and institutions.

It is important to point out, however, that the argument for modularization predates the advent of consumerism and in its original form had a strong equity dimension. The equity argument is that 'non-traditional students', that is those who have had poor prior educational backgrounds, those in full-time employment, and those with additional personal responsibilities would have a greater chance of access to, and success in, higher education if it was undertaken in smaller, independent chunks in a system with multiple points of entry and exit. At a later period, however, an economic dimension of the argument emerged which has been tied to the necessity for universities to make educational programmes more relevant to the world of work. This argument has been linked to pressures for universities to shift knowledge production from what has been termed 'Mode 1' knowledge, which is disciplinary bound, theoretical and evaluated by peer review, to 'Mode 2' knowledge, which is transdisciplinary, applied and evaluated by both internal and external stakeholders (see Gibbons et al. 1994). In this sense modularization has been presented as a mechanism to enable students to undertake a Mode 2 curriculum, which is more relevant to the world of work, by disaggregating year-long courses, eroding traditional disciplinary boundaries and ensuring greater portability and transferability through the development of modular programmes. The movement towards a Mode 2 curriculum is therefore expected to induct students into a problem-solving, applied and interdisciplinary curriculum required for a high skills economy (Ensor 2001).

However, it is an open question as to whether the changing structure of knowledge as indicated above is in accord with high quality learning or the discourse surrounding the notion of a knowledge economy. This is because increased pressures leading to the commodification of higher education may result in the development and combination of modules primarily around market incentives leading to a loss of coherence and induction mechanisms traditionally associated with disciplinary study. In post-apartheid South Africa, where the need for the educational achievement of black students from disadvantaged backgrounds is highly visible and urgent, the introduction of modularization has been questioned. The argument has been that a modular structure, with its lack of coherence and induction mechanisms, as well as its reliance on students' resources to make coherent choices, places students at a grave disadvantage. In particular, Muller (2001: 8) has argued that moving straight into a Mode 2 curriculum does not achieve high quality learning. He has argued that teaching applied knowledge directly 'before giving students the conceptual apparatus with which to "situate" that knowledge in its larger coherent pattern' may give students limited notions of application but does not equip students with conceptual skills relating to extension and innovation. The argument therefore appears to be that Mode 2 cognitive skills, understood in this elevated sense of developing interdisciplinary and applied thought, is only possible on the foundation of having acquired Mode 1 disciplinary knowledge. In addition, the mushrooming of programmes, particularly, but not exclusively, in non-elite institutions, which link in a direct manner to students' everyday lives, may also pose particular dangers. Sociologists of education including Muller (2000) and Young (2003) have warned that such approaches to the curriculum, which erode the distinction between the type of knowledge acquired in universities and the type of knowledge acquired in everyday life, may not have the capacity to enhance students' existing capabilities or induct students into complex intellectual work. Further research is required to investigate in what way changes in the curriculum designed to offer students greater choice and more accessible and 'relevant' programmes impact on learning.

While the outcomes of modularization and credit accumulation according to market principles may not accord with the rhetoric about the knowledge economy, it may in fact correspond with practice. Brown and Lauder (2003) have argued that the knowledge economy seeks a talented elite of what Reich (1991) has called 'symbolic analysts' and that many former 'knowledge' jobs are being routinized. They argue that the competitive pressures created by economic globalization and the global nature of knowledge based industries have led companies to substitute highly skilled workers at home with skilled, but less costly workers in developing countries. In addition, where knowledge is routinized, the discretion of knowledge workers is curtailed. While knowledge workers may be required to handle greater complexity, they are given little freedom to use their initiative. One of the conclusions drawn by Brown and Lauder (2003) is that the expansion of higher education may create a substantial wastage of talent amongst college and university graduates, which may in turn lead to a greater dispersion in incomes as graduates are forced into accepting sub-graduate work.

When linked to our analysis of the acquisition and transmission of knowledge in higher education, it may be that Mode 2 knowledge, as presently conceptualized and 'delivered' through modules and curriculum packages, provides the labour market with graduates for those jobs that are often paid at a sub-graduate level. Furthermore, drawing from our analysis of the field of university education, we would hypothesize that universities at the top of the hierarchy, which generally recruit students from advantaged backgrounds, would continue to teach disciplinary knowledge and feed into the elite end of the labour market, while those focusing more on Mode 2 knowledge in a highly modularized curriculum would feed into the labour market for intermediate skills. The implication therefore is that the most corrosive effects of the commodification of higher education are likely to be felt more strongly in vulnerable institutions which admit students from disadvantaged backgrounds. If the concerns expressed about changes in knowledge content and structure are valid, then rather than gaining access to powerful forms of knowledge, the majority of disadvantaged students will receive an education that has been reduced to narrowly defined core competencies which have been legitimated on the bandwagon of consumer choice. The result may be a higher education system that produces what Castells (2001) has termed a small elite of 'self programmable' workers who have learnt how to learn and are occupationally mobile, together with a large mass of 'generic workers' who are exchangeable and disposable and unable to adapt to a changing and volatile labour market.

Research Questions

Given the above discussion, what are the key areas that require investigation? First, theoretical frameworks and empirical data capable of analyzing how pressures for commodification may be transformed by a logic and structure that is particular to the institutional context of universities are essential for advancing the course of this research programme. Traditionally, research on higher education has been dominated by analyses which have either been pitched at a macro level or which have focused on the internal functioning of universities in isolation from socio-political and economic forces. Relatively less attention has been paid to the interaction between macro forces such as those associated with commodification and the internal functioning of the universities, particularly with regard to teaching and learning. As we have illustrated with Bourdieu's work in previous sections, the internal culture of the university is likely to form a crucial mediating context through which the forces associated with commodification may be displaced, restructured or even subverted. It is therefore by no means clear that the application of a business model to educational processes will inevitably result in the outcomes envisaged such as better quality and a more direct link to economic productivity. The North American literature has already revealed worrying trends in students' motivation and attitudes towards learning. In addition, sociological research carried out in other public sector institutions has indicated that attempts to restructure professional cultures through market and neo-managerial frameworks could result in a plethora of consequences which may be the opposite of what policy makers intended (see Power 1999; Clarke et al. 2000). Further research is therefore required to investigate the impact of commodification on pedagogical relationships and on professional identities and how this in turn impacts on the acquisition of skills and knowledge, and perhaps more importantly, on the disposition to learn.

A further important area for investigation is the changing form and structure of the curriculum under pressures for commodification. A focus on knowledge and the curriculum has generally been excluded from analyses of change in higher education. The work of Basil Bernstein (1996) on the structuring of knowledge suggests that differential knowledge structures have a decisive impact on the social relations and academic products in any given field. Bernstein's proposition that sociological accounts of the relationship between education and society need to incorporate both symbolic structures and social relations as part of one system for the purposes of analysis is therefore crucial to the further development of the effects of commodification on learning.

While sociologists such as Muller (2001) have raised questions about the erosion of disciplinary knowledge, the danger is that such analyses may lock teaching and research into an uncritical endorsement of traditional disciplinary boundaries. Such analyses therefore need to be extended to include the influence of consumerism on the transformation of knowledge and the emerging of new disciplines.

Finally, the relationship between commodificadon and the massification and democratization of higher education is an area that needs to be explored. An enduring limitation in relation to the social theory of higher education is that researchers have tended to conceptualize institutions of higher education in an overly homogenous way. However, as shown above, the outcomes of forces for commodification may differ substantially across different types of universities and subject areas. In an era where both academic and economic forces exert powerful structuring effects on universities, the field of higher education is likely to become the locus of power struggles over the legitimate capital required to attain dominance. An in-depth analysis of the impact of commodification on different types of universities may play an important role in contributing to sociological understandings of the impact of commodification on labour market destinations and social equity.

Conclusion

Consumerism was introduced in order to address the perceived problems of translating an elite system into a mass system of higher education. To do so, the New Labour Government in the UK has sought to change the incentives for academic work and has assumed a different model of the motivation of academics. The broad question is whether in seeking to address this problem through consumerism it has thrown the baby out with the bath water. Paradoxically and in this limited sense it may have facilitated a system of higher education that has some continuity with the demands of the labour market.

However it has been hypothesized in this [chapter] that rather than empowering students, consumerism may, perversely, threaten innovation and academic standards and further entrench academic privilege. Attempts to restructure professional cultures to comply with consumerist frameworks may unintentionally deter innovation and promote passive and instrumental attitudes to learning. However, these hypotheses need investigation because it is unlikely that the changes wrought by consumerism will be precisely of this kind. We know from previous studies of educational change (for example Bowe et al. 1992) that academics and perhaps students will seek to graft these consumerist changes onto existing professional ideologies and practices, making the outcomes unpredictable.

Whether the range of related hypotheses articulated [here] is borne out by subsequent empirical analysis remains to be seen. However, in our view it is essential for the research to be undertaken because it raises broad questions about the nature of academic professionalism, the identity and nature of learners, inequality and of the impact of higher education on the labour market and economic competitiveness. In terms of the sociology of education it attempts to show how social-structural issues and class and ethnicity can combine with policy to produce institutional changes to the meaning and nature of learning in higher education. Finally, the [chapter] raises the question that may need to be addressed, as a result of this research programme, of how an alternative mass higher education policy may be developed which counters the problems posed by consumerism.

NOTES

We are indebted to Hugh Lauder for critical commentary on an earlier draft of this [chapter]. We would also like to thank the two anonymous referees for helpful comments.

Educating for Privilege

Robert Perrucci and Earl Wysong

It is often asserted that new technologies will equalize learning opportunities for the rich and poor. It is devoutly to be wished for, but I doubt it will happen.

Neil Postman, *Nation*, 9 October 1995

Princeton versus Podunk: Getting 'Creamed'?

[Elsewhere (Perrucci and Wysong 1999)] we have demonstrated the strong influence schooling has on the reproduction of class inequality. Contrary to the beliefs contained in the American Dream, education is not the means for providing equality of opportunity to all Americans regardless of their social position at birth. Schooling serves to reproduce inequality through the power of the myth of the American Dream and through the effects of tracking and streaming as the way to deny equal access to the means for upward mobility. We [further] our analysis of schooling by examining the question of who goes to college and where they go.

[. . .] Rates of college attendance have increased dramatically in the past fifty years. In 1940, 216,000 degrees were awarded by American colleges and universities. By the mid-1990s, some 1.5 million degrees were being awarded. A total of 14,306,000 students were enrolled in 3,494 higher education institutions in 1993. These institutions consist of 2,106 four-year institutions, and 1,388 two-year institutions.

The expansion in college enrollments has had the effect of introducing greater diversity into the college environment. It is probably safe to assume that in the era of small enrollments, the college population was composed of persons with similar social and economic backgrounds. Only the sons and daughters of the most privileged classes attended college. But what are we to say about a time when 14 million young people are in college? Although they do not represent all of those persons from lower economic backgrounds who would go to college but cannot afford to, it must surely contain some of them. Perhaps what we have is a modified form of the American Dream, where at least some persons from the nonprivileged classes do get access to equality of opportunity. Perhaps.

The main argument of this section is that although the expansion of enrollments at the college level has resulted in larger proportions of nonprivileged youth attending colleges and universities, there has been at the same time movement toward a more rigidly class-based system of inequality within the framework of higher education. This more subtle and less visible form of inequality is reflected in the schools that privileged and nonprivileged students attend and in the areas in which they choose to specialize. The consequences of a class-based system of inequality within higher education are as serious in terms of wasted human resources as the class-based system of tracking and streaming that determines who goes to college.

Let us begin with the approximately thirty-five hundred institutions of higher education that are

From R. Perucci and E. Wysong, *The New Class Society* (Oxford: Rowman & Littlefield, 1999), 194–200. Reprinted with permission.

available to serve the needs of America's aspiring youth. Approximately 40 percent of those institutions are two-year colleges that students typically attend either because they lack the academic credentials to be admitted to a four-year institution or because they lack the money to pay for tuition, room, and board. Some enrollees at two-year colleges are nontraditional students who are already employed and are trying to improve their credentials and career opportunities.

The remaining 60 percent, the twenty-one hundred four-year institutions, are also highly differentiated. About two hundred of these institutions are the larger and more prestigious research universities that award almost all the professional and advanced degrees in the United States. These institutions graduate the doctors, lawyers, engineers, scientists, economists, and managers that populate the privileged class. These two-hundred 'top' universities can be further subdivided into the Ivy League (Brown, Columbia, Cornell, Dartmouth, Harvard, Pennsylvania, Princeton, and Yale), the so-called Big Ten (Illinois, Indiana, Iowa, Michigan, Michigan State, Minnesota, Northwestern, Ohio State, Penn State, Purdue, and Wisconsin), and other state universities. And then there are the small 'elite' liberal arts colleges that provide high-quality education, strong social ties (the basis of social capital), and very high tuition (Amherst, Bates, Bowdoin, Clark, Colby, Franklin and Marshall, Hamilton, Haverford, Hobart, Oberlin, Reed, William Smith, Swarthmore, Tufts, etc.).

The point of this little exercise (aside from the fact that we have probably misclassified many schools) is to indicate that higher education is highly differentiated, with a small number of schools that are very selective about their admissions and consistently rated among the elite colleges and universities. [...] Elite schools in the United States that confer great advantages on their graduates probably number about thirty, or less than 1 percent of all the colleges and universities in the country. If you are admitted to one of these thirty elite schools, after graduation you will be able to be admitted to one of the elite graduate or professional schools. And when schooling is completed, the graduates of elite schools will assume high-level positions in the major institutions of American society and join the privileged class. Students admitted to the 'elite 1 percent' are getting 'creamed,' which is the positive meaning of this term used at the beginning of this section. Those who rise to the top in this system will enjoy the 'good life' with all of its material and psychological benefits.

Students who are enrolled at the 1,388 community colleges, and at most of the 2,100 nonelite schools, are getting 'creamed' in the negative meaning of the term—that is, they are getting 'clobbered.' Most of these students are caught between a rock and a hard place. They choose to go to college because it is their only hope for getting a decent job. The absence of good jobs for people with only a high school diploma drives most into college. Their parents cannot really afford to cover the costs of college, and so students work and take out loans in the hope that all the debt and sacrifice will pay off in the end. They forgo income for four years and incur debt, yet when they graduate, all they may find is a job paying $6–10 an hour, or $12,000–21,000 a year. The median starting salary for 1993 college graduates was $22,968 (about $19,000 for education majors and $31,000 for computer science and engineering majors). About 40 percent of these graduates reported that the job they held did not require a college degree (only 17 percent of engineering graduates said this, but about 50 percent of graduates in humanities and social sciences said a college degree was not required for their current job).[1] To be sure, there is a small minority of graduates of the 2,100 nonelite schools that do better. They are usually graduates in engineering or business or those with teaching certificates who have the skill capital and credentials to command better incomes. But they will not be joining the privileged class.

This two-tiered system of schooling for privilege is summarized in Figure 61.1. On the extreme left of the figure is the secondary school system [...]. The children of the most wealthy members of the privileged class enter the stream in the elite prep schools that prepare students primarily for Harvard, Princeton, and Yale. The remaining children of the privileged class are being educated in the resource-rich suburban high schools that are homogeneous in terms of the economic class of their students and are well funded from their property taxes. These students from the privileged class compete among themselves for admission to a small number (about fifty) elite universities and liberal arts colleges. They are elite because they are well endowed by financial contributions from wealthy alumni and because their admissions procedures are highly selective (i.e., they get applications from many more students than they can ever admit). Some of the graduates of these elite schools go on to the elite schools of law, medicine, business, and engineering, and most of the rest go into entry-level positions in America's major corporations.

The lower panel of Figure 61.1 is where most students are located. In 1994, 2.5 million students graduated from high school, of whom about 300,000 graduated from private schools. Enrollments in the fifty elite colleges and universities are a small fraction of the millions enrolled in higher education, with the overwhelming proportion of students enrolled in the 2,100 nonelite colleges and universities and the 1,388 community colleges. A very small percentage of these students 'escape' their nonprivileged paths and are admitted to elite schools, usually owing to their academic achievements and their performance on the Scholastic Aptitude Tests (SAT) that are used with all applications for college.[2] A study of Harvard's admission process indicates that the school does attempt to admit a small number of 'working-class' students and 'students of color' who have academic merit, based on scores on the SAT and other achievement tests.[3] This possibility of 'moving up' describes the small amount of 'creaming' from the bottom tier of Figure 61.1 into the schooling streams of the privileged class.

The interesting thing about this two-tiered system of schooling for privilege is that the way it works has not changed very much in the past forty years. Graduates of the elite colleges and universities have always obtained better jobs (in terms of prestige, opportunities, and income) than graduates of the nonelite schools, and this is true independent of merit. The prestige of the degree-granting institution has an effect on postcollege jobs and incomes over and above the ability of their individual graduates.

In the 1950s, research compared the incomes of graduates from Ivy League schools, prestigious 'technical' schools (e.g., Cal Tech, Carnegie, MIT), elite private colleges, the Big Ten, other midwestern colleges, and other eastern colleges. The findings indicated that the median incomes of male graduates are directly related to the prestige ranking of the

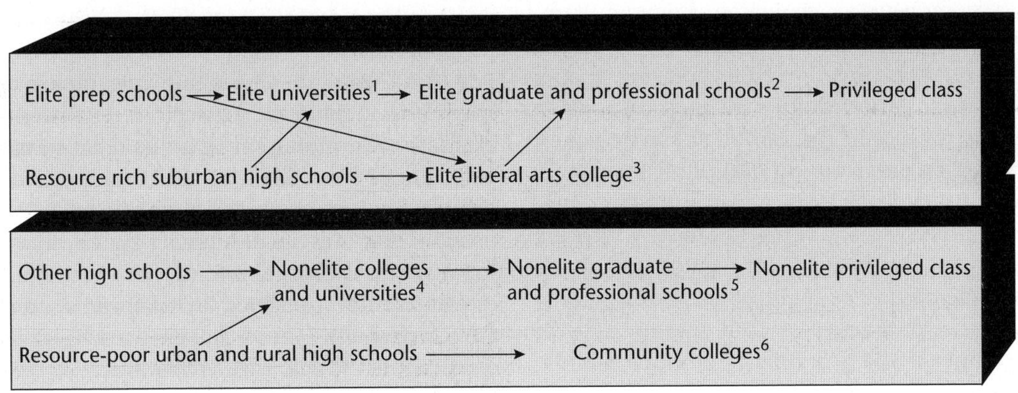

Fig. 61.1 Two-tiered system of schooling for privilege

1. Elite universities: Approximately 20, including Harvard, Yale, Princeton, Chicago, Stanford, Northwestern, California-Berkeley, Michigan, Wisconsin, UCLA, North Carolina, Columbia, Duke, Pennsylvania.
2. Elite graduate and professional schools: Approximately 15, including Harvard, California-Berkeley, Yale, Chicago, Wisconsin-Madison, Michigan, Columbia, Stanford, Princeton, Cornell, Illinois-Urbana, Pennsylvania.
3. Elite liberal arts colleges: Approximately 30, including Amherst, Bates, Bowdoin, Brown, Bryn Mawr, Reed, Swarthmore, Tufts, Colgate, Smith, Wellesley, Williams, Oberlin, Hamilton, Franklin and Marshall, Wesleyan of Connecticut, Barnard, Brandeis, Mount Holyoke, Haverford, Hobart, Skidmore, Union.
4. Nonelite colleges and universities: there are approximately 2,100 schools in this group.
5. Nonelite graduate and professional schools: there are approximately 200 schools in this group.
6. Community colleges: there are 1,388 schools in this group.

schools, and this pattern was found across different fields of study. The following summary from the researchers is important for its historic value, given that this was a period before higher education became as differentiated by prestige as it is today.

> Although we have noted that good grades may at least sometimes lead to good incomes, it develops that even the poorest students from the Ivy League share in the general prosperity—and do better than the best students from other schools. Of the Ivy Leaguers who just got by—the C and D students—42 percent had reached the [highest income] level. Of the A students from the Big Ten, only 37 percent had hit that mark, and only 23 percent of the A students from 'all other Midwest' colleges. Even the great financial disadvantage of a general education, rather than a specific one, does not seem to hold back the Ivy Leaguers. Of the Ivy League humanities majors, 46 percent had reached the [highest income] bracket, and of the social scientists 50 percent. But even among the Big Ten's engineering graduates, with their highly specific training and all the advantages that go with it, only 23 percent had reached the [highest income] level. [At the time of this study, the 'highest income' was about three times the median income for all U.S. men. A comparable 'highest income' figure in 1998 would be $108,000.]

What all this amounts to is that the differences in earning power between graduates of rich and famous schools and those from small obscure schools are so great that they override everything else. Earning power rises steadily with each increase in wealth and prestige of the school. At the extremes, the Ivy League graduates do best of all financially even when they make poor grades and take a general rather than specific course, both of which are ordinarily handicaps—while the graduates of the smallest schools do not get up to the averages even when they make fine grades and take the type of specific courses which ordinarily produce the biggest incomes.[4]

The pattern of advantage for graduates of elite schools observed more than forty years ago is still in operation today. Students from privileged-class backgrounds are more likely to enroll in the most prestigious schools, and they choose programs of study that have the greatest potential for high income.[5] In fact, the effects of privilege on who goes where to college may be greater today than they were forty years ago. Sons and daughters of the privileged class go to better high schools (if not private schools) and are provided with an educational experience that is geared to satisfy entrance requirements at the most selective elite colleges. And if that is not enough, privileged-class families have the money to help their children prepare for college entrance exams.

The final barrier for even the brightest working-class high school graduate is the cost of attending an elite college. How can a family earning the median national income of $34,000 a year afford to pay $27,000 a year for tuition, room, and board? Lacking funds, such students go to state colleges with lower costs, and they obtain financial aid and work to cover expenses. Choosing a major is often driven by practical considerations, such as the need to get a job after graduation. This can lead to vocationally oriented programs such as education, nursing, and technology degree programs, which assure jobs after the baccalaureate degree but allow limited opportunities for achieving high income or for accumulating wealth.

Findings such as those reported above indicate a clear lack of correspondence between the expectations derived from the American Dream and the actual experiences of college graduates. Ability and merit are important for a person's success after college, but where one goes to school is also important.

In the 1960s, there was growing interest in the science-based professions, such as engineering, as examples of a profession that was open to talented people, regardless of their social and economic origins. In the professions of medicine and law it is possible that a graduate's family background could influence postcollege success by providing the money to start a practice or the social contacts for attracting wealthy clients. But engineers work in large corporations where their scientific and technical expertise determines their movement up the corporate ladder. An engineer's social and economic background should have less significance for his or her success than might be the case in medicine or law.

Once again, contrary to the myth of equality of opportunity and the belief that engineering is a career open to talent, engineering graduates from higher social origins (based on their father's occupation) were more likely to hold engineering positions that provided greater prestige, power, and income.[6] This finding was based on a study of the graduates from a single university of moderate prestige, not part of the elite schools. When the research was expanded to a national sample of engineering graduates, it was found that engineers with upper social origins earned more money and held more-responsible positions than engineers from lower social origins. Moreover, this class difference was found to be true even among engineers who had the highest grades in college and had attended the most selective engineering schools.[7] Thus, even when working-class high school graduates are 'creamed' (i.e., are recruited to elite universities), their final rewards of income and position may not put them in the privileged class.

The Future: Continuing Inequality and Corporations in the Classroom

> *Corporations and their foundations have become sacred cows to university administrators. Few professors are willing to jeopardize their standing in universities by publishing research articles critical of these donors.*
>
> Lawrence C. Soley, *Leasing the Ivory Tower*, 1996

The main argument of this chapter is that the American educational system operates in a way that reproduces the existing structure of inequality in the larger society. It achieves this end, first of all, by promoting an ideology that proclaims schooling to be the great equalizer and the main avenue for upward mobility. Second, inequality is perpetuated through a multitiered system of education made up of elite schools, average schools, and horrible schools. The different quality of these schools is directly linked to the social- and economic-class level of their students. The quality of the educational experience in primary and secondary schools helps to determine a student's chances for attending college.

The inequality in primary and secondary schools that is linked to the social-class position of students is likely to be reinforced and extended in the years ahead. The most notable innovations in public education that are currently on the public agenda are the voucher system and the charter school. The voucher system provides families each school year with a voucher ($2,000 to $4,000) that can be used to enroll their children in nonreligious private schools. There have been attempts to extend the use of vouchers to religious schools, but such efforts have been blocked by lawsuits. Charter schools enable groups of parents, teachers, and community members to propose a new way of providing education for their children. For example, they might wish to emphasize self-paced learning, cross-disciplinary education, or traditional back-to-basics programs. Such groups apply for a charter from the local school board or state Board of Education to create the new school, and, if approved, they receive public funding on a per pupil basis similar to funding for public schools.

Vouchers and charter schools are attractive ideas because they appear to empower parents who have become frustrated with the public school system's failure to educate their children. Many parents in low-income inner cities have come to view these new ideas as the only way to provide their children with a better education. Unfortunately, only a fragment of inner-city families will be able to take advantage of vouchers or charter schools. Charter schools are not obligated to take all students who apply, and the ability to use a voucher may be dependent on the availability of transportation and other resources to get children to schools outside of their neighborhood. The main impact of vouchers and charter schools will be to siphon money away from public schools, leaving those left behind with even poorer facilities. The more affluent will take advantage of vouchers to move to private schools, leading to greater segregation in schools.

Students from resource-rich schools receive the kind of preparation that enables them to compete for admission to elite colleges and universities. Students from resource-poor schools are more likely to drop out or to terminate their education with the high school diploma. Those who do go to college attend community colleges and a wide variety of average to good state colleges and universities.

Based on everything we know today about the US economy and the actions of corporations [. . .] the inequality described above will not only continue, but in all likelihood, it will get worse. Students from families in the bottom of the double-diamond class structure will find it increasingly difficult to pay the costs of attending college. Moreover, it will become increasingly apparent that large numbers of college graduates will be unable to find any but the lowest-level jobs available in the service sector. It will become apparent that there is a significant mismatch between the kinds of job that colleges prepare students to enter and the kinds of job that are actually available.

In addition to continuing inequality in schooling, we expect greater involvement in private-sector corporations in the educational system at all levels. At the primary and secondary levels, there will be continuing interest in alternative ways of 'delivering' education to the young. The current antiunion, antibureaucracy, antigovernment climate will stimulate proposals to 'privatize' education. Private-sector firms, perhaps in cooperation with universities, will attempt to provide higher-quality education and at lower costs. The CEOs from *Fortune 500* firms have become involved in school reform efforts at the state and national levels.[8] Since these business leaders are used to thinking in terms of the 'bottom line,' productivity, and efficiency, their involvement gives one pause as to the kind of educational 'reforms' that may appear on the nation's agenda. In addition to 'for-profit' private schools, we should expect great attention to new educational technology that will reduce the need for teachers and increase dependence on telecommunications-based instruction.

Corporations have already recognized the potential for advertising commercial products to the millions of schoolchildren who are today's consumers as well as the consumers of the future.[9] Classroom films, television, and weekly papers are owned by large corporations, and the products developed for schoolroom use are accompanied by corporate logos and advertising material.[10]

Many of the proposals to bring corporate expertise and technology into the classroom are based on the assertion that the telecommunications revolution will be available to rich and poor alike. Schooling will therefore be able to deliver on its promise as the 'equalizer,' as all students will have access to the same educational resources, the same information, and the same master teachers, on the information superhighway. Once again, a technological fix to the problem of class inequality. [...] The life experiences of class inequality will not disappear because of the information superhighway.

Finally, we need to consider corporate penetration of higher education.[11] Private firms are no stranger to higher education. Corporate CEOs are prominent as trustees of most major universities but especially the elite schools. Such representation helps to encourage corporate-university relations that result in corporate funding of research and a variety of university programs. In return, corporations get access to the latest knowledge that can be converted into patents on products and processes that benefit the corporations providing the funding. Often, corporations that provide funds for research by faculty or graduate students are able to obtain agreements guaranteeing that the results of the funded research will remain secret for and agreed-upon period of time. The doctoral dissertation in bio-medical engineering or pharmacology of a student whose research has had corporate funding can be kept from public disclosure until such time as the corporation that funded the research can realize its expected benefits. Students and professors may not be able to publish the results of such research until given permission to do so by the corporation. This practice of secret or confidential research may have started during the Cold War era, when the Department of Defense funded research that involved national security interests. Today, the private corporations can prevent publication because of private financial interests.

Many faculty members at major research universities are active participants in corporate–university relations. Those whose work may have commercial possibilities are actively pursued by corporations with substantial research grants or consulting fees. Some faculty members are able to double their incomes through their consulting agreements, especially in several fields in engineering, science, and the business schools. Those faculty with a more entrepreneurial bent often start their own firms in a research park near the university while retaining their academic positions and salary. Faculty at large research universities may receive e-mail message from their research offices with titles such as 'Leveraging Your Research by Starting a Business.' This 'call-out' to faculty, staff, and students is an attempt to stimulate interest in starting a business by offering information on university guidelines for faculty-owned businesses and discussions of where to find capital. These cyberspace messages are supplemented with hard-copy slick brochures with announcements like the following: 'The climate for starting technology-based businesses has never been better. Owing to steady or dwindling budgets, coupled with increasing demand of and competition for funds, government support for university research projects is harder to secure. University research programs are seeking alternative funding sources, such as funneling research ideas with commercial potential into start-up businesses. The bottom-line: becoming an entrepreneur is not only "in" but is encouraged.'[12] Universities generally look the other way when confronted with the active corporate pursuit of faculty. They usually have regulations stipulating that faculty may be involved in 'outside activities' for one or more days per week or month, depending on the university. There is no stipulation as to how much they may earn as consultants, and no requirement that the university must be reimbursed for the time taken away from university responsibilities. Universities encourage these relationships in part because they hope to increase the flow of dollars from the private sector into the university's budget.

In recent years there has been a decline in federal money coming to universities for their research programs. This money often comes with agreements to cover overhead costs that allow universities to support other activities. In addition to the decline of federal dollars, many public universities have not been able to obtain more state funds or raise tuition. The only source for new money has been the private sector, which has been only too willing to help—but at a price. The price might be confidential research (as noted above). Private-sector funding might give the corporation the right to select researchers for projects and define the research topics to be pursued. It might even give corporations a voice on matters of promotions and tenure of faculty who work on corporate projects.

And it is also possible that corporate penetration of academe will have a chilling effect on those faculty in the liberal arts whose inclinations or disciplines tend to raise questions about corporations in American life, about the relative merits of capitalism versus socialism, or about the impact of unrestrained technology on the environment and our communities. Just as downsizing and plant closings serve to depress wages and discourage unionization, corporate penetration of academe could serve to create a climate of 'corporate correctness' that will dominate the minds of students and faculty alike.

NOTES

1. US Department of Education, National Center for Education Statistics, *The Condition of Education*, 1996, NCES 96-304, ed. Thomas Smith (Washington, DC: US Government Printing Office, 1996).
2. James Hearn, 'Academic and Nonacademic Influences on the College Destinations of 1980 High School Graduates', *Sociology of Education* 64 (July 1991): 158–71.
3. David Karen, 'Toward a Political-Organizational Model of Gatekeeping: The Case of Elite Colleges', *Sociology of Education* 63 (1990): 227–40.
4. Ernest Haveman and Patricia Salter West, *They Went to College* (New York: Harcourt, Brace, 1952), 180.
5. Scott Davies and Neil Guppy, 'Fields of Study, College Selectivity, and Student Inequalities in Higher Education', *Social Forces* 75 (1997): 1417–38.
6. Robert Perrucci, 'The Significance of Intra-Occupational Mobility', *American Sociological Review* 26 (1961): 874–83.
7. Carolyn Cummings Perrucci and Robert Perrucci, 'Social Origins, Educational Contexts, and Career Mobility', *American Sociological Review* 35 (1970): 451–63.

8. Douglas D. Noble, 'Schools as "Instructional Delivery Systems"', *In These Times*, 30 November 1992, 28–9.
9. Marianne Manilov, 'Channel One, Joe Camel, Potato Chips, and ABC', *Extra!*, July–August 1996, 18–19.
10. Luke Mines, 'Globalization in the Classroom', *Nation*, 1 June 1998, 22–4; William Hoynes, 'News for a Captive Audience: An Analysis of Channel One', *Extra!*, May–June 1997, 11–17.
11. For an expanded discussion, see Lawrence C. Soley, *Leasing the Ivory Tower: The Corporate Takeover of Academia* (Boston: South End, 1996).
12. Purdue Research Foundation, Home for High-Tech Business (West Lafayette, Ind.: Purdue Research Park, 1998).

National and Global Competition in Higher Education

Simon Marginson

[. . .]

The Global Element

The traditional equality of opportunity project, like the Keynesian policies of national economic management that nurtured it, was premised on a sealed national economy and social polity. Just as national financial regulation was broken open by world financial flows in the 1980s, and techniques of business and government became increasingly shaped by cross-border imitations, national higher education systems became irreversibly affected by globalisation. Between 1990 and 2002 the number of international students enrolled in Australian universities increased from 24,998 to 185,058 (DEST 2003). Cross-border flows do not necessarily render the pursuit of equality of opportunity impossible, but the education of a growing number of international students not part of the egalitarian equation of national equality of opportunity policies tends to change the conditions under which these policies are pursued, as well as posing new problems of global inequality. Here international education was also coloured by the marketised form in which it was developed, which worked against the logic of the equality project.

In 1985 it was decided to offer international student places on a full-fee basis, additional to the domestic enrolment, at prices designed to ensure profitability. In 1988 it was decided to phase out the existing international education program premised on foreign aid objectives, with a limited number of subsidised places subject to quota, and confirm the full-fee market as the dominant framework for cross-border education. Universities were allowed to set the prices they chose and expand the number of students without limit. The growing scarcity of public funding for universities encouraged the rapid growth of international education. This subordinated egalitarian considerations within the international program and fed the more general corporatisation and marketisation of the university sector (Marginson and Considine 2000). Australian universities are more entrepreneurially aggressive than American doctoral universities (Slaughter and Leslie 1997), and there is little subsidisation by either governments or universities. While the USA provides scholarships to a quarter of its international students (IIE 2003), in Australia in 2002 the ratio of full-fee-paying places to scholarship places was 61 to 1 (DEST 2003).

This [chapter] explores economic competition in higher education in both the national and global dimensions, up to and including the likely effects of the Nelson reforms, reflecting on the implications for the equality of opportunity project. The [chapter] does not focus on the implications of marketisation for the distribution of opportunities to access university between social groups—as noted, this element is widely understood (albeit inadequately

From the *Australian Educational Researcher* 31/2, August 2004. Reprinted.

monitored by governments) and there are no new data to report here—but explores the element less discussed elsewhere: the implications of national and global markets for the producer hierarchy of universities.

The National Market in Australia

A market is an economic system of coordination on the basis of buyer–seller relations, as distinct from a system of bureaucratic planning and administration, or communities of scholars, or democratic communal forms of education (Marginson 1997*b*: 27–50). Markets incorporate five distinctive features: a defined field of production/consumption; competition between producers; identifiable products ('commodities'); prices and monetary exchange between producers and consumers; and the human behaviours and values—entrepreneurship and cost minimisation in production, utility maximisation in consumption, contractual relations and so on—consistent with economic self-interest. Real life education systems normally incorporate some but not all of these features. Higher education systems typically consist of a set of producer institutions ('the market') together participating in several interlocking markets based on distinct products: undergraduate education, research degrees, research and consultancy and other services.

It is helpful to distinguish between *simple commodity production* in education—where the market is the means but not the end of production, and non-market objectives such as social access, or the formation of social leaders, or the reproduction of academic disciplines, may also come into play—and *fully capitalist production*, where the producer has no intrinsic interest in educational or social effects as such, only loyalty to the economic bottom line. The expansion of the production of individualised commodities and the accumulation of capital are ends in themselves.

Fully capitalist production is fundamentally subversive of the equality of opportunity project and other common goods. It fulfils non-capitalist objectives only by accident, not by design.

In 2002, the publicly funded national Australian system covered 896,621 students enrolled in thirty-eight public universities, three private universities and three small private colleges, with 98.2 per cent of these students in public institutions (DEST 2003). A 1999 survey identified a further 31, 212 students enrolled in seventy-nine accredited private institutions outside the national system (Watson 1999). The principal economic competitions are first, for research funding, via competitive academic schemes based on merit, and targeted research projects in the government and corporate sectors; and second, for tuition revenues from international and postgraduate students. Institutions also sell services in short courses, continuing professional education and consultancy; and compete for philanthropic support. International education is provided on a full-fee basis and designed to raise revenues. On the other hand, in undergraduate education Australian universities have been less market-like than American higher universities (though the Nelson reforms will change this: see below). The USA provides student loans for tuition, enabling a high level of student mobility and creating a quasi-voucher national market. In Australia there is a choice-based competition between universities in each capital but little national mobility. In 2002, 97 per cent of domestic undergraduates paid HECS to the government[1] rather than being subject to buyer–seller relations with their university. The cost of HECS-based courses is shared by students and the government, and the number of HECS places is capped by the government. There are three standardised levels of HECS based on field of study, at AUD $3,680–6,136 per full-time student per annum in 2003. HECS is a substantial charge in world terms but modified by its income-contingent character. In 2003 repayments began at an annual income of $24,365 (Nelson 2003*a*). HECS debts are indexed to prices with no real interest rate. This contrasts with direct fees and commercial loans in the USA.

Positional Goods and Positional Competition

Teaching services are standardised on the basis of credentials. All programs of study offered by accredited tertiary institutions are lodged in the

Australian Qualifications Framework. Here the degrees offered in all institutions are formally equivalent. Nevertheless, in the real world—in the minds of students, their families and employers of graduates—the degrees offered by different institutions are ranked hierarchically on the basis of institution and field of study. Higher education is a 'positional good' (Hirsch 1976) in which some student places are seen to offer better social status and lifetime opportunities than other places. A 1999 study of factors influencing the choices of prospective undergraduates found that 'applicants focus on broadly conceived course and institutional reputations when making their selections'.

Further, 'course entry scores, and by implication university scores, serve as a proxy for quality in prospective students' eyes' (James et al. 1999: p. ix). Applicants had low detailed knowledge of the teaching quality and lifelong earnings potential of particular courses, suggesting that the student-centred piety of the quality assurance movement is largely misplaced: in a positional market choice making is focused primarily on the status of universities and degrees, not the quality of teaching.

Positional goods confer advantages on some by denying them to others. 'Positional competition... is a zero-sum game. What winners win, losers lose' (Hirsch 1976: 52). Within any one nation (though 'within any one nation' is a significant qualification, as discussed below) there is an absolute limit on the number of positional goods at a given level of value. The number of such goods cannot be expanded without reducing unit value. For example, when everyone can enrol in medicine and become a doctor, medicine ceases to be a high-income-earning, high-status profession. Given the absolute limitation on the number of high-value positional goods, there is also a limit on the number of high-value producer institutions, and on the size of individual elite institutions. Elite institutions cannot expand production to meet the full demand, like capitalist businesses—while they enjoy higher revenues, for these institutions the lodestone is not maximum market share or maximum revenue; it is consumer preferment and social status. Thus, in a positional market, there is both competition among producers and competition among consumers. Producer universities compete for the custom of the most preferred 'customers', while student customers compete for entry to the most preferred institutions. Prestige sustains high student entry scores, and this very scarcity reproduces the prestige of the elite universities. Wealth follows prestige: wealthy families invest in high-value positions in education to maintain social leadership. Positional markets in higher education are a matching game in which the hierarchy of students/families becomes synchronised with the hierarchy of universities. In a high scarcity regime, with only a small number of high-quality/high-value institutions, the stakes in educational competition are much increased; and the more powerful social groups always enjoy advantages in that competition. When the element of positional competition dominates university, social equality of opportunity becomes almost impossible to achieve. The steeper the hierarchy of producers, the more the educational market becomes segmented vertically, the smaller the number of world-class universities becomes, and further hopes of equality of opportunity must recede.

Vertical segmentation is, however, inevitable in positional competition. The production of positional goods *necessarily* combines competition with oligopoly and market closure. Whether high tuition is charged or not, the university market is never a freely competitive market. In elite institutions, the more intense consumer competition for entry is, the *less* the elite institutions are required to court the consumer in the conventional manner, by dropping prices or providing more and better services, providing that they sustain their prestige (which again undermines the contemporary policy focus on improving teaching). Once a university obtains elite status, where it has a limited number of high value competitors, and its very status maintains student custom and research resources, to reproduce that status requires no more than ordinary prudence. At the top, the positional hierarchy in higher education tends to be very stable over time. In Australia the leading institutions are all 45 years old or more. At the bottom end of the market the positional competition operates differently. Institutions must compete hard to attract students to fill their places and secure revenues; and success is always provisional and contestable. But these institutions do not receive full recognition for the quality of good programs, because in a positional market their educational quality is over-determined by low social status. Intermediate institutions, combining some high-value scarce places with low-value access places, find it difficult to move up the ladder because of the limit to the number of high-prestige producers. They cluster as 'second choice' producers, or specialists. Positional markets segment into different groupings, with the segments aligned in a vertical hierarchy and firm barriers limiting upward movement between segments. There are four distinct segments in the Australian system. Geiger (2003: 6) cites seven in the United States.

Market Segmentation in Australia

The market Segmentation of the Australian system has been shaped by history and funding. The elite institutions, the 'Sandstones' or Group of 8—Queensland, Sydney, NSW, Melbourne, Monash, Adelaide, WA and ANU—are the older foundations in the capital cities (excluding Hobart and Darwin).[2] They are defined primarily by the pattern of school leaver preferment as measured by entry scores, and research prestige and performance as measured by the quantity of research grants, publications and research students. The older universities, especially Sydney, Western Australia and Melbourne, also enjoy what are in Australian terms relatively high levels of income from donors and private investments, further insulating them from market forces.

Below the Sandstones (Table 62.1), the further segments of the Australian market are

- the 'Gumtrees', mostly the second or later universities established in each state, prior to the Dawkins reforms that began in 1987;
- the 'Unitechs', large universities of technology in each state capital, which had longstanding status as vocational institutions, and became universities after 1987;
- the 'New Universities', other institutions that also achieved university status after 1987. Some are specialist regional and/or distance education providers;[3]
- private universities. Bond has no HECS places and like Notre Dame is small and marginal to the national system (the Nelson reforms will change this: see below).

Table 62.1 Elite higher education in the USA and Australia

United States (leading 30 institutions only, in rank order)	Australia ('Group of 8')
Princeton	Australian National
Harvard, Yale	Melbourne
Caltech, Duke, Massachusetts IT, Stanford, Pennsylvania	*Sydney*
Dartmouth	*Queensland*
Columbia, Northwestern	*Western Australia*
Chicago, Washington (St Louis)	*New South Wales*
Cornell	*Monash*
Johns Hopkins, Rice	*Adelaide*
Brown	
Emory, Notre Dame	
U California Berkeley	
Carnegie Mellon, Vanderbilt	
Virginia	
Georgetown	
U California Los Angeles, Michigan—Ann Arbor, Wake Forest	
Tufts, North Carolina—Chapel Hill	
William and Mary	

Italics indicates public university.

Sources: *US News and World Report* (2003: 82–3).

The national government's Institutional Grants Scheme (IGS), which is allocated competitively on the basis of research performance,[4] provides a useful indicator of segmentation (Nelson 2003*a*: 103–4). In 2003 the Sandstones received between \$24.8 million (Melbourne) and \$15.3 million (Adelaide) in IGS grants: next were Flinders, Newcastle and Tasmania—Gumtrees with medical faculties—each with \$7.0 million (see Table 62.2). The allocation of Australian Research Council Discovery grants follows a similar pattern. Research activity is open to merit-based contestation, but like school-leaver status it is also open to prestige-generates-prestige effects, and it is sensitive to the funding base. Before 1987 the Gumtrees were funded by government to conduct common good basic research in all disciplines. They now find it difficult to sustain this given that public funding is down, revenues are more dependent on competitive position, and the Sandstones are better

Table 62.2 Segments of the positional market, Australian universities, 2001–2003 data

Segments and universities	Med Total students 2002	Flexible delivery share 2002%	Total income 2002 $millions	Internat'l fee share income 2002%	*Research students 2002 number*	*share%*	New ARC Disc 2003	NCG per EFT staff 2001 ($)	IGS funds 2003 $millions
SANDSTONES									
U Melbourne	Y 39 378	3.0	856.3	13.1	3,908	9.9	104	29,788	29.8
U Queensland	Y 37 498	7.5	814.5	8.0	3,669	9.8	81	21, 452	28.3
U Sydney	Y 42 305	3.9	816.3	9.5	3,473	8.2	98	22, 943	27.1
U New South Wales	Y 42 333	10.1	701.5	16.5	2,669	6.3	81	23, 529	25.4
Monash U	Y 52 010	23.8	735.4	15.1	2,935	5.6	56	15, 786	19.3
Australian National U	Y 11 979	0	461.7	4.3	1,491	12.5	137	**—	16.6
U Western Australia	Y 15 885	0	360.4	8.0	1,830	11.5	46	31, 157	16.1
U Adelaide	Y 16 188	7.5	334.2	8.3	1,512	9.3	36	32, 382	15.3
GUMTREES									
U Tasmania	Y 13 750	10.9	199.7	7.1	1,030	7.5	22	20, 499	7.0
U Wollongong	N 18 764	1.1	210.1	20.5	1,024	5.5	14	14, 931	7.0
La Trobe U	N 24 930	0.7	314.0	8.1	1,359	5.5	24	10, 332	6.3
Macquarie U	N 27 239	17.5	295.9	18.9	1,031	3.8	23	12, 409	6.2
Griffith U	Y 30 969	7.5	350.7	11.6	1,283	4.1	22	7,996	6.1
U Newcastle	Y 23 502	7.5	256.9	10.9	1,236	5.3	22	13, 835	5.4
James Cook U	Y 13 189	17.0	173.5	6.2	679	5.1	6	11, 040	4.9
Flinders U	Y 13 644	10.9	177.2	7.8	905	6.6	10	18, 192	4.5
Murdoch U	N 12 734	24.1	156.0	10.4	761	6.0	7	14, 954	4.3
U New England	N 18 202	81.9	148.3	3.9	820	4.5	9	13, 880	3.8
Deakin U	N 33 033	54.7	325.8	8.5	899	2.7	11	6,624	2.9
UNITECHS									
Curtin U Technology	N 33 240	11.5	360.9	23.3	1,592	4.8	11	6,432	5.2
Queensland UT	N 39 192	15.1	365.2	15.6	1,105	2.8	13	5,121	4.9
U South Australia	N 30 627	22.0	286.1	15.8	1,741	5.7	13	5,297	4.5
Royal Melbourne IT	N 38 280	3.7	478.2	21.5	1,831	4.8	15	3,346	4.5
U Technology Sydney	N 29 290	0	287.7	17.1	918	3.1	13	6,892	3.6
NEW UNIS									
U Western Sydney	N 35 361	4.5	296.7	12.9	942	2.7	4	5,159	3.2
U Canberra	N 10 419	(0.04)	105.8	11.5	265	2.5	2	7,332	1.7
Swinburne UT	N 14 404	(0.01)	233.2	14.6	537	3.7	10	6,294	1.7
Victoria U Technology	N 19 475	1.9	277.8	10.5	654	3.4	1	4,372	1.7
Edith Cowan U	N 23 829	24.4	202.9	12.1	824	3.5	3	3,289	1.4
Northern Territory U	N 5612	26.3	91.6	2.8	213	3.8	2	7,885	1.2
Southern Cross U	N 11 961	52.9	89.7	7.6	449	3.8	1	5,920	1.2
Charles Sturt U	N 39 776	83.4	187.4	5.4	434	1.1	5	4,132	1.2
Central Queensland	N 21 763	40.9	210.6	37.7	316	1.5	0	2,995	1.0
Southern Queensland	N 24 271	81.0	118.6	13.3	326	1.3	3	3,832	0.9
U Ballarat	N 6615	0	106.9	4.9	187	2.8	3	3,754	0.5

Table 62.2 *(Continued)*

Segments and universities	Med Total students 2002	Flexible delivery share 2002%	Total income 2002 $millions	Internat'l fee share income 2002%	Research *students 2002 number*	*share%*	New ARC Disc 2003	NCG per EFT staff 2001 ($)	IGS funds 2003 $millions
U Sunshine Coast	N 3947	11.3	32.5	12.0	62	1.6	0	98	0.1
PRIVATE UNIS									
Aust Catholic U*	N 11 894	8.9	104.4	4.3	338	2.8	1	1,496	0.5
U Notre Dame Aust	N 2832	1.7	20.2	17.7	27	1.0	0	0	0.1
Bond U	N n.a.	n.a.	n.a.	n.a.	51	n.a.	0	n.a.	0.1
MINOR SITES									
(various)	– 6250	—	69.4	—	377	—	12	—	0.4
Total	– 896 621	19.2	11 614.1	12.5	45 703	5.1	921	15 165	277.6

* Private university funded as public universities. Med = medicine faculty (Y = yes, N = no). Dollar amounts in current prices. Flexible delivery share = % of students external (distance) students and multi-modal students, distinct from Internal (wholly campus-based). Research student share = number of research students as % of all students. IGS = Institutional Grants Scheme, awarded competitively on the basis of research performance (see note). NCR per EFT staff = national competitive research grants per effective full-time member of staff, teaching/research staff research only.

** Not all ANU staff eligible as funded separately for research. New ARC Discov = new Australian Research Council Discovery grants, awarded on academic merit across all fields except medical sciences.

Sources: DEST (2003), Nelson (2003a), Australian Vice-Chancellors Committee, Australian Research Council.

placed to attract competitive research funding and student fees. Nevertheless, the Gumtrees mostly perform much better than the post-1987 universities in national competitive research grants per effective staff member. The Sandstones can internationalise while sustaining universal research intensity. In the other segments, when institutions concentrate on specialist areas such as fee-based international education and distance education, major ventures in either domain tend to cut into potential research capacity.

All else being equal, the steeper the hierarchy of institutions in terms of resources and status, the greater will be the vertical variation in the value of the positional goods produced in higher education, and the more positional competition will structure student and university behaviours. In Australia economic competition in higher education sustains Sandstone hegemony, to an increasing degree, at the expense of the resources and prestige of all other universities. 'True quality' is seen to be centred on fewer institutions than at any time since the formation of mass higher education. In a market where institutions draw on their competitive position to pay their own way, it is no longer possible for all universities to be world-class. There is '*comparison* in place of real commonality and generality' (Marx 1973: 161). The producer hierarchy has become steeper than before, and the dominance of the elite institutions more difficult to contest.

Implications of the Nelson Reforms

The next round of marketisation, the Nelson reforms from 2005 (Nelson 2003*b*), will enhance these trends. In December 2003 the national parliament adopted a package of further market reforms in higher education as negotiated by the Minister for Education, Science and Training, Brendan Nelson. The new system [began] in 2005. There are three main changes. First, though the HECS remains a payment from students to government, covering only a part of the cost of the student place with the balance paid by government, it will move closer to the forms of a market fee. The level of HECS will be varied freely by the universities, at up to 25 per cent above current levels, becoming $0–7,670 per annum in 2005. All prestigious

Table 62.3 Annual full-time undergraduate tuition costs in the USA and Australia

USA private universities (2002–3)	21% of students pay over $36,000, 68% pay over $22,500
USA public universities in-state (2002–3)	22% of students pay over $7,500, 75% pay over $4,500
Australian HECS (2003)	Varies by course between $3680 and 6136
Australian HECS + 25% variation (2005)	Varies by course between $4,600 and 7,670 (watch this space)
Australian full-fees (2005)	

All data in Australian dollars with USD $1.00 = AUD $1.50; 2005 Australian charges expressed in 2003 prices.

Source: For American data: Geiger (2003: 14).

universities have opted for the maximum possible HECS. Second, public universities can charge direct tuition fees at whatever level they like for up to 35 per cent of the places in each course. Third, fee-paying students in both the public universities and accredited private institutions will be eligible for income-contingent loans under the government-backed FEE-HELP. Repayments under both HECS-HELP and FEE-HELP[5] will be income contingent, with no real interest rate, though students taking loans under FEE-HELP will be subject to an additional annual surcharge of $2,000.

These new arrangements will create a differentiated price-based undergraduate market, based on a voucher-like system of subsidised loans. With the cost gap between full-fee places and HECS places reduced, many students will opt for fee-paying places in prestigious universities and courses rather than HECS places in less desired courses. The cost gap between HECS places in public universities and fee places in private institutions will also narrow, making a large-scale private sector viable for the first time. For students overall, costs will rise sharply. There are two compensatory policies. First, scholarships of up to $24,000 per course will be offered to a small number of students from low socioeconomic status or isolated backgrounds. Second, and much more substantially, there will be a higher income threshold for repayments under HECS and FEE-HELP. This has been fixed at an indexed $35,000 per year (a higher repayment threshold also helps to make full-fee places economically viable). Later, the government can create a unified undergraduate market, with variable levels of public subsidy per place, by lifting the cap on maximum HECS, extending HECS to the private sector, and abolishing the surcharge on FEE-HELP places.

Post-Nelson the HECS will be redefined from a student contribution to the costs of a publicly funded place to a public subsidy ('scholarship') that covers part of the private cost of fees. The Nelson package abandons the purpose that guided the HECS, namely user charges without deterrent effects. Meanwhile the Nelson reforms bring Australian cost levels and structures closer to those of the United States. The cost gap between an Australian HECS place and an American in-state public university place is largely closed; and in the longer term, full-fee places supported by FEE-HELP will allow prestige Australian universities to charge fees approaching American private sector levels in sought after faculties such as law, medicine and dentistry. A University of Sydney or Melbourne law degree at $25,000 per year exceeds the production costs but students would pay the difference as it reflects the positional value of the degree, given that most law graduates from these universities enter high-income earning careers. Thus the Nelson package tends to join the markets in elite university places in the two nations; one effect of increasing the domestic price of prestige Australian degrees will be to encourage investment in American university degrees. If families have to pay $20,000–25,000 per annum for prestige positional goods in Australia then an American doctoral university looms as an increasingly attractive alternative.After 2005, the number of fee-based places underpinned by FEE-HELP can be expected to increase rapidly (Chapman 2003). This will expand the public subsidisation of positional investments by individuals—mostly from socially advantaged groups—through unpaid loans and administrative costs,[6] and further reduce funding for the direct grants to institutions vital to the common research and teaching infrastructure. No doubt much of the

Table 62.4 Principal exporters and importers of tertiary education, 2001

OECD exporter nations	International students		Nations importing from OECD	International students	
	No.	Proportion of all students		No.	Proportion of all students
USA	475,169	3.5	China	124,000	n/a
UK	225,722	10.9	Korea	70,523	2.3
Germany	199,132	9.6	India	61,179	n/a
France	147,402	7.3	Greece	55,074	11.4
Australia	110,789	13.9	Japan	55,041	1.4
Japan	63,637	1.6	Germany	54,489	2.6
Canada	40,667	4.6	France	47,587	2.0
Spain	39,944	2.2	Turkey	44,204	2.6
Belgium	38,150	10.6	Morocco	43,063	n/a
Austria	31,682	12.0	Italy	41,485	2.3

Source: OECD (2003).

additional fee revenue will be squandered on the costs of competition, such as marketing. At the same time, fees and variable HECS will widen the resource gap between the Sandstones and other universities, as the Sandstones are best placed to charge high prices. Drawing new private investments from families used to investing in secondary education, most of the Sandstones, at least, will strengthen their resource base. Part of this will be ploughed into research capacity, including remuneration for high performers, because research is the global source of prestige and competitiveness, again widening their advantage over other universities. At the lower levels of the hierarchy, there will be a 'race to the bottom' as institutions struggle to fill their places. Both of their strategic options—varying HECS charges downwards, and investing resources in marketing—will reduce the resources for teaching and learning, and thin out their research capacity.

The overall effect is to stretch the vertical hierarchy and widen the gaps between segments. Price variation enables a more differentiated set of economic choices, but matched by steep variations in educational quality. Because high-value course choices in the research-intensive universities command higher prices, and research-intensive provision itself—once government dependent, but now increasingly market dependant—is more firmly restricted, it becomes more difficult than before to access world-class education. Thus the protection and extension of market relations in education helps those with prior economic, social and cultural advantages to consolidate their position. The driving force of the Nelson reforms is the economisation of social privilege in education. Elite university education becomes continuous with independent private schooling at secondary level. First the Sandstones are restructured as a high-cost segment dependent on private investment. Second, the price mechanism is installed to mediate access and redifferentiate both consumption and production. The social pyramid becomes more closely aligned to the educational pyramid. The outcome is a neater, tighter (and fiscally cheaper) positional market: one more closed, with less competition for the Sandstones from below. The Sandstones will not need to become great innovators to maintain their domestic edge: the extent to which they are under pressure to innovate will depend on their openness to global competition. Closer market relations with leading Anglo-Australian families, and less reliance on international fee revenues, might encourage greater insularity. But unlike the USA Australia is not an imperial power; and in the longer term its university quality will be globally referenced. At the bottom of the market costs will be low, as well as quality. Total participation may not fall. The more important effect is the stratification of participation. The rising cost of HECS, fees and income-contingent loans will stream low-income families away from the high-cost, high-value places. In terms of equality of opportunity, the crucial questions become not so much whether or not there is access to higher education, but 'access to *what?*', and '*who* obtains it'? (Bastedo and Gumport 2003).

Global Markets in Higher Education

There are two forms of global market in higher education. First, there is the market that has developed out of student movement across national borders, such as full-fee undergraduate and Masters coursework programs provided to international students in Australia. With one significant exception—international education in the leading American research universities and a handful of British institutions—this kind of global market does not replace the national markets in higher education. There is not one single unified world market with all students choosing freely between different nations. For the most part students continue to be educated within national systems, with a small but growing minority moving between national systems. The size of that minority varies by nation. In 2001, 2 per cent of students from OECD nations accessed foreign education, and foreign students constituted just over 5 per cent of students in the OECD nations. However in Malaysia in 2001 6 per cent of tertiary students moved offshore (OECD 2003); and in Australia in 2003 international students, of whom three quarters were located within Australia, constituted 22.6 per cent of all higher education students (DEST 2004).

The economic character of international education also varies. It is fully commercial in the UK, Australia and New Zealand, heavily subsidised in Japan and the USA, and free of tuition charges in parts of Germany. Nevertheless, it is meaningful to refer to a global market. There is a defined field of production (higher education) with identifiable products (degrees and diplomas) that increasingly conform to a Bachelor/Masters/Doctoral structure along American lines. Most international students pay fees. Nations and institutions compete for the status and/or revenues they bring, with some competing more vigorously than others. Students make choices between competing offerings, in which they seek to maximise individual outcomes. Essentially, what export nations provide are the positional advantages gained from global mobility, in three spheres, albeit varying by field of study. First, back in the home nation a foreign education provides skills and prestige. Second, there may be prospects of working in and migrating to the nation where the foreign education is acquired. American immigration policies encourage high-skilled graduates to stay, for example in ICTs and research. Third, there are a growing number of globally mobile jobs in fields such as business, ICTs, engineering and technologies and scientific research (OECD 2002). The language of international business and global academic life is English, so all English-speaking education systems are targeted and there is particularly strong demand for American education (Mazzarol et al. 2001). The global market is especially important in nations where opportunities for upward mobility are constrained, but even where the number of tertiary places of good quality is adequate to meet demand, as in Korea and Japan, there is strong positional demand for an English-language foreign education.[7]

Within the national dimension, as noted, the number of high-value positional goods is subject to absolute limitations. This constrains the potential for high-fee, high-value places, sets limits on the number of elite producers, and rules out the potential for expansionary commercial production that at the same time enjoys high status. In the global dimension no such limits apply. As long as educational border crossing creates positional goods—as long as a foreign education leverages upward social mobility within and between nations—there is no foreseeable limit to the growth of the global positional market. The export market can expand freely without devaluing the unit value of global positional goods within producer nations such as Australia and the UK. Thus the market in international education can operate on a fully capitalist basis without immediately changing the character of the higher education of domestic students. International education has become Australia's third largest services export, and provides significant fiscal relief. In 2002, universities earned \$1.45 billion in student fees, 13 per cent of revenues (DEST 2003); and Australia earned about \$5 billion in total from international student spending on fees, food, transport, accommodation, living costs and entertainment, on and offshore (Nelson 2003*a*: 35).

International education in the American research universities and a handful of British institutions plays a special role within the market in cross-border education. In the global era, in which all research universities are networked and visible, and the leading institutions have a powerful presence throughout the world as both ideal-exemplars and practical leaders of the sector, these universities have come to constitute a worldwide market of elite institutions, attracting bright students and high achieving academic staff from every nation. The Ivy League universities value their hegemonic role, though it is largely subordinate to their national role in leadership selection and training, especially in the United States. Thus while only a small number of foreign students actually access Harvard, Stanford and Oxford each year, these universities exercise great symbolic power as producers of the highest value positional goods on offer. Increasingly, their global status overshadows the leading universities within national systems outside the USA/UK. This worldwide market does not replace the national markets, but it does subordinate them.

The second global market is constituted by doctoral training. Here there are signs that a single world market is emerging, not only subordinating the status of national systems of doctoral training but also substituting for them to an increasing extent. High achieving research students, not only from developing nations but in nations such as Australia with a viable national system of research training, are increasingly drawn to the 'world graduate school' based on the American universities and Oxford and Cambridge. 'Doctoral education, particularly in the sciences, is perhaps the most perfectly competitive market in higher education' (Geiger 2003: 3–4). It is a classic positional competition. Departments compete for the highest scoring students and students seek places in the preferred departments. Student places are scarce and are subsidised by scholarship funding, rather than subject to the expansionary capitalist dynamic of the market in vocational Masters degrees. American universities compete for the best students from everywhere: more than half their doctoral graduates in engineering are foreign, and over 30 per cent in the natural sciences. A study by the OECD notes that, of the doctoral students in American institutions, 60 per cent or more from each of India, China, the UK, Peru, Iran, Greece, Argentina and Germany had 'firm plans' to stay in the US after finishing their studies (Tremblay 2002: 44).

Student Flows in the Global Markets

The global markets are structured by student flows that are uneven and asymmetrical between nations. Some nations are primarily exporters, others are primarily importers; while a third group, including Japan and parts of Europe, exhibit a pattern of more balanced two-way exchange. The diagram simplifies the picture by leaving out Latin America, Africa and central Asia, concentrating on the dynamic parts of the global market. It illustrates:

- the magnetic attraction of American higher education, which is associated with globally superior positional opportunities;
- the UK, Australia, Canada and New Zealand sitting in the American slipstream, operating on a more entrepreneurial basis than American institutions. They gain a referred power as lesser English-language educational providers and sites

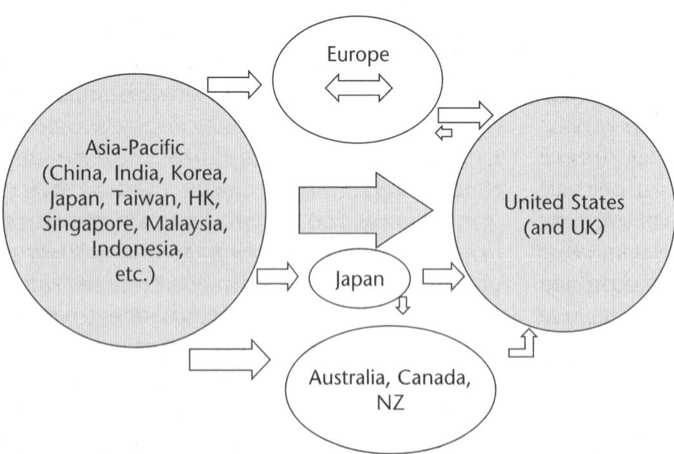

Fig. 62.1 Student flows in the worldwide environment of higher education
Source: Author.

for migration, sometimes as a transitional stage in passage to the USA;

- the massive demand for foreign education in the Asia-Pacific. Despite the frequent movement between contiguous European countries, four of the five largest importing nations are in the Asia-Pacific—China, Korea, India and Japan—and Malaysia, Indonesia, Hong Kong and Singapore are also in the top twenty importing nations. In 2001 the English-speaking countries enrolled 71.6 per cent of international students from Asia (OECD 2003);
- the extensive student flows within Europe, largely of a non-commercial nature. European universities also educate many students from the developing world.

In the Asia-Pacific region there is immense potential for the further growth of demand for education as a global positional good. The Asia-Pacific nations constitute well over half of the world's population, including three of the four largest nations: China, India and Indonesia. Ten of the world's sixteen cities with over ten million people are in the Asia-Pacific, representing immense concentrations of present and future demand for education. In China there have been two decades of high economic growth and the nation could produce one-fifth of world GDP by 2050. Expenditure on tertiary education is relatively low, and in 2000 only 8 per cent of the school leaver age group entered degree-level courses in China, a third of the level in Australia. Unmet demand in China will increase steeply because, though China will expand and upgrade domestic provision, the growth of middle-class demand for tertiary education will outstrip the roll-out of new institutions and places. Thailand and Indonesia are other countries where unmet demand can be expected to be high even without the extra incentive constituted by the positional value of foreign education. In much of the Asia-Pacific the habit of private investment is entrenched. In Korea 70 per cent of domestic expenditure on tertiary institutions is private spending, in Japan 56 per cent, in Indonesia 56 per cent, in China 43 per cent (OECD 2003).

Table 62.5 Principal sources of international students, USA and Australia (2002)

USA 2002–3		Australia 2002	
India	74,603	Singapore	29,956
China	64,757	Hong Kong China	26,956
Korea	51,519	Malaysia	23,725
Japan	45,960	China mainland	19,596
Taiwan	28,107	Indonesia	11,981
Canada	26,513	India	8,390
Mexico	12,801	USA	8,325
Turkey	11,601	UK	5,752
Indonesia	10,432	Thailand	5,202
Thailand	9,982	Taiwan	3,977

Sources: IIE (2003), DEST (2003).

Implications for National Markets

The growth of global markets has a number of implications for national markets and the national hierarchy of universities. First, in more entrepreneurial export nations such as Australia it has encouraged the installation of business cultures within universities, with potential to transform local as well as foreign operations. In some universities, especially the more recently established ones, corporatisation is associated with the weakening of academic cultures, with negative long-term implications for research capacity (Marginson and Considine 2000). Second, the emergence of a large-scale market sector serving international students, alongside domestic students, introduces a fatal ambiguity into the old national project of equalising educational opportunities between social groups. Monitoring the social patterns of access on a national scale becomes less meaningful, especially given the increasing leakages from the national pool. The social elite has the superior option of investment in American education, and exercises it to a growing degree; the large number of international students muddies the waters of local merit-based competition for places; and entrepreneurial global markets popularise the notion that opportunities can be bought, encouraging the installation of local fee systems on supposed 'equity' grounds. Notwithstanding the provision of loans and scholarships, systems in which there is direct charging for tuition always favours those families with a superior capacity to pay.

Third, and on the other hand, global markets offer all institutions, elite or not, a wider set of strategic options, identities and development paths. They can specialise in international partnerships, ICT-based linkages, international marketing or a more cosmopolitan curriculum. Suddenly institutions find themselves operating in more than one sphere at the same time, using the outcomes of strategies in one sphere (resources, networks, reputation) as inputs in the other. They also face new tensions between domestic investment and global investment options. Nevertheless, and while elite status is an advantage in the global as well as national markets, universities locked out of the elite segment of their national systems can position themselves as providers of high-value positional goods for students from elsewhere. At the same time, there are limits to this. Most revenues continue to be sourced not globally, but nationally and locally, from government grants for research and teaching, and from student fees. Even in export-oriented Australia, only 13 per cent of revenues derived from international students in 2003; and institutions spend more on globally linked research activity than they generate in international research funding. Universities that have placed especially high emphasis on the global dimension, such as RMIT and Central Queensland in Australia, risk over-exposure and resource instability.

Fourth, the global market also has another and profound implication for universities in all nations other than the USA. By bringing a new and superior layer of high-value positional opportunities within view (if not necessarily within reach) of middle-class families everywhere, it relativises the local Ivy League, disturbing the traditional conservatism of national positional markets. Suddenly, venerable and unchallengeable universities become less attractive and more vulnerable; undermined by the gravitational pull of the global markets; the global character of research and judgments about the value of knowledge; and the in-your-face visibility of American institutions in a networked era. This affects both leading universities in nations such as Australia—which at least can become global players in their own right—and in developing countries, where institutions lack the capacity in research and communications technologies and the national geo-strategic power to make a ready transition into the global era, facing fewer options and more constraints (Marginson and Sawir, forthcoming). Nevertheless, some local/national university traditions are more robust than others, some nations and institutions are more open to global influences than others, and the capacity to pursue a proactive global strategy is unevenly distributed throughout the world. Certain national governments underpin the forward strategies of their institutions in the global higher education environment (much the wisest policy), some offer their universities domestic protection from those same global market forces, and others leave it to the market to sort their universities out. Australian policies largely fall between categories two and three.

Thus, in relation to equality of opportunity, global markets have mixed effects. On the one hand, they offer the potential to free up the national hierarchy of universities, to at least some extent, while providing new positional options for middle-class families in developing nations. On the other hand, global markets undermine the old project of equalising social opportunities within national borders, and reproduce new patterns of global hierarchy and inequality in universities. Within developing nations, like global business activity, global higher education also fosters globally connected local elites, creating inequalities of opportunity between haves and have nots.

Global University Hierarchy

The global markets are subject to global segmentation, in which the world market is constituted by a small number of major players, and all developed nations subordinate all developing nations: 93.5 per cent of international students are enrolled in the OECD nations. English-language nations enjoy a post-imperial advantage, and American universities are unchallengeable—at least until there are global shifts in economic and cultural power, for example through the growth of East and Southeast Asian nations, especially China. American universities dominate institution-to-institution networking. Universities in the different global regions tend to have partial linkages with other regions but are always linked to universities in the United States, which is the global communications and business hub (Castells 2001). Recently the Shanghai Jiao Tong University Institute of Higher Education (2003) compiled a ranking of world universities based on research and academic performance.[8] The Shanghai Jiao Tong University Institute rankings found that:

- of the top twenty universities, fifteen were from the USA and four from the UK. There was only one other nation in the top twenty, Japan via the University of Tokyo;
- of the top fifty universities, thirty-five—*more than two-thirds*—were from the USA;
- of the top 101 universities, almost three-quarters were from the English-speaking nations: fifty-eight from the USA, nine from the UK, four from Canada and two from Australia: the Australian National University and the University of Melbourne.[9] There were also five universities from Japan, and twenty-three from Western European and Israel including five from Germany, and three each from Switzerland, Sweden and the Netherlands (see Table 62.6).

Given the market power of the American universities it is ironic that Americans mostly see international education as a form of foreign aid and cultural exchange, rather than as a source of revenue. There is an intense domestic competition between the American universities for top students, leading academic staff and research reputations; but American universities do not approach global competition with the same vigour. American global hegemony is exercised without entrepreneurial marketing. It is sustained by American economic, technological, cultural and military power; by the extraordinary resources US universities command, and by their academic prestige. These universities do not have to adjust their programs or cultural ambiance to attract international support. American universities do not sell an internationalised curriculum; they freely offer themselves as the global standard. Foreign students flock to them, like the crowds of tourists streaming into Disneyland. Globalisation—in education as in other sectors—is what America does to the world, not what the world does to America.

In sum, global education is produced and consumed in terms of a worldwide university hierarchy in which not only is global equality of opportunity absent, *global educational inequality is necessary to* the commercial market in international education (though not to non-commercial educational exchange, as the heavy traffic of students in Western Europe demonstrates). Global hierarchy creates global positional goods, making it worthwhile to invest in border crossing and worthwhile for Australian universities to grow their international education enrolments. It is global socioeconomic inequality not educational quality that drives the market: 'Capital invested in foreign trade can yield a higher rate of profit ... because it competes with commodities produced by other countries with less well developed production facilities, so that the more advanced country sells its goods above their value' (Marx 1981: 344–5). Correspondingly the global educational market tends to reproduce these global inequalities of power. It maintains the unequal value of education in the developing world compared to the developed world, and sustains asymmetries in student flows, capital flows, cultural engagement and cultural respect. Students from developed nations rarely enrol in developing countries. Economic revenues flow from the developing countries to the export nations, and aid dollars rarely compensate. By spreading English language and Americanised practises, global education markets colonise non-English cultures and identities. The half a million Asian students who enter the English-speaking education systems each year come from very diverse linguistic backgrounds. Apart from English, in the Asia-Pacific there are fourteen languages that are each spoken by 65 million people or more, including Putonghua (Mandarin) by 1,000 million, Hindi and Urdu by 900 million, Bengali by 250 million and Indonesian/Malay by 160 million (Linguasphere Observatory 2003). All of these languages could become alternative global mediums, but the global university markets relentlessly reproduce the hegemony and homogeneity of English. The bedrock assumption of English-language universities is that native English speakers have little to learn in other

Table 62.6 World's top 101 universities ranked on research and publications, according to the Shanghai Jiao Tong University Institute of Higher Education, 2003

	Institution	Nation
1	Harvard	USA
2	Stanford	USA
3	California IT	USA
4	California—Berkeley	USA
5	Cambridge	UK
6	Massachusetts IT	USA
7	Princeton	USA
8	Yale	USA
9	Oxford	UK
10	Columbia	USA
11	Chicago	USA
12	Cornell	USA
13	California—San Francisco	USA
14	California—San Diego	USA
15	California—Los Angeles	USA
16	Washington, Seattle	USA
17	Imperial College	UK
18	Pennsylvania	USA
19	Tokyo	Japan
20	University College London	UK
21	Michigan—Ann Arbor	USA
22	Washington, St Louis	USA
23	Toronto	Canada
24	Johns Hopkins	USA
25	Swiss Fed. IT Zurich	Switzerland
26	California—Santa Barbara	USA
27	Wisconsin Madison	USA
28	Rockefeller	USA
29	Northwestern	USA
30	Kyoto	Japan
31	Colorado—Boulder	USA
32	Vanderbilt	USA
32	Duke	USA
34	Texas—SW Med. Centre	USA
35	British Columbia	Canada
36	California—Davis	USA
37	Minnesota—Twin Cities	USA
38	Rutgers—New Brunswick	USA
39	Karolinska I—Stockholm	Sweden
40	Pennsylvania S—U Park	USA
40	Utrecht	Netherlands
40	Southern California	USA
43	Edinburgh	UK
44	California—Irvine	USA
45	Illinois—Urbana Champ.	USA
45	Zurich	Switzerland
47	Texas—Austin	USA
48	Munich	Germany
49	Brown	USA
49	Australian National	Australia
50		
51	Case Western Reserve	USA
52	North Carolina—Chapel Hill	USA
53	Osaka	Japan
53	Pittsburgh	USA
55	Arizona	USA
55	Bristol	UK
55	New York	USA
58	Heidelberg	Germany
59	Uppsala	Sweden
60	Technical U Munich	Germany
61	Rice	USA
61	Carnegie Mellon	USA
63	Oslo	Norway
64	Tohoku	Japan
65	Paris 06	France
65	Copenhagen	Denmark
67	Virginia	USA
68	Nagoya	Japan
68	Sheffield	UK
70	Roma—La Sapienza	Italy
70	Texas A & M U College Station	USA
72	Rochester	USA
72	Paris 11	France
74	Helsinki	Finland
75	Maryland—College Park	USA
75	Florida	USA
75	King's College London	UK
78	Leiden	Netherlands
79	McGill	Canada
80	Purdue—West Lafayette	USA
81	Ohio State—Columbia	USA
81	Utah	USA
83	Tufts	USA
84	Vienna	Austria
84	Groningen	Netherlands
86	McMaster	Canada
87	Michigan State	USA
88	California—Riverside	USA

Table 62.6 *(Continued)*

	Institution	Nation
89	Manchester	UK
90	Iowa	USA
91	Gottingen	Germany
92	Melbourne	Australia
93	Lund	Sweden
94	Hebrew U Jerusalem	Israel
95	Free U Berlin	Germany
96	Basel	Switzerland
96	Illinois—Chicago	USA
98	Boston	USA
99	North Carolina State—Raleigh	USA
100	Ghent	Belgium
101	Emory	USA

Source: SJTUIHE (2003).

languages. Along with global hegemony comes global insularity, a blindness to other languages and the cultures embedded in them, regardless of the immense richness these entail.

Yet some global educational flows are two-way; and, as emerging nations strengthen, more of their international graduates return or invest in the country of origin and feed their knowledge and skills into the national university system. In the longer term nations must develop their own national capacity in higher education to modify Americanisation and maximise their strategic options within the worldwide university network. As Singapore and Taiwan have shown, robust emerging nations can reverse the brain drain and transform their educational position. The clear losers in the global education market are those developing nations that are too weak to sustain their own national and university identities or provide sufficient opportunities to draw back their foreign-educated graduates.

For the lesser English-language providers such as Australia, the Americanised market presents more subtle difficulties for national identity and strategy. Australia has positioned itself as a high growth provider by good marketing and management, inventive off-shore engagement, a specialisation in high-volume standard-cost training in business and IT, improving non-academic services, proximity to Southeast Asia, a friendly climate and a peaceful social atmosphere, and a price advantage over the USA and UK deriving from a weak Australian dollar. IDP (2001) estimates that the average total cost of fees and living expenses in the American public universities was $19,427. It was $19,159 in the UK, where living costs are relatively high. In Australia it was $12,482, and in New Zealand $11,712. Australia's costs were therefore less than two-thirds of those in the UK and the American public universities. It is not surprising that Australian international education is price dependent rather than quality dependent given that average student-staff ratios have risen from 12 to 21 since the mid-1980s (DEST 2004). But such a price advantage is not secure in the long term. In addition, the discipline base and countries of origin are narrowly targeted; there is no product differentiation—Australian education in business and IT is much the same as American or British education—and, because there are few educational aid dollars to finance international research degrees, the research student strand is weak. Most bright international students prefer to study in the USA and the UK. The danger for Australia is that by selling itself as 'America on the cheap' it has boxed itself into a market niche, that of the global polytechnic.

For Asia-Pacific countries, Australian international education is associated with a downgrading of global equity and other global public goods. The dichotomy of 'trade versus aid', and the policy decision to opt for the, former at the expense of the latter—rather than pursue both in balanced fashion—guaranteed that. The production of global common goods in education is more effectively addressed by forms of internationalisation other than market exchange, such as scholarship programs, noncommercial student exchange, and cooperative research projects.

NOTES

This [chapter] is a revised version of the Radford Lecture delivered to the NZARE/AARE Joint Conference, Auckland, New Zealand, 29 November to 3 December 2003.

1. Institutions are reimbursed for an amount equivalent to the HECS obligations of their students, as part of government funding.
2. The Sandstone group here includes the Australian National University, Monash University and the University of New South Wales, although these are more recent post-Second World War foundations for which (following the architectural metaphor) the title 'Redbrick' might seem more appropriate. Redbricks is the term used in Marginson and Considine (2000). However, in popular usage the term 'Sandstones' has come to include these three, sharing as they do the prestige of the older foundations, and common membership of the elite segment in the 'Group of 8'.
3. For detailed discussion of the segments in the Australian system see Marginson and Considine (2000: 175–232).
4. The IGS formula is income from research grants (60 per cent of the IGS), the number of higher degree research students (30 per cent) and publications over the previous two years (10 per cent): see Nelson (2003*b*: 103–4).
5. The new fees/loans system from 2005 absorbs the PELS system of loans for fee-charging postgraduate courses introduced in 2002.
6. In the first full year of operation of the Commonwealth government's Postgraduate Education Loan Scheme (PELS) in 2002, 11,387 students, constituting 33 per cent of all fee-paying domestic postgraduates, took out a PELS loan at an average liability per full-time equivalent student of $10,076 for one year (Nelson 2003*b*: 68).
7. Like participation in higher education itself, once the acquisition of foreign education becomes a normal practice of middle-class families, it becomes not so much a method of gaining a special advantage, as a 'defensive necessity' (Hirsch 1976) for maintaining social position and retaining the effectiveness of the family business.
8. The criteria were the number of Nobel laureates associated with the university, the number of highly cited researchers (1981–99), articles in *Nature* and *Science* (2000–2), articles cited in the science index and the social science index, and academic performance per academic staff member using the above indicators.
9. The Shanghai Jiao Tong University Institute did not give precise rankings after 101, but bracketed the universities in groups of fifty. It included a total of twelve Australian universities in the top 500, including Sydney and Queensland (between 102 and 151), Monash, NSW and Western Australia (152–200), Adelaide (201–50), Macquarie (301–50), Newcastle and Tasmania (351–400) and La Trobe (401–50). There were 160 American doctoral universities in the top 500.

Issues in the Expansion of Higher Education in the People's Republic of China

Henry M. Levin and Zeyu Xu

[...]

Introduction

The current expansion of higher education in the People's Republic of China is unprecedented in magnitude. In this [chapter] we wish to speculate on some of the issues that have arisen in a situation of rapid growth and numerical expansion in enrolments that is incomparably greater that historical experience elsewhere. The purpose of this [chapter] is to suggest issues and areas that might be explored in a way to encourage maximization of effectiveness of available resources,[1] a challenge that is especially acute when ambitious plans for expansion are proposed. The work will be organized in the following way: In the next section we will present the background to the present organization and growth of higher education in China as well as future plans. We will also review the actual accomplishments that have taken place in recent years. The following section will suggest the magnitudes of faculty and staff needed to accommodate expansion. Finally, we will review some specific issues with major emphasis on the establishment of a qualified teaching and research staff that can keep pace with enrolment increases.

A note of caution is in order. Changes in higher education in China are taking place rapidly in terms of both the organization of the higher education industry and expansion of student enrolments, faculty and staff, and facilities. The fact that these changes are dynamic means that precise information at any point in time is difficult to obtain. In addition, raw data from nationwide higher education establishment surveys are not publicly available at the time of this report. Thus, we see this [chapter] as exploratory, with an attempt to capture the larger trends and to suggest their implications. At some later point we may be able to achieve greater precision.

Higher Education in China: Organization and Plans

The structure of higher education in China has evolved through three stages of development. Modern higher education first emerged in China at the turning point of the twentieth century, mainly following the European model.[2] By 1949, when the People's Republic of China was founded, in terms of the number of institutions 60.4% of the colleges were public, 29.8% were private and 9.7% were missionary.[3] The second stage started at the end of 1952, when all institutions were integrated into the public sector.[4] During this stage, Chinese higher education followed the Soviet model and was an integrated part of highly centralized national planning.

From the *China Review* 5/1 (Spring, 2005), 33–59. Reprinted with permission.

Comprehensive universities were discouraged from developing, and the structural focus was on over-specialized institutes that were dominated by the demands of specific industrial sectors, enterprises and even the needs for certain products.[5] Chinese higher education in this period was dominated by small-scale science and engineering institutions. In 1962, only 6.8% of college students were majoring in arts and humanities.[6]

Beginning in the 1980s, Chinese higher education started a new structural reshuffle, representing a shift from a centrally planned scheme to a more market-oriented scheme.[7] Two major changes reshaped the landscape. First, more schooling types became available to cater to the differential demands of a large population. Along the dimension of ownership, private tertiary education re-emerged alongside the existing public sector in the 1990s. By the end of 2003, there were 175 regular private higher education institutions that were recognized by the Ministry of Education, with 1,104 other types of private higher education groups or organizations.[8] The private sector, however, is still modest in size, almost all of the institutions being two-year colleges. The higher education system consists of regular institutions and adult institutions. In 2001, there were 1,225 regular colleges and universities and 686 adult colleges.[9] Regular institutions are further divided into four-year universities and two-year colleges. Adult tertiary education takes more diversified forms, ranging from radio/TV universities, workers' colleges and independent correspondence colleges, to evening schools run by regular universities. In the past several years, the adult tertiary education sector has been shrinking quickly in terms of both the number of schools and the number of full-time teachers. Within three years, from 1999 to 2001, the number of adult colleges dropped 28.7% and the number of full-time teachers dropped by 8.7%.

The second major change occurred with the administrative structure of higher education. The previous development stage resulted in small school sizes, redundant establishment of majors and low education and research efficiency. Before the 'Ninth Five-Year Plan' (1996–2000), there were two types of institutions in terms of administrative affiliations: national universities and regional universities. National universities included those directly administered by the Ministry of Education, and those reporting to their corresponding specialized national ministries, state-owned enterprises and national associations. For example, Beijing University was under the administration of the Ministry of Education, Petroleum University belonged to China Petroleum and Natural Gas Corporation, and China Central Academy of Music reported to the Ministry of Culture. Similarly, some regional universities were administered by the local education bureaus, and others by local ministries and state-owned enterprises. This structure of sponsorship applied to both regular and adult colleges and universities.

Since the 'Ninth Five-Year Plan,' this administrative structure has become regionalized and simplified. Although not yet fully completed, the reform assigned universities under two types of administrative authorities: those under the Ministry of Education or the education departments at the provincial level, and those administered by local governments. Specialized ministries and state-owned enterprises no longer assume administrative responsibilities for higher education, a major shift. Private institutions are usually established under the local municipalities.

Ten-Year Plans

The central government defined two new strategic development goals for higher education at the beginning of the 'Tenth Five-year Plan' (2001–2005): *expand substantially the scale of higher education*, and *establish world-class universities*. These goals were motivated by two considerations: the increasing demand for high-level human resources and technological innovations due to rapid economic growth and globalization, and the need for a developed tertiary education sector to strengthen the international profile of China as a prospering nation.

Before 1995, the higher education gross enrolment ratio (using full-time student equivalent numbers) had been consistently below 7%. Even in 2001, less than 4% of the labour force in China had tertiary degrees. In order to undertake the heavy burden of providing a large population with human resource advantages, the Ministry of Education stipulated that by 2005, the end of the 'Tenth Five-year Plan,' higher education enrolment should reach 16 million, among which 0.6 million are graduate students. The gross enrolment ratio of the age group (18–22 years old) will reach 15%. By 2010, higher education enrolment should reach 23 million, with nearly 1 million graduate students, and the gross enrolment ratio should reach around 20%.[10] To give some idea of the magnitudes of these numbers, consider that the US had about 13 million undergraduates and about 2 million graduate and professional students in the year 2000, with projections of undergraduates to about 15 million in 2010, the growth largely reflecting the increase in youth demography.[11]

Higher education in China is expected to shift from 'elitist education' to 'mass education.' To ensure the realization of such goals, provisions have been made to promote: (a) the resources devoted to higher education, including both increasing the national effort for higher education and diversifying the sources of funding; (b) the establishment and refining of higher education laws and regulations, and the evaluation, monitoring and accountability systems; and (c) the quality of higher education from both the teaching and the learning sides so that the expansion in quantity is accompanied by the improvement of the quality of high-level human resources.[12]

The expansion goals focusing on the teaching and learning in colleges and universities and the establishment of world-class universities mainly target research carried out by higher education institutions. The earliest mention of the goal was in 1995 and 1998. A 'world-class' university must have four characteristics: It is the cradle of high-quality researchers with outstanding creativity. It is the frontier of scientific research. It is an important force to transform research and innovation into higher productivity. And finally, it is a bridge for international academic and cultural exchange.[13] Two major governmental projects, the '211 project' and the '985 project,' give substantial financial support for a small group of selected universities that aspire to become world-class universities. Since the standards of 'world-class universities' are dynamic, no specific goals have been set for 2005 or 2010. However, the current leading universities will improve on the following aspects: the number of academic achievements, advanced laboratories, and world-renowned scientists, the amount of research funds, the number of graduate students and post-doctoral positions, modern administration, student quality, and active international exchange. With the increasing availability of government research funds and competitive funds, it is expected that in ten years, teaching and research budgets of leading universities in China will approach those of world-class universities. Academic staff members at Beijing University and Tsinghua University are expected to publish around ten articles each year in top journals such as *Nature* and *Science*. It is also expected that in 2025, Beijing University and Tsinghua University will be able to join the world's top 100 universities.[14]

Actual Accomplishments

The actual accomplishments in the past several years are as impressive as the plans, whether measured by the increases in resources or the preliminary results of such increased efforts.

The per-student recurrent expenditure each year in regular institutions of higher education increased by 65.5% between 1992 and 2000, from RMB 6,178 to RMB 10,230.[15] The major part of the expansion came from personnel recurrent expenditures for the teaching and research core, which increased by 78.6% in that period (Figure 63.1). Non-core expenditures for administration, external relationships and maintenance expenses that are not directly linked to teaching and research were kept under careful control. The relatively flat growth of these non-core recurrent expenditures is the result of two adjustments: the reduction of support staff, and the reshuffling of administrative structures. The decreasing ratio of non-personnel expenditure is a sign of improving efficiency to the degree that it reflects a reduction in redundant employees and multiple administrative structures. Per student expenditure in regular higher education institutions, however, decreased in more recent years. The explosive expansion of higher education around the beginning of the twenty-first century, and the relatively stagnant, if not shrinking, national effort (as measured by educational expenditure as a percentage of GDP), might have contributed to such a change. These two points will be discussed later.

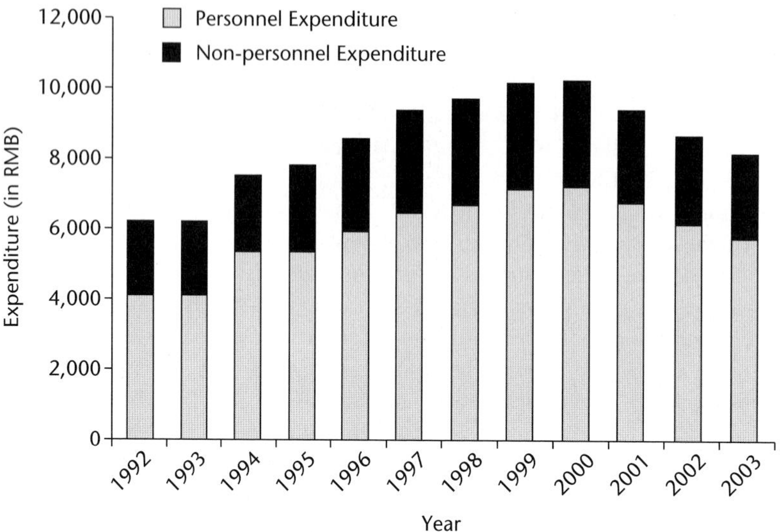

Fig. 63.1. Regular Institutions of Higher Education per student within-budget expenditure (unit: RMB, US$1 = RMB 8.3)
Source: China Ministry of Education, *Statistical Report on Educational Expenditures of Regular Higher Education Institutions* (2001). Available: http://www.moe.edu.cn/Stat/index.htm [2003, 1/17].

Total government spending on higher education increased from RMB 54.5 billion (US$ 6.7 billion) in 1998 to RMB 111.4 billion (US$ 13.6 billion) in 2001, doubling in three years.[16] The budgets and resources for research have increased substantially. For example, in 1999, the science and technology expenditure of regular higher education institutions was RMB 9.9 billion. Within one year, this figure jumped by 43.68% to reach 14.27 billion in 2000.[17] Both government funds and contract research funds increased substantially (Figure 63.2). Although government investments provide much stronger support to Beijing University and Tsinghua University than any other higher education institutions, some of the other universities managed to raise comparable amounts of science and technology funds from diversified resources. For example, Zhejiang University raised a total amount of RMB 610 million for science and technology research in 2000, ranking second in total budgets after Tsinghua. A total of 74.2% of the funds came from research contracts with enterprises and administrative organizations. As a comparison, 67.9% of Tsinghua's funds came from government direct investment.[18]

Increased governmental investment, diversified resources and improved efficiency have produced rapid expansion in terms of both teaching and research in the past several years. For a long time, the college entrance examination has been the most ferocious battlefield for Chinese students, and the gross enrolment ratio has been consistently below 7%. It has been especially difficult to get into national key universities, where the ratio of admissions to acceptances is even more selective. Within six years from 1996 to 2002, this ratio has more than doubled. In 2002, the gross enrolment ratio reached more than 15% of the corresponding age group (18–22) for the first time in history. In terms of absolute numbers of undergraduate students, from 1998–2001 the number of entrants more than doubled to reach 4.64 million; enrolments rose 88.6% to reach about 12 million, and graduates increased to nearly 2 million in 2001 (Figure 63.4).[19]

Graduate education has also expanded rapidly. From 1999 to 2001, the numbers of entrants, enrolments and graduates rose 79.2%, 68.4% and 23.9% respectively (Figure 63.5). After several years of very rapid increases in undergraduate enrolments, the 2003 higher education plan was designed to slow the pace of expansion to a 10% annual increase, while boosting the number of graduate students at a faster rate of 30%. In 2005, the number of graduate school entrants is projected to reach 370,000, which is nearly four times as many as the number of graduate entrants in 1999.

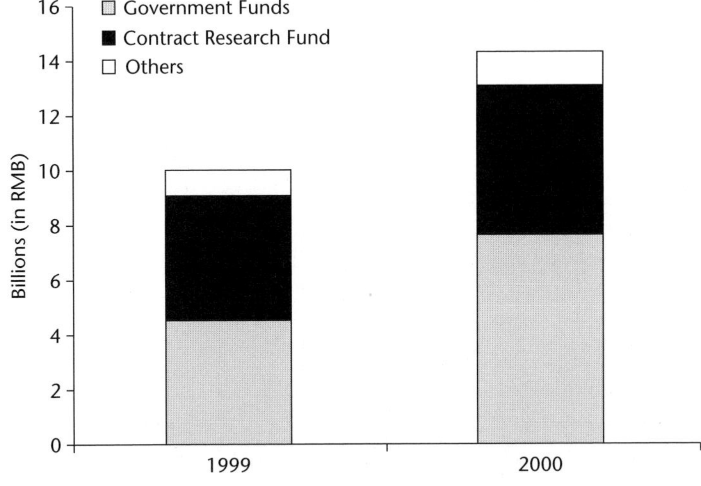

Fig. 63.2 Science and technology budgets in regular HEIs (units: RMB1 billion)
Source: China Ministry of Education, *Educational Statistics Yearbook of China*, 2001.

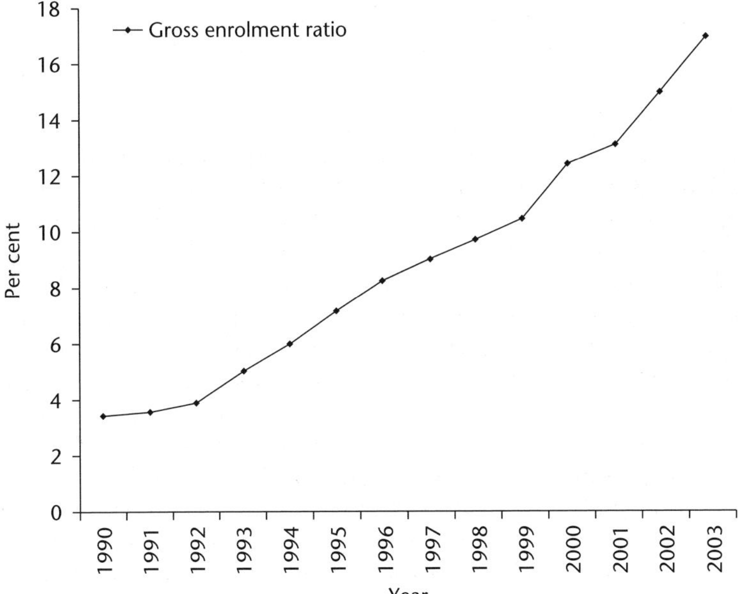

Fig. 63.3 Gross enrolment ratio (Age Group 18–22)
Sources: China Ministry of Education, *Statistical Report on National Educational Development*, 1999–2004.

Thus far, the expansion of higher education has met the ambitious levels set out in the plans. In contrast, there is little information on the quality of teaching in this expansionary phase. There are indications that the efficiency of higher education has improved. First, university size has increased to take advantage of scale. The old Soviet model resulted in very small university sizes. As late as 1992, regular higher education institutions only enrolled 2,074 students on average. By 2001, this number rose to 5,870 (Figure 63.6). At the same time, the student-teacher ratio has also increased. In 1990, the ratio was 5.2, mainly due to the large number of redundant and usually low-quality teaching staff. Today, this ratio has reached 13.5 (Figure 63.7).

Efforts have also been made to meet the goal of building world-class universities. Since this goal mainly targets research, the effects will take a longer time to achieve. However, based on the available data, some preliminary improvements are already

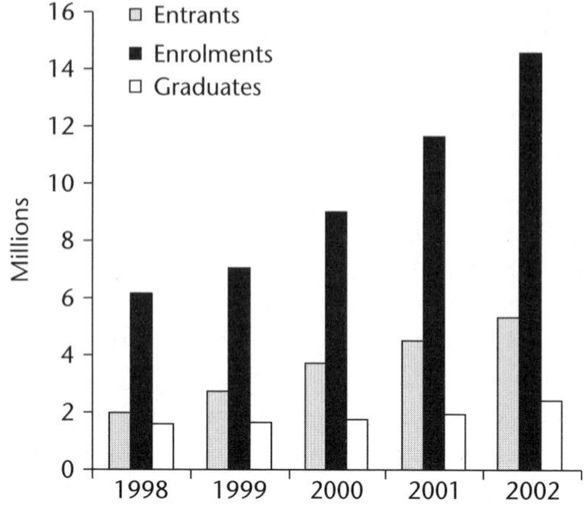

Fig. 63.4 Undergraduate enrolments
Sources: China Ministry of Education, *Statistical Report on National Educational Development*, 1999, 2000, 2001.

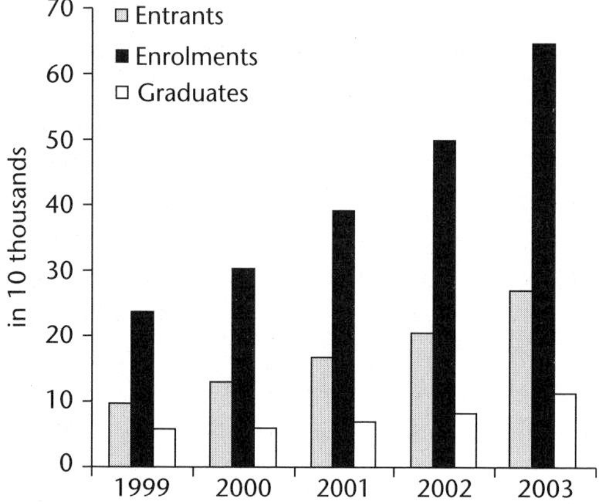

Fig. 63.5 Graduate school enrolments
Sources: China Ministry of Education, *Statistical Report on National Educational Development*, 1999, 2000, 2001.

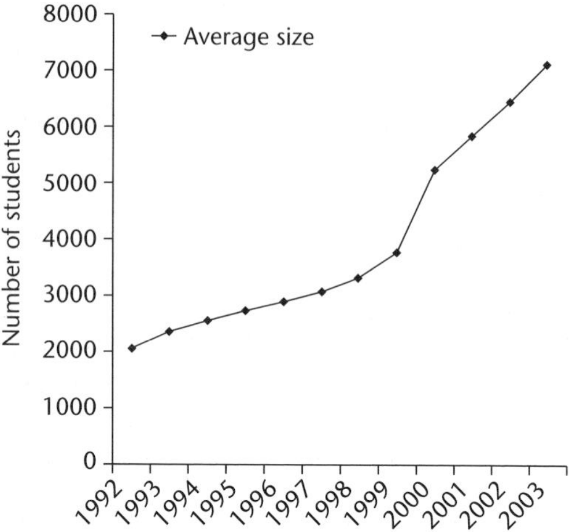

Fig. 63.6 Average size of regular HEIs
Sources: China Ministry of Education *Statistical Report on National Educational Development*, 1999–2003.

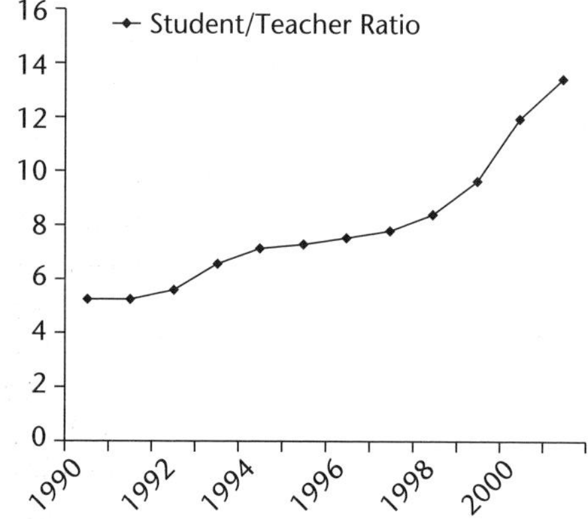

Fig. 63.7 Student/teacher ratio
Sources: *Educational Statistics Yearbook of China*, 2001.

obvious in terms of the number of publications, patents, and technological transfer contracts. The number of monographs published rose from 4,986 in 1999 to 5,347 in 2000. Published papers increased from 269,689 to 284,135, and the number of patents rose from 1,273 to 1,952. The revenue generated by selling patents rose from RMB 70 million in 1999 to 125.4 million in 2000. Similar patterns can be found with the number of technological transfer contracts and the revenue from those contracts. In 1999, regular higher education institutions received 3,973 contracts, with RMB 695 million in revenue. In 2000, the number of contracts reached 4,946, generating RMB 1.2 billion in revenue, a 73% increase from the previous year.[20]

In sum, since the start of the 'Tenth Five-year Plan,' higher education in China has expanded at a rate and magnitude that is unprecedented in the history of the country. The absolute expansion is unparalleled anywhere.

Challenges

In terms of expansion of enrolments, both the plan and actual accomplishments have been impressive.

The changes in rules and regulations governing higher education have also been substantial, although their impacts on overall educational results cannot be ascertained at this time. But, beyond these ambitious plans there has been a persistent concern for quality such that the major institutions would be comparable to world-class universities in both the quality of teaching and learning and in research. Substantial and continuing expansion of enrolments entails both massive capital construction and expenditure for classrooms, residential facilities, and research space and equipment as well as both professional and support personnel. All of these resource demands represent challenges. In this section, we raise a number of issues that must be addressed to fulfil the qualitative aspirations of the Chinese plan for higher education.

Because the qualitative aspirations for a group of selected Chinese higher education institutions are to meet world-class standards in teaching and research, we refer below to a specific public institution in the United States for purposes of comparing practices. That institution is the University of California at Los Angeles (UCLA), one of nine major campuses of the University of California.[21] UCLA, along with its sister institutions, the University of California at Berkeley, and the University of California at San Diego, are considered to be world-class universities in both teaching and research. Although a state institution, only a minority of its funding comes from the state, with the remainder derived from student fees, research grants and contracts, gifts, and other types of income. We will refer briefly to some features of UCLA in what follows.

Teaching Personnel

Obtaining adequate numbers of appropriately trained faculty can be a serious bottleneck to rapid expansion in enrolments. From the US experience, poor faculty quality is found to adversely affect graduation rates at four-year colleges[22] and reduce the likelihood of continuous enrolment in classes.[23] On the other hand, the presence of well-paid senior faculty produces students with significantly higher earnings later in life.[24] Therefore, we raise this issue as the first and foremost challenge in sustaining the current higher education expansion while ensuring its quality.

As part of the higher educational reforms, the hiring and contractual relations regarding teaching personnel have been modified dramatically. In the period following the Cultural Revolution, university faculty had employment commitments from the State that were not very different from other workers in the PRC. Once hired, they could expect to be employed continuously until retirement, a policy that was commonly termed 'the iron ricebowl.' Faculty hired during the Cultural Revolution often had no intellectual qualifications at all, and many highly qualified faculties lost their jobs during this period. Poor quality teaching and lack of research productivity were not uncommon in the past because there were few sanctions.

That policy has been largely reversed. Under the new arrangements for new hires, all contracts are granted for a specific term, usually one year. This means that, based upon performance and needs, they can be renewed or terminated, imparting great flexibility to adjusting the teaching force. In a time of rapid expansion, the practical impact of the new policies may be minimal because of the great need for additional faculty. It is very difficult to evaluate and release faculty with mediocre performance at a time when there is a shortage of qualified applicants. But, in the longer run the use of contracts of relatively short duration may have some negative consequences.

First, the lack of security for faculty is likely to mean higher voluntary turnover for those who can find more permanent positions outside teaching. The attractions of non-teaching positions may be greatest for those who are considered most productive, especially in the areas of science and technology, where both domestic and multinational firms are able to pay much higher salaries than can be found in teaching. Since China's accession to the WTO, domestic higher education institutions face direct competition from international education groups and multinational corporations for talent.[25] Faculty turnover not only limits the potential of higher education expansion but is also very costly. According to Ehrenberg et al., the cost of replacing departing senior scientists and engineers by highly talented, new assistant professors is often in the

$300,000 to $500,000 range.[26] Such costs have not yet included less quantifiable costs such as faculty morale or academic reputation. Second, at present hiring is largely in the hands of the key faculty in each field of specialization at each institution. This gives an enormous amount of power to relatively few persons in determining who will be hired and terminated, and will inhibit freedom of expression as teaching personnel are careful not to displease their decision-making benefactors. Intellectually there are many disputes and differences within most fields of specialization, and all or most should be represented in a first-class university. But, by concentrating decision-making power in the hands of relatively few senior faculty, it is likely that the views represented will echo those of the decision-makers. Indeed, this feature will invite considerable inbreeding as intellectuals with a narrow range of perspectives are produced by each university and hired to teach the next generation. Casual reports suggest that a very high proportion of teaching faculty is employed in the institutions at which they were trained. The undesirability of faculty inbreeding received a considerable amount of interest from researchers from the 1930s to the 1970s, and that research consistently found adverse impacts, such as lower research productivity of inbred faculty as compared to other faculty.[27]

In contrast with these policies, universities like UCLA follow very different procedures in selecting their faculties. UCLA delegates a committee of faculty from the pertinent department to carry out a search for a new faculty member. A national or international search is convened to attract a pool of the best candidates in terms of previous accomplishments, including teaching and research and representation of diverse specialties and perspectives. Top candidates from the search are reviewed by departmental faculty. If they are recommended by the department, they are evaluated by the deans of the School in which the department is located, and, ultimately, the university administration. An attempt is made to ensure that similar criteria are used for appointments and promotions throughout the University. New faculty is evaluated with two comprehensive reviews in their first seven years in consideration for a permanent appointment. Evaluations must include student assessments of teaching as well as internal and external letters from noted scholars that provide a critical appraisal of research accomplishments. For every available position, several hundred applications might be received. Even with this rigorous selection process for new appointees, typically about half or less are granted tenure or a permanent appointment. Thus, the process of faculty hiring and continuing employment is a very extensive one that must meet university standards and requires considerable internal and external evaluation.

Staff Qualifications

The plan for higher education in the PRC states that both the quantity and the quality of faculty members are to be improved to meet the goals of university expansion and research advancement. However, in terms of the number of full-time teachers, the growth of teaching staff could hardly keep up with that of the student population. Between 1998 and 2001, the number of full-time teachers in all public tertiary institutions increased by 18.7%, to 0.62 million.[28] The same period saw undergraduate entrants more than double, and total enrolments jumped by nearly 90%. In order to improve quality, redundant and under-qualified faculty was released. At the same time it was necessary to increase class size to accommodate expansion. For instance, the targeted student/full-time faculty ratio of the 'Tenth Five-year Plan' was set at 14 : 1.[29] With a goal of 16 million students by 2005, the higher education system will need about 1.14 million full-time teachers by then. With 0.62 million teachers in 2001, the goal implies an 84% increase within the next four years, a speed four and a half times that of the previous four-year phase. Even this does not take account of the hiring needed just to replace retirements, resignations, terminations, and deaths.

To evaluate the need of a world-class public university for full-time teachers, we can examine the situation of UCLA. Since it is a university in the public education system, we assume it is somewhat comparable to universities in China. In the autumn of 2001, UCLA's FTE student/FTE faculty ratio was 17 : 1.[30] Assuming Chinese universities will increase class size by 2005 to the level of UCLA, faculty size still has to increase by 51.8% during the four years from 2001 to 2004, a speed nearly 2.8 times that of the current pace. If the class size becomes comparable with UCLA's level in 2010, by that time 1.4 million full-time faculty members would be necessary to serve 23 million college students. And, if existing turnover is in the US range of 5–10% a year, that means that the total number of new persons hired could be as much as double this number to ensure a faculty of this size. Consider that this number is far greater than the numbers of graduate students completing advanced degrees, including those students who are studying abroad and returning to take faculty positions. Even these projections do not take account of research staff who do not occupy teaching positions, so our concern is understated; and clearly only a portion of the postgraduate population will be of the highest quality for the most selective institutions.

Second, it is not only the number of teachers that is a serious concern, but their quality as well. First, in 2000, of the 0.46 million full-time faculty members in regular higher education institutions, 6.5% carried no teaching load.[31] Further, more than one-fifth of these people were employed for reasons unrelated to research or training. Second, of the full-time faculty members in regular institutions, 18.7% are assistants, a position that is very close to the teaching assistants in US universities.[32] This ratio rose to 19.5% in 2000 (Figure 63.8). Finally, in 2000, only 6% of the faculty members in regular higher education institutions had doctoral degrees, 23.4% had master's degrees, and 70.6% had no graduate degrees at all. More strikingly, 16.3% of the faculty, and 30.3% of the full professors had not even completed a bachelor's degree (Figure 63.8)! The quality of faculty, however, varies significantly among universities.[33] As a comparison, 98% of the full-time instructional faculty in UCLA have a doctorate, first professional, or other terminal degrees.[34]

Improving the quality of teaching and research staff while expanding their numbers dramatically is a major challenge to all Chinese higher education institutions; one recent study shows that maintaining teaching quality poses more challenges to institutions located in economically less developed provinces in central, western, and remote regions.[35] The pressure to fill new positions must necessarily lead to the hiring of many who are not qualified to teach or do research. Even among those who have some qualifications, relatively few will be at the level of those at the leading universities in other countries with which China aspires to compete (e.g. UCLA). Pressure to fill openings also leads to inbreeding through hiring one's own graduates, a practice that makes institutions parochial by limiting cross-fertilization of ideas found at other institutions.

Suggested directions for consideration include:

- Reducing the rate of growth of enrolments until the employment of qualified faculty can keep pace.
- Making concerted efforts to attract Chinese nationals with valuable qualifications who did not return after completing graduate studies in other countries.

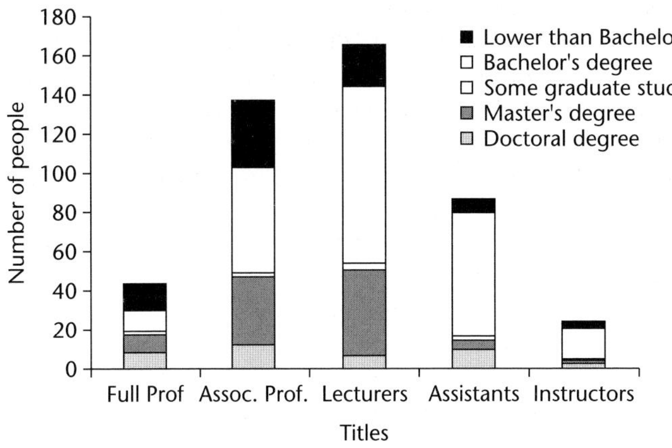

Fig. 63.8 Full-time faculty members in regular HEIs by academic qualifications and Titles (2000)

Source: Educational Statistics Yearbook of China, 2000.

- Recruiting highly qualified 'visiting' professors from abroad.
- Exploring, developing, and employing educational technologies such as multi-media courses, videotaped lectures, and distance education, to disseminate the teaching of the most qualified faculty members and the most effective instructional approaches.
- Continuing to raise student–faculty ratios to the levels of UCLA to ease pressure on hiring.
- Establishing effective evaluation systems for instruction to identify best practices and effective teaching and teachers, and using this information for personnel selection and improvement of teaching.
- Providing intensive professional development as needed on instructional strategies and subject-matter knowledge.
- For lower-level courses, considering the use of advanced undergraduate and graduate students who have demonstrated mastery of subject matter and can demonstrate good teaching skills with a standard curriculum. These personnel would work under the strict guidance of expert senior faculty.

Labour Markets

Rapid enrolment growth may also create distortions in labour markets. Even with high rates of economic growth, the economy is unlikely to expand according to the precise patterns of growth in graduates of different academic specialties. Counter-intuitively, with less than 4% of its labour force having tertiary education experience as of 2000, China increasingly finds itself facing the problem of college graduate unemployment in recent years. Higher education and labour market researchers are aware of this dilemma and trying to address it, based on cross-country and longitudinal experience from developed countries.[36] No clear patterns from the literature have been established about the relationship between higher education expansion, graduate employment and wage rates, and the developmental stage of a country. The unprecedented rate of higher educational expansion in the PRC makes it highly unrepresentative of historical patterns elsewhere.

The issue of college graduate unemployment can be explored from three aspects: the supply and demand of college graduates, and the characteristics of the labour market, such as market segmentation and incomplete information.[37] It should be noted that there are tremendous structural adjustments taking place in the Chinese economy. In general, these represent shifts from agriculture, state enterprises and traditional industries to private and joint ventures and movements into goods and services that are based upon computers and new technologies. Structural economic adjustment in China between 1997 and 2001 has generated 22 million laid-off workers from the state-owned enterprises, and a huge agricultural population shifting to industry, many not fully employed. Registered urban unemployment in 2001 reached 3.6%. The figure in 1992 was 2.3%.

Adding to this general labour market context, the number of college graduates has increased from 1.15 million in 2001, to 1.45 million in 2002, and finally to 2.12 million in 2003. It is projected that in 2004 there will be 2.5 million graduates. As of 15 June 2002, the rate of employment upon graduation was 83% for MOE institutions and 45% for local institutions. A third of those unemployed were preparing for graduate school applications. Three trends are emerging from the labour market for college graduates: (a) two-year college graduates are facing more challenges than four-year college students. The rate of employment upon graduation was only 44.3% for two-year college students in 2000. (b) Graduates from different majors face very different labour market demands. In 2000, philosophy graduates had the highest employment percentage, followed by law, history, science, engineering and medicine. Graduates in economics, education, literature and agriculture were among those for whom finding employment was most difficult. On average, 76.06% of students from four-year colleges found jobs upon graduation. (c) The percentage of employment upon graduation also varies with type of institutions. In 2000, 82.75% of the national key university graduates found jobs upon graduation, as compared with 68.2% of graduates from non-key universities. The situation of non-key universities further deteriorated in 2002, and we believe that the recent acceleration in production of graduates will further reduce these employment rates, at least in the short and medium term.

It is argued by some advocates of higher education expansion that the supply of college graduates is still far below the total demand. Their view is that current tension in the job market is due to high concentrations in economically developed areas and high expectations of college students.[38] There have been an increasing number of mismatches between demand and supply in the college graduate labour market.[39] A report from the Xinhua News Agency on job market conditions shows that supply by far exceeded demand in major cities in the fourth quarter of 2002 (Figure 63.9).

College unemployment is becoming one of the major challenges for higher education expansion in China as well as for Chinese society. Families may find themselves facing the dilemma of letting their teenagers become jobless right after high school, or delaying such unemployment by paying extra tuition to colleges. Without sufficient private returns to college education, weak demand for higher education may not justify the rapid pace of expansion. The World Bank report identified two main 'rigidities' that might cause an awkward situation where less-developed regions which need college graduates the most cannot attract sufficient numbers, while graduates in major cities remain unemployed.[40] The first cause of this is the rigidity of the curriculum and over-specialization. Under current arrangements, students are classified into narrowly defined fields long before they can adjust their own interests to market demand. Within a fast-growing economy, the lack of flexibility has resulted in numerous mismatches between supply and demand. The second cause is the rigidity in the labour market, which manifests itself in the relative lack of sufficient wage differentials to encourage individuals to acquire more skills, the residential restrictions of the *hukou* system, and the current occupation classification system that also defines the qualifications needed for each of the large number of narrowly defined occupations. Therefore, post-college unemployment is not only a higher education problem, but also a social problem. To some extent, allowing more young people to go to college is a strategy to postpone instant pressure on the labour market.[41]

Policy suggestions from the Ministry of Education and researchers as to the handling of the job market problem include improving the quality of teaching and learning. Some leading national universities have established an evaluation and monitoring system to ensure regular examinations of teaching quality and student performance[42] breaking down the borders and rigidity of over-specialized majors and allowing students to choose their specializations freely in the early years of college, as is happening in present experiments at Beijing University and Fudan University. This would move Chinese

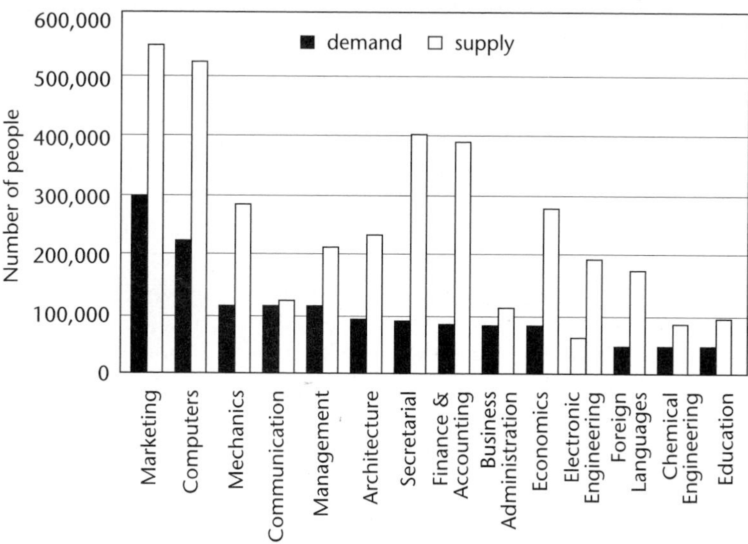

Fig. 63.9 Labour market demand and supply across professions in major cities (4th Quarter, 2002)

universities in the direction of UCLA, with its liberal arts and service courses in the first two years, prior to specialization. The purpose of this kind of experiment is to allow students to acquire more general knowledge as well as the capacity for life-long learning, so that they will be more versatile and flexible in the future labour market. Indeed, theory and evidence find general human capital carries more transferable values than specific human capital.[43] Beyond the improved labour market prospects for individuals, less specialized undergraduate training also improves social efficiency by reducing labour market mismatch between jobs and training. It is suggested that the state still has a role to play in improving labour market efficiency by, for example, providing policy guidance and information services to correct for market imperfections and information lag.[44]

Expansion Strategies

A repeated theme in the higher education development literature from the 1990s is expansion through improvement of internal efficiency and economies of scale.[45] It is argued that, by expanding the size of existing institutions, per student cost could be reduced by the pooling of resources and sharing governance and teaching capacity. For example, Tsang and Min found enrolment size was inversely related to per student recurrent expenditure.[46] The effect size was large and statistically significant.

The potential of such an expansion strategy might have been largely exhausted. The above evidence of economies of scale is valid only when interpreted within the context in which the study was carried out. At that time, in 1989, the average size of Chinese higher education institutions was less than 2,000. As shown in Figure 63.6, the current average college size has reached 6,000. To give a better idea of this size, New Zealand has an average college size of about 7,000, and the United Kingdom has about 4,500. These are the two examples given by the World Bank in 1997 as policy targets for Chinese higher education. It appears that China has already attained such a level. Comparing UCLA and leading universities in China, we find they are also very close in size. Currently UCLA has a student population of 37,494. The corresponding figure for Beijing University is 36,982. Tsinghua has 24,063 students, Fudan 36,100, and Zhejiang University has 40,000 full-time students, plus 43,000 part-time students. Even a local key university like Suzhou University has 28,400 full-time students and 16,600 part-time students. When school sizes reach this level, the effect of economies of scale diminishes significantly when controlled for quality.[47] Further expansion at the current pace will inevitably adopt a second strategy, of external expansion by establishing new institutions, which can be more costly.

Equity Issues

Although higher education expansion increases college access for high school graduates, another important question is whether such expansion benefits all high school graduates from various socioeconomic backgrounds equally. In order to finance higher education expansion, college resources have been decentralized, both from the central government to the local government, and from purely governmental subsidies to funding contributions from students and their families. At present, more than 20% of the total operational budgets of Chinese higher education institutions are covered by tuition and fees.[48] In the period when college education was virtually free, it was always harder for rural students to be admitted; but through adequate effort and achievement, they could become college students. The public higher education system in China thus represented a significant catalyst for social mobility. Charging significant tuition at a time when no credit mechanism for borrowing has been established denies poor students access to college that was previously attainable through conscientious study and achievement. In addition, the burden on families of tertiary education tuition for some of their children may reduce demand for secondary education for other offspring in poor rural regions, harming the average rural education attainment and perpetuating poverty. Students from families of high socioeconomic status are over-represented in the college student population.[49] And since most inequalities in China derive from rural-urban disparities,[50] regional inequality in terms of the number of college students per 10,000 population and expenditure per student is pronounced.[51] According to the World Bank's calculation,[52] if tuition is designed to recover 24% (which is very close to the reality) of the average cost of college education per student, it will require 109% of the annual income of a rural family where there is one wage-earner. By comparison, such an amount is only 56% of a similar (one wage-earner) family in the city. Such a differential economic burden on rural and urban households can, and should, be adjusted by government effort: Based on previous research, Tsang pointed out that the Chinese government has the financial potential and capacity to increase education investment.[53] Indeed, China's national effort (government education expenditure as a percentage of GDP) has been consistently below even some of the lowest national effort levels in the world. In fact, China's national effort decreased from 2.86% in 1991 to 2.49% in 1997.[54] Although China increased its national effort after 2000 to above 3%, educational expenditure as a percentage of GDP decreased from 3.32% in 2002 to 3.28% in 2003.

In addition to the impact of tuition and fees, there are other trends associated with massive expansion that are driving Chinese higher education towards a more socio-economically stratified system. Of the 2,000 or so higher education institutions in China, only about 80 belong to its top tier of national universities, all affiliated with the national Ministry of Education. Although these are distributed across the country in the major regions and cities, they are more heavily concentrated in the wealthier coastal regions and in Beijing. Without question these are considered to comprise the most prestigious segment of higher education. It is within this group that the Chinese government expects to create 'world class institutions', the equal of the best universities anywhere. These are the most competitive institutions with regard to admissions, drawing on the most privileged students economically and academically.

Even among these national institutions only a relatively small portion of funding is derived from the central government, with institutions reliant on tuition and income from other sources to cover their budgets. Some of the most prestigious universities such as Beijing and Tsinghua universities receive considerably greater support from the central government than do other universities, and these are two of the most sought institutions among highly qualified applicants. Highly prestigious and competitive universities in Shanghai, such as Fudan University, receive considerable support from the Shanghai government as do universities in prosperous Guanjhou. Many of these universities also derive income from ownership of businesses of which some of their business entities are substantial. In general, those universities that are able to select the most competitive students and that are located in the wealthier areas of the country are obtaining the highest levels of funding from both government and private sources. Thus, even within the most elite sector of higher education, there is considerable stratification of students by tuition, competitive admissions, and substantial differences in funding and resources.

Below this segment are the vast majority of institutions in higher education, constituting regional, local, and private institutions, each less selective than the national universities. These are usually institutions of second or third choice with family resources limiting students to institutions closer to their homes. In the case of the private institutions they can select their students only after other institutions have decided their admissions. Among these institutions there is a pecking order of prestige and competitiveness that is highly recognized among parents, students, and employers.

These differences are visited upon labor markets where the prestige of the institution awarding the degree weighs heavily in competition for jobs. With the supply of college graduates exceeding dramatically the demand in response to the vast expansion of higher education, the source of a degree has taken on added importance in labor markets. For all of these reasons, it seems clear that the stratification of students by socioeconomic background is already substantial and will become more important over time. In a society where connections are important, it is likely to be associated with differential advantages in peers and network connections in the attainment of economic and social opportunities.

Other Issues

A further area for scrutiny is whether all universities, including the national universities, need to have schools and departments of specialization in every field. For example, does every national university require a medical school, school of architecture, law school, engineering school, and research institutions that cover all of the academic fields? Some academic planners and administrators in China believe that a world-class university is incomplete without including all of the academic and professional specialities. This conception is also widely accepted in academic research that compares leading universities in the US and China.[55] Certainly, this is not the philosophy in the US where relatively few of the top universities have schools of dentistry and architecture. Princeton, for example, a [university] with high prestige, lacks medical, business, and law schools, yet no one would argue that Princeton is not of world class because of these omissions. Yale has a very small engineering programme that covers only a limited number of specialities, yet it too is a university that has great prestige. What we are suggesting is that beyond a broad comprehensiveness, universities can make choices about which fields they will cover. Not every university needs to cover all fields in teaching and research centres. Personnel and facilities are costly, and having too many centres dilutes the available talent pool so that most centres may not be able to maintain the depth and quality that is sought for the university. It may be better to choose 'fields of excellence' and to establish cooperative agreements or consortia with other universities to cover other fields.

Finally, there is a widespread belief in China that the 'top' students must enrol in one of the 82 national universities or major research institutions. Professor Bruce Johnstone of the State University of New York at Buffalo has suggested, correctly in our view, that this will place great pressure on the enrolments of those institutions, making it even more difficult to marshal resources to accommodate growth in the future. In the US a large proportion of the top students attend institutions that are known for the high quality of instruction rather than research, the liberal arts colleges. These four-year colleges specialize in small classes and strong teaching, personal mentoring, and general academic support, and they have greater success in placing their graduates in the most highly ranked graduate schools than the major universities.[56] The question that arises is whether, in long-term planning, a role might be considered for a new tier of institutions that might fill a specialized niche for talented students. These institutions could specialize in teaching of the highest quality and could act as teaching laboratories for improving instruction at the universities while taking some enrolment pressures off the latter. They could also be affiliated to specific universities to link students to research training during their period of specialization.

NOTES

1. For an analysis in a more stable situation, see H. M. Levin, 'Raising Productivity in Higher Education', *Journal of Higher Education* 62/3 (January 1991), 241–62.
2. Weifang Min, *Historical Perspectives and Contemporary Challenges: The Case of Chinese Universities*, mimeo (Beijing University, 2005).
3. D. Yang, *Higher Education of China* (China Education and Research Network [CERNET], 2001). Available: <http://www.edu.cn/20010827/208329> [16 Jan. 2003].
4. Higher education development during this period was interrupted by two mass social movements: the 'Great Leap Forward' (1958–60) and the 10-year 'Cultural Revolution' (1966–76). During the 'Great Leap Forward' the Chinese higher education system saw a

period of hectic expansion, with the number of higher education institutions increasing from 229 to 1,289 in three years. By 1965, the system was back on track after difficult system reorganization. But in the following years the 'Cultural Revolution' struck. This disrupted higher education again, negated almost everything existing in the higher education system, and reduced total enrolments by about 14 times. See Min, *Historical Perspectives*.

5. See ibid.

6. See Yang, *Higher Education*.

7. Weifang Min, 'Global Challenges and the Chinese Response', in *Higher Education in the 21st Century*, edited by Philip Altbach and Patti McGill Peterson (New York: Institute of International Education and Council on International Exchange of Scholars, 1999), 11–17.

8. Ministry of Education, *List of People-run Regular Higher Education Institutions* (2003). Available: <http://www.moe.edu.cn/highedu/gxtz/mbgx_20030121.htm> [16 Jan. 2003].

9. Ministry of Education, *2001 Statistical Report on National Educational Development* (2002). Available: <http://www.moe.edu.cn> [16 Jan. 2003].

10. The latest information from the 2003 National Regular Higher Education Admission Affairs Conference has raised the 2010 goal of gross enrolment ratio to 23%. Ministry of Education, *2000 Statistical Report on National Educational Development* (2001). Available: <http://www.moe.edu.cn> [16 Jan. 2003].

11. See National Center for Education Statistics, US Department of Education, *The Condition of Education 2002*, NCES 2002–025 (Washington, DC: US Government Printing Office, 2002), 130, 131. The rate of enrolment of the 18–24 year age group was about 31%.

12. Ministry of Education, abstracts from 'The Education Goals of the 10th Five-Year Plan', *Continuing Education* 5 (2001), 15–18.

13. For more discussions, see Ruth Hayhoe and Qiang Zha, 'Becoming World Class: Chinese Universities Facing Globalization and Internationalization', *Harvard China Review* 5/1 (2004), 87–92.

14. J. Liu, 'Women li shijie daxue haiyou duoyuan' (How Far Are We Away from World-Class Universities), *Zhongguo jiaoyu bao* (China Education Daily), 12 March 2002, p. 1.

15. It is not clear whether these numbers taken from the statistical yearbooks have been adjusted for inflation. However, from the early 1990s up to today, China has been experiencing slight deflation. Ministry of Education, *Statistical Report on Educational Expenditures of Regular Higher Education Institutions* (2001). Available: <http://www.moe.edu.cn/Stat/index.htm> [17 Jan. 2003].

16. Min, *Historical Perspectives*.

17. *Zhongguo jiaoyu tongji nianjian* (*Educational Statistics Yearbook of China*) (Beijing: People's Education Press, 2001).

18. Ministry of Education, *2000 Ranking of Science and Technology-Related Activities in National Key Universities* (2002). Available: <http://www.cer.net> [16 Jan. 2003].

19. Ministry of Education, *1999 Statistical Report on National Educational Development* (2000). Available: <http://www.moe.edu.cn> [16 Jan. 2003].

20. *Educational Statistics Yearbook of China*, 2001.

21. See <www.ucla.edu>.

22. R. G. Ehrenberg and L. Zhang, 'Do Tenured and Tenure-Track Faculty Matter?' *Cornell Higher Education Research Institute Working Paper 53* (Ithaca, NY: Cornell University, 2004).
23. E. Bettinger and B. T. Long, *Do College Instructors Matter?: The Effects of Adjuncts and Graduate Assistants on Students' Interests and Success*. NBER Working Paper No. W 10370 (Cambridge, Mass.: National Bureau of Economic Research, 2004).
24. J. R. Behrman, M. R. Rosenzweig, and P. Taubman, 'College Choice and Wages: Estimates Using Data on Female Twins', *The Review of Economics and Statistics* 78/4 (1996), 672–85.
25. H. Wang, 'Jiaru shimao dui Zhongguo jiaoyu shichang de yingxiang' (Influence of the WTO on the Chinese Education Market), *Higher Education* (Gaodeng Jiaoyu) 1 (2003), 46–9.
26. R. G. Ehrenberg, M. Rizzo, and G. H. Jakubson, 'Who Bears the Growing Cost of Science at Universities?' *Cornell Higher Education Research Institute Working Paper 35* (Ithaca, NY: Cornell University, 2003).
27. S. A. Clark and R. F. Larson, 'Mobility, Productivity, and Inbreeding at Small Colleges: A Comparative Study', *Sociology of Education* 45/4 (1972), 426–34.
28. Ministry of Education (Note 19).
29. Ministry of Education. *On Personnel Adjustment* (1999). Available: <http://www.moe.edu.cn> [20 Jan. 2003].
30. Reporting the autumn 2001 ratio of full-time equivalent students (full-time plus 1/3 part-time) to full-time equivalent instructional faculty (full-time plus 1/3 part-time). Excluded from the ratio calculations, are both faculty and students in stand-alone graduate or professional programmes such as medicine, law, veterinary science, dentistry, social work, business, or public health, in which faculty teach virtually only graduate level students. Undergraduate or graduate student teaching assistants do not count as faculty (UCLA Common Data Set 2001–02). Available: <http://www.apb.ucla.edu/apbtoc.htm>.
31. *Educational Statistical Yearbook of China*, 2001.
32. S. Liu, 'Over-expansion of Higher Education Is Not Desirable', *Higher Education Studies* 1 (1998), 61–4.
33. Min, *Historical Perspectives*.
34. UCLA 'Common Data Set 01–02', <http:// www.apb.ucla.edu/apbtoc.htm>.
35. W. Ma, 'Kuozhao hou gaodeng xuexiao jiaoxue zhiliang zhuangkuang fenxi' (Analysis of Teaching Quality of Institutions of Higher Learning after Enrolment Expansion), *Higher Education* 2 (2003), 21–6.
36. D. Wen, 'Gaodeng jiaoyu guimo kuozhan yu biyesheng jiuye' (Higher Education Expansion and College Graduates Employment), *Higher Education Exploration* (Gaojiao Tansuo), 4 (2000), 30–3.
37. S. Jiang, 'Woguo gaoxiao biyesheng jiuye wenti de chengyin yanjiu' (An Economical Model for the Explanation of Graduate Unemployment), *Tsinghua Journal of Education* (Qinghua Daxue Jiaoyu Yanjiu) 25/4 (2004), 57–63.
38. Ibid.
39. Min, 'Global Challenges'.
40. The World Bank, *Strategic Goals for Chinese Education in the 21st Century* (Washington, DC: The World Bank, 1999).
41. An interesting comparative perspective is provided by what Philip Altbach calls the University of Buenos Aires model, where the university successfully 'absorbs demand' [for higher education] at the same time that it dampens potential social unrest by offering

young people the widest possible access to higher education, although very few eventually earn a degree (see a discussion at <http://www.bc.edu/bc_org/avp/soe/cihe/index.html>.

42. Ma, 'Kuozhao hou'.

43. The literature on general and specific human capital is applied to the field of workplace training studies. Some of the recent studies include: E. Leuven, 'Studies in the Economics of Training' (Doctoral dissertation, University of Amsterdam, Amsterdam, 2001); P. Cappelli, *Why Do Employers Pay for College*? NBER Working Paper No. W9225 (Cambridge, Mass.: National Bureau of Economic Research, 2002).

44. Min, *Historical Perspectives*.

45. M. Tsang and W. Min, 'Expansion, Efficiency, and Economies of Scale of Higher Education in China', *Higher Education Policy* 5/2 (1992), 61–6. The World Bank, 'Financing Higher Education: Diversification of Resources', *China Higher Education Reform* (Washington, DC: The World Bank, 1997) and The World Bank, *Strategic Goals*.

46. Tsang and Min, ibid.

47. Liu, 'Over-expansion'.

48. Min, *Historical Perspectives*.

49. Min, 'Global Challenges'.

50. J. Heckman, *China's Investment in Human Capital*. NBER Working Paper Series, 9296 (Cambridge Mass.: National Bureau of Economic Research, 2002).

51. Min, 'Global Challenges'.

52. The World Bank, 'Financing Higher Education'.

53. M. Tsang and Y. Ding, 'Financial Challenges in Compulsory Education and Intergovernmental Education Grants', *Peking University Education Review* (Beijing Daxue Jiaoyu Pinglun) 1/1 (2003), 84–94.

54. Ibid.

55. For example, D. Wen, 'A Comparative Study of the Scale and Structure of Leading Universities in the US and China', *China Higher Education Research* (Zhongguo Gaojiao Yanjiu) 6 (2002), 46–7.

56. For further details, see Steven Koblik and Stephen R. Graubard (eds.), *Distinctively American: The Residential Liberal Arts College* (New Brunswick, NJ: Transaction, 2000).

History, Biography and Place in the Learning Society: Towards a Sociology of Life-Long Learning

Gareth Rees, Ralph Fevre, John Furlong, and Stephen Gorard

The principal aim of this [chapter] is to begin to shift the debate on the Learning Society away from the *normative* focus which has predominated hitherto. We take the development of an adequate social theory of life-long learning to be a necessary condition of creating a Learning Society, however conceived. Accordingly, rather than beginning with questions about what a Learning Society *ought* to constitute, we seek to engage initially with issues of what patterns of participation in learning through the life-course actually *are* and of how best to understand their determinants. More specifically, we wholly agree with Coffield's (1997) argument that: 'we need a more powerful social theory of learning which will encompass not only the cognitive processes within the heads of individuals but also the *social relationships and arrangements* which stimulate learning' (p. 9; emphasis added). Our analytical emphasis is thus on life-long learning as a set of social relations, which can be illuminated by insights drawn from sociological analysis. Indeed, in some respects, our project is to counterpose sociological reasoning about the Learning Society against other, more dominant forms of theory.

Our discussion begins with a brief examination of the way in which the official discourse of the Learning Society is dominated by a *particular* social theory of life-long learning: human capital theory. For this reason alone, the critical evaluation of the latter is a serious undertaking. What we demonstrate is that human capital theory involves an unwarranted abstraction of economic behaviour from social relations more widely; participation in life-long learning cannot be understood in terms of the narrow calculation of utility maximisation. This critique provides the basis for the development of at least the lineaments of a more satisfactory theoretical account, in which learning behaviour is conceived as the product of individual calculation and active choice, but within parameters set by both access to learning opportunities and collective norms. Moreover, these parameters, by their very nature, vary

Gareth Rees, Ralph Fevre, John Furlong, and Stephen Gorard, 'History, Biography and Place in the Learning Society: Towards a Sociology of Life-Long Learning', *The Journal of Educational Policy*, 12, 6, 485–97 <http://tandf.co.uk/journals>

systematically over space and time: accordingly, place and history must play a central role in any adequate theorisation. We conclude that this kind of theoretical approach has important implications not only for empirical research, but also for strategies aimed at creating a Learning Society.

The Official Discourse of the Learning Society

Coffield (1997) has drawn attention to the marked commonalities in state policies with respect to the building of a Learning Society. The latter is conceived in terms of objectives of economic growth. More particularly, he emphasises the crucial role accorded to the individual actor in this official discourse and the limitations which this imposes on effective strategy. Economic competitiveness, it is argued, is dependent on a highly skilled labour-force; and, hence, economic growth primarily reflects the capacities of individual workers to acquire these necessary skills and competences (for example, European Commission, 1996; Department for Education and Employment, 1995).

These arguments can be developed by locating this emphasis on the individual actor within the wider relationships between education and training and economic development, of which it forms part. This wider analysis, we suggest, is that derived from human capital theory.[1] In Schultz's (1961) initial formulation, the crucial benefits of investment in human capital are set out: where returns to other forms of capital are constant or decreasing, the development of human capital, primarily through education and training, will constitute the prime source of economic growth. Accordingly, it is in the interests of employers and, where necessary, the state to ensure that such investment in human capital takes place. Crucially, it also follows that for individuals seeking access to desirable employment opportunities, their self-interest will be served by personal investment in the acquisition of qualifications and experience. Indeed, as Becker (for example, 1975) argues, participation in education and training may be considered as a form of market behaviour, involving the rational calculation of the total benefits to be derived, setting real income foregone (through, for example, remaining in education) against enhanced opportunities of future rewards (such as better job prospects, higher wages and so on).

What this implies is that the scope for effective state intervention is circumscribed. Basic educational provision clearly needs to be guaranteed. Some employers may require encouragement to provide the most effective forms of training. However, the participation of the bulk of (prospective) employees in education and training will follow automatically from a 'natural' calculation of the benefits which will flow to them in the future. The role of the state in this context is to ensure that they are fully aware of the nature of the learning opportunities which are available and the specific advantages which will derive from their participation. In short, therefore, market mechanisms—albeit facilitated by limited state interventions—will ensure the achievement of the desired patterns of life-long learning at some point in the future. Indeed, the Learning Society itself comes to be conceived exclusively as a desirable *future* state: a target to be achieved, where maximum social benefits will be ensured through the effective operation of market processes.

We wish to argue, on the contrary, that participation in education and training cannot be understood as being determined within a *sui generis* economic realm. Human capital theory involves an unwarranted abstraction of life-long learning from the social relations in which it is encompassed. This, in turn, provides the analytical basis for an over-simplified view of strategy and a conception of the Learning Society itself which is impoverished.

The Sociological Critique of Human Capital Theory

Human capital theory has implications, then, for both wider patterns of economic development and the market behaviour of individuals. It is the latter which is of principal concern here (although the former poses important questions with respect to strategies for building a Learning Society too: see G. Rees, 1997*a*). To simplify somewhat, this aspect of human capital theory shares many of the characteristics of more general neo-classical analysis of market behaviour (Fevre *et al.*, 1999). In particular, human capital theory reflects the following assumptions which underpin the wider analysis of market behaviour: individuals seek to maximise their material well-being (or utility) in economic transactions; they possess full knowledge of market conditions; and they act rationally to achieve their preferences in the light of this knowledge (see, for example, Martinelli and Smelser, 1990: 29). Accordingly, individuals will choose to undertake education and training to the extent that they are aware of the opportunities available and that they are able to maximise material returns through doing so.

Contemporary developments in the sociology of economic life have renewed the critique of such neo-classical economic theory (for example, Granovetter and Swedberg, 1992). The absolute differentiation between economic and social life which it implies, and the consequent tendency for individuals to be governed by material motivations, are rejected. What are emphasised are the *continuities* between economic action and institutions, on the one hand, and wider social networks and organisations, on the other. Hence, behaviour in economic markets is, in Polanyi's (1957) term, 'embedded' in systems of social relations, particularly networks of interpersonal relations. Moreover, as Durkheim argued in his famous critique of utilitarian approaches as a whole (Fevre *et al.*, 1999), economic markets have characteristic *normative* bases (in the same way as the more obvious cases of exchange based on 'reciprocity' or 'redistribution') (Polanyi, 1957). And to these might be added the pervasive influence of differential power between social groups.

This dissolution of the boundary between economic action and social relations more widely has specific consequences for the ways in which the determinants of individual behaviours are conceptualised. The neo-classical formulation ignores the possibility that individuals may pursue ends (or have preferences) which are different from maximisation of material well-being. This potential for a diversity of preferences may be conceived, in Weberian terms, as reflecting different value positions (although the latter, in turn, may be shaped within normative structures: see below). For example, an employee may undertake a programme of training because he or she prizes the intrinsic pleasure obtained from the programme or from the enhanced capacity to do a job, even where the material benefits to be derived are negligible. This action would be 'rational', even though the ends which are sought deviate from those assumed in the conventional economic model of preferences. Indeed, a research programme (of a characteristically Weberian kind) might investigate the circumstances—presumably, derived from the wider context of social networks, etc.—in which deviations from 'economic' rationality occur. This, in turn, would open up the possibility of analysing individual behaviour with respect to learning opportunities not in terms of some *universal* economic rationality, but rather of alternative rationalities which are *socially constituted*.[2]

The critique of neo-classical theory also raises the question of the extent to which behaviour in markets may be conceived as the product of individual choice and decision-making *at all*. A conventional sociological approach emphasises that individuals are socialised into determinate normative structures and these, in turn, shape not only the preferences held by individuals, but also their perceptions of feasible options. For example, most sociologists of education would be comfortable with the notion that, in Gambetta's (1987: 15) words: 'class-related inertial forces can affect the preference structure by altering the values attached to any given option: the working-class belief, for instance, that academically oriented schools are not "for people like us"'. In this context, the exercise of choice by the individual is constrained by a structure of taken-for-granted presuppositions with respect to what is available and appropriately sought after. Moreover, this structure of presuppositions is systematic, in the sense that it is associated with a given location within—in this case—the relations of social class. What this suggests is that there are definable relationships between individual preferences and the choices based upon them, normative systems and the locations in the social structure within which socialisation occurs. Tracing out these relationships would be a major element in uncovering how alternative rationalities come to be socially constituted.

Nevertheless, it is important not to overstate the effects of socialisation: to avoid an *over*-socialised conception of the individual, where his or her action is viewed as a passive reflection of wider social forces. We should not substitute the neo-classical 'asocial rational egotist' with a sociological 'cultural dupe' (Ingham, 1996: 554). Even where the range of possible courses of action is perceived to be highly restricted, individuals remain able to compare options and to choose 'rationally' between them. Individuals are able to reject the preference structures into which they are socialised, as, for instance, any analysis of participation in adult education programmes demonstrates. Actors remain autonomous through exercising choice over the courses of action which they pursue, even though their choices are made within parameters which are set externally. Analytically, therefore, the task is to produce an account of the *interaction* of individual choice with its parameters (Swedberg, Himmelstrand and Brulin, 1990: 70).

These external parameters are not, however, confined to the effects of socialisation. Individual choices are not simply constrained by socially constituted preferences, but also reflect the social structure of actually available opportunities. Preferences themselves may be shaped—whether through socialisation or more directly—by the reality of feasible alternative actions. Moreover, the scope of autonomy and choice is not neutral in the face of processes of social exclusion and integration, but is structured by these wider social relations. Individuals do not enjoy a level playing-field in access to opportunities for education and training (as for other goods and services); and this is true, in principle, irrespective of how people understand these opportunities. For example, changes in state provision of educational opportunities (consequent, say, on the 1944 Education Act) or in the organisation of economic production (leading to the expansion of women's employment) have resulted in structural changes in learning opportunities, whose implications have, arguably, only partially been absorbed into people's social understanding and normative structures; in fact, one of the interesting analytical issues here is precisely the disjuncture between these dimensions (for example, T. Rees, 1992: chs. 3 and 4).

This implies a much more complex set of social processes through which participation in life-long learning is determined, than is derived from human capital theory. At best, the latter may be conceived as a partial account, which may apply in rather specific circumstances. In the next section, we begin to outline a more general analytical framework, which attempts to build on the critique which has been sketched here.

Towards a Social Theory of Life-Long Learning

A major part of the sociological analysis of participation in education and training presents almost a mirror image of human capital theory and neo-classical economic analysis more widely. Here, the emphasis has been overwhelmingly on the *constraints* within which individual actors operate.[3] For example, patterns of attainment in schools or of participation in post-compulsory areas of education have characteristically been analysed in terms of the changing structure of opportunities (through state policies, etc.) and the differentiation of individuals' access to these opportunities according to their location within the social structure, particularly their class, gender and ethnic backgrounds. Many accounts of the shift from an elite to a mass system of higher education or of participation in adult education programmes illustrate this mode of analysis (for example, Power *et al.*, 2003; Sargant and Aldridge, 2003). And much the same can be said of a great deal of the research on the take up of opportunities for vocational training, whether supplied by the state or (although the analysis is far less developed) by employers (for example, Rees, Fielder and Rees, 1992; Rainbird, 2000).

Frequently, this conceptualisation in terms of the restriction of individual choice over courses of action has been used to permit the reduction of the complexities of individual biographies to characteristic educational 'pathways' or 'trajectories' (the term which we shall use here). Precisely because autonomy is bounded by external conditions, it is possible to identify regularities in individuals' educational experiences as they proceed through the life course. Hence, for example, Halsey, Heath and Ridge (1980) identified different routes through compulsory schooling, based on performance at key junctures such as the '11+' or 'common entrance' examinations, and were concerned to elaborate on the nature and effects of the flows of individuals from different social backgrounds through them. Similarly, Banks *et al.* (1992) develop the notion of 'career trajectories' to encapsulate the contrasting experiences of young people during the years after they have passed the minimum school-leaving age; and again, these are related to key features of social background and previous education.

At one level, what is involved here is no more than the attempt to *describe* patterns of educational attainment, participation and so on. Individual educational experiences are simply aggregated into typologies, which may then be related to the opportunities provided and the social resources available from different backgrounds. However, the concept of 'trajectory' embodies a clear *analytical* element too. Our argument here has been elaborated by Hodkinson, Sparkes and Hodkinson (1996) through their invocation of Strauss's (1962) well known discussion of the metaphors used in discussions of such 'trajectories'. On the one hand, there is the predictability of progression up a 'career ladder'. On the other, just as an egg remains an egg, irrespective of how it is cooked, so an individual's background restricts the career opportunities available to him or her.

What this highlights is that there are two elements involved. Firstly, the 'trajectory' which people join is largely determined by the resources which they derive from their social backgrounds. Hence, to extend one of Strauss's (1962) examples, working-class males' experience of initial schooling and subsequent education and training differs systematically from that of middle-class females; their access to learning opportunities is differentiated by the social resources or capital available to them. Secondly, an individual's capacity to take up whatever learning opportunities are available is constrained by his or her previous history in this respect. Accordingly, once an individual has started out on a given 'trajectory', then the probability of proceeding through its subsequent stages is relatively high; the sequence of educational experiences is to a considerable extent *cumulative*. For example, if someone leaves school at 16 with no qualifications, this itself restricts subsequent access to further or higher education and to anything other than very limited vocational training.

This concept of 'trajectory' is integral to the development of an adequate social theory of life-long learning. By extension from previous research, it is possible—although empirically complex—to identify a range of characteristic sequences of learning experiences through the life course ('trajectories'), which constitute the core of the *explanandum* of such a theory.[4] However, whilst these 'trajectories' do certainly reflect an externally constituted structure of learning opportunities and socially differentiated access to them—as our earlier discussion suggests—it is necessary to elaborate a more nuanced account of their determinants. We need to explore more fully the ways in which 'trajectories' are 'embedded' in social relations; and to take proper account of the interaction of individual choices and constraining parameters in the determination of courses of educational action.

In locating 'trajectories' at the core of our theoretical concerns, attention is necessarily focused on processes of *social change*. Most immediately, this relates to the sequences of educational experiences which occur through individual biographies. However, in addition, characteristic 'trajectories' are themselves transformed over time; the kinds of 'trajectories' which are typical currently are significantly different from those of earlier (and, indeed, by implication, future) epochs. Hence, there is also a process of historical or inter-generational change, within which individual biographies may be located. Accordingly, it is possible to mark out historical periods in terms of their pattern of typical 'trajectories' (as, for example, Antikainen *et al.*, 1996: 14, do for Finland).

Transformations in the structure of available opportunities for education and training are key influences here. Changes in state education policies, in employers' strategies with respect to training provision or in community-based programmes of informal learning are all examples of ways in which characteristic 'trajectories' may be restructured over time, through expanding or contracting the learning opportunities which are available. Such changes also impact upon the role played by individuals' social backgrounds in differentiating access to such opportunities. For example, the post-war expansion of secondary and higher education in Britain, along with marked changes in employment structures, have contributed significantly to changing women's educational profile relative to that of men (for example, T. Rees, 1992).

These inter-generational changes in characteristic 'trajectories' underpin most strategies for building a Learning Society. What the latter involve is generating a set of typical 'trajectories' (however defined) in the future which is significantly different from the present one. For instance, official strategies at the moment are predominantly concerned with shifting the mix of 'trajectories' towards a situation where a much higher proportion of the population engage in the renewal of skills and competences throughout their working lives. In characterising policy in these terms, the partial nature of conceptualising the Learning Society *simply* as a desirable future objective is exposed. Viewed in this way, building a Learning Society becomes abstracted from the long-term processes of historical change through which patterns of learning ('trajectories') have been transformed. By focusing exclusively on a teleology of ends which remain to be achieved, a proper analysis of these processes of change may be avoided; indeed, this is precisely our claim with respect to current strategies derived from human capital theory. This future orientation also permits the presentation of a kind of 'Whig history' of the development of life-long learning, in which the weaknesses of the present are conceived as the necessary preconditions of the achievement of a desired state of learning in the future. The possibility that elements of past practice were superior to the present or, to put it another way, that the development of participation in education and training may be distinctly non-linear, especially for particular population groups, is discounted, through a failure to engage with the complexities of the social processes involved. For example, in a region like South Wales, the collapse of employment in the nationalised industries, where initial and continuing training were provided for all employees and were integral to the internal labour markets leading to supervisory and managerial jobs, may have brought about a significant deterioration in learning opportunities, at least for men. There is a real sense, then, in which substantial sections of the population now have learning opportunities which are significantly worse than their parents (or, more correctly, their fathers) enjoyed (G. Rees, 1997*b*).

This emphasis on the necessity of locating the concept of the Learning Society within an analysis of the complexities of change in social patterns of participation in learning necessarily draws attention to the specificities of *place* too. Quite simply, as our South Wales example begins to suggest, characteristic 'trajectories' vary from one locality to another. It is widely recognised that there are substantial variations in patterns of, for instance, educational attainment and participation more widely, between different regions of Britain and even between more local areas (for example, Sargant *et al.*, 1997). However, the theorisation of such differentiation is much less developed. Analytical concerns have focused on what are presented as national patterns and the location of individuals within a spatially undifferentiated social structure of class, gender and ethnic backgrounds (but see, for example, Coffield, Borrill and Marshall, 1986). Certainly, there have been very few (if any) attempts to relate historical or inter-generational changes in patterns of educational participation ('trajectories') to regionally and locally specific processes of social and economic development.

In the terms of our earlier discussion, precisely because characteristic 'trajectories' are 'embedded' in wider social relations, they reflect the spatial and temporal differentiation of the latter. Most obviously, the structure of learning opportunities and the impacts of its transformation are sharply differentiated between places. For example, although changes in state provision have been instigated largely at the national level, their effects have frequently been experienced most acutely in local contexts. Not only have many policy changes been implemented primarily at the local level, but also the interaction of national policies with local conditions has produced highly variable local outcomes. For instance, the national policy of expanding learning opportunities for younger adults through Youth Training in reality had very different effects according to the local context; and this is reflected in wide differences in take-up, completion, and eventual outcomes for young people (for example, Rees, Williamson and Istance, 1996). Moreover, the effects of changes in industrial structure and associated employment opportunities, whilst deriving from wider national and international economic developments, are experienced in local labour markets and the educational and training opportunities associated with them (Ashton, Maguire and Spilsbury, 1990). For instance, colliery closures in South Wales were the result of shifts in international energy markets and national state policies, but their impact was to remove from particular local areas jobs and the training which went with them (Rees and Thomas, 1991).

Equally, whilst the processes of social differentiation of access to learning opportunities are pervasive, the *form* which these processes take may be affected by the local context (a point which has not been adequately recognised in conventional studies of educational participation and attainment). For example, the significance of someone's gender to their education and training is *partly* determined by the structure of local employment opportunities, as the collapse of a male-dominated employment structure in South Wales has illustrated (Istance and Rees, 1994); although this is clearly mediated by class background and the consequent extent of dependence on local opportunities (Lovering, 1990). Accordingly, there are complex *interactions* between people's locations within the social structure, their spatial locations, and their access to learning opportunities. In short, then, the structure of learning opportunities to which individuals have access is not uniform from place to place; teasing out the precise empirical significance of this spatial differentiation is a major, albeit complex, part of the required analysis of characteristic patterns of 'trajectories'. And this, in turn, raises the possibility that strategies for building a Learning Society will have to take account of what may be significant variations between localities in learning resources.

Characteristic 'trajectories' do not, however, *simply* reflect the constraining effects of structures of learning opportunities. The individual educational experiences of which they are comprised are simultaneously the products of personal choices between alternative actions. This is seen most clearly where an individual opts to pursue a course of action which deviates from an established 'trajectory'; what Ahleit (1994) refers to as the 'biographical discontinuities' which result when, say, a redundant miner or a mother whose children have left home chooses to enter a university access programme (see, for example, Crossan *et al.*, 2003). However, even where individuals' behaviour is *consistent* with typical patterns of learning ('trajectories'), it is always possible for them to do something else; their actions thus remain the product of choices. To reiterate a point made earlier, the analytical puzzle is to unravel the *interaction* of individual choices and constraining social parameters. This is, of course, a perennial problem in social analysis; and, in what follows, we do not claim any definitive contribution to resolving it. Rather, our concern is to make an essentially pragmatic contribution to exploring the salience of these issues to an understanding of patterns of learning through the life-course.

At the most basic level, then, the choices which individuals exercise over their participation in education and training reflect the kinds of knowledge which they possess of the learning opportunities available. More interestingly, their actions are chosen in respect of preferences which are defined within what we referred to earlier as *socially constituted rationalities*; that is to say, individual choices are made over courses of action to be followed, but not in random ways. In the particular context of educational experience through the life-course, we suggest that a key concept in understanding the latter is that of 'learner identity'. As Weil (1986) puts it, 'learner identities' refer to:

> . . . the ways in which adults come to understand the conditions under which they experience learning as 'facilitating' or 'inhibiting', 'constructive' or 'destructive'. Learner identity suggests the emergence or affirmation of values and beliefs about 'learning', 'schooling' and 'knowledge'. The construct incorporates personal, social, sociological, experiential and intellectual dimensions of learning, as integrated over time. (p. 223)

'Learner identity' encapsulates how individuals come to understand themselves as learners and, thus, their relationships to learning opportunities. Accordingly, it provides the framework through which alternative courses of educational action are evaluated.[5] Moreover, as Weil (1986) indicates, an individual's 'learner identity' is essentially personal, with emotional as well as intellectual dimensions (Sennett and Cobb, 1972). And yet, however personal 'learner identities' may be, they remain the products of individuals' *social* experience. And here too, we wish to emphasise the ways in which the latter is pervaded by history and place.

Most obviously, compulsory schooling is a powerful source of 'learner identity'. Those who have had a successful experience of learning at school are more likely to have developed a positive 'learner identity' and therefore be readier to engage with learning opportunities in later life. But 'learner identity' is not simply a matter of success or failure at school; it is also the product of more complex processes. For example, the forms of curriculum, pedagogy and assessment associated with the 1960s grammar schools, served to construct the learner in quite different ways from those made available within the secondary moderns of the same period or the progressive comprehensives of the 1970s. The 'learner identities' that educational institutions aspire to engender in their students vary both between different types of institution and historically too. These factors thus underlie the ways in which the structure of learning opportunities has been evaluated differently by successive generations. To use a specific example from our current research, it may well be that the training opportunities which became available after coal nationalisation in 1947 were regarded very differently by the first generations of miners to experience them, whose schooling was overwhelmingly confined to elementary levels, compared with those who entered the industry subsequently, following what by then was universal secondary education. Indeed, for the earlier generations, the work-place training which they received, far from being understood in narrowly vocational terms, may well have constituted the most significant element of their *educational* experience as a whole.

'Learner identities' are not simply the product of formal education, however; they also emerge in relation to informal learning opportunities, with rather different implications for the evaluation of alternative courses of action. Traditionally, the fields of sport and music have provided a minority of young people with the opportunity to develop a different conception of their own abilities from that gained through formal education (Furlong, 1991). For older learners, experience within political and community organisations can have a similar effect (Weil, 1986). Indeed, in particular places and epochs, this latter kind of activity has been much more significant in shaping 'learner identities' than the formal education system. For example, historically in industrial South Wales, there is evidence of conflict between well-articulated ideological systems, within which individual 'learner identities' were developed, whose origins were very much in community-based activity. Hence, Non-conformism gave rise to a conception of education as individual cultural accomplishment, which contrasted sharply with the collectivism associated with what Lewis (1993) terms 'workers' education' through the Workers' Educational Association, the National Labour College and so on. It remains to be seen, however, the extent to which the actual learning opportunities which these ideological systems supported were appropriated by individuals for their own particular projects; as, for instance, where miners used workers' education as a route to individual occupational mobility, rather than the collective advancement of the working class (G. Rees, 1997*b*).

What these brief examples illustrate is the *complexity* of the social experience within which 'learner identities' are rooted. Certainly, such experience extends beyond the formal institutions of education and, indeed, community-based learning too. The workplace is one key arena within which the 'learner identities' forged through the formal education system may be renegotiated (or, alternatively, reinforced). As the experience of the coal industry suggests, what is involved here can extend beyond the specifically vocational; as we have suggested, nationalisation may have contributed as significantly to shifting characteristic *educational* experiences in places like South Wales as did the changes in education policy which comprised part of the same post-war settlement (G. Rees, 1997*b*). Similarly, the development in recent years of a significant advanced manufacturing sector in the region, based to a great extent on foreign direct investment, may in due course contribute towards an equivalent redefinition of educational experience and associated 'learner identities'. Moreover, these changes may have particular impacts on specific social groups: most obviously, women.

These latter arguments also pose in an acute way the issue of changes in 'learner identities' over time. 'Educational and training cultures', embodying distinctive dispositions amongst peers towards education and training, may develop to reflect not only current socio-economic circumstances in a given area, but also the residue of the past. For instance, willingness to undertake job-related training may reflect both the traditions of such provision in a locality, as well as the requirements of current employment patterns. Moreover, family life is a key vehicle through which such inter-generational transmission occurs. Some young people have grown up in families where continuing education and training is part of the routine cycle of employment life for family members; it is a naturalised form of experience. For others—currently the majority—the opposite is true. In these circumstances, then, participating in learning after compulsory schooling, when it does take place, demands a re-working of personal history (Hodkinson, Sparkes and Hodkinson, 1996).

What all of this suggests is a much more nuanced social theory of life-long learning than that offered by the dominant discourse of human capital theory. As should be clear, however, much of the foregoing remains tentative; it provides the basis for a systematic programme of empirical research, rather than a fully finished analysis. Nevertheless, we believe that it offers some insights into the nature of the Learning Society, which we set out briefly in the concluding section [. . .]

Concluding Comments

At one level, our discussion suggests no more than the need to transcend conceptions of the Learning Society which are rooted in economistic models of market behaviour. Although such conceptions currently dominate official discourse, this conclusion may, nevertheless, be regarded as unexceptional. However, what is significant is that it is rooted in an analysis of the social relations of life-long learning, rather than simply expressing an alternative set of normative preferences. Hence, choices with respect to participation in learning opportunities may be *rational*, without conforming to the preferences presumed in human capital theory.

It is recognition of this simple point that, at least in part, explains well documented reluctance to take up learning opportunities (as, for instance, in the case of Youth Training). More generally, there is no reason to expect a simple consensus over the implications of education and training programmes: opportunities provided by the state or by employers may well not be construed as such by potential trainees or employees, for example. And this point, moreover, also problematises simplistic distinctions between education and vocational preparation; as we have seen, even workplace training may be constructed as significant educational experiences, given particular 'learner identities'.

We have emphasised the way in which individual biographies of participation in life-long learning are embedded in the *specificities* of history and place; and contrasted this with the over-simplifications of *universalising* perspectives such as human capital theory. However, our stress on the complexity of the social relations of life-long learning is more than some postmodern celebration of diversity for its own sake. In particular, locating these social relations within a framework which embraces both change over time and differentiation between places, has important implications for strategies for building a Learning Society. Most obviously, the inadequacies of conceiving the Learning Society simply as something to be achieved in the future are exposed. To be effective, strategies need to take account of the actual processes of change in learning opportunities which different social groups have experienced. In doing so, the differentiation in this experience between both social groups and localities cannot be ignored. Indeed, rather than a uniform Learning Society, the aim of development is better conceived as the creation of a diversity of Learning Societies, which build upon the real-world complexity of the social relations within which life-long learning takes place.

NOTES

This [chapter] derives from a research project funded by the ESRC (grant number L123 25 1041) and by the Training and Enterprise Councils of Gwent, Mid Glamorgan and West Glamorgan. None of these bodies is responsible for the views expressed.

1. For an elaboration of these comments, see Fevre *et al.* (1999).
2. See Rees, Williamson and Istance (1996) for an attempt to apply these ideas to the decisions of school-leavers to reject Youth Training.
3. Ingham (1996: 554) cites Duesenberry's well-known observation that 'economics is about how people make choices and sociology is about how people don't really have any'.
4. For an account of such 'trajectories' derived from our fieldwork, see Gorard and Rees (2002).
5. For a further exploration of these ideas, see Rees *et al.*, 2000.

Adult Education and Cohesion

Kjell Rubenson

Does there exist a distinguishable Nordic adult education model that other countries might try to duplicate? A recent Nordic study, the NOMAD-project, tries to answer this question (Tuijnman and Hellström, 2001) using data on participation in adult education in 22 countries from the International Adult Literacy Survey (OECD, 2000). This [chapter] discusses these findings within a political economic framework and draws conclusions for public policy and private sector strategies in adult education and training. As a background to the analysis the main findings and conclusions as offered by the NOMAD study will be briefly presented.

NOMAD: Main Findings and Conclusions

The Nordic countries are characterized by a very high participation in adult education and training (see Figure 65.1). The average participation rate in the Nordic block was 53 percent compared to 32 percent for all IALS [International Adult Literacy Survey] countries. However, a comparison with other highly industrialised countries in the IALS might be more appropriate. Thus, the average Nordic participation rate is about 14 percentage points higher (53 versus 39) than that of the following group of Anglo-Saxon countries: Australia, Canada, New Zealand, United Kingdom and United States.

Another distinguishable characteristic of Nordic adult education is that the ever-present law of inequality is less severe in this region than in other countries, see Figure 65.2. This has to do with an unusually high participation rate among those with a short formal education, particularly those in the employed population. However, as noted in the NOMAD report, those with a short formal education are still far behind the well educated. The Nordic level of inequality is also linked to a more equal age distribution among participants. Although there was a wide gap in participation rates between age groups in all countries, those aged 56–65 in the Nordic countries participated more often than their counterparts in other countries. The training of professional categories in the Nordic countries does not

From Kjell Rubenson (2003), 'Adult Education and Cohesion', *Lifelong Learning in Europe* 8/1. Reprinted with permission.

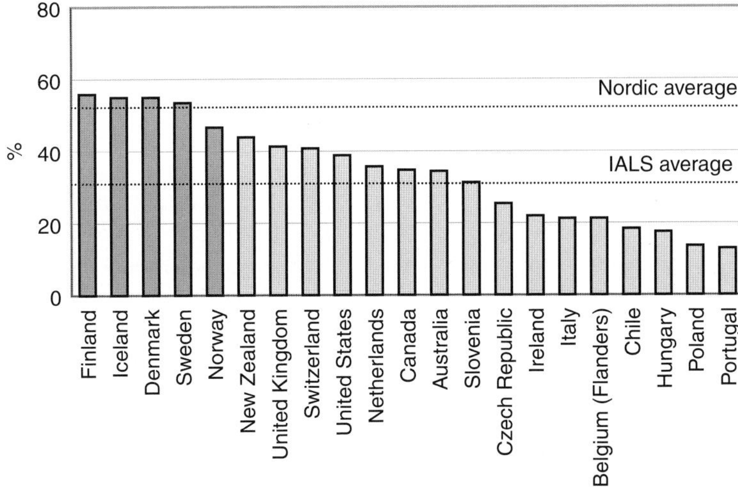

Fig. 65.1 Participation in adult education and training, population aged 25–65, 1994–1998

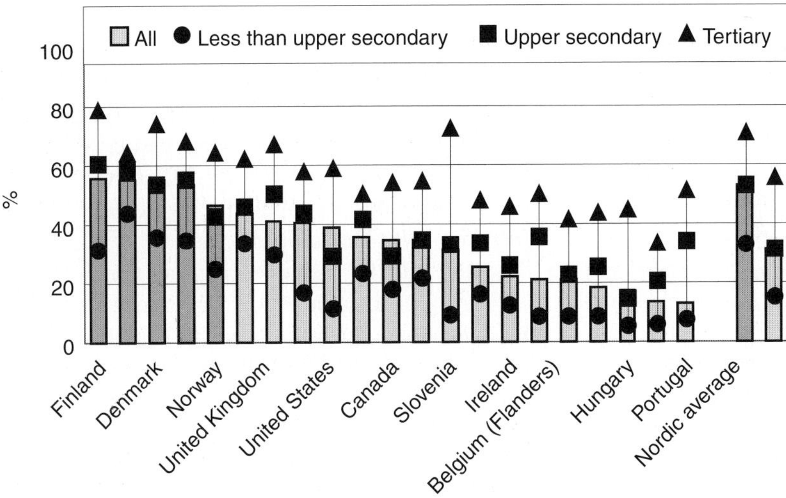

Fig. 65.2 Participation in adult education and training by educational attainment, population aged 25–65, 1994–1998
After Tuijman and Hellström, 2001

stand out. There was an as high or even higher rate of training in some other countries.

The IALS provides central information on public and private support for participation in adult education and training. The data show that employers are the primary source of financial support for that in all IALS countries. In the Nordic countries an average of 73 percent of those who had participated in some form of adult education and training reported that they had received financial support from the employer. This is slightly higher than the average for all the countries in the IALS, 69 percent.

The NOMAD report provides an in-depth analysis of the impact of level of public support for adult education. The study found no relationship between the level of public support for adult education and training and participation rates. However, NOMAD found that public support seems to have a crucial effect on the participation of those least likely to enrol in adult education and training. The authors conclude (ibid. 9): 'Thus it may be the case, more generally, that public support for disadvantaged groups is the main, defining characteristic of Nordic approaches to adult education.' The relatively high supply of adult education provided by public institutions in the Nordic countries makes the participants become less dependent on commercial providers.[1] The report notes that previous authors commenting on the Nordic model tend to point to a great diversity in institutional make-up and content of adult education. Nonetheless they generally conclude that the Nordic countries, viewed in an international perspective, have certain common values and basic assumptions that manifest themselves in the way in which adult learning is planned and designed (ibid. 13.)

In contrast the overall conclusion of NOMAD is that there does not seem to exist a one-dimensional Nordic model of adult education. Yet, the report notes that there are distinguishing Nordic patterns of adult education such as: a high participation rate; a high public share in financing; a high share of public suppliers; and a high share of personal-interest education. 'What does exist therefore is a Nordic "standard" in terms of participation rates, volume and orientation, and the role of the public sector' (ibid. 10).

What NOMAD refers to as the Nordic 'standard' might in a political economic terminology be referred to as the Nordic welfare regime, which will be the focus of this [chapter]. However, it should be noted that while there might not be a Nordic model of adult education there are certain common elements in all the Nordic countries. Thus, adult education is a highly visible phenomenon in the Nordic societies and far from the poor cousin that it is commonly referred to in many countries. A visit to a small community shows the central part of daily life the various forms of adult education have. This refers not only to bricks and mortar but also traditions of adult learning and teaching. Today's culture of adult education partly reflects an old tradition in all Nordic countries of a popular adult education sector with close links to social movements. What differ between the countries are the philosophical roots and institutional arrangements.

Adult education has since the 1960s evolved as a distinct and central public policy area across the Nordic countries, with a strong presence of the state. This also helps explain its current presence at all levels of society. Again, we find that specific policy designs, although aiming for the same goals, may differ. Another common element is the close involvement of the social partners in matters concerning adult education and a strong link between adult education and labour market policies. However, the thesis of this [chapter] is that we should anchor the analyses at the macro level rather than look at specific elements of the adult education system and pedagogical traditions. This makes it possible to reflect on how the broader institutional arrangements are creating conditions for adult education whereby at least some movement in the direction of lifelong learning for all becomes a possibility.

The Nordic Welfare-State Regime

Esping-Andersen (1991) identifies three distinct welfare state regimes characterised by different arrangements between state, market and the family. The Anglo-Saxon countries follow what he calls a liberal welfare-state regime where means-tested assistance, modest universal transfers, or modest social-insurance plans predominate. The benefits are mostly moderate and often associated with stigma. There is distrust towards the state, in both its willingness and its capability, as well as a strong belief in market-led solutions.

Another distinguishable regime-type can be found in nations such as Austria, France, Germany and Italy. Strongly influenced by the church and with old corporatist traditions there is less concern with market efficiency and granting of social rights have seldom been a contested issue in these countries. The tendency for the state is to [refrain from interfering] until the family capacity to help its members is exhausted.

The third category of countries follow what Esping-Andersen labels the social-democratic or Nordic regime-type. In this group of countries we find less dualism between state and market and between working class and middle class. The state sets a very demanding equity standard, rather than equity of minimal needs as pursued elsewhere. The citizen's right to services and benefits has traditionally been defined according to the pattern of the middle class. This model restricts the market and constructs an essentially universal solidarity in favour of the welfare state. A defining character of the social democratic state is the integration of welfare and work. While truly committed to a full-employment guarantee the Nordic model is at the same time entirely dependent on having a very extensive proportion in gainful employment as the massive cost of maintaining the welfare state forces it to minimize the social problems and maximize revenue income.

Esping-Andersen's classification of welfare-state regime was written more than ten years ago. During the 1990s the Nordic welfare model was under threat from ideological shifts and a severe economic crisis. In the beginning of the 1990s Finland and Sweden faced the worst economic downturn of any Western country since the great depression (Kautto, 2000). As the IALS data cover the middle of the 1990s we have to ask what kind of Nordic welfare state there was during that period. Despite all references to the death of the Nordic welfare-state regime it is therefore of interest to note that an in-depth analysis of how the two countries managed economic crises of the early 1990s shows that the Nordic welfare model not only survived the test, but that it mainly remains intact after the crisis (Kautto, 2000). 'It may be concluded here that in both countries the welfare state functioned as it should in a time of economic crisis and was able to soften its effects at the individual level' (ibid. 108). Several of the ideal-type characteristics of the Nordic welfare state are still visible, high taxation and high public spending as percentage of GDP, income inequality, although increasing, remains on a relatively lower level than elsewhere and full employment is still a central goal. However, as a response to the severe budgetary situation the principle of universalism is now, according to Kautto, weaker than before the economic downturn. But as he notes (p. 117): 'Yet in comparison to developments in other European countries Nordic distinctiveness in transfers and services seems to have persisted'.

When we try to understand the formation of adult learning in a time of economic and social challenges it is important that the Nordic welfare state is still in place with its institutional arrangements and traditions. A founding pillar in this strategy is the full employment concept, which has profound effects on adult education policies.

Full Employment, Human Capital Emphasis and Participation

The Nordic welfare-state model has been associated with a distinct labour market regime. An active labour market policy is a principal factor of economic stability and full employment, and the foundation for the building of a welfare state. The goal has been to achieve full employment while minimizing consumer price inflation and wage drift (Ryner, 2002). The provision of education and training arose out of the need to act swiftly against imbalances in the labour market. First, it helped underemployed and unemployed workers to improve their employability in occupations with better opportunities. Second, full employment prevented a fiscal overload on social policy programmes such as unemployment insurance and raised the general tax revenue. Third, it increased the supply of skills in industries where a shortage of suitably trained personnel tends to exacerbate inflationary pressures. Consequently not only the special labour market training programs but reforms in adult education generally have been heavily influenced by human capital thinking (Rubenson, 2002).

A very hierarchical and selective educational system had not produced the human capital necessary for modernizing the economy and ultimately wealth production. In the 1970s and 1980s, special post-compulsory options for adults at the secondary and tertiary levels were introduced, as well as major increases of funds for popular adult education. There was also a desire to promote democracy and to compensate for earlier injustices. The human capital concerns eased in the 1980s but returned a decade later with a vengeance to the fore of adult education policy, [which] was now driven by the challenges of the economic crises that took place in an environment shaped by concerns over how to adapt to the emergence of an information economy and the forces of globalisation.

With labour market conditions quickly eroding in the early 1990s the debate shifted to the role of adult education and training in the attack on unemployment. As an example, the Social Democratic government of Sweden introduced the Adult Education Initiative (AEI) (Sweden, Government Bill

1995/97: 222), not as an educational bill but as a cornerstone in its policy platform, 'Special Strategies Introduced in Order to Halve the Unemployment by Year 2000'. This was a gigantic five-year program for adult education focusing mainly on providing the equivalent of a three-year secondary education to unemployed adults. Over the five years, its aim was to reach 15 percent of the labour force. With an average yearly cost of ECU 3,700 per student the total investment in the five-year program was to be close to ECU 2 billion. The AEI signals a fundamental broadening of the Nordic tradition of active labour market policy. Instead of expanding labour market training programs with their strong vocational focus, the AEI is attempting to raise the general level of education of unemployed adults. Similar emphasis can be found in the other Nordic countries. The so-called Competence Reform in Norway (NOU, 1997: 25, OECD, 2001*a*), a far-reaching initiative to expand learning opportunities for adults as part of a national competence building, contains special provision for the education of adults at primary and secondary level. The 2000 adult education reform in Denmark saw public financing being targeted to a higher degree towards adult education and training that can contribute to giving formal qualification in the regular education and training system (OECD, 2001*b*: 73). Finally, Finland has recently launched a program to raise the educational level of adults aged 30–54 [who are] lacking a full secondary education. In accordance with the Nordic welfare-state model the education and training offered the unemployed in these reforms are quite extensive and not of the minimalist nature found in many other countries, particularly the Anglo-Saxon.

The close link between an active labour market policy and adult education can also be seen in the Swedish 2001 Bill on adult education. Unemployment is under control, and for future demographic changes and demands on the welfare system the Government's concern has shifted the focus onto how to raise the rate of participation in the economy. At the end of 2000 the rate stood at 77.5 percent for the labour force in ages 20–64. The goal is to raise this level to 80 percent by 2004. The Minister states: 'Adult education can in a considerable way help to make this a reality', (Sweden, Government Bill, 2000/01: 72, p. 22). Similar thinking is evident in Finland.

Recent Nordic policy documents reflect a growing understanding that while the New Economy holds the promise of increased productivity and an improved standard of living it also introduces a new set of transitions and adjustment challenges for society, industry, and individuals. If not met these challenges could increase the permanent exclusion or marginalisation of segments of the population and exacerbate socio-economic divisions. It should be noted that there is a strong objection also in the Nordic countries to the economistic paradigm driving adult education. However, it is of interest to note that not only governments influenced by the hegemony of neo-liberal thinking but also progressive welfare researchers promote lifelong learning as a solution to economic and social pressures (Esping-Andersen 1996: 259). While there is an understanding that adult education in itself does not create jobs, learning can promote competencies to adapt to the demands of the new economy and allow full participation in social and economic life. Lifelong learning can help provide citizens with the chance to acquire adequate skills to prevent low-paid jobs in the services from becoming life-cycle traps.

The recent shifts in adult education and human capital developments in the Nordic countries could be seen as a movement towards what Esping-Andersen (1996: 260) labels: 'A Pareto optimal welfare state of the future might very well be one that shifts the accent of social citizenship from its present preoccupation with income maintenance towards a menu of rights to lifelong learning and qualification.' It is interesting to note that while the state has been very keen to use labour market and educational policy to promote human capital development it has, despite strong pressures from the unions, been reluctant to regulate employer-sponsored education and training and [has] largely left this to be settled by the social partners at the bargaining table. This brings us to the Nordic model of industrial relations, which is an integrated part of the welfare-state regime.

The Nordic Model of Industrial Relations and Participation

The Nordic countries have seen partly different developments of industrial relations over the last fifteen years. A centrally co-ordinated decentralization trend has been visible in Sweden and Denmark while Finland and Norway have seen a revival of tripartite concentration at the central level (Dølvik and Stokke, 1998; Lilja, 1998; Scheuer, 1998). Despite these trends, continuing similarities between the Nordic countries and their differences to other countries still justify the notion of a Nordic model of industrial relations (Kjellberg, 1998).

There are some fundamental characteristics of this model that have been very conducive to the promotion of adult education and training. Firstly, a highly developed corporatist structure has fostered a tradition of collaboration between the state and the labour market organisations. Dølvik and Stokke (1998: 31), speaking from a Norwegian perspective, but relevant to the Nordic model of industrial relations, argue that contrary to commonly stated assumptions that globalization will undermine national corporatism, the Norwegian example suggests that renationalised co-operative practices can be a viable strategy for coping with such pressures. Thus they see the radical decentralization that has taken place in the Anglo- Saxon countries as the outcome of strong political agendas, rather than reflections of structural change in working life. This has helped develop a comparatively high degree of consensus on issues like productivity, the introduction of new technology and training (Qvale and Øverland, 2001).

Secondly, not only the trade unions, which boast the highest union density rates in industrial societies, but also the employers have a very large membership and are highly organised into large confederations of unions and employer associations with representation at national as well as local level. This provides the social partners with a strong research capacity and enables them to analyse and engage in public debates around vital policy issues. In the context of this [chapter] it is of interest to note that both trade unions and employers' confederations have, over the last thirty years, continuously paid close attention to education and training issues. The traditional three-tier system of collective bargaining corresponds to a four-level system of union organization: the workplace; local union branches; national unions; and union confederations. The local clubs that are fully integrated in the national unions and the local branches are involved in local bargaining selection of health and safety representatives, participation in project groups influencing the work environment and the design of work organization and new technology clubs also organize study circles. This reflects a unique combination of centralisation and decentralisation, a central feature in Nordic industrial relations. This has strengthened the position of workers at the political level through close links between social-democratic parties and unions while it at the same time also facilitates the union's presence at the workplace and allows direct contact with workers (Kjellberg, 1998: 75.). Thus, while The Confederation of Blue-Collar Workers (LO) is engaged in the production of research-based policy documents on adult education and training aimed at influencing public policy, it is at the same time, through its local representation, busy at the workplaces organising study circles for its membership. This helps to explain the unusually high participation in adult education and training among blue-collar workers in the Nordic countries.

The central involvement of the trade unions in adult education, at all levels of the organisation, helps adult education become part of a worker's individual and collective identity. In the struggle for individual and/or collective change the structure encourages [the worker] to reflect on the role adult education may or may not play. At the same time the corporatist institution provides a structure whereby adult education and training can become part of negotiations on changes in production processes and work organisation, introduction of new technology and economic democracy.

Civil Society, Popular Adult Education and Participation in Adult Education

The high and relatively more equal participation rates can partly be explained by the structure of the Nordic Adult education sector. In contrast to the situation in most other countries there exists a publicly supported sector of popular adult education. To many foreign observers knowledge of popular movements and popular adult education is an important source [for] the understanding of Nordic social development (Battail, 1988). The late nineteenth early twentieth century saw the emergence of strong popular movements that promoted their ideas through various forms of popular adult education, e.g. folk high schools and adult education associations. Over time this developed into a relatively unique and highly institutionalised popular adult education system whose distinguishing characteristics, despite considerable state and municipal subsidies, are that it is free and voluntary. Historically, popular adult education has been part of the labour movement's counter-hegemonic ambition and the movement's ambition to heighten individual members' consciousness and commitment to its dreams and goals for social change and justice.

Popular adult education can be seen as a part of the corporate state, lying at the crossroads between civil society and the state. State subsidies for popular adult education are motivated by the desire to support an enterprise that aims to make it possible for people individually and collectively to influence their position in life and promote commitment to participate in the development of society. Today popular adult education has three roles: as an agency of popular movements, an adult educator, and as a supporter of culture. The study associations reach an overwhelming proportion of people in popular adult education. These associations are motivated by the desire to support an enterprise that aims to make it possible for people to influence their position in life and promote commitment to participate in the development of society. The studies are supposed to grow out of the interests and needs of the participants, should encourage position taking and decision making and act as a counterforce to the increased commercialisation and technocratisation of culture and social life.

Through the existence of a publicly supported popular adult education, individuals in the Nordic countries have access to a form of adult education that can respond to different aspirations and needs than [can] the formal educational system or the education and training supplied by the employer. The existence of study associations and folk high schools within the labour movement promotes an offering of study circles and courses that focus on the needs and aspirations of groups that traditionally do not participate in adult education and that are not interested to enhance their formal level of education. These needs are not age-specific to the extent that career-oriented motives are and this might explain the fact that participation in adult education and training among those [aged] 55 and older is comparatively high in the Nordic countries. Social class and ethnicity come into play also in participation in popular adult education. Yet, the system provides a content and form of adult education that has greater appeal to those traditionally not participating than other forms of general adult education (Rubenson, 1996).

In addition to the broad impact of the welfare-state regime, industrial relations and existence of a publicly supported popular adult education sector, I shall briefly address how the funding regime affects participation by non-traditional groups in the Nordic countries.

Recruitment-Enhancing Programs and Participation

Funding regime is one of the key policy instruments available for influencing participation. As noted in the NOMAD report, the existence of public funding for adult education did not affect the overall participation rates in the IALS countries but seemed to be one of the reasons for the high participation rates in the Nordic countries. An explanation for this is that potential participants had access to publicly funded adult education, which was free or had very low tuition fees.

A crucial issue related to the funding regime is the link between supply of and demand for adult education on the one hand, and the processes that govern who gets what kind of adult education on the other. In order to understand why the effects of adult education on equity are so small we have to look at the way demand determines what the adult education organizations supply. In a market-driven system it is obvious that advantaged groups will strongly influence patterns of provision.

There is evidence to suggest that even organisations with pronounced ambitions to reach disadvantaged groups, unless there is earmarked funding for the target groups, actually provide a service that corresponds better to the demands of the advantaged. This is a result of existing funding regimes not compensating for the increased costs involved in recruiting the underprivileged. In a time when government policies seek to increase efficiency through the adoption of a more market-oriented approach and outcomes-based funding, there is a growing likelihood that the organisation goes after those easiest to recruit and more likely to succeed (see McIntyre, Brown, and Ferrier, 1996). In this perspective the comparatively successful recruitment of less well educated to adult education in the Nordic countries is a result, not of public funding as such, but [of the] availability of targeted funding for recruiting disadvantaged groups. Nordic adult education policies over the last 25 years show that general policies have limited effects on the recruitment of disadvantaged groups as traditionally strong groups are consuming more than their fair share of the resources. Instead it has been earmarked funding for targeted strategies, like outreach and special study aid, which have been most successful (Rubenson, 1996). These measures are based on the assumption that certain groups will 'consume' a supply and the challenge is to stimulate the demands among those groups for which the measure is taken.

Funding regimes bring up crucial issues around the relationship between the state and its citizens, and what understanding of democracy informs state interventions (see Rothstein, 1998). Dworkin (1977: 180 ff.) argues that the state should treat citizens not just with concern and respect but with equal concern and respect. In accordance with this principal both Rawls and Dworking argue for justice in resource allocation. However, as Amytag Sen (1982) stresses, the resource argument is not a sufficient condition for a just society. Instead he introduces the concept of basic capability equality referring, among other things, to the need to take into account differences in those abilities that are crucial for citizens to function in society.

Nussbaum (1990) discusses the fundamental problem caused by the fact that people living under difficult conditions tend to come to accept their fate, as they do not imagine any reasonable alternative. She argues that instead of accepting this situation, it is the duty of the state, with due respect of citizens' right to choose different ways of life, to see to it that citizens are in a position to make well-considered choices. In relation to what is being discussed in this [chapter], the issue is whether or not one possesses the basic capability to make choices with regard to participating in adult education. Sen's concept helps us to understand why a 'system' of adult education that implicitly takes for granted that the adult possesses vital instruments to make use of the available adult education possibilities by necessity widens, rather than narrows, the educational and cultural gaps in society. Instead the distribution of basic capabilities points to discrepancies in readiness to engage in organised forms of adult learning. The question is to what extend there are programs in place to help develop the basic capabilities.

Concluding Remarks

The Nordic participation patterns in adult education and training strongly support Martin Carnoy's point that there are crucial differences in what adult education attempts to do and can do in different social-political structures. He states (Carnoy, 1995: 3): 'Ultimately, these differences depend heavily on the possibilities and limits of the state, since it is the state that defines adult education and is the principal beneficiary of its effective implementation. These possibilities and limits of the state are, then, a key issue understanding the form and content of adult education.' In this context it is of interest to note that the International Literacy Survey (OECD, 2000) found that there is a strong relationship between economic inequality in a country on the one hand, and literacy and adult education participation inequalities on the other hand (see Figure 65.3). Where one is high the other two are also rampant. Second, the countries tend to group themselves in three distinguishable clusters. There are the Nordic countries with relatively speaking low economic and literacy inequalities. In the middle we can detect a continental European cluster with Germany and the Netherlands with slightly higher inequalities than in the first group. And then there is the Anglo-Saxon group which show the highest level of inequality. The finding seems to suggest that inequalities in basic capabilities, as defined by literacy, are part of national structures and can be understood in terms of various forms of welfare-state regimes. Thus, the high participation

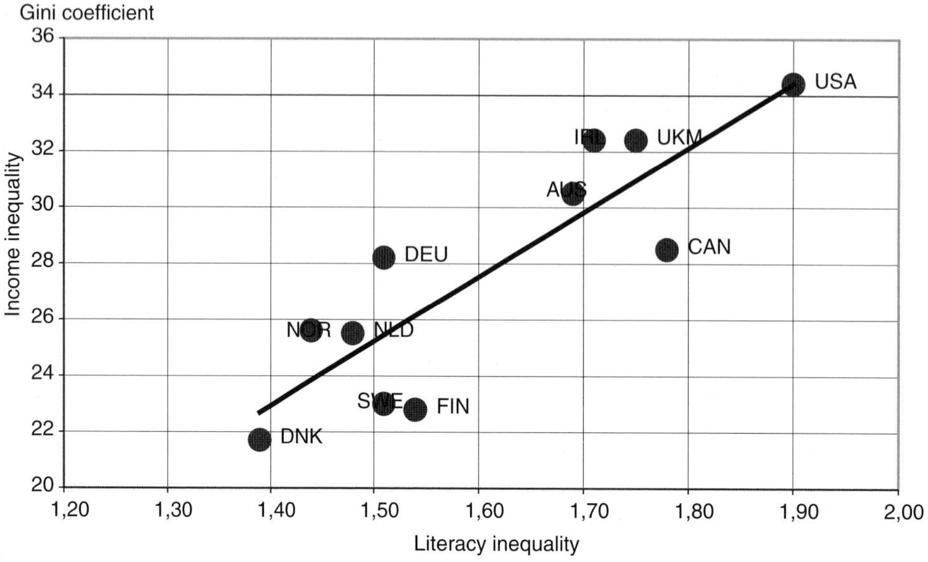

Fig. 65.3 Relationship between economic inequality (Gini coefficient) and the inequality in the distribution of literacy within selected countries. (Adapted from OECD, 2000).

rates in the Nordic countries are in line with what can be expected according to the Nordic welfare regime and reflect an active state concerned about inequalities in participation.

Accounts of globalisation often posit policy and institutional convergence towards reliance on individual and market incentives, rather than political or institutional mechanisms (Ohmae, 1990; Clayton and Pontusson, 1998). Yet the characteristics of the Nordic model of adult education seem to support findings in other studies that there is little convergence in the areas of labour market strategy, including the education and training systems and welfare-state role (McBride and Williams, 2001; Garrett, 1998; Rueda and Pontusson, 2000; Thelen and Kume, 1999). Distinct models of capitalism (Vogel 2001; Thelen, 2000), welfare state (Rieger and Leibfried, 1998; Regini, 2000), and skills formation systems (Brown et al., 2001; Ashton and Green, 1996) persist.

The assertion that the Nordic model of adult education persists should not be interpreted as an absence of hegemonic pressures from neoliberalistic ideas on current adult education policy. The demands of the market and individuals' responsibility to adapt to the challenges of the knowledge economy are themes that run through recent policy documents. Thus, in a shift from the traditional Nordic position on adult education, recent policy documents stress that it is essential to begin with the needs of the individual as the starting point for planning social measures. The recent reform Bill in Sweden notes that adult education and training has so far been too concentrated on treating the individual as part of a collective with a common background and common needs, with teaching organised in pre-packaged forms. Therefore, the challenge for state-supported education and training is to cater to everyone on the basis of individual wishes, needs and requirements. Some of the language in the Bill is reminiscent of the general neo-liberal discourse that has informed the policy directions of lifelong learning.

Marginson (1997) notes that the revolutionaries of the right do not restrict themselves to cutting public expenditure but in accordance with their basic values, emphasise as well the creation of quasi-markets in the educational sector. Increasingly, competition is enhanced in the Nordic countries by transferring public funds to private sector educational providers. While the notion of a training market is central in the 2001 Bill, the discourse is partly different to the neo-liberal one in that the state is clearly a player. Resources allocated for outreach activities, counselling, availability of courses and financial support can be seen as the base of a state-supported infrastructure for lifelong learning.

In the discussion above I made a case for a link between the existence of a viable sector of popular adult education and the high participation rate in adult education. Policy makers continue to stress that popular adult education has an important role to play in lifelong learning and that it can and should function as a counterweight to the commercialised, elitist and segregating forces that are so apparent in today's society. However, the actual public resources for popular adult education are decreasing. Further, by stressing lifelong learning as an individual project, the collective efforts of the social movements through their study associations are further being reduced and the traditional link between civil society and popular adult education is weakened. This development, at play in all the Nordic countries, is particularly visible in Denmark. In the 1980s labour market related training and education programs, as well as in the so-called 'Ten-Item Plan for Recurrent Education', there was a strong concern for securing basic education and broad competences for the less-well-educated groups through the means of collective efforts. This has now been replaced by a privileging of the individual and formal educational institutions while sharply reducing the resources for the collective ambitions of social movements, particularly the labour movement. The collective ethos is further being eroded by the shift in the Nordic countries from a concern about adult education to a preoccupation with lifelong learning which naturally puts the focus on the individual.

Another threat comes from the major shift that has occurred in the adult education landscape. While the balance between popular adult education and formal adult education has shifted, with the latter growing in importance, the most dramatic change is the enormous growth that has occurred in employer-sponsored activities. To understand adult education today is to understand the impact of the 'long arm of the job.' While employer sponsored adult education may be more equally distributed than in most other countries it is still the fact that there are major inequalities in access to this kind of education which is linked to work hierarchy and the nature of the job. Not only does the rate of participation differ greatly by the level of occupation but so does also the nature of the educational training. Those in higher positions more often follow academically oriented, often externally organised courses, while unskilled workers receive some shorter form of on-the-job training. Further, higher positions provide better and richer chances to learn new things on the job. These differences are more marked in the private sector than in the public (Xu, 2000). With the state unwilling to regulate workplace learning the future development will largely depend on the union's capacity to fulfil their aspirations at the bargaining table. However, the intervention by the Norwegian state in the 1999 central bargaining process to secure employees' right to study leave is an interesting exception.

The Nordic debate on adult education has mainly centred on whether or not the disadvantaged participate, and less on the type of adult education in which they participate. In other words, discussion has addressed only one of the two prerequisites for a redistribution of economic and cultural resources: participation. Whether or not this participation leads to a more equal distribution of resources has not received careful attention. In assessing the actual effects either in the creation of resources or in the intention of overcoming educational inequalities, it is worthwhile noting that most adult activities are in the form of short courses. The voluntary associations' study circle activities, the main component of popular adult education, usually last a maximum of 30 hours and the employer-sponsored activities are equally short. Thus, with a certain amount of exaggeration, it can be argued that more than 80 percent of Nordic participation in adult education has little or no effect on educational disparities in terms of the number of years of education people acquire. However, a strong argument can also be made about their importance for the general ability of the citizens. As Hartman (2000) has shown, popular adult education has remained important for the day-to-day work in popular movements. Further, popular adult education has an ability to reach and activate groups with little or an insufficient education. Most importantly it is thanks to such a large [proportion] of Nordic adults being involved in these shorter courses organised by study associations and the employer that the literacy levels among citizens in the Nordic countries with a short formal education is higher than in any other OECD country (OECD, 2000).

The present shift in the Nordic debate from recurrent education to lifelong learning as the organising principal for policy making further highlights the issue of the wider benefits, not only of formal and non-formal learning but now also of informal learning. To think about lifelong learning in this broad, all-encompassing way is a change of Copernican magnitude with broad consequences for how the Nordic countries address lifelong learning for all. It raises enormous challenges for public policy. Within this perspective the very core of lifelong learning is the informal or 'everyday' learning, positive or negative, which occurs in day-to-day life. Here, the issue is the nature and structure of everyday experiences, and their consequences for a person's learning processes, ways of thinking, and competencies. What challenges do people face? What possibilities do these challenges create, not only for restrictive forms of learning, but also for investigative learning promoting new ways of acting (see Engeström, 1994)?

It is interesting to note that during the progressive era of Danish adult education in the 1980s the discussions about everyday learning focused on possibilities and limitations caused by conditions of working life (see Salling-Olsen, 1989). This seems to be a more fruitful way to approach lifelong learning than what can be found in the present discussion where the informal aspects are being reduced to technical discussions on how to assess what has been learned in informal settings. Thus, the question ought to be, to what extent do working life, civil society and democratic traditions lead to a curriculum of everyday life inspiring and requiring all Nordic citizens to be active learners? And to what extent do social movements and educational institutions organise and support this learning?

NOTE

1. For a good overview of the national systems of adult education in Denmark, Finland, Norway, and Sweden see country reports prepared for OECD Thematic Review of Adult Learning (<http://www.oecd.org/EN/links_abstract/0,,EN-links_abstract-602–5-no-no-1240–0,00.html>).

Part Ten

Education and Development

Debates over issues of development in education have centred on neo-classical economic models which elevated the concepts of free trade and human capital theory (Becker, Ch. 19) to a central position in the policies of the multilateral agencies. The issue of free trade impinges on education in two ways. There are questions to be raised as to whether free trade produces the economic benefits to create greater income equality between societies (Wade 2004) and there are also questions about the way free trade policies destroy industries and the skills of indigenous workers (Buffie 2001). The fundamental problem with the theory of free trade as it has been applied to developing countries is that it fails to take into account inequalities of resources between developed and developing economies. Indeed as we have suggested in the general introduction, too often mercantilist policies that seek to advantage corporations in the developed world are advanced under the guise of free trade. What in effect has often occurred is that developing countries are forced to open their economies to Western corporations in return for various kinds of aid.

Buffie (2001) documents the consequences of trade liberalization in which the latter was followed by a surge in imports and a decline in exports, citing the examples of Senegal, Côte d'Ivoire, Nigeria, Sierra Leone, Zambia, Zaire, Uganda, Tanzania, Malawi, Cameroon, and Mozambique, and, in Latin America, Peru, Nicaragua, Ecuador, and Brazil all experienced large job losses in the formal sector and a substantial worsening of underemployment. The result for education has been a loss of the possibility of greater funding in the countries affected and a loss of skills, as viable industries have been unable to compete with overseas corporations.

The educational counterpart to the doctrine of free trade has been human capital theory, the idea that if countries invest in the education and skills of the population then this will equip them for the rigours of a free trade environment. The theory has had many critics both in the developed and developing world. A leading critic whose arguments apply to both contexts is

Amartya Sen (Ch. 66). Central to his account is the view that individuals should have the capacity to make considered choices about how to live their lives. A view which sees education as simply a branch of economic policy is unlikely to be able to achieve what, for Sen, is this prior and more important issue. Sen's account of the development of such a capacity is now being taken up in the educational literature (Unterhalter 2003; Saito 2003; Flores-Crespo 2004).

Stromquist (Ch. 67) examines the various global, national, and local factors that impact differentially on the influence of poverty on girls' education in Latin America. Her account highlights the complexities involved in seeking to address issues of poverty for girls through education. As she concludes, if schooling is to make a difference for poor women it has to be accompanied by changes in social and economic life, some of which are national and others international.

What Stromquist draws attention to are the various complex strands that need to be addressed if education is to be effective. This requires rethinking many of the dominant theories about the alleviation of poverty in developing countries. Mazawi (Ch. 68) also argues that in the West the kind of thinking about education in Arab states is coloured by assumptions that simply do not hold. The issues, he argues, are far more complex than Western commentators have assumed.

Given the limitations to the theories and policies of the multinational agencies and the complexities involved in developing an effective education to alleviate poverty, Mundy and Murphy (Ch. 69) examine the prospects of transnational advocacy networks (TANs) which bring together a wide grouping of Non-Governmental Organizations, citizens associations, and trade unions to apply pressure to global institutions. What they explore is the possibility that these TANs, as examples of an emerging global civil society, have the potential to act effectively to counter the more top-down approaches to educational policy employed by, for example, the World Bank, among others.

Pauline Rose's (Ch. 70) focus is on what she describes as the impact of the post-Washington consensus on education in Malawi. The post-Washington consensus recognized that the structural adjustment programmes of the 1980s had a negative impact as Buffie has described in relation to many developing economies. The post-Washington consensus took on board the need to look at the role of the state rather than just the market, but did so within broadly the same neo-liberal framework which in education gave priority to human capital theory. While she notes there has been a significant expansion in primary education in Malawi under the guiding hand of human capital theory, many problems remain, especially education's role relating to social integration and cohesion and the creation of a new national identity.

The final chapter in this section, and indeed the book, raises some of the most intellectually demanding and poignant issues concerning education. We have seen a growing recognition that children are often the victims of violence in both developed and developing countries. Lynn Davies (Ch. 71) argues that national systems of education have much to answer for in perpetuating violence but that at the local level of an education for refugees there is much that can be done. The global media has done much to draw our attention to the plight of the victims of violence at a time when the hope has been that the world might advance morally and socially beyond violence. Davies's argument about the causes of much of this violence is an invitation to rethink the relationships between the national and the global in the future.

Poverty as Capability Deprivation

Amartya Sen

In analyzing social justice, there is a strong case for judging individual advantage in terms of the capabilities that a person has, that is, the substantive freedoms he or she enjoys to lead the kind of life he or she has reason to value. In this perspective, poverty must be seen as the deprivation of basic capabilities rather than merely as lowness of incomes, which is the standard criterion of identification of poverty.[1] The perspective of capability-poverty does not involve any denial of the sensible view that low income is clearly one of the major causes of poverty, since lack of income can be a principal reason for a person's capability deprivation.

Indeed, inadequate income is a strong predisposing condition for an impoverished life. If this is accepted, what then is all this fuss about, in seeing poverty in the capability perspective (as opposed to seeing it in terms of the standard income-based poverty assessment)? The claims in favor of the capability approach to poverty are, I believe, the following.

1. Poverty can be sensibly identified in terms of capability deprivation; the approach concentrates on deprivations that are *intrinsically* important (unlike low income, which is only *instrumentally* significant).
2. There are influences on capability deprivation—and thus on real poverty—*other* than lowness of income (income is not the only instrument in generating capabilities).
3. The instrumental relation between low income and low capability is *variable* between different communities and even between different families and different individuals (the impact of income on capabilities is contingent and conditional).[2]

The third issue is particularly important in considering and evaluating public action aimed at reducing inequality or poverty. Various reasons for conditional variations have been discussed in the literature, and it is useful to emphasize some of them specifically in the context of practical policy making.

First, the relationship between income and capability would be strongly affected by the age of the person (e.g., by the specific needs of the old and the very young), by gender and social roles (e.g., through special responsibilities of maternity and also custom-determined family obligations), by location (e.g., by proneness to flooding or drought, or by insecurity and violence in some inner-city living), by epidemiological atmosphere (e.g., through diseases endemic in a region) and by other variations over which a person may have no—or only limited—control.[3] In making contrasts of population groups classified according to age, gender, location and so on, these parametric variations are particularly important.

Second, there can be some 'coupling' of disadvantages between (1) income deprivation and (2) adversity in converting income into functionings.[4] Handicaps, such as age or disability or illness, reduce one's ability to earn an income.[5] But they also make it harder to convert income into capability, since an older, or more disabled, or more seriously ill person may need more income (for assistance, for prosthesis, for treatment) to achieve

From A. Sen, *Development as Freedom* (Oxford: Oxford University Press, 2001). Reprinted with permission.

the same functionings (even when that achievement is at all possible).[6] This entails that 'real poverty' (in terms of capability deprivation) may be, in a significant sense, more intense than what appears in the income space. This can be a crucial concern in assessing public action to assist the elderly and other groups with 'conversion' difficulties in addition to lowness of income.

Third, distribution within the family raises further complications with the income approach to poverty. If the family income is used disproportionately in the interest of some family members and not others (for example, if there is a systematic 'boy preference' in the family allocation of resources), then the extent of the deprivation of the neglected members (girls in the example considered) may not be adequately reflected in terms of family income. This is a substantial issue in many contexts; sex bias does appear to be a major factor in the family allocation in many countries in Asia and North Africa. The deprivation of girls is more readily checked by looking at capability deprivation (in terms of greater mortality, morbidity, undernourishment, medical neglect, and so on) than can be found on the basis of income analysis.[7]

This issue is clearly not as central in the context of inequality and poverty in Europe or North America, but the presumption—often implicitly made—that the issue of gender inequality does not apply at the basic level to the 'Western' countries can be, to some extent, misleading. For example, Italy has one of the highest ratios of 'unrecognized' labor by women vis-à-vis recognized labor included in the standard national accounts.[8] The accounting of effort and time expended, and the related reduction of freedom, has some bearing on the analysis of poverty even in Europe and North America. There are also other ways in which intrafamily divisions are important to include among the considerations relevant for public policy in most parts of the world.

Fourth, *relative* deprivation in terms of *incomes* can yield *absolute* deprivation in terms of *capabilities*. Being relatively poor in a rich country can be a great capability handicap, even when one's absolute income is high in terms of world standards. In a generally opulent country, more income is needed to buy enough commodities to achieve the *same social functioning*. This consideration—pioneeringly outlined by Adam Smith in *The Wealth of Nations* (1776)—is quite central to sociological understandings of poverty, and it has been analyzed by W. G. Runciman, Peter Townsend and others.[9]

For example, the difficulties that some groups of people experience in 'taking part in the life of the community' can be crucial for any study of 'social exclusion.' The need to take part in the life of a community may induce demands for modern equipment (televisions, videocassette recorders, automobiles and so on) in a country where such facilities are more or less universal (unlike what would be needed in less affluent countries), and this imposes a strain on a relatively poor person in a rich country even when that person is at a much higher level of income compared with people in less opulent countries.[10] Indeed, the paradoxical phenomenon of hunger in rich countries—even in the United States—has something to do with the competing demands of these expenses.[11]

What the capability perspective does in poverty analysis is to enhance the understanding of the nature and causes of poverty and deprivation by shifting primary attention away from *means* (and one particular means that is usually given exclusive attention, viz., income) to *ends* that people have reason to pursue, and, correspondingly, to the *freedoms* to be able to satisfy these ends. The examples briefly considered here illustrate the additional discernment that results from this basic extension. The deprivations are seen at a more fundamental level—one closer to the informational demands of social justice. Hence the relevance of the perspective of capability-poverty.

Income Poverty and Capability Poverty

While it is important to distinguish conceptually the notion of poverty as capability inadequacy from that of poverty as lowness of income, the two perspectives cannot but be related, since income is such an important means to capabilities. And since enhanced capabilities in leading a life would tend, typically, to expand a person's ability to be more productive and earn a higher income, we would also expect a connection going from capability improvement to greater earning power and not only the other way around.

The latter connection can be particularly important for the removal of income poverty. It is not only the case that, say, better basic education and health care improve the quality of life directly; they also increase a person's ability to earn an income and be free of income-poverty as well. The more inclusive the reach of basic education and health care, the more likely it is that even the potentially poor would have a better chance of overcoming penury.

The importance of this connection was a crucial point of focus of my recent work on India, done jointly with Jean Drèze, dealing with economic reforms.[12] In many ways, the economic reforms have opened up for the Indian people economic opportunities that were suppressed by overuse of control and by the limitations of what had been called the 'license Raj.'[13] And yet the opportunity to make use of the new possibilities is not independent of the social preparation that different sections of the Indian community have. While the reforms were overdue, they could be much more productive if the social facilities were there to support the economic opportunities for all sections of the community. Indeed, many Asian economies—first Japan, and then South Korea, Taiwan, Hong Kong, and Singapore, and later post-reform China and Thailand and other countries in East Asia and Southeast Asia—have done remarkably well in spreading the economic opportunities through an adequately supportive social background, including high levels of literacy, numeracy, and basic education; good general health care; completed land reforms; and so on. The lesson of opening of the economy and the importance of trade has been more easily learned in India than the rest of the message from the same direction of the rising sun.[14]

India is, of course, highly diverse in terms of human development, with some regions (most notably, Kerala) having much higher levels of education, health care and land reform than others (most notably, Bihar, Uttar Pradesh, Rajasthan and Madhya Pradesh). The limitations have taken different forms in the different states. It can be argued that Kerala has suffered from what were until recently fairly anti-market policies, with deep suspicion of market-based economic expansion without control. So its human resources have not been as well used in spreading economic growth as they could have been with a more complementary economic strategy, which is now being attempted. On the other hand, some of the northern states have suffered from low levels of social development, with varying degrees of control and market-based opportunities. The need for seizing the relevance of complementarity is very strong in remedying the diverse drawbacks.

It is, however, interesting that despite the rather moderate record in economic growth, Kerala seems to have had a faster rate of reduction in income poverty than any other state in India.[15] While some states have reduced income poverty through high economic growth (Punjab is the most notable example of that), Kerala has relied a great deal on expansion of basic education, health care and equitable land distribution for its success in reducing penury.

While these connections between income poverty and capability poverty are worth emphasizing, it is also important not to lose sight of the basic fact that the reduction of income poverty alone cannot possibly be the ultimate motivation of antipoverty policy. There is a danger in seeing poverty in the narrow terms of income deprivation, and then justifying investment in education, health care and so forth on the ground that they are good means to the end of reducing income poverty. That would be a confounding of ends and means. The basic foundational issues force us, for reasons already discussed, toward understanding poverty and deprivation in terms of lives people can actually lead and the freedoms they do actually have. The expansion of human capabilities fits directly into these basic considerations. It so happens that the enhancement of human capabilities also tends to go with an expansion of productivities and earning power. That connection establishes an important indirect linkage through which capability improvement helps both directly and indirectly in enriching human lives and in making human deprivations more rare and less acute. The instrumental connections, important as they are, cannot replace the need for a basic understanding of the nature and characteristics of poverty.

Inequality of What?

The treatment of inequality in economic and social evaluation involves many dilemmas. Substantial inequalities are often hard to defend in terms of models of 'fairness.' Adam Smith's concern with the interests of the poor (and his outrage at the tendency for those interests to be neglected) related naturally to his use of the imaginative device of what it would look like to an 'impartial spectator'—an inquiry that offers far-reaching insights on the requirements of fairness in social judgment.[16] Similarly, John Rawls's idea of 'justice as fairness' in terms of what can be expected to be chosen in a hypothetical 'original position' in which people do not yet know who they are going to be provides a rich understanding of the demands of equity, and yields the anti-inequality features that are characteristic of his 'principles of justice.'[17] Patent inequalities in social arrangements can also be difficult to justify in terms of reasonableness to actual members of the society (for example, the case for these inequalities being one that others 'cannot reasonably reject': a criterion that Thomas Scanlon has proposed—and powerfully used—for ethical evaluation).[18] Certainly, severe inequalities are not socially attractive, and momentous inequalities can be, some would argue, downright barbaric. Furthermore, the sense of inequality may also erode social cohesion, and some types of inequalities can make it difficult to achieve even efficiency.

And yet attempts to eradicate inequality can, in many circumstances, lead to loss for most—sometimes even for all. This kind of conflict can arise in mild or severe form depending on the exact circumstances. Models of justice—involving the 'impartial spectator,' or the 'original position,' or not-reasonable-rejection—have to take note of these diverse considerations.

Not surprisingly, the conflict between aggregative and distributive considerations has received a remarkable amount of professional attention among economists. This is appropriate since it is an important issue.[19] Many compromise formulas have been suggested for evaluating social achievements by taking note simultaneously of aggregative and distributive considerations. A good example is A. B. Atkinson's 'equally distributed equivalent income,' a concept that adjusts the aggregate income by reducing its accounted value according to the extent of inequality in income distribution, with the tradeoff between aggregative and distributive concerns being given by the choice of a parameter that reflects our ethical judgment.[20]

There is, however, a different class of conflicts that relates to the choice of 'space'—or of the focal variable in terms of which inequality is to be assessed and scrutinized—and this relates to the subject matter of the previous chapter. Inequality of incomes can differ substantially from inequality in several other 'spaces' (that is, in terms of other relevant variables), such as well-being, freedom and different aspects of the quality of life (including health and longevity). And even aggregative achievements would take different forms depending on the space in which the composition—or the 'totaling'—is done (for example, ranking societies in terms of average income may differ from ranking them according to average health conditions).

The contrast between the different perspectives of income and capability has a direct bearing on the space in which inequality and efficiency are to be examined. For example, a person with high income but no opportunity of political participation is not 'poor' in the usual sense, but is clearly poor in terms of an important freedom. Someone who is richer than most others but suffers from an ailment that is very expensive to treat is obviously deprived in an important way, even though she would not be classified as poor in the usual statistics of income distribution. A person who is denied the opportunity of employment but given a handout from the state as an 'unemployment benefit' may look a lot less deprived in the space of incomes than in terms of the valuable—and valued—opportunity of having a fulfilling occupation. Since the issue of unemployment is particularly important in some parts of the world (including contemporary Europe), this is another area where there is a strong need to seize the contrast between income and capability perspectives in the context of inequality assessment.

Unemployment and Capability Deprivation

That the judgments of inequality in the space of incomes can be quite different from those related to important capabilities can easily be illustrated with examples of some practical importance. In the European context, this contrast is particularly significant because of the wide prevalence of unemployment in contemporary Europe.[21] The loss of income caused by unemployment can, to a considerable extent, be compensated by income support (including unemployment benefits), as it typically is in Western Europe. If income loss were all that were involved in unemployment, then that loss could be to a great extent erased—for the individuals involved—by income support (there is, of course, the further issue of social costs of fiscal burden and incentive effects involved in this compensation). If, however, unemployment has other serious effects on the lives of the individuals, causing deprivation of other kinds, then the amelioration through income support would be to that extent limited. There is plenty of evidence that unemployment has many far-reaching effects other than loss of income, including psychological harm, loss of work motivation, skill and self-confidence, increase in ailments and morbidity (and even mortality rates), disruption of family relations and social life, hardening of social exclusion and accentuation of racial tensions and gender asymmetries.[22]

Given the massive scale of unemployment in contemporary European economies, the concentration on income inequality only can be particularly deceptive. Indeed, it can be argued that at this time the massive level of European unemployment constitutes at least as important an issue of inequality, in its own right, as income distribution itself. An exclusive focus on income inequality tends to give the impression that Western Europe has done very much better than the United States in keeping inequality down and in avoiding the kind of increase in income inequality that the United States has experienced. In the space of incomes, Europe does indeed have a clearly better record both in terms of levels and trends of inequality, as is brought out by the careful investigation reported in the OECD (Organization for Economic Cooperation and Development) study prepared by A. B. Atkinson, Lee Rainwater, and Timothy Smeeding.[23] Not only are the usual measures of income inequality higher in the United States than is the case, by and large, on the European side of the Atlantic, but also the US income inequality has gone up in a way that has not happened in most countries in Western Europe.

And yet if we shift our gaze from income to unemployment, the picture is very different. Unemployment has risen dramatically in much of Western Europe, whereas there has been no such trend in the United States. For example, in the period 1965–1973, the unemployment rate was 4.5 percent in the United States, while Italy had 5.8 percent, France 2.3 percent, and West Germany below 1 percent. By now [2001] all three—Italy, France, and Germany—have unemployment rates that hover around 10 to 12 percent, whereas the US unemployment rate is still between 4 and 5 percent. If unemployment batters lives, then that must somehow be taken into account in the analysis of economic inequality. The comparative trends in *income* inequality give Europe an excuse to be smug, but that complacency can be deeply misleading if a broader view is taken of inequality.[24]

The contrast between Western Europe and the United States raises another interesting—and in some ways a more general—question. American social ethics seems to find it possible to be very non-supportive of the indigent and the impoverished, in a way that a typical Western European, reared in a welfare state, finds hard to accept. But the same American social ethics would find the double-digit levels of unemployment, common in Europe, to be quite intolerable. Europe has continued to accept worklessness—and its increase—with remarkable equanimity. Underlying this contrast is a difference in attitudes toward social and individual responsibilities.

[...]

Poverty and Deprivation in India and Sub-Saharan Africa

Extreme poverty is now heavily concentrated in two particular regions of the world: South Asia and sub-Saharan Africa. They have among the lowest levels of per capita income among all the regions, but that perspective does not give us an adequate idea of the nature and content of their respective deprivations, nor of their comparative poverty. If poverty is seen, instead, as the deprivation of basic capabilities, then a more illuminating picture can be obtained from information on aspects of life in these parts of the world.[26] A brief analysis is attempted below, based on a joint study with Jean Drèze, and on two follow-up works of this author.[27]

Around 1991 there were fifty-two countries where the expectation of life at birth was below sixty years, and those countries had a combined population of 1.69 billion.[28] Forty-six of these countries are in South Asia and sub-Saharan Africa—only six are outside these two regions (viz. Afghanistan, Cambodia, Haiti, Laos, Papua New Guinea and Yemen), and the combined population of these six is only 3.5 percent of the total population (1.69 billion) of the fifty-two low-life-expectancy countries. The *whole* of South Asia except Sri Lanka (i.e., India, Pakistan, Bangladesh, Nepal and Bhutan) and the *whole* of sub-Saharan Africa except South Africa, Zimbabwe, Lesotho, Botswana, and a collection of tiny islands (e.g., Mauritius and the Seychelles) belong to the group of the other forty-six low-life-expectancy countries. Of course, there are variations *within* each country. Well-placed sections of the population of South Asia and sub-Saharan Africa enjoy high longevity, and as was discussed earlier, parts of the population of countries even with very high average life expectancy (such as the United States), may have survival problems that compare with conditions in the third world. (For example, American black men in US cities such as New York, San Francisco, St. Louis, or Washington, DC, have life expectancies well below our cut-off point of sixty years.[29]) But in terms of country averages, South Asia and sub-Saharan Africa do indeed stand out as the regions where short and precarious lives are concentrated in the contemporary world.

Indeed, India alone accounts for more than half of the combined population of these fifty-two deprived countries. It is not by any means the worst performer on average (in fact, average life expectancy in India is very close to sixty years and according to latest statistics has just risen above it), but there are large regional variations in living conditions *within* India. Some regions of India (with populations as large as—or larger than—most countries in the world) do as badly as any country in the world. India may do significantly better on average than, say, the worst performers (such as Ethiopia or Zaire, now renamed the Democratic Republic of Congo) in terms of life expectancy and other indicators, but there are large areas within India where life expectancy and other basic living conditions are not very different from those prevailing in these most-deprived countries.[30]

Table 66.1 compares the levels of *infant mortality* and *adult literacy* in the least-developed regions of sub-Saharan Africa and India.[31] The table presents the 1991 estimates of these two variables not only for India and sub-Saharan Africa as a whole (first and last rows), but also for the three worst-performing countries of sub-Saharan Africa, the three worst-performing Indian states, and the worst-performing districts of each of these three states. It is remarkable that there is no country in sub-Saharan Africa—or indeed in the world—where estimated infant mortality rates are as high as in the district of Ganjam in Orissa, or where the adult female literacy rate is as low as in the district of Barmer in Rajasthan. Each of these two districts, incidentally, has a larger population than Botswana or Namibia, and the combined population of the two is larger than that of Sierra Leone, Nicaragua or Ireland. Indeed, even entire states such as Uttar Pradesh (which has a population as large as that of Brazil or Russia) do not do much better than the worst-off among the sub-Saharan countries in terms of these basic indicators of living quality.[32]

It is interesting that if we take India and sub-Saharan Africa as a whole, we find that the two regions are not very different in terms of either adult literacy or infant mortality. They do differ in terms of life expectancy, though. The expectation of life in India around 1991 was about sixty years, while it was much below that figure in sub-Saharan Africa (averaging about fifty-two years).[33] On the other hand, there is considerable evidence that the extent of undernourishment is much greater in India than in sub-Saharan Africa.[34]

There is thus an interesting pattern of contrast between India and sub-Saharan Africa in terms of the different criteria of (1) mortality and (2)

Table 66.1 India and Sub-Saharan Africa: selected comparisons (1991)

	Infant mortality rate comparisons		
	Region	Population (millions)	Infant mortality rate (per 1,000 live births)
INDIA	India	846.3	80
'Worst' three Indian states	Orissa	31.7	124
	Madhya Pradesh	66.2	117
	Uttar Pradesh	139.1	97
'Worst' district of each of the 'worst' Indian states	Ganjam (Orissa)	3.2	164
	Tikamgarh (Madhya Pradesh)	0.9	152
	Hardoi (Uttar Pradesh)	2.7	129
'Worst' three countries of sub-Saharan Africa	Mali	8.7	161
	Mozambique	16.1	149
	Guinea-Bissau	1.0	148
Sub-Saharan Africa	Sub-Saharan Africa	488.9	104

Note: The age cutoff is 15 years for African figures, and 7 years for Indian figures. Note that in India, the 7+ literacy rate is usually higher than the 15+ literacy rate (e.g., the all-India 7+ literacy rate in 1981 was 43.6%, compared with 40.8% for the 15+ literacy rate).

	Adult literacy rate comparisons	
Region	Population (millions)	Adult literacy rate* (female/male)
India	846.3	39/64
Rajasthan	44.0	20/55
Bihar	86.4	23/52
Uttar Pradesh	139.1	25/56
Barmer (Rajasthan)	1.4	8/37
Kishanganj (Bihar)	1.0	10/33
Bahraich (Uttar Pradesh)	2.8	11/36
Burkina Faso	9.2	10/31
Sierra Leone	4.3	12/35
Benin	4.8	17/35
Sub-Saharan Africa	488.9	40/63

nutrition. The survival advantage in favor of India can be brought out not only by comparisons of life expectancy, but also by contrasts of other mortality statistics. For example, the median age at death in India was about thirty-seven years around 1991; this compares with a weighted average (of median age at death) for sub-Saharan Africa of a mere five years.[35] Indeed, in as many as five African countries, the median age at death was observed to be three years or below. Seen in this perspective, the problem of premature mortality is enormously sharper in Africa than in India.

But we get a very different balance of disadvantages if we look at the prevalence of *undernourishment* in India via-à-vis Africa. Calculations of general undernourishment are much higher in India than in sub-Saharan Africa on the average.[36] This is so despite the fact that it is India, rather than sub-Saharan Africa, that is self-sufficient in food. Indian 'self-sufficiency' is based on the fulfillment of market demand, which can be, in normal years, easily met by domestically produced supply. But the market demand (based on purchasing power) understates the food needs. Actual undernourishment seems to be much higher in India than in sub-Saharan Africa. Judged in terms of the usual standards of retardation in weight for age, the proportion of undernourished children in Africa is 20 to 40 percent, whereas the proportion of undernourished children in India is a gigantic 40 to 60 percent.[37] About half of all Indian children are, it appears, chronically undernourished. While Indians live longer than sub-Saharan Africans, and have a median age at death much higher than Africans have, nevertheless there are many more undernourished children in India than sub-Saharan Africa—not just in absolute terms but also as a proportion of all children.[38] If we add to it the fact that gender bias at death is a substantial problem in India, but not so in sub-Saharan Africa, we see a picture that is much less favorable to India than to Africa.[39]

There are important policy issues related to the nature and complexity of the respective patterns of deprivation in the two most acute regions of poverty in the world. India's advantage over sub-Saharan Africa in survival relates to a variety of factors that have made Africans especially prone to premature mortality. Since independence, India has been relatively free of the problems of famine and also of large-scale and persistent warfare, which has periodically ravaged a large number of African countries. India's health services—inadequate as they are—have been less overwhelmed by political and military turmoil. Furthermore, many countries of sub-Saharan Africa have had specific experiences of economic *decline*—partly related to wars, unrest and political disorder—which make it particularly hard to improve living standards. A comparative assessment of the achievements and failures of the two regions would have to take note of these and other aspects of their respective development experiences.[40]

One should also note that one problem that India and sub-Saharan Africa have in common is the persistence of endemic illiteracy—a feature that, like low life expectancy, sets South Asia and sub-Saharan Africa apart from most of the rest of the world. As Table 66.1 indicates, literacy rates are very similar in the two regions. Both in India and in sub-Saharan Africa, every other adult is illiterate.

The three focal features of deprivation of basic capabilities on which I have concentrated in comparing and contrasting the nature of deprivation in India and in sub-Saharan Africa (viz., *premature mortality, undernourishment* and *illiteracy*) do not, of course, provide a comprehensive picture of capability-poverty in these regions. However, they bring out some striking failures and some crucial policy issues that demand immediate attention. I have also not attempted to produce an 'aggregate' measure of deprivation, based on 'weighting' the different aspects of capability deprivation.[41] A constructed aggregate may often be far less interesting for policy analysis than the substantive pattern of diverse performances.

Gender Inequality and Missing Women

I turn now to a specific aspect of a general inequality that has drawn much attention lately; this section draws on my article 'Missing Women' published in the *British Medical Journal* in 1992.[42] I refer to the terrible phenomenon of excess mortality and artificially lower survival rates of women in many parts of the world. This is a crude and sharply visible aspect of gender inequality, which often manifests itself in more subtle and less gruesome forms. But despite its crudeness, the artificially higher female mortality rates reflect a very important capability deprivation of women.

In Europe and North America, women tend, generally, to outnumber men by substantial numbers. For example, in the United Kingdom, France and the United States, the ratio of women to men exceeds 1.05. The situation is quite different in many countries in the third world especially in Asia and North Africa, where the female–male ratio can be as low as 0.95 (Egypt), 0.94 (Bangladesh, China, West Asia), 0.93 (India), or even 0.90 (Pakistan). The significance of these differences is of interest in analyzing female–male inequalities across the world.[43] Figure 66.1 presents this comparative information.

In fact, more boys than girls are born everywhere (typically about 5 percent more). But there is much evidence that women are 'hardier' than men and, given symmetrical care, survive better. (Indeed, it appears that even female fetuses have a higher survival rate than do the male fetuses; the proportion of male fetuses in conception is even higher than that in birth.[44]) It is through the lower mortality rates of females that the high female–male ratio of the 'West' comes about. There are also other causes for this preponderance of women. There is some remaining impact of deaths of males in past wars. There has been, in general, a greater incidence of smoking among men and also greater proneness toward violent death. But it seems clear that even when these other effects are taken out, women would tend to outnumber men, given symmetrical care.

The low female–male ratios in countries in Asia and North Africa indicate the influence of social factors. It is easily calculated that if these countries had the female–male ratio that obtains in Europe and the United States, there would have been millions more women in these countries (given the number of men).[45] In China alone the number of 'missing women,' calculated on the basis of the European or American ratio, would be more than 50 million, and on that basis, for these countries taken together, many more than 100 million women may be seen as 'missing.'

It may not, however, be appropriate to use the European or American ratio, not just because of such special features as wartime deaths. Because of lower mortality rates of females in Europe and America, the female–male ratio rises gradually with age. A lower ratio would be expected in Asia or North Africa partly because of the lower general life expectancy and higher fertility rate. One way of dealing with this issue is to take as the basis of comparison not the female–male ratio in Europe or America, but that in sub-Saharan Africa, where there is little female disadvantage in terms of relative mortality rates, but where life expectancy is no higher and fertility rates are no lower (quite the contrary), Taking the sub-Saharan female–male ratio of 1.022 as the benchmark (used in my earlier studies and in those with Jean Drèze) yields an estimate of 44 million missing women in China, 37 million in India, and a total for these countries still in excess of 100 million.[46]

Another way of dealing with this problem is to calculate what the expected number of females

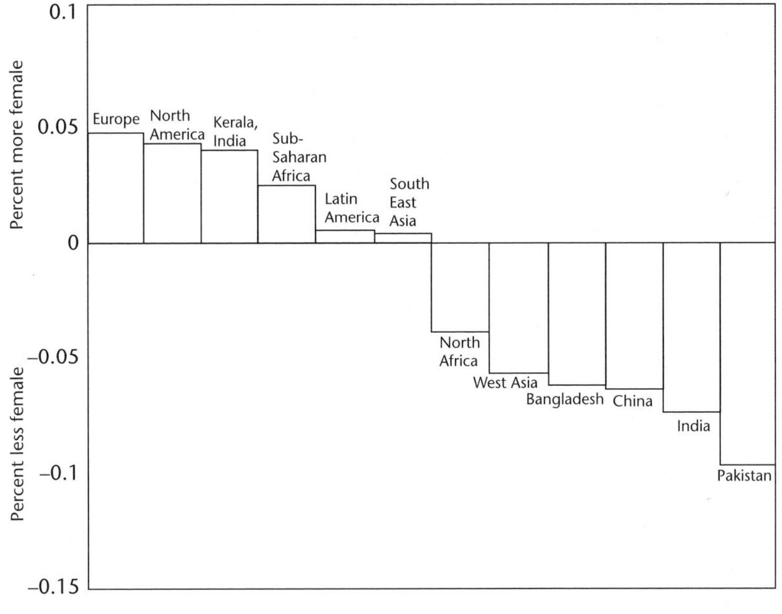

Fig. 66.1 Female-male ratios in total population in selected communities
Source: Calculated from *UN Population Statistics.*

would be had there been no female disadvantage in survival, given the actual life expectancy and the actual fertility rates in these respective countries. It is not easy to calculate that directly, but illuminating estimates have been made by Ansley Coale, through using model population tables based on the historical experience of 'Western' countries. This procedure yields 29 million 'missing women' in China, 23 million in India, and a total for these countries of around 60 million.[47] While these are lower numbers, they too are fiercely large. More recent estimates, based on the use of more scrutinized historical data, have tended to yield rather larger numbers of missing women (about 90 million, as estimated by Stephan Klasen).[48]

Why are overall mortality rates for females higher than for males in these countries? Consider India, where the age-specific mortality rate for females consistently exceeds that for males until the late thirties. While the excess mortality in the child-bearing age may be partly the result of maternal mortality (death during or just after childbirth), obviously no such explanation is possible for female disadvantage in survival in infancy and childhood. Despite occasional distressing accounts of female infanticide in India, that phenomenon, even if present, cannot do anything to explain the magnitude of extra mortality, nor its age distribution. The main culprit would seem to be the comparative neglect of female health and nutrition, especially—but not exclusively—during childhood. There is indeed considerable direct evidence that female children are neglected in terms of health care, hospitalization and even feeding.[49]

Even though the Indian case has been studied more extensively than others (there are more researchers working on this issue in India than in any other country), similar evidence of relative neglect of the health and nutrition of female children can be found in the other countries as well. In China there is even some evidence that the extent of neglect may have increased sharply in recent years, particularly since the compulsory family restrictions (such as the one-child policy in some parts of the country) were introduced, along with other reforms, around 1979. There are also some new, ominous signs in China, such as a radical increase in the reported ratio of male births to female births—quite out of line with the rest of the world. It can, quite possibly, indicate 'hiding' of newborn female children (to avoid the rigors of compulsory family restriction), but it can, no less plausibly, also reflect a higher female infant mortality —whether or not induced (with new births and new deaths both going unreported). However, recently, the brunt of the antifemale bias in family composition seems to be in sex-selective abortion, which has become quite widespread in China with the progress of technology.

Concluding Remarks

Economists are sometimes criticized for concentrating too much on efficiency and too little on equity. There may be some ground for complaint here, but it must also be noted that inequality has received attention from economists throughout the history of this discipline. Adam Smith, who is often thought of as 'the Father of Modern Economics,' was deeply concerned with the gulf between the rich and the poor [. . .]. Some of the social scientists and philosophers who are responsible for making inequality such a central subject of public attention (such as Karl Marx, John Stuart Mill, B. S. Rowntree, and Hugh Dalton, to take writers belonging to very different general traditions) were, in terms of substantive involvement, devoted economists, no matter what else they might also have been. In recent years, economics of inequality as a subject has flourished, with major leadership coming from such writers as A. B. Atkinson.[50] This is not to deny that the focus on efficiency to the exclusion of other considerations is very evident in some works in economics, but economists as a group cannot be accused of neglecting inequality as a subject.

If there is a reason to grumble, it rests more on the relative importance that is attached, in much of economics, to inequality in a very narrow domain, viz., *income inequality*. This narrowness has the effect of contributing to the neglect of other ways of seeing inequality and equity, which has far-reaching bearing on the making of economic policy. Policy debates have indeed been distorted by overemphasis on income poverty and income inequality, to the neglect of deprivations that relate to other variables, such as unemployment, ill health, lack of education, and social exclusion. Unfortunately, the identification of economic inequality with income inequality is fairly common in economics, and the two are often seen as effectively synonymous. If you tell someone that you are working on economic inequality, it is quite standardly assumed that you are studying income distribution.

To some extent, this implicit identification can be found in the philosophical literature as well. For example, in his interesting and important paper 'Equality as a Moral Ideal,' Harry Frankfurt, the distinguished philosopher, provides a closely reasoned and powerful critique of what he calls 'economic egalitarianism,' defining it as 'the doctrine that there should be no inequalities in the distribution of money.'[51]

The distinction, however, between income inequality and economic inequality is important.[52] Many of the criticisms of economic egalitarianism as a value or a goal apply much more readily to the narrow concept of income inequality than they do to the broader notions of economic inequality. For example, giving a larger share of income to a person with more needs—say, due to a disability—can be seen as militating against the principle of equalizing *incomes*, but it does not go against the broader precepts of economic equality, since the greater need for economic resources due to the disability must be taken into account in judging the requirements of economic equality.

Empirically, the relationship between income inequality and inequality in other relevant spaces can be rather distant and contingent because of various economic influences other than income that affect inequalities in individual advantages and substantive freedoms. For example, in the higher mortality rates of African Americans vis-à-vis the much poorer Chinese, or Indians in Kerala, we see the influence of factors that run in the opposite direction to income inequality, and that involve public policy issues with strong economic components: the financing of health care and insurance, provision of public education, arrangements for local security and so on.

Mortality differences can, in fact, serve as an indicator of very deep inequities that divide races, classes and genders, as the various illustrations in this chapter bring out. For example, the estimations of 'missing women' show the remarkable reach of female disadvantage in many parts of the contemporary world, in a way that other statistics may not adequately reflect. Also, since the incomes earned by family members are shared by others in the family, we cannot analyze gender inequality primarily in terms of income differences. We need much more information than is usually available on the division of resource use within the family to get a clearer idea of inequalities in economic affluence. However, statistics on mortality rates as well as other deprivations (such as undernourishment or illiteracy) can directly present a picture of inequality and poverty in some crucial dimensions. This information can also be used to relate the extent of relative deprivation of women to the existing inequalities in opportunities (in earning outside income, in being enrolled in schools and so on). Thus, both descriptive and policy issues can be addressed through this broader perspective on inequality and poverty in terms of capability deprivation.

Despite the crucial role of incomes in the advantages enjoyed by different persons, the relationship between income (and other resources), on the one hand, and individual achievements and freedoms, on the other, is neither constant nor in any sense automatic and irresistible. Different types of contingencies lead to systematic variations in the 'conversion' of incomes into the distinct 'functionings' we can achieve, and that affects the lifestyles we can enjoy. I have tried to illustrate in this chapter the different ways in which there can be systematic variations in the relationship between incomes earned and substantive freedoms (in the form of capability to lead lives that people have reason to value). The respective roles of personal heterogeneities, environmental diversities, variations in social climate, differences in relational perspectives and distributions within the family have to receive the serious attention they deserve for the making of public policy.

The argument is sometimes made that income is a homogeneous magnitude, whereas capabilities are diverse. This sharp contrast is not entirely correct, in the sense that any income evaluation hides internal diversities with some special—and often heroic—assumptions.[53] Also [...], interpersonal comparisons of real income give us no basis for interpersonal comparisons even of utility (though that hiatus is often ignored in applied welfare economics through the imposition of wholly arbitrary assumptions). To get from the comparison of the means in the form of income differences to something that can be claimed to be valuable in itself (such as well-being or freedom), we have to take note of circumstantial variations that affect the conversion rates. The presumption that the approach of income comparison is a more 'practical' way of getting at interpersonal differences in advantages is hard to sustain.

Furthermore, the need to discuss the valuation of diverse capabilities in terms of public priorities is, I have argued, an asset, forcing us to make clear what the value judgments are in a field where value judgments cannot be—and should not be—avoided. Indeed, public participation in these valuational debates—in explicit or implicit forms—is a crucial part of the exercise of democracy and responsible social choice. In matters of public judgment, there is no real escape from the evaluative need for public discussion. The work of public valuation cannot be replaced by some cunningly clever assumption. Some assumptions that give the appearance of working very nicely and smoothly operate through concealing the choice of values and weights in cultivated opaqueness. For example, the assumption—often implicitly made—that two persons with the same demand function must have the same relation between commodity bundles and well-being (no matter whether one is ill and the other not, one disabled and the other not, and so on) is basically a way of evading the need to consider many significant influences on well-being [. . .]. That evasion becomes transparent, as I have tried to illustrate, when we supplement income and commodity data with information of other types (including matters of life and death).

The issue of public discussion and social participation is thus central to the making of policy in a democratic framework. The use of democratic prerogatives—both political liberties and civil rights—is a crucial part of the exercise of economic policy making itself, in addition to other roles it may have. In a freedom-oriented approach, the participatory freedoms cannot but be central to public policy analysis.

NOTES

1. This view of poverty is more fully developed in my *Poverty and Famines* (Oxford: Clarendon Press, 1981) and *Resources, Values and Development* (Cambridge, Mass.: Harvard University Press, 1984), and also in Jean Drèze and Amartya Sen, *Hunger and Public Action* (Oxford: Clarendon Press, 1989), and in Sudhir Anand and Amartya Sen, 'Concepts of Human Development and Poverty: A Multidimensional Perspective', in *Human Development Papers 1997* (New York: UNDP, 1997).
2. These claims and their implications are more fully discussed in my 'Poverty as Capability Deprivation', mimeographed, Rome: Bank of Italy.
3. For example, hunger and undernutrition are related both to food intake and to the ability to make nutritive use of that intake. The latter is deeply affected by general health conditions (for example, by the presence of parasitic diseases), and that in turn depends much on communal health care and public health provisions; on this see Drèze and Sen, *Hunger and Public Action* (1989), and S. R. Osmani, ed., *Nutrition and Poverty* (Oxford: Clarendon Press, 1993).
4. See, for example, James Smith, 'Healthy Bodies and Thick Wallets: The Dual Relationship between Health and Socioeconomic Status', *Journal of Economic Perspectives* 13 (1999). There is also another type of 'coupling' between (1) undernutrition generated by income-poverty and (2) income-poverty resulting from work deprivation due to undernutrition. On these connections, see Partha Dasgupta and Debraj Ray, 'Inequality as a Determinant of Malnutrition and Unemployment: Theory', *Economic Journal* 96 (1986); 'Inequality as

a Determinant of Malnutrition and Unemployment: Policy', *Economic Journal* 97 (1987); and 'Adapting to Undernourishment: Biological Evidence and Its Implications', in *The Political Economy of Hunger*, edited by Jean Drèze and Amartya Sen (Oxford: Clarendon Press, 1990). See also Partha Dasgupta, *An Inquiry into Well-Being and Destitution* (Oxford: Clarendon Press, 1993), and Debraj Ray, *Development Economics* (Princeton: Princeton University Press, 1998).

5. The large contribution of such handicaps to the prevalence of income poverty in Britain was sharply brought out by A. B. Atkinson's pioneering empirical study, *Poverty in Britain and the Reform of Social Security* (Cambridge: Cambridge University Press, 1970). In his later works, Atkinson has further pursued the connection between income handicap and deprivations of other kinds.

6. On the nature of these functional handicaps, see Dorothy Wedderburn, *The Aged in the Welfare State* (London: Bell, 1961); Peter Townsend, *Poverty in the United Kingdom: A Survey of Household Resources and Standards of Living* (Harmondsworth: Penguin Books, 1979); J. Palmer, T. Smeeding and B. Torrey, *The Vulnerable: America's Young and Old in the Industrial World* (Washington, DC: Urban Institute Press, 1988); among other contributions.

7. I have tried to investigate the perspective of capability deprivation for analyzing gender inequality in *Resources, Values and Development* (1984; 1997); *Commodities and Capabilities* (Amsterdam: North-Holland, 1985); and 'Missing Women', *British Medical Journal* 304 (March 1992). See also Pranab Bardhan, 'On Life and Death Questions', *Economic and Political Weekly* 9 (1974); Lincoln Chen, E. Huq and S. D'Souza, 'Sex Bias in the Family Allocation of Food and Health Care in Rural Bangladesh', *Population and Development Review* 7 (1981); Jocelyn Kynch and Amartya Sen, 'Indian Women: Well-Being and Survival', *Cambridge Journal of Economics* 7 (1983); Pranab Bardhan, *Land, Labor, and Rural Poverty* (New York: Columbia University Press, 1984); Drèze and Sen, *Hunger and Public Action* (1989); Barbara Harriss, 'The Intrafamily Distribution of Hunger in South Asia', in Dreze and Sen, *The Political Economy of Hunger*, i. (1990); Ravi Kanbur and L. Haddad, 'How Serious Is the Neglect of Intrahousehold Inequality?' *Economic Journal* 100 (1990); among other contributions.

8. On this, see United Nations Development Programme, *Human Development Report* 1995 (New York: Oxford University Press, 1995).

9. See W. G. Runciman, *Relative Deprivation and Social Justice: A Study of Attitudes to Social Inequality in Twentieth-Century England* (London: Routledge, 1966); and Townsend, *Poverty in the United Kingdom* (1979).

10. On this see my 'Poor, Relatively Speaking', *Oxford Economic Papers* 35 (1983), reprinted in *Resources, Values and Development* (1984).

11. The connection is analyzed in my *Inequality Reexamined* (Oxford: Clarendon Press; and Cambridge, Mass.: Harvard University Press, 1992), ch. 7.

12. Jean Drèze and Amartya Sen, *India: Economic Development and Social Opportunity* (Delhi: Oxford University Press, 1995).

13. See the collection of papers in Isher Judge Ahluwalia and I. M. D. Little, eds., *India's Economic Reforms and Development: Essays for Manmohan Singh* (Delhi: Oxford University Press, 1998). See also Vijay Joshi and Ian Little, *Indian Economic Reforms*, 1991–2001 (Delhi: Oxford University Press, 1996).

14. These arguments are more fully developed in Drèze and Sen, *India: Economic Development and Social Opportunity* (1995).

15. See G. Dart, *Poverty in India and Indian States: An Update* (Washington, DC: International Food Policy Research Institute, 1997). See also World Bank, *India: Achievements and Challenges in Reducing Poverty*, report no. 16483 IN, 27 May 1997 (see particularly figure 2.3).

16. Adam Smith, *The Theory of Moral Sentiments* (1759; rev. edn., 1790); republished, edited by D. D. Raphael and A. L. Macfie (Oxford: Clarendon Press, 1976).

17. John Rawls, *A Theory of Justice* (Cambridge, Mass.: Harvard University Press, 1971). See also Stephen Darwall, ed., *Equal Freedom: Selected Tanner Lectures on Human Values* (Ann Arbor: University of Michigan Press, 1995), with contributions by G. A. Cohen, Ronald Dworkin, John Rawls, T. M. Scanlon, Amartya Sen and Quentin Skinner.

18. Thomas Scanlon, 'Contractualism and Utilitarianism', in *Utilitarianism and Beyond*, ed. Amartya Sen and Bernard Williams (Cambridge: Cambridge University Press, 1982.). See also his *What We Owe Each Other* (Cambridge, Mass.: Harvard University Press, 1998).

19. See, for example, James Mirrlees, 'An Exploration in the Theory of Optimal Income Taxation', *Review of Economic Studies* 38 (1971); E. S. Phelps, ed., *Economic Justice* (Harmondsworth: Penguin Books, 1973); Nicholas Stern, 'On the Specification of Modes of Optimum Income Taxation', *Journal of Public Economics* 6 (1976); A. B. Atkinson and Joseph Stiglitz, *Lectures on Public Economics* (London: McGraw-Hill, 1980); D. A. Starrett, *Foundations of Public Economics* (Cambridge: Cambridge University Press, 1988); among many other contributions.

20. A. B. Atkinson, 'On the Measurement of Inequality', *Journal of Economic Theory* 2 (1970), and *Social Justice and Public Policy* (Brighton: Wheatsheaf; Cambridge, Mass.: MIT Press, 1983). See also S. Ch. Kolm, 'The Optimum Production of Social Justice', in *Public Economics*, edited by J. Margolis and H. Guirton (London: Macmillan, 1969); Amartya Sen, *On Economic Inequality* (Oxford: Clarendon Press, 1973; expanded edn., including an annex with James Foster, 1997); Charles Blackorby and David Donaldson, 'A Theoretical Treatment of Indices of Absolute Inequality', *International Economic Review* 21 (1980), and 'Ethically Significant Ordinal Indexes of Relative Inequality', *Advances in Econometrics*, iii, ed. R. Basmann and G. Rhodes (Greenwich, Conn.: JAI Press, 1984).

21. In my paper 'Inequality, Unemployment and Contemporary Europe' (presented at the Lisbon conference on 'Social Europe' of the Calouste Gulbenkian Foundation, 5–7 May 1997, published in *International Labour Review*, 1997), I have discussed the relevance of this contrast for contemporary policy issues in Europe. The importance that the unemployed themselves attach to the loss of freedom and capability as a result of unemployment is illuminatingly analyzed (with Belgian data) by Eric Schokkaert and L. Van Ootegem, 'Sen's Concept of Living Standards Applied to the Belgian Unemployed', *Recherches Économiques de Louvain* 56 (1990).

22. See the literature cited in my 'Inequality, Unemployment and Contemporary Europe' (1997). On the psychological and other 'social harms' of unemployment, see Robert Solow, 'Mass Unemployment as a Social Problem' in *Choice, Welfare and Development*, ed. K. Basu, P. Pattanaik and K. Suzumura (Oxford: Clarendon Press, 1995), and A. Goldsmith, J. R. Veum and W. Darity Jr., 'The Psychological Impact of Unemployment and Joblessness', *Journal of Socio-Economics* 25 (1996), among other contributors. See also the related literature on 'social exclusion'; good introductions to the literature can be found in Gerry Rodgers, Charles Gore and J. B. Figueiredo, eds., *Social Exclusion: Rhetoric, Reality, Responses* (Geneva: International Institute for Labour Studies, 1995); Charles Gore et al., *Social Exclusion and Anti-Poverty Policy* (Geneva: International Institute for Labour Studies, 1997); Arjan de Haan and Simon Maxwell, *Poverty and Social Exclusion in North and South*, special number, *Institute of Development Studies Bulletin* 29 (January 1998).

23. A. B. Atkinson, Lee Rainwater and Timothy Smeeding, *Income Distribution in OECD Countries* (Paris: OECD, 1996).

24. The need for new policy initiatives is particularly strong at this time. See Jean-Paul Fitoussi and R. Rosanvallon, *Le Nouvel âge des inégalités* (Paris: Sevil, 1996); Edmund S. Phelps,

Rewarding Work: How to Restore Participation and Self-Support to Free Enterprise (Cambridge, Mass.: Harvard University Press, 1997). See also Paul Krugman, *Technology, Trade and Factor Prices*, NBER Working Paper no. 5355 (Cambridge, Mass.: National Bureau of Economic Research, 1995); Stephen Nickell, 'Unemployment and Labor Market Rigidities: Europe versus North America', *Journal of Economics Perspectives* 11 (1997); Richard Layard, *Tackling Unemployment* (London: Macmillan, 1999); Jean-Paul Fitoussi, Francesco Giavezzi, Assar Lindbeck, Franco Modigliani, Beniamino Moro, Dennis J. Snower, Robert Solow and Klaus Zimmerman, 'A Manifesto on Unemployment in the European Union', mimeographed, 1998.

26. On this see my *Commodities and Capabilities* (1985). UNDP's *Human Development Reports* have provided important information and assessment regarding this way of seeing poverty, especially in *Human Development Report* 1997. See also Sudhir Anand and Amartya Sen, 'Concepts of Human Development and Poverty: A Multidimensional Perspective' (1997).

27. Drèze and Sen, *India: Economic Development and Social Opportunity* (1995); Amartya Sen, 'Hunger in the Modern World', Dr Rajendra Prasad Memorial Lecture, New Delhi, June 1997; and 'Entitlement Perspectives of Hunger', World Food Programme, 1997.

28. For sources of this information and of other information used in this section, see Drèze and Sen, *India: Economic Development and Social Opportunity* (1995), ch. 3 and statistical appendix. The picture here focuses on 1991, for reasons of data availability. There has, however, been a considerable increase in literacy just reported in the latest Indian National Sample Survey. There are also some important policy departures announced by some of the state governments, such as West Bengal and Madhya Pradesh.

29. See C. J. L. Murray et al., *U.S. Patterns of Mortality by County and Race: 1965–1994* (Cambridge, Mass.: Harvard Center for Population and Developmental Studies, 1998), table 6d, p. 56.

30. The severity of India's failure to devote resources and efforts to social development is convincingly and movingly discussed by S. Guhan, 'An Unfulfilled Vision', *IASSI Quarterly* 12 (1993). See also the collection of essays in his honor: Barbara Harriss-White and S. Subramanian, eds., *Illfare in India: Essays on India's Social Sector in Honour of S. Guhan* (Delhi: Sage, 1999).

31. This is taken from table 3.1 in Drèze and Sen, India: *Economic Development and Social Opportunity* (1995). See also Saraswati Raju, Peter J. Atkins, Naresh Kumas and Janet G. Townsend, *Atlas of Women and Men in India* (New Delhi: Kali for Women, 1999).

32. See also A. K. Shiva Kumar, 'UNDP's Human Development Index: A Computation for Indian States', *Economic and Political Weekly*, 12 October 1991, and Rajah J. Chelliah and R. Sudarshan, eds., *Indian Poverty and Beyond: Human Development in India* (New Delhi: Social Science Press, 1999).

33. See World Bank, *World Development Report* 1994 (Oxford: Oxford University Press, 1994), table 1, p. 163.

34. On this see the extensive comparison made by Peter Svedberg, *Poverty and Undernutrition: Theory and Measurement* (Oxford: Clarendon Press, 1997). Svedberg also scrutinizes alternative approaches to measuring undernutrition, and the conflicting pictures generated by different statistics, but arrives at a firm conclusion against India in terms of undernutrition vis-à-vis sub-Saharan Africa.

35. See World Bank, *World Development Report* 1993 (Oxford: Oxford University Press, 1993), table A.3. Mortality rates have worsened with the spread of the AIDS epidemic.

36. See Svedberg, *Poverty and Undernutrition* (1997). See also C. Gopalan, ed., *Combating Undernutrition* (New Delhi: Nutrition Foundation of India, 1995).

37. See Nevin Scrimshaw, 'The Lasting Damage of Early Malnutrition', in R. W. Fogel et al., *Ending the Inheritance of Hunger* (Rome: World Food Programme, 1997). See also the papers of Robert W. Fogel, Cutberto Garza and Amartya Sen in the same volume.

38. This is not to deny that each of the standard criteria of undernourishment admits some room for doubt, but indicators based on health and physique do have some advantages over measures that simply look at food input. It is also possible to make use of the available medical and functional knowledge to improve the criteria to be used. On these and related issues, see Dasgupta, *An Inquiry into Well-Being and Destitution* (1993); Osmani, ed., *Nutrition and Poverty* (1993); Scrimshaw, 'The Lasting Damage of Early Malnutrition', and Robert W. Fogel, 'The Global Struggle to Escape from Chronic Malnutrition since 1700', in Fogel et al., *Ending the Inheritance of Hunger* (1997).

39. See Svedberg, *Poverty and Undernutrition* and the literature cited there. See also United Nations Development Programme, *Human Development Report* 1995 (New York: Oxford University Press, 1995).

40. Africa also suffers from a much greater burden of international debt, which is now gigantic. There is also the difference that African countries have been much more subjected to dictatorial governance, partly as a result of being caught in the cold war, with the West and Soviet Union both being willing to provide support to military coups and other takeovers by their nondemocratic allies. The penalties of dictatorship in terms of loss of voice by the vulnerable underdog and loss of transparency and accountability will be discussed [elsewhere (Amartya Sen, *Development as Freedom* (Oxford: Oxford University Press, 2001), chs. 6 and 7)]. Even the inclination to run into heavy debt to meet military and other priorities is encouraged by dictatorial rules.

41. The UNDP has produced since 1990 interesting and important detailed data on the nature of deprivation in the different parts of the world in its annual *Human Development Reports*, initiated by Dr Mahbub ul Haq. They have also proposed and presented some aggregate measures, in particular the Human Development Index (HDI) and the Human Poverty Index (HPI). These aggregate indices have tended to draw much more public attention than the detailed and diverse empirical pictures emerging from the tables and other empirical presentations. Indeed, getting public attention has clearly been a part of UNDP's objective, particularly in its attempt to combat the overconcentration on the simple measure of GNP per head, which often serves as the only indicator of which the public takes any notice. To compete with the GNP, there is a need for another—broader—measure with the same level of crudeness as the GNP. This need is partly met by the use of the HDI, just as the HPI has been offered by the UNDP as a rival to the standard measures of income poverty. It is not my intention to question the merits of such competitive use, in the context of getting public attention (I have, in fact, provided technical help to the UNDP to devise both these indices). The fact remains, nevertheless, that the *Human Development Reports* are much richer in relevant information than can be obtained from an exclusive concentration on the aggregative indicators such as HDI and HPI.

42. Amartya Sen, 'Missing Women' (1992).

43. See also my *Resources, Values and Development* (1984); Barbara Harriss and E. Watson, 'The Sex Ratio in South Asia', in *Geography of Gender in the Third World*, ed. J. H. Momson and J. Townsend (London: Butler & Tanner, 1987); Jocelyn Kynch, 'How Many Women Are Enough? Sex Ratios and the Right to Life', *Third World Affairs* 1985 (London: Third World Foundation, 1985); Amartya Sen, 'Women's Survival as a Development Problem', *Bulletin of the American Academy of Arts and Sciences* 43/2 (1989), 14–29; Ansley Coale, 'Excess

Female Mortality and the Balances of the Sexes in the Population: An Estimate of the Number of "Missing Females"', *Population and Development Review* 17/3 (1991), 517–23; Stephan Klasen, 'Missing Women Reconsidered', *World Development* 22 (1994).

44. See I. Waldron, 'The Role of Genetic and Biological Factors in Sex Differences in Mortality', in *Sex Differences in Mortality*, ed. A. D. Lopez and L. T. Ruzicka (Canberra: Department of Demography, Australian National University, 1983).

45. On this see my 'Women's Survival as a Development Problem', *Bulletin of the American Academy of Arts and Sciences* (November 1989); rev. version, 'More Than a Hundred Million Women Are Missing', *The New York Review of Books*, Christmas number (20 December), 1990.

46. See Drèze and Sen, *Hunger and Public Action* (1989), table 4.1, p. 52. See also my 'Missing Women' (1992).

47. Coale, 'Excess Female Mortality'.

48. Stephan Klasen, 'Missing Women Reconsidered', *World Development* 22 (1994).

49. Chen, Huq, and D'Souza, 'Sex Bias in the Family Allocation of Food and Health Care in Rural Bangladesh' (1981), 7; Sen, *Commodities and Capabilities* (1985), appendix B, and the empirical literature cited there (also Coale, 'Excess Female Mortality', 1991).

50. See particularly Atkinson, *Social Justice and Public Policy* (1983), and his *Poverty and Social Security* (New York: Wheatsheaf, 1989).

51. Harry Frankfurt, 'Equality as a Moral Ideal', *Ethics* 98 (1987), 21.

53. On this see my 'The Welfare Basis of Real Income Comparisons', *Journal of Economic Literature* 17 (1979), reprinted in *Resources, Values and Development* (1984).

What Poverty Does to Girls' Education: The Intersection of Class, Gender and Policy in Latin America

Nelly P. Stromquist

[. . .]

Introduction

Latin America is the region of the world where the colonial mode of social organisation remained in force the longest—about 300 years since the arrival of the Spanish conquerors (1492) to the first wars of independence (1810). The social mix of subjugated populations (Indians), African slaves, and a dominant white minority that persisted was not conducive to the establishment of fair relations of social and economic exchange (Filgueira, 1983; Rama, 1983; Alcalde, 1999). Large holdings by wealthy descendants of the colonists and subsistence agriculture by the exploited and powerless peasantry still characterise the region. Over time, export-based agrarian capitalism led to the emergence of a powerful landed elite capable of using the power of the state to advance its goals (Grindle, 1986). With current trends toward economic competitiveness and the need to develop comparative advantages among countries, it is likely that Latin America will keep up its agro-industrial production, which does not bode well for the resolution of social disparities.

Poverty[1] increased during the 1980–1990 decade in Latin America, growing from 46 to 60% in urban areas and from 80 to 85% in the countryside. Extreme poverty increased from 22 to 27% in urban areas and from 50 to 52% in rural areas, according to statistics gathered by the Economic Commission for Latin America and the Caribbean, also known as CEPAL. In Brazil, the industrial giant of Latin America, 1990 urban poverty stood at 39%, or 9% above its 1979 level and 5% above its 1987 level (CEPAL, 1994). More recently, from 1990 to 1997, according to CEPAL, the proportion of poor households in Latin America dropped from 41% to 36%. Not only are these gains small but the number of people who are poor increased from 136 million in the 1980s to 207 million in 1997 (CEPAL, 1998: 17).

Government expenditures on social benefits in the region remain largely regressive and will likely continue to be so in order to maintain investor

Nelly P. Stromquist, 'What Poverty Does to Girls' Education: the intersection of class, gender and policy in Latin America', *Compare*, 31, 1, 39–56 confidence. Tax reforms and minimum wage policies have not been used to redistribute income to any significant degree (Oxhorn, 1998; Bejar, 1999; Acosta, 1999). Policies designed to deal with the structural causes of poverty and inequality, particularly through investment in education and health care, are sacrificed to the short-term priorities of maintaining economic equilibrium under the assumption that programs targeted to the neediest of the needy will buy the time necessary for the economy to produce more jobs (Oxhorn, 1998).

Although peasants and small agricultural producers continue to comprise the populations most seriously affected by poverty, in a number of countries the largest proportion of poor people are rural wage-earners, whether engaged in agriculture or working in other sectors, especially commerce and service (CEPAL, 1994: 24). The Latin American region has seen an increase in the share of income going to wage-earners with professional or technical qualifications, but not to less qualified earners.

In Latin America, thus, poverty is not a question of stubborn pockets of uneducated or untrained people but is rather inherent in the social and economic structure of the region. This structure is both the effect and cause of asymmetrical power relations between urban and rural areas, between indigenous peoples and mestizo subcultures, between men and women, and, of course, between the North and the South.

This [chapter] deals with poverty and its effect on education in the context of Latin America. Its examination gives special attention to the question of gender, an important social dimension that greatly compounds the impact of poverty. It highlights the interaction between gender and two other important variables: social class and public policy, exploring the features of policies that emerge or fail to emerge to address serious educational disparities in society. To do so, this [chapter] blends descriptions of school functioning at the micro-level with features and measures taken at national level through governmental action.

Intractable Poverty

At one level, poverty is essentially a normative concept, specific to each society. At another level, there is what has been called an 'irreducible core of absolute deprivation' comprising starvation, malnutrition, and visible hardship (Altimir, 1981). As is repeatedly stated in both academic and mass media reports, without much horror by now, in the world today about 3 billion people live on US$ 2 a day or less and some 800 million people suffer from malnutrition.

What else do we know about the lives of the poor as a group? Very little, since beyond a few statistics we do not really have detailed studies of the poor. Nor do we know much about the rich, since they can easily avoid scrutiny. The fact that we know little of the lives of poor people greatly handicaps our understanding of the dynamic nature of poverty and how the lives of the rich and the poor intersect in functional and, often, inescapable ways.

In all countries of the world, we are making progress with key social indicators: life expectancy is going up, infant mortality is down, and illiteracy is also down. Yet poverty remains. What does this suggest in terms of the power of education as a tool for change? Could it be that we are ignoring those forces that indeed determine poverty? Probably we spend too much time defining poverty through statistical indicators while paying insufficient attention to the mechanisms and processes that create and sustain it. Further, currently favoured indicators of poverty do not tell us the distribution of income or wealth within the household (Kabeer, 1996). Poverty refers to what the poor lack, but their lack may be the result of a condition created or at best uncorrected by the upper and middle classes. Omnipresent as the concept of poverty is, it has not been sufficiently theorised in our understanding of how nations advance socially and politically and whether poverty represents an obstacle or is, on the contrary, a byproduct of unchecked 'advancement'. Work by feminist scholars question current initiatives by international organisations that call for 'poverty alleviation'. In their view, it is not alleviation that is needed, but instead drastic changes in power relations reflected in trade, the external debt, investments, and international development assistance (Townsend *et al.*, 1999).

The State and Education

Most nation-states make an effective and yet paradoxical use of education. On the one hand, education is defended in official discourse as a social good open to all. On the other hand, public education is treated with neglect as budgets are held with a tight rein and the children of the poor receive the lowest quality of education. Unquestionably, the function of education as an easily-made promise to reduce poverty serves to foster confidence and stability in society in the meantime.

Now, in the day of the minimalist state, the emphasis is on short-term solutions. Opportunities for the poor are complemented by the state in its subsidiary role of providing certain public goods and income transfers targeted directly at the poorest in society. As public policies to ensure social welfare seemed to have reached a nadir, the market is supposed to determine the best set of opportunities for the poor (Oxhorn, 1998).

With the present form of globalization (which emphasises commercial and technological features), the external debt, and structural adjustment programs, Latin America finds itself in an extraordinary moment of civil fragmentation. The growing social inequality has created a visible demobilisation of organised groups and has weakened the influence of labour unions, making it thus difficult for civil society to struggle for the expansion of citizenship rights (Oxhorn, 1998). In addition, austerity policies have brought reductions to sectors of governmental budgets with the weakest constituencies and yet the greatest potential for addressing the poor: education, health, social security and public housing.

Social expenditures in Latin America, of which education is traditionally a substantial part, decreased on a per capita basis by more than 20% in 1977–1981 and again in 1982–1985 (de Janvry and Sadoulet, 1993). The situation improved in the 1990s, when education as a percentage of the GNP rose in the region from 2.8% in 1990–1991 to 3.7% in 1996–1997 and per capita expenditures in education rose from $251 to $380 in the same period for the population 5–17 years of age (CEPAL, 1998: 126).

Schooling and Poverty

Liberal ideology presents education as 'a system that can do much to further social mobility and redistribution of opportunities, while becoming an efficient mechanism of equalisation and social justice in accordance with meritocratic equality criteria' (Filgueira, 1983: 60). Liberal ideology also portrays public education as free and compulsory worldwide. This latter assertion is far from reality: it is seldom completely free as parents must buy school materials, books, and uniforms—a substantial expenditure for the poor—and rarely does an educational system in developing countries enforce school attendance.

Educational statistics for Latin America at first glance show an ideal situation with many countries evincing rates of nearly 100% in gross primary school enrolment. An examination of secondary school enrolment shows a much lower figure, comparable to that of Africa, which means that a large number of young people leave primary school, often without completing it. When educational statistics are contrasted between urban and rural populations, enrolment rates among the latter populations are consistently much lower (UNESCO, 1998).

When the statistics are compared by sex, the degree of access to schooling and retention among girls and boys does not appear to be very different. In fact, in several countries, aggregate data indicate that girls enrol in and complete primary and secondary schooling in greater numbers than boys (CEPAL, 1997; UNESCO, 1998). If one looks at crude indicators of educational attainment, in seven of nine Latin American countries the rates of primary school enrolment increased in favour of girls during the 1990s and repetition decreased more among girls than boys. In nine out of ten countries, the proportion of girls that finished fourth grade stayed the same or increased, and in eight of those ten countries the proportion of girls that finished sixth grade stayed the same or increased (CEPAL, 1997). So, a first impression is that girls are doing even better than boys in schooling.

While most countries rely on UNESCO statistics (which are themselves produced by member states), there is growing evidence that these statistics grossly underestimate the number of children out of school. These alternative readings of educational participation derive from household surveys, census data, or from computations carried out by UNICEF, whose concern for street children has led it to focus on out-of-school children and children in the labour force. Recognised as a major problem are the low rates of primary school completion. One of four major regional goals for 2000 (and unlikely to be met) was to attain at least 70% primary school completion (CEPAL, 1998). There are few educational statistics broken down simultaneously by sex and ethnicity. Those that exist (e.g. Post, 1998, for Mexico; Montero and Tovar, 1999, for Peru) show a clear disadvantage for indigenous and particularly school-age girls living in poverty.

In the countryside, girls tend to enter primary school slightly older than boys and to leave at earlier grades. The low school participation rates are primarily a function of family or work obligations that render the individual unable to take advantage of available school offerings, but they are also due to a lack of school facilities. In rural areas, there are many single-classroom schools that usually serve only up to third or fourth grade (cases of Peru, Bolivia, Guatemala). The precise features and functioning of these 'multigrade' schools remains poorly documented in official statistics.[2] A study focusing on rural schools in Peru found that 90% of these schools operated in single rooms and that 37% had only one teacher, which suggests a high number of incomplete primary schools (Montero and Tovar, 1999). In urban areas, public schools sometimes cannot meet the demand. Thus, one observes the common phenomenon of parents having to stand in line for long hours to ensure that their children will be enrolled before the school reaches its limit (cases of Brazil, Peru, among others).

Life in rural schools, for both students and teachers, tends to be harsh. A large number of these schools have no water, electricity, or sanitation facilities. Girls are frequently called upon to perform domestic tasks for teachers. Teachers in rural areas in Peru are usually younger and less experienced than urban teachers and not trained to deal with multigrade classrooms; their average stay in the poorest rural areas is about two years (Montero and Tovar, 1999). The school year is much shorter than officially planned due to absences by both teachers and students. The learning hours per day are also shorter than they should be as time is spent in tangential activities such as long breaks or preparations for various extra-curricular events (Hornberger, 1987; Montero and Tovar, 1999). While boys and girls are equally affected by these practices, domestic and school factors combine to produce more women than men without schooling or with incomplete primary. In the case of Peru, data for 1997 show that while 28% of rural men 15–24 years of age have either no schooling or incomplete primary, the figure reaches 39% in the case of women (Montero and Tovar, 1999: 7).

At the macro-level, there exists a strong tie between the inequity in educational capital distribution and the inequality of income distribution inequality (CEPAL, 1997). In other words, population groups tend to have levels of school attainment proportional to their income. Most poor and extremely poor children in the region have parents with less than nine years of schooling (72 and 96%, respectively) (CEPAL, 1997: 143). On the other hand, as Rama (1983) has observed, in Latin America education has expanded more extensively than any other social good but this development has been 'inconsistent with the opportunities afforded by the social order in respect to income and participation in power' (p. 24).

The assumption of causality between poverty and education may be misread. It is not that parents are poor because they have no education; rather, they have no education because they are poor. Moreover, it appears that education in Latin America increasingly needs more years of schooling to be marketable in the labour force. According to studies by CEPAL (1994), it is 'necessary to have 10 years of schooling, and in many cases complete secondary to have an income above the poverty line' (p. 31). The level of education needed for a well-paying job will probably increase because globalisation trends in the labour force build upon differentiated schooling: university-level education especially with technical and scientific degrees for the highly-paid occupations and low levels of schooling for the provision of semi-skilled services in low-paid jobs.

Poor Families and Schooling

Public education at primary and secondary levels, not being free beyond tuition and the provision of some textbooks, represents high expenditures for low-income families. In principle, all families recognise the importance of education. Poor families try to give their children at least several years of education, but in the end withdraw them early. Since the children of the poor attend low-quality and incomplete primary schools, they tend to withdraw from school without having reached a solid literacy threshold; thus, many of them regress in their reading and numeracy skills.

For poor people, education means a trade-off, usually between obtaining food and going to school. From the perspective of the indigenous groups in rural areas, it might mean 'having to sell chickens to buy notebooks' (CEIMME, 1995). Having children go to school also means losing an income-earner. For instance, working in the tobacco crops of Nicaragua, adults earn US$ 11 dollars every two weeks; children are often paid half the salary of an adult, but poor parents still need that income (Havelin, 1999). Further evidence from Nicaragua illustrates the effect of deteriorating economic conditions for poor people in the late 1990s. Many poor Nicaraguan families found themselves with no disposable money for such public school expenses as pencils, notebooks, uniforms, shoes, exams, and even fees for security guards (Havelin, 1999). With an annual per capita income in Nicaragua of about US$ 340 in 1992, a family with two children in primary school and two in high school would need to pay some $60 per year, over one-sixth of its total income (Havelin, 1999: 27, citing Copling).

Low educational attainment does not always occur because children are taken out of school. Often, it happens because the children fall behind in their studies, as in cases when members of the family fall ill and children have to help in their care, or when the children themselves get sick and parents have to take them out of school to pay for medicine. Students from poor backgrounds, especially in cases where father abandonment is coupled with poverty, also develop serious emotional and social needs. Children of rural parents sometimes lack birth certificates and without such papers they have a difficult time enrolling in school (Montero and Tovar, 1999). Teachers of the poor often report having students who come to school tired, withdrawn, or overly aggressive. In many urban centres, it is common for teachers to find children who show up unannounced on the school's doorstep, their educational history a mystery, or cases where they leave with little or no notice, never to be seen again. These problems affect both girls and boys.

Teachers and Poor Children

It is sometimes forgotten that teachers of poor children are often poor themselves. In Bolivia and Ecuador, 65 to 70% of the teachers live in either poor or vulnerable homes (CEPAL, 1998).[3] In Mexico and Paraguay, 35 to 40% of teachers live in vulnerable homes (CEPAL, 1998).

For many years, one of the strongest conflicts regarding public education has concerned the salary of teachers who, compared to people in occupations with similar years of schooling, end up earning much less (CEPAL, 1998).[4] In the past seven years, Latin American teachers have received significant raises, as about 70–80% of the (modest) increase in educational budgets have gone to better salaries for primary and secondary school teachers (CEPAL, 1998). Yet, the fact remains that teachers' salaries are seldom sufficient to have comfortable lives.

The public/private divide in education has significant consequences upon teacher salaries and consequently on the quality of education that is provided to poor as well as non-poor students. On average, private teachers earn more than public school teachers in primary schools by 10–20%; this gap increases to about 30–45% in secondary schools (data for Brazil, Chile, Costa Rica, Ecuador, and Paraguay; CEPAL, 1998). The wage differential between public and private is substantial enough to foster a migration of the best qualified teachers toward the private system, thus augmenting the difficulties experienced by poor children. According to the World Bank (1993), one-third of the region's teachers lack professional certificates or degrees. It is well known that these teachers are usually assigned to work in rural areas, thus compounding the negative effects of poverty among rural children.

In comparing the salaries of teachers in Latin America with those of OECD countries in terms of the national 'level of effort' (defined as the teacher's salary as a percentage of GNP per capita), it has been found that Latin American teachers receive a share comparable to teachers in Northern countries (i.e.

about 1% of the GNP). This point is of interest because it suggests that in Latin America it is the countries' level of poverty which creates difficult conditions for their teachers (1995 data, CEPAL, 1998).

In short, poverty not only prevents poor children from gaining access to schooling, but it imposes limits on the number of years of school attainment. The state contributes to this situation by the provision of incomplete primary schools and inexperienced teachers in the countryside.

Poverty and Women

Feminist perspectives assert and have empirically demonstrated that gender is an element of social relationships that operates at multiple levels, affecting everyday interactions, public institutions, work, and the household. The consequences of gender distinctions are reflected in political, economic, and cultural spheres. Within the cultural sphere, gender asymmetries are expressed and reproduced through definitions of femininity and masculinity (including prescribed types and range of emotions) supported by such mechanisms as ideology, sexuality, language, law, schooling, and the mass media, among many others.

Feminist perspectives maintain that gender is a social marker that affects men and women. They also maintain that it affects all women negatively regardless of social class and ethnicity. Rather than argue which social marker is the strongest discriminant, feminist views are sensitive to the effects of the interaction of these markers and do not underestimate the specificity of gender.

Some societies defend gender differences on the basis of their own cultural values and preferences. But as Kabeer (1996: 16) notes, 'culture has profound material consequences, not only in shaping priorities and perceptions ... but also in shaping allocative behavior and practice'. For instance, in societies influenced by fundamentalist religious beliefs, culture tends to create norms that restrict women's physical and mental space. Across social classes, girls tend to have less physical mobility than boys and thus less freedom to move to larger towns or other countries to continue their education. Norms of femininity and masculinity restrict their choice of fields of study and later their choice of occupations. Women receive less remuneration for their years of education than men. Finally, women tend to aspire to political positions of less prestige and responsibility than men.

Among poor families, especially those in the rural areas, the sexual division of labour is of fundamental importance. Because girls in poor homes and in rural areas conduct the bulk of the domestic chores, parents perceive school knowledge as moving their daughters away from essential tasks. In communities lacking basic domestic facilities (e.g. electricity, potable water, sanitation facilities, rubbish collection), girls and women assume these chores. Since the poor have less possibility of regular medical attention, typically women and girls must assume these services, which usually translate into special diets and rest for the ill members of the family. In indigenous areas of Latin America, it is women who traditionally weave the clothing for their families. This is an activity that demands considerable skill and time. Its direct and indirect consequence on the availability of rural girls for schooling has not been analysed.

Poverty, in the Latin American context, also reflects itself in migration, from rural areas to major cities within the country or to foreign countries. Challenged by poverty, the cultural norm of women's restricted mobility has weakened. A major reason women migrate is to improve the quality of life for themselves and their families. In some cases, this is accomplished by taking menial jobs, in which case education levels are of relative unimportance. In fewer cases, women are forced to engage in prostitution, which, again, has no particular educational correlate.

While human capital assumes that salaries are a good measure of productivity, there is mounting evidence that women are given lower salaries than men for similar years of schooling. It has been asserted that women earn less because they are in fields that are less important and thus less well remunerated, but this is itself a reflection of societal values that discriminate against women's work. Another argument explaining these differences has been that women tend to work fewer hours than men, but a study comparing salary levels in terms of value per working hour found that women in urban areas earned between 66 and 80% of men's salaries with the same levels of education in eight of ten countries analyzed (CEPAL, 1994, citing 1992 data).

Education certainly helps women, but studies conducted by CEPAL several years ago found that, on average, a woman needed four more years of education than a man to earn a comparable salary. It should be observed that this statistic was presented at that time as an interesting finding rather than as a major social problem. Education is statistically associated with socio-cultural background and with income. The first association (socio-cultural background and education) indicates that education is not completely meritocratic; the second (education and income) suggests that education nonetheless is an important tool for social mobility. Competition in the labour market is imperfect and, thus, women need to be protected by labour legislation if their education is to be instrumental to their advancement.

While far from a perfect correlation, higher levels of education generally lead to higher levels of income for women. On the other hand, improvement in the economic well-being of women does not necessarily translate into greater autonomy and decision making in the domestic sphere, especially concerning decisions over their own body. This disjuncture suggests that higher levels of schooling are not a sufficient ingredient to foster autonomy and self-assertiveness in women. Thus, it would appear that there is a need to work on the content and experience of schooling to make education more responsive to women's feelings and practice of empowerment.

Highlighting the connection between poverty and women's education, the following points can be made:

(1) Poverty is a strong manifestation of inequity in society but it is not the only one. As Kabeer succinctly puts it, 'Not all women are poor, and not all poor people are women, but all women suffer from discrimination' (1996: 20). Gender differences operate in extremely important ways and serve to create and sustain poverty in society.

(2) In Latin America, men and women do not seem to show drastically different rates of enrolment and educational attainment compared to other regions of the Third World, but when analyses are made considering ethnicity and high levels of poverty, Latin American women are certainly at a disadvantage compared to men in terms of access to and completion of schooling.

(3) Owing to the current course of technological development and the presence of foreign firms with a greater sense of gender equality in many developing countries, some new opportunities are being opened to women, but gender inequity is not going away; it is being reinscribed in new ways. For instance, more women are moving into low-tech jobs regardless of social class.

(4) In debating the demands for greater access by girls to schools, it is usually forgotten by policy-makers that what is actually learned in school tends to be quite gendered. Gendered knowledge is acquired via the formal and the hidden curriculum, conditions that exist in all schools regardless of the quality of schooling. There is very little research of an ethnographic nature documenting the lived experience of girls and boys in Latin American schools. The comments by Longwe, reflecting on her experience as a teacher in African schools, seem equally applicable to Latin America. She states: 'Women with less schooling are likely to develop a clear perception of the asymmetries in the gender division of labour. The nearer they are to the poverty line, the less they can protect themselves by exploiting the labour of women even poorer than themselves. Being unschooled, they cannot rise by becoming honorary males' (1998: 26).

(5) Contrary to the argument that it is quality of schooling that causes poor girls to drop out (see, for instance, O'Gara *et al.*, 1998), poor girls are much more likely to leave school because domestic responsibilities at home do not allow them the free time necessary for schooling and because poor families must rely on the labour of their children from early years. Poor parents rarely know enough of what goes on in schools to be able to judge their quality. If quality were a factor, this would affect boys more than girls, since it is the schooling of boys that tends to be seen as an investment. In some cases, the 'relevance' of what is learned in school may be contested by rural families. The school's lack

of relevance, however, is not prominent in decisions to take girls out of school.

(6) It is incorrect to see women as merely one among several disadvantaged groups, next to rural, unemployed, street children, handicapped, etc. and to limit gender policies to the plight of poor women. This characterisation ignores the gender dimension of disadvantage and sees it as a less ingrained and pervasive social distinction.

(7) It is important to move away from identifying symptoms that affect the participation of girls in schooling and try, instead, to understand and correct the underlying causes of gender asymmetries in power. This implies a substantial use of feminist theory to move toward an understanding of the fundamental and interrelated causes of gender-based discrimination in society and an examination of schooling as a site where gender asymmetry is reproduced and yet may also be contested.

The Role of Governmental Policies

Education is considered a universal right in the UN Declaration of Human Rights. It is also a legal obligation since there is a convention that sustains this principle, the 1989 Convention on the Rights of the Child. Surprisingly, no state in the Third World has been sued by its citizens for failing to provide schooling to children, a right also enshrined in most constitutions.[5]

In an ideal world, economic policies that protect fair wages and fair terms of trade for products and services would obviate the need for special measures to ensure the minimum social welfare of citizens. In other words, in a fair economic world, social policies would be redundant. But if the world is not ideal, compensatory policies and their concomitant programs for the poor are needed.

The Economic Commission for Latin America and the Caribbean has long recognised the importance of educational equity. But educational equity is construed, first and foremost, as the equal distribution of schooling across social classes (proxied through income levels); a distant second in the concern for equity are urban/rural differences (see, for example, the arguments developed by Iglesias, a former executive director of CEPAL (Iglesias, 1981); see also Martin, 1997). In the 1990s, shortly before the Fourth World Conference on Women, CEPAL produced its second plan on gender and education (following one enacted in 1977). This plan recognised 'insufficient opportunities for large sectors of the female population to enter and stay in the education system; maintenance of school curricula and teaching practices that limit women's opportunities to participate in society and reinforce the lack of equity between women and men' (ECLAC, 1995: 23). The plan proposed a series of 'strategic actions' to be adopted by governments. It is not precisely known to what extent this regional plan has become reality. What is known is that while all Latin American countries have by now governmental units in charge of women in development, these are clearly understaffed and underfunded to comply with their mandate.

Two observations can be raised on the relation between equity and social class. First, Latin America indeed faces a serious problem of distribution of schooling according to income. In Brazil, the country with the highest income disparity in the region, 65% of the school-age children in the top income-per-capita quartile complete eight years of schooling by age 16 in contrast to only 14% in the bottom quartile (CEPAL, 1994: 89). CEPAL (1997) predicts that in Brazil by the year 2000 40% of lowest income quartile in urban areas will never complete fourth grade, so conditions exist to perpetuate extreme poverty. In Costa Rica, where income distribution is one of the most equal in Latin America, educational inequalities are still quite visible: 84% of young people in the highest income per capita quartile in urban areas complete eight years of schooling by age 16, in contrast with only 40% of those in the bottom quartile (CEPAL, 1994: 89).

Second, the official discourse about education is still cast in apolitical terms, leaving the ideological function of schooling unquestioned. While both global agreements (e.g. the Platform for Action emanating from the Fourth World Women's Conference in Beijing, 1995) and regional documents (e.g. ECLAC, 1995) recognise the need for intervening in school curricula and teacher practices to correct women's subordinations, few governments in Latin America have acted on these recommendations, much less altered the ways the hidden curriculum functions. Countries with large ethnic and rural populations, and thus with substantial poverty, have not engaged in these forms of educational transformation; these countries include Mexico (Gonzalez and Villaescusa, 1998), Peru (PROMUDEH, 2000), and Guatemala (Stromquist *et al.*, 2000), although Ecuador seems to be making inroads (GEO and REPEM, 1999). The belief in the neutrality of education is so widespread that it permeates even the demands for schooling of low-income groups, who also tend to be acritical of the gendered messages the school transmits. Some indigenous NGOs, notably those in Ecuador, Guatemala and Mexico (Chiapas), have contested the negative portrayal of native peoples, but even they remain silent regarding the gendered content of the schooling experience.

Several Latin American governments have enacted policies to address the question of equity. These policies include:

- Increasing subsidies and resources to schools for their day-to-day functioning (being attempted in Bolivia, Chile, Mexico, Peru).
- Lengthening the school day in schools that perform poorly in achievement tests and increasing the number of hours per week of those attending basic and intermediate education (carried out in Bolivia, Chile, Colombia, Costa Rica and Peru).
- Transferring (presumably trained and credentialled) teachers to critical areas.
- Expanding school meals and scholarships (Chile).
- Developing field-oriented schools in various disciplines (scientific, technical, artistic) (CEPAL, 1994: 118).

As can be seen, all of these measures seek to increase the effectiveness and efficiency of schools. Yet they are gender-blind, focusing primarily on poor communities and their schools. To undertake analyses that examine the distribution of education only by income levels and to fail to look at finer studies that consider the compound effects of gender and ethnicity is tantamount to considering social class as the key determinant of social outcomes and to ignore the role of ideology (regarding gender, ethnic and 'racial' differences) in the formation of social distinctions. The disregard of gender and 'racial' variables has proved a major weakness in current theories of national development and social change.

Through support to a few countries, particularly Guatemala, Bolivia, and Paraguay, several bilateral and multilateral agencies are acting to improve the conditions of girls' education (Cortina and Stromquist, 2000). It is important to remark that it is *girls'* and not women's education because international support tends to be concerned almost exclusively with the basic education of girls. When dealing with adult women, agencies give priority to reproductive health issues and local political participation, and, to a lesser extent, to income-generation skills. One of the few gender-focused compensatory efforts (not a policy) was attempted in Guatemala under USAID auspices in 1993–1996. Conducted as an experimental project, scholarships were found to increase the attendance of girls in rural areas (see Stromquist *et al.*, 2000). It should be noted that many of the governmental policies on gender often exist through the support of international development agencies. So in fact, such policies are not nationwide efforts but rather small projects, in many instances operating as pilot projects.[6]

Paradoxically, today gender equity is an accepted term and focus in public policy. There is new legislation on such issues such as domestic violence, rape, and representation quotas favouring women candidates for public office. There are also numerous initiatives to foster awareness of the use of contraceptives and of the spread of sexually transmitted diseases. But in the area of formal education, there still prevails the narrow vision of looking at it as the provision of access for women, particularly to basic education. Schooling as a fundamental site for the formation of gender ideologies passes unquestioned and thus governments do not seek to reform its overt and hidden curriculum or to train teachers for non-sexist and anti-sexist practices.[7] In fact, the first step in any kind of public policy development, the procurement of data, is missing. There is a serious need to acquire more data disaggregating gender by social class, ethnicity, and residence (rural/urban).

Two fundamental challenges to the successful design and implementation of public policies on gender come from within and outside Latin American countries.

The Challenge from Within: A Bifurcated Educational System

In Latin America, any enactment and implementation of educational policies to serve the marginalised social groups will be difficult. As Rama (1983) argues, in societies whose historical characteristic was the exclusion of the broad masses from education, and where there is radical socio-cultural discontinuity between them and the elite, 'the middle classes attach themselves to the upper class as a means of defending the small spaces at their disposal and tend to build up educational systems with the same peculiar features of social selectivity and ascriptions that characterised the traditional oligarchies' (p. 35).

In concrete terms, the imitation of upper-class norms has resulted in the existence of private schooling for groups who aspire to social mobility or who seek to keep their high status. In all countries of Latin America, there is a bifurcated educational system, with private elite schools catering to the wealthy classes and to middle-classes seeking higher mobility, and public schools serving mostly poor children. The higher-quality academic circuits function in a very closed manner, with entry usually beginning from pre-school in private and very selective institutions and moving into similarly exclusive universities.[8] The continuous deterioration of the public school system (persistently subjected to very low resource allocations) has also led to the emergence of non-elite private schools, attended by children of middle- and low-income families. De facto, this means that public schools in Latin American increasingly serve poor children whose families have low leverage on the political system.

Does this mean that states will not engage in equitable educational policy-making? No. What it means is that many policies will acquire symbolic rather than material character. It means also that policies will have a very narrow focus and will be short-term. Unless the heterogeneity of the colonial past is resolved through a profound social pact, such policies can be expected to play only a weak role in the reconfiguration of society.

The Challenge from Without: Missing Global Equity

Attempts to solve the problem of poverty cannot avoid dealing with structural factors; otherwise, we will continue indefinitely the pretense of taking poverty seriously.[9] To 'alleviate' poverty, several Latin American countries have established emergency funds and social investment funds in areas of health, education, and water and sewage systems. These funds, which have been established at different times, from 1971 onwards, have had a 'limited role in launching long-term anti-poverty programs' (CEPAL, 1994: 114).

To address structural poverty, certain changes are needed in the global market and would be complementary to other government sectors at the national level. In the case of Latin America, as is true for several African and Asian countries, the terms of trade that render agricultural products increasingly less valuable compared to technology-rich products place poor countries in a losing battle for the creation of national wealth. The burdens of excessive external debt further render national budgets very weak in social welfare (Alcalde, 1999; Acosta, 1999). Unequal terms of trade create differential living standards across countries; with globalisation, emigration of highly educated personnel out of the Third World is facilitated by constant demand in major industrial countries to enhance their industrial competitiveness.[10] In addition to improving the terms of trade, DAWN, a major global feminist NGO, proposes: changing the taxation system and making its functioning more effective, engaging in agrarian reform, and fostering the existence of NGOs as active counter-hegemonic elements of civil society (DAWN, 1995).

For compensatory educational policies to succeed, it is essential to affect other areas of the economy, particularly those pertaining to employment and health. Making the design of public policy even more difficult is the realisation that labour-intensive growth strategies will benefit poor women only if efforts are made to address the sexual division of labour at home and in the marketplace (Kabeer, 1996: 20). If no other social mechanisms for equalisation obtain, problems of over-education, devaluation of educational credentials, and competition for education 'goods' emerge (Filgueira, 1983). If educational policies do not remain in place until a stable solution is attained, good efforts may be short-lived. One case in point is Nicaragua: illiteracy before the Sandinista revolution (1979) was at 54%. With the subsequent literacy campaign it was supposedly reduced to 25%, yet estimates in 1996 put it back up to about 50% (Havelin, 1999).

Political Action from Civil Society

In trying to explain why some oppressed groups rebel to secure better conditions for themselves, Moore observes that 'there is no guarantee that exploitation, or just plain misery, will somehow secrete its own antidote ... Human beings have to create their own moral standards of condemnation and their own forms of collective action to change such situations' (1978: 457).

The first ones to take on the politics of poverty seriously will thus be the poor themselves. This requires that groups within civil society must be organised to put pressure on the state to implement corrective public policies and to engage in self-support initiatives. What Moore calls 'moral standards of condemnation' in my view implies a very strong knowledge foundation. One has to know the conditions that affect oneself as a poor person or poor group and the conditions that more privileged groups enjoy in order to develop some awareness of inequality and thus of injustice.

It has been remarked by some political observers and several feminists (activists and scholars) in the region, that the transition toward democracy in several Latin American countries was dominated by political parties and elite actors, a condition that, as a whole, has retarded the development of non-governmental organisations and grassroots groups (Oxhorn, 1998). In several cases, notably Chile and Argentina, women have been incorporated into the state bureaucracy but under the state's parameters that women should be professionals and technical experts, not advocates of feminist issues. International support for the more democratic states has been increased by withdrawing and transferring support from NGOs, including the women-led NGOs.

Overall, the women's movement in Latin America has had a limited impact on gender equity policies for formal systems of education (see Cortina and Stromquist, 2000, for an account of recent gender equity policies in the region). The work of women-led NGOs has typically concentrated on the education of adult women. Their efforts have addressed educating them in such issues as reproductive health, labour conditions and legislation, human rights (particularly domestic violence and rape), and political participation at local and national levels. The contributions that women-led NGOs have made to the development of new forms of citizenship among women are impressive. Surprisingly, however, their work has not questioned the ideological nature of the formal education system to the same degree that they have attacked the more visible welfare policies. A regional network, *Red de Educación Popular entre Mujeres de América Latina y el Caribe* (REPEM), has advocated the development of non-sexist education in the schools since 1990. This network has been able to conduct several training workshops for NGO personnel and teachers throughout the region and has fostered greater gender consciousness through short-story contests. However, its reduced funding has not allowed it to have a major impact on formal school systems.

The potential for women-led NGOs to address formal education is significant if we consider the multi-class composition of the feminist movement and its many organised groups. As Rama observes, 'Education contains in embryo a principle of social homogenisation and meritocratic selection, provided that it is itself effectively homogeneous, of scientific quality, and capable of developing personalities with independent criteria' (1983: 38). A major challenge for the feminist movement is to become more aware of formal education as a major political terrain and become more active in it.

International Co-operation and Gender-Sensitive Education

International agencies, with the collaboration of many NGOs, took a very positive step when they endorsed universal primary education, crystallised later in the Education for All Declaration, signed in

Jomtien, 1990. While the declaration acknowledged that two-thirds of the illiterate adults were women and stated among its key strategies that 'the most urgent priority is to ensure access to, and improve the quality of, education of girls and women and to remove every obstacle that hampers their active participation' (Interagency Commission WCEFA, 1990: 45), the governmental and donor agency action that ensued was not sufficient to meet either quantitative or qualitative goals (Torres, 2000). The World Education Forum, which met in Dakar in April 2000 to renew commitment to EFA, reiterated commitment to formal education for women, stating as a (repeated) goal: 'eliminating gender disparities in primary and secondary education by 2005, and achieving gender equality in education by 2015, with a focus on ensuring girls' full and equal access to and achievement in basic education of good quality' (WEF, 2000: 2). It remains unclear how the new timelines will enable countries to satisfy commitments not honoured in the past.

Literacy and adult basic education programmes, which are those most likely to be needed by the poor, have received very little attention. Weakening the possibilities for transforming the educational situation confronting poor women is the fact that structural adjustment programmes have also reduced national education priorities to cover only basic education and only for ages 7–14 years. This has been observed particularly in the case of Brazil, the Latin American country with the largest number of illiterates (Di Pierro, 2000). Agencies such as the World Bank, which play leading roles in shaping educational policies in the Third World, have adopted a view that illiteracy is a problem of the past and that as long as we keep making younger generations more able to go to school, illiteracy problems will disappear.

As to the policies pursued by international agencies, it is worthwhile to recognise that very few studies have been made of their actual effects. The expansion of pre-school in Brazil since the 1980s through the intense support of UNICEF offers important lessons. Through the use of census and household survey data, Rosemberg (2000) notes that approximately 86% of the pre-school expansion in Brazil took place through the hiring of women teachers who had only primary education, and were thus saddled with weak preparation and low salaries. She also found a large group of students of ages 7 to 9 in pre-school (11% by 1993), most of whom were black and poor. Rosemberg interprets this over-age preponderance as a reflection of the length of time they are retained in pre-school. Remarking that the pre-school women teachers receive low salaries and that the black children are being placed in dead-end schooling, Rosemberg concludes that there is 'an intricate game of subordination of class, race, and gender' going on through these 'low-cost compensatory educational programs'. She observes that a programme with a low financial cost may come with a high social cost.

Conclusions

Poverty is endemic in Latin America and affects a large segment of its population. While the region is more democratic than in the past, it has also become more unequal (Oxhorn, 1998). With globalisation, there has been a revival of the importance of education; this education is framed in terms of economic competitiveness, not social justice. In fact, however, the need for highly trained technical personnel may not create the atmosphere required to increase attention to poor and disadvantaged groups.

There continues a tendency to look at educational systems as self-contained, focusing on access to and completion of basic education, or as a means to achieve economic competitiveness, giving priority to the question of efficiency over equity. After years of considerable neglect, education in Latin America is emerging as a major policy concern (see, for instance the work of the Inter-American Dialogue, reflected in Puryear, 1997). This concern, unfortunately, is framed in terms of effectiveness and evinces a narrow definition of quality. By no means is quality being defined in terms of developing civic understanding in youth and adults, not to mention understanding of inequities and inequalities in society. Under such circumstances, it must be concluded that new educational policies emerging in Latin America are gender-blind.

Problems of access and attainment are still present and affect mostly rural areas, most of which are inhabited by groups of Indian or African (in the case of Brazil) descent. Much work remains to provide them with complete primary schools of good quality. Nonetheless, the fundamental educational problem for women, whether poor or rich, concerns the unquestioned, non-problematised gender-biased nature of schooling. Educational statistics focusing on access are not only likely to be overstated but they fail to capture the dynamics of discrimination that girls and women continue to face in the educational systems of their respective countries in terms of their everyday experience and what is learned in school. In this regard, more studies based on qualitative research methods are urgently needed.

Governmental policies in education have tended to respond to demand forces, albeit mostly urban, for greater access to schooling. These responses have not met the ambitious quantitative goals set by Jomtien but have permitted greater participation by the poor. Simultaneously, the expansion of schooling has not been accompanied by explicit recognition of the underlying factors that create the disadvantage in access and completion of rural and indigenous women, and has not been characterised by interventions to modify significantly the gendered nature of textbooks, teaching, and the overall schooling experience.

Public policies face particular tensions in the solution of the education of poor girls. Access, completion, and quality goals for the schooling of girls remain unfulfilled. While compensatory policies focusing on the poor make sense, as they prioritise the group most in need, policies that focus on poor girls have the effect of circumscribing gender problems only to the poor. Further, policies that concentrate on school access and completion, while reasonable from the perspective of social equality, leave the school untouched as a venue where undemocratic forms of femininity and masculinity are created and sustained.

Countries suffering structural poverty, such as those in Latin America, require a more comprehensive prescription. Education, as a form of socially legitimated knowledge, certainly helps individuals to obtain better jobs and higher salaries. But in bifurcated educational systems such as those characterising the region, education brings disproportionately higher rewards to the wealthier social classes. For schooling to make a substantial difference in the lives of poor women, not only does it have to be redesigned but it has to be accompanied by measures in other sectors of social and economic life, some national and some international.

NOTES

1. There are many ways of defining poverty. According to Kabeer (1996), two common conceptualisations of poverty are: (a) as a means, in which income levels are used as key proxies for well-being, and (b) as an end, which concentrates on the actual satisfaction of basic needs, including educational attainment. CEPAL defines poverty as the income below the poverty line, which in turn is defined as the amount of income relative to the 'basic food basket' required to cover nutritional needs, taking into account consumption habits, availability of goods and relative prices, plus the resources required for the satisfaction of non-food needs (CEPAL, 1998: 51). It defines as *indigentes* or people in extreme poverty 'those whose income is so low that it does not cover even nutritional expenditures' (CEPAL, 1998: 51). Perhaps because of different formulas used to measure poverty, it is not uncommon to find inconsistent statistics (sometimes produced by the same agency) concerning the poor and the extremely poor.
2. A welcome effort to address the need for greater understanding of multi-grade schools is the cross-country study being coordinated by Angela Little (1999) and her associates.
3. CEPAL defines vulnerable households as those whose total incomes are between 0.9 and 1.25 times the value of the poverty line (CEPAL, 1994: 12).
4. Teachers earn less than other professionals with equal years of schooling in all Latin American countries, with the exception of Costa Rica (CEPAL, 1998).

5. In Brazil, where basic education is protected by its latest Constitution, there was an unsuccessful attempt by an NGO to sue the government in 1994.
6. An example of the tendency to confuse externally funded projects with national policies is reflected in King and Hill, 1993.
7. Following Streitmatter (1994), we define non-sexist teaching as that attempting to question stereotypes and representations of men and women in different spheres of society, while anti-sexist teaching would be those efforts more proactive in nature seeking to develop an alternative view of society, with both men and women in equally important and valued roles and functions.
8. There has been a tendency by the elites to send their children to public universities that enjoy excellent reputations, in countries such as Brazil, Mexico and Chile. This situation is changing, however, with the emergence of high-prestige new private universities; these are also expensive but their high fees create a selective social environment that wealthy families prefer.
9. Helder Camera, a Brazilian bishop who worked with the poor of Northeastern Brazil for many years, is reported to have stated, 'When I give food to the poor, they call me a saint; when I ask why the poor don't have food, they call me a communist' (Selbin, 1998).
10. Brain-drain is increasing at a substantial rate. Not only are countries losing their people trained in science and technology, as medical doctors and computer engineers go North to secure better jobs, but also people trained in less technical fields or with little education leave to get menial (but higher paid) jobs abroad.

Educational Expansion and the Mediation of Discontent: The Cultural Politics of Schooling in the Arab States

André Elias Mazawi

Introduction

[This chapter] probes in a comparative approach, the socioeconomic and political underpinnings underlying the expansion of schooling in the Arab states.[1] [It] critically reviews studies and analyses already published. The review aims to redress the imbalance found in the literature dealing with the Arab states between the overemphasised modernising effects of schooling, and the more marginalised civil society processes ultimately affecting educational expansion.

The point of departure of [this chapter] is that schools represent 'terrains' (or arenas) mediating—through their structures, contents and dynamics—what others have termed as 'identity politics', classified by Davies and Guppy (1997: 455) as 'the struggles among groups for recognition, accommodation, and validation of their symbolic representations and world outlooks in institutions'. These two authors have also argued that '[i]dentity politics have spawned a revival of ethnicity and localism, with an attendant revival of particularism and attachments to local cultures and traditions', noting that '[t]his revival cannot be considered autonomous and individualised responses of isolated communities'. Rather, '[c]ommentators have likened the worldwide revival of fundamentalism in its myriad forms as a response to global culture—largely a commercial culture of Western origin—and its perceived threats to identity and heritage'. Hence, they conclude that '[s]chools have become a prime arena for these culture wars because they can promote or erode a group's cultural identity' (Davies and Guppy, 1997: 455).

Applied to developing states, the above contention implies that the 'modernising' or 'globalising' effects of school systems act ultimately as proxies of multilevel and conflict-laden sociocultural and political processes, rather than as a mere expression of social progress and transition to modernity (cf. Fägerlind and Saha, 1983; Larrain, 1989: 1–17; Taylor, 1979: 3–41). Most importantly, the concept of 'identity politics' also implies that the expansion of schooling

André Elias Mazawi, 'Educational Expansion and the Mediation of Discontent: The Cultural Politics of Schooling in the Arab States', *Discourse: Studies in the Cultural Politics of Education*, 23, 1, 59–74 © 2002 Taylor & Francis Ltd. <http://tandf.co.uk/journals>.

is closely associated with a rise in political contestation of the established order. It may be argued that in deeply divided societies an expanding public education is likely to bolster attempts by local communities and marginalised groups alike to uphold their cultural frames of reference, whether by devising alternative educational platforms, or through attempts to act directly on public education by instrumentalising its provision towards broader political gains. Such a dialectical dynamic boosts educational expansion along a multiplicity of institutional forms. Yet, it also plunges the school into the realm of ethnic politics and their cultural expressions.[2] Hence, state systems—or, more precisely, state-entrenched elites—are not the sole corporate actors determining educational expansion. Rather, civil society processes constitute an integral part of educational change and cannot be left outside the equation (see Davies, 1999; Gillborn, 1994).

Thus, if the consolidation of the contemporary state is perceived by established elites as possible through the subordination of mass schooling, it is also necessary to view how the expansion of school systems mediates social processes that, at times, jeopardise the dominant position of state-entrenched elites, or disclose resistance to their policies. This double-bind dynamic affects the outcomes of educational policies and the extent to which the acquisition of educational resources is perceived as pertinent by different social groups (Archer, 1984; Craig and Spear, 1982*a*, 1982*b*; Fernandes, 1988; Ramirez and Boli, 1987; Ray, 1988).

On this very issue, studies of educational expansion in the Arab states have remained largely silent, with a few outstanding exceptions mainly by anthropologists (see e.g. Eickelman, 1985; Starrett, 1998). Deeply immersed in modernisation, human capital and development narratives or in policy-oriented speculations (see e.g. Ansari, 1985; Birks and Rimmer, 1984; Massialas and Jarrar, 1983, 1991; Tansel and Kazemi, 2000; Zawdie, 1995), studies have highlighted essentially the structural outcomes of state policies (Mazawi, 1999). Others have investigated the school's reproduction of social inequalities and authoritarian patriarchal systems (Al-Saeed *et al.*, 2000; El Hachem, 1989; Haidar, 1997). Massialas and Jarrar (1991: 144–5) observed in this respect that 'the values of the patriarchal family are replicated in the school', and that the 'Arab classroom teaches reverence to authority figures and complete submission to their will; it teaches not to question traditional sources of knowledge and wisdom; and it teaches cooperation, not competition'.

Studies, however, tend to conceptualise the expansion of schooling in Arab societies as associated with structural strains due to their transition from 'conservatism'/'traditionalism' to 'modernity' (see Al-Saeed *et al.*, 2000; Christina *et al.*, 1999: 355). Much less research effort has been invested in understanding the extent to which educational expansion in Arab societies is linked to the emergence of competing political agenda, and the extent to which the context in which expansion occurs mediates not just reproduction but also civil resistance with far-reaching sociocultural and political implications (Eickelman, 1992; Farag, 1994; Faust *et al.*, 1991; Starrett, 1998).[3]

In the present [chapter] it is argued that development and modernisation approaches, as well as class reproduction theories, remain largely limited in their account of the complex web of factors affecting the expansion of schooling in the Arab states. Both approaches fail to point to the articulation of multi-level processes ultimately shaping the social and cultural underpinnings of educational expansion. It is further argued that these theoretical approaches, beyond their paradigmatic differences, have confined Arab civil societies essentially to the structural outcome of state policies. Consequently, processes of civil dissent and resistance and their effects on educational expansion are naively conceptualised in terms of 'forces of tradition' versus 'forces of change' (see the typology elaborated by Massialas and Jarrar [1987]). The community-based and conflict-laden power conjunctures shaping educational expansion in the Arab states have been largely left outside the analysis and the voices they represent often discarded. Critical aspects of sociopolitical dissent and contestation in Arab societies are thus decontextualised and dismissed from an analysis that, hence, addresses symptoms as if they were underlying causes (Eickelman, 1992: 643).

As stated, the present [chapter] does not report new data, but rather reviews existing research on education in the Arab states. First, the aim is to point to major macrostructural and historical factors affecting levels of literacy and access to educational resources in different states. Secondly, the [chapter] reviews published fieldwork research undertaken into diverse community-based settings. The aim is to explore points of articulation between state policies, civil society processes and their underlying sociopolitical and cultural effects on patterns of educational expansion. Thirdly, in the frame of a concluding discussion, the major implications of the above dynamics are discussed and possible research paths are pointed to.

Educational Expansion and the Rise of Public School Systems

The expansion of educational services in the contemporary Arab states occurred initially during post-independence periods (1920s–1970s). The expansion of schooling met with the basic barriers imposed by high illiteracy rates, estimated at 80–95% at the start of the 1940s. In some rural areas, illiteracy estimates in general, and among women in particular, could well have reached around 99%. Historical factors, cultural belief systems and practices, as well as explicit colonial policies, all cumulatively contributed to the maintenance of marginal rates of literacy. In Algeria, Egypt, Sudan and Palestine, for instance, colonial policies directly contributed to a large extent to sustain or otherwise reproduce marginal rates of literacy, as far as this was functional mainly to the bureaucratic needs of the imposed colonial systems, or as part of colonial attempts to prevent or suppress the formation of national movements (Starrett, 1998; Szyliowicz, 1973; Tibawi, 1956; Williamson, 1987).

State policies in a post-independence period were largely directed towards the promotion of an integrated economy and the training of an indigenous local professional labour force. Notwithstanding this, the recruitment of the needed human capital was very much affected by the lack of a sufficiently broad literate infrastructure. In this context, literacy campaigns, the expansion of formal schooling and the establishment of higher education institutions had to operate simultaneously. According to Massialas and Jarrar (1983, 1991), this exerted considerable structural strains on planning priorities, the allocation of national resources, the quality of training programmes and the economic viability of many school and higher education systems (see also Al-Saeed *et al.*, 2000).

In the mid-1990s, Arab states exhibited still relatively high illiteracy rates, though literacy rates have systematically increased since the early 1950s. UNESCO (1995) statistics show that, depending on the state concerned, between one-fifth and one-half of a state's population was estimated to be illiterate. Illiteracy rates are still much higher among women and among inhabitants of rural areas, with women in rural areas exhibiting the highest illiteracy rates. Literacy rates among adults (15 years of age and over) in all Arab states combined were estimated at 56.8% (68.4% for males and 44.2% for females). Notwithstanding this, Arab states ranked higher than most developing countries on this measure (UNESCO, 1995: 19).

Literacy policies in many Arab states, while reducing the percentage of illiterates in the general population, did not altogether succeed, with some exceptions, in reducing their absolute number. UNESCO estimates show that in spite of a net decrease in the percentage of illiterates during the period 1970–1990, the absolute number of illiterates in many cases rose during that same period. In some states the absolute number of illiterates increased by about 27%, such as in Egypt. In other states, the increase was more dramatic and attained almost 51% in Sudan and over 92% in Kuwait. Yet, the same estimates suggest that the increase was significantly more moderate during the period 1980–1990, and stood, in most cases, at half the increase of the whole 1970–1990 period.

Natural demographic increase, paralleled by insufficient expansion of primary or basic educational services, constitutes an important impediment to a decrease in illiteracy rates and in the absolute number of illiterates. In Egypt, as a matter of example, one UNESCO (1995: 30–1) report observed that, while literacy rates among adults are 'estimated to have increased from 40 to 51% in the 1980–1995 period, the absolute number of illiterate adults (both males and females) increased from nearly 16 million to nearly 19 million over the same period'. Fergany (1994: 19) concluded his empirical study on this issue by stating that 'Egypt finds itself in an absolute setback compared to Arab countries, and in a still greater one compared to the rest of the third world as far as girls' literacy is concerned. In other words, compared to the Arab and other third world countries, Egypt registers a setback in the eradication of female illiteracy and in the primary schooling of girls.'

The expansion of formal schooling was much affected by this basic set of parameters. The 'democratisation of education', in the sense of broadening access of various social groups to educational resources, became a major feature of educational policies in most Arab states (Massialas and Jarrar, 1991). By the mid-1990s, enrolment of the 6–11 age group in all Arab states was about 83.9% for males and 71.6% for females. For the 12–17 age group, percentages stood at 59.2 and 47.1, respectively (UNESCO, 1995: 36). These statistics imply that actual access to formal schooling is still not universal, in spite of state policies to the contrary. Significant inequalities of educational opportunities still persist mainly between urban and rural regions, but also between various social groups along gender and socioeconomic lines.

While females have significantly improved their school-life expectancies in many Arab states, they still have a significantly more restricted set of educational opportunities compared with males. For instance, between 1965 and 1992, females improved their school-life expectancy by 7 years in Jordan, 4.8 years in Syria, 4.4 years in Egypt and 3.7 years in Iraq. The respective figures for males were 3.9 years in Jordan, 1.1 years in Syria, 3.5 years in Egypt and 0.9 year in Iraq (UNESCO, 1995: 41). Yet, in most Arab states school-life expectancy and school survival remain significantly higher for males compared with females (UNESCO, 1995: 38).

Investment in education varies between Arab states, being largely conditioned by their GNP, economic structure, foreign hard currency indebtedness and dependency upon International Monetary Fund (IMF) and World Bank structural adjustment policies (see e.g. Tansel and Kazemi, 2000). For some states, such as Algeria, UNESCO statistics show that governmental expenditure on education amounted in 1993 to about one-fifth of all governmental expenditures and to 7.2% of the GNP. In other North African Arab states, such as Morocco, government expenditure on education constituted about 26.7% of all governmental expenditures and about 5.8% of the Moroccan GNP in 1992. By contrast, for Sudan, a country with an annual per capita GNP not exceeding US$ 300 (1986) and already overburdened by external debts and internal political fragmentation and instability, expenditure on education constituted about 9% of all government expenditures and 4.8% of the Sudanese GNP in 1980. Gulf states, by contrast, were able since the start of the 1970s to invest a considerable percentage of their significantly higher GNP in the provision of educational services due to revenues from oil exports (between 2% in the UAE and 6.1% in Kuwait in 1993). This wide range of investment capabilities of the different Arab states not only conditions the quality of educational provision in each state, but also affects the broader relevance of formal schooling to social mobility.

In almost all Arab states, public education remains free of charge and subsidised by the state. Some have observed that the provision of social welfare services, including education, is an integral part of the state's policy to ensure its legitimacy and maintain the dominant position of its elites and their repressive hegemony (Kamrava and Mora, 1998: 904–8). This is especially so with regard to access of holders of educational credentials into state bureaucracies (Shaw, 1996). In this respect, several writers have investigated the close linkage existing in several Arab states, such as Egypt, Syria, and the Gulf region, between educational credentials and entry to the state bureaucracy. Such a linkage, as in the case of post-1952 Egypt, is officially endorsed, and higher education graduates were, until very recently, secured jobs within state apparatus (Hargreaves, 1997; Sanyal *et al.*, 1982). In the Gulf states, the ability of nationals to secure access to educational credentials, and especially higher education degrees, is an important resource for their entry into state positions (Ghabra, 1997).

One of the surprisingly more marginalised aspects of education in Arab states concerns the scarce attention within the relevant research literature given to the effects exerted by political conflicts, wars and economic instability on national educational systems, their expansion and viability. More often than assumed, political conflicts have destabilised and hampered the operation and efficiency of educational systems in Algeria (Cheriet, 1996), Iraq ('Allaq, 1997), Lebanon (Oweini, 1998), Palestine (Rigby, 1995) and Sudan (Graham-Brown, 1991). The direct effects of context-specific political and economic circumstances were largely felt in terms of dramatic downward flows in school enrolment and literacy rates, and an increased shortage in teachers, textbooks and basic educational materials. Moreover, many indications suggest that in such deeply divided and internally fragmented societies, educational institutions have become powerful tools in the mobilisation of the younger generations into the conflict (Africa and Human Rights Watch, 1995). The lack of any meaningful educational policy and the breakdown of basic educational services and development schemes further accentuate already existing regional and class-related disparities.

Civil Society, Local Communities, and Educational Expansion

The emergence and expansion of public school systems in the Arab states have not therefore been devoid of inherent contradictions. The preceding review clearly suggests that given geographic, socio-economic, cultural and ethnic multi-level cleavages within Arab societies, the expansion of public school systems drained into them increasingly powerful loads of conflicting interests. This was more so because the expansion of public schools meant the marginalisation, if not the state's actual expropriation and appropriation, of community-based patterns of education, such as the largely ungraded and loosely coupled *madrasa, kuttab, zawiya* or *khalwa* types of education, which were organised around and in relation to religious institutions (see Al-Radi *et al.*, 1998; Grandin and Gaboricau, 1997; Lynch *et al.*, 1992; Tibawi, 1972; Wagner, 1993). It also meant the imposition of a paradigmatic alternative, namely, the graded, uniform and state-controlled public school system. Such a transformation is not a mere 'modernisation', 'structural change' or 'transition'. It rather expresses a more basic, often radical and certainly conflict-loaded, transformation of the existing bases of power, the determination of new sources of authority (political and social) and the definition of what valid (and therefore politically connoted) knowledge is. This is largely true in the case of Egypt, Syria, Iraq, Jordan, Sudan and the Maghreb states.[4]

With respect to Egypt, Starrett (1998: 9) conceptualises this process in terms of 'functionalisation', which he defines as a 'translation in which intellectual objects from one discourse come to serve the strategic or utilitarian ends of another discourse'. In this sense, Starrett (1998: 10) argues, for instance, that the 'functionalisation' of Islamic discourse within Egyptian public schools has enabled state-entrenched elites to put Islam 'consciously to work for various types of social and political projects' with far-reaching counter-implications. Peninsular Arab states, such as Saudi Arabia, Bahrain, Kuwait, Oman, Qatar and the UAE are also cases in point.

In peninsular states as well, the creation and expansion of state apparatus, mainly since the late 1960s and early 1970s, was heavily associated with local rivalries and political competition. It necessitated the reconceptualisation of earlier (religious) patterns of education, their reorganisation under diverse forms of state supervision as part of their 'functionalisation' in ways consonant with the state's ability to maintain and manage various conflictual processes while maintaining its legitimacy (see Al-Misnad, 1985; El-Sanabary, 1992). In many of these states, special arrangements had to be found to accommodate the *kuttab* or *madrasa* settings already in operation, institutionalising their operation within a broader state-controlled system of education. In some instances, such as in Algeria, Egypt, Iraq, Jordan and Syria, but less so in Lebanon, redefining the state's position on and relation to private, largely Western parochial schools was also indicative of the interests at stake, with far-reaching implications for the ability of local communities to access or maintain an alternative education to that offered by the state.[5]

Thus, the very expansion of public school systems was part of a comprehensive social, political and economic transformation of the power structures regulating intergroup relations in many Arab societies. This also implies considerable resistance and opposition by groups that perceive the state's increasing monopoly of educational services as jeopardising their own position within the broader power structure. The case of post-independence Algeria remains pertinent to briefly illustrate the argument. Cheriet (1996: 9), writing about Algeria, has argued in this respect that state-entrenched elites, 'in their bid to construct a new individual and a new society', perceived the development of a culturally diversified educational system as a means to coopt elites of various sociolinguistic and cultural traditions. However, by so doing, Cheriet continues, 'nation-state builders in Algeria have inadvertently caused the demise of their own legitimation devices'. Within this context, the current Algerian civil war placed the educational system, and particularly universities, at the forefront of the mediation of civic dissent and the transformation of existing power structures (Cheriet, 1996: 13). According to others (Abu-Absi, 1984; Burgat, 1988; Chevit, 1994; Moatassime, 1992; Sebaa, 1996), it further meant a radical shift in the cultural politics underlying educational policies, especially with respect to the Arabisation of school and university curricula.[6]

It is also possible to ponder on the cases of Lebanon and Egypt. In these two cases—though within largely different contexts—school systems mediate the formation or reproduction of competing social and political constructs. In Lebanon, the largely private provision of educational services, within the context of a weak(ened) public system, contributed to strengthening the association between specific socioeconomic indicators, type of education pursued and social opportunities. Such a process further intensified primary conflicting and colliding sectarian cleavages strengthening the school's role as reproducer of particularistic social and cultural identities that considerably overlap distinct political constituencies (Charafeddine, 1996; Wehbé and El Amine, 1980). On this point, El Hachem (1989: 99) poignantly observed that

> we can see two main educational elements in the production and reproduction of plurality in Lebanon: first, confessional schools, and second, family and social influences. Reinforced by geographic segmentation both these elements play important roles in the indoctrination of youth along sectarian lines, and thus both contribute to reinforcing inter-communal differences. In this way Lebanon has developed an identity as a patchwork of incompatible sociocultural and socioreligious semi-independent communities.

In Egypt, by contrast, the over-subordination of the public school system to regulations and control of state apparatus leads to the gradual formation of a community-based web of loosely coupled, but ideologically identifiable, Islamic, private or other formal and informal educational settings (Herrera, 1998; Starrett, 1998). This institutional web stands, too often, in considerable opposition to (if not direct competition with) the state's control over the definition of educational policies and the provision of educational services. According to Starrett (1998), it invites 'radical criticism and increases the hunger for religious resources that cannot be met solely by the public sector'. In a scholarly *tour de force*, Farag (1994) retraced how educational discourses are deeply rooted in the broader mediation of regional, ideological, political and class-related cleavages. Painstakingly analysing a wide array of Egyptian newspaper reports (both local and national), she skillfully reconstructs competing narratives about education, their vehement clash in given socio-political circumstances, and divergent social and cultural interpretations they acquire in given power constellations between state-entrenched elites and various opposition groups.

Quite differently, in Oman, Palestine and Yemen, the expansion of schooling mediated at times different modalities of civil dissent and political contestation. For example, a fieldwork-based anthropological study carried out by Chatty (1996) in Oman is quite revealing in terms of the activism of marginalised nomad communities in their persistent attempts to provide educational resources for their children. Chatty documents how Bedouin women affiliated to the Harasiis tribe undertook a radical reorganisation of their mobile households in order to secure their girls' access to a newly built remote school As no school dormitories were provided for girls in spite of repeated Harasiis demands to that effect, several Harasiis women undertook a radical reorganisation of their camp, split households and relocated them near the school so that their daughters could overcome the difficulties of distance and attend school. Chatty also shows the extent to which such innovative behaviour of Harasiis women was still met with conservative attitudes on the part of the urban expatriate (Egyptian) male headteacher, who 'explained that it was unbecoming for two such mature girls to be in the same place as adolescent boys' (Chatty, 1996: 161). In this sense, Harasiis women have been shown to promote their daughters' education much more actively than previous studies would lead to us to believe. Chatty (1996: 163) sums up:

> The assumption that Harasiis families would not permit girls to board has been proven to be based on misunderstandings of the tribe, its men, its women, and, most pointedly, its children. The way government policy was initially interpreted tended to exclude these girls from the benefits of education, and even hinted at a physical segregation of the sexes that the Harasiis themselves never required. The fact that education now fully extends to both girls and boys is a tribute to the spirited efforts of a handful of women and their supportive spouses. Harasiis women, through a concerted cooperative effort to help themselves and their daughters, really have been able to demand formal schooling. At another level this action clearly reveals that women as they view themselves—and as their men regard them—are actors, with the power to determine their own needs and those of their families and the authority to control their lives and those of their children.

Chatty's study demonstrates that the drive towards educational expansion can be identified also within marginalised communities,[7] and as such departs from centralist accounts of educational expansion. The latter have mainly narrated how, in different contexts, state policies towards nomad societies have affected their transition to modernity while, at the same time, integrating them into mainstream society. Within this type of account, the lower academic achievement of pupils of nomadic origin in general, and girls more particularly, has been attributed essentially to cultural factors related to their society's traditionalism (see e.g. Ben-David, 1994) and family structure (Al-Krenawi and Lightman, 2000; cf. Elbedour *et al.*, 2000). In her account, Chatty therefore breaks with the discourse and assumptions of modernisation and development theories. She clearly shows that marginalised communities are able to contextually generate, and institutionally sustain innovative modes of behaviour with respect to the consumption of educational resources.

Elsewhere, on the Palestinian West Bank and Gaza Strip, starting from late 1987 onward as part of the *Intifada* (Uprising), loosely coupled and largely clandestine community-based educational settings challenged the closure of educational institutions by the Israeli military apparatus. Banned and outlawed by the Israeli military, such activism offered alternative and empowering political platforms to Palestinians, through which civil dissent against Israeli occupation was further promoted (Mahshi and Bush, 1989; Rigby, 1995: 15–33). In this respect, the Palestinian case illustrates the ability of individuals and groups to pursue the implications of their own perceptions of sociopolitical reality, actively promoting their own socialisation and education (Mazawi, 1998). The Palestinian case also suggests that, under specific political circumstances, educational resources may be perceived as relevant tools for the mediation of broader resistance against state apparatus. In such cases, 'educational expansion' is politically connoted in the sense that it reflects essentially resistance and opposition rather than cooptation within state-sponsored systems (see e.g. Badran, 1980; Mazawi, 1994*b*; Nakhleh, 1979).

Quite differently, in post-1990 unified (the national-oriented North and the socialist-oriented South) Yemen, the parliamentary debates over the 1992 Education Bill were indicative of the intensive power struggles between the Yemeni Socialist Party (YSP) and the Yemen Reform Grouping (YRG). The YSP managed a successful parliamentary vote, in spite of Islamist opposition, in view of creating a secular educational programme for the unified state. The programme stressed a broader citizenship affiliation for all Yemenis, while discarding primary tribal and other sectarian solidarities. However, beneath the surface the YSP was also seeking to end YRG control over the 'scientific institutes', which were state-funded Islamic institutions. In many respects, the struggle over the 1992 Education Bill served as a significant power test between the YSP and YRG and other groupings over the drafting of the Yemeni constitution and election law (Kostiner, 1996: 29). The Yemeni case sheds light on the internal conflicts underlying power struggles among state-entrenched elites. The latter are far from presenting a monolithic and unified mode of behaviour. Rather, state policies in general, and educational policies in particular, express antagonistic outcomes of a political system too often fragmented internally (on state–civil-society relations in Yemen, see Carapico [1998]).

The above cases suggest that the expansion of schooling systems in the Arab states cannot be reduced to the sum total of state-initiated policies. Rather, expansion reflects, in addition, a wide array of intervening factors related to civil society processes. The latter are associated with the ability of various social groups to generate and devise alternative platforms within the broader transformation of power structures regulating intergroup relations. Building on Appadurai's (1996: 184) notion of 'context generative' changes, it is therefore possible to argue, using his words, that the communities presented above 'produce contexts against which their own intelligibility takes shape'. For researchers this 'provides the beginnings of a theoretical angle on the relationship between local and global realities' underlying the expansion of schooling among various social groups in Arab societies.

Conclusion

Macro-structural research on the expansion of schooling in the Arab states is largely policy driven, and depicts an omnipotent and centralised state system that regulates various aspects of the public provision of education (see e.g. Christina *et al.*, 1999; Massialas and Jarrar, 1983, 1991; Tansel and Kazemi, 2000). Educational expansion is accounted for in terms of the emergence of state apparatus in the post-independence period and as the outcome of state-building policies. Community-level ethnographic studies suggest, however, that educational expansion in the Arab states operates within a multifaceted context that mediates its ultimate political and cultural implications. Beyond geographic particularities, the expansion of schooling is affected, in addition, by factors closely associated with community-based processes. In many respects it may be argued that educational expansion eventually channels, under specific sociopolitical circumstances, modes of civil participation in state systems characterised by limited participatory opportunities. In other words, educational settings—*qua* societal 'fields' (Bourdieu, 1984) or 'contexts' (Appadurai, 1996)—enable distinct constituencies to attempt and act on the broader distribution of power by enhancing their access to public education, or, alternatively, by generating their own power base and devising educational settings outside the direct control of the state.

Contextually situating the expansion of schooling in the Arab states enables therefore a more sensitive account of the social transformations involved, their cultural reinterpretation in diverse situations and their political implications for the broader power structure. At community level, modernisation and development approaches remain limited in their explanatory power. Their implied progress-entrenched metanarrative—as suggested by models of 'world systems' (Adick, 1992), 'social transition' (Massialas and Jarrar, 1987, 1991), 'dual perception' or even 'parallel growth' (Moghaddam and Taylor, 1985)—expresses essentially an explanatory syntax that reproduces, by and large, a hegemonic Western politico-cultural and value-laden discourse. Elsewhere, I have argued at length that such models account for educational expansion in developing states in general, and in Arab states in particular, in terms of rationalising the discourse and perspectives of state-entrenched elites (Mazawi, 1999: 335–8, 350–2).

Apple (1996: 42) has observed that beyond their ideological premises and assumptions, educational policies are deeply embedded in a society's socio-economic structure and political conflicts. As such, they cannot be comprehended outside the immediate political and cultural context in which they are constantly formulated and negotiated. Thus, 'contexts' become critical to comprehend the interplay between state policies and local and global processes. Appadurai (1996: 187) has already stressed that '[c]ontexts are produced in the complex imbrication of discursive and nondiscursive practices', with each context implying 'a global network of contexts'. From this vantage point, what becomes clear is that the expansion of schooling in the Arab states cannot be reduced to its modernising effects or to nation-building processes or even to the mere reproduction of social stratification. There is much more to add. The expansion of schooling plays a significant role in a constant reformulation and transformation of sociopolitical power. By implication it *generates* interpretations of 'tradition' and 'culture' which enable competing groups to differentially frame schooling and educational resources and their perceived values (see e.g. Starrett, 1998). If that is the case, then focusing on the contribution of schooling to the 'transition' of Arab societies into modernity becomes largely an intellectual exercise in futility, and a misleading one, at best. The problematic does not lie so much between 'forces of tradition' versus 'forces of change', as has been suggested by Massialas and Jarrar (1987) and to a more limited extent by Khaleefa, Erdos and Ashria (1997) and others, but beyond such a unidimensional spectrum and the questionable disputes it raises. It rather lies, as Appadurai (1996) suggests, within the generative capabilities of individuals and groups to promote 'locales' through which they could negotiate or act upon the social and cultural underpinnings of the political order.

At this particular junction, Davies and Guppy's (1997: 455) contention on 'identity politics' is very relevant in order to grasp the fuller meaning of the expansion of schooling in the Arab states. Schools have much more to do with the mediation of civil discontent and the distribution of sociopolitical power than with the reductionist and redundant tale of traditionalism versus modernisation. Indeed, the cases reviewed in the second part of this [chapter]—be they the Egyptian, Lebanese, Palestinian and Sudanese cases, or the Harasiis women in Oman, or the Yemeni debates over the 1992 Education Bill—all illustrate distinct dimensions of 'identity politics'. In all these cases, schools—as locales, are associated with the generation of culturally framed and politically connoted modalities of discontent much more than they are with the external features of traditionalism and modernity.

Whether one probes the emergence and expansion of various modes of Islamic or private education in Egypt, or the post-civil-war expansion of sectarian educational settings in Lebanon, or the community-based classrooms during the Palestinian *Intifada*, one is bound to acknowledge the association between educational expansion in each of these cases and the mediation of contextually situated sociopolitical dissent. This process occurs, however, in constant relation to cultural frames of reference (be they nationalist, religious or other ideologies), mobilised to legitimise its various institutional outcomes. The Harasiis and the Yemeni cases strongly suggest that such a dynamic may be also mediated from *within* the public school systems. Accounting for the expansion of schooling necessitates therefore a reference to what McLaren (1988) calls 'modes of subjectivity' and the extent to which they are related to the drives, perceptions and actions of individuals and groups in relation to the acquisition of educational resources.

What can the present review offer in terms of theoretical insights into the case of educational expansion in the Arab states? First, a comparative approach becomes essential if research is to gain some critical insights into the multiplicity and interwoven complexity of voices within a given geopolitical region, in this case the Arab states. Comparative studies reveal that in spite of their relative sociocultural homogeneity, there nonetheless exists a polyphonic and multifaceted web of circumstances resulting in divergent institutional and behavioural outcomes across the Arab states (Hovsepian, 1995). As far as the expansion of schooling in these states is concerned, its occurrence is necessarily conditioned by a wide array of contextual factors, in relation to which state-entrenched elites are only one of the parties involved.

Secondly, McLaren's 'modes of subjectivity' and the concept of 'identity politics' become critical theoretical tools if researchers are to break the vicious cycle of macro-structural and policy-oriented studies, so frequently upheld in studies of education in the Arab states and in third world states in general (see Saha, 1991: 249). This implies that educational expansion be conceptualised within a wider area of theoretical approaches, sensitive to the different levels of action in which expansion occurs. This also implies, in the words of Hey (1996: 360), that more attention is given to 'people's reactions and resistances inside homes, communities, schools and classrooms' and how such contestation ultimately mediates patterns of schooling with counter-hegemonic implications for the broader distribution of political power.

NOTES

1. The [chapter] discusses the expansion of access to school in the Arab states. The term 'Arab states' refers to countries formally affiliated to the League of Arab States. The present [chapter] refers mainly to Algeria, Bahrain, Egypt, Iraq, Jordan, Kuwait, Lebanon, Libya, Morocco, Oman, Palestine, Qatar, Tunisia, Saudi Arabia, Sudan, Syria, the United Arab Emirates (UAE) and Yemen (North and South unified since 1990). Their combined territories extend over some 12 million km^2 with a population amounting to slightly over 220 million inhabitants at the start of the 1990s. Arab states vary considerably in the size of their populations, their social structure, and the volume of their economics.
2. The expansion of schooling in Israel is an interesting case in point, to illustrate the argument. Peled (1998) studied the rise of *El ha-Ma'ayan* Sepharadic school network, associated with the Shas party, as an empowering alternative to public education. Shas' constituency comprises mostly socioeconomically less established strata within Jewish society, of Middle Eastern and North African origin. The emergence of Shas, and especially the expansion of its school network, is strongly associated with perceived traits of Sepharadic culture and heritage and their mobilisation into a culturally embedded political platform. Their emergence clearly represents an example of 'identity politics' managed through the structuration of an alternative educational system in view of consolidating a distinct constituency. By contrast, Palestinian citizens of Israel seem to exhibit a different strategy. While bolstering community institutions at the national level since the mid-1970s, no alternative school system (including a university) has been established so far, though the issue of an Arab university in Israel remains highly debated. Currently, the state-managed public school system and public Israeli universities remain the mainstream venues for Palestinians in Israel. Regarding the formal school system, repeated demands were put forth stressing the need to accommodate the cultural and national background of Palestinian pupils (Mazawi, 1994*a*, 1997). Notwithstanding this, since the late 1980s some culturally specific educational platforms have emerged among Palestinians in Israel, mainly Islamic religious training institutions associated with various political currents. These have rather been more instrumental in reinforcing intra-social power politics *vis-à-vis* other groups within the Palestinian polity in Israel (Mazawi, 1997: 33). In both cases, it should be noted, the end result is further expansion of educational provision, yet through greater fragmentation and the emergence of a kaleidoscopic myriad of institutional outcomes, each rooted in a different cultural frame of reference.
3. On the spirited debates and controversies regarding state–civil-society relations in the Arab states, compare the positions of Ayubi (1995), Ibrahim (1995, 1996), Ismail (1997), Kamrava and Mora (1998), and the various papers edited by Norton (1995). While some have supported the existence of civil society in the various Arab states, others have expressed doubts as to its very existence.
4. An interesting case study was carried out during the early 1980s in the 'Allan area of Jordan (Wåhlin, 1982). The case study reconstructed the introduction and expansion patterns of public schools among essentially rural and nomad communities. The study reveals the scope and intensity of the social transformations that took place in this area, especially following Palestine's partition in 1948 and the exodus of Palestinian refugees into this area. Other processes were related to the establishment and differential expansion of public schools for boys and girls. The findings show that the state gradually monopolised and standardised educational provision, at the expense of eradicating previously existing community-based *kuttab* settings. The study also documents 'how eagerly education was sought, at least by some parts of the population' (Wåhlin, 1982: 66). See also Eickelman's (1985: 161–80) case study and his description of the decline of

community-based education in Morocco and the expansion of public education. By contrast, Haeri (1997) addressed the appropriation of symbolic cultural capital through the differential acquisition of literary Arabic in Egypt. In many Arab states, Arabisation of school curricula and the imposition of Arabic as the language of instruction reveal the extent to which the state has monopolised the mechanisms of cultural production, by implication situating the school at the juncture of competing conceptions of culture and tradition.

5. For instance, Abecassis (1994) studied the cultural politics and institutional change of foreign (mainly Western) schools in pre-1952 Egypt. By contrast, Al-Burak (1985) narrated the emergence and political roles of schools serving the Jewish and Iranian communities in Iraq. His narrative, though heavily ideologised and deterministic in scope, nonetheless reveals the intensity of political conflicts involved around the operation of such schools between the Iraqi state and various local communities. It also depicts the effects of broader geopolitical conflicts—with the Zionist movement on the one hand and with the Iranian Islamic regime on the other—on the ability of the Jewish and Iranian or Shi'a communities in Iraq to maintain and operate these schools.

6. Arabisation policies are powerful mediators of ethnico-cultural conflicts in the Maghreb states and Sudan, or, though quite differently, in Lebanon and Syria. In the Maghreb states, and particularly Algeria, the language issue (a structural residue of colonial regimes) has acquired highly sensitive political ramifications that extended far beyond the school and the university. As Cheriet (1996) rightly noted with regard to Algeria, the imposition of Arabic, for instance, does have comprehensive implications for the social opportunities available to social groups who do not master the Arabic language. The same can be said about Arabisation policies in Sudan (Douglas, 1986; Taha, 1990). In Syria and Lebanon, the language issue is rooted in a different problematic, but one that nonetheless mediates divergent political and ideological constructs (Badinjki, 1994).

7. Similar observations were often reported on the margins of other studies. In her review of educational expansion in rural Palestine in the 1940s, Miller (1985: 186 n. 22) notes that in many impoverished rural localities, where the mandatory government did not open or finance schools, villagers would erect the school building and maintain teachers at their own expense. Melitz (1995) reports the same practice among Bedouins in Israel following that state's institution in 1948. Some tribes would build and maintain schools at their own expense while pressuring the government to expand educational provision. Bénot (1972: 18–19, 19 n. 7) referred to some African societies where villagers would institute a regional fundraising, extending beyond village limits, in order to finance the studies of one of their children.

Transnational Advocacy, Global Civil Society? Emerging Evidence from the Field of Education

Karen Mundy and Lynn Murphy

It is now possible to speak of an international system of influence powerful enough to bind up the educational destinies of the world's peoples. If such a network of global influence limits the discretion of peoples to shape their own educational destinies and imposes its own solution to the material-moral dilemma facing educational policy, then it is worthy of investigation.

(Phillip Jones, *World Bank Financing of Education*)

The argument that a widening and increasingly influential 'international architecture' has developed in the field of education has been made with relative frequency in recent years as interest in and research on international organizations in the field of education have grown.[1] As reflected in the above quotation from Phillip Jones's masterful study of the World Bank, much of this work has tended to focus on (and question) the hegemonic influence of formal intergovernmental organizations, both as these directly influence domestic educational policies and as they construct a global interpretation of, and set of responses to, worldwide educational 'needs.'

At the same time, a mounting literature on globalization and the changing nature of international relations has provided convincing evidence that an increasingly strong and complex array of international nongovernmental actors and new nongovernmental organizational (NGO) forms is emerging. Described variously as 'transnational advocacy networks' (TANs) or 'transnational social movements' (TSMs), these new organizational forms bring together a wide array of nongovernmental organizations, citizens' associations, and trade unions in forms of activism that target global-level institutions and issues while they attempt to use global-level visibility to level changes at the national level. These TANs or TSMs are the focus of a thriving and often ethically inspired literature that sets out to study the origins, strength, influence, and long-term implications of their activities on the broader development of a world-level political

Karen Mundy and Lynn Murphy, 'Transnational Advocacy, Global Civil Society? Emerging Evidence from the Field of Education', *Comparative Education Review*, 45, 1.

system.[2] They are frequently portrayed as the building blocks of a prototypical 'global civil society,' with the power to influence, and perhaps democratize, the structure of world politics, both through their increasing influence within existing international institutions and through their capacity to use this influence to leverage change in individual nation-states.

This [chapter] brings together these two lines of research: one concerned with the evolution of an international system of influence in education, the other with the broader possibility of a more democratic form of global governance. Our focus is on the emergence and evolution of nongovernmental actors and organizational forms engaged in transnational advocacy in the field of education.[3] We ask whether or not there has been a deep, qualitative change in the involvement of nongovernmental actors in the field of international educational cooperation over the past decade, one parallel to trends described in the burgeoning literature on transnational advocacy networks, international nongovernmental organizations, and global civil society. The answer to this question, as we hope to show, is yes. There are clear signs of a new and qualitatively different wave of transnational nongovernmental advocacy initiatives in education, especially around the idea of 'education for all.' This can be seen by comparing nongovernmental participation in international educational forums over time, by looking more closely at the recent genesis of an NGO-led 'Global Campaign for Education,' and by analyzing nongovernmental activism at the most recent international meeting on education, the World Education Forum (WEF), which was held in April 2000 in Dakar, Senegal, as a 10-year follow-up to the Jomtien World Conference on Education for All.

Our goals in this [chapter] are twofold. First, we present an exploratory account of the trends suggestive of a new kind of nongovernmental activism in the field of education, drawing on over two dozen interviews and documentary data; and second, we set out an analytical framework for assessing the significance of that activism, drawing on concepts from research on new social movements and from current theoretical debates about global civil society. Here we hope to raise larger questions about the future of international cooperation in education and the potential for new and more democratic structures of global governance.

Transnational Advocacy Networks and Global Civil Society: Toward a Conceptual Framework

The end of the Cold War; rising evidence of global economic, social, and cultural integration; and the increasingly visible activities of networks of transnational social movements focused on such issues as the environment, women's rights, human rights, Third-World debt, and globalization have given impetus to a renewed interest in the influence of nonstate actors in the world system over the past decade. From a purely empirical stance, studying the growing complexity and volume of international relations among nonstate actors (and between nonstate actors and states) and characterizing the way these interact to structure a single, world-level political system has become a major challenge to the entire field of international relations.[4] At the same time, an ethical or normative question lies at the core of a growing interest in the capacity of nongovernmental networks to influence world order. Whether framed by liberal or critical traditions of political thought, the key question here is, To what extent can networks of nongovernmental actors influence the development of a more just world order that is both equitable and representative?

Collective action among nongovernmental actors at the international level is, of course, not an entirely new phenomenon. International links between nongovernmental organizations, citizens groups, expert communities, and trade unions began to thicken in the middle of the nineteenth century, often stimulated by the desire to share information and offer mutual support and solidarity for national reform movements. Once an international link was made, many of these organizations played a key role in the establishment of formal intergovernmental agreements and institutions—key examples include the antislavery movement of the nineteenth century, the child survival movement of the early twentieth century, and the work of the international labor movement in the formation of the International

Labor Organization and its conventions.[5] Yet because international nongovernmental organizations were largely dependent on resources provided by nation-states and because they were often marginalized in the decision-making processes of international organizations during the Cold War era, there was a widely shared sense that these organizations were not significant or sufficiently autonomous players in international politics. Until quite recently, political scientists have viewed transnational nongovernmental actors as marginal to state-based power politics.

Today that sense of insignificance has evaporated, for two broad reasons. The first set of factors influencing the new salience of international nongovernmental actors is largely contextual. This century has seen the steady institutionalization of new global structures of governance and political power that have 'transformed world politics into a global politics of agenda setting, coalition building and multilateral regulation.'[6] Moreover, recent intensification of processes of economic, political, and cultural globalization raises questions for each about the appropriate locus of political decision making in an increasingly complex, interdependent world. The problem is of a world order in which decisions made by centers of power (states, multilateral institutions, and, increasingly, international corporations and financial capital) have repercussions beyond national boundaries, while forms of democratic participation and societal compromise remain territorially grounded in increasingly hollowed-out welfare states. In this context, it can be argued, the rise of new technologies, increasing pressure on nongovernmental actors to fill in the social service vacuum left by the state, and the historical accumulation of models and spaces for transnational collective action have combined to create a unique 'opportunity' for the development of new effective forms of transnational nongovernmental contestation.

Second, in simple empirical terms, 'the number, size, professionalism, and the speed, density and complexity of international linkages among [international nongovernmental organizations] has grown dramatically in the last three decades.'[7] This growth is especially marked around the issues of women's rights, the environment, peace, development, and human rights, where a variety of nonstate actors have come together as advocates of major social and political change in what scholars have described variously as 'transnational advocacy networks,' 'principled issue networks,' and 'transnational social movements.' These networks are increasingly visible—one need only think, for example, of the nongovernmental activism at the United Nations conferences of the 1990s;[8] the Jubilee 2000 campaign against Third-World debt;[9] the international campaign against the Multilateral Agreement on Investment; the antilandmine campaign;[10] and the broad coalition movement mobilized for the fall 1999 meetings of the World Trade Organization (WTO) and the spring 2000 meetings of the World Bank and the International Monetary Fund.[11]

The expansion and visibility of such transnational nongovernmental advocacy networks have raised two key questions for international relations scholars. First, how do these networks work? Second, are they effective, autonomous actors in world politics? On the first point, there is broad consensus: working without significant financial or electoral resources, these new collective actors use telecommunications and transportation technologies to build networks and generate international public interest in an issue. They develop highly publicized campaigns that target international organizations or intergovernmental regimes, and they link domestic and international groups in collective protests against both governments and international organizational policies in what Margaret Keck and Kathryn Sikkink describe as a common 'boomerang' strategy designed to provide domestic movements greater leverage against their home governments. These networks have had a cumulative impact: they increasingly interact, use similar strategies and repertoires for action, and mobilize around overlapping collective action frames.[12]

Less agreement exists, however, about the long-term influence of these nongovernmental networks on world politics. Most scholars agree that their greatest impact to date has been 'at the level of agenda setting, the spreading norms and changes in intergovernmental and governmental discourse.'[13] But very different assessments have been offered of their success in holding nations and international organizations accountable to new agendas, or in achieving the deeper democratization of international organizations and intergovernmental forums, which is so often a key part of their agenda. Thus, while many scholars have gone so far as to describe these new nongovernmental networks as the harbingers of 'global civil society' (which they conceptualize as a redemptive, semiautonomous political space in which popular organizations come together to create and participate in institutions of global governance), others raise serious questions about the long-term capacities and representativeness of the new advocacy movements. They prefer to think of them as uneven transnational (rather than global) networks whose development into an effective global civil society needs to be empirically studied rather than naively assumed.[14]

Our framework for researching and thinking about transnational advocacy in the field of education draws extensively from this broader literature and its debates. The first stage of our research has been an effort to describe and explain the appearance of new forms and types of collective action among nongovernmental actors in the field of education. In what follows, [. . .] we borrow from recent research on new social movements and transnational advocacy to organize a case study of the key organizations involved in the genesis of a recently launched nongovernmental advocacy initiative, the Global Campaign for Education.[15] Here we look at two key processes. First, we build on Marie-Claude Smout's observation that international nongovernmental organizations (INGOs) derive 'their legitimacy from their ability to make demands in terms of collective needs . . . [and] from their innovative capacity to suggest ways to meet these needs' by focusing on the 'mobilizing frames' or ways in which global educational problems and their solutions are talked about and used to legitimate and motivate collective action among nongovernmental actors.[16] Second, we look at the 'repertoires of contention' that each advocacy initiative utilizes, defined here as the set of practices and strategies being developed by international nongovernmental actors to leverage educational change.[17]

The second step in our framework involves addressing the 'so what' question that underlies recent debates about transnational advocacy and global civil society. To do so, we follow in the footsteps of international relations scholars who have transposed the concept of civil society from its more common usage in political theories of the nation-state. Like them, we recognize that the absence of a supranational state makes the transposition of theories of 'civil society' problematic, but we think that the current world context—characterized by powerful international institutions and mounting popular recognition of the need for greater international oversight of the world economy—makes it imperative that we consider the potential emergence of global civil society and find ways of studying it empirically.

Two theoretical traditions have been used by scholars in the field of international relations to generate a loose evaluative template for thinking about transnational advocacy networks and the extent to which they approximate global civil society. The liberal tradition emphasizes the importance of a pluralistic political order; it values civil society in two ways, both as a check on the excesses of the state and governmental bureaucracy and as the arena responsible for producing the degree of consensus and civility necessary for the functioning of formal, representative democracy and a pluralist society. Gramscian and other critical traditions are more interested in understanding the opportunities for counterhegemony and contention that exist within civil society. Here it is assumed that civil society is the space in which consent to a capitalist system is culturally constructed by a variety of actors (including the state) and, therefore, that it is also a key location for its opposition.[18]

Overall, theories of international civil society drawn from the literature on domestic politics 'envision a dense exchange among individuals, groups, and organizations in the public sphere, separate from state dominated action'.[19] Thus civil society can influence government in two ways: 'It enhances political responsiveness by aggregating and expressing the wishes of the public through a wealth of nongovernmental forms of association; and it safeguards public freedom by limiting the government's ability to impose arbitrary rule by force.'[20]

Three concepts, 'civility,' 'democracy,' and 'contention,' seemed especially central to either one or both of these literatures. We developed them into a set of questions that can be asked both of specific international nongovernmental advocacy initiatives in education and of the nature of collective efforts and interrelationships as a whole:

1. To what extent and in what ways are these initiatives building global 'civility'? By 'civility' we refer to the development of a dense pattern of sustained interaction and collaboration among international nongovernmental actors around a coherent framing of the issue of education. This notion draws from the ideas of Alexander de Tocqueville and Robert Putnam in focusing on the extent to which the capacity and habit of participation, reciprocity, and social pluralism is being cultivated, expanded, and sustained at an international level.[21] In the transnational sphere, authors have argued that the establishment of regularized interactions between transnational actors and international organizations and nation-state governments can also be used as a measure of global civility.[22]

2. To what extent and in what ways are these initiatives 'democratic' in the sense of representative of, and accountable to, those for whom they purport to advocate? One measure of this might be the extent to which efforts promote horizontal linkages, through new forms of communication, decision making, and direct participation, rather than new patterns of hierarchy or exclusion.[23] Another measure might be the extent to which regularized structures for global (geographically representative) participation are encouraged over the reproduction of existing inequalities between citizens of rich and poor nations. The ideal of 'democracy,' as used in both liberal and left-liberal theories of civil society, can imply quite different ideal forms for global governance, ranging along a spectrum from radical participatory democracy to a more institutionalized form of constitutional, representative governance.[24] Thus, in answering this question, it will also be interesting to ponder the kind of democracy that the practices of each advocacy initiative embodies.

3. To what extent are these initiatives 'contentious' in the sense of advocating fundamental social change, independent of, or in opposition to, existing structures and initiatives organized by states and international governmental organizations? Based on the literature on social movements and Gramscian theories of civil society, one key measure of contention will be the extent to which initiatives are autonomous and provide forceful alternatives to the current structure of world order. Another measure might be the extent to which transnational initiatives have a self-reflexive strategy that targets changing global decision-making structures and supporting local level struggles.[25]

In asking these three sets of questions about transnational advocacy efforts in education, we do not intend to imply that they all fit neatly together. For example, the ideal of 'civility' may well be at odds with the ideal of 'contention,' while, as noted above, democracy can take on dramatically different institutional forms.[26] Nonetheless, looking at each of these questions should allow us to examine the nature, shape, and extent to which something approaching a new transnational political space, and new collective actors, are emerging around the issue of education.

[...]

Education International: A New International Advocacy Effort among Teachers Unions

By the middle of 1999, Education International, the recently formed international association of teachers trade unions, emerged as Oxfam's chief partner in global educational advocacy. It later became the coordinator and headquarter organization for the Global Campaign for Education. Education International's participation marks two novel events in the field of nongovernmental activism in education. First, it suggests a renewed solidarity and internationalism among teachers unions, which have for decades been sharply divided into rival international associations.[27] Second, it marks the beginning of a new era of cooperation between international trade union associations and other international nongovernmental actors around a common agenda for global change.[28] For both these reasons, it is important to consider the mobilizing frames and repertoires for contention that Education International brings to the new educational advocacy.

In 1993, 97 percent of the members of the International Federation of Free Teachers Unions and the World Confederation of Organizations of the Teaching Profession agreed to a merger of the two organizations, ending decades of fierce rivalry and ideological disagreement.[29] The new association, Education International, is 'a world-wide trade union organization of education personnel' that is committed to both the expansion of trade unionism among teachers and the development of a unified, professional vision of global educational issues.[30] Education International has 23 million individual members, drawn from 294 national trade unions and associations in 152 countries and territories. It is governed by policy resolutions made at triennial World Congresses, and it has an elected executive board. Its activities are implemented by a secretariat based in Brussels and through six regional offices.[31]

Historically, the central concern of international teachers associations has been the establishment of international standards on the status of teachers.[32] This concern has continued to be a major focus for the activities of Education International, but the new organization has also reorganized its aims and goals around the threat to teachers, and to public education more generally, posed by austerity and the new policy agenda. Education International's new mobilizing frame is captured well in the address of Fred Van Leeuwen, the organization's general secretary, at Education International's founding congress. He promised that Education International would wage a battle with neoliberalism, step up efforts to influence the IMF and the World Bank, and target the 'international education crisis ... [as marked] by austerity measures in the South and by neo-liberal schemes in the North, put forth to destroy free compulsory education and replace it with some form of fragmented semi-public or private system.'[33] Van Leeuwen concluded, 'Let there be no misunderstandings about our intentions to use this organization as a tool to intensify the North–South dialogue, to help establish a more just international economic order, to pursue the active involvement of trade unions, and to reform the significant role that public education plays in democratic development, economic growth and social progress.'[34]

Thus, alongside its more traditional advocacy of the right of teachers to collective bargaining, Education International, like Oxfam, has become engaged in broader debates about economic globalization. Indicative of this, it has expanded its activities to include research and lobbying related to the World Trade Organization.[35] Education International is also active in the defense of children's rights and the promotion of human rights more generally (especially as related to discrimination against women, racism, homophobia, promotion of the rights of indigenous peoples, and child labor).[36] It has played an active role in the child labor movement and is a founding member and international convener of the Global March against Child Labor, the fourth INGO to join the Global Campaign on Education.

Early in 1999, Education International officially launched a campaign calling for 'Quality Public Education for All' after it was given the mandate to do so by resolution of its 1998 World Congress. The ideological centerpiece of its mobilizing frame is an unequivocal commitment to the notion of publicly funded and provided free education. In the view of Education International, public education is a necessary safeguard against the growth of economic and social inequality. Education International argues that public education (as compared with privatized education) is also more likely to encompass a humanistic, plural, and democratically oriented curriculum. The Education International campaign has also argued for the right of teachers (and other civil society actors) to participate in national and international educational policy-making arenas. Here Education International builds on such earlier efforts as its 1994 report on the inclusion of teachers in the Education for All initiatives of the nine most populous countries.[37] Finally, the Education International campaign takes up specific policy issues related to what it describes as the neoliberal policy agenda in education: it questions existing approaches to national standardized testing, decentralization, privatization, and civil service reform. Each of these issues is taken up in the newsletters and journals Education International circulates to its membership, and in research and policy documents it posts on its popular web site.

Education International's decision to help launch the Global Campaign for Education in fall 1999 brought to new nongovernmental advocacy in education both a distinctive mobilizing frame and a new and extensive repertoire for contention. Although Education International's capacity to mobilize its membership has not yet been tested, the organization represents the largest membership-based international nongovernmental actor with an interest in educational issues. It also boasts extensive formal affiliations to other international union movements and formal consultative status with many United Nations organizations. Its status as a trade union movement suggests a capacity for disciplined and coherent activism.[38]

ActionAid, the Global March against Child Labor, and the Launching of the Global Campaign

During 1999, two other organizations and several Southern NGO networks joined with Oxfam and Education International to launch the Global Campaign. The most distinctive and active in shaping the Campaign platform was ActionAid, a British NGO, which is not only among the largest UK development NGOs, but also a member of a family of NGOs with affiliates in Ireland, France, Italy, and Greece. ActionAid emphasizes community development and partnership with Southern NGOs and citizens organizations; since 1990, it has engaged in advocacy work, with current campaigns on the issues of education for all, ending the sex trade, and the threat to Third-World agriculture posed by genetically engineered seeds.[39] Unlike Oxfam, ActionAid has worked extensively in the field of education in developing countries, and it is well known for its development of community-based methods for teaching adult literacy and for its early involvement in such nonformal and non-governmental educational initiatives as the Bangledesh Rural Action Committee (BRAC).[40]

Not only was ActionAid an early partner in the Global Campaign but it also launched its own distinctive education campaign, 'Elimu: Education for Life,' in 1999. The Elimu campaign is focused on building the capacities of local NGOs and civil society organizations to participate in national education policies. It operates as a coalition of national campaigns and regional networks in the South, producing its own newsletter and giving rise to many opportunities for South–South collaboration. Its objective is to 'increase the participation of poor people in the design and implementation of education policy and practice by organizing people around education issues, forming strong alliance with civil society and influencing governments and donors.'[41]

Global March against Child Labor, a Southern-based coalition of NGOs that views itself as the world's largest social movement in defense of exploited children, also joined the leadership of the Global Campaign in 1999.[42] Launched in 1997, the Global March was initially organized around a highly publicized series of national demonstrations and a worldwide march in which both national policies and international agreements related to child labor were the lobbying target. The campaign appears to have played an important role in getting governments to agree to the development of the new international Convention on the Worst Forms of Child Labor. The Global March coalition placed education high on its agenda, going so far as to argue that free education is 'the best way of ending child labor.'[43]

Both ActionAid's Elimu campaign and the Global March Coalition brought to the Global Campaign for Education a unique opportunity for partnership with a large number of Southern NGOs. Several Southern coalitions subsequently joined the campaign, some of which include the South African NGO Coalition; the Campaign for Popular Education (Bangladesh); the Brazilian National Campaign for the Right to Education; the Citizen's Education Initiative in India; the Ghana National Education Campaign Coalition; the Civil Society Action Committee on EFA, Nigeria; Association du Sahel d'Aide à la Femme et à l'Enfance, Mali; Cadre de Concertation en Basic Education, Burkina Faso; Consultation of Adult Education in Latin America, Mexico; Forum for African Women Educationalists, Mozambique; and Tanzania Education Network.[44] The campaign's eight-person steering committee reflects this widening membership: four positions are held by representatives of ActionAid, Oxfam, Education International, and the Global March against Child Labor. The other four are held by four Southern NGO coalitions, including a representative from CAMPE, Bangladesh; Education International, Togo; the Brazilian National Campaign for the Right to Education; and the South African National NGO Coalition.

With these new partners, the Global Campaign for Education promised to mobilize 'public pressure on governments to fulfil their promises to provide free, quality education for all people, in particular for our children and for women.'[45] Each of the campaign's sponsoring organizations continued to develop its own independent campaign, while joining in a series of joint efforts leading up to the Dakar world forum. These included a 'millennium appeal' letter sent to heads of states calling for high-level participation in the EFA review and commitment to the goal of education for all; and a 'Global Week of Action' in April 2000 to engage NGOs and teachers unions around the world in advocacy activities the week prior to the Dakar meeting.[46] Campaigners also joined Unesco in hosting an NGO parallel conference at the Africa regional EFA pre-conference meetings in 1999. By March 2000, the campaign claimed the affiliation of over 400 non-governmental members.

Overall, the campaigners' preparations for the Dakar meeting suggested a new kind of coherence and mobilization among nongovernmental actors in the field of education. In November 1999, they began a heated and contentious exchange with the intergovernmental agencies sponsoring the EFA review. Campaign sponsors sent a strongly worded letter to World Bank president James Wolfensohn signaling their intention to make the Dakar forum a key event in their campaign. The letter described the interagency EFA forum as 'failing to galvanize governments and build a constituency around the EFA project,' and it demanded 'evidence of a concrete global plan of action through which the resources needed to achieve the goal of education for all can be mobilized; and through which civil society and local communities are given a greater voice in the development of education policies.'[47] In February 2000, Oxfam (with the backing of other campaigners) announced that it would leave the EFA Forum Steering Committee in protest of its failure to organize an effective EFA effort with concrete targets and commitments, a new kind of international financial mechanism for delivering educational assistance, and a better organized and more democratic EFA secretariat.[48]

Just before the Dakar meeting, a clear, nine-point platform was adopted and widely circulated among campaign members, which they planned to use as the basis for lobbying at the Dakar declaration (see Table 69.1).[49] Press conferences were held in Tokyo and Washington, DC.[50] Meetings with members of national delegations and other important actors such as the European Union were held.[51] Throughout the week before the Dakar conference, electronic messages were shared among Global Campaign participants as they tried to identify which high-level leaders would be attending Dakar and which delegations would meet with them in Dakar. All of these efforts took place in the face of the relative disorganization of the World Forum organizers, who both attempted to keep a tight limit on NGO invitations to Dakar and failed to establish explicit procedures or mechanisms for the amendment of the Dakar declaration.[52]

The New Educational Advocacy in Action: The World Education Forum, April 2000

What kind of interim assessment can we offer of these admittedly relatively new trends toward coalition building, advocacy, and contention in the field of international educational cooperation? One way of answering this question is to look more closely at nongovernmental activism at the Dakar 2000 World Education Forum, the most recent in a long line of international meetings held to discuss global educational problems and the culminating meeting of the United Nations Education for All decade. In what follows, we do not claim to provide an exhaustive account of the outcomes of the Dakar meetings. Rather we follow in the footsteps of other scholars who have attempted to understand the issue of transnational advocacy and global civil society by focusing on the changing nature of nongovernmental participation at international conferences.[53] Much of what we report here is drawn from our own experience of participating in and observing the Dakar forum, as well as from the interviews we conducted while at the conference.

The Dakar meeting was somewhat different from the Jomtien conference, where nongovernmental actors participated alongside other delegates and where only a small, UNESCO-hosted NGO

Table 69.1 Global Campaign On Education: partners, repertoires, and mobilizing frames

	Core Mobilizing Frame	Strategic Repertoires
Education for All: Official Frame	Education is a basic right and a requirement for national development. It depends on national political will and better 'partnerships'.	• Global declarations: persuade developing country governments to sign on to the goal of education for all.
		• Shift educational aid to target basic education.
		• Provide better technical solutions and more careful data for monitoring progress.
Oxfam International: Education Now	The achievement of the right to education depends on debt relief, reform of international organizations, and a clear commitment by governments to the provision of free, quality public education to all.	• Use aggressive popular media campaign and high-level lobbying to expose failure of Western governments to meet their Jomtien commitments.
		• Link efforts to other campaigns for debt relief (Jubilee 2000). Form broad coalition of nongovernmental organizations (NGOs) and international non-governmental organizations (INGOs).
		• Focus on lack of resources at global level.
Education International: Quality Public Education for All	Quality, free, and equal publicly provided education for all is a global priority. To achieve this goal the working conditions and rights of teachers must be protected and teachers must become part of the policy-making process, and neo-liberal reforms must be fought.	• Union-like structure with access to wide geographic membership.
		• Utilize formal links to the International Labor Organization, Unesco, the United Nations, and other international trade union bodies for high-level lobbying.
		• Uses language of trade unionism and labor rights.
ActionAid: Elimu (Education for Life)	Expand definition of public education to include right to literacy and adult education. Involvement of local communities and NGOs in educational decision making is crucial.	• Brings distinctive record in community-based literacy and adult education programs.
		• Strong local NGO partnerships and commitment to giving poor and marginalized populations a voice in national policy making.

preconference was held. Dakar was also much smaller in scale than the major UN conferences of the 1990s, with fewer than 800 issued invitations and no formal United Nations oversight.[54] Members of the conference's interagency steering committee hoped to channel NGO participation into regional preparatory conferences, and thus they kept tight control over a highly limited number of invitations to the World Forum. These were primarily given to national delegations. As a result, nongovernmental participants formally invited to participate in the World Education Forum numbered only 55 (as compared with 125 NGOs represented at Jomtien, 3,000 at the 1995 Beijing World Conference on Women, and 248 at the 1993 Vienna Conference on Human Rights). Less than 300 invitations were issued to the Dakar NGO preconference (as compared with approximately 300,000 attenders who flooded Beijing and the 598 NGOs who officially attended the Vienna preconference).[55] The World Education Forum was, nonetheless, similar to many other UN conferences in that it included both an officially sponsored preconference for nongovernmental actors (something that had not happened at Jomtien) and a series of drafting and roundtable meetings intended to produce a new framework for action as well as a set of intergovernmental commitments on the theme of 'education for all.'[56]

Nongovernmental actors—both those belonging to the Global Campaign and others—took their participation in Dakar very seriously, and they used the event as an occasion to develop their advocacy networks, as well as their repertoires for contention. Dakar, therefore, provides an important opportunity to consider the nature and extent of the 'civility,' 'democracy,' and 'contention' exhibited in the new educational advocacy efforts among nongovernmental organizations.

Civility

Both the character of nongovernmental participation at Dakar and the kinds of nongovernmental activism leading up to it suggest a growing density of transnational nongovernmental activities around the theme of 'education for all,' indicative of the kind of civility that Anne Marie Clark, Elisabeth Friedman, and Kathryn Hochsteltler describe in their account of NGO activism at other major United Nations Conferences during the 1990s.[57] The Dakar conference saw the participation of a slightly larger number of nongovernmental actors than did the WCEFA in 1989. Continuing the shift begun at Jomtien, large development and relief organizations, as well as a few nonprofit consulting groups, held a disproportionate number of invitations, while members of literacy and adult education groups participated in smaller numbers and with less coherence.[58]

But the real change between the two conferences can primarily be found in the development of a highly cohesive strategy for coordination among nongovernmental participants. Focused primarily around the leadership of the Global Campaign for Education, nongovernmental actors held preconference strategy sessions, met daily for debriefings, huddled around the campaign's media table, argued over the content of their formal report to the World Education Forum, and held meetings to elect nongovernmental representatives to the two key committees formed for the conference, the Declaration Drafting Committee and the Futures Committee.[59] Even though many points of disagreement between campaigners and noncampaigners emerged, the nine-point 'Bottom Line' platform prepared by the Global Campaigners became the recognized mobilizing frame for intra-NGO discussions and for general lobbying efforts.[60] The coherence of the campaign's mobilizing frame is suggested in the fact that Global Campaign members were elected for the large majority of NGO seats on the Drafting and Futures Committees.[61] Among the NGOs participating in the campaign, Dakar saw a high degree of frame alignment and the development of widely shared understandings about the 'rules of the game,' each suggestive of a widening civility.[62]

New levels and kinds of civility among international nongovernmental actors, governments, and intergovernmental organizations emerged at Dakar. Initial efforts to limit the numbers of nongovernmental organizations attending the preconference and the formal proceedings of the World Education Forum were ultimately reversed in a last-minute decision by the UNESCO director general on the eve of the first day of the forum.[63] At the forum itself, nongovernmental actors were also integrated in various ways into the conference proceedings: they read a statement of their demands at the opening of the forum, addressed several of the plenary sessions, elected a total of ten representatives to the Steering and Futures Committees, and had a plenary and strategy session devoted to the sole issue of future EFA participation with civil society. Southern NGOs were invited to special meetings with national delegates from Britain and the Netherlands.[64] Speeches by officials from intergovernmental organizations and governments formally endorsed the Global Campaign and recognized a new role for what was commonly referred to as 'civil society' in achieving education for all.[65] Official recognition of the Global Campaign was carried further when several high-level officials held individual meetings with the campaigners.[66] The character of this civility, however, varied. Among intergovernmental bodies, for example, the World Bank showed the strongest interest in working with campaigners.[67] UNESCO, on the other hand, did not formally endorse the campaign or hold a separate meeting with the campaigners, at least partly because its EFA secretariat was criticized by many of the participating nongovernmental organizations.[68]

All of these factors suggest a more formalized recognition of nongovernmental actors at Dakar than at Jomtien, a new acceptance of their role as policy-level interlocutors, and new degrees of coordination and coalition building among NGOs themselves. Of course this new civility was not 'complete,' and below we discuss some of the rivalries and uncivil behavior which did occur. Potential threats to the campaign's contributions to global civility can be seen in competition among campaign sponsors and the possibility of serious disputes over their various visions of education. For example, there would seem to be a likely tension between ActionAid's emphasis on local community control of education and the assumption by Education International and its teachers unions that educational decision making is properly concentrated at the national level. But there are also signs that the patterns of civility initiated by the campaign at Dakar are continuing to widen: in early May the popular web site Oneworld.net launched a new portal to cover Education for All, and the Global Campaign has also launched a web site and list-serve for all civil society actors interested in supporting the campaign.[69]

Democracy

How democratic, that is, representative and accountable, was the participation and activism of nongovernmental actors at Dakar? Perhaps what is most interesting here is that these questions were among the most frequently raised issues at nongovernmental meetings during the Dakar conference, as well as in our individual interviews with Dakar participants. In Dakar, both nongovernmental participants and some officials were quick to criticize the dominant role played by the Global Campaign at the conference, pointing out in particular that the campaign is led by a few Northern-based organizations, several with limited experience in the field of education and with less than altruistic motives.[70] Some Southern NGO participants, as well as members of the Global Campaign itself, questioned whether this dominance had led to too great a campaign focus on Northern governments and international organizations at the expense of building self-sufficient Southern coalitions.[71] Reflecting this, Southern organizations voiced less satisfaction than others about the accomplishments of the campaigners at Dakar, because these did not include serious targets for Southern government expenditure on education.[72] Leaders from Save the Children Alliance, Care, and World Vision (the first two of which belong to a sizeable number of nongovernmental actors that were not affiliated with the campaigners at Dakar) faulted the campaign's overemphasis on resource mobilization and its narrow definition of schooling.[73] Others regretted the loss of real discussion about education-specific matters and criticized the campaigners for importing a slick lobbying machinery into the EFA process.

Attention to the question of democracy was also carried through to the final meetings among the Global Campaigners, the group that became, at least in official eyes, the de facto representative of civil society. For example, tensions emerged between campaigners who preferred more fluid approaches to representation versus those who preferred the more formal, centralized, and hierarchical model of organizing used by Education International (which has a union-like membership structure). At one point, a rift opened up between Oxfam and other campaigners when Oxfam endorsed the World Bank's 'fast track plan' for EFA on behalf of the campaign without consulting other members.[74] ActionAid and Southern affiliates argued for greater attention to the inclusion of Southern actors and for the mobilization of Southern networks. Campaign leaders appeared to take these debates seriously, announcing that they would include more Southern representatives on the campaign steering committee and would make the mobilization of regional and national NGO networks a key part of future activities.[75]

One of the major constraints to democracy and accountability among nongovernmental actors at Dakar was rooted in the official structure of the conference itself. Dakar followed a common UN model for international meetings that is structured around the goal of achieving consensus among governmental delegations and that is only gradually developing a common approach to the integration of nongovernmental actors in the process. At Dakar, this model was evidenced in efforts to control NGO invitations and in the absence of transparent and preestablished processes for amending the declaration.[76] The official intergovernmental community provided no direct funding for NGO participation, and official organizers felt very limited responsibility for ensuring that a wide, or representative, sample of NGOs participated. In this context, what happened at Dakar is not surprising: the loudest voices among the nongovernmental participants became recognized as the common voice for civil society at the conference.

The very fact that the issue of NGO participation was so openly debated might be seen as an indication that a certain criterion of democratic practice was achieved at Dakar. However, the overall pattern of relationships among NGOs at Dakar tended to mimic the structure of center–periphery relations in the world system, in which Northern actors play leadership and coordination roles. Furthermore, NGO criticisms of the EFA structure and their efforts to formalize their role in future EFA activities seem to have been sidetracked. According to the July 2000 newsletter of ActionAid's Elimu Campaign, 'no concrete alternative to existing EFA structures was agreed . . . UNESCO Director General Matsuura made a change to the Framework after it had been adopted by the plenary, giving a negative message as to UNESCO's intentions to become more transparent and accountable. . . . No explicit steps were proposed to increase coordination and cooperation by the international community.'[77]

Ultimately the test of democracy lies in the realization of NGO commitments to collaborate with a broader range of partners and to engage Southern and smaller NGOs in educational advocacy. Even if this should occur, however, careful empirical study will be needed to ascertain whether a greater representation of ideas from the grassroots occurs. Increased levels of interaction might also cause rising levels of disagreement and competition in ways that will test the formal commitment to 'democratizing' relationships among actors, or it could produce a top-down socialization of new and weaker partners in which authentic participation is lost.[78]

Contention

How far has the development of new international nongovernmental activity in the field of education gone toward meeting the idealized criteria of contention? One way of answering this question is to consider the extent to which these new initiatives—both in their mobilizing frames and in their repertoires of contention—promote fundamental social change and alternative visions of world order that are in opposition to, or independent of, existing structures and activities organized by states and intergovernmental organizations. More concretely, we can try to weigh the success of their contention by looking at the effects nongovernmental advocacy appears to have had on the decisions made at Dakar.

Campaigners brought a clear platform of demands to the Dakar conference. As can be seen in Table 69.2, at least some of their demands were met: inclusion of the wording 'free' education; endorsement of the idea of national educational forums and an expanded definition of education that includes commitment to early childhood education and adult literacy; and a commitment to annual high-level EFA review meetings. Perhaps not so surprisingly, the campaigners did not wield sufficient influence to achieve commitments on issues that cut more closely into the prerogatives of existing international organizations or nation-states, especially those of the more powerful donor states. Thus, demands for a clear commitment of resources by rich country governments were again sidestepped (as they had been at Jomtien). No

Table 69.2 Demands made by the Global Campaign and their effects on the Dakar Declaration

Mobilizing Frame	Effect on Final Declaration
Clear, time-bound commitments by governments and international organizations (IGOs) to providing free and compulsory basic education	Change from affordable education to free and compulsory education by 2015 in final text. However, there is no mention of sanctions for countries that do not meet goals and targets.
Clear and time-bound process for countries to agree to their own plans of action for achieving education for all (EFA), with binding mechanisms for civil society participation	National plans to be developed with civil society by 2002. Plans will 'be time-bound and action-oriented'. Commitment to building National EFA Forums, with mandatory civil society engagement.
Clearer and measurable commitment to an expanded vision of basic education—especially in quality, gender equity, literacy, and non-formal education	National plans to address six goals of Education for All with 50% improvement in adult literacy by 2015, commitment to early childhood education, and gender equity
A clear international financial commitment to EFA, both through binding commitments from governments and through a financial Global Action Plan with a special provision for sub-Saharan Africa. The suggested target is 8% of all bilateral aid earmarked for basic education.	The final document mentions a 'global initiative aimed at developing strategies and mobilizing resources needed'. Several donors (Canada, the United States, and the World Bank) announced unilateral funding increases, but do not earmark a specific percentage.
A new code of conduct to improve aid itself	The framework makes references to improving donor coordination, strengthening sector-wide approaches, and providing debt relief and/or cancellation. Sub-Sahara Africa is named as one of neediest areas.
'Democratization, decentralization, and empowerment of the present Education for All structures and mechanisms.' Campaigners seek to 'empower' future EFA mechanisms with civil society participation, and call for the reform of Unesco in particular.	Unesco reinstated as lead in EFA (wording to reform and strengthen Unesco was omitted by its director general without consultation of the futures' committee); also a new commitment to the development of national EFA forums with civil society participation.
A commitment to a mid-term global review of EFA in 2006 and an official United Nations conference in 2010.	Framework calls for an annual review, led by DG of Unesco and made up of high-level officials to hold the global community accountable for commitments made in Dakar.

Sources: Global Campaign for Education, *The Global Action Plan for Education* (Brussels: Global Campaign for Education and Education International, 2000), and *The World Education Forum in Dakar, Success or Failure? Our Bottom Line Position* (Brussels: Global Campaign for Education and Education International, 2000), 6. *World Education Forum—Dakar Senegal, Outcomes and Next Steps*, 2000 (<http://www.elimu.org/newstestl.html>, 5 May 2000); World Education Forum, *The Dakar Framework for Action, Education for All: Meeting our Collective Commitments, Revised Final Draft* (Dakar: World Education Forum, 2000), 5, and 'WEF Press Releases: 181 Governments Adopt Framework for Action at the World Education Forum', 28 April 2000 (<http://www2.unesco.org/en-press/elea_dak_0428_1940.shtm>, 1 May 2000).

minimum investment targets were set by governments or the international community. Wording related to the necessary reform and strengthening of UNESCO was removed. The key innovation proposed by the campaigners in their Global Action Plan—the establishment of a new international funding mechanism for education development under joint IO, government, and civil society oversight—was also left aside, in part because rich country governments prefer to deliver resources bilaterally, on a country-by-country basis.[79]

On the other hand, several things about the repertoires of contention utilized by NGOs participating in the Global Campaign for Education suggest that this was a more deeply contentious form of nongovernmental participation than has previously been seen in the international educational arena. Strategically, the campaigners were better and more professionally organized, they utilized high-level technologies to support the sharing of information, and they did, indeed, mobilize a wide coalition of nongovernmental and civil society actors. Thus,

Education International argues that 'the difference between Jomtien and Dakar is not in the final declaration. Hundreds of thousands of activists, teachers and parents have made governments and world institutions sit up and listen. We will not go away until every child is in school and adult illiteracy is dramatically reduced. That is the difference.'[80]

Some aspects of the mobilizing frame of the campaign were also effectively contentious. As we have noted earlier, the campaigners have distinguished themselves from other nongovernmental participants at Dakar by embedding the problem of education within a larger agenda for changing North–South, center–periphery relations and by taking the view that education can be used as a venue for enlarging national and transnational civic action. The campaigners clearly view their efforts against the backdrop of a much larger wave of transnational advocacy efforts that urge the development of what Michael Edwards et al. call 'new social contracts' between citizens and authorities at various levels of the world.[81] The Global Campaigners thus link the crisis of basic education to problems of economic globalization, debt relief, structural adjustment, and declining aid from G7 nations, and they make demands for free, publicly provided, mass education and an expanded voice for nongovernmental organizations, unions, and peoples organizations in domestic educational policy-making arenas. The impact of this mobilizing frame on the Dakar Framework for Action is evident in its stronger recognition of the right to free (not just 'affordable') education, in the direct attention paid to the responsibilities of the state and the value of teachers, and in the official recognition of civil society's right to participate in education policy making.

Nonetheless, the choice of education as a venue for transnational advocacy raises important questions about the contention. Our case studies suggest that large INGOs went 'venue shopping' in the mid-1990s and that they chose education precisely because it was an issue already adopted by governments and intergovernmental organizations and thus capable of providing them increased legitimacy and leverage. Clearly, the popularity of education as a field for international activism is conditioned by the fact that schooling is one of the most highly legitimated avenues for the provision of public welfare within Anglo-American societies and liberal political theory. In important ways, the choice of education is a reflection of the continuing hegemony of the United States within the international arena and is an indicator of the erosion of the United Nations as a forum for more politicized demands for global economic redistribution.

Being deeply contentious in this context would seem to require a fine balancing act between more general demands for greater international and national expenditure on education and a critical effort to rethink the models and purposes of schooling and its relationship to other means of ensuring social security, welfare, and solidarity on both a global and a national scale.[82] Some observers believe that the Global Campaign has already done a poor job of preserving this balance—they point to its limited focus on educational matters and to its endorsement of the use of international sanctions that may further infringe upon the right of Southern countries to design their own educational plans, and they worry about the somewhat surprising bedfellow that the campaign's hard-edged approach to the achievement of EFA has found in the World Bank.[83]

Although such judgments are premature, they do suggest some measures of contention in educational advocacy for future research. In this category, we would also include the following questions and tensions. First, how will the campaigners deal with the tension between the fact that NGOs themselves are implicated in the new policy agenda as service providers for marginal and poor populations and their vision of an expanding, state-provided and state-guaranteed education (most forcefully advocated by Education International)? Second, will they continue to advocate for new mechanisms for channeling untied international finance for education to the developing world?[84] Finally, as their framing of global educational solutions develops, will these organizations continue to push inward toward new models of learning and educational governance, as well as outward toward new forms of societal compromise and redistributive justice at a world level?

Conclusion

In this [chapter], we have explored the emergence and evolution of nongovernmental organizational forms and actors engaged in transnational advocacy in the field of education. Our purpose was to bring a new awareness of the significance of transnational organization and the contention in world politics to existing research on the evolution of global structures influencing education. Our goals were both to describe what we suggest is a 'new wave' of transnational advocacy in education and to assess its implications for the evolution of a 'global civil society.'

In our view, there has been an important qualitative change in the involvement of nongovernmental actors in the field of international educational cooperation over the past decade. Five key trends are suggestive of this wider development (see appendix). Development and relief organizations are becoming more interested in education, and in advocacy, and they increasingly link these two together. Virtual nongovernmental coalitions have increasingly taken up the theme of education as a component of their agendas for global governance, linking it to the issue of debt relief and to an interlocking frame of international and national responsibilities for social security and solidarity. Teachers unions around the globe have committed themselves to a renewed internationalism, and through their newly formed organ, Education International, they are launching a campaign in support of public education for all. There are clear signs of new forms of cross-organizational collaboration and of unprecedented levels of interaction between INGOs and intergovernmental bodies around the theme of education.

The heart of this [chapter] focuses on a paradigmatic instance of this new transnational advocacy in education—the genesis of a nongovernmentally sponsored Global Campaign for Education and its efforts to shape the World Education Forum held in Dakar and the future of the education for all activities of international organizations. Organizations involved in this campaign have moved into the international educational arena, not as service providers but, rather, as advocates mobilized around a well-developed action frame that links the problem of educational access to the wider issues of debt relief, human rights, and global equity and targets the erosion of national commitments to free, publicly provided educational services. To realize their demands, campaigners have employed a remarkable repertoire of strategies drawn from the experience of other transnational advocacy initiatives. They work at both international and national levels, attempting to build strong national coalitions of NGOs and civil society actors that are capable of bringing grassroots demands home to Southern governments while also generating the international support capable of altering the policies and resource allocations made to education by international organizations and the Northern governments who dominate them.

The density and coherence of these efforts is something new to the international educational arena. The Global Campaign has shown that it has much to contribute to the development of civility and democracy at the international level, and it has introduced a potentially contentious reframing of global educational needs. Should the campaign continue to develop, it promises to bring about a major reshaping of decision-making processes in the field of international educational cooperation. But the new transnational advocacy in international education is not without its limitations and tensions, which we have illustrated by considering the patterns of civility, democracy, and contention that played out between campaigners, other nongovernmental actors, governments, and intergovernmental organizations at the Dakar World Education Forum. These limits and possibilities deserve the sustained attention of scholars in the field of comparative education, offering us an opportunity to join in vital debates about new forms of collective action and societal compromise in our emergent global polity.

Appendix: Key Trends among Nongovernmental Actors in Education after 1990

1. Development and relief organizations take up or expand education sector work and move into advocacy work;
2. Virtual coalitions and advocacy networks on women, human rights, development, and debt relief take up education as a component of their agenda for global justice;

3. International teachers associations renew their commitments to internationalism;
4. Unprecedented levels of interaction emerge between nongovernmental actors and intergovernmental bodies like UNESCO, UNICEF, and the World Bank; and
5. New forms of cross-organizational collaboration emerge, as in the Global Campaign on Education.

NOTES

This research was supported by the National Academy of Education and the Spencer Foundation, through a postdoctoral fellowship awarded to Karen Mundy, 1998–99.

1. Miriam Henry, Bob Lingard, Fazal Rizvi, and Sandra Taylor, *The OECD, Globalization and Education Policy* (Oxford: Pergamon, 2000); Phillip Jones, 'UNESCO and the Politics of Global Literacy', *Comparative Education Review* 34 1 (1988): 41–60, *World Bank Financing of Education* (New York: Routledge, 1992), and *International Policies for Third World Education: Unesco, Literacy and Development* (New York: Routledge, 1988); Connie McNeely and Yun-Kyung Cha, 'Worldwide Educational Convergence through International Organizations: Avenues for Research', *Educational Policy Analysis Archives* 2 14 (1994), available at <http://epaa.asu.edu/epaa/v2nl4.html>; Karen Mundy, 'Educational Multilateralism and World (Dis)Order', *Comparative Education Review* 42 4 (1998), 448–78, and 'Unesco and the Limits of the Possible', *International Journal of Educational Development* 19 1 (1999), 27–52; Francisco Ramirez and John Boli, 'Global Patterns of Educational Institutionalization', in *Institutional Structure: Constituting State, Society and the Individual*, ed. George Thomas, John W. Meyer, Francisco O. Ramirez, and John Boli (Beverly Hills, Calif.: Sage, 1987), 150–72.
2. John Boli and George Thomas, eds., *Constructing World Culture: International Nongovernmental Organizations since 1875* (Stanford, Calif.: Stanford University Press, 1999); Margaret Keck and Kathryn Sikkink, *Activists beyond Borders* (Ithaca, NY: Cornell University Press, 1998); Ronnie Lipschutz, 'Reconstructing World Politics: The Emergence of Global Civil Society', in *International Society after the Cold War*, ed. Rich Fawn and Jeremy Larkins (New York: St Martin's Press, 1996), 101–31; James Rosenau, *Along the Domestic-Foreign Frontier* (New York: Cambridge University Press, 1997); Jackie Smith, ed., *Transnational Social Movements, Solidarity beyond the State* (Syracuse, NY: Syracuse University Press, 1997).
3. It is not our intention to review the literature on nongovernmental organizations in domestic educational arenas, although this has been a thriving theme of debate in recent years in the field of comparative education. See, e.g., David Archer, 'The Changing Roles of Non-governmental Organizations in the Field of Education', *International Journal of Educational Development* 14 3 (1994), 223–32; and also articles by Robert Arnove and Rachel Christina ('NGO-State Relations: An Argument in Favor of the State and Complementarity Efforts'), Steve Klees ('NGO's: A Progressive Force or Neoliberal Tool'), and Nelly Stromquist ('NGOs in a New Paradigm of Civil Society'), all in *Current Issues in Comparative Education* 1 1 (November 1998), an electronic journal (<http://www.tc.columbia.edu/~academic/ice/>, March 10, 1999).
4. James Nye and Robert Keohane, *Power and Interdependence: World Politics in Transition* (Boston: Little Brown, 1977); James Rosenau, 'Governance, Order and Change in World Politics', in *Governance without Government*, ed. James N. Rosenau and Ernst O. Czempiel (New York: Cambridge University Press, 1992), 1–291, and *Along the Domestic-Foreign Frontier*.
5. For historical case studies, see Boli and Thomas; Lyman Cromwell White, *International Nongovernmental Organizations: Their Purposes, Methods and Accomplishments*

(New Brunswick, NJ: Rutgers University Press, 1951); Martha Finnemore, *National Interests in International Society* (Ithaca, NY: Cornell University Press, 1996); and Smith.

6. David Held and Anthony McGrew, *Global Transformations: Politics, Economics and Culture* (Stanford, Calif.: Stanford University Press, 1999), quote on p. 431. See also Manuel Castells, *The Power of Identity, The Information Age: Economy, Society and Culture*, vol. ii (Oxford: Blackwell, 1997); Rosenau, 'Governance, Order and Change in World Politics'.

7. Keck and Sikkink, p. 11. Also, strong empirical evidence of the overall growth of international nongovernmental actors is provided by Boli and Thomas; also see Smith.

8. Anne Marie Clark, Elisabeth J. Friedman, and Kathryn Hochsteltler, 'The Sovereign Limits of Global Civil Society: A Comparison of NGO Participation in UN World Conferences on the Environment, Human Rights, and Women', *World Politics* 51 1 (October 1998), 1–35; Alison Van Rooy, 'The Frontiers of Influence: NGO Lobbying at the 1974 World Food Conference, the 1992 Earth Summit and Beyond', *World Development* 25 1 (1997), 93–114; L. Gordenker and T. G. Weiss, 'NGO Participation in the International Policy Process', *Third World Quarterly* 16 3 (1995), 543–613.

9. Jubilee 2000 is a 'worldwide movement to cancel the crushing international debt of impoverished countries by the new millennium' (<http://www.oneworld.org/jubilee2000>). The campaign is led by a coalition of church-based and development organizations and has achieved significant prominence through worldwide lobbying of national governments and a direct action campaign that utilizes the formation of 'human chains' around the sites of key intergovernmental conferences, most recently at the G7 interministerial meetings in June 1999. See John Mihevc, 'Jubilee 2000: Starting from Scratch', *New Internationalist* 312 (May 1999), 22–4.

10. Richard Price, 'Reversing the Gun Sights: Transnational Civil Society Targets Land Mines', *International Organization* 52 3 (Summer 1998), 613–44.

11. Cecilia Lynch, 'Social Movements and the Problem of Globalization', *Alternatives* 23 (1998), 149–73. For extensive coverage of World Trade Organization events, see *Seattle Times* (26 November - 3 December 1999); and World Bank, *Development News* (26–30 November 1999) (<http://www.devnews@ worldbank.org>). For protests in Washington, DC, see World Bank, *Development News* (17 April 2000); or 'IMF and World Bank Carry on Meeting Even with Protests', *Washington Post* (17 April 2000), p. A07. Several web sites also hosted extensive coverage of the protests and the coalitions that have formed to monitor them, such as A16 (<http://www.al6.org>) and WTOwatch (<http://www.wtowatch.org>). The A16 (or August 16) web site is run by a consortium of antiglobalization NGOs and citizen organizations under the title 'Mobilization for Global Justice'. The WTOwatch is a web site devoted to news and analysis on the World Trade Organization, trade, and sustainable development. It is operated by the Institute of Agriculture and Trade Policy, a nonprofit research organization based in Minneapolis that was formed in 1986.

12. Keck and Sikkink (n. 2 above), 12; Smith (n. 2 above); Price; Lipschutz (n. 2 above); Clark, Friedman, and Hochstelter, 'Sovereign Limits of Global Civil Society'; Boli and Thomas (n. 2 above); Lynch. For an overarching assessment of the normative potential held by such organizations, see Martha Finnemore and Kathryn Sikkink, 'International Norm Dynamics and Political Change', *International Organization* 52 4 (autumn 1998), 887–917.

13. Keck and Sikkink, 12.

14. Clark, Friedman, and Hochsteltler, 'Sovereign Limits of Global Civil Society'; Lipschutz; Mustapha Pasha and David Blaney, 'Elusive Paradise: The Promise and Peril of Global Civil Society', *Alternatives* 23 (1998), 417–50; Diane Otto, 'Nongovernmental Organizations in the United Nations System: The Emerging Role of International Civil Society', *Human*

Rights Quarterly 18 1 (1996), 107–14; W. Andy Knight, 'Engineering Space in Global Governance: The Emergence of Civil Society in Evolving "New" Multilateralism', in *Future Multilateralism*, ed. Michael G. Schechter (New York: St Martin's Press, 1999), 255–91; M. Smouts, 'Multilateralism from Below: A Prerequisite for Global Governance', in Schechter, ed., 292–311; Lisa Jordan and Peter van Tuijl, 'Political Responsibility in NGO Advocacy: Exploring Emerging Shapes of Global Democracy', Novib web site, April 1998 (<http>//www.oneworld.org/euoric/novib/novibl.htm>, 12 July 1999); Michael Edwards, David Hulme, and T. Wallace, 'NGOs in a Global Future: Marrying Local Delivery to World Wide Leverage' (Ford Foundation, 1999, mimeographed); Blair Rutherford, 'Civil (Dis)Obedience and Social Development in the New Policy Agenda: Research Priorities for Analyzing the Role of Civil Society Organizations in Social Policy Reform, with Particular Attention to Sub-Saharan Africa and Latin America', 1998 (<http://www.idrc.ca/socdev/pub/documents/civilsociety.html>, 8 April 1999), International Development Research Center; Alison Van Rooy, *Civil Society and the Aid Industry: The Politics and Promise* (London: Earthscan, 1998). For an official account of the significance of 'global civil society', see the United Nations Commission on Global Governance, *Our Global Neighborhood* (New York: Oxford University Press, 1995).

15. See John McCarthy, 'The Globalization of Social Movement Theory', in Smith, ed., 243–57; Dieter Rucht, 'The Transnationalization of Social Movements: Trends, Causes, Problems', in *Social Movements in a Globalizing World*, ed. Hanspeter Kriesi, Dieter Rucht, and Donatella della Porta (New York: St Martin's Press, 1999), 206–22; and Sydney Tarrow, 'Transnational Contention', in *Power in Movement: Social Movements and Contentious Politics*, ed. Sidney Tarrow (Cambridge: Cambridge University Press, 1998), 176–95.

16. See Smouts, 304. The idea of 'framing' is drawn from David Snow and Robert Benford, 'Master Frames and Cycles of Protest', in *Frontiers of Social Movement Theory*, ed. Aldon Morres and Carol Mueller (New Haven, Conn.: Yale University Press, 1992), 133–55. Smith (n. 2 above) transposes this to the study of transnational social movements and describes framing as the development of interpretive frames that 'process political information, interpreting certain conditions as problems in need of attention and conveying the need and potential efficacy of collective attempts to address the problem' (p. 73). See also, Clark, Friedman, and Hochsteltler, 'Sovereign Limits of Global Civil Society'.

17. See Sidney Tarrow, 'Cycles of Collective Action: Between Moments of Madness and Repertoires of Contention', in his *Repertoires and Cycles of Collective Action* (Durham, NC: Duke University Press 1995), 91.

18. John Hall, ed., *Civil Society: Theory, History, Comparison* (Cambridge: Blackwell, 1995); Andrew Arato and Jean Cohen, *Civil Society and Political Theory* (Cambridge, Mass.: MIT Press, 1992).

19. Clark, Friedman, and Hochsteltler, 'Sovereign Limits of Global Civil Society' (n. 8 above), 3.

20. Ibid.

21. Robert Putnam, *Making Democracy Work: Civic Traditions in Modern Italy* (Princeton, NJ: Princeton University Press, 1993); Alexander de Tocqueville, *Democracy in America* (New York: Doubleday, 1969).

22. See Clark, Friedman, and Hochsteltler, 'Sovereign Limits of Global Civil Society'.

23. Jordan and van Tuijl; see also Johannes Galtung, *True Worlds: A Transnational Perspective* (New York: Free Press, 1980), and 'Self-Reliance: An Overriding Strategy for Transition', in *Toward a Just World Order*, ed. Richard Falk, Samuel Kim, and Saul Mendlovitz (Boulder, Colo.: Westview, 1982).

24. For discussion, see, e.g., Galtung, *True Worlds*; Richard Falk, *On Humane Governance: Toward a New Global Politics* (University Park: Pennsylvania State University Press, 1995); Held, *Democracy and the Global Order* (n. 6 above); Held and McGrew (n. 6 above); and Smouts (n. 14 above).

25. See discussions by Robert Cox, 'Social Forces, States and World Order: Beyond International Relations Theory', *Millennium* 10 2 (1981), 126–55; Jordan and van Tuijl (n. 14 above); Lynch (n. 11 above); Claus Offe, 'New Social Movements: Challenging the Boundaries of Institutional Politics', *Social Research* 52 4 (1985), 817–69; Smith (n. 2 above); McCarthy (n. 15 above); and Tarrow, 'Transnational Contention' (n. 15 above), and 'Cycles of Collective Action'. See also Antonio Gramsci, *Selections from the Prison Notebooks:* 1929–35, ed. Quintin Hoare and Geoffrey Novell Smith (London: Lawrence & Wishart, 1971).

26. As Lynch and Pasha and Blaney (n. 14 above) point out, discussions about civil society from Hegel and Gramsci onward intermarry liberal and critical ideas about the possibility of governance, notions of economic causality, and notions about economic causality and public morality. Tensions and contradictions between liberal and critical notions of international civil society are especially marked around the issue of economic globalization.

27. Education International, *Congress Highlights: Speeches from the Constituent Congress of Education International*, ed. Nick Patrice and Vezina Grieswood (Morges, Switzerland: Education International, 1993), 35; Thompson (n. 32 above).

28. Indicative of this, the WCOTP, one of Education International's predecessor organizations, is described by Thomas-Fontaine (n. 35 above) as having 'never taken part (except very briefly from 1984–85) in the work of the [Unesco Collective NGO] Consultation, owing to internal crisis, on the one hand, and, on the other, the difficulty of broadening the scope of literacy problems beyond teachers concerns' (p. 5).

29. Education International, *Congress Highlights*, 35.

30. These and other quotations, where not cited, are drawn from the Education International web site at <http://www.ei-ie.org/main/english/index.html>. See also its two periodical publications, *Education International Magazine* and the *Monitor*.

31. Regional offices include one in Africa (Lome, Togo); two in Asia/Pacific (Kuala Lumpur, Fiji); and one each in Latin America (Costa Rica), North America (Washington, DC), and the Caribbean (St Lucia). The Brussels secretariat has five departments: education, trade union and human rights, development cooperation, information, and administration. According to its web site, the three main focuses of Education International activities since its formation in 1993 are the (1) right to quality public education for all, (2) the protection of international standards of human and trade union rights, and (3) the improvement of the status of women.

32. For a full history, see Education International, 'The Recommendation on the Status of Teachers', at <http://www.ei-e.org/educ/english/eed1966rec.htm>.

33. Education International, *Congress Highlights*.

34. Fred Van Leeuwen, quoted ibid. 30.

35. Education International argues that the WTO-sponsored liberalization of trade in educational services will threaten public education, and it also wants to see the WTO create a working group on international labor standards. See Education International, 'The WTO and the Millennium Round: What Is at Stake for Public Education?' in *Questions for Debate* 2 (Brussels: Education International, May 1999, <http://www.ei-ie.org/educ/

english/eedQD3_june99.html>), and 'After Seattle: Vigilance Is Necessary', 15 December 1999 (<http://www.ei-ie.org/action/english/Globalisation/etrseattle.htm>).

36. See, e.g., resolutions on these issues made at the first (1995) and second (1998) Education International World Congresses. These resolutions can be found on the Educational International web site (<http://www.ei-ie.org/main/english/index.html>), respectively, at <http://www.ei-ie.org/edu/english/eeires95index.html> and <http://www.ei-ie.org/edu/english/eeires98index.html>. See also the annual publication, Education International, *Barometer on Trade Union and Human Rights in the Education Sector, 1998* (Brussels: Education International, July 1998). Child Labor is the focus for one of the three campaigns Education International is currently conducting. A 1995 resolution of the World Congress mandates Education International to hold regional meetings among indigenous educators and commits the organization to the promotion of indigenous peoples' rights.

37. See Education International, 'Education for All', *Questions for Debate* 3, (Brussels: Education International, June 1999, available at <www.ei-ie.org/main/english/index.html>), 'Quality Public Education for All', *Education International Quarterly Magazine* (Brussels: Education International, October 1999), and *Defending Teacher Union Rights* (Brussels: Education International, 1994).

38. Education International ascribes to the general policies of the International Confederation of Free Trade Unions and works especially closely with the Public Service International. It also holds category 1, NGO consultative status, with Unesco, the International Labor Organization (ILO), the IBE, the World Bank, the OECD, and the Economic and Social Committee of the United Nations.

39. Interview nos. 17a and 17b, representative of ActionAid, Reality of Aid project, and Global Campaign for Education Steering Committee, respectively, 28 July 1999, and 31 January 2000, London; see also ActionAid's web site at <http://www.actionaid.org>.

40. See Archer (n. 3 above). ActionAid is also cross-networked: it was a lead agency in the Reality of Aid project and is a lead agency in Unesco's Collective Consultation.

41. The Elimu campaign documents and statements can be found at <http://www.elimu.org/issue.htm>. Some of these coalitions, such as Tanzania, Ghana, Burkina Faso, Mali, Bangladesh, India, Brazil, and Senegal, have already launched an education campaign (*Education Now* 3 [n. 72 above]; ActionAid, *Elimu Update: July 2000* (London: ActionAid United Kingdom, 1999 and 2000); Interview no. 8a, representative of Oxfam United Kingdom and current cochair of Global Campaign for Education, June 24, 1999, Oxford; Interviews nos. 17a and 17b, representative of ActionAid, Reality of Aid project, and Global Campaign for Education Steering Committee, 28 July 1999, and 31 January 2000, London).

42. The mission of the Global March is 'to mobilize world-wide efforts to protect and promote the rights of all children, especially the rights to receive a free, meaningful education and to be free from economic exploitation and from performing any work that is likely to be damaging to the child's physical, mental, spiritual, moral and social development' (cited from the Global March web site at <www.globalmarch.org/about_the_march/index.html>). Among its originators were NOVIB (Oxfam in the Netherlands) in conjunction with Anti-slavery International, the International Labor Rights Fund, ChristianAid, Casa Alianza, ECPAT (End Child Prostitution, Pornography, and Trafficking), Fundação Abrinq, Education International, Network against Child Labor, and the South Asia Coalition on Child Servitude. See documentation provided at <http://www.globalmarch.org>.

43. See Global March web site at <http://www.globalmarch.org>.

44. See Actionaid, *Elimu Update: Winter* 1999 (London: Actionaid United Kingdom, 1999). For a complete list of organizations who have joined the campaign, see Global Campaign for Education, 'Organizations Active in the Global Campaign for Education, Listed per Country', 29 March 2000 (<http://www.campaignforeducation.org/who_is/who_is.html, 1 May 2000>).

45. See the mission statement 'What Is the Global Campaign?' (<http://www.campaignfor education.org/what is/what_is.html>, n.d.).

46. Education International, 'Quality Education for All-Make It Happen Now! The Global Action Week: A Resounding Success! Press Release', March 2000 (<http://www.ei-ie.org/main/English/index.html>, 1 May 2000).

47. Letter from James D. Wolfensohn, president of World Bank, October 20, 1999 (<http://www.ei_ie.org/main/english/index.html>, 15 December 1999).

48. Charlotte Denny, 'Oxfam Quits Campaign in Protest', *The Guardian* (10 February 2000). See also Global Campaign for Education, *Speech and Media Brief, April 19, 2000* (Brussels: Global Campaign for Education, 2000); for e-mail distribution list, see: mailing_list_global_edu_campaign@ei-ie.org.

49. See Global Campaign for Education, *The Global Action Plan for Education* (Brussels: Global Campaign for Education/Education International, 2000), 5, *The World Education Forum in Dakar, Success or Failure? Our Bottom Line Position* (Brussels: Global Campaign for Education/Education International, 2000), 6, and 'Global Campaign on Education, Mission Statement and Common Purpose', October 1999 (<http://www.ei-ie.org/camp/English/efa/GlobalCamp/eed_missionstat.htm>, 1 April 2000).

50. Education International/Global Campaign for Education, 'Symposium on the Educational Situation in G8 Countries: Tokyo', 4 April 2000 (<http://www.ei-ie.org/ressourc/speeches/gcetokoyo_40400.htm>, 20 April 2000); Education International/Global Campaign for Education, 'Transcript of the Washington Press Conference: Global Campaign to Get Every Child in the World into School', 3 April 2000 (<http://www.ei-ie.org/ressourc/speeches/er_spe_gcewash_030400.htm>, 20 April 2000).

51. For example, Oxfam Great Britain, ActionAid, and a host of other British NGOs, including Save the Children Fund/UK, made a (failed) bid to get Tony Blair to come to Dakar and take a stand on EFA similar to that taken by the United Kingdom in the Highly Indebted Poor Country (HIPC) initiative. See *Guardian Weekly*, 'Blair Declines to Lead Fight for Education' (3 April 2000), 2; and *Guardian Weekly*, 'Blair's March on Downing Street' (21 April 2000), 10. See also Global Campaign for Education, 'European Union Position', 18 April 2000 (Global Campaign for Education, 2000); e-mail distribution list at: mailing_list_global_edu_campaign@ei-ie.org.

52. See, e.g., 'More on DFID' on the Global Campaign for Education e-mail distribution list available at: mailing_list_global_edu_campaign@ei-ie.org, 19 April 2000.

53. Clark, Friedman, and Hochstelter, 'Sovereign Limits of Global Civil Society' (n. 8 above); Van Rooy 'Frontiers of Influence' (n. 8 above); and Gordenker and Weiss, 'NGO Participation in the International Policy Process' (n. 8 above). See also Gordenker and Weiss, 'Pluralizing Global Governance: Analytical Approaches and Dimensions', *Third World Quarterly* 16 3 (1995), 357–89; and Anne Marie Clark, Elisabeth Friedman, and Kathryn Hochstetler, 'Sovereignty, Global Civil Society, and the Social Conferences: NGOs and States at the UN Conferences on Population, Social Development, and Human Settlements' (paper presented at the International Studies Association, Washington, DC, 16–20 February 1999), 19.

54. Private communication, EFA Steering Committee Member, 5 February 2000, and 30 April 2000. Ultimately, an estimated 1,500 persons attended the closed forum. See World Education Forum (WEF), *Provisional List of Participants* (Dakar: World Education Forum, 2000).

55. Clark, Friedman, and Hochstelter, 'Sovereign Limits of Global Civil Society'.

56. Clark, Friedman, and Hochstelter ('Sovereign Limits of Global Civil Society', 8) note that 'All UN world conferences share similar goals and format. A central focus of official business at each conference and its preparatory meetings is the creation of a final conference document to be endorsed by state participants. At regional preparatory meetings, governments develop regional positions on specific conference issues. The additional meetings of the Preparatory Commission ... focus on drafting the conference document. The wording of the final document is invariably the focus of intense politicking among state and between NGOs and states.'

57. Ibid.

58. World Education Forum (WEF), 'List of NGO Participants' (Paris: International Consultative Forum of NGOs, March 2000), *Provisional List of Participants*, and 'Newsletter of the World Education Forum in Dakar, No. 2' (Dakar: International Consultation Forum on Education, 2000). On the opening day of the conference, Southern NGOs waited most of the day for their registration forms to be processed because the communication that NGOs were invited to register and participate had not reach the registration desk until midday. Meanwhile, several Northern NGOs who were officially invited entered along with the rest of the official delegates. In contrast, the Jomtien conference only had two large development NGOs present, World Vision and the International Save the Children Alliance. See Inter-agency Commission (n. 46 above). At Dakar, these INGOs also attended, but there was a new participation by more radical INGOs, such as Oxfam and ActionAid.

59. Interview no. 23a, representative of ActionAid, 4 May 2000, London. Each of these events was also attended and observed by one of the authors. The efforts made by the International Consultation of NGOs and the UNESCO Collective Consultation of NGOs to coordinate a nongovernmental platform before and during the NGO preconference were overshadowed throughout the week by the efforts of Oxfam, ActionAid, and Education International. The week's events were also listed on the Global Campaign for Education web site at <http://www.campaignforeducation.org>, 5 June 2000.

60. See Global Campaign for Education, *World Education Forum in Dakar, Success or Failure?* (n. 49 above), 6. See also Global Campaign for Education, *The Global Action Plan for Education* (n. 49 above). In our observations we noted that even noncampaigners used the nine points and the Global Action Plan idea in lobbying efforts. Moreover, the NGO declaration prepared for the WEF bore a strong resemblance to the platform of the Global Campaign. See International Consultation of NGOs, *NGO Declaration on Education for All* (Dakar: International Consultation on Education for All, 2000), 4.

61. The drafting committee had four NGO representatives, which included a representative from the Global March against Child Labor, the Brazilian National Campaign for the Right to Education, Oxfam United Kingdom, and the Council of Non-governmental Organizations in Support of Government (CONGAD), Senegal. All four representatives are members of the Global Campaign, and two serve on its steering committee. The futures group had six NGO representatives, from ActionAid, Acuo Educativa (the parent organization of the Brazilian National Campaign for the Right to Education), Education International, the Arab Resource Collective, the Civil Society Action Committee on EFA, and the Asian-South Pacific Bureau of Adult Education. Of these ten representatives, eight

are members of the Global Campaign for Education. No representative from the UNESCO NGO Collective Consultation was elected to either body.

62. It is important to note, however, that some NGOs found the campaigners distinctly 'uncivilized.' For example, one representative of a larger, Northern-based development organization with a long history of work in education told us: 'Here [at Dakar] we're seeing the ugly side of NGOs. They are screaming and pushing their way into things . . . .For us, advocacy comes from our demonstrated experience' (Interview no. 3b, Save the Children [United States] representative, 27 April 2000, Dakar, Senegal).

63. Originally 55 NGOs were invited to send a single delegate each to the World Forum. This was in keeping with the EFA Steering Committee's objective of limiting and keeping tight control over attendance at the conference. About 150 nongovernmental participants ultimately attended the WEF. Our interviews with Southern NGOs and teachers' unions revealed that many others had hoped to attend the WEF but had not done so after being denied an official invitation to the conference (Interview no. 25a, representative of Brazilian Education Network, 24 April 2000, Dakar, Senegal). Like them, we were denied official permission to attend or observe the conference by the UNESCO EFA secretariat.

64. Interview no. 23a, representative of ActionAid, 4 May 2000, London; Interview no. 17c, representative of ActionAid, 5 May 2000, London; Interview no. 24a, representative of Oxfam International, 5 May 2000; Interview no. 22a, representative of Citizen's Initiative on Education India, 30 April 2000, Dakar, Senegal.

65. See World Education Forum, *WEF, News and Views-Speeches-Carol Bellamy: Plenary Address by Unicef*, 27 April 2000 (<http://www2.unesco.org/wef/en-news/coverage_speech_belamy.shtm>, 2 May 2000); World Education Forum, 'WEF, News and Views, Online Coverage, Speeches: A Time for Action: Placing Education at the Core of Development', by James D. Wolfensohn, president, the World Bank, 27 April 2000 (<http://www2.unesco.org/wef/en_news/coverage_speech_wolfen.shtm>, 1 May 2000), 'UN Secretary General, Address to the World Education Forum: Building a Partnership for Girls' Education' (Dakar: World Education Forum, 2000), and 'Address by Mark Malloch Brown, Administrator of the UNDP to the World Education Forum' (Dakar: World Education Forum, 2000). These speeches and other press releases are available at the World Education Forum web site (<http://www2.unesco.org/wef/en-news/latest.shtm>), 5 June 2000.

66. Interview no. 17c, representative of ActionAid, 5 May 2000, London; Interview no. 24a, representative of Oxfam International, 5 May 2000, Washington, DC. Some of these meetings were also attended by one of us.

67. Oxfam has played a leading role in lobbying the World Bank, which has more sustained contact with the campaigners than any other international organization (Interview no. 9b, representative of Oxfam United Kingdom and former member of EFA Steering Committee, 23 April 2000, Washington, DC; Interview no. 24a, representative of Oxfam International, 5 May 2000, Washington, DC).

68. Camilla Crosa-Silva and Kailash Sathyarti, 'What We Achieved at Dakar', *Elimu Update* (London: July 2000), 1.

69. The Global Campaign has its own web site at <http://www.campaignforeducation.org> on which one can join an active list-serve in which information about campaign plans and events are shared. Oneworld.net, a popular portal for news about the Third World, international development, and new social movements, is sponsored by about 685 organizations, mainly nongovernmental. Its page on education allows readers to send letters to members of the World Education Forum Drafting Committee, join Oxfam's Education Now campaign, and to join the Global Campaign for Education e-mail

list-serve. The Oneworld.net page can be found at <http://www.oneworld.net/campaigns/education/index.html>.

70. UNESCO representatives in particular raised this question; some NGO informants interviewed felt that Unesco had kept too tight a control over NGO participation and had tried to demonize the Global Campaign as an attempt by Oxfam to control international funds (Interviews nos. 17b and 17c, representative of ActionAid, 31 January 2000, and 5 May 2000, both in London). Frustrations with the limited invitations to the preconference were aired publicly at the open house the Global Campaign held on the eve of the preconference.

71. This issue was also discussed openly at several of the NGO meetings and in private communication among the authors and the campaign members throughout the week. It is a point of contention between Oxfam and ActionAid, with ActionAid demanding more attention to the development of national networks and regional coalitions in the South. The campaign steering committee addressed these tensions in their last meeting in Dakar, where both Northern and Southern partners expressed the need for the campaign to focus on building Southern coalitions.

72. Global Campaign for Education, 'Final Press Release and Speech by Tom Bediako', 28 April 2000, with distribution list (8 May 2000). In a debriefing meeting held at the end of the week for the NGOs, the achievements throughout the week were discussed. Individuals from Northern NGOs expressed that while they did not achieve all that they had hoped to, they were organized, highly visible, and able to influence parts of the framework. As one Southern NGO representative present at the debriefing expressed, 'I am not so quick to pat myself on the back before I go ... We are leaving without real commitments from governments and donors to finance basic education'.

73. Among the NGOs we identified as not affiliating with the campaign at Dakar are: Save the Children (United States), Save the Children (the Netherlands), the UNESCO Collective Consultation and several of its members such as the Summer Institute for Linguistics, the Asia-South Pacific Bureau of Adult Education, and the International Council on Adult Education, CARE, and Plan International.

74. The World Bank's fast-track proposal focuses on offering quick disbursing money for education to governments that have acceptable national education plans. See World Bank, 'Draft Proposal World Bank for Consideration for Inclusion in the Framework for Action' (Dakar: World Bank, 2000); World Education Forum, *WEF Press Releases: A Time for Action, Placing Education at the Core of Development*, 27 April 2000 (<http://www2.unesco.org/wef/en-press/relea_dak_0427_18h.shtm>, 1 May 2000).

75. Interview no. 17c, representative of ActionAid, 5 May 2000, London; Interview no. 23a, representative of ActionAid, 4 May 2000, London; Interview no. 24a, representative of Oxfam International, 5 May 2000, Washington, DC.

76. Interview no. 20a, prior secretary of Inter-agency Commission, 27 April 2000, Dakar, Senegal; Interview no. 23a, representative of ActionAid, 4 May 2000, London. One NGO representative we interviewed (personal communication, 25 April 2000) explained that the invitation process for him was quite extensive, including a written statement of the desired goals and objectives for the forum and an extensive phone call with one of the conveners.

77. Crosa-Silva and Sathyarti (n. 68 above).

78. For discussion, see Boli and Thomas' (n. 2 above), 3–6.

79. Education International, 'Campaigners Say "Don't Let Dakar Repeat the Decade of Failure"', 28 April 2000 (<http://www.ei-ie.org/main/english/index.html>, 1 May 2000);

Global Campaign for Education, 'Final Press Release and Speech by Tom Bediako' (n. above). Clare Short, the UK Minister for Development Cooperation was adamant on this point (see *Guardian Weekly*, 'World Summit Clash on Education of Poor' (26 April 2000), 2.

80. Elie Jouen, of Education International, as quoted in Global Campaign for Education, 'Final Press Release'.

81. Edwards, Hulme, and Wallace, 'NGOs in a Global Future' (n. 14 above), 2.

82. Here it seems reasonable to echo Galtung's warning of more than two decades ago that a focus on schooling may lead us down the path of narrow, technical solutions to the problem of global inequality, and away from larger questions about structural inequalities and responsibilities; see Galtung, 'Literacy, Education, and Schooling—For What?' in *A Turing point for Literacy*, ed. Leon Bataille (Oxford: Pergamon, 1976), 93–105. *True Worlds* (n. 23 above), 150, and 'Self-Reliance' (n. 23 above).

83. The campaign's hard-edged approach revolves around its efforts to have binding sanctions placed on governments who don't make EFA plans and meet EFA targets. Reflecting on this, a member of the steering committee noted that 'things get kind of funny when you hear the World Bank talking about a soft touch and Oxfam talking about taking a hard edge' (Interview no. 21a, EFA Steering Committe member, 27 April 2000, Dakar, Senegal).

84. In the world of foreign aid, 'tying' refers to the practice of stipulating that donated funds are used to purchase goods or services from the donating country.

From the Washington to the Post-Washington Consensus: The Influence of International Agendas on Education Policy and Practice in Malawi

Pauline Rose

[...]

Introduction

It is widely recognised that the World Bank, along with other Washington institutions, has dominated development practice over the past two decades. This dominance is evident both in the intellectual role it has sought to play, as well as the policy prescriptions it has placed on borrowing countries since the 1980s. World Bank operations have continuously been influenced by economic considerations which determine the activities of a bank. Its role has, however, evolved and expanded over time to incorporate the perception of itself as a development agency during McNamara's presidency in the 1970s, to being a self-styled 'knowledge bank' in the 1990s (Mason and Asher, 1973; Stern with Ferreira, 1997; World Bank, 1999a; Mundy, 2002; Klees, 2004). Although tensions between its different activities as a development agency on the one hand and a bank on the other hand are evident, it is undeniable that the World Bank has played, and continues to play, a catalytic role in determining and reinforcing a particular development agenda. While there are differences of opinion of the extent to which the World Bank is a creator of ideas, its influential role in disseminating, promoting and applying a particular dominant view of economic development is generally acknowledged (Stern with Ferreira, 1997; Waelbroeck, 1998; Wade, 2001; Standing, 2000; Fine *et al.*, 2001).

Dominance of the World Bank in setting the development agenda is clearly reflected in the education sector, given the intellectual and financial role it has attained over the past two decades (Jones, 1992; Samoff, 1992; Mundy, 2002).[1] This [chapter]

Pauline Rose, 'From the Washington to the Post-Washington Consensus: the influence of international agendas on education policy and practice in Malawi', *Globalisation, Societies and Education*, 1, 1, 67–86 © 2003 Taylor & Francis Ltd. <http://tandf.co.uk/journals>.

examines changing debates in World Bank educational priorities, with emphasis on the financing of education, an area in which the World Bank has played a particularly influential role, in the context of broader shifts in the development agenda. These shifts are illustrated by examining the experience in Malawi. The Malawi case is of particular interest because it was the first country in which primary school fees were increased in the 1980s based on World Bank advice. As this [chapter] will show, while shifts in World Bank policies towards education are evident, one thing has remained consistently resilient to change—an uncritical faith in the notion of human capital.

The [chapter] begins by indicating the origins of the concept of human capital in the 1960s. It then illustrates how human capital has risen to prominence since the 1980s in conjunction with the Washington consensus neo-liberal agenda. It examines the implications of the adoption of human capital for national educational policy and practice in Malawi, particularly in relation to advocacy for user fees. This is followed by an investigation of the shift in development agenda in the 1990s to address governance issues to facilitate implementation of Washington consensus principles, and the implications of this for the education sector. The [chapter] concludes by examining more recent trends towards a 'global education industry'.

The Human Capital Revolution

Initially adopted by T. W. Schultz in 1960, and rising to prominence with its further development in particular by his own work and that of Gary Becker throughout the 1960s and onwards, human capital has allowed an economic approach based on the calculation of costs and benefits of education to predominate. According to the notion of human capital, people acquire skills and knowledge which is perceived as a form of capital, and a substantial part of this acquisition is a deliberate investment (Schultz, 1960). Human capital, therefore, provided education with an explicit economic value, seeing it as an important explanation for economic progress. Increased productivity as a result of education was perceived to benefit individuals as well as society as a whole. In particular, Schultz (1960) and Becker (1993) illustrated the importance of investment in human capital through the application of rates of return showing that, taking total costs of education into account (including earnings forgone as a result of time spent in school or college), rates of return to education are relatively attractive, and larger than returns in physical capital. Since the 1960s, proponents of human capital have continued to use calculations of rates of return as empirical justification to show that education is a good investment. Thus, the rise of human capital theory grew out of the more specific application of cost–benefit analysis to calculation of rates of return. As such, it has nothing to do with education specifically. Exactly the same methodology can be applied to any factor with an economic effect (Fine and Rose, 2001).

From the early 1960s, simultaneous with Schultz's discovery of human capital, the World Bank began a cautious exploration of possibilities for involving itself in education. From the outset, it was made clear that only economic factors should be taken into consideration for Bank lending in education, despite acknowledgement of its social and cultural objectives. In 1960, the prospect of introducing lending for education projects was initially dismissed, on the grounds that it was neither revenue-generating nor capital-intensive (Kapur *et al.*, 1997). Schultz's work allowed this view to be refuted, as education could now be seen as an investment. However, the human capital revolution initially had little impact on the World Bank. World Bank staff were still reluctant to get involved in education, on the basis of the World Bank's perceived comparative advantage in other areas, the 'inherent subjectivities of a soft sector', and the potential for political issues (Kapur *et al.*, 1997: 168–9).

Gradual acceptance that certain types of education were productive resulted in approval of investment in vocational and technical training at higher and secondary levels. This was based on needs identified by manpower gaps revealed by other Bank projects in the country. An initial antipathy towards support for primary education was apparent, based on the 'bizarre rationale' that it would make unlimited demands as far as finance was concerned, and self-provision should be relied upon because of the high demand for it (Jones, 1992: 99).

It was only by the 1970s, with the expansion of the Bank's identity as a development agency and adoption of the basic needs approach under McNamara's presidency, that education began to be taken more seriously, with a shift in emphasis to primary education. Proponents of the basic needs approach were, however, expected to justify their proposals in terms of cost and economic return and to show that economic growth would not be impaired (Kapur *et al.*, 1997).

The increasing emphasis on education over the 1970s is evident by changing priorities in World Bank lending. There was a notable expansion and diversification of lending for education during the early 1970s. Commitments for education increased from an average of $154 million during the years 1963–9 to $528 million per annum on average during the period 1970–4, and continued to increase during the latter half of the 1970s (Table 70.1). Furthermore, greater priority to primary education was also apparent, with its allocation increasing from 4% of education lending in the 1960s to almost one-quarter by the late 1970s.

Washington Consensus and Education: The Rise of Human Capital

The term 'Washington consensus' was coined by Williamson (1990) to define the set of policy instruments associated with World Bank structural adjustment programmes and IMF stabilisation programmes in the early 1980s, the main objective of which was to stabilise economies in severe disequilibrium and promote economic growth. These policy instruments were advocated as a reaction against interventionist policies which were perceived to be the cause of the economic crisis that many countries were facing. The policy instruments of the Washington consensus were embodied in the conditionalities of stabilisation and structural adjustment programmes imposed on countries accepting IMF and World Bank loans during the 1980s. Market-oriented principles and policies of neo-liberal economists were influential in informing these programmes.

Williamson summarises the economic policies 'that Washington urges on the rest of the world' as 'prudent macroeconomic policies, outward orientation, and free-market capitalism' (Williamson, 1990: 20). The list of policy instruments includes ten elements of reform: fiscal discipline, public expenditure priorities towards education and health (particularly primary), tax reform to broaden the tax base and cut marginal tax rates, market-determined interest rates, unified and competitive exchange rates, trade liberalisation, encouragement of foreign direct investment, promotion of privatisation, deregulation and securing of property rights. Broadly, the Washington consensus believes that markets would work best if left to themselves as they will allocate resources more efficiently than alternative mechanisms, and policies aimed at privatisation and trade liberalisation are advocated. In the view of the Washington consensus, the state is seen to reflect inappropriate economic interests, such as rent-seeking, whereas the market is unaffected by

Table 70.1 Trends in World Bank lending to education (US$ million, average per year)

	1963–69	1970–74	1975–79	1980–84	1985–89	1990–94	1995–99
Total education (constant $)	154	528	794	977	1,091	2,024	1,878
Education as % total lending	3.0	5.1	4.4	4.5	4.5	8.2	7.6
% of education lending to pre-primary and primary	4.2	10.6	23.6	22.9	26.3	36.1	37.8

Source: Adapted from Mundy (2001: Table 1).

such influences. Thus, the aim is to rely on market forces and reduce state intervention and expenditure to a minimum (Fine, 2001*a*; Fine, 2001*b*).

Human capital took two decades to achieve prominence within the World Bank, finally coming into its own from the early 1980s. The appointment of George Psacharopoulos to head the Education Department's Research Unit established in 1981 was instrumental in this significant shift. Emphasis on the analysis of rates of return to education became increasingly evident within the Bank, supported in particular by Psacharopoulos's numerous surveys and summaries of studies (1973; 1981; 1985; 1994). Investment in primary education was promoted on the basis that estimates of rates of return to education were highest, and the difference between social and private returns greatest, at that level, particularly for girls. Rates of return to investment in education were also estimated to be above the 10% yardstick used as the opportunity cost of capital in developing countries. As Jones (1992) suggests, Psacharopoulos brought to the Bank the type of educational research that was organisationally necessary for research to have an influence over the character and quality of lending in education.

It is not coincidental that the ascendancy of human capital in conjunction with the application of rates of return corresponded with the advent of the Washington consensus. Human capital provided the opportunity for the neo-liberal agenda to be applied to education, allowing the World Bank to continue its involvement, and even increase its influence, in the education sector despite austerity packages adopted as part of structural adjustment programmes. Although basic education and health were seen as areas for public expenditure priority even during the Washington consensus era, in practice this conflicted with the principle of reducing overall government expenditure. This meant that, in reality, education expenditure often suffered, even though governments made considerable efforts to protect the education budget where possible (Stewart, 1994; Woodhall, 1994).

Productivity benefits associated with human capital permitted an expansion of World Bank loans to education. World Bank lending to education increased dramatically, doubling between the early 1980s and early 1990s (Table 70.1). Furthermore, World Bank lending played an even greater role internationally, increasing from 16% to 30% of the amount spent on education by bilateral agencies (which remained relatively unchanged) over the period (Mundy, 1998; World Bank, 1999*b*)—indicative of the increasing financial dominance of the World Bank in education internationally. The share of primary education remained relatively stable over the 1980s at around one-quarter of total education lending, despite proclamations of a focus on this level during the period.

At the same time as the rise of human capital allowed the World Bank to justify its own involvement in education, it also provided a rationale for the World Bank to reassess the relative role of states and markets in education. World Bank-supported research put forward efficiency and equity arguments to justify setting a price for consumers (see, for example, Thobani, 1984; Mingat and Tan, 1986; Jimenez, 1986; 1987; Psacharopoulos *et al.*, 1986). While the payment of fees for the use of education services was not new, market principles were formally adopted in the 1980s to justify cost-recovery in public education. A total retreat of the state was, however, never supported in education given the acceptance of externalities, such as education's benefits to society through improved health, reduced fertility etc., imperfections in capital and labour markets, and inadequate information about anticipated future benefits (Colclough, 1996).

As Fine and Rose (2001) argue, however, acknowledgement of externalities and market imperfections undermine the operation of the model in the first place. The appropriateness of allowing the market to set the price for education, even once externalities and market imperfections are accounted for, is further weakened once the validity of conditions underpinning the application of the model are questioned, as the experience of Malawi illustrates (see below). In particular, in order to justify the charging of fees, conditions of excess and inelastic demand is required. Based on these conditions, it is proposed that unmet demand can be met by expanding the coverage of education through the receipt of fees, and that the fall in demand will be less than proportionate than the increase in price. Alternatively, additional resources will be used to improve the quality of education. It

Table 70.2 Malawian government expenditure on education, 1973/4–1997 (Kwacha, 1995 prices)

	Total	Primary		
	recurrent education expenditure as % total government	Enrolment	Recurrent expenditure	Unit costs
1973/74	16.2	481,461	140,503,467	292
1975/76	14.2	576,377	137,764,538	239
1980/81	11.4	754,590	154,874,450	205
1985/86	8.8	890,523	184,149,524	207
1990/91	11.6	1,267,009	233,341,409	184
1995/96	28.3	2,887,107	562,925,757	195
1997	21.9	2,905,950	556,049,062	191

Source: Author's calculations from Ministry of Education Education Statistics, various years; and Malawi Government Approved and Revised Estimates of Expenditure on Recurrent Account, various years. GDP deflator (IMF 1999).

is also argued that equity would not be adversely affected, as the extended coverage would benefit those in more remote areas of a country where coverage and quality of education are anticipated to be most constrained.

Washington Consensus and Education in Malawi

Similar to many other African countries, the Malawian economy was in crisis in the late 1970s, resulting in its adoption of a structural adjustment programme in 1981. Conditions were set according to Washington consensus principles, emphasising liberalisation in smallholder agriculture in particular (see Harrigan, 2001 and Gulhati, 1989 for a description of the programmes). Inadequate human capital was identified as one of the factors contributing to the economic crisis at the end of the 1970s (Gulhati, 1989). As a result, although the main focus during the 1980s was on economic reforms, the education sector also received attention. In principle, public expenditure on education was prioritised. However, in practice, recurrent expenditure on education was a small proportion of total government recurrent expenditure over the decade falling from around 14% in the mid-1970s to below 9% in the mid-1980s (Table 70.2).

Despite the intended prioritisation of recurrent expenditure to primary education in the structural adjustment programme, expenditure only increased at around the same rate as enrolment. As a result, by the beginning of the 1990s, expenditure per primary pupil was lower than at the beginning of the previous decade, and was substantially lower compared with the early 1970s. During this period, public recurrent expenditure at the primary level was almost exclusively allocated to teacher costs. The pupil/teacher ratio remained high, fluctuating between 65 : 1 and 70 : 1 over the decade (Ministry of Education, various years). Furthermore, despite nominal increases in teachers' salaries, these failed to keep pace with inflation resulting in their decline by one-third in real terms over the decade. As a result, teachers' salaries were just half of their real value in the early 1970s (Malawi Government Approved and Revised Estimates on Recurrent Account, various years).

Although it is often the case that development expenditure in social sectors was adversely affected in countries undertaking structural adjustment programmes because this could be most easily cut (Stewart, 1994; Woodhall, 1994), this was not apparent in Malawi in the 1980s due to high levels of World Bank lending to the sector. Mainly as a result of the increase in IDA funds, expenditure on the development programme increased at 6% per annum, resulting in a doubling of expenditure over the decade. The local contribution remained at around 15–20% of the development programme (based on conditions set for counterpart funds) and, therefore, also doubled in real terms. However, only 1% of the government's development programme was allocated to the primary level at the end of the decade, with primary school construction relying on self-help. Thus, the proposed prioritisation of primary schooling by the World Bank and government in the 1980s was not evident in their development funding commitments.

Given falling public expenditure per primary pupil, alternative sources of resources needed to be identified in order to fulfil the objective of prioritising primary schooling. According to World Bank research, Malawi fulfilled the conditions of having excess and inelastic demand, including at the primary level (Thobani, 1984; Mingat and Tan, 1986). Thobani proposed that evidence of overcrowded classrooms (an average of 66 students compared with the government's target of 50) was an indication of excess demand for education. Moreover, he noted that the enrolment rate was highest in the Northern Region, which was perceived to be the poorest region, compared with the Southern and Central Regions. He, therefore, suggested that, where children were not enrolled, this was not due to inability to pay, but rather to insufficient school places in the South and Centre, which was further evidence of excess demand.

Thobani also hypothesised that opportunity cost of time spent in school of the child in richer households would be higher as the child could usefully be employed on the family farm so their expected return to education would be likely to be lower than for a poorer person. He proposed that an increase in primary school fees would discourage those whose opportunity cost of time is high the most and, since they would not necessarily be the poorest, an increase in fees would not be inequitable. It is notable that no attempt was made to estimate opportunity costs in order to support the hypothesis. However, more recent estimates support Klees's (1984) view that it is far more likely that it is the poor who drop out or do not attend school because of their higher opportunity costs. Furthermore, when unpaid household work is included, opportunity costs of time spent in school are substantially higher for girls than boys. However, despite subsequent interest in promoting girls' education due to perceived social benefits, the implications for gender equity of a fee increase were not considered by the World Bank economists in the 1980s.

Thobani (1984: 417) further proposed that higher fees would improve internal efficiency of the system in Malawi. In particular, he noted the high dropout in the first two years due to low quality by which time children would not have achieved basic literacy and 'their time could probably have been better spent elsewhere'. Thus, although he recognised that the higher fees might discourage some from entering school, he considered that dropout among those who do enter should fall as they expect higher returns from the improved quality. Thobani's analysis acknowledged that enrolment would decline, indicating that he was not concerned with the need to increase enrolment in a country where half of primary school-aged children were not in school.

Proposals for increasing primary school fees in Malawi were not based on an appropriate analysis of the political, economic and social conditions of the country. For example, educational development was strongly influenced by missionary involvement in the North (McCracken, 1977). By contrast, expansion in the Southern and Central Regions was slower partly due to deep-rooted cultural practices (Kadzamira and Chibwana, 2000). Furthermore, given that fees were increased at the same time as households were suffering from economic crisis, excess and inelastic demand was not evident, as claimed. Interestingly, advocacy of fees as part of the first structural adjustment programme in 1981 predated Thobani's analysis (see, for example, World Bank, 1982), implying that the technical model was developed post-factum, and was undertaken to support a decision that had already been made.

As a result of the inadequate analysis primary school fees were increased based on World Bank advice and education was adversely affected. In the two years following the increase in fees (1982–4), enrolment fell by 2% per annum. The initial decline in primary enrolment affected standard 1 the most, where enrolment almost halved over a period of two years (Figure 70.1). As a result, the primary gross enrolment ratio declined from 70% to 63%. Furthermore, enrolment declined in the regions where it was already lowest (Southern and Central Regions) suggesting that excess and inelastic demand was not evident in these regions, as predicted, while it continued to rise in the North.

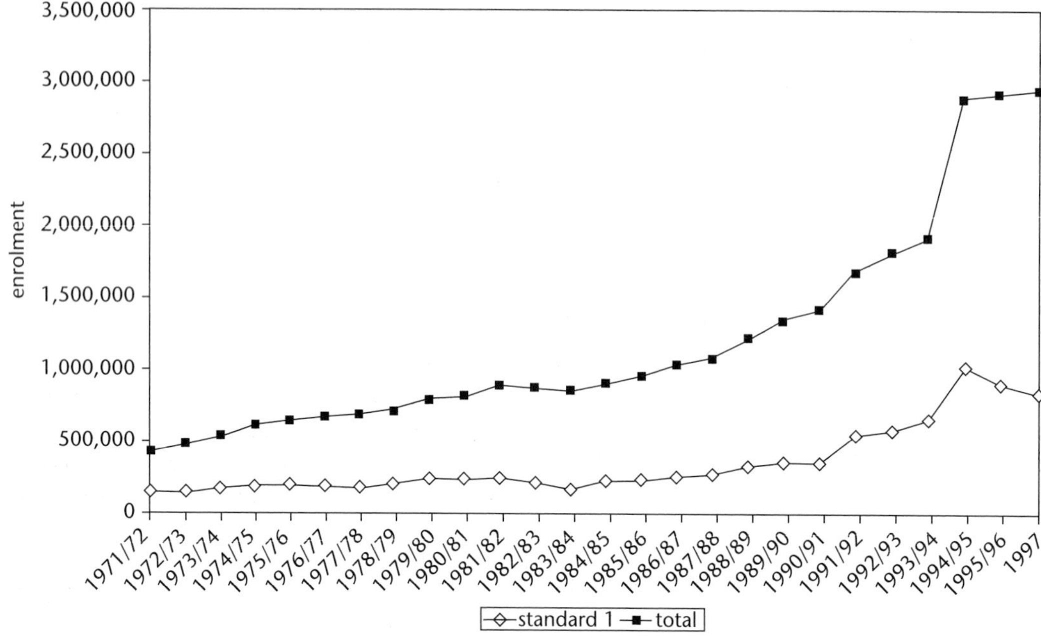

Fig. 70.1 Primary enrolment in Malawi, 1971/72–1997
Source: Ministry of Education Education Statistics.

Although enrolment subsequently increased, so that by the end of the 1980s the gross enrolment ratio reached 84%, the government's goal of universal primary education was not attained. Furthermore, by the early 1990s, girls from poorest households were least likely to be in school, suggesting that the payment of fees had not resulted in an equitable outcome (Table 70.3).

Since publicly financed expenditure per pupil was declining, fee income was used to replace public expenditure rather than supplement it. Thus, it was not used to create additional school places or increase quality which was required for the intended efficiency and equity outcomes of the model. Contrary to Thobani's expectations, the proportion of children dropping out of school increased following the fee increase, indicating a deterioration in internal efficiency in the system. Survival rates in primary school which were already low, worsened after the fee increase in 1982. As a result, by the mid-1980s, only 13% of girls and 23% of boys enrolling in standard 1 could expect to complete the primary cycle. The fall in demand for primary schooling and increase in dropout has been attributed to the combined effect of the fee increase together with the decline in real incomes of the poorest households due to drought, falling agricultural output and an increase in price of maize as a result of the structural adjustment programme (Fuller, 1989; Moyo, 1992).

Table 70.3 Primary gross and net enrolment rates by income quintiles and gender

	GER				NER			
	1990/91		1997		1990/91		1997	
	Boys	Girls	Boys	Girls	Boys	Girls	Boys	Girls
I—Poorest	65	51	115	106	34	31	70	72
II	83	69	125	111	50	45	75	75
III	88	83	124	116	52	57	76	78
IV	104	89	127	117	66	61	78	79
V—Richest	113	106	124	115	76	75	81	79
All	86	75	123	112	52	50	76	76

Source: Castro-Leal (1996); Al-Samarrai and Zaman (2002).

Post-Washington Consensus and Education: Neo-Liberalism with a Human Face

By the end of the 1980s, policy instruments of structural adjustment programmes associated with the Washington consensus were being severely criticised due to their observed negative social impact (see, for example, Cornia, Jolly and Stewart, 1987). In addition, there was growing recognition that the success of East Asian Newly Industrialised Countries (NICs) was due to an active role of the state including in relation to regulation of trade and domestic markets and public ownership, as well as high levels of investment in education. While NICs did participate in the world market, they did so on terms that they manipulated in their favour (Fine *et al.*, 2001).

These factors contributed to the shift in the 1990s to what Stiglitz (1998), former Chief Economist at the World Bank, has termed the 'post-Washington consensus'.[2] Rhetorically at least, the post-Washington consensus proposes an extended focus from economic growth to more instruments and broader objectives with a transition from a states versus markets approach to a complementary relationship between states and markets. The transition to the post-Washington consensus in the 1990s occurred due in part to an awareness of the need to address the political realities of borrowing countries. However, the post-Washington consensus is not built on a critical analysis or a careful internal reconsideration of the Washington consensus (Hildyard, 1997; Standing, 2000; Fine, 2001*a*; 2001*b*). The basic policy instruments continue to be based on Washington consensus principles of free trade and privatisation, with the only significant change being a reassessment of a role for the state to ensure that they can be implemented effectively and humanely (Hildyard, 1997; Gore, 2000).[3] While acknowledgement of market imperfections indicates an incorporation from development economics that preceded the Washington consensus, the post-Washington consensus differs from this by reducing everything to market and non-market imperfections, rather than looking at broad structures of the economy and broad processes of development, and how these interact with each other (Fine, 2001*b*).

The notion of human capital continues to be the motivation for investing in education with, if anything, the role of rates of return analysis in shaping World Bank educational priorities increasing over time (Bennell, 1996). Despite growing criticisms of the approach, the most recent World Bank (1999*b*) *Education Sector Strategy* continues to rely on evidence on rates of return to justify investment in education. The Strategy paper indicates a continued uncritical adherence to the importance of the notion of human capital and the application of rates of return analysis in the post-Washington consensus era: 'The rise of human capital theory since the 1960s, and its widespread acceptance now after thorough debate, has provided conceptual underpinnings and statistical evidence. Estimates by Nobel-laureate economists have shown that education is one of the best investments, outstripping the returns from many investments in physical capital' (World Bank 1999*b*: 6).

Despite the continued adherence to human capital, emphasis of the post-Washington consensus on more instruments and broader objectives provides an even greater opportunity for the prioritisation of education, seeing it as both a means to, and end of, development. Stiglitz (1997: 22) proposes, for example, that promoting human capital can advance economic development, equality, participation and democracy and, as such, sees education as 'the core of development'. Primary education has continued as a central priority for the World Bank, with even greater emphasis given to the focus of the World Bank's mission on poverty reduction in the 1990s. This focus supports the more general acceptance of the importance of primary education by international agencies and national governments, as articulated at the 1990 and 2000 World Conferences on Education for All in Jomtien and Dakar, with both rights-based as well as economic arguments used in its favour. For the World Bank, the latter continue to predominate. As a result, a global consensus in education is evident, as articulated by the Millennium Development Target of achieving universal primary education by 2015.

The priority towards primary education is evident in changing lending priorities of the World Bank. Together with a doubling of total education lending between the 1980s and 1990s, the proportion allocated to primary education has also increased from one-quarter to one-third (see Table 70.1). However, a small number of countries (17) account for three-quarters of the World Bank's education lending in the late 1990s (World Bank, 1999*b*). Furthermore, according to Colclough *et al.* (forthcoming) total World Bank lending for education has fallen dramatically over the 1990s (falling by 15.5%), with lending to sub-Saharan Africa being the most seriously affected (declining by 44%), suggesting that it has not been possible to sustain the growth in lending despite the fact that the goal of achieving universal primary education is most elusive in this region. Moreover, despite the increasing importance of World Bank resources to education internationally, the 1995 World Bank Review notes that World Bank spending is small compared with spending on education by developing countries themselves, accounting for only 0.6% of the total. Thus, it suggests without apparent irony: 'This low share of total spending means that the Bank should concentrate on providing advice designed to help governments develop education policies suitable for the circumstances of their own countries' (World Bank, 1995: 153).

The increased prioritisation of primary education, in principle at least, has allowed an image to be presented of the World Bank being more attuned to welfare, poverty alleviation, gender issues and community participation (Ilon, 1996; Puiggros, 1997; Klees, 2002). The World Bank's interpretation of these issues is, however, narrow and are at best strategies to achieve its more conventional goals related to global markets (Ilon, 2002). For example, in the post-Washington consensus era, participation is seen as a means of improving educational outcomes, and education is perceived to improve participation (Stiglitz, 1997). The new focus is, however, integrated into the more traditional human capital dialogues: 'Since we accept human capital theory and the outcomes approach, then our focus naturally becomes poverty reduction . . . Or in other words, empowering the poor by improving their productivity . . . is the World Bank's goal in education' (Burnett and Patrinos, 1996: 276).

Although the World Bank and other international agencies no longer directly support payment of fees at the primary level, the reality for many poor countries is that the state faces problems in financing education. This is particularly true in countries such as Malawi where, as a result of the Education for All agenda, education systems have expanded rapidly in the 1990s, raising challenges for the quality of primary schooling. Thus, the problems of pricing of educational services have remained at the core of the World Bank's research on education (Mundy, 2002). On the one hand, the view persists that household contributions to schooling are restricted by the existing financing arrangements, resulting in underinvestments in education and 'an untapped willingness of households to pay for education' (Patrinos, 1999: 6). On the other hand, free public primary schooling is advocated, with demand-side financing mechanisms (such as vouchers, matching grant schemes etc.) proposed to encourage contributions from users of the service. The need to cushion those on low incomes is increasingly recognised. Targeted stipends are advocated, paid directly to households that cannot afford to enrol their children (Patrinos and Ariasingam, 1997; World Bank, 1995). Furthermore, for the World Bank (2001*b*), financial incentives that make it affordable for children to attend school are considered the most effective strategy for overcoming exploitative forms of child labour which is considered to be on the increase as a result of trade liberalisation arising from the neo-liberal agenda since the 1980s.

The U-turn in primary school fees does not appear to be based on an acknowledgement of the problems associated with the theoretical basis of the 1980s neo-liberal model. While the model is no longer explicitly referred to in World Bank documents, the assumptions and concepts on which it is based are implicit in the more recent forms of cost-sharing that are advocated. Investment in human capital continues to be the driving motivation for the pricing policy. The role of the state, in this context, is unresolved and uncertain. While increasing attention is placed on the role of the private sector in education in the post-Washington consensus, a role for the state continues to be envisaged in the setting of national objectives and maintaining educational standards (World Bank, 1999*b*). Governments are still expected to play a part in the financing of education, particularly at the primary level. However, recognition that governments face financial pressures prevails: 'Fiscal considerations, including competing claims on the public purse, make it difficult for most governments—even those whose philosophies might push them in this direction—to be the sole provider of "free" education to all who seek it at every level' (World Bank 1999*b*: 18).

In this context, a change in cost-sharing approaches has occurred from a narrow focus on sharing of costs between the government and households in the 1980s, to more diverse and indirect cost-sharing mechanisms in the 1990s. In particular, a shift in focus from the individual/household to the community as the unit of analysis is evident. For the World Bank (1995: 105, emphasis added):

> Public schools should not, of course, be prohibited from mobilizing resources, in cash or in kind, from local communities when public financing is inadequate and such resources constitute the only means to achieving quality... *Cost-sharing with communities is normally the only exception to free basic education.* Even poor communities are often willing to contribute toward the cost of education, especially at the primary level.

As Dale (1997: 275) points out, a role for communities in school governance and financing has always been evident, with the state never solely responsible for funding, regulation and provision/delivery of education. However, as he suggests, the respective roles for states and communities is changing, with the role of communities becoming formalised and more responsibility being passed to them. Although the rationale for community participation is couched in terms of ownership and accountability, the main objective for the World Bank is to mobilise, and make more efficient use of, resources.

Community participation is likely to be most strongly advocated where the demand for schooling is high, but government inputs are inadequate. It is not coincidental, therefore, that a more explicit emphasis on community participation has corresponded with economic crises which adversely affected education systems in sub-Saharan African countries since the 1980s together with rapid expansion of school systems in the context of the drive for achieving universal primary education and advocacy for the abolition of fees in the 1990s, necessitating the search for alternative sources of resources (Bray, 1996). The post-Washington consensus era has adopted a particular, top-down interpretation of community participation, formalising it through its inclusion in international agreements and promoting it in national policy. Recent international agency interest has changed the nature of community participation by integrating it into the market system through valuing contributions previously made by communities voluntarily (Rose, 2003). Such marketisation is likely to affect the dynamics within a community which could result in further fragmentation, as members compete for resources available, rather than encouraging co-operation (Sayed, 1999). As a result, a shift in the perception of community participation as collective action to individual responsibility is promoted, contradicting the intended goals of accountability, ownership and empowerment. This implies that the focus on education in the post-Washington consensus era continues to support neoliberal principles of individual responsibility for meeting social needs, as previously evident in the support for user fees in the 1980s.

Post- Washington Consensus and Education in Malawi

While the World Bank played less of a direct role in Malawian educational policy in the 1990s compared with previously (partly because of an increase in involvement of other international agencies), the shifts evident in the dominant international agenda continue to be reflected in changes that have occurred in Malawi since the 1990s. There is general acceptance, including by the World Bank and IMF, that reforms undertaken in the 1980s did not have a positive impact on the Malawian economy. By the end of the 1980s, real GDP growth was below the rate of population growth and, in some years, was negative (Harrigan, 2001). The lack of success in implementing proposed reforms during the 1980s was attributed by the World Bank to failure by the government to comply with the programme. Therefore, political reform was considered necessary. Democratic elections were held in 1994, following pressure from international agencies, including the World Bank, who were threatening to withdraw non-humanitarian aid.

With the election of a new government in 1994, a World Bank-supported poverty alleviation programme was established (Ministry of Economic

Planning and Development, 1995). The poverty alleviation programme placed attention on the importance of education in reducing poverty. However, neo-liberal principles continue to predominate. Despite the government's hostility to the programmes, the country had little choice but to continue with liberalisation and privatisation reforms supported by the IMF and World Bank into the 1990s, given its dependence on balance of payments support (Harrigan, 2001). An important aspect of the election promise was the abolition of primary school fees. Following their election, the new government fulfilled this promise, implementing a programme of non-fee primary education. Given that this corresponded with the international agenda, support from donors was forthcoming. Following the abolition of fees, enrolment increased by 50% (Figure 70. 1), with a similar proportionate increase in the number of teachers—the majority of whom were now untrained.

Following the total abolition of fees in 1994, government resources faced the dual challenge of needing to provide additional resources for the massive increase in enrolment, as well as to compensate for the loss in fee income. The government met this challenge by increasing resources available to education, particularly at the primary level. Total government recurrent expenditure to education increasing from less than 10% in the late 1980s to 21% by 1994, over 60% of which was allocated to primary schooling (Table 70.2). This was largely achieved as a result of the support of international agencies, which were providing up to 40% of the resources for education. The increase in expenditure at the primary level was not, however, initially sufficient to compensate for the increase in enrolment. This resulted in a decline in expenditure per pupil by one-quarter, although subsequently increasing to a similar level to the early 1990s (Table 70.2).

Although children are entering school in vast numbers, and almost all children now spend some time in school, many leave before they are likely to have obtained basic literacy and numeracy skills. Given, existing dropout and repetition rates through the primary cycle, only half of all children who start school reach standard 3, and less than one-fifth are expected to complete the primary cycle. Fewer girls than boys are completing. As mentioned, low retention rates were, however, evident even before the introduction of FPE, and worsened after the fee increase in 1982. Therefore, despite these low survival rates, the absolute number of children completing the primary cycle has almost doubled following the abolition of fees. Although coverage improved, quality, which was already low, deteriorated even further. In addition, the emphasis on primary schooling has implications for other levels of education where resources have become even more constrained. Private schooling has grown at the primary level by default rather than design, mainly because of low quality of government schools. However, the extent of growth is unknown because many of these schools are unregistered and, therefore, unregulated by the government.

Community participation in education has been receiving increased attention in Malawi through various routes, including the World Bank-supported cross-sectoral Malawi Social Action Fund, the Poverty Reduction Strategy Paper (PRSP), DFID and USAID-supported community school programmes, and the Education Policy Investment Framework. Concerns about financial pressures following the abolition of fees have resulted in the national education policy giving explicit attention to the role that communities can and should play in delivering education. Paradoxically, the continued and intensified focus on community participation in policy has occurred without the involvement of different stakeholders, including teachers, parents, communities, local leaders and NGOs involved in education, in policy formulation, with the Ministry of Education and international agencies continuing to dominate decision-making and planning (Kadzamira and Rose, 2001). Thus, decisions about the forms of participation are being made in a top-down fashion. As recent evidence shows, rather than resulting in increased ownership and accountability as intended, community participation in Malawi has continued to be a way to extract resources in the 1990s (Rose, 2003).

Post-post Washington Consensus?: Global Education Industry

Education is increasingly seen as big business in the context of a global economy in the twenty-first century. Presentations by World Bank staff, for example, point out that the global education market place is equal to $2 trillion, with 15% of the global education market in developing countries (Patrinos, 2000). Most of the trade in education services has been in foreign students attending higher education and training institutions in other countries and, more recently, enrolled in distance education programmes at universities in other countries. Despite the apparent prioritisation of primary education since the 1990s, the 'global education industry' has placed a renewed emphasis by the World Bank on technical and higher education. This is evident, for example, in the 1998/9 World Development Report on Knowledge for Development which proposes that basic education 'should not monopolize a nation's attention as it becomes a player in global markets' (World Bank, 1999*a*: 42). Rather, it is proposed that higher levels of education deserve increased attention because of the need to adapt to and apply new information-based technologies.

As a result of the focus on a global education industry, even greater emphasis has been placed on privatisation of education in the international arena in recent years. This has occurred with respect to the promotion of free trade in goods and services (WTO, 1998; Patrinos, 1999). The World Bank (2000), for example, calls for a 'lighter touch' in regulating higher education suggesting that countries remove restrictions of private provision of education services. The World Trade Organisation's (WTO) General Agreement on Trade in Services (GATS) is influential in promoting the market in education. Its memo on Education Services (1998) indicates the intention to create the conditions for greater liberalisation of the trade in education and to create a market system of educational provision, particularly in higher education. The WTO and World Bank consider that it is important for countries to remove barriers to trade in education in order to promote competition (see, for example, Patrinos 1999). The WTO is, however, defensive about its intentions in the education sector (WTO, 2001). As it points out, fewer than fifty of WTO members have made commitments to education which it suggests, reflecting the fact that education is regarded as essentially a function of the state in many countries. While little is known of the implications of the WTO's role in the education sector in practice, it is evident that it is reinforcing a discourse of a market for education goods and services.

In Malawi, where there are only four telephone lines per 1,000 people, a nine-year waiting list for a telephone, 1.2 personal computers per 1,000 people (compared with an average of 9.2 in sub-Saharan Africa) and just 15,000 of the population of 10 million have ISP registered addresses (World Bank, 2002), it is questionable whether ICTs will play a major role for the majority of the population in the foreseeable future. This suggests that the international emphasis on the role of ICTs in education could widen local and global inequality with poor countries such as Malawi suffering, an issue which warrants urgent investigation.

Conclusion

> ***The flame of human capital theory has been kept alight in the corridors of the Bank partially through the devotion of those analysts committed to manifesting its pertinence through cost-benefit analyses of educational expenditures... human capital theory has served a useful institutional purpose, irrespective of its dated and limited theoretical character. (Jones, 1992: 234)***

The notion of human capital through the application of rates of return analysis has permitted the Bank to justify its role in education since the 1980s. This emphasis is not surprising given that the Bank is regulated by the rules of a bank which means it has to find economic justification for its loans. However, the narrow focus on economic efficiency and equity aspects risks neglecting important features of education. The processes of teaching and learning, which transform inputs into outputs, remain outside the scope of the Bank's approach to education, leaving the black box of educational provision firmly shut. For countries such as Malawi, the emphasis on human capital and prioritisation of primary schooling has resulted in a significant expansion of education systems. However, this has been at the expense of quality which has not been adequately addressed.

Furthermore, a focus on human capital has shifted from a traditional view of education as cultivating social integration and cohesion, and forging new notions of national citizenship and identity, to a means of individual and collective economic advancement (Green, 1997).

Although human capital theory has not been as uncontroversial as World Bank documents imply (see, for example, Bowles and Gintis, 1976; Blaug, 1976), criticism has been less forthcoming than might be anticipated. By treating educational provision as a stream of costs and benefits, both to individuals and society as a whole, which ignores the social relations within and around education, neo-liberal economists show no understanding of the educational process. The black box of how education is provided remains firmly shut other than in the labelling of financial costs and benefits (Fine and Rose, 2001).

As noted, social factors have been increasingly recognised in relation to education since the 1990s. Just as the post-Washington consensus has permitted a populist notion of neo-liberalism more generally, within education, the terms such as 'participation' are touted to provide a human face to World Bank operations in education. However, the notion of human capital and associated application of rates of return has continued to permit an economic rationale for the World Bank's involvement in education. The more this occurs, the more human capital theory undermines its own analytical starting point in terms of understanding education in terms of costs and benefits. Human capital exponents have attempted to bring social factors back in, rather than addressing the broader historical, political, economic and social environment in which education operates, resulting in continued emphasis on individual responsibility for meeting social needs.

NOTES

1. A focus on the World Bank in this [chapter] does not intend to underplay the role played by other international agencies, but rather to highlight the central role played by a key actor in the global development process. See, for example, Mundy (1998) and Jones (1988) for UNESCO's influence in international educational priorities. However, by the 1980s, the World Bank had taken the lead both in terms of its own research and superior access to other information and other research, as well as in relation to the volume of loans which had grown substantially. It is also recognised that the World Bank is not a monolithic organisation. However, as Samoff (1992) points out, although there may be internal disagreements about approaches within the World Bank, the general orientation and consequences of World Bank-supported research and funding have important implications for developing countries.
2. The controversial resignation of Stiglitz from the World Bank in November 1999 raises a question about the status of the post-Washington consensus in his absence. On the one hand, the continued close ties between the 1998 Nobel Prize winner for economics, Amartya Sen, and President James Wolfensohn, indicates that Sen's broader view of development is influential, at least at a rhetorical level. On the other hand, the subsequent resignation of Ravi Kanbur as editor of the 2000/1 World Development Report on 'Attacking Poverty' has highlighted the continued domination of the World Bank by the US treasury (headed at the time by the former World Bank chief economist, Lawrence Summers) which sought editorial control of the report. This has reinforced the view that the World Bank has never really let go of the Washington consensus, with a strengthening of progrowth arguments at the expense of attention to post-Washington consensus concepts such as empowerment in redrafting (Wade, 2001).
3. The post-Washington consensus has resonances with the views put forward by McNamara, former President of the World Bank, over two decades previously, in the context of a focus on the basic needs approach to development.

Education for Positive Conflict and Interruptive Democracy

Lynn Davies

This chapter summarises the 'lessons learned' from exploring the relationship between education and conflict, and sets out my proposals for a type of education which can begin to address them. The insights and concepts from complexity theory have formed the basis for this analysis. A bald summary of my argument is that education indirectly does more to contribute to the underlying causes of conflict than it does to contribute to peace. This is through reproduction of economic inequality and the birfurcation of wealth/poverty; through magnifying ethnic and religious segregation or intolerance; through the promotion of a particular version of hegemonic masculinity and gender segregation; and through competitive individualism rather than cooperation. In complexity terms, schools and education systems are adaptive, but they tend towards equilibrium rather than radical emergence; hence at best they do not challenge existing social patterns which are generative of conflict. At worst, they act as amplifying mechanisms.

At the direct interface between conflict and education, some contradictions can however be found. Schools are obviously gravely affected by national or international conflict, but some are resilient; and while most schools are at root engaged in war education through militarisation and competitiveness, some are also engaged in peace education through particular emphases in their curricula or through the organisation of their school. There is evidence of human agency and resistance to prevailing trends. Lessons can also be learned from specific educational endeavours during times of conflict or post-conflict; one clear one is that these have to be aimed at 'emergence', not at returning to the situation which contributed to the conflict in the first place. At the individual level, people can be helped to find personal emergence from trauma or from the experience of war; and at the societal level, groups can be enabled to reconstruct new relationships and new forms of governance. The equally plain message is that such emergence in the end has to come from within. While outside intervention can facilitate the process of change, the creativity, the self-organized criticality, comes from enhanced connectivities *within* an organisation or group. Top-down, imposed packages, even of peace education, will generate adaptivity, but this is not guaranteed to shift a complex system to new forms of working and thinking unless most or all are somehow involved in finding a 'fitness of purpose'.

I would propose a theory of 'complexity shutdown'—that negative and sustained conflict is caused by a breakdown in connectivity and in complex information processing. This would indeed explain the paradox that has emerged from exploring education and conflict: that formal education in peace-time is more likely to add to conflict than is non-formal education in conflict-time. This is

This chapter has been adapted from Davies, C. (2003), the conclusion to *Conflict and Education: Complexity and Chaos* (London: Routledge).

because much formal education is about destroying connectivity—between the wealthy and the poor, between different ethnic or religious groups, between males and females, between the 'able' and the 'less able'. Educational initiatives post-conflict on the other hand can be genuinely about inclusion: trying to heal and reintegrate the traumatised, the child soldiers or the refugees, and trying to build cohesive political and public cultures. It can be seen that post-conflict education is less about selection and 'standards' and more about co-operation and encounters.

I am not optimistic therefore that formal schooling as currently constructed can ever 'solve' problems of world peace. Without a massive dismantling of the whole examination system and a radical rethinking of the goals of education, the most it could achieve—probably—is to do no further harm (as we have argued for school leadership, Harber and Davies 2003). But complexity theory does talk about amplification and the butterfly effect. Small steps *might* achieve an evolutionary breakthrough, or at least a curb on the current seemingly inexorable trends towards warfare through schooling. One does not want to see schools increasing their military spending (on steel barriers, detention units and weapons of mass boredom).

Greater expenditure on peace is unlikely—and how this would be done is not always clear (National Lottery funds for peace groups?). But in a formal education system one has already a massive potential resource. Mostly we have blown it in favour of the deep fries of academic competition, the safety play, the comfort food, the portion control. If one accepts the underlying premise that there is an urgency in finding a 'fitness of purpose' for education that will help to challenge destructive conflict—globally, nationally and organisationally—then we should try to identify some means towards this. How can we get schools out of the 'attractor state' of fostering negative conflict? How can schools reach the edge of chaos to become something new? How can young (and older) people emerge from educational institutions more inclined to challenge injustice and violence?

The answer to this is that in order to restore complexity and connectivity, schools should foster *positive* conflict. My argument will be that a particular form of democracy, which I shall term 'interruptive democracy' is the best way to foster such positive conflict. First, I outline the case for positive conflict as, paradoxically, the best way to counter negative conflict.

Positive/Constructive Conflict

Positive conflict has a number of backers, although not so many within educational circles. There is a long tradition of the use of conflict within organisations generally (De Dreu 1997), but perhaps educational organisations have been less swift to espouse this, given that actual and potential relationships with pupils make conflict a daily feature more akin to prison management rather than civil service management. Conflict is seen as dysfunctional, with harmony as the official goal, and uneasy truce as the unofficial one. There is a dilemma for schools in that the control function is so visible. Increasingly nowadays, as for other organisations, there is a focus on not just harmony but on harmonisation, standardisation, compliance. Inspection and quality control will look for congruent procedures. There is little room for creative individuality or agreement to differ. Yet of course conflict resolution is not just an end in itself, but a creative force for overall positive change. In theory, resolving a conflict, say between teachers and pupils, should not just be about minimising that particular disruption but about leading to better ways of interacting, so that negative conflicts occur less often.

Yet many writers on conflict have pointed out the difficulty that people have in seeing it as a positive force. This can be because of media concentration on violent events (Fountain 1995); because of people being unaccustomed to confronting conflict and a cultural tendency to avoid uncomfortable situations (Folger et al. 1993); and in schools, because of its association with psycho-pathology, social disorder and war (Deutsch 1991).

Étienne Grosjean, in writing about cultural specificity, is quite dogmatic about this: Conflict

> Cannot be seen as a mere accident that can be removed or reduced, if it arises, by wisdom or prudence. It must now be recognized as an ordinary 'force field'. In other words, conflict is part of the nature of things and is inextricably linked with all forms of development and the working out of human destiny. Peace can never again be equated with the absence of conflict.

It will either take the form of creative, positive and constructive conflict management or not exist at all. (1995: 22)

Similarly, for Rupesinghe, peace building can be seen as 'Transforming violence into creative, militant, positive non-violence' (1995: 90) in contrast to pacifism or just a cease-fire.

In looking at conflict theory and Marxist theory, Adams (1991) celebrates their bringing of conflict to a position of prominence. But 'it may still be difficult to avoid viewing protest as abnormal, an aberration or disturbance' (p. 15). For complexity theory, disturbance is indeed important—but it is disturbance as a normal event in the process of change. Murphy contends that confronting change, stress and conflict is central to human experience:

Children thrive on change and novel experience, and are traumatized critically by the crude, aggressive, violent and violating repression of their attempts at freedom of experience, perception and expression, and the heavy-handed imposition of pre-set norms, perceptions and practices. If, as children, our learning experiences promoted continuous cultural transformation as a value, and nurtured our natural inclination to participate in and thrive on change, there would be little trauma attached to living in a society in which change was accepted as a cultural norm. (1999: 82)

What would this mean for educational policy? Fisher et al. (2000) make a significant distinction between *intensifying conflict* and *escalating conflict. Intensifying conflict* means making a hidden conflict more visible and open, for purposeful, non-violent ends (e.g. when people are doing well and have enough power and resources, and do not notice—or refuse to acknowledge—that others are disadvantaged or marginal). *Escalating conflict* refers to a situation in which levels of tension and violence are increasing (because of inadequate channels for dialogue, instability, injustice and fear in the wider community). It would seem that 'intensifying conflict' has a purposive aim to shake people from complacency or apathy, passivity or fatalism. Linked to Murphy's argument, it is about the promotion of cultural transformation as a norm, not a problem.

I quite like another sort of relevant distinction made, that between *negative duties* and *positive duties*. Writers on educational leadership such as Hwang (2001) go back to Kantian philosophy for this demarcation. Negative duties are those that simply require abstention from action (do not kill, do not harm, do not steal). This is a legitimate reason to restrain free will. Because they are compulsory, negative duties are also known as 'perfect duties' in Kant's analysis of morality. Positive duties on the other hand are 'imperfect duties', as they are basically duties of 'commission' rather than omission. They are difficult to define and predict: and not everyone can perform positive duties because of lack of opportunity and skill. And in Western individualism, an individual has a right to choose whether to perform certain positive duties (Miller 1994). Yet we may want to look at shifting school rules more from negative prohibitions ('do not run in the corridors') to positive duties ('think of ways that increase safety for others').

Civic education and peace education need to act as a reminder that all of us are 'co-creators of history' and could have a part to play in the resolution of problems that afflict us. 'There will be no peace in Afghanistan, for example, unless transitional authorities work out ways in which they can consult with and incorporate the views of a broad cross-section of Afghani ethnic, age and gender diversity into the discussions' (Clements 2001: 15). Peace and security have to become everyone's business—for ownership and for the practice of positive duties.

[...]

Democracy and Complexity

Before looking at education and democracy, I want to link the theoretical framework of complexity with democracy generally, as complexity theory enables us to see what versions of democracy would be valuable in promoting peace. There is no guarantee that democracy will prevent armed conflict. The USA, UK, France, Sweden are all supposedly democratic countries and yet still contribute to the arms race and to making conflict in other countries more likely. They have elected governments that need to stay in power and will do so by various means. Complexity theory shows us how non-linear political systems such as democracy can have unpredictable outcomes. The problem with the types of democracy that do not challenge war is that they do not have sufficiently active civil societies nor mechanisms for constant challenge and public accountability. It is not as if there is a silenced intellectual class—for the universities also make a living from 'defence' research.

While there is then with representative democracy the possibility of electing or removing leaders, the major question for global survival is how we can elect leaders that are not bent on destruction. The majority of people may see war as 'winnable'. At the height of the India–Pakistan tension in 2002, Burke and Beaumont quoted a former Indian Chief of Staff as saying that 'War is one game that you cannot lose or draw, especially if you are the bigger country'. Crushing victories are not just possible but essential. At that stage, both sides were psychologically committed to conflict, and had entered a 'war mindset', neither seeing any sense (Burke and Beaumont 2002). Even when the electorate do not support a war, four-year cycles of voting are too slow to remove belligerent leaders, as was found with leadership on the Iraq war in UK.

In his discussion of complexity theory with regard to development, Rihani (2002) interestingly dismisses democracy as 'too vague for the present purpose' (p. 165). His critique seems to stem from the fact that democracy as a concept has been abused throughout history; that so-called democratic states act undemocratically outside their own territory; that there is a danger of oppression by the majority; that it is perceived as a Western concept that cannot be transplanted to other cultures. All this may be true, but this is the equivalent of saying we should not accede to notions of 'freedom' or to 'rights', because people use the notion of freedom or rights falsely and for their own ends. The problem is not with democracy (and rights) itself nor its underpinning principles; it is a problem of how it is used, taught, learned, interpreted (Davies 1999). Rihani obviously accedes to the centrality of rights, but for the development of a country pays more attention to the freedom and capability to interact for members of populations, to be able to exercise flexibility and pragmatism. He acknowledges that change in complex adaptive systems (CAS) can lead to inequality and the emergence of elites, as those with the 'greatest complexity' stand to make the greatest gain. But monitoring is important, as the management of a CAS is essentially a 'reiterative' process leading to frequent but minor adjustments to encourage local interactions to proceed optimally. Rigid long-term plans, and command and control economies are counter-indicated. For me, the democratic process is actually the one most likely to lead to the necessary 'frequent but minor adjustments'.

This responsiveness and 'reiteration' links with a number of characteristics of a complex democracy. Alex de Waal (1996) claims that India (unlike parts of Africa) has not suffered famine for more than forty years, because it has a free press and democratic or adversarial political institutions which mean pressure on government to do something about it. Collier posits that 'democratisation is worth around half a century of income growth in terms of its contribution to peace' (1998: 18). This would be not just because of adversarial politics (far from it), but because of various sorts of transparencies and procedural claims. In our work on democratisation of teacher education (Davies, Harber and Schweisfurth 2002) we outlined four principles: equity, rights, informed choice and active participation in decision-making. All of these overlap, but all are essential. Participation without respect for rights can be non-challenging (there was massive popular participation in Hitler's Germany); and simply giving choices of voting without information is no real choice. Demanding rights without a concern for equity and reciprocity in those rights is also inimical to democracy.

Complexity theory can therefore actually explain the success of particular *modes* of democracy. One is the localisation of decision-making. For Rihani, the logic of complexity is that 'healthy' change in social, political and economic life takes place at the local level and is driven by local actors. I enjoy the banners saying 'Join the World wide movement against globalization': there is a tension of wanting local interactions yet needing wider networks. But certainly the notion of only one 'fitness landscape' which matches some versions of globalization (McDonaldisation) does not meet the demands for creativity and emergence. It seems a cry for decentralisation; but also for transparency and democracy in those local interactions, if national self-serving or corrupt elites are not to be replaced by local self-serving or corrupt elites. A CAS will not just be a massive amount of internal interaction, but freedom to interact *within rules that command support*. How can it arrive at such rules without some sort of democratic process? Without them, interaction and innovation on their own can simply feed inequality and power differentials—leading to negative conflict. The Brazilian model of participatory democracy, while grassroots and localised, has a strong value base as well as linkages to the centre (Hatcher 2002). Those organisations or countries that have created ombudsmen to represent the interests of citizens or children (as citizens) provide the central arrangements for local redress (for example the Instituto Libertad y Democracia in Peru, or the Children's Ombudsman in Norway). Here and elsewhere (Davies and Kirkpatrick 2000) I therefore argue for national legislation around student voice and pupil democracy, to ensure the universal rules by which local voices can be heard.

Another link between complexity and democracy is the exploitation of diversity. Complex adaptive systems, for evolution and emergence, need diversity in order to be able to test ideas, experiment, have new combinations. The notion of diversity therefore has to be protected, although—and this is a significant point—not necessarily all the actual components within each diverse body. If aspects of that diversity are redundant, then new creative forms emerge. In social terms, this means that cultural diversity is not to be retained unthinkingly and at all costs. All aspects of a culture need constant examining and possible revision to establish fitness. So there is no such thing as a cultural imperative. Everything is conditional. This is highly uncomfortable for many people, although a great relief to others caught in the 'frozen accidents' of gender, religion or caste.

[...]

The arguments for democracy in terms of a complex adaptive system that can both survive and move forward are, in summary, fourfold:

- the localisation of decision-making;
- very high participation and connectivity, with rich information channels;
- a system of agreed rules that apply to all (and therefore a respect for rights); and
- the ever-present possibility of making changes to rules, procedures, cultures and leaders to provide a better fitness landscape.

Interruptive Democracy in Education

It is particularly this last point which leads to me to propose a notion of 'interruptive democracy' as the basis for the complex adaptive school. I define interruptive democracy as '*the process by which people are enabled to break into practices which continue injustice*'. It is an 'in-your-face' democracy—not just taking part, but having the disposition to challenge. It is the democracy of the hand shooting up, the 'excuse-me' reflex. It is the 'outrage' against social injustice identified by OXFAM in their definition of the global citizen. It is by definition non-linear, finding spaces for dissent, resilience and action. A host of challenges have emerged from the analysis of the relationship between education and conflict: challenges to quasi-market ideologies, class injustice, ethnic oppression, war-like masculinity, essentialist identities, the militarisation of the mind, runaway norms, frozen struggles, threat inflation. For education, interruptive democracy combines four elements: the handling of identity and fear; the need for deliberation and dialogue; the need for creativity, play and humour, and the impetus for a defiant agency. [...]

Identity Building and the Handling of Difference

Let me look first of all at the immense question of identity, which permeates the whole discussion of the roots and effects of conflict. What emerges always is the paradox that a secure identity is needed in order to be less likely to be aggressive towards others; and yet that the 'essentialising' of identity can equally be a cause of conflict. While it is convenient to be able to say that we should all acknowledge our multiple identities, it is not as simple as that. We do need a base to start.

Ozacky-Lazar (2001) argues in her work bringing together Jewish and Arab young people that you need to build internal culture. 'We realized that when someone is very sure about his/her own culture, it's much easier to meet the other side. We first build Jewish national identity—as Jews from whatever region. For Palestinians this is a serious problem. They've never had their own state, but identify themselves as Muslims, Christians or a minority' (p. 21). Initially one might feel uneasy about such culture building—could it not so easily spill over into nationalism? Yet it might be true that hostility comes from insecurity about one's culture or nation, from the desire and need to prove and mark an identity. If one is secure, one can take a joke. If not, it is perceived as insult, which I return to later. Identities can be complementary, those that one wants to be engaged with; or a self can invoke a wholly alien other, with a voice that is heard as 'sickness, inferiority or evil' (Connolly 1991: 64). As Cockburn points out, 'if you lack a secure self, are caught up in inner conflict, you are likely to disown the hated or feared parts of yourself and project them onto the unknown "other"' (1998: 214). We can see this clearly in the discussion of masculinity, where young men disown any tendency towards a female or homosexual inclination within themselves and react adversely or violently towards others who display such identities more obviously. There seems initially a contradiction here: I have argued that schools promote masculinity; yet this does not seem to make boys secure. What in fact happens is that by *not* interrupting hegemonic, idealised versions, schools reinforce boys' aspirations to what are actually unattainable goals.

The obvious message for a school community is to provide that sense of secure self which does not project deficiency onto others. It will not do this while it labels some pupils as low ability, or exclusionary material. The coercive labelling is actually getting worse in UK under the targetting regime. We all fear failure, isolation, ostracism; but in schools this is played on by teachers and students alike. The result is *exclusionary* collective identities, rather than overlapping or cooperative ones. Schools are actually probably better at affirming cultural diversity than they are at affirming 'academic' diversity, as the latter is in fact impossible under any rationing or screening function. Yet the negative, fearful identities that emerge from this are those that are hostage to the securities of various sorts of fundamentalisms.

[...]

The next part is then the handling of difference and diversity. Here I might debate with Cockburn. She argues that for democracy to work, universalism must transcend difference, defining all subjects as equal before the law. But she then says you need to 'reinstate' difference as a higher-order value which encompasses equality through 'a relational and dialogical ethic of care, compassion and responsibility'. This is not diametrically opposed but 'embedded'. Yet I am not sure why difference has to be a 'higher-order value' rather than a parallel one: it seems to me the old rights-and-responsibilities dualism: rights are the universals, responsibilities acknowledge the differences. Democracy does not revert to cultural relativism, or 'anything goes', but—precisely because of the universal principles of rights and equity—is able to provide the mechanism to *question* culture and difference when these appear to do harm. Democracy is not only a principled politics, but a practical one: built into the process is the means to mount a challenge when the differences get too big, and when the claims around diversity takes over from the common rights. This is the 'interruptive' part.

To avoid essentialism, the argument by Yuval-Davis (1997) is that we need 'transversal politics' rather than 'identity politics'. This denies that *social* positioning (for example, being a woman) can automatically be conflated with *personal* values (for example, being a feminist). Transversal politics, across very complex divides, is based on the recognition that each positioning (say, of an ethnicity, or gender) produces specific situated 'knowledges'; but that these knowledges *cannot but be unfinished*—and therefore dialogue should take place in order to reach a common perspective. Transversal dialogue should be based on the principles of 'rooting and shifting'—that is, being centred (rooted) in one's own experiences while being empathetic (able to shift) to the differential positionings of the partners in the dialogue. I think this notion of 'unfinished knowledge' is a crucial aspect of good democratic education: schools all too often present knowledge as finished (and individuals as lacking if they do not have it), rather than everything as tentative—even identities. There are strong parallels to Freire: 'Problem-posing education affirms men and women as beings in the process of becoming—as unfinished, uncompleted beings in and with a likewise unfinished reality' (2001: 77). A hybrid identity is also unfinished too, with hybridity not a complete form, but recombinant, in the genetic analogy. In dialogue, the key would seem to be to replace 'who one is' with 'what one's experiences are'. This sharing of experience and pain has been seen as crucial in dialogue across conflict lines.

The issues for education are to recognise subtleties and unfinishedness in complex identity, and not to portray the apparent 'absence' of one strand of a possible identity as an 'empty space'. There are no empty spaces, only different configurations. Atheism is a positive identity as much as religion. By providing avenues for voice, interruptive democracy in schools would constantly call into question who supposedly 'lacks' what in terms of learning and contribution.

The implications are for a 'critical pedagogy', or the 'border pedagogy' of Giroux (1991). A pedagogy of difference surfaces quite blatantly all aspects of our hybridity, and enables young people to analyse class, 'race', gender, 'ability' or 'special needs' in order to understand the sources of inequality and the sources of conflict. Carrim argues that an anti-racist pedagogy of 'difference' would not compromise theoretical and academic rigour even if rationality is 'pluralised' and differences in meanings are allowed. This would, however, entail 'a more skills driven, instead of a content driven, form of assessment' (1995: 33).

So interrupting essentialist identities in schools is done through

- surfacing and valuing hybrid identities in all of us (including teachers);
- providing means to belong, but *not* giving essentialist or exclusionary academic identities, and particularly not 'empty' ones;
- a good social science or political education curriculum which enables critical discussion of identity and difference, and of different experience across borders;
- *not* having a multicultural curriculum that presents cultures as finished and untouchable and impermeable by others;
- a transversal politics of learning which means the constant responsibility of learners towards each other, through mentors, guardians, peer tutors, cooperative groups and so on.

Creativity, Play, Humour and Anti-Dogmatism

[Next] Creativity [. . .] was one of Dimitrov's 'fuzzy' components of a human CAS, together with willingness to engage in dialogue and willingness to act together. The components of creativity involve fresh ideas and new formulations (including metaphors, imagery, paradoxes, humour, jokes and story telling). This not only helps the enrichment and the variety of options, but begins the process of moving together in a group and acting together in a world where relativity, complexity and uncertainty are 'inevitable companions'.

Porter (1999) argues for the 'reflexive school' and the reflective teacher training college, which can enable young people to cope with globalisation and the threat to self-identity and even survival which comes from competitive economies that prevent democracies establishing a global consensus around human concerns and rights. Such reflexiveness requires acknowledgement of multiple intelligences and in particular, emotional intelligence. It requires a professional teaching force, not one that is deskilled and controlled. For Porter, decentralisation is essential, to provide a flexibility and creativity released from political agendas and dogmas, as well as for a more participant democracy.

But I think we need to establish how 'reflexivity' happens. As well as the furthering of emotional intelligence that comes from dialogue and encounter, I would argue for play and humour. The huge importance of play in the process of healing has been revealed; and the 'child soldiers' of so-called normal schools in normal societies also need this on a daily basis to counter hurt. It is significant that Adams analyses pupil protest as, in part, a 'game'—locating it with expressive rather than purely instrumental concerns. Protest as a game 'challenges the reality of the institutionalised process of schooling in several ways.' It is voluntary and superfluous, and may interrupt the competitiveness of the curriculum or reinforce it. Like play, protest is 'played out' with its own course and meanings. And acts of protest, once finished, 'become part of pupils' memories, and like other games, are transmissable as traditions' (1991: 11).

[. . .]

The Doing Word: Agency

The components of interruptive democracy so far (identity work, deliberation and, creativity) are not then enough without this disposition to act. Interrupting dogma within the school is logically linked to the capacity to protest in a range of arenas. Salmi reports confidently that 'authoritarian governments have been overthrown, for instance in Korea and Thailand, as a result of student protest' (1999: 12). This cannot surely be the only cause of government decline, but does it give grounds for hope and agency?

For Byrne (1998), the idea of citizenship must include within it the possibility that the political actions of citizens matter in terms of determining the course of events. He claims that increasingly this is not true. There is a crisis of political engagement, both in terms of visible actions by people, most notably in the decline in voting, and in relation to the actual content of politics itself. Labour is seeking 'to replace the deliberative democracy of its annual policy forming conference with a combination of fan club rally and "policy forums" [sic]. ... In these processes the citizen who acts becomes replaced by the passive consumer whose action is confined to choice among available product suppliers, with the produce being distinguished by superficial packaging rather than essential content' (Byrne 1998: 151). In contrast, interruptive democracy and action would stem from the engagement or outrage mentioned earlier, not just from passive 'choosing'. So perhaps every day we should do a small thing. I remember the buzz when I found out you could email Ariel Sharon directly (in my case to protest about the destruction of olive trees on Palestinian land). It will make not a jot of difference, I know; but I *felt* agentic, and this spreads to other areas of life.

In education, a particular form of critical pedagogy becomes the key to a disposition to act. Apple (2002) describes teaching immediately after 9/11 and how he wanted his students to appreciate fully the fact that the US-led embargo of Iraq had caused the death of thousands upon thousands of children each year that it had been in place. He wanted them to understand how US policies in the Middle East and in Afghanistan itself had helped create truly murderous consequences. However, he realised too that unless their feelings of anger and their understandings were voiced and taken seriously, the result could be 'exactly the opposite of what any decent teacher wants'.

> Instead of a more complicated understanding of the lives of people who are among the most oppressed in the world—often as a result of Western and Northern economic policies ... students could be led to reject any critical contextual understanding largely because the pedagogical politics seemed arrogant. In my experiences both as an activist and a scholar, this has happened more often than some theorists of 'critical pedagogy' would like to admit. (Apple 2002: 4).

Fortunately, the majority of students were willing to re-examine their anger, to put themselves in the place of the oppressed, to take their more critical and nuanced understandings and put them into action. A striking result was a coalition of students being forced to engage in concrete action in their own schools and communities to interrupt the growing anti-Islamic and jingoistic dynamics that were present even in progressive areas.

Conclusion: The Interruptive School

Education on its own will not solve world peace. Nor will a school be able to heal and control children living in violent or drug-related communities. I am not over-romanticising the possibilities for schools. But I do think they can interrupt the processes towards more violence. Putting all the above together, the features of the interruptive school are tenfold:

1. The existence of a wide range of forums for positive conflict (councils, circle time, representation on governing bodies, representation on curriculum committees, going to Youth Parliaments, support for school student unions).
2. The provision of organised and frequent ways to generate dialogue, deliberation, connectivity, argument, information exchange, empathy, feedback and listening between students, between teachers in front of students, and between teachers and students *as encounters between equals*.

3. The encouragement of avenues for belonging which are not exclusionary or segregated, and the promotion of identity which values hybridity, not purity.
4. A critical pedagogy and political education which surfaces inequalities such as class, ethnicity, gender and (dis)ability as well as global inequality, and which contains language and media analysis.
5. An emphasis on human rights, and on active responsibilities to other learners.
6. The learning of conflict mapping and conflict resolution skills and dispositions (for students and teachers) which lead to new behaviours and new reflection.
7. The acknowledgement of unfinished knowledge and unfinished cultures, of fuzzy logic.
8. Creativity, play and humour, both to heal people and to interrupt dogma.
9. The modelling by teachers of protest and resistance, of imperfect duties, of sins of commission, and encouragement of students; to exercise agency against injustice.
10. Risk taking and limit-testing which pushes the school towards the edge of chaos and to creative emergence.

I know schools which do some or all of the above, and am thankful for their inspiration and 'possibility space'. But they are by no means enough at the moment. I do not know whether, if we had enough complex adaptive schools across the world, this would at least *help* to avert conflict and produce generations attuned to alternatives to violence; but I am clear that as they are at the moment, the majority of schools will just be doing their bit for the war effort.

Bibliographical References

Abécassis, F. (1994), 'Approche d'un champ: l'enseignement étranger en Egypte d'après la statistique scolaire de l'Egypte, 1921–1951', *Egypte/Monde Arabe* 18–19: 169–95.

Abrahamson, J. (1974), *Classroom constraints and teacher coping strategies: A way to conceptualize the teaching task*, Ph.D. thesis, University of Chicago.

Abu-Absi, S. (1984), 'Language Planning and Education in the Arab World', *International Education Journal* 1/2: 113–32.

Abu-Lughod, L. (1989), *Before European Hegemony: The World System A.D. 1250–1350* (New York: Oxford University Press).

Acemoglu, D. (2002), 'Technical Change, Inequality and the Labour Market', *Journal of Economic Literature* 40 (March), 7–72.

Acheson, D. (1998), *Independent Inquiry into Inequalities in Health* (London: HM Stationery Office).

Achieving the Lisbon Goal: The Contribution of VET (2004) (London: Qualifications and Curriculum Authority).

Achtenhagen, F., and Grubb, W. N. (2001), 'Vocational and Occupational Education: Pedagogical Complexity, Institutional Indifference', in V. Richardson (ed.), *Handbook of Research on Teaching*, 4th edn. (Washington, DC: American Educational Research Association), 176 206.

Acker, S. (1996), 'Teachers and Gender', in M. Apple (ed.), *Review of Research in Education* 21 (Washington: American Educational Research Association).

—— (2000), *Realities of Teaching: Never a Dull Moment* (London: Cassell).

—— and Feureverger, G. (1997), 'Doing Good and Feeling Bad: The Work of Women University Teachers', *Cambridge Journal of Education* 26/3: 401–22.

Acosta, A. (1999), 'La increible y triste historia de America Latina y su perversa deuda externa', *Socialismo y Participación* 85, August, 29–48.

Adair, V. C. (2002), 'Branded with Infamy: Inscriptions of Poverty and Class in the United States', *Signs: Journal of Women in Culture and Society* 27: 451–71.

Adams, H., and Marshall, A. (1998) 'Off-target Messages: Poverty, Risk and Sexual Rights', *Agenda* 39: 87–92.

Adams, R. (1991), *Protests By Pupils: Empowerment, Schooling and the State* (London: Falmer).

Adamson, B., and Auyeung-Lai, W. (1997), 'Language and the Curriculum in Hong Kong: Dilemmas of Triglossia', in M. Bray and W. O. Lee (eds.), *Education and Political Transition: Implications of Hong Kong's Change of Sovereignty* (Hong Kong: Comparative Education Research Centre, Hong Kong University).

Adelzadeh, A., Alvillar, C., and Mather, C. (2001), 'Poverty Alleviation, Employment Creation and Sustainable Livelihoods in South Africa', in M. M. Khosa (ed.), *Empowerment through Economic Transformation* (Durban: African Millennium Press), 229–48.

Adick, Ch. (1992), 'Modern Education in "Non-Western" Societies in the Light of the World Systems Approach in Comparative Education', *International Review of Education* 38/3: 242–55.

Africa and Human Rights Watch (1995), *Children in Sudan: Slaves, Street Children and Child Soldiers* (New York: Human Rights Watch).

Aggleton, P. (1987), *Rebels without a Cause* (London: Falmer).

Aglietta, M. (1979), *A Theory of Capitalist Regulation: The US Experience* (London: New Left Books).

Agre, P. E. (1997), 'Computing as a Social Practice', in P. E. Agre and D. Schuler (eds.), *Reinventing Technology, Rediscovering Community: Critical Explorations of Computing as a Social Practice* (Greenwich, Conn: Ablex Publishing).

Ahier, J., and Moore, R. (1999), 'Post 16 Education, Semi-Dependent Youth and the Privatisation of Inter-age Transfers: Re-theorising Youth Transition', *British Journal of Sociology of Education*, 20/4: 515–30.

Ahleit, P. (1994), *Taking the Knocks: Youth Unemployment and Biography—a Qualitative Analysis* (London: Cassell).

Ahmad, A. (1987), 'Jameson's Rhetoric of otherness and the "National Allegory"', *Social Text* 17: 3–25.

Ainley, P., Gokulsing, M., and Tysome, T. (1996), *Beyond Competence: The NCVQ Framework and the Challenge to Higher Education in the New Millenium* (Aldershot: Avebury).

Al-Burak, F. (1985), *Al-madares al-Yahudiya wal-Iraniya fil 'Irak* [Jewish and Iranian schools in Iraq], 2nd rev. edn. (Baghdad: Al-Dar Al-'Arabiya) (Arabic).

Al-Hibri, Azizah Y. (1999), 'Is Western Patriachal Feminism Good for Third World/Minority Women?', in Susan Moller Okin, *Is Multiculturalism Bad for Women?*, ed. Joshua Cohen, Matthew Howard, and Martha C. Nussbaum (Princeton: Princeton University Press), 41–7.

Al-Krenawi, A., and Lightman, E. S. (2000), 'Learning Achievement, Social Adjustment, and Family Conflict Among Bedouin-Arab Children from Polygamous and Monogamous Families', *Journal of Social Psychology* 140/3: 345–55.

Al-Misnad, Sh. (1985), *The Development of Modern Education in the Gulf* (London: Ithaca Press).

Al-Radi, S., Porter, V., and Barnes, R. (1998), *The Amiriya: A Sixteenth-Century Madrasa in Yemen* (Oxford: Oxford University Press).

Al-Saeed, M., Shaw, K. E., and Wakelam, A. (2000), 'Issues of Educational Administration in the Arab Gulf Region', *Middle Eastern Studies* 36/4: 63–74.

Alarcon, R. (1999), 'Recruitment Processes Among Foreign-Born Engineers and Scientists in Silicon Valley', *American Behavioural Scientist* 42/9: 1381–97.

Alberdi, Ines (1994), *Informe Sobre la Situacion de la Familia en España* (Madrid: Ministerio de Asuntos Sociales).

Albert, S., and Bradley, K. (1997), *Managing Knowledge: Experts, Agencies, and Organizations* (Cambridge: Cambridge University Press).

Albrow, M. (1996), *The Global Age* (Cambridge: Polity).

Alcalde, J. (1999) 'Desarrollo, subdesarrollo y decadencia social', *Socialismo y Participación* 85, August, 9–25.

Alcorn, N. (1999), *To the Fullest Extent of His Powers; C.F. Beeby's Life in Education* (Wellington: Victoria University Press)

Alekeson, V. (2005), *Spending on Education and Training over the Life Course. Have We Got the Balance Right?* (London: Social Market Foundation).

Alexander, J. C. (ed.) (1990), *Durkheimian Sociology: Cultural Studies* (Cambridge: Cambridge University Press).

Alexander, K. L., Entwisle, D. R., and Dauber, S. L. (1993), 'First-grade Classroom Behavior: Its Short- and Long-Term Consequences for School Performance', *Child Development* 64: 801–14.

Alexander, R. J. (1997), *Policy and Practice in Primary Education: Local Initiative, National Agenda* (London: Routledge).

—— (2001), *Culture and Pedagogy: International Comparisons in Primary Education* (Malden, Mass.: Blackwell).

—— (2004), 'Still No Pedagogy? Principle, Pragmatism and Compliance in Primary Education', *Cambridge Journal of Education* 341: 7–33.

—— (2005), *Towards Dialogic Teaching: Rethinking Classroom Talk* (York: Dialogos).

—— Rose, A. J., and Woodhead, C. (1992), *Curriculum Organisation and Classroom Practice in Primary Schools: A Discussion Paper* (London: Department for Education and Science).

Allan, G. (1989), *Friendship: Developing a Sociological Perspective* (Hemel Hempstead: Harverster Wheatshea).

'Allaq, 'A. (1997), 'The Dialogue of Ink, Blood and Water: Modernity and Higher Education in Iraq', in K. Shaw (ed.), *Higher Education in the Gulf: Problems and Prospects* (Exeter : Exeter University Press).

Allman, P., McLaren, P., and Rikowski, G., (2003), 'After the Box People: The Labour-Capital Relation as Class Constitution and Its Consequences for Marxist Educational Theory and Human Resistance' in J. Freeman-Moir, and A. Scott, (eds.), (2003) Yesterday's Dreams: International and Critical Perspectives on Education and Social Class, (Christchurch (NZ) University of Canterbury Press).

Althusser, L. (1971), 'Ideology and Ideological State Apparatus', in L. Althusser (ed.), *Lenin and Philosophy and Other Essays* (London: New Left).

—— (1972) Ideology and Ideological State Apparatuses, in B. Cosin, (ed.), *Education, Structure and Society* (Milton Keynes: Open University Press).

Altimir, O. (1981), 'Poverty in Latin America. A Review of Concepts and Data', *CEPAL Review*, April, 65–91.

Altman, R. (1987), *The American Film Musical* (Bloomington: Indiana University Press).

Alvermann, D. E., and Hagood, M. C. (2000), 'Fandom and Critical Media Literacy', *Journal of Adolescent & Adult Literacy* 43/5: 436–46.

Alvesson, M. (2001), 'Knowledge Work: Ambiguity, Image and Identity', *Human Relations* 54/7: 863–86.

Ambert, A. M. (1995), 'Toward a Theory of Peer Abuse', in A. Ambert (ed.), *Sociological Studies of Children* (Greenwich, Conn.: JAI), vii. 177–205.

Amin, S. (1980), *Class and Nation: Historically and in the Current Crisis* (New York: Monthly Review Press).

Anderson, B., (1991), *Imagined Communities: Reflections on the Origin and Spread of Nationalism* (London: Verso).

Anderson-Levitt, K. (2001), 'Teaching Culture as National and Transnational', *Educational Researcher* 31/3: 19–21.

Andrews, M., Duncombe, W., and Yinger, J. (2002), 'Revising Economies of Size in American Education: Are We Any Closer to a Consensus?' *Economics of Education Review* 21: 195–210.

Angus, L. (1993), 'The Sociology of School Effectiveness', *British Journal of the Sociology of Education* 14/3: 333–45.

Ansari, Gh. (1985), 'Modernization in the Arabian Gulf States: A Paradigm of Cultural Changes', *Eastern Anthropologist* 38: 189–205.

Antikainen, A., Houtsonen, J., Kauppila, J., and Huotelin, H. (1996), *Living a Learning Society: Life Histories, Identities and Education* (London: Falmer).

Anyon, J. (1983), 'Intersections of Gender and Class: Accommodation and Resistance by Working-Class and Affluent Females to Contradictory Sex-Role Ideologies', in S. Walker and L. Barton (eds.), *Gender, Class and Education.* (Lewes: Falmer 19–37).

—— (1994) 'The Retreat of Marxism and Socialist Feminism: Postmodern and Poststructuralist Theories in Education', *Curriculum Inquiry* 24/2: 114–34.

—— (1995), 'Race, Social Class, and Educational Reform in an Inner-City School', *Teachers College Record* 97/1: 4–21.

—— (1997), *Ghetto Schooling: A Political Economy of Urban Education Reform* (London: Teachers College Press).

Appadurai, A. (1986), 'Introduction: Commodities and the Politics of Value', in A. Appadurai (ed.), *The Social Life of Things* (New York: Cambridge University Press).

—— (1990), 'Disjuncture and Difference in the Global Cultural Economy', in M. Featherstone (ed.), *Global*

Culture. Nationalism, Globalization and Modernity (New York: Sage).

—— (1993), 'Patriotism and Its Futures', *Public Culture* 5/3: 418–28.

—— (1996), *Modernity at Large: Cultural Dimensions of Globalization* (Minneapolis: University of Minnesota Press).

Appelbaum, E., Bailey, T., Berg, P., and Kalleberg, A. (2000), *Manufacturing Advantage: Why High Performance Work Systems Pay Off* (Ithaca: Cornell University Press).

Apple, M. (1990), *Ideology and Curriculum* (London: Routledge).

—— (1996), 'Power, Meaning and Identity: Critical Sociology of Education in the US', *British Journal of Sociology of Education* 17: 125–44.

—— (2002), 'Pedagogy, Patriotism and Democracy: On the Educational Meanings of September 11', *Education and Social Justice* 4/2: 2–8.

—— (ed.) (1982), *Cultural and Economic Reproduction in Education* (London: Routledge).

Apple, M. W. (1996), *Cultural Politics and Education* (New York: Columbia University Teachers College Press).

Arat, Yesim (2002), 'Gender and Citizenship in Turkey', in Suad Joseph (ed.), *Gender and Citizenship in the Middle East* (Syracuse: Syracuse University Press).

Archer, J. (1992), 'Childhood Gender Roles: Social Context and Organisation', in H. McGurk (ed.), *Childhood and Social Development* (Hove: Lawrence Erlbaum), 31–61.

Archer, M. S. (1984), *Social Origins of Educational Systems* (London: Sage).

Archibugi, D. (1998), 'Principles of Cosmopolitan Democracy', in D. Archibugi, D. Held, and M. Köhler (eds.), *Reimagining Political Community* (Cambridge: Polity/ Blackwell), 198–228.

Argyris, C., and Schön, D. (1974), *Theory in Use: Increasing Professional Effectiveness* (San Francisco: Jossey-Bass).

Aristotle (1941), *Politics*, in *Basic Works of Aristotle*, ed. Richard McKeon, trans. Benjamin Jowett (New York: Random House).

Arneson, R. J. (2000), 'Perfectionism and Politics', *Ethics* 111/1: 37–63.

Arnette, J. (2004), *Emerging Adulthood: The Winding Road from the Late Teens through the Twenties* (Oxford: Oxford University Press).

Arnot, M. (1980), 'Socio-cultural Reproduction and Women's Education', in R. Deem (ed.), *Schooling for Women's Work* (London: Routledge).

—— (1981), 'Culture and Political Economy: Dual Perspectives in the Sociology of Women's Education', *Educational Analysis*, 3: 97–116.

—— (1982), 'Male Hegemony, Social and Women's Education', *Journal of Education* 164/1: 64–89.

—— (1991), 'Equality and Democracy: A Decade of Struggle over Education', *British Journal of Sociology of Education* 12/ 3: 447–66.

—— (1993), 'A Crisis in Patriarchy? British Feminist Educational Politics and State Regulation of Gender', in M. Arnot and K. Weiler (eds.), *Feminism and Social Justice in Education* (London: Falmer).

—— Araújo, H., Deliyanni-Kouimtzi, K., Rowe, G., and Tomé, A. (1996), 'Teachers, Gender and the Discourses of Citizenship', *International Studies in Sociology of Education* 6/1: 3–35.

—— and Dillabough, J. (1999), 'Feminist Politics and Democratic Values in Education', *Curriculum Inquiry* 29: 159–89.

—— (2002), *Reproducing Gender? Essays on Educational Theory and Feminist Politics* (London: Routledge Falmer).

—— (2004), 'Freedom's' Children: A Gender Perspective on the Education of the Learner Citizen, Paper to the Plenary Session for the Nordic Educational Research Association, Reykjavik, March.

—— and Reay, D. (2004), 'The Framing of Pedagogic Encounters: Regulating the Social Order of Classroom Learning', in J. Muller, B. Davies, and A. Morais (eds.), *Reading Bernstein, Researching Bernstein* (London, Routledge Falmer).

—— (forthcoming, 2005), 'Power, Pedagogic Voices and Pedagogic Encounters: The Implications for Pupil Consultation as Transformative Practice', in R. Moore, M. Arnot, J. Beck, and H. Daniels (eds.), *Knowledge, Power and Social Change* (London: Routledge).

—— McIntyre, D., Pedder, D., and Reay, D. (2004), *Consultation in the Classroom: Pupil Perspectives on Teaching and Learning* (Cambridge: Pearson).

—— Weiner, G., and David, M. (1999), *Closing the Gender Gap: The Post War Era and Social Change* (Cambridge: Polity).

Aronowitz, S. and Giroux, H. A. (1985), *Education under Siege* (South Hadley, Mass.: Bergin & Garvey).

Aronowitz, S., and De Fazio, W. (1994), *The Jobless Future: Sci-Tech and the Dogma of Work* (Minneapolis: University of Minnesota).

Arthur, M. B., and Rousseau, D. M. (eds.) (1996), *The Boundaryless Career: A New Employment Principle for a New Organisational Era* (New York: Oxford University Press).

Asante, M. (1993), *Malcolm X as Cultural Hero and Other Afrocentric Essays* (Trenton NJ: Africa World Press).

—— (1996), *Education, Training and the Global Economy* (Aldershot: Edward Elgar).

Ashton, D., and Green F. (1996), *Education, Training and the Global Economy* (Aldershot: Edward Elgar).

—— Maguire, M., and Spilsbury, M. (1990), *Restructuring the Labour Market: The Implications for Youth* (London: Macmillan).

Ashton, P., and Webb, R. (1986), *Making a Difference: Teachers' Sense of Efficacy and Student Achievement* (New York: Longman).

Asplund, R., and Leijola, L. (2005), 'Education and Wage Inequality in Finland: A Review of the Empirical Evidence', in R. Asplund and E. Barth (eds.) *Education and Wage Inequality in Europe* (Helsinki: ETLA B206).

ATKearney (2003), 'U.S. Financial Services Firms to Move More Than 500,000 Jobs Overseas Over the Next Five Years', Current News Release at <http://www.atkearney.com/main>.

Atkinson, A. B. (1970), 'On the Measurement of Inequality', *Journal of Economic Theory* 2.

—— L. Rainwater, and T. Smeeding (1996), *Income Distribution in OECD Countries* (Paris: OECD).

—— Maynard, A., and Trinder, C. (1983), *Parents and Children: Incomes in Two Generations* (London: Heineman).

Atkinson, E. (2001), 'Deconstructing Boundaries: Out on the Inside?', in *International Journal of Qualitative Studies in Education*, 14/3: 307–16.

—— (2002), 'Education for Diversity in a Multisexual Society: Negotiating the Contradictions of Contemporary Discourse', in *Sex Education* 2/2: 119–32.

Atkinson, J. (1985), 'The Changing Corporation', in D. Clutterbuck (ed.), *New Patterns of Work* (Aldershot: Gower).

Atkinson, P., and Delamont, S. (1977), 'Mock Ups and Cock Ups: The Stage Management of Guided Discovery', in M. Hammersley and P. Woods (eds.), *School Experience* (London: Croom Helm).

Atkinson, R. C. (1996a), 'Universities and the Knowledge-Based Economy', California State Fiscal Retreat, Berkeley, 3 Feb. Retrieved 10 May 1998, from <www.ucop/ucophome/pres/comments/science/html>.

—— (1996*b*), 'The California Solution', California Coalition for Science and Technology Summit, Sacramento, 26 May. Retrieved 10 May 1998, from <www.ucop/ucophome/pres.comments/science/html>.

Authers, J. (1999), 'Keeping company with the campus: Recent mergers have enhanced the role of corporate universities', *Financial Times* (London), 26 April.

Avis, J., Bloomer, M., Esland, G., Gleeson, D., and Hodkinson, P. (1996), *Knowledge and Nationhood: Education, Politics and Work* (London: Cassell).

Ayubi, N. N. (1995), *Overstating the Arab State. Politics and Society in the Middle East* (London: Tauris).

Bénot, Y. (1972), *Idéologies des independences africaines*, 2nd edn. (Paris: François Maspéro).

Bacchi, C. (1997), *The Politics of Affirmative Action* (London: Sage).

Badinjki, T. (1994), 'Research Notes: The Challenge of Arabization in Syria', *American Journal of Islamic Social Sciences* 1/1: 108–12.

Badran, N. (1980), 'The Means of Survival: Education and the Palestinian Community, 1948–1967', *Journal of Palestine Studies* 36: 44–74.

Bagley, C., Woods, P. A., and Glatter, R. (2001), 'Implications of School Choice Policy: Interpretation and Response by Parents of Students with Special Educational Needs', *British Education Research Journal* 27/3: 287–307.

Baker, C. (ed.) (1997), *Foundations of Bilingual Education and Bilingualism* (Clevedon: Multilingual Matters).

Baker, D. (1997), 'Surviving TIMSS'. *Phi Delta Kappan* (December) 79/4: 295–300.

Baker, D. P., and Stevenson, D. L. (1986), 'Mothers' Strategies for Children's School Achievement: Managing the Transition to High School', *Sociology of Education* 59: 156–66.

Baker, J., Lynch, K., Cartillon, S., and Walsh, J. (2004), *Equality: From Theory to Action* (Basingstoke: Palgrave).

Bakker, I., and Miller, R. (1996), 'Escape from Fordism: The Emergence of Alternative Forms of State Administration and Output', in R. Boyer and D. Drache (eds.), *State Against Markets: The Limits of Globalization* (New York: Routledge).

Baldock, C. (1990), 'Award Restructuring for Women: Tool of Change?', *Feminist Studies* 12 (Summer): 43-9.

Ball, S. (1994), *Education Reform: A Critical and Post-Structuralist Perspective* (Buckingham: Open University Press).

—— (2003), 'The Teacher's Soul and the Terrors of Performativity', *Journal of Education Policy* 18/2: 215–28.

—— (2003), *Class Strategies and the Education Market: The Middle Classes and Social Advantage* (London: Routledge Falmer).

—— and Vincent, C. (2001), 'New Class Relations in Education: the Strategies of the "Fearful" Middle Classes', in J. Demaine (ed.), *Sociology of Education Today* (Baskingstoke: Palgrave).

Ball, S. J. (1981), *Beachside Comprehensive* (Cambridge: Cambridge University Press).

—— (1990), 'Introducing Monsieur Foucault', in: S. J. Ball (ed.), *Foucault and Education: Disciplines and Knowledge* (London: Routledge), 1–8.

—— (1990), *Politics and Policy Making in Education* (London: Routledge).

—— (1994), *Education Reform: A Critical and Post-Structural Approach* (Buckingham: Open University Press).

—— (1994), *Education Reform* (Buckingham: Open University Press).

—— (1997), 'Good School/Bad School', in *British Journal of Sociology of Education* 18/3: 317–36.

—— (1999), 'Global Trends in Educational Reform and the Struggle for the Soul of the Teacher!', Education Policy series: Occasional Paper, Chinese University of Hong Kong.

—— (1999), 'Labour, Learning and the Economy: A "policy sociology" perspective', *Cambridge Journal of Education*, 29/2: 195–206.

—— (2001) 'Performativities and Fabrications in the Education Economy: Towards the Performative Society', in D. Gleeson and C. Husbands (eds.), *The Performing School* (London: Routledge Falmer).

—— Thrupp, M., Vincent, C., Marques-Cardoso, C., Neath, S., and Reay, D. (forthcoming), 'L'Angleterre', in C. Maroy (ed.), École, regulation et marche ; Une comparaison de six espaces scolaires en Europe (Paris: Presses Universitares de France).

—— (2003), *Class Strategies and the Education Market: The Middle Classes and Social Advantage* (London: Routledge Falmer).

Bankston, C. L., and Zhou, M. (1995), 'Effects of Minority-Language Literacy on the Academic Achievement of Vietnamese Youths in New Orleans', *Sociology of Education* 68: 1–17.

Barbarin, O., and Richter, L. M. (2001), *Mandela's Children: Growing Up in Post-Apartheid South Africa* (New York: Routledge).

Barber, B. (2004), *Fear's Empire: War, Terrorism and Democracy* (New York: W. W. Norton).

Barber, K. (1987), 'Popular Arts in Africa', *African Studies Review* 30/3 (September): 1–78.

Barlow, M., and Robertson, H-J. (1994), *Class Warfare: The Assault on Canada's Schools* (Toronto: Key Porter Books).

Barrett, M. (1980), *Women's Oppression Today: Problems in Marxist Feminist Analysis* (London: Verso).

—— and Dillabough, J. (eds.) (2000), *Education, Democracy and Citizenship: Emerging International Feminist Perspectives* (London: Routledge).

Bartholomew, D. J. (2004), *Measuring Intelligence: Facts and Fallacies* (Cambridge: Cambridge University Press).

Barton, L., Barrett, E., Whitty, G., Miles, S., and Furlong, J. (1994), 'Teacher Education and Teacher Professionalism in England: Some Emerging Issues', *British Journal of Sociology of Education* 15/4: 520–44.

Baruah, S. (1986), 'Immigration, Ethnic Conflict and Political Turmoil, Assam 1979–1985', *Asian Survey* 26/11 (November): 1184–1206.

Bassey, M. (1978), *Nine Hundred Primary School Teachers* (Slough: NFER).

Bastedo, M., and Gumport, P. (2003), 'Access to What? Mission Differentiation and Academic Stratification in US Public Higher Education', *Higher Education* 46: 341–59.

Battail, J.-F. (1988), 'Folkbildning har inte spelat ut sin roll' [Popular Adult Education Has Not Completed its Role], *Artes* 6: 126–36.

Battu, H., and Sloane, P. (2000), 'Overeducation and Crowding Out in Britain,' in L. Borghans and A. De Grip (eds.), *The Overeducated Worker?: The Economics of Skill Utilization* (Cheltenham: Edward Elgar).

Bauman, Z. (2002), *Society Under Siege* (Cambridge: Polity Press).

Baylies, C., and Bujra, J. (2000), *AIDS, Sexuality and Gender in Africa: Collective Strategies and Struggles in Tanzania and Zambia* (London: Routledge).

Bayly, C. A. (1989), *Imperial Meridian: The British Empire and the World, 1780–1830* (London: Longman).

Beck, J. (1999), ' Makeover or Takeover? The Strange Death of Educational Autonomy in Neo-Liberal England', *British Journal of Sociology of Education* 20/2: 223–38.

Beck, U. (1992), *Risk Society: Towards a New Modernity* (London: Sage).

—— *The Reinvention of Politics: Rethinking Modernity in the Global Social Order* (Cambridge: Polity).

—— (1992), *The Risk Society* (London: Polity).

Becker, G. (1964*a*), *A Theoretical and Empirical Analysis with Special Reference to Education* (New York: National Bureau of Economic Research).

—— (1964b), *Human Capital* (New York: Columbia University Press).

—— (1975), *Human Capital*, 2nd edn. (Chicago: Chicago University Press).

—— (1993), *Human Capital: A Theoretical and Empirical Analysis with Special Reference to Education*, 3rd edn. (Chicago: University of Chicago).

—— (2002), 'The Age of Human Capital', in E. P. Lazear (ed.), *Education in the Twenty-First Century*, The Hoover Institute, available at <http://www.hoover.org/publications/books/fulltext/ed21st/>

—— and Tomes, N. (1979), 'An Equilibrium Theory of the Distribution of Income and Intergenerational Mobility' *Journal of Political Economy* 87: 1153–89.

—— —— (1986), 'Human Capital and the Rise and Fall of Families', *Journal of Labor Economics* 4: 1–39.

—— (1981), *A Treatise on the Family* (Cambridge, Mass.: Harvard University Press).

Becker, H. S. (1967), 'Whose Side Are We On?', *Social Problems* 12: 239–47.

Beitz, C. (1979), *Political Theory and International Relations* (Princeton, NJ: Princeton University Press).

Bejar, H. (1999), Deuda externa y deuda social; legitimidad y derechos humanos, *Socialismo y Participación* 85, August, 49–75.

Belfield, C. R. (2003), 'Democratic Education across School Types: Evidence from the NHES', Working Paper, <www.ncspe.org>.

—— and Levin, H. M. (2002), 'The Effects of Competition on Educational Outcomes: A Review of the U.S. Evidence', *Review of Educational Research* 27: 279–341.

—— —— (2003), 'The Economics of Tuition Tax Credits for US Schools', *NTA Proceedings*, 95th Annual Conference on Taxation, 1–15.

—— —— and Schwartz, H. J. (2003), 'School Choice and the Supply of Private Schooling Places: Evidence from the Milwaukee Parental Choice Program'. Working Paper, <www.ncspe.org>.

Bell, D. (1953), 'America's Un-Marxist Revolution', in R. Bendix and S. M. Lipset (eds), *Class, Status and Power: A Reader in Social Stratification* (Glencoe, Ill.: The Free Press).

—— (1973), *The Coming of the Post-Industrial Society* (New York: Basic Books)

—— (1979), *Cultural Contradictions of Capitalism* (New York: Basic Books)

—— (1999), 'Foreword: The Axial Age of Technology', in *The Coming of the Post Industrial Society*, Special Anniversary Edition (New York: Basic Books).

—— (2003), *Inequality and Education: Must Urban Schools Fail?* Anniversary lecture of Ofsted report *Access and Achievement in Urban Education*, 20 November.

—— (2003), *Speech* to the City of York Council's annual education conference 28 Feb. 2003, <http://www.ofsted.gov.uk/news/index.cfm?fuseaction = news.details&id = 1402> accessed 25 June 2005.

Bellamy, R., and Castiglione, D. (1998), 'Between Cosmopolis and Community: Three Models of Rights and Democracy within the European Union', in D. Archibugi, D. Held, and M. Köhler (eds.), *Reimagining Political Community* (Cambridge, Polity/Blackwell), 152–78.

Bempechat, J., and Drago-Severson, E. (1999), 'Cross-cultural Differences in Academic Achievement: Beyond Etic Conceptions of Children's Understanding', *Review of Educational Research* 69/3: 287–314.

Ben-David, Y. (1994), 'Adaptation through Crisis: Social Aspects of Urbanisation of Negev Bedouins', in D. Grossman and A. Meir (eds.), *The Arab Locality in Israel: Geographical Processes* (Tel-Aviv, Ramat-Gan, and Beer-Sheva: University Presses) (Hebrew).

Beneton de Morange, E.C., *Dissertations sur les Tentes*, 1735. *Histoire de la guerre*, 1741.

Benhabib, S. (1995*a*), 'Feminism and Postmodernism', in S. Benhabib, J. Butler, D. Cornell, and N. Fraser (eds.), *Feminist Contentions: A Philosophical Exchange* (New York: Routledge), 17–57.

—— (1995*b*), 'The Debate over Women and Moral Theory Revisited', in J. Meehan (ed.), *Feminists Read Habermas: Gendering the Subject of Discourse* (New York: Routledge), 181–204.

Bennell, P. (1996), 'Using and Abusing Rates of Return: A Critique of the World Bank's 1995 Education Sector Review', *International Journal of Educational Development*, 16/3: 235–48.

Bennett, W. J. (1987), *The Book of Virtues* (New York: Simon and Schuster).

Bénot, Y. (1972) *Idéologies des independences africaines*, 2nd edn. (Paris: François Maspéro).

Beresford, E. (1996), *How Do We Provide Effective Education/Training for Staff Related Work with Parents?* Paper presented to Education is Partnership Conference, Copenhagen, November.

Berg, I. (1970), *Education and Jobs: The Great Training Robbery* (New York: Praeger).

Berghman, J. (1995), 'Social Exclusion in Europe: Policy Context and Analytical Framework', in G. Room (ed.), *Beyond the Threshold: The Measurement and Analysis of Social Exclusion* (Bristol: Policy Press), 10–28.

Berliner, D. C., and Biddle, B. J. (1995), *The Manufactured Crisis: Myths, Frauds and the Attack on America's Public Schools* (Cambridge, Mass.: Perseus).

Berman, E., and Machin, S. (2000), 'Skill-Biased Technology Transfer Around the World', *Oxford Review of Economic Policy* 16/3.

Bernstein, B. (1970), 'Education Cannot Compensate for Society', *New Society* 387 (26 February), 344–7.

—— (1971), *Class, Codes and Control* (London: Routledge & Kegan Paul), i.

—— (1975), *Class, Codes and Control*, (London: Routledge & Kegan Paul), iii.

—— (1971), 'Education Cannot Compensate for Society', in B. Cosin et al. (eds.), *School and Society* (London: Routledge & Kegan Paul)..

—— (1973), *Class, Codes and Control*, i. *Theoretical Studies Towards a Sociology of Language* (St Albans: Paladin).

—— (1977), *Class, Codes and Control*, iii. *Towards a Theory of Educational Transmissions*, 2nd edn. (London: Routledge & Kegan Paul).

—— (1990), *Class, Codes and Control*, iv. *The Structuring of Pedagogic Discourse*: (London: Routledge).

—— (1996), *Pedagogy, Symbolic Control and Identity: Theory, Research, Critique*, 1st edn. (London: Taylor & Francis).

—— (2000), *Pedagogy, Symbolic Control and Identity: Theory, Research, Critique*, rev. edn. (Oxford: Rowman & Littlefield).

—— (1974), *Class, Codes and Control: Theoretical Studies towards a Sociology of Language* (New York: Schocken).

—— (1977), *Class Codes and Control*, 3rd edn. (London: Routledge & Kegan Paul).

—— (1990), *The Structuring of Pedagogic Discourse: Class, Codes, and Control* (London: Routledge).

—— (1977), *Class, Codes and Control*, iii. *Towards a Theory of Educational Transmissions* (London: Routledge & Kegan Paul).

—— (2000), *Pedagogy, Symbolic Control and Identity: Theory, Research, Critique*, 2nd edn. (London: Taylor & Francis; Oxford: Rowman & Littlefield).

—— (1990), *Class, Codes and Control: The Structuring of Pedagogic Discourse* (London: Routledge).

—— (1996), *Pedagogy, Symbolic Control and Identity: Theory, Research, Critique* (London: Taylor & Francis).

—— (1997), 'Class and Pedagogies: Visible and Invisible' in A. H. Halsey, H. Lauder, P. Brown, and A. Stuart Wells, (eds.), *Education, Culture, Economy and Society*, (Oxford: Oxford University Press).

—— (1997) 'Class and Pedagogies: Visible and Invisible', in Halsey et al. (eds.) 59–79.

—— (2000), *Pedagogy, Symbolic Control and Identity*, (Lanham, Md.: Rowman & Littlefield).

Bhaskar, R. (1993), *Dialectic: The Pulse of Freedom* (London: Verso).

Bhorat, H., Liebbrandt, M., Maziya, M., van den Berg, S., and Wooland, I. (2001), *Fighting Poverty: Labour Markets and Inequality in South Africa* (Cape Town: University of Cape Town Press).

Biagoli, M. (1998). 'The Instability of Authorship: Credit and Responsibility in Contemporary Biomedicine', *FASEB Journal* 12: 13–16.

Bidwell, C., and Dreeben, R. (1992), 'School Organization and Curriculum'. in P. Jackson (ed.), *Handbook of Research on Curriculum* (New York: Macmillan), ch. 13.

Bifulco, R., and Ladd, H. (2003), 'Charter School Impacts on Student Performance: Evidence from North Carolina', APPAM Paper, November 2003.

Bigelow, B. (1997), 'The Human Lives Behind the Labels: The Global Sweatshop, Nike, and the Race to the Bottom', *Phi Delta Kappa* 79/2: 112–19.

Billig, M. (1987), *Arguing and Thinking: A Rhetorical Approach to Social Psychology* (Cambridge: Cambridge University Press).

Birks, J. S., and Rimmer, J. A. (1984), *Developing Education Systems in the Oil States of Arabia: Conflicts of Purpose and Focus* (University of Durham: Centre for Middle Eastern and Islamic Studies).

Bishop, P., and Mulford, W. (1996), 'Empowerment in Four Primary Schools: They Don't Really Care', *International Journal of Educational Reform* 5/2: 193–204.

Bishops' Conference (1999), *Foundations for Excellence: Catholic Primary Schools in Urban Poverty Areas* (London: Bishops' Conference of England and Wales).

Bjorklund, A., and Jantti, M. (1997), 'Intergenerational Income Mobility in Sweden Compared to the United States', *American Economic Review* 87: 1009–18.

Black, D., Morris, J., Smith, C., and Townsend, P. (1980), *Inequalities in Health: Report of a Research Working Group* (London: Department of Health and Social Security).

Blackmore, J. (1996), 'Doing "Emotional Labour" in the Education Market Place: Stories from the Field of Women in Management', *Discourse* 17/3: 337–51.

—— (1997*a*), 'The Gendering of Skill in Australian State Education 1900–80', in E. Halsey et al. (eds.), *Education, Culture, Economy and Society* (Oxford: Oxford University Press).

—— (1997*b*), 'The Level Playing Field? The Restructuring and Regendering of Educational Work', *International Review of Education* 43/5–6: 1–23.

—— (1998), *Troubling Women: Feminism, Leadership and Educational Change* (Buckingham: Open University Press).

—— and Angwin, J. (1997), 'Educational Outworkers: The Impact of Educational Restructuring upon the Work of Women Educators'. *Forum of Education* 52/2: 1–23.

—— and Sachs, J. (1997), '"All Worked Out"—Gender, Restructuring and the Psychic Economy of Universities', Paper presented to the Australian Association for Research in Education Annual Conference, Brisbane, December, 1–5.

—— Bigum, C., Hodgens, J., and Laskey, L. (1996), 'Managed Change and Self Management in Schools of the Future', *Leading and Managing* 3/3: 195–220.

Blackmore, J., and Sachs, J. (1997), 'Worried, Weary and Just Plain Worn Out: Gender, Restructuring and the Psychic Economy of Higher Education', Brisbane: AARE Annual Conference.

—— —— (1999), 'Performativity, Passion and the Making of the Academic Self: Women Leaders in the Restructured and Internationalized University', in A. McKinnon and A. Grant (eds.), *Academic Women*.

Blackstone, T. (1999), *'Students Are Now 'Critical Consumers'*, DfEE press release, 16 September.

Blackstone, W. (1979), *Commentaries on the Laws of England* (Chicago: University of Chicago Press).

Blair, T. (1999), Speech delivered 14 January, IPPR <www.number-10.gov.uk>.

Blanden J., Goodman A., Gregg P., and Machin S. (2004), 'Changes in Intergenerational Mobility in Britain', in M. Corak (ed.), *Generational Income Mobility in North America and Europe* (Cambridge: Cambridge University Press).

—— Gregg, P., and Machin, S. (2005), *Intergenerational Mobility in Europe and North America: Differences Across Countries and Over Time* (London: Sutton Trust).

Blase, J. J. (1987), 'The Politics of Teaching: The Teacher–Parent Relationship and the Dynamics of Diplomacy', *Journal of Teacher Education* 38/2: 53–60.

Blau, D. (2001), *The Childcare Problem* (New York: Russell Sage).

Blaug, M. (1976), 'The Empirical Status of Human Capital Theory: a Slightly Jaundiced Survey', *Journal of Economic Literature* 14: 827–55.

Block, F. (1990), *Postindustrial Possibilities: A Critique of Economic Discourse* (Berkeley: University of California).

Blommaert, J. (ed.) (1999), *Language Ideological Debates* (Berlin: Mouton de Gruyter).

Blöndal, S., Field, S., and Girouard, N. (2002), 'Investment in Human Capital Through Post-Compulsory Education and Training: Selected Efficiency and Equity Aspects', OECD Economic Department Working Papers 333. <http://www.oils.oecd.org/oils/2002doc.nsf/linkto/eco-wkp>.

Bloom, A. (1997) 'Introduction: On Virtue', in Halsey et al. (eds.), 498–508.

Bloom, L. R. (1999), 'Interpreting Interpretation: Gender, Sexuality and the Practice of Not Reading Straight', in *International Journal of Qualitative Studies in Education* 12/4: 331–45.

Bluestone, Barry, and Rose, Stephen (1997), 'The Growth in Work Time and the Implications for Macro Policy'. *Working Paper 204* (New York: Jerome Levy Economics Institute of Bard College).

Blumenstyk, G. (1998b), 'Royalties on Inventions Bring $336 Million to Top Research Universities', *Chronicle of Higher Education* (27 Feb.), A44.

Blunkett, D. (2000), 'Transforming Secondary Education', speech to the Social Markets Foundation, London, 15 March.

Bock, G. R., Goode, J. A., and Webb, K. (eds.) (2000), *The Nature of Intelligence* (Chichester: Wiley).

Bok, D. (2000), *The Trouble with Government* (Cambridge, Mass.: Harvard University Press).

Bonder, G. (1997), 'Young Girls' Construction of the Citizen in Argentina', Paper presented to the Gender and Education Conference, Warwick, England.

Bonnet G. (2002), 'Reflections in a Critical Eye: On the Pitfalls of International Assessment', *Assessment in Education* 9/3: 387–400.

Boorstin, D. (1975), *The Image: A Guide to Pseudo-events in America* (New York: Atheneum).

Borjas, G. (1995), 'Ethnicity, Neighbourhoods, and Human Capital Externalities', *American Economic Review* 85: 365–90.

Börjesson, M. (1997), *Om skolbarns olikheter: diskurser kring 'särskilda behov' i skolan—med historiska jämförelsepunkter* [On Differences between Children: Discourses About 'Special Needs' in the School—with Historical Comparisons] (Stockholm: Liber).

Bornstein, M. H., and Bradley, R. H. (eds.) (2003), *Socioeconomic Status, Parenting and Child Development* (Hillsdale, NJ: Lawrence Erlbaum Associates).

Boscagli, M. (1996), 'The Resisting Screen: Multicultural Politics in a Global Perspective', *Diaspora* 5/3.

Boston, J., Martin, J., Pallot, J., and Walsh, P. (1996), *Public Management: The New Zealand Model.* (Auckland: Oxford University Press).

Boudon, R. (1973), *Education, Opportunity and Social Inequality: Changing Prospects in Western Society* (New York: John Wiley).

Bloom, A. (1997), 'Introduction: On Virtue', in Halsey et al. (eds.), 498–508.

Bound, J., and Johnson, G. (1995), 'What Are the Causes of Rising Wage Inequality?' *Federal Reserve Bank of New York Economic Policy Review*, 1: 9–17.

Bourdieu, P. (1974), 'The School as a Conservative Force: Scholastic and Cultural Inequalities', in J. Eggleston (ed.), Contemporary Research in the Sociology of Education (London: Methuen).

—— (1977), *Outline of a Theory of Practice* (Cambridge: Cambridge University Press).

—— (1982), 'Les rites d'institution', *Actes de la recherche en sciences sociales* 43: 58–63.

—— (1984), *Distinction: A Social Critique of the Judgment of Taste*, trans. R. Nice (Cambridge, Mass.: Harvard University Press).

—— (1986), 'The Forms of Capital', in J. G. Richardson (ed.), *Handbook of Theory and Research for the Sociology of Education* (New York Greenwood), 241–58.

—— (1988), *Homo academicus* (Cambridge: Polity).

—— (1990), *The Logic of Practice* trans. R. Nice (Stanford, Calif.: Stanford University Press).

—— (1991), *Language and Symbolic Power* (Cambridge: Polity).

—— (1994), *Language and Symbolic Power*, trans. C. Raymond and M. Adamson (Cambridge, Mass.: Harvard University Press).

—— (1996) *The State Nobility: Elite Schools in the Field of Power*, trans. L. C. Clough (Cambridge: Polity).

—— (1998), *Acts of Resistance Against the New Myths of our Time* (Cambridge: Polity).

—— (1998), *Practical Reason: On the Theory of Action* (Cambridge: Polity).

—— (2000) *Pascalian Meditations* (Cambridge: Polity).

—— (2003), *Firing Back: Against the Tyranny of the Market* (London: Verso), ii.

—— and Boltanski, L. (1978), 'Changes in Social Structure and Changes in the Demand for Education', in S. Giner and M. Archer (eds.), *Contemporary Europe: Social Structure and Cultural Change* (London: Routledge & Kegan Paul).

—— and Passeron, J. (1977), *Reproduction in Education, Society and Culture*, trans. R. Nice (Thousand Oaks, Calif.: Sage).

—— —— (1977), *Reproduction in Education, Society and Culture* (London: Sage).

—— and Passeron, J-C. (1990), *Reproduction in Education, Society and Culture*, 2nd edn., trans. R. Nice (London: Sage). 1st edn. 1976.

—— and Wacquant, L. (1992), *An Invitation to Reflexive Sociology* (Chicago: University of Chicago Press).

Bourne, J. (2000), 'New Imaginings of Reading for a New Moral Order. A Review of the Production, Transmission and Acquisition of a New Pedagogic Culture in the UK', *Linguistics and Education* 11/1: 31–45.

Bowe, R., Ball, S., and Gold, A. (1992), *Reforming Education and Changing Schools: Case Studies in Policy Sociology* (London: Routledge).

Bowker, G. C., and Star, S. L. (1999), *Sorting Things Out—Classification and Its Consequences* (Cambridge, Mass.: MIT).

Bowlby, R. (1985), *Just Looking: Consumer Culture in Dreiser, Gissing and Zola* (London: Methuen).

Bowles, S., and Gintis, H. (1976), Schooling in Capitalist America (London: Routledge and Kegan Paul).

—— —— and Osborne, M. (2001) 'The Determinants of Earning: A Behavioural Approach, *Journal of Economic Literature* 30: 1137–76.

Boyle, J. (1996), *Shamans, Software and Spleens: Law and the Construction of the Information Society* (Cambridge, Mass: Harvard University Press).

Bozzoli, B. (1983), 'Marxism, Feminism and South African Studies', *Journal of Southern African Studies* 9: 139.

Braaten, J. (1995), 'From Communicative Rationality to Communicative Thinking: A Basis for Feminist Theory and Practice', in J. Meehan (ed.), *Feminists Read Habermas: Gendering the Subject of Discourse* (New York Routledge), 139–162.

Bradbury, B., Jenkins, S., and Micklewright, J. (2001), *The Dynamics of Child Poverty in Industrialised Countries* (Cambridge: Cambridge University Press).

Bradley, K., and Ramirez, F. (1996), 'World Polity and Gender Parity; Women's Share of Higher Education 1965–85', *Sociology of Education and Socialisation* 11: 63–91.

Brah, A. (1996), *Cartographies of Diaspora: Contesting Identities* (London: Routledge).

—— and Minhas, R. (1985), 'Structural Racism or Cultural Difference: Schooling for Asian Girls', in G. Weiner (ed.), *Just a Bunch of Girls: Feminist Approaches to Schooling* (Milton Keynes: Open University).

Brandom, R. (2000), *Articulating Reasons: An Introduction to Inferentialism* (Cambridge, Mass.: Harvard University Press).

Brannen, J., Heptinstall, E., and Bhopal, K. (2000), *Connecting Children: Care and Family Life in Later Childhood* (London: Routledge Falmer).

Bratlinger, E., Majd-Jabbari, M., and Guskin, S. L. (1996), 'Self-interest and Liberal Educational Discourse: How Ideology Works for Middle-Class Mothers', *American Educational Research Journal* 33/3: 571–98.

Braudel, F. (1981–4), *Civilization and Capitalism, 15th–18th Century* (3 vols.) (London: Collins).

Bray, M. (1996), *Decentralization of Education: Community Financing* (Washington DC: World Bank).

—— (1996), *Education and Political Transition: Themes and Experiences in East Asia* (Hong Kong: Comparative Education Research Centre, University of Hong Kong).

Bredo, I., Foersom T., and Laursen, P. F. (1993), 'Student Choice: A Model', *Higher Education Review*, 26/1: 64–73.

Breen, R. (2001), 'A Rational Choice Model of Educational Inequality', *Instituto Juan March Working Paper* 166 (October).

Brenner, N. (1997), 'Global, Fragmented, Hierarchical: Henri Lefebvre's Geographies of Globalization', *Public Culture* 10/1: 135–67.

Breton, A. (1964), 'The Economics of Nationalism', *Journal of Political Economy* 72: 376–86.

Bridges, W. (1995), *Jobshift: How to Prosper in a Workplace without Jobs* (London: Nicholas Brealey).

Brint, S. (2001), 'Professionals and the "Knowledge Economy": Rethinking the Theory of Post Industrial Society', *Current Sociology* 49/4: 101–32.

—— Contreras, M. F. and Matthews, M. T. (2001), 'Socialization Messages in Primary Schools: An Organizational Analysis', *Sociology of Education* 74: 157–80.

British Journal of Sociology of Education (2002), *Special Issue: Basil Bernstein's Theory of Class, Educational Codes and Social Control*, 23/4.

Brito, S., and Waller, H. (1993), 'Partnership at What Price?', in R. Merttens, D. Mayers, A. Brown, and J. Vass (eds.), *Ruling the Margins: Problematising Parental Involvement* (London: University of North London Press).

Britzman, D. (1991), *Practice Makes Practice: A Critical Study of Learning to Teach* (Albany, NY: SUNY Press).

Britzman, D. (1995), 'Is There a Queer Pedagogy? Or Stop Reading Straight', in *Educational Theory*, 45: 151–65.

Broadfoot, P. (1996), *Education, Assessment and Society* (Buckingham: Open University Press).

Brocker, L. (2002), *Starting School: Young Children Learning Cultures* (Buckingham: Open University Press).

Brodie, J. (1996), 'New State Forms, New Political Spaces', in R. Boyer and D. Drache (eds.), *State Against Markets: The Limits of Globalization* (New York: Routledge).

Bromme, R. (1987), 'Teachers' Assessments of Students' Difficulties and Progress in Understanding in the Classroom', in J. Calderhead (ed.), *Exploring Teacher Thinking* (Eastbourne: Holt-Saunders).

Bronfenbrenner, U. (1979), *The Ecology of Human Development* (Cambridge, Mass.: Harvard University Press).

—— (1986), 'Ecology of the Family as a Context for Human Development: Research Perspectives', *Developmental Psychology* 22: 723–42.

—— and Crouter, N. (1983), 'The Evolution of Environmental Models in Developmental Research', in W. Kessen (ed.), *History, Theory, and Methods* (New York: Wiley), i. 357–414).

Bronner, E. (1998), 'Universities giving less financial aid on basis of need', *The New York Times*, 21 June, p. A1 +.

Brooks, A. (1997), *Academic Women* (Buckingham: SRHE and Open University Press).

Brooks, R. (2003), 'Young People's Higher Education Choices: The Role of Family and Friends', *British Journal of Sociology of Education* 24/3: 283–97.

Brown, C., and Campbell, B. (2002), 'The Impact of Technological Change on Work and Wages', *Industrial Relations* 41/1: 1–33.

Brown, G. (2004), Full text: Gordon Brown's Confederation of British Industry Speech, 9 November. <http://news.ft.com/cms/s/eb4dc42a-3239-11d9-8498-00000e2511c8.html>.

Brown, P. (1990), 'The "Third Wave": Education and the Ideology of Parentocracy', *Journal of Sociology of Education* 11: 65–85.

—— (1995), 'Cultural Capital and Social Exclusion: Some Observations On Recent Trends in Education, Employment and the Labour Market', *Work, Employment and Society* 9: 29–51.

—— (2000), 'The Globalization of Positional Competition?', *Sociology* 34/4: 633–53.

—— (2003) 'The Opportunity Trap: Education and Employment in a Global Economy', *European Education Research Journal* 2/1: 142–80.

—— Green, A., and Lauder, H. (2001), *High Skills: Globalization, Competitiveness and Skill Formation* (Oxford: Oxford University Press).

—— and Hesketh, A. (2004), *The Mismanagement of Talent: Employability and Jobs in the Knowledge Economy* (Oxford: Oxford University Press).

—— and Hesketh, A. with Williams, S. (2004), *The Mismanagement of Talent: Employability and Jobs in the Knowledge Economy* (Oxford: Oxford University Press).

—— and Lauder, H. (1991), *Education for Economic Survival* (London: Routledge).

—— —— (1997), 'Education, Globalization and Economic Development', in A. Halsey *et al.* (eds.), *Education, Culture, Economy and Society* (Oxford: Oxford University Press).

—— —— (2000), 'Education, Child Poverty and the Politics of Education', in S. J. Ball (ed.) *Sociology of Education: Major Themes*, iv. *Policies and Practices* (London: Routledge Falmer), 1753–79.

—— —— (2003), *Globalization and the Knowledge Economy: Some Observations on Recent Trends in Employment, Education and the Labour Market*, Cardiff School of Social Science, Working Paper Number 43.

—— and Scase, R. (1994), *Higher Education and Corporate Realities* (London: UCL Press).

—— and Scase, R. (1997), 'Universities and Employers: Rhetoric and Realities', in A. Smith and F. Webster (eds.), *The Postmodern University?* (Buckingham: Open University Press).

Brown, W. (1995), *States of Injury: Studies in Power and Freedom in Late Modernity* (Princeton: Princeton University Press).

Bruegger, U., and Knorr Cetina, K. (2000), 'Global Microstructures: The Interactional Order of Financial Markets'. *Canadian Journal of Sociology* 25/2: 141–68.

Brun-Rovet, Marianne (2000), 'A Perspective on the Multiculturalism Debate: "L'affaire foulard" and *laicite* in France, 1989–1999', Seminar paper submitted to Professor Benhabib's class "Nations, States, and Citizens", Harvard University, Department of Government. On file with the author.

Bruner, J. S. (1968), *Toward a Theory of Instruction* (New York: Norton).

—— and Haste J. E. (ed.) (1987), *Making Sense: The Child's Construction of the World* (London: Routledge).

Brynin, M. (2002) 'Graduate Density, Gender and Employment', *British Journal of Sociology* 53/3: 363–81.

—— (2002*a*), 'Overqualification in Employment', *Work, Employment and Society* 16/4: 637–54.

Bryson, L. (1996), 'The Proletarianisation of Women: Gender Justice in Australia?', *Social Justice* 16/3: 87–101.

Buckingham, D. (1996), 'Critical Pedagogy and Media Education: A Theory in Search of a Practice', *Journal of Curriculum Studies* 28: 627–50.

Buck-Morss, S. (1991), *The Dialectics of Seeing: Walter Benjamin and the Arcades Project*, first published 1989 (Cambridge, Mass.: MIT).

Buddin, R., and Zimmer R., (2003), 'Student Achievement in Charter Schools: New Evidence from California', APPAM Paper, November 2003.

Buffie, E. (2001), *Trade Policy in Developing Countries* (Cambridge: Cambridge University Press).

Bull, H. (1977), *The Anarchical Society* (New York: Columbia University Press).

Bullough, R. V. Jr., and Gitlin, A. D. (1994), 'Challenging Teacher Education as Training: Four Propositions', *Journal of Education for Teaching* 20/1: 67–81.

—— Knowles, J. G., and Crow, N. (1991), *Emerging as a Teacher* (London: Routledge).

Bunting, M. (2004), *Willing Slaves: How the Overwork Culture is Ruling Our Lives* (London: Harper Collins).

Burbules, N., and Torres, C. A. (eds.) (2000), 'Globalization and Education: An Introduction', in *Globalization and Education: Critical Perspectives* (New York: Routledge).

Burgat, F. (1988), 'L'Algérie: de la laicité islamique à l'Islamisme', *Monde Arabe: Maghreb-Machrek*, 121: 43–57.

Burgess, R., Herphes, C., and Moxan, S. (1991), 'Parents Are Welcome: Headteachers and Mothers' Perspectives on Parental Participation in the Early Years', *Qualitative Studies in Education* 4/2: 95–107.

Burke, J., and Beaumont, P. (2002), 'Nuclear neighbours teeter on the brink of Armageddon', *Sunday Times*, June, 2, p. 17.

Burnett, N., and Patrinos, H. A. (1996), 'Response to Critiques of Priorities and Strategies for Education: A World Bank Review', *International Journal of Educational Development*, 16/3: 273–6.

Burnheim, J. (1985), *Is Democracy Possible?* (Cambridge: Cambridge University Press).

—— (1986), 'Democracy, Nation-States, and the World System', in D. Held and C. Pollitt (eds.), *New Forms of Democracy* (London: Sage), 218–39.

—— (1995), 'Power-Trading and the Environment', *Environmental Politics* 4/4: 49–65.

Burns, K. (2002), 'Sexuality Education in a Girls' School in Eastern Uganda', *Agenda* 53: 81–8.

Burris, V. (1987), 'The Neo-Marxist Synthesis of Marx and Weber on Class', in N. Wiley (ed.), *The Marx–Weber Debate* (Newbury Park, Calif: Sage).

Burton, C. (1990), *The Promise and the Price: The Struggle for Equal Opportunity in Women's Employment* (Sydney: Allen & Unwin).

Butler, J. (1990), *Gender Trouble: Feminism and the Subversion of Identity* (New York: Routledge).

—— (1995), 'Contingent Foundations', in S. Benhabib, J. Butler, D. Cornell, and N. Fraser (eds.), *Feminist Contentions: A Philosophical Exchange* (New York: Routledge), 35–58.

—— (1999), *Gender Trouble. Feminism and the Subversion of Identity* (Tenth Anniversary edition) (London: Routledge).

Butler, T., and Savage, M. (eds.) (1995), *Social Change and the Middle Classes* (London: UCL Press).

Bynner, J., and Parsons, S. (1997), *Does Numeracy Matter? Evidence from the National Child Development Study on the Impact of Poor Numeracy on Adult Life.* (London: Social Statistics Research Unit, City University, on behalf of The Basic Skills Agency).

Bynner, J., Ferri, E., and Shepherd, P. (eds.) (1997), *Twenty-Something in the 1990s: Getting On, Getting By, and Getting Nowhere*, (Aldershot: Ashgate).

Calhoun, C. (2000), 'Resisting Globalization or Shaping It?' *Prometheus*, 4: 29–47.

——, LiPuma, F., and Postone, M. (eds.) (1993), *Bourdieu: Critical Perspectives* (Chicago: University of Chicago Press).

Calhoun, D. (1973), *The Intelligence of a People* (Princeton, NJ: Princeton University Press).

Callinicos, A. (1998), *Social Theory: A Historical Introduction London* (Cambridge: Polity).

Camilli, G., and Bulkley, K. (2001), 'Critique of "An Evaluation of the Florida A-Plus Accountability and School Choice Program" '. *Education Policy Analysis Archives* 9: 7.

Campbell, D. E. (2001), 'Making Democratic Education Work', in P. E. Peterson and D.E. Campbell (eds.), *Charters, Vouchers and American Education* (Washington, DC: Brookings Institution).

Campbell, R. J. (1985), *Developing the Primary Curriculum* (London: Holt, Rinehart, & Winston).

—— Neill, S. R. St. J. (1994), *Primary Teachers at Work* (London: Routledge).

Capello, C. (2004), 'Blowing the Whistle on the Texas Miracle: An interview with Robert Kimball', *Rethinking schools*, available on line at <www.rethinkingschools.org>.

Cappelli, P. (1999), *Employment Practices and Business Strategies* (Oxford: Oxford University Press).

Carapico, Sh. (1998), *Civil Society in Yemen: The Political Economy of Activism in Modern Arabia* (Cambridge: Cambridge University Press).

Carbonaro, W. J. (1998), 'A Little Help from My Friends' Parents: Intergenerational Closure and Educational Outcomes'. *Sociology of Education* 771: 295–313.

—— (1999), 'Opening the Debate on Closure and Schooling Outcomes'. *American Sociological Review* 64: 682–6.

Card, D. (1999), 'The Causal Effect of Education on Earnings', in O. Ashenfelter and D. Card, (eds.), *Handbook of Labor Economics* (New York: Elsevier), iii.

Carlen, P., Gleeson, D., and Wardhaugh, J. (1992), *Truancy: The Politics of Compulsory Schooling* (Buckingham: Open University Press).

Carnevale, A. P., and Porro, J. D. (1994), *Quality Education: School Reform for the New American Economy* (Washington, DC: US Department of Education).

Carney, D. (1998), 'Visas for skilled immigrants finds home in the senate', *Congressional Quarterly Weekly Report*, 4 April, 891.

Carnoy, M. (1995), 'Foreword: How Should We Study Adult Education?' in C. A. Torres (ed.), *The Politics of Nonformal Education in Latin America* (New York: Praeger).

—— (2000), *Sustaining the New Economy: Work, Family, and Community in the Information Age* (Cambridge, Mass.: Harvard University Press).

—— and Marshall, Jeffery (2005), 'Cuba's Academic Performance in Comparative Perspective', *Comparative Education Review* 49/2: 230–61.

Carr, W. (1989), 'Understanding Quality in Teaching', in W. Carr (ed.), *Quality in Teaching: Arguments for a Reflective Profession* (London, Falmer), 1–20.

Carrim, N. (1995), 'Working With and Through Difference in Antiracist Pedagogies', *International Studies in Sociology of Education* 5/1: 25–39.

—— (2001), 'From Teachers to Educators: Homogenizing Tendencies in Contemporary South African Educational Reforms', *International Journal of Educational Development* 21: 45–51.

Casey, K. (1990), 'Teacher as Mother: Curriculum Theorising in the Life Histories of Contemporary Women Teachers', *Cambridge Journal of Education* 20: 301–20.

—— (1993), *I Answer With My Life* (New York: Routledge).

Caspi, A., Moffitt, T. E., Entner Wright, B. R., and Silva, P. A. (1998), 'Early Failure in the Labour Market: Childhood and Adolescent Predictors of Unemployment in the Transition to Adulthood', *American Sociological Review* 63: 424–51.

Castells, M. (1996), *The Information Age: Economy, Society and Culture*, i. *the Rise of the Network Society*. (Oxford: Blackwell).

—— (1996), *The Rise of Network Society* (Cambridge: Blackwell).

—— (1996), *The Rise of the Network Society*, i. *The Information Age: Economy, Society and Culture* (London: Macmillan).

—— (1997), *The Information Age: Economy, Society and Culture*, ii. *the Power of Identity* (Oxford: Blackwell).

—— (1998), *The Information Age: Economy, Society, and Culture*, iii. *End of Millennium* (Oxford: Blackwell)

—— (2000), *The Rise of the Network Society*, 2nd edn. (Oxford: Blackwell).

—— (2001), 'Information Technology and Global Development', in J. Muller, N. Cloete, and S. Badat (eds.), *Challenges of Globalisation: South African Debates with Manuel Castells* (Cape Town: Maskew Miller/Longman).

—— (2001), *The Internet Galaxy: Reflections on the Internet, Business and Society* (Oxford: Oxford University Press).

CBI (1989), *Towards a Skills Revolution* (London: CBI).

CEIMME (1995), *Mujer Indigena y Participación Politica* (Guayaquil: Centro de Estudios e Investigación sobre el Maltrato a la Mujer Ecuatoriana).

Center for the Study of Public Policy (1970), *Education Vouchers, a Report on Financing Elementary Education by Grants to Parents* (Cambridge, Mass.: CSPP).

Central Advisory Council for Education (1967), *Children and Their Primary Schools* (London: HMSO).

Central Advisory Council for Education (England) (1967), *Children and Their Primary Schools* (Plowden Report) (London: HMSO).

CEPAL (1994), *Social Panorama of Latin America 1994* (Santiago: Comision Economica para America Latina y el Caribe).

—— (1997), *Panorama Social 1997* (Santiago: Comision Economica para America Latina y el Caribe).

—— (1998) *Panorama Social 1998* (Santiago: Comision Economica para America Latina y el Caribe).

CERI (1995), *Education at a Glance. The OECD Indicators* (Paris: OECD).

—— (2001), *The Well-Being of Nations: The Role of Human and Social Capital* (Paris: OECD).

—— (2003*a*), *Knowledge Management: New Challenges for Educational Research* (Paris: OECD).

—— (2003*b*), *Schooling for Tomorrow—Networks of Innovation* (Paris: OECD).

—— (2004*a*), *Innovation in the Knowledge Economy: Implications for Education and Learning* (Paris: OECD).

—— (2004*b*), *Measuring Knowledge Management in the Business Sector: First Steps* (Paris: OECD).

Cerny, P. (1990), *The Changing Architecture of Politics: Structure, Agency and the Future of the State* (London: Sage).

Chadwick, E. (1842), *General Report on the Sanitary Conditions of the Labouring Population of Great Britain* (Edinburgh: Edinburgh University Press, 1965).

Chamberlain, R., and Davey, A. (1976), 'Cross-Sectional Study of Developmental Test Items in Children aged 94–97 Weeks: Report of the British Births Child Study', *Developmental Medicine and Child Neurology* 18: 54–70.

Chan, J. (1995), 'A Decade of Education in Hong Kong', in J. Chan (ed.), *Prospect of Education in Hong Kong* (Hong Kong: Hong Kong Teachers' Association).

Chapman, B. (2003), 'Hidden Costs the Big Burden', *The Australian*, 10 December, 36.

Charafeddine, F. (1996), 'Social Change in Lebanon after the Recent War and Perspectives for a Solution', Paper presented at the UNESCO Conference on the Management of Social Transformations in the Arab States Region, Tunis, 26–8 February.

Charlesworth, S. (2000), 'Bourdieu, Social Suffering and Working Class Life', in B. Fowler (ed.), *Reading Bourdieu on Society and Culture* (Oxford: Blackwell).

Chatterjee, P. (1986), *Nationalist Thought and the Colonial World: A Derivative Discourse?* (London: Zed Books).

—— (1993), *The Nation and Its Fragments: Colonial and Postcolonial Histories* (Princeton, NJ: Princeton University Press).

Chatty, D. (1996), *Mobile Pastoralists: Development, Planning and Social Change in Oman* (New York: Columbia University Press).

Cheah, P. (1998), 'Introduction, part II: the cosmopolitical—today', in P. Cheah and B. Robbins (eds.), *Cosmopolitics: Thinking and Feeling Beyond the Nation* (Minneapolis: University of Minnesota Press).

Cheriet, B. (1996), 'The Evaluation of the Higher Education System in Algeria', in R. Cowen (ed.), *The Evaluation of Higher Education Systems* (London: Kogan Page).

Cheung, B. L. (2001), 'English, Mother Tongue and Putonghua—What to Value? Ming Pao, 21 November, in *Educational News* 11 (Hong Kong: Hong Kong Educational Information Centre) 27.

Chevalier, A., and Conlon, G. (2003), *Does it Pay to Attend a Prestigious University?* (London: Centre for the Economics of Education, London School of Economics).

Chevit, B. (1994), 'Politique linguistique: un processus de dépossession', *Les Cahiers de L'Orient* 35: 133–61.

Chisholm, L. (1990), 'Gender and Deviance in South African Industrial Schools and Reformatories for Girls, 1911–34', in C. Walker (ed.), *Women and Gender in Southern Africa to 1945* (Cape Town: David Philip).

—— (2001), 'Gender and Leadership in South African Educational Leadership Administration', *Gender and Education* 13/4: 387–99.

Christina, R., Mehran, G., and Mir, Sh. (1999), 'Education in the Middle East: Challenges and Opportunities', in R. F. Arnove and C. A. Torres (eds.), *Comparative Education: The Dialectic of the Global and the Local* (New York: Rowman & Littlefield).

Chua, A., (2003), *World on Fire: How Exporting Free-Market Democracy Breeds Ethnic Hatred and Global Instability* (London, Random House).

Chubb, J., and Moe T., (1990), *Politics, Markets, and America's Schools* (Washington, DC: The Brookings Institution).

—— and Moe, T. (1997), 'Politics, Markets, and the Organization of Schools', in Halsey et al. (eds.), 363–81.

Cladis, M. (ed.) (1999), *Durkheim and Foucault: Perspectives on Education and Punishment* (Oxford: Durkheim Press).

Clark, C. M., and Peterson, P. L. (1986), 'Teachers' Thought Processes', in M. C. Wittrock (ed.), *Handbook of Research on Teaching*, 3rd edn. (New York: Macmillan).

Clark, J., Dyson, A., et al. (1999), *Housing and Schooling—A Case Study in Joined Up Problems* (York: Joseph Rowntree Foundation).

Clark, L. (1976), 'The Rights of Women: The Theory and Practice of the Ideology of Male Supremacy', in W. R. Shea and J. King-Farlow (eds.), *Contemporary Issues in Political Philosophy* (New York: Science History Publications).

Clark, N. (2003), 'The Play of the World', in M. Pryke, G. Rose, and S. Whatmore (eds.), *Using Social Theory* (London: Sage).

Clarke, J. Gerwitz, S., Hughes, G., and Humphrey, J. (2000), 'Guarding the Public Interest? Auditing Public Services', in: J. Clarke, S. Gerwitz, and E. McLauchline (eds.), *New Managerialism, New Welfare* (London: Open University/Sage).

Clarke, P. (2001), *Teaching and Learning: The Culture of Pedagogy* (New Delhi: Sage).

Clayton, R., and Pontusson, J. (1998), 'Welfare-State Retrenchment Revisited: Entitlement Cuts, Public Sector Restructuring and Inegalitarian Trends in Advanced Capitalist Societies', *World Politics* 51: 67–98.

Clayton, T. (2000), *Education and the Politics of Language: Hegemony and Pragmatism in Cambodia, 1979–1989* (Hong Kong: Comparative Education Research Centre, HKU).

Clements, K. (2001), 'Peace Education in Conflict Zones', *SangSaeng*, Asia Pacific Centre of Education for International Understanding (Winter 2001), 2: 9–16.

Clifford, J. (1997), *Routes: Travel and Translation in the Late Twentieth Century* (Cambridge, Mass.: Harvard University Press).

Cock, J. (1980), *Maids and Madams: A Study in the Politics of Exploitation* (Johannesburg: Ravan).

Cockburn, C. (1992), 'Equal Opportunities: The Short and Long Agenda', *Industrial Relations Journal*, 213–25.

—— (1998), *The Space Between Us: Negotiating Gender and National Identities in Conflict* (London: Zed Books).

Codd, J. (1993), 'Managerialism, Market Liberalism and the Move to Self Managing Schools in New Zealand', in J. Smyth (ed.), *A Socially Critical View of the Self Managing School* (London: Falmer).

Coffey, M. (1999), 'The State of Culture: Institutional Patrimony in Post-Revolutionary Mexico'. Unpublished Ph.D. Dissertation, Department of Art and Design, University of Illinois at Urbana-Champaign).

Coffield, F. (1997), 'A Tale of Three Little Pigs: Building the Learning Society with Straw', *Evaluation and Research in Education* 11: 1–15.

Coffield, F., Borrill, C., and Marshall, S. (1986), *Growing Up at the Margins: Young Adults in the North East* (Milton Keynes: Open University Press).

Cohen, J. L., and Arato, A. (1992), *Civil Society and Political Theory* (Cambridge, Mass.: MIT).

Cohen, M. (1996), 'Democracy and the Future of Nations: Challenges of Disadvantaged Women and Minorities', in R. Boyer and D. Drache (eds.), *State Against Markets: The Limits of Globalization* (New York: Routledge).

Cohen, P. (1998), 'On Teaching Arts and 'Race' in the Classroom', in D. Buckingham (ed.), *Teaching Popular Culture: Beyond Radical Pedagogy* (London: UCL).

Colclough, C. (1996), 'Education and the Market: Which Parts of the Neo-Liberal Solution are Correct?', *World Development* 24/4: 589–610.

—— Al-Samarrai, S., Rose, P., and Tembon, M. (2003), *Achieving Schooling for All in Africa: Costs, Commitment and Gender* (Aldershot: Ashgate).

Coleman, J. (1968), 'The Concept of Equality of Educational Opportunity', *Harvard Educational Review*, 38 (Winter): 7–22.

Coleman, J. S. (1969), *Equality of Educational Opportunity* (Cambridge, Mass.: Harvard University Press).

—— (1988), 'Social Capital and the Creation of Human Capital', *American Journal of Sociology* 94 (Suppl.): S95–S120.

—— (1990), *Foundations of Social Theory* (Cambridge, Mass.: Harvard University Press).

Collier, P. (1998), *The Political Economy of Ethnicity*, Annual World Bank Conference on Development Economics, 20–1 April 1998.

Collins, A., Brown, J., and Newman, S. (1989), 'Cognitive Apprenticeship: Teaching the Craft of Reading, Writing, and Mathematics', in L. Resnick (ed.), *Knowing, Learning, and Instruction: Essays In Honour of Robert Glaser* (Hillsdale, NJ: Erlbaum), 453–94.

Collins, R. (1979), *The Credential Society: An Historical Sociology of Education and Stratification* (New York: Academic Press).

—— (1990), 'The Durkheimian Tradition in Conflict Sociology', in J. C. Alexander (ed.), *Durkheimian Sociology: Cultural Studies* (Cambridge: Cambridge University Press).

—— (1994), *Four Sociological Traditions* (Oxford: Oxford University Press).

—— (1997), 'A Sociological Guilt Trip: Comment on Connell', *American Journal of Sociology* 102/6: 1558–64.

—— (2000), *The Sociology of Philosophies: A Global Theory of Intellectual Change* (Cambridge, Mass: Harvard University Press).

—— (2002), 'Credential Inflation and the Future of Universities', in S. Brint (ed.), *The Future of the City of Intellect: The Changing American University* (Stanford, Calf.: Stanford University Press).

Collins, T., and Tillman, S. (1998), 'Global Technology Diffusion and the American Research University', in J. T. Kenny (ed.), *Research Administration and Technology Transfer* (San Francisco: Jossey Bass).

Comaroff, J., and Comaroff, J. (1992), *Ethnography and the Historical Imagination* (Boulder: Westview).

Comedu-Kirschner, C. (2000), 'The Sharing Culture', *Management Review* 89/1 (January).

Connell, R. (1997) 'Why is Classical Theory Classical?', *American Journal of Sociology* 102/6: 1511–57.

Connell, R. W. (1985), *Teachers' Work* (Sydney: George Allen & Unwin).

—— (1987), *Gender and Power* (Cambridge: Polity).

—— (1990), 'The State, Gender and Sexual Politics', *Theory and Society* 19: 507–44.

—— (1995), *Masculinities* (London: Polity).

Connor, H., and Dewson, S. (2001), *Social Class and Higher Education: Issues Affecting Decisions on Participation by Lower Social Class Groups*, DfEE Research Report RR267 (London: HMSO).

—— Burton, R., Pollard, E., Regan, J., and Pearson, R. (1999), *How students Choose Universities and Colleges* (London: Institute for Employment Studies and CVCP).

Cooke, K. (1994), *Real Gorgeous: The Truth about Body and Beauty* (St Leonards, NSW: Allen & Unwin).

Coole, D. (1993), *Women in Political Theory: From Ancient Misogyny to Contemporary Feminism* (New York: Harvester Wheatsheaf).

Coons, J. E. and Sugarman, S. D., (1978), *Education by Choice: The Case for Family Control* (Berkeley: University of California Press).

Cooper, D. H., and Farran, D. C. (1988), 'Behavioral Risk Factors in Kindergarten', *Early Childhood Research Quarterly* 3: 1–19.

Cope, B., and Kalantzis, M. (1997), *Productive Diversity* (Annandale: Pluto).

Corak, M. (2001), 'Are the Kids All Right? Intergenerational mobility and child well-being in Canada', *Working Paper* 171, Family and Labour Studies, Statistics Canada.

—— (ed) (2004), *The Dynamics of Intergenerational Income Mobility* (Cambridge: Cambridge University Press).

Corbridge, S. and Harriss, J. (2000), *Reinventing India: Liberalization, Hindu Nationalism and Popular Democracy* (Cambridge: Polity).

Corcoran, M., Gordon, R., Laren, D., and Solon, G. (1992), 'The Association between Men's Economic Status and their Family and Community Origins', *Journal of Human Resources* 27: 575–601.

Corlett, W. (1993), *Community Without Unity: A Politics of Derridean Extravagance* (Durham: Duke University Press).

Cornia, G., Jolly, R., and Stewart, F. (1987), *Adjustment with a Human Face* (Oxford: Clarendon).

Corrigan, P. (1979), *Schooling the Smash Street Kids* (London: Macmillan).

—— and Sayer, D. (1985), *The Great Arch: English State Formation as Cultural Revolution* (Oxford: Basil Blackwell).

Cortada, J. W. (ed.) (1998), *Rise of the Knowledge Worker* (Oxford: Butterworth-Heinemann).

Cortina, R., and Stromquist, N. P. (eds.) (2000), *Distant Alliances: Gender Equity Policies in Education in Latin America* (New York: Garland).

Court, M. (1993), '1898–1993: How Far Have We Come in Women's Employment in Education', *New Zealand Annual Review of Education* 3: 81–126.

Cowen, R. (1996), 'Last Past the Post: Comparative Education, Modernity and Perhaps Postmodernity', *Comparative Education* 3/2.

Cox, M. (2003), 'America and the World'. In R. Singh (ed.), *Governing America: The Politics of a Divided Democracy* (Oxford: Oxford University Press).

Cox, R. (2004), 'Navigating Community College Demands: Contradictory Goals, Expectations, and Outcomes in Composition'. Unpublished doctoral dissertation, School of Education, University of California, Berkeley, USA.

Craig, J. E., and Spear, N. (1982*a*), 'Rational Actors, Group Processes, and the Development of Educational Systems', in M. S. Archer (ed.), *The Sociology of Educational Expansion* (London: Sage), 65–90.

—— (1982*b*), 'Explaining Educational Expansion: An Agenda for Historical and Comparative Research', in M. S. Archer (ed.), *The Sociology of Educational Expansion* (London: Sage).

Critchley, S. (1999), 'Habermas and Derrida Get Married' in *The Ethics of Deconstruction*, 2nd edn. (Edinburgh: Edinburgh University Press), 267–80.

—— 'Globalization and Education: Demonstrating a "Common World Educational Culture" or Locating a "Globally Structured Educational Agenda"', *Educational Theory*, 50/4: 427–67.

Crompton, R. (ed.) (1999), *Restructuring Gender Relations and Employment: The Decline of the Male BreadWinner* (Oxford: Oxford University Press).

Cross, M. (1986), 'A Historical View of Education in South Africa: Towards an Assessment' *Comparative Education* 22/3: 185–200.

Crossan, B., Field, J., Gallacher, J., and Merrill, B. (2003), 'Understanding Participation in Learning for Non-traditional Adult Learners: Learning Careers and the Construction of Learning Identities', *British Journal of Sociology of Education*, 24/1: 55–67.

Cuban, L. J. (1984), *How Teachers Taught: Constancy and Change in American Classrooms, 1890–1990* (New York: Longman).

—— (1990), 'Reforming Again and Again and Again', *Educational Researcher* 19/1 (Jan.—Feb.) 3–13.

—— (1992). "Curriculum Stability and Change", in P. Jackson (ed.), *Handbook of Research on Curriculum* (New York: Macmillan), ch. 8.

Cummins, J. (1998), 'Language Issues and Educational Change', in A. Hargreaves, A. Lieberman, M. Fullan, and D. Hopkins (eds.), *International Handbook of Educational Change* (Dordrecht:, Kluwer Academic).

Cunha, F., Heckman, J., Lochner, L. and Masterov, D. (2005), 'Interpreting the Evidence on Life Cycle Skill Formation', in E. Hanushek and F. Welch (eds.), *The Handbook of the Economics of Education* (New York: North-Holland).

Curriculum Development Council (2001) *Learning to Learn: the way forward in curriculum development* (Hong Kong: Government Printer).

Curtin, P. (1984), *Cross-Cultural Trade in World History* (Cambridge: Cambridge University Press).

Curtis, B. (1988), *Building the Educational State: Canada West* (New York: Falmer).

Curtis, P. (2003), 'Raising standards "impossible" in some schools', *The Guardian*, 5 February.

Dølvik, J. E., and Stokke, T. A. (1998), 'Norway: The Revival of Centralized Concentration', in A. Ferner and R. Hyman (eds.), *Changing Industrial Relations in Europe* (Oxford: Blackwell).

Dahl, R. (1999), 'Can International Organizations be Democratic?: A Sceptic's View', in I. Shapiro and C. Hacker-Cordon (eds.), *Democracy's Edges* (Cambridge: Cambridge University Press).

Dahloff, U., and Lundgren, U. P. (1970), *Macro and Micro Approaches Combined for Curriculum Process Analysis: A Swedish Education Field Project*, Report (Institute of Göteborg, Sweden).

Dahrendorf, R. (1990), *The Modern Social Conflict* (Berkeley: University of California).

Dale, R. (1988), 'Implications for Progressivism of Recent Changes in the Control and Direction of Education Policy', in A. Green (ed.), *Progress and Inequality in Comprehensive Education* (London, Routledge) 39–62.

—— (1989), *The State and Education Policy* (Buckingham: Open University Press).

Dale, R. (1992), 'Recovering from a Pyrrhic Victory? Quality, Relevance and Impact in the Sociology of Education', in M. Arnot and L. Barton (eds.), *Voicing Concerns: Sociological Perspectives on Contemporary Educational Reforms* (Wallingford: Triangle Books).

—— (1997), 'The State and the Governance of Education: An Analysis of the Restructuring of the state–education Relationship', in A. Halsey, et al., *Education, Culture, Economy, and Society* (Oxford: Oxford University Press).

—— (2000), 'Globalization and Education: Demonstrating a "Common World Educational Culture" or Locating a "Globally Structured Educational Agenda"', *Educational Theory* 50/4: 427–67.

—— and Robertson, S. (1996), 'Resiting the Nation, Reshaping the State: Globalization Effects on Education Policy in New Zealand', in M. Olssen and K. Morris (eds.), *Education Policy in New Zealand: The 1990s and Beyond* (Palmerston North: Dunmore).

—— —— (2002), 'The Varying Effects of Regional Organisations as Subjects of Globalisation of Education', *Comparative Education Review* 46/1: 10–36.

Daly, M., Büchel, F., and Duncan, G. (2000), 'Premiums and Penalties for Surplus and Deficit Education: Evidence from the United States and Germany', *Economics of Education Review* 19: 169–78.

Daniels, H. (2001), *Vygotsky and Pedagogy* (London: Routledge Falmer).

Danmarks Statistik (1997), *Statistical Yearbook 1997* (Copenhagen: Danmarks Statistik).

—— Socialforskningsinstituttet (1992), *Living Conditions in Denmark: Compendium of Statistics 1992* (Copenhagen: Danmarks Statistik).

Danziger, S., and Waldfogel, J. (2000), *Securing the Future: Investing in Children from Birth to College* (New York: Russell Sage).

Darling-Hammond, L. (2000), 'Teacher Quality and Student Achievement: A Review of State Policy Evidence', *Education Policy Analysis Archives*, 8. Available at <http://olam.ed.asu.edu/epaa/v8n1/>.

Darwall, S. (ed.) (1995), *Equal Freedom: Selected Tanner Lectures on Human Values* (Ann Arbor: University of Michigan Press).

Davies, B. (1989), *Frogs Snails and Feminist Tales* (Sydney: Allen and Unwin)

Davies, C. (1993), 'Concentric, Overlapping and Competing Loyalties and Identities', in K. Schleicher (ed.), *Nationalism in Education* (Frankfurt: Peter Lang).

—— (1996), 'The Sociology of Professions and the Profession of Gender', *Sociology* 30: 661–78.

Davies, J. (1996), *Educating Students in a Media-Saturated Culture* (Lancaster, Pa.: Technomic).

Davies, L. (1999), 'Comparing Definitions of Democracy in Education', *Compare* 29/2.

—— and Kirkpatrick, G. (2000), *The Euridem Project: A Review of Pupil Democracy in Europe* (London: The Children's Rights Alliance).

—— Harber, C., and Schweisfurth, M. (2002), *Democracy Through Teacher Education: A Guidebook for Use with Student Teachers* (Birmingham: Centre for International Education and Research, University of Birmingham).

Davies, R. (1979), *Capital, State and White Labour in South Africa, 1900–1960* (Brighton: Harvester).

—— Kaplan, D., Morris, M., and O'Meara, D. (1976), 'Class Struggle and the Periodisation of the South African State', *Review of African Political Economy* 7: 4–30.

Davies, S. (1999), 'From Moral Duty to Cultural Rights: A Case Study of Political Framing in Education', *Sociology of Education* 72: 1–21.

—— and Guppy, N. (1997), 'Globalization and Education Reforms in Anglo-American Democracies', *Comparative Education Review* 41/4: 435–59.

Davin, A. (1978), 'Imperialism and Motherhood', *History Workshop Journal* 5: 9–65.

Davis, E. and Pratt, V. (1993) *Making the Link. Affirmative Action and Industrial Relations* (Canberra: AGPS).

Davis, J., and Ridge, T. (1997), *Same Scenery, Different Lifestyle: Rural Children on a Low Income* (London: The Children's Society).

Davis, K., and Moore, W. E. (1945), 'Some Principles of Stratification', *American Sociological Review* 10: 242–9.

DAWN (1995), 'Rethinking Social Development: DAWN's Vision', *World Development* 23/11: 2001–4.

Day, C. (1999), *Developing Teachers: The Challenges of Lifelong Learning* (London: Falmer).

de Beauvoir, Simone (1949), *Le Deuxième Sexe* (Paris: Éditions Gallimard).

De Dreu, C. (1997), 'Productive Conflict: The Importance of Conflict Management and Conflict Issue', in C. De Dreu and E. Van De Vliert, (eds.), *Using Conflict in Organisations* (London: Sage).

De gado Gaitan, C (1992), 'School Mattus in the Maxican-American Home: Socializing Children to Education, *American Educational Research Journal* 29: 495513.

—— (200), 'Teacher Quality and Student Achievement: A Review of State Policy evidence;, *Education Policy Analysis Archiness*, 8. Available at <http://olam.ed.asu.edu/epaa/v8n1/>.

de Graaf, P., et al. (1998), 'Parents' Financial and Cultural Resources, Grades, and Transitions to Secondary School', *European Sociological Review* 4: 209–21.

De Janvry, A., and Sadoulet, E. (1993), 'Market, State, and Civil Organizations in Latin America Beyond the Debt Crisis: The Context for Rural Development', *World Development* 21/4: 659–74.

de Lauretis, T. (1986), 'Feminist Studies/Critical Studies: Issues, Terms and Contexts', in T. de Lauretis (ed.), *Feminist Studies/Critical Studies* (Bloomington: University of Indiana Press).

de Waal, A. (1994), 'Genouide in Rwanda', *Anthropology Today*10/3:1-2

—— (1996), 'Famine and Human Rights', in D. Eade (ed.), *Development in States of War* (Oxford: Oxfam).

de Witte, M., and Stein, B. (2000), 'Automation, Job Content, and Underemployment', *Work, Employment and Society* 14/2: 245–64.

Dean, M. (1994), '"A Social Structure of Many Souls": Moral Regulation, Government, and Self Formation', in *Canadian Journal of Sociology* 19/2: 145–68.

—— (1999), 'Normalizing Democracy: Foucault and Habermas on Democracy, Liberalism and Law', in S. Ashenden and D. Owen (eds.), *Foucault contra Habermas* (London: Sage), 166–94.

Deary, I. J. (2000), *Looking Down on Human Intelligence, from Psychometrics to the Brain* (Oxford: Oxford University Press).

de Waal, A. (1994), 'Genocide in Rwarda', *Anthropology Today* 10/3: 1–2.

Deem, R. (2001), 'Globalisation, New Managerialism, Academic Capitalism and Entrepreneuralism in Universities: Is the Local Dimension Still Important?', *Comparative Education*, 37/1: 7–20.

—— Brehony, K and Heath, S. (1995) *Active Citizenship and the Governing of Schools*. (Buckingham: Open University Press).

Dehli, K. (1996), 'Between "market" and "state": Engendering Education in the 1990s', *Discourse: Studies in the Cultural Politics of Education* 17/3: 363–76.

—— Januario, I. (1994), *Parent Activism and School Reform in Toronto* (Toronto: The Department of Sociology, The Ontario Institute for Studies in Education at the University of Toronto).

Delamont, S. (1984*a*), 'Debs, Dollies, Swots and Weeds: Classroom Styles at St Luke's', in G. Walford (ed.), *British Public Schools* (London: Falmer).

—— (1984*b*), 'The Old Girl Network', in R. G. Burgess (ed.), *Fieldwork in Educational Settings* (London: Falmer).

Delanty, G. (2001), *Challenging Knowledge* (Buckingham: Open University Press).

Deleuze, G. (1992), 'Postscript on the Societies of Control', 59 (Oct.): 3–7.

—— and Guattari, F. (1987), *A Thousand Plateaus: Capitalism and Schizophrenia*, trans. B. Massumi (Minneapolis: University of Minnesota Press).

Delgado-Gaitan, C. (1992), 'School Matters in the Mexican-American Home: Socializing Children to Education', *American Educational Research Journal* 29: 495–513.

—— (2001), *The Power of Community: Mobilizing for Family and Schooling* (New York: Rowman & Littlefield).

Demia, C., *Règlement pour les écoles de la ville de Lyon*, 1716.

Dennett, D. (1987), *The Intentional Stance* (Cambridge, Mass.: MIT).

Department for Education and Employment (1995), *Life-long Learning: A Consultation Document* (London: HMSO).

Department for Education and Employment (DfEE) (1998*a*), *Higher Education for the Twenty-First Century: Response to the Dearing Report* (London: HMSO).

—— (1998*b*), *The Learning Age: A Renaissance for a New Britain. Higher Education: Meeting the Challenge* (London: HMSO).

Department for Education and Employment (DfEE) (2000), *Sex and Relationship Education Guidance. DfEE ref. 0116/2000* (London: Department for Education and Employment).

Department for Education and Skills (2003), *Statistics of Education: Pupil Progress by Pupil Characteristics: 2002* (London: HMSO).

—— (2004), *Department for Education and Skills: Five Year Strategy for Children and Learners*, Cm 6272 (London: HMSO).

Department for Education and Skills (2003), *Excellent and Enjoyment: A Strategy for Primary Schools* (London: DfES).

Department for Education and Skills (DfES) (2003), *The Future of Higher Education* (London: HMSO).

Department of Education (2000), *Implementation Plan for Tirisano* (Pretoria: Department of Education).

Department of Education and Science (1967), *Children and Their Primary Schools*, Report of the Plowden Committee (London: HMSO).

Department of Education, Science and Training (2003, 2004), Selected higher education statistics, viewed 2 December 2003, 21 June 2004, <http://www.dest.gov.au/highered/statinfo.htm>.

Derrida, J. (1994) *Specters of Marx: The State of the Debt, the Work of Mourning, and the New International* (London: Routledge).

Deutsch, C. H. (1989), 'The Powerful Push for Self-Service', *The New York Times* (9 April), 3: 1.

Deutsch, M. (1991), 'Subjective Features of Conflict Resolution: Psychological, Social and Cultural Influences', in R. Vayrynen, (ed.) *New Directions in Conflict Theory* (London: Sage).

Devine, F. (1999), 'Class Analysis and the Stability of Class Relations', *Sociology* 33: 23–42.

—— Savage, M., Scott, J. and Cromption, R. (eds.) (2005) *Rethinking Class: Culture, Identities and Lifestyles* (Basingstoke: Palgrave Macmillan).

Devine, J. (1997), *Maximum Security: The Culture of Violence in Inner-City Schools* (Chicago: Chicago University Press).

Devroye, D., and Freeman, R. (2002), *Does Inequality in Skills Explain Inequality in Earnings Across Advanced Countries?* (London: London School of Economics and Political Science, Centre for Economic Performance).

Dewey, J. (1916), *Democracy and Education* (New York: Macmillan).

—— (1976/1910), 'How We Think', in J. Boydston (ed.), *The Collected Works, Middle Works 6*.

—— and Dewey, E. (1915), *Schools of Tomorrow* (New York: E. P. Dutton).

DfEE (1998), *From Targets to Action* (London: DfEE).

DfEE (1998), *The Learning Age* (London: The Stationery Office).

DfES (2001), *Schools: Achieving Success* (London: DfES).

—— (2002*a*), *Education and Skills: Delivering Results. A Strategy to 2006* (London: DfES).

—— (2002*b*), *14–19: Extending Opportunities, Raising Standards* (London: DfES).

—— (2003*a*), *Technical Note on the New Education Funding System*, <www.dfes.gov.uk/efsg/docs/THENEWFUNDINGSYSTEMtechnicalnote.doc>.

—— (2003*b*) *14–19: Opportunity and Excellence* (London: DfES).

DfES (2003), *The Future of Higher Education*, White Paper (London: HMSO).

DfES (2003*a*), *Excellence and Enjoyment* (London: HMSO).

—— (2003*b*), *Guidance for LEAs on Target-Setting at Key Stages 2, 3 and 4* (London: DfES).

Di Pierro, M. C. (2000), 'Public Policy and Adult Education for Women in Brazil', in R. Cortina and N. P. Stromquist (eds.), *Educational Policies for Gender Equity in Latin America* (New York: Garland).

Diamond, J., (2005), *Collapse: How Societies Choose to Fail or Survive*, (London: Allen Lane).

Diaz, M. (2001), 'Subject, Power and Pedagogic Discourse', in A. Morais et al. (eds.), *Towards a Sociology of Pedagogy: The Contribution of Basil Bernstein to Research* (New York: Peter Lang).

Dickens, W. T., and Flynn, J. (2001), 'Heritability Estimates Versus Large Environmental Effects: The IQ Paradox Resolved', *Psychological Review* 108/2: 346–69.

Dietz, M. G. (1985), 'Citizenship with a Feminist Pace: The Problem with Maternal Thinking', *Political Theory*, February: 19–37.

—— (2003), 'Current Controversies in Feminist Theory', *Annual Review of Political Science*, 6, 399–431.

Dika, S. I., and Singh, K. (2002), 'Applications of Social Capital in Educational Literature: A Critical Synthesis', *Review of Educational Research* 72: 31–60.

Dill, D. D. (1997), 'Higher Education Markets and Public Policy', *Higher. Education Policy* 10: 167–85.

Dillabough, J. (1998), 'Gender Politics and Conceptions of the Modern Teacher: Women, Identity, and Professionalism', Paper under review.

—— (2000), 'Theorising Women's Diverse Feminist Political Identities in British Teacher Education', in M. Arnot and J. Dillabough (eds.), *Gender, Education and Citizenship: An International Feminist Reader* (London: Routledge).

—— and Arnot, M. (1998), 'Feminist Perspectives in the Sociology of Education', in D. Levinson, R. Sadovnik and P. Cookson (eds.), *Sociology of Education: An Encyclopaedia* (New York: Taylor and Francis).

—— —— (2001), 'Feminist Sociology of Education: Dynamics, Debates and Directions', in J. Demaine (ed.), *Sociology of Education Today* (Basingstoke: Palgrave).

Dillon, S. (2004), 'Good schools or bad? Ratings baffle parents', *New York Times*, 5 Sept. 2004.

DiMaggio, P. (1982), 'Cultural Capital and School Success', *American Sociological Review* 47: 189–201.

—— and Mohr, J. (1985), 'Cultural Capital, Educational Attainment and Marital Selection', *American Journal of Sociology* 90: 231–61.

Dimitriadis, C., and Kamberelis, G. (1997), 'Shifting Terrains: Mapping Education within a Global Landscape', *The Annals of the American Academy of Political and Social Science* 551: 137–50.

Disney, M. (2001), 'Qualities of the K-Professional', *Malaysian Business*, 16 March, 11.

Dizard, W. (1997), *Meganet: How the Global Communications Network Will Connect Everyone on Earth* (Boulder: Westview).

Dolby, N. (2001), *Constructing Race: Youth, Identity and Popular Culture in South Africa* (Buffalo: State University of New York Press).

Dølvik, J. E., and Stokke, T. A. (1998), 'Norway: The Revival of Centralized Concentration', in A. Femer and R. Hyman (eds.), *Changing Industrial Relations in Europe* (Oxford: Blackwell).

Donald, J. (1992), *Sentimental Education* (London: Verso).

Dore, R. (1976), *The Diploma Disease: Education, Qualification and Development* (London: George Allen & Unwin).

Doremus, Paul N., Keller, William W., Pauly, Louis W. and Reich, Simon (1998), *The Myth of the Global Corporation* (Princeton: Princeton University Press).

Douglas, D. (1986), 'From School to University: Language Policy and Performance at the University of Khartoum', *International Journal of the Sociology of Language* 61: 89–112.

Douglas, J. W. B. (1964), *The Home and the School* (London: Macgibbon & Kee).

Douglas, M. (1969), *Purity and Danger* (London: Routledge & Kegan Paul).

—— (1986), *How Institutions Think* (London: Routledge & Kegan Paul).

Dow, A. (1996), *Status Quo? Post-Fordism, Knowledge and Power at Gallipoli High School*, Paper presented at the Annual Meeting of the American Educational Research Association, New York, April.

Doz, Y., Santos, J., and Williamson, P. (2001), *From Global to Metanational* (Boston: Harvard Business School Press).

Dreze, J., and Sen, A. (1995), *India: Economic Development and Social Opportunity* (Delhi: Oxford University Press).

Drucker, P. (1969), *The Age of Discontinuities* (London: Transaction Publications).

—— (1993), *Post-Capitalist Society* (London: Butterworth/Heinemann).

Dryzek, J. S. (1995), 'Political and Ecological Communication', *Environmental Politics* 4/4: 13–30.

DSS (1999), *A New Contract for Welfare: Children's Rights and Parent's Responsibilities* (London: DSS).

du Gay, P. (1996), *Consumption and Identity at Work* (London: Sage).

Ducatel, K. (ed.) (1994), *Employment and Technical Change in Europe: Work Organization, Skills and Training* (Aldershot: Edward Elgar).

Duncan, G., and Brooks-Gunn, J. (1997), *Consequences of Growing up Poor* (New York: Russell Sage Foundation).

—— et al. (1998), 'The Effects of Childhood Poverty on the Life Chances of Children', *American Sociological Review* 63: 406–23.

Dunleavy, P. (1980), 'The Political Implications of Sectoral Cleavages and the Growth of State Employment: Part 2, Cleavage Structures and Political Alignment', *Political Studies* 28: 527–49.

Dupont-Ferrier, *Du collége de Clermont au lycée Louis-le-Grand*, i.

Durkheim, É. (1933), *The Division of Labour In Society*, Trans. G. Simpson (New York: Macmillan).

—— (1933), *The Division of Labour in Society* (London: Collier-Macmillan).

—— (1952), *Suicide* (London: Routledge & Kegan Paul).

—— (1956), *Education and Sociology*, trans. S. D. Fox (New York: Free Press).

—— (1961), *Moral Eduation* (New York: Free Press).

—— (1973), *Émile Durkheim on Morality and Society*, ed. R. Bellah (Chicago: University of Chicago Press).

—— (1977), *The Evolution of Educational Thought* (London: Routledge).

—— (1995), *The Elementary Forms of Religious Life* (New York: Free Press).

Dworkin, R. (1977), *Taking Rights Seriously* (London: Duckworth).

Dyehouse, C. (1976), 'Social Darwinistic Ideas and the Development of Women's Education in England 1880–1920', *History of Education* 5/1: 41–58.

Earl, L., and Lemahieu, P. (1997), 'Rethinking Assessment and Accountability', in A. Hargreaves (ed.), *Rethinking Educational Change with Heart and Mind: The 1997 ASCD Yearbook* (Alexandria, Va.: Association for Supervision and Curriculum Development).

Earl, L., et al. (2001), *Watching and Learning 2: OISE/UT Evaluation of the Implementation of the National Literacy and Numeracy Strategies* (Toronto: Ontario Institute for the Study of Education) (for the Standards and Effectiveness Unit of the DfES; ref.: DfES 0617/2001).

EC (2001), *Lifelong Learning Memorandum*. (Brussels: EC).

Eccles. J. S., and Gootman, J. (eds.) (2002), *Community Programs to Promote Youth Development* (Washington DC: National Academy Press).

ECLAC (1995), *Regional Programme of Action for the Women of Latin America and the Caribbean, 1995–2001* (Santiago: Economic Commission for Latin American and the Caribbean).

Edwards, M., and Magarey, S. (eds.) (1995), *Women in a Restructuring Australia* (Sydney: Allen & Unwin).

Edwards, R. (1994), 'From a Distance? Globalization, Space-Time Compression and Distance Education', *Journal of Open Learning* 9/3.

Edwards, T., Fitz, J., and Whitty, G. (1989), *The State and Private Education* (London: Falmer).

—— Whitty, G., and Wigfall, V. (2003), *Education and the Middle Class* (Buckingham: Open University Press).

—— Whitty, G., Edwards, T., and Wigfall, V. (1998), 'Schools, Families and Academically Able Children: Contrasting Modes of Involvement in Secondary Education', *British Journal of Sociology of Education* 19/2: 157–76.

Ehrenreich, B. (1990), *Fear of Falling: The Inner Life of the Middle Class* (New York: HarperPerennial).

—— and Ehrenreich, J. (1979), 'The professional and managerial class', in P. Walker (ed.) *In Between Labor and Capital* (Cambridge MA: Southend Press).

Eickelman, D. F. (1985), *Knowledge and Power in Morocco: The Education of a Twentieth-Century Notable* (Princeton: Princeton University Press).

—— (1992), 'Mass Higher Education and the Religious Imagination in Contemporary Arab Societies', *American Ethnologist*, 19: 643–55.

Eisenstein, H. (1992), *Gender Shock. Feminism on Two Continents* (Sydney: Allen & Unwin).

—— (1995), *Inside Agitators: Australian Femocrats and the State* (Sydney: Allen & Unwin).

El Hachem, B. (1989), 'Education and Plurality in Lebanon', in A. Badran (ed.), *At the Crossroads: Education in the Middle East* (New York: Paragon House).

El-Sanabary, N. (1992), *Education in the Arab Gulf States and the Arab World: An Annotated Bibliography* (New York: Garland).

Elbedour, S., Bart, W. M. and Hektner, J. M. (2000), 'Scholastic Achievement and Family Marital Structure: Bedouin-Arab Adolescents from Monogamous and Polygamous Families in Israel', *Journal of Social Psychology* 140/4: 503–14.

Elias, P., and Purcell, K. (2003) *Measuring Change in the Graduate Labour Market, Researching Graduate Careers Seven Years On*, Research Report No. 1 (Warwick: Warwick

Institute for Employment Research and the Employment Studies Research Unit, University of West of England).

Elkind, D. (1997), 'Schooling in the Postmodern World', in A. Hargreaves (ed.), *Rethinking Educational Change with Heart and Mind: The 1997 ASCD Yearbook* (Alexandria, Va.: Association for Supervision and Curriculum Development).

Elliott, J. (1996), 'Quality Assurance, the Educational Standards Debate, and the Commodification of Educational Research', BERA Annual Conference: University of Lancaster.

—— (1996), 'Quality Assurance, the Educational Standards Debate, and the Commodification of Educational Research', *Curriculum Journal* 8/6: 63–83.

Elliott, L., and Atkinson, D. (1998), *The Age of Insecurity* (London: Verso).

Ellsworth, E. (1997), *Teaching Positions: Difference, Pedagogy and the Power of Address* (New York: Teachers College).

Engeström, Y. (1994), *Training for Change*. (Geneva: ILO).

Englund, T. (1996), 'Are Professional Teachers a Good Thing?', in I. Goodson and A. Hargreaves (eds.), *Teachers' Professional Lives* (London: Falmer).

Ensor, P. (2001), 'Curriculum', in N. Cloete, R. Fehnel, P. Maassen, T. Moja, H. Perold, and T. Gibbon (eds.), *Transformation in Higher Education: Global Pressures and Local Realities* (Cape Town: CHEPS/Juta).

Epstein, D. (1994), 'Introduction: Lesbian and Gay Equality in Education—Problems and Possibilities', in D. Epstein (ed.), *Challenging Lesbian and Gay Inequalities in Education* (Buckingham: Open University Press).

—— (1997), 'Boyz' Own Stories: Masculinities and Sexualities in Schools', in *Gender and Education* 9/1: 105–15.

—— and Johnson, R. (1998), *Schooling Sexualities* (Buckingham: Open University Press).

—— O'Flynn, S., and Telford, D. (2003), *Silenced Sexualities in Schools and Universities* (Stoke-on-Trent: Trentham Books).

—— and Unterhalter, E. (1999), 'Gendering Education for Reconciliation: "Femininity", Memory and Silence in the South African Truth and Reconciliation Commission Report', Paper presented at Second International Gender and Education Conference, University of Warwick, April.

Epstein, J. (1995), 'School/family/Community Partnerships', *Phi Delta Kappan* 76: 701–12.

Erault, M. (ed.) (1991), *Education and the Information Society* (London: Cassell).

Eraut, M. (2004), 'Informal Learning in the Workplace', *Studies in Continuing Education* 26/2: 247–73.

Erikson, R., and Goldthorpe, J. (1992), *The Constant Flux: A Study of Class Mobility in Industrial Societies* (Oxford: Clarendon).

—— and Jonsson, J. (1996), *Can Education be Equalised? The Swedish Case in Comparative Perspective* (Boulder: Westview).

Ermisch, J., and Francesconi, M. (2002), 'The Effect of Parents' Employment on Children's Educational Attainment', *ISER Working Paper* 21 (Colchester: University of Essex).

—— and Francesconi, M. (2002), *Intergenerational Social Mobility and Assortative Mating in Britain*, Discussion Paper No 465 (Bonn: Institute for the Study of Labour).

Errante, A. (2003) 'Where in the World Do Children Learn "Bloody Revenge"? Cults of Terror and Counter Terror and their Implications for Child Socialisation', *Globalisation, Societies and Education* 1/2: 131–52.

Esping Andersen, G. (1990), *The Three Worlds of Welfare Capitalism* (Princeton: Princeton University Press).

—— (1999), *Social Foundations of Postindustrial Economies* (Oxford: Oxford University Press).

—— (2004), 'Untying the Gordian Knot of Social Inheritance', *Research in Social Stratification and Mobility* 21: 115–39.

—— and Sarasa, S. (2002), 'The Generational Conflict Revisited', *Journal of European Social Policy* 12: 5–22.

—— (1996) The Three Words of Welfare Capitalism (Cambridge: Polity).

—— (1991) 'Positive-Sum Solutions in a World of Trade-Offs?' in G. Esping-Andersen (ed.), *Welfare States in Transition: National Adaptations in Global Economies* (London: Sage).

Estevez-Abe, M., Iversen, T., and Soskice, D. (2001), 'Social Protection and the Formation of Skills: A Reinterpretation of the Welfare State', in Hall and Soskice (eds.).

Etzioni, A. (1969), *The Semi-Professions and Their Organization* (New York: Free Press).

—— (1993), *The Spirit of Community: Rights, Responsibilities and the Communitarian Agenda* (New York: Croan).

Etzkowitz, H. (1997), 'The Entrepreneurial University and the Emergence of Democratic Corporatism', in H. Etzkowitz and L. Leydesdorff (eds.), *Universities and the Global Knowledge Economy* (London: Pinter).

—— and Leydesdorff, L. (1997*a*), 'Introduction: Universities in the Global Knowledge Economy', in H. Etzkowitz and L. Leydesdorff (eds.), *Universities and the Global Knowledge Economy* (London: Pinter).

—— —— (eds.) (1997*b*), *Universities and the Global Knowledge Economy: A Triple Helix of University-Industry-Government Relations* (London: Pinter).

European Commission (1996), *Teaching and Learning: Towards the Learning Society* (Luxembourg: Office for Official Publications of the EC).

European Union Commission for Research on Education and Training (1996), *White Paper on Education and Training: Teaching and Learning; Towards the Learning Society*, (Brussels: European Commission).

Evans, P. (1992), 'Indian Informatics in the 1980s: The Changing Character of State Involvement', *World Development* 20/1: 1–18.

Evetts, J. (2002), 'New Directions in State and International Professional Occupations: Discretionary Decision-Making and Acquired Regulation', *Work, Employment and Society* 16/2: 341–53.

Ewen, S. (1988), *All Consuming Images: The Politics of Style in Contemporary Culture* (New York: Basic Books).

Fabian, J. (1983), *Time and the Other: How Anthropology Makes Its Object* (New York: Columbia University Press).

Fabos, B., and Young, M. (1999), 'Telecommunications in the Classroom: Rhetoric Versus Reality', *Review of Educational Research* 69/3:, 217–60.

Fägerlind, I., and Saha, L. J. (1983), *Education and National Development: A Comparative Perspective* (Oxford: Pergamon Press).

Fairbrother, P. (2000), *Unions at the Crossroads* (London: Mansell).

Fairclough, N. (1992), *Discourse and Social Change* (Cambridge: Polity).

Fairlie, R. W., and Resch, A. M. (2002), 'Is There "White Flight" into Private Schools? Evidence from the National Educational Longitudinal Survey', *Review of Economics and Statistics* 84: 21–33.

Farag, I. (1994), 'L'Enseignement en question—enjeux d'un débat', *Egypt/Monde Arabe* 18–19: 241–329.

Faulkner, W., and Senker, J. (1995), *Knowledge Frontiers: Public Sector Research and Industrial Innovation in Biotechnology, Engineering Ceramics, and Parallel Computing* (Oxford: Clarendon).

Faust, K., Bach, R., Gadalla, S., Khattab, H., and Gulick, J. (1991), 'Mass Education, Islamic Revival, and the Population Problem in Egypt', *Journal of Comparative Family Studies* 22: 329–41.

Featherman, D., and Hauser, R. (1976), 'Prestige or Socio-economic Scales in the Study of Occupational Achievement?', *Sociological Methods and Research* 4/4: 403–22.

——Jones, F., and Hauser, R. (1975) 'Assumptions of Social Mobility Research in the United States: The Case of Occupational Status', *Social Science Research* 4: 329–60.

Federal Immigration and Naturalization Service (1986, 1987), *Statistical Yearbook* (Washington DC: US Government Printing Office).

Feinstein, L. (2003), 'Inequality in the Early Cognitive Development of British Children in the 1970 Cohort', *Economica* 70/277: 73–98.

——and Bynner, J. (2004), 'The Importance of Developmental Trajectories in Mid-Childhood: Effects on Adult Outcomes in the UK 1970 Birth Cohort', *Child Development*. 75/5.

——and Duckworth, K. (April 2005), 'The Contributions of Cognitive and Behavioural Development at School Entry to School Performance and Adult Outcomes', in G. Duncan (Chair), *Hard Skills and Socioemotional Behaviour at School Entry: What Matters Most for Subsequent Achievement?* Symposium conducted at the biennial meeting of the Society for Research on Child Development, Atlanta, Georgia.

——and Symons, J. (1999), 'Attainment in Secondary School', *Oxford Economic Papers* 51: 300–21.

Feld, S. (1988), Notes on World Beat, *Public Culture* 1/1: 31–7.

Felstead, A., Gallie, D., and Green, F. (2002), *Work Skills in Britain, 1986–2001* (London: Department for Education and Skills).

————(2003), 'Job Complexity and Task Discretion: Tracking the Direction of Skills at Work in Britain', in C. Warhurst, E. Keep, and I. Grugulis (eds.), *The Skills That Matter* (Basingstoke: Palgrave).

————(2002), *Work Skills in Britain 2001* (London: DfES).

Ferber, M., and Nelson, J. (1993), *Beyond Economic Man. Feminist Theory and Economics* (Chicago: Chicago University Press).

Fergany, N. (1994), 'L'Education féminine en Egypte', *Egypte/Monde Arabe*, 18–19: 101–13.

Ferguson, N. (2004), *Colossus: The Rise and Fall of the American Empire* (London, Penguin).

Fernandes, J. V. (1988), 'From the Theories of Social and Cultural Reproduction to the Theory of Resistance', *British Journal of Sociology of Education* 9: 169–80.

Fevre, R. (1998), 'Labour Migration and Freedom of Movement in the European Union: Social Exclusion and Economic Development', *International Planning Studies*, 3/1: 75–92.

——(2003), *Economy and Morality: The Sociology of Economic Behaviour* (London: Sage).

—— Rees, G., and Gorard, S. (1999), 'Some Sociological Alternatives to Human Capital Theory and their Implications for Research on Post-Compulsory Education and Training', *Journal of Education and Work* 12/2: 117–40.

Feyerabend, P. (1987), *Farewell to Reason* (London: Verso).

Fielding, T. (1995), 'Migration and Middle-Class Formation in England and Wales, 1981–91', in T. Butler and M. Savage (eds.), *Social Change and The Middle Classes* (London: UCL Press).

Figlio, D., and Ludwig, J. (2001), 'Sex, Drugs and Catholic Schools: Private Schooling and Adolescent Behaviors', NCSPE Working Paper 30.

—— and Stone, J. A. (1999), 'Are Private Schools Really Better?', *Research in Labor Economics* 18: 115–40.

Filgueira, C. (1983), 'To Educate or Not to Educate. Is That the Question?' *CEPAL Review* 21: 56–86.

Filmer, R (1991), *Patriarcha and Other Writings* (Cambridge: Cambridge University Press).

Fine, B. (2001*a*), 'Neither the Washington nor the post-Washington Consensus. An Introduction', in B. Fine, C. Lapavitsas, and J. Pincus (eds.), *Development Policy in the Twenty-First Century: Beyond the Post-Washington Consensus* (London: Routledge).

—— (2001*b*), *Social Capital versus Social Theory. Political Economy and Social Science at the Turn of the Millennium* (London: Routledge).

—— and Rose, P. (2001), 'Education and the Post-Washington Consensus', in B. Fine, C. Lapavitsas, and J. Pincus (eds.), *Development Policy in the Twenty-First Century: Beyond the Post-Washington Consensus* (London: Routledge).

—— Lapavitsas, C., and Pincus, J. (2001), Preface, in B. Fine, C. Lapavitsas, and J. Pincus (eds.), *Development Policy in the Twenty-First Century: Beyond the Post-Washington Consensus* (London, Routledge).

Fine, M., and Wiess, L. (1998), *The Unknown City: Lives of Poor and Working-Class Young Adults* (Boston, Mass.: Beacon).

Finegold, D. (1999), 'Creating Self-Sustaining High Skill Ecosystems', *Oxford Review of Economic Policy* 15/1: 60–81.

—— and Soskice, S. (1988), 'The Failure of Training in Britain: Analysis and Prescription', *Oxford Review of Economic Policy* 4/3.

Finnegan, W. (1998), *Cold New World: Growing Up in a Harder Country* (New York: Random House).

Fischer, C. S. (1982), *To Dwell among Friends: Personal Networks in Town and City* (Chicago: University of Chicago Press).

Fischer, C., Hout, M., Jankowski, M. S., Lucas, S., Swidler, A., and Voss, K. (1996), *Inequality by Design: Cracking the Bell Curve Myth* (Princeton: Princeton University Press).

Fisher, S., Abdi, D., Ludin, J., Smith, R., Williams, S., and Williams, S. (2000), *Working with Conflict: Skills and Strategies for Action* (London: Zed Books).

Fishman, J. A. (1980), 'Bilingualism and Biculturalism as Individual and as Societal Phenomena', *Journal of Multilingual and Multicultural Development* l: 3–15.

Fiske, E. B., and Ladd, H. F. (2003), 'School Choice in New Zealand: A Cautionary Tale', in D. N. Plank and G. Sykes (eds.), *Choosing Choice: School Choice in International Perspective* (New York: Teachers College Press).

Fiske, J. (1996), *Media Matters: Everyday Culture and Political Change* (Minneapolis: University of Minnesota Press).

Fletcher, R. (1974), *The Crisis of Industrial Civilization: The Early Essays of Auguste Comte* (London: Heinemann).

Flinders, D. J. (1988), 'Teachers' Isolation and the New Reforms', *Journal of Curriculum and Supervision* 4/1: 17–29.

Flores-Crespo, P. (2004), 'Situating Education in the Human Capabilities Approach', Fourth Conference on the Capability Approach: Enhancing Human Security, September, University of Pavia, Italy.

Floud, J. and Halsey, A.H. (1961) 'English Secondary Schools and the Supply of Labour', in A.H. Halsey, J. Floud, and J. Anderson (eds.), *Education, Economy and Society* (New York: Free Press).

Floud, J. E., Halsey, A. H., et al. (1956), *Social Class and Educational Opportunity* (London: Heinemann).

Flynn, J. R. (1987), 'Massive Gains in 14 Nations: What IQ Tests Really Measure', *Psychological Bulletin* 101/2: 171–91.

—— (2004), 'The Sociology of IQ: Enhancing Cognitive Skills', in M. Olssen (ed.), *Culture and Learning: Access and Opportunity in the Classroom* (Greenwich, Conn.: Information Age Publishing), 257–78.

Flynn, J. R. (2004), 'The Sociology of IQ: Enhancing Cognitive Skills', in M. Olssen (ed.), *Culture and Learning: Access and Opportunity in the Classroom* (Greenwich, Conn.: Information Age Publishing), 257–78.

Folger, J., Poole, M., and Stutman, R. (1993), *Working Through Conflict* (New York: HarperCollins).

Fordham, S. (1996), *Blacked Out: Dilemmas of Race, Identity, and Success in Capital High* (Chicago: University of Chicago Press).

Foster, M. (1997), *Black Teachers on Teaching* (New York: The New Press).

Foucault, M. (1972), *The Archaeology of Knowledge* (London: Tavistock/Routledge).

—— (1979), *The History of Sexuality*, i. *An Introduction* (Harmondsworth: Penguin).

—— (1980), *Power and Strategies*, in *Power/Knowledge: Selected Interviews and Other Writings, 1972–1977* (New York: Pantheon).

—— (1991), 'Governmentality', in G. Burchell, C. Gordon, and P. Miller (eds.), *The Foucault Effect: Studies in Governmentality* (Chicago: University of Chicago).

—— (1980), *Two Lectures: Power/Knowledge* (New York: Pantheon Books).

—— (1983), 'On the Genealogy of Ethics: An Overview of Work in Progress', in H. Dreyfus and P. Rabinow (eds.), *Michel Foucault: Beyond Structuralism and Hermeneutics* (Chicago: University of Chicago Press).

—— (1997), *Ethics: Subjectivity and Truth (Essential Works of Michel Foucault)*, P. Rainbow (New York: New Press),:.

—— (1988), *The Ethic of the Care for the Self as a Practice of Freedom*, in J. Bernauer and D. Rasmussen (eds.), The Final Foucault (Cambridge Mass.: MIT).

—— (1991), *Discipline and Purnish: The Birth of the Prison*, trans. A. Sheridan (London: Penguin).

—— (2001), *Fearless Speech* (Los Angeles: Semiotext(e)).

Fountain, S. (1995), *Education for Development: A Teacher's Resource for Global Learning* (London: Hodder & Stoughton).

Francis, B., and Skelton, C. (2001), 'Men Teachers and the Construction of Hetero-sexual Masculinity in the Classroom', in *Sex Education* 1/1: 9–21.

Frank, A. (1991), 'For a Sociology of the Body: An Analytical Review', in M. Featherstone, M. Hepworth, and B. Turner (eds.) *The Body* (London: Sage).

Frank, R. H., and Cook, P. J. (1995), *The Winner-Take-All Society* (New York: Penguin).

Frankfurt, H. (1987), 'Equality as a Moral Ideal', *Ethics* 98: 21.

Franzway, S., Court, D., and Connell, R. (1989), *Staking a Claim. Feminism, Bureaucracy and the State* (Sydney: Allen & Unwin)

Fraser, N. (1995), 'What's Critical about Critical Theory?', in J. Meehan (ed.), *Feminists Read Habermas: Gendering the Subject of Discourse* (New York, Routledge), 21–56.

—— (1996), 'Equality, Difference and Radical Democracy', in D. Trend (ed.), *Radical Democracy: Identity, Citizenship and the State* (New York: Routledge), 197–208.

—— and Gordon, L. (1994), 'A Genealogy of Dependency: Tracing a Keyword of the US Welfare State', *Signs* 19/2: 309–36.

—— and Nicholson, L. (1990), 'Social Criticism without Philosophy: An Encounter Between Feminism and Post-modernism', in L. Nicholson (ed.), *Feminism and Postmodernism* 242–61.

—— and Nicholson, L. (1995), 'Social Criticism Without Philosophy: An Encounter Between Feminism and Post-Modernism, S. Siedman in (ed.), *The Postmodern Turn: New Perspectives on Social Theory* (Cambridge: Cambridge University Press).

—— (2000), 'Rethinking Recognition'. *New Left Review*, 3 (May/June): 107–120.

Freire, P. (1973), *Pedagogy of the Oppressed* (New York: Seabury).

—— (2001), *The Paulo Freire Reader*, ed. Ana Freire and Donaldo Macedo (New York: Continuum).

Friedman, M. (1962), 'The Role of Government in Education', in M. Friedman, *Capitalism and Freedom* (Chicago: Chicago University Press).

—— and Friedman, R. (1980), *Free to Choose* (London: Penguin).

Friedman, T. (1999), *The Lexus and the Olive Tree* (New York: Farrar Straus Giroux).

—— (2005), *The World is Flat* (New York: Farrar, Straus & Giroux).

Friedson, E. (1986), *Professional Powers* (Chicago: University of Chicago Press).

—— (1994), *Professionalism Reborn* (Chicago, Ill. University of Chicago Press).

Friere, P. and Macedo, D. (1987), *Literacy: Reading the Word and the World* (South Hadley, Mass.: Bergin & Garvey).

Frith, S. (1981), *Sound Effects: Youth, Leisure, and the Politics of Rock 'n' Roll* (New York: Pantheon Books).

Fromm, E. (1942), *The Fear of Freedom* (London: Routledge & Kegan Paul).

Fullan, M. (1991), with S. Stiegelbauer, *The New Meaning of Educational Change* (New York: Teachers College Press).

—— and Connelly, M. (1990), *Teacher Education in Ontario: Current Practices and Options for the Future* (Toronto: Ontario Ministries of Colleges and Universities and of Education and Training).

—— and Hargreaves, A. (1996), *What's Worth Fighting For in Your School?*, 2nd edn. (New York: Teachers' College Press).

Fuller, B. (1989), 'Eroding Economy, Declining School Quality: The Case of Malawi', *IDS Bulletin* 20/1: 11–16.

Fuller, Bruce, Coonerty, Casey, Kipnis, Fran, and Choong, Yvonne (1997), *An Unfair Head Start* (Berkeley: Policy Analyses for California Education (PACE)).

Furlong, A., and Cartmel, F. (1997), *Young People and Social Change: Individualization and Risk in Late Modernity* (Buckingham: Open University Press).

Furlong, J. (1991), 'Disaffected Pupils: Reconstructing the Sociological Perspective', *British Journal of Sociology of Education* 12/3: 293–307.

Furnham, A. (1989), 'Friendship and Personal Development', in R. Porter and S. Tomaselli (eds.), *The Dialectics of Friendship* (London: Routledge), 92–110.

Gage, N. (1978), *The Scientific Basis of the Art of Teaching* (New York: Teachers College Press).

Gaines, J. 1991. *Contested culture: The image, the voice and the law.* Chapel Hill: University of North Carolina Press.

—— (1995), 'Reincarnation as the Ring On Liz Taylor's Finger: Andy Warhol and the Right of Publicity', in A. Sarat and T. Kearns (eds.), *Indentities, Politics and Rights* (Ann Arbor: University of Michigan Press).

Gaitskell, D., Kimble, J., Maconachie, M., and Unterhalter, E. (1983), 'Class, Race and Gender: Domestic Workers in South Africa', *Review of African Political Economy* 27–8: 86–107.

Galindo-Rueda, F., and Vignoles, A. (2003), *Class Ridden or Meritocratic? An Economic Analysis of Recent Changes in Britain* (London: LSE Centre for Economics of Education).

—— Marcenaro-Gutierrez, O., and Vignoles, A. (2004), 'The Widening Socio-economic Gap in UK Higher Education', *Centre for the Economics of Education Discussion Paper* 44 (London: London School of Economics).

Galloway, D. (1985), 'Pastoral Care and School Effectiveness', in D. Reynolds (ed.), *Studying School Effectiveness* (Lewes: Falmer).

Galton, M., Simon, B., and Croll, P. (1980), *Inside the Primary Classroom* (London, Routledge & Kegan Paul).

Gambetta, D. (1987), *Were They Pushed Or Did They Jump? Individual Decision Mechanisms in Education* (Cambridge: Cambridge University Press).

Gamoran, A. (1996), 'Student Achievement in Public Magnet, Public, Comprehensive and Private City Schools', *Education Evaluation and Policy Analysis* 18/1: 1–18

Gans, E. (1985), *The End of a Culture: Toward a Generative Anthropology* (Berkeley: University of California Press).

Gardner, H. (1983), *Frames of Mind: The Theory of Multiple Intelligences* (New York: Basic Books).

Garrett, G. (1998), 'Global Markets and National Policies: Collision Course or Virtuous Circle?' *International Organisation* 52/4: 791–823.

Garrison, E. K. (2000), 'US Feminism—Grrrl Style! Youth (Sub)cultures and the Technologics of the Third Wave, *Feminist Studies* 26/1: 141–70.

Gaspard, Françoise, and Khosrokhavar, Farhad (1995), *Le Foulard et la Republique* (Paris: Découverte).

Geiger, R. (2003), 'Market Coordination in United States Higher Education'. Paper presented at the seminar 'Markets in Higher Education—Mature Economies', Douro, Portugal, October.

Gelb, S. (ed.) (1991), *South Africa's Economic Crisis* (Cape Town: David Philip).

Gellner, E. (1983), *Nations and Nationalism*, (Oxford, Blackwell).

—— (1992), *Reason and Culture* (Oxford: Blackwell).

—— (1994), *Conditions of Liberty: Civil Society and Its Rivals* (London: Hamish Hamilton).

GEO and REPEM (1999), *Education in Motion: Educational Watch on Gender and Education* (Montevideo: Gender and Education Office of the International Council for Adult Education and Red de Educación Popular entre Mujeres de América Latina y el Caribe).

Gephart, W. (1999), 'The Realm of Normativity in Durkheim and Foucault', in M. Cladis (ed.), *Durkheim and Foucault: Perspectives on Education and Punishment* (Oxford: Durkheim Press).

Gerschenkron, A. (1962), *Economic Backwardness in Historical Perspective* (Cambridge, Mass.: Harvard University Press).

Gerth, H., and Mills, C. W. (1947), *From Max Weber: Essays in Sociology* (New York: Oxford University Press).

Gevisser, M., and Cameron, E. (eds.) (1994), *Defiant Desire: Gay and Lesbian Lives in South Africa* (Johannesburg: Ravan).

Gewirtz, S. (1997), 'Post-Welfarism and the Reconstruction of Teachers' Work in the UK', *Journal of Educational Policy* 12: 217–23.

—— (1998), 'Can All Schools be Successful? An Exploration of the Determinants of School "Success"', *Oxford Review of Education* 24/4: 439–57.

—— (2002), 'Can Managerial Means be Harnessed to Social Democratic Ends? Critical Reflections on New Labour's 'Third Way' policies for Schooling in England', *Prospero: A Journal for New Thinking in Philosophy for Education* 8/3: 36–47.

—— (2002), The Managerial School (London: Routledge).

—— Ball, S. J. and Bourer (1995), *Markets, Choice and Equity in Education* (Buckingham: Open University Press).

Giddens, Anthony (ed.) (1972), *Émile Durkheim: Selected Writings*, (Cambridge: Cambridge University Press).

—— (1973), *The Class Structure of Advanced Societies* (London: Hutchinson).

—— (1984), *The Constitution of Society* (Cambridge: Polity).

—— (1991), *Modernity and Self-Identity: Self and Society in the Late Modern Age* (Cambridge: Polity).

—— (1994), *Beyond Left and Right: the Future of Radical Politics* (Cambridge: Polity).

—— (1998), *The Third Way: The Renewal of Social Democracy* (Cambridge: Polity Press).

Ghabra, Sh. (1997), 'Kuwait and the Dynamics of Socio-economic Change', *Middle East Journal* 51: 358–72.

Ghosh, A. (1993), *In an Antique Land* (New York: A. A. Knopf).

Gibbons, M., Limoges, C., Newtony, H., Schwartsman, S., Scott, P., and Trow, M. (1994), *The New Production of Knowledge: The Dynamics of Science and Research in Contemporary Societies* (California: Sage).

—— (1994). *New Production of Knowledge* (London: Sage).

Gibbons, S. (2001), *Paying for Good Neighbours? Neighbourhood Deprivation and the Community Benefits of Education* (London: Centre for Economic Performance, London School of Economics).

Gibson, A., and Asthana, S. (1998), 'School Performance, School Effectiveness and the 1997 White Paper', *Oxford Review of Education* 24/2: 195–210.

Gilborn, D., and Mirza, H. (2000), *Educational Inequality: Mapping Race, Class and Gender* (London: Office for Standards in Education).

Giliomee, H., and Simkins, C. (eds.) (1999), *The Awkward Embrace: One-Party Domination and Democracy* (Cape Town: Tafelberg).

Gill, B., Timpane, P. M., Ross, K. E., and Brewer, D. J. (2001), *Rhetoric versus Reality: What we Know and What we Need to Know about Vouchers and Charter Schools* (Washington, DC: Rand).

Gillberg, C. (1991), 'Nordisk enighet om MBD-bedömning. Termen otidsenlig och olämplig' [Nordic Consensus on MBD-Assessment. The Term is Out of Date and Inappropriate], *Läkartidningen* 88/9: 713–17.

Gillborn, D. (1990), *'Race', Ethnicity and Education: Teaching and Learning in Multi-ethnic Schools* (London: Unwin Hyman).

—— and Gipps, C. (1996), *Recent Research on the Achievements of Ethnic Minority Pupils*, Report for the Office for Standards in Education (London: HMSO).

—— and Youdell (2000), *Rationing Educaton: Policy, Practice, Reform and Equity* (Buckingham: Open Univesity Press).

—— ——(2000), 'Intelligence, "Ability" and the Rationing of Education', in J. Demaine (ed.), *Sociology of Education Today* (London: Palgrave).

—— ——(1994), 'The Micro-Politics of Macro Reforms', *British Journal of Sociology of Education* 15: 147–64.

—— ——(1998), 'Racism and the Politics of Qualitative Research: Learning from Controversy and Critique', in P. Connolly and B. Troyna (eds.), *Researching Racism in Education: Politics, Theory and Practice* (Buckingham: Open University Press).

Gilligan, C. (1982), *In a Different Voice: Psychological Theory and Women's Development* (Cambridge, Mass.: Harvard University Press).

——(1986), 'Moral Orientation and Moral Development', in Eva Kitty and D. Meyers (eds.), *Women and Moral Theory* (New Jersey: Rowman & Littlefield).

Gilloch, G. (1996), *Myth and Metropolis: Walter Benjamin and the City* (Cambridge: Polity).

Girdwood, A. (2004), 'The Formulation and Implementation of Policy for Tertiary Education Reform in Ghana, 1986–1998: A Case Study', University of Bath, Ph.D.

Giroux, H. (1991), 'Democracy and the Discourse of Cultural Difference: Towards a Politics of Border Pedagogy', *British Journal of Sociology of Education* 12/4: 501–19.

——(1996), *Fugitive Cultures: Race, Violence, and Youth* (London: Routledge).

Giroux, H. A. (1983), *Theory and Resistance in Education: A Pedagogy for the Opposition* (South Hadley, Mass.: Bergin & Garvey).

Gitlin, A., Buenida, E., Crosland, K., Dumbia, F. (2003), 'The Production of Margin & Centre: Welcoming-Unwelcoming of Immigrant Students', *American Educational Review Journal* 40/1: 91–122.

Glennerster, H. (2002), 'United Kingdom Education 1997–2001', *Oxford Review of Economic Policy* 18/2: 120–36.

Godwin, K., and Kemerer, F. R. (2002), *School Choice Trade-offs*. (Austin: University of Texas Press).

——Deng Z., Martinez V., Wolf P., and Wood, S. (2001) *Comparing Tolerance in Public, Private, and Evangelical Schools* (Denton, Tex.: Department of Political Science, North Texas State University).

Goldstein H. (2004), 'International Comparisons of Student Attainment: Some Issues Arising from the PISA Study', *Assessment in Education* 11/3: 319–30.

Goldstein, P. (1992), 'Copyright' *Law and Contemporary Problems* 55/2: 79–92.

Goldthorpe, J. (2003), 'The Myth of Education-Based Meritocracy: Why the Theory Isn't Working', *New Economy*, 10/4: 234–9.

——, Llewellyn, C., and Payne, C. (1987), *Social Mobility and Class Structure in Modern Britain*, 2nd edn. (Oxford: Clarendon).

Gonzalez, E. J. (ed.) (2003), *PIRLS 2001 User Guide for the International Database* (Boston, Mass.: International Association for the Evaluation of Educational Achievement (IEA), International Study Center Lynch School of Education, Boston College).

Gonzalez, R. M., and Villaescusa, M. E. (1998), 'Politicas publicas en genero y educación: analisis del caso Mexicano'. Paper presented at the seminar on Seguimiento de las Conferencias Beijing y Hamburgo: Genero, Educación y Ciudadania. Influencias en Politicas Publicas, Santa Cruz, Bolivia, 22–6 June.

Good, C. (1959), 'Curriculum', in *Dictionary of Education* (New York: McGraw Hill).

Goodlad, J. I. (1984), *A Place Called School: Prospects for the Future* (New York: McGraw-Hill).

Goodman, N. (1978), *Ways of Worldmaking* (Indianapolis: Hackett).

Goodman, P. (1956), *Growing Up Absurd* (New York: Vintage Books).

Goodson, I. (1997), 'Chariots of Fire: Etymologies, Epistemologies and the Emergence of Curriculum', in G. Milburn, I. Goodson, and R. Clark (eds.), *Reinterpreting Curriculum Research: Images and Arguments* (Ontario: Althouse).

Goodson, I. F. (1988), *The Making of Curriculum* (New York: Falmer).

Goodwin, C., and Opper, S. (1992), 'Rethinking Context: An Introduction', in A. Duranti and C. Goodwin (eds.), *Rethinking Context. Language as an Interactive Phenomenon*. (Cambridge: Cambridge University Press), 1–42.

Gorard, S., and Fitz, J. (2000), 'Investigating the Determinants of Degregation between Schools', *Research Papers in Education* 15: 115–32.

Gorard, S., Fitz, J. and Taylor, C. (2003) *Schools, Markets and Choice Policies* (London: Routledge Falmer).

Gorard, S., and Rees, G. (2002), *Creating a Learning Society? Learning Careers and Policies for Lifelong Learning* (Bristol: Policy Press).

Gordon, L. (1990), 'The New Feminist Scholarship on the Welfare State', in L. Gordon (ed.), *Women, the State, and Welfare* (Madison: University of Wisconsin Press)

—— (1991), 'The State, Devolution and Educational Reform in New Zealand', *Journal of Education Policy* 7/2: 187–203.

—— (1994*a*) 'Whatever Happened to the National Policy for Girls and Women in New Zealand?' Unpublished paper, University of Canterbury.

—— (1994*b*) '"Rich" and "Poor" Schools in Aotearoa', *New Zealand Journal of Educational Studies* 29/1–2: 129–36.

Gordon, W. (1993), 'A Property Right in Self-Expression: Equality and Individualism in the Natural Law of Intellectual Property', *Yale Law Journal* 102: 1533–609.

Gore, C. (2000), 'The Rise and Fall of the Washington Consensus as a Paradigm for Developing Countries', *World Development* 28/5: 789–804.

Government Information Services (various issues), *Hong Kong Annual Report* (Hong Kong: Printing Department).

—— (2001), *Hong Kong Annual Report* (Hong Kong: Printing Department).

Gow, J. (1993), 'Music Video as Persuasive Form: The Case of the Pseudo-Reflexive Strategy', *Communication Quarterly* 41/3: 318–27.

Goyette, K. A., and Conchas, G. Q. (forthcoming). 'Should Families be Praised or Blamed? A Look at the Relative Influences of Family and Non-family Social Capital on Vietnamese and Mexican Americans' Study Habits', in B. Fuller and E. Hannum (eds.), *Research in the Sociology of Education*, xiii. *Schooling and Social Capital in Diverse Cultures* (Oxford: Elsevier).

Grace, G. (1994), 'Education is a Public Good: On the Need to Resist the Domination of Economic Science', in D. Bridges and T. Mclaughlin (eds.), *Education and the Market Place* (London: Falmer).

—— —— (1994), 'Urban Education and the Culture of Contentment: The Politics, Culture and Economics of Inner-City Schooling', in N. Stromquist (ed.), *Education in Urban Areas: Cross-National Dimensions* (Westport, Conn.: Praeger).

—— (1995), *School Leadership: Beyond Educational Management* (London: Falmer).

Graddol, D. (1997), *The Future of English: A Guide to Forecasting the Popularity of the English Language in the 21st Century* (London: British Council).

Graham-Brown, S. (1991), *Education in the Developing World: Conflict and Crisis* (London: and Longman).

Gramsci, A. (1971), *Selections from Prison Notebooks*, trans. Q. Moare and G. Nowell-Smith (London: Lawrence & Wishart).

Grandin, N., and Gaboricau, M. (eds.) (1997), *Madrasa: les transmissions du savoir dans le monde musulman* (Paris: Éditions Arguments).

Granovetter, M., and Swedberg, R. (eds.) (1992), *The Sociology of Economic Life* (Boulder: Westview).

Grassby, R. (1970), 'English Merchant Capitalism in the Late Seventeenth Century: The Composition of Business Fortunes', *Past and Present* 46: 87–107.

Gray, J. (1990), 'The Quality of Schooling: Frameworks for Judgement', *British Journal of Educational Studies* 38/3: 204–23.

—— (1998), *False Dawn: The Delusions of Global Capitalism* (London: Granta Books).

Gray, M. (1997), 'Web growth summary', online at <http://www.mit.edu/people/mkgray/net/web-growth-summary.html>.

Green, A. (1990), *Education and State Formation: The Rise of Education Systems in England, France and the USA* (Basingstoke: Macmillan).

—— (1996), 'Education, Globalization and the Nation state' Paper presented to the World Congress of Comparative Education Societies, University of Sydney, 1–6 July.

—— (1997), *Education, Globalization and the National State* (London: Macmillan).

—— and Steedman, H. (1993), *Educational Provision, Educational Attainment and the Needs of Industry: A Review of the Research for Germany, France, Japan, the USA and Britain*, Report Series 5 (London: National Institute of Economic and Social Research).

—— Preston, J., and Sabates, R., (2003), 'Education, Equality and Social Cohesion: A Distributional Approach', *Compare*, 33/4, 451–68.

Green, D.A., and Riddell, W. C. (2000), 'Literacy, Numeracy and Labour Market Outcomes in Canada', unpublished paper, Department of Economics, University of British Columbia (May).

Green, F. (2006), *Demanding Work: The Paradox of Job Quality in the Affluent Economy* (Princeton: Princeton University Press).

Greenfield, L., (2003) *The Spirit of Capitalism: Nationalism and Economic Growth* (Cambridge, Mass: Harvard University Press).

Greene, J. P. (2001), 'An Evaluation of the Florida A-Plus Accountability and School Choice Program', Working Paper, The Manhattan Institute, New York.

—— Peterson P. E. , and Du, J. (1998), 'School Choice in Milwaukee: A Randomized Experiment', in P. E. Peterson, and B. C. Hassel (eds.) (1998), *Learning from School Choice* (Washington: Brookings Institution).

Gregg, P., and Wadsworth, J. (eds.) (1999), *The State of Working Britain* (Manchester: Manchester University Press).

——Harkness, S., and Machin, S. (1999), *Child Development and Family Income* (York: Joseph Rowntree Foundation).

Grenfell, M., and Kelly, M. (eds). (1999), *Pierre Bourdieu: Language, Culture and Education: Theory into Practice* (Berne: Peter Lang).

Grewal, I., and Kaplan, C. (eds.) (1994), *Scattered Hegemonies: Postmodernity and Transnational Feminist Practices* (Indianapolis: University of Minnesota Press).

Grimmett, P., and Crehan, E. P. (1992), 'The Nature of Collegiality in Teacher Development', in M. Fullan and A. Hargreaves (eds.), *Teacher Development and Educational Change* (London: Falmer).

Grindle, M. (1986), *State and Countryside Development Policy and Agrarian Politics in Latin America* (Baltimore: The Johns Hopkins University Press).

Grissmer, D., Flanagan, A., and Williamson, S. (1998), 'Does Money Matter for Minority and Disadvantaged Students? Assessing the New Empirical Evidence', in W. J. Fowler (ed.), *Developments in School Finance*, NCES Publications, No. 98–212.

Grosjean, É. (1995), 'Cultural Identity: A Key Element of the Democratic Society', in D. Dadsi (ed.), *Specificities and Universality* (Strasbourg: Council of Europe).

Grosse, R., and Kujawa, D. (1988), *International Business: Theory and Management Applications* (Homewood, Ill.: Irwin).

Grossman, P. (1996), 'Of Regularities and Reform: Navigating the Subject Specific Territory of High School', in M. McLaughlin and I. Oberman (eds.), *Professional Development in the Reform Era* (New York: Teachers' College Press).

Grubb, W. N. (ed.) (1995), *Education Through Occupations in American High Schools* (New York: Teachers College Press). i and ii.

—— (2004), *The Anglo-American Approach to Vocationalism: The Economic Roles of Education in England*, Research Paper 52 (Oxford: Oxford University Centre on Skills, Knowledge, and Organisational Performance).

—— and Lazerson, M. (2004), *The Education Gospel: The Economic Value of Schooling* (Cambridge Mass.: Harvard University Press).

—— and Sweet, R. (2005), 'Alternative to Universities Revisited', *Education Policy Analysis 2004* (Paris: OECD).

Grusky, D., and Hauser, R. (1984), 'Comparative Social Mobility Revisited', *American Sociological Review* 49.

Guile, D. (2002), 'Work, Skill, and Work Experience in the European Knowledge Economy', *Journal of Education and Work* 15/1: 25–76.

—— (2006), *Knowledge and Learning in the Knowledge Economy* (Amsterdam: Sense).

—— (forthcoming), *Knowledge, Reflection and Higher Education: A 'Holy' Yet Problematic Trinity?*

Gulhati, R. (1989), 'Malawi. Promising Reforms. Bad Luck', *EDI Development Policy Case Series*, Analytical Case Study 3 (Washington, DC: Economic Development Institute, World Bank).

Gupta, U. (1989), 'US-India Satellite Link Stands to Cut Software Costs', *The Wall Street Journal* (6 March), B2.

Guttman, A. (1987), *Democratic Education* (Princeton, NJ: Princeton University Press).

Haas, E. (1990), *When Knowledge is Power: Three Models of Change in International Organizations* (Berkeley: University of California Press).

Habermas, J. (1974), 'On Social Identity', *Telos* 19: 91–103.

—— (1987), *Theory of Communicative Action*, ii. *System and Lifeworld: A Critique of Functionalist Reason* (Boston: Beacon).

—— (1993), *The Theory of Communicative Action* trans. T. McArthy (Boston, Mass.: Beacon), ii.

—— (1995), *Postmetaphysical Thinking* (Cambridge: Polity).

Hacking, I. (1986), 'Making People Up', in T. Heller, M. Sosna, and D. Wellbery (eds.), *Autonomy, Individuality and the Self in Western Thought* (Stanford Calif.: Stanford University Press), 222–36.

—— (1999). *The Social Construction of What?* Cambridge, MA: Harvard University Press.

Haeri, N. (1997), 'The Reproduction of Symbolic Capital: Language, State and Class in Egypt', *Current Anthropology* 38: 795–816.

Hagberg, B. (1975), 'Minimal Brain Dysfunction—vad innebär det för barnets utveckling ochanpassning?' [Minimal Brain Dysfunction—What Does It Mean for the Child's Development and Adaptation?], *Läkartidningen* 72/36: 3296–300.

Haidar, 'A.-L. (1997), 'Al'ilaqa al-batraqiya fil-ittijahat al-'ilmiya lida tullab al-marhala al-thanawiya fil-Yaman' [Patriarchal relations and their effects on the scientific orientations of secondary school pupils in Yemen], *Al-Mustaqbal Al-'Arabi* [Arab Future], 214: 87–106 (Arabic).

Haig, B. (1987), 'Scientific Problems and the Conduct of Research', *Educational Philosophy and Theory* 19/2:, 22–32.

Hall, M. (2001), 'Education and the Margins of the Network Society', in J. Muller, N. Cloete, and S. Badat (eds.), *Challenges of Globalization: South African Debates with Castell* (Cape Town: Maskew Miller/Longman).

Hall, P., and Soskice, D. (eds.) (2001), *Varieties of Capitalism: The Institutional Foundations of Comparative Advantage* (Oxford: Oxford University Press).

Hallam, S. (2002), *Ability Grouping in Schools* (London: Institute of Education).

Halsey, A. H. (1975), 'Sociology and the Equality Debate', *Oxford Review of Education* 1: 9–23.

—— (ed.) (1972), *Educational Priority* (London: HMSO).

—— with Webb, J. (eds.) (2000) *Twentieth Century British Social Trends* (Basingstoke: Macmillan).

—— and Floud, J. (1961) 'Introduction' in A. H. Halsey, J. Floud, and J. Anderson (eds.) Education, Economy and Society (New York: Free Press).

—— and Anderson, C. A. (1961), *Education, Economy, and Society* (New York: The Free Press).

—— Heath, A. F., and Ridge, J. M. (1980), *Origins and Destinations: Family, Class and Education in Modern Britain* (Oxford: Clarendon).

——Lauder, H., Brown, P., and Wells, A. Stuart (1997) *Education, Culture, Economy and Society* (Oxford: Oxford University Press).

Halstead, J. M., and Waite, S. (2001), '"Living in Different Worlds": Gender Differences in the Developing Sexual Values and Attitudes of Primary School Children', in *Sex Education* 1/1: 59–76.

Hamel, G., and Prahalad, C. K. (1994), *Competing for the Future* (Boston: Harvard Business School Press).

Hamelink, C. (1983), *Cultural Autonomy in Global Communications* (New York: Longman).

Hamilton, D. (1989), *Towards a Theory of Schooling* (New York: Falmer).

Hamilton, D. (1999), 'The Pedagogic Paradox (or Why No Didactics in England?)', *Pedagogy, Culture and Society* 7/1: 135–52.

Hammersley, M. (1974), 'The Organization of Pupil Participation', *Sociological Review* 22/3: 355–68.

—— (1976), 'The Mobilization of Pupil Attention', in M. Hammersley and P. Woods (eds.), *The Process of Schooling* (London: Routledge & Kegan Paul).

—— (1977), 'The Cultural Resources Required to Answer a Teacher's Question', in P. Woods and M. Hammersley (eds.), *School Experience* (London: Croom Helm).

Hammersley, M., and Gomm, R. (1997), 'Bias in Social Research', *Sociological Research Online* 2/1.

Hammons, C. W. (2001), 'The Effects of Town Tuitioning in Vermont and Maine', Mimeo, Milton and Rose D. Friedman Foundation, <www.friedmanfoundation.org>.

Handler, R. (1988), *Nationalism and the Politics of Culture in Quebec* (Madison: University of Wisconsin Press).

Haney, W. (2000), 'The Myth of the Texas Miracle in Education', *Education Analysis Policy Archives*, 8/41. Available online at: <http://epaa.asu.edu/epaa/v9n2.html> (accessed 20 April 2005).

—— (2003), 'Attrition of Students from New York Schools', invited testimony at public hearing, 'Regents Learning Standards and High School Graduation Requirements', before the New York Senate Standing Committee on Education , Senate Hearing Room, New York, 23 September.

Hanlon, G. (1998), 'Professionalism as Enterprise: Service Class Politics and the Redefinition of Professionalism', *Sociology*, 32/1: 43–63.

—— (1998), 'Professionalism as Enterprise', in *Sociology* 32/1: 43–63.

Hannay, L., and Ross, J. (1997), 'Initiating Secondary School Reform', *Educational Administration Quarterly* 33: 576–603.

Hannerz, U. (1987), 'The World in Creolization', *Africa* 57/4: 546–59.

—— (1989), 'Notes on the Global Ecumene', *Public Culture* 1/2 (Spring): 66–75.

Hanson, D., and Herrington, M. (1976), *From College to Classroom: The Probationary Year* (London: Routledge & Kegan Paul).

Hanson, F. Allan (1993), *Testing Testing: Social Consequences of the Examined Life* (Berkeley, Calif.: University of California Press).

Hanushek, E. A. (1994), *Making Schools Work* (Washington, DC: Brookings Institution).

—— (1998), 'Conclusions and Controversies about the Effectiveness of Schools', *Federal Reserve Bank of New York Economic Policy Review* 4. 1–22.

—— Kain, J., and Rivkin, S. (2003), 'New Evidence on the Impact of Charter Schools on Academic Achievement', APPAM Paper, November 2003.

Haraway, D. (1988), 'Situated Knowledges: The Science Question in Feminism and the Privilege of the Partial Perspective', *Feminist Studies* 14: 575–96.

Harber, C., and Davies, L. (2003), 'Educational Leadership for War and Peace', in M. Brunswick, N. Burton, and R. Smith (eds.), *Leadership in Education* (London: Sage).

Harding, D., Jencks, C., Lopoo, L., and Mayer, S. (2002), 'The Changing Effects of Family Background on the Incomes of American Adults', in S. Bowles, H. Gintis, and M. Osborne (eds.), *Family Background and Economic Success* (New York: Russell Sage).

Hargreaves, A. (1977), 'Progressivism and Pupil Autonomy', *Sociological Review* 25: 3.

—— (1978), 'The Significance of Classroom Coping Strategies', in L. Barton and R. Meighan (eds.), *Sociological Interpretations of Schooling and Classrooms: A Reappraisal* (Driffield: Nafferton Books).

—— (1979), 'Strategies, Decisions and Control', in J. Eggleston (ed.), *Teacher Decision-Making in the Classroom* (London: Routledge & Kegan Paul).

—— (1982), 'The Rhetoric of School-Centred Innovation', *Journal of Curriculum Studies*, June, 251–66.

—— (1989), *Curriculum and Assessment Reform* (Milton Keynes: Open University Press).

—— (1994), *Changing Teachers, Changing Times: Teachers' Work and Culture in the Postmodern Age* (London: New York, and Toronto: Cassell, Teachers' College Press, and University of Toronto Press).

—— (1994), 'Restructuring Restructuring: Postmodernity and the Prospects of Education Change', *Journal of Education Policy* 9/1: 47–65.

—— (1997), 'Rethinking Educational Change', in A. Hargreaves (ed.), *Rethinking Educational Change with Heart and Mind: The 1997 ASCD Yearbook* (Alexandria, Va.: Association for Supervision and Curriculum Development).

—— (1998), 'Teachers Role in Renewal', *Orbit* 129/1: 10–13.

—— and Fullan, M. (1998), *What's Worth Fighting For Out There?* (Toronto, New York, and Buckingham: Elementary Teachers Federation of Ontario, Teachers' College Press, and Open University Press).

—— and Goodson, I. (1996), 'Teachers Professional Lives: Aspirations and Actualities', in I. Goodson and A. Hargreaves (eds.), *Teachers' Professional Lives* (London: Falmer).

—— and Jacka, N. (1995), 'Induction or Seduction?', *Peabody Journal of Education* 70/3: 41–63.

—— Earl, L., and Ryan, J. (1996), *Schooling for Change: Reinventing Education for Early Adolescents* (London: Falmer).

—— Leithwood, K., Gerin-Lajoie, D., et al. (1993), *Years of Transition: Times for Change* (Toronto: The Ontario Institute for Studies in Education).

—— Davis, J., Fullan, M., Wignall, R., Stager, M., and Macmillan, R. (1992), *Secondary School Work Cultures and Educational Change* (Toronto: The Ontario Institute for Studies in Education at the University of Toronto).

—— (1980), 'The Occupational Culture of Teaching', in P. Woods (ed.), *Teacher Strategies* (London: Croom Helm).

—— (1994), 'The New Professionalism: The Synthesis of Professional and Institutional Development', *Teaching and Teacher Education* 10/4: 423–38.

Hargreaves, D. (1967), *Social Relations in a Secondary School* (London: Routledge & Kegan Paul).

—— (1996), 'Teaching as a Research-based Profession: Possibilities and Prospects' *TTA Annual Lecture* (London: TTA).

Hargreaves, E. (1997), 'The Diploma Disease in Egypt: Learning, Teaching and the Monster of the Secondary Leaving Certificate', *Assessment in Education: Principles, Policy & Practice* 4/1: 161–76.

Harrigan, J. (2001), *From Dictatorship to Democracy. Economic Policy in Malawi 1964–2000* (Hampshire: Ashgate).

Harris, A. (2004), *Future Girl: Young Women in the Twenty-First Century* (New York: Routledge).

Harris, D. B. (1963), *Children's Drawings as Measures of Intellectual Maturity* (New York: Harcourt, Brace and World).

Harrison, A., Xaba, N., Kunene, P., and Ntuli, N. (2001), 'Understanding Young Women's Risk for HIV/AIDS: Adolescent Sexuality and Vulnerability in Rural KwaZulu/Natal', *Society in Transition*, 32/1: 69–78.

Harrison, P. R. (1993), 'Bourdieu and the Possibility of a Postmodern Sociology', *Thesis Eleven* 35: 36–50.

Hartog, J. (2000), 'Over-education and Earnings: Where Are We, Where Should We Go?', *Economics of Education Review* 19:131–47.

Hartup, W.W. (1992), 'Friendships and their Developmental Significance', in H. McGurk (ed.), *Childhood and Social Development* (Hove: Lawrence Erlbaum), 175–206.

Harvey, D. (1989), *The Condition of Postmodernity* (Cambridge: Polity).

Harvey, D. (1989), *The Postmodern Condition* (Cambridge: Blackwell).

Harvey, D. (1996), *Justice, Nature and the Geography of Difference* (Cambridge, Mass.: Blackwell).

Hasan, R. (2001), 'The Ontogenesis of Decantextualized Language: Some Achievements of Classification and Framing', in A Morais et al. (eds.), *Towards a Sociology of Pedagogy: The Contribution of Basil Bernstein to Research* (Oxford: Peter Lang).

—— (2002), 'Ways of Meaning, Ways of Learning: Code as an Explanatory Concept, *British Journal of Sociology of Education* 23/4: 537–48.

Hatcher, R. (2002), 'Participatory Democracy and Education: The Experience of Porto Alegre and Rio Grande do Sul, Brazil', *Education and Social Justice* 4/2: 47–64.

Havelin, J. (1999), 'Education and Campesinas in Nicaragua, 1960–1997', Los Angeles, Center for International Studies, USC, mimeo, April.

Haveman, R., and Wolfe, B. (1995), 'The Determinants of Children's Attainments: A Review of Methods and Findings' *Journal of Economic Literature* 33: 1829–78.

Hawe, P., and Schiell, A. (2000), 'Social Capital and Health Promotion: A Review', *Social Science and Medicine* 51:. 871–85.

Hayakawa, S. I. (1965), *Language in Thought and Action* (London: George Allen & Unwin).

Haycock, K. (1998), 'Good Teaching Matters ... a Lot', *OAH Magazine of History* 13: 61–3.

Hayden, M., Thompson, J., and Walker. G. (eds.) (2002), *International Education in Practice: Dimensions for National and International schools* (London: Kogan Page).

Hayek, F., (1976), *Law, Legislation and Liberty* (London: Routledge).

Haywood, C., and Mac an Ghaill, M. (1996), 'Schooling Masculinities', in M. Mac an Ghaill, (ed.), *Understanding Masculinities* (Buckingham: Open University Press) 50–61.

Heater, D. (1990), *Citizenship: The Civic Ideal in World History, Politics and Evaluation* (London: Longman).

Heath, A., and McMahon, D. (1997), 'Education and Occupational Attainments: The Impact of Ethnic Origins', in A. H. Halsey, H. Lauder, P. Brown, and A. Stuart Wells, *Education, Culture, Economy and Society* (Oxford: Oxford University Press).

Hebdige, D. (1988), *Hiding in the Light: On Images and Things* (London: Routledge-Comedia).

Hechter, M. (1975), *Internal Colonialism: The Celtic Fringe in British National Development, 1536–1966* (Berkeley: University of California Press).

Heckman, J. (1999), 'Doing it Right: Job Training and Education', *The Public Interest* (Spring), 86–106.

Hekman, S. (1996), *Feminist Interpretations of Michel Foucault* (London: Routledge).

Held, D. (1995), *Democracy and the Global Order: From Modern State to Cosmopolitan Governance* (Cambridge: Cambridge University Press).

—— and McGrew, A. (2000), *The Global Transformations Reader: An Introduction to the Globalization Debate* (Cambridge: Polity).

Helms, M. W. (1988), *Ulysees' Sail: An Ethnographic Odyssey of Power, Knowledge, and Geographical Distance* (Princeton, NJ: Princeton University Press).

Helsby, G. (1995), 'Teachers' Construction of Professionalism in England in the 1990s', *Journal of Education for Teaching* 21/3: 317–32.

—— (2000), *Changing Teachers' Work and Culture* (Buckingham: Open University Press).

—— and McCulloch, G. (eds.), (1997), *Teachers and the National Curriculum* (London: Cassell).

Henig, J. R., and Sugarman, S. D. (1999), 'The Nature and Extent of School Choice', in S. D. Sugarman and F. R. Kemerer (eds.), *School Choice and Social Controversy: Politics, Policy and Law* (Washington, DC: Brookings Institute).

Henry, M. E. (1994), 'Parent-School Partnerships: Public School Reform from a Feminist Perspective'. Paper presented at the Annual Meeting of the American Educational Research Association, New Orleans.

Henry, M., Lingard, B., Rizvi, F., and Taylor, S. (2000), *The OECD, Globalization and Education Policy* (Oxford: Pergamon).

Heritage, J. (1984), *Garfinkel and Ethnomethodology* (Cambridge: Polity).

Herrera, L. (1998), 'Song without Music: Islamism and Education—a Case from Egypt', *Revue du Monde Musulman et de la Méditerrannée* 85–6: 149–59.

Herrnstein, R., and Murray, C. (1994), *The Bell Curve: Intelligence and Class Structure in American Life* (New York: The Free Press).

Herzfeld, M. (1982), *Ours Once More: Folklore, Ideology and the Making of Modern Greece* (Austin: University of Texas Press).

Hesketh, A. J., and Knight, P. T. (1999), 'Postgraduates' Choice of Programme: Helping Universities to Market and Postgraduates Choose', *Studies in Higher Education* 24/2: 151–63.

Hess, F., Maranto, R., and Milliman, S. (2001), 'Small Districts in Big Trouble: How Four Arizona School Systems Responded to Charter Competition', *Teachers College Record* 103: 1102–24.

Hester, S. (1991), 'The Social Facts of Deviance in School: A Study of Mundane Reason', *British Journal of Sociology of Education* 42: 443–463.

Hey, V. (1996), '"A Game of Two Halves"—a Critique of Some Complicities: Between Hegemonic and Counter-Hegemonic Discourses Concerning Marketisation and Education', *Discourse* 17/3: 351–62.

—— (1997), *The Company She Keeps: An Ethnography of Girls' Friendship* (Buckingham: Open University Press).

—— (1994), *Teaching to Transgress: Education as the Practice of Freedom* (London: Routledge).

Heyman, S. (1992), 'Positive and Negative Liberty', *Chicago-Kent Law Review* 68/1: 81–98.

Heyneman, S. (2001) 'The Growing International Commercial Market for Educational Goods and Services', *International Journal of Educational Development*, 21: 345–59.

Hildyard, N. (1997), *The World Bank and the State: A Recipe for Change?* (London: Bretton Woods Project).

Hills, J. (2004), 'Tax and Welfare', *Inequality and the State* (Oxford: Oxford University Press), ch. 7.

—— (2004) *Inequality and the State* (Oxford: Oxford University Press).

Hilts, P. (1993*a*), 'Lab limits plan to give company its discoveries', *New York Times* (13 July), A8.

—— (1993*b*), 'U.S. seeks to protect fruits of tax-supported research', *New York Times* (17 June), A12.

Hindess, B. (2000), 'Democracy and the Neo-Liberal Promotion of Arbitrary Power', *Critical Review of International Social and Political Philosophy* 3/4: 68–84.

Hinshaw, S. P. (1992), 'Externalizing Behavior Problems and Academic Underachievement in Childhood and Adolescence: Causal Relationships and Underlying Mechanism'. *Psychological Bulletin* 111: 127–55.

Hirsch, E. D., Jr. (1987), *Cultural Literacy: What Every American Needs to Know* (New York: Houghton-Mifflin).

Hirsch, F. (1976), *Social Limits to Growth*, (Cambridge, Mass: Harvard University Press).

Hirschman, A. (1989), *Rival Views on the Market* (Cambridge, Mass.: Harvard University Press).

Hirschman, A. O. (1970), *Exit, Voice, and Loyalty* (Cambridge, Mass.: Harvard University Press).

Hirst, P. (2000*b*) 'Globalization, the Nation State and Political Theory', in N. O'Sullivan (ed.), *Political Theory in Transition* (London: Routledge), 172–89.

—— and Thompson, G. (1996), *Globalization in Question* (Cambridge: Polity).

HM Government (1994), *Competitiveness: Helping Business to Win*, Cm 2563 (London: HMSO).

HM Government (2003), *Every Child Matters*, Cm 5860 (London: HMSO).

—— (2004), *Children's Workforce Strategy: A Strategy to Build a World-Class Workforce for Children and Young People*, Consultation (Document London: HMSO).

HM Treasury (2004), *Choice for Parents, the Best Start for Children: A Ten-Year Strategy for Childcare* (Norwich: HMSO).

Hobbes, T. (1881), *Leviathan* (Oxford: James Thornton).

—— (1961), 'Of the Natural Condition of Mankind', in T. Parsons, E. Shils, K. Naegele, and J. Pitts (eds.), *Theories of Society* (New York: Free Press), i.

—— (1968), *Leviathan* (London: Pelican).

Hobcraft, J. N. (2002), 'Social Exclusion and the Generations', in J. Hills, J. LeGrand, and D. Piachaud (ed.), *Understanding Social Exclusion*, (Oxford: Oxford University Press).

Hobhouse, L. T. (1911), *Liberalism* (London: Williams & Norgate).

Hobsbawm, E. (1994), *Age of Extremes* (London: Abacus).

—— (2005), *The Guardian*, 15 January.

Hobsbawm, E. J. (1968), *Industry and Empire* (Harmondsworth: Penguin).

Hobsbawm, E. J. (1990), *Nations and Nationalism since 1780: Programme, Myth, Reality* (Cambridge: Cambridge University Press).

—— and Ranger, T. (eds.) (1983), *The Invention of Tradition* (New York: Columbia University Press).

Hobson, J., and Ramesh., M., (2002), 'Globalisation Makes of States What States Make of It: Between Agency and Structure in the State/Globalisation Debate', *New Political Economy*, 7/1:5–22.

Hochschild, A. (1987), *The Time Bird* (New York: Metropolitan).

Hochschild, J. L., and Scovronick, N. (2003), *The American Dream and the Public Schools* (New York: Oxford University Press).

Hodgson, M. (1974), *The Venture of Islam, Conscience and History in a World Civilization*, 3 vols. (Chicago: University of Chicago Press).

Hodkinson, P., Sparkes, A., and Hodkinson, H. (1996), *Triumphs and Tears: Young People, Markets and the Transition From School to Work* (London: David Fulton).

Hoetker, J., and Ahlbrand, W. P. (1969), 'The Persistence of the Recitation', *American Educational Research Journal* 6.

Hofferth, S. L., Stanhope, S., and Harris, K. M. (2002), 'Exiting Welfare in the 1990s: Did Public Policy Influence Recipients' Behavior?' *Population Research and Policy Review* 21: 433–72.

Holland, A., and Andre, T. (1994), 'Athletic Participation and the Social Status of Adolescent Males and Female', *Youth and Society* 25: 388–407.

Holland, J., Lahelma, E., and Gordon, T. (2000), 'The Abstract Individual and School Processes', in M. Arnot and J. Dillabough's (eds.), *Education, Democracy and Citizenship: Emerging International Feminist Perspectives* (Routledge: London).

Holloway, S. and Valentine, G. (2004), Spatiality and the New Social Studies of Chidhood'. *Sociology* 34/4: 763–83.

Holly, D. (1974), 'The Invisible Ruling Class', in D. Holly (ed.), *Education or Domination?* (London: Arrow).

Holt, J. (1969), *How Children Fail* (Harmondsworth: Penguin).

—— (1971), *The Underachieving School* (Harmondsworth: Penguin).

Holusha, J. (1995), 'First to college, then to the mill', *New York Times*, 22 August, p. D1.

Hong Kong Education Commission (1994), *Language Proficiency Working Group Report* [in Chinese] (Hong Kong: Government Printer).

Hong Kong Education Commission (1995), *Consultation Paper on Enhancing Language Proficiency: A Comprehensive Strategy, Education Commission Report No. 6: Main Report* (Hong Kong: Government Information Services).

—— (1997), *Quality School Education, Education Commission Report No. 7* (Hong Kong: Government Information Services).

—— (1999), A general summary of the public views received on the 'Review of Academic System: Aims of Education', retrieved 29 September 1999, from <http://www.e-c.edu.hk/eng/aims/summary.html>.

—— (2000), *Education Blueprint for the 21st Century: Learning for Life, Learning through Life* (Hong Kong: Printer Department).

Hong Kong Education Department (1997), *Medium of Instruction: Guidance for Secondary Schools* (Hong Kong: Government Printer).

Hong Kong Federation of Youth Groups (1997), *Mother Tongue Education: An Attitudinal Study on Secondary School Students and Parents* [in Chinese] (Hong Kong: Hong Kong Federation of Youth Groups).

Honohan, I. (2002), *Civic Republicanism* (London: Routledge).

Hooks, B. (1989), *Talking Back—Talking Feminist, Talking Black* (London: Sheba).

Horio, T. (1988), *Educational Thought in Modern Japan*, ed. and trans. S. Platzer (Tokyo: University of Tokyo Press).

Horkheimer, M. (1947), *Eclipse of Reason* (New York: Oxford University Press).

Hornberger, N. (1987), 'Schooltime, Classtime, and Academic Learning Time in Rural Highland Puno, Peru', *Anthropology of Education Quarterly* 18: 207–21.

Hovsepian, N. (1995), 'Competing Identities in the Arab World', *Journal of International Affairs* 49/1: 1–24.

Howarth, C. (2002), '"So, You're from Brixton?": The Struggle for Recognition and Esteem in a Stigmatised Community', *Ethnicities* 2/2: 120–36.

Howarth, D., and Norval, A. (eds.) (1998), *South Africa in Transition: New Theoretical Perspectives* (London: Macmillan).

Howe, M. J. A. (1990), *The Origins of Exceptional Abilities* (Oxford: Blackwell).

Howe, W. (2001), *A Brief History of the Internet* online <http://www.walthowe.com/navnet/history.html>.

Howell, D. (2002), 'Increasing Earnings, Inequality and Unemployment in Developed Countries: Markets, Institutions and the "Unified Theory"', *Politics and Society* 30/2: 193–243.

Howell, W. G., and Peterson, P. E. (2002), *The Education Gap. Vouchers and Urban Public Schools* (Washington: Brookings).

Hoxby, C. M. (2000) 'Does Competition among Public Schools Benefit Students and Taxpayers?' *American Economic Review* 90: 1209–38.

—— (ed.) (2003), *The Economics of School Choice* (Chicago: University of Chicago and NBER Press).

Hoyle, E. (1974), 'Professionality, Professionalism and Control in Teaching', *London Educational Review* 3: 13–19.

Huerta, L., and Gonzalez, M.-F. (2003), 'Cyber and Home School Charter Schools: How States are Defining New Forms of Public Schooling', Working Paper, <www.ncspe.org>.

Human Rights Watch (2001), 'Scared at School: Sexual Violence against Girls in South African Schools' (New York: Human Rights Watch) Available at <www.hrw.org>.

Hunter, L., Bernhardt, A., Hughes, L., and Skuratowicz, E. (2001), 'Its Not Just the ATMs: Technology, Firm Strategies, Jobs and Earnings in Retail Banking', *Industrial and Labour Relations Review*, 54/2A: 402–24.

Hursh, D. (2005), 'The Growth of High-Stakes Testing in the US: Accountability, Markets and the Decline in Educational Equality', *British Educational Research Journal* 31/5.

Hwang, K. (2001), 'Introducing Human Rights Education in the Confucian Society of Taiwan: Its Implications for Ethical Leadership in Education', *International Journal of Educational Leadership* 4/4: 321–32.

Hyman, P. (1994), *Women and Economics: A New Zealand Feminist Perspective* (Wellington: Bridget Williams Books).

Hymes, D. (1995), 'Bernstein and Poetics', in P. Atkinson, B. Davies, and S. Delamont (eds.), *Discourse and Reproduction: Essays in Honour of Basil Bernstein* (Cresskill, NJ: Hampton Press).

Hyslop, J. (1999), *The Classroom Struggle: Policy and Resistance in South Africa 1940–1990* (Pietermaritzburg: University of Natal Press).

Ibrahim, S. E. (1995), 'Civil Society and Prospects of Democratization in the Arab World', in A. R. Norton (ed.), *Civil Society in the Middle East* (Leiden: E. J. Brill).

—— (1996), *Management and Mismanagement of Diversity: The Case of Ethnic Conflict and State Building in the Arab World* (Paris: UNESCO).

IDP Education Australia, with Australian Education International (2001), *Comparative Costs of Higher Education Courses for International Students in Australia, New Zealand, the United Kingdom, Canada and the United States*, (Sydney: IDP).

Iglesias, E. (1981), 'Development and Equity: The Challenge of the 1980s', *CEPAL Review* 1/15: 7–46.

Ikenberry, J. (2001), *After Victory: Institutions, Strategic Restraint and the Rebuilding of Order after Major Wars* (Princeton: Princeton University Press).

Illich, I. (1971), *Deschooling Society* (New York: Harper & Row).

—— and Verne, E. (1976), *Imprisoned in the Global Classroom* (London: Writers and Readers).

Ilon, L. (1996), 'The Changing Role of the World Bank: Education Policy as Global Welfare', *Policy and Politics* 24/4: 413–24.

—— (2002), 'Agents of Global Markets or Agents of the Poor? The World Bank's Education Section Strategy Papers', *International Journal of Educational Development* 22.

Ingham, G. (1996), 'The "New Economic Sociology"', *Work, Employment and Society*, 10/3: 549–64.

Ingvarsson, L. (1992), 'Educational Reform Through Restructuring Industrial Awards: A Study of the Advanced Skills Teacher', mimeograph (Melbourne: Melbourne University School of Education).

Ikenberry, J., (2001), *After Victory, Institutions, Strategic Restraint and the rebuilding of Order after Major Wars* (Princeton: Princeton University Press).

Institut National de la Statistique et des Études Économiques (INSEE) (1996), *Données Sociales 1996: La Société française* (Paris: INSEE).

Institute for International Education (2003), Data on international education in the USA, viewed 11 December 2003, <http://www.iie.org/>.

Interagency Commission WCEFA (UNDP, UNESCO, UNICEF, and World Bank) (1990), *Final Report. World Conference on Education for All: Meeting Basic Learning Needs* (Jomtien: Interagency Commission WCEFA).

International Motor Vehicles Program (1989) (Cambridge, Mass.: MIT).

Ireson, J., and Hallam, S. (2001), *Ability Grouping in Education* (London: Paul Chapman).

Ismail, T. Y. (1997), 'Civil Society in the Arab World: Historical Traces, Contemporary Vestiges', *Arab Studies Quarterly* 19: 77–87.

Istance, D., and Rees, T. (1994), *Women in Post-Compulsory Education and Training in Wales* (Manchester: Equal Opportunities Commission).

Ivy, M. (1988), 'Tradition and Difference in the Japanese Mass Media', *Public Culture* 1/1: 21–9.

Iyer, P. (1988), *Video Night in Kathmandu* (New York: Knopf).

Jagger, A. M. (1983), *Feminist Politics and Human Nature* (Lanham, Md.: Rowman & Littlefield).

—— and Epstein, D. (1996), Introduction to special edition, 'Feminist Analysis of Marketization', *Discourse* 17/3.

James, A. (1993) *Childhood Identities: Social Relationships and the Self in Children's Experiences* (Edinburgh: Edinburgh University Press).

——Jenks, C., and Prout, A. (1998), *Theorizing Childhood* (Cambridge: Polity).

James, E. (1987), 'The Public/Private Division of Responsibility for Education: An International Comparison', in T James and H. M. Levin (ed.), *Comparing Public and Private Schools* (New York: Falmer).

—— (1993), 'Why Do Different Countries Choose a Different Public–Private Mix of Educational Services?', *Journal of Human Resources* 28: 571–92.

James, H. (2001), *The End of Globalization: Lessons from the Great Depression* (Cambridge Mass: Harvard University Press).

James, P., Veit, W. and Wright, S. (eds.) (1997), *Work of the Future: Global Perspectives* (St. Leonards, NSW: Allen & Unwin).

James, R., Baldwin, G., and McInnis, C. (1999), *Which University? The Factors Influencing the Choices of Prospective Undergraduates*, Evaluations and Investigations Program, Higher Education Division, Department of Education, Science and Training (DEST), Canberra, viewed 21 June 2004, <http://www.dest.gov.au/archive/highered/eippubs/99-3/whichuni.pdf>.

James, T., and Levin, H. M. (1983), *Public Dollars for Private Schools: The Case of Tuition Tax Credits* (Philadelphia: Temple University Press).

Jameson, Fredric (1983), 'Postmodernism and Consumer Society', in H. Foster (ed.), *The Anti-Aesthetic: Essays on Post-Modern Culture* (Port Townsend, Wash.: Bay Press), 111–25.

—— (1991), 'Nostalgia for the Present', in *Postmodernism, or, the Cultural Logic of Late Capitalism* (Durham, NC: Duke University Press).

Jamieson, L. (2001), *Intimacy, Personal Relationships in Modern Society* (Cambridge: Polity).

Jayasuriya, K. (2001), 'Globalization, Sovereignty, and the Rule of Law: from Political to Economic Constitutionalism?', *Constellations* 8/4: 442–59.

Jaynes, Gerald, and Williams, Robin (eds.) (1990), *A Common Destiny* (Washington, DC: National Academy of Sciences).

Jeffrey, B., and Woods, P. (1998), *Testing Teachers: The Effect of School Inspections on Primary Teachers* (London: Falmer).

Jencks, C. (1972), *Inequality: A Reassessment of the Effect of Family and Schooling in America* (New York: Basic Books).

—— and Phillips, M. (1998), *The Black-White Test Score Gap* (New York: Russell Sage).

—— Smith, M., Acland, H., Bane M. J., Cohen, D., Gintis, H., Heyns, B., and Michelson, S. (1972), *Inequality: A Reassessment of Family and Schooling in America* (New York: Basic Books).

Jensen, A. (1998), *The g Factor: The Science of Mental Ability* (New York: Praeger).

Jensen, J. (1998), *Passage from India: Asian Indian Immigrants in North America* (New Haven, Conn.: Yale University Press).

Jerrome, D. (1984), 'Good Company: The Sociological Implications of Friendship', *The Sociological Review*, 10: 117–28.

Jhally, S. (1990), *The Codes of Advertising: Fetishism and the Political Economy of Meaning in Consumer Society* (New York: Routledge).

Jimenez, E. (1986), 'The Public Subsidization of Education and Health in Developing Countries. A Review of Equity and Efficiency', *World Bank Research Observer* 1/1: 110–29.

—— (1987), *Pricing Policy in the Social Sectors: Cost Recovery for Education and Health in Developing Countries* (Baltimore: Johns Hopkins University Press).

Johnson, C., (2004), *The Sorrows of Empire: Militarism, Secrecy and the Fall of the Republic* (London: Verso).

Johnson, M. (1999), *Failing School, Failing City: The Reality of Inner City Education* (Charlbury: Jon Carpenter).

Johnson, M. (2003), *Schooling in London: An Overview* (London: Institute of Public Policy Research).

Johnson, S. M. (1990), *Teachers at Work* (New York: Basic Books).

Johnson, W., Packer, A., et al. (1987), US Bureau of the Census Current Population Reports Series P23/138, tables 2.1, 4.6, in *Workforce 2000: Work and Workers for the 21st Century* (Indianapolis: Hudson Institute).

Jones, C., and Mahony, P. (eds.) (1989), *Learning Our Lines: Sexuality and Social Control in Education* (London: The Women's Press).

Jones, K. (1993), *Compassionate Authority. Democracy and the Representation of Women*. (New York: Routledge).

—— and Epstein, D. (1996), 'The Marketisation of School Education: Feminist Studies and Perspectives', *Discourse* 17/3: 301–14.

—— Bigum, C., and Fitzclarence, L. (1993), 'Marketing Education in the Post-Modern Age', *Journal of Education Policy* 8/2: 105–22.

Jones, L., and Moore, R. (1993), 'Education, Competence and the Control of Expertise', *British Journal of Sociology of Education* 14: 385–98.

Jones, P. (1992), *World Bank Financing of Education. Lending, Learning and Development* (London: Routledge).

Jones, S. (1993), *Assaulting Childhood: Children's Experiences of Migrancy and Hostel Life in South Africa* (Johannesburg: Witwatersrand University Press).

Jorgensen, S. (2001), 'Analyser of Indkomstfordelingen', *Working Paper* 2001:6, from Det Okonomiske Raad Sekretariatet, Copenhagen.

Joyce, B., and Showers, B. (1988), *Student Achievement Through Staff Development* (New York: Longman).

—— Weil, M. (1980), *Models of Teaching*, 2nd edn. (Englewood Cliffs, NJ: Prentice-Hall).

Kabeer, N. (1996), 'Agency, Well-being, and Inequality: Reflections on the Gender Dimensions of Poverty', *IDS Bulletin* 27/1: 11–25.

Kadesjö, B. (2000). 'Neuropsychiatric and Neurodevelopmental Disorders in a Young School-Age Population. Epidemiology and Comorbidity in a School Health Perspective'. Diss., Göteborg University, Göteborg.

—— and Gillberg. C. (1998), 'Attention Deficits and Clumsiness in Swedish 7-year-old Children', *Developmental Medicine and Child Neurology*, 40: 796–804.

Kadzamira, E. C., and Chibwana, M. (2000), 'Gender and Primary Schooling in Malawi', *IDS Research Report* 40 (Brighton: IDS).

—— & Rose, P. (2001), 'Educational Policy Choice and Policy Practice in Malawi: Dilemmas and Disjunctures' *IDS Working Paper* 124 (Brighton: IDS).

Kaim, B. (2002), 'Auntie Stella: Teenagers Talk about Sex, Life and Relationships'. Retrieved 15 April 2002 from <www.auntiestella.org>.

Kakar, Sudhir (1990), *Intimate Relations: Exploring Indian Sexuality* (Chicago: University of Chicago Press).

Kalecki, M. (1993), *Developing Economies* (Oxford: Clarendon).

Kallaway, P. (ed.) (1984), *Apartheid and Education* (Johannesburg: Ravan).

—— (ed.) (2002), *The History of Education under Apartheid, 1948–1994: the doors of learning and culture shall be opened*. New York: Peter Lang.

—— Kruss, G., Fataar, A., and Donn, G. (eds.) (1997), *Education after Apartheid: South African Education in Transition* (Cape Town: University of Cape Town Press).

Kamrava, M., and Mora, F. O. (1998), 'Civil Society and Democratisation in Comparative Perspective Latin America and the Middle East', *Third World Quarterly* 19/5: 893–916.

Kane, P. R., and Lauricella, C. J. (2001), 'Assessing the Growth and Potential of Charter School', in H. M. Levin (ed.), *Privatizing Education* (Boulder: Westview), 203–33.

Kane, T. J. and Staiger, D. O. (2002), 'The Promise and Pitfalls of Using Imprecise School Accountability Measures', *Journal of Economic Perspectives* 16: 91–114.

Kant, I. (1932), *Perpetual Peace* (Los Angeles: US Library Association).

Kanter, R.M. (1991), 'The Future of Bureaucracy and Hierarchy in Organisational Theory: A Report from the Field', in P. Bourdieu and J. Coleman (eds.), *Social Theory for a Changing Society* (Boulder: Westview).

Kanter, R. (1995) 'Nice Work If You Can Get It', *The American Prospect*, 6/23, 21 Sept.

Kapur, D., Lewis, J., et al. (1997), *The World Bank. Its First Half Century*, i. *History* (Washington, DC: The Brookings Institute).

Karabel, J., and Halsey, A. H. (eds.) (1977), *Power and Ideology in Education* (New York: Oxford University Press).

Karrier, T. (1994), 'Competition and American Enterprise', *Challenge* 37/1 (Jan.–Feb.), 40–5.

Karsten, S. (1994), 'Policy on Ethnic Segregation in a System of Choice: The Case of the Netherlands', *Journal of Education Policy* 9: 211–25.

Katz, L., and Revenga, A. (1989), 'Changes in the Structure of Wages: US and Japan', *Calculations of Current Population Surveys* (National Bureau of Economic Research, Sept.).

Kärfve, E. (2000), *Hjärnspöken. Damp och hotet mot folkhälsan* [Figments of Brain. DAMP and the Threat to Popular Health] (Stockholm: Brutus Östling).

Kautto, M. (2000), 'Two of a Kind', *Balance Sheet for Welfare of the 1990s. SOU 2000:83* (Stockholm: Fritzes).

Keatinge, M. W. (1896), *The Great Didactic of Comenius* (London: A. and C. Black).

Keep, E. (2000), *Creating a Knowledge Driven Economy—Definitions, Challenges and Opportunities* (Warwick: Centre for Skills, Knowledge and Organizational Performance, University of Warwick).

Keep, W., and Mayhew, K. (1993), *UK Training Policy: Assumptions and Reality*, ESRC Seminar Paper, December.

—— and Mayhew, K. (2004), 'The Economic and Distributional Implications of Current Policies in Higher Education', *Oxford Review of Economic Policy* 20: 298–314.

Kehily, M. J., and Nayak, A. (1997), '"Lads and Laughter': Humour and the Production of Heterosexual Identities', in *Gender and Education* 9/1: 69–87.

Kelchtermans, G. (1996), 'Teacher Vulnerability: Understanding its Moral and Political Roots', *Cambridge Journal of Education*.

Kellner, D. (2004), *From 9/11 to Terror War: The Dangers of the Bush Legacy* (Lanham, Md.: Rowman & Littlefield).

Kelly, L. (1992), 'Not in Front of the Children: Responding to Right Wing Agendas On Sexuality and Education', in M. Arnot and L. Barton (eds.), *Voicing Concerns: Sociological Perspectives on Contemporary Education Reforms* (Wallingford: Triangle Books), 20–40.

Kennedy, D. (1997), *Academic Duty* (Cambridge, Mass: Harvard University Press).

Kennedy, H. (2004), 'Take no comfort in this warm blanket of security', *Guardian*, 15 March, 15.

Kent, A. (2002), 'A Study of Pupil and Teacher Attitudes with Regard to the Gender Implications on HIV and AIDS Education in KwaZulu Natal, South Africa', MA Dissertation, University of London Institute of Education.

Kenway, J. (1992), *Marketing Education in the Post-Modern Age*, Paper to the AARE Conference in San Francisco.

—— and Bullen, E. (2001), *Consuming Children* (Bukingham: Open University Press).

—— Bigum, C. and Fitzclarence, L. (1993), 'Marketing Education in the Post-Modern Age', *Journal of Education Policy* 8/2 105–22.

—— and Epstein, D. (1996), 'The Marketisation of School Education: Feminist Studies and Perspectives', *Discourse* 17/3 301–14.

—— and Langmead, D. (2000), 'Cyberfeminism and Citizenship? Challenging the Political Imaginary', in M. Arnot and J. Dillabough (eds.), *Challenging Democracy: International Perspectives on Gender, Education and Citizenship* (London: Routledge).

—— Willis, S., with Blackmore, J., and Rennie, L. (1997), *Answering Back: Girls, Boys and Feminism* (Sydney: Allen & Unwin).

Kerr, C., Dunlop, J., Harbinson, F. and Myers, C. (1973), *Industrialism and Industrial Man* (Harmondsworth: Penguin).

Khaleefa, O., Erdos, G., and Ashria, I. H. (1997), 'Traditional Education and Creativity in an Afro-Arab Islamic Culture: The Case of Sudan', *Journal of Creative Behavior* 31/3: 201–11.

Khilnani, S. (1997), *The Idea of India* (London: Hamish Hamilton).

Khosa, M. (2001), 'Public Appraisal of Social and Economic Infrastructure Delivery', in M. M. Khosa (ed.), *Empowerment through Economic Transformation* (Durban: African Millennium Press), 377–408.

Kickert, W. (1991), 'Steering at a Distance: A New Paradigm of Public Governance in Dutch Higher Education', Paper presented to European Consortium for Political Research, University of Essex.

Kimble, J. (1983), 'Runaway Wives: Basotho Women, Chiefs and the Colonial State c. 1890–1920', Unpublished seminar paper, Institute of Commonwealth Studies, London.

King, E., and Hill, A. (eds.) (1993), *Women's Education in Developing Countries. Barriers, Benefits, and Policies* (Baltimore: The Johns Hopkins University Press).

King, K. (1993), 'Education Policy in a Climate of Entitlement: The South African Case'. Unpublished discussion paper.

Kjellberg, A. (1998), 'Sweden: Restoring the Model', in A. Ferner, and R. Hyman (eds.), *Changing Industrial Relations in Europe* (Oxford: Blackwell).

Klasen, S. (1994), 'Missing Women Reconsidered', *World Development* 22.

Klees, S. (1984), 'The Need for a Political Economy of Educational Finance: A Response to Thobani', *Comparative Education Review* 28/3.

Klees, S. (2000), 'The Implications of the World Bank' Private Sector Development Strategy', *Transnational Women's and Gender Studies* (15 Aug.).

Klein, N. (2000), *No Logo*. (London: Flamingo).

—— (2003), 'Fortress Continents', *Guardian*, 16 January, 23.

Klienfield, N. (2002), 'The elderly man and the sea? Test sanitizes literacy texts', *New York Times*, 31 July, 1.

Knight, J., and de Wit, H. (1995), 'Strategies for Internationalization of Higher Education: Historical and Conceptual Perspectives', in H. de Wit (ed.), *Strategies for Internationalization of Higher Education* (Amsterdam: EAIE).

Knorr Cetina, K. (1997), *Sociality with Objects. Social Relations in Postsocial Knowledge Societies, Theory, Culture and Society* 14/4: 1–30.

—— (1999), *Epistemic Communities* (Harvard: Harvard Education Press).

Kobrin, S. (2000), 'Development after Industrialization: Poor Countries in an Electronically Integrated Global Economy', in N. Hood and S. Young (eds.), *The Globalization of Multinational Enterprise Activity and Economic Development* (Basingstoke: Macmillan).

Koppitz, E. M. (1968), *Psychological Evaluation of Children's Human Figure Drawings* (New York: Grune & Stratton).

Korten, D. (1996), *When Corporations Rule the World* (London: Earthscan).

Kostiner, J. (1996), *Yemen: The Tortuous Quest for Unity, 1990–1994* (London: Royal Institute of International Affairs).

Kothari, R. (1989) *State against Democracy: In Search of Humane Governance* (New York: New Horizons).

Koven, S., and Michel, S. (1994), *Mothers of a New World: Maternalistic Politics and the Origins of Welfare States* (London: Routledge).

Kraak, A. and Young, M. (2005), Special Issue on Skill Formation in South Africa, *Journal of Education and Work* 181 (March).

Krasner, S. (1993), 'Westphalia and All That', in J. Goldstein and R O. Keohane (eds.), *Ideas and Foreign Policy: Beliefs, Institutions and Political Change* (Ithaca, NY: Cornell University Press).

Kristol, I. (2003), 'The neoconservative persuasion: What it was, and what it is ', *The Weekly Standard*, 25 August.

Kros, C. (1990/91),' "Deep Rumblings": Z. K. Matthews and African Education before 1955', *Perspectives in Education* 12/ 1: 21–40.

Krueger, A. B., and Zhu P., (2004*a*), 'Another Look at the New York City School Voucher Experiment', *American Behavioral Scientist* 47: 658–98.

—— —— (2004*b*), 'Inefficiency, Subsample Selection Bias, and Nonrobustness: A Response to Paul E. Peterson and William G. Howell', *American Behavioral Scientist* 47: 718–28.

Krugman, P. (1997), 'Technology's Revenge', *Pop Internationalism* (Boston: MIT).

Kuiper, E., and Saps, P. (1995), *Out on the Margins: A Feminist Economics* (London: Routledge).

Kumar, K. (1991), *Political Agenda of Education: A Study of Colonialist and Nationalist Ideas* (Delhi: Sage).

Kupermintz, H. (2001), 'The Effects of Vouchers on School Improvement: Another Look at the Florida Data', *Education Policy Analysis Archives* 9: 8.

Kwo, W. Y. (1992), 'The Teaching of Putonghua in Hong Kong Schools: Language Education in a Changing Economic and Political Context', in G. A. Postiglione (ed.), *Education and Society in Hong Kong—Toward One Country and Two Systems* (Hong Kong: Hong Kong University Press).

Kwok, H. K (1998), 'Mother Tongue Education and Changing Language Environments of Hong Kong', in H. K. Kwok and S. L. Chan (eds.), *The Theory and Practice of Mother Tongue Education* (Hong Kong: Hong Kong Teachers' Association).

Kymlicka, W. (1999), 'Liberal Complacencies', in S. Moller Okin (ed.), *Is Multiculturalism Bad for Women?* (Princeton, NJ: Princeton University Press).

Labaree, D. (1992), 'Power, Knowledge and the Rationalization of Teaching: A Genealogy of the Movement to Professionalize Teaching', *Harvard Educational Review*, 62/2: 123–54.

Lacan, J. (1977), 'The Mirror Stage as Formative of the Function of the Eye', in *Écrits* (New York: Norton).

Lacerino-Paquet, N., Holyoke, T. T., Moser, M., and Henig, J. R., (2002), 'Creaming versus Cropping: Charter School Enrollment Practices in Response to Market Incentives', *Educational Evaluation and Policy Analysis* 24: 145–58.

Lacey, C. (1970), *Hightown Grammar* (Manchester: Manchester University Press).

—— (1977), *The Socialization of Teachers* (London: Methuen).

Ladson-Billings, G. (1991), *The Dreamkeepers: Successful Teachers of African-American Children* (San Francisco: Jossey-Bass).

—— (2004), 'Landing on the Wrong Note: The Price we Paid for Brown', *Educational Researcher* 33/7:3–13.

Lakoff, G., and Johnson, M. (1980), *Metaphors We Live By* (Chicago: University of Chicago Press).

Lamore, C. (1999), 'The Moral Basis of Political Liberalism', *Journal of Philosophy*, 96/12: 599–625.

Lanauze, M., & Snow, C. (1989), 'The Relation between First and Second Language Writing Skills', *Linguistic and Education* 1: 323–39.

Landau, R. T., Taylor, T., and Wright, G. (1996), *The Mosaic of Economic Growth* (Stanford: Stanford University Press).

Landes, D. (1999), *The Wealth and Poverty of Ntions* (London: Abacus).

Lang, R. E., and S. P. Hornburg (1998), 'What is Social Capital and Why is it Important to Public Policy?' *Housing Policy Debate* 9: 1–16.

Lange, D. (1981), 'Recognizing the Public Domain', *Law and Contemporary Problems* 44/4: 147–78.

Lareau, A. (1987), 'Social Class Differences in Family/School Relationships—The Importance of Cultural Capital', *Sociology of Education* 60/1: 73–85.

—— (1989), *Home Advantages: Social Class and Parental Intervention in Elementary Education* (Washington DC: Falmer).

—— (1997), 'Social Class Difference in Family–;School Relationships: The Importance of Cultural Capital', in J. Karabel and A. H. Halsey (eds.), *Power and Ideology in Education* (London: Oxford University Press).

—— (2000), *Home Advantage: Social Class and Parental Intervention in Elementary Education* (Lanham, Md.: Rowman & Littlefield).

—— (2001). *Social Capital: A Theory of Social Structure and Action* (Cambridge: Cambridge University Press).

Larrain, J. (1989), *Theories of Development* (Cambridge: Polity).

Larsen, K. and Vincent-Lancrin, S. (2002), 'International Trade in Educational Services: Good or Bad?' *Higher Education Policy and Management* 14/3: 9–4s.

Larson, M. S. (1977), *The Rise of Professionalism* (Berkeley: University of California Press).

—— (1994), *Economies of Signs and Space* (London: Sage).

—— (1987), *The End of Organized Capitalism* (Cambridge: Polity).

Lasonen, J., and Young, M. (1998), *Strategies for Achieving Parity of Esteem in European Upper Secondary Education*, The Leonardo da Vinci Project, Post-16 Strategies (Jyväskylä: Institute for Education Research, University of Jyväskylä).

Lather, P. (1992), *Getting Smart* (New York: Routledge).

Latour, B., and Woolgar, S. (1979), *Laboratory Life: The Social Construction of Scientific Facts* (Beverly Hills: Sage).

Lauder H. (1994), *The Creation of Market Competition for Education in New Zealand* (Wellington: Smithfield Project).

—— (2001), 'Globalization, Multinationals, and the Labour Market', in P. Brown, A. Green, and H. Lauder, *High Skills: Globalization, Competitiveness and Skill Formation* (Oxford: Oxford University Press).

—— Brown, P. and Halsey, A. H. (2004), 'Sociology and Political Arithmetic: Some Principles of a New Policy Science', *British Journal of Sociology* 55/1:

—— and Hughes, D., et al. (1999), *Trading in Futures: Why Markets in Education Don't Work* (Buckingham: Open University Press).

—— Brown, P., and Egerton, M., (2005), *A Report on Graduate Earnings: Theory and Empirical Analysis* (Cardiff: National Assembly of Wales).

Lave, J., and Wenger, E. (1991), *Situated Learning: Legitimate Peripheral Participation* (New York: Cambridge University Press).

Lawn, M. (1990), 'From Responsibility to Competency: A New Context for Curriculum Studies in England and Wales', *Journal of Curriculum Studies* 22/4: 388–92.

—— (2001), 'Borderless Education: Imagining a European Education Space in a Time of Brands and Networks', *Discourse: Studies in the Cultural Politics of Education* 22/2: 173–84.

—— and Lingard, B. (2002), 'Constructing a European Policy Space in Educational Governance: The Role of 'Transnational Policy Actors', *European Educational Research Journal*, 1/2: 290–307.

—— and Ozga, J. (1981), *Teachers, Professionalism and Class* (Lewes: Falmer).

Lawton, D. (1980), *The Politics of the School Curriculum* (London: Routledge & Kegan Paul).

Lawton, S. (1992), 'Why Restructure? An International Survey of Roots of Reform', *Journal of Education Policy* 7/2: 139–54.

Lazonick, W. (1993), *Business Organization and the Myth of the Market Economy* (Cambridge: Cambridge University Press).

Lefebvre, H. (1991), *The Production of Space* (Cambridge, Mass.: Blackwell).

Le Grand, J. (1997), 'Knights, Naves or Pawns? Human Behaviour and Social Policy', *Journal of Social Policy* 26/2: 149–69.

Le Tendre, G., Baker, D. P., Akiba, M., Goesling, B., and Wiseman, A. (2001), 'Teachers' Work: Institutional Isomorphism and Cultural Variation in the US, Germany and Japan', *Educational Researcher* 306: 3–15.

Lenskyj, H. (1990), 'Beyond Plumbing and Prevention: Feminist Approaches to Sex Education', in *Gender and Education* 2: 217–30.

Lenti, L. (2003), 'New Wave of Voucher Programs? The Colorado Opportunity Contract Pilot Program', Occasional Paper, National Center for the Study of Privatization in Education.

Leonard, K. (1997), *The South Asian Americans* (Westport, Conn.: Greenwood).

Levi, M., and Ziegler, S. (1991), *Making Connections: Guidance and Career Education in the Middle Years* (Toronto: The Ontario Ministry of Education).

Levin, B., and Riffel, P. (1997), *Schools in a Changing World* (London: Falmer).

Levin, H. M. (1998), 'Educational Vouchers: Effectiveness, Choice and Costs', *Journal of Policy Analysis and Management* 17: 373–92.

—— (1999), 'The Public–Private Nexus in Education', *American Behavioral Scientist* 43: 124–137.

—— (2001*a*), *Privatizing Education: Can the Market Deliver Freedom of Choice, Productive Efficiency, Equity and Social Cohesion?* (Boulder: Westview).

—— (2001*b*), 'Thoughts on For-Profit School', Occasional Paper, National Center for the Study of Privatization in Education, <www.ncspe.org>.

—— (2002), 'A Comprehensive Framework for Evaluating Educational Vouchers', *Educational Evaluation and Policy Analysis* 24: 159–74.

—— and Driver, C. (1997), 'Costs of an Educational Voucher System', *Education Economics* 5: 303–11.

—— and Kelley, C. (1997), 'Can Education Do it Alone?', in A. H. Halsey, H. Lauder, P. Brown, and A. Stuart Wells, (eds.), *Education, Culture, Economy, and Society* (Oxford: Oxford University Press).

Levine, D. (1995), *Reinventing the Workplace: How Business and Employees can Both Win* (Washington DC: Brookings).

Levinson, M., and Levinson, S. (2003), '"Getting Religion": Religion, Diversity, and Community in Public and Private Schools', in A Wolfe (ed.), *School Choice: A Moral Debate* (Princeton: Princeton University Press).

Lévi-Strauss, Claude (1969), *Elementary Structures of Kinship* (Boston: Beacon).

Levy, A. (2000), Diasporas through Anthropological Lenses: Contexts of Postmodernity, *Diaspora* 9/1.

Lewis, J., and Astrom, G. (1992), 'Equality, Difference: State Welfare Labor Market Policies and Family Polities in Sweden', *Feminist Studies* 18/1: 59–87.

Lewis, R. (1993), *Leaders and Teachers: Adult Education and the Challenge of Labour in South Wales, 1906–1940* (Cardiff: University of Wales Press).

Li, J. (2003), 'US and Chinese Cultural Beliefs about Learning', *Journal of Educational Psychology* 952: 258–67.

Lieberman, A. (1996), 'Practices that Support Teacher Development: Transforming Conceptions of Professional Learning', in M. W. Mclaughlin and I. Oberman (eds.), *Teacher Learning: New Policies, New Practices* (New York, Columbia University: Teachers College Press), 185–201.

—— and Miller, L. (2000), *Teachers Transforming Their World and Their Work* (New York: Teachers College Press).

Lilja, K. (1998), 'Finland: Continuity and Modest Moves towards Company-Level Corporatism', in A. Ferner and R. Hyman (eds.), *Changing Industrial Relations in Europe* (Oxford: Blackwell).

Lin, N. (2001), Social Capital: *A Theory of Social Structure and Action* (Cambridge: Cambridge University Press).

Lindensjö, B., and Lundgren, U. P. (2000), *Utbildningsreformer Och Politisk Styrning* [Educational Reforms and Political Steering] (Stockholm: HLS).

Lingard, B., and Blackmore, J. (1997), 'The "Performative" State and the State of Educational Research' (Editorial), in *The Australian Educational Researcher* 24/3: 1–20.

—— and Porter, P. (eds.) (1997), *A National Approach to Schooling in Australia*? (Canberra: Australian College of Education).

—— Rawolle, S., and Taylor, S. (2005), 'Globalising Policy Sociology in Education: Working with Bourdieu', *Journal of Education Policy* 20/6.

Linguasphere Observatory (2003), Data on world language use, viewed 15 July 2003, <http://www.linguasphere.org/>.

Lipman, P. (2004), *High-Stakes Education: Inequality, Globalization, and Urban School Reform* (New York: Routledge Falmer).

Litman, J. (1990), 'The Public Domain', *Emory Law Journal* 39/4: 965–1023.

Little, A. (1999), 'Multi-grade Teaching: Why is it Important to Take Seriously?' Paper presented at the Fifth Oxford Conference on Education and Development, 9–13 September.

Little, J. W. (1990), 'The Persistence of Privacy: Autonomy and Initiative in Teachers' Professional Relations', *Teachers' College Record* 91/4: 509–36.

—— (1993), 'Teachers' Professional Development in a Climate of Educational Reform', *Educational Evaluation and Policy Analysis* 15/2: 129–51.

—— and Mclaughlin, M. W. (eds.), (1994), *Teachers' Work: Individuals, Colleagues and Contexts* (New York: Teachers' College Press).

Livingstone, D. (1998), *The Education–Jobs Gap: Underemployment or Economic Democracy* (Boulder: Westview).

Llewellyn, M. (1980), 'Studying Girls at School: The Implications of Confusion', in R. Deem (ed.), *Schooling for Women's Work* (Boston: Routledge & Kegan Paul), 42–51.

Lloyd, C., and Payne, J. (2003), 'What is the 'High Skills Society'? Some Reflections on Current Academic and Policy Debates in the UK', *Policy Studies* 24/2–3: 115–33.

Lloyd, G. (1986), 'Selfhood, War and Masculinity', in C. Pateman and E. Gross (eds.), *Feminist Challenges: Social and Political Theory* (Sydney: Allen & Unwin).

Lortie, D. (1975), *Schoolteacher: A Sociological Study* (Chicago, Il., University of Chicago Press).

Lovering, J. (1990), 'A Perfunctory Sort of Post-Fordism: Economic Restructuring and Labour Market Segmentation in Britain in the 1980s', *Work, Employment and Society*, Special Issue, 9–28.

Low, L. (2002), 'Globalization and the Political Economy of Singapore's Policy on Foreign Talent and High Skills', *Journal of Education and Work* 15/4: 409–26.

Lowe, J. (2000), 'International Examinations, National Systems and the Global Market', *Compare* 29/3: 317–30; 363–77.

Lowen, R. (1996), *Creating the Cold War University: The Transformation of Stanford* (Berkeley: University of California Press).

Lubeck, S., and Garrett, P. (1990), 'The Social Construction of the "At-Risk" Child', *British Journal of Sociology of Education* 11/3: 327–41.

Lucas, S. R. (1999), *Tracking Inequality: Stratification and Mobility in American High Schools* (New York: Teachers College Press).

Luke, C. (1997), 'Quality Assurance and Women in Higher Education', *Higher Education* 33: 433–51.

Luke, C., and Gore, J. (eds.) (1989), *Feminisms and Critical Pedagogy* (New York: Routledge).

Lukes, S. (1973), *Émile Durkheim, His Life and Works: A Historical and Critical Study* (London: Allen Lane).

Lupton, R. (2003*a*), 'Secondary Schools in Disadvantaged Areas: The Impact of Context on School Processes and Quality', Ph.D. thesis, Department of Social Policy, London School of Economics.

—— (2003*b*), *Poverty Street: The Dynamics of Neighbourhood Decline and Renewal* (Bristol: The Policy Press).

—— (2005), 'Social Justice and School Improvement: Improving the Quality of Schooling in the Poorest Neighbourhoods', *British Educational Research Journal* 31/5.

Luria, A. R. (1978), *Cognitive Development: Its Cultural and Social Foundations*, ed. M. Cole (Cambridge, Mass.: Harvard University Press).

Lury, C. (1996), *Consumer Culture* (Cambridge: Polity).

Luttrell, W. (1996), 'Taking Care of Literacy: One Feminist's Critique, *Educational Policy* 10: 342–65.

Lynch, K., and Baker, J. (2005), 'Equality in Education: An Equality of Condition Perspective', *Theory and Research in Education* 3/2:131–64.

Lynch, P. Saifilislam, M. O., and Abasalih, A. Q. (1992), 'Educational Change and the "Khalwa" in the Sudan: Reform Reformed', *Journal of Educational Administration* 30:53–62.

Lyotard, J. F. (1984), *The Postmodern Condition: A Report on Knowledge* (Manchester: Manchester University Press).

Mac an Ghaill, M. (1988), *Young, Gifted and Black* (Milton Keynes.: Open University Press).

—— (1989), 'Beyond The White Norm: The Use of Qualitative Methods in the Study of Black Youths' Schooling in England', *Qualitative Studies in Education* 2/3: 175–89.

—— (1994), *The Making of Men: Masculinities, Sexualities and Schooling* (Buckingham: Open University Press).

—— (ed.) (1996), *Understanding Masculinities: Social Relations and Cultural Arenas* (Buckingham: Open University).

MacCormick, N. (1999), *Questioning Sovereignty* (Oxford: Clarendon).

Macedo, D. (1999), 'Our Common Culture: A Poisonous Pedagogy', in M. Castells, R. Flecha, P. Freire, H. A. Giroux, and P. Willis (eds.), *Critical Information in the New Information Age* 117–138. (Lanham, Md.: Rowman & Littlefield).

Machin, S. (1998), 'Childhood Disadvantage and Intergenerational Transmissions of Economic Status', in A. Atkinson and J. Hills (eds.), *Exclusion, Employment and Opportunity* (London: London School of Economics (CASE)).

MacKinnon, and Westbury, I. (1975), 'Stability and Change in the Public Schools of Gary, Indiana: 1940–1970', in W. Reid and D. Walker (eds.), *Case Studies in Curriculum Change*. Great Britain and the United States.

Mackintosh, N. J. (1998), *IQ and Human Intelligence* (Oxford: Blackwell).

Maclean's (1999), 'How teens got the power: Gen Y has the cash, the cool—and a burgeoning consumer culture', Maclean's, 22 March. <www.web4.infotrac.galegroup.com>, Article A54833728.

MacLeod, C. (1988), *Inventing the Industrial Revolution: The English Patent System, 1660–1800* (Cambridge: Cambridge University Press).

MacPhail, C., and Campbell, C. (2000), 'I Think Condoms Are Good but, aai, I Hate Those Things': Condom Use among Adolescents and Young People in a Southern African Township', *Social Science and Medicine* 52: 1613–27.

Macrae, S., Maguire, M., and Ball, S. J. (1996), 'Opportunity Knocks: Choice in the Post-16 Education and Training Market', *Proceedings of Markets in Education: Processes and Practices*. University of Southampton, 4–5 July.

Madaus, G. F. (1994), 'Testing's Place in Society: An Essay Review of "Testing Testing: Social Consequences of the Examined Life", by F. A. Hanson', *American Journal of Education* 102: 222–34

Mahoney, P., and Hextall, I. (1997), 'Social Justice and the Reconstruction of Teacher Education', Paper presented to the British Educational Research Association, York, UK.

Mahshi, Kh., and Bush, K. (1989), 'The Palestinian Uprising and Education for the Future', *Harvard Education Review* 59: 470–83.

Majone, G. (1996), 'Regulatory Legitimacy', in G. Majone (ed.), *Regulating Europe* (London: Routledge).

Mäkitalo, Å. (2002), *Categorizing Work: Knowing, Arguing, and Social Dilemmas in Vocational Guidance*, Göteborg Studies in Educational Sciences, 177 (Göteborg: Acta Universitatis Götheburgensis).

—— and Säljö, R. (2002), 'Talk in Institutional Context and Institutional Context in Talk: Categories as Situated Practices', *Text* 22/1: 57–82.

Malawi Government (various years), *Approved and Revised Estimates of Expenditure on Recurrent Account* (Zomba: Government Press).

Mandel, E. (1978), *Late Capitalism* (London: Verso).

Mann, M. (1993), *The Sources of Social Power*, ii. *The Rise of Classes and Nation-States, 1760–1914* (Cambridge: Cambridge University Press).

Mann, M. (2003), *Incoherent Empire* (London, Verso).

Manson, H. (2004), 'Parliament? Does it mean a Bunch of People in a Big House? Conceptions of Citizenship of the Pre-First Time Voter—Background and a Preliminary Sampling', Education Department, University of Bath.

Marais, H. (1998), 'South Africa: Limits to Change', *The Political Economy of Transformation* (London: Zed Books).

Mare, R. (1993), 'Educational Stratification and Observed and Unobserved Components of Family Background', in Y. Shavit, and H.P. Blossfeld (eds.), *Persistent Inequality* (Boulder: Westview), 351–76.

Marginson, S. (1997), *Educating Australia: Government, Economy and Citizen Since 1960* (Melbourne: Cambridge University Press).

—— (1997), *Markets in Education* (St Leonards: Allen & Unwin).

—— and Considine, M. (2000), *The Enterprise University: Power, Governance and Reinvention in Australia* (Cambridge: Cambridge University Press).

—— and Sawir, E. (2004), 'The Global University and its Future: Beyond National States, Markets, and Systems of Higher Education' *Higher Education* 43: 281–309.

Markley, M. (2004), 'TAAS scores rose as SAT's fell', *Houston Chronicle*, 1 April.

Marks, S., and Rathbone, R. (eds.) (1982), *Industrialisation and Social Change in South Africa: African Class Formation, Culture and Consciousness 1870–1930* (London: Longman).

Marquez, G. G. (1982), *One Hundred Years of Solitude* (New York: Penguin).

—— (1988), *Herein the Time of Cholera* (New York: Penguin).

Marriott, M. (1993), 'Hard core rap lyrics stir backlash', *New York Times*, 15 August, 1.

Marshall, H. (2003), 'Global Education — A Re-emerging Field', *British Journal of Sociology of Education* 24/3: 397–405.

Marshall, T.H., (1950), *Citizenship and Social Class and Other Essays* (Cambridge: Cambridge University Press).

Marshall, G., Swift, A., and Roberts, S. (1997), *Against the Odds: Social Class and Social Justice in Industrial Societies* (Oxford: Clarendon).

Martens, K., Balzer, C., Sackmann, R., and Waymann, A. (2004), *Comparing Governance of International Organizations: The EU, The OECD and Educational Policy* (Bremen: Univeristat Bremen).

Martin, J. (1997), 'La equidad en el presupuesto publico', *CEPAL Review*, December, 17–27.

Martin, M. O., Mullis, I. V. S., Gonzalez, E. J., and Chrostowski, S. J. (2004), *Findings from IEA's Trends in International Mathematics and Science Study at the Fourth and Eighth Grades: Science Report* (Chestnut Hill, Mass.: TIMSS and PIRLS International Study Center, Boston College), <http://timss.bc.edu/timss2003i/scienceD.html>, accessed 20 June 2005.

—— Kennedy, A. M. (2003*a*), *PIRLS 2001 International Report: IEA's Study of Reading Literacy Achievement in Primary Schools* (Chestnut Hill, Mass.: Boston College), <http://timss.bc.edu/pirls2001i/PIRLS2001_Pubs_IR.html>, accessed 20 June 2005.

—— and Chrostowski, S. J. (2003*b*), *Findings From IEA's Trends in International Mathematics and Science Study at the Fourth and Eighth Grades: Maths Report* (Chestnut Hill, Mass.: TIMSS and PIRLS International Study Center, Boston College), <http://timss.bc.edu/timss2003i/mathD.html>, accessed 20 June 2005.

Martinelli, A., and Smelser, N. (eds.) (1990), 'Economy and Society: Overviews in Economic Sociology', *Current Sociology* 38/2–3.

Martinez, V., Godwin, K., and Kemerer, F., (1996), 'Public School Choice in San Antonio: Who Chooses and with What Effects?', in B. Fuller and R. Elmore (eds.), *Who Chooses? Who Loses? Culture, Institutions, and the Unequal Effects of School Choice* (New York: Teachers College Press).

Marx, K. (1843/1972), *On the Jewish Question*, in R. C. Tucker. *The Marx-Engels Reader*, (ed.), (New York: Norton).

—— (1973), *Grundrisse: Foundation to the Critique of Political Economy* (Harmondsworth: Penguin).

—— (1976), *Capital: A Critique of Political Economy* (Harmondsworth: Penguin) i.

—— (1981), *Capital* (Harmondsworth: Penguin), iii.

Mason, A., and Palmer, A. (1996), *Queer Bashing: A National Survey of Hate Crimes against Lesbians and Gay Men* (London: Stonewall).

Mason, E., and Asher, R. (1973), *The World Bank since Bretton Woods* (Washington, DC: The Brookings Institute).

Mason, G. (2002), 'High Skills Utilization Under Mass Higher Education: Graduate Employment in Service Industries', *Journal of Education and Work* 15/4: 427–56.

—— and Wilson, R. (2003), *Employers' Skill Survey, New Analyses and Lessons Learned* (London: National Institute of Economic and Social Research).

Massey, D. (1994), *Space, Place, and Gender* (Minneapolis: University of Minnesota Press).

—— (1995), *Spatial Divisions of Labour* (London: Macmillan).

—— (1999), 'Imaging Globalization: Power-Geometries of Time-Space', in A. Brah, M.Hickman, and M. Mac an Ghaill (eds). *Global Futures: Migration, Environment and Globalization* (Basingstoke: Macmillan).

Massey, D. S., and Denton, N. (1993), *American Apartheid: Segregation and the Making of the Underclass* (Cambridge, Mass.: Harvard University Press).

Massialas, B. G., and Jarrar, S. A. (1983), *Education in the Arab World* (New York: Praeger).

—— (1987), 'Conflicts in Education in the Arab World: The Present Challenge', *Arab Studies Quarterly* 9: 35–53.

—— (1991), *Arab Education in Transition* (New York: Garland).

Masterman, L. (1990), *Teaching the Media* (New York: Routledge).

Matkin, G. (1990), *Technology Transfer and the University* (New York: Macmillan).

Mattelart, A. (1983), *Transnationals and the Third World: The Struggle for Culture* (South Hadley, Mass.: Bergin & Garvey).

Maurer, R. (1996), *Beyond the Wall of Resistance* (Austin, Tex.: Band Books).

Maxwell Hamilton, J. (1989), 'A Bit Player Buys Into the Computer Age', *The New York Times Business World* (3 December), 14.

May, J. (ed.) (2000), *Poverty and Inequality in South Africa: Meeting the Challenge* (Cape Town: David Philip).

Mayer, S. (1997), *What Money Can't Buy* (Cambridge, Mass.: Harvard University Press).

Mazawi, A. E. (1994*a*), 'Palestinians in Israel: Educational Expansion, Social Mobility and Political Control', *Compare* 24/3: 277–84.

—— (1994*b*), 'Teachers' Role Patterns and the Mediation of Sociopolitical change: The Case of Palestinian Arab School Teachers', *British Journal of Sociology of Education* 15: 497–514.

—— (1997), 'Culture and Ethnicity in the Curricula of Arab Education in Israel: On the Dimensions and Limits of Political Discourse', *Mifneh*, December, 32–3 (Hebrew).

—— (1998), 'Contested Regimes, Civic Dissent, and the Political Socialization of Children and Adolescents: The Case of the Palestinian Uprising', in O. Ichilov (ed.), *Citizenship and Citizenship Education in a Changing World* (London: Woburn).

—— (1999), 'The Contested Terrains of Education in the Arab States: An Appraisal of Major Research Trends', *Comparative Education Review* 43/3: 332–52.

Mazzarol, T., Soutar, G., Smart D., and Choo, S. (2001), *Perceptions, Information and Choice: Understanding How Chinese Students Select a Country for Overseas Study*, Australian Education International, Canberra, viewed 15 July 2003, <www.dest.gov.au>.

McBride, S., and Williams, R. (2001), 'Globalization, the Restructuring of Labour Markets and Policy Convergence: The OECD "Jobs Strategy"'. *Global Social Policy* 1/3.

McCarthy, C. (1990), *Race and Curriculum: Social Inequality and the Theories and Politics of Difference in Contemporary Research on Schooling*, (London: Falmer).

—— (1998), *The Uses of Culture: Education and the Limits of Ethnic Affiliation* (New York: Routledge).

—— (2002), 'Understanding the Work of Aesthetics in Modern Life: Thinking about the Cultural Studies of Education in a Time of Recession', Paper presented at the annual meeting of the American Educational Research Association, New Orleans, April.

—— and Apple, M. W. (1988), 'Race, Class and Gender in American Educational Research: Toward a Nonsynchronous Parallelist Position', in L. Weis (ed.), *Class, Race and Gender in American Education* (Albany, NY: State University of New York Press), 9–39.

McClelland, M., and Morrison, F. J. (2003), 'The Emergence of Learning-Related Social Skills in Preschool Children', *Early Childhood Research Quarterly* 18: 206–24.

McCracken, J. (1977), *Politics and Christianity in Malawi* (Cambridge: Cambridge University Press).

McCulloch, A., and Joshi, H. (2002), 'Child Development and Family Resources: Evidence from the Second. Generation of the 1958 British Birth Cohort', *Journal of Population Economics* 15/2: 283–304.

McCulloch, G. (1997), 'Marketing the Millennium: Education for the Twenty-First Century', in A. Hargreaves and R. Evans (eds.), *Beyond Educational Reform: Bringing Teachers Back In* (Buckingham: Open University Press).

McEwan, P. J. (2001), 'Comparing the Effectiveness of Public and Private Schools: A Review of Evidence and Interpretations', Occasional Paper, National Center for the Study of Privatization in Education, <www.ncspe.org>.

—— (2003), 'Peer Effects on Student Achievement: Evidence from chile', *Economics of Education Review* 22: 131–41.

—— and Carnoy, M. (2000), 'Effectiveness and Efficiency of Private Schools in Chile's Voucher System', *Educational Evaluation and Policy Analysis* 22: 213–40.

McGrew, A. (2000), 'Democracy Beyond Borders?', in D. Held and A. McGrew (eds.), *The Global Transformations Reader: An Introduction to the Globalization Debate* (Cambridge: Polity), 405–19.

McIntyre, J., Brown, A., and Ferrier, F. (1996), *The Economics of ACE Delivery* (Sydney: BACE).

McKay, D. (1994), *American Politics and Society* (Malden, Mass.: Blackwell).

McLaren, P. (1988), 'Schooling the Postmodern Body: Critical Pedagogy and the Politics of Enfleshment', *Journal of Education* 170/3: 53–83.

—— (1998), *Life in Schools: An Introduction to Critical Pedagogy in the Foundations of Education* (New York: Longman).

—— and Hammer, R. (1995), 'Media Knowledges, Warrior Citizenry, and Postmodern Literacies', in P. McLaren, R. Hammer, D. Scholle and S. Reilly (eds.), *Rethinking Media Literacy: A Critical Pedagogy of Representation* (New York: Peter Lang).

McLaughlin, M. W. (1997), 'Rebuilding Teacher Professionalism in the United States', in A. Hargreaves and R. Evans (eds.), *Buying Teachers Back* (Buckingham: Open University Press).

McLean, I. (1986), 'Mechanisms for Democracy', in D. Held and C. Pollitt (eds.), *New forms of Democracy* (London: Sage/Open University Press).

McLeod, J. (2005),'Feminists Rereading Bourdieu: Old Debates and New Questions about Gender Habitus and Gender Change', *Theory and Research in Education* 3: 7–9.

McLuhan, M., and Powers, B. R. (1989), *The Global Village: Transformations in World, Life and Media in the 21st Century* (New York: Oxford University Press).

McMillan, R. (2000), 'Competition, Parental Involvement, and Public School Performance'. Ph.D. Thesis, Stanford University.

McMullin, E. (1985), 'Openness and Secrecy in Science: Some Notes on Early History', *Science, Technology, and Human Values* 10/2: 14–23.

McNay, L. (2000), *Gender and Agency: Reconfiguring the Subject in Feminist Social Theory* (Cambridge: Polity).

McNeal, R. B. (1999), 'Parental Involvement as Social Capital: Differential Effectiveness on Science Achievement, Truancy, and Dropping Out', *Social Forces* 78: 117–44.

McNiece, R., Bidgood, P., and Soan, P. (2004), 'An Investigation into Using National Longitudinal Studies to Examine Trends in Educational Attainment and Development', *Educational Research* 46: 119–36.

McNeil, L. (2000), *Contradictions of School Reform: Educational Costs of Standardized Testing* (New York: Routledge).

McQueen, H. (1988), 'The Australian Stamp: Image, Design and Ideology', *Arena* 84 (Spring): 78–96.

McTaggart, R. (1989), 'Bureaucratic Rationality and the Self-Educating Profession: The Problem of Teacher Privatism', *Journal of Curriculum Studies* 21/4: 345–61.

McWilliam, E., Hatcher, C. et al. (1999), 'Developing Professional Identities: Re-making the Academic for Corporate Time' (Queensland: Queensland University of Technology).

Mehan, H. (1992), 'Understanding Inequality in Schools: The Contribution of Interpretive Studies', *Sociology of Education*, 65/1: 1–20.

—— (1993), 'Beneath the Skin and Between the Ears: A Case Study in the Politics of Representation', In S. Chaiklin and J. Lave (eds.), *Understanding Practice: Perspectives on Activity and Context* (Cambridge: Cambridge University Press), 241–69.

—— Hertweck, A., and Meihls, J. L. (1986), *Handicapping the Handicapped: Decision Making in Students' Educational Careers* (Stanford, Calif.: Stanford University Press).

—— Villanueva, I., Hubbard, L., and Lintz, A. (1996), *Constructing School Success: The Consequences of Untracking Low-Achieving Students* (New York: Cambridge University Press).

Mehralizadeh, Y. (1999), 'The Relationship Between Schools and the Demands of Paid Work', Ph.D. thesis, University of Bath.

Meier, D. (1998), 'Authenticity and Educational Change', in A. Hargreaves, A. Lieberman, M. Fullan and D. Hopkins (eds.), *International Handbook of Educational Change* (Dordrecht: Kluwer Academic).

Meighan, R. (1981), *A Sociology of Educating* (London: Holt, Rhinehart & Winston.

Meister, J. C. (1998), *Corporate Universities: Lessons in Building a World-Class Work Force* (revised) (New York: McGraw-Hill).

Melitz, A. (1995), *Changes in the Bedouin Education System* (Beer-Sheva, Israel: Authority for Bedouin Education, Southern District of the Ministry of Education, Culture and Sport) (Hebrew).

Mentor, I., Muschamp, Y., Nicholls, P. Ozga, J., and Pollard, A. (1997), *Work and Identity in the Primary School: A Post-Fordist Analysis* (Buckingham: Open University Press).

Merton, R. K. (1973), 'The Perspectives of Insiders and Outsiders', in N. W. Storer (ed.), *The Sociology of Science: Theoretical and Empirical Investigations* (Chicago: University of Chicago Press, 1973).

Metcalf, K. K., West, S. D., Legan, N. A., Paul, K. M., and Boone, W. J. (2003), *Evaluation of the Cleveland Scholarship and Tutoring Program*, Summary Report 1998–2002 (Bloomington: Indiana University School of Education).

Metz, M. (1978), 'Order in the Secondary School: Strategies for Control and their Consequences', *Sociological Inquiry* 48/1: 59–69.

—— (1991), 'Real School: A Universal Drama Amid Disparate Experience', in D. Mitchell and M. Gnesta (eds.), *Education Politics for the New Century, The Twentieth Anniversary Yearbook of the Politics of Education Association* (Philadelphia: Falmer).

Meyer, J. (1977), 'The Effects of Education as an Institution', *American Journal of Sociology* 83/1: 55–77.

—— and Rowan, B. (1977), 'Institutional Organizations: Formal Structure as Myth and Ceremony', *American Journal of Sociology* 83: 340–63.

—— —— (1978), 'The Structure of Educational Organizations', in M. W. Meyer et al. (eds.), *Environments and Organizations* (San Francisco: Jossey-Bass), 78–109.

Meyrowitz, J. (1985), *No Sense of Place: The Impact of Electronic Media on Social Behavior* (New York: Oxford University Press).

Michaels, E., Handfield-Jones, H., and Axelrod, B. (2001), *The war for Talent* (Boston: Harvard Business School Press).

Michie, J., and Padayachee, V. (eds.) (1997), *The Political Economy of South Africa's Transition* (London: Dryden).

Middleton, C. (2000), 'Models of State and Market in the Modernisation of Higher Education', *British Journal of Sociology of Education* 21/4: 537–54.

Middleton, S. (1998), *Disciplining Sexuality: Foucault, Life Histories, and Education* (New York: Teachers College).

—— Ashworth, K., and Braithwaite, I. (1997), *Small Fortunes* (York: Joseph Rowntree Foundation).

—— —— and Walker, R. (1994), *Family Fortunes* (London: Child Poverty Action Group).

Midwinter, E. (1972), *Priority Education* (London: Longman).

Milberg, (1994), 'Market Competition and the Failure of Competitiveness Enhancement Policies in the United States', *Journal of Economic Issues* 28/2 (June) 587–96.

Miles, S. (1996), 'Use and Consumption in the Construction of Identities', Paper presented at 'British Youth Research: The New Agenda' conference, 26–8 January, Glasgow.

Mill, J. S. (1975), *Three Essays: John Stuart Mill* (London: Oxford University Press).

Miller, D. (2000), *Citizenship and National Identity* (Cambridge: Polity).

Miller, J. G. (1994), 'Cultural Diversity in the Morality of Caring: Individuality-Oriented Versus Duty-Based Interpersonal Moral Codes', *Cross-Cultural Research* 28: 3–39.

Miller, T. (1998), *Technologies of Truth: Cultural Citizenship and the Popular Media* (Minneapolis: University of Minnesota Press).

Miller, Y. (1985), *Government and Society in Rural Palestine: 1920–1948* (Austin: University of Texas, Center for Middle Eastern Studies).

Mills, C. (1995), 'Managerial and Professional Work Histories', in T. Butler and M. Savage (eds.), *Social Change and the Middle Classes* (London: UCL Press).

Mingat, A. & Tan, J.-P. (1986), 'Expanding Education through User Charges: What Can be Achieved In Malawi and Other LDCs?' *Economics of Education Review* 5/3: 273–86.

Ministry of Economic Planning And Development (1995), *Policy Framework for Poverty Alleviation Programme* (Lilongwe: MEPD).

Ministry of Education And Culture (various years), *Education Statistics* (Lilongwe: Planning Unit, Ministry of Education).

Miron, G., and Nelson, C., (2002), *What's Public about Charter Schools?* (Thousand Oaks, Calif.: Corwin Press).

Mirza, H. (1992), *Young, Female, and Black*. Milton Keynes: Open University Press.

Mishel, L., and Bernstein, J. (1998), 'Technology and the Wage Structure: Has Technology's Impact Accelerated Since the 1970s?', *Research in Labor Economics*, 17: 305–55.

—— —— and Boushey, (2003), *The State of Working America 2002/2003*, (Ithaca, NY: Cornell University Press).

—— —— and Schmitt, J. (1999), *The State of Working America, 1998-99* (Ithaca, NY: Cornell University Press).

—— —— and Schmitt, J. (2003), *The State of Working America 2002/2003* (Ithaca, NY: Cornell University Press).

Mitchell, K. (2001), 'Education for Democratic Citizenship: Transnationalism, Multiculturalism and the Limits of Liberalism', *Harvard Educational Review* 71/1: 51–78.

—— (1988), *Social Closure: The Theory of Monopolization and Exclusion* (Oxford: Oxford University Press).

Moatassime, A. (1992), *Arabisation et Langue Française au Maghreb* (Paris: Presses Universitaires de France).

Moe, T. M. (1995), *Private Vouchers* (Stanford, Calif.: Hoover Institution Press).

—— (2001), *Schools, Vouchers and the American Public* (Washington, DC: Brookings Press).

Moghaddam, F., and Taylor, D. (1985), 'Psychology in the Developing World: An Evaluation through the Concepts of Dual Perception and Parallel Growth', *American Psychologist* 40: 1144–6.

Mohanty, C. (1990), 'Cartographies of Struggle: Third World Women and the Politics of Feminism', in C. Mohanty, A. Risso. and L. Torres (1990), *Third World Women and the Politics of Feminism* (Minneapolis: Indiana University Press).

Moletsane, R., Morrell, R., Unterhalter, E., and Epstein, D. (2002), 'Instituting Gender Equality in Schools: Working in an HIV/AIDS Environment', *Perspectives in Education* 20/2: 37–53.

Moll, L. C., Amanti, C., Neff, D., and Gonzalez, N. (1992), 'Funds of Knowledge for Teaching: Using a Qualitative Approach to Connect to Homes and Classrooms', *Theory into Practice* 31: 132–41.

Monbiot, G. (2001), *The Captive State* (London: Pan).

—— (2003), 'Stronger than ever', *Guardian*, 28 January, 19.

Monk, Sipple, and Killeen (2001), 'Adoption and Adaptation, New York State School Districts' Responses to State Imposed High School Graduation Requirements: An Eight-Year Retrospective', Education Finance Research Consortium, available online at: <www.albany.edu/edfin/CR01_MSk_Report.pdf> (accessed 3 March 2002).

Montero, C., and Tovar, T. (1999), *Agenda Abierta para la Educación de las Niñas Rurales* (Lima: CARE Peru, Instituto de Estudios Peruanos, and Foro Educativo).

Montesquieu, Charles de Secondat, Baron de (1900), *The Spirit of Laws* (New York: Colonial).

Montgommery, J. de, *La Milice française*, ed. 1636.

Moore, Jr., B. (1978), *Injustice: The Social Bases of Obedience and Revolt* (White Plains, NY: M. E. Sharper).

Moore, R. (1996), 'Back to the Future: The Problem of Change and the Possibilities of Advance in the Sociology of Education', *British Journal of Sociology of Education*, 17: 145–61.

—— and Maton, K. (2001), 'Founding the Sociology of Knowledge: Basil Bernstein, Intellectual fields and the Epistemic Device', in A. Morais et al. (eds.), *Towards a Sociology of Pedagogy: The Contribution of Basil Bernstein to Research* (New York: Peter Lang).

—— and Muller, J. (1999), 'The Discourse of "Voice" and the Problem of Knowledge and Identity in the Sociology of Education', *British Journal of Sociology of Education*, 20/2: 189–206.

—— —— (2002), 'The Growth of Knowledge and the Discursive Gap', *British Journal of Sociology of Education*, Special Issue: Basil Bernstein's Theory of Class, Educational Codes and Social Control, 23/4: 627–38.

—— and Young, M. F. D. (2001), 'Knowledge and the Curriculum: Towards a Reconceptualisation', *British Journal of the Sociology of Education* 22/4: 445–61.

Morais, A., Neves, I., Davies, B., and Daniels, H. (eds.) (2001), *Towards a Sociology of Pedagogy: The Contribution of Basil Bernstein to Research* (New York: Peter Lang).

Morgan, S. (1993), 'Coastal disturbances', *Mirabella* (March): 46.

Morgan, S. L., and Sørensen, A. B. (1999), 'Parental Networks, Social Closure, and Mathematics Learning: A Test of Coleman's Social Capital Explanation of School Effects', *American Sociological Review* 64: 661–81.

Morrell, R. (2001*a*), *From Boys to Gentlemen: Settler Masculinity in Colonial Natal, 1880–1920* (Pretoria: UNISA Press).

—— (2001*b*), 'Corporal Punishment and Masculinity in South African Schools', *Men and Masculinities* 4/2: 140–57.

—— (2001*c*) 'Corporal Punishment in South African Schools: A Neglected Explanation for Its Persistence', *South African Journal of Education* 21/4: 292–9.

—— (2002), 'On a Knife's Edge: Masculinity in Black Working-Class Schools in Post-Apartheid Education', in B. Frank and K. Davison (eds.), *Masculinity and Schooling: International Practices and Perspectives* (Black Point, Nova Scotia: Fernwood).

—— Unterhalter, E., Moletsane, R., and Epstein, D. (2001), 'Missing the Message: HIV/AIDS Interventions and Learners in South African Schools', *Canadian Woman Studies* 21/2: 90–6.

Morris, P. (1996), *The Hong Kong School Curriculum: Development, Issues and Policies*, 2nd edn. (Hong Kong: Hong Kong University Press).

Morrison, A. (1992), *The New Leaders: Guidelines On Leadership Diversity in America* (San Francisco: Jossey-Bass).

Morrow, R. A., and Torres, C. A. (1998*a*), 'Education and the Reproduction of Class, Gender, and Race: Responding to the Postmodern Challenges', in C. A. Torres and T. R. Mitchell (eds.), *Sociology of Education: Emerging Perspectives* (Albany: State University of New York Press).

—— —— (1998*b*), 'Social Closure, Professional Domination, and the New Middle Strata: Rethinking Credentialist Theories of Education', in C. A. Torres and T. R. Mitchell (eds.), *Sociology of Education: Emerging Perspectives* (Albany: State University of New York Press).

Morrow, R. and Torres, C. A. (2000), 'The State, Globalization and Education Policy', in N. Burbules and C. Torres (eds.), *Globalization and Education: Critical Perpsectives* (New York: Routledge).

Morrow, V. (1999), 'Conceptualizing Social Capital in Relation to the Well-being of Children and Young People: A Critical Review', *Sociological Review* 47: 744–66.

—— (2000), '"Dirty Looks" and "Trampy Places" in Young People's Accounts of Community and Neighborhood: Implications for Health Inequalities', *Critical Public Health* 10: 141–53.

Mortimore, P., and Mortimore, J. (1994), *Managing Associate Staff Innovation in Primary and Secondary Schools* (London: Paul Chapman).

Moss, G. (2004), 'Text and Technologies of Regulation: Using Bernstein's Theory to Explore the National Literacy Strategy as a Performance Pedagogy for New Times', Paper presented at the 3rd International Basil Bernstein Conference, Cambridge.

Motala, E., and Pampallis, J. (eds.) (2001), *Education and Equity: The Impact of State Policies on South African Education* (Sandown: Heinemann).

Motala, S. (2002), 'From Policy to Practice: Achieving Quality Education in Postapartheid South Africa', in S. Marks (ed.), *Siyafunda: Partners in Learning* (London: Canon Collins Educational Trust for Southern Africa), 127–34.

—— and Perry, H. (2001), 'The 2000 Senior Certificate Examinations', *Quarterly Review of Education and Training in South Africa* 8/1: 1–11.

Mouffe, C. (1992*a*), 'Feminism, Citizenship and Radical Democratic Politics', in J. Butler and J. W. Scott (eds.), *Feminists Theorise the Political* (New York: Routledge).

—— (2000), 'For an Agonistic Model of Democracy', in N. O'Sullivan (ed.), *Political Theory in Transition* (London: Routledge), 113–30.

Mouzelis, N. (2000), 'The Subjectivist-Objectivist Divide: Against Transcendence', *Sociology* 34/4: 741–62.

Moyo, C. (1992), 'Formal Education Policy and Strategy In Malawi, 1964–1990', in G. Mhone (ed.), *Malawi at the Crossroads: The Post-Colonial Political Economy* (Harare: Sapes Books).

Mukerji, C. (1989), *A Fragile Power: Scientists and the State* (Princeton: Princeton University Press).

Mulgan, R. (2000), 'Was Aristotle an "Aristotelian Social Democrat"', *Ethics* 111/1: 79–101.

Muller, C. (1995), 'Parental Ties to the School and Community and Mathematics Achievement', in Peter W. Cookson, Jr., and Barbara Schneider (eds.), *Transforming Schools* (New York: Garland), 57–79.

—— and Ellison, C. G. (2001), 'Religious Involvement, Social Capital, and Adolescents' Academic Progress: Evidence from the National Education Longitudinal Study of 1988', *Sociological Focus* 34: 155–83.

Muller, J. (2000), *Reclaiming Knowledge: Social Theory, Curriculum and Education Policy* (London: Routledge Falmer).

—— (2001), 'Return to User: Responsivity and Innovation in Higher Education', Paper commissioned by N. Cloete, R. Fehnel, P. Maassen, T. Moja, H. Perold, and T. Gibbon (eds.), *Transformation in Higher Education: Global Pressures and Local Realities* (Cape Town: CHEPS/Juta).

Mullis, I. V. S., Martin, M. O., Gonzalez, E. J. and Kennedy, A. M. (2003*a*), *PIRLS 2001 International Report: IEA's Study of Reading Literacy Achievement in Primary Schools* (Chestnut Hill, Mass.: Boston College), <http://timss.bc.edu/pirls2001i/PIRLS2001_Pubs_IR.html>, accessed 20 June 2005.

—— —— —— and Chrostowski, S.J. (2003*b*), *Findings from IEA's Trends in International Mathematics and Science Study at* *the Fourth and Eighth Grades: Maths Report* (Chestnut Hill, Mass.: TIMSS and PIRLS International Study Center, Boston College), <http://timss.bc.edu/timss2003i/mathD.html>, accessed 20 June 2005.

Mundy, K. (1998), 'Educational Multilateralism and World (Dis)Order', *Comparative Education Review*, November, 448–78.

—— (2002), 'Retrospect and Prospect: Education in a Reforming World Bank', *International of Educational Development* 22/5: 483–508.

Mundy, K., and Iga, M. (2003), 'Hegemonic Exceptionalism and Legitimating Bet Hedging: Paradoxes and Lessons from the US and Japanese Approaches to Education Services under the GATs, *Globalisation, Societies and Education*, 1/3: 281–319.

Muraskin, L., and Stullich, S. (1998), *Barriers, Benefits, and Costs of Using Private Schools to Alleviate Overcrowding in Public Schools*, US Department of Education, Planning and Evaluation Service.

Murphy, B. (1999), *Transforming Ourselves, Transforming the World: A Open Conspiracy for Social Change* (London: Zed Books).

Murphy, J., and Adams, J. (1998), 'Reforming America's Schools 1980–2000', *Journal of Educational Administration* 36/5: 426–44.

Murphy, R. (1984), 'The Structure of Closure: A Critique and Development of the Theories of Weber, Collins and Parkin', *British Journal of Sociology* 35: 547–67.

—— (1988), *Social Closure: The Theory of Monopolization and Exclusion* (Oxford: Clarendon).

Murray, C. E. (1992), 'Teaching as a Profession: The Rochester Case in Historical Perspective', *Harvard Educational Review* 62/4: 494–519.

Murray, M. (1994), *The Revolution Deferred: The Painful Birth of Post-Apartheid South Africa* (London: Verso).

Musgrove, F. (1979), *School and the Social Order* (Chichester: John Wiley).

Nader, R. (1996), *Children First: A Parent's Guide to Fighting Corporate Predators* (Washington, DC: Corporate Accountability Research Group).

Nagel, J. (2000), 'Sexualising the Sociological: Queering and Queerying the Intimate Substructure of Social Life', Presidential address to the Midwest Sociological Society, in *The Sociological Quarterly* 41/1: 1–17.

Naidoo, R. (2003), 'Repositioning Higher Education as a Global Commodity: Opportunities and Challenges for Future Sociology of Education Work', *British Journal of Sociology of Education*, 24(2), 249–259.

—— (2004), 'Fields and Institutional Strategy: Bourdieu on the Relationship between Higher Education, Inequality and Society', *British Journal of Sociology of Education* 4/25: 457–72.

Nakhleh, Kh. (1979), *Palestinian Dilemma: Nationalist Consciousness and University Education in Israel* (Detroit: Association of Arab-American University Graduates).

Nandy, A. (1989), 'The Political Culture of the Indian State', *Daedalus* 118/4: 1–26.

Nash, R. (1990), *Intelligence and Realism: A Materialist Critique of IQ* (London: Macmillan).

—— (1997), *Inequality/Difference: A Sociology of Education* (Palmerston North: ERDC).

—— (1999*a*) *School Learning: Conversations with the Sociology of Education*, Delta Studies in Education, 3 (Palmerston North: Delta).

Nash, R. (1999*b*), 'Social Capital, Class Identity, and Progress at School: Case Studies, *New Zealand Journal of Educational Studies* 34/2: 267–80.

—— (2001), 'Class, "Ability" and Attainment: A Problem for the Sociology of Education', *British Journal of Sociology of Education* 22/2: 189–202.

—— (2003), 'Social Explanation and Socialization: On Bourdieu and the Structure, Disposition, Practice Scheme', *Sociological Review* 51/1: 43–62.

—— (2004), 'Beyond Reproduction Theory: A Multi-level Explanation of Inequality/Difference in Education', in M. Olssen (ed.), *Culture and Learning: Access and Opportunity in the Classroom* (Greenwich, Conn: Information Age Publishing), 95–116.

—— (2005*a*). 'Cognitive *Habitus* and Collective Intelligence: Concepts for the Explanation of Educational Opportunity', *Journal of Education Policy* 20/1: 3–21.

—— (2005*b*) 'Explanation and Quantification in Educational Research: The Arguments of Critical and Scientific Realism', *British Educational Research Journal* 31/2: 185–204.

Nash, R., and Harker, R. (2005), 'The Predicable Failure of School Marketization: The Limitations of Policy Reform', in J. Codd and K. Sullivan (eds.), *Education Policy Directions in Aotearoa New Zealand* (Melbourne: Thomson-Dunmore).

National Progressive Primary Health Care Network/UNICEF (1997), *Youth Speak Out: A Study on Youth Sexuality* (Braamfontein: NPPHCN/UNICEF).

National Research Council (2002), *Scientific Research in Education* (Washington, DC: National Academy Press).

National Research Council (2003), *Engaging Schools: Fostering High School Students' Motivation to Learn* (Washington, DC: National Academies Press).

Nayak, A. (1999), 'White English Ethnicities: Racism, Anti-racism and Student Perspective', *Race, Ethnicity and Education*, 2/2: 177–202.

NCE (1996), *Success Against the Odds—Effective Schools in Disadvantaged Areas* (London: Routledge).

NCES. (2003), *A Brief Portrait of Private Schools*, National Center for Educational Statistics, <www.ed.nces.gov>.

Neave, G. (1988), 'Education and Social Policy: Demise of an Ethic or Change of Values?', *Oxford Review of Education* 14/3: 273–82.

—— (1988), 'On the Cultivation of Quality, Efficiency and Enterprise, an Overview of Recent Trends in Higher Education in Western Europe 1986–88', in *European Journal of Education* 23/1: 7–23.

Neef, D. (Ed.) (1998), *The Knowledge Economy* (Boston: Butlerworth Heinemann).

Neligan, G. A., and Prudham, D. (1969), 'Norms for Four Standard Development Milestones by Sex, Social Class and Place in Family', *Developmental Medicine and Child Neurology*, 11: 413.

Nelson, B. (2003*a*), *Higher Education: Report for 2003 to 2005 Triennium*, Department of Education, Science and Training, Canberra, viewed 10 February 2004, <http://www.dest.gov.au/highered/he_report/2003_2005/pdf/triennium2003_2005.pdf>.

—— (2003*b*), *Our Universities: Backing Australia's Future*, Commonwealth of Australia, Canberra, viewed 21 June 2004, <http://www.backingaustraliasfuture.gov.au/policy_paper/policy_paper.pdf>.

Nelson, R., and Winter, S. (1972), 'In Search of a Useful Theory of Innovation', *Research Policy* 6/1: 36–77.

New York State School Boards Association (2002), Title I accountability status updated for 10 March, 2003. Available online at <http://www. nyssba.org/adnews/misc/thenewaccountability-5.htm> (accessed 28 August 2003).

Newman, F. M. (1994), *School-Wide Professional Community: Issues in Restructuring Schools*, (Madison, Wis.: Centre on Organization and Restructuring of Schools), vi.

—— and Wehlage, G. (1995), *Successful School Restructuring* (Madison, Wis.: Center on Organization and Restructuring of Schools).

Ng-Lun, N. H. (1984), *Interactions of West and East: Development of Public Education in Early Hong Kong* (Hong Kong: CUHKP).

Nias, J., Southworth, G., and Yeomans, R. (1989), *Staff Relationships in the Primary School* (London: Cassell).

—— —— and Campbell, P. (1992), *Whole School Curriculum Development in the Primary School* (London: Falmer).

Nichols. S., and Berliner, D. (2005), 'The Inevitable Corruption of Indicators and Educators through High-Stakes Testing (Arizona State University, Tempe, AZ, Education Policy Studies Laboratory). Available online at <http://edpolicylab.org> (accessed 5 April 2005).

Nickell, Stephen, and Bell, Brian (1996), 'The Collapse in Demand for the Unskilled and Unemployment Across the OECD', *Oxford Review of Economic Policy* 11: 40–62.

Nicoll, F. (1989), 'My Trip to Alice', *Criticism, Heresy and Interpretation* 3: 21–32.

Nieto, S. (1998), 'Cultural Difference and Educational Change', in A. Hargreaves, M. Fullan, A. Lieberman, and D. Hopkins (eds.), *International Handbook of Educational Change* (Dordrecht: Kluwer).

Nietzsche, F. (1967), *On the Genealogy of Morals* (New York: Vintage).

Nixon, J., Martin, J. Mckeown, P., and Ranson, S. (1997), 'Towards a Learning Profession: Changing Codes of Occupational Practice Within the New Management of Education', *British Journal of Sociology of Education* 18: 5–28.

Nixon, S. (1997), 'Exhibiting Masculinity', in S. Hall (ed.), *Representation: Cultural Representations and Signifying Practices* (London: Sage).

Nkomo, M. (ed.) (1990), *Pedagogy of Domination: Toward a Democratic Education in South Africa* (Trenton, NJ: Africa World Press).

Noble, D. (1979), *America by Design: Technology and the Rise of Corporate Capitalism* (Oxford: Oxford University Press).

—— (1999), *The Religion of Technology: The Divinity of Man and the Spirit of Invention* (London: Penguin).

Noddings, N. (1996), 'Stories and Affect in Teacher Education', *Cambridge Journal of Education* 26: 435–47.

Nonaka, I., and Takeuchi, H. (1995), *The Knowledge Creating Company* (New York: Oxford University Press).

Norton, A. (ed.) (1995), *Civil Society in the Middle East* (Leiden: E. J. Brill), i.

NOU (1997), *Ny kompetens* (New Competence)

Nowotony, H., Scott, P., and Gibbons, M. (2002), *Re-Thinking Science* (London: Polity).

Nozick, R. (1974), *Anarchy, State and Utopia* (Oxford: Blackwell).

NTIA (National Telecommunications and Information Administration) (2002), *A Nation Online: How Americans are Expanding Their Use of the Internet* (available online at <ntia.doc.gov/ntiahome/dn/index.html>).

Nunberg, G. (1995), 'Virtual Rialto', *Fresh Air* (national public radio programme).

Nurden, R. (1999), 'Corporate Universities Threaten the Old Guard', *The Independent* (London) 18 April, p. 3.

Nussbaum, M. (1990), 'Aristotelian Social Democracy', in R. B. Douglass, G. M. Mara, and H. S. Richardsson (eds.), *Liberalism and the Good* (New York: Routledge).

—— (1992), 'Human Functioning and Social Justice: In Defence of Aristotelian Essentialism', *Political Theory* 20/2: 202–46.

—— (2000*a*), *Women and Human Development: The Capabilities Approach* (Cambridge: Cambridge University Press).

—— (2000*b*) 'Aristotle, Politics, and Human Capabilities: A Response to Antony, Arneson, Charlesworth and Mulgan', *Ethics* 111/1: 102–40.

Nuttall, S., and Coetzee, C. (eds.) (1998), *Negotiating the Past: The Making of Memory in South Africa* (Cape Town: Oxford University Press).

Nystrand, M., with Gamoran, A., Kachur, R., and Prendergast, C. (1997), *Opening Dialogue: Understanding the Dynamics of Teaching and Learning in the English Classroom* (New York: Teachers College Press).

O'Gara, C., Benoliel, S., Sutton, M., and Tietien, K. (1998), *More, But Not Yet Better. USAID's Programs and Policies to Improve Girls' Education in Developing Countries*. Draft (Washington: Center for Development Information and Evaluation, USAID), December.

O'Neill, A. (1996), 'Privatizing Public Policy: Privileging Market Man and Individualizing Equality through Choice within Education in Aotearoa/New Zealand', *Discourse* 17/3: 403–16

O'Neill, O. (1988), 'Ethical Reasoning and Ideological Pluralism', *Ethics* 98/4: 705–22.

—— (2000), 'Transnational Justice', in D. Held and A. McGrew (eds.), *The Global Transformations Reader: An Introduction to the Globalization Debate* (Cambridge: Polity), 442–52.

Oakes, J., Wells, A., Yonezawa, S., and Ray, K. (1997), 'Equity Issues from Detracking Schools', in A. Hargreaves (ed.), *Rethinking Educational Change with Heart and Mind: The 1997 ASCD Yearbook* (Alexandria, Va.: ASCD).

Oakley A. (2003), 'Research Evidence, Knowledge Management and Educational Practice: Early Lessons from a Systematic Approach', *London Review of Education* 1/1: 21–33.

OECD (1995), *Governance in Transition: Public Management Reforms in OECD Countries* (Paris: OECD).

—— (1996*a*), *Globalization and Linkages to 2030: Challenges and Opportunities for OECD Countries* (Paris: OECD).

—— (1996*b*), *Lifelong Learning for All* (Paris: OECD).

—— (1996*c*), *The Knowledge Based Economy* (Paris: OECD).

—— (1997), *Education at a Glance: OECD Indicators* (Paris: OECD).

—— (1998), *Annual Report 1997* (Paris: OECD).

—— (1998), *Redefining Tertiary Education* (Paris: OECD).

—— (2001*a*), *Science and Technology Labour Markets* (Paris: OECD).

—— (2001*b*), *The Wellbeing of Nations* (Paris: OECD).

—— (2004), *Internationalization of Higher Education: Policy Brief* (Paris: OECD). <http://www.oecd.org/dataoecd/33/60/33734276.pdf>.

—— (2005), *OECD Work on Education 2005–2006* (OECD website).

—— (2001*a*), *Education Policy Analysis: Education and Skills* (Paris: OECD).

—— (2001*b*), *Knowledge and Skills for Life: First Results from PISA 2000* (Paris: OECD).

—— (2001*c*), *Early Childhood Education and Care Policy in Finland* (Paris: OECD).

—— (2005). *Career Guidance and Public Policy: Bridging the Gap* (Paris: OECD).

—— (2000), *Literacy in the Information Age* (Paris: OECD).

—— (2001*a*), *Norway: Country Note* (Paris: OECD).

—— (2001*b*), *Denmark: Country Report* (Paris: OECD).

OECD (2000), *Literacy in the Knowledge Society* (Paris: OECD).

—— (2001), *Education at a Glance* (Paris: OECD).

—— (2001), *Knowledge and Skills for Life* (Paris: OECD).

—— (2002), *Education At a Glance* (Paris: OECD).

—— (2004*a*), *Learning for Tomorrow's World: First Results from PISA 2003* (Paris: OECD), <http://www.pisa.oecd.org/dataoecd/1/60/34002216.pdf>, accessed 20 June 2005.

—— (2004*b*), *Messages from PISA 2000* (Paris: OECD) (available from OECD website: <http://www.oecd.org/home>, accessed 20 June 2005).

Offe, C. (1976), *Industry and Inequality* (London: Edward Arnold).

—— —— (1984), *Contradictions of the Welfare State* (London: Hutchinson).

Office of National Statistics. (2003), 'Work and joblessness. June assessment: Claimant count up', in *National Statistics Online*. Retrieved 2 July 2003 from <http://www.statistics.gov.uk/cci/nugget.asp?id = 12> (Last updates 11 June 2003.)

OFSTED (1993) *Access and Achievement in Urban Education* (London: OFSTED).

—— (2001), *National Summary Data Report for Secondary Schools 2001 Data* (London: OFSTED).

—— (2002), *Annual Report 2000–1* (London: OfSTED).

—— (2003) *Excellence in Cities and Education Action Zones: Management and Impact* (London: OFSTED).

—— (2003), *Annual Report* of HMCI 2001–2 (London: HMSO).

Ohlander, M. (1956), *Hjälpskolan i Göteborg 1906–1956* [Remedial School in Göteborg 1906–1956] (Borås: Aktiebolaget J F Björsell).

Ohmae, K. (1990), *The Borderless World* (London: Collins).

—— (1996), *The End of the Nation State: The Rise of Regional Economics* (London: HarperCollins).

Okin, Susan Moller (1999), 'Is Multiculturalism Bad for Women?', in Susan Moller Okin, *Is Multiculturalism Bad for Women?*, ed. Joshua Cohen, Matthew Howard, and Martha C. Nussbaum (Princeton: Princeton University Press), 41–7.

Olson, D. S. (1994), *The World on Paper: The Conceptual Implications of Writing and Reading* (Cambridge: Cambridge University Press).

Olssen, M. (2002), 'Michel Foucault as "Thin" Communitarian: Difference, Community, Democracy', *Cultural Studies-Critical Methodologies* 2/4: 483–513.

—— (2004), 'Foucalt and Marxism: Rewriting the Theory of Historical Materialism', *Policy Futures in Education* 2/3–4: 454–82.

—— Codd, J., and O'Nell, A-M. (2004), *Education Policy: Globalisation, Citizenship and Democracy* (London: Sage).

'One in Five Young People May Drop Out, says OFSTED' (2003), *London Times Higher Education Supplement*, 6 March, 6.

Ong, A. (1999), *Flexible Citizenship: The Cultural Logics of Transnationality* (Durham, NC: Duke University Press).

Orfield, G., Losen, D., Wald, J. and Swanson, C. (2004), *Losing our Future: How Minority Youth Are Being Left Behind by the Graduation Rate Crisis* (Cambridge, Mass.: The Civil Rights Project at Harvard University).

Organisation for Economic Cooperation and Development (OECD) (1992), *Information and Technology Outlook*, 1992 (Paris OECD).

Organization for Economic Cooperation and Development (2002), *International Mobility of the Highly Skilled* (Paris: OECD).

—— (2003), *Education at a Glance* (Paris: OECD).

Orloff, A. S. (1993), 'Gender and the Social Rights of Citizenship: The Comparative Analysis of Gender Relations and Welfare States', *American Sociological Review* 58: 303–28.

Ortner, S. (2002), 'Burned Like a Tattoo: High School Social Categories and "American culture"', *Ethnography* 3: 115–48.

Ortner, Sherry (1974), 'Is Female to Male as Nature is to Culture?', in M. Z. Rosaldo and L. Lamphere (eds.), *Woman, Culture, and Society* (Stanford, Calif.: Stanford University Press).

Osborn M., et al. (2000), *What Teachers Do: Changing Policy and Practice in Primary Education* (London: Continuum).

—— Rees, T., et al. (2000), *Science Policy in the European Union* (Brussels: European Commission).

Osborne, T. (1998), *Aspects of Enlightenment* (London: University College Press).

Ostroff, F. (1999), *The Horizontal Organization: What the Organization of the Future Actually Looks Like and How it Delivers Value to Customers* (New York: Oxford University Press).

Oweini, A. A. (1998), 'How Students Coped with the War: the Experience of Lebanon', *Journal of Higher Education* 69/4: 406–23.

Oxhorn, P. (1998), 'Social Inequality, Civil Society and the Limits of Citizenship in Latin America', Paper presented at the annual meeting of the Latin American Studies Association. Chicago, 24–6 September.

Ozacky-Lazar, S. (2001), 'The Jewish-Arab Center for Peace at Givat Haviva', *SangSaeng*, Asia Pacific Centre of Education for International Understanding (Winter 2001), 2: 17–22.

Pahl, R. (1998), 'Friendship: The Glue of Contemporary Society?', in J. Franklin (ed.), *The Politics of Risk Society* (Cambridge: Polity) 99–119.

—— (2000), *On Friendship* (Cambridge, Polity).

—— and Spencer, L. (1997), 'Friends and Neighbours', *New Statesman*, 10/472: 36–7.

Papadopoulos, G. S. (1994), *Education 1960–1990: The OECD Perspective* (Paris: OECD)

Parekh, Bhikhu (2000). *Rethinking Multiculturalism: Cultural Diversity and Political Theory* (Cambridge, Mass.: Harvard University Press).

Parker, I. (1990), 'Discourse: Definitions and Contradictions', *Philosophical Psychology*, 3/2: 189–204.

Parkes, J. (2002), '"Children Also Have Rights, but Then Who Wants to Listen to Our Rights?": Children's Perspectives on Living with Community Violence in South Africa', *Educate* 2/2: 59–71.

Parkin, F. (1979), *Marxism and Class Theory: A Bourgeois Critique* (London: Tavistock).

—— (ed.), (1974), *The Social Analysis of Class Structure* (London: Tavistock).

Parsons, T. (1961), 'The School Class as a Social System: Some of its Functions in American Society, in A. H. Halsey, J. Floud, and J. Anderson (Eds.), *Education, Economy and Society* (New York: Free Press).

—— and Platt, G. M. (1973), *The American University* (Cambridge, Mass.: Harvard University Press).

Passmore, J. (2000), *The Perfectibility of Man*, 3rd edn. (Indianapolis: The Liberty Fund).

Pateman, C. (1988), *The Sexual Contract* (Cambridge: Polity).

—— (1989), *The Disorder of Women* (Cambridge: Polity).

—— (1992), 'Equality, Difference, Subordination: The Politics of Motherhood and Women's Citizenship'. In G. Bock and S. James (eds.), *Beyond Equality and Difference: Citizenship, Feminist Politics, Female Subjectivity* (New York: Routledge).

Patrinos, H. (1999), 'Market Forces in Education', Mimeo (Washington, DC: World Bank).

—— (2000), 'Global Education Market', Available online at: <http//www.worldbank.org/edinvest/>.

—— and Ariasingam, D. L. (1997), *Decentralization of Education: Demand-Side Financing* (Washington, DC: World Bank).

Paulle, B. (2003), 'Contest and Collaboration: Embodied Cultural Responses of Adolescents in an "Inner City" School in the Bronx (New York) and a "Zwarte" School in the Bijlmer (Amsterdam)', in J. C. C. Rupp and W. Veugelers (eds.), *Moreel politieke heroriëntatie in het onderwijs* (Leuven, Garant), 17–51.

Paxton, W., and Dixon, M. (2004), *The State of the Nation: An Audit of Injustice in the UK*, (London: Institute of Public Policy Research).

Payne, I. (1980), 'A Working-Class Girl in a Grammar School', in D. Spender and E. Sarah (eds.), *Learning to Lose: Sexism and Education* (London: Women's Press), 12–19.

Peled, Y. (1998), 'Towards a Redefinition of Jewish Nationalism in Israel? The Enigma of Shas', *Ethnic and Racial Studies* 21: 703–27.

Penrose, E. (1959), *The Theory of Growth of the Firm* (Oxford: Blackwell).

Perkin, H. (1989), *The Rise of Professional Society: England since 1800* (London: Routledge).

Perrucci, R., and Wysong, E. (1999), *The New Class Society* (Oxford Rowman & Littlefield).

—— (1999), *The New Class Society* (Lanham, M: Rowman & Littlefield).

Peshkin, A. (1986), *God's Choice: The Total World of a Fundamentalist Christian School* (Chicago: University of Chicago Press).

Peters, M., and Marshall, J. (1996), *Individualism and Community Education and Social Policy in the Post Modern Condition* (London: Falmer).

Peterson, P. E., and Hassel, B. C. (eds.) (1998), *Learning from School Choice* (Washington, DC: Brookings Institution).

—— and Howell, W. (2004), 'Efficiency, Bias and Classification Schemes: Estimating Private-School Impacts on Test Scores in the New York City Voucher Experiment', *American Behavioral Scientist* 47/5: 699–717.

Pettit, P. (1993), *The Common Mind: An Essay on Psychology, Society, and Politics* (Oxford: Oxford University Press).

—— (1997), *Republicanism: A Theory of Freedom and Government* (Oxford: Oxford University Press).

Phillips, A. (1991*a*), *Engendering Democracy* (Cambridge: Polity).

—— (1991*b*), 'Citizenship and Feminist Theory', in G. Andrews (ed.), *Citizenship* (London: Lawrence & Wishart).

—— (1992), *Democracy and Difference* (Cambridge: Polity).

Phillipson, R. (1996), 'Globalizing English: Are Linguistic Human Rights an Alternative to Linguistic Imperialism?' Paper presented at the International Conference on Language Rights, the Hong Kong Polytechnic University, 22–24 June.

Pierson, H. (1992), 'Cantonese, English or Putonghua—Unresolved Communicative Issue in Hong Kong's Future', in G. A. Postiglione (ed.), *Education and Society in Hong Kong—Toward One Country and Two Systems* (Hong Kong: Hong Kong University Press).

Pieterse, Jan Nederveen, and Parekh, Bhikhu (eds.) (1995), *The Decolonization of Imagination: Culture, Knowledge and Power* (London: Zed Books).

Pignatelli, F. (1993), 'What Can I do? Foucault on Freedom and the Question of Teacher Agency', in *Educational Theory* 43/4: 411–32.

Pillow, W. (1997), 'Exposed Methodology: The Body as a Deconstructive Practice', in *International Journal of Qualitative Studies in Education* 10/3: 349–63.

—— (2003), '"Bodies are Dangerous": Using Feminist Genealogy as Policy Studies Methodology', in *Journal of Education Policy* 18/2: 145–59.

Pindyck, D., and Rubinfeld, R. (2000), *Microeconomics*, 5th ed. (New York: Macmillan).

Pinzur, M. (2003), 'State schools fail to meet new federal test standards: federal, state results differ', *Miami Herald*, 8 August.

Plato (1968), *The Republic*, ed. and trans. Allan Bloom (New York: Basic Books).

Plowden, B. (1967), *Children and their Primary Schools: A Report of the Central Advisory Council for Education [England]* (London: HMSO).

Pocock, J. G. A. (1975), *The Machiavellian Moment: Florentine Political Theory and the Atlantic Republican Tradition* (Princeton, NJ: Princeton University Press).

Poggi, G. (1972), *Images of Society: Essays on the Sociological Theories of Tocqueville, Marx and Durkheim* (Stanford, Calif.: Stanford University Press).

Poiner G., and Wills, S. (1990), *The Gifthorse* (Sydney: Allen & Unwin).

Polanyi, K. (1957), *The Great Transformation* (Boston: Beacon).

Polanyi, M. (1958 [1973]), *Personal Knowledge: Towards a Post-Critical Philosophy* (London: Routledge & Kegan Paul).

Pollard, A. (1982), 'A Model of Coping Strategies', *British Journal of Sociology of Education* 3/1: 19–37.

—— (1997), 'Learning and a New Curriculum for Primary Schooling', paper presented to the SCAA conference on Developing the Primary School Curriculum: The Next Steps, June (London: SCAA).

—— and Filer, A. (1996), *The Social World of Children's Learning* (London: Cassell).

—— Broadfoot, P., Croll, P., Osborn, M., and Abbott, D. (1994), *Changing English Primary Schools? The Impact of the Educational Reform Act at Key Stage One* (London: Cassell).

Pollitt C. (1990), *Managerialism and the Public Services: The Anglo-American Experience* (Oxford: Basil Backwell).

Pollock, S., Bhabha, H., Breckenridge, C., and Chakrabarty, D. (2000), 'Cosmopolitanisms', *Public Culture* 12/3.

Popkewitz, T. (1998), *Struggling for the Soul: The Politics of Schooling and the Construction of the Teachers* (New York: Teachers College Press).

Porio, E. (1988), 'State, Class and Education Reform in the Philippines', Ph.D. dissertation, Department of Sociology, University of Hawaii at Manoa.

Porter, J. (1999), *Reschooling and the Global Future* (Oxford: Symposium Books).

Porter, M. (1990), *The Competitive Advantage of Nations* (London: Mcmillan).

Portes, A. (1998), 'Social Capital: Its Origins and Applications in Modern Sociology', *Annual Review of Sociology* 24: 1–24.

—— and Sensenbrenner, J. (1993), 'Embeddedness and Immigration: Notes on the Social Determinants of Economic Action', *American Journal of Sociology* 98: 1320–50.

—— (ed.) (1995), *The Economic Sociology of Immigration: Essays on Networks, Ethnicity and Entrepreneurship* (New York: Russell Sage).

Post, D. (1998), 'Educational Inequality in Mexico', Paper presented at the annual Comparative and International Education Society conference, Buffalo, April.

Postiglione, G. (1997), 'Schooling and Social Stratification', in G. A. Postiglione and W. O. Lee (eds.), *Schooling in Hong Kong: Organization, Teaching and Social Context* (Hong Kong: Hong Kong University Press).

Postman, N., and Weingarter, C. (1969), *Teaching as a Subversive Activity* (New York: Delacorte).

Poulantzas, N. (1973), *Political Power and Social Class* (London: NLD and Sheed & Ward).

Power, M. (1999), *The Audit Society: Rituals of Verification* (Oxford: Oxford University Press).

Power S. (forthcoming), 'Markets and Misogyny: Educational Research on Educational Choice', *British Journal of Educational Studies*.

——, Aggleton, P., Brannen, J., Brown, A., Chisholm, L., and Mace, J. (eds.) (2001), *A Tribute to Basil Bernstein* (London: Institute of Education).

—— —— and Edwards, T. (2005 forthcoming), 'Success Sustained? A Follow-up Study of the 'Destined for Success?' Cohort', *Research Papers in Education*.

—— —— —— and Wigfall, V. (1998), 'Schools, Families and Academically Able Children: Contrasting Modes of Involvement in Secondary Education', *British Journal of Sociology of Education* 19/2: 157–76.

——, Edwards, T., Whitty, G., and Wigfall, V. (2003), *Education and the Middle Class* (Buckingham: Open University Press).

—— and Whitty, G. (1996), 'Teaching New Subjects? The Hidden Curriculum of Marketised Education Systems', Unpublished paper, London Institute of Education.

—— —— (2002) 'Bernstein and the Middle Class', *British Journal of Sociology of Education*, 23 (4), 595–606.

Praissac, *Les Discours militaries*, 1623.

Prashad, V. (1996), 'Emergency Assessments', *Social Scientist* 24/9, 36–68.

—— (2000), *The Karma of Brown Folk* (Minneapolis: University of Minnesota Press).

Prashad, V., and Mathew, B. (2000), 'Satyagraha in America: The Political Culture of South Asian Americans', *Amerasia Journal* 25/3: ix–xv.

Prawat, R. S. (1999), 'Cognitive Theory at the Crossroads: Head Fitting, Head Splitting, or Somewhere in Between?', *Human Development* 42/2: 59–77.

Prestoungrange, G., et al. (eds.) (2000), *The Virtual Learning Organization: Learning at the Workplace Campus* (London: Continuum).

Pringle, J., and Timperley, H. (1995), 'Gender and Educational Management in New Zealand', in B. Limerick, and B. Lingard, (eds.) *Gender and Changing Educational Management* (Sydney: Hodder & Stoughton).

—— and Watson, S. (1992), ' "Women's Interests" and the Post-structuralist State', in M. Barrett and A. Phillips (eds.), *Destabilising Theory. Contemporary Feminist Debate* (Cambridge: Polity).

Probert, B. (1995), 'A Restructuring World?', in M. Edwards and S. Magarey (eds.), *Women in a Restructuring Australia* (Sydney: Allen & Unwin).

PROMUDEH (2000), *Plan Nacional de Igualdad de Oportunidades entre Mujeres y Hombres 2000–2005* (Lima: Ministerio de Promoción de la Mujer y del Desarrollo Humano) [Ministry for the Promotion of Women and Human Development].

Pryor, F., and Schaffer, D. (2000), *Who's Not Working and Why? Employment, Cognitive Skills, Wages and the Changing U.S. Labour Market* (Cambridge: Cambridge University Press).

Psacharopoulos, G. (1973), *Returns to Education: An International Comparison* (Amsterdam: Elsevier).

—— (1981), 'Returns to Education: An Updated International Comparison', *Comparative Education* 17/3: 321–41.

—— (1985), 'Returns to Education: A Further International Update and Implications', *Journal of Human Resources* 20/4: 583–604.

—— (1994), 'Returns to Investment in Education: a Global Update', *World Development* 22/9: 1325–43.

—— Tan, J.-P., and Jimenez, E. (1986), *Financing Education in Developing Countries* (Washington, DC: World Bank).

Public Agenda (1999), *On Thin Ice* (New York: Public Agenda Inc.).

Puiggros, A. (1997), 'World Bank Education Policy: Market Liberalism Meets Ideological Conservatism', *International Journal of Health Services* 27/2 217–26.

Pun, S. H. (1997), 'Hegemonic Struggle in the Language Policy Development of Hong Kong, 1982–1994', in W. O. Lee and M. Bray (eds.), *Education and Political Transition: Perspectives and Dimensions in East Asia* (Hong Kong: Comparative Education Research Centre, Hong Kong University).

Punt, T. (1975), 'Social Pressures', in J. Morrell (ed.), *Britain in the 1980s* (London: Henley Centre for Forecasting).

Puryear, J. (1997), *Education in Latin America: Problems and Challenges* (Washington, DC: Inter-American Dialogue).

Putnam, R. (2000), *Bowling Alone: The Collapse and Revival of American Community* (New York: Simon & Schuster).

—— (1996), 'The Strange Disappearance of Civic America', *The American Prospect* 24: 34–48.

Quality Assurance Agency (2000), *Code of Practice for the Assurance of Quality and Standards in Higher Education* (Gloucester: Quality Assurance Agency).

Qvale, T. U., and Øverland, E. F. (2001), 'Norway: Out of Europe', in G. Széll (ed.), *European Labour Relations* (Aldershot: Gower), ii.

Qvortrup, L. (1998), 'From Teleworking to Networking: Definitions and Trends', in P. Jackson and J. van der Wielien (eds.), *Teleworking: International Perspectives* (London: Routledge), ch 2.

Rainbird, H. (ed.) (2000), *Training in the Workplace: Critical Perspectives on Learning at Work* (Basingstoke: Macmillan).

Raissiguier, C. (1995), 'The Construction of Marginal Identities: Working-Class Girls of Algerian Descent in a French School', in M. H. Marchand and J. L. Parpart (eds.), *Feminism/Postmodernism/Development* (London: Routledge), 79–93.

Rajchman, J. (1985), *Michel Foucault: The Freedom of Philosophy* (New York: Columbia University Press).

Rama, G. (1983), 'Education in Latin America: Exclusion or Participation', *CEPAL Review* 21: 13–38.

Ramazanogluc (1993), *Up Against Foucault. Explorations of Some Tensions between Foucault and Feminism* (London: Routledge).

Ramirez, F. O., and Boli, J. (1987), 'The Political Construction of Mass Schooling: European Origins and Worldwide Institutionalization', *Sociology of Education* 60/1: 2–17.

Ranson, S. (1994), *Towards a Learning Society* (London: Cassell).

Ratnesar, R. (1997), 'The next big divide', *Time*, 1 December: 52.

Rawls, J. (1971), *A Theory of Justice* (Cambridge, Mass.: Harvard University Press).

—— (1985), 'Justice as Fairness: Political not Metaphysical', *Philosophy and Public Affairs* 14/3: 223–51.

Ray, R. (1988), 'The Contested Terrain of Reproduction: Case and Gender in Schooling in India', *British Journal of Sociology of Education* 9: 387–401.

Read, A. W. (1974), 'What is "Linguistic imperialism"?', *Geolinguistics*, 1: 5–10.

Reay, D. (1998), 'Engendering Social Reproduction: Mothers in the Educational Marketplace', *British Journal of Sociology of Education* 19: 195–209.

—— (1998), *Class Work: Mothers' Involvement in their Children's Primary Schooling* (London: UCL Press).

—— (2001), ' "Spice Girls", "Nice Girls", "Girlies", and "Tomboys": Gender Discourses, Girls' Cultures and Femininities in the Primary Classroom', in *Gender and Education* 13/2: 153–66.

—— and Arnot, M. (2004), 'Participation and Control in Learning: A Pedagogic Democratic Right?', in L. Poulson (ed.), *Learning to Read Critically in Teaching and Learning* (London: Sage).

Reboul-Sherrer, F. (1989), *Les Premiers Instituteurs, 1833–1882* (Paris: Hachette).

Rees, G. (1997*a*) 'Vocational Education and Training and Regional Development: An Analytical Framework', *Journal of Education and Work* 10/2: 141–9.

—— (1997*b*), 'Making a Learning Society: Education and Work in Industrial South Wales', *Welsh Journal of Education* 6/2: 4–16.

—— and Thomas, M. (1991), 'From Coal-Miners to Eentrepreneurs? A Case-Study in the Sociology of Re-industrialization', in M. Cross and G. Payne (eds.), *Work and the Enterprise Culture* (Lewes: Falmer).

—— Fielder, S., and Rees, T. (1992), 'Employees' Access to Training Opportunities: Shaping the Social Structure of Labour Markets'. Paper presented at the ESRC Seminar on Training and Recruitment, Royal Society of Arts, 3 April, mimeo.

—— Williamson, H., and Istance, D. (1996), ' "Status Zero": Jobless School-Leavers in South Wales', *Research Papers in Education* 11/2: 219–35.

—— Gorard, S., Fevre, R. and Furlong, J. (2000), 'Participating in the Learning Society: History, Place and Biography', in F. Coffield (ed.), *Differing Visions of a Learning Society: Research Findings* (Bristol: Policy Press) ii.

Rees, T. (1992), *Women and the Labour Market* (London: Routledge).

Regini, M. (2000), 'Between Deregulation and Social Pacts: The Responses of European Economies to Globalization', *Politics and Society* 28/1.

Reich, R. (1991), *The Work of Nations: A Blueprint for the Future* (New York: Vintage).

—— (1992), *The Work of Nations: Preparing Ourselves for 21st Century Capitalism* (New York: Vintage).

—— (2002), *Bridging Liberalism and Multiculturalism in American Education* (Chicago: University of Chicago Press).

Reid, A., (ed.) (2005), 'Natural Capital: Metaphor, Learning and Human Behaviour', Special Issue, *Environmental Educational Research* 11/1 (Feb.)

Reid, W. (1999), *Curriculum as Institution and Practice* (Mahwah, NJ: Lawrence Erlbaum).

Renihan, F. I. and Renihan, P. (1992), 'Educational Leadership: A Renaissance Metaphor', *Education Canada* 11 (Spring): 4–12.

Renold, E. (1999), 'Presumed Innocence: An Ethnographic Exploration into the Construction of Sexual and Gender Identities in the Primary School', Unpublished Ph.D. thesis, University of Wales, Cardiff.

—— (2000), ' "Coming Out": Gender, (Hetero)sexuality and the Primary School', in *Gender and Education* 12/3: 309–26.

—— (2002), 'Presumed Innocence: Sexualised Bullying and Harassment in the Primary School', Unpublished paper, University of Wales, Cardiff.

Reynolds, D., and Farrell, S. (1996), *Worlds Apart? A Review of International Surveys of Educational Achievement Involving England* (London: TSO).

—— and Stringfield, S. (1996), 'Failure-Free Schooling is Clear for Take Off', *Times Educational Supplement Management Update*, 19 January, 10.

—— Creemers, B., Nesselrodt, P., Schaffer, E., Stringfield, S., and Teddlie, C. (1994), *Advances in School Effectiveness Research and Practice* (Oxford: Pergamon).

—— Sammons, P. et al. (1996), 'School Effectiveness and School Improvement in the UK', *School Effectiveness and School Improvement* 7/2: 133–58.

Ricardo, D. (1966), *The Works and Correspondence of David Ricardo*, i. *On the Principles of Political Economy and Taxation* (Cambridge: Cambridge University Press).

Richardson, K. (1998), *The Origins of Human Potential: Evolution, Development and Psychology* (London: Routledge).

Ridge, T., and Millar, J. (2000), 'Excluding Children: Autonomy, Friendship and the Experience of the Care System', *Social Policy and Administration* 34/2: 160–75.

Rieger, E., and Liebfried, S. (1998), 'Welfare State Limits to Globalization,' *Politics and Society*, 26/3.

Rigby, A. (1995), *Palestinian Education: The Future Challenge* (Jerusalem: Palestinian Academic Society for the Study of International Affairs).

Rihani, S. (2002), *Complex Systems Theory and Development Practice* (London: Zed Books).

Rizvi, F. (2003), Democracy and Education After September 11, *Globalisation, Societies and Education* 1/1: 13–23.

—— (2004) 'Transnational Identity and the Uses of International Education', paper presented to the Globalisation, Culture, Society and Education seminar, American Educational Research Association Conference, San Diego.

—— (2005) 'Theorizing the Global Convergence of Restructuring Policies in Education', in S. Lindale and T. Popkewitz (eds.), *Educational Restructuring: International Perspectives on Travelling Policies* (Greenwich, Conn.: Information Age Publishing), 91–108.

—— (1991), *The Work of Pierre Bourdieu: Recognising Society* (Milton Keynes: Open University Press).

Robbins, D. (1991), *The Work of Pierre Bourdieu* (Boulder: Westview).

Roberts, K. (2001), *Class in Modern Britain* (Basingstoke: Palgrave).

Robertson, D., and Symons, J. (2003), 'Do Peer Groups Matter? Peer Group versus Schooling Effects on Academic Attainment', *Economica* 70: 277.

Robinson, S. (1997). 'Individualism, identity and community in globalising society', Symposium Paper presented to the Learned Societies, Ottawa, Canada.

Robinson, W. (2004), *A Theory of Global Capitalism* (Baltimore: Johns Hopkins University Press).

Roid, G. H., and Barram, R. A. (2004), *Essentials of Stanford-Binet Scales (SB5) Assessment* (New York: Wiley).

Roland Martin, J. (1994), 'Excluding Women from the Educational Realm', (First published in 1982). in L. Stone *The Education Feminism Reader* (New York: Routledge).

Roman, L. (1992), 'The Political Significance of Other Ways of Narrating Ethnography, A Feminist Materialist Approach', in M. D. Lecompte, W. Milroy, and J. Priessle (eds.), *The Handbook of Qualitative Research in Educational Theory* (San Diego, Calif.: Academic Press), 43: 279–308.

Romei, S. (2000), 'Who Wants To Be a Voyeur?', *The Weekend Australian*, 1–2 July.

Room, G. (1995), 'Poverty and Social Exclusion: The New European Agenda for Policy and Research', in G. Room (ed.), *Beyond the Threshold: The Measurement and Analysis of Social Exclusion* (Bristol: Policy Press), 1–9.

—— (2000), 'Globalisation, Social Policy and International Standard Setting: The Case of Higher Education Credentials', *International Journal of Social Welfare* 9: 103–19.

Rorty, R. (1998), 'Justice as a Larger Loyalty', in P. Cheah and B. Robbins (eds.), *Cosmopolitics: Thinking and Feeling Beyond the Nation* (Minneapolis: University of Minnesota Press), 45–58.

Rose, M. (1993), *Authors and Owners: The Invention of Copyright* (Cambridge, Mass.: Harvard University Press).

Rose, N. (1989), *Governing the Soul: The Shaping of the Private Self* (London: Routledge).

—— (1992), 'Governing the Enterprising Self', in P. Heelas and P. Morris (eds.), *The Values of the Enterprise Culture* (London: Routledge).

—— (1996), 'Governing "Advanced" Liberal Democracies', in A. Barry, T. Osborne, and N. Rose (eds.), *Foucault and Political Reason: Liberalism, Neo-Liberalism and Rationalities of Government* (London: UCL Press).

—— (1999), *Governing the Soul: The Shaping of the Private Self*, 2nd edn. (London: Free Association Press).

—— (1999), *Powers of Freedom: Reframing Political Thought* (Cambridge: Cambridge University Press).

Rose, S. (2005), *The 21st Century Brain: Explaining, Mending and Manipulating the Mind* (London: Jonathan Cape).

Rosemberg, F. (2000), 'Ambiguities in Compensatory Policies: A Case Study from Brazil', in R. Cortina and N. P. Stromquist (eds.), *Educational Policies for Gender Equity in Latin America* (New York: Garland).

Rosenblatt, R. (1993), 'Government denounces Scripps-Sandoz deal', *Los Angeles Times* (18 June), D2.

Rosencrarze, R. (1999), *The rise of the Virtual State* (New York: Basic Books).

Rosenholtz, S. (1989), *Teachers' Workplace* (New York: Longman).

Ross, A. (1989), *No Respect: Intellectuals and Popular Culture* (New York: Routledge).

Ross, J. A. (1995), 'Strategies for Enhancing Teachers' Beliefs in Their Effectiveness: Research on a School Improvement Hypothesis', *Teachers' College Record* 97/2: 227–51.

Rothstein, B. (1998), *Just Institutions Matter: The Moral and Political Logic of the Welfare State* (Cambridge: Cambridge University Press).

Rouse, C. E. (1998), 'Private School Vouchers and Student Achievement: An Evaluation of the Milwaukee Parental Choice Program', *Quarterly Journal of Economics* 113: 553-602.

Rouse, J., and Smith, G. (1999), 'Accountability', in M. Powell (ed.), *New Labour, New Welfare State* (Bristol: Policy), 235–55.

Rowan, B., and Miskel, C. (1999), 'Institutional Theory and the Study of Educational Organizations', in J. Murphy and K. Louis (eds.), *Handbook of Research on Educational Administration*, 2nd edn. (San Francisco: Jossey-Bass), ch. 17, 359–83.

Rowthorn, R. E. and Wells, J. R. (1987), *De-industrialization and Foreign Trade* (Cambridge: Cambridge University Press).

Rubenson, K. (1996), 'The Role of Popular Adult Education: Reflections in Connection to an Analysis of Surveys on Living Conditions, 1975 to 1993', *Parliamentary Commission on Popular Adult Education: Three Studies on Popular Adult Education* (Stockholm: Fritzes).

—— (2002), *Measuring Motivation and Barriers in the AETS: A Critical Review* (Ottawa: HRDC).

Ruddock G., et al. (2004), *Where England Stands in the Trends in International Mathematics and Science Study (TIMSS) 2003: Summary National Report for England* (London: NfER/DfES), <http://www.nfer.ac.uk/publications>, accessed 20 June 2005.

Rueda, D., and Pontusson, J. (2000), 'Wage Inequality and Varieties of Capitalism', *World Politics* 52: 350–83.

Rugman, A., and D'Cruz, J. (2000), *Multi-Nationals as Flagship Firms* (Oxford: Oxford University Press).

—— and Verbeke, A. (2004), 'A Perspective on Regional and Global Strategies of Multinational Enterprises', *Journal of International Business Studies* 35/1: 3–8.

Runciman, W. G. (1966), *Relative Deprivation and Social Justice: A Study of Attitudes to Social Inequality in Twentieth-Century England* (London: Routledge).

Rupesinghe, K. (1995), (ed.) *Conflict Transformation* (London: Macmillan).

Rutter, M. (1990), 'Psychosocial Resilience and Protective Mechanisms', in J. Rolf, A. S. Masten, D. Cicchetti, K. H. Nuechterlein, and S. Weintraub, (eds.), *Risk and Protective Factors in the Development of Psychopathology* (Cambridge: Cambridge University Press).

—— Maughan, B., Mortimore, P., and Ouston, J. (1979), *Fifteen thousand Hours: Secondary Schools and their Effects on Children* (Cambridge Mass.: Harvard University Press).

Ryan, B. (1992), *Feminism and the Women's Movement: Dynamics of Change in Social Movement Ideology and Activism*, (New York: Routledge)

Ryan, J. (1995), 'Organizing for Teaching and Learning in a Culturally Diverse School Setting', Paper prepared for the Annual Conference of the Canadian Society of the Study of Education, June.

Rydelius, P.-A. (1999), 'Bokstavsbarn—gengångare från förr med ny beteckning' [Letter Children—Ghosts from Earlier Times in a New Terminology], *Läkartidningen* 96/30–1: 3332–8.

Ryner, M. J. (2002), *Capitalism Restructuring. Globalization and the Third Way* (London: Routledge).

Saboulin, Michel de, and Thave, Suzanne (1993), 'La Vie en couple marie: Un modele qui s'affablit', in *Données Sociales 1996: La Société française* (Paris: INSEE).

Sacks, H. (1992), *Lectures on Conversation* (Oxford: Blackwell), i.

Sacks, P. (1996), *Generation X Goes to College: An Eye Opening Account of Teaching in Postmodern America* (Chicago: Open Court).

Saha, L. (1991), 'Universities and National Development Issues and Problems in Developing Countries', *Prospects* 21/2: 248–57.

Said, E. (1979), *Orientalism* (London: Vintage).

Sainsbury, M., Schagen, I., and Hammond, P. (2004), 'What Did PIRLS Tell Us about Reading Skills?' Paper presented to the International Association for Educational Assessment, Philadelphia, June 2004, <http://www.nfer.ac.uk/publications>, accessed 20 June 2005.

Saito, M. (2003), 'Amartya Sen's Capability Approach to Education: A Critical Exploration', *Journal of Philosophy of Education* 37/1: 17–33.

Salling-Olsen, H. (1989), *Everyday Learning* (Roskilde: Roskilde University Press).

Sameroff, A., Bartko, W. T., Baldwin, A., Baldwin, C., and Seifer, R. (1998), 'Family and Social Influences on the Development of Child Competence', in M. Lewis and C. Feiring (eds.), *Families, Risk, and Competence* (Mahwah, NJ: Lawrence Erlbaum) 161–86.

Sammons, P. (1999), *School Effectiveness: Coming of Age in the 21st Century* (Abingdon: Swets and Zeitlinger).

Samoff, J. (1992), 'The Intellectual/Financial Complex of Foreign Aid', *Review of African Political Economy* 19/53.

—— Stromquist, N. (2001)' 'Managing Knowledge and Storing Wisdom? New Forms of Foreign Aid?', *Development and Change* 32: 631–56.

Sanyal, B., El-Koussy, A., Noonan, R., Harby, M., Balbaa, Sh., and Yaici, L. (1982), *University Education and the Labour Market in the Arab Republic of Egypt* (Oxford: UNESCO International Institute for Educational Planning and Pergamon Press).

Sargant, N., and Aldridge, F. (eds.) (2003), *Adult Learning and Social Division: A Persistent Pattern* (Leicester: NIACE), ii.

—— Field, J., Francis, H., Schuller, T., and Tuckett, A. (1997), *The Learning Divide* (Leicester: NIACE).

Sassen, S. (1988), *Cities in the World Economy* (Thousand Oaks, Calif.: Pine Forge).

—— (1996), 'Beyond Sovereignty: Immigrant Policy Making Today', *Social Justice* 23/3: 9–20.

—— (2005), 'New Global Classes: Implications for Politics', in A. Giddens, and P. Diamond (eds.), *The New Egalitarianism* (Cambridge: Polity).

Saunders, C. (1988), *The Making of the South African Past: Major Historians on Race and Class* (Cape Town: David Philip).

Saunders, P. (1995), 'Might Britain be a Meritocracy?' *Sociology* 29: 23–41.

—— (1996), *Unequal but Fair? A Study of Class Barriers in Britain* (London: Institute of Economic Affairs, Choice and Welfare Unit).

Savage, M., Barlow, J., Dickens, P., and Fielding, T. (1992), *Property, Bureaucracy and Culture: Middle-Class Formation in Contemporary Britain* (London: Routledge).

—— and Egerton, M. (1997), 'Social Mobility, Individual Ability and the Inheritance of Class Inequality', *Sociology* 31: 645–72.

Sawer, M. (1991), 'Why Has the Women's Movement Had More Influence on Government in Australia than Else-where', in F. Castles (ed.), *Australia Compared. People, Policies and Politics* (Sydney: Allen & Unwin).

—— (1994) 'Feminism and the State: Theory and Practice in Australia and Canada', *Australian-Canadian Studies* 12/1: 49–68.

Saxenian, A. (1994), *Regional Advantage, Culture and Competition in Silicon Valley and Route 128* (Cambridge, Mass.: Harvard University Press).

—— A. (2000*a*), 'The Bangalore Boom: From Brain Drain to Brain Circulation?', in K. Kenniston, and D. Kumar, (eds.), *Bridging the Digital Divide, Lessons from India* (Bangalore: National Institute of Advanced Study).

—— (2000*b*), 'Bangalore: The Silicon Valley of East Asia?', Paper presented at the Conference on Indian Eonomic Prospects, Stanford, May.

—— (2002), 'Transnational Communities and the Evolution of Global Production Networks: The Case of Taiwan, China and India', *Industry and Innovation*, Special Issue on Global Production Networks (Fall).

Sayed, Y. (1999), 'Discourses of the Policy of Educational Decentralisation in South Africa since 1994: An Examination of the South Africa Schools Act', *Compare* 29/2: 141–52.

—— and Jansen, J. (eds.) (2001), *Implementing Education Policies: The South African Experience* (Cape Town: University of Cape Town Press).

Scanlon, T. (1982), 'Contractualism and Utilitarianism', in A. Sen and B. Williams (eds.), *Utilitarianism and Beyond*, (Cambridge: Cambridge University Press).

Scarbrough, H. (1999), 'Knowledge as Work: Conflicts in the Management of Knowledge Workers', *Technology Analysis and Strategic Management* 11/1: 5–16.

Scarth, J. (1987), 'Teacher Strategies: A Review and Critique', *British Journal of Sociology of Education* 8/3: 245–62.

Schafer, E. (1963), *Golden Peaches of Samarkand: A Study of T'ang Exotics* (Berkeley: University of California Press).

Scheff, T. J. (1994), *Bloody Revenge: Emotions, Nationalism and War* (Boulder: Westview).

Scheffler, I. (1971), *The Language of Education* (Springfield, Ill.: Thomas).

Schempp, P. G., Sparkes, A., and Templin, T. (1993), 'The Micropolitics of Teacher Induction', *American Education Research Journal* 30/3: 447–72.

Scheuer, S. (1998), 'Denmark: A Less Regulated Model', in A. Ferner and R. Hyman (eds.), *Changing Industrial Relations in Europe* (Oxford: Blackwell).

Scheurich, J. J., and Young, M. D. (1997), 'Coloring Epistemologies: Are Our Research Epistemologies Racially Biased?', in *Educational Researcher* 26/4: 4–16.

Schiller, D. (1997), 'The Information Commodity: A Preliminary View', in J. Davis, T. Hirschal, and M. Stack (eds.), *Cutting Edge Technology: Information Capitalisms and Social Revolution* (Cambridge, Mass: MIT).

—— (1999), *Digital Capitalism: Networking the Global Market System* (Cambridge, Mass: MIT).

Schiller, H. (1976), *Communication and Cultural Domination* (White Plains, NY: International Arts and Sciences).

Schirato. A., and Webb, J. (2003), *Understanding Globalization* (London: Sage).

Schmaus, W. (1994), *Durkheim's Philosophy of Science and the Sociology of Knowledge* (Chicago: University of Chicago Press).

Schmidt, M., Esser, G., Allehoff, W., Geisel, B., Laucht, M., and Woerner, W. (1987), 'Evaluating the Significance of Minimal Brain Dysfunction—Results of an Epidemiologic Study', *Journal of Child Psychology and Psychiatry* 28: 803–21.

Schneider, M., Teske, P., and Marschall, M. (2000), *Choosing Schools: Consumer Choice and the Quality of American Schools* (Princeton: Princeton University Press).

Schön, D. (1987), *Educating the Reflective Practitioner* (San Francisco: Jossey-Bass).

Schoppa, J. (1991), *Education Reform in Japan: A Case of Immobilist Politics* (London: Routledge).

Schultz, T. (1961), 'Investment in Human Capital', *American Economic Review*, 51/1: 1–17.

Schultz, T. W. (1960), 'Capital Formation in Education', *Journal of Political Economy* 68/6: 571–83; reproduced in T. W. Schultz (1993), *Investing in People: The Economics of Population Quality* (Berkeley: University of California Press).

Schultze, Q. J., Ankar, R. M., Bratt, J. D., Romanowski, W. D., Worst, J. W., and Zuidervaart, L. (1991), *Dancing in the Dark: Youth, Popular Culture and the Electronic Media* (Grand Rapids: Midwest).

Schumpeter, J. (1976), *Capitalism, Socialism and Democracy* (London: Routledge).

Scott, P. (1995), *The Meanings of Mass Higher Education* (Buckingham: Open University Press).

Scott, W., and Gough, S. (2003), *Sustainable Development and Learning: Framing the Issues* (London: Routledge Falmer).

Scruton, R. (1984), *The Meaning of Conservatism* (London: Macmillan).

Scruton, R. (1997), *Kant*, Oxford Past Masters: German Philosophers (Oxford: Oxford University Press).

Seang, G. (2001), 'Defining knowledge worker', *New Strait Times* (Malaysia), 28 July, p. 4-EX.

Sebaa, R. (1996), *L'Arabisation des Sciences Sociales: le cas de l'université algérienne* (Paris: Harmattan).

Seebach, L. (2001), 'Management visionary sees new future of work', *Rocky Mountain News*, 17 November, p. 5B.

Seely Brown, J., and Duguid, P. (2000), *The Social Life of Information* (Cambridge, Mass.: Harvard Business Press).

Segal, L. (1990), *Slow Motion: Changing Masculinities, Changing Men* (London: Virago).

Selbin, E. (1998), 'Social Justice in Latin America: Dilemmas of Democracy and Revolution', Paper presented at the annual meeting of the Latin American Studies Association, Chicago, 24–6 September.

Seltzer, K., and Bentley, T. (1999), *The Creative Age: Knowledge and Skills for the New Economy* (London: Demos).

Selznick, P. (1992), *The Moral Commonwealth: Social Theory and the Promise of Community* (Berkeley: University of California Press).

Sen, A. (1979), 'Utilitarianism and Welfarism', *Journal of Philosophy* 76: 463–89.

—— (1982), *Choice, Welfare and Measurement* (Cambridge, Mass.: MIT).

—— (1992), 'Missing Women', *British Medical Journal* 304: 587–8.

—— (1985), *Commodities and Capabilities* (Amsterdam: North-Holland).

—— (1988), *On Ethics and Economics* (Oxford: Blackwell).

—— (1992), *Inequality Reexamined* (Oxford: Clarendon).

—— (1993), 'Capability and Well Being' in M. Nussbaum and A. Sen (eds.), *Quality of Life* (Oxford: Clarendon), 30–53.

—— (1999), *Development as Freedom* (Oxford: Oxford University Press).

—— (2002), *Rationality and Freedom* (Cambridge, Mass.: Belknap).

Sennett, R., and Cobb, J. (1972), *The Hidden Injuries of Class* (New York: Norton).

—— (1998), *The Corrosion of Character: The Personal Consequences of Work in the New Capitalism* (New York: W. W. Norton).

—— (2003), *Respect: The Formation of Character in an Age of Inequality* (London: Penguin).

Sergiovanni, T. (1994), *Building Community in Schools* (San Francisco: Jossey-Bass).

SEU (1998) *Truancy and Schools Exclusion*, Cm 3957 (London: The Stationery Office).

Sewell, T. (1997), *Black Masculinities and Schooling: How Black Boys Survive Modern Schooling* (London: Trentham Books).

—— (2002), 'I know why black boys fail at school—and racism isn't to blame', *Mail on Sunday*, 15 December, 59.

Sewell, T. (1997), *Black Masculinities and Schooling: How Black Boys Survive Modern Schooling* (Stoke-on-Trent: Trentham).

—— (1998), 'Loose Canons: Exploding the Myth of the 'Black Macho' Lad', in D. Epstein, J. Elwood, V. Hey, and J. Maw (eds.), *Failing Boys? Issues in Gender and Achievement* (Buckingham: Open University Press).

Shachar, Ayelet (2000), 'The Puzzle of Interlocking Power Hierarchies: Sharing the Pieces of Jurisdictional Authority', *Harvard Civil Rights-Civil Liberties Law Review* 35/2 (Summer 2000), 387–426.

Shain, F., and Ozga, J. (2001), 'Identity Crisis? Sociology of Education', *British Journal of Sociology of Education* 22/1 (March), 109–20.

Shanghai Jiao Tong University Institute of Higher Education (2003), Academic ranking of world universities—2003, viewed 22 May 2004, <http://ed.sjtu.edu.cn/ranking.htm>.

Shapin, S. (1994), *A Social History of Truth: Civility and Science in Seventeenth Century England* (Chicago: University of Chicago Press).

—— (1996), *The Scientific Revolution* (Chicago: University of Chicago Press).

Sharp, G. (1985), 'Constitutive Abstraction and Social Practice', *Arena* 80: 42–82.

Sharp, R. (1980), *Knowledge, Ideology and the Politics of Schooling: Towards a Marxist Analysis of Education* (London: RKP).

Shavit, Y., and Blossfeld, H. P. (1993), *Persistent Inequality* (Boulder: Westview).

Shaw, K. (1996), 'Cultural Issues in Evaluation Studies of Middle Eastern Higher Education', *Assessment and Evaluation in Higher Education* 21/4: 313–24.

Shimahara, K., and Sakai, A. (1995), *Learning to Teach in Ttwo Cultures: Japan and the United States* (New York: Galard).

Shipler, D. (2005), *The Working Poor: Invisible in America* (New York: Vintage).

Sholle, D., and Denski, S. (1995), 'Critical Media Literacy: Reading, Remapping, Rewriting', in P. McLaren, R. Hammer, D. Scholle, and S. Reilly (eds.), *Rethinking Media Literacy: A Critical Pedagogy of Representation.* (New York: Peter Lang).

Shotter, J. (1993), *Conversational Realities* (London: Sage).

Shukor, R. (2001), 'Producing knowledge workers', *New Strait Times* (Malaysia), 16 April, p. 17, *Computimes* section.

Shumar, W. (1997), *College for Sale: A Critique of the Commodification of Higher Education* (London: Falmer).

Shweder, R. A., (1991), *Thinking Through Cultures* (Cambridge, Mass.: Harvard University Press).

Sidhu, R., (2002) 'Educational Brokers in Global Educational Markets', *Journal of Studies in International Education*, 6/1 16–43.

Sikes, G. (1997), *8 Ball Chicks: A Year in the Violent World of Girl Gangsters* (New York: Bantam).

Silberman, C. E. (1970), *Crisis in the Classroom: The Revaluing of American Education* (New York: Random House).

Silva, E., and Smart, C. (1999), 'The "New" Practices and Politics of Family Life', in E. Silva and C. Smart (eds.), *The 'New' Family?* (London: Sage), 1–12.

Simmel, G. (1990) [1907], *The Philosophy of Money*, ed. David Frisby (London: Routledge).

Simon, B. (1981), 'Why No Pedagogy in England?', in B. Simon and W. Taylor (eds.), *Education in the Eighties: The Central Issues* (London: Batsford).

—— (1994), *The State and Educational Change: Essays in the History of Education and Pedagogy* (London: Lawrence & Wishart), 147–61.

Simons, H. J., and Simons, R. (1969), *Class and Colour in South Africa, 1850–1950* (Harmondsworth: Penguin).

Sinclair, J., and Coulthard, M. (1974), *Towards an Analysis of Discourse: The English Used by Teachers and Pupils* (Oxford: Oxford University Press).

Singh, A., and Weisse B. (2001), 'Deindustrialization', in Jonathan Michie (ed.), *Reader's Guide to the Social Sciences* (London: Fitzroy Dearborn), i.

Siskin, L. (1994), *Realms of Knowledge* (New York: Falmer).

Sizer, T. (1992), *Horace's School: Redesigning the American High School* (Boston: Houghlin Mifflin).

Skelton, C. (2001), *Schooling the Boys: Masculinities and Primary Education* (Buckingham: Open University Press).

Skidelsky, R. (1979), 'The Decline of Keynesian Politics', in C. Crouch (ed.), *State and Economy in Contemporary Capitalism* (London: Croom Helm).

Skinner, Q. (1978), *The Foundations of Modern Political Thought* (Cambridge: Cambridge University Press).

Sklair, L. (2001), *The Transnational Capitalist Class* (Oxford: Blackwell).

Slaughter, S., and Leslie, L. (1997), *Academic Capitalism: Politics, Policies, and the Entrepreneurial University* (Baltimore: Johns Hopkins University Press).

Smith, A. (1976), *An Inquiry into the Nature and Causes of the Wealth of Nations*, ed R. H Campbell and W. Todd (Oxford: Clarendon).

Smith, A. M. (1994), *New Right Discourse on Race and Sexuality. Britain, 1968–1990* (Cambridge: Cambridge University Press).

Smith, B., Stanley, W., and Shores, J. (1957), *Fundamentals of Curriculum Development* (Yonkers, NY: World Books).

Smith, K. B. (2003), *The Ideology of Education: The Commonwealth, the Market, and America's Schools* (Buffalo: State University of New York Press).

Smith, L., and Keith, P. (1971), *Anatomy of Educational Innovation: An Organizational Analysis of an Elementary School* (New York: Wiley).

Smith, M. H., Beaulieu, L. J., and Seraphine, A. (1995), 'Social Capital, Place of Residence, and College Attendance', *Rural Sociology* 60: 363–80.

Smith, N. (1997), 'The Satanic Geographies of Globalization: Uneven Development in the 1990s', *Public Culture* 10/1: 169–89.

Smith, P. K., and Sharp, S. (eds.) (1994), *School Bullying: Insights and Perspectives* (London: Routledge).

Smyth, J. (ed.) (1995), *Critical Discourses in Teacher Development* (London: Cassell).

So, D. W. C. (1992), 'Language-Based Bifurcation of Secondary Schools in Hong Kong: Past, Present and Future', in K. K. Luke (ed.), *Issues of Language in Education in Hong Kong* (Hong Kong: Linguistic Society of Hong Kong).

Socialstyrelsen (2002), *ADHD hos barn och vuxna* [ADHD among children and Adults] (Stockholm: Modin-Tryck).

Soder, R. (1990), 'The Rhetoric of Teacher Professionalism', in J. Goodlad, R. Soder, and K. Sirotnik (eds.), *The Moral Dimensions of Teaching* (San Francisco: Jossey-Bass).

Solon, G. (1992), 'Intergenerational Income Mobility in the United States', *American Economic Review* 82: 393–408.

—— (1999), 'Intergenerational Mobility in the Labor Market', 1762–1800 in O. Ashenfelter and D. Card (eds.), *Handbook of Labor Economics* (New York: Elsevier), iii A.

—— Page, M., and Duncan, G. (2000), 'Correlations between Neighbouring Children in their Subsequent Educational Attainment', *Review of Economics and Statistics* 82: 83–92.

SOU (2000), *Från dubbla spår till elevhälsa i en skola som främjar lust att lära, hälsa och utveckling* [From Double Tracks to Pupils' Health in a School Promoting the Will to Learn, Health and Development] (Stockholm: Liber).

Soudien, C., Jacklin, H., and Hoadley, U. (2001), 'Policy Values: Problematising Equity and Redress in Education', in Y. Sayed and J. Jansen (eds.), *Implementing Education Policies: The South African Experience* (Cape Town: University of Cape Town Press).

Spady, W. G. (1970), 'Lament for the Letterman: Effects of Peer Status and Extracurricular Activities on Goals and Achievement, *American Journal of Sociology* 75: 680–702

Sparkes, A. C. (1996), 'Interrupted Body Projects and the Self in Teaching: Exploring an Absent Presence', in *International Studies in Sociology of Education* 6/2: 167–89.

Sparkes, J. (1999), *Schools, Education and Social Exclusion*, CASE Paper 29 (London: Centre for the Analysis of Social Exclusion, London School of Economics and Political Science).

Spearman, C. (1904), 'General Intelligence, Objectively Determined and Measured', *American Journal of Psychology* 15/201–93.

—— (1927), *The Nature of Intelligence and the Principles of Cognition* (London: Macmillan).

Spender, J.-C. (1996), 'Competitive Advantage from Tacit Knowledge: Unpacking the Concept and its Strategic Implications', in B. Moingeon and A. Edmondson (eds.), *Organizational Learning and Competitive Advantage* (London: Sage).

Spivak, G. (1993), *Outside in the Teaching Machine* (London: Routledge).

Stam, R. (1992), *Reflexivity in Film and Literature: From Don Quixote to Jean-Luc Goddard* (New York: Columbia University Press).

Standing, G. (2000), 'Brave New Words? A Critique of Stiglitz's World Bank Rethink', *Development and Change* 31: 737–63.

Stanton-Salazar, R. (1997), 'A Social Capital Framework for Understanding the Socialization of Racial minority Children and Youths', *Harvard Educational Review* 67:. 1–40.

—— and Dornbusch, S. M. (1995), 'Social capital and the Reproduction of Inequality: Information Networks among Mexican-Origin High School Students', *Sociology of Education* 68: 116–35.

Starrett, G. (1998), *Putting Islam to Work: Education, Politics, and Religious Transformations in Egypt* (Berkeley: University of California Press).

Starrin, B., Rantakeisu, U., and Hagquist, C. (1997), 'In the Wake of Recession—Economic Hardship, Shame and Social Disintegration', *Scandinavian Journal of Work and Environmental Health* 23/4: 47–54.

Steedman, C. (1985), '"The Mother Made Conscious": The Historical Development of a Primary School Pedagogy', *History Workshop Journal* 20: 149–63.

Steele, S. (1990), *Content of Our Character: A New Vision of Race in America* (New York: St Martins Press).

Stehr, N. (1994), *Knowledge Societies* (London: Sage).

Steinberg, S., and Kincheloe, J. (eds.) (1997), *Kinderculture: The Corporate Construction of Youth* (Boulder: Westview).

Stern, N., and Ferreira, F. (1997), 'The World Bank as "Intellectual Actor"', in D. Kapur, P. Lewis, and R. Webb (eds.), *The World Bank. Its First Half Century*, ii. *Perspectives* (Washington, DC: The Brookings Institution).

Sternberg, R. J. (1985), *Beyond IQ* (New York: Cambridge University Press).

Stevenson, H. W., and Stigler, J. (1992), *The Learning Gap. Why Our Shools Are Failing and What We Can Learn from Japanese and Chinese Education* (New York: Summit Books).

Stewart, F. (1994), 'Education and Adjustment: The Experience of the 1980s and Lessons for the 1990s', in R. Prendergast and Stewart (eds.), *Market Forces and World Development* (London: Macmillan Press).

Stewart, M. (1986), *Keynes and After* (London: Penguin).

Stewart, T. A. (2001), *The Wealth of Knowledge* (London: Nicholas Brealey).

Stigler, J.W., and Hiebert, J. (1999), *The Teaching Gap: Best Ideas from the World's Teachers for Improving Education in the Classroom*. (New York: The Free Press).

—— Gallimore, R., and Hierbert, J. (2000), 'Using Video Surveys to Compare Classrooms and Teaching Across Cultures: Examples and Lessons from the TIMSS Video Studies', *Educational Psychologist* 352: 81–100.

Stiglitz, J. (1997), 'An Agenda for Development for the Twenty-First Century', *Ninth Annual Bank Conference on Development Economics* (Washington, DC: World Bank).

Stiglitz, J. (1998), 'More Instruments and Broader Goals: Moving Toward the Post-Washington Consensus', *The 1998 WIDER Annual Lecture* (Helsinki: WIDER).

Stiglitz, J. (2002), *Globalization and Its Discontents* (London: Penguin).

Stone, L. (ed.), (1994) *The Education Feminism Reader* (New York: Routledge).

Storm, A. K. (1995), 'The Psychology of Cyberspace', *The Chronicle of Higher Education* 41/29: B1-B3.

Strange, S. (1996), *The Retreat of the State: The Diffusion of Power in the World Economy* (Cambridge: Cambridge University Press).

Strathdee, E. (2005), *Social Exclusion and the Remaking of Social Networks* (Aldershot: Ashgate).

Straus, T. (2000), 'Baby Steps to a Global revolution?': Barbara Ehrenreich and Juliette Beck discuss the new activism, Alternet.org, 27 April. <www.alternet.org/print.html?StoryID = 9060> (accessed 22 August 2000).

Strauss, A. (1962), 'Transformations of Identity', in A. Rose (ed.), *Human Behaviour and Social Processes: An Interactionist Approach* (London: Routledge & Kegan Paul).

Streeck, W. (1997), 'German Capitalism: Does it Exist? Can it Survive?', *New Political Economy*, 2/2: 237–56.

Street, B. V. (1984), *Literacy in Theory and Practice* (Cambridge: Cambridge University Press).

—— (1994), 'What is Meant by Local Literacies?', *Language and Education* 8/1 and 2: 9–17.

Steinberg, S., and Kincheloe, J. (eds.) (1997), *Kinderculture: The Corporate Construction of Youth* (Boulder: Westview).

Streitmatter, J. (1994), *Toward Gender Equity in the Classroom* (Albany: State University of New York Press).

Stromquist, N. (1992), 'Sex Equity Legislation in Education: The State as the Promoter of Women's Rights', *Review of Educational Research* 63/4: 379–408.

Stromquist, N. P., Klees, S., and Miske, S. (2000), 'USAID Efforts to Expand and Improve Girls' Primary Education in Guatemala', in: R. Cortina and N. P. Stromquist (eds.), *Educational Policies for Gender Equity in Latin America* (New York: Garland).

—— and Monkman, K. (eds.) (2000), 'Defining Globalization and Assessing its Implications on Knowledge and Education', in *Globalization and Education: Integration and Contestation Across Cultures* (New York: Rowman & Littlefield).

Sugarman, S. D. (2002), 'Charter School Funding Issues', *Education Policy Analysis Archives* 10/34, <www.epaa.asu.edu/epaa/v10n34>.

Sugrue, C. (1996), 'Student Teachers' Lay Theories: Implications for Professional Development', in I. Goodson and A. Hargreaves (eds.), *Teachers' Professional Lives* (London: Falmer).

Sundkvist, M. (1994), *De vanartade barnen. Mötet mellan barn, föräldrar och Norrköpings barnavårdsnämnd 1903–1925* [The Degenerate Children. The Encounter between Children, Parents and the Child Welfare Board of Norrköping] (Södertälje: Hjelm).

Sutz, J. (1997), 'The New Role of the University in the Productive Sector', in H. Etzkowitz and L. Leydesdorff (eds.), *University and the Global Knowledge Economy* (London: Pinter).

Swain, J. (2000), '"The Money's Good, the Fame's Good, The Girls are Good": The Role of Playground Football in the Construction of Young Boys' Masculinity in a Junior School', in *British Journal of Sociology of Education* 21/1: 95–109.

—— (2002), 'The Right Stuff: Fashioning an Identity Through Clothing in a Junior School', in *Gender and Education* 14/1: 53–69.

Swain, M., and Lapkin, S. (1991), 'Additive Bilingualism and French Immersion Education: The Roles of Language Proficiency and Literacy', in A. G.Reynolds (ed.), *Bilingualism, Multiculturalism and Second Language Learning* (Hillsdale, NJ: Lawrence Erlbaum).

Swartz, D. (1997), *Culture and Power: The Sociology of Pierre Bourdieu* (Chicago: University of Chicago Press).

Swedberg, R., Himmelstrand, U., and Brulin, G. (1990), 'The Paradigm of Economic Sociology', in S. Zukin and P. DiMaggio (eds.), *Structures of Capital: The Social Organization of the Economy* (Cambridge: Cambridge University Press).

Sydney Morning Herald (2000), 'Sweatshops make McDonald's toys', *Sydney Morning Herald*, 28 August.

Szyliowicz, J. (1973), *Education and Modernization in the Middle East* (Ithaca, NY: Cornell University Press).

Taft, D., and Glascock, S. (1999), 'In the heat of the battle, Microsoft regroups', *Computer Reseller News* 836, 5 April.

Taha, T. (1990), 'The Arabicisation of Higher Education: The Case of Khartoum University', *Journal of Multilingual and Multicultural Development* 11/4: 291–305.

Talbert, J., and Mclaughlin, M. (1994), 'Teacher Professionalism in Local School Contexts', *American Journal of Education* 102: 123–53.

Tanner, D. (1998), *The Argument Culture: Moving from Debate to Dialogue* (New York: Random House).

—— and Tanner, L. (1980), *Curriculum Development: Theory into Practice* (New York: Macmillan).

Tansel, A., and Kazemi, A. (2000), 'Educational Expenditure in the Middle East and North Africa', *Middle Eastern Studies* 36/4: 75–98.

Tawney, R. (1982), *The Acquisitive Society* (Brighton: Wheatsheaf).

Taylor, C. (1989), *Sources of the Self: The Making of the Modern Identity* (Cambridge, Mass: Harvard University Press).

Taylor, Frederick Winslow (1911), *The Principles of Scientific Management* (New York: Harper & Bros.).

Taylor, J. J. (1979), *From Modernization to Modes of Production: A Critique of the Sociologies of Development and Underdevelopment* (London: Mcmillan).

Taylor, S. (1991), 'Equity and the Politics of Change: Education Policy Making in Context', Paper presented to the Australian Sociological Association Conference, Perth, 1–3 Dec.

—— and Henry, M. (1994), 'Equity and the New Post Compulsory Education and Training Policies in Australia: A Progressive or Regressive Agenda', *Journal of Education Policy* 2: 105–27.

—— Rizvi, F., Lingard, B., and Henry, M. (1997), *Education Policy and the Politics of Change* (London: Routledge).

Teach for America (1994a), *America Needs Both of You* (New York: Teach For America).

—— (1994b), *Teach For America—Recruitment Manual* (New York: Teach For America).

Teachman, J. D., Paasch, K., and Carver, K. (1997), 'Social Capital and the Generation of Human Capital', *Social Forces* 75: 1343–59.

Teske, P., and Schneider, M. (2001), 'What Research Can Tell Policymakers about School Choice', *Journal of Policy Analysis and Management* 20: 609–32.

Thelen, K. (2000), 'Why German Employers Cannot Bring Themselves to Dismantle the German Model', in T. Iversen, J. Pontusson, and D. Soskice (eds.), *Unions, Employers and Central Banks* (New York: Cambridge University Press).

—— and Kume, I. (1999), 'The Effects of Globalization On Labour Revisited', *Politics and Society* 27/4: 477–8.

Thobani, M. (1984), 'Charging User Fees for Social Services: Education in Malawi', *Comparative Education Review*, August, 402–23.

Thompson, J. (1998), 'Community Identity and World Citizenship', in D. Archibugi, D. Held, and M. Köhler (eds.), *Re-imagining Political Community* (Cambridge: Polity/Blackwell), 179–97.

Thompson, P. (2002), *Schooling the Rustbelt Kids* (London: Trentham Books).

—— and Warhurst, C. (eds.) (1998), *Workplaces of the Future* (Basingstoke: Macmillan).

Thornton, S. (1995), *Club Cultures* (Cambridge: Polity).

Thorpe, C. (1999), 'Science Against Modernism: The Relevance of the Social Theory of Michael Polanyi', *British Journal of Sociology* 52/1: 19–35.

Thorpe, M. (2002), 'Masculinity in an HIV Intervention', *Agenda* 53: 61–8.

Thrupp, M. (1999), *Schools Making a Difference: Let's Be Realistic* (Milton Keynes: Open University Press).

—— (2005), *School Improvement: An Unofficial Approach* (London: Continuum).

—— and Tomlinson, S. (2005), 'Introduction: Education Policy, Social Justice and "Complex Hope" ', *British Educational Research Journal* 31/5:

—— and Willmott, R. (2003), *Education Management in Managerialist Times: Beyond the Textual Apologists* (Maidenhead: Open University Press).

—— Ball S. J., Vincent, C., Marques-Cardoso, C., Neath, S., and Reay, D. (2004), 'Additive and Hyper-regulation of Schooling in England: The Case of Wyeham, *Recherches Sociologiques* 35: 65–81.

Tibawi, A.-L. (1956), *Arab Education in Mandatory Palestine: A Study in Three Decades of British Administration* (London: Luzac).

—— (1972), *Islamic Education: Its Traditions and Modernization into the Arab National Systems* (London: Luzac).

Tiebout, C. (1956), 'A Pure Theory of Local Expenditures', *Journal of Political Economy* 64: 416–24.

TIMSS (2003*a*), Homepage, <http://timss.bc.edu/timss2003.html>, accessed 20 June 2005.

—— (2003*b*), 'Highlights', <http://timss.bc.edu/timss2003i/conference_IR.html>, accessed 20 June 2005.

Tobin, J. J. (1999), 'Method and Meaning in Comparative Classroom Ethnography', in R. J. Alexander, P. Broadfoot, and D. Phillips (eds.), *Learning from Comparing: New Directions in Comparative Educational Research*, i. *Contexts, Classrooms and Outcomes* (Oxford: Symposium Books).

Todorov, T. (2003), *Hope and Memory: Reflections on the Twentieth Century* (London: Atlantic).

Toffler, A. (1990), *Power Shift: Knowledge, Wealth and Violence at the Edge of the 21st Century* (New York: Bantam).

Tölölyan, K. (1996), 'Rethinking Diaspora(s): Stateless Power in the Transnational Moment', *Diaspora* 5/1.

Tomlinson, S. (2001), *Education in a Post-welfare Society* (Buckingham: Open University Press).

Torrance, H. (2003), 'Assessment of the National Curriculum in England', in T. Kellaghan and D. Stufflebeam (eds.),

International Handbook of Educational Evaluation (Dordrecht: Kluwer), 905–28

—— (2004), 'Targeting Tests: Time to Move on', *Keynote Presentation* to UK Literacy Association Annual Conference, 8 July 2004, Manchester.

Torres, R. M. (2000), *One Decade of Education for All: The Challenge Ahead* (Buenos Aires: International Institute of Educational Planning and UNESCO).

Touraine, A. (1995), *Critique of Modernity* (Oxford: Blackwell).

Townsend, J., Zapata, E., Rowlands, J., Alberti, P., and Mercado, M. (1999), *Women and Power: Fighting Patriarchy and Poverty* (London: Zed Books).

Traube, Elizabeth G. (1996), '"The Popular" in American Culture', *Annual Review of Anthropology* 25: 127–51.

Tremblay, K. (2002), 'Student Mobility between and towards OECD Countries: A Comparative Analysis' in OECD, *International Mobility of the Highly Skilled* (Paris: OECD).

Trenchard, L., and Warren, H. (1984), *Something To Tell You* (London: London Gay Teenage Group).

Trent, J. W. (1994), *Inventing the Feeble Mind: A History of Mental Retardation in the United States* (Berkeley: University of California Press).

Troman, G. (2000), 'Teacher Stress in the Low Trust Society', *British Journal of Sociology of Education* 21/3: 331–53.

Tuijnman, A., and Hellström, Z. (eds.) (2001), *Curious Minds—Nordic Adult Education Compared.* (Copenhagen: Nordic Council).

Tung. C. H. (2001), CE Speaks at HKU Anniversary Dinner, Speech delivered at the 90th anniversary dinner of the University of Hong Kong, 18 December, retrieved 23 December 2001 from <http://www.Info.gov. hk.gia/general/200112/18/1218246.htm>.

Turkle, S. (1995), *Life on the Screen: Identity in the Age of the Internet* (New York: Simon & Schuster).

Turnbull, S. (1998), 'Dealing with Feeling: Why Girl Number Twenty Still Doesn't Answer', in D. Buckingham (ed.), *Teaching Popular Culture: Beyond Radical Pedagogy* (London: UCL).

Turner, R. (1961), 'Modes of Social Ascent Through Education: Sponsored and Contest Mobility' in Halsey, Floud, and Anderson (eds.).

Turoff, M., and Hiltz, S. (1983), 'Working at Home or Living at the Office?' *Information Processing*, September.

Turpin, T., and Garrett-Jones, S. (1997), 'Innovation Networks in Australia and China', in H. Etzkowitz and L. Leydesdorff (eds.), University and the Global Knowledge Economy (London: Pinter).

Twist, L., et al. (2003), *Reading All Over the World: PIRLS National Report for England* (London: NfER/DfES), <http://www.nfer.ac.uk/publications/other-publications/downloadable-reports/pdf_docs/PIRLSPrelims.pdf>, accessed 20 June 2005.

Tyack, D. B. (1974), *The One Best System: A History of American Urban Education* (Cambridge, Mass.: Harvard University Press).

Tyack, D., and Cuban, L. (1995), *Tinkering Towards Utopia: A Century of Public School Reform* (Cambridge, Mass.: Harvard University Press).

—— and Tobin, W. (1994), 'The Grammar of Schooling: Why Has It Been So Hard to Change?', *American Educational Research Journal* 31/3: 453–80.

Tye, B. (1985), *Multiple Realities: A Study of 13 American High Schools* (Lanham, Md.: University Press of America).

Tymms, P. (2004), 'Are Standards Rising in English Primary Schools?', *British Educational Research Journal* 30/4: 477–94.

Unemployment Unit (1999), *Working Brief 107, August/September* (London: Unemployment Unit and Youth-Aid Research, Information, Campaigning).

UNESCO (1995), *World Education Report* (Paris: UNESCO).

—— (1998), *Statistical Yearbook 1998* (Paris: UNESCO).

Unicef (2005) 'The Big Picture', <http://www.unicef.org/earlychildhood/index_bigpicture.html> accessed 23 September 2005.

Unterhalter, E. (1991), 'The Impact of Apartheid on Women's Education in South Africa', *Review of African Political Economy* 48: 66–75.

—— (1996), 'States, Households and Markets in World Bank Discourses 1985–1995', *Discourse* 17/3: 389–402.

—— (1999), 'The Schooling of South African Girls', in C. Heward and S. Bunwaree (eds.), *Gender, Education and Development: Beyond Access to Empowerment* (London: Zed Books).

—— (2000), 'The Work of the Nation: Heroic Masculinity in South African Autobiographical Writing of the Anti-Apartheid Struggle', *European Journal of Development Research* 12/3: 157–78.

—— (2002*a*), 'Gender, Race and Different Lives: South African Women Teachers' Autobiographies and the Analysis of Education Change', in P. Kallaway, *The History of Education under Apartheid, 1948–1994: The Doors of Learning and Culture Shall Be Opened* (New York: Peter Lang).

—— (2002*b*), 'Gender Justice and the Transformation of Apartheid Education', in S. Marks (ed.), *Siyafunda: Partners in Learning* (London: Canon Collins Educational Trust for Southern Africa), 127–34.

—— (2003), 'The Capabilities Approach and Gendered Education: An Examination of South African Complexities', *Theory and Research in Education* 1/1: 5–22.

—— (2003), 'Gender, Basic Education and Development: An Overview of the Literature', Institute of Education, London University. Prepared for the Introductory Seminar of the Institute of Education/Oxfam, Gender, Development and Education: Beyond Access Project, London, 30th June 2003.

—— (2003), 'Crossing Disciplinary Boundaries: The Potential of Sen's Capability Approach for Sociologists of Education', *British Journal of Sociology of Education* 24/5: 665–9.

—— Wolpe, H., Botha, T., et al. (1991), *Apartheid Education and Popular Struggles* (Johannesburg: Ravan).

US Department of Education (2003), *Identifying and Implementing Educational Practices Supported by Rigorous Evidence: A User-Friendly Guide*, US Dept. of Education (NCEE 2004-3000).

US Department of Education, Office of Elementary and Secondary Education (2002*a*) *No Child Left Behind: A Desk Reference* (Washington, DC: US Department of Education).

US Department of Education, Office of the Secretary (2002*b*), *What to Know and Where to Go: A Parents' Guide to No Child Left Behind* (Washington, DC: US Department of Education).

US Department of Labor, Bureau of Labor Statistics (1986), 'Re-employment Increases Among Displaced Workers', *BLS News* (USDL, 14 October), 86–414: table 6.

US Government Printing Office (1989), *Statistical Abstract of the United States* (Washington DC), 416: table 684.

US News and World Report (2003), 'America's Best Colleges', *US News and World Report*, special annual edition.

Useem, E. (1992), 'Middle Schools and Math Groups: Parents' Involvement in Children's Placement', *Sociology of Education* 65: 263–79.

Usher, R., and Edwards, R. (1994), *Postmodernism and Education: Different Voices, Different Worlds* (London: Routledge).

Vachani, L. (1989), 'Narrative, Pleasure and Ideology in the Hindu Film: An Analysis of the Outsider Formula'. MA thesis, Annenberg School of Communication, University of Pennsylvania.

Vail, L. (ed.) (1989), *The Creation of Tribalism in Southern Africa* (London: James Currey).

Valenzuela, A. (1999), *Subtractive Schooling: U.S.-Mexican Youth and the Politics of Schooling* (New York: State University of New York Press).

—— and Dornbusch, S. M. (1994), 'Familism and Social Capital in the Academic Achievement of Mexican Origin and Anglo Adolescents', *Social Science Quarterly* 75: 18–36.

Valery, P. (1943), *Tel Quel*, ii. 73.

Veblen, T. (1918/1965), *The Higher Learning in America: A Memorandum on the Conduct of Universities by Businessmen* (New York: A. M. Keller).

Verespej, M. (1999) 'Global Quandary'. *Industry Week*, 15 November, 9–10.

Verhoeven, J. C. (1989), *Methodological and Metascientific Problems in Symbolic Interactionism*, (Leuven: Department of Sociology, Catholic University.

Vidal, J. (2002), 'Florence builds a bridge to a brand new social paradise', *Guardian*, 11 November, 18.

Villanueva, I. (1996), 'Change in the Educational Life of Chicano Families across Three Generations', *Education and Urban Society* 29: 13–34.

Vincent, C. (1996), *Parents and Teachers: Power and Participation* (London: Falmer).

Vinz, R. (1999), 'Learning from the Blues: Beyond Essentialist Readings of Cultural Texts', in C. McCarthy, G. Hudak, S. Miklaucic, and P. Saukko (eds.), *Sound Identities* (New York: Peter Lang).

Vitteriti, J. P. (1999), *Choosing Equality* (Washington, DC: Brookings Institution).

Vogel, S. (2001), 'The Crisis of German and Japanese Capitalism', *Comparative Political Studies* 34/10.

Vygotsky, L. S. (1978), *Mind in Society*. (Cambridge, Mass.: Harvard University Press).

—— (1994), *The Vygotsky Reader*, ed. R. van der Veer and J. Valsiner (Oxford: Blackwell).

Wade, R. (2001), 'Showdown at the World Bank', *New Left Review* 7 (Jan.–Feb.), 124–37.

Wade, R. H. (2003), 'The Invisible Hand of the American Empire' Ethics and International Affairs 17/2: 77–88.

—— (2004), 'On the Causes of Increasing World Poverty and Inequality, or Why the Matthew Effect Prevails'. *New Political Economy* 9/2: 163–88.

Waelbroeck, J. (1998), 'Half a Century of Development Economics: A Review Based on the *Handbook of Development Economics, World Bank Economic Review'* 12/2: 323–52.

Wagner, D. A. (1993), *Literacy, Culture, and Development: Becoming Literate in Morocco* (Cambridge: Cambridge University Press).

Wåhlin, L. (1982), *Education as Something New: The Introduction of Village Schools and a Study of Two Student Cohorts 1948–1980* (Stockholm: University of Stockholm: Department of Human Geography).

Waldfogel, J. (2002), 'Child care, women's employment, and child outcomes', *Journal of Population Economics* 15: 527–48.

Walker, C. (ed.) (1990), *Women and Gender in Southern Africa to 1945* (Cape Town: David Philip).

Walker, R. B. J. (1988), *One World, Many Worlds: Struggles for a Just World Peace* (Boulder: Lynne Rienner).

—— (1991) 'On the Spatio-Temporal Alternatives of Democratic Practice', *Alternatives* 16/2: 243–62.

—— (1994), *Inside/Outside* (Cambridge: Cambridge University Press).

—— (1995), 'International Relations and the Concept of the Political', in K. Booth and S. Smith (eds.), *International Relations Theory Today* (Cambridge: Polity), 306–27.

Walkerdine, V. (1984), 'Developmental Psychology and the Child-Centred Pedagogy: The Insertion of Piaget into Early

Education', in J. Henriques, W. Holloway, C. Urwin, C. Venn and V. Walkerdine (eds.), *Changing the Subject* (London: Methuen).

—— (1986), 'Post-Structuralist Theory and Everyday Social Practices', in V. Walkerdine (ed.), *Feminist Social Psychology* (Milton Keynes: Open University Press).

—— (1990), *School Girl Fictions* (London: Verso).

—— (1997), *Daddy's Girl: Young Girls and Popular Culture* (London: Macmillan).

—— and Lucey, H. (1989), *Democracy in the Kitchen: Regulating Mothers and Socialising Daughters* (London: Virago).

Wall Street Journal (16 February 1990), A5.

Wallace, M. (1993), 'Discourse of Derision: The Role of the Mass Media within the Education Policy Process', *Journal of Education Policy* 8/4: 321–37.

—— and Denham, C. (1996), *The ONS Classification of Local and Health Authorities of Great Britain* (London: HMSO).

Waller, W. (1932), *The Sociology of Teaching* (New York: Wiley).

Wallerstein, I. (1974), *The Modern World System*, 2 vols. (New York: Academic Press).

Walshok, M. (1995), *Knowledge without Boundaries: What America's Research Universities Can Do for the Economy, the Workplace, and the Community*, Foreword by Daniel Yankelovich (San Francisco: Jossey Bass).

Ward, S. (1996), *Reconfiguring Truth* (Lanham Md: Rowan & Littlefield).

Warner, M. (1990), *The Letters of the Republic: Publication and the Public Sphere in Eighteenth-Century America* (Cambridge, Mass.: Harvard University Press).

Warren, J., Hauser, R., and Sheridan, J. (2002), 'Occupational Stratification across the Life Course', *American Sociological Review* 67: 432–55.

Waters, M. (1995), *Globalization* (London: Routledge).

Watkins, D. A., and Biggs, J. B. (eds.) (1996), *The Chinese Learner: Cultural, Psychological and Contextual Influences* (Hong Kong and Melbourne.: Comparative Education Research Centre, and The Australian Council of Educational Research).

Watkins, P. (1996), 'Decentralizing Education to the Point of Production: Sloanism, the Market and Schools of the Future', *Discourse* 17/1: 85–99.

Watson, L. (1999), *Survey of Private Providers in Australian Higher Education 1999*, 00/4, Evaluations and Investigations Program, Higher Education Division, Department of Education, Science and Training, Canberra, viewed 11 December 2003, <http://www.dest.gov.au/archive/highered/eippubs/eip00_4/survey.pdf>.

Wattenberg, B. (1991), *The First Universal Nation* (New York: The Free Press).

Webb, R., and Vulliamy, G. (1993), 'A Deluge of Directives: Conflict Between Collegiality and Managerialism in the Post ERA Primary School', *British Education Research Journal* 22/4: 441–58.

Weber, E. (1979), *Peasants into Frenchmen: The Modernization of Rural France, 1870–1914* (London: Chatto).

Weber, M. (1945), *From Max Weber*, ed. H. Gerth and C. W. Mills (London: Routledge).

—— (1968), *Economy and Society*, 3 vols. ed. G. Roth and C. Wittich (New York: Bedminster).

Weber, S., and Mitchell, C. (1996), 'Using Drawings to Interrogate Professional Identity and the Popular Culture of Teaching', in I. F. Goodson and A. Hargreaves (eds.), *Teachers' Professional Lives* (Washington, DC: Falmer). 109–26.

Webster, A., and Packer, K. (1997), 'When Worlds Collide: Patents in Public Sector Research', in H. Etzkowitz and L. Leydesdorff (eds.), *University and the Global Knowledge Economy* (London: Pinter).

Webster, F. (1997), 'Information, Urbanisms and Identity: Perspectives on the Current Work of Manuel Castells', *City* 7: 105–21.

Weedon, K. (2002) 'Why Do Some Occupations Pay More than Others? Social Closure and Earnings Inequality in the United States', *American Journal of Sociology* 108/1:55–101.

Weeks, J., Heaphy, B., and Donovan, C. (2001), *Same Sex Intimacies: Families of Choice and Other Life Experiments* (London: Routledge).

Wehbé, N., and El Amine, A. (1980), *Système d'Enseignement et Division Sociale au Liban* (Paris: Le Sycomore).

Weiher, G. R., and Tedin, K. L. (2002), 'Does Choice Lead to Racially Distinctive Schools? Charter Schools and Household Preferences', *Journal of Policy Analysis and Management* 21/1: 79–92.

Weil, S. W. (1986), 'Non-Traditional Learners within Traditional Higher Education Institutions: Discovery and Disappointment', *Studies in Higher Education* 11/3: 219–35.

Weiler, D. (1974), *A Public School Voucher Demonstration: The First Year at Alum Rock* (Santa Monica, Calif.: Rand).

Weiler, K. (1988), *Women Teaching for Change*, Critical Educational Series (Granby, Mass.: Bergin & Harvey).

—— (1993), 'Feminism and the Struggle for Democratic Education: A View from the United States', in M. Arnot and K. Weiler (eds.), *Feminism and Social Justice in Education* (London: Falmer).

—— (1994), 'Freire and a Feminist Pedagogy of Difference', in P. McLaren and C. Lankshear (eds.), *Politics of Liberation: Paths from Freire* (New York: Routledge). (First Published 1991).

Weinbaum, E. (1999), 'Organizing Labor in an Era of Contingent Work and Globalization', in B. Nissen (ed.),

Which Direction for Organized Labor? (Detroit: Wayne State University Press), ch. 2, 37–58.

Weiner, G. (1995), *Feminism and Education* (Buckingham: Open University Press).

Weir, A. (1997), *Sacrificial Logics: Feminist Theory and the Critique of Identity* (New York: Routledge).

Weis, L. (1983), 'Schooling and Cultural Production: A Comparison of Black and White Lived Culture', in M. Apple and L. Weis (eds.), *Ideology and practice in Schooling* (Philadelphia: Temple University Press).

—— (1990), *Working Class without Work: High School Students in a De-industrializing Economy* (New York: Routledge).

—— and Fine, M. (1996), 'Narrating the 1980s and 1990s: voice of Poor and Working-Class White and African American Men', *Anthropology and Education Quarterly* 27:493-516.

Wells, A. S., and Oakes, J. (1998), 'Tracking, De-tracking, and the Politics of Educational Reform: A Sociological Perspective', in C. A. Torres and T. R. Mitchell (eds.), *Sociology of Education: Emerging Perspectives* (Albany: University of New York Press).

—— and Serna, I. (1997), 'The Politics of Culture: Understanding Local Political Resistance to De-tracking in Racially Mixed Schools', in J. Karabel and A. H. Halsey (eds.), *Power and Ideology in Education* (London: Oxford University Press).

Wells, A., Carnochan, S., Slayton, J., Allen, R., and Vasudeva, A. (1998), 'Globalization and Educational Change', in A. Hargreaves et al. (eds.), *International Handbook of Educational Change* (Dordrecht: Kluwer), 322–84.

Wells, G. (1986), *The Meaning Makers: Children Learning Language and Using Language to Learn* (London: Heinemann).

Wertsch, J. V. (1991), *Voices of the Mind: A Sociocultural Approach to Mediated Action.* (Cambridge, Mass.: Harvard University Press).

—— (1998), *Mind as Action* (New York: Oxford University Press).

West, E. G. (1967), 'Tom Paine's Voucher Scheme for Public Education', *Southern Economic Journal* 33: 378–82.

—— (1991), 'Public Schools and Excess Burdens', *Economics of Education Review* 10: 159–69.

Westbury, I. (1973), 'Conventional Classrooms "Open" Classrooms, and the Technology of Teaching', *Journal of Curriculum Studies* 5/2: 99–121.

—— (1973), 'Conventional Classrooms, Open Classrooms and the Technology of Teaching', *Journal of Curriculum Studies* 5/2.

Westergaard, J. (1995), *Who Gets What? The Hardening of Social Class in the Late Twentieth Century* (Oxford: Polity).

Weston, P. (1979), *Negotiating the Curriculum* (Slough: NFER).

Whelehan, I. (1995), *Modern Feminist Thought* (Edinburgh: Edinburgh University Press).

White, M. (1987), *The Japanese Educational Challenge* (London: Macmillan).

Whitney, I., and Smith, P. K. (1993), 'A Survey of the Nature and Extent of Bullying in Junior/Middle School and Secondary School', *Educational Research* 35/1: 3–25.

Whitty, G. (1985), *Sociology and School Knowledge: Curriculum Theory, Research and Politics* (London: Methuen).

—— (1996), 'Creating Quasi-Markets in Education: A Review of Recent Research On Parental Choice and School Autonomy in Three Countries', *Review of Research in Education* 22: 3–48.

—— (1997), 'Marketization, the State, and the Re-Formation of the Teaching Profession', in A. Halsey, H. Lauder, P. Brown, and A. Well (eds.), *Education: Culture, Economy and Society* (Oxford, Oxford University Press), 299–310.

—— (2000), 'Education and Social Inclusion: Possibilities and Limits', *Education Review* 13/2: 5–14.

—— (2001), 'Education, Social Class and Social Exclusion', *Journal of Education Policy*, 16/4: 287–95.

—— Power, S., and Halpin, D. (1998), *Devolution and Choice in Education: The School, the State and the Market* (Melbourne: ACER).

Wideen, M., Mayer-Smith, J., and Moon, B. (1996), 'Knowledge, Teacher Development and Change', in I. Goodson and A. Hargreaves (eds.), *Teachers' Professional Lives* (New York: Falmer).

Wiener, J. (2001), 'Globalization and Disciplinary Neoliberal Governance', *Constellations* 8/4: 462–79.

Wiliam, D. (2001), *Level Best? Levels of Attainment in National Curriculum Assessment* (London: The Association of Teachers and Lecturers).

Will, G. (1989), 'Eurocentricity and the school curriculum', *Baton Rouge Morning Advocate*, 18 December: 3.

Williams, G. (1997), 'The Market Route to Mass Higher Education: British Experience 1979–1996', *Higher Education Policy* 10: 275–89.

Williams, R. (1976), *Keywords* (New York: Oxford University Press).

—— (1983), *Keywords* (London: Flamingo).

Williamson, B. (1981), 'Class Bias', in D. Warren-Piper (ed.), *Is Higher Education Fair?* (Guildford: Society for Research in Higher Education).

Williamson, B. (1987), *Educational Change and Social Change in Egypt and Turkey: A Study in Historical Sociology* (New York: Macmillan).

Williamson, J. (1990), 'What Washington Means by Policy Reform', in J. Williamson (ed.), *Latin American Adjustment. How Much Has Happened?* (Washington, DC: Institute for International Economics).

Willis, P. (1977), *Learning to Labour: How Working Class Kids Get Working Class Jobs* (Farnborough: Saxon House).

—— (2000), *The Ethnographic Imagination* (Cambridge: Polity).

—— Bekenn, A., Ellis, T., and Whitt, D. (1988), *The Youth Review* (Aldershot: Avebury).

—— Jones, S., Cannan J., and Hurd, G. (1990), *Common Culture: Symbolic Work at Play in the Everyday Cultures of the Young* (Milton Keynes: Open University Press).

Willmott, H. (1992), 'Postmodernism and Excellence: The De-differentiation of Economy and Culture', in *Journal of Organisational Change and Management* 5/1: 58–68.

Willms, J. D. (1996), 'School Choice and Community Segregation: Findings from Scotland', in A Kerckhoff (ed.), *Generating Social Stratification: Toward a New Research Agenda* (Boulder: Westview).

Wilmott, R. (1999), 'Structure, Agency and School Effectiveness: Researching a "Failing School"', *Educational Studies* 25/1: 5–18.

Wilson, A. (1983), *A Consumers Guide to Bill 82: Special Education in Ontario* (Toronto: Ontario Institute for Studies in Education).

Wilson, E. (1992), 'The Invisible Flaneur', *New Left Review* 191 (January/February): 90–110.

—— (1995), *Hidden Agendas: Theory, Politics, and Experience in the Women's Movement* (London: Tavistock Publications). (First published 1986.)

Wilson, William J. (1987), *The Truly Disadvantaged* (Chicago: University of Chicago).

Wilson, W.J. (1997), 'Studying Inner-city Social Dislocation: The Challenge of Public Agenda Research', in Halsey, et al. (eds.), 750–64.

Winerip, M. (2003), 'The "zero dropout" miracle: Alas! Alack! A Texas tall tale', *New York Times*, 13 August, B7.

Winter, G. (2004), 'Worst rates of graduation are in New York', *New York Times*, Feb 26 February.

Witte, J. F. (1999), *The Market Approach to Education* (Princeton: Princeton University Press).

—— (2003), 'Charter Schools in Wisconsin: Assessing Form and Performance', APPAM Paper, November 2003.

Wittgenstein, L. (1953), *Philosophical Investigations* (Oxford: Blackwell).

Wolf, A. (1989), 'Markets and Society as Modes of Moral Obligation', *Acta Sociologica* 32: 221–36.

—— (2002), *Does Education Matter?: Myths About Education and Economic Growth* (London, Penguin).

Wolf, E. (1982), *Europe and the People without History* (Berkeley: University of California Press).

Wolfe, A. (ed.) (2003), *School Choice. The Moral Debate* (Princeton: Princeton University Press).

Wolfe, Alan (2001), 'Alien Nation', *New Republic* (26 March, 2001).

Wollstonecraft, M. (1992), *Vindication of the Rights of Women* (London: Penguin) (First published in 1792).

Wolpe, A. M. (1988), *Within School Walls: The Role of Discipline, Sexuality and the Curriculum* (London: Routledge).

Wolpe, A., Quinlan, O., and Martinez, L. (1997), *Gender Equity in Education: A Report of the Gender Equity Task Team* (Pretoria: Department of Education).

Wolpe, H. (1988), *Race, Class and the Apartheid State* (London: James Currey).

Wood, A. (1998), 'Kant's Project for Perpetual Peace', in P. Cheah and B. Robbins (eds.), *Cosmopolitics: Thinking and Feeling Beyond the Nation* (Minneapolis: University of Minnesota Press).

Woodhall, M. (1994), 'The Effects of Austerity and Adjustment on the Allocation and Use of Resources: A Comparative Analysis of Five Case Studies', in J. Samoff (ed.), *Coping with Crisis. Austerity, Adjustment and Human Resources* (London: Cassell).

Woodhead, C. (1995), 'Education—the Elusive Engagement and the Continuing Frustration', *Times Educational Supplement* 3: 7.

—— (1996), 'Boys who learn to be losers', *The Times*, 6 March, 18.

Woods Ngaire, (2001), 'International Political Economy in an Age of Globalization', in J. Baylis and S. Smith (eds.), *The Globalization of World Politics* (Oxford University Press), ch. 13.

—— (2003), The United States and the International Financial Institutions: Power and Influence within the World Bank and IMF', in R. Foot, N. McFarlane, N. and M. Mastanduno (eds.), *US Hegemony and International Organisations* (Oxford: Oxford University Press).

Woods, P. (1977), 'Teaching for Survival', in P. Woods and M. Hammersley (eds.), *School Experience* (London: Croom Helm).

—— (1990), *Teacher Skills and Strategies* (London: Falmer).

—— Jeffrey, R., Troman, G., and Boyle, M. (1997), *Restructuring Schools, Reconstructing Teachers: Responding to Changes in the Primary School* (Buckingham: Open University Press).

Woolcock, M. (1998), 'Social Capital and Economic Development: Toward a Theoretical Synthesis and Policy Framework', *Theory and Society* 27: 151–208.

—— (2005), 'The Shifting Politics of Global Aid;, *International Affairs* 81/2 (March), 393–409.

World Bank (1982), 'Malawi. Growth and Structural Change. A Basic Economic Report', Report No. 3082a-MAI (Washington, DC: World Bank).

—— (1993), *Human Resources in Latin America and the Caribbean: Priorities and Action* (Washington, DC: The World Bank).

—— (1995), *Priorities and Strategies for Education: A World Bank Review* (Washington, DC: World Bank).

—— (1999*a*), *World Development Report. Knowledge for Development* (Washington, DC: World Bank).

—— (1999*b*), *Education Sector Strategy* (Washington, DC: World Bank).

—— (2002), <http://www.worldbank.org/data/countrydata/countrydata.html> (accessed 17 June 2002).

World Book Knowledge Source (2002), Article on American Federation of Labor and Congress of Industrial Organizations (online <http://newfirstsearch.oclc.org/webZ/FSFETCH, accession #fw00am0838000a>).

World Education Forum (WEF) (2000), *The Dakar Framework for Action. Education for All: Meeting Our Collective Commitments* (Dakar: WEF), 26–8 April.

Wright, C. (1992), *Race Relations in the Primary School* (London: David Fulton).

Wright, E. O. (1979), *Class Structure and Income Determination* (New York: Academic Press).

Wright, E. O. (1982), 'Class boundaries and contradicting class locations' in A. Giddens and D. Held (eds.) *Classes, Power and Conflict* (London: Macmillan Press).

Wright, F. O. (1997), *Class Counts: Comparative Studies in Class Analysis* (Cambridge: Cambridge University Press).

Wright, M. (1992), *International Theory: The Three Traditions* (New York: Holmes & Meier).

WTO (1998), 'Education Services: Background Note by the Secretariat', S/C/W/49, 23 September 1998 (Geneva: WTO).

—— (2001), *GATS—Fact and Fiction* (Geneva, WTO).

Wylie, C. (1995), 'Contrary Currents: The Application of Public Sector Reform Framework in Education', *New Zealand Journal of Educational Studies* 30/2: 149–64.

Wyness, M. C. (1996), *Schooling, Welfare and Parental Responsibility* (London: Falmer).

Xu, G. (2000), *Participation in Employer-Sponsored Adult Education and Training in Sweden (1975–1995)*, Dissertation Series (Vancouver: UBC).

Yamamoto, M. (2004), 'Will India Price Itself Out of Offshore Market?', at <http://news.com.com/Will-+India+price+itself+out+of|+offshore+market/2100-10223-5180589.html>

Yates, L. (1993), 'Feminism and Australian State Policy', in N. Amot and K. Weiler (eds.), *Feminism and Social Justice* (London: Falmer)

Yeatman, A. (1992), 'Women's Citizenship Claims. Labour Market Policy and Globalization', *Australian Journal of Political Science* 27: 449–61.

—— (1994), *Postmodern Theorisings of the Political* (London: Routledge).

—— (1998) 'Trends and Opportunities in the Public Sector: A Critical Assessment', *Australian Journal of Public Administration* 57/4: 138–47.

Yeung, W. J., Linver, M. R., and Brooks-Gunn, J. (2002), 'How Money Matters for Young Children's Development: Investment and Family Process', *Child Development* 73: 1861–79.

Yoshimoto, M. (1989), 'The Postmodern and Mass Images in Japan', *Public Culture*, 1/2: 8–25.

Young, I. (1990), *Justice and the Politics of Difference* (Princeton: Princeton University Press).

—— (1994), 'Polity and Group Difference: A Critique of the Ideal of Universal Citizenship', in B. Turner and P. Hamilton (eds.), *Citizenship: Critical Concepts* (London: Routledge), ii.

Young, I. M. (1995), 'Gender as Seriality: Thinking About Women as a Social Collective', in L. Nicholson and S. Seidman (eds.), *Social Postmodernism* (Cambridge: Cambridge University Press).

Young, M. (1961), *The Rise of the Meritocracy* (Harmondsworth: Penguin).

Young, M. F. O. (1998), *The Curriculum of the Future* (London: Falmer).

—— (2003), 'Curriculum Studies and the Problem of Knowledge: Updating the Enlightenment?' Paper presented to the Education, Policy, Innovation and Change Research Group (EPIC), Department of Education, University of Bath, 14 March.

—— (ed.) (1971), *Knowledge and Control: New directions for the Sociology of Education* (London: Collier MacMillan).

—— and McGheery, P. (1970), *Parents are Welcome* (London: Longman).

Young, R. (1992), 'The Idea of a Chrestomathic University', in R. Rand (ed.), *Logomachia: The Conflict of Faculties* (Lincoln: University of Nebraska Press).

Yuval-Davis, N. (1997), *Gender and Nation* (London: Sage).

—— and Anthias, F. (1989), *Woman-Nation-State*, (London: Macmillan).

Zarilli, P. (1995), 'Repositioning the Body: An Indian Martial Art and its Pan-Asian Publics', in C. A. Breckenridge (ed.), *Consuming Modernity: Public Culture in a South Asian World* (Minneapolis: University of Minnesota Press).

Zawdie, G. (1995), 'Tertiary Education and Technological Progress in Transitional Economies: Whither Demand Pull?' *Science, Technology and Development* 13/3: 89–104.

Zelman vs. *Simmons-Harris*, 00–751, US Supreme Court Ruling (2002).

Zetlin, D., and Whitehouse, G. (1996), 'Citizenship and Industrial Regulation: A Feminist Perspective', Paper presented to the Culture and Citizenship Conference, Griffith University, 30 Sept. 2 Oct.

Zielinsky, A. K., and Hoy, W. K. (1983), 'Isolation and Alienation in the Elementary Schools', *Education Administration Quarterly* 19/2: 27–45.

Zimmer, R. (ed.) (2003), *Charter School Operations and Performance. Evidence from California* (Santa Monica: Rand Publications).

—— and Toma, E. (2000), 'Peer Effects in Private and Public Schools across Countries', *Journal of Policy Analysis and Management* 19: 75–92.

Zipp, J. F., and Plutzer, F. (1996), 'Wives and Husbands: Social Class, Gender, and Class Identification in the U.S.', *Sociology* 30: 235–52.

Zuboff, S. (1988), *In the Age of the Smart Machine: The Future of Work and Power* (New York: Basic Books).

Index

A

B

D

H

I

J

L

N

O

Q

R

S

T

U

V

W

Z